Volume 97 • Number 1 • January 2026

SRL

Seismological Research Letters

SSA
Seismological Society of America

SRL Seismological Research Letters

Volume 97 • Number 1 • January 2026

Opinion

Are Short-Term Low-Probability Earthquake Forecasts Useful? An Emergency Management Perspective 1
James D. Goltz

Articles

Coseismic and Postseismic Displacements of the 2024 M_w 7.0 Wushi, China, Earthquake Observed from SAR Images 4
Xing Li, Jihong Liu, Shuai Wang, Nan Fang, Meng Duan, and Alexandros Savvaidis

Incorporating Directly Observed Rotational Seismic Data into Moment Tensor Inversion for the 2019 M_w 6.2 Hualien Earthquake 15
Beibei Xu, Yong Zhang, Wei Li, Chang Chen, and Yun Wang

Complex Multifault Rupture During the 2016–2025 Dingri Earthquakes, Southern Tibetan Plateau, Unraveled by Multisource InSAR Observations 28
Jiuyuan Yang, Yangmao Wen, Caijun Xu, and Qingfeng Hu

Investigation of the Foreshock Characteristics of the 2014 M_s 6.5 Ludian Earthquake 38
Shiguang Deng, Haikun Jiang, Yawei Ma, Zhiwei Liu, Shaowei Kang, and Yue Wang

High-Resolution Shear-Wave Velocity Model of the Source Region of the 1970 M_s 7.7 Tonghai Earthquake, Yunnan, China 54
Di Zhong, Jianping Wu, Changzai Wang, Lihua Fang, Guangyao Cai, Jing Liu, and Yaning Liu

The Role of Earthquake Interaction in Hydraulic-Fracturing-Induced Seismicity in Sichuan Basin, Southwest China 67
Yangtianli Zhou and Fenglin Niu

On the Cover

The beautiful Dead Sea coastline graces this issue's cover. A paper by Lellouch in this issue uses data from stations initially installed for earthquake early warning (go back and read your old issues of *SRL* if you want more information on that) to improve earthquake locations and gain some insight into the relation between faults and seismic activity in the region.

Image credit: iStock.com/NickolayV

Underestimates of Magnitudes in Real Time Lead to Underestimates of Earthquake Disasters 81
Max Wyss

Clock Error Detection for Decade-Long Seismic Monitoring Network in Marapi Volcano, Indonesia 86
Mingye Feng, Shengji Wei, Benoit Taisne, Yukuan Chen, Christina Widiwijayanti, and Sulistiyani

Deep Learning–Based Footfall Detection and Anthropogenic Activity Characterization Using Fiber-Optic Distributed Acoustic Sensing 100
Yuming Yuan, Bin Luo, and Zhen Guo

Detecting Urban Earthquakes with the San Fernando Valley Nodal Array and Machine Learning 111
Joses Omojola and Patricia Persaud

Seismic Lessons from the Implosion of Reser Stadium's Western Stands and the Dense 177-Node Corvallis Array 126
Pieter-Ewald Share, Anne M. Tréhu, Armin Stuedlein, Hannah R. Reinhard, Aurélien Mordret, and Rachel A. M. Way

Readapting PhaseNet to Laboratory Earthquakes: AEsNet, a Robust Acoustic Emission Picker Illuminating Seismic Signatures of Different Fault Gouge Materials 141
Giacomo Mastella, Giulio Poggiali, Federico Pignalberi, and Marco Scuderi

A Mixed Efficient AWENO Scheme to Model Cross-Fault Ground Motions and Its Applications 161
Tianhong Xu, Houyun Yu, Wenqiang Wang, Zijia Wang, and Zhenguo Zhang

Improving the Transportability of a Deep Learning Denoising Model Using Transfer Learning Techniques 173
Louis Quinones and Rigobert Tibi

Deep-Learning-Based Catalog of Background Seismicity and Aftershocks of the 2020–2021 Large Earthquakes Along the Alaska Peninsula 187
Yaqi Jie, Songqiao Shawn Wei, Weiqiang Zhu, Jeffrey Freymueller, and Julie Elliott

Mailing & Subscription Information

Subscriptions to *Seismological Research Letters* (SRL): Information regarding institutional subscriptions can be found at https://www.seismosoc.org/publications/institutional-subscribers/. Members of the Seismological Society of American receive online access to SRL and may purchase a print subscription. For membership information visit https://www.seismosoc.org.

Seismological Research Letters (ISSN: 0895-0695) is published bimonthly in January, March, May, July, September, and November by the Seismological Society of America, 400 Evelyn Avenue, Suite 201, Albany, California 94706. Periodicals postage paid at Berkeley, California and at additional mailing offices.

Postmaster: Send address changes to Seismological Research Letters, 400 Evelyn Avenue, Suite 201, Albany, California 94706.

For information on submissions and instructions for authors, visit https://www.seismosoc.org/publications/srl. Communications regarding the journal apart from submission of manuscripts should be addressed to the Seismological Society of America at info@seismosoc.org.

Lahar Early Warning at Volcano Santiaguito, Guatemala: A Standard and a Deep Learning Approach 204
Dario Jozinović, Frederick Massin, John Clinton, and Amilcar Roca

Testing FinDer in New Zealand for Earthquake Early Warning 217
Jen Andrews, Yannik Behr, Maren Böse, Anna Kaiser, and Bill Fry

Improving Magnitude Estimates in the EPIC Earthquake Early Warning Algorithm 233
Amy Williamson, Angela Lux, and Richard M. Allen

An Updated Seismicity View of the Dead Sea Transform Using an Early Warning Network 246
Ariel Lellouch

Attention-Based Neural Network for Onsite Peak Ground Velocity Earthquake Early Warning 256
Ting-Chung Huang, Tzu-Ling Liu, Benjamin Ming Yang, and Yih-Min Wu

Reducing Frequency Bias of Fourier Neural Operators in 3D Seismic Wavefield Simulations Through Multistage Training 272
Qingkai Kong, Caifeng Zou, Youngsoo Choi, Eric M. Matzel, Kamyar Azizzadenesheli, Zachary E. Ross, Arthur J. Rodgers, and Robert W. Clayton

Short-Term Forecasting of Aftershock Ground-Motion Hazards Within a Few Hours After a Large Earthquake in Japan 283
Hisahiko Kubo and Katsuhiko Shiomi

On the Lagged Coherence Estimation for Seismic Ground Motions 295
Xizhong Cui

Peak Ground Velocity and Shaking Duration Control Coseismic Surficial Sediment Remobilization on Lacustrine Slopes and Emplacement of Seismoturbidites 309
Katleen Wils, Gonzalo Montalva, Maarten Van Daele, Marc De Batist, and Jasper Moernaut

Pre- and Postseismic Variations of Crustal 3D Velocity Structure Around the Ludian Earthquake Zone in Southwest China Revealed by Time-Lapse Ambient Noise Tomography 323
Yang Chen, Lianghui Guo, Xueyang Bao, and Xiang Wang

Mechanisms and Implications of Lower Crust Earthquakes and Shallow Events Beneath Yanzhou Coal Mining Area, North China 340
Guangwei Zhang, Enyuan Wang, Luyuan Huang, Yujiang Li, and Xingping Hu

Lateral Viscosity Heterogeneity of Mantle Wedge and Back-Arc Mantle: Implications from the 2010 M_w 8.8 Maule and 2011 M_w 9.0 Tohoku-Oki Postseismic Deformation 354
Hyeon-Seob Kim, Byung-Dal So, and Sung-Joon Chang

A Single-Station Earthquake Catalog for the Endeavour Segment of the Juan de Fuca Ridge (2011–2016): Challenges and Implications for the Spreading Cycle 369
Zoe Krauss, Christian Baillard, William S. D. Wilcock, Martin Heesemann, Angela Schlesinger, and Jacob Kukovica

Seismogenic Potential of Hydraulic Fracturing in the South Montney Play, Northeast British Columbia: A Seismogenic Index Approach 383
Ramin M. H. Dokht, Honn Kao, and Ryan Visser

Systematics of the Fault-Zone Seismogenic Width of Strike-Slip Plate Boundaries 399
Shaked Engelberg, Amotz Agnon, Amir Sagy, and Nadav Wetzler

Illuminating Subsurface Structures Beneath Lake George Fault Zone, Southeast Australia with Traffic Noise 409
Chengxin Jiang and Meghan S. Miller

Unsupervised Deep Clustering of Microseismic Signals from the Dalk Glacier in East Antarctica 425
Lei Zhao, Lei Fu, Jingxue Guo, Yanlan Hu, Zefeng Li, Kai Lu, Ruijia Wang, and Xiangyun Hu

Characterizing Seismic Events in an Industrial Corridor of the Chicago Area 439
Ann Mariam Thomas, Omkar Ranadive, and Suzan van der Lee

Revisiting Seismological Discoveries of the Inner Core 451
Adam T. Ringler, Pritwiraj Moulik, Thomas Lee, David C. Wilson, and Robert E. Anthony

Evaluation of Seismic Artificial Intelligence with Uncertainty 471
Samuel Myren, Nidhi Parikh, Rosalyn Rael, Garrison Flynn, Dave Higdon, and Emily Casleton

Electronic Seismologist

Cardinal: Seismic and Geoacoustic Array Processing 487
Miro Ronac Giannone, Stephen J. Arrowsmith, and Elizabeth A. Silber

MaxMagMod: A Web-Based Application for Next Largest Magnitude Forecasting in Enhanced Geothermal Systems 501
Sadegh Karimpouli, Tomasz Balawajder, Joanna Kocot, and Grzegorz Kwiatek

***PySolate*: A Python-Based Thresholding Tool to Denoise or Designal Seismic Waveforms Based on the Continuous Wavelet Transform** 514
Ana C. Aguiar, Andrea Chiang, and Stephen C. Myers

HypoNet Nankai: Rapid Hypocenter Determination Tool for the Nankai Trough Subduction Zone Using Physics-Informed Neural Networks 524
Ryoichiro Agata, Satoru Baba, Ayako Nakanishi, and Yasuyuki Nakamura

Parallel Seismic Data Processing Performance with Cloud-Based Storage 537
Sasmita Mohapatra, Weiming Yang, Zhengtang Yang, Chenxiao Wang, Jinxin Ma, Gary L. Pavlis, and Yinzhi Wang

Historical Seismologist

Reflections on a Trio of North American Earthquakes in 1925 548
Susan E. Hough, Maurice Lamontagne, John Ebel, and Laurie Baise

Early Macroseismic Intensity Observations, Isoseismal Maps, and Instrumental Recordings of Earthquakes in Mexico (1888–1934): A Review 564
Max Suter

Eduquakes

Introducing Novices to Active-Source Seismology via SeismicUnixGui 578
Juan M. Lorenzo, Mike Hubenthal, Nathan W. Benton, and Emilio E. Vera

Data Mine

LAB2022: A New Nodal Seismic Array Spanning the Los Angeles Basin 585
Fan-Chi Lin, Robert W. Clayton, Heather A. Ford, Amir Allam, Konstantinos Gkogkas, Valeria Villa, and HyeJeong Kim

Active and Passive Seismic Surveys over the Grounding Zone of Eastwind Glacier, Antarctica 591
Ronan S. Agnew, Emma Pearce, Marianne Karplus, Meghana Ranganathan, Andrew O. Hoffman, Madeline Hunt, Andrew Pretorius, Sooraj E. Shanly, Mitchel Beres, Kaushik K. Pradhan, Yeshey Seldon, Adam D. Booth, Roger A. Clark, and Tun Jan Young

Preliminary Analysis of Distributed Acoustic Sensing (DAS) Data Using a Submarine Fiber-Optic Cable Across the North Anatolian Fault 606
Ji Zhang, Aitaro Kato, Ahmet Anil Dindar, Wei Wang, Shigeki Nakagawa, Yosuke Aoki, Masanao Shinohara, Yoshiyuki Kaneda, and Süleyman Tunç

SSA News and Notes 616

Opinion

Are Short-Term Low-Probability Earthquake Forecasts Useful? An Emergency Management Perspective

James D. Goltz*[1]

The **M** 8.8 Kamchatka earthquake and tsunami of 29 July 2025 were preceded by 50 M_w 5.0+ earthquakes, 3 M_w 6.6 earthquakes, and an M_w 7.4 earthquake on 20 July 2025 (U.S. Geological Survey [USGS], 2025). This earthquake was the largest since the 11 March 2011 Great East Japan earthquake and tsunami which also had prominent foreshocks immediately prior to the **M** 9.1 event. These earthquakes once again raise the question of whether preshocks, particularly those in subduction zones should prompt a public alert about possible follow-on major tsunamigenic earthquakes. Some, perhaps most, scientists would say no, that the short-term probabilities are extremely low that any moderate-to-large foreshock or other seismic activity like slow-slip events, would justify social and economic interventions that could be both socially disruptive and financially costly. In a provocative set of articles that appeared in this journal in the middle of last decade, the pros and cons of operational earthquake forecasting (OEF) were debated (Jordan, 2013; Jordan *et al.*, 2014; Wang and Rogers, 2014; Goltz, 2015; Wang, 2015) and those who argued against such forecasts held that the only useful actions would be evacuations of vulnerable structures. They cautioned that such actions based on low-probability forecasts would be both disruptive and costly and thus unjustified, given the overwhelming likelihood that a large earthquake would not follow such a forecast, at least in a short-term time frame (Wang and Rogers, 2014). In this essay, I will argue that there are considerations that justify some limited interventions following possible precursory seismic activity that may or may not be considered operational forecasts.

In making this argument, perspective is important and I should identify myself as a social scientist and former emergency manager of a state-level earthquake, tsunami, and volcanic hazards program. This background carries with it certain considerations that shape my views regarding low-probability, high-consequence natural hazards. These considerations suggest that consequences as well as probability must be considered in any public policy. Furthermore, state and local governments share responsibility for seismic safety and, based on organizational culture, are inclined to have contingency plans for hazards, even those that are infrequent and for which there are no reliable prediction systems. In addition, from a social science perspective, perceptions, and beliefs, rooted in culture have implications for seismic safety policy that must be part of the conversation including how risk is defined and managed. Thus, in addition to considerations that are purely scientific—recurrence rates, fault modeling, subduction zone physics, and so forth—are societal factors that include risk perception, organizational cultures, and role obligations, and the beliefs and local understanding about hazards that may or may not align with those of scientists and public officials.

I think it appropriate to begin with consequences, which, in the context of this essay, constitutes the flip side of probabilities. Following the 2011 Great East Japan earthquake and tsunami, the Japanese government established an OEF system for the Nankai region. This region, consisting of 68 million people in 29 prefectures and 723 municipal governments, was defined as having in common an estimated 6+ shaking intensity on the Japanese Shindo scale based on the occurrence of an **M** 9 earthquake. A total of 139 of these municipalities are located on the Pacific Coast with vulnerability to tsunamis that would be generated by an **M** 9 event or multiple **M** 8s. The OEF system is scenario-driven and based on the occurrence of possible precursory seismic activity, an **M** 7 or a slow-slip event will trigger a notice from the Japan Meteorological Agency (JMA) entitled "Nankai Megathrust Attention" and an **M** 8 will cause a higher-level notice, a "Nankai Megathrust Alert" to be issued within the region. The decision to implement an OEF system was likely motivated by the occurrence in 1854 of two earthquakes of **M** 8.6, 32 hr apart and another set of **M** 8s in the Nankai trough in 1944 and 1946. Foreshocks and multiple slow-slip events preceded the **M** 9.1 earthquake in March 2011 that claimed the lives of 20,000 people. The current loss estimates for a recurrence of a great earthquake and tsunami in the Nankai trough include casualties that could approach 300,000. Most municipalities in the Nankai region have plans to respond to megathrust

1. Berkeley Seismological Lab, University of California, Berkeley, California, U.S.A., https://orcid.org/0000-0003-0723-3811 (JDG)

*Corresponding author: jamesgoltz_5@berkeley.edu

Cite this article as Goltz, J. D (2025). Are Short-Term Low-Probability Earthquake Forecasts Useful? An Emergency Management Perspective, *Seismol. Res. Lett.*, **97**, 1–3, doi: 10.1785/0220250273.

notifications from the JMA by recommending the evacuation of vulnerable populations (very elderly, persons with disabilities, and those unlikely to be able to exit tsunami inundation zones within 30 min) and mobilizing municipal staff with roles in disaster response. These limited measures are arguably consistent with a short-term (5–7 days) low-probability forecast, and though statistically low, may be significantly greater than levels of background seismicity in the Nankai region.

Communities that have experienced earthquakes and tsunamis over generations develop what social scientists refer to as “disaster subcultures.” (Wenger and Weller, 1973; Bankoff, 2017). Within these subcultures are embedded experiences and narratives that ascribe meaning to the natural hazards typical of a region as well as coping strategies. These coping strategies and historical memories may resonate with scientific understanding of hazards and official definitions of best practices for personal safety, or may be at variance with them. Consider, for example, the recommendation to drop, cover, and hold on during an earthquake. Recent research (Goltz *et al.*, 2020, 2024; Nakayachi *et al.*, 2024) suggests that few people have implemented this strategy during moderate and severe shaking and that the more salient actions are exiting buildings, remaining in place, and standing in doorways. There may also be popular understandings regarding the frequency of large earthquakes, the events that precede large events, damage scenarios, and means of coping with risk that may, or may not, be consistent with scientific understanding and official best practices.

The Pacific Northwest region of the United States and Canada is at risk of a major earthquake and tsunami posed by proximity to the Cascadia subduction zone (CSZ). During the last decade, the states of Washington, Oregon, and California, in cooperation with tribal nations, the Canadian province of British Columbia and the Federal Emergency Management Agency developed response plans for a major tsunamigenic earthquake in the CSZ (Federal Emergency Management Agency, 2022). These plans assumed a “no notice” major earthquake and tsunami, in other words, a major event and tsunami with no detectable foreshocks or seismic activity that might presage a major event, in the short-to-intermediate time frame. But, what if there is a “notice” in the form of potential foreshocks, swarms of earthquakes, or slow-slip events? An **M** 7–7.5 earthquake in the plate interface, for example, would be widely felt in the Pacific Northwest and people in the region would reasonably ask of scientists, what does this mean in terms of larger more dangerous events? Residents would undoubtedly turn to state, provincial, and local governments in the region and ask if plans have been implemented to keep them safe and informed of new developments as they emerge. Plans may call for partial activation of first responders, the possible evacuation of persons with disabilities or others who would be unable to evacuate quickly if a tsunami is generated, providing public information on preparedness, evacuation routes, household hazard mitigation, and other measures consistent with a low probability, but consequential hazard.

In response to skeptics of these measures, advocates of OEF have argued (Jordan *et al.*, 2014; Field *et al.*, 2016) that short-term low-probability forecasts, can be justified as an opportunity to emphasize the importance of individual, community, and regional earthquake preparedness in a compressed time frame when public attention is focused on the hazards associated with a large earthquake and tsunami. OEF advocates cite social science evidence that adverse societal responses like large-scale self-motivated evacuations from the region, unnecessary closures of schools, and businesses and rumor-induced social disruption occasioned by an alert are unlikely. However, more extreme social reactions are indeed more likely if the response by scientists and emergency managers to the occurrence of anomalous seismic activity in the CSZ is ad hoc, poorly coordinated and unplanned. And at this point, there are no plans that provide for a rapid assessment of seismic activity in the CSZ, nor is there a protocol for a coordinated pre-event response between scientists who monitor seismic activity in the CSZ and state and local governments in the region. Even if such a plan and protocol fell short of a full-scale scenario-driven OEF system such as that now in place in Japan, there should be a conversation about providing a rapid and coordinated risk assessment of potential precursors and scientifically sound public information regarding what is known and unknown about seismic activity that is either widely felt or is broadly discussed within the region.

Data and Resources

All data used in this article came from published sources listed in the references.

Declaration of Competing Interests

The author acknowledges that there are no conflicts of interest recorded.

Acknowledgments

The author would like to thank Chris Goldfinger, Lori Dengler, Richard Allen and a reviewer selected by *SRL* for helpful comments on the original draft of this article.

References

Bankoff, G. (2017). Living with hazard: disaster subcultures, disaster cultures and risk-mitigating strategies, in *Historical Disaster Experiences. Transcultural Research—Heidelberg Studies on Asia and Europe in a Global Context*, G. Schenk (Editor), Springer, Cham, doi: 10.1007/978-3-319-49163-9_2.

Federal Emergency Management Agency (2022). Region 10 Cascadia subduction zone (CSZ) earthquake and tsunami plan, Bothell, Washington.

Field, E. H., T. H. Jordan, L. M. Jones, A. J. Michael, and M. L. Blanpied (2016). The potential uses of operational earthquake forecasting, *Seismol. Res. Lett.* **87,** no. 2A, 313–322.

Goltz, J. D. (2015). A further note on operational earthquake forecasting: An emergency management perspective, *Seismol. Res. Lett.* **86,** no. 5, 1231–233.

Goltz, J. D., H. Park, G. Nakano, and K. Yamori (2020). Earthquake ground motion and human behavior: Using DYFI data to assess behavioral response to earthquakes, *Earthq. Spectra* doi: 10.1177/8755293019899958.

Goltz, J. D., D. J. Wald, S. K. McBride, E. Reddy, V. Quitoriano, and J. Saunders (2024). The Ojai California earthquake of August 20, 2023: Earthquake early warning performance and alert recipient response in the M5.1 event, *Seismol. Res. Lett.* doi: 10.1785/0220240023.

Jordan, T. H. (2013). Lessons of L'Aquila for operational earthquake forecasting, *Seismol. Res. Lett.* **84,** no. 1, doi: 10.1785/0220120167.

Jordan, T. H., W. Marzocchi, A. J. Michael, and M. C. Gerstenberger (2014). Operational earthquake forecasting can enhance earthquake preparedness, *Seismol. Res. Lett.* **85,** no. 5, 955–959.

Nakayachi, K., R. Yokoi, and J. Goltz (2024). Human behavioral response to earthquake early warnings (EEW): Are alerts received on mobile phones inhibiting protective actions? *Int. J. Disaster Risk Reduct.* **105,** 104,401, doi: 10.1016/j.ijdrr.2024.104401.

U.S. Geological Survey (USGS) (2025). M 8.8-2025 Kamchatka Peninsula, Russia earthquake, available at https://earthquake.usgs.gov/earthquakes/eventpage/us6000qw60/executive (last accessed August 2025).

Wang, Z. (2015). Predicting or forecasting earthquakes and the resulting ground-motion hazards: A dilemma for earth scientists, *Seismol. Res. Lett.* **86,** no. 1, 1–5.

Wang, K., and G. C. Rogers (2014). Earthquake preparedness should not fluctuate on a daily or weekly basis, *Seismol. Res. Lett.* **85,** 569–571.

Wenger, D., and J. Weller (1973). Disaster subcultures: The residue of community disasters, The Disaster Research Center, University of Delaware, Preliminary Paper #9, Newark, Delaware.

Manuscript received 20 August 2025
Published online 20 October 2025

Coseismic and Postseismic Displacements of the 2024 M_w 7.0 Wushi, China, Earthquake Observed from SAR Images

Xing Li[1], Jihong Liu[2], Shuai Wang[3], Nan Fang[4], Meng Duan[*5], and Alexandros Savvaidis[1]

Abstract

On 23 January 2024, a magnitude (M_w) 7.0 earthquake struck Wushi County (China) in the southwestern Tian Shan orogen. Both Sentinel-1 and Advanced Land Observation Satellite-2 radar images were used to obtain coseismic displacements with interferometry and pixel offset-tracking techniques. We calculated coseismic 3D displacements with a prevailing strain model and variance component estimation method and then inverted the source model of this earthquake. The results reveal a high-angle (58°) thrust fault with a significant strike-slip component. The maximum slip of 3.3 m is concentrated at 13 km depth, and the estimated seismic moment is 4.01×10^{19} N·m, equivalent to an M_w 7.04 event. The postseismic slip inverted from 10-month Interferometric Synthetic Aperture Radar displacements exhibits a spatial pattern complementary to the coseismic slip, suggesting that the coseismic rupture was likely inhibited by rate-strengthening zones. Integrated analysis of inter-, co-, and postseismic geodetic data further reinforces the evidence that the southwestern Tian Shan region is characterized by slip partitioning, with ongoing compression and left-lateral motion in the intermontane areas.

Cite this article as Li, X., J. Liu, S. Wang, N. Fang, M. Duan, and A. Savvaidis (2025). Coseismic and Postseismic Displacements of the 2024 M_w 7.0 Wushi, China, Earthquake Observed from SAR Images, *Seismol. Res. Lett.* **97**, 4–14, doi: 10.1785/0220250062.

Supplemental Material

Introduction

The Tian Shan Mountain, a reactivated orogenic belt triggered by the Cenozoic India–Eurasia collision, stretches ~2500 km from east to west and measures 250–350 km in width from north to south (Molnar and Tapponnier, 1975; Tapponnier and Molnar, 1979). This region has undergone profound crustal shortening and thickening and has a history of strong and large earthquakes, including several events with moment magnitudes >7.0 (Mellors *et al.*, 1997; Molnar and Ghose, 2000; Delvaux *et al.*, 2001; Crosby *et al.*, 2007). The southwestern Tian Shan stands out as one of the most active zones in central Asia, characterized by well-developed active faults and intense seismicity (Nelson *et al.*, 1987; Yin *et al.*, 1998; Allen *et al.*, 1999; Burchfiel *et al.*, 1999; Sloan *et al.*, 2011). The north–south convergence is estimated to be ~20 mm/yr across the southwestern Tian Shan from geodetic observations (Abdrakhmatov *et al.*, 1996; Yang *et al.*, 2008; Zubovich *et al.*, 2010; Zheng *et al.*, 2017; Wang and Shen, 2020). Apart from the pervasive foreland folds-and-thrust belts between the mountain front and the Tarim basin, a series of east–northeast-trending faults, including the Kemin–Chilik fault (KCF), the Nalati fault (NLTF), and the Maidan fault (MDF), are well developed within the interior mountain range (Fig. 1). The interior of the range has witnessed several historical earthquakes, marked by oblique thrusting with substantial strike-slip components. Notable examples include the 1889 M_s 8.3 Chilik earthquake and the 1911 M_s 8.2 Kemin earthquake along the KCF (Delvaux *et al.*, 2001; Abdrakhmatov *et al.*, 2016). The seismic activity along the MDF zone was relatively weak in the past century (Sloan *et al.*, 2011; Wu *et al.*, 2019). Nevertheless, earlier studies based on paleoearthquakes suggest that the MDF is active with a late Quaternary crustal shortening rate of ~1.1 mm/yr and a sinistral-slip rate of ~1.5 mm/yr (Wu *et al.*, 2019). These findings align closely with geodetic observations that reveal a similar shortening rate of 1–2 mm/yr and sinistral-slip rate of 1.8–3.5 mm/yr. (Li *et al.*, 2022; Qiu *et al.*, 2022; Wu *et al.*, 2023; Wang *et al.*, 2024). Because it is capable of storing significant elastic energy, the MDF remains a potential site for large earthquakes.

On 23 January 2024, an M_w 7.0 earthquake struck Wushi County in Aksu Prefecture, Xinjiang Uygur autonomous

1. Bureau of Economic Geology, The University of Texas at Austin, Austin, Texas, U.S.A., https://orcid.org/0000-0002-4018-8920 (XL); https://orcid.org/0000-0001-6373-5256 (AS); 2. King Abdullah University of Science and Technology (KAUST), Thuwal, Saudi Arabia, https://orcid.org/0000-0003-1528-3771 (JL); 3. School of Geomatics Science and Technology, Nanjing Tech University, Nanjing, China; 4. School of Geoscience and Info-Physics, Central South University, Changsha, China, https://orcid.org/0000-0001-6461-7219 (NF); 5. College of Advanced Interdisciplinary Studies, Central South University of Forestry and Technology, Changsha, China

*Corresponding author: T20222604@csuft.edu.cn

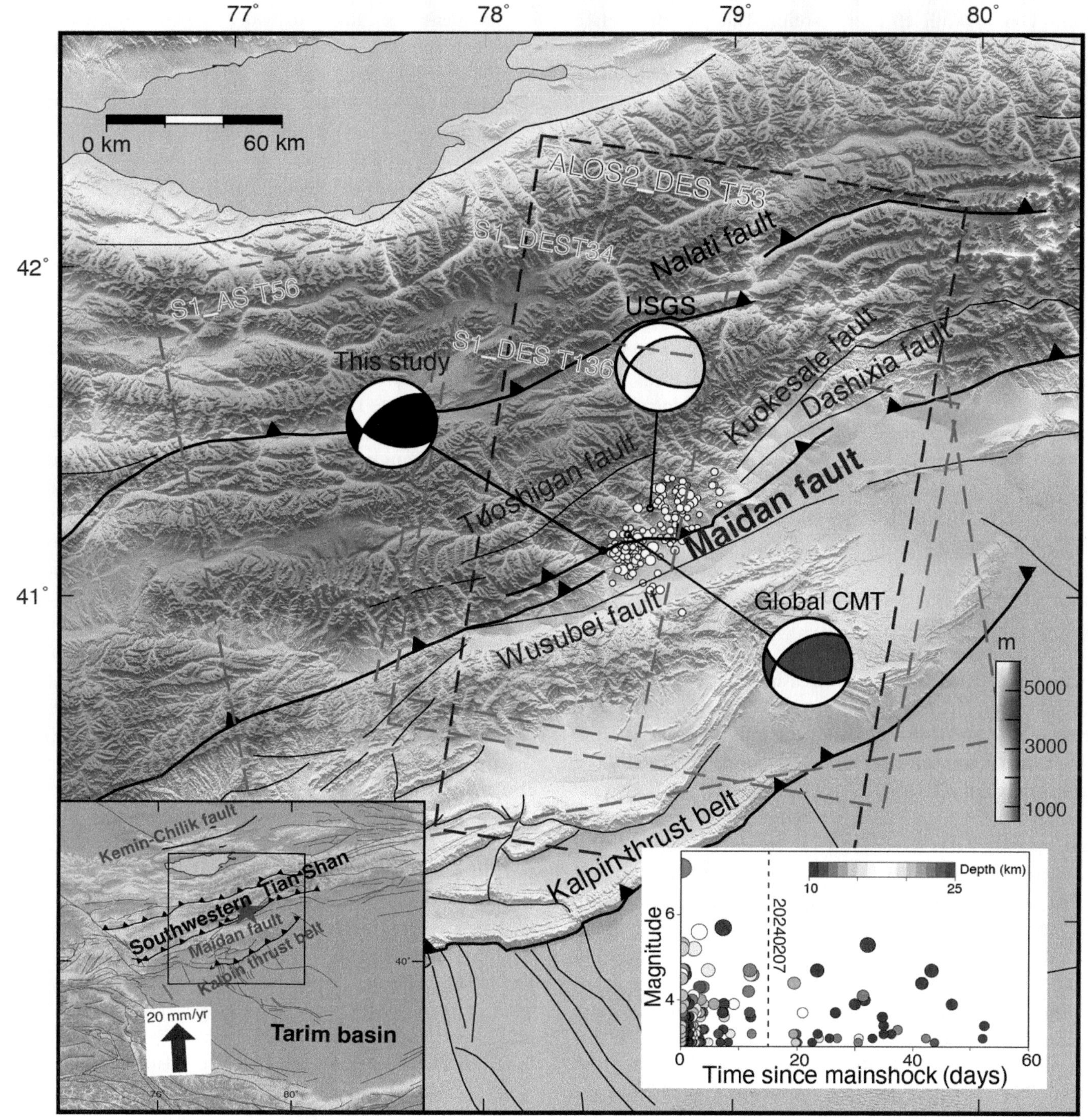

region, China. This earthquake was the most significant earthquake around the Tian Shan orogen in the past 40 yr. Field investigations unveiled limited ground-surface ruptures (Zhang *et al.*, 2024). During the two months after the earthquake, >160 aftershocks were recorded, including seven M_w > 5 events, as reported by the China Earthquake Networks Center. The focal mechanisms from the U.S. Geological Survey (USGS) and Global Centroid Moment Tensor (Global CMT) solutions indicate that the main M_w 7.0 event occurred on a north-northeast–south-southwest fault plane, with a minimal non–double-couple component and characterized by thrust

Figure 1. Tectonic setting of the 2024 Wushi earthquake. The dashed rectangles depict the footprint of Synthetic Aperture Radar (SAR) data used in this study. The focal mechanism plots represent the focal mechanisms and epicenter locations from the U.S. Geological Survey (USGS) (yellow), Global Centroid Moment Tensor (Global CMT) (red), and this study (black). The white circles indicate aftershocks recorded by the China Earthquake Networks Center (CENC) following 60 days after the mainshock. The lower-left panel shows the study area outlined by the black rectangle, and the lower-right panel illustrates the temporal evolution of the recorded aftershocks, with colors indicating their focal depths. ALOS2, Advanced Land Observation Satellite; S1, Sentinel-1. The color version of this figure is available only in the electronic edition.

faulting coupled with left-lateral motion. This event took place in the intermontane region, close to the MDF in space, distinguishing itself from the majority of large earthquakes ($M_w > 7.0$) that have typically occurred along the southern foreland fold-and-thrust belt. The Kalpin thrust belt, ~80–100 km to the south of the MDF (Fig. 1), is considered to be more active than the MDF because the former is situated within the foreland basin of southwestern Tian Shan, but the latter is the intermontane basement-rooted fault. As the first strong intermontane earthquake around Tian Shan with good co- and postseismic geodetic observations, this Wushi earthquake has the potential to provide insights into the tectonic activities and seismic hazards in the intermontane region of southwestern Tian Shan.

To better understand the fault geometry and kinematics of the 2024 Wushi earthquake, we use high-resolution satellite Synthetic Aperture Radar (SAR) images to measure the coseismic 3D surface displacements and as the postseismic displacements, which are then used to constrain and interpret the fault location, geometry, and slip distribution of this event. Combining analysis with these geodetic data provides insights about the rupture behavior of this Wushi earthquake and the regional seismogenic structure in the southwestern Tian Shan. Although previous studies have analyzed the coseismic deformation pattern using Differential Interferometric SAR (DInSAR) displacements (Ding *et al.*, 2024; Qiu *et al.*, 2024; Zhao *et al.*, 2024), this study incorporates Advanced Land Observation Satellite (ALOS)-2 data and the pixel-offset tracking method (POT) to complement the widely used Sentinel-1 dataset, enhancing the optimization of the surface fault trace and slip model. In addition, we examine the 10-month postseismic deformation following the earthquake, providing valuable insights to deepen our understanding of regional tectonics.

Data and Methods

We use both Sentinel-1 and ALOS-2 satellite SAR images (Table S1, available in the supplemental material to this article) to generate coseismic ground displacements of the 2024 Wushi earthquake. The ascending Sentinel-1 and descending Sentinel-1 (T34) SAR images were freely acquired three days after the earthquake, but the descending image can only cover part of the earthquake. Hence, we additionally collect descending ALOS-2 images to derive the complete displacement field of this earthquake. Another descending Sentinel-1 image (T136) was not available until 25 February 2024, which would suffer more decorrelation noises and include more postseismic displacements. We process the SAR images with GAMMA software using a 30 m digital elevation model (DEM) to remove the phase of topography and to assist the image coregistration. The interferograms are multilooked to about $50 \times 50\ m^2$. Here, the DInSAR, POT and burst-overlap interferometry (BOI) methods are used to process the SAR images. DInSAR-derived displacements are limited to two distinct geometries, that is, ascending and descending line-of-sight (LoS) directions. POT and BOI methods can obtain displacement observations along the satellite azimuth direction, which effectively compensates for the absence of north–south displacement information in DInSAR LoS observations. Although BOI-derived azimuth observations are only available in the burst overlaps of Sentinel-1 SAR data, they play a crucial role in constraining 3D displacements when other azimuth observations are unavailable (Grandin *et al.*, 2016; Li *et al.*, 2021; Ma *et al.*, 2022).

Figure 2 shows the coseismic displacement observations in four different viewing geometries based on the three aforementioned data processing methods. We have identified asymmetric displacement distributions in both ascending and descending orbits, extending ~110 km along the north-northeast–south-southwest direction. The pronounced disparity between displacements from ascending and descending orbits suggests a considerable amount of horizontal motion associated with the 2024 Wushi earthquake. Although we try to unwrap all DInSAR interferograms from the four pairs of SAR images, the two descending Sentinel-1 DInSAR displacements (Fig. 2h,l) have serious unwrapping errors because of interferometric fringes that are too dense. In general, displacement observations with similar geometry but from different SAR data and different methods are consistent with each other. The POT amplitude-based displacements have higher-level noises than the DInSAR xand BOI phase-based results, and the high spatial resolution dimension of the pixel corresponds to the POT-obtained displacement with high accuracy. The BOI displacement is limited within the burst overlaps but is still capable of revealing a displacement pattern with opposite directions across the fault. However, the BOI displacement of descending T34 (Fig. 2k) shows localized signals near the fault, which may be due to aftershocks or other undistinguished errors. Given that two descending Sentinel-1 obtained displacements have either a long time span or incomplete coverage, only the descending ALOS-2 and ascending Sentinel-1 displacements (Fig. 2a,c–f) are combined to calculate the coseismic 3D displacements.

Coseismic 3D surface displacements provide an intuitional view for the kinematics interpretation of earthquakes (Wang and Jónsson, 2015; Gan *et al.*, 2018; Xu *et al.*, 2020) and provide stronger constraint for the distributed slip inversion than original SAR-based observations (Text S1). In this study, we used the strain model and variance component estimation (SM-VCE) method to calculate 3D displacements of the Wushi earthquake based on SAR displacement observations (Liu *et al.*, 2018, 2022). Typically, 3D displacements are computed at a target point using a weighted least-squares (WLS) method, in which weights are determined from far-field observations or from the standard deviation of observations in a 5×5 pixel window around the target point (Hu *et al.*, 2012). However, this traditional approach ignores the correlation between ground surface displacements at

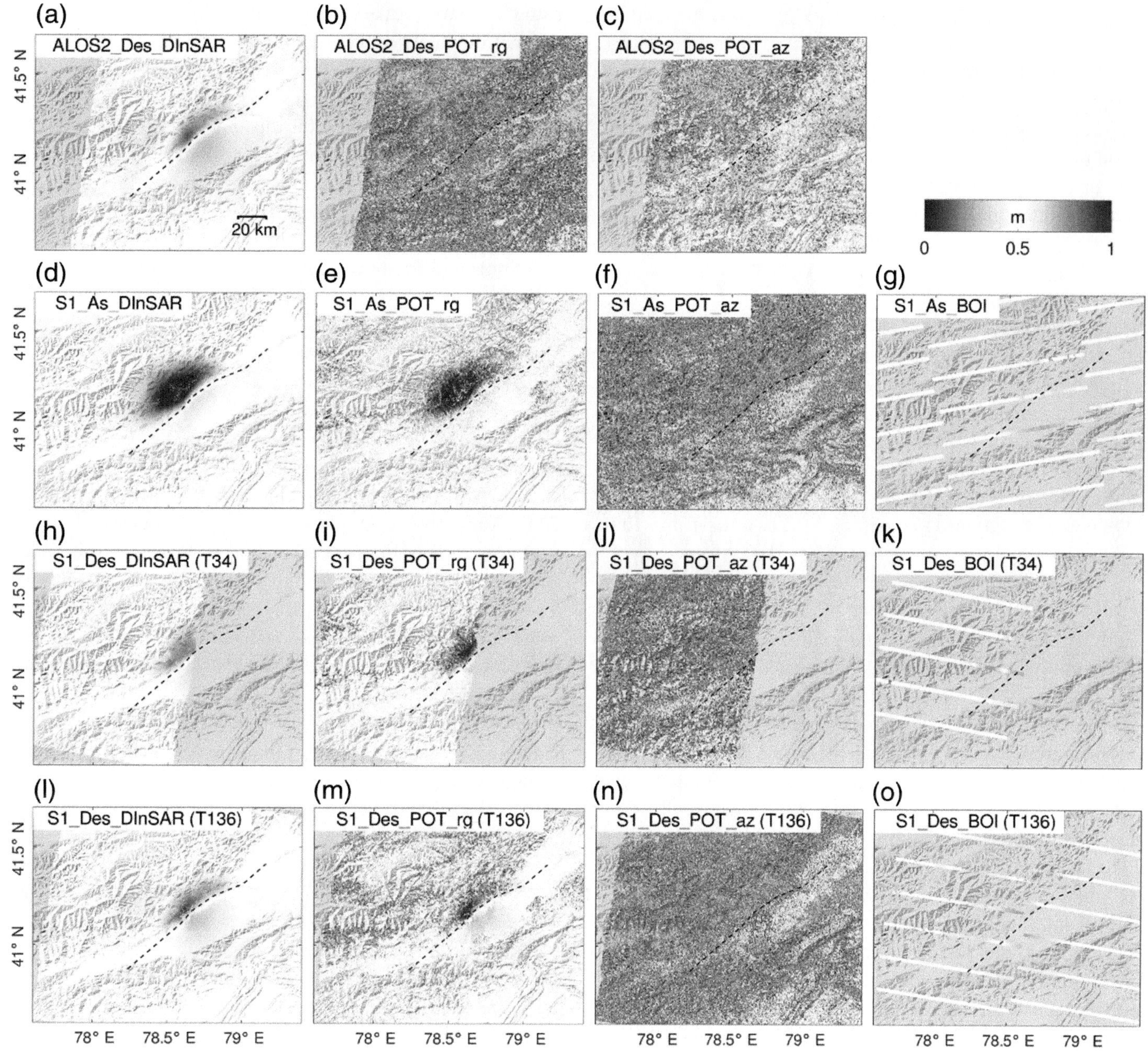

Figure 2. Coseismic displacement observations obtained from (a–c,h–o) descending (Des) and (d–g) ascending (As) S1 and ALOS-2 SAR data based on Differential Interferometric SAR (DInSAR), pixel-offset tracking (POT), and burst-overlap interferometry (BOI) methods. The dashed black line in each panel shows the surface fault trace used in this study. az, azimuth direction; rg, range direction. The color version of this figure is available only in the electronic edition.

adjacent points and cannot determine the weight of different observations accurately. The SM-VCE method addresses these issues using the strain model to represent the correlation between adjacent points' displacements (Guglielmino *et al.*, 2011) and using the VCE algorithm to determine the weight in an iterative posterior way (Hu and Xiao, 2016). The SM-VCE method has been proven to be superior to the WLS method in calculating 3D displacements, and the relevant MATLAB code can be freely accessed online (Liu *et al.*, 2022). One key parameter required to be set is the window size of using the SM to represent the spatial correlation of adjacent point displacements. Based on the noise level of POT observations and the spatial range of this earthquake, the window size of 41×41 pixels ($\sim 2 \times 2$ km^2) is used in this study.

To map the evolutions of the postseismic deformation and potential postseismic slip, we process ascending (T56) and descending (T34 and T136) Sentinel-1 SAR images in 10 months after the earthquake. The SIGMA (Liu *et al.*, 2021) and DetrendInSAR (Liu *et al.*, 2024) methods are used to derive the postseismic InSAR displacement time series. The SIGMA method extracts the InSAR phase time series from wrapped interferograms using an iterative WLS algorithm combined with an SM, effectively suppressing decorrelation noise. Subsequently, the DetrendInSAR method models and corrects atmospheric delays in the phase time series to produce the final InSAR displacement time series. These two advanced techniques ensure the accuracy and reliability of our InSAR displacement results.

Slip Model Inversion

The 3D coseismic displacement datasets were first downsampled using the quadtree algorithm (Jónsson *et al.*, 2002). The fault geometry inversion for the causative fault of the 2024 Wushi earthquake is performed by assuming elastic dislocations in a homogeneous linear elastic half-space (Okada, 1985). The inversion process is constrained by a total of 3299 points, including 1104 vertical, 1104 east–west, and 1091 north–south displacement points.

First, we used the Geodetic Bayesian Inversion Software (GBIS) for the nonlinear search of spatial position, length, width, strike, and dip angles of a uniform-slip fault to determine the geometry of the seismogenic fault (Bagnardi and Hooper, 2018; Wen *et al.*, 2021). Based on the InSAR coseismic displacement information presented in Figure 2, the magnitude of the displacement on the northern side of the fault exceeds that on the southern side; thus, we determine that the causative fault dips in the northwest direction. Accordingly, the search ranges for fault strike are set between 20° and 80°, dip between 40° and 89°, length between 6 and 65 km, width between 5 and 20 km, and depth between 5 and 15 km. Subsequently, by randomly generating 106 sets of samplings, the Monte Carlo method is used to estimate the uncertainty of fault geometric parameters. The results indicate that under the constraint of uniform slip, the seismogenic fault is 35×10.8 km^2 at a depth of 8 km. The strike is 229°, and the dip is 63°. The joint probability distribution of different parameters from the GBIS is shown in Figure S1, and the downsampled 3D displacement observations, predictions, and residuals are shown in Figure S2.

After we obtained the optimal geometric parameters of the causative fault, we inverted for the distributed slip model (both strike slip and dip slip) using the nonnegative least-square method. By extending the GBIS-obtained underground fault patch to the ground surface, it can be observed that the fault line is generally in line with the displacement boundary (Fig. S2). However, in some local near-fault areas, there are significant residuals of the modeled 3D displacements. Therefore, we manually selected the surface fault line based on the GBIS-obtained parameters, 3D displacements, and geomorphology (Figs. S2 and S3) and then used it to construct the fault plane of the distributed slip model. The final fault plane is ~90 km along the fault strike and 40 km in depth. To obtain the optimal dip angle of this new fault under the distributed slip model, we used the grid-search method for the dip angle between −50° and −70° with a search step of 1°, and the minimum residual is achieved at the dip angle of −58° (Fig. S4). The smoothing condition is realized by minimizing the difference between the slip value of the target patch and the mean slip value of its surrounding patches, and the smoothing factor of 6.31 is determined based on the trade-off between the slip roughness and the observation misfit (Fig. S5).

Results and Discussions

Coseismic 3D displacements and slip model

Figure 3a–c presents the coseismic 3D displacements obtained from the SM-VCE method by combining Sentinel-1 and ALOS-2 DInSAR and POT observations. The overall pattern is consistent with the focal mechanism of thrust faulting coupled with left-lateral slip reported by USGS and Global CMT. More obvious displacement signals are observed in the northwest side of the fault compared with the southeast side, which is expected with the fault plane dipping to the northwest. The vertical displacement, with uplift as large as 0.65 m, is more dominant than the east–west and north–south displacement components, whereas the largest horizontal displacement is ~0.43 m.

The coseismic slip distribution for the earthquake is shown in Figure 3d. The results indicate that the coseismic slip did not rupture to the Earth's surface, and the primary slip zone is $\sim 40 \times 20$ km^2, with the predominant slip occurring in a depth range of 10–18 km. At the depth of 13 km, the maximum slip reaches 3.3 m, resulting in a seismic moment release of 4.01×10^{19} N · m, equivalent to an M_w 7.04 event. The downsampled 3D displacement observations, simulations, and residuals are shown in Figure S7. The root mean square (rms) value of residuals for the vertical, east–west, and north–south components are 1.5, 1.5, and 4.3 cm, respectively. The larger rms value for the north–south component is due to the large uncertainty of POT-obtained displacements along the azimuth direction (i.e., approximately the north–south direction). Nevertheless, the rms values for both vertical and east–west components are much smaller compared with the magnitude of observations.

Based on the distributed slip model, we derived the focal mechanism as shown in Figure 1. Notably, the double-couple component accounts for 97% of the moment tensor. This simplicity suggests that the seismogenic fault exhibits minimal complexity in its slip pattern and interactions with adjacent faults, in contrast to other large earthquakes characterized by complex fault geometries and rupture processes (Zhang *et al.*, 2009; Wang *et al.*, 2018).

Postseismic displacements and slip model

We investigate 10-month postseismic displacements following the Wushi earthquake with Sentinel-1 SAR data. Given that

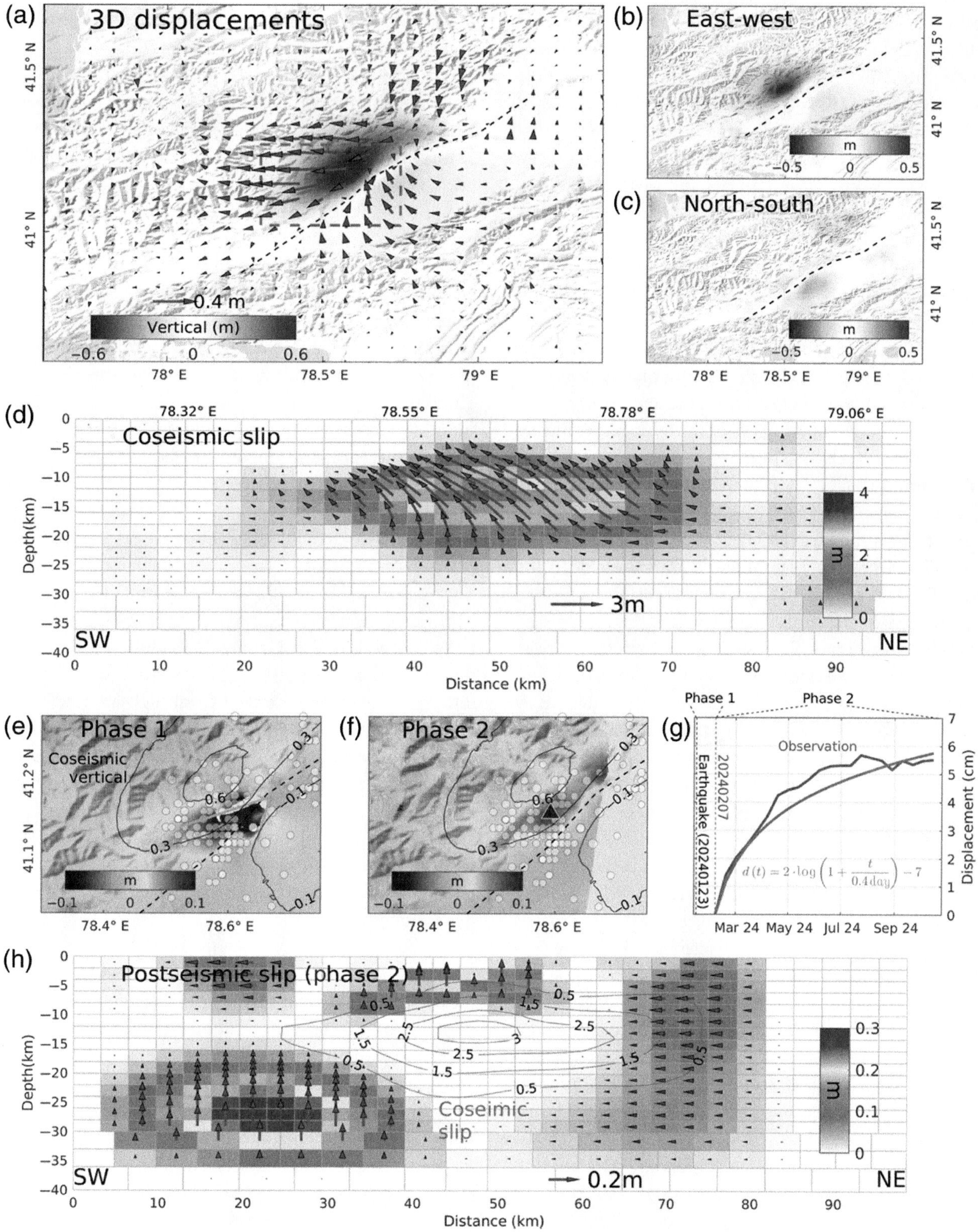

Figure 3. (a–c) Coseismic 3D displacements and (d) the slip model of the 2024 Wushi earthquake. In (a), the arrow and the color represent the downsampled horizontal displacement and the vertical displacement, respectively. The dashed red rectangle outlines the range of (e,f). In (d), the arrow and the color represent the slip vector and slip magnitude for each patch, respectively. The strike-slip and dip-slip components are shown in Figure S6. (e,f) Postseismic displacement field in the periods of 2024/01/26–2024/02/07 (phase 1) and 2024/02/07–2024/10/16 (phase 2), respectively (yyyy/mm/dd). (e) The ascending line-of-sight (LoS) displacement. (f) Quasi-vertical displacements by averaging ascending and descending observations to increase the signal-to-noise ratio. (g) Quasi-vertical displacement time series at the blue triangle in panel (f). The white circles are aftershocks from CENC (see Data and Resources). (h) The postseismic slip model. The color version of this figure is available only in the electronic edition.

there are dense and strong aftershocks during the span time (2024/01/26–2024/02/07, yyyy/mm/dd, phase 1) of the first postseismic interferogram, we processed the first postseismic interferogram of tracks T56 and T34 with the standard DInSAR workflow (Fig. S8) and obtained the afterward displacements (2024/02/07–2024/10/16, phase 2) with the time-series methods as described in the Data and Methods section. We use the same method mentioned in Section 2.4 and invert the postseismic slip model. During phase 1 (2024/01/26–2024/02/07) (Fig. 3e, Figs. S8–S10), the displacement occurred mainly near the mainshock's epicenter but involved different seismogenic faults (yellow lines in Fig. 3e) from those in the coseismic rupture (dashed black line in Fig. 3). This deformation signal was dominated by slip on the minor faults (Figs. S8–S10), although minor contributions from the main fault cannot be entirely ruled out. Notably, ~80% of the aftershocks during the first two months, including four $M_w > 5.0$ events, occurred during this period (Fig. 1), and the displacement magnitude reached 30 cm (Fig. 3e).

In contrast, during phase 2 (Fig. 3f,g, 2024/02/07–2024/10/16), the observed displacements were more likely nucleated on the coseismic fault plane because the inverted slip on the coseismic fault can well explain the surface displacement (Figs. S11–S12). The spatial characteristics of displacement are temporally consistent (Figs. S13–S15), and the temporal feature of the deformation (Fig. 3g) aligns with the commonly observed logarithmic decay process ($d = \alpha \times \log(1 + t/\tau) + \beta$, in which α is the scaling factor, t is the measurement time from the earthquake occurrence, τ is the decay time, and β is the offset of the fitted curve). Compared with the postseismic creep decay processes of large strike-slip faults documented in previous studies (Zhao *et al.*, 2021; Xiong *et al.*, 2022), the logarithmic decay time τ for the postseismic deformation of this thrust fault is only 0.4 ± 14 days, indicating a much faster postseismic creep relaxation process. Given that the temporal deformation reference for phase 2 is 2024/02/07, the estimated offset $\beta = -7$ cm indicates that the postseismic displacement during the first two weeks (2024/01/23–2024/02/07) can reach 7 cm. Although the deformation caused by aftershocks during phase 1 obscures the 7 cm postseismic displacement signal from the corresponding period, the aftershock, with surface displacements of up to 0.3 m (Fig. 3e) during phase 1, can also be interpreted as evidence of the rapid postseismic relaxation process. During phase 2, spanning nine months, the maximum vertical displacement reached ~6 cm. Although the magnitude of deformation during phase 2 is smaller than that in phase 1, the spatial extent of deformation in phase 2 is significantly larger. Inversion of the slip model further confirms that the energy released during phase 2 (4.62×10^{18} N · m, Fig. S12) is about an order of magnitude greater than that released during phase 1 (7.95×10^{17} N · m, Fig. S10). Our results demonstrate that afterslip remains the dominant relaxation mechanism following this earthquake. Aftershocks are primarily driven by afterslip, as evidenced by their alignment with regions of elevated Coulomb stress changes (Fig. S16b), consistent with observations from other earthquakes (Guo *et al.*, 2025).

The phase 2 postseismic slip model reveals a strong spatial complementarity between the postseismic and coseismic slip areas, with postseismic slip zones closely aligning with regions of increased Coulomb stress (Fig. S16). Notably, the postseismic slip model exhibits distinct separation between strike-slip and dip-slip components (Fig. S12), a phenomenon rarely observed in previous postseismic slip models. The combined analysis of coseismic and postseismic slip models reveals that postseismic slip fills coseismic slip gaps while maintaining consistent slip directions throughout the fault plane. In this context, postseismic slip zones act as a complement to coseismic slip rather than resulting from distinct tectonic processes. These findings suggest that the postseismic slip regions correspond to rate-strengthening zones, which likely inhibited further rupture propagation during the coseismic phase. Rate-strengthening zones, characterized by increased frictional resistance with higher sliding velocities, exhibit stable, aseismic slip, effectively acting as strength barriers that limit dynamic rupture propagation (Guo *et al.*, 2020; Zheng *et al.*, 2024). This behavior is significant for seismic hazard assessment because it relaxes stress aseismically, reducing the seismic potential within these zones. In addition, these identified rate-strengthening zones align well with the distribution of interseismic coupling derived from high-accuracy, high-resolution InSAR interseismic displacement data (Wang *et al.*, 2024), further validating our conclusions. Our study advances the understanding of the Wushi earthquake through a higher-resolution 3D slip model, integration of postseismic processes, and refined Coulomb stress changes analyses, yet it also aligns with prior work (Yu *et al.*, 2024; Famiglietti *et al.*, 2025), providing a more comprehensive view of the earthquake's dynamics.

Slip partitioning in southwestern Tian Shan

Strike-slip faulting and slip partitioning represent crucial components of crustal deformation in the Tian Shan region (Molnar and Tapponnier, 1975; Tapponnier and Molnar, 1979; Wu *et al.*, 2023); however, they were paid less attention than the north–south compression. To address the questions regarding how deformation is distributed and accommodated in Tian Shan, we used the latest Global Navigation Satellite Systems data (Fig. 4b) to calculate the principal strain rate and maximum shear strain rate (Shen *et al.*, 2015; Cai *et al.*, 2024). The compression strain rate in the southwestern Tian Shan is ~30 nstrain/yr. However, moving to the eastern Tian Shan, the compression strain decreases to <10 nstrain/yr. The overall deformation of the Tian Shan orogen exhibits a spatial distribution pattern of strengthening in the west and weakening in the east (Fig. 4a). The eastward shortening reduction (Avouac *et al.*, 1993; Wang and Shen, 2020) suggests the oblique thrusting between the Tarim basin and the Tian Shan

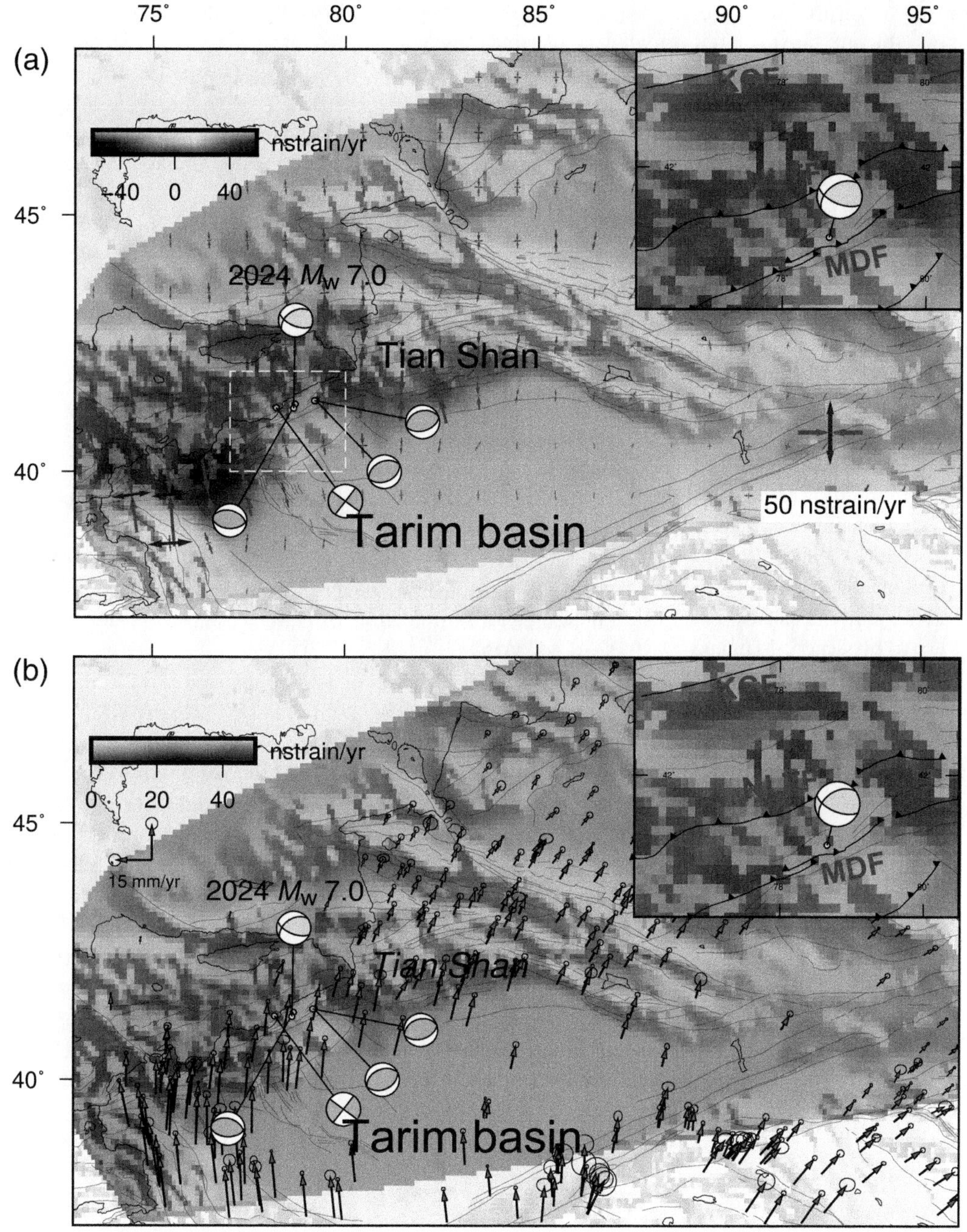

Figure 4. Global Navigation Satellite Systems (GNSS)–derived strain rate maps. (a) The principal strain rate is shown by arrows; red arrows indicate compression, and blue arrows indicate extension. The shaded color denotes the dilatation rate. The gray focal mechanism plots represent the focal mechanisms of historical events from 1969 to 2009 (Sloan *et al.*, 2011). (b) The arrows indicate GNSS velocities from Wang and Shen (2020), and the shaded color denotes the maximum shear strain rate. The upper right plots (the white rectangle in panel a) show the details of strain rates along the Kemin–Chilik fault (KCF), Maidan fault (MDF), and Nalati fault (NLTF). The color version of this figure is available only in the electronic edition.

and the clockwise rotation of the Tarim basin, which contribute to the observed strike slip within the Tian Shan orogen. The maximum shear-strain rate (Fig. 4b) indicates that the lateral motion should be significant around the southwest Tian Shan orogen, particularly along major inherited high-angle thrust faults (e.g., the MDF, NLTF, and KCF) (Wu *et al.*, 2014, 2019) where significant historical events have occurred (Thompson *et al.*, 2002; Wu *et al.*, 2019). Besides, analysis of historical $M_w > 5.0$ events (Fig. 4a,b, Table S3) also reveals that the pattern consists of both compression and left-lateral motion within the vicinity of the MDF (Sloan *et al.*, 2011). Furthermore, the co- and postseismic slip we derived for the 2024 Wushi earthquake also demonstrates a combination of compressional and lateral components. In summary, these inter-, co-, and postseismic displacements strengthen the indication that the southwestern Tian Shan is characterized by slip partitioning with ongoing compression and left-lateral motion in the intermontane region.

Conclusions

The 2024 Wushi earthquake represents the most significant seismic event around the Tian Shan orogen in the past 40 yr. This study obtained the coseismic 3D displacements associated with the Wushi earthquake by leveraging SAR images from both C-band Sentinel-1 and L-band ALOS-2 satellites based on a prevailing SM-VCE method. The vertical displacement as large as 0.65 m uplift is more dominant than the east–west and north–south displacement components, and the largest horizontal displacement is ~0.43 m. The slip model inverted from the 3D displacements reveals that the focal mechanism is characterized by high-angle (58°) thrust faulting with comparable left-lateral motion, with the maximum slip reaching 3.3 m at 13 km depth. The 10-month postseismic displacements reveal that the afterslip persisted for a short period after the earthquake. The complementary pattern of the coseismic and postseismic slip model indicates that rate-strengthening zones likely contributed to halting the coseismic rupture. Interseismic GNSS observations reveal that the oblique thrusting between the Tarim basin and Tian Shan results in significant north–south compression coupled with a left-lateral strike-slip component in the southwestern Tian Shan. Combined analysis on these geodetic observations demonstrates that the 2024 Wushi earthquake directly reflects partitioned fault behavior in the southwestern Tian Shan.

Data and Resources

The raw Sentinel-1 and Advanced Land Observation Satellite-2 data were downloaded from the Alaska Satellite Facility (https://vertex.daac.asf.alaska.edu, last accessed March 2024) and Japan Aerospace Exploration Agency (JAXA) (https://gportal.jaxa.jp/gpr/index, last accessed February 2024), respectively. The aftershocks were obtained from the China Earthquake Networks Center (https://data.earthquake.cn, last accessed May 2024). The Global Navigation Satellite Systems (GNSS) data used in this article came from published sources listed in the references. Data postprocessing was performed using MATLAB (MathWorks, Inc., https://www.mathworks.com/products/matlab, last accessed February 2025). All figures were drawn by Generic Mapping Tools (Wessel *et al.*, 2013). The supplemental material includes three tables and 18 figures that supplement the main article.

Declaration of Competing Interests

The authors acknowledge that there are no conflicts of interest recorded.

Acknowledgments

The Sentinel-1 and Advanced Land Observation Satellite (ALOS)-2 data were provided by the Alaska Satellite Facility and Japan Aerospace Exploration Agency, respectively. This work was supported by the National Natural Science Foundation of China under Grant 42404051 and University of Texas at Austin by Grant 201503664. The authors thank the editor and two anonymous reviewers for their insightful feedback.

References

Abdrakhmatov, K. E., R. T. Walker, G. E. Campbell, A. S. Carr, A. Elliott, C. Hillemann, J. Hollingsworth, A. Landgraf, D. Mackenzie, A. Mukambayev, *et al.* (2016). Multisegment rupture in the 11 July 1889 Chilik earthquake (M_w 8.0–8.3), Kazakh Tien Shan, interpreted from remote sensing, field survey, and paleoseismic trenching, *J. Geophys. Res.* **121,** 4615–4640.

Abdrakhmatov, K. Y., S. A. Aldazhanov, B. H. Hager, M. W. Hamburger, T. A. Herring, K. B. Kalabaev, V. I. Makarov, P. Molnar, S.V. Panasyuk, M.T. Prilepin, *et al.* (1996). Relatively recent construction of the Tien Shan inferred from GPS measurements of present-day crustal deformation rates, *Nature* **384,** 450–453.

Allen, M. B., S. J. Vincent, and P. J. Wheeler (1999). Late Cenozoic tectonics of the Kepingtage thrust zone: Interactions of the Tien Shan and Tarim basin, northwest China, *Tectonics* **18,** 639–654.

Avouac, J. P., P. Tapponnier, M. Bai, H. You, and G. Wang (1993). Active thrusting and folding along the northern Tien-Shan and late Cenozoic rotation of the Tarim relative to Dzungaria and Kazakhstan, *J. Geophys. Res.* **98,** 6755–6804.

Bagnardi, M., and A. Hooper (2018). Inversion of surface deformation data for rapid estimates of source parameters and uncertainties: A Bayesian approach, *Geochem. Geophys. Geosys.* **19,** 2194–2211.

Burchfiel, B., E. Brown, Q. D. Deng, X. Y. Feng, J. Li, P. Molnar, J. B. Shi, W. Zhangming, and Y. Huichuan (1999). Crustal shortening on the margins of the Tien Shan, Xinjiang, China, *Int. Geol. Rev.* **41,** 665–700.

Cai, J. F., Y. M. Wen, K. F. He, X. H. Wang, and C. J. Xu (2024). Strain partitioning, interseismic coupling, and shallow creep along the Ganzi-Yushu fault from Sentinel-1 InSAR data, *Geophys. Res. Lett.* **51,** e2024GL111469, doi: 10.1029/2024GL111469.

Crosby, C., J. Arrowsmith, A. Korjenkov, B. Guralnik, E. Mamyrov, and I. Povolotskaya (2007). The hunt for surface rupture from the 1889 M_s 8.3 Chilik earthquake, northern Tien Shan, Kyrgyzstan and Kazakhstan, *AGU* (Fall Meet.) Abstracts T23D-1635.

Delvaux, D., K. Abdrakhmatov, I. Lemzin, and A. Strom (2001). Landslides and surface breaks of the 1911 M_s 8.2 Kemin Earthquake, Kyrgyzstan, *Russian Geol. Geophys.* **42,** no. 10, 1583–1592.

Ding, Y. R., X. Liu, X. F. Dai, G. Y. Yin, Y. Yang, and J. Guo (2024). D-InSAR-based analysis of slip distribution and coulomb stress implications from the 2024 M_w 7.01 Wushi earthquake, *Remote Sens.* **16,** 4319.

Famiglietti, N. A., D. Cheloni, R. Caputo, and A. Vicari (2025). Geodetic model of the 2024 January 22 M_w 7.0 Wushi (northwestern China) earthquake and M_w 5.7 aftershock from inversion of InSAR data, *Geophys. J. Int.* **241,** 941–953.

Gan, J., J. Hu, Z. Li, C. Yang, J. Liu, Q. Sun, and W. Zheng (2018). Mapping three-dimensional co-seismic surface deformations associated with the 2015 M_W 7.2 Murghab earthquake based on InSAR and characteristics of crustal strain, *Sci. China Earth Sci.* **61,** 1451–1466.

Grandin, R., E. Klein, M. Métois, and C. Vigny (2016). Three-dimensional displacement field of the 2015 8.3 Illapel earthquake (Chile) from across- and along-track Sentinel-1 TOPS interferometry, *Geophys. Res. Lett.* **43,** 2552–2561.

Guglielmino, F., G. Nunnari, G. Puglisi, and A. Spata (2011). Simultaneous and integrated strain tensor estimation from geodetic and satellite deformation measurements to obtain three-dimensional displacement maps, *IEEE Trans. Geosci. Remote Sens.* **49,** 1815–1826.

Guo, R., X. Tang, Y. Zhang, W. Zhang, M. Qin, J. Xu, J. Zhou, X. Zou, and H. Sun (2025). Seismic versus aseismic slip for the 2023 Kahramanmaraş earthquake doublet, *Nat. Commun.* **16,** 959.

Guo, R., Y. Zheng, and J. Xu (2020). Stress modulation of the seismic gap between the 2008 M_s 8.0 Wenchuan earthquake and the 2013 M_s 7.0 Lushan earthquake and implications for seismic hazard, *Geophys. J. Int.* **221,** 2113–2125.

Hu, J., and B. Xiao (2016). *Modern Theory and Application of Surveying Data Processing*, Surveying and Mapping Press, Beijing, China.

Hu, J., Z. Li, X. Ding, J. Zhu, L. Zhang, and Q. Sun (2012). 3D coseismic displacement of 2010 Darfield, New Zealand earthquake estimated from multi-aperture InSAR and D-InSAR measurements, *J. Geod.* **11,** 1029–1041.

Jónsson, S., H. Zebker, P. Segall, and F. Amelung (2002). Fault slip distribution of the 1999 M_w 7.1 Hector Mine, California, earthquake, estimated from satellite radar and GPS measurements, *Bull. Seismol. Soc. Am.* **92,** 1377–1389.

Li, J., Y. Yao, R. Li, S. Yusan, G. Li, J. T. Freymueller, and Q. Wang (2022). Present-day strike-slip faulting and thrusting of the Kepingtage fold-and-thrust belt in southern Tianshan: Constraints from GPS observations, *Geophys. Res. Lett.* **49,** e2022GL099105, doi: 10.1029/2022GL099105.

Li, X., S. Jónsson, and Y. M. Cao (2021). Interseismic deformation from Sentinel-1 burst-overlap interferometry: Application to the southern Dead Sea fault, *Geophys. Res. Lett.* **48,** doi: 10.1029/2021GL093481.

Liu, J. H., J. Hu, R. Bürgmann, Z. Li, and S. Jónsson (2024). Mitigating atmospheric delays in InSAR time series: The DetrendInSAR method and its validation, *J. Geophys. Res.* **129,** e2024JB028920, doi: 10.1029/2024JB028920.

Liu, J. H., J. Hu, R. Bürgmann, Z. Li, Q. Sun, and Z. Ma (2021). A strain-model based InSAR time series method and its application to the geysers geothermal field, California, *J. Geophys. Res.* **126,** e2021JB021939, doi: 10.1029/2021JB021939.

Liu, J. H., J. Hu, Z. W. Li, Z. F. Ma, L. X. Wu, W. P. Jiang, G. C. Feng, and J. Zhu (2022). Complete three-dimensional coseismic displacements due to the 2021 Maduo earthquake in Qinghai Province, China from Sentinel-1 and ALOS-2 SAR images, *Sci. China Earth Sci.* **65,** 687–697.

Liu, J. H., J. Hu, Z. W. Li, J. J. Zhu, Q. Sun, and J. Gan (2018). A method for measuring 3-D surface deformations with InSAR based on strain model and variance component estimation, *IEEE Trans. Geosci. Remote Sens.* **56,** 239–250.

Ma, Z. F., S. J. Wei, X. Li, Y. Aoki, J. H. Liu, X. J. Liu, W. F. Mao, S. Yang, N.X. Wang, Q.H. Huang, *et al.* (2022). Challenges and prospects to time series burst overlap interferometry (BOI): Some insights from a new BOI algorithm test over the Chaman fault, *IEEE Trans. Geosci. Remote Sens.* **60,** 1–19.

Mellors, R., F. Vernon, G. Pavlis, G. Abers, M. Hamburger, S. Ghose, and B. Iliasov (1997). The $M_s = 7.3$ 1992 Suusamyr, Kyrgyzstan, earthquake: 1. Constraints on fault geometry and source parameters based on aftershocks and body-wave modeling, *Bull. Seismol. Soc. Am.* **87,** 11–22.

Molnar, P., and S. Ghose (2000). Seismic moments of major earthquakes and the rate of shortening across the Tien Shan, *Geophys. Res. Lett.* **27,** 2377–2380.

Molnar, P., and P. Tapponnier (1975). Cenozoic tectonics of Asia: Effects of a continental collision: Features of recent continental tectonics in Asia can be interpreted as results of the India-Eurasia collision, *Science* **189,** 419–426.

Nelson, M. R., R. McCaffrey, and P. Molnar (1987). Source parameters for 11 earthquakes in the Tien Shan, central Asia, determined by *P* and *SH* waveform inversion, *J. Geophys. Res.* **92,** 12,629–12,648.

Okada, Y. (1985). Surface deformation due to shear and tensile faults in a half-space, *Bull. Seismol. Soc. Am.* **75,** 1135–1154.

Qiu, J., J. Sun, and L. Ji (2024). The 2024 M_w 7.1 Wushi earthquake: A thrust and strike-slip event unveiling the seismic mechanisms of the South Tian Shan's thick-skin tectonics, *Remote Sens.* **16,** 2937.

Qiu, J. T., L. Y. Ji, L. Y. Zhu, and Q. L. Wang (2022). Present-day tectonic deformation partitioning across South Tian Shan from satellite geodetic imaging, *Front. Earth Sci.* **9,** doi: 10.3389/feart.2021.793890.

Shen, Z. K., M. Wang, Y. Zeng, and F. Wang (2015). Optimal interpolation of spatially discretized geodetic data, *Bull. Seismol. Soc. Am.* **105,** 2117–2127.

Sloan, R., J. Jackson, D. McKenzie, and K. Priestley (2011). Earthquake depth distributions in central Asia, and their relations with lithosphere thickness, shortening and extension, *Geophys. J. Int.* **185,** 1–29.

Tapponnier, P., and P. Molnar (1979). Active faulting and Cenozoic tectonics of the Tien Shan, Mongolia, and Baykal regions, *J. Geophys. Res.* **84,** 3425–3459.

Thompson, S. C., R. J. Weldon, C. M. Rubin, K. Abdrakhmatov, P. Molnar, and G. W. Berger (2002). Late Quaternary slip rates across the central Tien Shan, Kyrgyzstan, central Asia, *J. Geophys. Res.* **107,** ETG 7-1–ETG 7-32.

Wang, M., and Z. K. Shen (2020). Present-day crustal deformation of continental China derived from GPS and its tectonic implications, *J. Geophys. Res.* **125,** doi: 10.1029/2019JB018774.

Wang, T., and S. Jónsson (2015). Improved SAR amplitude image offset measurements for deriving three-dimensional coseismic displacements, *IEEE J. Sel. Top. Appl. Earth Observ. Remote Sens.* **8,** 3271–3278.

Wang, T., S. Wei, X. Shi, Q. Qiu, L. Li, D. Peng, R. J. Weldon, and S. Barbot (2018). The 2016 Kaikōura earthquake: Simultaneous rupture of the subduction interface and overlying faults, *Earth Planet. Sci. Lett.* **482,** 44–51.

Wang, X., C. Xu, Y. Wen, X. Zhao, S. Wang, and G. Xu (2024). Distribution of interseismic coupling along the Maidan fault in Tianshan before the 2024 M_w 7.0 Wushi earthquake, *Geophys. Res. Lett.* **51,** e2024GL111472, doi: 10.1029/2024GL111472.

Wen, Y., Z. Xiao, P. He, J. Zang, Y. Liu, and C. Xu (2021). Source characteristics of the 2020 M_w 7.4 Oaxaca, Mexico, earthquake estimated from GPS, InSAR, and teleseismic waveforms, *Seismol. Res. Lett.* **92,** 1900–1912.

Wessel, P., W. H. Smith, R. Scharroo, J. Luis, and F. Wobbe (2013). Generic mapping tools: Improved version released, *Eos Trans. AGU* **94,** 409–410.

Wu, C. Y., G. Wu, J. Shen, J. Chen, and X. Chang (2014). The late-Quaternary activity of the Nalati fault and its implications for the crustal deformation in the interior of the Tianshan mountains, *Quat. Sci.* **34,** 269–280.

Wu, C. Y., P. Z. Zhang, Z. Q. Zhang, W. J. Zheng, B. B. Xu, W. T. Wang, Z. Y. Yu, X. Dai, B. Zhang, and K. Zang (2023). Slip partitioning and crustal deformation patterns in the Tian Shan orogenic belt derived from GPS measurements and their tectonic implications, *Earth Sci. Rev.* **238,** 104362.

Wu, C. Y., W. Zheng, P. Zhang, Z. Zhang, Q. Jia, J. Yu, H. Zhang, Y. Yao, J. Liu, G. Han, *et al.* (2019). Oblique thrust of the Maidan fault and late Quaternary tectonic deformation in the southwestern Tian Shan, northwestern China, *Tectonics* **38,** 2625–2645.

Xiong, W., W. Chen, D. Wang, Y. Wen, Z. Nie, G. Liu, W. Dijin, P. Yu, X. Qiao, and B. Zhao (2022). Coseismic slip and early afterslip of the 2021 M_w 7.4 Maduo, China earthquake constrained by GPS and InSAR data, *Tectonophysics* **840,** 229558.

Xu, X., D. T. Sandwell, and B. Smith-Konter (2020). Coseismic displacements and surface fractures from Sentinel-1 InSAR: 2019 Ridgecrest earthquakes, *Seismol. Res. Lett.* **91,** 1979–1985.

Yang, S., J. Li, and Q. Wang (2008). The deformation pattern and fault rate in the Tian Shan Mountains inferred from GPS observations, *Sci. China Earth Sci* **51,** 1064–1080.

Yin, A., S. Nie, P. Craig, T. Harrison, F. Ryerson, X. L. Qian, and G. Yang (1998). Late Cenozoic tectonic evolution of the southern Chinese Tian Shan, *Tectonics* **17,** 1–27.

Yu, S., Z. Li, P. Zhao, J. Luo, and Y. Yang (2024). Source parameters and seismogenic fault model of the 2024 M_w 7.0 Wushi (Xinjiang, China) earthquake revealed by InSAR observations, *Pure Appl. Geophys.* **182,** 1149–1162.

Zhang, B. X., L. Qian, T. Li, J. Chen, J. H. Xu, Y. Yao, L. H. Fang, C. Xie, J. Chen, and G. Liu (2024). Geological disasters and surface ruptures of January 23, 2024 M_s 7.1 Wushi earthquake, Xinjiang, China, *Seismol. Geol.* **46,** 220–234.

Zhang, Y., W. Feng, L. Xu, C. Zhou, and Y. Chen (2009). Spatio-temporal rupture process of the 2008 great Wenchuan earthquake, *Sci. China Earth Sci* **52,** 45–154.

Zhao, D. Z., C. Y. Qu, R. Bürgmann, W. Y. Gong, and X. J. Shan (2021). Relaxation of Tibetan lower crust and afterslip driven by the 2001 M_w 7. 8 Kokoxili, China, earthquake constrained by a decade of geodetic measurements, *J. Geophys. Res.* **126,** e2020JB021314, doi: 10.1029/2020JB021314.

Zhao, L., Z. D. Chen, L. Xie, Z. H. Zhu, and W. B. Xu (2024). Coseismic deformation and slip model of the 2024 M_W 7.0 Wushi earthquake obtained from InSAR observation, *Rev. Geophys.* **55,** 453–460, doi: 10.19975/j.dqyxx.2024-010.

Zheng, G., H. Wang, T. J. Wright, Y. D. Lou, R. Zhang, W. X. Zhang, C. Shi, J. Huang, and N. Wei (2017). Crustal deformation in the India-Eurasia collision zone from 25 years of GPS measurements, *J. Geophys. Res.* **122,** 9290–9312.

Zheng, Y., R. Guo, and D. Liu (2024). Present status and prospective on the seismic hazard studies of major seismic gaps in the Sichuan-Yunnan region, *Sci. China Earth Sci.* **67,** 3339–3366.

Zubovich, A. V., X. Q. Wang, Y. G. Scherba, G. G. Schelochkov, R. Reilinger, C. Reigber, O. I. Mosienko, P. Molnar, W. Michajljow, V. I. Makarov, *et al.* (2010). GPS velocity field for the Tien Shan and surrounding regions, *Tectonics* **29,** doi: 10.1029/2010TC002772.

Manuscript received 21 February 2025
Published online 15 August 2025

Incorporating Directly Observed Rotational Seismic Data into Moment Tensor Inversion for the 2019 M_w 6.2 Hualien Earthquake

Beibei Xu[1,2], Yong Zhang[*1,2], Wei Li[3,4], Chang Chen[3,4], and Yun Wang[3]

Abstract

Rotational observations offer significant benefits in various fields of seismology. In recent years, fiber-optic rotational seismometers have recorded high-quality rotational waveform data, which could be used for seismological researches. In this study, we introduce directly observed rotational data into moment tensor inversion for the first time. In inversions of the 2019 M_w 6.2 Hualien earthquake, we confirm the improved constraints on moment tensor solutions and centroid depth achieved with the additional use of rotational data. Particularly, inversions of six-component (6C) records from 1 to 2 stations yield acceptable results, indicating potential applications of sparse-network observations to planetary seismology. With the increasing deployment of rotational seismometers, as well as the improvements of these seismographs in sensitivity and frequency range, rotational records will further contribute to seismological researches on Earth and other solid planets, playing a crucial role in probing deep structures and refining source parameters.

Cite this article as Xu, B., Y. Zhang, W. Li, C. Chen, and Y. Wang (2025). Incorporating Directly Observed Rotational Seismic Data into Moment Tensor Inversion for the 2019 M_w 6.2 Hualien Earthquake, *Seismol. Res. Lett.* **97**, 15–27, doi: 10.1785/0220240470.

Supplemental Material

Introduction

The complete seismic wavefield is composed of three parts: translation, rotation, and strain (Aki and Richards, 2002). Most current seismological researches are based on translational observations, occasionally supplemented by strain measurements. Because of technique limitations, rotational observations have not been widely used. According to continuum mechanics, rotational ground motion is mathematically expressed as half the spatial curl of the translational ground-motion field, that is, $\vec{\omega} = \frac{1}{2}\nabla \times \vec{u}$, in which $\vec{\omega}$ and $\vec{u}$ denote the rotational and translational ground motion, respectively. Theoretical investigations through forward syntheses have provided us with many meaningful insights into seismic rotational components. The rotational components can complement the information derived from translational components, and the combined use of both translational and rotational components enables the acquisition of complete surface-wave dispersion curves, which holds significance for the detection of localized shallow-velocity anomalies (Zhang *et al.*, 2020; Sun *et al.*, 2022; Li *et al.*, 2023). The rotational ground motion shows sensitivity to anisotropism, and the qP wave associated with rotation is independent of variations in the Thomsen parameter γ, facilitating related research of anisotropic parameters (Pham *et al.*, 2010; Sun, Wang, Li, and Wei, 2021). In the early stage, the rotational ground motions were mainly measured indirectly by calculating spatial or temporal derivatives of translational records from seismic arrays, named array-derived rotations (ADR) (Oliveira and Bolt, 1989; Spudich *et al.*, 1995; Huang, 2003; Suryanto *et al.*, 2006; Ichinose *et al.*, 2021; Kislov and Gravirov, 2021). Compared with direct measurement, the ADR are limited to lower frequencies due to the inevitable sensor spacing (Cochard *et al.*, 2006; Poppeliers and Evans, 2015). The available frequency range of ADR depends on the spatial extent of the array, and under proper conditions the ADR could substitute direct measurement (Langston, 2007; Poppeliers and Evans, 2015; Donner *et al.*, 2017; Ichinose *et al.*, 2021). Nevertheless, the reliability of ADR is affected by many factors such as topography, structural heterogeneities, picking time error, and the spatial average on site effects (Suryanto *et al.*, 2006; Donner, 2021). Therefore, the direct measurement is still essential to further study and utilize rotational ground motion. In recent years, rotational seismometers that measure the rotational ground motions directly have developed rapidly. According to the measuring principle, they can be classified into mechanical, electrochemical, and

1. School of Earth and Space Sciences, Peking University, Beijing, China, https://orcid.org/0009-0000-5840-4049 (BX); 2. State Key Laboratory of Earthquake Dynamics and Forecasting, Beijing, China; 3. Key Laboratory of Intraplate Volcanoes and Earthquakes, China University of Geosciences, Beijing, Ministry of Education, Beijing, China, https://orcid.org/0000-0002-6450-5249 (CC); https://orcid.org/0000-0002-7543-4677 (YW); 4. MWMC research group, School of Geophysics and Information Technology, China University of Geosciences Beijing, Beijing, China

*Corresponding author: zhang-yong@pku.edu.cn

optical types (Lee *et al.*, 2009; Nigbor *et al.*, 2009; Lin *et al.*, 2011; Bernauer *et al.*, 2012; Zembaty *et al.*, 2013; Chen *et al.*, 2023). The optical rotational seismometers, including ring-laser gyroscopes and fiber-optic gyroscopes, have gradually become mainstream due to their high sensitivity and large dynamic range. The ring-laser gyroscopes have high accuracy, large dynamic range, and ability to record teleseismic signals, but are expensive and challenging to maintain (Igel *et al.*, 2005, 2007; Belfi *et al.*, 2017; Igel *et al.*, 2021). In contrast, the fiber-optic gyroscopes are simpler and more economical, with sensitivity and dynamic range generally meeting the seismological requirements (Bernauer *et al.*, 2018; Cao *et al.*, 2021; Kislov and Gravirov, 2021; Sun, Wang, Yang, Zhang, and Wang, 2021). With the development of observational technology, high-quality rotational data are expected to contribute in various fields of seismology, including source inversion, free oscillation analysis, and tilt correction (Igel *et al.*, 2011; Bernauer *et al.*, 2014; Reinwald *et al.*, 2016; Schmelzbach *et al.*, 2018; Bernauer, Wassermann, *et al.*, 2020; Lin, Ku, *et al.*, 2022).

Moment tensor inversion is an effective way to determine focal mechanism, providing crucial information for both earthquake source studies and disaster response. For medium-to-large earthquakes, centroid moment tensors are preferred for describing the point sources (Dziewonski *et al.*, 1981; Dziewonski and Woodhouse, 1983). Currently, moment tensor inversions are mainly based on translational seismograms (Kanamori and Rivera, 2008; Duputel *et al.*, 2012; Ekström *et al.*, 2012). Theoretically, introducing rotations into moment tensor inversion would be helpful. As mentioned earlier, the 3C rotations can be expressed as

$$\begin{pmatrix} \omega_x \\ \omega_y \\ \omega_z \end{pmatrix} = \frac{1}{2} \begin{pmatrix} \partial_y u_z - \partial_z u_y \\ \partial_z u_x - \partial_x u_z \\ \partial_x u_y - \partial_y u_x \end{pmatrix}, \tag{1}$$

and when the receiver is at the free surface, the zero-traction boundary condition leads to

$$\omega_x^{\mathrm{FS}} = -\partial_z u_y, \omega_y^{\mathrm{FS}} = \partial_z u_x. \tag{2}$$

Equations (1) and (2) suggest that the rotations carry information on the spatial gradient of seismic wavefield, especially the vertical gradient related to the depth, which is not available with conventional measurements of translation due to the limitation of instrument deployment. Besides, the radiation patterns of translations and rotations are orthogonal (Cochard *et al.*, 2006), which means adding rotational measurements could effectively improve the data coverage. Several numerical experiments have explored the potential applications of rotational records to moment tensor inversions (Donner *et al.*, 2016, 2018, 2020; Hua and Zhang, 2022). Ichinose *et al.* (2021) used the indirectly observed rotational data, that is, the ADR records, in moment tensor inversion for real earthquakes. These studies suggest that, under suitable conditions, adding rotational data to moment tensor inversion can improve the resolution of depth-related elements and the constraints on the centroid depths, which is exactly a key challenge for traditional moment tensor inversion techniques (Dziewonski *et al.*, 1981; Kanamori and Given, 1981; Xu and Zhang, 2023). In addition, rotational data can provide supplementary wavefield information in situations for which the station networks are sparse. These results are in line with theoretical expectations.

In recent years, Chen *et al.* (2023) deployed broadband and fiber-optic seismometers at two stations on different sides of the Taiwan Strait and succeeded in recording six-component seismograms (three components of translation and three of rotation, 6C) of the 2019 M_w 6.2 Hualien earthquake. In this study, we apply these directly measured rotational data to moment tensor inversion for the first time. Our aim is to validate the value of rotational data in seismic source inversion, as predicted by previous numerical experiments, and to gain new insights and discoveries on this topic.

Methods

Assuming all moment tensor elements share the same time history, the equation for moment tensor inversion can be expressed as

$$u_n(t) = \sum_i [G_{ni}(t) * s(t)] M_i, \tag{3}$$

in which $u_n(t)$ is the nth observation (either translation or rotation), M_i is the ith element of the moment tensor, $G_{ni}(t)$ is the Green's function corresponding to the nth station and the ith moment tensor element, and $s(t)$ is the source time function (moment rate history). For each observational record, the amplitude is normalized to prevent the inversion from being dominated by certain stations. The normalization factor for the ith record $u_i(t)$ is calculated as

$$\omega_i = 1/\sqrt{\int [u_i(t)]^2 dt}. \tag{4}$$

When using two data sets (translations and rotations), the quantities of available records might differ largely because rotational observations are quite rare compared to translations. In this case, two additional weighting factors are applied to ensure that the square-root energy of each data set is balanced (Chen *et al.*, 2019). They are calculated as

$$\lambda_{\mathrm{Tra}} = 1/\sqrt{\int [u_{\mathrm{Tra}}(t)]^2 dt},\ \lambda_{\mathrm{Rot}} = 1/\sqrt{\int [u_{\mathrm{Rot}}(t)]^2 dt}, \tag{5}$$

in which $u_{\mathrm{Tra}}(t)$ and $u_{\mathrm{Rot}}(t)$ are concatenated normalized translational records and rotational records, respectively. These factors are also applied to the corresponding Green's functions.

The waveform fitting misfit ρ_n for the nth record is defined as the relative root mean square

$$\rho_n = ||u_n - d_n||/||u_n||, \tag{6}$$

in which d_n is the nth synthetic seismogram, and $||\cdot||$ denotes the L2 norm. Similarly, the total misfit for all stations is defined as

$$\chi = \sqrt{\sum_n ||u_n - d_n||^2 / \sum_n ||u_n||^2}, \quad (7)$$

and the variance reduction (VR) is calculated as

$$\mathrm{VR} = 1 - \chi^2. \quad (8)$$

To compare results with different inversion settings the normalized VR (nVR) is used in our study,

$$\mathrm{nVR} = \frac{\mathrm{VR} - \min(\mathrm{VR})}{\max(\mathrm{VR}) - \min(\mathrm{VR})}. \quad (9)$$

To evaluate the inversion results, we also calculate the deviation angles (Kagan, 1991; Duputel *et al.*, 2012) between our obtained moment tensor solutions and those from other studies or institutes. The detailed calculation is described in the appendix of Duputel *et al.* (2012).

For Green's function calculations, we use the QSSP program developed by Wang *et al.* (2017). The QSSP can generate both translational and rotational seismograms based on a 1D spherical Earth model. Given the regional scale of our study area, we employ the CRUST1.0 model (Laske *et al.*, 2013) at the source location for the crust part, and the AK135 model (Kennett *et al.*, 1995) for the mantle and core parts.

The inversion process follows the common practice for centroid moment tensor inversion. We constrain the isotropic components of the moment tensor to zero considering the Hualien earthquake to be a tectonic event, in which case the isotropic component from full moment tensor inversion should come from inversion error rather than actual physical meaning. The source time function (STF, referring to moment rate function in this study) is modeled as a simple area-normalized isosceles triangle with a half duration t_h equal to the centroid time τ_c. The long-period data used in moment tensor inversion are not sensitive to the source duration, yet they have resolution for the centroid time (Kanamori and Rivera, 2008; Duputel *et al.*, 2012). A series of trial STFs with varying values of τ_c is generated. The search range of centroid depth is 12–40 km with a step of 2 km. For each candidate depth, we convolve the Green's functions with each trial STF and solve equation (3) in the least-square sense. The trial STF and depth yielding the lowest misfit χ are selected as the optimal STF and the centroid depth h_c, respectively. Given the rupture scale of this event (10–20 km), we do not perform further searches for its horizontal centroid location.

Data

We use source information of the 2019 M_w 6.2 Hualien earthquake released by the U.S. Geological Survey (USGS), that is, the hypocenter is located at 24.037 N 121.650° E, with a depth of 20 km, and the origin time is 18 April 2019 05:01:06.493 UTC. Rotational records from stations NA01 and QS01 provided by Chen *et al.* (2023) are used in moment tensor inversions. These records were recorded by the blueSeis-3A seismometer, one of the most accurate fiber-optic rotational seismographs, with a flat response in frequency range of 0.001–50 Hz (Bernauer *et al.*, 2018). It should be noted that the original rotational records at QS01 station contain a time discrepancy of 18 s due to the leap seconds. To compare our results with the traditional moment tensor inversion using translational records, we also collect three-component (3C) broadband translational records from seven stations within an epicentral distance of 50–150 km from the Incorporated Research Institutions for Seismology website (Fig. 1). Broadband stations within 50 km are excluded to satisfy the point-source approximation required in moment tensor inversion, whereas those beyond 150 km are also omitted to minimize the effects of lateral variations in velocity structure.

First, we perform several trial inversions to determine a suitable period band for waveform filtering and to check the quality of records. We find it difficult to fit the translational waveforms at the northern stations. For this event, previous studies have suggested that the earthquake rupture propagated to the north with a high speed (Lee *et al.*, 2020; Lin, Wen, and Yen, 2022). Similar to previous observation in the 2016 Meinong earthquake (Kanamori *et al.*, 2017), the directivity effect caused by the northward rupture propagation, as well as other factors like source radiation pattern and path–site effects, might have resulted in significantly strong ground motions in the north, leading to severe drifts and amplitude clipping at stations YHNB and TATO. Although it is possible to recover real signals from these records, the point-source model used in moment tensor inversion may still struggle to interpret them. Thus, we exclude these two broadband stations from inversion. For the rotational records, the vertical component (RoZ) at station QS01 decreases rapidly at lower frequency bands (see Fig. S1, available in the supplemental material to this article), becoming nearly invisible below 0.5 Hz. Therefore, we do not use the RoZ component at QS01 in our inversions. Equation (1) indicates that the vertical rotation is related to spatial derivative of the transverse displacement, and the latter can be further transformed into the transverse velocity multiplied by the phase velocity (Igel *et al.*, 2005). Thus, the vertical component of rotational ground motion is related to the *SH* wave, and the low amplitude of RoZ component at QS01 station might be related to *SH*-wave propagation with large takeoff angle. A similar phenomenon was observed during the 2008 Wenchuan earthquake in rotational records across the Taiwan Strait, possibly due to the island-strait structure that blocks the propagation of the horizontal *SH* wave (Lin *et al.*, 2011).

For translational data, we use velocity records and apply a fourth order Butterworth filter with a period band of 30–100 s, whereas for rotational data, we use rotation rate records and a period band of 10–100 s. To avoid amplification of long-period

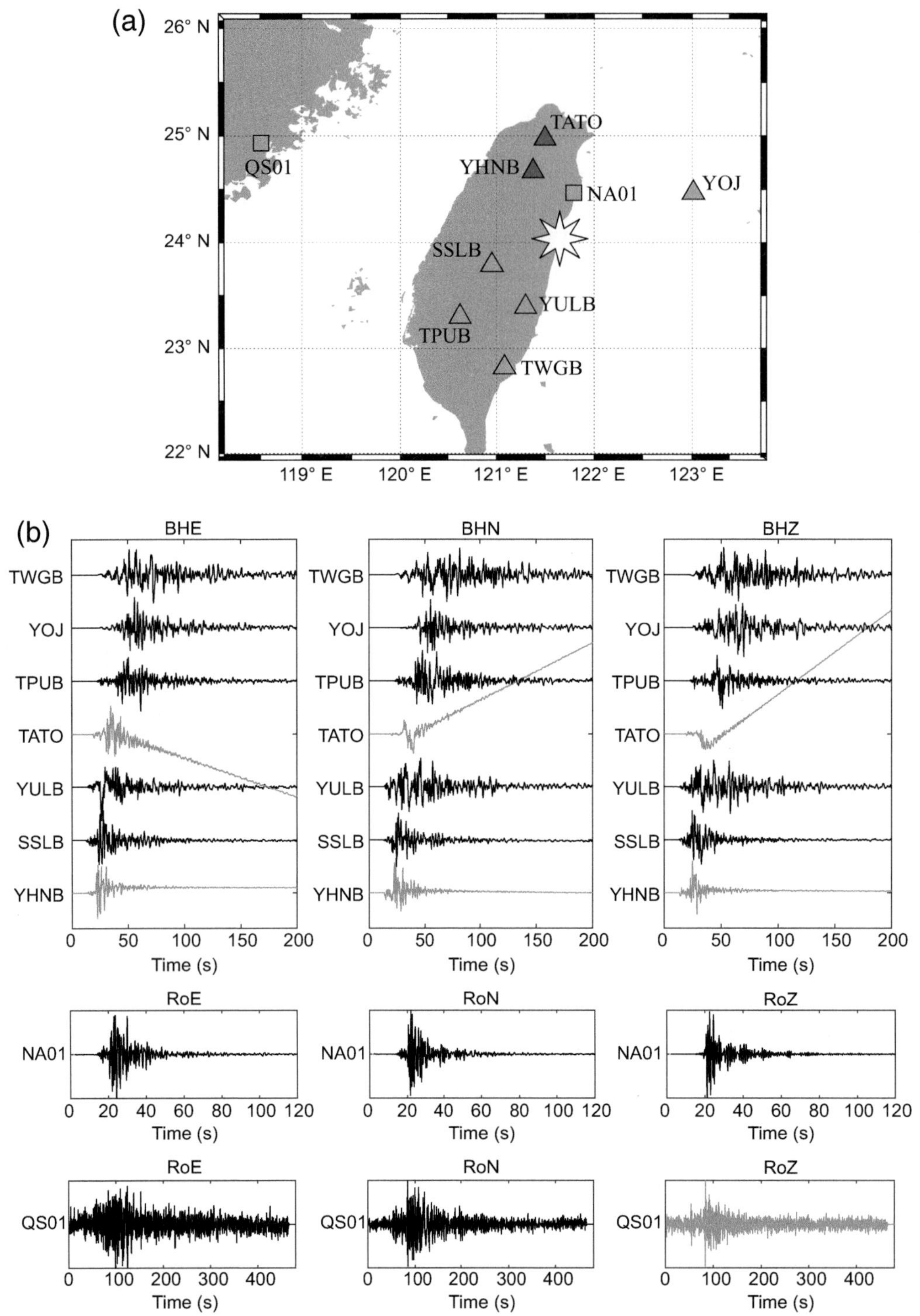

Figure 1. Locations and records of the translational and rotational stations. (a) Epicenter and station locations. The white star denotes the epicenter, triangles represent translational stations, and squares indicate rotational stations from Chen *et al.* (2023). (b) Translational and rotational waveforms. The amplitude–normalized three-component (3C) velocity (unfiltered) and 3C rotation rate (low-pass filtered at 1 Hz) records are displayed. The time axes begin at the earthquake origin time. Stations TATO and YHNB are removed from the inversions, and the corresponding records are shown as gray lines in panel (b). The color version of this figure is available only in the electronic edition.

noises, we do not integrate the rotation rate into rotation. As the amplitude spectra in Figure S1 suggest, in rotational records the major energy of the event signals focuses on short periods and decays rapidly as the period grows over ~30 s. Therefore, we use a higher frequency range for rotation rate records.

Results

The moment tensor inversion is conducted in two different scenarios based on the station amount used in inversion. The first is the multistation scenario in which more than three stations are used, whereas the second is the sparse-network scenario in which only 1–2 stations are used.

Scenario 1: Multistation scenario

In the first scenario, we consider adding rotational observation into existing broadband seismic observation. The moment tensor inversion is carried out in three schemes:

1. using only broadband translational records;
2. using both translational and rotational records, without applying the weighting factors in equation (5); and
3. using both translational and rotational records with the weighting factors applied.

In Figure 2, we show the nVR contours of three inversion schemes. The parameter A_{95} for each contour denotes the area proportion of nVR over 0.95, corresponding to the area surrounded by a dashed contour line. Although the final centroid depths of three schemes are close, the contours of schemes

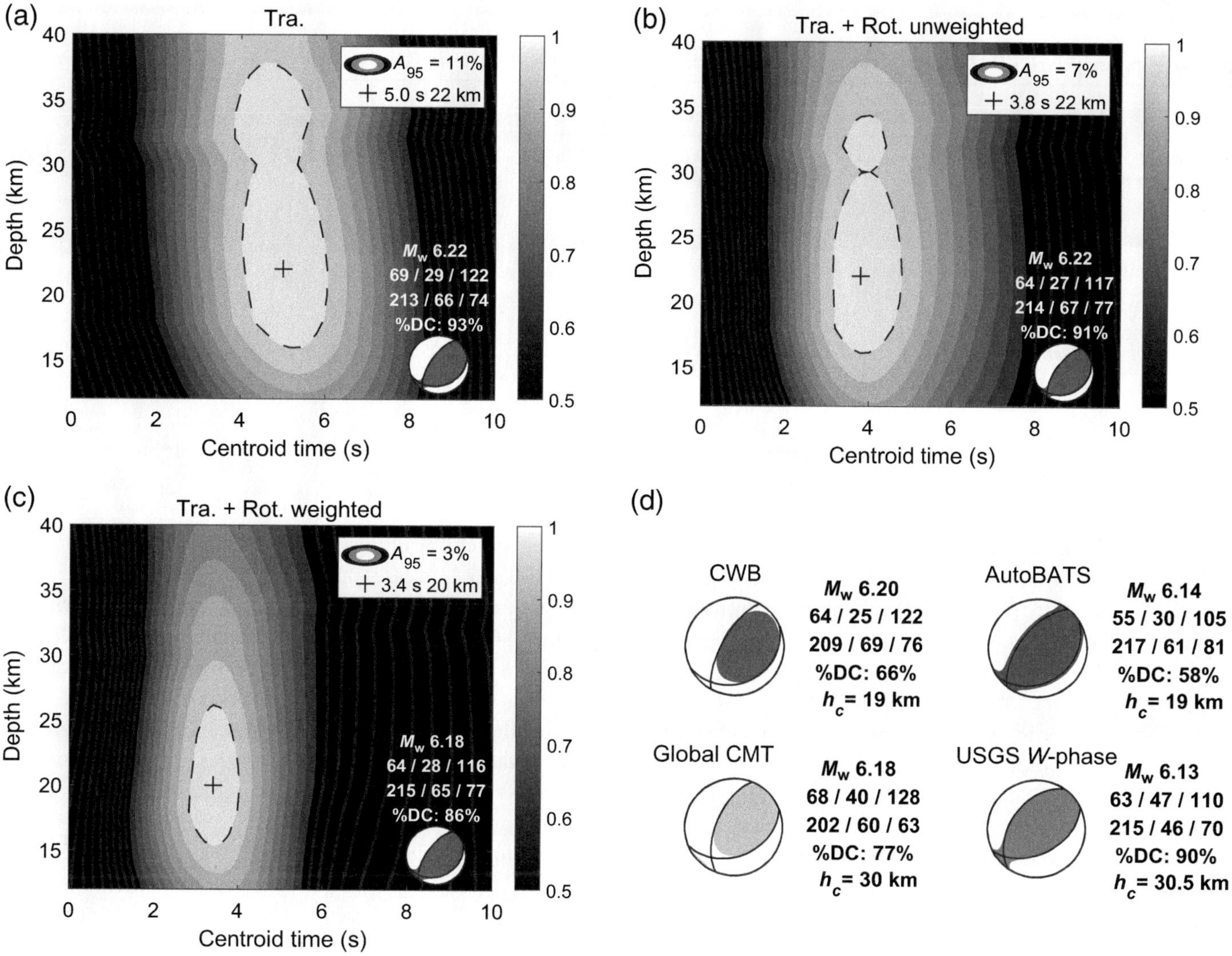

Figure 2. Inversion results for scenario 1. The contour denotes normalized variance reduction (nVR) variation with depth and centroid time. A_{95} is the area proportion of nVR over 0.95, which is outlined by the dashed contour line. The cross marker denotes the final centroid depth and centroid time with highest VR, and the corresponding moment tensor is plotted at the bottom right. (a) Scheme (1): using only translational records. (b) Scheme (2): using both translational and rotational records, without applying the weighting factors. (c) Scheme (3): using both translational and rotational records with the weighting factors applied. (d) Moment tensors from other studies as references. CWB, Central Weather Bureau; Global CMT, Global Centroid Moment Tensor; USGS, U.S. Geological Survey. The color version of this figure is available only in the electronic edition.

(1) and (2) both show large uncertainty for depth and a second local minimum at about 32 km, which is close to the centroid depths from Global Centroid Moment Tensor (Global CMT) and USGS *W*-phase results. The multiple local minima in centroid depth estimation were also observed in previous studies (Donner *et al.*, 2013, 2016; Xu and Zhang, 2023), which might be related to various factors like data coverage and velocity model errors.

By jointly inverting both translational and rotational data and equally weighting them, we obtain a centroid depth of 20 km in scheme (3), aligning well with near-field inversion results, including 19 km from the Taiwan Central Weather Bureau (CWB) solution, 19 km from the AutoBATS solution (Jian *et al.*, 2018), 19.2 km from the finite-fault model (Lee *et al.*, 2020), and 22.5 km from the source-scanning algorithm technique inversion (Lin *et al.*, 2018; Lin, Wen, and Yen, 2022). The nVR distribution becomes more concentrated and the A_{95} drops to 3%, indicating improved constraint on centroid depth provided by the rotational data. This improvement is consistent with previous synthetic tests (Donner *et al.*, 2016; Hua and Zhang, 2022), which found that the centroid depth could benefit from additional rotational data even if the translational data coverage was already good. As we mentioned in the Introduction, the horizontal rotation data are related to the spatial derivatives of translational motions with respect to depth, which makes them particularly sensitive to depth, and this information could not be obtained from conventional translational observations.

TABLE 1
Deviation Angles (°) Between Moment Tensor Solutions Involved in This Study

Reference		Scenario 1 Scheme (1)	Scenario 1 Scheme (2)	Scenario 1 Scheme (3)	CWB	AutoBATS	Global CMT	USGS
Scenario 1	Scheme (1)	–	3.0	3.2	5.8	8.3	13.2	20.2
	Scheme (2)	3.0	–	2.1	6.7	5.5	15.0	19.6
	Scheme (3)	3.2	2.1	–	5.1	6.7	15.8	21.6
Scenario 2	Case (i)	29.6	31.6	32.1	29.8	34.3	17.1	29.7
	Case (ii)	26.3	27.2	29.0	30.8	28.0	18.5	13.8
	Case (iii)	21.7	19.0	20.4	24.8	14.2	28.7	19.2
	Case (iv)	21.0	20.6	22.6	25.1	19.2	16.2	2.0

CWB, Central Weather Bureau; Global CMT, Global Centroid Moment Tensor; USGS, U.S. Geological Survey.

All three schemes obtain similar moment tensor solutions, which are close to those from CWB and AutoBATS, with deviation angles of ~6° (Table 1, Table S1), showing the reliability of our inversion. The waveform fitting is displayed in Figure S2.

Scenario 2: Sparse-network scenario

In the second scenario, we examine the improvements gained from including rotational data under sparse network—that is, when only a few stations are available. This scenario is relevant in practical cases such as rapid earthquake warning, in which moment tensor inversion is performed in real time as soon as data from any station become available, and in planetary seismology, in which instrument deployment times and locations are limited by spaceflight resources (Donner *et al.*, 2018). Previous numerical experiments (Donner *et al.*, 2018; Hua and Zhang, 2022) have demonstrated that moment tensors can be recovered with only one or two 6C stations, though centroid depth remains challenging to resolve.

In Chen *et al.* (2023), they also deployed collocated broadband translational seismometers with the rotational seismometers. It would have been handy if direct 6C observation at a certain station was available for this event. Unfortunately, the collocated translational records at NA01 were clipped. Therefore, only the collocated translational records at QS01 can be used in inversion. In this section, the record numbers of rotation and translation are close, and thus the weighting is unnecessary.

We perform inversions for four cases:

(i) using NA01 rotations only;
(ii) using NA01 rotations and QS01 rotations;
(iii) using QS01 translations only; and
(iv) using NA01 rotations, QS01 rotations, and QS01 translation.

For each case, the records not used are still predicted to evaluate the results. The nVR results are shown in Figure 3 and the waveform fittings in Figure S3, with deviation angles listed in Table 1. In case (i), the centroid depth extending toward the Earth's surface is barely constrained, and the waveform prediction at QS01 is poor (Fig. S3a), showing that it is challenging to resolve the moment tensor with only one rotational station. Inversion with QS01 rotations alone was also tried but failed, which might be due to the longer epicentral distance and the lower data quality compared with NA01. Case (ii) demonstrates that an acceptable moment tensor solution can be obtained using two rotational stations, which is promising. In this case, the waveform prediction for translations at QS01 is much better than case (i). In these two cases, the overestimation of moment magnitudes might be caused by the large amplitude of the RoZ record at NA01, which is not well fitted in other inversions with translational records involved. In case (iii), the moment tensor solution and prediction for rotational records are quite good. However, in these three cases, the centroid depth is not well constrained due to the limited data amount and coverage. When we combine rotations and translations in case (iv), both the moment tensor solution and depth constraint become favorable. The focal mechanism from case (iv) has an average deviation angle of 15.6° relative to other studies, which is quite good given the sparse-network condition. It is surprisingly close to the result of USGS, with a deviation angle of only 2°. Considering the significant differences in data, crust models, and inversion settings, the mechanism consistency is likely coincidental. As a test for single-station 6C inversion at QS01 (actually it is 5C because the RoZ is excluded), the inversion with both translations and rotations at QS01 also shows improvement on depth constraint (Fig. S4).

Numerical Tests

To elaborate the benefit of adding rotational data into moment tensor inversion, we perform numerical tests in this section. The source-station locations of the 2019 Hualien earthquake are used to simulate a realistic condition. We use the QSSP

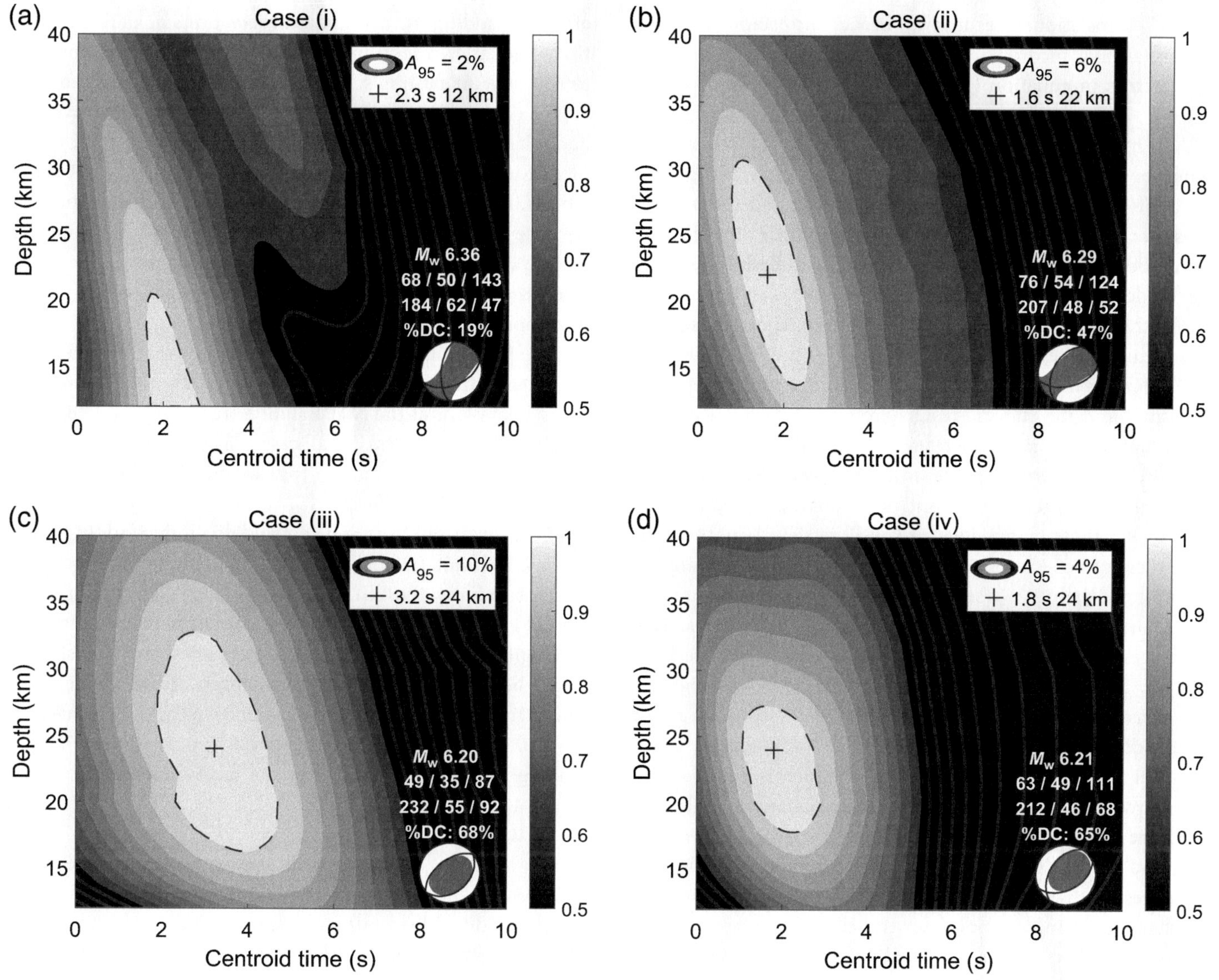

Figure 3. Inversion results for scenario 2. The figure caption is the same as Figure 2. (a) Case (i): using NA01 rotations only. (b) Case (ii): using NA01 rotations and QS01 rotations. (c) Case (iii): using QS01 translations only. (d) Case (iv): using NA01 rotations, QS01 rotations, and QS01 translations. The color version of this figure is available only in the electronic edition.

to synthesize translational and rotational records at these stations. The input moment tensor is a pure double-couple (DC) source with the same nodal planes as the Global CMT solution (202°/60°/63°), and a seismic moment of 2.5×10^{18} N · m (M_w 6.20). The input depth is 20 km, and the input STF is a triangle with half duration of 3 s. Gaussian white noises are added to the synthetic observations according to designated signal-to-noise ratio (SNR, defined as the power ratio of signal to noise). The inversion follows the process described in the Methods section.

Test 1: Multistation test

Similar to the above scenario 1 for real data inversion, for test 1 we use the five broadband translational stations and the two additional stations (NA01 and QS01) from Chen *et al.* (2023). For the broadband stations, only translational records (15 translations) are synthesized. For the additional stations, both translational and rotational records (five translations or five rotations with no vertical components) are synthesized. The vertical rotation at QS01 station is excluded to stay consistent with real data inversion, and the vertical translation at QS01 is also excluded to keep the same numbers of translations and rotations. In this test, the moment tensor inversion is carried out in four schemes:

(A) 15 translational records at broadband stations;
(B) 15 translational records at broadband stations and 5 translational records at additional stations;
(C) 15 translational records at broadband stations and 5 rotational records at additional stations, without weighting factors applied;

(D) 15 translational records at broadband stations and 5 rotational records at additional stations, with weighting factors in equation (5) applied.

Scheme (A) is the basic reference, and in the other three schemes the data amount and station coverage are improved by the two additional stations. Schemes (C) and (D) further illustrate the results of adding rotations compared with extra translations. To test the performance under different noise levels, we designate the SNR at 20, 10, 5 dB. Lower SNR levels can reflect the influence of practical factors to some extent, such as lower earthquake magnitudes and velocity model errors. For each SNR level, the generation of random noises is repeated 30 times, and the statistic results are analyzed.

In Figure 4, we show the results of deviation angle, moment magnitude, DC percentage, centroid time, centroid depth, area proportion of nVR over 0.95, and nodal plane parameters from test 1. All these parameters are well retrieved in the tests regardless of noise level. Comparing the results of scheme (A) with other schemes, we see that for all parameters, the results are improved by a greater amount of data and better station coverage. Comparing scheme (C) with scheme (B), we infer that for most parameters adding rotations without weighting is not as good as adding extra translations. However, as the results of scheme (D) suggest, once the two data sets are properly weighted, the profit of adding rotations is no less than extra translations. In general, for the deviation angle, the moment magnitude, the centroid time, the nVR area proportion and the dip angle, adding weighted rotations yields even better results than extra translations. The improvement in focal mechanism mainly comes from the constraints provided by rotations on depth-related moment tensor elements (M_{xz}, M_{yz}, and M_{zz}), especially the M_{zz}, which is directly linked to the dip angle. The sensitivity for centroid time might be due to the higher frequency for rotation rate. The lower A_{95}-values for schemes (C) and (D) benefit from both the factors above. An example of grid-search contours, waveform fittings, and noise-added waveforms from test 1 is shown in Figures S5 and S6. Comparing Figure S5(b) with Figure S5(c) and (d), we see that for a fixed centroid time, the depth-dependent VR is still better constrained by adding rotations than extra translations, which is consistent to the real data inversion in the multistation scenario.

Test 2: Sparse-network test

In this test, we synthesize only 6C observations from 1 to 2 stations for each inversion. The 6C observations are composed of 3C translations at NA01 station and 3C translations at a broadband station, or both the 3C translations and 3C rotations at NA01 station. This setting simulates the scenario in which we already have a seismic station (NA01) with 3C translational observations, and then we aim to compare the effects of adding another 3C broadband translational station with the effects of adding 3C rotational observations at the NA01 station. The latter, which means adding rotational seismometers to augment an existing seismic station, would be more convenient to deploy for tasks like moment tensor real-time inversion and planetary seismology. Different broadband stations are picked to compose the 6C observations with the NA01 translations, to reduce the impact of the source radiation pattern. Because the record numbers of translations and rotations are the same, the weighting in equation (5) is not applied here. The SNR is fixed at 10 dB in test 2, and the generation of random noise is also repeated 30 times.

As shown in Figure 5, compared with adding another broadband translational station (plotted as blue point sets), adding rotations at the NA01 station (red point sets) generally produces better results. For all cases, the centroid depth is well recovered due to the simple forward model, whereas adding rotations shows the lowest A_{95}-values, indicating better constraint on centroid time and centroid depth than adding translations. It should be noted that among the optional broadband stations, adding the SSLB station or the YOJ station yields results as good as rotations for parameters relevant to focal mechanism. The strong performances of these two stations might be related to the radiation pattern of the source. With azimuths of 249° and 70°, these two stations are located close to the strike direction of the auxiliary nodal plane (68°/39°/128°), making them more sensitive to the focal mechanism.

Discussion

In two scenarios, the numerical tests show an increase in the DC component percentage of obtained moment tensors with rotations added. Previous study using ADR also suggested significant improvement for DC components with rotational data (Ichinose *et al.*, 2021). However, this improvement is absent in our results of real data inversion, especially for the sparse-network inversion in scenario 2. The non-DC components in moment tensor inversion are related to many factors, including station coverage, modeling errors, epicenter uncertainty, data quality, and source complexity (Frohlich, 1995; Adamova and Sileny, 2010, 2013; Jian *et al.*, 2018), which might account for this discrepancy.

In our inversion, the obtained centroid time seems to be shorter when rotational records are used. The rupture directivity might account for this phenomenon because the rupture propagated northward with a high speed (Lee *et al.*, 2020). Because of the directivity effect, apparent source time functions at stations in the rupture direction have shorter durations and larger amplitudes than those from a stationary source (Huang *et al.*, 2017), and the high rupture speed intensifies this effect. In the low-frequency range that we use for source inversion with translational records, the effect on amplitudes is reduced, and the effect on source duration remains as variant time shifts of waveforms at different stations. For this study, the NA01 rotational station is the only station that locates in the rupture direction, and we use

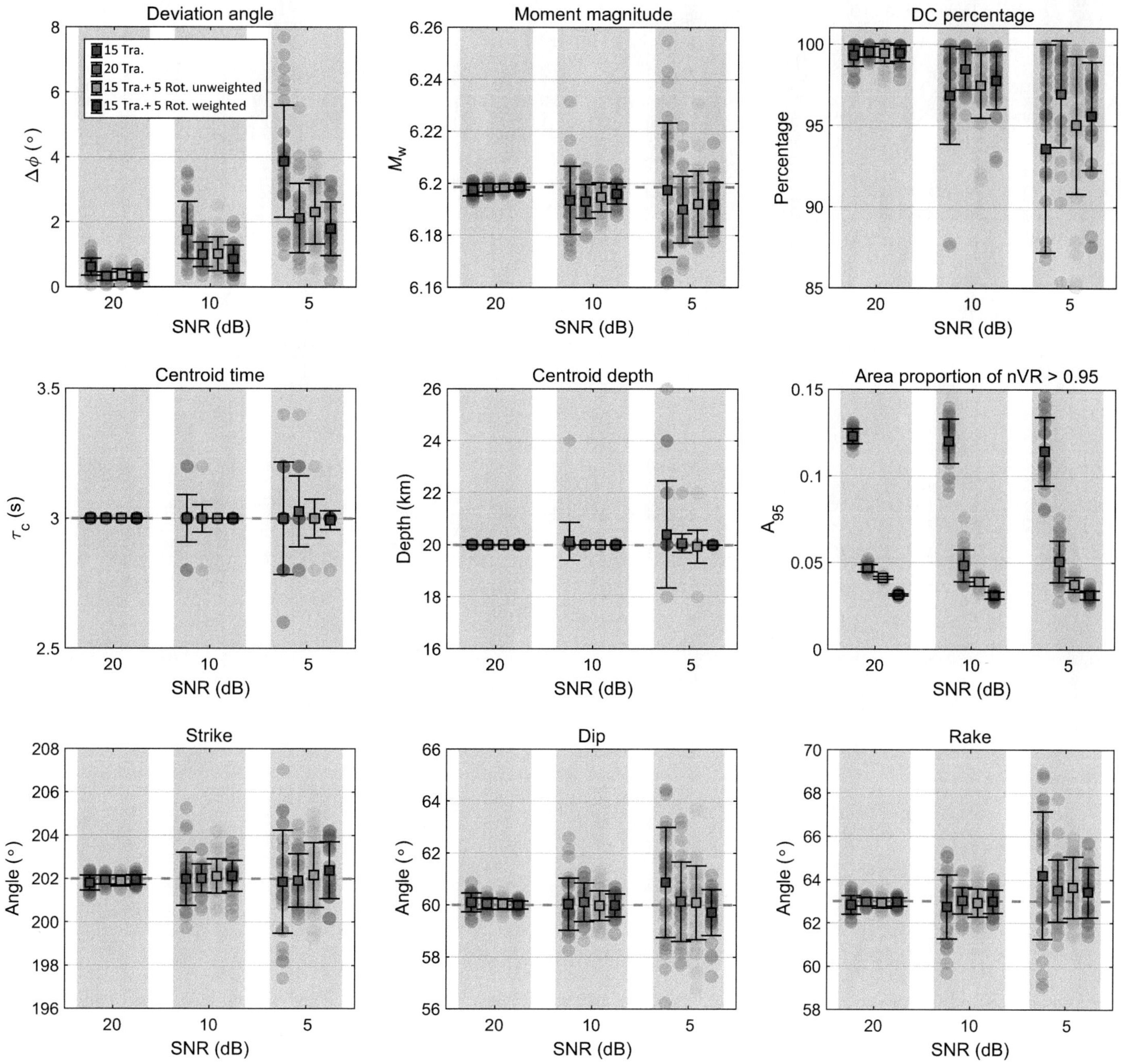

Figure 4. Statistical results for test 1. For each signal-to-noise ratio (SNR) level, inversion results of four schemes are dotted as point sets with different colors, and the mean value and standard deviation of each point set are marked out as error bar. The legend is shown in the top left subfigure. The green dashed lines denote the input value for forward simulation. The color version of this figure is available only in the electronic edition.

a higher filtering frequency band for rotations, thus leading to strongly shortened centroid time shift. Theoretically, using a lower frequency band could mitigate such directivity effect in inversion, which makes the data better meet the point-source requirement. Unfortunately, the amplitudes of rotations decay rapidly with periods growing over ~30 s (Fig S1). Although the nominal lower frequency limit of the instrument is 0.001 Hz, the sensitivity limitation and self-noise make it challenging to use long-period signals. It should be reasonable to transfer the experience of picking period band from translational data processing, but it would be better to summarize a new set of criteria for rotational data from further study and instrument tests. Especially, if we aim to use rotational data to study large earthquakes (**M** > 7.5), the available long periods would be important and decisive. Many efforts are being made to raise the upper boundary of the available frequency band of rotational seismometers by instrument developers, but what we need in studying the seismic source is reliable low-frequency information. Therefore, it is also crucial to broaden the lower cutoff frequency of the instrumental response.

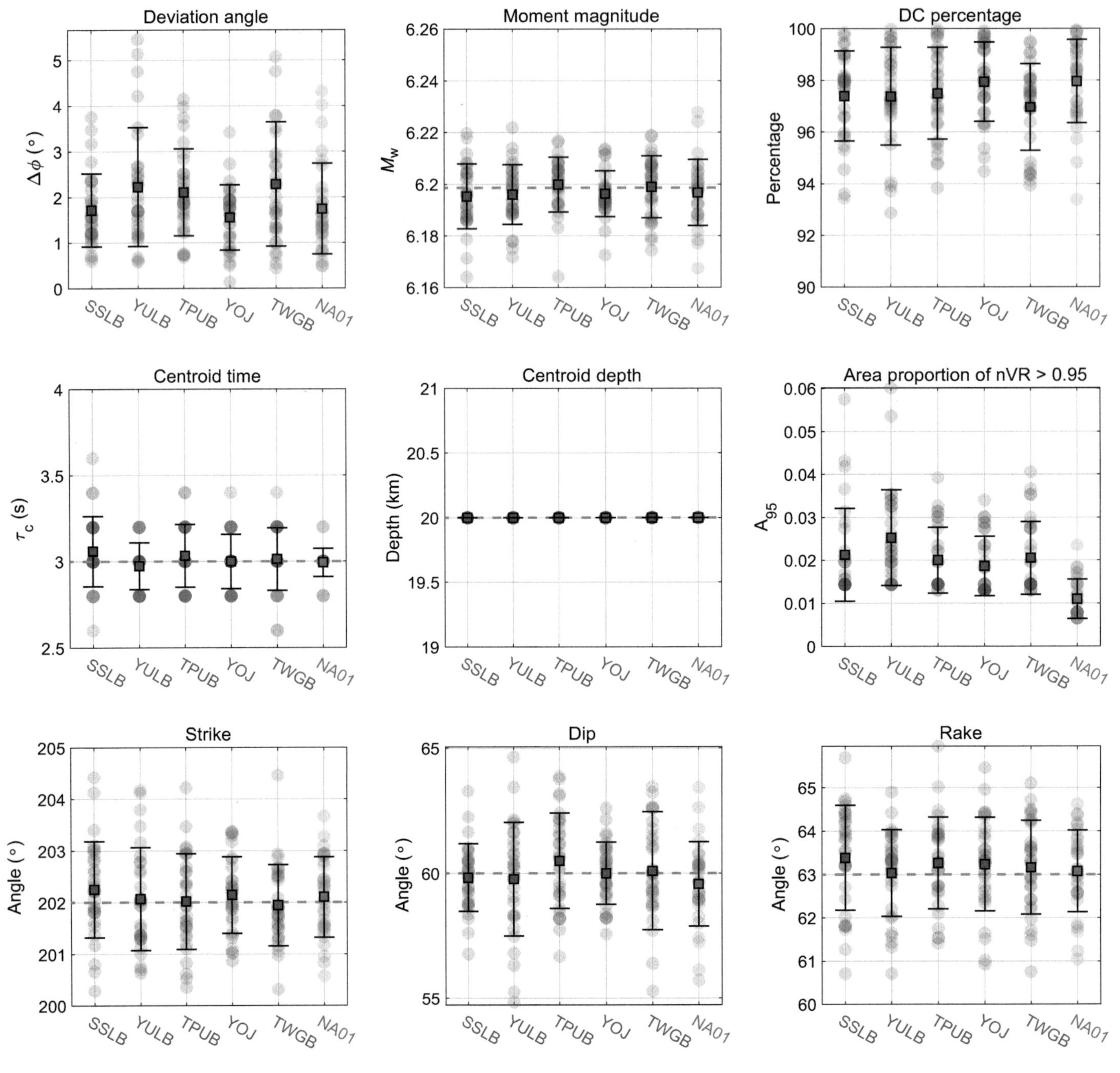

Figure 5. Statistical results for test 2. The blue point sets show the results of adding a broadband station with 3C translations to compose the 6C observations with 3C translations at the NA01 station. The red point sets show the results of adding 3C rotations at the NA01station to compose the 6C observations. The mean value and standard deviation of each point set are marked out as error bar. The green dashed lines denote the input value for forward simulation. The labels for *X*-axis denote the name of the station added to compose the 6C observations. The color version of this figure is available only in the electronic edition.

In scenario 2, we obtain encouraging results for using rotations with sparse network, which is often the case for planetary seismology. For example, currently there is only one set of seismic observational instruments on Mars, the Seismic Experiment for Interior Structure carried by the National Aeronautics and Space Administration's InSight lander (Lognonné *et al.*, 2019; Knapmeyer-Endrun and Kawamura, 2020). Therefore, studies on focal mechanisms of Marsquakes have to be conducted with only one station (Brinkman *et al.*, 2021; Maguire *et al.*, 2023). In such a case, it would cost less to deploy a rotational seismometer at the same station, compared with another translational seismometer at a different spot. The PIONEERS project in Europe also focuses on measuring rotations on the planets, which aims to develop two types of six degree-of-freedom sensors with different accuracy (Bernauer, Garcia, *et al.*, 2020). Extra rotational observations can significantly improve the application potential of single station or sparse network, which is helpful in source inversion, epicenter location, and velocity structure investigation on the planets.

Conclusions

In this study, for the first time we use rotational data recorded by fiber-optic seismometers to perform moment tensor inversion. As predicted by previous numerical experiments, incorporating rotational data improves moment tensor solutions and the constraint on centroid depth. Inversions using only rotational data show acceptable results, indicating potential applications of sparse-network observations to earthquake early warning and planetary seismology. To make rotational data more practical for source inversion, further studies are needed on more instances with real rotational records. By summarizing experience such as the relationship between seismic magnitude and suitable frequency band, we can fully use rotational data in seismological studies. In addition, the feedback will be valuable for improving the future design of rotational seismometers.

Data and Resources

The broadband seismic data were downloaded through the EarthScope Consortium Wilber 3 system (https://ds.iris.edu/wilber3/) or EarthScope Consortium webservices (https://service.iris.edu/), including the following seismic networks: (1) the TW (Institute of Earth Sciences, Academia Sinica, Taiwan, 1996); (2) the JP (Japan Meteorological Agency, Japan, 1994, http://www.jma.go.jp/en/quake/). The rotational and translational records at stations NA01 and QS01 are provided by Chen *et al.* (2023). The finite-fault model of the 2019 M_w 6.2 Hualien event is requested from Lee *et al.* (2020). The map in Figure 1 is plotted using the MATLAB package M_Map (Pawlowicz, 2020). All websites were last accessed in September 2024. The supplemental material includes Table S1 for moment tensor solutions obtained in this study, Figure S1 for rotational records with different frequency bands, Figures S2 and S3 for waveform fitting results, Figure S4 for a supplementary case in scenario 2, and Figure S5 for an example from the numerical tests for scenario 1.

Declaration of Competing Interests

The authors acknowledge that there are no conflicts of interest recorded.

Acknowledgments

The authors sincerely thank Bor-Shouh Huang, Chin-Jen Lin, Yongxiang Wei, Chunqi Liao for the help of obtaining 6C seismic data in Taiwan and Fujian. This study used the Centroid Moment Tensor (CMT) solution from the Global CMT catalog, event origin, and *W*-phase CMT solution from the U.S. Geological Survey (USGS), CMT solution from Taiwan Central Weather Bureau (CWB), and CMT solution form AutoBATS catalog. This work was supported by the National Natural Science Foundation of China (42150201, 62127815, U1839208).

References

Adamova, P., and J. Sileny (2010). Non-double-couple earthquake mechanism as an artifact of the point-source approach applied to a finite-extent focus, *Bull. Seismol. Soc. Am.* **100,** no. 2, 447–457, doi: 10.1785/0120090097.

Adamova, P., and J. Sileny (2013). Disputable non-double-couple mechanisms of several strong earthquakes: Second-degree moment approach, *Bull. Seismol. Soc. Am.* **103,** no. 5, 2836–2849, doi: 10.1785/0120130014.

Aki, K., and P. Richards (2002). *Quantitative Seismology*, Second Ed., University Science Books, California.

Belfi, J., N. Beverini, F. Bosi, G. Carelli, D. Cuccato, G. De Luca, A. Di Virgilio, A. Gebauer, E. Maccioni, A. Ortolan, *et al.* (2017). Deep underground rotation measurements: GINGERino ring laser gyroscope in Gran Sasso, *Rev. Sci. Instrum.* **88,** no. 3, 034502, doi: 10.1063/1.4977051.

Bernauer, F., R. F. Garcia, N. Murdoch, V. Dehant, D. Sollberger, C. Schmelzbach, S. Stähler, J. Wassermann, H. Igel, A. Cadu, *et al.* (2020). Exploring planets and asteroids with 6DoF sensors: Utopia and realism, *Earth Planets Space* **72,** no. 1, 191, doi: 10.1186/s40623-020-01333-9.

Bernauer, F., J. Wassermann, F. Guattari, A. Frenois, A. Bigueur, A. Gaillot, E. de Toldi, D. Ponceau, U. Schreiber, and H. Igel (2018). BlueSeis3A: Full characterization of a 3C broadband rotational seismometer, *Seismol. Res. Lett.* **89,** no. 2A, 620–629, doi: 10.1785/0220170143.

Bernauer, F., J. Wassermann, and H. Igel (2012). Rotational sensors—A comparison of different sensor types, *J. Seismol.* **16,** no. 4, 595–602, doi: 10.1007/s10950-012-9286-7.

Bernauer, F., J. Wassermann, and H. Igel (2020). Dynamic tilt correction using direct rotational motion measurements, *Seismol. Res. Lett.* **91,** no. 5, 2872–2880, doi: 10.1785/0220200132.

Bernauer, M., A. Fichtner, and H. Igel (2014). Reducing nonuniqueness in finite source inversion using rotational ground motions, *J. Geophys. Res.* **119,** no. 6, 4860–4875, doi: 10.1002/2014JB011042.

Brinkman, N., S. C. Stähler, D. Giardini, C. Schmelzbach, A. Khan, A. Jacob, N. Fuji, C. Perrin, P. Lognonné, E. Beucler, *et al.* (2021). First focal mechanisms of marsquakes, *J. Geophys. Res.* **126,** no. 4, e2020JE006546, doi: 10.1029/2020JE006546.

Cao, Y., Y. Chen, T. Zhou, C. Yang, L. Zhu, D. Zhang, Y. Cao, W. Zeng, D. He, and Z. Li (2021). The development of a new IFOG-based 3C rotational seismometer, *Sensors* **21,** no. 11, 3899, doi: 10.3390/s21113899.

Chen, C., Y. Wang, L. Sun, C. J. Lin, Y. Wei, C. Liao, B. Lin, and L. Qin (2023). Six-component earthquake synchronous observations across Taiwan strait: Phase velocity and source location, *Earth Space Sci.* **10,** no. 12, e2023EA003040, doi: 10.1029/2023EA003040.

Chen, Y.-T., Y. Zhang, and L.-S. Xu (2019). Inversion of earthquake rupture process: Theory and applications, *La Riv. Del Nuovo Cimento* **42,** no. 8, 367–406, doi: 10.1393/ncr/i2019-10162-4.

Cochard, A., H. Igel, B. Schuberth, W. Suryanto, A. Velikoseltsev, U. Schreiber, J. Wassermann, F. Scherbaum, and D. Vollmer (2006). Rotational motions in seismology: theory, observation, simulation, in *Earthquake Source Asymmetry, Structural Media and Rotation Effects*, R. Teisseyre, E. Majewski, and M. Takeo (Editors), Springer-Verlag, Berlin/Heidelberg, 391–411, doi: 10.1007/3-540-31337-0_30.

Donner, S. (2021). Rotational ground motion measurements for regional seismic moment tensors: A review, *Adv. Geophys.* **62,** 141–186, doi: 10.1016/bs.agph.2021.06.002.

Donner, S., M. Bernauer, and H. Igel (2016). Inversion for seismic moment tensors combining translational and rotational ground motions, *Geophys. J. Int.* **207,** no. 1, 562–570, doi: 10.1093/gji/ggw298.

Donner, S., H. Igel, C. Hadziioannou, and , and The Romy Group (2018). Retrieval of the seismic moment tensor from joint measurements of translational and rotational ground motions: Sparse networks and single stations, in *Moment Tensor Solutions*, S. D'Amico (Editor), Springer International Publishing, Cham, 263–280, doi: 10.1007/978-3-319-77359-9_12.

Donner, S., C. J. Lin, C. Hadziioannou, A. Gebauer, F. Vernon, D. C. Agnew, H. Igel, U. Schreiber, and J. Wassermann (2017). Comparing direct observation of strain, rotation, and displacement with array estimates at piñon flat observatory, California, *Seismol. Res. Lett.* **88,** no. 4, 1107–1116, doi: 10.1785/0220160216.

Donner, S., M. Mustać, B. Hejrani, H. Tkalčić, and H. Igel (2020). Seismic moment tensors from synthetic rotational and translational ground motion: Green's functions in 1-D versus 3-D, *Geophys. J. Int.* **223,** no. 1, 161–179, doi: 10.1093/gji/ggaa305.

Donner, S., D. Rößler, F. Krüger, A. Ghods, and M. R. Strecker (2013). Segmented seismicity of the M_w 6.2 Baladeh earthquake sequence (Alborz Mountains, Iran) revealed from regional moment tensors, *J. Seismol.* **17,** no. 3, 925–959, doi: 10.1007/s10950-013-9362-7.

Duputel, Z., L. Rivera, H. Kanamori, and G. Hayes (2012). W phase source inversion for moderate to large earthquakes (1990-2010): *W* phase inversion for $M_w \geq 6.0$ earthquakes, *Geophys. J. Int.* **189,** no. 2, 1125–1147, doi: 10.1111/j.1365-246X.2012.05419.x.

Dziewonski, A. M., and J. H. Woodhouse (1983). An experiment in systematic study of global seismicity: Centroid-moment tensor solutions for 201 moderate and large earthquakes of 1981, *J. Geophys. Res.* **88,** no. B4, 3247–3271, doi: 10.1029/JB088iB04p03247.

Dziewonski, A. M., T.-A. Chou, and J. H. Woodhouse (1981). Determination of earthquake source parameters from waveform data for studies of global and regional seismicity, *J. Geophys. Res.* **86,** no. B4, 2825–2852, doi: 10.1029/JB086iB04p02825.

Ekström, G., M. Nettles, and A. M. Dziewoński (2012). The global CMT project 2004–2010: Centroid-moment tensors for 13,017 earthquakes, *Phys. Earth Planet. In.* **200–201,** 1–9, doi: 10.1016/j.pepi.2012.04.002.

Frohlich, C. (1995). Characteristics of well-determined non-double-couple earthquakes in the Harvard CMT catalog, *Phys. Earth Planet. In.* **91,** no. 4, 213–228, doi: 10.1016/0031-9201(95)03031-Q.

Hua, S., and Y. Zhang (2022). Numerical experiments of moment tensor inversion with rotational ground motions, *Chin. J. Geophys.* **65,** no. 1, 197–213, doi: 10.6038/cjg2022P0668 (in Chinese).

Huang, B. (2003). Ground rotational motions of the 1999 Chi-Chi, Taiwan earthquake as inferred from dense array observations, *Geophys. Res. Lett.* **30,** no. 6, doi: 10.1029/2002GL015157.

Huang, H.-H., N. Aso, and V. C. Tsai (2017). Toward automated directivity estimates in earthquake moment tensor inversion, *Geophys. J. Int.* **211,** no. 2, 1062–1076, doi: 10.1093/gji/ggx354.

Ichinose, G. A., S. R. Ford, and R. J. Mellors (2021). Regional moment tensor inversion using rotational observations, *J. Geophys. Res.* **126,** no. 2, e2020JB020827, doi: 10.1029/2020JB020827.

Igel, H., A. Cochard, J. Wassermann, A. Flaws, U. Schreiber, A. Velikoseltsev, and N. Pham Dinh (2007). Broad-band observations of earthquake-induced rotational ground motions, *Geophys. J. Int.* **168,** no. 1, 182–196, doi: 10.1111/j.1365-246X.2006.03146.x.

Igel, H., M.-F. Nader, D. Kurrle, A. M. G. Ferreira, J. Wassermann, and K. U. Schreiber (2011). Observations of Earth's toroidal free oscillations with a rotation sensor: The 2011 magnitude 9.0 Tohoku-Oki earthquake: Ring laser free oscillations, *Geophys. Res. Lett.* **38,** no. 21, doi: 10.1029/2011GL049045.

Igel, H., K. U. Schreiber, A. Gebauer, F. Bernauer, S. Egdorf, A. Simonelli, C. J. Lin, J. Wassermann, S. Donner, C. Hadziioannou, *et al.* (2021). ROMY: A multicomponent ring laser for geodesy and geophysics, *Geophys. J. Int.* **225,** no. 1, 684–698, doi: 10.1093/gji/ggaa614.

Igel, H., U. Schreiber, A. Flaws, B. Schuberth, A. Velikoseltsev, and A. Cochard (2005). Rotational motions induced by the M 8.1 Tokachi-Oki earthquake, September 25, 2003, *Geophys. Res. Lett.* **32,** no. 8, 2004GL022336, doi: 10.1029/2004GL022336.

Institute of Earth Sciences, Academia Sinica, Taiwan (1996). Broadband array in Taiwan for seismology [SEED data], International Federation of Digital Seismograph Networks, doi: 10.7914/SN/TW.

Jian, P., T. Tseng, W. Liang, and P. Huang (2018). A new automatic full-waveform regional moment tensor inversion algorithm and its applications in the Taiwan Area, *Bull. Seismol. Soc. Am.* **108,** no. 2, 573–587, doi: 10.1785/0120170231.

Kagan, Y. Y. (1991). 3-D rotation of double-couple earthquake sources, *Geophys. J. Int.* **106,** no. 3, 709–716, doi: 10.1111/j.1365-246X.1991.tb06343.x.

Kanamori, H., and J. W. Given (1981). Use of long-period surface waves for rapid determination of earthquake-source parameters, *Phys. Earth Planet. In.* **27,** no. 1, 8–31, doi: 10.1016/0031-9201(81)90083-2.

Kanamori, H., and L. Rivera (2008). Source inversion of *W* phase: Speeding up seismic tsunami warning, *Geophys. J. Int.* **175,** no. 1, 222–238, doi: 10.1111/j.1365-246X.2008.03887.x.

Kanamori, H., L. Ye, B.-S. Huang, H.-H. Huang, S.-J. Lee, W.-T. Liang, Y.Y. Lin, K.F. Ma, Y.M. Wu, and T.Y. Yeh (2017). A strong-motion hot spot of the 2016 Meinong, Taiwan, earthquake ($M_w = 6.4$), *Terr. Atmos. Ocean. Sci.* **28,** no. 5, 637–650, doi: 10.3319/TAO.2016.10.07.01.

Kennett, B. L. N., E. R. Engdahl, and R. Buland (1995). Constraints on seismic velocities in the Earth from travel times, *Geophys. J. Int.* **122,** no. 1, 108–124, doi: 10.1111/j.1365-246X.1995.tb03540.x.

Kislov, K. V., and V. V. Gravirov (2021). Rotational seismology: Review of achievements and outlooks, *Seism. Instrum.* **57,** no. 2, 187–202, doi: 10.3103/S0747923921020262.

Knapmeyer-Endrun, B., and T. Kawamura (2020). NASA's InSight mission on Mars—First glimpses of the planet's interior from seismology, *Nat. Commun.* **11,** no. 1, 1451, doi: 10.1038/s41467-020-15251-7.

Langston, C. A. (2007). Wave gradiometry in two dimensions, *Bull. Seismol. Soc. Am.* **97,** no. 2, 401–416, doi: 10.1785/0120060138.

Laske, G., G. Masters, Z. Ma, and M. Pasyanos (2013). Update on CRUST1.0 - A 1-degree global model of earth's crust, *Geophys. Res. Abstracts*, available at https://igppweb.ucsd.edu/~gabi/crust1/laske-egu13-crust1.pdf (last accessed September 2024).

Lee, S., T. Wong, T. Liu, T. Lin, and C. Chen (2020). Strong ground motion over a large area in northern Taiwan caused by the northward rupture directivity of the 2019 Hualien earthquake, *J. Asian Earth Sci.* **192,** 104095, doi: 10.1016/j.jseaes.2019.104095.

Lee, W. H. K., H. Igel, and M. D. Trifunac (2009). Recent advances in rotational seismology, *Seismol. Res. Lett.* **80,** no. 3, 479–490, doi: 10.1785/gssrl.80.3.479.

Li, W., Y. Zhang, L. Sun, R. Qian, and Y. Wang (2023). Seismic wavefield characteristics in translational and rotational components for isolated velocity-anomaly bodies in two-dimensional shallow media, *J. Appl. Geophys.* **217,** 105190, doi: 10.1016/j.jappgeo.2023.105190.

Lin, C., H. Huang, N. D. Pham, C. Liu, W. Chi, and W. H. K. Lee (2011). Rotational motions for teleseismic surface waves, *Geophys. Res. Lett.* **38,** no. 15, doi: 10.1029/2011GL047959.

Lin, C.-J., C.-S. Ku, T.-C. Chi, B.-S. Huang, H.-H. Huang, and C.-C. Liu (2022). Correcting the background tilt signal of the horizontal seismometer using a rotation sensor, *Seismol. Res. Lett.* **93,** no. 3, 1564–1572, doi: 10.1785/0220210185.

Lin, Y., Y. Wen, and Y. Yen (2022). Source properties of the 2019 M_L 6.3 Hualien, Taiwan, earthquake, determined by the local strong motion networks, *Geophys. J. Int.* **229,** no. 3, 1665–1679, doi: 10.1093/gji/ggac003.

Lin, Y., T. Yeh, K. Ma, T. Song, S. Lee, B. Huang, and Y. Wu (2018). Source characteristics of the 2016 Meinong (M_L 6.6), Taiwan, earthquake, revealed from dense seismic arrays: Double sources and pulse-like velocity ground motion, *Bull. Seismol. Soc. Am.* **108,** no. 1, 188–199, doi: 10.1785/0120170169.

Lognonné, P., W. B. Banerdt, D. Giardini, W. T. Pike, U. Christensen, P. Laudet, S. De Raucourt, P. Zweifel, S. Calcutt, M. Bierwirth, *et al.* (2019). SEIS: Insight's seismic experiment for internal structure of mars, *Space Sci. Rev.* **215,** no. 1, 12, doi: 10.1007/s11214-018-0574-6.

Maguire, R., V. Lekić, D. Kim, N. Schmerr, J. Li, C. Beghein, Q. Huang, J. C. Irving, F. Karakostas, P. Lognonné, *et al.* (2023). Focal mechanism determination of event S1222a and implications for tectonics near the dichotomy boundary in southern Elysium Planitia, Mars, *J. Geophys. Res.* **128,** no. 9, e2023JE007793, doi: 10.1029/2023JE007793.

Nigbor, R. L., J. R. Evans, and C. R. Hutt (2009). Laboratory and field testing of commercial rotational seismometers, *Bull. Seismol. Soc. Am.* **99,** no. 2B, 1215–1227, doi: 10.1785/0120080247.

Oliveira, C. S., and B. A. Bolt (1989). Rotational components of surface strong ground motion, *Earthq. Eng. Struct. Dynam.* **18,** no. 4, 517–526, doi: 10.1002/eqe.4290180406.

Pawlowicz, R. (2020). M_Map: A mapping package for MATLAB (Version 1.4m), available at www.eoas.ubc.ca/~rich/map.html (last accessed October 2024).

Pham, N. D., H. Igel, J. De La Puente, M. Käser, and M. A. Schoenberg (2010). Rotational motions in homogeneous anisotropic elastic media, *Geophysics* **75,** no. 5, D47–D56, doi: 10.1190/1.3479489.

Poppeliers, C., and E. V. Evans (2015). The effects of measurement uncertainties in seismic-wave gradiometry, *Bull. Seismol. Soc. Am.* **105,** no. 6, 3143–3155, doi: 10.1785/0120150043.

Reinwald, M., M. Bernauer, H. Igel, and S. Donner (2016). Improved finite-source inversion through joint measurements of rotational and translational ground motions: A numerical study, *Solid Earth* **7,** no. 5, 1467–1477, doi: 10.5194/se-7-1467-2016.

Schmelzbach, C., S. Donner, H. Igel, D. Sollberger, T. Taufiqurrahman, F. Bernauer, M. Häusler, C. Van Renterghem, J. Wassermann, and J. Robertsson (2018). Advances in 6C seismology: Applications of combined translational and rotational motion measurements in global and exploration seismology, *Geophysics* **83,** no. 3, WC53–WC69, doi: 10.1190/geo2017-0492.1.

Spudich, P., L. K. Steck, M. Hellweg, J. B. Fletcher, and L. M. Baker (1995). Transient stresses at Parkfield, California, produced by the *M* 7.4 Landers earthquake of June 28, 1992: Observations from the UPSAR dense seismograph array, *J. Geophys. Res.* **100,** no. B1, 675–690, doi: 10.1029/94JB02477.

Sun, L., Y. Wang, W. Li, and Y. Wei (2021). The characteristics of seismic rotations in VTI medium, *Appl. Sci.* **11,** no. 22, 10845, doi: 10.3390/app112210845.

Sun, L., Y. Wang, and X. Qiu (2022). Rayleigh-wave dispersion analysis and inversion based on the rotation, *Sensors* **22,** no. 3, 983, doi: 10.3390/s22030983.

Sun, L., Y. Wang, J. Yang, Y. Zhang, and S. Wang (2021). Progress in rotational seismology, *Earth Sci. J. China Univ. Geosci.* **46,** no. 4, 1518, doi: 10.3799/dqkx.2020.113.

Suryanto, W., H. Igel, J. Wassermann, A. Cochard, B. Schuberth, D. Vollmer, F. Scherbaum, U. Schreiber, and A. Velikoseltsev (2006). First comparison of array-derived rotational ground motions with direct ring laser measurements, *Bull. Seismol. Soc. Am.* **96,** no. 6, 2059–2071, doi: 10.1785/0120060004.

Wang, R., S. Heimann, Y. Zhang, H. Wang, and T. Dahm (2017). Complete synthetic seismograms based on a spherical self-gravitating Earth model with an atmosphere–ocean–mantle–core structure, *Geophys. J. Int.* **210,** no. 3, 1739–1764, doi: 10.1093/gji/ggx259.

Xu, B., and Y. Zhang (2023). Joint inversion of centroid moment tensor for large earthquakes by combining teleseismic P-wave and W-phase records, *Geophys. J. Int.* **234,** no. 2, 1143–1156, doi: 10.1093/gji/ggad128.

Zembaty, Z., S. Kokot, and P. Bobra (2013). Application of rotation rate sensors in an experiment of stiffness "reconstruction," *Smart Mater. Struct.* **22,** no. 7, 077001, doi: 10.1088/0964-1726/22/7/077001.

Zhang, Z., L. Sun, G. Tang, T. Xu, Y. Wang, M. Wang, and X. Guo (2020). Numerical simulation of the six-component elastic-wave field, *Chin. J. Geophys.* **63,** no. 6, 2375–2385, doi: 10.6038/cjg2020N0392 (in Chinese).

Manuscript received 5 December 2024
Published online 14 July 2025

Complex Multifault Rupture During the 2016–2025 Dingri Earthquakes, Southern Tibetan Plateau, Unraveled by Multisource InSAR Observations

Jiuyuan Yang[1], Yangmao Wen[*2], Caijun Xu[2], and Qingfeng Hu[1]

Abstract

During 22 May 2016 to 7 January 2025, three significant earthquakes (2016 M_w 5.4, 2020 M_w 5.7, and 2025 M_w 7.1 Dingri earthquakes) progressively ruptured the Shenza-Dingjie fault system, southern Tibetan plateau, effectively closing a remarkable seismic gap. We use Sentinel-1, Lutan-1, and Advanced Land Observation Satellite-2 Synthetic Aperture Radar images to extract coseismic deformation of the three events and the first-month postseismic deformation of 2025 event. Coseismic modeling demonstrates that the 2025 earthquake ruptured one west-dipping strike-variable moderate-angle main normal fault while the 2016 and 2020 earthquakes activated two shallow-dipping secondary normal faults, highlighting a complex synthetic–antithetic seismogenic structure. Further time-dependent postseismic analysis not only documents prominent postseismic signal of up to ~5 cm closely following 2025 earthquake, but also resolves discrete coseismic signals of ~3–4 cm related to three $M_s \geq 4.6$ aftershocks. By the comprehensive analysis of geodetic inversion, fault distribution, and topography, we deduce that 2025 earthquake nucleation is likely driven by elevated gravitational potential energy within the southern Tibetan plateau extensional regime.

Cite this article as Yang, J., Y. Wen, C. Xu, and Q. Hu (2025). Complex Multifault Rupture During the 2016–2025 Dingri Earthquakes, Southern Tibetan Plateau, Unraveled by Multisource InSAR Observations, *Seismol. Res. Lett.* **97**, 28–37, doi: 10.1785/0220250095.

Supplemental Material

Introduction

As the largest high-elevation and seismically active region in Tibetan plateau, its southern region has been undergoing the east–west extensional deformation and the nearly north–south-oriented crustal shortening and thickening in response to the unremitting collision between the Indian and Eurasian tectonic plates. As a result, there forms a series of typical east–west-striking thrust fault zones, such as the Main frontal thrust, Main boundary thrust, and Main central thrust zones, and north–south-trending rift systems, including Nyalam-Coqen rift, Yadong-Gulu rift, Nima-Dingri rift, and Shenza-Dingjie rift (SDR) (Molnar and Tapponnier, 1978; Yin, 2006; Taylor and Yin, 2009; Almeida *et al.*, 2018; Bai *et al.*, 2025; Shi *et al.*, 2025; Xu *et al.*, 2025; Fig. 1a,c). As a tectonically active large fault system located at the SDR, the ~300-km-long Shenza-Dingjie fault system (SDFS), mainly including the northern and southern Shenza-Dingjie fault segments, plays a crucial role in accommodating the east–west extension of southern Tibetan plateau and thus is easily prone to long-term strain accumulation (Shi *et al.*, 2025; Fig. 1c). However, in comparison with that the December 1934 M_w 7.3 and January 1935 M_w 6.5 earthquakes nucleated at the northern segment of the SDFS, the lack of historical $M_w > 6.5$ strong earthquakes in the southern segment of the SDFS presents an seismic gap (Shi *et al.*, 2025; Fig. 1c), which hampers our insight into the regional strain partitioning and seismogenic structure.

On 7 January 2025 (UTC time 01:05), an M_w 7.1 shallow earthquake occurred around the Dengme Co fault (DMF, the southern segment of the SDFS), nucleating ~40 km southeast of the Dingri county in Xizang Province, China (Fig. 1b). As the most destructive event to strike the southern part of the SDR, the 2025 Dingri earthquake not only caused 126 casualties, 188 injuries, and 3612 houses collapsed (Wei *et al.*, 2025), but also led to serious secondary phenomena, such as debris flow, landslide, surface rupture, and ground fissure (Shi *et al.*, 2025; Tie *et al.*, 2025), and was rapidly followed by an intense aftershock sequence with magnitudes ranging from M_L 0.5 to 5.1 (Yao *et al.*, 2025; Fig. 1b). The general aftershock distribution that occurred between 8 and 18 January 2025 (Fig. 1b,d–g) seems to delineate a continuous roughly south-trending

1. College of Surveying and Geo-informatics, North China University of Water Resources and Electric Power, Zhengzhou, China; 2. School of Geodesy and Geomatics, Wuhan University, Wuhan, China, https://orcid.org/0000-0001-8746-8615 (YW); https://orcid.org/0000-0002-3459-7824 (CX)

*Corresponding author: ymwen@sgg.whu.edu.cn

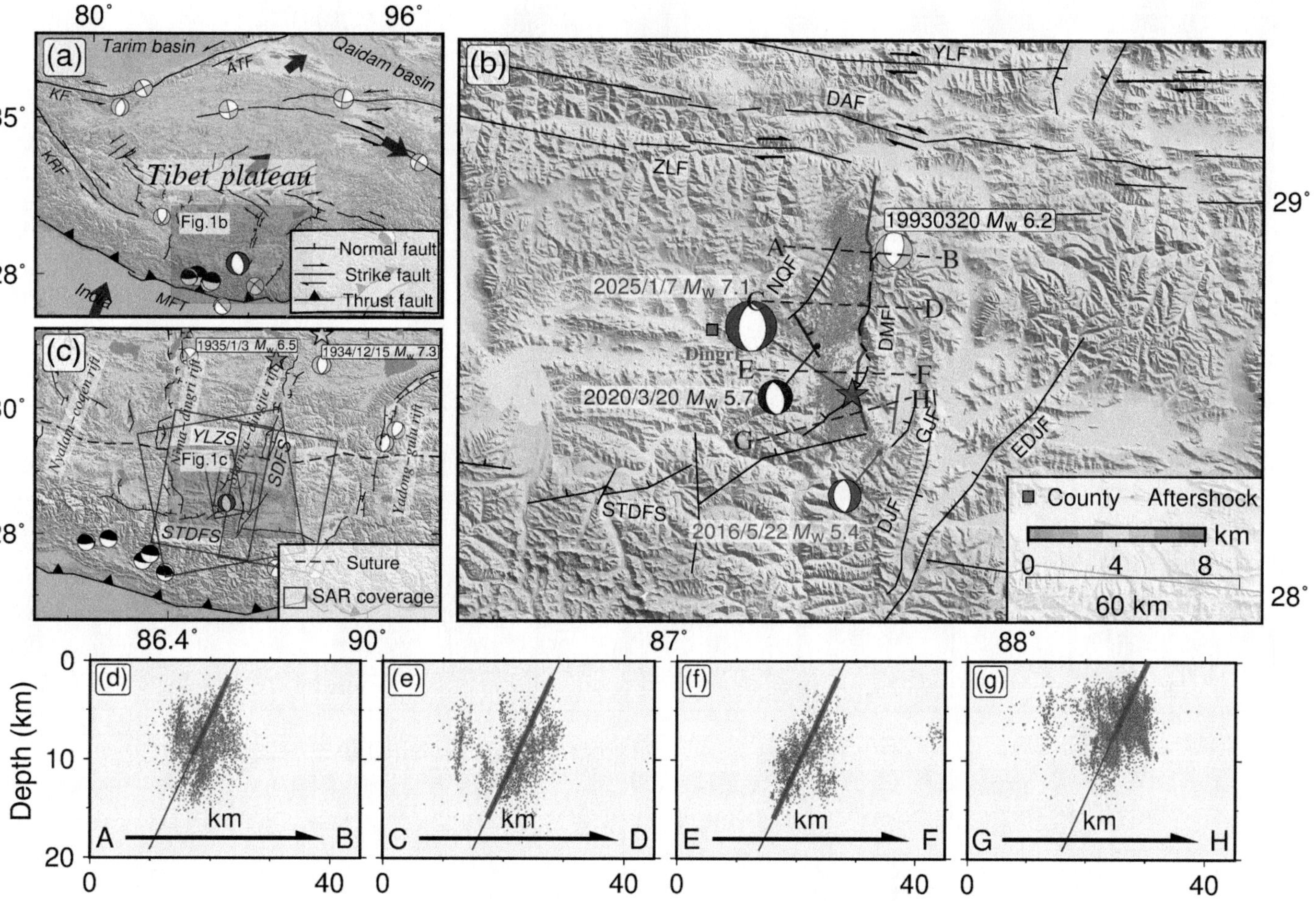

Figure 1. (a–c) Tectonic background of the Tibetan plateau, southern Tibetan plateau and 2025 Dingri earthquake, respectively. The red large arrows show the plate motion (Xu *et al.*, 2013). The green short lines represent the surface rupture from field investigation (Shi *et al.*, 2025), and black small circles are relocated aftershocks from Yao *et al.* (2025). The red, blue, and purple thick lines indicate the coseismic fault surface traces of the 2025, 2020, and 2016 Dingri earthquakes, respectively. ATF, Altyn Tagh fault; DAF, Dajilin-Angren-Renbu fault; DJF, Dingjie fault; DMF, Dengme Co fault; EDJF, East Dingjie fault; GJF, Guojia fault; KF, Karakash fault; KRF, Karakoram fault; MFT, Main frontal thrust; NQF, Nongqu fault; SDFS, Shenza-Dingjie fault system; STDFS, Southern Tibetan detachment fault system; YLF, Yarlung-Zangbo fault; YLZS, Yarlung-Zangbo suture zone; ZLF, Zhada-Lazi fault. The light blue, black, and focal mechanism plots denote the focal mechanisms of historical normal, thrust, and strike-slip earthquakes [$M_w > 6.5$ in (a) and $M_w > 6.0$ in (b) and (c)], respectively, from Global Centroid Moment Tensor (Global CMT). (d–g) The relocated aftershocks along the profiles AB, CD, EF, and GH, respectively. The red thin line represents the constructed fault plane during the linear inversion while thick red line depicts the main coseismic slip area. SAR, Synthetic Aperture Radar. The color version of this figure is available only in the electronic edition.

strike-variable fault, highlighting a complex rupture behavior during the 2025 Dingri earthquake. In comparison with two moderate normal-faulting earthquakes (22 May 2016 M_w 5.4 and 20 March 2020 M_w 5.7 Dingri earthquakes) located around the middle-south segment of the known DMF (Fig. 1b, Tables S1 and S2, available in the supplemental material to this article), the coseismic surface rupture from field investigation (Shi *et al.*, 2025; Fig. 1b) and focal mechanism solutions from the Global Centroid Moment Tensor Project (Global CMT) and U.S. Geological Survey (USGS) (Table S3) indicate that the large 2025 Dingri earthquake ruptured on the mapped west-dipping normal DMF, which is broadly in line with the overall spatial distribution of aftershocks (Fig. 1b,d–g). The Dingri earthquake sequence offers a valuable opportunity to improve our understanding of the regional strain partitioning and seismogenic structure with modern satellite geodetic data. Many geodetic studies (Hou *et al.*, 2020; Wang *et al.*, 2021; Li *et al.*, 2022, 2024) consistently support the activation of one buried simple planar normal fault during the 2016 and 2020 Dingri earthquakes without complex fault segmentation and geometrical structure. However, the subsurface fine seismogenic fault structure related to the 2025 Dingri event have not been fully explored in early studies (Wang *et al.*, 2025; Yang *et al.*, 2025; Yu *et al.*, 2025). For example, Wang *et al.* (2025), Yu *et al.* (2025), and Yang *et al.* (2025) believe one roughly south-striking (west-dipping) planar normal fault to be responsible for the 2025 Dingri earthquake. But they only exploit the Sentinel-1 ascending and descending and Lutan-1 ascending

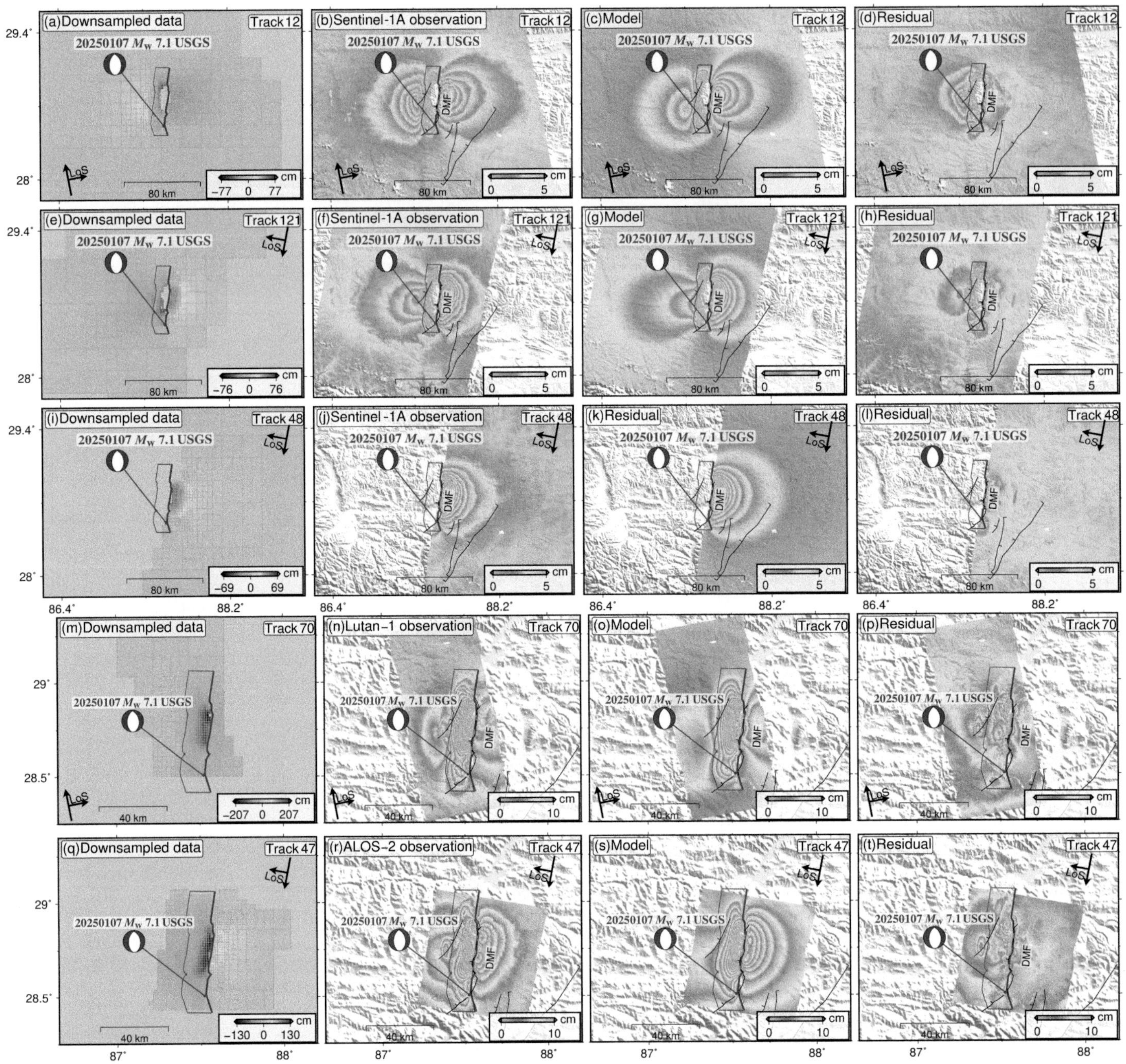

Figure 2. (a,e,i,m,q) Downsampled line-of-sight (LoS) deformation. (b,f,j,n,r) The observed coseismic interferograms covering the 2025 Dingri earthquake from the Sentinel-1A, Lutan-1, and Advanced Land Observation Satellite (ALOS)-2 satellites, respectively. (c,g,k,o,s) Modeled interferograms. (d,h,l,p, t) Residuals. The red thick line represents the coseismic fault surface trace. USGS, U.S. Geological Survey. The color version of this figure is available only in the electronic edition.

Synthetic Aperture Radar (SAR) images covering the major deformation area of the 2025 event to construct the seismogenic fault plane and ignore other available SAR images with different imaging geometries, relocated aftershocks, and field investigation data. Furthermore, their established straight planar fault segment is too simple to match the actual strike-variable surface trace outlined by the multisource deformation fringe pattern and relocated aftershocks (Figs. 1b and 2), which will result in some significant residuals in the near field of coseismic deformation (e.g., Yang *et al.*, 2023) and an inaccurate assessment of stress transfer (e.g., Mildon *et al.*, 2016). Besides, the previous researches only focus on the coseismic deformation of the 2025 Dingri earthquake as well as the relevant source model but overlook the coseismic deformation of the 2016 and 2020 Dingri events and large aftershocks and postseismic deformation of the 2025 Dingri event along with its related mechanism.

In this study, we first utilize Sentinel-1 SAR data to image the coseismic surface deformation of the 2016 and 2020 Dingri earthquake and then make full use of the Sentinel-1, Lutan-1,

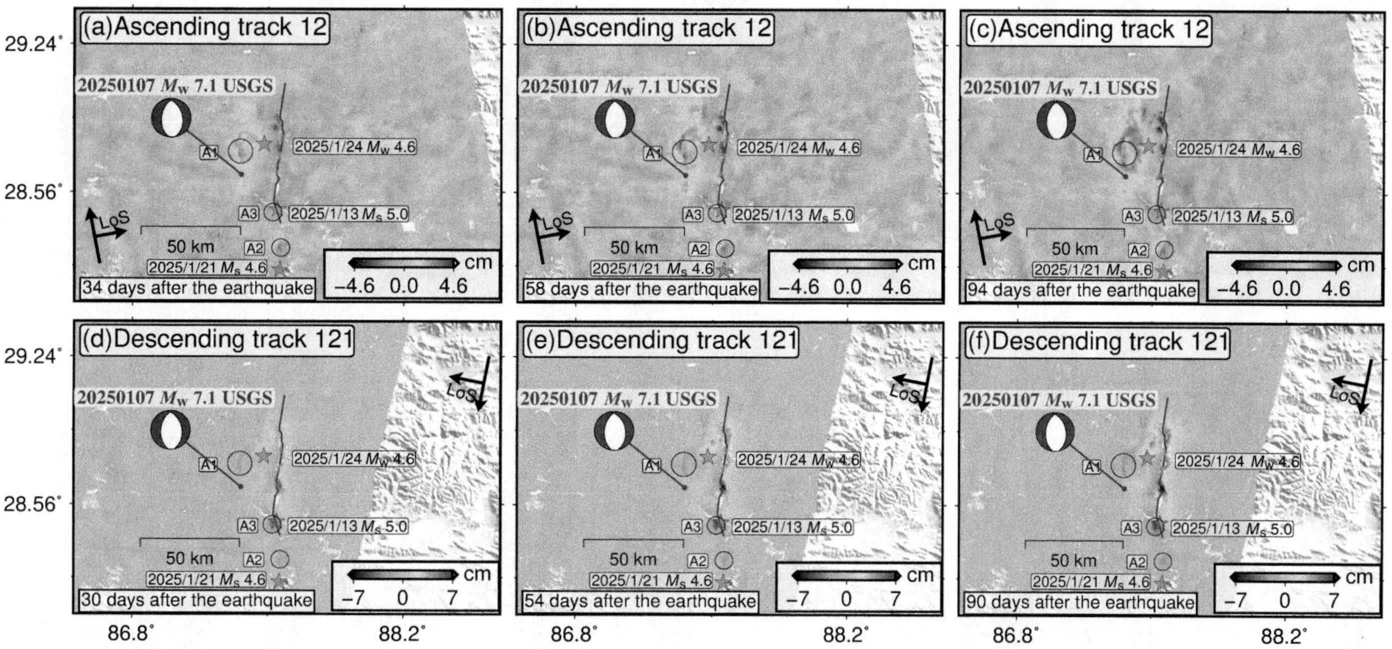

Figure 3. (a–c) Ascending postseismic time series of the 2025 Dingri earthquake. (d–f) Descending postseismic time series of the 2025 Dingri earthquake. The magenta stars represent the large aftershocks and the black circles show the deformation regions of these aftershocks. The color version of this figure is available only in the electronic edition.

and Advanced Land Observation Satellite (ALOS)-2 SAR data to extract the coseismic surface deformation of the 2025 Dingri earthquake. Furthermore, the early postseismic deformation of the 2025 Dingri event and coseismic deformation associated with three large aftershocks are also investigated in detail. Subsequently, we retrieve the coseismic slip of the 2016 and 2020 Dingri earthquakes according to the in-depth analysis of geodetic modeling and pay more attention to exploring the fine fault structure of the 2025 Dingri earthquake through the combined analysis of coseismic slip model, field observations, and relocated aftershocks. We further analyze which postseismic mechanisms, mostly consisting of poroelastic rebound, afterslip, and viscoelastic relaxation, play a key role in the observed postseismic deformation over a period of the first month following the 2025 Dingri event and deeply investigate the subsurface seismogenic structure of the known DMF as well as the possible seismogenic mechanism of the 2025 event. Finally, the influence of coseismic Coulomb stress changes triggered by the 2016, 2020, and 2025 Dingri earthquakes on the vicinal faults is quantified to discuss the potential for seismic hazard.

InSAR Observations and analysis

Benefitting from the relatively short revisit period of the Sentinel-1A, Lutan-1, and ALOS-2 satellites, we acquire a valuable chance to investigate the 2016, 2020, 2025 Dingri earthquakes. Nine pairs of the Sentinel-1, Lutan-1, and ALOS-2 Single Look Complex SAR images are utilized to construct coseismic interferograms of the three earthquakes by means of the Gamma software (Wegnüller *et al.*, 2016; Fig. 2, Figs. S1 and S2, Tables S4–S6). In addition, to detect the early postseismic deformation related to the 2025 Dingri earthquake and coseismic deformation of large aftershocks, we use eight Sentinel-1A ascending images spanning the time period from 17 January 2025 to 11 April 2025 and eight descending images spanning the time period from 13 January 2025 to 7 April 2025 to construct the postseismic time series of the 2025 event based on the small baseline method (Fig. 3, Figs. S3–S4, Table S7). Detailed data processing method and analysis are described in Text S1.

Geodetic Modeling

Coseismic modeling

To describe the subsurface seismogenic structure, we make use of the resolution-based resampling scheme (Lohman and Simons, 2005) to downsample the coseismic deformation of the 2016 M_W 5.4, 2020 M_W 5.7, and 2025 M_W 7.1 Dingri earthquakes (Fig. 2a,e,i,m,q). The extracted deformation is utilized to retrieve detailed slip on the rectangular dislocation embedded within an elastic, homogeneous and isotropic half-space (Okada, 1985). First, a nonlinear inversion is executed to solve for the best-fit fault geometrical parameters and locations with uniform slip. We also utilize the 100 datasets disturbed with random noise to evaluate the uncertainty of each inferred fault geometrical parameter according to the Monte Carlo simulation technique (Parsons *et al.*, 2006) (Tables S1–S3). Subsequently, a linear inversion is implemented to image the spatially variable slip distribution on the determined fault plane subdivided into square subpatches of the proper sizes (1 by 1 km or 2 by 2 km). Moreover, we append a best-fit smoothing weight factor during

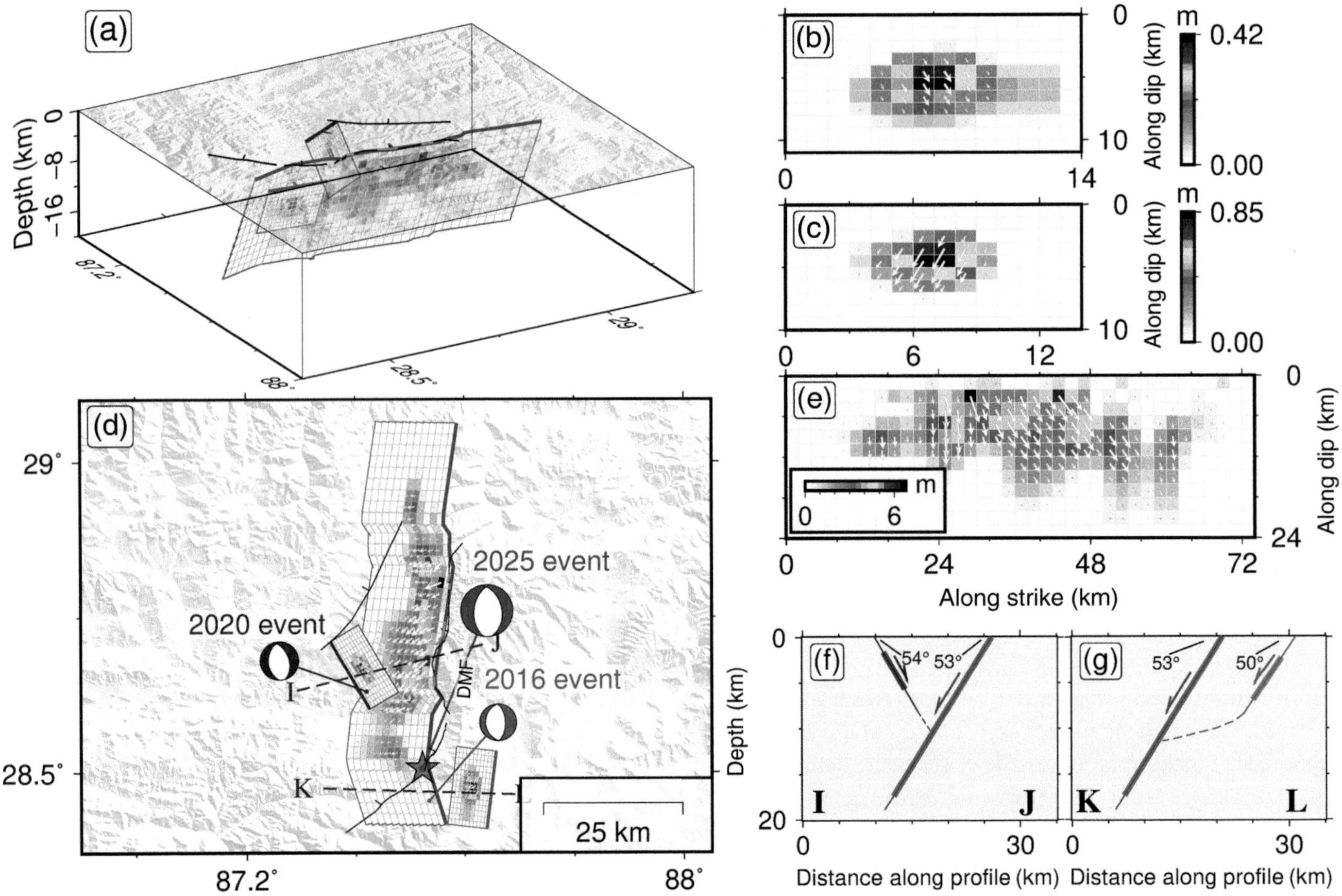

Figure 4. (a,d) 3D and 2D map views of coseismic slip distribution of the 2016–2025 Dingri earthquakes, respectively. (b,c,e) The projection of coseismic slip distribution of the three earthquakes along the strike and dip directions. (f,g) Subsurface fault structure along the profiles IJ and KL, respectively. The thin line indicates the established fault plane during the linear inversion and thick line represents the main coseismic slip area of three earthquakes. The dashed line denotes the inferred fault structure. The color version of this figure is available only in the electronic edition.

the slip distribution inversion so as to avoid slip oscillations (Figs. S5–S7).

22 May 2016 Dingri earthquake

According to the detailed analysis of the coseismic ascending and descending interferograms (Text S1), we regard the west-dipping fault to be the seismogenic fault accounting for the 2016 Dingri earthquake. Detailed inversion procedures and discussion are provided in Text S2 (Fig. S8). Our best-fit coseismic slip distribution reveals that the rupture fault is mainly characterized by normal faulting with slight left-lateral strike-slip motion and that the majority of coseismic slip propagates at depths between 2.3 and 6.9 km, peaking at ~0.42 m at 4.2 km depth (Fig. 4a,b,d). The seismic moment generated by the slip distribution model is $\sim 2.6 \times 10^{17}$ N · m, corresponding to an M_w 5.6 earthquake. The coseismic observations can be well recovered with the root mean square (rms) of ~3.5 mm (Fig. S1).

20 March 2020 Dingri earthquake

Under the guidance of the coseismic ascending and descending deformation described in Text S2, we consider the seismogenic fault to be a northeast-dipping normal fault. Detailed inversion procedures and discussion are provided in Text S2. The spatially variable slip distribution (Fig. 4c,d) highlights that the rupture fault is dominated by normal dip-slip motion accompanied by minor right-lateral strike-slip component and that most coseismic slip distributes at a depth of 1.6–5.7 km with the maximum slip of 0.85 m at 4.7 km depth. The location of the epicenter relative to the retrieved coseismic slip distribution implies that the coseismic rupture propagates northwestward unilaterally. The geodetic moment yielded by the coseismic slip distribution reaches $\sim 3.65 \times 10^{17}$ N · m, equivalent to an M_w 5.7 earthquake. The detected coseismic ascending and descending observations can be well explained with rms of 4.1 and 6.3 mm, respectively (Fig. S2).

7 January 2025 Dingri earthquake

Based on the deformation fringe patterns in the multisource coseismic interferograms (Fig. 2b,f,j,n,r), surface rupture from field investigation (Fig. 1b), postseismic deformation

(Fig. S4), overall spatial distribution of relocated aftershocks (Fig. 1b,d–g), and the mapped surface trace of DMF, we identified one strike-variable west-dipping normal fault with a dip angle of 53° and an average strike angle of 182° during 2025 Dingri event. Detailed inversion strategies and analysis are provided in Text S2 (Figs. S9–S12). Our favored coseismic slip distribution model (Fig. 4a,d,e) illustrates that the rupture fault is characterized by normal faulting with minor left-lateral strike-slip motion and that the prominent coseismic slip is concentrated at depths between 0 and 14 km with the peaking slip of ~6.8 m at a depth of 2.4 km. Some significant shallow slip patches of up to ~2.0 m are identified at the top of the rupture fault, which basically coincides with the surface rupture from field investigation (Fig. 4d). The resolution test results (Fig. S13) verify that our used multisource coseismic observations can well identify the fault slip of the 2025 Dingri earthquake. Considering that the location, strike, and slip sense of our inverted rupture fault are basically consistent with the known DMF, we conclude that the mapped DMF, together with its previous unidentified northern and southern continuations, is the seismogenic fault responsible for the 2025 Dingri earthquake. The hypocentral location relative to the inverted slip distribution highlights that the coseismic rupture mainly propagates northward unilaterally. The coseismic slip distribution releases a geodetic moment of $\sim 4.95 \times 10^{19}$ N · m, which amounts to M_w 7.1, and fits the observed ascending and descending coseismic deformation well (Fig. 2). In the whole, compared with a relatively large residual fringe left by the single planar fault model (Fig. S11), our established strike-variable fault model exhibits a noticeably better fit to the Interferometric Synthetic Aperture Radar (InSAR) observations (Fig. 2).

Postseismic modeling

Poroelastic deformation, afterslip, and viscoelastic relaxation are believed to be three major postseismic deformation mechanisms. Taking into consideration the short-period, localized postseismic deformation (Figs. S3 and S4) and shallow source depth of the January 2025 Dingri earthquake, we rule out the viscoelastic relaxation as a driving mechanism accounting for the early postseismic deformation. To explore whether the poroelastic rebound is the main mechanism of the observed postseismic deformation, we subtract the expected deformation under undrained conditions (Poisson ratio values of 0.28) from that under the drained conditions (Poisson ratio values of 0.25) with the purpose to estimate the surface deformation of poroelastic rebound (e.g., Wang and Fialko, 2014). The predicted surface deformation magnitude and patterns caused by poroelastic rebound (Fig. S14) are obviously inconsistent with the observed postseismic deformation (Figs. S3 and S4), indicating that afterslip may be the driving mechanism for the accumulated postseismic deformation. Then, we utilize the cumulative ascending and descending postseismic deformation to carry out the afterslip inversion. The result (Fig. S15) shows that afterslip is dominated by normal faulting and that most slip is confined at shallow part of the seismogenic fault. Considering the location of aftershocks (Figs. S3 and S4), postseismic deformation analysis (section 1.2 in Text S1), afterslip distribution (Fig. S15), and modeling result (Fig. S16), we deduce that the central postseismic slip may be associated with the 2025 Dingri event and the northern and southern postseismic slip may be related with the large aftershocks (Fig. S15). More detailed postseismic investigations will be required in the future research.

Discussion

Complex subsurface seismogenic structure of the DMF revealed by the 2016 M_w 5.4, 2020 M_w 5.7, and 2025 M_w 7.1 Dingri earthquakes

Finely identifying subsurface seismogenic structure of the moderate-to-large normal-faulting earthquake sequence can help us better understand the evolution of the regional geological structures such as basins, grabens, and rift valleys. Thereinto, a large earthquake is of great significance because it can directly reflect the overall structure information of a main fault. Nevertheless, a moderate earthquake on a secondary or auxiliary fault is equally significant because it is able to complement some additional structural information associated with a main fault, offering a more detailed and complete view of a large fault system (Yang *et al.*, 2023). In the vicinity of the mapped DMF, two moderate earthquakes (2016 M_w 5.4 and 2020 M_w 5.7 Dingri earthquakes) and a strong earthquake (2025 M_w 7.1 Dingri earthquake) occurred successively (Fig. 1b). Our well-constrained inversion result indicates that the 2016 Dingri earthquake ruptured an unknown west-dipping normal fault with tiny sinistral strike-slip component, whereas 2020 Dingri earthquake nucleated on an unmapped east-dipping normal fault with minor right-lateral strike-slip motion and that the 2025 Dingri earthquake disrupted the mapped normal DMF as well as its previous unidentified continuations with slight left-lateral strike-slip faulting (Fig. 4). Around the epicenter of 2016 and 2020 Dingri earthquakes, DMF is the closest and subparallel structure to the identified causative faults of these two events (Fig. 1b). The prominent coseismic slip of the 2016 Dingri earthquake propagates within a 8-km-long and 6-km-wide rupture plane and stops before the junction of the seismogenic fault and DMF, whereas the significant coseismic slip of the 2020 Dingri earthquake transmits within a 7-km-long and 5-km-wide rupture plane and also stops before the junction of the rupture fault and DMF (Fig. 4f,g). The lack of coseismic slip in the deep part of the two rupture faults implies that the seismogenic faults do not pass through the known DMF (Fig. 4f,g). For an active major continental normal fault, it often exists in a planar, listric, or ramp-flat geometry and develops associated with smaller, secondary antithetic, or synthetic faults (e.g., Yang *et al.*, 2022). Given that the eastern west-dipping moderate-angle (a dip of 50°) normal fault (the seismogenic fault of 2016 event) and the western east-dipping moderate-angle (a dip of 54°) normal fault (the causative fault of 2020 event) are only ~12 and 14 km away from the normal DMF (the source fault of 2025 event with a dip of 53°), respectively, and that each inferred fault is characterized by minor strike-slip motion toward the north direction, we think that the seismogenic faults of 2016 and 2020 earthquakes, which act as secondary fault branches, are likely to merge into the seismogenic fault (DMF) of 2025 earthquake at depth, revealing the complex antithetic and synthetic seismogenic structures associated with the main DMF (Fig. 4f,g).

Cause of the 2025 Dingri earthquake

Our geodetic modeling indicates that the January 2025 normal-faulting Dingri earthquake nucleated on a roughly north-striking west-dipping DMF fault in the Dengme Co garden, which lies at the average elevation of ~4500 km (Fig. 1b; Yang *et al.*, 2025). For such an east–west extensional earthquake for which epicenter is located at the high-altitude area in Tibetan plateau, the stepover model or gravitational spreading model is usually applied to explain its occurrence (e.g., Molnar and Tapponnier, 1978; Elliot *et al.*, 2010; Fang *et al.*, 2024). For example, the occurrence of the March 2008 M_w 7.1 Yutian earthquake in northwest Tibetan plateau is interpreted to the release of extensional stress in a stepover zone controlled by the northeast-trending left-lateral strike-slip Altyn Tagh fault and Longmu-Gazga Co fault (Furuya and Yasuda, 2011; Bie and Ryder, 2014). Similarly, the July 2020 M_w 6.3 Nima earthquake striking the Yibug Caka basin in the central Tibetan plateau is also attributed to the release of regional tectonic stress in an extensional stepover zone controlled by the nearby "en echelon" sinistral strike-slip fault system (Yang *et al.*, 2022). However, the stepover fault model is often proposed to explain the occurrence of a normal-faulting earthquake in a tectonic region mainly characterized by strike-slip structures, where normal faults act as secondary or auxiliary fault branches (Molnar and Tapponnier, 1978; Furuya and Yasuda, 2011), but it is not generally suitable for explaining all the normal-faulting earthquakes that occur in high-altitude geological structure regions. In contrast, the gravitational spreading model is used to account for the cause of a normal-faulting earthquake in an active tectonic region dominated by extensional structures, where strike-slip faults are sparse (Molnar and Tapponnier, 1978; Furuya and Yasuda, 2011). The 2025 Dingri earthquake, manifested as normal faulting, struck the southern segment of the large normal SDFS in southern Tibetan plateau, where the circumambient tectonic structures are dominated by nearly east–west extensional motion. For this roughly west-dipping shallow normal-faulting event lying at the extremely high elevation of the southern Tibetan plateau, we speculate that the regional high gravitational potential energy may be the seismogenic cause of the 2025 Dingri earthquake (e.g., Elliot *et al.*, 2010).

Stress adjustment and regional hazard assessment

To study stress transfer among the 2016, 2020, and 2025 Dingri earthquakes, we quantify the influence of coseismic coulomb failure stress (CFS) changes due to previous earthquakes on the subsequent events with a typical friction coefficient of 0.4 (e.g., Freed, 2005), noticing that positive stress value usually promotes rupture, whereas negative one prevents rupture. Our result indicates that the 2016 earthquake induces limited effect (~0.002 MPa) on the 2020 earthquake (Figs. S17a) and positive stress values of up to 0.014 MPa on the 2025 earthquake (Fig. S17b) and that 2020 earthquake gives arise to 0.005 MPa on the 2025 earthquake (Fig. S17c). Therefore, we think that the 2016 event has no effect on the occurrence of the 2020 event, but raises the probability of the occurrence of 2025 event (e.g., Stein *et al.*, 1997). Figure S17d shows a total of ~0.02 MPa stress value at the epicenter of the 2025 Dingri event induced by the 2016 and 2020 Dingri events, suggesting that the 2016 and 2020 event promotes the rupture of 2025 event. To further evaluate the effect of the recent three earthquakes on the neighboring faults, we exploit the inverted coseismic slip distributions of the three events to acquire the coseismic CFS changes on the mapped faults. Given the fault distribution and kinematics (Fig. 1b), the receiver mechanisms (Table S8) are set for the calculation of coseismic CFS changes on the mapped nearby active faults. The results (Fig. 5) reveal stress unloading on the entire segment of the STDFS. By contrast, the western segment of the ZLF, DAF, and YLF (a stress value of up to ~0.15, 0.1, and 0.07 MPa, respectively), the entire segment of the GJF and DJF (maximum ~0.18 and 0.08 MPa, respectively) and the southern segment of the DMF and EDJF (maximum ~3.0 and 0.05 MPa, respectively) exhibit stress loading of more than 0.01 MPa commonly known as an earthquake triggering threshold (e.g., Ziv and Rubin, 2000). Considering the large positive CFS change (Fig. 5), strong tectonic activity and decades of earthquake quiescence along the western segment of the ZLF, DAF, and YLF, the entire segment of the GJF and DJF and the southern segment of the DMF and EDJF, we believe that these fault segments represent an important hazard in the region.

Conclusion

We exploit multisource coseismic InSAR observations supplemented with relocated aftershocks and field investigation data to study the source models of the 2016, 2020, and 2025 Dingri earthquakes. Our results highlight that at least three moderate-angle normal faults are activated, including one west-dipping strike-variable main fault for the 2025 event, one synthetic west-dipping secondary fault for the 2016 event and one antithetic northeast-dipping fault for 2020 event. Further postseismic observation of the 2025 earthquake not only shows prominent postseismic signal closely following the 2025 earthquake, but also reveals localized coseismic signals related to three large aftershocks. We also discuss the possible cause

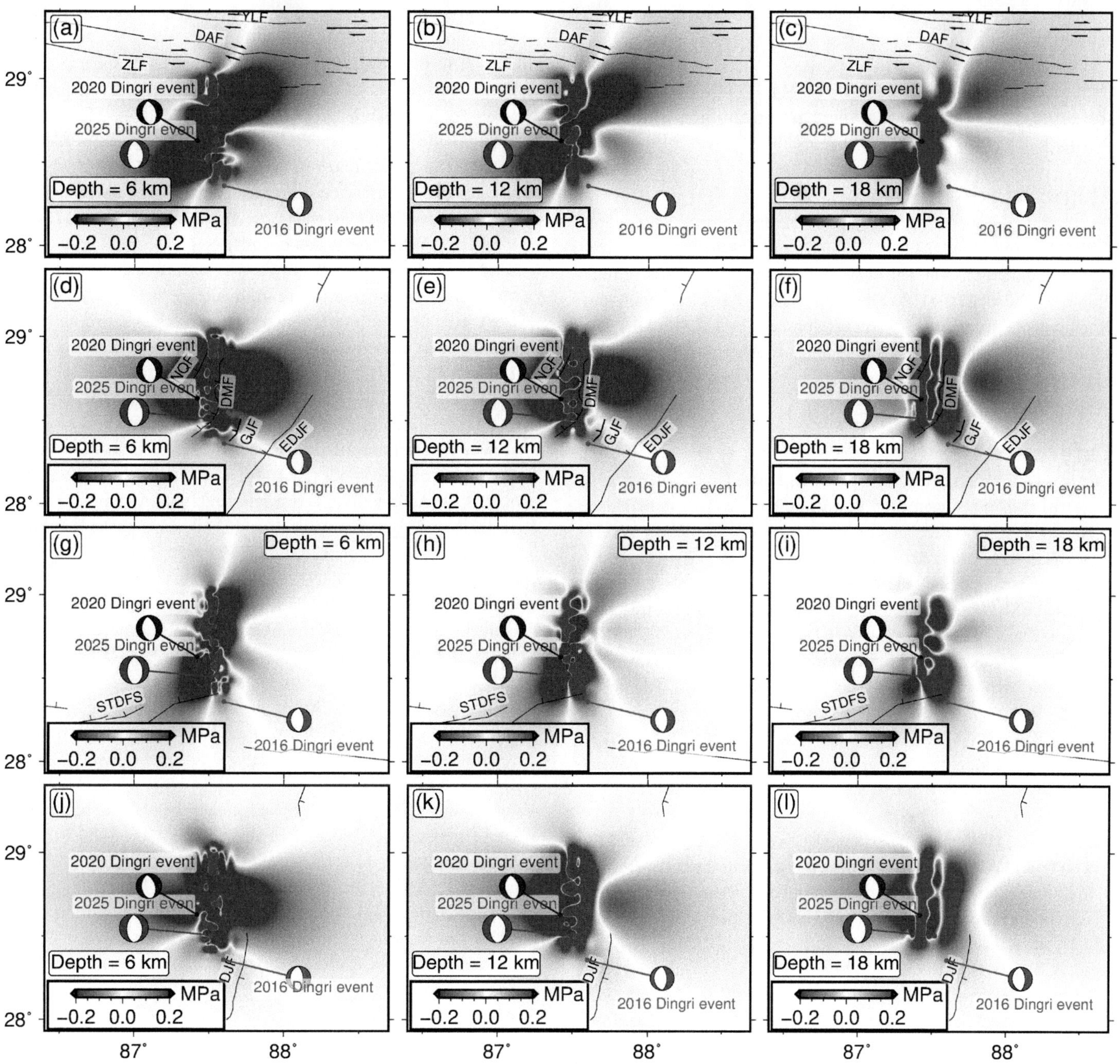

for the occurrence of the 2025 event through the joint analysis of geodetic inversion, fault distribution, and topography and suggest that the occurrence of 2025 Dingri earthquake may be attributed to the regional high gravitational potential energy. Furthermore, we should focus on the western segment of the ZLF, DAF, and YLF, the entire segment of the GJF and DJF and the southern segment of the DMF and EDJF because of the large CFS change and the lack of seismicity.

Figure 5. (a–c) Coseismic CFS changes along the DAF, YLF and ZLF caused by the 2016–2025 Dingri earthquakes. (d–f) Coseismic CFS changes along the NQF, DMF, GJF and EDJF caused by the 2016–2025 Dingri earthquakes. (g–i) Coseismic CFS changes along the STDFS caused by the 2016–2025 Dingri earthquakes. (j–l) Coseismic CFS changes along the DJF caused by the 2016–2025 Dingri earthquakes. The color version of this figure is available only in the electronic edition.

Data and Resources

The European Space Agency Sentinel-1 Synthetic Aperture Radar (SAR) data are downloaded from the Alaska Satellite Facility (https://search.asf.alaska.edu/). The Lutan-1 SAR data are required from Natural Resources Satellite Remote Sensing Cloud Service Platform (http://sasclouds.com/english/home). The Advanced Land Observation Satellite (ALOS)-2 SAR data are acquired from the Japan Aerospace Exploration Agency (https://satpf.jp/spf/?lang=en). Focal mechanism solutions are acquired from the Global Centroid Moment Tensor Project (https://www.globalcmt.org/) and U.S. Geological Survey (https://www.usgs.gov/). All websites were last accessed in August 2025. The supplemental material includes two texts, eight tables, and seventeen figures.

Declaration of Competing Interests

The authors acknowledge that there are no conflicts of interest recorded.

Acknowledgments

This work is cosupported by the National Natural Science Foundation of China (Numbers 42304007, 42374003, and 42130101), the Henan Science Foundation for Distinguished Young Scholars of China (Number 242300421041), and the Henan Key Research and Development Program of China (Number 241111321100). The authors thank the editor, one anonymous reviewer, and the reviewer J. Jara for their constructive comments and also thank Yongsheng Li for his helpful suggestions.

References

Almeida, R. V., J. Hubbard, L. Liberty, A. Foster, and S. N. Sapkota (2018). Seismic imaging of the Main Frontal Thrust in Nepal reveals a shallow décollement and blind thrusting, *Earth Planet. Sci. Lett.* **494,** 216–225.

Bai, L., Z. Chen, and S. Wang (2025). The 2025 Dingri M_S 6.8 earthquake in Xizang: Analysis of tectonic background and discussion of source characteristics, *Rev. Geophys. Planet. Phys.* **56,** no. 3, 258–263.

Bie, L., and I. Ryder (2014). Recent seismic and aseismic activity in the Ashikule stepover zone, NW Tibet, *Geophys. J. Int.* **198,** no. 3, 1632–1643.

Elliott, J. R., R. J. Walters, P. C. England, J. A. Jackson, Z. Li, and B. Parsons (2010). Extension on the Tibetan plateau: Recent normal faulting measured by InSAR and body wave seismology, *Geophys. J. Int.* **183,** no. 2, 503–535.

Fang, J., G. A. Houseman, T. J. Wright, L. A. Evans, T. J. Craig, J. R. Elliott, and A. Hooper (2024). The dynamics of the India-Eurasia collision: Faulted viscous continuum models constrained by high-resolution Sentinel-1 InSAR and GNSS velocities, *J. Geophys. Res.* **129,** no. 6, e2023JB028571, doi: 10.1029/2023JB028571.

Freed, A. M. (2005). Earthquake triggering by static, dynamic, and post-seismic stress transfer, *Annu. Rev. Earth Planet. Sci.* **33,** 335–367.

Furuya, M., and T. Yasuda (2011). The 2008 Yutian normal faulting earthquake (M_w 7.1), NW Tibet: Non-planar fault modeling and implications for the Karakax fault, *Tectonophysics* **511,** nos. 3/4, 125–133.

Hou, L., X. Shan, W. Gong, Y. Zhang, H. Luo, and D. Zhao (2020). Characterizing seismogenic fault of 2016 Dingjie earthquake based on multitemporal DInSAR, *Chin. J. Geophys.* **63,** no. 4, 1357–1369.

Li, C., Q. Li, K. Tan, Y. Huang, and X. Lu (2022). Ground deformation and source fault model of the M_w 5.7 Xegar (Tibetan plateau) 2020 earthquake, based on InSAR observation, *Pure Appl. Geophys.* **179,** no. 10, 3589–3603.

Li, Q., C. Li, B. Zhao, Y. Huang, Y. Wan, K. Tan, and Q. Dong (2024). Estimated seismic source parameters for 2020 Dingri M_W 5.6 earthquake in Xizang and study on the stress triggering, *Chin. J. Geophys.* **67,** no. 1, 172–188.

Lohman, R. B., and M. Simons (2005). Some thoughts on the use of InSAR data to constrain models of surface deformation: Noise structure and data downsampling, *Geochem. Geophys. Geosys.* **6,** no. 1, doi: 10.1029/2004GC000841.

Mildon, Z. K., S. Toda, J. P. Faure Walker, and G. P. Roberts (2016). Evaluating models of Coulomb stress transfer: Is variable fault geometry important?, *Geophys. Res. Lett.* **43,** 12,407–12,414.

Molnar, P., and P. Tapponnier (1978). Active tectonics of Tibet, *J. Geophys. Res. Solid Earth* **83,** no. B11, 5361–5375.

Okada, Y. (1985). Surface deformation due to shear and tensile faults in a half-space, *Bull. Seismol. Soc. Am.* **75,** no. 4, 1135–1154.

Parsons, B., T. Wright, P. Rowe, J. Andrews, J. Jackson, R. Walker, M. Khatib, M. Talebian, E. Bergman, and E. R. Engdahl (2006). The 1994 Sefidabeh (eastern Iran) earthquakes revisited: New evidence from satellite radar interferometry and carbonate dating about the growth of an active fold above a blind thrust fault, *Geophys. J. Int.* **164,** no. 1, 202–217.

Shi, F., M. Liang, Q. Luo, J. Qiao, D. Zhang, X. Wang, W. Yi, J. Zhang, Y. Zhang, H. Zhang, *et al.* (2025). Seismogenic fault and coseismic surface deformation of the Dingri M_S 6.8 earthquake in Tibet, *China Seismol. Geol.* **47,** no. 1, 1–15.

Stein, R. S., A. A. Barka, and J. H. Dieterich (1997). Progressive failure on the North Anatolian fault since 1939 by earthquake stress triggering, *Geophys. J. Int.* **128,** no. 3, 594–604.

Taylor, M., and A. Yin (2009). Active structures of the Himalayan-Tibetan orogen and their relationships to earthquake distribution, contemporary strain field, and Cenozoic volcanism, *Geosphere* **5,** no. 3, 199–214.

Tie, Y., Y. Gao, X. Zhang, A. Shi, W. Huang, Y. Qin, Z. Li, L. Dong, and Z. Ning (2025). Study on the development laws and mitigation of geological hazards in Dingri M_S 6.8 earthquake region, Xizang automomous region, *Sediment. Geol. Tethyan Geol.* 1–20.

Wang, K., and Y. Fialko (2014). Space geodetic observations and models of postseismic deformation due to the 2005 M7.6 Kashmir (Pakistan) earthquake, *J. Geophys. Res.* **119,** no. 9, 7306–7318.

Wang, N., Y. Li, W. Shen, W. Jiang, Q. Li, and Q. Jiao (2025). Source parameters and rapid simulation of strong ground motion of the MS 6.8 earthquake on January 7, 2025 in Dingri (Xizang, China) derived from InSAR observation, *Geomat. Inf. Sci. Wuhan Univ.* **50,** no. 2, 404–411.

Wang, Y., S. Chen, and K. Chen (2021). Source model and tectonic implications of the 2020 Dingri M_w 5.7 earthquake constrained by InSAR data, *Earthquake* **41,** no. 1, 7306–7318.

Wegnüller, U., C. Werner, T. Strozzi, A. Wiesmann, O. Frey, and M. Santoro (2016). Sentinel-1 support in the GAMMA software, *Procedia Comput. Sci.* **100,** 1305–1312.

Wei, B., Y. Zhang, F. Shi, J. Qiao, X. Wang, and D. Zhang (2025). Analysis of building damage and casualties of the Dingri M_S 6.8 earthquake in Xizang based on field investigation, *Seismol. Geol.* **47,** no. 1, 64–79.

Xu, X., X. Tan, G. Yu, G. Wu, W. Fang, J. Chen, H. Song, and J. Shen (2013). Normal-and oblique-slip of the 2008 Yutian earthquake: evidence for eastward block motion, northern Tibetan plateau, *Tectonophysics* **584,** 152–165.

Xu, X., S. Wang, J. Cheng, and X. Wu (2025). Shaking the Tibetan Plateau: Insights from the M_w 7.1 Dingri earthquake and its implications for active fault mapping and disaster mitigation, *npj Nat. Hazards.* **2,** no. 1, 16.

Yang, J., M. Jin, B. Ye, L. Li, and Q. Li (2025). Source rupture mechanism and stress changes to the adjacent area of January 7, 2025, MS 6.8 Dingri earthquake, Xizang China, *Seismol. Geol.* **47,** no. 1, 64–79.

Yang, J., C. Xu, and Y. Wen (2023). Coseismic and early postseismic deformation associated with the January 2022 M_w 6.6 Menyuan earthquake, NE Tibet, revealed by InSAR Observations, *Tectonophysics* **868,** 230,090.

Yang, J., C. Xu, Y. Wen, and G. Xu (2022). The July 2020 M_w 6.3 Nima earthquake, central Tibet: A shallow normal-faulting event rupturing in a stepover zone, *Bull. Seismol. Soc. Am.* **93,** no. 1, 45–55.

Yao, J., D. Yao, F. Chen, M. Zhi, L. Sun, and D. Wang (2025). A preliminary catalog of early aftershocks following the 7 January 2025 M_S 6.8 Dingri, Xizang earthquake, *J. Earth Sci.* 1–5.

Yin, A. (2006). Cenozoic tectonic evolution of the Himalayan orogen as constrained by along-strike variation of structural geometry, exhumation history, and foreland sedimentation, *Earth Sci. Rev.* **76,** nos. 1/2, 1–131.

Yu, C., Z. Li, X. Hu, C. Song, S. Li, H. Liu, *et al.* (2025). Source parameters and induced hazards of the 2025 M_w 7.1 Dingri earthquake on the southern Tibetan plateau (Xizhang), China, as revealed by imaging geodesy, *J. Earth Sci.* 1–5.

Ziv, A., and A. M. Rubin (2000). Static stress transfer and earthquake triggering: No lower threshold in sight?, *J. Geophys. Res.* **105,** no. B6, 13,631–13,642.

Manuscript received 14 March 2025
Published online 16 September 2025

Investigation of the Foreshock Characteristics of the 2014 M_S 6.5 Ludian Earthquake

Shiguang Deng[1], Haikun Jiang[*2], Yawei Ma[2], Zhiwei Liu[1], Shaowei Kang[3,4], and Yue Wang[2]

Abstract

Foreshocks play a crucial role in providing insights into the earthquake nucleation process. Analyzing the foreshock characteristics of typical earthquake cases is essential for enhancing our understanding of the mechanisms behind earthquake nucleation. Although most case studies focus on earthquakes with significant foreshocks, studies of earthquakes with less obvious or initially undetected foreshocks can broaden our perspective on the earthquake nucleation process. The 2014 M_S 6.5 Ludian earthquake is a typical intraplate earthquake that was initially cataloged without obvious foreshocks. In this study, we first used the hypoDD method to accurately relocate earthquakes near the M_S 6.5 Ludian earthquake and then applied the match-and-locate method to detect and locate missing events from 65 days before to 29 days after the mainshock. The updated catalog included 4285 seismic events, nearly doubling the original catalog. The number of foreshocks increased from 19 to 155, with magnitudes ranging from M_L−0.3 to 2.7. We found that the b value of the foreshock sequence is significantly higher than that of the aftershocks, which is likely due to differences in the fault segments associated with the foreshock and aftershock activity zones, as well as the incomplete release of stress along the fault during the mainshock. The spatiotemporal evolution of the foreshocks revealed a migration trend toward the mainshock, followed by a period of quiescence. Observations of migrating foreshocks and repeating earthquakes indicate that aseismic slip plays an important role in the initial nucleation process. Considering existing research on earthquake rupture processes and Global Positioning System observations, we suggest that cascading stress transfer also contributes to the nucleation process. Therefore, we propose that multiple mechanisms can work together, and the rate-dependent cascade-up model better explains the nucleation process of the Ludian earthquake.

Cite this article as Deng, S., H. Jiang, Y. Ma, Z. Liu, S. Kang, and Y. Wang (2025). Investigation of the Foreshock Characteristics of the 2014 M_S 6.5 Ludian Earthquake, *Seismol. Res. Lett.* **97**, 38–53, doi: 10.1785/0220250022.

Supplemental Material

Introduction

Foreshock activity provides important information for studying the process of earthquake nucleation and is considered one of the most effective indicators for earthquake prediction (Chen, 1978; Jones and Molnar, 1979; Dodge *et al.*, 1995, 1996; Chen *et al.*, 1999; Ben-Zion, 2008). Early research results show that about 10%–40% of moderate-to-strong earthquakes are accompanied by foreshocks (Chen, 1978; Jones and Molnar, 1979; Zhu and Wang, 1996; Reasenberg, 1999; Wang *et al.*, 2005; Xue *et al.*, 2012). However, there remains a significant gap between this proportion and the laboratory results (Jiang and Zhou, 2020). Numerous rock fracture experiments have consistently demonstrated that the onset of macroscopic fracture or instability in a rock sample is almost always preceded by precursor sliding events, analogous to foreshocks (Goebel *et al.*, 2013; Johnson *et al.*, 2013; Bolton *et al.*, 2019; Jiang and Zhou, 2020). In addition, theoretical studies suggest that there is a gradual acceleration of the pre-sliding process before the dynamic instability of faults, with foreshocks being one of the typical manifestations of the earthquake nucleation process (Dieterich, 1994; Dodge *et al.*, 1996; Marone, 1998; Ma *et al.*, 2004; Ampuero and Rubin, 2008; He *et al.*, 2023).

The template matching method based on waveform cross-correlation (CC) technology is effective in detecting missing

1. Chinese Academy of Geological Sciences, Beijing, China, https://orcid.org/0009-0003-5021-5026 (SD); https://orcid.org/0000-0003-3438-771X (ZL); 2. China Earthquake Networks Center, Beijing, China; 3. Key Laboratory of Coal Resources Exploration and Comprehensive Utilization, Ministry of Natural Resources, Xi'an, China; 4. Oil and Gas Drilling Company, Shaanxi Coalfield Geological Bureau, Xi'an, China

*Corresponding author: jianghaikun@sohu.com

microearthquakes (Peng and Zhao, 2009; Zhang and Wen, 2015a) and has been widely and successfully applied to the detection of foreshock and aftershock sequences (Feng *et al.*, 2021; Deng and Jiang, 2022; Liu, Zhang, and Li, 2022; Zhou *et al.*, 2022; Yan *et al.*, 2023). Ross *et al.* (2019) systematically detected missing earthquakes in Southern California from 2008 to 2017 using the template matching method, resulting in a new earthquake catalog (quake template matching [QTM]) that contained ten times the number of earthquakes compared to the Southern California Seismic Network (SCSN) catalog. The completeness magnitude (M_c) was reduced from M 1.7 in the SCSN catalog to M 0.3. Trugman and Ross (2019) examined the foreshock activity preceding earthquakes with magnitudes of 4 and above using the QTM catalog. Their analysis revealed that 72% of these earthquakes were preceded by foreshock activity exhibiting significantly higher levels than the background seismicity, leading to a 20% increase in the foreshock detection rate compared to the SCSN catalog. These findings suggest that the prevalence of foreshock phenomena in nature exceeds previous understanding, and many earthquakes previously thought to lack foreshocks may have been undetected due to inadequate monitoring capabilities (Jiang and Zhou, 2020).

The interaction between foreshocks and their role in mainshock nucleation is still under debate (Gomberg, 2018). Traditionally, the cascade-up and pre-slip models are considered two end-member mechanisms to explain the triggering relationship between foreshocks and the mainshock (Ellsworth and Beroza, 1995; Dodge *et al.*, 1996; Mignan, 2014). The cascade model characterizes the seismic sequence as a chain reaction of isolated asperity failures, with each event triggered by the stress transfer from the previous earthquake (Ellsworth and Beroza, 1995; Beroza and Ellsworth, 1996; Ellsworth and Bulut, 2018). In contrast, the pre-slip model interprets foreshocks as by-products of the mainshock nucleation process, driven by aseismic slip (Dodge *et al.*, 1996). Observations of repeating earthquakes and the migration of foreshocks are generally considered supporting evidence for the pre-slip model (Bouchon *et al.*, 2011; Kato *et al.*, 2012; Chen and Shearer, 2013; Tape *et al.*, 2018; Uchida and Bürgmann, 2019). More recently, McLaskey (2019) proposed a rate-dependent cascade-up model that incorporates contributions from both cascade and pre-slip mechanisms based on laboratory observations. Recent studies have shown that using template matching to identify a greater number of foreshocks can substantially enhance our understanding of the earthquake nucleation process (Yoon *et al.*, 2019; Durand *et al.*, 2020; Yao *et al.*, 2020; Feng *et al.*, 2021; Deng and Jiang, 2022; Liu, Li, *et al.*, 2022; Liu, Zhang, and Li, 2022; Zhou *et al.*, 2022; Yan *et al.*, 2023). However, most studies focus on earthquakes with significant foreshocks, whereas many earthquakes occur without obvious foreshocks (Ruan *et al.*, 2017; Neves *et al.*, 2022; Kwiatek *et al.*, 2023; Picozzi *et al.*, 2023). The selection bias in foreshock case studies may skew our understanding of earthquake nucleation mechanisms.

On 3 August 2014, an M_s 6.5 earthquake struck Ludian, Yunnan, China, at 16:30 Beijing standard time (Fig. 1). In the two months before the mainshock, 19 events with magnitudes ranging from M_L 1.0 to 2.7 were recorded in the local catalog. These events were not pronounced compared to the background seismicity, which recorded an average of 18 events with $M_L \geq 1.0$ every two months, based on the local catalog over the three years prior to the mainshock. Aftershocks are distributed in a conjugate pattern along the north-northwest and northeast-east directions. Studies based on the focal mechanism, distribution of strong aftershocks, and field geological surveys have identified the Baogunao–Xiaohe fault (BGN-XHF), which exhibits left-lateral strike-slip faulting in the north-northwest direction, as the focal fault of the M_s 6.5 Ludian earthquake (Wang *et al.*, 2014, 2018; Xu *et al.*, 2014). In the short term before the mainshock, the seismic area exhibited prominent anomalous activity, likely resulting from an increase in regional stress levels (Fu *et al.*, 2015; Liu *et al.*, 2015; Li *et al.*, 2017). Because the mainshock occurred near the Xiluodu Reservoir (closest distance ~40 km), there is debate over whether the M_s 6.5 Ludian earthquake was triggered by the reservoir's impoundment (Qiu, 2014). Hou and Wang (2017) detected a significant number of missing events in the earthquake sequence. Based on the b value characteristics and earthquake frequency before and after impoundment, they suggested that the M_s 6.5 Ludian earthquake was not reservoir-induced. However, the nucleation process of the M_s 6.5 Ludian earthquake remains unclear.

To further analyze the foreshock characteristics and the nucleation process of the M_s 6.5 Ludian earthquake, this study first employed the hypoDD method (Waldhauser, 2000; Waldhauser and Ellsworth, 2002) to relocate seismic events in the study area. Subsequently, the graphics processing unit (GPU)-based match-and-locate (M&L) method (Zhang and Wen, 2015a; Liu *et al.*, 2020) was applied to detect and locate missing earthquakes before and after the mainshock. The study then proceeded to investigate the spatiotemporal evolution of foreshock activity and the b value characteristics using the newly detected earthquake catalog. The nucleation process was discussed based on the observation results.

Data

We collected seismic phase data for 5354 events ($M_L \geq 1.0$) that occurred in the vicinity of the mainshock (26.7°–27.5° N, 102.9°–103.7° E) from January 2014 to February 2016, obtained from the China Earthquake Networks Center (CENC), for hypoDD analysis. The phase data included arrival times from 69 seismic stations within the national network, 4 stations from the Zhaotong network, 5 stations from the Qiaojia array, and 3 temporary stations deployed after the mainshock (Fig. S1, available in the supplemental material

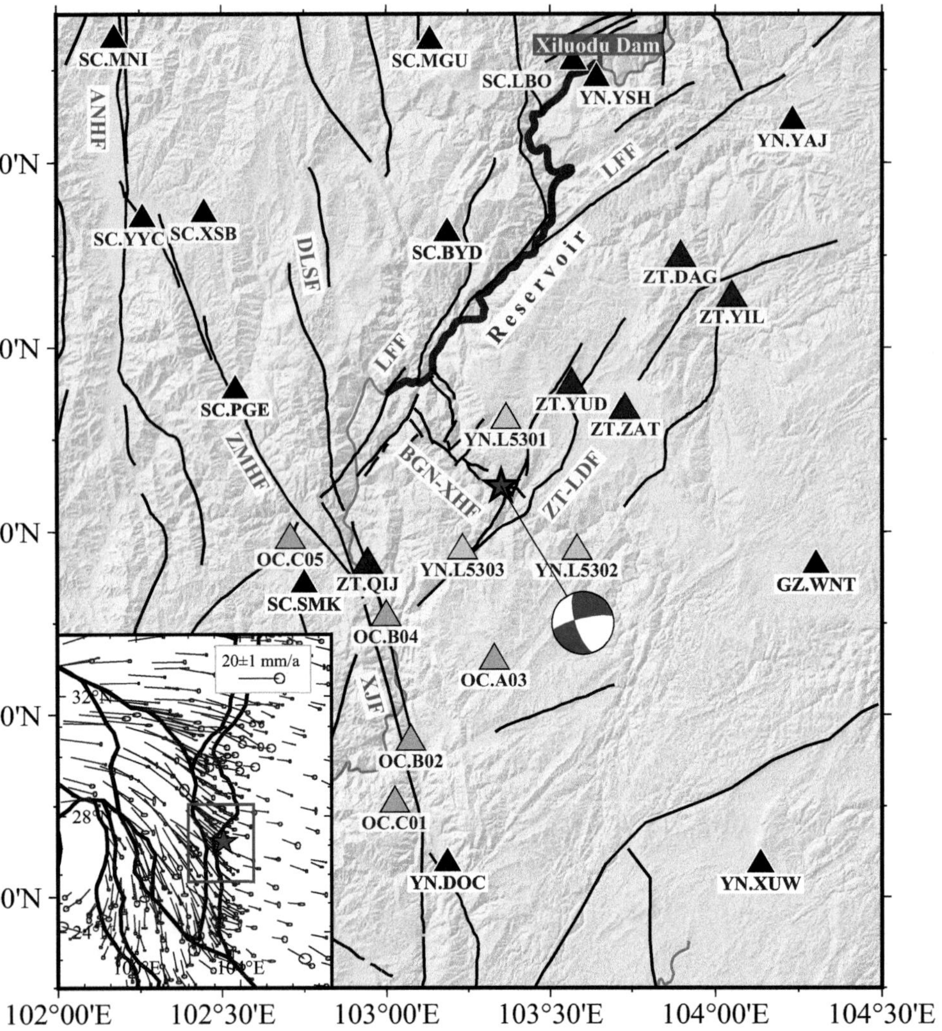

Figure 1. Tectonic background and distribution of seismic stations. In the main plot, fault traces are shown as black lines: ANHF, Anninghe fault; BGN-XHF, Baogunao-Xiaohe fault; DLSF, Daliangshan fault; LFF, Lianfeng fault; XJF, Xiaojiang fault; ZMHF, Zemuhe fault; and ZT-LDF, Zhaotong-Ludian fault. The epicenter and focal mechanism of the M_S 6.5 Ludian earthquake are represented by a red star and a focal mechanism plot, respectively (Zhang *et al.*, 2014). Black triangles represent national seismic stations, blue triangles represent stations of the Zhaotong network, orange triangles represent the Qiaojia seismic array, and light-blue triangles represent temporary seismic stations deployed after the mainshock. A short, brown line marks the Xiluodu Dam, and a thick, blue line outlines the reservoir. The inset in the lower-left corner shows the location of the study area. Blue arrows represent the Global Positioning System (GPS) velocity field with respect to the Eurasian plate (Zhao *et al.*, 2015), the red rectangle outlines the area covered by the main map, and thick black lines represent block boundaries. The color version of this figure is available only in the electronic edition.

to this article). In addition, continuous waveform data were collected from four national network stations (GZ.WNT, SC.BYD, SC.PGE, and SC.SMK) and five Zhaotong network stations (ZT.DAG, ZT.QIJ, ZT.YIL, ZT.YUD, and ZT.ZAT) within a 100 km radius of the epicenter from June to August 2014 to detect and locate missing earthquakes. The stations used for the M&L procedure are equipped with three-component velocity meters, operating at a sampling rate of 100 Hz. The lower cutoff frequencies vary across stations, ranging from 60 to 120 s, whereas the higher cutoff frequency is 50 Hz for all stations. The daily average proportion of available stations during the study period was 98.9% (Fig. S2).

Method

Earthquake relocation

The hypoDD method calculates the relative earthquake locations by pairing seismic events within a defined spatial range and analyzing the differences between the observed arrival times of seismic phases and the theoretical arrival times for each pair. This approach effectively mitigates positioning errors caused by inaccuracies in the velocity model and has been widely applied in various studies (Waldhauser and Ellsworth, 2002; Wang *et al.*, 2014; Fang *et al.*, 2018; Wan *et al.*, 2023).

This study utilizes the collected original phase data and applies a travel-time curve fitting method to exclude seismic travel-time data that deviates by more than 2 s from the fitted line (Fig. S3). During the matching of seismic pairs, it is ensured that each event is recorded by at least five stations, with a maximum distance of 10 km between pairs. Each earthquake can be paired with up to 15 other events. In addition, we calculated the *P*- and *S*-wave differential arrival times between earthquake pairs through waveform CC. To ensure data quality, we retained only differential times with CC coefficients ≥ 0.7. In total, 5131 seismic events were selected, yielding 392,577 catalog differential times (201,021 *P* wave and 191,556 *S* wave) and 6466 CC differential times (2202 *P* wave and 4264 *S* wave) for hypoDD relocation. Wang *et al.* (2014) constructed a 1D velocity model for the Ludian region based on receiver function $H - \kappa$ stacking and the explosive refraction profile from Xiong *et al.* (1993). This study primarily relies on this velocity model, while also referencing other existing research (Zhao and Sun, 2014; Wang *et al.*,

2018) to construct a 1D velocity model (Table S1) for hypoDD analysis in the study area.

Earthquake detection and location

To further investigate seismic activity near the focal area prior to the mainshock, we used relocated earthquakes as templates and applied the GPU-accelerated M&L method to detect and locate small earthquakes within the study area (Zhang and Wen, 2015a; Liu *et al.*, 2020). Before performing CC stacking, the M&L method scans a 3D space surrounding the template events to calculate the relative travel-time differences between potential earthquake locations and reference locations at the same station. These travel-time differences are then used to calibrate and stack the cross-correlated waveforms. This computational approach enables the M&L method to detect lower-magnitude seismic events, including those located relatively far from the template events. Furthermore, this method exhibits lower dependency on the accuracy of the velocity model while simultaneously providing spatial location information for the detected events (Zhang and Wen, 2015a). Compared to sequential location methods (matched-filter + CC-based hypoDD), the M&L method can detect a greater number of events and provide more precise location results (Liu, Zhang, and Li, 2022).

This study collected continuous waveform data from nine seismic stations (GZ.WNT, SC.BYD, SC.PGE, SC.SMK, ZT.DAG, ZT.QIJ, ZT.YIL, ZT.YUD, and ZT.ZAT) within a 100 km radius of the epicenter from June to August 2014 (Fig. 1). After detrending and removing the mean from the continuous waveform data, a four-pole, two-channel Butterworth band-pass filter with a frequency range of 2–12 Hz was applied to enhance the signal-to-noise ratio (SNR).

We selected 859 seismic events as template events, including $M_L \geq 1.0$ earthquakes that occurred before the mainshock and $M_L \geq 2.0$ earthquakes that occurred after it (Fig. S4). The *S*-wave SNR is calculated for each station across all templates. The noise window is set as the 3–1 s interval before the *P*-wave arrival, whereas the signal window spans from 2 s before to 5 s after the *S*-wave arrival. We visually inspected all templates and removed stations with SNR < 3 or multiple events within the template waveforms. The CC window is defined as 2 s before to 5 s after the *S*-wave arrival time of the template. During the detection process, a spatial search grid is established with the template event at its center. The travel-time differences between the grid points and the template event at each station are then calculated. After correcting the travel times of the template, the sliding CC (SCCs) coefficients at the searched grid are calculated according to the following equation:

$$\mathrm{SCC}(t) = \sum_{S,C} W_{S,C} \frac{\sum_{n=1}^{N} T_{S,C}(\tau_n) C_{S,C}(t + \tau_n + \Delta t_{S,C})}{\sqrt{\sum_{n=1}^{N} T_{S,C}(\tau_n) T_{S,C}(\tau_n)} \sqrt{\sum_{n=1}^{N} C_{S,C}(t + \tau_n) C_{S,C}(t + \tau_n + \Delta t_{S,C})}}, \quad (1)$$

in which $W_{S,C}$ represents the SNR weights for each component at each station, with their sum equal to one. $T_{S,C}$, and $C_{S,C}$ represent the template and continuous seismic waveforms, respectively. N denotes the number of sampling points within the template time window. The variables n, S, and C correspond to the sampling point index, station, and component, respectively (Liu *et al.*, 2020). Δt represents the relative travel-time difference between the grid points and the template event, calculated using the velocity model applied in hypoDD (Table S1). By applying the aforementioned calculations to each grid point, the grid point with the highest CC value is selected as the hypocenter location of the detected earthquake. Because of the sparse distribution of seismic stations available for Match and Locate, the focal depth could not be accurately constrained. Therefore, during the detection process, we fixed the focal depth and searched within a 0.015° × 0.015° area surrounding the template event, using a search interval of 0.0005°.

We selected segments of the template autocorrelations within a fixed time window (ranging from 3 to 5 s on both sides) and calculated their mean absolute value as the background CC value (0.02094; Zhang and Wen, 2015a,b; Yao *et al.*, 2018). The average peak prominence for all selected segments across all templates is 0.1264, with a maximum of 0.289, indicating that the selected segments are not influenced by sidelobes. Nine times the background CC value was suggested as the detection threshold (Zhang and Wen, 2015a); however, to reduce the chance of false detections, we applied a stricter threshold of 11 times the background CC value in this study (Fig. S5). When the computed CC exceeded this threshold (0.23), it was considered a valid detection of an earthquake event. The magnitude of the detected event (M_d) can be determined as

$$M_d = M_t + c \log_{10}(\alpha), \quad (2)$$

in which M_t is the magnitude of the best-matching template, α is the amplitude ratio (AR) between the detected and template event, and c is a constant that describes the amplitude–magnitude scaling. The value of c is conventionally set to 1.0 for local magnitude (M_L) scales. However, for relatively small events, for which corner frequencies dominantly lie above the band-pass range of 2–12 Hz (Shelly *et al.*, 2016), the measured AR for this band-passed data should reflect the ratio of seismic moments (Hanks and Boore, 1984). Furthermore, the relationship between log moment and M_L is found to change in slope at small magnitudes (Hanks and Boore, 1984; Ben-Zion and Zhu, 2002). Given that we are working with relatively small events, recalibration of c is essential to ensure consistency in magnitude scales

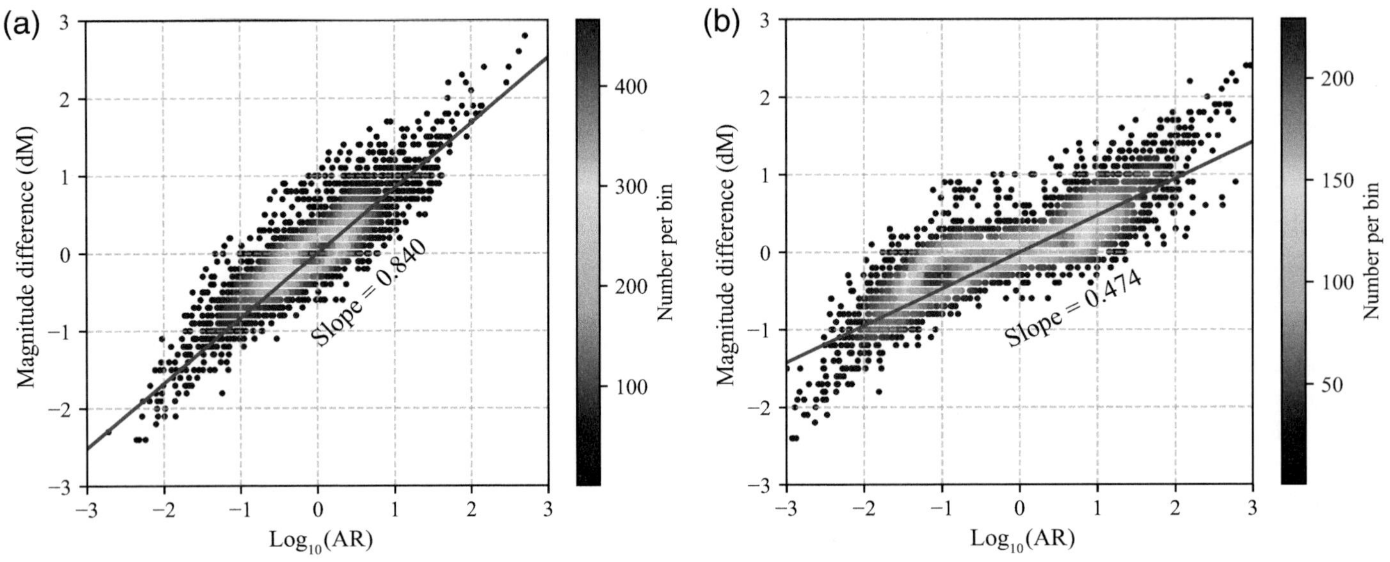

Figure 2. Magnitude differences versus the logarithmic amplitude ratio (AR) for template pairs, color-coded by their densities. In panel (a), the AR is measured as the median peak AR across all channels, whereas in panel (b), the AR is determined as the median slope estimated through principal component fitting across all channels. The color version of this figure is available only in the electronic edition.

between newly detected and cataloged earthquakes (Shelly *et al.*, 2016). We calculated the AR and magnitude difference for all template events and selected event pairs with an average CC greater than 0.2 to estimate the c value. We compared two methods for calculating the AR: peak amplitude and principal component fitting (Fig. 2). Our analysis shows that the AR derived from peak amplitude exhibits a more linear relationship with magnitude differences in this dataset (Fig. 2a). Although principal component fitting can mitigate the influence of noise when estimating ARs (Shelly *et al.*, 2016), this method requires relatively high waveform similarity. When estimating the AR of waveforms with lower CC values, using peak amplitude is more robust (Fig. S6). In addition, the magnitudes in the local catalog are also determined using peak amplitude measurements (Liu *et al.*, 2018). Therefore, using peak amplitude to estimate AR can enhance the consistency in magnitude scales between newly detected and cataloged earthquakes. Consequently, we used $c = 0.84$ to compute the magnitudes of newly detected earthquakes, with the AR measured as the median peak AR across all channels. We also compared the magnitudes of common events between the hypoDD catalog and the newly detected catalog. The results indicate that magnitudes computed using $c = 0.84$ exhibit better agreement with the hypoDD catalog (Fig. S7).

Results

HypoDD result

We relocated a total of 4702 earthquakes using the hypoDD method. The relative location uncertainties were estimated using the bootstrap method with 200 iterations, and the average horizontal and vertical relative location uncertainties were 184.72 and 451.68 m, respectively (Fig. S8a,b). The average root mean square (rms) residuals for CC and catalog data were 4.37 and 26.77 ms, respectively (Fig. S8c,d). The average rms of absolute travel-time residuals decreased from 622.51 to 245.15 ms after relocation (Fig. S9a). The absolute location uncertainties were estimated by the covariance matrix calculated with absolute travel times (Klein, 2002), and the average horizontal and vertical absolute location uncertainties were 2.14 and 8.97 km, respectively (Fig. S9b,c). The relocated earthquakes show a greater convergence toward the source faults (Fig. 3a). Prior to relocation, the focal depths were largely influenced by the sparse distribution of seismic stations and the simplicity of the velocity model, with depths predominantly concentrated in the range of 5–15 km (Fig. 3b). In contrast, the distribution of relocated focal depths more closely approximates a normal distribution (Fig. 3c).

M&L result

Following the procedures outlined for earthquake detection and location, and after removing events common with the hypoDD catalog, we detected 2679 new earthquakes in the focal area (26.9°–27.35° N, 103.1°–103.55° E) from 1 June to 31 August 2014. We then augmented the HypoDD catalog within the same spatiotemporal range by incorporating the newly detected earthquakes to create the M&L catalog, which contains a total of 4275 events. This number is approximately 1.9 times the number of events recorded in the CENC catalog, which documented 2261 events over the same spatiotemporal range. We cataloged 155 foreshocks with magnitudes ranging from $M_L - 0.3$ to 2.7, which is approximately 8.2 times the 19 events recorded in the CENC catalog for the same

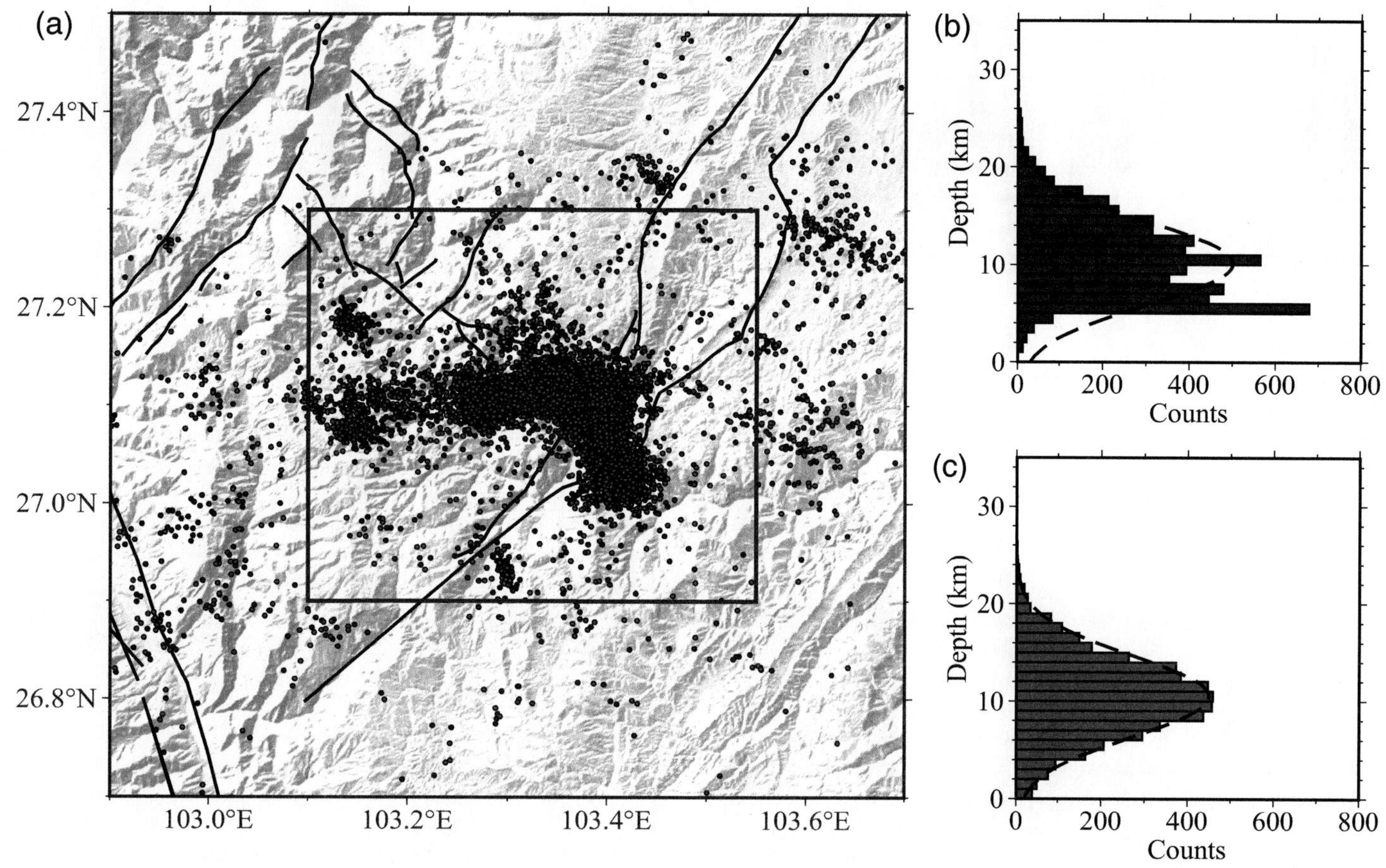

Figure 3. Comparison of earthquake distributions before and after relocation. (a) Epicenter distributions before (blue points) and after (red points) relocation. The black-solid lines represent the main faults, and the blue rectangle outlines the focal area where the match-and-locate (M&L) procedure was applied. (b) Depth distribution before relocation. (c) Depth distribution after relocation. The black dashed lines indicate the fitted normal distribution curves. The color version of this figure is available only in the electronic edition.

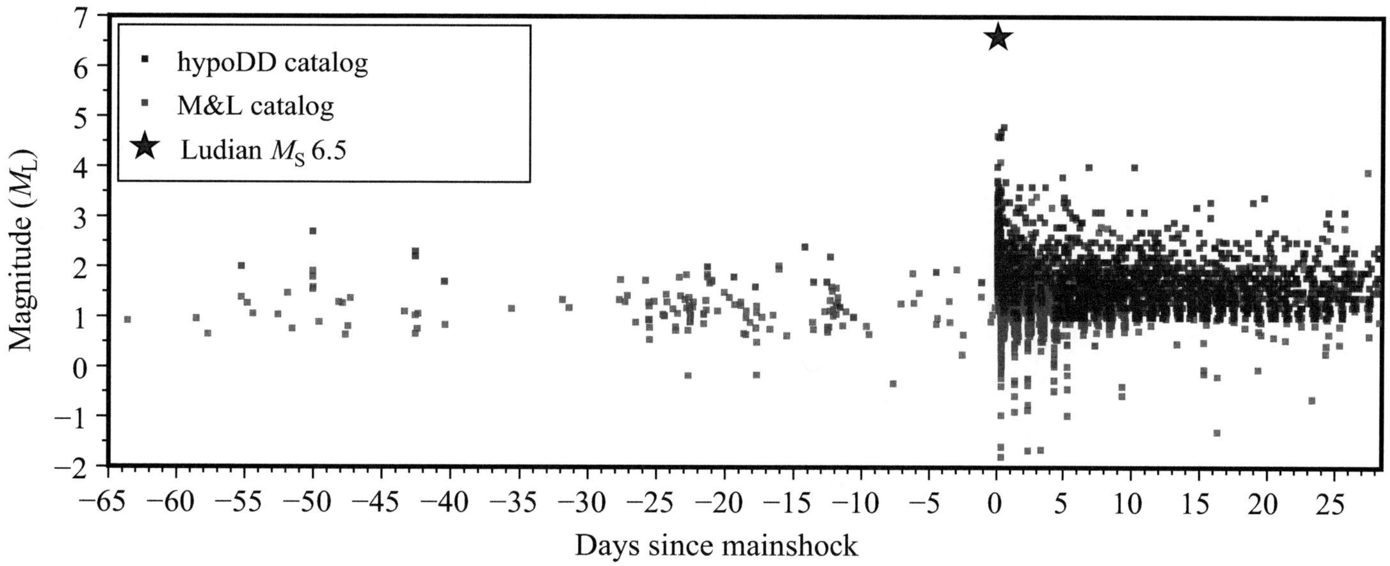

Figure 4. Magnitude–time diagram of the M_S 6.5 Ludian earthquake sequence. The dark-red star marks the mainshock, and the blue and red dots represent the events in the hypoDD and M&L catalogs, respectively. The color version of this figure is available only in the electronic edition.

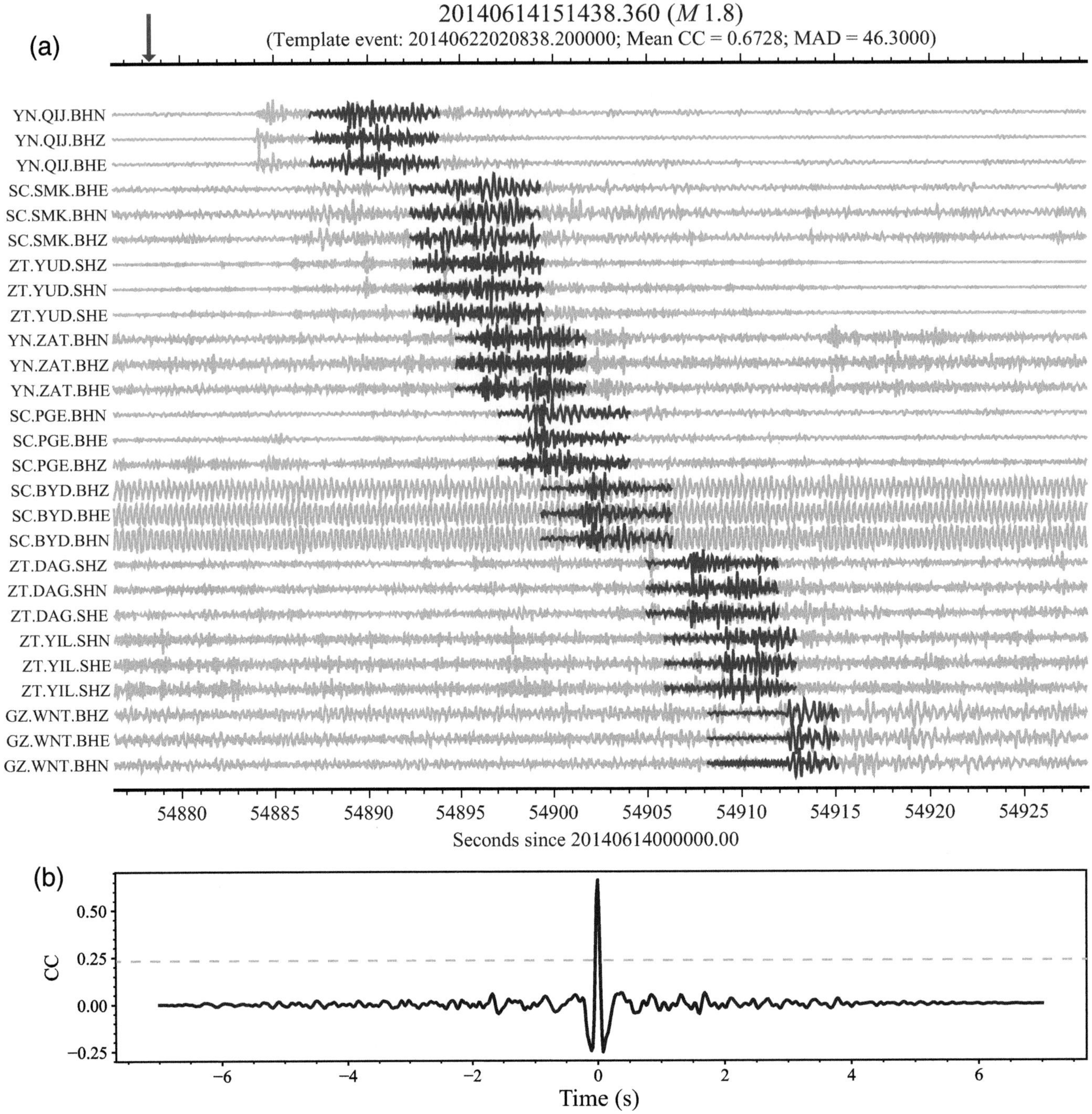

Figure 5. Detection results for the M_S 1.8 earthquake on 14 June 2014, using the M&L method. (a) Comparison of the template earthquake waveform (red) and the detected earthquake waveform (gray), with the red arrow indicating the determined origin time of the detected earthquake. (b) Stacked cross-correlation (CC) function (blue) between the template and the detected earthquake, with a maximum CC value of 0.6728, exceeding the detection threshold of 0.23 (gray dashed line). The color version of this figure is available only in the electronic edition.

spatiotemporal range (Fig. 4). We detected slightly more foreshocks than those detected by Hou and Wang (2017) over the same time period, possibly due to the use of additional seismic stations. Figure 5 illustrates the waveform and the stacked CC function for an M_L 1.8 earthquake detected using the M&L method.

Using the maximum curvature method, we calculated the magnitude of completeness (M_c) of the earthquake catalogs by determining the maximum of the first derivative of the magnitude–frequency curve (Wiemer and Katsumata, 1999). The results show that by supplementing the catalog with newly detected earthquakes, the M_c of the overall catalog decreased from M_L 1.5 to 1.3, whereas the M_c of the foreshock sequence decreased from M_L 1.7 to 1.1 (Fig. 6). This indicates a significant reduction in the issue of missing small earthquakes in the catalog.

Discussions

Higher *b* value for foreshock sequence

The *b* value in the Gutenberg–Richter relationship characterizes the ratio between large and small earthquakes and is an important parameter in seismicity analysis (Gutenberg and Richter, 1944). It is generally considered that the *b* value is related to stress changes and heterogeneity of the medium (Scholz, 1968; Wiemer and Wyss, 1997; Meng *et al.*, 2021). Both laboratory experiments and field earthquake observations have widely recognized and applied the inverse relationship between the *b* value and stress (Scholz, 1968; Schorlemmer *et al.*, 2005; Yi *et al.*, 2006, 2008, 2013; Meng *et al.*, 2018; Shi *et al.*, 2018; Gulia and Wiemer, 2019; Morales-Yáñez *et al.*, 2022; Yan *et al.*, 2023). The *b* value is typically higher in creeping segments of faults and lower in asperity segments (Wiemer and Wyss, 1997; Yi *et al.*, 2008; Meng *et al.*, 2021). Meng *et al.* (2021), summarizing previous earthquake case studies, pointed out that although the temporal evolution of the *b* value before different earthquakes varies, the low *b* value feature before large earthquakes is a commonly observed phenomenon.

The background *b* value for the study region was calculated using the maximum-likelihood method (Aki, 1965; Utsu, 1966; Marzocchi and Sandri, 2003), with the CENC catalog covering the period from 2004 until the occurrence of the mainshock (Fig. S10). The *b* values for the foreshocks (within 63 days prior to the mainshock) and aftershocks (within 27 days following the mainshock) were calculated using the M&L catalog (Fig. 6). The results show that the *b* value of the foreshock sequence is 1.12 ± 0.13, higher than both the background *b* value (0.94 ± 0.06) and the *b* value of the aftershock sequence (0.91 ± 0.02). The difference in the *b* value between the foreshocks and aftershocks is statistically significant at the 91.2% confidence level, as determined by the Utsu test (Utsu, 1966). The higher *b* value for the foreshock sequence, compared to the aftershock sequence, observed in this study, is consistent with previous findings (Hou and Wang, 2017). To assess whether this result is influenced by the inclusion of missed earthquakes, we also calculated the *b* values for the foreshock and aftershock sequences using the CENC catalog. The results again show that the *b* value of the foreshock sequence is higher than that of the aftershock sequence (Fig. S10).

The higher *b* value observed in the Ludian foreshock sequence contrasts with the typically lower *b* value observed before large earthquakes (Meng *et al.*, 2021). It is worth noting that the foreshock *b* value discussed earlier was calculated over the 65 days prior to the mainshock. According to Jiang *et al.* (2024), the *b* value of the foreshock sequence, calculated over a longer timescale (8 months prior to the mainshock) using data from the Qiaojia seismic network, is lower than both the *b* value of the aftershock sequence and the background *b* value. Notably, the foreshocks are primarily located within the swarm activity zone, whereas aftershocks mainly occur in the seismogenic zone. This suggests that the *b* values of foreshocks and

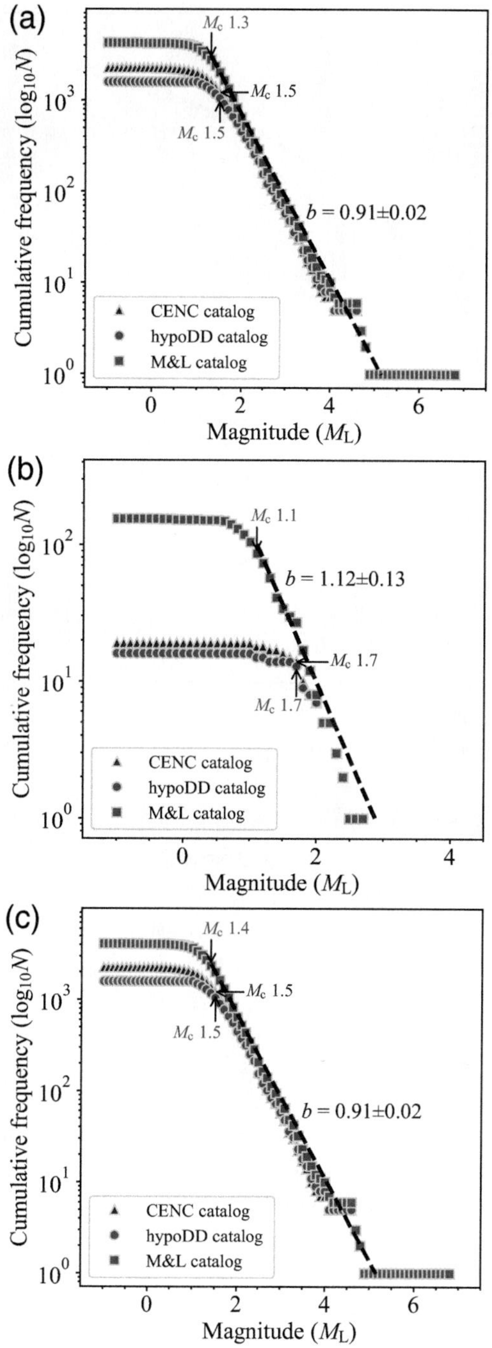

Figure 6. Comparison of magnitude–frequency distributions among the M&L catalog (red squares), hypoDD catalog (green circles), and China Earthquake Networks Center (CENC) catalog (blue triangles). (a) Cumulative frequency for the entire sequence, (b) cumulative frequency for the foreshock sequence, and (c) cumulative frequency for the aftershock sequence. Black dashed lines represent the best-fit Gutenberg–Richter relationships for the M&L catalog. The text colors of the M_c values correspond to the colors of the respective catalogs. Panel (b) is enlarged for clarity while maintaining the *x*/*y* axis ratio consistent with panels (a) and (c). By supplementing the catalog with newly detected earthquakes, the M_c for the entire sequence decreased from M_L 1.5 to 1.3, and theM_c for the foreshock sequence decreased from M_L 1.7 to 1.1. The color version of this figure is available only in the electronic edition.

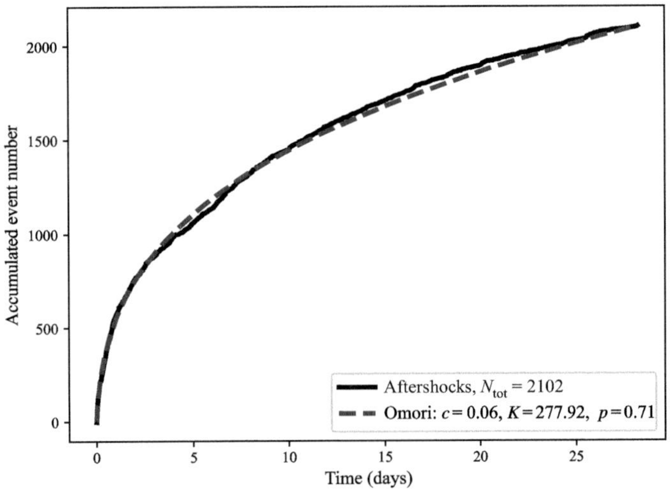

Figure 7. Cumulative frequency of the aftershock sequence, with the red dashed line representing the best-fit curve based on the modified Omori law. The color version of this figure is available only in the electronic edition.

aftershocks may reflect the stress states in different fault segments. The high b value of the foreshock sequence suggests that the fault segment associated with the swarm is weakly coupled, with a lack of strong asperities to accumulate significant stress. Meanwhile, frequent small earthquakes facilitate stress release along the fault. In contrast, the sparse foreshock activity near the mainshock fault suggests a highly locked fault, where stronger asperities allow for greater stress accumulation. If the fault contains numerous moderate-to-strong asperities, the mainshock may not fully release the long-term accumulated stress, which could result in a low aftershock b value and slow aftershock decay. The aftershock b value time series calculated by Hou and Wang (2017) confirms the relatively low b value observed during the early stages of aftershock activity. Using the modified Omori formula (Utsu, 1961; Ogata, 1999), we estimated the decay parameters for aftershocks with magnitudes above the M_c (M_L 1.4). The obtained p value (0.71) is significantly lower than the global median of 1.1 (Utsu *et al.*, 1995), indicating a slower aftershock decay rate (Fig. 7). Furthermore, the occurrence of numerous moderate-to-strong late-stage aftershocks (Wang *et al.*, 2018) further supports the assumption that the mainshock did not fully release the accumulated stress along the fault. Therefore, we propose that the higher b value observed in the foreshock sequence, compared to the aftershock sequence, likely results from differences in the fault segments associated with the foreshock and aftershock activity zones, as well as the incomplete release of stress along the fault during the mainshock.

Spatiotemporal evolution of the foreshocks

Using the M&L catalog, we mapped the spatial distribution of seismic events over the 65 days leading up to the mainshock (Fig. 8a). The results show that the foreshocks are primarily distributed in two regions: the aftershock zone (Z1) and the earthquake swarm zone (Z2). The earthquake frequency histogram (Fig. 8b) shows that seismic activity across the entire region began to increase 28 days before the mainshock, followed by a significant decline 11 days prior to the mainshock. Seismic activity in Z1 became relatively quiescent 16 days before the mainshock, and five days later, seismic activity in Z2 also significantly decreased. This relatively low level of seismicity persisted until the occurrence of the mainshock.

To investigate seismic activity along the conjugate seismogenic fault, while considering the relative positions of the swarms and the mainshock, we defined a seismic projection line (AA′) along the BGN-XHF (Fig. 8a) and projected the seismic events in the study area onto this line. The projected spatiotemporal evolution of the foreshocks shows a migration trend toward the mainshock in Z1, occurring 24–17 days before the mainshock, with an apparent migration velocity of approximately 1.5 km/day. Seismic activity then gradually decreased, and Z1 remained relatively quiescent until the mainshock (Fig. 8c). He *et al.* (2023) revealed the expansion and contraction of the weakening-zone core (WZcore), where a higher seismicity rate can be observed, during the nucleation process through numerical simulation. Jiang *et al.* (2024) conducted a simulation based on the fault conditions of the Ludian earthquake, revealing that the WZcore exhibited accelerated contraction in the final nucleation stage. These findings are consistent with the foreshock migration and contraction observed in our study. Similar phenomena of foreshock migration, contraction, and subsequent seismic quiescence have also been reported in other studies (Yagi *et al.*, 2014; Liu *et al.*, 2019; Deng and Jiang, 2022; Yan *et al.*, 2023). These phenomena are generally considered to be related to fault creep (Ma *et al.*, 2004; Liu *et al.*, 2019; Yao *et al.*, 2020), suggesting that aseismic slip plays a role in the nucleation process.

There is debate about whether the Ludian earthquake was reservoir-induced (Qiu, 2014). Water infiltration is an important trigger for reservoir-induced earthquakes (Hou and Wang, 2017). Based on the spatiotemporal evolution of foreshock activity (Fig. 8c), we did not observe expanding foreshocks driven by fluid diffusion (Du *et al.*, 2024; Lei *et al.*, 2024; Liu *et al.*, 2025), indicating that the impoundment of the Xiluodu Reservoir did not cause fluid infiltration or diffusion into the Ludian earthquake region. Our observation supports that the Ludian earthquake was not a reservoir-triggered earthquake.

Repeating earthquakes

Repeating earthquakes, which are characterized by high waveform similarity and small spatial separation, are typically regarded as the repeated rupture of the same fault patch driven by fault creep (Uchida and Bürgmann, 2019). The criteria for identifying repeating earthquakes vary across different studies (Uchida, 2019). In this study, we adopted a commonly used

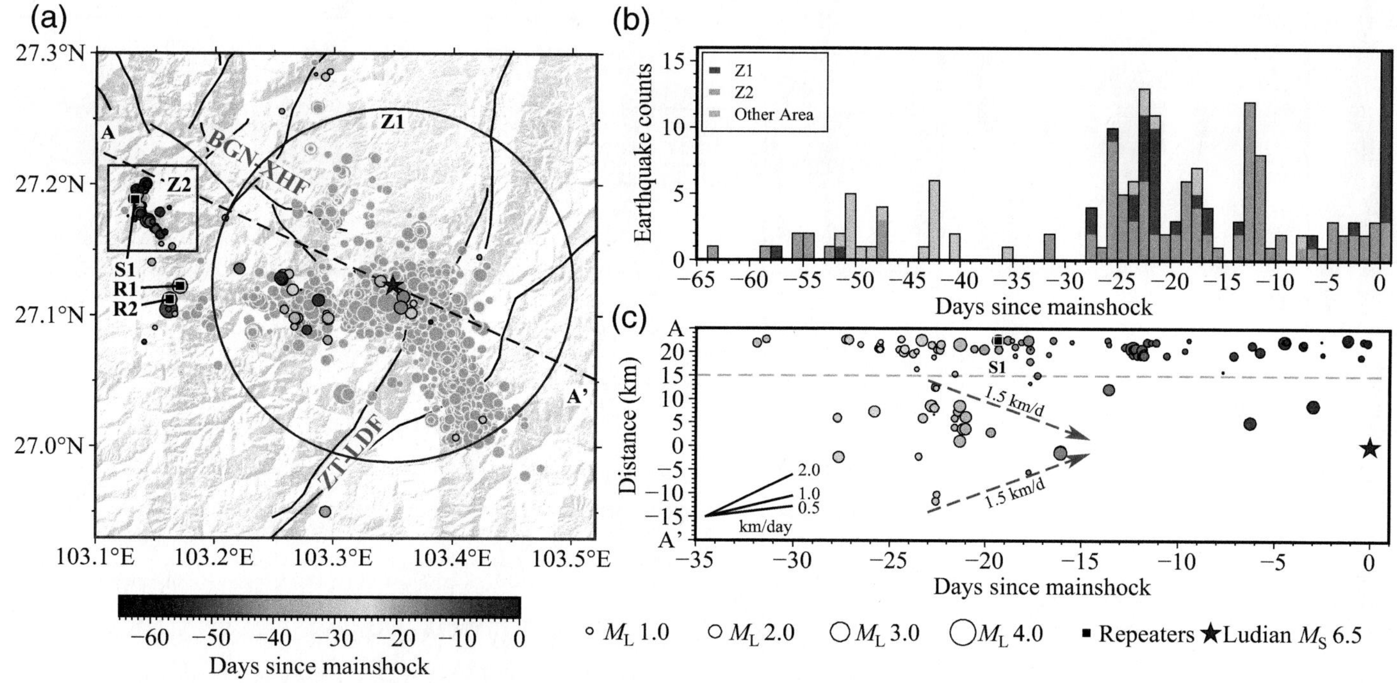

Figure 8. (a) Spatial distribution of foreshocks, (b) daily frequency of foreshocks, and (c) projection of earthquakes along the AA′ direction in the study area. The dark-red pentagram represents the mainshock, colored circles denote foreshocks, and gray circles indicate aftershocks that occurred within 10 days of the mainshock. The black-solid lines represent the main faults: BGN-XHF and ZT-LDF. Similar and repeating earthquakes are marked by black squares. In panel (b), the seismic frequency bar is cumulative, with different colors representing different areas. In panel (c), earthquakes below the gray dashed line are primarily located in Z1, whereas those above are mainly located in Z2. The color version of this figure is available only in the electronic edition.

criterion to identify repeating earthquakes: event pairs with an average CC greater than 0.9 and a horizontal location separation less than the maximum of the rupture radii of the two earthquakes (Gardonio *et al.*, 2015; Yao *et al.*, 2017; Uchida, 2019; Zhou *et al.*, 2022).

Because of the low SNR at distant stations for small-magnitude earthquakes, we selected two nearby stations, ZT.QIJ (~47 km from the mainshock) and SC.SMK (~66 km from the mainshock), for the detection of repeating earthquakes. We first applied a band-pass filter to the waveforms between 1 and 12 Hz, and then measured the waveform similarity within a 16-s time window starting 1 s before the *P* arrival, ensuring that the *P*, *S*, and major coda waves are covered (Liu, Li, *et al.*, 2022; Zhou *et al.*, 2022). We identified three pairs of similar earthquakes in the foreshock sequence, with CC greater than 0.9 at most stations (Fig. 9). Typically, event pairs with an average $\Delta(S-P)$ of less than 0.01 s can limit the location separation to approximately 0.1 km, which is smaller than the typical rupture radius of an M_L 1.0 event (Zhou *et al.*, 2022). However, considering the similar azimuths from the events to the two seismic stations (ZT.QIJ and SC.SMK), it is essential to accurately determine the relative locations of the similar earthquakes using additional stations. Therefore, we applied waveform CC to calculate the differential *P*- and *S*-wave arrival times for each similar earthquake pair across nine stations. These differential times were then used in the hypoDD relocation procedure, employing the singular value decomposition method. Based on the circular crack model, we calculated the rupture radius using the empirical relationship between seismic moment and rupture radius proposed by Kanamori and Anderson (1975). The seismic moment was estimated by the formula of Abercrombie (1996), and the stress drop was set to 3 MPa based on statistical results from the Yunnan region (Liu *et al.*, 2010). The results show that one pair of similar earthquakes did not meet the criteria for repeating earthquakes due to relatively small overlap in the rupture areas (Fig. 9a), whereas the other two pairs satisfied the criteria for repeating earthquakes (Fig. 9c–f). It is worth noting that the repeating earthquakes, though located outside Z1, are situated at the western end of the northeast-east-trending seismogenic fault delineated by the aftershocks (Fig. 8a).

Insights for the nucleation process

Previous studies have shown that the Ludian earthquake is a complex conjugate-ruptured event (Wang *et al.*, 2014; Xu *et al.*, 2014; Zhang *et al.*, 2014, 2015; Cheng *et al.*, 2016). From the joint inversion of local and teleseismic data, Zhang *et al.* (2015) revealed that the ruptures first initiated on the northeast-east-trending fault, and two seconds later, the north-northwest-trending fault began to rupture. From the spatial distribution of foreshocks, a notable observation is that foreshocks in Z1 are

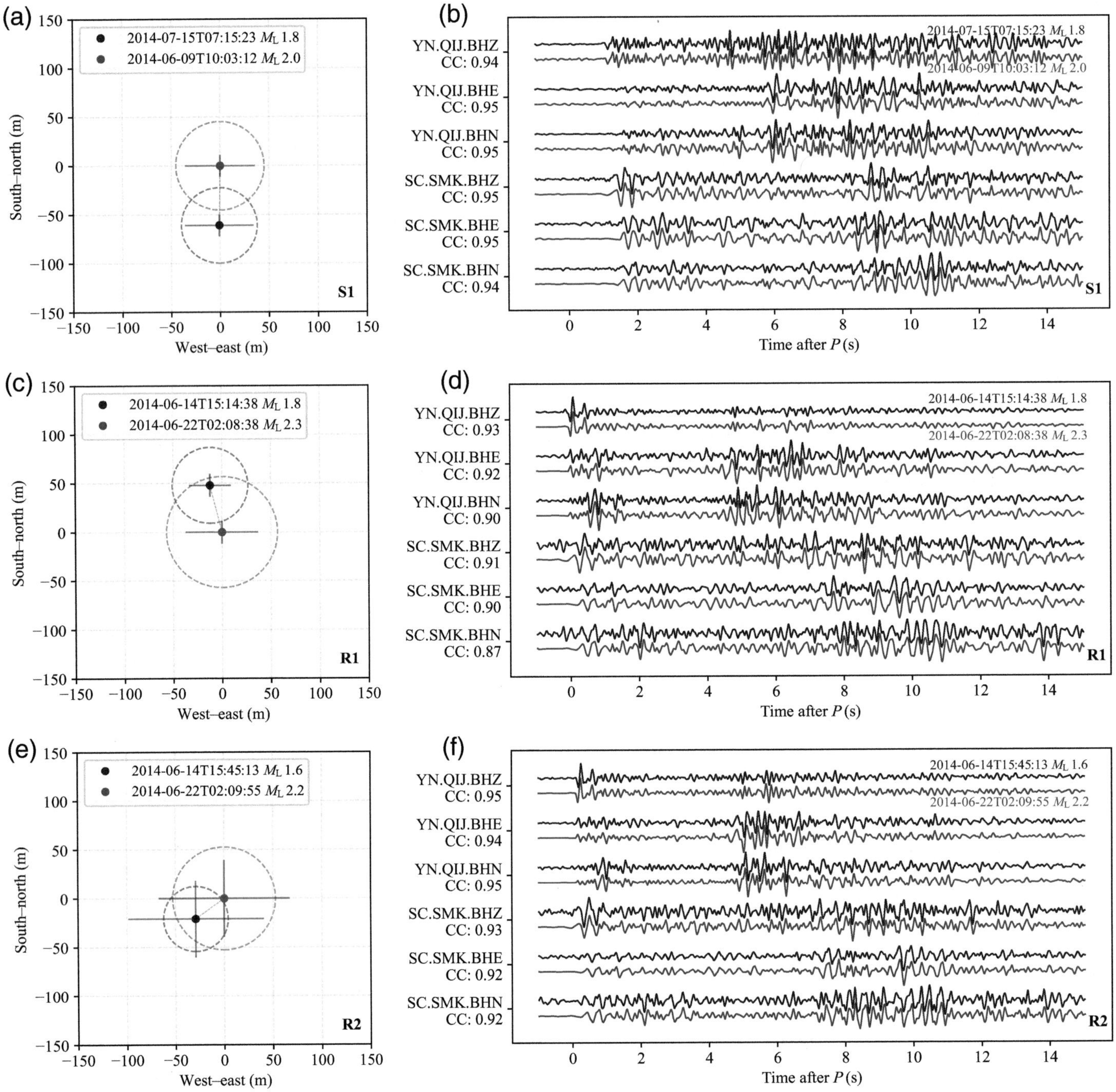

primarily located along a near northeast-east-trending branch of the aftershock distribution (Fig. 8a). This suggests that the nucleation process of the mainshock could also begin along the northeast-east-trending fault (Jiang *et al.*, 2024). Cheng *et al.* (2016) calculated that the rupture of the northeast-east-trending fault would result in positive Coulomb stress changes, which exceeds the triggering threshold of 0.01 MPa, on the north-northwest-trending fault. Based on Global Positioning System (GPS) data observed before the mainshock, Xu *et al.* (2014) calculated that the left-lateral strain rate of the BGN-XHF was approximately 3 mm/a, along with a nearly east–west tensile strain rate of about 1 mm/a. Wen *et al.* (2013) observed

Figure 9. Relative location and waveform comparison (1–12 Hz) of three pairs of earthquakes. In the relative location plots (a,c,e), location uncertainties are represented by crosses, and the size of the dashed circles indicates the approximate rupture area under a 3 MPa stress drop. In the waveform comparison plots (b,d,f), the waveform colors are consistent with those in the relative location plots, and corresponding station names with CC values are marked on the left. The similar earthquake group name (S1) and repeating earthquake group names (R1, R2) are marked in the lower right corner of each subplot. The color version of this figure is available only in the electronic edition.

that the deformation rates decreased significantly closer to the Zhaotong–Ludian fault (ZT-LDF) on the northwest side, indicating that the ZT-LDF was highly locked. The north-north-west-trending seismogenic fault, located at the southern end of the BGN-XHF and adjoining the ZT-LDF, may be constrained by the ZT-LDF and be in a heavily locked state. This is further supported by the observation that fewer foreshocks occurred along the north-northwest-trending fault (Fig. 8a) and that the rupture of the north-northwest-trending fault released the majority of the seismic moment of the mainshock (Zhang *et al.*, 2015). Considering the heavily locked state of the north-northwest-trending fault prior to the mainshock and the significant elastic stress triggering, we suggest that cascading stress transfer plays an important role in the nucleation process of the north-northwest-trending fault. However, the locking of the BGN-XHF near the ZT-LDF could potentially facilitate slipping in the northeast-east-trending branch fault to accommodate the accumulated strain energy, as indicated by the observation of a nearly east–west tensile strain rate (Xu *et al.*, 2014). The observed repeating earthquakes and migrating foreshocks on the northeast-east-trending fault (Fig. 8a) further support the presence of aseismic slip.

Martínez-Garzón and Poli (2024) argued that both preslip and cascade-up models may oversimplify the complexity of earthquake nucleation in nature. Marty *et al.* (2023) conducted a quantitative analysis of laboratory earthquakes, highlighting that the nucleation process begins as a fully aseismic process and evolves into a cascading process at the onset of dynamic rupture. This is consistent with the rate-dependent cascade-up model proposed by McLaskey (2019). An increasing number of studies have revealed that multiple physical processes can operate simultaneously (Yao *et al.*, 2020; Cabrera *et al.*, 2022; Liu, Li, *et al.*, 2022; Zhou *et al.*, 2022; Peng and Lei, 2024; Wang *et al.*, 2024). Based on observations of foreshock activity and other existing research, we propose that the nucleation process of the Ludian earthquake likely initiated on the northeast-east-trending fault, where aseismic slip played a significant role. Following the rupture of the northeast-east-trending fault, the north-northwest-trending fault ruptured due to stress triggering, releasing the majority of the seismic moment. During this phase, cascading stress transfer predominated. Thus, the rate-dependent cascade-up model is preferred for explaining the nucleation process of the Ludian earthquake.

Conclusions

This study employs the hypoDD and GPU-accelerated M&L methods to detect and locate earthquakes in the M_s 6.5 Ludian earthquake sequence. The approach significantly improves the completeness of the earthquake catalog, lowering the M_c from M_L 1.5 to 1.3. A total of 155 foreshocks, with magnitudes ranging from M_L − 0.3 to 2.7, were cataloged. The spatiotemporal evolution of the foreshocks and the b value characteristics are discussed in detail based on the augmented catalog.

Observations of foreshock migration and repeating earthquakes indicate that aseismic slip plays a role in the nucleation process. Furthermore, by incorporating existing research on rupture processes and GPS observations, we suggest that multiple mechanisms can operate together, and the rate-dependent cascade-up model better explains the nucleation process of the Ludian earthquake. In addition, no expanding foreshocks associated with fluid diffusion were observed, indicating that the Ludian earthquake was not reservoir-triggered. This study highlights that earthquakes initially lacking obvious foreshocks could provide insights that may broaden our understanding of the earthquake nucleation process.

Data and Resources

Seismic data used in this study can be requested from the China Earthquake Networks Center (CENC; http://www.csndmc.ac.cn/newweb/index.jsp, last accessed July 2023). Figures in this article are plotted with Matplotlib and Generic Mapping Tools (GMT). The graphics processing unit (GPU)-based match-and-locate (M&L) code is available on GitHub (https://github.com/MinLiu19/GPU-MatchLocate1.0, last accessed August 2023). The supplemental material for this article includes the velocity model of the study area, distribution of seismic stations, data continuity of the stations used in the M&L, *P*- and *S*-wave travel-time fitting and selection result, template events distribution, autocorrelation of template earthquakes, examples of amplitude ratio (AR) estimation, comparison of magnitudes for common events between the hypoDD catalog and the M&L catalog, statistical distributions of relative and absolute location uncertainties and travel-time residuals, magnitude–frequency distribution and b value fitting results for the foreshock and aftershock sequences based on the CENC catalog.

Declaration of Competing Interests

The authors acknowledge that there are no conflicts of interest recorded.

Acknowledgments

The authors would like to thank the Zhaotong Earthquake Disaster Reduction Bureau of Yunnan Province for providing continuous waveform data from the Zhaotong seismic network. Constructive comments from two anonymous reviewers improved this article. This research is co-supported by the Chinese Academy of Geological Sciences Basal Research Fund (Grant Number JKY202407), the National Key R&D Program of China (Grant Numbers 2021YFC3000705 and 2018YFC1503305), and the Key Laboratory of Coal Resources Exploration and Comprehensive Utilization, Ministry of Natural Resources (Grant Number SMDZ-2023ZD-13).

References

Abercrombie, R. E. (1996). The magnitude-frequency distribution of earthquakes recorded with deep seismometers at Cajon pass, southern California, *Tectonophysics* **261,** no. 1, 1–7, doi: 10.1016/0040-1951(96)00052-2.

Aki, K. (1965). Maximum likelihood estimate of B in the formula Log N = a-bM and its confidence limits, *Bull. Earthq. Res. Inst.* **43,** 237–239, doi: 10.15083/0000033631.

Ampuero, J., and A. M. Rubin (2008). Earthquake nucleation on rate and state faults—Aging and slip laws, *J. Geophys. Res.* **113,** no. B1, 2007JB005082, doi: 10.1029/2007JB005082.

Ben-Zion, Y. (2008). Collective behavior of earthquakes and faults: Continuum-discrete transitions, progressive evolutionary changes, and different dynamic regimes, *Rev. Geophys.* **46,** no. 4, 2008RG000260, doi: 10.1029/2008RG000260.

Ben-Zion, Y., and L. Zhu (2002). Potency-magnitude scaling relations for southern California earthquakes with 1.0 < ML < 7.0, *Geophys. J. Int.* **148,** no. 3, F1–F5, doi: 10.1046/j.1365-246X.2002.01637.x.

Beroza, G. C., and W. L. Ellsworth (1996). Properties of the seismic nucleation phase, *Tectonophysics* **261,** nos. 1/3, 209–227, doi: 10.1016/0040-1951(96)00067-4.

Bolton, D. C., P. Shokouhi, B. Rouet-Leduc, C. Hulbert, J. Rivière, C. Marone, and P. A. Johnson (2019). Characterizing acoustic signals and searching for precursors during the laboratory seismic cycle using unsupervised machine learning, *Seismol. Res. Lett.* **90,** no. 3, 1088–1098, doi: 10.1785/0220180367.

Bouchon, M., H. Karabulut, M. Aktar, S. Özalaybey, J. Schmittbuhl, and M.-P. Bouin (2011). Extended nucleation of the 1999 M_w 7.6 Izmit earthquake, *Science* **331,** no. 6019, 877–880, doi: 10.1126/science.1197341.

Cabrera, L., P. Poli, and W. B. Frank (2022). Tracking the spatio-temporal evolution of foreshocks preceding the mw 6.1 2009 L'aquila earthquake, *J. Geophys. Res.* **127,** no. 3, e2021JB023888, doi: 10.1029/2021JB023888.

Chen, X., and P. M. Shearer (2013). California foreshock sequences suggest aseismic triggering process, *Geophys. Res. Lett.* **40,** no. 11, 2602–2607, doi: 10.1002/grl.50444.

Chen, Y. (1978). Consistency of focal mechanism as a new parameter in describing seismic activity, *Chin. J. Geophys.* **21,** no. 2, 142–159 (in Chinese).

Chen, Y., J. Liu, and H. Ge (1999). Pattern characteristics of foreshock sequences, *Pure Appl. Geophys.* **155,** 395–408.

Cheng, J., X. Xu, and J. Liu (2016). Cause and rupture characteristics of the 2014 Ludian M_S 6.5 mainshock and its aftershock distribution using the Coulomb stress changes, *Chin. J. Geophys.* **59,** no. 2, 556–567, doi: 10.6038/cjg20160214 (in Chinese).

Deng, S., and H. Jiang (2022). Investigation of the foreshock activity of the 2020 M_S 6.4 Jiashi earthquake, *Chin. J. Geophys.* **65,** no. 9, 3322–3334, doi: 10.6038/cjg2022P0488 (in Chinese).

Dieterich, J. (1994). A constitutive law for rate of earthquake production and its application to earthquake clustering, *J. Geophys. Res.* **99,** no. B2, 2601–2618, doi: 10.1029/93JB02581.

Dodge, D. A., G. C. Beroza, and W. L. Ellsworth (1995). Foreshock sequence of the 1992 Landers, California, earthquake and its implications for earthquake nucleation, *J. Geophys. Res.* **100,** no. B6, 9865–9880, doi: 10.1029/95JB00871.

Dodge, D. A., G. C. Beroza, and W. L. Ellsworth (1996). Detailed observations of California foreshock sequences: Implications for the earthquake initiation process, *J. Geophys. Res.* **101,** no. B10, 22,371–22,392, doi: 10.1029/96JB02269.

Du, K., H. Li, Y. Li, Z. Ma, J. Lei, J. Jiang, and Z. Sun (2024). Investigation of the 2011 Yingjiang, Yunnan, China Ms. 5.8 earthquake sequence: Seismic migration, seismogenic mechanism, and hazard implication, *Tectonophysics* **890,** 230507, doi: 10.1016/j.tecto.2024.230507.

Durand, V., S. Bentz, G. Kwiatek, G. Dresen, C. Wollin, O. Heidbach, P. Martínez-Garzòn, F. Cotton, M. Nurlu, and M. Bohnhoff (2020). A two-scale preparation phase preceded an M_W 5.8 earthquake in the Sea of Marmara Offshore Istanbul, Turkey, *Seismol. Res. Lett.* **91,** no. 6, 3139–3147, doi: 10.1785/0220200110.

Ellsworth, W. L., and G. C. Beroza (1995). Seismic evidence for an earthquake nucleation phase, *Science* **268,** no. 5212, 851–855, doi: 10.1126/science.268.5212.851.

Ellsworth, W. L., and F. Bulut (2018). Nucleation of the 1999 Izmit earthquake by a triggered cascade of foreshocks, *Nature Geosci.* **11,** no. 7, 531–535, doi: 10.1038/s41561-018-0145-1.

Fang, L., J. Wu, J. Su, M. Wang, C. Jiang, L. Fan, W. Wang, C. Wang, and X. Tan (2018). Relocation of mainshock and aftershock sequence of the M_S 7.0 Sichuan Jiuzhaigou earthquake, *Chin. Sci. Bull.* **63,** no. 7, 649–662, doi: 10.1360/N972017-01184 (in Chinese).

Feng, T., J. Wu, L. Fang, X. Guo, Y. Cai, and W. Wang (2021). Foreshocks of the 2018 M_L 4.0 Shimian earthquake in the Anninghe fault and its implications for earthquake nucleation, *Seismol. Res. Lett.* **92,** no. 3, 1937–1949, doi: 10.1785/0220200332.

Fu, H., X. Qian, Y. Mao, Y. Su, X. Liu, Q. Li, L. Zhang, X. Zhao, and C. Wu (2015). Anomaly and forecast of Yunnan Ludian M_S 6.5 earthquake in 2014, *J. Seismol. Res.* **38,** no. 2, 181–188 (in Chinese).

Gardonio, B., D. Marsan, O. Lengliné, B. Enescu, M. Bouchon, and J. Got (2015). Changes in seismicity and stress loading on subduction faults in the Kanto region, Japan, 2011–2014, *J. Geophys. Res.* **120,** no. 4, 2616–2626, doi: 10.1002/2014JB011798.

Goebel, T. H. W., D. Schorlemmer, T. W. Becker, G. Dresen, and C. G. Sammis (2013). Acoustic emissions document stress changes over many seismic cycles in stick-slip experiments, *Geophys. Res. Lett.* **40,** no. 10, 2049–2054, doi: 10.1002/grl.50507.

Gomberg, J. (2018). Unsettled earthquake nucleation, *Nature Geosci.* **11,** no. 7, 463–464, doi: 10.1038/s41561-018-0149-x.

Gulia, L., and S. Wiemer (2019). Real-time discrimination of earthquake foreshocks and aftershocks, *Nature* **574,** no. 7777, 193–199, doi: 10.1038/s41586-019-1606-4.

Gutenberg, B., and C. F. Richter (1944). Frequency of earthquakes in California, *Bull. Seismol. Soc. Am.* **34,** no. 4, 185–188, doi: 10.1785/BSSA0340040185.

Hanks, T. C., and D. M. Boore (1984). Moment-magnitude relations in theory and practice, *J. Geophys. Res.* **89,** no. B7, 6229–6235, doi: 10.1029/JB089iB07p06229.

He, C., L. Zhang, P. Liu, and Q. Chen (2023). Characterizing the final stage of simulated earthquake nucleation governed by rate-and-state fault friction, *J. Geophys. Res.* **128,** no. 5, e2023JB026422, doi: 10.1029/2023JB026422.

Hou, J., and B. Wang (2017). Temporal evolution of seismicity before and after the 2014 Ludian M_S 6.5 earthquake, *Chin. J. Geophys.* **60,** no. 4, 1446–1456, doi: 10.6038/cjg20170418 (in Chinese).

Jiang, H., and S. Zhou (2020). Foreshock, predicting significance and distinguishing methods, *Seismol. Geomagn. Obs. Res.* **41,** no. 5, 222–225, doi: 10.3969/j.issn.1003-3246.2020.05.028 (in Chinese).

Jiang, H., S. Deng, Q. Yao, J. Song, and J. Wang (2024). Integrated interpretation on the precursory process evolution in the meta-instability stage of the earthquake: A case study on 2014 ludian M_S 6.5 earthquake, *Seismol. Geol.* **46,** no. 3, 513–535 (in Chinese).

Johnson, P. A., B. Ferdowsi, B. M. Kaproth, M. Scuderi, M. Griffa, J. Carmeliet, R. A. Guyer, P. Le Bas, D. T. Trugman, and C. Marone

(2013). Acoustic emission and microslip precursors to stick-slip failure in sheared granular material, *Geophys. Res. Lett.* **40,** no. 21, 5627–5631, doi: 10.1002/2013GL057848.

Jones, L. M., and P. Molnar (1979). Some characteristics of foreshocks and their possible relationship to earthquake prediction and premonitory slip on faults, *J. Geophys. Res.* **84,** no. B7, 3596–3608, doi: 10.1029/JB084iB07p03596.

Kanamori, H., and D. L. Anderson (1975). Theoretical basis of some empirical relations in seismology, *Bull. Seismol. Soc. Am.* **65,** no. 5, 1073–1095.

Kato, A., K. Obara, T. Igarashi, H. Tsuruoka, S. Nakagawa, and N. Hirata (2012). Propagation of slow slip leading up to the 2011 M_w 9.0 Tohoku-Oki earthquake, *Science* **335,** no. 6069, 705–708, doi: 10.1126/science.1215141.

Klein, F. W. (2002). User's guide to HYPOINVERSE-2000, a Fortran program to solve for earthquake locations and magnitudes, *U.S. Geol. Surv. Open-File Rept. 2002-171*.

Kwiatek, G., P. Martínez-Garzón, D. Becker, G. Dresen, F. Cotton, G. C. Beroza, D. Acarel, S. Ergintav, and M. Bohnhoff (2023). Months-long seismicity transients preceding the 2023 MW 7.8 Kahramanmaraş earthquake, Türkiye, *Nat. Commun.* **14,** no. 1, 7534, doi: 10.1038/s41467-023-42419-8.

Lei, X., Z. Wang, S. Ma, and C. He (2024). Step-over of strike-slip faults and overpressure fluid favor occurrence of foreshocks: Insights from the 1975 Haicheng fore-main-aftershock sequence, China, *Earthq. Res. Adv.* **4,** no. 1, 100237, doi: 10.1016/j.eqrea.2023.100237.

Li, Y., L. Chen, and X. Chen (2017). Enhancement of seismicity recorded by the Qiaojia seismic network before the 2013 Lushan and 2014 Ludian earthquakes, *Earthquake* **37,** no. 3, 95–106 (in Chinese).

Liu, L., Y. Su, J. Liu, and J. Yang (2010). Study on temporal and spatial features of stress drop for low-to-moderate earthquakes in Sichuan and Yunnan region, *J. Seismol. Res.* **33,** no. 3, 314–319 (in Chinese).

Liu, M., H. Li, L. Li, M. Zhang, and W. Wang (2022). Multistage nucleation of the 2021 Yangbi M_S 6.4 earthquake, Yunnan, China and its foreshocks, *J. Geophys. Res.* **127,** no. 5, e2022JB024091, doi: 10.1029/2022JB024091.

Liu, M., H. Li, M. Zhang, and T. Wang (2020). Graphics processing unit-based match and locate (GPU-M&L): An improved match and locate method and its application, *Seismol. Res. Lett.* **91,** no. 2A, 1019–1029, doi: 10.1785/0220190241.

Liu, M., Y. J. Tan, H. Guo, H. Li, R. Lu, and J. Jiang (2025). Fluids and fault structures underlying the complex foreshock sequence of the 2021 Mw 6.1 Yangbi earthquake, *Earth Planet. Sci. Lett.* **651,** 119173, doi: 10.1016/j.epsl.2024.119173.

Liu, M., M. Zhang, and H. Li (2022). Using the match-and-locate method to characterize foreshocks of the July 2019 MW6.4 Ridgecrest, California earthquake, *Earthq. Sci.* **35,** no. 4, 213–242, doi: 10.1016/j.eqs.2022.08.005.

Liu, R., Y. Chen, F. Xue, and E. Li (2018). How to use the new national standard of magnitude correctly, *Seismol. Geomagn. Obs. Res.* **39,** no. 4, 1–11, doi: 10.3969/j.issn.1003-3246.2018.04.001 (in Chinese).

Liu, S., C. Tang, C. Chen, and R. Xu (2019). Spatiotemporal evolution of the 2018 M_W 6.4 Hualien earthquake sequence in Eastern Taiwan, *Seismol. Res. Lett.* doi: 10.1785/0220180389.

Liu, Y., H. Ren, L. Zhang, H. Fu, X. Sun, D. He, H. Yu, Z. Zhou, and G. Zhang (2015). Underground fluid anomalies and the precursor mechanisms of the Ludian M_S 6.5 earthquake, *Seismol. Geol.* **37,** no. 1, 307–318, doi: 10.3969/j.issn.0253-4967.2015.24 (in Chinese).

Ma, S., H. Jiang, X. Hu, and J. Ba (2004). A discussion on mechanism for seismic quiescence before large earthquakes based on experimental results of acoustic emission, *Seismol. Geol.* **26,** no. 3, 426–435 (in Chinese).

Marone, C. (1998). Laboratory-derived friction laws and their application to seismic faulting, *Annu. Rev. Earth Planet. Sci.* **26,** no. 1, 643–696, doi: 10.1146/annurev.earth.26.1.643.

Martínez-Garzón, P., and P. Poli (2024). Cascade and pre-slip models oversimplify the complexity of earthquake preparation in nature, *Commun. Earth Environ.* **5,** no. 1, 120, doi: 10.1038/s43247-024-01285-y.

Marty, S., A. Schubnel, H. S. Bhat, J. Aubry, E. Fukuyama, S. Latour, S. Nielsen, and R. Madariaga (2023). Nucleation of laboratory earthquakes: Quantitative analysis and scalings, *J. Geophys. Res.* **128,** no. 3, e2022JB026294, doi: 10.1029/2022JB026294.

Marzocchi, W., and L. Sandri (2003). A review and new insights on the estimation of the b-valueand its uncertainty, *Ann. Geophys.* **46,** no. 6, doi: 10.4401/ag-3472.

McLaskey, G. C. (2019). Earthquake initiation from laboratory observations and implications for foreshocks, *J. Geophys. Res.* **124,** no. 12, 12882–12904, doi: 10.1029/2019JB018363.

Meng, X., H. Yang, and Z. Peng (2018). Foreshocks, *b* value map, and aftershock triggering for the 2011 M_W 5.7 Virginia earthquake, *J. Geophys. Res.* **123,** no. 6, 5082–5098, doi: 10.1029/2017JB015136.

Meng, Z., J. Liu, Z. Xie, and Y. Lü (2021). Analysis of the correlation between the temporal-spatial distribution of b-value and seismic hazard: A review, *Prog. Geophys.* **36,** no. 1, 30–38, doi: 10.6038/pg2021EE0025 (in Chinese).

Mignan, A. (2014). The debate on the prognostic value of earthquake foreshocks: A meta-analysis, *Sci. Rep.* **4,** no. 1, 4099, doi: 10.1038/srep04099.

Morales-Yáñez, C., L. Bustamante, R. Benavente, C. Sippl, and M. Moreno (2022). B-value variations in the Central Chile seismic gap assessed by a Bayesian transdimensional approach, *Sci. Rep.* **12,** no. 1, 21,710, doi: 10.1038/s41598-022-25338-4.

Neves, M., Z. Peng, and G. Lin (2022). A high-resolution earthquake catalog for the 2004 mw 6 parkfield earthquake sequence using a matched filter technique, *Seismol. Res. Lett.* **94,** no. 1, 507–521, doi: 10.1785/0220220206.

Ogata, Y. (1999). Seismicity analysis through point-process modeling: A review, *Pure Appl. Geophys.* **155,** no. 2, 471–507, doi: 10.1007/s000240050275.

Peng, Z., and X. Lei (2024). Physical mechanisms of earthquake nucleation and foreshocks: Cascade triggering, aseismic slip, or fluid flows? *Earthq. Res. Adv.* **5,** 100349, doi: 10.1016/j.eqrea.2024.100349.

Peng, Z., and P. Zhao (2009). Migration of early aftershocks following the 2004 Parkfield earthquake, *Nature Geosci.* **2,** no. 12, 877–881, doi: 10.1038/ngeo697.

Picozzi, M., A. G. Iaccarino, and D. Spallarossa (2023). The preparatory process of the 2023 Mw 7.8 Türkiye earthquake, *Sci. Rep.* **13,** no. 1, 17,853, doi: 10.1038/s41598-023-45073-8.

Qiu, J. (2014). Chinese data hint at trigger for fatal quake, *Nature* **513,** no. 7517, 154–155, doi: 10.1038/513154a.

Reasenberg, P. A. (1999). Foreshock occurrence before large earthquakes, *J. Geophys. Res.* **104,** no. B3, 4755–4768, doi: 10.1029/1998JB900089.

Ross, Z. E., D. T. Trugman, E. Hauksson, and P. M. Shearer (2019). Searching for hidden earthquakes in Southern California, *Science* **364,** no. 6442, 767–771, doi: 10.1126/science.aaw6888.

Ruan, X., X. Meng, Z. Peng, F. Long, and R. Xie (2017). Microseismic activity in the last five months before the mw 7.9 Wenchuan earthquake, *Bull. Seismol. Soc. Am.* **107,** no. 4, 1582–1592, doi: 10.1785/0120160332.

Scholz, C. H. (1968). Microfracturing and the inelastic deformation of rock in compression, *J. Geophys. Res.* **73,** no. 4, 1417–1432, doi: 10.1029/JB073i004p01417.

Schorlemmer, D., S. Wiemer, and M. Wyss (2005). Variations in earthquake-size distribution across different stress regimes, *Nature* **437,** no. 7058, 539–542, doi: 10.1038/nature04094.

Shelly, D. R., W. L. Ellsworth, and D. P. Hill (2016). Fluid-faulting evolution in high definition: Connecting fault structure and frequency-magnitude variations during the 2014 long valley caldera, California, earthquake swarm, *J. Geophys. Res.* **121,** no. 3, 1776–1795, doi: 10.1002/2015JB012719.

Shi, H., L. Meng, X. Zhang, Y. Chang, Z. Yang, W. Xie, K. Hattori, and P. Han (2018). Decrease in b value prior to the Wenchuan earthquake (M_S 8.0), *Chin. J. Geophys.* **61,** no. 5, 1874–1882, doi: 10.6038/cjg2018M0024 (in Chinese).

Tape, C., S. Holtkamp, V. Silwal, J. Hawthorne, Y. Kaneko, J. P. Ampuero, C. Ji, N. Ruppert, K. Smith, and M. E. West (2018). Earthquake nucleation and fault slip complexity in the lower crust of central Alaska, *Nature Geosci.* **11,** no. 7, 536–541, doi: 10.1038/s41561-018-0144-2.

Trugman, D. T., and Z. E. Ross (2019). Pervasive Foreshock Activity Across Southern California, *Geophys. Res. Lett.* **46,** no. 15, 8772–8781, doi: 10.1029/2019GL083725.

Uchida, N. (2019). Detection of repeating earthquakes and their application in characterizing slow fault slip, *Prog. Earth Planet. Sci.* **6,** no. 1, 40, doi: 10.1186/s40645-019-0284-z.

Uchida, N., and R. Bürgmann (2019). Repeating earthquakes, *Annu. Rev. Earth Planet. Sci.* **47,** no. 1, 305–332, doi: 10.1146/annurev-earth-053018-060119.

Utsu, T. (1961). A statistical study on the occurrence of aftershocks, *Geophys. Mag.* **30,** no. 4, 521–605.

Utsu, T. (1966). A statistical significance test of the difference in b-value between two earthquake groups, *J. Phys. Earth* **14,** no. 2, 37–40, doi: 10.4294/jpe1952.14.37.

Utsu, T., Y. Ogata, and R. S. Matsu'ura (1995). The centenary of the Omori formula for a decay law of aftershock activity, *J. Phys. Earth* **43,** no. 1, 1–33, doi: 10.4294/jpe1952.43.1.

Waldhauser, F. (2000). A Double-difference earthquake location algorithm: Method and application to the Northern Hayward Fault, California, *Bull. Seismol. Soc. Am.* **90,** no. 6, 1353–1368, doi: 10.1785/0120000006.

Waldhauser, F., and W. L. Ellsworth (2002). Fault structure and mechanics of the Hayward Fault, California, from double-difference earthquake locations, *J. Geophys. Res.* **107,** no. B3, doi: 10.1029/2000JB000084.

Wan, Y., S. Huang, F. Wang, Y. Xu, and H. She (2023). Fault geometry and slip characteristics revealed by the 2022 Menyuan earthquake sequence, *Chin. J. Geophys.* **66,** no. 7, 2796–2810, doi: 10.6038/cjg2022Q0345 (in Chinese).

Wang, G., X. Zhao, H. Fu, Z. Liu, and Q. Wang (2018). Relocation of the 2014 Ludian M_S 6.5 earthquake and its large aftershock sequence, *Acta Seismol. Sin.* **40,** no. 5, 582–594, doi: 10.11939/jass.20170180 (in Chinese).

Wang, K., Z. Peng, S. Liang, J. Luo, K. Zhang, and C. He (2024). Migrating foreshocks driven by a slow slip event before the 2021 M_W 6.1 Yangbi, China earthquake, *J. Geophys. Res.* **129,** no. 1, e2023JB027209, doi: 10.1029/2023JB027209.

Wang, L., P. Chen, Z. Wu, and T. Bai (2005). Characteristics of foreshock and its identification, *Acta Seismol. Sin.* **27,** no. 2, 171–177, doi: 10.1007/s11589-005-0065-1 (in Chinese).

Wang, W., J. Wu, L. Fang, and G. Lai (2014). Double difference location of the Ludian M_S 6.5 earthquake sequences in Yunnan province in 2014, *Chin. J. Geophys.* **57,** no. 9, 3042–3051, doi: 10.6038/cjg20140929 (in Chinese).

Wen, X., F. Du, G. Yi, F. Long, J. Fan, P. Yang, R. Xiong, X. Liu, and Q. Liu (2013). Earthquake potential of the Zhaotong and Lianfeng fault zones of the eastern Sichuan-Yunnan border region, *Chin. J. Geophys.* **56,** no. 10, 3361–3372, doi: 10.6038/cjg20131012 (in Chinese).

Wiemer, S., and K. Katsumata (1999). Spatial variability of seismicity parameters in aftershock zones, *J. Geophys. Res.* **104,** no. B6, 13,135–13,151, doi: 10.1029/1999JB900032.

Wiemer, S., and M. Wyss (1997). Mapping the frequency-magnitude distribution in asperities: An improved technique to calculate recurrence times? *J. Geophys. Res.* **102,** no. B7, 15,115–15,128, doi: 10.1029/97JB00726.

Xiong, S., Y. Zheng, Z. Yin, X. Zeng, Y. Quan, and K. Sun (1993). The 2-D structure and it's tectonic implications of the crust in the Lijiang-Pan-Zhihua-Zhehai region, *Chin. J. Geophys.* no. 4, 434–444 (in Chinese).

Xu, X., G. Jiang, G. Yu, X. Wu, J. Zhang, and X. Li (2014). Discussion on seismogenic fault of the Ludian M_S 6.5 earthquake and its tectonic attribution, *Chin. J. Geophys.* **57,** no. 9, 3060–3068, doi: 10.6038/cjg20140931 (in Chinese).

Xue, Y., J. Liu, H. Yu, and S. Liu (2012). Seismicity characteristics of the 2011 M 9.0 Tohoku earthquake near the East Coast of Honshu in Japan, *Chin. Sci. Bull.* 57, no. 8, 634–640, doi: 10.1360/csb2012-57-8-634 (in Chinese).

Yagi, Y., R. Okuwaki, B. Enescu, S. Hirano, Y. Yamagami, S. Endo, and T. Komoro (2014). Rupture process of the 2014 Iquique Chile earthquake in relation with the foreshock activity, *Geophys. Res. Lett.* **41,** no. 12, 4201–4206, doi: 10.1002/2014GL060274.

Yan, K., W. Wang, L. Feng, F. Peng, H. Kou, A. Yuan, and G. Fu (2023). The foreshock temporal-spatial evolutionary patterns of the strong earthquakes since 2012 in Yutian, Xinjiang, China, *Chin. J. Geophys.* **66,** no. 1, 245–259, doi: 10.6038/cjg2022Q0020 (in Chinese).

Yao, D., Y. Huang, Z. Peng, and R. R. Castro (2020). Detailed investigation of the foreshock sequence of the 2010 M_W 7.2 El Mayor-Cucapah earthquake, *J. Geophys. Res.* **125,** no. 6, e2019JB019076, doi: 10.1029/2019JB019076.

Yao, D., J. I. Walter, X. Meng, T. E. Hobbs, Z. Peng, A. V. Newman, S. Y. Schwartz, and M. Protti (2017). Detailed spatiotemporal evolution of microseismicity and repeating earthquakes following the 2012 M_W 7.6 Nicoya earthquake, *J. Geophys. Res.* **122,** no. 1, 524–542, doi: 10.1002/2016JB013632.

Yao, J., D. Tian, Z. Lu, L. Sun, and L. Wen (2018). Triggered seismicity after North Korea's 3 September 2017 Nuclear Test, *Seismol. Res. Lett.* **89,** no. 6, 2085–2093, doi: 10.1785/0220180135.

Yi, G., X. Wen, and Y. Su (2008). Study on the potential strong-earthquake risk for the eastern boundary of the Sichuan-Yunnan active faulted-block, China, *Chin. J. Geophys.* **51,** no. 6, 1719–1725, doi: 10.1002/cjg2.1311 (in Chinese).

Yi, G., X. Wen, S. Wang, F. Long, and J. Fan (2006). Study on fault sliding behaviors and strong-earthquake risk of the Longmenshan-Minshan fault zones from current seismicity parameter, *Earthq. Res. China* **22,** no. 2, 117–125 (in Chinese).

Yi, G., X. Wen, H. Xin, H. Qiao, S. Wang, and Y. Gong (2013). Stress state and major-earthquake risk on the southern segment of the Longmen Shan fault zone, *Chin. J. Geophys.* **56,** no. 4, 1112–1120, doi: 10.6038/cjg20130407 (in Chinese).

Yoon, C. E., N. Yoshimitsu, W. L. Ellsworth, and G. C. Beroza (2019). Foreshocks and mainshock nucleation of the 1999 M_W 7.1 Hector Mine, California, earthquake, *J. Geophys. Res.* **124,** no. 2, 1569–1582, doi: 10.1029/2018JB016383.

Zhang, G., J. Lei, S. Liang, and C. Sun (2014). Relocations and focal mechanism solutions of the 3 August 2014 Ludian, Yunnan M_S 6.5 earthquake sequence, *Chin. J. Geophys.* **57,** no. 9, 3018–3027, doi: 10.6038/cjg20140926 (in Chinese).

Zhang, M., and L. Wen (2015a). An effective method for small event detection: match and locate (M&L), *Geophys. J. Int.* **200,** no. 3, 1523–1537, doi: 10.1093/gji/ggu466.

Zhang, M., and L. Wen (2015b). Earthquake characteristics before eruptions of Japan's Ontake volcano in 2007 and 2014, *Geophys. Res. Lett.* **42,** no. 17, 6982–6988, doi: 10.1002/2015GL065165.

Zhang, Y., Y. Chen, L. Xu, X. Wei, M. Jin, and S. Zhang (2015). The 2014 M_W 6.1 Ludian, Yunnan, earthquake: A complex conjugated ruptured earthquake, *Chin. J. Geophys.* **58,** no. 1, 153–162, doi: 10.6038/cjg20150113 (in Chinese).

Zhao, B., Y. Huang, C. Zhang, W. Wang, K. Tan, and R. Du (2015). Crustal deformation on the Chinese mainland during 1998–2014 based on GPS data, *Geodes. Geodynam.* **6,** no. 1, 7–15, doi: 10.1016/j.geog.2014.12.006.

Zhao, X., and N. Sun (2014). Simultaneous inversion for focal location of Yunnan Ludian M_S 6.5 earthquake sequence in 2014 and velocity structure in the source region, *J. Seismol. Res.* **37,** no. 4, 523–531 (in Chinese).

Zhou, Y., C. Ren, A. Ghosh, H. Meng, L. Fang, H. Yue, S. Zhou, and Y. Su (2022). Seismological characterization of the 2021 Yangbi foreshock-mainshock sequence, Yunnan, China: More than a triggered cascade, *J. Geophys. Res.* **127,** no. 8, e2022JB024534, doi: 10.1029/2022JB024534.

Zhu, C., and L. Wang (1996). Study on the characteristics of foreshock and ID identification, *Chin. J. Geophys.* **39,** no. 1, 80–88 (in Chinese).

Manuscript received 16 January 2025
Published online 10 September 2025

High-Resolution Shear-Wave Velocity Model of the Source Region of the 1970 M_s 7.7 Tonghai Earthquake, Yunnan, China

Di Zhong[1], Jianping Wu[*1,2], Changzai Wang[1,2], Lihua Fang[1,3,4], Guangyao Cai[5], Jing Liu[1,2], and Yaning Liu[1,2]

Abstract

The M_S 7.7 Tonghai earthquake, which struck the southeastern margin of the Tibetan Plateau on 5 January 1970, along the Qujiang fault (QJF), led to a high number of casualties and severe economic losses. However, research about the high-resolution velocity structure and seismotectonics around this seismogenic fault remains limited. To fill this gap, we deployed 110 short-period seismometers around the QJF from March to September 2023 to construct an *S*-wave velocity (V_S) model of the source region, adopting ambient noise tomography. The V_S structure is mainly characterized by relatively high velocities in the western part of the study area and relatively low velocities in the eastern part. The significant low-velocity anomalies in the shallow eastern portion of the fault zone, which align with the broader isoseismic lines in the southeastern section of the main rupture zone, suggest a strong-motion amplification effect due to shallow structures. The correlation between the velocity structure and surface rupture displacement indicates that the inhomogeneous characteristics of the deep medium significantly influenced the rupture process of the Tonghai earthquake. The initial rupture nucleated at the intersection between the QJF and the high- and low-velocity anomaly boundary, a location likely prone to stress accumulation. At depths of 7.5–9.0 km, a prominent low-velocity anomaly is imaged in the eastern study area. We attribute this anomaly to geothermal fluids within the upper-crustal fault system and high temperatures within the crust caused by mantle-derived thermal activity. Along the southern side of the QJF within the same depth range, a narrow velocity anomaly correlates with the granitic intrusion. This research improves our understanding of the seismotectonics of the strong Tonghai earthquake.

Cite this article as Zhong, D., J. Wu, C. Wang, L. Fang, G. Cai, J. Liu, and Y. Liu (2025). High-Resolution Shear-Wave Velocity Model of the Source Region of the 1970 M_s 7.7 Tonghai Earthquake, Yunnan, China, *Seismol. Res. Lett.* **97**, 54–66, doi: 10.1785/0220240293.

Supplemental Material

Introduction

In 1970, an M_s 7.7 earthquake occurred in the Tonghai area at the southeastern end of the Sichuan–Yunnan active tectonic block (SYB), China. The earthquake produced a maximum magnitude of X and affected a wide area. This event was one of the largest and most destructive earthquakes of the twentieth century in China, causing over 15,000 deaths and over 26,700 injuries (Liu *et al.*, 1999). From the perspective of regional structure, the SYB, located in the southeastern margin of the Tibetan Plateau, is bounded by the Xianshuihe–Xiaojiang fault system and Jinshajiang–Red River fault, and represents the front of the tectonic extrusion zone of the Tibetan Plateau. According to Global Positioning System data, crustal movement in this region is exhibiting clockwise rotation around the eastern Himalayan syntaxis (cyan arrows in the inset of Fig. 1; Tapponnier and Molnar, 1976; Zhang *et al.*, 2004). Since the Cenozoic Era, the tectonic extrusion of the Tibetan Plateau has generated an intersection between the southern section of the Xiaojiang fault (XJF) and the Qujiang fault (QJF) at the SYB, forming a unique and complex tectonic pattern. This pattern, referred to as "wedge-shaped fracture-block tectonics," is proposed to exert strict control over crustal deformation and to drive strong seismic activity in the region (He *et al.*, 1992).

1. Institute of Geophysics, China Earthquake Administration, Beijing, China, https://orcid.org/0009-0008-8723-5879 (DZ); https://orcid.org/0000-0003-2156-4406 (LF); https://orcid.org/0000-0003-4519-5019 (JL); 2. Beijing Baijiatuan Earth Science National Observation and Research Station, Beijing, China; 3. Key Laboratory of Earthquake Forecasting and Risk Assessment, Ministry of Emergency Management, Beijing, China; 4. Institute of Earthquake Forecasting, China Earthquake Administration, Beijing, China; 5. Geophysical Exploration Center, China Earthquake Administration, Zhengzhou, China

*Corresponding author: wjpwu@cea-igp.ac.cn

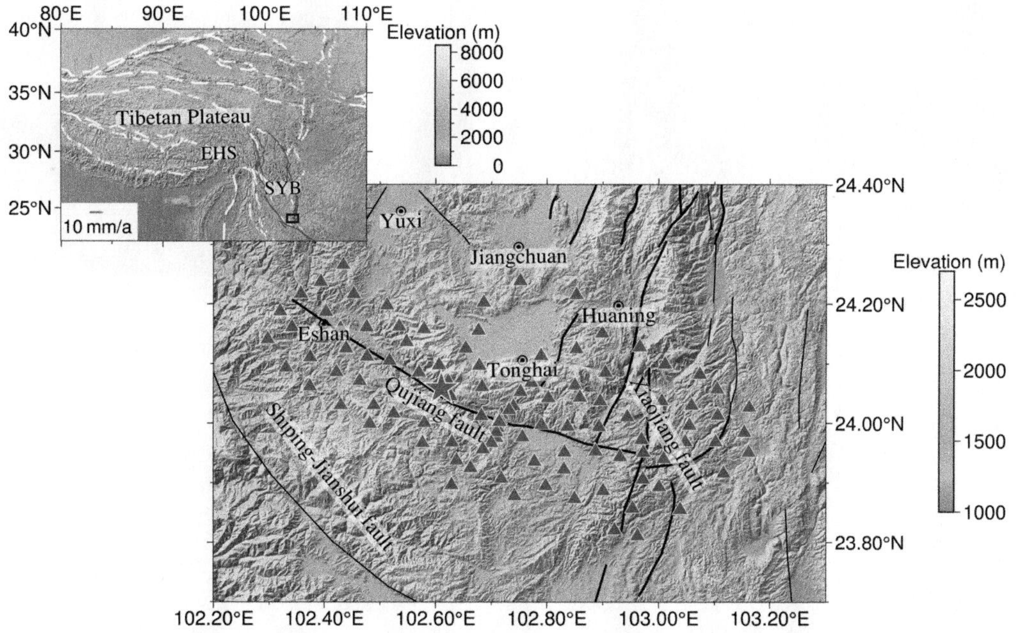

Figure 1. Topographic of the study area and distribution of seismic stations. The black-solid lines represent active faults (Xu *et al.*, 2016), blue triangles mark the locations of seismic stations, and the dark-pink star marks the epicenter of the M_S 7.7 Tonghai earthquake (Liu, 1983). The inset in the upper-left corner indicates the location of the study area relative to the Tibetan Plateau; white-dashed lines represent the boundary of the active tectonic blocks, cyan arrows indicate the surface velocity fields relative to the stable Eurasian plate (Zhang *et al.*, 2004), red-dashed lines represent the boundary faults of the Sichuan–Yunnan active tectonic block, EHS indicates the eastern Himalayan syntaxis, and SYB indicates the Sichuan–Yunnan active tectonic block. The color version of this figure is available only in the electronic edition.

The seismogenic fault of the Tonghai earthquake is the QJF (Fig. 1), which began to develop in the Paleozoic Variscan and exhibited characteristics of predominantly right-lateral strike-slip movement with compressional thrusting due to southeastward movement of the SYB since the Cenozoic (Zhang and Liu, 1978; Liu *et al.*, 1999; Wen *et al.*, 2011). Since the Tonghai earthquake, extensive research has been conducted on the seismic-geological and fault-activity characteristics of this region (Zhang and Liu, 1978, 1982; Zhu, 1978; Zhou *et al.*, 1983; Wen *et al.*, 2011; Wang *et al.*, 2014; Yu, Zhang, *et al.*, 2020). However, the tomographic studies of the deep structures have been limited to regional scales. The results of body-wave tomography reveal that the XJF zone exhibits low-velocity anomalies in the middle and upper crust (Wu *et al.*, 2013, 2024; Feng *et al.*, 2022); surface-wave tomography by Zhang *et al.* (2020) shows the QJF zone exhibits obvious low-velocity anomalies from the crust to the upper mantle. These studies remain insufficient to reveal the fine structures of the Tonghai earthquake source region. Determining the high-resolution 3D velocity structure is crucial for understanding the seismotectonics of strong earthquakes and can serve as an essential reference model for numerical simulations of strong ground motions. Luo *et al.* (2023) employed a fine velocity model for scenario earthquake simulations and showed that the horizontal peak ground acceleration increased by 25%–50% compared to that using a smooth regional velocity model. This highlights the importance of fine velocity structures in assessing the risk of large earthquakes.

Ambient noise tomography technique has rapidly developed over the past decade and is widely used to study crustal and mantle velocity structures (Shapiro *et al.*, 2005; Yao *et al.*, 2006, 2008, 2011; Lin *et al.*, 2007, 2008; Yang *et al.*, 2007, 2008; Fang *et al.*, 2009; Luo *et al.*, 2015; Shen *et al.*, 2016). With the development of seismic observation technology, the short-period dense seismic array ambient noise tomography technique has emerged as a key tool for studying high-resolution shallow velocity structures. This method has been widely applied to analyze urban spatial environments, fault-zone structures, and mineral resource exploration (Ranasinghe *et al.*, 2018; Yang *et al.*, 2020; Chen *et al.*, 2023; Liang *et al.*, 2023; Luo *et al.*, 2023; Zhao *et al.*, 2023; Wang *et al.*, 2024).

Shallow high-resolution velocity structure can be obtained using the short-period dense seismic array ambient noise tomography technique. Therefore, in this study, we apply this method to approximately six months of continuous waveform data from 110 short-period nodal seismometers to construct a high-resolution 3D *S*-wave velocity (V_S) model of the M_s 7.7 Tonghai earthquake source region. We then combine the results of previous geological, geochemical, and geophysical research to discuss the tectonic significance of the imaging results.

Data Analysis and Inversion Method

Data acquisition

The data used in this study were collected from a dense array of 110 short-period seismometers (Smartsolo IGU-16HR 3C, natural frequency 5 Hz; sampling rate 250 Hz) deployed in the source region of the M_s 7.7 Tonghai earthquake. Figure 1 shows the distribution of stations, with an average spacing of approximately 5 km and covering an area of approximately 94.5 km × 51.0 km. This array recorded continuous waveform data for over six months, from 11 March to 18 September 2023.

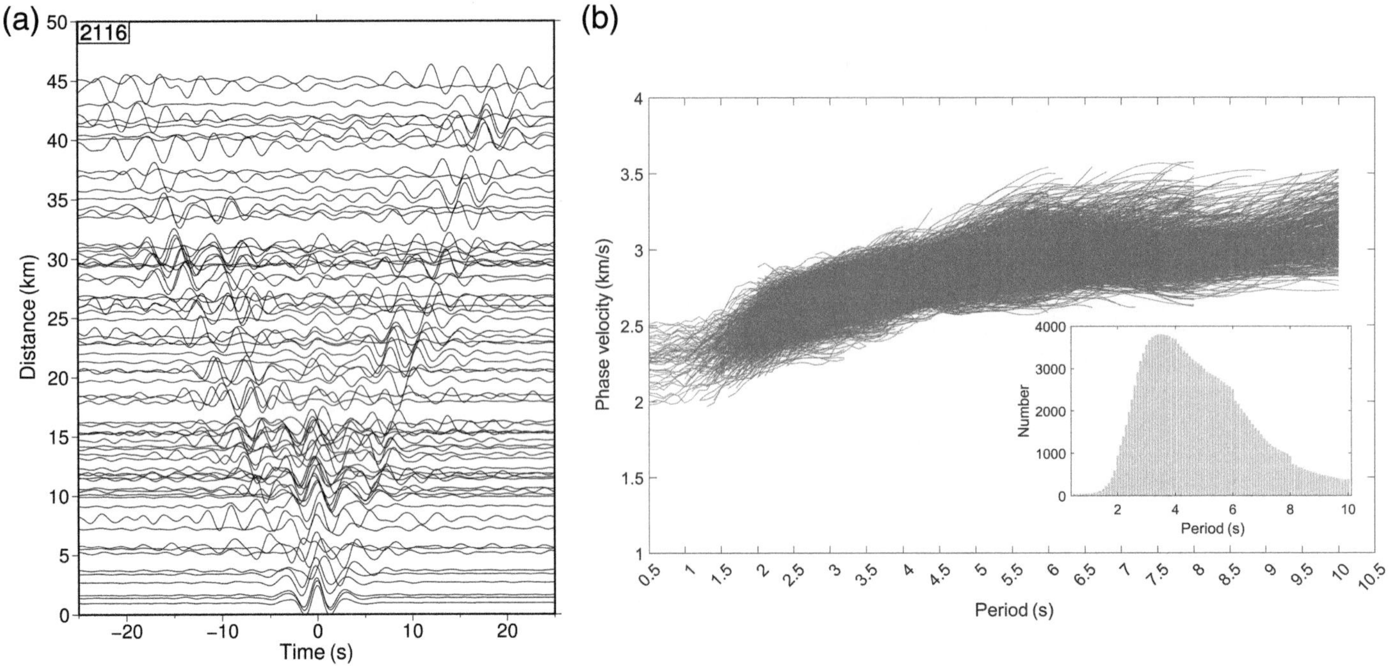

Figure 2. (a) Cross-correlation functions (CCFs) of station 2116 with all other stations, within a filtered range of 2–5 s. (b) Rayleigh-wave phase velocity dispersion curves. The inset panel shows the total number of measurements for each period. The color version of this figure is available only in the electronic edition.

Ambient noise data processing

Ambient noise data processing was performed according to the procedure outlined by Bensen *et al.* (2007). Specifically, we cut the vertical component into daily segments, resampled the data to 25 Hz, removed the mean and trend, and band-pass filtered the data in a frequency range of 0.1–10.0 s. To suppress the effects of man-made and other natural seismic signals, we applied temporal normalization and spectral whitening. Then, we calculated the cross-correlation function (CCF) for each station (Levshin and Ritzwoller, 2001). To improve the signal-to-noise ratio, the CCFs for each day were stacked using the time–frequency phase weighted stacking method (Schimmel *et al.*, 2011), and a total of 5995 CCFs were obtained. The surface-wave signal from the stacked CCFs in the filtering band of 2–5 s was clearly visible (Fig. 2a).

In practical observations, asymmetry in the causal and anticausal branches of the CCF often occurs because of the uneven distribution of noise sources. To remove interference from asymmetric CCF branches in the dispersion curve measurement, we averaged the causal and anticausal branches of CCF. Then, we used the image analysis method of Yao *et al.* (2006, 2011) to manually pick phase velocity dispersion curves of the Rayleigh wave for periods of 0.5–10.0 s.

To eliminate outliers in the dispersion curves, we conducted path clustering analysis and quality control (Zhang *et al.*, 2018; Text S1 and Fig. S1, available in the supplemental material to this article). After quality control, we finally obtained 3980 dispersion curves for the inversion (Fig. 2b). Figure 3 shows the ray-path coverage for periods of 2, 4, 7, and 9 s. Ray-path coverage was densest at 3–6 s then became sparser after 8 s. Considering the relatively sparse ray-path coverage before 2 s and after 9 s, we propose that dispersion data between 2 and 9 s are more reliable for constraining underground structures.

Inversion method and model resolution tests

Fang *et al.* (2015) developed a surface-wave direct inversion method that avoids the intermediate step of inverting 2D phase velocity or group velocity structures in traditional surface-wave tomography. The method considers the influence of nongreat-circular path propagation of surface waves in complex media. For short-period surface waves with complex propagation paths, the accuracy of inversion results was effectively improved. A fast marching method was used to calculate surface-wave travel times and ray paths given the 3D V_S model (Rawlinson and Sambridge, 2004).

The selection of an initial model is a crucial step in the inversion process. A proper initial model can accelerate the iteration and ensure better results. In this study, we obtained a 1D V_S model for the shallow and middle depths of the study area by converting the measured average phase velocity for each period to the V_S at one-third depth using the following empirical equation (Shearer, 2019):

$$V_s = 1.08c; \quad h = \frac{1}{3}cT, \tag{1}$$

in which c is the average phase velocity, h is the depth, and T is the period. We then used the CSES_VM1.0 velocity model

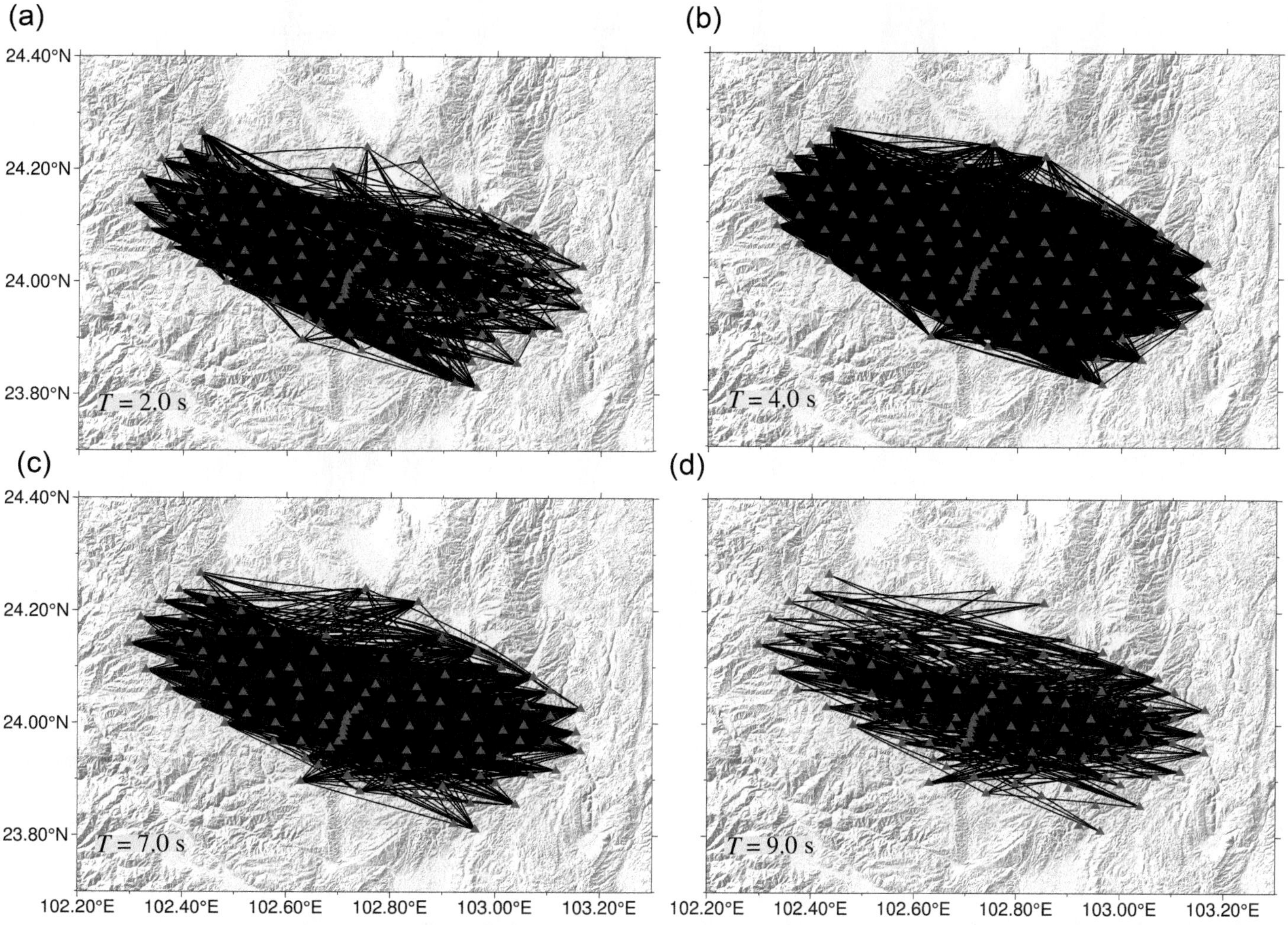

Figure 3. Rayleigh-wave ray-path coverage at different periods. (a–d) Ray-path coverage for periods of 2.0, 4.0, 7.0, and 9.0 s, respectively. The black lines show the ray paths, and blue triangles mark the locations of seismic stations. The color version of this figure is available only in the electronic edition.

(Wu *et al.*, 2024) after interpolation and averaging to 1D as a deep constraint to obtain a 1D V_S model of the study area (Fig. 4). Considering that our data set is more sensitive to shallower depth, the depth grid was set to 0, 0.5, 1.0, 1.5, 2.0, 2.5, 3.0, 4.0, 5.0, 6.0, 7.5, 9.0, 10.5, 12.0, 15.0, and 20.0 km, and the horizontal grid was set to 0.03° × 0.03°.

To determine the spatial resolution and recoverability of the 3D velocity model, we conducted checkerboard tests on two V_S models with horizontal anomaly sizes of 0.09° × 0.09° and 0.12° × 0.12° and vertical anomaly sizes of 0–4 and 5–20 km, using ±15% velocity perturbation and 2% Gaussian noise. After 10 iterations, the anomalies within most of the study area were effectively recovered, as shown in Figures 5 and 6. The checkerboard tests indicate that our dispersion data can effectively resolve 0.09° × 0.09° V_S anomalies at depths shallower than 4 km. However, at the 4–9 km depth range, the resolution capability for 0.09° × 0.09° anomalies becomes limited, but it performs better for the 0.12° × 0.12° anomalies. Considering that model resolution is affected by several factors, the checkerboard test should only be used as a reference and not as an indicator of the true recoverability of the model (Rawlinson and Spakman, 2016; Luo *et al.*, 2023).

Results and Discussion

Error analysis and reliability of the results

In the inversion, the input parameters are consistent with the checkerboard tests, and the inversion is iterated 10 times. The standard deviation of travel-time residuals decreases from 0.46 to 0.18 s after 10 iterations (Fig. 7). The travel-time residuals after the initial inversion are centered around 0.4 s, whereas those after the final inversion are centered around 0 s and exhibit a normal distribution (inset panel in Fig. 7).

To verify the reliability of our V_S model, we performed the same inversion process on the waveform data recorded by the seismic array in our study area during the first phase (March to June), the second phase (June to September), and the entire six-month period. The V_S inversion results shown in Figure S2 are generally consistent, with only minor differences observed in areas with less ray coverage and low resolution at the edge of the array, indicating that our V_S model is reliable.

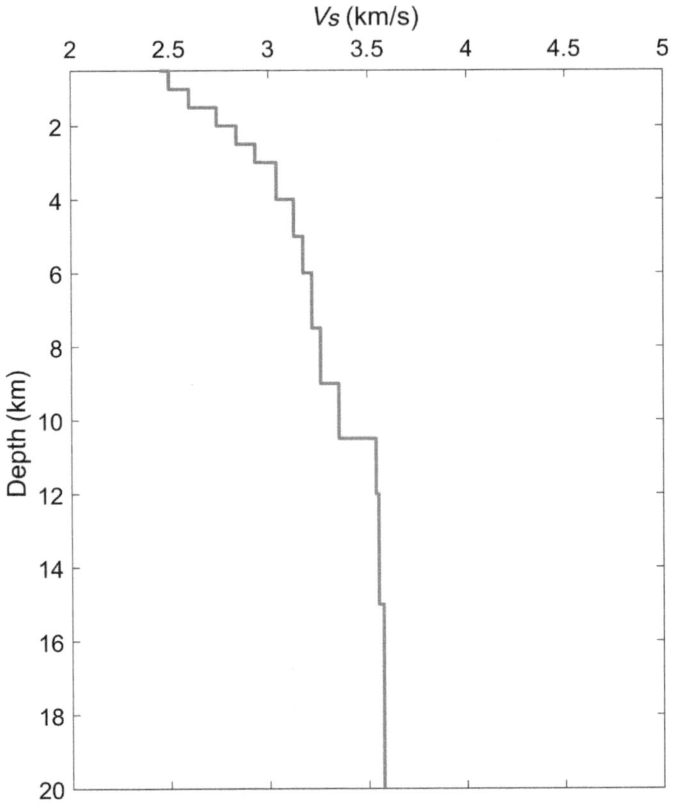

Figure 4. One-dimensional initial velocity model. The color version of this figure is available only in the electronic edition.

In addition, we also inverted the surface-wave phase velocity for different periods using the fast marching surface tomography method (Rawlinson and Sambridge, 2003, 2005) (Text S2 and Figs. S3, S4). Overall, the phase velocity images for each period reveal high-velocity anomalies in the northwest section of the QJF and low-velocity anomalies at the intersection of the QJF and XJF.

3D *S*-wave velocity structure

Figure 8 shows horizontal slices of V_S at depths of 1.0, 2.5, 5.0, 6.0, 7.5, and 9.0 km in the source region of the 1970 M_S 7.7 Tonghai earthquake. Along the QJF, four fault basins are located: Eshan, Ledejiu, Gaoda, and Quxi basins (Fig. 8a). The Tonghai basin, developed on the northeast side of the QJF, has a thin and unevenly distributed sedimentary layer, with a maximum thickness of approximately 450 m (He *et al.*, 2013). The Quxi basin, although smaller than the Tonghai basin, has a thicker sedimentary layer, with a maximum thickness of up to 700 m (Wang *et al.*, 2014). At a depth of 1 km, the Quxi basin shows a low-velocity anomaly, whereas the Tonghai basin shows a relatively weak high-velocity anomaly because of the thin sedimentary layer. A distinct low-velocity anomaly on the south side of the Tonghai basin corresponds to Devonian and Carboniferous sandstone and siliceous mudstone exposed on the surface (Ma *et al.*, 2002). The three additional basins (Eshan, Ledejiu, and Gaoda basins) are small in area, our resolution is insufficient to identify them, and therefore they are not discussed in this study. Generally, the V_S structure shallower than 9 km depth in the study area shows lateral consistency, mainly characterized by relatively high velocities in the western part of the study area and relatively low velocities in the eastern part. This characteristic is more pronounced below a depth of 6 km. Wu *et al.* (2013) studied the 3D *P*-wave velocity structure in the area around the XJF system using travel-time tomography. Their results showed the presence of low-velocity zones in the upper and middle crust at the intersection zone of the XJF and QJF, which is consistent with our results.

Figure 9 shows the V_S structure for three vertical profiles: profile AA′ along the strike of the QJF, profile BB′ parallel to the strike of the QJF, and profile CC′ along a latitude of 24.1° N. Both the profiles AA′ and BB′ show the presence of a local high-velocity anomaly in the northwest section of the QJF at depths below 4 km. Profile CC′ shows higher *S*-wave velocity characteristics in the west and lower *S*-wave velocity characteristics in the east of the study area.

Influence of shallow V_S structures on the seismic intensity distribution

The epicenter of the M_S 7.7 Tonghai earthquake on 5 January 1970, was located at 102.61° E, 24.06° N, with a focal depth of 13 km, and the seismogenic fault was the QJF (Zhang and Liu, 1978; Liu, 1983; Liu *et al.*, 1999). Although the focal depth may be uncertain due to limited seismic station data available in the 1970s, it is consistent with the focal depth range of 9–12 km for $M \geq 3$ earthquakes in Yunnan during 1999–2001, as determined by Wu *et al.* (2004) using waveform fitting. Therefore, we consider this focal depth to be a reasonable reference. As shown in Figure 8a,b, the area enclosed by the southeast part of the M_S 7.7 Tonghai earthquake's isoseismic lines is larger than that of the northwest part, with the IX and X isoseismic lines being especially prominent (Zhang and Liu, 1982). Geological investigations revealed that fault horizontal displacement during the Tonghai earthquake was significantly larger than the vertical displacement, reaching a maximum of 3.25 m, whereas vertical displacements were generally less than 0.5 m. In addition, the distribution of horizontal displacement along the seismic fault is uneven, with the southeast section showing a larger overall horizontal displacement than the northwest section (Fig. 8a,b).

Numerical simulations on the dynamic rupture process of the M_S 7.7 Tonghai earthquake revealed the influence of several different rupture processes on the distribution of seismic intensity (Yu, Zhang, *et al.*, 2020). However, the resolution of the velocity model used in these simulations was insufficient to ensure more detailed simulation results. The V_S images at depths of 1.0 and 2.5 km (Fig. 8a,b) reveal pronounced low-velocity anomalies in the eastern part of the rupture zone, which align with the wider isoseismic line distribution to the

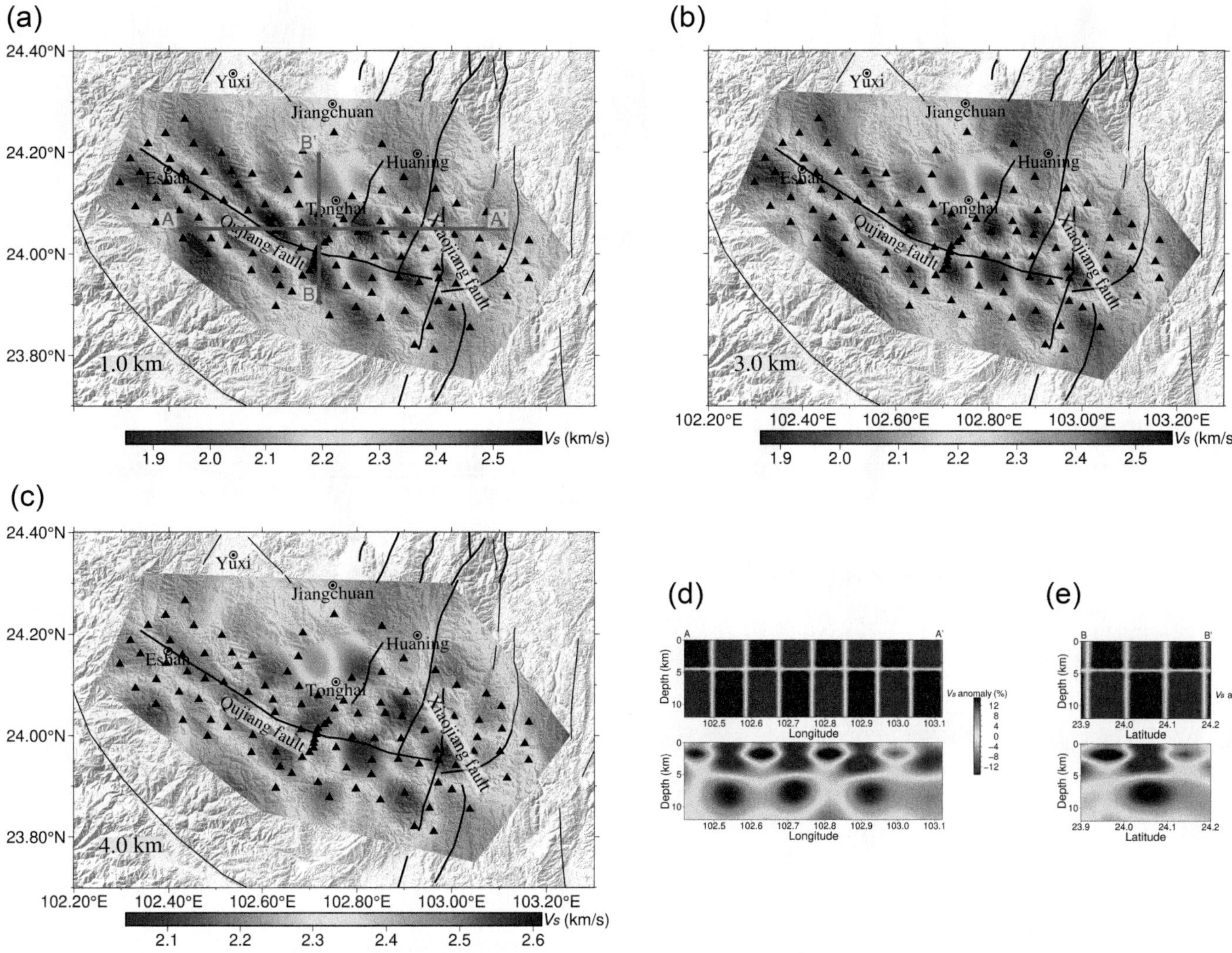

Figure 5. Checkerboard test results for velocity anomaly bodies with horizontal size of 0.09° × 0.09°. (a–c) The recovered checkerboard models at depths of 1.0, 3.0, and 4.0 km, respectively. (d,e) The input and recovery models along the profile AA′ and the profile BB′. The color version of this figure is available only in the electronic edition.

southeast of the main rupture. The studies of Borcherdt and Gibbs (1976) and Langston (2003) demonstrate that the near-surface loose overburden layer, which is characterized by low density and low moduli, can cause multiple reflections of seismic waves within the layer. This leads to significant amplification of seismic ground motions. This phenomenon has been observed in numerous subsequent studies (Kurzon *et al.*, 2014; Wirth *et al.*, 2019; Chen and Yang, 2020). We suggest that the distribution of M_S 7.7 Tonghai earthquake intensity is influenced not only by the larger horizontal displacement in the southeastern segment compared to the northwestern one, but also by the amplification effect of the near-surface low-velocity medium on ground motions. The combined effect of these two factors caused severe damage in the southeastern region of the rupture zone. Thus, our model can be used to obtain more reliable strong ground-motion simulation results.

Influence of upper-crustal structure on the mainshock rupture process

A clear surface rupture zone was observed during the Tonghai earthquake (Zhang and Liu, 1978; Liu *et al.*, 1999). The rupture stopped east of Eshan without propagating across the entire QJF. The source process exhibited an asymmetric bilateral rupture pattern, with seismic energy mostly concentrated in the southeastern part of the study area (Zhang and Liu, 1982; Zhou *et al.*, 1983; Yu, Zhang, *et al.*, 2020). Simulations of the dynamic rupture process of the Tonghai earthquake revealed that regional stress rotation, increased cohesion, and fault absence could have led to the northwestern segment of the QJF remaining unbroken (Yu, Zhang, *et al.*, 2020).

Coseismic rupture of the M_S 7.7 Tonghai earthquake occurred mainly in the upper crust. Velocity structures are important for understanding its rupture process. Our findings (Fig. 8, profiles AA′ and BB′ in Fig. 9) reveal that the V_S in the western part of the study area is considerably higher

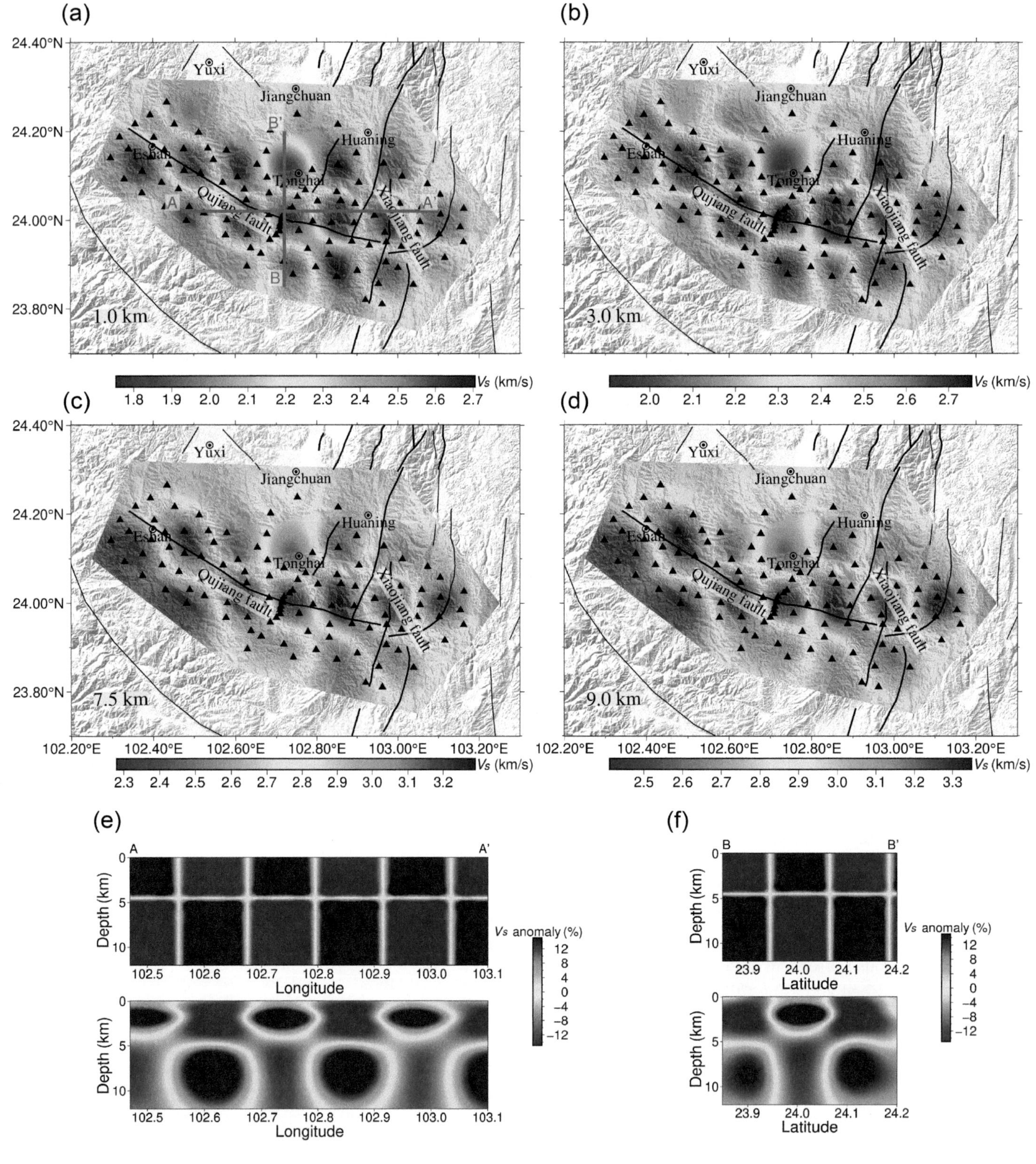

Figure 6. Checkerboard test results for velocity anomaly bodies with horizontal size of 0.12° × 0.12°. (a–d) The recovered checkerboard models at depths of 1.0, 3.0, 7.5, and 9.0 km, respectively. (e,f) The input and recovery models along the profile AA′ and the profile BB′. The color version of this figure is available only in the electronic edition.

than that in the eastern part. The epicenter of the Tonghai earthquake was located at the intersection of the QJF and the boundary of high- and low-velocity anomalies. We propose that this intersection zone facilitated the stress accumulation, which likely triggered the initial rupture of the Tonghai earthquake at this location. Once the initial rupture took place, it quickly propagated in both directions. To the

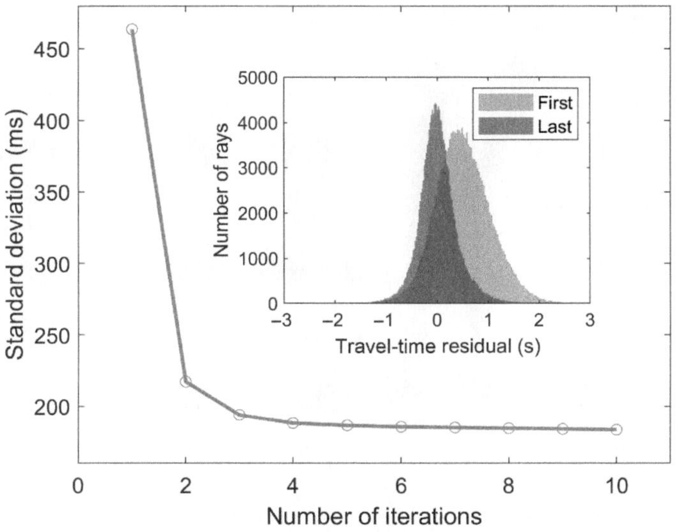

Figure 7. Variation of the standard deviation of travel-time residuals with iteration number. The inset panel shows the distribution of travel-time residuals for both initial and final inversions. The color version of this figure is available only in the electronic edition.

west, the rupture advanced into a high-velocity zone, where it was restrained by the high-velocity and high-cohesive medium. This restriction caused the fault slip to progressively decrease, eventually halting the rupture. Extension of the rupture to the east was less hindered by the cohesion of the medium, resulting in a relatively large slip (Fig. 9a). However, as the rupture propagated farther eastward, the fault slip gradually decreased due to the relatively lower energy accumulation in the eastern low-velocity zone, which is influenced by mantle-derived thermal activity and geothermal fluid. The influence will be elaborated in the subsequent discussion. In addition, the northeast-striking XJF also exhibits a barrier effect on the propagation of the rupture, ultimately causing the rupture to terminate at the obvious surface trace of the XJF (Fig. 8). Therefore, we infer that the inhomogeneity characteristics of the deep medium structure in the area played a significant role in shaping the rupture process of the Tonghai earthquake.

Eastern area low-velocity anomalies: Related to mantle-derived thermal processes and geothermal fluids

The eastern part of the research area contains the intersection of the southern section of the XJF with the northwest-trending QJF. Low-velocity anomalies observed in the area exhibit a distinct vertical variation. Specifically, the near surface shows low velocity, which decreases gradually with increasing depth. Notably, the low velocity becomes significant again at depths of 7.5–9.0 km (Fig. 8). The shallow low-velocity anomalies are attributed to the lithological characteristics of the rocks. The area is predominantly composed of sandstone and siliceous mudstone (Ma *et al.*, 2002). Sandstone generally has relatively higher porosity, facilitating water retention and resulting in lower *S*-wave velocities. However, the causes of the significantly low-velocity anomalies at depths of 7.5–9.0 km remain ambiguous. Are these anomalies related to changes in the composition of the medium, or are they associated with deep fluid activities, geothermal processes, and other internal dynamic processes of the Earth? An accurate understanding of this issue will contribute to a deeper insight into the tectonic evolution process in this region.

In the eastern low-velocity anomaly area (3.0–3.1 km/s) of the depth range of 7.5–9.0 km, the *P*-wave velocities obtained from the deep seismic sounding are 5.7–5.8 km/s (Pan *et al.*, 2015), with corresponding *P-to-S*-wave velocity (V_P/V_S) ratios of 1.84–1.93 and Poisson's ratios of 0.29–0.32. The laboratory measured seismic-wave velocities of rocks in the southeastern Tibetan Plateau and global continental crust show rocks with *P*-wave velocities of 5.7–5.8 km/s at 200 MPa (about a depth of 8 km) have SiO_2 contents of about 70% (Christensen and Mooney, 1995; Miao *et al.*, 2022). The Poisson's ratio of a rock is inversely proportional to the SiO_2 content when the SiO_2 content of the rock exceeds 55%, usually less than 0.25 with SiO_2 content higher than 70% (Christensen, 1996). Therefore, the low *S*-wave velocity and high-V_P/V_S ratio in the study area are unlikely to be caused by a medium with a high SiO_2 content.

The regional scale *S*-wave velocity structure (Zhang *et al.*, 2020) also shows low-velocity anomalies in the crust and upper mantle near the QJF zone, reaching a depth of 235 km. High surface heat flow (Tang *et al.*, 2020), high-mantle helium (H_e) values (Shao *et al.*, 2024), and low resistivity within a depth of 82 km (Yu, Unsworth, *et al.*, 2020) are also observed in this area, suggesting the intrusion of mantle-derived material into the crust (Shao *et al.*, 2024). The geochemical characteristics of geothermal fluids in the southeast Yunnan show that the maximum circulation depth of thermal springs in the eastern part of the study area is approximately 10 km (Wang *et al.*, 2018). Higher temperatures and the existence of fluids can lead to a higher Poisson's ratio (Zandt and Ammon, 1995; Owens and Zandt, 1997; Chevrot and Van Der Hilst, 2000; Xu *et al.*, 2007; Ji *et al.*, 2009). Therefore, we infer that the *S*-wave low-velocity anomaly and high Poisson's ratio at a depth of 7.5–9.0 km in the eastern part of the study area are mainly attributed to mantle-derived thermal processes and the geothermal fluids within the upper-crustal fracture system. This low-velocity anomaly zone spatially correlates with the structural intersection of the QJF and XJF, for which multiple parallel branching faults are observed. Such a tectonic configuration facilitates upward heat transfer from the mantle, resulting in increased crustal temperatures, enhanced fluid circulation, and significant medium deformation and disruption, ultimately reducing seismic-wave propagation velocities.

Another significant feature of the *S*-wave velocity structure at the depth range of 7.5–9.0 km is a narrow velocity anomaly with basically consistent velocity values (approximately 3.4 km/s)

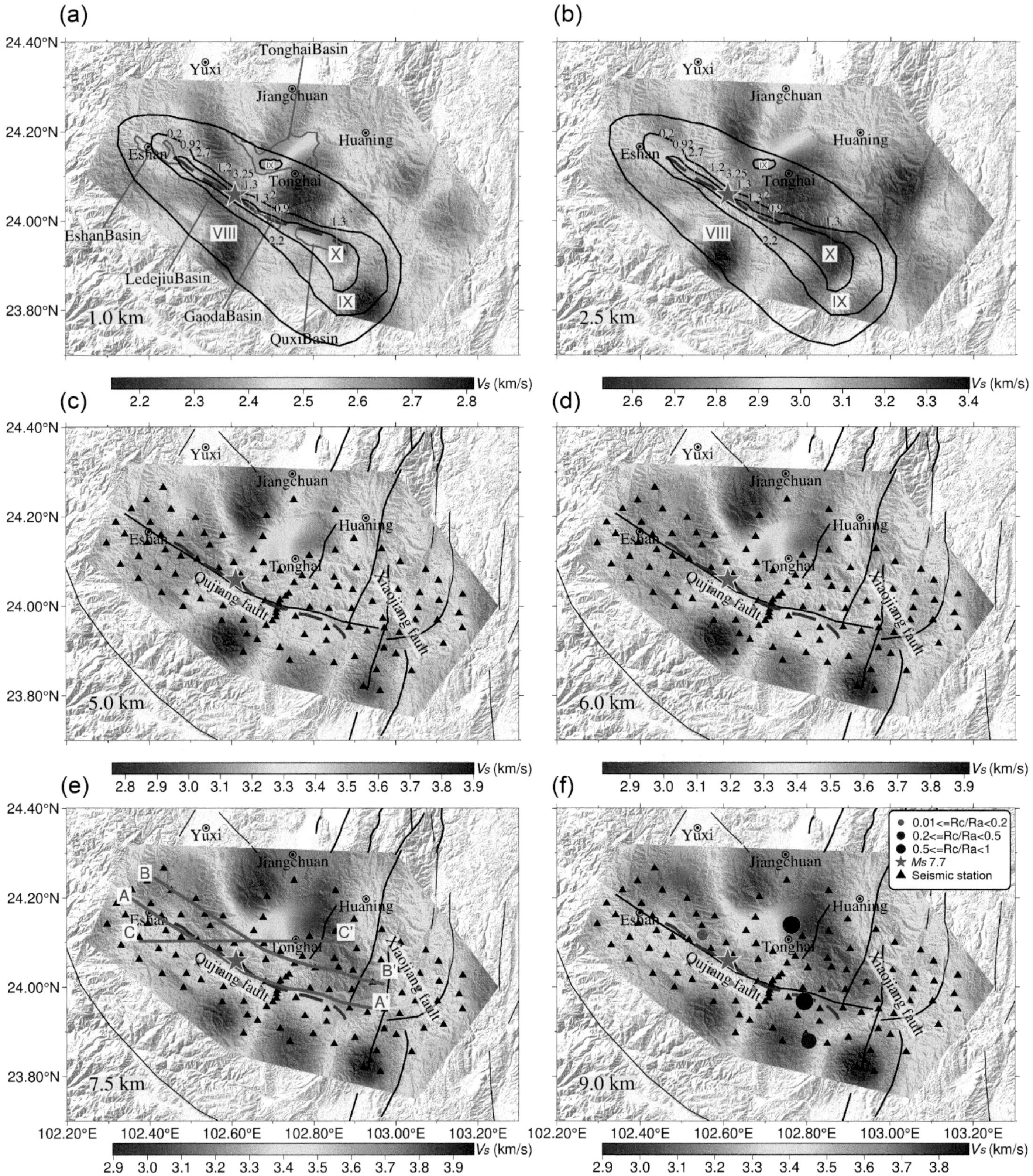

Figure 8. V_S images at different depths. (a–f) V_S images at depths of 1.0, 2.5, 5.0, 6.0, 7.5, and 9.0 km, respectively. The purple-dashed line represents the approximate rupture range of the Tonghai earthquake (Yu, Zhang, *et al.*, 2020). The black-solid lines in panels (a) and (b) denote the isoseismic lines of the Tonghai earthquake, with Roman numerals indicating the earthquake intensity and Arabic numerals representing the horizontal displacements at different positions along the Qujiang fault (QJF). The isoseismic lines are modified from Yu, Zhang, *et al.* (2020) and reference therein, the fault horizontal displacements are derived from Zhang and Liu (1978) and Liu *et al.* (1999). The red lines in panel (e) represent the location of profiles in Figure 9. The blue dots in panel (f) represent the helium (H_e) isotope correction value, Rc/Ra, in the thermal spring gases (Shao *et al.*, 2024). The color version of this figure is available only in the electronic edition.

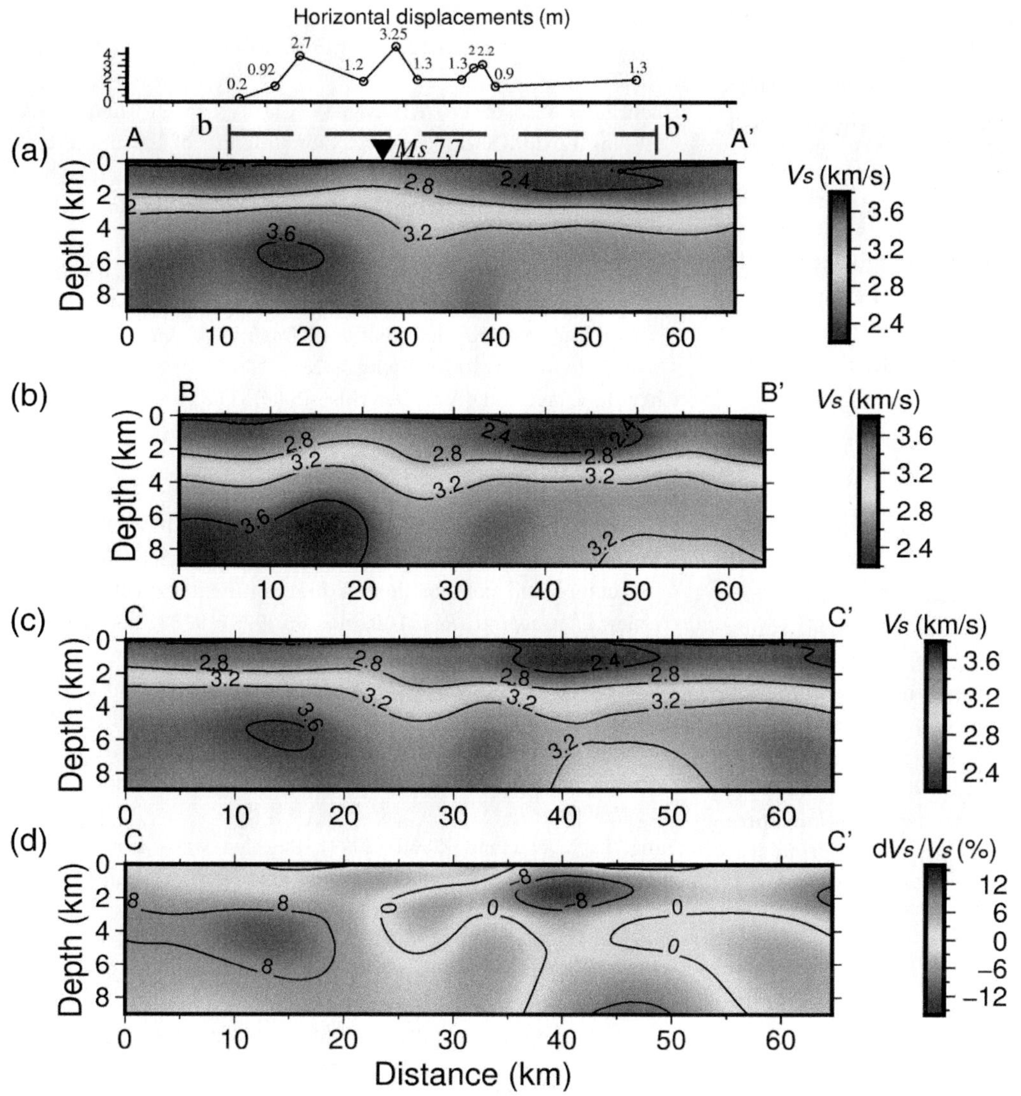

Figure 9. V_S structure of (a) profile AA′, (b) profile BB′, and (c,d) profile CC′. The purple-dashed line bb′ in panel (a) indicates the surface rupture range of the M_S 7.7 Tonghai earthquake, with the plot above showing the horizontal displacement, and the black-inverted triangle marking the epicenter. The color version of this figure is available only in the electronic edition.

along the southern side of the QJF, which exhibits relatively low velocities in the western high-velocity area and relatively high velocities in the eastern low-velocity area. Most granites generally have an SiO_2 content ranging between 65% and 78%. Some research indicates that the *P*-wave velocity is approximately 5.8 km/s for rock containing around 70% SiO_2 at a depth of around 8 km (Christensen and Mooney, 1995; Miao *et al.*, 2022). The corresponding *S*-wave velocity is 3.45 km/s, calculated using an empirical formula by Brocher (2005). The velocity value of this narrow anomaly aligns closely with the above value. Therefore, we infer that the narrow anomaly is likely associated with granitic intrusion. However, the formation age of this narrow anomaly is unclear.

Zhu (1978) revealed the tectonic evolution of landforms in the southern Yunnan region by analyzing the sedimentary development characteristics and tectonic deformation of the region in different epochs. They inferred that the QJF began to develop approximately during the Paleozoic Variscan. Whether the narrow velocity anomaly observed south of the QJF predated its formation and influenced its development, or whether this anomaly intruded along the fault after the QJF had formed, remains unsupported by evidence and requires further investigation. Given the relatively limited geological information currently available for this region and the QJF, geophysical information is particularly significant. We believe that these preliminary findings can provide valuable insights for future research and promote a deeper understanding of the tectonic evolution of the area.

Conclusion

In this study, we constructed a high-resolution V_S model in the depth range of 0.0–9.0 km using the ambient noise tomography method based on waveform data recorded by a short-period dense array deployed in the M_S 7.7 Tonghai earthquake source area. By combining the modeling results with the regional geology, active faults, and historical earthquakes, we drew the following three main conclusions.

1. Our results reveal a significant low-velocity anomaly in the eastern shallow area of the QJF, which aligns with the characteristic of wider isoseismic lines in the southeastern section of the main rupture zone of the M_S 7.7 Tonghai earthquake. This suggests that this low-velocity medium plays a significant role in amplifying the ground motions generated by this seismic event.
2. The epicenter of the M_S 7.7 Tonghai earthquake was located at the intersection of the QJF and the boundary between high- and low-*S*-wave velocity anomalies. This location could represent a zone favorable for stress accumulation, as well as for the initial rupture of the event. Following the initial

rupture, it rapidly propagated in both eastward and westward directions, with inhomogeneities in the deep medium structure leading to differences in rupture length and slip displacements between the northwestern and southeastern sections of the QJF.

3. Within the depth range of 7.5–9.0 km, we observed an apparent low-velocity anomaly in the eastern part of the study area, which we interpreted as the combined effects of mantle-derived thermal activity and geothermal fluids. In addition, a narrowbanded anomaly occurs on the south side of the QJF, likely associated with the granitic intrusion.

Data and Resources

The data collected in this project are currently managed by Changzai Wang; any collaborative work with this data set is welcome. For those interested in the data set, please contact Changzai Wang (wangchangzai@cea-igp.ac.cn). Figures were generated using Generic Mapping Tools (GMT; Wessel *et al.*, 2019). The supplemental material for this article includes the following: the path clustering analysis of the dispersion curve (Text S1 and Fig. S1); Rayleigh-wave phase velocity for different periods (Text S2 and Fig. S4); V_S images obtained by inverting the waveform data recorded at the array in the study area for the initial three months, the following three months, and the full six-month period (Fig. S2); and the depth sensitivity kernels of the Rayleigh-wave phase velocity for different periods (Fig. S3).

Declaration of Competing Interests

The authors acknowledge that there are no conflicts of interest recorded.

Acknowledgments

The authors would like to express their gratitude to all those who participated in deploying the short-period dense array, Huajian Yao for providing the dispersion curve extraction program, Hongjian Fang for providing the surface-wave direct inversion program, and Zhenyu Wang for his valuable suggestions. The authors are also grateful to Editor-in-Chief Allison Bent and two anonymous reviewers for their constructive comments and suggestions that greatly improve this article. This study was supported by the National Key R&D Program of China (Grant Numbers 2022YFF0800601 and 2021YFC3000600) and the National Natural Science Foundation of China (Grant Number U2039204).

References

Bensen, G. D., M. H. Ritzwoller, M. P. Barmin, A. L. Levshin, F. Lin, M. P. Moschetti, N. M. Shapiro, and Y. Yang (2007). Processing seismic ambient noise data to obtain reliable broad-band surface wave dispersion measurements, *Geophys. J. Int.* **169,** no. 3, 1239–1260, doi: 10.1111/j.1365-246X.2007.03374.x.

Borcherdt, R. D., and J. F. Gibbs (1976). Effects of local geological conditions in the San Francisco Bay region on ground motions and the intensities of the 1906 earthquake, *Bull. Seismol. Soc. Am.* **66,** no. 2, 467–500, doi: 10.1785/BSSA0660020467.

Brocher, T. M. (2005). Empirical relations between elastic wavespeeds and density in the Earth's crust, *Bull. Seismol. Soc. Am.* **95,** no. 6, 2081–2092.

Chen, S., R. Gao, Z. Lu, Y. Liang, W. Cai, L. Cao, Z. Chen, and G. Wang (2023). Shear wave velocity structure of the upper crust in north Xiaojiang fault zone in SE Tibet via short-period ambient noise dense seismic array, *Phys. Earth Planet. In.* **344,** doi: 10.1016/j.pepi.2023.107110.

Chen, X., and H. Yang (2020). Effects of seismogenic width and low-velocity zones on estimating slip-weakening distance from near-fault ground deformation, *Geophys. J. Int.* **223,** no. 3, 1497–1510, doi: 10.1093/gji/ggaa385.

Chevrot, S., and R. D. Van Der Hilst (2000). The Poisson ratio of the Australian crust: Geological and geophysical implications, *Earth Planet. Sci. Lett.* **183,** nos. 1/2, 121–132.

Christensen, N. I. (1996). Poisson's ratio and crustal seismology, *J. Geophys. Res.* **101,** no. B2, 3139–3156, doi: 10.1029/95JB03446.

Christensen, N. I., and W. D. Mooney (1995). Seismic velocity structure and composition of the continental crust: A global view, *J. Geophys. Res.* **100,** no. B6, 9761–9788, doi: 10.1029/95JB00259.

Fang, H., H. Yao, H. Zhang, Y. C. Huang, and R. D. Van Der Hilst (2015). Direct inversion of surface wave dispersion for three-dimensional shallow crustal structure based on ray tracing: Methodology and application, *Geophys. J. Int.* **201,** no. 3, 1251–1263, doi: 10.1093/gji/ggv080.

Fang, L., J. Wu, and Z. Lü (2009). Rayleigh wave group velocity tomography from ambient seismic noise in North China, *Chin. J. Geophys.* **52,** no. 3, 663–671 (in Chinese).

Feng, T., M. Zhang, L. Xu, J. Wu, and L. Fang (2022). Machine learning-based earthquake catalog and tomography characterize the middle-northern section of the Xiaojiang Fault Zone, *Seismol. Res. Lett.* **93,** no. 5, 2484–2497, doi: 10.1785/0220220116.

He, H. L., P. Li, and Z. Fang (1992). Analysis of seismogenic conditions in the wedge tectonic region of southeast Yunnan Province, *Seismol. Geol.* **14,** no. 3, 217–226 (in Chinese).

He, Z., G. Hu, L. Lu, W. Zhang, T. Ye, and K. Shen (2013). The shallow velocity structure for the Tonghai basin in Yunnan, *Chin. J. Geophys.* **56,** no. 11, 3819–3827, doi: 10.6038/cjg20131123 (in Chinese).

Ji, S., Q. Wang, and M. H. Salisbury (2009). Composition and tectonic evolution of the Chinese continental crust constrained by Poisson's ratio, *Tectonophysics* **463,** nos. 1/4, 15–30, doi: 10.1016/j.tecto.2008.09.007.

Kurzon, I., F. L. Vernon, Y. Ben-Zion, and G. Atkinson (2014). Ground motion prediction equations in the San Jacinto Fault Zone: Significant effects of rupture directivity and fault zone amplification, *Pure Appl. Geophys.* **171,** no. 11, 3045–3081, doi: 10.1007/s00024-014-0855-2.

Langston, C. A. (2003). Local earthquake wave propagation through mississippi embayment sediments, part I: Body-wave phases and local site responses, *Bull. Seismol. Soc. Am.* **93,** no. 6, 2664–2684, doi: 10.1785/0120030046.

Levshin, A. L., and M. H. Ritzwoller (2001). Automated Detection, Extraction, and Measurement of Regional Surface Waves, in *Monitoring the Comprehensive Nuclear-Test-Ban Treaty: Surface Waves*, A. L. Levshin and M. H. Ritzwoller (Editors), Birkhäuser, Basel, Switzerland, 1531–1545, doi: 10.1007/978-3-0348-8264-4_11.

Liang, Y., T. Xie, Z. Lu, Q. Li, X. Zhang, G. Wang, G. Wang, S. Chen, and C. Chang (2023). Shear wave velocity structure in the middle segment of the Xiaojiang fault zone using ambient noise tomography, *Front. Earth. Sci.* **11,** 1161989, doi: 10.3389/feart.2023.1161989.

Lin, F., M. P. Moschetti, and M. H. Ritzwoller (2008). Surface wave tomography of the western United States from ambient seismic noise: Rayleigh and Love wave phase velocity maps, *Geophys. J. Int.* **173,** no. 1, 281–298, doi: 10.1111/j.1365-246X.2008.03720.x.

Lin, F., M. H. Ritzwoller, J. Townend, S. Bannister, and M. K. Savage (2007). Ambient noise Rayleigh wave tomography of New Zealand, *Geophys. J. Int.* **170,** no. 2, 649–666, doi: 10.1111/j.1365-246X.2007.03414.x.

Liu, S. (1983). Aftershock activity and seismogenic mechanism of the Tonghai earthquake—An attempt at using aftershock sequence, *J. Seismol. Res.* **6,** no. 2, 141–150 (in Chinese).

Liu, Z., F. Huang, and Z. Jin (1999). *The 1970 Tonghai Earthquake*, Seismological Press, Bejing, China (in Chinese).

Luo, S., H. Yao, J. Wen, H. Yang, B. Tian, and M. Yan (2023). Apparent low-velocity belt in the Shallow Anninghe Fault Zone in SW China and its implications for seismotectonics and earthquake hazard assessment, *J. Geophys. Res.* **128,** no. 3, doi: 10.1029/2022JB025681.

Luo, Y., Y. Yang, Y. Xu, H. Xu, K. Zhao, and K. Wang (2015). On the limitations of interstation distances in ambient noise tomography, *Geophys. J. Int.* **201,** no. 2, 652–661, doi: 10.1093/gji/ggv043.

Ma, L., X. Qiao, and N. Liu (2002). *Geological Atlas of China*, Geology Press, Bejing, China (in Chinese).

Miao, S., Y. Zhou, X. Ma, and J. Dang (2022). Lithologic structure of the Anninghe fault zone: constraints from high-pressure wave velocity experiments, *Front. Earth. Sci.* **10,** doi: 10.3389/feart.2022.853474.

Owens, T. J., and G. Zandt (1997). Implications of crustal property variations for models of Tibetan plateau evolution, *Nature* **387,** 37–43, doi: 10.1038/387037a0.

Pan, S., F. Wang, Y. Duan, X. Deng, Y. Zang, X. Song, Y. Duan, Y. Sun, C. Zhang, and Y. Yang (2015). Basement structure of southern Yunnan and adjacent areas: The Zhenkang-Luxi deep seismic sounding profile, *Chin. J. Geophys.* **58,** no. 11, 3917–3927, doi: 10.6038/cjg20151103 (in Chinese).

Ranasinghe, N. R., L. L. Worthington, C. Jiang, B. Schmandt, T. S. Finlay, S. L. Bilek, and R. C. Aster (2018). Upper-crustal shear-wave velocity structure of the south-central Rio Grande rift above the Socorro magma body imaged with ambient noise by the large-N Sevilleta seismic array, *Seismol. Res. Lett.* **89,** no. 5, 1708–1719, doi: 10.1785/0220180074.

Rawlinson, N., and M. Sambridge (2003). Seismic travel time tomography of the crust and lithosphere, *Adv. Geophys.* **46,** 81–199, doi: 10.1016/S0065-2687(03)46002-0.

Rawlinson, N., and M. Sambridge (2004). Wave front evolution in strongly heterogeneous layered media using the fast marching method, *Geophys. J. Int.* **156,** no. 3, 631–647, doi: 10.1111/j.1365-246X.2004.02153.x.

Rawlinson, N., and M. Sambridge (2005). The fast marching method: An effective tool for tomographic imaging and tracking multiple phases in complex layered media, *Explor. Geophys.* **36,** no. 4, 341–350, doi: 10.1071/EG05341.

Rawlinson, N., and W. Spakman (2016). On the use of sensitivity tests in seismic tomography, *Geophys. J. Int.* **205,** no. 2, 1221–1243, doi: 10.1093/gji/ggw084.

Schimmel, M., E. Stutzmann, and J. Gallart (2011). Using instantaneous phase coherence for signal extraction from ambient noise data at a local to a global scale, *Geophys. J. Int.* **184,** no. 1, 494–506, doi: 10.1111/j.1365-246X.2010.04861.x.

Shao, W., Z. Liu, Y. Li, Z. Chen, C. Lu, C. Zhao, Y. Wang, Q. Li, Z. Gao, Y. Luo, *et al.* (2024). Geochemical characteristics of thermal springs and insights into the intersection between the Xiaojiang Fault and the Red River Fault, Southeastern Tibet Plateau, *Geochem. Geophys. Geosys.* **25,** no. 3, doi: 10.1029/2023GC011431.

Shapiro, N. M., M. Campillo, L. Stehly, and M. H. Ritzwoller (2005). High-resolution surface-wave tomography from ambient seismic noise, *Science* **307,** 1615–1618, doi: 10.1126/science.1108339.

Shearer, P. M. (2019). *Introduction to Seismology*, Cambridge University Press, Cambridge, United Kingdom.

Shen, W., M. H. Ritzwoller, D. Kang, Y. Kim, F. C. Lin, J. Ning, W. Wang, Y. Zheng, and L. Zhou (2016). A seismic reference model for the crust and uppermost mantle beneath China from surface wave dispersion, *Geophys. J. Int.* **206,** no. 2, 954–979, doi: 10.1093/gji/ggw175.

Tang, H., L. Guo, and Y. Fang (2020). Estimation of heat flow in southeastern margin of Tibetan Plateau and its analysis of the correlation with earthquake activity, *Chin. J. Geophys.* **63,** no. 3, 1056–1069, doi: 10.6038/cjg2019N0045 (in Chinese).

Tapponnier, P., and P. Molnar (1976). Slip-line field theory and large-scale continental tectonics, *Nature* **264,** no. 5584, 319–324, doi: 10.1038/264319a0.

Wang, J., H. Li, Y. Zhang, H. Li, Y. Li, Z. Ma, and Y. Xiang (2024). Shallow crustal structure of the northern Longmen Shan fault zone revealed by a dense seismic array with ambient noise analysis, *J. Asian Earth Sci.* **276,** doi: 10.1016/j.jseaes.2024.106338.

Wang, Y., B. Zhang, J. Hou, and X. Xu (2014). Structure and tectonic geomorphology of the Qujiang fault at the intersection of the Ailao Shan–Red River fault and the Xianshuihe–Xiaojiang fault system, China, *Tectonophysics* **634,** 156–170, doi: 10.1016/j.tecto.2014.07.031.

Wang, Y., C. Zhao, Q. Li, Y. Liu, C. E. Administration, and Y. E. Agency (2018). Study on geochemical characteristics of geothermal fluid in the wedge-shaped tectonics, Southeast Yunnan, *J. Seismol. Res.* **41,** no. 4, 534–543 (in Chinese).

Wen, X., F. Du, F. Long, J. Fan, and H. Zhu (2011). Tectonic dynamics and correlation of major earthquake sequences of the Xiaojiang and Qujiang-Shiping fault systems, Yunnan, China, *Sci. China Earth Sci.* doi: 10.1007/s11430-011-4231-0.

Wessel, P., J. F. Luis, L. Uieda, R. Scharroo, F. Wobbe, W. H. F. Smith, and D. Tian (2019). The Generic Mapping Tools Version 6, *Geochem. Geophys. Geosys.* **20,** no. 11, 5556–5564, doi: 10.1029/2019GC008515.

Wirth, E. A., J. E. Vidale, A. D. Frankel, T. L. Pratt, N. A. Marafi, M. Thompson, and W. J. Stephenson (2019). Source-dependent amplification of earthquake ground motions in deep sedimentary basins, *Geophys. Res. Lett.* **46,** no. 12, 6443–6450, doi: 10.1029/2019GL082474.

Wu, J., Y. Cai, W. Wang, W. Wang, C. Wang, L. Fang, Y. Liu, and J. Liu (2024). Three dimensional velocity model and its tectonic implications at China seismic experimental site, eastern margin of the Tibetan Plateau, *Sci. China Earth Sci.* doi: 10.1007/s11430-023-1293-4.

Wu, J., Y. Ming, and C. Wang (2004). Source mechanism of small-moderate earthquakes and tectonic stress field in Yunnan Province, *Acta. Seismol. Sin.* **17,** 509–517, doi: 10.1007/s11589-004-0032-2 (in Chinese).

Wu, J., T. Yang, W. Wang, Y. Ming, and T. Zhang (2013). Three dimensional P-wave velocity structure around Xiaojiang fault system and its tectonic implications, *Chin. J. Geophys.* **56,** no. 7, 2257–2267, doi: 10.6038/cjg20130713 (in Chinese).

Xu, L., S. Rondenay, and R. D. Van Der Hilst (2007). Structure of the crust beneath the southeastern Tibetan Plateau from teleseismic receiver functions, *Phys. Earth Planet. In.* **165,** nos. 3/4, 176–193, doi: 10.1016/j.pepi.2007.09.002.

Xu, X., Z. Han, X. Yang, G. Yu, B. Zhou, F. Li, B. Ma, G. Chen, and Y. Ran (2016). *Seismotectonic Map in China and its Adjacent Regions*, Seismological Press, Beijing, China (in Chinese).

Yang, Y., S. Hu, H. Yao, L. Fang, and J. Wu (2020). Crustal shear wave velocity and radial anisotropy in the Xiaojiang fault zone system (SE Tibet) revealed by ambient noise interferometry, *Tectonophysics* **792,** no. 5, doi: 10.1016/j.tecto.2020.228594.

Yang, Y., A. Li, and M. H. Ritzwoller (2008). Crustal and uppermost mantle structure in southern Africa revealed from ambient noise and teleseismic tomography, *Geophys. J. Int.* **174,** no. 1, 235–248, doi: 10.1111/j.1365-246X.2008.03779.x.

Yang, Y., M. H. Ritzwoller, A. L. Levshin, and N. M. Shapiro (2007). Ambient noise Rayleigh wave tomography across Europe, *Geophys. J. Int.* **168,** no. 1, 259–274, doi: 10.1111/j.1365-246X.2006.03203.x.

Yao, H., C. Beghein, and R. D. Van Der Hilst (2008). Surface wave array tomography in SE Tibet from ambient seismic noise and two-station analysis-II. Crustal and upper-mantle structure, *Geophys. J. Int.* **173,** no. 1, 205–219, doi: 10.1111/j.1365-246X.2007.03696.x.

Yao, H., P. Gouédard, J. A. Collins, J. J. McGuire, and R. D. Van Der Hilst (2011). Structure of young East Pacific Rise lithosphere from ambient noise correlation analysis of fundamental- and higher-mode Scholte-Rayleigh waves, *C. R. Geosci.* **343,** nos. 8/9, 571–583, doi: 10.1016/j.crte.2011.04.004.

Yao, H., R. D. Van Der Hilst, and M. V. De Hoop (2006). Surface-wave array tomography in SE Tibet from ambient seismic noise and two-station analysis—I. Phase velocity maps, *Geophys. J. Int.* **166,** no. 2, 732–744, doi: 10.1111/j.1365-246X.2006.03028.x.

Yu, H., W. Zhang, Z. Zhang, Z. Li, and X. Chen (2020). Investigation on the dynamic rupture of the 1970 Ms 7.7 Tonghai, Yunnan, China, earthquake on the Qujiang Fault, *Bull. Seismol. Soc. Am.* **110,** no. 2, 898–919, doi: 10.1785/0120190185.

Yu, N., M. Unsworth, X. Wang, D. Li, E. Wang, R. Li, Y. Hu, and X. Cai (2020). New insights into crustal and mantle flow beneath the red river fault zone and adjacent areas on the southern margin of the Tibetan Plateau revealed by a 3-D magnetotelluric study, *J. Geophys. Res.* **125,** no. 10, doi: 10.1029/2020JB019396.

Zandt, G., and C. J. Ammon (1995). Continental crust composition constrained by measurements of crustal Poisson's ratio, *Nature* **374,** 152–154, doi: 10.1038/374152a0.

Zhang, P., Z. Shen, M. Wang, W. Gan, R. Bürgmann, P. Molnar, Q. Wang, Z. Niu, J. Sun, J. Wu, *et al.* (2004). Continuous deformation of the Tibetan Plateau from global positioning system data, *Geology* **32,** no. 9, 809–812, doi: 10.1130/G20554.1.

Zhang, S., and B. Liu (1978). Seismic geological characteristics of Tonghai earthquake in 1970, *Chin. J. Geol.* **13,** no. 4, 323–335 (in Chinese).

Zhang, Y., H. Yao, H. Yang, H. Cai, H. Fang, J. Xu, X. Jin, H. Kuo-Chen, W. Liang, and K. Chen (2018). 3-D crustal shear-wave velocity structure of the Taiwan strait and Fujian, SE China, revealed by ambient noise tomography, *J. Geophys. Res.* **123,** no. 9, 8016–8031, doi: 10.1029/2018JB015938.

Zhang, Z., and S. Liu (1982). The focal characteristics of the Tonghai earthquake, Yunnan Province, on January 5,1970, *Chin. J. Geophys.* **25,** no. 5, 440–447 (in Chinese).

Zhang, Z., H. Yao, and Y. Yang (2020). Shear wave velocity structure of the crust and upper mantle in Southeastern Tibet and its geodynamic implications, *Sci. China Earth Sci.* **63,** 1278–1293, doi: 10.1007/s11430-020-9625-3.

Zhao, Y., J. Li, J. Xu, H. Yao, G. Zhu, H. Yang, J. Zhang, and R. Lu (2023). High-resolution velocity structure and seismogenic potential of strong earthquakes in the Bamei-Kangding segment of the Xianshuihe fault zone, *Sci. China Earth Sci.* **66,** no. 9, 1960–1978, doi: 10.1007/s11430-022-1133-y.

Zhou, H., C. R. Allen, and H. Kanamori (1983). Rupture complexity of the 1970 Tonghai and the 1973 Luhuo earthquakes, China, from P-wave inversion, and relationship to surface faulting, *Bull. Seismol. Soc. Am.* **73,** no. 6A, 1585–1597, doi: 10.1785/BSSA07306A1585.

Zhu, C. (1978). Cenozoic tectonic development in southern Yunnan and the geological background of the Tonghai earthquake, *J. Seismol. Res.* **1,** no. 3, 32–43 (in Chinese).

Manuscript received 23 July 2024
Published online 14 July 2025

The Role of Earthquake Interaction in Hydraulic-Fracturing-Induced Seismicity in Sichuan Basin, Southwest China

Yangtianli Zhou*[1] and Fenglin Niu[1,2]

Abstract

Earthquake interaction plays an important role in both tectonic and human-induced seismicity. Numerous studies have documented elevated background seismicity rates and earthquake swarms in areas of induced seismicity, which may be associated with distinctive earthquake interaction behaviors. The Sichuan basin and surrounding regions in southwestern China contain seismicity driven by both human-induced and tectonic mechanisms. We utilized the nearest-neighbor distance clustering approach to analyze earthquake interaction features in the Sichuan basin and conduct a careful comparison with the surrounding regions. After distinguishing background events from earthquake clusters, we measured background seismicity rates and categorized clusters into repeat, couple, star, chain, and complex based on their structure. Three quantitative attributes: mainshock relative node depth, mainshock relative edge productivity, and normalized average leaf depth, were employed to characterize the features of earthquake interaction within complex clusters. Our findings include the following: (1) the Sichuan basin exhibits a notably high background seismicity rate; (2) many clusters associated with mainshocks of magnitude 4.0 or greater display complex structural patterns; (3) a significant proportion of earthquake clusters within the Sichuan basin exhibit swarm-like characteristics, characterized by multiple stages of foreshocks and low-mainshock productivity. We conclude that earthquake interactions, especially foreshocks, play a pivotal role in triggering seismic events in the Sichuan basin and should be carefully incorporated into future models of induced earthquake rupture and risk assessment.

Cite this article as Zhou, Y., and F. Niu (2025). The Role of Earthquake Interaction in Hydraulic-Fracturing-Induced Seismicity in Sichuan Basin, Southwest China, *Seismol. Res. Lett.* **97**, 67–80, doi: 10.1785/0220250006.

Supplemental Material

Introduction

Earthquakes can be induced by injecting water through boreholes into underground reservoirs (Healy *et al.*, 1968). The primary triggering mechanisms of hydraulic-fracturing (HF)-induced earthquakes include pore-pressure diffusion, poreelastic coupling, aseismic slip, and earthquake interactions (Schultz *et al.*, 2020; Moein *et al.*, 2023). Pore-pressure diffusion refers to the increasing pore pressure that expands outward from injection wells if there is a permeable hydrologic connection between the fracturing site and nearby faults (Azad *et al.*, 2017). Aseismic slip triggering involves gradual fault movement and requires a fault intersecting the fracturing system (Eyre *et al.*, 2019). Poroelastic coupling refers to the instantaneous stress changes on the fault due to the coupling between the pressurized water and the rock matrix (Segall and Lu, 2015). Earthquake interaction is the process by which stress changes associated with an earthquake can induce or retard seismic activity in the surrounding region and potentially trigger other earthquakes at great distances (Freed, 2005). It plays an important role in inducing earthquakes (Karimi and Davidsen, 2021, 2023). A minor earthquake induced by either pore-pressure diffusion, poroelastic coupling, or aseismic slip can end up triggering a larger earthquake with unfavored orientation through a cascading process (Kyriakopoulos and Oglesby, 2024). On a regional scale, the interaction between earthquakes can be characterized by their clustering features. Background earthquakes are independent from each other, whereas earthquake clusters are associated with a hierarchical triggering process.

Numerous studies have tried to characterize the different clustering features of induced earthquakes with respect to tectonic earthquakes. For instance, many studies have identified swarmlike characteristics in induced seismicity (Špičák, 2000; Schultz *et al.*, 2020; Sirorattanakul *et al.*, 2025). Although the

1. Department of Earth, Environmental and Planetary Sciences, Rice University, Houston, Texas, U.S.A., https://orcid.org/0009-0009-3810-4503 (YZ); 2. School of Earth and Space Sciences, University of Science and Technology of China (USTC), Hefei, China

*Corresponding author: yz182@rice.edu

mechanism behind earthquake swarms remains unclear, they are commonly associated with triggering processes facilitated by fluid migration and aseismic slip (Mogi, 1963; Hill, 1977; Yamashita, 1997; Vidale and Shearer, 2006; Vidale *et al.*, 2006; Lohman and McGuire, 2007). In addition, many studies separated earthquakes into background and clustered events, and comparisons have been conducted on the background ratio and cluster features. A high background rate of induced seismicity has been commonly observed, indicating that these earthquakes are externally triggered and largely independent of one another (Llenos and Michael, 2013; Schoenball *et al.*, 2015; Zaliapin and Ben-Zion, 2016; Goebel *et al.*, 2019). On top of this, features of induced clusters, including b-value, aftershock productivity, and spatial footprint, have been measured and compared to the natural fluid-driven clusters (Karimi and Davidsen, 2021, 2023).

The nearest-neighbor distance (NND) method has been widely used in this separation. The NND clustering method analyzes an earthquake catalog by converting it into an ancestry tree, or spanning tree, and then separates it into a spanning forest (Baiesi and Paczuski, 2004; Zaliapin *et al.*, 2008). Within this framework, some earthquakes are isolated as single events, whereas others form subtrees composed of a root event and multiple node events (Zaliapin and Ben-Zion, 2013a). These subtrees represent earthquake clusters, with edges between nodes depicting interevent triggering or cascading processes. However, the topological structure of earthquake clusters has not been utilized in most cases.

The objective of this study is to characterize not only the background events and clusters but also the interaction within the clusters. We aim to separate earthquake clusters, categorize cluster types, measure cluster topological features, compare them between induced and tectonic seismicity, and eventually, summarize the features of induced seismicity. We applied the NND method to seismicity in the Sichuan region, an area with contrasting geological conditions and a mix of tectonic and induced earthquakes. By comparing the clustering characteristics of regions dominated by tectonic and induced seismicity, we analyzed temporal variations in background seismicity rates and classified the clusters into four structural types: couple, star, chain, and complex. For complex clusters, we quantified swarmlike features using three attributes. First, we introduced the normalized average leaf depth (NALD), an adaptation of the Zaliapin and Ben-Zion (2013b) average leaf depth, to describe the elongation of earthquake sequences. In addition, we proposed two new indices: the mainshock relative node depth (MRND) and the mainshock relative edge productivity (MREP), which quantify a cluster's deviation from a typical mainshock–aftershock sequence.

The following sections outline the structure of this study. The Data and study region section provides an overview of the geological background of the Sichuan region and describes the data utilized. The Methods section reviews the NND clustering method and introduces three attributes designed to characterize cluster features. The Results section presents the application of NND clustering in the Sichuan region. This includes extracting background events and earthquake sequences, comparing the temporal variation in background seismicity rates, and examining the characteristics of earthquake clusters between the Sichuan basin and surrounding regions. We also test various parameters and data sets to evaluate the robustness of our findings. In the Discussion section, we confirm our findings with some extended analysis, interpret the results using a case example, compare with findings from previous studies, and address the limitations of this study.

Data and Study Region

As shown in Figure 1, the study region spans latitudes 26°–34° N and longitudes 100°–108° E, encompassing a geologically diverse area. The collision between the Indian and Eurasian plates has driven the uplift and eastward extrusion of the Tibetan Plateau, releasing strain energy through tectonic earthquakes. In the north, this tectonic activity led to the uplift and shortening that formed the Longmenshan (LMS) thrust fault. To the south, the extrusion was accommodated by clockwise rotation, resulting in the formation of the left-lateral Xianshuihe-Anninghe-Zemuhe (XSH-ANH-ZMH) fault system (Royden *et al.*, 2008). These fault systems delineate the western boundary of the stable Sichuan basin.

The Sichuan basin is part of the Yangtze craton with a low-strain rate and lower seismicity rate compared with the surrounding region (Chen *et al.*, 2015; Lei *et al.*, 2020). However, as a resource-rich basin, various industrial activities—including salt mining, wastewater disposal, conventional oil and gas extraction, and HF—have been conducted and linked to seismic activity over the past decades (Lei *et al.*, 2017, 2020; Schultz *et al.*, 2020; Sheng *et al.*, 2020, 2022; Tan *et al.*, 2020; Yang *et al.*, 2020). Many of these earthquakes occurred on blind structures that are unfavorably oriented to the background stress field (Lei *et al.*, 2020). Considering that many industrial sites are in operation and have been associated with earthquakes inside the Sichuan basin, whereas no water-injection related industrial sites or induced earthquakes are reported in the surrounding areas, we infer that seismicity inside the basin is primarily driven by different mechanisms than in the surrounding regions. Accordingly, we separate the earthquakes into two groups for comparison. As shown in Figure 1, the yellow dots represent earthquakes inside the Sichuan basin, dominated by induced events, and the red dots are earthquakes in the surrounding regions, dominated by tectonic events. The green circles are centered at two HF sites, Changning and Weiyuan, with a radius of around 35 km. According to the 2000–2019 China Earthquake Administration (CEA) earthquake catalog, 58.84% of earthquakes ($\mathbf{M} \geq 2.0$) in the Sichuan basin occurred in these two circles after 2014, suggesting that they are linked to HF.

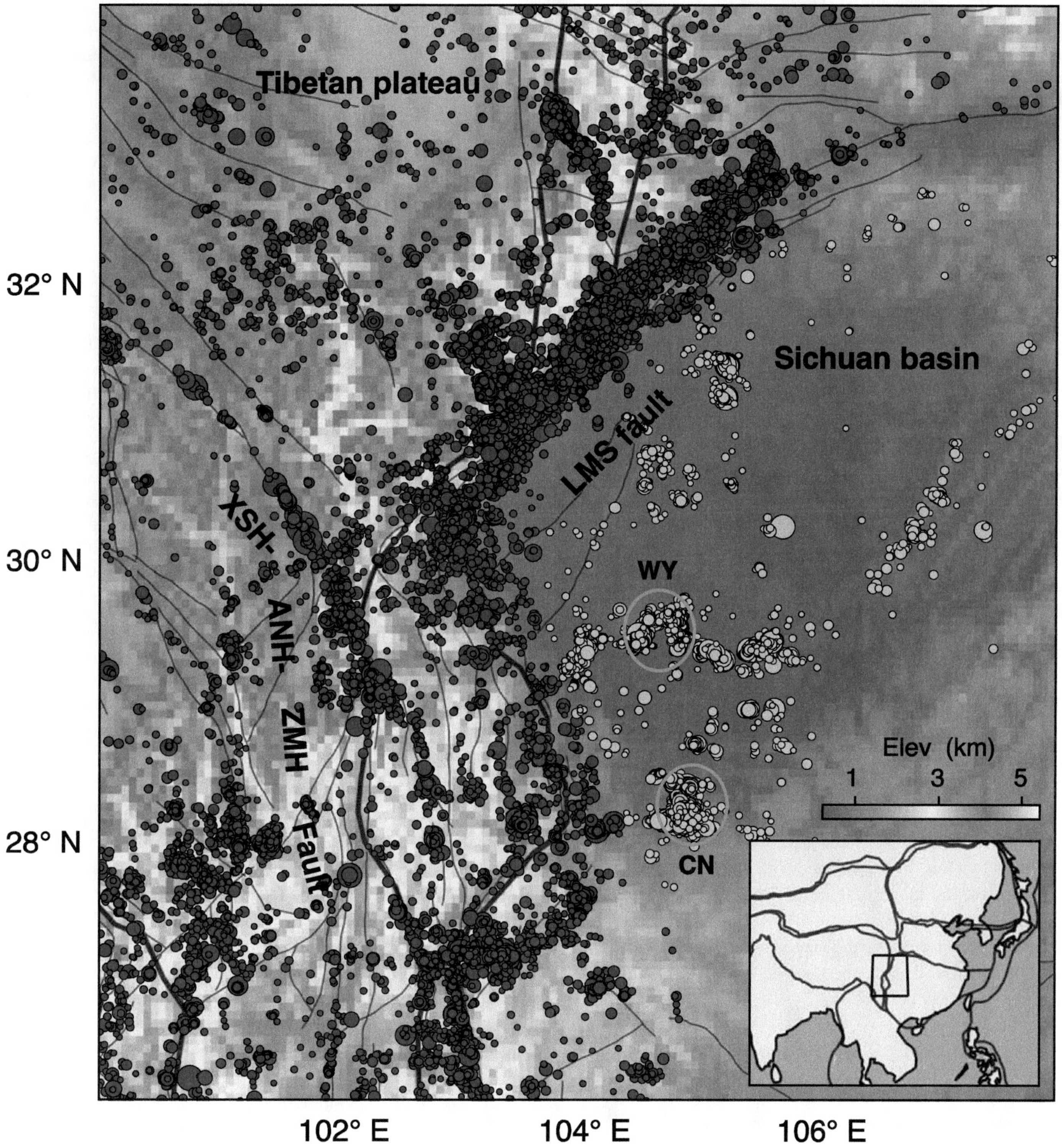

Figure 1. Map of the study region. The background color represents the elevation; thin-black lines are the faults observed on the surface; the thick lines are the boundary between the tectonic blocks of the Tibetan plateau and the Sichuan basin. Earthquakes from China Seismic Experimental Site (CSES) with a magnitude larger than 2.0 that occurred between 1 January 2009 and 31 March 2019 are shown as points. Events inside the Sichuan basin dominated by induced events are colored yellow, whereas events in the other regions dominated by tectonic events are colored red. The sizes of the points are scaled by the magnitude. Two major fault zones formed the Y-shape fault system. The XSH-ANH-ZMH fault represents the Xianshuihe-Anninghe-Zemuhe fault zone, and the LMS fault represents the Longmenshan fault zone. The green circles with 0.3° radius cover two well-studied hydraulic fracturing (HF) sites: CN, Changning; WY, Weiyuan. The inset map offers a regional context, with the study area delineated by blue squares and significant geological blocks indicated by thick black lines. The color version of this figure is available only in the electronic edition.

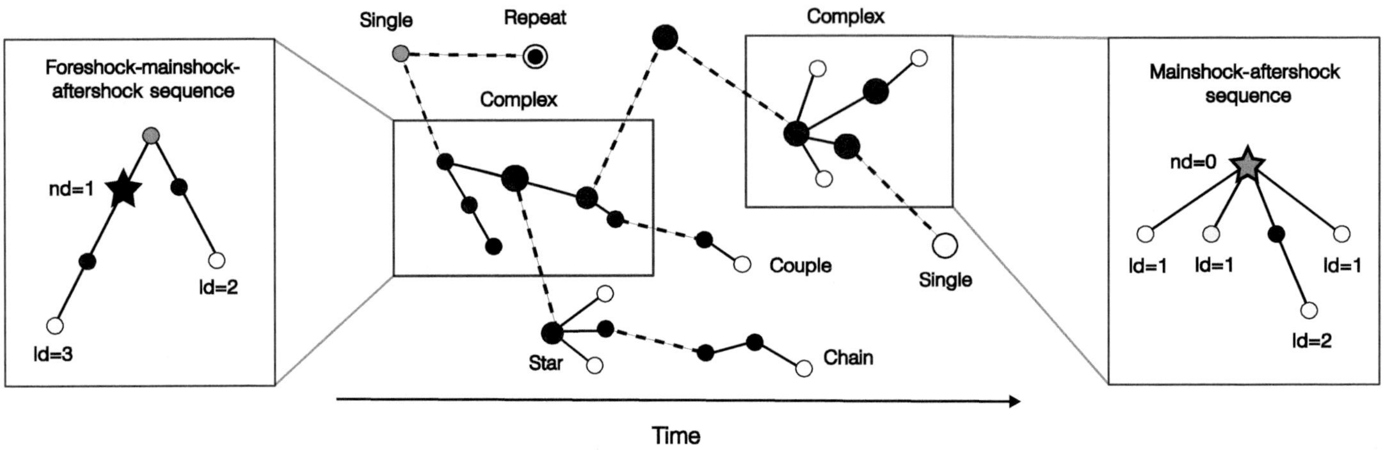

Figure 2. Schematic diagram of the nearest-neighbor distance (NND) method. This figure illustrates the terminology used in this study. The main part of this feature is a spanning tree. The dots with different colors represent earthquakes or nodes, and the lines connecting these events are edges. The gray and white dots represent the root and leaf nodes of the spanning tree individually. The solid and dashed lines represent the edges with an NND shorter or longer than the threshold. When cutting down the dash lines, this spanning tree turns into a spanning forest, including singles and clusters. The types of clusters include single, repeat, couple, star, and complex. Two examples of complex clusters are shown in this figure. The gray and white colors still represent the root and leaf nodes in the clusters. In addition, the mainshock with the largest magnitude is labeled as a star. The "nd" represents the node depth of the mainshocks, and the "ld" represents the node depth of the leaves or leaf depth.

This study utilizes a relocated earthquake catalog published by the China Seismic Experimental Site (CSES), covering events from 1 January 2009 to 31 March 2019. To validate our results, we also employed a standard catalog from the CEA. Though the CEA catalog has slightly lower location precision, it covers a longer period, from 1 January 2000 to 31 March 2019. We choose to analyze earthquakes with a magnitude greater than 2.0, and the estimated magnitude of completeness is shown in Figure S1, available in the supplemental material to this article. After the magnitude truncation, the CSES catalog retains 33,554 events, and the CEA catalog retains 57,095 events in total.

Methods

Earthquake clustering is a method for categorizing earthquakes based on their spatial, temporal, and magnitude relationships. This study employs the NND method, originally introduced by Baiesi and Paczuski (2004) and further refined by Zaliapin *et al.* (2008) and Zaliapin and Ben-Zion (2013a,b). NND clustering integrates information on origin time, epicenter or hypocenter, and magnitude of earthquakes to compute neighbor distances, identify nearest-neighbor pairs, and construct a spanning tree for an earthquake catalog.

The neighbor distance between an earthquake pair of earthquakes i and j is defined as

$$\eta_{ij} = \begin{cases} t_{ij} r_{ij}^{d_f} 10^{-bm_i}, & t_{ij} > 0 \\ \infty, & t_{ij} < 0 \end{cases}, \qquad (1)$$

in which b is the b-value of the frequency–magnitude distribution, d_f is the fractal dimension, $t_{ij} = t_j - t_i$ is the difference between the origin time of the two earthquakes in years, and r_{ij} is the spatial distance between the epicenters or hypocenters in kilometers. After calculating the neighbor distance for every earthquake pair (i,j), we can find the nearest neighbor k for every earthquake j, and their distance is $\mathrm{NND}_j = \eta_{kj} = \min(\eta_{ij})$.

Figure 2 presents a schematic diagram of a spanning tree along with its associated terminologies. In this framework, each earthquake within the spanning tree represents a node, and the connection between two nodes is referred to as an edge. For any edge, the predecessor and descendant nodes act as the parent and child nodes, respectively. The first earthquake in a cluster, located at the top of the tree, is designated as the root node, whereas an earthquake with no children is referred to as a leaf node. Assuming that related earthquakes are spatially or temporally closer, a threshold η_c can be established to determine whether a pair of earthquakes is related. To ensure objectivity, this threshold η_c can be inferred from the data. Assuming the histogram of NND follows a Gaussian mixture distribution with two components, threshold η_c can be defined as the intersection of the two Gaussian modes (Hicks, 2011; Zaliapin and Ben-Zion, 2016). These two modes are more distinct when represented in the joint domain of the temporal and spatial distances (T_j, R_j):

$$T_j = t_{kj} 10^{-bm_k/2}; R_j = r_{kj}^{d_f} 10^{-bm_k/2}. \qquad (2)$$

To test the robustness of the estimated threshold, we followed the method proposed by Karimi and Davidsen (2023) and Sirorattanakul *et al.* (2025) to create shuffled catalogs by randomly permuting the order of the magnitude and locations, and then calculating the NND distribution for these shuffled catalogs. The threshold is chosen appropriately if the majority of shuffled events are located at the independent mode.

After clustering, a spanning tree can be converted to a spanning forest by breaking edges that are further than this threshold. Earthquakes that are independent of any other earthquakes will become single-leaf nodes or singles. Triggered earthquakes will stay in subtrees or clusters with their parent events. The background seismicity rate and features of earthquake clusters can be measured after this separation. Background events consist of singles and the first events of clusters. The cumulative background event number can be counted over time, and the background seismicity rate can be calculated by the derivative after fitting the cumulative curve by a second-order polynomial function (Marsan *et al.*, 2017).

Terms to describe the spanning tree are also applied to the subtrees in the spanning forest. In addition, the number of edges from the root to a node is the depth of that node. To distinguish it from the real depth of an earthquake, we call it the node depth in this study. The depth of the leaf node is the leaf depth. Earthquakes with the same node depth are in the same layer. The productivity of a parent node is the number of direct children or edges it has. A subtree can grow by increasing the number of edges or the number of layers. The earthquake with the maximum magnitude inside a cluster is the mainshock. If multiple earthquakes have the same magnitude, the one that occurred first will be the mainshock. To better describe the clustering results, we also label any earthquake that occurs before the mainshock as a foreshock and after as an aftershock. It is worth noting that foreshock in this study is a general definition, including the real foreshocks that participate in triggering the mainshock and those events that are triggered by real foreshocks before the mainshock.

To better categorize the clusters, we introduce repeat, couple, chain, star, and complex to describe the shape of the tree structure, and examples are shown in Figure 2. Repeat clusters result from low location precision and are more common in the early earthquake catalog. Earthquakes inside this type of cluster are all located at the same spot (distance < 100 m), and their structure cannot be measured. The rest of the clusters cover at least two spots in space. A couple is a cluster with only two earthquakes. A chain is a cluster of events that trigger each other one by one and only has one leaf node. Couples are very common, whereas chains are rare. Both may result from the incompleteness of the catalog. A star cluster only has one parent node because all aftershocks are triggered by the mainshock. This study focuses on complex clusters, including their ratio and shape. In a complex cluster, an earthquake can be both a parent and a child, which represents a multistage rupture process. Three indices are used to measure their features. First, the MRND $\in[0,1]$ is proposed to describe when the mainshock occurred:

$$\text{MRND} = \frac{\text{mainshock node depth}}{\text{maximum node depth}}. \tag{3}$$

Second, the MREP $\in[0,1]$ is designed to describe how much the mainshock contributes to spreading the cluster tree:

$$\text{MREP} = \frac{\text{number of children of the mainshock}}{\text{number of leaf nodes}}. \tag{4}$$

Third, this study uses the NALD $\in(0,1)$, which normalizes the average leaf depth proposed by Zaliapin and Ben-Zion (2013b). A high-average leaf depth represents that this earthquake cluster grows more layers than edges, which may be related to brittle–ductile rupture resulting from high heat flow (Zaliapin and Ben-Zion, 2013b). Considering that the average leaf depth depends on the size of the cluster, we normalize it with the maximum depth a cluster can reach. If a cluster is a chain that only grows layers, the average leaf depth will reach the maximum: cluster size minus one as follows:

$$\text{NALD} = \frac{\text{average leaf depth}}{\text{cluster size} - 1}. \tag{5}$$

For the cluster shown on the left panel of Figure 2, the mainshock node depth is 1, and the maximum node depth is 3. Therefore, the MRND is 1/3 = 0.33. The mainshock only has one child, and the cluster has two leaf nodes. The MREP is 1/2 = 0.50. The average leaf depth is (3 + 2)/2 = 2.50, and the cluster size is 6. The NALD then is (3 + 2)/2/(6−1) = 0.50. Similarly, in the cluster at the right panel of Figure 2, the mainshock node depth is 0, and the maximum node depth is 2. Therefore, the MRND is 0/2 = 0. The mainshock has four children, the same as the leaf nodes. So, the MREP is 4/4 = 1. The average leaf depth is (1 + 1 + 1 + 2)/4 = 1.25, and the cluster size is 6. The NALD then is (1 + 1 + 1 + 2)/4/(6−1) = 0.25.

The types of earthquake clusters have a spectrum from mainshock–aftershock sequences to swarms. A typical mainshock–aftershock sequence starts with a strong mainshock. This mainshock triggers a series of aftershocks that follow Omori's law (Ōmori, 1894) and Båth's law (Richter, 1958) in observation. When foreshocks occur, an earthquake sequence deviates from the mainshock–aftershock type and becomes a foreshock–mainshock–aftershock sequence. If the mainshock wanes, the sequence will end up as a swarm with blurred boundaries, an uncertain mainshock, and distributed energy. These three attributes can describe the swarmlike feature of a cluster by measuring how much a sequence deviates from a mainshock–aftershock sequence. Assuming an earthquake sequence has a bell-shaped time–energy curve: the NALD represents the width of the bell, the MRND labels where the peak is located, and the MREP is the height of the peak. When a cluster deviates from the aftershock sequence to swarm, the bell grows smoother, and the peak moves to the middle. In this case, the MRND increases whereas the MREP decreases. The NALD indicates the mechanism of swarms. A swarm caused by brittle–ductile rupture under high heat flow tends to have a larger average leaf depth, which may affect their NALD (Zaliapin and Ben-Zion, 2013b).

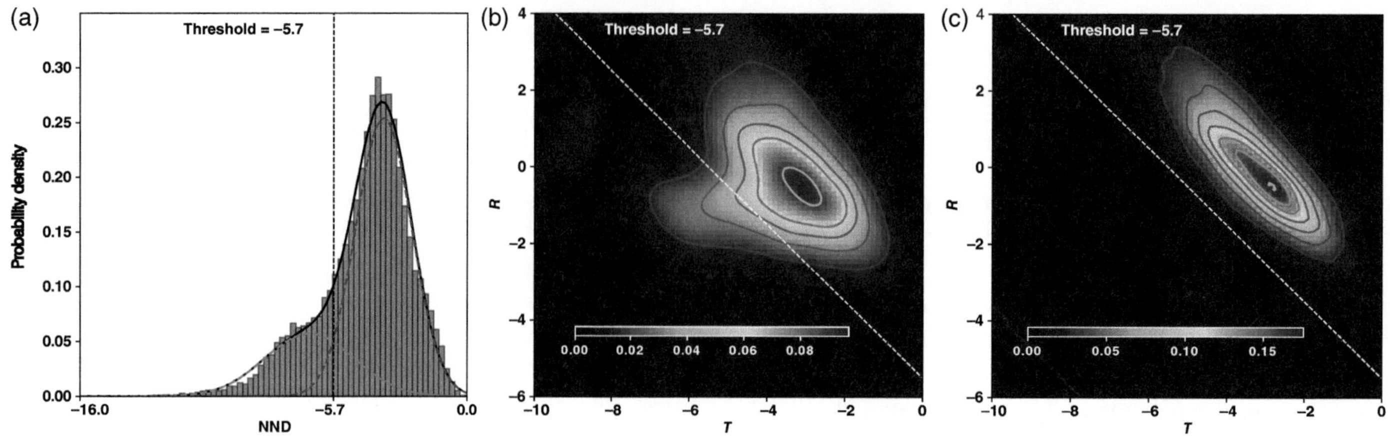

Figure 3. NND distribution of the Sichuan region. The values are normalized to sum to unity. (a) Histogram of the NND. The magenta and cyan curves are the two best-fit components of the Gaussian mixture with mean values of −6.8 and −3.7. The best-fit threshold −5.7 is labeled as the black-vertical dashed line. (b) The joint distribution of the rescaled time and space components (T, R). The best-fit threshold −5.7 is labeled as the white-dashed line. (c) The joint distribution of the rescaled time and space components (T, R) of the shuffled catalog. The NNDs are concentrated at the outer side of the threshold, which indicates that threshold = −5.7 is a reasonable choice. The color version of this figure is available only in the electronic edition.

Results

Figure 3 shows the 1D and 2D NND distribution with parameters $b = 1.0$ and $d_f = 2.0$. The earthquake hypocenters are used in the calculation. Figures S2 and S3 show the fitting of the b-value and fractal dimension. In Figure 3a, the mean of the clustered mode is −6.8, and the mean of the single mode is −3.7. The best-fit threshold η_c is −5.7 and has been approved by the NND distribution of the shuffled catalog in Figure 3c. Figure 4 shows the clustering process from a spanning tree to a spanning forest of earthquakes with a magnitude greater than 4.0. All earthquakes are connected in the spanning tree, whereas in the spanning forest, the long edges are defective, and the earthquakes are separated into singles and clusters. Figure 5 and the first row of Table 1 present the clustering result in time–latitude and time–magnitude coordinates. Among the 33,554 events in the catalog, 72.0% are single earthquakes. The remaining events form 2491 clusters, comprising 5848 aftershocks and 1056 foreshocks. Mainshocks, aftershocks, and foreshocks account for 7.42%, 17.43%, and 3.15% of the total events, respectively.

Figure 6 shows the comparison of the cumulative event number and background seismicity rate of the Sichuan basin and the surrounding regions. The cumulative event number is counted daily whereas the seismicity rate is calculated over a 30-day sliding window. The background seismicity rate of the Sichuan basin was low and stable before late 2014. After 2018, the background seismicity rate of the Sichuan basin has sharply increased and exceeded the other regions, reaching more than 2000 events per month with a magnitude larger than 2.0. On the contrary, the background seismicity rate of the other regions has decreased since 2009 after being increased by the **M** 8.0 Wenchuan earthquake.

The comparison of types of clusters is shown in the first row of the Sichuan basin and the other regions in Table 2. Only clusters with a mainshock magnitude larger than 4.0 are considered because the grandchildren of smaller mainshocks are likely to have a magnitude smaller than the cutoff magnitude. The results show that no repeat cluster is observed in this catalog, which indicates a high location accuracy. The Sichuan basin has more complex clusters (52.94%) compared with the other regions (32.95%). Among these complex clusters, 50.00% of the complex clusters in the Sichuan basin have foreshocks, labeled as F-cluster in Table 2. In contrast, the ratio of the F-cluster for the other region is only 33.33%. Most of the clusters in the other regions are couples (34.10%) and stars (30.06%). In the Sichuan basin, the ratios of couples and stars are around 10% less. The violin plot in Figure 7 shows the distribution of the three attributes of all complex clusters in the Sichuan basin and the other regions. The complex clusters of the Sichuan basin have relatively higher MRND, lower MREP, and comparable NALD with respect to the other regions. These results show that the clusters in the Sichuan basin have comparable length but more swarmlike shapes compared with the other regions.

Tables 1 and 2 also include six more tests with various catalogs, methods, and parameter sets of b, d_f, and η_c. The fitting of parameters is shown in Figures S2 and S3, and their NND distribution and thresholds are shown in Figure S4. Regardless of different parameters and catalogs, the percentage of different earthquakes remains similar. The first four tests use the catalogs that cover the same time period from 1 January 2009 to 31 March 2009, and the calculations are based on their best-fitting parameters. The difference is that the first two rows used relocated earthquake catalogs, whereas the following two rows used the original catalogs. In addition, the first and third rows used the hypocenters, whereas the second and fourth rows used

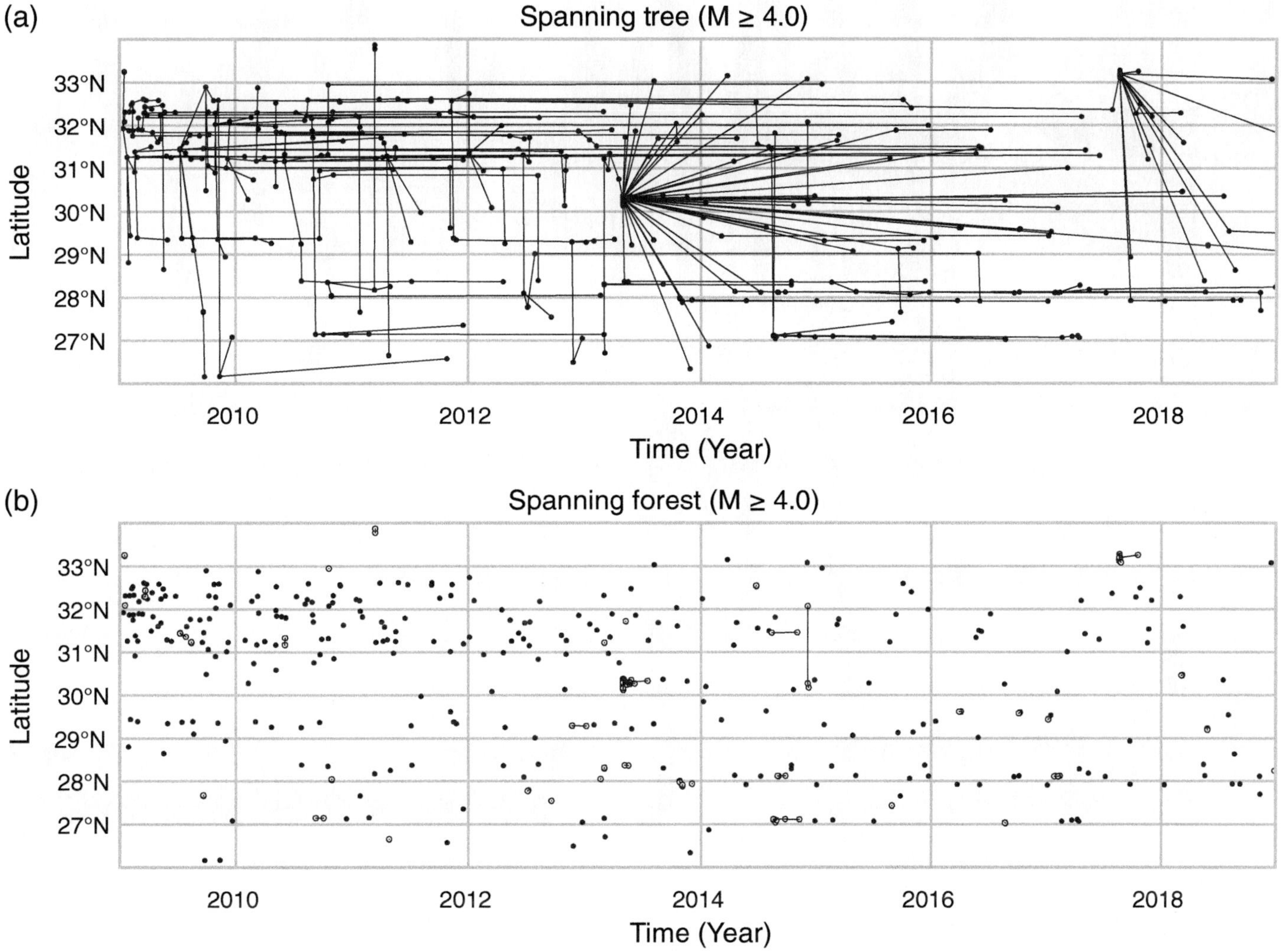

Figure 4. Spanning tree and forest of earthquakes with **M** ≥ 4 in the Sichuan region. The nearest-neighbor links are shown by gray lines. (a) Spanning tree of nearest neighbors. (b) The nearest-neighbor forest is obtained by removing the weak links from the spanning tree. Open circles represent clustered events, and filled circles represent singles.

TABLE 1
Clustering Results for Seven Tests

Test ID	Catalog	Period	b and d_f	η_c	2D/3D	Number	b	d_f	η_c	Single (%)	Mainshock (%)	Aftershock (%)	Foreshock (%)
1	09-19 R	09-19	F	F	3D	33554	1.0	2.0	−5.7	72.00%	7.42%	17.43%	3.15%
2	09-19 R	09-19	F	F	2D	33554	1.0	1.4	−6.3	70.78%	7.54%	18.60%	3.08%
3	09-19 O	09-19	F	F	3D	31785	1.0	2.3	−5.2	75.32%	6.06%	15.35%	3.27%
4	09-19 O	09-19	F	F	2D	31785	1.0	1.6	−6.1	70.48%	7.98%	16.79%	4.76%
5	00-19 O	00-19	E	E	2D	31785	1.0	1.6	−6.1	70.51%	7.97%	16.74%	4.75%
6	00-19 O	00-19	F	F	2D	31785	0.8	1.8	−6.5	79.49%	6.87%	9.82%	3.81%
7	00-19 O	00-19	E	F	2D	31785	1.0	1.6	−7.0	77.58%	6.75%	11.83%	3.84%

The 2D/3D column represents whether the depth information is included or not; the % columns are the percentage of their previous columns. E, empirical; F, fitting; O, original; R, relocated.

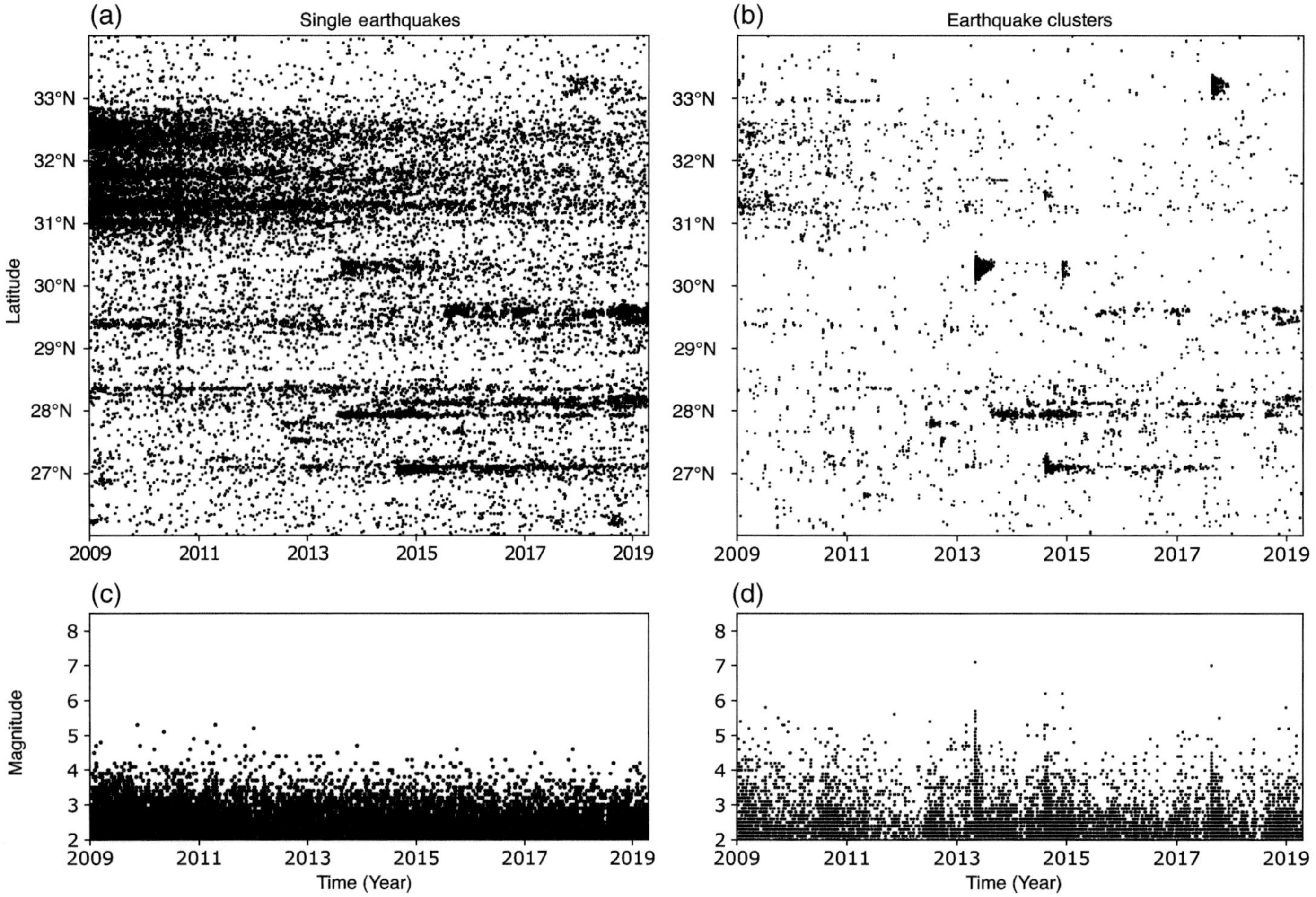

Figure 5. Clustering results. (a) Time–latitude diagram of single earthquakes, (b) time–latitude diagram of earthquake clusters, (c) time–magnitude diagram of single earthquakes, and (d) time–magnitude diagram of earthquake clusters.

epicenters. The comparison between rows with the same catalog but different location types estimates the importance of depth information. Despite the altered fractal dimension and threshold η_c, the results are nearly identical. Slightly more (~5%) earthquakes are clustered as single when considering the depth information because many earthquakes for which epicenters are in the same region may be located at different depths. This indicates that location errors have a minor effect on the clustering results in this region. The comparison between the rows with the same location type but different resource estimates shows the effect of location accuracy. The calculation based on the same location type of the two catalogs resulted in almost the same numbers, which suggests that the difference in location accuracy between these catalogs does not play an important role in this study.

The comparison between the fourth test and the last three tests highlights the effect of historical events and parameter types. These calculations are conducted on the original 20 yr CEA catalog, but only the period from 1 January 2009 to 31 March 2009 was analyzed. In the fifth row, the same parameters are used on the 20 yr catalog. The events that occurred before 1 January 2009 are removed after clustering. The NND distributions in Figure S4 are strongly affected by the historical events that occurred from 2000 to 2009. Some aftershocks were reclassified as single events when historical events were ignored because they were leaf nodes in earlier clusters. However, the overall results remained identical. This indicates that the historical events have little influence on NND clustering with the same parameters. The fifth and sixth rows followed the same approach as the fourth but used different parameter settings. The sixth row re-estimated the threshold η_c, whereas the seventh row re-estimated all parameters based on the 20 yr catalog. More aftershocks are categorized as singles when using the best-fitting parameters in the fifth test, whereas the ratio of foreshocks and mainshocks is consistent with the previous test. This is because the very low location accuracy from 2000 to 2009 biased the threshold analysis.

Moreover, the ratio of cluster types and the attributes measured on complex clusters remained stable despite changes in catalogs and parameters. The distributions of mean MRND, MREP, and NALD of the seven tests are presented in Table 2 and the box plots in Figure 7. Consistent with the first test, the complex clusters in the Sichuan basin have larger MRND and smaller MREP. Considering that clusters that have

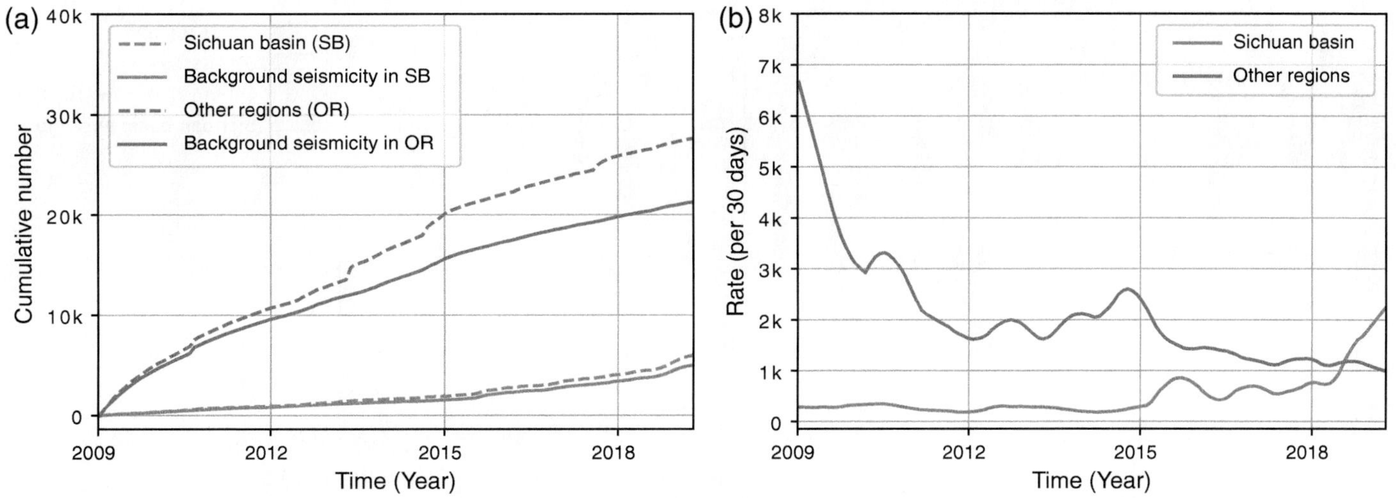

Figure 6. Temporal variation of background events. (a) Cumulative number of all events and background events in the Sichuan basin and the other regions. (b) Background seismicity rate in the Sichuan basin and the other regions. The color version of this figure is available only in the electronic edition.

a mainshock magnitude larger than 3.0 are more common, we measured their cluster structure and show it in Figure S5. Regardless of the potential incompleteness, the result is consistent with the **M** 4.0 clusters in Figure 7.

Discussion

In this study, we applied the NND clustering approach to multiple catalogs using different parameter sets to compare the seismicity characteristics of the Sichuan basin with other regions. Our results reveal an increasing background seismicity rate in the Sichuan basin, consistent with observations from industrial sites in the region (Lei *et al.*, 2017, 2019a,b, 2020; Tan *et al.*, 2020) and with patterns of induced seismicity in other regions (Llenos and Michael, 2013; Schoenball *et al.*, 2015; Zaliapin and

TABLE 2
Comparison of Types of Clusters with Mainshock Magnitude Larger Than M 4.0 Between the Sichuan Basin and the Other Regions

Region	Test ID	Single	Cluster	Repeat (%)	Couple (%)	Star (%)	Chain (%)	Complex (%)	F-Cluster (%)	MRND	MREP	NALD
OR	1	115	173	0.00	34.10	30.06	2.89	32.95	33.33	0.14	0.84	0.11
	2	104	180	0.00	36.11	31.11	2.78	30.00	29.63	0.13	0.83	0.09
	3	130	164	0.61	29.88	35.37	4.88	29.27	25.00	0.11	0.82	0.08
	4	118	176	8.52	20.45	32.39	7.95	30.68	33.33	0.15	0.90	0.11
	5	120	173	9.25	20.81	32.37	6.36	31.21	33.33	0.15	0.90	0.11
	6	159	153	11.76	22.80	30.72	7.19	27.45	26.19	0.12	0.91	0.12
	7	175	150	14.67	24.00	22.67	8.67	30.00	33.33	0.17	0.88	0.13
SB	1	25	34	0.00	20.59	23.53	2.94	52.94	50.00	0.28	0.79	0.14
	2	24	36	0.00	22.22	19.44	5.56	52.78	52.63	0.31	0.79	0.14
	3	22	37	0.00	24.32	24.32	10.81	40.54	46.67	0.22	0.76	0.12
	4	24	36	11.11	16.67	19.44	0.00	52.78	42.11	0.20	0.79	0.12
	5	35	28	17.86	17.86	21.43	3.57	39.29	45.45	0.23	0.69	0.20
	6	29	33	15.15	27.27	15.15	3.03	39.39	38.46	0.20	0.69	0.17
	7	24	36	11.11	16.67	19.44	0.00	52.78	42.11	0.20	0.79	0.12

MREP, mainshock relative edge productivity; MRND, mainshock relative node depth; NALD, normalized average leaf depth; OR, other region; SB, Sichuan basin; F-cluster represents a complex cluster with at least one foreshock.

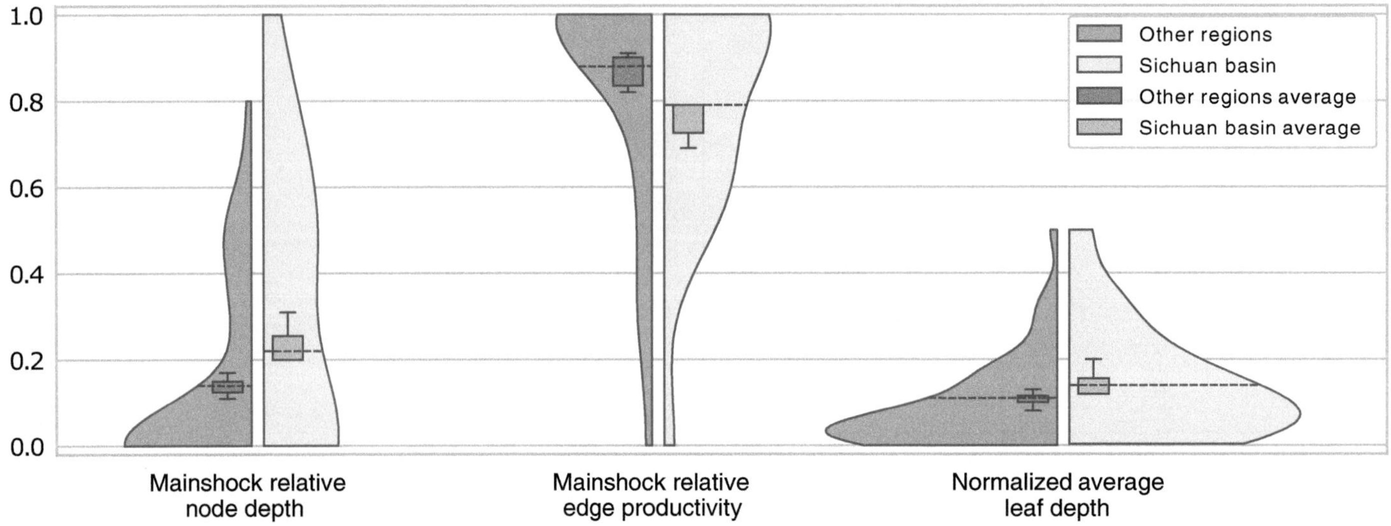

Figure 7. Comparison between complex clusters with mainshock magnitude greater than 4.0 in the Sichuan basin and the other regions. The split violin plots show the comparison of cluster attributes between the Sichuan basin and the other regions. The dashed lines represent the average of the cluster attributes. The inserted boxplot is the average attribute of all tests. The color version of this figure is available only in the electronic edition.

Ben-Zion, 2016; Goebel *et al.*, 2019). High background rate of induced seismicity may be attributed to the external forces such as fluid migration or stage-by-stage stimulation (Cochran *et al.*, 2020; Schultz *et al.*, 2020). The increasing background rate in the Sichuan basin, which has surpassed that of other regions since 2018, supports the idea of an external origin rather than being driven by background tectonic forces or the aftereffects of the 2008 **M** 8.0 Wenchuan earthquake. This result, in turn, supports our assumption that seismicity in the two regions is driven by different mechanisms.

After quantitative analysis, we found more complex clusters in the Sichuan basin, and they are more swarmlike in nature. Many studies have highlighted the swarmlike characteristics of induced seismicity (Zaliapin and Ben-Zion, 2016; Špičák, 2000; Schultz *et al.*, 2020). However, a clear definition of earthquake swarm remains elusive, and a widely accepted criterion to distinguish it is absent. Attempts have been made to distinguish swarms with mainshock–aftershock sequences through manual selection (Vidale and Shearer, 2006), anomalous with respect to the epidemic-type aftershock sequence model (Hainzl and Ogata, 2005), magnitude–time distribution (Zhang and Shearer, 2016), and the average leaf depth of the cluster topological tree (Sirorattanakul *et al.*, 2025). In this study, we provide a quantitative measure of the swarmlike behavior in complex clusters to better characterize this phenomenon. The higher MRND in the Sichuan basin indicates that mainshocks always occur later in a cluster after several stages of foreshocks. The lower MREP suggests that mainshocks are relatively weak because many earthquakes are children of foreshocks or aftershocks. The similar NALD values imply that the clusters in the Sichuan basin and surrounding regions have an elongated structure at comparable levels. This is not surprising, as Zaliapin and Ben-Zion (2013b) proposed high average leaf depth as an indicator of brittle–ductile rupture in regions with high heat flow, and the heat flow of the Sichuan basin is similar to the surrounding region (Hu *et al.*, 2000). In addition, the swarmlike feature is also characterized by the smaller magnitude difference between the mainshock and the largest aftershock. As shown in Figure S6, the complex clusters show a smaller magnitude difference, whereas the other clusters roughly follow Båth's Law. This swarmlike feature indicates that they may be related to fluid migration or aseismic slip instead of purely tectonic stress release.

We avoid categorizing the clusters into either mainshock–aftershock sequences but use swarmlike to describe their feature because the structure of complex clusters exists as a spectrum in our observation. As shown in Figure S7, this spectrum can partially be described by the three attributes we propose in this study. The endpoint is the star clusters with MRND $= 0$, MREP $= 1$, and NALD $= 1/\text{number of aftershocks} \approx 0$. When moving away from this endpoint, MRND increases (mainshocks occur later), MRND decreases (cluster elongates), and MREP decreases (mainshock becomes less productive). When simply dichotomizing the spectrum to aftershock sequences and swarms with MRND $= 0.3$ and MREP $= 0.7$, the magnitude difference of the swarmlike sequence is less than the aftershock-like sequences. This comparison is shown in Figures S7 and S8. As aforementioned, all types of clusters roughly follow Båth's law except complex clusters. This very preliminary dichotomy indicates that clusters with larger MREP and lower MRND tend to violate Båth's law.

By studying the topological structure of an earthquake cluster, we can learn not only about the number of events but also the triggering process among potential foreshocks,

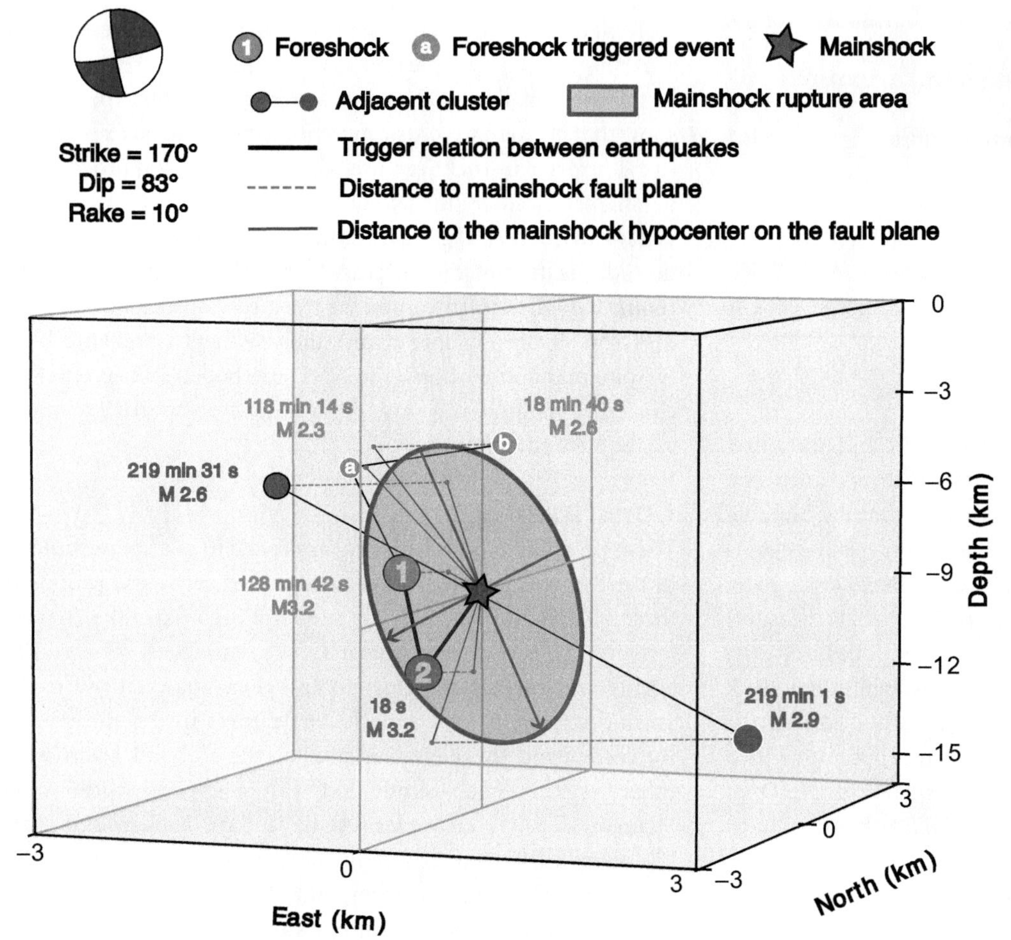

Figure 8. Foreshock sequences of the Xingwen earthquake. The focal mechanism refers to Lei *et al.* (2019a). The red circle represents the estimated mainshock rupture area with a radius of 4.5 km. Two red arrows show the strike and dip. The foreshocks are shown as dots with different numbers and colors. The origin time with respect to the mainshock and magnitude are labeled next to the dots with the same color. The triggered relations are labeled as black and gray lines. The black lines represent the triggering process between different stages, whereas the gray lines represent the same stage. The projection of earthquakes to the fault plane is shown as small gray dots and connects the event with its projection with gray-dashed lines. The distances from the projections to the mainshocks are shown as red lines. The two blue dots consist of an adjacent cluster and can be part of the foreshocks if the threshold is chosen through the shuffled catalog (−5.3). The color version of this figure is available only in the electronic edition.

mainshocks, and aftershocks within the earthquake cluster. We find that foreshocks of complex clusters, indicative of multistage nucleation processes, are more prevalent in the Sichuan basin. Glasgow *et al.* (2023) observed multistage rupture processes in induced earthquakes, and this study further demonstrates that such processes are common in HF-induced seismicity in the Sichuan basin. In addition, the cascading nucleation process may play a significant role in the development of the swarmlike feature. For example, Figure 8 and Table 3 show the foreshock sequence of the 16 December 2018 **M** 5.8 Xingwen earthquake, one of the largest HF-induced earthquakes in the Sichuan basin. This strike-slip earthquake occurred on a north–south blind fault (Lei *et al.*, 2019a). The estimated rupture area, shown in Figure 8, is approximately 4.5 km. Two foreshocks within the rupture area are recorded and labeled as numbers 1 and 2 in Figure 8. The sequence began with an **M** 3.2 earthquake approximately 2 hr before the mainshock. These two foreshocks occurred almost on the same plane, located 400 m west of the fault and parallel to it. The first foreshock was closest to the mainshock but did not trigger it until the second foreshock ruptured the deeper part of the fault plane. These foreshocks also triggered small events on both sides of the fault plane. For example, the foreshock-triggered event "b" occurred at the upper boundary of the rupture area. The cascading nucleation process may be facilitated by a complex fault zone with a high density of secondary faults (Im and Avouac, 2023), which is common in the Sichuan basin (Lei *et al.*, 2019b; Liu and Zahradník, 2020; Liu *et al.*, 2023; Wang *et al.*, 2020). In this case, a minor earthquake triggered the moderate mainshock through a foreshock chain on a complex fault zone. This suggests that the potential impact region of fracturing operations may be larger than initially estimated. Earthquake interactions should be considered in future models of induced earthquake rupture and risk estimation.

Some challenges still exist for this method. It is clear that the NND clustering results depend on the threshold η_c, and maybe other parameters. Zaliapin and Ben-Zion (2013a, 2022) mentioned that NND clustering is not sensitive to the parameters b and d_f, but to location accuracy. To minimize the ambiguity, we try to calculate every parameter from the data instead of using an empirical value and test a series of parameters on different catalogs. We find the result remains stable under different parameters and processing flows. Although the uncertainties caused by different event numbers, local b-values, and fractal dimensions in the two regions cannot be ruled out, applying

TABLE 3
Foreshock Sequences of the Xingwen Earthquake

Edge	Magnitude	Distance (km)	Time	NND
1-2	3.2	2.9	128 min 26 s	−5.8
2-M	3.2	2.6	18 s	−8.6
1-a	3.2	3.9	20 min 30 s	−6.4
a-b	3.2	1.5	99 min 32 s	−5.7

NND, nearest-neighbor distance.

the same parameter sets to the Sichuan basin and the other regions can minimize the effect of location errors and bias. Other challenges of the NND method include that the bimodal distribution is not evident in some regions, especially regions with induced earthquakes (Zaliapin and Ben-Zion, 2016; Vasylkivska and Huerta, 2017; Kothari *et al.*, 2020; Glasgow *et al.*, 2021). In most cases, a perfect threshold does not exist due to the overlapping of two modes (Schoenball *et al.*, 2015; Aden-Antoniów *et al.*, 2022). The current method to find the threshold either considering the intersection point of two Gaussian mixtures (Hicks, 2011) or boundary of NND of shuffled catalog (Karimi and Davidsen, 2023). In this study, the thresholds recommended by the shuffled catalog are consistently larger than the intersection point and close to the average of the mean value of the two Gaussian mixtures. If this threshold is chosen, more events will be categorized into the clustered mode. For example, with a threshold of −5.3, recommended by the shuffled catalog, the adjacent couple cluster, with an **M** 2.6 mainshock that occurred 3 hr before 1.5 km west of the Xingwen earthquake, will be part of its foreshock chain.

As a data-driven statistical method, the triggering relationship is identified only by a spatial–temporal closeness instead of a physical or numerical model (Hill *et al.*, 2024). In this case, all earthquakes are regarded as points, regardless of the size of their rupture surfaces. The events that occurred much later at the edge of the rupture surface of the mainshock are not considered as aftershocks but as background events. This caused the evident increase of background events after the **M** 8.0 Wenchuan earthquake. This phenomenon is illustrated in Figure S9. If an earthquake occurred a year after an **M** 8.0 mainshock, it would need to be within a 15 km radius of the mainshock to be considered as an aftershock of the latter. This means that events that occurred a year after, 15 km away, are considered as background events, even though they are located at the rupture area of the mainshock. Improvements of the NND method are needed in the future to address this limitation. In addition, high-level randomness together with the very long memory makes the reconstruction of tree ancestry quite unreliable (Sornette and Utkin, 2009). Under the NND method, static stress triggering in close spatial distance or dynamic triggering at a close time can both be identified as a triggering relation. Nucleation processes that are compact in both time and space should be clearly identified by the method. Observations on acoustic emission experiments show that clustered events can be triggered by local or nonlocal stress transfer in rock fracture, and this triggering process can be characterized by the NND method (Xiong and Hampton, 2020; Davidsen *et al.*, 2021). Future studies are needed to connect the statistical measurement with the physical model to refine the physical meaning of the nearest-neighbor pair in the NND-spanning forest and analyze their systematic bias. Despite many limitations, the NND method is still an efficient clustering method and provides a unique perspective to study earthquake interaction.

Conclusions

We applied the NND clustering approach to analyze seismicity in the Sichuan region and its surrounding areas and proposed three indices to quantitatively measure the swarmlike characteristics of earthquake clusters. We extracted background events and earthquake clusters and then analyzed the background seismicity rate and cluster features in the study area. By comparing the characteristics of the Sichuan basin with other regions, we found that (1) seismicity within the Sichuan basin is characterized by a high background rate, (2) many clusters with a mainshock magnitude greater than 4.0 exhibit complex structures, and (3) many earthquake clusters in the Sichuan basin display swarmlike features. Our findings suggest that earthquake interaction, especially foreshocks, plays a significant role in inducing seismicity in the Sichuan basin, and should be considered in future models of induced earthquake rupture and risk estimation.

Data and Resources

The original catalog used in this study is from the China National Earthquake Data Center (https://data.earthquake.cn/index.html, last accessed August 2023), and the relocated earthquake catalog is from the China Seismic Experimental Site (CSES; http://124.17.4.85/sjcp/ggmx/2021/132.shtml, last accessed September 2024). The supplemental material for this article includes the calculation of the complete magnitude, *b*-value, and fractal dimension, the nearest-neighbor distance (NND) distributions for tests in Table 1, and other tests mentioned in the main article.

Declaration of Competing Interests

The authors acknowledge that there are no conflicts of interest recorded.

Acknowledgments

The authors would like to thank the China National Earthquake Data Center and China Seismic Experimental Site (CSES) for providing the earthquake catalogs. The authors would like to thank Brandon Schmandt, Le Li, and Haichao Chen for the helpful discussion. The authors would like to thank Krittanon Sirorattanakul and another anonymous reviewer for their helpful suggestions.

References

Aden-Antoniów, F., W. B. Frank, and L. Seydoux (2022). An adaptable random forest model for the declustering of earthquake catalogs, *J. Geophys. Res.* **127,** no. 2, e2021JB023254, doi: 10.1029/2021JB023254.

Azad, M., D. I. Garagash, and M. Satish (2017). Nucleation of dynamic slip on a hydraulically fractured fault, *J. Geophys. Res.* **122,** no. 4, 2812–2830.

Baiesi, M., and M. Paczuski (2004). Scale-free networks of earthquakes and aftershocks, *Phys. Rev. E* **69,** no. 6, 066,106.

Chen, F., L. Ta, and J. Chen (2015). Deformation-strain field in Sichuan and its surrounding areas based on GPS data, *Geod. Geodynam.* **6,** no. 3, 203–209.

Cochran, E. S., A. Wickham-Piotrowski, K. B. Kemna, R. M. Harrington, S. L. Dougherty, and A. F. Peña Castro (2020). Minimal clustering of injection-induced earthquakes observed with a large-n seismic array, *Bull. Seismol. Soc. Am.* **110,** no. 5, 2005–2017.

Davidsen, J., T. Goebel, G. Kwiatek, S. Stanchits, J. Baró, and G. Dresen (2021). What controls the presence and characteristics of aftershocks in rock fracture in the lab? *J. Geophys. Res.* **126,** no. 10, e2021JB022539, doi: 10.1029/2021JB022539.

Eyre, T. S., D. W. Eaton, D. I. Garagash, M. Zecevic, M. Venieri, R. Weir, and D. C. Lawton (2019). The role of aseismic slip in hydraulic fracturing–induced seismicity, *Sci. Adv.* **5,** no. 8, eaav7172, doi: 10.1126/sciadv.aav7172.

Freed, A. M. (2005). Earthquake triggering by static, dynamic, and postseismic stress transfer, *Annu. Rev. Earth Planet. Sci.* **33,** no. 1, 335–367.

Glasgow, M., B. Schmandt, R. Wang, M. Zhang, S. L. Bilek, and E. Kiser (2021). Raton Basin induced seismicity is hosted by networks of short basement faults and mimics tectonic earthquake statistics, *J. Geophys. Res.* **126,** no. 11, e2021JB022839, doi: 10.1029/2021JB022839.

Glasgow, M. E., B. Schmandt, and S. L. Bilek (2023). Cascading multi-segment rupture in an injection-induced earthquake sequence with a Mw 5.3 mainshock, *Earth Planet. Sci. Lett.* **620,** 118335.

Goebel, T. H. W., Z. Rosson, E. E. Brodsky, and J. I. Walter (2019). Aftershock deficiency of induced earthquake sequences during rapid mitigation efforts in Oklahoma, *Earth Planet. Sci. Lett.* **522,** 135–143.

Hainzl, S., and Y. Ogata (2005). Detecting fluid signals in seismicity data through statistical earthquake modeling, *J. Geophys. Res.* **110,** no. B5, doi: 10.1029/2004JB003247.

Healy, J. H., W. W. Rubey, D. T. Griggs, and C. B. Raleigh (1968). The Denver earthquakes, *Science* 161, 1301–1310.

Hicks, A. L. (2011). *Clustering in Multidimensional Spaces With Applications to Statistical Analysis of Earthquake Clustering*, University of Nevada, Reno, Nevada.

Hill, D. P. (1977). A model for earthquake swarms, *J. Geophys. Res.* **82,** no. 8, 1347–1352.

Hill, R. G., D. T. Trugman, and M. Weingarten (2024). Separating injection-driven and earthquake-driven induced seismicity by combining a fully coupled poroelastic model with interpretable machine learning, *Geophys. Res. Lett.* **51,** no. 18, e2024GL109802, doi: 10.1029/2024GL109802.

Hu, S., L. He, and J. Wang (2000). Heat flow in the continental area of China: A new data set, *Earth Planet. Sci. Lett.* **179,** no. 2, 407–419.

Im, K., and J. P. Avouac (2023). Cascading foreshocks, aftershocks and earthquake swarms in a discrete fault network, *Geophys. J. Int.* **235,** no. 1, 831–852.

Karimi, K., and J. Davidsen (2021). Aftershock triggering and spatial aftershock zones in fluid-driven settings: Discriminating induced seismicity from natural swarms, *Geophys. Res. Lett.* **48,** no. 15, e2020GL092267, doi: 10.1029/2020GL092267.

Karimi, K., and J. Davidsen (2023). Separating primary and secondary mechanisms for seismicity induced by hydraulic fracturing, *Bull. Seismol. Soc. Am.* **113,** no. 5, 1982–1991.

Kothari, S., R. Shcherbakov, and G. Atkinson (2020). Statistical modeling and characterization of induced seismicity within the Western Canada Sedimentary Basin, *J. Geophys. Res.* **125,** no. 12, e2020JB020606, doi: 10.1029/2020JB020606.

Kyriakopoulos, C., and D. D. Oglesby (2024). Direct dynamic triggering scenarios of the southern San Andreas Fault by moderate-magnitude cross-fault earthquakes in the Brawley Seismic Zone, California, *Seismol. Res. Lett.* **95,** no. 5, 2859–2873.

Lei, X., D. Huang, J. Su, G. Jiang, X. Wang, H. Wang, X. Guo, and H. Fu (2017). Fault reactivation and earthquakes with magnitudes of up to Mw4. 7 induced by shale-gas hydraulic fracturing in Sichuan Basin, China, *Sci. Rep.* **7,** no. 1, 7971.

Lei, X., J. Su, and Z. Wang (2020). Growing seismicity in the Sichuan Basin and its association with industrial activities, *Sci. China Earth Sci.* **63,** 1633–1660.

Lei, X., Z. Wang, and J. Su (2019a). The December 2018 ML 5.7 and January 2019 ML 5.3 earthquakes in South Sichuan basin induced by shale gas hydraulic fracturing, *Seismol. Res. Lett.* **90,** no. 3, 1099–1110.

Lei, X., Z. Wang, and J. Su (2019b). Possible link between long-term and short-term water injections and earthquakes in salt mine and shale gas site in Changning, south Sichuan Basin, China, *Earth Planet. Phys.* **3,** no. 6, 510–525.

Liu, G., R. Lu, D. He, W. Tao, P. Su, W. Zhang, X. Guo, and H. Fu (2023). Detailed imaging of a seismogenic fault that potentially induced the two 2019 Weiyuan moderate earthquakes in the Sichuan Basin, China, *Seismol. Res. Lett.* 94, no. 3, 1379–1391.

Liu, J., and J. Zahradník (2020). The 2019 MW 5.7 Changning earthquake, Sichuan Basin, China: A shallow doublet with different faulting styles, *Geophys. Res. Lett.* **47,** no. 4, e2019GL085408, doi: 10.1029/2019GL085408.

Llenos, A. L., and A. J. Michael (2013). Modeling earthquake rate changes in Oklahoma and Arkansas: Possible signatures of induced seismicity, *Bull. Seismol. Soc. Am.* **103,** no. 5, 2850–2861.

Lohman, R. B., and J. J. McGuire (2007). Earthquake swarms driven by aseismic creep in the Salton Trough, California, *J. Geophys. Res.* **112,** no. B4, doi: 10.1029/2006JB004596.

Marsan, D., M. Bouchon, B. Gardonio, H. Perfettini, A. Socquet, and B. Enescu (2017). Change in seismicity along the Japan trench, 1990–2011, and its relationship with seismic coupling, *J. Geophys. Res.* **122,** no. 6, 4645–4659.

Moein, M. J., C. Langenbruch, R. Schultz, F. Grigoli, W. L. Ellsworth, R. Wang, A. P. Rinaldi, and S. Shapiro (2023). The physical mechanisms of induced earthquakes, *Nat. Rev. Earth Environ.* **4,** no. 12, 847–863.

Mogi, K. (1963). Some discussions on aftershocks, foreshocks and earthquake swarms-the fracture of a semi finite body caused by an inner stress origin and its relation to the earthquake phenomena, *Bull. Earthq. Res. Inst.* **41,** 615–658.

Ōmori, F. (1894). *On the After-Shocks of Earthquakes*, Vol. 7, The Journal of the College of Science, Imperial University, Tokyo, Japan.

Richter, C. (1958), *Elementary Seismology*, W. H. Freeman and Co, San Francisco, California.

Royden, L. H., B. C. Burchfiel, and R. D. Hilstvan der (2008). The geological evolution of the Tibetan Plateau, *Science* **321,** no. 5892, 1054–1058.

Schoenball, M., N. C. Davatzes, and J. M. Glen (2015). Differentiating induced and natural seismicity using space-time-magnitude statistics applied to the Coso Geothermal field, *Geophys. Res. Lett.* **42,** no. 15, 6221–6228.

Schultz, R., R. J. Skoumal, M. R. Brudzinski, D. Eaton, B. Baptie, and W. Ellsworth (2020). Hydraulic fracturing-induced seismicity, *Rev. Geophys.* **58,** no. 3, e2019RG00069, doi: 10.1029/2019RG000695.

Segall, P., and S. Lu (2015). Injection-induced seismicity: Poroelastic and earthquake nucleation effects, *J. Geophys. Res.* **120,** no. 7, 5082–5103.

Sheng, M., R. Chu, S. Ni, Y. Wang, L. Jiang, and H. Yang (2020). Source parameters of three moderate size earthquakes in Weiyuan, China, and their relations to shale gas hydraulic fracturing, *J. Geophys. Res.* **125,** no. 10, e2020JB019932, doi: 10.1029/2020JB019932.

Sheng, M., R. Chu, Z. Peng, Z. Wei, X. Zeng, Q. Wang, and Y. Wang (2022). Earthquakes triggered by fluid diffusion and boosted by fault reactivation in Weiyuan, China due to hydraulic fracturing, *J. Geophys. Res.* **127,** no. 5, e2021JB022963, doi: 10.1029/2021JB022963.

Sirorattanakul, K., J. D. Wilding, M. Acosta, Y. Li, Z. E. Ross, S. J. Bourne, J. van Elk, and J.P. Avouac (2025). Bursts of fast propagating swarms of induced earthquakes at the Groningen gas field, *Seismol. Res. Lett.* **96,** no. 1, 130–146.

Sornette, D., and S. Utkin (2009). Limits of declustering methods for disentangling exogenous from endogenous events in time series with foreshocks, main shocks, and aftershocks, *Phys. Rev. E* **79,** no. 6, 061110.

Špičák, A. (2000). Earthquake swarms and accompanying phenomena in intraplate regions: a review, *Stud. Geophys. Geod.* **44,** 89–106.

Tan, Y., J. Hu, H. Zhang, Y. Chen, J. Qian, Q. Wang, H. Zha, P. Tang, and Z. Nie (2020). Hydraulic fracturing induced seismicity in the southern Sichuan Basin due to fluid diffusion inferred from seismic and injection data analysis, *Geophys. Res. Lett.* **47,** no. 4, e2019GL084885, doi: 10.1029/2019GL084885.

Vasylkivska, V. S., and N. J. Huerta (2017). Spatiotemporal distribution of Oklahoma earthquakes: Exploring relationships using a nearest-neighbor approach, *J. Geophys. Res.* **122,** no. 7, 5395–5416.

Vidale, J. E., and P. M. Shearer (2006). A survey of 71 earthquake bursts across southern California: Exploring the role of pore fluid pressure fluctuations and aseismic slip as drivers, *J. Geophys. Res.* **111,** no. B5, doi: 10.1029/2005JB004034.

Vidale, J. E., K. L. Boyle, and P. M. Shearer (2006). Crustal earthquake bursts in California and Japan: Their patterns and relation to volcanoes, *Geophys. Res. Lett.* **33,** no. 20, doi: 10.1029/2006GL027723.

Wang, M., H. Yang, L. Fang, L. Han, D. Jia, D. Jiang, and B. Yan (2020). Shallow faults reactivated by hydraulic fracturing: The 2019 Weiyuan earthquake sequences in Sichuan, China, *Seismol. Res. Lett.* **91,** no. 6, 3171–3181.

Xiong, Q., and J. C. Hampton (2020). Non-local triggering in rock fracture, *J. Geophys. Res.* **125,** no. 11, e2020JB020403, doi: 10.1029/2020JB020403.

Yamashita, T. (1997). Mechanical effect of fluid migration on the complexity of seismicity, *J. Geophys. Res.* **102,** no. B8, 17,797–17,806.

Yang, H., P. Zhou, N. Fang, G. Zhu, W. Xu, J. Su, F. Meng, and R. Chu (2020). A shallow shock: the 25 February 2019 ML 4.9 earthquake in the Weiyuan shale gas field in Sichuan, China, *Seismol. Res. Lett.* **91,** no. 6, 3182–3194.

Zaliapin, I., and Y. Ben-Zion (2013a). Earthquake clusters in southern California I: Identification and stability, *J. Geophys. Res.* **118,** no. 6, 2847–2864.

Zaliapin, I., and Y. Ben-Zion (2013b). Earthquake clusters in southern California II: Classification and relation to physical properties of the crust, *J. Geophys. Res.* **118,** no. 6, 2865–2877.

Zaliapin, I., and Y. Ben-Zion (2016). Discriminating characteristics of tectonic and human-induced seismicity, *Bull. Seismol. Soc. Am.* **106,** no. 3, 846–859.

Zaliapin, I., and Y. Ben-Zion (2022). Perspectives on clustering and declustering of earthquakes, *Seismol. Res. Lett.* **93,** no. 1, 386–401.

Zaliapin, I., A. Gabrielov, V. Keilis-Borok, and H. Wong (2008). Clustering analysis of seismicity and aftershock identification, *Phys. Rev. Lett.* **101,** no. 1, 018501.

Zhang, Q., and P. M. Shearer (2016). A new method to identify earthquake swarms applied to seismicity near the San Jacinto Fault, California, *Geophys. J. Int.* **205,** no. 2, 995–1005.

Manuscript received 2 January 2025
Published online 23 July 2025

Underestimates of Magnitudes in Real Time Lead to Underestimates of Earthquake Disasters

Max Wyss*[1]

Abstract

Near-real-time magnitude, M1, estimates for earthquakes are strongly different from M2, the final estimate, as a function of magnitude band and time. For potentially fatal earthquakes, M1 estimates are approximately correct for the bands M2 < 7.0. For the band 7.0 ≤ M ≤ 7.9, M1 is approximately equal to M2 since October 2015. For great earthquakes with M2 > 8.2, M1 is always strongly underestimated, leading to initial underestimates of the earthquake consequences. These underestimates are due to saturation of the magnitude scale used in near-real-time estimates of earthquake size. If source parameter estimates based on records by local to regional seismograph networks were accepted, then manual quantitative estimates of fatalities and other consequences could be issued at least 15 min earlier than the current 25 min delay.

Cite this article as Wyss, M. (2025). Underestimates of Magnitudes in Real Time Lead to Underestimates of Earthquake Disasters, *Seismol. Res. Lett.* **97**, 81–85, doi: 10.1785/0220250081.

Introduction

To recognize the extents of earthquake disasters as fast as possible, Quake Loss Assessment for Response and Mitigation (QLARM) and Prompt Assessment of Global Earthquakes for Response (PAGER) issue alerts within 25 min, median, of large ruptures worldwide. The key parameter is the number of fatalities, which implies that several times as many were injured and may be saved by rapid intervention. These earthquake alerts are based on the magnitudes **M**1 estimated by the GeoForschungsZentrums and the U.S. Geological Survey (USGS) within 8 and 22 min, median, respectively. If the **M**1 estimates are wrong, the fatality estimates are wrong. For great earthquakes (**M** ≥ 8), the fatality estimates are especially important, but the magnitude is almost always underestimated at first, preventing a correct estimate of the severity of large earthquake disasters in near-real time. The difference between first, **M**1, and later, **M**2, estimates, and the consequences for fatality estimates, are shown here for different magnitude bands from 6 to 9 plus and as a function of time.

This study does not address the differences of magnitude scales. **M**1 is simply defined as the first magnitude estimates that are distributed within minutes, based on worldwide network records. **M**2 is the magnitude that is listed later, within months, on international lists of earthquakes.

Data

The bulk of the data used consists of (1) the 79 alerts for earthquakes with **M** ≥ 7, issued by QLARM between October 2002 and January 2025, plus (2) for medium-size earthquakes, 6 ≤ **M** < 7, the 50 QLARM alerts issued during the years 2022, 2023, and 2024 were used to serve as a sample of the magnitude difference for moderate size earthquakes. To add more data from other years in this earthquake band would not add information, thus they were not included.

The initial **M**1 used is that issued by the National Earthquake Information Center of the USGS in near-real time and **M**2 is the final value, currently found on the website of "Significant Earthquakes" of the USGS. By comparing **M** values by the same institution, consistency is assured.

Supplemental data for nine relatively recent well-known great earthquakes (**M** ≥ 8) were added for which an original **M**1 could be found in the literature. These initial magnitude estimates are compared to today's values, **M**2, found on the USGS website of significant earthquakes.

Difference in Magnitude Estimates as a Function of Earthquake Size

The sum of **M** differences is shown in Figure 1 as a function of **M** rank. The range of given magnitudes is defined in that figure because several earthquakes have the same M. For medium-size earthquakes of **M** < 7 (events 1–50 in Fig. 1), the sum of the **M** differences oscillates around zero, indicating that the rapid initial **M** estimates are judged to have been correct by the final estimates in this magnitude band.

1. International Centre for Earth Simulation Foundation, Geneva, Switzerland, https://orcid.org/0000-0002-7250-3649 (MW)

*Corresponding author: max@maxwyss.ch

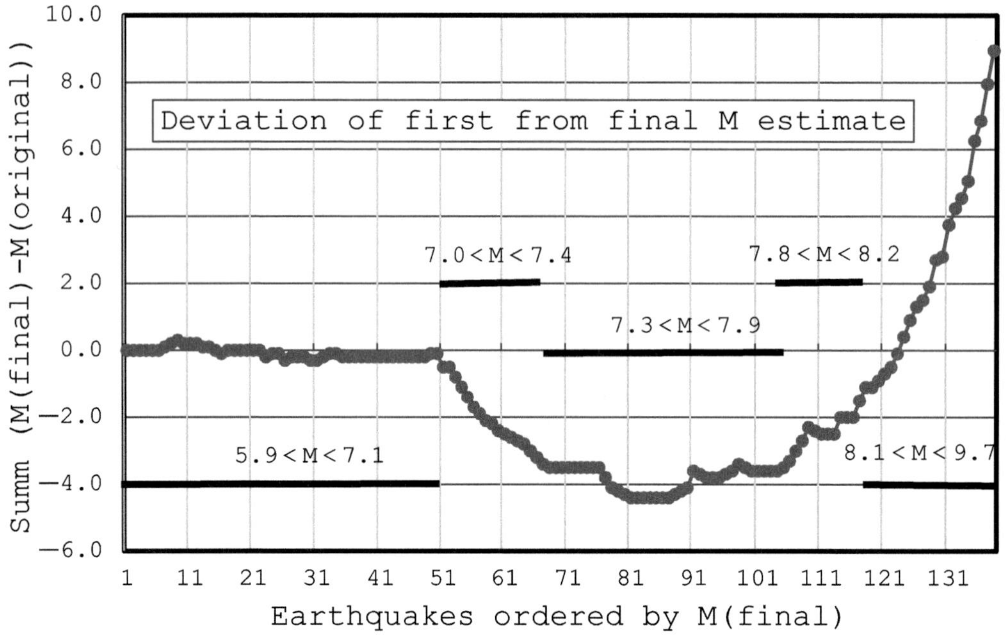

Figure 1. Sum of the difference of final, **M**2, minus initial, **M**1, magnitude estimates as a function of magnitude. Ranges of the same **M** are marked. In each **M** range, earthquakes are ordered as a function of time. Slopes provide a measure of the systematic difference between **M**1 and **M**2, a slope of 0 indicates no difference. Changes in slope mark changes in the relationship between **M**1 and **M**2.

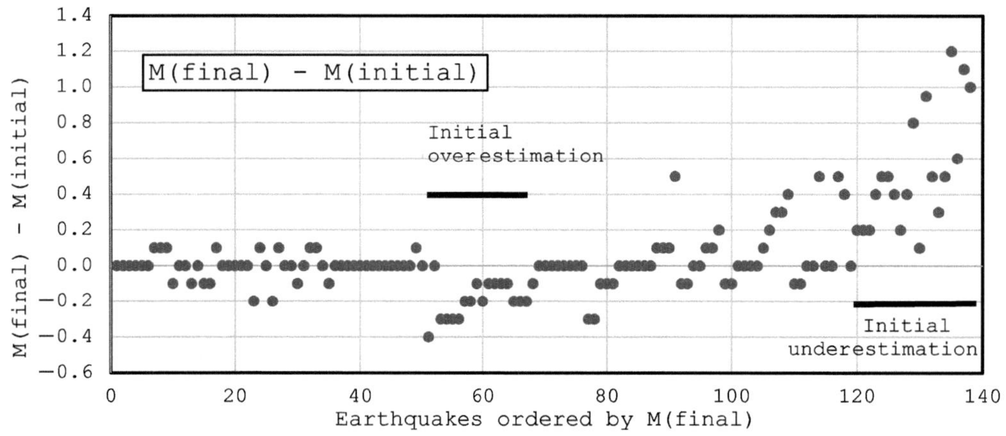

Figure 2. Difference between initial and final **M** of each earthquake as a function of event size. Sections of special interest are labeled. The abscissa has the same scale as in Figure 1, for which magnitude segments are explicitly defined.

The most important part of Figure 1 is the steep rise of the curve seen at the right in the band of **M** ≥ 8 (event 116 and larger). This means that for all great earthquakes the initial estimate **M**1 is smaller or equal to the final, more correct, estimate **M**2.

In the magnitude band 7.3 ≤ **M** ≤ 7.9 (events 68–107), the differences do not vary much and show no trend.

In the magnitude band of 7.1 ≤ **M** < 7.4 (events 51–67), initial estimates of **M** are consistently larger by about 0.2 magnitude units per earthquake. This is shown by a consistently negative trend in the sum for these magnitude differences (Fig. 1).

The individual magnitude differences **dM** are shown in Figure 2 as a function of earthquake size, as in Figure 1. This view is presented to draw attention to the segment between events 108 (**M** ≥ 7.8) and 189 (**M** ≤ 8.2), in which the initial estimate of **M** is sometimes correct and in other instances it is underestimated.

In Figure 2, it can also be seen that (1) **dM** is approximately correct within ±0.1 on average for earthquakes with **M** < 7 (numbers 1–50); (2) **dM** is consistently negative with an average value of −0.2 for the magnitude range 7.1 ≤ **M** ≤ 7.4 (events 51–67); (3) in the magnitude band 7.5 ≤ **M** ≤ 7.9 (events 68–104), the differences show no trend and are about ±0.1, on average; and (4) the preponderance of positive, and sometimes large, **dM** values is clear for **M** ≥ 8.2 earthquakes (event numbers larger than 119). However, between events 104 and 118 (magnitude band 7.9–8.2), some events show no differences, whereas for others **dM** shows positive values from 0.2 to 0.5 magnitude units.

Difference in Estimated Numbers of Fatalities Due to Differences in M Estimates

Alerts are important for first responders, even for moderate **M** earthquakes. In the example of the 2008 **M** 7.5 and 7.9 Wenchuan, China, earthquake according to initial and final estimates, respectively (original email from USGS and later values in significant earthquakes), the maps of mean damage (Fig. 3) that would be presented to first responders would be quite different depending on which **M** is known or accepted.

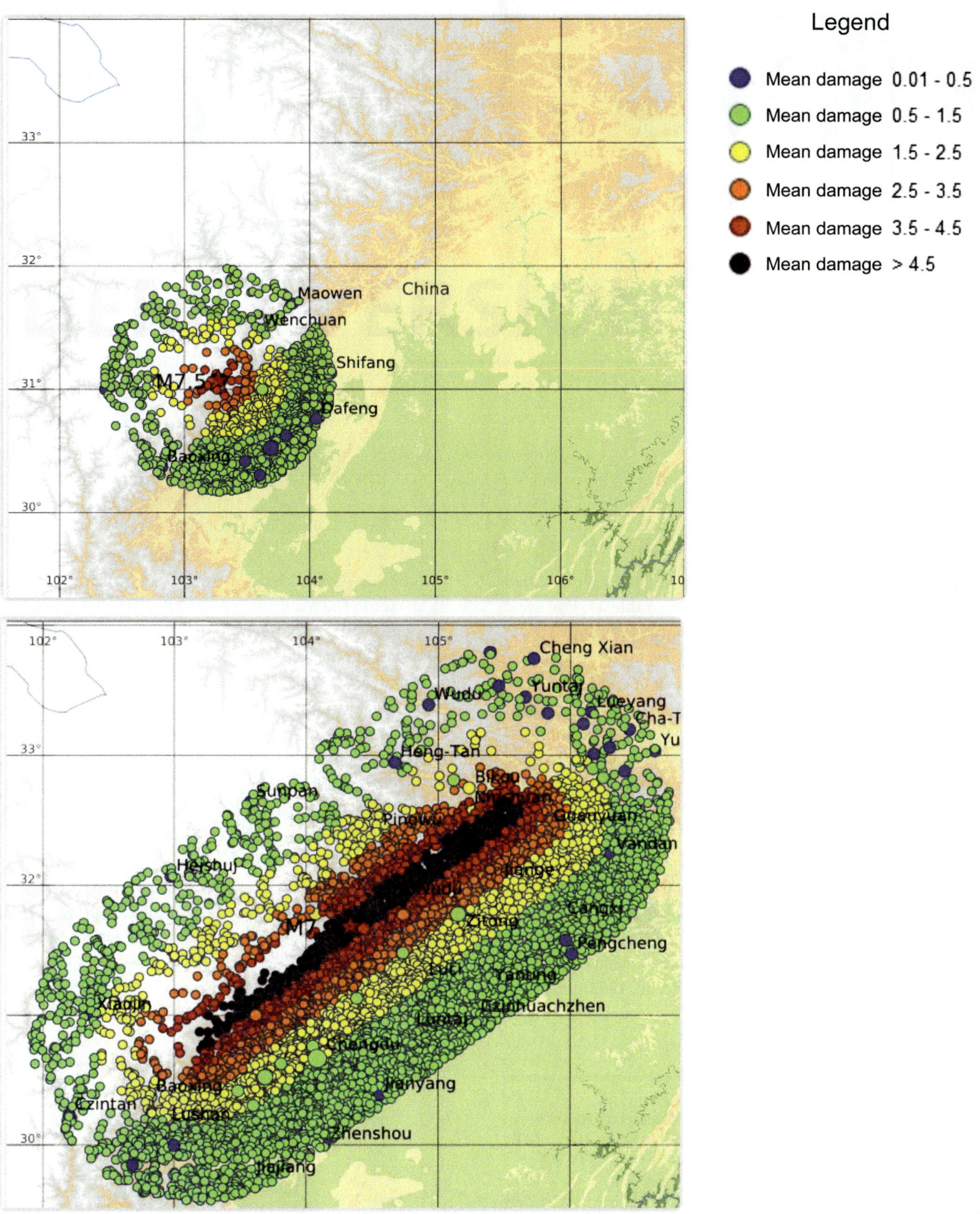

Figure 3. Maps of calculated mean damage in settlements (dots) for the 2008 Wenchuan, China, earthquake with two **M** estimates. The above results based on the **M** 7.5 estimate distributed by the U.S. Geological Survey (USGS) 27 min after the earthquake, yielding an estimate of 7700 fatalities on average, and below results based on an estimate of **M** 7.9 modeled as a line source, yielding an estimate of 199,000 fatalities on average. Although both Quake Loss Assessment for Response and Mitigation (QLARM) alerts would be judged as in the highest category (color red), the difference seen on the map for guiding rescuers is strong.

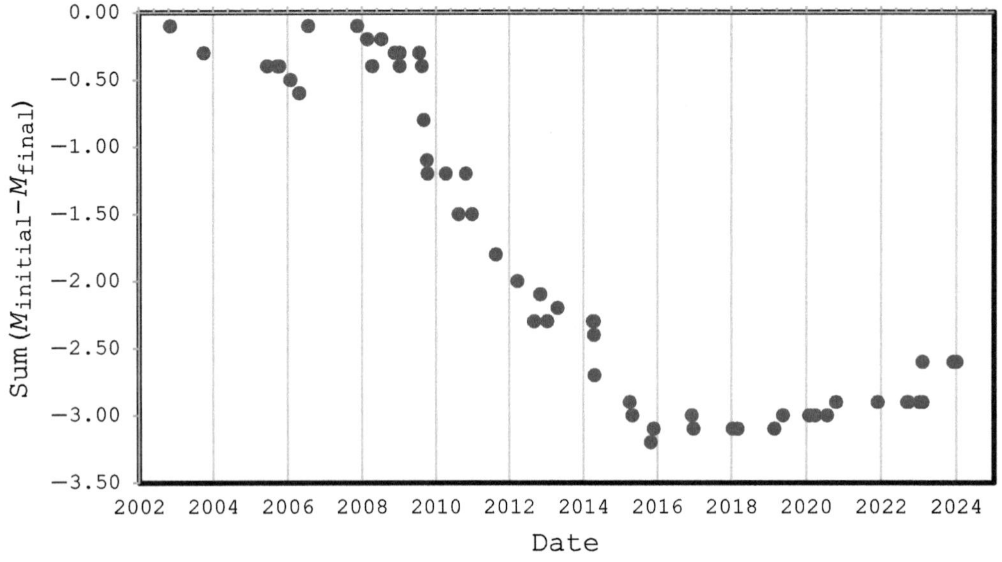

Figure 4. Sum of the difference d**M** = **M**1 − **M**2 as a function of time since late 2002 to 2024 for 7.0 ≤ **M**2 ≤ 7.8. This presentation makes it clear that for the period from May 2009 to 2016 M_{initial} was consistently underestimate, but from 2016 onward it is correct.

The difference between the numbers of fatalities calculated for the two cases is about a factor of 26 (Table 1). For great earthquakes (**M** 8–9), such large differences are standard.

Discussion

The consistently small difference between initial and final **M** estimates in the magnitude band **M** < 7 (Figs. 1, 2) is comforting: fatality estimates can be expected to be reliable and thus rescue plans are on a solid basis, when responding to alerts for moderate magnitude earthquakes.

For great earthquakes (**M** > 8.2), the **M**1 is always an underestimate (Figs. 1, 2), only it is not known by how much, at first. It is important to realize this fact, when planning a response to earthquake disasters in case of great magnitudes. The time it takes for the correct **M** to become known varies. The great Alaska earthquake of 28 March 1964 was understood to have been an **M** 8.1 rupture (e.g., Wyss and Brune, 1967) for 49 yr, until its **M** was updated to **M**2 9.2 on 7 November 2016 (see Data and Resources). In this case, the difference was 1.1 units on the logarithmic **M** scale. Although near-real-time alerts for great earthquakes are always based on underestimates of M, QLARM has classified all recent such cases as red alerts.

It is encouraging to observe that for earthquakes with **M** < 7, the rapid estimates **M**1 are always within 0.2 units of the final **M**2 determination. This means that the extents of disasters for **M** < 7 earthquakes are correctly estimated as far as **M** is concerned. However, mislocations of the epicenter can cause large errors in fatality estimates, even for moderate-size earthquakes with correct estimates of M. That problem is discussed elsewhere (e.g., Wyss *et al.*, 2006; Wyss and Rosset, 2024).

Magnitude differences, d**M** = **M**1−**M**2, for potentially fatal earthquakes in the magnitude band 7.0 ≤ **M** ≤ 7.8 are shown in Figure 4 as the sum as a function of time. In this presentation, it is seen that d**M** was slightly negative, but constant between the end of the year 2002 and about 2010, from 2010 to 2016 d**M** was consistently negative by 0.13 units, average, and since 2016 d**M** = 0, approximately. For operators who need to estimate numbers of fatalities based on **M**1, it is comforting to know that since 2016, **M**1 given initially, is correct, not expected to be changed later. Therefore, for this magnitude band, fatality estimates based on **M**1 may be trusted.

The project GOBEYOND aims at moving response to natural disasters to a higher efficiency level by involving local civil protection groups. GOBEYOND focuses on speeding up quantitative estimates of the extents of disasters in western Mediterranean countries. The disaster estimating services by QLARM and PAGER are based on teleseismic wave arrivals, which mean their estimates of **M**1, coordinates and depth become available within 8 and 22 min, respectively. However, epicenter estimates based on local to regional seismograph networks, for which the recorded waves travel much shorter distances, become available within 2–3 min (Wyss and Rosset, 2024, their table 6 and fig. 5). This means that automatic earthquake disaster alerts could be issued within about 5 min, if regional seismological observatories of the world would collaborate with QLARM and PAGER. Opinions differ on whether or not a speed up of earthquake alerts by about 15 min is worth the increased risk of errors.

The largest magnitude earthquakes have the potential to generate the greatest disasters, but their true **M** is not recognized, at first (Figs. 1, 2). Civil defense should therefore be instructed to put special procedures in place in case of

TABLE 1
Fatality Estimates by QLARM (Average) Using the Real-Time Epicenter and M1 (7.5) Estimates (Fig. 3a) and the Final Line Source Estimate with M2 (7.9), Both Magnitude Estimates by the USGS

Wenchuan M Data Source	M	Fat(Average)
USGS real-time message	7.5	7,700
USGS significant earthquakes	7.9	199,000

QLARM, Quake Loss Assessment for Response and Mitigation; USGS, U.S. Geological Survey.

near-real-time alerts for earthquakes with **M** > 7.5 because consequences may be underestimated, implying potentially differences in the locations of great damage as seen in Figure 3.

The most promising way to derive **M**1 for great earthquakes, in my opinion, is the Finder analysis (e.g., Böse *et al.*, 2012, 2024). In this method, the true **M** and rupture length of great earthquakes have been demonstrated to be obtainable within the seconds it takes for the rupture to finish. These analyses have been done after-the-fact, that is, years after the earthquakes, with the purpose to demonstrate the capability of the method. However, two conditions are required to implement this method in real time: (1) local to regional strong-motion stations must be available, which is fulfilled in only a few countries; and (2) an operator must be willing to perform the analysis within minutes of the initial alert, but such people are not available in the majority of earthquake-prone countries.

Another powerful method to determine fault length and location, and hence the true M, is satellite interferometry for which observations before and after the event are required. The resulting maps of the ruptures are detailed, but in the typical case of the Türkiye earthquake of 6 February 2023 a suitable satellite image became available on 10 February 2023, only (see Data and Resources), that is, four days after the disaster, at a time when no victims can be found alive beneath collapsed buildings.

For smaller earthquakes, the exact location, rather than the rupture lengths of earthquakes, can be critical in estimating the number of fatalities. For the 26 December 2003 **M** 6.6 Bam earthquake, the first available epicenters were approximately 10 km too far west in the desert, whereas satellite interferometry would have revealed the correct location of the rupture to within meters, if available rapidly after the earthquake. This difference in epicenter estimates maps into a great difference in estimated numbers of fatalities in this case: instead of about 500, more than 20,000 fatalities would have been estimated (Wyss *et al.*, 2006), much closer to the ultimate approximative report of 25,000.

Conclusions

Information to consider concerning magnitude quality by seismologists issuing earthquake alerts in near-real time, by first responders and authorities involved in rescue is the following.

- Magnitude band **M** < 7: initial **M**1 estimates are correct within approximately ±0.1 magnitude units.
- Magnitude band 7.5 ≤ **M** ≤ 7.9: initial **M**1 estimates are correct within approximately ±0.2 magnitude units.
- Magnitude band 7.9 ≤ **M** ≤ 8.2: sometimes initial **M**1 values are correct, sometimes they underestimate the true M.
- Magnitude band **M** > 8.2: initial **M**1 values are always underestimates, sometimes by large amounts.

Rapid fatality estimates for **M** > 8 earthquakes are of first-rate importance. However, their magnitudes, and hence the likely numbers of fatalities generated by them, are initially underestimated. This is due to the fact that **M** is based on amplitudes of waves with lengths of about 5–50 km, much shorter than the rupture lengths of great earthquakes, which are 300 km and longer. M_s is based, by definition, on amplitudes of exactly 20 s period Rayleigh waves. Estimates of M_w would help to estimate fatalities more correctly, if they became available rapidly. First responders and governments must realize that most likely rapid calculations of numbers of fatalities in great earthquakes are underestimates. Even if not giving a full picture of the seriousness of a disaster due to **M** > 8 earthquakes in the first minutes, red alerts issued for such events must be taken seriously and followed up. Although first responders must mobilize immediately, the full extent of the disaster will become known as they deploy in the area.

Data and Resources

All data used in this article came from published sources listed in the references. The **M**2 of the great Alaska earthquake of 28 March 1964 is available at https://earthquake.usgs.gov/earthquakes/eventpage/official19640328033616_30/executive. The information on the 6 February 2023 Pazarcik-Kahramanmaraş, Türkiye, earthquake is available at https://earthquake.usgs.gov/earthquakes/eventpage/us6000jllz/finite-fault. Both websites were last accessed in April 2015.

Declaration of Competing Interests

The author acknowledges that there are no conflicts of interest recorded.

Acknowledgments

The author thanks M. Speiser, M. Böse, Ph. Rosset, T. Zadeh, and S. Tolis and especially Mustafa Comoglu for helpful suggestions. This work was funded in part by the Swiss State Secretariat for Education, Research, and Innovation, in the framework of the European Union (EU) Research Project GOBEYOND under the umbrella of the EU Horizon 17 309 Europe program Grant Number 101121135 and in part by the International Centre for Earth Simulation (ICES) Foundation, Geneva.

References

Böse, M., S. Ceylas, J. Andrews, F. Massin, J. Clinton, J. K. Saunders, O. Tatar, and M. Türkoğlu (2024). Rapid finite-fault models for the 2023 Mw 7.8 Kahramanmaraş, Türkiye, earthquake sequence, *Seismol. Res. Lett.* **95,** no. 3, 1–18, doi: 10.1785/0220230426.

Böse, M., T. H. Heaton, and E. Hauksson (2012). Real-time Finite Fault Rupture Detector (FinDer) for large earthquakes, *Geophys. J. Int.* **191,** no. 2, 803–812.

Wyss, M., and J. N. Brune (1967). The Alaska earthquake of 28 March 1964: A complex multiple rupture, *Bull. Seismol. Soc. Am.* **57,** no. 5, 1017–1023.

Wyss, M., and P. Rosset (2024). Rapid fatality estimates after earthquakes in Western Mediterranean countries for first response, *Bull. Seismol. Soc. Am.* **114,** 2791–2803, doi: 10.1785/0120240078.

Wyss, M., R. Wang, J. Zschau, and Y. Xia (2006). Earthquake loss estimates in near real-time, *Eos Trans. AGU* 477–479.

Manuscript received 5 March 2025
Published online 13 August 2025

Clock Error Detection for Decade-Long Seismic Monitoring Network in Marapi Volcano, Indonesia

Mingye Feng[1], Shengji Wei[*1,2,3], Benoit Taisne[1,3], Yukuan Chen[1], Christina Widiwijayanti[1], and Sulistiyani[4]

Abstract

Accurate seismometer timing is crucial for seismic studies that rely on arrival time, such as earthquake relocation and subsurface velocity change monitoring—both are essential for understanding volcanic systems. To assess the timing accuracy in the decadal seismic records from the monitoring network at the Marapi volcano, Indonesia, we apply both teleseismic *P*-wave waveform cross-correlation function and ambient seismic noise cross-correlation function methods. These methods derive consistent clock error estimates, revealing both constant and nearly linear drifting time errors at two stations, PCAK and GGSL. Our results indicate a ~1 s constant time error at PCAK for approximately nine months (2019–2020) and at GGSL for about one month (2018). In addition, at both stations, time drifted nearly linearly over three to five months in 2016 at a rate of ~4 to 5 ms/day. Synthetic tests show that an ~1 s constant time shift in current network configuration leads to an ~1.5 km depth error for an event at ~10 km depth beneath the crater. The linearly drifting time error causes an artificial downward migration of seismicity that should remain stationary, potentially leading to misinterpretations of magma transport and storage variations. Timing error estimations are essential for future seismic studies using this dataset, and the workflow developed here can be generalized to other long-term seismic monitoring networks.

Cite this article as Feng, M., S. Wei, B. Taisne, Y. Chen, C. Widiwijayanti, and Sulistiyani (2025). Clock Error Detection for Decade-Long Seismic Monitoring Network in Marapi Volcano, Indonesia, *Seismol. Res. Lett.* **97**, 86–99, doi: 10.1785/0220250143.

Supplemental Material

Introduction

Accurate absolute timing of seismic record is fundamental for seismic studies, such as earthquake location, travel-time tomography, subsurface velocity variation monitoring, and temporal change analysis of Earth's core (e.g., Ringler *et al.*, 2021; Yang *et al.*, 2022; Takano and Nishida, 2024). To acquire high-precision timing, seismometers are designed to synchronize with the atomic clocks of Global Navigation Satellite System (GNSS) satellites (Ringler *et al.*, 2021). However, when the GNSS signal reception is lost, seismometers rely on their internal quartz clocks, which naturally drift over time, leading to timing errors (Le *et al.*, 2018; Ringler *et al.*, 2021; Cabieces *et al.*, 2024). Although this issue is more common for ocean-bottom seismometers (OBSs; Le *et al.*, 2018; Abbas *et al.*, 2023; Cabieces *et al.*, 2024), significant time errors have also been reported in land-based seismometers for various reasons (Ringler *et al.*, 2021; Sens-Schönfelder, 2008; Yang *et al.*, 2022; Hirose and Ueda, 2023).

Timing issues are particularly critical for seismic monitoring networks around volcanoes, which typically consist of multiple expensive broadband seismometers and operate over long periods at high cost. These networks are designed to capture microseismic signals and low-frequency earthquakes associated with volcanic unrest (Shapiro *et al.*, 2017; Hotovec-Ellis *et al.*, 2018; Sigmundsson *et al.*, 2022), detect precursory velocity changes associated with volcanic eruptions (Ratdomopurbo and Poupinet, 1995; Liu *et al.*, 2022; Kupres *et al.*, 2024), or image the magmatic plumbing architecture (Huang *et al.*, 2015; Koulakov *et al.*, 2016; Li *et al.*, 2023). These methods rely on precise timing of seismic phase arrivals; however, significant timing issues have often been reported in volcanic monitoring networks (Sens-Schönfelder, 2008; Hirose and Ueda, 2023). Such timing errors can create false spatiotemporal variation patterns of seismicity, potentially leading to

1. Earth Observatory of Singapore, Nanyang Technological University, Singapore, Singapore, https://orcid.org/0000-0002-4960-4791 (MF); https://orcid.org/0000-0002-0319-0714 (SW); https://orcid.org/0000-0002-3205-6485 (BT); https://orcid.org/0009-0004-6646-6900 (YC); https://orcid.org/0000-0001-8505-5200 (CW); 2. Key Laboratory of Deep Petroleum Intelligent Exploration and Development, Institute of Geology and Geophysics, Chinese Academy of Sciences, Beijing, China; 3. Asian School of the Environment, Nanyang Technological University, Singapore, Singapore; 4. Center of Volcanology and Geologic Hazard Mitigation (CVGHM), Bandung, Indonesia, https://orcid.org/0000-0003-3626-5388 (Sulistiyani)

*Corresponding author: shjwei@gmail.com

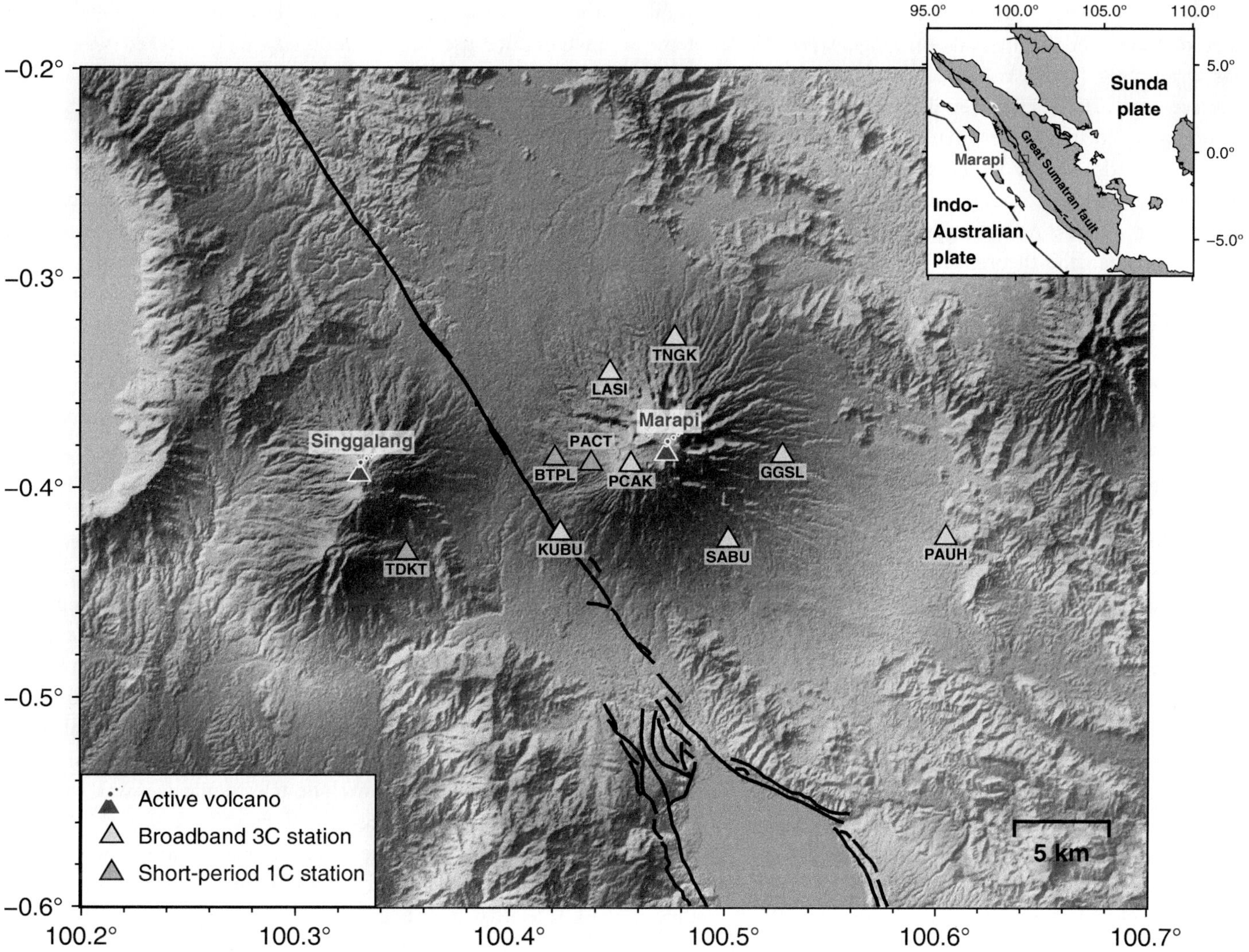

Figure 1. Seismometer distribution for Marapi volcano monitoring network. Yellow and green triangles show three-component broadband stations and one-component short-period stations, respectively. The insert in top right corner shows the location of the Marapi volcanic zone (red box) and the tectonic background of the Sumatran subduction zone. The color version of this figure is available only in the electronic edition.

misinterpretation of the magmatic plumbing system and the underlying magma storage dynamics (Syracuse *et al.*, 2017).

Marapi volcano is a typical arc volcano located in the western Sumatra, Indonesia, where the Indo-Australian plate subducts beneath the Sunda plate (Fig. 1). In recent years, Marapi volcano has become increasingly active, with two VEI-2 and three VEI-1 eruption events since 2015 (Global Volcanism Program, 2024). The volcano's most recent eruption began in December 2023 and has continued for over a year, resulting in dozens of casualties and posing significant hazards to the surrounding communities (Global Volcanism Program, 2024). To monitor its volcanic activities, the Earth Observatory of Singapore (EOS) and Indonesia's Center for Volcanology and Geological Hazard Mitigation (CVGHM) have collaborated to maintain a seismic monitoring network around the volcano since December 2014 (Table S1, available in the supplemental material to this article). These onsite observations provide a high-quality dataset for detecting precursory signals of eruptions and imaging the transcrustal magmatic system (Nurfiani *et al.*, 2021). However, potential timing errors in the records may hinder further seismic analysis, including local earthquake relocation and seismic velocity change monitoring (e.g., Takano and Nishida, 2024).

To detect time errors, various seismic methods have been proposed, including those based on collocated sensors (Ringler *et al.*, 2021), moderate magnitude repeating earthquakes (Yang *et al.*, 2022), teleseismic waveforms (Xie *et al.*, 2018), and ambient noise (Stehly *et al.*, 2007). Because of the absence of collocated sensors in the Marapi network, the first method is not applicable. The second method, which relies on repeating earthquakes, is also limited because such events are rare and provide insufficient temporal sampling. The most widely used approach is the ambient noise cross-correlation function (NCCF) method. This method identifies time errors based on the broken symmetry of NCCFs averaged over several days, daily, or subdaily intervals, offering near continuous temporal sampling (Hable *et al.*, 2018; Hirose and Ueda, 2023; Cabieces *et al.*, 2024). However, this method may produce fluctuations in clock error estimate particularly for long-term seismic records, due to periodical migrations of microseism sources (e.g., Stehly *et al.*, 2007) or sudden changes of the dominant noise sources. Another approach is based on the comparison between the theoretical and observed *P*-wave arrival times to identify the presence of time error (Le *et al.*, 2018; Abbas *et al.*, 2023). However, this method cannot allow for precise corrections because theoretical *P*-wave arrivals can have bias of several seconds due to imperfect velocity model used. Teleseismic *P*-waveform cross-correction functions (PCCFs) have been used to estimate time errors of closely spaced seismometers with greater precision (Xie *et al.*, 2018; Zhu *et al.*, 2019). Despite its high accuracy, this method is typically used to provide auxiliary information for short-term seismic deployments, due to the limited number of high-quality teleseismic waveforms (Xie *et al.*, 2018; Zhu *et al.*, 2019). Given that both the PCCF and NCCF methods have their own disadvantages, it is critical to combine both methods to minimize the overall limitations, which, to our knowledge, has not been conducted.

In this study, we jointly use the NCCF and PCCF methods to evaluate clock error for records from the Marapi volcano seismic network. Different from previous studies that treat PCCF estimates as auxiliary or preliminary information, we demonstrate that the PCCF method provides time error estimates comparable to those obtained from the NCCF method. Furthermore, results from the two independent methods cross validate each other, enhancing reliability of estimation while reducing bias from their inherent uncertainties. In the following sections, we first introduce the seismic data used in this analysis, describe the methodology, then show our results and followed by discussions and conclusions.

Data

We analyze data from 10 seismometers, with records between January 2015 and September 2024. These stations were jointly installed by EOS, Nanyang Technological University, Singapore, and CVGHM, Indonesia. Seven stations are equipped with three-component broadband sensors, whereas the remaining three are one-component short-period stations that record only the vertical component (Fig. 1; Table S1). The network was established in late 2014 and has been operating with a sampling rate of 100 Hz.

For the teleseismic method, we select earthquakes with magnitudes ≥5.7 and epicentral distance between 28° and 92°. This magnitude threshold ensures a high signal-to-noise ratio (SNR) of direct *P* waveforms. The waveforms are first trimmed between −50 and 150 s relative to the theoretical *P*-wave arrival time calculated by the TauP software based on the IASP91 global velocity model (Kennett and Engdahl, 1991). The data are then downsampled to 20 Hz. For the ambient noise method, we use three-component daily stacked waveforms, excluding the days without continuous records.

Method

Teleseismic *P*-wave cross-correlation method

We measure time drift by performing cross correlation between a reference station and other stations. For the same teleseismic events, the ray paths to these stations are highly similar, resulting in almost identical waveforms (Fig. 2). Without clock errors, the time lag derived from PCCFs should remain a small constant, reflecting minor velocity differences between the ray paths (Fig. 3). However, in the presence of a clock error, the time lag deviates from the constant, which can be used to estimate the time error (Fig. 4).

The teleseismic waveforms are preprocessed by removing the mean, detrending, and tapering. Instrument responses are removed for short-period stations to expand the frequency range. The waveforms are then band-pass filtered between 0.05 and 0.5 Hz to balance resolution and the SNR (e.g., Wang *et al.*, 2016). We only use the vertical component because it generally exhibits larger amplitudes than horizontal components for the *P* waves. For cross-correlation calculation, the time axis is set between −20 and 20 s relative to the first *P*-wave arrival. Time lag estimates with cross-correlation coefficients (CCCs) ≤ 0.70 are discarded. We also exclude teleseismic *P* waves with low SNR (<2.5), in which SNR is defined as $\sqrt{|S|/|N|}$, with $|S|$ and $|N|$ representing the quadratic sum of amplitudes within the signal window of −2 to 6 s and the noise window of −10 to −2 s relative to the theoretical *P*-wave arrival, respectively. Final time error estimations are determined using a weighted averaging scheme (Hable *et al.*, 2018) (Fig. 5),

$$E(t) = \frac{\sum_{i=1}^{N} c_i^2(t)e_i(t)}{\sum_{i=1}^{N} c_i^2(t)}, C(t) = \frac{\sum_{i=1}^{N} c_i^3(t)}{\sum_{i=1}^{N} c_i^2(t)}, \quad (1)$$

in which N is the number of estimates for a teleseismic event at time t, c is the CCC used as a weighting factor, e is the time error estimated from each station pairs, and E and C are the weighted averaged time error and CCC, respectively.

Ambient seismic noise cross-correlation method

NCCFs, calculated between station pairs, are primarily sourced from background oceanic microseism. If there is no timing errors or temporal variations in velocity, the causal and acausal components will be symmetric in arrival time over time (Shapiro and Campillo, 2004; Yao *et al.*, 2006; Stehly *et al.*, 2007). Whereas, the presence of a clock error disrupts the expected symmetry, allowing the error to be estimated using cross correlation of the NCCFs (Stehly *et al.*, 2007; Fig. 6). We compute NCCFs on a daily basis, providing higher temporal resolution than the PCCF method (Abbas *et al.*, 2023) and the previous studies that stack NCCFs over approximately

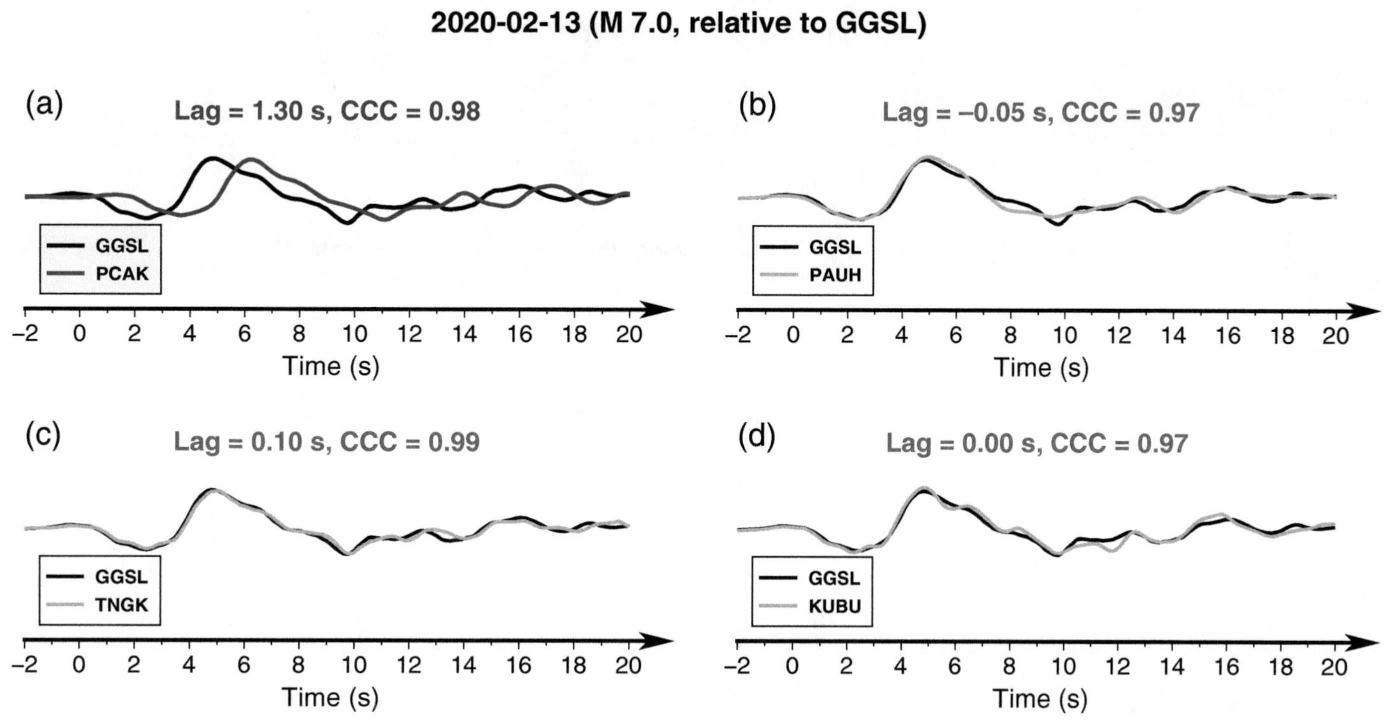

Figure 2. Teleseismic waveform cross-correlation method to detect time error, using GGSL as the reference station. Panels (a–d) show the cross correlation between GGSL and PCAK, PAUH, TNGK, and KUBU stations, respectively. The waveforms are normalized. PCAK station shows a time lag (Lag) of 1.30 s with the waveform highlighted in red. CCC, cross-correlation coefficient. The color version of this figure is available only in the electronic edition.

10 days (e.g., Stehly *et al.*, 2007; Hable *et al.*, 2018; Le *et al.*, 2018). We calculate NCCFs for north-to-north (NN), east-to-east (EE), and vertical-to-vertical (ZZ) components between station pairs, and only use those that have CCCs > 0.7 in the analysis (Figs. 7, 8). To compute NCCFs, we first segment daily seismic records into 60 min windows with a 15 min overlap. The data are then preprocessed with mean removing, detrending, and tapering. To suppress transient signals, we apply time-domain normalization and perform spectral whitening in the 0.01–5 Hz frequency range using a running-mean method (Bensen *et al.*, 2007). We discard segments with the maximum amplitude larger than 10 times the standard deviation in amplitude and with zero or problematic records. Cross-correlation functions between temporally overlapping segments are computed in the frequency domain. We apply a 40 s shift at each fold along the time axis. Finally, we stack all segments to generate daily NCCFs. To increase the SNR, we apply a band-pass filter between 0.1 and 0.2 Hz. The NCCF symmetry is then analyzed over one year using cross correlation with 10 s maximum allowed time shift, referencing to the stacked NCCF during the periods without significant time shifts, as identified by the PCCF method. Outliers are removed, and interpolation is applied when the NCCF measurements are less scattered. The final estimates are obtained using the same weighted averaging scheme (equation 1) as used for the PCCF method. The interpolated points are marked at the lowest CCC of 0.7 (Fig. 8).

Cross validation and joint estimation

The PCCF and NCCF methods each have distinct advantages and inherent limitations. The PCCF method relies on event waveforms and therefore is computationally efficient. In contrast, the NCCF method, based on continuous noise waveforms, is more computationally expensive, especially for long-term monitoring networks and large station numbers. In this study, we first apply the PCCF method to check potential clock issues and assess data quality across all stations throughout the entire study period. Then, we apply the NCCF method to data acquired in a selected time window to estimate clock error with higher temporal resolution. NCCF results sometimes exhibit fluctuations due to periodical variations of ambient noise sources (Stehly *et al.*, 2007; Abbas *et al.*, 2023). To ensure reliable estimates, we compare estimates from the two independent methods to check their consistency. The final estimate is defined as the average of the results from the two methods to mitigate their inherent uncertainties. The onset and the end of timing issues are primarily determined by the NCCF method, leveraging on its higher temporal resolution. Combining the two methods presents advantages over single-method analysis: less computational cost, high-temporal resolution, robust cross validation, and improved accuracy at the same time.

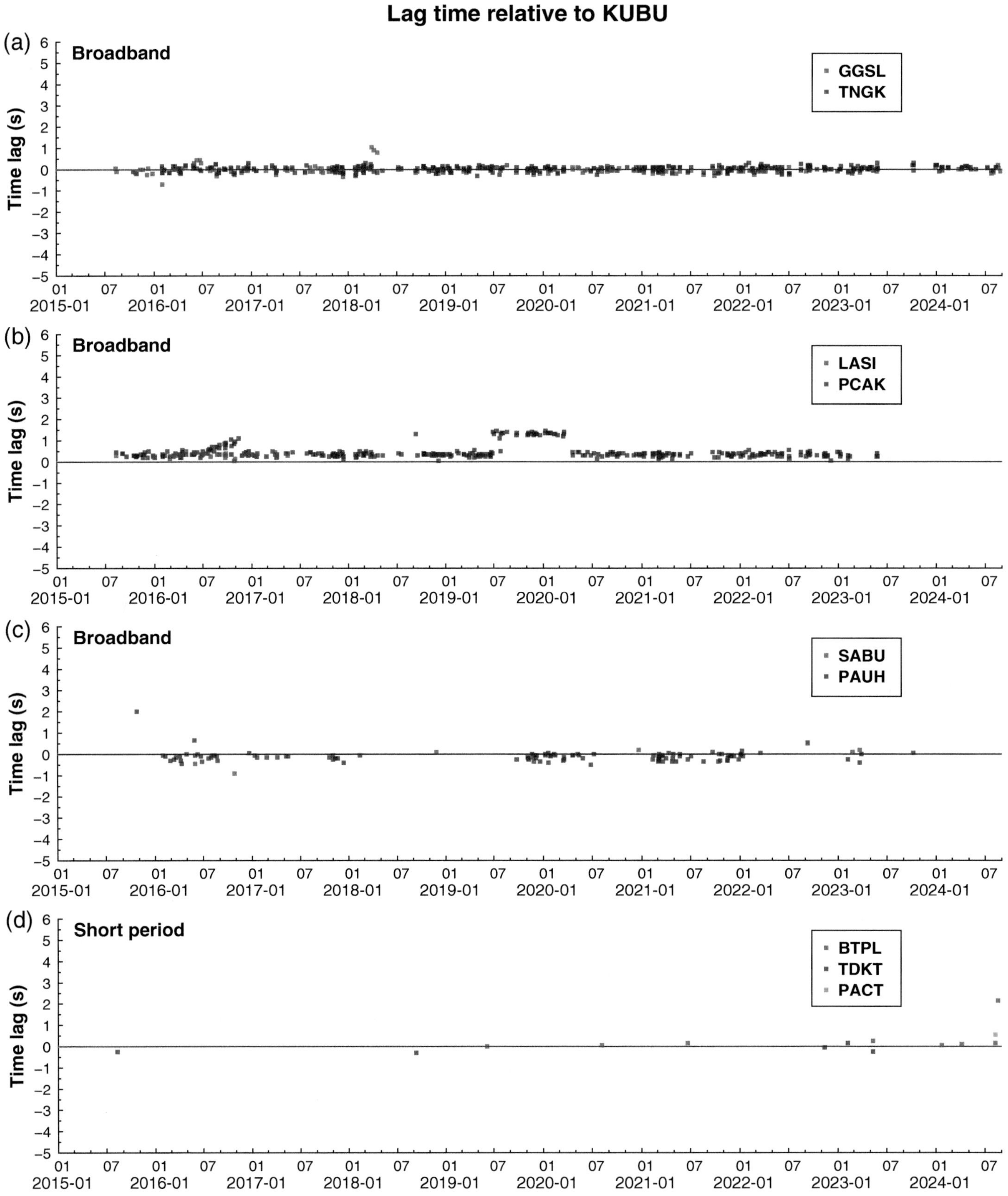

Figure 3. Time lag temporal variations derived by the *P*-waveform cross-correction function (PCCF) method with station KUBU as the reference. Panels (a–c) show results of broadband stations, whereas panel (d) shows results of short-period stations. Different stations in each subplot are marked in different colors. The color version of this figure is available only in the electronic edition.

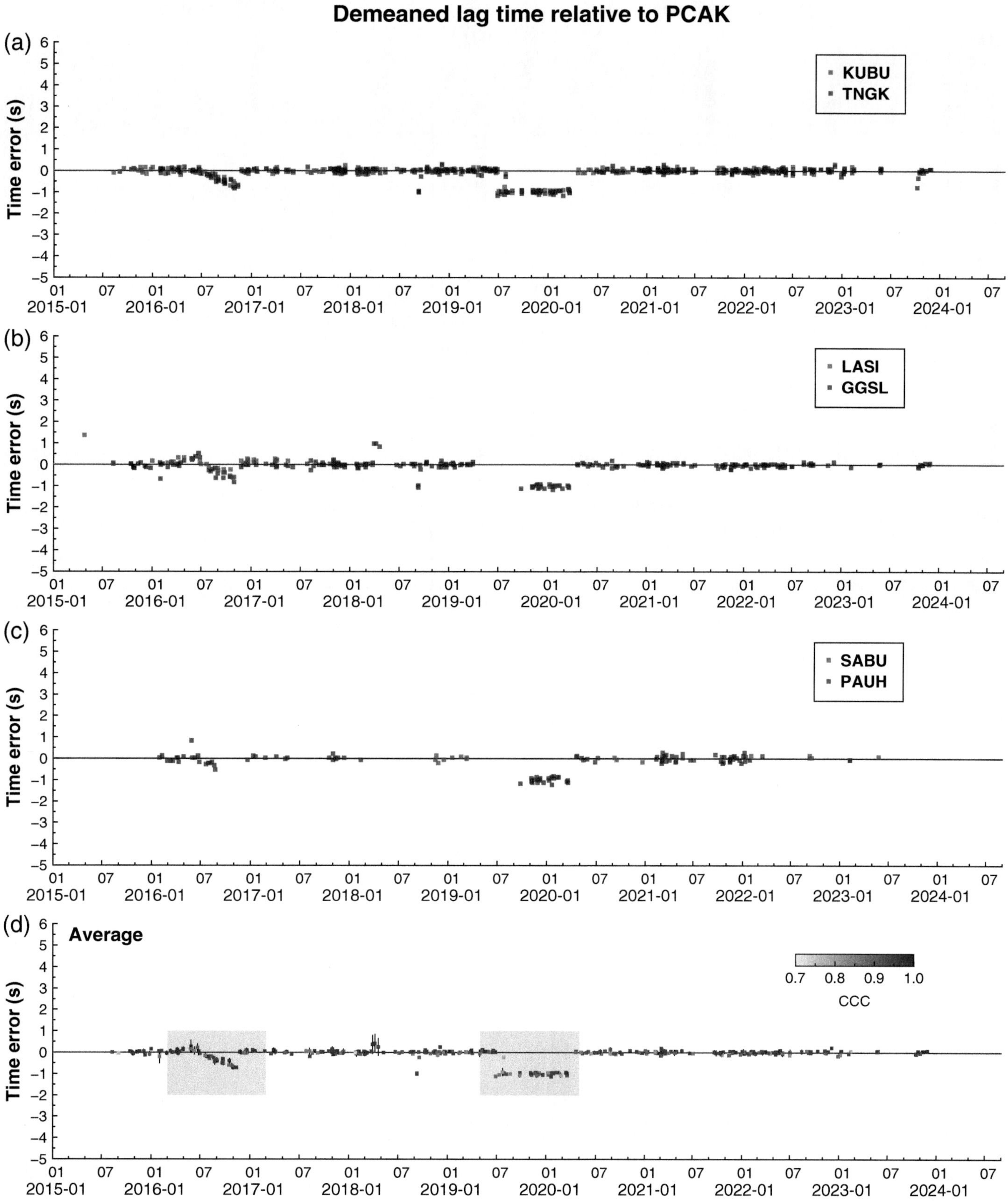

Figure 4. (a–c) Time errors estimated by the PCCF method with the problematic station PCAK as the reference station. (d) The weighted average of time error estimates, calculated after outliers removed across different station pairs. Standard deviations for each estimate are indicated by black bars. The color bar shows the weighted averaged CCCs. Blue boxes mark the identified time errors. The color version of this figure is available only in the electronic edition.

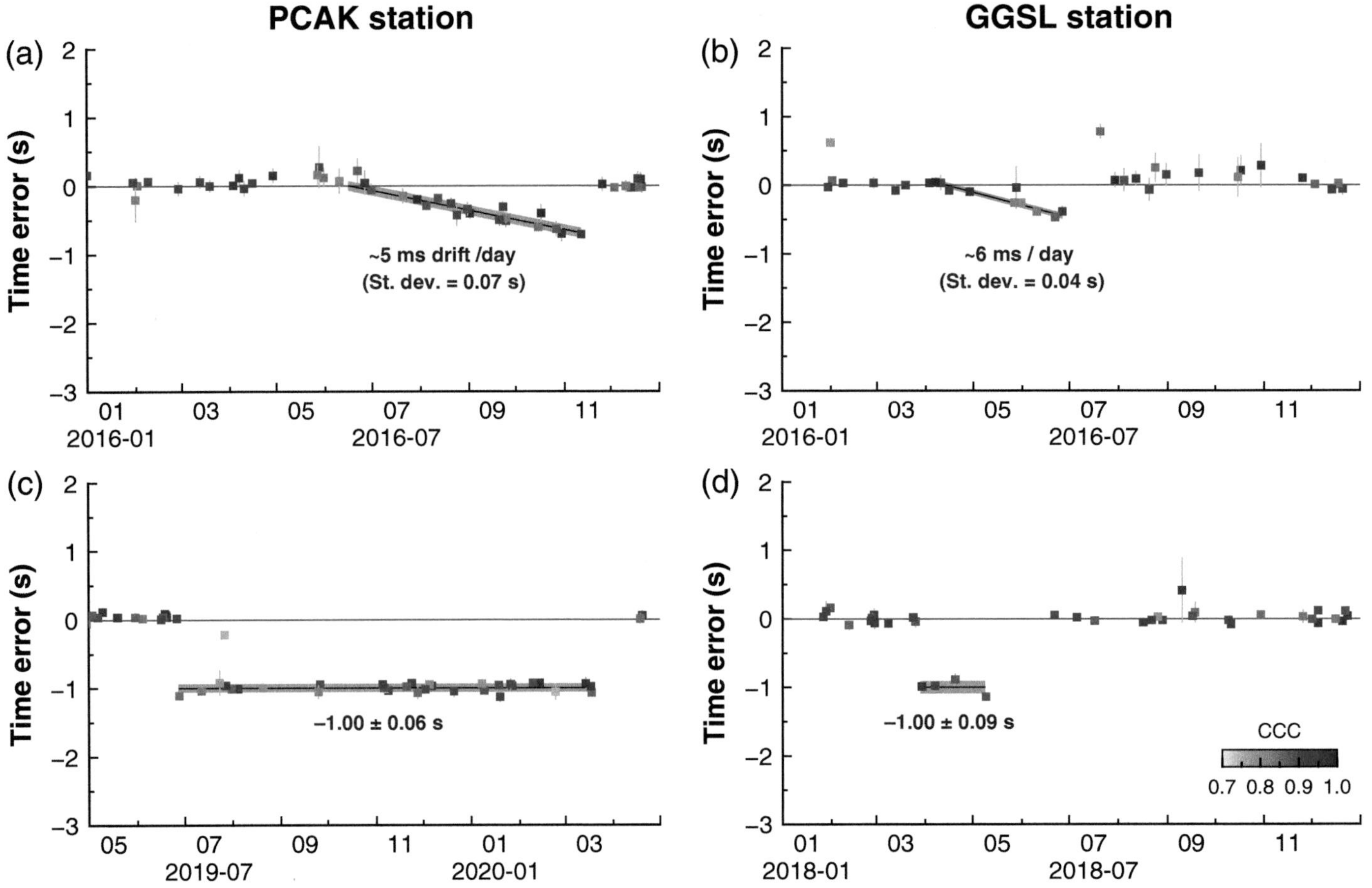

Figure 5. Two types of time errors detected at (a,c) PCAK and (b,d) GGSL stations, marked by blue lines. (a,b) The drifting time error fitted by the least-squares linear regression method. (c,d) The constant time error. CCC is shown by the color bar. The color version of this figure is available only in the electronic edition.

Results

Figure 3 and Figure S1 show the time lag measurements relative to stations KUBU and TNGK, respectively. The time lag between the two stations mainly keeps a constant, indicating that the two stations are free from significant timing issues. Therefore, KUBU and TNGK are set as reference stations to identify time errors of other stations (Fig. 3a, Fig. S1a). Both reference stations consistently reveal potential time errors in 2016 and 2018 at GGSL, and in 2016 and during 2019–2020 at PCAK. To estimate the time errors, we set PCAK and GGSL as reference stations and cross correlate with other broadband stations, removing the mean time lag to isolate the timing discrepancies (Fig. 4, Fig. S2). At PCAK, PCCF estimates by different station pairs all show a gradual drifting time error during 2016 and a constant time error in 2019–2020 (Fig. 4). Similar time error patterns are observed at GGSL (Fig. S2). Using weighted averaging and least-squares linear fitting methods, we show that PCAK and GGSL experienced time drifts of ~5 ms/day (July to November 2016) and ~6 ms/day (May to June 2016), respectively (Fig. 5). In addition, both stations show a nearly constant time error of ~1 s for PCAK from June 2019 to March 2020 and for GGSL in April 2018, with standard deviation of 0.06–0.09 s. Such nearly constant time offset of ~1 s has also been detected in previous studies (Stehly *et al.*, 2007; Xia *et al.*, 2015).

The number of the selected teleseismic events is 5–15 per month. This uneven and insufficient temporal sampling makes it difficult to pinpoint the exact onset and end of clock errors. To improve temporal resolution, we apply the NCCF method, which provides daily-scale resolution (Fig. 6, Fig. S3). The NCCF method reveals a constant time error of 0.96 ± 0.07 s at PCAK between 27 June 2019 and 28 March 2020, and a 0.99 ± 0.16 s constant time error at GGSL between 28 March 2018 and 03 May 2018. In addition, the NCCF method detects a drifting time error of ~4 ms/day at PCAK from 06 July 2016 to 24 November 2016, and ~5 ms/day at GGSL from 01 April 2016 to 01 July 2016. The standard deviations are 0.06 s at PCAK and 0.13 s at GGSL. The higher standard deviation at GGSL likely results from poorer SNRs in NCCF (Fig. 7, Fig. S4). The NCCF estimates at both stations exhibit fluctuations (Figs. 7, 8, and Figs. S4, S5), which could be associated with periodic variations of oceanic microseism sources (Stehly *et al.*, 2007). The NCCF between stations KUBU and PCAK exhibits a drastic shift of the symmetry around 16 October 2019 (Fig. 6), which could be related to a sudden change of

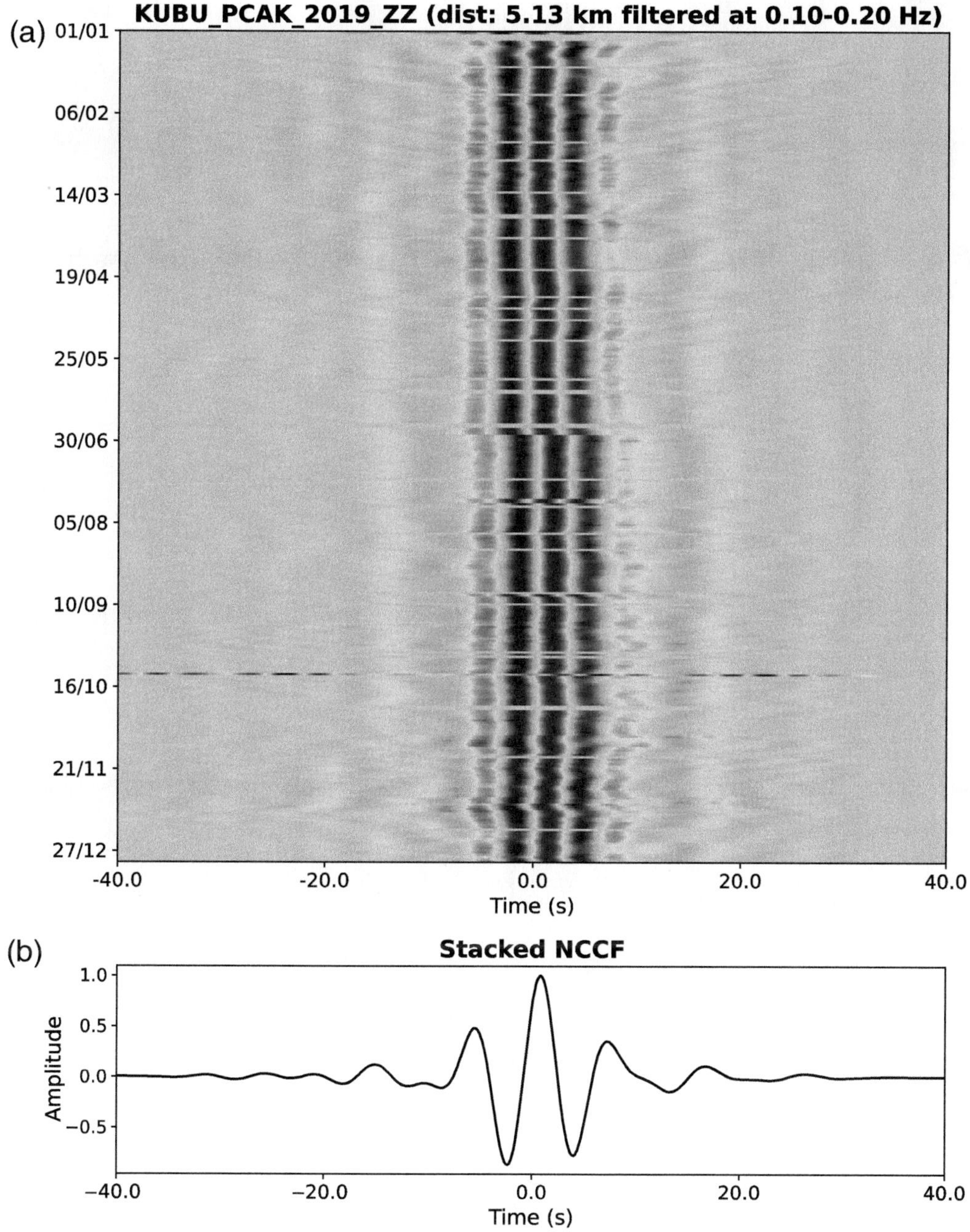

Figure 6. Noise cross-correlation functions (NCCFs) in 2019 between stations KUBU and PCAK (ZZ components) located ~5 km apart. (a) Each row shows a daily stacked NCCF; days without continuous records or without high-quality overlapping segments for cross correlation are shown as empty. (b) The stacked NCCF from 1 January to 15 June, representing a period without time error. The observed asymmetry in the NCCF, such as around 30 January, indicates a timing issue. The color version of this figure is available only in the electronic edition.

the dominant ambient noise source or the low SNR of the NCCF. Such outliers have also been observed in Abbas *et al.* (2023).

The NCCF and PCCF methods derive consistent time error estimates, except for the drifting time error at station GGSL (Figs. 7c, 8c, and 9). At GGSL, the PCCF method estimates a drifting rate of 6.0 ms/day, whereas the NCCF method derives a lower rate of 4.7 ms/day. Because the NCCF result is more consistent to those derived at PCAK (4.2 ms/day by NCCF and 4.6 ms/day by PCCF), we adopt the NCCF result as the final estimate for the drifting behavior (Fig. 9).

In summary, we identify a constant time error of 0.98 ± 0.07 s at PCAK between 27 June 2019 and 28 March 2020, and 0.99 ± 0.13 s at GGSL between 28 March 2018 and 9 May 2018. From 06 July 2016 to 24 November 2016, the drifting time error at PCAK is best described by the equation $y = -0.0044 x - 0.1694$, in which x represents the relative time in days (24 × 3600 s), and y is the drifted time error in second, corresponding to a drifting rate of ~4 ms/day. From 1 April 2016 and 1 July 2016, the drifting time error at GGSL is best fitted by $y = -0.0047 x + 0.0004$, indicating a drifting rate of ~5 ms/day. The similarity in both the drifting rates and constant time errors at PCAK and GGSL suggests these errors may have been caused by the same reasons.

Discussions

Analysis on time error reasons

We identify two types of time error at stations PCAK and GGSL in the Marapi seismic monitoring network: drifting time error and constant time error. The drifting time error follows a linear trend, similar to that observed in the OBS datasets (e.g., Hable *et al.*, 2018; Cabieces *et al.*, 2024). This error may be caused by prolonged synchronization failures with GNSS satellites. Specifically, the potential GNSS disconnection persisted for about three months at GGSL and five months at PCAK during 2016. The ~1 s constant time errors likely result from the mixed use of observation systems with different

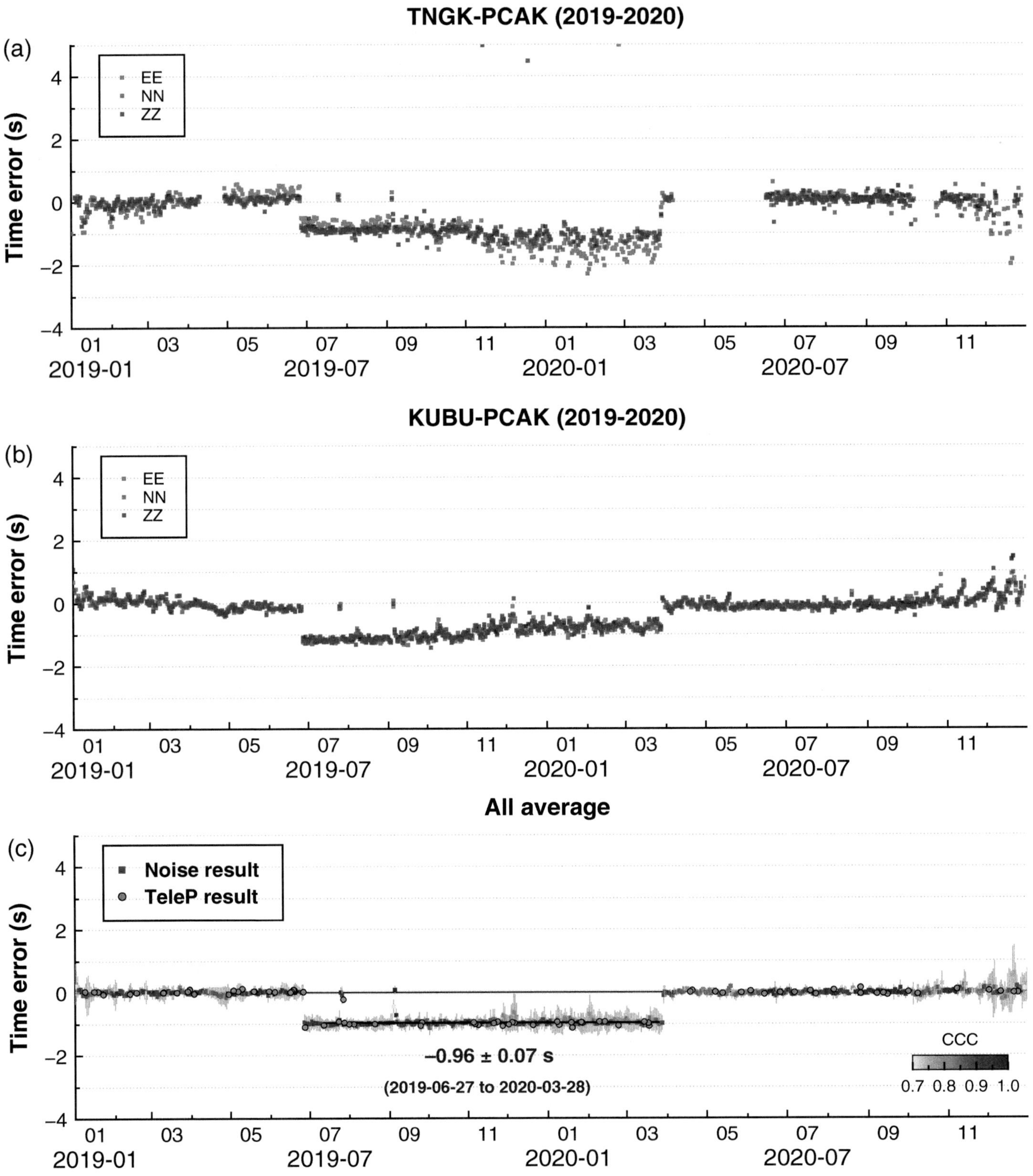

Figure 7. (a,b) Time errors estimated using NCCF for station pairs TNGK–PCAK and KUBU–PCAK across three components between 2019 and 2020. Only estimates with CCCs > 0.7 are shown. (c) Weighted averaging results are represented by squares, color coded by CCC values. PCCF results with standard deviations < 0.5 s, derived from more than two stations, are shown as green dots. Gray bars show standard deviations of individual estimates. The color version of this figure is available only in the electronic edition.

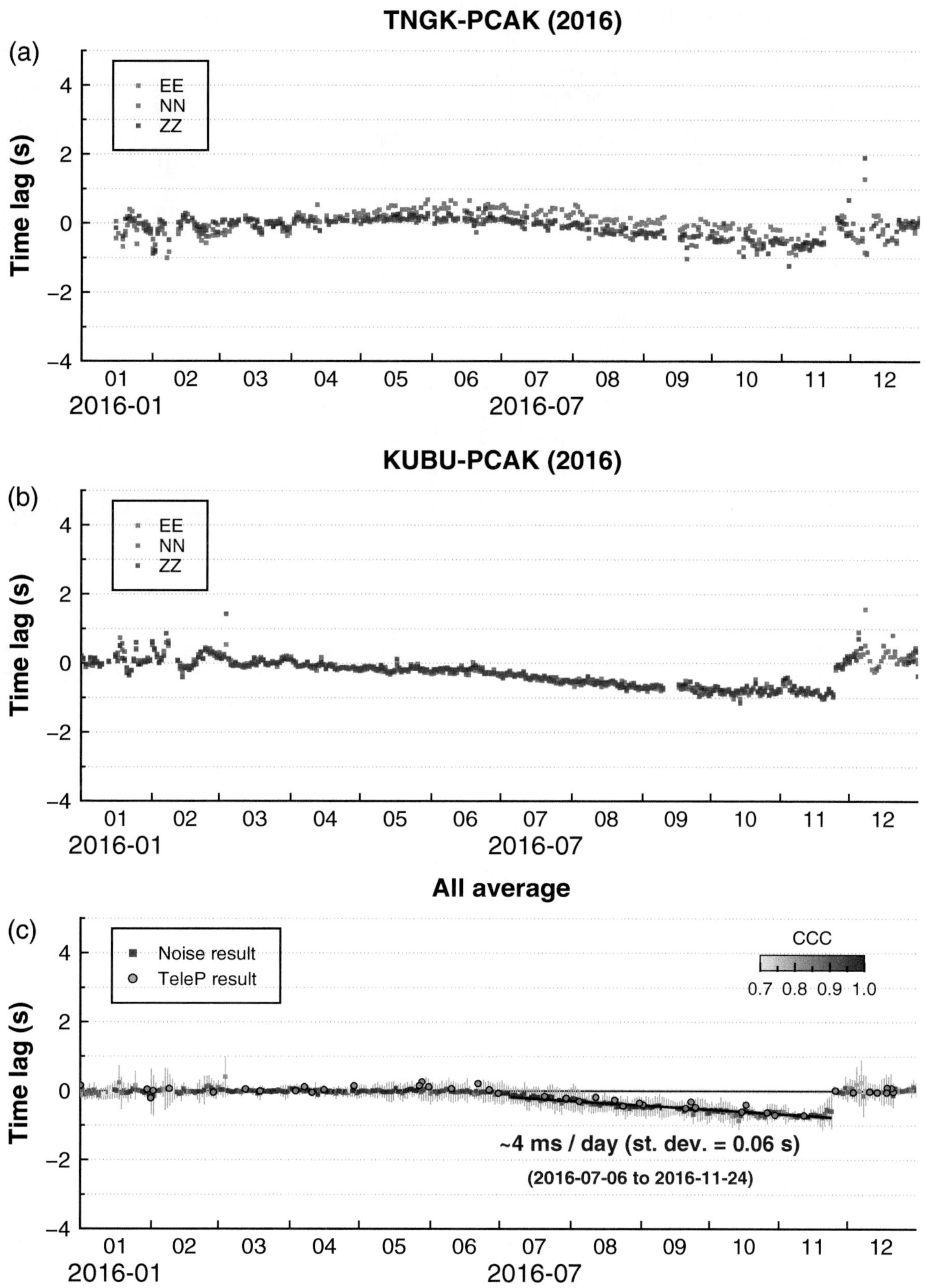

Figure 8. Drifting time errors detected at station pairs TNGK–PCAK and KUBU–PCAK in 2016. Other descriptions are the same as in Figure 7. The color version of this figure is available only in the electronic edition.

internal clock settings or instrument firmware or software problems (Xia *et al.*, 2015) that wrongly corrected the UTC leap second. Constant clock errors associated with system or instrument maintenance were also reported in other seismic networks (Stehly *et al.*, 2007; Ringler *et al.*, 2021; Takano and Nishida, 2024).

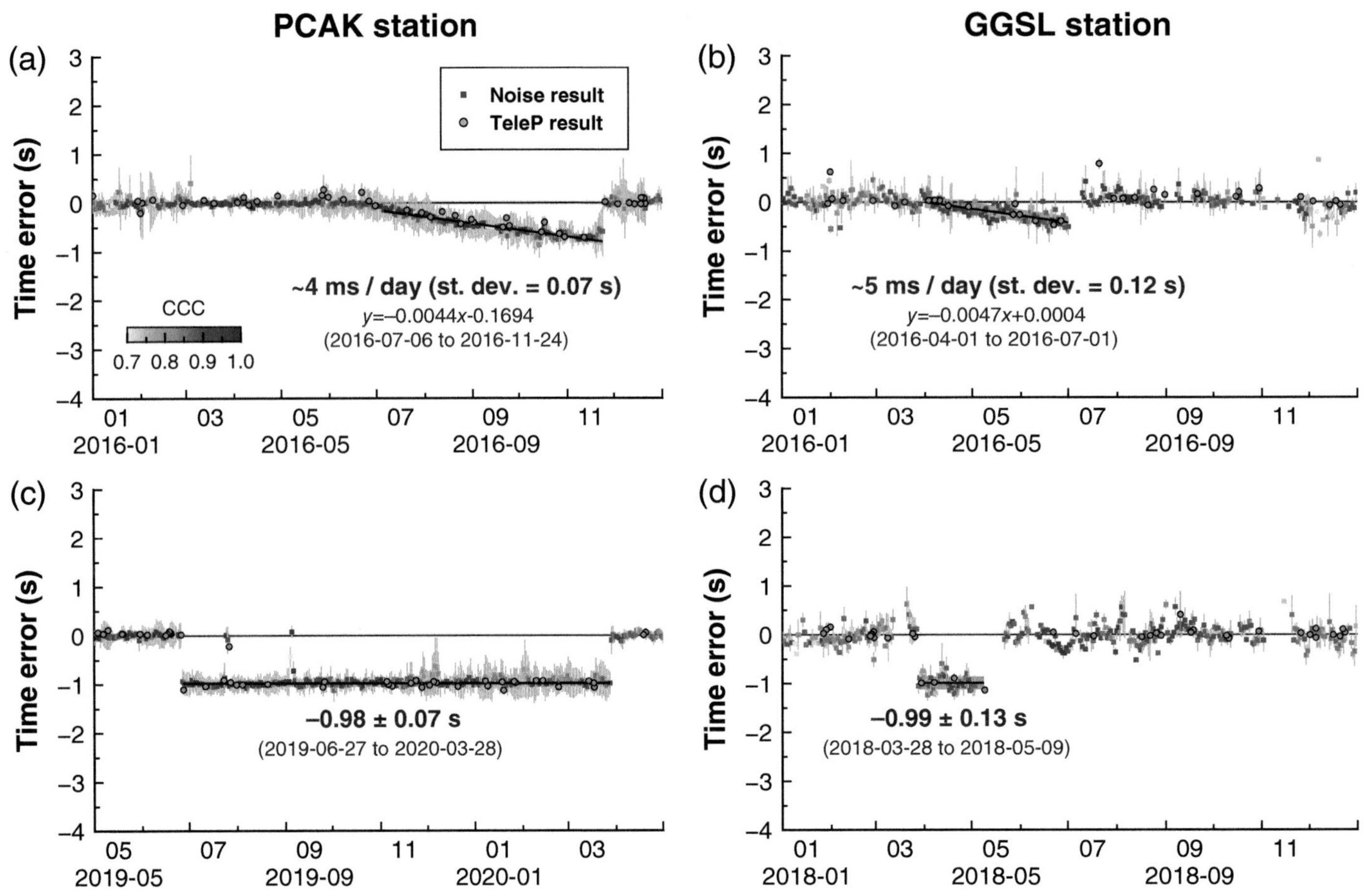

Figure 9. Final time error estimates for stations (a,c) PCAK and (b,d) GGSL, shown by black-thin lines with labeled values. Blue-thick lines mark the uncertainty. (a,b) Drifting time errors and (c,d) constant time errors. The NCCF (noise-based) results are shown by squares color coded by CCCs. The PCCF (teleseismic, TeleP) results are shown by green dots. The color version of this figure is available only in the electronic edition.

In addition to these long-term time errors, we also detect frequent abrupt time jumps exceeding 1 s (Fig. 4). Similar clock jumps, sometimes reaching amplitudes of ~25 s, have been reported in other seismic networks (Stehly *et al.*, 2007; Sens-Schönfelder, 2008; Xie *et al.*, 2018). These jumps are likely caused by misinterpreted GNSS timing signals due to adverse meteorological conditions (Sens-Schönfelder, 2008). Although such transient timing anomalies are short-lived and can be filtered out through standard quality control procedures, our findings underscore the importance of timing assessment to better understand the data quality in future seismic analyses. We acknowledge that the clock errors can be stemmed from very complicated instrument, system, or global GNSS issues, and our analysis cannot cover all possibilities.

Potential influence on volcanoseismological studies

The importance of identifying time errors could be shown with their influences on volcanoseismological studies, such as generating earthquake catalogs and estimating subsurface temporal velocity variations, both are critical for understanding the volcanos and mitigating the eruption impacts (e.g., Ratdomopurbo and Poupinet, 1995; Hotovec-Ellis *et al.*, 2018; Kupres *et al.*, 2024). Precise and complete earthquake catalogs are fundamental for focal mechanism inversion, swarm analysis, and travel-time tomography, relying on accurate and absolute arrival-time pickings for event association and location (e.g., Lomax *et al.*, 2000, 2014; Zhang *et al.*, 2019). Temporal variations of subsurface velocity, linked to magma pressurization, provide critical insights into pre-eruption and coeruption volcanic processes (e.g., Kupres *et al.*, 2024).

To quantitatively evaluate the impact of time errors on earthquake location in the volcanic region, we conduct an illustrative synthetic test, in which we simulate a gradual time drift at station PCAK. We assess the resulting earthquake location errors for a hypothetical event located at a depth of 10 km beneath the network center, or the summit (Fig. 10). Travel times are calculated using the Crust 1.0 model sampled at the Marapi region (Laske *et al.*, 2012). To simulate observational uncertainties, we add random noise that uniformly distributed between −0.1 and 0.1 s to the synthetic *P*- and *S*-wave arrival-time data. We also introduce a gradual time drift to the arrival times at PCAK, increasing in 0.1 s increment up to 1.0 s. Using the NonLinLoc location method (Lomax

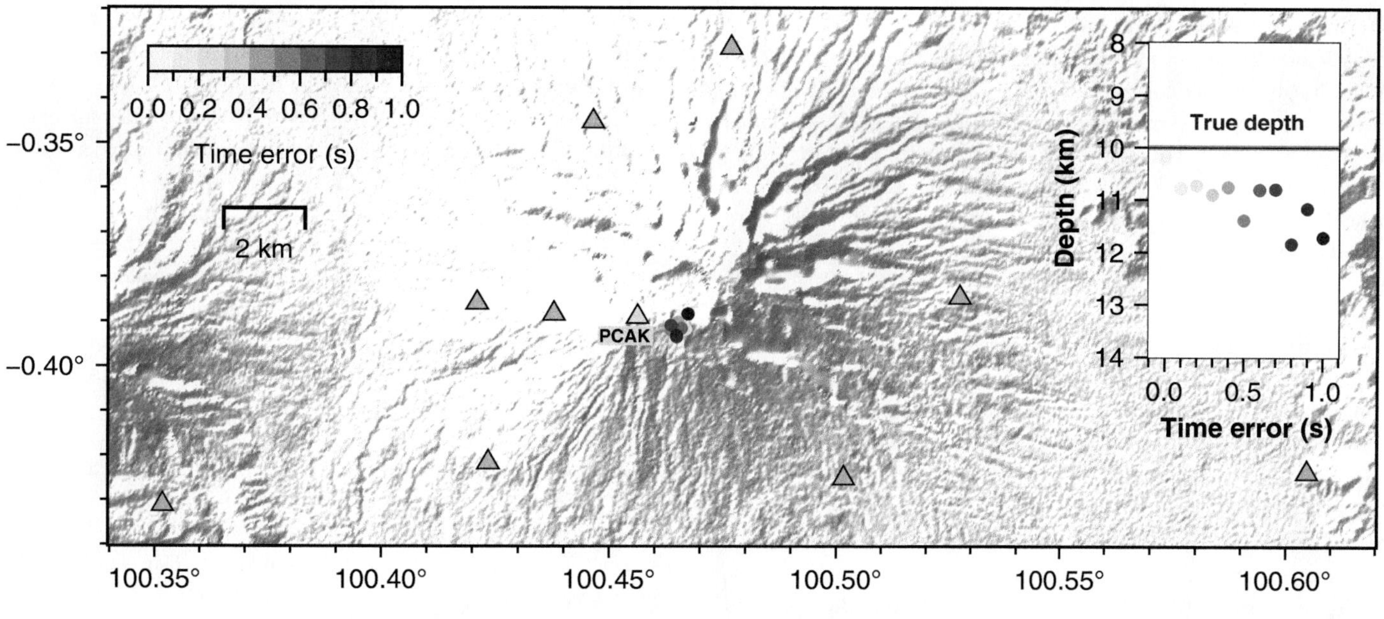

Figure 10. Synthetic tests illustrating the impact of time errors on earthquake location at a depth of 10 km beneath the volcano's summit. Seismic stations are represented by triangles, with the yellow one highlighting station PCAK. The right (inset) panel shows variations in the estimated earthquake depth (true depth: 10 km) as a function of introduced time errors at PCAK, which range from 0.0 to 1.0 s in 0.1 s increments, represented by colored dots. The color version of this figure is available only in the electronic edition.

et al., 2000, 2014), we find that such time drift can cause depth mislocation up to ~1.5 km (Fig. 10). Notably, a time drift ranging from 0.0 to 1.0 s results in an artificial downward migration of seismicity (Fig. 10), a pattern resembling magma transport (Hotovec-Ellis *et al.*, 2018). Therefore, such time drift error could likely lead to a misinterpretation of magma transportation if not corrected. Errors in earthquake location can further affect focal mechanism determination, especially when relying on the *P*-wave first-motion polarity distribution of few stations (e.g., Hardebeck and Shearer, 2002).

Subsurface velocity changes are typically measured by relative travel-time perturbations (dt/t) in repeating earthquake coda waves or NCCFs (Ratdomopurbo and Poupinet, 1995; Brenguier, Shapiro, *et al.*, 2008). Detecting such perturbations requires measuring subtle time shift (dt) at subsecond scales (e.g., <100 ms; Brenguier, Shapiro, *et al.*, 2008), making these methods sensitive to clock errors as small as tens of milliseconds (Takano and Nishida, 2024). For example, Brenguier, Campillo, *et al.* (2008) corrected up to 30 ms clock errors to ensure reliable dv/v estimates. In our study, the drifting time errors of ~4 to 5 ms/day could introduce a systematical delay of ~40 to 150 ms or decreased SNR of NCCFs when using stacking windows of 10–30 days, as in Brenguier, Campillo, *et al.* (2008) and Brenguier, Shapiro, *et al.* (2008). These timing errors will consequently affect the accuracy of dv/v estimates and their interpretations. A systematic assessment on how clock errors influence dv/v and other seismological measurements is recommended for future studies.

Conclusion

In this study, we combine teleseismic *P*-wave cross correlation and ambient noise cross-correlation methods to detect potential time errors in the long-term seismic monitoring network at Marapi volcano, Indonesia. Both methods consistently reveal two types of time errors at the PCAK and GGSL stations: constant time error and drifting time error. The constant time errors, averaging ~1 s, persist for periods ranging from one to nine months. The drifting time errors span three to five months, with drifting rates of ~4 to 5 ms/day. We attribute the constant time errors to potential observation system or instrument issues, whereas the drifting time error is likely due to failed synchronization with GNSS satellites. Our synthetic tests show that such time errors can produce an artificial downward migration of volcanic seismicity beneath the crater, potentially leading to misinterpretations of temporal magma storage dynamics.

Data and Resources

The supplemental material for this article includes: (1) raw time lag measurements relative to station TNGK (Fig. S1); (2) demeaned and weighted averaging time error estimates relative to station GGSL (Fig. S2); (3) noise cross-correlation function (NCCF) between the KUBU–PCAK station pair in 2019 (Fig. S3); (4) time error estimated by the NCCF method at GGSL station in 2018 and in 2016 (Figs. S4, S5, respectively); and (5) station information (Table S1).

Declaration of Competing Interests

The authors acknowledge that there are no conflicts of interest recorded.

Acknowledgments

The authors sincerely thank two anonymous reviewers, Associate Editor Adam Ringler, and Editor-in-Chief Allison Bent for their helpful comments that improve the quality of the article. This research is supported by the Ministry of Education (MOE), Singapore, under its MOE Academic Research Fund Tier 3 (Award MOE-MOET32021-0002, component D and E). The authors thank the Centre for Geohazard Observations (CGO) of Earth Observatory of Singapore (EOS) for installing and maintaining the seismic network and managing the dataset. The authors thank CGO staffs for providing information about the instrument status and helpful discussions on potential causes of clock errors. The authors thank Wei Xu, Zhangfeng Ma, Ling Chen, Jurgen Neuberg, Tania Espinosa-Ortega, Yizhou Luo, and the Center for Volcanology and Geological Hazard Mitigation (CVGHM) staffs for helpful discussions.

References

Abbas, A., G. Zhu, J. Zi, H. Chen, and H. Yang (2023). Evaluating and correcting short-term clock drift in data from temporary seismic deployments, *Earthq. Res. Adv.* **3,** no. 2, 100199, doi: 10.1016/j.eqrea.2022.100199.

Bensen, G. D., M. H. Ritzwoller, M. P. Barmin, A. L. Levshin, F. Lin, M. P. Moschetti, N. M. Shapiro, and Y. Yang (2007). Processing seismic ambient noise data to obtain reliable broad-band surface wave dispersion measurements, *Geophys. J. Int.* **169,** no. 3, 1239–1260, doi: 10.1111/j.1365-246X.2007.03374.x.

Brenguier, F., M. Campillo, C. Hadziioannou, N. M. Shapiro, R. M. Nadeau, and É. Larose (2008). Postseismic relaxation along the San Andreas fault at Parkfield from continuous seismological observations, *Science* **321,** no. 5895, 1478–1481.

Brenguier, F., N. M. Shapiro, M. Campillo, V. Ferrazzini, Z. Duputel, O. Coutant, and A. Nercessian (2008). Towards forecasting volcanic eruptions using seismic noise, *Nature Geosci.* **1,** no. 2, 126–130.

Cabieces, R., K. Harris, A. M. G. Ferreira, M. Tsekhmistrenko, and S. P. Hicks (2024). Clock drift corrections for large aperture ocean bottom seismometer arrays: application to the UPFLOW array in the mid-Atlantic Ocean, *Geophys. J. Int.* **239,** 1709–1728, doi: 10.1093/gji/ggae354.

Global Volcanism Program (2024). [Database] Volcanoes of the World (v. 5.2.7; 21 Feb 2025), Distributed by Smithsonian Institution, compiled by E. Venzke (Editor), doi: 10.5479/si.GVP.VOTW5-2024.5.2.

Hable, S., K. Sigloch, G. Barruol, S. C. Stähler, and C. Hadziioannou (2018). Clock errors in land and ocean bottom seismograms: High-accuracy estimates from multiple-component noise cross-correlations, *Geophys. J. Int.* **214,** no. 3, 2014–2034, doi: 10.1093/GJI/GGY236.

Hardebeck, J. L., and P. M. Shearer (2002). A new method for determining first-motion focal mechanisms, *Bull. Seismol. Soc. Am.* **92,** no. 6, 2264–2276.

Hirose, T., and H. Ueda (2023). Continuous monitoring of instrumental clock errors at 50 volcanoes in Japan based on seismic interferometry, *Earth Planets Space* **75,** no. 1, doi: 10.1186/s40623-023-01798-4.

Hotovec-Ellis, A. J., D. R. Shelly, D. P. Hill, A. M. Pitt, P. B. Dawson, and B. A. Chouet (2018). Deep fluid pathways beneath mammoth mountain, California, illuminated by migrating earthquake swarms, *Sci. Adv.* **4,** no. 8, eaat5258, doi: 10.1126/sciadv.aat5258.

Huang, H., F. Lin, B. Schmandt, J. Farrell, R. B. Smith, and V. C. Tsai (2015). The Yellowstone magmatic system from the mantle plume to the upper crust, *Science* **348,** no. 6236, 773–776.

Kennett, B. L. N., and E. R. Engdahl (1991). Traveltimes for global earthquake location and phase identification, *Geophys. J. Int.* **105,** no. 2, 429–465, doi: 10.1111/j.1365-246X.1991.tb06724.x.

Koulakov, I., E. Kasatkina, N. M. Shapiro, C. Jaupart, A. Vasilevsky, S. El Khrepy, N. Al-Arifi, and S. Smirnov (2016). The feeder system of the Toba supervolcano from the slab to the shallow reservoir, *Nat. Commun.* **7,** 1–12, doi: 10.1038/ncomms12228.

Kupres, C. A., X. Yang, M. Haney, and D. C. Roman (2024). Sustained co-eruptive increase in seismic velocity below Great Sitkin Volcano due to magma extrusion, *Geophys. Res. Lett.* **51,** no. 15, e2024GL108991.

Laske, G., G. Masters, Z. Ma, and M. E. Pasyanos (2012). CRUST1.0: An updated global model of earth's crust, *Geophysical Research Abstracts EGU General Assembly*, Vol. 14, 2012–3743.

Le, B. M., T. Yang, Y. J. Chen, and H. Yao (2018). Correction of OBS clock errors using Scholte waves retrieved from cross-correlating hydrophone recordings, *Geophys. J. Int.* **212,** no. 2, 891–899, doi: 10.1093/gji/ggx449.

Li, J., Y. Tian, D. Zhao, D. Yan, Z. Li, and H. Li (2023). Magmatic system and seismicity of the Arxan Volcanic Group in Northeast China, *Geophys. Res. Lett.* **50,** no. 6, doi: 10.1029/2022GL101105.

Liu, Z., C. Liang, H. Huang, C. Wang, and F. Cao (2022). Seismic velocity variations at different depths reveal the dynamic evolution associated with the 2018 Kilauea eruption, *Geophys. Res. Lett.* **49,** no. 3, e2021GL093691.

Lomax, A., A. Michelini, and A. Curtis (2014). Earthquake location, direct, global-search methods, in *Encyclopedia of Complexity and Systems Science*, R. Meyers (Editor), Springer, New York, New York, doi: 10.1007/978-3-642-27737-5_150-2.

Lomax, A., J. Virieux, P. Volant, and C. Berge-Thierry (2000). Probabilistic earthquake location in 3D and layered models, in *Advances in Seismic Event Location*, C. H. Thurber and N. Rabinowitz (Editors), Springer, Dordrecht, The Netherlands, 101–134.

Nurfiani, D., X. Wang, H. Gunawan, H. Triastuty, D. Hidayat, S. J. Wei, B. Taisne, and C. B. de Maisonneuve (2021). Combining petrology and seismology to unravel the plumbing system of a typical arc volcano: An example from Marapi, West Sumatra, Indonesia, *Geochem. Geophys. Geosys.* **22,** no. 4, 1–25, doi: 10.1029/2020GC009524.

Ratdomopurbo, A., and G. Poupinet (1995). Monitoring a temporal change of seismic velocity in a volcano: Application to the 1992 eruption of Mt. Merapi (Indonesia), *Geophys. Res. Lett.* **22,** no. 7, 775–778.

Ringler, A. T., R. E. Anthony, D. C. Wilson, D. Auerbach, S. Bargabus, P. Davis, M. Gunnels, K. Hafner, J. F. Holland, A. Kearns, *et al.* (2021). A review of timing accuracy across the global seismographic network, *Seismol. Res. Lett.* **92,** no. 4, 2270–2281, doi: 10.1785/0220200394.

Sens-Schönfelder, C. (2008). Synchronizing seismic networks with ambient noise, *Geophys. J. Int.* **174,** no. 3, 966–970, doi: 10.1111/j.1365-246X.2008.03842.x.

Shapiro, N. M., and M. Campillo (2004). Emergence of broadband Rayleigh waves from correlations of the ambient seismic noise, *Geophys. Res. Lett.* **31,** no. 7, 2–5, doi: 10.1029/2004GL019491.

Shapiro, N. M., D. V. Droznin, S. Y. Droznina, S. L. Senyukov, A. A. Gusev, and E. I. Gordeev (2017). Deep and shallow long-period volcanic seismicity linked by fluid-pressure transfer, *Nature Geosci.* **10,** no. 6, 442–445, doi: 10.1038/ngeo2952.

Sigmundsson, F., M. Parks, A. Hooper, H. Geirsson, K. S. Vogfjörd, V. Drouin, B. G. Ófeigsson, S. Hreinsdóttir, S. Hjaltadóttir, K. Jónsdóttir, *et al.* (2022). Deformation and seismicity decline before the 2021 Fagradalsfjall eruption, *Nature* **609,** no. 7927, 523–528, doi: 10.1038/s41586-022-05083-4.

Stehly, L., M. Campillo, and N. M. Shapiro (2007). Traveltime measurements from noise correlation: Stability and detection of instrumental time-shifts, *Geophys. J. Int.* **171,** no. 1, 223–230, doi: 10.1111/j.1365-246X.2007.03492.x.

Syracuse, E. M., W. S. Phillips, M. Maceira, and M. L. Begnaud (2017). Identifying and correcting timing errors at seismic stations in and around Iran, *Seismol. Res. Lett.* **88,** no. 6, 1472–1479, doi: 10.1785/0220170113.

Takano, T., and K. Nishida (2024). Estimation of seismometer clock time offsets using Kalman Filter toward accurate seismic velocity change, *Geophys. J. Int.*, 1087–1102, doi: 10.1093/gji/ggae322.

Wang, X., Q. F. Chen, J. Li, and S. Wei (2016). Seismic sensor misorientation measurement using P-wave particle motion: An application to the NECsaids array, *Seismol. Res. Lett.* **87,** no. 4, 901–911, doi: 10.1785/0220160005.

Xia, Y., S. Ni, X. Zeng, J. Xie, B. Wang, and S. Yuan (2015). Synchronizing intercontinental seismic networks using the 26 s persistent localized microseismic source, *Bull. Seismol. Soc. Am.* **105,** no. 4, 2101–2108.

Xie, J., S. Ni, R. Chu, and Y. Xia (2018). Assessing the short-term clock drift of early broadband stations with burst events of the 26 s persistent and localized microseism, *Geophys. J. Int.* **212,** no. 1, 324–332, doi: 10.1093/gji/ggx401.

Yang, Y., X. Song, and A. T. Ringler (2022). An evaluation of the timing accuracy of global and regional seismic stations and networks, *Seismol. Res. Lett.* **93,** no. 1, 161–172, doi: 10.1785/0220210232.

Yao, H., R. D. van der Hilst, and M. V. de Hoop (2006). Surface-wave array tomography in SE Tibet from ambient seismic noise and two-station analysis - I. Phase velocity maps, *Geophys. J. Int.* **166,** no. 2, 732–744, doi: 10.1111/j.1365-246X.2006.03028.x.

Zhang, M., W. L. Ellsworth, and G. C. Beroza (2019). Rapid earthquake association and location, *Seismol. Res. Lett.* **90,** no. 6, 2276–2284.

Zhu, G., H. Yang, J. Lin, Z. Zhou, M. Xu, J. Sun, and K. Wan (2019). Along-strike variation in slab geometry at the southern Mariana subduction zone revealed by seismicity through ocean bottom seismic experiments, *Geophys. J. Int.* **218,** no. 3, 2122–2135, doi: 10.1093/gji/ggz272.

Manuscript received 7 May 2025
Published online 26 August 2025

Deep Learning–Based Footfall Detection and Anthropogenic Activity Characterization Using Fiber-Optic Distributed Acoustic Sensing

Yuming Yuan[1], Bin Luo[*1], and Zhen Guo[1]

Abstract

Fiber-optic distributed acoustic sensing (DAS) has been found effective for vibration-based monitoring of human activities with high resolution in space and time. Here, we use deep learning–based computer vision algorithms for footfall signal extraction from the 2D array like DAS data. Unlike previous studies that primarily focused on detecting linear walker movement features along the fiber, we treat each individual footstep as an independent event target for picking. Using the effective algorithm, we detect a massive amount of footstep signals from a month-long DAS recording. We also correct for the polarity reversal characteristics of DAS and use backprojection techniques to determine each footstep location and reconstruct anonymous walking trajectories of walkers along the coastline, revealing unique walking behaviors under different weather conditions. This seismic experiment demonstrates the potential of combining DAS with advanced deep learning algorithms to achieve precise signal recognition and real-time monitoring, thereby opening new possibilities for characterizing anthropogenic activities.

Cite this article as Yuan, Y., B. Luo, and Z. Guo (2025). Deep Learning–Based Footfall Detection and Anthropogenic Activity Characterization Using Fiber-Optic Distributed Acoustic Sensing, *Seismol. Res. Lett.* **97**, 100–110, doi: 10.1785/0220250120.

Supplemental Material

Introduction

Human activities can induce seismic excitation and generate propagating seismic waves on the ground. Collecting these seismic signals to characterize human activities, especially tracking the dynamic location of the source, may provide essential information of public activity to help city planners better understand the occupancy of city facilities and make appropriate decisions. Many studies have presented human activity monitoring using conventional seismic sensors (Vidale *et al.*, 1995; Díaz *et al.*, 2017; Lecocq *et al.*, 2020; Zhao *et al.*, 2021). Yet the nature of uncertain emergence of human activity poses great challenge to expansive, sparsely distributed seismic instrumentation. This can be addressed by an emerging sensing technique called distributed acoustic sensing (DAS), which transforms existing telecommunication fiber-optic cables into ultra-dense sensing arrays. As a distributed sensor, DAS can exploit full fiber length to cover city-scale distances but at the same time provide dense sample spacing to capture sporadic emergence of small-scale human activity–induced seismic signals. Along with its low cost in deployment and maintenance, DAS has demonstrated its advantage in urban monitoring applications in a number of previous studies, such as detecting walking pedestrians (Jakkampudi *et al.*, 2020; Zhou *et al.*, 2024); tracking traffic flows (Lindsey *et al.*, 2020; Wang *et al.*, 2021); and monitoring parades, concerts, and other cultural events (Wang *et al.*, 2020; Zhu *et al.*, 2021). The success of detecting the significant change of traffic volume during the coronavirus disease 2019 (COVID-19) pandemic lockdown measure (Lindsey *et al.*, 2020; Shen and Zhu, 2021; Wang *et al.*, 2021) proved that DAS can become an ideal sensing tool for city planners to acquire crucial information for emergency decision-making.

DAS-transformed fiber-optic cables acquire vibration signals with extremely high spatial resolution (Ajo-Franklin *et al.*, 2019; Zhan, 2019), which opens up the possibility of conducting accurate geophysical study in various earthquake monitoring scenarios, such as volcanoes, glaciers, and the seafloor (e.g., Walter *et al.*, 2020; Hudson *et al.*, 2021; Jousset *et al.*, 2022; Landrø *et al.*, 2022). Although natural earthquakes commonly shake up a significant portion of the DAS array, human activity–induced seismic waves, such as those excited by the foot stepping of walking pedestrians, commonly manifest as weak signals with limited impact ranges. Therefore, the direct use of DAS for

1. Department of Ocean Science and Engineering, Southern University of Science and Technology, Shenzhen, China, https://orcid.org/0009-0005-1866-7342 (YY); https://orcid.org/0000-0002-4155-9746 (BL)

*Corresponding author: luob@sustech.edu.cn

human activity monitoring is challenged by not only the transient nature of these induced seismic signals in a long-term, continuous recording in time but also by the sporadic emergence of these small-scale signals along the long-range cable in space. Meanwhile, the high spatiotemporal resolution feature of DAS yields a large volume of dynamic strain dataset, which drives the need for new processing methods to extract these small-scale, transient signals generated by humans.

Deep learning models are a promising solution that has seen rapid development in recent years for geophysical data analysis. Compared with traditional methods, deep learning has a significant advantage in large-scale data processing. Many important studies have combined deep learning with geophysical applications (Linville *et al.*, 2019; Titos *et al.*, 2019; Zhong *et al.*, 2021; Lv *et al.*, 2022). In the field of seismic phase picking, PhaseNet by Zhu and Beroza (2019) and EQtransformer by Mousavi *et al* (2020) have both made significant progress compared with traditional earthquake phase picking methods. Advancements have also been seen in using deep learning to address geophysical problems related to distributed fiber optics, such as using the You Only Look Once (YOLO) algorithm for microseismic monitoring on DAS data (Stork *et al.*, 2020) and using convolutional neural network (CNN) for monitoring human footsteps (Jakkampudi *et al.*, 2020; Zhou *et al.*, 2024). Min *et al.* (2024) applied machine learning methods to recognize and extract vehicle signals from DAS data. Zhou *et al.* (2024) proposes a new artificial intelligence (AI)–based footfall detection method using DAS.

In this study, we proposed a deep learning–based workflow to analyze pedestrian trajectories from the DAS seismic recording. The workflow is applied to a DAS dataset acquired from an outdoor cable deployed in the vicinity of the Xinfengjiang artificial water reservoir in Guangdong, China. The reservoir, sitting next to the Heyuan city in Guangdong Province, is a popular location for visiting tourists. Human activities may pose a potentially significant impact on the fragile ecological system of the reservoir (Chi *et al.*, 2022). Using DAS cables as an efficient and cost-effective means to monitor human activity has been explored in this study, which can help reconstruct the human activity scenario at the moment of monitoring and improve our understanding of human interaction with the environment.

Data Acquisition

The DAS data analyzed in this work were collected from a 3 km long fiber-optic cable buried along the northeast shoreline of the Xinfengjiang Reservoir in southeast China, which is one of the largest artificial water reservoirs in the region (Fig. 1). The cable is deployed horizontally on the surface and buried at ~20 cm deep. The data were acquired at a sampling rate of 300 Hz, with a channel spacing of 1 m and a gauge length of 10 m. We analyzed the data recorded from 27 April 2022 to 21 May 2022. The experiment site is remote and quiet, and the major environmental seismic sources are human footsteps. To improve signal quality, we first demean the raw data and remove linear trends and then apply a band-pass filter to the DAS data within the frequency range of 1–140 Hz to eliminate both low- and high-frequency background noises. Tap tests were conducted to confirm channel locations, during which we struck the fiber-optic cable twice at specific locations, generating signals significantly stronger than human footsteps. As shown in Figure S1, available in the supplemental material to this article, whereas tapping with a shovel produces two strong signals propagating laterally over 150 m, people walking nearby induced footstep signals that propagated 50–100 m. The location of the reservoir and the cable layout are shown in Figure 1a. Among the 3000 channels of the full DAS array, 1900 channels, from 300 to 2200, are considered valid for data analysis because the channels before 300 are spooled up and those after 2200 mostly stay loose on the ground.

YOLO-Based Object Detection Method on DAS Data

DAS enables ultra-dense sampling of ground vibration in both space and time domain, which leads to a 2D nature of its output strain or strain rate data. The 2D DAS data format resembles digital images with a representation of a 2D matrix of pixels, except that each pixel of the DAS data represents a true measurement of the optical phase change from the laser pulse instead of color indices. Therefore, unlike conventional seismic signal detection methods that rely on waveform features in the seismic recordings, DAS-based signal detection may exploit the spatiotemporal features of the seismic signals embedded in the 2D DAS data format. Several attempts have been made for such purposes, especially in the downhole monitoring environment for induced microseismic events (Binder and Tura, 2020; Stork *et al.*, 2020; Huot *et al.*, 2022).

In the field of computer vision, object detection is a branch that involves detection and identification of different objects in images or videos, which is a critical task for modern applications such as self-driving vehicles, security systems, and robotics. A number of sophisticated algorithms have been developed, including the Viola–Jones algorithm, the region-based CNN (R-CNN) family of algorithms, and the YOLO algorithm. In this work, we apply a transfer learning strategy to retrain the pretrained YOLO model for DAS data analysis. In particular, we retrain the model to search for human footstep signal detection in DAS data images, the most commonly seen signal in the DAS recording, to reveal their patterns and characteristics from the dataset. We adopt a YOLO v. 5 model (Jocher *et al.*, 2022) that has shown robust and excellent performance in both calculation speed and accuracy in numerous computer vision applications.

We experiment with the length of the time window and determine that the choice of a 6 s time window is suitable for human footstep event detection purposes because the duration of a typical single event is ~0.5 s, that is, it is ~5%–10% of such a window length, similar to the percentage of the effective propagation

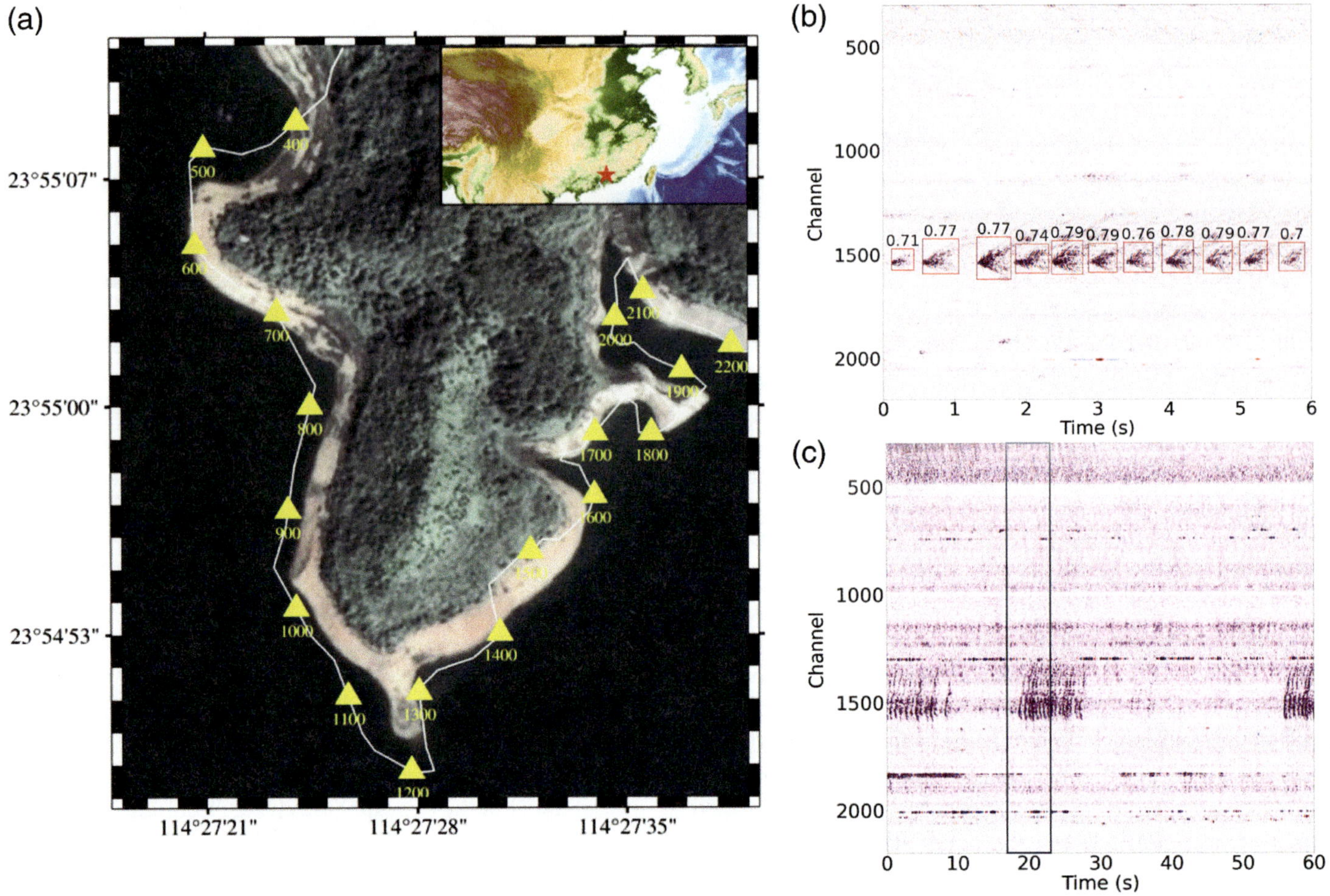

Figure 1. A map of the study region and footstep signals examples in 2D image form of distributed acoustic sensing (DAS) data and the catalog and analysis of detected results. (a) The fiber-optic cable deployed at the reservoir shown as a white line with yellow triangles that mark channel number for every 100 channels. The inset on the top right corner shows a map of China in which the red star in the south marks the site of this study. (b) A 6 s DAS data example. The red rectangles highlight the footstep signals detected by You Only Look Once (YOLO) v. 5. Scores are provided above each rectangle. (c) A 60 s DAS example with blurry illustration of footfall signals that are unsuitable for image-based detection. The black rectangle shows the same 6 s data in panel (b).

distance of the wavefield (~200 m) to the length of this cable section (1900 m). With this reasonable aspect ratio of 1900 m/6 s = 316 m/s being comparable to near-surface shear-wave velocity and a 10% ratio between the event size and the data image dimension, the seismic events are visually balanced in both space and time, with their wavefield details clearly presented in the data image, as illustrated in Figure 1b. In addition, the event interval in a sequence is on average about the same as or slightly longer than the event duration, resulting in a clear separation between events that further facilitates event identification.

A 60 s long data example is shown in Figure 1c, which is of 18,000 × 1,900 time–space dimension and initially used for labeling and retraining purposes. However, we noticed that the targeted human footstep signals are highly compressed and blurry for the given aspect ratio, losing sufficient distinctive details for signal identification purposes. In addition, events that occurred within a short period of time are clustered and become a challenge for labeling. Initial retraining attempts of the YOLO model based on such an image dataset yield unsatisfactory performance.

Deep Learning Model Training and Performance

In the data labeling step, we manually draw rectangular bounding boxes around the visually picked signals as a ground truth for model training. In the training step, to compare a bounding box output from a YOLO model with the ground-truth bounding boxes, we use the concept of intersection over union (IoU) to evaluate the level of overlapping between two bounding boxes, which is schematically shown in Figure 2a. Therefore, the IoU value is the loss function for model training and is computed as $\mathrm{IoU} = \frac{A \cap B}{A \cup B}$, ranging from 0 to 1, in which A and B denote the two bounding boxes to be compared. A threshold is chosen to decide if a bounding box output from the model is sufficiently close to the desired ground-truth bounding box. Varying the IoU threshold yields the classical precision–recall curve that measures the performance of the model. We use the average precision (AP) score, that is, the area under the precision–recall curve, for model performance evaluation.

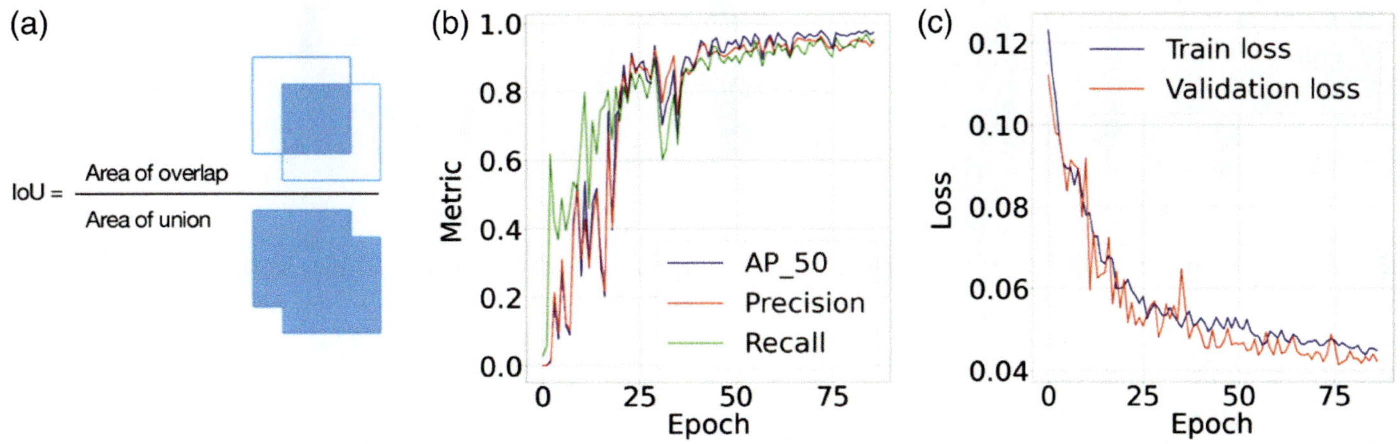

Figure 2. Summary of the DAS footfall recognition retraining performance, showing the schematic diagram of the (a) intersection over union (IoU) metric, (b) model performance (in which AP_50 means the AP score when IoU threshold is 0.5), and (c) model loss during the transfer learning process.

Three types of loss functions are used in the YOLO algorithm: box loss, object loss, and class loss. Given that our problem is a one-class object detection task, we only focus on the object loss and box loss. The box loss is the difference between the predicted box and the ground-truth box, and the object loss represents the binary cross-entropy loss of the probability of an object's presence within the box to the ground truth. Because the trends of box loss and object loss are similar, for simplicity, we opt to showcase only the box losses. The AP performance and the box loss of the retrained model are shown in Figure 2b,c, respectively. We can observe that the AP metric stabilizes above 0.95 after 40 epochs. In addition, both the validation and training loss tend to flatten out after 40 epochs. Moreover, the fact that the validation loss and training loss remain close to each other indicates that the dataset of 300 images is sufficient to train a model capable of detecting human footsteps. Subsequent applications have also demonstrated that this small dataset, when trained for a short duration, can effectively detect human footsteps.

To retrain the YOLO model as a footstep signal classifier for DAS data, we create a catalog of 300 DAS data images of the aforementioned space–time dimension (1900 channels in space and 6 s in time), with two-thirds of them being manually selected event images containing multiple footstep signals; the rest are background noise images selected from random time windows in the DAS dataset. In each of the 200 event images, we visually pick all of the footstep signals and manually draw rectangular bounding boxes around them, resulting in >1500 labeled events in total. The 300 labeled images are then randomly divided into training and validation sets with a 2:1 ratio, whereas in each set the ratio between event and noise images is also set to 2:1. The data labeling procedure takes about one hour for a graduate student to complete. The model retraining procedure takes ~10 min on an RTX 3090 Graphics Processing Unit (GPU).

Using the trained model to detect footstep signals on all the DAS data images results in identification of ~300,000 footsteps from the 4 TB continuous DAS recording, with a processing speed of 30 ms per image. After undergoing a quality check, the model demonstrates accurate detection of human footsteps. True positive and false alarm examples are shown in Figure 3. The detection examples in Figure 3 are mostly true positives that demonstrate the effectiveness of the retrained model in almost exhaustively searching all the clear footstep signals in a DAS data image. The false positive in Figure 3a shows that some background noises may confuse the model with a shape that is similar to the footstep signals. Weak footstep signals in Figure 3b with a low signal-to-noise ratio may exhibit an incomplete shape compared with a regular footstep signal and may become false negatives that are missed by the retrained model.

Statistical analysis of the detection output show consistency with onsite observation. Figure 4a illustrates the distribution of signals on all days along the cable. Two peaks, each with >60,000 signals per 200 m, can be seen at the 1250 and 1850 m bins in the histogram, which indicate two hot spots that people commonly visit for recreational activities. Figure 4b shows the distribution of daily detected signals along the whole cable over the experiment period compared with the contemporary history of daily precipitation and the daily increment of the water level of the reservoir. Peaks at around 2 May 2022, correspond strongly to a public holiday in China, when tourists visit the shoreline for recreational purposes more often than usual, and the trough on 1 May corresponds to heavier rainfall. Meanwhile, one can notice a significant drop of the footstep signal volume from 6 to 8 May and the extremely low volume of the detected signals that lasts for 9 days until 17 May. This distinctive change in the number of detected signals is found to correlate negatively with the daily increment of reservoir water level, which reflects the heavy rainfall and the resulting surge of water level of the reservoir during the week from 9 to 14 May. An intuitive explanation is that the adverse weather condition prevents people from accessing the area, and thus, there are fewer vibration events at the cable

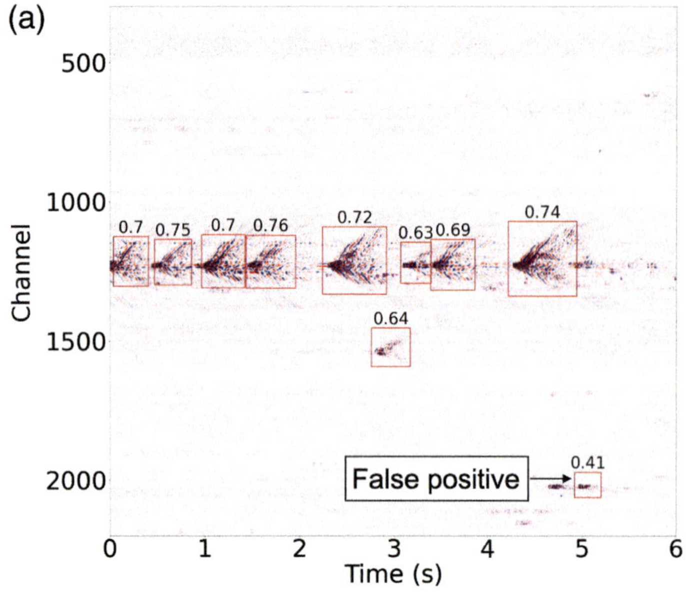

Figure 3. Footstep detections from the model inference highlighted by red rectangles. Examples of (a) false-positive detection and (b) false -negative detection are shown.

location, whereas before and after the heavy rainfall, the water level increment stays at a low level, and a large volume of human footstep signals are detected, indicating a fairly large amount of human activities and the significantly busy human interaction with the shoreline cable.

Figure 4c illustrates a detailed depiction of detected events occurring between 12:00 and 17:00 on 27 April. Scattered points represent detected footstep events at various moments and channel locations, offering insights into the migration patterns of human footstep events. Four categories of event patterns can be identified: unilaterally migrating events, bilaterally migrating events, stationary random events, and sporadically dispersed "noisy" events. The red rectangle in Figure 4c highlights events migrating unilaterally in this time period, when the footstep events are seen moving from around 1200 m toward 1800 m and then moving backward after a brief pause. These events occur in one place at a time and move continuously from one place to another in one direction only. We also observe bilateral migration of the detected events, highlighted by the green rectangle in Figure 4c. These events occur simultaneously at two locations and move from a "center" point outward in both directions along the cable. In the time period shown in Figure 4c, five bilateral migration clusters can be seen, and they are all centered at around 1200 m. Besides the migrating events, the dots within the blue rectangle in Figure 4c indicate stationary random stomping within the hot spot region centered at 1250 m. Finally, the data points within the yellow rectangle highlight randomly scattered "noisy" events.

Footfall Seismic Characteristics and Source Location Determination

Further examination of the detected seismic signals reveals that although all footsteps manifest as exciting point sources radiating seismic waves that propagate across the DAS channels, some exhibit contemporary low-frequency components highly localized within the source area. An example sequence of this type of footstep signal is shown in Figure 5a, in which the transient footstep seismic waves appear to radiate from a long-lasting low-frequency signal around channel 1262. We interpret the coexistence of the highly localized low-frequency signal and the source location of seismic radiation as an implication of the low-frequency signal being directly related to the foot stomping. Apparently, these low-frequency signals exhibit a limited impact range (<10 m) across the DAS channels and thus can be observed only when the footstep falls very close to or directly on top of the cable. We therefore identify such a low-frequency signal as a response of the fiber to near-field deformation of the footsteps. A contradictory example is shown in Figure 5b, in which no localized low-frequency signals are found along with the footstep sequences, suggesting the footstep source is far from the cable.

A time–frequency analysis of selected channels in Figure 5a,b is shown in Figure 5c,d, respectively. Distinct differences can be observed in the time–frequency field that the signals of footsteps on the cable comprise both significant low- (<5 Hz) and high-frequency components (>70 Hz), whereas the off-cable footsteps show a lack of these frequency components. Previous studies on human footsteps have shown that the seismic particle velocity response to footsteps is site specific, with a characteristic frequency band of 20–90 Hz (Ekimov and Sabatier, 2006). The emergence of highly localized low-frequency strain and the preservation of high-frequency seismic components together signifies a near-field observation of the footstep signal by DAS. These distinctive seismic features of near-cable footsteps can become physical constraints to qualitative determine whether footsteps fall near the cable (e.g., in <10 m in our dataset), and their

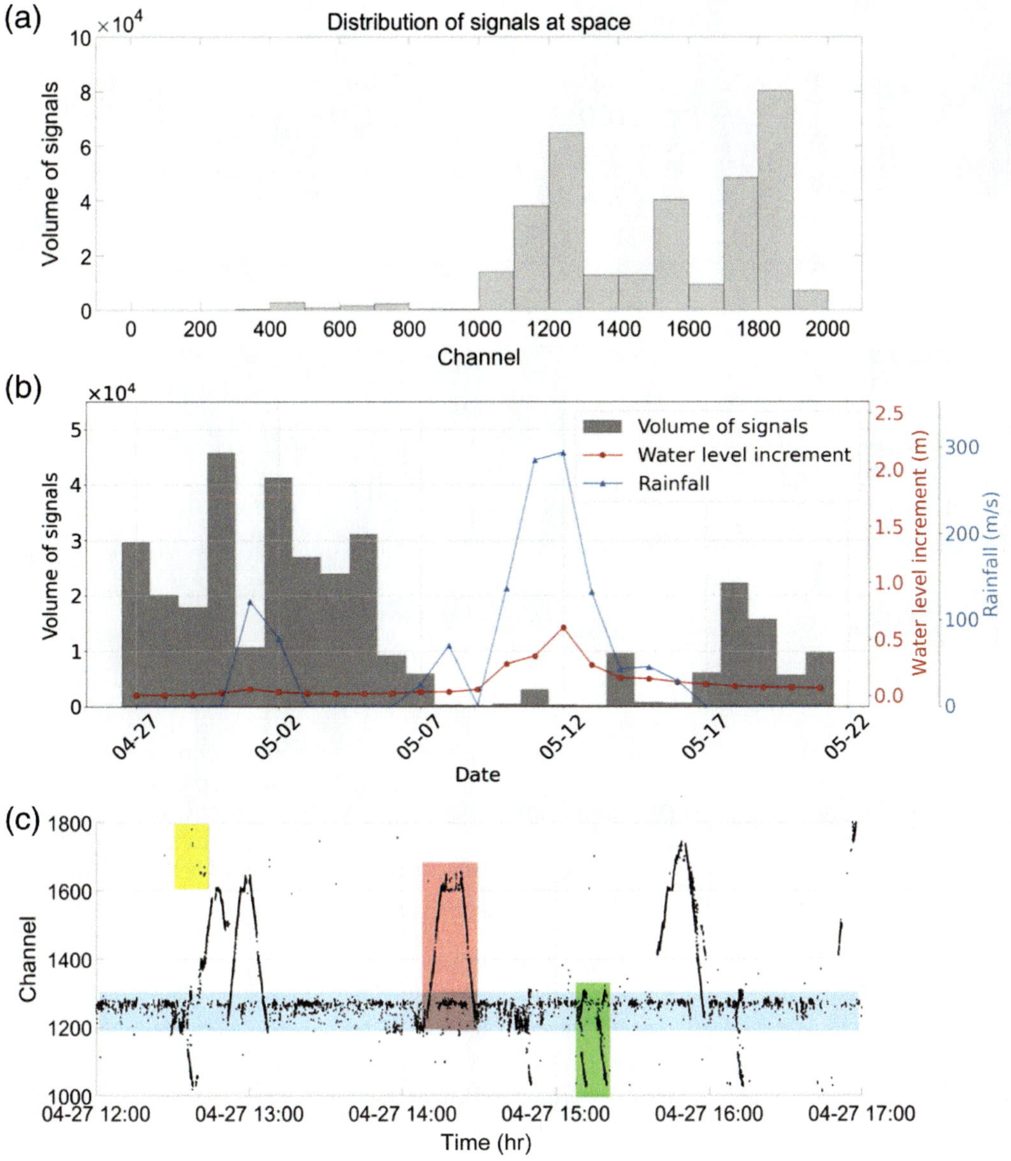

Figure 4. Statistical analysis of the detected footfall signals from the DAS data. (a) The histogram shows the distribution of signals in space. (b) The temporal variation of human activity compared with the variation of precipitation and reservoir water level increment. The histogram shows the change in the number of signal detections, the red line shows the change in the amount of water level change, and the blue line shows the change of rainfall. (c) The scatter that plots human footsteps from 12:00 to 17:00 on 27 April, where the red, green, blue, and yellow shading areas highlight examples of unilaterally migrating events, bilaterally migrating events, stationary random events, and sporadically dispersed "noisy" events, respectively.

locations can be precisely determined by the channel number of the localized low-frequency strain. The unilaterally migrating events mostly present these low-frequency components and thus can be easily interpreted as a typical movement of a person along the trajectory of the cable.

On the contrary, we notice that the newly observed bilaterally migrating event groups in the green rectangle in Figure 4c mostly consist of off-cable footsteps. Either converging or diverging migration of the events is detected in our dataset. Figure 6a is such an example illustrating two parallel sequences of off-cable footstep signals at two adjacent cable segments, which will eventually merge at one single location after a few minutes. After meticulous examination, these bilateral movement patterns of footstep event groups are found to be a result of off-cable human movement surrounded by a semi-enclosing cable geometry. This distinctive type of migration pattern occurs exclusively at around channels 1200 and 1800. As evident in Figure 1a, these two specific locations exhibit a U-shape DAS array geometry, enabling registration of seismic waves at multiple cable segments at the same time.

It appears that the pairs of seismic events in the parallel sequences always emerge simultaneously at two different cable segments, suggesting that they share the same off-cable origin of source excitation. We hereby adopt a backprojection procedure for footstep source determination by assuming a surface point source, a series of surface DAS virtual receivers along the cable, and a constant velocity subsurface medium. We estimate the travel times for all DAS channel locations, which can be simply put as $\tau_i(S_x,S,V) = \sqrt{(x_i - S_x)^2 + (y_i - S_y)^2}/V$, in which (x_i, y_i) denotes the ith channel location, (S_x, S_y) denotes the point-source location on the ground, and V denotes the seismic-wave velocity of the medium.

When stacking the DAS waveforms, we observe a unique polarity reversal feature among the footstep signals that could hamper the process. Such a feature has been reported by a previous experiment (Ku and Duckworth, 2013) as a consequence of the dipole nature of the footfall, which emits *SH* waves that show different DAS responses for fiber orientations and relative azimuth from the walker. It was found that the waveform

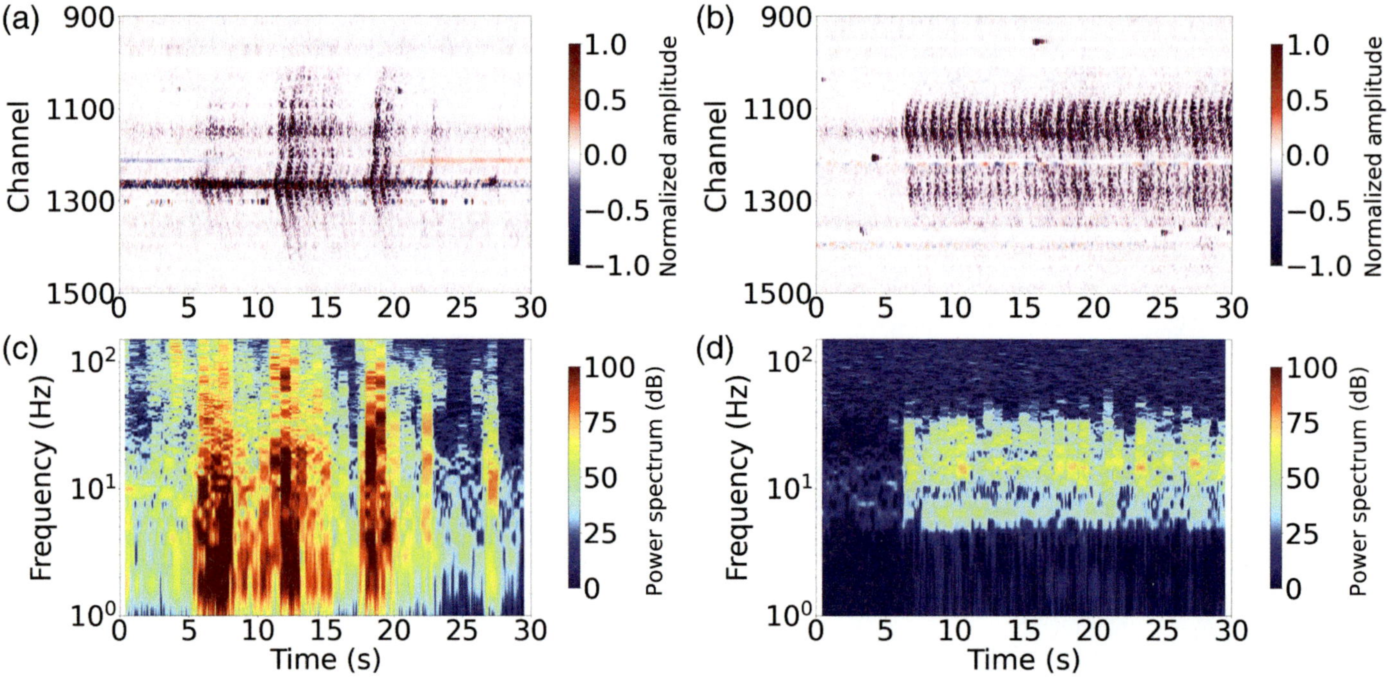

Figure 5. Comparison of detected human footstep DAS signals before and after the fiber-optic cable was submerged. (a) The DAS data from 29 April 2022, with the spectrogram for DAS channel 1262 shown in (c). (b) The DAS data from 21 May 2022, with the spectrogram for DAS channel 1180 shown in (d).

polarity flips at the waveform apex when the walker travels in a parallel direction to the cable, but when traveling toward a transversed cable in the front, there is no such polarity reversal phenomenon in the signal. In essence, there are nodal points at the broadsides of a walker, showing polarity reversal when emitting waves perpendicular to the traveling direction. To account for such a property, we calculate the differential azimuth between the traveling direction θ of the walker and the wave propagation direction toward the ith channel θ_i. We then design a differential azimuth-based coefficient

$$\gamma(\theta) = \begin{cases} 1, & 0° < \theta < 180° \\ -1, & 90° < \theta < 180° \end{cases}, \qquad (1)$$

to reverse the DAS record of ith channel in the back of the walker to ensure coherence of the waveforms of all channels. Because of the symmetry, one only needs to consider the range of footstep direction from 0° to 180°. Then we apply the estimated travel times for moveout correction to the DAS traces and calculate the corresponding semblance value ϕ as follows:

$$\phi(S_x, S_y, V, \theta) = \frac{\sum_t [\sum_i \gamma(\theta - \theta_i) \cdot d_i(t + \tau_i(S_x, S_y, V))]^6}{\sum_t [\sum_i d_i(t)]^6}, \qquad (2)$$

where $d_i(t)$ denotes the DAS time series data at the ith channel. We apply a grid-search strategy to target the optimal source location (S_x, S_y), as well as the velocity V and the traveling direction θ that maximize the semblance $\phi(S_x, S_y, V, \theta)$ and best explain the moveout of a pair of events. The backprojection location determination procedure of a two second example of the bilaterally migrating events is illustrated in Figure 6. The waveform of the data is shown in Figure 6a, along with the predicted arrival-time curves of the best solution, which match the actual data remarkably well. Figure 6a also illustrates the polarity reversal feature of human footsteps in DAS data, of which a zoom-in version is provided in Figure S2. Figure 6b illustrates the direction of the footstep and the channels in which polarity needs to be reversed. The semblance distribution of each pair of the target parameters is presented in Figure 6c–h. Figure 6d shows that the phase velocity of the event is ~300 m/s. One can estimate from Figure 6a, for example, the slope of the lower part of the fitted black line (channel 1300–1500 with 1 m spacing, taking 1.2 − 0.55 = 0.65 s to travel, yielding 307 m/s of wavespeed).

Subsequently, we can apply the same procedure to bilateral sequences of footstep signals and track human movement trajectories. Two examples of converging and diverging bilateral movements are illustrated in Figure 7a,b. Using channel stacking and 2 Hz narrowband filtering, we divide the DAS data into individual footstep events. From the DAS record in Figure 7a, we obtained 252 independent DAS records; Figure 7b produces 324 independent records. Using the backprojection method, we can determine the location of each footstep with meter-scale uncertainties, enabling precise tracking of human movement trajectories. Figure 7c,d shows the computed movement trajectories from the data in Figure 7a,b, respectively. The two data examples are also selected for before and after rainfall comparison, respectively. The prerainfall trajectory (Fig. 7c)

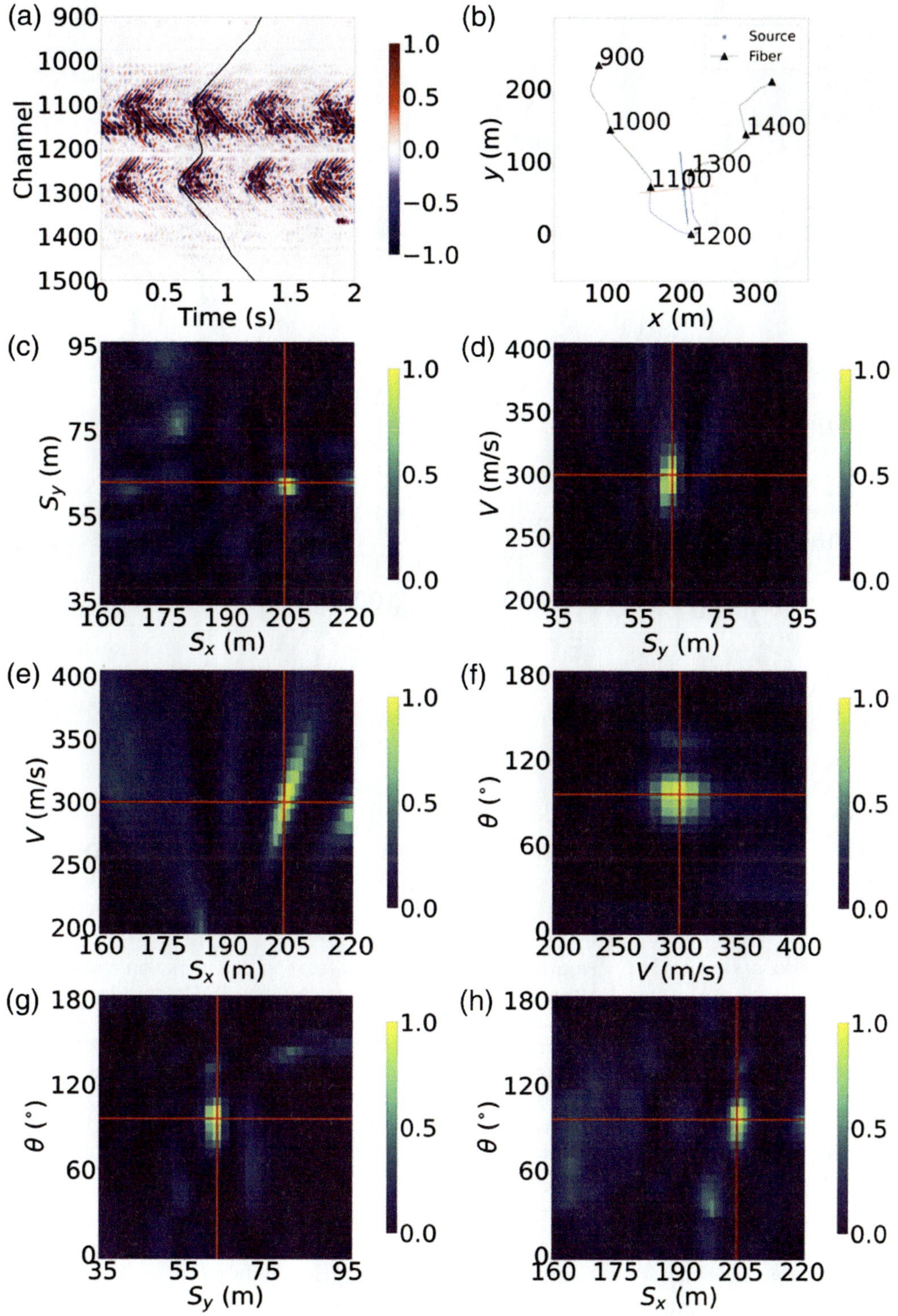

Figure 6. The exhibition of semblance. (a) The 2 s DAS record and the predicted arrival time (black curve) calculated by the parameters $S_x, S_y = (204, 63)$, $V = 300$, and $\theta = 96$. (b) The source location of the footstep in panel (a), marked by the crossing of a blue and a red line, where the blue line is the direction of footstep, and the red line shows the perpendicular direction to the blue line, which divides the potential DAS data recording of footsteps of different polarities. A solid curve representing part of the cable trajectory from 900 to 1400 is shown in black on the northern side of the red line and in dark blue on the southern side, differentiating opposite directions that the footstep points at. The black triangles denote locations of every 100 channels. Panels (c–h) are the semblance value distribution of different parameter pairs.

shows movement crossing the fiber, whereas the postrainfall record (Fig. 7d) shows the movement ended at a distance away from the fiber. The endpoints of these trajectories are hypothesized as the docking location of boats where human footsteps appear or disappear. The shift of the docking location of the trajectories matches our field observation that the cable has been submerged because of rising water levels following the rainfall, and thus, no direct crossing of the walker and the cable can be seen.

Discussion

The fiber-optic DAS technique has been widely applied in seismic detection because of its advantages of high sampling rate, dense sensor distribution, and higher sensitivity. However, the generation of a large volume of data has become a bottleneck for DAS data processing, making deep learning methods very suitable for addressing DAS-related problems. Our work focuses on the real-time detection of human activities using a DAS cable. The trained model predicts >300,000 footstep signals from the 4 TB continuous recording collected from 1900 DAS channels, with a processing speed of less than half an hour for each day's data. Our method could still achieve real-time monitoring of human activities on a large cable scale when extending the total number of channels to 10 times or more. Our research has captured >300,000 human signals within a 25-day period. The database created from these signals can be further used to study the characteristics of human footstep signals and to investigate seismic attenuation

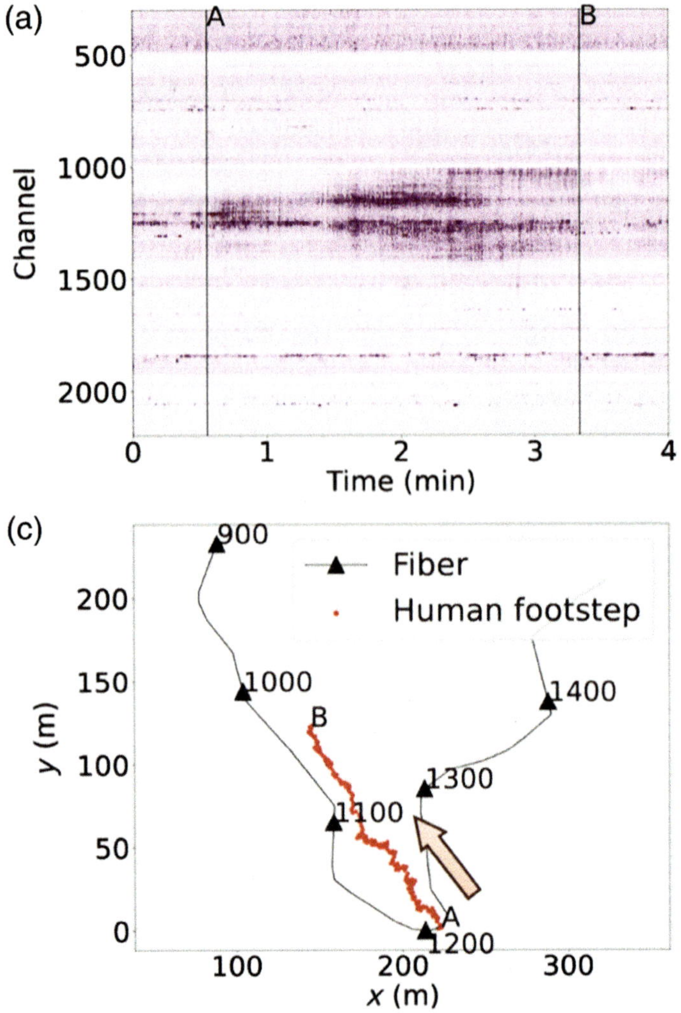

Figure 7. The illustration of location determination and human movement tracking results. (a) A 4 min DAS record for the divergence pattern is used to track human footsteps. (b) A 4 min DAS record for the convergence pattern is used to track human footsteps. (c,d) The movement inferred from the arrival time through an inversion process to determine the source location. The black lines with A and B annotations in (a) marks the moments when the walker is located at points A and B in (c). Same for panels (b) and (d).

phenomena. The Xinfengjiang Reservoir is also a seismically active area well known for reservoir-induced seismicity, detecting human activities on the ground may facilitate the removal of these unwanted ambient noise from microseismic signal recordings.

By introducing DAS technology, we can achieve unprecedented spatial resolution over long distances. Previous research on human footsteps has extensively used time-domain and time–frequency methods to analyze footstep data. However, the inherent spatial resolution limitations of traditional seismic nodal sensors pose a challenge for a comprehensive understanding of human footstep phenomena. Conventional time-domain methods struggle to provide accurate results in low signal-to-noise scenarios. Our study indicates that the time–frequency characteristics of human footstep signals vary significantly at different distances. Therefore, signals that are difficult to identify with traditional nodal arrays can be more easily recognized by DAS systems and can thus provide richer and more accurate information. This information includes not only temporal but also spatial variations, significantly enhancing geophysical monitoring capabilities. Because of the large volume of data, combining this technology with deep learning algorithms for monitoring is highly effective. Using object detection technology to identify events with similar spatiotemporal characteristics helps us explore and recognize signals with specific features that are currently hidden in DAS data but have not yet been studied.

Because of the high resolution of DAS, our study treats each footfall as a single seismic event rather than considering the overall characteristics of human movement. This approach offers several advantages. First, by taking each footfall as a fundamental unit, we can detect not only the signals arising from movement across the fiber but also all the footsteps of nearby individuals. Capturing the footsteps taking place around the cable offers a comprehensive perspective of the entire movement in the proximity of the cable because we can capture each footfall within a specific area. Second, treating each footfall as a basic unit provides deeper insights into human movement. Using special geometric shape of fiber-optic cables, this method can be used for tracking human movements more accurately, applicable in both indoor and outdoor scenarios. Finally, treating each footfall as a basic unit allows us to use hundreds of thousands of human footsteps as active sources to determine the subsurface velocity structure. There are many direct footfalls on our fiber, and from these signals, the spread of the wavefield is clear. We can use this information to determine the subsurface velocity structure. It is of great utility because we are able to use and identify numerous "semi-active" sources that are always recognized as ambient noise.

The proposed workflow may indeed face challenges when being extended to DAS application scenarios with poor cable coupling and thus poor data quality. Footstep signals may be significantly attenuated or distorted, rendering unrecognizable seismic waveform patterns in the DAS data that hinders the application of YOLO identification and the backprojection location method. Therefore, in urban space with additional noise interference (such as those from traffic), the proposed workflow may miss more signals than what we can observe in this study, and the detection range of footstep from the cable might not be as far as that we have seen in this study. In addition, the footstep detection method using seismic signals is by nature not as straightforward as vision-based methods. Inference of walker numbers is conditionally possible when there are separated trajectories constructed from the picked events. However, when people are walking together, it seems quite unlikely for DAS to be able to separate individuals and identify the number of people walking.

Conclusion

DAS technology, with its high spatial resolution, has significant advantages in monitoring small-scale weak vibration signals. In the field of urban seismology, DAS technology has achieved many meaningful results. We deployed optical fibers for seismic monitoring in the Xinfengjiang Reservoir and observed a large number of human footstep vibration events. In this study, we develop a deep learning method to capture signals with specific characteristics in DAS images, enabling precise spatiotemporal localization of these events. By retraining YOLO v. 5, we achieve a real-time object detection model to detect human footstep signals in DAS images. Through time–frequency analysis, it is found that human footstep signals have a strong high-frequency component (>10 Hz). Therefore, we hope to capture the complete wavefield of human footsteps. Compared with traditional methods, this study focuses on using a single human footstep as the basic detection unit. The model used in this study can extract clearly visible human footstep signals from DAS data, and the average accuracy exceeds 90%. Using this model, we extracted >300,000 human footstep signals from 21 day DAS data. By analyzing the spatiotemporal distribution of the detected signals, we found that the temporal changes of the detected human footstep signals are consistent with the weather changes, and the spatial changes are consistent with our actual local observations. Furthermore, by analyzing the spatiotemporal changes of human footsteps, we found that in the area where the optical fiber presents a characteristic geometric shape, the human footstep signals will be detected by DAS on both sides at the same time. Using this characteristic, combined with the polarity correction and backprojection methods, we successfully obtained the source locations of a series of human footstep signals and realized the tracking of human movement trajectories using DAS data.

Data and Resources

Distributed acoustic sensing (DAS) data were acquired using a Silixa iDAS-MG interrogator. The DAS records used in this study are available at doi: 10.5281/zenodo.14020647, and source codes for footfall event location calculation can be downloaded from https://figshare.com/articles/software/footstep_das/28656212 (last accessed March 2025). The supplemental material for this article includes validation of DAS footstep signals and highlight of polarity reversal feature in Figure 6a.

Declaration of Competing Interests

The authors acknowledge that there are no conflicts of interest recorded.

Acknowledgments

The authors are thankful to all the people who participated in the field experiment of the Xinfengjiang fiber-optic distributed acoustic sensing (DAS) observation. This work is supported in part by the National Key Research and Development Program of China (Grant Number 2023YFB2905300), in part by the National Science Foundation (NSF) of China (Grant Numbers 4247040345, 41890814, and U1901602), and in part by Shenzhen Science and Technology Program (Grant Number 20231116133945002)

References

Ajo-Franklin, J. B., S. Dou, N. J. Lindsey, I. Monga, C. Tracy, M. Robertson, V. Rodriguez Tribaldos, C. Ulrich, B. Freifeld, T. Daley, *et al.* (2019). Distributed acoustic sensing using dark fiber for near-surface characterization and broadband seismic event detection, *Sci. Rep.* **9,** no. 1, 1328, doi: 10.1038/s41598-018-36675-8.

Binder, G., and A. Tura (2020). Convolutional neural networks for automated microseismic detection in downhole distributed acoustic sensing data and comparison to a surface geophone array, *Geophys. Prospect.* **68,** no. 9, 2770–2782, doi: 10.1111/1365-2478.13027.

Chi, M., Q. Li, Z. Cao, J. Fang, B. Wu, Y. Zhang, S. Wei, X. Liu, and Y. Yang (2022). Evaluation of water resources carrying capacity in ecologically fragile mining areas under the influence of underground reservoirs in coal mines, *J. Clean. Prod.* **379,** 134,449.

Díaz, J., M. Ruiz, P. S. Sánchez-Pastor, and P. Romero (2017). Urban Seismology: On the origin of earth vibrations within a city, *Sci. Rep.* **7,** no. 1, 15,296, doi: 10.1038/s41598-017-15499-y.

Ekimov, A., and J. M. Sabatier (2006). Vibration and sound signatures of human footsteps in buildings, *J. Acoust. Soc. Am.* **120,** no. 2, 762–768, doi: 10.1121/1.2217371.

Hudson, T. S., A. F. Baird, J. M. Kendall, S. K. Kufner, A. M. Brisbourne, A. M. Smith, A. Butcher, A. Chalari, and A. Clarke (2021). Distributed Acoustic Sensing (DAS) for natural microseismicity studies: A case study from Antarctica, *J. Geophys. Res.* **126,** no. 7, e2020JB021493 , doi: 10.1029/2020JB021493.

Huot, F., A. Lellouch, P. Given, B. Luo, R. G. Clapp, T. Nemeth, K. T. Nihei, and B. L. Biondi (2022). Detection and characterization of microseismic events from fiber-optic das data using deep learning, *Seismol. Res. Lett.* **93,** no. 5, 2543–2553, doi: 10.1785/0220220037.

Jakkampudi, S., J. Shen, W. Li, A. Dev, T. Zhu, and E. R. Martin (2020). Footstep detection in urban seismic data with a convolutional neural network, *The Leading Edge* **39,** no. 9, 654–660, doi: 10.1190/tle39090654.1.

Jocher, G., A. Chaurasia, A. Stoken, J. Borovec, Y. Kwon, K. Michael, J. Fang, Z. Yifu, C. Wong, and D. Montes (2022). ultralytics/yolov5: v7. 0-yolov5 sota realtime instance segmentation, *Zenodo*, doi: 10.5281/zenodo.7347926.

Jousset, P., G. Currenti, B. Schwarz, A. Chalari, F. Tilmann, T. Reinsch, L. Zuccarello, E. Privitera, and C. M. Krawczyk (2022). Fibre optic distributed acoustic sensing of volcanic events, *Nat. Commun.* **13,** no. 1, 1753, doi: 10.1038/s41467-022-29184-w.

Ku, E. M., and G. L. Duckworth (2013). Tracking a human walker with a fiber optic distributed acoustic sensor, *Proc. of Meetings on Acoustics*, ASA, 70053, doi: 10.1121/1.4800575.

Landrø, M., L. Bouffaut, H. J. Kriesell, J. R. Potter, R. A. Rørstadbotnen, K. Taweesintananon, S. E. Johansen, J. K. Brenne, A. Haukanes, O. Schjelderup, *et al.* (2022). Sensing whales, storms, ships and earthquakes using an Arctic fibre optic cable, *Sci. Rep.* **12,** no. 1, 19,226, doi: 10.1038/s41598-022-23606-x.

Lecocq, T., S. P. Hicks, K. van Noten, K. van Wijk, P. Koelemeijer, R. S. M. de Plaen, F. Massin, G. Hillers, R. E. Anthony, M. T. Apoloner, *et al.* (2020). Global quieting of high-frequency seismic noise due to COVID-19 pandemic lockdown measures, *Science* **369,** no. 6509, 1338–1343, doi: 10.1126/science.abd2438.

Lindsey, N. J., S. Yuan, A. Lellouch, L. Gualtieri, T. Lecocq, and B. Biondi (2020). City-scale dark fiber DAS measurements of infrastructure use during the COVID-19 pandemic, *Geophys. Res. Lett.* **47,** no. 16, e2020GL089931 , doi: 10.1029/2020GL089931.

Linville, L., K. Pankow, and T. Draelos (2019). Deep learning models augment analyst decisions for event discrimination, *Geophys. Res. Lett.* **46,** no. 7, 3643–3651.

Lv, H., X. Zeng, F. Bao, J. Xie, R. Lin, Z. Song, and G. Zhang (2022). ADE-Net: A deep neural network for DAS earthquake detection trained with a limited number of positive samples, *IEEE Trans. Geosci. Remote Sens.* **60,** 1–11.

Min, R., Y. Chen, H. Wang, and Y. Chen (2024). DAS vehicle signal extraction using machine learning in urban traffic monitoring, *IEEE Trans. Geosci. Remote Sens.* **62,** 1–10, doi: 10.1109/TGRS.2024.3371052.

Mousavi, S. M., W. L. Ellsworth, W. Zhu, L. Y. Chuang, and G. C. Beroza (2020). Earthquake transformer—An attentive deep-learning model for simultaneous earthquake detection and phase picking, *Nat. Commun.* **11,** no. 1, 3952, doi: 10.1038/s41467-020-17591-w.

Shen, J., and T. Zhu (2021). Seismic noise recorded by telecommunication fiber optics reveals the impact of COVID-19 measures on human activity, *Seism. Record* **1,** 46–55, doi: 10.1785/0320210008.

Stork, A. L., A. F. Baird, S. A. Horne, G. Naldrett, S. Lapins, J. M. Kendall, J. Wookey, J. P. Verdon, A. Clarke, and A. Williams (2020). Application of machine learning to microseismic event detection in distributed acoustic sensing data, *Geophysics* **85,** no. 5, KS149–KS160, doi: 10.1190/geo2019-0774.1.

Titos, M., A. Bueno, L. García, C. Benítez, and J. C. Segura (2019). Classification of isolated volcano-seismic events based on inductive transfer learning, *IEEE Geosci. Remote Sens. Lett.* **17,** no. 5, 869–873.

Vidale, J. E., S. Goes, and P. G. Richards (1995). Near-field deformation seen on distant broadband seismograms, *Geophys. Res. Lett.* **22,** no. 1, 1–4, doi: 10.1029/94GL02893.

Walter, F., D. Gräff, F. Lindner, P. Paitz, M. Köpfli, M. Chmiel, and A. Fichtner (2020). Distributed acoustic sensing of microseismic sources and wave propagation in glaciated terrain, *Nat. Commun.* **11,** no. 1, 1–10, doi: 10.1038/s41467-020-15824-6.

Wang, X., E. F. Williams, M. Karrenbach, M. G. Herráez, H. F. Martins, and Z. Zhan (2020). Rose parade seismology: Signatures of floats and bands on optical fiber, *Seismol. Res. Lett.* **91,** no. 4, 2395–2398, doi: 10.1785/0220200091.

Wang, X., Z. Zhan, E. F. Williams, M. G. Herráez, H. F. Martins, and M. Karrenbach (2021). Ground vibrations recorded by fiber-optic cables reveal traffic response to COVID-19 lockdown measures in Pasadena, California, *Commun. Earth Environ.* **2,** no. 1, 160, doi: 10.1038/s43247-021-00234-3.

Zhan, Z. (2019). Distributed acoustic sensing turns fiber-optic cables into sensitive seismic antennas, *Seismol. Res. Lett.* **91,** no. 1, 1–15, doi: 10.1785/0220190112.

Zhao, Y., Y. E. Li, E. Nilot, and G. Fang (2021). Urban running activity detected using a seismic sensor during COVID-19 pandemic, *Seismol. Res. Lett.* **93,** no. 1, 181–192, doi: 10.1785/0220210147.

Zhong, T., M. Cheng, S. Lu, X. Dong, and Y. Li (2021). RCEN: a deep-learning-based background noise suppression method for DAS-VSP records, *IEEE Geosci. Remote Sens. Lett.* **19,** 1–5.

Zhou, Y., J. K. W. Yeoh, Y. E. Li, and W. Solihin (2024). Large scale indoor occupant tracking using distributed acoustic sensing and machine learning, *Build. Environ.* **247,** 111,005, doi: 10.1016/j.buildenv.2023.111005.

Zhu, T., J. Shen, and E. R. Martin (2021). Sensing earth and environment dynamics by telecommunication fiber-optic sensors: An urban experiment in Pennsylvania, USA, *Solid Earth* **12,** no. 1, 219–235, doi: 10.5194/se-12-219-2021.

Zhu, W., and G. C. Beroza (2019). PhaseNet: A deep-neural-network-based seismic arrival-time picking method, *Geophys. J. Int.* **216,** no. 1, 261–273, doi: 10.1093/gji/ggy423.

Manuscript received 22 April 2025
Published online 2 September 2025

Detecting Urban Earthquakes with the San Fernando Valley Nodal Array and Machine Learning

OPEN ACCESS

Joses Omojola*[1] and Patricia Persaud[1]

Abstract

The San Fernando Valley (SFV), part of the Los Angeles metropolitan area, is a seismically active urban environment. Large-magnitude earthquakes, such as the 1994 M_w 6.7 Northridge event that occurred on a blind fault beneath the valley, caused significant infrastructure damage in the region, underscoring the need for enhanced seismic monitoring to improve the identification of buried faults and hazard evaluation. Currently, the Southern California Earthquake Data Center operates four broadband instruments within the valley; however, the network's ability to capture small earthquakes beneath the region may be limited. To demonstrate how this data gap can be filled, we use recordings from the SFV array, comprised of 140 nodal instruments with interstation distances ranging from 0.3 to 2.5 km that recorded for one month. High-anthropogenic noise levels in urbanized areas tend to conceal earthquake signals; therefore, we applied a previously developed machine learning model fine-tuned on similar waveforms to detect events and pick seismic phases. In a two-step event association workflow, isolated phase picks were first culled, which eliminated false positive detections and reduced computational runtime. We located 62 events within a 209 km radius of our array with magnitudes ranging from M_L 0.13 to 4, including 36 new events that were undetected by the regional network. One event cluster reveals a previously unidentified (5.3 km × 4 km) blind fault zone located ~5 km beneath the southern part of the valley. Seismicity from this zone is rare in the regional catalog (< 3 events per year), despite producing a M_b 4.4 event in 2014. Our results highlight the benefits of detecting small-magnitude seismicity for hazard estimation. Temporary nodal arrays can identify critical gaps in regional monitoring and guide site selection for permanent stations. In addition, our workflow can be applied to complement seismic monitoring in other urban settings.

Cite this article as Omojola, J., and P. Persaud (2025). Detecting Urban Earthquakes with the San Fernando Valley Nodal Array and Machine Learning, *Seismol. Res. Lett.* **97**, 111–125, doi: 10.1785/0220250124.

Supplemental Material

Introduction

The San Fernando Valley (SFV) in the greater Los Angeles area is a densely populated urbanized valley that is prone to damaging shaking from earthquakes (Fig. 1; Vidale and Helmberger, 1988; Hartzell *et al.*, 1997; Krishnan *et al.*, 2005). The SFV basin initiated during an extensional period in the Miocene, following which the tectonic regime was altered to transpression during the evolution of the San Andreas fault (SAF; Crowell, 1979; Ingersoll, 2001; Levy *et al.*, 2020). Because of the critical role that sedimentary basin structure plays in seismic-wave amplification (e.g., Liu and Heaton, 1984; Graves and Wald, 2004; Day *et al.*, 2012), the region is one of several in Southern California where substantial effort is being dedicated to advance knowledge of sedimentary basin structure and rock properties to improve preparedness for a future large earthquake on the SAF system (Persaud *et al.*, 2016; Liu *et al.*, 2018; Ghose *et al.*, 2023; Villa *et al.*, 2023; Yang and Clayton, 2024). In addition, two of the most devastating earthquakes in the Los Angeles area, the 1971 M_w 6.7 San Fernando and 1994 M_w 6.7 Northridge earthquakes, occurred on blind thrust faults beneath the SFV (Fig. 1; Baldwin *et al.*, 2000; Fuis *et al.*, 2003), revealing large earthquake source regions as close as 25 km from downtown Los Angeles. Using information from the Northridge event, the U.S. Geological Survey (USGS) constructed new seismic hazard maps for Southern California that would account for the presence of blind faults (Updike *et al.*, 1996). A study after the Northridge event showed that site amplification was largest for stations on softer

1. Department of Geosciences, University of Arizona, Tucson, Arizona, U.S.A., https://orcid.org/0000-0001-5807-2953 (JO); https://orcid.org/0000-0003-3462-7023 (PP)

*Corresponding author: jomojo1@arizona.edu

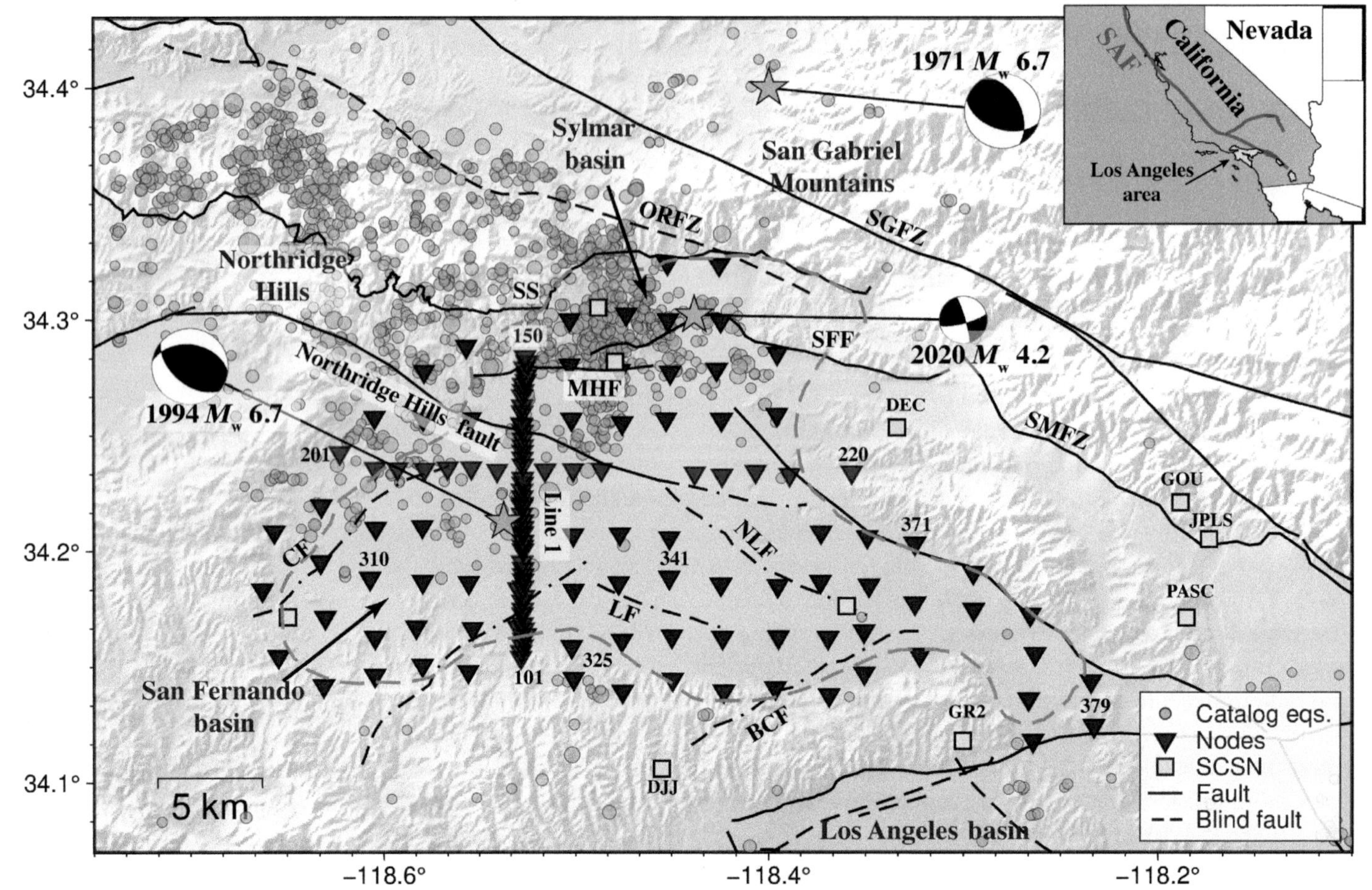

soils, and site amplification estimates show a better correlation with the detailed geology compared to a general geology classification (Catchings and Lee, 1996; Bonilla *et al.*, 1997; Hartzell *et al.*, 1997). The San Fernando and Northridge events have had far-reaching impacts on earthquake risk reduction (Hough *et al.*, 2024) and underscore the need for improved understanding of both the seismic structure of sedimentary basins and hazardous faults in urban areas with high-seismic risk (Islam *et al.*, 2025).

Utilizing gravity and magnetic data, well logs, and 2D seismic reflection profiles, Langenheim *et al.* (2011) mapped the major faults across the SFV basin. The basin can be subdivided into the San Fernando basin in the south and the Sylmar sub-basin in the north, which sits at a higher topographic elevation than the rest of the valley south of the Mission Hills fault (Levy *et al.*, 2020). Basin depths from ambient noise tomography and gravity modeling show the detailed structure of the SFV basin with its deepest part in the Sylmar sub-basin, and strong velocity contrasts characterizing the major faults (Juárez-Zúñiga and Persaud, 2025). The southern edge of the basin hosts normal faults from the extensional episode, whereas the northern part has thrust faults from the transpressional episodes (Levy *et al.*, 2020). The two major thrust faults beneath the SFV are the Oak Ridge fault zone (ORFZ) and the San Fernando fault, which dip to the south and north, respectively, and the ORFZ is overthrust by the Santa Susana fault (Fig. 1; Jennings *et al.*, 2010). Movement along the thrust faults is uplifting the Sylmar basin at a faster rate than the SFV, and causing seismicity beneath the basin (Langenheim *et al.*, 2011; Levy *et al.*, 2020).

Figure 1. Topographic map of the study area showing the San Fernando Valley (SFV) nodal array and the Southern California Seismic Network (SCSN) stations used in this study, with selected stations labeled. Black-solid lines are fault traces, and dashed lines are blind faults from the Statewide California Earthquake Center (SCEC) Community Fault Model (CFM) 6.1 (Marshall *et al.*, 2023). Focal mechanisms of the 1971 San Fernando and 1994 Northridge earthquakes are shown (USGS, 2025). Brown circles are the $M_w > 2.5$ earthquakes from the Hauksson *et al.* (2012) catalog from 1981 to 2018. The yellow fill in the inset map represents the outline of the major sedimentary basins in Southern California. Major faults and fault zones: MHF, Mission Hills fault; ORFZ, Oak Ridge fault zone or Northridge thrust; SAF, San Andreas fault; SFF, San Fernando fault; SGFZ, San Gabriel fault zone; SMFZ, Sierra Madre fault zone; SS, Santa Susana fault. The outline of the SFV (blue dashed line) and additional faults (black dashed–dotted lines; BCF, Benedict Canyon fault; CF, Chatsworth fault; LF, Leadwell fault; NLF, North Leadwell fault) are from Juárez-Zúñiga and Persaud (2025). The color version of this figure is available only in the electronic edition.

The seismicity forms diffuse clusters around the surface traces of the major faults in and around the northern part of the basin (Fig. 1). Regional catalogs indicate that the majority of these events are a subset of the 1994 Northridge event aftershock sequence (Hauksson *et al.*, 2012). Although the seismic hazard north of the basin is better understood, less is known about the seismicity and structural characterization in the southern part of the valley.

Local seismicity is useful for improving our understanding of earthquake statistics and seismic hazards; however, small-magnitude events (M $<\sim$1.8) can be routinely missed by regional networks in sparsely instrumented areas (Hutton *et al.*, 2010). In a study in metropolitan Los Angeles, Walls *et al.* (1998) suggest that small-magnitude seismicity along short fault segments is more likely to stimulate seismic moment release compared to infrequent large-magnitude events along major faults. The short recurrence intervals of small–medium magnitude events also make them useful in other urban seismic hazard studies, such as evaluating site effects (Islam *et al.*, 2025), mapping seismic scattering and absorption (Nardoni and Persaud, 2024), and developing high-resolution velocity models for improved ground-motion simulation studies. Within the SFV, the Southern California Earthquake Data Center (SCEDC) currently operates four broadband instruments under the CI network (Fig. 1) for monitoring seismicity (Caltech and USGS, 1926). Additional broadband stations can be costly to install and maintain, and have a large footprint; however, temporary dense nodal arrays can be employed to supplement broadband instruments and address monitoring gaps. The advancement of nodal seismometers, which are less expensive and easier to install, has made nodal experiments and large-*N* arrays (>100 instruments) more commonplace. Their autonomous operation makes nodes ideal for short-term experiments such as monitoring aftershocks and complementing regional networks (Farrell *et al.*, 2018; Catchings *et al.*, 2020; Lythgoe *et al.*, 2021).

There is general agreement that cataloging small-magnitude events is useful, but the task of detecting these events in metropolitan areas is limited by both our ability to adequately instrument high-density built environments and the challenges of extracting small-magnitude earthquake signals from data with high-anthropogenic noise levels. High-urban noise levels combined with seismic scattering in the shallow sedimentary layers, such as in the SFV, can mask seismic signals, complicating event detection and phase picking (Fiori *et al.*, 2023; Castillo *et al.*, 2024; Vassallo *et al.*, 2024). Although dense nodal deployments can improve the chances of event detection, relatively large datasets can further complicate the manual analysis of small-magnitude events (Liu *et al.*, 2020; Di Luccio *et al.*, 2021; Yang and Clayton, 2023). Recent advancements in machine learning (ML) models for automated event detection and phase picking have demonstrated their efficiency at processing large datasets (Zhu and Beroza, 2019; Mousavi *et al.*, 2020). Compared to other automated methods such as template matching and short-term average/long-term average (STA/LTA), ML techniques provide an optimal trade-off between processing speed and detection accuracy (Münchmeyer *et al.*, 2022; Kubo *et al.*, 2024). They generalize well to new datasets and can be readily fine-tuned to improve prediction accuracy on complex datasets (Woollam *et al.*, 2022). Detecting small events in high-noise urban sedimentary basins presents a new opportunity to adapt ML-based methods that are traditionally applied in quieter, sparsely populated settings, to urban nodal arrays. By leveraging these advancements, we can improve the detectability of small-magnitude events in densely populated metropolitan areas and shed light on the limitations of such detection efforts. In October to November 2023, an array of three-component SmartSolo nodal seismometers was installed across the SFV to test the feasibility of addressing seismicity monitoring gaps and to develop a high-resolution 3D seismic velocity model of the sedimentary basin. Here, we apply a pretrained ML model for automated processing of the dataset to evaluate the limitations of detecting small-magnitude events in an urban setting and improving seismic hazard characterization beneath the SFV.

Dataset

The SFV array was installed by teams of volunteers that included individuals from universities in Arizona, California, Louisiana, Texas, and Mexico, as well as nonacademic volunteers. The teams discussed the objectives of the project with residents and business owners and obtained permission to install the instruments on their properties or installed them in public places (Persaud *et al.*, 2024). The nodes were buried in ~20 cm deep holes to reduce traffic noise. In total, 140 three-component SmartSolo IGU-16HR 3C nodal seismometers were installed across the SFV over an area of ~520 km^2. The instruments were split into three subarrays (Fig. 1), with the first subarray being a dense line of 49 stations installed along a 15 km profile spaced ~300 m apart. This subarray was installed near the epicenter of the 1994 Northridge earthquake to improve seismic characterization across the Northridge Hills and Northridge thrust faults. A second 15-node linear subarray was installed along a west–east profile, and a grid of 76 stations with an interstation distance of ~2500 m was installed across the rest of the valley. The nodes recorded at 500 Hz from 21 October to 22 November 2023, and the recordings were manually downloaded from the nodes after they were retrieved. We also analyzed data from 10 broadband stations deployed within and around the SFV. These stations are part of the CI network and continuously record data at 100 Hz. Instrument response files for the nodal and broadband stations were obtained from the Earthscope Seismological Facility for the Advancement of Geoscience (SAGE) Data Management Center (DMC), and the waveforms were converted to displacement. The dataset is available at the Earthscope SAGE DMC (Persaud, 2023). We also utilized several existing datasets to provide context for our analysis and evaluate potential relationships with known fault structures. We obtained catalogs of relocated seismicity (1981–2018) and focal mechanisms in Southern California from the SCEDC special datasets (Hauksson *et al.*, 2012; Yang *et al.*, 2012). The aftershock catalog of the 1971 San Fernando earthquake was accessed through the SCEDC (Mori *et al.*, 1995), and 3D fault-plane representations were obtained from the Statewide California Earthquake Center (SCEC) Community Fault Model (CFM) 6.1 (Marshall *et al.*, 2023). Fault names correspond to those in the SCEC CFM 6.1.

Methodology

Event detection

We began our analysis by creating a catalog of seismic phases associated with events recorded by the nodal array. ML models are reliable for automating earthquake phase detection, and they generalize well to unseen datasets (e.g., Kubo *et al.*, 2024). Compared to traditional methods such as STA/LTA and template-matching cross-correlation catalogs, ML models provide an optimal trade-off between phase detection accuracy and computational runtimes (Kubo *et al.*, 2024). For phase detection, we used the hybrid autoencoder ML model of Omojola and Persaud (2024) that was developed to detect small-magnitude seismicity in high-noise industrial settings, hereafter referred to as microearthquake-Unet (MUnet). The MUnet model was developed to achieve high-quality phase detection for microearthquakes, which are important for accurate event locations while minimizing false positives caused by non-earthquake signals. It was first trained on small-magnitude earthquakes ($M_w < 3$), then fine-tuned on microearthquakes ($M_L < 2$) recorded by nodal arrays in an industrial area. Compared to other popular ML phase pickers, MUnet produced smaller mean errors for *P*- and *S*-phase picks (Omojola and Persaud, 2024) and is well suited for the SFV dataset. The model processes three-component waveforms downsampled to 100 Hz and outputs phase pick probabilities for both *P*- and *S*-wave arrivals. Following the waveform preprocessing steps applied in the original MUnet implementation, we cut our waveforms into 6-s-long windows with 25% overlap. A pick probability threshold of 0.4 was used for selecting phase picks based on tests carried out to detect known SCEDC catalog events across the SFV array.

Event association and location

Following phase identification, the *P*- and *S*-phase picks were processed in an event association workflow. Pick association is a process of merging phase arrivals from multiple stations to create a catalog of events. Simple association techniques such as grouping the number of picks within a time window (e.g., 2 s) generate subpar association results because of the moveout time across the entire array, especially for *S* waves that are slowed by the sediments. More robust association techniques that utilize velocity models are more accurate for phase association but trade off computational speed for accuracy. As the number of picks per event and the total number of events increase, these association algorithms can stall for several days without recovering or develop segmentation faults (Münchmeyer, 2024). Preliminary tests with the Gaussian Mixture Model Association (GaMMA) algorithm did not provide encouraging runtime results for known SCEDC catalog events (Zhu *et al.*, 2022); therefore, we did not test it on the entire dataset. In this study, we tested both the Rapid Earthquake Association and Location (REAL; Zhang *et al.*, 2019) and PyOcto algorithms for event association (Münchmeyer, 2024; Text S2, available in the supplemental material to this article). REAL and PyOcto produced similar results for synthetic tests that we executed using the SFV array station configuration (Text S2). PyOcto's computational runtime was shorter than REAL, so we opted to apply it to our full dataset.

The high volume of picks across the 140 stations (~1400 phase picks per station per day) required a computation time of over 24 hr with the PyOcto algorithm. To improve the runtimes, we developed an association preprocessing algorithm (Fig. 2a,b). Our algorithm first sorts all the phase pick arrival times and uses a cached table of interstation distances to estimate interstation apparent seismic velocities based on consecutive travel times. Minimum apparent seismic velocities (V_P 3.5 km/s and V_S 2 km/s) were then used to eliminate slow uncorrelated picks, and a minimum of 12 consecutive picks were further required for event identification. The minimum apparent velocity cutoff enables identification of pick clusters with interstation travel times that fit reasonable body-wave speeds for rays traveling through both sedimentary and crystalline rocks (Christensen and Mooney, 1995). This eliminates isolated or random picks from cultural noise sources and significantly reduces the number of input picks to the association algorithm (Fig. 2b,c). After preprocessing, the association computational time reduced from >24 to <8 hr. We proceeded to locate events using a 1D velocity model for southern California (Hadley and Kanamori, 1977). Increasing the minimum number of associated picks can reduce computational runtimes even further (<1 hr) at the expense of skipping small microearthquakes.

The association algorithm provides preliminary locations; however, we use the HYPOINVERSE (Klein, 2002) and HYPODD (Waldhauser, 2001) programs to improve the event locations. Python wrappers were developed around binary executables for both programs to enable easier location and relocation of the events in a single environment. We refined our initial event locations from HYPOINVERSE using the HYPODD double-difference relocation method. This helped to reduce our travel-time residuals to below 0.06 s and improved our catalog locations. Distant, larger magnitude regional events (farther than 30 km from our array) recorded by our nodal array did not form sufficient relocation clusters. For these events, we used initial location estimates from HYPOINVERSE with travel-time residuals <1 s in our catalog.

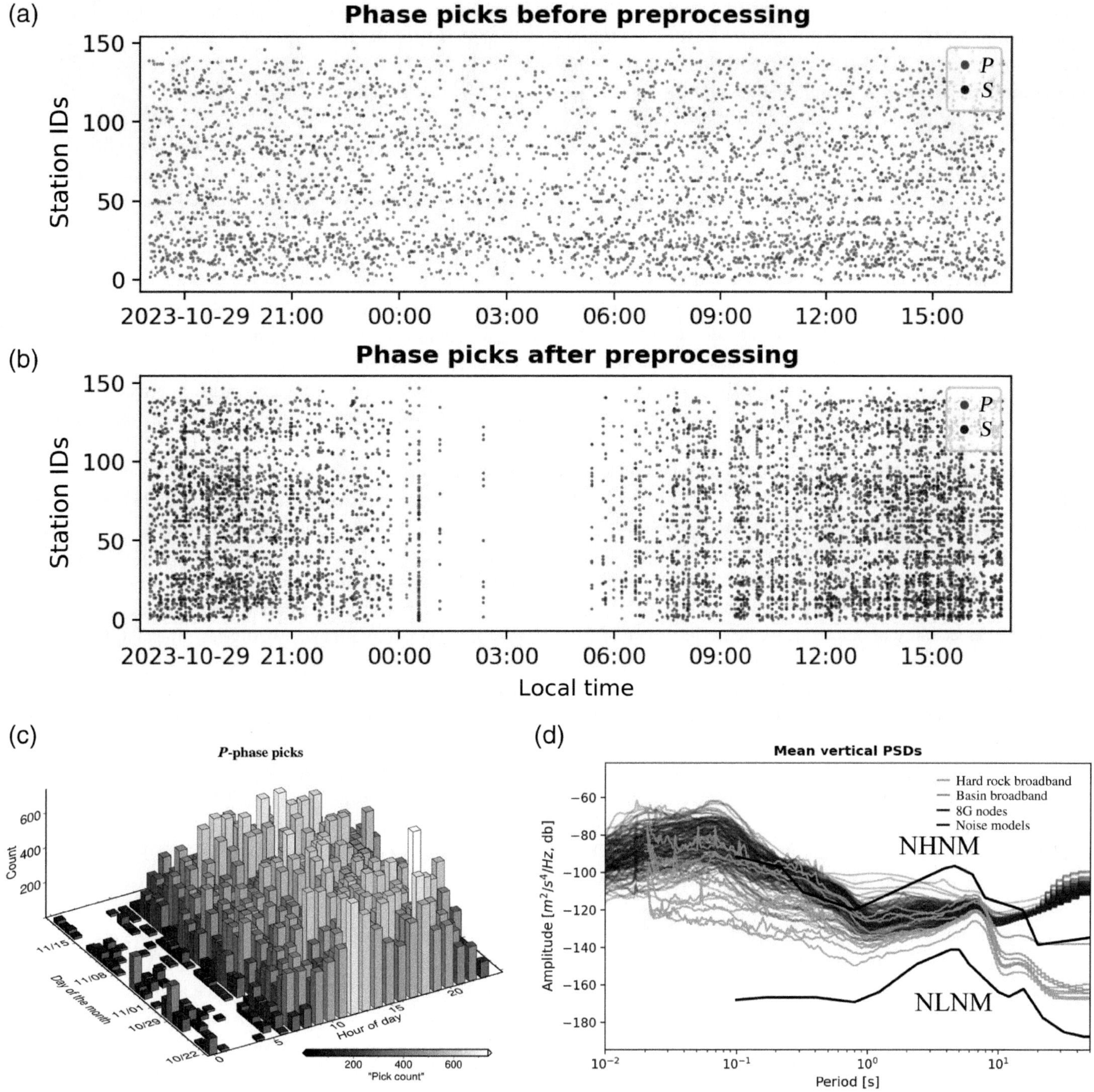

Figure 2. Preprocessing of phase picks for event association and comparison of noise levels of the node and broadband stations. (a) Raw picks before preprocessing from 30 October 2023 (UTC) with the *x* axis shown in local time. (b) Preprocessed picks after removing isolated detections. Fewer picks speed up the association process. Similar plots for 25 October, 5 November, and 17 November 2023 (UTC) are shown in Figures S3–S5. (c) 3D visualization of preprocessed *P* picks for the 140 SFV array and 10 SCSN stations used in this study. For each hour, the total number of consecutive phase picks that were detected by 12 or more stations is shown. The hour of the day is shown in local time. Note that the higher frequency of picks from 6 a.m. to 8 p.m. local time is influenced by the higher noise levels from human activity in the SFV. A similar plot including *S*-wave picks is shown in Figure S6. (d) Mean noise levels for vertical components of nodal and broadband stations for the full recording period. Relatively quiet broadband instruments are outside the SFV basin, and collocated nodal and broadband instruments within the basin have similar noise levels for periods below 10 s. NHNM, new high noise model; NLNM, new low noise model; PSD, power spectral density (Peterson, 1993). The color version of this figure is available only in the electronic edition.

Event magnitudes and detectability

Local magnitudes M_L of relocated events were estimated using a regression equation (1) that is dependent on the maximum amplitude of the P wave, A in millimeters, and the epicentral distance Δ for each event-station pair (Richter, 1935):

$$M_L = \log_{10} A + a \log_{10} \Delta + b. \quad (1)$$

Eighteen events from our relocated catalog, with known magnitudes from the SCEDC catalog were used to calibrate local magnitude values. Optimal estimates of the empirical values a and b were obtained by linear regression, and our best-fit results were $a = 1.7175$ and $b = 6.1777$. Magnitudes of local events detected by our array that are not in the SCEDC catalog were estimated using equation (1), and the median value across all recording stations was used to calculate the catalog magnitudes.

Seismic transient influences on urban recordings due to local site conditions, while having negligible effects on relatively long-period regional and teleseismic events (Liu *et al.*, 2018), play a key role in detecting local events by our array. Event detectability at individual stations depends on different factors, including but not limited to local geology, nearby noise sources, station coupling, event magnitude, and hypocentral distance (Inbal *et al.*, 2024). To evaluate the detectability of our array, we began by assessing the background noise levels using the probabilistic power spectral density (PPSD) of individual stations. The PPSDs were calculated by slicing continuous waveforms into 30-min windows with 50% overlap, and the power spectrum was estimated using the routines of McNamara and Buland (2004) in the ObsPy package (Krischer *et al.*, 2017). The mean PPSDs provide insights into local noise levels for different instruments (Fig. 2d). To estimate noise levels at specific times for detected events, the background seismic noise at 15 min intervals was converted to displacement using the routines of Lecocq *et al.* (2020).

Given that the SFV array recorded both local and regional events, using only epicentral distance or magnitude cutoffs to determine detectability limits can be inefficient. To assess the seismic signal at individual stations, we rely on ground-motion prediction equations (GMPE) because they are useful for estimating ground-shaking intensity while accounting for earthquake properties such as magnitude, distance to site, and spectral period (Boore and Atkinson, 2008). The peak amplitude of displacement (P_d), which is an example of a GMPE, provides a regression-based estimate of ground motion and is derived from the empirical relationships between magnitude and hypocentral distance (Wu and Zhao, 2006). Using 684 vertical-component records, Wu and Zhao (2006) derived regression estimates of P_d empirical coefficients for $M_w < 7$ events in Southern California as

$$\log(P_d) = -3.463 + 0.729M - 1.374 \log(\mathrm{R}) \pm 0.305, \quad (2)$$

in which M is the event magnitude, R is the hypocentral distance, and the unit of P_d is centimeters. The P_d of relocated events was converted from displacement $\mathrm{disp}_{\mathrm{cm}}$ to decibels, $\mathrm{amp}_{\mathrm{db}}$, at individual stations using the following equation:

$$\mathrm{amp}_{\mathrm{db}} = 20 \log_{10}(\mathrm{disp}_{\mathrm{cm}}). \quad (3)$$

The detectability threshold is calculated by subtracting the empirical signal amplitude from the nearest background noise amplitude at frequencies between 1 and 20 Hz. Examples of the detectability threshold are shown in Figure S7. When the signal amplitude exceeds the background noise amplitudes, the event is classified as being detectable at that station. The integration of event magnitudes, hypocentral distances, and noise levels at individual stations allows estimation of dynamic detectability thresholds. These thresholds are adaptive to temporal changes in noise levels, which are expected for an urban area such as SFV, and provide a robust estimate of event detectability at each station.

Results

We detected and located 62 events within a 209 km radius of the SFV array, during the month-long recording period (Dataset S2). The median signal-to-noise ratio (SNR) for daytime events across all stations was 0.34 compared to 4.2 for nighttime events, and many of our catalog events (61%) were detected at night between 8 p.m. and 5 a.m. Los Angeles time. Thirty-six events were relocated, with 17 of them occurring near faults within 10 km of our array. Average location errors for our relocated catalog were 108 and 152 m in the horizontal and vertical directions, respectively, with average travel-time residuals of ~10 ms. Location errors were relatively higher for the full catalog, which includes events outside our array's coverage. Our relocated events are shown in Figure 3, and our full catalog is shown in Figure S8. During the same period, the SCEDC catalog lists 10 events within 10 km of our array, and we recorded nine of those events. The 10th undetected M 1.48 event is considered a spurious event because its location is ~3 km from our array, but nearby nodal and broadband stations show no evident waveforms for this event (Fig. 3, Fig. S9). We also detected 15 additional events that were undetected by the SCEDC but could not be relocated reliably within the SFV (Fig. S8). These events were generally smaller, recorded on fewer stations (<24) in our array, and had higher travel-time residual errors. The station density of our nodal array provides improved constraints on our computed locations within the valley, giving us better resolved hypocenters and depth estimates compared to the SCEDC catalog (Fig. 4).

Our relocated event magnitudes around the SFV range between M_L 0.13 and 2.04, with a median magnitude of M_L 1.27. Event depths range between 6 and 25 km, forming miniclusters along major thrust faults such as the ORFZ and the Santa Susana faults north of the SFV (Figs. 3, 5a–c). Three of these events were located south of our array, in an area without any mapped active faults, and we designate these events as cluster 1 (Fig. 3). The events are located within proximity of prior seismicity in the Hauksson *et al.* (2012) catalog and a concealed Pre-Quaternary

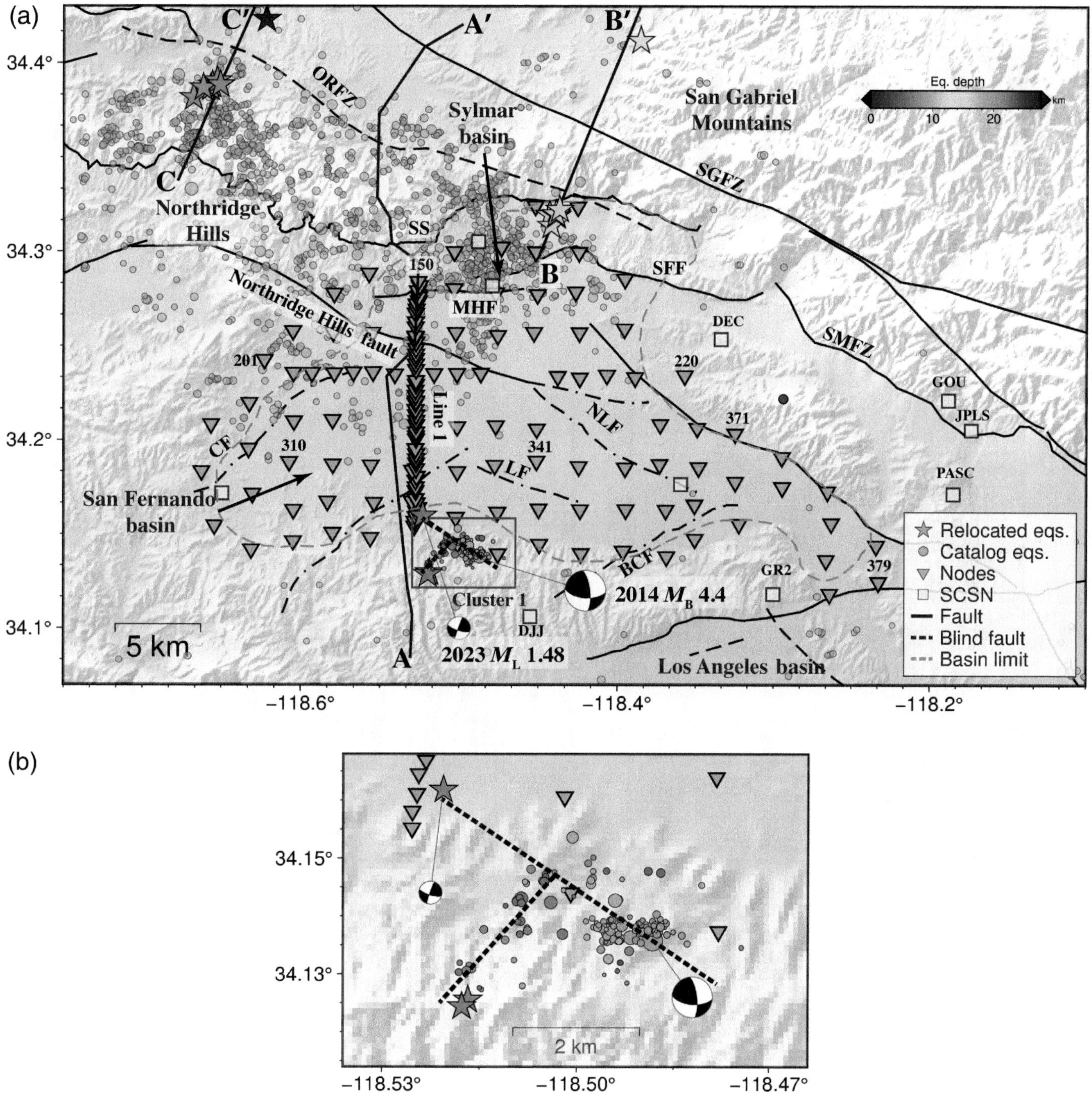

fault in the California Geologic Survey records (Jennings *et al.*, 2010; Hauksson *et al.*, 2012). Map and cross-section estimates of the fault zone indicate potential intersecting fault branches with a dimension of ~5.3 km × 4 km.

We estimated the focal mechanisms for one event in cluster 1 using the HASH method (Hardebeck and Shearer, 2003) and a 1D velocity model (Hadley and Kanamori, 1977) to calculate fault-plane orientations with uncertainty bounds. This approach required a minimum of eight stations with alternating polarity directions to obtain high-quality focal mechanism solutions. Our focal mechanism solution for the largest (M_L 1.48) event in cluster 1 is well constrained with a

Figure 3. Map of relocated local events within 10 km of installed stations colored by hypocentral depth. (a) Relocated events are shown as stars. The locations of the A–A′, B–B′, and C–C′ cross sections in Figure 5 are shown with solid dark blue lines. The fault names, background seismicity, and stations are the same as Figure 1. The red circle near node station 371 marks the location of the spurious Southern California Earthquake Data Center (SCEDC) catalog event, with waveforms shown in Figure S9. Cluster 1, with three relocated events, is highlighted with the brown rectangle. (b) A zoomed-in map of the cluster 1 events. A representative fault plane that aligns with the 17 March 2014 13:25:36 M 4.4 (event ci15476961; USGS, 2025) and the aftershock seismicity from Hauksson *et al.* (2012) is shown with the black dashed line. The color version of this figure is available only in the electronic edition.

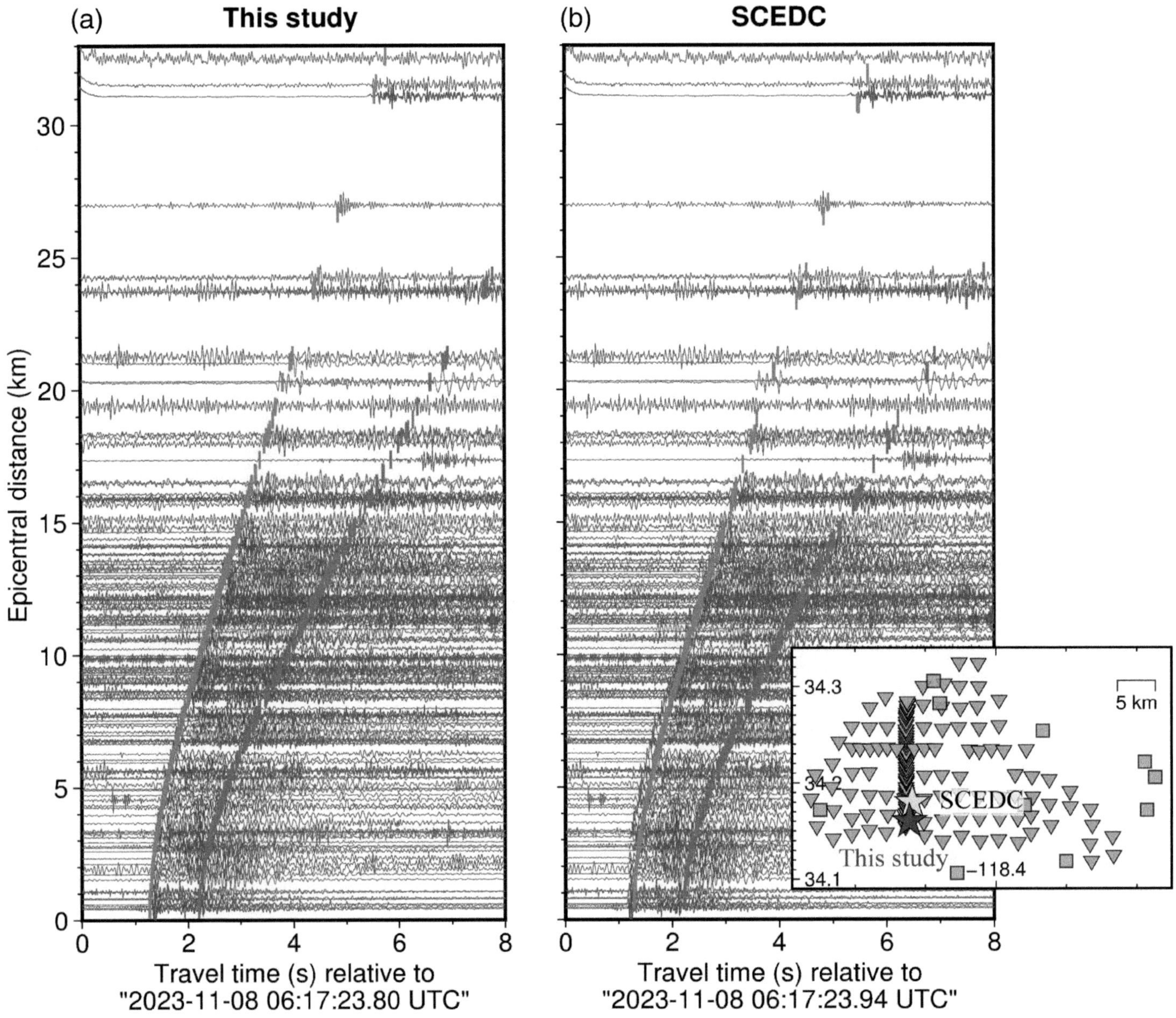

HASH quality of "B", and has a strike, dip, and rake of 108°, 73°, and 176°, respectively (Fig. 3b). The event is located 7.04 km beneath the basin (Fig. 5a) and can be interpreted as a dominantly strike-slip fault with a minor thrust component. The other two events had magnitudes of M_L 0.13 and 0.44, and reliable focal mechanisms could not be computed for these events due to insufficient opposite first polarity measurements.

The remaining 19 events in our relocated catalog were a combination of local and regional events from outside the SFV area. Epicentral distances ranged between 29 and 209 km, and local magnitudes for these events ranged between M_L 0.77 and 4.0. The SCEDC catalog contained 12 of these 19 events, and all relocated events were recorded by at least six stations in our study.

We reviewed the SCEDC catalog seismicity in the SFV from the last decade (2010–2023), to evaluate the earthquake statistics around the SFV. We selected a time period for which no major aftershocks or magnitude modifications were implemented to reduce the risk of masking natural changes in seismicity (Tormann *et al.*, 2010). A total of 2510 events were included in our search criteria, and the magnitude of

Figure 4. Comparison of predicted *P*- and *S*-wave arrival times for two different event locations for the M_L 1.48 event shown in Figure 3. Waveforms are band-pass filtered between 1 and 40 Hz. *P*- and *S*-wave arrivals in red and blue, respectively, were calculated using a 1D velocity model (Hadley and Kanamori, 1977) to compare event locations from (a) our study and (b) the SCEDC catalog shown in the inset map. Waveforms are sorted by epicentral distance. The SCEDC hypocenter gives a poor match and appears later than observed arrivals for stations <10 km from the epicenter. Different start times were used to crop the waveforms to ensure consistency with both catalogs. Epicentral locations from the SCEDC and this study for the M_L 1.48 event are included in the inset map. Nodal and broadband stations are shown as blue triangles and gray squares, respectively. The color version of this figure is available only in the electronic edition.

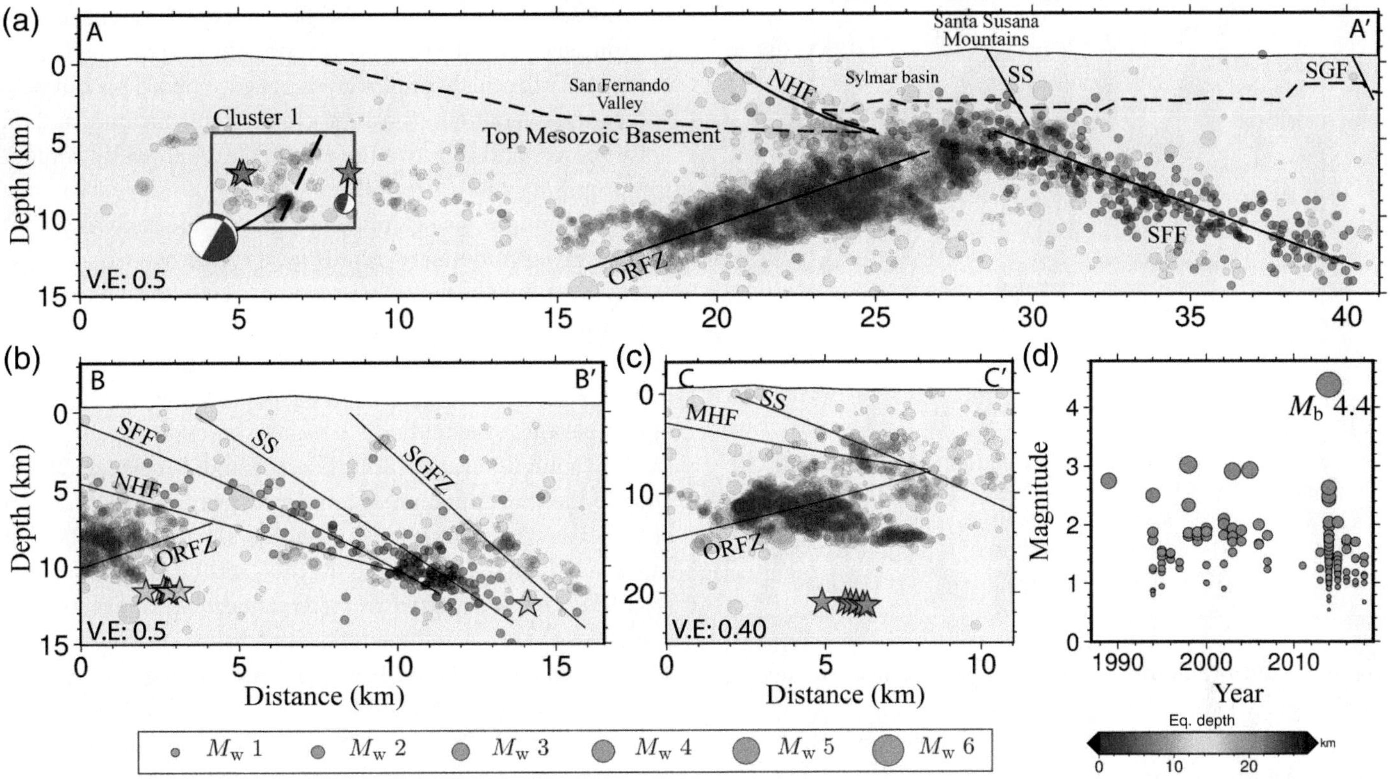

completeness (M_c) of the catalog is 2.5 (Fig. 6). This indicates that the regional network is capable of reliably detecting M 2.5 events and greater. The b-value for our catalog was calculated using the Gutenberg–Ritcher relationship, which is a function of the relative proportion of small-to-large earthquakes (Geffers *et al.*, 2022). The estimated b-value of 0.85 is on par with regional studies of seismicity in southern California (Hutton *et al.*, 2010; Tormann *et al.*, 2010), and relative differences may be attributed to catalog incompleteness due to the short deployment period. Although the time period of our catalog is too restricted to allow a meaningful comparison to M_c, the magnitude–frequency distribution of our catalog includes a higher proportion of smaller magnitude events M < 0.5 (Fig. 6). This suggests that the smaller magnitude events below 0.5 may be routinely undetected by the regional array, and additional permanent stations can help lower the overall magnitude of completeness within the SFV.

Figure 5. Cross sections showing our relocated events with stars colored by hypocentral depth, the background seismicity with red circles (Hauksson *et al.*, 2012), and aftershocks from the 1971 San Fernando earthquake with blue circles (Mori *et al.*, 1995). Profile locations are shown in Figure 3. (a) Projected seismicity within 4 km of profile A–A′. The ORFZ and SFF faults converge beneath the SFV. Basin depth and known faults are modified after Langenheim *et al.* (2011). The background seismicity shows the interpreted dip of the cluster 1 fault zone. Focal mechanisms for our M_L 1.48 event and the 17 March 2014 M_b 4.4 event (USGS, 2025) indicate an oblique strike-slip fault, with a dip ranging between 71° and 72°, and a minor reverse component. (b) Projected background seismicity within 2 km of profile B–B′. Projected fault locations from the SCEC CFM 6.1 are shown as solid lines. Relocated events are linked to seismicity along the SGFZ and ORFZ. (c) Projected seismicity and faults along profile C–C′. Our relocated events lie below the major event clusters. (d) Magnitude versus time distribution of events from Hauksson *et al.* (2012) in the cluster 1 fault zone showing quasi-continuous and ongoing activity. The color version of this figure is available only in the electronic edition.

Discussion

A major challenge in urban seismic monitoring is the high background noise levels caused by anthropogenic activities such as transportation, construction, and industrial operations (Inbal *et al.*, 2018; Bao *et al.*, 2024). Temporal differences in noise levels (Fig. S10) can complicate earthquake detection, reinforcing a need to estimate event detectability, which can be used to modify event detection strategies. For example, the M_L 0.13 event in cluster 1 occurred at night and was recorded at a maximum epicentral distance of 18 km, whereas the M_L 0.44 event, which occurred during the day, was recorded at a maximum epicentral distance of 9 km. In the SFV, higher daytime noise levels impact event detection as evidenced by the lower median SNR we observed for daytime events (0.34) compared to nighttime events (4.2). Similar issues have been encountered in other urban studies, such as in Auckland, New Zealand; London, United Kingdom; and the Long Beach and Seal Beach areas of Southern California (Boese *et al.*, 2015; Green *et al.*, 2016; Yang and Clayton, 2023). To address noise contamination, some authors focus on analyzing

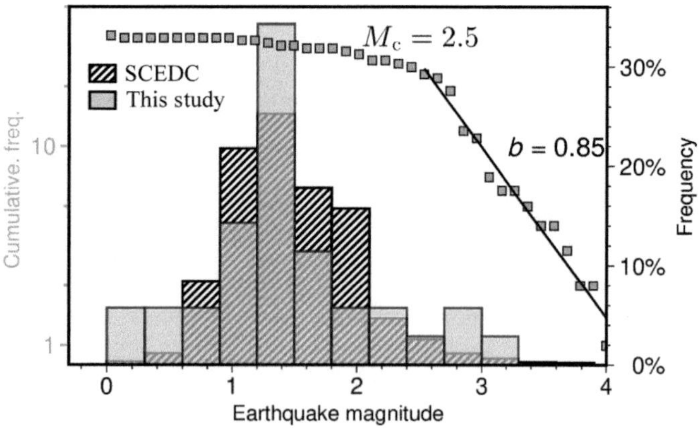

Figure 6. Magnitude–frequency distribution for our catalog compared to the SCEDC catalog of events around SFV (2010–2023). The blue histogram includes all 36 relocated events detected in this study. The color version of this figure is available only in the electronic edition.

mainly nighttime events, deploying borehole instruments, or employing ML denoisers (Boese *et al.*, 2015; Yang *et al.*, 2022; Yang and Clayton, 2023). But borehole instruments are expensive to install, and employing trace-by-trace ML denoisers can attenuate coherent signals in waveforms, reducing the overall quality of phase picks and detected events (Yang and Clayton, 2023). In addition, spectrogram stacking detection methods have also been applied to a dense seismic array dataset (Lythgoe *et al.*, 2021). This approach entails compromises between accurate event detection, the rate of false positive detections, and computational complexity (Lythgoe *et al.*, 2021). Other techniques include exploiting subarray similarity (Meng and Ben-Zion, 2017), and combined detection-location methods (Poiata *et al.*, 2016). Li *et al.* (2018) also applied correlation and stacking methods to dense nodal array data. Although many of these methods are robust, they are often computationally expensive and require additional dependencies such as duplication of input waveforms and consistent station spacing (Li *et al.*, 2018). Combined detection-location methods can also be affected by uncertainties in velocity models (Li *et al.*, 2020).

In urban settings such as the SFV, consistent station spacing is not feasible. We therefore adopted the MUnet model that was fine-tuned on noisy event waveforms for event detection and phase picking. This allows detection of small-magnitude events with the trade-off of a high number of phase detections (Fig. 2a). We designed our preprocessing algorithm to optimize the computational efficiency of event association, eliminate spurious phase detections, and reduce the association runtime without sacrificing accuracy (Text S1). Using our initial catalog of detected events and station noise estimates from PPSD calculations, we were able to estimate event detectability for the M_L 1.48 event at local stations, which compares well to the observed detectability (Fig. S7e,f). When applied in a permanent network scenario, computed detection thresholds can be used to dynamically adjust the ML picker probabilities at different times of the day when higher noise levels are expected. This can help reduce the overall false positive events from daytime cultural noise sources and improve the event detection quality without compromising catalog completeness by omitting real daytime events or compromising coherent signals with denoising. Our dense array also routinely records local events over shorter distances that would be typically attenuated across the longer interstation distances of regional stations.

The magnitude of completeness of a catalog provides insights into the network's detection capability. A lower magnitude of completeness can indicate a higher detection capability for small-magnitude events (Schorlemmer and Woessner, 2008). Despite the short duration of our deployment, the high station density resulted in our array detecting a large proportion of small-magnitude events within the SFV, across multiple stations (Fig. S8). This is expected to increase the ratio of events with magnitudes <1.5 over time, contributing to an overall lower M_c. For some events outside of our array coverage, our relocation workflow gave deeper locations than seismicity in the SCEDC catalog. This may be due to the sparse azimuthal coverage in the phase arrivals used to locate these events (C–C′ in Fig. 5). Within the SFV, increased *P*- and *S*-phase picks from our dense network potentially improves constraints on our locations including event depths, which results in a better fit of predicted arrival times for near epicentral stations.

The importance of our results extends beyond event detection and association. Prior studies of fault activity highlight detailed shallow crustal structures (<5 km) using a combination of well logs, geophysical data, and forward structural modeling (Langenheim *et al.*, 2011; Levy *et al.*, 2020). Although these structures are generally important, the large-magnitude earthquakes in the SFV occur on deeper faults >10 km, where the geometry and interfault relationships are not as clearly defined. Fault traces from the U.S. Geological Survey (USGS) (2025) and 3D fault planes from SCEC CFM attempt to capture these relationships using earthquake data (Marshall *et al.*, 2023; Fig. S11). However, improvements can be achieved by integrating high-resolution relocated catalogs. Besides the major fault planes, minor faults in and around the SFV are illuminated by small-magnitude seismicity such as cluster 1 (Fig. 3).

Our focal mechanism solution for the largest event in cluster 1 (M_L 1.48) suggests strike-slip faulting with a minor thrust component, consistent with the regional tectonic setting (Fig. 5a). This demonstrates that the potential of dense nodal arrays to resolve small-scale fault structures and kinematics, providing valuable inputs for seismic hazard models. The cluster 1 fault zone is ~5.3 km × 4 km, and the Hauksson *et al.* (2012) catalog shows that it has produced M_w 3 events every few years since 1988 (Fig. 5d). In 2014, it produced a moderate magnitude M_b 4.4 event, indicating a potential for nucleating larger magnitude events. In our one month of recordings, we

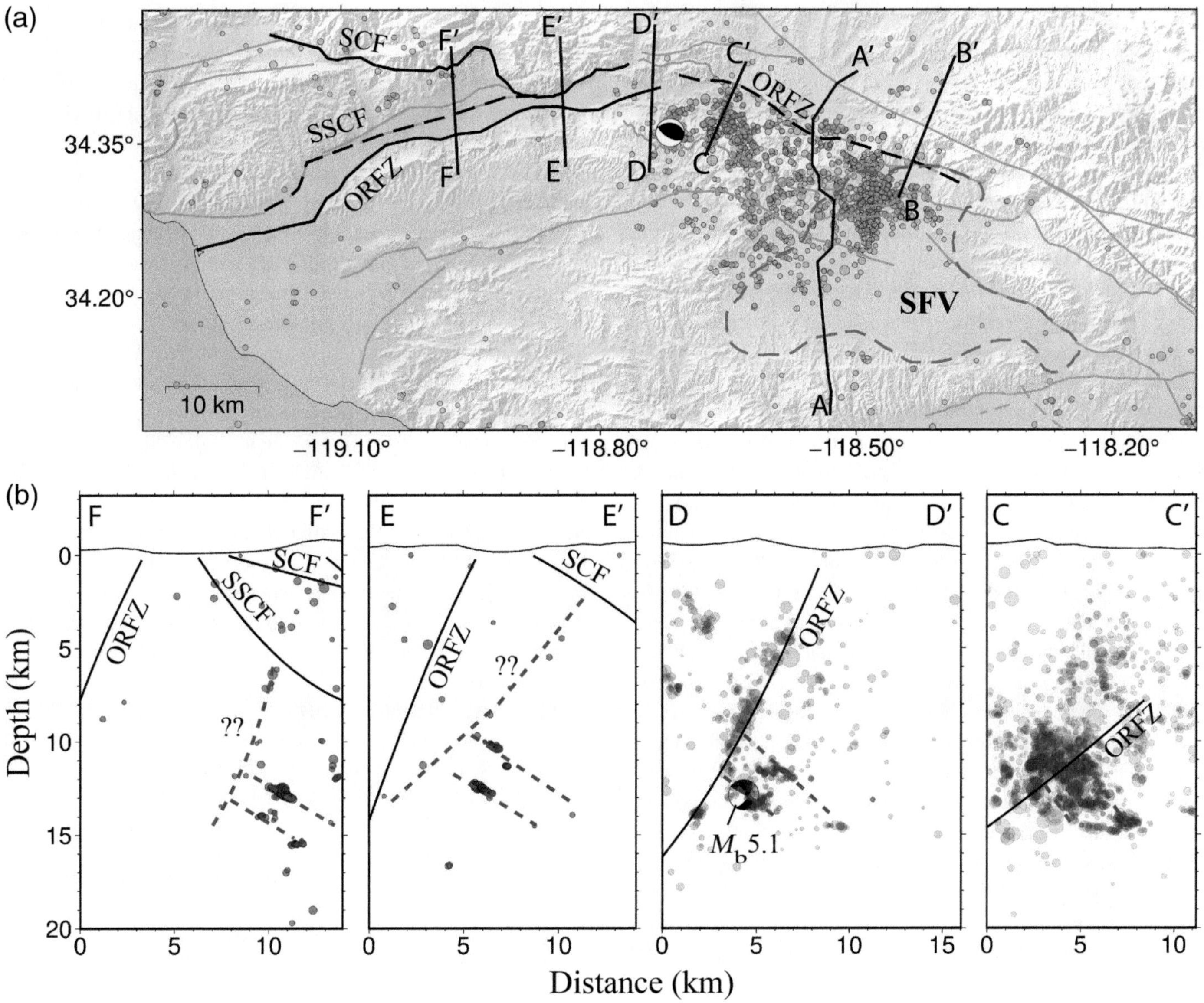

Figure 7. Improving fault geometry estimates with small-magnitude seismicity. (a) Topographic relief map showing the ORFZ geometry. Earthquakes ($M_w > 2.5$) from Hauksson *et al.* (2012) are shown as brown circles. Selected cross sections (dark-blue lines) are drawn across the ORFZ. The SFV basin is outlined with the light-blue dashed line. The M_b 5.1 (19 January 1994 21:09:28) focal mechanism is from Yang *et al.* (2012). Major faults and fault zones: ORFZ, Oak Ridge fault zone or Northridge thrust; SCF, San Cayetano fault; SSCF, Southern San Cayetano fault. (b) Interpreted antithetic faults or secondary structures are shown with blue dashed lines. Projected seismicity and SCEC CFM fault planes are similar to Figure 5. A time-lapse view of the seismicity from 1981 to 2018 along profiles C–F is shown in Video S1. The color version of this figure is available only in the electronic edition.

detected three events along the cluster 1 fault zone compared to the SCEDC catalog annual average of 2.3 events. These events, often overlooked in regional catalogs, can serve as indicators of larger seismic moment releases and offer critical insights into fault interactions and stress accumulation in urban basins. Temporal and spatial clustering of small events can indicate areas of stress concentration that may eventually culminate in larger ruptures. This phenomenon has been documented in several major earthquake sequences, for which retrospective analysis revealed accelerated microseismicity preceding the mainshock (Kato *et al.*, 2012; Bouchon *et al.*, 2013). By improving detection capabilities in urban areas, we can better identify such potential nucleation zones, providing critical inputs for time-dependent seismic hazard models. The spatial distribution of these small-magnitude events also helps constrain fault segmentation and interaction zones, where stress transfer between adjacent structures may facilitate or inhibit rupture propagation during larger events.

For example, the ORFZ associated with the 1994 Northridge earthquake is a blind thrust fault that extends from the western SFV to the Santa Barbara channel (Jennings *et al.*, 2010; Fig. 7a). Geologic interpretation of structural features and fault interactions along the ORFZ, northwest of the SFV has been a subject of controversy with earlier studies before the Northridge earthquake suggesting thin-skinned deformation (Yeats *et al.*, 1988), and post-Northridge cross-section balancing studies indicating thick-skinned deformation structures (Huftile and Yeats, 1995, 1996; Carena and Suppe, 2002). The ORFZ is represented within the 3D SCEC CFM as a simple thrust fault plane (Fig. S11); however, cross-section views of relocated seismicity along the fault from Hauksson *et al.* (2012), highlights northward-dipping seismicity possibly along a secondary fault plane that is antithetic to the main thrust (Fig. 7b). We interpret this and other off-fault seismicity trends in the cross-sections as secondary fault planes (blue dashed lines in Fig. 7b). Although, a potential proto-ORFZ has been highlighted in geologic studies (Huftile and Yeats, 1995), these faults have not been included in any major databases including the SCEC CFM and California Geological Survey. The antithetic faults branch from the main ORFZ around 10 km depth and have continuity along strike for >20 km (Fig. 7b). Multifault interactions like this create structural complexity that can potentially lead to larger magnitude earthquakes (Aochi and Kato, 2010). Early aftershocks of the Northridge earthquake reactivated the antithetic faults (Video S1), and additional seismic sequences can be observed in the updated Hauksson *et al.* (2012) catalog up until 2015. These faults can host moderate magnitude seismicity, such as the M_b 5.1 Northridge aftershock on profile D–D′ (Fig. 7b). The focal mechanism for the M_b 5.1 event indicates dominantly thrust faulting with a minor strike-slip component, dipping at 32°. Incorporating these secondary faults into a refined 3D fault representation can provide improved fault rupture estimates during seismic hazard evaluations. Improved fault geometries would help to better capture the strain partitioning between the main thrust and antithetic faults, providing more accurate rupture propagation barriers and segment boundaries, and account for potential multifault rupture scenarios that could cause larger earthquakes that are currently unaccounted for in hazard models (Kyriakopoulos *et al.*, 2017). These refinements are particularly important for dynamic rupture simulations, as complex fault interactions can amplify shaking intensity and duration in areas at risk of seismic damage, such as the SFV (Carena and Suppe, 2002).

Finally, the proportion of small-to-large earthquakes in a catalog is crucial for seismic hazard estimation (Geffers *et al.*, 2022). The central portions of the SFV are devoid of CI network stations (Fig. 1). Installing two additional stations, which can be node stations, west and east of Line 1 within the SFV, close to the proposed locations in Figure S12, would potentially improve the detectability of the regional network to capture low-magnitude seismicity and improve the hypocentral estimates for events in the SCEDC catalog.

Conclusion

Our study utilizes a dense nodal array with ML techniques to detect and characterize small-magnitude seismicity in the urban environment of the SFV. We effectively address the challenges of high-anthropogenic noise by omitting uncorrelated phase picks while preserving coherent seismic signals, thus improving computational efficiency for event association. This approach identified 62 events within a month-long period, 36 of which were relocated to obtain improved location estimates. The increased number of event phase picks from our dense array improved our constraints on event locations. Travel-time estimates from our catalog hypocenters match observed event arrivals better when compared to shared regional catalog events, demonstrating the potential for reducing location uncertainties. We highlight new insights into fault activity and seismic hazard within the SFV and along the ORFZ, where fault interactions should be examined for their potential to promote rupture propagation, increasing the risk of seismic hazard beneath the SFV. Finally, we evaluated monitoring limitations of the regional network for detecting small-magnitude events and proposed infill permanent station locations that can address these issues. These findings highlight how dense nodal deployments can address monitoring gaps in seismically active urban areas, though challenges remain in processing large datasets and differentiating legitimate seismic signals from cultural noise sources.

Data and Resources

The earthquake catalog and associated data archived at the Southern California Earthquake Data Center (SCEDC) were collected by the Southern California Seismic Network (SCSN), a cooperative project of Caltech and the U.S. Geological Survey (USGS). The facilities of EarthScope Consortium were used for access to some waveforms, related metadata, and/or derived products used in this study. These services are funded through the National Science Foundation's (NSF) Seismological Facility for the Advancement of Geoscience (SAGE) Award under Cooperative Agreement EAR-1724509. The published catalog of relocated seismicity in Southern California from 1981 to 2018 (Hauksson *et al.*, 2012), focal mechanisms for the relocated events (Yang *et al.*, 2012), and the aftershock catalog of the 1971 San Fernando earthquake (Mori *et al.*, 1995) were obtained from the SCEDC website special datasets. The focal mechanism of the 17 March 2014 13:25:36 M 4.4 was obtained from the USGS catalog (event ci15476961; USGS, 2025). Three-dimensional fault planes from the Statewide California Earthquake Center (SCEC) Community Fault Model (CFM) 6.1 (Marshall *et al.*, 2023) were accessed using the SCEC CFM explorer website. Additional faults are from Juárez-Zúñiga and Persaud (2025). Hyperlinks are embedded in the electronic version. Figures were created using Matplotlib and PyGMT in Python (Hunter and Dale, 2007; Uieda *et al.*, 2021). Associated algorithms tested in this study include Gaussian Mixture Model Association (GaMMA), PyOcto, and Rapid Earthquake Association and Location (REAL) (Zhang *et al.*, 2019; Zhu *et al.*, 2022; Münchmeyer, 2024). The supplemental material for this article includes 12 figures, 1 video, text, and 3 csv files. A zenodo archive with the preprocessing scripts is included at https://zenodo.org/records/15875900 (last accessed July 2025).

Declaration of Competing Interests

The authors acknowledge that there are no conflicts of interest recorded.

Acknowledgments

The authors thank the San Fernando Valley (SFV) residents and business owners for hosting the seismic stations and the 29 volunteers for dedicating their time to install and retrieve the nodal instruments—including Young Ho Aladro, James Atterholt, Ettore Biondi, Alex Clayton, Doug Clayton, Robert Clayton, Alex Goseyun, Catherine Hanagan, Alan Juarez-Zuniga, Sandra Juarez-Zuniga, Yida Li, Adam Margolis, Joses Omojola, Patricia Persaud, Katleho Ramotso, Samantha Rios, Benjamin Sadler, Ashlyn Schneida, Rajani Shrestha, Elaine Tagge, Valeria Villa, Matthew Wang, Debbie White, Xiaozhuo Wei, Yan Yang, Yifan Yu, and Caifeng Zou. The authors thank two anonymous reviewers, the Associate Editor, and Editor-in-Chief Allison Bent for their valuable comments and suggestions. This work was supported by the U.S. Geological Survey (USGS) Award G24AP00067, Statewide California Earthquake Center Award 24148, and the National Science Foundation (NSF) Awards 2105320 and 2317154. The Statewide California Earthquake Center (SCEC) Contribution Number is 14192. The nodal seismic instruments were provided by the EarthScope Consortium through the EarthScope Primary Instrument Center at New Mexico Tech. The data collected is available through EarthScope. These services are funded through the NSF's Seismological Facility for the Advancement of Geoscience (SAGE) Award under Cooperative Agreement EAR-1724509.

References

Aochi, H., and A. Kato (2010). Dynamic rupture of crosscutting faults: A possible rupture process for the 2007 M 6.6 Niigata-ken Chuetsu-Oki earthquake, *J. Geophys. Res.* **115,** no. B5, doi: 10.1029/2009JB006556.

Baldwin, J. N., K. I. Kelson, and C. E. Randolph (2000). Late Quaternary fold deformation along the Northridge Hills fault, Northridge, California: Deformation coincident with past Northridge blind-thrust earthquakes and other nearby structures? *Bull. Seismol. Soc. Am.* **90,** no. 3, 629–642.

Bao, W., Q. An, Y. Guo, L. Wang, and J. Gao (2024). Ambient noise levels of seismic stations located in urban agglomerations in central Inner Mongolia, China, *PloS One* **19,** no. 12, e0315004, doi: 10.1371/journal.pone.0315004.

Boese, C. M., L. Wotherspoon, M. Alvarez, and P. Malin (2015). Analysis of anthropogenic and natural noise from multilevel borehole seismometers in an urban environment, Auckland, New Zealand, *Bull. Seismol. Soc. Am.* **105,** no. 1, 285–299, doi: 10.1785/0120130288.

Bonilla, L. F., J. H. Steidl, G. T. Lindley, A. G. Tumarkin, and R. J. Archuleta (1997). Site amplification in the San Fernando Valley, California: Variability of site-effect estimation using the S-wave, coda, and H/V methods, *Bull. Seismol. Soc. Am.* **87,** no. 3, 710–730, doi: 10.1785/bssa0870030710.

Boore, D. M., and G. M. Atkinson (2008). Ground-motion prediction equations for the average horizontal component of PGA, PGV, and 5%-damped PSA at spectral periods between 0.01 s and 10.0 s, *Earthq. Spectra* **24,** no. 1, 99–138, doi: 10.1193/1.2830434.

Bouchon, M., V. Durand, D. Marsan, H. Karabulut, and J. Schmittbuhl (2013). The long precursory phase of most large interplate earthquakes, *Nature Geosci.* **6,** no. 4, 299–302, doi: 10.1038/ngeo1770.

Caltech and USGS (1926). Southern California Seismic Network [Data set], *International Federation of Digital Seismograph Networks,* doi: 10.7914/SN/CI.

Carena, S., and J. Suppe (2002). Three-dimensional imaging of active structures using earthquake aftershocks: The Northridge thrust, California, *J. Struct. Geol.* **24,** no. 4, 887–904, doi: 10.1016/S0191-8141(01)00110-9.

Castillo, E., D. Siervo, and G. A. Prieto (2024). Colombian seismic monitoring using advanced machine-learning algorithms, *Seismol. Res. Lett.* **95,** no. 5, 2971–2985.

Catchings, R. D., and W. H. K. Lee (1996). Shallow velocity structure and Poisson's ratio at the Tarzana, California, strong-motion accelerometer site, *Bull. Seismol. Soc. Am.* **86,** no. 6, 1704–1713, doi: 10.1785/bssa0860061704.

Catchings, R. D., M. R. Goldman, J. H. Steidl, J. H. Chan, A. A. Allam, C. J. Criley, Z. Ma, D. S. Langermann, G. J. Huddleston, A. T. McEvilly, *et al.* (2020). Nodal seismograph recordings of the 2019 Ridgecrest earthquake sequence, *Seismol. Res. Lett.* **91,** no. 6, 3622–3633, doi: 10.1785/0220200203.

Christensen, N. I., and W. D. Mooney (1995). Seismic velocity structure and composition of the continental crust: A global view, *J. Geophys. Res.* **100,** no. B6, 9761–9788, doi: 10.1029/95JB00259.

Crowell, J. (1979). The San Andreas fault system through time, *J. Geol. Soc.* **136,** no. 3, 293–302.

Day, S. M., D. Roten, and K. B. Olsen (2012). Adjoint analysis of the source and path sensitivities of basin-guided waves, *Geophys. J. Int.* **189,** no. 2, 1103–1124, doi: 10.1111/j.1365-246X.2012.05416.x.

Di Luccio, F., P. Persaud, L. Cucci, A. Esposito, R. Carniel, G. Cortés, D. Galluzzo, R. W. Clayton, and G. Ventura (2021). The seismicity of Lipari, Aeolian Islands (Italy) from one-month recording of the LIPARI array, *Front. Earth Sci.* **9,** doi: 10.3389/feart.2021.678581.

Farrell, J., S. M. Wu, K. M. Ward, and F. C. Lin (2018). Persistent noise signal in the Fairfield Nodal three-component 5-Hz geophones, *Seismol. Res. Lett.* **89,** no. 5, 1609–1617.

Fiori, R., J. Vergne, J. Schmittbuhl, and D. Zigone (2023). Monitoring induced microseismicity in an urban context using very small seismic arrays: The case study of the Vendenheim EGS project, *Geophysics* **88,** no. 5, WB71–WB87, doi: 10.1190/geo2022-0620.1.

Fuis, G. S., R. W. Clayton, P. M. Davis, T. Ryberg, W. J. Lutter, D. A. Okaya, E. Hauksson, C. Prodehl, J. M. Murphy, and M. L. Benthien (2003). Fault systems of the 1971 San Fernando and 1994 Northridge earthquakes, southern California: Relocated aftershocks and seismic images from LARSE II, *Geology* **31,** no. 2, 171–174.

Geffers, G.-M., I. G. Main, and M. Naylor (2022). Biases in estimating b-values from small earthquake catalogues: How high are high b-values? *Geophys. J. Int.* **229,** no. 3, 1840–1855, doi: 10.1093/gji/ggac028.

Ghose, R., P. Persaud, and R. W. Clayton (2023). Basin structure for earthquake ground motion estimates in Urban Los Angeles mapped with nodal receiver functions, *Geosci.* **13,** no. 11, 320.

Graves, R. W., and D. J. Wald (2004). Observed and Simulated Ground Motions in the San Bernardino Basin Region for the Hector Mine, California, earthquake, *Bull. Seismol. Soc. Am.* **94,** no. 1, 131–146, doi: 10.1785/0120030025.

Green, D. N., I. D. Bastow, B. Dashwood, and S. E. J. Nippress (2016). Characterizing broadband seismic noise in Central London, *Seismol. Res. Lett.* **88,** no. 1, 113–124, doi: 10.1785/0220160128.

Hadley, D., and H. Kanamori (1977). Seismic structure of the transverse ranges, California, *Geol. Soc. Am. Bull.* **88,** no. 10, 1469–1478.

Hardebeck, J. L., and P. M. Shearer (2003). Using S/P amplitude ratios to constrain the focal mechanisms of small earthquakes, *Bull. Seismol. Soc. Am.* **93,** no. 6, 2434–2444, doi: 10.1785/0120020236.

Hartzell, S., E. Cranswick, A. Frankel, D. Carver, and M. Meremonte (1997). Variability of site response in the Los Angeles urban area, *Bull. Seismol. Soc. Am.* **87,** no. 6, 1377–1400, doi: 10.1785/bssa0870061377.

Hauksson, E., W. Yang, and P. M. Shearer (2012). Waveform relocated earthquake catalog for southern California (1981 to June 2011), *Bull. Seismol. Soc. Am.* **102,** no. 5, 2239–2244.

Hough, S. E., R. W. Graves, E. S. Cochran, C. E. Yoon, L. Blair, S. Haefner, D. J. Wald, and V. Quitoriano (2024). The 17 January 1994 Northridge, California, earthquake: A retrospective analysis, *Seism. Rec.* **4,** no. 3, 151–160, doi: 10.1785/0320240012.

Huftile, G. J., and R. S. Yeats (1995). Convergence rates across a displacement transfer zone in the western Transverse Ranges, Ventura basin, California. *J. Geophys. Res.* **100,** no. B2, 2043–2067, doi: 10.1029/94JB02473.

Huftile, G. J., and R. S. Yeats (1996). Deformation rates across the Placerita (Northridge Mw = 6.7 aftershock zone) and Hopper Canyon segments of the western transverse ranges deformation belt, *Bull. Seismol. Soc. Am.* **86,** no. 1B, S3–S18, doi: 10.1785/bssa08601b00s3.

Hunter, J., and D. Dale (2007). The Matplotlib 0.90.0 user's guide, *Comput. Sci. Eng.* **9**, no. 3, 90–95, doi: 10.1109/MCSE.2007.55.

Hutton, K., J. Woessner, and E. Hauksson (2010). Earthquake monitoring in southern California for seventy-seven years (1932–2008), *Bull. Seismol. Soc. Am.* **100,** no. 2, 423–446, doi: 10.1785/0120090130.

Inbal, A., J. P. Ampuero, and R. Clayton (2024). Earthquake detectability and depth resolution with dense arrays in long beach, California: Further evidence for upper-mantle seismicity within a continental setting, *Seismol. Res. Lett.* doi: 10.1785/0220240035.

Inbal, A., T. Cristea-Platon, J. P. Ampuero, G. Hillers, D. Agnew, and S. E. Hough (2018). Sources of long-range anthropogenic noise in Southern California and implications for tectonic tremor detection, *Bull. Seismol. Soc. Am.* **108,** no. 6, 3511–3527, doi: 10.1785/0120180130.

Ingersoll, R. V. (2001). Tectonostratigraphy of the Santa Monica mountains, Southern California, doi: 10.32375/2001-GB77.5.

Islam, M. M., P. Persaud, M. Thant, K. Win, and E. Sandvol (2025). Estimating site amplification variability in Yangon, Myanmar, from a dense nodal seismic array, *Earthq. Spectra* **0,** no. 0, 87552930251352843, doi: 10.1177/87552930251352843.

Jennings, C. W., W. A. Bryant, G. J. Saucedo, and S. California Geological (2010). Fault activity map of California, *California Geol. Surv.* Retrieved July 2025 from https://ngmdb.usgs.gov/Prodesc/proddesc_96751.htm

Juárez-Zúñiga, A., and P. Persaud (2025). New insights into the crustal structure of the San Fernando Valley, California, from a Dense nodal seismic array, *Seismol. Res. Lett.* doi: 10.1785/0220240473.

Kato, A., K. Obara, T. Igarashi, H. Tsuruoka, S. Nakagawa, and N. Hirata (2012). Propagation of slow slip leading up to the 2011 Mw 9.0 Tohoku-Oki earthquake, *Science* **335,** no. 6069, 705–708, doi: 10.1126/science.1215141.

Klein, F. W. (2002). User's guide to HYPOINVERSE-2000, a Fortran program to solve for earthquake locations and magnitudes (2331-1258), doi: 10.3133/ofr02171.

Krischer, L., T. Megies, E. Sales de Andrade, R. Barsch, and J. MacCarthy (2017). ObsPy: A Python Toolbox for Seismology, *EGU General Assembly Conference Abstracts*, Vienna, Austria.

Krishnan, S., C. Ji, D. Komatitsch, and J. Tromp (2005). Performance of 18-story steel moment-frame buildings during a large San Andreas earthquake—A Southern California-wide end-to-end simulation, *Tech. Rept. EERL 2005*, 1 pp., available at https://authors.library.caltech.edu/records/4qemw-m0q51 (last accessed July 2025).

Kubo, H., M. Naoi, and M. Kano (2024). Recent advances in earthquake seismology using machine learning, *Earth Planets Space* **76,** no. 1, 36.

Kyriakopoulos, C., D. D. Oglesby, G. J. Funning, and K. J. Ryan (2017). Dynamic rupture modeling of the M7.2 2010 El Mayor-Cucapah Earthquake: Comparison with a geodetic model, *J. Geophys. Res.* **122,** no. 12, 10,263–210,279, doi: 10.1002/2017JB014294.

Langenheim, V., T. Wright, D. Okaya, R. Yeats, G. Fuis, K. Thygesen, and H. Thybo (2011). Structure of the San Fernando Valley region, California: Implications for seismic hazard and tectonic history, *Geosphere* **7,** no. 2, 528–572.

Lecocq, T., S. P. Hicks, K. Van Noten, K. van Wijk, P. Koelemeijer, R. S. M. PlaenDe, F. Massin, G. Hillers, R. E. Anthony, M.-T. Apoloner, *et al.* (2020). Global quieting of high-frequency seismic noise due to COVID-19 pandemic lockdown measures, *Science* **369,** no. 6509, 1338–1343, doi: 10.1126/science.abd2438.

Levy, Y., T. Rockwell, S. Minas, A. Hughes, and D. Rood (2020). Geological structure of the Sylmar basin: Implications for slip distribution along the Santa Susana/Hospital and Mission Hills Fault System in the San Fernando Valley, CA, USA, *Front. Earth Sci.* **8,** 560,081.

Li, L., J. Tan, B. Schwarz, F. Staněk, N. Poiata, P. Shi, L. Diekmann, L. Eisner, and D. Gajewski (2020). Recent advances and challenges of Waveform-based seismic location methods at multiple scales, *Rev. Geophys.* **58,** no. 1, e2019RG000667, doi: 10.1029/2019RG000667.

Li, Z., Z. Peng, D. Hollis, L. Zhu, and J. McClellan (2018). High-resolution seismic event detection using local similarity for Large-N arrays, *Sci Rep* **8,** no. 1, 1646, doi: 10.1038/s41598-018-19728-w.

Liu, G., P. Persaud, and R. W. Clayton (2018). Structure of the Northern Los Angeles basins revealed in teleseismic receiver functions from short-term nodal seismic arrays, *Seismol. Res. Lett.* **89,** no. 5, 1680–1689, doi: 10.1785/0220180071.

Liu, H.-L., and T. Heaton (1984). Array analysis of the ground velocities and accelerations from the 1971 San Fernando, California, earthquake, *Bull. Seismol. Soc. Am.* **74,** no. 5, 1951–1968, doi: 10.1785/bssa0740051951.

Liu, M., H. Li, M. Zhang, and T. Wang (2020). Graphics processing unit-based match and locate (GPU-M&L): An improved match and locate method and its application, *Seismol. Res. Lett.* **91,** no. 2A, 1019–1029, doi: 10.1785/0220190241.

Lythgoe, K., A. Loasby, D. Hidayat, and S. Wei (2021). Seismic event detection in urban Singapore using a nodal array and frequency domain array detector: Earthquakes, blasts and thunderquakes, *Geophys. J. Int.* **226,** no. 3, 1542–1557, doi: 10.1093/gji/ggab135.

Marshall, S., A. Plesch, and J. Shaw (2023). SCEC Community Fault Model (CFM), doi: 10.5281/zenodo.8327463.

McNamara, D. E., and R. P. Buland (2004). Ambient noise levels in the continental United States, *Bull. Seismol. Soc. Am.* **94,** no. 4, 1517–1527.

Meng, H., and Y. Ben-Zion (2017). Detection of small earthquakes with dense array data: example from the San Jacinto fault zone, Southern California, *Geophys. J. Int.* **212,** no. 1, 442–457, doi: 10.1093/gji/ggx404.

Mori, J., D. J. Wald, and R. L. Wesson (1995). Overlapping fault planes of the 1971 San Fernando and 1994 Northridge, California earthquakes, *Geophys. Res. Lett.* **22,** no. 9, 1033–1036.

Mousavi, S. M., W. L. Ellsworth, W. Zhu, L. Y. Chuang, and G. C. Beroza (2020). Earthquake transformer—An attentive deep-learning model for simultaneous earthquake detection and phase picking, *Nat. Commun.* **11,** no. 1, 1–12, doi: 10.1038/s41467-020-17591-w.

Münchmeyer, J. (2024). PyOcto: A high-throughput seismic phase associator, *Seismica* **3,** no. 1, doi: 10.26443/seismica.v3i1.1130.

Münchmeyer, J., J. Woollam, A. Rietbrock, F. Tilmann, D. Lange, T. Bornstein, T. Diehl, C. Giunchi, F. Haslinger, and D. Jozinović (2022). Which picker fits my data? A quantitative evaluation of deep learning based seismic pickers, *J. Geophys. Res.* **127,** no. 1, e2021JB023499., doi: 10.1029/2021JB023499.

Nardoni, C., and P. Persaud (2024). Evidence for faulting and fluid-driven earthquake processes from seismic attenuation variations beneath metropolitan Los Angeles, *Sci Rep* **14,** no. 1, 17,595, doi: 10.1038/s41598-024-67872-3.

Omojola, J., and P. Persaud (2024). Monitoring salt domes used for energy storage with microseismicity: Insights for a Carbon-Neutral Future, *Geochem. Geophys. Geosys.* **25,** e2024GC011573, doi: 10.1029/2024GC011573.

Persaud, P. (2023). San Fernando Valley, California Nodal Array [Data set], *International Federation of Digital Seismograph Networks*, doi: 10.7914/7xh3-5a25.

Persaud, P., Y. Ma, J. M. Stock, J. A. Hole, G. S. Fuis, and L. Han (2016). Fault zone characteristics and basin complexity in the southern Salton Trough, California, *Geology* **44,** no. 9, 747–750, doi: 10.1130/g38033.1.

Persaud, P., A. Schneida, H. Shepard, S. Rios, L. Franklin, C. Nardoni, A. Juarez-Zuñiga, A. Goseyun, B. Sadler, E. C. Ferré, *et al.* (2024). Volunteer-led, short-term, geophysical field experiment: Lessons for inviting broader participation, building public trust, and com, *GSA Today* **34,** no. 10, 4–6.

Peterson, J. R. (1993). Observations and modeling of seismic background noise, *Open-File Report 2331-1258*, doi: 10.3133/ofr93322.

Poiata, N., C. Satriano, J.-P. Vilotte, P. Bernard, and K. Obara (2016). Multiband array detection and location of seismic sources recorded by dense seismic networks, *Geophys. J. Int.* **205,** no. 3, 1548–1573, doi: 10.1093/gji/ggw071.

Richter, C. F. (1935). An instrumental earthquake magnitude scale, *Bull. Seismol. Soc. Am.* **25,** no. 1, 1–32, doi: 10.1785/bssa0250010001.

Schorlemmer, D., and J. Woessner (2008). Probability of detecting an earthquake, *Bull. Seismol. Soc. Am.* **98,** no. 5, 2103–2117, doi: 10.1785/0120070105.

Tormann, T., S. Wiemer, and E. Hauksson (2010). Changes of reporting rates in the Southern California earthquake catalog, introduced by a new definition of ML, *Bull. Seismol. Soc. Am.* **100,** no. 4, 1733–1742, doi: 10.1785/0120090124.

Uieda, L., D. Tian, W. Leong, L. Toney, W. Schlitzer, M. Grund, D. Newton, M. Ziebarth, M. Jones, and P. Wessel (2021). PyGMT: A Python interface for the generic mapping tools, doi: 10.5281/zenodo.5607255.

Updike, R. G., W. M. Brown III, M. L. Johnson, E. M. Omdahl, P. S. Powers, S. Rhea, and A. C. Tarr (1996). USGS response to an urban earthquake, Northridge'94, available at https://pubs.usgs.gov/of/1996/0263/report.pdf (last accessed July 2025).

U.S. Geological Survey (USGS) (2025). Catalog webservice for recent and historic significant earthquakes, available at https://www.usgs.gov/programs/earthquake-hazards/earthquakes (last accessed June 2025).

Vassallo, M., G. Cultrera, A. Esposito, A. Mercuri, A. Bobbio, G. Di Giulio, G. Milana, P. Bordoni, M. G. Ciaccio, and F. Cara (2024). Temporary seismic network in the metropolitan area of Rome (Italy): New insight on an urban seismology experiment, *Seismol. Res. Lett.* **95,** no. 4, 2554–2569, doi: 10.1785/0220230290.

Vidale, J. E., and D. V. Helmberger (1988). Elastic finite-difference modeling of the 1971 San Fernando, California earthquake, *Bull. Seismol. Soc. Am.* **78,** no. 1, 122–141, doi: 10.1785/bssa0780010122.

Villa, V., Y. Li, R. W. Clayton, and P. Persaud (2023). Three-dimensional basin depth map of the Northern Los Angeles basins from gravity and seismic measurements, *J. Geophys. Res.* **128,** no. 7, e2022JB025425, doi: 10.1029/2022JB025425.

Waldhauser, F. (2001). HypoDD-A program to compute double-difference hypocenter locations, doi: 10.3133/ofr01113.

Walls, C., T. Rockwell, K. Mueller, Y. Bock, S. Williams, J. Pfanner, J. Dolan, and P. Fang (1998). Escape tectonics in the Los Angeles metropolitan region and implications for seismic risk. *Nature* **394,** no. 6691, 356–360, doi: 10.1038/28590.

Woollam, J., J. Münchmeyer, F. Tilmann, A. Rietbrock, D. Lange, T. Bornstein, T. Diehl, C. Giunchi, F. Haslinger, D. Jozinović, *et al.* (2022). SeisBench—A toolbox for machine learning in seismology, *Seismol. Res. Lett.* **93,** no. 3, 1695–1709, doi: 10.1785/0220210324.

Wu, Y. M., and L. Zhao (2006). Magnitude estimation using the first three seconds P-wave amplitude in earthquake early warning, *Geophys. Res. Lett.* **33,** no. 16, doi: 10.1029/2006GL026871.

Yang, L., X. Liu, W. Zhu, L. Zhao, and G. C. Beroza (2022). Toward improved urban earthquake monitoring through deep-learning-based noise suppression, *Sci Adv* **8,** no. 15, eabl3564, doi: 10.1126/sciadv.abl3564.

Yang, W., E. Hauksson, and P. M. Shearer (2012). Computing a large refined catalog of focal mechanisms for Southern California (1981–2010): Temporal stability of the style of faulting, *Bull. Seismol. Soc. Am.* **102,** no. 3, 1179–1194, doi: 10.1785/0120110311.

Yang, Y., and R. W. Clayton (2023). Shallow seismicity in the long beach–seal beach, California Area, *Seismol. Res. Lett.* **94,** no. 4, 1948–1956, doi: 10.1785/0220220358.

Yang, Y., and R. W. Clayton (2024). Mapping Los Angeles basin depth with sp converted phases, *Geophys. Res. Lett.* **51,** no. 18, e2024GL111135, doi: 10.1029/2024GL111135.

Yeats, R. S., G. J. Huftile, and F. B. Grigsby (1988). Oak Ridge fault, Ventura fold belt, and the Sisar decollement, Ventura basin, California, *Geology* **16,** no. 12, 1112–1116.

Zhang, M., W. L. Ellsworth, and G. C. Beroza (2019). Rapid earthquake association and location, *Seismol. Res. Lett.* **90,** no. 6, 2276–2284, doi: 10.1785/0220190052.

Zhu, W., and G. C. Beroza (2019). PhaseNet: A deep-neural-network-based seismic arrival-time picking method, *Geophys. J. Int.* **216,** no. 1, 261–273, doi: 10.1093/gji/ggy423.

Zhu, W., I. W. McBrearty, S. M. Mousavi, W. L. Ellsworth, and G. C. Beroza (2022). Earthquake phase association using a Bayesian Gaussian mixture model, *J. Geophys. Res.* **127,** no. 5, e2021JB023249, doi: 10.1029/2021JB023249.

Manuscript received 18 April 2025
Published online 22 August 2025

Seismic Lessons from the Implosion of Reser Stadium's Western Stands and the Dense 177-Node Corvallis Array

Pieter-Ewald Share*[1], Anne M. Tréhu[1], Armin Stuedlein[2], Hannah R. Reinhard[1], Aurélien Mordret[3], and Rachel A. M. Way[1]

Abstract

On the morning of 7 January 2022, the Western Stands of Reser Stadium, Corvallis, Oregon, was demolished. To capture this unique seismic event and inform local upper-crustal structure, we deployed a 177-node array for approximately three weeks with circular geometry centered on the stadium and a >5 km quasi-linear portion west of it and across the Corvallis fault (CF). We estimate an equivalent earthquake magnitude of M_w~2.3 for the implosion. The stadium toppling toward the southwest and its shape generated two to three times higher peak ground accelerations (>0.1g <80 m away), and the most impulsive signals (>5 Hz) in that direction and longer duration elevated shaking (>60 s) to the northwest and southeast. Using implosion P first arrivals, we model shallow V_P along the >5-km-long profile and invert Rayleigh- and Love-wave phase velocities derived from ambient noise to obtain V_S on an overlapping ~3.6 km section. Both models show a 300–500 m deep basin ($V_P < 3$ km/s, $V_S < 1$ km/s) spanning ~2 km of the profile and starting near the stadium where Spencer Formation basement is locally uplifted. This transition from shallow basement rock to deeper basin coincides with a rapid reduction in prolonged high-amplitude shaking and high-frequency content from the implosion. The basin shallows around the CF before giving way to high-velocity Siletz basalts in the west. Analyses of teleseismic P waveforms pinpoint a rapid change in crustal structure >300 m east of the mapped CF, and an uncataloged shallow local event, identified with EQTransformer, has an epicenter west of it. These results highlight the need for more widespread near-field observations of seismic sources; a concerted effort to identify the most recently active locus within the CF zone; and more broadly, better understanding the heterogeneous crust of the Willamette Valley and its unique seismic response.

Cite this article as Share, P.-E., A. M. Tréhu, A. Stuedlein, H. R. Reinhard, A. Mordret, and R. A. M. Way (2025). Seismic Lessons from the Implosion of Reser Stadium's Western Stands and the Dense 177-Node Corvallis Array, *Seismol. Res. Lett.* **97**, 126–140, doi: 10.1785/0220250098.

Supplemental Material

Introduction

As part of a $153 million U.S. renovation to Reser Stadium on the Oregon State University campus in Corvallis, Oregon, its Western Stands was scheduled to be imploded on the morning of 7 January 2022. To record this unique event as well as other seismic signals during an approximate three-week-long period, we deployed a dense three-component nodal array in and around campus and a >5-km-long quasi-linear profile west and out of Corvallis (Fig. 1a, Tréhu and Share 2022). Soon after 7:53 a.m. local time (15:53 UTC), the implosion started with the detonation of a sequence of explosives positioned to remove structural support for the Western Stands, bringing the >2500 ton structure to the ground ~5 s later (Fig. 1b). P-, S-, and surface-wave signals generated by the explosions and the subsequent lower-frequency ground impact were observed across the entire array (Fig. 2 and Fig. S1, available in the supplemental material to this article).

Although near-field seismic observations of earthquake sources, including small-magnitude ones (e.g., Yamada *et al.*, 2007; Klinger and Werner, 2022), are rare, they can provide unique and novel constraints on the physics of earthquake rupture (Ben-Zion, 2019). Moreover, the widespread occurrence of seismicity at shallow depths, in response to the proliferation of geothermal energy production, hydraulic fracturing, underground mining, and so forth, means that surface shaking is now more often experienced at close distances (Atkinson,

1. College of Earth, Ocean, and Atmospheric Sciences, Oregon State University, Corvallis, Oregon, U.S.A., https://orcid.org/0000-0001-6674-1491 (P-ES); 2. College of Engineering, Oregon State University, Corvallis, Oregon, U.S.A., https://orcid.org/0000-0002-6265-9906 (AS); 3. Geological Survey of Denmark and Greenland, GEUS, Copenhagen, Denmark, https://orcid.org/0000-0002-7998-5417 (AM)

*Corresponding author: pieter.share@oregonstate.edu

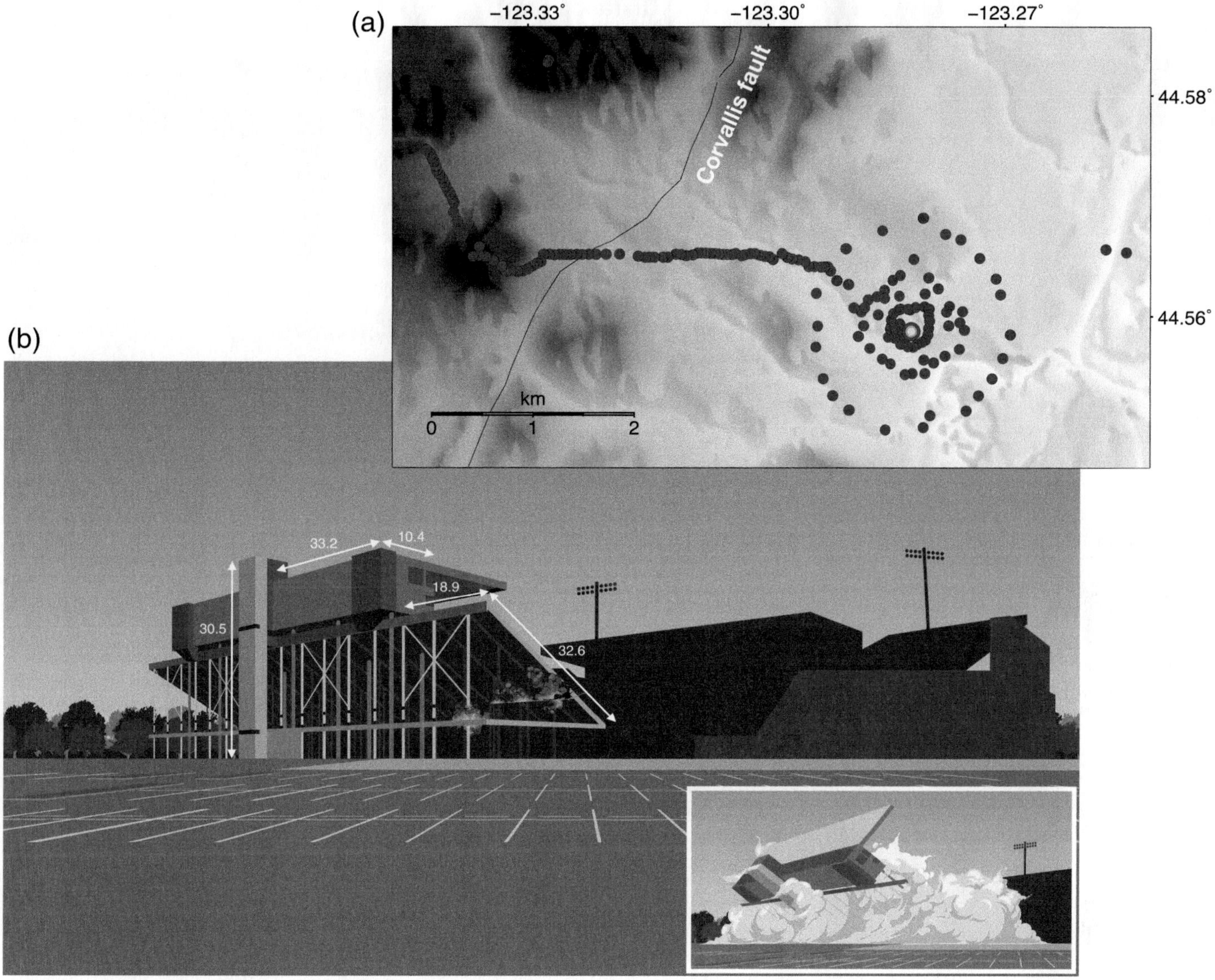

Figure 1. The Corvallis array and Reser Stadium. (a) Layout of the 177-node Corvallis array (dark circles) overlain on local topography with the first explosion (bright circle) centered on the circular portion of the array. The linear portion of the array transects the mapped Corvallis fault (CF) in the west before gaining elevation. (b) Graphic depiction of Reser Stadium's Western Stands looking northward with the first explosions starting in the south. Black strips on foundational pillars and the concrete elevator shaft (30.5 m high) detonated later in the explosion sequence. Several measures of length (in meters) are shown for reference. After the explosions, the building pivoted and collapsed toward the southwest (inset), hitting the ground ~5 s later. The color version of this figure is available only in the electronic edition.

2015; Atkinson *et al.*, 2016), making near-field ground-motion studies a timely focus. Even for small-magnitude ($M_w < 3$) events, peak ground accelerations (PGAs) at <1 km distances can exceed 1*g* (e.g., Atkinson and Viegas, 2023). We analyze seismic signals generated by the explosions and implosion for PGAs, peak ground velocities (PGVs), shaking duration, attenuation, and frequency content at epicentral distances as close as 65 m. Although it was not an earthquake, the seismic source provided by the implosion of the Stadium's Western Stands provides insights into near-source ground motions.

The data also provide new information on the structure of the upper crust beneath Corvallis. Most of the area is covered by a ~5-m-thick layer of Willamette Silt, which was deposited ~14,000 yr ago by the Missoula Floods (Wiley, 2008). This is overlain locally by younger alluvium from various creeks and rivers (e.g., Oak Creek [OC], Marys River). Beneath the Willamette Silt are layered deposits of clay, silt, sand, and gravel estimated to extend several tens of meters before more competent sedimentary bedrock of the Late Eocene Spencer and Middle Eocene Tyee Formations are encountered (Wiley, 2008). These formations form a series of discontinuous hills along the boundary between the Willamette Valley and the Coast Range in the west (Fig. 3).

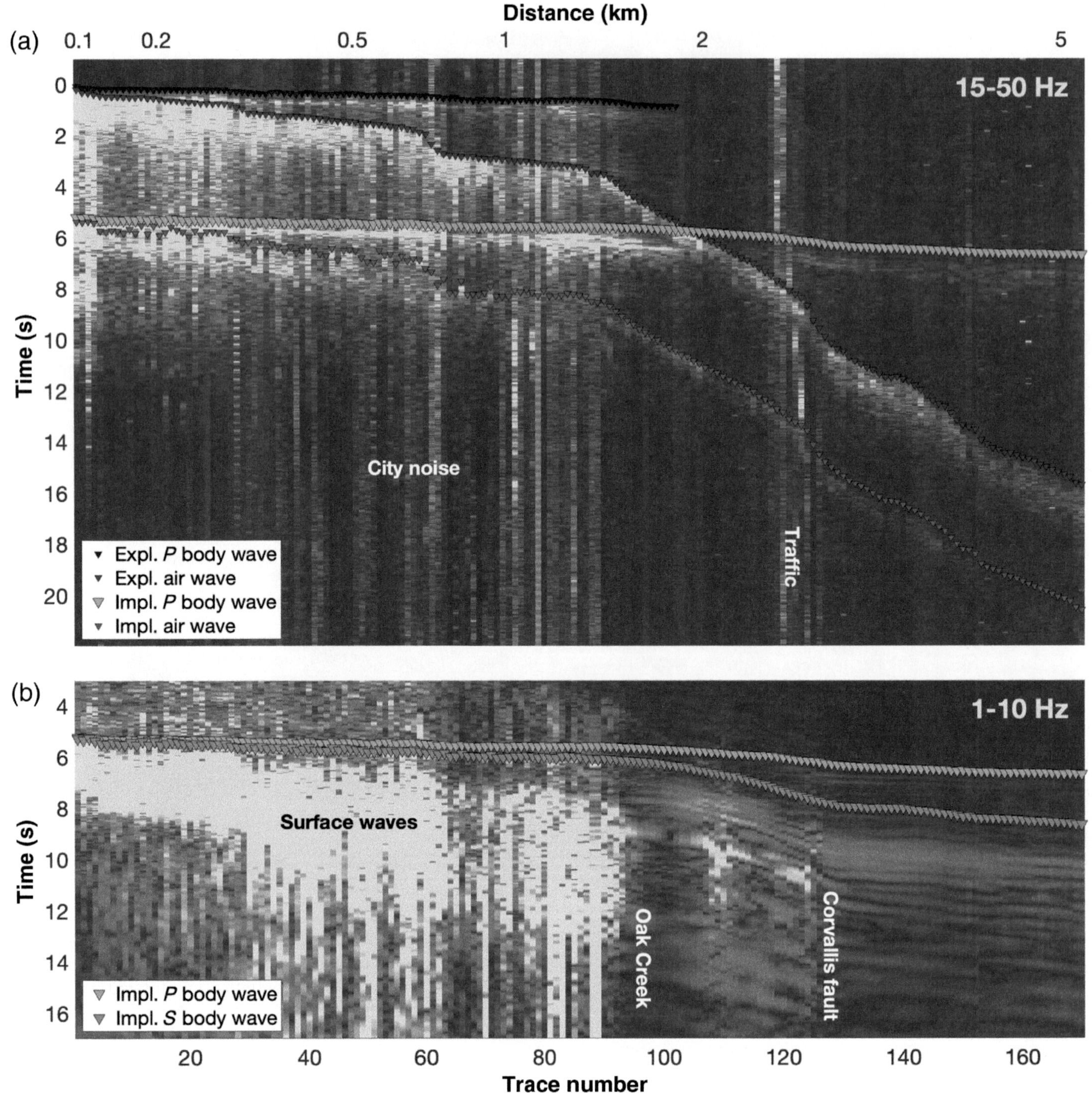

Early Eocene volcanic rocks of the Siletz terrane (e.g., Duncan, 1982; Wells *et al.*, 1998, 2014) underlie the Tyee formation beneath both the Coast Range, where they are uplifted and widely exposed, and beneath the Willamette Valley, where drilling and geophysical data suggest that they are at a depth of ~2 km (Goldfinger, 1990). Seismic and potential field data across the Willamette Valley indicate that the Siletz terrane provides an approximately flat floor to the valley from the Coast Range to (and beneath) the western Cascades (Tréhu *et al.*, 1994; Ward *et al.*, 2018). We would therefore expect the response of the Willamette Valley to seismic waves to differ

Figure 2. Energy envelopes (vertical traces) for the explosion–implosion event at (a) high and (b) low frequencies. The *y*-axis is time relative to the first explosion and traces are ordered by distance from it. Each trace is amplified by a distance-proportional factor to compensate for geometrical spreading attenuation. Manual air and body-wave picks are indicated with colored triangles. Explosion *P* body waves disappear beneath the noise floor at 1.8 km. Self-normalized traces plotted versus distance are shown in Figure S1. The color version of this figure is available only in the electronic edition.

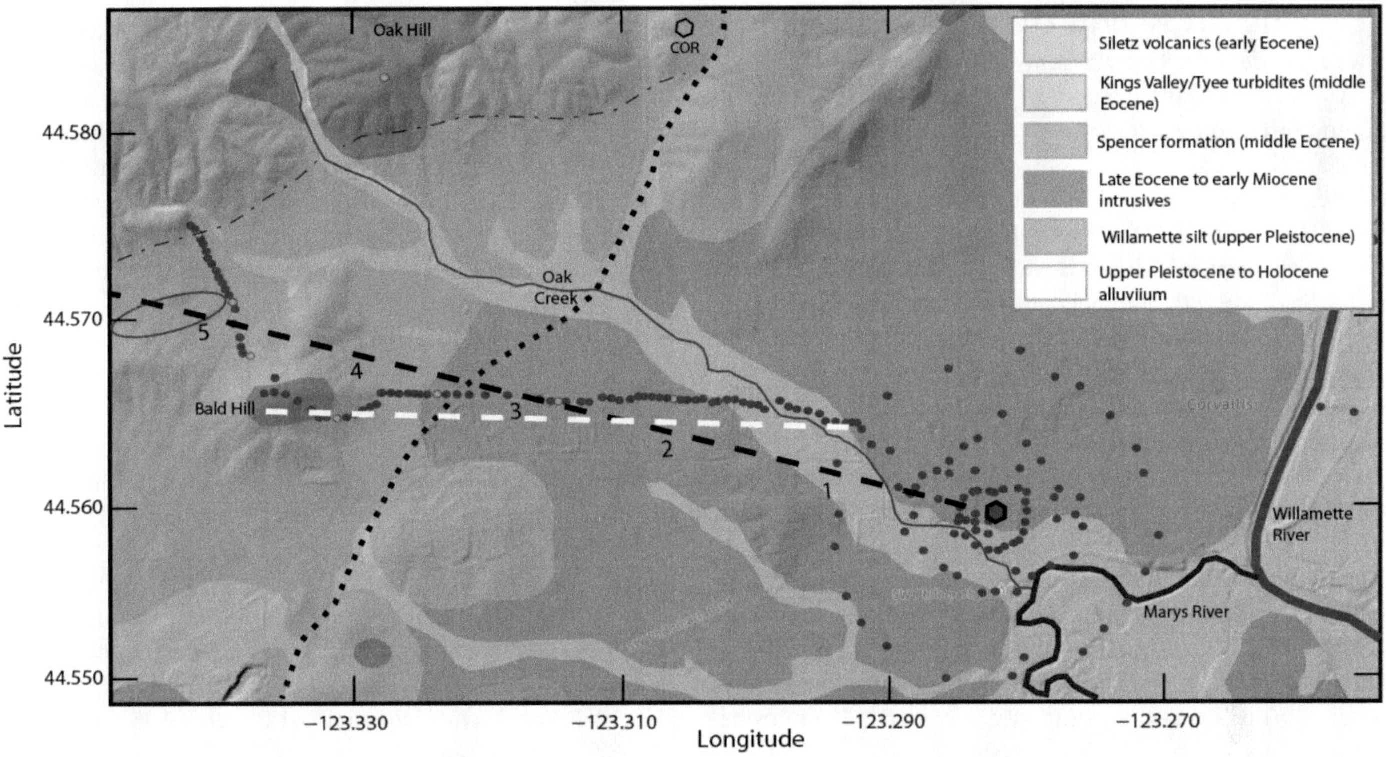

Figure 3. Geologic setting around Corvallis and the dense array. Geology is simplified from Wiley (2008). Underlying shaded relief is bare earth light detection and ranging (lidar) from the Oregon Department of Geology and Mineral Industries (DOGAMI) lidar viewer (DOGAMI Oregon Department of Geology and Mineral Industries Lidar Program Data, 2025). Node locations are shown as brown dots. The location of the Reser implosion is shown as a red hexagon. The dotted line is the mapped CF. *P*- and *S*-wave velocity cross sections in Figures 5c and 6d are indicated by bold and dashed black and white lines, respectively. The orange hexagon shows the location of the permanent seismic station COR. Orange dots indicate nodes that were used to locate the event found by beamforming using first arrivals and the oval northeast of Bald Hill shows the likely source location determined from this analysis (see discussion accompanying Figs. S12 and S13). The faint dashed–dotted line in the northwest corner of the map shows the location of a topographic step in the lidar bare earth image that may represent the most recent activity within the CF zone. This feature swings to the southwest parallel to the mapped CF beyond the western edge of the map shown here. The color version of this figure is available only in the electronic edition.

from that of the much deeper Seattle and Tualatin basins (e.g., Snelson *et al.*, 2007; McPhee *et al.*, 2014), highlighting the need for better quantification of the local structure of the upper crust and its seismic response.

In west Corvallis, the boundary between the uplifted Siletz terrane and overlying Eocene-age sedimentary rocks and the Willamette Valley is thought to be controlled by the northeast-trending and northwestward-dipping Corvallis fault (CF; Goldfinger, 1990; Fig. 1a). Its location has been directly identified in only a few areas where Siletz terrane rocks are observed in fault contact with Tyee Formation sandstone (Goldfinger, 1990), and its strike and dip are inferred in regions of sediment cover, including where our seismic profile crosses it (Fig. 3).

Goldfinger (1990) presented a model for the subsurface structure of the CF based on gravity data. However, the gravity models are nonunique, and the thicknesses of the post-Eocene sedimentary and Eocene sedimentary rock horizons as they approach the Coast Range are not well constrained. Consequently, their impact on the seismic response of this complex basin edge (e.g., Brissaud *et al.*, 2020) is unknown. Focusing mainly on the >5-km-long profile, we image the structure of the upper crust by analyzing waveform property changes from the implosion and for teleseisms (e.g., Qin *et al.*, 2021; Qiu *et al.*, 2021; Share *et al.*, 2022), modeling *P*-wave first-arrival times and inverting Rayleigh- and Love-wave phase velocities from ambient noise (e.g., Morfret *et al.*, 2013, 2015). We also identify several possible local earthquakes that are not in the Pacific Northwest Seismic Network(PNSN) catalog.

The following section describes the acquisition parameters of the nodal array and the data preprocessing applied. Analysis results focusing on converting the implosion to an earthquake-equivalent magnitude and key characteristics of its generated wavefield are discussed in the Implosion source and signal properties section. The Subsurface structure section focuses on waveform property changes from signals throughout the entire acquisition window, including the implosion, and how it informs subsurface structure. We discuss the implications of these results in the Discussion and Conclusions section.

Corvallis Array and Data Preprocessing

The first node of the Corvallis array (Fig. 1a) was deployed on 1 January 2022, and the majority of the array was operating by the end of day on 4 January, with the last node installed on 6 January. The complete array consisted of 177 SmartSolo three-component 5 Hz geophones recording at 1000 Hz. Retrieval of nodes started on 21 January and finished on 24 January. The array configuration included three concentric circles, centered on the Stadium, with nominal radii of 200 m, 500 m, and 1 km. Each circle contained 24 nodes. In addition, four nodes were positioned at distances <200 m from the implosion as well as six others within the 200–500 m range and at different azimuths. The remaining nodes comprised the >5 km profile to the west with sensors spaced on average 64 m apart along that line and four others placed at various locations around town (Fig. 1a). The latter four nodes were excluded from analysis in this particular study because they did not add significant value to source or structure estimation, and other noisy channels were discarded from each data analysis step as needed. To fully capture the 7 January event while minimizing clipping (saturation) of signals, the sensitivity of sensors ≤500 m from the stadium was set to 12 dB and those farther away to 24 dB.

All recordings were corrected for instrument response and rotated, where needed, into geographic north–south and east–west. The resultant velocity recordings for 7 January were then analyzed to quantify the implosion source (next section) and differentiated to produce accelerograms. For all days, two down-sampled datasets were then created, one at 100 Hz and another at 50 Hz, using Python ObsPy software (Krischer *et al.*, 2015). The 100 Hz recordings were used for deep-learning-based detection of unknown local earthquakes (EQTransformer, Mousavi *et al.*, 2020) and the 50 Hz data for teleseismic arrival and ambient noise analyses. For the latter, using MSNoise (Lecocq *et al.*, 2014), cross correlations (CCs) were computed for all days and interstation ZZ and TT component pairs (Z, vertical; T, transverse). The CCs were then stacked to produce one representative trace per station and component pair.

Implosion Source and Signal Properties

Most of the explosives (~90 kg total) were placed on the southwest-facing side of Reser Stadium ~6 m above ground on critical structural support members on the concourse level, including on an elevator shaft (Fig. 1b). Another set of explosives was attached to the same elevator shaft but 21.6 m above ground. Despite the deployment of elevated charges, the entire elevator shaft, the second and third viewing levels that it serviced, and the Western Stands' roof all pivoted as essentially a single unit around 6 m elevation as it fell to the ground (Fig. 1b, inset). In addition, a line of explosives was placed ~1/4 of the way up the rows of concrete seats to initiate collapse of that structure (Fig. 1b). The latter pivoted around that line as it fell, settling at the concourse level immediately prior to the contact of the elevator shaft with the ground below.

Air waves from the sequence of explosions propagated across town with little anelastic attenuation (Fig. 2a), were impulsive and wide band (1–500 Hz), and with most energy focused around 1–100 Hz (Fig. S2). On the other hand, the <100 m length-scale of the imploding stadium produced generally lower frequency and less impulsive signals, with most energy below 10 Hz (Fig. S2). For these signals, we calculated representative PGVs and PGAs per station over the entire 1–500 Hz band using the geometric mean (GM; e.g., Boore *et al.*, 2006) as follows:

$$GM(H) = \sqrt{\max(H_1) \times \max(H_2)}, \quad (1)$$

in which H_1 and H_2 denote two orthogonal horizontal recordings of either velocity or acceleration. For eight nearby stations, signals from the implosion were clipped on at least one horizontal trace. To be conservative, PGVs and PGAs were not calculated for these stations, but it should be noted that they experienced ground motions exceeding the maxima of the remaining stations. Maximum PGV and PGA for the implosion, calculated with equation (1), were 0.95 cm/s and 88 cm/s^2 (0.09g), respectively (Fig. 4a,b). These maxima were associated with the same station 80 m from the center of the elevator shaft after impact (Fig. 4a,b). In the case of the explosions (essentially a series of point sources), PGV and PGA maxima for the more impulsive air waves were 0.71 cm/s and 360 cm/s^2 (0.37g), respectively, at distances <200 m from the blast (Fig. S3). Because most explosives were on the southwest-facing side, these waves propagated relatively unobstructed in that direction, resulting in more than two times more shaking in the near field (<250 m away) compared with the northeast side of the stadium's Western Stands (Fig. S3).

To convert the implosive source to total available energy and an equivalent earthquake magnitude, we focused on stadium structures where most of the mass was concentrated. These were the rows of seats, the elevator shaft, and the bases and floors of viewing levels two and three, all composed of concrete (density = 2403 kg/m^3). Total volumes (masses) calculated for these structures were 746 (1793 tons), 93 (223 tons), and 115 m^3 per level (275 tons times 2), respectively. Their centers of mass were located at 16, 21.4, 25.4 (level two), and 29.3 m (level three) above ground, respectively. Because the elevator shaft and viewing levels fell as a single unit, we considered them as such during calculation (structure 1) with a combined center of mass of 25.6 m above ground prior to collapse (rows of seats = structure 2). Conservation of energy was used to quantify the energy imparted to the ground with the assumption that all initial (i) potential energy (U) was entirely converted to final (f) rotational kinetic energy (K) prior to impact,

$$U_{i1} + U_{i2} = U_{f1} + U_{f2} + K_{f1} + K_{f2}, \quad (2)$$

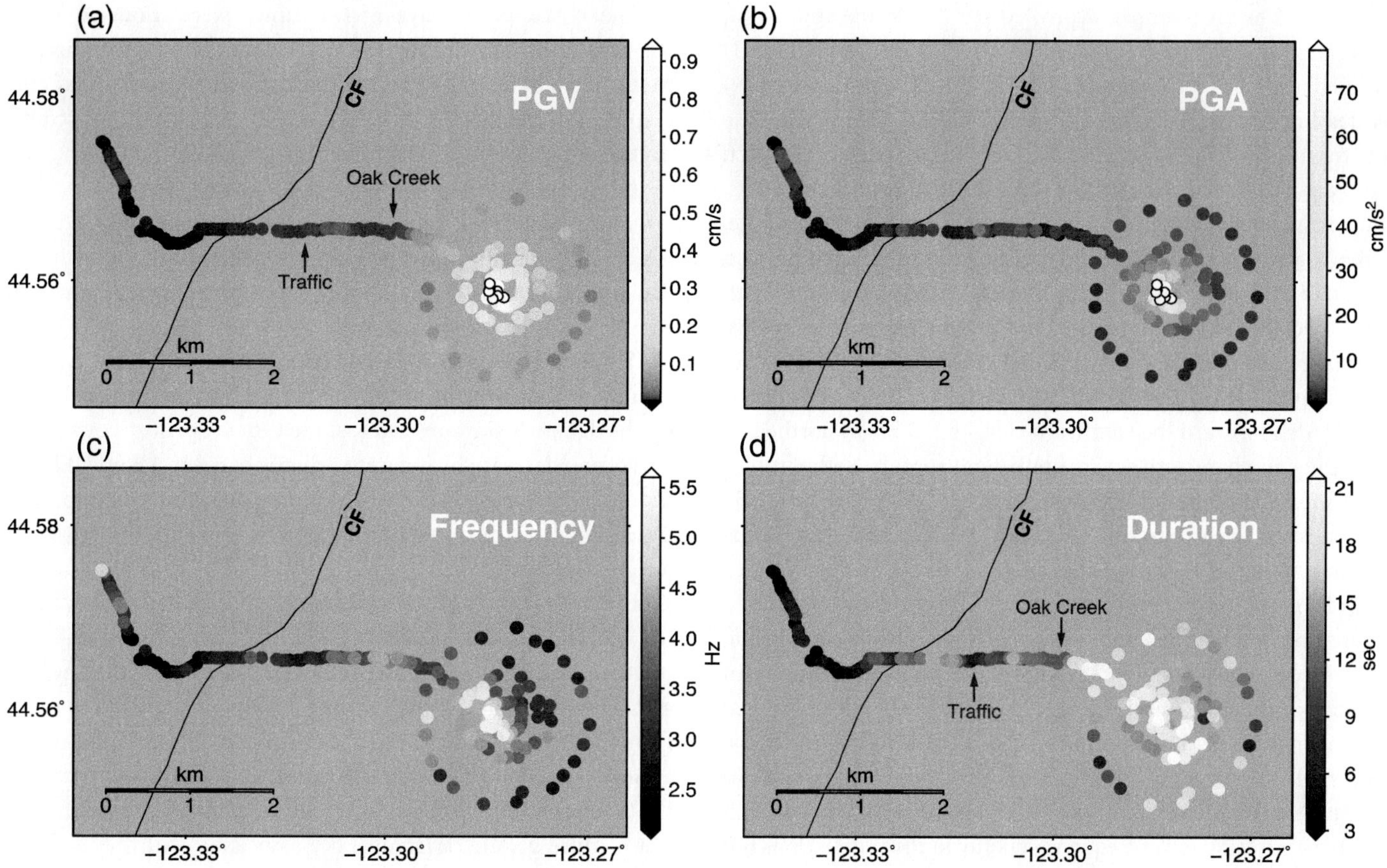

Figure 4. (a) Peak ground velocities (PGVs) and (b) peak ground accelerations (PGAs) generated by the implosion of Reser Stadium's Western Stands across the Corvallis array. The black outlined white circles show stations with clipped signals. (c) Dominant frequencies and (d) elevated shaking duration in radial velocity components and the 1–10 Hz band highlight azimuthal anisotropic properties of the implosion. During calculation of panels (a–d), high-frequency air wave signals from the explosions (Fig. 2a) were muted using a 2 s zeroed window. The color version of this figure is available only in the electronic edition.

in which subscripts 1 and 2 denote the two main stadium structures, and

$$U = m \times g \times h \quad \text{and} \quad K = \frac{1}{2} I \times \omega^2, \tag{3}$$

with m being the mass of a body centered at height h; g denoting gravitational acceleration (9.81 $\mathrm{m/s^2}$); and I and ω are the moment of inertia and rotational speed of a body, respectively. Using equations (2) and (3), the rotational kinetic energies transferred to the ground on impact for structures 1 and 2 were 1.487×10^8 J and 1.744×10^8 J, respectively, noting that their centers of mass were both around 6 m above ground on impact because structure 2 came to rest at the concourse level, whereas structure 1, with its irregular shape, had a center of mass a few meters above the elevator shaft on impact (in front of it to the northeast prior to collapse). We also note that because of various aspects of an imperfect impact, the values calculated for structures 1 and 2 are overestimates of energies transferred to the ground. However, numerous other structures were not included in the calculation (roof, metal pillars and support, and so on) but did contribute to the total energy budget. Thus, we consider 3.23×10^8 J an appropriate estimate. The empirical relationship of Båth (1966) between energy (E) and moment magnitude (M_w), that is, $\log_{10} E = 5.24 + 1.44 M_w$, ties this total energy to an equivalent implosion M_w 2.27.

Ground motions across the array match well predictions made using an empirically derived equation suitable for small magnitude events (Atkinson, 2015; Fig. S4), suggesting $M_w \sim 2.3$ is an appropriate estimate for the implosion and that its seismic efficiency (ratio of total available energy to radiated energy, e.g., Kanamori, 2001) was similar to earthquakes of that size. Compared with large-magnitude events, a PGA of $\sim 0.1g$ would be the peak value expected at a hard rock site ~70 km from an M_w 8 Cascadia earthquake (Silva *et al.*, 1991). However, the intense shaking would be more prolonged and PGVs significantly elevated for such events. The direction and style of the stadium impact also help explain the azimuthally uneven distribution of ground motion. For stations at distances <250 m, the impact produced PGVs and PGAs more than two and more than three times larger to the southwest, respectively, compared with the northeast (Fig. 4a,b). All clipped sensors were also located to the southwest. Taking structure 1 as an example, it pivoted and fell to the southwest, reaching $\omega = 0.94\ \mathrm{s}^{-1}$ ($I = 3.380 \times 10^8\ \mathrm{kg\,m}^2$, equation 3) immediately prior to impact (Fig. 1b, inset). Linear speed (v) scales linearly with distance (r) (i.e., $v = \omega r$); thus, the base of structure 1 was moving at near zero linear speed on impact, whereas the top of the elevator shaft hit the ground at 29 m/s, injecting considerably more energy into the earth than its base. This is akin to a unilateral earthquake rupture, initiating at a point (~0 m slip), propagating mostly in one direction (with increased slip and strain release) and producing more impulsive and larger amplitude shaking in that direction. This impulsiveness manifested as signals with the highest dominant frequencies (>5 Hz) toward the southwest (Fig. 4c, ~3 Hz to northeast). Mapping all characteristics of a unilateral rupture to the implosion source is nontrivial, though, because overlapping reverberations from the explosions (Fig. 2a), the less impulsive initial impact of structure 2, and the irregular shape of the Western Stands complicate the extraction of first-motion polarities, source time functions, and so forth from the early implosion waveforms (Fig. S5a). For example, the longest durations of intense shaking (>20 times pre-explosion level) were observed orthogonal to the direction of collapse, that is, to the northwest and southeast (Fig. 4d and Fig. S5b). This could be because of a longer structure 1 source length (shaft height = 30.5 m vs. width = 5.6 m) emitting lower frequency energy in those directions but could also be due to local northwest–southwest-trending shallow low-velocity zones (Edmonds, 2025). In terms of the combined explosion–implosion event, some stations to the northwest and southeast experienced elevated shaking (more than two times the pre-explosion level) for more than a minute. Next, we turn our focus to structure.

Subsurface Structure

High-frequency body waves from the implosion

To determine shallow velocity structure, we manually picked P- and S-body-wave first arrivals generated by the implosion and recorded along the >5-km-long profile (Fig. 2 and Fig. S1). Because of the source type, S arrivals were not impulsive; therefore, the picks in Figure 2b and Figure S1 are tentative. In general, apparent velocities increase from east to west as deeper structures are sampled. Overlain on this are local apparent velocity changes caused by lateral velocity variations, a prominent one being the broad decrease in shallow velocity between 1.8 and 3 profile km (e.g., Fig. S1).

To better understand the relationship between horizontal and vertical variations in velocity, we projected the observations onto the black dashed line in Figure 3 and conducted 2D forward modeling of the P-wave first arrivals. The resulting model represents the P-wave velocity (V_P) characteristic of a swath up to 300 m wide around the dashed line, and structures that are oblique to the dashed line are smeared. The travel time picks were corrected for topography assuming a velocity of 2 km/s (Fig. 5a).

The corrected P-wave arrival times were modeled using Rayinvr (Zelt and Smith, 1992). The model was specified by three layers of laterally varying thickness and velocity that correspond to changes in the V_P gradient. No velocity discontinuities were included. The travel time through the upper 1 km of the model is shown in Figure 5b and shows that the shallow structure leads to P-wave travel time perturbations of up to 0.1 s. The maximum depth of ray coverage is overlain on the preferred model in Figure 5c, showing which parts of the model are well constrained.

A rapid increase in apparent velocity around 1.6 km is modeled by a shallowing of the basement sedimentary rocks defined by the 3.5 km/s contour and assumed to be Spencer Formation. The broad decrease in apparent velocity between 1.8 and 3 km is modeled by a basin with a maximum depth of ~500 m. The transition from near-surface basement rocks to the relatively deep basin immediately west of OC correlates with rapid reductions in peak amplitude (~order of magnitude; Figs. 2, 4a), shaking duration (50% reduction; Fig. 4d), and high-frequency content (Fig. S5c) from the implosion. Beyond 4 km, there is a shallowing of the 5 km/s velocity contour, interpreted to result from uplift of Siletz terrane rocks along the CF. The basin appears to extend beneath the eastern limit of Siletz rocks on the geologic map, which indicates that our V_P model does not capture geometric complexity associated with the fault.

Mid-frequency ambient noise tomography

Because of the larger uncertainties in implosion S-wave first arrival times (Fig. 2b), we did not try to resolve S-wave velocities (V_S) using these data. Instead, we estimated shallow V_S by deriving and then inverting frequency-dependent surface-wave phase velocities from stacked ambient noise CCs at frequencies <4 Hz. During analysis, only the relatively straight (and flat) ~3.6-km-long section of the profile was used (Fig. 3) because of the sensitivity of the methodology to irregular array geometry. In addition, we focused on fundamental-mode surface waves only as higher order modes, although expected in a basin-like environment, were not clearly observed, likely because of high-intrinsic attenuation. The steps to produce Rayleigh (ZZ)- and Love (TT)-wave 2D phase velocity maps were as follows.

1. A zero-phase band-pass (0.7–3.5 Hz) filter was applied to all CCs (Fig. 6a).
2. Negative and positive time CCs (Fig. 6a) were folded and averaged to produce single-sided broadband CCs.
3. CCs were ordered with stations east of a virtual source at negative distances and ones to the west positive.
4. A Hann window was applied to each CC to ensure that all phases with moveout velocities <0.8 km/s (starting at $t = 0.8$ s at $x = 0$ km to capture entire waveforms at close distances) or >1.8 km/s were muted.
5. Frequency-dependent phases were calculated with the fast Fourier transform.

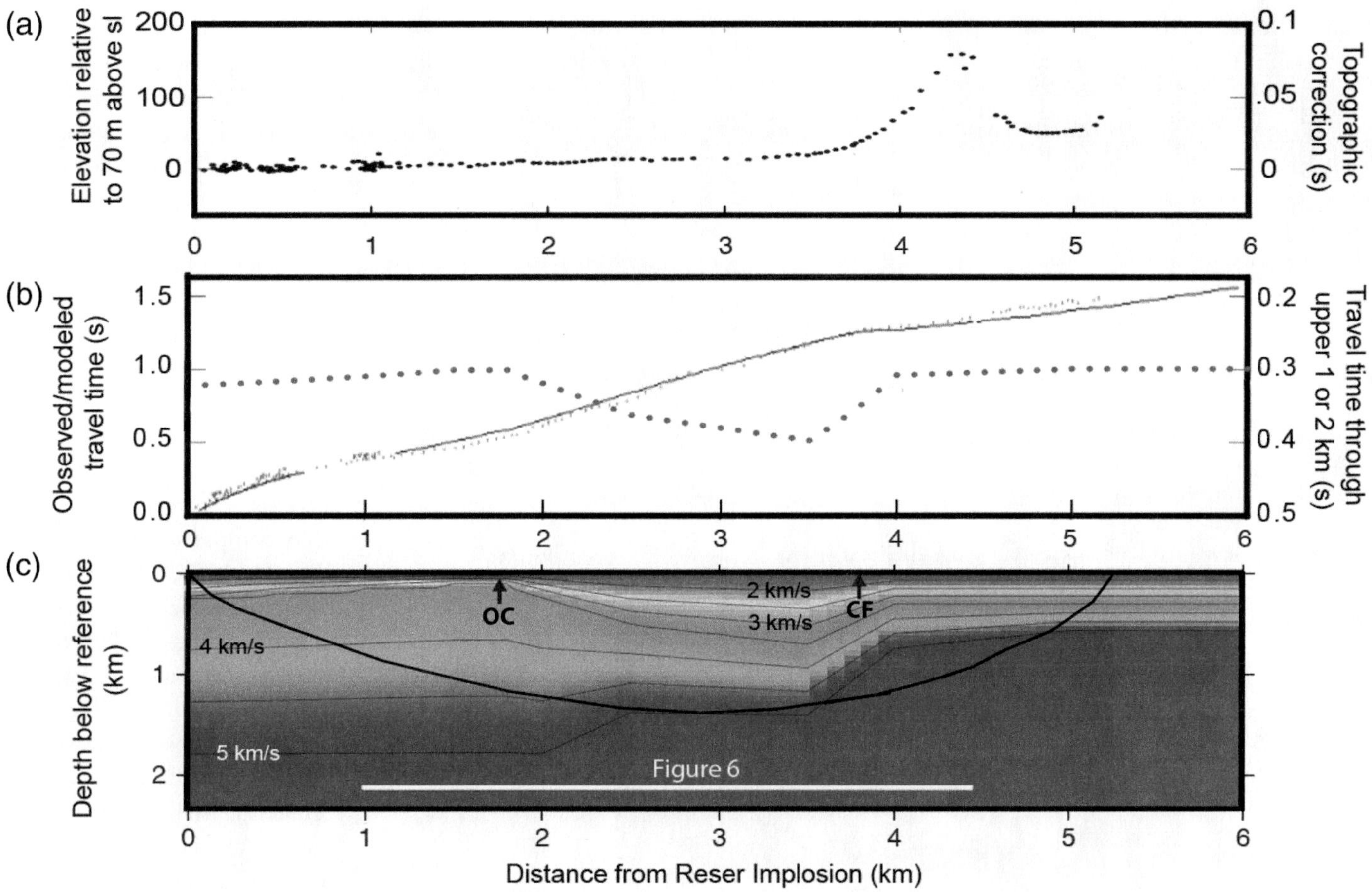

Figure 5. V_P forward model from first arrivals generated by the Reser Stadium implosion. The *x* axis for all figures is the distance between the centroid of the implosion and the observation. (a) Elevation along the profile (left axis) relative to the reference elevation and the topographic correction applied to the data for modeling (right axis). (b) The observed (small red vertical dashes) and modeled (black line) travel times (left axis) and the total time through the upper 1 km (red dots and right axis). (c) V_P below the reference depth. Contours are at intervals of 0.5 km/s. The dark-black line shows the lower limit of ray coverage. The portion of the model that is based on the same set of nodes as were used for Figure 6 is indicated by a white line. The locations of Oak Creek (OC) and the mapped CF are also shown. The color version of this figure is available only in the electronic edition.

6. All phases within one wavelength of a virtual source or at large distances where SNR is low were excluded. Based on visual inspection, these distances for 3.5 and 0.7 Hz were 0.5 and 1.4 km and 1.3 and 3.6 km, respectively, interpolating between those bounds to produce distances for intermediate frequencies.
7. An unwrapping step was applied to correct for $\pm\pi$ phase cycle skipping.
8. Travel time (t) was calculated from phase (φ) and frequency (f) using $t = \frac{-\varphi}{2\pi f}$.
9. Calculated travel times were interpolated onto a regular spatial grid (spacing = 80 m) and smoothed using a mean filter of length 480 m.
10. Phase velocity (c) as a function of distance from a virtual source (x) was derived using the 1D Eikonal equation (Aki and Richards, 2002), that is, $|\frac{dt}{dx}|^2 = \frac{1}{c^2}$.

After computing phase velocity maps for each virtual source, we shifted sources to their appropriate profile locations and combined all maps to produce median Rayleigh- and Love-wave phase velocity maps (Fig. 6b,c). These generally exhibit low uncertainty (~0.1 km/s median absolute deviations) and significant lateral variability (0.7–2.7 km/s). In particular, as in Figure 5c, the intersection of our profile and OC marks an east-to-west transition from shallow Spencer Formation (1.5–2 km/s) to a low-velocity feature (<1 km/s) that becomes less prominent around the mapped CF and gives way to the high phase velocities (>2 km/s) of outcropping Siletz basalts (Bald Hill) in the west.

Next, we jointly inverted the Rayleigh- and Love-wave results to produce a V_S cross section using the general approach of Mordret *et al.* (2015, 2019) and the neighborhood algorithm (NA, Sambridge, 1999; Wathelet, 2008). At each point in space along the profile, we extracted a local ZZ and TT phase velocity dispersion curve, which we inverted into a local 1D V_S profile. The lateral concatenation of these 1D profiles produces the final 2D V_S model (Fig. 6d). The general parameterization of the problem consisted of four

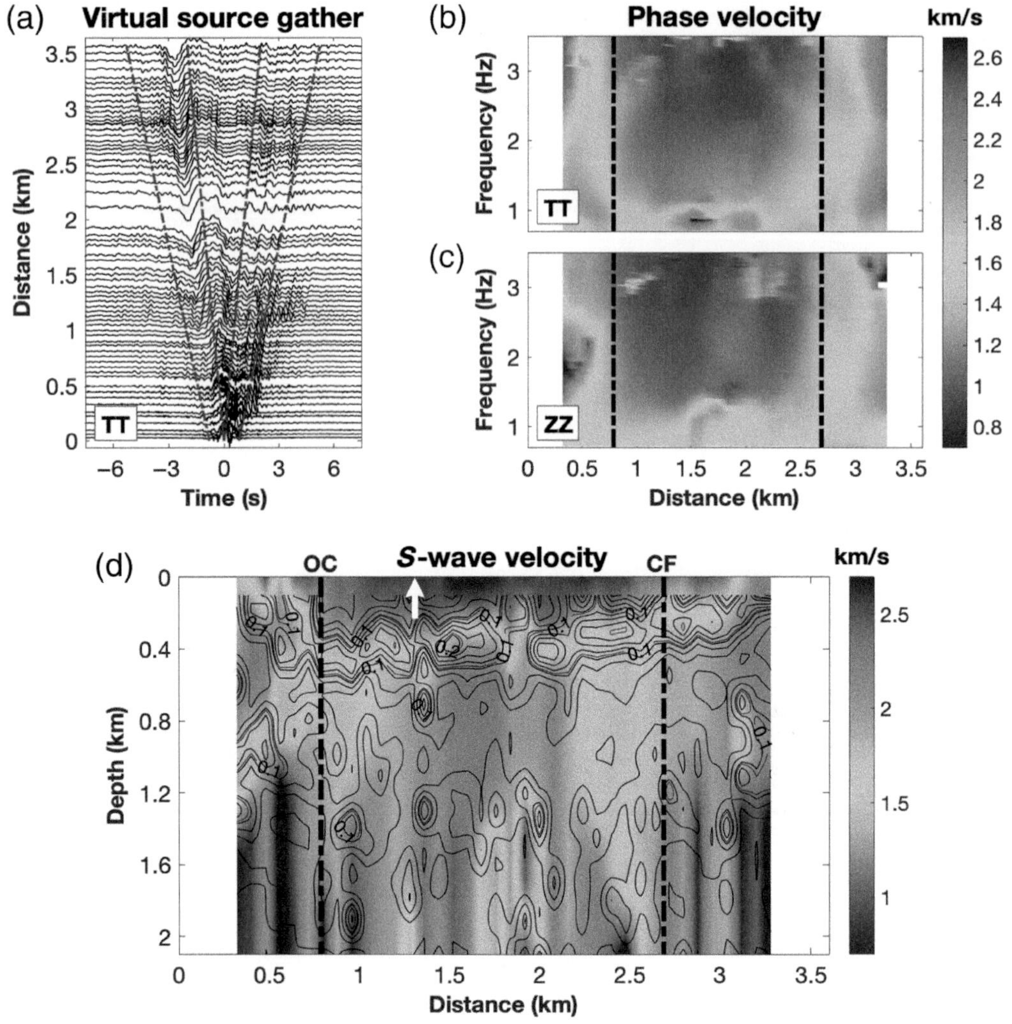

Figure 6. V_S properties derived from ambient noise cross correlations (CCs). (a) TT-pair CCs (0.7–3.5 Hz) for the easternmost virtual source along the ~3.6 km profile. ~1 Hz-ocean noise, originating in the west, manifests in negative time, whereas higher frequency anthropogenic noise from Corvallis dominates in positive time. Steep and less-steep red lines represent moveouts of 1.8 and 0.8 km/s, respectively; 0.8 km/s lines start at ±0.8 s to capture the entire near-field wave packet. (b,c) Median Love- (TT) and Rayleigh- (ZZ) wave phase velocities of all virtual source gathers. Black lines indicate OC (left) and the mapped CF (right). (d) Final 2D V_S model with interface probability (see Fig. S7b for full details) contours superimposed. The arrow highlights the intersection of white (V_P) and black (V_P) profiles in Figure 3. The color version of this figure is available only in the electronic edition.

homogeneous layers above a half-space. The velocities and thicknesses of these layers were allowed to vary within the ranges described in Table 1. The top of the half-space was fixed at 8000 m depth with a velocity of 2.9 km/s. During the inversion, V_P was scaled to V_S using a V_P/V_S ratio of $\sqrt{3}$. Density was scaled to V_P using the Brocher (2005) empirical relationship. The ZZ and TT dispersion curves were jointly inverted with the same weight in the misfit calculation. The misfit was computed, after Mordret *et al.* (2014), as the ratio of the area of the modeled dispersion curve outside of the area delimited by the measured dispersion curve and its standard deviation, divided by the area of the measured dispersion curve and its standard deviation. Finally, to run the NA, the parameter space sampling was done with 10,000 initial random samples followed by the resampling of the neighborhood of the best 3000 models with two random samples each during 10 iterations. At each location along the profile, a total of 70,000 models were sampled and the best 3000 kept for further analysis.

A comparison of measured (Fig. 6b,c) and modeled (Fig. S6) phase velocities shows that only the edges of the profiles were poorly fitted, likely the effect of nonlinear array segments at those edges, with the low-velocity zone at the center of the profile reproduced especially well. The modeled phase velocities also illustrate the different depth sensitivities between Rayleigh and Love waves at the same period, or conversely, the sensitivity of the same depth at longer periods for Love waves compared with Rayleigh waves.

To build the final velocity profile, we followed the probabilistic approach of Lu *et al.* (2018). We used the 3000 best models to extract the posterior probability distribution of the S-wave velocity at each depth, accompanied by the probability of presence of a layer interface at each depth. We see that the range of possible velocities fitting the data increases with depth, from ±50 m/s near the surface to ±100 m/s above 1.3 km depth and ±200 m/s below 1.3 km depth. From this probability distribution, we compute a smoothed most probable model and its uncertainties (example point in Fig. S7a) that we use to construct the final model (Fig. 6d).

The main feature of this model is the 300–400 m deep (Fig. S7b) $V_S < 1$ km/s basin feature west of the profile-OC intersection that pinches out on approach to the CF and Siletz terrane (Fig. 6d). Its thickness is consistent with the

TABLE 1
Parameter Ranges for the V_S Inversion in the Mid-Frequency Ambient Noise Tomography Section

Parameter	Description	Minimum	Maximum	Units
$V0$	Shear-wave velocity in the first layer	300	2000	m/s
$V1$	Shear-wave velocity in the second layer	500	2500	m/s
$V2$	Shear-wave velocity in the third layer	1300	2800	m/s
$V3$	Shear-wave velocity in the fourth layer	1500	2850	m/s
$D1$	Thickness of the first layer	1	800	m
$D2$	Thickness of the second layer	1	1300	m
$D3$	Thickness of the third layer	1	1500	m

V_P results (Fig. 5c). The second layer is characterized by a velocity around 1.8 km/s down to 1.2–1.4 km depth with a potentially higher velocity (2–2.2 km/s) between 1.5 and 2 km along the profile. The third layer, starting at 1.2–1.4 km depth beneath the profile, may represent Siletz basement (Edmonds, 2025). Velocities in this layer are more uncertain, though, because of lower data sensitivity (e.g., Fig. S7a).

Low-frequency teleseisms

As with most seismic tomograms, the results in Figures 5 and 6 represent smoothed versions of the true subsurface. Locating sharp interfaces and lateral changes in structure (e.g., faults) requires other seismic signals. Teleseismic arrivals have been successfully used (e.g., Qin *et al.*, 2021; Share *et al.*, 2022) to pinpoint the locations of such fault-related rapid changes. Resolution scales with frequency, so these low-frequency arrivals are mostly sensitive to large-scale (~kilometer length) structures, but because they are vertically incident and are modulated differently by the disparate crustal blocks on either side of a near-vertical fault, subtle across-fault shifts in signal phase, amplitude, and complexity can be used to pinpoint its location to within interstation distances.

Three teleseismic events with clear arrivals were analyzed. The first had magnitude *M* 6.8, an epicenter south of the Aleutian Islands and Alaska (52.342 −167.755, depth = 20 km) and occurred at 11:35:43 (all times in UTC) on 11 January (Fig. 7a). The second, an *M* 6.6 event near Labuan, Indonesia (−6.860 105.289, depth = 33 km), occurred at 09:05:41 on 14 January (Fig. S8a). The last event analyzed occurred deep beneath southern Japan (*M* 6.3, 32.728 132.039, depth = 39 km) at 16:08:37 on 21 January (Fig. S9a). We manually picked *P* arrivals for each event and profile station on vertical component recordings. A different band-pass filter and time window for each event was selected prior to CC to account for different source and path effects. For the Alaska event, a bandpass of 0.5–2 Hz was applied, and a 3.1 s early *P*-wave window was selected (1.2 s before and 1.9 s after manual *P* picks). For the Indonesia event, these parameters were 1–2 Hz and 4.7 s (1.5 s before and 3.2 s after), and for the Japan event, they were 0.5–2 Hz and 4 s (1 s before and 3 s after).

For each event and recording component, the processed and selected *P* window at a given station was correlated with the *P* windows of all other stations along the profile, and the correlation coefficient maxima were plotted (Fig. 7b–d and Figs. S8b–d, S9b–d). Ideally, if the CF laterally separates two different crustal blocks that are internally uniform at a scale commensurate with teleseismic wavelengths, then this type of CC operation would result in coefficients of ~1 for stations west of the fault compared with ones on the same side and the same for station groups east of the fault but coefficients <1 when across-fault stations are compared. Taking the Alaska event as an example (Fig. 7), this is generally the case (especially in Z components in which *P* is strongest), but there is greater variability in correlations within station groups to the west and east of the CF, respectively, reflecting smaller-scale changes within each block (e.g., Figs. 5c and 6d). More critically though, the location where early *P* waves recorded in the east become highly dissimilar to ones in the west is consistently >300 m east of the mapped CF (red indicators in Fig. 7). A similar conclusion can be drawn from the other two events (Figs. S8 and S9). The CF location in this part of Corvallis is inferred because of a lack of outcropping rock. This inference may require an update if this rapid lateral change in upper-crustal structure is also found to be the presently active strand within the CF zone. To explore present-day activity within this fault zone and beyond, we next search the array dataset for any uncataloged seismicity.

Detection and properties of local earthquakes

Compared with other subduction zones, the Cascadian margin has low ambient seismicity rates (e.g., Tréhu *et al.*, 2015; Bostock *et al.*, 2019). Capturing more of the infrequent seismicity that does occur requires denser seismic networks and cutting-edge detection tools. Toward this aim, we applied EQTransformer to the Corvallis array as a final analysis step to detect unknown small events.

Local events were detected in downsampled (100 Hz) continuous seismic data with EQTransformer as implemented in SeisBench (Woollam *et al.*, 2022). The model was used with pretrained weights from the Stanford Earthquake Dataset (Mousavi *et al.*, 2019). After application, a total of 2441

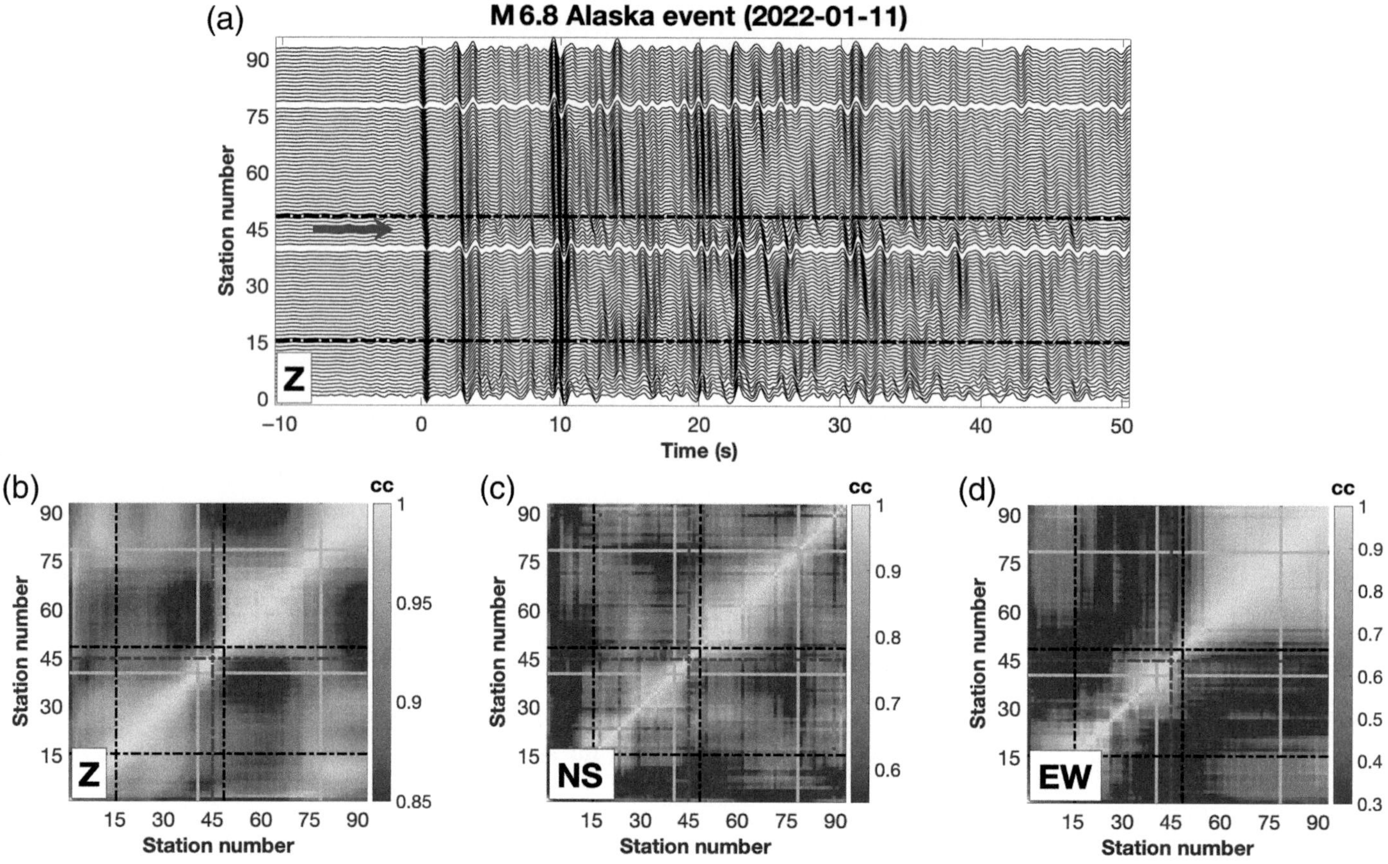

detections were returned across all 177 three-component sensors, representing time picks for possible *P*- or *S*-wave arrivals. Visual inspection of the waveforms yielded at least one event that may be a previously uncataloged local earthquake (Fig. 8a). A borehole broadband seismometer at global network station COR (Fig. 3) confirms that this event generated distinct *P* and *S* arrivals, with an *S*-*P* time of ~2.6 s, implying a local source.

Beamforming (*f*-*k* analysis) was performed with the circular portion of the Corvallis array on this event using the array processing functions in ObsPy (Krischer *et al.*, 2015). The target frequency ranges were chosen to be 1–3 Hz for the horizontal components and 1–7 Hz for the vertical components to reduce the effect of anthropogenic noise. Beamforming was performed on the 8 s surrounding the event using a 1 s sliding window and a 0.1 s step. Figure 8b shows the resulting beams for each component. The array transfer functions for these frequency ranges were also calculated and show no significant azimuthal dependence or side lobes (Fig. S10).

Based on the beamforming results, the event in Figure 8 appears to be shallow with an epicenter west of campus. For comparison, we also attempted to locate the event using high-frequency *P*- and *S*-wave first arrivals observed at COR as well as on approximately every 10th station from the western half of the linear array (Fig. 3), where impulsive *P*-wave arrivals were observed. Consistent with the beamforming results, this exercise also indicates a very shallow source (<2 km depth) west of Corvallis. Given the shallow source depth and well-developed surface-wave energy (see supplemental material), this could be a quarry blast. The general trend of *P* and *S* phases arriving first in the west and last in the east across the linear profile is in line with an event located to the west. However, some local variations in these moveouts reflect subsurface structure. For example, the earliest arriving body waves are observed atop Bald Hill, the most elevated part of the array (>200 m above sea level; Fig. 5a) but also the structure with fastest seismic velocity (Fig. 5c). The summed travel time effect of topography on the structure in the upper 1 km is shown in Figure 5b. Another example detection, which is likely not a classic earthquake but rather a tremor-like arrival, has similar arrival-time

Figure 7. Example teleseismic arrival along the linear profile. (a) First *P*-wave arrival on vertical component (Z) recordings for an event south of Alaska (latitude = 52.342, longitude = −167.755, depth = 20 km). Blue triangles are manual *P* picks. The top dotted–dashed line is the mapped CF and bottom one OC. The red arrow highlights the station around which most rapid waveform changes occur. (b–d) CC coefficients between profile stations and the vertical (Z), north–south (NS), and east–west (EW) components. The black dotted–dashed lines have the same meaning as in panel (a), whereas the red dotted–dashed line tracks the arrow station location in panel (a). Gray lines represent missing (or not operational) stations. Note the different color bars in panels (b) and (d). The color version of this figure is available only in the electronic edition.

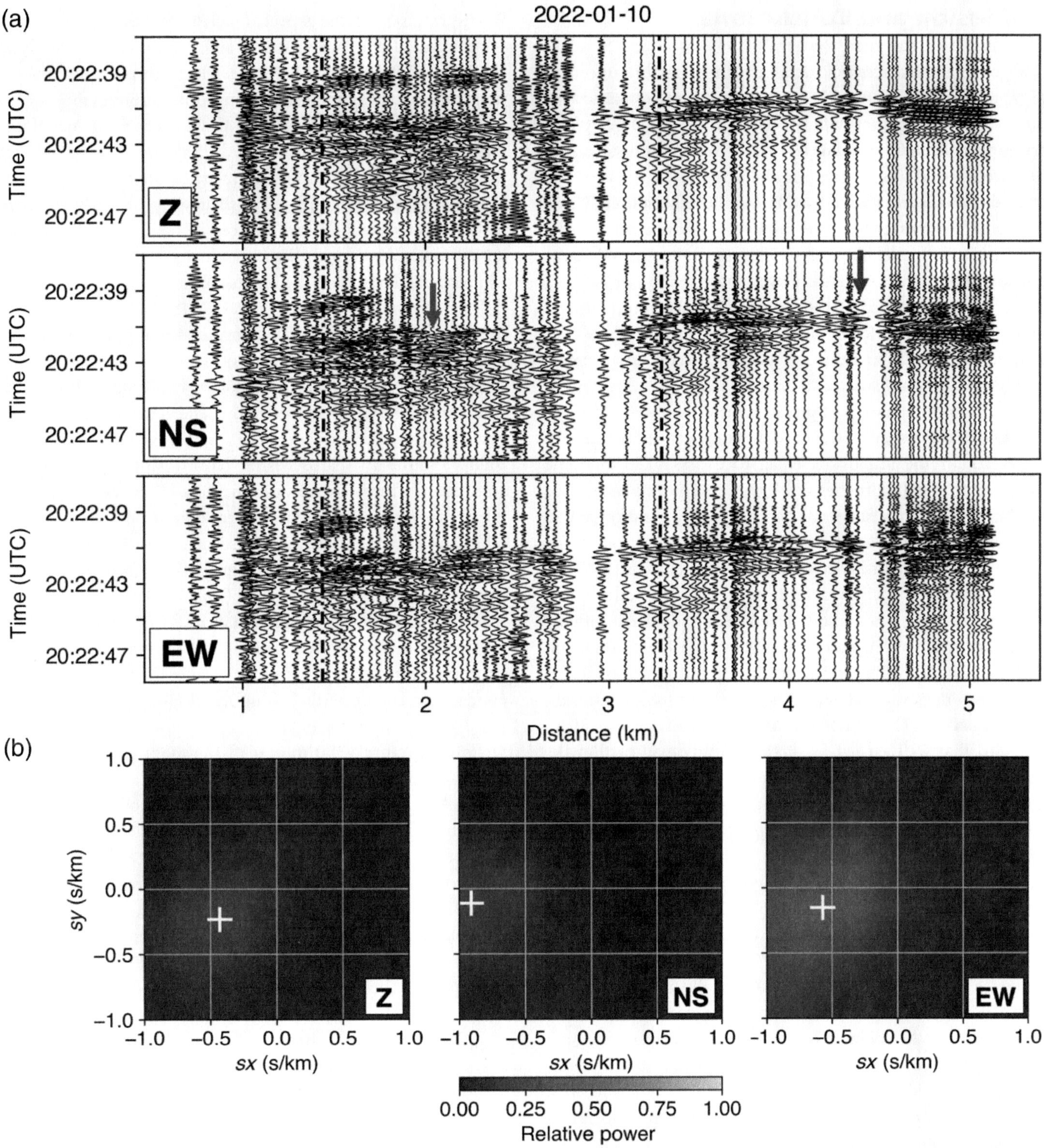

trends (Fig. S11a). It originated beneath campus and was deep, as evidenced by a stronger beam (more coherent incident plane wave; Fig. S11b). Despite occurring beneath the eastern end of the linear array and lowest elevation (~60 to 70 m) stations, signals from this event again arrived first around Bald Hill, ~4.5 km west of campus, and last through the low-velocity basin west of OC (Fig. S11a). This corroborates the structural features illuminated in Figures 5c and 6d.

Figure 8. A likely uncataloged local earthquake close to but west of Corvallis. (a) *P* and *S* arrivals (2–7 Hz) on Z, NS, and EW recordings along the linear profile (km 0 is Reser Stadium). Blue and red arrows show stations with earliest and latest arriving *S* body waves. Dotted–dashed lines are OC (~1.4 km) and the CF (~3.3 km). (b) Beams for each component (constructed with the circular array portion only) showing energy arriving from the southwest with large horizontal slowness (likely shallow). The color version of this figure is available only in the electronic edition.

Discussion and Conclusions

The implosion of the Western Stands of Reser Stadium (Oregon State University) presented an opportune moment to capture ground motions in the near field from a smaller seismic event and, together with the deployed 177-node Corvallis array, provided a unique dataset to inform upper-crustal structure around and west of campus and across the CF zone. Data from the entire array were used to quantify the source. Using isolated *P* body waves from the implosion, we were able to generate a 2D V_P model along the >5 long east–west quasi-linear portion of the array. A partially overlapping ~3.6-km-long V_S section was derived from ambient seismic noise recorded over the three-week-long deployment window. The analysis of teleseismic earthquake arrivals and newly detected local events provided additional structural constraints.

Based on the major Stadium structures involved as well as the style of collapse, we calculated an equivalent magnitude of $M_w \sim 2.3$ for the implosion, equal to the Seattle Kingdome implosion in 2000 (Brocher *et al.*, 2002). The implosion was similar in ways to an earthquake with directivity and generated more impulsive and higher frequency energy to the southwest, in line with the main tower of the toppled stadium (Figs. 1b, 4a–c). Moreover, owing to finite-source length-scale effects and/or heterogeneous shallow structure, it had an azimuthally nonuniform radiation pattern and generated longer duration high-amplitude shaking in the northwest and southeast directions (Fig. 4d; elevated shaking for >60 s). Similar to Atkinson and Viegas (2023), with PGAs of >0.1*g* at distances <80 m (Fig. 4b) that well exceed predictions from small-earthquake ground motion prediction equations (Fig. S4), this event had point source–like characteristics (Hassani and Atkinson, 2018) and produced highly energetic ground accelerations in the near field. Unlike that study, though, our sensors were installed in wet surface silts and sediments instead of intact bedrock, indicating that near-field high-PGAs are a ubiquitous seismic hazard in diverse geologic settings. Despite producing even larger ground accelerations (PGAs > 0.37*g*, Fig. S3b), the sequence of explosions, triggered in air, did not couple well with the ground (Fig. 2a) and cannot be used as indicators for waveform behavior from subsurface seismic sources. Focusing on the far field, node recordings can now be combined with regional network data (e.g., Figs. S12 and S13) to allow the implosion source, with a well-constrained radiation pattern (Fig. S5a), to be used as a template for the characteristic arrival time, amplitude, frequency, and reach of shallow $M_w > 2$ earthquakes in the Willamette Valley. We suggest that this should be the focus of future works.

Both the V_P (Fig. 5c) and V_S (Fig. 6e) models indicate the presence of a 300–500 m deep basin ($V_P < 3$ km/s, $V_S < 1$ km/s) between where OC crosses the profile and Bald Hill. The V_P model also shows a thinning of sediment between Reser Stadium and OC, which corresponds to locally uplifted Spencer Formation basement. The basin west of OC is superimposed on the expected increase in velocity with depth (Goldfinger, 1990; Wiley, 2008), and it terminates abruptly at the base of Bald Hill, where the Siletz terrane volcanics are uplifted along CF. Implosion waveforms around the eastern edge of the basin show an east-to-west order of magnitude reduction in peak ground motions, a 50% reduction in shaking duration, and reduced high-frequency power at the surface (Figs. 2b, 4 and Fig. S5c). The shallowing of basement rock between Reser Stadium and the crest of the Spenser Formation anticline, combined with the low-velocity basin, likely result in trapping of energy from the implosion in the east and markedly different ground motions in the west. More regionally, the intermittent presence of generally northeast-trending outcrops of Spencer and Tyee formation rocks (Fig. 3) suggests that basin structure within a band of a few kilometers wide on the southeast flank of the CF varies both along and across strike. Its interplay with local creeks and rivers in the western Willamette Valley and the associated seismic hazard is poorly constrained and requires further investigation. As a start, we suggest that future work on seismic hazard incorporate the Corvallis and other similarly dense arrays to estimate near-surface intrinsic attenuation using freight train signals (Brenguier *et al.*, 2019; Zhang *et al.*, 2023) in the area (e.g., Portland and Western Railroad) and ambient noise (Liu *et al.*, 2015).

The V_P and V_S models also suggest a thinning of the basin structure around the mapped location of the CF (Figs. 5c and 6b–d). Teleseismic arrivals (Fig. 7 and Figs. S8, S9) point to a rapid change along a near-vertical boundary in the deeper seismic structure >300 m east of the mapped fault (Fig. 3). Taken together, these results indicate that although the CF is deeply rooted and controls the location of the basin, the basin has formed since major activity on the fault. A subtle topographic discontinuity in recent light detection and ranging (lidar) data (DOGAMI Oregon Department of Geology and Mineral Industries Lidar Program Data, 2025) is located west of the mapped fault (Fig. 3) and may represent the most recent activity within the CF zone. One of the potential local earthquakes (not in the PNSN catalog) identified in this study (Fig. 8) also locates near this topographic feature (Fig. 3 and Fig. S13). These results support an interpretation of the CF as a broad zone of deformation with a long history of complex uplift and deformation. Identifying the most recent locus of activity within the CF zone is important for improving ground failure hazard maps and other geotechnical foci targeting the high-relief western edge of the Willamette Valley.

Our study demonstrates the value of dense nodal deployments for better understanding the impact of structure on ground motion in the Willamette Valley and other similar terrains within active tectonic zones. Future deployments of this type will help produce more complete earthquake catalogs, improved fault maps, and accurate subsurface velocity images of the heterogeneous crust in the Pacific Northwest.

Data and Resources

The nodal array data and associated metadata are publicly available for download from the EarthScope Consortium DMC (doi: 10.7914/SN/YM_2022: Tréhu and Share, 2022). The supplemental material contains supporting figures and a description on newly detected event location efforts.

Declaration of Competing Interests

The authors acknowledge that there are no conflicts of interest recorded.

Acknowledgments

The authors thank Oregon State University (OSU), the City of Corvallis, the Greenbelt Land Trust, and numerous private owners for allowing them to install seismic nodes on their property. The authors truly appreciate the help of geology, geophysics, and geotechnical engineering students Besrat Alemu, Tifong Chin, Ali Dadashiserej, Nathaniel Edmonds, Jintana Happala, Elizabeth Hayden, Weston Hustace, Kirill Ivanov, Amalesh Jana, Alaina Keller, Jackson Kilger, Joshua Love, Jesus Magdaleno, Charity Mann, Sarah Nolan, Ezra (Kyle) Nunley, Ann Olesh, Lance Parson, Sanjaya Paudel, Talenta Pisto, Raied Refaei, Hannah Reinhard, Joel Scott, Chase Strang, Owen Strid, Nikolo Vo, Hao Wang, Haskelle White, and Ehsan Yazdani during scouting, deploying, and pickup of nodes. Discussions with Mark Rado from Hoffman Construction were invaluable in quantifying the implosion. Figure 1b was created by Oliver Day and Lam Long from OSU University Relations and Marketing. The others were made with Generic Mapping Tools (GMT; Wessel *et al.*, 2013), MATLAB (www.mathworks.com/products/matlab, last accessed July 2025), and Python. The seismic nodes were provided by the EarthScope Primary Instrument Center. The article benefitted greatly from the comments and suggestions of two anonymous reviewers.

References

Aki, K., and P. G. Richards (2002). *Quantitative Seismology*, University Science Books, Melville, New York700 pp.

Atkinson, G. M. (2015). Ground-motion prediction equation for small-to-moderate events at short hypocentral distances, with application to induced-seismicity hazards, *Bull. Seismol. Soc. Am.* **105,** no. 2A, 981–992.

Atkinson, G. M., and G. Viegas (2023). Point-source decay of ground-motion amplitudes at <10 km, *Seism. Record* **3,** no. 1, 21–28.

Atkinson, G. M., E. Yenier, N. Sharma, and V. Convertito (2016). Constraints on the near-distance saturation of ground-motion amplitudes for small-to-moderate induced earthquakes, *Bull. Seismol. Soc. Am.* **106,** no. 5, 2104–2111.

Båth, M. (1966). Earthquake energy and magnitude, *Phys. Chem. Earth* **7,** 115–165.

Ben-Zion, Y. (2019). A critical data gap in earthquake physics, *Seismol. Res. Lett.* **90,** no. 5, 1721–1722.

Boore, D. M., J. Watson-Lamprey, and N. A. Abrahamson (2006). Orientation-independent measures of ground motion, *Bull. Seismol. Soc. Am.* **96,** no. 4A, 1502–1511.

Bostock, M. G., N. I. Christensen, and S. M. Peacock (2019). Seismicity in Cascadia, *Lithos* **332–333,** 55–66.

Brenguier, F., P. Boué, Y. Ben-Zion, F. Vernon, C. W. Johnson, A. Mordret, O. Coutant, P.-E. Share, E. Beaucé, D. Hollis, and T. Lecocq (2019). Train traffic as a powerful noise source for monitoring active faults with seismic interferometry, *Geophys. Res. Lett.* **46,** 9529–9536, doi: 10.1029/2019GL083438.

Brissaud, Q., D. C. Bowden, and V. C. Tsai (2020). Extension of the Basin Rayleigh-wave amplification theory to include basin-edge effects, *Bull. Seismol. Soc. Am.* **110,** no. 3, 1305–1322.

Brocher, T. M. (2005). Empirical relations between elastic wavespeeds and density in the Earth's crust, *Bull. Seismol. Soc. Am.* **95,** no. 6, 2081–2092.

Brocher, T. M., T. L. Pratt, C. S. Weaver, C. M. Snelson, and A. D. Frankel (2002). Implosion, earthquake, and explosion recordings from the 2000 Seattle Kingdome Seismic Hazards Investigation of Puget Sound (SHIPS), Washington, *Open-File Rept. 2002-123*, doi: 10.3133/ofr02123.

Duncan, R. A. (1982). A captured island chain in the Coast Range of Oregon and Washington, *J. Geophys. Res.* **87,** no. B13, 10,827–10,837.

DOGAMI Oregon Department of Geology and Mineral Industries Lidar Program Data (2025). Distributed by OpenTopography, doi: 10.5069/G9QC01D1.

Edmonds, N. (2025). Upper crustal shear-wave velocities and structure in Corvallis, Oregon, from ambient noise tomography, *M.S. Thesis*, Oregon State University.

Goldfinger, C. (1990). Evolution of the Corvallis fault, and implications for the Oregon Coast Range, *M.S. Thesis*, Oregon State University, Corvallis, Oregon, 129 pp.

Hassani, B., and G. M. Atkinson (2018). Adjustable generic ground-motion prediction equation based on equivalent point-source simulations: Accounting for kappa effects, *Bull. Seismol. Soc. Am.* **108,** no. 2, 913–928.

Kanamori, H. (2001). Energy budget of earthquakes and seismic efficiency, *Int. Geophys.* **76,** 293–305.

Klinger, A. G., and M. J. Werner (2022). Stress drops of hydraulic fracturing induced microseismicity in the Horn River basin: Challenges at high frequencies recorded by borehole geophones, *Geophys. J. Int.* **228,** no. 3, 2018–2037.

Krischer, L., T. Megies, R. Barsch, M. Beyreuther, T. Lecocq, C. Caudron, and J. Wassermann (2015). ObsPy: A bridge for seismology into the scientific Python ecosystem, *Comput. Sci. Discov.* **8,** no. 1, 014003.

Lecocq, T., C. Caudron, and F. Brenguier (2014). MSNoise, a Python package for monitoring seismic velocity changes using ambient seismic noise, *Seismol. Res. Lett.* **85,** no. 3, 715–726.

Liu, X., Y. Ben-Zion, and D. Zigone (2015). Extracting seismic attenuation coefficients from cross-correlations of ambient noise at linear triplets of stations, *Geophys. J. Int.* **203,** no. 2, 1149–1163.

Lu, Y., L. Stehly, A. Paul, and , and AlpArray Working Group (2018). High-resolution surface wave tomography of the European crust and uppermost mantle from ambient seismic noise, *Geophys. J. Int.* **214,** no. 2, 1136–1150.

McPhee, D., V. E. Langenheim, R. Wells, and R. J. Blakely (2014). Tectonic evolution of the Tualatin basin, northwest Oregon, as revealed by inversion of gravity data, *Geosphere* doi: 10.1130/GES00929.1.

Mordret, A., M. Landès, N. M. Shapiro, S. C. Singh, and P. Roux (2014). Ambient noise surface wave tomography to determine the shallow shear velocity structure at Valhall: Depth inversion with a neighbourhood algorithm, *Geophys. J. Int.* **198,** no. 3, 1514–1525.

Mordret, A., M. Landès, N. M. Shapiro, S. C. Singh, P. Roux, and O. I. Barkved (2013). Near-surface study at the Valhall oil field from ambient noise surface wave tomography, *Geophys. J. Int.* **193,** no. 3, 1627–1643.

Mordret, A., D. Rivet, M. Landès, and N. M. Shapiro (2015). Three-dimensional shear velocity anisotropic model of Piton de la Fournaise Volcano (La Réunion Island) from ambient seismic noise, *J. Geophys. Res.* **120,** no. 1, 406–427.

Mordret, A., P. Roux, P. Boué, and Y. Ben-Zion (2019). Shallow three-dimensional structure of the San Jacinto fault zone revealed from ambient noise imaging with a dense seismic array, *Geophys. J. Int.* **216,** no. 2, 896–905.

Mousavi, S. M., W. L. Ellsworth, W. Zhu, L. Y. Chuang, and G. C. Beroza (2020). Earthquake transformer—An attentive deep-learning model for simultaneous earthquake detection and phase picking, *Nat. Commun.* **11,** no. 1, 3952.

Mousavi, S. M., Y. Sheng, W. Zhu, and G. C. Beroza (2019). STanford EArthquake Dataset (STEAD): A global data set of seismic signals for AI, *IEEE Access* **7,** 179,464–179,476.

Qin, L., P.-E. Share, H. Qiu, A. A. Allam, F. L. Vernon, and Y. Ben-Zion (2021). Internal structure of the San Jacinto fault zone at the Ramona Reservation, north of Anza, California, from dense array seismic data, *Geophys. J. Int.* **224,** no. 2, 1225–1241.

Qiu, H., Y. Ben-Zion, R. Catchings, M. R. Goldman, A. A. Allam, and J. Steidl (2021). Seismic imaging of the Mw 7.1 Ridgecrest earthquake rupture zone from data recorded by dense linear arrays, *J. Geophys. Res.* **126,** no. 7, e2021JB022043, doi: 10.1029/2021JB022043.

Sambridge, M. (1999). Geophysical inversion with a neighbourhood algorithm—I. Searching a parameter space, *Geophys. J. Int.* **138,** no. 2, 479–494.

Share, P., H. Qiu, F. L. Vernon, A. A. Allam, Y. Fialko, and Y. Ben-Zion (2022). General seismic architecture of the Southern San Andreas Fault Zone around the Thousand Palms Oasis from a Large-N Nodal Array, *Seism. Record* **2,** no. 1, 50–58.

Silva, W. J., I. G. Wong, R. B. Darragh, and , and U.S. Geological Survey (1991). Engineering characterization of earthquake strong ground motions with applications to the Pacific Northwest, *Open-File Rept. 91-441-H*, doi: 10.3133/ofr91441H.

Snelson, C. M., T. M. Brocher, K. C. Miller, T. L. Pratt, and A. M. Tréhu (2007). Seismic amplification within the Seattle Basin, Washington State: Insights from SHIPS seismic tomography experiments, *Bull. Seismol. Soc. Am.* **97,** 1432–1448.

Tréhu, A., and P.-E. Share (2022). Recording signals from the Reser stadium implosion for site response and structure at the western edge of the Willamette Valley [Data set], *International Federation of Digital Seismograph Networks*, doi: 10.7914/SN/YM_2022.

Tréhu, A. M., I. Asudeh, T. M. Brocher, J. Luetgert, W. D. Mooney, J. L. Nabelek, and Y. Nakamura (1994). Crustal architecture of the Cascadia forearc, *Science* **266,** 237–243.

Tréhu, A. M., J. Braunmiller, and E. Davis (2015). Seismicity of the Central Cascadia Continental Margin near 44.5° N: A decadal view, *Seismol. Res. Lett.* **86,** no. 3, 819–829.

Ward, K. M., F. Lin, and B. Schmandt (2018). High-resolution receiver function imaging across the Cascadia subduction zone using a dense nodal array, *Geophys. Res. Lett.* doi: 10.1029/2018GL079903.

Wathelet, M. (2008). An improved neighborhood algorithm: Parameter conditions and dynamic scaling, *Geophys. Res. Lett.* **35,** no. 9, doi: 10.1029/2008GL033256.

Wells, R., D. Bukry, R. Friedman, D. Pyle, R. Duncan, P. Haeussler, and J. Wooden (2014). Geologic history of Siletzia, a large igneous province in the Oregon and Washington Coast Range: Correlation to the geomagnetic polarity time scale and implications for a long-lived Yellowstone hotspot, *Geosphere* **10,** no. 4, 692–719.

Wells, R. E., C. S. Weaver, and R. J. Blakely (1998). Fore-arc migration in Cascadia and its neotectonic significance, *Geology* **26,** no. 8, 769–762.

Wessel, P., W. H. F. Smith, R. Scharroo, J. F. Luis, and F. Wobbe (2013). Generic Mapping Tools: Improved version released, *Eos Trans. AGU* **94,** 409–410.

Wiley, T. J. (2008). Preliminary geologic maps of the Corvallis, Wren, and Marys Peak 7.5' quadrangles, Benton, Lincoln, and Linn Counties, Oregon, *Oregon Department of Geology and Mineral Industries Open-File Rept. O-08-14*, 10 pp.

Woollam, J., J. Münchmeyer, F. Tilmann, A. Rietbrock, D. Lange, T. Bornstein, T. Diehl, C. Giunchi, F. Haslinger, D. Jozinović, *et al.* (2022). SeisBench—A Toolbox for machine learning in seismology, *Seismol. Res. Lett.* **93,** no. 3, 1695–1709.

Yamada, T., J. J. Mori, S. Ide, R. E. Abercrombie, H. Kawakata, M. Nakatani, Y. Iio, and H. Ogasawara (2007). Stress drops and radiated seismic energies of microearthquakes in a South African gold mine, *J. Geophys. Res.* **112,** no. B3, doi: 10.1029/2006JB004553.

Zelt, C. A., and R. B. Smith (1992). Seismic traveltime inversion for 2-D crustal velocity structure, *Geophys. J. Int.* **108,** 16–34.

Zhang, H., H. Meng, and Y. Ben-Zion (2023). Lateral variations across the southern San Andreas Fault zone revealed from analysis of traffic signals at a dense seismic array, *Geophys. Res. Lett.* **50,** no. 14, e2023GL103759, doi: 10.1029/2023GL103759.

Manuscript received 18 March 2025
Published online 10 September 2025

Readapting PhaseNet to Laboratory Earthquakes: AEsNet, a Robust Acoustic Emission Picker Illuminating Seismic Signatures of Different Fault Gouge Materials

OPEN ACCESS

Giacomo Mastella*[1], Giulio Poggiali[1], Federico Pignalberi[1,2], and Marco Scuderi[1]

Abstract

Laboratory acoustic emissions (AEs) represent microslip events analogous to small-scale earthquakes, providing valuable insights into the mechanics of frictional instabilities. With technological advancements in acoustic monitoring, thousands of AE waveforms can now be collected in minutes of experimental time, requiring efficient methods for their detection and analysis. In this study, we introduce a deep learning model for automatically detecting AEs in laboratory shear experiments. Our dataset consists of about 30,000 manually picked AE waveforms collected under different experimental boundary conditions using two fault gouge materials: Min-U-Sil quartz gouge and glass beads. By adapting the PhaseNet model, originally developed for natural earthquake phase detection, we train AEsNet, a robust AE picker that outperforms pre-existing picking methods for the tested materials. To investigate whether trained models can generalize across different boundary conditions and materials, and overcome the limitations of small, manually labeled datasets, we apply transfer learning to analyze performance relative to training size and material diversity. Our results indicate that model performance is largely independent of experimental conditions but strongly dependent on material type. This finding suggests that direct transfer of models trained on one material to another is often ineffective due to distinct frequency characteristics of AEs, which are closely linked to the microphysical processes driving emissions in the different granular materials. However, quick fine-tuning significantly enhances pretrained AEsNet performance, even surpassing that of a fine-tuned PhaseNet model pretrained on natural earthquakes. This underscores the importance of customizing models to the specific attributes of laboratory-generated AEs—a conclusion consistent with findings from transfer learning applications in natural seismicity. In conclusion, our approach provides an efficient tool for enhancing AE detection, even with limited data from diverse laboratory conditions, enabling the creation of reliable AE catalogs that can significantly advance our understanding of fault mechanics in controlled experimental settings.

Cite this article as Mastella, G., G. Poggiali, F. Pignalberi, and M. Scuderi (2025). Readapting PhaseNet to Laboratory Earthquakes: AEsNet, a Robust Acoustic Emission Picker Illuminating Seismic Signatures of Different Fault Gouge Materials, *Seismol. Res. Lett.* **97**, 141–160, doi: 10.1785/0220250025.

Supplemental Material

Introduction

Acoustic emissions (AEs) represent elastic waves generated by the release of energy from micromechanical processes (fractures or frictional sliding) within a material under deformation. Given their small source, AEs emit high-frequency seismic signals ranging from tens of kilohertz to megahertz (Lei and Ma, 2014), requiring the use of high central-frequency transducers such as piezoelectric sensors (PZTs) to capture them effectively. Since the 1960s, AEs observed during rock deformation experiments have been recognized as microslip events analogous to natural earthquakes, and have been used to study seismogenic processes in controlled laboratory

1. Department of Earth Sciences, Sapienza University of Rome, Rome, Italy, https://orcid.org/0000-0002-9052-4873 (GM); https://orcid.org/0009-0008-4723-5954 (GP); https://orcid.org/0000-0002-4153-379X (FP); https://orcid.org/0000-0001-5232-0792 (MS); 2. Department of Engineering Geology and Hydrogeology, RWTH Aachen University, Aachen, Germany

*Corresponding author: giacomo.mastella@uniroma1.it

settings (Mogi, 1962, Scholz, 1968; Lockner *et al.*, 1991; Johnson *et al.*, 2013). Large AE catalogs have demonstrated that these events follow statistical distributions similar to those of natural earthquakes, including power-law size-frequency distributions (Gutenberg and Richter, 1944; Mogi, 1962, Scholz, 1968), and aftershock sequences governed by Omori's law (Omori, 1894; Mogi, 1966). Analyzing the rate and amplitude of AEs throughout the seismic cycle can yield valuable insights into fault dynamics. These microslip events, which often precede the main failure, exhibit nonrandom patterns that provide critical information about the nucleation process leading to dynamic rupture. Statistical analyses of AE parameters, such as the *b*-value (Main *et al.*, 1989; Main, 1992; McLaskey and Kilgore, 2013; Kwiatek *et al.*, 2014; Goebel *et al.*, 2017; Rivière *et al.*, 2018; Shreedharan *et al.*, 2019; Dresen *et al.*, 2020; Bolton *et al.*, 2021; Korkolis *et al.*, 2021; Bianchi *et al.*, 2024), along with the spatiotemporal evolution of AE waveforms (Bolton *et al.*, 2023; Kwiatek *et al.*, 2024), suggest that the increase of these events and their tendency to cluster both spatially and temporally might signal the initiation of an instability (Marty *et al.*, 2023; Goebel *et al.*, 2024). In gouge faults, during this phase, the deformation is initially distributed within the gouge, becoming increasingly concentrated along pre-existing localized slipping zones, in which microscale frictional asperities fail and potentially coalesce, ultimately triggering larger failures (Yamashita *et al.*, 2021; Bolton *et al.*, 2023), similar to what is observed in natural seismicity (Ben-Zion and Zaliapin, 2020), in which also the geometry of asperities has been interpreted as a key parameter controlling failures characteristics (Chatterjee *et al.*, 2024; Lee *et al.*, 2024). These asperity-scale processes (Shreedharan *et al.*, 2020) often lead to an exponential increase in acoustic power before failure—a characteristic that enables machine learning models to predict laboratory earthquakes (Rouet-Leduc *et al.*, 2017, 2018; Lubbers *et al.*, 2018; Hulbert *et al.*, 2019; Wang *et al.*, 2022; Karimpouli *et al.*, 2023). AEs can thus be viewed as stress meters (Goebel *et al.*, 2013; Bolton *et al.*, 2020), providing real-time insight into stress evolution. Moreover, removing the influence of the monitoring system (commonly referred to as the instrument apparatus response) from the AE signals allows for source characterization through seismological spectral analysis (McLaskey and Glaser, 2012; McLaskey *et al.*, 2015; Pignalberi *et al.*, 2024), providing valuable information on source properties and energy partitioning during dynamic rupture events. This analysis is essential for scaling observations from laboratory experiments to natural earthquakes (Goodfellow and Young, 2014; Selvadurai, 2019; Blanke *et al.*, 2021).

Acoustic monitoring systems, capable of operating at megahertz sampling rates, enable the collection of thousands of AEs within minutes of experimental time (Lockner *et al.*, 1991; Rivière *et al.*, 2018), highlighting the ongoing need for fast and reliable detection and analysis methods. However, in laboratory experiments, several factors complicate their detection. A major challenge is experimental noise, often generated by hydraulic power supplies or electrical motors in laboratory earthquake machines. Furthermore, depending on the material tested and boundary conditions—such as normal stress, loading rate, surface roughness, or grain size/shape—AEs often occur in large numbers and close succession. This is observed both on bare rock surfaces (Fryer *et al.*, 2022; Marty *et al.*, 2023) and in gouge materials (Bolton *et al.*, 2020; Casas *et al.*, 2025), frequently resulting in overlapping waveforms and scattering that can hinder the clear identification of first arrivals. AEs detection accuracy is also heavily influenced by PZT characteristics, particularly their inherent polarization, which leads to preferential sensitivity to either *P* or *S* waves. Due to the aperture effect—which depends on the sensor's dimensions and the wave frequency—the angle of wave incidence relative to the sensor orientation can significantly influence arrival amplitude and clarity, leading to variations in detection performance across different source locations. In addition, while PZTs operate across a broad-frequency spectrum, they typically work in resonance and lack a flat response, which can significantly influence the recorded AE waveforms, making first-arrival picking even more challenging.

Standard amplitude-based picking methods include the short-term/long-term averages (STA/LTA) method (Allen, 1978), which detects seismic arrivals by tracking the ratio of seismic amplitude in two time windows. The STA window focuses on capturing sudden increases in signal amplitude, whereas the long-term window establishes the baseline noise level. When the STA/LTA ratio surpasses a predefined threshold, it indicates the arrival of a *P* or *S* wave. Another common technique involves joint autoregressive (AR) modeling of noise and seismic signals, using the Akaike Information Criterion (AIC) to identify seismic signal onset (Sleeman and Van Eck, 1999). Although generally efficient, these methods are susceptible to noise and may lack accuracy when precise arrival times are required. They are particularly challenging to apply when target waveforms are closely spaced in time, a common occurrence with AEs during laboratory experiments on granular materials (Johnson *et al.*, 2013; Bolton *et al.*, 2020). In addition, all these methods require the tuning of numerous empirical hyperparameters, which are dependent on factors such as monitoring rate, sensor types, waveform characteristics, experimental noise, and, most importantly, user input trial-and-error adjustments. This makes the picking procedure tedious and highly user-dependent because optimal parameter settings must be tailored to each specific experimental condition.

Recently, deep learning (DL) has shown promise in overcoming some of these challenges in the context of natural earthquakes. In earthquake seismology, DL methods have become standard for phase picking (Perol *et al.*, 2018; Ross *et al.*, 2018; Zhu and Beroza, 2019; Mousavi *et al.*, 2020; Soto and Schurr, 2021), significantly enhancing the detection of smaller events and thereby improving the completeness and resolution of earthquake catalogs (e.g., Tan *et al.*, 2021). Trugman *et al.* (2020) were the first to apply DL for detecting AEs in laboratory shear experiments, despite working with a model trained on natural earthquakes and a limited catalog not manually labeled. Recently, Shi *et al.* (2024) proposed a workflow to enhance the performance of pretrained seismic picking models on out-of-distribution datasets without requiring retraining, by applying data rescaling, filtering, and prediction ensembling. The method, which employs DL models trained on natural earthquakes, has been tested on various seismic datasets across different spatial and temporal scales, as well as on AEs recorded during a triaxial rock deformation experiment on Berea sandstone.

Despite these advancements, there remains a lack of well-established ML models specifically for AE detection in laboratory settings, likely due to the scarcity of large, manually annotated AEs catalogs. To address this gap, we leverage an extensive dataset of manually revised AEs picks from shear experiments conducted under various boundary conditions, using different types of PZTs sensors and with different gouge materials, glass beads, and quartz granular gouge. We train an adapted version of the PhaseNet model (Zhu and Beroza, 2019) originally developed for earthquake phase detection, to enable automatic AEs detection. We demonstrate that our model, which we call AEsNet, outperforms pre-existing picking techniques. To address the challenge of limited training datasets, we propose a transfer learning approach. We evaluate the prediction performance and limitations of our models in relation to the underlying physical behaviors of the different granular materials generating AEs. AEsNet results in a robust and adaptable tool that enhances AE detection and analysis in experimental seismology, improving efficiency and accuracy in processing large event catalogs.

Data and Methods

Experimental procedure

In this study, we rely on AEs detected during laboratory experiments run with the biaxial apparatus, BRAVA2, housed in the Rock Mechanics and Earthquake Physics Laboratory at Sapienza University of Rome (Fig. 1a). The biaxial apparatus consists of two orthogonal servocontrolled hydraulic pistons used to apply normal and shear load on the samples. Each piston is equipped with a strain gauge load cell to measure the applied forces with a precision of ± 0.03 MPa. Displacement transducers (linear variable differential transformers, LVDTs) are fixed between the load frame and the moving piston to measure piston movement with submicron resolution, less than 0.1 μm/s.

Experiments were performed in a double direct-shear configuration, in which two 3-mm-thick gouge layers are sandwiched between three steel forcing blocks characterized by two stationary side blocks (friction area 50×50 mm^2) and a central forcing block (80×50 mm^2, see inset in Fig. 1a). The forcing blocks have grooves perpendicular to the shear direction (0.8 mm high and 2 mm spacing) to ensure shear localization within the gouge layers and not at the boundary with the steel blocks. The vertical ram moves at a constant displacement rate, applying shear stress and inducing shear deformation within the sample. On the central block, an on-board LVDT is mounted to directly measure fault displacement. All mechanical signals (stress and displacement) are recorded and digitized in real time at 1 kHz using a multichannel analog-to-digital converter (NI-9403) with 24-bit resolution. Four acoustic sensors (PZTs from Physik Instrument Ceramic, made from modified lead zirconate–lead titanate, PIC 255) are mounted on each of the forcing blocks to capture high-frequency AEs, resulting in a total of eight sensors in the double direct shear configuration. The PZT array on each block consists of two axial disk polarized parallel to the sensor surface, specifically more sensitive to compressional *P* waves, and two shear plates polarized perpendicular to the sensor surface, with one rotated 90° relative to the other to enhance sensitivity to shear *SV* waves (moving vertically in the imposed shear direction) and shear *SH* waves (moving along the block plane but perpendicular to the vertical direction) (Fig. 1b). Accordingly, we refer to them as *P*, *SV*, and *SH* sensors. This configuration simulates a three-component seismic station on each side block. Sensor axial resonances occur at 2.47 MHz for *P*-wave sensors and 826 kHz for *S*-wave sensors. The *P*-wave sensor also exhibits a weaker radial resonance at 600 kHz. These resonance frequencies are generally outside the frequency content of the AEs generated in both the Minusil and the glass bead experiments (Pignalberi *et al.*, 2024).

We performed experiments using two different types of fault gouges: fine-grained quartz (Min-U-Sil 40 US Silica Company, average grain size 10 μm) and glass beads (class IV spheres, average grain size 150 μm). We chose these two gouges since they have been widely used in past laboratory experiments (e.g., Johnson *et al.*, 2013; Leeman *et al.*, 2016), as discussed in the next section. Figure 1c shows a typical experiment. The gouge material is sheared at a constant sliding velocity of 10 μm/s. After a first elastic loading phase, during which the shear stress builds up, two unload–reload cycles are performed to promote shear localization and the formation of a steady-state shear fabric (Fig. 1c). With accumulated deformation, we observe the spontaneous emergence of unstable stick-slip behavior, typical of this material for which stress drop and recurrence time are controlled by the applied normal stress (e.g., Leeman *et al.*, 2016). Because the stick-slip instabilities begin, experiments are acoustically monitored using the eight PZTs mounted on the two lateral blocks. The PZT analog signals are digitized by four two-channel TiePie Handyscope HS5 digital oscilloscopes with 16-bit resolution and a sampling rate of 3.125 or 6.25 MHz (Fig. 1b).

TiePie oscilloscopes also record shear stress to synchronize acoustic and mechanical data. Figure 2a,d shows 7 s of raw acoustic and shear stress data for quartz and glass beads, respectively. Further details of the monitoring system and experimental procedure are provided in Pignalberi *et al.* (2024).

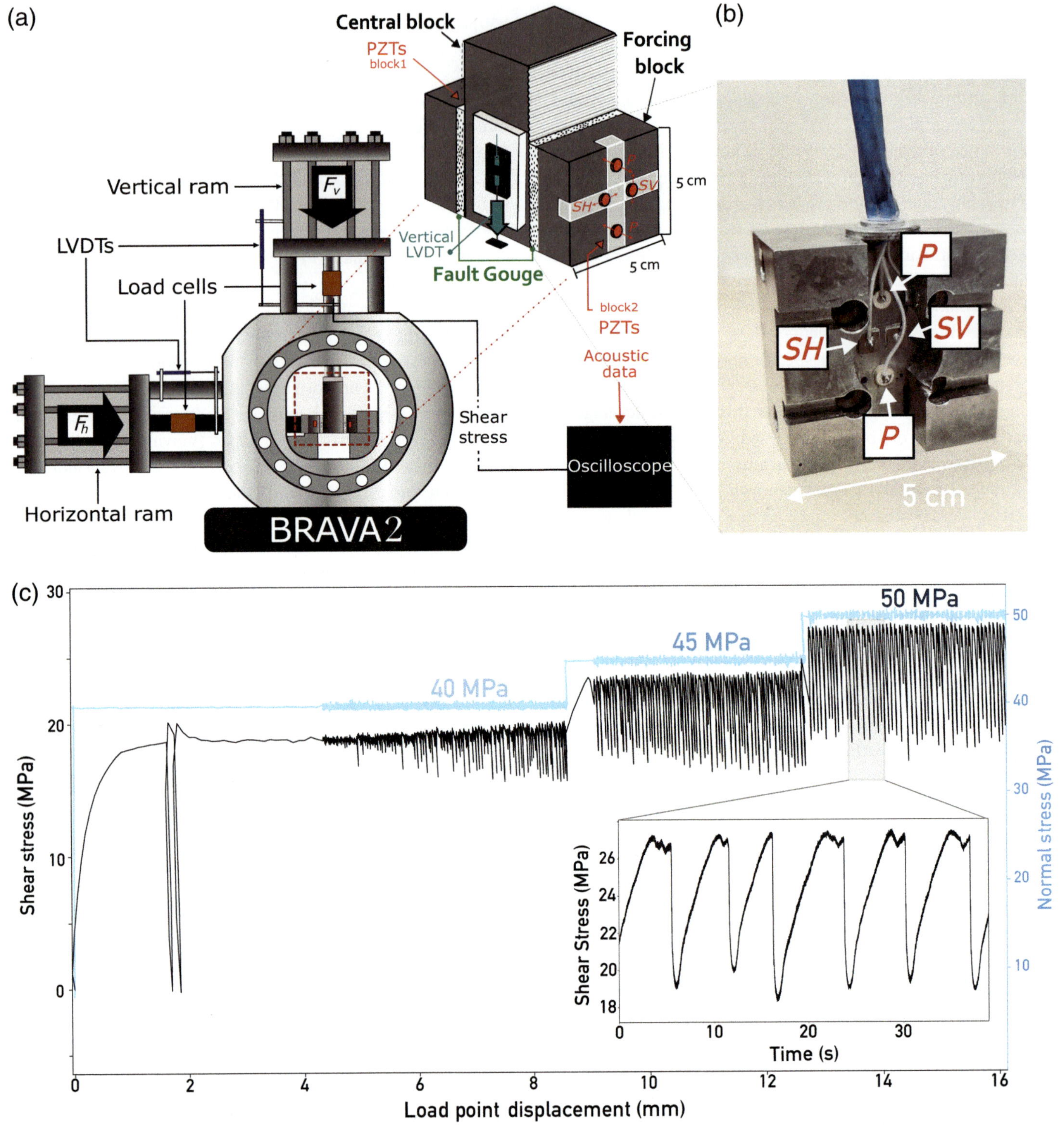

Figure 1. (a) The BRAVA2 biaxial apparatus. (b) Rear view of the side blocks showing the piezoelectric sensor positions. (c) Shear stress–displacement curve for a laboratory experiment using Min-U-Sil as the fault shearing material at different normal stress values. The inset on the right shows a zoomed-in view of some seismic cycles. LVDT, linear variable differential transformers; PZTs, piezoelectric sensors.

Acoustic emission dataset

Our dataset comprises AEs collected from double direct shear experiments using Min-U-Sil quartz powder and glass beads to simulate fault gouge. Min-U-Sil has been extensively studied to reproduce the full spectrum of slip behaviors from slow to fast stick-slip and explore the role of strain localization in controlling fault stability (e.g., Leeman *et al.*, 2016; Scuderi *et al.*, 2017; Bedford and Faulkner, 2021). Furthermore, it has been acoustically monitored to investigate laboratory earthquake

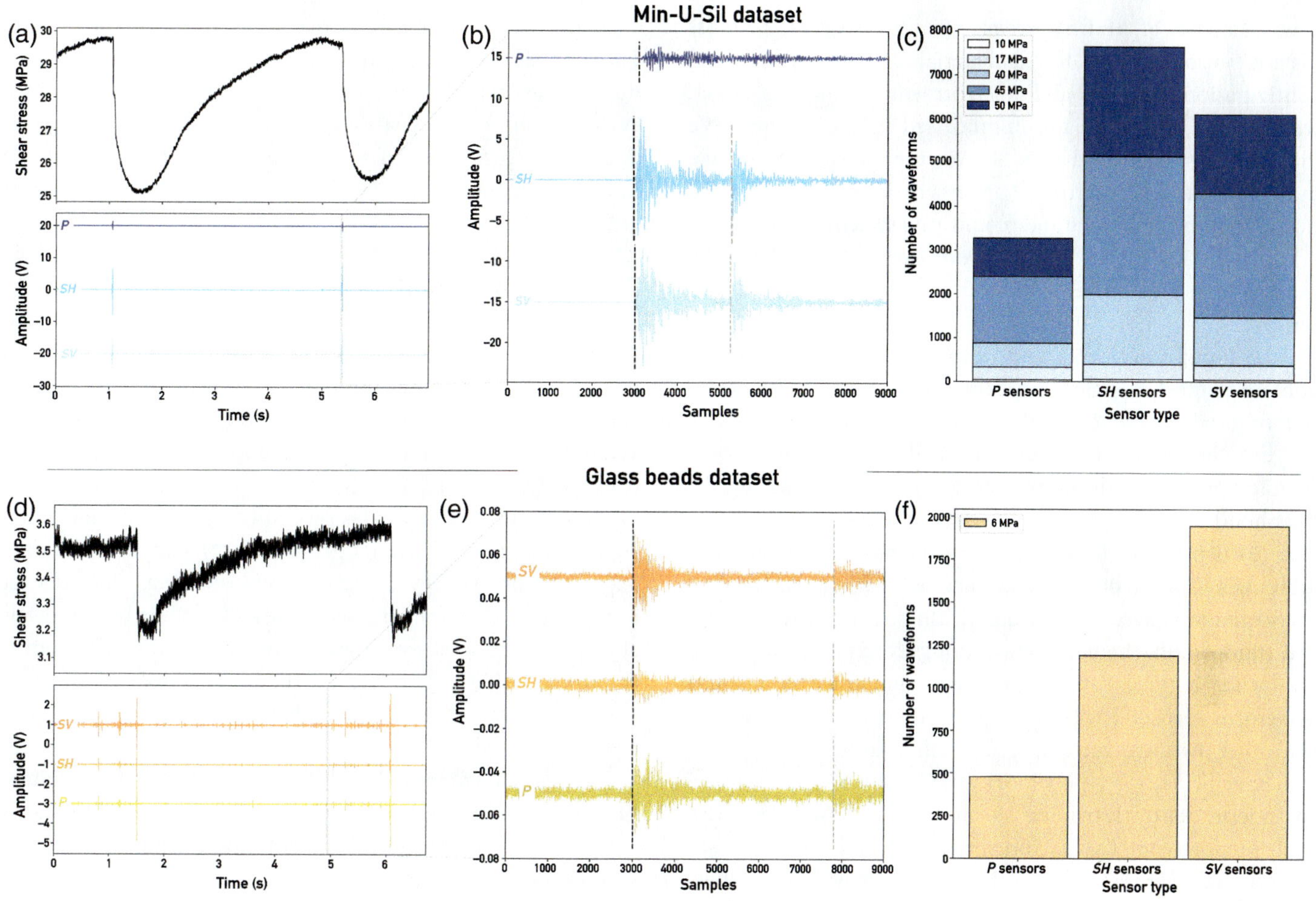

nucleation processes (e.g., Bolton *et al.*, 2020). Similarly, glass beads have been extensively employed to explore the microphysics of frictional instabilities. The physics of this material is governed by force chain interactions (Mair *et al.*, 2002; Scuderi *et al.*, 2014), which are encoded in AE's activity and control stress accumulation and release during fault stick-slip motion (e.g., Johnson *et al.*, 2013; Rivière *et al.*, 2018). Our dataset of AEs generated in Min-U-Sil consists of 22,000 manually picked AE waveforms, generated from different experiments, performed under a range of applied normal loads (from 10 to 50 MPa). For glass beads, the dataset consists of 3200 waveforms, all collected at a normal load of 6 MPa to avoid grain breakage during deformation (Mair *et al.*, 2002). AE waveform first arrivals have been manually picked by seven different operators using Snuffler, a seismogram browser that allows fast visualization and picking of seismic waveforms (Heimann *et al.*, 2017). Our analysis focuses only on *P*-wave first arrivals, excluding *S* waves, because the short 1.5 cm distance between the possible AE source and PZT sensors in our setup hinders their clear separation.

Each manually picked waveform in our dataset is classified according to the gouge material, applied normal stress, and, because the same AE event is recorded using different PZTs, also by sensor type and orientation, as illustrated in Figure 2c,f.

Figure 2. Experimental data and waveform distribution for the Min-U-Sil (a–c) and glass beads (d–f) datasets. Panels (a) and (d) depict the shear stress evolution alongside continuous acoustic emission (AE) activity recorded by three PZTs (*P*, *SH*, and *SV*). Panels (b) and (e) provide a zoomed-in view of the acoustic data, showing an example waveform used for training AEsNet, in which vertical dashed lines represent the manual target picks. Panels (c) and (f) illustrate the distribution of AE waveforms, categorized by material, applied normal stress, and sensor type.

The number of picks for *P* sensors is smaller than for *SV* and *SH* because *P* sensors are more sensitive to hydraulic noise from the horizontal servohydraulic piston.

Model setup

As in the original PhaseNet model, manually picked arrivals are converted into probabilities, assigning the highest probability to the time point identified by the analysts, with nearby points receiving progressively lower probabilities based on a Gaussian distribution. This probabilistic representation of manual picks helps the algorithm mitigate the impact of picking errors within the dataset. We set the standard deviation of the Gaussian to 40 samples (6.4 or 12.8 microseconds at 6.25 MHz or 3.125 of sampling rate), reflecting the maximum time difference of AE first arrivals recorded between the most distant sensors for the tested materials in our experimental configuration. The probabilities represent the model's target, whereas the inputs are the unprocessed AE waveforms. We intentionally avoid band-pass filtering the waveforms to make our picker model more robust against hydraulic and electrical noise from the apparatus and monitoring system. These noises arise from the feedback control hydraulic system applying the normal load and power line interference affecting the PZT sensors.

The input waveforms and output probability sequences contain 9000 data points, in contrast to the 3000 points of the original PhaseNet version for natural earthquakes. A longer window offers two advantages: (1) it helps the model handle examples with multiple target picks by increasing the likelihood of having multiple events in the same waveform, and (2) it provides better sampling of the noise before and after AEs. The positions of the arrivals within the window are varied to ensure that the algorithm does not simply learn the windowing scheme. Each training example in our setup comprises a three-component array: one trace is a single waveform recorded with a single-component PZT, whereas the other two are zero-padded. Each channel corresponds to a specific sensor type (*P*, *SH*, or *SV*), enabling the model to independently learn waveform features associated with each sensor type. This is fundamental because each sensor type has a different response that may alter waveform characteristics and is more sensitive to either *P* or *S* waves due to the piezoelectric polarization (Pignalberi *et al.*, 2024). Each waveform is normalized by removing its mean and dividing it by its standard deviation. To enhance the model's generalization capability during training, we randomly stacked event waveforms by shifting, scaling their amplitude, and flipping their polarity. Amplitude scaling was performed based on estimated noise and signal amplitudes from the two input waveforms (amp_noise1, amp_signal1, amp_noise2, and amp_signal2). Specifically, waveform2 was scaled by a randomly selected factor within bounds designed to ensure that (1) the scaled signal from waveform2 remains distinguishable from the noise in waveform1 (minimum scaling derived from $\frac{\text{amp\_noise1}}{\text{amp\_signal2}}$), and (2) the scaled noise from waveform2 does not overwhelm the signal in waveform1 (maximum scaling derived from $\frac{\text{amp\_signal1}}{\text{amp\_noise2}}$). Overlapping event regions were avoided through the application of masks on phase, event, and polarity features, along with careful shifting to maintain distinct event boundaries.

An example of training waveforms for the same AE recorded by different PZT sensors for the different tested materials is shown in Figure 2b,e. We divided both the glass beads and Min-U-Sil datasets into training (60%), validation (10%), and testing (30%) subsets. The training and validation sets were used for model training and hyperparameter tuning, respectively, whereas the testing set was reserved for evaluating the final performance of AEsNet. For the testing set, we added an equal number of noise waveforms collected during our experiments, enabling the model performance evaluation on both signals and noise. The data split was conducted independently of waveform characteristics. Separate models were trained for the glass beads and Min-U-Sil quartz gouge datasets.

Deep learning model

In this work, we use an adapted version of the original PhaseNet model (Zhu and Beroza, 2019), which is based on the U-Net convolutional autoencoder architecture (Ronneberger *et al.*, 2015) for processing 1D time-series data. We reuse the PhaseNet implementation code from the EQNet package (Zhu *et al.*, 2022), with slight modifications. This implementation incorporates several enhancements, including support for multiple events per waveform sample and a data augmentation strategy based on event stacking. Our AEsNet model takes AE waveforms as input and outputs binary probability distributions for *P* waves and noise, ranging from 0 (noise) to 1 (AE). The loss function is defined using cross-entropy between the true probability distribution ($p(x)$) and predicted distribution ($q(x)$).

We maintained the original PhaseNet autoencoder architecture, using four downsampling and four up-sampling stages with 1D convolutions and Rectified Linear Unit (ReLU) activations. Downsampling compresses the data, whereas up-sampling converts it into probability distributions for *P* waves and noise. Skip connections enhance training convergence. The convolution filter size is seven data points, with a stride of four for downsampling. Deconvolution expands the layers by a factor of four for up-sampling. Padding is added to maintain sequence length. The softmax function is used in the final layer. All models were trained for 500 epochs using a learning rate of 0.01 and a batch size of 256.

The *P* arrival times are identified by extracting the picks of the output probability distributions after applying a threshold. For more detailed and technical specifications, we refer to the original PhaseNet article (Zhu and Beroza, 2019).

Results

AEsNET performance evaluation

We evaluate the performance of our trained models following a binary classification framework. The models produce "positive" or "negative" outcomes based on the accuracy of the predicted result, identifying either noise or a pick. Four scenarios are possible: true positive (TP), true negative (TN), false positive (FP), and false negative (FN). We calculate precision, recall, and $F1$-score for each trained model.

Precision is:

$$P = \frac{\text{TP}}{\text{TP} + \text{FP}},$$

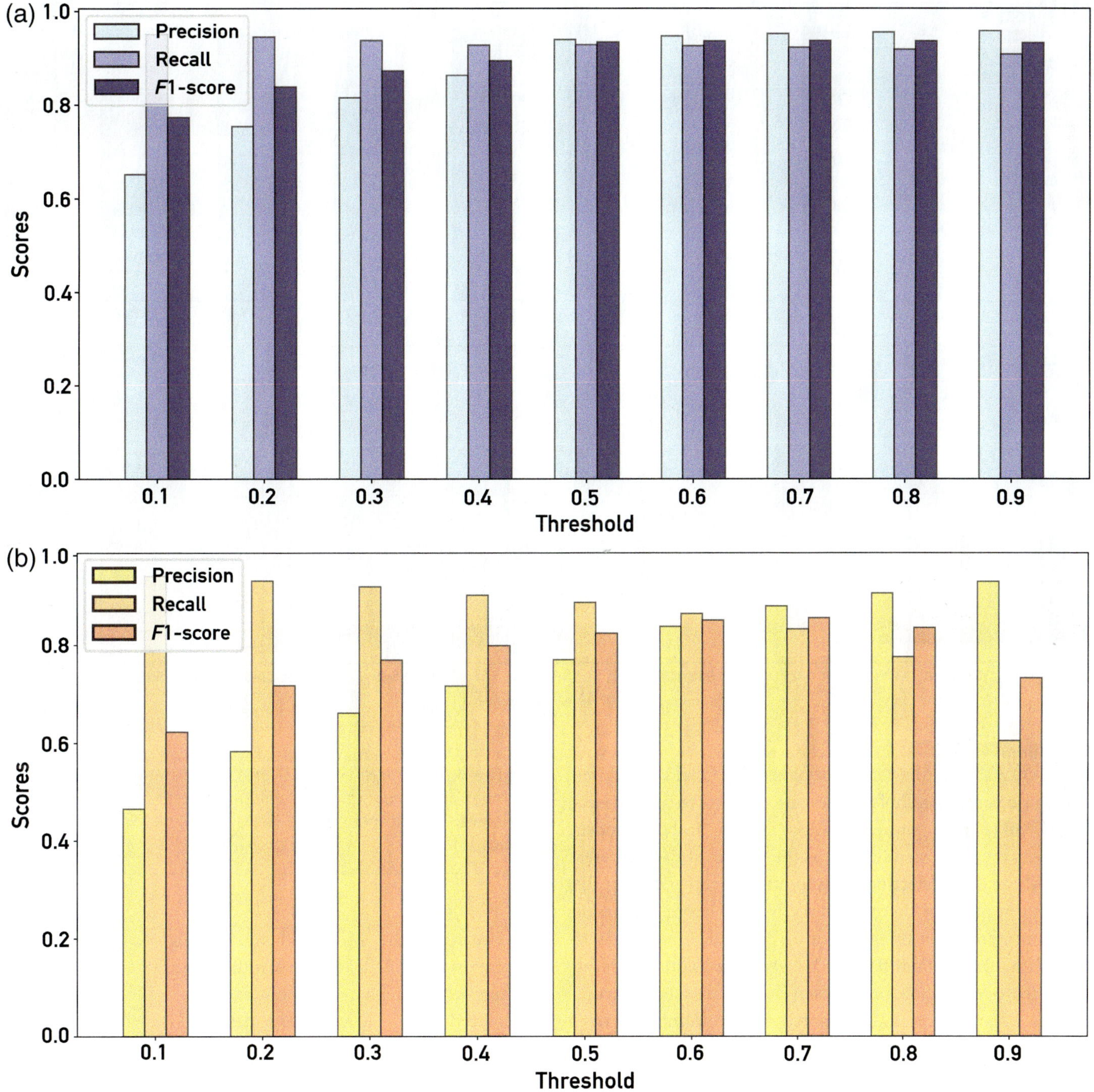

Figure 3. Performance of AEsNet on the testing dataset as a function of the phase score threshold used to extract picks from output probabilities for Min-U-Sil (a) and glass beads (b).

representing the proportion of positive identifications that were actually correct. Recall measures the ability to identify all relevant instances:

$$R = \frac{\mathrm{TP}}{\mathrm{TP} + \mathrm{FN}},$$

and the $F1$-score combines both precision and recall to provide a balanced evaluation:

$$F1 = 2 \cdot \frac{P \times R}{P + R}.$$

Considering TPs, we additionally calculate the mean (μ) and standard deviation (σ) of time residuals (Δt) between AEsNet and analyst picks to further assess the picks' precision. Arrival-time residuals Δt of less than 6.4 μs (40 samples at 6.25 MHz), are classified as TPs, with larger residuals counted as FPs.

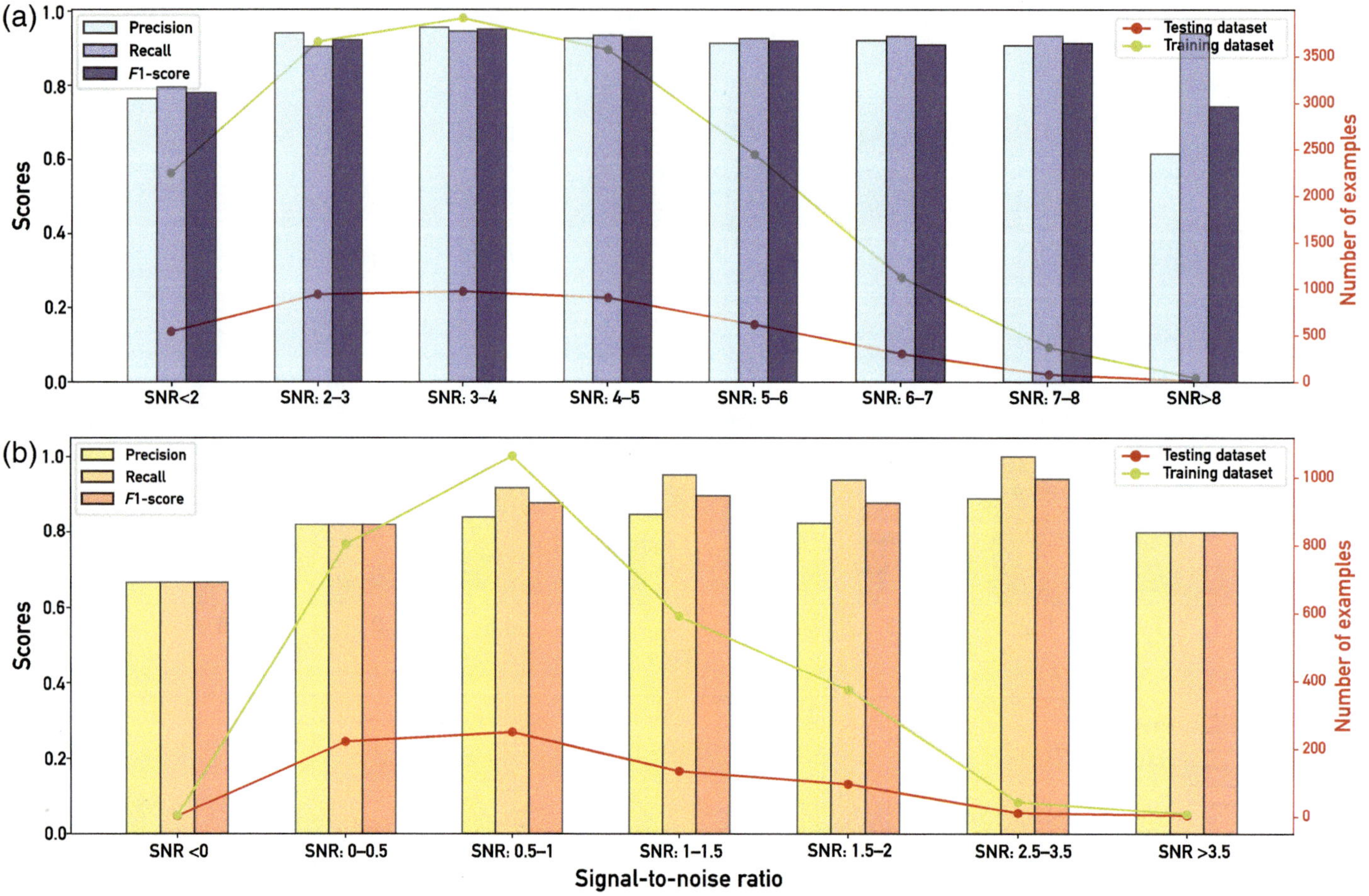

Figure 4. Performance of AEsNet on the testing dataset and number of examples in the training and testing datasets across different signal-to-noise ratios (SNRs) for Min-U-Sil (a) and glass beads (b).

Figure 3 shows AEsNet performance as a function of different phase score threshold values for the two tested datasets, Min-U-Sil (Fig. 3a) and glass beads (Fig. 3b). In both models, precision increases significantly as the threshold rises, whereas recall decreases, reflecting a trade-off between reducing FPs and the number of detected picks. The $F1$-score reaches its maximum around a threshold of 0.5 for both models, identifying it as the optimal balance between precision and recall. Thus, the 0.5 threshold was chosen for all subsequent investigations because it provides a practical compromise between accurately identifying true positives and minimizing FNs. Importantly, the performance of the glass beads model consistently falls short compared to the Min-U-Sil model across all evaluated metrics.

Figure 4 shows how AEsNet performance varies across different signal-to-noise ratio (SNR) levels. The test set is categorized into 10 groups based on the value of ln(SNR), with precision, recall, and $F1$-score computed for each category. SNR is calculated as the ratio of the standard deviations of 500 samples following the P arrival (the signal) to the 500 samples preceding it (the noise). The SNR can be negative for certain AEs waveforms due to the short moveout between phase arrivals. In such cases, noise windows contain the coda of AEs that occurred before, a phenomenon particularly noticeable in glass beads waveforms.

Regarding the Min-U-Sil model (Fig. 4a), performance improves as the SNR increases, with all metrics achieving higher values in the higher SNR ranges. This reflects the model's enhanced ability to accurately identify TPs when signals are clearer. Remarkably, even at very low SNR levels (<2), the model maintains solid performance, achieving an $F1$-score of 0.8, demonstrating its robustness under challenging conditions. On the other hand, when the SNR becomes extremely high (>8), precision drops significantly. Although this might seem counterintuitive, it is attributable to the very small number of examples in this SNR bin within the training dataset (<5, right y-axis in Fig. 4a). Figure 4b shows a similar trend for the testing glass beads dataset, with performance metrics improving as the SNR increases. Although the model does not perform exceptionally well, it is not entirely unreliable even at negative SNR values (<0). At higher SNR (>3.5), performance slightly declines, likely due to the scarcity of training examples in this SNR bin, consistent with the trend observed in the Min-U-Sil model. These observations highlight that the model primarily learns to identify AEs based on their unique frequency content rather than their amplitude or SNR, emphasizing the importance of having a well-distributed dataset in terms of frequency range and SNR, for robust performance. The dependence of the trained model on the frequency content is a feature we will revisit later, as other observations further corroborate this finding.

Comparison with existing models

The performance of our AEsNet model is compared against standard picking algorithms, including the STA/LTA and AIC algorithms, both implemented in the ObsPy library (Beyreuther *et al.*, 2010). Both of these "classic" methods for picking first arrivals require extensive user tuning, which we have attempted to optimize (Fig. S1, available to the supplemental material to this article). In addition, we benchmark our models against the Quakephase approach (Shi *et al.*, 2024). Quakephase employs advanced preprocessing techniques to improve the performance of pretrained DL picking models on out-of-distribution datasets. Quakephase has already been tested on AEs collected during a triaxial rock deformation experiment performed on Berea sandstone samples. In our work, we apply Quakephase through Seisbench (Woollam *et al.*, 2022) by applying four different pretrained models—the original PhaseNet, the original EQTransformer (Mousavi *et al.*, 2020), and the two models retrained on the STEAD dataset (Mousavi *et al.*, 2019). The models are applied after a series of preprocessing techniques. The first procedure involves applying a rescaling factor to the AE waveform, given by $R = t_m/t_i = s_i/s_m$, in which t_m and t_i are the time-window lengths of the ML model used during training and the actual input data, respectively, and s_m and s_i are the data sampling rates used for training the ML model and the designated sampling rate of the actual input data, respectively. Subsequently, bandwidth filtering is applied with a low cutoff frequency of 20 kHz and a high cutoff of 2 MHz to eliminate low-frequency noise from the hydraulic power supply and the high-frequency electrical noise that characterizes our experimental data (Pignalberi *et al.*, 2024). A sliding-window approach with an overlap ratio of 0.9 is used to enhance model performance by exposing seismic events in multiple prediction windows at different positions. The windows contain the same number of points as those used during the training of the applied DL models. At the end, the prediction results of the four different models are combined using principal component analysis, which selects the first principal component maximizing data variance as the final ensemble output. This approach automatically assigns greater weight to models with consistent predictions while downweighting outlier-like models.

Figure 5 illustrates the performance of AEsNet compared to all benchmark models across different PZTs sensor types. For Min-U-Sil (Fig. 5a,b), AEsNet demonstrates robust performance across all PZTs, with $F1$-scores consistently exceeding 0.9. These results are significantly higher than those of the AIC, STA/LTA, and Quakephase. This last method, although showing good performance, achieved a smaller $F1$-score of around 0.7. An example of the picks obtained using the different tested methods for a complicated Min-U-Sil waveform containing nine AEs manually picked (marked by dashed vertical lines) is shown in Figure 6. The AIC method results in numerous missed picks, whereas the STA/LTA method performs reasonably well but introduces a noticeable delay in the automatically identified picks compared to the target picks (Fig. 6c,d). Quakephase misses the smaller picks and often misinterprets P-wave arrivals as S waves. AEsNet clearly outperforms all other methods, producing accurate, high-confidence picks. This strong performance is further evidenced when examining the distribution of time residuals between the automated and human-labeled P picks (Fig. 5b). The residual distributions for AEsNet are noticeably narrower and show fewer biases compared to those obtained using the other methods.

Figure 5c,d reports the same statistics for the glass beads dataset. As with the Min-U-Sil dataset, the AIC method again shows the worst performance, followed by the STA/LTA and then the DL-based methods. Despite its acceptable performance, the STA/LTA method exhibits a strongly asymmetric distribution of residuals, with picks occurring later than the true ones, indicating some bias in its predictions. Quakephase and AEsNet show very similar performance for this dataset, with AEsNet performing slightly better, particularly for SV and P sensors, as evidenced by the standard deviation (μ) of the residuals (Fig. 5d). Overall, the SH sensors exhibit the poorest performance, likely due to their lower sensitivity to the imposed shear direction, which favors microslip AEs with vertical directivity.

Figures S2–S6 show additional examples of the application of the different employed methods to AEs waveforms in the testing dataset. Figure S2 presents an example from Min-U-Sil with a low SNR of 0.7. The AIC method detects too many picks, whereas the STA/LTA method shows delayed picks. Quakephase and AEsNet perform similarly, with Quakephase showing slightly better residuals; however, it sometimes incorrectly interprets the P-wave first arrival as an S wave. Figure S3 provides an example with low SNR for glass beads, where AEsNet clearly outperforms the other methods, particularly in terms of phase scores. Figure S4 highlights that AEsNet excels even in the presence of strong low-frequency background noise, which in our setup is caused by the hydraulic power supply imposing a constant normal load. AEsNet accurately detects first-arrival picks without the need for filtering, demonstrating its robustness in handling noisy conditions. Figure S5 shows an example where the amplitude of the AEs is clipped (due to exceeding the 4 V voltage range), yet AEsNet successfully picks the first arrivals. Figure S6 shows two glass beads AEs for which manual analysts did not identify any picks, whereas AEsNet outputs probability functions with values above 0.75. Although these are classified as false picks in our statistics, they are likely genuine events that were overlooked by analysts due to their low visibility and that AEsNet has correctly detected.

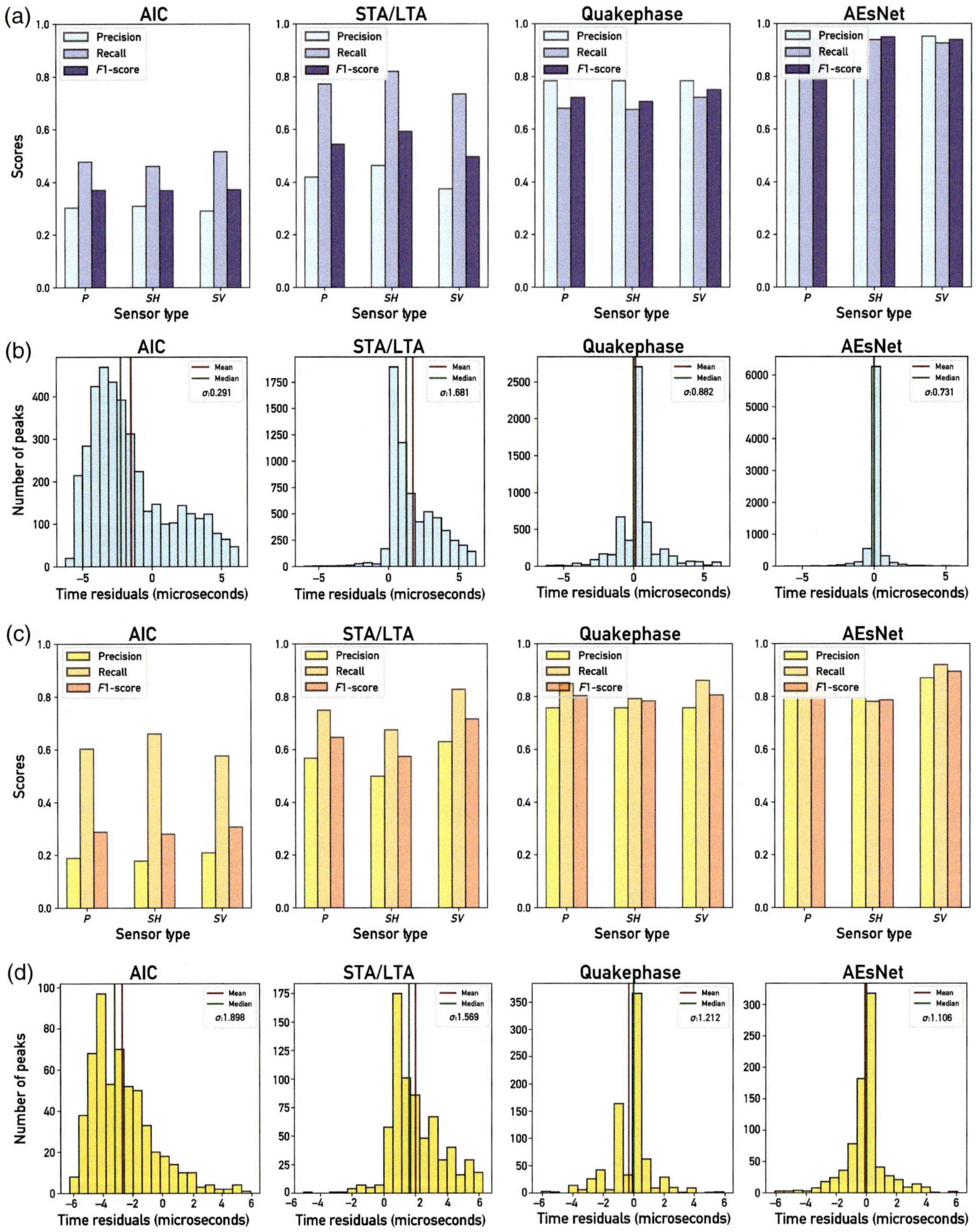

Figure 5. Benchmarking AEsNet performance. Precision, recall, and *F*1-score of each picking method (Akaike Information Criterion [AIC], short-term average [STA]/long-term average [LTA], Quakephase, and AEsNet) across different PZT types (*P*, *SH*, and *SV*) are shown for Min-U-Sil (a) and glass beads (c). Distributions of time residuals for each picking method are presented for Min-U-Sil (b) and glass beads (d). AEsNet consistently outperforms the other benchmark methods for the Min-U-Sil dataset, and for glass beads, it only slightly outperforms Quakephase.

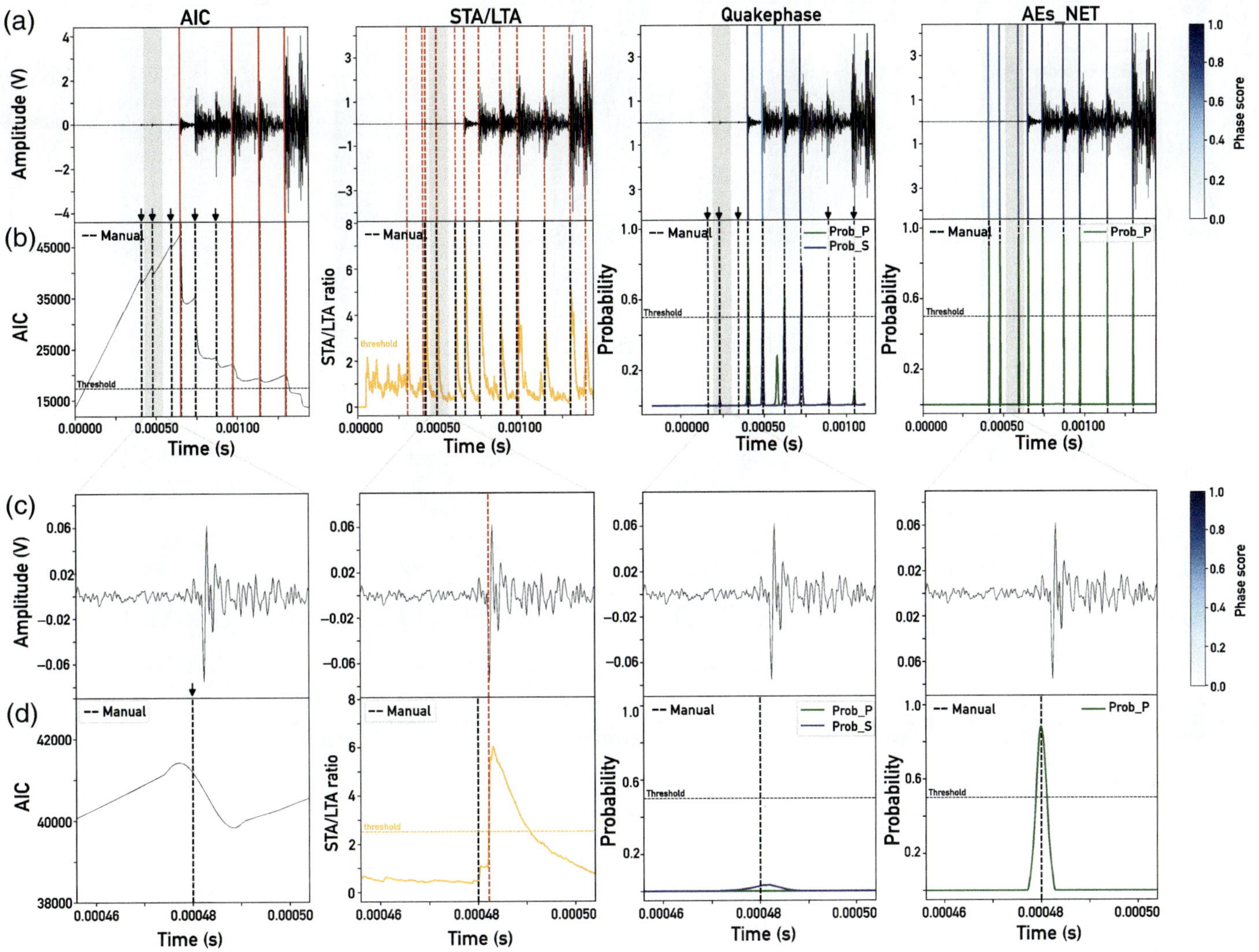

Figure 6. Comparison of picking methods on Min-U-Sil testing dataset. (a) Examples of picks obtained from different methods for a challenging waveform with nine AEs (black dashed vertical lines). The raw waveform is shown in panel (a), with a zoomed view presented in (c). (b) The output probabilities, with a detailed zoom shown in (d). The black arrows highlight missed picks. The AIC method misses many picks, and STA/LTA produces delayed picks relative to the targets. Quakephase struggles to detect smaller picks and often misinterprets *P*-wave arrivals as *S* waves. In contrast, AEsNet demonstrates superior performance, delivering accurate and high-confidence picks.

Discussions

Models generalization: how much training data is necessary for optimal performance?

A major challenge in developing ML models for AE detection is the scarcity of labeled AE datasets in laboratory settings, along with the need for models capable of generalizing across different experiments and conditions. Understanding how training dataset size and different experimental boundary conditions affect model performance is crucial for optimizing detection in data-limited scenarios. This section examines AEsNet's performance in relation to these factors. Regarding the Min-U-Sil dataset that includes around 16,000 training examples, QuakePhase performs reasonably well, but it is significantly outperformed by AEsNet in overall accuracy and reliability. In addition, QuakePhase faces two main challenges. First, its extensive preprocessing pipeline, including filtering, rescaling, and the aggregation of multiple DL models, significantly slows its application. Although this approach avoids the need for extensive hyperparameter tuning, as required by standard picking methods, it still requires manual threshold selection (Shi *et al.*, 2024). For instance, applying AEsNet to a 1 s AE recording on a MacBook Air with an Apple M1 chip takes 4 s, whereas QuakePhase (applied with only PhaseNet as the inference model and no overlapping windows and therefore with not optimal performance) takes 25 s. Second, QuakePhase's reliance on models trained on local natural earthquakes with clear, long (relative to window size) *P*–*S* moveouts often results in frequent misinterpretation of first-arrival AEs as *S* waves.

Figure 7a shows AEsNet's performance for the different normal loads applied in the Min-U-Sil experiments present

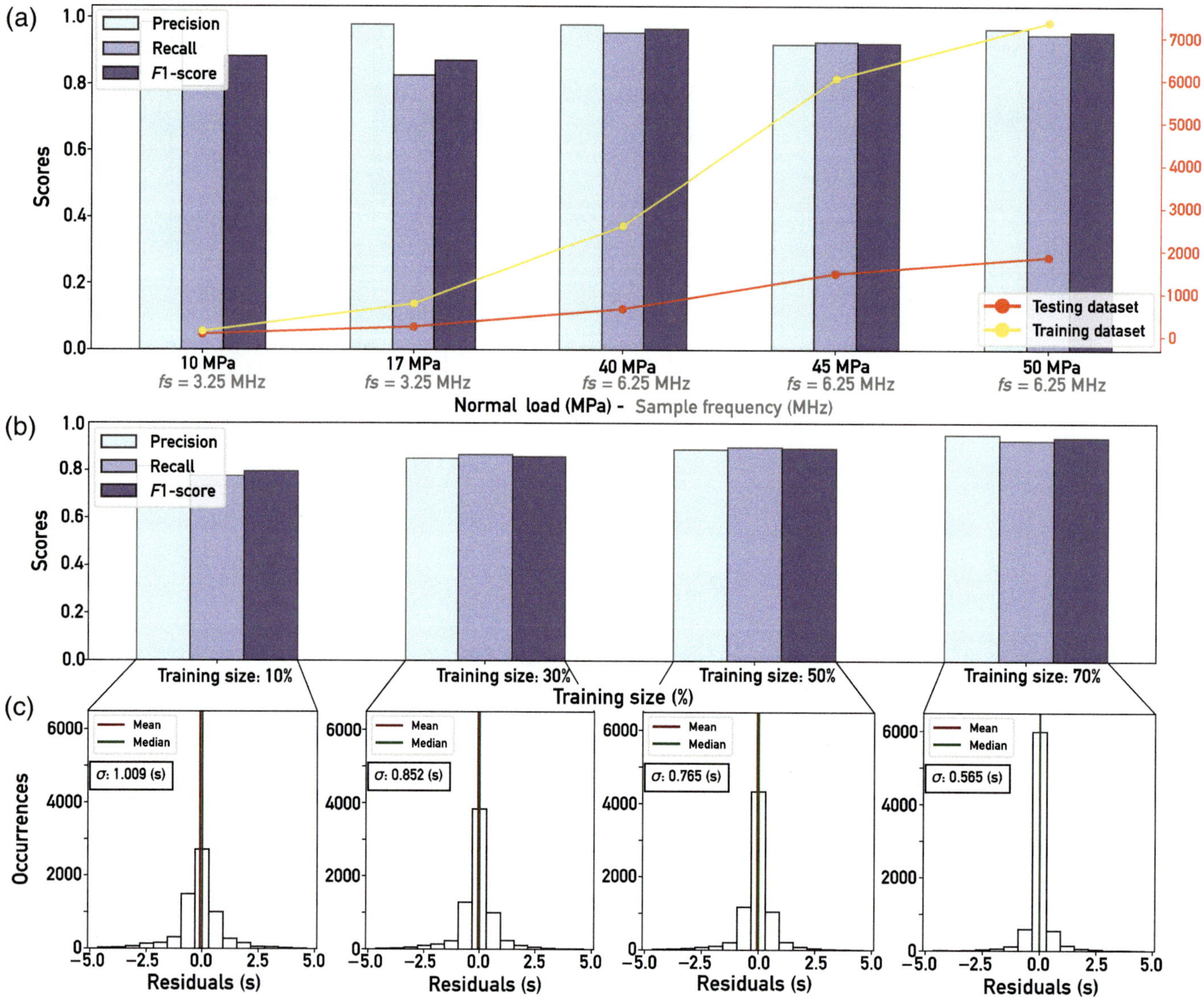

in the testing dataset. AEsNet generally shows a good generalization across different normal loads. However, performance is lower for the 10 and 17 MPa loads, which have fewer training examples. It is important to note that these experiments were conducted at a sampling rate of 3.125 MHz, compared to the 6.25 MHz used for the majority of the experiments. This overlap makes it challenging to determine whether the slight drop in performance is due to the lower sampling rate or the reduced normal load. However, the performance drop is minimal (~0.08 in *F*1-score), with values above 0.94 at normal loads >40 MPa and around 0.85 at loads <17 MPa, highlighting that the model's performance remains robust and significantly surpasses the results achieved with Quakephase.

For the glass beads dataset, Quakephase and AEsNet perform very similarly, with reasonable performances, but never reach the very high scores of the Min-U-Sil model (Fig. 5c). Why is this the case? On the one hand, this can be attributed to the lower average SNR values of glass beads AEs, which do not have very large amplitudes with respect to the noise (Fig. S7). However, as suggested by AEsNet performance as a function of the SNR, the model primarily relies on waveform frequency content rather than amplitude. The dependence of DL pickers on frequency content is well established and has been robustly demonstrated

Figure 7. Analyzing the generalizability of AEsNet on the Min-U-Sil dataset. (a) Performance of AEsNet in terms of precision, recall, and *F*1-score in the testing dataset, and number of examples in the training and testing datasets across different normal loads and sampling frequencies. Lower performance is observed for 10 and 17 MPa, likely due to fewer training examples and a lower sampling frequency (3.125 MHz) compared to 6.25 MHz for most other loads. (b) Performance of AEsNet and residual distributions for different training dataset sizes, ranging from 10% to 70%, illustrating the impact of dataset size on AEsNet's performance. (c) Corresponding residual distributions for each training size, showing a reduction in the spread of prediction errors (standard deviation decreasing from 1.009 s to 0.565 s) as more training data are used, indicating improved temporal accuracy and generalizability.

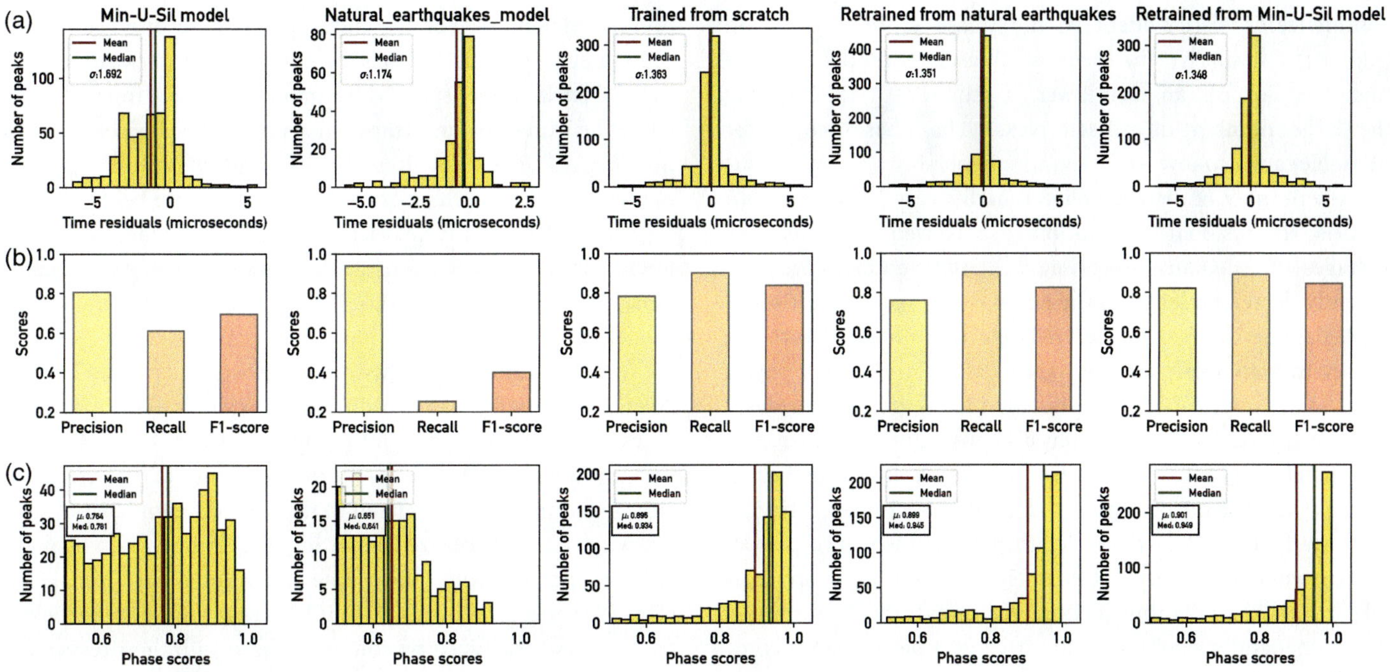

Figure 8. Performance of various deep learning (DL) models on the glass beads testing dataset. (a) The residual distributions of predicted picks relative to manual picks for five models: the Min-U-Sil model, the original PhaseNet model trained on natural earthquakes, the glass beads model trained from scratch, and two fine-tuned models (Min-U-Sil retrained on glass beads and PhaseNet retrained on glass beads). Mean and median residuals are indicated for each distribution. (b) Precision, recall, and $F1$-score metrics for each model, showing that fine-tuned models achieve significantly improved performance. (c) Phase score distributions, highlighting the confidence of picks made by each model. In general, retraining the Min-U-Sil model on glass beads yields optimal performance.

through complementary techniques that enhance the interpretability of convolutional pickers (Majstorović *et al.*, 2022; Shi *et al.*, 2024). Therefore, the less optimal performance of the Glass Beads model is likely due to the lower number of training examples, rather than the actual SNR values.

To further investigate this, we examine the performance of the Min-U-Sil model as a function of the training dataset size, reducing it from the initial 60% (16,000 examples) to 10% (1,600 examples) in steps of 20%. Performance, along with pick-time residuals, is reported in Figure 7b. As expected, reducing the number of training examples leads to a decrease in performance. However, even with a small training dataset, the Min-U-Sil AEsNet performs decently, achieving an $F1$-score of 0.8, still slightly better than Quakephase. This result demonstrates that with just 1600 examples, a newly trained Min-U-Sil model can outperform the Quakephase approach. Performance is slightly lower than that achieved with the glass beads dataset, likely due to the smaller number of training examples for Min-U-Sil (2200 versus 1600). To achieve a more stable model with an $F1$-score higher than 0.9, around 11,000 AEs examples are necessary.

Our results indicate that, in general, QuakePhase performs comparably to AEsNet for glass beads. However, for Min-U-Sil, AEsNet outperforms QuakePhase, even when a smaller training dataset is used. These results raise some interesting questions: why do we observe different performances for different materials? Is it possible to improve AEsNet performance with smaller AEs training datasets?

Improving glass beads detection performance: a transfer learning approach

In laboratory settings, we must address the challenge of a small training dataset, because the scientist may investigate, performing a number of experiments, different materials under different boundary conditions, to draw solid scientific conclusions, and does not have the time to manually pick thousands of waveforms for each experiment. In this context, for glass beads, we attempt to apply the transfer learning technique through the use of pretrained models. Specifically, we first apply the Min-U-Sil model and the original PhaseNet model, which was trained on natural earthquakes from the Northern California Earthquake Data Center Catalog by Northern California Earthquake Data Center (NCEDC) (2014), without any additional fine-tuning. Performance results are presented in Figure 8, which includes residuals (Fig. 8a), performance metrics (Fig. 8b), and phase score distributions of the transfer learning models (Fig. 8c), contrasted with the glass beads AEsNet model trained from scratch for which performance has been shown in previous sections (e.g., Fig. 5c,d).

When applied to glass beads, the Min-U-Sil model achieves a good precision of 0.8, but the $F1$-score is only 0.7, indicating that it misses a significant number of picks. This lack of picking confidence is also evident in the phase score distribution (Fig. 8c). Similarly, the original PhaseNet model exhibits high precision but an even lower $F1$-score of 0.4, highlighting the large number of missed picks. The phase scores for PhaseNet are also low, and even when applying a lower threshold, the number of detected picks remains very small. For both models, the residual distributions are skewed, with negative averages and medians, indicating that predicted picks are consistently delayed relative to the target ones. Examples of high-SNR glass bead AEs with delayed detection obtained with the model trained solely on Min-U-Sil, along with their power spectral density (PSD), are represented in Figure S8. This delay may be linked to the microphysical mechanisms generating AEs in glass beads, a topic that will be explored further in the next discussion paragraph. The Min-U-Sil model, having been trained on AEs data, demonstrates reasonable performance, whereas the original PhaseNet model, trained on natural earthquakes, fails almost entirely. However, both pretrained models generally exhibit significantly lower performance compared to the glass beads model trained from scratch.

Given the low initial performance, we further fine-tune the two pretrained models using the glass beads training dataset. The last two columns of Figure 8 illustrate the resulting performances. Fine-tuning substantially improves the performance of both the original PhaseNet model and the retrained Min-U-Sil model, bringing them closer to the performance of the glass beads model trained from scratch. The fine-tuned PhaseNet model shows slightly lower precision, larger residuals, and marginally lower phase scores. In contrast, the retrained Min-U-Sil model outperforms the glass beads model, demonstrating higher precision, smaller residuals, and improved phase scores, indicating greater confidence in its picks.

Figure 9a shows an example of an AE from the testing dataset, along with the picks obtained with the different models. The original PhaseNet model misses all picks, whereas the original Min-U-Sil model identifies some FPs. The retrained models and the glass beads model trained from scratch all perform very well, with no noticeable macroscopic differences between them in this specific example.

We discuss the modest results of our transfer learning exercise in the next section, in which we explore the causes of this behavior and interpret the model's performance in relation to the microphysical processes driving acoustic emissions in different granular materials.

Interpreting model performance: variability in AE signatures across different granular materials

The results of our transfer learning exercise demonstrate that a model trained on natural earthquakes does not perform well when directly applied to laboratory AE data without preprocessing. Techniques like rescaling, filtering, and model aggregation used in QuakePhase can enhance performance but still present challenges. For instance, QuakePhase often misinterprets first arrivals as S waves, and it does not perform as well as AEsNet, a model specifically trained for AEs. Interestingly, while the Min-U-Sil model performs better on glass beads than the original PhaseNet, it still falls short of optimal performance. This highlights a crucial finding: despite being trained on a large dataset, the characteristics of AEs generated by different physical mechanisms in different granular gouge materials, glass beads, and Min-U-Sil, vary significantly, influencing model accuracy.

To better understand this outcome, we analyze the PSD of AE waveforms for the two different materials. The PSD provides valuable insights into their distinct characteristics because it reflects the distribution of energy across frequencies—a feature directly related to the underlying microphysical processes and source size generating AEs. Figure 10a,b displays AE waveforms with the same amplitude for Min-U-Sil (Fig. 10a) and glass beads (Fig. 10b) across different piezoelectric sensors (organized by column), along with their respective PSDs (Fig. 10c). Despite the similar amplitude, the difference in PSD shapes between the two materials is evident. Glass beads AEs show a much narrower frequency band in which all the energy is distributed when compared with Min-U-Sil that is characterized by a much more widespread frequency range. This contrast becomes even more pronounced when examining the distribution of all normalized PSDs for all AEs in the dataset, shown for Min-U-Sil (Fig. 10d) and glass beads (Fig. 10e). For glass beads, the median PSD exhibits a relatively evident concentration in the midfrequency range (150–400 kHz), with two evident picks (with the first being more energetic at 150 kHz), followed by a gradual, almost linear decline as the frequency increases. Conversely, the average Min-U-Sil PSD spans a much broader frequency range, exhibiting a higher concentration of energy at lower frequencies compared to glass beads. This is followed by a relatively flat energy plateau that drops off more steeply at higher frequencies, culminating in a distinct high-frequency bump around 1 MHz. The distinct frequency content of AEs generated by glass beads and Min-U-Sil reflects their different deformation mechanisms. The deformation in glass beads is fundamentally governed by the physics of force chains—a network of interconnected particles that transmit concentrated stress or force along specific paths through the system (Morgan and Boettcher, 1999; Ferdowsi *et al.*, 2013; Johnson *et al.*, 2013; Scuderi *et al.*, 2015). AEs predominantly correspond to the volumetric breaking of force chains, which, under the low normal stress experimental conditions we tested, do not involve the breakage and comminution of single beads (Mair *et al.*, 2002). The maximum size of force chains, and consequently of AE sources, is inherently dictated by the gouge layer thickness (3 mm) (Anthony and Marone, 2005). Because frequencies are, to a first approximation, inversely proportional to seismic source size, this limitation likely explains the sharp

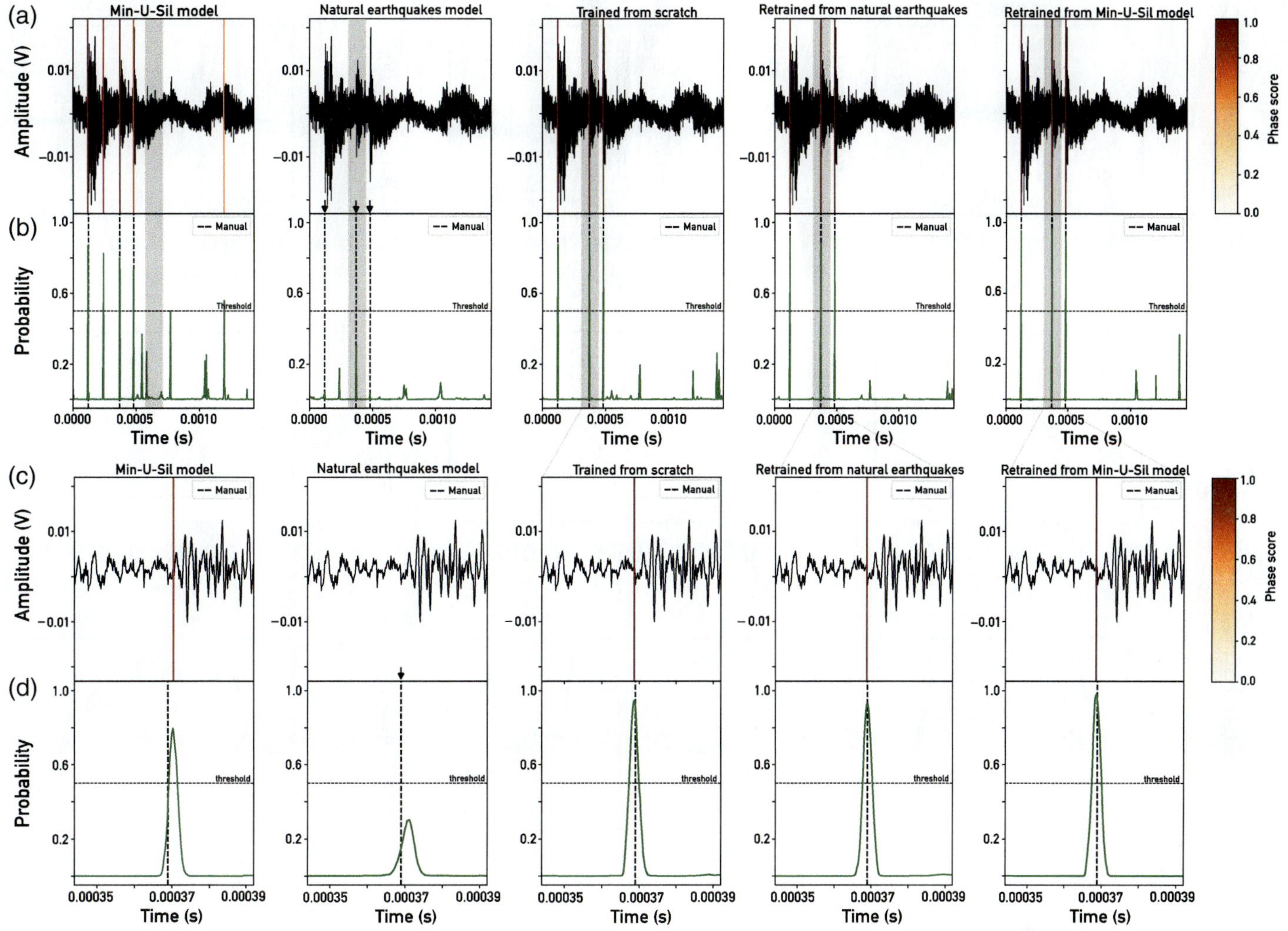

Figure 9. Example of AE waveform from the glass beads testing dataset, comparing picks obtained using different DL models. (a) The raw waveform, with a zoom presented in (c). (b) The output probabilities, with a zoom provided in (d). Manual picks are displayed as black dashed lines. Extracted picks are those with a phase score higher than 0.5. The black arrows highlight missed peaks. The original PhaseNet model trained on natural earthquakes demonstrates poor performance, missing many picks. The Min-U-Sil model identifies some false positives but provides better results. Fine-tuned models, including those retrained from the original PhaseNet and Min-U-Sil models, achieve significantly improved performance. These models produce accurate picks with high confidence, similar to the glass beads model trained from scratch.

drop in AE frequencies below 100 kHz, which reflects the largest force chain that can form within the layer. In contrast, deformation in Min-U-Sil is dominated by shear localization, in which most of the accumulated strain is accommodated along narrow, localized slip planes parallel to the shear direction. These planes are formed through microphysical processes such as grain comminution, breakage, and microslip. AEs in this material exhibit higher energy with respect to glass beads at lower frequencies, indicating, in general, larger seismic sources compared to glass beads. These events are likely associated with the failure of millimeter- to centimeter-size asperities along the localized slipping surfaces, as evidenced by AE location data (Trugman *et al.*, 2020), frequency content analysis (Bolton *et al.*, 2020, 2022), waveform similarities (Bolton *et al.*, 2023), seismic source spectral estimates (Pignalberi *et al.*, 2024), active acoustic imaging (Shreedharan *et al.*, 2020), and microstructural observations (Scuderi *et al.*, 2017). AEs in Min-U-Sil can involve ruptures spanning the entire sample plane, potentially reaching the full sample size of 5 cm, resulting in larger seismic sources and broader frequency content. It is important to emphasize that AE source size, and consequently the energy released at lower frequencies, is also influenced by the normal stress acting on the fault gouge. Higher normal stresses promote larger strike-slip instabilities and greater seismic energy release (Leeman *et al.*, 2016; Tinti *et al.*, 2016; Scuderi *et al.*, 2017; Bolton *et al.*, 2022; Pignalberi *et al.*, 2025). This relationship is clearly illustrated in Figure S9, which shows average PSDs from Min-U-Sil experiments conducted under varying normal stresses. Because normal stress increases, AEs exhibit a marked increase in low-frequency

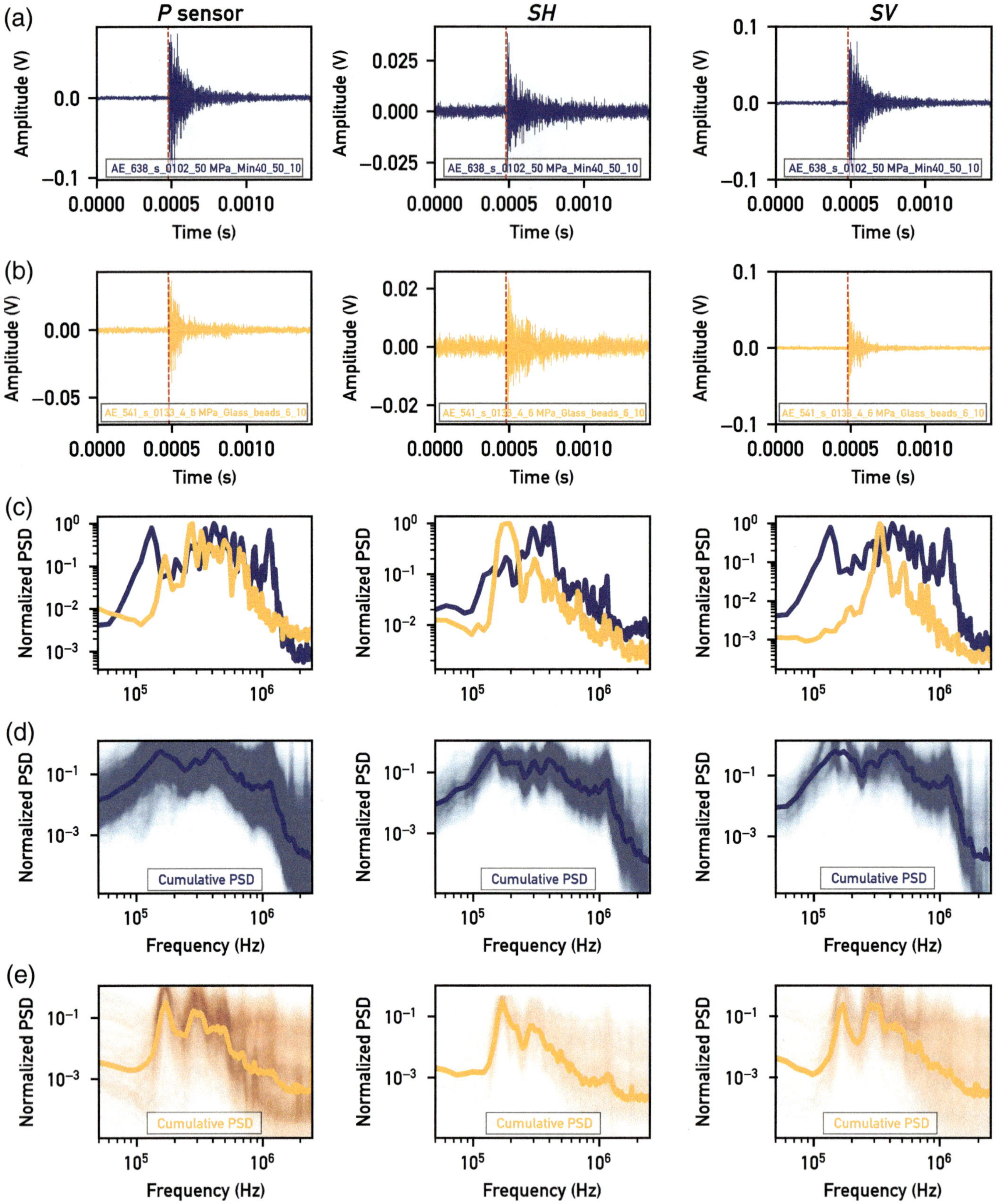

Figure 10. Comparison of AEs waveforms and their corresponding power spectral density (PSD) for Min-U-Sil quartz gouge and glass beads materials. (a,b) Different example waveforms with similar amplitudes recorded by different piezoelectric sensors (*P*, *SH*, and *SV*, respectively) for Min-U-Sil (a, in blue) and glass beads (b, in orange). (c,d) The normalized PSDs of those waveforms for each material. (d,e) The median of all normalized PSDs for the AEs generated by the two materials, highlighting differences in frequency content governed by their microphysical behavior.

energy. Simultaneously, high-frequency content is also enhanced, likely due to intensified shear-enhanced compaction, grain-scale damage, comminution, and cataclasis (Casas *et al.*, 2025), processes particularly active during the breakdown phase of slip events (Scuderi *et al.*, 2020) and known to generate high-frequency radiation. Together, the presence of larger seismic sources and the amplification of high-frequency-generating mechanisms lead to a broadening of the PSD with increasing normal stress. Despite these stress-dependent variations, the frequency characteristics of AEs in Min-U-Sil remain consistently distinct from those observed in glass beads across all tested conditions. Indeed, even at low normal stresses (10–17 MPa; Fig. S9a,b), Min-U-Sil exhibits a broader PSD, with two clear energy peaks: one at 200–250 kHz, exceeding the primary peak of glass beads at 150 kHz, and another, often more pronounced, near 600 kHz. Because normal stress increases, the PSD of Min-U-Sil broadens further, reflecting a wider range of active frequencies. Therefore, although we observe differences in the frequency content of AEs in Min-U-Sil as a function of normal stress, normal stress alone cannot explain the differences between Min-U-Sil and glass beads. The dominant frequency range of AEs remains material specific—and primarily dependent on the fundamentally different micromechanical deformation mechanisms in glass beads and Min-U-Sil, consistent with previous observations (Bolton *et al.*, 2022). Our interpretation that the spectral content of AEs is the key factor driving model performance, and explaining why the model trained on Min-U-Sil does not generalize well to waveforms from glass beads, is further supported by the fact that the majority of AEs in the Min-U-Sil dataset originate from relatively high normal stresses (>40 MPa). We propose that the observed differences in PSD may also explain why the AE detection model trained on Min-U-Sil signals tends to delay onset picks when applied to glass bead data (see pick residuals in Fig. 8a). Min-U-Sil AEs contain relatively strong high-frequency components, which, particularly above 400 kHz, are largely absent in glass beads. Specifically, glass bead AEs lack the high-frequency signatures typically associated with the first microsecond of the recorded AE waveform (Bolton *et al.*, 2023), as also evidenced by wavelet analysis (Pignalberi *et al.*, 2024). The Min-U-Sil-trained model has likely learned to associate these early high-frequency features with AE onset. When applied to glass beads, which lack such spectral features, the model may delay its pick while searching for familiar patterns. This leads to systematic negative residuals, with predicted onsets lagging behind the observed ones —a behavior also apparent in high-SNR AEs waveforms (Fig. S8). It is important to note that the spectral differences described here are somewhat qualitative because the frequency content of raw waveforms is certainly influenced by the instrument response of the PZT sensors, which was not accounted for in this study. Although this warrants further investigation, the use of the same sensors across all experiments supports the validity of our spectral comparison. Our results clearly show that Min-U-Sil and glass beads produce distinct AE PSDs. These spectral differences likely reflect material-specific acoustic signatures shaped by the underlying mechanical and microphysical deformation processes. Future studies will be essential to fully characterize these differences as a function of parameters such as normal stress, strain, and strain rate, to better link them to the micromechanical mechanisms governing energy release in sheared granular materials under varying conditions.

Conclusion

In this study, we introduce AEsNet—a PhaseNet-based picker designed to detect AEs generated during laboratory experiments from two different granular materials: Min-U-Sil and glass beads. We demonstrate its superior performance compared to all previously existing picking methods, including other DL models trained on natural earthquakes. AEsNet achieves better results for Min-U-Sil than for glass beads, reflecting the impact of training dataset size. Our findings suggest that picking performance is influenced by the number of training examples and is primarily driven by the signal frequency content, rather than their absolute amplitude or SNR, highlighting the importance of the physics of the source properties.

When transfer learning is applied to address the limited dataset size for glass beads, the model's reliance on frequency content becomes even more evident. Applying the Min-U-Sil model to glass beads yields unsatisfactory performance, underscoring the strong dependence of picker models on the specific granular material they are trained on, particularly the microphysical processes generating AEs. This observation aligns with findings from DL pickers for natural earthquakes. Although such models can sometimes be successfully transferred to different regions of the world (Cianetti *et al.*, 2021), they often exhibit performance degradation when generalized across distinct tectonic settings, requiring retraining to maintain accuracy (Chatterjee *et al.*, 2025) or the use of self-supervised training strategies based on rule-based picks as training labels (Zhou *et al.*, 2025). Furthermore, these models typically perform poorly when applied to datasets involving significant changes in scale, such as transferring between regional and teleseismic distances (Münchmeyer *et al.*, 2022). This underscores the importance of adapting picker models to the specific characteristics of the seismic signals and environments they are intended to analyze, whether for natural earthquakes or laboratory AEs. Additional fine-tuning can significantly enhance the performance of pretrained models and is often necessary for specific environments, as has been observed for seismic signals collected in Antarctica (Ho *et al.*, 2024).

In our experiments, retraining the Min-U-Sil model on the glass beads dataset resulted in significantly improved performance. Despite the distinct micromechanical processes generating AEs in these materials, our results indicate that fine-tuning a model pretrained on Min-U-Sil AEs performs better at detecting AEs in glass beads than using a fine-tuned model pretrained on natural earthquake data, even when the latter is trained on a substantially larger dataset. This finding highlights that, while preprocessing techniques such as rescaling can improve the performance of earthquake pickers on AEs data, inherent temporal differences between AEs and natural earthquakes critically influence AEs picker performance. Importantly, our findings highlight that training a new PhaseNet model for AE detection does not require large datasets; a few thousand waveforms are sufficient, and potential fine-tuning can further reduce this requirement, making it a practical and efficient strategy for AE detection across diverse laboratory conditions. This aligns with the findings of Chai *et al.* (2020), who successfully adapted the original PhaseNet model, trained on local seismic data, for mesoscale hydraulic fracturing experiments. Their study showed that only a few thousand waveforms were sufficient to bridge the three orders of magnitude difference in both spatial and temporal scales between the original training data and the target data. In conclusion, our approach provides a flexible, robust, and fast framework for enhancing AE detection, even with limited datasets from diverse laboratory conditions. This capability enables the rapid generation of reliable AE catalogs, offering critical insights into fault micromechanics and potential applications for understanding fault behavior in natural settings.

Data and Resources

The dataset used in this study, along with the trained models and a Jupyter notebook for reproducing the figures presented in the article, is available at https://zenodo.org/records/14639594. The complete codebase will be made available on GitHub upon publication at https://github.com/jekmasto. Both websites were last accessed in July 2025. The GitHub repository will also include explanatory Jupyter notebooks demonstrating how to use our models and train new models from scratch. The supplemental material contains Figures S1–S9.

Declaration of Competing Interests

The authors acknowledge that there are no conflicts of interest recorded.

Acknowledgments

This research was funded by European Research Council ERC g.a. n.o. 101040600 (HYQUAKE) to MMS and PRIN giovani PREVENT to MMS. G. Poggiali acknowledges support from European Research Council Advanced Grant 835012 (TECTONIC). The authors thank Luca Coppola, Aurora Perrella, Michele De Solda, Giovanni Guglielmi, and Michele Mauro (from Sapienza University) for their valuable contributions in manually picking many acoustic emission (AE) waveforms.

References

Allen, R. (1978). Automatic earthquake recognition and timing from single traces, *Bull. Seismol. Soc. Am.* **68,** no. 5, 1521–1532.

Anthony, J. L., and C. Marone (2005). Influence of particle characteristics on granular friction, *J. Geophys. Res.* **110,** no. B8, doi: 10.1029/2004JB003399.

Bedford, J. D., and D. R. Faulkner (2021). The role of grain size and effective normal stress on localization and the frictional stability of simulated quartz gouge, *Geophys. Res. Lett.* **48,** e2020GL092023, doi: 10.1029/2020GL092023.

Ben-Zion, Y., and I. Zaliapin (2020). Localization and coalescence of seismicity before large earthquakes, *Geophys. J. Int.* **223,** no. 1, 561–583.

Beyreuther, M., R. Barsch, L. Krischer, T. Megies, Y. Behr, and J. Wassermann (2010). Obspy: A python toolbox for seismology, *Seismol. Res. Lett.* **81,** no. 3, 530–533.

Bianchi, P., P. A. Selvadurai, L. Dal Zilio, M. Rast, C. Madonna, and S. Wiemer (2024). Effects of energy dissipation on precursory seismicity during earthquake preparation, *Seismica* **3,** no. 2, 1417.

Blanke, A., G. Kwiatek, T. H. W. Goebel, M. Bohnhoff, and G. Dresen (2021). Stress drop-magnitude dependence of acoustic emissions during laboratory stick-slip, *Geophys. J. Int.* **224,** no. 2, 1371–1380.

Bolton, D. C., C. Marone, D. Saffer, and D. Trugman (2023). Foreshock properties illuminate nucleation processes of slow and fast laboratory earthquakes, *Nat. Commun.* **14,** 3859.

Bolton, D. C., S. Shreedharan, G. C. McLaskey, J. Rivière, P. Shokouhi, D. T. Trugman, and C. Marone (2022). The high-frequency signature of slow and fast laboratory earthquakes, *J. Geophys. Res.* **127,** e2022JB024170, doi: 10.1029/2022JB024170.

Bolton, D. C., S. Shreedharan, J. Rivière, and C. Marone (2020). Acoustic energy release during the laboratory seismic cycle: Insights on laboratory earthquake precursors and prediction, *J. Geophys. Res.* **125,** e2019JB018975, doi: 10.1029/2019JB018975.

Bolton, D. C., S. Shreedharan, J. Rivière, and C. Marone (2021). Frequency-magnitude statistics of laboratory foreshocks vary with shear velocity, fault slip rate, and shear stress, *J. Geophys. Res.* **126,** e2021JB022175.

Casas, N., C. Giorgetti, F. Pignalberi, and M. M. Scuderi (2025). The role of grain size on shear localization illuminated by acoustic emissions, *J. Geophys. Res.* **130,** no. 4, e2024JB030448, doi: 10.1029/2024JB030448.

Chai, C., M. Maceira, H. J. Santos-Villalobos, S. V. Venkatakrishnan, M. Schoenball, W. Zhu, G. C. Beroza, C. Thurber, and , and EGS Collab Team (2020). Using a deep neural network and transfer learning to bridge scales for seismic phase picking, *Geophys. Res. Lett.* **47,** e2020GL088651, doi: 10.1029/2020GL088651.

Chatterjee, A., C. N. Pennington, D. T. Trugman, and W. R. Walter (2025). A deep learning-aided workflow for decoding the stress regime of southern Nevada, *Seismol. Res. Lett.* doi: 10.1785/0220240443.

Chatterjee, A., D. T. Trugman, G. Hirth, J. Lee, and V. C. Tsai (2024). High-frequency ground motions of earthquakes correlate with fault network complexity, *Geophys. Res. Lett.* **51,** no. 12, e2024GL109418, doi: 10.1029/2024GL109418.

Cianetti, S., R. Bruni, S. Gaviano, D. Keir, D. Piccinini, G. Saccorotti, and C. Giunchi (2021). Comparison of deep learning techniques for the investigation of a seismic sequence: An application to the 2019, m_w 4.5 Mugello (Italy) earthquake, *J. Geophys. Res.* **126,** e2021JB023405, doi: 10.1029/2021JB023405.

Dresen, G., G. Kwiatek, T. Goebel, and Y. Ben-Zion (2020). Seismic and aseismic preparatory processes before large stick-slip failure, *Pure Appl. Geophys.* **177,** 5741–5760.

Ferdowsi, B., M. Griffa, R. A. Guyer, P. A. Johnson, C. Marone, and J. Carmeliet (2013). Microslips as precursors of large slip events in the stick-slip dynamics of sheared granular layers: A discrete element model analysis, *Geophys. Res. Lett.* **40,** no. 16, 4194–4198.

Fryer, B., C. Giorgetti, F. Passelègue, S. Momeni, B. Lecampion, and M. Violay (2022). The influence of roughness on experimental fault mechanical behavior and associated microseismicity, *J. Geophys. Res.* **127,** no. 8, e2022JB025113, doi: 10.1029/2022JB025113.

Goebel, T. H., G. Kwiatek, T. W. Becker, E. E. Brodsky, and G. Dresen (2017). What allows seismic events to grow big?: Insights from b-value and fault roughness analysis in laboratory stick-slip experiments, *Geology* **45,** 815–818.

Goebel, T. H. W., D. Schorlemmer, T. W. Becker, G. Dresen, and C. G. Sammis (2013). Acoustic emissions document stress changes over many seismic cycles in stick-slip experiments, *Geophys. Res. Lett.* **40,** 2049–2054.

Goebel, T.H., V. Schuster, G. Kwiatek, K. Pandey, and G. Dresen (2024). A laboratory perspective on accelerating preparatory processes before earthquakes and implications for foreshock detectability, *Nat. Commun.* **15,** 5588.

Goodfellow, S. D., and R. P. Young (2014). A laboratory acoustic emission experiment under in situ conditions, *Geophys. Res. Lett.* **41,** no. 10, 3422–3430.

Gutenberg, B., and C. F. Richter (1944). Frequency of earthquakes in California, *Bull. Seismol. Soc. Am.* **34,** no. 4, 185–188.

Heimann, S., M. Kriegerowski, M. Isken, S. Cesca, S. Daout, F. Grigoli, C. Juretzek, T. Megies, N. Nooshiri, A. Steinberg, *et al.* (2017). Pyrocko—An open-source seismology toolbox and library, *GFZ Data Services*, doi: 10.5880/GFZ.2.1.2017.001.

Ho, L. M., J. I. Walter, S. E. Hansen, J. L. Sánchez-Roldán, and Z. Peng (2024). Evaluating automated seismic event detection approaches: An application to Victoria land, east Antarctica, *J. Geophys. Res.* **1,** e2024JH000185, doi: 10.1029/2024JH000185.

Hulbert, C., B. Rouet-Leduc, P.A. Johnson, C.X. Ren, J. Rivière, D.C. Bolton, and C. Marone (2019). Similarity of fast and slow earthquakes illuminated by machine learning, *Nature Geosci.* **12,** 69–74.

Johnson, P. A., B. Ferdowsi, B. M. Kaproth, M.A.R.C.O. Scuderi, M. Griffa, J. Carmeliet, R.A. Guyer, P.Y. Le Bas, D.T. Trugman, and C. Marone (2013). Acoustic emission and microslip precursors to stick-slip failure in sheared granular material, *Geophys. Res. Lett.* **40,** 5627–5631.

Karimpouli, S., D. Caus, H. Grover, P. Martínez-Garzón, M. Bohnhoff, G. C. Beroza, G. Dresen, T. Goebel, T. Weigel, and G. Kwiatek (2023). Explainable machine learning for labquake prediction using catalog-driven features, *Earth Planet. Sci. Lett.* **622,** 118,383.

Korkolis, E., A. R. Niemeijer, H. Paulssen, and J. Trampert (2021). A laboratory perspective on the Gutenberg-Richter and characteristic earthquake models, *J. Geophys. Res.* **126,** no. 8, e2021JB021730, doi: 10.1029/2021JB021730.

Kwiatek, G., T. H. W. Goebel, and G. Dresen (2014). Seismic moment tensor and b value variations over multiple seismic cycles in laboratory stick-slip experiments, *Geophys. J. Int.* **198,** 273–286.

Kwiatek, G., P. Martínez-Garzón, T. Goebel, M. Bohnhoff, Y. Ben-Zion, and G. Dresen (2024). Intermittent criticality multi-scale processes leading to large slip events on rough laboratory faults, *J. Geophys. Res.* **129,** e2023JB028411, doi: 10.1029/2023JB028411.

Lee, J., V.C. Tsai, G. Hirth, A. Chatterjee, and D.T. Trugman (2024). Fault-network geometry influences earthquake frictional behavior, *Nature* **631,** 106–110.

Leeman, J.R., D.M. Saffer, M.M. Scuderi, and C. Marone (2016). Laboratory observations of slow earthquakes and the spectrum of tectonic fault slip modes, *Nat. Commun.* **7,** 11,104.

Lei, X., and S. Ma (2014). Laboratory acoustic emission study for earthquake generation process, *Earthq. Sci.* **27,** 627–646.

Lockner, D., J.D. Byerlee, V. Kuksenko, A. Ponomarev, and A. Sidorin (1991). Quasi-static fault growth and shear fracture energy in granite, *Nature* **350,** 39–42.

Lubbers, N. E., D. C. Bolton, J. Mohd-Yusof, C. Marone, K. M. Barros, and P. A. Johnson (2018). Earthquake catalog-based machine learning identification of laboratory fault states and the effects of magnitude of completeness, *Geophys. Res. Lett.* **45,** 13,269–13,276.

Main, I. G. (1992). Damage mechanics with long-range interactions: Correlation between the seismic b-value and the fractal two-point correlation dimension, *Geophys. J. Int.* **111,** no. 3, 531–541.

Main, I. G., P. G. Meredith, and C. Jones (1989). A reinterpretation of the precursory seismic b-value anomaly from fracture mechanics, *Geophys. J. Int.* **96,** 131–138.

Mair, K., K. M. Frye, and C. Marone (2002). Influence of grain characteristics on the friction of granular shear zones, *J. Geophys. Res.* **107,** no. B10, ECV 4-1–ECV 4-9.

Majstorović, J., S. Giffard-Roisin, and P. Poli (2022). Interpreting convolutional neural network decision for earthquake detection with feature map visualization, backward optimization and layer-wise relevance propagation methods, *Geophys. J. Int.* **232,** no. 2, 923–939.

Marty, S., A. Schubnel, H. S. Bhat, J. Aubry, E. Fukuyama, S. Latour, S. Nielsen, and R. Madariaga (2023). Nucleation of laboratory earthquakes: Quantitative analysis and scalings, *J. Geophys. Res.* **128,** e2022JB026294, doi: 10.1029/2022JB026294.

McLaskey, G., and S. Glaser (2012). Acoustic emission sensor calibration for absolute source measurements, *J. Nondestr. Eval.* **31,** 157–168.

McLaskey, G. C., and B. D. Kilgore (2013). Foreshocks during the nucleation of stick-slip instability, *J. Geophys. Res.* **118,** 2982–2997.

McLaskey, G. C., D. A. Lockner, B. D. Kilgore, and N. M. Beeler (2015). A robust calibration technique for acoustic emission systems based on momentum transfer from a ball drop, *Bull. Seismol. Soc. Am.* **105,** no. 1, 257–271.

Mogi, K. (1962). Study of elastic shocks caused by the fracture of heterogeneous materials and its relations to earthquake phenomena, *Bull. Earthq. Res. Inst. Univ. Tokyo* **40,** 125–173.

Mogi, K. (1966). Earthquakes and fractures, *Tectonophysics* **5,** no. 3, 1–8.

Morgan, J. K., and M. S. Boettcher (1999). Numerical simulations of granular shear zones using the distinct element method: 1. Shear zone kinematics and the micromechanics of localization, *J. Geophys. Res.* **104,** no. B2, 2703–2719.

Mousavi, S. M., W. L. Ellsworth, W. Zhu, L. Y. Chuang, and G. C. Beroza (2020). Earthquake transformer—An attentive deep-learning model for simultaneous earthquake detection and phase picking, *Nat. Commun.* **11,** 3952.

Mousavi, S. M., Y. Sheng, W. Zhu, and G. C. Beroza (2019). Stanford earthquake dataset (stead): A global data set of seismic signals for AI, *IEEE Access*, doi: 10.1109/ACCESS.2019.2947848.

Münchmeyer, J., J. Woollam, A. Rietbrock, F. Tilmann, D. Lange, T. Bornstein, T. Diehl, C. Giunchi, F. Haslinger, D. Jozinović, *et al.*

(2022). Which picker fits my data? A quantitative evaluation of deep learning based seismic pickers. *J. Geophys. Res.* **127,** e2021JB023499, doi: 10.1029/2021JB023499.

Northern California Earthquake Data Center (NCEDC) (2014). Northern California Earthquake Data Center, Dataset, UC Berkeley Seismological Laboratory, doi: 10.7932/NCEDC.

Omori, F. (1894). On after-shocks of earthquakes, *J. Coll. Sci. Imp. Univ. Tokyo* **7,** 111–200.

Perol, T., M. Gharbi, and M. Denolle (2018). Convolutional neural network for earthquake detection and location, *Sci. Adv.* **4,** no. 2, e1700578, doi: 10.1126/sciadv.1700578.

Pignalberi, F., G. Mastella, C. Giorgetti, C. Marone, and M. M. Scuderi (2025). Understanding fault slip modes through AE scaling and seismic partitioning, *EGU General Assembly 2025*, Vienna, Austria, 27 April–2 May 2025, EGU25-5800.

Pignalberi, F., G. Mastella, C. Giorgetti, and M. M. Scuderi (2024). Estimating lab-quake source parameters: Spectral inversion from a calibrated acoustic system, *Sensors* **24,** 5824.

Rivière, J., Z. Lv, P. A. Johnson, and C. Marone (2018). Evolution of b-value during the seismic cycle: Insights from laboratory experiments on simulated faults, *Earth Planet. Sci. Lett.* **482,** 407–413.

Ronneberger, O., P. Fischer, and T. Brox (2015). *U-net:* Convolutional networks for biomedical image segmentation, in N. Navab, J. Hornegger, W. M. Wells, and A. F. Frangi (Editors), *Medical Image Computing and Computer-Assisted Intervention—MICCAI 2015*, Springer International Publishing, Cham, 234–241.

Ross, Z. E., M. Meier, E. Hauksson, and T. H. Heaton (2018). Generalized seismic phase detection with deep learning, *Bull. Seismol. Soc. Am.* **108,** no. 5A, 2894–2901.

Rouet-Leduc, B., C. Hulbert, D. C. Bolton, C. X. Ren, J. Riviere, C. Marone, and P. A. Johnson (2018). Estimating fault friction from seismic signals in the laboratory, *Geophys. Res. Lett.* **45,** 1321–1329.

Rouet-Leduc, B., C. Hulbert, N. Lubbers, K. Barros, C. J. Humphreys, and P. A. Johnson (2017). Machine learning predicts laboratory earthquakes, *Geophys. Res. Lett.* **44,** no. 18, 9276–9282.

Scholz, C. H. (1968). The frequency-magnitude relation of microfracturing in rock and its relation to earthquakes, *Bull. Seismol. Soc. Am.* **58,** no. 1, 399–415.

Scuderi, M., C. Collettini, C. Viti, E. Tinti, and C. Marone (2017). Evolution of shear fabric in granular fault gouge from stable sliding to stick slip and implications for fault slip mode, *Geology* **45,** no. 8, 731–734.

Scuderi, M. M., B. M. Carpenter, P. A. Johnson, and C. Marone (2015). Poromechanics of stick-slip frictional sliding and strength recovery on tectonic faults, *J. Geophys. Res.* **120,** no. 10, 6895–6912.

Scuderi, M. M., B. M. Carpenter, and C. Marone (2014). Physicochemical processes of frictional healing: Effects of water on stick-slip stress drop and friction of granular fault gouge, *J. Geophys. Res.* **119,** no. 5, 4090–4105.

Scuderi, M. M., E. Tinti, M. Cocco, and C. Collettini (2020). The role of shear fabric in controlling breakdown processes during laboratory slow-slip events, *J. Geophys. Res.* **125,** no. 11, e2020JB020405, doi: 10.1029/2020JB020405.

Selvadurai, P. A. (2019). Laboratory insight into seismic estimates of energy partitioning during dynamic rupture: An observable scaling breakdown, *J. Geophys. Res.* **124,** no. 11, 11,350–11,379.

Shi, P., M.-A. Meier, L. Villiger, K. Tuinstra, P. A. Selvadurai, F. Lanza, S. Yuan, A. Obermann, M. Mesimeri, J. Münchmeyer, *et al.* (2024). From labquakes to megathrusts: Scaling deep learning based pickers over 15 orders of magnitude, *J. Geophys. Res.* **1,** no. 4, e2024JH000220, doi: 10.1029/2024JH000220.

Shreedharan, S., D. C. Bolton, J. Rivière, and C. Marone (2020). Preseismic fault creep and elastic wave amplitude precursors scale with lab earthquake magnitude for the continuum of tectonic failure modes, *Geophys. Res. Lett.* **46,** doi: 10.1029/2020GL086986.

Shreedharan, S., J. Rivière, P. Bhattacharya, and C. Marone (2019). Frictional state evolution during normal stress perturbations probed with ultrasonic waves, *J. Geophys. Res.* **124,** 5469–5491.

Sleeman, R., and T. Van Eck (1999). Robust automatic p-phase picking: An on-line implementation in the analysis of broadband seismogram recordings, *Phys. Earth Planet. In.* **113,** 265–275.

Soto, H., and B. Schurr (2021). Deepphasepick: A method for detecting and picking seismic phases from local earthquakes based on highly optimized convolutional and recurrent deep neural networks, *Geophys. J. Int.* **227,** no. 2, 1268–1294.

Tan, Y. J., F. Waldhauser, W. L. Ellsworth, M. Zhang, W. Zhu, M. Michele, L. Chiaraluce, G. C. Beroza, and M. Segou (2021). Machine-learning-based high-resolution earthquake catalog reveals how complex fault structures were activated during the 2016-2017 central Italy sequence, *Seism. Rec.* **1,** no. 1, 11–19.

Tinti, E., M. M. Scuderi, L. Scognamiglio, G. Di Stefano, C. Marone, and C. Collettini (2016). On the evolution of elastic properties during laboratory stick-slip experiments spanning the transition from slow slip to dynamic rupture, *J. Geophys. Res.* **121,** no. 12, 8569–8594.

Trugman, D. T., I. W. McBrearty, D. C. Bolton, R. A. Guyer, C. Marone, and P. A. Johnson (2020). The spatiotemporal evolution of granular microslip precursors to laboratory earthquakes, *Geophys. Res. Lett.* **47,** e2020GL088404, doi: 10.1029/2020GL088404.

Wang, K., C. W. Johnson, K. C. Bennett, and P. A. Johnson (2022). Predicting future laboratory fault friction through deep learning transformer models, *Geophys. Res. Lett.* **49,** no. 19, e2022GL098233, doi: 10.1029/2022GL098233.

Woollam, J., J. Münchmeyer, F. Tilmann, A. Rietbrock, D. Lange, T. Bornstein, T. Diehl, C. Giunchi, F. Haslinger, D. Jozinović, *et al.* (2022). Seisbench—A toolbox for machine learning in seismology, *Seismol. Res. Lett.* **93,** no. 3, 1695–1709.

Yamashita, F., E. Fukuyama, S. Xu, and K. Mizoguchi (2021). Two end-member earthquake preparations illuminated by foreshock activity on a meter-scale laboratory fault, *Nat. Commun.* **12,** no. 1, 4302.

Zhou, Y., H. Ding, A. Ghosh, and Z. Ge (2025). AI-PAL: Self-supervised AI phase picking via rule-based algorithm for generalized earthquake detection, *J. Geophys. Res.* **130,** no. 4, e2025JB031294, doi: 10.1029/2025JB031294.

Zhu, W., and G. C. Beroza (2019). Phasenet: A deep-neural-network-based seismic arrival-time picking method, *Geophys. J. Int.* **216,** no. 1, 261–273.

Zhu, W., K. S. Tai, S. M. Mousavi, P. Bailis, and G. C. Beroza (2022). An end-to-end earthquake detection method for joint phase picking and association using deep learning, *J. Geophys. Res.* **127,** no. 3, e2021JB023283, doi: 10.1029/2021JB023283.

Manuscript received 21 January 2025
Published online 13 August 2025

A Mixed Efficient AWENO Scheme to Model Cross-Fault Ground Motions and Its Applications

Tianhong Xu[1], Houyun Yu[1], Wenqiang Wang[2], Zijia Wang[1], and Zhenguo Zhang[*1,3,4]

Abstract

Cross-fault ground motions play a crucial role in conducting seismic response analysis for engineering projects or regional seismic hazard assessment and also help to constrain the properties of faults. However, high-frequency nonphysical oscillations often manifest near faults in the seismic numerical simulations as a result of the discontinuity of the fault plane, which is attributed to the Gibbs phenomenon. In this work, a graphic processing units-based program for simulating cross-fault ground motions has been developed that mixed the standard Alternative flux finite-difference Weighted Essentially Non-Oscillatory (AWENO) scheme with another more efficient AWENO scheme, resulting in a significant reduction in memory usage and improved computational efficiency. Whether dynamic rupture sources (taking the benchmark model TPV10 and a scenario earthquake on the Shunyi–Liangxiang fault as examples) or the kinematic rupture sources (taking the 2022 M_w 6.6 Menyuan earthquake as an example) could be discretized into a set of moment tensor sources for strong ground motion simulations, yielding accurate and reliable cross-fault ground-motion records and permanent displacements. The potential high-frequency nonphysical oscillations in the seismic simulations are limited reasonably, and the cross-fault ground motions are modeled efficiently and accurately. The cross-fault ground motions performed by the proposed method can be directly applied to engineering designs or inversion works.

Cite this article as Xu, T., H. Yu, W. Wang, Z. Wang, and Z. Zhang (2025). A Mixed Efficient AWENO Scheme to Model Cross-Fault Ground Motions and Its Applications, *Seismol. Res. Lett.* **97**, 161–172, doi: 10.1785/0220250047.

Introduction

Engineering works often inevitably cross active faults, such as bridges, highways, tunnels, and pipelines. When an earthquake occurs, significant displacements can result in damage to the aforementioned projects. On 8 January 2022, an M_w 6.6 earthquake struck Menyuan, Qinghai Province, China (37.77° N, 101.26° E). The event generated extensive surface ruptures along the Lenglongling fault (LLLF), causing significant damage to the Lanzhou–Urumqi high-speed railway traversing the fault zone. Consequently, railway operations were suspended for nine months. Advance prediction of potential surface displacements near faults enables the incorporation of prospective seismic events into project construction planning, thereby mitigating potential losses. Similarly, accurate and rapid ground-motion estimation is critical for seismic risk assessment, facilitating prompt government deployment of disaster relief efforts (Li *et al.*, 2022).

The determination of cross-fault permanent displacements typically relies on pairs of ground-motion records from both sides of the fault or onsite surveys conducted postearthquake. The significance of near-fault ground motions has been recognized ever since their initial observation during the 1966 Parkfield earthquake. The seismic response analysis of engineering projects necessitates the evaluation of cross-fault ground motions and permanent displacements, which is crucial for understanding the potential impact on structures and ensuring their safety (Stewart *et al.*, 2002; Kalkan and Kunnath, 2006). Unfortunately, accurately predicting the timing, location, and magnitude of earthquakes is a challenging task. In addition, near-fault instruments are susceptible to being damaged during seismic events. As a result, acquiring these records poses a formidable challenge. The current state of knowledge indicates that there are only a limited number of earthquakes with well-documented records of ground motions near the

1. Department of Earth and Space Sciences, Southern University of Science and Technology, Shenzhen, China, https://orcid.org/0000-0002-7717-1428 (TX); https://orcid.org/0000-0002-2909-2741 (ZW); https://orcid.org/0000-0002-0059-1766 (ZZ); 2. High Performance Computing Department, National Supercomputing Center in Shenzhen, Shenzhen, China, https://orcid.org/0000-0002-8842-6465 (WW); 3. Guangdong Provincial Key Laboratory of Geophysical High-resolution Imaging Technology, Southern University of Science and Technology, Shenzhen, China; 4. Key Laboratory of Earthquake Forecasting and Risk Assessment, Ministry of Emergency Management, Southern University of Science and Technology, Shenzhen, China

*Corresponding author: zhangzg@sustech.edu.cn

fault, whereas the postearthquake surface displacements across faults that can be measured are also very limited.

The available records are insufficient for conducting a comprehensive analysis of the seismic hazard associated with any active fault worldwide. Instead, the simulated seismograms are widely used to achieve the above purpose. The simulation of near-fault ground motions generally employs three distinct methodologies, namely theoretical, mathematical, and numerical. There are two typical characteristics of near-fault ground motion; one is called fling step, and the other is called forward directivity, which is mainly determined by the nature of the rupture propagation. Most theoretical and mathematical methods are used to fit the fling step. The fling step is a typical waveform of near-fault ground motions, representing a permanent displacement like the form of a step function, which may pose significant risks to linear infrastructure projects and buildings. Dreger *et al.* (2011) consider it as an intermediate term of the elastodynamics equations of motion (Aki and Richards, 1980). Hisada and Bielak (2003) and Hisada and Tanaka (2021) perceive it as the contribution of the static Green's function in the representation theorem. The theoretical solution, although highly precise and possessing clear physical implications, is constrained by the current state of development in elastodynamics theory. As a result, its applicability is limited to specific cases such as the half-space layered medium model. The elastic half-space dislocation model (Okada, 1992; Meade, 2007; Nikkhoo and Walter, 2015) can efficiently calculate the static displacements on the surface. However, this model can only obtain the final displacement rather than a displacement time series. Incorporating topography and 3D complex media into such calculations is exceedingly challenging.

An alternative approach involves a parameterization process that aims to optimize the fit between the waveform shape and its mathematical or empirical representation. Mavroeidis and Papageorgiou (2003) utilize a modified Gabor wavelet to accurately and comprehensively characterize the properties of near-fault pulsed ground motion, employing parameters with clear physical significance associated with magnitude. The utilization of analogous parameterization procedures has also been employed by other researchers (Dabaghi and Der Kiureghian, 2017; Yadav and Gupta, 2017). In recent years, machine-learning-based methods have also been utilized for predicting strong ground motions (Alimoradi and Beck, 2015; Withers *et al.*, 2020; Joshi *et al.*, 2024), and the prospective implementation of such techniques in near-fault pulse-like ground-motion prediction is highly anticipated. These mathematical methods are primarily phenomenological models, and their accuracy diminishes when applied to active faults beyond the databases for which they were trained or calibrated.

The near-fault pulse-like ground motions generated by the seismic behavior of any active fault can be influenced by various factors, including the complexities of 3D media, fluctuating surface conditions, intricate source processes, and so forth. It is of great importance to obtain more sophisticated, realistic, and physics-based near-fault ground motions, necessitating the utilization of 3D numerical simulations. Although numerous endeavors have been made in this aspect (Stupazzini *et al.*, 2009; Dreger *et al.*, 2011; Liu *et al.*, 2012), their progress is often hindered by the constraints of simplistic models and exorbitant computational costs. Moreover, the strong ground motion simulations are usually performed with a kinematic source (Zhang *et al.*, 2008; Ba *et al.*, 2022; Sangeetha and Raghukanth, 2022), whereas the dynamic source model is undoubtedly more in line with physics (Zhang *et al.*, 2017; Liu and Duan, 2018; Li *et al.*, 2023, 2024).

However, there is another challenge to obtaining cross-fault ground motions and permanent displacements accurately by numerical simulations, specifically, the fault planes anchored in the computational domain are discontinuous surfaces, and numerical solutions on these surfaces can result in significant high-frequency nonphysical oscillations (known as the Gibbs phenomenon). To solve this issue, Xu and Zhang (2024) developed a 3D seismic wavefield simulation program based on the Alternative flux finite-difference Weighted Essentially Non-Oscillatory (AWENO) scheme. This program employs the AWENO scheme based on substencil weights to mitigate high-frequency nonphysical oscillations near the fault and utilizes characteristic boundary conditions and conservative mapping techniques to accurately fit the free surface in the body-fitted grid (Bayliss *et al.*, 1986; Jiang and Shu, 1996; Jiang *et al.*, 2014; Dong *et al.*, 2023). The efficacy of the program has been demonstrated through comparison with the Generalized Reflection/Transmission coefficients Method proposed by Chen *et al.* (1996) and the CGFDM3D-EQR developed by Wang *et al.* (2022) based on the curve-grid finite-difference method (CGFDM).

Furthermore, we observe that the intricate nonlinear computations associated with the Weighted Essentially Non-Oscillatory (WENO) process necessitate a substantial amount of computational time and lead to a significant increase in memory usage due to the requirement of storing numerous intermediate variables for obtaining the Riemann solvers and higher-order terms within the entire scheme. A more efficient AWENO scheme proposed by Chu *et al.* (2023) modifies the approximations of the high-order terms in the standard AWENO scheme, enabling the utilization of the previously obtained Riemann solvers instead of flux terms, which significantly reduces memory consumption and enhances computational efficiency to a certain extent.

In this study, we developed a graphic processing units (GPU)-based program, for which the numerical scheme is mixed with the standard AWENO scheme and the more efficient AWENO scheme proposed by Chu *et al.* (2023), to model cross-fault ground motions and permanent displacements. This hybrid scheme, called Mixed Efficiency AWENO (ME-AWENO), reduces memory usage and computation time to meet the requirements of ground-motion simulation while maintaining the computational accuracy and nonoscillatory properties of the standard AWENO scheme. This article is structured as follows: In the Methods section, we outline the numerical schemes, boundary conditions, and implementation specifics of the ME-AWENO scheme. In the Numerical experiments section, a series of numerical experiments were conducted. We assess the accuracy, memory consumption, and computational efficiency of the proposed method, and we subsequently verify the effectiveness of the method using a rupture source of benchmark model TPV10. In the Applications section, we perform numerical simulations of the 2022 M_w 6.6 Menyuan earthquake and a scenario earthquake on the Shunyi–Liangxiang fault (SLF) as applications for generating accurate cross-fault ground motions and permanent displacements. In the Conclusions section, we summarize this work and forecast its pivotal role in seismic response analysis of cross-fault projects and earthquake disaster assessments.

Methods

In this study, we have proposed an ME-AWENO scheme for simulating cross-fault ground motions. This scheme is a hybrid of the standard AWENO scheme and a more efficient AWENO scheme proposed by Chu *et al.* (2023), ensuring computational accuracy while reducing memory consumption and enhancing computational efficiency. In the following three (AWENO scheme, WENO interpolation, and A more efficient AWENO scheme) sections, we will sequentially present each of these numerical schemes. Subsequently, in the Free-surface boundary conditions section, we concisely introduce the characteristic boundary conditions utilized for the accurate fitting of free surfaces. Finally, we present a comprehensive description of the specific implementation of the proposed approach in the Implementation of the ME AWENO scheme section.

AWENO scheme

The AWENO scheme incorporates the WENO scheme within the alternative flux finite-difference framework, ensuring that the reconstructed flux remains free from oscillations, whereas various approximate or exact Riemann solvers can be employed to enhance the accuracy and efficiency of the scheme (Jiang *et al.*, 2014). Xu and Zhang (2024) used this scheme to model 3D seismic-wave propagation and verified its accuracy. Here, we give a brief overview of the whole scheme.

The velocity–strain equations of 3D elastic waves can be expressed in the form of the following conservation law (LeVeque, 2002):

$$\partial_t u + \partial_x f + \partial_y g + \partial_z h = 0, \tag{1}$$

in which $u = (\rho v_x, \rho v_y, \rho v_z, \epsilon_{xx}, \epsilon_{yy}, \epsilon_{zz}, 2\epsilon_{yz}, 2\epsilon_{xz}, 2\epsilon_{xy})^T$ is called conservative variables, $f = (\tau_{xx}, \tau_{xy}, \tau_{xz}, v_x, 0, 0, 0, v_z, v_y)^T$, $g = (\tau_{xy}, \tau_{yy}, \tau_{yz}, 0, v_y, 0, v_z, 0, v_x)^T$, and $h = (\tau_{xz}, \tau_{yz}, \tau_{zz}, 0, 0, v_z, v_y, v_x, 0)^T$ are called flux terms. The strain terms in the conservative variables are related to the stress terms in the flux terms by the constitutive relation, which is described by Hooke's law in this article to apply linear elasticity:

$$\tau_{ij} = \lambda \varepsilon_{kk} \delta_{ij} + 2\mu \varepsilon_{ij}. \tag{2}$$

In general, we need to solve the problem in a curved grid that fits the boundary to reduce the difficulty of imposing boundary conditions. In the generalized Cartesian coordinate system, conservation laws can be systematically extended to

$$\partial_t \tilde{u} + \partial_\xi \tilde{f} + \partial_\eta \tilde{g} + \partial_\zeta \tilde{h} = 0, \tag{3}$$

in which $\tilde{u} = \frac{u}{J}$ and $\tilde{f} = n_x f + n_y g + n_z h$. $\tilde{g}$ and $\tilde{h}$ are in the same form, and the corresponding direction vector (n_x, n_y, n_z) is chosen according to the direction of the calculation. The Jacobian is given by $J^{-1} = |\frac{\partial(x,y,z)}{\partial(\xi,\eta,\zeta)}| = \begin{vmatrix} x_\xi & x_\eta & x_\zeta \\ y_\xi & y_\eta & y_\zeta \\ z_\xi & z_\eta & z_\zeta \end{vmatrix}$.

The finite-difference methods involve computing dimension by dimension, specifically, when calculating for 1D, we keep the others fixed. Taking the 1D calculation as an example, we consider the semidiscrete form of the conservation law:

$$\partial_t u_i + \frac{1}{\Delta x}(\hat{f}_{i+\frac{1}{2}} - \hat{f}_{i-\frac{1}{2}}) = 0. \tag{4}$$

in which $\hat{f}_{i+\frac{1}{2}}$ is so-called numerical flux reconstructed on the interface of elements and given by

$$\hat{f}_{i+\frac{1}{2}} = f_{i+\frac{1}{2}} + \sum_{k=1}^{\frac{m-1}{2}} a_{2k} \Delta x^{2k} \partial_x^{2k} f, \tag{5}$$

to guarantee mth-order accuracy, in which a_{2k} are some coefficients obtained by Taylor expansion and truncated at a certain precision. The first term in equation (5) is approximated by

$$f_{i+\frac{1}{2}} = F(u^-_{i+\frac{1}{2}}, u^+_{i+\frac{1}{2}}), \tag{6}$$

with the values $u^{\pm}_{i+1/2}$ obtained by the WENO interpolation procedure (Jiang and Shu, 1996), and function F is based on an approximate or exact Riemann solver. The remaining higher-order terms in equation (5) are constructed by the simple central differences to ensure the accuracy of the scheme. Normally fifth-order precision expansion is used in the AWENO scheme, so the approximation of higher-order terms is given by

$$\begin{aligned} \Delta x^2 \partial_x^2 f &\approx \tfrac{1}{48}(-5f_{i-2} + 39f_{i-1} - 34f_i - 34f_{i+1} + 39f_{i+2} - 5f_{i+3}), \\ \Delta x^4 \partial_x^4 f &\approx \tfrac{1}{2}(f_{i-2} - 3f_{i-1} + 2f_i + 2f_{i+1} - 3f_{i+2} + f_{i+3}). \end{aligned} \tag{7}$$

WENO interpolation

Equation (6) needs us to supply the interpolation result $u^{\pm}_{i+1/2}$ to the Riemann solver. A standard fifth-order WENO interpolation procedure proposed by Jiang and Shu (1996) is performed on each component of the conservative variable u to obtain the corresponding component of $u^{\pm}_{i+1/2}$.

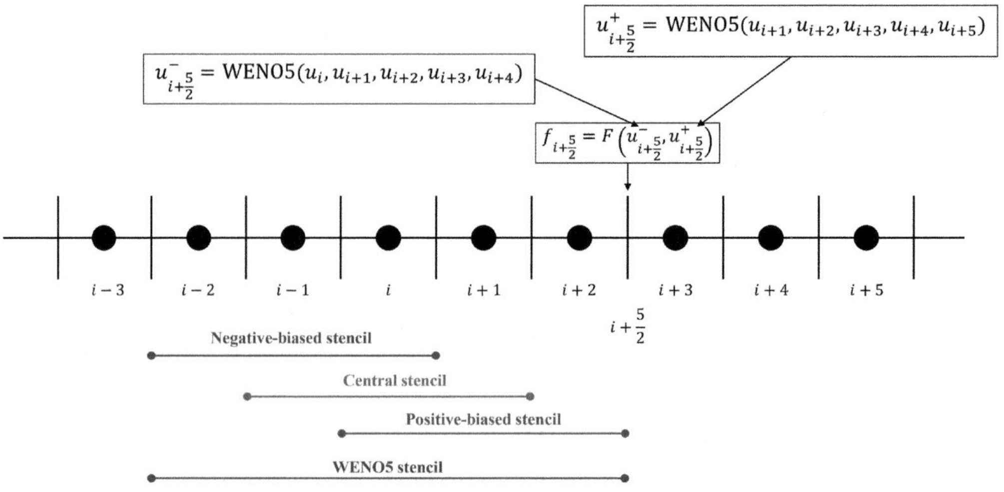

Figure 1. The fifth-order Weighted Essentially Non-Oscillatory (WENO) interpolation stencil consists of a negative-biased stencil, a center stencil, and a positive-biased stencil. The stencil needed to calculate the numerical flux at the point $i + 5/2$ is also shown. The color version of this figure is available only in the electronic edition.

a. Three substencils with negative bias, center bias, and positive bias were selected to calculate the interpolation respectively as $S^{(0)} = \{x_{i-2}, x_{i-1}, x_i\}$, $S^{(1)} = \{x_{i-1}, x_i, x_{i+1}\}$, $S^{(2)} = \{x_i, x_{i+1}, x_{i+2}\}$, as shown in Figure 1:

$$u^{(0)}_{i+\frac{1}{2}} = \frac{3}{8}u_{i-2} - \frac{5}{4}u_{i-1} + \frac{15}{8}u_i,$$
$$u^{(1)}_{i+\frac{1}{2}} = -\frac{1}{8}u_{i-1} + \frac{3}{4}u_i + \frac{3}{8}u_{i+1},$$
$$u^{(2)}_{i+\frac{1}{2}} = \frac{3}{8}u_i + \frac{3}{4}u_{i+1} - \frac{1}{8}u_{i+2}. \tag{8}$$

In fact, these substencils can be linearly weighted together into a long stencil:

$$u^{-}_{i+\frac{1}{2}} = \sum_{r=0}^{2} d_r u^{(r)}_{i+\frac{1}{2}}, \tag{9}$$

with the linear weights being $d_0 = \frac{5}{16}, d_1 = \frac{5}{8}, d_2 = \frac{1}{16}$, which are also called ideal weights and have the best spectral properties.

b. Compute nonlinear weights ω_r from the linear weights d_r

$$\omega_r = \frac{\alpha_r}{\alpha_0 + \alpha_1 + \alpha_2}, \alpha_r = \frac{d_r}{(\beta_r + \epsilon)^2}, r = 0,1,2, \tag{10}$$

in which $\epsilon = 10^{-6}$ is used to avoid division by zero, which is a value of experience, and the smoothness indicators β_r are given by

$$\beta_0 = \frac{1}{3}(4u^2_{i-2} - 19u_{i-2}u_{i-1} + 25u^2_{i-1} + 11u_{i-2}u_i - 31u_{i-1}u_i + 10u^2_i),$$
$$\beta_1 = \frac{1}{3}(4u^2_{i-1} - 13u_{i-1}u_i + 13u^2_i + 5u_{i-1}u_{i+1} - 13u_iu_{i+1} + 4u^2_{i+1}),$$
$$\beta_2 = \frac{1}{3}(10u^2_i - 31u_iu_{i+1} + 25u^2_{i+1} + 11u_iu_{i+2} - 19u_{i+1}u_{i+2} + 4u^2_{i+2}). \tag{11}$$

c. The WENO interpolation is defined by

$$u^{-}_{i+\frac{1}{2}} = \sum_{r=0}^{2} \omega_r u^{(r)}_{i+\frac{1}{2}}, \tag{12}$$

The process to obtain $u^{+}_{i+\frac{1}{2}}$ is mirror-symmetric and requires a bias of one point in the positive direction. That is, a complete fifth-order AWENO scheme requires a total of seven points on both sides of the points to be solved. In the smooth region, the nonlinear weights ω_r degenerate into ideal weights to ensure the scheme has better spectral properties, whereas in the discontinuous region, the smoothest substencil is chosen to ensure the nonoscillatory properties.

A more efficient AWENO scheme

Generally, the aforementioned calculations suffice for addressing the requirements of most scenarios. However, it is worth noting that the Riemann solver in equation (5) relies on the interpolation of conservative variables, whereas the approximation of higher-order terms is achieved through interpolating flux terms. This implies that before the whole implementation of the scheme, it is necessary to address the flux terms, a process that not only consumes computational resources but also demands significant memory allocation for storage. This poses challenges in seismic-wave numerical simulations, particularly when simulating larger regions or employing finer grids.

Chu *et al.* (2023) have devised a more efficient AWENO scheme, which effectively approximates higher-order terms by leveraging the Riemann solvers, which have been calculated and stored in memory by the first term in equation (5), achieving computational accuracy equivalent to the central difference approximation of flux terms. The approximations of higher-order terms in the efficient AWENO scheme proposed by Chu *et al.* (2023) are given by

$$\begin{aligned}\Delta x^2\partial_x^2 f &\approx \frac{1}{12}\left(-f_{i-\frac{3}{2}}+16f_{i-\frac{1}{2}}-30f_{i+\frac{1}{2}}+16f_{i+\frac{3}{2}}-f_{i+\frac{5}{2}}\right),\\ \Delta x^4\partial_x^4 f &\approx \left(f_{i-\frac{3}{2}}-4f_{i-\frac{1}{2}}+6f_{i+\frac{1}{2}}-4f_{i+\frac{3}{2}}+f_{i+\frac{5}{2}}\right).\end{aligned} \tag{13}$$

Compared with the standard scheme of equation (7), the calculation and storage of flux terms f, g, h are reduced, and the calculation accuracy is not affected. We will prove it in numerical validation later in the article.

Free-surface boundary conditions

To fit the free surface accurately in complex terrain, we use a conservative mesh mapping process to generate body-fitted grids. A simple coordinate rotation is considered and then free-surface boundary conditions based on 1D characteristic analysis are applied. The implementation of the characteristic boundary condition involves two steps: first, obtaining the values at the ghost points through interpolation, and subsequently correcting the variables at the boundary (Bayliss *et al.*, 1986; Kosloff *et al.*, 1990; Dong *et al.*, 2023; Xu and Zhang, 2024). The corrections for the free surface of the 3D linear elastic wave equation are given by

$$\begin{aligned}\tau_{xx}^{\text{new}} &= \tau_{xx}^{\text{old}} - \frac{\lambda}{\lambda+2\mu}\tau_{zz},\\ \tau_{yy}^{\text{new}} &= \tau_{yy}^{\text{old}} - \frac{\lambda}{\lambda+2\mu}\tau_{zz},\\ \tau_{xy}^{\text{new}} &= \tau_{xy}^{\text{old}},\\ v_x^{\text{new}} &= v_x^{\text{old}} + \frac{1}{\rho v_s}\tau_{xz},\\ v_y^{\text{new}} &= v_y^{\text{old}} + \frac{1}{\rho v_s}\tau_{yz},\\ v_z^{\text{new}} &= v_z^{\text{old}} + \frac{1}{\rho v_p}\tau_{zz}.\end{aligned} \tag{14}$$

The superscript "old" represents the variables calculated using the complete stencil obtained by interpolation, which only meets the requirements of the stencil and does not take into account the actual physical conditions. The points on the boundary can then be time integrated as normal as the points inside. The corrections are then used to obtain the "new" values of these variables, which are derived based on the 1D characteristic analysis of the elastic wave equation in the standard Cartesian coordinate system. However, if the local coordinate system of the points on the boundary is rotated to the normal direction and then rotated back after corrections, good results can be obtained in the generalized Cartesian coordinate system. For technical details of this part, please refer to Xu and Zhang (2024).

Implementation of the ME AWENO scheme

Although Chu *et al.* (2023) proposed a more efficient AWENO scheme to solve the hyperbolic conservation law, the simulation

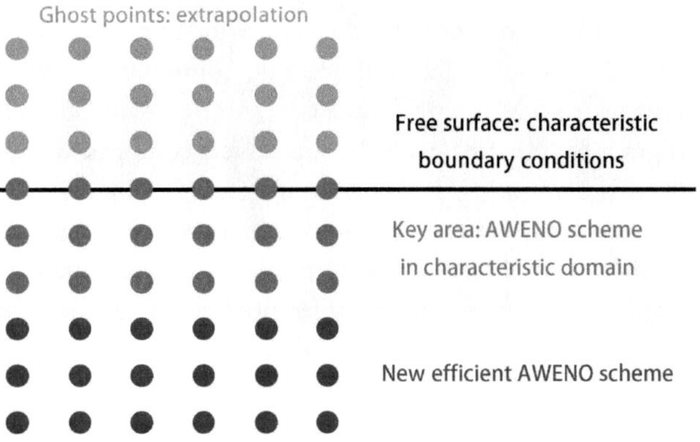

Figure 2. The Mixed Efficiency Alternative flux finite-difference Weighted Essentially Non-Oscillatory (ME-AWENO) numerical scheme. The black-solid line represents the free surface, whereas the ghost points above it are extrapolated (depicted as gray circles). The points on the free surface are adjusted based on the wavefield to meet physical requirements through characteristic boundary conditions. The three layers near the free surface are referred to as the key area (red circles), where the standard AWENO scheme is employed to solve the equations in the characteristic domain, thereby enhancing the accuracy and stability of the scheme. The remaining portion of the wavefield is resolved using the new efficient AWENO scheme to optimize computational efficiency (green circles). The color version of this figure is available only in the electronic edition.

of strong ground motions also needs to consider the fitting of free-surface boundary conditions accurately. However, we can find that it requires Riemann solvers at $x = i + \frac{5}{2}$, which relies on a WENO interpolation procedure to obtain $q^{\pm}_{i+5/2}$, requiring a seven-point stencil around it. This means that the values of at least five additional ghost points in the direction normal to the free surface need to be processed to satisfy the requirements of the full stencil, as shown in Figure 1. The calculation accuracy of the several layers near the free surface is crucial, which affects the accuracy of the whole simulation of strong ground motion, and we call it the key areas.

With that in mind, we design the mixed scheme in accordance with the following principles: (a) maximize the efficiency in smooth regions and (b) maximize computational accuracy in key areas. The efficient AWENO scheme proposed by Chu *et al.* (2023) is preferred across the entire computing domain to optimize computational resource utilization, building upon our previous introduction to numerical schemes. And we employ the standard AWENO scheme and enhance the stability and precision of the computation in this region by mapping the calculation of numerical flux in the direction normal to the free surface to the characteristic domain. The increase in computing resource consumption resulting from such a transformation is practically negligible, given that this area constitutes only a small fraction of the overall computing domain. The comprehensive numerical scheme of ME-AWENO is outlined in Figure 2.

The simulations of ground motions and permanent displacements necessitate rapid and accurate computation. We utilize message passing interface and CUDA C/C++ to optimize the program for efficient execution on servers equipped with multiple GPU computing cards. Using if statements in a GPU kernel function to determine the scheme is not recommended because it can lead to thread blocking until the slowest calculation is completed or thread warp differentiation. Therefore, we opt to conduct an initial comprehensive calculation of the entire area, followed by targeted recalculations in key areas to enhance the precision of our calculations, which ensures load balancing.

Numerical Experiments

Memory and efficiency

In this section, the memory and computational efficiency of the proposed scheme are evaluated using a Ricker-wavelet point-source model to simulate the propagation of seismic waves in 3D half-space with homogeneous media. The moment tensor is applied to the stress terms to simulate the propagation of the explosion source in space. We established multiple calculation domains with varying grid sizes and evaluated the normalized memory usage and computational time of both the standard AWENO scheme and the ME-AWENO scheme based on the memory occupancy and time consumption of the CGFDM3D-EQR (Wang *et al.*, 2022), as presented in Table 1. The tests in this research were all run on an 8x Nvidia A100 SXM4 80 GB dual-channel GPU server running on CentOS 7.

TABLE 1
Computation Time and Memory of Each Scheme in Cases of Various Grid Sizes, for Which They Are Quantified in Terms of Multiples of CGFDM3D-EQR (CGFDM Scheme)

Grid Size	Scheme	Memory	Time
200 × 200 × 200	CGFDM	1.00	1.00
	AWENO	5.11	2.33
	ME-AWENO	4.72	2.00
400 × 400 × 200	CGFDM	1.00	1.00
	AWENO	3.69	3.00
	ME-AWENO	2.97	2.50
800 × 800 × 400	CGFDM	1.00	1.00
	AWENO	2.46	4.20
	ME-AWENO	1.42	3.51
1200 × 1200 × 400	CGFDM	1.00	1.00
	AWENO	2.35	4.34
	ME-AWENO	1.26	3.59

AWENO, Alternative flux finite-difference Weighted Essentially Non-Oscillatory; CGFDM, curve-grid finite-difference method; ME-AWENO, Mixed Efficiency Alternative flux finite-difference Weighted Essentially Non-Oscillatory.

We observed that, when the computational scale is small, the AWENO and ME-AWENO schemes necessitate a greater number of intermediate variables for storage and computation of the Riemann solvers. This results in a significant memory overhead compared to the CGFDM scheme. However, as the computational scale increases to that required for actual seismic calculations, this count has already been reduced to an acceptable level. When the grid size is 1200 × 1200 × 400, the memory usage of the AWENO scheme is approximately 2.35 times that of the CGFDM. In contrast, the ME-AWENO scheme exhibits a mere 1.26 times increase, and the memory usage is reduced by half compared with the AWENO scheme. Although this number remains roughly 25% higher than that of CGFDM, it reaches a satisfactory outcome for practical applications.

Furthermore, due to the conservative finite-difference method employed in the AWENO and ME-AWENO schemes, a significant number of nonlinear weight calculations are introduced, along with solving the Riemann problem. This results in a notable increase in computation time compared to CGFDM. Although this increase may not be readily apparent at smaller calculation scales, it becomes pronounced as the scale increases to 1200 × 1200 × 400; at this scale, the AWENO scheme consumes approximately 4.34 times more computation time than the CGFDM scheme. The ME-AWENO scheme mitigates this by about 17.2%, reducing it to only 3.59 times. It is noteworthy that, due to the efficient GPU calculation, the single-timestep computation time is only about 0.316 s even in this scenario. In addition, the high-frequency nonphysical oscillations are effectively eliminated in the wavefield simulation while maintaining calculation accuracy, as will be demonstrated in subsequent simulations.

3D benchmark model TPV10

TPV10 is a 3D dynamic rupture benchmark model that describes the spontaneous rupture of a 60° dipping planar normal fault (Harris *et al.*, 2009). We obtained the finite-fault source using dynamic simulation (Zhang *et al.*, 2014, 2020), which is discretized as a set of point moment tensor sources. The transformation strain caused by the moment tensor is obtained by the constitutive relation described in equation (2) and then applied to the conservative variable u. This dynamic model is employed to simulate strong ground motion using CGFDM3D-EQR and the ME-AWENO scheme. The final surface displacements U_z are depicted in Figure 3a. It can be observed that both CGFDM3D-EQR and the ME-AWENO scheme accurately simulate the propagation of strong ground motion, with static displacements calculated by the Okada model (Okada, 1992) according to the slip distribution on the fault serving as a reliable reference. However, near the fault, CGFDM3D-EQR exhibited significant oscillations whereas the ME-AWENO scheme did not demonstrate such behavior. To provide a clearer depiction of the fault vicinity, we established five survey lines (L0–L4) perpendicular to the fault, as illustrated

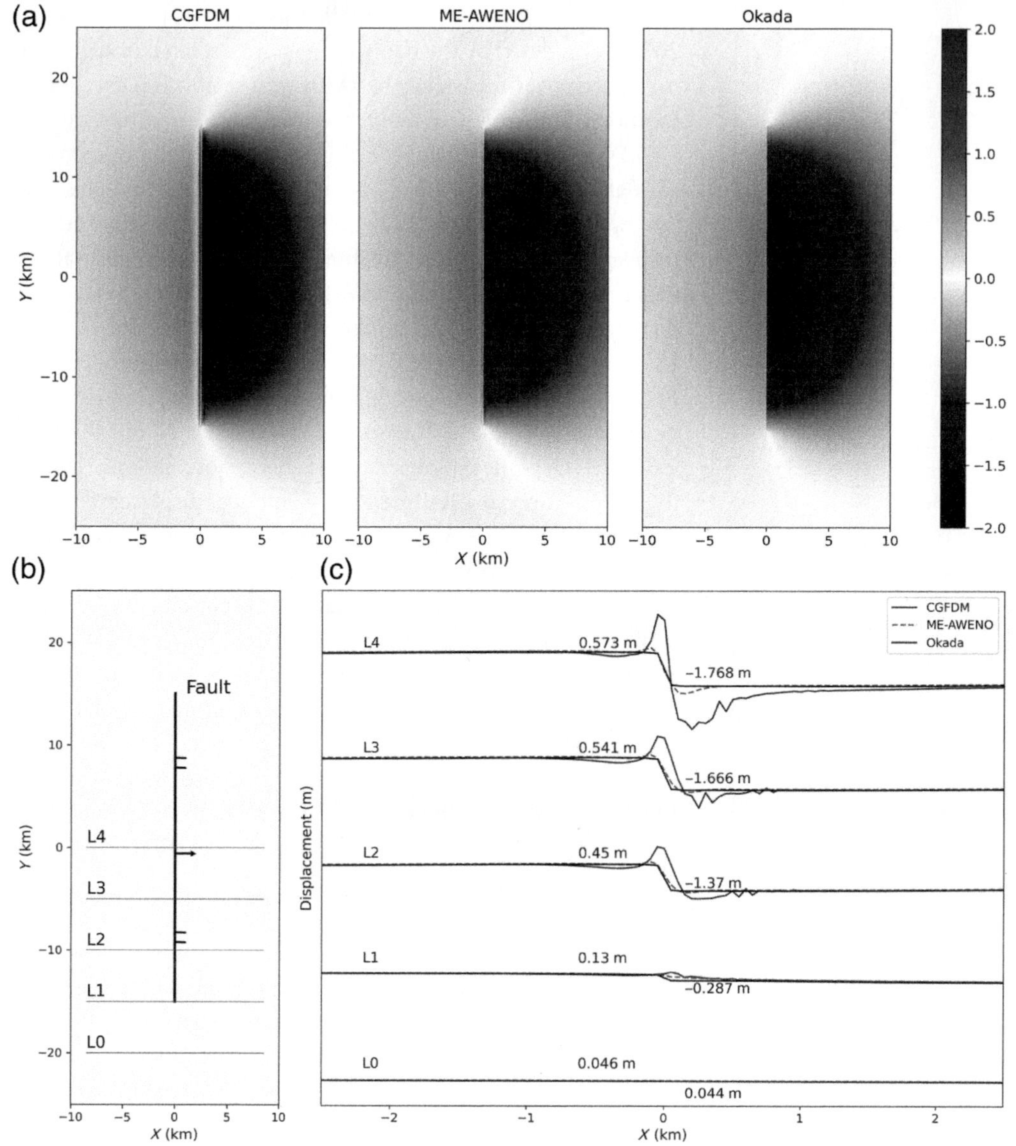

Figure 3. Final surface displacements U_z simulated by CGFDM3D-EQR, the ME-AWENO scheme, and the Okada model are shown in panel (a). The cross-fault survey lines L0–L4 are shown in panel (b), and the corresponding surface displacements U_z obtained along them are shown in panel (c). The black numbers represent the surface displacements on both sides of the fault calculated by the Okada model. CGFDM, curve-grid finite-difference method. The color version of this figure is available only in the electronic edition.

in Figure 3b, accompanied by the corresponding surface displacement U_z measurements displayed in Figure 3c. The numbers in the figure represent the surface displacements on both sides of the fault calculated by the Okada model. It is clear that they both demonstrate good agreement with the static displacements calculated by the Okada model in regions far from the fault; however, within a proximity of 1.5 km to the fault (approximately 30 grid points), significant oscillations are observed in the former, whereas the latter remains almost unaffected by such oscillations.

We set up 10 stations labeled 0–9 in Figure 4a along the L4 survey line, which exhibited the most significant oscillation, and the corresponding waveforms captured by these stations are depicted in Figure 4b. We also mark the static displacements calculated by the Okada model with black-dashed lines for intuitive comparison with the two schemes. The waveforms demonstrate that as the fault proximity increases, the CGFDM3D-EQR migration becomes more pronounced in comparison to the ME-AWENO scheme. Notably, the final surface displacements at stations 5–7, which are closest to the fault, exhibit nearly twice the magnitude compared to those of the latter. The displacements given by the ME-AWENO scheme are closer to the reference displacements calculated by the Okada model. The aforementioned comparison reveals that our method significantly improves the precision of near-fault ground motions, enabling us to obtain the displacement waveforms without oscillations.

Applications

2022 M_w 6.6 Menyuan earthquake

As we mentioned in the Introduction, the 2022 M_w 6.6 Menyuan earthquake seriously jeopardized the safety of the local community and engineering projects. The source physical process of this earthquake is not the primary focus of our research, and our main concern lies in analyzing the near-fault surface displacements resulting from strong ground motions, which may play a more important role in the field of earthquake engineering. We construct the 3D model in the study area using elevation from the Shuttle Radar Topography Mission (SRTM, see Data and Resources) and the Chinese 3D V_S reference model proposed by Shen *et al.* (2016), whereas other medium parameters are derived from the empirical relations proposed by Brocher (2005). The coseismic rupture process of this earthquake was jointly inverted by Lyu *et al.* (2022) using Interferometric Synthetic Aperture Radar and high-frequency Global Navigation

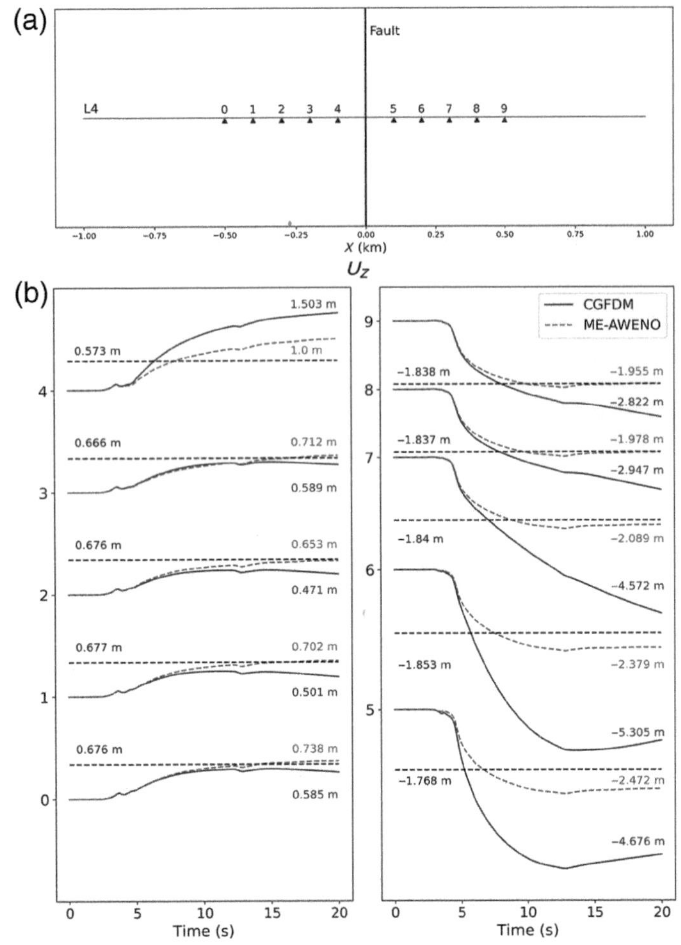

Figure 4. Several stations arranged along the cross-fault survey line L4 marked in Figure 3b are shown in panel (a), and their recorded U_z waveforms are shown in panel (b). The numbers preceding the waveform indicate the names of the stations. The blue-solid line and red-dashed line represent the waveforms recorded by the CGFDM3D-EQR and ME-AWENO schemes at the stations, with their final displacement U_z values indicated by corresponding colored numbers. The black-dashed line represents the static displacements of the corresponding station calculated by the Okada model, with the static displacement U_z indicated by black numbers. The color version of this figure is available only in the electronic edition.

Satellite Systems displacement waveforms, which are utilized to construct a finite-fault seismic source model. The model consists of a total of 12,000 subfaults, for which the source time function of each subfault is approximated by a Gauss-shaped function. All the subfaults are projected and interpolated onto the corresponding grid points. The simulation region is 160 km × 120 km × 80 km, and the grid size is 200 m. The timestep is 0.013 s, and the total time is 60 s.

The elevation variations within the research area are depicted in Figure 5a, with the solid-black line denoting the surface trace of the LLLF and the Tuolaishan fault (TLSF), whereas the blue-dashed line indicates the path of the Lanzhou–Urumqi high-speed railway across the LLLF. The wavefield snapshots at about 26 s, as simulated by the two schemes, are depicted in Figure 5b, c, respectively. Consistency between both methods is excellent in locations far from the fault; however, close to the fault, the CGFDM3D-EQR method exhibits pronounced nonphysical oscillations, whereas this phenomenon is absent in the ME-AWENO scheme, as anticipated. We acquired the final surface displacements along the Lanzhou–Urumqi high-speed railway and presented it in Figure 5d. The horizontal axis denotes the distance from each point on the railway to its intersection with LLLF, whereas the vertical axis represents corresponding displacement values. The conclusion remains consistent with previous findings. At the intersection of the railway and the fault, CGFDM3D-EQR exhibits high-frequency oscillations, leading to a significant overestimation of surface displacements. As anticipated, the ME-AWENO method reveals notable displacement disparities on either side of the fault, enabling accurate estimation of cross-fault permanent displacements resulting from seismic activity. In Figure 5a, the final horizontal displacements of the ME-AWENO scheme along the railway are denoted by red arrows, clearly illustrating the displacement changes on both sides of the fault. The estimated horizontal displacement of the Lanzhou–Urumqi high-speed railway and the LLLF intersection by the ME-AWENO scheme is approximately 3.2 m, closely aligning with the measured value of 2.7 ± 0.2 m by Niu *et al.* (2023).

Scenario earthquake on the SLF

To demonstrate the capability of the ME-AWENO scheme in obtaining cross-fault ground motions and permanent displacements, which might be utilized for future seismic response analysis in engineering, we conduct a scenario earthquake simulation of the SLF. The fault has an overall strike of N40°E, a total length of approximately 36 km, and a fault width of 19 km along the dip. The fault plane dips to the southeast with a dip angle of 75°. We constructed a finite-fault model based on dynamic rupture simulation (Zhao *et al.*, 2025), for which spatial–temporal evolution of the slip rate and slip distribution is shown in Figure 6, and the solid-blue lines represent the rupture isochrons with an interval of 1 s. The source has a moment magnitude of M_w 6.73.

The 3D model of the study area is constructed utilizing SRTM data and the Chinese 3D V_S reference model proposed by Shen *et al.* (2016). In the simulation, we employed a grid size of 100 m to provide a more detailed characterization of cross-fault ground motions, and the simulation region is 100 km × 100 km × 60 km. The timestep is 0.00746 s, and the total time is 30 s.

Figure 7a depicts the topography of the research area, with the surface trace of the SLF delineated by a continuous black line. To capture the cross-fault ground motions and permanent displacements, we have established two survey lines intersecting the fault, A–A′ and B–B′ (indicated by the blue-dashed line), and have also

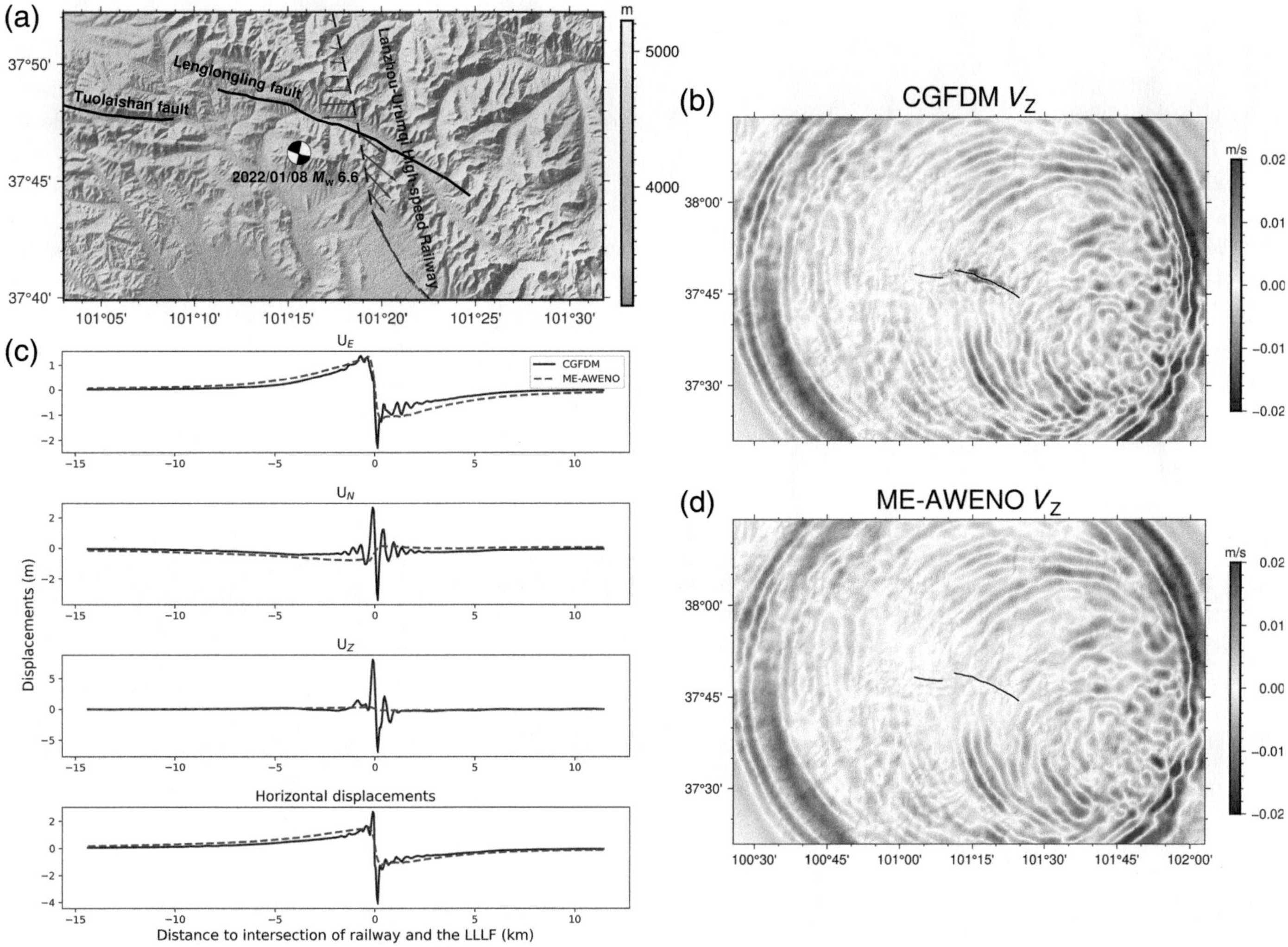

strategically positioned multiple stations on both sides of the fault (marked by white circles). The horizontal displacements along these two survey lines, resulting from the coseismic process, are illustrated in Figure 7b, which displays the extent of displacements on both sides of the fault. Displacements exhibit a smooth pattern along both survey lines, with the anticipated noticeable slip occurring at the intersection of the survey lines and the fault, without high-frequency nonphysical oscillations.

The three-component wavefield snapshots of the study area at about 15 s are shown in Figure 8a–c, respectively, revealing that the ME-AWENO scheme demonstrates excellent performance in accurately modeling strong ground motions without any stray oscillations. Figure 8d,e illustrates the fault-normal velocity component V_{FN} and the fault-parallel velocity component V_{FN} recorded at the stations indicated in Figure 7a, respectively. These records are shown as pulses in the velocity waveform, thus well recording the characteristics of cross-fault strong ground motions. The absence of any high-frequency nonphysical oscillations in the records, as anticipated, enables their direct application to seismic response analysis cross-fault engineering works in the seismogenic fault region with minimal additional processing of the waveforms.

Figure 5. The elevation changes in the study area are depicted in panel (a), along with the surface trace of the Lenglongling fault (LLLF) and Tuolaishan fault (TLSF) represented by the black-solid line, and the blue-dashed line representing the Lanzhou–Urumqi high-speed railway. The red vector illustrates the final horizontal displacements on both sides of the fault calculated by the ME-AWENO scheme. Panels (b) and (c) depict the wavefield snapshots obtained from the simulations conducted by the two methods at about 26 s. The final surface displacements along the Lanzhou–Urumqi high-speed railway, including three-component and horizontal displacements, resulting from simulations using both methods are depicted in panel (d), for which the horizontal axis represents the distance of points along the railway from its intersection with the LLLF (an increase in latitude is considered positive). The color version of this figure is available only in the electronic edition.

Conclusions

In this work, we have developed an accurate numerical simulation program for cross-fault ground motions and permanent displacements, which avoids high-frequency nonphysical oscillations caused by discontinuities of faults and sufficiently takes

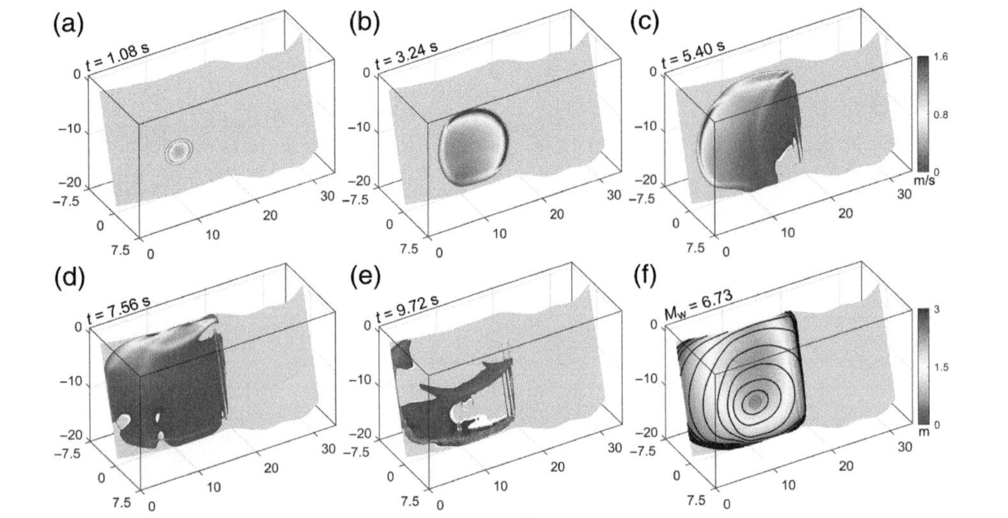

Figure. 6. (a–e) Spatial–temporal evolution of the slip rate in the finite-fault model. The slip distribution of the dynamic source is shown in panel (f), for which solid-blue lines represent the rupture isochrons with an interval of 1 s. The source has a moment magnitude of M_W 6.73. The color version of this figure is available only in the electronic edition.

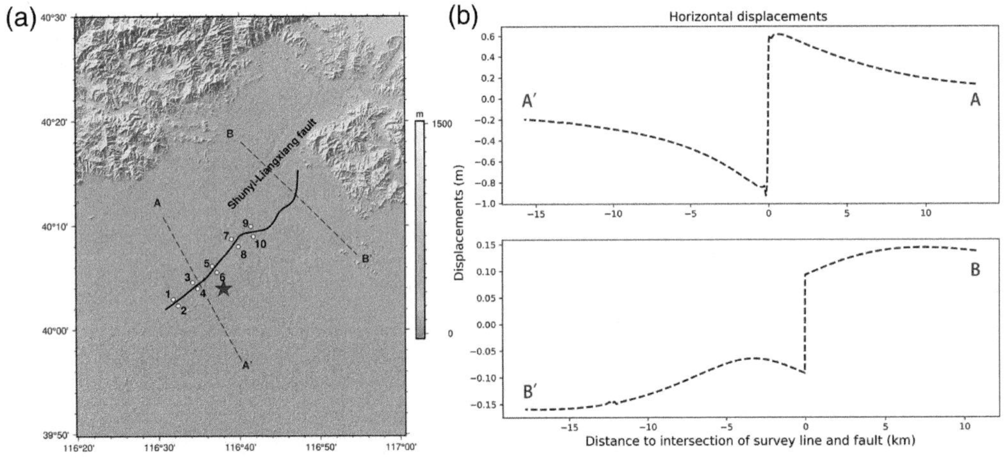

Figure 7. The topography of the study area is illustrated in panel (a), with the black-solid lines depicting the surface trace of the Shunyi–Liangxiang fault, and the red stars indicating the epicenter location. The white circles represent symmetrically located strong ground motion stations on both sides of the fault, with numbers beside them indicating station names. The two blue-dashed lines denote cross-fault survey lines, and their corresponding measurements are depicted in panel (b), for which the horizontal axis represents distances from survey line points to its intersection with the fault (an increase in latitude is considered positive). The color version of this figure is available only in the electronic edition.

into account the effects of irregular terrains and 3D complex media. The ground motions and permanent displacements obtained by this program can be used to determine the seismic response of cross-fault engineering works or seismic risk assessments and also help to constrain the properties of faults in the process of inversion. In this way, more accurate predictions of earthquake disasters can be made to design the seismic performance of the projects or invert the coseismic rupture process more accurately. The noteworthy point is that our simulation performs effectively even in more refined velocity structures, which is a prominent advantage of finite-difference methods. In future studies, we will focus on the optimization of the program and consider more complex cases such as viscoelastic and elastoplastic media. Furthermore, we anticipate that the proposed approach can be utilized for simulating dynamic ruptures to address the potential shock wave issue arising from the rupture front on the fault plane and to mitigate the high-frequency nonphysical oscillations.

Data and Resources

The Chinese 3D V_S reference model is obtained from Shen *et al.* (2016) (http://chinageorefmodel.org). The elevations are obtained from the Shuttle Radar Topography Mission (SRTM, https://srtm.csi.cgiar.org/srtmdata). The strong ground motion simulation software CGFDM3D-EQR is available at https://github.com/wenqiangwang sustech/CGFDM3D-EQR and archived on Zenodo at https://zenodo.org/records/10531266. The software CGFDM3D-EQR-SC including the Mixed Efficiency Alternative flux finite-difference Weighted Essentially Non-Oscillatory (ME-AWENO) scheme for modeling the cross-fault ground motions used in this work is available at https://github.com/nightassert/CGFDM3D-EQR-SC and archived on Zenodo at https://zenodo.org/records/13382014. All websites were last accessed in September 2024.

Declaration of Competing Interests

The authors acknowledge that there are no conflicts of interest recorded.

Acknowledgments

The authors express their gratitude to Editor-in-Chief Allison Bent, Eric Dunham, and an anonymous reviewer for their valuable constructive

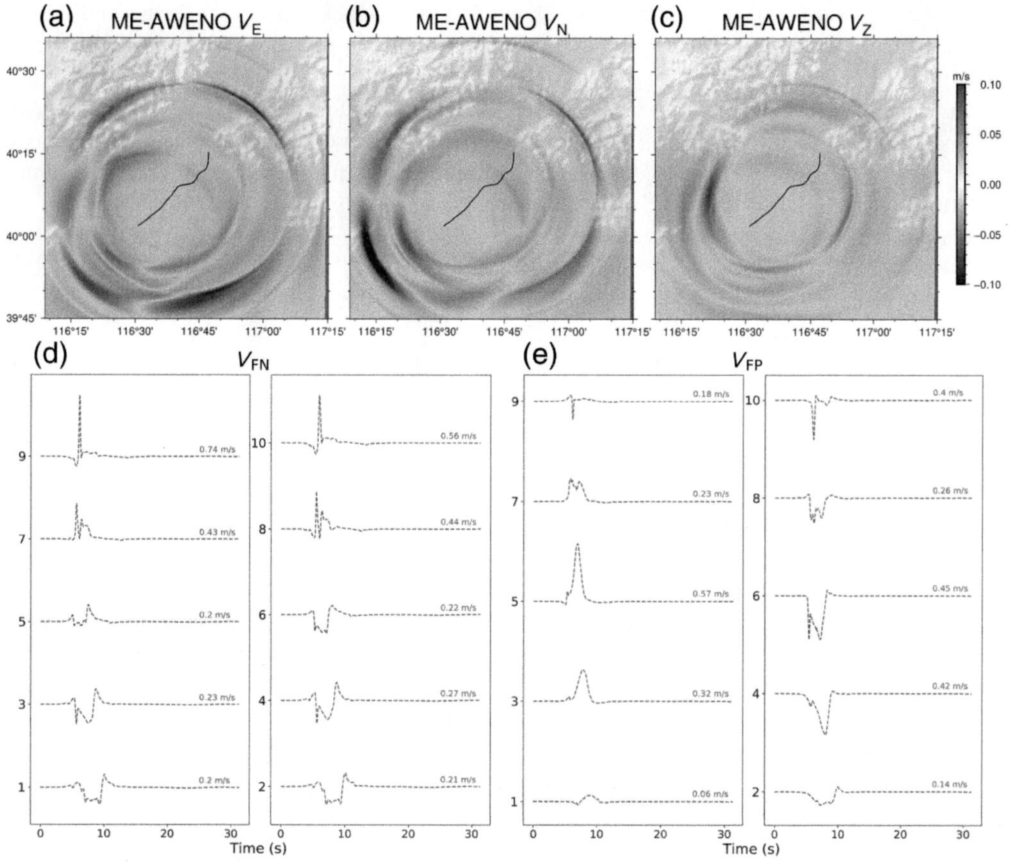

Figure 8. The three-component seismic wavefields snapshots at approximately 15 s simulated by the ME-AWENO scheme are depicted in panels (a–c), for which the solid-black line denotes the surface trace of the Shunyi–Liangxiang fault. The fault-normal velocity component V_{FN} and the fault-parallel velocity component V_{FP}, recorded at each station indicated in Figure 7a, are depicted in panels (d) and (e), respectively. The values following the waveform indicate the corresponding maximum absolute velocity. The color version of this figure is available only in the electronic edition.

feedback. This work is supported by the National Key R&D Program of China (2023YFC300 7402), Shenzhen Science and Technology Program (JCYJ2024 1202125759001), Guangdong Provincial Key Laboratory of Geophysical High-resolution Imaging Technology (2022B12 12010002), and High Level Special Funds (G03050K001). This work is supported by the Center for Computational Science and Engineering at the Southern University of Science and Technology.

References

Aki, K., and P. G. Richards (1980). The double-couple solution in an infinite homogeneous medium, in *Quantitative Seismology, Theory and Methods*, J. Ellis (Editor), Vol. 1, Univeristy Science Books, Sausalito, California, 77–84.

Alimoradi, A., and J. L. Beck (2015). Machine-learning methods for earthquake ground motion analysis and simulation, *J. Eng. Mech.* **141,** no. 4, 04014147, doi: 10.1061/(ASCE)EM.1943-7889.0000869.

Ba, Z., J. Zhao, J. Liang, Y. Zhang, and Y. Zhang (2022). Simulation of strong ground motion in Beijing area based on finite fault source model: Taking the 1679 Sanhe-Pinggu M8 earthquake as an example, *J. Seismol. Res.* **45,** no. 03, 479–488 (in Chinese).

Bayliss, A., K. E. Jordan, B. J. LeMesurier, and E. Turkel (1986). A fourth-order accurate finite-difference scheme for the computation of elastic waves, *Bull. Seismol. Soc. Am.* **76,** no. 4, 1115–1132.

Brocher, T. M. (2005). Empirical relations between elastic wavespeeds and density in the Earth's crust, *Bull. Seismol. Soc. Am.* **95,** no. 6, 2081–2092.

Chen, X., Y. Quan, and J. M. Harris (1996). Seismogram synthesis for radially layered media using the generalized reflection/transmission coefficients method: Theory and applications to acoustic logging, *Geophysics* **61,** no. 4, 1150–1159.

Chu, S., A. Kurganov, and R. Xin (2023). New more efficient A-WENO schemes, available at https://ssrn.com/abstract=4486288 (last accessed July 2024).

Dabaghi, M., and A. Der Kiureghian (2017). Stochastic model for simulation of near-fault ground motions, *Earthq. Eng. Struct. Dynam.* **46,** no. 6, 963–984.

Dong, S., X. W. Yu, and W. B. Zhang (2023). Modified characteristic variable method and its application to seismic source dynamics, *Chin. J. Geophys.* **66,** no. 05, 2051–2068 (in Chinese).

Dreger, D., G. Hurtado, A. Chopra, and S. Larsen (2011). Near-field across-fault seismic ground motions, *Bull. Seismol. Soc. Am.* **101,** no. 1, 202–221.

Harris, R. A., M. Barall, R. Archuleta, E. Dunham, B. Aagaard, J. P. Ampuero, H. Bhat, V. Cruz-Atienza, L. Dalguer, and P. Dawson (2009). The SCEC/USGS dynamic earthquake rupture code verification exercise, *Seismol. Res. Lett.* **80,** no. 1, 119–126.

Hisada, Y., and J. Bielak (2003). A theoretical method for computing near-fault ground motions in layered half-spaces considering static offset due to surface faulting, with a physical interpretation of fling step and rupture directivity, *Bull. Seismol. Soc. Am.* **93,** no. 3, 1154–1168.

Hisada, Y., and S. Tanaka (2021). What is fling step? Its theory, simulation method, and applications to strong ground motion near surface fault ruptures, *Bull. Seismol. Soc. Am.* **111,** no. 5, 2486–2506.

Jiang, G.-S., and C.-W. Shu (1996). Efficient implementation of weighted ENO schemes, *J. Comput. Phys.* **126,** no. 1, 202–228.

Jiang, Y., C.-W. Shu, and M. Zhang (2014). Free-stream preserving finite difference schemes on curvilinear meshes, *Methods Appl. Anal.* **21,** no. 1, 1–30.

Joshi, A., B. Raman, C. K. Mohan, and L. R. Cenkeramaddi (2024). Application of a new machine learning model to improve earthquake ground motion predictions, *Nat. Hazards.* **120,** no. 1, 729–753.

Kalkan, E., and S. K. Kunnath (2006). Effects of fling step and forward directivity on seismic response of buildings, *Earthq. Spectra* **22,** no. 2, 367–390.

Kosloff, D., D. Kessler, A. Q. Filho, E. Tessmer, A. Behle, and R. Strahilevitz (1990). Solution of the equations of dynamic elasticity by a Chebychev spectral method, *Geophysics* **55,** no. 6, 734–748.

LeVeque, R. J. (2002). *Finite Volume Methods for Hyperbolic Problems,* Cambridge University Press, Cambridge, United Kingdom.

Li, B., A. Gabriel, T. Ulrich, C. Abril, and B. Halldorsson (2023). Dynamic rupture models, fault interaction and ground motion simulations for the segmented Húsavík-Flatey fault zone, northern Iceland, *J. Geophys. Res.* **128,** no. 6, e2022JB025886, doi: 10.1029/2022JB025886.

Li, Y., Z. Wang, Z. Zhang, Y. Gu, and H. Yu (2024). A physics-based seismic risk assessment of the Qujiang fault: From dynamic rupture to disaster estimation, *Int. J. Disast. Risk Sci.* **15,** no. 1, 165–177.

Li, Y., Z. Zhang, W. Wang, and X. Feng (2022). Rapid estimation of earthquake fatalities in mainland China based on physical simulation and empirical statistics—A case study of the 2021 Yangbi earthquake, *Int. J. Environ. Res. Publ. Health.* **19,** no. 11, 6820.

Liu, D., and B. Duan (2018). Scenario earthquake and ground-motion simulations in North China: Effects of heterogeneous fault stress and 3D basin structure, *Bull. Seismol. Soc. Am.* **108,** no. 4, 2148–2169.

Liu, T., Y. Luan, and W. Zhong (2012). A numerical approach for modeling near-fault ground motion and its application in the 1994 Northridge earthquake, *Soil Dynam. Earthq. Eng.* **34,** no. 1, 52–61.

Lyu, M., K. Chen, H. Chai, J. Geng, S. Zhang, and L. Fang (2022). Joint inversion of InSAR and high-rate GNSS displacement waveforms for the rupture process of the 2022 Qinghai Menyuan M 6.9 earthquake, *Chin. J. Geophys.* **65,** no. 12, 4725–4738 (in Chinese).

Mavroeidis, G. P., and A. S. Papageorgiou (2003). A mathematical representation of near-fault ground motions, *Bull. Seismol. Soc. Am.* **93,** no. 3, 1099–1131.

Meade, B. J. (2007). Algorithms for the calculation of exact displacements, strains, and stresses for triangular dislocation elements in a uniform elastic half space, *Comput. Geosci.* **33,** no. 8, 1064–1075.

Nikkhoo, M., and T. R. Walter (2015). Triangular dislocation: An analytical, artefact-free solution, *Geophys. J. Int.* **201,** no. 2, 1119–1141.

Niu, P., Z. Han, K. Li, L. Lyu, and P. Guo (2023). The 2022 Mw 6.7 Menyuan earthquake on the northeastern margin of the Tibetan Plateau, China: Complex surface ruptures and large slip, *Bull. Seismol. Soc. Am.* **113,** no. 3, 976–996.

Okada, Y. (1992). Internal deformation due to shear and tensile faults in a half-space. *Bull. Seismol. Soc. Am.* **82,** no. 2, 1018–1040.

Sangeetha, S., and S. T. G. Raghukanth (2022). Broadband ground motion simulations for Northeast India, *Soil Dynam. Earthq. Eng.* **154,** 107,120.

Shen, W., M. H. Ritzwoller, D. Kang, Y. Kim, F.-C. Lin, J. Ning, W. Wang, Y. Zheng, and L. Zhou (2016). A seismic reference model for the crust and uppermost mantle beneath China from surface wave dispersion, *Geophys. J. Int.* **206,** no. 2, 954–979.

Stewart, J. P., S.-J. Chiou, J. D. Bray, R. W. Graves, P. G. Somerville, and N. A. Abrahamson (2002). Ground motion evaluation procedures for performance-based design, *Soil Dynam. Earthq. Eng.* **22,** nos. 9/12, 765–772.

Stupazzini, M., R. Paolucci, and H. Igel (2009). Near-fault earthquake ground-motion simulation in the Grenoble valley by a high-performance spectral element code, *Bull. Seismol. Soc. Am.* **99,** no. 1, 286–301.

Wang, W., Z. Zhang, W. Zhang, H. Yu, Q. Liu, W. Zhang, and X. Chen (2022). CGFDM3D-EQR: A platform for rapid response to earthquake disasters in 3D complex media, *Seismol. Res. Lett.* **93,** no. 4, 2320–2334.

Withers, K. B., M. P. Moschetti, and E. M. Thompson (2020). A machine learning approach to developing ground motion models from simulated ground motions, *Geophys. Res. Lett.* **47,** no. 6, e2019GL086690, doi: 10.1029/2019GL086690.

Xu, T., and Z. Zhang (2024). Numerical simulation of 3D seismic wave based on alternative flux finite-difference WENO scheme, *Geophys. J. Int.* **238,** no. 1, 496–512.

Yadav, K. K., and V. K. Gupta (2017). Near-fault fling-step ground motions: Characteristics and simulation, *Soil Dynam. Earthq. Eng.* **101,** 90–104.

Zhang, W., Y. Shen, and X. Chen (2008). Numerical simulation of strong ground motion for the Ms 8.0 Wenchuan earthquake of 12 May 2008, *Sci. China Earth Sci.* **51,** no. 12, 1673–1682.

Zhang, W., Z. Zhang, M. Li, and X. Chen (2020). GPU implementation of curved-grid finite-difference modelling for non-planar rupture dynamics, *Geophys. J. Int.* **222,** no. 3, 2121–2135.

Zhang, Z., W. Zhang, and X. Chen (2014). Three-dimensional curved grid finite-difference modelling for non-planar rupture dynamics, *Geophys. J. Int.* **199,** no. 2, 860–879.

Zhang, Z., W. Zhang, X. Chen, P. Li, and C. Fu (2017). Rupture dynamics and ground motion from potential earthquakes around Taiyuan, China, *Bull. Seismol. Soc. Am.* **107,** no. 3, 1201–1212.

Zhao, S., Z. Yu, H. Yu, D. Xu, X. Chen, Z. Zhang, X. Lyu, J. Sun, F. Wang, and G. Luo (2025). Evaluation of earthquake dynamic rupture simulation parameters: A case study on the northern segment of the Shunyi-Liangxiang fault, *Chin. J. Geophys.* doi: 10.6038/cjg2025S0478 (in Chinese).

Manuscript received 12 February 2025
Published online 8 July 2025

Improving the Transportability of a Deep Learning Denoising Model Using Transfer Learning Techniques

Louis Quinones*[1] and Rigobert Tibi[1]

Abstract

The adoption of machine learning techniques in the seismology community has led to great performance improvements in several areas, including signal processing. Specifically, the development of deep learning–based seismic waveform denoising models has the potential to yield improvements in signal detection capabilities for networks operating in particularly noisy environments. Recent advancements in the design of these deep learning denoising models have included the incorporation of continuous and discrete wavelet transform functions into the network architecture to improve the learning capabilities and efficiency of said models. These wavelet transform–based seismic denoising models have shown improved denoising capabilities in regions where there is good agreement between the data features present in the training and evaluation datasets. However, questions remain about the overall transportability of these models to other monitoring regions. Here, we will determine the baseline transportability of a newly developed multilevel wavelet-transform convolutional neural network (MWCNN) seismic denoising model. We accomplish this by taking a version of the MWCNN denoising model trained on data collected from the Utah region and evaluating its denoising performance on datasets collected from the neighboring Nevada region, which differ with regard to monitoring sensor types and event histories. We find that there is a notable variability in denoising performance related to the degree of similarity between the initial and new target datasets. The most notable difference in denoising performance is the ability of the denoising model to preserve accurate amplitude information associated with the signal energy present in the waveform data. Finally, we evaluate the ability of transfer learning techniques to improve the transportability of the MWCNN denoising model. We find that although there is still a performance gap present in the denoising results of the MWCNN model, transfer learning did yield improved results.

Cite this article as Quinones, L., and R. Tibi (2025). Improving the Transportability of a Deep Learning Denoising Model Using Transfer Learning Techniques, *Seismol. Res. Lett.* **97**, 173–186, doi: 10.1785/0220250053.

Introduction

Advancements in the applications of machine learning (ML) methods in the field of seismology have led to sharp increases in the overall usage of ML models across the entire seismic data processing pipeline. From the incorporation of signal detection models (Ross *et al.*, 2018; Mousavi *et al.*, 2019, 2020; Zhu and Beroza, 2019) to association algorithms (McBrearty *et al.*, 2019; Ross *et al.*, 2019; Le Bras *et al.*, 2021) to including work on improving waveform denoising techniques (Zhu *et al.*, 2019; Tibi *et al.*, 2021; Quinones and Tibi, 2024), the use of ML algorithms has become a necessary consideration when designing and performing seismic experiments. As such, it can often be overwhelming for those unfamiliar with the intricate details of each individual ML model to determine which model is best suited for their experiments. It can be tempting to simply apply a previously trained version of a model that appears to perform well on other datasets to one's own, believing that the model should achieve comparable results without the need to retrain it. Studies comparing the performance of various models have been conducted and found that significant performance gaps exist between different models pertaining to factors such as model architecture, initial training datasets, and discrepancies between initial and target dataset feature distributions (Duro *et al.*, 2012; Srivastava *et al.*, 2021; Wang *et al.*, 2021; Münchmeyer *et al.*, 2022). The process of curating a dataset

1. Sandia National Laboratories, Albuquerque, New Mexico, U.S.A., https://orcid.org/0000-0003-3659-0447 (LQ); https://orcid.org/0000-0002-4784-3940 (RT)

*Corresponding author: laquino@sandia.gov

suitable for ML model training is expensive because it requires significant investments in terms of both time and effort. For this reason, one must make careful considerations to ensure that the datasets used to train new models are representative of the task the model is designed for (Paullada *et al.*, 2021; Paleyes *et al.*, 2022). The question of how transportable any previously developed ML model is to other datasets is a fundamental question that must be considered before the model is used. As we demonstrate in this study, the transportability of any ML model is heavily reliant on the differences of the features present and their overall distributions between the initial training and target evaluation datasets. Techniques such as transfer learning (Dai *et al.*, 2007; Pan and Yang, 2010; Weiss *et al.*, 2016; Niu *et al.*, 2020; Zhuang *et al.*, 2020) can be implemented to try to improve the transportability of ML models by bridging the gaps that may exist between initial and target datasets. Transfer learning techniques can be separated into categories dealing with attempting to either train a model to perform a new task or training a model to better perform on a new dataset (Dai *et al.*, 2007). For our purposes, we are primarily concerned with the latter type of transfer learning, referred to as homogeneous transfer learning techniques (Dai *et al.*, 2007; Jiang and Zhai, 2007; Pan and Yang, 2010), wherein our initial and target datasets are composed of the same type of features but contain different distributions of said features. This difference in feature distributions can hinder the performance of an ML model. Specifically, our goal is to examine the baseline transportability of our previously developed deep learning seismic denoising model (Quinones and Tibi, 2024) and whether transfer learning techniques can improve it.

ML-based seismic denoising models offer the potential to improve signal detection capabilities across monitoring networks through the application of time-dependent filters that also retain accurate phase arrival time and signal amplitude information (Zhu *et al.*, 2019; Tibi *et al.*, 2021; Quinones and Tibi, 2024). Our previously developed multilevel wavelet-transform convolutional neural network (MWCNN) seismic denoising model was able to achieve excellent denoising results in the Utah region (Quinones and Tibi, 2024). In the case of the initial study, we both trained and evaluated the performance of the MWCNN model on data collected from the same set of stations over different periods of time, meaning that our initial training and target evaluation datasets were, as to be expected, highly similar to one another in terms of feature distributions. In the case of the seismic denoising models, the features we are primarily concerned with are the frequency bands for which there is signal or noise energy present because this is how our model interacts with our datasets. Thus, for our purposes, we would consider two datasets to have similar feature distributions if both waveform datasets have consistent frequency bands where signal or noise energy is present. However, if two waveform datasets have entirely different frequency bands where signal or noise energy is present, we would consider these datasets to have different feature distributions. Here, we seek to first establish the baseline transportability of the MWCNN model by evaluating the model's denoising performance on two other datasets from the neighboring Nevada region (University of Nevada, Reno, 1971; dePolo, 2008; Mendoza and Hartzell, 2009; Ruhl *et al.*, 2016; Bormann *et al.*, 2021). The first of these datasets is one in which we intentionally seek to collect data that differ in terms of feature distributions when compared with the initial training dataset from the Utah region. The purpose in this case is to evaluate model transportability to regions with sensor types that differ from those used to train the initial Utah data-based MWCNN (UT) model. The second dataset instead comprises data collected from stations from the Nevada region, which the initial UT model was not trained on but that has similar feature distributions, such as signal and noise frequency content, to that of the initial Utah training dataset. To better assess the performance of the UT model on these two Nevada datasets, we also train a new version of the MWCNN model on solely data collected from the Nevada region, hereafter referred to as the Nevada (NV) model. Using the denoising results achieved by both the UT and NV models, we establish how large a performance gap currently exists when examining both dissimilar and similar datasets and thus quantify the transportability of denoising models created using the MWCNN model architecture. Finally, we experimented with transfer learning techniques to assess whether a seismic denoising model that was initially trained on data from the Utah region can achieve better results when examining data collected from the Nevada region. The denoising results of this new transfer learning model, hereafter referred to as the UT–TL model, along with the results of the UT and NV models are all compared with one another to determine the overall transportability of models created using the MWCNN architecture and to give guidance on cases for which the incorporation of transfer learning techniques may be necessary.

Methods and Data

The original MWCNN denoising model was trained on data from the Utah region recorded by the University of Utah Seismograph Stations (UUSS) network (Fig. 1). The waveform data were composed of local to near-regional distance scale earthquake and explosion recordings from a selected number of stations that ranged from those installed in quiet rural areas to those in noisy urban environments (The University of Utah, 1962; Tibi *et al.*, 2021). All the selected stations were three-component broadband or short-period sensors recording at 100 Hz sampling rate, which were active over the period 2009–2018. For this model, the initial training data and target evaluation datasets had high degrees of similarity to one another because both datasets came from the same set of stations in the same monitoring environments. To assess and

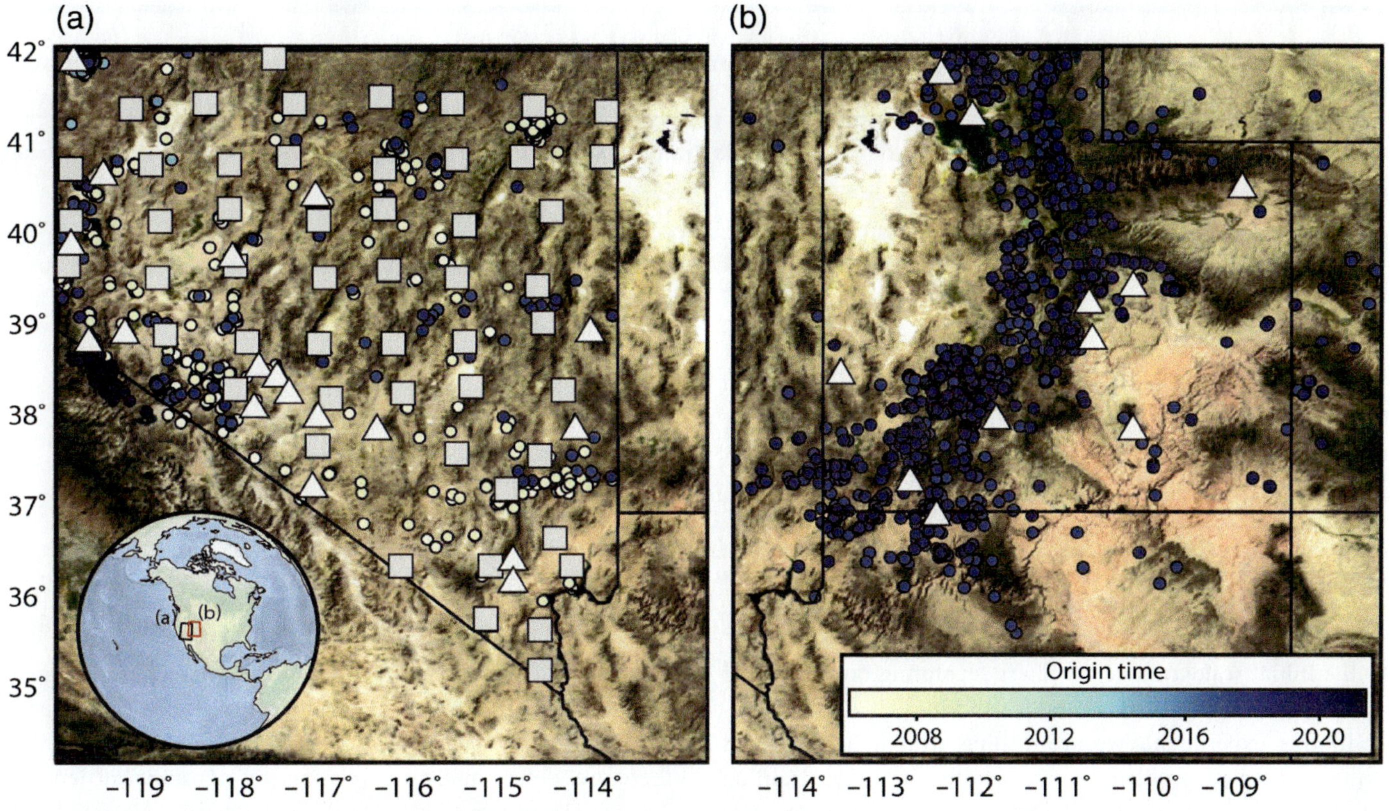

Figure 1. Map views of the (a) Nevada and (b) Utah regions showing the locations of the earthquakes and explosions (circles) whose recordings are used in this study. Also shown are the selected stations from the UU, NN, LB (triangles), and TA (squares) networks. The events are color coded based on their origin times as shown by the color bar in (b). The global context of the two monitoring regions is depicted in the inset in (a).

quantify the transportability of the denoising models created using the MWCNN architecture, we gathered two new datasets from the recordings of the neighboring Nevada region. These datasets are meant to represent two potential cases to use a previously trained version of a model on a new dataset. These two potential cases are one wherein the new evaluation dataset has the same set of features in a similar distribution to that of the initial training dataset and one wherein the distributions of the features are highly dissimilar to that of the initial training dataset. Both datasets collected from the Nevada region (Fig. 1) are composed of waveform data from earthquakes and explosions recorded at local to near-regional scale distances with a few key differences. In the case of the dataset with similar feature distributions to the Utah training data, the data are collected from three-component broadband and short-period sensors at uniform 100 Hz sampling rates, with the stations located in a similar mix of rural and urban environments around areas of high seismic activity. Meanwhile, the dataset with dissimilar feature distribution is composed of waveform data collected from the transportable array (TA) broadband stations, which were active in Nevada from 2006 to 2008. In this case, the data from stations installed at a set of uniform distances from one another across the entirety of the state (Meltzer *et al.*, 1999) were uniformly sampled at 40 Hz. This uniform station distribution led to a greater degree of near-regional distance waveform recordings compared with the Utah training dataset, further decreasing the overall similarity of the feature distributions between the two datasets. The exact number of waveforms along with information about the stations used to create each of these three datasets is reported in Table 1.

Model architecture and training

The development of the MWCNN model architecture and model training procedure followed to create the UT, NV, and UT–TL models are described by Quinones and Tibi (2024) and are summarized here.

The MWCNN network has a U-net style architecture (Ronneberger *et al.*, 2015) that incorporates discrete wavelet transform functions as substitutes for traditional pooling layers common to other convolutional neural networks (Liu *et al.*, 2019; Tian *et al.*, 2023). Each model is trained in a supervised manner with a defined set of labeled data representing the model targets. Training time is controlled by early stopping with a patience of 30 epochs. The model inputs are the real and imaginary parts of scalogram of the "noisy" waveform segment, consisting of a mixture of signal and noise energy. The model outputs are a pair of mask operators that when applied

TABLE 1
Waveform Counts and Metadata Information Associated with Each of the Datasets Used to Train and Evaluate the Denoising Models

Parameter	Utah Training Dataset	Nevada Training Dataset	Nevada Real-World Waveform Dataset
Signal waveforms	4,463	1,590	–
Noise waveforms	10,672	11,201	–
Waveform count	267,780	159,000	55,530
Station count	11	70	13
Time period	2009–2018	2006–2008	2014–2021
Networks	UU	NN, TA	NN, LB
Station types	BB, SP	BB, SP	BB, SP
Sampling rate (Hz)	100	40, 100	100

Network codes follow abbreviations used by the Incorporated Research Institutes of Seismology (IRIS) and are the University of Utah Seismograph Stations Network (UU, The University of Utah, 1962), Western Great Basin/Eastern Sierra Nevada Network (NN, University of Nevada, Reno, 1971), and the Leo Brady Network (LB). Station types are abbreviated as broadband (BB) and short-period (SP).

to the initial scalogram act as filters separating out the signal and noise energy present in the waveform.

In this experiment, we are dealing with a homogenous transfer learning problem, wherein both our initial training and new target datasets contain the same sets of features but with differing distributions of said features (Pan and Yang, 2010). Our goal with transporting our model to new monitoring regions is not to retrain our model to complete some entirely different tasks but rather to achieve similar levels of performance on different datasets. In addition, transfer learning processes can help in lowering the computational and dataset generation costs associated with training the denoising models from scratch for regions where there may be limited data. Here, to create the UT–TL model, we use an instance transfer learning procedure, wherein we use the model weights generated from the training of the model on the Utah-based training datasets because our new initial model weights rather than generating a new random initialization of model weights (Pan and Yang, 2010). Next, we use data from our new target dataset—the Nevada-based training dataset—to adjust and reassign the model weight values to better adapt to the differing feature distributions of the target dataset. Because our initial model weights come from a model previously trained to handle data of the same domain, the training time and required amounts of data are greatly reduced during this retraining process. The result of this instance transfer learning process is a new model that has the same structure as our initial denoising model but is better suited for the analysis of the new target dataset.

Data collection and construction

Each version of the MWCNN seismic denoising model is trained on what we define as noisy waveform datasets, which contain both signal and noise energy. Here, we define a signal as being a high-quality recording of a *P* phase arrival (signal-to-noise ratio [SNR] >4.0) associated with either an earthquake or explosion source at local to near-regional distances. We therefore define noise as relating to nontransient energy. The process of constructing both the Utah- and Nevada-based noisy waveform training datasets is the same and follows the procedure outlined by Quinones and Tibi (2024). First, all clean signal waveforms are 60 s segments from events that occurred within 250 km distance. The signal waveforms are initially band-pass filtered between 1 and 20 Hz using a filter order of 4. Second, the timing of the *P* phase is allowed to vary across the entirety of the noisy waveform segment. Finally, the amplitudes of the noise waveforms used are randomly scaled to diversify the SNR values of the constructed noisy waveforms (Quinones and Tibi, 2024). The total number of constructed noisy waveforms associated with each dataset is reported in Table 1.

The process of converting the constructed noisy waveforms into scalogram representations is outlined by Quinones and Tibi (2024) and is summarized here. First, our sets of noisy waveforms are separated into training, validation, and test datasets following a 70-15-15 distribution of waveforms for each set. All of the waveforms in the training and validation datasets, along with their associated clean signal and noise waveforms, are converted into scalograms using a continuous wavelet transform. The scalograms created from the clean signal and noise waveforms are then used with the scalogram of the noisy waveforms to calculate the mask operators used as labels for the supervised training purposes (Quinones and Tibi, 2024). The scalograms are treated as 2D arrays of data points for which initial size is based on the number of time samples present in the waveform segment (6000 time samples for 100 Hz data and 2400 time samples for 40 Hz data). To lower the memory cost needed to train and run the model, all scalograms are downsampled to 128 evenly spaced time and scale samples to fit the 128 × 128 input size parameter set by the MWCNN architecture. For model evaluation, we use the test datasets, wherein we follow the same procedure of converting the waveforms into scalogram representations to be input into the model. To generate the denoised signal and designaled noise scalograms, we take the output signal and noise masks and multiply them individually with the scalogram of the noisy waveform. Finally, we use the inverse wavelet transform to convert these scalogram products back into waveforms. For our purposes, we will focus on the denoising performance of each denoising model on the Nevada datasets.

In addition to evaluating each denoising model's performance using a set of constructed waveform data, we also evaluate the denoising performance of each model on real-world waveform recordings. Here, we gather a separate set of waveform data collected from a set of 19 stations operated by the University of Nevada, Reno (NN) network active from 2014 to 2021. These stations are a mixture of three-component broadband and short-period sensors and the waveforms collected from these stations represent consist of 1655 recordings from local to near-regional distances. In contrast to constructed waveforms for which the signal and noise components are perfectly known, for the real-world data these components are unknown; therefore, the denoising performance is evaluated using only the SNR gain achieved after denoising. For analysis purposes, we treat the real-world waveform dataset as a separate test dataset that is different to that of the training, validation, and test datasets associated with the constructed waveform dataset.

Dataset comparison

The primary factor to consider when assessing the transportability of our denoising models is the degree of similarity between our initial and target datasets. Here, we define initial dataset as the dataset used to train the model and define the target dataset as the dataset used to evaluate the model performance. Our goal is to create a highly transportable model, meaning that even in cases in which large differences exist between the initial and target datasets, we expect the model to perform at a high level. To accurately assess the transportability of our denoising models, we first assess how similar the initial and target datasets are to one another. The differences between the datasets come from each dataset containing different distributions of the features. Specifically, because of differences in monitoring sensor types, differences in network coverage, and recording periods (Table 1), we expect there to be differences in the characteristics (e.g., frequency contents) of the signal and noise recordings across the different datasets.

The datasets analyzed as part of this study can be classified as belonging to one of the two regions of origin, Utah or Nevada. In addition, datasets can be further classified as consisting of either constructed or real-world waveforms. We evaluate each model's denoising performance on both a set of constructed noisy waveform data from Nevada, referred to as the Nevada test dataset, and a set of real-world data, referred to as the Nevada real-world waveform dataset (Table 1). When comparing each dataset, we are primarily considering the distributions in the peak frequency value associated with the signal and noise energy present in each dataset (Fig. 2). For the constructed datasets, the peak frequency corresponds to the frequency of the peak amplitude in the spectrograms of the clean signal and noise waveforms associated with each noisy waveform. For the real-world event waveforms, the peak signal frequency values were determined by generating the spectrogram of each waveform and finding the frequency corresponding to the peak amplitude value within a 9 s window beginning at the signal arrival time. The peak noise frequency corresponds to the frequency of the spectrogram peak amplitude within the window prior to the phase arrival. We believe these two specific features associated with each waveform in each dataset are key in characterizing the datasets because the models are trained to identify different frequency bands along the time axis as consisting of signal energy, noise energy, or some combination of the two. Therefore, if the two datasets were to have large overlaps in the distributions of which frequencies contain signal or noise energy, then it could be said that those datasets are similar to one another, and it would be expected that the models have good transportability across the two datasets. However, it is important to note that these are not the sole defining features associated with each of the datasets. Other features, such as event-to-station distances, event magnitudes, noise characteristics, or propagation and station site effects, may also affect the transportability of the models. When we plot out the distributions of these features for the Nevada and Utah constructed waveforms, which encompass the training, validation, and test datasets from each region, we find that the Utah datasets contain a much wider band of signal frequency content than that of the Nevada datasets (Fig. 2a,b). Inversely, the Nevada constructed waveform dataset appears to have a more consistent distribution of noise energy present than the Utah dataset. In addition, the Nevada constructed waveform dataset has a much narrower frequency band of peak signal energy, which can be attributed to the fact that most of the events used to pull the signal waveforms are of near-regional distances from broadband sensors with lower 40 Hz sampling rates. This contrasts to the signal waveforms pulled for the Utah constructed waveform dataset, which primarily came from local distance events recorded on 100 Hz sampling short-period or broadband sensors (Quinones and Tibi, 2024). This could lead to issues when attempting to use a model trained on the Utah datasets in Nevada because the model could become either less restrictive or too conservative in defining what is signal or noise. This difference in peak frequency distribution is not present between the real-world datasets from both regions, though the Nevada dataset is significantly larger than the Utah dataset (Fig. 2c,d). This is because the real-world waveforms from both regions are coming

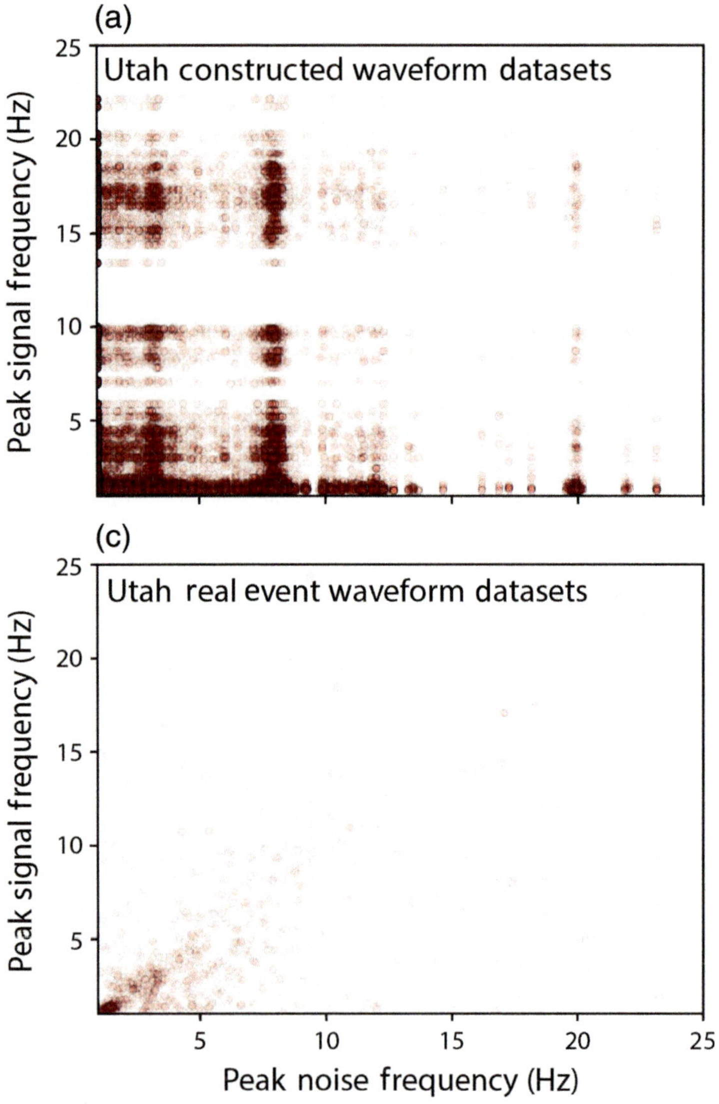

Figure 2. Comparison of the peak noise and signal frequency values associated with each of the waveforms. (a,b) Constructed waveform data, comprising the training, validation, and test datasets used in model training and evaluation. (c,d) Real event waveform data used to evaluate model performance. In (a, c) and (b, d), the data points for the Utah dataset are colored in red, and those for the Nevada dataset are colored in blue.

from similar sensor types that are in similar monitoring environments (Table 1). Thus, we should expect that a model that performs well on one dataset should also perform well on the other dataset because of the similarity between the datasets. It should be noted that both real-world datasets are more similar to the Utah constructed waveform dataset than the Nevada constructed waveform dataset. Although here we focus on these two specific features of the datasets to serve as measures of similarity, as mentioned earlier, it is possible that other features within the datasets also play significant roles in affecting the transportability of our models.

Performance evaluation

To evaluate the performance of our denoising models on the constructed Nevada test dataset, we use the normalized cross-correlation (CC) coefficient and signal-to-distortion ratio (SDR) metric values. Because in the case of the constructed test waveforms, we know what our desired output signal and noise waveforms should be, so we can compute CC coefficient values between the model outputs and ground-truth (GT) waveforms to quantify how well the model is able to reproduce the shapes of the GT waveforms. Meanwhile, we can also assess the denoising model's ability to preserve the amplitude information associated with the signal and noise energy using the SDR metric values, which are calculated using the following equation (Nakajima *et al.*, 2018):

$$\mathrm{SDR} = 10\log_{10}\frac{\|W_{\mathrm{GT}}\|^2}{\|W - W_{\mathrm{GT}}\|^2}. \tag{1}$$

In this equation, the array of amplitudes of the model output waveforms are denoted as W, and the array of amplitudes of the GT signal or noise waveform are denoted as W_{GT}. The structure of this equation means that the SDR value goes to infinity as the W and W_{GT} become increasingly equal. A well-trained and highly transportable denoising model would be able to maintain high performance with regards to these metrics with CC coefficient values near 1.0 and SDR values ≥10.0.

In the case of the real-world waveform evaluation datasets, we lack information on what our GT signal or noise waveforms should be, meaning we cannot truly measure the change in waveform shape or the amplitude distortion effects caused by the denoising process; thus, instead we measure the denoising model's ability to improve the SNR values of the waveforms. The SNR value of each of the real-world event waveforms is calculated using the following equation:

$$\mathrm{SNR} = 20\log_{10}\frac{A_S}{A_N}. \qquad (2)$$

Here, we define A_S as the root mean square (rms) value of the waveform amplitudes over a 9 s time window beginning at the signal arrival time. The A_N term represents the rms value of the waveform amplitudes over a 9 s time window ending 1 s before the signal arrival time. Theoretically, higher SNR values should correspond to waveforms with clear detectable signal arrivals. Although solely relying on SNR values will not entirely capture the denoising performance in the same way as using the CC and SDR metrics, it is still a useful representation of improvements in signal detection capabilities associated with using the MWCNN denoising model. A transportable denoising model would be able to achieve similar levels of SNR improvement across different datasets.

Results and Discussion

Evaluation of baseline model transportability

To evaluate the baseline transportability of our MWCNN denoising models, we compare the denoising performance of models trained on data from the Utah and Nevada regions on separate datasets collected from the Nevada region. Our goal is to determine whether the UT model can achieve similar levels of denoising performance on Nevada data compared with the NV model. By examining the performance of the NV model, we establish a target performance level for the UT model to be measured against and quantify what potential performance gaps exist between the models. In addition, if any consistent behaviors exist within the results across the different model versions, we could gain insight into potential weaknesses or research avenues that could be implemented to improve the MWCNN denoising model.

Baseline Nevada test waveform dataset results

The first dataset to be examined is the Nevada test waveform dataset. The denoising results of the UT and NV denoising models on the signal waveforms of the Nevada test dataset are shown in histogram form in Figure 3. Here, we observe that both the NV and UT denoising models were able to accurately preserve the shapes of the signal waveforms used to construct the Nevada test waveforms with the NV model achieving slightly better average CC (0.92) results compared with the UT model (0.87). The larger performance gap between the two model versions is found when examining the SDR metric values, in which we observe that on average, the UT model (14.0 dB) achieved significantly worse results than the NV model (20.1 dB). In fact, the average SDR metric value associated with the UT model results is slightly lower than that of the raw noisy Nevada test dataset waveforms (14.2 dB), meaning that the UT model introduced significant amplitude distortion. This behavior is most clearly illustrated with the peak near 0 dB in the SDR histogram (Fig. 3d), which, according to equation (1), implies that the UT model was generating distorted waveforms with amplitude values close to zero. The observed underperformance of the UT model may be traced back to the large differences in the distributions of frequency bands between the Utah and Nevada training datasets (Fig. 2). An example of a Nevada test waveform and its denoising results are shown in Figure 4, in which we can observe that the UT model introduced various artifacts into the output denoised waveform. These artifacts include significant amounts of noise energy on the edges of the waveform being passed through as being signal energy and a far more emergent signal arrival when compared to the GT. These artifacts likely arose because the UT model was not able to properly separate out the signal and noise energy present in the waveform because of conflicts between the characteristics (e.g., frequency contents) of said signal and noise energy present in this example waveform and the expected characteristics learned by the UT model from its initial training dataset. This implies that denoising models built using the MWCNN architecture are prone to issues of amplitude distortion when the feature distributions of training datasets differ from those of the target datasets. This results in missing signal energy (signal leakage; see Chen and Fomel, 2015) in some frequency bands or introduction of artifacts in other frequency bands. This same issue can be observed in the designaled noise waveforms in which the average SDR values associated with UT model (−2.7 dB) are far lower than those associated with the NV model (7.7 dB) (Fig. 5). However, we also observe that there is now also a large performance gap regarding the CC metric values. This larger performance gap between the two models can be attributed to the Utah training dataset having a wider band of frequencies associated with noise energy than the Nevada training dataset (Fig. 2a,b). In addition, the noisy waveforms from the Nevada test dataset were dominated primarily by signal energy rather than noise energy as can be inferred when comparing the average CC values with respect to the signal (0.80) and noise (0.35) components of the raw test data. The dominant component, signal in this case, is recovered with higher level of fidelity compared with the less dominant component (the noise) (Tibi *et al.*, 2021).

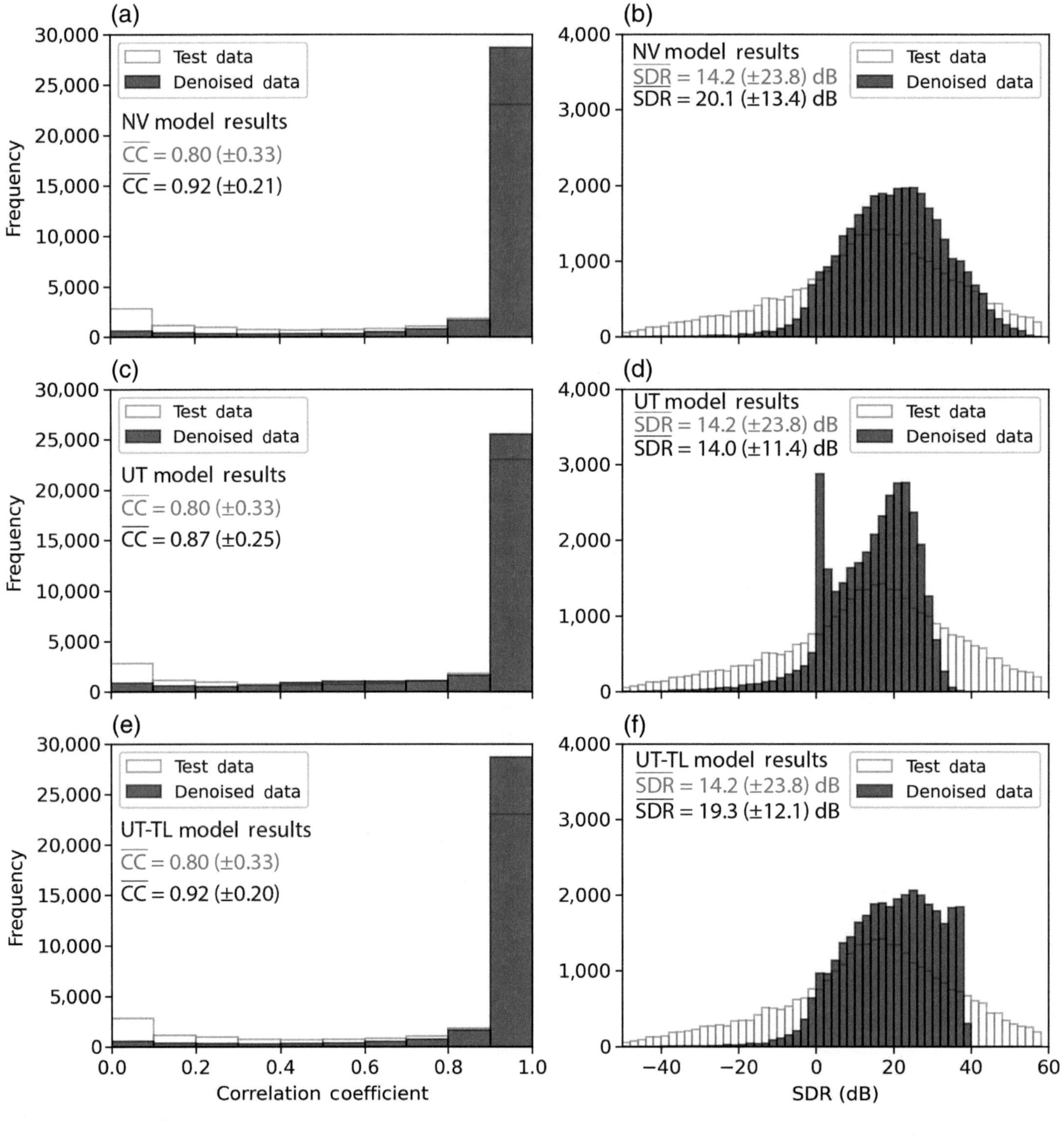

Figure 3. Histogram plots showing the model evaluation results on the Nevada test signal dataset for the (a,b) NV, (c,d) UT, and (e,f) UT–TL models. The left column (a,c,e) shows the cross-correlation (CC) coefficient values of the noisy test data (white bars) and denoised waveforms (dark gray bars) when cross correlated with the ground-truth (GT) signal waveforms used to construct the noisy test data. The right column (b,d,f) shows the signal-to-distortion ratio (SDR) values of the noisy test data (white bars) and denoised waveforms (dark gray bars), which are calculated by comparing the amplitude values of these waveforms to that of the GT signal waveforms used to construct the noisy test data. Noted in each plot are the average CC and SDR metric values for each dataset.

Baseline Nevada real-world waveform dataset results

The second dataset we examined was the set of real-world event recordings, referred to as the Nevada real-world waveform dataset. Here, we are looking to improve the waveform SNR values, which can translate to improved signal detection capabilities. The resulting distributions of SNR values associated with the output denoised signal waveforms are shown in Figure 6. Here, we observe that the average SNR values of waveforms output from the UT model (21.2 dB) are higher

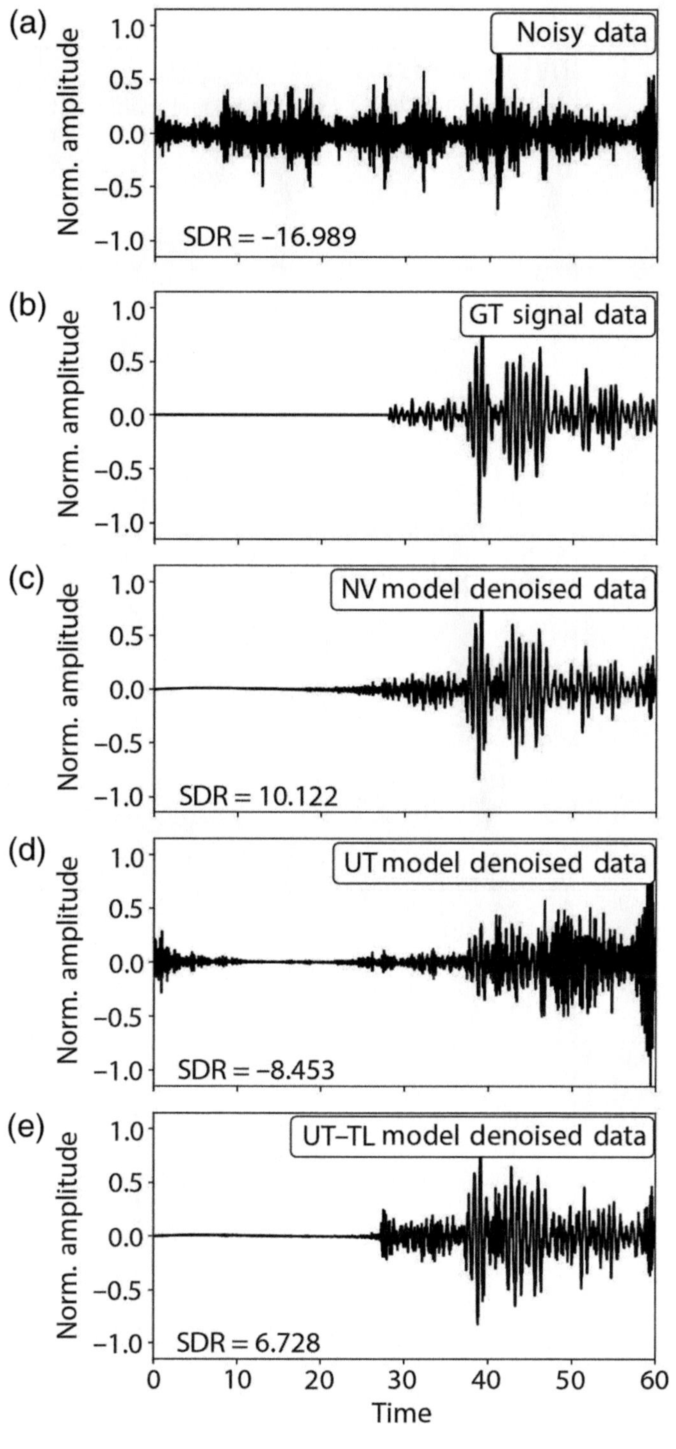

Figure 4. Plot of a noisy test data waveform (a) and the associated clean signal waveform (b) that was used to construct it. The plots of the denoised waveform created using the NV model (c), UT model (d), and UT–TL model (e) are also shown. The SDR metric values associated with the noisy and denoised waveforms calculated with respect to the clean signal waveform are noted for each waveform.

than those of the NV model (18.8 dB). This is noteworthy, considering that the Nevada real-world waveform and Nevada training datasets collected data from some of the same stations. This behavior can be traced back to the issue of differences in feature distributions between the datasets. Here, the distribution of the frequency bands, wherein peak signal and noise energy occurs that defines each dataset, suggests that the Nevada real-world waveform dataset is more similar to the Utah training dataset than it is to the Nevada training dataset (Fig. 2). This can be attributed to the fact that the majority of the Nevada training dataset is composed of data collected from the 40 Hz sampling broadband TA stations that were installed in a highly uniform distribution that are not present in the Nevada real-world waveform dataset. Meanwhile, both the Nevada real-world waveform and Utah training datasets are entirely composed of waveform data collected from 100 Hz sampling short-period and broadband sensors at similar monitoring distances and array patterns (Fig. 1). Again, this points to the direct correlation between the transportability of the MWCNN denoising models and the similarity in feature distributions of waveform datasets. This means that the denoising models do not necessarily need to be trained on data coming from a specific set of stations to achieve good denoising results if the frequency bands of signal and noise energy are similar to those of the initial training dataset. Furthermore, if a model is trained using collected data from a specific region of interest, one may not achieve better results if the training data have discrepancies with the target dataset.

In this case, both the UT and NV models were able to achieve high denoising performance on the Nevada real-world data, with both models being able to cleanly separate out the signal component of raw waveforms, as shown in the example waveform of Figure 7.

Evaluation of transfer learning techniques

We have observed that model performance degrades when there are discrepancies between the distributions of features in the initial and target datasets. Here, we investigate whether the incorporation of transfer learning techniques can yield a model that is better able to analyze disparate datasets using mixed training data. The UT model has good transportability when examining the later 2014–2021 Nevada data, but there exist transportability issues relating to significant amplitude distortion effects when examining the earlier 2006–2008 Nevada test dataset. We have incorporated transfer learning techniques (Pan and Yang, 2010) to determine whether we can train a denoising model that maintains high performance on the Nevada real-world waveform data while alleviating amplitude distortion issues that were observed when using the UT model on this dataset. We used instance transfer learning procedures taking the UT model weights as our new model initialization before feeding in the Nevada constructed waveforms in as our new training dataset to create the UT–TL model. We chose the UT model weights as our new initialization due to the Utah-based dataset being the larger of the two available training datasets and being more like the Nevada real-

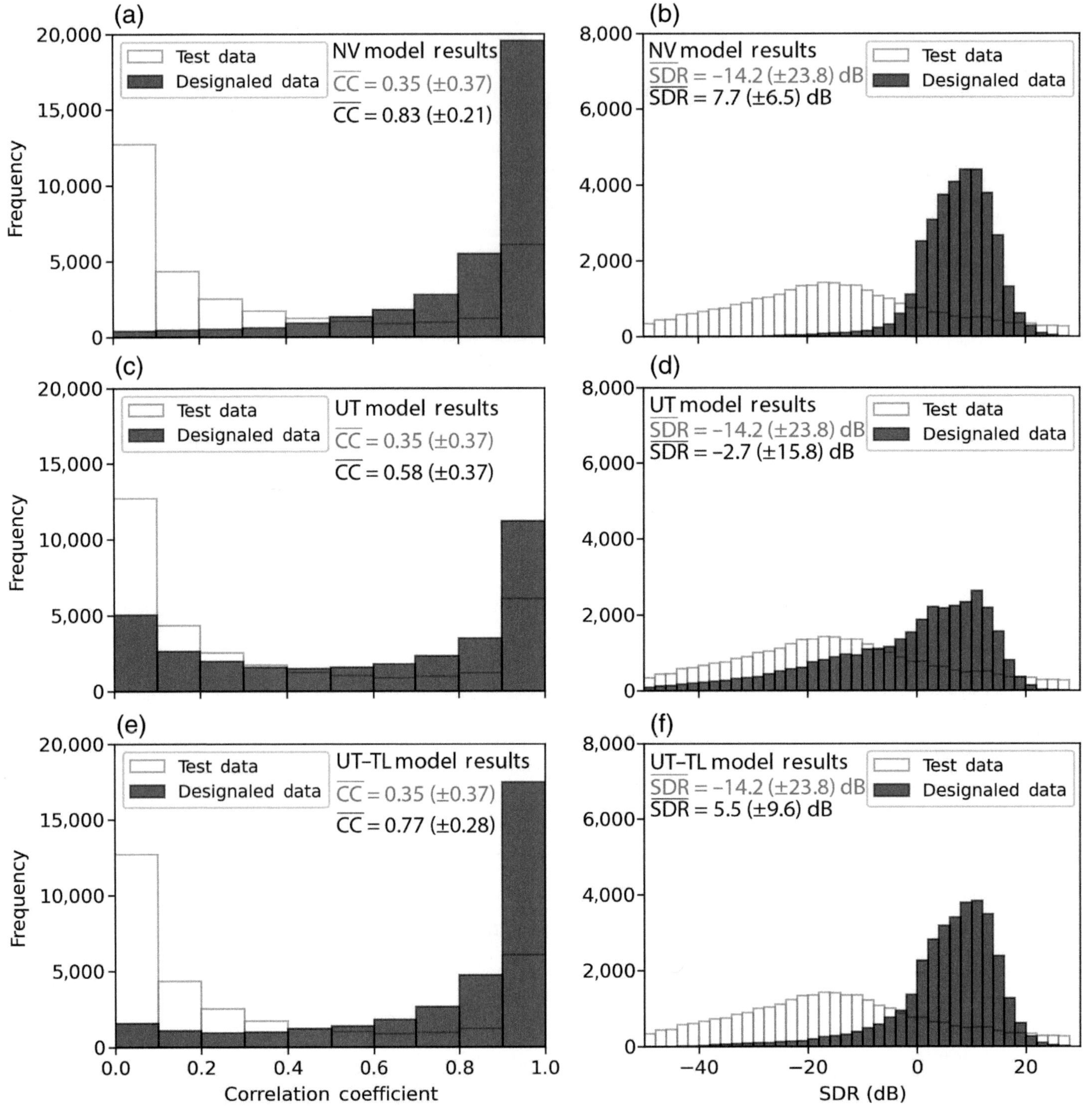

Figure 5. Histogram plots showing the model evaluation results on the Nevada test noise dataset for the NV (a,b), UT (c,d), and UT–TL (e,f) models. The left column (a,c,e) shows the cross-correlation (CC) values of the noisy test data (white bars) and denoised waveforms (dark gray bars) when cross correlated with the GT noise waveforms used to construct the noisy test data. The right column (b,d,f) shows the signal-to-distortion ratio (SDR) values of the noisy test data (white bars) and denoised waveforms (dark gray bars), which are calculated by comparing the amplitude values of these waveforms to that of the GT noise waveforms used to construct the noisy test data. Noted in each plot are the average CC and SDR metric values for each dataset.

world dataset. For this experiment, we used all available training data waveforms (159,000) from the Nevada training dataset, although further experimentation could focus on analyzing how much new training data would be required to achieve adequate performance results through transfer learning. Model training followed the same methodology as that conducted for both the UT and NV models and used the same hyperparameters, including learning rate settings, as those used for the initial MWCNN denoising model training (Quinones and Tibi, 2024). Overall, the training time required for the UT–TL model is significantly shorter than that required

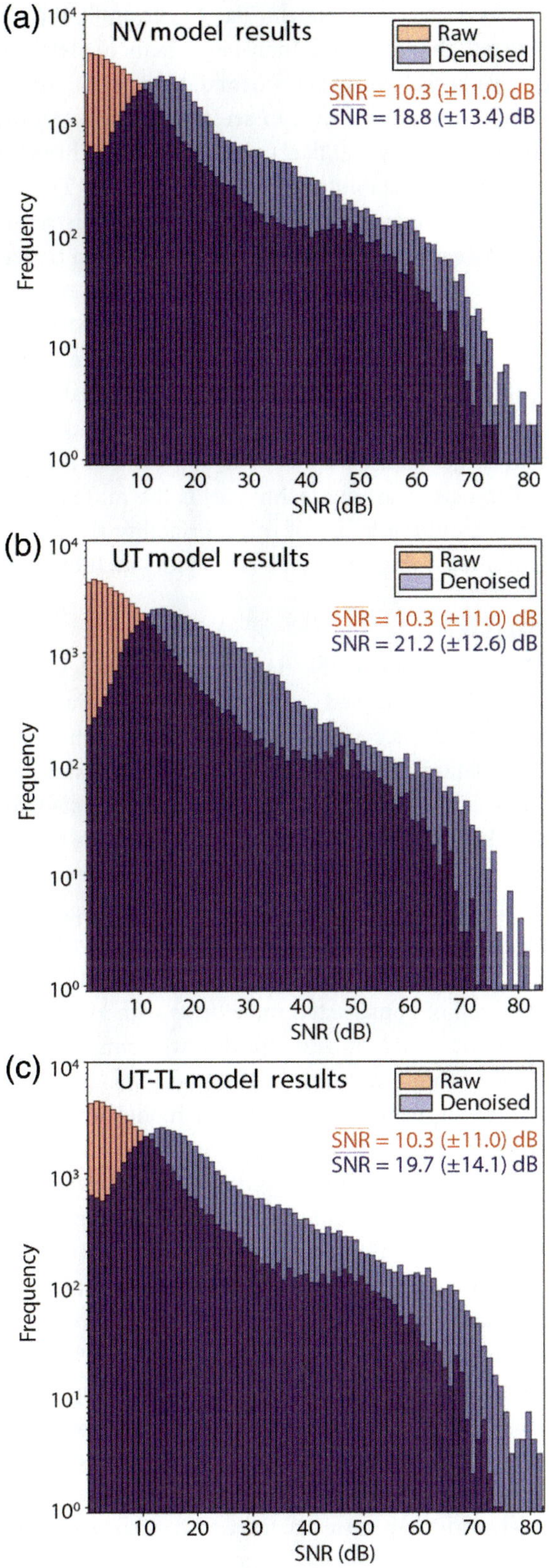

Figure 6. Histogram plots comparing the signal-to-noise ratio (SNR) values of the Nevada real-world raw waveform data (orange bars) and denoised waveform data (blue bars) created using (a) the NV model, (b) UT model, and (c) UT–TL model. The average SNR values of the raw and denoised waveform datasets are noted for each model.

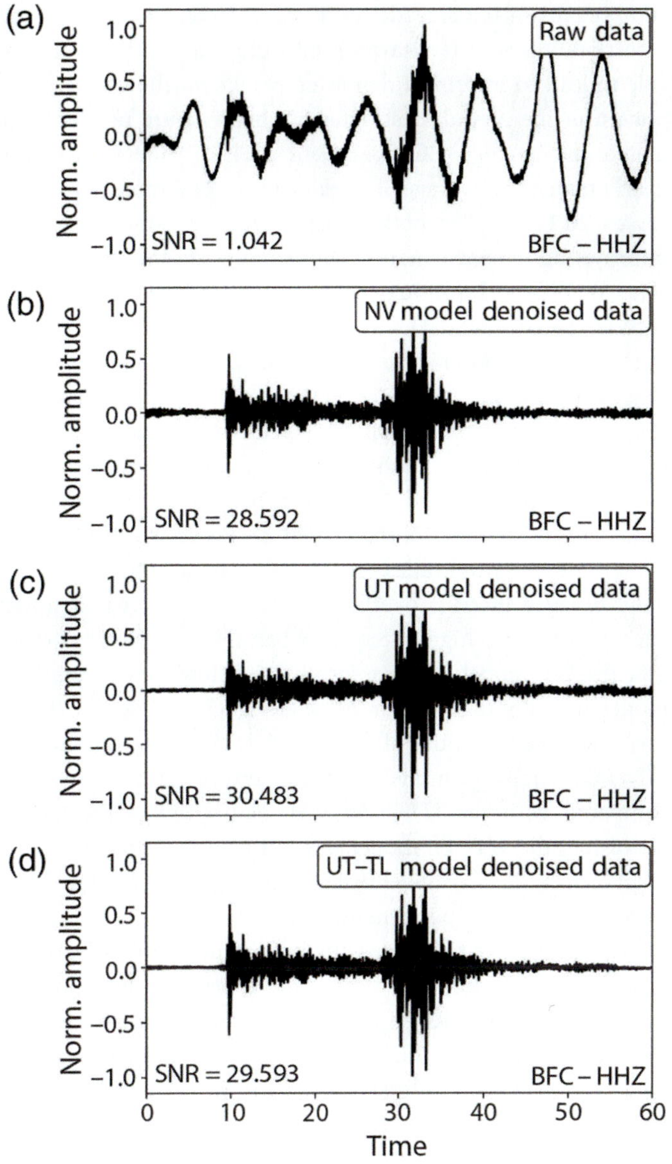

Figure 7. Waveform plots of an event recorded within the Nevada region showing (a) the raw waveform along with (b) the denoised versions of this same seismogram as obtained using the NV model, (c) the UT model, and (d) the UT–TL model. The associated SNR values calculated for each version of the waveform are noted.

for the UT model training (~4 versus 18 hr using four 32 GB central processing unit cores on a graphic processing units-accelerated machine) and required fewer epochs (38 versus 87) to reach its early stopping patience of 20 epochs.

Transfer learning Nevada test waveform dataset results

The UT–TL denoising model performance results are presented alongside those of the UT and NV denoising models in Figures 3 and 5. Our primary focus was on resolving the amplitude distortion issues associated with the signal and noise components of the Nevada test dataset. Here, we observe that incorporating transfer learning into the training process was able to lead to improved denoising results on the signal component of the Nevada test dataset, where we are now able to match the average CC coefficient metric value (0.92) and nearly match the average SDR value of the NV model (19.3 dB versus 20.1 dB). For both metrics, we were able to greatly improve upon performance compared with the UT model (Fig. 3). When examining our example waveform along with broader swaths of data, we note that the edge effects and unclear signal onset observed when using the UT model (Fig. 4d) have been removed and better defined, respectively (Fig. 4e). The denoised signal waveform produced by the UT–TL model does contain more low-frequency energy compared with the NV model waveform but still has a high SDR value (6.73). In addition, the UT–TL denoised waveform does contain higher amplitudes on the initial signal arrival, potentially because there is overlap between the signal and noise energy within this higher frequency band. We previously noted that the UT model performance is far below that of the NV model in both metrics for noise designaling (Fig. 5). Here too, the incorporation of transfer learning has led to the UT–TL denoising model showing improved performance compared with the UT model. However, unlike the signal denoising, the UT–TL model was not able to match the performance of the NV model in either average metric value. This may be because the performance gap between the UT and NV models is too large to bridge with the instance transfer learning process we incorporated. It can also be the case that some of the training data included in the Utah training dataset is detrimental to achieving high performance on the Nevada test dataset because of differences in features. More advanced transfer learning techniques, such as boosting transfer learning (Dai *et al.*, 2007), which assess the suitability of data points included as part of the initial training dataset for use in training a model to evaluate a different target dataset, could yield improved results. However, these boosting transfer learning techniques may require having greater knowledge about feature distributions in each dataset or having greater amounts of data than what we have available.

Transfer learning Nevada real-world waveform dataset results

Our secondary focus with incorporating transfer learning techniques was to ensure that our newly created UT–TL model would still perform well on the Nevada real-world waveform dataset. A drop in denoising performance on the Nevada real-world waveform dataset was expected because of the inclusion of the Nevada training data as part of the transfer learning process. We did record a slight drop in denoising performance for the UT–TL model compared with the UT model when examining the average SNR values of the denoised waveforms (19.7 dB versus 21.2 dB); however, the UT–TL model still outperformed the NV model (Fig. 6). Overall, the UT–TL denoising model achieved high-performance metric values on the Nevada real-world waveform dataset. When examining our example waveform, we can see that all three model versions produced very similar output, with all three models improving the detectability of the signal (Fig. 7). This implies that incorporating training data with a different distribution of features may lead to a minor performance drop on target datasets that are similar to the original training dataset. However, improvements in performance on target datasets that are dissimilar to that original training dataset are far more pronounced. This in combination with the comparatively lower computational cost of training an entirely new model to handle dissimilar target datasets leads us to suggest that the incorporation of transfer learning techniques is the more economical solution to handling issues of transportability associated with models trained using the MWCNN model architecture.

Conclusions

Here, we have explored the transportability issues related to denoising models trained using the MWCNN architecture, assessed performance issues that can arise when examining dissimilar datasets, and assessed whether transfer learning techniques can improve the transportability of said models. We trained three different denoising models, with two models trained on separate datasets from the Utah and Nevada regions and the third model trained on both datasets using transfer learning. We have evaluated the denoising performance of all three model versions on two different evaluation datasets, one composed of constructed waveforms with known components and the other of real-world waveforms from known events. We found that the performance of the denoising models created using the MWCNN model architecture is highly reliant on the training and target datasets having similar feature distributions, with large differences between the two resulting in decreased model performance. Specifically, we found that the UT denoising model performed worse than the NV denoising model on the Nevada test dataset. This is likely because of discrepancies between the peak frequency values of the noise and signal energy between the Nevada test and Utah training datasets. However, the UT denoising model outperformed the NV model on the Nevada real-world dataset even though the Nevada training dataset contained waveform data from some of the same stations that were used to compile the real-world waveform dataset. This showed that the MWCNN denoising models do not need to be trained on data from a specific set of stations to perform well on them if the initial training dataset was representative. We then explored the capabilities of transfer learning techniques to create a model that can achieve high performance on datasets that are either similar or dissimilar to the initial training dataset. We found that the transfer learning–based model was the most generally applicable model, able to achieve high performance on both evaluation datasets. However, it could not achieve the same level of performance on the individual Nevada test and real-world waveform datasets as the NV and UT models, respectively. In addition, training a model using transfer learning techniques was computationally less expensive than training an entirely new denoising model from scratch. Future avenues of research pertaining to improving the transportability of denoising models trained using the MWCNN architecture could focus on establishing the amount of new training data that would be required to achieve satisfactory results using transfer learning, exploring more advanced transfer learning techniques such as boosting transfer learning, or evaluating the effects of using broader initial training datasets that may contain dissimilar features on the overall performance of MWCNN denoising models.

Data and Resources

Waveform data were obtained from the EarthScope Consortium database available at http://ds.iris.edu/ds using network codes NN, UU, LB, and TA. The model architecture was constructed using the Keras Python library available at https://github.com/fchollet/keras. All websites were last accessed in June 2025.

Declaration of Competing Interests

The authors acknowledge that there are no conflicts of interest recorded.

Acknowledgments

This Low Yield Nuclear Monitoring (LYNM) research was funded by the National Nuclear Security Administration, Defense Nuclear Nonproliferation Research and Development (NNSA DNN R&D). The authors acknowledge important interdisciplinary collaboration with scientists and engineers from Los Alamos National Laboratories (LANL), Lawrence Livermore National Laboratories (LLNL), Nevada National Security Sites (NNSS), Pacific Northwest National Laboratories (PNNL), and Sandia National Laboratories (SNL). Sandia National Laboratories are a multimission laboratory managed and operated by National Technology and Engineering Solutions of Sandia, LLC, a wholly owned subsidiary of Honeywell International, Inc., for the U.S. Department of Energy's National Nuclear Security Administration under Contract Number DE-NA-0003525. The views expressed in the article do not necessarily represent the views of the U.S. Department of Energy or the U.S. Government. The authors thank Clinton Koch and all anonymous reviewers for their comments and suggestions that helped improve the article.

References

Bormann, J. M., E. A. Morton, K. D. Smith, G. M. Kent, W. S. Honjas, G. L. Plank, and M. C. Williams (2021). Nevada Seismological Laboratory rapid seismic monitoring deployment and data availability for the 2020 M_{ww} 6.5 Monte Cristo Range, Nevada, earthquake sequence, *Bull. Seismol. Soc. Am.* **92,** no. 2A, 810–822.

Chen, Y., and S. Fomel (2015). Random noise attenuation using local signal-and-noise orthogonalization, *Geophysics* **80,** WD1–WD9.

Dai, W., Q. Yang, G. Xue, and Y. Yu (2007). Boosting for transfer learning, *Proc. 24th Intl Conf. ML*, Oregon State University in Corvallis, Oregon, 20–24 June 2007, 193–200.

dePolo, C. M. (2008). Observations and reported effects of the February–April, 2008 Mogul-Somersett, Nevada earthquake sequence, *Nevada Bureau of Mines and Geology Open-File Rept. 2515.*

Duro, D. C., S. E. Franklin, and M. G. Dubé (2012). A comparison of pixel-based and object-based image analysis with selected ML algorithms for the classification of agricultural landscapes using SPOT-5 HRG imagery, *Remote Sens. Environ.* 118.

Jiang, J., and C. Zhai (2007). Instance weighting for domain adaptation in NLP, *Proc. 45th Ann. Meeting of the Assoc. Computational Linguistics*, Prague, Czech Republic, 23–30 June 2007, 264–271.

Le Bras, R., N. Arora, N. Kushida, P. Mialle, I. Bondar, E. Tomuta, F. K. Alamneh, P. Feitio, M. Villarroel, B. Vera, and A. Sudakov (2021). NET-VISA from cradle to adulthood. A machine-learning tool for seismo-acoustic automatic association, *Pure Appl. Geophys.* **178,** 2437–2458.

Liu, P., H. Zhang, W. Lian, and W. Zuo (2019). Multi-level wavelet convolutional neural networks, *IEEE Access* **7,** 74,973–74,985.

McBrearty, I. W., J. Gomberg, A. A. Delorey, and P. A. Johnson (2019). Earthquake arrival association with backprojection and graph theory, *Bull. Seismol. Soc. Am.* **109,** no. 6, 2510–2531, doi: 10.1785/0120190081.

Meltzer, A., R. Rudnick, P. Zeitler, A. Levander, G. Humphreys, K. Karlstrom, E. Ekstrom, C. Carlson, T. Dixon, M. Gurnis, *et al.* (1999). The USArray initiative, *Geol. Soc. Am. Today* **9,** 8–10.

Mendoza, C., and S. Hartzell (2009). Source analysis using regional empirical Green's functions: The 2008 Wells, Nevada, earthquake, *Geophys. Res. Lett.* **36,** no. 11, doi: 10.1029/2009GL038073.

Mousavi, S. M., W. L. Ellsworth, W. Zhu, L. Y. Chuang, and G. C. Beroza (2020). Earthquake transformer—An attentive deep-learning model for simultaneous earthquake detection and phase picking. *Nature Commun.* **11,** no. 1, 1–12.

Mousavi, S. M., W. Zhu, Y. Sheng, and G. C. Beroza (2019). Cred: A deep residual network of convolutional and recurrent units for earthquake signal detection, *Scientific Reports* **9,** no. 1, 1–14, doi: 10.1038/s41598-019-45748-1.

Münchmeyer, J., J. Woollam, A. Rietbrock, F. Tilmann, D. Lange, T. Bornstein, T. Diehl, C. Giunchi, F. Haslinger, D. Jozinović, *et al.* (2022). Which picker fits my data? A quantitative evaluation of deep learning based seismic pickers, *J. Geophys. Res.* **127,** no. 1, e2021JB023499.

Nakajima, H., Y. Takahasi, K. Kondo, and Y. Hisaminato (2018). Monaural source enhancement maximizing source-to-distortion ratio via automatic differentiation, available at http://arXiv.org/abs/1806.05791v1 (last accessed October 2024).

Niu, S., Y. Liu, J. Wang, and H. Song (2020). A decade survey of transfer learning (2010–2020), *IEEE Trans. Artif. Intellig.* **1,** no. 2, 151–166.

Paleyes, A., R. G. Urma, and N. D. Lawrence (2022). Challenges in deploying ML: A survey of case studies, *ACM Comput. Surv.* **55,** no. 6, 1–29.

Pan, S. J., and Q. Yang (2010). A survey on transfer learning, *IEEE Trans. Knowledge Data Eng.* **22,** no. 10, 1345–1359.

Paullada, A., I. D. Raji, E. M. Bender, E. Denton, and A. Hanna (2021). Data and its (dis) contents: A survey of dataset development and use in ML research, *Patterns* **2,** no. 11.

Quinones, L., and R. Tibi (2024). Denoising seismic waveforms using a wavelet-transform-based machine-learning method, *Bull. Sismol. Soc. Am.* **114,** 1777–1788, doi: 10.1785/0120230304.

Ronneberger, O., P. Fischer, and T. Brox (2015). U-Net: Convolutional networks for biomedical image segmentation, *Proc. Int. Conf. Med. Image Comput. Comput. Assist. Intervent*, 234–241.

Ross, Z. E., M.-A. Meier, E. Hauksson, and T. H. Heaton (2018). Generalized seismic phase detection with deep learning, *Bull. Seismol. Soc. Am.* **108,** no. 5A, 2894–2901, doi: 10.1785/0120180080.

Ross, Z. E., Y. Yue, M.-A. Meier, E. Hauksson, and T. H. Heaton (2019). PhaseLink: A deep learning approach to seismic phase association, *J. Geophys. Res.* **124,** 856–869, doi: 10.1029/2018JB016674.

Ruhl, C. J., R. E. Abercrombie, K. D. Smith, and I. Zaliapin (2016). Complex spatiotemporal evolution of the 2008 M_w 4.9 Mogul earthquake swarm (Reno, Nevada): Interplay of fluid and faulting, *J. Geophys. Res.* doi: 10.1002/2016JB013399.

Srivastava, S., A. V. Divekar, C. Anilkumar, I. Naik, V. Kulkarni, and V. Pattabiraman (2021). Comparative analysis of deep learning image detection algorithms, *J. Big Data* **8,** no. 1, 66.

The University of Utah (1962). University of Utah regional seismic network, International Federation of Digital Seismograph Networks, doi: 10.7914/SN/UU.

Tian, C., M. Zheng, W. Zuo, B. Zhang, Y. Zhang, and D. Zhang (2023). Multi-stage image denoising with the wavelet transform, *Pattern Recognit.* **134,** 109050.

Tibi, R., P. Hammond, R. Brogan, C. J. Young, and K. Koper (2021). Deep learning denoising applied to regional distance seismic data in Utah, *Bull. Seismol. Soc. Am.* **111,** 775–790, doi: 10.1785/0120200292.

University of Nevada, Reno (1971). Nevada seismic network [Data set], International Federation of Digital Seismograph Networks, doi: 10.7914/SN/NN.

Wang, P., E. Fan, and P. Wang (2021). Comparative analysis of image classification algorithms based on traditional ML and deep learning, *Pattern Recogn. Lett.* **141,** 61–67.

Weiss, K., T. M. Khoshgoftaar, and D. Wang (2016). A survey of transfer learning, *J. Big Data* **3,** 1–40.

Zhu, W., and G. C. Beroza (2019). Phasenet: A deep-neural-network-based seismic arrival-time picking method, *Geophys. J. Int.* **216,** no. 1, 261–273.

Zhu, W., S. M. Mousavi, and G. C. Beroza (2019). Seismic signal denoising and decomposition using deep neural networks, *IEEE Trans. Geosci. Remote Sens.* **57,** no. 11, 9476–9488, doi: 10.1109/TGRS.2019.2926772.

Zhuang, F., Z. Qi, K. Duan, D. Xi, Y. Zhu, H. Zhu, H. Xiong, and Q. He (2020). A comprehensive survey on transfer learning, *Proc. IEEE* **109,** no. 1, 43–76.

Manuscript received 17 February 2025
Published online 29 July 2025

Deep-Learning-Based Catalog of Background Seismicity and Aftershocks of the 2020–2021 Large Earthquakes Along the Alaska Peninsula

Yaqi Jie*[1,2], Songqiao Shawn Wei[1,2], Weiqiang Zhu[3], Jeffrey Freymueller[1], and Julie Elliott[1]

Abstract

The Alaska Peninsula section of the Alaska-Aleutian subduction zone shows significant along-strike variations in seismic activity and interseismic plate coupling. This region experienced the 2020 M_w 7.8 Simeonof megathrust, M_w 7.6 Sand Point strike-slip, and 2021 M_w 8.2 Chignik megathrust earthquakes. This study, utilizing deep learning techniques, presents a high-precision earthquake catalog, providing insights into background seismicity, aftershocks, and slab geometry. An abrupt change in the slab dip angle at 30–40 km depths in the Shumagin segment acted as a barrier to the Simeonof and Sand Point earthquake ruptures. The Simeonof event triggered more aftershocks in the overriding plate than the Chignik event, suggesting the overriding plate is more deformed and hydrated in the Shumagin segment. The Sand Point earthquake triggered numerous aftershocks in the overriding plate, delineating a fault in the overriding plate with similar geometry as the intraslab mainshock fault, but activated around seven days after the mainshock.

Cite this article as Jie, Y., S. S. Wei, W. Zhu, J. Freymueller, and J. Elliott (2025). Deep-Learning-Based Catalog of Background Seismicity and Aftershocks of the 2020–2021 Large Earthquakes Along the Alaska Peninsula, *Seismol. Res. Lett.* **97**, 187–203, doi: 10.1785/0220250072.

Supplemental Material

Introduction

The Alaska-Aleutian subduction zone is the most tectonically and seismically active convergent margin in North America. The Alaska Peninsula section of this subduction zone, with its diverse seismicity patterns, has been identified by the scientific community as a top site to address fundamental questions of subduction processes. This region, comprising several distinct segments identified through slip deficit distribution and seismic imaging, exhibits notable along-strike variations in both interseismic plate coupling and seismicity (Fig. 1). In particular, the "Shumagin seismic gap" first identified by Davies *et al.* (1981) remained unruptured by any $M > 8$ earthquakes for at least 200 yr, whereas the megathrust was ruptured by an M_w 8.3 earthquake in 1938 (Freymueller *et al.*, 2021) to the northeast and an M_w 8.6 earthquake in 1946 to the southwest (Davies *et al.*, 1981). In the fore-arc region between Kodiak Island and Shumagin Islands, the slip deficit decreases from northeast to southwest (Drooff and Freymueller, 2021; Xiao *et al.*, 2021), and slab dehydration and overriding plate hydration also become more extensive and intensive to the southwest (Wang *et al.*, 2025). These variations reflect the heterogeneous nature of the megathrust, likely influenced by sedimentary and crustal structures of the subducting slab, such as pre-existing fault systems (Shillington *et al.*, 2015), sediment layer thickness (Wei *et al.*, 2021), and the rigidity of the overriding plate (Shillington *et al.*, 2022).

Since 2020, a new megathrust sequence, including the 2020 M_w 7.8 Simeonof earthquake and the 2021 M_w 8.2 Chignik earthquake occurred offshore the Alaska Peninsula. Several coseismic slip models indicate that the 2020 Simeonof event ruptured the eastern part of the Shumagin gap at 25–45 km depths (Crowell and Melgar, 2020; Xiao *et al.*, 2021; Ye *et al.*, 2021). The slip occurred in localized patches, likely related to the rheological heterogeneity revealed by active-source *P*-wave tomography (Shillington *et al.*, 2022). Subsequently, the 2021 Chignik earthquake, located northeast of the 2020 Simeonof event and potentially triggered by it, ruptured the megathrust at 25–45 km depths and farther east into the 1938 M_w 8.3 earthquake rupture area (Elliott *et al.*, 2022; Liu *et al.*, 2022; Ye *et al.*, 2022). Active-source studies have identified significant changes in the plate interface dip angle and width (Shillington *et al.*,

1. Department of Earth and Environmental Sciences, Michigan State University, East Lansing, Michigan, U.S.A., https://orcid.org/0000-0003-3431-6583 (YJ); https://orcid.org/0000-0002-6217-0545 (SSW); https://orcid.org/0000-0003-0614-0306 (JF); https://orcid.org/0000-0001-6996-5706 (JE); 2. Department of Computational Mathematics, Science and Engineering, Michigan State University, East Lansing, Michigan, U.S.A.; 3. Department of Earth and Planetary Science, University of California, Berkeley, California, U.S.A., https://orcid.org/0000-0003-2889-1493 (WZ)

*Corresponding author: jieyaqi@msu.edu

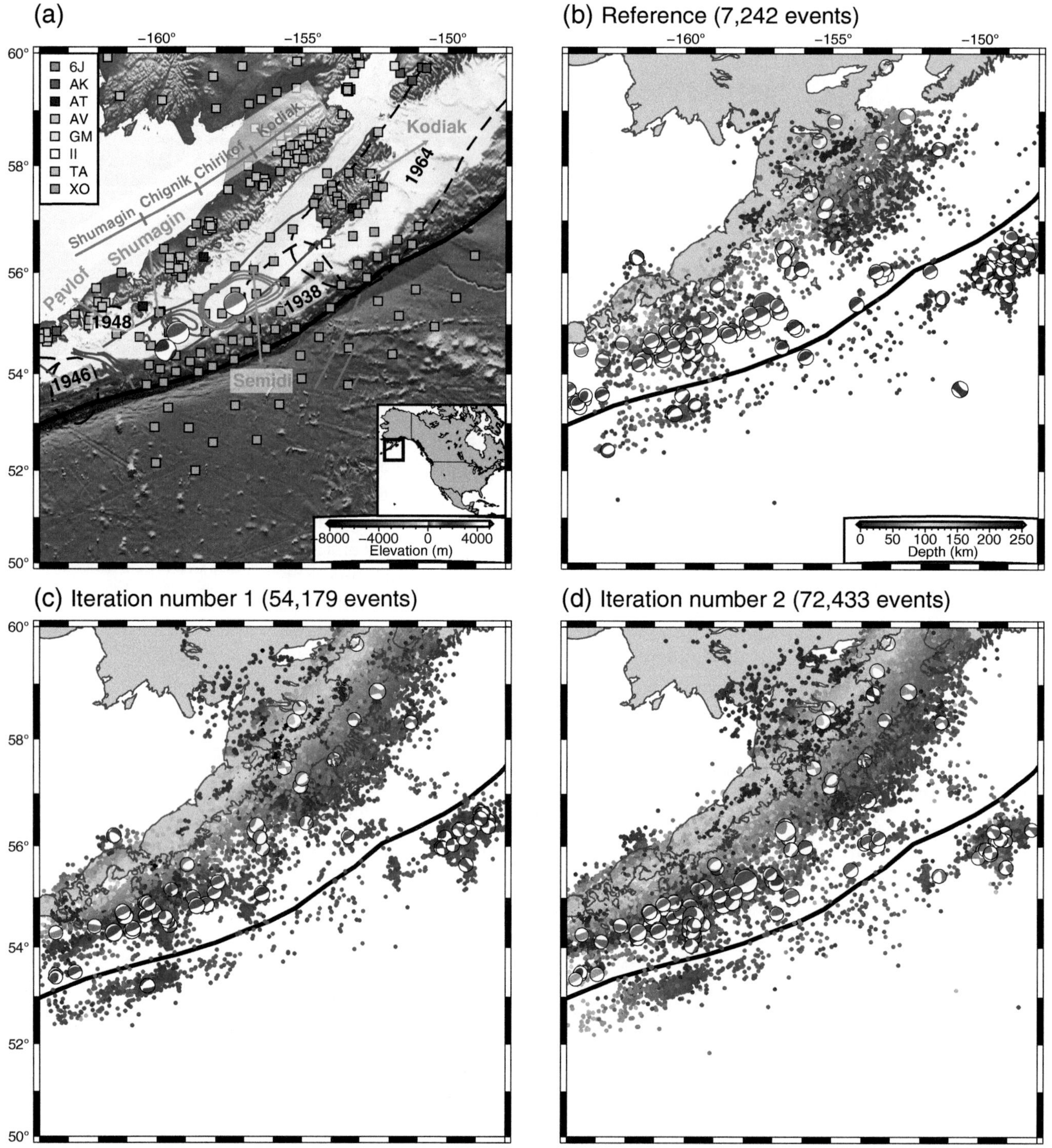

Figure 1. Maps of seismic stations and events. (a) Bathymetry and topography of the Alaska Peninsula and adjacent region. The squares represent seismic stations of various networks. The red, blue, and green focal mechanism plots indicate the 2020 M_w 7.8 Simeonof, 2020 M_w 7.6 Sand Point, and 2021 M_w 8.2 Chignik earthquakes, respectively. The coseismic slip models for the 2020 Simeonof and 2021 Chignik earthquakes are shown with 1, 1.5, and 2 m contours in red and green, respectively (Xiao *et al.*, 2021; Elliott *et al.*, 2022). The solid brown curves outline terrane boundaries and known faults in this region (Horowitz *et al.*, 1989). The black dashed contours outline the rupture zones of previous megathrust earthquakes (Davies *et al.*, 1981) and the 1 m contour of the 1938 M_w 8.3 earthquake slip model (Freymueller *et al.*, 2021). The light blue bars illustrate the four segments discussed in this article, following Wang *et al.* (2024), and the pink arrows denote the islands mentioned in the text. The inset map shows the location of the study area. Gray shading denotes the North America Plate, and the black box outlines the study region. (b) The reference catalog from May 2018 to August 2019 manually examined by the Alaska Earthquake Center (AEC). Earthquakes are color-coded by depth with Global Centroid Moment Tensor (Global CMT) focal mechanisms shown as focal mechanism plots. The bold black line represents the trench, and the gray lines depict the coastline. (c) Iteration number 1 output catalog. (d) Iteration number 2 output as the final catalog. The color version of this figure is available only in the electronic edition.

2022), potentially providing rupture barriers to the Simeonof and Chignik earthquakes.

About three months after the Simeonof earthquake, an M_w 7.6 strike-slip event, called the Sand Point, occurred nearby. It originated inside the subducting slab with the fault plane nearly aligned with the slab dip. This event has been attributed to several causes, including stress changes produced by the Simeonof earthquake (Jiang *et al.*, 2022; Yang *et al.*, 2023; Senapati *et al.*, 2024), abrupt coupling changes (Herman and Furlong, 2021; Jiang *et al.*, 2022), and pre-existing structures from the incoming and overriding plate (Clarke *et al.*, 2024). This strike-slip event generated an unexpected tsunami with wave heights higher than those produced by the larger Simeonof megathrust event. Bai *et al.* (2023) proposed a three-fault coseismic model to fit the tsunami data, although after including more Global Positioning Sys data (Grapenthin *et al.*, unpublished manuscript, see Data and Resources) favored a single-fault model with additional contributions from slip on the plate interface.

In this study, we explore the three 2020–2021 earthquakes by building a high-precision regional earthquake catalog powered by deep learning techniques. Deep learning has demonstrated its ability to detect an order of magnitude more events than conventional catalogs examined by human analysts (Mousavi and Beroza, 2022). The resulting increase in detected earthquakes enables more detailed spatial and temporal analysis of aftershocks and helps delineate fault systems (Park *et al.*, 2020; Tan *et al.*, 2021). With more information about the background seismicity and aftershocks of these earthquakes, we provide new insights into the three mainshocks as well as subduction zone processes.

Data and Methods

Data and reference catalog

We used seismic data recorded by 218 stations from January 2018 to December 2022 (Fig. 1a). These stations include those from permanent networks (network codes: II, GM, AK, AT, and AV), as well as temporary stations from the EarthScope USArray (network code: TA), ocean-bottom seismographs (OBSs) and land-based seismic stations from the Alaska Amphibious Community Seismic Experiment (AACSE, network code: XO), and a 1-year temporary seismic array deployed immediately after the 2021 M_w 8.2 Chignik earthquake (network code: 6J). Only data from broadband stations were utilized.

We assembled a reference catalog of local earthquakes, consisting of 7,242 events, 212,853 *P*-wave arrivals, and 100,292 *S*-wave arrivals from May 2018 to August 2019, which were manually picked by the Alaska Earthquake Center (AEC) (Ruppert *et al.*, 2022; Fig. 1b). Based on this reference catalog, we created a reference dataset by selecting 5 min before and after each *P*-wave arrival, ensuring to include the corresponding *S*-wave arrival from the same event. Time windows containing only *S* phases without *P* phases were discarded to maintain data quality. Traces with missing data were filled with zeros, and missing channels were also replaced with zero-filled traces. All three-component waveforms were detrended, demeaned, tapered, and resampled to 40 Hz. Because about half of the stations were operated with a sample rate of 100 Hz, this downsampling approach potentially leads to the loss of high-frequency signals recorded by some stations. However, because all the training, validation, testing, and continuous data are consistently resampled to 40 Hz, this approach should not introduce systematic bias to phase picking.

We also assembled a continuous dataset from January 2018 to December 2022 by cutting waveforms into 10-day segments and processing them in the same manner as the reference dataset. Given the large data volume, exceeding 2 TB in miniSEED format, the dataset construction was facilitated by the mseedindex package and ObsPy wrapper (Beyreuther *et al.*, 2010) to ensure efficient data access and improved input/output performance.

Earthquake detection and relocation

To develop a new earthquake catalog, we use a semi-supervised learning workflow (Xi *et al.*, 2024) starting with PhaseNet-TF to pick phases, then associating phases with GaMMA-1D, and finally relocating earthquakes with tomoDD. This process is iterated twice. We use the reference dataset for training in iteration number 1, and use the output of iteration number 1 for training in iteration number 2. Previous experience (Xi *et al.*, 2024) shows that two iterations are sufficient to obtain a nearly complete catalog.

PhaseNet-TF was initially trained and applied to a dataset in the Tonga subduction zone (Xi *et al.*, 2024) and showed a much better performance in picking *S* waves at OBSs and land stations compared to its predecessor PhaseNet (Zhu and Beroza, 2019). Because the tectonic setting, instrument types, and earthquake mechanisms at the Alaska Peninsula differ from those in Tonga, we retrain the PhaseNet-TF model using the reference dataset to optimize performance. The PhaseNet-TF Alaska model is trained for a maximum of 400 epochs with potential early stopping to prevent overfitting, achieving an F1 score higher than 0.97 on the test dataset. We then apply this model to the continuous dataset to obtain probabilities for *P*- and *S*-wave arrivals. Peak probabilities higher than 0.5 are considered positive picks, resulting in more than 9,000,000 picks. In iteration number 1, training and predicting took 37 and 163 hr on eight graphic processing units (GPUs), respectively. In iteration number 2, with a 6 times larger training dataset, training and predicting took 185 hr on 16 GPUs and 163 hr on 8 GPUs, respectively.

Next, we associate PhaseNet-TF output picks using GaMMA-1D, a Bayesian Gaussian Mixture Model Associator with a 1D velocity structure. Compared to its predecessor GaMMA (Zhu *et al.*, 2022), this new version utilizes a 1D velocity model, which is necessary for associating arrivals of events deeper than 30 km. In this study, the velocity model comes from averaging previous 3D shallow (0–240 km; Wang *et al.*, 2024) and deep (240–400 km; Wang *et al.*, 2025) tomography models in this region. Events with fewer than ten picks are discarded before further relocation. Associating more than 9,000,000 picks took only 2 hr on 20 central processing units, resulting in a preliminary catalog of over 150,000 events. After the initial association, we then refine the earthquake locations using a resampling strategy adapted from the Random Sample Consensus algorithm (Zhu *et al.*, 2025). For each event, we locate it with random subsets of the associated picks to identify and exclude outlier picks. Because of the large uncertainties associated with estimating magnitudes of small earthquakes, we excluded the magnitude information from the new catalog to avoid additional uncertainties.

We use tomoDD (Zhang and Thurber, 2003), a double-difference tomography and relocation package, to relocate earthquakes. We fix the 3D velocity structure as the combined model from Wang *et al.* (2024) and Wang *et al.* (2025) and only invert for the locations and origin times of earthquakes. We estimate uncertainties with a bootstrap resampling strategy. We create 100 datasets, each consisting of 80% random *P*- and *S*-wave arrivals for relocation. The output catalog is relocated using the complete dataset, whereas the uncertainties of location and origin time of each event are computed from the standard deviations of the 100 bootstrap resampling inversions. We discard events with uncertainties exceeding 0.05° in longitude, 0.1° in latitude, 5 km in depth, or 1 s in origin time for future discussion. In addition, we also discard events with station azimuthal gaps greater than 270°, many of which are offshore events before or after the AACSE deployment.

After iteration number 1, the output catalog contains 110,147 events, of which 32,036 events fall within the same time range as the reference catalog (May 2018 to August 2019). 54,177 events, along with 1,253,058 *P*- and 528,190 *S*-wave arrivals, are retained to construct the training dataset for iteration number 2 (Fig. 1c). Because of our high-quality control requirements, 31,316 *P*- and 17,231 *S*-wave manually picked arrivals in the reference catalog are not included in the iteration number 1 output catalog. By combining these arrivals, we have a new dataset consisting of 59,968 events, 1,284,374 *P*-, and 545,421 *S*-wave arrivals with a size of 692 GB, 6 times larger than the reference dataset. We then use this dataset to retrain PhaseNet-TF and conduct a second iteration of phase picking, phase association, and event relocation to produce the final catalog (Fig. 1d). In addition, we associate the final catalog with the Global Centroid Moment Tensor (Global CMT) catalog (Dziewonski *et al.*, 1981; Ekström *et al.*, 2012) to obtain the moment magnitude and focal mechanism parameters of large events.

Results

Final catalog and assessments

The final catalog, output of iteration number 2, contains 117,151 events with 2,631,256 *P*- and 1,091,693 *S*-wave arrivals in 2018–2022, about 30 times larger than the International Seismological Center (ISC) Reviewed Bulletin (Bondár and Storchak, 2011; International Seismological Center [ISC] Bulletin, 2018) during the same period. In addition, our catalog contains about 5 times more events than the AEC catalog (Ruppert *et al.*, 2022) during the overlap time from May 2018 to August 2019. 72,434 of these events have a spatial uncertainty (square root of the sum of the squares of horizontal and vertical uncertainties) lower than 5 km (Fig. 1d) and are used for the following discussions. Figure 2 shows examples of spectrograms, waveforms, and prediction probabilities for both shallow (< 50 km) and deep earthquakes (> 50 km) at one land station and one OBS, highlighting the robustness of the PhaseNet-TF Alaska model in accurately identifying phase arrivals.

We evaluate the earthquake detection/relocation performance against the AEC-picked reference catalog from May 2018 to August 2019 (Table 1). The recall, precision, and F1 metrics are calculated based on the numbers of true positives, false positives, and false negatives. An arrival with a time difference of 3 s or less compared to the reference is considered a true positive, whereas an event is treated as a true positive if it has a majority of matching phases and its origin time is within 15 s compared to the reference. Iteration number 1 achieves recall rates of 0.93 for *P*-wave arrivals, 0.94 for *S*-wave arrivals, and 0.95 for events. After iteration number 2, the final catalog successfully autodetects 95% of the earthquakes from the AEC-picked reference catalog. 5% of the events are missed because each of them has less than 10 phases or has large relocation uncertainty, and we do not use all AEC stations out of the Alaska Peninsula. More metrics are listed in Table 1.

Although many offshore earthquakes in our catalog lack offshore constraints, we are still confident in most of their depths. From a methodological perspective, the double-difference relocation algorithm integrates the 5-year onshore data with the 15-month AACSE offshore data into the same inversion, so that the OBS data can help constrain the earthquakes that occurred before or after the AACSE deployment. More importantly, the relocated hypocenters of the Simeonof and Chignik mainshocks and most aftershocks (see the Aftershocks in the overriding plate section) coincide with the plate interface independently determined by active-source seismic studies (Kuehn *et al.*, 2024). This coincidence provides strong independent evidence for the reliability of the majority of our relocated earthquake depths and locations. About 10 events located deeper than 50 km beneath the fore-arc seem tectonically impossible. Careful manual examinations suggest that these events are false detections. Because our methods are based on statistics and these events constitute only 0.01% of the entire catalog, we avoid using a subjective way to discard them.

Comparing different deep learning methods

We first assess the associator by applying different versions of GaMMA to the AEC manually labeled phase arrivals (Fig. 3,

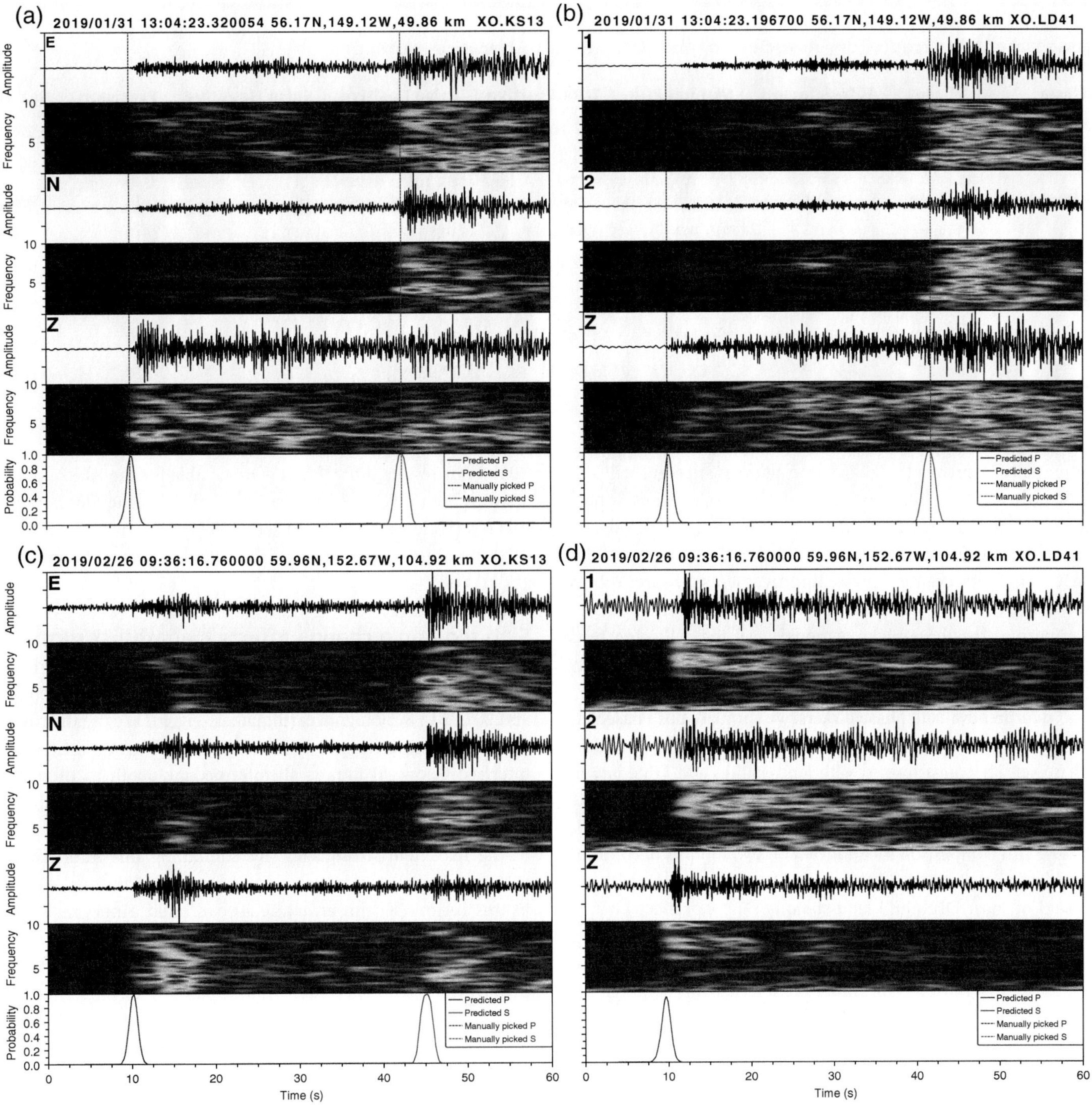

Table 2). When using GaMMA-1D, the performance of both association and relocation improves significantly, as seismic velocity changes dramatically with respect to depth in a subduction zone. For instance, GaMMA incorrectly splits single earthquakes into multiple events in the outer-rise, resulting in numerous artificially deep earthquakes (Fig. 3c). GaMMA-1D addresses this issue by generating more accurate synthetic travel-time estimates using a 1D velocity model, which enhances the reliability of phase association and improves the precision of earthquake locations. Using a 3D velocity model

Figure 2. Examples of PhaseNet-TF picking on continuous data. Each panel displays the event origin time, event latitude, longitude, depth, and network station in the title. (a) A shallow event (<50 km) recorded by a land station. (b) The same shallow event recorded by an ocean-bottom seismometer (OBS). (c) A deeper event (>50 km) recorded by a land station. (d) The same deeper event recorded by an OBS. The color version of this figure is available only in the electronic edition.

TABLE 1

Assessment for Prediction, Association, and Relocation in Iteration Number 2

Stage	Phases	Autodetected	Manual Pick	True Positive	False Positive	False Negative	Precision	Recall
Phase picking	*P* phase	4,815,991	212,853	207,207	4,608,784	5,646	0.04	0.97
	S phase	952,109	100,292	99,585	852,524	707	0.10	0.99
Association	*P* phase	1,135,419	212,853	198,817	936,602	14,036	0.18	0.93
	S phase	435,284	100,292	82,361	352,923	17,931	0.19	0.82
	Event	43,719	7242	7,153	36,566	89	0.16	0.99
Relocation	*P* phase	971,284	212,853	191,939	779,345	20,914	0.20	0.90
	S phase	399,031	100,292	80,427	318,604	19,865	0.20	0.80
	Event	34,834	7,242	6,845	27,989	397	0.20	0.95

Performance is evaluated against the Alaska Earthquake Center (AEC)-picked reference catalog from May 2018 to August 2019.

potentially improves the association performance but will significantly increase the computational demand, which is unnecessary at this stage. The use of an Alaska-specific velocity model further enhances the association performance, particularly for deep events. These improvements ensure robust association and relocation, providing a solid foundation for comparing the phase-picking models. All the following tests in this section use GaMMA-1D with a 1D Alaska velocity model and the same relocation processes.

To further evaluate phase pickers, we compare our PhaseNet-TF Alaska model with two other deep learning models: PhaseNet-TF Tonga trained with land-station and OBS data in the Tonga subduction zone (Xi *et al.*, 2024) and Earthquake Transformer (EQT) trained with global data (Mousavi *et al.*, 2020). This comparison is conducted on two months of continuous data from January to February 2019, during the operation period of most OBSs and land stations (Fig. 4, Table 3).

The new PhaseNet-TF Alaska model significantly improves the performance, not only detecting more events, but also achieving a recall of 0.98, much higher than the EQT global model's recall of 0.81 and the PhaseNet-TF Tonga model's recall of 0.67 (Fig. 4, Table 3), even though the PhaseNet-TF Tonga and EQT models pick more arrivals. The comparison between the PhaseNet-TF Alaska (Fig. 4b) and PhaseNet-TF Tonga (Fig. 4d) models highlights the importance of training with local data. Although the Tonga model is trained with data after removing instrumental responses, the performance difference is minimal when applied to data with or without instrumental response (recall of 0.98 versus 0.98, Table 3). Thus, removing the instrumental response does not significantly impact the performance, saving computational resources in future catalog building.

Neither the EQT nor the PhaseNet-TF Tonga model is trained with local data, but the latter obviously outperforms the former (Fig. 4c,d). Although EQT's deep encoder and attention layers may reduce phase arrival uncertainty (Mousavi *et al.*, 2020), our results show that it is unsuitable for the Alaska dataset with both OBS and land stations and thus generates numerous false picks and events. PhaseNet-TF performs better due to incorporating spectrograms in the time–frequency domain.

Discussion

Slab dip angle change affects megathrust rupture

The new catalog shows the background seismicity before June 2020 and abundant aftershocks of the 2020 M_w 7.8 Simeonof and 2021 M_w 8.2 Chignik earthquakes (Fig. 5). We use the background seismicity (black dots in Fig. 5) to determine the plate interface below 40 km, as all intermediate-depth earthquakes occur in the slab crust and mantle. We also estimated the dip angle uncertainty by considering the spatial uncertainty of the relocated earthquakes. By combining this information with previous active-source seismic images of the top 40 km in this region (Kuehn *et al.*, 2024), we build a new model of the plate interface geometry shown as red dashed curves in Figure 5. In addition, we define the aftershocks of these three major events following Tape and Lomax (2022). The relationship between coseismic rupture and aftershock distribution has been discussed in many previous studies and still remains controversial. Traditionally, aftershock distributions are used to outline mainshock rupture areas (e.g., Davies *et al*, 1981; Tape and Lomax, 2022). On the other hand, Wetzler *et al.* (2018) suggest that regions of high coseismic slip often exhibit fewer aftershocks, resulting in a generally complementary pattern between the two. In this study, the aftershocks within 30 days after the mainshocks, combined with the coseismic slip models by Elliott *et al.* (2022) and Xiao *et al.* (2021), shed light on the coseismic and postseismic deformation of the three major events. We also compared the aftershocks with the coseismic slip models from Ye *et al.* (2021, 2022) in Figure S1, available in the supplemental material to this article, leading to the same interpretations.

The new plate interface model shows a rapid change in the slab dip angle at 30–40 km depths in the Shumagin segment

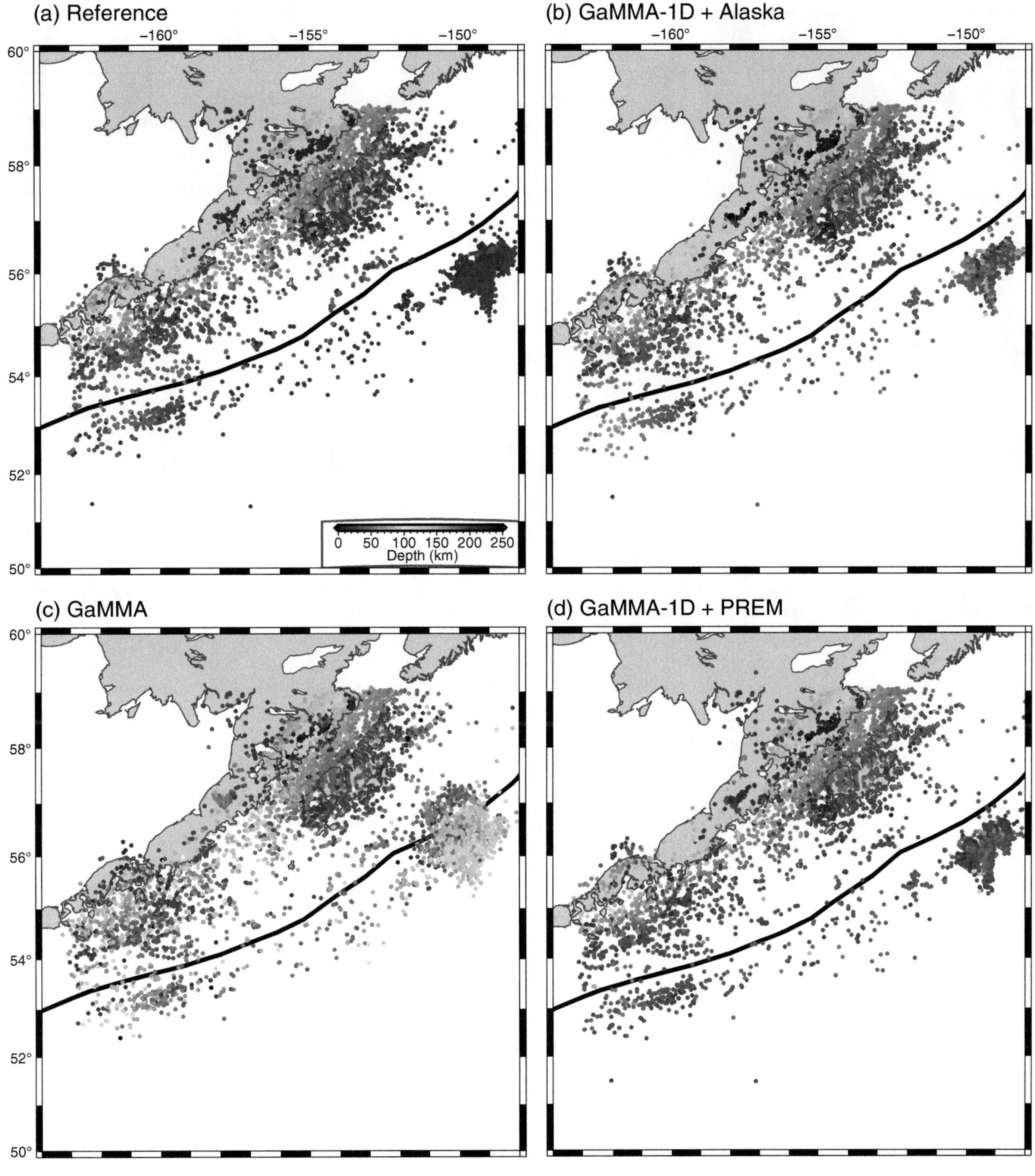

Figure 3. Catalogs from manual pick tests. All the catalogs are generated using AEC manually labeled phase arrivals, applying different associators but following the same relocation process. All other features are the same as Figure 1b. (a) The reference catalog from May 2018 to August 2019 was manually examined by the Alaska Earthquake Center (AEC). (b) Catalog associated using GaMMA-1D with the Alaska velocity model. (c) Catalog associated using GaMMA. (d) Catalog associated using GaMMA-1D with the PREM velocity model. The color version of this figure is available only in the electronic edition.

TABLE 2
Association and Relocation Result for Alaska Earthquake Center (AEC) Manual Picks in Iteration Number 2

Method	Phase	Relocated	Reference Catalog	True Positive	False Positive	False Negative	Precision	Recall	F1
GaMMA	*P* phase	139,863	212,850	137,451	2,412	75,399	0.98	0.65	0.78
	S phase	67,507	100,292	66,184	1323	34,108	0.98	0.66	0.79
	Event	6,944	7,242	6,767	177	475	0.97	0.93	0.95
GaMMA-1D with PREM model	*P* phase	201,512	212,850	201,294	218	11,556	1.00	0.95	0.97
	S phase	90,226	100,292	90,134	92	10,158	1.00	0.90	0.95
	Event	6,957	7,242	6,945	12	297	1.00	0.96	0.98
GaMMA-1D with Alaska model	*P* phase	202,503	212,850	202,281	222	10,569	1.00	0.95	0.97
	S phase	93,341	100,292	93,249	92	7,043	1.00	0.93	0.96
	Event	6,978	7,242	6,967	11	275	1.00	0.96	0.98

Performance is evaluated against the AEC-picked reference catalog from May 2018 to August 2019. PREM, preliminary reference Earth model.

(Fig. 5 C–C′ and D–D′), in which the dip angle increases from 13.4° above 30 km depth to 30.6 ± 2.1° at 40–100 km depths. Although Kuehn *et al.* (2024) do not estimate the slab dip uncertainty above 30 km depth, the lower bound of the slab dip angle below 40 km is significantly greater than the shallow dip angle. This dip angle change is most prominent in the western Shumagin segment, gradually fading away toward the east until it becomes indistinguishable in the Chignik segment. This feature is also observed in active-source seismic reflection images along ALEUT lines 4 and 5 (Shillington *et al.*, 2022; Fig. S2). Recent studies suggest that slab dip is controlled by subduction duration, with additional influence from the nature of the overriding plate and convergence rate, where thicker lithosphere with faster convergence tends to produce flatter dips (Hu and Gurnis, 2020). Given the similar subduction duration along the Alaska Peninsula and the existence of the Shumagin Islands, we suspect that the thicker continental crust of the Shumagin Islands than the surrounding fore-arc crust may be responsible for the slab dip angle change.

This slab dip angle change at 30–40 km depths coincides with changes in the aftershock distribution and coseismic deformation of the 2020 M_w 7.8 Simeonof earthquake. Coseismic modeling indicates that the mainshock ruptured the megathrust at 20–45 km depth, with the most slip concentrating in a narrow zone at 25–40 km depth, propagating primarily to the west from the hypocenter (Crowell and Melgar, 2020; Xiao *et al.*, 2021; Ye *et al.*, 2021). Most megathrust aftershocks were confined in the Shumagin segment, extending westward and landward from the mainshock hypocenter and coseismic peak slip area. On the western end of the rupture area, most aftershocks concentrated at 30–40 km depths along the plate interface (Fig. 5 C–C′), whereas on the eastern side, aftershocks extended up-dip to about 25 km depth (Fig. 5 E–E′). Therefore, our results, along with coseismic slip models, show that the coseismic and postseismic deformation of the western portion of the 2020 M_w 7.8 Simeonof rupture area was mainly confined at 30–40 km depths on the megathrust, where the slab dip angle changes rapidly. In contrast, the 2021 M_w 8.2 Chignik earthquake ruptured a wider portion of the megathrust along-dip at 20–45 km depths without an obvious change in the slab dip angle. Similarly, the aftershock distribution is wider than that of the 2020 event, ranging from 20 to 45 km depth, although most aftershocks are up-dip. In sum, both coseismic slip models and aftershock distributions suggest that the western portion of the 2020 M_w 7.8 Simeonof earthquake ruptured the megathrust in a relatively narrow zone along the dip (30–40 km depths), whereas the 2021 M_w 8.2 Chignik event rupture area was much wider.

The contrast between the Simeonof and Chignik rupture areas suggests that the slab dip angle change may play a role in controlling rupture propagation. Fault geometry significantly influences seismicity and slip distribution (Segall and Pollard, 1980; Ben-Zion and Rice, 1995) because bends and segmentations often act as barriers to rupture propagation (Aki, 1979). Various global earthquakes support this phenomenon; for example, the 2007 M_w 7.7 Tocopilla earthquake rupture was likely inhibited by an abrupt dip angle change (Contreras-Reyes *et al.*, 2012), and a lateral change in the dip angle limited the rupture propagation of the 2015 M_w 7.8 Gorkha earthquake (Zhang *et al.*, 2017). Along the Alaska Peninsula in the Shumagin segment, the abrupt slab dip angle change at 30–40 km depths likely inhibited the seaward propagation of the Simeonof earthquake rupture and triggered stress release in the overriding plate (see the Aftershocks in the overriding plate section). In contrast, the megathrust to the east, where the dip angle change was less pronounced, experienced less restriction and allowed for slightly shallower rupture during the Chignik earthquake. Other factors, such as plate interface roughness, slab hydration, and variations in the overriding

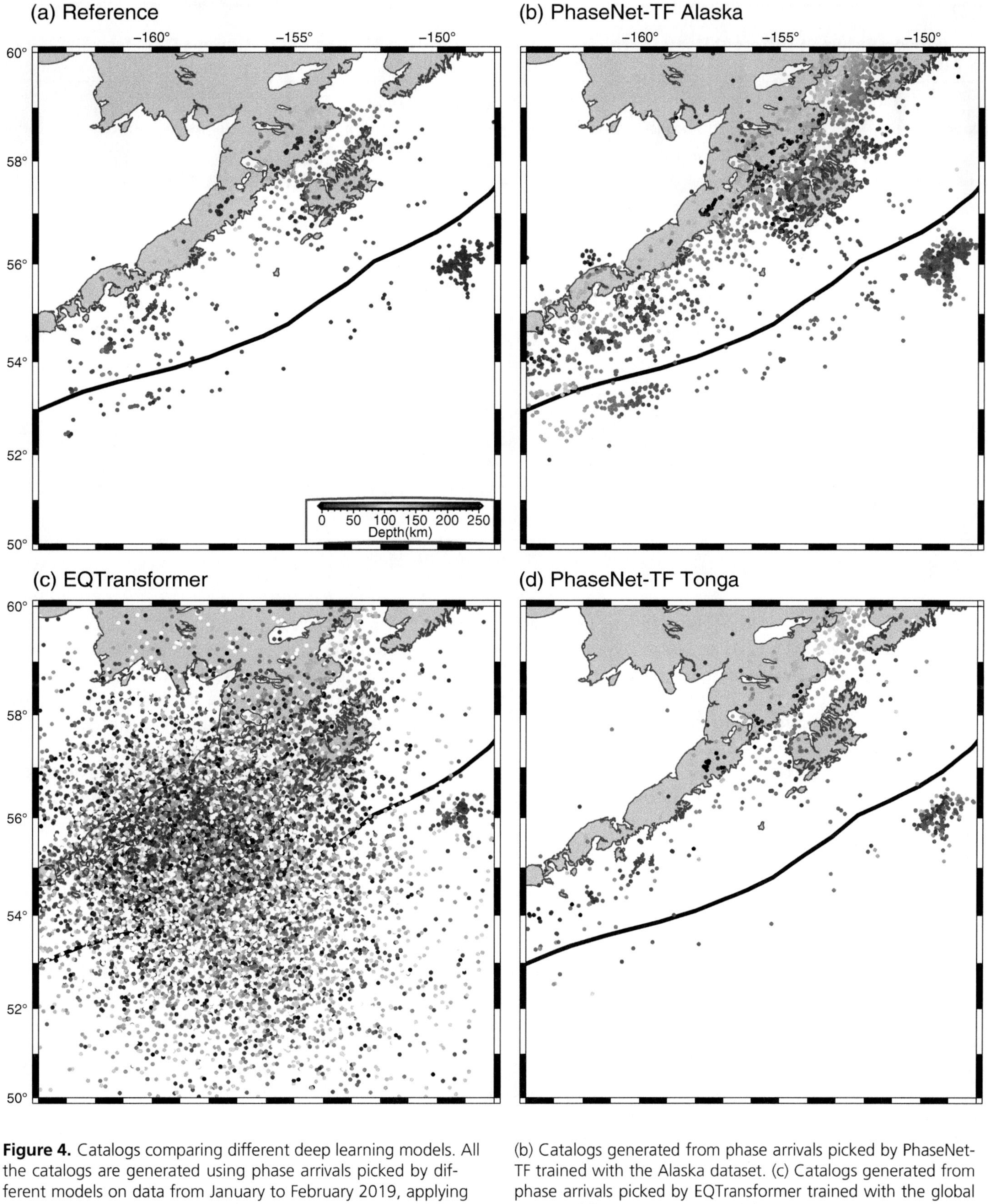

Figure 4. Catalogs comparing different deep learning models. All the catalogs are generated using phase arrivals picked by different models on data from January to February 2019, applying GaMMA-1D with the Alaska velocity model and the same relocation process. All other features are the same as Figure 1b. (a) The reference catalog from January to February 2019 was manually examined by the Alaska Earthquake Center (AEC). (b) Catalogs generated from phase arrivals picked by PhaseNet-TF trained with the Alaska dataset. (c) Catalogs generated from phase arrivals picked by EQTransformer trained with the global dataset. (d) Catalogs generated from phase arrivals picked by PhaseNet-TF trained with the Tonga dataset. The color version of this figure is available only in the electronic edition.

TABLE 3

Comparison Between Different Deep Learning Phase Pickers on Two Months of Continuous Data from January to February 2019

Model	Phases	Autodetected	Manual Pick	True Positive	False Positive	False Negative	Precision	Recall
PhaseNet-TF Alaska	*P* phase	128,825	25,028	23,991	104,834	1,037	0.19	0.96
	S phase	54,752	11,754	10,922	43,830	832	0.20	0.93
	Events	4,467	740	728	3,739	12	0.16	0.98
PhaseNet-TF Alaska (Instrument response removed)	*P* phase	118,288	25,028	22,977	95,311	2,051	0.19	0.92
	S phase	52,801	11,754	10,164	42,637	1,590	0.19	0.86
	Events	4,251	740	728	3,523	12	0.17	0.98
PhaseNet-TF Tonga	*P* phase	21,036	24,965	10,523	10,513	14,442	0.50	0.42
	S phase	15,684	11,754	4,619	11,065	7,135	0.29	0.39
	Events	929	740	499	430	241	0.54	0.67
EQT Global	*P* phase	219,440	25,028	10,891	208,549	14,137	0.05	0.44
	S phase	125,044	11,754	2,262	122,782	9,492	0.02	0.19
	Events	27,910	740	595	27,315	145	0.02	0.80

Performance is evaluated against the Alaska Earthquake Center (AEC)-picked reference catalog. EQT, Earthquake Transformer.

plate strength and thickness, likely also play important roles (e.g., Shillington *et al.*, 2022; Liu *et al.*, 2023). These combined factors limited the Simeonof rupture propagation.

Aftershocks in the overriding plate

In addition to along-strike variations in the plate interface, the distribution of aftershocks within the overriding plate also shows significant differences. Within 30 days following the 2020 M_w 7.8 Simeonof mainshock, our catalog shows at least four distinct aftershock clusters extending from the plate interface to the overriding plate (Fig. 5 C–C′, D–D′, and E–E′). These aftershocks suggest the Simeonof mainshock activated a complex fault system within the overriding plate in the Shumagin segment, consistent with active-source images (Shillington *et al.*, 2022). This type of dynamic triggering has been observed globally. For instance, the 2010 Maule megathrust earthquake (M_w 8.8) in Chile triggered seismic slip on a normal fault within the overriding plate (Hicks and Rietbrock, 2015). In contrast, after the 2021 M_w 8.2 Chignik mainshock, fewer aftershocks occurred in the overriding plate during the first 30 days (Fig. 5 F–F′, G–G′, and H–H′, Fig. 6c,d).

The activation of the fault system in the overriding plate after the 2020 M_w 7.8 Simeonof earthquake indicates that the overriding plate in the Shumagin segment is weaker compared to that in the Chignik segment. Previous seismic tomography studies show extremely low-velocity and high-V_P/V_S anomalies in the overriding plate of the Shumagin segment, suggesting a high degree of deformation and hydration in this region (Li *et al.*, 2024; Wang *et al.*, 2024). Therefore, we attribute the abundant aftershocks in the relatively weak overriding plate of the Shumagin segment to intensive and extensive deformation and hydration because the fluids from slab dehydration increase pore pressure, inducing microcracking, and triggering earthquakes.

At the megathrust depths, the fluids released from slab dehydration primarily originate from water stored in pore spaces and loosely bound water within sediments and the upper oceanic crust. This process is largely determined by plate hydration in the outer-rise region and the thickness of sediments (Faccenda, 2014). Because the subduction of the Zodiac sediment fan influences both the Shumagin and Chignik segments, the primary along-strike change in hydration arises from the outer-rise geology. Shillington *et al.* (2015) proposed that the existing fabrics on the incoming plate intersect the trench at a smaller angle (<30°) in the Shumagin segment than in the Semidi segment, thereby promoting the development of outer-rise faults. This hypothesis is supported by recent bathymetric mapping results, which show the Shumagin segment with more extensive and larger faults compared to the Chignik segment (Clarke *et al.*, 2024). In agreement with these observations, our catalog also shows a significant number of outer-rise events in the Shumagin segment, whereas only a few such events are observed in the Chignik segment.

In sum, the aftershock distributions of the 2020 and 2021 major earthquakes confirm that the slab dehydration and overriding plate hydration are more intensive and extensive in the

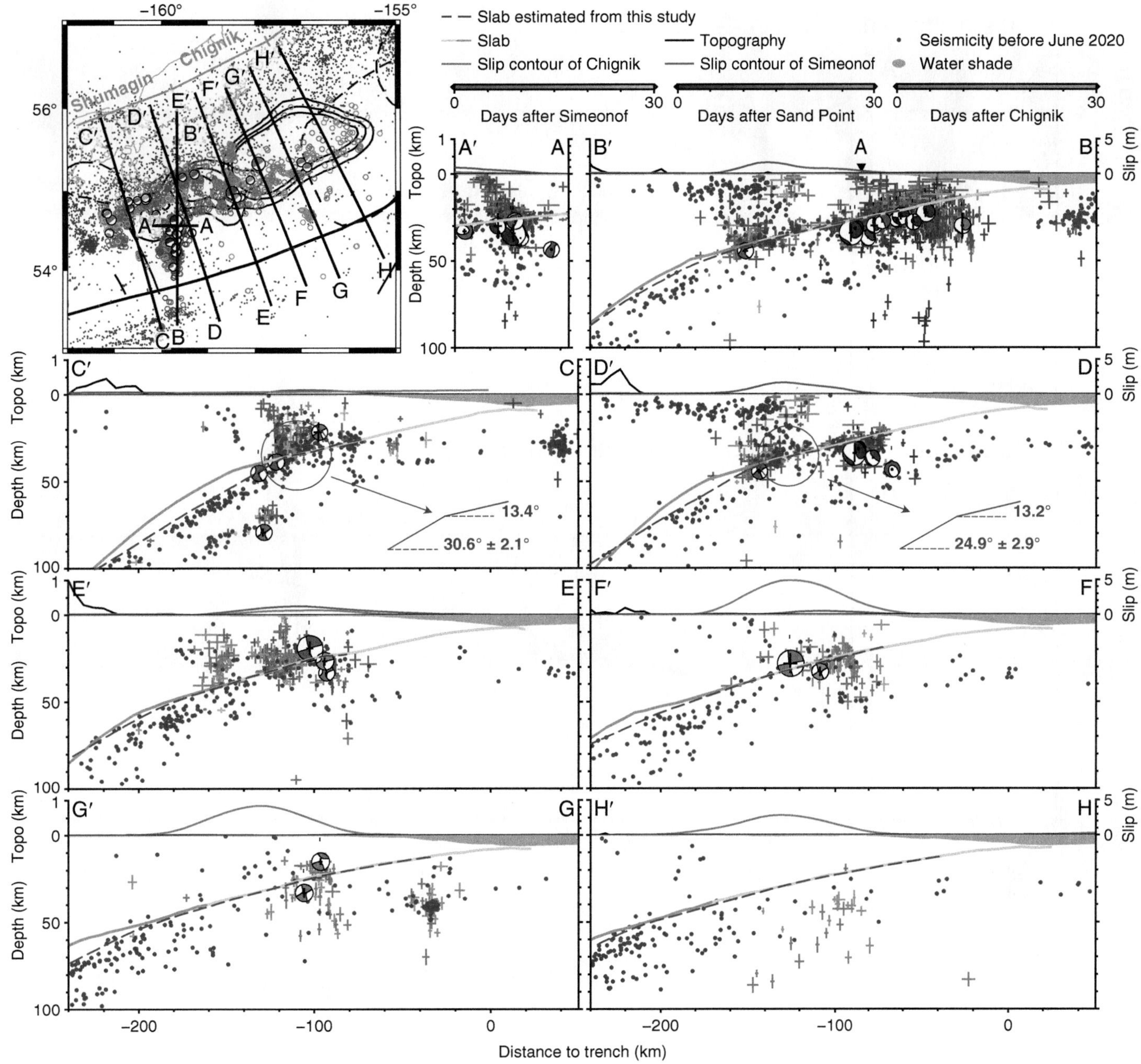

Figure 5. Map and cross sections of the final (iteration number 2) catalog. On the map, red, blue, and green circles represent aftershocks occurring within 30 days of the Simeonof, Sand Point, and Chignik mainshocks, respectively. The black dots indicate background seismicity before June 2020. On the map, straight lines indicate the cross sections shown in other panels, and other features are the same as in Figure 1b. The trench-normal cross sections have the same length from the trench, focusing on the main rupture areas at 20–50 km depths and 80–190 km from the trench. In each cross-section panel, crosses show the aftershocks of the three mainshocks with horizontal and vertical uncertainties (1-sigma). The black dots indicate the background seismicity before June 2020. The black curve and gray area on the top represent topography and bathymetry, whereas the red and green curves show the coseismic slip distributions for the Simeonof (from Elliott *et al.*, 2022) and Chignik (from Xiao *et al.*, 2021) earthquakes, respectively. The pink and gray curves illustrate the slab surface (top of the plate interface) from Wang *et al.* (2024), based on a model constrained by active-source seismic experiments (pink, Kuehn *et al.*, 2024) combined with the Slab2 model (gray, Hayes *et al.*, 2018). The red, dashed curve indicates the revised plate interface based on the background seismicity relocation in this study. The color version of this figure is available only in the electronic edition.

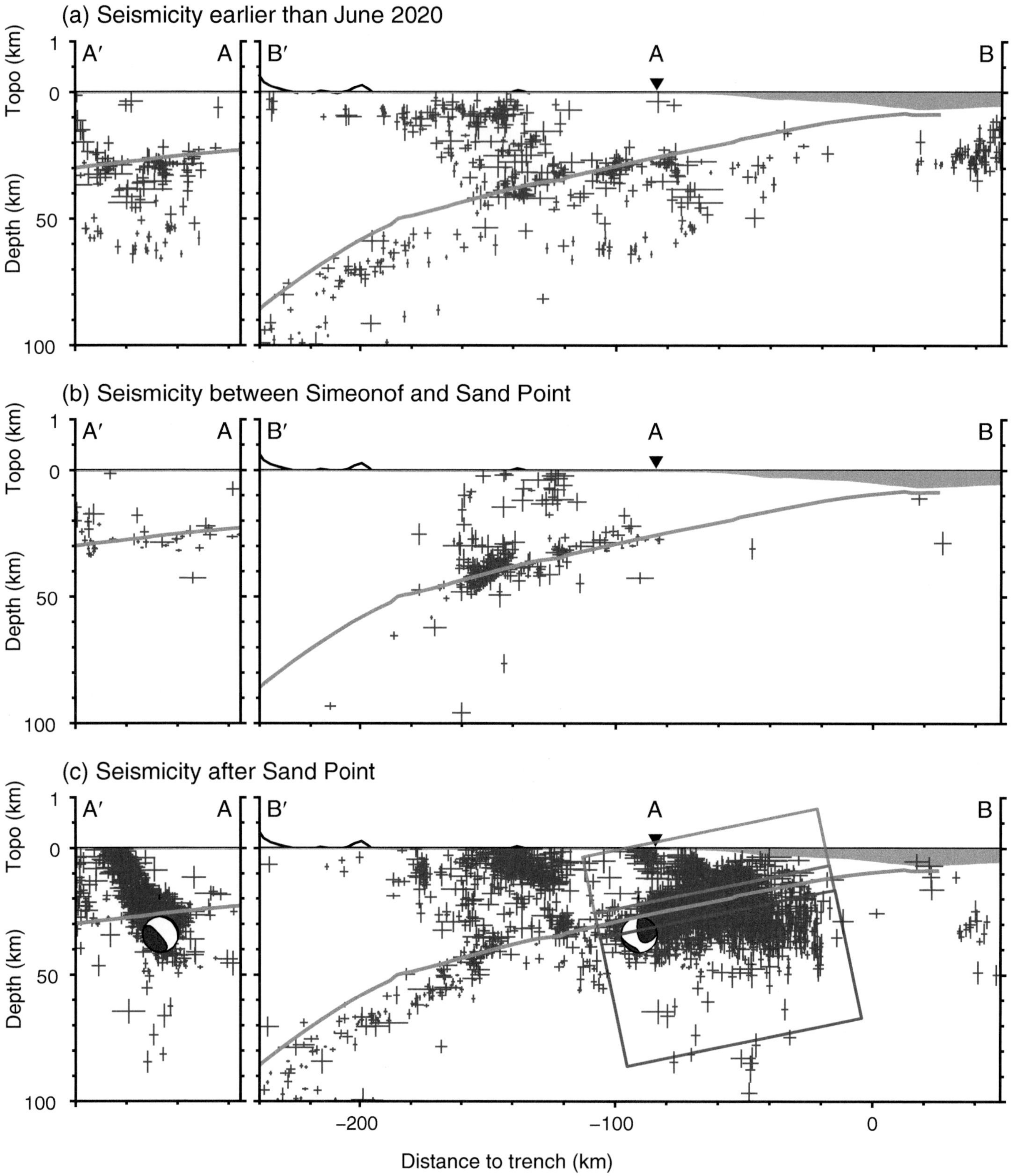

Figure 6. (a–c) Background seismicity and aftershocks of the 2020 Sand Point earthquake. The black crosses represent events with horizontal and vertical uncertainties. Other features are the same as in Figure 5. The green, red, and blue boxes in (c) denote the regions of the overriding plate, plate interface, and intraslab, respectively, used for estimating temporal changes in Figure 7. Given the hypocenter uncertainties and plate interface thickness (Kuehn *et al.*, 2024), we assume all events within 5 km above or below the slab surface occurred on the plate interface. The color version of this figure is available only in the electronic edition.

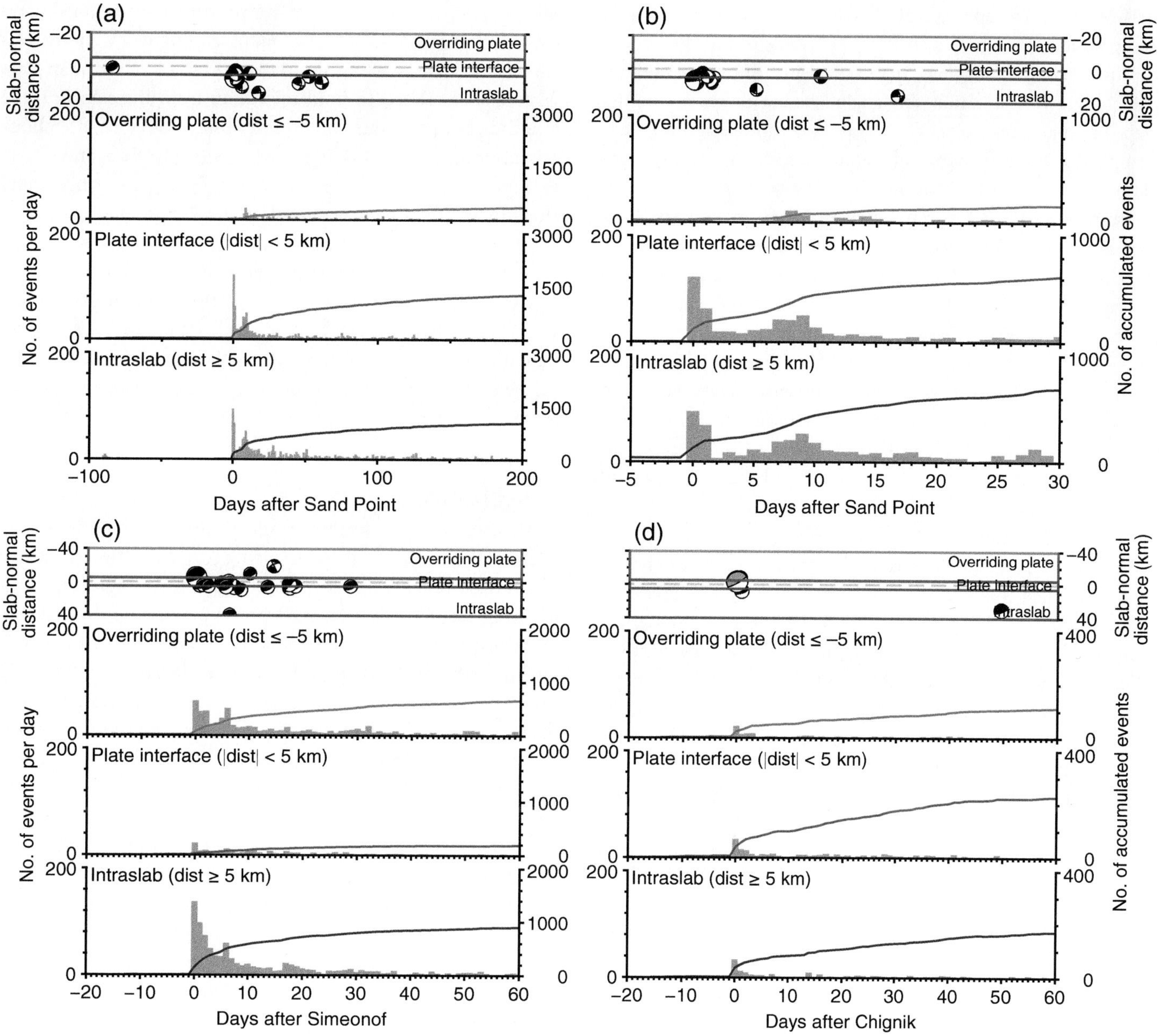

Shumagin segment than in the Chignik segment, as observed in previous tomography images (Shillington *et al.*, 2022; Li *et al.*, 2024; Wang *et al.*, 2024).

Complex fault system of the 2020 M_w 7.6 Sand Point strike-slip earthquake

The 2020 M_w 7.6 strike-slip event ruptured within the slab and unexpectedly generated a notable tsunami. Contrary to previous studies that mainly focus on the slab interior (Herman and Furlong, 2021), our catalog shows two clusters of aftershocks delineating two previously unmapped faults with almost identical strike and dip angles, one within the slab and the other in the overriding plate (Fig. 5 A–A′ and B–B′). The intraslab fault is responsible for the mainshock, extending 10–15 km downward from the plate interface. Based on the distribution of the first-day aftershocks, the intraslab fault has a strike of 1° and a dip angle of 70°. The aftershocks in the overriding plate extended from the plate interface at ~25 km depth to the Earth's surface. If all of them occurred on a single fault, it would have a

Figure 7. Cumulative number of events and daily event rates before and after the three events. The top panels show events with Global CMT solutions plotted at their origin time and distance from the slab surface. Lower panels show event rates for the overriding plate, on the interface, and inside the subducting plate. (a) Number of events 100 days before and 200 days after the Sand Point earthquake. (b) Zoomed-in view of (a), showing 5 days before and 30 days after the Sand Point earthquake. (c) Number of events 20 days before and 60 days after the Simeonof earthquake. (d) Number of events 20 days and 60 days after the Chignik earthquake. The color version of this figure is available only in the electronic edition.

strike of 5° and a dip angle of 52° on the first day of activation, and gradually change to a strike of 14°. Some of the aftershocks ruptured along the plate interface, with the lower bound coinciding with the slab dip angle change discussed in the Slab dip angle change affects megathrust rupture section, suggesting that the dip change also influenced the rupture propagation of the Sand Point intraslab earthquake.

Examining the background seismicity from January 2018 through June 2020 reveals few events along these faults. To further investigate the nature of these unmapped faults, we relocate all events with Global CMT solutions in the aftershock region back to 1970 with our catalog using the same setting and find that none align with the geometry of the two fault planes, indicating a long history of seismic quiescence. These faults are not identified in previous active-source studies or regional tectonic maps (Bruns *et al.*, 1987; Bécel *et al.*, 2017; Shillington *et al.*, 2022) in which most identified faults dip northward. Based on Coulomb stress change studies (Herman and Furlong, 2021; Elliott *et al.*, 2022; Yang *et al.*, 2023), the Simeonof earthquake likely caused a maximum stress change of four bars in this region, insufficient to initiate a new fault plane in the overriding plate. Thus, we suspect that the aftershocks in the overriding plate delineate a pre-existing, unmapped fault system, possibly related to the backstop splay fault zone along the trench (von Huene *et al.*, 2021).

To better understand the deformation in this region south of the Shumagin Islands, we plot the temporal evolution of seismicity before and after the M_w 7.8 Simeonof and M_w 7.6 Sand Point mainshocks (Fig. 6a–c). In addition, our high-precision catalog enables us to distinguish events in the slab from those in the overriding plate (Figs. 6c and 7b). The Simeonof earthquake on 22 July 2020 triggered overriding plate aftershocks near but more seaward of background seismicity and more plate-interface aftershocks down-dip to 40 km depth (Fig. 6a,b). After the Simeonof event, seismic activity did not increase significantly in the region where the Sand Point earthquake occurred. The Sand Point mainshock on 19 October 2020 triggered numerous aftershocks in a previously seismically quiet region closer to the trench (Fig. 6c). After the Sand Point mainshock, aftershock activity surged immediately in the slab and plate interface, with a second peak of activity seven days after the mainshock (Fig. 7b). This second peak coincides with the onset of aftershocks in the overriding plate. No big ($M > 5.5$) earthquake occurred on day 7 that could be potentially linked to this activation of faults in the slab, plate interface, and overriding plate.

Given the temporal and spatial distributions of aftershocks, we propose that the M_w 7.6 Sand Point ruptured within the slab and triggered slip along the megathrust. Shallow megathrust slip during or shortly after the main M_w 7.6 slip, possibly with a low amplitude, could generate a tsunami, as suggested by geodetic modeling and tsunamic simulation (Grapenthin *et al.*, unpublished manuscript, see Data and Resources). Intriguingly, the overriding plate remained silent for 7 days after the mainshock before being ruptured by numerous aftershocks. We suspect this 7-day delay of overriding plate seismicity is related to fluid migration from the slab into the fore-arc crust, although we do not observe obvious aftershock migration in the overriding plate (Movie S1). We acknowledge that our catalog is probably incomplete, and some small aftershocks could have occurred within 7 days after the mainshock. However, given the same detection capability across the system, we are confident to conclude that the overriding plate was seismically inactive compared to the slab and plate interface immediately after the mainshock. Therefore, we suggest that the slip within the overriding plate was not responsible for generating the tsunami on 19 October 2020, in contrast to some studies that invoke overriding plate faults (e.g., Bai *et al.*, 2023).

Conclusions

In this study, we examine complex seismic behaviors in the Alaska Peninsula region, focusing on the aftershocks of major earthquakes in 2020 and 2021. By integrating deep learning techniques, advanced phase picking, and improved association and relocation methods, we develop a high-precision earthquake catalog with 36 times more events than the ISC Reviewed Bulletin. Our findings suggest that slab geometry, particularly an abrupt dip angle change at 30–40 km depths in the Shumagin segment, may influence rupture propagation during both megathrust and intraslab events. The 2020 M_w 7.8 Simeonof earthquake rupture appears to have been inhibited from propagating up-dip by this dip change, likely inducing stress release in the overriding plate. In contrast, the 2021 M_w 8.2 Chignik earthquake ruptured a smoother megathrust, possibly facilitating more extensive up-dip rupture. Aftershocks in the overriding plate are more abundant and widespread in the Shumagin segment than in the nearby Chignik segment. We suggest that this contrast reveals a more deformed and hydrated overriding plate, likely resulting from more extensive and intensive slab dehydration in the Shumagin segment. The 2020 M_w 7.6 Sand Point aftershocks delineate two previously unmapped faults in the slab and overriding plate with nearly identical strikes and dip angles. The overriding plate fault was activated 7 days after the mainshock, but no big ($M > 5.5$) earthquakes could be linked to the onset of this fault activation.

Data and Resources

All data and codes associated with this study are publicly accessible and built on open-source platforms. PhaseNet-TF can be accessed at doi: 10.5281/zenodo.14877592, and GaMMA-1D is available at doi: 10.5281/zenodo.14877602. The compiled dataset is hosted on Hugging Face at doi: 10.57967/hf/4498, with model weights available at doi: 10.57967/hf/4499. The supplemental material includes cross sections of the final catalog with coseismic slip model from Ye *et al.* (2021, 2022; Fig. S1), cross sections of the final catalog along ALEUT Line 3, 4,

5 (Li *et al.*, 2015; Fig. S2), final earthquake catalog (Data Set S1), and a movie showing temporal evolution of seismicity before and after the 2020 M_w 7.6 Sand Point mainshock (Movie S1). Data processing and visualization were carried out using open-source packages, including ObsPy (https://github.com/obspy/obspy/) and GMT (https://docs.generic-mapping-tools.org/latest/). All seismic data used in this study were downloaded from EarthScope Consortium Web Services (https://service.iris.edu/) including the following seismic networks: (1) the II (Scripps Institution of Oceanography, 1986); (2) the GM (U.S. Geological Survey [USGS], 2016); (3) the AK (Alaska Earthquake Center, University of Alaska Fairbanks, 1987); (4) the AT (National Oceanic and Atmospheric Administration [NOAA], 1967); (5) the AV (Alaska Volcano Observatory/USGS, 1988); (6) the TA (Incorporated Research Institutions for Seismology [IRIS] Transportable Array, 2003); (7) the XO (Abers *et al.*, 2018); and (8) the 6J (Abers *et al.*, 2021). The unpublished manuscript by Grapenthin *et al.* (in revision), "Late triggered megathrust slip following the 2020 M_W 7.6 Sand Point Alaska strike-slip earthquake explains its tsunami," submitted to *Seismica*.

Declaration of Competing Interests

The authors acknowledge that there are no conflicts of interest recorded.

Acknowledgments

The authors thank Yihe Huang and Demian Saffer for constructive discussions. This work was made possible by the support of National Science Foundation grants EAR-1942431 to S. S. W., EAR-2052558 and EAR-2152253 to S. S. W., J. T. F., and J. E. National Science Foundation Grant EAR-2147422 to J. T. F. and J. E. supported the rapid earthquake response to the Chignik earthquake, resulting in network 6J. The computing resources were made available through the ACCESS (Advanced Cyberinfrastructure Coordination Ecosystem: Services and Support) Grant EES240096, utilizing the Delta graphic processing units (GPU) system at the University of Illinois. The facilities of the EarthScope Consortium were used for access to waveforms and related metadata. These services are funded through the National Science Foundation's Seismological Facility for the Advancement of Geoscience (SAGE) Award under Cooperative Agreement EAR-1724509. Additional computational support was provided by the Institute for Cyber-Enabled Research (ICER) at Michigan State University.

References

Abers, G., S. Schwartz, A. Sheehan, D. Wiens, and J. Freymueller (2021). RAPID: Response to the 29 July 2021 Chignik earthquake [SEED data], International Federation of Digital Seismograph Networks, doi: 10.7914/SN/6J_2021.

Abers, G., D. Wiens, S. Schwartz, A. Sheehan, D. Shillington, L. Worthington, *et al.* (2018). AACSE: Alaska Amphibious Community seismic Experiment [SEED data], International Federation of Digital Seismograph Networks, doi: 10.7914/SN/XO_2018.

Aki, K. (1979). Characterization of barriers on an earthquake fault, *J. Geophys. Res.* **84,** no. B11, 6140–6148, doi: 10.1029/JB084iB11p06140.

Alaska Earthquake Center, University of Alaska Fairbanks (1987). Alaska Geophysical Network [SEED data], *International Federation of Digital Seismograph Networks*, doi: 10.7914/SN/AK.

Alaska Volcano Observatory/U.S. Geological Survey (USGS) (1988). Alaska Volcano Observatory [SEED data], *International Federation of Digital Seismograph Networks*, doi: 10.7914/SN/AV.

Bai, Y., C. Liu, T. Lay, K. F. Cheung, and Y. Yamazaki (2023). Fast and slow intraplate ruptures during the 19 October 2020 magnitude 7.6 Shumagin earthquake, *Nat. Commun.* **14,** no. 1, 2015, doi: 10.1038/s41467-023-37731-2.

Bécel, A., D. J. Shillington, M. Delescluse, M. R. Nedimović, G. A. Abers, D. M. Saffer, *et al.* (2017). Tsunamigenic structures in a creeping section of the Alaska subduction zone, *Nature Geosci.* **10,** no. 8, 609–613, doi: 10.1038/ngeo2990.

Ben-Zion, Y., and J. R. Rice (1995). Slip patterns and earthquake populations along different classes of faults in elastic solids, *J. Geophys. Res.* **100,** no. B7, 12,959–12,983, doi: 10.1029/94JB03037.

Beyreuther, M., R. Barsch, L. Krischer, T. Megies, Y. Behr, and J. Wassermann (2010). ObsPy: A Python toolbox for seismology, *Seismol. Res. Lett.* **81,** no. 3, 530–533, doi: 10.1785/gssrl.81.3.530.

Bondár, I., and D. Storchak (2011). Improved location procedures at the International Seismological Centre, *Geophys. J. Int.* **186,** no. 3, 1220–1244, doi: 10.1111/j.1365-246X.2011.05107.x.

Bruns, T. R., R. von Huene, S. D. Lewis, and J. W. Ladd (1987). Geology and Petroleum Potential of the Shumagin Margin, Alaska, available at https://archives.datapages.com/data/circ_pac/0007/0157_f.htm (last accessed January 2025).

Clarke, J., D. J. Shillington, C. Regalla, J. B. Gaherty, J. Estep, D. A. Wiens, *et al.* (2024). Controls on bending-related faulting offshore of the Alaska Peninsula, *Geochem. Geophys. Geosyst.* **25,** no. 3, e2023GC011271, doi: 10.1029/2023GC011271.

Contreras-Reyes, E., J. Jara, I. Grevemeyer, S. Ruiz, and D. Carrizo (2012). Abrupt change in the dip of the subducting plate beneath north Chile, *Nature Geosci.* **5,** no. 5, 342–345, doi: 10.1038/ngeo1447.

Crowell, B. W., and D. Melgar (2020). Slipping the Shumagin gap: A kinematic coseismic and early afterslip model of the M_w 7.8 Simeonof Island, Alaska, earthquake, *Geophys. Res. Lett.* **47,** no. 19, e2020GL090308, doi: 10.1029/2020GL090308.

Davies, J., L. Sykes, L. House, and K. Jacob (1981). Shumagin seismic gap, Alaska Peninsula: History of great earthquakes, tectonic setting, and evidence for high seismic potential, *J. Geophys. Res.* **86,** no. B5, 3821–3855, doi: 10.1029/JB086iB05p03821.

Drooff, C., and J. T. Freymueller (2021). New constraints on slip deficit on the Aleutian megathrust and inflation at Mt. Veniaminof, Alaska from repeat GPS measurements, *Geophys. Res. Lett.* **48,** no. 4, e2020GL091787, doi: 10.1029/2020GL091787.

Dziewonski, A. M., T.-A. Chou, and J. H. Woodhouse (1981). Determination of earthquake source parameters from waveform data for studies of global and regional seismicity, *J. Geophys. Res.* **86,** no. B4, 2825–2852, doi: 10.1029/JB086iB04p02825.

Ekström, G., M. Nettles, and A. M. Dziewoński (2012). The global CMT project 2004–2010: Centroid-moment tensors for 13,017 earthquakes, *Phys. Earth Planet. Int.* **200–201,** 1–9, doi: 10.1016/j.pepi.2012.04.002.

Elliott, J. L., R. Grapenthin, R. M. Parameswaran, Z. Xiao, J. T. Freymueller, and L. Fusso (2022). Cascading rupture of a megathrust, *Sci. Adv.*, **8,** no. 18, eabm4131, doi: 10.1126/sciadv.abm4131.

Faccenda, M. (2014). Water in the slab: A trilogy, *Tectonophysics* **614,** 1–30, doi: 10.1016/j.tecto.2013.12.020.

Freymueller, J. T., E. N. Suleimani, and D. J. Nicolsky (2021). Constraints on the slip distribution of the 1938 M_W 8.3 Alaska Peninsula earthquake from tsunami modeling, *Geophys. Res. Lett.* **48,** no. 9, e2021GL092812, doi: 10.1029/2021GL092812.

USGS (2016). U.S. Geological Survey Networks [SEED data], *International Federation of Digital Seismograph Networks*, doi: 10.7914/SN/GM.

Hayes, G. P., G. L. Moore, D. E. Portner, M. Hearne, H. Flamme, M. Furtney, and G. M. Smoczyk (2018). Slab2, a comprehensive subduction zone geometry model, *Science* **362,** no. 6410, 58–61, doi: 10.1126/science.aat4723.

Herman, M. W., and K. P. Furlong (2021). Triggering an unexpected earthquake in an uncoupled subduction zone, *Sci. Adv.* **7,** no. 13, doi: 10.1126/sciadv.abf7590.

Hicks, S. P., and A. Rietbrock (2015). Seismic slip on an upper-plate normal fault during a large subduction megathrust rupture, *Nature Geosci.* **8,** no. 12, 955–960, doi: 10.1038/ngeo2585.

Horowitz, W. L., P. J. Hoose, D. A. Steffy, and R. F. Turner (1989). *Geologic Report for the Shumagin Planning Area, Western Gulf of Alaska*, U.S. Department of the Interior, Minerals Management Service, Alaska OCS Region.

Hu, J., and M. Gurnis (2020). Subduction duration and slab dip, *Geochem. Geophys. Geosyst.* **21,** no. 4, e2019GC008862, doi: 10.1029/2019GC008862.

Incorporated Research Institutions for Seismology (IRIS) Transportable Array (2003). USArray Transportable Array [SEED data], *International Federation of Digital Seismograph Networks*, doi: 10.7914/SN/TA.

International Seismological Centre (ISC) Bulletin (2018). [Data set], International Seismological Centre, doi: 10.31905/D808B830.

Jiang, Y., P. J. González, and R. Bürgmann (2022). Subduction earthquakes controlled by incoming plate geometry: The 2020 M > 7.5 Shumagin, Alaska, earthquake doublet. *Earth Planet. Sci. Lett.* **584,** 117,447, doi: 10.1016/j.epsl.2022.117447.

Kuehn, H., M. R. Nedimovic, D. J. Shillington, and A. Bécel (2024). Variations in reflection signature and slip behavior. Tectonics and seismic structure of Alaska and Northwestern Canada, *EarthScope and Beyond*, 419.

Li, J., D. J. Shillington, A. Bécel, M. R. Nedimović, S. C. Webb, D. M. Saffer, *et al.* (2015). Downdip variations in seismic reflection character: Implications for fault structure and seismogenic behavior in the Alaska subduction zone, *J. Geophys. Res.* **120,** no. 11, 7883–7904, doi: 10.1002/2015JB012338.

Li, Z., D. A. Wiens, W. Shen, and D. J. Shillington (2024). Along-strike variations of Alaska subduction zone structure and hydration determined from amphibious seismic data, *J. Geophys. Res.* **129,** no. 3, e2023JB027800, doi: 10.1029/2023JB027800.

Liu, C., Y. Bai, T. Lay, Y. Feng, and X. Xiong (2023). Megathrust complexity and the up-dip extent of slip during the 2021 Chignik, Alaska Peninsula earthquake, *Tectonophysics* **854,** 229,808, doi: 10.1016/j.tecto.2023.229808.

Liu, C., T. Lay, and X. Xiong (2022). The 29 July 2021 M_W 8.2 Chignik, Alaska Peninsula earthquake rupture inferred from seismic and geodetic observations: Re-rupture of the western 2/3 of the 1938 rupture zone, *Geophys. Res. Lett.* **49,** no. 4, e2021GL096004, doi: 10.1029/2021GL096004.

Mousavi, S. M., and G. C. Beroza (2022). Deep-learning seismology, *Science* **377,** no. 6607, eabm4470, doi: 10.1126/science.abm4470.

Mousavi, S. M., W. L. Ellsworth, W. Zhu, L. Y. Chuang, and G. C. Beroza (2020). Earthquake transformer—An attentive deep-learning model for simultaneous earthquake detection and phase picking, *Nat. Commun.* **11,** no. 1, 3952, doi: 10.1038/s41467-020-17591-w.

National Oceanic and Atmospheric Administration (NOAA). (1967). National Tsunami Warning Center Alaska Seismic Network [SEED data], *International Federation of Digital Seismograph Networks*, doi: 10.7914/SN/AT.

Park, Y., S. M. Mousavi, W. Zhu, W. L. Ellsworth, and G. C. Beroza (2020). Machine-learning-based analysis of the Guy-Greenbrier, Arkansas earthquakes: A tale of two sequences, *Geophys. Res. Lett.* **47,** no. 6, e2020GL087032, doi: 10.1029/2020GL087032.

Ruppert, N. A., G. Barcheck, and G. A. Abers (2022). Enhanced regional earthquake catalog with Alaska amphibious community seismic experiment data, *Seismol. Res. Lett.* doi: 10.1785/0220220226.

Scripps Institution of Oceanography (1986). Global Seismograph Network - IRIS/IDA [SEED data], *International Federation of Digital Seismograph Networks*, doi: 10.7914/SN/II.

Segall, P., and D. D. Pollard (1980). Mechanics of discontinuous faults, *J. Geophys. Res.* **85,** no. B8, 4337–4350, doi: 10.1029/JB085iB08p04337.

Senapati, B., E. O. Lindsey, B. Kundu, D. Panda, D. K. Tiwari, and R. K. Yadav (2024). 'Double Puzzle' at the Shumagin seismic gap, Alaska Peninsula: Intraslab strike-slip faulting loaded by lateral variations in megathrust fault friction, *Geophys. J. Int.* **236,** no. 3, 1471–1483, doi: 10.1093/gji/ggae002.

Shillington, D. J., A. Bécel, and M. R. Nedimović (2022). Upper plate structure and megathrust properties in the Shumagin gap near the July 2020 M 7.8 Simeonof event, *Geophys. Res. Lett.* **49,** no. 2, e2021GL096974, doi: 10.1029/2021GL096974.

Shillington, D. J., A. Bécel, M. R. Nedimović, H. Kuehn, S. C. Webb, G. A. Abers, *et al.* (2015). Link between plate fabric, hydration and subduction zone seismicity in Alaska, *Nature Geosci.* **8,** no. 12, 961–964, doi: 10.1038/ngeo2586.

Tan, Y. J., F. Waldhauser, W. L. Ellsworth, M. Zhang, W. Zhu, M. Michele, *et al.* (2021). Machine-learning-based high-resolution earthquake catalog reveals how complex fault structures were activated during the 2016–2017 central Italy sequence, *Seism. Rec.* **1,** no. 1, 11–19, doi: 10.1785/0320210001.

Tape, C., and A. Lomax (2022). Aftershock regions of Aleutian-Alaska megathrust earthquakes, 1938–2021, *J. Geophys. Res.* **127,** no. 7, e2022JB024336, doi: 10.1029/2022JB024336.

von Huene, R., J. J. Miller, and A. Krabbenhoeft (2021). The Alaska convergent margin Backstop Splay fault zone, a potential large tsunami generator between the frontal prism and continental framework, *Geochem. Geophys. Geosyst.* **22,** no. 1, e2019GC008901, doi: 10.1029/2019GC008901.

Wang, F., S. S. Wei, C. Drooff, J. L. Elliott, J. T. Freymueller, N. A. Ruppert, and H. Zhang (2024). Fluids control along-strike variations in the Alaska megathrust slip, *Earth Planet. Sci. Lett.* **633,** 118,655, doi: 10.1016/j.epsl.2024.118655.

Wang, F., S. S. Wei, N. A. Ruppert, H. Zhang, and J. Wu (2025). Slab morphology, dehydration, and sub-arc melting beneath the Alaska Peninsula revealed by body-wave tomography, *J. Geophys. Res.* **130,** no. 3, e2024JB029814, doi: 10.1029/2024JB029814.

Wei, S. S., P. Ruprecht, S. L. Gable, E. G. Huggins, N. Ruppert, L. Gao, and H. Zhang (2021). Along-strike variations in intermediate-depth seismicity and arc magmatism along the Alaska Peninsula, *Earth Planet. Sci. Lett.* **563,** 116,878, doi: 10.1016/j.epsl.2021.116878.

Wetzler, N., T. Lay, E. E. Brodsky, and H. Kanamori (2018). Systematic deficiency of aftershocks in areas of high coseismic slip for large subduction zone earthquakes, *Sci. Adv.* **4,** no. 2, eaao3225, doi: 10.1126/sciadv.aao3225.

Xi, Z., S. S. Wei, W. Zhu, G. C. Beroza, Y. Jie, and N. Saloor (2024). Deep learning for deep earthquakes: Insights from OBS observations of the Tonga subduction zone, *Geophys. J. Int.* **238,** no. 2, 1073–1088, doi: 10.1093/gji/ggae200.

Xiao, Z., J. T. Freymueller, R. Grapenthin, J. L. Elliott, C. Drooff, and L. Fusso (2021). The deep Shumagin gap filled: Kinematic rupture model and slip budget analysis of the 2020 M_w 7.8 Simeonof earthquake constrained by GNSS, global seismic waveforms, and floating InSAR, *Earth Planet. Sci. Lett.* **576,** 117,241, doi: 10.1016/j.epsl.2021.117241.

Yang, L., J. Wang, and C. Xu (2023). Coseismic Coulomb stress changes induced by the 2020–2021 Alaska earthquake sequence in and around the Shumagin gap and their influence on the Alaska-Aleutian subduction interface, *Geod. Geodyn.* doi: 10.1016/j.geog.2023.04.007.

Ye, L., Y. Bai, D. Si, T. Lay, K. F. Cheung, and H. Kanamori (2022). Rupture model for the 29 July 2021 M_W 8.2 Chignik, Alaska earthquake constrained by seismic, geodetic, and tsunami observations, *J. Geophys. Res.* **127,** no. 7, e2021JB023676, doi: 10.1029/2021JB023676.

Ye, L., T. Lay, H. Kanamori, Y. Yamazaki, and K. F. Cheung (2021). The 22 July 2020 M 7.8 Shumagin seismic gap earthquake: Partial rupture of a weakly coupled megathrust, *Earth Planet. Sci. Lett.* **562,** 116,879, doi: 10.1016/j.epsl.2021.116879.

Zhang, H., and C. H. Thurber (2003). Double-difference tomography: The method and its application to the Hayward fault, California, *Bull. Seismol. Soc. Am.* **93,** no. 5, 1875–1889, doi: 10.1785/0120020190.

Zhang, Y., R. Wang, T. R. Walter, W. Feng, Y. Chen, and Q. Huang (2017). Significant lateral dip changes may have limited the scale of the 2015 M_w 7.8 Gorkha earthquake, *Geophys. Res. Lett.* **44,** no. 17, 8847–8856, doi: 10.1002/2017GL074095.

Zhu, W., and G. C. Beroza (2019). PhaseNet: A deep-neural-network-based seismic arrival-time picking method, *Geophys. J. Int.* **216,** no. 1, 261–273, doi: 10.1093/gji/ggy423.

Zhu, W., I. W. McBrearty, S. M. Mousavi, W. L. Ellsworth, and G. C. Beroza (2022). Earthquake phase association using a Bayesian Gaussian mixture model, *J. Geophys. Res.* **127,** no. 5, e2021JB023249, doi: 10.1029/2021JB023249.

Zhu, W., B. Rong, Y. Jie, and S. S. Wei (2025). Robust earthquake location using random sample consensus (RANSAC), arXiv, doi: 10.48550/arXiv.2502.10933.

Manuscript received 26 February 2025
Published online 10 September 2025

Lahar Early Warning at Volcano Santiaguito, Guatemala: A Standard and a Deep Learning Approach

OPEN ACCESS

Dario Jozinović*[1], Frederick Massin[1], John Clinton[1], and Amilcar Roca[2]

Abstract

Santiaguito is an active volcano located in Guatemala. Among its many hazards, frequent lahar flows impact the infrastructure and the population living and working downstream among the wide river channel network. Lahars are flows comprising large amounts of water and pyroclastic debris which can rapidly initiate and reach speeds of tens of meters per second down the channels making them highly destructive. Lahars are commonplace in the long rainy season. Recently, the agency responsible for monitoring earthquake and volcanic activity in Guatemala (INSIVUMEH), has built and operates a dense real-time seismic network around the volcano. This study shows how seismic data can be used to provide early warning for lahars. We used the 2022 and 2023 seismic data to create a lahar catalog with a total of 50 lahars. We use the seismic records of lahars from 2022 (91 waveforms from 25 events) to train a Siamese Neural Network (SNN) that uses 5 min waveforms to produce a lahar detection. We use the same data to optimize a classical lahar detector that uses ratios between two different short-term/long-term average (STA/LTA) characteristic functions. We test and compare both approaches on continuous data from 2023. Both algorithms operate as single-station detectors but require detection from at least two stations. The tests show that the STA/LTA method misses fewer events, whereas the SNN provides earlier warnings. We show that the two methods could be combined for an optimal lahar early warning that could be faster than the individual methods and operate on a single station. In a move toward operational use, the STA/LTA method (implemented through SeisComP) is used to operate a real-time early warning messaging system at INSIVUMEH. Furthermore, we demonstrate the usefulness of SNNs for developing deep learning models when little training data is available.

Cite this article as Jozinović, D., F. Massin, J. Clinton, and A. Roca (2025). Lahar Early Warning at Volcano Santiaguito, Guatemala: A Standard and a Deep Learning Approach, *Seismol. Res. Lett.* **97**, 204–216, doi: 10.1785/0220250097.

Supplemental Material

Introduction

The Santiaguito-Santa Maria volcanic complex is located in Guatemala's western volcanic highlands, along the westernmost section of the central American volcanic arc and in the southern rim of Xela caldera (Bennati *et al.*, 2011). Lying between the Quetzaltenango and Retalhuleu departments, this volcanic complex is 115 km west of Guatemala City. Formed during four different growth periods between 102,000 and 35,000 yr ago, in 1902 Santa Maria's towering stratovolcano produced a Plinian eruption, one of the biggest and most violent of the twentieth century (Williams and Self, 1983). Just 20 yr later, in June 1922, volcanic activity resumed with the growth of a dacitic dome in the crater left by the 1902 eruption (Sapper, 1926; Rose, 1973). This dome, "Caliente," is the first of four dacitic domes that together form the Santiaguito dome complex. The 1929 Caliente dome collapse produced pyroclastic density currents (PDCs) in a volume of 1.5×10^7 cubic meters that traveled 10 km to the south, sweeping across plantations and rural communities, causing an estimated 5000 deaths. Since its formation, activity at the complex has migrated between the four domes and alternated between periods of increased explosive or extrusive activity and some resting periods. Since 1986, however, activity has become localized exclusively to the Caliente dome.

Since 1922, minor eruptions have continued to occur (volcanologists usually consider this period as one long-lived

1. Swiss Seismological Service, ETH Zurich, Zurich, Switzerland, https://orcid.org/0000-0001-7443-3915 (DJ); https://orcid.org/0000-0002-7532-5139 (FM); https://orcid.org/0000-0001-8626-2703 (JC); 2. Instituto Nacional de Sismología, Vulcanologia, Meteorologia e Hidrología (INSIVUMEH), Guatemala City, Guatemala, https://orcid.org/0000-0002-7920-1141 (AR)

*Corresponding author: dario.jozinovic@sed.ethz.ch

eruption). Other significant eruptions and/or collapses that generated PDCs up to 5–7 km long occurred in 1989, 2010, 2016, 2020, 2021, and 2022 (Lamb *et al.*, 2019; Global Volcanism Program, 2023). It is hypothesized that magma is continuously extracted from a stratified storage zone ~25–12 km deep formed during the ~25,000 yr of quiescence that preceded the 1902 eruption (Scott, 2016; Wallace *et al.*, 2020), whereas a 150–600 m shallow plug (Holland *et al.*, 2011) traps gases arising from the magma before it erupts in small explosions (Lamb *et al.*, 2019; Carter *et al.*, 2020) and/or dacite lava flows. After erupting, the plug reseals, and pressure begins to rise again. The dome shows a periodic (26 ± 6 min; Johnson *et al.*, 2014) pattern of inflation and deflation which reflects gas accumulation and release cycles, with some releases occurring explosively, and others contributing to the extrusion dome complex that is growing at a rate of ~0.56 m^3/s since 1967 (Rose, 1973; Harris *et al.*, 2003). Typical volcanic activity at Caliente dome includes many hazards such as PDCs, lava flows, lahars, explosions and avalanches, and ash dispersal and fall.

Because of the multiple hazards, as well as the level of exposure with 1.6 million people living within 30 km (including the fifth largest city of Guatemala, Quetzaltenango, with about 180,000 inhabitants), Santiaguito-Santa Maria's volcanic complex is currently listed in first place (i.e., the most dangerous) in the relative threat volcanic ranking of Guatemalan volcanoes (Roca *et al.*, 2021), developed between 2019 and 2020 by the Guatemalan National Institute of Seismology, Volcanology, Meteorology and Hydrology (INSIVUMEH; *Instituto Nacional de Sismología, Vulcanologia, Meteorologia e Hidrología*). Pyroclastic and lahar flows pose a threat to workers and infrastructure in farms harvesting the fertile volcanic soils of the southwest flank (Fig. 1). Consequently, the southern slopes of the Santiaguito-Santa Maria volcanic complex are the priority target for the installation of geophysical instruments to support the volcanic surveillance efforts by INSIVUMEH.

Lahars are among the most threatening volcanic hazards. The 1985 eruption of Nevado del Ruiz in Colombia, which triggered lahars, left an estimated 25,000 victims (Sigurdsson and Carey, 1986), and the 1980 cataclysmic Plinian eruption of Mount St. Helens in Washington, United States, and subsequent lahars resulted in 57 casualties (Lipman and Mullineaux, 1981). Their early detection is essential for mitigating volcanic hazards at Santiaguito (and other volcanoes). Five of the eight river channels shown in Figure 1 have recorded lahar flows in 2022 and 2023. All the channels merge at one point—15 km south-southwest from the crater, generating recurrent impacts over the same area. Lahars can drastically modify the topography of the southern flank of the volcano. They can cause significant damage and even casualties (Global Volcanism Program, 2023). For example, the El Palmar community (Fig. 1) was strongly impacted in 1982–1983 and 1997–1998, and was finally permanently evacuated. Lahars are commonplace in the rainy season and can last up to several hours.

Seismic monitoring should be an essential component of any volcano observatory (Sparks *et al.*, 2012; Wassermann, 2012; De Angelis *et al.*, 2019). It provides the capability to track the evolution of volcanic activity in terms of eruptive rate, style, and location. As an example, seismological monitoring at a volcano observatory can support continuous tracking of lahar pathways and dimensions, gas and ash explosions, and volcano–tectonic (VT) seismic activity (De Angelis *et al.*, 2016; Gottschämmer *et al.*, 2021; Rohnacher *et al.*, 2021).

Recently, low-frequency acoustic monitoring (infrasound) has become routinely used to detect the infrasounds associated with debris flows, including lahars, as well as with pyroclastic flows (e.g., Yamasato, 1997, at Unzen, Japan; Ripepe *et al.*, 2009, at Soufrière Hills, Montserrat). Unfortunately, an infrasound sensor array was not available at Santiaguito. Furthermore, seismic monitoring of debris flows has also gained traction in recent years (Allstadt *et al.*, 2018; Hürlimann *et al.*, 2019). Kramer *et al.* (2024) detailed lahar monitoring advancements made since 2016 at Mount Rainier to improve the detection latency of events underway. Indeed, they justified the discontinuation of acoustic flow monitors (LaHusen, 2005) in favor of an expanded broadband network alongside cameras and infrasound for reference. Although conventional seismic methods have been demonstrated to characterize debris and pyroclastic flow parameters (Coviello *et al.*, 2019), innovative new methods based on machine learning (ML) could bring improvements in terms of the number of lahars detected and, most importantly, in the timeliness of the lahar detection allowing for better integration in future lahar early warning systems.

In this study, we present a new seismic network built around Santiaguito, which is being used to manually build a catalog of lahar signals by INSIVUMEH technical staff. In this study, we revised and extended the catalog for the 2022 and 2023 seasons. With the extended catalog, we investigated the use of a classical technique based on the short-term/long-term average (STA/LTA) ratio and a deep learning model to detect lahars from continuous seismic data. We compare their performances and assess their capability to provide lahar early warning, focusing on both the number of lahars detected and the timeliness of the provided warning. Finally, we describe an operational lahar early warning based on the STA/LTA method developed and described in this study, which is running in real time at INSIVUMEH.

Seismic network and the lahar signals catalog

In 2022, motivated by the VolcSat project funded by the Swiss Agency for Development and Cooperation (COSUDE), a permanent multiparametric network (including seismic sensors) began to be installed. All stations are installed and operated by INSIVUMEH within the Guatemala seismic network (GI; see Data and Resources), and hardware was funded from

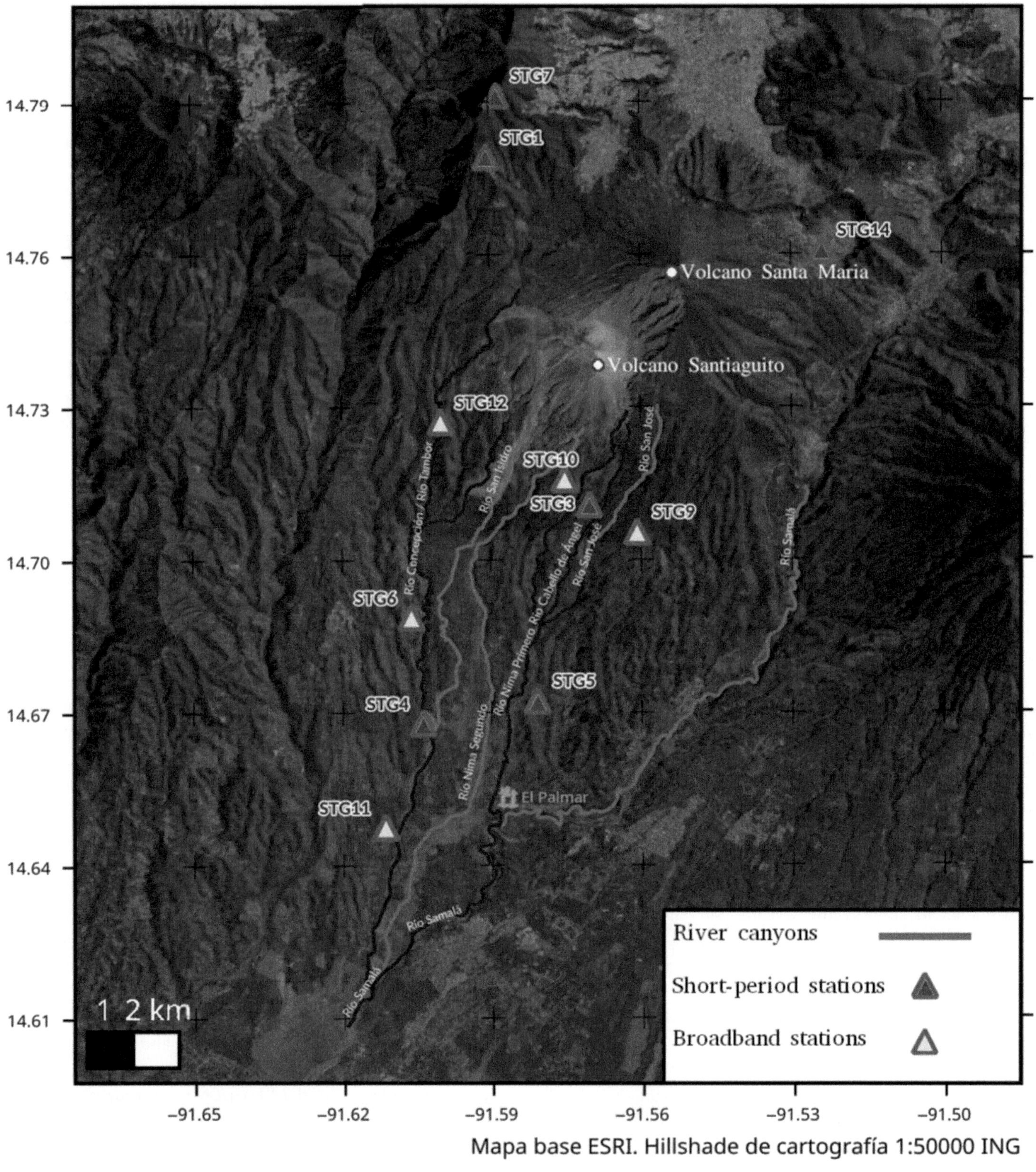

Figure 1. The Santiaguito-Santa Maria volcanic complex and the river channels through which lahars descend, including the stations from the seismic network. The broadband (yellow) and short-period (red) stations are shown as triangles. The blue paths show the channels through which the lahars can propagate. The darker blue paths show the channels through which had lahar flows in 2022 and 2023. The lahars propagate from north to south, with population numbers increasing as the flow moves downstream. The abandoned El Palmar community is shown in orange. The color version of this figure is available only in the electronic edition.

INSIVUMEH as well as donations from COSUDE and Volcano Disaster Assistance Program (VDAP)/United States Agency for International Development (USAID)/U.S. Geological Survey. Today, the INSIVUMEH network available for this study comprises 11 multiparametric stations, with 5 broadband (3-component) and 6 short-period seismic sensors, shown in Figure 1 and further described in Table S1, available in the supplemental material to this article (technical summary). Data are sampled at 100 Hz. Stations are predominantly situated toward the south of the volcano because the main goal of the network was to monitor lahar and pyroclastic flows. Stations were selected to cover the entire lahar catchment area, with four stations located as close to the Santiaguito dome complex as possible, and four stations located further downstream, closer to the population centers. Three additional stations are located North of Santa Maria. Stations typically have solar power and cell phone or radio communications. The eight sites south of Santa Maria are located relatively close to river channels, but not so close that they are at risk. A priority is achieving station security so stations are often located in or around small buildings on farms, which often leads to higher site noise. The stations vary in quality, both in terms of sensor and datalogger quality and robustness. Sample noise power spectral densities for the vertical component of stations for 2023 are included in Figures S1–11 and the data availability summary is in Figure S13. It is clear that at high frequencies, noise across the network is similarly high, near to or even exceeding the high noise model between 1 and 10 Hz. The data are continuously streamed to INSIVUMEH headquarters in Guatemala City and integrated into a SeisComP system. Challenging environmental conditions and almost continuous ash fall at some of the sites where the stations are located sometimes lead to gaps in the data completeness (Fig. S13). However, the performance of the whole network is still satisfactory, allowing for high uptime of the lahar detectors, with the case of having the whole network out occurring extremely rarely.

Most lahars initiate at the upper flanks of the volcano. During the 2022 and 2023 rainy seasons, the majority of lahars occurred in the channel Rio Cabello de Ángel, since a major lava flow on the southwest flank of Santiaguito in 2021 partially blocked the channels on the western side. The seismic records from a lahar within Cabello de Ángel are shown in Figure 2. The lahar is seen across the network as a long and emergent cigar-like signal with frequencies predominantly between 1 and 15 Hz. The lahar can first be identified at the stations near the upper parts of the river channel (STG12, STG10, and STG3) at ~18:40 UTC, with concurrent detection at the stations to the north (SGT1 and SGT7). High-frequency, high-amplitude signals are observed at the stations with higher elevation. Because the flow progresses, the seismic signal at the downstream STG5 station transitions to a higher frequency as the flow is close by, estimated at 19:13 UTC, 30 min after a possible first detection. The lahar is less visible at stations located near other channels.

In 2023, lahars were also observed in the channel Rio Tambor on the western flank; an example set of seismograms is in Figure S16. For this lahar, the signal is not as strong across the network, and although more stations are missing clear signals, the event is identifiable.

During office hours, an on-duty seismologist at INSIVUMEH is observing spectrograms and seismic amplitude trends from the Santiaguito network stations in real time and identifies lahars as they occur. Because the majority of lahars occur following afternoon rains during the season, this means most lahars are identified and catalogued as they occur. Furthermore, the local community and COLRED (community civil defense organization; *Coordinadoras Locales para la Reducción de Desastres*) report lahar occurrences (and their location) through a WhatsApp (WhatsApp Inc., 2020) messaging group. Via these detections, INSIVUMEH curates a catalog of lahars. A complete catalog is a prerequisite to any work to optimize a lahar detector, and as a part of this work, we manually reviewed daily spectrograms from each station. Lahar signals can be complex depending on flow conditions and proximity to the flow, among other factors, though they have in common an emergent, long-duration signal that excites a narrow bandwidth typically between 1 and 10 Hz. Hence, these events can be readily identified and distinguished from other strong signals such as local and regional seismicity, volcano explosions, or weather-related noise. An example of a daily spectrogram is shown in Figure S12. The lahar catalog used in this study is a combination of the information from INSIVUMEH, the local community, and our review. This catalog consisted of 25 events from 2022 and 25 events from 2023. Additional events detected by the SNN model, which were not used for training, have been added later to the final catalog, bringing the final number of events to 28 (2022) and 29 (2023). All events occur during a window from March to November. The catalog also contains the manually picked onset times at the stations that have a clear lahar signal (Tables S2 and S3). It should be noted, however, that the lahars' signals are very emergent, making it hard to pick the exact onset time. When picking manually, we opted for a more conservative criterion by picking the onset when the signal was coming from a lahar. Because of the reasons mentioned earlier, it can be expected that all the manual picks could have an error of ±5 min. Figures S14 and S18 provide an insight into the manual detections at each station (ordered from north to south), allowing us to understand which stations record the most lahars. In addition to the lahar onset times, we also added manually determined times of significant flow at station STG5 (e.g., Fig. 2), to be used as a proxy for warning time provided to communities downstream. The events missing the significant flow timing were either not flowing in the eastern part of the channel network (e.g., Fig. S16) or were not significant enough to be clearly seen downstream. The impact of the lahar on the population does not just depend on the warning provided but

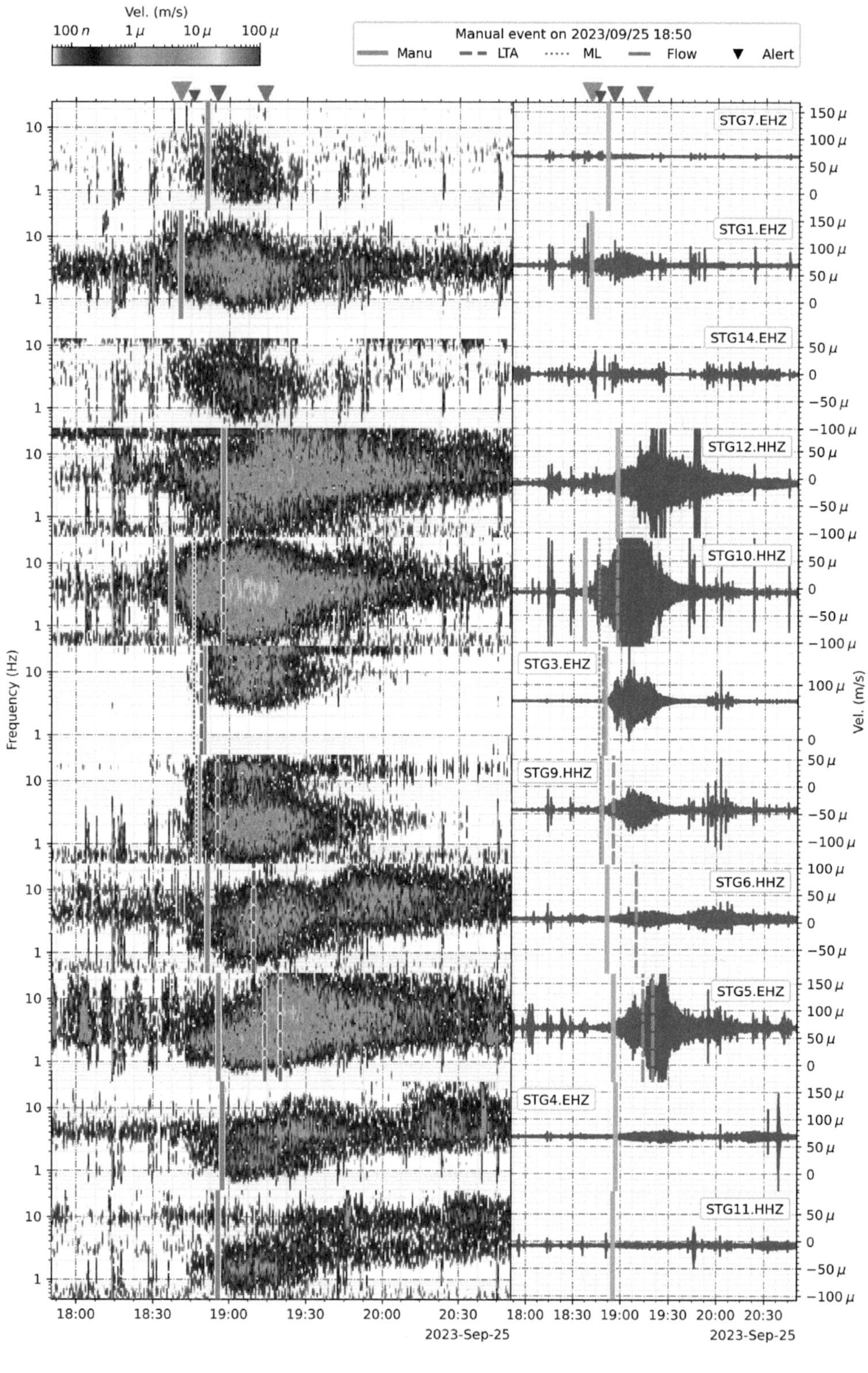

Figure 2. An example of a lahar signal captured by the Santiaguito seismic network on 25 September 2023. Station names are indicated and are ordered from north to south (see Fig. 1). The summit of Santiaguito volcano lies between SGT1 and SGT10. The gain-corrected vertical component in velocity, meters per second, is shown as a seismogram and continuous wavelet transform scalogram (as defined in Kristeková *et al.*, 2006). At each station, orange, green, and red vertical bars indicate the manually picked first observation and machine learning (ML) and short-term average/long-term average (STA/LTA) trigger times. The second earliest networkwide observation (which represents the event detection time for ML and STA/LTA), is indicated by the triangles at the top, using the same color as for the bars for each method. The manually interpreted arrival of the lahar flow front on STG5 is indicated by the purple dashed bar and the purple triangle on top. The color version of this figure is available only in the electronic edition.

also on the size of the lahar itself. We therefore classified the lahars (through visual observation) into small and large ones (which can be dangerous), which is further explained in the discussion.

Methods

In this section, we describe how we can detect lahars at Santiaguito using two different approaches: a simple trigger ratio algorithm and a deep learning algorithm. Each approach consists of an independent single-station algorithm. To reduce false alarms, a common algorithm is used to combine the single-station alerts and declare a network-based alert. From the lahar catalog, we selected events from 2022 to train the deep learning model and optimize the STA/LTA detector parameters. The trained ML model and the STA/LTA detector were then applied to the continuous data from 2023 and compared with the catalog to provide a measure of the performance of the two methods, thus ensuring the independence and reliability of our test results. For all the stations, we use only the data from the vertical component in both algorithms because some of the stations have only those components available (see Table S1). Our study also provides a comparison of the traditional network seismology approach to the formalism of the deep learning community.

Trigger ratio algorithm

The trigger ratio algorithm for lahar detection relies on the ratio between two STA/LTA ratios (Allen, 1982; Baer and Kradolfer, 1987; Küperkoch

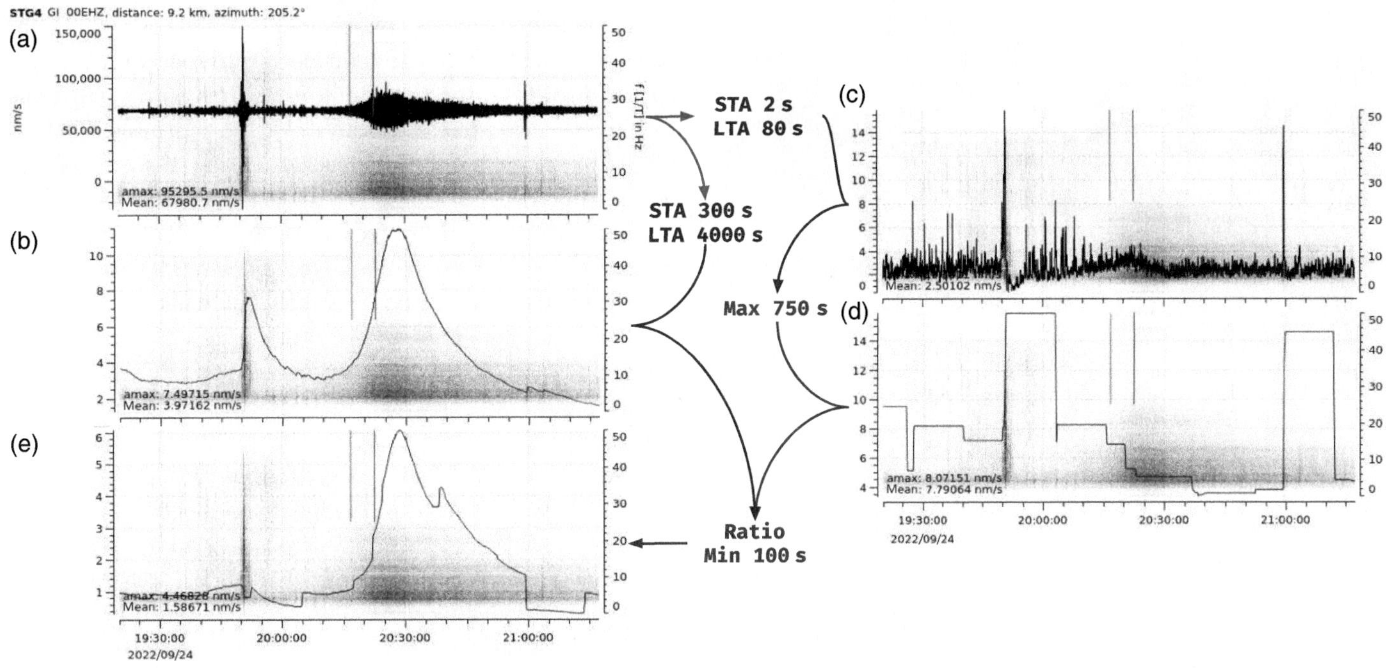

Figure 3. Illustration of the trigger ratio algorithm, using a lahar on 24 September 2022 at station STG4. (a) Raw seismic vertical component velocity time series (gain corrected), with spectrogram shown in the background. A volcanic explosion occurs at 19:50, and a lahar emerges at 20:17 (green vertical line). (b) Emerging STA/LTA function. (c) Impulsive STA/LTA function. (d) Sliding maximum of (c) over 750 s. (e) characteristic function F, the ratio of (b) over (d). For stability, F must exceed the detection threshold for at least 100 s to trigger a detection. The time of the trigger based on F is represented by a red vertical line. The color version of this figure is available only in the electronic edition.

et al., 2012; Lomax *et al.*, 2012) configured using observed characteristics of the lahars from the 2022 catalog and of the signals that are noise to this analysis (e.g., earthquakes). The method is illustrated in Figure 3, using a typical lahar signal that occurs in a noisy time window. The data from the vertical component are first preprocessed by applying a 2 Hz high-pass filter (Fig. 3a). We then calculate the emerging STA/LTA function, with the STA duration of 5 min (corresponding to the observed typical duration of the emergent onset of lahar signal) and the LTA duration of about one hour (4000 s, corresponding to only a little more than 10 times the STA to limit memory usage, while ensuring a reliable measure of the current noise level at time of onset, as suggested in Earthworm and SeisComP3; Allen, 1982; Baer and Kradolfer, 1987; Lomax *et al.*, 2012). The emerging long-duration STA/LTA allows for the detection of slowly rising signals with long duration, such as lahars (Fig. 3b), which would not be detected with a short-duration STA/LTA. However, high-amplitude short-duration events (e.g., earthquakes or explosions) can still affect the emerging STA value and produce false detections. To combat this, we introduce an impulsive STA/LTA (Fig. 3c), with STA duration of 2 s (corresponding to the typical observed onset duration of local and regional earthquakes) and LTA duration of 80 s (40 times the STA, corresponding to the typical suggestions in Earthworm and SeisComP3; Allen, 1982; Baer and Kradolfer, 1987; Lomax *et al.*, 2012), that detects only the impulsive signals. We combine both emerging and impulsive STA/LTA in a characteristic function, F (Fig. 3e), that divides the emerging STA/LTA (Fig. 3b) by the 12.5 min sliding maximum window of the impulsive STA/LTA to mute emerging onset for 12.5 min after any impulsive onset and the minimum over 100 s sliding window is used for detection to ensure that our threshold is exceeded for that long and avoid triggering from any remaining peculiar filtering effect such as those from gaps and electronic step signal (Fig. 3d). The function F is sensitive to long-duration average amplitude increase and not to short-duration average amplitude increase. A lahar signal onset trigger is declared if $F > 1.9$ which corresponds to about 1 unit over the envelope of the noise level of F ensuring any flow will trigger, confident that only those events can trigger. Indeed, reprocessing all the continuous data from 2022 and 2023 did not produce a single false detection. The method is implemented in SeisComP software, using a custom-made station trigger associator (see Data and Resources), and is operating in real time at INSIVUMEH.

Deep Learning

Siamese neural networks (Bromley *et al.*, 1993; SNNs) are a type of deep metric learning (Bellet *et al.*, 2015) based on automatic learning of a similarity measure suitable for a specific task. SNNs contain two identical subnetworks (twin networks) that share weights (Chopra *et al.*, 2005). The features extracted by applying these two subnetworks to the input data are then

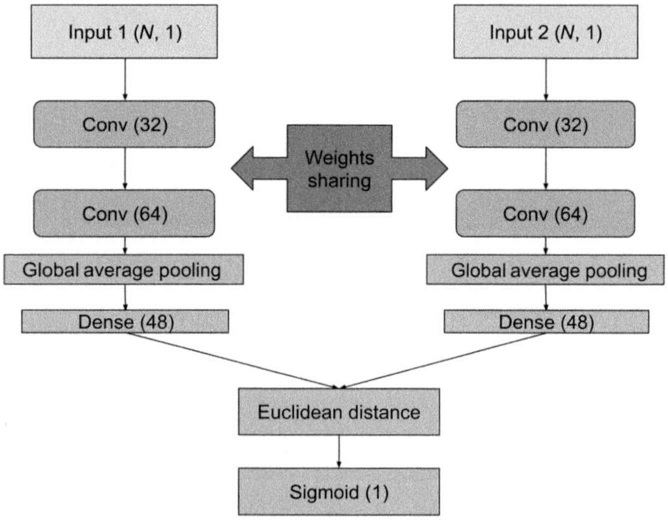

Figure 4. Siamese neural network (SNN) architecture. The number in brackets shows the dimensions of the layer. Further details about the layers are in the text. The color version of this figure is available only in the electronic edition.

used to measure the distance between a pair of input data (e.g., two images or two time series) by some predefined distance measure. Training SNNs aim to teach the two subnetworks how to extract features from the input data that will lead to the successful qualification of a pair of input data as similar or different while providing a quantitative measure of similarity. The architecture of the subnets is not strictly defined, and fully connected layers, convolutional layers, and so forth can be used to generate features relevant to similarity (distance) measurement.

The number of waveforms in the lahar (91 vertical-component waveforms from 25 lahars) and noise (102 waveforms randomly selected from the rainy season) classes of our dataset is far too small for any supervised deep learning classification method that uses waveforms (or their transformations) as an input. However, the SNNs are using pairs of waveforms as inputs, allowing us to make 19,947 different waveform combinations as inputs to the model for training. This significantly improves the possibility of the model converging to the minimum of the loss function during training, allowing the network to be trained with only a few examples of a specific class (few-shot learning). Therefore, we use SNNs as our deep learning architecture because they allow us to alleviate the problem of a small number of training samples.

The model we choose to employ (Fig. 4) consists of two convolutional neural networks (CNNs) that share weights. The inputs to the CNNs are 280-s-long one-component (vertical) waveforms. Two convolutional layers with a kernel size of 4 samples, a stride of 2 samples, and 32 and 64 filters, respectively, are then used to transform the input waveform. The output of the second convolutional layer is then processed through a global average pooling layer and then fed to a fully connected layer with 48 neurons, producing the embedding for the distance calculation. The Euclidean distance between the embeddings from the two input waveforms is calculated and then fed to the output layer with a sigmoid activation function, providing a measure of similarity of the two waveforms bounded between 0 and 1. We opted for the use of a global pooling layer to significantly reduce the number of trainable parameters in the model to tackle the small number of training data further, and have a positive side effect of accepting waveforms of any length bigger than 25 s as inputs. The exponential linear unit (ELU) activation function is applied to each layer except the output, in which the sigmoid activation function is used.

The data we used for the SNN training and validation are 280-s-long waveforms from 2022, downsampled to 50 Hz. We choose to downsample the data because we do not expect any necessary information loss (lahars have limited energy above 20 Hz) while reducing the training and inference time of the model, which can be relevant when many waveform pairs are compared. We first select 5 min windows (300 s) before resampling and then trim the 10 s of data from waveform edges to avoid any possible artifacts of resampling, leading to a 280 s long input window. To select the noise data to train the model, we select random samples from days not containing lahars that satisfy the criteria of having the absolute maximum of the last 30 s of the waveform twice as high as the absolute maximum of the first 30 s of the waveform. This selection criterion is used to select the noise waveforms that are similar to the lahar waveforms in terms of an increase in amplitude over the 280 s window. It also means that the SNN model would only be trained on the data satisfying that criterion. However, the lahar waveforms used all satisfy that criterion, and running the model in inference mode on continuous data would already include this criterion during preprocessing without any significant loss of information. The waveforms are then normalized by their input maximum and used for training the model.

The data are split into 85% training and 15% validation sets. The validation set is used to optimize the model's parameters, and testing the model is done later using the continuous data from 2023. We train the model for a maximum of 32 epochs using a batch size of 32, stopping the training if the validation accuracy does not improve for 10 epochs. The learning rate of the model is set to 0.1 in the first epochs, then to 0.01 in the subsequent epochs. If the validation accuracy does not improve for 4 epochs, the learning rate is reduced using a factor of 0.2, with a minimum learning rate of 10^{-7}. Although training the model, we had problems with the model not reaching any convergence (i.e., having a constant training and validation accuracy) when the model weights were initialized randomly. This is probably a consequence of the small number of data in the training dataset and the susceptibility of SNNs to the model hyperparameter value selection (Alkhalid, 2022; Chakraborty *et al.*, 2020). By a manual (ad hoc) trial-and-error approach to optimize the model parameters, we have trained a model that was able to converge, and then used that model to initialize the model's convolutional layers' weights for all further model training and hyperparameter optimization. Our final model converged to the minimum after 17 training epochs (taking 41 min to train on a personal laptop without a dedicated graphics processing unit), having a validation accuracy of 86%. Keras framework (Chollet *et al.*, 2015) was used to train and apply the model.

The trained model was then applied to the continuous data from 2023. We split the continuous data into 280 s waveforms with a step of one minute (i.e., data windows have a 220 s overlap). The preprocessing used for the training data (downsampling to 50 Hz, normalizing the waveforms with their maximum, and preselecting them based on the ratio between the maximums of the beginning and end of the waveform) has also been applied to the test data. The similarity score between the waveforms and the lahar templates from 2022 is then calculated on a station-by-station basis. To declare a waveform as similar to a lahar at a station, the mean similarity between all the templates for that station and the waveform must be higher than 75%. To reduce the possibility of false detections, we require the similarity to be higher than 75% in at least four consecutive 5 min (see above for the waveform trimming to 280 s) windows (with 4 min of overlap) before declaring a lahar onset at a station (thus making sure that the emerging pattern can be seen in several consecutive windows; see Fig. S17 for an example). This, in practice, means that we are using 8 min long windows for lahar detection. It should be noted, however, that the lahar start can be at any place inside those windows (i.e., the lahar onset does not have to be at the beginning of the input window), allowing us to have detections earlier than 8 min after the lahar onset (Table S1). The SNN lahar detector provides positive detections at a station for several minutes after the earliest onset detection, due to having more and more of a lahar signal in the detection window.

Trigger association

The two methods produce single-station triggers, which are then used to produce a network-wide lahar detection. We declare a lahar detection if it is triggered (i.e., detected) on at least two stations within 30 min. The same procedure is used for both the STA/LTA and the SNN. To further increase the method's robustness, we require the detection times at two stations to have at least 30 s of difference, allowing us to reduce the possibility of false detection from an earthquake that would have the onset times at different stations very close in time. The same is applied to the testing of the hybrid method in which we allow the usage of two triggers from any of the methods to produce a detection.

Both algorithms provide only the information that a lahar onset has been detected. Any other interpretation, analysis, and decision-making is left to INSIVUMEH staff, who can use all the available data (not just seismic) to analyze the ongoing lahar and take further steps (describing the lahar, declaring the end of the alert, etc.).

Algorithm Performance and Discussion

We test both methods on the entire continuous data from 2023. For detected lahars, we calculate the difference between the earliest time of the first manually picked onset, and the detection time coming from the two algorithms (Fig. 5). In addition to this, we also calculate the same difference for a hybrid detection algorithm, in which a hybrid detection would be achieved by having one detection coming from the SNN and the other from the STA/LTA algorithm. When available, we also compare the detection times with the time of significant energy onset at station STG5, which is 7.5 km downstream of the Caliente crater and close to the abandoned village of El Palmar, with the first manually picked onset at the network. We define the significant energy onset time close to station STG5 as the time of a sudden jump in dominant frequency on the spectrogram (see Fig. 2), which suggests that the lahar front begins to pass near the station. Given the location of STG5 in the lower parts of the volcano, this method allows us to approximate the warning time T_w, defined as the difference between the method detection time (two triggers) and the significant onset time on STG5, which could be given to the communities downstream of STG5. Modeling the time needed for lahars to further reach any point of interest downstream of STG5 is beyond the scope of this article. It should also be noted that the arrival on STG5 can only be seen for 16 out of the 29 lahars catalogued in 2023, corresponding to the lahars that can be mainly or only seen on the stations in the eastern part of the volcano. The time T_w, therefore, does not give us an indication of the possible warning times of lahars propagating in the other channels, but still provides valuable insight into the possible usefulness of the described methods.

"Our early warning system is designed to provide the earliest possible alert to INSIVUMEH, who are then responsible for determining the alert content and identifying the communities to be alerted. The confluence point of the main river channels descending from the southern flank of the volcano, where they join the Samalá River approximately 15 km from the volcano's summit and 7 km downstream of the STG5 seismic station, is one such location where the impact of lahars is strong and people are threatened. It is an area that can be considered as one of the targets of the system, based on high probabilities of flooding (due to river channel shallowing) and severe topographic changes (identified previously by INSIVUMEH staff), which lead to increased impacts on people and infrastructure. For this site and all sites below STG5, the alert time at STG5 provides a useful lower time threshold that can be used to estimate arrival times that are earlier than other downstream stations (such as STG11), and also earlier than for any nearby communities located close to or beyond the confluence point.

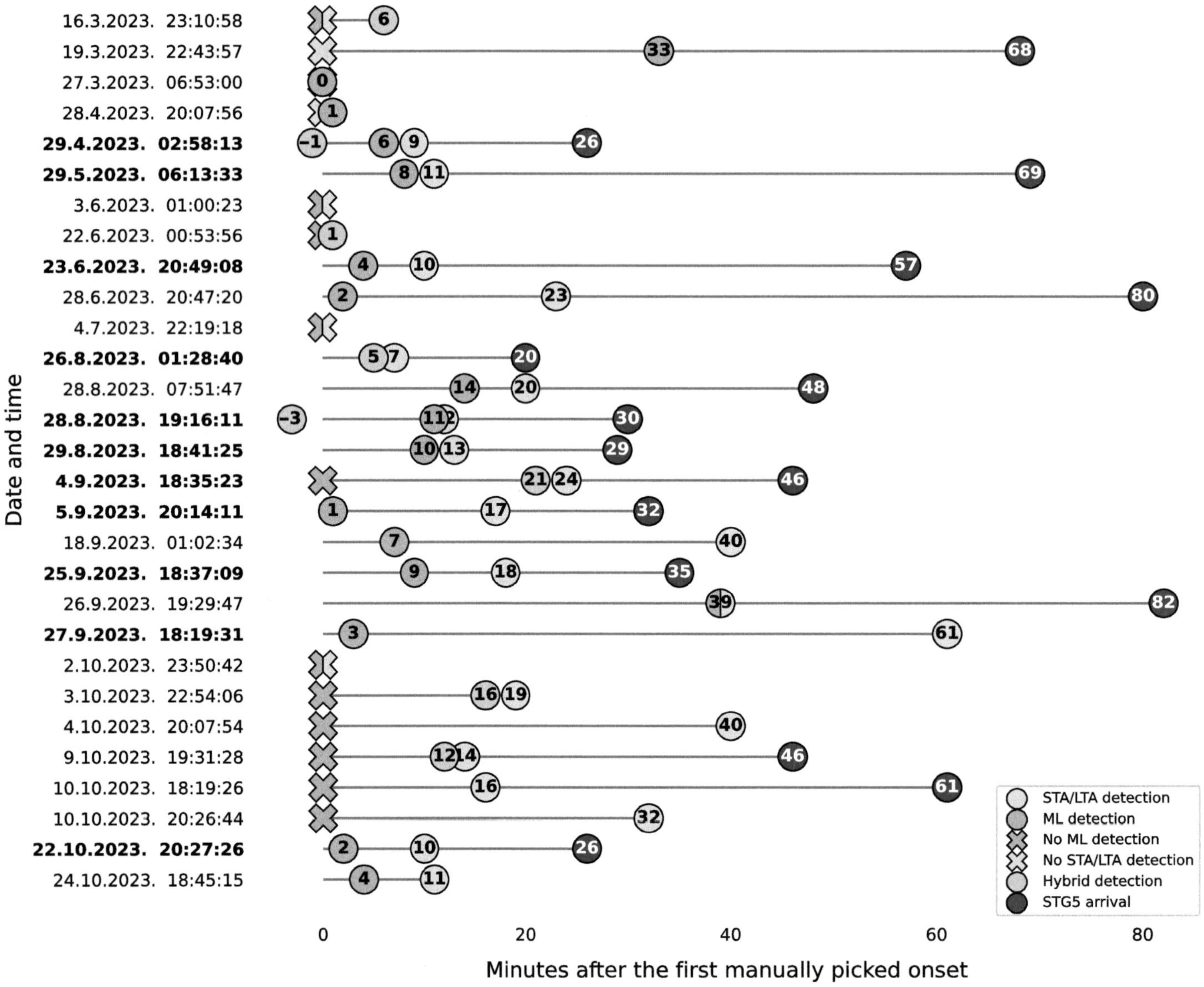

Figure 5. The detection times for the ML (blue) and STA/LTA (yellow) algorithms (in minutes after the first manually picked onset) for all 29 lahars from 2023 (testing period). A hybrid method of detection is also shown (pink) if it is faster than any of the individual algorithms. In two cases, the hybrid method is also faster than the first manually picked onset, which can be attributed to the uncertainty of the manual picks of the emerging lahar signals. In addition to the detections, the lahar flow arrival time on the station STG5 (red) is plotted for the 16 times it has been observed. The color version of this figure is available only in the electronic edition.

Another target of our early warning system is the workers on the farms who are endangered when they cross the river channels as part of their work or to get home from work. They are, however, highly mobile and spread out around the wide area of the southwestern flanks of the volcano, making the warning time for each of them very individual."

The performance of the methods is shown in Figure 5. The STA/LTA method performs better in terms of event detection —it misses 8 of 29 catalog events, whereas the SNN method misses 11 events. We classified the lahars into small and large ones (see the Seismic network and the lahar signals catalog section), which can be seen in Figure 5 in where we bolded the large events. It can be seen that, out of 11 events classified as large, the STA/LTA does not miss any while the SNN misses one. The station STG5, located by an inhabited building, provided a large number of false triggers (in both SNN and STA/LTA) when applied to the continuous data, causing five SNN false alarms in 2022 when its false triggers were paired with a false trigger on another station. On the other hand, it did not prove important for the detection of true events (which is expected given the location in the lower part of the volcano). As is standard in network seismology, we then excluded the faulty station (STG5) from the detection process. Following this, the STA/LTA and SNN did not cause any false alarms. Furthermore, we observe that all the SNN detections except one were coming from the stations in the upper parts of

Santiaguito (STG1, STG10, STG7, STG3, and STG9), meaning that the use of stations in the lower parts of Santiaguito (STG4 and STG6) did not provide significant benefits to the detection capability of the method. However, the stations STG4 and STG6 from the lower parts of Santiaguito were important for many of the STA/LTA detections. When applying the SNN, we have been using only the stations with templates from 2022 (STG1, STG3, STG5, STG6, STG7, STG9, STG10, and STG4). The hybrid system produced one false alarm (STG5 was not used). It should be noted, however, that the ML and the hybrid method detected two new events each in 2023, which were not part of the original catalog and were confirmed as (weak) lahars upon manual review (and added to the final catalog). These events have not been detected by STA/LTA.

The advantage of the SNN is that it provides earlier detection times than STA/LTA for most of the events. The mean improvement in warning time T_w, compared to the STA/LTA detection times, is 7 min, and the median improvement is 5 min. The two methods, however, complement each other as the later warning times of the STA/LTA are compensated by their higher reliability with fewer events missed. Furthermore, a hybrid system, using two single-station detections from either of the algorithms, possibly even from a single station, could provide even earlier warning times for some of the lahars (Fig. 5). Another benefit of the SNN when compared to the STA/LTA is the possibility of detecting events in sequence with short temporal differences (e.g., the events on 3 November 2022 which are two hours apart, see Table S3). The STA/LTA relies on a 4000 s long window to calculate the LTA, which means that the STA (300 s) of the second event would not be significantly higher than the LTA unless the second event is significantly stronger. Furthermore, impulsive signals (earthquakes, explosions) can further delay the STA/LTA detection due to the 750-s-long mute time (after impulsive signals) incorporated in the algorithm. The SNN does not have those problems because it relies on 5 min long waveforms only.

Figure 5 and Table S2 also show that the mean of the warning time T_w (the difference between an algorithm detection time and the STG5 flow onset)—a proxy for lahar impact on a larger population—is 29 (STA/LTA) and 35 (SNN) min, whereas the median is 21 (STA/LTA) and 31 (SNN) min. It should be noted that the mean and median for the two methods have not been calculated on the same set of lahars, but only those that had the T_w calculated for the respective methods. If we were to use only the lahars that have T_w for both methods, the mean T_w would be 35 (SNN) and 29 (STA/LTA), and the median would be 29 (SNN) and 19 (STA/LTA). When we compare the mean improvement in detection speed of the SNN (5 min faster than the STA/LTA) with the absolute warning times the systems provide, it is clear that the faster detection coming from the SNN is providing significant benefit to the system. This long warning time of both methods is very encouraging for the system because there are significant lead times for messages to get to the populations and for them to react appropriately. We expect that these are the significant lahars that reach the local population centers below. The arrival time of the lahar at STG5 is dependent on many variables, primarily the lahar initialization point, the river channel, and the flow dynamics, meaning that the detection time is not only dependent on the seismic network and the algorithm but also on the lahar itself. We therefore provided normalized (relative) arrival times (T_{wn}) in Tables S2 and S3 to give more context for algorithm performance.

In addition to running the methods on the continuous data from 2023 (testing year), we performed the same test on the continuous data from 2022 to check how many false alarms, if any, the methods would produce in 2022. The results show (chapter 2 of the supplemental material) that both methods perform well, and that the SNN even detected three smaller new events (i.e., new detections are confirmed as lahars upon review). However, the SNN also produced one false alarm. It is, however, interesting that the STA/LTA fails to detect one and SNN three of these (significant) events. Notably, these are all different events, further supporting the complementarity of the two methods.

The stations without templates (STG11, STG12, and STG14) have not been used by SNN, while they were used in the testing year (2023) with STA/LTA (they were set up at the end of 2022, so they were not included in the results of STA/LTA for 2022). This means that the STA/LTA has the advantage of using more stations than the SNN in 2023. This, on one hand, biases the results toward STA/LTA, but on the other hand, the advantage of STA/LTA is that it does not need any templates and can be run on a station from the moment it is installed and streaming. The results reported in Figure 5 and Table S2 for the STA/LTA use all the stations available (except STG5). To give more insight into the algorithms' performance, we also calculate the warning times if the stations without templates were not used with STA/LTA, and add a column in Table S2, which shows the difference in detection time between the two cases. We can see that the exclusion of stations without templates would affect the STA/LTA detections in six events, making it slower from 1 to 31 min and missing one event previously detected. It should be noted that the larger events affected would be delayed by 1 or 2 minutes, and that the significant change in detection happens on smaller events.

The performance of both methods makes us confident that they are robust and that the results achieved on the test data (2023) can be expected in future years. Furthermore, a large majority of the lahars from 2022 seem to have originated and propagated in the eastern part of the channel network, producing a specific cross-station waveform pattern. In 2023, however, many of the lahars can be seen propagating in the west side of the channel network (e.g., Fig. S16), which did not significantly influence the performance of the algorithms trained and optimized on 2022 data.

The methods used here have been developed and optimized using a limited amount of data from 2022. Using data from both 2022 and 2023 to optimize the methods for 2024 could further improve the results. For example, using the data from both 2022 and 2023, the SNN method could be even more reliable and robust by significantly increasing the number of templates from the stations and using stations that were missing templates from 2022 (STG11, STG12, and STG14). These additional data can further be used to significantly increase the amount of training data and improve the SNN model itself. All these optimizations do not require significant (or any) changes in the software used, making it an easy target for future improvements.

The 2022 training data had all the lahars in the eastern part of the volcano, in only one river channel (*Rio Nima Primero*; confirmed by the observers in the field close to the channels and INSIVUMEH technicians on duty). In 2023 (the testing year), the lahars also appeared in the western part of the channel network, and both methods still performed well on those. This indicates that the methods could also detect lahars that appear in other channels or potentially even other volcanoes with some adaptations and fine-tuning of the methods. The STA/LTA method can be readily transferred to any other volcano through SeisComP, and we expect that it is general enough to work on other volcanic settings threatened by lahars as long as there is a relevant seismic monitoring infrastructure in operation. We expect the same for the SNN because it has been trained and applied to different stations from Santiaguito, which should allow it to generalize to other unseen stations. Furthermore, no site-specific or region-specific preprocessing has been done on the data when training the SNN (e.g., filtering at a specific band), and the input data are normalized by the input waveform maximum. We have also successfully tested the SNN at a station without templates (STG4—not using the templates from the station) using templates from other stations, indicating that it could be applied to a new station without lahar records. Thorough optimization of the STA/LTA and the SNN parameters could allow the methods to work as hybrid single-station detectors (requiring triggers from both methods) with very few false alarms, for volcanoes with only a single station available. However, such conclusions cannot be made without further testing, which is beyond the scope of our work.

At INSIVUMEH, the STA/LTA implemented in SeisComP has been connected to a messaging system capable of sending alerts. Since mid-2023, the alerts have been sent through the Telegram (Telegram FZ LLC and Telegram Messenger Inc., 2019) app to a limited number of key stakeholders in the region. Around 100 persons are directly receiving the messages, including local civil defense (COLRED), community leaders, local government officials, and business owners. Further public rollout will be coordinated by INSIVUMEH and CONRED (national civil defense organization; *Coordinadora Nacional para la Reducción de Desastres*). Two technical meetings (2023 and 2024) have been held with each user to explain the capabilities and limitations of the warning system. A fully operational system that reaches more vulnerable people will require further investment and should include additional methods of providing warning, such as sirens, as well as a clear communication policy on how to react upon receiving a warning, and relevant training for the affected populations.

Conclusion

In the rainy season, lahars are a regular occurrence and pose a major hazard for the populations working and living near the channels downstream of Volcano Santiaguito. An early detection of lahar flows will have a significant impact on the mitigation of one of the key volcanic hazards at Santiaguito. We used seismic data from a new dense seismic network to generate a complete lahar catalog spanning two seasons in 2022 and 2023. We develop two different approaches to lahar detection, based on traditional detection and deep learning approaches, and evaluate their performance. Data from 2022 was used to train/optimize, and from 2023 to test our algorithms. Each algorithm operates as a single-station detector, and good performance is reached when at least two stations trigger. Hence, the approach is resistant to the failure of individual or clusters of stations, an asset in such a challenging operational environment. A hybrid version that combines both algorithms can provide a robust warning using only a single station. The algorithms we developed operate effectively with minor differences: the STA/LTA approach provides a more robust detector with few missed alarms, whereas the deep learning detector provides earlier warning times, but misses more events. The STA/LTA algorithm has been implemented within the SeisComP monitoring platform at INSIVUMEH, providing a prototype lahar early warning with the first users receiving alerts. We expect that the methods developed here are portable to other volcanic areas, with the STA/LTA SeisComP implementation providing a ready-to-use product for lahar monitoring. In addition to this, we show how the deep learning techniques (SNN) can be used to improve the lahar detection speed, and how they can be applied even for problems with a low number of training data available.

Data and Resources

The data that we use in this study are provided by the Santiaguito array from the GI network (Instituto Nacional de Sismologia, Vulcanologia, Meteorologia e Hidrologia, INSIVUMEH, 1976, doi: 10.7914/SN/GI). To obtain the continuous data for a time period of interest INSIVUMEH should be contacted. The Santiaguito lahar early warning is implemented within the SeisComP framework (Helmholtz Centre Potsdam GFZ German Research Centre for Geosciences and Gempa GmbH, 2008). The station trigger associator that we developed for

SeisComP within this study is documented at https://scdummyloc.readthedocs.io. The spectrograms and seismogram figures are drawn with Matplotlib (Hunter, 2007) and ObsPy (Beyreuther *et al.*, 2010). The supplemental material contains additional figures that describe the seismic network and the description of the performance of the algorithms in 2022 and 2023. The figures of the catalogued lahars are available at https://zenodo.org/doi/10.5281/zenodo.13348111. All the code and the data used for training the model are available at https://github.com/djozinovi/SNN_laharEW. All websites were last accessed in July 2025.

Declaration of Competing Interests

The authors acknowledge that there are no conflicts of interest recorded.

Acknowledgments

This work was funded by the Swiss Development and Cooperation, Nicaragua Office (COSUDE), under project 7F-10296.01.54, "Technical Support for Improving Seismic Monitoring of Santiaguito, Volcano, Guatemala." The authors would like to thank the staff at Departamento de Investigación y Servicios Geofísicos—INSIVUMEH—for setting up and maintaining the Santiaguito seismic network, managing and curating the seismic data, and generating the lahar catalog. The authors would also like to thank our colleagues at ETH for their insightful comments and suggestions, especially Pilar Sánchez-Pastor, Sin-Mei Wu, and Maria Mesimeri. The authors also thank the reviewers and the editors who helped us significantly improve our article.

References

Alkhalid, F. (2022). The effect of optimizers on Siamese neural network performance, *International Conf. on Industrial Engineering and Operations Management*, 5084–5089.

Allen, R. V. (1982). Automatic phase pickers: Their present use and future prospects, *Bull. Seismol. Soc. Am.* **72,** S225–S242.

Allstadt, K. E., R. S. Matoza, A. B. Lockhart, S. C. Moran, J. Caplan-Auerbach, M. M. Haney, W. A. Thelen, and S. D. Malone (2018). Seismic and acoustic signatures of surficial mass movements at volcanoes, *J. Volcanol. Geotherm. Res.* **364,** 76–106.

Baer, M., and U. Kradolfer (1987). An automatic phase picker for local and teleseismic events, *Bull. Geol. Soc. Am.* **77,** 1437–1445.

Bellet, A., A. Habrard, and M. Sebban (2015). Metric learning, in *Synthesis Lectures on Artificial Intelligence and Machine Learning*, Springer International Publishing, doi: 10.1007/978-3-031-01572-4.

Bennati, L., A. Finizola, J. A. Walker, D. L. Lopez, I. C. Higuera-Diaz, C. Schütze, F. Barahona, R. Cartagena, V. Conde, R. Funes *et al.* (2011). Fluid circulation in a complex volcano-tectonic setting, inferred from self-potential and soil CO2 flux surveys: The Santa María–Cerro Quemado–Zunil volcanoes and Xela caldera (northwestern Guatemala), *J. Volcanol. Geotherm. Res.* **199,** nos. 3/4, 216–229.

Beyreuther, M., R. Barsch, L. Krischer, T. Megies, Y. Behr, and J. Wassermann (2010). ObsPy: A python toolbox for seismology, *Seismol. Res. Lett.* **81,** no. 3, 530–533.

Bromley, J., I. Guyon, Y. LeCun, E. Säckinger, and R. Shah (1993). Signature verification using a "siamese" time delay neural network, *Adv. Neural Inform. Process. Syst.* **6.**

Carter, W., A. Rietbrock, Y. Lavallée, E. Gottschämmer, A. D. Moreno, J. E. Kendrick, O. D. Lamb, P.A. Wallace, G. Chigna, and S. De Angelis (2020). Statistical evidence of transitioning open-vent activity towards a paroxysmal period at Volcán Santiaguito (Guatemala) during 2014–2018, *J. Volcanol. Geotherm. Res.* **398,** 106891.

Chakraborty, N., A. Dan, A. Chakraborty, and S. Neogy (2020). Effect of dropout and batch normalization in Siamese network for face recognition, *Int. Conf. Innov. Comput. Commun. Proc. of ICICC 2019*, Vol. 2, 21–37, Springer, Singapore.

Chollet, F. (2015). Keras, available at https://keras.io (last accessed July 2025).

Chopra, S., R. Hadsell, and Y. LeCun (2005). Learning a similarity metric discriminatively, with application to face verification, *2005 IEEE computer society conference on computer vision and pattern recognition (CVPR'05)*, Vol. 1, IEEE, 539–546.

Coviello, V., M. Arattano, F. Comiti, P. Macconi, and L. Marchi (2019). Seismic characterization of debris flows: Insights into energy radiation and implications for warning, *J. Geophys. Res.* **124,** no. 6, 1440–1463.

De Angelis, S., O. D. Lamb, A. Lamur, A. J. Hornby, F. W. Von Aulock, G. Chigna, Y. Lavallée, and A. Rietbrock (2016). Characterization of moderate ash-and-gas explosions at Santiaguito volcano, Guatemala, from infrasound waveform inversion and thermal infrared measurements, *Geophys. Res. Lett.* **43,** no. 12, 6220–6227, doi: 10.1016/j.jvolgeores.2020.106891.

De Angelis, S., A. Rietbrock, Y. Lavallee, W. Carter, P. Wallace, E. Gottschämmer, and A. Rohnacher (2019). An international partnership to develop volcano monitoring capacities in Guatemala, *SEG Technical Program Expanded Abstracts 2019*, 4782–4785, Society of Exploration Geophysicists.

Global Volcanism Program (2023). Santa María (342030) in [Database] Volcanoes of the World (v. 5.1.5; 15 Dec 2023), Distributed by Smithsonian Institution, compiled by Venzke, E., doi: 10.5479/si.GVP.VOTW5-2023.5.1.

Gottschämmer, E., A. Rohnacher, W. Carter, A. Nüsse, K. Drach, S. De Angelis, Y. Lavallée, J. E. Kendrick, A. Roca, P. Castellanos, *et al.* (2021). Volcanic emission and seismic tremor at Santiaguito, Guatemala: New insights from long-term seismic, infrasound and thermal measurements in 2018–2020, *J. Volcanol. Geotherm. Res.* **411,** 107154.

Harris, A. J., W. I. Rose, and L. P. Flynn (2003). Temporal trends in lava dome extrusion at Santiaguito 1922–2000, *Bull. Volcanol.* **65,** 77–89, doi: 10.1007/s00445-002-0243-0.

Helmholtz Centre Potsdam GFZ German Research Centre for Geosciences and gempa GmbH (2008). The SeisComP seismological software package, *GFZ Data Services*. doi: 10.5880/GFZ.2.4.2020.003.

Holland, A. P., I. M. Watson, J. C. Phillips, L. Caricchi, and M. P. Dalton (2011). Degassing processes during lava dome growth: Insights from Santiaguito lava dome, Guatemala, *J. Volcanol. Geothermal Res.* **202,** nos. 1/2, 153–166.

Hunter, J. D. (2007). Matplotlib: A 2D graphics environment, *Comput. Sci. Eng.* **9,** no. 3, 90–95.

Hürlimann, M., V. Coviello, C. Bel, X. Guo, M. Berti, C. Graf, J. Hübl, S. Miyata, J. B. Smith, and H. Y. Yin (2019). Debris-flow monitoring and warning: Review and examples, *Earth Sci. Rev.* **199,**102981.

Instituto Nacional de Sismologia, Vulcanologia, Meteorologia e Hidrologia (INSIVUMEH) (1976). Red Sismologica Nacional [Data set], International Federation of Digital Seismograph Networks, doi: 10.7914/SN/GI.

Johnson, J. B., J. J. Lyons, B. J. Andrews, and J. M. Lees (2014). Explosive dome eruptions modulated by periodic gas-driven inflation, *Geophys. Res. Lett.* **41,** no. 19, 6689–6697.

Kramer, R. L., W. A. Thelen, A. M. Iezzi, S. C. Moran, and B. A. Pauk (2024). Recent expansion of the Cascades volcano observatory geophysical network at Mount Rainier for improved volcano and lahar monitoring, *Seismol. Res. Lett.* **95,** no. 5, 2707–2721.

Kristeková, M., J. Kristek, P. Moczo, and S.M. Day (2006). Misfit criteria for quantitative comparison of seismograms, *Bull. Seismol. Soc. Am.* **96,** no. 5, 1836–1850.

Küperkoch, L., T. Meier, and T. Diehl (2012). Automated event and phase identification, in *New Manual of Seismological Observatory Practice 2 (NMSOP-2),* Deutsches GeoForschungsZentrum GFZ, Potsdam, Germany1–52, doi: 10.2312/GFZ.NMSOP-2_ch16.

LaHusen, R. (2005). Acoustic flow monitor system-user manual, *U.S. Geol. Surv. Open-File Rept. 2002-429.*

Lamb, O. D., A. Lamur, A. -MorenoDíaz, S. De Angelis, A. J. Hornby, F. W. von Aulock, J. E. Kendrick, P. A. Wallace, E. Gottschämmer, A. Rietbrock, *et al.* (2019). Disruption of long-term effusive-explosive activity at Santiaguito, Guatemala, *Front. Earth Sci.* **6,** doi: 10.3389/feart.2018.00253.

Lipman, P. W., and D. R. Mullineaux (1981). The 1980 eruptions of Mount St. Helens, Washington, *U.S. Geol. Surv. Rept. Profess. Pap. 1250,* Warehouse Publications.

Lomax, A., C. Satriano, and M. Vassallo (2012). Automatic picker developments and optimization: FilterPicker—A robust, broadband picker for real-time seismic monitoring and earthquake early warning, *Seismol. Res. Lett.* **83,** 531–540, doi: 10.1785/gssrl.83.3.531.

Ripepe, M., S. De Angelis, G. Lacanna, P. Poggi, C. Williams, E. Marchetti, D. D. Donne, and G. Ulivieri (2009). Tracking pyroclastic flows at Soufrière hills volcano, *Eos Trans. AGU* **90,** no. 27, 229, doi: 10.1029/2009eo270001.

Roca, A., E. R. M. Boogher, C. M. F. C. Quinillo, D. M. E. G. Domínguez, G. A. C. Marroquin, F. J. J. Cacao, and P. D. A. Ordoñez (2021). Volcano observatories and monitoring activities in Guatemala, *Volcanica* **4,** no. S1, 203–222.

Rohnacher, A., A. Rietbrock, E. Gottschämmer, W. Carter, Y. Lavallée, S. De Angelis, J. E. Kendrick, and G. Chigna (2021). Source mechanism of seismic explosion signals at Santiaguito volcano, Guatemala: New insights from seismic analysis and numerical modeling, *Front. Earth Sci.* **8,** 603441, doi: 10.3389/feart.2020.603441.

Rose, W. I. (1973). Pattern and mechanism of volcanic activity at the Santiaguito volcanic dome, Guatemala, *Bull Volcanol* **37,** 73, doi: 10.1007/BF02596881.

Sapper, K. (1926). Die Vulkanische Tätigkeit in Mittelamerika im 20, *Jahrhundert I Teil Z. Vulk.* **9,** 156–203 (in German).

Scott, J. (2016). Origin and evolution of the Santiaguito lava dome complex, Guatemala, *Ph.D. Thesis,* Oxford University, United Kingdom.

Sigurdsson, H., and S. Carey (1986). Volcanic disasters in Latin America and the 13th November 1985 eruption of Nevado del Ruiz volcano in Colombia, *Disasters* **10,** no. 3, 205–216.

Sparks, R. S. J., J. Biggs, and J. W. Neuberg (2012). Monitoring volcanoes, *Science* **335,** no. 6074, 1310–1311.

Telegram FZ LLC and Telegram Messenger Inc. (2019). Telegram, available at https://telegram.org (last accessed July 2025).

Wallace, P. A., O. D. Lamb, S. De Angelis, J. E. Kendrick, A. J. Hornby, A. MorenoDíaz, P. J. González, F. W. von Aulock, A. Lamur, J. E. Utley, *et al.* (2020). Integrated constraints on explosive eruption intensification at Santiaguito dome complex, Guatemala, *Earth Planet. Sci. Lett.* **536,** 116139, doi: 10.1016/j.epsl.2020.116139.

Wassermann, J. (2012). Volcano seismology, in *New Manual of Seismological Observatory Practice 2 (NMSOP-2),* Deutsches GeoForschungsZentrum GFZ, Potsdam, Germany, 1–77, doi: 10.2312/GFZ.NMSOP-2_ch13.

WhatsApp Inc. (2020). WhatsApp, available at https://whatsapp.com (last accessed July 2025).

Williams, S. N., and S. Self (1983). The October 1902 Plinian eruption of Santa Maria volcano, Guatemala, *J. Volcanol. Geotherm. Res.* **16,** 33–56, doi: 10.1016/0377-0273(83)90083-5.

Yamasato, H. (1997). Quantitative analysis of pyroclastic flows using infrasonic and seismic data at Unzen Volcano, Japan, *J. Phys. Earth* **45,** no. 6, 397–416, doi: 10.4294/jpe1952.45.397.

Manuscript received 17 March 2025
Published online 11 August 2025

Testing FinDer in New Zealand for Earthquake Early Warning

Jen Andrews*[1], Yannik Behr[2], Maren Böse[3], Anna Kaiser[1], and Bill Fry[1]

Abstract

Early warning systems are one tool for mitigating earthquakes' devastating human and economic impacts. A diversity of earthquake early warning (EEW) approaches (sensors and methodologies) has been implemented or tested in many regions over recent years, each having different capability in terms of accuracy, maximum warning time, and system configurability. Despite high seismic hazard, New Zealand (NZ) does not as yet have a national EEW system (though some products are available within the country), and high cost is perceived as one barrier. National seismic monitoring infrastructure is maintained and operated by the GeoNet program within GNS Science, and a recent initiative (GNS Science–led program "Rapid Characterization of Earthquake and Tsunami") has tested and implemented a suite of rapid earthquake characterization tools for use in event response. One of these tools is the Finite-fault rupture Detector (FinDer), which is used internationally in EEW systems. In NZ, FinDer is currently only configured and operated for rapid assessment of rupture extent and location. Here, we explore whether this existing infrastructure can be leveraged for EEW, providing one perspective when considering the cost–benefit ratio for NZ. Combining real-time observations from the current FinDer implementation with testing of historic earthquakes, we assess the potential for the FinDer algorithm to provide actionable EEW alerts for NZ using the currently available GeoNet sensor network.

Cite this article as Andrews, J., Y. Behr, M. Böse, A. Kaiser, and B. Fry (2025). Testing FinDer in New Zealand for Earthquake Early Warning, *Seismol. Res. Lett.* **97**, 217–232, doi: 10.1785/0220250092.

Supplemental Material

Introduction

The implementation of operational earthquake early warning (EEW) systems has seen global acceleration during recent years, driven by advances in ground-motion sensors, communications, and computing (e.g., summaries in Cremen and Galasso, 2020, and Allen and Stogaitis, 2022). These systems aim to provide data and information in the first seconds after an earthquake rupture begins to give impacted populations short time windows for protective actions to be taken before strong shaking arrives (Strauss and Allen, 2016; Allen and Melgar, 2019). Currently, more than 25 countries have operational systems (either national, regional, or delivering to specific users) or are running prototypes (e.g., summary in Cremen and Galasso, 2020).

Despite its high onshore and offshore seismic hazard (e.g., Clark *et al.*, 2019; Howarth *et al.*, 2021; Gerstenberger *et al.*, 2024; Pizer *et al.*, 2024), New Zealand (NZ) as yet has no national EEW system. Recent events such as the 2010–2011 Canterbury sequence (**M** 7.1 Darfield and **M** 6.2 Christchurch) and 2016 **M** 7.8 Kaikōura earthquakes had significant human and economic impacts (Potter *et al.*, 2015; Stevenson *et al.*, 2017). A national EEW system could potentially play an important role in reducing the impact of future earthquakes. Furthermore, several NZ-based studies suggest strong public support for a national EEW system (Becker, Potter, Prasanna, *et al.*, 2020; Becker, Potter, Vinnell, *et al.*, 2020; Tan *et al.*, 2021). However, NZ's relatively small population (Worldbank, 2022), Google's test operation of Android earthquake alerts (AEA) in the country (Allen and Stogaitis, 2022), and other commercial operations (e.g., *P* alert from Jenlogix, 2024) mean that proposed implementation of a national system must demonstrate both additional capability and favorable cost-benefit ratio.

A range of EEW approaches has been developed internationally, and potential implementations for a national system in NZ include leveraging the existing national sensor network operated by GeoNet (GNS Science, 2025a), low-cost EEW technologies (Prasanna *et al.*, 2022; Chandrakumar *et al.*, 2024, 2025), or a hybrid of these similar to directions taken in China (Peng *et al.*, 2021) and Taiwan (Wu *et al.*, 2021). Here, we explore aspects of using the existing GeoNet network with the operational Finite-fault rupture Detection (FinDer)

1. GNS Science, Lower Hutt, Wellington, New Zealand, https://orcid.org/0000-0002-5679-5565 (JA); https://orcid.org/0000-0002-0458-5451 (AK); https://orcid.org/0000-0003-3753-6928 (BF); 2. GNS Science, Taupō, New Zealand, https://orcid.org/0000-0002-6047-5396 (YB); 3. Swiss Seismological Service (SED), ETH Zürich, Zurich, Switzerland, https://orcid.org/0000-0003-4639-719X (MB)

*Corresponding author: jen.andrews@gns.cri.nz

algorithm (Böse *et al.*, 2012, 2023; Böse, Smith, *et al.*, 2018) for EEW in NZ.

FinDer compares the evolving spatial pattern of high-frequency ground motions (peak ground acceleration [PGA]) with precomputed template maps to estimate rupture length (and therefore magnitude), position, and orientation. It is part of several operational and prototype EEW systems around the world. It has been part of the ShakeAlert EEW system for the West Coast of the United States since 2018 (Kohler *et al.*, 2020). It is running real time in central America (Porras *et al.*, 2021) and Switzerland (Massin *et al.*, 2021) and is being tested in Taiwan. In addition, testing has been undertaken by replaying historic data from central Italy (Böse, Colombelli, *et al.*, 2018), Japan (Meier *et al.*, 2020), China (Li *et al.*, 2021), and Türkiye (Böse *et al.*, 2024), as well as at a global scale using European–Mediterranean Seismological Centre felt reports (Böse *et al.*, 2021). The FinDer algorithm has been running operationally in NZ since early 2023 for the purpose of rapid rupture characterization and to support improved mapping of strong shaking for post-event response and recovery (Andrews *et al.*, 2024; Kaiser *et al.*, 2024). Although the NZ configuration and operation of the algorithm are not designed to generate or distribute EEW alerts at present, the real-time performance combined with testing using replays of historic data allows us to explore the potential for FinDer to contribute to EEW in NZ.

Here, we report on metrics of the real-time performance, such as source characterization accuracy and detection time, that indicate the capability for EEW of the existing FinDer implementation and current GeoNet sensor network, as well as considering possible alert frequency. We also replay a set of historic earthquakes and compute EEW performance metrics to analyze possible warning times and ground-motion accuracy for moderate- to large-magnitude earthquakes.

Data and Analysis

Earthquake detection and source characterization accuracy

The NZ implementation of FinDer is described in detail by Andrews *et al.* (2024) and is summarized in the supplemental material, available to this article. It uses the SeisComP seismic monitoring platform for data ingestion and preprocessing. The only change to the FinDer configuration outlined by Andrews *et al.* (2024) is the set of crustal PGA templates. For this study, we have created updated templates using a scaling relation based on those used in the recent updates to the NZ Seismic Hazard Model (Gerstenberger *et al.*, 2024), which is better suited for the largest **M** 7.5+ earthquakes. We use an area scaling relation of the form $M_w = \log A + C$ following Stirling *et al.* (2023) with a C-value of 4.2 (which is within the enveloping equation ranges for all crustal earthquakes in Stirling *et al.*, 2023) and convert area to length using the aspect ratio of Chiou and Youngs (2006) for crustal strike-slip earthquakes. The new templates were deployed for real-time operation in August 2024, and for the smaller-magnitude earthquakes, the change is not expected to have a noticeable impact on FinDer solutions. In addition to the rupture solution from template matching, FinDer also assigns an approximate origin time based on the PGA timestamp at the closest station and assigns an epicenter equal to early centroid estimates, updating only if the fault length is still estimated to be <20 km.

Event detection within FinDer is currently configured to require four stations to exceed 2 cm/s^2 within a window of 60 s, and criteria for spatial and temporal coherence thresholds must be met (Böse *et al.*, 2023). Using these earthquake detection criteria, Andrews *et al.* (2024) calculated that the current GeoNet network geometry (strong motion and broadband sites) allows detection of most **M** 4.5+ earthquakes across the whole country, though earthquakes down to **M** 3 should be detected in regions with dense instrumentation such as Christchurch, Wellington, and the Taupō volcanic zones. Although this magnitude detection threshold is sufficient for EEW purposes, the network geometry also affects potential first detection times, as do the configuration of network components and telemetry. Approximate first detection times for shallow crustal earthquakes can be estimated for the current GeoNet network if we assume that the ground-motion threshold of 2 cm/s^2 is exceeded at all four stations in the *S* wave using an *S*-wave velocity of 3.5 km/s (ignoring packetization and data transfer latencies). Figure 1 shows that areas with high station density such as around Wellington, Christchurch, Marlborough, and Taupō should have first detection times below 10 s, most of the rest of the country would be in the 10–20 s range, and a few regions would be up to 30 s. (For larger-magnitude earthquakes, faster detections may be possible because the ground-motion threshold could be exceeded within the *P* wave.)

FinDer has been running in real time in NZ since 25 January 2023 and in the period up until 1 February 2025 has detected 90 earthquakes (Fig. 2), with GeoNet catalog magnitudes in the range from 2.9 to 6.0. FinDer magnitudes show good agreement with catalog values, with a median 0.1 underprediction compared with M_w-values (GNS Science, 2025b) and median 0.3 underprediction compared with catalog-authoritative values (M_L or $M_w(m_B)$; GNS Science, 2025c). The median first detection time for shallow (<40 km) crustal earthquakes is 12.8 s, and it is 14.4 s for all earthquakes. Rapid first detections within 6.7–10 s are regularly observed for earthquakes in the Christchurch and Wellington regions. As expected, the longest detection times are for deep subduction-related earthquakes and can reach 100 s.

A few **M** 4.5+ earthquakes in the GeoNet catalog were not detected by FinDer and are marked as "missed" in Figure 2 and clearly fall in areas of lower station density. During the 2 yr observation period, there were no false detections with magnitudes >5.5 and just four false detections (all during 2023) with FinDer solutions that had magnitudes >**M** 4.5. These were caused by environmental noise in the network, and two of the

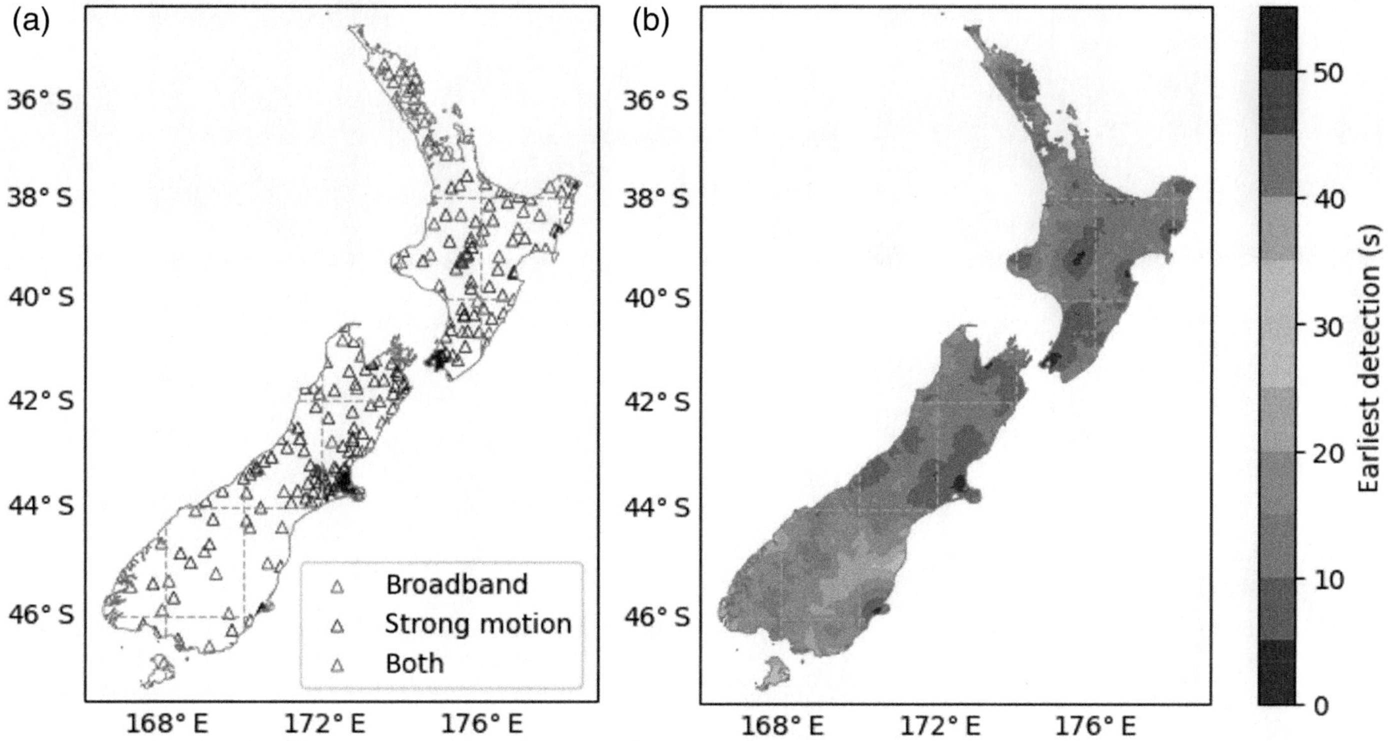

Figure 1. (a) GeoNet station network strong motion and broadband sites. (b) Approximate detection time for a hypothetical earthquake occurring at each grid point using finite-fault rupture detector (FinDer) detection criteria of four stations exceeding 2 cm/s^2, assuming that occurs within the *S*-wave and an *S*-wave velocity of 3.5 km/s. The color version of this figure is available only in the electronic edition.

false detections coincided with high winds. A further challenge is deep (>100 km) earthquakes related to the subducting Pacific plate, which have strong path effects that complicate the spatial ground-motion pattern. For these very deep earthquakes, FinDer epicentral errors can exceed 100 km.

These real-time observations are in good agreement with the expectations described earlier for detection magnitude and first detection time based on current GeoNet sensor density. This demonstrates that performance in some parts of the country is already comparable to that achieved in other international EEW networks (e.g., 4–8 s within the ShakeAlert U.S. West Coast system; Lux *et al.*, 2024).

EEW Alert and Warning Time Performance

To quantitatively assess potential EEW performance in terms of warning time and ground-motion accuracy, we can use historic data. To simulate the real-time system, we have replayed data for a selection of larger magnitude historic earthquakes through the SeisComP FinDer pipeline. This mimics the real-time set up and captures data processing and calculation times but neglects data latencies, that is, the time taken for data to reach the central processing system. Furthermore, our replay system delivers data to the processing system in packets containing ~2–3 s of waveform. This is likely shorter than the current sensor network configuration in NZ, but it is longer than the 1 s configuration for the ShakeAlert EEW system (Stubailo *et al.*, 2020).

Thirty-five earthquakes were selected from the GeoNet catalog from the time period 2007 to 2023 (Fig. 3, Table S1). This includes all onshore and near-shore M 6.0+ and three lower-magnitude earthquakes to expand testing locations: 2015 **M** 5.8 Wanaka, 2020 **M** 5.8 Whanganui, and 2022 **M** 5.7 Taupō. Sixteen of the earthquakes have offshore epicenters, the majority either in the southwest tip of the South Island (mixture of crustal faults and Puysegur subduction related) or northeast of East Cape (related to the Kermadec subduction zone). Two deep subduction-related earthquakes—the 2012 **M** 6.2 Whanganui and 2018 **M** 6.2 Taumarunui earthquakes—are included to explore the effect on FinDer performance of the slab path effects mentioned earlier. The Kaikōura earthquake and several of its aftershocks are also included.

FinDer is designed to begin issuing solutions as soon as event detection criteria are met and will continue to issue updated solutions as rupture evolves (i.e., rupture geometry and magnitude will update in real time; see Andrews *et al.*, 2024 for NZ examples). For each FinDer solution that exceeded a chosen magnitude threshold, we define alert regions for selected modified Mercalli intensity (MMI) thresholds. The alert regions are polygons at an appropriate radius around the FinDer rupture (line) geometry, equivalent to the contour product issued by the U.S. ShakeAlert EEW system (e.g., Given *et al.*, 2018; Thakoor *et al.*, 2019).

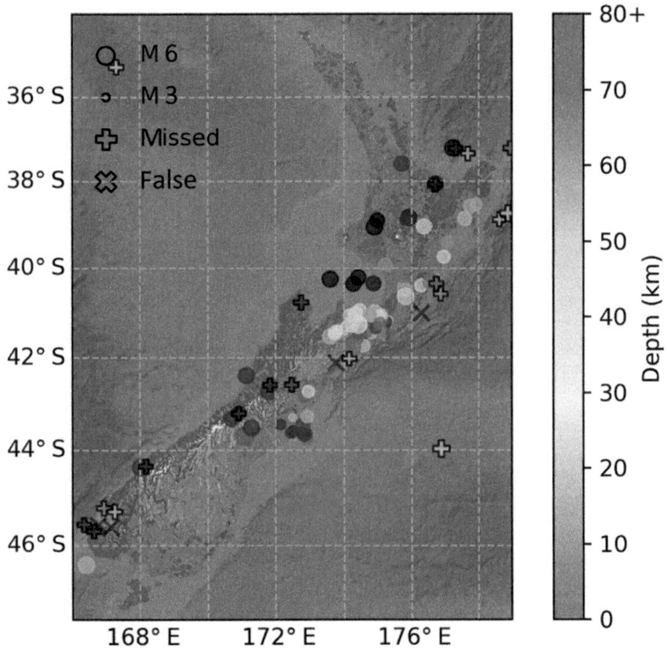

Figure 2. Map of earthquakes detected by FinDer in real time between 25 January 2023 and 1 February 2025, sized by catalog magnitude and colored by catalogue depth according to the legends shown. Earthquakes of **M** 4.5+ in the GeoNet catalog that FinDer did not detect ("missed," plus sign) are also shown, as well as false detections by FinDer that had solutions with **M** 4.5+ ("false," cross). The color version of this figure is available only in the electronic edition.

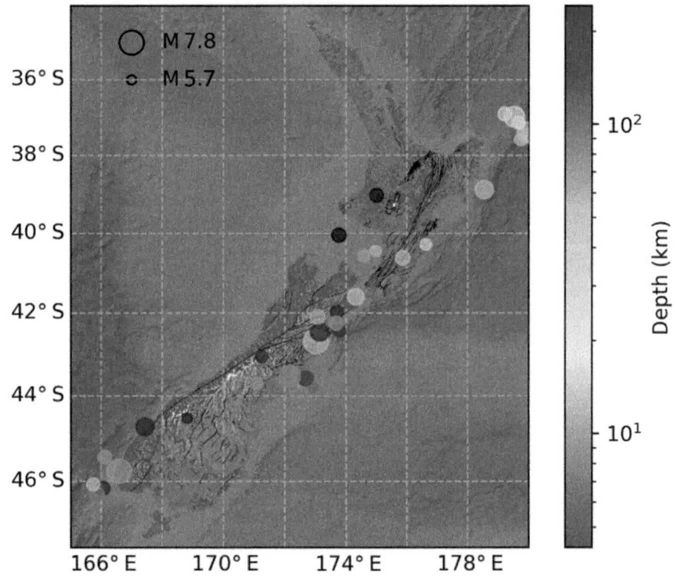

Figure 3. The 35 historic earthquakes from the GeoNet catalog used to test earthquake early warning (EEW) potential of FinDer in New Zealand (NZ). Earthquakes are from the time period 2007 to 2023 and are sized by magnitude and colored by depth according to the scales shown. Faults from the NZ Active Fault Database (Morgenstern *et al.*, 2024) are shown in black. The color version of this figure is available only in the electronic edition.

Alert radii were computed for given magnitude and MMI and are shown in Table 1. To compute the alert radii, we used the OpenQuake software (Pagani *et al.*, 2014; Silva *et al.*, 2014) to calculate median peak ground velocity (PGV) and PGA at selected magnitudes and a range of distances. Our configuration used a set of crustal-source ground-motion prediction equations, equally weighted between the Next Generation Attenuation-West2 (Bozorgnia *et al.*, 2014) models of Abrahamson *et al.* (2014), Boore *et al.* (2014), Campbell and Bozorgnia (2014), Chiou and Youngs (2014) and the NZ-adapted model of Bradley (2013), as discussed further in Andrews *et al.* (2024). These models were found to work well in NZ (Lee *et al.*, 2024) and are similarly incorporated into the ground-motion logic tree of the National Seismic Hazard model (Bradley *et al.*, 2024; Gerstenberger *et al.*, 2024). We used a fixed V_{S30} of 400 m/s, approximately the median of estimated V_{S30}-values at GeoNet strong-motion stations (Kaiser, HoutteVan, *et al.*, 2017). Ignoring local site effects leads to some under- and overestimation of alerted regions (Saunders *et al.*, 2024); however, we adopt this simplification in our analysis because it is faster in real-time implementations (Thakoor *et al.*, 2019). PGA and PGV were converted to MMI using the NZ-specific ground-motion intensity conversion equations (GMICE) of Moratalla *et al.* (2020) (their equation 2 and table 2), and we took the mean of the two values.

TABLE 1
Alert Distances (Joyner–Boore Distance (R_{JB}) from the Rupture) for Indicative Magnitudes and MMI Thresholds, Computed Using Median Ground Motions Predicted by GMPEs (Equally Weighted Between the Active Crustal Models of Abrahamson *et al.*, 2014; Boore *et al.*, 2014; Campbell and Bozorgnia, 2014; Chiou and Youngs, 2014; Bradley, 2013) at Fixed V_{S30}-Value of 400 m/s, Converted to MMI Using Moratalla *et al.* (2020) GMICE

	Alert R_{JB} Distance (km)		
Magnitude M_w	**MMI 6.0**	**MMI 5.0**	**MMI 4.0**
7.5	62	156	320
7.0	46	116	254
6.5	32	80	189
6.0	23	53	131
5.5	15	33	84
5.0	9	20	48
4.5	4	10	25
4.0	–	4	13

GMICE, ground-motion intensity conversion equations; GMPE, ground-motion prediction equation; MMI, modified Mercalli intensity.

We interpolated the resultant magnitude–distance–MMI data to extract alert radii at chosen magnitudes and MMI levels. For each FinDer solution, we use the appropriate radius to create the alert polygon around the FinDer rupture (line) geometry.

Selecting an alert strategy is a balance of meeting end-user requirements and system and algorithm capability. The chosen magnitude threshold and target MMI level will determine how many alerts are issued and also influence maximum possible warning time. Here, we test a few possible combinations. We test minimum alert magnitudes of 4.5 and 5.5, selected based on ShakeAlert threshold discussion of McGuire *et al.* (2025). Using FinDer's solutions for the 35 historic earthquakes, this would lead to 34 or 24 earthquakes being alerted, respectively. We have selected the target warning MMI threshold (MMI_tw) of 5.0, consistent with the onset of light damage and the preferences expressed by potential NZ recipients to be alerted at MMI 5–6 (e.g., Becker, Potter, Prasanna, 2020; Becker, Potter, Vinnell, *et al.*, 2020). We aim to alert all sites that exceed the MMI 5.0 level, and warning times are calculated relative to the first time this MMI level is observed at a site. Because of the ground-motion variability, we may choose to issue alerts when the predicted MMI is less than or equal to the target warning MMI threshold (Minson *et al.*, 2019). We have used alert MMI thresholds of 4.0 and 5.0.

We have computed the ground motion–based alert metrics introduced by Meier (2017), which use observed and predicted MMI at station sites. We calculate observed MMI every second by computing per-channel PGA and PGV, converting them to MMI using the GMICE of Moratalla *et al.* (2020), and taking the mean. We calculate predicted MMI at the station for each FinDer solution and the time at which the station would be alerted for each MMI threshold by comparing the distance between the station and the FinDer rupture with the alert radius. Performance categories are then assigned to each site for each earthquake tested using the following classifications: "TP timely" sites have maximum observed MMI of ≥5.0 and receive an alert before that shaking intensity is reached (i.e., true positive, timely), "TP timely < MMI_tw" sites have maximum observed MMI between MMI alert threshold and 5.0 and receive an alert before the *S* wave arrives (only possible if alert threshold is below MMI 5.0), "TP untimely" sites have maximum observed MMI of the MMI alert threshold or greater but receive an alert after MMI 5.0 is reached, "FP" sites receive an alert but have a maximum observed MMI below the MMI alert threshold (i.e., false positive), "FN" sites do not receive an alert but have a maximum observed MMI above the alert threshold (i.e., false negative), and "TN" sites do not receive an alert and have a maximum observed MMI below the alert threshold (i.e., true negative). This performance is computed for station locations to use direct ground-motion observations, and we do not interpolate for impacted population or infrastructure.

Our offline replay tests do not directly account for data transmission, alert delivery latencies, or alert creation time (generation of end-user message). These delays may only be subsecond to seconds, but this can have a significant impact on performance given the small time frame when EEW is possible. To present a realistic measure of performance, a fixed latency time is added to all replay test results. Stubailo *et al.* (2020) reported on data latencies observed within the southern California seismic network and reported that the majority of the network had median data transmission latencies of 2 s. Potential EEW alert pathways include delivery to mobile phones through apps, messages, or the operating system (e.g., AEA; see Data and Resources), traditional media notifications through television or radio, or dedicated systems such as sirens or alarms. Some studies of the U.S. ShakeAlert system have investigated alert delivery latency for internet systems (McGuire and de Groot, 2020), the MyShake app (Patel and Allen, 2022), and wireless emergency alerts (WEA; McBride *et al.*, 2023). Internet-connected systems are the fastest with delivery in <1 s; app alerts had a median delivery time of 2 s, and the WEA alerts had a median delivery time of 6–12 s. Additional computation time for alert generation is likely to be small (subsecond) (Thakoor *et al.*, 2019). We therefore consider that an additional latency of 5 s for these combined factors is reasonable. This is consistent with reported values from the United States for the faster pathways, though significant variation is possible (McGuire *et al.*, 2025), and latencies would hopefully decrease in the future as technologies develop. A summary of alert parameters tested is given in Table 2.

EEW has the greatest potential for success for higher-magnitude earthquakes when the impacted region is large. The highest magnitude event in our dataset is the 2016 **M** 7.8 Kaikōura earthquake (Clark *et al.*, 2017; Kaiser, Balfour, *et al.*, 2017), and EEW performance metrics are shown in Figure 4 for alert magnitude 5.5, alert MMI 4.0 and 5.0, and added latency 5 s. These parameters result in a "no alert" zone of ~20 km around the epicenter, but high ground-motion sites (MMI 8.0+) beyond this distance still receive several seconds of warning. Between 70% and 100% of sites with observed MMI between 5.0 and 7.0 would receive alerts, and many of these sites would have long warning times (even reaching 2 min) for the lower MMI 4.0 alert threshold or several tens of seconds for the higher MMI 5.0 alert threshold.

Figure 4 also demonstrates a number of effects of using ground-motion prediction and alert thresholds on EEW performance. As expected because of ground-motion variability, the MMI 5.0 threshold leads to more "missed" sites when the observed ground motion is MMI 5.0+, but the median prediction based on distance from rupture is lower. The scatter plots clearly show the impact of this ground-motion variability in generating both "missed" (FN) and overpredicted (FP) sites, with a spread of ± 2 MMI units about the equality line. Furthermore, the asymmetry of the spatial distribution of these site types in the map plots indicates directivity, path, or site effects. Warning times are also affected for sites near the alert threshold MMI,

TABLE 2
Alert Strategy Parameters Used in Historic Testing for EEW Performance

Alert Parameter	Parameter Explanation	Values
Magnitude threshold	FinDer magnitude estimates must meet or exceed this threshold for an alert to be issued.	4.5, 5.5
MMI alert	MMI used to determine the alert region (often set lower than MMI target because of ground-motion variability)	4.0, 5.0 (alert distance at MMI 4.0 is ~2.5 times that for MMI 5.0)
MMI target, MMI_tw	Target MMI used for computation of warning time and onset of damage	5.0 (equivalent to PGA 43 cm/s^2 and PGV 4.0 cm/s using Moratalla *et al.*, 2020)
Latency	Added system latency to account for time taken for data transmission and alert transmission	0, 5 s

EEW, earthquake early warning; MMI, modified Mercalli intensity; PGA, peak ground acceleration; PGV, peak ground velocity.

with a lower percentage of sites alerted and shorter warning times.

The interplay of EEW system alert thresholds and ground-motion variability are discussed by Minson *et al.* (2019, 2022), and trade-offs between system settings and maximum warning times are discussed by Minson *et al.* (2018) and McGuire *et al.* (2025). Although system setting details become a question of user preferences and tolerance to different behaviors, these results demonstrate very promising performance for delivery of actionable EEW alerts to a significant fraction of the region with potentially damaging ground motions.

Performance for the next largest earthquake, the 2010 M 7.2 Darfield earthquake (Gledhill *et al.*, 2011), is also encouraging, with high fractions of the MMI 5.0–7.0 sites alerted and warning times reaching a few tens of seconds. However, the MMI 8.0–9.0 sites were all located within 26 km of the epicenter, and alerts are not timely, with success only possible if system latencies are lower than the assumed 5 s added in this testing (or sensor networks or algorithms are improved). As seen for Kaikōura, using a higher alert MMI of 5.0 increases the "no alert" radius and reduces warning times for the highest MMI sites. For sites with observed MMI 7.0–8.0, using alert MMI 4.0 provides up to 10 s of warning for nearly 90% of sites, but using the smaller alert radius for MMI 5.0 reduces that to just a few seconds at <20% of sites (Fig. 5).

For earthquakes in the magnitude **M** 6.0–7.0 range, the EEW system needs to be faster to provide useful warning at MMI 5.0+ sites because of the smaller impacted region, making performance more strongly dependent on epicentral station density and earthquake-specific ground-motion variability. For seven of the onshore earthquakes with magnitudes in the lower half of the range (**M** 6.0–6.5), very small numbers of sites observed MMI 5.0+, making statistics unhelpful. In general, warning times of a few seconds could be received by some of the MMI 5.0+ sites only if using an MMI 4.0 alert threshold. Three earthquakes were tested with magnitudes between **M** 6.5 and 7.0 (2013 **M** 6.5 Cook Strait, 2013 **M** 6.6 Lake Grassmere, Holden *et al.*, 2013, and 2016 **M** 6.7 Hanmer Springs). For the two 2013 earthquakes located offshore between the two main islands of NZ, an alert threshold of MMI 4.0 produced alerts at between 70% and 100% of MMI 5.0–7.0 sites with warning times up to 10 s, but an alert threshold of MMI 5.0 produced no successful alerts. Performance for the 2016 earthquake (an aftershock of the 2016 Kaikōura earthquake) is less successful, with only 20% of MMI 5.0–6.0 sites given a few seconds of warning using an alert threshold of MMI 4.0 and no successful alerts for an alert threshold of MMI 5.0.

The most challenging scenarios for EEW are for moderate (**M** 6.0–6.5) earthquakes with epicenters within populated areas, where every second counts. In our dataset, the 2011 **M** 6.2 and 6.0 Christchurch earthquakes (Bannister and Gledhill, 2012; Kaiser *et al.*, 2012) are in this category. None of the MMI 7.0–9.0 sites would be successfully alerted even with no latency added to our performance calculations, but high fractions of MMI 5.0–7.0 sites could be alerted with a few seconds' warning. Adding the 5 s of system latency reduces alerting of MMI 6.0–7.0 sites to <20% (Fig. 6). The current GeoNet sensor network now has more stations close to the epicenter of the **M** 6.2 Christchurch earthquake, reducing the distance to the fourth station from 4.7 to 3.7 km, which would potentially reduce the time to first alert by less than half a second.

For earthquakes outside (or on the boundary) of the instrument network, FinDer's current methodology tends to poorly characterize the source, usually placing it within the instrument network and with lower magnitude (Böse *et al.*, 2022). This occurs because the simplified ground-motion pattern used by FinDer cannot easily discriminate between smaller, in-network earthquakes and larger, out-of-network earthquakes. In NZ, this may also be exacerbated by sparse and/or limited azimuthal station coverage (e.g., Warren-Smith *et al.*, 2024). Nearly half of our dataset (16 earthquakes) is in this category, mostly offshore (Kermadec or Puysegur subduction zones). Of these earthquakes, one was not detected by FinDer

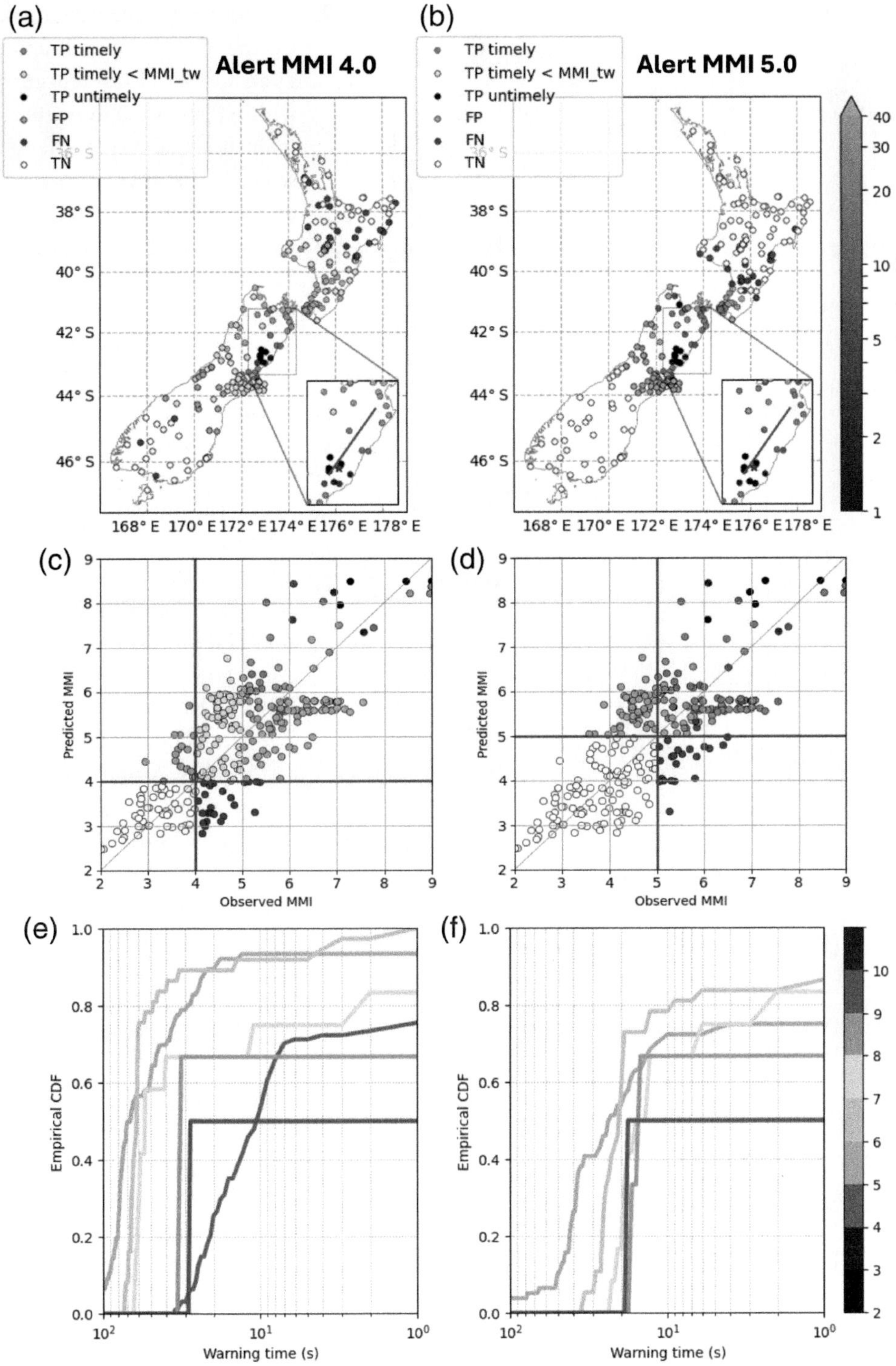

Figure 4. EEW performance metrics for a FinDer replay of the 2016 **M** 7.8 Kaikōura earthquake using an alert magnitude threshold of 5.5 and target modified Mercalli intensity (MMI) of 5.0. The alert MMI thresholds are 4.0 (a,c,e) and 5.0 (b,d,f). An assumed alert delay of 5 s has been added. (a,b) Map of alerts, categorized according to the legend, with sites that have timely alerts colored by the warning time. Site classifications are explained in the text. The inset shows the source region, with the GeoNet catalog epicenter marked as a red star and the FinDer rupture line from the last timestep as a red line. (c,d) Scatter plot of the observed and maximum predicted MMI, with sites colored following the map. (e,f) Cumulative distribution functions for warning times grouped by observed MMI (according to color scale shown). Sites with no warning time are included in the calculation such that the intersection of each trend line with the right axis gives the percentage of sites with a timely alert. The color version of this figure is available only in the electronic edition.

(2009 **M** 6.1 Puysegur), and eight have no sites with observed ground motion of ≥MMI 5.0. Five of these earthquakes would have no alert for a magnitude threshold of **M** 5.5 and small onshore alerted regions for **M** 4.5. For the remaining seven offshore earthquakes, even with poor source characterization, FinDer alerts provide timely warnings to some of the few sites (<10 in each case) with observed MMI of ≥5.0. For the earthquakes with magnitudes up to low **M** 7, alerting at MMI 4.0 could give a few seconds' warning but generally not with an alerting threshold at MMI 5.0. For the two earthquakes with larger **M** 7+ magnitudes—the 2009 **M** 7.8 Dusky Sound (Fry *et al.*, 2010) and 2021 **M** 7.3 East Cape (Okuwaki *et al.*, 2021) earthquakes—alerts would be issued at all thresholds to most MMI 5.0 sites, with slightly higher warning times and percentage of sites reached for the MMI 4.0 alert threshold. Overall, this suggests that even for earthquake location scenarios that challenge FinDer's methodology and result in erroneous source parameters, useful ground-motion alerting is still possible (i.e., true positives), and we see no significant incorrect alerting for sites with unfelt shaking levels (i.e., false positives). This is consistent with previous international studies (Böse *et al.*, 2023). Performance for the two deep earthquakes can be summarized in an identical way as for the out-of-network events. In these cases, FinDer source characterization is degraded because of the use of template sets for shallow crustal earthquakes.

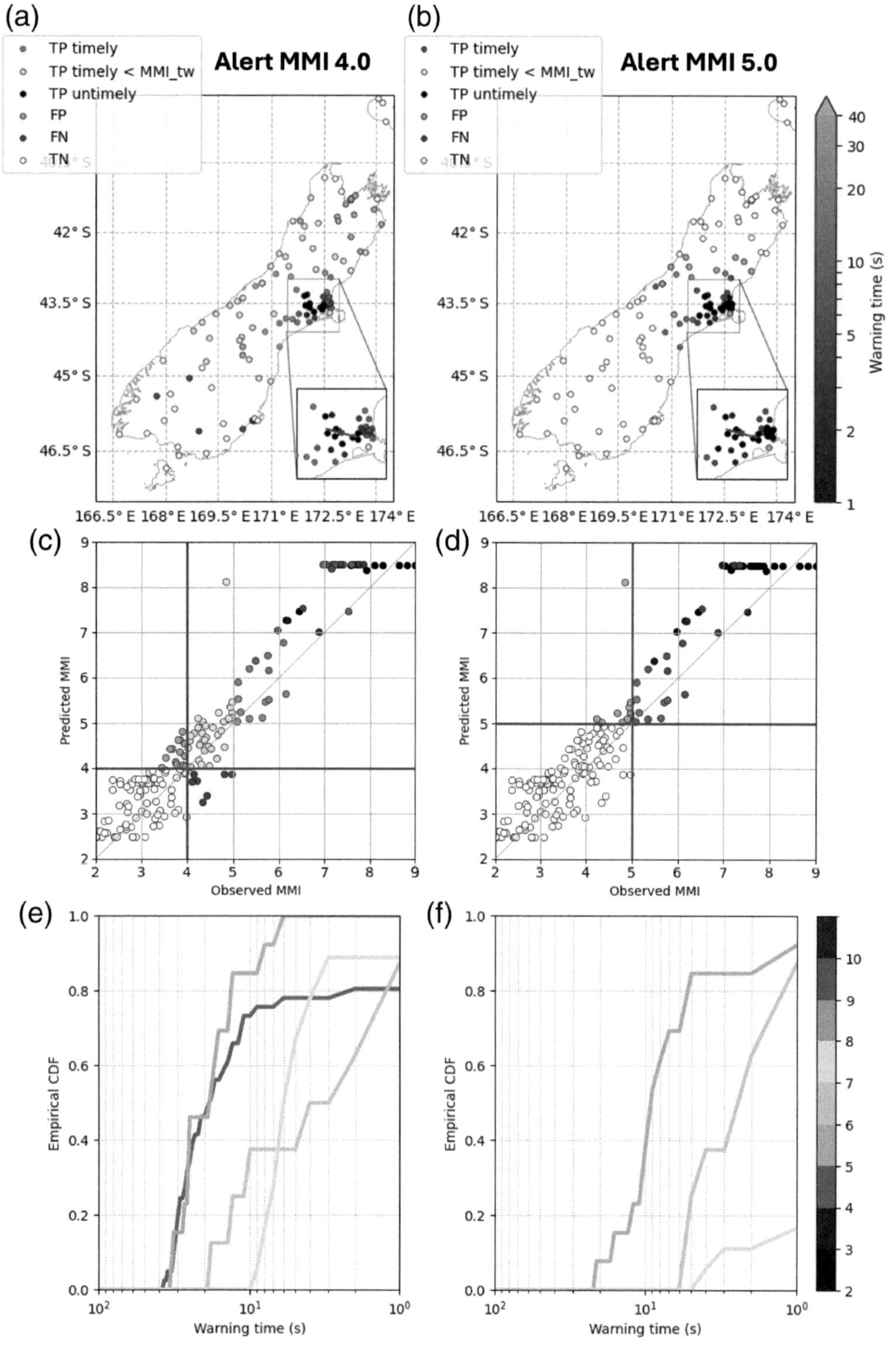

Figure 5. EEW performance metrics for a FinDer replay of the 2011 M 7.1 Darfield earthquake using an alert magnitude threshold of 5.5 and target MMI of 5.0. The alert MMI thresholds are 4.0 (a,c, e) and 5.0 (b,d,f). An assumed alert delay of 5 s has been added. (a,b) Map of alerts, categorized according to the legend, with sites that have timely alerts colored by the warning time color scale. Site classifications are explained in the text. The inset shows the source region, with the GeoNet catalog epicenter marked as a red star and the FinDer rupture line from the last timestep as a red line. (c,d) Scatter plot of the observed and maximum predicted MMI, with sites colored following the map. (e,f) Cumulative distribution functions for warning times grouped by observed MMI (according to color scale shown). Sites with no warning time are included in the calculation such that the intersection of each trend line with the right axis gives the percentage of sites with a timely alert. The color version of this figure is available only in the electronic edition.

The final three earthquakes in the dataset are Kaikōura aftershocks that occurred within the first 30 min after the mainshock, a very challenging scenario because of overlapping aftershocks and high levels of ground motion. Two **M** 6.0 earthquakes occurred within the first 10 min after the mainshock and for these FinDer merged earthquake detections as seen in previous studies (Böse *et al.*, 2022), whereas results for the third **M** 6.2 earthquake at ~30 min produced no actionable alerts.

This historic testing indicates that the existing network and FinDer algorithm already offer potential for successful EEW for the largest, most damaging earthquakes. For **M** 7+ earthquakes, source characterization is excellent, and EEW alerts for MMI 5.0–7.0 sites can range from seconds to minutes. Even sites experiencing MMI 8.0–9.0 could be alerted at distances >20 km. For earthquakes in the **M** 6–7 range, successful alerting should be possible for some fraction of MMI 5.0–7.0 sites with a few seconds of warning time (depending on system thresholds) and would still be useful where population centers are situated just beyond the epicentral "no alert" zone. Greater success would require a faster system, achieved through latencies below the estimated 5 s used in this study (e.g., very rapid alert distribution), changes to the FinDer configuration (e.g., reducing the number of stations required for initial earthquake detection), or a different EEW approach (e.g., point-source algorithms, Lux *et al.*, 2024). For the dataset tested here, using a lower MMI

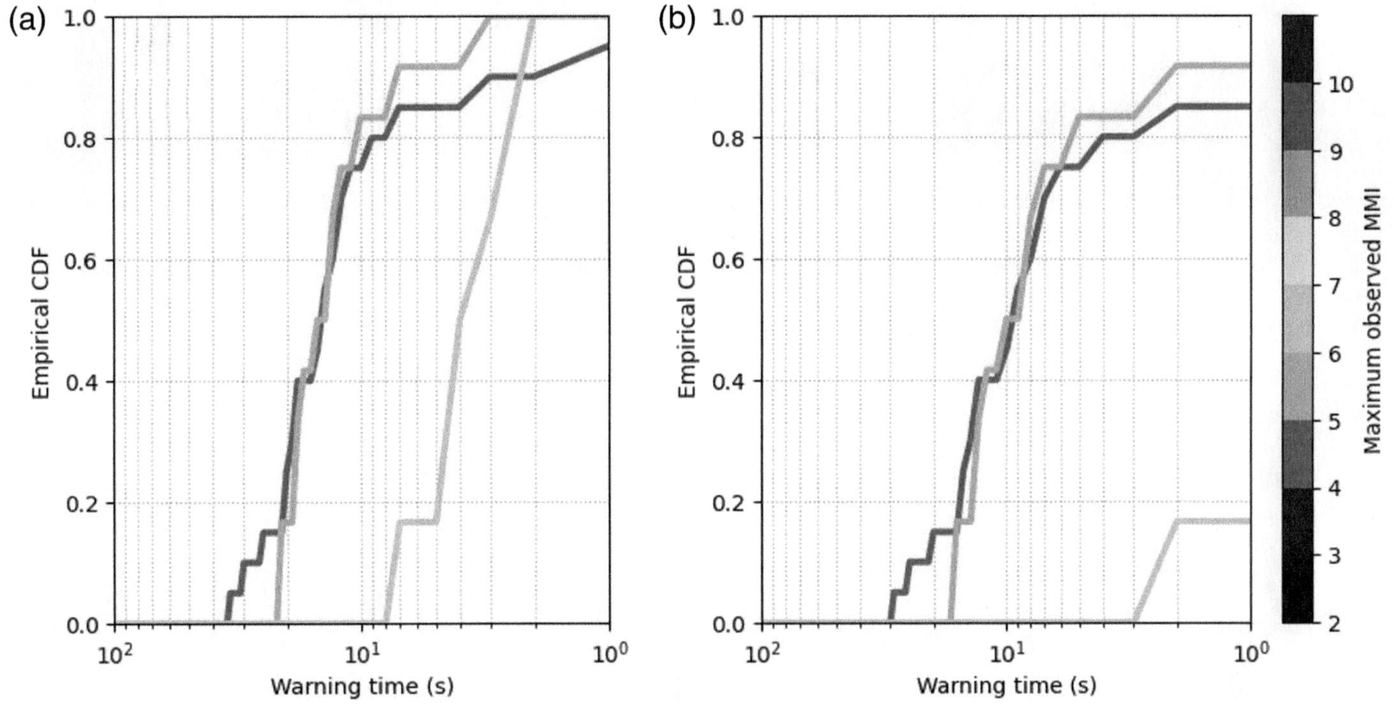

Figure 6. EEW performance metrics for a FinDer replay of the 2010 **M** 6.2 Christchurch earthquake, using an alert magnitude threshold of 4.5, target MMI of 5.0, alert MMI threshold of 4.0, and added alert latency of 0 s (a) and 5.0 s (b). Cumulative distribution functions for warning times grouped by observed MMI (according to color scale shown). Sites with no warning time are included in the calculation such that the intersection of each trend line with the right axis gives the percentage of sites with a timely alert. The color version of this figure is available only in the electronic edition.

alert threshold of 4.0 enables a greater number of sites to be alerted and longer warning times, but a higher alert magnitude of **M** 5.5 gives almost identical performance to the lower **M** 4.5 threshold. Most of the offshore earthquakes tested would not warrant EEW (i.e., no onshore damaging ground motions), but performance was adequate to maintain trust in the system (i.e., alerts may be issued in regions with felt shaking levels).

EEW Alert Frequency and Configuration

Although lower alerting thresholds for magnitudes and MMI may be attractive in providing longer warning times for large earthquakes, it will also have the effect of increasing the frequency of alerts distributed by the system. Previous studies (Allen *et al.*, 2017; Orihuela *et al.*, 2023; Goltz *et al.*, 2024) have suggested that recipients are generally happy to receive alerts for nondamaging shaking, seeing it as an opportunity to practice, but data are limited and vary by country. We expect long-term operational systems to continuously learn how to balance regular exercising of the system and public familiarity with receiving alerts while avoiding frequent alerting in which users experience nondamaging levels of shaking, which (we speculate) may make them less likely to act during infrequent high-impact earthquakes.

We can use the observations from the real-time FinDer instance to explore alert frequency for earthquakes that may have met lower magnitude and MMI EEW alert thresholds. Data from the 2 yr of operation resulted in 26 earthquakes when FinDer solutions met or exceeded a magnitude threshold of **M** 4.5, of which 6 earthquakes met or exceeded a magnitude threshold of **M** 5.5. (N.B. because of the evolution of FinDer solutions, the final alert magnitude may be below the threshold.) As previously noted, FinDer source characterization has been generally good, and there is an agreement between predicted and observed MMI 4.0 when comparing both with shaking layers contours (GNS Science, 2025d; Goded *et al.*, 2025; Horspool *et al.*, 2023; see Fig. S1) and felt reports (GNS Science, 2025e; Goded *et al.*, 2021; see Fig. S2 and Table S2), though it is less accurate for earthquakes offshore or with low station density (e.g., southwest and west coast of the South Island).

Based on national estimated population data (StatsNZ, 2023), Table S3 gives estimates for the number of people who reside within the alerted region for these earthquakes. For the lower magnitude threshold of **M** 4.5 and lower alert threshold of MMI 4.0, these numbers range from zero to ~800,000 people for an earthquake that occurred offshore in the Whanganui basin and would have alerted larger population centers, including Wellington. Some areas would have received multiple alerts (e.g., the Wairarapa, Wellington coast, Taranaki, and Marlborough) with the maximum being seven alerts received by about 1000 people (Fig. 7). Larger regions in those same areas could have received between two and six

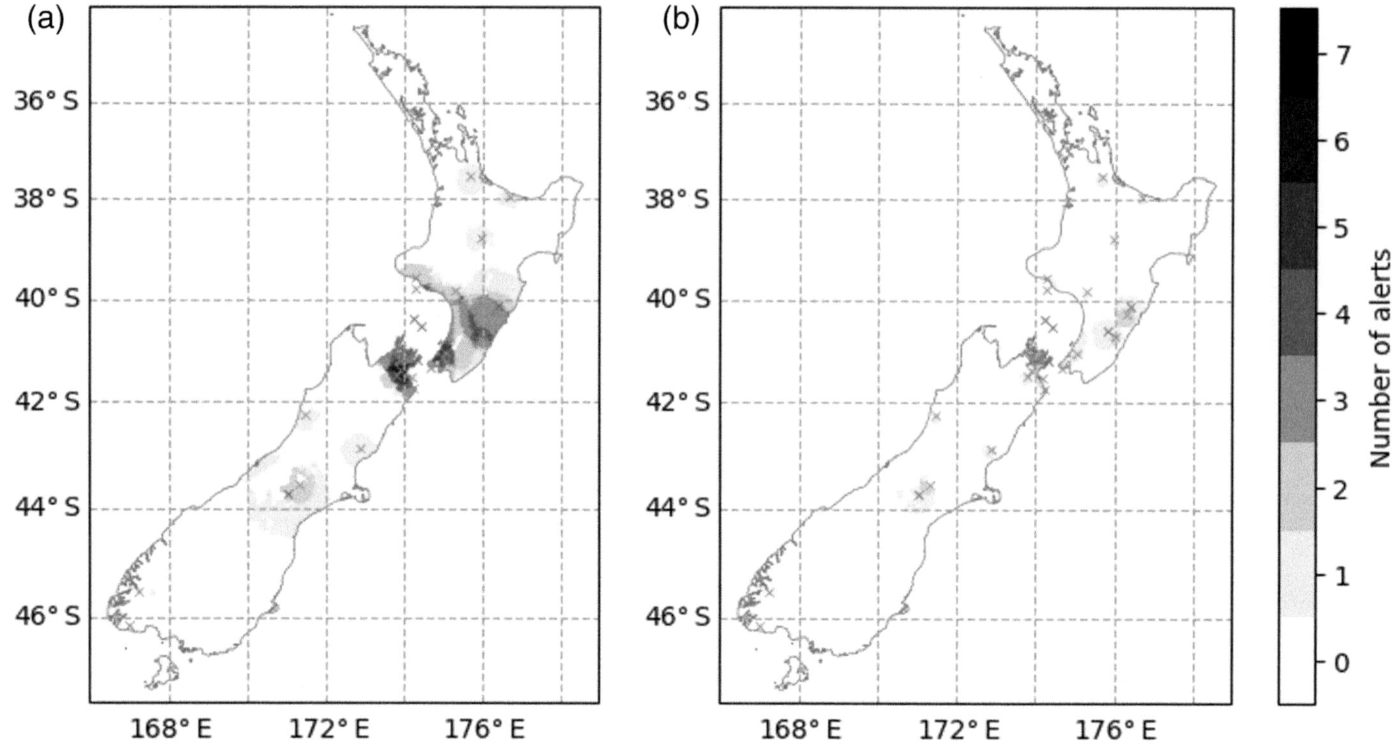

Figure 7. Simulated population experience of FinDer EEW alerts for the period February 2023 to February 2025 using real-time performance data. Populated areas are colored according to the number of alerts received using alert thresholds of (a) MMI 4.0 or (b) MMI 5.0. Earthquake epicenters are shown as magenta (**M** 5.5+) and green (**M** 4.5+) crosses. The color version of this figure is available only in the electronic edition.

alerts, with nearly 200,000 people receiving four alerts. Using the higher ground-motion threshold of MMI 5.0 would reduce alerts significantly (Fig. 7), with the same Whanganui basin earthquake alerts reaching only 185,000 people and only about 28,000 people receiving two alerts over the time period. If the alert magnitude threshold is **M** 5.5, then only ~170 people (in the Marlborough area) might have received two alerts during the time period.

The open question is whether people would want a system with lower thresholds, in which alerts are more frequent and are received for shaking that is potentially felt but not damaging but that has a higher chance of success and longer warning times for higher levels of shaking in rarer larger magnitude earthquakes. Note that we have analyzed these alerts in a naïve way, assuming alert delivery to all the population and regardless of whether the alert might arrive late. A delivery system that would suppress alerts if they were received at a location where strong ground shaking is already computed to have arrived would potentially reduce alerting for smaller earthquakes where the affected zone is very close to the epicenter. Alternatively, the messaging within alerts could be modified as severity escalated (magnitude and/or MMI) to better handle the trade-offs between higher thresholds and longer warning times and user response (e.g., description of AEAs in Chung *et al.*, 2020). However, any such measure to reduce overalerting will be affected by the high uncertainty in EEW algorithm solutions (because of the nature of very rapid assessments using limited data), and some undesirable behavior should be expected.

To test the effect of suppressing late alerts, we have repeated the calculations, but now any alerts issued after a theoretical *S*-wave traveling at 3 km/s (a slightly slower *S* wave is assumed here to be conservative in issuing alerts) has arrived at a location are assumed to not be delivered to that location. This results in no alerts being issued when using the higher ground-motion threshold of MMI 5.0 (i.e., all alerts are untimely). For the MMI 4.0 threshold, only nine earthquakes would have any alerts issued and to smaller numbers of people, with the maximum number of alerts received by any area now reduced to four. We note that although this strategy perhaps most effectively reduces alerts that may be deemed unnecessary (Fig. 8), it may incorrectly suppress alerts if the origin time or location are incorrect, and it may not align with user preferences around receiving alerts even after shaking has arrived (Goltz *et al.*, 2024).

Discussion

In this study, we have used seismic data from the GeoNet network between 2007 and 2025 to assess the potential for successful EEW for NZ using the FinDer algorithm. Instrument density and geometry have changed through this period, and only parts of the network meet the requirements set by other regions that use network-based EEW (e.g., Japan; United

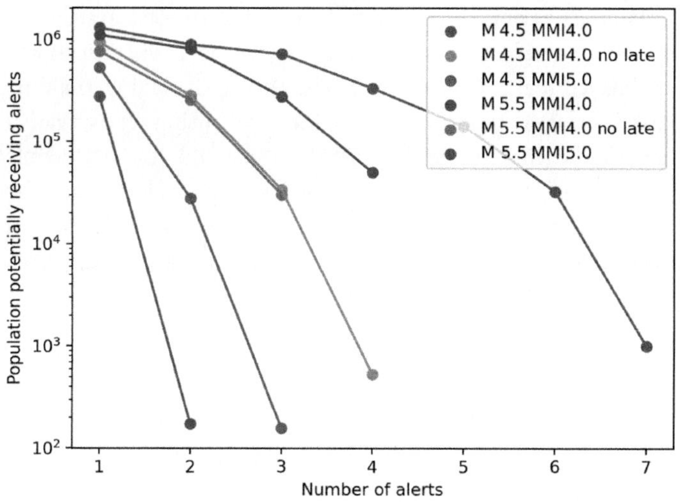

Figure 8. Simulated size of recipient population and number of alerts delivered by FinDer EEW for the period February 2023 to February 2025 using real-time performance data for different alert criteria. The color version of this figure is available only in the electronic edition.

States, Given *et al.*, 2018; Switzerland, Massin *et al.*, 2021). Even so, assuming that just a few seconds are sufficient for some protective actions to be taken to reduce injury (e.g., Fujinawa and Noda, 2013; Porter and Jones, 2018), we find that the current network should be capable of successful EEW for the most damaging **M** 7+ earthquakes. Using more conservative estimates of the time needed for protective action (e.g., 5–15 s; McGuire *et al.*, 2025) suggests useful EEW could be challenging for **M** 7–7.5 earthquakes but still possible for **M** 7.5+ earthquakes. Targeted increases of station density could potentially help for moderate **M** 6–7 earthquakes occurring within urban areas and might be achieved by combining with low-cost sensor networks (e.g., Wu *et al.*, 2021; Prasanna *et al.*, 2022; Chandrakumar *et al.*, 2024). Quick wins may also be achieved in reducing system latencies by optimizing data packetization and delivery (Stubailo *et al.*, 2020). Our real-time testing suggests that false alerts should not be a significant problem, but further work could be undertaken to ensure noise levels across the network are sufficiently well characterized and accounted for in EEW algorithms so that false alerts are minimized further (Given *et al.*, 2018).

Our analysis of EEW performance is somewhat limited by the use of historic data (because of the small number of instrumentally recorded large-magnitude earthquakes) and the computation of metrics only at sensor locations. This reduces our ability to understand impact for rare large earthquakes or to comprehensively consider populations and infrastructure. Studies that compute metrics at a grid of target sites (Cochran *et al.*, 2018) using long-duration synthetic catalogs (Minson *et al.*, 2022) or large-magnitude synthetic scenarios (Thompson *et al.*, 2024) permit a more comprehensive analysis of alert frequency, network and algorithm optimization, and population impact. Conversely, synthetic studies may struggle to capture the observed ground-motion variability against which the performance of a real EEW system would be measured.

The recent real-time implementation of FinDer in NZ provides a continuous dataset for us to begin exploring detection capability, source characterization, and alert frequency for EEW implementation. However, FinDer is only one EEW approach and is not used internationally as the sole EEW algorithm within a system (Massin *et al.*, 2021; Porras *et al.*, 2021; Lux *et al.*, 2024). The real-time characterization of rupture extent gives FinDer significant advantages over other methodologies for larger ruptures (**M** 6.5+), but it is often slightly slower to detect earthquakes and will initially underestimate magnitude compared with point-source algorithms that rely on faster portions of the seismic wavefield (Chung *et al.*, 2020; Massin *et al.*, 2021; Lux *et al.*, 2024). To derive the greatest societal benefit from an EEW system, we should strive to improve performance for the highest impacted epicentral sites. To that end, the following avenues could be explored:

1. Reduce the number of stations required for FinDer earthquake detection or increase sensor density in and around urban regions (Li *et al.*, 2021).
2. Test a combined EEW system that uses mixed regional approaches (e.g., FinDer alongside a point-source or ground-motion-based approach such as VS, Cua and Heaton, 2007; EPIC, Chung *et al.*, 2019; or PLUM, Kodera *et al.*, 2018) or combine regional and on-site approaches (Wu *et al.*, 2021).
3. Explore and minimize any latencies in the EEW system, especially potential alert distribution mechanisms. Although NZ already has a system for distributing emergency alerts (EMA; NEMA, 2024), we have not assessed if latencies would be sufficiently low for EEW delivery, nor have we investigated other potential alert delivery pathways that would be vital to a successful national system.

As a source characterization algorithm, FinDer can support detailed alert broadcasts (e.g., earthquake magnitude and origin time, multiple alert regions at different MMI levels). This permits end users to tune their systems for different thresholds (Given *et al.*, 2018), for thresholds to vary geographically, or for alert messaging to evolve as magnitude or ground-motion severity increases, even if the information presented to users is necessarily short and targeted (Sutton *et al.*, 2020; Dallo *et al.*, 2022). This may be a further reason for exploring mixed approaches, combining FinDer with simpler, faster, less detailed methods that target the closest epicentral regions.

It is not our intention to suggest an optimum alert strategy in this study, though we have used stated user preferences from social science research to inform our test parameters. EEW system design is a social, political, and economic challenge as much as it is a seismological one, and further work for the

NZ context would be required prior to any implementation. As discussed in several studies (e.g., Minson *et al.*, 2019; McGuire *et al.*, 2025), optimum alert strategies are likely to be user specific and will depend on tolerance to inaccurate alerts (i.e., ground-motion prediction accuracy or false alerts when no earthquake occurs), required warning time, and costs of taking action. In line with previous work (McGuire *et al.*, 2021, 2025; Thompson *et al.*, 2024), we find that increasing the MMI alert threshold makes timely EEW alerting much more challenging, and using a higher alert magnitude may be the better way to approach the preference to receive alerts only for damaging shaking expressed by New Zealanders (Becker, Potter, Prasanna, *et al.*, 2020; Becker, Potter, Vinnell, *et al.*, 2020). Further study is needed to explore if potentially alerting people once or several times per year for felt but nondamaging shaking, as our study suggests might be the case based on the most recent 2 yr of data, would encourage trust in the system or cause frustration.

Conclusions

Here, we have explored the capability of existing infrastructure and methods to contribute to a future national EEW system for NZ as a means of mitigating potential implementation costs (Given *et al.*, 2018; Wanigarathna *et al.*, 2023). Based on real-time observations from 2 yr of continuous operation, supplemented with testing using a suite of historic moderate to large earthquakes, we find that the current GeoNet network combined with the FinDer algorithm (operational for NZ as described in Andrews *et al.*, 2024) already has the potential to generate actionable EEW alerts for the most damaging (**M** 7+) earthquakes for a significant fraction of the areas with potentially damaging shaking (MMI 5.0+) and provide warning times between seconds and up to two minutes. For moderate (**M** 6–7) earthquakes, we find that some MMI 5.0+ sites may be alerted with a few seconds of warning times, but alerts are too late for the most strongly shaken sites in the epicentral region. Although offshore and deep earthquakes challenge FinDer's methodology, resulting in lower accuracy source characterization, our results suggest that MMI 5.0+ regions could still be provided with a few seconds of warning, and there would not be significant incorrect alerting for unfelt shaking levels.

Providing successful EEW for the highest impacted epicentral region is an ongoing global research challenge. Potential avenues to be explored for NZ include optimized network densification using observatory-grade or low-cost sensors targeted to exposed populations and chosen EEW approaches. In addition, alternative EEW methods such as point-source or ground motion–based ones may also have the potential to provide faster alerts for the epicentral region. Faster alert creation will only be useful if alert distribution pathways are also effective.

Finally, an EEW system is only useful if it prompts recipients to take effective protective actions, whether manual or automated. Any EEW system must therefore be trusted and meet users' expectations. Social science research suggests New Zealanders prefer higher-magnitude and MMI alert thresholds, but with current approaches, this may come at the cost of late or delayed alerts for sites with potentially damaging shaking. Based on real-time data, we find that using conservative thresholds (magnitude 4.5, MMI 4.0), could lead to people in the most seismic regions to receive a few alerts per year for felt but nondamaging shaking. Further work is needed to understand if this behavior is acceptable to NZ recipients or if it could become so with greater familiarity or experience with EEW systems.

Data and Resources

GeoNet data for analysis were downloaded through the International Federation of Digital Seismograph Networks (FDSN) webservices data service: https://www.geonet.org.nz/data/access/FDSN (last accessed March 2025). The authors acknowledge the New Zealand GeoNet program and its sponsors Natural Hazards Commission (NHC), GNS Science, Land Information New Zealand (LINZ), National Emergency Management Agency (NEMA), and Ministry of Business, Innovation, and Employment (MBIE) for providing data/images used in this study. Codes to create the earthquake early warning (EEW) analysis plots (Figs. 4–6) are available at https://github.com/jenrandrews/FinDer_EEW_plots (last accessed June 2025). Further information on Android earthquake alerts (AEA) can be found at https://crisisresponse.google/android-alerts (last accessed June 2025). The supplemental material includes details of finite-fault rupture detector (FinDer) configuration, a table of earthquake information for the historic events used to test FinDer EEW performance, a map comparing shaking layers (observed, modeled) and FinDer (predicted) shaking regions for earthquakes used in the real-time analysis of potential FinDer EEW alerting, a map showing felt reports and FinDer (predicted) shaking regions for earthquakes used in the real-time analysis of potential FinDer EEW alerting, a table of the percentage of felt reports falling within the FinDer (predicted) shaking regions for earthquakes used in the real-time analysis of potential FinDer EEW alerting, and a table of population numbers that could have received alerts for earthquakes in the real-time analysis of potential FinDer EEW alerting depending on configuration.

Declaration of Competing Interests

The authors acknowledge that there are no conflicts of interest recorded.

Acknowledgments

J. Andrews, Y. Behr, A. Kaiser, and B. Fry are supported by New Zealand Ministry of Business, Innovation and Employment Contract C05X2003 for the Rapid Characterization of Earthquakes and Tsunami (RCET) program. M. Böse is supported by the U.S. Geological Survey under Grant/Cooperative Agreement Number G19AC00414 to ETH Zurich. Many thanks to Katie Jacobs and Florent Aden of GNS Science and the associate editor and two anonymous reviewers for their thorough and insightful reviews which significantly improved this article.

References

Abrahamson, N. A., W. J. Silva, and R. Kamai (2014). Summary of the ASK14 ground motion relation for active crustal regions, *Earthq. Spectra* **30**, no. 3, 1025–1055.

Allen, R. M., and D. Melgar (2019), Earthquake early warning: Advances, scientific challenges, and societal needs, *Annu. Rev. Earth Planet. Sci.* **47,** 361–388, doi: 10.1146/annurev-earth-053018-060457.

Allen, R. M., and M. Stogaitis (2022). Global growth of earthquake early warning, *Science* **375,** no. 6582, 717–718.

Allen, R. M., E. S. Cochran, T. Huggins, S. Miles, and D. Otegui (2017). Quake warnings, seismic culture, *Science* **358,** no. 6367, 1111, doi: 10.1126/science.aar4640.

Andrews, J., Y. Behr, M. Böse, F. Massin, A. Kaiser, and B. Fry (2024). Rapid earthquake rupture characterization for New Zealand using the FinDer algorithm, *Bull. Seismol. Soc. Am.* **114,** 775–793, doi: 10.1785/0120230213.

Bannister, S., and K. R. Gledhill (2012). Evolution of the 2010-2012 Canterbury earthquake sequence, *New Zeal. J. Geol. Geophys.* **55,** no. 3, 295–304, doi: 10.1080/00288306.2012.680475.

Becker, J. S., S. H. Potter, R. Prasanna, M. L. Tan, B. A. Payne, C. Holden, N. Horspool, R. Smith, and D. M. Johnston (2020). Scoping the potential for earthquake early warning in Aotearoa New Zealand: A sectoral analysis of perceived benefits and challenges, *Int. J. Disaster Risk Reduct.* **51,** 1–16, doi: 10.1016/j.ijdrr.2020.101765.

Becker, J. S., S. H. Potter, L. J. Vinnell, K. Nakayachi, S. K. McBride, and D. M. Johnston (2020). Earthquake early warning in Aotearoa New Zealand: A survey of public perspectives to guide warning system development, *Humanit. Soc. Sci. Commun.* **7,** 1–12, doi: 10.1057/s41599-020-00613-9.

Boore, D. M., J. P. Stewart, E. Seyhan, and G. M. Atkinson (2014). NGA-West2 equations for predicting PGA, PGV, and 5% damped PSA for shallow crustal earthquakes, *Earthq. Spectra* **30,** no. 3, 1057–1085, doi: 10.1193/070113EQS184M.

Böse, M., J. Andrews, R. Hartog, and C. Felizardo (2023). Performance and next-generation development of the finite-fault rupture detector (FinDer) within the United States West Coast ShakeAlert warning system, *Bull. Seismol. Soc. Am.* doi: 10.1785/0120220183.

Böse, M., J. Andrews, C. O'Rourke, D. Kilb, A. Lux, J. Bunn, and J. McGuire (2022). Testing the ShakeAlert earthquake early warning system using synthesized earthquake sequences, *Seismol. Res. Lett.* **94,** no. 1, 243–259, doi: 10.1785/0220220088.

Böse, M., S. Ceylan, J. Andrews, F. Massin, J. Clinton, J. K. Saunders, O. Tatar, and M. Türkoğlu (2024). Rapid finite-fault models for the 2023 M_w 7.8 Kahramanmaraş, Türkiye, earthquake sequence, *Seismol. Res. Lett.* **95,** no. 5, 2761–2778, doi: 10.1785/0220230426.

Böse, M., S. Colombelli, A. Emolo, S. Nazeri, S. Tarantino, S. Cesca, N. Nooshiri, and A. Michelini (2018). D28.1 Report on methodologies for the real-time, automatic determination of fault geometry, source duration size parameters, *Deliverable of EU H2020 Project SERA, Contract no. 730900*, available at http://www.sera-eu.org/export/sites/sera/home/.galleries/Deliverables/SERA_D28.1_Fault_geometry_size.pdf (last accessed February 2025).

Böse, M., T. H. Heaton, and E. Hauksson (2012). Real-time finite fault rupture detector (FinDer) for large earthquakes, *Geophys. J. Int.* **191,** no. 2, 803–812, doi: 10.1111/j.1365-246X.2012.05657.x.

Böse, M., S. Julien-Laferrière, R. Bossu, and F. Massin (2021). Near real-time earthquake line-source models derived from felt reports, *Seismol. Res. Lett.* **92,** no. 3, 1961–1978, doi: 10.1785/0220200244.

Böse, M., D. Smith, C. Felizardo, M.-A. Meier, T. H. Heaton, and J. Clinton (2018). FinDer v.2: Improved real-time ground-motion predictions for M2–M9 with seismic finite-source characterization, *Geophys. J. Int.* **212,** doi: 10.1093/gji/ggx430.

Bozorgnia, Y., N. A. Abrahamson, L. A. Atik, T. D. Ancheta, G. M. Atkinson, J. W. Baker, A. Baltay, D. M. Boore, K. W. Campbell, B. S.-J. Chiou, *et al.* (2014). NGA-West2 research project, *Earthq. Spectra* **30,** no. 3, 973–987, doi: 10.1193/072113EQS209M.

Bradley, B. A. (2013). A New Zealand-specific pseudospectral acceleration ground-motion prediction equation for active shallow crustal earthquakes based on foreign models, *Bull. Seismol. Soc. Am.* **103,** 1801–1822.

Bradley, B. A., S. S. Bora, R. L. Lee, E. F. Manea, M. C. Gerstenberger, P. J. Stafford, G. M. Atkinson, G. Weatherill, J. Hutchinson, C. A. de la Torre, *et al.* (2024). The ground-motion characterization model for the 2022 New Zealand National Seismic Hazard Model, *Bull. Seismol. Soc. Am.* **114,** no. 1, 329–349, doi: 10.1785/0120230170.

Campbell, K. W., and Y. Bozorgnia (2014). NGA-West2 ground motion model for the average horizontal components of PGA, PGV, and 5% damped linear acceleration response spectra, *Earthq. Spectra* **30,** no. 3, 1087–1115, doi: 10.1193/062913EQS175M.

Chandrakumar, C., M. L. Tan, C. Holden, M. Stephens, A. Punchihewa, and R. Prasanna (2024). Estimating S-wave amplitude for earthquake early warning in New Zealand: Leveraging the first 3 seconds of P-wave, *Earth Sci. Inform.* **17,** 4527–4554, doi: 10.1007/s12145-024-01403-6.

Chandrakumar, C., M. L. Tan, C. Holden, M. T. Stephens, and R. Prasanna (2025). Evaluating P-wave detection algorithms for earthquake early warning: Insights from GeoNet data in Canterbury, Aotearoa New Zealand, *Earth. Sci. Inform.* **18,** 46, doi: 10.1007/s12145-024-01519-9.

Chiou, B., and R. R. Youngs (2006). PEER-NGA empirical ground motion model for the average horizontal component of peak acceleration and pseudo-spectral acceleration for spectral periods of 0.01 to 10 seconds, available at https://apps.peer.berkeley.edu/research/lifelines/nga_docs/jul_10_06/Chiou_Youngs_NGA_2006.pdf (last accessed June 2025).

Chiou, B. S.-J., and R. R. Youngs (2014). Update of the Chiou and Youngs NGA model for the average horizontal component of peak ground motion and response spectra, *Earthq. Spectra* **30,** no. 3, 1117–1153, doi: 10.1193/072813EQS219M.

Chung, A. I., I. Henson, and R. M. Allen (2019). Optimizing earthquake early warning performance: ElarmS-3, *Seismol. Res. Lett.* **90,** no. 2A, 727–743, doi: 10.1785/0220180192.

Chung, A. I., M.-A. Meier, J. Andrews, M. Böse, B. W. Crowell, J. J. McGuire, and D. E. Smith (2020). ShakeAlert earthquake early warning system performance during the 2019 Ridgecrest earthquake sequence, *Bull. Seismol. Soc. Am.* **110,** no. 4, 1904–1923, doi: 10.1785/0120200032.

Clark, K. J., J. D. Howarth, N. J. Litchfield, U. A. Cochran, J. Turnbull, L. Dowling, A. Howell, K. Berryman, and F. Wolfe (2019). Geological evidence for past large earthquakes and tsunamis along the Hikurangi subduction margin, *New Zeal. Mar. Geol.* **412,** 139–172, doi: 10.1016/j.margeo.2019.03.004.

Clark, K. J., E. K. Nissen, J. D. Howarth, I. J. Hamling, J. J. Mountjoy, W. F. Ries, K. E. Jones, S. Goldstein, U. A. Cochran, P. Villamor, *et al.* (2017). Highly variable coastal deformation in the 2016 M_W 7.8 Kaikoura earthquake reflects rupture complexity along a transpressional plate boundary, *Earth Planet. Sci. Lett.* **474,** 334–344, doi: 10.1016/j.epsl.2017.06.048.

Cochran, E. S., M. D. Kohler, D. D. Given, S. Guiwits, J. Andrews, M.-A. Meier, M. Ahmad, I. Henson, R. Hartog, and D. Smith (2018). Earthquake early warning ShakeAlert system: Testing and certification platform, *Seismol. Res. Lett.* **89,** no. 1, 108–117, doi: 10.1785/0220170138.

Cremen, G., and C. Galasso (2020). Earthquake early warning: Recent advances and perspectives, *Earth Sci. Rev.* **205,** 103184, doi: 10.1016/j.earscirev.2020.103184.

Cua, G., and T. Heaton (2007). The virtual seismologist (VS) method: A Bayesian approach to earthquake early warning, in *Earthquake Early Warning Systems*, P. Gasparini, G. Manfredi, and J. Zschau (Editors), Springer, Berlin, Heidelberg, doi: 10.1007/978-3-540-72241-0_7.

Dallo, I., M. Marti, J. Clinton, M. Böse, F. Massin, and S. Zaugg (2022). Earthquake early warning in countries where damaging earthquakes only occur every 50 to 150 years—The societal perspective, *Int. J. Disaster Risk Reduct.* **83,** no. 103, doi: 10.1016/j.ijdrr.2022.103441.

Fry, B., S. Bannister, R. J. Beavan, L. Bland, B. A. Bradley, S. C. Cox, W. J. Cousins, N. H. Gale, G. T. Hancox, C. Holden, *et al.* (2010). The M_W 7.6 Dusky Sound earthquake of 2009: Preliminary report, *Bull. New Zeal. Soc. Earthq. Eng.* **43,** no. 1, 24–40, doi: 10.5459/bnzsee.43.1.24-40.

Fujinawa, Y., and Y. Noda (2013). Japan's earthquake early warning system on 11 March 2011: Performance, shortcomings, and changes, *Earthq. Spectra* **29,** S341–S368, doi: 10.1193/1.4000127.

Gerstenberger, M. C., S. S. Bora, B. A. Bradley, C. DiCaprio, A. E. Kaiser, E. F. Manea, A. Nicol, J. C. Rollins, M. W. Stirling, K. K. S. Thingbaijam, *et al.* (2024). The 2022 Aotearoa New Zealand National seismic hazard model: Process, overview, and results, *Bull. Seismol. Soc. Am.* **114,** no. 1, 7–36, doi: 10.1785/0120230182.

Given, D. D., R. M. Allen, A. S. Baltay, P. Bodin, E. S. Cochran, K. Creager, R. M. de Groot, L. S. Gee, E. Hauksson, T. H. Heaton, *et al.* (2018). Revised technical implementation plan for the ShakeAlert system—An earthquake early warning system for the West Coast of the United States, *U.S. Geol. Surv. Open-File Rept. 2018-1155*, 42 pp., doi: 10.3133/ofr20181155 [Supersedes USGS Open-File Report 2014-1097].

Gledhill, K. R., J. Ristau, M. E. Reyners, B. Fry, and C. Holden (2011). The Darfield (Canterbury, New Zealand) M_W 7.1 earthquake of September 2010: A preliminary seismological report, *Seismol. Res. Lett.* **82,** no. 3, 378–386, doi: 10.1785/gssrl.82.3.378.

GNS Science (2025a). GeoNet Aotearoa New Zealand stations metadata repository [Dataset], GNS Science, GeoNet, doi: 10.21420/0VY2-C144.

GNS Science (2025b). GeoNet Aotearoa New Zealand earthquake moment tensor solutions [Dataset], GNS Science, GeoNet, doi: 10.21420/MMJ9-CZ67.

GNS Science (2025c). GeoNet Aotearoa New Zealand earthquake catalogue [Dataset], GNS Science, GeoNet, doi: 10.21420/0S8P-TZ38.

GNS Science (2025d). GNS Science shaking layers dataset [Dataset], GNS Science, GeoNet, doi: 10.21420/J856-2J84.

GNS Science (2025e). GeoNet Aotearoa New Zealand felt rapid dataset [Dataset], GNS Science, GeoNet, doi: 10.21420/RS7F-VE53.

Goded, T., N. Horspool, A. Kaiser, M. Chadwick, J. Groom, J. Houltham, S. Harvey, D. Charlton, H. Wu, B. Peng, *et al.* (2025). The shaking layers project: Near real-time shaking intensity maps for New Zealand earthquakes: Project overview, *Bull. New Zeal. Soc. Earthq. Eng.* (accepted).

Goded, T., M. L. Tan, J. S. Becker, N. Horspool, S. Canessa, R. Huso, J. Hanson, and D. M. Johnston (2021). Using citizen data to understand earthquake impacts: Aotearoa New Zealand's earthquake Felt Reports, *Australas. J. Disaster Trauma Stud.* **25,** no. 3, 61–78.

Goltz, J. D., D. J. Wald, S. K. McBride, E. Reddy, V. Quitoriano, and J. K. Saunders (2024). The Ojai California earthquake of 20 August 2023: Earthquake early warning performance and alert recipient response in the M_w 5.1 event, *Seismol. Res. Lett.* **95,** no. 5, 2745–2760, doi: 10.1785/0220240023.

Holden, C., A. E. Kaiser, R. J. Van Dissen, and R. Jury (2013). Sources, ground motion and structural response characteristics in Wellington of the 2013 Cook Strait earthquakes, *Bull. New Zeal. Soc. Earthq. Eng.* **46,** no. 4, 188–195, doi: 10.5459/bnzsee.46.4.188-195.

Horspool, N. A., A. E. Kaiser, T. Goded, D. H. Charlton, J. M. Moratalla, M. P. Chadwick, J. Groom, J. Houltham, E. R. Abbott, J. R. Andrews, *et al.* (2023). GNS Shaking layers tool: Guidelines for end users, *GNS Science Rept. 2023/13*, GNS Science, Lower Hutt, New Zealand, 64 pp., doi: 10.21420/VZKK-TP35.

Howarth, J. D., N. C. Barth, S. J. Fitzsimons, K. Richards-Dinger, K. J. Clark, G. P. Biasi, U. A. Cochran, R. M. Langridge, K. R. Berryman, and R. Sutherland (2021). Spatiotemporal clustering of great earthquakes on a transform fault controlled by geometry, *Nature Geosci.* **14,** 314–320, doi: 10.1038/s41561-021-00721-4.

Jenlogix (2024). Available at https://jenlogix.co.nz/home/seismic-sensors/ (last accessed February 2025).

Kaiser, A., C. HoutteVan, N. Perrin, L. Wotherspoon, and G. McVerry (2017). Site characterisation of GeoNet stations for the New Zealand strong motion database, *Bull. New Zeal. Soc. Earthq. Eng.* **50,** no. 1, 39–49, doi: 10.5459/bnzsee.50.1.39-49.

Kaiser, A. E., J. R. Andrews, B. Fry, N. A. Horspool, B. Lukovic, C. I. Massey, E. Warren-Smith, T. Godet, and C. Chamberlain (2024). Dynamic shaking layer models for large New Zealand earthquakes (M 6.5+): From rapid source characterization to landslide and impact forecasting, *Proc. of the 2024 New Zealand Society for Earthquake Engineering Annual Technical Conference*, Wellington, New Zealand, April 2024.

Kaiser, A. E., N. J. Balfour, B. Fry, C. Holden, N. J. Litchfield, M. C. Gerstenberger, E. D'Anastasio, N. A. Horspool, G. H. McVerry, J. Ristau, *et al.* (2017). The 2016 Kaikoura, New Zealand, earthquake: Preliminary seismological report, *Seismol. Res. Lett.* **88,** no. 3, 727–739, doi: 10.1785/0220170018.

Kaiser, A. E., C. Holden, R. J. Beavan, R. D. Beetham, R. A. Benites, A. Celentano, D. Collet, W. J. Cousins, M. Cubrinovski, G. D. Dellow, *et al.* (2012). The M_w 6.2 Christchurch Earthquake of February 2011: Preliminary report, *New Zeal. J. Geol. Geophys.* **55,** no. 1, 67–90, doi: 10.1080/00288306.2011.641182.

Kodera, Y., Y. Yamada, K. Hirano, K. Tamaribuchi, S. Adachi, N. Hayashimoto, M. Morimoto, M. Nakamura, and M. Hoshiba (2018). The propagation of local undamped motion (PLUM) method: A simple and robust seismic wavefield estimation approach for earthquake early warning, *Bull. Seismol. Soc. Am.* **108,** no. 2, 983–1003, doi: 10.1785/0120170085.

Kohler, M., D. Smith, J. Andrews, A. Chung, R. Hartog, I. Henson, D. Given, R. Groot, and S. Guiwits (2020). Earthquake early warning

ShakeAlert 2.0: Public rollout, *Seismol. Res. Lett.* **91,** doi: 10.1785/0220190245.

Lee, R. L., B. A. Bradley, E. F. Manea, J. A. Hutchinson, and S. S. Bora (2024). Evaluation of empirical ground motion models for the 2022 New Zealand National Seismic Hazard Model revision, *Bull. Seismol. Soc. Am.* **114,** no. 1, 311–328, doi: 10.1785/0120230180.

Li, J., M. Böse, Y. Feng, and C. Yang (2021). Real-time characterization of finite rupture and its implication for earthquake early warning: Application of FinDer to existing and planned stations in Southwest China, *Front. Earth Sci.* **9,** 699560, doi: 10.3389/feart.2021.699560.

Lux, A. I., D. Smith, M. Böse, J. J. McGuire, J. K. Saunders, M. Huynh, I. Stubailo, J. Andrews, G. Lotto, B. Crowell, *et al.* (2024). Status and performance of the ShakeAlert earthquake early warning system: 2019–2023, *Bull. Seismol. Soc. Am.* **114,** no. 6, 3041–3062, doi: 10.1785/0120230259.

Massin, F., J. F. Clinton, and M. Böse (2021). Status of earthquake early warning in Switzerland, *Front. Earth Sci.* **9,** 707654, doi: 10.3389/feart.2021.707654.

McBride, S. K., D. F. Sumy, A. L. Llenos, G. A. Parker, J. McGuire, J. K. Saunders, M.-A. Meier, P. Schuback, D. Given, and R. de Groot (2023). Latency and geofence testing of wireless emergency alerts intended for the ShakeAlert earthquake early warning system for the West Coast of the United States of America, *Safety Sci.* **157,** 105898, doi: 10.1016/j.ssci.2022.105898.

McGuire, J. J., and R. M. de Groot (2020). What if the ShakeAlert earthquake early warning system had been operating during the M 6.7 1994 Northridge earthquake, available at https://www.shakealert.org/wp-content/uploads/2024/01/Northridge_ShakeAlertOrg_FINAL_a_20240116.pdf (last accessed June 2025).

McGuire, J. J., D. E. Smith, A. D. Frankel, E. A. Wirth, S. K. McBride, and R. M. de Groot (2021). Expected warning times from the ShakeAlert earthquake early warning system for earthquakes in the Pacific Northwest (ver. 1.1, March 24, 2021), *U.S. Geol. Surv. Open-File Rept. 2021-1026*, 37 pp., doi: 10.3133/ofr20211026.

McGuire, J. J., C. W. Ulberg, A. I. Lux, M. Böse, J. R. Andrews, D. E. Smith, B. W. Crowell, J. R. Murray, I. Henson, R. Hartog, *et al.* (2025). ShakeAlert Version 3: Expected performance in large earthquakes, *Bull. Seismol. Soc. Am.* doi: 10.1785/0120240189.

Meier, M.-A. (2017). How "good" are real-time ground motion predictions from earthquake early warning systems, *J. Geophys. Res.* **122,** 5561–5577, doi: 10.1002/2017JB014025.

Meier, M.-A., Y. Kodera, M. Böse, A. Chung, M. Hoshiba, E. Cochran, S. Minson, E. Hauksson, and T. Heaton (2020). How often can earthquake early warning systems alert sites with high-intensity ground motion? *J. Geophys. Res.* **125,** no. 2, 1–17, doi: 10.1029/2019JB017718.

Minson, S. E., A. S. Baltay, E. S. Cochran, T. C. Hanks, M. T. Page, S. K. McBride, K. R. Milner, and M.-A. Meier (2019). The limits of earthquake early warning accuracy and best alerting strategy, *Sci. Rep.* **9,** 2478, doi: 10.1038/s41598-019-39384-y.

Minson, S. E., E. S. Cochran, J. K. Saunders, S. K. McBride, S. Wu, A. S. Baltay, and K. R. Milner (2022). What to expect when you are expecting earthquake early warning, *Geophys. J. Int.* **231,** no. 2, 1386–1403, doi: 10.1093/gji/ggac246.

Minson, S. E., M.-A. Meier, A. S. Baltay, T. C. Hanks, and E. S. Cochran (2018). The limits of earthquake early warning: Timeliness of ground motion estimates, *Sci. Adv.* **4,** eaaq0504, doi: 10.1126/sciadv.aaq0504.

Moratalla, J. M., D. A. Tatiana Goded, S. C. Rhoades, and M. C. Gerstenberger (2020). New ground motion to intensity conversion equations (GMICEs) for New Zealand, *Seismol. Res. Lett.* **92,** no. 1, 448–459, doi: 10.1785/0220200156.

Morgenstern, R., N. J. Litchfield, R. M. Langridge, D. W. Heron, D. B. Townsend, P. Villamor, D. J. A. Barrell, W. F. Ries, R. J. Van Dissen, K. J. Clark, *et al.* (2024). New Zealand active faults database: The high-resolution dataset v2.0, *New Zeal. J. Geol. Geophys.* doi: 10.1080/00288306.2024.2427396.

NEMA (2024). Emergency Mobile Alert. Matohi waea pūkoro ohotata, National Emergency Management Agency, available at https://mcdem4.cwp.govt.nz/prepared/ema (last accessed October 2024).

Okuwaki, R., S. P. Hicks, T. J. Craig, W. Fan, S. Goes, T. J. Wright, and Y. Yagi (2021). Illuminating a contorted slab with a complex intraslab rupture evolution during the 2021 M_w 7.3 East Cape, New Zealand earthquake, *Geophys. Res. Lett.* **48,** e2021GL095117, doi: 10.1029/2021GL095117.

Orihuela, B., I. Dallo, J. Clinton, W. Strauch, M. Protti, R. Yani, G. Marroquin, J. Sanchez, F. Vega, M. Floribeth, *et al.* (2023). Earthquake early warning in central America: The societal perspective, *Int. J. Disaster Risk Reduct.* **97,** 103982, doi: 10.1016/j.ijdrr.2023.103982.

Pagani, M., D. Monelli, G. Weatherill, L. Danciu, H. Crowley, V. Silva, P. Henshaw, L. Butler, M. Nastasi, L. Panzeri, *et al.* (2014). OpenQuake Engine: An open hazard (and risk) software for the Global Earthquake Model, *Seismol. Res. Lett.* **85,** no. 3, 692–702, doi: 10.1785/0220130087.

Patel, S. C., and R. M. Allen (2022). The MyShake App: User experience of early warning delivery and earthquake shaking, *Seismol. Res. Lett.* **93,** no. 6, 3324–3336, doi: 10.1785/0220220062.

Peng, C., P. Jiang, Q. Ma, P. Wu, J. Su, Y. Zheng, and J. Yang (2021). Performance evaluation of an earthquake early warning system in the 2019–2020 M 6.0 Changning, Sichuan, China, seismic sequence, *Front. Earth Sci.* **9,** 699941, doi: 10.3389/feart.2021.699941.

Pizer, C. O., J. D. Howarth, K. J. Clark, A. R. Orpin, S. E. Tickle, L. J. Strachan, P. Barnes, S. Camp, M. Mckeown, and E. Twort (2024). Integrated onshore–offshore paleoseismic records show multiple slip styles on the plate interface, central Hikurangi subduction margin, Aotearoa New Zealand, *Quat. Sci. Rev.* **344,** 108942, doi: 10.1016/j.quascirev.2024.108942.

Porras, J., F. Massin, M. Arroyo-Solórzano, I. Arroyo, L. Linkimer, M. Böse, and J. Clinton (2021). Preliminary results of an earthquake early warning system in Costa Rica, *Front. Earth Sci.* **9,** 700843, doi: 10.3389/feart.2021.700843.

Porter, K., and J. Jones (2018). How many injuries can be avoided in the HayWired scenario through earthquake early warning and drop, cover, and hold on? in *The HayWired Earthquake Scenario—Engineering Implications, Scientif. Investig. Rept. 2017-5013-I-Q*, U.S. Geological Survey, Reston, Virginia, 429 pp., doi: 10.3133/sir20175013v2.

Potter, S. H., J. S. Becker, D. M. Johnston, and K. P. Rossiter (2015). An overview of the impacts of the 2010-2011 Canterbury earthquakes, *Int. J. Disaster Risk Reduct.* **14,** 6–14, doi: 10.1016/j.ijdrr.2015.01.014.

Prasanna, R., C. Chandrakumar, R. Nandana, C. Holden, A. Punchihewa, J. S. Becker, S. Jeong, N. Liyanage, D. Ravishan, R. Sampath, *et al.* (2022). "Saving precious seconds"—A novel approach to implementing a low-cost earthquake early warning system with node-level detection and alert generation, *Informatics* doi: 10.3390/informatics9010025.

Saunders, J. K., A. S. Baltay, S. E. Minson, and M. Böse (2024). Uncertainty in ground-motion-to-intensity conversions significantly affects earthquake early warning alert regions, *Seism. Rec.* **4,** no. 2, 121–130, doi: 10.1785/0320240004.

Silva, V., H. Crowley, M. Pagani, D. Monelli, and R. Pinho (2014). Development of the OpenQuake engine, the Global Earthquake Model's open-source software for seismic risk assessment, *Nat. Hazards* **72,** 1409–1427, doi: 10.1007/s11069-013-0618-x.

StatsNZ (2023). Metadata for the New Zealand 2022 estimated resident population grid 1 km, 2023, available at www.stats.govt.nz (last accessed March 2025).

Stevenson, J. R., J. Becker, N. Cradock-Henry, S. Johal, D. Johnston, C. Orchiston, and E. Seville (2017). Economic and social reconnaissance: Kaikōura earthquake 2016, *Bull. New Zeal. Soc. Earthq. Eng.* **50,** no. 2, 343–351.

Stirling, M., M. Fitzgerald, B. Shaw, and C. Ross (2023). New magnitude–area scaling relations for the New Zealand National Seismic Hazard Model 2022, *Bull. Seismol. Soc. Am.* **114,** 137–149, doi: 10.1785/0120230114.

Strauss, J. A., and R. M. Allen (2016). Benefits and costs of earthquake early warning, *Seismol. Res. Lett.* **87,** no. 3, 765–772, doi: 10.1785/0220150149.

Stubailo, I., M. Alvarez, G. Biasi, R. Bhadha, and E. Hauksson (2020). Latency of waveform data delivery from the southern California seismic network during the 2019 Ridgecrest earthquake sequence and its effect on ShakeAlert, *Seismol. Res. Lett.* **92,** no. 1, 170–186, doi: 10.1785/0220200211.

Sutton, J., L. Fischer, L. E. James, and S. E. Sheff (2020). Earthquake early warning message testing: Visual attention, behavioral responses, and message perceptions, *Int. J. Disaster Risk Reduct.* **49,** 101664, doi: 10.1016/j.ijdrr.2020.101664.

Tan, M., R. Prasanna, J. Becker, A. Brown, K. Stock, C. Kenney, E. Lambie, D. Johnston, and D. De Alwis (2021). Outlook for earthquake early warning for Aotearoa New Zealand: Insights from initiating a community-of-practice, *Proc. of the 2021 New Zealand Society for Earthquake Engineering Annual Technical Conference*, Christchurch, New Zealand, April 2021.

Thakoor, K., J. Andrews, E. Hauksson, and T. Heaton (2019). From earthquake source parameters to ground-motion warnings near you: The ShakeAlert earthquake information to ground-motion (eqInfo2GM) method, *Seismol. Res. Lett.* **90,** no. 3, 1243–1257, doi: 10.1785/0220180245.

Thompson, M., J. R. Hartog, and E. A. Wirth (2024). A population-based performance evaluation of the ShakeAlert earthquake early warning system for M 9 megathrust earthquakes in the Pacific Northwest, USA, *Bull. Seismol. Soc. Am.* **114,** no. 2, 1103–1123, doi: 10.1785/0120230055.

Wanigarathna, N., K. Jones, F. Mulder, B. Borzi, F. Bozzoni, and E. Festa (2023). Economic appraisal standards for planning earthquake early warning infrastructure acquisition, *IOP Conf. Ser. Earth Environ. Sci.* **1176,** 012030.

Warren-Smith, E., K. Jacobs, C. Rollins, C. J. Chamberlain, D. Eberhart-Phillips, and C. Williams (2024). A quantitative assessment of GeoNet earthquake location quality in Aotearoa New Zealand, *New Zeal. J. Geol. Geophys.* doi: 10.1080/00288306.2024.2421309.

Worldbank (2022). Available at https://databank.worldbank.org/source/world-development-indicators/Series/EN.POP.DNST (last accessed March 2025).

Wu, Y.-M., H. Mittal, D.-Y. Chen, T.-Y. Hsu, and P.-Y. Lin (2021). Earthquake early warning systems in Taiwan: Current status, *J. Geol. Soc. India* **97,** 1525–1532, doi: 10.1007/s12594-021-1909-6.

Manuscript received 12 March 2025
Published online 17 July 2025

Improving Magnitude Estimates in the EPIC Earthquake Early Warning Algorithm

Amy Williamson*[1], Angela Lux[1], and Richard M. Allen[1]

Abstract

Earthquake early warning (EEW) programs, such as the U.S. ShakeAlert system, provide users with critical and time-sensitive earthquake information with seconds to tens of seconds of lead time prior to experiencing strong ground motions. ShakeAlert has been active on the U.S. West Coast since 2018, amassing a large dataset of detected earthquakes. Using information about these earthquakes and how they are observed at regional seismic stations, we can improve on established EEW algorithms. Here, we propose an update to the scaling relationship used in the Earthquake Point-Source Integrated Code (EPIC) algorithm to calculate real-time magnitudes. This update is based on an analysis of over 15,000 earthquakes detected through EPIC. Our reconfiguration calculates station magnitudes using one scaling relationship for stations located within 30 km of the epicenter and another scaling relationship for mid- to far-field stations. When tested against a large dataset of past events, our new scaling methodology reduces EPIC's magnitude error from 0.41 to 0.27 magnitude units with additional improvements possible if improved epicentral location information is available. Applying the new scaling to the past event catalog reduces cases in which EPIC's magnitude erroneously triggers an alert, without introducing many missed alerts due to underestimates. The time it takes to reach an alertable magnitude under the new scaling is also unchanged. In addition, because the new scaling accommodates the inclusion of *S*-wave data, rather than filters for their removal, no new delays related to processing are incurred in EPIC. This work is motivated by a goal to lower the current magnitude overestimate as a means to increase confidence in future alerts.

Cite this article as Williamson, A., A. Lux, and R. M. Allen (2025). Improving Magnitude Estimates in the EPIC Earthquake Early Warning Algorithm, *Seismol. Res. Lett.* **97**, 233–245, doi: 10.1785/0220240453.

Supplemental Material

Introduction

Earthquake early warning (EEW) is the process to detect, characterize, and warn areas that may experience damaging ground motions immediately following an earthquake (Allen *et al.*, 2009; Allen and Melgar, 2019). In a well-functioning system, seconds to tens of seconds of warning may be provided to affected communities. Although limited, this amount of time allows for people to take simple protective measures such as to drop, cover, and hold on, thereby mitigating their seismic risk (McBride *et al.*, 2022). Numerous countries have developed or are in the testing phase of public EEW systems. For example, Mexico and Japan both have long-standing early warning programs (Espinosa-Aranada *et al.*, 2009; Hosiba *et al.*, 2011). Other countries have developed regional EEW systems, including Taiwan, Israel, Costa Rica, El Salvador, Nicaragua, Switzerland, Italy, and Peru (Satriano *et al.*, 2011; Strauch *et al.*, 2018; Nof *et al.*, 2021; Porras *et al.*, 2021; Wu *et al.*, 2021; Lara *et al.*, 2025). In addition, Android Earthquake Alerts is also delivering alerts in a total of 98 countries, including the United States (Allen and Stogaitis, 2022; Allen *et al.*, 2025).

The United States' ShakeAlert EEW system, developed and implemented by the U.S. Geological Survey (USGS) and partnering academic institutions, provides alerts for earthquakes in the states of California, Oregon, and Washington (Given *et al.*, 2018; Kohler *et al.*, 2020). ShakeAlert's operation has three components: (1) a data layer ingesting ground-motion data from seismic and Global Navigation Satellite Systems (GNSS) stations, (2) a production layer containing vetted algorithms to automatically determine the earthquake's location, magnitude, and origin time, and (3) an alert layer that assesses the quality of the information from the production layer and allows the issuances of alert if certain preset magnitude and ground-motion conditions are met. Public alerts are issued for earthquakes with magnitudes as low as **M** 4.5 and to areas with expected shaking as low as modified Mercalli intensity (MMI) 3 through the use of licensed-to-operate third-party applications such as the MyShake App (Allen *et al.*, 2020; Patel and Allen, 2022) and Android Alerts (Allen and Stogaitis, 2022).

1. UC Berkeley Seismology Laboratory, University of California, Berkeley, California, U.S.A., https://orcid.org/0000-0003-1481-725X (AW); https://orcid.org/0000-0002-3767-6018 (AL); https://orcid.org/0000-0003-4293-9772 (RMA)

*Corresponding author: amy.williamson@berkeley.edu

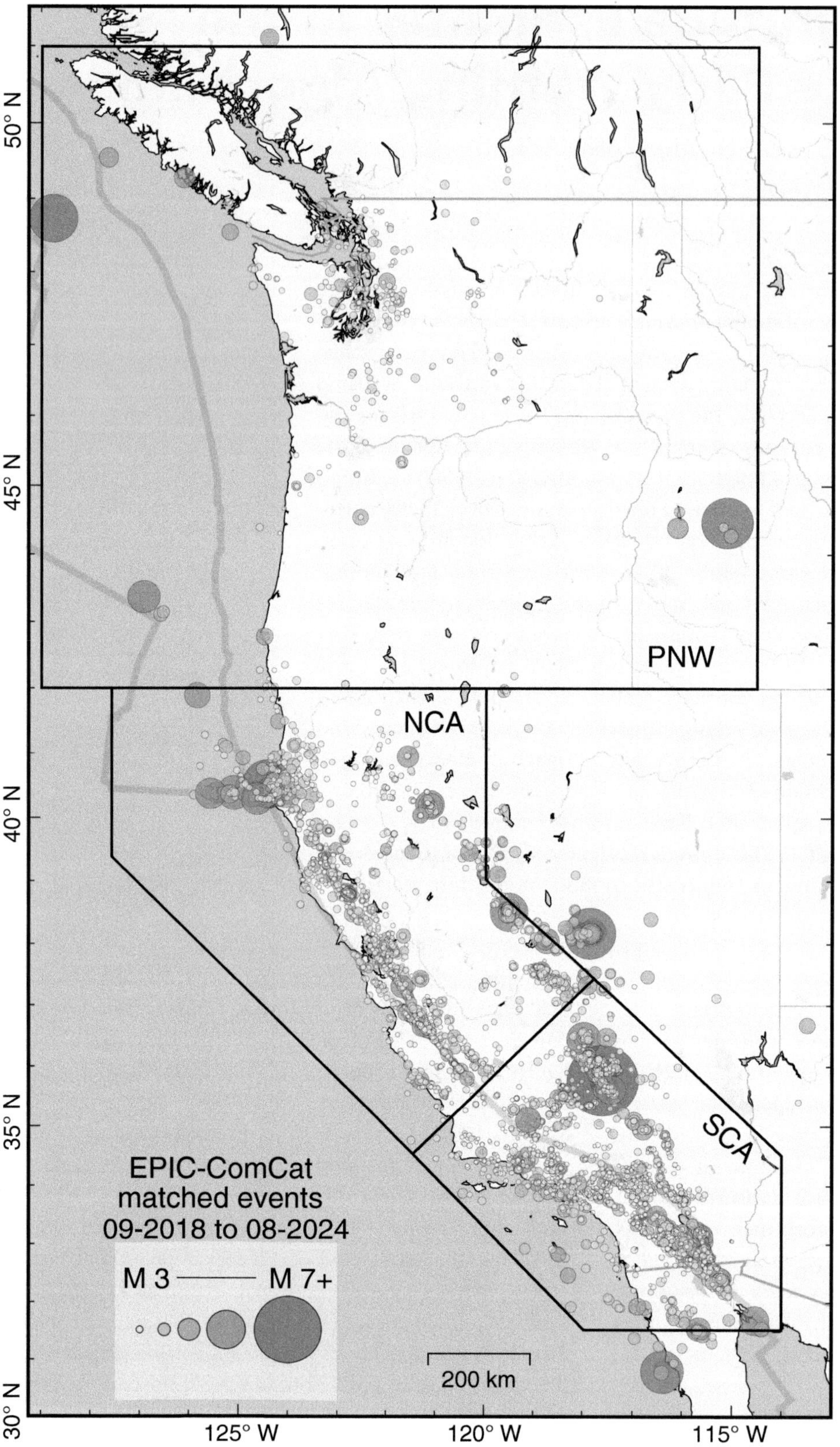

Figure 1. Seismicity detected by Earthquake Point-Source Integrated Code (EPIC) and matched to a Comprehensive Catalog (ComCat) database entry from September 2018 to August 2024. Southern California, northern California, and the Pacific Northwest generalized subregions are outlined and marked with SCA, NCA, and PNW, respectively. The color version of this figure is available only in the electronic edition.

Wireless emergency alerts are created for M 5 and greater earthquakes to the MMI 4 shaking intensity region (Kohler *et al.*, 2020). Events that fall below these magnitude and intensity thresholds are not published as alerts but are logged within the ShakeAlert system. To date, the Earthquake Point-Source Integrated Code (EPIC), which is one of the three algorithms that provides real-time information to ShakeAlert (Allen *et al.*, 2009; Chung *et al.*, 2019), has detected and characterized over 15,000 earthquakes, shown in map view in Figure 1. Data collected at these lower magnitude ranges can be used by scientists to analyze and improve the system.

The timeliness of EEW alerts is dependent in part on the density of the geodetic and seismic systems that detect the earthquake close to the source, the efficiency of the earthquake characterization algorithms, and the effectiveness of the alerting methodology to notify people or systems (Patel and Allen, 2022; McBride *et al.*, 2023). In addition to timeliness, a good EEW alert should be as accurate as possible, despite the inherent trade-off between the two (Lin *et al.*, 2021). This study focuses on the efficiency of the earthquake characterization from EPIC. Through the analysis of a multiyear dataset of detected events, we identify higher errors in magnitude estimates when using near-field stations at small-to-moderate-magnitude ranges. To reduce these errors, we develop a revised magnitude-scaling methodology based on a new calibration dataset that is reflective of the real-time data included in EPIC. We validate performance of this new magnitude-scaling system against the current production system using a dataset of earthquakes detected through EPIC since the public rollout of ShakeAlert. This performance analysis highlights both improvements to the magnitude estimates as well as identifies resolved and continuing sources of error.

Background

Overview of ShakeAlert

ShakeAlert utilizes three algorithms designed to characterize features of an earthquake in real time: EPIC, Finite-Fault Rupture Detector (FinDer), and Geodetic First Approximation of Size and Time (GFAST). EPIC, the topic of this study, is a network-based point source algorithm that uses up to 4 s of data from seismic stations to calculate the earthquake's epicenter, magnitude, and origin time (Chung *et al.*, 2019). It is often the fastest algorithm, contributing source parameters to all but one of the published ShakeAlert detections since public rollout (Lux *et al.*, 2024). FinDer compares observations of ground motion at nearby seismic stations against precalculated templates to determine fault rupture extent (Böse *et al.*, 2012, 2018). GFAST uses ground deformation data recorded over a network of GNSS stations to estimate magnitude (Murray *et al.*, 2023). Because GNSS data do not saturate, it is ideal for estimating magnitudes for large earthquakes. Because of its infancy as an active operational algorithm in ShakeAlert, GFAST has yet to contribute to a solution. Earthquake parameter estimates from one, all, or a combination of these algorithms are combined through a Solution Aggregator module. Decisions about if and when to issue an alert based on the information provided by the Solution Aggregator are governed by the decision module (Kohler *et al.*, 2020). Although public-facing alerts are issued for events with magnitudes as low as **M** 4.5, the decision module accepts solutions at a lower **M** 3.5 threshold. A more detailed explanation of the end-to-end ShakeAlert system can be found in Lux *et al.* (2024) and McGuire *et al.* (2025).

EPIC, FinDer, and GFAST use complementary data and methodologies, targeting different earthquake magnitude ranges. EPIC excels at characterizing small-to-moderate-size earthquakes, but as a point-source algorithm, it may underestimate magnitudes of large earthquakes where the finiteness of the source becomes a contributing factor (Kuyuk and Allen, 2013; Chung *et al.*, 2020). In addition, the short-time window of data used in EPIC can limit the maximum magnitude attained through peak displacement measurement methods (Trugman *et al.*, 2019). Because of these limitations, the Solution Aggregator caps the maximum magnitude that EPIC can contribute to a solution to M 7.5 (McGuire *et al.*, 2025). FinDer uses a finite-length solution, rather than point source, and is designed for characterizing larger earthquakes. As such, the Solution Aggregator does not include solutions from FinDer below **M** 5.5. Similarly, GFAST has a lower magnitude limit of **M** 6.0.

EPIC's magnitude calculation

This study focuses entirely on magnitude estimates created by EPIC, before its potential combination with FinDer and GFAST within the Solution Aggregator. EPIC runs continuously in real time, receiving information about triggered stations provided by a waveform processor. EPIC calculates magnitudes using a methodology developed by Kuyuk and Allen (2013), shortened in this study to KA2013. Using an empirically derived linear scaling relation, shown in equation (1):

$$M_{\mathrm{sta}} = a \times \log_{10}(P_d) + b \times \log_{10}(R) + c, \quad (1)$$

the magnitude at an individual station is calculated using the station's distance to the epicenter, R, and the peak absolute amplitude displacement measured within the first 4 s following P-wave arrival at triggered stations. This peak value is shortened to peak displacement (P_d).

To develop this relation, KA2013 used a calibration dataset combining P_d data previously used by Wurman *et al.* (2007), Tsang *et al.* (2007), and Brown *et al.* (2011) from northern California, southern California, and Japan, respectively. KA2013 developed their scaling relationship using a linear best fit to the calibration dataset, yielding the values of coefficients a, b, and c to be 1.23, 1.38, and 5.39, respectively. Notably, the calibration dataset used in KA2013 is developed by processing the dataset in non-real time and removes P_d measurements related to the S wave, even if they occur within the first 4 s following trigger time.

The station magnitudes, M_{sta}, calculated from equation (1), are combined through a weighted average to determine the event magnitude, M_{EPIC}, following equation (2):

$$M_{\mathrm{EPIC}} = M_{\mathrm{sta}_1} \frac{t_{\mathrm{sta}_1}}{T} + M_{\mathrm{sta}_2} \frac{t_{\mathrm{sta}_2}}{T} + \ldots + M_{\mathrm{sta}_N} \frac{t_{\mathrm{sta}_N}}{T}. \quad (2)$$

EPIC weighs station magnitude estimates by the amount of data available at each station, up to a maximum of 4 s. The weighted event magnitude is a recent change incorporated into the EPIC algorithm (Lux *et al.*, 2024). In equation (2), T is the sum of the durations of the time windows of data from all participating stations $T = t_{\mathrm{sta}_1} + t_{\mathrm{sta}_2} + \ldots + t_{\mathrm{sta}_N}$. When applied, stations with less data will have a lower impact on the event magnitude. Stations with closer to the maximum of 4 s of data will have a larger overall impact. Stations are excluded from contributing to the event magnitude if they are located more than 200 km away from the epicenter or if they fail a signal-to-noise ratio check.

EPIC continuously recalculates source parameters as more stations trigger and associate with an event. This means that EPIC produces a time series of evolving source parameters. All triggers and event parameter data are written into daily log files. Each event detected by EPIC is given its own unique event ID within the daily log file. These events are retrospectively matched with events from the Advanced National Seismic System Comprehensive Catalog (ComCat) based on distance and timing criteria. The solutions matched in

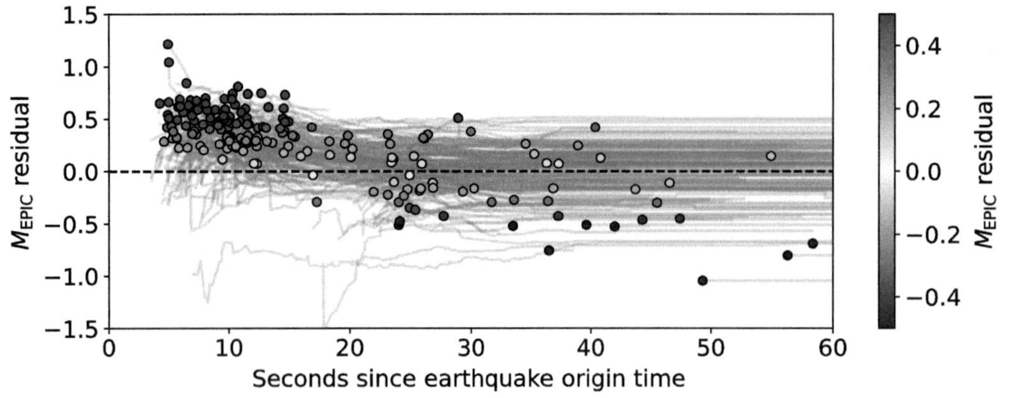

Figure 2. Magnitude residuals for EPIC real-time events. The gray overlaid lines are time series of M_{EPIC} residuals for alertable level earthquakes with respect to the time since earthquake origin. All earthquake magnitudes are calculated using the corrected station epicentral distances. The time when the maximum magnitude occurs for each event is marked with a circle. The color of the circle indicates the residual, with red colors indicating an overestimate and blue circles indicating an underestimate. The color version of this figure is available only in the electronic edition.

ComCat are held as the ground-truth value for all performance analyses. Specifically, we focus on the ComCat magnitude (M_C) and the epicentral location. For an individual earthquake, M_C can vary slightly depending on which magnitude type was preferred. For example, some earthquakes are published using a moment magnitude (M_w), whereas smaller events may use a local magnitude (M_L). Using the ComCat solution when calculating performance metrics aligns our study results with the quantitative objectives that are part of ShakeAlert's Revised Technical Implementation Plan (Given *et al.*, 2018; McGuire *et al.*, 2025). However, it bears noting that the ComCat database is not an EEW database; catalog entries are unavailable until minutes after the each event.

The KA2013 magnitude-scaling relationship was developed before the inclusion of operational real-time data streams for EEW and without knowledge of the current architecture used in both ShakeAlert and EPIC. As such, the relation operates under the assumption that all incoming P_d measurements are related to the *P* wave. Although the waveform processor that feeds data into the EPIC algorithm discriminates between *P*- and *S*-wave triggers through an initial horizontal to vertical check, it does not discriminate between *P*- and *S*-wave information post-trigger and does not currently have a mechanism in place to do so. This means that the KA2013 scaling relationship, which focuses on only displacements related to the *P* wave, is applied to a dataset that has the potential to include both *P*- and *S*-wave displacement measurements, if they occur within the 4 s post-trigger.

Using the current KA2013 scaling, we present a view of the magnitude estimate performance with respect to time after earthquake origin in Figure 2. What this shows is a common trend over many magnitude time series: an early overestimate of the magnitude that, with time and the inclusion of more stations further from the source, reduces and stabilizes to a lower residual magnitude. The residual here is calculated as the difference between M_{EPIC} and the catalog magnitude (M_C). We suspect that the early overestimate is due to the inclusion of peak displacements drawn from *S*-wave energy at stations close to the epicenter. This suspicion will be further explored within this study.

We present a methodology in this article that reframes the scaling relations to account for the potential of both *P*- and *S*-wave displacement information. The goal of this new approach is to reduce overestimates in the maximum event magnitude (M_{EPIC}) without increasing EPIC's computational load and through utilizing as much of the available data as possible.

Data and Methods

To estimate magnitude while utilizing the data coming into EPIC, we develop a new calibration dataset, following the general methodology of the Global P_d relationship developed in KA2013 but adapted to fit the needs of our real-time system. All earthquakes in the new calibration dataset originate inside the ShakeAlert reporting area and were detected by EPIC. Although this no longer would be considered a global dataset, it will best reflect the tectonic environment where the algorithm is employed. Similar local calibrations have been completed in other places where the EPIC algorithm is used (Nof and Allen, 2016).

Our calibration dataset uses 119,985 P_d observations stemming from 1,979 earthquakes. The calibration dataset that we developed uses data from earthquakes with magnitudes ranging from **M** 3.0 to 7.1. Although EPIC has detected earthquakes below **M** 3.0, we do not want to bias our fit to earthquakes that are far below ShakeAlert alerting thresholds. The KA2013 dataset uses 16,711 observations from 2,066 earthquakes. The model space covered by the KA2013 calibration dataset and the calibration dataset developed in this study are shown side-by-side in Figure 3. We do not include data from the original KA2013 dataset in this updated scaling dataset. This is because of the differences in scaling and preprocessing (i.e., the exclusion of *S*-wave observations) done by the authors of the KA2013 dataset, which no longer reflects the current processing used in real time by EPIC.

A notable difference between the two calibration datasets is the inclusion of low-magnitude (**M** < 3.0) earthquakes in the KA2013 dataset. An additional difference is the increased number

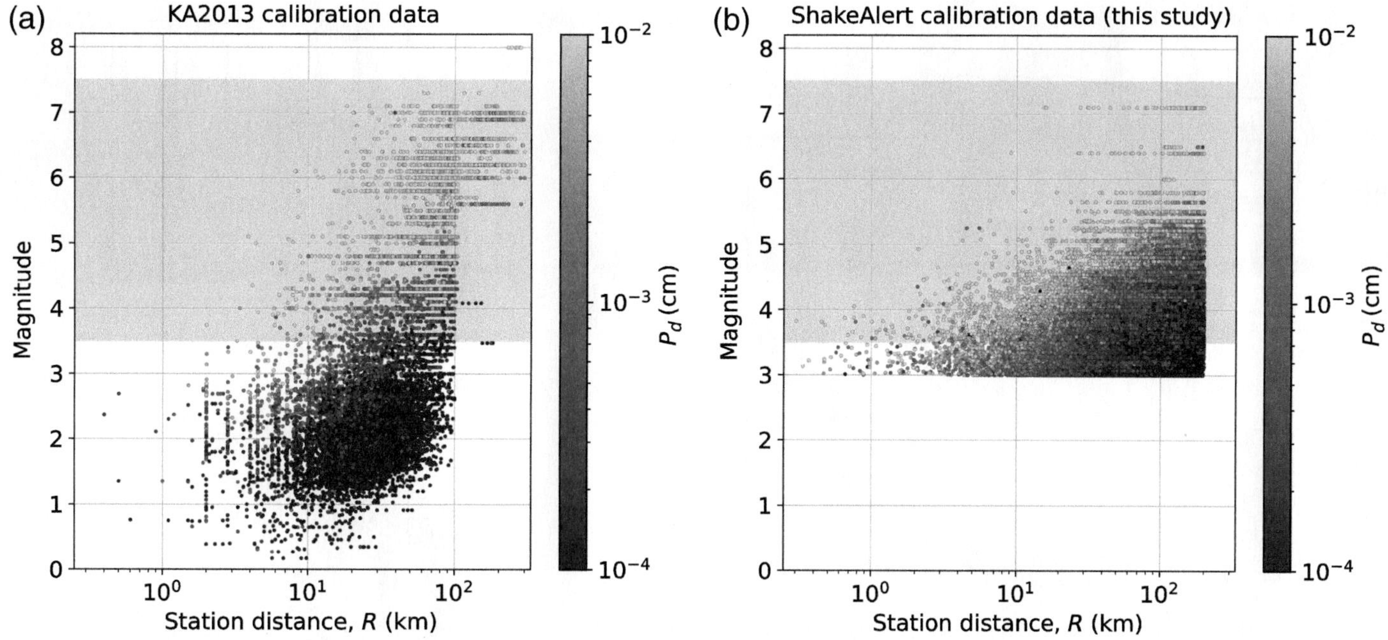

Figure 3. Calibration data used (a) in the KA2013 scaling and (b) in this study. Each point represents a single observation of peak displacement related to an earthquake of known magnitude from a single seismic station at known epicentral distance, R. Dots are colored based on the peak displacement value. The gray shaded region highlights **M** 3.5–7.5, the range in magnitudes where EPIC contributes a solution to the Solution Aggregator. The color version of this figure is available only in the electronic edition.

of near-station observations ($R < 30$ km) in our calibration dataset, particularly in the **M** 3.0–5.0 magnitude range. This is due to the seismic network densification since ShakeAlert's public rollout. Our new calibration dataset shows higher P_d-values at near-field distances compared to the data included in KA2013. As shown in Figure 4, this is due to the sampling of the S wave at close epicentral distances. In fact, the majority of P_d measurements up to a station distance of 30 km are based on the S wave, not the P wave. For example, over 70% of the P_d picks made at a distance of 16 km were likely associated with the S-wave arrival.

We could follow a similar approach as KA2013 and exclude these identified S wave picks, generating a new scaling relationship based only on P-wave information. However, the result would not be representative of the data that enters the EPIC algorithm and would require additional new processing of the data to exclude S waves post-trigger. An alternative approach would be to account for the dominant dataset in the near field and modify the model rather than to modify the data. Therefore, we depart from the methodology of KA2013 and develop two scaling relationships: a first scaling relationship in which both P- and S-wave peak displacements are present and a second for which we expect only P-wave displacements. The division between these two scaling relationships is based on the station distance, R. We divide our dataset at 30 km, the dividing distance where the majority of the displacement measurements are related to the P wave, and not the S wave, as shown in Figure 4. Similar to KA2013, we also fit our calibration data through two multivariate linear least-squares regressions. Specifically, we fit our dependent variable, P_d, against two independent variables: the catalog magnitude, M_C, and station distance, R. We then analyze our results to identify if this change adversely affects our station and event magnitude results, first isolated from other potential sources of error, such as a poor location estimate. Then, results are compared with all known sources of uncertainty.

The near-field regression fits 14,995 observations from stations located as far as 30 km from the epicenter. The far-field regression fits 104,989 observations from stations located between 30 and 200 km away from the epicenter. We do not include further stations as EPIC does not utilize stations with distances greater than 200 km in the magnitude estimate. The near- and far-field station-magnitude relations are shown in equations (3) and (4), respectively.

$$M_{\mathrm{sta}} = 1.03\log_{10}(P_d) \times 1.106\log_{10}(R) + 5.026 \quad \text{if } R \leq 30 \text{ km}, \tag{3}$$

$$M_{\mathrm{sta}} = 1.195\log_{10}(P_d) \times 1.298\log_{10}(R) + 5.475 \quad \text{if } 30 \text{ km} < R \leq 200 \text{ km}. \tag{4}$$

The event magnitude remains a weighted average of all station magnitudes at all distances, following equation (2).

Results

The dual scaling relations produce M_{sta}-values that better estimate M_C than if using the single scaling relation presented in

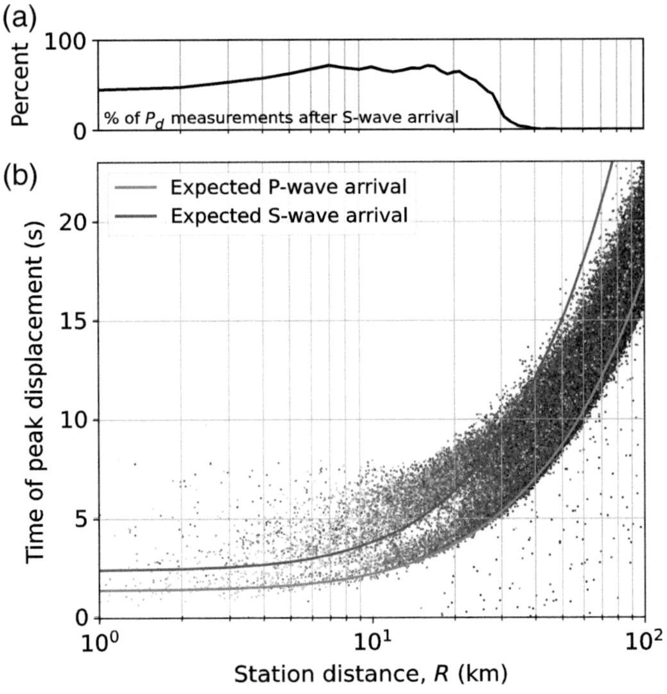

Figure 4. Estimate of *S*-wave occurrence in EPIC input data. (a) Estimated percentage of *S*-wave peak displacement measurements at 1 km station distance spacing. (b) Distribution of peak displacement measurements from calibration dataset, as shown in Figure 3b. The dots plot the time of the peak displacement pick with respect to their known station distance and a known origin time. The orange and purple lines are estimated *P*- and *S*-wave arrival times based on an assumed perfect location with an 8 km source depth. The dots are colored based on the absolute peak displacement values and use the same color scale, as shown in Figure 3. The color version of this figure is available only in the electronic edition.

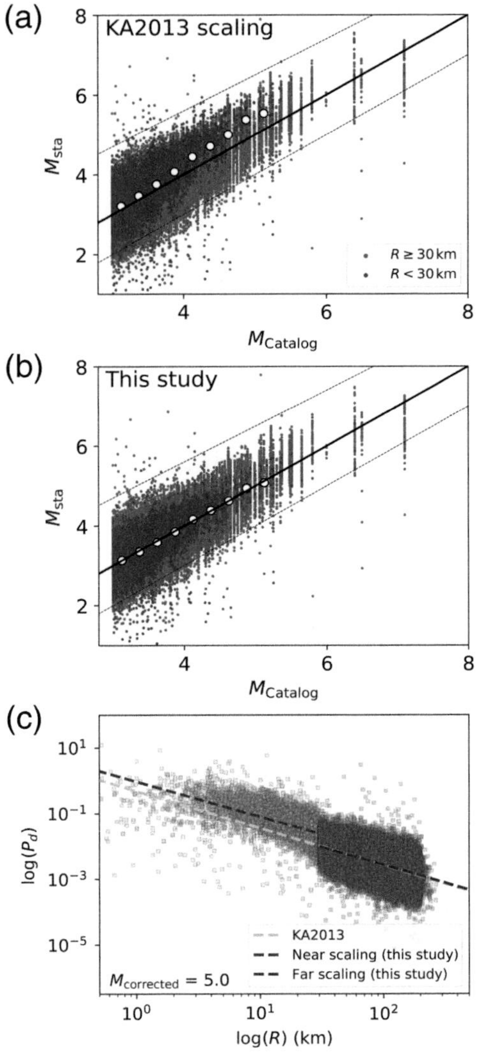

Figure 5. Fit of station magnitudes (M_{sta}) derived from (a) the calibration data using the current KA2013 scaling and (b) the dual scaling proposed in this study. Station magnitudes are colored based on their station epicenter distance. Near-field stations located less than 30 km from the known epicenter are colored in red. Far-field stations located 30 km or further from the epicenter are colored in blue. Station magnitudes are plotted against the catalog magnitude ($M_{Catalog}$). The white circles show the average station magnitude at 0.25 magnitude unit spacing. The black thick line shows 1:1 relation. The black thin dotted line shows 1 magnitude unit above and below. (c) Scaling relationship between station distance, R, and peak displacement, P_d, for all observations in calibration dataset. Note, because the fit is based on three variables (P_d, R, and magnitude), we need to correct for one to plot in a 2D space. Therefore, we rescale all peak displacement data to a magnitude 5.0. Similar studies typically correct based on station distance R (see fig. 1b in Kuyuk and Allen, 2013); however, as that is an attribute we wish to highlight, we choose instead to correct based on magnitude. The blue and green dots represent individual station observations at near- and far-field distances, respectively. The best-fit lines to the new EPIC scaling datasets are shown as blue and green lines, fitting the near- and far-field individual observations. The yellow-dashed line shows the fit of the current KA2013 regression to the EPIC real-time data. The color version of this figure is available only in the electronic edition.

KA2013 (Fig. 5). Here, the calibration data are separated into near- and far-field stations based on whether the true epicentral distances are less than or greater than 30 km. When using the KA2013 single scaling relation, the near- and far-field data have R^2-values of 0.50 and 0.61, respectively. When using the dual scaling proposed in this study, the near-field R^2-value increases to 0.57. The far-field R^2-value also increases a small amount to 0.62. This indicates that the introduction of additional parameters via the dual scaling relations fit the near-field calibration data better than the KA2013 scaling. The fit at the far-field stations is similar between the two methodologies. As shown in Figure 5a, the near-field stations overestimate the magnitude using the KA2013 relation. This overestimate increases with an increasing catalog magnitude and is exemplified by the average station magnitude, calculated at 0.25 magnitude unit bins. Because there are multiple variables included in the analysis (P_d, M_C, and R), it can be difficult to show the fit of all variables in one figure. Therefore, we also plot the data in Figure 5c by means of correcting the dependent variable, P_d, to a target magnitude. An additional analysis using binned magnitudes is

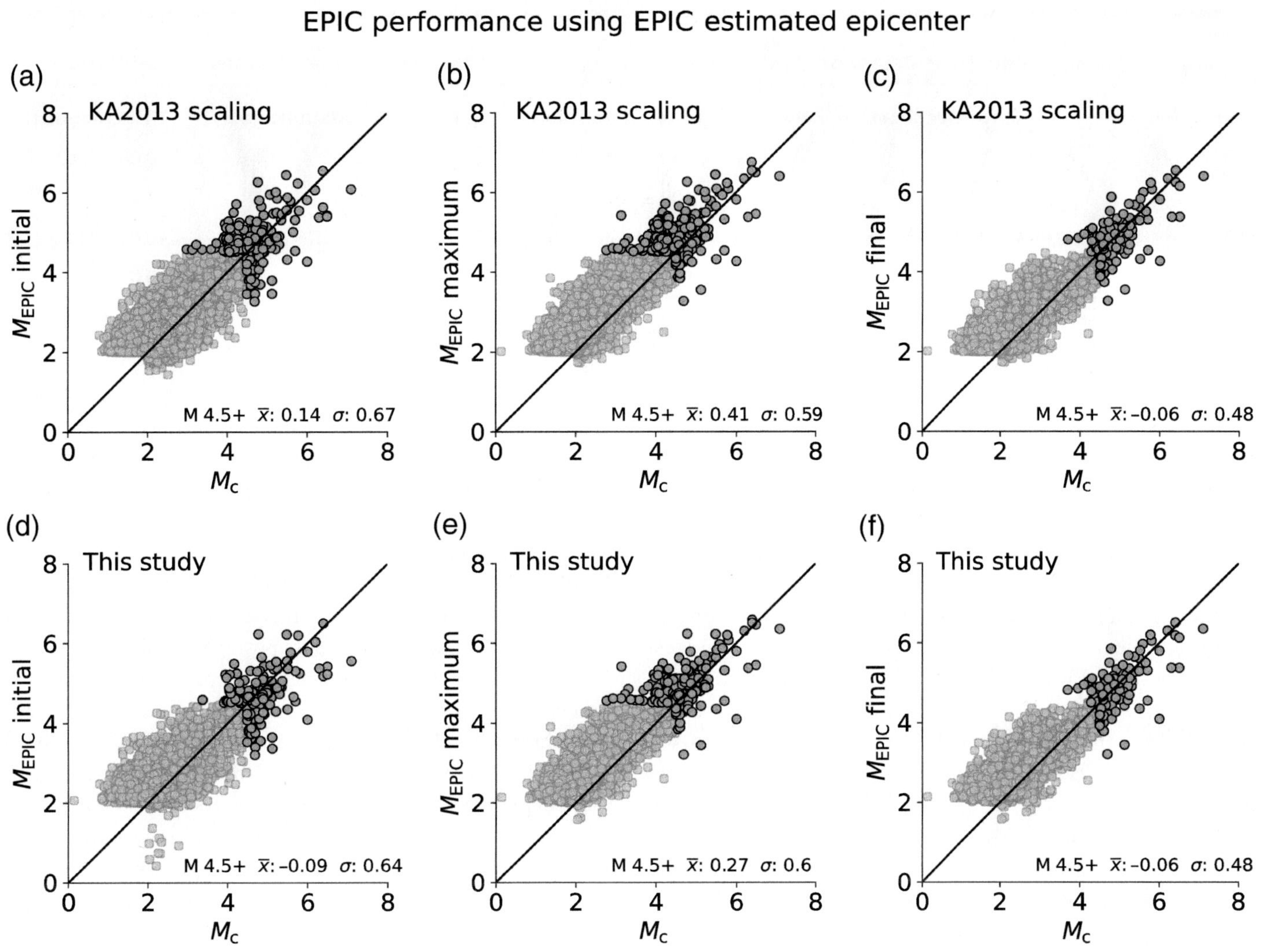

Figure 6. EPIC event magnitude performance at initial, maximum, and final epochs using (a–c) the EPIC real-time locations using KA2013 scaling and (d–f) the dual scaling in this study. Results are further summarized in Table 1. The bright, fully saturated, orange circles mark earthquakes where either M_{EPIC} or M_C calculates a magnitude equal to or exceeding **M** 4.5. The color version of this figure is available only in the electronic edition.

also available in Figure S01, available in the supplemental material to this article.

The improvement in M_{EPIC} estimates is shown in Figure 6 through a recalculation of the event magnitude time series of the real-time events detected by EPIC since the public rollout of ShakeAlert. Performance is quantified through a residual defined here as M_{EPIC} subtracted by M_C. A positive residual indicates an overestimate by EPIC; a negative residual indicates an underestimate. Although there is one static M_C-value for each earthquake, the EPIC magnitude is calculated as a time series. Therefore, we calculate the magnitude residual for three points in time: at the initial alert, at the time when the maximum magnitude is recorded, and at the last alert. In addition, we present performance results for earthquakes that exceed the lower limit of ShakeAlert alerting (**M** 4.5), calculating the mean of the residuals and the variation at one standard deviation. First, performance results of EPIC using the KA2013 scaling are shown in Figure 6a–c and summarized in Table 1. EPIC currently overestimates the magnitude for alerting events at initial and maximum alerts by 0.14 and 0.41 magnitude units, respectively. At the time of the final alert, EPIC underestimates the magnitude by 0.06 magnitude unit. The residual values, particularly among the alerting earthquakes, are broadly distributed, indicating some events where the event magnitudes have large over- and underestimates. The event magnitudes using the dual scaling relationship developed in this study are shown in Figure 6d–f. The new scaling reduces the initial alert overestimate to an underestimate of 0.09 magnitude unit, reduces the maximum overestimate from 0.41 to 0.27 magnitude units, and maintains the same small underestimate (0.06 magnitude unit) at the final alert timestep. This amounts to a reduction in the maximum magnitude residual of 34%.

Noticeable in Figure 6 is an increase in the underestimate at the time of the initial alert. A potential concern is that the new scaling, which primarily lowers the magnitude at near-field stations, will slow down the magnitude growth for **M** 4.5 and larger

TABLE 1
Summary of Magnitude Error Based on Scaling Relation Used, Epicenter Location, and Measurement Type

Scaling Relation	Epicenter Location Used	Initial Magnitude	Maximum Magnitude	Final Magnitude
KA2013	EPIC	0.14 ± 0.67	0.41 ± 0.59	−0.06 ± 0.48
This study	EPIC	−0.09 ± 0.64	0.27 ± 0.6	−0.06 ± 0.48
KA2013	ComCat	0.09 ± 0.43	0.25 ± 0.37	−0.04 ± 0.31
This study	ComCat	−0.1 ± 0.4	0.1 ± 0.33	−0.07 ± 0.3

KA2013 indicates the current scaling relationship used in Earthquake Point-Source Integrated Code (EPIC). This is compared to the formulation presented in this study. The EPIC and Comprehensive Catalog (ComCat) locations used affect the station-epicenter distance as presented in equations (3) and (4). The initial magnitude, maximum magnitude, and final magnitudes are measurements made over the duration of the earthquake characterization in EPIC.

earthquakes, delaying alerts. Through a comparison of **M** 4.5+ earthquakes using the old and new scaling, we do not find this to be the case (Fig. 7). The mean delay in alert time due to the initial underestimate is 0.7 s. However, this is largely due to two outliers. There is no change in the median alert time.

The reduction in the overestimate of the magnitudes translates to a reduction in the number of false positive events. A false positive occurs when M_{EPIC} exceeds **M** 4.5, but M_{C} does not. Using the KA2013 scaling, EPIC produced 112 false positive events in the real-time dataset. With the new scaling applied here, the number of false positives reduces to 60 (46% reduction). However, a caveat is that the number of true positive events reduced from 92 to 90 (2% reduction). A true positive occurs when M_{EPIC} and M_{C} both exceed **M** 4.5. Despite the slight reduction in the true positive rate, we believe that the larger reduction in false positives indicates a net performance improvement. The new scaling relation's effect on false positive overestimates at alertable magnitudes is further summarized in Table 2.

Discussion

As is common when using real-time data, there are many sources of error operating simultaneously. Coexisting in the performance analysis thus far has been a large source of unaccounted error: the estimated epicenter location, R. Both the KA2013 scaling and the dual scaling proposed in this study require knowledge of R, derived from EPIC's epicenter location algorithm. EPIC estimates epicenters through a 2D grid search using P-wave trigger times and a 1D velocity model. The station–epicenter distance for all triggered stations is then calculated before the start of the magnitude estimate. Because more stations trigger, the location estimate updates, updating station distances used in the magnitude estimate. A station distance that is erroneously large will lead to a larger station magnitude. The opposite is also true; if the station distance is miscalculated to be too close, the station magnitude will be underestimated.

To demonstrate the impact of location errors on the magnitude error, we recalculated the magnitude time series for all real-time events using the ground-truth station distance based on the ComCat epicenter. The results are presented in Figure 8. Using a fixed value for R, the magnitude residual is reduced in both the KA2013 scaling and the dual scaling proposed here. At the maximum magnitude epoch, the KA2013 overestimates 0.41 magnitude unit is reduced to 0.25 magnitude unit (39% reduction). If using the new dual scaling and the fixed location, the overestimate is further reduced to 0.1 magnitude unit. These results are also summarized in Table 1. The effect that the location error has on false positive alerts is summarized in Table 2. Although the expectation of perfect real-time location estimates is unrealistic at this time, we present these results to highlight that between the new dual scaling, which fixes a poor estimate of near-field peak displacements, and the location estimate, most errors related to the magnitude are accounted for. Although location errors are outside the direct control of the magnitude estimator, recent work to improve location estimates for earthquakes in the offshore and edge of network areas has shown a reduction in error that would reduce errors in magnitude estimates as well (Williamson *et al.*, 2023).

The dual scaling methodology presented here best reflects the data ingested into EPIC, which includes peak displacements related to both P and S waves, with the latter being the dominant data used at near-field station distances (Fig. 4). This is a departure from the previous scaling, which was developed under the assumption that only P_d-values from P waves would be included. However, because the density of seismic stations included in ShakeAlert has increased, the chances of including near-field stations have also increased. Therefore, the inclusion of the previously ignored S-wave data must be accounted for in some way.

Rather than account for the S waves as part of the calibration data and scaling relation, an alternative is to employ techniques to remove them. The simplest approach would prohibit near-field stations from contributing to the magnitude calculation due to the potential risk of including an unwanted displacement value based on the S wave. Although easy to implement, this would greatly increase the time to first alert (Fig. 9), which is not ideal in an EEW setting.

In a second approach, EPIC could dynamically scale the amount of data used in the P_d measurement to exclude data at the S-wave arrival. One way would be to utilize the already known station–epicenter distance, R, to quickly calculate the

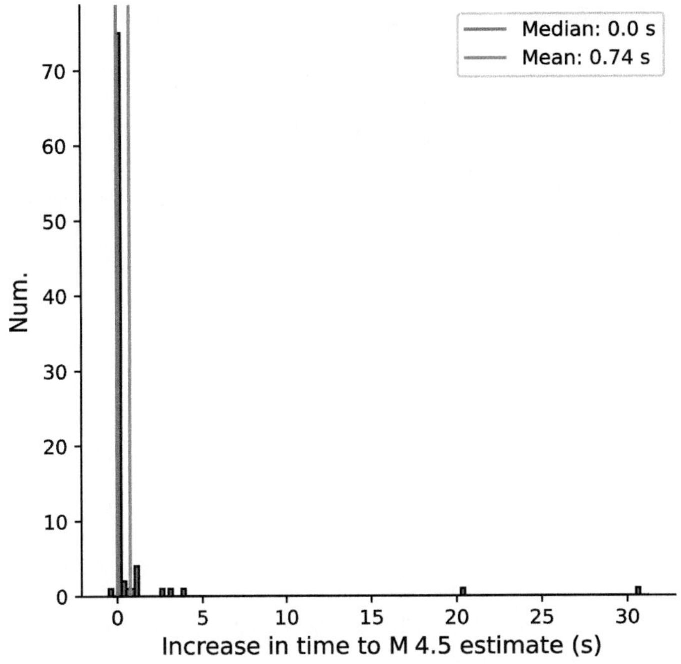

Figure 7. Increase in time to reach **M** 4.5 magnitude using new scaling. Distribution shows the increase in time to reach **M** 4.5 for all events where the catalog magnitude equaled or exceeds **M** 4.5. Mean and median increases in time are indicated by the red and blue vertical lines, respectively. The color version of this figure is available only in the electronic edition.

expected *S*-wave arrival-time post-trigger. Then, the largest P_d-value up to the *S*-wave arrival would be used. A limitation of this approach is the need for a low-error epicenter estimate. If the station–epicenter distance, *R*, is overestimated, then the maximum allowable time will be too large, meaning that an *S* wave will likely still be picked (Fig. 9). If *R* is underestimated, only a subset of the *P*-wave window is included in the peak displacement measurement, leading to a potential underestimate.

Similar in concept, the incoming window of data could be truncated through the identification of the *S* wave through a continuous vertical to horizontal check applied to the waveform prior to its inclusion in EPIC (Nakamura, 1988). Although this would not rely on knowledge of the station–epicenter distance and errors associated therein, it would create its own potential sources of error if the *S*-wave pick time is not perfect. Although of potential use in real time, this method would require significant analyses before use in an operational system. In the meantime, we view our approach to be easy to implement, and it achieves a ShakeAlert goal of reducing overalerting without increasing computation time or imposing far-reaching changes in the architecture of the EPIC algorithm.

The calibration dataset developed here utilizes data originating within the ShakeAlert reporting boundaries. This approach guarantees that the scaling relation used accounts for the type of seismicity and attenuation observed on the West Coast of the United States. Studies that incorporate EPIC, or EPIC's predecessor ElarmS, sometimes use locally derived data to recalculate the KA2013 scaling data, providing a better fit for their individual EEW systems (Nof and Allen, 2016). The ShakeAlert reporting area is large and includes detected earthquakes in California, Oregon, and Washington, as well as earthquakes outside of these three states but close enough to be detected with stations at the edge of the network. However, due to different rates in seismicity, the calibration dataset is heavily weighted to California earthquakes. We explore the fit of our scaling relation on generalized subregions of the ShakeAlert zone: northern California, southern California, and the Pacific Northwest in Figures S2–S3.

A final identified source of error affecting the magnitude is the inclusion of stations with site-specific observational biases. Some stations will consistently over- or underestimate the magnitude, independent of the inclusion of the *S* wave or a poor epicentral location. Because EPIC's event magnitude is an average of station magnitudes, a large deviation in one station can cause a large error in the event magnitude. This is particularly problematic early in an event solution when the number of associated stations is limited. An example of this occurred during the October 2023 Isleton, California, earthquake (Fig. 10). Although the earthquake was later determined to be M_w 4.2, EPIC's initial alert was an **M** 5.7. This large overestimate was not due to a poor location. EPIC's location error at the time was 4 km, which, while not perfect, is considered within EEW systems as accurate and would not be the leading cause for such an overestimate. Stations close to the epicenter had larger than expected magnitudes due to the inclusion of *S* waves in the trigger window. Upon applying the new scaling from this study, the overestimate at station magnitudes near the source was reduced, and the overall event magnitude overestimate was also lowered. However, despite this improvement, the magnitude residual was still anomalously high with an initial and maximum magnitude of **M** 5.2.

It appears that the nearest station, BK.TWIT, reported a very high station magnitude (**M** 6.0 under old scaling and **M** 5.6 under our proposed scaling). The inclusion of this station's magnitude estimate early in the solution, when only a few stations are associated with the event, is the reason for the large initial over alert. Investigating further, we identify that this was not an isolated event. By compiling the station magnitude residuals for BK.TWIT across all events where that station contributed magnitude information, we observe a consistent overestimate of station magnitudes (Fig. 10c). It is possible that the station's locality is contributing to the overestimate; the station is located in a sediment-rich marsh environment, which may amplify shaking compared to neighboring stations. Indeed, a handful of sites within ShakeAlert appear to display strong deviations in station magnitude that are independent of station distance, location errors, and the employed scaling relations (see example in Fig. S4). An additional, under-

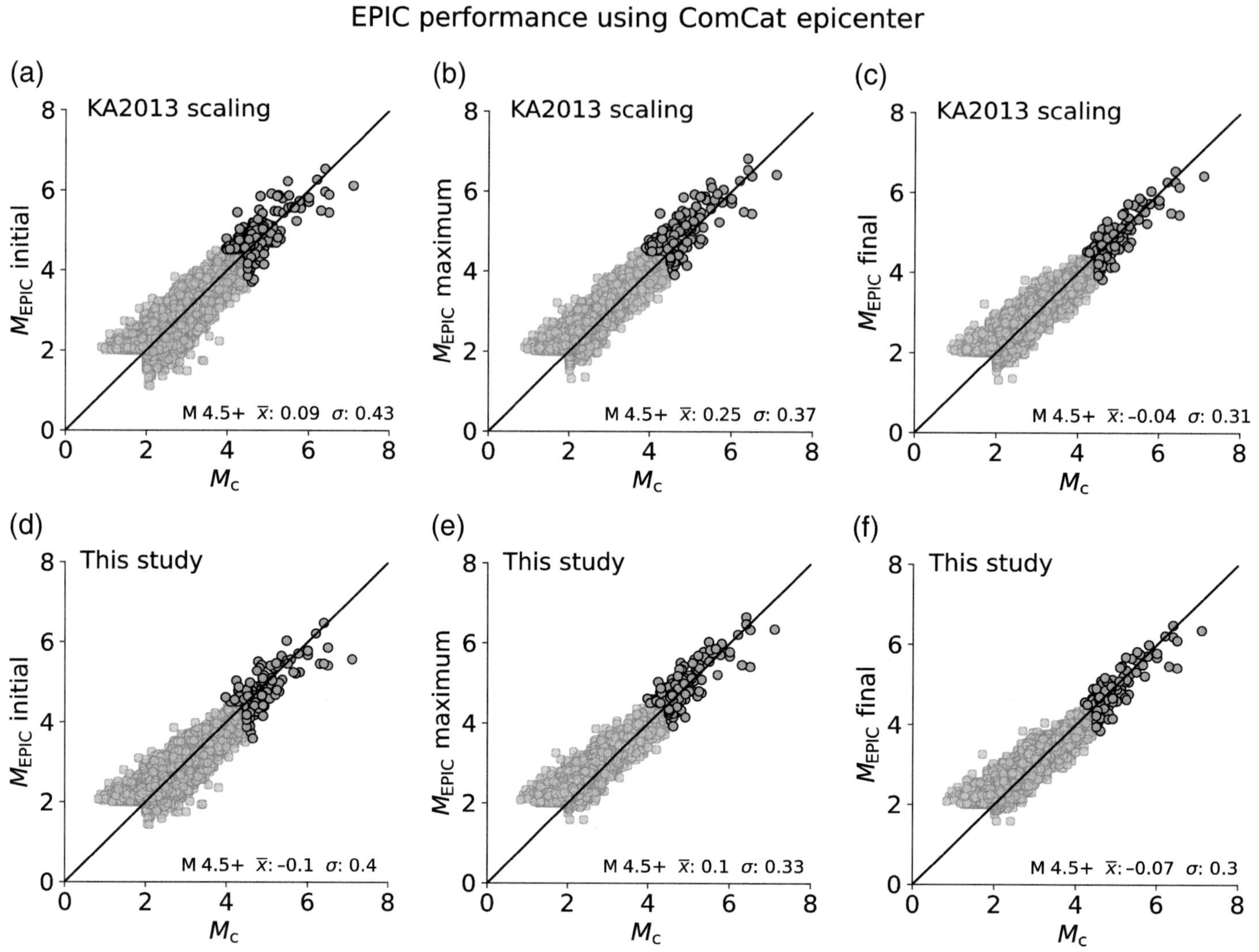

Figure 8. EPIC event magnitude performance at initial, maximum, and final epochs using (a–c) the ComCat-derived epicentral locations using KA2013 scaling and (d–f) the dual scaling in this study. Results are further summarized in Table 1. The bright, fully saturated, orange circles mark earthquakes where either M_{EPIC} or M_C calculates a magnitude equal to or exceeding **M** 4.5. The color version of this figure is available only in the electronic edition.

TABLE 2

Event over, Under, and Matched Alerts at the M 4.5 Threshold Using the Current KA2013 Scaling and the New Scaling Proposed Here

Scaling	Epicenter Location Used	True Positive M_{EPIC}≥4.5 and M_C≥4.5	False Positive (Over Alert) M_{EPIC}≥4.5 and M_C<4.5	False Negative (Under Alert) M_{EPIC}<4.5 and M_C≥4.5
KA2013	EPIC	92	112	20
KA2013	ComCat	89	75	18
This study	ComCat	88	38	19
This study	EPIC	90	69	22

The location used is either the Earthquake Point-Source Integrated Code (EPIC) real-time epicenter locations or a fixed Comprehensive Catalog (ComCat) epicenter. M_C is the reference ground-truth magnitude, and M_{EPIC} is the maximum magnitude obtained from EPIC for that event.

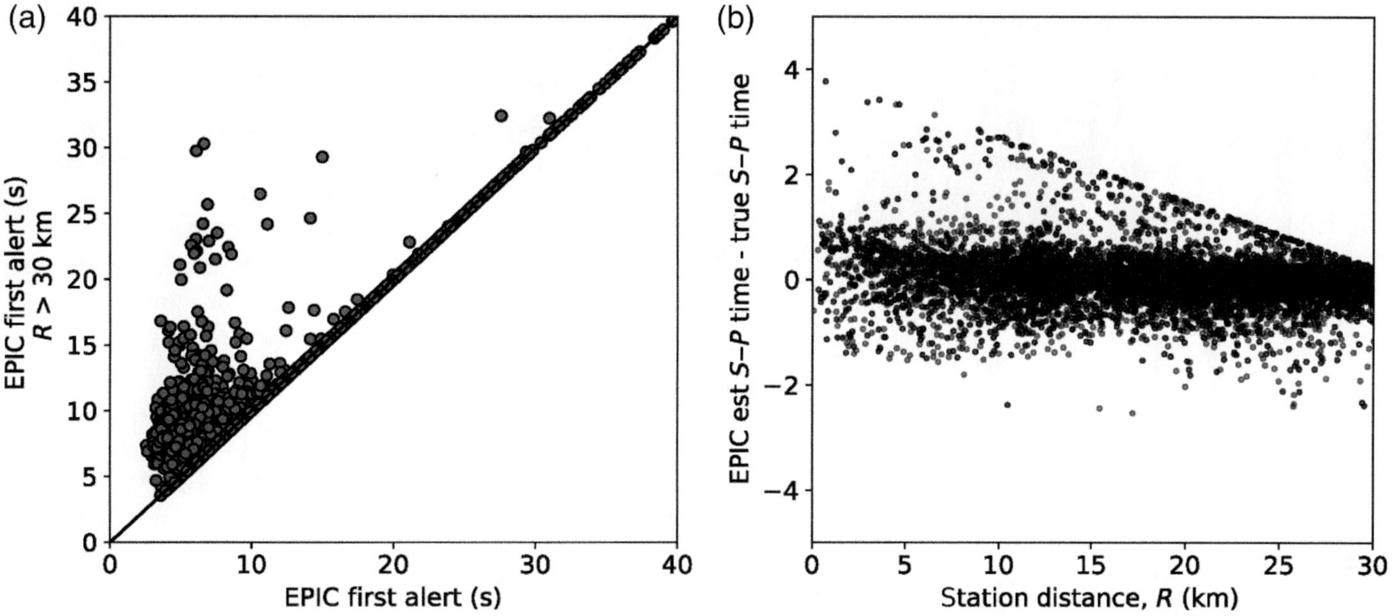

Figure 9. Investigation of *S*-wave mitigation strategies as an alternative to include them in the scaling relation. (a) Comparison of the time of first alert between EPIC's current configuration and a version of EPIC where stations within the nearest 30 km are forbidden from contributing to the magnitude. (b) Differencing between EPIC's estimated *S–P* timing and true *S–P* timing at near-field station distances. Positive values indicate instances when EPIC's estimate may still include *S*-wave data into the peak displacement observation.

investigated effect on per-station and per-event magnitudes is the potential for directivity.

Individual station corrections due to probable site effects or source radiation patterns are not currently employed in any of the early warning algorithms in ShakeAlert. The implementation of per-station corrections in EPIC would require sufficient observations at each station to distinguish between a consistent deviation in magnitude versus aleatoric uncertainty based on other unknowns in the rupture process and recording of the data at that station. This may be challenging for many newer stations, which may not have enough data available to make such a calculation. Because of the individualized nature of these potential corrections, they are out of scope of this study, which focuses on generalized improvements to the magnitude methods that can be applied over the entire network.

Conclusion

EEW systems can alert communities to damaging ground motions with seconds to tens of seconds of lead time. The efficiency of EEW programs relies on proximal, good-quality data, tolerant detection, and characterization algorithms, and a reliable means to disseminate alerts. This study focuses on assessing the performance of one part of the ShakeAlert EEW system: the algorithm used to calculate magnitude in EPIC, one of the three currently supported earthquake characterization algorithms. Using a large database of EPIC-detected events, we identified sources of error related to the earthquake's estimated location and the inclusion of *S*-wave energy at near-field distances.

The epicenter location used in the magnitude calculation directly affects the station magnitude. This is because the equation used requires knowledge of the station's epicentral distance. If a mislocation of an earthquake leads to an increase in the station–epicenter distance, then the magnitude will increase. Conversely, a shortened station–epicenter distance will cause the station magnitude to decrease. Most epicenter estimates from EPIC have small location errors of a few kilometers; however, when substantial location errors are present, as is sometimes the case for offshore and edge of network events, the magnitude estimate suffers. Improvements to EPIC's location algorithm, limiting the instances of large mislocations, are underway.

Through an analysis in this study using accurate ground-truth locations, we further identified that stations located within the first 30 km from an earthquake tend to overestimate the magnitude. The new scaling proposed here largely remedies this overestimate. We propose two sets of scaling relations, one for near-field stations ($R \leq 30$ km) and another for mid- to far-field stations ($30 < R < 200$ km). This new formulation lowers the magnitude residual at the maximum magnitude epoch from 0.41 to 0.27 magnitude units.

Importantly, our new scaling reduces false alerts due to magnitude overestimation. False alerts are defined here as instances with EPIC estimates a magnitude to be greater than 4.5 when the final ComCat magnitude is below 4.5. False alerts are reduced over our dataset from 112 to 69 instances. It should be noted that some of these remaining false alerts are heavily influenced by poor locations. Under the fixed location schema, the number of false alerts is further reduced to 38 instances.

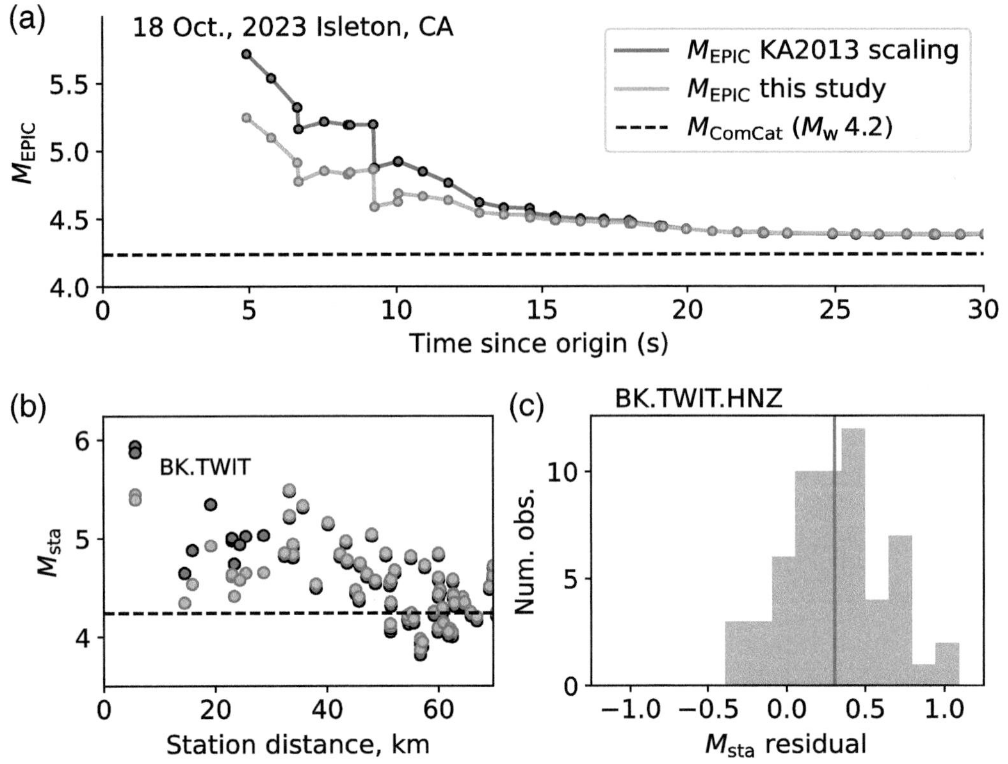

Figure 10. EPIC event and station magnitude calculations for the October 2023 Isleton, California earthquake. (a) Time series of EPIC's magnitude estimate using current KA2013 configuration (black line) and proposed scaling (gold line). The ComCat M_w 4.2 magnitude of this event is marked with the black-dashed line. (b) Station magnitudes as a function of station distance for the event. The black and gold dots are calculated using KA2013 and this study's configurations, respectively. (c) Magnitude residuals from station BK.TWIT over 72 separate events where the station was included in the magnitude calculation. The dark orange line represents the mean station residual. The color version of this figure is available only in the electronic edition.

The reduction in false alerts is not accompanied by a large increase in missed alerts, and these only increase from 20 to 22.

Although the magnitude calculated in EPIC represents one piece of a large workflow within the ShakeAlert reporting system, we believe that the new scaling relationship proposed here would greatly improve the overall system by reducing the number of false alerts. EPIC is often the fastest algorithm to report a solution, providing the timeliest alert information. An increase in accuracy, both with EPIC as a standalone algorithm or combined with FinDer and GFAST for larger magnitude events, would greatly improve community trust of the EEW system.

Data and Resources

Data used in this study, including event parameters pertaining to earthquakes in the EPIC catalog and scaling dataset, are accessible at doi: 10.5281/zenodo.11200256. EPIC-detected events were matched to events in the Advanced National Seismic System (ANSS) Comprehensive Earthquake Catalog (ComCat): https://earthquake.usgs.gov/data/comcat/ (last accessed May 2025). Some figures were made using PyGMT (https://zenodo.org/record/6702566, last accessed October 2024; Wessel *et al.*, 2019; Uieda *et al.*, 2022). The supplemental material containing additional data fit visualizations, regional variations in magnitude residuals, and per-station magnitude deviations is available alongside this article.

Declaration of Competing Interests

The authors acknowledge that there are no conflicts of interest recorded.

Acknowledgments

The authors would like to thank the three anonymous reviewers for their thoughtful and detailed comments. Their contributions have greatly strengthened this study. The authors would also like to acknowledge the useful conversations with Fabia Terra of UC Berkeley related to per-station corrections and the use of local networks. This research was supported by the U.S. Geological Survey under Grant Agreement Number G21AC10525 awarded to UC Berkeley.

References

Allen, R. M., and D. Melgar (2019). Earthquake early warning: Advances, scientific challenges, and societal needs, *Annu. Rev. Earth Planet. Sci.* **47,** 361–388.

Allen, R. M., and M. Stogaitis (2022). Global growth of earthquake early warning, *Science* **375,** no. 6582, 717–718.

Allen, R. M., P. Gasparini, O. Kamigaichi, and M. Bose (2009). The status of earthquake early warning around the world: An introductory overview, *Seismol. Res. Lett.* **80,** no. 5, 682–693.

Allen, R. M., Q. Kong, and R. Martin-Short (2020). The myshake platform: A global vision for earthquake early warning, *Pure Appl. Geophys.* **177,** 1699–1712.

Allen, R. M., A. Barski, M. Berman, R. Bosch, Y. Cho, X. S. Jiang, Y. L. Lee, *et al.* (2025). Global earthquake detection and warning using Android phones, *Science* **389,** no. 6757, 254–259, doi: 10.1126/science.ads4779.

Böse, M., T. H. Heaton, and E. Hauksson (2012). Real-time finite fault rupture detector (FinDer) for large earthquakes, *Geophys. J. Int.* **191,** no. 2, 803–812.

Böse, M., D. E. Smith, C. Felizardo, M. A. Meier, T. H. Heaton, and J. F. Clinton (2018). FinDer v. 2: Improved real-time ground-motion predictions for M2–M9 with seismic finite-source characterization, *Geophys. J. Int.* **212,** no. 1, 725–742.

Brown, H. M., R. M. Allen, M. Hellweg, O. Khainovski, D. Neuhauser, and A. Souf (2011). Development of the ElarmS methodology for earthquake early warning: Realtime application in California and offline testing in Japan, *Soil Dynam. Earthq. Eng.* **31,** no. 2, 188–200.

Chung, A. I., I. Henson, and R. M. Allen (2019). Optimizing earthquake early warning performance: ElarmS-3, *Seismol. Res. Lett.* **90,** no. 2A, 727–743.

Chung, A. I., M. A. Meier, J. Andrews, M. Böse, B. W. Crowell, J. J. McGuire, and D. E. Smith (2020). ShakeAlert earthquake early warning system performance during the 2019 Ridgecrest earthquake sequence, *Bull. Seismol. Soc. Am.* **110,** no. 4, 1904–1923.

Espinosa-Aranda, J. M., A. Cuellar, A. Garcia, G. Ibarrola, R. Islas, S. Maldonado, and F. H. Rodriguez (2009). Evolution of the Mexican seismic alert system (SASMEX), *Seismol. Res. Lett.* **80,** no. 5, 694–706.

Given, D. D., R. M. Allen, A. S. Baltay, P. Bodin, E. S. Cochran, K. Creager, R. M. de Groot, L. S. Gee, E. Hauksson, T.H. Heaton, *et al.* (2018). Revised technical implementation plan for the ShakeAlert system—An earthquake early warning system for the West Coast of the United States, *U.S. Geol. Surv. Open-File Rept. 2018-1155.*

Hoshiba, M., K. Iwakiri, N. Hayashimoto, T. Shimoyama, K. Hirano, Y. Yamada, Y. Ishigaki, and H. Kikuta (2011). Outline of the 2011 off the Pacific coast of Tohoku earthquake (M_w 9.0)—Earthquake early warning and observed seismic intensity, *Earth Planets Space* **63,** no. 7, 547–551.

Kohler, M. D., D. E. Smith, J. Andrews, A. I. Chung, R. Hartog, I. Henson, D.D. Given, R. de Groot, and S. Guiwits (2020). Earthquake early warning ShakeAlert 2.0: Public rollout, *Seismol. Res. Lett.* **91,** no. 3, 1763–1775.

Kuyuk, H. S., and R. M. Allen (2013). A global approach to provide magnitude estimates for earthquake early warning alerts, *Geophys. Res. Lett.* **40,** no. 24, 6329–6333.

Lara, P., H. Tavera, Q. Bletery, J. P. Ampuero, A. Inza, D. Portugal, B. Orihuela, and F. Meza (2025). Implementation of the Peruvian earthquake early warning system, *Bull. Seismol. Soc. Am.* **115,** no. 1, 191–209.

Lin, J. T., D. Melgar, A. M. Thomas, and J. Searcy (2021). Early warning for great earthquakes from characterization of crustal deformation patterns with deep learning, *J. Geophys. Res.* **126,** no. 10, e2021JB022703, doi: 10.1029/2021JB022703.

Lux, A. I., D. Smith, J. J. McGuire, J. K. Saunders, M. Huynh, I. Stubailo, J. Andrews, G. Lotto, B. Crowell, S. Crane, *et al.* (2024). Status and performance of the ShakeAlert® earthquake early warning system: 2019–2023, *Bull. Seismol. Soc. Am.* doi: 10.1785/0120230259.

McBride, S. K., H. Smith, M. Morgoch, D. Sumy, M. Jenkins, L. Peek, A. Bostrom, D. Baldwin, E. Reddy, R. De Groot, *et al.* (2022). Evidence-based guidelines for protective actions and earthquake early warning systems, *Geophysics* **87,** no. 1, WA77–WA102.

McBride, S. K., D. F. Sumy, A. L. Llenos, G. A. Parker, J. McGuire, J. K. Saunders, M.A. Meier, P. Schuback, D. Given, and R. de Groot (2023). Latency and geofence testing of wireless emergency alerts intended for the ShakeAlert® earthquake early warning system for the West Coast of the United States of America, *Saf. Sci.* **157,** 105898.

McGuire, J. J., C. W. Ulberg, A. I. Lux, M. Bose, J. R. Andrews, D. Smith, B.W. Crowell, J.R. Murray, I. Henson, R. Hartog, *et al.* (2025). ShakeAlert® version 3: Expected performance in large earthquakes, *Bull. Seismol. Soc. Am.* **115,** no. 2, 531–561, doi: 10.1785/0120240189.

Murray, J. R., B. W. Crowell, M. H. Murray, C. W. Ulberg, J. J. McGuire, M. A. Aranha, and M. T. Hagerty (2023). Incorporation of real-time earthquake magnitudes estimated via peak ground displacement scaling in the ShakeAlert earthquake early warning system, *Bull. Seismol. Soc. Am.* **113,** no. 3, 1286–1310.

Nakamura, Y. (1988). On the urgent earthquake detection and alarm system (UrEDAS), *Proc. of the 9th World Conf. Earthquake Engineering,* Vol. 7, 673–678.

Nof, R. N., and R. M. Allen (2016). Implementing the ElarmS earthquake early warning algorithm on the Israeli seismic network, *Bull. Seismol. Soc. Am.* **106,** no. 5, 2332–2344.

Nof, R. N., I. Lior, and I. Kurzon (2021). Earthquake early warning system in Israel—Towards an operational stage, *Front. Earth Sci.* **9,** 684421.

Patel, S. C., and R. M. Allen (2022). The MyShake App: User experience of early warning delivery and earthquake shaking, *Seismol. Soc. Am.* **93,** no. 6, 3324–3336.

Porras, J., F. Massin, M. Arroyo-Solórzano, I. Arroyo, L. Linkimer, M. Böse, and J. Clinton (2021). Preliminary results of an earthquake early warning system in Costa Rica, *Front. Earth Sci.* **9,** 700843.

Satriano, C., Y. M. Wu, A. Zollo, and H. Kanamori (2011). Earthquake early warning: Concepts, methods and physical grounds, *Soil Dyn. Earthq. Eng.* **31,** no. 2, 106–118, doi: 10.1016/j.soildyn.2010.07.007.

Strauch, W., E. Talavera, V. Tenorio, J. Ramírez, G. Argüello, M. Herrera, A. Acosta, and A. Morales (2018). Toward an earthquake and tsunami monitoring and early warning system for Nicaragua and central America, *Seismol. Res. Lett.* **89,** no. 2A, 399–406.

Tsang, L. L., R. M. Allen, and G. Wurman (2007). Magnitude scaling relations from P-waves in southern California, *Geophys. Res. Lett.* **34,** no. 19, doi: 10.1029/2007GL031077.

Trugman, D. T., M. T. Page, S. E. Minson, and E. S. Cochran (2019). Peak ground displacement saturates exactly when expected: Implications for earthquake early warning, *J. Geophys. Res.* **124,** no. 5, 4642–4653.

Uieda, L., D. Tian, W. J. Leong, M. Jones, W. Schlitzer, and S. Grund (2022). PyGMT: A Python interface for the generic mapping tools [Software], Zenodo.

Wessel, P., J. F. Luis, L. Uieda, R. Scharroo, F. Wobbe, W. H. Smith, and D. Tian (2019). The generic mapping tools version 6, *Geochem. Geophys. Geosyst.* **20,** no. 11, 5556–5564.

Williamson, A., A. Lux, and R. Allen (2023). Improving out of network earthquake locations using prior seismicity for use in earthquake early warning, *Bull. Seismol. Soc. Am.* **113,** no. 2, 664–675.

Wu, Y. M., H. Mittal, D. Y. Chen, T. Y. Hsu, and P. Y. Lin (2021). Earthquake early warning systems in Taiwan: Current status, *J. Geol. Soc. India* **97,** 1525–1532.

Wurman, G., R. M. Allen, and P. Lombard (2007). Toward earthquake early warning in northern California, *J. Geophys. Res.* **112,** no. B8, doi: 10.1029/2006JB004830.

Manuscript received 19 November 2024
Published online 7 August 2025

An Updated Seismicity View of the Dead Sea Transform Using an Early Warning Network

Ariel Lellouch*[1]

Abstract

A network of strong-motion sensors typically used for early warning can be incorporated into an earthquake location workflow. By leveraging machine-learning-generated travel-time picks, validated through existing catalog information, stable and naturally coalescing locations are obtained. I apply this methodology to 6.5 yr of data from a dense array installed along the Dead Sea Transform (DST). In this time period, the seismogenic zone is, on average, deeper by about 4 km than previously estimated. In addition, new locations indicate depth localization of fault-related seismicity along the Dead Sea, Sea of Galilee, and Arava basins, as well as event migration toward the Faria fault system along a 70 km section of the DST. In the Northern Arava valley, event locations are surprisingly primarily perpendicular to mapped faults, indicating complex subsurface structures. Despite the limited period of analysis, these results may have significant implications for the tectonic understanding and seismic hazard assessment of the region.

Cite this article as Lellouch, A. (2025). An Updated Seismicity View of the Dead Sea Transform Using an Early Warning Network, *Seismol. Res. Lett.* **97**, 246–255, doi: 10.1785/0220250164.

Introduction

The Dead Sea Transform (DST) is a left-lateral transform boundary separating the Arabian plate to the east and the Sinai subplate to the west (Garfunkel *et al.*, 1981; Garfunkel, 2014). It spans approximately 1000 km, from the Red Sea spreading center to the convergent plate boundaries in Southern Türkiye (Fig. 1). The DST slip rate varies from 5 mm/yr in the south to 4 mm/yr in the north (Sadeh *et al.*, 2012). It contains three major pull-apart basins: the Gulf of Eilat (Aqaba), the Sea of Galilee, and the Dead Sea basin. Modern seismic activity along the DST has been documented by Wetzler and Kurzon (2016). The most destructive recorded earthquake happened in 1927, led to 285 deaths and about a thousand injured, and was estimated at M_L 6.2 (Shapira *et al.*, 1993; Avni *et al.*, 2002). In 1995, a Gulf of Aqaba M_w 7.2 occurred at the southernmost segment of the DST and was interpreted as strike-slip rupture (Baer *et al.*, 2008). Paleoseismic and archaeological studies indicate earthquakes larger than M_w 7 (Ellenblum *et al.*, 1998; Ken-Tor *et al.*, 2001; Marco *et al.*, 2003; Marco, 2008; Hamiel *et al.*, 2009; Lu *et al.*, 2020). The DST, with its northern branches of the Roum and Yamouneh faults, and potentially with the Carmel fault, poses a significant risk to the population in Syria, Lebanon, Jordan, Israel, and the Palestinian Authority. In response to this risk and the increase in population density living in proximity to the DST, the Israeli government has commissioned "TRUAA," an earthquake early warning system (Kurzon *et al.*, 2020; Nof and Kurzon, 2020). The project, started early 2018, included a significant improvement of the Israeli Seismological Network (ISN) mostly by installing new strong-motion accelerometers and modernizing broadband seismometer stations. Currently, the network consists of 124 strong-motion accelerometers and 26 broadband seismometers (see Fig. 1 for network geometry), some of which are collocated. Although instrument coverage has increased, strong-motion data remain somewhat underutilized in seismological studies. Lellouch *et al.* (2024) utilized the dense strong-motion network for the inversion of surface waves generated by the 2023 Kahramanmaraş earthquake sequence in Türkiye, and demonstrated its usefulness and similarity to broadband seismometers. In this study, we aim to leverage the significant increase of usable seismological data (see Fig. 1) to refine the earthquake catalog in the area of DST because these stations were primarily used for early warning and were not routinely incorporated into earthquake bulletins.

The structure and seismicity of the DST have been the topic of many studies (Ben-Avraham *et al.*, 1996; Braeuer *et al.*, 2012; ten Brink and Flores, 2012; ten Brink *et al.*, 2023). The existing seismological network has been used with a regional 1D velocity model to derive event locations (Wetzler and Kurzon, 2016). However, due to geopolitical constraints, permanent monitoring networks are primarily installed on one side of the transform, leading to estimation biases and

1. Department of Geophysics, Tel-Aviv University, Tel Aviv, Israel, https://orcid.org/0000-0002-9913-7191 (AL)

*Corresponding author: ariellel@tauex.tau.ac.il

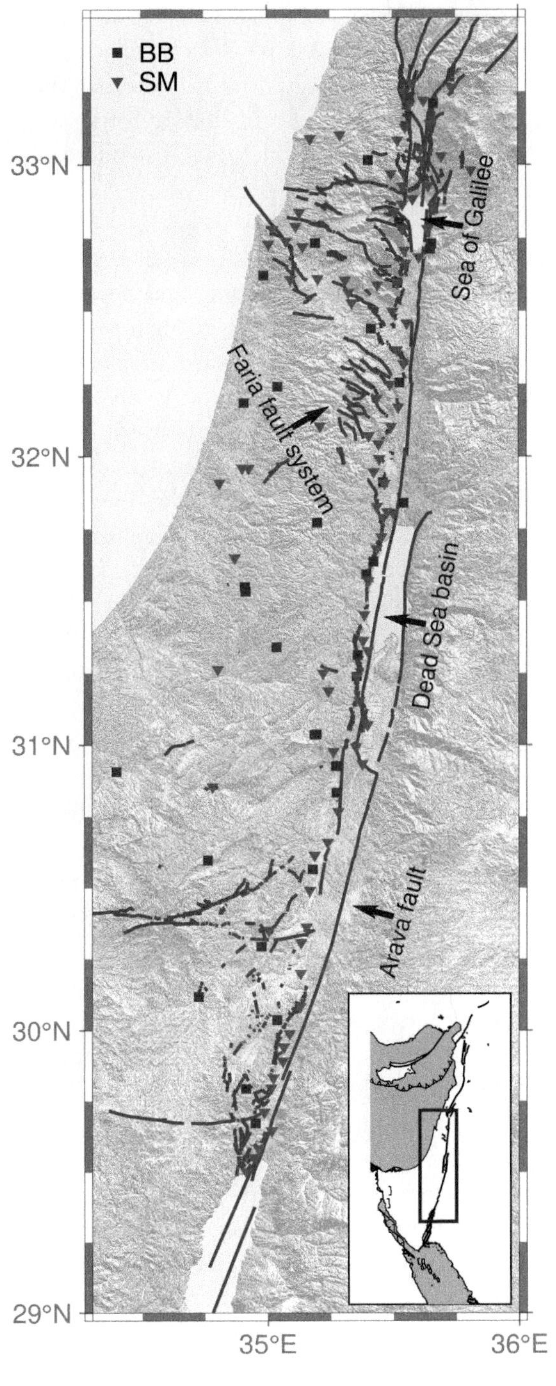

Figure 1. Overview of the study area. Mapped surface faults (Sharon *et al.*, 2020) are in red. Broadband stations are marked by green triangles, and strong-motion stations by inverted purple triangles. Major geological features are denoted in blue. The inset shows major faults on a larger scale, including strike-slip faults (black lines), intrarift faults (notches along lines), and a subduction zone (triangles along line), as well as the study area in a blue rectangle. The color version of this figure is available only in the electronic edition.

difficulties in accurately estimating out-of-network events, especially in the Gulf of Aqaba (Wetzler and Kurzon, 2016). The seismogenic depth is generally in agreement with heat flux interpolation (Shalev *et al.*, 2013) and significantly varies along the transform. Temporary dense deployments, primarily along the Dead Sea basin, have been used for local 3D velocity tomography, event relocation, and seismicity analysis (Braeuer *et al.*, 2012, 2014; Braeuer and Bauer, 2015). They show the east–west asymmetry of the basin in terms of structure and activity, with sediments reaching deeper along the more seismically active eastern boundary. In the Sea of Galilee, seismic activity had been relatively limited until 2013, during which an earthquake swarm occurred. Another swarm happened in 2018, and both have been attributed to groundwater extraction (Wetzler *et al.*, 2019).

Accurately locating earthquakes is one of the most fundamental tasks in experimental seismology. Traditional earthquake bulletins derive earthquake locations based on picked arrival times (Grigoli *et al.*, 2018), from which the most probable source location can be derived given a certain velocity model of the study area. It is usually considered that uncertainties in earthquake locations are dominated by three key factors (Pavlis, 1986; Garcia-Aristizabal *et al.*, 2020): errors in picking, velocity model errors that influence predicted travel times, and nonlinearity of the location problem. The topic of accurate waveform picking has been the focus of numerous studies, with recent developments shifting the trend toward machine-learning (ML)-based picking (Zhu and Beroza, 2019; Mousavi *et al.*, 2020; Mousavi and Beroza, 2022). Velocity model quality varies greatly among different areas, but 1D depth-dependent models remain the predominant case (Yu *et al.*, 2024). Relative relocation methods, such as Waldhauser and Ellsworth (2000) and Michelini and Lomax (2004), are popular because they can partially circumvent velocity model uncertainty. However, in addition to potentially inducing biases in the absolute locations, they also impose certain conditions upon the relocated earthquakes, mostly similar locations and focal mechanisms, and are thus not necessarily available for all earthquakes. In this study, I show how PhaseNet (Zhu and Beroza, 2019) can be used to leverage strong-motion stations in refining an earthquake catalog that informs our understanding of an important transform boundary, similarly to other study areas around the globe (Becker *et al.*, 2024; Castillo *et al.*, 2024).

Data and Location Methodology

I use publicly available data from the ISN, between 1 January 2018 and 1 September 2024. We study 6260 earthquakes reported in the Geological Survey of Israel (GSI) bulletin within the region of study, which extends between 34°18′ E and 36°30′ E and between 29°0′ N and 33°30′ N. The catalog was primarily built using broadband stations. The network expanded significantly from 2018 to 2020 as early warning stations became operational (Kurzon *et al.*, 2020). However, I chose to study earthquakes as early as 2018, when only 6–7 strong-motion stations were active, to include the important 2018 sequence in the Sea of Galilee (Wetzler *et al.*, 2019) and to increase the overall number of analyzed events. Between 2018 and 2020, the number of strong-motion sensors increased to 100, after which the improvement rate slowed considerably until reaching the current state. Hence, events from 2020 and onward are considered to be reliably recorded by the strong-motion network, whereas the 2018–2020 period offers partial recording. In this study, I only attempt to locate cataloged earthquakes rather than detect new ones.

Therefore, for each cataloged event, I download raw waveforms available for the entire network from 10 s before to 100 s after the origin time. For each set of waveforms, I apply a PhaseNet (Zhu and Beroza, 2019) picker with a sensitivity threshold of 0.3. Then, I apply my own associator based on existing catalog locations to filter out unreliable picks, instead of standard associators that are agnostic to catalog information (Zhang *et al.*, 2022; Zhu *et al.*, 2022). For that purpose, I use an Eikonal solver (scikit-fmm) to predict *P*- and *S*-arrival times based on cataloged location and origin time, taking into account receiver elevation information and a velocity model of the area. At each station, I accept all PhaseNet *P*-wave picks within $\pm$ 2.5 s of the predicted arrival time and *S*-wave picks within $\pm$ 4.0 s of the predicted arrival time. If multiple picks fall within those boundaries, I choose the one with the highest confidence as estimated by PhaseNet. After ordering all stations by increasing distance from the catalog location, I identify the first two consecutive stations yielding no acceptable picks (either *P* or *S*). All stations farther from the source are then automatically discarded from the location process because picks beyond this distance are likely to be unreliable. I also limit the maximal source–receiver distance to 200 km. I emphasize that using an existing catalog is not mandatory, and applying standard associators is possible. However, using cataloged information simplifies and generally improves such association, especially under conditions of low signal-to-noise ratio, as the predicted travel times stem from constrained and manually validated locations and origin times.

The location itself is a straightforward travel-time minimization error using an exhaustive search on a $250 \times 250 \times 250$ m grid, using precomputed travel-time tables, for all events that have a total of four or more picks. Events are searched within $\pm$ 30 km northwest and southeast from the catalog location, at depths of 0–40 km. The relatively limited search area allows for the computationally expensive grid search. I use the L1 norm to avoid strong outlier effects because the picks were not manually validated and the association process may still allow for erroneous picks. I linearly weight picks based on their PhaseNet-computed confidence. It is also possible to penalize picks that are temporally distant from the predicted arrival times, but I did not apply this to avoid a bias to the existing catalog. *P* and *S* waves are weighed equally.

For both association and location, I use the 1D *P*-wave velocity model used by the GSI (Wetzler and Kurzon, 2016). The upper layer is extended to account for station elevation. Whereas the shallow (< 2 km) *S*-wave velocity along the DST has been shown to be significantly lower than the existing velocity model (Lellouch *et al.*, 2024), I use a constant $V_P/V_S = \sqrt{3}$ at all depths, which is the standard model for the area of study.

Results

The comparison between the existing and new catalog is in Figure 2, with zoomed-in versions in Figure 3. Generally, I observe a coalescence of events toward simpler, quasi-linear fault structures. Along the DST, focusing on the four main areas marked in Figure 1, events appear shifted westward. Depth distributions are also more regular, especially near the Arava fault. Except for the Sea of Galilee, most events originate to the east of the network, causing an expected deepening of the estimated hypocenters to compensate for the shorter source–receiver ray paths due to their westward shift. I emphasize that for the new catalog each event is located independently and did not undergo any relocation or postprocessing procedure.

Along the Sea of Galilee (Fig. 3a,b), seismicity is concentrated along a predominantly north–south structure to the north of the basin, with an angle slightly different from the existing catalog. There is no clear surface expression of that structure. Because the earthquakes occur beneath the lake, Global Navigation Satellite Systems (GNSS) measurements cannot directly validate changes in faulting patterns. However, Hamiel and Piatibratova (2023) postulate that deformation in the area was released aseismically, and thus earthquakes do not originate along the mapped faults. Along the Faria fault system (Fig. 3c,d), the new catalog clearly indicates that the activity is not on the main DST fault and instead has migrated to the Faria fault system. In the Dead Sea basin (Fig. 3e,f), the seismicity appears to primarily align along the center of the basin. However, shallower and more scattered seismic activity is also observed on the western edge. In the Northern Arava (Fig. 3g,h), we observe a clear trend of concentrated seismicity.

In the new catalog, depth distribution appears to be more clustered, especially near the Northern Arava and Dead Sea basins. The new catalog positions events approximately 4 km deeper on average. We filter out events in proximity of the DST by defining a polygon, and compute the moving average of event depth versus latitude. The moving average is weighted by the square of the catalog magnitude and a spatial Gaussian decay function around the center of the window, with $\sigma = 200$ m. Results are in Figure 4 and show that the new catalog follows a very similar north–south trend but with average deepening of the events. In the Sea of Galilee, whereas the majority of events are shallow, there appears to be a deeper (>18 km) structure that is also active, with a gap in the 10–18 km range. For the Faria fault system, the depth

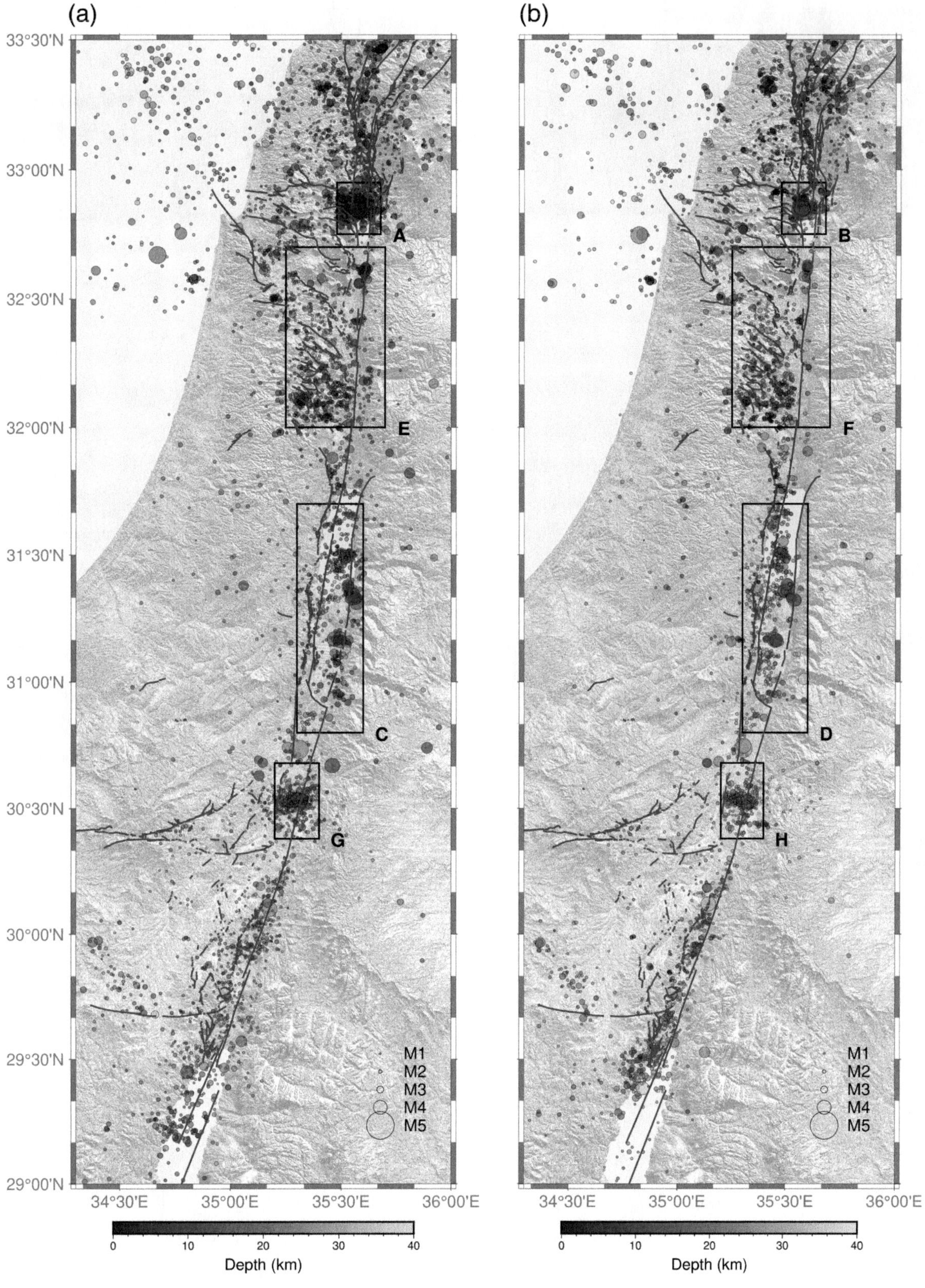

distribution is wide, indicating a complex subsurface structure. In the Dead Sea basin, the deep seismicity agrees with previous studies of the area, attributing the deep activity to the structure of the basin. The Northern Arava region shows minimal shallow seismicity, suggesting a single deep active zone.

Figure 2. Comparison of the (a) original and (b) new earthquake locations in the study area. The size of each event is proportional to the magnitude in the original catalog, and color indicates depth. Mapped surface faults (Sharon *et al.*, 2020) are in red. Black rectangles marked in A–H highlight key regions analyzed in Figure 3. The color version of this figure is available only in the electronic edition.

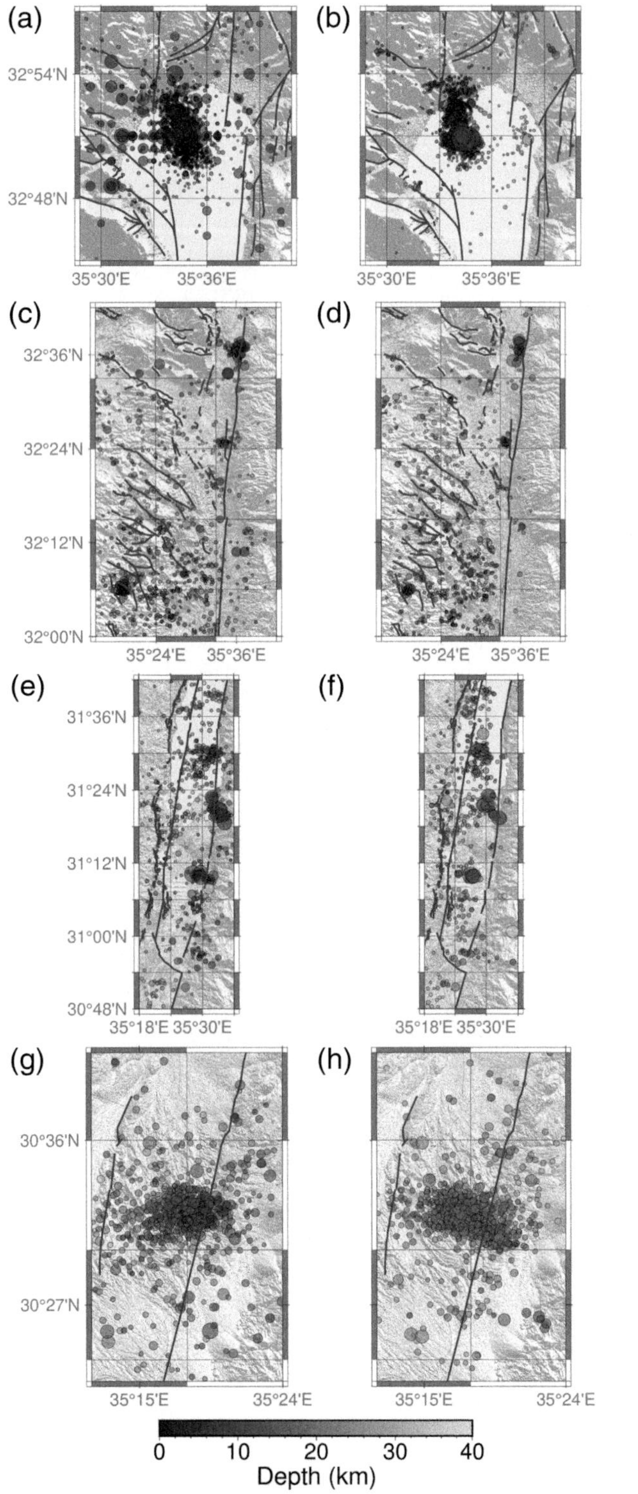

Figure 3. Detailed view of seismicity in key regions from Figure 2: (a,b) Sea of Galilee, (c,d) Faria fault system, (e,f) Dead Sea basin, and (g,h) Northern Arava valley. The (a,c,e,g) original catalog is compared with the (b,d,f,h) new locations, in accordance with A–H in Figure 2. The new catalog exhibits tighter horizontal clustering and more consistent depth distributions compared to the existing catalog, along with a general westward shift in locations and deepening of the estimated depths. The color version of this figure is available only in the electronic edition.

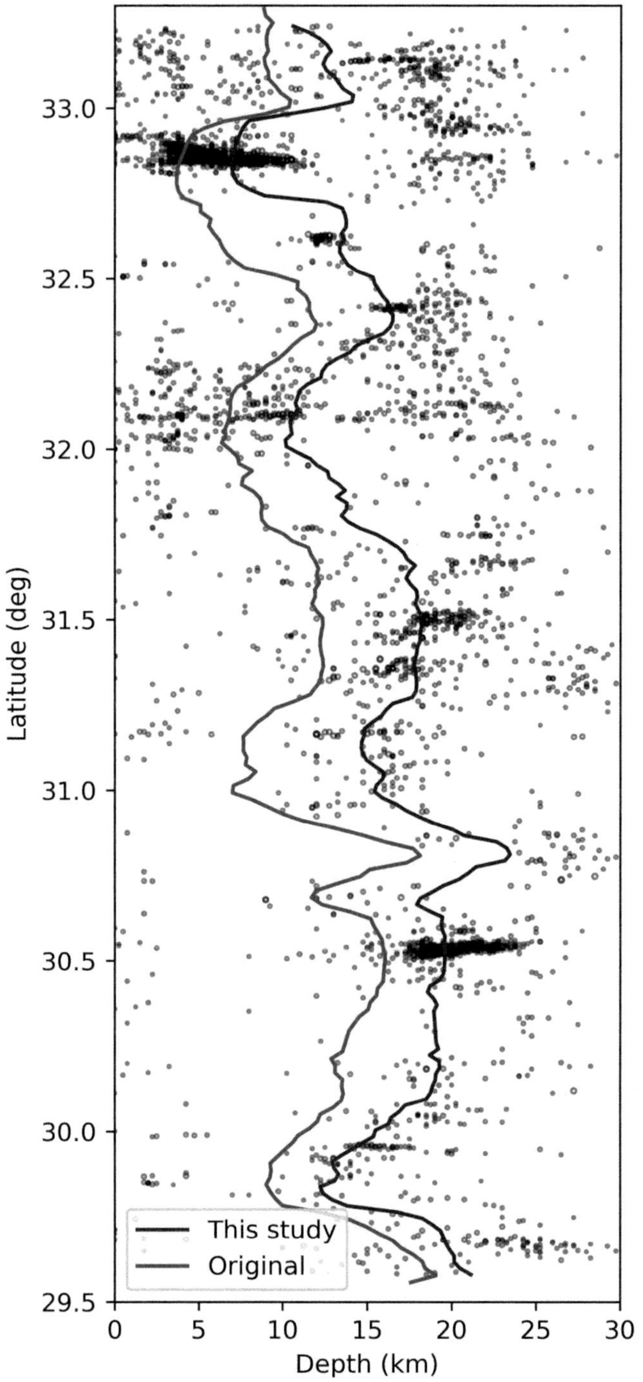

Figure 4. Depth distribution of events along the Dead Sea Transform (DST) in the new catalog (black). The moving average, weighted by the square of the cataloged magnitude, is in blue (new catalog) and red (existing catalog). Main features are marked on the right. The color version of this figure is available only in the electronic edition.

Discussion and Conclusions

There are several factors to which the differences between the catalogs can be attributed. A major difference between the catalogs is the number of stations and ensuing picks used for

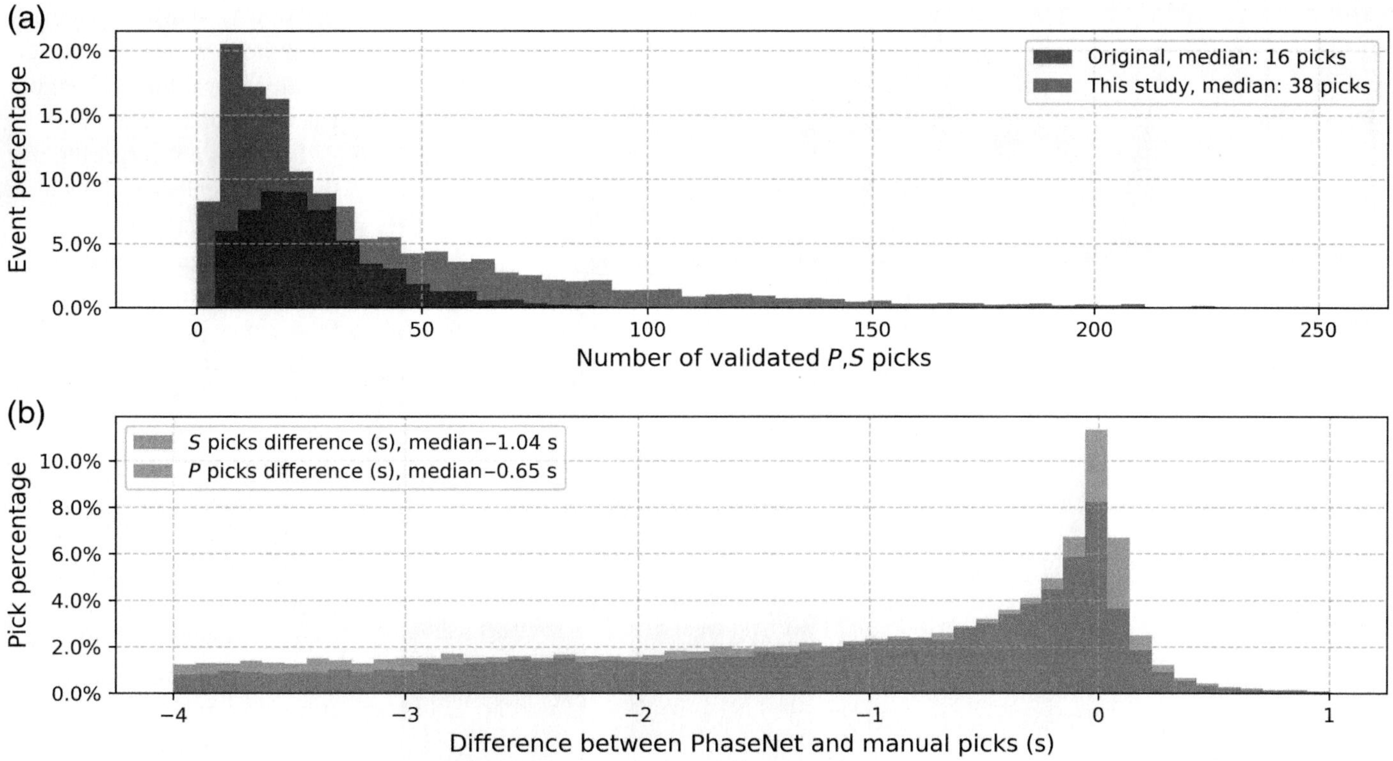

Figure 5. (a) Comparison of the number of picks used for location in the original (red) and new (blue) catalogs. The median number of used picks is 16 in the original catalog and 38 in the new catalog. (b) Difference between PhaseNet and manual picks, for *S* (orange) and *P* (light blue) arrivals. Median PhaseNet arrivals precede manual picks by 0.65 (*P* waves) and 1.04 s (*S* waves). The color version of this figure is available only in the electronic edition.

location. Figure 5a summarizes the number of *P* and *S* picks used for location in both cases. The PhaseNet picks reported here are validated ones, limited to a distance of 200 km from the catalog epicenter and within a reasonable time error from the predicted arrival time, thus effectively limiting their number. For the existing catalog, all picks are used. The added benefit of the early warning network is noticeable, more than doubling the median number of picks used for location. Some stations have collocated broadband and strong-motion sensors, but the additional strong-motion picks were not considered in this calculation. The statistical analysis also includes years with a partial network, starting with as little as 7–8 strong-motion sensors in 2018. Since 2020–2021, when the early warning network became fully operational, the gap between existing and new catalogs is thus even wider than shown in this figure.

Another possible cause for the discrepancy between the catalogs is the difference between PhaseNet and manual picks. Figure 5b shows that manual picks are consistently lagging behind ML-assisted picks, with a median delay of 0.65 s for *P* waves and 1.04 s for *S* waves. This analysis was conducted for all existing, manually cataloged picks and the temporally closest PhaseNet pick of the same phase. The primary explanation for this lag is that PhaseNet is more sensitive than manual picking and can detect early onset phases better than an analyst. Whereas the difference between manual and automatic picking is pronounced, it is not immediately obvious how it translates to a location difference due to the nonlinear nature of the problem. However, for comparison, I also repicked all cataloged events between 1984 and 2018, before the addition of the early warning network, with PhaseNet. Relocating these events yielded a seismicity map that is slightly worse or equivalent to the cataloged locations, based on visual inspection of coalescence patterns and depth distributions. This indicates that the picking difference is not, by itself, sufficient to significantly improve the catalog. However, I emphasize that for many of these stations, the original sampling rate was only 40 Hz, whereas PhaseNet is designed for 100 Hz data. Although I solved this technical limitation by upsampling the data, it is possible that this somewhat deteriorates PhaseNet's performance.

Finally, the broad choice of location method and objective function can also influence results. The existing catalog was built using the VELEST (Kissling *et al.*, 1994) software, which attempts to solve for both location and velocity. In this study, I do not attempt to change the velocity model. In addition, I apply an exhaustive search within a dense grid around the cataloged source location, thus increasing search resolution and avoiding sampling issues in the model space. I also use the L1 norm instead of L2 to account for picking errors. Picking weights are from PhaseNet and are computed differently in the existing catalog. Notwithstanding, I estimate that it is rather

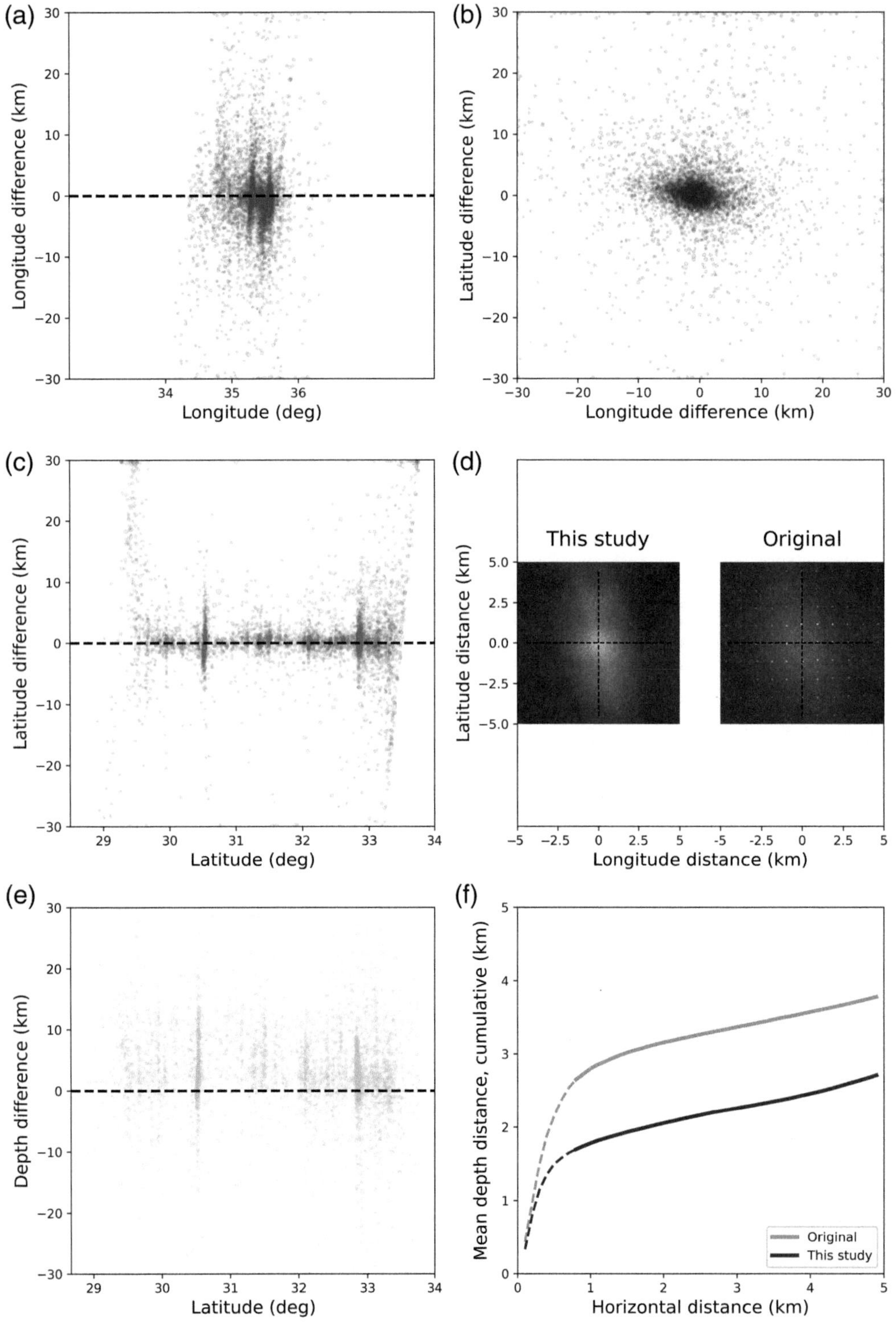

Figure 6. Comparison of original and new catalogs across different parameters: (a) longitude differences, (b) cross plot of longitude versus latitude differences, (c) latitude differences, (d) 2D histogram of latitude and longitude differences, computed in 100 × 100 m bins and clipped at 500 events, (e) depth differences, and (f) cumulative mean depth difference as a function of horizontal separation. The existing catalog is in orange, and the new catalog is in purple. Dashed lines represent the area where there are less than 5% of the maximum number of event pairs used in the plot. The color version of this figure is available only in the electronic edition.

unlikely that systematic differences arise due to the location algorithm and parameters of choice.

It is thus not surprising that there are significant differences between the catalogs. Yu *et al.* (2024) recognize that algorithm-driven uncertainty quantification tends to be underestimated and is not necessarily a reliable way to estimate actual errors. There is also a significant source of error due to the 1D velocity model approximation, which cannot be directly quantified. Therefore, I seek alternative validation of the new catalog, summarized in Figure 6. First, there is no clear bias in either longitude or latitude, with the median and mean differences falling under 1 km in both directions. There are some significant changes for out-of-network events, located at high or low latitudes, and we thus do not analyze the results in those areas. A cross plot (Fig. 6d) of the differences between the catalogs indicates that changes are primarily along the longitude, which makes sense as the network, either with or without the strong-motion sensors, is much better sampled along the latitude than the longitude. Therefore, we expect larger changes along the longitude. Our catalog also shows much better spatial coalescence (Fig. 6e) than the existing catalog, with the event cloud collapsing along the horizontal axis. The larger degree of smearing along the latitude in Figure 6e is due to the events being primarily distributed along a north–south trend, as opposed to a random distribution. Depth differences between the catalogs are significant, with an average deepening of about 4 km in the new catalog. In the new catalog, horizontally closed events are also closer in depth than in the existing catalog (Fig. 6f).

Under the absence of independent geodetic or geologic information, it is hard to validate the correctness of the locations. Whereas spatial coalescence is not always an indicator of more accurate locations, simple faulting models do favor it, on average. Whereas this is not necessarily true for individual faults, and for lack of a better validation approach, I attribute the overall higher spatial coalescence to more reliable locations, which are reasonable given the significant increase in the number of reliable picks.

The new catalog clearly shows reduced activity on the DST to the north of the Dead Sea basin, and that seismicity has migrated to the Faria fault system. Engelberg *et al.* (2025) recognize this gap, but in their study it is not continuous. Whereas they use the existing catalog, they also take into account many more years of data; hence, it is difficult to directly compare the two studies. Nonetheless, and based on the short-span new catalog only, I observe that the gap, where the fault is locked, extends approximately 70 km from the north of the Dead Sea basin. Hamiel, Piatibratova, *et al.* (2018) showed that the southern part of this region is locked for strike-slip motion at a depth of 16.6 ± 7.8 km and a slip rate of 4.8 ± 0.7 mm/yr. Slip transfer toward the Faria fault system has been postulated by Hamiel *et al.* (2016), who observed a reduction of slip rate in the northern part of the seismic gap.

In the Dead Sea basin, I show localization at depth toward a single fault close to the central axis of the Dead Sea basin. This has been recognized in a previous study of the area using a 3D tomographic velocity model (Braeuer *et al.*, 2012; Hofstetter *et al.*, 2012). There is also activity on the western boundary of the basin, but it is more scattered. I do not observe the relatively shallow events attributed to the eastern boundary of the basin (Braeuer *et al.*, 2012). However, due to the asymmetry of the basin, a westward shifting of the events in the new catalog could be due to the use of 1D velocity model.

The new catalog shows an interesting event distribution in the Northern Arava region, with events clustering primarily perpendicularly to mapped faults. I note that the western fault, although marked here (Sharon *et al.*, 2020), is less clearly mapped, and GNSS measurements can be fitted without it (Masson *et al.*, 2015). Their depth is consistent around 18–25 km, in accordance with the locking depth shown by previous studies (Masson *et al.*, 2015; Hamiel, Masson, *et al.*, 2018). Event distribution does not seem to align with a simple strike-slip faulting along the eastern edge of the basin. This could indicate the activity of east–west faults with no surface expression or of a fault along the edge of the pull-apart basin, similar to other faults along the basins of the DST (Weber *et al.*, 2009). More data, possibly along with a local 3D velocity model, are required for a more thorough understanding of the faulting structure at depth.

I emphasize that, in general, the currently used 1D velocity model is inadequate. The area is geologically complex, including major basins. The existing *P*-wave velocity model was estimated as an average for all of Israel, calibrated using explosions and using a constant V_P/V_S to estimate *S*-wave velocity (Wetzler and Kurzon, 2016). Thus, building and utilizing a 3D velocity model is expected to significantly influence results. For example, local tomography studies along the Dead Sea basin show that updated velocity models lead to an eastward migration of event locations, toward the edge of the fault (Braeuer *et al.*, 2014). Building such a model for the entire region of study should be, in my opinion, the focus of further studies.

This study spans only 6.5 yr of monitoring, including four years with a fully operational early warning network. Because of the low seismicity rate of the DST, this period is insufficient for a reliable interpretation of subsurface structures, especially because previous studies along the DST have shown changes in faulting regimes. Therefore, findings from this study should be treated with caution. Nonetheless, I show that incorporating the existing network of stations into standard seismological bulletins has significant potential to influence our understanding of the region. In addition, the average deepening of the estimated depths may influence seismic hazard models in the region. Although out of the scope of this study, moment tensor inversion is also expected to be significantly improved, thanks to both new locations and denser sampling of the focal sphere.

Data and Resources

Seismic data (broadband and strong motion), auxiliary information, and existing catalogs are provided by the Geological Survey of Israel (GSI). They can be accessed using standard ObsPy routines (Beyreuther *et al.*, 2010) with the client defined as https://seis.gsi.gov.il/ (last accessed July 2025). The existing and new catalogs, for a one-to-one comparison, have been uploaded to doi: 10.5281/zenodo.15045222.

Declaration of Competing Interests

The author acknowledges that there are no conflicts of interest recorded.

Acknowledgments

The deployment and maintenance of the Israeli network are conducted by the Geological Survey of Israel (GSI), which the author thanks for their continuous effort and for making the data available. The author is deeply thankful to Shaked Engelberg for stimulating discussions and useful comments. Conversations with Shmulik Marco have greatly enriched this article. This research was supported by the Israeli Science Foundation under Grant Number 2775/21.

References

Avni, R., D. Bowman, A. Shapira, and A. Nur (2002). Erroneous interpretation of historical documents related to the epicenter of the 1927 Jericho earthquake in the Holy Land, *J. Seismol.* **6,** no. 4, 469–476, doi: 10.1023/A:1021191824396.

Baer, G., G. J. Funning, G. Shamir, and T. J. Wright (2008). The 1995 November 22, Mw 7.2 Gulf of Elat earthquake cycle revisited, *Geophys. J. Int.* **175,** no. 3, 1040–1054, doi: 10.1111/j.1365-246X.2008.03901.x.

Becker, D., I. W. McBrearty, G. C. Beroza, and P. Martínez-Garzón (2024). Performance of AI-based phase picking and event association methods after the large 2023 Mw 7.8 and 7.6 Türkiye doublet, *Bull. Seismol. Soc. Am.* **114,** no. 5, 2457–2473, doi: 10.1785/0120240017.

Ben-Avraham, Z., U. ten Brink, R. Bell, and M. Reznikov (1996). Gravity field over the Sea of Galilee: Evidence for a composite basin along a transform fault, *J. Geophys. Res.* **101,** no. B1, 533–544, doi: 10.1029/95JB03043.

Beyreuther, M., R. Barsch, L. Krischer, T. Megies, Y. Behr, and J. Wassermann (2010). ObsPy: A Python toolbox for seismology, *Seismol. Res. Lett.* **81,** no. 3, 530–533, doi: 10.1785/gssrl.81.3.530.

Braeuer, B., and K. Bauer (2015). A new interpretation of seismic tomography in the southern Dead Sea basin using neural network clustering techniques, *Geophys. Res. Lett.* **42,** no. 22, 9772–9780, doi: 10.1002/2015GL066559.

Braeuer, B., G. Asch, R. Hofstetter, C. Haberland, D. Jaser, R. El-Kelani, and M. Weber (2012). High-resolution local earthquake tomography of the southern Dead Sea area: Tomography of the southern DSB, *Geophys. J. Int.* doi: 10.1111/j.1365-246X.2012.05668.x.

Braeuer, B., G. Asch, R. Hofstetter, C. Haberland, D. Jaser, R. El-Kelani, and M. Weber (2014). Detailed seismicity analysis revealing the dynamics of the southern Dead Sea area, *J. Seismol.* **18,** no. 4, 731–748, doi: 10.1007/s10950-014-9441-4.

Castillo, E., D. Siervo, and G. A. Prieto (2024). Colombian seismic monitoring using advanced machine-learning algorithms, *Seismol. Res. Lett.* **95,** no. 5, 2971–2985, doi: 10.1785/0220240036.

Ellenblum, R., S. Marco, A. Agnon, T. Rockwell, and A. Boas (1998). Crusader castle torn apart by earthquake at dawn, *Geology* **26,** no. 4, 303–306, doi: 10.1130/0091-7613(1998)026<0303:CCTABE>2.3.CO;2.

Engelberg, S., N. Wetzler, and A. Agnon (2025). Earthquake swarms and seismic gaps along the Dead Sea Fault System, *Seismol. Res. Lett.* doi: 10.1785/0220240414.

Garcia-Aristizabal, A., S. Danesi, T. Braun, M. Anselmi, L. Zaccarelli, D. Famiani, and A. Morelli (2020). Epistemic uncertainties in local earthquake locations and implications for managing induced seismicity, *Bull. Seismol. Soc. Am.* **110,** no. 5, 2423–2440, doi: 10.1785/0120200100.

Garfunkel, Z. (2014). Lateral motion and deformation along the Dead Sea Transform, in *Dead Sea Transform Fault System: Reviews*, Z. Garfunkel, Z. Ben-Avraham, and E. Kagan (Editors), Modern Approaches in Solid Earth Sciences, Springer, Dordrecht, the Netherlands, 109–150, doi: 10.1007/978-94-017-8872-4_5.

Garfunkel, Z., I. Zak, and R. Freund (1981). Active faulting in the Dead Sea rift, *Tectonophysics* **80,** no. 1, 1–26, doi: 10.1016/0040-1951(81)90139-6.

Grigoli, F., L. Scarabello, M. Böse, B. Weber, S. Wiemer, and J. F. Clinton (2018). Pick- and waveform-based techniques for real-time detection of induced seismicity, *Geophys. J. Int.* **213,** no. 2, 868–884, doi: 10.1093/gji/ggy019.

Hamiel, Y., and O. Piatibratova (2023). Transient behavior and interplay between seismic and aseismic deformation near the tip of a creeping segment: Insights from the Northern Jordan Valley Segment of the Dead Sea Fault, *Geophys. Res. Lett.* **50,** no. 3, e2022GL100584, doi: 10.1029/2022GL100584.

Hamiel, Y., R. Amit, Z. B. Begin, S. Marco, O. Katz, A. Salamon, E. Zilberman, and N. Porat (2009). The seismicity along the Dead Sea Fault during the last 60,000 years, *Bull. Seismol. Soc. Am.* **99,** no. 3, 2020–2026, doi: 10.1785/0120080218.

Hamiel, Y., F. Masson, O. Piatibratova, and Y. Mizrahi (2018). GPS measurements of crustal deformation across the southern Arava Valley section of the Dead Sea Fault and implications to regional seismic hazard assessment, *Tectonophysics*, **724–725,** 171–178, doi: 10.1016/j.tecto.2018.01.016.

Hamiel, Y., O. Piatibratova, and Y. Mizrahi (2016). Creep along the northern Jordan Valley section of the Dead Sea Fault, *Geophys. Res. Lett.* **43,** no. 6, 2494–2501, doi: 10.1002/2016GL067913.

Hamiel, Y., O. Piatibratova, Y. Mizrahi, Y. Nahmias, and A. Sagy (2018). Crustal deformation across the Jericho Valley Section of the Dead Sea Fault as resolved by detailed field and geodetic observations, *Geophys. Res. Lett.* **45,** no. 7, 3043–3050, doi: 10.1002/2018GL077547.

Hofstetter, R., C. Dorbath, and M. Calò (2012). Crustal structure of the Dead Sea Basin from local earthquake tomography, *Geophys. J. Int.* **189,** no. 1, 554–568, doi: 10.1111/j.1365-246X.2012.05369.x.

Ken-Tor, R., A. Agnon, Y. Enzel, M. Stein, S. Marco, and J. F. W. Negendank (2001). High-resolution geological record of historic earthquakes in the Dead Sea basin, *J. Geophys. Res.* **106,** no. B2, 2221–2234, doi: 10.1029/2000JB900313.

Kissling, E., W. L. Ellsworth, D. Eberhart-Phillips, and U. Kradolfer (1994). Initial reference models in local earthquake tomography, *J. Geophys. Res.* **99,** no. B10, 19,635–19,646, doi: 10.1029/93JB03138.

Kurzon, I., R. N. Nof, M. Laporte, H. Lutzky, A. Polozov, D. Zakosky, H. Shulman, A. Goldenberg, B. Tatham, and Y. Hamiel (2020). The "TRUAA" seismic network: Upgrading the Israel Seismic Network—Toward national earthquake early warning system, *Seismol. Res. Lett.* **91,** no. 6, 3236–3255, doi: 10.1785/0220200169.

Lellouch, A., A. Inbal, and A. Ziv (2024). Shear-wave velocity model for the Dead Sea Transform from multimode inversion of surface waves excited by the February 2023 Southeast Türkiye earthquake sequence, *Seismol. Res. Lett.* **95,** no. 3, 1926–1938, doi: 10.1785/0220230303.

Lu, Y., N. Wetzler, N. Waldmann, A. Agnon, G. P. Biasi, and S. Marco (2020). A 220,000-year-long continuous large earthquake record on a slow-slipping plate boundary, *Sci. Adv.* **6,** no. 48, eaba4170, doi: 10.1126/sciadv.aba4170.

Marco, S. (2008). Recognition of earthquake-related damage in archaeological sites: Examples from the Dead Sea fault zone, *Tectonophysics* **453,** no. 1, 148–156, doi: 10.1016/j.tecto.2007.04.011.

Marco, S., M. Hartal, N. Hazan, L. Lev, and M. Stein (2003). Archaeology, history, and geology of the A.D. 749 earthquake, Dead Sea transform, *Geology* **31,** no. 8, 665–668, doi: 10.1130/G19516.1.

Masson, F., Y. Hamiel, A. Agnon, Y. Klinger, and A. Deprez (2015). Variable behavior of the Dead Sea Fault along the southern Arava segment from GPS measurements, *C. R. Geosci.* **347,** no. 4, 161–169, doi: 10.1016/j.crte.2014.11.001.

Michelini, A., and A. Lomax (2004). The effect of velocity structure errors on double-difference earthquake location, *Geophys. Res. Lett.* **31,** no. 9, doi: 10.1029/2004GL019682.

Mousavi, S. M., and G. C. Beroza (2022). Deep-learning seismology, *Science* **377,** no. 6607, eabm4470, doi: 10.1126/science.abm4470.

Mousavi, S. M., W. L. Ellsworth, W. Zhu, L. Y. Chuang, and G. C. Beroza (2020). Earthquake transformer—An attentive deep-learning model for simultaneous earthquake detection and phase picking, *Nat. Comm.* **11,** no. 1, 3952, doi: 10.1038/s41467-020-17591-w.

Nof, R. N., and I. Kurzon (2020). TRUAA—Earthquake early warning system for Israel: Implementation and current status, *Seismol. Res. Lett.* **92,** no. 1, 325–341, doi: 10.1785/0220200176.

Pavlis, G. L. (1986). Appraising earthquake hypocenter location errors: A complete, practical approach for single-event locations, *Bull. Seismol. Soc. Am.* **76,** no. 6, 1699–1717, doi: 10.1785/BSSA0760061699.

Sadeh, M., Y. Hamiel, A. Ziv, Y. Bock, P. Fang, and S. Wdowinski (2012). Crustal deformation along the Dead Sea Transform and the Carmel Fault inferred from 12 years of GPS measurements, *J. Geophys. Res.* **117,** no. B8, doi: 10.1029/2012JB009241.

Shalev, E., V. Lyakhovsky, Y. Weinstein, and Z. Ben-Avraham (2013). The thermal structure of Israel and the Dead Sea Fault, *Tectonophysics* **602,** 69–77, doi: 10.1016/j.tecto.2012.09.011.

Shapira, A., R. Avni, and A. Nur (1993). A new estimate for the epicenter of the Jericho earthquake of 11 July 1927, *Isr. J. Earth Sci.* **42,** no. 2, 93–96.

Sharon, M., A. Sagy, I. Kurzon, S. Marco, and M. Rosensaft (2020). Assessment of seismic sources and capable faults through hierarchic tectonic criteria: Implications for seismic hazard in the Levant, *Nat. Hazards Earth Syst. Sci.* **20,** no. 1, 125–148, doi: 10.5194/nhess-20-125-2020.

ten Brink, U. S., and C. H. Flores (2012). Geometry and subsidence history of the Dead Sea basin: A case for fluid-induced mid-crustal shear zone? *J. Geophys. Res.* **117,** no. B1, doi: 10.1029/2011JB008711.

ten Brink, U. S., E. Levi, C. H. Flores, I. Koulakov, N. Bronshtein, and Z. Ben-Avraham (2023). Crustal structure across the Central Dead Sea Transform and surrounding areas: Insights into tectonic processes in continental transforms, *Tectonics* **42,** no. 8, e2023TC007799, doi: 10.1029/2023TC007799.

Waldhauser, F., and W. L. Ellsworth (2000). A double-difference earthquake location algorithm: Method and application to the Northern Hayward Fault, California, *Bull. Seismol. Soc. Am.* **90,** no. 6, 1353–1368, doi: 10.1785/0120000006.

Weber, M., K. Abu-Ayyash, A. Abueladas, A. Agnon, Z. Alasonati-Tašárová, H. Al-Zubi, A. Babeyko, Y. Bartov, K. Bauer, M. Becken, *et al.* (2009). Anatomy of the Dead Sea Transform from lithospheric to microscopic scale, *Rev. Geophys.* **47,** no. 2, doi: 10.1029/2008RG000264.

Wetzler, N., and I. Kurzon (2016). The earthquake activity of Israel: Revisiting 30 years of local and regional seismic records along the Dead Sea Transform, *Seismol. Res. Lett.* **87,** no. 1, 47–58, doi: 10.1785/0220150157.

Wetzler, N., E. Shalev, T. Göbel, F. Amelung, I. Kurzon, V. Lyakhovsky, and E. E. Brodsky (2019). Earthquake swarms triggered by groundwater extraction near the Dead Sea fault, *Geophys. Res. Lett.* **46,** no. 14, 8056–8063, doi: 10.1029/2019GL083491.

Yu, Y., W. L. Ellsworth, and G. C. Beroza (2024). Accuracy and precision of earthquake location programs: Insights from a synthetic controlled experiment, *Seismol. Res. Lett.* doi: 10.1785/0220240354.

Zhang, M., M. Liu, T. Feng, R. Wang, and W. Zhu (2022). LOC-FLOW: An end-to-end machine learning-based high-precision earthquake location workflow, *Seismol. Res. Lett.* **93,** no. 5, 2426–2438, doi: 10.1785/0220220019.

Zhu, W., and G. C. Beroza (2019). PhaseNet: A deep-neural-network-based seismic arrival-time picking method, *Geophys. J. Int.* **216,** no. 1, 261–273, doi: 10.1093/gji/ggy423.

Zhu, W., I. W. McBrearty, S. M. Mousavi, W. L. Ellsworth, and G. C. Beroza (2022). Earthquake phase association using a Bayesian Gaussian mixture model, *J. Geophys. Res.* **127,** no. 5, e2021JB023249, doi: 10.1029/2021JB023249.

Manuscript received 15 May 2025
Published online 12 September 2025

Attention-Based Neural Network for Onsite Peak Ground Velocity Earthquake Early Warning

Ting-Chung Huang*[1], Tzu-Ling Liu[1], Benjamin Ming Yang[1], and Yih-Min Wu[1,2]

Abstract

To improve on-site earthquake early warning for peak ground velocity (PGV), we leverage a machine learning approach. We propose a novel attention-based transformer architecture to address this challenging problem. A series of comparisons with other methods, including the traditional peak *P*-wave displacement amplitude approach and long short-term memory neural networks, is conducted. In addition, we demonstrate that the influence of building effects can be mitigated by incorporating station corrections to peak values in the seismograms as additional features during training. Finally, we discuss how the shape of the label can serve as a proxy to indicate the reliability of PGV determination within the first few seconds after the arrival time.

Cite this article as Huang, T.-C., T.-L. Liu, B. Ming Yang, and Y.-M. Wu (2025). Attention-Based Neural Network for Onsite Peak Ground Velocity Earthquake Early Warning, *Seismol. Res. Lett.* **97**, 256–271, doi: 10.1785/0220240496.

Introduction

Earthquake early warning (EEW) relies on the speed difference between *P* waves and *S* waves ($V_P > V_S$) to deliver warnings of destructive earthquakes before significant ground motion occurs. In practice, to maximize warning time and enhance effectiveness, EEW systems must determine whether an earthquake is destructive within the first few seconds (Wu and Kanamori, 2005). This quasi-deterministic approach, which involves assessing the earthquake's destructiveness based on the initial behavior of ground motion, has been widely adopted. The parameters used for estimation may include magnitude (Wu and Zhao, 2006), peak ground acceleration (PGA), or peak ground velocity (PGV) (Chandrakumar *et al.*, 2024).

There are two types of EEW systems: regional EEW and onsite EEW. Regional EEW uses ground-motion data from stations near the hypocenter to estimate key earthquake parameters, including the earthquake's location and magnitude. After determining these parameters, the regional EEW takes advantage of the fact that internet transmission speeds are much faster than the speeds of *P* waves and *S* waves ($V_{\text{internet}} \gg V_P > V_S$), enabling it to deliver warnings to regions before the arrival of the largest seismic wave.

Regional EEW systems are highly reliable, with both low false alarm rates and low missed alarm rates. There are several operating regional EEW around the world, for example, in Japan (Kamigaichi *et al.*, 2009) and Mexico (Vaiciulyte *et al.*, 2024). However, regional EEW systems have a significant limitation: they require seismic data from multiple stations, and collecting these data take time. In addition, processing the data to estimate parameters and broadcasting warnings also requires time. As a result, issuing a regional warning typically takes ~10–20 s, depending on the event's coverage (Wu *et al.*, 2025). This delay creates what is known as the "blind zone," where regions close to the epicenter cannot receive warnings in time (Wald, 2020). The absence of warnings in the blind zone is particularly critical because these areas often experience the most severe damage.

To address the challenge of providing timely warnings within the blind zone, onsite EEW systems have been proposed and developed (Allen *et al.*, 2009; Satriano *et al.*, 2011; Wu and Mittal, 2021). These systems aim to deliver faster alerts by focusing on real-time seismic data from single stations, enabling them to function effectively in the most vulnerable areas.

The onsite EEW system uses seismic information from a single station to estimate the intensity of an upcoming wave. If the estimated wave exceeds a predefined threshold, the system directly issues a warning from that station.

The key advantages of the onsite EEW system are its speed and independence. Because the warning is issued solely based on ground motion observed at the station, the system avoids delays caused by transmitting ground-motion data and warnings back and forth. In addition, the onsite system can continue to function even during internet outages.

However, these advantages come with certain trade-offs. The primary disadvantage of the onsite EEW system is its reduced accuracy. This limitation arises from the reliance

1. Department of Geosciences, National Taiwan University, Taipei, Taiwan, https://orcid.org/0000-0002-8039-952X (T-CH); https://orcid.org/0000-0003-2954-1997 (BMY); https://orcid.org/0000-0003-4542-1741 (Y-MW); 2. Institute of Earth Sciences, Academia Sinica, Taipei, Taiwan

*Corresponding author: tingchunghuang@gmail.com

on data from only one seismic station. Because biases in seismic records between stations cannot be averaged out, the uncertainty in ground-motion estimation is relatively high when using data from a single station.

Over the past decade, there have been significant advancements in EEW systems worldwide. Currently, operating EEW systems can be classified into three categories: (1) public alerts distributed through broadcasts or cellphones, (2) limited alerts provided to select users, and (3) systems still in the testing and development stage.

Among the three categories of EEW, Taiwan falls into the first category. The regional EEW system is operated by the official agency, the Central Weather Administration (CWA) of Taiwan. Taiwan is located in a seismically active region, experiencing ~3000 felt earthquakes per year. To mitigate earthquake damage, the development of EEW systems in Taiwan has been thriving.

The primary provider of the regional EEW system in Taiwan is the CWA. For the onsite EEW system, the *P*-alert seismic network plays a significant role. The *P*-alert network consists of a large number of low-cost microelectromechanical system (MEMS) accelerometers (Mittal *et al.*, 2021; Wu and Mittal, 2021). As of 2024, ~800 *P*-alert stations have been installed. Because the primary focus of the *P*-alert network is to provide onsite EEW to the public, the stations are deliberately located in public facilities where people gather. To minimize interference from human activity and noise, most *P*-alert stations are installed inside buildings. However, this introduces additional complexities because building effects must be addressed alongside the effects of varying geological settings.

The *P*-alert network provides onsite EEW using peak ground-motion displacement (P_d). Previous studies (Wu *et al.*, 2003, 2004; Wu and Kanamori, 2005; Wu and Zhao, 2006) have shown that the P_d measured during the first 3 s after the seismic wave's arrival correlates with the earthquake magnitude. The computational requirements for determining P_d are minimal, enabling the calculation to be performed efficiently by the station's microchip. Although the P_d indicator offers a reasonable warning time and acceptable warning accuracy (Hsieh *et al.*, 2015), its overall performance is insufficient to meet the demands of current-generation advancements.

Significant changes in the landscape of EEW systems have occurred following the implementation of the *P*-alert network. First, the intensity scale used in Taiwan has been revised by the CWA. Details about this revision were disclosed in a press release (in Chinese), and discussions regarding the new intensity scale can be found in several studies (Yang *et al.*, 2021; Liu and Wu, 2024). The updated scale incorporates both PGA and PGV to determine seismic intensity. For smaller ground motions, the revised scale primarily uses PGA, whereas for larger ground motions, it relies on PGV. This approach allows the revised scale to assign higher intensity values based on PGV, reflecting the observed correlation between PGV and building damage identified in previous studies (Yamaguchi and Yamazaki, 2001; Mittal *et al.*, 2021). Second, the computational capabilities of the *P*-alert stations are improving significantly. The next generation of *P*-alert devices is expected to feature computational power comparable to that of the fourth-generation Raspberry Pi. This substantial enhancement in processing power will enable more complex data processing and even allow the deployment of trained machine learning (ML) models.

As a response to the major changes in the landscape of onsite EEW, we aim to address the following questions in this study:

1. Because the revised intensity scale relies on PGV to identify higher intensities, can we develop an onsite EEW method for PGV that outperforms the traditional P_d method (Hsieh *et al.*, 2015)?
2. Given the upcoming upgrades in computational hardware and recent advancements in the application of ML in seismology (Li *et al.*, 2018; Mousavi and Beroza, 2020; Zhang *et al.*, 2021), can we use similar ML techniques to address the onsite EEW problem?
3. Considering the inhomogeneity between stations due to varying geological settings and installation conditions (Huang and Wu, 2023a), can we identify suitable ML features that effectively represent these differences between stations?

In this article, we use the attention mechanism (Vaswani *et al.*, 2017) to solve the onsite EEW of PGV problem. The attention method is a ML method that determines the importance of certain parts of the sequence of data. The advantage of the attention mechanism lies in its ability to identify the most crucial part of the seismic record and focus on it to improve estimation of the incoming peak velocity. We manage to answer all the aforementioned questions. The key points of our work are as follows:

- We describe in detail the proposed attention-based model for the onsite PGV EEW problem (the Methodology section).
- We demonstrate the effectiveness of including the station corrections as a feature in the training (the Results section).
- We show the test results of the proposed attention-based model against several independent medium to large events (the Results section).
- We compare the accuracy of the warning of the attention-based model with that of the other two methods, including the P_d method and the long short-term memory (LSTM) model (see the Results section).
- We discuss the shape of the optimized label can reflect the credibility of PGV determination (see the Testing with various shapes of label section).

Data

Figure 1 illustrates the dataset used in this study, including events in Taiwan, events in Japan, stations of *P*-alert network

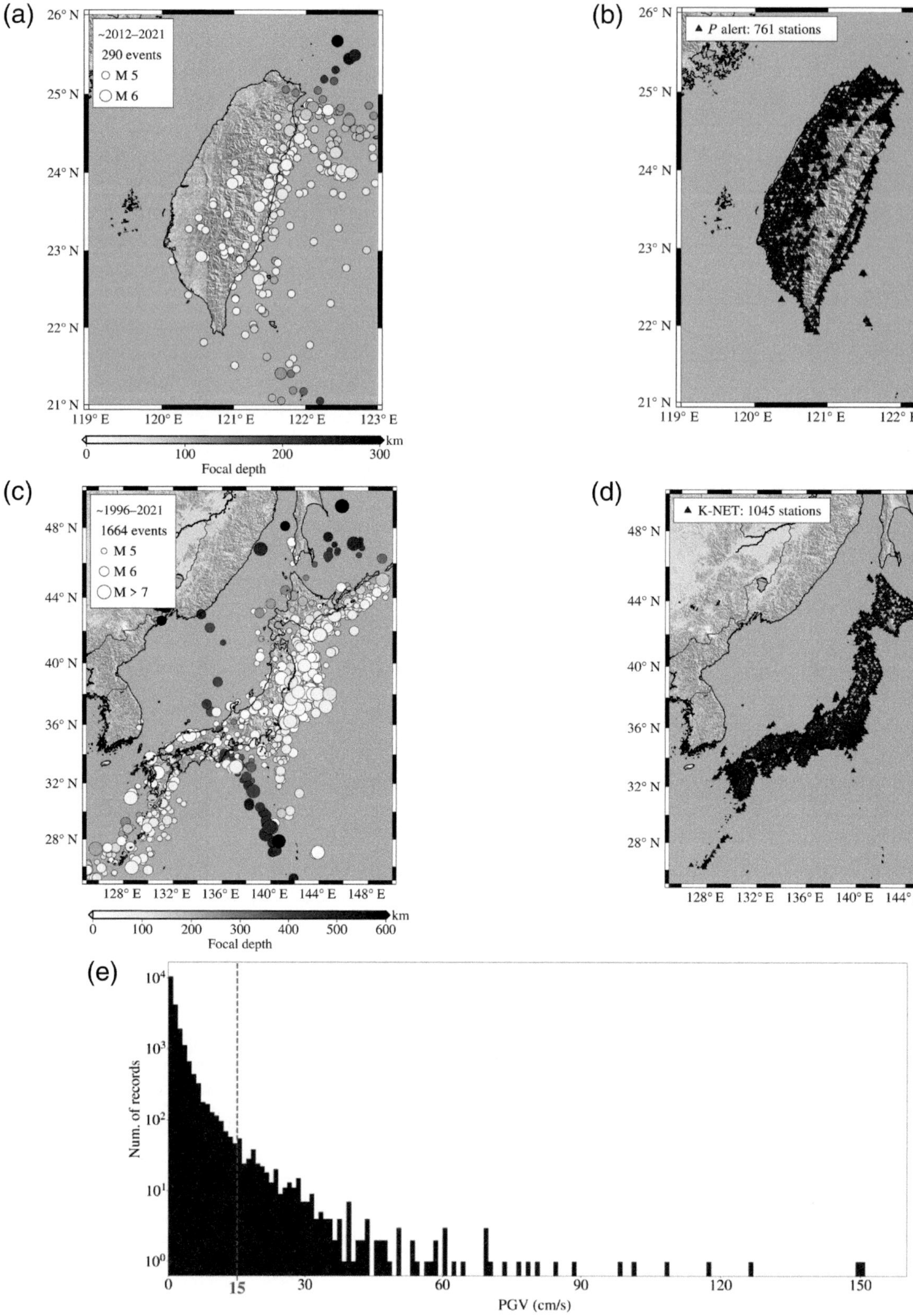

Figure 1. Illustrations of dataset used in this study. (a) 290 Taiwan events recorded by the *P*-Alert network. (b) 761 stations used in the *P*-alert network. (c) 1664 Japan events recorded by the Kyoshin-net (K-NET) network. (d) 1045 stations used in the K-NET network. (e) Histogram of the peak ground velocity (PGV) for all records in the dataset. The color version of this figure is available only in the electronic edition.

in Taiwan, stations of Kyoshin net (K-NET) network in Japan, and the PGV histogram of all the events combined.

P-alert dataset

The *P*-alert network consists of low-cost MEMS sensors designed to record real-time ground motion in Taiwan. Currently, there are ~800 operational stations, which enables the network to achieve ultra-high density. Each *P*-alert station is equipped with a three-component MEMS accelerometer capable of providing 16-bit readings at a sampling rate of 100 Hz. The amplitude range that a *P*-alert station can record spans from −2g to +2g.

For this project, we collected all events with $M_L > 5.0$ recorded by the *P*-alert network between 2012 and 2021. A total of 290 medium to large events were identified, all located within the coordinates 21°–26° N and 119°–123° E. Notice that the choice of $M_L > 5.0$ for our dataset is based on the observation that records with higher PGV are extremely rare in smaller magnitude events.

K-NET dataset

Because of the rarity of higher PGV records, we also collected K-NET data from Japan with $M_{JMA} > 5.0$ between 1996 and 2021 as part of a data enhancement and transfer learning backup plan. A total of 1664 medium to large events were included. A similar transfer learning plan has been implemented and proven successful for the PGA-based onsite EEW problem in a previous study (Wang *et al.*, 2022). Details of the performance of transfer learning using K-NET data are provided in the Discussion section, in which we compare the performance of the original training dataset (*P*-alert records only) with that of the enhanced training dataset (*P*-alert records combined with K-NET records).

Methodology

Data preprocessing

The primary goal of onsite EEW is to address the insufficient warning time within the blind zone. Therefore, we selected records from within the blind zone for training. Generally speaking, the area within 50–60 km of the epicenter is considered the blind zone for regional EEW systems in Taiwan. Note that it is a rough estimation, and the exact region of blind zone depends on several parameters, including depth, V_S, alert calculation time, broadcasting time, and more. In this study, we focused exclusively on records with an epicentral distance <70 km.

Following the data selection based on epicentral distance, a series of data quality checks was implemented. Records with missing or abnormal data (e.g., records with large noisy spikes) were excluded. After preliminary data cleaning, we proceeded to pick arrival times. We chose to use the local extrema scalogram (LES) picker (Huang and Wu, 2019) because of its robustness in noisy environments. After obtaining the preliminary *P* arrivals, we used the SNR_d method (Huang and Wu, 2023b), which calculates the signal-to-noise ratio based on the logarithm of the summation of vertical displacement squared after the *P* arrival ($\sum_{t=0}^{3} d^2[t]$) divided by the summation of vertical displacement squared before the *P* arrival ($\sum_{t=-3}^{0} d^2[t]$). Records with excessively low SNR ($SNR_d < 1$) were discarded because they were contaminated by noise. Finally, we manually verified the quality of the arrival times in the remaining records by comparing the performance of the LES picker with the traditional short-term average (STA)/long-term average (LTA) picker. A 10 s time window from the curated records was selected as a training feature. In addition, velocity and displacement values derived from the acceleration records were included as candidates for training features. Figure 2 summarizes the preprocessing procedures described earlier. The three components of velocity are derived from the three components of acceleration by integration in time and a high-pass Butterworth filter of 0.075 Hz. The three components of displacement are derived from the three components of velocity by integration in time and a high-pass Butterworth filter of 0.075 Hz.

Station corrections of initial peak ground motion

To account for the differences in ground motion at *P*-alert stations due to overall station effects, including site effects, topographic effects, and building effects, we incorporated station corrections of initial peak ground motion (Huang and Wu, 2023a) as candidates for training features. Station corrections of initial peak ground motion are statistical parameters estimated using the iterative regression (IR) method (Huang and Wu, 2021). IR treats the station corrections as missing data. IR alternatively uses a seismic dataset to perform two types of estimation, including (1) given the station corrections, estimation of attenuation model, and (2) given the attenuation model, estimation of station corrections. After several iterations, both estimations will converge to true values. The convergence of station corrections to their true values is guaranteed by the corresponding statistical theory. In practice, convergence is typically achieved within a few iterations of estimation. In this project, we included three types of station corrections as candidates for training features: the station correction of initial peak acceleration (SC_a), the station correction of initial peak velocity (SC_v), and the station correction of initial peak displacement (SC_d).

Data labeling

Data labeling is crucial in supervised learning because it provides ground truth for the given features, enabling the machine to learn. In this project, the label for onsite EEW is associated with the decision to issue a warning. In other words, the label reflects the legitimacy of sending out a warning. In practice, we consult the revised intensity scale by the CWA and set the judging criterion at PGV = 15 cm/s, which distinguishes milder ground motions from severe ground motions. Records with

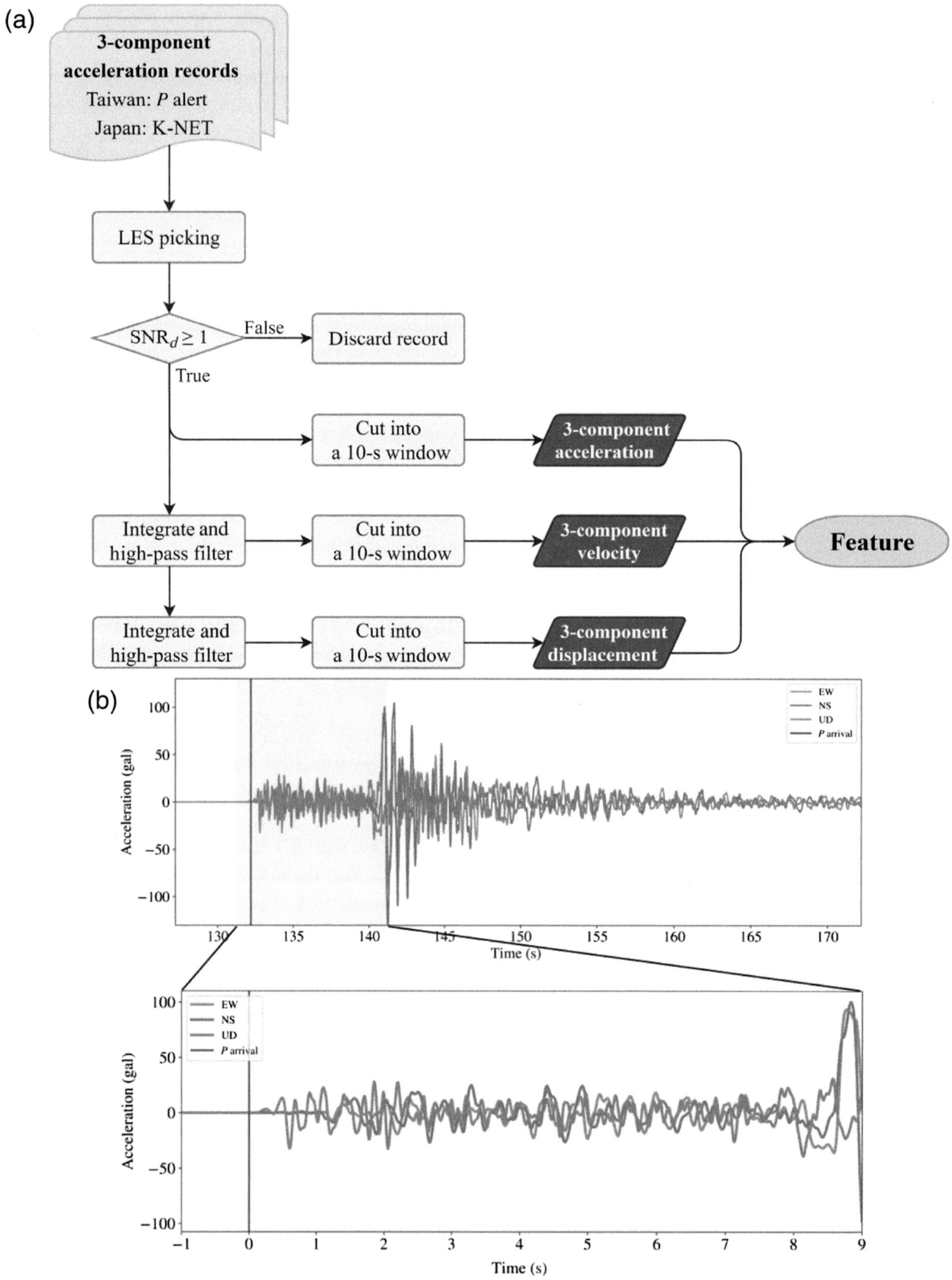

Figure 2. The preprocessing procedure and its output feature. (a) The preprocessing procedure used in this study. (b) An example of the features used for training, showing a 10 s window from one acceleration channel. EW, east–west; LES, local extrema scalogram; NS, north–south; UD, up–down. The color version of this figure is available only in the electronic edition.

PGV >15 cm/s are labeled as 1 (100% credibility to issue a warning), and the remaining records are labeled as 0 (0% credibility to issue a warning). It is important to note that we treat the records as time series, and because a warning can be issued at any time after the *P*-wave arrival, time introduces an additional degree of complexity to the labeling. For example, consider a record with PGV > 15 cm/s. Its label should also be represented as a time series. The beginning and ending of the label are straightforward: before the arrival of the *P* wave, the credibility is 0 because no information is available. After the *P*-wave arrival, the credibility is 1. An interesting question is how the label transitions from 0 to 1. To maximize lead time, we start with a step function–shaped label that jumps at the *P*-wave arrival, similar to the approach used in the case of PGA-based EEW. In the Discussion section, we compare the performance of different label functions.

Note that theoretically, it is possible to have records exceeding 15 cm/s that are outside the 70 km epicentral distance region. One may be concerned that the training dataset does not include these records because of the 70 km criterion. However, records exceeding 15 cm/s are fairly rare. In practice, we do not observe any of such records yet in the *P*-alert catalog. Therefore, we think our dataset captures most of the large PGV records.

Data imbalance and data augmentation

One of the inevitable difficulties in applying ML to the EEW problem is data imbalance, a very common challenge in ML tasks (Sun *et al.*, 2009; Fan *et al.*, 2020; Thabtah *et al.*, 2020). Specifically, if all available records are included in the training dataset, the predictions will be heavily biased toward "no warning," reflecting the rarity of large PGV records. To address this data imbalance, we use data augmentation techniques to "create" additional large PGV records. In this work, we adopt three common data augmentation methods (Fan *et al.*, 2020): (1) adding background noise to the signal, (2) shifting the arrival time to simulate the uncertainty in determining the *P*-wave arrival, and (3) flipping the signal's polarity. By combining these three data augmentation techniques, we successfully increased the number of large PGV records by eightfold.

ML methods for onsite PGV problem

In this work, we have adopted two types of ML architectures in solving the onsite PGV problem. The first one is the LSTM architecture (Sutskever *et al.*, 2014), which was used to solve the onsite PGA problem in the previous study (Wang *et al.*, 2022). The second one is an attention-based architecture designed to predict the time series based on the "context" of the time series (Vaswani *et al.*, 2017).

The LSTM model. The LSTM architecture (Hochreiter and Schmidhuber, 1997; Gers *et al.*, 2002) consists of two sets of memories: short-term memory and long-term memory. The architecture can forecast anomalies from the sequential data based on comparing long-term trends with short-term trends. In the context of using the LSTM architecture to solve the onsite EEW problem, we follow closely with our previous study by Wang *et al.* (2022), in which we proposed an LSTM model for onsite EEW.

Conceptually, the LSTM model for onsite EEW operates similarly to the STA/LTA picker in that it compares information in the long-term memory with information in the short-term memory to determine specific targets. In the case of the STA/LTA picker, the target is to distinguish seismic signals from noise, which can be achieved using a simple average of the time series. However, if the target is to identify the incoming intensity of a seismic wave, the required function would be far more complex than a simple average. This complexity makes it appealing to use a neural network to derive such a function. The LSTM model is a viable candidate because of its proven effectiveness in predicting onsite PGA. In this project, we adapt a modified LSTM model, originally designed for the onsite PGA problem, to fit our onsite PGV problem.

The attention-based model. The attention-based model (transformer layers) is one of the latest and most popular architectures developed for solving natural language processing (NLP) tasks. It can learn context by tracking specific relationships within sequential data (Luong *et al.*, 2015). The attention-based model has achieved success in many otherwise challenging tasks, including language translation (Cho *et al.*, 2014; Bahdanau *et al.*, 2015), sound-to-text conversion, and various NLP applications such as chatbots. Among all applications involving the attention-based model, Chat Generative Pre-trained Transformer (ChatGPT) is perhaps the most well-known example (Brown *et al.*, 2020). ChatGPT is a powerful chatbot capable of interpreting commands, understanding their context and meaning, and generating appropriate feedback as an output.

The ability to learn context is enabled by the mechanism of attention, which comprises an encoder and a decoder. In our project, we use a simplified version of the attention mechanism (Wu *et al.*, 2020) to enable the architecture to identify which parts of the seismic signal are significant for predicting subsequent PGV. The attention model can be viewed as a generalization of the LSTM model, extending the short-term memory of the current signal to specific, significant portions of the signal. We anticipate performance enhancements with the addition of the attention mechanism.

Figure 3 illustrates the attention-based model adopted in our study. The architecture was originally designed for time-series prediction (Wu *et al.*, 2020). In our implementation, we feed the sequential seismic signal (the x_1 to x_t in Fig. 3) into both the encoder and decoder parts of the architecture. The output is the probability of the PGV surpassing the 15 cm/s threshold (the y_1 to y_t in Fig. 3).

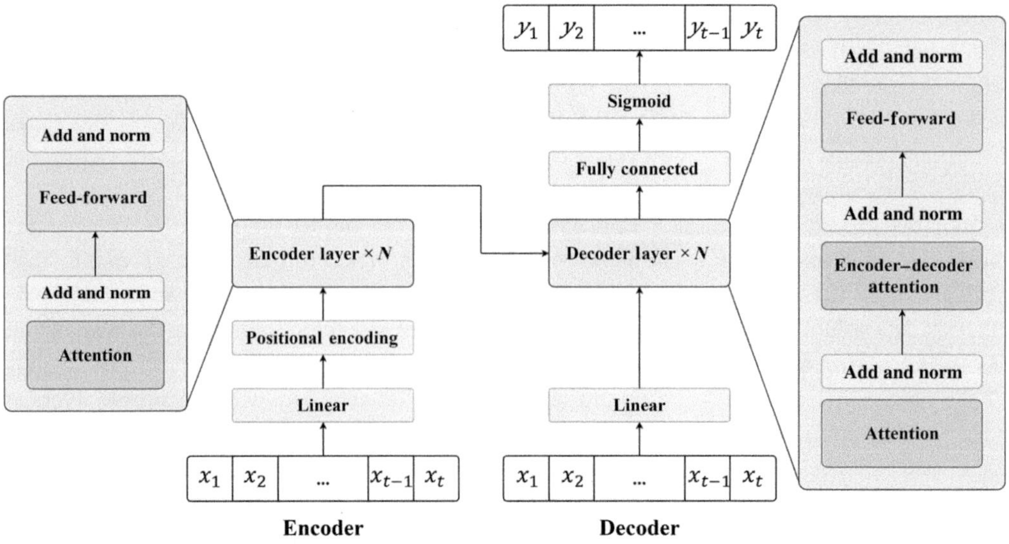

Figure 3. The proposed attention-based architecture. One encoder is on the left side, and one decoder is on the right side. The inputs are sequential seismic data $x_1 \ldots x_t$, in which the subscript denote the timesteps. The outputs are warning probabilities at every time steps $y_1 \ldots y_t$. The color version of this figure is available only in the electronic edition.

To reduce the computational complexity, we design our attention-based model to update every second, not every sampling period. For example, at $t = 2$, the model already knows the records from −1 to 1. Then we further input the records from 1 to 2. Now the model knows updated records from −1 to 2. Finally, the model will output a probability of the alert at $t = 2$. The prompt for calculating alert probability is once every second.

Results

Model score based on performance metrics

We use two metrics to evaluate performance. The first metric measures how good the alert classification is. In ML, the common used metrics are the precision and the recall, which depict the effect of type I and type II errors. They are defined as

$$\text{Precision} = \frac{\text{TP}}{\text{TP} + \text{FP}}, \quad (1)$$

$$\text{Recall} = \frac{\text{TP}}{\text{TP} + \text{FN}}, \quad (2)$$

in which TP denotes the true positive cases, FP denotes the false positive cases, and FN denotes the false-negative cases. To have a combined measure of the two types of errors, we used the F1-score. The F1-score is the harmonic mean of precision and recall, and it is defined as

$$\text{F1} = 2 \times \frac{\text{Precision} \times \text{Recall}}{\text{Precision} + \text{Recall}}. \quad (3)$$

The second metric assesses the effectiveness of the warnings. An effective warning should be issued early enough to provide the recipient with sufficient time for proper preparation. The effectiveness is commonly depicted through the lead time of the warnings, defined as the time difference between when the velocity exceeds the threshold and when the warning is issued. The lead time (T_{lead}) is defined as

$$T_{\text{lead}} = T_{V \geq 15\text{cm/s}} - T_{\text{alert}}, \quad (4)$$

in which $T_{V \geq 15\text{cm/s}}$ denotes the time when the velocity first exceeds 15 cm/s and T_{alert} denotes the time when the model issues alert.

Our goal is to identify a model that generates both accurate warnings and warnings issued as quickly as possible. To achieve this, we introduce a combined model score that incorporates both metrics (Wang *et al.*, 2022). The model score is defined as

$$\text{Model score} = 0.5 \times \text{PR(F1)} + 0.5 \times \text{PR(mean lead time)}, \quad (5)$$

in which the two metrics are normalized to a range of 0–100 based on their performance through a population of models with different hyperparameters and settings. The normalization is done by using percentile rank (PR), which is commonly used for student performance assessment in education (Crawford and Garthwaite, 2009). The 0.5 and 0.5 coefficients are assigned to give equal importance to both metrics. The highest attainable model score is 100, corresponding to the best possible F1-score and mean lead time. We acknowledge that there are other ways to combine different metrics into one single overall metric. Another possible approach is to use *t*-scores. However, we opted for the current design of the model score instead of *t*-scores because of the lack of normality in the distributions of both metrics.

Feature selection

Feature selection is a common practice in ML. The primary goal is to identify the features most relevant to the target variables. This process enhances model performance by eliminating irrelevant and redundant features. In this project, we adopt an exhaustive search method from the wrapper approach to determine the optimal combination of features. The dataset used in the feature selection are confined to the training dataset and the validation dataset.

We examine combinations of six types of features, including the following: three components of acceleration (A), three

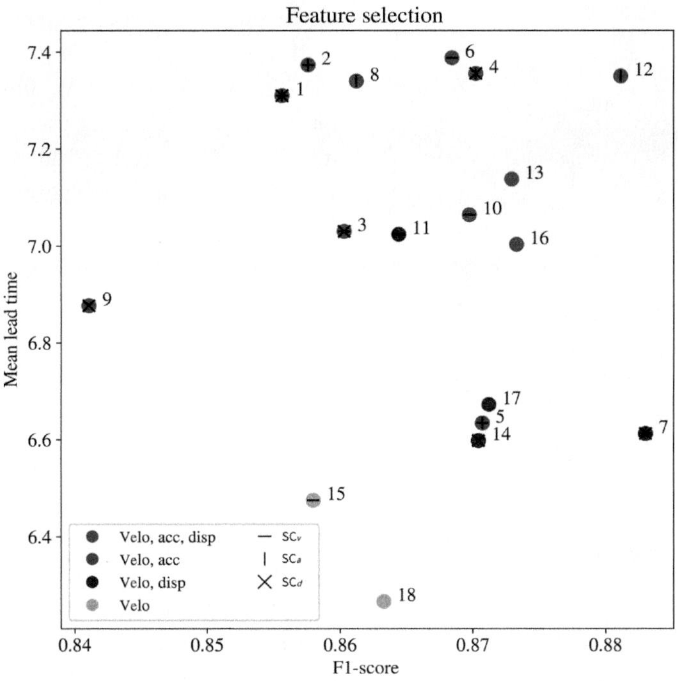

Figure 4. Distribution of performance using different subsets of features. The *x*-axis represents the F1-score, and the *y*-axis represents the lead time. A feature set with better performance corresponds to points located toward the upper-right corner of the figure. SC_a, the station correction of initial peak acceleration; SC_d, the station correction of initial peak displacement; SC_v, the station correction of initial peak velocity. The color version of this figure is available only in the electronic edition.

components of velocity (V), three components of displacement (D), station correction for initial peak acceleration (SC_a), station correction for initial peak velocity (SC_v), and station correction for initial peak displacement (SC_d).

Figure 4 presents the results of all the feature combinations considered. The figure indicates that the best F1-score performance is achieved when the model includes velocity, displacement, SC_v, and SC_d. Conversely, the best lead-time performance is observed when the model incorporates acceleration, velocity, displacement, and SC_v. Finally, the highest model score performance occurs when the model includes acceleration, velocity, and SC_a. The optimal feature combination for model score appears reasonable for several reasons: (1) it includes acceleration, which captures raw ground-motion data; (2) it incorporates velocity, a derivative of acceleration, which has also been used as a sensitivity modulator in previous studies; and (3) it includes station corrections to address the heterogeneity among *P*-alert stations. Notably, the selection of SC_a station correction reflects its compatibility with acceleration ground-motion data.

Hyperparameter selection

We use the same model score to select the hyperparameters for the architectures, including both the LSTM architecture and the attention-based architecture. The datasets used in the hyperparameter selection are confined to the training dataset and the validation dataset.

For attention-based architectures, we explore three aspects of hyperparameters: the dimension of the hidden layer, the scaling factor of the feedforward neural networks, and the number of layers in the encoder and decoder. Generally, the dimension of the hidden layer determines the resolution of the learned features; models with higher dimensions typically capture more details. Similarly, the scaling factor of the feedforward neural networks and the number of encoder and decoder layers influence the model's complexity. Although increased complexity often enhances performance, it also raises the risk of overfitting. After finding the model with the highest model score, we determined that the optimal hyperparameters are as follows:

1. Dimension of the hidden layer: 20
2. Scaling factor of the feedforward neural networks: 40
3. Number of layers in the encoder and decoder: 1

For LSTM architectures, we investigate three hyperparameter aspects: the number of hidden layers (N), the scaling ratio of dimensions between hidden layers (U), and the width factor of the final layers (i). The output dimension of the LSTM hidden layers is calculated as

$$\dim = U^{N+i}. \quad (6)$$

After evaluation, we identified the optimal hyperparameters as follows:

1. Number of hidden layers (N): 4
2. Scaling ratio of dimensions between layers (U): 2
3. Width factor of the final layers (i): 0

The performance of testing events

To ensure a fair performance assessment, we selected a testing dataset that is independent of both the training and validation datasets. The testing dataset comprises four medium to large events. Three of these events occurred on the eastern side of Taiwan, and one event took place on the western side. Notably, all the selected events have larger magnitudes because, otherwise, they would not produce ground motions with PGV > 15 cm/s.

We have selected four independent earthquake events in the testing dataset. These earthquakes represent four active seismic locations in Taiwan. The first event is the 2016 Meinong earthquake, which had a local magnitude of 6.6 and a PGA >400 gal. This earthquake caused the collapse of one building and damaged several others. The death toll was 117, making it the most destructive earthquake in Taiwan since the 1999 Jiji earthquake. The second event is the 2022 Hualien earthquake, with a local magnitude of 6.7. This earthquake caused damage to several

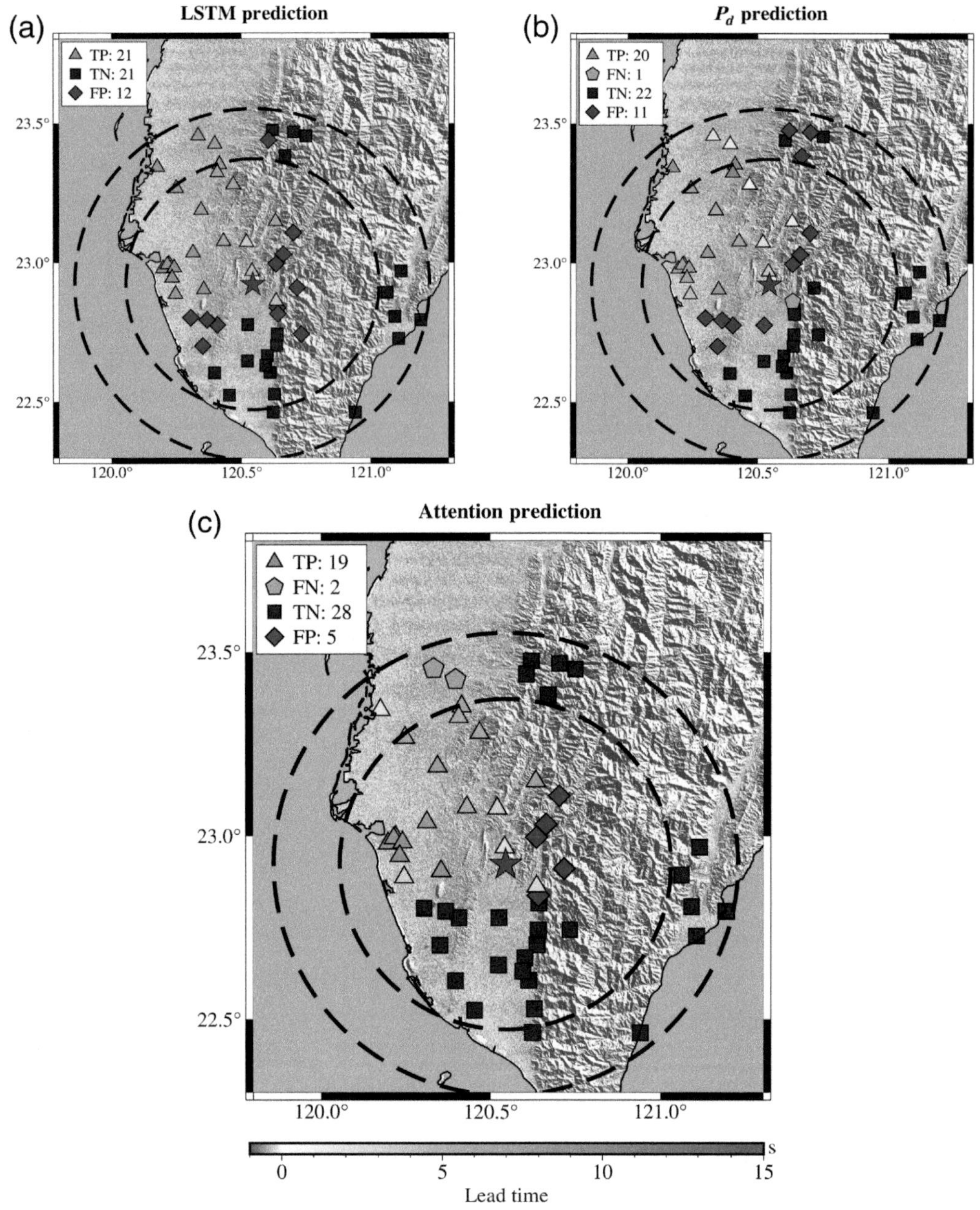

Figure 5. Earthquake early warning (EEW) performance for the 2016 Meinong earthquake. The triangles represent the true positive (TP) stations, with color fillings indicating the lead time. The squares represent the true negative (TN) stations. The diamonds represent the false positive (FP) stations. The pentagons represent the false negative (FN) stations. The two dashed circles around the epicenter (star) illustrate the 50 and 70 km radii around the epicenter. (a) The results of the long short-term memory (LSTM) model. (b) The results of the P_d method. (c) The results of the proposed attention-based model. The color version of this figure is available only in the electronic edition.

buildings, bridge failures, and gas leaks. The third event is the 2022 Guanshan earthquake, which had a local magnitude of 6.6. The fourth and final event is the 2022 Chishang earthquake, with a local magnitude of 6.8. The 2022 Guanshan earthquake is considered the largest foreshock of the 2022 Chishang earthquake. It is important to note that the last three events occurred outside the temporal scope of the training dataset, ensuring there is no data leakage. The first event was deliberately chosen to include a representative earthquake from western Taiwan. We combine all the records in all the testing events into one whole testing dataset, without extra weighting imposed.

Figure 5 illustrates the warning results for the 2016 Meinong earthquake. The triangle labeled TP represents stations with TP warnings, meaning that the PGV exceeds 15 cm/s, and the system successfully issues a warning. The color filling of the triangle indicates the lead time for each station. The pentagon labeled FN represents stations with FN warnings (missed alarms), in which the PGV exceeds 15 cm but the system fails to issue a warning. The square labeled TN represents stations with true negative warnings, indicating that the PGV does not exceed 15 cm and the system correctly does not issue a warning. The diamond labeled FP represents stations with FP warnings (false alarms), in which the PGV does not exceed 15 cm, yet the system still issues a warning. The F1-scores for the three models—attention-based model, LSTM model, and P_d method—are 0.844, 0.778, and 0.769, respectively. The mean lead times (arithmetic mean of the TP cases) for the three models are 5.95, 7.03, and 4.18 s, respectively. Notably, we examined all five FP cases in the attention-based model and found that they all exhibited PGA values exceeding 80 gal. These FP cases are considered challenging to classify because of the ambiguity between PGV-based and PGA-based intensity measures.

Figure 6 presents the warning results for the 2022 Hualien earthquake. The F1-scores for the three models—attention-based model, LSTM model, and P_d method—are 0.727, 0.586, and 0.692, respectively. The mean lead times (arithmetic mean of the TP cases) for the three models are 6.78, 7.12, and 5.62 s,

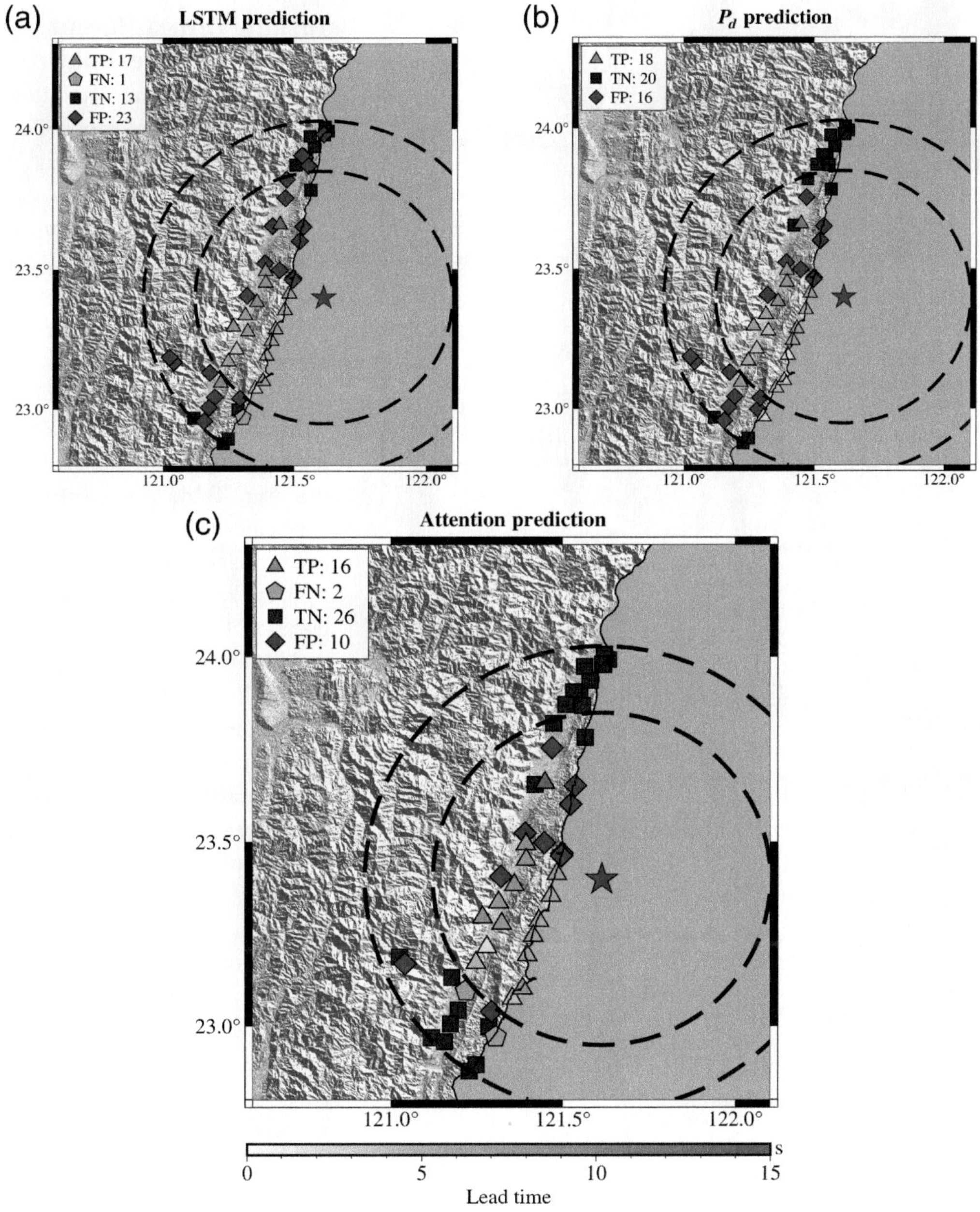

Figure 6. EEW performance for the 2022 Hualien earthquake. The triangles represent the TP stations, with color fillings indicating the lead time. The squares represent the TN stations. The diamonds represent the FP stations. The pentagons represent the FN stations. The two dashed circles around the epicenter (star) illustrate the 50 and 70 km radii around the epicenter. (a) The results of the LSTM model. (b) The results of the P_d method. (c) The results of the proposed attention-based model. The color version of this figure is available only in the electronic edition.

respectively. Among the 10 FP cases, 9 have PGA values ranging from ~100 to 400 gal.

Figure 7 illustrates the warning results for the 2022 Guanshan earthquake. The F1-scores of the three models—attention-based model, LSTM model, and P_d method—are 0.561, 0.469, and 0.511, respectively. The mean lead times (arithmetic mean of the TP cases) for the three models are 5.11, 5.33, and 5.42 s, respectively. We observe more TP cases in the south of the epicenter and more FP cases in the north of the epicenter. We think one possible explanation for the observation could be related to the empirical southward directivity seen in the evolution of the ShakeMap. The directivity effect (Doppler effect) enhances the shaking for records associated with incoming rupture. These larger initial signals are making themself more distinguishable from the noise, and it is thus easier to perform classification. This results in more true cases, including TPs. On the other hand, the records associated with outgoing rupture have smaller shaking. Those records are less distinguishable from the noise and thus more difficult to identify possible large PGVs.

Figure 8 presents the warning results for the 2022 Chishang earthquake. The F1-scores of the three models—attention-based model, LSTM model, and P_d method—are 0.756, 0.643, and 0.704, respectively. The mean lead times (arithmetic mean of the TP cases) for the three models are 8.26, 8.84, and 7.42 s, respectively. A close examination of the FN case for the attention-based model within 50 km reveals that this case is a "late bloomer." It takes 16.78 s to reach the 15 cm/s threshold after the *P*-wave arrival. Because our protocol only employs a 10 s window during training, this specific case highlights a limitation of the current approach. We believe this issue can be mitigated by incorporating longer training windows.

Table 1 presents the overall performance of the three methods across all four testing events. The overall F1-scores of the three models—attention-based model, LSTM model, and P_d method—are 0.694, 0.594, and 0.645, respectively. The overall mean lead times for the three models are 6.35, 6.97, and 5.68 s, respectively. Figure 9 illustrates the distributions of lead times. In summary, we find the improvement in the F1-score of the attention-based model to be significant. This model notably reduces the number

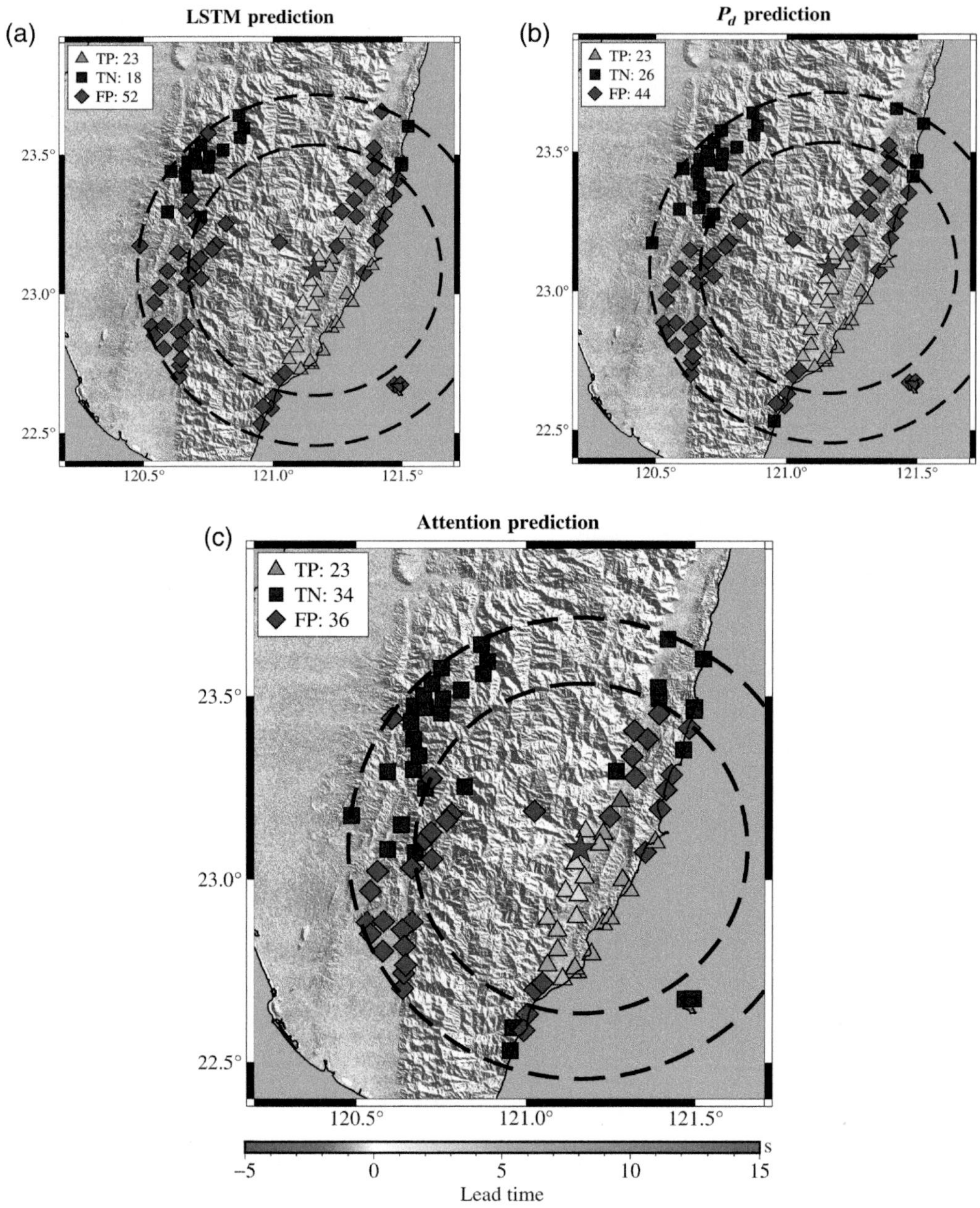

Figure 7. EEW performance for the 2022 Guanshan earthquake. The triangles represent the TP stations, with color fillings indicating the lead time. The squares represent the TN stations. The diamonds represent the FP stations. The pentagons represent the FN stations. The two dashed circles around the epicenter (star) illustrate the 50 and 70 km radii around the epicenter. (a) The results of the LSTM model. (b) The results of the P_d method. (c) The results of the proposed attention-based model. The color version of this figure is available only in the electronic edition.

of false alarms. Regarding lead time, both the LSTM model and the attention-based model perform well. The LSTM model slightly outperforms the attention-based model in lead time. However, the larger lead time and higher number of FP cases suggest that the LSTM model is more easily triggered.

Discussion

In this section, we discuss extra tests and their implications found in the proposed attention-based model.

Testing with different probability threshold

The output of the attention-based model is the probability of a large PGV, represented as a number between 0 and 1. By default, we set the probability threshold for issuing a warning to 0.5. When the probability of a large PGV exceeds 50% (0.5), the system issues a warning. This probability threshold is a metaparameter that can be adjusted by the user. Table 2 presents the performance results for different probability thresholds.

The results highlight the trade-off between the F1-score and lead time. Setting the probability threshold to higher values requires the model to have greater confidence before issuing a warning. Consequently, this increases the confirmation time but improves warning accuracy. In our metrics, this trade-off is evident: because the probability threshold increases, the F1-score improves while the lead time decreases. Conversely, lowering the probability threshold makes the model more sensitive to changes in ground motion. This reduces the confirmation time but compromises warning accuracy.

In practice, the optimal probability threshold can often be determined by identifying the "corner" of the trade-off curve—a common approach in seismic inversion. In our case, the corner of the trade-off curve is close to 0.6.

Testing with different composition subset of training datasets

Because of the scarcity of large PGV records in the *P*-alert network, we use the concept of transfer learning, building on the experience of a previous study, and incorporate large PGV records from events in Japan. This approach may raise concerns about the validity of using events from Japan. To address this,

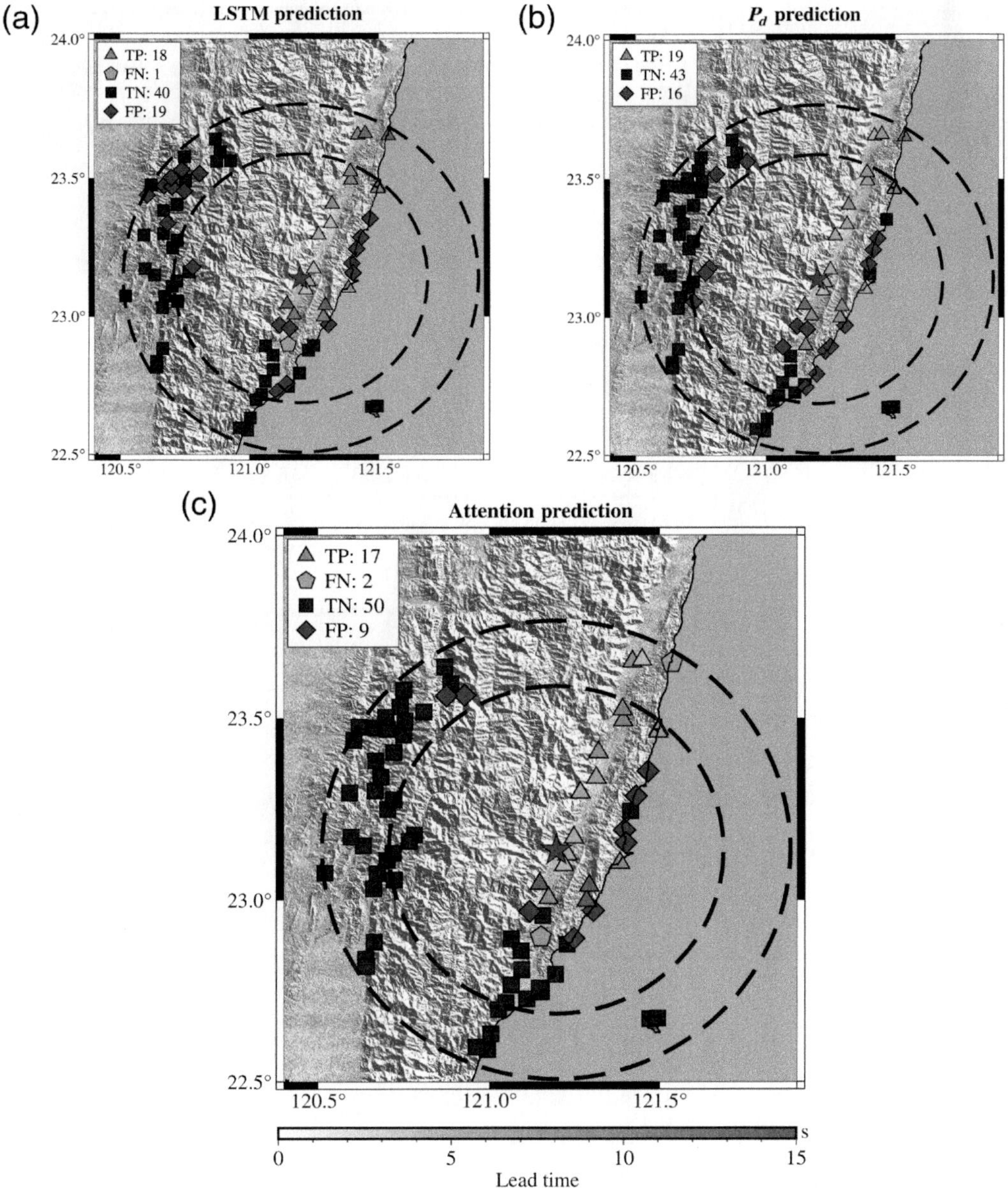

Figure 8. EEW performance for the 2022 Chishang earthquake. The triangles represent the TP stations, with color fillings indicating the lead time. The squares represent the TN stations. The diamonds represent the FP stations. The pentagons represent the FN stations. The two dashed circles around the epicenter (star) illustrate the 50 and 70 km radii around the epicenter. (a) The results of the LSTM model. (b) The results of the P_d method. (c) The results of the proposed attention-based model. The color version of this figure is available only in the electronic edition.

we conducted a sanity test by training the model using only events from Taiwan.

The results indicate that while the accuracy of the warnings increases, the lead time decreases. Specifically, the F1-score improves from 0.694 to 0.779, and the lead time reduces from 6.35 to 4.96 s. In terms of overall model performance, the model using transfer learning outperforms the model trained solely on events in Taiwan.

By comparing these results, we draw the following conclusions:

1. The optimal dataset for training would consist of all events in Taiwan with a sufficient number of large PGV records. However, the transfer learning strategy incorporating events from Japan proves to be a viable and effective alternative given the current limitations.
2. The improvement in the F1-score highlights differences in seismic records between Japan and Taiwan. Because all testing events are from Taiwan, a dataset with similar conditions allows the model to better capture the nuances of seismic records.
3. The reduction in lead time underscores the significant impact of a lack of large PGV records in the training dataset on the speed of recognition.

Testing with various shapes of label

In our proposed attention-based model and the LSTM model, we adopt the step-function label approach used in a previous study, in which the label reaches a probability of 1 at the *P*-wave arrival for all true records. Although this labeling choice pushes the limit of lead time, it raises concerns that the model may require additional time to make reliable decisions.

To investigate the effect of label shapes on performance, we trained the attention-based model using different label shapes and conducted comparisons. Figure 10 illustrates three alternative label shapes. The first label follows a sigmoid function. The second label adopts a similar pattern but saturates earlier. The third label follows a linear function.

The performance results reveal a trade-off tendency between the F1-score and lead time. Delaying the time at which the probability reaches 1 by 3 s generally increases the F1-score while reducing the lead time. Among the three label shapes, the linear

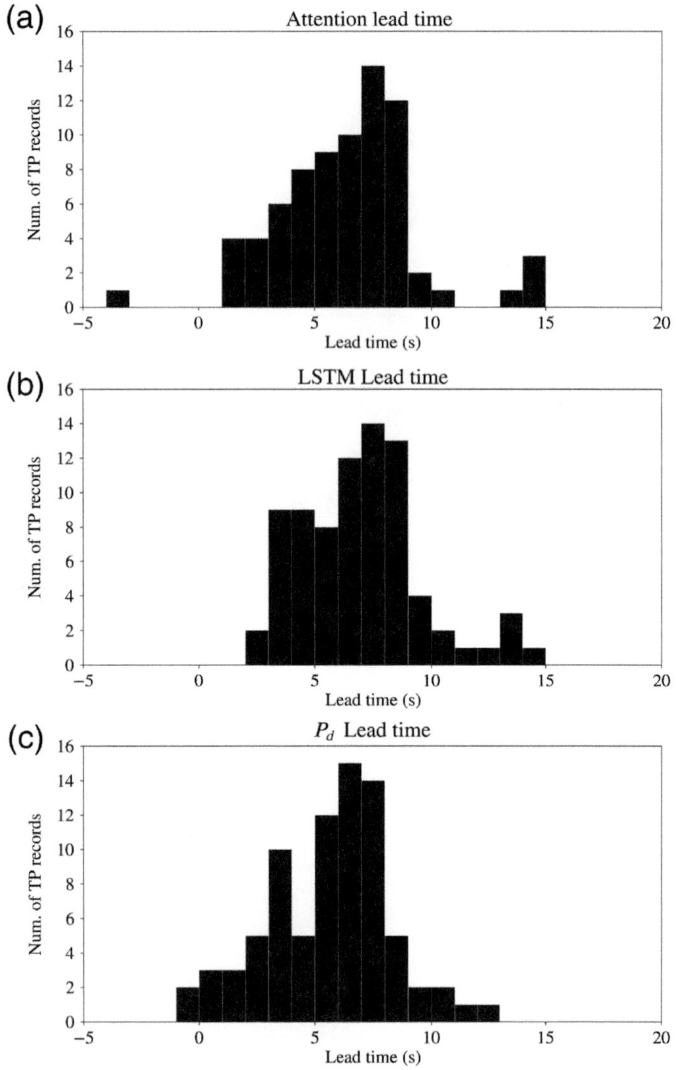

Figure 9. Lead time histogram of all three methods. (a) Results from the proposed attention-based model. (b) Results from the LSTM model. (c) Results from the P_d method. The color version of this figure is available only in the electronic edition.

TABLE 1
Performance Results of All Four Testing Events

	Attention	**LSTM**	P_d
TP	75	79	80
FN	6	2	1
TN	138	92	111
FP	60	106	87
Miss alarm rate	7.4%	2.5 %	1.2 %
False alarm rate	30.3%	53.5%	43.9%
F1-score	0.694	0.594	0.645
Mean lead time	6.35 ± 2.96	6.97 ± 2.64	5.68 ± 2.63

FN, false negative; FP, false positive; TN, true negative; TP, true positive.

TABLE 2
Performance Results with Different Threshold

Threshold	**F1-Score**	**Lead Time**
0.1	0.576	7.36 ± 2.69
0.2	0.619	7.16 ± 2.54
0.3	0.653	6.87 ± 2.62
0.4	0.679	6.76 ± 2.69
0.5	0.694	6.35 ± 2.96
0.6	0.706	6.04 ± 3.15
0.7	0.731	5.39 ± 3.42
0.8	0.762	5.06 ± 3.04
0.9	0.763	3.66 ± 2.96

label achieves the highest F1-score (0.764) but also the shortest lead time (4.35 s). The second label (early saturation) has the longest lead time (5.67 s) but a comparatively lower F1-score. In terms of overall model performance, the best label is the first label (sigmoid-shaped increasing function), which achieves a balanced F1-score (0.72) and lead time (5.24 s). However, none of the alternative labels surpass the original step-function label in terms of model score.

Based on these results, we offer the following observations:

1. The original step-function-at-arrival label is validated as an effective choice within the context of our model because it achieves a balanced trade-off between the F1-score and lead time.
2. Just as model performance can reveal the best feature sets, identifying the optimal label shape may also enhance our understanding of how the credibility of EEW systems evolves over time because the label is a sequential of probabilities for warning. For instance, one could investigate the ideal label shape to maximize the F1-score while maintaining fixed values at both endpoints (0.5 at 0 s and 1.0 at 3 s).
3. Among the three alternative labels, we think the linear label corresponds more closely to real-world scenarios of credibility changes over time, owing to its superior F1-score.

Testing on adding noise and changing epicenter criterion in training dataset

Finally, we tested two possible modulations of the training dataset selection. The first involves expanding the dataset with additional noise records. The performance results show a marginal increase in the F1-score (0.696) and a moderate increase in lead time (6.78 s). Overall, we observed an improvement in the model score.

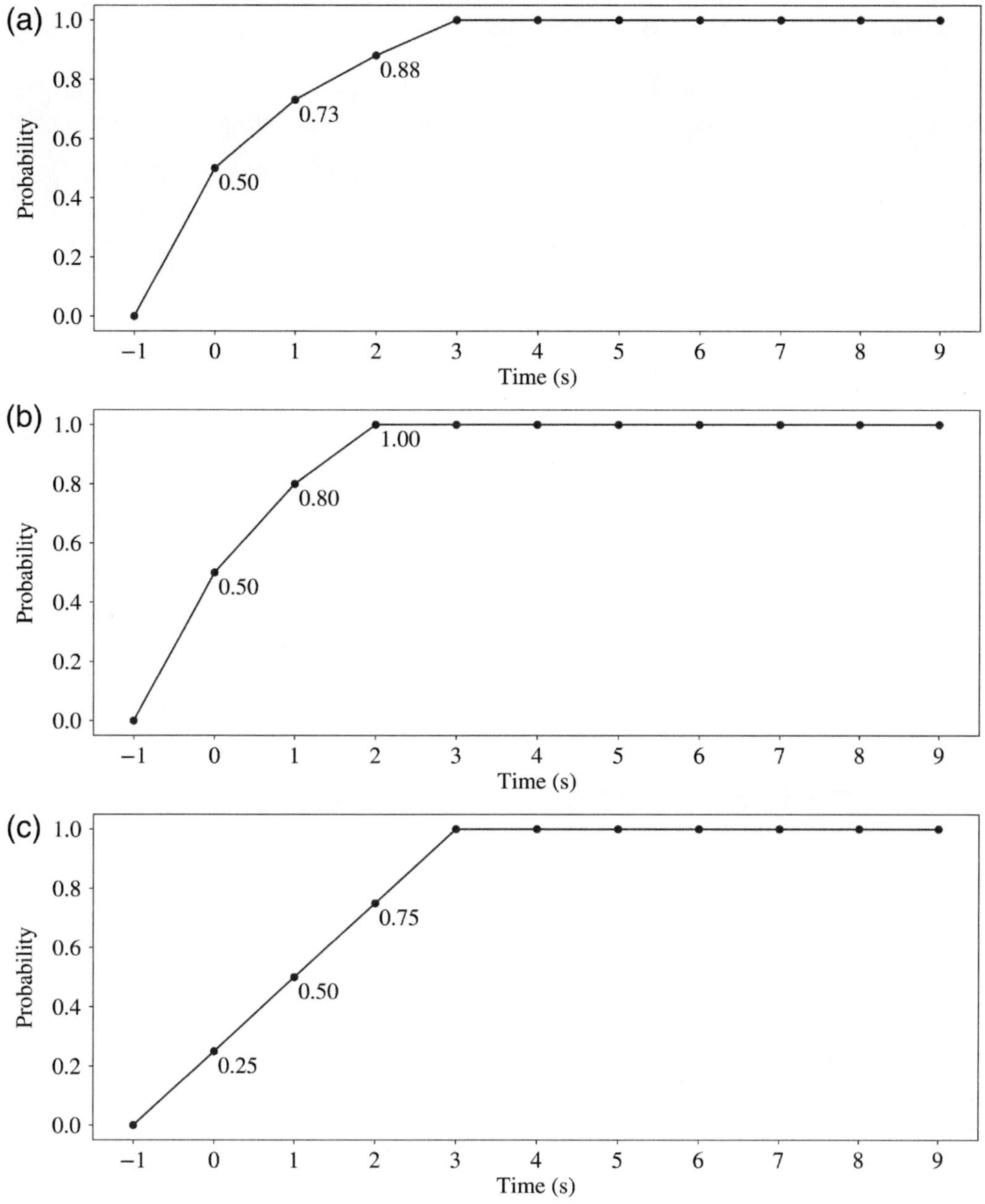

Figure 10. (a–c) Various shapes of labels used in the discussion. The color version of this figure is available only in the electronic edition.

The second approach involves increasing the dataset by relaxing the record selection criterion for the epicenter. Specifically, the new dataset includes records that were previously excluded for being too far from the epicenter. The performance results show an increase in the F1-score (0.712) but a notable decrease in lead time (5.74 s).

In summary, we believe that enlarging the current training dataset with noise records from the *P*-alert stations can be beneficial. This approach may help the model better capture detailed features hidden within the records. However, adding excessive noise records to the training dataset could exacerbate the existing data imbalance problem.

Performance difference between onsite PGV and onsite PGA

Compared with the previous study on onsite PGA ML, we observed that the overall performance is lower for onsite PGV. We believe there are two main reasons for this performance difference. The primary reason is the lack of TP records for large PGV. Specifically, there are relatively few records exceeding 15 cm/s in the *P*-alert dataset, which likely impacts the classification performance. The second reason relates to the nature of velocity evolution over time. We have identified a significantly higher number of "late bloomer"—records that start with mild motion but gradually exhibit more substantial velocity at later times. This phenomenon can occasionally confuse the trained ML model. Interestingly, the "late bloomers" are less observed in the PGA dataset.

Limitations

In the testing events, we only use the records with normal behavior. These are records without missing data and abnormal data. The proposed model cannot properly issue alerts with abnormal records. The proposed model might give unpredictable results.

Another limitation lies in the bias in the training dataset regarding the types of seismic sources the events have. Because of the rarity of the large PGV records, the corresponding events are also limited. The trained model could potentially have worse alert performance if the records come from events with very different source parameters, including source mechanisms, rupture dynamics, source depths, and so forth.

Computational specification

The ML training was conducted on a server equipped with an NVIDIA Tesla T4 Tensor Core graphic processing units. The Tesla T4 features 2560 CUDA cores and 16 GB of RAM.

Subsequently, we present some benchmarks for ML performance using the Tesla T4. For a one-layer attention mechanism architecture, the training time is ~1.5 hr, with each epoch taking about 100–110 s. In contrast, for a four-layer LSTM architecture, the training time is significantly shorter at around 20 min, with each epoch taking ~6–8 s.

Conclusions

In this project, we adopt an attention-based neural network to address the onsite PGV EEW problem. The attention-based architecture demonstrates its feasibility in delivering fast and reliable early warnings based on the eventual PGV. Our findings indicate a noticeable improvement in the accuracy of onsite PGV predictions using the attention-based model. The mean lead time is slightly better than the LSTM model. In addition, the feature selection results highlight the importance of station corrections in accounting for the inhomogeneity of stations.

Furthermore, we have explored the optimized label for achieving the best performance. We think the optimized label illustrates how the credibility of EEW grows over time, potentially providing an alternative approach to assessing the validity of EEW systems.

We believe that our prototype attention-based model can contribute to the future development of onsite EEW systems. In addition, our project raises several novel interesting questions for future exploration. For instance, what is the most suitable architecture for the PGV EEW problem? What are the common characteristics of optimized labels? How should we define the best model? What makes the most reasonable model score?

Data and Resources

The strong-motion waveform records from the *P*-alert networks can be downloaded at http://palert.earth.sinica.edu.tw/db/. The strong-motion waveform records from the Kyoshin net (K-NET) networks can be downloaded at National Research Institute for Earth Science and Disaster Resilience website https://www.kyoshin.bosai.go.jp/kyoshin, doi: 10.17598/NIED.0004. All websites were last accessed in June 2025.

Declaration of Competing Interests

The authors acknowledge that there are no conflicts of interest recorded.

Acknowledgments

This work was supported by the Ministry of Science and Technology (MOST) of Taiwan under MOST 106-2116-M-002-019-MY3 and MOST 109-2116-M-002-030-MY3. T. C. H. thanks Lily Wong for her hospitality during the making of the article. T. C. H. initiated the project, developed the machine learning (ML) model, and wrote the article. T. L. L. conducted the data analysis, trained and tested the ML, and developed the code for processing. T. C. H. and T. L. L. share the first authorship of this article. B. M. Y. trained and tested the ML and supported the hardware of the server. Y. M. W. supervised this work and advised. All authors discussed the training results and contributed to the final article.

References

Allen, R. M., P. Gasparini, O. Kamigaichi, and M. Bose (2009). The status of earthquake early warning around the world: An introductory overview, *Seismol. Res. Lett.* **80,** 682–693, doi: 10.1785/gssrl.80.5.682.

Bahdanau, D., K. Cho, and Y. Bengio (2015). Neural machine translation by jointly learning to align and translate, *Proc. of the 3rd International Conf. on Learning Representations (ICLR)*, San Diego, California, 7–9 May 2015.

Brown, T., B. Mann, N. Ryder, M. Subbiah, J. D. Kaplan, P. Dhariwal, A. Neelakantan, P. Shyam, G. Sastry, A. Askell, *et al.* (2020). Language models are few-shot learners, *Advances in Neural Information Processing Systems*, Vol. 33, 1877–1901.

Chandrakumar, C., M. L. Tan, C. Holden, M. Stephens, A. Punchihewa, and R. Prasanna (2024). Estimating S-wave amplitude for earthquake early warning in New Zealand: Leveraging the first 3 seconds of P-wave, *Earth Sci. Inf.* **17**, 4527–4554, doi: 10.1007/s12145-024-01403-6.

Cho, K., B. van Merrienboer, C. Gulcehre, D. Bahdanau, F. Bougares, H. Schwenk, and Y. Bengio (2014). Learning phrase representations using RNN encoder-decoder for statistical machine translation, 1724–1734.

Crawford, J. R., and P. H. Garthwaite (2009). Percentiles please: The case for expressing neuropsychological test scores and accompanying confidence limits as percentile ranks, *Clin. Neuropsychol.* **23,** no. 2, 193–204, doi: 10.1080/13854040801968450.

Fan, J., C. Sun, C. Chen, X. Jiang, X. Liu, X. Zhao, L. Meng, C. Dai, and W. Chen (2020). EEG data augmentation: Towards class imbalance problem in sleep staging tasks, *J. Neural Eng.* **17,** 056017, doi: 10.1088/1741-2552/abb5be.

Gers, F. A., N. N. Schraudolph, and J. Schmidhuber (2002). Learning precise timing with lstm recurrent networks, *J. Machine Learn. Res.* **3,** no. 1, 115–143, doi: 10.1162/153244303768966139.

Hochreiter, S., and J. Schmidhuber (1997). Long short-term memory, *Neural Comput.* **9,** no. 8, 1735–1780, doi: 10.1162/neco.1997.9.8.1735.

Hsieh, C. Y., W. A. Chao, and Y. M. Wu (2015). An examination of the threshold-based earthquake early warning approach using a low-cost seismic network, *Seismol. Res. Lett.* **86**, 1664–1667, doi: 10.1785/0220150073.

Huang, T.-C., and Y.-M. Wu (2019). A robust algorithm for automatic P-wave arrival-time picking based on the local extrema scalogram, *Bull. Seismol. Soc. Am.* **109,** no. 1, 413–423, doi: 10.1785/0120180127.

Huang, T.-C., and Y.-M. Wu (2021). Revisiting M_L determination in Taiwan based on the expectation-maximization algorithm, *J. Seismol.* **25,** 1077–1087, doi: 10.1007/s10950-021-10013-4.

Huang, T.-C., and Y.-M. Wu (2023a). Improving earthquake early warning initial peak ground motion magnitude estimation with station corrections: A case study using the P-alert network in Taiwan, *J. Earthq. Eng.* **28,** no. 6, 1532–1551, doi: 10.1080/13632469.2023.2245498.

Huang, T.-C., and Y.-M. Wu (2023b). Revisiting the initial peak P-wave displacement and the ground motion characteristic period with signal-to-noise ratios: A case study using a low-cost sensor network in Taiwan, *J. Earthq. Eng.* **27,** no. 16, 4694–4704, doi: 10.1080/13632469.2023.2190416.

Kamigaichi, O., M. Saito, K. Doi, T. Matsumori, S. Tsukada, K. Takeda, T. Shimoyama, K. Nakamura, M. Kiyomoto, and Y.

Watanabe (2009). Earthquake early warning in Japan: Warning the general public and future prospects, *Seismol. Res. Lett.* **80,** no. 5, 717–726, doi: 10.1785/gssrl.80.5.717.

Li, Z., M. A. Meier, E. Hauksson, Z. Zhan, and J. Andrews (2018). machine learning seismic wave discrimination: Application to earthquake early warning, *Geophys. Res. Lett.* **45,** 4773–4779, doi: 10.1029/2018GL077870.

Liu, P.-H., and J.-H. Wu (2024). New methodology for assessing seismic ground vulnerability based on microtremor and Taiwan seismic intensity scale, *J. Earthq. Eng.* doi: 10.1080/13632469.2024.2415992.

Luong, M. T., H. Pham, and C. D. Manning (2015). Effective approaches to attention-based neural machine translation, *Proc. of the 2015 Conf. on Empirical Methods in Natural Language Processing (EMNLP),* 1412–1421.

Mittal, H., B. M. Yang, T. L. Tseng, and Y. M. Wu (2021). Importance of real-time PGV in terms of lead-time and shakemaps: Results using 2018 M_L 6.2 and 2019 M_L 6.3 Hualien, Taiwan earthquakes, *J. Asian Earth Sci.* **220,** 104936, doi: 10.1016/j.jseaes.2021.104936.

Mousavi, S. M., and G. C. Beroza (2020). A machine-learning approach for earthquake magnitude estimation, *Geophys. Res. Lett.* **47,** e2019GL085976, doi: 10.1029/2019GL085976.

Satriano, C., Y. M. Wu, A. Zollo, and H. Kanamori (2011). Earthquake early warning: Concepts, methods and physical grounds, *Soil Dynam. Earthq. Eng.* **31,** no. 2, 687–719, doi: 10.1016/j.soildyn.2010.07.007.

Sun, Y., A. K. Wong, and M. S. Kamel (2009). Classification of imbalanced data: A review, *Int. J. Pattern Recognit. Artif. Intell.* **23,** no. 4, 687–719, doi: 10.1142/S0218001409007326.

Sutskever, I., O. Vinyals, and Q. V. Le (2014). Sequence to sequence learning with neural networks, *Advances in Neural Information Processing System,* Vol. 2, 3104–3112.

Thabtah, F., S. Hammoud, F. Kamalov, and A. Gonsalves (2020). Data imbalance in classification: Experimental evaluation, *Inform. Sci.* **513,** 429–441, doi: 10.1016/j.ins.2019.11.004.

Vaiciulyte, S., D. A. Novelo-Casanova, and A. L. Husker (2024). Demystifying response to eew in Mexico: Socio-technical motivations in protective action, *Saf. Sci.* **174,** 106469, doi: 10.1016/j.ssci.2024.106469.

Vaswani, A., N. Shazeer, N. Parmar, J. Uszkoreit, L. Jones, A. N. Gomez, L. Kaiser, and I. Polosukhin (2017). Attention is all you need, *Advances in Neural Information Processing Systems,* Vol. 30, 5998–6008.

Wald, D. J. (2020). Practical limitations of earthquake early warning, *Earthq. Spectra* **36,** no. 3, 1412–1447, doi: 10.1177/8755293020911388.

Wang, C.-Y., T.-C. Huang, and Y.-M. Wu (2022). Using LSTM neural networks for onsite earthquake early warning, *Seismol. Res. Lett.* **93,** 814–826, doi: 10.1785/0220210197.

Wu, N., B. Green, X. Ben, and S. O'Banion (2020). Deep transformer models for time series forecasting: The influenza prevalence case, *Proc. of the 37th International Conf. on Machine Learning,* Vienna, Austria, 13–18 July 2020.

Wu, Y. M., and H. Kanamori (2005). Rapid assessment of damage potential of earthquakes in Taiwan from the beginning of P waves, *Bull. Seismol. Soc. Am.* **95,** no. 3, 1181–1185, doi: 10.1785/0120040193.

Wu, Y. M., and H. Mittal (2021). A review on the development of earthquake warning system using low-cost sensors in Taiwan, *Sensors* **21,** 7649, doi: 10.3390/s21227649.

Wu, Y.-M., and L. Zhao (2006). Magnitude estimation using the first three seconds P-wave amplitude in earthquake early warning, *Geophys. Res. Lett.* **33,** no. 16, L16312, doi: 10.1029/2006GL026871.

Wu, Y. M., N. C. Hsiao, and T. L. Teng (2004). Relationships between strong ground motion peak values and seismic loss during the 1999 Chi-Chi, Taiwan earthquake, *Nat. Hazards* **32,** 357–373, doi: 10.1023/B:NHAZ.0000035550.36929.d0.

Wu, Y.-M., Y.-H. Lin, B. M. Yang, and S.-S. Ke (2025). Performance of the P-alert real-time shakemaps system and onsite warning during the 2025 M_L 6.4 Dapu earthquake, *Terr. Atmos. Ocean. Sci.* **36,** no. 3, doi: 10.1007/s44195-025-00086-w.

Wu, Y. M., T. L. Teng, T. C. Shin, and N. C. Hsiao (2003). Relationship between peak ground acceleration, peak ground velocity, and intensity in Taiwan, *Bull. Seismol. Soc. Am.* **93,** no. 1, 386–396, doi: 10.1785/0120020097.

Yamaguchi, N., and F. Yamazaki (2001). Estimation of strong motion distribution in the 1995 Kobe earthquake based on building damage data, *Earthq. Eng. Struct. Dynam.* **30,** no. 6, 787–801, doi: 10.1002/eqe.33.

Yang, B. M., H. Mittal, and Y.-M. Wu (2021). Real-time production of PGA, PGV, intensity, and Sa Shakemaps using dense MEMS-based sensors in Taiwan, *Sensors* **21,** no. 3, 943, doi: 10.3390/s21030943.

Zhang, X., M. Zhang, and X. Tian (2021). Real-time earthquake early warning with deep learning: Application to the 2016 M 6.0 Central Apennines, Italy earthquake, *Geophys. Res. Lett.* **48,** 2020GL089394, doi: 10.1029/2020GL089394.

Manuscript received 30 December 2024
Published online 1 August 2025

Reducing Frequency Bias of Fourier Neural Operators in 3D Seismic Wavefield Simulations Through Multistage Training

Qingkai Kong*[1], Caifeng Zou[2], Youngsoo Choi[1], Eric M. Matzel[1], Kamyar Azizzadenesheli[3], Zachary E. Ross[2], Arthur J. Rodgers[1], and Robert W. Clayton[2]

Abstract

The recent development of neural operator (NeurOp) learning for solutions to the elastic wave equation shows promising results and provides the basis for fast large-scale simulations for different seismological applications. In this article, we use the Fourier neural operator (FNO) model to directly solve the 3D Helmholtz wave equation for fast seismic ground-motion simulations on different frequencies and show the frequency bias of the FNO model, that is, it learns the lower frequencies better comparing to the higher frequencies. To reduce the frequency bias, we adopt the multistage FNO training, that is, after training a stage 1 FNO model for estimating the ground motion, we use a second FNO model as the stage 2 to learn from the residual, which greatly reduced the errors on the higher frequencies. By adopting this multistage training, the FNO models show reduced biases on higher frequencies, which enhanced the overall results of the ground-motion simulations. Thus the multistage training FNO improves the accuracy and realism of the ground-motion simulations.

Cite this article as Kong, Q., C. Zou, Y. Choi, E. M. Matzel, K. Azizzadenesheli, Z. E. Ross, A. J. Rodgers, and R. W. Clayton (2025). Reducing Frequency Bias of Fourier Neural Operators in 3D Seismic Wavefield Simulations Through Multistage Training, *Seismol. Res. Lett.* **97**, 272–282, doi: 10.1785/0220250085.

Introduction

Partial differential equations (PDEs) play an important role in scientific and engineering simulations to help scientists understand complex physical systems or processes. Few of them can have analytical solutions, thus many numerical methods are developed to approximate the solutions, such as finite-difference, finite element, finite volume methods, spectral element methods and so on (Evans *et al.*, 2012; Simmons, 2016). Many of the numerical methods discretize both space and time demanding high-resolution grids to achieve an accurate solution. Therefore, even with the aid of high-performance computing (HPC), the heavy computational costs prohibit some applications, such as uncertainty quantifications that rely on the generation of many simulations, real-time applications that require fast simulations, and so on.

Recent efforts on using the neural-network-based approaches to speed up the simulations show promising results over the traditional numerical solvers (Greenfeld *et al.*, 2019; Blechschmidt and Ernst, 2021; Kasim *et al.*, 2021). More recently, a type of new data-driven approach called neural operators (NeurOps) emerged as a great tool to solve PDEs. Compared to the neural-network-based approaches, the NeurOp-based models can learn the mapping between infinite dimensional function spaces, thus achieving mesh independence, that is, trained models with the same parameters can be applied on different discretizations (Li *et al.*, 2020a,b; Kovachki, Li, *et al.*, 2021). In particular, the Fourier neural operator (FNO) and its variants demonstrated both computational efficiency as well as good accuracy in solving various PDEs compared to the numerical methods based on HPC (Li *et al.*, 2020a; Kovachki, Lanthaler, and Mishra, 2021; Kovachki, Li, *et al.*, 2021; Azizzadenesheli *et al.*, 2024; Tang *et al.*, 2024; Choy *et al.*, 2025;). For example, Wen *et al.* (2023) uses a nested FNO model for real-time CO_2 geological storage prediction and achieves a speedup of 700,000 times compared to existing numerical solvers. The FourCastNet (Kurth *et al.*, 2023), which utilizes an adaptive FNO model, achieves a speed of up to 10,000 times in global weather forecasting. Furthermore, the mesh-independent property allows the

1. Lawrence Livermore National Laboratory, Livermore, California, U.S.A., https://orcid.org/0000-0001-8797-7970 (YC); https://orcid.org/0000-0002-6784-5695 (AJR); 2. Seismological Laboratory, California Institute of Technology, Pasadena, California, U.S.A., https://orcid.org/0000-0001-9445-7594 (CZ); https://orcid.org/0000-0002-6343-8400 (ZER); https://orcid.org/0000-0003-3323-3508 (RWC); 3. Nvidia, Santa Clara, California, U.S.A., https://orcid.org/0000-0001-8507-1868 (KA)

*Corresponding author: kong11@llnl.gov

trained FNO model to evaluate solutions on higher resolution grids than the training resolution grids.

A similar trend appears in the field of seismology. The seismic-wave propagations in 3D Earth media that are governed by the wave equations can be solved by numerical methods with heavy computational cost (Igel, 2017). Therefore, machine learning approaches are developed as surrogate models to speed up the simulations (Karimpouli and Tahmasebi, 2020; Moseley *et al.*, 2020; Song and Wang, 2022; Tamhidi *et al.*, 2022; Song *et al.*, 2023). Recently, efforts to use the NeurOp-based models show promising results in solving the wave equations (Yang *et al.*, 2021, 2023; Sun *et al.*, 2022; Wei and Fu, 2022; Li *et al.*, 2023; Shi *et al.*, 2024) both in the acoustic and elastic version, but due to the computational cost as well as the graphic processing units (GPU) memory usage limitation, most of these are on relatively small scales or 2D problems. There are also efforts to use the NeurOps on 3D problems (Kong and Rodgers, 2023; Lehmann *et al.*, 2024) in the time domain, as well as to decompose the seismic wavefield into the frequency domain using the Helmholtz equations to overcome the memory required for the 3D time domain equations (Zou *et al.*, 2024).

Meanwhile, the machine learning communities identified many of the neural network models that share the limitation of the frequency biases (Rahaman *et al.*, 2019; Xu *et al.*, 2019, 2024), which show that the neural networks are good at learning low frequencies yet struggle in learning high frequencies. Even the FNO models show similar frequency bias in solving the Navier–Stokes and Darcy equations (Qin *et al.*, 2024). Different approaches are proposed to reduce this bias, and multistage training shows promising results on neural networks as well as FNO models (Qin *et al.*, 2024; Wang and Lai, 2024). In this article, we show that frequency biases also exist with FNO models in solving 3D seismic-wave equations. Inspired by Qin *et al.* (2024) and Wang and Lai (2024), we used multistage training, specifically similar to the so-called spectral-boosted FNO (Qin *et al.*, 2024) to reduce discrepancies in learning the high frequencies. We show an improvement in the overall performance of FNO models, either to train the model with different frequencies, or one FNO model for each individual frequency, in the forward modeling. Meanwhile, we also show the potential improvement of the inversion of subsurface structure imaging as well.

Methods

Elastic wave equations

The propagation of the waves in the elastic media is governed by the second-order hyperbolic elastic wave equations. The 3D time-domain wave equation can be transformed to the Fourier domain and solve as a set of Helmholtz equations:

$$\begin{aligned}
&\omega^2\rho U_x+\frac{\partial}{\partial x}\left[\lambda\left(\frac{\partial U_x}{\partial x}+\frac{\partial U_y}{\partial y}+\frac{\partial U_z}{\partial z}\right)+2\mu\frac{\partial U_x}{\partial x}\right]\\
&+\frac{\partial}{\partial y}\left[\mu\left(\frac{\partial U_x}{\partial y}+\frac{\partial U_y}{\partial x}\right)\right]+\frac{\partial}{\partial z}\left[\mu\left(\frac{\partial U_x}{\partial z}+\frac{\partial U_z}{\partial x}\right)\right]+F_x\\
&=0,\omega^2\rho U_y\ +\frac{\partial}{\partial y}\left[\lambda\left(\frac{\partial U_x}{\partial x}+\frac{\partial U_y}{\partial y}+\frac{\partial U_z}{\partial z}\right)+2\mu\frac{\partial U_y}{\partial y}\right]\\
&+\frac{\partial}{\partial x}\left[\mu\left(\frac{\partial U_x}{\partial y}+\frac{\partial U_y}{\partial x}\right)\right]+\frac{\partial}{\partial z}\left[\mu\left(\frac{\partial U_y}{\partial z}+\frac{\partial U_z}{\partial y}\right)\right]+F_y\\
&=0,\omega^2\rho U_z+\frac{\partial}{\partial z}\left[\lambda\left(\frac{\partial U_x}{\partial x}+\frac{\partial U_y}{\partial y}+\frac{\partial U_z}{\partial z}\right)+2\mu\frac{\partial U_z}{\partial z}\right]\\
&+\frac{\partial}{\partial x}\left[\mu\left(\frac{\partial U_x}{\partial z}+\frac{\partial U_z}{\partial x}\right)\right]+\frac{\partial}{\partial y}\left[\mu\left(\frac{\partial U_y}{\partial z}+\frac{\partial U_z}{\partial y}\right)\right]+F_z=0,
\end{aligned} \tag{1}$$

in which ρ is the material density, ω is the angular frequency, and $\hat{U}_i$ and $\hat{F}_i (i = x,y,z)$ are the displacements and body forces in the frequency domain, respectively. λ and μ are the Lamé parameter and shear modulus related to the medium properties, which they can be linked to the *P*- and *S*-wave velocities through the following relationship:

$$\alpha = \sqrt{\frac{\lambda + 2\mu}{\rho}}, \qquad \beta = \sqrt{\frac{\mu}{\rho}}. \tag{2}$$

Multistage FNO structure and training setup

We mainly used the original FNO model developed in Li *et al.* (2021), which is shown mathematically as a universal approximator for any arbitrary nonlinear continuous operators (Kovachki, Lanthaler, and Mishra, 2021). The FNO model has the property of learning the mappings between infinite-dimensional function spaces, a key difference to the traditional neural network, which only maps finite-dimensional vector spaces. Thus, in the context of solving a PDE, the FNO $\mathcal{G}_\theta$ attempts to learn a mapping between the input field $\mathcal{A}$ that usually consists of a function space containing coefficients, initial or boundary conditions of the PDE and the coordinates as the features, and a function space $\mathcal{U}$ containing the output of the PDE

$$\mathcal{G}_\theta : \mathcal{A} \rightarrow \mathcal{U}, \tag{3}$$

in which θ is the parameterization of the FNO model that can be learned through the training. Figure 1 broadly sketches the experimental setup for this study.

As a neural network, the FNO model uses an iterative architecture to learn this mapping. The model first lifts the input function $a(x)$, in which it includes equation coefficients, initial or boundary conditions, forcing, grids, and so on, via a P operator into higher dimension space, which can be achieved by pointwise transformation on each point along the feature dimension. This lifted space subsequently passes through a series of FNO layers until a Q operator to project it back to

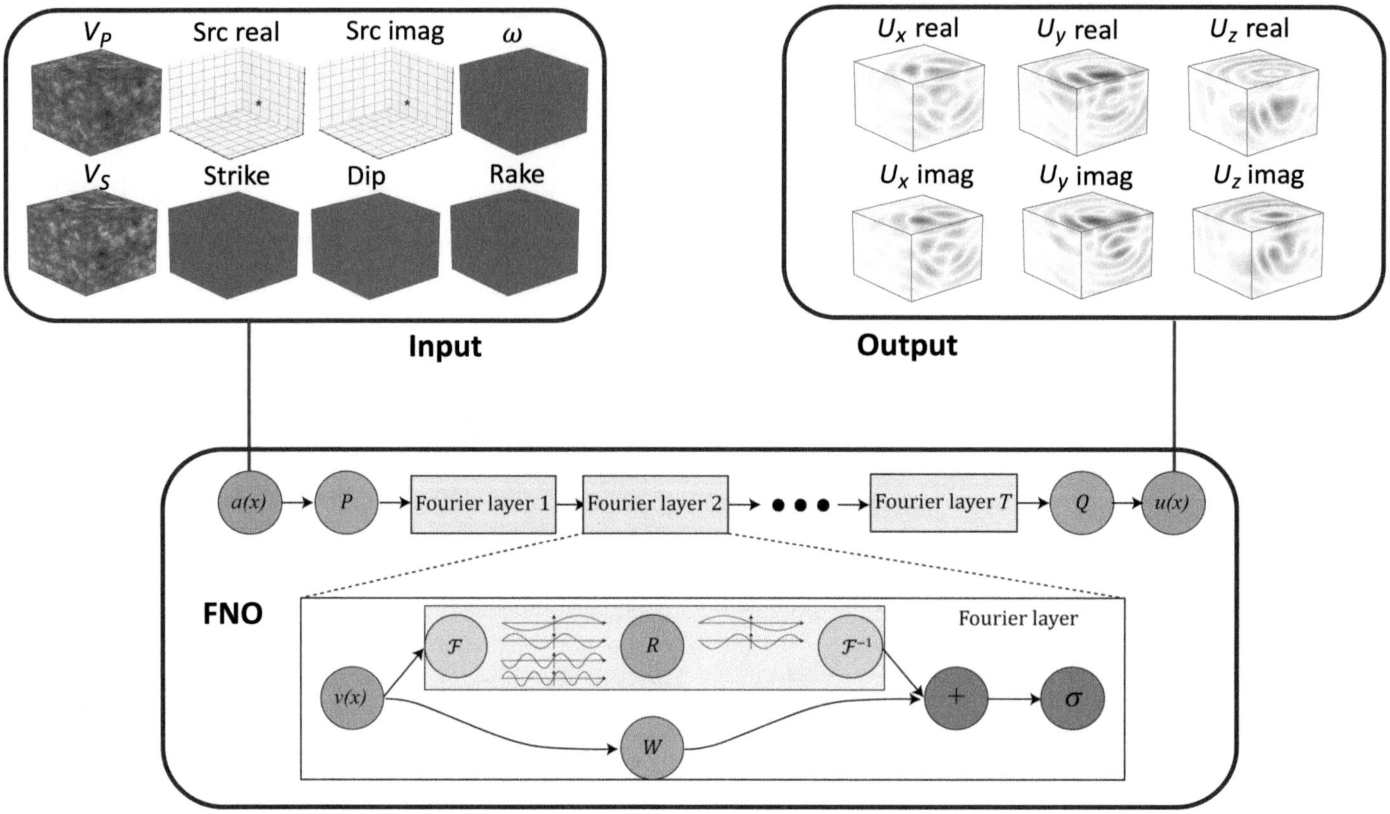

Figure 1. Fourier neural operator (FNO) model for seismic forward simulation. The 3D *P*- and *S*-wave speeds (V_P and V_S), the source distribution in frequency domain, strike, dip, rake, as well as the angular frequency (ω) are used as the input which are fed into the FNO model to approximate the 3D ground motions in frequency domain as output. The color version of this figure is available only in the electronic edition.

the output dimension. The bottom part of Figure 1 shows a schematic of the FNO model structure. Each of the FNO layers can be written as

$$v_{k+1}(x) = \sigma(Wv_k(x) + (\mathcal{K}(\phi)v_k)(x)), \quad (4)$$

in which v_k is the kth layer, σ is a nonlinear activation function, W is the linear transformation weights to be learned along the feature dimension, and $\mathcal{K}(\phi)$ is the kernel integral operator with the parameters ϕ to be learned. The so-called FNO model employs Fourier transform $\mathcal{F}$ to approximate the kernel operator, as shown in the following equation:

$$(\mathcal{K}(\phi)v_k)(x) = \mathcal{F}^{-1}(R_\phi \cdot (\mathcal{F}v_k))(x), \quad (5)$$

in which R_ϕ is a restriction operator, which truncates the Fourier modes to lower frequencies, essentially a low-pass filter, with the pointwise weight parameter ϕ to be learned. A user can define how many Fourier modes to keep in each feature dimension. More detailed information about FNO can be found in the article (Li *et al.*, 2021).

To solve the Helmholtz wave equation, we use discretized pairs of data (A, U), as shown in the upper part of Figure 1, in which A is the input data includes 3D *P*- and *S*-wave velocities, the amplitude distribution of the source in frequency domain, source characteristics (strike, dip, and rake) as well as the frequency component (omega in the figure) we are solving for. The solution from the PDE is U, which consists of three-component real and imaginary parts of the displacements at each of the spatial grid ($64 \times 64 \times 64$) that generated using the spectral element method (see more details in the Data section). The normal flow of the forward estimation using the FNO model is shown in Figure 1. The estimation of the three-component ground motions on the 3D volumes by the FNO model (with the parameters initialized randomly) is used to obtain the errors matching the ground truth Y. The loss function we used here is a combination of pointwise L2 and L1 norm, which is the same as that used in (Yang *et al.*, 2021, 2023; Zou *et al.*, 2024), to strike a balance between accuracy and robustness based on tests, as follows:

$$\text{loss} = 0.9L_1 + 0.1L_2. \quad (6)$$

This loss can be propagated back through the network via an Adam optimizer (Kingma and Ba, 2014); we use 0.01 as the learning rate, and shrink it to half every 30 epochs to update the FNO model. As for the FNO model, we used the original FNO structure described in Li *et al.* (2021), with width 48 and modes 30 for the X, Y, and Z directions.

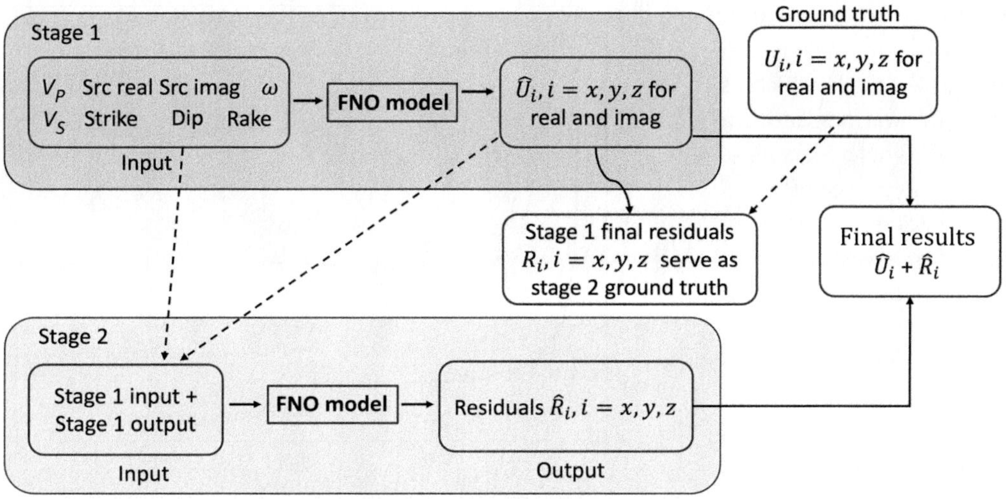

Figure 2. Setup of the multistage FNO model. The blue-shaded box contains stage 1 whereas the orange-shaded box contains the stage 2 input and output of the FNO model. The final results are a combination of the output from the two stages. The color version of this figure is available only in the electronic edition.

Multistage FNO model

Figure 2 shows the setup of a stage 2 FNO model to improve the model's capability on modeling the high-frequency contents, reducing the frequency biases that present using the FNO model. Stage 1 trains a FNO model as we described in the previous section, the only difference is that after getting the final-trained model and the estimated ground motion $\hat{U}$, we compute the residuals by comparing it to the ground truth U. The frequency-dependent residuals from stage 1 are used as the target to be fit by the stage 2 model (see Fig. 3). Thus, in stage 2 we have another FNO model to try to capture the residuals left from stage 1. The input for the stage 2 model includes both the input and output from the stage 1 model, which provide information about the output status of stage 1. With the guidance of the residuals from stage 1 R, the FNO model in the stage 2 estimates the residuals $\hat{R}$ that missed by the previous model, mostly from high frequencies and a little from low frequencies as well. After the training of the stage 2 model, the final solution for the wave equation can be represented by the sum of the results from both of the stages, that is, $\hat{U} + \hat{R}$. We use the same FNO structure, loss function as well as the optimization algorithm through the two stages.

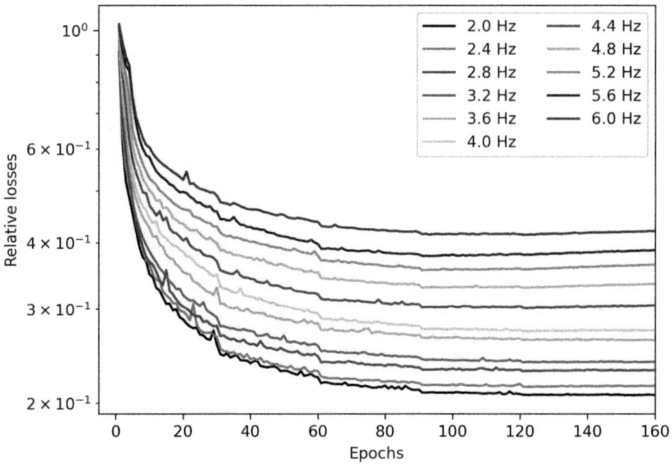

Figure 3. Relative validation losses versus training epoch for different frequencies training. Each FNO model is trained using single-frequency data (15,000 samples) and validated on 1000 samples. The color version of this figure is available only in the electronic edition.

Data parallel on multinodes

The overall pipeline is implemented in a data parallel fashion to use a multinode computing environment. We use Lawrence Livermore National Laboratory's (LLNL) Tioga computing platform: each node consists eight AMD MI-250X GPU (128 GB memory each) for training the FNOs. For training the FNO model in each stage for a single frequency (the FNO-11 model described in the discussion session), we use 5 nodes with 40 GPUs in total, whereas for training the FNO model for all frequencies (the FNO-1 model described in the discussion session), we use 12 nodes with 96 GPUs to accelerate the training.

Data

A 3D seismic-wave propagation simulation dataset is generated using Salvus, a spectral element method (Afanasiev *et al.*, 2019), for model training with a split 15,000, 1000, and 500 as training, validation, and testing, respectively. Each data simulation is on a discretized 3D domain with a 64 × 64 × 64 grids and 5 km in X, Y, and Z directions. As suggested by the Salvus documentation, we take one element per wavelength at the maximum frequency and a fourth-order polynomial for the simulations. This computational domain contains a free-surface boundary condition at the top boundary with other five sides as absorbing boundary conditions. For each simulation the P- and S-wave velocities, and a randomly located earthquake source in the domain with strike, dip, and rake randomly draw from 0° to 360°, 0° to 90°, 0° to 180° are specified. For demonstration purposes, we use a Ricker wavelet with a central frequency of 3 Hz as the source time function. We use a background of 3 km/s with stochastic

Von Kármán random field perturbations (Hurst exponent of 0.5, correlation length of 8 grid cells) with a standard deviation of 10% to generate the velocities of S-wave (V_S) fields, which its power spectral density function follows a power law and can accurately represent the distribution of Earth's heterogeneity as shown in Yang *et al.* (2023). The velocity ratio between P and S (V_P/V_S) is generated by perturbing a background ratio of 1.732 with the Gaussian random fields, which have 32 grid cells as the correlation length and a standard deviation of 2%. This allows some diversity in the travel times of P and S waves as is common in the Earth's crust and breaks any correlations in P- and S-wave speeds and travel time. The P-wave velocity can be computed as V_S multiply the V_P/V_S ratio. Of course, when applied in some applications, such as waveform inversion, we need make sure the variations of V_P and V_S in the training data are broad enough to cover the true variations. Though the training data only consist of stochastic random fields, prior studies show that the NeurOp models trained by it can generalize well to realistic Earth models (Yang *et al.*, 2021, 2023; Zou *et al.*, 2024). A constant density 2.7 g/cm^3 is utilized in the simulations. We use 0.002 s timestep for the simulations to ensure the Courant–Friedrichs–Lewy condition (Courant *et al.*, 1967). The three-component displacements are then sampled to the $64 \times 64 \times 64$ grid points in 3D for a total of 2.5 s with a timestep of 0.04 s. It takes about 2 min to generate one simulation on a Nvidia RTX 6000 GPU. After obtaining the Salvus simulations, the source time function as well as the time series of the displacement fields are transformed into the Fourier domain, and 11 discrete frequencies (2–6 Hz with 0.4 Hz step) are used for the Helmholtz equation, from which we eliminate the frequencies with little energy in the wavefield spectrum. Using the Helmholtz equation with discrete frequencies is a natural data parallel approach and provides a significant reduction in computational cost comparing to the time-domain approach. But to simulate the broadband spectra one can use the time-domain 3D FNO model described in previous studies (Kong and Rodgers, 2023; Lehmann *et al.*, 2024). The P- and S-wave velocity distributions, the complex source term indicating source location, source characteristics (strike, dip, and rake), and the frequency desired are fed into the FNO model to train it to generate the 3D wavefield (complex values) as shown in Figure 1.

Results

We start our experiment by training individual FNO models (as shown in Fig. 1), each focused on the solution within a separate frequency band. When the results are summed together from the different models, these solutions should reproduce the full wavefield. Figure 3 shows the frequency bias from the FNO model, for which the model tends to learn how to reproduce the lower frequencies more quickly than the higher frequencies. Part of the reasons attribute to the physics, where higher frequency contents correspond to wavefields with shorter wavelengths, thus being harder to model. Another reason attributed to the tendency of neural networks to generate smooth output using the nonlinear activation function to increase the generalization capability of the model, thus causing the model to fit the lower frequency content easier (Neal *et al.*, 2018; Yang *et al.*, 2020; Xu *et al.*, 2024).

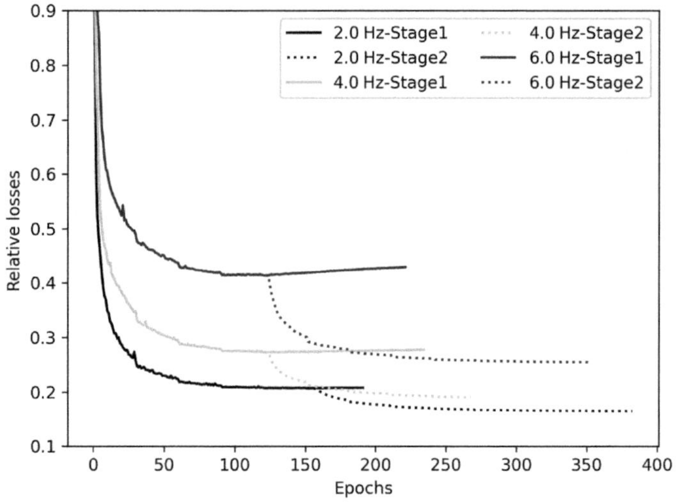

Figure 4. Multistage training validation curves with relative losses. The solid lines are the stage 1 training whereas the dotted lines are from the stage 2 training colored by the frequencies. The stage 2 trainings start from the best-trained models from stage 1. The color version of this figure is available only in the electronic edition.

To address the frequency bias of the FNO model in seismic forward simulations, we adopt the multistage training (Qin *et al.*, 2024; Wang and Lai, 2024), that is, after the FNO models finish the estimation of the ground motion, the residuals between the estimation and target are calculated, which become the target of the stage 2 of training new FNO models to model these residuals. The idea is that the stage 1 FNO models focus on fitting the main characteristics of the data, the small residuals for the stage 2 will be more highlighted in the training data thus easier to be fitted for a new FNO model. To illustrate the effectiveness of the stage 2 training, Figure 4 shows the validation curves for three frequencies training for both stages. We only show three frequencies here, but the other frequencies do have similar trends. We can see after the convergence of the stage 1 training and stage 2 models can further reduce the errors that were left in the previous training. Furthermore, the higher the frequencies, the more errors can be reduced by the stage 2 models. This indicates that the lower frequencies are relatively easy to fit by the stage 1 model, thus not leaving much room to improve on as opposed to the higher frequencies. Figures 5 and 6 show some specific examples from test data (source at 22, 50, and 25) between the performance of single-stage training versus the multistage training. In both cases, we can see the residuals from the

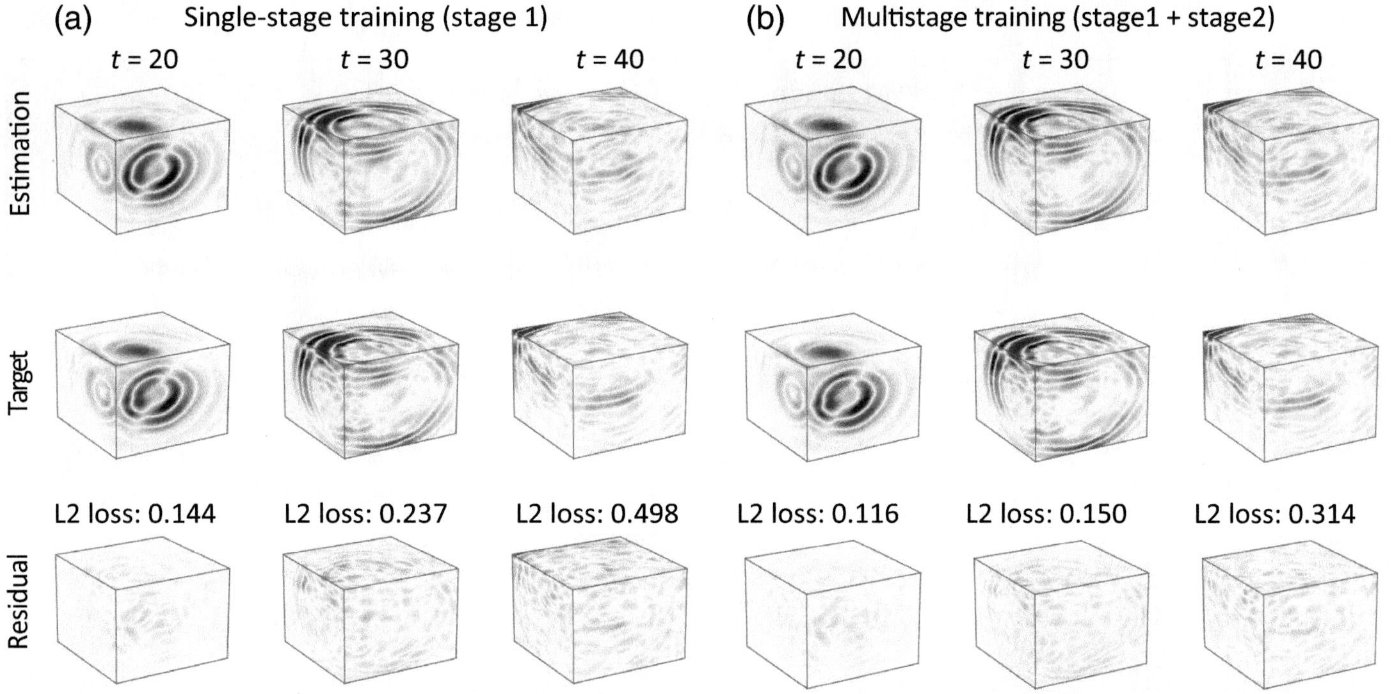

Figure 5. Ground-motion snapshots at t = 10, 20, 30. (a) Stage 1 results and (b) multistage training results. The estimation from FNO models, target, and residuals are shown in the three rows. Relative L2 loss is shown at the top of the last row for each snapshot. The color version of this figure is available only in the electronic edition.

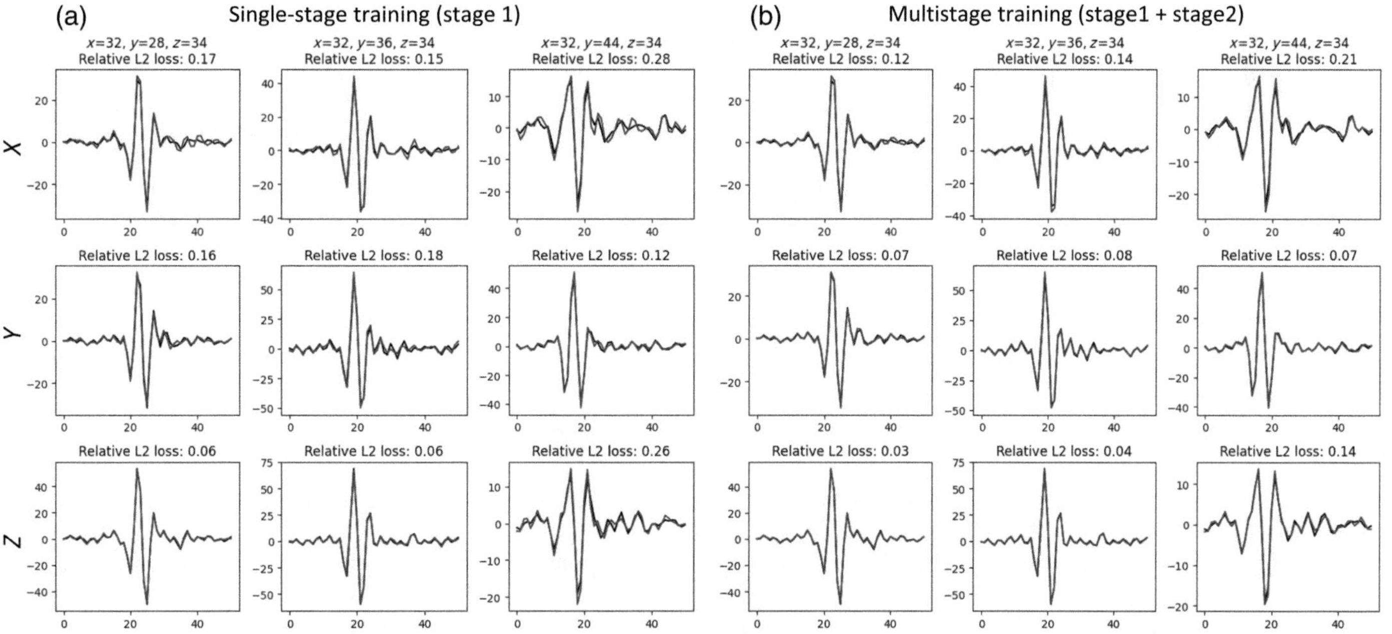

Figure 6. Comparison of the three-component seismic waveforms at different grid locations. The Red and black lines are results from the FNO model and that of the spectral element solver respectively. The top row titles show the grid locations (x, y, and z). The relative L2 losses between the FNO estimation and the spectral element solver are shown in the title as well. In each panel, horizontal axis is index of the samples, whereas vertical axis is the amplitude. X, Y, and Z components are shown in the three rows. (a) Stage 1 results and (b) multistage training results. The color version of this figure is available only in the electronic edition.

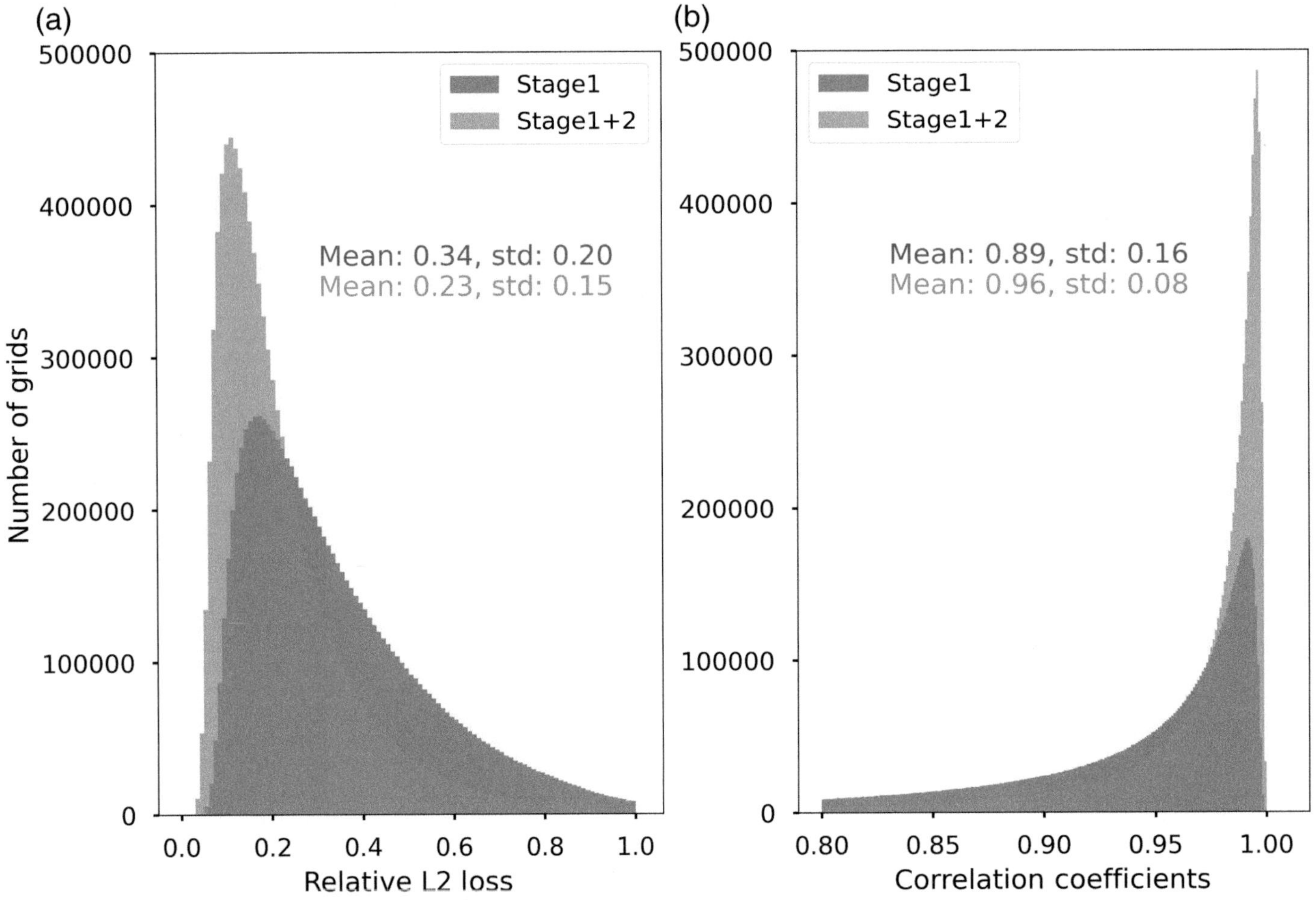

Figure 7. Distribution of relative L2 loss as well as the correlation coefficient for every other grid in the domain for all the three components. Stage 1 model results are shown in blue color whereas the multistage model results are shown in orange color, with mean and standard deviation are shown in the legend. The bins for (a) relative L2 losses are 0–1 with 0.01 as the bin width, and (b) 0.8–1 with 0.001 for correlation coefficients. The color version of this figure is available only in the electronic edition.

multistage training are smaller compared to the single-stage training, thus the higher frequency changes have better fitting.

We use 100 test simulations to evaluate the performance of the trained model on every other grid. On each of these grids, the metrics of the time series of the x, y, and z components are computed and then aggregated to generate the histograms as shown in Figure 7, which shows the relative L2 loss and correlation coefficients. Stage 1 metrics are shown in blue, whereas stage 1+2 metrics are shown in orange. The multistage training improves both metrics, that is, reducing the mean of the L2 loss about one-third and improving the correlation coefficients from 0.89 to 0.96. To show the performance metrics on each frequency and get a better understanding of the different gains on individual frequencies, we flatten the corresponding frequency output and ground-truth simulation data into vectors, and compute the relative L2 loss and correlation coefficients directly, without converting them back to the time domain. The mean and standard deviation of these metrics against frequencies are illustrated in Figure 8. From the figure, we can clearly see that the single-stage model learns the low frequencies better than the high frequencies, for example, the relative L2 losses are getting higher with the increasing of the frequencies, whereas the correlation coefficients are generally dropping (the blue curves with shading area). With adding the stage 2 training, the multistage training metrics (orange curve with its shading) show significant improvement on high frequencies compared to the single-stage model, as the relative L2 losses are mostly flat across different frequencies, showing a slightincrease with frequency. The correlation coefficients also show a flat pattern and remain at high values across different frequencies for the multistage models. This all demonstrates the effectiveness of the multistage training in reducing the frequency biases.

Conclusion and Discussion

In this article, we use the FNO model to solve the 3D elastic wave equation in the frequency domain with earthquake source represented using the strike, dip, and rake. Using 15,000 simulations from spectral element methods, the FNO models are

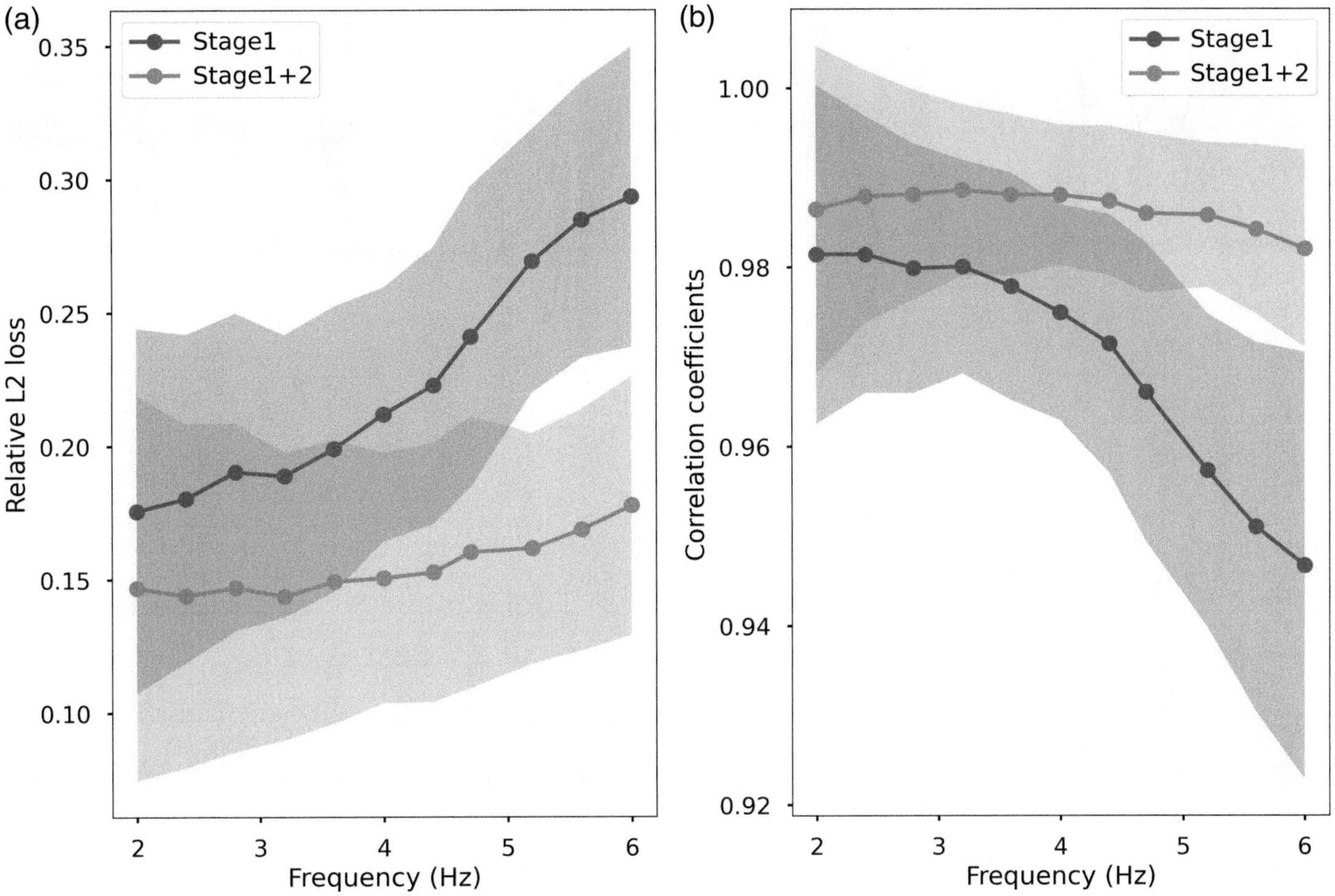

Figure 8. Performance metrics against frequencies for single- and multistage training. (a) Relative L2 losses and (b) correlation coefficients. Dots with solid lines show the mean values for each frequency, whereas the shaded areas are the standard deviations. The color version of this figure is available only in the electronic edition.

trained in a supervised way to estimate the ground motion. The trained FNO models show the tendency of fitting the lower frequency better but not the higher frequencies. Using the multistage training, for which new FNO models are used to fit the residuals from the first stage FNO models, the errors in the higher frequencies can be reduced and the overall performance can be improved. The test results show with the multistage training, the errors across different frequencies are mostly flat, with only a slight increase with frequencies.

To further test the multistage training, we also test a stage 3 using new FNO model to train on the stage 2 residuals in the hope that it will reduce the error even more. Figure 9a shows the stage 3 validation error for 6.0 Hz test, we can see it drops only about 4% which is not significant, and thus we decide only to use stage 2 training.

The main purpose of the article is to show the frequency biases of FNO models can be reduced using the multistage training, thus we only use 15,000 samples to train the FNO models for the consideration of computational cost. We could use more training data to reduce the error even more if we need a better model. Figure 9b shows the stage 2 training validation losses for three different frequencies using 30,000 simulations. It shows we can further reduce the error by adding more data.

In each stage, we use 11 FNO models to learn each of the 11 frequencies (let us call these models as FNO-11 models), in contrast of using only one FNO model for all the frequencies (let us call this model FNO-1). One consideration we have is that individual model that is specifically learning only one frequency may capture better characteristics of the wavefield. The second consideration is mainly for computational purposes; it is easier to train 11 models because each model only sees 1/11 of the data, the training can be done with a relatively small number of GPUs that are easier to request in a multiuser cluster environment. For example, to train the FNO-11, the training takes about 200 s per epoch with 40 GPUs, whereas to train the FNO-1 model for all the 11 frequencies, the training takes about 800 s per epoch with 96 GPUs. Thus requiring smaller sets of GPUs with shorter running time is a big advantage on multi-user clusters without waiting in a queue too long. To test if there are performance differences between training FNO-11 and FNO-1, we further train one FNO-1 model to learn all the frequencies with 15,000 simulations. Figure 10 shows the test relative L2 losses on every other grid for 100 simulations for the

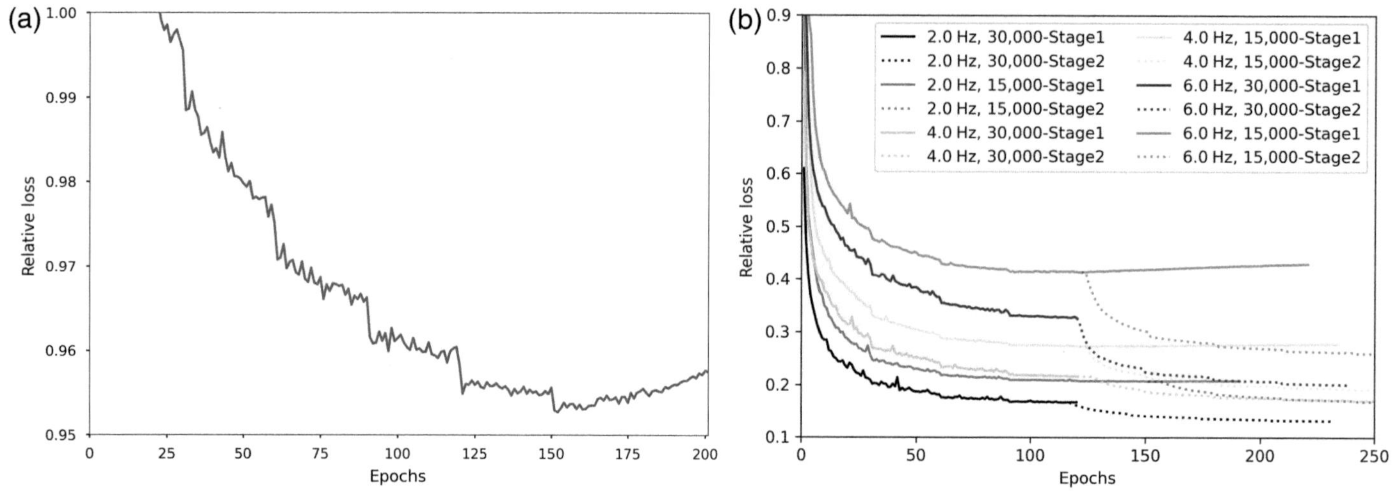

Figure 9. (a) Validation loss with training epochs for 6.0 Hz FNO model for stage 3. (b) Comparison of multistage training using 15,000 and 30,000 simulations for frequencies 2.0, 4.0, and 6.0 Hz. The solid lines are validation curves for stage 1 whereas dotted lines are for stage 2. The color version of this figure is available only in the electronic edition.

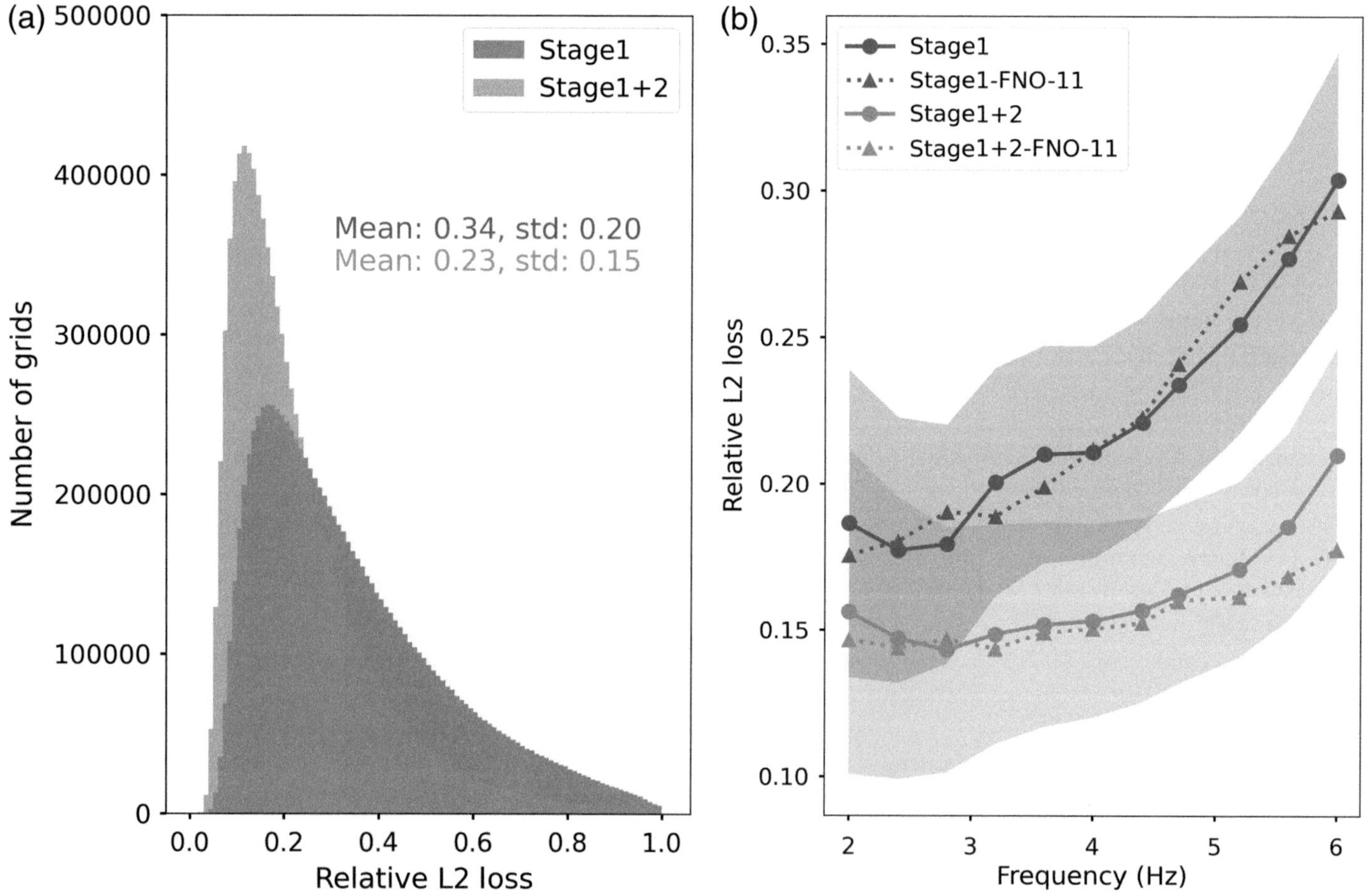

Figure 10. Performance metrics for only training one FNO model (FNO-1) for all frequencies. (a) Histograms of relative L2 losses for FNO-1 model. The bins are from 0 to 1 with 0.01 as bin width. The mean and standard deviation for the FNO-11 model are the same as shown here. (b) Relative L2 losses against frequencies for FNO-1 model. Dots with solid lines show the mean values for each frequency, whereas the shaded areas are the standard deviations. The triangles and dotted lines are from mean values of the FNO-11 models for comparison. The color version of this figure is available only in the electronic edition.

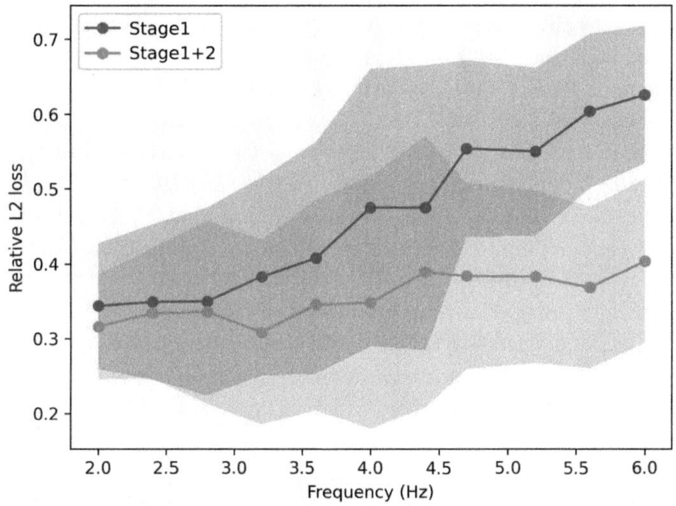

Figure 11. Relative L2 losses against frequencies for applying the multistage models (refined using transfer learning) to 50 test cases of 128 × 128 × 128 simulations. Dots with solid lines show the mean values for each frequency, whereas the shaded areas are the standard deviations. The color version of this figure is available only in the electronic edition.

trained FNO-1 model. Comparing to Figure 7 and 8, we can see the relative L2 losses histograms are basically the same, whereas the relatively L2 losses on different frequencies are a little higher for the FNO-1 model at high-frequency end. Thus this illustrates the FNO-11 and FNO-1 models are very similar, but the FNO-11 models perform slightly better, which may be due to simpler tasks for the model, that is, only paying attention to one frequency at each time.

Because the FNO model has the property of grid invariance, that is, when trained on coarse resolution simulations, the model can directly be applied to the higher resolution simulations. When we apply the multistage-trained models directly to simulations with resolution 128 × 128 × 128 (same physical domain, but denser spacing), the results only show a small improvement using the proposed approach. As shown in our previous studies (Kong and Rodgers, 2023; Tang *et al.*, 2024), transfer learning can make the FNO model perform more reliably when applied to higher resolution simulations. We use 500 128 × 128 × 128 simulations to fine tune the multistage models that pretrained with 15,000 64 × 64 × 64 simulations, and apply the derived models to the higher resolution simulations, as shown in Figure 11. We can see similar results of these fine-tuned multistage models effectively reducing the higher frequency errors.

Data and Resources

The datasets used to train the Fourier neural operator (FNO) model are generated using the Salvus. The main code developed for this research can be obtained at https://github.com/qingkaikong/multi-stage_FNO-SeismicSimulations (last accessed July 2025).

Declaration of Competing Interests

The authors acknowledge that there are no conflicts of interest recorded.

Acknowledgments

This research has been funded by the Laboratory Directed Research & Development at Lawrence Livermore National Laboratory (LLNL), under 24-ERD-012. This research was performed in part under the auspices of the U.S. Department of Energy by the LLNL under Contract Number DE-AC52-07NA27344. This is LLNL Contribution LLNL-JRNL-2002877. The authors also thank the useful discussions by colleagues from LLNL, Tim Lin, Claire Doody, Bill Walter, Stephen C. Myers, Arben Pitarka, Hewei Tang, Joshua A. White, and Graham Bench. The authors thank the two reviewers (Filippo Gatti and an anonymous reviewer) and Editor-in-Chief Allison Bent who provided constructive suggestions to improve the article.

References

Afanasiev, M., C. Boehm, M. van Driel, L. Krischer, M. Rietmann, D. A. May, M. G. Knepley, and A. Fichtner (2019). Modular and flexible spectral-element waveform modelling in two and three dimensions, *Geophys. J. Int.* **216,** no. 3, 1675–1692.

Azizzadenesheli, K., N. Kovachki, Z. Li, M. Schiaffini-Liu, J. Kossaifi, and A. Anandkumar (2024). Neural operators for accelerating scientific simulations and design, *Nature Reviews Phys.* **6,** no. 5, 320–328, doi: 10.1038/s42254-024-00712-5.

Blechschmidt, J., and O. G. Ernst (2021). Three ways to solve partial differential equations with neural networks—A review, *GAMM-Mitteilungen* **44,** no. 2, e202100006, doi: 10.1002/gamm.202100006.

Choy, C., A. Kamenev, J. Kossaifi, M. Rietmann, J. Kautz, and K. Azizzadenesheli (2025). Factorized implicit global convolution for automotive computational fluid dynamics prediction, available at http://arxiv.org/abs/2502.04317 (last accessed July 2025).

Courant, R., K. Friedrichs, and H. Lewy (1967). On the partial difference equations of mathematical physics, *IBM J. Res. Develop.* **11,** no. 2, 215–234.

Evans, G., J. Blackledge, and P. Yardley (2012). *Numerical Methods for Partial Differential Equations*, Springer Science & Business Media, Heidelberg, Germany.

Greenfeld, D., M. Galun, R. Basri, I. Yavneh, and R. Kimmel (2019). Learning to optimize multigrid PDE solvers, *Proceedings of the 36th International Conference on Machine Learning*, Long Beach, California, 2415–2423.

Igel, H. (2017). *Computational Seismology: A Practical Introduction*, Oxford University Press, Oxford, United Kingdom.

Karimpouli, S., and P. Tahmasebi (2020). Physics informed machine learning: Seismic wave equation, *Geosci. Front.* **11,** no. 6, 1993–2001.

Kasim, M. F., D. Watson-Parris, L. Deaconu, S. Oliver, P. Hatfield, D. H. Froula, G. Gregori, M. Jarvis, S. Khatiwala, J. Korenaga, *et al.* (2021). Building high accuracy emulators for scientific simulations with deep neural architecture search, *Machine Learn. Sci. Tech.* **3,** no. 1, 015013, doi: 10.1088/2632-2153/ac3ffa.

Kingma, D. P., and J. Ba (2014). Adam: A method for stochastic optimization, arXiv:1412.6980, doi: 10.48550/arXiv.1412.6980.

Kong, Q., and A. Rodgers (2023). Feasibility of using Fourier neural operators for 3D elastic seismic simulations (LLNL-TR-854521, 2001189, 1082411), available at https://www.osti.gov/servlets/purl/2001189/ (last accessed July 2025).

Kovachki, N., S. Lanthaler, and S. Mishra (2021). On universal approximation and error bounds for Fourier neural operators, available at https://arxiv.org/abs/2107.07562v1 (last accessed July 2025).

Kovachki, N., Z. Li, B. Liu, K. Azizzadenesheli, K. Bhattacharya, A. Stuart, and A. Anandkumar (2021). Neural operator: Learning maps between function spaces, available at https://arxiv.org/abs/2108.08481v3 (last accessed July 2025).

Kurth, T., S. Subramanian, P. Harrington, J. Pathak, M. Mardani, D. Hall, A. Miele, K. Kashinath, and A. Anandkumar (2023). FourCastNet: Accelerating global high-resolution weather forecasting using adaptive Fourier neural operators, Paper Presented at the *Proceedings of the Platform for Advanced Scientific Computing Conference*, Davos, Switzerland, doi: 10.1145/3592979.3593412.

Lehmann, F., F. Gatti, M. Bertin, and D. Clouteau (2024). 3D elastic wave propagation with a Factorized Fourier Neural Operator (F-FNO), *Comput. Meth. Appl. Mech. Eng.* **420,** 116718, available at https://www.sciencedirect.com/science/article/pii/S0045782523008411 (last accessed July 2025).

Li, B., H. Wang, S. Feng, X. Yang, and Y. Lin (2023). Solving seismic wave equations on variable velocity models with Fourier neural operator, *IEEE Trans. Geosci. Remote Sens.* **61,** 1–18.

Li, Z., N. Kovachki, K. Azizzadenesheli, B. Liu, K. Bhattacharya, A. Stuart, and A. Anandkumar (2020a). Fourier neural operator for parametric partial differential equations, available at https://arxiv.org/abs/2010.08895v3 (last accessed July 2025).

Li, Z., N. Kovachki, K. Azizzadenesheli, B. Liu, K. Bhattacharya, A. Stuart, and A. Anandkumar (2020b). Neural operator: Graph kernel network for partial differential equations, available at https://arxiv.org/abs/2003.03485v1 (last accessed July 2025).

Li, Z., N. Kovachki, K. Azizzadenesheli, B. Liu, K. Bhattacharya, A. Stuart, and A. Anandkumar (2021). Fourier neural operator for parametric partial differential equations, available at https://arxiv.org/abs/2010.08895 (last accessed July 2025).

Moseley, B., T. Meyer-Nissen, and A. Markham (2020). Deep learning for fast simulation of seismic waves in complex media, *Solid Earth* **11,** no. 4, 1527–1549.

Neal, B., S. Mittal, A. Baratin, V. Tantia, M. Scicluna, S. Lacoste-Julien, and I. Mitliagkas (2018). A modern take on the bias-variance tradeoff in neural networks, available at https://arxiv.org/abs/1810.08591 (last accessed July 2025).

Qin, S., F. Lyu, W. Peng, D. Geng, J. Wang, N. Gao, X. Liu, and L. L. Wang (2024). Toward a better understanding of Fourier neural operators: Analysis and improvement from a spectral perspective, available at https://arxiv.org/abs/2404.07200 (last accessed July 2025).

Rahaman, N., A. Baratin, D. Arpit, F. Draxler, M. Lin, F. Hamprecht, Y. Bengio, and A. Courville (2019). On the spectral bias of neural networks, Paper Presented at the *International Conference on Machine Learning*, Long Beach, California, 9–15 June 2019, 5301–5310.

Shi, Y., G. Lavrentiadis, D. Asimaki, Z. E. Ross, and K. Azizzadenesheli (2024). Broadband ground-motion synthesis via generative adversarial neural operators: Development and validation, *Bull. Seismol. Soc. Am.* **114,** no. 4, 2151–2171.

Simmons, G. F. (2016). *Differential Equations with Applications and Historical Notes*, CRC Press, Boca Raton, Florida.

Song, C., and Y. Wang (2022). High-frequency wavefield extrapolation using the Fourier neural operator, *J. Geophys. Eng.* **19,** no. 2, 269–282.

Song, C., Y. Liu, P. Zhao, T. Zhao, J. Zou, and C. Liu (2023). Simulating multicomponent elastic seismic wavefield using deep learning, *IEEE Geosci. Remote Sens. Lett.* **20,** 1–5.

Sun, H., Y. Yang, K. Azizzadenesheli, R. W. Clayton, and Z. E. Ross (2022). Accelerating time-reversal imaging with neural operators for real-time earthquake locations, available at https://arxiv.org/abs/2210.06636 (last accessed July 2025).

Tamhidi, A., N. Kuehn, S. F. Ghahari, A. J. Rodgers, M. D. Kohler, E. Taciroglu, and Y. Bozorgnia (2022). Conditioned simulation of ground-motion time series at uninstrumented sites using Gaussian process regression, *Bull. Seismol. Soc. Am.* **112,** no. 1, 331–347.

Tang, H., Q. Kong, and J. P. Morris (2024). Multi-fidelity Fourier neural operator for fast modeling of large-scale geological carbon storage, *J. Hydrol.* **629,** 130641, available at https://www.sciencedirect.com/science/article/pii/S0022169424000350 (last accessed July 2025).

Wang, Y., and C.-Y. Lai (2024). Multistage neural networks: Function approximator of machine precision, *J. Comput. Phys.* **504,** 112865, available at https://www.sciencedirect.com/science/article/pii/S0021999124001141 (last accessed July 2025).

Wei, W., and L.-Y. Fu (2022). Small-data-driven fast seismic simulations for complex media using physics-informed Fourier neural operators, *Geophysics* **87,** no. 6, T435–T446, doi: 10.1190/geo2021-0573.1.

Wen, G., Z. Li, Q. Long, K. Azizzadenesheli, A. Anandkumar, and S. M. Benson (2023). Real-time high-resolution CO2 geological storage prediction using nested Fourier neural operators, *Energy Environ. Sci.* **16,** no. 4, 1732–1741.

Xu, Z.-Q. J., Y. Zhang, and T. Luo (2024). Overview frequency principle/spectral bias in deep learning, *Comm. Appl. Math. Comput.* doi: 10.1007/s42967-024-00398-7.

Xu, Z.-Q. J., Y. Zhang, T. Luo, Y. Xiao, and Z. Ma (2019). Frequency principle: Fourier analysis sheds light on deep neural networks, available at https://arxiv.org/abs/1901.06523 (last accessed July 2025).

Yang, Y., A. F. Gao, K. Azizzadenesheli, R. W. Clayton, and Z. E. Ross (2023). Rapid seismic waveform modeling and inversion with neural operators, *IEEE Trans. Geosci. Remote Sens.* **61,** 1–12.

Yang, Y., A. F. Gao, J. C. Castellanos, Z. E. Ross, K. Azizzadenesheli, and R. W. Clayton (2021). Seismic wave propagation and inversion with neural operators, *Seism. Record* **1,** no. 3, 126–134, doi: 10.1785/0320210026.

Yang, Z., Y. Yu, C. You, J. Steinhardt, and Y. Ma (2020). Rethinking bias-variance trade-off for generalization of neural networks, Paper Presented at the *International Conference on Machine Learning*, Online, 12–18 July 2020.

Zou, C., K. Azizzadenesheli, Z. E. Ross, and R. W. Clayton (2024). Deep neural Helmholtz operators for 3-D elastic wave propagation and inversion, *Geophys. J. Int.* **239,** no. 3, 1469–1484, doi: 10.1093/gji/ggae342.

Manuscript received 7 March 2025
Published online 17 July 2025

Short-Term Forecasting of Aftershock Ground-Motion Hazards Within a Few Hours After a Large Earthquake in Japan

OPEN ACCESS

Hisahiko Kubo*[1] and Katsuhiko Shiomi[1]

Abstract

A large earthquake is typically followed by numerous aftershocks, which generate further ground shaking that can cause additional damage in disaster-stricken areas. Therefore, the early estimation of aftershock seismic hazards after the initial event is crucial for saving lives and resources. This study proposes a scheme for forecasting the short-term hazard of ground motions from aftershocks in Japan using event catalog data from the first few hours after an initial event. This scheme was validated on data from four large crustal earthquakes, including the largest foreshock and mainshock (MS) of the 2016 Kumamoto earthquake sequence. We found that the forecasts roughly reproduced the observed trends, demonstrating the usefulness of this scheme. Our findings revealed that the seismic hazard immediately after the 2016 Kumamoto largest foreshock was significantly higher than that of the MS, although the largest foreshock was approximately one order of magnitude smaller. Our study highlights the importance of hazard assessments based on actual trends in aftershock activity and provides a useful framework for rapid short-term forecasts.

Cite this article as Kubo, H., and K. Shiomi (2025). Short-Term Forecasting of Aftershock Ground-Motion Hazards Within a Few Hours After a Large Earthquake in Japan, *Seismol. Res. Lett.* **97**, 283–294, doi: 10.1785/0220250113.

Supplemental Material

Introduction

After a large earthquake, aftershocks typically cause further shaking in the vicinity of the source, where damage has already been caused by initial strong ground motions. Early response during disaster mitigation, such as evacuation, rescue, and emergency response, is crucial for saving the most lives. During this phase, short-term (multiday) forecasts of aftershock hazards could aid in planning resource allocation. Several studies have forecasted aftershock activity based on event catalogs (Reasenberg and Jones, 1989; Ogata and Katsura, 2006; Omi *et al.*, 2013, 2016; van der Elst, 2021; Hardebeck *et al.*, 2024; Mizrahi *et al.*, 2024), evaluated the seismic hazards of ground motions posed by aftershocks (Wiemer, 2000; Gerstenberger *et al.*, 2005; Yeo and Cornell, 2009; Gee *et al.*, 2022; Hsieh *et al.*, 2024), and estimated the shaking potential of future aftershocks directly from observed seismic records (Lippiello *et al.*, 2016; Sawazaki *et al.*, 2016; Sawazaki, 2021, 2025). However, only a few studies have attempted to assess the short-term seismic hazards posed by aftershocks. This study aimed to forecast the hazard of ground motions due to aftershocks in the days following a large earthquake in Japan, based on event catalog data for the initial postevent period.

Kamaya *et al.* (2017) summarized the current approach to forecasting aftershock hazards in Japan according to the Japan Meteorological Agency (JMA), which was revised following the 2016 Kumamoto earthquake sequence. For approximately 1 week after a large earthquake, the JMA issues alerts for strong motions with the same level as the initial large earthquake, highlighting examples previously hit by successive large events and nearby active source faults. If the aftershocks continue to actively occur, the JMA issues an aftershock probability estimated from event catalog data using a stochastic earthquake approach based on the Omori–Utsu (O-U) formula (Utsu, 1961; Utsu *et al.*, 1995) and Gutenberg–Richter (G-R) formula (Gutenberg and Richter, 1944). This time lag stems from two factors: the need to provide public-oriented information with clear messages for disaster prevention—even when the probability is low—and technical difficulties in reliably estimating model parameters from an incomplete event catalog following a large earthquake (this point will be discussed later). Although shortening the time lag may be difficult for general public communication, it is valuable to provide probabilistic information about ground-motion hazards of aftershocks to experts and disaster-response agencies as early as possible. In the first 24 hr after the initial large earthquake, the occurrence of a secondary disaster incurs a large probability in and around the

1. National Research Institute for Earth Science and Disaster Resilience, Ibaraki, Japan, https://orcid.org/0000-0002-1933-7899 (HK); https://orcid.org/0000-0003-3566-0749 (KS)

*Corresponding author: hkubo@bosai.go.jp

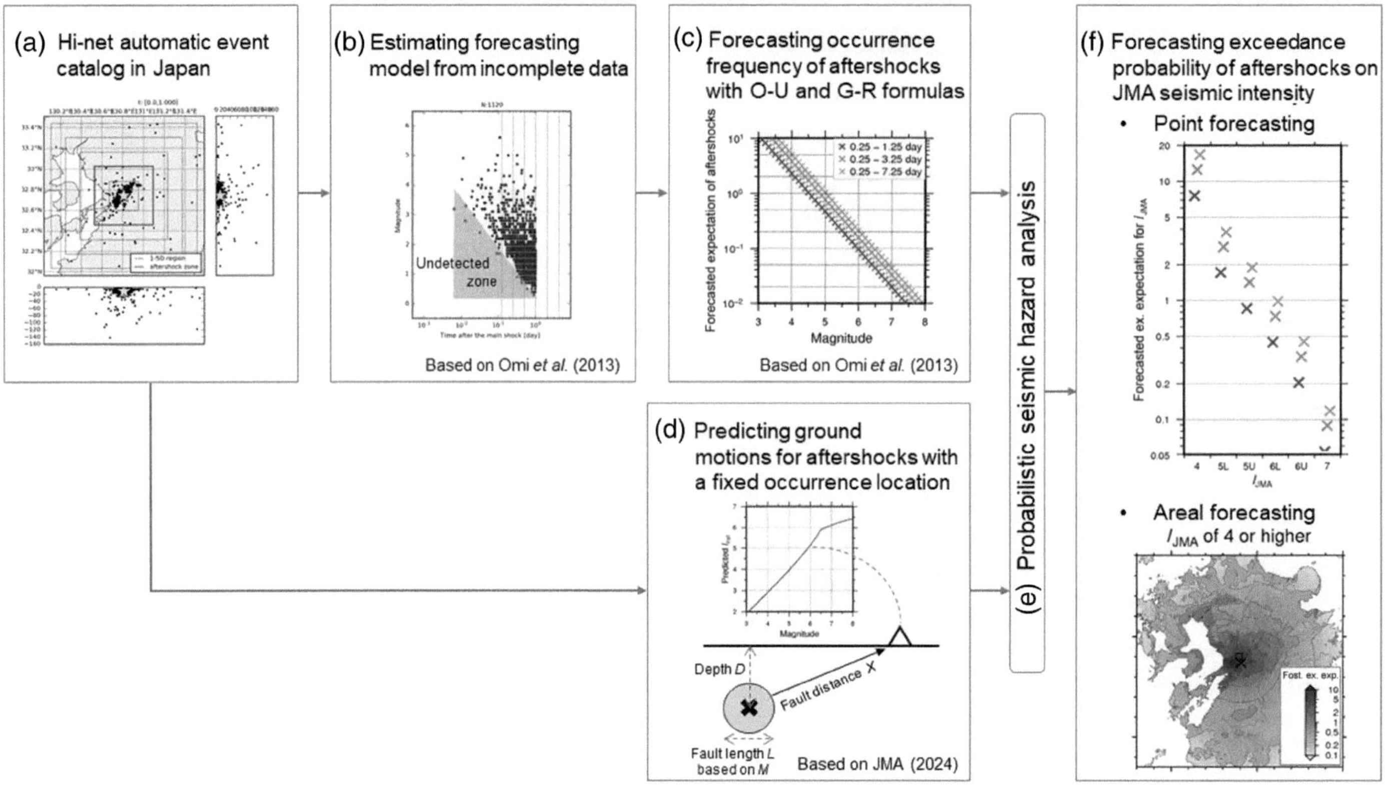

Figure 1. Schematic diagram of the proposed forecast scheme. G-R, Gutenberg–Richter; JMA, Japan Meteorological Agency; O-U, Omori–Utsu. The color version of this figure is available only in the electronic edition.

focal area. Therefore, early forecasts of aftershock hazards are essential for rapid disaster response and mitigation.

Figure 1 shows a schematic diagram of the forecast scheme proposed in this study. The challenge associated with rapid short-term forecasts is the incompleteness of catalog data for the hours or days after a large earthquake (Ogata and Katsura, 2006; Omi *et al.*, 2013; van der Elst, 2021). Following a large earthquake, ongoing strong shaking caused by the initial event and large aftershocks inhibit the detection of smaller aftershocks, followed by a gradual recovery of the detection rate. This sudden deterioration in seismic detection rates leads to a deterioration in the quality and quantity of event catalogs immediately following a large earthquake. Because statistical forecasting methods typically assume a constant detection rate, they are inappropriate for data affected by variations in the aftershock detection rate. To address this issue, we adopted the approach of Omi *et al.* (2013, 2016; steps (b) and (c) in Fig. 1), which accounts for temporal changes in the seismic detection rate with respect to the parameter estimation of the seismic activity model and subsequent forecasts. The scheme proposed in this study targets crustal earthquakes in Japan. Because of the semi-real-time data requirements for monitoring earthquake activity, we used event catalog data from the automatic hypocenter determination system based on the nationwide dense high-sensitive seismograph network, Hi-net of the National Research Institute for Earth Science and Disaster Resilience (NIED; Aoi *et al.*, 2020; step (a) in Fig. 1).

Our proposed scheme provides customized forecast information for each target location. Currently, the shaking potential for aftershocks issued from the JMA only contains information on the maximum shaking around the source fault of the initial event (Kamaya *et al.*, 2017). The aftershock hazard varies depending on the distance from the aftershocks and the site condition of the target location. Therefore, an approach is needed that can forecast aftershock hazard at arbitrary locations. In this study, we adopted the approach used for early earthquake warning (EEW) in Japan (step (d) in Fig. 1), which has been operational for over 10 yr and is expected to be a highly robust ground-motion prediction method even for unknown earthquakes with limited source information. We applied a probabilistic seismic hazard analysis (PSHA; Baker *et al.*, 2021; Fujiwara *et al.*, 2023) to estimate the probability and expectation of ground-motion exceedance, for which aftershock ground motions exceeded a threshold value of seismic intensity, based on aftershock forecast and ground-motion prediction information (step (e) in Fig. 1).

Methods

Our aftershock forecasting approach followed that of Omi *et al.* (2013, 2016) (steps (b) and (c) in Fig. 1). In their model, the occurrence of aftershocks follows an inhomogeneous Poisson process that combines the O-U formula for the aftershock decay and the G-R formula for the magnitude–frequency relationship. Therefore, the occurrence rate of aftershocks of magnitude M at time t after the initial large earthquake can be presented as follows:

$$\lambda(t,M) = \frac{K}{(t+c)^p}\beta e^{-\beta(M-M_0)}, \tag{1}$$

in which parameters K, c, and p of the O-U formula and parameter β of the G-R formula ($\beta = b\ln 10$) should be estimated and M_0 represents the magnitude of the initial large earthquake. The K-, c-, and p-values in the O-U formula correspond to the productivity of the aftershock sequence, the time delay before the onset of the power-law aftershock decay rate, and the slope of the power-law aftershock decay rate, respectively. The b-value in the G-R formula corresponds to the relative frequency of large-magnitude events compared to small-magnitude events; a small b-value implies a relatively large number of large-magnitude events. Because of the reduced quality and quantity of catalog data after large earthquakes, Omi *et al.* (2013) introduced a seismic detection rate that varies with the elapsed time since the initial event (Ringdal, 1975; Ogata and Katsura, 1993, 2006) and estimated the temporal change in the seismic detection rate as well as the parameters of the O-U and G-R formulas simultaneously from an incomplete catalog. The detection rate of an aftershock of magnitude M at time t after the initial large earthquake is assumed as follows:

$$\Phi(M|\mu(t),\sigma) = \int_{-\infty}^{M} \frac{1}{\sqrt{2\pi\sigma^2}} e^{-\frac{(x-\mu(t))^2}{2\sigma^2}} dx, \tag{2}$$

in which $\mu(t)$ represents the magnitude with a 50% detection rate varying in time t, and σ represents the magnitude range of partially detected earthquakes. From the aftershock sequence data based on the hypocenter catalog, the parameter set $\theta = (K,c,p,\beta,\mu(t),\sigma)$ was estimated using the Bayesian framework with the Markov chain Monte Carlo method (Omi *et al.*, 2013, 2016). Although Omi *et al.* (2013, 2016) estimated the occurrence frequency of aftershocks of a magnitude greater than a threshold from the estimated parameter set θ, we estimated the expectation (occurrence frequency) of aftershocks, v, with a magnitude range between M_1 and M_2 in the forecasting period between t_1 and t_2 as follows:

$$v(t_1 \sim t_2, M_1 \sim M_2|\theta) = \int_{t_1}^{t_2} dt \int_{M_1}^{M_2} dM\lambda(t,M|\theta)$$
$$= \begin{cases} \frac{-K}{1-p}[e^{-\beta(M_1-M_0)} - e^{-\beta(M_2-M_0)}][(t_2+c)^{1-p} - (t_1+c)^{1-p}] & (p \neq 1) \\ -K[e^{-\beta(M_1-M_0)} - e^{-\beta(M_2-M_0)}][\ln(t_2+c) - \ln(t_1+c)] & (p = 1). \end{cases} \tag{3}$$

NIED has developed and operated the nationwide high-sensitivity seismograph network in Japan, Hi-net (Okada *et al.*, 2004; Aoi *et al.*, 2020), which consists of nearly 800 stations with an average spacing of 20 km in land. To achieve stable high-sensitivity seismic observation avoiding surface ground noise, seismographs are placed at the bottom of boreholes at depths of 100 m or more at each Hi-net station. Using Hi-net data, earthquakes in Japan are automatically detected and located in real time by NIED (Okada *et al.*, 2004). On average, earthquakes are registered in the Hi-net catalog 6–7 min after their occurrence. Omi *et al.* (2016, 2019) developed a system for which the scheme of Omi *et al.* (2013) is applied to the automatic hypocenter catalog data of NIED Hi-net for automatic short-term aftershock forecasting in Japan. This system estimates θ and forecasts the earthquake occurrence probability every hour, starting 3 hr after an earthquake of magnitude ≥5.0, based on the data in Hi-net catalog for aftershocks that occurred within a defined zone during a given estimation period. To calculate v in equation (3), we used θ obtained by this system in which the zone for an initial large earthquake of magnitude M_0 is a square centered at the initial large earthquake with a side length of $2 \times 0.01 \times 10^{0.5M_0-1.8°}$. This side length was set to be twice as large as that of the Utsu–Seki aftershock zone length ($0.01 \times 10^{0.5M_0-1.8°}$; Utsu, 1969). This is because the Hi-net automatic catalog has large location errors during the early stage of aftershock sequences, and the relatively large aftershock zone is necessary to make the best use of the aftershock data (Omi *et al.*, 2016). Depth criteria are not adopted here due to large uncertainties in estimated focal depth in the early stage of aftershock sequences in the Hi-net automatic catalog. The estimation period was set to be the time from the occurrence of the initial large earthquake to the time of the analysis.

As the target ground-motion index, we adopted the JMA seismic-intensity scale I_{JMA} (Japan Meteorological Agency [JMA], 1996; Hoshiba *et al.*, 2010; Kodera *et al.*, 2018). This scale is a discrete representation that divides the JMA scale into 10 degrees ranging from 0 to 7, with 5 and 6 further subdivided into 2 degrees: 5-lower (5L), 5-upper (5U), 6-lower (6L), and 6-upper (6U). Each degree corresponds to the level of earthquake damage and human perception. The I_{JMA} is calculated from the JMA instrumental seismic intensity I_{inst}-a continuous representation of the JMA scale. The details of I_{JMA} and I_{inst}, including the relationship with the modified Mercalli scale, are explained in Hoshiba *et al.* (2010) and Kodera *et al.* (2018).

Generally, the aftershock area is spatially finite. For simplicity, we assumed that aftershocks will occur at the same location as the hypocenter of the initial large earthquake. This assumption enables ground-motion prediction with a fixed spatial relationship between the earthquake and predicted target location. In the ground-motion prediction of I_{inst} (step (d) in Fig. 1), we mostly followed the ground-motion prediction method using earthquake source information in the JMA EEW system, which uses the ground-motion prediction equation (GMPE) of Si and Midorikawa (1999). The input parameters are the source information of the initial large earthquake (earthquake magnitude listed in the Hi-net catalog M_{Hi-net}, hypocentral distance X_0, and source depth D) and average S-wave velocity up to a depth of 30 m at the target site

V_{S30}. Because the GMPE of Si and Midorikawa (1999) uses M_w as one of the explanatory variables, the conversion between $M_{\text{Hi-net}}$ and M_w is needed. First, because $M_{\text{Hi-net}}$ and the JMA magnitude M_{JMA} are both local magnitudes based on the maximum amplitude of seismic waveforms, we assumed that they are equivalent:

$$M_{JMA} \approx M_{\text{Hi-net}}. \quad (4)$$

Following Utsu (1977, 1982) and Sato *et al.* (1989), M_{JMA} was converted to M_w as follows:

$$M_w = M_{JMA} - 0.171. \quad (5)$$

To consider the effect of earthquake-fault finiteness, JMA (2024) used the shortest distance from the fault of the target aftershock X, not the hypocentral distance X_0. JMA (2024) assumed that the source is a sphere with diameter L, which is the fault length based on the source scaling of Utsu (1977):

$$\log_{10} L = 0.5 \times M_w - 1.85. \quad (6)$$

Based on L, X can be obtained as follows:

$$X = \max(X_0 - 0.5 \times L, 3). \quad (7)$$

Here, X was assumed to be saturated at 3 km. Using the GMPE for crustal earthquakes proposed by Si and Midorikawa (1999), the peak ground velocity (PGV) at the engineering bedrock with an average S-wave velocity of 600 m/s PGV_{600} was calculated as follows:

$$\log_{10}\text{PGV}_{600} = 0.58 \times M_w + 0.0038 \times D - 1.29 - \log_{10}(X + 0.0028 \times 10^{0.50 \times M_w}) - 0.002X. \quad (8)$$

To account for site amplification due to shallow soft soils at the target point, we used the relationship between V_{S30} and the site amplification factor ARV_{600} (amplitude ratio of PGV at the ground surface relative to the engineering bedrock of average S-wave velocity 600 m/s), proposed by Fujimoto and Midorikawa (2006):

$$\text{ARV}_{600} = 2.367 - 0.852 \times \log_{10} V_{S30}. \quad (9)$$

Accordingly, PGV_{600} was converted to the PGV on the surface, PGV_s, as follows:

$$\text{PGV}_s = \text{PGV}_{600} \times \text{ARV}_{600}. \quad (10)$$

PGV_s was converted to I_{inst}, using the empirical relationship from Midorikawa *et al.* (1999):

$$I_{\text{inst}} = 2.68 + 1.72 \times \log_{10} \text{PGV}_s. \quad (11)$$

The prediction based on the GMPE naturally includes variability. Accordingly, to calculate the exceedance probability of ground motions, we adopted the ordinary logarithmic standard deviation expressed as follows:

$$\sigma = \begin{cases} 0.23 & (X \le 20 \text{ km}) \\ 0.23 - 0.03\frac{\log_{10}(\frac{X}{20})}{\log_{10}(\frac{30}{20})} & (20 \text{ km} < X \le 30 \text{ km}) \\ 0.20 & (30 \text{ km} < X) \end{cases}. \quad (12)$$

This prediction variation depends on the fault distance, which is the same as that used by Fujiwara *et al.* (2023).

Using the PSHA approach (Baker *et al.*, 2021; Fujiwara *et al.*, 2023), we estimated the probability that the aftershock ground motion exceeded a threshold seismic intensity during the target period (step (e) in Fig. 1). For each degree in the I_{JMA}, we calculated the exceedance probability and exceedance expectation to forecast shaking beyond the threshold. Generally, the PSHA considers variations in earthquake location, magnitude, and mechanism type. However, because we assumed a fixed location for the aftershocks and focused on crustal earthquakes, only variations in the earthquake magnitude were considered. The probability of the seismic intensity exceeding y at least once during period t at the forecast location $P(Y > y;t)$ is expressed as follows:

$$P(Y > y; t) = 1 - \prod_k \{1 - P_{M_k}(Y > y; t)\}, \quad (13)$$

in which $P_{M_k}(Y > y; t)$ is the probability that the seismic intensity will exceed y at least once during period t from an earthquake of magnitude M_k. M_k denotes the representative magnitude of the kth interval obtained by discretizing the overall magnitude range into equal-width bins. When the occurrence of aftershocks is modeled using inhomogeneous Poisson processes, as in this study, $P_{M_k}(Y > y; t)$ can be written as follows:

$$P_{M_k}(Y > y; t) = 1 - e^{-\nu_{M_k}(Y > y; t)}, \quad (14)$$

in which $\nu_{M_k}(Y > y; t)$ is the frequency at which the seismic intensity exceeds y due to an earthquake of magnitude M_k during period. Here, $\nu_{M_k}(Y > y; t)$ can be transcribed to the following:

$$\nu_{M_k}(Y > y; t) = \nu(M_k; t)P(Y > y|M_k), \quad (15)$$

in which $\nu(M_k; t)$ is the frequency of earthquakes of magnitude M_k during period t and $P(Y > y|M_k)$ is the conditional probability of the seismic intensity exceeding y under the condition of one earthquake of M_k. Here, $\nu(M_k; t)$ is comparable to equation (3) in steps (b) and (c) of Figure 1, and $P(Y > y|M_k)$ is obtained based on equations from equations (4) to (10) in step (d) of Figure 1. Although the parameters in the O-U and G-R formulas are estimated based on aftershock activity within a certain spatial range, ground-motion prediction and hazard assessment in our scheme are performed under the assumption that the aftershock sequence expressed by these parameters occurs at

TABLE 1
Source Information of the Four Crustal Earthquakes to Which the Proposed Scheme Was Applied in This Study

		Source Information of Hi-Net Catalog				
Earthquake Number	Earthquake Name	Origin Time (JST) (yyyy/mm/dd hh:ss)	Latitude (°)	Longitude (°)	Depth (km)	M_{Hi-net}
1	2016 Kumamoto Largest Foreshock (LFS)	2016/04/14 21:26	32.742	130.809	11	6.5
2	2016 Kumamoto Mainshock (MS)	2016/04/16 01:25	32.755	130.763	12	7.3
3	2018 Northern Osaka	2018/06/18 07:58	34.843	135.623	13	6.2
4	2019 off Yamagata	2019/06/18 22:22	38.606	139.488	12	6.6

TABLE 2
Estimated Parameters of the Omori–Utsu (O-U) and Gutenberg–Richter (G-R) Formulas for the Four Earthquakes Estimated by the Aftershock Forecasting System (Omi *et al.*, 2019) with Their Credible Interval Between the 25th and 75th Percentiles, As Well As the Generic-Model Parameters of Omi *et al.* (2016)

	Parameters			
Earthquake Number	*K*	*c*	*p*	*b*
1	0.197 [0.143–0.292]	0.080 [0.060–0.115]	1.01 [0.93–1.10]	0.69 [0.66–0.72]
2	0.007 [0.003–0.011]	0.140 [0.083–0.171]	1.01 [0.92–1.08]	1.02 [0.99–1.12]
3	0.018 [0.011–0.030]	0.062 [0.039–0.078]	0.96 [0.84–1.02]	0.71 [0.67–0.75]
4	0.012 [0.010–0.024]	0.040 [0.030–0.058]	1.08 [0.99–1.16]	0.78 [0.73–0.80]
Generic model	0.008	0.018	1.05	0.85

a fixed location (the location of the initial event). Using equations (13) and (14), the expectation of the seismic intensity exceeding y at least once during period t at the forecast location $n(Y > y; t)$ is expressed as follows:

$$n(Y > y; t) = \sum_k \nu_{M_k}(Y > y; t) = \ln\left(\frac{1}{1 - P(Y > y;)}\right). \quad (16)$$

Application to Real Data

The proposed scheme was applied to four crustal earthquakes in Japan: the largest foreshock (M_{Hi-net} 6.5) and mainshock (M_{Hi-net} 7.3) of the 2016 Kumamoto earthquake sequence (Kubo *et al.*, 2016; Suzuki *et al.*, 2017; Omi *et al.*, 2019; hereafter, the former is referred to as the 2016 Kumamoto largest foreshock [LFS] and the latter as the 2016 Kumamoto mainshock [MS], respectively), the 2018 northern Osaka earthquake (M_{Hi-net} 6.2; Hallo *et al.*, 2019; Kato and Ueda, 2019; Omi *et al.*, 2019), and the 2019 off Yamagata earthquake (M_{Hi-net} 6.6; Yoshida *et al.*, 2020; Ueda *et al.*, 2021). Table 1 lists their source information, and Figure S1, available in the supplement material to this article shows their locations. Here, M_{Hi-net} is the earthquake magnitude listed in the Hi-net catalog. Notably, the Kumamoto MS occurred 28 hr (~1.17 day) after the 2016 Kumamoto LFS. For parameter estimation, the event catalog up to 6 hr (0.25 day) after the initial event was used. The parameters of the O-U and G-R formulas for the four events, which were estimated by the aftershock forecasting system (Omi *et al.*, 2019), are listed in Table 2; this table also lists the credible interval between the 25th and 75th percentiles of the estimated parameters. The magnitude range of the assumed aftershocks in the PSHA was set between 3.0 and 8.0 in increments of 0.1. The lower and upper limits of the magnitude range corresponded to the earthquake of which predicted seismic intensity does not reach the target intensity (4 or higher) and to the largest inland earthquake that has occurred in Japan (1891 *M* 8.0 Nobi earthquake; Usami *et al.*, 2013), respectively. For comparison, we used the seismic intensity records, extracted from original data in the JMA seismic intensity database (Ishigaki and Takagi, 2000) under the condition that the seismic intensity was recorded within 1.25 day following the initial large event.

First, we conducted the point forecasting of aftershock ground-motion hazard at stations with hypocentral distances of 13–15 km (Table 3). The V_{S30} at each station was obtained from the V_{S30} map of Japan in Matsuoka and Wakamatsu (2008), publicly available on the NIED Japan Seismic Hazard Information Station (J-SHIS) website (Fujiwara *et al.*, 2013; National Research Institute for Earth Science and Disaster Resilience [NIED], 2019).

TABLE 3
Station Information for Each Point Forecasting

Earthquake Number	Station Code	Hypocentral Distance (km)	V_{S30} (m/s)
1	KMM006	13.3	268.5
2	KMM006	13.6	268.5
3	OSK002	13.5	445.2
4	YMT004	14.9	641.3s

The point-forecasting results for the aftershocks of the 2016 Kumamoto LFS at KMM006 at 1, 3, and 7 days from 6 hr after the LFS are shown in Figure 2. The forecasted occurrence frequency of the aftershocks, which was obtained from equation (3) (step (c)), based on the estimated parameters in Table 2, increased with the forecasting time and tended to decay over time according to the O-U formula (Fig. 2a). The predicted JMA seismic intensity, which was obtained from equations (4) to (10) (step (d)), increased with an increase in M (Fig. 2b). The predicted value of I_{JMA} corresponded to 6U for events of $M \sim 7$. The relationship between the magnitude and seismic intensity changed at an M of approximately 6.5, which corresponded to the saturation of the shortest fault distance. The forecasted exceedance expectation, which was obtained from equations (13) to (16) (step (e)), was greater than 5 for $I_{JMA} \geq 4$ at 0.25–1.25 day, near 1 for $I_{JMA} \geq$ 5U, and approximately 0.2 for $I_{JMA} \geq$ 6U (Fig. 2c). The observed frequency at KMM006 is shown in Figure 2d. Within 0.25–1.25 day, an $I_{JMA} \geq 4$ was frequently observed. An I_{JMA} of 6U was also observed once, corresponding to the Kumamoto MS that occurred 28 hr (~1.17 day) after the Kumamoto LFS.

Figure 3 shows the point-forecasting results at 0.25–1.25 day for the four events. The forecasted occurrence frequencies of aftershocks (Fig. 3a) suggest that the aftershock activities of the 2018 northern Osaka and 2019 off Yamagata earthquakes were forecasted to be low. Although the 2016 Kumamoto LFS had a magnitude similar to the 2018 northern Osaka and 2019 off Yamagata earthquakes (Table 1), the forecasted activity of its aftershocks was significantly higher and comparable to that of the 2016 Kumamoto MS, which was approximately one magnitude larger than that of the LFS. This is mainly due to the high productivity of the aftershocks, which is indicated as the large estimated K-value in the O-U formula for the 2016 Kumamoto LFS (Table 2). Moreover, because of the low estimated b-value in the O-U formula (Table 2), the occurrence probability of large-magnitude aftershocks following the LFS was higher than that of the MS. The predicted JMA seismic intensity was similar for the four events (Fig. 3b) because the target stations had similar hypocentral distances (Table 3). The slight differences in the predicted seismic intensity were caused by differences in V_{S30} among the stations. The exceedance expectation for I_{JMA} (Fig. 3c) was forecasted to be low in the 2018 northern Osaka and 2019 off Yamagata earthquake due to the lower forecasted aftershock seismicity. The 2016 Kumamoto LFS had a higher forecasted exceedance expectation than the MS, reflecting the increased likelihood of large-magnitude aftershocks following the 2016 Kumamoto LFS and the associated stronger ground motions. These forecasted expectations of ground-motion exceedance were roughly consistent with the trend in the observed JMA seismic intensity at their target points during the forecasting period (Fig. 3d): higher forecasted expectations with more frequent ground motion. Moreover, the trend in the observed frequency of aftershocks (Fig. 3e) was consistent with the forecasted frequency of aftershock occurrence (Fig. 3a), including the occurrence of larger-magnitude aftershocks following the 2016 Kumamoto LFS compared to that of the MS.

We also conducted areal forecasts of the 2016 Kumamoto LFS and MS for 0.25–1.25 day. Figure 4a,c shows their areal-forecasting results (spatial distribution of the forecasted exceedance expectation of aftershock ground motions). Here, the forecast calculations were performed in 1 km mesh units based on the V_{S30} map covering Japan (Matsuoka and Wakamatsu, 2008). The forecasted exceedance expectation decreased as the distance from the epicenter of the initial large event increased and was high in plains and basins with poor ground conditions (low V_{S30}). Figure 4c,d shows the spatial distributions of the observed exceedance frequency of the seismic intensity. Strong motions were frequently observed in areas with a high-forecasted exceedance expectation. The Kumamoto LFS had a higher overall exceedance expectation than the MS, consistent with the seismic intensity observations.

The relationship between the forecasted exceedance expectation and observed exceedance frequency at observation stations for the 2016 Kumamoto LFS and MS is shown in Figure 5. Forecasted values are continuous, whereas observations are discrete integers. Therefore, a direct comparison between them in Figure 5 may not be appropriate. Nevertheless, their overall trends can still be identified from this figure. In both events, a higher forecasted exceedance expectation corresponded to more frequent strong motions. When the forecasted exceedance expectation exceeded 0.1, the likelihood of encountering at least one instance of strong motions increased. In the 2016 Kumamoto MS, our forecasts generally explain the observations, although some variability was found. In the 2016 Kumamoto LFS, there was a tendency to relatively underestimate strong motions, which was particularly pronounced for $I_{JMA} \geq$ 5U.

The aftershock activity following the 2016 Kumamoto MS extended beyond the Kumamoto region, where the source fault was located, into the Aso and Oita regions, which were distant from the MS source fault (dotted ellipses in Fig. 4c,d; Yano and Matsubara, 2017). At some stations in these areas, seismic intensity ≥ 4 was recorded several times at several locations (yellow crosses with gray circle in the left plot of Fig. 5b). Because we assumed that aftershocks occur at the same location as the

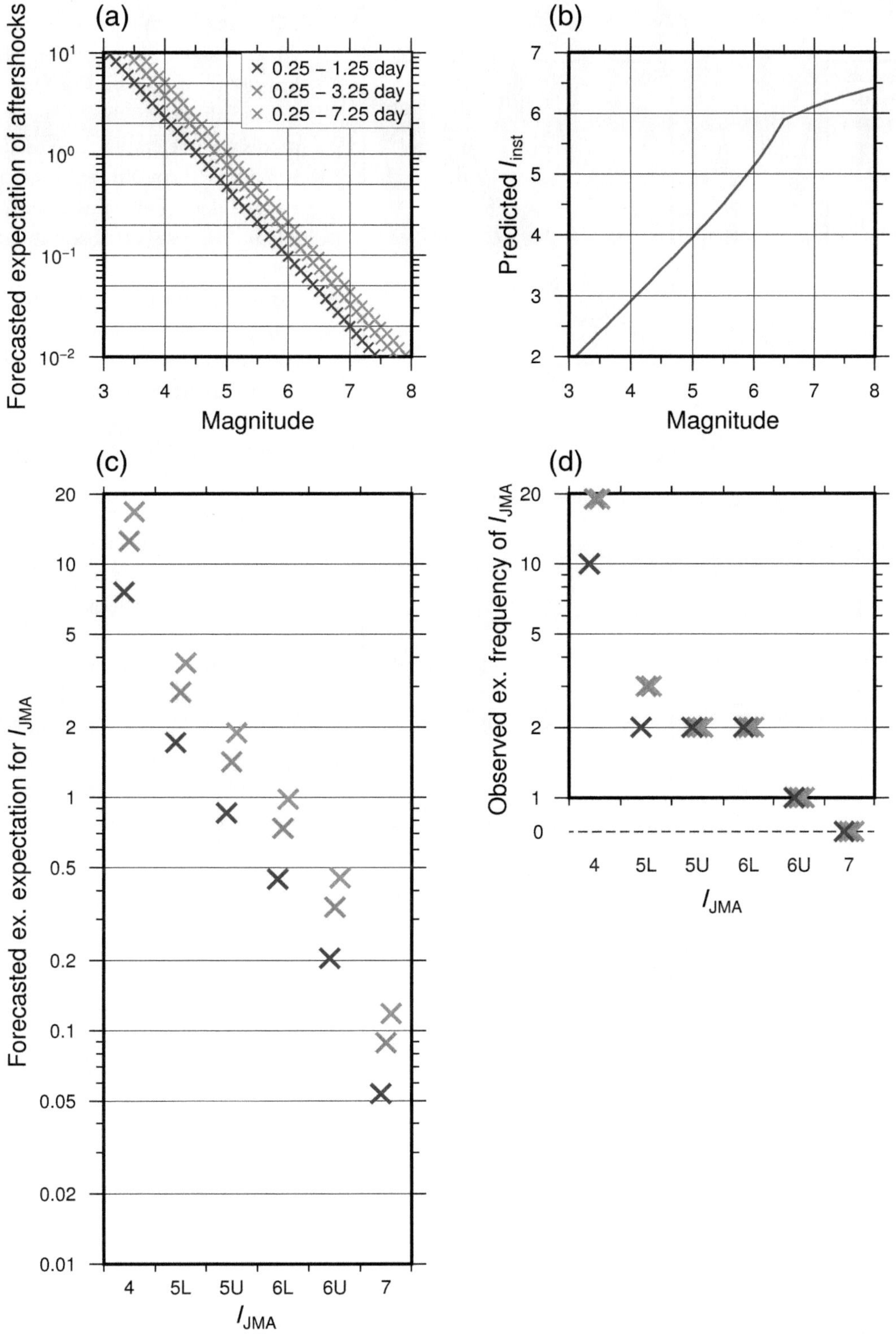

Figure 2. Point-forecasting results for aftershocks of the 2016 Kumamoto largest foreshock (LFS) at KMM006 for 0.25–1.25 day (red cross), 0.25–3.25 day (purple cross), and 0.25–7.25 day (blue cross). (a) Forecasted expectation of aftershocks by magnitude. (b) Predicted JMA seismic intensity of aftershocks by magnitude. (c) Forecasted exceedance expectation for JMA seismic intensity. (d) Observed exceedance frequency of JMA seismic intensity at KMM006. The crosses are layered in the following order: blue, purple, and red. The color version of this figure is available only in the electronic edition.

MS, our forecast scheme did not account for the spatial spread of aftershock activity. Therefore, our scheme underestimated the hazard in the Aso and Oita regions.

Discussion and Conclusions

This study proposed a scheme to forecast the exceedance expectation of aftershock ground motions in the days immediately following a large earthquake using event catalog data for the initial postevent hours. Through the application of the proposed method to real data, we demonstrated the usefulness of our scheme: the forecasts of ground-motion exceedance roughly reproduced the observed trends.

We also performed hazard assessment of aftershock ground motions based on the generic-model parameters in the O-U and G-R formulas (bottom row of Table 2) as proposed by Omi *et al.* (2016) based on the analysis results for 38 aftershock sequences in Japan in Omi *et al.* (2015). The forecast results are represented by gray symbols in Figures 3 and 5. The forecasts for the 2016 Kumamoto LFS using the generic-model parameters were close to those for the 2019 northern Osaka earthquake and the 2019 off Yamagata earthquake, significantly underestimating the observations. The *K*- and *b*-values in the generic model were significantly different from the estimated values of the 2016 Kumamoto LFS (Table 2), resulting in the underestimation of aftershock hazards. We also found a tendency to underestimate even for the 2016 Kumamoto MS. Our forecasts using the parameters

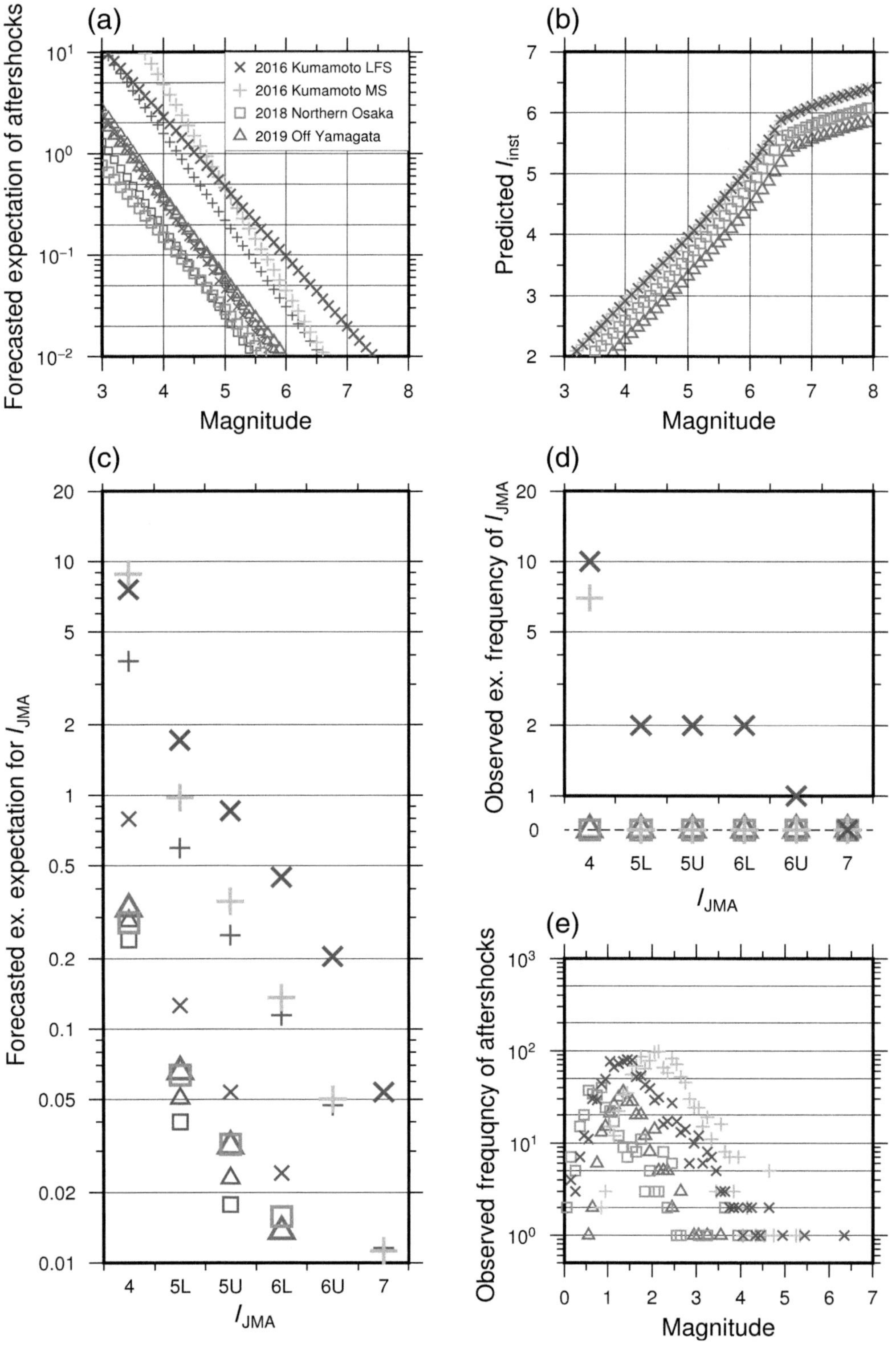

Figure 3. Point-forecasting results for 0.25–1.25 day following the 2016 Kumamoto LFS (red cross), 2016 Kumamoto mainshock (MS; yellow plus), 2018 northern Osaka earthquake (green square), and 2019 off Yamagata earthquake (blue triangle). (a) Forecasted expectation of aftershocks by magnitude. (b) Predicted JMA seismic intensity of aftershocks by magnitude at target points. (c) Forecasted exceedance expectation for JMA seismic intensity at target points. (d) Observed exceedance frequency of JMA seismic intensity at target points. (e) Observed frequency of aftershocks. Gray symbols in panels (a) and (c) indicate the forecast results based on the generic-model parameters. The color version of this figure is available only in the electronic edition.

estimated from the observed seismicity significantly improved these underestimations. Although the generic-model parameters are often used when there is insufficient observation data (Mizrahi *et al.*, 2024), the use of observation data, even for short periods, is worthwhile for evaluating aftershock activity. Some studies have evaluated seismic activity using short-term seismicity data to assess aftershock hazards (Hsieh *et al.*, 2024; Mizrahi *et al.*, 2024). However, immediately after an earthquake, the event catalog often suffers from incompleteness, necessitating the use of an analysis method that can address this issue, as in this study.

This study demonstrated that our approach successfully forecasted the observed trend, in which the seismic hazards from aftershocks immediately following the 2016 Kumamoto LFS were significantly higher than that of the MS, despite the LFS being approximately one order of magnitude smaller. This was due to the significant active seismicity of aftershocks for the 2016 Kumamoto LFS, in which large magnitude events likely occurred, corresponding to the large K- and small b-values estimated in the evaluation of its aftershock activity (Table 2). This result suggests that, when evaluating the seismic hazard of aftershocks, we should consider not only the magnitude of the initial large earthquake, but also the nature of the aftershock activity itself.

Our scheme assumed that aftershocks occur at the same location as the initial large event. However, for earthquakes with magnitudes exceeding 7,

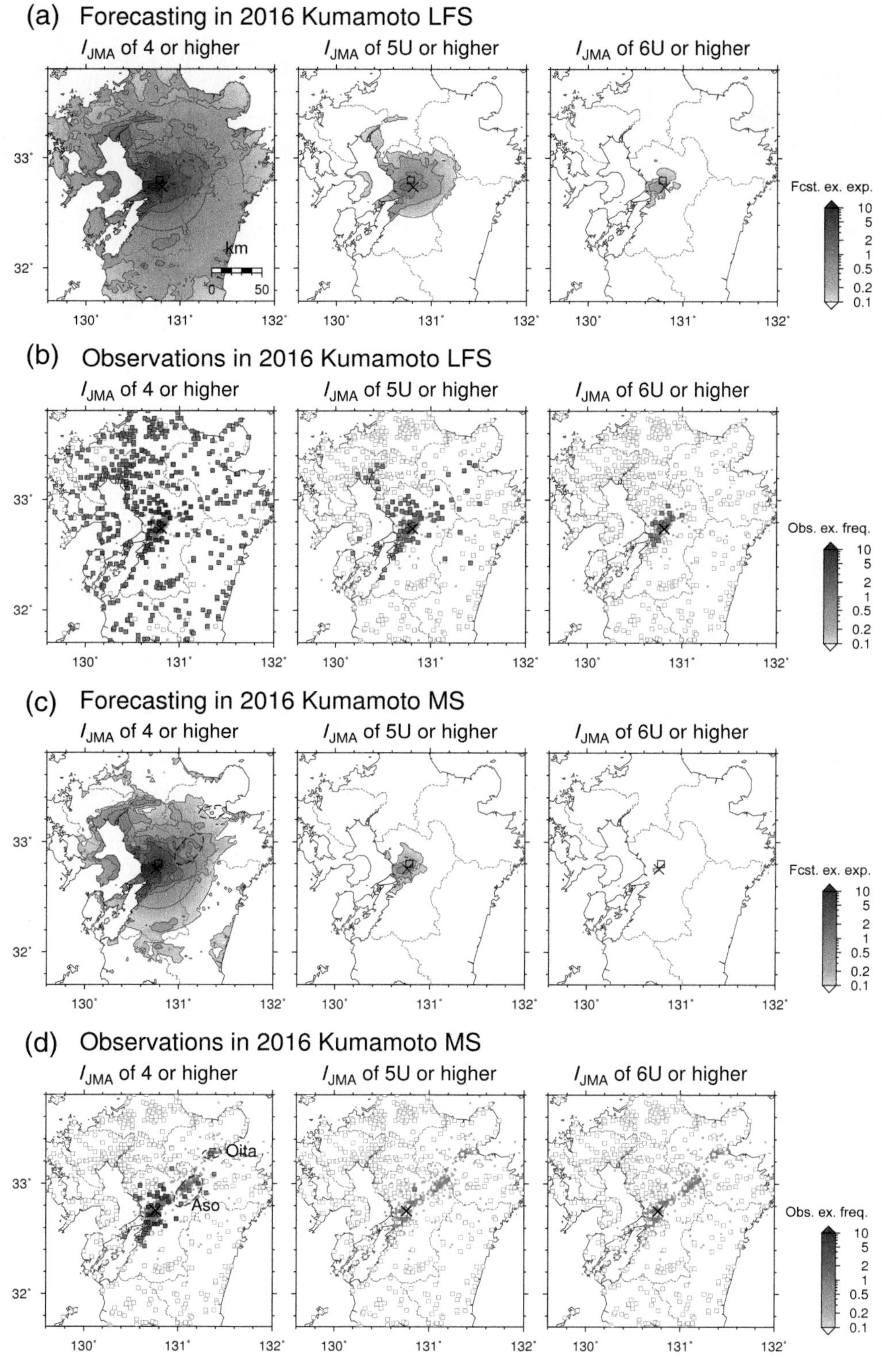

Figure 4. Spatial distributions of the forecasted exceedance expectation for 0.25–1.25 day according to JMA seismic intensities of ≥4, ≥5U, and ≥6U for the (a) 2016 Kumamoto LFS and (c) MS. The spatial distributions of the observed exceedance frequency of the JMA seismic intensities (squares) for the (b) 2016 Kumamoto LFS and (d) MS. Crosses denote epicenters. Squares in panels (a) and (c) denote the location of KMM006, of which the point forecasting results are shown in Figures 2 and 3. Blue circles in panels (b) and (d) denote the epicenters of the aftershocks within the forecast period. Squares are filled with colors corresponding to the scale bar if at least one record is available. If there is no record, the square is left blank. The color version of this figure is available only in the electronic edition.

the finiteness of the source fault and associated aftershock distribution should be accounted for. Moreover, aftershock seismicity can be activated even at locations far from the source fault, as in the case of the 2016 Kumamoto MS. Ignoring the spatial extent of aftershocks in our proposed method could lead to an underestimation of aftershock hazards in areas near the aftershock zone and far from the epicenter of the initial event, as discussed earlier, and an overestimation near the epicenter of the initial event. To consider the spatial extent of aftershocks, future studies should estimate the major aftershock area from an event catalog during the first few hours after the initial large event. This is a major challenge due to the limited number of earthquakes and lower quality of the initial event catalog automatically detected.

There are cases for which continuous seismic records from observation stations are interrupted by power outages and/or communication failures after a large earthquake. In such cases, a site-specific forecast of seismic hazard based directly on the observed seismic records (Lippiello *et al.*, 2016; Sawazaki *et al.*, 2016; Sawazaki, 2021, 2025) is not applicable to the stations where seismic data are unavailable. However, our approach based on the event catalog is robust as long as data from a regional network consisting of many seismometers are used to detect and locate earthquakes; the deterioration of earthquake detection due to data loss at observation stations can be treated as a deterioration of seismic detection in our approach

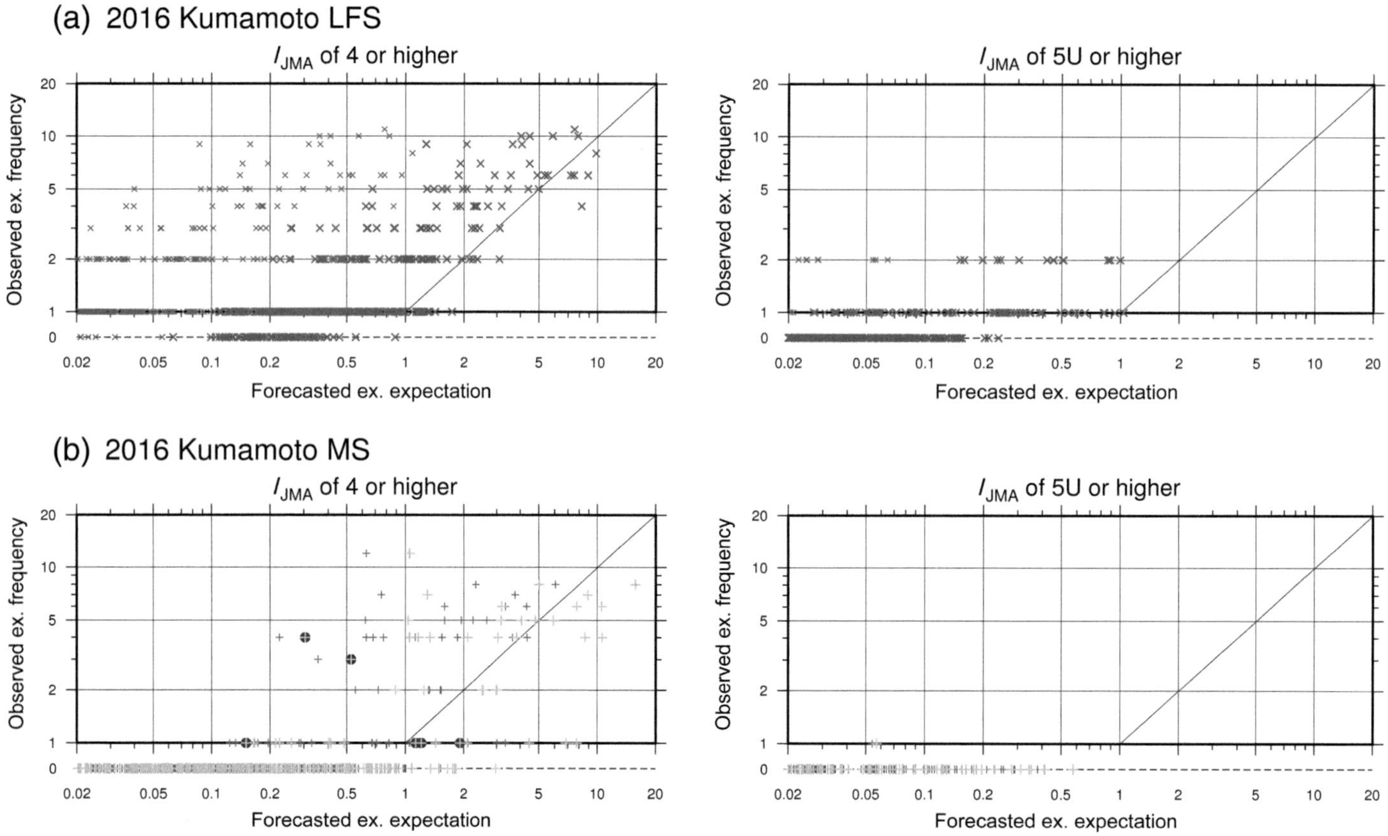

Figure 5. Relationship between the forecasted exceedance expectation in the proposed method and observed exceedance frequency of the JMA seismic intensities at observation stations for 0.25–1.25 day following the (a) 2016 Kumamoto LFS (red cross) and (b) MS (yellow plus). Here, the relationships at the stations shown in Figure 4b,d are plotted. The left and right plots correspond to JMA seismic intensities of ≥4 and ≥5U, respectively. Gray symbols indicate the forecast results in using the generic model parameters. Yellow pluses with a gray circle in the left plot of panel (b) indicate the forecast results in the proposed method at stations located in the Aso and Oita regions, which are shown by the dashed ellipse in Figure 4d. The diagonal gray line indicates the 1:1 ratio line, for which the forecasted exceedance expectation perfectly matches the observed exceedance frequency. The color version of this figure is available only in the electronic edition.

based on Omi *et al.* (2013). In contrast, a site-specific forecast can manage peculiar ground motions due to local subsurface structures and local seismic phenomena. Thus, the site-specific forecast and the event catalog-based forecast are complementary; their combination should lead to more robust and accurate forecasts.

Previous studies have used long-term observation records (Miyazawa and Mori, 2009; Mak and Schorlemmer, 2016; Gee *et al.*, 2022) to evaluate the validity of the PSHA. However, a similar verification approach is difficult for short-term forecasts given the short observation window, requiring the analyses of more earthquakes and different case data. Further studies should evaluate the validity of our scheme for subduction earthquakes. In addition, accelerating and optimizing our computational algorithm is important for implementing probabilistic aftershock hazard assessment in semi real time. This study used an event catalog covering 6 hr after the initial large earthquake. Although the use of shorter-period event catalogs would allow for earlier seismic hazard assessments of aftershocks, investigating the relationship between the forecast accuracy and stability over time and improving the automatically determined event catalog both in terms of quality and quantity are important.

Data and Resources

The original code of Omi *et al.* (2013) is available at https://github.com/omitakahiro/AftFore. The automatic hypocenter catalog data of Hi-net is available at https://hinetwww11.bosai.go.jp/auth/hinet_hypolist/. The Japan Meteorological Agency (JMA) seismic intensity database (Ishigaki and Takagi, 2000) is available at https://www.data.jma.go.jp/eqev/data/bulletin/shindo.html. The V_{S30} map of Japan in Matsuoka and Wakamatsu (2008) is available at https://www.j-shis.bosai.go.jp/. The Generic Mapping Tools (GMT; Wessel and Smith, 1998) were used to draw the figures. All websites were last accessed in July 2025. The supplemental material for this article includes Figure S1 to plot the locations of the four crustal earthquakes to which the proposed scheme was applied in this study.

Declaration of Competing Interests

The authors acknowledge that there are no conflicts of interest recorded.

Acknowledgments

The authors thank three anonymous reviewers for their helpful comments. The authors also would like to thank Yosihiko Ogata, Takahiro Omi, Kaoru Sawazaki, Shinichi Kawai, and Takahiro Shiina for their insightful comments. This study was supported by Ministry of Education, Culture, Sports, Science and Technology (MEXT) Project for Seismology toward Research Innovation with Data of Earthquake (STAR-E) Grant Number JPJ010217.

References

Aoi, S., Y. Asano, T. Kunugi, T. Kimura, K. Uehira, N. Takahashi, H. Ueda, K. Shiomi, T. Matsumoto, and H. Fujiwara (2020). MOWLAS: NIED observation network for earthquake, tsunami and volcano, *Earth Planets Space* **72,** no. 1, 126, doi: 10.1186/s40623-020-01250-x.

Baker, J., B. Bradley, and P. Stafford (2021). *Seismic Hazard and Risk Analysis*, Cambridge University Press, London, UK.

Fujimoto, K., and S. Midorikawa (2006). Relationship between average shear-wave velocity and site amplification inferred from strong motion records at nearby station pairs, *J. Jpn. Assoc. Earthq. Eng.* **6,** no. 1, 11–22, doi: 10.5610/jaee.6.11.

Fujiwara, H., N. Morikawa, T. Maeda, A. Iwaki, S. Senna, S. Kawai, H. Azuma, K. X. Hao, M. Imoto, K. Wakamatsu, *et al.* (2023). Improved seismic hazard assessment after the 2011 great East Japan earthquake (Part 2), *Technical Note of the National Research Institute for Earth Science and Disaster Resilience, no. 489*, 1–391, doi: 10.24732/nied.00003933.

Fujiwara, H., N. Morikawa, and T. Okumura (2013). Seismic hazard assessment for Japan: Reconsiderations after the 2011 Tohoku earthquake, *J. Disaster Res.* **8,** no. 5, 848–860, doi: 10.20965/jdr.2013.p0848.

Gee, R., L. Peruzza, and M. Pagani (2022). The power of the little ones: Computed and observed aftershock hazard in Central Italy, *Earthq. Spectra* 38, no. 1, 702–724, doi: 10.1177/87552930211036913.

Gerstenberger, M. C., S. Wiemer, L. M. Jones, and P. A. Reasenberg (2005). Real-time forecasts of tomorrow's earthquakes in California, *Nature* **435,** no. 7040, 328–331, doi: 10.1038/nature03622.

Gutenberg, B., and C. F. Richter (1944). Frequency of earthquakes in California, *Bull. Seismol. Soc. Am.* **34,** no. 4, 185–188, doi: 10.1785/bssa0340040185.

Hallo, M., I. Opršal, K. Asano, and F. Gallovič (2019). Seismotectonics of the 2018 northern Osaka M6.1 earthquake and its aftershocks: Joint movements on strike-slip and reverse faults in inland Japan, *Earth Planets Space* **71,** 34, doi: 10.1186/s40623-019-1016-8.

Hardebeck, J. L., A. L. Llenos, A. J. Michael, M. T. Page, M. Schneider, and N. J. van der Elst (2024). Aftershock forecasting, *Annu. Rev. Earth Planet. Sci.* **52,** no. 1, 61–84, doi: 10.1146/annurev-earth-040522-102129.

Hoshiba, M., K. Ohtake, K. Iwakiri, T. Aketagawa, H. Nakamura, and S. Yamamoto, (2010). How precisely can we anticipate seismic intensities? A study of uncertainty of anticipated seismic intensities for the Earthquake Early Warning method in Japan, *Earth Planets Space* **62,** no. 8, 611–620, doi: 10.5047/eps.2010.07.013.

Hsieh, M.-C., C.-H. Chan, K.-F. Ma, Y.-T. Yen, C.-T. Chen, D.-Y. Chen, and Y.-W. Mika Liao (2024). Toward real-time ground-shaking-intensity forecasting using ETAS and GMM: Insights from the analysis of the 2022 Taitung earthquake sequence, *Seismol. Res. Lett.* **95,** no. 6, 3264–3277, doi: 10.1785/0220240180.

Ishigaki, Y., and A. Takagi (2000). JMA seismic intensity data base and several operational utility examples, *Q. J. Seismol.* **63,** 75–92.

Japan Meteorological Agency (JMA) (1996). *Seismic Intensity*, Gyosei, Tokyo, Japan.

JMA (2024). Technical reference materials on the overview and processing methods of earthquake early warning, Japan Meteorological Agency.

Kamaya, N., K. Takeda, and T. Hashimoto (2017). New Japanese guidelines for the information of the prospect of seismic activity after large earthquakes and their applications, *J. Disaster Res.* **12,** no. 6, 1109–1116, doi: 10.20965/jdr.2017.p1109.

Kato, A., and T. Ueda (2019). Source fault model of the 2018 Mw 5.6 northern Osaka earthquake, Japan, inferred from the aftershock sequence, *Earth Planets Space* **71,** 11, doi: 10.1186/s40623-019-0995-9.

Kodera, Y., Y. Yamada, K. Hirano, K. Tamaribuchi, S. Adachi, N. Hayashimoto, M. Morimoto, M. Nakamura, and M. Hoshiba (2018). The propagation of local undamped motion (PLUM) method: A simple and robust seismic wavefield estimation approach for earthquake early warning, *Bull. Seismol. Soc. Am.* 108, no. 2, 983–1003, doi: 10.1785/0120170085.

Kubo, H., W. Suzuki, S. Aoi, and H. Sekiguchi (2016). Source rupture processes of the 2016 Kumamoto, Japan, earthquakes estimated from strong-motion waveforms, *Earth Planets Space* **68,** 161, doi: 10.1186/s40623-016-0536-8.

Lippiello, E., A. Cirillo, G. Godano, E. Papadimitriou, and V. Karakostas (2016). Real-time forecast of aftershocks from a single seismic station signal, *Geophys. Res. Lett.* **43,** no. 12, 6252–6258, doi: 10.1002/2016gl069748.

Mak, S., and D. Schorlemmer (2016). A comparison between the forecast by the United States national seismic hazard maps with recent ground-motion records, *Bull. Seismol. Soc. Am.* **106,** no. 4, 1817–1831, doi: 10.1785/0120150323.

Matsuoka, M., and K. Wakamatsu (2008). Site amplification capability map based on the 7.5-arc-second Japan engineering geomorphologic classification map, National Institute of Advanced Industrial Science and Technology, Intellectual property management, No.H20PRO-936.

Midorikawa, S., K. Fujimoto, and I. Muramatsu (1999). Instrumental seismic intensity with former J.M.A. seismic intensity and ground motion parameters, *J. Soc. Saf. Sci.* **1,** 51–56, doi: 10.11314/jisss.1.51.

Miyazawa, M., and J. Mori (2009). Test of seismic hazard map from 500 years of recorded intensity data in Japan, *Bull. Seismol. Soc. Am.* **99,** no. 6, 3140–3149, doi: 10.1785/0120080262.

Mizrahi, L., I. Dallo, N. J. van der Elst, A. Christophersen, I. Spassiani, M. J. Werner, P. Iturrieta, J. A. Bayona, I. Iervolino, M. Schneider, *et al.* (2024). Developing, testing, and communicating earthquake forecasts: Current practices and future directions, *Rev. Geophys.* **62,** no. 3, e2023RG000823, doi: 10.1029/2023rg000823.

National Research Institute for Earth Science and Disaster Resilience (NIED) (2019). J-SHIS Japan seismic hazard information station, doi: 10.17598/nied.0010.

Ogata, Y., and K. Katsura (1993). Analysis of temporal and spatial heterogeneity of magnitude frequency distribution inferred from earthquake catalogues, *Geophys. J. Int.* **113,** no. 3, 727–738, doi: 10.1111/j.1365-246x.1993.tb04663.x.

Ogata, Y., and K. Katsura (2006). Immediate and updated forecasting of aftershock hazard, *Geophys. Res. Lett.* **33,** L10305, doi: 10.1029/2006gl025888.

Okada, Y., K. Kasahara, S. Hori, K. Obara, S. Sekiguchi, H. Fujiwara, and A. Yamamoto (2004). Recent progress of seismic observation networks in Japan—Hi-net, F-net, K-NET and KiK-net, *Earth Planets Space* **56,** no. 8, xv–xxviii, doi: 10.1186/bf03353076.

Omi, T., Y. Ogata, Y. Hirata, and K. Aihara (2013). Forecasting large aftershocks within one day after the main shock, *Sci. Rep.* **3,** 2218, doi: 10.1038/srep02218.

Omi, T., Y. Ogata, Y. Hirata, and K. Aihara (2015). Intermediate-term forecasting of aftershocks from an early aftershock sequence: Bayesian and ensemble forecasting approaches, *J. Geophys. Res.* **120,** no. 4, 2561–2578, doi: 10.1002/2014jb011456.

Omi, T., Y. Ogata, K. Shiomi, B. Enescu, K. Sawazaki, and K. Aihara (2016). Automatic aftershock forecasting: A test using real-time seismicity data in Japan, *Bull. Seismol. Soc. Am.* **106,** no. 6, 2450–2458, doi: 10.1785/0120160100.

Omi, T., Y. Ogata, K. Shiomi, B. Enescu, K. Sawazaki, and K. Aihara (2019). Implementation of a real-time system for automatic aftershock forecasting in japan, *Seismol. Res. Lett.* **90,** no. 1, 242–250, doi: 10.1785/0220180213.

Reasenberg, P. A., and L. M. Jones (1989). Earthquake hazard after a mainshock in California, *Science* **243,** no. 4895, 1173–1176, doi: 10.1126/science.243.4895.1173.

Ringdal, F. (1975). On the estimation of seismic detection thresholds, *Bull. Seismol. Soc. Am.* **65,** no. 6, 1631–1642, doi: 10.1785/bssa0650061631.

Sato, R., K. Abe, Y. Okada, K. Shimazaki, and Y. Suzuki (1989). *Handbook of Earthquake Fault Parameters in Japan*, Kajima Institute Publishing Co., Ltd., Tokyo, Japan.

Sawazaki, K. (2021). Early forecast of maximum amplitude due to aftershocks by applying extreme value statistics to a single continuous seismogram, *Bull. Seismol. Soc. Am.* **111,** no. 5, 2825–2845, doi: 10.1785/0120200365.

Sawazaki, K. (2025). Integration of extreme value statistics and Bayesian estimation for early forecasting of aftershock shaking: Application to main shock–aftershock sequences in inland Japan, *Geophys. J. Int.* **241,** no. 3, 1518–1534, doi: 10.1093/gji/ggaf109.

Sawazaki, K., H. Nakahara, and K. Shiomi (2016). Preliminary estimation of high-frequency (4–20 Hz) energy released from the 2016 Kumamoto, Japan, earthquake sequence, *Earth Planets Space* **68,** no. 1, doi: 10.1186/s40623-016-0557-3.

Si, H., and S. Midorikawa (1999). New attenuation relationships for peak ground acceleration and velocity considering effects of fault type and site condition, *J. Struct. Constr. Eng. (Trans. AIJ)* **64,** no. 523, 63–70, doi: 10.3130/aijs.64.63_2.

Suzuki, W., S. Aoi, T. Kunugi, H. Kubo, N. Morikawa, H. Nakamura, T. Kimura, and H. Fujiwara (2017). Strong motions observed by K-NET and KiK-net during the 2016 Kumamoto earthquake sequence, *Earth Planets Space* **69,** 19, doi: 10.1186/s40623-017-0604-8.

Ueda, T., A. Kato, Y. Ogata, and L. Yamaya (2021). Spatial variations in seismicity characteristics in and around the source region of the 2019 Yamagata-Oki Earthquake, Japan, *Earth Planets Space* **73,** 40, doi: 10.1186/s40623-020-01325-9.

Usami, T., H. Ishii, T. Imamura, M. Takemura, and R. S. Matsu'ura (2013). *The Catalogue of Disaster Earthquake in Japan 599–2012*, University of Tokyo Press, Tokyo, Japan.

Utsu, T. (1961). A statistical study on the occurrence of aftershocks, *Geophys. Mag.* **30,** 521–605.

Utsu, T. (1969). Aftershocks earthquake statistics (1): Some parameters which characterize aftershock sequence interrelations, *J. Fac. Sci. Hokkaido* **3,** 129–195.

Utsu, T. (1977). *Seismology*, Kyoritsu Shuppan, Tokyo, Japan.

Utsu, T. (1982). Relationships between earthquake magnitude scales, *Bull. Earthq. Res. Inst. Univ. Tokyo* **57,** 465–497.

Utsu, T., Y. Ogata, and R. Matsu'ura (1995). The centenary of the Omori formula for a decay law of aftershock activity, *J. Phys. Earth* **43,** no. 1, 1–33, doi: 10.4294/jpe1952.43.1.

van der Elst, N. J. (2021). *B-positive*: A robust estimator of aftershock magnitude distribution in transiently incomplete catalogs, *J. Geophys. Res.* **126,** no. 2, e2020JB021027, doi: 10.1029/2020jb021027.

Wessel, P., and W. H. F. Smith (1998). New, improved version of generic mapping tools released, *Eos Trans. AGU* **79,** no. 47, 579–579, doi: 10.1029/98eo00426.

Wiemer, S. (2000). Introducing probabilistic aftershock hazard mapping, *Geophys. Res. Lett.* **27,** no. 20, 3405–3408, doi: 10.1029/2000gl011479.

Yano, T. E., and M. Matsubara (2017). Effect of newly refined hypocenter locations on the seismic activity recorded during the 2016 Kumamoto Earthquake sequence, *Earth Planets Space* **69,** 74, doi: 10.1186/s40623-017-0656-9.

Yeo, G. L., and C. A. Cornell (2009). A probabilistic framework for quantification of aftershock ground-motion hazard in California: Methodology and parametric study, *Earthq. Eng. Struct. Dynam.* **38,** no. 1, 45–60, doi: 10.1002/eqe.840.

Yoshida, K., N. Uchida, S. Hiarahara, T. Nakayama, T. Matsuzawa, T. Okada, Y. Matsumoto, and A. Hasegawa (2020). 2019 M6.7 Yamagata-Oki earthquake in the stress shadow of 2011 Tohoku-Oki earthquake: Was it caused by the reduction in fault strength? *Tectonophysics* **793,** 228609, doi: 10.1016/j.tecto.2020.228609.

Manuscript received 3 April 2025
Published online 13 August 2025

On the Lagged Coherence Estimation for Seismic Ground Motions

Xizhong Cui*[1,2]

Abstract

This article questioned and examined the adequacy of using the Fourier transform (FT) to estimate the frequency-dependent but time-independent lagged coherence of ground motions following evolutionary theory, which was widely used in the stochastic ground-motion modeling. Accurate estimation of lagged coherence is paramount for understanding the spatial variability and model development of seismic ground motions. FT was widely applied in the estimation of lagged coherence and for coherence model development, whereas its adequacy was never investigated. First, by assuming the ground motions as evolutionary processes, this study critically examines the application of the FT for estimating frequency-dependent only coherency and lagged coherence. Notably, the investigation reveals the FT's limitations in accurately calculating lagged coherence for nonstationary ground motions, demonstrating an inconsistent bias across ground motions with different nonstationary characteristics, thus rendering it unsuitable for reliable lagged coherence estimation of ground motions. To address this critical issue, a new method based on the *S* transform is proposed for the estimation of time-independent lagged coherence between evolutionary processes, designed to yield a consistent and negligibly small bias for ground motions with different nonstationary characteristics. The comparison of the estimated time-independent lagged coherence from real records using FT and the proposed method is also shown and substantiates the above examination. Further, by jumping out of the concept of evolutionary theory, the study also investigates both the calculated time-independent and time-dependent lagged coherence of actual historical ground motion records, providing valuable observations and discussions that contribute to a more robust understanding of the spatial and temporal dependencies inherent in seismic excitations. This research offers a more reliable approach for characterizing the complex coherence structure of nonstationary ground motions, crucial for advanced seismic risk and resilience assessments.

Cite this article as Cui, X. (2025). On the Lagged Coherence Estimation for Seismic Ground Motions, *Seismol. Res. Lett.* **97**, 295–308, doi: 10.1785/0220250111.

Introduction

Seismic ground motions are known as nonstationary stochastic processes for which statistical properties (e.g., mean, variance, and spectral content) change with time and with spatial variation along the ground surface and depth (Zerva, 2016). The spatial variation of ground motions is crucial for understanding the risk of a group of regional structures (Goda and Hong, 2009) with extended foundations or supports. Seismic ground motions are complex phenomena that arise from the propagation of seismic waves generated by earthquake ruptures. These waves can travel vast distances, interacting with the geologic conditions and structural properties along their path. As a result, ground motions recorded at different locations or time intervals exhibit significant variability and irregularities. One of the spatial variability and irregularities of ground motions is the phase variation of the ground-motion records at different sites (Kiureghian, 1996). The phase variation of ground-motion records may have significant implications on the responses of structures with multiple supports or extended rigid foundations, for which the energy distribution variation in space may be negligible. The spatial variation of ground excitations will increase the internal forces or maximum displacement of structures with multiple supports (Li *et al.*, 2014) and amplify the rocking or torsional responses of structures with rigid foundation (Abrahamson *et al.*, 1991).

1. School of Intelligent Civil and Ocean Engineering, Harbin Institute of Technology, Shenzhen, China, https://orcid.org/0000-0002-3734-1066 (XC); 2. Guangdong Provincial Key Laboratory of Intelligent and Resilient Structures for Civil Engineering, Shenzhen, China

*Corresponding author: xzcui824@163.com

The quantity used for describing the phase difference variation between ground motions is usually known as coherency, or coherence, or lagged coherence. Coherency is a theoretical definition without smoothing and, in some literature, is also known as complex coherence (Carter, 1980), and coherence is usually known as the squared magnitude of coherency (Benignus, 1969a; Torrence and Compo, 1998; Zoubir, 2005). The coherency and coherence represent different quantitative measures, yet in some studies in earthquake engineering or seismology, coherence is usually used interchangeably with coherency. The lagged coherence is widely used in earthquake engineering or seismology, and equals the square root of the coherence (Zerva, 2016), in which the wave passage effect is removed (Der Kiureghian, 1996). Considering a single pair of processes or records from an ideal constant parameter linear system, the value of the coherence or lagged coherence is always identical to the unit if the smoothing operation is not applied (Cohen and Walden, 2010; Zerva, 2016). Therefore, smoothing of the spectrum obtained from the transformed coefficients is usually suggested before calculating the coherence or lagged coherence (Zerva, 2016). Smoothing could help extract the true spectral trends by reducing high-frequency noise, resulting in a more stable and representative estimate of the underlying lagged coherence. It is known that the calculation of lagged coherence between stationary Gaussian processes after smoothing operation is always associated with positive bias (Benignus, 1969a; Nuttall and Carter, 1976), and the value of bias is both a function of "effective degrees of freedom" or known as the shape of the smoothing window and of the true coherence (Enochson and Goodman, 1965; Benignus, 1969a). Benignus (1969b) also discussed the coherence estimation of non-Gaussian processes.

Although earthquake ground motions are known as highly nonstationary processes and usually modeled as evolutionary process, the use of Fourier transform (FT) to assess the lagged coherence between historical ground motions from dense arrays is frequently used in the literature (Hao *et al.*, 1989; Abrahamson *et al.*, 1991; Liu and Hong, 2016; Zerva, 2016; Rodda and Basu, 2018), based on the records from dense arrays (mostly from Strong Motion Array in Taiwan [SMART-1] and Lotung Large-Scale Seismic Test [LSST] arrays). The lagged coherence estimated using FT is frequency-dependent only. And the reason for frequently using FT to assess the lagged coherence of nonstationary ground motions might be due to the wide application of evolutionary theory for modeling nonstationary processes, a pioneering work done by Priestley (1965), in earthquake engineering. Moreover, Priestley and Tong (1973) had mathematically proved that the coherency between evolutionary processes is frequency dependent but time independent. The evolutionary process is a popular subclass of nonstationary process and widely used in earthquake engineering to model the nonstationary ground motions; it is defined by applying a time–frequency-dependent amplitude modulation function over the spectrum of the stationary process (Priestley, 1965; Conte and Peng, 1997). Because the representation obtained from FT obeys the assumption of frequency-dependent coherence for evolutionary processes, using FT in assessing the lagged coherence and developing the model for ground motions was widely adopted in most developed lagged coherence models in the literature. As mentioned earlier, the calculated lagged coherence using FT is biased due to the smoothing operation. Among the literature, Abrahamson *et al.* (1991) include a bias correction factor in the calculated lagged coherence after the smoothing operation, whereas other studies rarely discuss the bias issue. In Abrahamson *et al.* (1991), the included bias correction factors are determined from the expected median lagged coherence for incoherent white noise, which is based on the stationary processes. Although parametric time series models (e.g., autoregressive models) are also widely used in ground-motion modeling (Rupakhety and Sigbjornsson, 2012) because the following bias analysis primarily focuses on evolutionary processes, such models are not further discussed here. The frequency-dependent only lagged coherence was widely used in earthquake engineering and mostly developed based on the estimated lagged coherence using FT. However, the bias of estimated lagged coherence using FT illustrated in Enochson and Goodman (1965) and Benignus (1969a) is adequate or not for the calculated lagged coherence between evolutionary processes using FT is unknown. This would be the first thing the author would like to examine in the present study. It is also followed by a suggested new method in estimating the time-independent lagged coherence between ground motions with consistent small and negligible bias.

The power spectral density (PSD) distribution of an evolutionary process is called evolutionary PSD (Priestley, 1965) and is usually estimated using the time–frequency decomposition method (Priestley, 1965; Hong, 2023). Although based on the evolutionary theory, the lagged coherence between evolutionary processes is theoretically time independent (Priestley and Tong, 1973), if jumping out the evolutionary theory, several recent studies found that the lagged coherence between ground motions is time dependent, using continuous wavelet transform (Abbas and Tezcan, 2019; Qiao *et al.*, 2020) and *S* transform (ST; Cui and Hong, 2021a; Xiao *et al.*, 2024). The use of the time–frequency decomposition method directly to estimate the time-dependent lagged coherence indeed drops the concept of evolutionary theory, which could be viewed as a transform pair-based analysis method (Hong and Cui, 2023).

In the present study, I will first quickly review the use of FT and ST to estimate the coherency and lagged coherence, which lays the theoretical foundation for the later investigation. After that, the effect of the smoothing window on the bias in the estimated lagged coherence between stationary processes is revisited and illustrated. The revisit serves to help the reader understand the source of the bias, which will facilitate the following investigation on nonstationary processes. This study examines the adequacy of using the FT to calculate lagged coherence between ground motions and finds that this approach leads to inconsistent bias among records with different nonstationary characteristics, even if their true coherence is the same. It is pointed out that the FT should not be used for the lagged coherence calculation and model development for nonstationary ground motions, even if evolutionary theory is adopted. To address the inconsistent bias issue of lagged coherence estimation between evolutionary processes using FT, a new method based on ST is suggested for the estimation of the frequency-dependent only lagged coherence with a consistent ignorable minor bias. Then, considering real records from the SMART-1 dense array, the comparison of the estimated lagged coherence using FT and the proposed method indicates once again that employing FT will result in significant and inconsistent bias. As a result, the adequacy of the developed lagged coherence model based on FT is doubtful. Finally, by dropping the evolutionary theory, the facts of time-dependent lagged coherence for nonstationary ground motions are investigated using actual historical records. Some observations and discussions are given.

Review of Lagged Coherence Estimation Based on FT and ST

Given two processes $x(t)$ and $y(t)$ with the same duration, the coherence between $x(t)$ and $y(t)$ is defined as

$$\gamma_{xy}(\Omega) = \frac{S_{xy}(\Omega)}{\sqrt{S_{xx}(\Omega)S_{yy}(\Omega)}}, \tag{1}$$

in which $S_{xy}(\Omega)$ and $S_{xx}(\Omega)$ (or $S_{yy}(\Omega)$) are the cross and auto PSDs in domain Ω in which the PSDs and the associated domain Ω are defined by different transform pairs (i.e., FT, ST, continuous wavelet transform, etc.) that will be further elaborated in the following. The cross PSD $S_{xy}(\Omega)$ is usually complex, and its real and imaginary parts are usually denoted as cospectral $S_{xy,\mathrm{Co}}(\Omega) = \mathrm{real}(S_{xy}(\Omega))$ and quadrature spectral $S_{xy,Q}(\Omega) = \mathrm{imag}(S_{xy}(\Omega))$ (Stull, 2012). Directly taking the absolute value of coherency always results in a value identical to unity (Percival and Walden, 2000). Therefore, the smoothing operation should be applied to the cross and auto PSD before calculating the lagged coherence,

$$|\gamma_{xy}(\Omega)| = \frac{|\tilde{S}_{xy}(\Omega)|}{\sqrt{\tilde{S}_{xx}(\Omega)\tilde{S}_{yy}(\Omega)}} = \frac{|\mathcal{S}[S_{xy}(\Omega)]|}{\sqrt{\mathcal{S}[S_{xx}(\Omega)]\mathcal{S}[S_{yy}(\Omega)]}}, \tag{2}$$

in which $\tilde{S}$ is the smoothed PSD and $\mathcal{S}[\bullet]$ denote the smoothing operation applied on the domain Ω. Different transform pairs could be used to estimate the coherence and result in a different domain Ω. Then, the key problem in estimating the coherency is the calculation of the auto and cross PSD. Moreover, the ground motions are usually given in discrete time series, therefore, in the following, the analyzed ground motions are considered as N-point length time series $x(k\Delta_t)$ and $y(k\Delta_t)$ (k = 0, 1, …, N-1) and Δ_t is the time increment. The duration of both time series is T and equals $N\Delta_t$.

Based on FT

By applying the discrete Fourier transform (DFT) to $x(k\Delta_t)$, the DFT coefficients are

$$\begin{aligned} x_F(p\Delta_f) &= \mathrm{DFT}_{k\to p}(x(k\Delta_t)) \\ &= \Delta_t \sum_{k=0}^{N-1} x(k\Delta_t)\exp(-i2\pi kp/N), \end{aligned} \tag{3}$$

in which $p = -N/2 + 1,\ldots,N/2$ and Δ_f is the frequency increment which is equal to $1/(N\Delta_t)$. The $x(k\Delta_t)$ could be reconstructed through inverse DFT (IDFT) with DFT coefficients $x_F(p\Delta_f)$,

$$\begin{aligned} x(k\Delta_t) &= \mathrm{IDFT}_{p\to k}(x_F(p\Delta_f)) \\ &= (N\Delta_t)^{-1} \sum_{p=-N/2+1}^{N/2} x_F(p\Delta_f)\exp(i2\pi pk/N). \end{aligned} \tag{4}$$

The DFT coefficients of $y(k\Delta_t)$ is $y_F(p\Delta_f)$ and obtained through equation (3) with x replaced by y. For DFT case, the domain Ω is the frequency domain and is denoted as $p\Delta_f$. The double-sided cross PSD of $x(k\Delta_t)$ and $y(k\Delta_t)$ is defined as (Zerva, 2016)

$$S_{xy}(p\Delta_f) = x_F(p\Delta_f)y_F^*(p\Delta_f)/T, \tag{5}$$

in which the * denotes the complex conjugate operation. The double-sided auto PSD of $x(k\Delta_t)$ or $y(k\Delta_t)$ can be obtained through equation (5) by substituting y with x or x with y, respectively. The smoothed cross PSD is calculated at discrete frequencies using

$$\tilde{S}_{xy}(p\Delta_f) = \sum_{m=-M}^{+M} W(m\Delta_f)S_{xy}(p\Delta_f + m\Delta_f), \tag{6}$$

in which $W(m\Delta f)$ is the window with $2M + 1$ points. Different types of windows, including boxcar, Hanning, and Hamming windows (Newland, 2012), could be used in the smoothing operation. The smoothed auto PSD $\tilde{S}_{xx}(p\Delta_f)$ and $\tilde{S}_{yy}(p\Delta_f)$ are obtained through applying the smoothing operation on the $S_{xx}(p\Delta_f)$ and $S_{yy}(p\Delta_f)$. The lagged coherence between $x(k\Delta_t)$ and $y(k\Delta_t)$ then becomes

$$|\gamma_{xy}(p\Delta_f)| = \frac{|\tilde{S}_{xy}(p\Delta_f)|}{\sqrt{\tilde{S}_{xx}(p\Delta_f)\tilde{S}_{yy}(p\Delta_f)}}, \tag{7}$$

in which the $\gamma_{xy}(p\Delta_f)$ denotes the calculated coherency and can be defined using equation (7) if the absolute and smoothing operations are not involved.

Based on ST

The FT only presents the frequency representation. To obtain the time–frequency characteristics from nonstationary processes, the ST for discrete time series $x(k\Delta_t)$ is (Stockwell *et al.*, 1996; Hong and Cui, 2023)

$$x_S(p\Delta_f,q\Delta_t) = ST_{k\rightarrow(p,q)}(x(k\Delta_t)) = \sum x(k\Delta_t)w_S(p\Delta_f,q\Delta_t - k\Delta_t)e^{-i2\pi pq/N}, \quad (8)$$

in which $x_S(p\Delta_f,q\Delta_t)$ is the ST coefficients and $w_S(p\Delta_f,q\Delta_t - k\Delta_t)$ is the Gaussian window that depends on both time and frequency,

$$w_S(p\Delta_f,q\Delta_t - k\Delta_t) = |p\Delta_f|e^{-p^2(q-k)^2/2N^2}/\sqrt{2\pi}. \quad (9)$$

If the window in equation (9) is frequency-dependent only, then the ST becomes the traditional short-time FT with a Gaussian window. The ST coefficient in equation (8) could be evaluated by taking advantage of fast Fourier transform to gain computational efficiency (Battisti and Riba, 2016) and equation (8) becomes

$$x_S(p\Delta_f,q\Delta_t) = ST_{k\rightarrow(p,q)}(x(k\Delta_t)) = \mathrm{IDFT}_{j\rightarrow q}\left(x_F((j+p)\Delta_f)\exp\left(-\frac{2\pi^2 j^2}{p^2}\right)\right). \quad (10)$$

The reconstruction of $x(k\Delta_t)$ through inverse ST (IST) with ST coefficients $x_S(p\Delta_f,q\Delta_t)$ is

$$x(k\Delta_t) = \mathrm{IST}_{(p,q)\rightarrow k}(x_S(p\Delta_f,q\Delta_t)) = \mathrm{IDFT}_{p\rightarrow k}\left(\Delta_t\sum_{q=0}^{N-1}x_S(p\Delta_f,q\Delta_t)\right). \quad (11)$$

The ST coefficients of $y(k\Delta_t)$ are denoted as $y_S(p\Delta_f,q\Delta_t)$. The cross PSD between $x(k\Delta_t)$ and $y(k\Delta_t)$ is (Cui and Hong, 2021a)

$$S_{S,xy}(p\Delta_f,q\Delta_t) = 2\sqrt{\pi}x_S(p\Delta_f,q\Delta_t)y_S^*(p\Delta_f,q\Delta_t)/|p\Delta_f|. \quad (12)$$

The double-sided auto PSD of $x(k\Delta_t)$ or $y(k\Delta_t)$ based on ST can be obtained through equation (12) by substituting y with x or y with x, respectively. The smoothed cross PSD is calculated at discrete frequencies using

$$\tilde{S}_{S,xy}(p\Delta_f,q\Delta_t) = \sum_{m=-M}^{+M}\sum_{h=-H}^{+H}W_S(m\Delta_f,h\Delta_t)S_{S,xy}(p\Delta_f + m\Delta_f,q\Delta_t + h\Delta_t), \quad (13)$$

in which $W_S(m\Delta_f,h\Delta_t)$ is a manually selected window with matrix size equal $(2M + 1) \times (2H + 1)$. In Cui and Hong (2021a), they adopted a rectangular window for the smoothing.

According to equation (1), the coherency is

$$\gamma_{xy}(p\Delta_f,q\Delta_t) = \frac{S_{S,xy}(p\Delta_f,q\Delta_t)}{\sqrt{S_{S,xx}(p\Delta_f,q\Delta_t)S_{S,yy}(p\Delta_f,q\Delta_t)}}. \quad (14)$$

The lagged coherence calculated based on ST then becomes both time and frequency dependent,

$$|\gamma_{xy}(p\Delta_f,q\Delta_t)| = \frac{|\tilde{S}_{S,xy}(p\Delta_f,q\Delta_t)|}{\sqrt{\tilde{S}_{S,xx}(p\Delta_f,q\Delta_t)\tilde{S}_{S,yy}(p\Delta_f,q\Delta_t)}}. \quad (15)$$

Estimation of Lagged Coherence for Stationary Processes

The bias of the estimated lagged coherence between stationary processes has been investigated in several studies, and they are found to be dependent on the true coherence and the used smoothing windows (Enochson and Goodman, 1965; Benignus, 1969a). In this section, the study of bias associated with estimated lagged coherence for stationary processes will be revisited, but from the perspective of earthquake ground motions. This will help the readers better understand the source of bias and build the basis analysis procedure for later analysis of nonstationary processes.

To see the effect of the smoothing operation on the bias of estimated lagged coherence, stationary coherent processes are first simulated with prescribed target PSD and coherence. The use of simulated stationary processes instead of real ground-motion signals is because the true coherency of simulated processes is known, which is unavailable from the real signals. The simulated ground motions could be more realistic if considering the real ground motions as conditions at some sites; however, the true coherence will deviate from the target due to Baysian updating effect (Cui and Hong, 2020). Therefore, the unconditional simulation is adopted in the following investigation. For the simulation, the Clough–Penzien PSD model is used as the target PSD (Clough and Penzien, 2003),

$$S_T(f) = S_0\frac{f_g^4 + 4\xi_g^2 f_g^2 f^2}{(f_g^2 - f^2)^2 + 4\xi_g^2 f_g^2 f^2}\frac{f^4}{(f_f^2 - f^2)^2 + 4\xi_f^2 f_f^2 f^2}, \quad (16)$$

in which f_g and ξ_g are the resonant frequency and damping ratio of the first filter and f_f and ξ_f are those of the second filter, respectively. Assuming a medium soil type, the values of the four parameters are $[f_g,\xi_g,f_f,\xi_f] = [1.59\ \mathrm{Hz},0.4,0.16\ \mathrm{Hz},0.6]$. The value of S_0 equals 0.201 and ensures the total energy of $S_T(f)$ equals unity. The target PSD is shown in Figure 1a. The Luco–Wong coherence function (Luco and Wong, 1986) is adopted as the target coherence,

$$\gamma(f,d) = e^{-\left(\frac{\alpha}{V_S}2\pi f d\right)^2}, \quad (17)$$

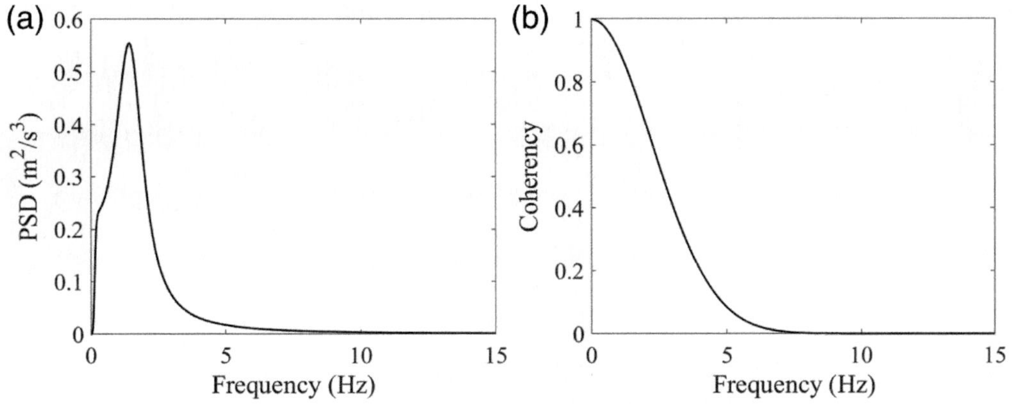

Figure 1. (a) Target power spectral density (PSD) and (b) target coherency.

in which d denotes the separation distance along the propagation distance and the parameter $\alpha/V_S = 5 \times 10^{-4}$ s/m. For the simulation, the separation distance d is assumed to be 100 m. The target coherency is shown in Figure 1b. Five hundred sets of samples are simulated using the spectral representation method (Shinozuka and Deodatis, 1991). The procedure for simulating coherent stationary processes was well illustrated in Shinozuka (1971) and a theoretical proof of the matching to the target PSD and coherency is already given in Liang *et al.* (2007). A set of samples is shown in Figure 2a,b. The coherency for each set of samples is first calculated using equation (1) based on FT without a smoothing operation. The real and imaginary parts of the coherency between the two signals shown in Figure 2a,b are displayed in Figure 2c,d, respectively. Large fluctuations are observed in both plots, and it is also found that the variability increases as the frequency increases or say as the target coherency decreases. It should be noted that the coherency shown in Figure 2c,d is without smoothing, therefore, the absolute value of the coherency is identical to unity for all frequencies as shown in Figure 2e. The real and imaginary parts of the mean of the coherency for 500 sets of simulated signals are also shown in Figure 2f,g, respectively. The comparison to the target indicates perfect matching to the target coherence, which has been verified in many studies in the literature. As the sample size increases, the value of the imaginary part will approach zero and the value of the real part will approach the target coherency.

In practical application, there is only one set of observed ground motions for the coherence investigation; the complex coherency for a single pair of records as shown in Figure 2c,d is not suitable for model development. Therefore, the lagged coherence is often used for the coherence model development. As mentioned in the Introduction, the estimation of lagged coherence is always associated with bias caused by smoothing operations. To see the effect of using different smoothing windows on the bias of estimated lagged coherence, two commonly adopted windows, the rectangular window and the Hamming window, are used for the examination.

The rectangular window is defined as

$$W_R(m\Delta_f) = \begin{cases} \frac{1}{2M+1} & -M \le m \le M \\ 0 & \text{otherwise} \end{cases}. \quad (18)$$

The Hamming window is defined as

$$W_H(m\Delta_f) = \begin{cases} 0.54 - 0.46\cos(2\pi m/M) & -M \le m \le M \\ 0 & \text{otherwise} \end{cases}, \quad (19)$$

in which M is the parameter to describe the width of the adopted window. M equal to 5, 9, and 13 are used for the investigation. The calculated lagged coherence between the two signals is shown in Figure 2a,b using equations (6) and (7), but they are shown in Figure 3 based on rectangular window and Hamming window with different parameters, respectively. It is observed that the fluctuation is less pronounced if the values of M increase. Moreover, using Hamming window will result in a smoother lagged coherence than using a rectangular window. By repeating the calculation for all the simulated 500 sets of signals, the mean of the estimated lagged coherence, but adopted different smoothing windows, is shown and compared in Figure 4. It is observed that as the value of M increases, the associated bias decreases. However, the increase of the width of the smoothing window will result in a more uncovered range at the lower frequency from zero frequency, as observed from the left-up corners of each plot in Figure 3. As demonstrated by the illustration shown in Figures 3 and 4, it is found that adjusting the smoothing bandwidth parameter directly influences the trade-off between bias and variance of the estimated lagged coherence: wider bandwidths reduce variance (stabilizing estimates) but introduce bias by oversmoothing true spectral features, whereas narrower bandwidths preserve detail but the variation trend is vague. However, the criteria for selecting the bandwidth of the smoothing window are unclear in the literature.

Estimation of Lagged Coherence for Evolutionary Processes

If the ground motions are assumed as evolutionary processes, the coherency is adequate to be assumed as time independent, as proved in Priestley and Tong (1973). Because only

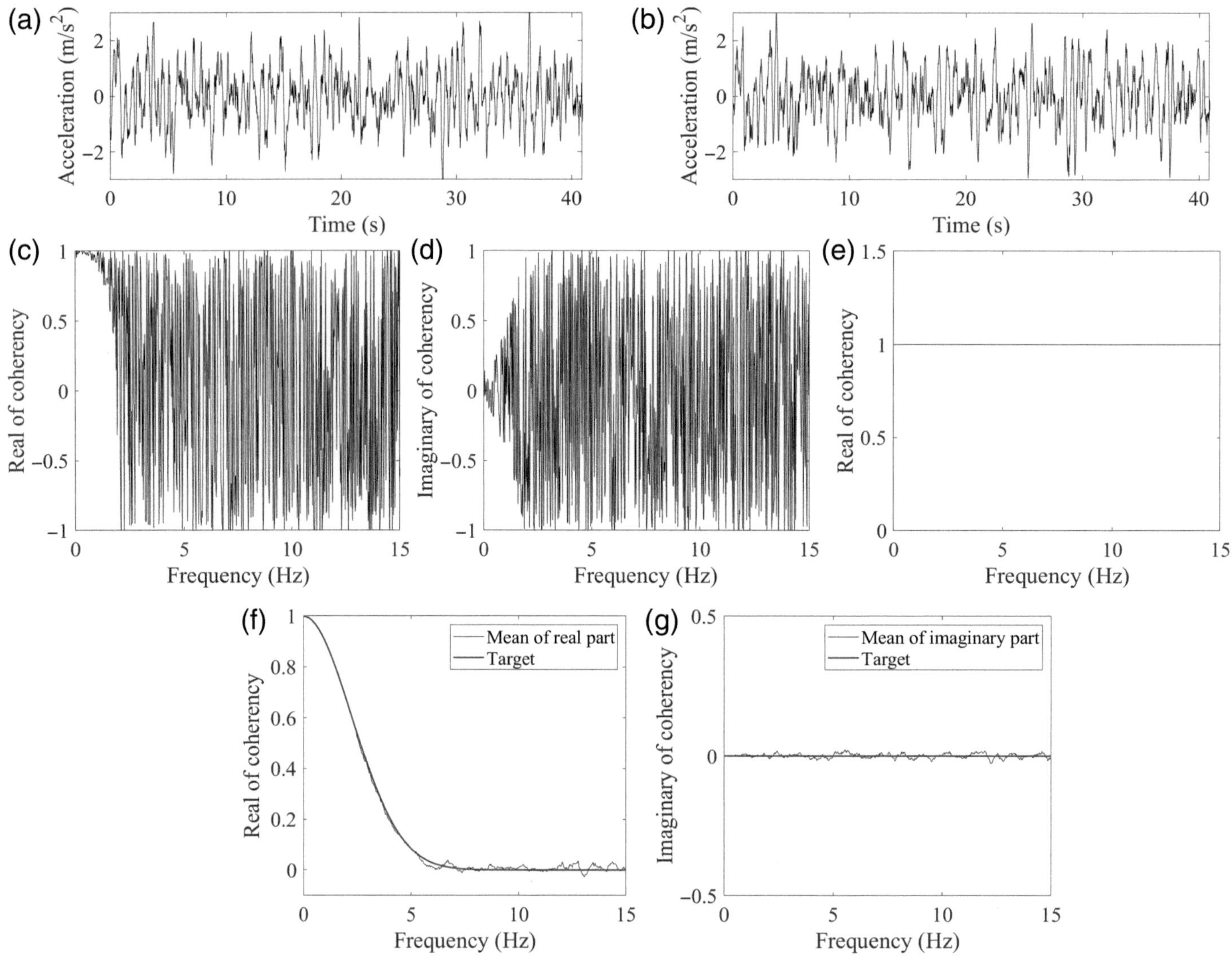

Figure 2. (a,b) A set of simulated samples, (c) real, (d) imaginary part, (e) absolute value of calculated coherency between the set of samples shown in panels (a) and (b) based on Fourier transform (FT), (f) real and (g) imaginary part of the mean of coherency between 500 sets of simulated samples. The color version of this figure is available only in the electronic edition.

frequency-dependent representations are desired, the FT is then widely used in the calculation of time-independent lagged coherence (Abrahamson *et al.*, 1991; Hao *et al.*, 1989; Liu and Hong, 2016; Zerva, 2016; Rodda and Basu, 2018). However, as mentioned in the Introduction, the adequacy of using FT in calculating the lagged coherence between nonstationary processes was never examined.

The true coherency between the historical ground-motion records is never known; therefore, the simulated nonstationary ground motions are used for the investigation. The target evolutionary poser spectral density function adopts the Clough–Penzien PSD model shown in equation (16) but including a time-varying envelope function,

$$S_T(f,t) = A(t)S_0 \frac{f_g^4 + 4\xi_g^2 f_g^2 f^2}{(f_g^2 - f^2)^2 + 4\xi_g^2 f_g^2 f^2} \frac{f^4}{(f_f^2 - f^2)^2 + 4\xi_f^2 f_f^2 f^2}, \quad (20)$$

in which the parameters are the same as those defined in equation (15). $A(t)$ is the time-varying envelope function (Boore, 2009),

$$A(t) = a(t/t_\eta)^b e^{(-c(t/t_\eta))}, \quad (21)$$

in which a, b, c, and t_η are the model parameters. For the investigation, three different envelope functions are considered and denoted as A1–A3, and their corresponding parameters in equation (21) are [1,1,3,10], [1,1,5,30], and [1,1,5,50], respectively. The shapes of the three considered envelope functions are shown in Figure 5a. For the simulation, the target coherence function shown in equation (17) with a distance equal to 100 m is used in the spectral representation method. Three sets of samples of simulated nonstationary ground motions are shown in Figure 5b,c with considered envelope functions A1–A3, respectively. For further analysis, 500 sets of samples for each considered envelope function are simulated. Again, the theoretical proof of the matching of the mean coherency

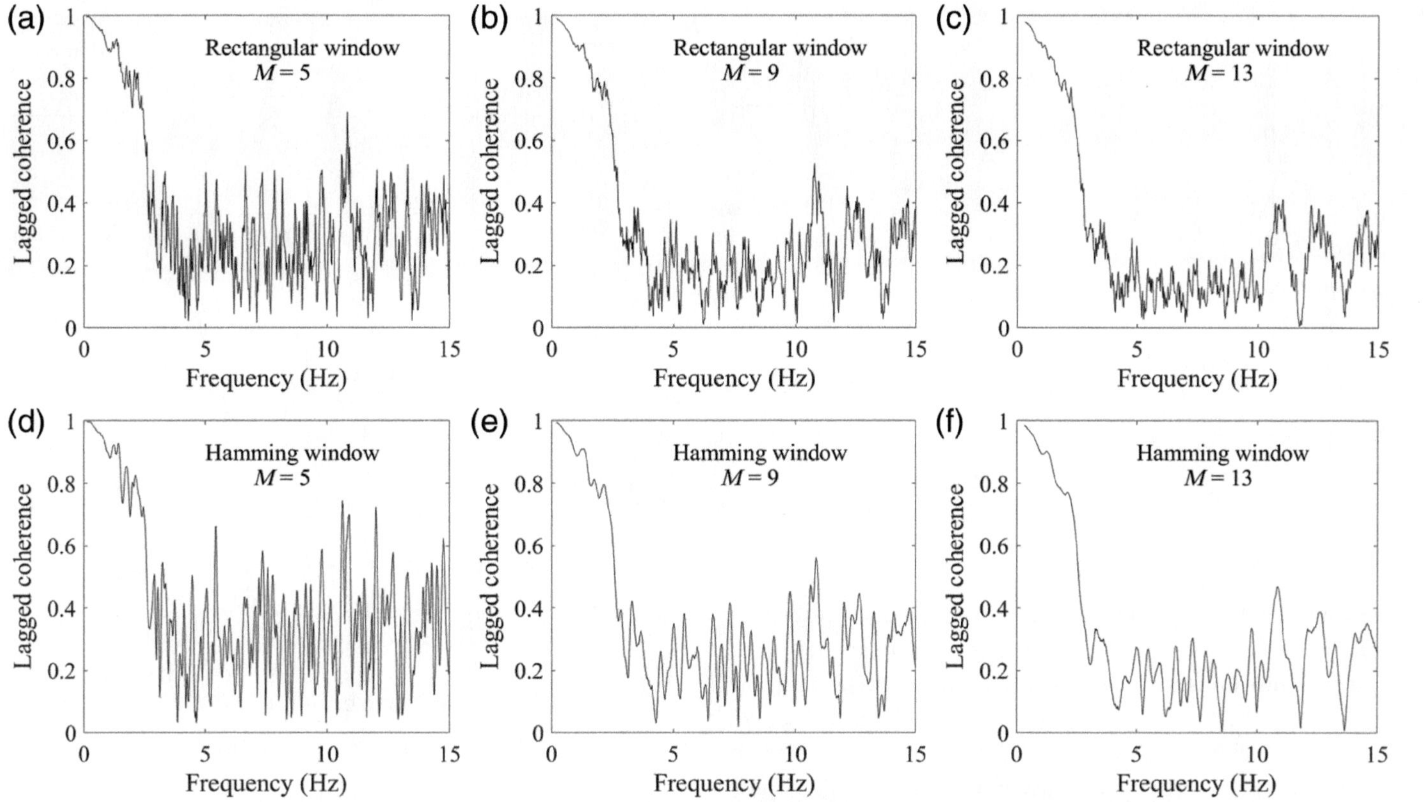

Figure 3. Calculated lagged coherence between the set of samples shown in Figure 2a,b smoothed using a rectangular window with M equals (a) 5, (b) 9, and (c) 13; (d–f) same as panels (a–c) but using a Hamming window.

between simulated samples to the target coherency is already given in Liang *et al.* (2007).

Bias of estimated time-independent lagged coherence using FT

As discussed in the Introduction, the FT is commonly employed to estimate lagged coherence between ground-motion records. This section investigates the bias inherent in this methodology when applied to nonstationary ground motions.

Specifically, we analyze the calculation of lagged coherence using simulated ground-motion datasets. It is well known that the choice of smoothing window significantly influences the bias of coherence estimates. For this analysis, the Hamming window is initially selected as the smoothing window. First, the Hamming window with M equals 5 is adopted, and the mean lagged coherence values calculated from the sets of simulated ground motions with three different envelope functions are displaced in Figure 6a and compared with the target. Notably, despite the simulated datasets being generated from identical target coherency models, the mean lagged coherence estimates vary systematically across different envelope functions, even when using the same smoothing

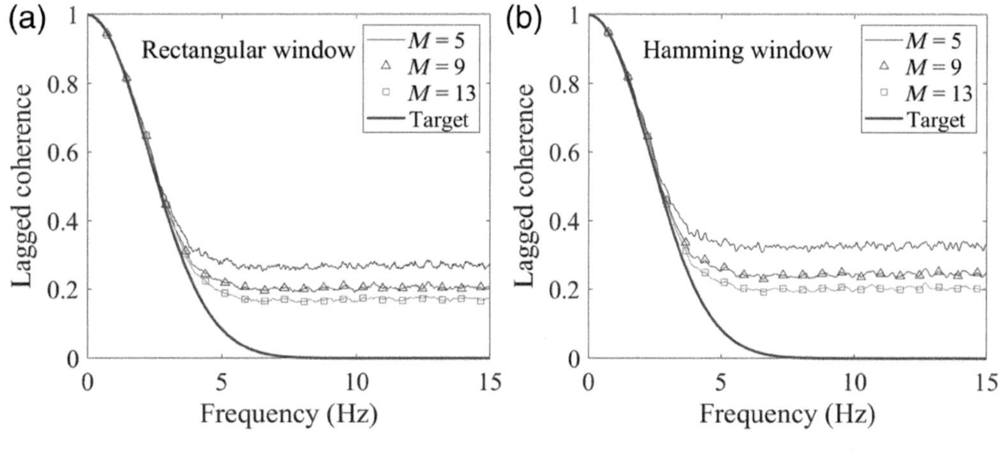

Figure 4. Mean of lagged coherence between 500 sets of samples. (a) Smoothed using a rectangular window with different parameters and compared with the target. (b) Smoothed using a Hamming window with different parameters and compared with the target. The color version of this figure is available only in the electronic edition.

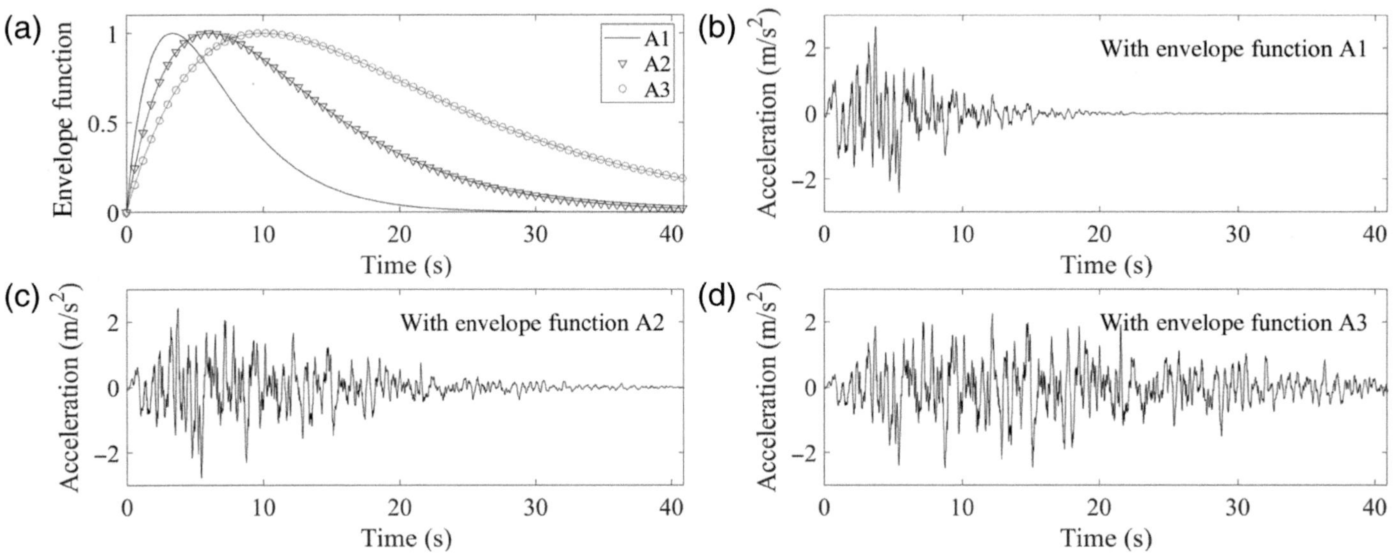

Figure 5. (a) Considered three envelope functions; simulated coherent ground motions at two sites with envelope function: (b) A1, (c) A2, and (d) A3. The color version of this figure is available only in the electronic edition.

window. A substantial bias is observed, which depends explicitly on the time-varying amplitude characteristics (i.e., envelope functions) of the ground motions. Repeating the analysis with a Hamming window of M equals 13, it is observed that the overall bias is reduced, yet the dependence of bias on amplitude characteristics remains clearly discernible. These findings demonstrate that the FT is improper for lagged coherence analysis of nonstationary ground motions because it introduces inconsistent bias depending on the specific nonstationary characteristics of the ground motions. Therefore, the lagged coherence model of ground motions developed based on the FT and ground-motion record datasets from various seismic events is not adequate because the time-varying amplitude characteristics are significantly different for different events, and they introduce inconsistent bias depending on the specific nonstationary characteristics of the signals.

A proposed new method for estimating the time-independent lagged coherence for evolutionary processes

Ground-motion signals exhibit significant nonstationarity, resulting in time-dependent frequency content. Unlike the FT, which is inherently suited for stationary processes, time–frequency analysis methods such as the ST are better equipped to handle the nonstationary ground-motion signals. Consider the simulated ground-motion set presented in Figure 5b, coherency between the two records was calculated using equation (14). The real and imaginary components of the coherency estimate are displayed in Figure 7a,b, respectively. Lagged coherence could be computed using equation (15) with parameters $M = H = 15$, as shown in Figure 7c. Both coherency and lagged coherence estimates demonstrated significant time-independent characteristics. Notable fluctuations observed in the time–frequency domain (Fig. 7a–c) were attributed to sample variability inherent in single-record pair estimation. Repeating the analysis for all the 500 record sets, the ensemble-averaged coherency and lagged coherence results are presented in Figure 7d–f. The mean real component of

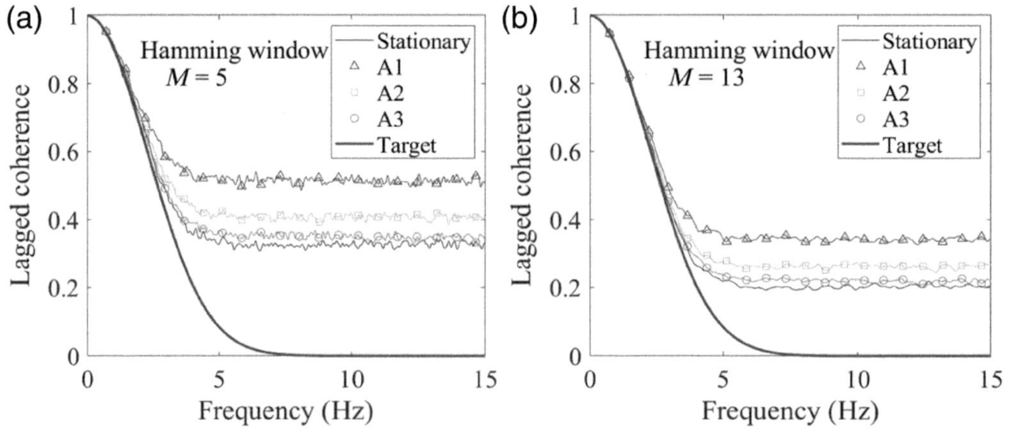

Figure 6. The mean of lagged coherence between the 500 sets of samples modulated with different modulation functions. (a) Smoothed using a Hamming window with M equals 5. (b) Smoothed using a Hamming window with M equals 13. The color version of this figure is available only in the electronic edition.

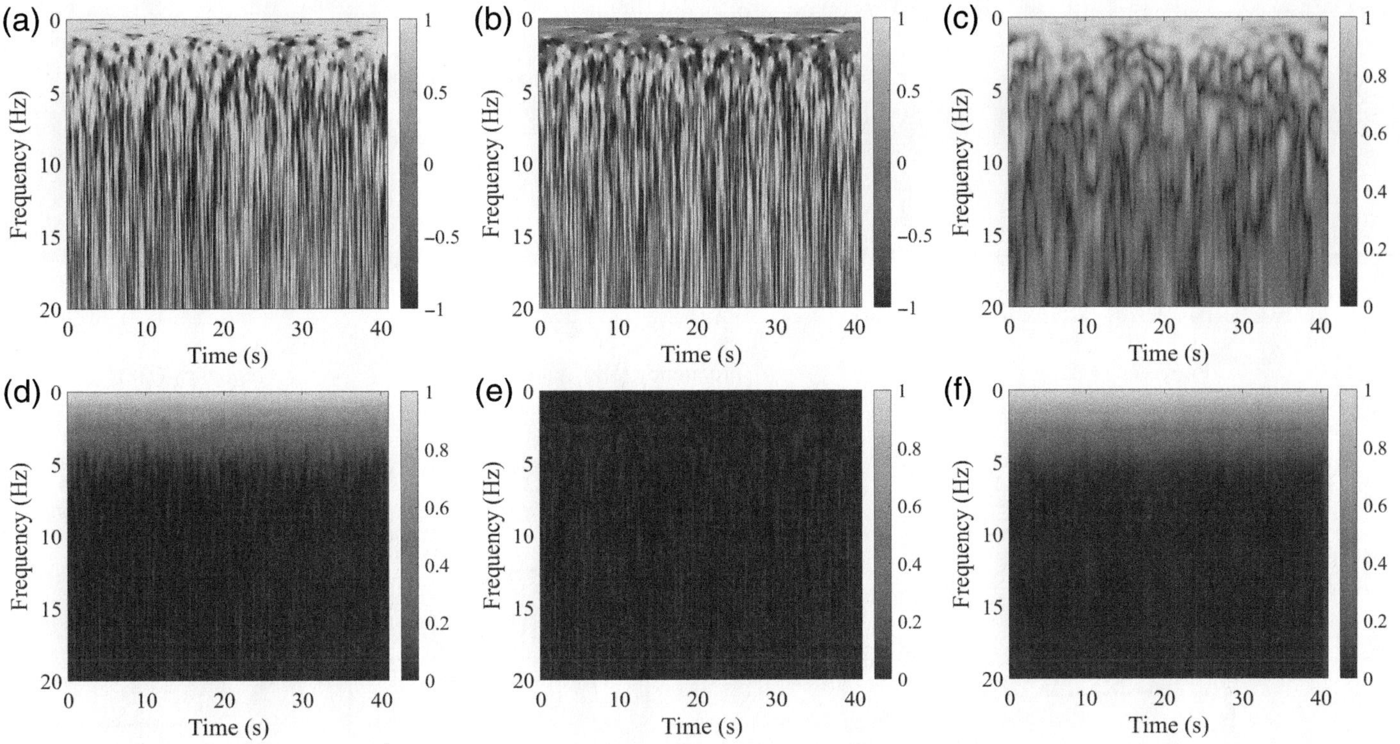

coherency closely matches the target coherency along the frequency axis for all the time instances, and the mean imaginary component approaches zero. Although the mean lagged coherence also remains time independent, its values exceed those of the real coherency mean, indicating a systematic bias introduced by the smoothing operation in equation (15).

The analyzed results and some prior coherence studies using ST (e.g., Cui and Hong, 2021a) primarily use time–frequency analysis to characterize fully time-dependent lagged coherence in nonstationary signals, treating coherence as a time–frequency-varying quantity without assuming evolutionary theory. As observed from Figure 7a,d, when the true coherency between ground motions is time independent, the ST produces consistent time-independent estimates. The reduced variability in the mean coherency (Fig. 7d) arises from ensemble averaging over 500 record pairs, in contrast to the single-record fluctuations observed in Figure 7a. This observation indicates that the ST is also applicable for time-independent lagged coherence estimation within the evolutionary process framework (Priestley, 1965; Zerva, 2016), for which lagged coherence is theoretically proven to be frequency dependent but time independent for evolutionary processes (Priestley and Tong, 1973). Building on this insight, we propose calculating frequency-dependent coherency by averaging over time:

$$\gamma_{xy}(p\Delta_f) = \frac{\sum_q S_{S,xy}(p\Delta_f, q\Delta_t)}{\sqrt{\sum_q S_{S,xx}(p\Delta_f, q\Delta_t)\sum_q S_{S,yy}(p\Delta_f, q\Delta_t)}}. \quad (22)$$

Figure 7. Calculated time–frequency-dependent coherency and lagged coherence using *S* transform (ST). (a) Real and (b) imaginary components of the calculated coherency between the records shown in Figure 5b, (c) the calculated lagged coherence between the records shown in Figure 5b, the (d) real and (e) imaginary mean of coherency, and (f) lagged coherence calculated using the 500 sets of simulated records with envelope function A1. The color version of this figure is available only in the electronic edition.

The frequency-dependent coherency $\gamma_{xy}(p\Delta_f)$ calculated using ST and equation (22) for the set of simulated ground motions as shown in Figure 5b is presented in Figure 8a,b for the real and imaginary parts, respectively. Taking the absolute value of $\gamma_{xy}(p\Delta_f)$, the frequency-dependent lagged coherence $|\gamma_{xy}(p\Delta_f)|$ is obtained, as shown in Figure 8c. When repeating this analysis for all 500 record sets with envelope function A1, the ensemble-averaged coherency and lagged coherence are shown in Figure 8d–f. The ensemble-averaged real part of coherency perfectly matches the target coherency, and the ensemble-averaged lagged coherence reveals only minor discrepancies compared against the target. This observation indicates that the bias in the estimated lagged coherence could be significantly reduced using equation (22), and the bias at the part with medium and high lagged coherence is small enough to be ignored.

Further, extending the analysis to record sets with envelope functions A2 and A3, the ensemble-averaged coherency and lagged coherence estimates are presented in Figure 8d–f. Notably, the proposed method yields nearly identical mean lagged coherence values across all three amplitude modulation scenarios, confirming its insensitivity to time-varying amplitude

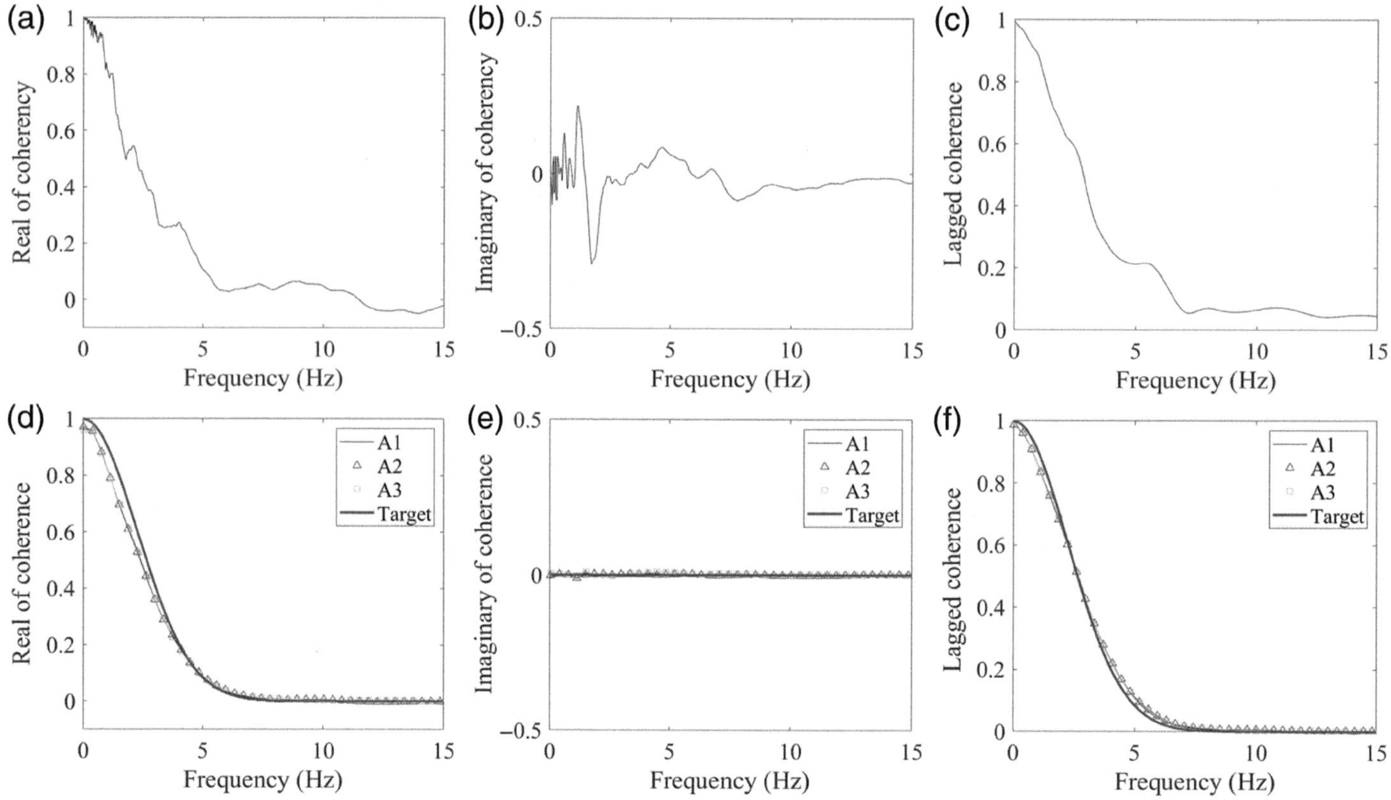

Figure 8. Calculated frequency-only dependent coherency and lagged coherence using the proposed equation (22). (a) Real and (b) imaginary components of the calculated coherency between the records shown in Figure 5b, (c) the calculated lagged coherence between the records shown in Figure 5b, the (d) real and (e) imaginary mean of coherency, and (f) lagged coherence calculated using the 500 sets of simulated records with three different envelope functions and compare to the target. The color version of this figure is available only in the electronic edition.

characteristics. Mechanistically, this approach shares conceptual similarities with multitaper FT techniques (or known as the p-Welch method; Welch, 2003) but incorporates a frequency-dependent Gaussian window to adaptively balance time–frequency resolution.

Comparison of the calculated lagged coherence between real records

The aforementioned analysis shows that the proposed methods for calculating the frequency-dependent lagged coherence between nonstationary processes (assuming evolutionary processes) yield consistent and negligible bias relative to the true coherence. In contrast, the bias from using the traditional FT is inconsistent across cases with different nonstationary characteristics. This analysis is entirely based on simulated ground motions. The rationale for selecting simulated records is that they enable us to know the true underlying coherence values, which is crucial for quantifying bias. Because the proposed method (equation 22) leads to consistent and negligible bias, the lagged coherence calculated via equation (22) can serve as a benchmark to show the bias introduced by FT when applied to real records.

For further analysis using real records, ground-motion records from the SMART-1 for five seismic events in Taiwan are utilized. Details of these five seismic events are provided in Table 1, and the records can be accessed from the Data Management Center for Strong Motion Seismology of the Institute of Earth Sciences, Taiwan. The layout of the stations is shown in Figure 9. These record sets are widely employed in lagged coherence model development, as seen in works by Abrahamson *et al.* (1991), Hao *et al.* (1989), Zerva (2016), Liu and Hong (2016), Rodda and Basu (2018), Cui and Hong (2021a), and Xiao *et al.* (2024). For more in-depth information about the records, readers are directed to Zerva (2016) or Cui and Hong (2021a).

Records from the same event with similar separation distances should display comparable lagged coherence variations. For comparison, for each event listed in Table 1, records from stations with separation distances between 90 and 110 m are chosen as samples, and they are assumed to belong to the group with a separation distance of 100 m. The proposed method (equation 22) is used to calculate the lagged coherence, acting as the benchmark. Subsequently, the traditional FT, along with a Hamming window with three different parameters ($M = 5$, 9, and 13), is used to calculate the lagged coherence. The resulting calculated lagged coherences are presented and compared in Figure 10a. It is observed that using FT with different parameters results in similar lagged coherence variations, and using $M = 5$ gives higher estimated lagged coherence

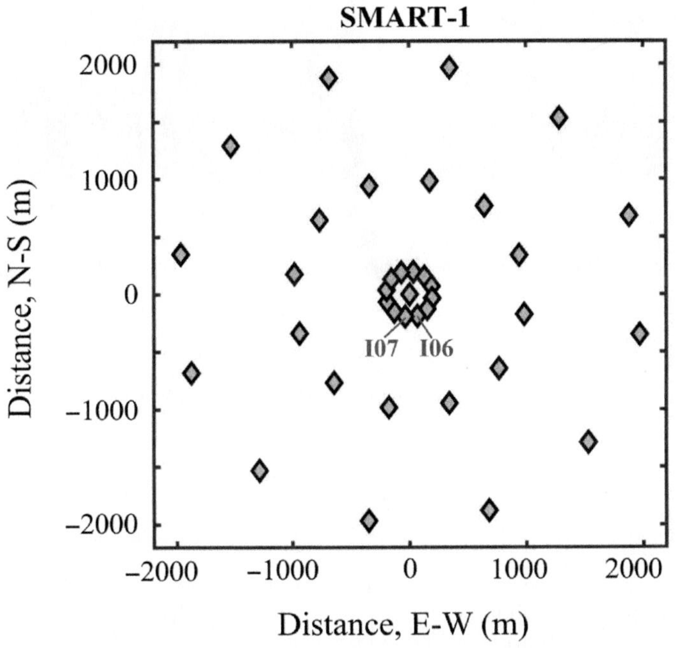

Figure 9. Layout of the stations in the Strong Motion Array in Taiwan (SMART-1) array. The color version of this figure is available only in the electronic edition.

values. However, all these estimates exhibit significant bias when compared with the benchmark (lagged coherence calculated via equation 22). Moreover, the bias differs across events. This confirms that the bias in lagged coherence estimation using FT is affected by the nonstationary characteristics of different events. For most events, the bias is smaller at low frequencies and larger at high frequencies; however, for event 1, the bias is significant across all frequencies. These findings indicate that FT is unsuitable for estimating the frequency-dependent lagged coherence between nonstationary ground motions, even when they are assumed to be evolutionary processes. In addition, the inconsistent bias across events with different nonstationary characteristics makes it difficult to eliminate. By repeating the same analysis with records from stations having separation distances between 180 and 220 m, the results (shown in Fig. 10b) reveal similar observations.

Some Observations and Discussion About Time-Dependent Lagged Coherence Between Nonstationary Ground Motions

The preceding analysis and discussions pertain to nonstationary ground motions modeled within the evolutionary process framework. In this context, coherency or lagged coherence between two evolutionary processes (Priestley and Tong, 1973) is theoretically frequency-only dependent. However, when considering sigma oscillatory evolutionary processes (i.e., superpositions of multiple evolutionary components; Conte and Peng, 1997) or from the perspective of a general nonstationary process, coherency or lagged coherence could become both time- and frequency-dependent. Alternatively, abandoning the evolutionary process framework altogether and directly analyzing time–frequency representations reveals that ground-motion coherency inherently exhibits both time and frequency dependence. This conclusion aligns with several recent advancements in the field (Abbas and Tezcan, 2019; Qiao *et al.*, 2020; Cui and Hong, 2021a). Wavelet-transform-based approaches for time-dependent lagged coherence analysis have been explored by Qiao *et al.* (2020) and Abbas and Tezcan (2019). The simulation of ground motions with time-dependent coherency is well discussed in Hong and Cui (2020) and Cui and Hong (2021b). Cui and Hong (2021a) and Xiao *et al.* (2024) investigated the time-dependent lagged coherence using the ST for tricomponents of ground motions recorded at LSST and SMART-1 arrays. Notably, among these studies, only Cui and Hong (2021a) and Xiao *et al.* (2024) systematically addressed bias in time–frequency-based lagged coherence estimates. Drawing inspiration from Abrahamson *et al.* (1991), who introduced a bias correction factor for FT-based lagged coherence, Cui and Hong (2021a) proposed a consistent bias correction factor applied in the hyperbolic transform domain of lagged coherence. Although theoretically more sophisticated time–frequency-dependent correction factors might exist, the consistent bias correction approach appears particularly efficient for time–frequency analysis tools. Supporting evidence arises from A proposed new method for estimating the time-independent lagged

TABLE 1
Detailed Information of the Considered Five Events

Seismic Event	Date (yyyy/mm/dd)	Latitude (°)	Longitude (°)	Magnitude (M_L)	Focal Depth
Event 1	1985/10/26	121.84	24.42	4.7	1.7
Event 2	1986/01/16	121.97	24.77	6.1	10.2
Event 3	1986/05/20	121.60	24.09	6.2	15.8
Event 4	1986/07/30	121.80	24.64	5.8	1.6
Event 5	1986/11/14	121.84	24.00	6.8	15

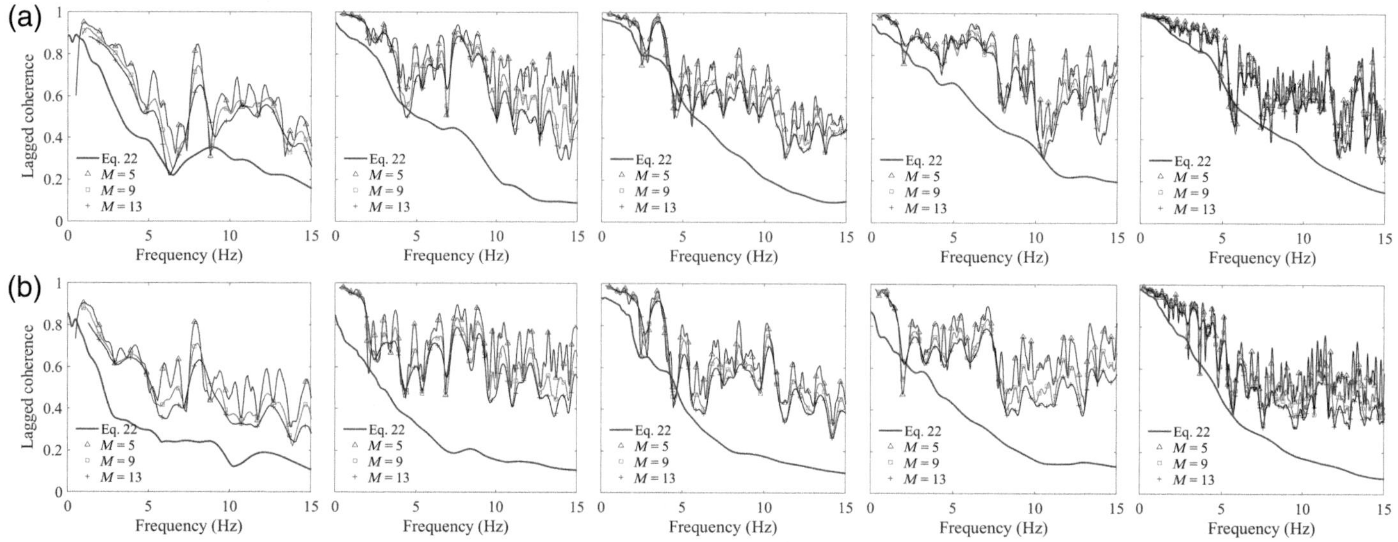

Figure 10. Comparison of the calculated lagged coherence between real ground motions from the SMART-1 array using the proposed equation (22) and traditional FT with different smoothing windows. (a) Calculated lagged coherences between records with separation distance around 100 m (90–110 m) for the five events and (b) calculated lagged coherences between records with separation distance around 200 m (180–220 m) for the five events. The color version of this figure is available only in the electronic edition.

coherence for evolutionary processes section, which shows that ST-based time-independent lagged coherence bias remains invariant to ground-motion time-varying characteristics.

In this section of the present study, I do not further investigate the bias associated with lagged coherence estimation from the ST or other time–frequency analysis tools. Instead, I focus on presenting the estimated time-dependent lagged coherence between ground motions and evaluating how different smoothing window parameters influence these estimates. Most importantly, show the time dependency of lagged coherence in the estimates using time–frequency analysis tool.

By considering two real records from the SMART-1 array, specifically those from the I06 and I07 stations (see Fig. 9), which have a separation distance of 97 m. These two records are depicted in Figure 11a,b. First, the FT is employed to calculate the frequency-only dependent lagged coherence smoothed by two rectangular windows with M equals 5 and 13 and shown in Figure 11c,d, respectively. For the sake of consistency in comparison, the calculated lagged coherences are represented in time–frequency space, although they are frequency-dependent only. Further, using equation (22), the frequency-only dependent lagged coherence is calculated and also represented in time–frequency space as shown in Figure 11e. It is evident that when time-independent lagged coherence for evolutionary processes is the objective, the proposed method (equation 22) yields smoother estimates. In addition, the negligible bias results in a more accurate estimation as discussed in the previous section. Subsequently, the time–frequency-dependent lagged coherence is calculated using the ST and smoothed with three different rectangular windows, in which $M = H = 5$, $M = H = 10$, and $M = H = 15$. The obtained results are shown in Figure 11f–h. It is observed that when a small smoothing window $M = H = 5$ is applied, significant fluctuations are observed, and the values are close to 1. This is reasonable because as the smoothing window size decreases, the calculated lagged coherence approaches unity and will be identical to unity if no smoothing operation is applied. As the smoothing window size increases, the time dependency of the lagged coherence becomes more pronounced. It is also noted that the time dependency of the lagged coherence is more significant in the medium and high-frequency regions, and the lagged coherence is larger in the time interval between 10 and 15 s, for which the intensity of the considered ground motions is at its peak. This observation indicates that the amplitude of the lagged coherence is related to the intensity of the ground motions, as already discussed by Cui and Hong (2021a). This phenomenon is understandable because ground motions with high intensity are likely to be less affected during propagation from the source to the sites, whereas ground motions with low intensity are more susceptible to contamination during the propagation process. Therefore, the time dependency of lagged coherence does exist in the ground motions, and the effect of the time-dependent characteristic on the structure responses shall be further investigated in further studies.

Conclusion

This study has critically examined the application of FT and ST in estimating coherency and lagged coherence. The revisited analysis of the smoothing window's effect on bias in stationary processes clarifies the origins of these biases. Furthermore, the investigation into the use of FT for calculating the lagged coherence of nonstationary ground motions reveals its limitations, demonstrating an inconsistency in the induced bias across different seismic events. Consequently, it is emphasized that FT is

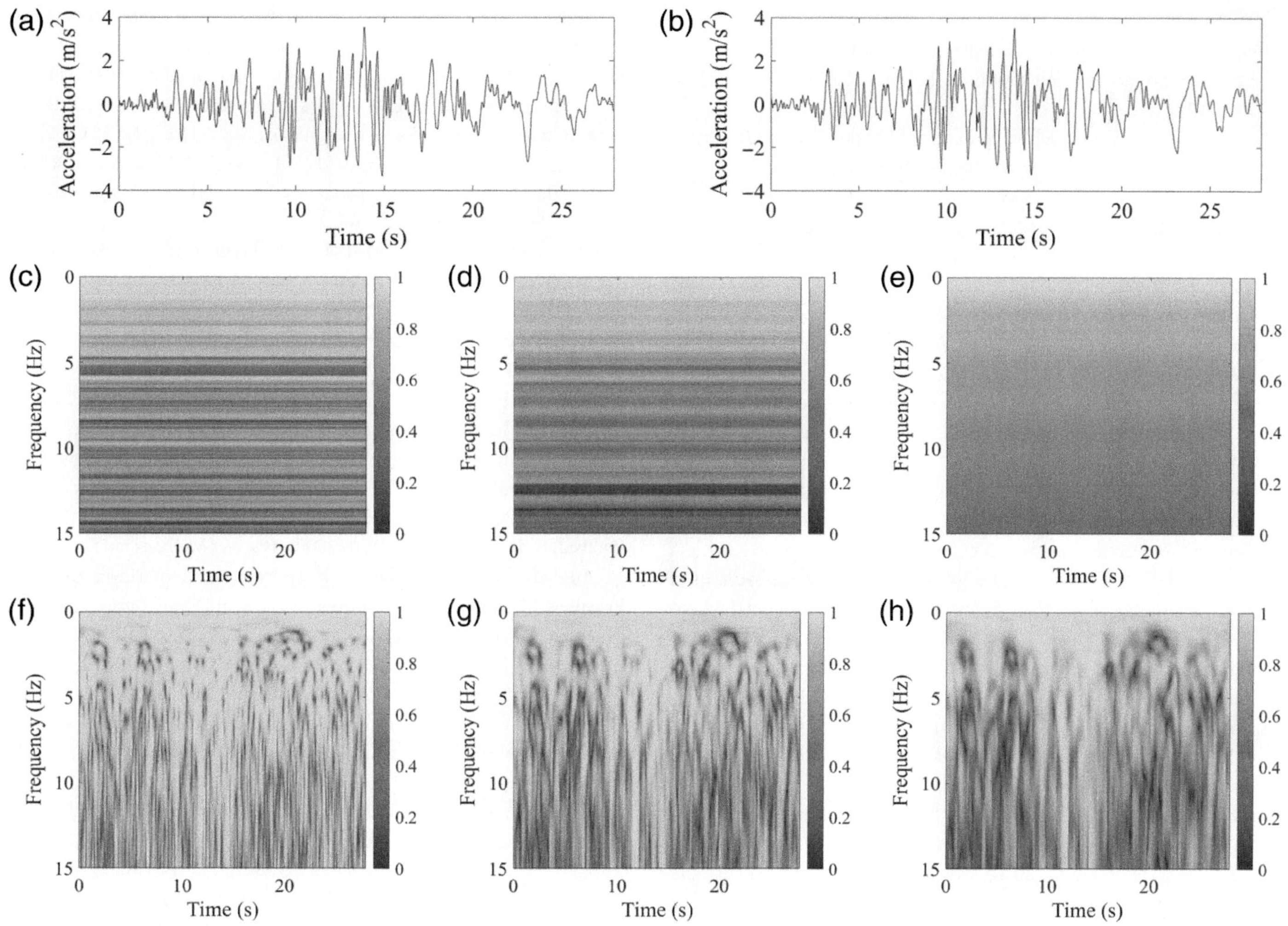

unsuitable for the accurate calculation and modeling of lagged coherence for nonstationary ground motions. To address this, a new method for estimating time-independent lagged coherence with a consistent and negligibly small bias is proposed, suggesting a more reliable approach for time-independent lagged coherence estimation for nonstationary ground motions. Considering real records from the SMART-1 dense array, the comparison of the estimated lagged coherence using FT and the proposed method indicates once again that employing FT will result in significant and inconsistent bias. As a result, the estimated lagged coherence using FT is not suitable for lagged coherence model development for ground motions. Finally, the time-independent and time-dependent lagged coherence of actual historical ground-motion records has been investigated and shows the existence of time-dependent characteristics of lagged coherence, yielding valuable observations and discussions that contribute to a better understanding of the spatial and temporal dependencies in seismic excitations.

Figure 11. (a,b) Considered two ground-motion records from SMART-1 array, the calculated frequency-dependent only lagged coherence using FT with rectangular smoothing window and M equals (c) 5 and (d) 13, and represent in time–frequency space, (e) the calculated frequency-dependent only lagged coherence using equation (22) and represent in time–frequency space; the calculated time–frequency-dependent lagged coherence using ST and smoothed by rectangular window with M and H equal (f) 5, (g) 10, and (h) 15. The color version of this figure is available only in the electronic edition.

Data and Resources

The ground-motion records from the Strong Motion Array in Taiwan (SMART-1) array are from http://www.earth.sinica.edu.tw/ (last accessed June 2023).

Declaration of Competing Interests

The author acknowledges that there are no conflicts of interest recorded.

Acknowledgments

The financial supports from the following institutions and agencies are appreciated: Harbin Institute of Technology (Shenzhen), National Natural Science Foundation of China (Grant Number 52408520), and the Shenzhen Science and Technology Program (Grant Number RCBS20231211090659100).

References

Abbas, H., and J. Tezcan (2019). Relevance vector machines modeling of nonstationary ground motion coherency, *Soil Dynam. Earthq. Eng.* **120,** 262–272.

Abrahamson, N. A., J. F. Schneider, and J. C. Stepp (1991). Empirical spatial coherency functions for application to soil-structure interaction analyses, *Earthq. Spectra* **7,** no. 1, 1–27.

Battisti, U., and L. Riba (2016). Window-dependent bases for efficient representations of the Stockwell transform, *Appl. Comput. Harmon. Anal.* **40,** no. 2, 292–320.

Benignus, V. (1969a). Estimation of the coherence spectrum and its confidence interval using the fast Fourier transform, *IEEE Trans. Audio Electroacoust.* **17,** no. 2, 145–150.

Benignus, V. (1969b). Estimation of coherence spectrum of non-Gaussian time series populations, *IEEE Trans. Audio Electroacoust.* **17,** no. 3, 198–201.

Boore, D. M. (2009). Comparing stochastic point-source and finite-source ground-motion simulations: SMSIM and EXSIM, *Bull. Seismol. Soc. Am.* **99,** no. 6, 3202–3216.

Carter, G. (1980). Bias in magnitude-squared coherence estimation due to misalignment, *IEEE Trans. Acoust. Speech Signal Process.* **28,** no. 1, 97–99.

Clough, R. W., and J. Penzien (2003). *Dynamics of Structures*, Third Ed., Computers and Structures, Inc., Berkeley, California.

Cohen, E. A., and A. T. Walden (2010). A statistical study of temporally smoothed wavelet coherence, *IEEE Trans. Signal Process.* **58,** no. 6, 2964–2973.

Conte, J. P., and B. F. Peng (1997). Fully nonstationary analytical earthquake ground-motion model, *J. Eng. Mech.* **123,** no. 1, 15–24.

Cui, X. Z., and H. P. Hong (2020). Conditional simulation of spatially varying multicomponent nonstationary ground motions: Bias and ill condition, *J. Eng. Mech.* **146,** no. 2, 04019129, doi: 10.1061/(ASCE)EM.1943-7889.0001700.

Cui, X. Z., and H. P. Hong (2021a). A time-frequency dependent coherence model for seismic ground motions, *Earthq. Eng. Struct. Dynam.* **50,** no. 3, 955–973.

Cui, X. Z., and H. P. Hong (2021b). Simulating nonstationary and non-Gaussian vector ground motions with time- and frequency-dependent lagged coherence, *Earthq. Eng. Struct. Dynam.* **50,** no. 9, 2421–2441.

Enochson, L. D., and N. R. Goodman (1965). Gaussian approximations to the distribution of sample coherence, *No. MAC-403-07*, Measurement Analysis Corp.

Goda, K., and H. P. Hong (2009). Deaggregation of seismic loss of spatially distributed buildings, *Bull. Earthq. Eng.* **7,** 255–272.

Hao, H., C. S. Oliveira, and J. Penzien (1989). Multiple-station ground motion processing and simulation based on SMART-1 array data, *Nucl. Eng. Des.* **111,** no. 3, 293–310.

Hong, H. P. (2023). On the estimation of the evolutionary power spectral density, *Mech. Syst. Sig. Process.* **190,** 110,131.

Hong, H. P., and X. Z. Cui (2020). Time–frequency spectral representation models to simulate nonstationary processes and their use to generate ground motions, *J. Eng. Mech.* **146,** no. 9, 04020106, doi: 10.1061/(ASCE)EM.1943-7889.0001827.

Hong, H. P., and X. Z. Cui (2023). Use of transform pairs to represent and simulate nonstationary non-Gaussian process with applications, *Struct. Saf.* **100,** 102,267.

Kiureghian, A. D. (1996). A coherency model for spatially varying ground motions, *Earthq. Eng. Struct. Dynam.* **25,** no. 1, 99–111.

Li, Y. G., F. Fan, and H. P. Hong (2014). Effect of support flexibility on seismic responses of a reticulated dome under spatially correlated and coherent excitations, *Thin Walled Struct.* **82,** 343–351.

Liang, J., S. R. Chaudhuri, and M. Shinozuka (2007). Simulation of nonstationary stochastic processes by spectral representation, *J. Eng. Mech.* **133,** no. 6, 616–627.

Liu, T. J., and H. P. Hong (2016). Assessment of spatial coherency using tri-directional ground motions, *J. Earthq. Eng.* **20,** no. 5, 773–794.

Luco, J. E., and H. L. Wong (1986). Response of a rigid foundation to a spatially random ground motion, *Earthq. Eng. Struct. Dynam.* **14,** no. 6, 891–908.

Newland, D. E. (2012). *An Introduction to Random Vibrations, Spectral and Wavelet Analysis*, Thirrd Ed., Courier Corporation, Massachusetts.

Nuttall, A., and G. Carter (1976). Bias of the estimate of magnitude-squared coherence, *IEEE Trans. Acoust. Speech Signal Process.* **24,** no. 6, 582–583.

Percival, D. B., and A. T. Walden (2000). *Wavelet Methods for Time Series Analysis*, Vol. 4, Cambridge University Press, Cambridge, England.

Priestley, M. B. (1965). Evolutionary spectra and non-stationary processes, *J. Roy. Stat. Soc.* **27,** no. 2, 204–229.

Priestley, M. B., and H. Tong (1973). On the analysis of bivariate non-stationary processes, *J. Roy. Stat. Soc.* **35,** no. 2, 153–166.

Qiao, D., X. Zhi, F. Fan, and H. Hong (2020). Estimation of wavelet coherence of seismic ground motions, *Bull. Seismol. Soc. Am.* **110,** no. 2, 613–628.

Rodda, G. K., and D. Basu (2018). Coherency model for translational and rotational ground motions, *Bull. Earthq. Eng.* **16,** 2687–2710.

Rupakhety, R., and R. Sigbjornsson (2012) Spatial variability of strong ground motion: novel system-based technique applying parametric time series modelling, *Bull. Earthq. Eng.* **10,** no. 4, 1193–1204

Shinozuka, M. (1971). Simulation of multivariate and multidimensional random processes, *J. Acoust. Soc. Am.* **49,** no. 1B, 357–368.

Shinozuka, M., and G. Deodatis (1991). Simulation of stochastic processes by spectral representation, *Appl. Mech. Rev.* **44,** no. 4, 191–204.

Stockwell, R. G., L. Mansinha, and R. P. Lowe (1996). Localization of the complex spectrum: The S transform, *IEEE Trans. Signal Process.* **44,** no. 4, 998–1001.

Stull, R. B. (2012). *An Introduction to Boundary Layer Meteorology*, Second Ed., Springer Science & Business Media, Heidelberg, Germany.

Torrence, C., and G. P. Compo (1998). A practical guide to wavelet analysis, *Bull. Am. Meteorol. Soc.* **79,** no. 1, 61–78.

Welch, P. (2003). The use of fast Fourier transform for the estimation of power spectra: A method based on time averaging over short, modified periodograms, *IEEE Trans. Audio Electroacoust.* **15,** no. 2, 70–73.

Xiao, M. Y., X. Z. Cui, and H. P. Hong (2024). Time-varying characteristics of coherence for tri-directional seismic ground motions, *Soil Dynam. Earthq. Eng.* **185,** 108,849.

Zerva, A. (2016). *Spatial Variation of Seismic Ground Motions: Modeling and Engineering Applications*, CRC Press, Florida.

Zoubir, A. M. (2005). On confidence intervals for the coherence function, *Proc. of the IEEE International Conf. on Acoustics, Speech, and Signal Processing*, Vol. 4, IEEE, IV–413.

Manuscript received 26 March 2025
Published online 29 July 2025

Peak Ground Velocity and Shaking Duration Control Coseismic Surficial Sediment Remobilization on Lacustrine Slopes and Emplacement of Seismoturbidites

OPEN ACCESS

Katleen Wils*[1], Gonzalo Montalva[2], Maarten Van Daele[1], Marc De Batist[1], and Jasper Moernaut[3]

Abstract

Lacustrine paleoseismology has evolved into one of the most prominent techniques to establish long and high-resolution records of past earthquakes, particularly in subduction zones. A thorough understanding of the relation between the various components of strong ground motion and the resulting sedimentary signature is, however, still missing. Therefore, characterization of the source parameters of paleoearthquakes, such as magnitude and location, up to now relies solely on qualitative or semiquantitative considerations, linking the occurrence or absence of coseismic imprints (e.g., turbidites) to seismic shaking strength. These intensity values are usually expressed on the macroseismic scale, as such information is more readily available compared to instrumental data, especially for the numerous historical earthquakes that outdate the first use of seismometers. However, these are relatively subjective ground-motion measures, unable to capture key aspects of strong ground motion (e.g., peak ground acceleration [PGA], peak ground velocity [PGV], and duration). In this study, we determine the relation between these quantitative ground-motion values calculated for the bottom of a lake and the sedimentary shaking imprints identified therein. To achieve this, we focus on the sedimentary signature of instrumentally recorded megathrust earthquakes in south-central Chile. This includes the 1960 M_w 9.5 Valdivia earthquake and the 2010 M_w 8.8 Maule earthquake. A compilation of existing sedimentological data shows that coseismic deposits related to either of these events are identified in over 20 lakes. For these deposits, PGV scales log–logistically to the relative abundance of turbidites in each lake (within a 13 and 40 cm/s minimum and maximum threshold, respectively), whereas the turbidite volume correlates to both strength (PGA and/or PGV) and duration of shaking. By linking lacustrine imprint characteristics for both earthquakes to local ground motions, we bridge the gap between sedimentology and seismology, opening perspectives toward quantitative characterization of paleoearthquakes based on the signature of their imprint in lake sediment sequences.

Cite this article as Wils, K., G. Montalva, M. Van Daele, M. De Batist, and J. Moernaut (2025). Peak Ground Velocity and Shaking Duration Control Coseismic Surficial Sediment Remobilization on Lacustrine Slopes and Emplacement of Seismoturbidites, *Seismol. Res. Lett.* **97**, 309–322, doi: 10.1785/0220240487.

Supplemental Material

Introduction

Accurate seismic hazard assessment strongly relies on paleoseismic research, which provides long timescales of earthquake recurrence and potentially also reveals earthquakes that were larger than the highest magnitude events known from historical or instrumental records. In this respect, lakes can provide long and highly sensitive shaking records (e.g., Schnellmann *et al.*, 2007; Strasser *et al.*, 2013; Howarth *et al.*, 2016; Moernaut *et al.*, 2018; Lu *et al.*, 2020; Daxer, Huang, *et al.*,

1. Department of Geology, Renard Centre of Marine Geology, Ghent University, Ghent, Belgium, https://orcid.org/0000-0003-4738-2002 (KW); https://orcid.org/0000-0002-8530-4438 (MVD); https://orcid.org/0000-0002-1625-2080 (MDB); 2. Departamento de Ingeniería Civil, Universidad de Concepción, Concepción, Chile, https://orcid.org/0000-0001-8598-7120 (GM); 3. Institute of Geology, University of Innsbruck, Innsbruck, Austria, https://orcid.org/0000-0003-3164-4274 (JM)

*Corresponding author: katleen.wils@ugent.be

2022; Fan *et al.*, 2022; Praet *et al.*, 2022; Gastineau *et al.*, 2023). They are particularly powerful in regions where more traditional paleoseismic techniques such as trenching or reconstructions of coastal land-level changes are not feasible, or cannot resolve the manifold earthquake sources within these settings (e.g., Kremer *et al.*, 2017; Praet *et al.*, 2022). Lacustrine paleoseismology has therefore proven to be an invaluable methodology for reliable inferences on earthquake recurrence intervals around the world (Moernaut, 2020). Most notably, it allows for estimations of the magnitude and rupture extent of paleoearthquakes (Howarth *et al.*, 2014; Kremer *et al.*, 2017; Vanneste *et al.*, 2018; Philibosian and Meltzner, 2020; Wils *et al.*, 2020; Howarth, Barth, *et al.*, 2021; Fan *et al.*, 2022; Oswald *et al.*, 2022; Lemot *et al.*, 2024; Moernaut *et al.*, 2025; Niederstätter *et al.*, 2025). Nevertheless, these estimates, however valuable they may be, are still mostly based on qualitative rather than quantitative assumptions that link the intensity of earthquake shaking to a resulting sedimentary imprint.

The coseismic sedimentary imprint identifiable in lakes may consist of direct fault-related deformation (e.g., Wils *et al.*, 2018; Oswald *et al.*, 2021), or shaking-induced secondary evidence. The latter includes (1) soft-sediment deformation structures (SSDS) (e.g., Molenaar *et al.*, 2021), (2) mass-transport deposits (MTDs) and MTD-evolved turbidites and megaturbidites (e.g., Praet *et al.*, 2017), (3) turbidites resulting from surficial remobilization of lacustrine slopes (e.g., Moernaut *et al.*, 2017), and (4) flood-evolved turbidites resulting from a catchment response to shaking (e.g., Howarth *et al.*, 2012). Previous studies have aimed at calibrating the lacustrine paleoseismic method by attributing the occurrence or absence of various coseismic imprints to threshold values of seismic shaking, either related to local intensities, or epicentral intensities or earthquake magnitude in combination with a distance dependency (e.g., Inouchi *et al.*, 1996; Monecke *et al.*, 2004; Strasser *et al.*, 2013; Moernaut *et al.*, 2014; Van Daele *et al.*, 2015, 2020; Avşar *et al.*, 2016; Wilhelm *et al.*, 2016; Kremer *et al.*, 2017; Daxer, Ortler, *et al.*, 2022; Singleton *et al.*, 2024). These intensity values are usually expressed on a macroseismic scale (e.g., modified Mercalli intensity [MMI] or Medvedev–Sponheuer–Karnik), as such reports are more readily available compared to instrumental data for many recent as well as historical earthquakes. Macroseismic intensity is, however, a relatively subjective ground-motion measure, unable to capture variability in the various aspects of strong ground motion, whereas characteristics such as the peak ground acceleration (PGA) and peak ground velocity (PGV) have a physical meaning. Nevertheless, studies linking lacustrine shaking imprints to measurable ground-motion parameters, even if determined using empirical ground-motion prediction equations (GMPEs), remain scarce (e.g., Avşar *et al.*, 2016; Lu *et al.*, 2020; Molenaar *et al.*, 2024).

This study aims to calibrate the lacustrine paleoseismic method by determining the relation between quantitative ground-motion measures (i.e., PGA, PGV, and duration of shaking) on the bottom of a lake and the sedimentary shaking imprints identified therein, thus determining the missing link needed for quantitative paleoearthquake characterization. To achieve this, we focus on turbidites resulting from surficial remobilization of lacustrine slope sediments during instrumentally recorded megathrust earthquakes in south-central Chile, for which the rupture parameters are well constrained and calibrated ground-motion models exist (Idini *et al.*, 2017; Montalva *et al.*, 2017, 2021). This includes the 1960 Valdivia earthquake, with a moment magnitude (M_w) of 9.5 the largest instrumentally recorded earthquake worldwide so far, and the 2010 M_w 8.8 Maule earthquake. Compiling existing sedimentological data shows that coseismic deposits related to either of these events have been identified in over 20 lakes (e.g., Moernaut *et al.*, 2014; Van Daele *et al.*, 2015).

Lacustrine Paleoseismology in South-Central Chile

Chile is situated on the western side of the South American continent, flanked along its coastline by a long, roughly north–south-oriented subduction zone. Here, the Nazca plate subducts beneath the South American plate (Fig. 1), resulting in frequent seismic activity. South-central Chile is characterized by the presence of several lakes and fjords that have been extensively studied for paleoseismological purposes over the last ~20 yr, covering a north–south transect of study sites of more than 1300 km distance along the Maule and Valdivia segments of the subduction zone. Particularly, the deposits related to the 1960 and 2010 earthquakes have been thoroughly investigated and are by now well documented (Bertrand, 2005; Chapron *et al.*, 2006; Moernaut *et al.*, 2007, 2014, 2017, 2018, 2019, 2021; Urrutia *et al.*, 2007; Bertrand *et al.*, 2008; St-Onge *et al.*, 2012; Van Daele *et al.*, 2015, 2019, Wils *et al.*, 2020). These deposits include SSDS, turbidites, megaturbidites, and/or MTDs and were robustly attributed to these two events by identification of the ^{137}Cs peak (corresponding to the year 1964/1965), varve counting, and comparison of the topmost sediments in cores retrieved before and after the 2010 earthquake. A compilation of all these studies shows that sedimentary imprints related to the 1960 earthquake have been identified in 18 different lakes and fjords, whereas those caused by the 2010 earthquake were found in 8 lakes (Table S1, available in the supplemental material to this article). These imprints show a clear tapering out beyond the respective rupture terminations: the more northern 2010 Maule earthquake is not recorded in the southernmost lakes, whereas the northern lakes do not show any identifiable imprint from the more southern 1960 Valdivia rupture (Van Daele *et al.*, 2015). This underscores the potential of lacustrine coseismic sedimentary imprints for quantitative paleoseismology, which is especially true when considering (seismo)turbidites. It has been shown that the number of turbidites resulting from remobilization of hemipelagic slope material (hereafter termed LT1 further suggested that the bracketed duration (BD) of strong ground motion can be correlated to the depth of surficial hemipelagic slope sediment remobilization, and thus to the CTT of LT1 turbidites (Molenaar *et al.*, 2021).

In this study, we aim to improve initial attempts at calibrating the lacustrine paleoseismic method by considering quantitative earthquake parameters (i.e., PGA, PGV, and BD) rather than macroseismic shaking intensity for both the 1960 and 2010 earthquakes. However, because not all the lakes and fjords in which an imprint of either of the two recent megathrust earthquakes could be identified show the same sedimentary characteristics and/or were studied with the same research methodologies, we made a comprehensive selection to avoid lithological or analytical bias as much as possible, and to ensure that the process resulting in turbidite emplacement can be considered equal (i.e., surficial remobilization of lacustrine slope sediments). Only information from short gravity cores in basins (thus excluding slope cores) is used from lakes with sediment-bearing slope segments of over 10 m long and a gradient of ≥2°, to allow for gravity-flow development (Molenaar *et al.*, 2021), so that slope-sourced turbidites should in theory be possible. As a result, a total of 15 lakes are considered here, including from north to south (Table 1): Negra, Lo Encañado, Laja, Villarrica, Calafquén, Pullinque, Pellaifa, Panguipulli, Neltume, Riñihue, Ranco, Maihue, Puyehue, Rupanco, and Llanquihue. Each of these lakes is divided into depositional areas in which the seismically induced event deposits resulting from a certain earthquake are similar (compare to Van Daele *et al.*, 2015). To isolate the lake response to seismic shaking, we only consider turbidites resulting from surficial remobilization of lacustrine slope sediments that are either hemipelagic or deltaic in origin (hereafter

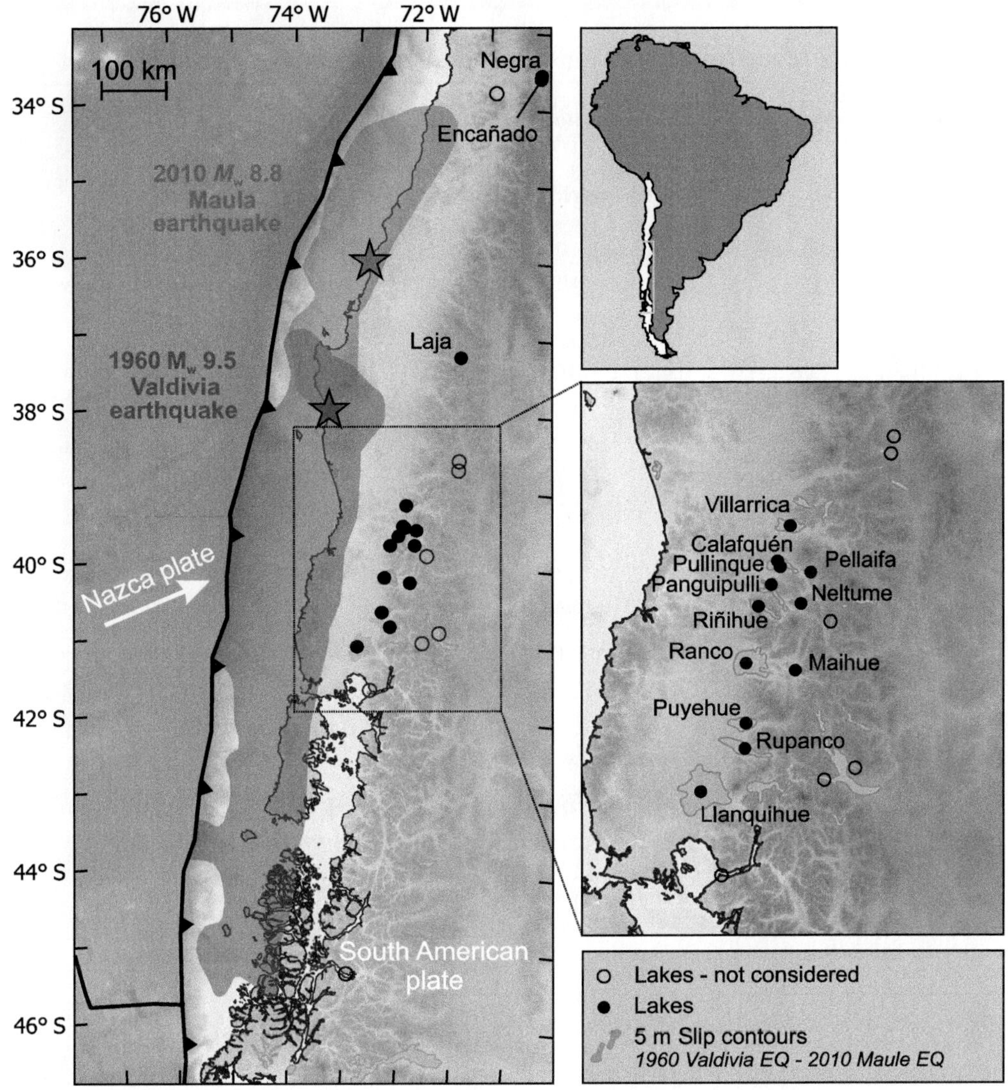

Figure 1. Overview of all lakes in south central Chile in which an imprint related to the 1960 Valdivia and/or 2010 Maule earthquake has been identified and their location with respect to rupture extent for both events (5 m slip contours in red and purple, respectively, after Moreno *et al.*, 2009, 2012). To avoid lithological or analytical bias and ensure that all turbidites result from surficial remobilization of lacustrine slope sediments, only a comprehensive selection of lakes (full dots) is considered for calibration purposes, whereas the others (hollow dots) are omitted. The color version of this figure is available only in the electronic edition.

turbidites, in contrast to LT2 turbidites that consist of more terrestrial material; after Moernaut *et al.*, 2014) in depositional areas adjacent to hemipelagic sediment-bearing slopes increases with increasing local seismic intensity between V¾ and VII½. Below and above this threshold intensity range, respectively none or all the depositional areas in the studied lakes show LT1 turbidites (Van Daele *et al.*, 2015). In addition, in one of the studied lakes, the cumulative turbidite thickness (CTT, which is a measure for turbidite volume) of LT2s in front of an alluvial fan was found to increase linearly with increasing shaking intensity (Moernaut *et al.*, 2014). A recent effort to define more quantitative shaking thresholds using data from two Chilean lakes

TABLE 1
Overview of Lacustrine Sedimentary Imprints Identified for Recent Earthquakes in South-Central Chile

			1960 Valdivia Earthquake		2010 Maule Earthquake		
Location	**Lat (°N)**	**Lon (°E)**	**1960 Imprint**	**Affected DAs**	**2010 Imprint**	**Affected DAs**	**References**
Negra	−33.64	−70.13	None	0/1	LT2	N.A.	Van Daele *et al.* (2015)
Encañado	−33.67	−70.13	None	0/1	LT2-intra, MTD	1/1	Van Daele *et al.* (2015) and (2019)
Laja	−37.32	−71.32	LT1	3/4	LT1	3/4	Van Daele *et al.* (2015)
Villarrica	−39.27	−72.14	LT1, LT2, MTD	6/8	LT1, LT2, MTD	3/6	Moernaut *et al.* (2014, 2017) and Van Daele *et al.* (2015)
Calafquén	−39.54	−72.18	LT1, LT2-intra, MTD	12/16	LT1, LT2-intra, MTD	5/8	Moernaut *et al.* (2014, 2021) and Van Daele *et al.* (2015)
Pullinque	−39.57	−72.16	LT1	1/2	Pre-2010 cores	N.A.	Van Daele *et al.* (2015)
Pellaifa	−39.60	−71.96	LT2	N.A.	Pre-2010 cores	N.A.	Van Daele *et al.* (2015)
Panguipulli	−39.68	−72.25	LT1, MTD	3/3	Pre-2010 cores	N.A.	Van Daele *et al.* (2015)
Neltume	−39.80	−71.98	LT2	N.A.	Pre-2010 cores	N.A.	Van Daele *et al.* (2015)
Riñihue	−39.81	−72.39	LT1, LT2-intra, MTD	6/6	LT2-intra	1/5	Moernaut *et al.* (2014), Van Daele *et al.* (2015) and Molenaar *et al.* (2021)
Ranco	−40.22	−72.47	LT1, MTD	6/7	LT1, LT2-intra, MTD	2/7	Van Daele *et al.* (2015)
Maihue	−40.29	−72.04	LT2, MTD	N.A.	Pre-2010 cores	N.A.	Van Daele *et al.* (2015)
Puyehue	−40.68	−72.50	LT1	5/5	None	0/5	Van Daele *et al.* (2015)
Rupanco	−40.87	−72.35	LT1, LT2	1/1	Pre-2010 cores	N.A.	Van Daele *et al.* (2015)
Llanquihue	−41.13	−72.90	LT1, LT2	1/1	None	0/1	Van Daele *et al.* (2015)

Overview of the types of sedimentary imprints (turbidite or mass transport deposit [MTD]) that have been identified in the lakes considered in this study for both the 1960 Valdivia and 2010 Maule earthquake as well as the relative number of depositional areas (DAs) near sediment-bearing (hemipelagic or deltaic) slopes where intrabasinal event deposits (LT1 or LT2-intra) could be identified. LT1 are turbidites resulting from remobilization of hemipelagic slope material, LT2 turbidites consist of more terrestrial material. In case the terrestrial material originates from within the lake (e.g., deltas), they are referred to as LT2-intra, all other cases (onshore or unclear origin) are labeled as LT2. Depositional areas where the presence of an LT1 or LT2-intra cannot be verified (e.g., due to the presence of a megaturbidite, MTD, or LT2 with unclear origin) are not considered. Lat, latitude; and Lon, longitude.

referred to as intrabasinal turbidites) and exclude those that are MTD-evolved or resulting from a catchment response. This means we consider the presence of LT1 turbidites as well as LT2 turbidites originating from deltaic slopes (LT2-intra), and exclude LT2 turbidites for which the origin is unclear or that can be related to onshore mass movements based on historical reports (Table 1). Although not all LT2-intra turbidites necessarily result from surficial remobilization, this is assumed to be the case in the lakes considered in this study (Moernaut *et al.*, 2014, 2017). Megaturbidites are also excluded from our analysis because they do not result from surficial remobilization but rather from large-scale mass wasting, which can occur either sub-aquatically and/or in the lake catchment, and would thus require a separate calibration study. We subsequently evaluated those depositional areas that are surrounded by gentle (≥2°, compare to Molenaar *et al.*, 2021), sediment-charged lacustrine slopes and determine in how many of those intrabasinal imprints related to the 1960 and/or 2010 earthquake can be identified. Finally, it is important to note Laguna del Laja has undergone lake-level fluctuations introduced by seasonal extraction of lake water for hydropower production since the early 1970s (Bevis *et al.*, 2004). Such fluctuations can strongly affect the susceptibility of hemipelagic slopes to remobilization of material (e.g., Tournier *et al.*, 2023). In addition, there is a considerable change in sediment composition and structure: sedimentation was more homogenous before 1960 and more layered, with strong contrasts, before 2010 (Van Daele *et al.*, 2015). Apart from the compositional change, this layering may also influence shear strength between layers and therefore surficial remobilization. Therefore, we do not consider the Laguna del Laja deposits for our lacustrine seismograph calibration, but merely include them here to show the potential impact of (anthropogenic) sediment variability on surficial remobilization.

TABLE 2
Overview of Ground Motions in Different Lakes for Recent Earthquakes in South-Central Chile

	1960 Valdivia Earthquake						2010 Maule Earthquake					
	Bedrock			Lake Sediments			Bedrock			Lake Sediments		
Location	PGA (g)	PGV (cm/s)	BD (s)	PGA (g)	PGV (cm/s)	BD (s)	PGA (g)	PGV (cm/s)	BD (s)	PGA (g)	PGV (cm/s)	BD (s)
Negra	0.18	5.82	45.14	0.20	12.22	109.92	0.17	9.94	37.20	0.19	20.92	90.61
Encañado	0.19	5.89	45.90	0.20	12.38	111.78	0.17	10.00	37.45	0.19	21.04	91.21
Laja	0.45	14.90	157.94	0.33	31.45	384.63	0.16	9.16	33.84	0.18	19.27	82.41
Villarrica	0.51	16.35	173.41	0.35	34.54	422.31	0.19	10.84	41.05	0.20	22.84	99.97
Calafquén	0.51	16.47	174.48	0.36	34.77	424.92	0.18	10.54	39.76	0.19	22.19	96.84
Pullinque	0.50	16.27	172.60	0.35	34.36	420.33	0.18	10.34	38.91	0.19	21.77	94.77
Pellaifa	0.46	15.15	160.87	0.34	31.99	391.78	0.16	9.39	34.84	0.18	19.76	84.84
Panguipulli	0.50	16.30	172.84	0.35	34.42	420.93	0.18	10.47	39.46	0.19	22.04	96.11
Neltume	0.45	14.82	157.07	0.33	31.29	382.52	0.16	8.98	33.06	0.17	18.89	80.52
Riñihue	0.51	16.39	173.70	0.35	34.60	423.03	0.18	10.56	39.86	0.19	22.24	97.07
Ranco	0.51	16.52	174.99	0.36	34.89	426.16	0.16	8.96	32.99	0.17	18.85	80.35
Maihue	0.46	15.12	160.53	0.34	31.93	390.94	0.13	7.69	27.55	0.16	16.16	67.09
Puyehue	0.51	16.42	174.07	0.35	34.68	423.91	0.13	7.21	25.55	0.15	15.15	62.23
Rupanco	0.50	16.19	171.80	0.35	34.19	418.40	0.11	6.41	22.30	0.14	13.47	54.31
Llanquihue	0.52	16.63	176.00	0.36	35.12	428.62	0.11	6.08	20.99	0.14	12.77	51.12

Overview of PGA, PGV, and BD values (with 1σ of 0.46 for ln(PGA), 0.59 for ln(PGV), and 1.09 for BD) for each lake considered in this study for both the 1960 Valdivia and 2010 Maule earthquake, calculated using V_{S30}-values for bedrock (1000 m/s) or lake sediments (175 m/s). Peak ground acceleration (PGA) and peak ground velocity (PGV) values are calculated using the ground-motion prediction equations (GMPEs) from Montalva *et al.* (2017) and Montalva *et al.* (2021), respectively, and bracketed duration (BD) is calculated according to the model of Céspedes *et al.* (2022).

Ground-Motion Characterization

For both the 1960 and 2010 earthquakes, we calculate the PGA, PGV, and BD in each lake considering a V_{S30}-value for bedrock as well as lake sediments for a first evaluation of the impact of site characteristics (Table 2). Although each depositional area would in principle experience a (slightly) different shaking strength (expressed either as PGA or PGV), we calculate only one value per lake. This simplified approach is necessary but reasonable, as, apart from small rupture distance variations, all other factors within that lake have to be considered the same because detailed site characterization is currently not available. For bedrock, we consider a value of 1000 m/s in accordance with the National Earthquake Hazards Reduction Program site classification. For lake sediments, in situ measurements of the V_S range only exist in Lake Lucerne, indicating a value of <100 m/s for pure lacustrine sedimentation (Shynkarenko *et al.*, 2021). To check the validity of these values for our Chilean lakes, we performed passive seismic measurements on lake sediment outcrops around Lago Llanquihue (Fig. S1). Although the uppermost 5 m of our measurements indeed indicate a V_S of around 75 m/s, values rise up to 270 m/s between 10 and 30 m of depth likely as a result of a change in sediment type or structure. This combination results in a V_{S30} of 175 m/s, which can thus be considered as a reasonable average for the subaquatic slopes in this study, taking into account that the thickness of the hemipelagic slope sediment cover in most of the lakes is also limited. For the values of PGA and PGV, we use the event-corrected estimates from the Chile-calibrated GMPEs from Montalva *et al.* (2017) and Montalva *et al.* (2021), respectively. This corresponds to

$$\text{PGA or PGV} = e^{\ln(\text{PGA or PGV}_{\text{GMPE}})+\delta B_e}, \quad (1)$$

in which δB_e is the event residual, representing the median difference between observed and predicted ground-motion values for all measured stations for the considered event. For the 2010 earthquake, δB_e is −0.013 for PGA and 0.258 for PGV (both in log units), whereas for the 1960 earthquake, the median of the models is considered ($\delta B_e = 0$) as an event residual cannot be determined due to the lack of seismometer registrations. Although the errors on these calculations are large (σ corresponds to 0.46 for ln(PGA) and 0.59 for ln(PGV)), they are currently the best-fitting models available for Chilean megathrust earthquakes.

For determination of the BD, defined as the time elapsed between the first and last time a location reaches 0.05*g* during a single event, we use the model developed by Céspedes *et al.* (2022). To minimize existing bias for large-magnitude events ($M_w > 8.0$), we correct it with a constant equal to the bias of the residuals. The latter are the model log residuals for which distributed $N(\mu,\sigma)$ were shifted to $N(0,\sigma)$, with μ −0.917 and σ 1.09 (log units). This bias is evident when computing residuals between observed (Bastías and Montalva, 2016) and predicted (Céspedes *et al.*, 2022) durations for earthquakes with $M_w > 8$, in which case the predicted values are consistently too large. Because both events have a similar source mechanism, the PGA/PGV and BD are strongly correlated (Céspedes *et al.*, 2022).

These calculated values show that high PGA is strongly attenuated in lake sediments, whereas lower values appear to be amplified (Table 2). Moreover, the obtained PGV values and durations are significantly higher in lake sediments compared to bedrock. Such trends can be expected from previously determined site-amplification factors (Wald and Allen, 2007). In addition, ground shaking was clearly more intense (in strength and duration) during the 1960 Valdivia earthquake compared to the 2010 Maule earthquake. This is not only due to the proximity of most lakes to the 1960 rupture area—as shown by ground-shaking values in Laguna del Laja, which is located at a similar rupture distance to both events (Fig. 1) but mostly reflects the considerable magnitude difference between both events. Also, Laguna Negra and Lago Lo Encañado show longer shaking duration and higher PGA for the 1960 earthquake, even though both are located north of the 2010 rupture area and thus even further from the more southern (but higher magnitude) 1960 earthquake.

Calibration of the Lacustrine Seismograph

Impact of site variability

Independent of the considered V_{S30}-values, the relative abundance of intrabasinal turbidites in depositional areas near sediment-bearing slopes increases with increasing PGA and PGV (Fig. 2a,c). However, previous studies consistently considered shaking intensities at the lake shores or nearest towns to evaluate whether a coseismic sedimentary imprint could be present, even though bedrock substrates clearly respond differently to shaking compared to lake sediments. This highlights the importance of considering site effects when evaluating a lacustrine seismic record. It is clear that both the PGA and PGV determined for lake sediments and bedrock material are not linearly related because of their different V_{S30}-values (Fig. 2a,c). This effect would be even further emphasized when considering additional (inevitable) site and seismic wavepath variability. This hampers a straightforward interpretation of what happens on the bottom of a lake based on the shaking registered in its catchment, meaning that the latter is not necessarily suitable to explain the presence or absence of lacustrine shaking imprints. For further interpretations, we will, therefore, only consider the values calculated for a subsurface consisting of material with a V_{S30} of 175 m/s, referred to as the PGA_{175}, PGV_{175}, and BD_{175}.

Linking turbidity current triggering to shaking strength

When comparing the PGA and PGV values for the 2010 and 1960 events for each lake to the number of intrabasinal deposits, it seems that increased shaking strength leads to more deposits (Fig. 2). Moreover, PGA and PGV values below or above a certain threshold value appear to never or always result in an imprint, respectively. This, however, does not necessarily mean that when a certain threshold value of seismic shaking is exceeded, all lacustrine slopes have been completely remobilized, especially considering that surficial remobilization is known to be a patchy process (Molenaar *et al.*, 2021). This means that, even for strong earthquakes, only part of the slopes would get affected, leaving enough material to become remobilized during a subsequent earthquake relatively shortly after (Moernaut *et al.*, 2017). As a result, their previous assumption that surficial remobilization allows for continuous shaking records that are not influenced by slope recharging likely remains valid.

To determine a meaningful regression, logarithmic transformations are performed, which required turbidite occurrences of 0% and 100% to be replaced by 5% and 95%, respectively. Because of the limited number of depositional areas with these values, a 5% error can be considered reasonable and not too constraining. Subsequent binning of lake evidence in PGA and PGV classes of 0.025*g* and 2.5 cm/s, respectively, shows that the relative amount of intrabasinal near-slope deposits scales log–logistically to PGV ($R^2 = 0.92$), whereas PGA shows more scatter and does not allow for meaningful regressions ($R^2 < 0.6$) to be determined. Similar regressions are obtained when only considering LT1 deposits (Fig. S2), again confirming that the LT2-intra deposits considered here are formed by the same process (i.e., surficial remobilization) as LT1 turbidites. Although binning boundaries can be set arbitrarily, grouping several lakes and depositional areas affected by similar shaking allows for a more statistically robust determination of shaking effects, provided that it results in a reasonable spreading of the data. At the same time, it (partly) accounts for the error in the calculated ground motions. Moreover, the log–logistic regression for PGV remains valid even without binning ($R^2 = 0.74$). This suggests a predominant influence of PGV rather than PGA on the triggering of coseismic lacustrine turbidites, underscoring the importance of surficial remobilization as the main driving factor for turbidity current triggering (Moernaut *et al.*, 2017). Namely, previous studies already hypothesized that surficial remobilization

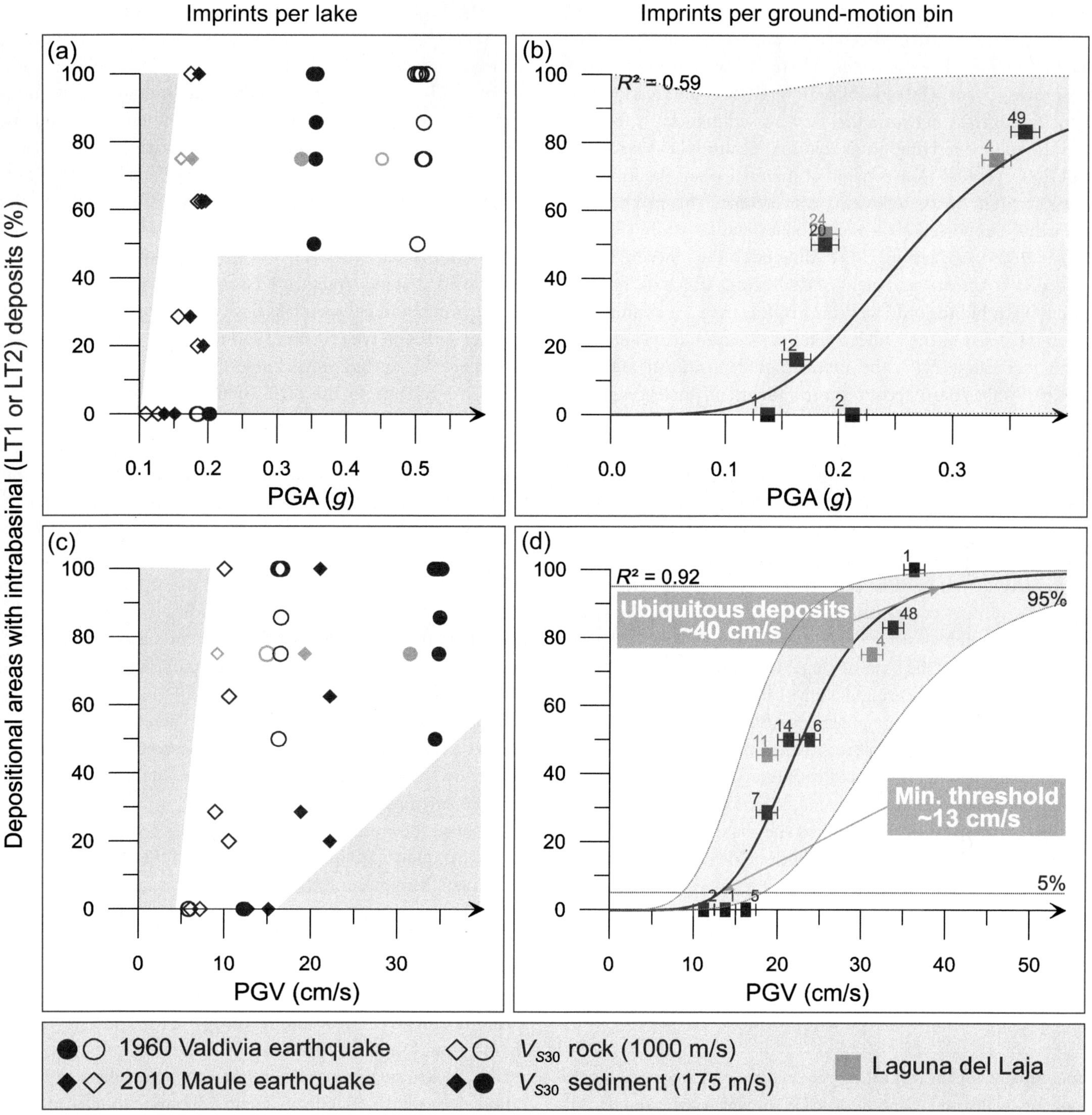

Figure 2. Percentage of depositional areas with intrabasinal (LT1 or LT2) turbidites near sediment-bearing (hemipelagic or deltaic) slopes in function of median (a,b) peak ground acceleration (PGA) and (c,d) peak ground velocity (PGV) for the 1960 Valdivia (circles) and 2010 Maule (diamonds) earthquakes using V_{S30}-values corresponding to bedrock material (hollow shapes) and lake sediments (filled shapes), either plotted per lake (left; a, c, with gray-shaded areas marking "forbidden zones") or with the lakes grouped with bin sizes of 0.025*g* or 2.5 cm/s (right; b, d). In plots (b) and (d), the number of depositional areas with sediment-bearing slopes that experienced this intensity of shaking is indicated per data point, along with the 95% confidence interval of the log–logistic regression (for PGV, this corresponds to equation 2). Points that include data from Laguna del Laja are indicated in gray, as they are not considered for the regressions due to anthropogenic influence on the lake's sedimentation.

is promoted by long durations of shaking at low frequencies (McHugh *et al.*, 2020; Molenaar *et al.*, 2021), which control the PGV values (Kramer, 1996). Therefore, we can assume that the process of surficial remobilization relies on the creation of a velocity contrast between the moving sedimentary substrate and the static overlying water column, resulting in shear stress and thus eventual resuspension of material when the inherent shear strength of the sediments is overcome. This mechanism is further supported by a recent experimental study (Seibert *et al.*, 2025). A certain PGV threshold thus needs to be exceeded to create sufficient shear stress, which is around 13 cm/s (turbidites only identified in less than 5% of the depositional areas) in the Chilean lakes considered here (Fig. 1D). With increasing PGV, the number of depositional areas in which intrabasinal deposits can be identified increases, until at around 40 cm/s, when deposits can be found in over 95% of the depositional area of each lake. For values in between 13 and 40 cm/s, turbidites could thus be identified, but not necessarily in every depositional area, which is then dependent on (1) factors affecting the local slope shear strength, such as cohesion or consolidation state, which is in turn governed by the sedimentation rate, compressibility, vertical permeability, and sediment composition, (2) factors increasing the static shear stress, such as slope angle, and (3) the distance between the coring site and the base-of-slope, which relates to whether a turbidity current of a certain volume can reach the site. In addition, factors such as slope angle or sediment composition may also create additional site effects that result in locally amplified or damped shaking. This could counteract or enhance the susceptibility of specific slopes to remobilization but can currently not be considered due to the limited site characterization knowledge of hemipelagic slopes. The chance of identifying a turbidite (P) in a specific sedimentary basin for a given PGV considering a V_{S30} value of 175 m/s, calibrated for lakes in south-central Chile, can thus be written as follows (Fig. 2d):

$$P = \frac{e^{-16.37\pm1.87+5.22\pm0.61\ln(\mathrm{PGV}_{175}(\frac{\mathrm{cm}}{\mathrm{s}}))}}{1+e^{-16.37\pm1.87+5.22\pm0.61\ln(\mathrm{PGV}_{175}(\frac{\mathrm{cm}}{\mathrm{s}}))}}. \quad (2)$$

Interestingly, the process behind surficial remobilization seemingly contrasts with the formation of SSDS, of which the amount and deformation degree appears more susceptible to variations in PGA and high-frequency shaking (Heifetz *et al.*, 2005; Wetzler *et al.*, 2010; Tuttle *et al.*, 2019; Lu *et al.*, 2020; Molenaar *et al.*, 2021, 2024). This would imply that these coseismic shaking-related traces can be regarded as proxies for different shaking-related parameters. Nevertheless, it should be noted that a potential influence of PGV on SSDS formation has, up to now, not been investigated.

Turbidite volume as a measure for shaking duration

Apart from increasing the chances for surficial remobilization and triggering of a turbidity current, higher shaking intensities have also been related to more extensive turbidites in an earlier study, using the CTT as a proxy for turbidity current volume (Moernaut *et al.*, 2014; Van Daele *et al.*, 2015). However, comparing CTT and shaking strength in multiple basins requires some form of normalization because sedimentation and the slope area available for remobilization is variable between lakes or even basins, as is the depositional area. This leads to different amounts of material with different geotechnical properties being available for remobilization, and thus variations in turbidite volume and eventually thickness that are independent of the seismic shaking strength. To account for such natural variability within and between lakes, we consider the CTT per lake and per turbidite type for the 1960 and 2010 earthquake (sum of the average turbidite thickness in each depositional area), expressed relative to the CTT of the 2010 or 1960 deposit, respectively, in that same lake (normalized CTT). This summation also aims to minimize the effect of MTD presence below some of the considered intrabasinal turbidites because this might result in locally thinner or thicker deposits. As a result, this can only be done using depositional areas in which we have data for both the 1960 and 2010 earthquakes, and for each lake we obtain two datapoints, which are the inverse of each other. Because the turbidite thickness is now expressed relatively (i.e., thicker or thinner deposits compared to the reference deposit), the ground-motion parameters should be normalized in the same way (i.e., stronger or weaker shaking compared to the reference earthquake). Therefore, we calculate relative PGV, PGA, and BD values for the 1960 and 2010 earthquakes by normalizing against the values obtained for the 2010 or 1960 earthquake, respectively.

Because the number of lakes in which both the 1960 and 2010 earthquakes left an imprint is limited (i.e., Laja, Villarrica, Calafquén, Riñihue, and Ranco), it is important to note that the resulting trends are less robust compared to those for turbidite occurrence. Nevertheless, it is obvious that higher PGV and PGA lead to overall thicker deposits (Fig. 3a). There is one exception: the LT1 turbidites in Laguna del Laja, for which the 2010 imprints seem to be anomalously thick or the 1960 deposits too thin. We infer that this apparent discrepancy is again related to the anthropogenic influence on the lake's sedimentation since the 1970s, likely affecting the susceptibility of hemipelagic slopes to remobilization of material. Indeed, not only the thickness of the 2010 turbidite seems to be anomalously high, also the relative amount of near-slope LT1 turbidites is slightly higher than would be expected based on the average trend, whereas that for the 1960 deposits fits better (Fig. 2d).

In cases in which stable sedimentation circumstances persisted, it is thus possible to determine if shaking that induced a specific intrabasinal turbidite was stronger or weaker compared to that for a reference deposit. To robustly quantify this relation, however, more data covering a better spread in ground-motion parameters would be required because a log–log regression on the current dataset would be anchored by

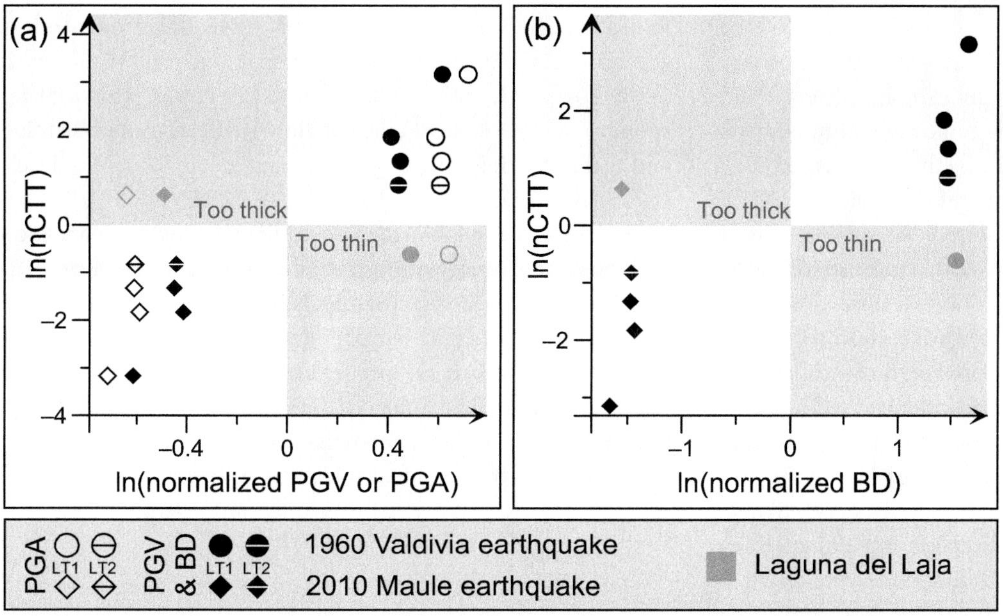

Figure 3. Normalized cumulative intrabasinal (LT1, uniform shapes, or LT2, strikethrough shapes) turbidite thicknesses (nCTT) as a function of (a) normalized PGA (hollow shapes) and PGV (filled shapes) and (b) normalized bracketed duration (BD, filled shapes) using a V_{S30} of 175 m/s for all lakes in which both the 1960 (circles) and 2010 (diamonds) earthquake triggered a turbidite. To avoid the impact of different amounts of sediment availability between lakes, the values are normalized to the thickness of either the 2010 or 1960 deposit, respectively, per lake. Points that include data from Laguna del Laja are indicated in gray because they are not considered for the regressions due to anthropogenic influence on the lake's sedimentation.

points at the extreme ends of the space with no data in between, resulting in artificially high R^2-values. This could be achieved by (1) having more lakes covering a larger geographical area that contain imprints resulting from both earthquakes, or (2) consider turbidite thickness and ground-motion data for more than two events. Although the former could be achieved in south-central Chile by collecting additional sediment cores in some of the lakes where a possible imprint of the 2010 earthquake could so far not be investigated (Table 1), the latter is unfeasible as no additional well-characterized earthquakes have affected our considered lakes.

Previous research by Molenaar *et al.* (2021) and McHugh *et al.* (2016) hypothesized that surficial remobilization depth correlates with the duration of strong shaking, which relates to earthquake magnitude (Hanks and McGuire, 1981; Meier *et al.*, 2017), rather than its shaking amplitude (in this case expressed as PGA). Because a deeper remobilization depth evidently results in more voluminous turbidity currents, this should also appear when comparing our BD data to the normalized CTT (Fig. 3b). Indeed, longer shaking seems to result in thicker turbidites, again except for in Laguna del Laja. Similar to the reasoning for shaking strength, meaningful regressions cannot be established with the current dataset.

The CTT is thus related to both shaking strength and duration, likely resulting from an interplay between both parameters. This is similar to the formation of SSDS, requiring a minimum duration to form and higher degrees of deformation with increasing duration, while also being susceptible to variations in PGA and high-frequency shaking (Molenaar *et al.*, 2024). A possible explanation could be that exceeding a certain threshold level of shaking strength (either PGV for turbidites or PGA for SSDS) allows for surficial remobilization or in situ deformation to start, whereas the duration of shaking above this threshold level determines how long the process continues and thus how much material is remobilized or how strongly it is deformed. This hypothesis can, however, not be verified at this point because existing GMPEs do not allow us to calculate shaking durations in such detail, and because the relation between PGV and BD is similar for the considered events. To disentangle the effects of PGV and BD, the imprints of earthquakes with a different PGV and BD relation would need to be compared, such as those of recent megathrust and intraslab events (Céspedes *et al.*, 2022), which is not possible with the current dataset. However, observed correlations between ground-motion evolution and marine turbidite structure as a result of the 2016 Kaikōura earthquake (Howarth, Barth, *et al.*, 2021) suggest a similar mechanism, thus supporting our interpretations.

Implications for Quantitative Paleoseismic Research

The importance of multilocation studies

In the previous section, normalization of the CTT was performed per lake to allow for interlake comparisons, assuming the process resulting in surficial remobilization—which is related to slope shear strength—is universal in all those lakes. Nevertheless, the distinct response to seismic shaking in Laguna del Laja (Figs. 2 and 3) already hints to an influence of sediment composition on shear strength. Sediment composition is therefore presumed to also affect surficial sediment remobilization, as is the case for SSDS generation (Molenaar *et al.*, 2024). Comprehensive and comparative studies investigating the impact of lithology on turbidity current triggering is therefore required, and would allow to correct for shear strength changes, either when comparing different lakes, or within a single lake when considering a paleorecord. To counteract such lithology dependence as much as possible, single-lake regressions could be established. When considering the imprints within a single depositional area (where sedimentation is thus considered consistent throughout space and the time window considered), CTT normalization should also not be required. To validate this, a lake with imprints related to other well-characterized earthquakes would be required. The only other example of such an event in the region is the 1575 earthquake, deemed similar to the 1960 event in location and size based on historical reports (Lomnitz, 2004) as well as on the spatial extent of sedimentary imprints (Wils *et al.*, 2020). Indeed, its deposit seems to support our interpretation, as each depositional area of Lago Villarrica and Lago Calafquén shows a turbidite of very similar thickness resulting from the 1960 and 1575 earthquakes, but a much thinner one related to the more distant and thus locally weaker 2010 earthquake (Moernaut *et al.*, 2014). This opens perspectives for quantitative determination of shaking strength and duration even when studying a single-lake basin, provided that sufficient coring locations are targeted to eliminate depositional variations resulting from a spatial change in lake bottom morphology, and that sedimentation stays consistent in rate as well as composition. For the relatively short and recent timeframe of our calibration study, this is a fair assumption, but for paleoseismology based on long sediment cores, timeframes of several thousands of years are often considered in which this presumed consistency is more difficult to verify. Apart from thorough evaluation of changes in sedimentation rate and composition, it requires additional seismic profiling to understand the basin evolution. To eliminate the influence of small-scale local variations as much as possible, it is thus recommendable to consider multiple basins or depositional areas when possible, or at least several cores, in each lake when performing quantitative paleoseismic studies. This is especially true when considering CTT, which is more susceptible to local variability, rather than turbidite occurrence.

Inferring paleoshaking intensities and rupture characteristics

Taking into account the established calibration of the natural lacustrine paleoseismograph, we surmise that a certain threshold value of PGV needs to be exceeded to start remobilizing surficial sediments on subaquatic slopes, but the time during which this value is exceeded determines the amount of material that gets remobilized and governs the eventual turbidite volume. In this way, the macroseismic intensity values that have so far been used for lacustrine calibration studies (e.g., Moernaut *et al.*, 2014; Van Daele *et al.*, 2015, 2020; Wilhelm *et al.*, 2016; Daxer, Ortler, *et al.*, 2022; Singleton *et al.*, 2024) could thus be regarded as representing a combination of both the PGV and duration of shaking. This is not surprising because the damage-related MMI scale intrinsically considers shaking duration (Wood and Neumann, 1931) and has been found to correlate closer to PGV than PGA in various studies, especially for high-intensity (≥VI) shaking (e.g., Wald *et al.*, 1999; Boatwright *et al.*, 2001; Wu *et al.*, 2003), which corresponds to the values relevant for surficial remobilization and turbidite triggering (e.g., Moernaut *et al.*, 2014; Van Daele *et al.*, 2020).

For the Chilean lakes considered here, using the proportion of depositional areas with intrabasinal turbidites (LT1 or LT2) near sediment-bearing (hemipelagic or deltaic) lacustrine slopes for a particular megathrust earthquake in each lake, hereafter referred to as "occurrence," of which values of 0% and 100% should be replaced by 5% and 95%, respectively, the PGV experienced by that lake ($V_{S30} = 175$ m/s) during this event can thus be determined as follows:

$$\mathrm{PGV}_{175}\left(\frac{\mathrm{cm}}{\mathrm{s}}\right) = e^{\left(\frac{\ln\left(\frac{\mathrm{Occurrence}}{1-\mathrm{Occurrence}}\right)-(3.13\pm0.05)}{0.18\pm0.02}\right)}. \quad (3)$$

This represents the inverse regression compared to equation (2), in which PGV values were considered to be known (calculated, independent X variable) and govern turbidite occurrence (dependent Y variable), whereas for paleoearthquakes, turbidite occurrence is known (measured, independent X variable) and the related PGV needs to be determined (dependent Y variable).

When considering the CTT, and if additional input data would be available to establish robust regressions, it is important to note that the effects of sediment compaction may result in an overestimation of the imprint thickness for recent earthquakes compared to those for older events because the uppermost sediments did not yet undergo significant natural compaction. This could be corrected for by considering the water content of the sediment. In addition, shortening or extension of sediment thickness that occurs during coring may counter or enhance the effects of natural sediment compaction and is not necessarily uniform throughout a sediment core (Morton and White, 1997). This underscores the importance of comparing sediment characteristics only in cores that have been retrieved by the same coring technique (e.g., piston coring).

By considering the determined PGV values in a depositional area or lake with site effects, magnitude and rupture distance for that site can be estimated for a single paleoearthquake when considering the original formulas used to calculate the ground motions in each of our lakes (Montalva *et al.*, 2017, 2021). Combining multiple lakes affected by the same event, in which correlated coseismic deposits have been identified, subsequently allows to further refine the paleorupture location. This should ideally be done probabilistically to take into account the error margins on each of these formulas. Such an approach has already been developed using the MMI thresholds linked to coseismic sedimentary imprints (e.g., Van Daele *et al.*, 2015), in which the most likely combinations of magnitude and location for prehistoric earthquakes are estimated by comparing the intensities calculated for a theoretical earthquake with a given magnitude and location to the threshold values assigned to multiple depositional areas or lakes (Vanneste *et al.*, 2018; Lemot *et al.*, 2024). These intensities are then calculated either by an intensity prediction equation (IPE), such as the one developed by Bakun and Wentworth (1997), or the combination of a GMPE and a ground-motion intensity conversion equation (GMICE), such as Worden *et al.* (2012), to convert the quantitative ground-motion measures determined by the GMPE back to intensity. As such, only a single ground-motion measure (preferably PGV) needs to be known, but additional constraints (such as BD values, should they be available) can easily be added. The latter is especially useful in case of different earthquake sources, for which PGV and BD may not correlate as well as they do for the 1960 and 2010 earthquakes (Table 2). The use of quantitative shaking parameters such as PGV entails a significant advancement from using MMI values because they no longer rely on the use of IPEs that do not consider any site effects (e.g., Howarth *et al.*, 2014; Vanneste *et al.*, 2018; Kremer *et al.*, 2020; Lemot *et al.*, 2024; Vervoort *et al.*, 2024), and avoid the need to convert site-dependent GMPE-determined PGV values back to intensity using a GMICE which would otherwise introduce another source of uncertainty (Vanneste *et al.*, 2024; Niederstätter *et al.*, 2025). As a result, the parameters established here have great potential to fine-tune the reconstruction of megathrust rupture variability that exists in south-central Chile and, by extension, for earthquakes around the world.

Considerations for worldwide applications

It is important to emphasize that, although the impact of PGV and shaking duration on turbidite triggering and deposition could be deemed consistent in all lakes around the world, the quantitative values and ground-motion models mentioned here are setting-dependent and cannot simply be applied to any other lake study. Apart from differences in lithology, the type of earthquake (i.e., megathrust, intraslab, or crustal) and the rigidity of the host rock will also impact the calibration because this results in different earthquake frequency content (e.g., Leyton *et al.*, 2009). Because sediments tend to amplify the low-frequency motions that are more common for megathrust earthquakes (Van Daele *et al.*, 2019), this will likely also affect the triggering thresholds for surficial remobilization. The herein established PGV thresholds might thus be different when considering intraplate events as the turbidite triggering mechanism because detailed site characterization and frequency dependency are not considered so far. This highlights the need for more of these calibration studies in the future, considering lakes with different lithologies, in different plate-tectonic contexts, and for different focal mechanisms. Furthermore, it needs to be noted that the presented threshold values are estimates based on empirically determined GMPEs (with considerable error margins) and assumptions on V_{S30}, which can thus deviate significantly from the actual ground-motion measures at the time of the earthquake. A way forward to improve estimates of strong ground motion parameters at lake sites consists of physics-based ground-motion modeling that captures source, path, and site effects, especially in situations in which these models can be calibrated for historical events using station data (Howarth, Barth, *et al.*, 2021). However, due to the sparsity of seismometer registrations for major earthquakes and a total lack of in situ earthquake registrations on the bottom of a lake, the actual site effects cannot be determined, and approximations are currently still necessary. With this in mind, we strongly encourage future efforts with respect to (long-term) in situ seismometer deployment in lakes, such as pioneered by Shynkarenko *et al.* (2021).

Conclusion

The wealth of available sediment cores throughout south-central Chilean lakes allowed us to, for the first time, establish a quantitative calibration of the lacustrine seismograph considering physically sound measures of shaking strength (i.e., PGA, PGV, and BD), improving on previously established relations that rely on rather subjective macroseismic shaking intensity values. This showed that a certain value of PGV needs to be exceeded to trigger turbidity currents resulting from surficial sediment remobilization, whereas the duration of strong shaking governs remobilization volume and thus determines the size of the resulting turbidite. Because the relative number of event deposits in a single basin can be variable based on local slope gradient and shear strength, higher PGV values increase the chances of encountering a turbidite within a considered sedimentary basin. The exact relations for PGV and BD are not only dependent on the seismic site response (here approximated by considering a V_{S30} for lake sediments), but are also setting-dependent (e.g., sedimentation rate, lithology, and basin morphology) and likely also differ when considering different earthquake source mechanisms. Therefore, the sedimentary system of each lake needs to be well-understood and stable throughout the timeframe of interest. Keeping these boundary conditions in mind, our study paves the way for more quantitative calibration studies in different tectonic settings and sedimentary environments around the world, ultimately advancing our understanding of the invaluable paleoseismic records that exist in lake sediments.

Data and Resources

This study is entirely based on published sedimentary lake records. The supplemental material includes a data compilation table with all considered lakes and the sedimentary imprints of both the 1960 and 2010 earthquakes, as well as an overview figure summarizing the V_{S30} measurements at the shores of Lago Llanquihue. Finally, additional regression plots for the occurrence of LT1 turbidites are presented.

Declaration of Competing Interests

The authors acknowledge that there are no conflicts of interest recorded.

Acknowledgments

This research was funded by the Research Foundation—Flanders (FWO) using Katleen Wils' fellowship 12ZC422N and travel Grant V435222N, the EASER project under Grant ACT240044 from Chilean Research and Development Agency (ANID), and the QuakeScene Chile project of the Austrian Science Fund (FWF) [10.55776/P34504]. The authors thank Jana Molenaar for inspiring brainstorm sessions on sediment remobilization and deformation processes, Gert Jan Weltje for enlightening insights into data analysis and statistics, and Markus Niederstätter for asking the right questions that improved our interpretations. The constructive comments of Jamie Howarth and one anonymous reviewer were greatly appreciated and helped further improve the article.

References

Avşar, U., S. Jónsson, Ö. Avşar, and S. Schmidt (2016). Earthquake-induced soft-sediment deformations and seismically amplified erosion rates recorded in varved sediments of Köyceğiz Lake (SW Turkey), *J. Geophys. Res.* **121,** 4767–4779, doi: 10.1002/2016jb012820.

Bakun, W., and C. Wentworth (1997). Estimating earthquake location and magnitude from seismic intensity data, *Bull. Seismol. Soc. Am.* **87,** 1502–1521.

Bastías, N., and G. A. Montalva (2016). Chile strong ground motion Flatfile, *Earthq. Spectra* **32,** 2549–2566, doi: 10.1193/102715eqs158dp.

Bertrand, S. (2005). *Sédimentation lacustre postérieure au Dernier Maximum Glaciaire dans les lacs Icalma et Puyehue (Chili méridional): Reconstitution de la variabilité climatique et des événements sismotectoniques,* University of Liège, Belgium (in French).

Bertrand, S., F. Charlet, E. Chapron, N. Fagel, and M. De Batist (2008). Reconstruction of the Holocene seismotectonic activity of the southern Andes from seismites recorded in Lago Icalma, Chile, 39°S, *Palaeogeogr. Palaeoclimatol. Palaeoecol.* **259,** 301–322, doi: 10.1016/j.palaeo.2007.10.013.

Bevis, M., E. Kendrick, A. Cser, and R. Smalley (2004). Geodetic measurement of the local elastic response to the changing mass of water in Lago Laja, Chile, *Phys. Earth Planet. In.* **141,** 71–78, doi: 10.1016/j.pepi.2003.05.001.

Boatwright, J., K. Thywissen, and L. C. Seekins (2001). Correlation of ground motion and intensity for the 17 January 1994 Northridge, California, earthquake, *Bull. Seismol. Soc. Am.* **91,** 739–752, doi: 10.1785/0119990049.

Céspedes, S., R. Boroschek, and R. O. Ruiz (2022). Strong motion models for duration and Arias intensity for strong motion records in Chile, *J. Earthq. Tsunami* doi: 10.1142/s1793431122500105.

Chapron, E., D. Ariztegui, S. Mulsow, G. Villarosa, M. Pino, V. Outes, E. Juvignié, and E. Crivelli (2006). Impact of the 1960 major subduction earthquake in northern Patagonia (Chile, Argentina), *Quat. Int.* **158,** 58–71, doi: 10.1016/j.quaint.2006.05.017.

Daxer, C., J. S. Huang, S. Weginger, M. Hilbe, M. Strasser, and J. Moernaut (2022). Validation of seismic hazard curves using a calibrated 14 ka lacustrine record in the eastern Alps, Austria, *Sci. Rep.* **12,** 19943, doi: 10.1038/s41598-022-24487-w.

Daxer, C., M. Ortler, S. C. Fabbri, M. Hilbe, I. Hajdas, N. Dubois, T. Piechl, C. Hammerl, M. Strasser, and J. Moernaut (2022). High-resolution calibration of seismically-induced lacustrine deposits with historical earthquake data in the eastern Alps (Carinthia, Austria), *Quat. Sci. Rev.* **284,** 107497, doi: 10.1016/j.quascirev.2022.107497.

Fan, J., H. Xu, W. Shi, Q. Guo, S. Zhang, X. Wei, M. Cai, S. Huang, J. Wang, and J. Xiao (2022). A ~28-kyr continuous lacustrine paleoseismic record of the intraplate, slow-slipping Fuyun fault in northwest China, *Front. Earth Sci.* **10,** 828801, doi: 10.3389/feart.2022.828801.

Gastineau, R., P. Sabatier, S. C. Fabbri, F. S. Anselmetti, P. Roeser, N. Findling, M. Şahin, S. Gündüz, F. Arnaud, S. O. Franz, *et al.* (2023). Lateral variations in the signature of earthquake-generated deposits in Lake Iznik, NW Turkey, *Depositional Rec,* doi: 10.1002/dep2.232.

Hanks, T. C., and R. K. McGuire (1981). The character of high-frequency strong ground motion, *Bull. Seismol. Soc. Am.* **71,** 2071–2095, doi: 10.1785/bssa0710062071.

Heifetz, E., A. Agnon, and S. Marco (2005). Soft sediment deformation by Kelvin Helmholtz Instability: A case from Dead Sea earthquakes, *Earth Planet. Sci. Lett.* **236,** 497–504, doi: 10.1016/j.epsl.2005.04.019.

Howarth, J. D., N. C. Barth, S. J. Fitzsimons, K. Richards-Dinger, K. J. Clark, G. P. Biasi, U. A. Cochran, R. M. Langridge, K. R. Berryman, and R. Sutherland (2021). Spatiotemporal clustering of great earthquakes on a transform fault controlled by geometry, *Nature Geosci.* **14,** 314–320, doi: 10.1038/s41561-021-00721-4.

Howarth, J. D., S. J. Fitzsimons, R. J. Norris, and G. E. Jacobsen (2012). Lake sediments record cycles of sediment flux driven by large earthquakes on the Alpine fault, New Zealand, *Geology* **40,** 1091–1094, doi: 10.1130/g33486.1.

Howarth, J. D., S. J. Fitzsimons, R. J. Norris, and G. E. Jacobsen (2014). Lake sediments record high intensity shaking that provides insight into the location and rupture length of large earthquakes on the Alpine fault, New Zealand, *Earth Planet. Sci. Lett.* **403,** 340–351, doi: 10.1016/j.epsl.2014.07.008.

Howarth, J. D., S. J. Fitzsimons, R. J. Norris, R. Langridge, and M. J. Vandergoes (2016). A 2000 yr rupture history for the Alpine fault derived from Lake Ellery, South Island, New Zealand, *Geol. Soc. Am. Bull.* **128,** 627–643, doi: 10.1130/b31300.1.

Howarth, J. D., A. R. Orpin, Y. Kaneko, L. J. Strachan, S. D. Nodder, J. J. Mountjoy, P. M. Barnes, H. C. Bostock, C. Holden, K. Jones, *et al.* (2021). Calibrating the marine turbidite palaeoseismometer using the 2016 Kaikōura earthquake, *Nature Geosci.* **14,** 161–167, doi: 10.1038/s41561-021-00692-6.

Idini, B., F. Rojas, S. Ruiz, and C. Pastén (2017). Ground motion prediction equations for the Chilean subduction zone, *Bull. Earthq. Eng.* **15,** 1853–1880, doi: 10.1007/s10518-016-0050-1.

Inouchi, Y., Y. Kinugasa, F. Kumon, S. Nakano, S. Yasumatsu, and T. Shiki (1996). Turbidites as records of intense palaeoearthquakes in Lake Biwa, Japan, *Sediment. Geol.* **104,** 117–125, doi: 10.1016/0037-0738(95)00124-7.

Kramer, S. L. (1996). *Geotechnical Earthquake Engineering,* Prentice Hall, Upper Saddle River, New Jersey.

Kremer, K., G. Gassner-Stamm, R. Grolimund, S. B. Wirth, M. Strasser, and D. Fäh (2020). A database of potential paleoseismic evidence in Switzerland, *J. Seismol.* **24,** 247–262, doi: 10.1007/s10950-020-09908-5.

Kremer, K., S. B. Wirth, A. Reusch, D. Fäh, B. Bellwald, F. S. Anselmetti, S. Girardclos, and M. Strasser (2017). Lake-sediment based paleoseismology: Limitations and perspectives from the Swiss Alps, *Quat. Sci. Rev.* **168,** 1–18, doi: 10.1016/j.quascirev.2017.04.026.

Lemot, F., P. Sabatier, M. L. Chevalier, A. L. Develle, Z. Fang, P. Rioual, S. Zhang, M. Bai, S. Wang, H. Li, *et al.* (2024). Building a multilake paleoseismometer for the Xianshuihe fault (Tibetan plateau, China), *Tectonics* **43,** doi: 10.1029/2024tc008508.

Leyton, F., J. Ruiz, J. Campos, and E. Kausel (2009). Intraplate and interplate earthquakes in Chilean subduction zone: A theoretical and observational comparison, *Phys. Earth Planet. In.* **175,** 37–46, doi: 10.1016/j.pepi.2008.03.017.

Lomnitz, C. (2004). Major earthquakes of Chile: A historical survey, 1535-1960, *Seismol. Res. Lett.* **75,** 368–378, doi: 10.1785/gssrl.75.3.368.

Lu, Y., N. Wetzler, N. Waldmann, A. Agnon, G. P. Biasi, and S. Marco (2020). A 220,000-year-long continuous large earthquake record on a slow-slipping plate boundary, *Sci. Adv.* **6,** eaba4170, doi: 10.1126/sciadv.aba4170.

McHugh, C. M., T. Kanamatsu, L. Seeber, R. Bopp, M.-H. Cormier, and K. Usami (2016). Remobilization of surficial slope sediment triggered by the A.D. 2011 M_w 9 Tohoku-Oki earthquake and tsunami along the Japan trench, *Geology* **44,** 391–394, doi: 10.1130/g37650.1.

McHugh, C. M., L. Seeber, T. Rasbury, M. Strasser, A. Kioka, T. Kanamatsu, K. Ikehara, and K. Usami (2020). Isotopic and sedimentary signature of megathrust ruptures along the Japan subduction margin, *Mar. Geol.* **428,** 106283, doi: 10.1016/j.margeo.2020.106283.

Meier, M.-A., J. P. Ampuero, and T. H. Heaton (2017). The hidden simplicity of subduction megathrust earthquakes, *Science* **357,** 1277–1281, doi: 10.1126/science.aan5643.

Moernaut, J. (2020). Time-dependent recurrence of strong earthquake shaking near plate boundaries: A lake sediment perspective, *Earth Sci. Rev*, doi: 10.1016/j.earscirev.2020.103344.

Moernaut, J., M. De Batist, F. Charlet, K. Heirman, E. Chapron, M. Pino, R. Brümmer, and R. Urrutia (2007). Giant earthquakes in south-central Chile revealed by Holocene mass-wasting events in Lake Puyehue, *Sediment. Geol.* **195,** 239–256, doi: 10.1016/j.sedgeo.2006.08.005.

Moernaut, J., J. D. Howarth, K. Kremer, and K. Wils (2025). Lacustrine records of past seismic shaking, in *Understanding Past Earthquakes*, C. G. Austin Elliott (Editor), Springer, Cham, 256 pp.

Moernaut, J., M. Van Daele, K. Fontijn, K. Heirman, P. Kempf, M. Pino, G. Valdebenito, R. Urrutia, M. Strasser, and M. De Batist (2018). Larger earthquakes recur more periodically: New insights in the megathrust earthquake cycle from lacustrine turbidite records in south-central Chile, *Earth Planet. Sci. Lett.* **481,** 9–19, doi: 10.1016/j.epsl.2017.10.016.

Moernaut, J., M. Van Daele, K. Heirman, K. Fontijn, M. Strasser, M. Pino, R. Urrutia, and M. De Batist (2014). Lacustrine turbidites as a tool for quantitative earthquake reconstruction: New evidence for a variable rupture mode in south central Chile, *J. Geophys. Res.* **119,** 1607–1633, doi: 10.1002/2013jb010738.

Moernaut, J., M. Van Daele, K. Heirman, G. Wiemer, A. Molenaar, T. Vandorpe, D. Melnick, I. Hajdas, M. Pino, R. Urrutia, *et al.* (2019). The subaqueous landslide cycle in south-central Chilean lakes: The role of tephra, slope gradient and repeated seismic shaking, *Sediment. Geol.* **381,** 84–105, doi: 10.1016/j.sedgeo.2019.01.002.

Moernaut, J., M. Van Daele, M. Strasser, M. A. Clare, K. Heirman, M. Viel, J. Cardenas, R. Kilian, B. Ladrón de Guevara, M. Pino, *et al.* (2017). Lacustrine turbidites produced by surficial slope sediment remobilization: A mechanism for continuous and sensitive turbidite paleoseismic records, *Mar. Geol.* **384,** 159–176, doi: 10.1016/j.margeo.2015.10.009.

Molenaar, A., M. Van Daele, T. Vandorpe, G. Degenhart, M. De Batist, R. Urrutia, M. Pino, M. Strasser, and J. Moernaut (2021). What controls the remobilization and deformation of surficial sediment by seismic shaking? Linking lacustrine slope stratigraphy to great earthquakes in South-Central Chile, *Sedimentology* **68,** 2365–2396, doi: 10.1111/sed.12856.

Molenaar, A., K. Wils, M. Van Daele, C. Daxer, N. Dubois, A. Grießer, P. Oswald, A. Ramisch, M. Strasser, and J. Moernaut (2024). Shaken and stirred: A comparative study of earthquake-triggered soft-sediment deformation structures in lake sediments, *Geochem. Geophys. Geosyst.* **25,** e2023GC011402, doi: 10.1029/2023GC011402.

Monecke, K., F. S. Anselmetti, A. Becker, M. Sturm, and D. Giardini (2004). The record of historic earthquakes in lake sediments of central Switzerland, *Tectonophysics* **394,** 21–40, doi: 10.1016/j.tecto.2004.07.053.

Montalva, G. A., N. Bastías, and F. Leyton (2021). Strong ground motion prediction model for PGV and spectral velocity for the Chilean subduction zone, *Bull. Seismol. Soc. Am.* **112,** 348–360, doi: 10.1785/0120210037.

Montalva, G. A., N. Bastías, and A. Rodriguez-Marek (2017). Ground-motion prediction equation for the Chilean subduction zone, *Bull. Seismol. Soc. Am.* **107,** 901–911, doi: 10.1785/0120160221.

Moreno, M., J. Bolte, J. Klotz, and D. Melnick (2009). Impact of megathrust geometry on inversion of coseismic slip from geodetic data: Application to the 1960 Chile earthquake, *Geophys. Res. Lett.* **36,** L16310, doi: 10.1029/2009gl039276.

Moreno, M., D. Melnick, M. Rosenau, J. Baez, J. Klotz, O. Oncken, A. Tassara, J. Chen, K. Bataille, M. Bevis, *et al.* (2012). Toward understanding tectonic control on the M_w 8.8 2010 Maule Chile earthquake, *Earth Planet. Sci. Lett.* **321–322,** 152–165, doi: 10.1016/j.epsl.2012.01.006.

Morton, R. A., and W. A. White (1997). Characteristics of and corrections for core shortening in unconsolidated sediments, *J. Coast. Res.* **13,** 761–769.

Niederstätter, M., K. Wils, A. Ramisch, J. N. Haas, H. Pomella, S. Szidat, M. Strasser, and J. Moernaut (2025). Strong earthquake in a low seismicity area of the European Southern Alps during Roman Times—A lacustrine paleoseismic evaluation, *Quat. Sci. Rev.* **357,** doi: 10.1016/j.quascirev.2025.109341.

Oswald, P., J. Moernaut, S. C. Fabbri, M. De Batist, I. Hajdas, H. Ortner, S. Titzler, and M. Strasser (2021). Combined on-fault and off-fault paleoseismic evidence in the postglacial infill of the inner-Alpine Lake Achensee (Austria, eastern Alps), *Front. Earth Sci.* **9,** 670952, doi: 10.3389/feart.2021.670952.

Oswald, P., M. Strasser, J. Skapski, and J. Moernaut (2022). Magnitude and source area estimations of severe prehistoric earthquakes in the western Austrian Alps, *Nat. Hazards Earth Syst. Sci.* **22,** 2057–2079, doi: 10.5194/nhess-22-2057-2022.

Philibosian, B., and A. J. Meltzner (2020). Segmentation and supercycles: A catalog of earthquake rupture patterns from the Sumatran Sunda megathrust and other well-studied faults worldwide, *Quat. Sci. Rev.* **241,** 106390, doi: 10.1016/j.quascirev.2020.106390.

Praet, N., J. Moernaut, M. Van Daele, E. Boes, P. J. Haeussler, M. Strupler, S. Schmidt, M. G. Loso, and M. De Batist (2017). Paleoseismic potential of sublacustrine landslide records in a high-seismicity setting (south-central Alaska), *Mar. Geol.* **384,** 103–119, doi: 10.1016/j.margeo.2016.05.004.

Praet, N., M. Van Daele, J. Moernaut, T. Mestdagh, T. Vandorpe, B. J. L. Jensen, R. C. Witter, P. J. Haeussler, and M. De Batist (2022). Unravelling a 2300 year long sedimentary record of megathrust and intraslab earthquakes in proglacial Skilak Lake, south-central Alaska, *Sedimentology* **69,** 2151–2180, doi: 10.1111/sed.12986.

Schnellmann, M., F. S. Anselmetti, D. Giardini, and J. A. McKenzie (2007). 15,000 years of mass-movement history in Lake Lucerne: Implications for seismic and tsunami hazards, *Eclogae Geol. Helv.* **99,** 409–428, doi: 10.1007/s00015-006-1196-7.

Seibert, C., C. McHugh, C. Paola, L. Seeber, and J. Tucker (2025). Surficial sediment remobilization by shear between sediment and water above tsunamigenic megathrust ruptures: experimental study, *Earth Surf. Dynam.* **13,** 341–348, doi: 10.5194/esurf-13-341-2025.

Shynkarenko, A., A. M. Lontsi, K. Kremer, P. Bergamo, M. Hobiger, M. Hallo, and D. Fäh (2021). Investigating the subsurface in a shallow water environment using array and single-station ambient vibration techniques, *Geophys. J. Int.* **227,** 1857–1878, doi: 10.1093/gji/ggab314.

Singleton, D. M., D. S. Brothers, P. J. Haeussler, R. C. Witter, and J. C. Hill (2024). Constraining the earthquake recording threshold of intraslab earthquakes with turbidites in south-central Alaska's lakes and fjords, in *Tectonics and Seismicity of Alaska and Western Canada: EarthScope and Beyond*, 389–418, doi: 10.1002/9781394195947.ch14.

St-Onge, G., E. Chapron, S. Mulsow, M. Salas, M. Viel, M. Debret, A. Foucher, T. Mulder, T. Winiarski, M. Desmet, *et al.* (2012). Comparison of earthquake-triggered turbidites from the Saguenay (eastern Canada) and Reloncavi (Chilean margin) Fjords: Implications for paleoseismicity and sedimentology, *Sediment. Geol.* **243–244,** 89–107, doi: 10.1016/j.sedgeo.2011.11.003.

Strasser, M., K. Monecke, M. Schnellmann, F. S. Anselmetti, and H. Weissurt (2013). Lake sediments as natural seismographs: A compiled record of late quaternary earthquakes in central Switzerland and its implication for Alpine deformation, *Sedimentology* **60,** 319–341, doi: 10.1111/sed.12003.

Tournier, N., S. C. Fabbri, F. S. Anselmetti, S. Y. Cahyarini, S. Bijaksana, N. Wattrus, J. M. Russell, and H. Vogel (2023). Climate-controlled sensitivity of lake sediments to record earthquake-related mass wasting in tropical Lake Towuti during the past 40 kyr, *Quat. Sci. Rev.* **305,** doi: 10.1016/j.quascirev.2023.108015.

Tuttle, M. P., R. Hartleb, L. Wolf, and P. W. Mayne (2019). Paleoliquefaction studies and the evaluation of seismic hazard, *Geosciences* **9,** doi: 10.3390/geosciences9070311.

Urrutia, R., A. Araneda, F. Cruces, L. Torres, L. Chirinos, H. C. Treutler, N. Fagel, S. Bertrand, I. Alvial, R. Barra, *et al.* (2007). Changes in diatom, pollen, and chironomid assemblages in response to a recent volcanic event in Lake Galletué (Chilean Andes), *Limnologica* **37,** 49–62, doi: 10.1016/j.limno.2006.09.003.

Van Daele, M., C. Araya-Cornejo, T. Pille, K. Vanneste, J. Moernaut, S. Schmidt, P. Kempf, I. Meyer, and M. Cisternas (2019). Distinguishing intraplate from megathrust earthquakes using lacustrine turbidites, *Geology* **47,** 127–130, doi: 10.1130/g45662.1.

Van Daele, M., P. J. Haeussler, R. Witter, N. Praet, and M. De Batist (2020). The sedimentary record of the 2018 Anchorage earthquake in Eklutna Lake, Alaska: Calibrating the lacustrine seismograph, *Seismol. Res. Lett.* **91,** 126–141, doi: 10.1785/0220190204.

Van Daele, M., J. Moernaut, L. Doom, E. Boes, K. Fontijn, K. Heirman, W. Vandoorne, D. Hebbeln, M. Pino, R. Urrutia, *et al.* (2015). A comparison of the sedimentary records of the 1960 and 2010 great Chilean earthquakes in 17 lakes: Implications for quantitative lacustrine palaeoseismology, *Sedimentology* **62,** 1466–1496, doi: 10.1111/sed.12193.

Vanneste, K., B. Neefs, and T. Camelbeeck (2024). Testing the applicability of ground motion prediction equations for the Hainaut region (Belgium) using intensity data, *Bull. Earthq. Eng.* doi: 10.1007/s10518-024-01958-1.

Vanneste, K., K. Wils, and M. Van Daele (2018). Probabilistic evaluation of fault sources based on paleoseismic evidence from mass-transport deposits: The example of Aysén Fjord, Chile, *J. Geophys. Res.* **123,** 9842–9865, doi: 10.1029/2018JB016289.

Vervoort, M., K. Wils, K. Vanneste, R. Urrutia, M. Pino, C. Kissel, M. De Batist, and M. Van Daele (2024). Co- and postseismic subaquatic evidence for prehistoric fault activity near Coyhaique, Aysén region, Chile, *Nat. Hazards Earth Syst. Sci.* doi: 10.5194/egusphere-2024-8.

Wald, D. J., and T. I. Allen (2007). Topographic slope as a proxy for seismic site conditions and amplification, *Bull. Seismol. Soc. Am.* **97,** 1379–1395, doi: 10.1785/0120060267.

Wald, D. J., V. Quitoriano, T. H. Heaton, and H. Kanamori (1999). Relationships between peak ground acceleration, peak ground velocity, and modified Mercalli intensity in California, *Earthq. Spectra* **15,** 557–564, doi: 10.1193/1.1586058.

Wetzler, N., S. Marco, and E. Heifetz (2010). Quantitative analysis of seismogenic shear-induced turbulence in lake sediments, *Geology* **38,** 303–306, doi: 10.1130/g30685.1.

Wilhelm, B., J. Nomade, C. Crouzet, C. Litty, P. Sabatier, S. Belle, Y. Rolland, M. Revel, F. Courboulex, F. Arnaud, *et al.* (2016). Quantified sensitivity of small lake sediments to record historic earthquakes: Implications for paleoseismology, *J. Geophys. Res.* **121,** 2–16, doi: 10.1002/2015jf003644.

Wils, K., M. Van Daele, C. Kissel, J. Moernaut, S. Schmidt, G. Siani, and G. Lastras (2020). Seismo-turbidites in Aysén Fjord (southern Chile) reveal a complex pattern of rupture modes along the 1960 megathrust earthquake segment, *J. Geophys. Res.* **125,** e2020JB019405, doi: 10.1029/2020JB019405.

Wils, K., M. Van Daele, G. Lastras, C. Kissel, F. Lamy, and G. Siani (2018). Holocene event record of Aysén Fjord (Chilean Patagonia): An interplay of volcanic eruptions and crustal and megathrust earthquakes, *J. Geophys. Res.* **123,** 324–343, doi: 10.1002/2017JB014573.

Wood, H. O., and F. Neumann (1931). Modified Mercalli intensity scale of 1931, *Bull. Seismol. Soc. Am.* **21,** 277–283, doi: 10.1785/bssa0210040277.

Worden, C. B., M. C. Gerstenberger, D. A. Rhoades, and D. J. Wald (2012). Probabilistic relationships between ground-motion parameters and modified Mercalli intensity in California, *Bull. Seismol. Soc. Am.* **102,** 204–221, doi: 10.1785/0120110156.

Wu, Y.-M., T.-L. Teng, T.-C. Shin, and N.-C. Hsiao (2003). Relationship between peak ground acceleration, peak ground velocity, and intensity in Taiwan, *Bull. Seismol. Soc. Am.* **93,** 386–396, doi: 10.1785/0120020097.

Manuscript received 18 December 2024
Published online 14 July 2025

Pre- and Postseismic Variations of Crustal 3D Velocity Structure Around the Ludian Earthquake Zone in Southwest China Revealed by Time-Lapse Ambient Noise Tomography

Yang Chen[1,2], Lianghui Guo*[1,2,3], Xueyang Bao[4], and Xiang Wang[1,2]

Abstract

The 2014 M_s 6.5 Ludian earthquake is a typical event in southwest China, resulting in extensive earthquake damage and disasters. Numerous geophysical observations have been conducted around the Ludian earthquake zone to reveal the seismogenic environment, but the underlying seismogenic mechanism remains a subject of debate. The spatiotemporal variation in crustal velocity is closely related to stress state and seismicity. In this article, we present an ambient noise time-lapse tomography algorithm based on the conventional surface-wave direct inversion method and the parallel difference strategy. We apply this algorithm to the ambient noise data recorded by 90 permanent seismic stations around the Ludian earthquake zone from 2011 to 2017, to construct a 3D time-lapse velocity model of the crust in this region. Based on the results, we find significant variations of crustal *S*-wave velocity (V_S) along most active fault zones of the study area. The V_S around the hypocenter of the Ludian earthquake decreased during the preseismic stage, reaching its largest variation of −0.015% ± 0.0027% between 2011 and 2014. This decrease in V_S is consistent with the time-lapse variations in the gravity and geomagnetic fields around this area, indicating their common responses to physical state variation in the subsurface. The V_S gradually increased during the postseismic stage; however, it had not returned to its preseismic levels by 4 August 2017. We deduce that material migration (such as partial melting or aqueous fluids) within the crust strengthened the interactions between rocks and fluids within the active fault zones and their creep behaviors, altering the stress and physical states and then causing variation in the velocity, gravity, and geomagnetic fields. Thus, our time-lapse model of crustal V_S could provide significant support for understanding the seismogenic mechanism of the Ludian earthquake.

Cite this article as Chen, Y., L. Guo, X. Bao, and X. Wang (2025). Pre- and Postseismic Variations of Crustal 3D Velocity Structure Around the Ludian Earthquake Zone in Southwest China Revealed by Time-Lapse Ambient Noise Tomography, *Seismol. Res. Lett.* **97**, 323–339, doi: 10.1785/0220240480.

Introduction

On 3 August 2014, at 16:30 local time (UTC + 8), a magnitude M_s 6.5 earthquake (hereafter referred to as the Ludian earthquake) struck Ludian County, Zhaotong City, Yunnan Province, China, resulting in a substantial loss of life and property. This earthquake was induced by the Baogunao–Xiaohe fault, a secondary fault within the Zhaotong–Ludian fault zone, and characterized by a left-lateral slip event with a steep dip angle (Xu *et al.*, 2014; Li *et al.*, 2015; Huang *et al.*, 2023). The aftershock sequence primarily propagated southeast and southwest (Fig. 1c), following a conjugate and asymmetric pattern (Fang *et al.*, 2014; Riaz *et al.*, 2017). Tectonically situated at the southeastern Tibetan plateau margin, the Ludian seismic zone comprises multiple active blocks and fault systems with differential slip rates (Fig. 1a). This region has been significantly shaped by the lateral extrusion of plateau materials, crustal shortening,

1. Key Laboratory of Intraplate Volcanoes and Earthquakes (China University of Geosciences, Beijing), Ministry of Education, Beijing, China, https://orcid.org/0009-0004-9460-0644 (YC); https://orcid.org/0000-0002-5149-232X (LG); https://orcid.org/0009-0001-2435-1898 (XW); 2. School of Geophysics and Information Technology, China University of Geosciences, Beijing, China; 3. State Key Laboratory of Geological Processes and Mineral Resources, China University of Geosciences, Beijing, China; 4. Department of Earth and Space Sciences, Southern University of Science and Technology, Shenzhen, China, https://orcid.org/0000-0002-5761-5837 (XB)

*Corresponding author: guolh@cugb.edu.cn

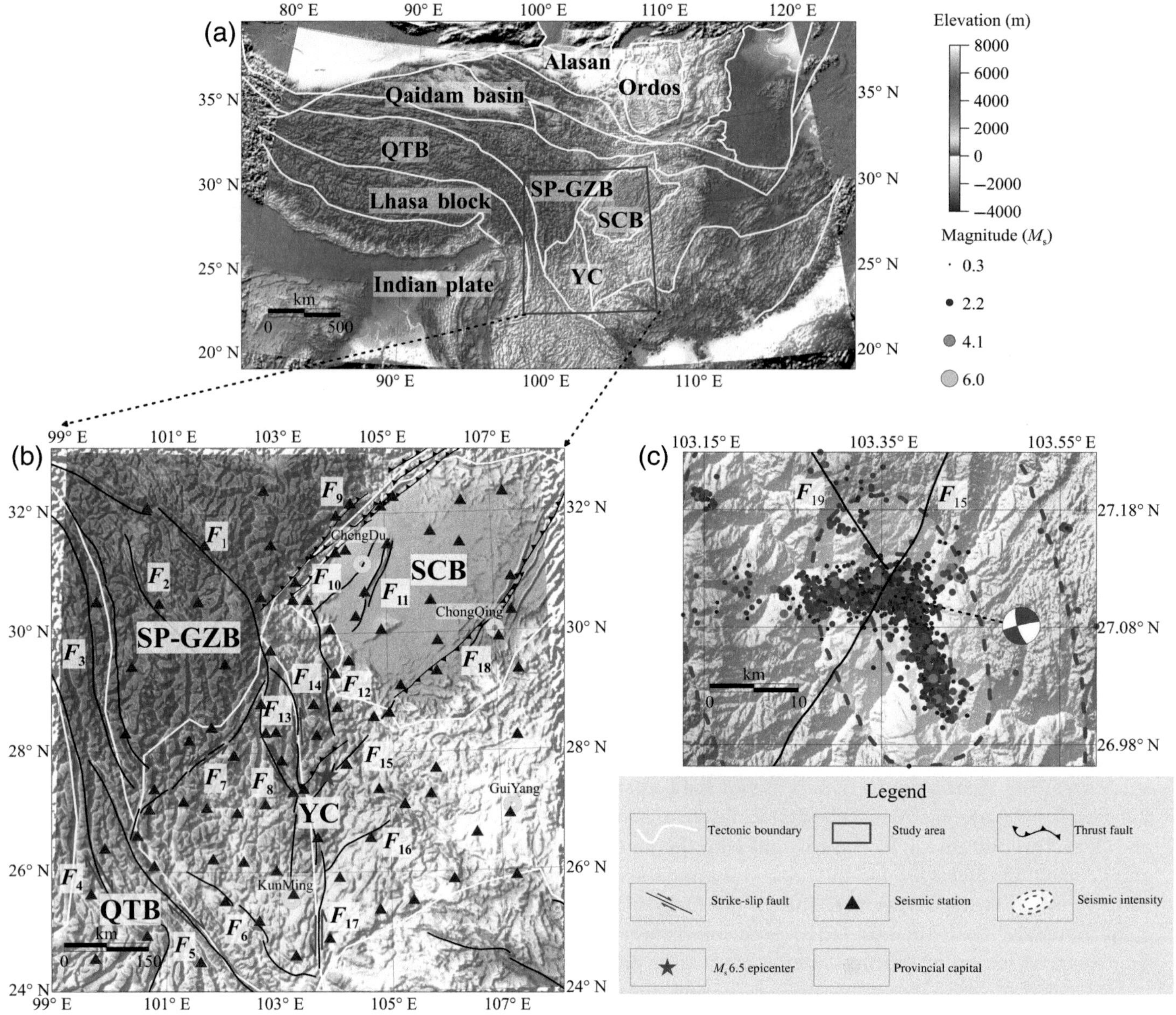

and gravitational slip-collapse processes (Xu *et al.*, 2003; Zhang *et al.*, 2003), resulting in an extensive tectonic deformation and frequent seismic activity. Therefore, understanding the seismogenic mechanism of the Ludian earthquake zone is essential for advancing earthquake research and for preventing disasters and reducing damage in this seismically active region.

The preparation and occurrence of earthquakes involve the deformation and rupture of active faults because they transition from stable, metastable, or marginally unstable states to fully unstable conditions (Ma, 2016). These processes affect the physical properties of the crust, such as wave velocity, density, magnetism, and electrical conductivity, thus influencing the observable spatiotemporal evolution of geophysical fields. Consequently, the physical structure of the crust and the evolution of regional geophysical fields serve as indicators of the earthquake preparation process, providing insights into stress variation within active faults and their metastable states.

Figure 1. Tectonic sketch map of the study area, locations of permanent seismic stations, and the Ludian earthquake sequence. (a) Regional tectonic location of the study area. (b) Major tectonic structures, active fault zones, and seismic stations. (c) The Ludian earthquake sequence and the spatial distribution of its intensity. Legend for the figure is as follows: ANH-ZMHF, Anninghe–Zemuhe fault zone (F_8); BGN-XHF, Baogunao–Xiaohe fault zone (F_{19}); CXF, Chuxiong fault zone (F_6); DLSF, Daliangshan fault zone (F_{13}); EB-JYF, Ebian–Jinyang fault zone (F_{12}); HHF, Honghe fault zone (F_5); HYSF, Huayingshan fault zone (F_{18}); JSJF, Jinshajiang fault zone (F_3); LCJF, Lancangjiang fault zone (F_4); LFF, Lianfeng fault zone (F_{14}); LJ-XJHF, Lijiang–Shiaojinhe fault zone (F_7); LMSF, Longmenshan fault zone (F_9); LQSF, Longquanshan fault zone (F_{11}); LTF, Litang fault zone (F_2); PJ-XJF, Pujiang–Xinjin fault zone (F_{10}); QTB, Qiangtang block; SCB, Sichuan basin; SP-GZB, Songpan–Ganzi block; XD-XWF, Xundian–Xuanwei fault zone (F_{16}); XJF, Xiaojiang fault zone (F_{17}); XSHF, Xianshuihe fault zone (F_1); YC, Yangtze craton; and ZT-LDF, Zhaotong–Ludian fault zone (F_{15}). The color version of this figure is available only in the electronic edition.

Seismic time-lapse tomography is a critical tool for examining and monitoring wave velocity variation in the subsurface, offering valuable information on seismogenic mechanisms.

Two principal methodologies exist for monitoring subsurface seismic wave velocity variation. The first method estimates velocity variation by analyzing arrival-time differences of repeated seismic sources at the same station, typically through cross-correlation of the passive or active seismic recordings from the consistent locations and source mechanisms (Poupinet *et al.*, 1984; Niu *et al.*, 2003, 2008). By measuring waveform delays, this method enables the study of velocity variation. A notable technique within this framework involves extracting body, surface, or coda waves via ambient noise cross-correlations or autocorrelations (Snieder *et al.*, 2002; Brenguier *et al.*, 2008, 2020; Liu *et al.*, 2014; Wang *et al.*, 2019; Mordret *et al.*, 2020; Nishida *et al.*, 2020; Mao *et al.*, 2022). For instance, Dai and Zhang (2016) employed the ambient noise cross-correlation to demonstrate stress-induced variation of seismic wave velocity in the subsurface of the Ludian earthquake zone, whereas Pang *et al.* (2017) applied the ambient noise autocorrelation to observe the decreased coseismic wave velocity, indicative of tectonic stress alteration due to interaction between the Tibetan plateau and the South China block. However, this type of method primarily focuses on velocity variation patterns between seismic stations, providing limited insights into deeper velocity structure variation.

Another type of method employs seismic wave arrival-time data from different time segments to image the temporal variation of the velocity structure. Asnaashari *et al.* (2015) and Hu (2020) outlined four implementation strategies for such imaging methods. The first strategy, the parallel difference strategy (PDS), involves independently inverting data from different time segments using the same initial model and subsequently calculating velocity variation for each time segment through differencing (Patanè *et al.*, 2006; Chiarabba *et al.*, 2009, 2020; Koulakov *et al.*, 2013, 2016; Koulakov and Vargas, 2018; Wang *et al.*, 2018; Baccheschi *et al.*, 2020). This strategy, however, proves sensitive to temporal variations in data quality and ray-path distributions (Julian and Foulger, 2010). The second strategy, the sequential difference strategy (SDS), uses inversion results from the first time segment as the initial model for subsequent time segments (Zhang and Zhang, 2015). Although this strategy is based on the results of the first inversion, it still faces challenges similar to those of the PDS, including error accumulation due to data inaccuracies, initial model biases, and inversion inconsistencies. The third strategy, the double-difference strategy (DDS), inverts for velocity variations by focusing on data differences between different time segments, provided that earthquake doublets occur within the same time frame (Qian *et al.*, 2018; Cao, Qian, Huang, and Huang, 2021; Cao, Qian, Huang, Zhang, and Fu, 2021). Using this strategy, Cao, Huang, Qian, and Fu (2021) observed a coseismic reduction in *P*-wave velocity (V_P) and a subsequent healing effect in the Ludian earthquake zone, attributing these changes to variations in stress. The last strategy, the joint inversion strategy (JIS), integrates multitemporal data into a single inversion system to jointly invert for seismic wave velocity variation, optimizing the fit by minimizing travel-time delays and model discrepancies (Pei *et al.*, 2019). Although the JIS tends to yield reliable results, it remains susceptible to variation in ray-path distribution.

In this study, we primarily focus on investigating the temporal variation of crustal V_S structure around the Ludian earthquake zone for understanding its seismogenic mechanism. To achieve this, we study the time-lapse ambient noise tomography algorithm based on the conventional surface-wave direct inversion method and the aforementioned PDS for deriving the crustal V_S time-lapse model. We collect the continuous waveform data recorded at 90 permanent seismic stations within the Ludian earthquake zone and surrounding regions, covering the time segments from 2011 to 2017. Then we utilize this algorithm to obtain the 3D variation model of crustal V_S around the Ludian earthquake zone. Based on these results, we further analyze the variation of V_S at the hypocenter of the Ludian earthquake and the correlations between our velocity variation model and the seismicity along the major active fault zones. In addition, we investigate the coupling relationship between our velocity variation model and the time-lapse gravity and magnetic fields. Collectively, these findings provide essential support for understanding the seismogenic mechanism of the Ludian earthquake zone.

Data and Method

Data

The continuous waveform data from 90 permanent seismic stations within the study area were collected from the Data Management Center of China National Seismic Network (Zheng *et al.*, 2009, 2010). These data were recorded from August 2011 to August 2017 (both in UTC + 8) at a sampling rate of 1 Hz. The seismic stations are uniformly distributed around the hypocenter of the Ludian earthquake, with an average spacing of ~100 km, as shown in Figure 1b.

Ambient noise tomography method

The ambient noise tomography method has been applied widespread in recent years for revealing the Earth's structure at various scales (Grêt *et al.*, 2006; Poli *et al.*, 2012; Lin *et al.*, 2013; Shen *et al.*, 2016), and is regarded as one of the most significant developments in seismology. This method is highly efficient, facilitating straightforward, repeatable observations, and yielding high imaging resolution independent of natural sources.

Fang *et al.* (2015) presented a direct inversion method for surface-wave dispersion data based on the ray tracing technique. Compared to the conventional two-step inversion method (Shapiro *et al.*, 2005; Yao *et al.*, 2006, 2008; Yang *et al.*, 2008; Luo *et al.*, 2013), this method eliminates intermediate steps, including phase or group velocity imaging. It directly inverts surface-wave dispersion data from various periods to delineate the 3D V_S structure of the crust and mantle. Notably, this method incorporates the influence of bending in the propagation paths of surface waves through complex media, resulting in accurate imaging outcomes even in regions with limited ray coverage (Yao *et al.*, 2023). Furthermore, this method accounts for the influence of V_P and density on the inversion results by integrating them with V_S.

The 3D travel-time tomography equations for the surface-wave direct inversion method are as follows (Fang *et al.*, 2015):

$$\Delta t_i(\omega) = \sum_{k=1}^{K}\left(-\frac{v_{ik}}{C_k^2(\omega)}\right)\sum_{j=1}^{J}\left[R_\alpha(z_j)\frac{\partial C_k(\omega)}{\partial \alpha_k(z_j)} + R_\rho(z_j)\frac{\partial C_k(\omega)}{\partial \rho_k(z_j)} + \frac{\partial C_k}{\partial \beta_k(z_j)}\right]\Bigg|_{\Theta_k}\Delta\beta_k(z_j). \quad (1)$$

Equation (1) can be rewritten as

$$\Delta t_i(\omega) = \sum_{l=1}^{M} G_{il} m_l, \quad (2)$$

in which J and K represent the number of grid nodes in the depth direction and in the horizontal direction, respectively, with $j = 1, 2, 3, ..., J$ and $k = 1, 2, 3, ..., K$ as the corresponding indices; thus, the total number of grid nodes is $M = KJ$. $\Delta t_i(\omega)$ represents the difference between the observed travel time and the calculated travel time of the surface wave for the ith ray path. $C_k(\omega)$ represents the phase velocity of the kth grid node in the horizontal direction at an angular frequency of ω. v_{ik} represents the bilinear interpolation coefficient of the ith surface-wave travel-time data along the ray paths. $\alpha_k(z_j)$, $\beta_k(z_j)$, and $\rho_k(z_j)$ are the V_P, V_S, and density at the kth grid node in the horizontal direction and the jth grid node in the depth direction, respectively. $R_\alpha(z_j)$ and $R_\rho(z_j)$ are P-wave and S-wave perturbation coefficients, respectively, based on the empirical formula (Brocher, 2005). Θ_k represents the 1D model below the kth grid node.

By expressing equation (2) as a linear forward problem $\boldsymbol{d} = \boldsymbol{Gm}$, the inverse objective function is then constructed as follows:

$$\phi(\boldsymbol{m}) = \|\boldsymbol{d} - \boldsymbol{Gm}\|_2^2 + \lambda\|\mathbf{L}\boldsymbol{m}\|_2^2, \quad (3)$$

in which $\boldsymbol{d}$ is the surface-wave travel-time delay vector encompassing all paths and frequencies. $\boldsymbol{G}$ is the sensitivity kernel matrix corresponding to the data. The vector $\boldsymbol{m}$ contains the model parameters, $\mathbf{L}$ is the model smoothing factor, and λ is the regularization parameter used to stabilize the inversion process.

The estimate of model parameter vector $\boldsymbol{m}^{\text{est}}$ can be obtained by minimizing the objective function $\phi(\boldsymbol{m})$ as follows:

$$\boldsymbol{m}^{\text{est}} = (\boldsymbol{G}^T\boldsymbol{G} + \lambda\boldsymbol{L}^T\boldsymbol{L})^{-1}\boldsymbol{G}^T\boldsymbol{d}. \quad (4)$$

This equation can be solved by utilizing the least-squares optimization algorithm (Paige and Saunders, 1982).

Ambient noise time-lapse tomography algorithm

We propose an ambient noise time-lapse tomography method based on the ambient noise direct inversion approach combined with the PDS. The algorithm framework, as outlined in Figure 2, comprises three key steps.

The first step involves data segmentation. The non-uniform spatial distribution and seasonal evolution characteristics of noise sources can cause the deviation of cross-correlation functions (CCFs), thereby affecting the quality of dispersion curves. Yang and Ritzwoller (2008) demonstrated that using noise data spanning one year or longer can effectively mitigate these effects. In addition, to effectively capture seismic wave velocity variation before and after the Ludian earthquake, we consider the earthquake's origin time as the segmentation point, with each time-lapse window spanning three years. As shown in Table 1, the data from 2011 to 2017 are divided into two time segments, labeled T_{pre} and T_{post}.

The second step is data processing. For each time segment, preprocessing tasks are conducted, including removing the instrument response, eliminating mean and trend components, band-pass filtering, time-domain normalization, and spectral whitening (Bensen *et al.*, 2007; Yang *et al.*, 2007). Following these processes, Rayleigh-wave dispersion curves are extracted using the time–frequency analysis method after calculating cross-correlations. A critical consideration is the impact of variations in ray paths on the inversion results. To minimize spurious velocity variation caused by differing ray paths, the ray paths were standardized based on the dispersion curves obtained from both time segments prior to inversion.

Figure 3a depicts the CCFs for the T_{pre} time segment, with station YN.ZAT acting as the source and other stations serving as receivers. The CCFs reveal distinct surface-wave signals, with both causal and acausal signals displaying symmetrical features. This symmetry confirms that the use of long-duration ambient noise data effectively mitigates the effects of uneven noise source distribution. The signal-to-noise ratio of the extracted dispersion curves exceeds 15, with surface-wave periods ranging from 6 to 40 s (Fig. 3b). The corresponding sensitivity depths range from ~5 to 30 km for periods between 5 and 25 s (Fig. 3d). Because the quality of dispersion curves directly impacts the accuracy of subsequent inversions, we estimate the uncertainties associated with these curves across different periods (Fig. 3d). The maximum error is 1.542×10^{-4} km/s, corresponding to a sensitivity depth of 30 km, which translates to an ~±0.0045% influence on the inversion results. In addition, over 2500 dispersion points within the 6–40 s range contribute to a robust dataset, ensuring the reliability of the inversion results (Fig. 3c).

The final step involves calculating the S-wave velocity variation. Here, $\frac{\Delta v}{v}$ is defined as the relative variation in V_S

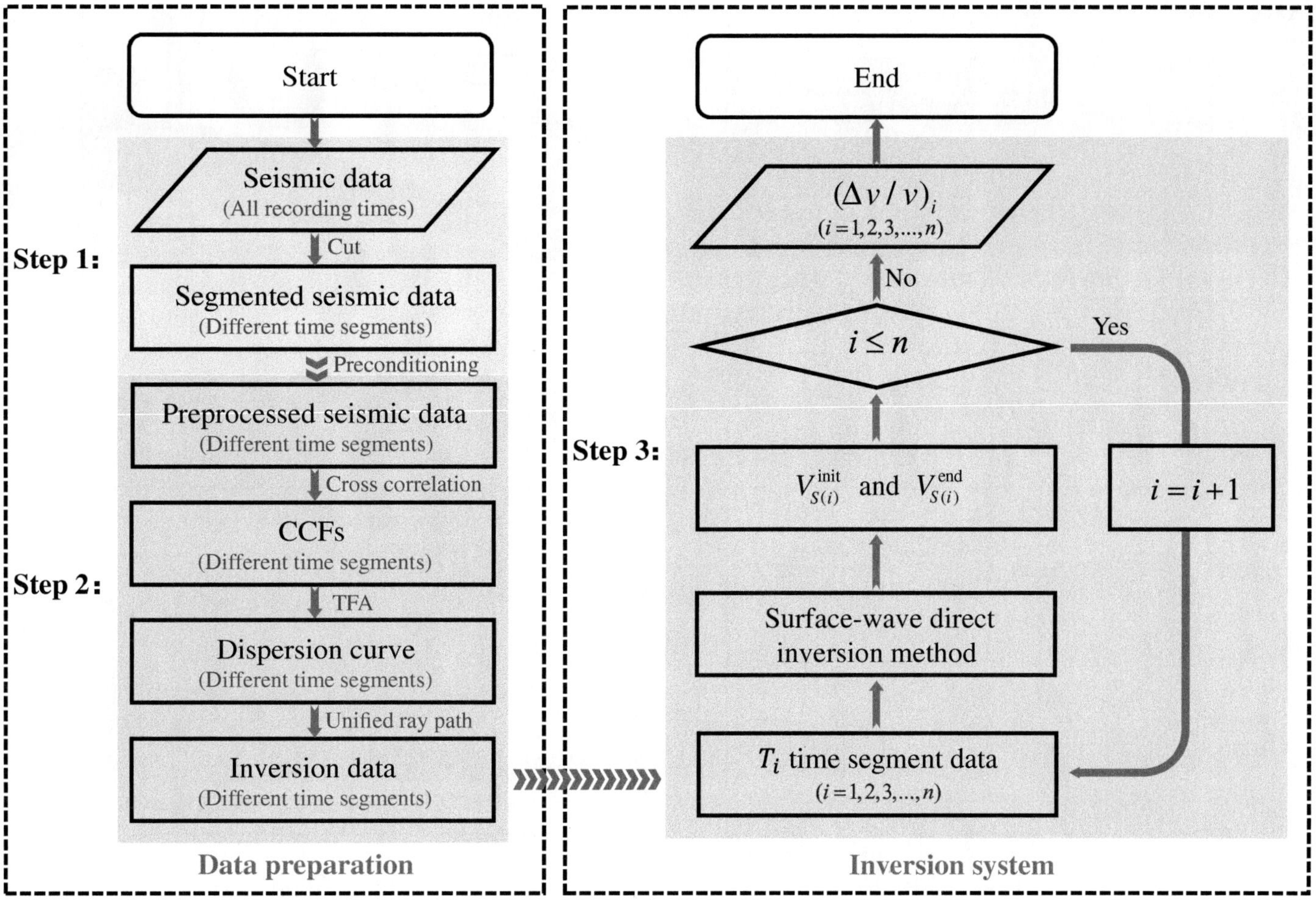

Figure 2. Framework and flowchart of the ambient noise time-lapse tomography algorithm. CCFs, cross-correlation functions; and TFA, time–frequency analysis; The color version of this figure is available only in the electronic edition.

between the end time and the initial time of a time segment. It is calculated using the following formula:

$$\frac{\Delta v}{v} = \frac{V_S^{init} - V_S^{end}}{V_S^{init}} \times 100\%, \quad (5)$$

in which V_S^{init} and V_S^{end} which correspond to the initial and end values of V_S within the time segment, respectively.

The earlier describes the stepwise flow of this algorithm. These three steps are applied to invert the data from the different time segments outlined in Table 1. Simultaneously, the initial model and inversion parameters are kept consistent for each time segment.

Results and Quality Evaluation

Inversion parameters and initial model

The Community Velocity Model version 1.0 of southwest China (Liu *et al.*, 2021) was used to construct the initial model of the crustal V_S structure in this study. The model has a grid spacing of 0.5° and depth intervals of 5 km between 0 and 40 km. As shown in Figure 4a, the initial model reveals a significantly broader distribution of V_S in the depth range of 20–30 km compared to other depths, reflecting the crustal heterogeneity in the study area. The model achieves a lateral resolution of at least 50 km in most areas and effectively delineates the complex low-velocity anomaly within the Sichuan–Yunnan crust.

The L-curve method was applied to determine the regularization parameter λ in equation (3). Usually, an optimal value of λ is typically identified at the inflection point of the L-curve, which balances data fitting and model resolution. In this case, we chose $\lambda = 10$ according to the L-curve shown in Figure 4b. In addition, the smoothing factor **L** stabilizes and refines the inversion results

TABLE 1
Temporal Segments and Corresponding Time Ranges

Time Segments	Time Range (UTC + 8) (yyyy/mm/dd)
T_{pre}	2011/08/02–2014/08/02
T_{post}	2014/08/04–2017/08/04

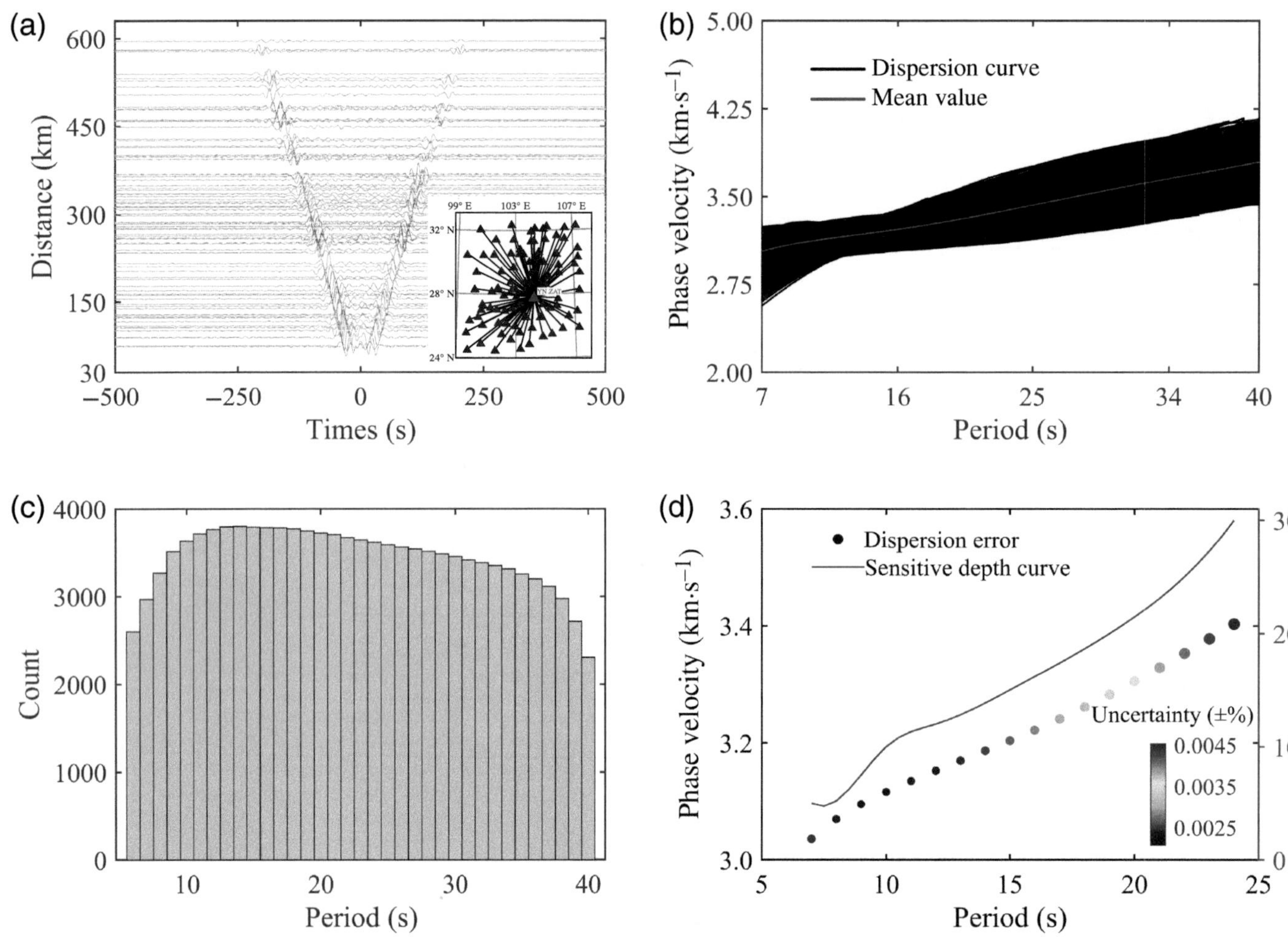

Figure 3. Surface-wave dispersion data and uncertainty estimation for the T_{pre} time segment. (a) The CCFs between YN.ZAT stations and other stations. The red station indicates the source station, and the blue stations represent the receiver stations. (b) Dispersion curves for the inversion, in which the black line represents the picked dispersion curve, and the red line denotes the average of all dispersion curves. (c) Distribution of surface-wave periods, ranging from 6 to 40 s. (d) Uncertainty and sensitivity depth of surface waves extracted at different periods, in which the red line represents the sensitivity depth curve, and the colored points indicate dispersion curve errors at varying depths. The color version of this figure is available only in the electronic edition.

(Tikhonov and Arsenin, 1977; Nolet, 1987; Simons *et al.*, 2002). Through trial and error, we identified 0.1 as the optimal smoothing factor for this study. Figure 4c,d illustrates the inversion convergence curve and travel-time delays distribution before and after the inversion of T_{pre} time segment inversion. The convergence curve shows the travel-time delays decreasing from 1.525 to 0.359 s after 10 iterations inversion. The travel-time delays in the final iteration are more centered around zero compared to the first iteration, whereas the root mean square value decreases from 9.044×10^{-1} s to 5.825×10^{-5} s. After strict quality control, the inversion will provide a high-quality and reliable model of V_S variation of the study area.

Resolution test

The checkerboard resolution test is a widely used method for assessing model recovery and resolution in seismic tomography. In this test, we introduce ±2% Gaussian white noise to the initial model, followed by an inversion process that uses the same grid sizes (0.5° × 0.5° horizontal discretization) and parameters ($\lambda = 10$, $\mathbf{L} = 0.1$) as those applied in the actual inversion. Through experiments with different checker sizes, we determined that the optimal checker size for recovery is 0.5°. The vertical node distribution spans a depth range of 0–30 km with non-uniform sampling: 2.5 km intervals in the upper crust (0–10 km), increasing to 5 km spacing in the mid-to-lower crust (10–30 km).

Figure 5 illustrates the surface-wave ray paths and their coverage densities for T_{pre} and T_{post} time segments. The study area is well covered by uniformly distributed ray paths within the network of seismic stations (Fig. 5a,b). The ray-path density is derived by discretizing all ray paths into points and subsequently computing the probability density of scattered points per unit area. The highest ray-path densities are observed in the central region, gradually decreasing toward the periphery (Fig. 5c,d). The probability density of the difference in ray

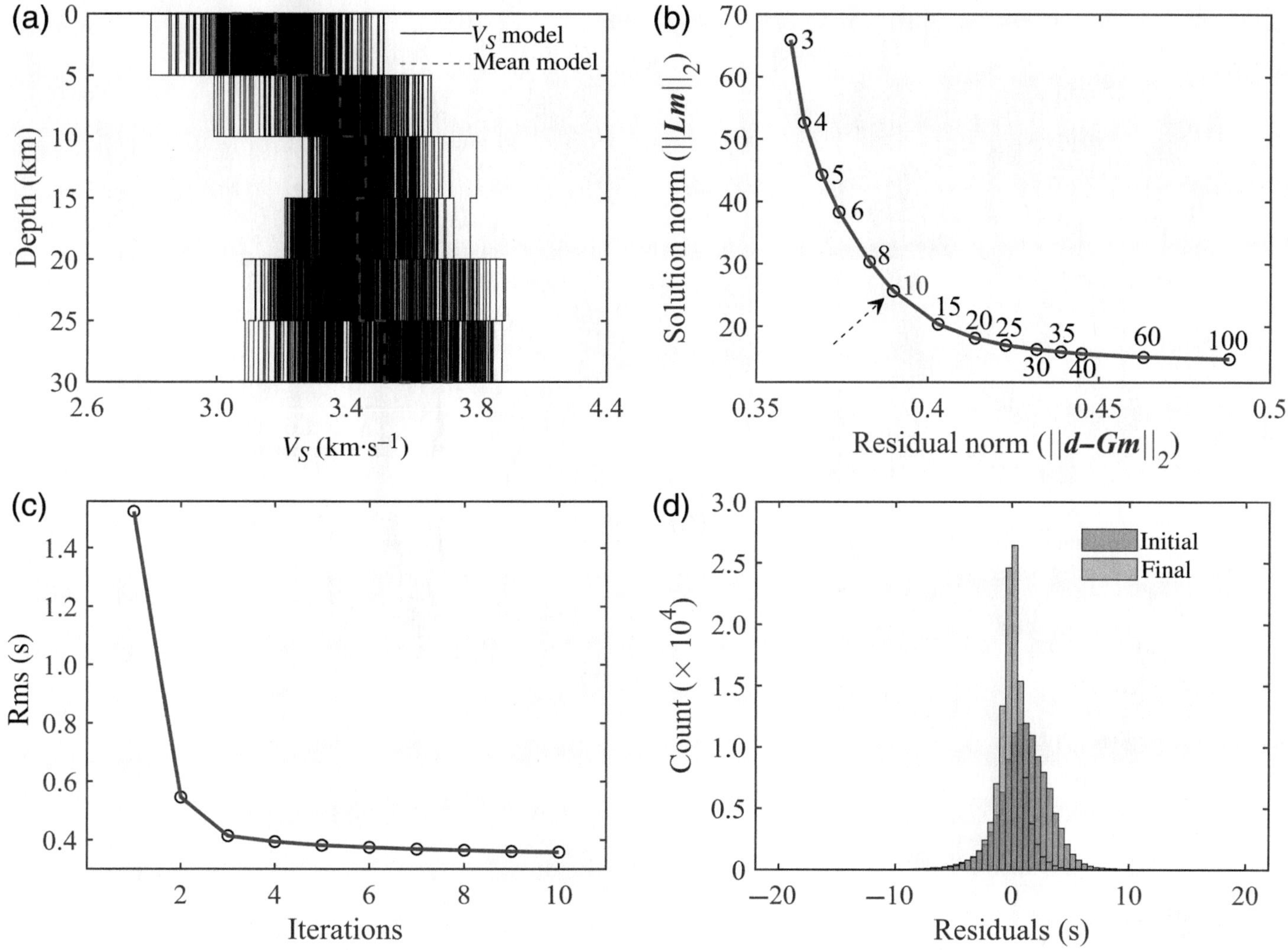

Figure 4. The initial model for the T_{pre} time segment and the choice of related inversion parameter, along with the error analysis. (a) The 1D models at each grid node and the mean model for the study area. (b) The L-curve for the regularization parameter λ. (c) The convergence curve of inversion iterations. (d) The travel-time delays distributions for the initial and ultimate inversions. Rms, root mean square. The color version of this figure is available only in the electronic edition.

paths between the T_{pre} and T_{post} time segments, which is only 0.001, significantly reduces the errors associated with ray-path differences (Fig. 5e,f). As shown in Figure 6, we present the checkerboard test slice results at depths of 5, 10, 15, and 30 km. According to the S-wave sensitive kernel in the study area, the selected depths correspond to the surface-wave periods of 7, 12, 14, and 23 s, respectively. The depth slices and profile sections indicate that regions with lower ray-path densities exhibit diminished velocity recovery in the test. In contrast, the resolution at depths of 15 and 30 km is superior to that at depths of 5 and 10 km (Fig. 6i,j).

The 3D time-lapse model of crustal V_S variation

The 3D variation of crustal V_S across the preseismic (T_{pre}) and postseismic (T_{post}) stages was computed through the application of equation (5). According to the earthquake catalog from the China Earthquake Network Center and studies by Fang et al. (2014), the hypocenters of the Ludian earthquake and its aftershocks are primarily distributed within a depth range of 0 to 30 km. Therefore, we primarily focus on analyzing the variation of crustal V_S around the Ludian earthquake zone, from the surface to a depth of 30 km.

Through a systematic comparison of the preseismic stage (T_{pre}) and postseismic adjustment stage (T_{post}) of the Ludian earthquake, we observed that the earthquakes analyzed in this study are primarily concentrated within a depth range of 5–15 km, exhibiting distinct depth-dependent spatial distribution characteristics. This indicates a significant coupling relationship between the spatial distribution of seismic events and V_S variation.

During the T_{pre} stage, shallow crustal seismicity (~5 km) is concentrated in zones of significant V_S increase (Fig. 7a), whereas mid-crustal events (10–15 km) correlate with regions of marked V_S decrease (Fig. 7b,c). This spatial pattern undergoes systematic reversal during the T_{post} stage: shallow

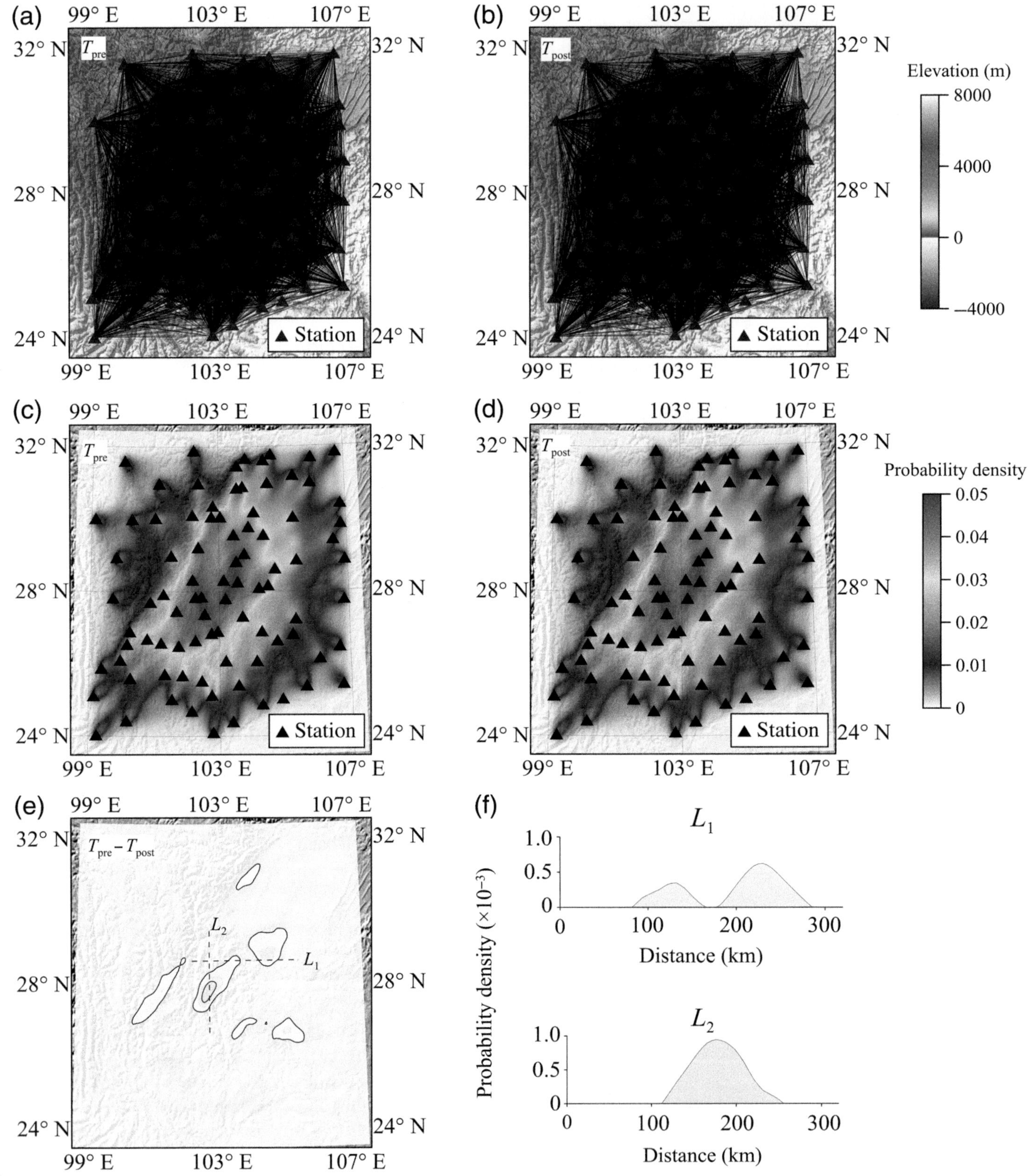

seismicity (~5 km) shifts to V_S decrease regions (Fig. 7g), whereas mid-crustal events (10–15 km) migrate to V_S increase regions (Fig. 7h,i). Notably, a consistent statistical pattern is observed across both stages: in areas with stable V_S, the earthquake occurrence rate is lower compared to regions with significant V_S variation, where seismicity is notably higher.

Figure 5. Surface-wave ray paths and coverage densities for T_{pre} and T_{post} time segments. (a,b) The ray paths for all periods are included in the inversion. (c,d) The coverage densities of the surface-wave ray paths for the corresponding periods in panels (a) and (b). (e,f) The differences in inversion ray paths between the T_{pre} and T_{post} time segments. The color version of this figure is available only in the electronic edition.

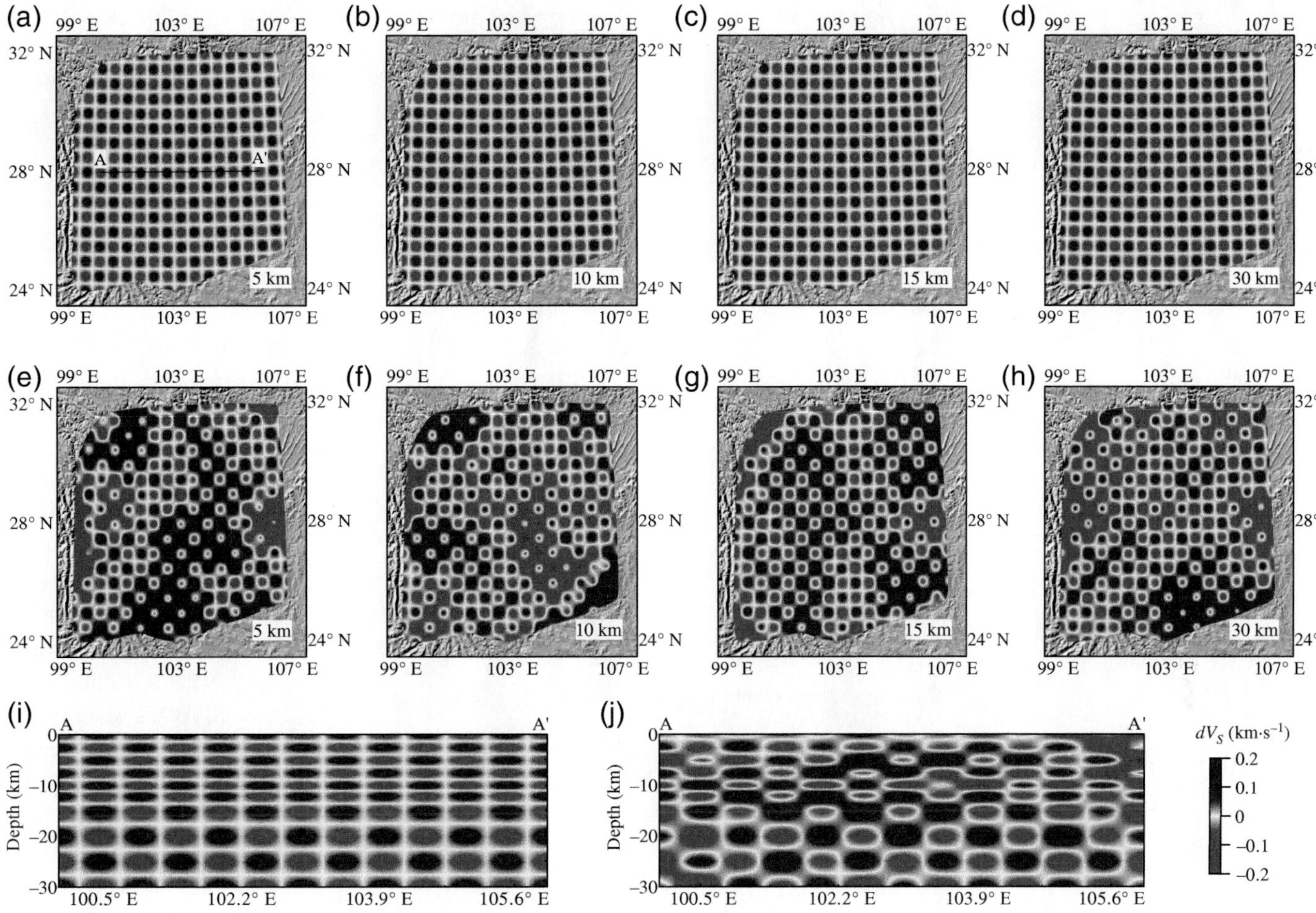

Figure 6. Checkerboard model resolution test. (a–d,i) The true checkerboard model depth slices and the A–A′ profile at depths of 5, 10, 15, and 30 km. (e–h,j) The corresponding model recovery for (a–d,i). The color version of this figure is available only in the electronic edition.

In addition, V_S variation exhibits a strong spatial correlation with specific fault zones, often displaying pronounced V_S variation along fault zones. The fault zones system composed of F_{12}–F_{14}–F_{15}–F_{18} exhibits a quasi-periodic response in V_S variation. During the T_{pre} stage, shallow crustal fault zones at ~5 km and deep crustal zones at 20–25 km correspond to regions of positive (Fig. 7a,e,f) and negative (Fig. 7b–d) V_S variation anomaly, respectively. However, in the T_{post} stage, this spatial configuration is completely reversed (Fig. 7g,k,l versus Fig. 7h–j). Such spatiotemporal reversals suggest that velocity recovery may reflect a staged adjustment of the regional stress field.

This coupling mechanism between seismic events, velocity fields, and fault zones implies that velocity gradient zones and persistently evolving anomalous regions along fault zones may serve as indicators of tectonically sensitive zones. These findings could provide dynamic constraints for understanding the earthquake nucleation process and constructing time-lapse predictive models. Furthermore, particular attention should be paid to regions along fault zones that exhibit significant velocity variation, as such areas are often accompanied by increased seismicity.

Previous studies have established that earthquakes and their aftershocks may result from the migration of crustal materials driven by tectonic stress (Bouchon *et al.*, 2011; Yukutake *et al.*, 2011; Kato *et al.*, 2012). Fluids, commonly present at various depths within the crust, play a crucial role in this migration, both in shallow and deep crustal regions. Furthermore, variation in seismic wave velocity is closely related to the expansion and closure of fractures in the subsurface (Brenguier *et al.*, 2014; Taira *et al.*, 2015; An *et al.*, 2023). Thus, the expansion and closure of fractures in the subsurface create favorable conditions for crustal fluid migration, which, in turn, significantly influence variations in seismic wave velocity. In the study area, the regional occurrence of seismic events, accompanied by the V_S variation, may also be closely linked to crustal fluid migration.

Discussion

Implications of velocity variation for seismogenesis in the Ludian earthquake zone

The pre- and postseismic V_S variation in the Ludian earthquake zone also has significant features in the empirical

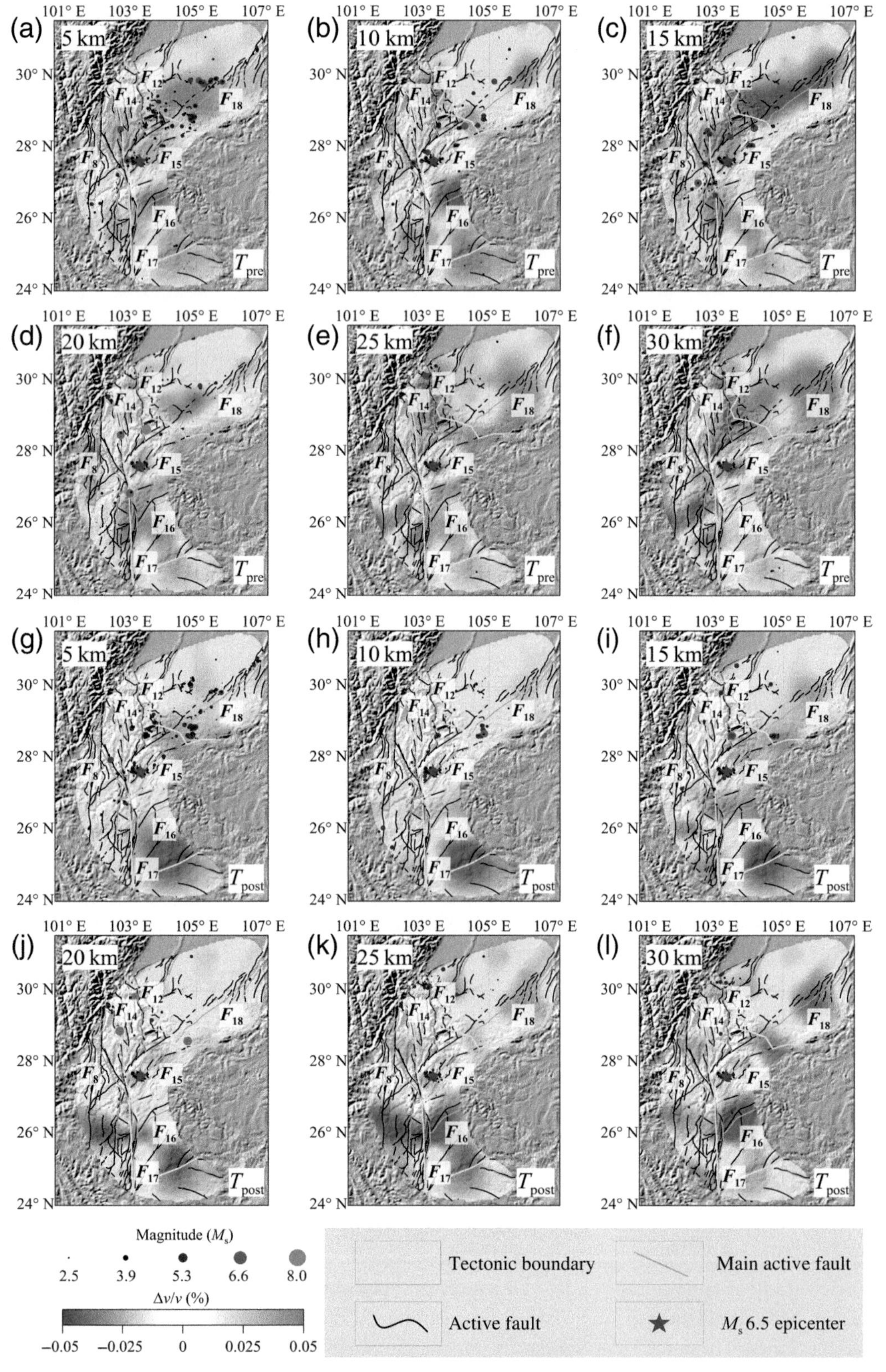

Figure 7. Depth slices of V_S variation at different depths for the T_{pre} and T_{post} time segments in the study area. (a–f) V_S variation at 5, 10, 15, 20, 25, and 30 km during the T_{pre} time segment, whereas (g–l) V_S variation at the corresponding depths for the T_{post} time segment. The color version of this figure is available only in the electronic edition.

Green's functions (EGFs). We obtained the EGFs through the CCFs using the following formula:

$$\hat{G}_{sr}(t) = -\frac{dC_{sr}(t)}{dt} \approx G_{sr}(t), \quad (6)$$

in which $C_{sr}(t)$ represents the CCFs, $G_{sr}(t)$ denotes the true Green's functions (TGFs), and $\hat{G}_{sr}(t)$ corresponds to the EGFs, all defined between the source and receiver. This formulation reveals that the time derivative of the CCFs corresponds to the EGFs, which serve as an approximation of the TGFs.

As illustrated in Figure 8a, we selected five station pairs, among which only the SC.PGE–GZ.WNT station pair passed through the epicentral region of the Ludian earthquake. The EGFs for these station pairs were subjected to band-pass filtering at the periods of 8–15 s, 20–25 s, and 30–35 s. The results indicate that only the waveforms from the SC.PGE–GZ.WNT station pair exhibited a notable phase shift during the preseismic and postseismic stages (Fig. 8b–d), whereas the phase variation in the other station pairs was minimal. Besides, the filtering results revealed a positive correlation between EGFs' phase shift magnitude and signal period, demonstrating that V_S variation amplitude escalates progressively with depth. These differential phase behaviors imply a postseismic decrease in V_S within the Ludian earthquake zone, indicating that the Ludian earthquake likely played a significant role in the observed velocity variation.

Similar features are also evident in the 3D time-lapse model of crustal V_S variation. At a depth of 15 km, V_S

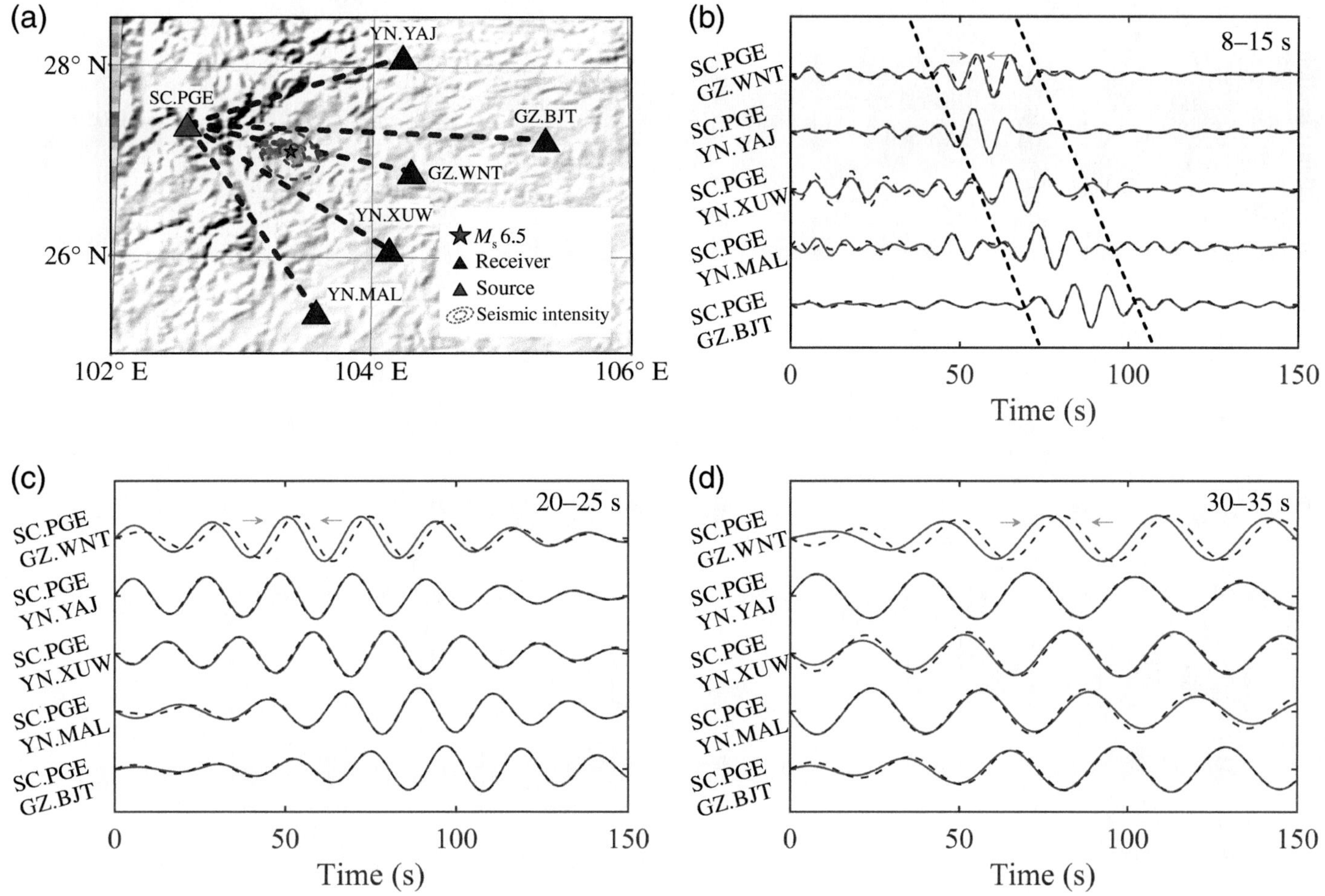

Figure 8. Comparison of empirical Green's functions (EGFs) for five station pairs before and after the Ludian earthquake. (a) Spatial distribution of seismic station pairs, in which red and blue symbols denote the seismic source and receiver stations, respectively. (b–d) Band-pass-filtered EGFs comparisons in three period bands: (b) 8–15 s, (c) 20–25 s, and (d) 30–35 s. The red curves represent preseismic EGFs measurements, and the blue curves indicate postseismic EGFs recordings. The color version of this figure is available only in the electronic edition.

variation shows different patterns along fault zones: the F_{15}–F_{18} fault zone demonstrates a prominent V_S decrease, whereas the F_{16}–F_{17} fault zone displays a significant V_S increase, forming alternating positive–negative anomaly couples (Fig. 7c). Notably, the Ludian earthquake occurred within an active fault zone characterized by a decrease of V_S (Fig. 7c). A decrease in apparent V_S is also observed over a larger depth range beneath the Ludian source region, particularly between 20 and 30 km (Fig. 7d–f). Within the depth range above the hypocenter, the majority of earthquakes occurred along the active fault zones associated with variation in V_S. In contrast, the areas exhibiting minimal or nearly unchanged V_S variation have significantly reduced probabilities of earthquake occurrence. Similarly, studies have shown that the 2013 M_s 7.0 Lushan earthquake (Wang *et al.*, 2020) in China also occurred along the active fault zones characterized by decrease of V_S.

Apart from the above results, a noticeable postseismic recovery phenomenon in the V_S is observed. The profiles A and B in Figure 9 reveal that during the preseismic stage, the source region of the Ludian earthquake was situated within an area of V_S decrease (Fig. 9a,c). In the postseismic stage, however, the magnitude of this decrease diminishes (Fig. 9b, d), suggesting partial V_S recovery following the seismic event. Nevertheless, this recovery is incomplete, and the Ludian earthquake source remains within a region of decreased V_S (Fig. 7i). Such a velocity recovery phenomenon observed after the Ludian earthquake is not unique because it has also been noted in other seismic events. For instance, Liu and Huang (2010) employed the ambient noise cross-correlation method to investigate the V_S variation in the 2008 M_s 8.0 Wenchuan earthquake zone in China, finding that seismic wave velocity at most stations began to recover to preseismic levels ~5 months after the mainshock. Similarly, Wang *et al.* (2016) utilized the ambient noise autocorrelation method to examine the spatiotemporal variation of crustal V_S within the 2013 M_s 7.0 Lushan earthquake zone in China, where they observed a decrease in V_S over 40–100 days after the mainshock, followed by a subsequent recovery phase.

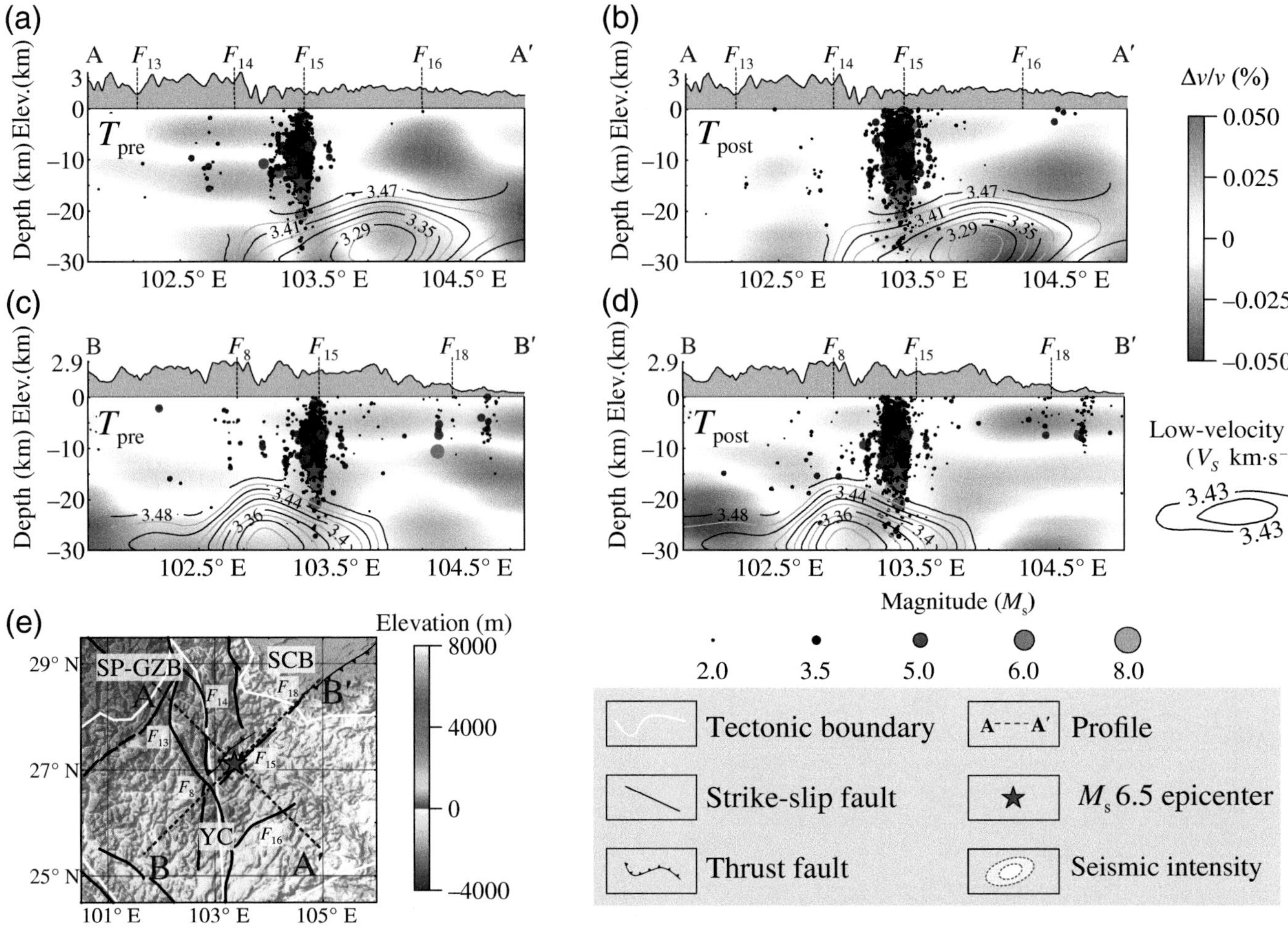

Figure 9. Crustal V_S variation along the A–A′ and B–B′ profiles from time segments T_{pre} to T_{post} in the Ludian earthquake zone. (a,c) V_S variation along A–A′ and B–B′ profiles during the preseismic stage of the Ludian earthquake. (b,d) The variation during the postseismic stage. (e) The position of the two profiles. The color version of this figure is available only in the electronic edition.

By comparing these results with previous studies on seismic velocity variation in the study area, we infer that stress variation within the Ludian earthquake zone constitutes a significant factor contributing to seismic wave velocity variation. Moreover, the interaction between the deep and shallow parts of the crust may play a crucial role in earthquake triggering. Seismicity is not only associated with the timing of stress accumulation but may also be influenced by fluid activity along fault zones, such as partial melting, viscous fluids containing water, or aqueous fluids (Zhong and Xiao, 1990; Lin, 1994; Cox, 1995; Klemperer, 2006; Che and Yu, 2014). Under the high-temperature and high-pressure conditions in the crust, these fluids can maintain connectivity (Hu *et al.*, 2024). The presence of fluids can elevate pore pressure within fault zones, thereby reducing their strength and promoting seismicity (Bao and Eaton, 2016; Tan *et al.*, 2020; Hennings *et al.*, 2021). As illustrated in Figure 9, the high-resolution crustal V_S model developed by Liu *et al.* (2023) reveals a prominent low-velocity zone beneath the hypocenter of the Ludian earthquake. Such crustal low-velocity anomalies are typically closely associated with fluid activity, and the presence of deep-seated fluids may have provided essential dynamic conditions for the nucleation of the Ludian earthquake. Therefore, we hypothesize that the velocity variation associated with the Ludian earthquake may result from the interaction mechanism between fluids and rocks within the fault zones. The presence of fluids in the fractures of fault zones leads to stress accumulation within these zones (earthquake preparation process). In the postseismic stage, the mechanism of fluid–rock interactions recurs, leading to the seismic wave velocity recovery phenomenon (postseismic recovery process). In addition to the primary deep underground factors, near-surface processes also influence seismic wave velocity. These include the destruction and healing of earthquake fault zones, surface damage caused by earthquakes, precipitation, atmospheric pressure changes, and tidal fluctuations, all of which can induce V_S variations (Rubinstein and Beroza, 2004, 2005; Xu and Song, 2009).

Coupling with time-lapse gravity and geomagnetic fields

The preparation and occurrence of moderate-to-strong earthquakes are often associated with spatiotemporal variations in

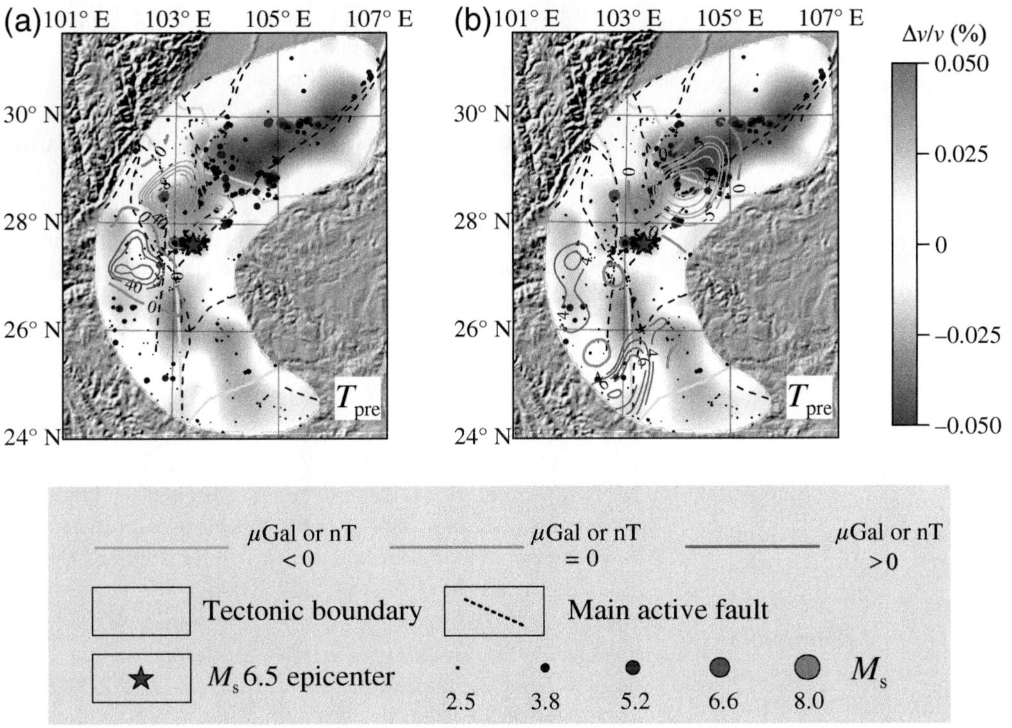

Figure 10. Preseismic coupling analysis of V_S variation with contemporaneous gravity and geomagnetic field anomalies preceding the Ludian earthquake. (a) Spatiotemporal correlation between the V_S variation and time-lapse gravity field perturbations (Zhu *et al.*, 2015), measured in μGal. (b) Corresponding analysis of V_S variation with time-lapse geomagnetic field fluctuations, quantified in nT. The color version of this figure is available only in the electronic edition.

regional gravity and geomagnetic fields (Zhang *et al.*, 2012; Chen *et al.*, 2015; Marchetti *et al.*, 2019; Zhu *et al.*, 2022). Thus, investigating the spatiotemporal coupling of seismic velocity variations with those of gravity and geomagnetic fields may provide a more comprehensive understanding of seismogenic mechanisms.

Zhu *et al.* (2015) analyzed the annual variation of the regional gravity field in the study area using mobile gravity data collected from 2011 to 2014, with an average precision exceeding 1μGal. The gravity variation at the Ludian earthquake epicenter presents a four-quadrant distribution, with the earthquake occurring in a region characterized by a high-gravity gradient. A clear correlation was observed between seismic wave velocity variation and gravity variation across the gravity data coverage area before the Ludian earthquake (Fig. 10a). Specifically, the areas with decreasing seismic wave velocity corresponded to weaker gravity fields, whereas the regions with an increasing velocity aligned with stronger gravity fields, indicating a positive correlation. In the literature, two primary factors are identified as contributing to gravity variation before and after an earthquake. First, gravity variation may arise from subsurface mass migration or significant surface deformations during the earthquake preparation and occurrence (Wang *et al.*, 2023). Second, gravity variations can result from coseismic or postseismic displacements (Fu *et al.*, 2010; Zhang *et al.*, 2015), with coseismic displacements typically exerting a stronger influence (Okubo, 1992). Thus, the observed gravity variation in the study area may be attributed to subsurface mass migration. When material accumulates and fills fractures in the subsurface medium, gravity increases, leading to a corresponding rise in V_S. Conversely, when the material disperses, gravity decreases, resulting in a reduction in V_S.

Regarding the geomagnetic field, we subsequently calculated the distribution of geomagnetic field variation in the lithosphere. As shown in Figure 10b, similar to the time-lapse gravity field, a positive correlation is also observed between temporal variation in the geomagnetic field and V_S variation. According to the electrokinetic effect (Fitterman, 1979; Dobrovolsky *et al.*, 1989; Song *et al.*, 2021), stress accumulation during the late stages of the Ludian earthquake induced fluid movement within the subsurface fractures under pressure. By the influence of the double-layer effect, electric currents are generated within the fluid, creating a potential difference that results in additional geomagnetic field variation. Therefore, in the Ludian earthquake zone, the accumulation of seismic stress accelerated fluid migration, causing the variation of the geomagnetic field.

In summary, we infer that the regional variation of V_S in the study area is hypothesized to result from the movement of crustal fluids through the fracture zones. This fluid migration simultaneously influences the gravity field, producing a positive coupling between the time-lapse V_S and the time-lapse gravity fields. In addition, fluid movement along the active fault fractures activates the fault zones, contributing to the occurrence of the Ludian earthquakes. The accumulation of seismic stress further accelerates fluid migration, inducing changes in the geomagnetic field. As a result, a positive coupling is also observed between the time-lapse V_S and the time-lapse geomagnetic field.

Conclusions

We developed an ambient noise time-lapse tomography algorithm based on the surface-wave direct inversion method and the PDS. The algorithm is applied to derive the 3D time-lapse velocity model of the crust around the Ludian earthquake zone from 2011 to 2017. The model reveals a correlation between the active fault zones and V_S variation across the study area. The V_S near the Ludian earthquake hypocenter exhibited a decline during the preseismic stage, with a maximum decrease of 0.015% ± 0.0027% between 2011 and 2014. This trend is corroborated by postseismic EGFs analyses revealing phase delays relative to preseismic signals. In addition, a positive coupling is observed between the V_S variation and the time-lapse gravity and geomagnetic field changes during the postseismic stage. A recovery of velocity around the Ludian earthquake hypocenter is observed during the postseismic stage; however, by 4 August 2017, V_S had not recovered to its preseismic levels. We infer that the migration of crustal materials, including partial melting, viscous fluids containing water, or aqueous fluids, intensified rock–fluid interactions, and the creep behavior of the fault zones, thereby activating these fault zones. This migration altered subsurface stress and physical states, influencing velocity, gravity, and geomagnetic fields. The time-lapse V_S model presented here offers valuable insights into crustal fluid migration and the seismogenic mechanisms of the Ludian earthquake zone.

Data and Resources

The continuous waveform data were obtained from the Data Management Center of China National Seismic Network (http://www.seisdmc.ac.cn/). The relocated catalog of $M_L \geq 1.5$ earthquakes released by the China Earthquake Science Experiment Field (http://cses.ac.cn/sjcp/ggmx/2021/132.shtml). The figures were generated using Golden Software Surfer (https://www.goldensoftware.com/) and MATLAB 2019 (https://ww2.mathworks.cn/). All websites were last accessed in April 2025.

Declaration of Competing Interests

The authors acknowledge that there are no conflicts of interest recorded.

Acknowledgments

This work is supported by the National Key R&D Program of China (2023YFF0803301) and the National Natural Science Foundation of China (41974101). The authors would like to thank the Data Management Center of China National Seismic Network for providing continuous seismic waveform data. The authors acknowledge A. Hongjian Fang from Sun Yat-sen University for sharing the *DSurfTomo* direct inversion software. The authors are grateful to Yiqing Zhu from the Second Monitoring and Application Center, China Earthquake Administration for providing the time-lapse gravity field data. Finally, the authors sincerely thank the editor and reviewers for their insightful comments and constructive suggestions, which have significantly improved the quality of this article.

References

An, Y., W. Wang, W. Yang, H. Jiang, J. Yang, X. Li, and R. Pan (2023). Using ambient noise to study the co-seismic and post-seismic velocity changes of the 2021 Yangbi M_s 6.4 earthquake in Yunnan, *Chin. J. Geophys.* **66,** no. 8, 3185–3201, doi: 10.6038/cjg2022Q0641 (in Chinese with English abstract).

Asnaashari, A., R. Brossier, S. Garambois, F. Audebert, P. Thore, and J. Virieux (2015). Time-lapse seismic imaging using regularized full-waveform inversion with a prior model: Which strategy? *Geophys. Prospect.* **63,** no. 1, 78–98, doi: 10.1111/1365-2478.12176.

Baccheschi, P., P. De Gori, F. Villani, F. Trippetta, and C. Chiarabba (2020). The preparatory phase of the M_w 6.1 2009 L'Aquila, Italy, normal faulting earthquake traced by foreshock time-lapse tomography, *Geology* **48,** no. 1, 49–55, doi: 10.1130/G46618.1.

Bao, X., and D. W. Eaton (2016). Fault activation by hydraulic fracturing in western Canada, *Science* **354,** no. 6318, 1406–1409, doi: 10.1126/science.aag2583.

Bensen, G. D., M. H. Ritzwoller, M. P. Barmin, A. L. Levshin, F. Lin, M. P. Moschetti, N. M. Shapiro, and Y. Yang (2007). Processing seismic ambient noise data to obtain reliable broad-band surface wave dispersion measurements, *Geophys. J. Int.* **169,** no. 3, 1239–1260, doi: 10.1111/j.1365-246X.2007.03374.x.

Bouchon, M., H. Karabulut, M. Aktar, S. Öalaybey, J. Schmittbuhl, and M.-P. Bouin (2011). Extended nucleation of the 1999 M_w 7.6 Izmit earthquake, *Science* **331,** no. 6019, 877–880, doi: 10.1126/science.1197341.

Brenguier, F., M. Campillo, C. Hadziioannou, N. M. Shapiro, R. M. Nadeau, and E. Larose (2008). Postseismic relaxation along the San Andreas fault at Parkfield from continuous seismological observations, *Science* **321,** no. 5895, 1478–1881, doi: 10.1126/science.1160943.

Brenguier, F., M. Campillo, T. Takeda, Y. Aoki, N. M. Shapiro, X. Briand, K. Emoto, and H. Miyake (2014). Mapping pressurized volcanic fluids from induced crustal seismic velocity drops, *Science* **345,** no. 6192, 80–82, doi: 10.1126/science.1254073.

Brenguier, F., R. Courbis, A. Mordret, X. Campman, P. Boué, M. Chmiel, T. Takano, T. Lecocq, W. Van der Veen, S. Postif, *et al.* (2020). Noise-based ballistic wave passive seismic monitoring. Part 1: Body waves, *Geophys. J. Int.* **221,** no. 1, 683–691, doi: 10.1093/gji/ggz440.

Brocher, T. M. (2005). Empirical relations between elastic wavespeeds and density in the Earth's crust, *Bull. Seismol. Soc. Am.* **95,** no. 6, 2081–2092, doi: 10.1785/0120050077.

Cao, Y., P. Huang, J. Qian, and H. Fu (2021). Application of time-lapse seismic tomography based on double-difference tomography to reveal P wave velocity changes related to the 2014 Ludian M_s 6.5 earthquake, *Chin. J. Geophys.* **64,** no. 5, 1569–1584, doi: 10.6038/cjg2021O0122 (in Chinese with English abstract).

Cao, Y., J. Qian, J. Huang, G. Zhang, and H. Fu (2021). P-wave velocity changes in hypocenter region of the 2014 Jinggu M_s 6.6 earthquake using time-lapse tomography based on double-difference tomography, *Seismol. Geol.* **43,** no. 6, 1563–1585, doi: 10.3969/j.issn.0253-4967.2021.06.012 (in Chinese with English abstract).

Cao, Y., W. Qian, J. Huang, and P. Huang (2021). P-wave velocity changes in the source area before and after two moderate strong earthquakes in Yingjiang, Yunnan in 2014, *Acta Seismol. Sinica* **43,** no. 6, 690–705, doi: 10.11939/jass.20200214.

Che, Y., and J. Yu (2014). Influence and controlling of fluid in the crust on earthquake activity, *Recent Develop. World Seismol.* **8,** 1–9, doi: 10.3969/j.issn.0235-4975.2014.08.001 (in Chinese with English abstract).

Chen, S., W. Xu, and C. Jiang (2015). Relationship between gravity variation and seismic hazards in western China, *Acta Seismol. Sinica* **37,** no. 4, 575–587, doi: 10.11939/jass.2015.04.005 (in Chinese with English abstract).

Chiarabba, C., P. De Gori, and E. Boschi (2009). Pore-pressure migration along a normal-fault system resolved by time-repeated seismic tomography, *Geology* **37,** no. 1, 67–70, doi: 10.1130/G25220A.1.

Chiarabba, C., P. De Gori, M. Segou, and M. Cattaneo (2020). Seismic velocity precursors to the 2016 M_s 6.5 Norcia (Italy) earthquake, *Geology* **48,** no. 9, 924–928, doi: 10.1130/G47048.1.

Cox, S. F. (1995). Faulting processes at high fluid pressures: An example of fault valve behavior from the Wattle Gully fault, Victoria, Australia, *J. Geophys. Res.* **100,** no. B7, 12841–12859, doi: 10.1029/95JB00915.

Dai, Z., and X. Zhang (2016). Characteristic analysis of seismic velocity changes associated with the 2014 Ludian M_s 6.5 earthquake, *Earthquake* **36,** no. 3, 34–45 (in Chinese with English abstract).

Dobrovolsky, I. P., N. I. Gershenzon, and M. B. Gokhberg (1989). Theory of electrokinetic effects occurring at the final stage in the preparation of a tectonic earthquake, *Phys. Earth. Planet. In.* **57,** no. 1–2, 144–156, doi: 10.1016/0031-9201(89)90224-0.

Fang, H., H. Yao, H. Zhang, Y. Huang, and R. D. van der Hilst (2015). Direct inversion of surface wave dispersion for three-dimensional shallow crustal structure based on ray tracing: Methodology and application, *Geophys. J. Int.* **201,** no. 3, 1251–1263, doi: 10.1093/gji/ggv080.

Fang, L., J. Wu, W. Wang, Z. Lu, C. Wang, T. Yang, and S. Zhong (2014). Relocation of the aftershock sequence of the M_s 6.5 Ludian earthquake and its seismogenic structure, *Seismol. Geol.* **36,** no. 4, 1173–1185, doi: 10.3969/j.issn.0253-4967.2014.04.019 (in Chinese with English abstract).

Fitterman, D. V. (1979). Theory of electrokinetic-magnetic anomalies in a faulted half-space, *J. Geophys. Res.* **84,** no. B11, 6031–6040, doi: 10.1029/JB084iB11p06031.

Fu, G, W. Sun, Y. Fukuda, and S. Gao (2010). Coseismic displacements caused by point dislocations in a three-dimensional heterogeneous, spherical earth model, *Geophys. J. Int.* **183,** no. 2, 706–726, doi: 10.1111/j.1365-246X.2010.04757.x.

Grêt, A., R. Snieder, and J. Scales (2006). Time-lapse monitoring of rock properties with coda wave interferometry, *J. Geophys. Res.* **111,** no. B3, B03305, doi: 10.1029/2004JB003354.

Hennings, P. H., J. -P. Nicot, R. S. Gao, H. R. DeShon, J. -E. Lund Snee, A. P. Morris, M. R. Brudzinski, E. A. Horne, and C. Breton (2021). Pore pressure threshold and fault slip potential for induced earthquakes in the Dallas-Fort Worth area of North Central Texas, *Geophys. Res. Lett.* **48,** no. 15, e2021GL093564, doi: 10.1029/2021GL093564.

Hu, H., C. Yin, L. Dai, J. Lai, Y. Chen, P. Wang, J. Zhu, and S. Han (2024). The role of $\alpha - \beta$ quartz transition in fluid storage in crust from the evidence of electrical conductivity, *J. Geophys. Res.* **129,** no, 9, e2024JB029140, doi: 10.1029/2024JB029140.

Hu, J. (2020). Development of region-scale seismic velocity and attenuation tomography methods and its applications, *Ph.D. Dissertation*, University of Science and Technology of China, 4–6, doi: 10.27517/d.cnki.gzkju.2020.001648 (in Chinese with English abstract).

Huang, Y., M. Moorkamp, J. Gao, and H. Zhang (2023). Seismogenic structure of the 2014 *M* 6.5 Ludian earthquake from three-dimensional joint inversion of magnetotelluric data and seismic arrival times, *J. Geophys. Res.* **128,** no. 7, e2022JB026151, doi: 10.1029/2022JB026151.

Julian, B. R., and G. R. Foulger (2010). Time-dependent seismic tomography, *Geophys. J. Int.* **182,** no. 3, 1327–1338, doi: 10.1111/j.1365-246X.2010.04668.x.

Kato, A., K. Obara, T. Igarashi, H. Tsuruoka, S. Nakagawa, and N. Hirata (2012). Propagation of slow slip leading up to the 2011 M_w 9.0 Tohoku-Oki earthquake, *Science* **335,** no. 6069, 705–708, doi: 10.1126/science.1215141.

Klemperer, S. L. (2006). *Crustal Flow in Tibet: Geophysical Evidence for the Physical State of Tibetan Lithosphere, and Inferred Patterns of Active Flow*, Vol. 268, Geological Society, Special Publications, London, doi: 10.1144/GSL.SP.2006.268.01.03.

Koulakov, I., and C. A. Vargas (2018). Evolution of the magma conduit beneath the Galeras volcano inferred from repeated seismic tomography, *Geophys. Res. Lett.* **45,** no. 15, 7514–7522, doi: 10.1029/2018GL078850.

Koulakov, I., V. Gladkov, S. El Khrepy, N. Al-Arifi, and I. H. Fathi (2016). Application of repeated passive source travel time tomography to reveal weak velocity changes related to the 2011 Tohoku-Oki M_w 9.0 earthquake, *J. Geophys. Res.* **121,** no. 6, 4408–4426, doi: 10.1002/2016JB013002.

Koulakov, I., E. I. Gordeev, N. L. Dobretsov, V. A. Vernikovsky, S. Senyukov, A. Jakovlev, and K. Jaxybulatov (2013). Rapid changes in magma storage beneath the Klyuchevskoy group of volcanoes inferred from time-dependent seismic tomography, *J. Volcanol. Geoth. Res.* **263,** 75–91, doi: 10.1016/j.jvolgeores.2012.10.014.

Li, X., X. Xu, Y. Ran, J. Cui, Y. Xie, and F. Xu (2015). Compound fault rupture in the 2014 M_s 6.5 Ludian, China, earthquake and significance to disaster mitigation, *Seismol. Res. Lett.* **86,** no. 3, 764–774, doi: 10.1785/0220140198.

Lin, F., D. Li, R. W. Clayton, and D. Hollis (2013). High-resolution 3D shallow crustal structure in Long Beach, California: Application of ambient noise tomography on a dense seismic array, *Geophysics* **78,** no. 4, Q45–Q56, doi: 10.1190/GEO2012-0453.1.

Lin, Y. (1994). Weakening effect of hot spring thermal storage temperature on rupture and its effect on seismic activity, *Acta Seismol. Sinica* **16,** no. 2, 251–257 (in Chinese).

Liu, Y., H. Yao, H. Zhang, and H. Fang (2021). The community velocity model V.1.0 of southwest China, constructed from joint body- and surface-wave travel-time tomography, *Seismol. Res. Lett.* **92,** no. 5, 2972–2987, doi: 10.1785/0220200318.

Liu, Y., Z. Yu, Z. Zhang, H. Yao, W. Wang, H. Zhang, H. Fang, and L. Fang (2023). The high-resolution community velocity model V2.0 of southwest China, constructed by joint body and surface wave tomography of data recorded at temporary dense arrays, *Sci. China Earth Sci.* **66,** no. 10, 2368–2385, doi: 10.1007/s11430-022-1161-7.

Liu, Z., and J. Huang (2010). Temporal changes of seismic velocity around the Wenchuan earthquake fault zone from ambient seismic noise correlation, *Chin. J. Geophys.* **53,** no. 4, 853–863, doi: 10.3969/j.issn.0001-5733.2010.04.010 (in Chinese with English abstract).

Liu, Z., J. Huang, Z. Peng, and J. Su (2014). Seismic velocity changes in the epicentral region of the 2008 Wenchuan earthquake measured from three-component ambient noise correlation techniques, *Geophys. Res. Lett.* **41,** no. 1, 37–42, doi: 10.1002/2013GL058682.

Luo, Y., Y. Xu, and Y. Yang (2013). Crustal radial anisotropy beneath the Dabie orogenic belt from ambient noise tomography, *Geophys. J. Int.* **195,** no. 2, 1149–1164, doi: 10.1093/gji/ggt281.

Ma, J. (2016). On "whether earthquake precursors help for prediction do exist", *Chin. Sci. Bull.* **61,** no. C1, 409–414, doi: 10.1360/N972015-01239 (in Chinese with English abstract).

Mao, S., A. Lecointre, R. D. van der Hilst, and M. Campillo (2022). Space-time monitoring of groundwater fluctuations with passive seismic interferometry, *Nat. Commun.* **13,** no. 1, 4643, doi: 10.1038/s41467-022-32194-3.

Marchetti, D., A. De Santis, S. D'Arcangelo, F. Poggio, A. Piscini, S. A. Campuzano, and W. V. J. O. De Carvalho (2019). Pre-earthquake chain processes detected from ground to satellite altitude in preparation of the 2016–2017 seismic sequence in central Italy, *Remote Sens. Environ.* **229,** 93–99, doi: 10.1016/j.rse.2019.04.033.

Mordret, A., R. Courbis, F. Brenguier, M. Chmiel, S. Garambois, S. Mao, P. Boué, X. Campman, T. Lecocq, W. Van der Veen, and D. Hollis (2020). Noise-based ballistic wave passive seismic monitoring—Part 2: Surface waves, *Geophys. J. Int.* **221,** no. 1, 692–705, doi: 10.1093/gji/ggaa016.

Nishida, K., Y. Mizutani, M. Ichihara, and Y. Aoki (2020). Time-lapse monitoring of seismic velocity associated with 2011 Shinmoe-Dake eruption using seismic interferometry: An extended Kalman filter approach, *J. Geophys. Res.* **125,** no. 9, e2020JB020180, doi: 10.1029/2020JB020180.

Niu, F., P. G. Silver, T. M. Daley, X. Cheng, and E. L. Majer (2008). Preseismic velocity changes observed from active source monitoring at the Parkfield SAFOD drill site, *Nature* **454,** no. 7201, 204–208, doi:10.1038/nature07111.

Niu, F., P. G. Silver, R. M. Nadeau, and T. V. McEvilly (2003). Migration of seismic scatterers associated with the 1993 Parkfield aseismic transient event, *Nature* **426,** no. 6966, 544, doi: 10.1038/nature02151.

Nolet, G. (1987). *Seismic Tomography: With Applications in Global Seismology and Exploration Geophysics*, D. Reidel Publishing Company, Netherlands, 49–83.

Okubo, S. (1992). Gravity and potential changes due to shear and tensile faults in a half-space, *J. Geophys. Res.* **97,** no. B5, 7137–7144, doi: 10.1029/92JB00178.

Paige, C. C., and M. Saunders (1982). LSQR: An algorithm for sparse linear equations and sparse least squares, *ACM Trans. Math. Software* **8,** no. 1, 43–71, doi: 10.1145/355984.355989.

Pang, W., R. Yang, Y. Xu, and Y. Shen (2017). Study on the crustal wave velocity variation around the 2014 Ludian M_s 6.5 earthquake area by background noise autocorrelation function, *J. Seismol. Res.* **40,** no. 3, 491–501, doi: 10.3969/j.issn.1000-0666.2017.03.027(in Chinese with English abstract).

Patanè, D., G. Barberi, O. Cocina, P. De Gori, and C. Chiarabba (2006). Time-resolved seismic tomography detects magma intrusions at Mount Etna, *Science* **313,** no. 5788, 821–823, doi: 10.1126/science.1127724.

Pei, S., F. Niu, Y. Ben-Zion, Q. Sun, Y. Liu, X. Xue, J. Su, and Z. Shao. (2019). Seismic velocity reduction and accelerated recovery due to earthquakes on the Longmenshan fault, *Nature Geosci.* **12,** no. 5, 387–392, doi: 10.1038/s41561-019-0401-z.

Poli, P., M. Campillo, and H. Pedersen (2012). Body-wave imaging of Earth's mantle discontinuities from ambient seismic noise, *Science* **338,** no. 6110, 1063–1065, doi: 10.1126/science.1228194.

Poupinet, G., W. L. Ellsworth, and J. Frechet (1984). Monitoring velocity variation in the crust using earthquake doublets: An application to the Calaveras fault, California, *J. Geophys. Res.* **89,** no. B7, 5719–5731, doi: 10.1029/JB089iB07p05719.

Qian, J., H. Zhang, and E. Westman (2018). New time-lapse seismic tomographic scheme based on double-difference tomography and its application in monitoring temporal velocity variation caused by underground coal mining, *Geophys. J. Int.* **215,** no. 3, 2093–2104, doi: 10.1093/gji/ggy404.

Riaz, M. S., Y. Zheng, X. Xiong, Z. Xie, Z. Li, and M. Song (2017). Refined 3D seismic-velocity structures and seismogenic environment of the M_s 6.5 Ludian earthquake, *Bull. Seismol. Soc. Am.* **107,** no. 6, 3023–3036, doi: 10.1785/0120170072.

Rubinstein, J. L., and G. C. Beroza (2004). Evidence for widespread nonlinear strong ground motion in the M_w 6.9 Loma Prieta earthquake, *Bull. Seismol. Soc. Am.* **94,** no. 5, 1595–1608, doi: 10.1785/012004009.

Rubinstein, J. L., and G. C. Beroza (2005). Depth constraints on nonlinear strong ground motion from the 2004 Parkfield earthquake, *Geophys. Res. Lett.* **32,** no. 14, L14313, doi: 10.1029/2005GL023189.

Shapiro, N. M., M. Campillo, L. Stehly, and M. H. Ritzwoller (2005). High-resolution surface-wave tomography from ambient seismic noise, *Science* **307,** no. 5715, 1615–1618, doi: 10.1126/science.1108339.

Shen, W., M. H. Ritzwoller, D. Kang, Y. Kim, F. Lin, J. Ning, W. Wang, Y. Zheng, and L. Zhou (2016). A seismic reference model for the crust and uppermost mantle beneath China from surface wave dispersion, *Geophys. J. Int.* **206,** no. 2, 954–979, doi: 10.1093/gji/ggw175.

Simons, F. J., R. D. van der Hilst, J. -P. Montagner, and A. Zielhuis (2002). Multimode Rayleigh wave inversion for heterogeneity and azimuthal anisotropy of the Australian upper mantle, *Geophys. J. Int.* **150,** no. 3, 738–754, doi: 10.1046/j.1365-246X.2002.01787.x.

Snieder, R., A. Grêt, H. Douma, and J. Scales (2002). Coda wave interferometry for estimating nonlinear behavior in seismic velocity, *Science* **295,** no. 5563, 2253–2255, doi: 10.1126/science.1070015.

Song, C., Z. Chen, S. Zhou, Y. Xu, and B. Chen (2021). Geomagnetic field change before and after 2021 Yangbi M_s 6.4 earthquake, *Seismol. Geol.* **43,** no. 4, 958–971, doi: 10.3969/j.issn.0253-4967.2021.04.014 (in Chinese with English abstract).

Taira, T., F. Brenguier, and Q. Kong (2015). Ambient noise-based monitoring of seismic velocity changes associated with the 2014 M_w 6.0 South Napa earthquake, *Geophys. Res. Lett.* **42,** no. 17, 6997–7004, doi: 10.1002/2015GL065308.

Tan, Y., J. Hu, H. Zhang, Y. Chen, J. Qian, Q. Wang, H. Zha, P. Tang, and Z. Nie (2020). Hydraulic fracturing induced seismicity in the southern Sichuan basin due to fluid diffusion inferred from seismic and injection data analysis, *Geophys. Res. Lett.* **47,** no. 4, e2019GL084885, doi: 10.1029/2019GL084885.

Tikhonov, A. N., and V. Arsenin (1977). *Solutions of Ill-Posed Problems*, John Wiley & Sons, New York, 87–94, doi: 10.1137/1021044.

Wang, J., D. Zheng, J. Zhang, X. Zhan, and T. Qian (2020). Seismic velocity changes in the epicentral region of the 2013 Lushan earthquake measured from ambient seismic noise, *Chin. J. Geophys.* **63,** no. 2, 517–531, doi: 10.6038/cjg2020N0275 (in Chinese with English abstract).

Wang, J., D. Zheng, J. Zheng, X. Zhan, H. Jiang, Z. Li, and J. Zhang (2016). Temporal velocity changes in the crust associated with the Lushan M_s 7.0 earthquake by auto-correlation function analysis of ambient noise, *Seismol. Geol.* **38,** no. 1, 152–168, doi: 10.3969/j.issn.0253-4967.2016.01.012 (in Chinese with English abstract).

Wang, L., S. Chen, J. Zhuang, B. Zhang, W. Shi, J. Yang, and W. Xu (2023). Gravity field changes reveal deep mass transfer before and after the 2013 Lushan earthquake, *Commun. Earth. Environ.* **4,** no. 1, 1–13, doi: 10.1038/s43247-023-00860-z.

Wang, Q. Y., M. Campillo, F. Brenguier, A. Lecointre, T. Takeda, and A. Hashima (2019). Evidence of changes of seismic properties in the entire crust beneath Japan after the M_w 9.0, 2011 Tohoku-Oki earthquake, *J. Geophys. Res.* **124,** no. 8, 8924–8941, doi: 10.1029/2019JB017803.

Wang, Z., X. Li, D. Zhao, X. Shang, and L. Dong (2018). Time-lapse seismic tomography of an underground mining zone, *Int. J. Rock. Mech. Min.* **107,** 136–149, doi: 10.1016/j.ijrmms.2018.04.038.

Xu, Z. J., and X. Song (2009). Temporal changes of surface wave velocity associated with major Sumatra earthquakes from ambient noise correlation, *Proc. Natl. Acad. Sci. Unit. States Am.* **106,** no. 34, 14,207–14,212, doi: 10.1073/pnas.0901164106.

Xu, X., G. Jiang, G. Yu, X. Wu, J. Zhang, and X. Li (2014). Discussion on seismogenic fault of the Ludian M_s 6.5 earthquake and its tectonic attribution, *Chin. J. Geophys.* **57,** no. 9, 3060–3068, doi: 10.6038/cjg20140931 (in Chinese with English abstract).

Xu, X., X. Wen, R. Zheng, W. Ma, F. Song, and G. Yu (2003). Recent patterns of tectonic changes of active blocks in Sichuan-Yunnan area and their power sources, *China. Sci. Earth Sci.* **33,** no. A1, 151–162 (in Chinese).

Yang, Y., and M. H. Ritzwoller (2008). Characteristics of ambient seismic noise as a source for surface wave tomography, *Geochem. Geophys. Geosys.* **9,** no. 2, Q02008, doi: 10.1029/2007GC001814.

Yang, Y., A. Li, and M. H. Ritzwoller (2008). Crustal and uppermost mantle structure in southern Africa revealed from ambient noise and teleseismic tomography, *Geophys. J. Int.* **174,** no. 1, 235–248, doi: 10.1111/j.1365-246X.2008.03779.x.

Yang, Y., M. H. Ritzwoller, A. L. Levshin, and N. M. Shapiro (2007). Ambient noise Rayleigh wave tomography across Europe, *Geophys. J. Int.* **168,** no. 1, 259–274, doi: 10.1111/j.1365-246X.2006.03203.x.

Yao, H., C. Beghein, and R. D. Van Der Hilst (2008). Surface wave array tomography in SE Tibet from ambient seismic noise and two-station analysis—II. Crustal and upper-mantle structure, *Geophys. J. Int.* **173,** no. 1, 205–219, doi: 10.1111/j.1365-246X.2007.03696.x.

Yao, H., S. Luo, C. Li, S. Hu, and H. Fang (2023). Direct surface wave tomography for three-dimensional structure based on surface wave travel times: Methodology review and applications, *Rev. Geophys. Planet. Phys.* **54,** no. 3, 231–251, doi: 10.19975/j.dqyxx.2022-063.

Yao, H., R. D. van der Hilst, and M. V. de Hoop (2006). Surface-wave array tomography in SE Tibet from ambient seismic noise and two-station analysis—I. Phase velocity maps, *Geophys. J. Int.* **166,** no. 2, 732–744, doi: 10.1111/j.1365-246X.2006.03028.x.

Yukutake, Y., H. Ito, R. Honda, M. Harada, T. Tanada, and A. Yoshida (2011). Fluid-induced swarm earthquake sequence revealed by precisely determined hypocenters and focal mechanisms in the 2009 activity at Hakone volcano, Japan, *J. Geophys. Res.* **116,** no. B4, B04308, doi: 10.1029/2010JB008036.

Zhang, G., G. Fu, X. Zhou, and C. Xu (2015). Retrieve post-seismic gravity changes induced by Sumatra earthquake (M_w 9.3) based on the viscoelastic dislocation theory, *Chin. J. Geophys.* **58,** no. 5, 1654–1665, doi: 10.6038/cjg20150517 (in Chinese with English abstract).

Zhang, P., Q. Deng, G. Zhang, J. Ma, W. Gan, W. Min, F. Mao, and Q. Wang (2003). Active tectonic blocks and strong earthquakes in the continent of China, *Sci. China Ser. D-Earth Sci.* **46,** no. Suppl 2, 13–24, doi: 10.1360/03dz0002.

Zhang, X., and H. Zhang (2015). Wavelet-based time-dependent travel time tomography method and its application in imaging the Etna volcano in Italy, *J. Geophys. Res.* **120,** no. 10, 7068–7084, doi: 10.1002/2015JB012182.

Zhang, X., X. Shen, M. Parrot, Z. Zeren, X. Ouyang, J. Liu, J. Qian, S. Zhao, and Y. Miao. (2012). Phenomena of electrostatic perturbations before strong earthquakes (2005–2010) observed on DEMETER, *Nat. Hazard Earth. Syst. Sci.* **12,** no. 1, 75–83, doi: 10.5194/nhess-12-75-2012.

Zheng, X., B. Ouyang, D. Zhang, Z. Yao, J. Liang, and J. Zheng (2009). Technical system construction of Data Backup Centre for China Seismograph Network and the data support to researches on the Wenchuan earthquake, *Chin. J. Geophys.* **52,** no. 5, 1412–1417, doi: 10.3969/j.issn.0001-5733.2009.05.031 (in Chinese with English abstract).

Zheng, X., Z. Yao, J. Liang, and J. Zheng (2010). The role played and opportunities provided by IGP DMC of China National Seismic Network in Wenchuan earthquake disaster relief and researches, *Bull. Seismol. Soc. Am.* **100,** no. 5B, 2866–2872, doi: 10.1785/0120090257.

Zhong, Y., and X. Xiao (1990). Preliminary study on spatial relationship between earthquakes and hot springs on Liaodong peninsula, *Seismol. Geol.* **12,** no. 4, 343–350 (in Chinese with English abstract).

Zhu, Y., G. Fu, W. Liang, and Y. Xu (2015). Earthquake predictions: Spatial-temporal gravity changes before the Ludian M_s 6.5, Lushan M_s 7.0 and Wenchuan M_s 8.0 earthquakes, *Seismol. Geol.* **37,** no. 1, 319–330, doi: 10.3969/j.issn.0253-4967.2015.01.025 (in Chinese with English abstract).

Zhu, Y., Y. Zhang, X. Yang, F. Liu, G. Zhang, Y. Zhao, S. Wei, J. Mao, and S. Zhang (2022). Progress of time-varying gravity in seismic research, *Rev. Geophys. Planet. Phys.* **53,** no. 3, 278–291, doi: 10.19975/j.dqyxx.2021-060 (in Chinese with English abstract).

Manuscript received 12 December 2024
Published online 14 July 2025

Mechanisms and Implications of Lower Crust Earthquakes and Shallow Events Beneath Yanzhou Coal Mining Area, North China

Guangwei Zhang[*1,2], Enyuan Wang[1,2], Luyuan Huang[3], Yujiang Li[4], and Xingping Hu[4]

Abstract

The Yanzhou Coal Mining area in North China has experienced a significant increase in shallow depth (< 2 km) seismic activity in recent years, particularly following the 2017 M 4 lower crust earthquake. However, the relationship between deep tectonic earthquakes and shallow seismicity remains poorly understood. This study employs seismic tomography to resolve a high-resolution 3D crustal velocity structure and inverts the source parameters of the 2017 M 4 event (22 km depth) to calculate static Coulomb stress changes. By integrating these analyses, we investigated the mechanical relationship between the lower crustal and shallow seismicity. The 2017 earthquake, which is spatially correlated with a low-velocity anomaly and the westward migration of the hypocenters in the lower crust, suggests that fluid-driven fault activation occurred where deep fluids from the upper mantle led to increased seismicity rates. In contrast, Coulomb stress changes generated by this event are insufficient to induce stress-triggering effects and lack a direct causative relationship with shallow seismic activity. Although our analysis rules out static stress transfer associated with the 2017 M 4 event, the possibility of remote dynamic triggering remains and cannot be definitively excluded. Instead, the statistically significant increase in shallow seismicity correlated temporally with extended subsurface resource extraction and the post-2017 use of new deep-mining methods under conditions of high stress and elevated temperatures, highlighting anthropogenic production behaviors as a primary driver. The study demonstrates that lower crustal seismicity and shallow mining-induced activity operate within distinct mechanical frameworks. Although deep fluids influence tectonic earthquakes by reducing the effective normal stress along the fault plane, shallow seismicity is dominantly controlled by the intensity of coal mine extraction. These findings highlight the necessity of distinguishing between tectonically driven and mining-induced seismic hazards.

Cite this article as Zhang, G., E. Wang, L. Huang, Y. Li, and X. Hu (2025). Mechanisms and Implications of Lower Crust Earthquakes and Shallow Events Beneath Yanzhou Coal Mining Area, North China, *Seismol. Res. Lett.* **97**, 340–353, doi: 10.1785/0220250125.

Supplemental Material

Introduction

The Yanzhou Coal Mining (YCM) area, located in the southern part of the North China basin, is a tectonically active region characterized by high seismic activity (Fig. 1). This seismic activity can be classified into two main categories: tectonic earthquakes, associated with regional fault systems, and mining-induced events, linked to anthropogenic subsurface extraction processes. Historical earthquake catalogs document three significant earthquakes, each with a magnitude exceeding 6.5, which have occurred in the past century (Li *et al.*, 2021). Notably, Heze City (HZ), within a 100 km radius of the YCM area, was struck by a devastating magnitude 7.0 earthquake in 1937 (Fig. 1a). This earthquake resulted in widespread damage and left a trail of destruction (Li *et al.*, 2021). In recent years, the YCM region has experienced a marked increase in shallow-depth (<2 km) seismic activity. This trend became particularly pronounced following the 2017 **M** 4 seismic event within the lower crust (>20 km) (Zhang *et al.*, 2024). The

1. School of Safety Engineering, China University of Mining and Technology, Xu Zhou, Jiangsu, China, https://orcid.org/0000-0001-7453-0539 (GZ); 2. Key Laboratory of Theory and Technology on Coal and Rock Dynamic Disaster Prevention and Control, National Mine Safety Administration, China University of Mining and Technology, Xuzhou, China; 3. Institute of Geophysics, China Earthquake Administration, Beijing, China; 4. National Institute of Nature Hazards, Ministry of Emergency Management of China, Beijing, China

*Corresponding author: zhanggw@cumt.edu.cn

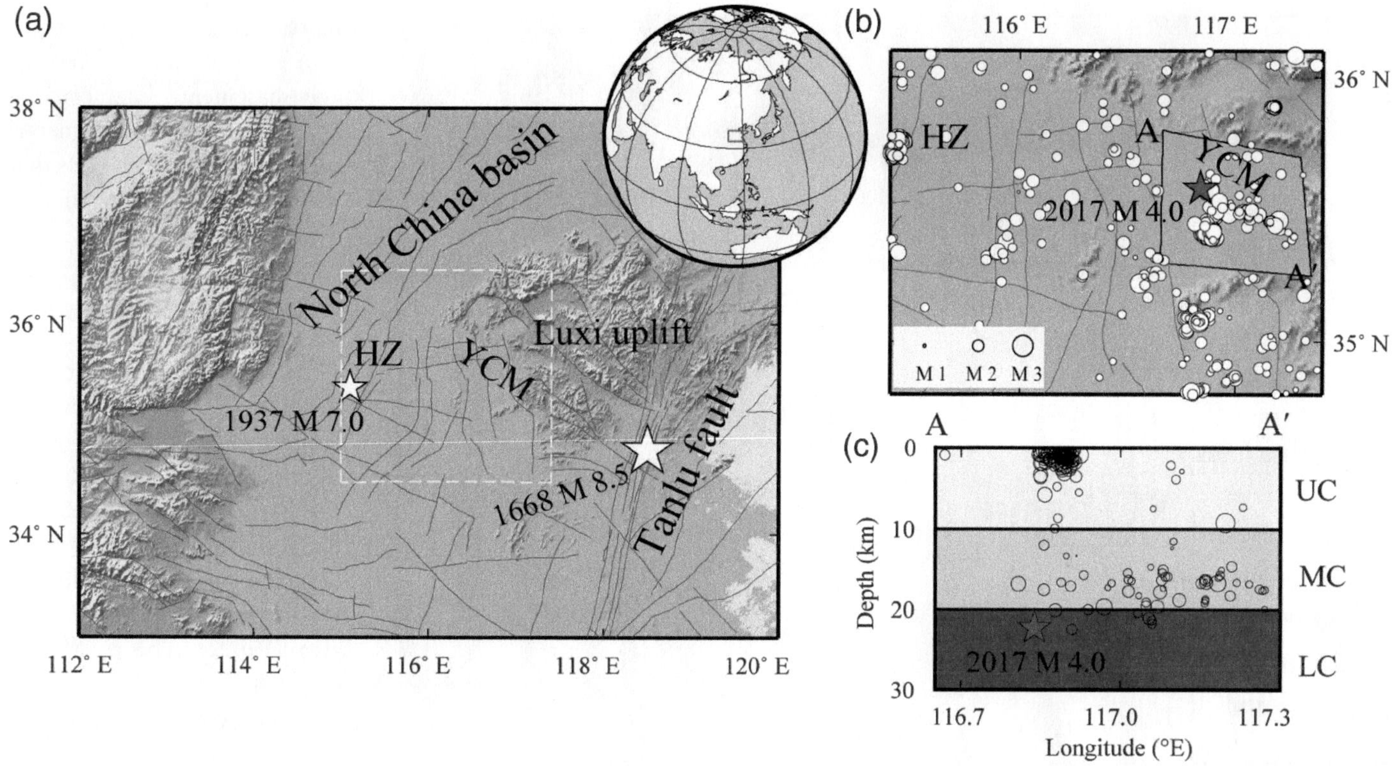

Figure 1. (a) Regional tectonic map illustrating major geological structures and historical seismic events with magnitudes ≥7.0 (white stars denote epicenters). The brown lines indicate the faults. The focal depths of the 1937 **M** 7.0 and 1668 **M** 8.5 earthquakes are recorded as zero, attributed to the absence of regional seismic stations. Yanzhou coal mining area (YCM) and Heze City (HZ) in white dashed box are annotated for spatial reference. (b) Location of seismicity in and around the YCM area. The shaded region demarcates the YCM area. And the 2017 *M* 4 lower crust earthquake is marked by a red star, and open circles represent **M** < 4.0 events. (c) Seismic profiles A–A′ across the YCM area in panel (b). Delineate crustal layers: upper crust (UC), middle crust (MC), and lower crust (LC) (from Crust1.0, Laske *et al.*, 2013). The color version of this figure is available only in the electronic edition.

spatial–temporal clustering of seismicity highlights that the region is in a complex geodynamic regime (Xu, 2004; Zheng *et al.*, 2008; Gu *et al.*, 2022), which is characterized by intersecting fault systems (Fig. 1b) and depth-dependent seismic clusters in the shallow and lower crust (Fig. 1c). Numerous studies have established that large tectonic earthquakes can remotely trigger microseismic events (Yao *et al.*, 2015; Liu *et al.*, 2017). However, most research has predominantly focused on long-range distances, such as plate subduction zones, intraplate large faults, and volcanic areas (Peng and Gomberg, 2010; Wu *et al.*, 2011). The localized triggering mechanisms between crustal tectonic earthquakes and shallow mining-induced seismicity remain poorly understood. Such interactions may enhance or suppress seismic activity in mining areas, with rapid increases in event frequency generally correlating with elevated seismic hazard. Thus, a comprehensive understanding of this knowledge is essential for accurately refining seismic risk assessments, particularly in regions like YCM where anthropogenic activities intersect with active tectonic settings.

To understand earthquake generation, it is crucial to obtain detailed information about the crustal velocity structure. The seismic velocity structure provides insight into the properties of crustal materials and plays a significant role in determining the spatial distribution of earthquakes (Zhang *et al.*, 2019; Zhang, Ji, *et al.*, 2022; Zhang, Li, and Hu, 2022). However, current knowledge regarding the crustal velocity model (0.5° × 0.5°) in the YCM region remains insufficient for accurately representing its 3D structure (Xin *et al.*, 2018). This lack of information hinders the precise identification of earthquake locations and the delineation of fault geometries. In the context of mining earthquakes, significant efforts have been directed toward understanding the stress perturbations resulting from industrial activities, solid earth tides, and tectonic earthquakes (Wang *et al.*, 2014, 2015; Zhang, Ji, and Wu, 2022; Ding *et al.*, 2023; Song *et al.*, 2024). Experimental and numerical investigations demonstrate that stress perturbations can change fault stress and trigger earthquakes (Huang *et al.*, 2023). However, the mechanism of stress transfer between lower crust earthquakes and shallow seismicity remains an elusive challenge.

Research on earthquake aftershocks suggests that even minor changes in the stress field can trigger fault failure when the stress level is critical (Kilb *et al.*, 2000). Azhari and Ozbay (2017) investigated the impact of earthquakes on open-pit mine slopes, suggesting that the open-pit mine slopes could experience significant failures when subjected to local

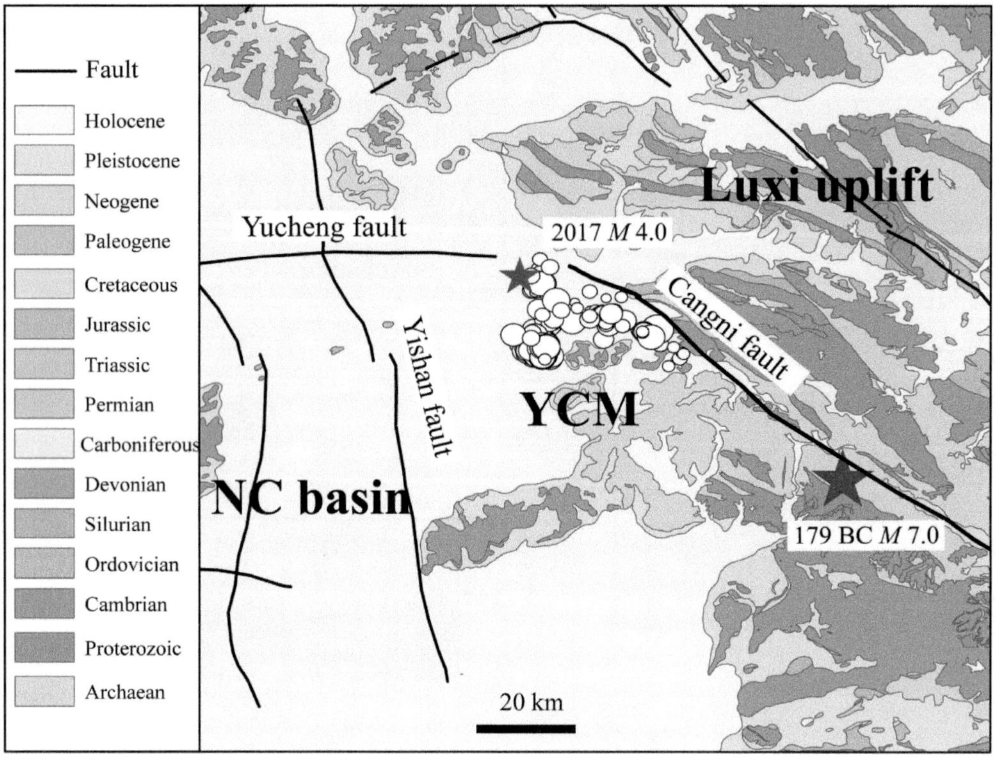

Figure 2. Geologic map of the YCM area and the adjacent area. The blue star represents the **M** 7.0 earthquake that occurred in 179 B.C. (Chao *et al.*, 2012), and the red star is the 2017 **M** 4.0 event. The open circles represent **M** < 4.0 events. The three main faults around the YCM area are east–west trending Yuncheng fault, the north–south-trending Yishan fault, and the northwest-striking Cangni fault. The NC basin refers to the North China basin. The color version of this figure is available only in the electronic edition.

earthquakes with depths of less than 40 km. In addition, stress changes may also affect fluid migration and potentially induce seismic activities through high-permeable pathways (Shelly *et al.*, 2013; Taira and Brenguier, 2016; Currenti *et al.*, 2017). This mechanism, which quantifies stress redistribution from earthquake ruptures to adjacent crustal structures, is well established as a critical factor in seismic triggering.

In this research, we focus on the YCM area—a region characterized by both lower crust earthquakes and mine-induced seismic events. Our objective is to explore the potential links between deep and shallow seismicity and to determine whether a triggering relationship exists between them. We began our study with seismic tomography to construct a 3D, fine-scale velocity model of the crust. This was followed by an inversion of the source parameters of the 2017 M 4 earthquake, enabling us to derive the static Coulomb stress distribution. By combining these results, we further investigate the interaction between lower crustal earthquakes and shallow seismic activities.

Geological background

The YCM area and its surrounding region comprise two distinct tectonic units: the Luxi uplift to the east and the North China basin to the west (Figs. 1 and 2). The Luxi uplift represents a significant exposure zone of Archean crystalline basement, characterized by extensive Mesozoic igneous rocks and Cenozoic basalts that are distributed along northwest-trending fault systems (Zheng *et al.*, 2008). The North China basin in the west has conjugate faults oriented approximately east–west and north–south. Three primary faults, including the east–west-trending Yuncheng fault, the north–south-trending Yishan fault, and the northwest-striking Cangni fault, delineate the boundaries of the YCM area (Fig. 2). The YCM displays a well-defined stratigraphic succession that ranges from Archean crystalline basement to Cenozoic sequences. The Upper Paleozoic strata contain significant coal-bearing formations, whereas Quaternary unconsolidated sediments dominate the surface materials in this region. In addition, the Cangni fault is noteworthy for its significant Quaternary activity, characterized by left-lateral strike-slip movement (Chao *et al.*, 1992). It has been identified as the seismogenic fault responsible for the **M** 7.0 earthquake that occurred in 179 B.C. (Chao *et al.*, 2012). Furthermore, we illustrate the hypocentral distribution of the 2017 **M** 4.0 earthquake sequence on the geological map and observe that these earthquakes are concentrated near the northern segment of the Cangni fault. This spatial correlation suggests a direct tectonic relationship associated with the earthquake sequence.

Data and Method

Seismic data

We collect seismic arrival-time data from provincial seismic observational bulletins of the China Seismic Networks Center to conduct seismic tomography. A total of 1138 earthquakes, including both deep and shallow events with at least 8 arrivals, were chosen from 2008 to 2023, and these earthquakes were recorded at 135 permanent seismic stations. The depths at which these earthquakes occur vary from 0 to 30 km, whereas the local magnitudes (M_L) range from 0.2 to 4. As shown in Figure 3a, the dense coverage of local seismic stations ensures the reliability of our results. The distribution of seismic ray

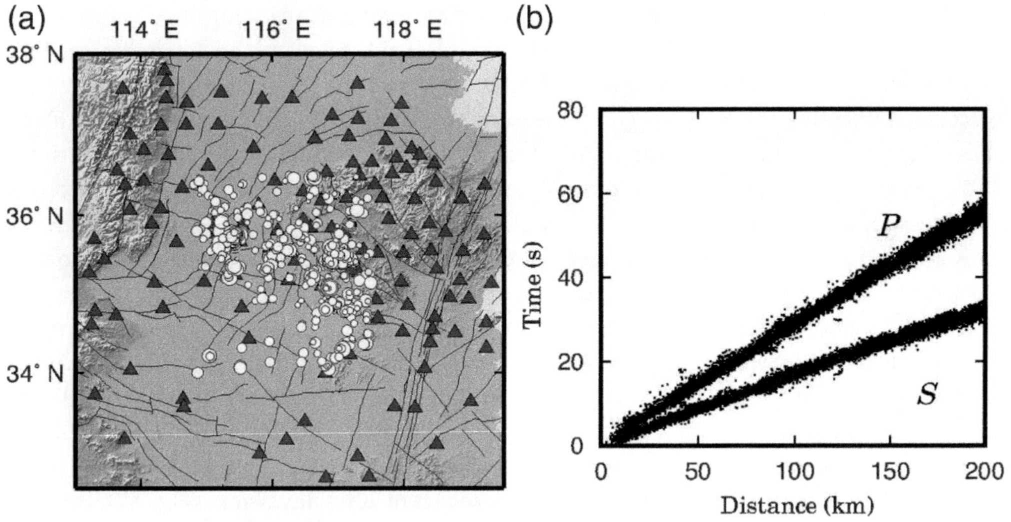

Figure 3. (a) Seismic stations (blue triangles) and earthquakes (open circles) used in this study. (b) Travel-time curve of *P* and *S* waves. The color version of this figure is available only in the electronic edition.

paths within the study area is shown in Figure S1, available in the supplemental material to this article. Most of the ray paths are dominant in the HZ and YCM areas. In addition, the ray paths from distant stations can pass through the lower crust, thereby providing a good ray path coverage for the lower crust. From the selected events, we obtain 6810 *P*-wave and 5325 *S*-wave absolute travel times for velocity inversion and hypocenter relocation (Fig. 3b). We further collect high-quality waveform data from seismic stations with epicentral distances less than 200 km to invert for the source parameters of the 2017 **M** 4 earthquake.

Seismic tomography

We employ the double-difference tomography (tomoDD) technique to obtain the event location and invert for velocity structure, as proposed by Zhang and Thurber (2003, 2006). This method has been widely applied to construct regional velocity models (Guo *et al.*, 2018; Zhang *et al.*, 2019; Zhang, Ji, *et al.*, 2022; Zhang, Li, and Hu, 2022). The tomoDD method utilizes not only absolute arrival times but also differential times between pairs of earthquakes to derive *P*- and *S*-wave velocity structures, as well as hypocenter locations. By calculating the difference in travel times between neighboring earthquakes, the structure near the source region can be well resolved. In the tomoDD inversion scheme, we construct 262,677 differential *P* times and 209,582 differential *S* times. The average separation of selected earthquake pairs is ~4 km. We investigate various grid spacing values of 0.1°, 0.2°, and 0.3° in both latitude and longitude directions. Based on previous tomography results (Zhang *et al.*, 2024), the study region is parameterized into grid points with intervals of 0.2° × 0.2° on the horizontal plane, and the depth layers are located at 0, 2, 5, 10, 15, 20, 25, and 30 km in the vertical direction. The initial reference model was taken from Xin *et al.* (2018). It is evident that the lateral structural variation of the initial velocity model is not pronounced (Fig. S2). We also selected the optimal values of damping and smoothing parameters through a trade-off analysis between data misfit and model variance, thereby improving the stability of the solution (Fig. S3).

Source parameter inversion

We first invert the focal mechanism of the 2017 **M** 4 earthquake using the general cut-and-paste method (Zhu and Ben-Zion, 2013). The inversion searches the best combination of strike, dip, and rake values to fit the real and synthetic waveforms, and it allows different time shifts for the *Pnl*- and *S* (or surface)-wave segments which can better reduce the dependence of the focal mechanism on velocity structure (Zhang, Ji, *et al.*, 2022). In our inversion, the synthetic waveforms are calculated by the frequency–wavenumber integration technique (Zhu and Rivera, 2002), and the *Pnl* waves are band-pass filtered between 0.05 and 0.5 Hz, whereas the *S* (or surface) segments are band-pass filtered between 0.02 and 0.2 Hz. Furthermore, to obtain the earthquake rupture length, we followed the methods of Lancieri *et al.* (2012) and Satriano (2024) to estimate the stress drop and source dimension. The displacement spectrum is expressed as

$$\Omega_0(f) = \frac{FR_{\theta,\varphi}}{4\pi\rho R\beta^3} \cdot \frac{M_0}{1 + \left(\frac{f}{f_c}\right)^2} \cdot e^{-\pi f t^*}, \tag{1}$$

in which M_0 is the seismic moment, and f_c denotes the corner frequency, $R_{\theta,\phi}$ is the radiation pattern, and R refers to the hypocentral distance, F is the free surface amplification factor, with ρ, β, and t^* representing density, wave velocity, and attenuation parameter, respectively. The inversion employs a truncated Newton algorithm to minimize the least-squares norm between the synthetic and observed spectra (Satriano, 2024). The source radius r is derived from the corner frequency f_c. k is a nondimensional parameter that depends on the source model. Subsequently, the static stress drop $\Delta\sigma$ is calculated based on the assumption of a circular rupture model:

$$r = \frac{k\beta}{f_c}, \tag{2}$$

$$\Delta\sigma = \frac{7}{16}\frac{M_0}{r^3}. \quad (3)$$

In this study, we use the *S* phase of each seismic station record to invert separately the spectrum. To accurately identify the *S* window, we manually picked the *S* phase arrival time. Finally, the seismic moment, stress drop, and source radius were computed by taking the average results of each seismic station.

Coulomb stress calculation

The Coulomb failure stress change (ΔCFS) is employed to explore earthquake triggering mechanisms (Toda and Stein, 2020). To compute Coulomb stress change on a receiver fault imposed by a source fault, the Coulomb 3.4 program is used in this study (Toda *et al.*, 2011). Stresses are computed in a homogeneous elastic half-space, and the shear modulus *G* was established as 3.2×10^5 bar, with a Poisson ratio of 0.25 according to the seismic velocity model derived from our tomography inversion analysis. The effective friction coefficient μ' is generally assumed to be between 0.4 and 0.8 for rough faults with relatively low cumulative slip, and between 0.0 and 0.4 for smooth faults with high cumulative slip or elevated pore pressure (Parsons *et al.*, 1999). In this study, we select $\mu' = 0.4$ as a conservative estimate, representing a midpoint between the possible extremes (Ma *et al.*, 2005). The ΔCFS calculation requires knowledge of the parameters of the source fault and the faulting mechanism of the receiver fault (Hainzl *et al.*, 2010; Cattania *et al.*, 2014). Because of the unknown faulting mechanism of the shallow small-magnitude earthquakes, we arbitrarily resolved the ΔCFS on receiver faults with the same mechanism as the mainshock, which is commonly adopted in previous studies (Toda and Stein, 2000). The source parameters derived from the above source parameter inversion are utilized to investigate the stress modulation following the 2017 *M* 4 earthquake.

Results

Tomography image and earthquake location

To evaluate the spatial resolution of the tomographic images, a checkerboard test is performed. The checkerboard models are arranged with alternating ±5% velocity anomalies based on the initial velocities. Synthetic arrivals are calculated using the same source-station geometry. These synthetic travel times are subsequently inverted to obtain the velocity anomalies using the same parameter setting. The results of the checkerboard tests for both *P* and *S* models demonstrate that the size (0.2° × 0.2°) and amplitude of both positive and negative anomalies can be effectively resolved from 0 to 25 km depths (Fig. 4). We conducted an additional checkerboard test by alternately inputting velocity anomalies with ±10% (Fig. S4). The results indicate that the pattern of anomalies can be effectively recovered. Although the amplitudes of the velocity anomalies are relatively poorly resolved, the overall pattern remains well defined. In addition, we show a vertical checkerboard profile traversing the HZ and YCM regions, demonstrating good resolution throughout these critical structural zones (Fig. S5). We also calculate the derivative weighted sum (DWS) values to assess the model quality. The DWS is a weighted measure of the ray path density near a given inversion point (Zhang *et al.*, 2019). The DWS values demonstrate that the HZ and YCM regions have good ray-path coverage (DWS > 100, Fig. S6; Thurber *et al.*, 2007), which aligns well with resolved regions from the checkerboard test. Based on the recovered patterns, we focus our discussions on the features within these areas.

We successfully relocated 1058 events using tomoDD with average errors in longitude and latitude of 120 and 105 m, respectively, and an average error in depth of 203 m. Notably, the *P*- and *S*-wave arrival-time residuals are more concentrated around zero after inversion (Fig. S7), and the average root mean square (rms) of the travel-time residuals decreased from 0.53 s before the inversion to 0.06 s after the inversion. Based on the comprehensive analysis presented earlier, we can conclude that the velocity structures and earthquake locations derived from our study are reliable.

Figure 5 illustrates the *P* and *S* velocity results at various depths. The *P*-wave and *S*-wave velocity structures exhibit significant lateral heterogeneity within the crust. The velocity structures, ranging from 2 to 5 km in depth, generally correlate with surface geology. This correlation is demonstrated by the higher V_P and V_S anomalies in the mountainous region to the east and the lower anomalies in the basin to the west (Figs. 1 and 5). From 10 to 25 km depth, the middle and lower crusts exhibit low-velocity anomalies beneath the YCM area, which gradually expand. This suggests that the low-velocity structures likely have deep extensions. Moreover, a prominent characteristic of relocated earthquakes is that most occur in the transition zone between high- and low-velocity anomalies from 5 to 20 km depth. In the YCM region, a significant proportion of earthquakes have been recorded at depths shallower than 2 km, indicating that seismic activity in this area is predominantly shallow and exhibits a clear clustering pattern.

To study the relationship between earthquake occurrences and velocity distribution, we present a vertical profile of *P*-wave and *S*-wave velocities across the YCM region. A significant observation from this profile is the presence of both low-*P*-wave and *S*-wave velocity anomalies within the lower crust beneath the HZ and YCM regions. These low-velocity anomalies represent upwelling of the deep hot materials induced by the lithospheric keel removal or delamination (He, 2020). Nevertheless, these velocity anomalies and the associated earthquakes exhibit complex patterns, characterized by variations in both velocity and focal depth (Fig. 6). In the HZ region, the relocated earthquakes reveal an almost vertical fault plane. This fault extends downward to a depth of 10 km and represents the southern segment of the north–south-trending Lanliao fault (Li *et al.*, 2021). In contrast, the earthquakes in the YCM area are categorized into two distinct clusters based on their depths: one cluster is deeper,

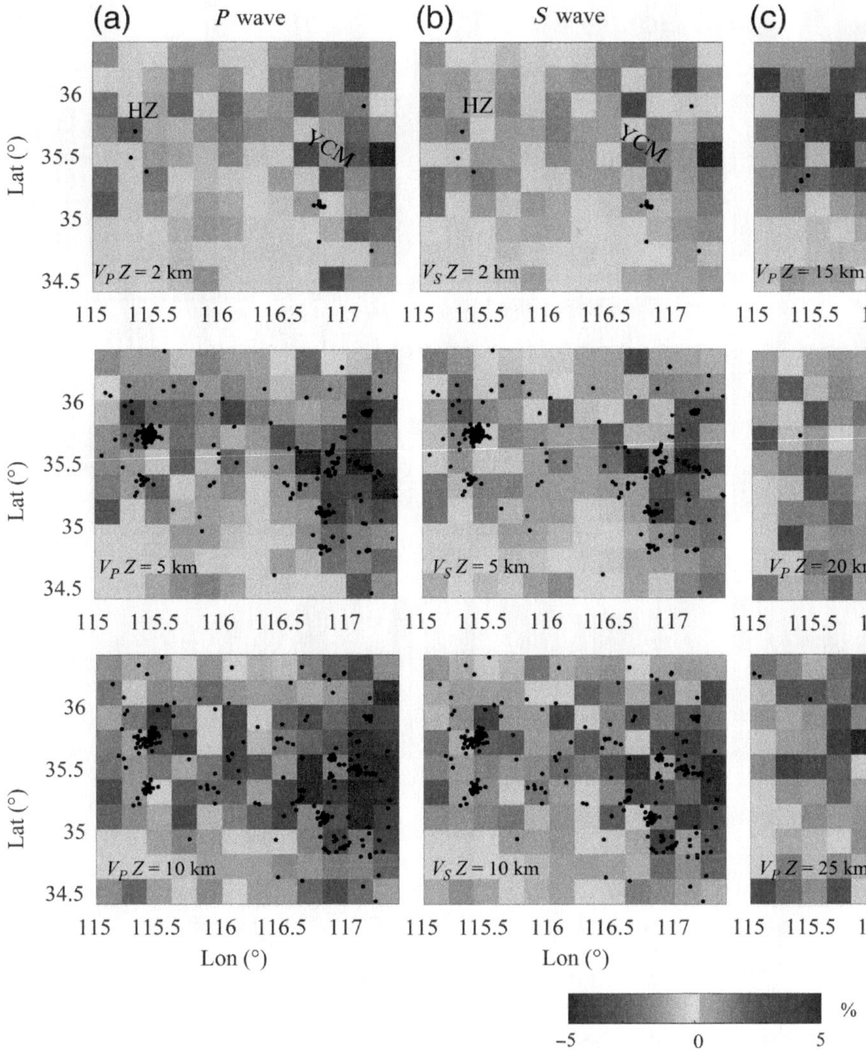

Figure 4. Checkerboard test on the (a,c) *P*- and (b,d) *S*-wave velocity anomalies at different depths. The cell size is 0.2° × 0.2°, and the depth of each layer is indicated in the lower-left corner of the corresponding panel. The velocity perturbation scale is shown at the bottom. Earthquakes occurring at a depth of 2 km were limited to a thickness of 2 km, and events at the other depths occurred within a layer of 5 km thickness bound to each slice. The color version of this figure is available only in the electronic edition.

with focal depths ranging from 15 to 23 km, and the 2017 **M** 4 earthquake is located in the lower crust (Fig. 6); the other cluster consists of shallow seismicity (<2 km), with a possibility of extending up to the surface. To explore the relationship between shallow and deep earthquakes, we will further examine the source parameters of the 2017 **M** 4 earthquake in the following discussions.

Source parameters of the 2017 M 4 earthquake

The waveform inversion of the 2017 **M** 4 earthquake yields a strike-slip focal mechanism, with estimated uncertainties in strike, dip, and rake all below 8° (Fig. 7). To further validate the reliability of the **M** 4 event depth, a grid-search scheme was employed to identify optimal solutions at various depths. The misfit function reaches its minimum value at 22 km (Fig. S8), which is consistent with the results obtained from the tomoDD method. The inversion results indicate that the best double-couple solution for the strike/dip/rake angle of nodal plane I is 311°/78°/22°, whereas that of nodal plane II is 216°/68°/162°. Given the refined earthquake locations (Fig. 8a), it is evident that nodal plane I aligns with the approximately northwest-west direction of the earthquake sequences, implying that the 2017 **M** 4 earthquake was caused by a rupture on a northwest-west fault. Further analysis, using waveform records from eight seismic stations (Fig. S9), reveals the stress drop and rupture size. The spectrum at each seismic station is inverted for both the M_0 and the f_c parameters. We observe that the M_0 and f_c at different stations exhibit azimuthal-dependent variations, with the inverted values being relatively higher in the southeast direction (Figs. S10 and S11). Although M_0 and f_c are influenced by path effects, rupture directivity, and the evolution of multiple sources (Schliwa and Gabriel, 2023), these azimuthal patterns indicate a southeastward rupture

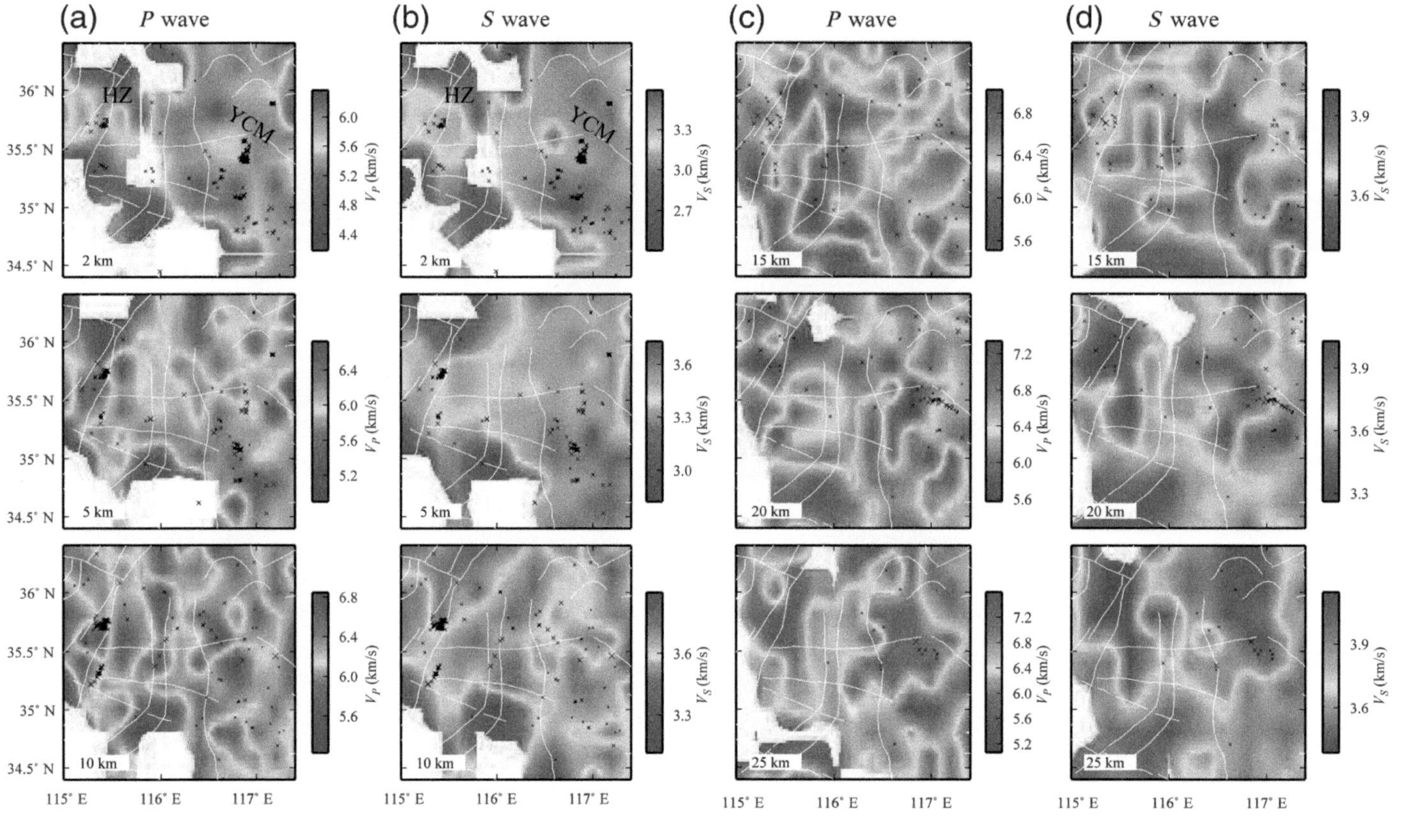

Figure 5. Map views of the (a,c) *P*- and (b,d) *S*-wave tomographic images at different depth slices. The white line segments represent the surface fault traces, and the black crosses denote the earthquakes. The layer depth is shown in the lower-left corner of the corresponding panel. The earthquakes represented on each slice correspond to those depicted in Figure 4. The color version of this figure is available only in the electronic edition.

directivity for the 2017 **M** 4 event. This inferred rupture direction aligns with the aftershock distribution (Fig. 8c). The final results are computed by averaging over the seismic stations. The source parameters that provide the best fit suggest a seismic moment of 1.7×10^{14} N · m and a corner frequency of 4.86 Hz (Fig. S12). Concurrently, the stress drop and source rupture radius are determined to be 8.3 MPa and 268 m, respectively. Previous studies have shown that the stress drop for earthquakes in the lower crust is about ∼4–9 MPa (Oth, 2013; Hauksson, 2014; Sunilkumar *et al.*, 2023), which is consistent with our results.

The spatiotemporal evolution of seismic sequences in the YCM region is illustrated in Figure 8. The vertical cross-section AB reveals hypocenter distributions predominantly clustered within two distinct depth intervals: 0–2 km (cluster 1) and 15–25 km (cluster 2). Using the 2017 **M** 4 earthquake as a reference event, we analyze the depth distributions of clusters 1 and 2 seismicity. Our observations reveal distinct spatiotemporal patterns: cluster 1 demonstrates consistent seismic activity throughout the study period, and cluster 2 exhibits a progressive westward migration of hypocenters at greater depths over time. The migration direction in cluster 2 aligns with the northwest-west-striking Cangni fault (Fig. 2). The hypocenters are spatially concentrated within a linearly distributed zone that deepens progressively westward. The deepening trend suggests rupture propagation along a planar fault structure. We consider the spatiotemporal evolution of cluster 2 as representative of deep-seated fault activation (Fig. 8b,c).

To further quantify variations in seismic activity before and after the 2017 event, we performed a magnitude–time analysis across the same period (Fig. 8d). The results indicate a significant increase in seismic frequency within cluster 1 following the **M** 4 earthquake. Meanwhile, we observed a notable decrease in seismicity frequency between 2019 and 2020 within cluster 1, a period that coincided with the COVID-19 pandemic. This decline may reflect a reduction in seismic activity due to diminished mining operations (Fig. 8d). In contrast, cluster 2 shows no statistically significant change in event frequency, highlighting divergent triggering mechanisms between the two clusters (Fig. 8e).

Coulomb stress change distribution

We calculated the ΔCFS imparted by the 2017 **M** 4 earthquake to assess the potential effects on shallow seismic activity. The nodal plane I (strike/dip/rake angle: 311°/78°/22°) is utilized to specify the strike, dip, and rake of the source fault and the receiver fault. Following the method described in the Coulomb stress calculation section, the ΔCFS is resolved along

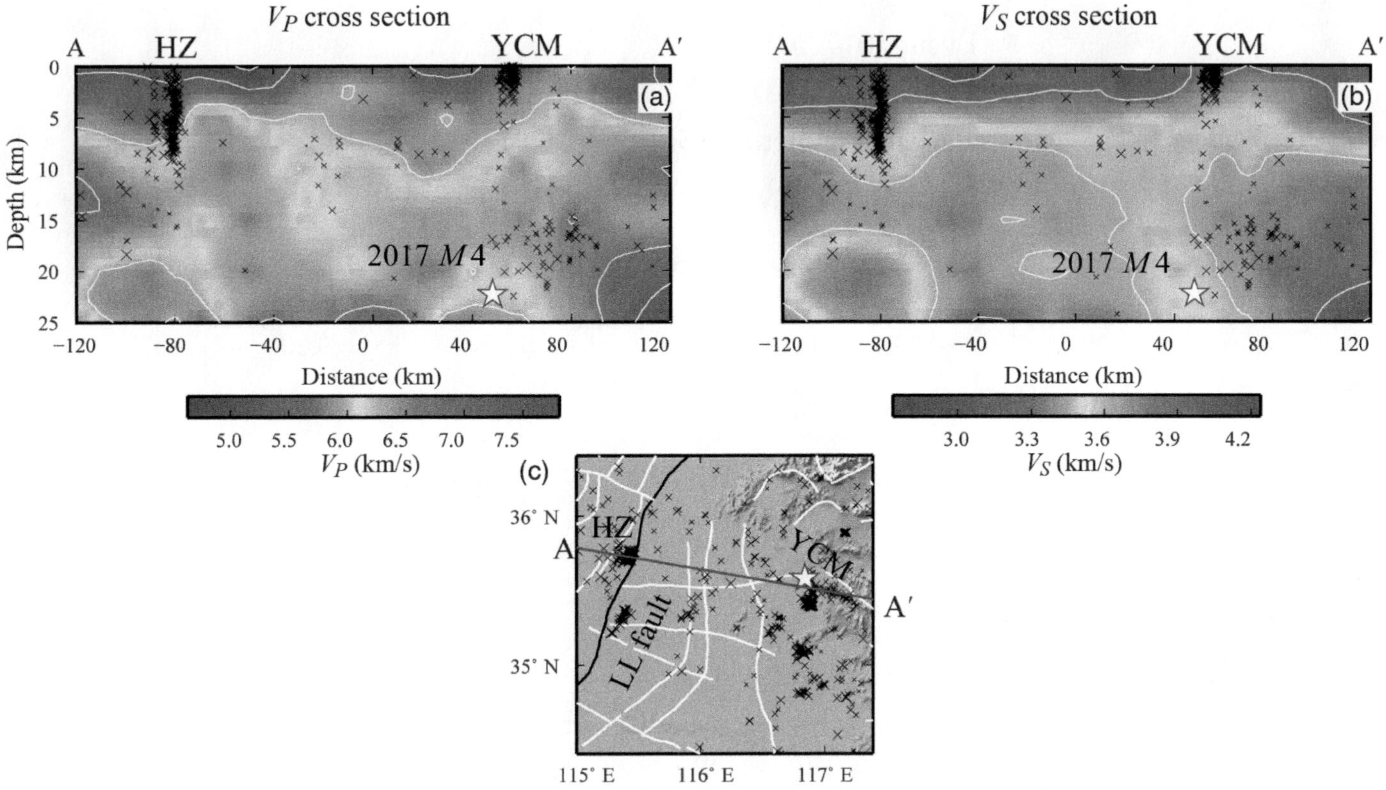

Figure 6. Cross sections of (a) *P*-wave and (b) *S*-wave tomography images. The white stars represent the locations of the 2017 *M* 4 earthquake, and the black crosses represent the **M** < 4.0 events. (c) The location of the cross-section A–A′. The LL fault refers to the north–south-trending Lanliao fault, as delineated by Li *et al.* (2021). The color version of this figure is available only in the electronic edition.

the fault that is approximately represented by profile A–B, as illustrated in Figure 8. Figure 9 shows that both the shallow seismicity and the deep earthquakes are located in areas of positive ΔCFS. However, the ΔCFS values at both depths are far below 0.1 bar, which is commonly accepted as the stress-triggering threshold (King *et al.*, 1994). Although the stress drop can reach up to 8.3 MPa, as previously mentioned, the ΔCFS level within the shallow depth is subtle. This is because the static stress change is known to decay according to r^{-3} (in which r is the distance between the observation point and the source point) in the far field for the case of a point source in an infinite elastic medium (Aki and Richards, 2002). To minimize uncertainties in the ΔCFS calculations, we conducted experiments with effective friction coefficient μ' values ranging from 0.0 to 0.8. The results within the shallow depth were found to be insensitive to changes in μ' (Fig. S13).

Discussion

Mechanism of the 2017 M 4 lower crust earthquake

Earthquakes within the continental crust of the North China basin typically occur at depths of up to 15 km (Zhang *et al.*, 2011). The physical mechanisms underlying earthquakes in the lower crust (>20 km) continue to be a topic of debate. This is primarily due to the expectation that the rock at these depths would exhibit ductile rather than brittle behavior. Proposed mechanisms include thermal-runaway plastic instabilities, Coulomb stress transfer between earthquakes, or deep fluid-induced failure (Prieto *et al.*, 2013; Alvizuri and Hetényi, 2019). In our 3D velocity models, pronounced low-velocity anomalies characterized by reductions in *P*- and *S*-wave velocities are found below 20 km in the HZ and YCM source areas. Previous studies have demonstrated that the velocities of rocks in the middle to lower crust are significantly influenced by fluid (Singh *et al.*, 2012; Zhang *et al.*, 2019; Fonzetti *et al.*, 2024).

The North China basin is located to the east of the North China craton. Numerous prior studies on seismic tomography have largely concurred that the destruction of the North China craton is associated with the westward deep subduction of the western Pacific plate (Huang and Zhao, 2006; An *et al.*, 2011; Lei, 2012; Tian and Zhao, 2013; He, 2020; Guo *et al.*, 2024). Deep dehydration reactions from the flat slab result in buoyant, hydrous upwelling, which can promote melting, subsequently leading to the thinning and fracturing of the underlying continental lithosphere beneath the North China basin (Fig. S14). Since the Mesozoic era, the North China basin has undergone considerable lithospheric thinning, with its thickness sharply decreasing from over 200 km during the Paleozoic to roughly 60–80 km at present (Xu, 2004). Because this thinning progresses, upwelling hot material

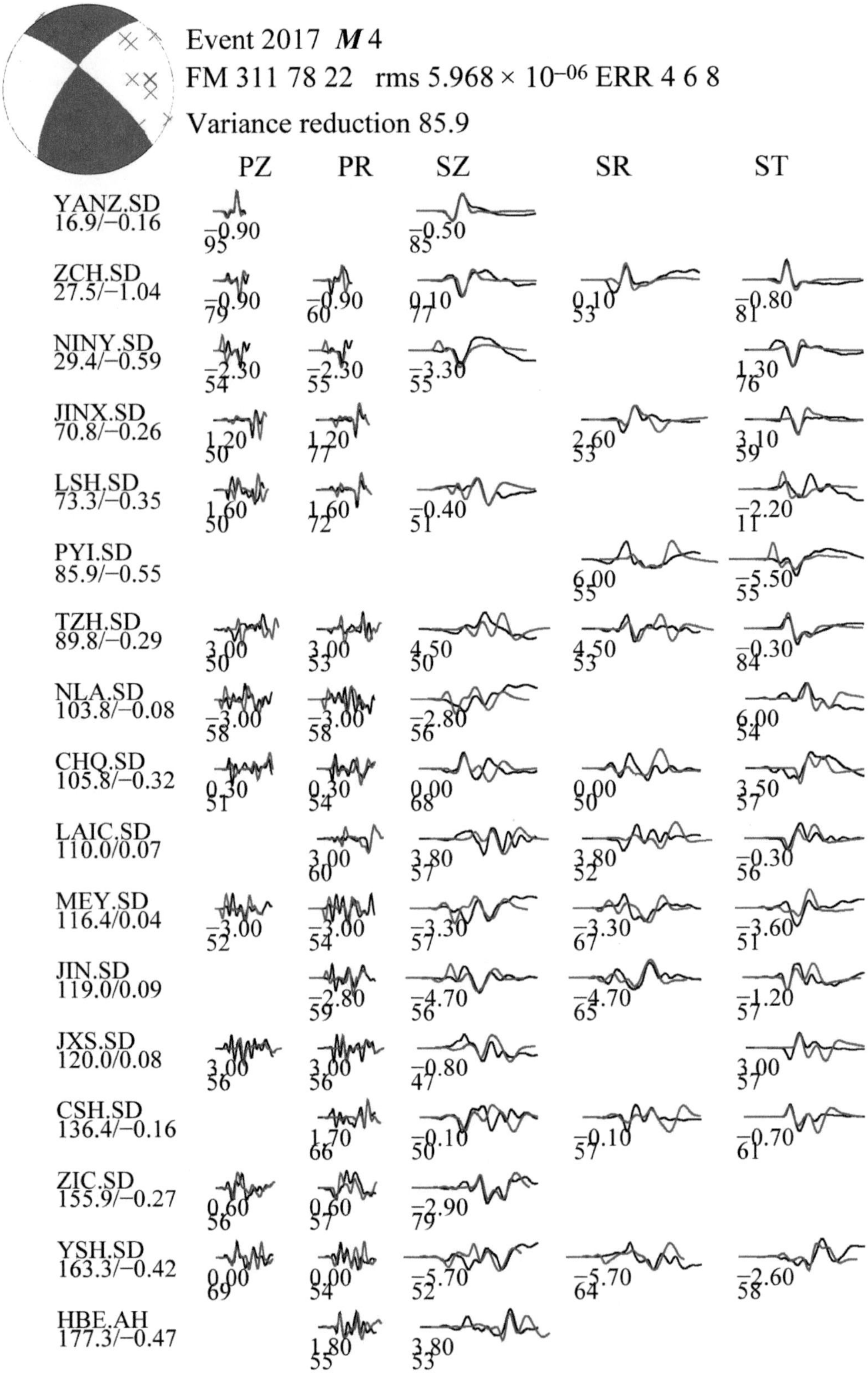

Figure 7. Focal mechanism of the 2017 *M* 4 earthquake and the comparison between synthetic (red) and observed (black) waveforms. The focal mechanism plot is the focal mechanism; the red crosses in the focal mechanism plot indicate the seismic station azimuth distribution. The right box provides the best-fitting fault nodal plane solution, along with the root mean square (rms) of the inversion and the variance reduction value of waveform fitting. The numbers below each trace are the relative time shift and cross-correlation coefficient in percentage; the five waveform columns from left to right are *Pnl* waves on the vertical (PZ), radial (PR) components, and surface waves on the vertical (SZ), radial (SR), and transverse (ST) components. The station names are given on the left, and the numbers below each station are the epicentral distance (kilometers) and relative time shift (seconds). The color version of this figure is available only in the electronic edition.

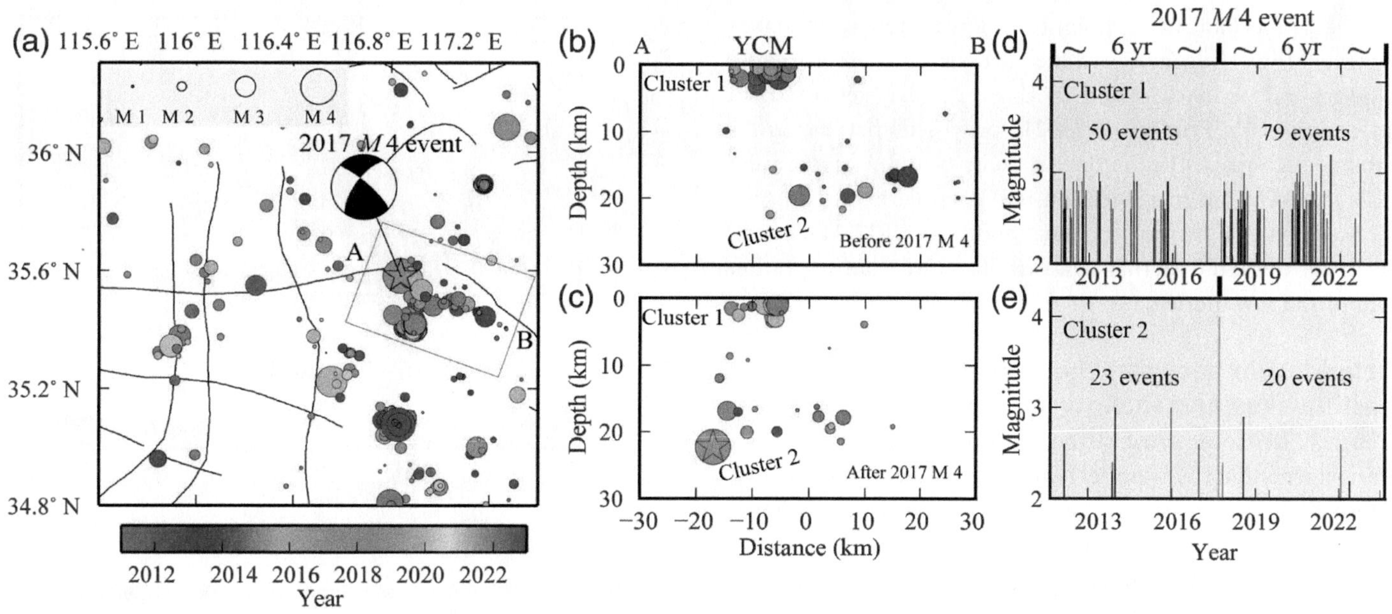

Figure 8. (a) Spatial location of relocated earthquakes in the horizontal plane. Vertical cross sections of earthquakes occurred before (b) and after (c) the 2017 **M** 4 event. Magnitude–time sequence diagram of the cluster 1 (d) and the cluster 2 (e). The numerical values in panels (d) and (e) represent the seismic events that occurred during the corresponding period. The color version of this figure is available only in the electronic edition.

induces thermal weakening of the crust, reducing its mechanical strength and enhancing extensional tectonic activity (Duan *et al.*, 2007). Local seismic velocity structures in the upper mantle and lower crust also reveal extensive low-velocity zones beneath our study region (Dong *et al.*, 2021; Feng *et al.*, 2022). In addition, receiver function analyses suggest a shallow Moho discontinuity (~30 km) and a relatively high Poisson's ratio within the crust, indicating the intrusion of hot materials from the mantle into the crust (Gu *et al.*, 2022). Furthermore, with the constraint of the upper-mantle temperature derived from seismic velocity and the surface temperature data from meteorological station observations, Sun *et al.* (2013) conducted a comprehensive calculation of the 3D thermal structure in the continental lithosphere beneath the North China basin. The findings reveal the presence of an extensive, weak ductile lower crust (Fig. S15). The pronounced brittle–ductile transition zone within the lower crust is prone to the accumulation of elastic strain, thereby serving as a seismogenic zone favoring earthquake nucleation. Moreover, previous studies have documented instances of deep crust earthquakes in the North China basin. For instance, the M 3.0 Wen'an earthquake of 19 April 2016 occurred at a depth of 18 km, whereas the **M** 4.3 Yongqing earthquake in 2018 had a focal depth of 19 km (Li *et al.*, 2020).

Thus, the low-velocity anomalies identified in this study indicate the presence of deep fluids within the middle-lower crust, providing critical evidence in support of the hypothesis that such fluids are localized at seismogenic depths, which correspond to the brittle–ductile transition zone (20–26 km) within the lower crust (Sun *et al.*, 2013). However, the lower crustal materials in the HZ and YCM areas exhibit structural heterogeneities. In the HZ region, seismic activity delineates a vertical dipping planar structure that is spatially correlated with the Lanliao fault (Fig. 6). We speculate that the sharp material contrast across the Lanliao fault results in seismicity extending from the surface to a depth of 10 km.

By contrast, in the YCM region, there are two earthquake clusters. One of them is beneath the coal mine area, and the other is located in the middle-lower crust (Fig. 8b,c, clusters 1 and 2). Cluster 1 exhibits a magnitude range of 1.0–3.2, and cluster 2 spans 0.2–4.0. The 2017 **M** 4 event belongs to the lower cluster occurring at the top of the low-velocity anomaly, significantly exceeding the hypocentral distribution observed in the HZ region. Based on the analysis of the surface fault trace distribution (Fig. 2) and the seismotectonic constraints derived from focal mechanism solutions (Fig. 7), we interpret this deep earthquake as resulting from the reactivation of the Cangni fault, which exhibits characteristic left-lateral strike-slip movement. The hypocentral parameters and nodal plane solutions are consistent with the slip along this pre-existing crustal fault.

The nucleation of this **M** 4 event is likely associated with deep fluids within the lower crust, as illustrated by tomographic anomalies shown in Figure 6 and the westward migration of hypocenters in Figure 8. Our analysis suggests that deep crustal fluids infiltrating the basement fault zone induce progressive increases in pore-fluid pressure, thereby reducing the effective normal stress along the fault plane (Zhang *et al.*, 2019). This process culminates in earthquake failure when critical fluid pressure thresholds are exceeded, consistent with fault reactivation models proposed by Katayama *et al.* (2018).

The same mechanism is presented in lower crust earthquakes beneath the Himalayas, where dehydration-driven stress changes induce crack opening (Alvizuri and Hetényi, 2019). In addition, La Rosa *et al.* (2021) proposed that the lower crustal earthquakes in the border faults of the Afar rift were also caused by magma intrusion into deep parts of the crust. Consequently, a plausible explanation for the 2017 **M** 4 earthquake in our study is that it was induced by fluid migration within the lower crust.

Relationship between the lower crust earthquakes and shallow seismicity

The 2017 M 4 lower crust earthquake provides a case for examining interactions between tectonic and coal mining seismicity. The possible mechanism can be grouped into two main categories: (1) the Coulomb stress changes resulting from the preceding earthquake may facilitate failure along favorably oriented faults, and (2) the long-term coal extraction activities contribute to the instability of pre-existing faults.

Studies such as those by King *et al.* (1994), Stein *et al.* (1999), and Toda *et al.* (2005) establish that ΔCFS perturbations of 0.1 bar can trigger failure on nearby faults, with delays in the response that may vary from seconds to years. In some cases, even the small stresses produced by solid earth tides (~0.01 bar) appear to play a role in the triggering of earthquakes (Métivier *et al.*, 2009). Within mining environments, this framework has also been adapted to explain how both earthquakes and induced stress changes interact. For example, Orlecka-Sikora (2010) demonstrated that mining-induced seismic events preferentially occurred in zones of stress amplification caused by prior earthquakes. Their findings revealed a lower stress threshold for triggering seismicity in mining areas, with statistically significant event clustering in regions experiencing ΔCFS values ≥0.05 bar. Similarly, Wang *et al.* (2015) observed a significant seismicity rate increase in the coal mine region during two tectonic earthquakes.

In the YCM region, the spatial clustering of shallow seismicity corresponds to areas characterized by positive Coulomb stress changes (ΔCFS) generated by the 2017 **M** 4 earthquake (Fig. 9). However, the calculated ΔCFS values at shallow depths are notably low (<0.001 bar), falling significantly below the commonly accepted stress-triggering threshold of 0.1 bar (King *et al.*, 1994). These results indicate that the stress perturbations induced by the 2017 **M** 4 earthquake are insufficient to induce stress-triggering effects and lack a direct causative relationship with subsequent shallow seismic activity. Numerous observations from dynamic triggering studies demonstrate that coseismic stress transfer predominantly occurs during the passage of seismic waves (e.g., Peng *et al.*, 2009; Wu *et al.*, 2011), with certain cases exhibiting a longer period of triggering (Peng *et al.*, 2011). Moreover, areas with induced seismicity are more sensitive to dynamic triggering processes (Van Der Elst *et al.*, 2013). Although our analysis excludes static stress transfer associated with the 2017 **M** 4 event as a viable mechanism, remote dynamic triggering effects remain plausible and cannot be conclusively ruled out.

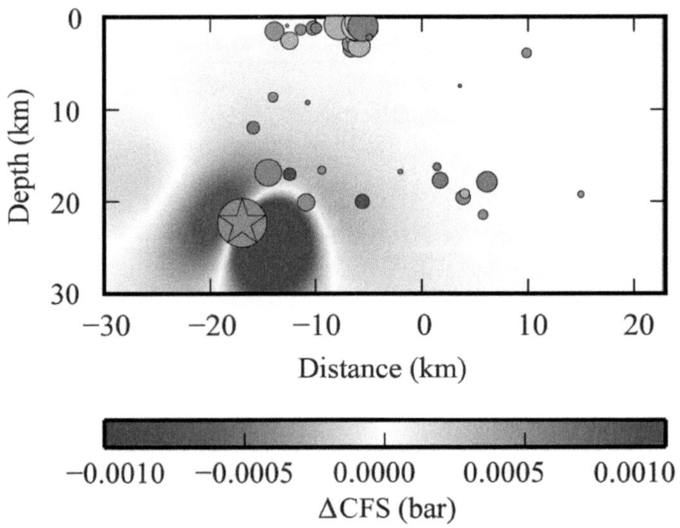

Figure 9. Coulomb failure stress change distribution generated by the 2017 **M** 4 earthquake along the cross section AB in Figure 8. The color of earthquakes is consistent with that shown in Figure 8. The color version of this figure is available only in the electronic edition.

In addition, mining extraction activities are widely recognized as the main factor for induced seismicity in the coal mine area (Li *et al.*, 2007; Wang *et al.*, 2014; Yan *et al.*, 2025). To advance this understanding, we further investigate the potential relationship between coal production and shallow seismicity within the YCM area. The shallow earthquakes typically occur at depths of less than 2 km and are predominantly concentrated in mining regions. Although granular monthly production data remain unavailable, operational reports from YCM Group (website accessible in Data and Resources) indicate a cumulative output increase of 6%–10% over the past six years, coinciding with the implementation of intelligent deep-mining technologies initiated in 2017 and the extraction of deep coal seams. Compared with shallow resource extraction, deep mining typically operates under conditions of high stress, elevated temperatures, and high water pressure. The disturbances generated by these activities may lead to sudden and unpredictable failures of the rockmass (Ranjith *et al.*, 2017). Meanwhile, this upward production trend exhibits a temporal correlation with a statistically significant rise in shallow seismic event frequency during the same period (Fig. 8d). As demonstrated in the Source parameters of the 2017 **M** 4 earthquake section, a significant decline in seismicity was observed between 2019 and 2020, coinciding with the onset of the COVID-19 pandemic. This reduction is likely attributable to decreased mining operations resulting from pandemic-induced disruptions. Li *et al.* (2007) conducted a systematic investigation of mining-induced seismicity in China, establishing a correlation between the increased seismic frequency and the intensity of natural resource extraction. Concurrently,

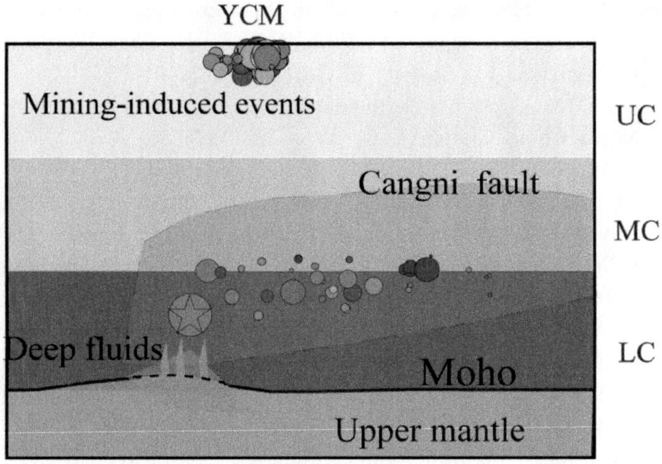

Figure 10. Simplified sketch showing the mechanism of the lower crust earthquakes and the shallow seismic activity. The color version of this figure is available only in the electronic edition.

Wang *et al.* (2023) identified that accelerated movement of thick and hard-rock strata directly contributes to enhanced seismicity through elastic energy accumulation. The spatial–temporal correlation between production intensity and seismic activity supports the hypothesis that coal extraction has a substantial impact on shallow seismicity in the YCM region.

Through an integrated analysis of Coulomb stress changes and observed swarm-like patterns of seismic activity, we propose that the static stress changes associated with the M 4 lower crustal earthquake exhibit negligible capacity to perturb shallow seismicity. The intensity of coal mine extraction, particularly when extended to greater depths, leads to a higher incidence of mining-induced events. Spatial and temporal seismicity rate anomalies correlate with the evolution of mining operations, suggesting a causative relationship between seismic events and mining operations.

Conclusion

This study provides new constraints on the mechanisms governing lower crustal and shallow seismic events in the YCM region through integrated analysis of seismicity patterns, velocity structure, and mining activities (Fig. 10). The observed westward migration of hypocenters within the lower crust, coupled with the spatial correlation of the 2017 M 4 earthquake with a pronounced low-velocity anomaly, supports a model of fluid-driven fault activation. Relocated seismicity and tomographic imaging indicate that deep crustal fluids facilitate fault weakening, promoting earthquake nucleation in the lower crust. In contrast, shallow seismic activity in the coal mining region exhibits minimal mechanical linkage to the 2017 **M** 4 lower crust event because Coulomb stress changes from the latter did not perturb the near surface. Instead, the statistically significant increase in shallow event frequency aligns temporally with decades of subsurface resource extraction and the implementation of advanced mining technologies post-2017. Because the intensity and depth of mining operations increase, mining causes significant seismic activity. This correlation highlights the profound influence of anthropogenic production behaviors on shallow seismicity, emphasizing the need to differentiate between tectonically driven and mining-induced seismic hazards.

Data and Resources

The seismic arrival-time data from the China Earthquake Network Center are available at https://www.cenc.ac.cn/. The waveform data of the 2017 *M* 4 earthquake are available at http://www.esdc.ac.cn. The 3D velocity models are available from Github (https://github.com/zhanggw08). The operational reports from Yanzhou Coal Mining Group are accessible via www.yanzhoucoal.com.cn. All websites were last accessed in April 2025 (login required). The supplemental material includes reliability tests for tomoDD inversion, source parameters of the 2017 **M** 4 earthquake, uncertainties in Coulomb failure stress calculations, and other figures mentioned in the main article.

Declaration of Competing Interests

The authors acknowledge that there are no conflicts of interest recorded.

Acknowledgments

The authors thank Editor-in-Chief Allison Bent and two anonymous reviewers for their insightful comments and suggestions. This work is supported by the National Natural Science Foundation of China (42374117 and 42274179) and the Deep Earth Probe and Mineral Resources Exploration-National Science and Technology Major Project (2024ZD1000707). Most figures were generated using the Generic Mapping Tools (GMT) software (Wessel and Smith, 1998).

References

Aki, A., and P. G. Richards (2002). Quantitative Seismology Second Ed., University Science Books, Sausalito, California.

Alvizuri, C., and G. Hetényi (2019). Source mechanism of a lower crust earthquake beneath the Himalayas and its possible relation to metamorphism, *Tectonophysics* **769,** 128,153.

An, M., Y. Zhao, M. Feng, Y. Yang, Q. Xu, J. Hao, and C. Tan (2011). What resulted in new tectonic activities in the eastern North China craton in the Neogene? *Earth Sci. Front.* **18,** no. 3, 121–140.

Azhari, A., and U. Ozbay (2017). Investigating the effect of earthquakes on open pit mine slopes, *Int. J. Rock Mech. Min. Sci.* **100,** 218–228.

Cattania, C., S. Hainzl, L. Wang, F. Roth, and B. Enescu (2014). Propagation of Coulomb stress uncertainties in physics-based aftershock models, *J. Geophys. Res.* **119,** no. 10, pp. 7846–7864.

Chao, H., Z. Cui, and J. Li (1992). The northwestward faults in the Lu-Zhong region and their seismic activity characteristics during the late Quaternary period, *Seismol. J.* **2** (in Chinese).

Chao, H., S. Diao, and Z. Wang (2012). Textual research of the Qi-Chu earthquake of 179 BC and discussion on its seismogenic structure, *Seismol. J.* **2,** 211–227 (in Chinese).

Currenti, G., R. Napoli, A. Coco, and E. Privitera (2017). Effects of hydrothermal unrest on stress and deformation: insights from numerical modeling and application to Volcano Island (Italy), *Bull. Volcanol.* **79,** 28.

Ding, Y., E. Wang, Z. Li, X. Liu, T. Huang, and J. Yao (2023). Comprehensive early warning method of microseismic, acoustic emission, and electromagnetic radiation signals of rock burst based on deep learning, *Int. J. Rock Mech. Min. Sci.* **170,** 105,519.

Dong, X., D. Yang, F. Niu, S. Liu, and P. Tong (2021). Adjoint traveltime tomography unravels a scenario of horizontal mantle flow beneath the North China craton, *Sci. Rep.* **11,** 12,523.

Duan, Q., W. Tan, C. Yang, Y. Zhang, and Z. Yan (2007). A review on the late Mesozoic extensional tectonics on the eastern North China craton, *Progr. Geophys.* **22,** no. 2, 403–410.

Feng, J., H. Yao, L. Chen, and C. Li (2022). Ongoing lithospheric alteration of the North China craton revealed by surface-wave tomography and geodetic observations, *Geophys. Res. Lett.* **49,** e2022GL099403, doi: 10.1029/2022GL099403.

Fonzetti, R., L. Valoroso, P. De Gori, and C. Chiarabba (2024). Localization of deformation on faults driven by fluids during the L'aquila 2009 earthquake, *J. Geophys. Res.* **129,** e2024JB029075, doi: 10.1029/2024JB029075.

Gu, Q., D. Li, Z. Ding, Q. Kang, Y. Yu, J. Wang, K. Meng, H. Yang, H. Zhang, and Y. Lü (2022). Crustal structure characteristics beneath the Shandong-Jiangsu-Anhui segment of the Tan-Lu fault zone and its adjacent regions using receiver functions, *Chin. J. Geophys.* **65,** no. 9, 3280–3296 (in Chinese).

Guo, H., H. Zhang, and B. Froment (2018). Structural control on earthquake behaviors revealed by high-resolution Vp/Vs imaging along the Gofar transform fault, East Pacific Rise, *Earth Planet. Sci. Lett.* **499,** 243–255.

Guo, H., D. Zhao, and Z. Ding (2024). Anisotropic tomography and mantle dynamics of the North China craton, *Geophys. J. Int.* **236,** no. 3, 1455–1470.

Hainzl, S., G. Zöller, and R. Wang (2010). Impact of the receiver fault distribution on aftershock activity, *J. Geophys. Res.* **115,** no. B5.

Hauksson, E (2014). Average stress drops of southern California earthquakes in the context of crustal geophysics: Implications for fault zone healing, *Pure Appl. Geophys.* **172,** no. 5, 1359–1370.

He, C. (2020). Upwelling mantle plume and lithospheric delamination beneath the North China craton, *Phys. Earth Planet. Int.* **306,** 106,548.

Huang, J., and D. Zhao (2006). High-resolution mantle tomography of China and surrounding regions, *J. Geophys. Res.* **111,** no. B9, doi: 10.1029/2005JB004066.

Huang, Y., S. Ma, X. Li, and Y. Shao (2023). Advances in experiments and numerical simulations on the effects of stress perturbations on fault slip, *Earthq. Res. Adv.* **3,** no. 3, 100,220.

Katayama, I., A. Nicolas, and A. Schubnel (2018). Fluid-induced fracturing of initially damaged granite triggered by pore pressure buildup, *Geophys. Res. Lett.* **45,** 7488–7495.

Kilb, D., J. Gomberg, and P. Bodin (2000). Triggering of earthquake aftershocks by dynamic stresses, *Nature* **408,** 570–574.

King, G., R. Stein, and J. Lin (1994). Static stress changes and the triggering of earthquakes, *Bull. Seismol. Soc. Am.* **78,** no. 3.

La Rosa, A., D. Keir, C. Doubre, F. San i, G. Corti, S. Leroy, A. Ayele, and C. Pagli (2021). Lower crustal earthquakes in the March 2018 sequence along the western Margin of Afar, *Geochem. Geophys. Geosyst.* **22,** e2020GC009614, doi: 10.1029/2020GC009614.

Lancieri, M., R. Madariaga, and F. Bonilla (2012). Spectral scaling of the aftershocks of the Tocopilla 2007 earthquake in northern Chile, *Geophys. J. Int.* **189,** no. 1, 469–480.

Laske, G., G. Masters, Z. Ma, and M. Pasyanos (2013). Update on CRUST1.0-A 1-degree Global Model of Earth's Crust, *Geophys. Res. Abstracts* **15,** Abstract EGU2013-2658.

Lei, J. (2012). Upper-mantle tomography and dynamics beneath the North China Craton, *J. Geophys. Res.* **117,** no. B06313, doi: 10.1029/2012JB009212.

Li, H., Y. Dong, Y. Wang, Y. Peng, S. Liu, and B. Wu (2020). Seismological evidence for a deep-seated shear zone in the Langgu Depression, *Chin. J. Geophys.* **63,** no. 2, 492–504, doi: 10.6038/cjg2020N0192 (in Chinese).

Li, T., M. Cai, and M. Cai (2007). A review of mining-induced seismicity in China, *Int. J. Rock Mech. Min. Sci.* **44,** 1149–1171.

Li, T., Y. Zhang, R. Lu, J. Gao, J. Sun, X. Zhao, X. Ma, and Z. Wang (2021). 3D geometry of the Lanliao fault revealed by seismic reflection profiles: Implications for earthquake clustering in the Dongpu Sag, North China, *Tectonophysics* **806,** 228,798.

Liu, G., C. Li, Z. Peng, X. Li, and J. Wu (2017). Detecting remotely triggered microseismicity around Changbaishan Volcano following nuclear explosions in North Korea and large distant earthquakes around the world, *Geophys. Res. Lett.* **44,** 4829–4838, doi: 10.1002/2017GL072511.

Ma, K. F., C. H. Chan, and R. S. Stein (2005). Response of seismicity to Coulomb stress triggers and shadows of the 1999 $M_w = 7.6$ Chi-Chi, Taiwan, earthquake, *J. Geophys. Res.* **110,** no. B5.

Métivier, L., O. de Viron, C. Conrad, S. Renault, M. Diament, and G. Patau (2009). Evidence of earthquake triggering by the solid earth tides, *Earth Planet. Sci. Lett.* **278,** 370–375.

Orlecka-Sikora, B. (2010). The role of static stress transfer in mining induced seismic events occurrence, a case study of the Rudna mine in the Legnica-Glogow Copper District in Poland, *Geophys. J. Int.* **182,** no. 2, 1087–1095.

Oth, A. (2013). On the characteristics of earthquake stress release variations in Japan, *Earth Planet. Sci. Lett.* **377,** 132–141.

Parsons, T., R. S. Stein, R. W. Simpson, and P. A. Reasenberg (1999). Stress sensitivity of fault seismicity: A comparison between limited-offset oblique and major strike-slip faults, *J. Geophys. Res.* **104,** no. B9, pp. 20,183–20,202.

Peng, Z., and J. Gomberg (2010). An integrated perspective of the continuum between earthquakes and slow-slip phenomena, *Nature Geosci.* **3,** 599–607.

Peng, Z., J. Vidale, A. G. Wech, R. M. Nadeau, and K. C. Creager (2009). Remote triggering of tremor along the San Andreas fault in central California, *J. Geophys. Res.* **114,** B00A06.

Peng, Z., C. Wu, and C. Aiken (2011). Delayed triggering of microearthquakes by multiple surface waves circling the Earth, *Geophys. Res. Lett.* **38,** L04306.

Prieto, G., M. Florez, S. Barrett, G. Beroza, P. Pedraza, J. Blanco, and E. Poveda (2013). Seismic evidence for thermal runaway during intermediate-depth earthquake rupture, *Geophys. Res. Lett.* **40,** 6064–6068.

Ranjith, P., J. Zhao, M. Ju, R. De Silva, T. Rathnaweera, and A. Bandara (2017). Opportunities and challenges in deep mining: A brief review, *Engineering* **3,** no. 4, 546–551.

Satriano, C. (2024). SourceSpec-Earthquake source parameters from P- or S-wave displacement spectra (X.Y), doi: 10.5281/ZENODO.3688587.

Schliwa, N., and A. Gabriel (2023). Equivalent near-field corner frequency analysis of 3D dynamic rupture simulations reveals dynamic source effects, *Seismol. Res. Lett.* **95,** no. 2A, 900–924.

Shelly, D., D. Hill, F. Massin, J. Farrell, R. Smith, and T. Taira (2013). A fluid-driven earthquake swarm on the margin of the Yellowstone caldera, *J. Geophys. Res.* **118,** 4872–4886.

Singh, A., O. Mishra, R. Yadav, and D. Kumar (2012). A new insight into crustal heterogeneity beneath the 2001 Bhuj earthquake region of Northwest India and its implications for rupture initiations, *J. Asian Earth Sci.* 31–42.

Song, Y., E. Wang, H. Yang, C. Liu, B. Li, and D. Chen (2024). Microseismic source location using deep learning: A coal mine case study in China, *J. Rock Mech. Geotech. Eng.* **16,** 3407–3418.

Stein, R., A. Barka, and J. Dieterich (1997). Progressive failure on the North Anatolian fault since 1939 by earthquake stress triggering, *Geophys. J. Int.* **128,** 594–604.

Sun, Y., S. Dong, T. Fan, H. Zhang, and Y. Shi (2013). 3D rheological structure of the continental lithosphere beneath China and adjacent regions, *Chin. J. Geophys.* **56,** no. 9, 2936–2946 (in Chinese).

Sunilkumar, T., V. Gahalaut, D. Srinagesh, and B. Naresh (2023). Seismotectonic significance of the December 1, 2020 Haridwar, India earthquake (*M* 4.3), a lower crust event near the Himalayan topographic front, *J. Earth Syst. Sci.* **132,** 46.

Taira, T., and F. Brenguier (2016). Response of hydrothermal system to stress transients at Lassen Volcanic Center, California, inferred from seismic interferometry with ambient noise, *Earth Planets Space* **68,** 162.

Thurber, C., T. Brocher, H. Zhang, and V. Langenheim (2007). Three-dimensional P wave velocity model for the San Francisco Bay region, California, *J. Geophys. Res.* **112,** 2006JB004682.

Tian, Y., and D. Zhao (2013). Reactivation and mantle dynamics of North China craton: Insight from P-wave anisotropy tomography, *Geophys. J. Int.* **195,** 1796–1810.

Toda, S., and R. S. Stein (2000). Did stress triggering cause the large off-fault aftershocks of the 25 March 1998 $M_w = 8.1$ Antarctic plate earthquake?, *Geophys. Res. Lett.* **27,** no. 15, pp. 2301–2304.

Toda, S., and R. Stein (2020). Long- and short-term stress interaction of the 2019 Ridgecrest sequence and Coulomb-based earthquake forecasts, *Bull. Seismol. Soc. Am.* **110,** no. 4, 1765–1780.

Toda, S., R. Stein, K. Richards-Dinger, and S. Bozkurt (2005). Forecasting the evolution of seismicity in southern California: Animations built on earthquake stress transfer, *J. Geophys. Res.* **110,** B05S16.

Toda, S., R. Stein, V. Sevilgen, and J. Lin (2011). Coulomb 3.3 graphic-rich deformation and stress-change software for earthquake, tectonic, and volcano research and teaching-user guide, *U.S. Geol. Surv. Open-File Rept. 2011-1060.*

Van Der Elst, N. J., H. M. Savage, K. M. Keranen, and G. A. Abers (2013). Enhanced remote earthquake triggering at fluid-injection sites in the midwestern United States, *Science* **341,** no. 6142, 164–167.

Wang, E., H. Jia, D. Song, N. Li, and W. Qian (2014). Use of ultra-low-frequency electromagnetic emission to monitor stress and failure in coal mines, *Int. J. Rock Mech. Min. Sci.* **70,** 16–25.

Wang, G., S. Zhu, X. Zhang, Y. Wen, Z. Zhu, Q. Zhu, L. Xie, J. Li, Y. Tan, and T. Yang, *et al.* (2023). Prediction of mining-induced seismicity and damage assessment of induced surface buildings in thick and hard key stratum working face: A case study of Liuhuanggou coal mine in China, *Front. Earth Sci.* **11,** 1238055.

Wang, W., X. Meng, Z. Peng, Q. Chen, and N. Liu (2015). Increasing background seismicity and dynamic triggering behaviors with nearby mining activities around Fangshan Pluton in Beijing, China, *J. Geophys. Res.* **120,** 5624–5638.

Wessel, P., and W. H. F. Smith (1998). New, improved version of generic mapping tools released, *Eos Trans. AGU* **79,** no. 47, 579, doi: 10.1029/98EO00426.

Wu, C., Z. Peng, W. Wang, and Q. Chen (2011). Dynamic triggering of shallow earthquakes near Beijing, China, *Geophys. J. Int.* **185,** 1321–1334.

Xin, H., H. Zhang, M. Kang, R. He, L. Gao, and J. Gao (2018). High-resolution lithospheric velocity structure of continental China by double-difference seismic travel-time tomography, *Seismol. Res. Lett.* **90,** no. 1, 229–241.

Xu, Y. (2004). Lithospheric thinning beneath North China: A temporal and spatial perspective (in Chinese), *Geol. J. China Univ.* **10,** no. 3, 324–331.

Yan, C., Y. Jiao, Y. Gu, J. Zou, Q. Zhang, and Z. Wu (2025). Strong mining-induced seismicity characteristics and precursor signals based on statistical seismology, *Int. J. Geomech.* **25,** no. 5, 04025070.

Yao, D., Z. Peng, and X. Meng (2015). Remotely triggered earthquakes in south-central Tibet following the 2004 M_w 9.1 Sumatra and 2005 M_w 8.6 Nias earthquakes, *Geophys. J. Int.* **201,** no. 2, 543–551.

Zhang, H., and C. Thurber (2003). Double-Difference tomography: The method and its application to the Hayward fault, California, *Bull. Seismol. Soc. Am.* **93,** no. 5, 1875–1889.

Zhang, H., and C. Thurber (2006). Development and applications of double-difference seismic tomography, *Pure Appl. Geophys.* 373–403.

Zhang, G., Y. Ji, H. Guo, and X. Ping (2022). Complex fault geometry of the 1976 Ms 7.8 Tangshan earthquake source region in North China, *Tectonophysics* **845,** 229,642.

Zhang, G., J. Lei, and D. Sun (2019). The 2013 and 2017 Ms 5 seismic swarms in Jilin, NEChina: Fluid-triggered earthquakes?, *J. Geophys. Res.* **124,** no. 12.

Zhang, G., J. Lei, F. Xie, Y. Guo, and C. Lan (2011). Precise relocation of small earthquakes occurred in North China and its tectonic implications, *Acta Seismol. Sinica* **33,** no. 6, 699–714.

Zhang, G., Y. Li, and X. Hu (2022). Nucleation mechanism of the 2021 M_w 7.4 Maduo earthquake, NE Tibetan plateau: Insights from seismic tomography and numerical modeling, *Tectonophysics* **839,** 229,528.

Zhang, Y., H. Ji, and H. Wu (2022). Triggering and relationship between mine earthquake activities and stress of earth tides during deep mining, *Front. Earth Sci.* **10,** 889,545.

Zhang, Z., J. Zheng, D. Yin, B. Li, Y. Guo, G. Chai, J. Wu, and Y. Wu (2024). Vertical high-velocity structures and seismic activity in western Shandong Rise, China: Case study inspired by double-difference seismic tomography, *Open Geosci.* **16,** no. 1, 20220699.

Zheng, T., L. Zhao, W. Xu, and R Zhu (2008). Insight into modification of North China Craton from seismological study in the Shandong Province, *Geophys. Res. Lett.* **35,** no. L22305, doi: 10.1029/2008GL035661.

Zhu, L., and Y. Ben-Zion (2013). Parameterization of general seismic potency and moment tensors for source inversion of seismic waveform data, *Geophys. J. Int.* **194,** no. 2, 839–843.

Zhu, L., and L. Rivera (2002). A note on the dynamic and static displacements from a point source in multilayered media, *Geophys. J. Int.* **148,** no. 3, 619–627.

Manuscript received 21 April 2025
Published online 12 September 2025

Lateral Viscosity Heterogeneity of Mantle Wedge and Back-Arc Mantle: Implications from the 2010 M_w 8.8 Maule and 2011 M_w 9.0 Tohoku-Oki Postseismic Deformation

Hyeon-Seob Kim[1], Byung-Dal So[*1,2], and Sung-Joon Chang[1,2]

Abstract

Dehydration during slab subduction plays an important role in controlling the rheological properties of the continental mantle. Fluid release from slab dehydration induces variations in rheological strength within the upper mantle, leading to a weak mantle wedge (MW) and a relatively strong back-arc mantle (BM). We quantitatively analyzed the effects of a weak MW and a strong BM on back-arc subsidence and parameterized a laterally heterogeneous viscous structure with the MW–BM rheological interface and corresponding viscosity contrast. A generalized model with key elements of the subduction zone (subducting slab, continental crust, lithospheric mantle, asthenosphere, deep mantle, and cold-nose) shows that the larger the viscosity contrast between the MW and BM, the larger the amplitude of subsidence around the MW–BM interface. The different viscoelastic relaxation times of MW and BM cause relative horizontal viscoelastic deformation expressed as surface subsidence. The postseismic quasi-static stress changes manifest as enhanced extensional stress in the crust above the weak MW. The rheological contrast between the MW and BM induces lateral variations in the postseismic stress distribution within the overriding plate. We simulated the back-arc subsidence following the 2010 M_w 8.8 Maure earthquake and the 2011 M_w 9.0 Tohoku-Oki earthquake, using the MW–BM structure. The inferred MW–BM interface in the Chile and Japan subduction zones was located at ~550 and 325 km from the trench, respectively. The spatial correlation between the location of the back-arc subsidence and the extent of the low-viscosity MW suggests localized dehydration of the subduction zone.

Cite this article as Kim, H.-S., B.-D. So, and S.-J. Chang (2025). Lateral Viscosity Heterogeneity of Mantle Wedge and Back-Arc Mantle: Implications from the 2010 M_w 8.8 Maule and 2011 M_w 9.0 Tohoku-Oki Postseismic Deformation, *Seismol. Res. Lett.* **97**, 354–368, doi: 10.1785/0220250153.

Supplemental Material

Introduction

Geodetic observations and numerical modeling of viscoelastic deformation have been integrated to improve our understanding of mantle rheology from postseismic deformation (Sun *et al.*, 2014; Pollitz, 2019). Numerical modeling to constrain horizontal postseismic motion has inferred an average mantle viscosity of 10^{18}–10^{20} Pa · s in the global subduction zones (e.g., Wang *et al.*, 2012). The obtained range of mantle viscosity has contributed to the modeling of long-term deformation of subducting plates (e.g., Yuen *et al.*, 1982) and stress on faults during earthquake cycles (So and Capitanio, 2017; Herman and Govers, 2020).

Geodetic measurements of vertical postseismic motion in subduction zones ubiquitously show substantial uplift in the fore-arc and relatively minor subsidence in the back-arc (Hu *et al.*, 2014; Klein *et al.*, 2016; Qiu *et al.*, 2018). The rheological contrast between the cold-nose and hot mantle wedge (MW), which is thermally controlled by subduction dynamics, influences the location of substantial fore-arc uplift during postseismic deformation (Luo and Wang, 2021). On the other hand, interpretations of back-arc subsidence are influenced by lateral variations in the mantle viscosity of subduction zones.

1. Interdisciplinary Program in Earth Environmental System Science and Engineering, Kangwon National University, Chuncheon, South Korea, https://orcid.org/0000-0002-9294-7570 (H-SK); https://orcid.org/0000-0002-9294-7896 (B-DS); https://orcid.org/0000-0003-1434-1132 (S-JC); 2. Department of Geophysics, Kangwon National University, Chuncheon, South Korea

*Corresponding author: bdso@kangwon.ac.kr

For example, postseismic back-arc subsidence following the 2010 M_w 8.8 Maule, 2004 M_w 9.2 Sumatra, and 2011 M_w 9.0 Tohoku-Oki earthquakes has been successfully constrained by numerical models, including the cratonic mantle (Li *et al.*, 2017), the back-arc spreading center (Wiseman *et al.*, 2015), and the volcanic arc (Muto *et al.*, 2016), respectively. The postseismic numerical simulations have included rheological heterogeneities derived from geophysical observations (e.g., gravity, seismic, and heat flow data; Pérez-Gussinyé *et al.*, 2008; Shapiro *et al.*, 2008; Muto, 2011). The incorporation of rheological heterogeneity inferred from these observations into postseismic deformation simulations required the conversion of the size and relative viscosity of the heterogeneity within the subduction zone mantle (Luo and Wang, 2021; Dhar *et al.*, 2023; Sun *et al.*, 2024). Therefore, it is essential to conduct systematic investigations using forward modeling to account for the effects of lateral rheological heterogeneities on postseismic back-arc subsidence.

Thermal structure and water content, influenced by slab-driven mantle flow and oceanic crust dehydration, control the viscosity structure across the MW and back-arc mantle (BM) (Dixon *et al.*, 2004; He, 2014). The MW temperature is modulated by a balance between hot mantle flow from the back-arc (Currie *et al.*, 2004) and cooling by thermal diffusion of the subducting slab (Arcay *et al.*, 2007). From a tectonic perspective, the temperature of the MW under steady-state conditions becomes similar to that of the BM (Syracuse *et al.*, 2010). However, the water content of the MW is primarily controlled by dehydration reactions, which depend on the stability of hydrous minerals in the slab under temperature and pressure conditions (Mibe *et al.*, 2011). Water influx into the MW from slab dehydration rises rapidly in a vertical direction through the pore matrix of the mantle (Cerpa *et al.*, 2017). Even without mantle partial melting, the incorporation of hydroxyl group at grain boundaries facilitates the formation of subgrain boundaries, leading to rheological weakening of the rocks (Hirth and Kohlstedt, 1996). The geochemical reactions of the mantle rocks with the released fluid cause partial melting (Iwamori, 1998) and the formation of hydrous minerals (Karato and Jung, 2003), which reduce the strength of the MW (Horiuchi and Iwamori, 2016). Thus, at regional scales (i.e., >300 km), water released along the subducting slab contributes to the rheological contrast between MW and BM (i.e., the lower viscosity of the MW) depending on the stability of hydrous minerals (van Keken *et al.*, 2011). Although previous studies have generally suggested a weak rheology for the BM based on high temperatures and the presence of melt (Currie and Hyndman, 2006; Nakajima *et al.*, 2013), in this study, we distinguish a hydrated, low-viscosity MW from a relatively dry and mechanically stronger BM located farther from the trench and MW.

A number of studies of postseismic deformation have included a localized low-viscosity block (Trubienko *et al.*, 2014) and hydrated channels above the slab (Klein *et al.*, 2016), both of which were weakened by slab dehydration. Spatial heterogeneity has also been inferred from viscoelastic inversions of geodetic data (Li *et al.*, 2018) and from power-law rheology models in which the effective viscosity varies with coseismic stress and thermal structure (Agata *et al.*, 2019; Muto *et al.*, 2019; Peña *et al.*, 2020). However, the power-law rheology model typically assumes a spatially uniform water content. Furthermore, the predominant approach in postseismic modeling has been to use laterally uniform viscosity mantle models (Sun *et al.*, 2014; Iinuma *et al.*, 2016) or depth-dependent layered models (Freed *et al.*, 2017; Suito, 2017) without the lateral viscosity variations induced by dehydration. Although the influence of effective viscosity variations on postseismic viscoelastic deformation has been extensively discussed (Pollitz, 2015; Masuti *et al.*, 2016; Dhar *et al.*, 2023), the frequent assumption of uniform water content, which can lead to an underestimation of lateral viscosity contrasts, remains a standard approach to modeling postseismic deformation. In this study, we divided the upper mantle into two distinct rheological domains: a hydrated MW and a relatively dry BM. The MW was assumed to be homogeneously hydrated by slab-derived fluids within the region bounded by the overlying crust and subducting slab. We investigated the influence of this laterally heterogeneous MW–BM structure on the spatial pattern of vertical displacement, particularly the back-arc subsidence observed after the 2011 M_w 9.0 Tohoku-Oki (Iinuma *et al.*, 2012) and 2010 M_w 8.8 Maule (Bedford *et al.*, 2016) earthquakes.

To systematically examine MW–BM structure on postseismic viscoelastic deformation, we evaluate the effect of lateral using generalized and regional postseismic models representing a 2D subduction zone. We developed regional postseismic models for the Chile and Japan subduction zones to quantify the effect of geometry and rheological contrasts of MW–BM structures on the back-arc subsidence observed after the M_w 8.8 Maule and M_w 9.0 Tohoku-Oki earthquakes, respectively. A series of numerical models demonstrated the relationship between the postseismic back-arc subsidence and the MW–BM structure, providing insight into the stress transfer between the interplate and intraplate regions, controlled by the strength of the BM during the postseismic period.

Methods

We constructed a 2D subduction zone model perpendicular to the trench using the finite-element software PyLith (Aagaard *et al.*, 2013), which is specialized for lithospheric and crustal deformation. The 2D model prescribes a trench-parallel MW–BM rheological contrast, allowing the investigation of the fundamental physical mechanism responsible for postseismic deformation in a simplified framework. For the generalized models (Fig. 1a,b), we designed a sufficiently wide domain extending 1500 km landward in the overriding crust and 500 km seaward from the trench with free-slip boundary conditions on the sidewalls. The depth of the domain was set to

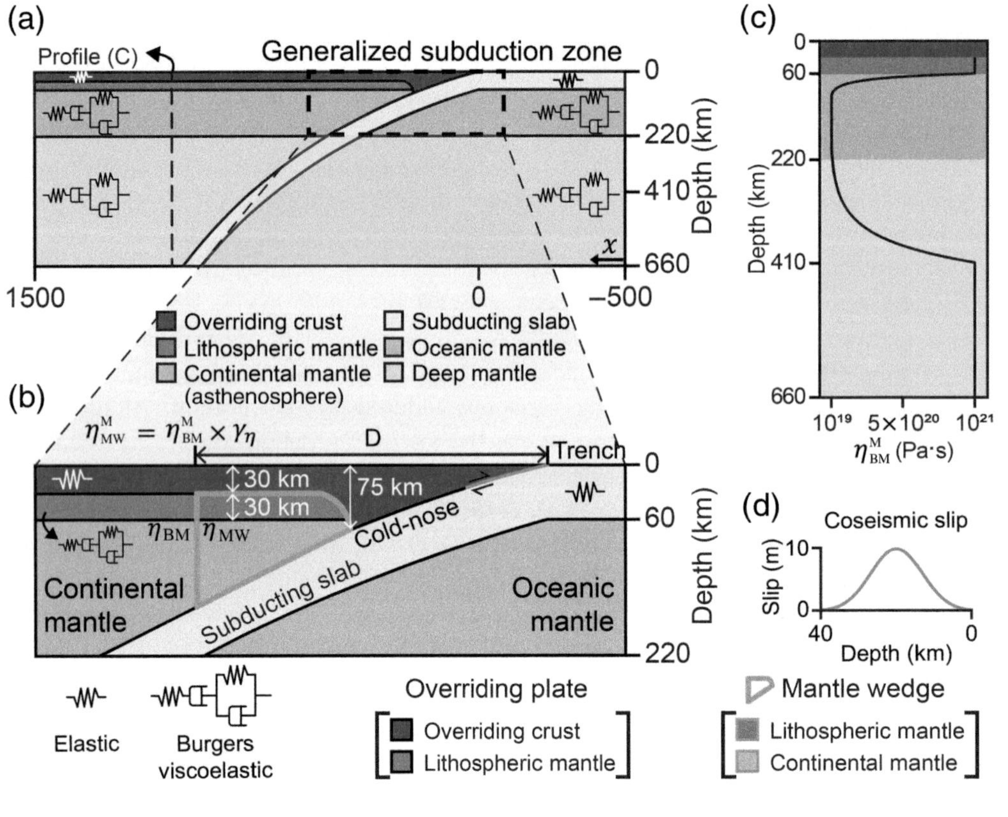

Figure 1. 2D generalized model setup. (a) The entire generalized model consists of an elastic overriding crust and slab (represented by a spring) and a viscoelastic mantle (comprising serially connected springs and dashpots), as shown in (b). The green line indicates a bell-shaped seismic slip (d). The parameter D denotes the interface (dashed line) between the mantle wedge (MW) and back-arc mantle (BM). (c) The Maxwell viscosity profile of the BM (η^{M}_{BM}) along the vertical line in (a) (black-dashed line). The viscosity profile represents the exponential decrease and increase in viscosity from the lithosphere to the asthenosphere and from the asthenosphere to the deep mantle, respectively. The color version of this figure is available only in the electronic edition.

660 km, corresponding to the boundary between the upper and lower mantle, to prevent the vertically fixed bottom surface from influencing the postseismic vertical deformation at the top free surface.

In the generalized model, we constructed the slab geometry, including the megathrust fault interface, in a curved configuration using a logarithmic function that effectively represents two different dips (~15° and 30°) depending on depth. Coseismic reverse slip was imposed kinematically with a bell-shaped distribution Wang and He, 2008) (Fig. 1d), and the maximum slip was set to 10 m at 20 km depth (green line in inset of Fig. 1b). We defined smaller mesh sizes (<2.5 km) in the vicinity of the fault interface, which mainly hosts coseismic and postseismic deformation, whereas mesh sizes >10 km were used in the oceanic mantle (see Fig. S1, available in the supplemental material to this article). The overriding plate consists of 30 km elastic crust and 30 km viscoelastic lithospheric mantle, whereas the subducting plate consists of 60 km of elastic crust. The cold-nose refers to a cooled mantle, which is decoupled from the mantle corner flow and the subducting slab (Wada and Wang, 2009). We defined the cold-nose as an elastic structure between 30 and 75 km depth (Fig. 1b).

We applied the Burgers rheology to the MW, BM, and oceanic mantle to provide a more physically consistent representation of the viscoelastic deformation process of crustal and mantle materials by distinguishing between transient and steady-state viscosity (Bürgmann and Dresen, 2008). In the Burgers model, the Kelvin (i.e., transient; η^{K}) viscosity is often assumed to be an order of magnitude lower than the Maxwell (i.e., steady-state; η^{M}) viscosity (e.g., Tian *et al.*, 2024). The lateral rheological heterogeneity was described by the rheological interface position (D value) and the MW–BM rheological contrast ($\gamma_\eta = \eta^{M}_{MW}/\eta^{M}_{BM} = \eta^{K}_{MW}/\eta^{K}_{BM}$). A large D value (i.e., a large MW) indicates that the spatial extent of the mantle-weakening mechanism (e.g., dehydration or concentrated corner flow) is large. An increase in γ_η indicates that the weakening mechanism is locally enhanced within the MW. We also applied the weakening mechanism to the lithospheric mantle to reflect the reduction in rheological strength of the lower lithosphere caused by slab dehydration (Hyndman and Peacock, 2003) (see the region enclosed by the orange curve in Fig. 1b). The asthenosphere and deep mantle correspond to depths of 100–220 km and 220–660 km, respectively (Thybo, 2006). The viscosity of the deep mantle increases exponentially up to 10^{21} Pa · s from 220 to 410 km depth (Fig. 1c).

In the regional models, the geometry of the subducting slab in central Chile (Fig. 2a,b) and northeastern Japan (Fig. 2c,d) was derived from Slab 1.0 (Hayes *et al.*, 2012) with thicknesses of 60 and 70 km, respectively. The structure of the overriding plate was defined based on the Moho depth and the thermal profile corresponding to temperatures of 1100°C–1200°C (Artemieva and Mooney, 2001), which includes an elastic crust and Burgers viscoelastic lithospheric mantle. The thicknesses of the overriding crust and lithospheric mantle were set to 60 and 20 km, respectively, for the Chile subduction zone (Oleskevich *et al.*, 1999), and 40 and 20 km, respectively,

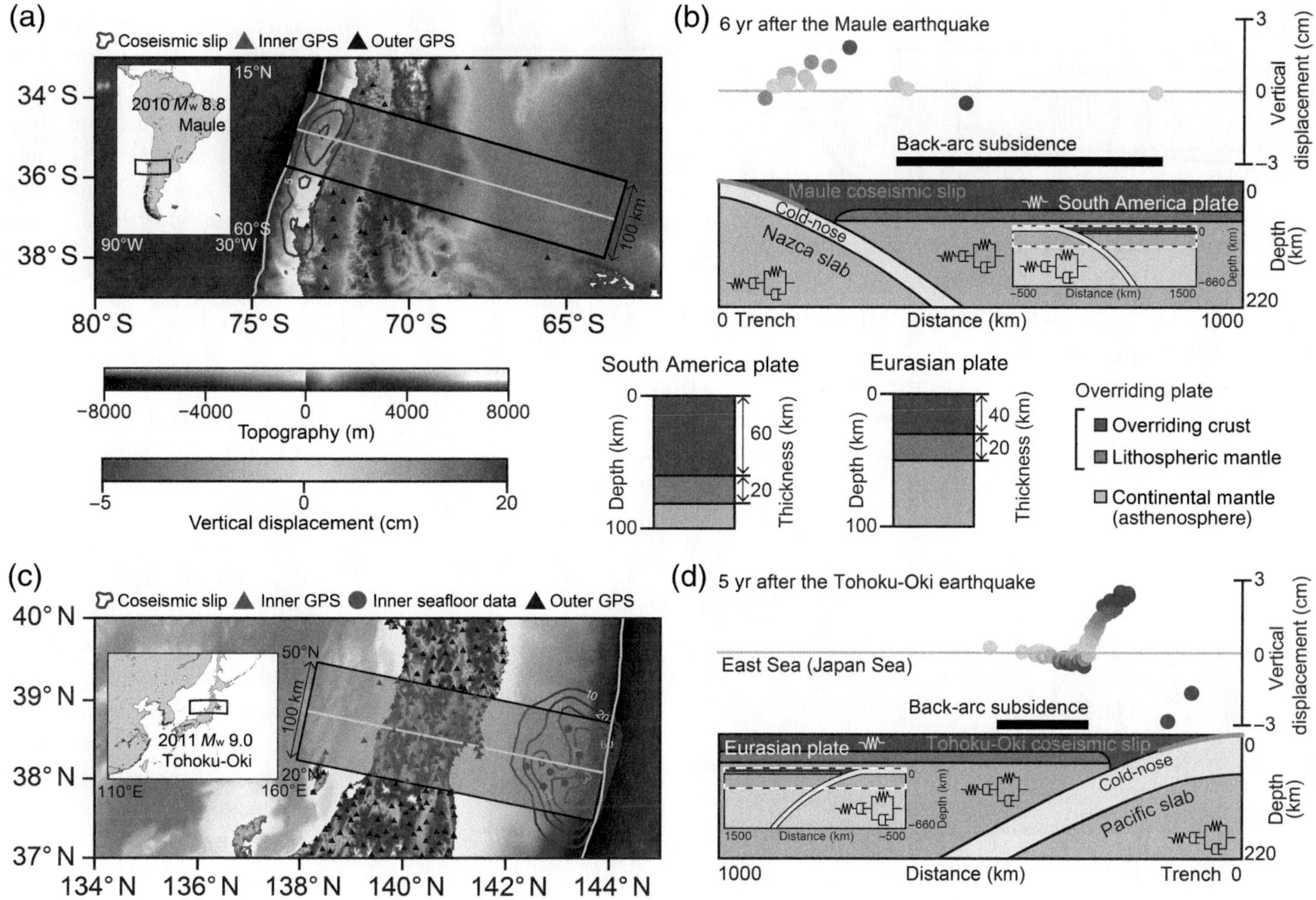

Figure 2. Postseismic vertical displacements after six years for the 2010 M_w 8.8 Maule and five years for the 2011 M_w 9.0 Tohoku-Oki earthquakes. (a,c) The topographic map with inland (triangles) and seafloor (circles) observation stations, which recorded the postseismic deformations after the Maule (Li *et al.*, 2017) and Tohoku-Oki (Muto *et al.*, 2019) earthquakes, respectively. Inner Global Positioning System (GPS) (red triangles and circles) within the gray-shaded boxes were used for grid search. The blue contours indicate coseismic slip, and the left inset marks earthquake epicenters (red stars). (b,d) Subduction zone geometries in central Chile and northeastern Japan, along with postseismic vertical displacements along the yellow lines in (a) and (c) (Slab1.0; Hayes *et al.*, 2012). The green line represents the rupture boundary, and black bars highlight back-arc subsidence. The color version of this figure is available only in the electronic edition.

for the Japan subduction zone (van Keken *et al.*, 2012). We applied the coseismic slip distributions of the 2010 M_w 8.8 Maule earthquake and the 2011 M_w 9.0 Tohoku-Oki earthquake along the megathrust faults (green lines in Fig. 2b,d), following the methods of Peña *et al.* (2019) and Muto *et al.* (2016). The original 3D slip distributions (blue contours in Fig. 2a,c) of Moreno *et al.* (2012) and Iinuma *et al.* (2012) were reduced to 2D distributions by averaging slip magnitudes along the megathrust fault. The assumption of dimensionally reduced fault-slip magnitude from 3D to 2D is generally used because most slip of large megathrust earthquakes occur predominantly occurring in the dip direction (e.g., Muldashev and Sobolev, 2020). Each regional model has the identical rheological structure as the generalized model, except for the location of the cold-nose at ~220 km (Völker and Stipp, 2015) and ~250 km (Freed *et al.*, 2017) from the trench in the Chile and Japan subduction zones, respectively.

We compiled geodetic data of cumulative surface displacements for five and six years after the 2010 Maule and 2011 Tohoku-Oki earthquakes, respectively, as reported by Li *et al.* (2017) and Muto *et al.* (2019). The postseismic displacements of the Maule earthquake observed at geodetic stations on the South American plate were provided by Li *et al.* (2017). Raw Global Positioning System (GPS) data from different South American networks were postprocessed by the Nevada Geodetic Laboratory (NGL) (Blewitt *et al.*, 2018). This processed dataset was openly provided by NGL, and postseismic displacements were subsequently extracted by time series analysis conducted by Li *et al.* (2017).

Inland geodetic data for the Tohoku-Oki postseismic displacements were obtained from two networks: GEONET (operated by the Geospatial Information Authority of Japan) and the network maintained by Tohoku University (Muto *et al.*, 2019).

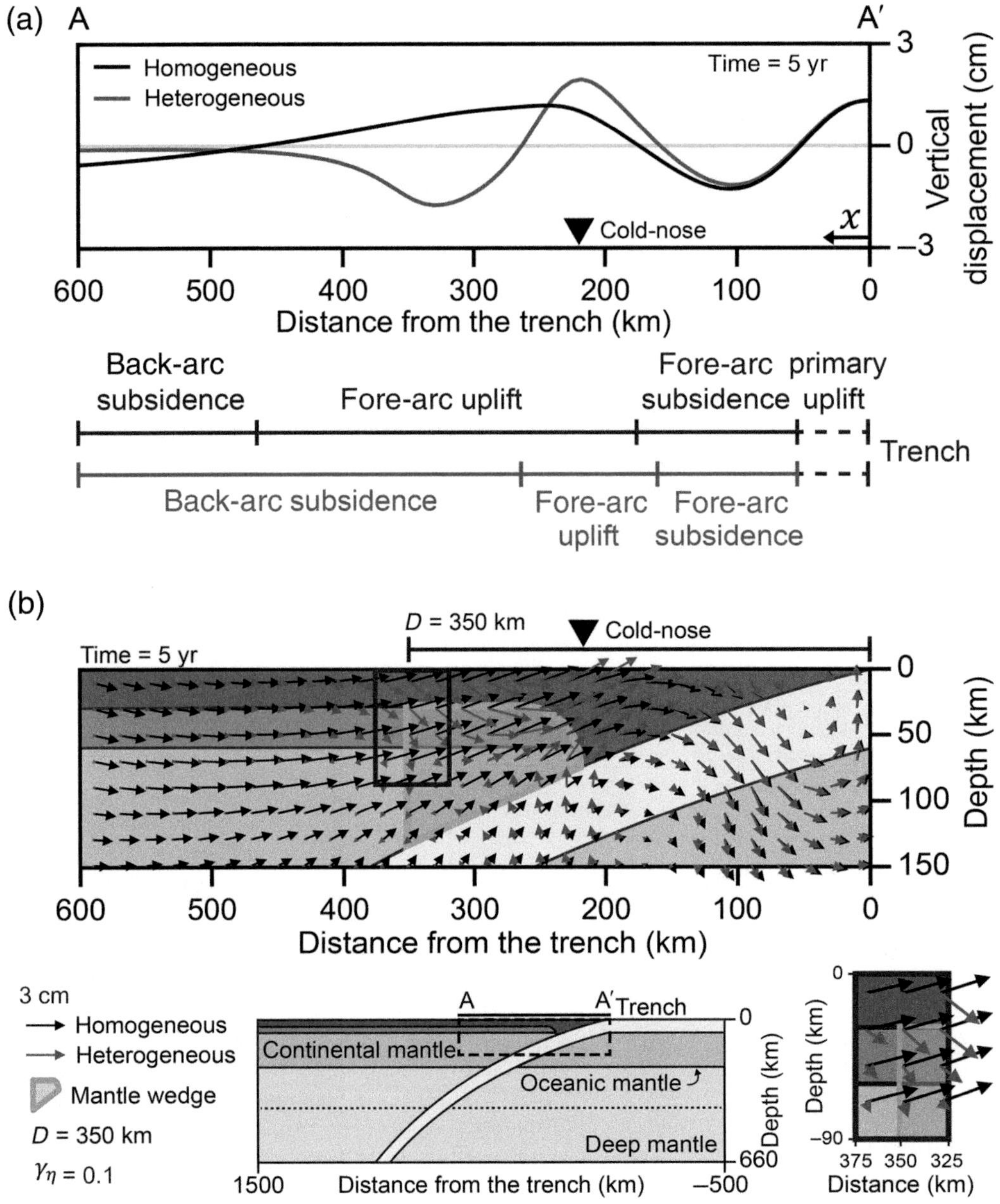

Figure 3. Postseismic deformation of the generalized models for five years. (a) Vertical displacement on profile A–A′ in homogeneous and heterogeneous models is represented by black and red lines, respectively. (b) The zoomed distribution of the postseismic deformation (black-dashed box in the inset). The black and red arrows indicate the deformation vectors in the homogeneous (without MW) and heterogeneous (with MW of $D = 350$ km) models, respectively. The orange curve shows the geometry of the MW. The blue box in (b) highlights the zoomed region around the MW–BM interface, as shown in the lower right inset. The color version of this figure is available only in the electronic edition.

Seafloor observations from the Japan Coast Guard (Watanabe *et al.*, 2014) and GNSS-A sites (Sun *et al.*, 2014) were also used to compile the fore-arc postseismic displacements. The postseismic displacement of the Tohoku-Oki earthquake was reported by Muto *et al.* (2019).

To verify the effect of the MW–BM structure on the postseismic back-arc subsidence, we applied a grid-search approach to compare the regional postseismic models and geodetic data of the back-arc subsidence. We quantitatively evaluated the root mean square error (rmse) between the numerical modeling results and the geodetic data. For comparison with the 2D subduction zone model, we stacked the geodetic observations (red triangles and closed circles in Fig. 2a,c) within a ~100 km wide box (shaded boxes), except for the outer GPS (black triangles).

Results

We investigated the mechanical effects of lateral viscosity contrast on postseismic deformation using a generalized model. The generalized model evaluated the physical influence of MW–BM viscosity structures on postseismic deformation by varying lateral viscosity parameters. Then, we performed regional modeling to estimate the MW–BM structures associated with the observed postseismic back-arc subsidence. The inferred lateral rheological heterogeneity represents the spatial distribution of weakened upper mantle in the Japan and Chile subduction zones.

Generalized model

We calculated the viscoelastic deformation in the generalized models to explore the influence of MW and BM viscosity on the deformation for five years (Fig. 3). The heterogeneous ($\eta^{M}_{BM} = 10^{20}$ Pa · s and $\eta^{M}_{MW} = 10^{19}$ Pa · s with D = 350 km and $\gamma_\eta = 0.1$) and homogeneous ($\eta^{M}_{BM} = \eta^{M}_{MW} = 10^{19}$ Pa · s) models represent the upper mantle with and without a lower viscosity MW, respectively. In both the heterogeneous and homogeneous models, fore-arc subsidence between the cold-nose and the trench (x = ~100 km) developed as viscoelastic deformation progressed in the oceanic mantle (black and red arrows in Fig. 3b). In the heterogeneous model, postseismic fore-arc

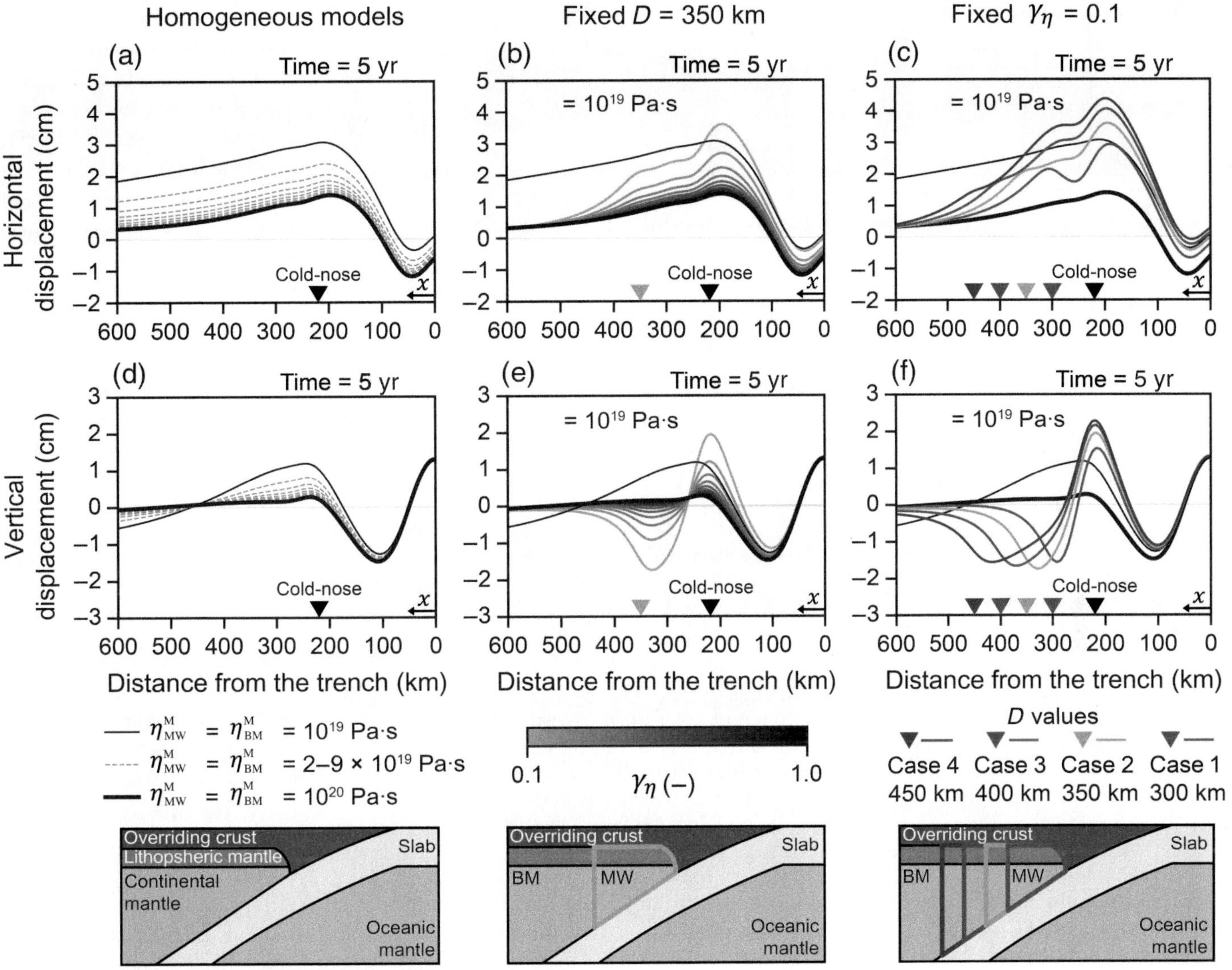

uplift ($x = \sim 200$ km) was more pronounced because the cold-nose redirected the postseismic seaward motion of the less viscous lithospheric mantle upward (Luo and Wang, 2021) (red arrows in Fig. 3b). Back-arc subsidence occurred in the heterogeneous and homogeneous models at $x = \sim 270$ km and $x = \sim 500$ km, respectively (Fig. 3a). In the BM (i.e., $x > 350$ km), the magnitude of viscoelastic deformation was smaller in the heterogeneous model (red arrows) than in the homogeneous model (black arrows) (Fig. 3b). In addition, we obtained a downward viscoelastic flow within the MW domain near $D = 350$ km in the heterogeneous model (blue box and inset in Fig. 3b), indicating that the rheological contrast between the BM and MW is associated with back-arc subsidence (Fig. 3a,b). The downward viscoelastic flow pattern around the MW–BM interface in the heterogeneous model was also observed in Muto *et al.* (2016), in which a short-wavelength (<50 km width), low-viscosity volcanic arc was applied to the postseismic model.

We investigated the effect of MW–BM viscosity contrast on postseismic displacements. Our analytical framework involves

Figure 4. Postseismic displacements in homogeneous and heterogeneous models. The left (a and d), middle (b and e), and right (c and f) columns show the homogeneous (black lines) models and heterogeneous models with different γ_η (black–orange lines) and D values (colored lines), respectively. The top and bottom rows show the horizontal and vertical displacements, respectively. The black thin and thick lines show the uniform mantle viscosity of 10^{19} and 10^{20} Pa · s, respectively. The fixed parameters for each model are shown in the schematic diagrams below. The black and colored triangles mark the cold-nose edge and MW–BM interfaces, respectively. The color version of this figure is available only in the electronic edition.

the variation of parameters such as viscosity contrast (γ_η) and location of the rheological interface (D). First, we examined displacement patterns within a continental mantle characterized by uniform viscosity, with a steady-state viscosity range of 10^{19}–10^{20} Pa · s. The lower viscosity of the homogeneous mantle causes an increase in trench-ward horizontal displacement (compare thin and thick lines in Fig. 4a). For vertical

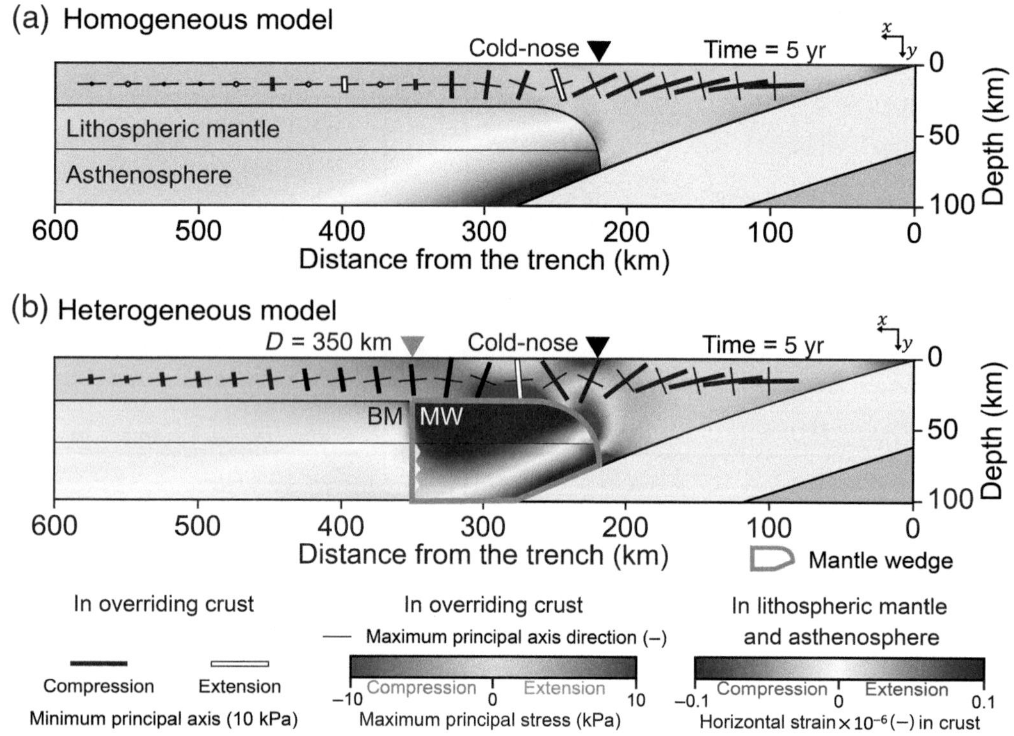

Figure 5. Postseismic strain and stress distribution for five years. (a,b) The maximum principal stress (colors and thin bar) in the overriding crust and the horizontal strain (colors) in the lithospheric mantle and asthenosphere. The white and black thick bars indicate the extension and compression of the minimum principal stress of the overriding crust, respectively. The black thin bar indicates the direction of the maximum stress axis. The orange box in (b) shows the shape of the MW (D = 350 km). The color version of this figure is available only in the electronic edition.

displacement, subsidence occurs for $x > \sim 450$ km, with an increasing magnitude because viscosity decreases (Fig. 4d). For example, in the homogeneous models with mantle viscosities of 10^{19} Pa · s (black thin line) and 10^{20} Pa · s (black thick line), subsidence at 600 km from the trench reaches ~0.5 and 0.1 cm, respectively.

The heterogeneous models with the smaller γ_η and larger D values yield the increase in horizontal displacements of both MW and BM (Fig. 4b,c). The horizontal displacements at x = 250 km were ~1.0 and 2.5 cm when γ_η was 1 and 0.1, respectively (Fig. 5b; black thick and light orange, respectively). For the heterogeneous models with D values of 300 km (case 1, red line in Fig. 4c) and D = 450 km (case 4, blue line), the horizontal displacement at x = 250 km was ~1.8–3.6 cm, respectively (Fig. 4c).

For vertical displacement, all heterogeneous models show back-arc subsidence closer to the trench (<300 km), compared to the homogeneous model where subsidence manifests at >~450 km from the trench. The heterogeneous models with smaller γ_η show a larger back-arc subsidence near the MW–BM rheological interface (Fig. 4e, compare light orange and black thick lines) because the increased viscosity contrast drives further relative horizontal motion across the MW and BM. We found that the surface point where maximum back-arc subsidence occurred was slightly seaward of the rheological interface (Fig. 4f). The maximum back-arc subsidence in case 1 (D = 300 km) and case 4 (D = 450 km) was located at x = ~290 km and x = ~420 km, respectively. We tested the effect of gradual rheological changes on the location of back-arc subsidence around the viscosity transition zone (see Fig. S2). We confirmed that the location of back-arc subsidence is independent of the gradual change in viscosity between MW and BM, which is represented by the finite width of the rheological transition zone.

Figure 5a,b illustrates the principal stress in the crust and the horizontal strain in the viscoelastic continental material for the homogeneous and heterogeneous models, respectively. The thin bars and background color represent the orientation and magnitude of the maximum principal stress, respectively. The white and black thick bars indicate the minimum extensional and compressional principal stresses, respectively. The extensional stress dominates in the back-arc crust because the mantle closer to the trench accommodates greater viscoelastic deformation in response to coseismic stress perturbations. In the heterogeneous model, the relative trenchward motion between MW and BM increases due to different viscoelastic deformation rates (see Fig. 3b), yielding a more localized distribution of horizontal strain within the MW compared to the homogeneous model (purple zone in Fig. 5b). The concentration of horizontal strain in the MW increases the trenchward-oriented maximum principal stress in the overlying crust (red zone above the MW in Fig. 5b). Furthermore, the horizontal extension of the MW exerts a downward pull on the overlying crust, causing the back-arc surface subsidence.

We explored the effect of a rheologically weak MW and strong BM configuration on postseismic stress accumulation in the crust by varying the values of γ_η and D (Fig. 6). In both homogeneous and heterogeneous models, the compressional and extensional stresses of the overriding crust dominated the seaward (black thick bars) and landward (background color) directions of the cold-nose, respectively (Fig. 6a). We plotted the maximum principal stresses, depending on values

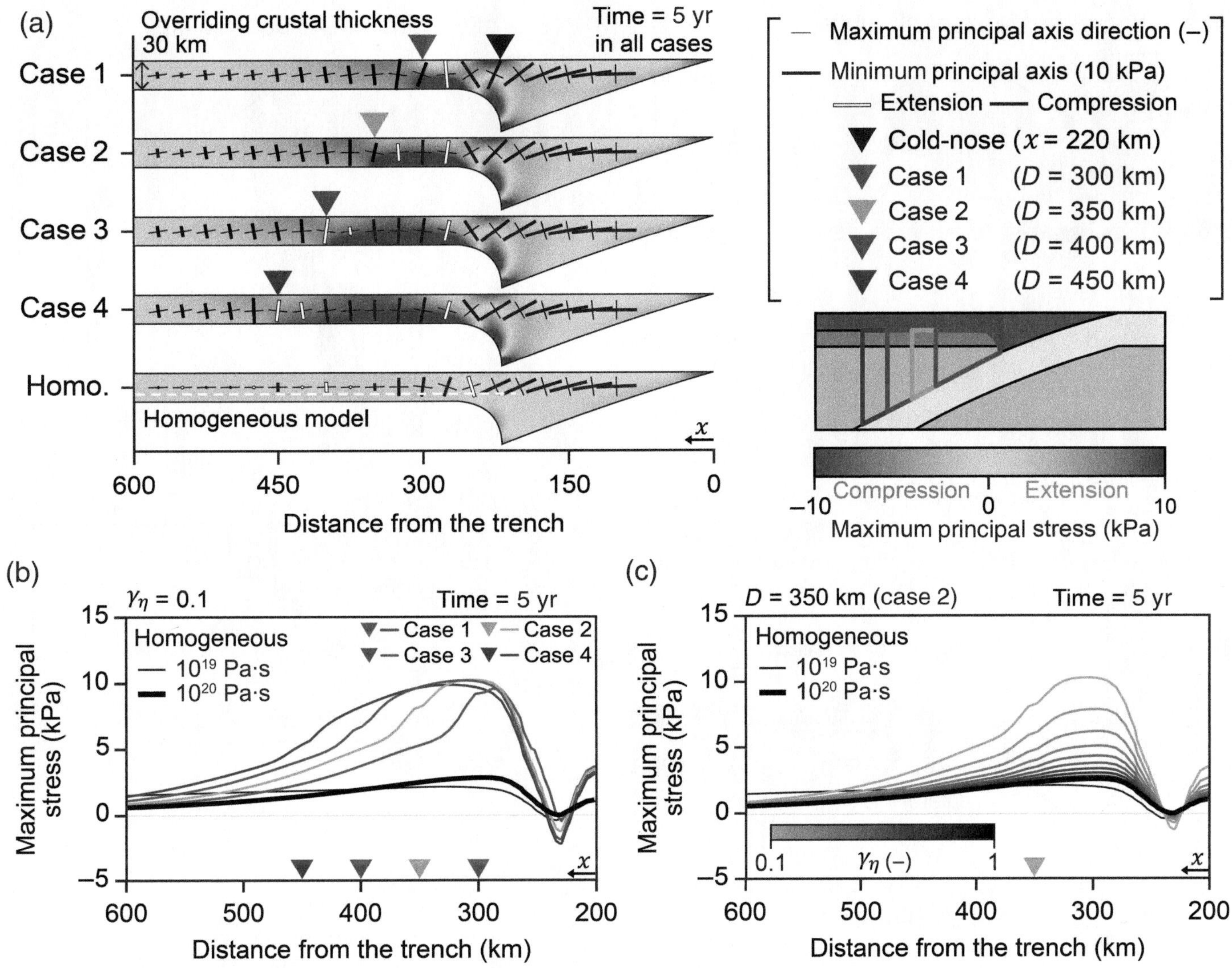

Figure 6. Postseismic principal stress and horizontal strain accumulation for five years. The black and colored triangles indicate the locations of the cold-nose and rheological interfaces, respectively. (a) Maximum and minimum principal stresses in the crust are shown as background shading colors and bars, respectively. (b,c) The stress along the horizontal line in (a) (white-dashed line) at 20 km depth, modeled with different γ_η (black–orange lines) and D values (colored lines), respectively. The black, thin, and thick lines in (b) and (c) represent the homogeneous models with uniform mantle viscosities of 10^{19} and 10^{20} Pa · s, respectively. The color version of this figure is available only in the electronic edition.

of D (Fig. 6b) and γ_η (Fig. 6c), along the horizontal line at a depth of 20 km (white dashed line in Fig. 6a), which corresponds to the brittle–ductile transition zone between the overriding crust and upper mantle in the generalized model. For the heterogeneous models (cases 1–4), the extensional stresses were localized near the MW–BM rheological interface (see regions around the colored triangles in Fig. 6a). For example, case 2 exhibited an extensional stress of ~10 kPa (red line in Fig. 6b), which was much higher than that of the homogeneous models (black thin and thick lines in Fig. 6b). The heterogeneous model with $\gamma_\eta =$ 0.1 and = 1 showed the maximum principal horizontal stress of ~7 and 3 kPa, respectively (Fig. 6c). In addition, the extensional stress of the heterogeneous models increases beyond the interface (350–600 km far from the trench), when the effective MW strength was lower (i.e., smaller γ_η), the far-field stress level increased more.

Regional model

We determine the values of the parameters D, η^{M}_{BM}, and γ_η that minimize the misfit with the back-arc subsidence observed after the 2010 M_w 8.8 Maule and 2011 M_w 9.0 Tohoku-Oki earthquakes (see Fig. 2a,c). We excluded observations from the near trench, where other mechanisms such as poroelastic rebound, afterslip, and relocking are dominant (Bedford *et al.*, 2016; Muto *et al.*, 2019; Peña *et al.*, 2022), from the rmse calculation. The viscoelastic relaxation model tends to provide a poor fit to near-field geodetic data without other postseismic mechanisms (Freed *et al.*, 2017).

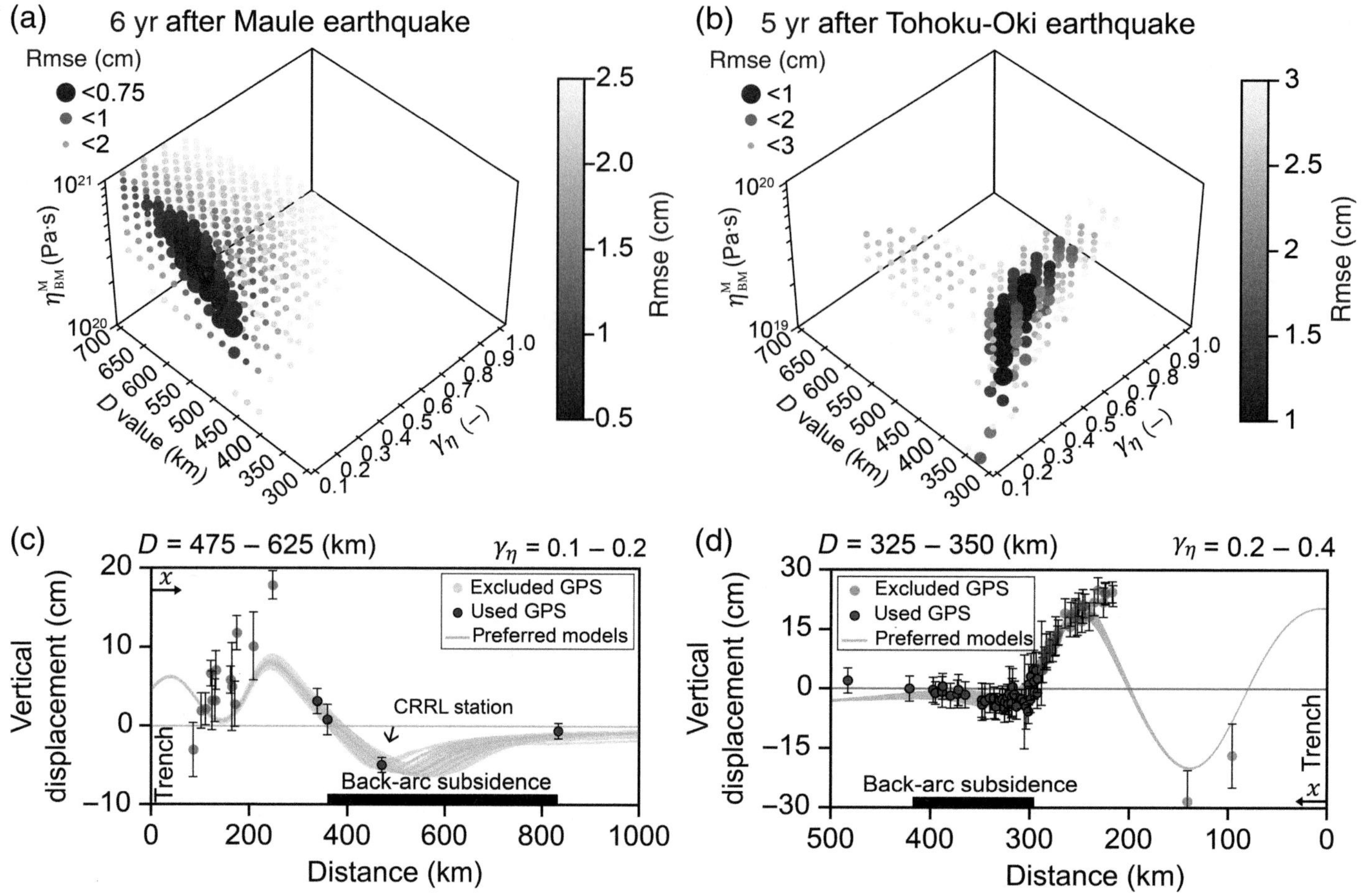

Figure 7. (a,b) Misfits with different values of η_{BM}^{M}, D, and γ_η for the Maule and Tohoku-Oki models, respectively. The size of the circles indicates the magnitude of the root mean square error (rmse) between the modeled and observed postseismic displacements. (c,d) Vertical displacement profiles of the Maule and Tohoku-Oki preferred models with rmse < 1 cm and <2 cm, respectively, superimposed with gray transparent lines. The colored, transparent, and solid circles indicate that the geodetic data were excluded and used to calculate the rmse, respectively. The colored, transparent, and solid circles indicate that the geodetic data were excluded and used to calculate the rmse, respectively. The arrow in (c) indicates the CRRL station where the maximum subsidence was recorded. The black bars in (c) and (d) indicate back-arc subsidence. The color version of this figure is available only in the electronic edition.

We performed a grid search by changing three parameters over the wide ranges of η_{BM}^{M} (and the associated transient viscosity), γ_η, and the D values to identify an optimized model with the lowest rmse (Fig. 7a). For the Maule postseismic deformation, we defined preferred models as those with parameter combinations for which the rmse was less than 1 cm (Fig. 7a). The preferred models were obtained in the ranges of D = 475–625 km, $\gamma_\eta = 0.1$–0.2, and $\eta_{BM}^{M} = 2$–8×10^{20} Pa · s. The preferred models show different wavelengths of back-arc subsidence as a function of D values (gray lines in Fig. 7c). Because only the CRRL station, located ~450 km from the trench, recorded back-arc subsidence, the D value indicating the rheological interface was constrained with low resolution. The range of η_{BM}^{M} in the preferred models is 2–8 × 10^{20} Pa · s (a fourfold difference), whereas γ_η varies by only a factor of two (0.1–0.2). The narrower range of γ_η compared to η_{BM} implies that the postseismic subsidence of the Maule case is more sensitive to the rheological contrast between the MW and BM than to the absolute viscosity of the BM. Although the MW–BM structure successfully reproduced back-arc subsidence more than 350 km from the trench following the Maule earthquake at locations, the residual displacement, where the observed displacement is larger than the modeled displacement, remained within 300 km in the fore-arc (Fig. 7c). Thus, the preferred models that accurately simulate the back-arc subsidence may underestimate postseismic deformation near the trench, suggesting that our preferred models may overestimate the viscosity of the MW.

We performed an additional numerical experiment incorporating a hydration-induced low-viscosity channel (hydrated channel; Klein *et al.*, 2016) and a bell-shaped afterslip distribution (Peña *et al.*, 2019) (see Fig. S5a and inset of Fig. S5a, respectively). This exploratory model (i.e., adding the hydrated channel and afterslip to the preferred model with the lowest rmse) explains residual displacements not captured by the MW–BM structure, particularly vertical uplift near the trench (within <200 km) and total horizontal displacement (Fig. S5b,c, respectively) remains at intermediate distances (~200–300 km), and vertical subsidence is overestimated at larger distances (>~300 km). The residual displacement between the exploratory model and the observation may be caused by the long-wavelength deformation induced by the assumed uniform thickness and viscosity of the hydrated channel in our model.

A grid search for the Tohoku-Oki postseismic displacement was performed using three parameters, that is, η_{BM}^{M} (10^{19}–10^{20} Pa · s), γ_η (0.1–1), and D (300–700 km) values. The preferred models, defined as those with an rmse of less than 2 cm, yielded D values concentrated in the range of 325–350 km (Fig. 7b). The range of D values is much narrower than the 150 km range estimated in the Maule postseismic model. The densely distributed geodetic observation points for the Tohoku-Oki postseismic deformation provide a high-resolution inversion for detecting the rheological heterogeneity between the MW and BM.

We constructed an exploratory model by integrating the low-viscosity asthenosphere–lithosphere boundary (LAB) beneath the oceanic plate (Sun *et al.*, 2024) and the bell-shaped afterslip (Fig. S6a and inset of Fig. S6a, respectively) with the preferred MW–BM model of lowest rmse. The exploratory model improved the agreement between observed and modeled displacements near the trench. The LAB structure enhanced subsidence near the trench, whereas the afterslip distribution moderately adjusted deformation at intermediate distances (Fig. S6b). The LAB also induced localized landward motion near the trench, whereas the afterslip produced a broader seaward displacement extending into the back-arc, effectively reducing the mismatch relative to the observation (Fig. S6c).

Discussion

The role of lateral heterogeneous viscoelastic relaxation has been noted in various numerical models using different approaches. The geodetic inversion models for viscoelastic deformation exhibited a larger amount of viscous strain in the MW than in the BM (Weiss *et al.*, 2019). The power-law viscosity models showed the reduced viscosity in the MW due to the coseismic stress perturbation during the early postseismic period (Agata *et al.*, 2019; Muto *et al.*, 2019; Peña *et al.*, 2020, 2022). As estimated in our model using Burgers viscoelasticity, the viscosity contrast between MW and BM is consistent with postseismic models with stress-driven power-law viscosity (Agata *et al.*, 2019; Peña *et al.*, 2020). For example, previous numerical simulations with power-law viscosity have demonstrated that MW viscosity can be reduced by more than an order of magnitude during the early postseismic period (Agata *et al.*, 2019; Peña *et al.*, 2020). In the model of Agata *et al.* (2019), lateral viscosity heterogeneity developed purely from the coseismic stress change because the MW had a uniform lateral water content. Despite generating localized viscoelastic deformation, this stress-driven heterogeneity showed limited influence on back-arc subsidence. In contrast, Peña *et al.* (2020) effectively reproduced back-arc subsidence by concentrating creep strain based on the thermal structure of MW.

The model of Peña *et al.* (2020) implied that the spatial distribution of deformation may be controlled by imposed lateral variations in the thermal structure, rather than by coseismic stress alone. If the viscosity reduction is caused solely due to the power-law rheology of the MW, then back-arc subsidence can hardly be induced at a finite distance from the trench because the largest viscosity reduction in the MW occurs near the trench with the largest coseismic stress perturbation. However, recent analyses of postseismic displacement observations suggest that the ratio of postseismic to coseismic displacement is only weakly correlated with earthquake magnitude (Boulze *et al.*, 2022). This pattern has been observed in earthquakes of varying magnitudes along the South American plate boundary (e.g., M_w 8.8 Maule, M_w 8.3 Illapel, and M_w 8.1 Iquique earthquakes) as well as in other subduction zones (e.g., M_w 9.0 Tohoku-Oki and M_w 9.2 Sumatra earthquakes; Trubienko *et al.*, 2014). In addition, the geodetic inversion of postseismic deformation (Qiu *et al.*, 2018) suggests that viscosity changes derived from viscous strain show a weak correlation with the spatial distribution of coseismic stress. This suggests that pre-existing rheological heterogeneities prior to the megathrust earthquakes are essential for the interpretation of postseismic deformation.

Forward modeling of the Tohoku-Oki postseismic back-arc subsidence included a volcanic arc structure geophysically constrained by low-velocity, high electrical conductivity, and high heat flow (Hu *et al.*, 2014; Muto *et al.*, 2016, 2019). Such volcanic arc models typically assume a very low-viscosity zone (at least ~10^{16} Pa · s) extending into the sub-arc mantle to depths of ~65 km. In contrast, the MW–BM model proposed in our study suggests a relatively wider (~100 km wide) and deeper (≥90–110 km) MW with comparatively higher viscosity (~8×10^{18} Pa · s).

Recent 3D modeling efforts have incorporated spatial variability that aligns more realistically with volcanic clustering (Dhar *et al.*, 2025), although the viscosity reduction is still located at shallow depths of <~65 km. However, the slow *S*-wave velocity distribution suggests that the origin of volcanic clustering is more strongly associated with fluids or partial melting rising from the slab (Nakajima *et al.*, 2013). The MW–BM structure of the Tohoku-Oki model provides complementary insights to the volcanic models by providing a deeper structural origin of the viscosity reduction associated with slab-derived dehydration processes. In the postseismic deformation modeling for the Maule, a hydrated channel was used to constrain the postseismic velocity using a low-velocity structure along the slab interface (Klein *et al.*, 2016). The hydrated channel, with an estimated thickness of ~30 km and a viscosity of $< \sim 10^{18}$ Pa · s, effectively explained the postseismic deformation observed from the trench to the Andes including far-field back-arc subsidence. However, hydrated channel models may overestimate subsidence compared to the observation in the ultra-far field (>~850 km), suggesting the need for a stronger rheological structure to suppress deformation at greater distances from the trench. Our MW–BM structure, characterized by a MW >~500 km wide and a viscosity of $\sim 6 \times 10^{19}$ Pa · s, successfully constrained the far-field vertical displacement. This suggests that a combination of low- and high-viscosity structures may be necessary to accurately capture the full spatial pattern of postseismic deformation. Although both our model and Klein *et al.* (2016) reproduced key aspects of postseismic deformation, neither provided a complete fit to the full spatial extent of the subduction zone. The hydrated channel showed limitations in constraining far-field observations, whereas the MW–BM model remained uncertain in the near-field.

Li *et al.* (2018) incorporate high-viscosity structures (i.e., cratons) to improve the fit to far-field postseismic vertical displacements. In this model, a fit focused on horizontal displacements is integrated with a craton to infer lateral variations in upper-mantle viscosity. In contrast, our model directly resolves the MW–BM viscosity contrast, which may exert a more dominant control on postseismic vertical deformation. The three heterogeneities (e.g., hydrated channel, craton, and MW–BM structure) differ in the definition of the local low-viscosity structures or lateral viscosity contrast, although all suggest that lateral viscosity heterogeneity is necessary to explain postseismic back-arc subsidence. Thus, the combination of these complementary rheological structures may provide a more accurate and comprehensive characterization of the complex rheological structure of the upper mantle beneath the Chile subduction zone.

The D value representing the MW–BM rheological boundary spans a wide range of 475–625 km in the Maule model, while the Tohoku model showed a relatively narrow range of 325–350 km. The wider range of the MW–BM boundary in the Maule model, which causes the uncertainty in interpreting the depth of fluid release in the subduction zone, is mainly due to sparse geodetic observations. Nevertheless, the MW width inferred from the Tohoku-Oki model (i.e., <350 km) remains smaller than that inferred from the Maule model (i.e., >475 km). Interestingly, the Chile and Japan subduction zones have different structural characteristics, despite similar slab angles (~30°; Syracuse *et al.*, 2010) at depths where slab dehydration transfers water into the MW. The Chile subduction zone contains a thinner subducting plate and a thicker overriding plate than the Japan subduction zone (Hayes *et al.*, 2012). The older and colder Pacific plate can preserve more hydrous minerals at greater depths (Mibe *et al.*, 2011), which should correspond to a larger MW width. However, the MW width inferred from the Tohoku-Oki postseismic model (i.e., <350 km) is smaller than that inferred from the Maule postseismic model (i.e., >500 km). This difference in the inferred MW width from postseismic models suggests that both hydrous mineral stability in the slab and tectonic plate interactions with mantle dynamics are important.

In the Japan subduction zone, rapid dehydration primarily from sediments and oceanic crust at shallow depths of ~100 km (van Keken *et al.*, 2011) likely triggers localized mantle weakening possibly enhanced by small-scale mantle convection (Lee and Wada, 2017). In contrast, the warmer Chile subduction zone is characterized by partial dehydration of the slab mantle at intermediate depths of ~150 km (van Keken *et al.*, 2011), potentially leading to fluid release. In particular, high-temperature mantle material ascending from the asthenosphere (Rosenbaum *et al.*, 2021) may have reacted with hydrated mantle due to slab dehydration, causing partial melting over a wide area.

In the Japan subduction zone, analyses of volcanic rocks distributed from the Quaternary front-arc to the rear-arc (Kimura and Yoshida, 2006) and xenoliths from the back-arc basin (Hirahara *et al.*, 2015) revealed a spatial distribution of hydrated mantle caused by slab-derived fluids. The geochemical evidence indicated that slab-derived fluids are pronounced near the trench and progressively decrease landward. In addition, thermodynamic modeling (van Keken *et al.*, 2012) shows that the BM gradually evolves into an equilibrium thermal structure over geological timescales. The continuous influx of the fluids derived from slab dehydration promotes the formation of a locally hydrated zone, referred to as the wet BM or weak MW (Horiuchi and Iwamori, 2016). Seismological studies have identified the zones of a low seismic velocity (Nakajima and Hasegawa, 2004) and high seismic attenuation (Nakajima *et al.*, 2013) within the BM, which are spatially consistent with the weak MW defined by our Tohoku model. Furthermore, the intraslab seismicity in the subducted Pacific slab is caused by the dehydration that extends to depths of ~100 km (Kita *et al.*, 2006). Consequently, the D values (325–375 km corresponding to ~90–110 km depth) estimated in the Tohoku model support the inferred MW–BM structure beneath the Japan subduction zone.

In the Chile subduction zone, electrical resistivity tomography models (Cordell *et al.*, 2019) suggest low electrical resistivity at depths of >~150 km (above the subducted slab), indicating widespread hydration of the MW. Despite the limitations of geophysical observations at greater depths, thermochemical simulations suggest that hydrous minerals in the lower crust and slab mantle continuously release water into the MW at depths of ~150–250 km in the south-central Chile subduction zone (van Keken *et al.*, 2011; Völker and Stipp, 2015). Recent seismic tomography models further support this, revealing pronounced low S-wave velocities in the MW above the Nazca slab (Gao *et al.*, 2021), extending eastward up to ~500 km from the trench, along with high V_P/V_S ratios (i.e., ~2.0; Rodriguez Piceda *et al.*, 2023), indicating significant fluid presence or partial melt. These geophysical observations and thermochemical simulations are spatially consistent with the inferred weak MW structure in our Maule model, reinforcing the interpretation that mantle weakening is driven by slab-derived fluids and subsequent partial melting.

Coseismic static stress changes temporarily relieve the horizontal compressional stress accumulated in the fault zone during the interseismic period, triggering reverse-fault activity (Toda *et al.*, 2011; Lange *et al.*, 2012). In contrast to the interseismic period, which is dominated by reverse faulting, the evolution of the stress regime after the megathrust earthquake is primarily associated with strike-slip fault and volcanic activity in the overriding crust (Lupi and Miller, 2014). Our generalized model shows that extensional stress, caused by viscoelastic relaxation, affects the upper crust above the MW (see Figs. 5 and 6). The extensional stress reduces seismic activity on reverse faults in the fore-arc region (Correa-Otto and Gianni, 2023) and potentially increases normal- and strike-slip-fault activity over longer timescales (Tagami *et al.*, 2024). However, even with the temporary release of compressional stress following the megathrust earthquake, reverse- or strike-slip-fault activity may persist in the overriding crust when the accumulated background stress during the interseismic interval remains sufficient (Dielforder *et al.*, 2023). A quantitative numerical analysis that includes stress accumulation, drop, and relaxation is required to validate the seismic cycle stress regime (Herman and Govers, 2020). A joint investigation of geodetic data and numerical modeling proposed that megathrust postseismic deformation alters the stress level in faults located >500 km from the trench (Shao *et al.*, 2016). In this study, the postseismic extensional stress in the intraplate fault (>400 km from the MW–BM interface) was higher in the homogeneous model than in the heterogeneous model. In the heterogeneous model, the high-viscosity BM causes a smaller amount of postseismic displacement, leading to less stress transfer to the intraplate fault. We argue that the rheology of the BM determines the degree of decoupling between intraplate seismicity and the subduction zone seismic cycle. For example, a megathrust earthquake in a subduction zone with a dry and strong BM has a negligible long-term effect on continental intraplate seismicity. This decoupling effect from a strong BM is consistent with the semianalytical viscoelastic model of intraplate seismotectonics (So and Capitanio, 2016, 2017), suggesting that the significant viscosity contrast between the two interacting strong and weak plates induces longer and shorter periods of earthquake recurrence, respectively.

Conclusions

In this study, we investigated the influence of viscosity contrast between a weaker MW and a stronger BM on postseismic deformation using the finite-element method. The contrast in viscoelastic deformation between the low-viscosity MW and the high-viscosity BM increases the relative horizontal deformation between the MW and the BM. Thus, localized horizontal extensional strain in the overriding plate (i.e., near the MW–BM interface) yielded the back-arc subsidence. The process of back-arc subsidence provides evidence that rheological boundaries can be inferred from postseismic vertical displacements. The observed back-arc subsidence following the 2010 Maule and 2011 Tohoku-Oki earthquakes was constrained by the MW–BM structure. The estimated MW–BM rheological boundary in the Chile and Japan subduction zones spanned a range of 475–625 km and 325–350 km, respectively. The lateral rheological heterogeneity is explained by the stability of hydrous minerals within the slab as well as additional tectonics (such as small-scale convection or ascending deep mantle flow). However, dense geodetic observations of back-arc subsidence are needed to clearly identify the rheological boundaries of the subduction zone. The viscoelastic deformation of the weak MW induces extensional stress in the overriding plate. Furthermore, the heterogeneous rheological strength beneath the overriding plate influences the stress transfer between inter- and intraplate faults after the megathrust earthquake.

Data and Resources

Model inputs in our numerical simulation are available on Zenodo at doi: 10.5281/zenodo.15365205. The 2D 2010 Maule coseismic slip distribution is illustrated in figure 2c of Peña *et al.* (2019). Time-series Global Positioning System (GPS) data for the Chilean subduction zone are available in the supporting information of Li *et al.* (2017) at doi: 10.1002/2016GL071995. The 2D coseismic slip distribution of 2011 Tohoku-Oki is presented in figure 5 of Muto *et al.* (2016) at doi: 10.1002/2016GL068113. Global Navigation Satellite Systems (GNSS) data in Japanese islands are displayed in figure 1b of Muto *et al.* (2019) at doi: 10.1126/sciadv.aaw1164. The slab geometries of the Chile and Japan subduction zones are based on the Slab 1.0 model of Hayes *et al.* (2012), with a recent version of Slab 2.0 is published at doi: 10.5066/F7PV6JNV. The supplemental material provided contains figures showing the mesh structure, postseismic displacement patterns across the viscosity transition zone, exploratory models for the Maule and Tohoku-Oki earthquakes, and a table summarizing the viscoelastic properties of the models examined.

Declaration of Competing Interests

The authors acknowledge that there are no conflicts of interest recorded.

Acknowledgments

The authors thank Editor-in-Chief Allison Bent, the Associate Editor, and two anonymous reviewers for their helpful and constructive comments. This work was supported by the National Research Foundation of Korea (NRF) grants (NRF-2022R1A2C1009742 and RS-2025-02293161), the Ministry of the Interior and Safety as Human Resource Development Project in Disaster management, and the Korea Institute of Marine Science and Technology Promotion (KIMST) funded by the Ministry of Oceans and Fisheries (RS-2023-00256330, RS-2023-00259686, and RS-2023-00254680).

References

Aagaard, B. T., M. G. Knepley, and C. A. Williams (2013). A domain decomposition approach to implementing fault slip in finite-element models of quasi-static and dynamic crustal deformation, *J. Geophys. Res.* **118,** no. 6, 3059–3079.

Agata, R., S. D. Barbot, K. Fujita, M. Hyodo, T. Iinuma, R. Nakata, T. Ichimura, and T. Hori (2019). Rapid mantle flow with power-law creep explains deformation after the 2011 Tohoku mega-quake, *Nat. Commun.* **10,** no. 1, 1385.

Arcay, D., E. Tric, and M.-P. Doin (2007). Slab surface temperature in subduction zones: Influence of the interplate decoupling depth and upper plate thinning processes, *Earth Planet. Sci. Lett.* **255,** nos. 3/4, 324–338.

Artemieva, I. M., and W. D. Mooney (2001). Thermal thickness and evolution of Precambrian lithosphere: A global study, *J. Geophys. Res.* **106,** 16387–16414.

Bedford, J., M. Moreno, S. Li, O. Oncken, J. C. Baez, M. Bevis, O. Heidbach, and D. Lange (2016). Separating rapid relocking, afterslip, and viscoelastic relaxation: An application of the postseismic straightening method to the Maule 2010 cGPS, *J. Geophys. Res.* **121,** no. 10, 7618–7638.

Blewitt, G., W. Hammond, and C. Kreemer (2018). Harnessing the GPS data explosion for interdisciplinary science, *Eos Trans AGU* **99,** no. 2, e2020943118, doi: 10.1029/2018EO104623.

Boulze, H., L. Fleitout, E. Klein, and C. Vigny (2022). Post-seismic motion after 3 Chilean megathrust earthquakes: A clue for a linear asthenospheric viscosity, *Geophys. J. Int.* **231,** no. 3, 1471–1478.

Bürgmann, R., and G. Dresen (2008). Rheology of the lower crust and upper mantle: Evidence from rock mechanics, geodesy, and field observations, *Annu. Rev. Earth Planet. Sci.* **36,** 531–567.

Cerpa, N. G., I. Wada, and C. R. Wilson (2017). Fluid migration in the mantle wedge: Influence of mineral grain size and mantle compaction, *J. Geophys. Res.* **122,** no. 8, 6247–6268.

Cordell, D., M. J. Unsworth, D. Diaz, V. Reyes-Wagner, C. A. Currie, and S. P. Hicks (2019). Fluid and melt pathways in the central Chilean subduction zone near the 2010 Maule earthquake (35–36°S) as inferred from magnetotelluric data, *Geochem. Geophys. Geosys.* **20,** no. 4, 1818–1835.

Correa-Otto, S., and G. M. Gianni (2023). Lower and upper plate controls on crustal seismicity in the southern central and Patagonian Andes, *Tectonics* **42,** no. 1, e2022TC007335, doi: 10.1029/2022TC007335.

Currie, C. A., and R. D. Hyndman (2006). The thermal structure of subduction zone back arcs, *J. Geophys. Res.* **111,** B08404.

Currie, C. A., K. Wang, R. D. Hyndman, and J. He (2004). The thermal effects of steady-state slab-driven mantle flow above a subducting plate: The Cascadia subduction zone and backarc, *Earth Planet. Sci. Lett.* **223,** nos. 1/2, 35–48.

Dhar, S., J. Muto, Y. Ohta, and T. Iinuma (2023). Heterogeneous rheology of Japan subduction zone revealed by postseismic deformation of the 2011 Tohoku-Oki earthquake, *Progr. Earth Planet. Sci.* **10,** no. 1, 9.

Dhar, S., Y. Takada, and J. Muto (2025). Inferring 3-D rheology of low-viscosity zone around quaternary volcanoes of NE Japan from post-seismic deformation of the 2011 Tohoku-Oki earthquake, *J. Geophys. Res.* **130,** no. 4, e2024JB029939, doi: 10.1029/2024JB029939.

Dielforder, A., G. M. Bocchini, K. Kemna, A. Hampel, R. M. Harrington, and O. Oncken (2023). Megathrust stress drop as trigger of aftershock seismicity: Insights from the 2011 Tohoku earthquake, Japan, *Geophys. Res. Lett.* **50,** no. 3, e2022GL101320, doi: 10.1029/2022GL101320.

Dixon, J. E., T. H. Dixon, D. R. Bell, and R. Malservisi (2004). Lateral variation in upper mantle viscosity: Role of water, *Earth Planet. Sci. Lett.* **222,** no. 2, 451–467.

Freed, A. M., A. Hashima, T. W. Becker, D. A. Okaya, H. Sato, and Y. Hatanaka (2017). Resolving depth-dependent subduction zone viscosity and afterslip from postseismic displacements following the 2011 Tohoku-Oki, Japan earthquake, *Earth Planet. Sci. Lett.* **459,** 279–290.

Gao, Y., X. Yuan, B. Heit, F. Tilmann, D. P. van Herwaarden, S. Thrastarson, and B. Schurr (2021). Impact of the Juan Fernandez Ridge on the Pampean flat subduction inferred from full waveform inversion, *Geophys. Res. Lett.* **48,** no. 21, e2021GL095509.

Hayes, G. P., D. J. Wald, and R. L. Johnson (2012). Slab1.0: A three-dimensional model of global subduction zone geometries, *J. Geophys. Res.* **117,** no. B1, doi: 10.1029/2011JB008524.

He, L. (2014). Numerical modeling of convective erosion and peridotite-melt interaction in big mantle wedge: Implications for the destruction of the North China craton, *J. Geophys. Res.* **119,** no. 4, 3662–3677.

Herman, M. W., and R. Govers (2020). Stress evolution during the megathrust earthquake cycle and its role in triggering extensional deformation in subduction zones, *Earth Planet. Sci. Lett.* **544,** 116,379.

Hirahara, Y., J. I. Kimura, R. Senda, T. Miyazaki, H. Kawabata, T. Takahashi, and S. Kodaira (2015). Geochemical variations in Japan Sea back-arc basin basalts formed by high-temperature adiabatic melting of mantle metasomatized by sediment subduction components, *Geochem. Geophys. Geosys.* **16,** no. 5, 1324–1347.

Hirth, G., and D. L. Kohlstedt (1996). Water in the oceanic upper mantle: implications for rheology, melt extraction and the evolution of the lithosphere, *Earth Planet. Sci. Lett.* **144,** nos. 1/2, 93–108.

Horiuchi, S., and H. Iwamori (2016). A consistent model for fluid distribution, viscosity distribution, and flow-thermal structure in subduction zone, *J. Geophys. Res.* **121,** no. 5, 3238–3260.

Hu, Y., R. Bürgmann, J. T. Freymueller, P. Banerjee, and K. Wang (2014). Contributions of poroelastic rebound and a weak volcanic arc to the postseismic deformation of the 2011 Tohoku earthquake, *Earth Planet. Space* **66,** no. 1, 106.

Hyndman, R. D., and S. M. Peacock (2003). Serpentinization of the forearc mantle. *Earth Planet. Sci. Lett.* **212,** nos. 3/4, 417–432.

Iinuma, T., R. Hino, N. Uchida, W. Nakamura, M. Kido, Y. Osada, and S. Miura (2016). Seafloor observations indicate spatial separation of coseismic and postseismic slips in the 2011 Tohoku earthquake, *Nat. Commun.* **7,** 13506.

Iinuma, T., R. Hino, M. Kido, D. Inazu, Y. Osada, Y. Ito, M. Ohzono, H. Tsushima, S. Suzuki, H. Fujimoto, and S. Miura (2012). Coseismic slip distribution of the 2011 off the Pacific Coast of Tohoku earthquake (M9.0) refined by means of seafloor geodetic data, *J. Geophys. Res.* **117.**

Iwamori, H. (1998). Transportation of H_2O and melting in subduction zones, *Earth Planet. Sci. Lett.* **160,** nos. 1/2, 65–80.

Karato, S., and H. Jung (2003). Effects of pressure on high-temperature dislocation creep in Olivine, *Phil. Mag.* **83,** no. 3, 401–414.

Kimura, J. I., and T. Yoshida (2006). Contributions of slab fluid, mantle wedge and crust to the origin of Quaternary lavas in the NE Japan arc, *J. Petrol.* **47,** no. 11, 2185–2232.

Kita, S., T. Okada, J. Nakajima, T. Matsuzawa, and A. Hasegawa (2006). Existence of a seismic belt in the upper plane of the double seismic zone extending in the along-arc direction at depths of 70–100 km beneath NE Japan, *Geophys. Res. Lett.* **33**, no. 24.

Klein, E., L. Fleitout, C. Vigny, and J. D. Garaud (2016). Afterslip and viscoelastic relaxation model inferred from the large-scale post-seismic deformation following the 2010 M_w 8.8 Maule earthquake (Chile), *Geophys. J. Int.* **205,** no. 3, 1455–1472.

Lange, D., F. Tilmann, S. E. Barrientos, E. Contreras-Reyes, P. Methe, M. Moreno, and S. Beck (2012). Aftershock seismicity of the 27 February 2010 M_w 8.8 Maule earthquake rupture zone, *Earth Planet. Sci. Lett.* **317**, 413–425.

Lee, C., and I. Wada (2017). Clustering of arc volcanoes caused by temperature perturbations in the back-arc mantle, *Nat. Commun.* **8,** no. 1, 15,753.

Li, S., J. Bedford, M. Moreno, W. D. Barnhart, M. Rosenau, and O. Oncken (2018). Spatiotemporal variation of mantle viscosity and the presence of cratonic mantle inferred from 8 years of postseismic deformation following the 2010 Maule, Chile, earthquake, *Geochem. Geophys. Geosyst.* **19,** no. 9, 3272–3285.

Li, S., M. Moreno, J. Bedford, M. Rosenau, O. Heidbach, D. Melnick, and O. Oncken (2017). Postseismic uplift of the Andes following the 2010 Maule earthquake: Implications for mantle rheology, *Geophys. Res. Lett.* **44,** no. 4, 1768–1776.

Luo, H., and K. Wang (2021). Postseismic geodetic signature of cold forearc mantle in subduction zones, *Nature Geosci.* **14,** no. 2, 104–109.

Lupi, M., and S. A. Miller (2014). Short-lived tectonic switch mechanism for long-term pulses of volcanic activity after mega-thrust earthquakes, *Solid Earth* **5,** 13–24.

Masuti, S., S. D. Barbot, S. Karato, L. Feng, and P. Banerjee (2016). Upper-mantle water stratification inferred from observations of the 2012 Indian Ocean earthquake, *Nature* **538,** no. 7625, 373–377.

Mibe, K., T. Kawamoto, K. N. Matsukage, Y. Fei, and S. Ono (2011). Slab melting versus slab dehydration in subduction-zone magmatism, *Proc. Natl. Acad. Sci. Unit States Am.* **108,** no. 20, 8177–8182.

Moreno, M., D. Melnick, M. Rosenau, J. Baez, J. Klotz, O. Oncken, A. Tassara, J. Chen, K. Bataille, M. Bevis, *et al.* (2012). Toward understanding tectonic control on the M_w 8.8 2010 Maule Chile earthquake, *Earth Planet. Sci. Lett.* **321,** 152–165.

Muldashev, I. A., and S. V. Sobolev (2020). What controls maximum magnitudes of giant subduction earthquakes? *Geochem. Geophys. Geosys.* **21,** no. 9, e2020GC009145, doi: 10.1029/2020GC009145.

Muto, J. (2011). Rheological structure of northeastern Japan lithosphere based on geophysical observations and rock mechanics, *Tectonophysics* **503,** nos. 3/4, 201–206.

Muto, J., J. D. P. Moore, S. Barbot, T. Iinuma, Y. Ohta, and H. Iwamori (2019). Coupled afterslip and transient mantle flow after the 2011 Tohoku earthquake, *Sci. Adv.* **5,** no. 9, eaaw1164, doi: 10.1126/sciadv.aaw1164.

Muto, J., B. Shibazaki, T. Iinuma, Y. Ito, Y. Ohta, S. Miura, and Y. Nakai (2016). Heterogeneous rheology controlled postseismic deformation of the 2011 Tohoku-Oki earthquake, *Geophys. Res. Lett.* **43,** no. 10, 4971–4978.

Nakajima, J., S. Hada, E. Hayami, N. Uchida, A. Hasegawa, S. Yoshioka, T. Matsuzawa, and N. Umino (2013). Seismic attenuation beneath northeastern Japan: Constraints on mantle dynamics and arc magmatism, *J. Geophys. Res.* **118,** no. 11, 5838–5855.

Nakajima, J., and A. Hasegawa (2004). Shear-wave polarization anisotropy and subduction-induced flow in the mantle wedge of northeastern Japan, *Earth Planet. Sci. Lett.* **225,** nos. 3/4, 365–377.

Oleskevich, D. A., R. D. Hyndman, and K. Wang (1999). The updip and downdip limits to great subduction earthquakes: Thermal and structural models of Cascadia, south Alaska, SW Japan, and Chile, *J. Geophys. Res.* **104**, 14,965–14,991.

Peña, C., O. Heidbach, M. Moreno, J. Bedford, M. Ziegler, A. Tassara, and O. Oncken (2019). Role of lower crust in the postseismic deformation of the 2010 Maule earthquake: Insights from a model with power-law rheology, *Pure Appl. Geophys.* **176,** no. 9, 3913–3928.

Peña, C., O. Heidbach, M. Moreno, J. Bedford, M. Ziegler, A. Tassara, and O. Oncken (2020). Impact of power-law rheology on the viscoelastic relaxation pattern and afterslip distribution following the 2010 M_w 8.8 Maule earthquake, *Earth Planet. Sci. Lett.* **542,** 116,292.

Peña, C., S. Metzger, O. Heidbach, J. Bedford, B. Bookhagen, M. Moreno, O. Oncken, and F. Cotton (2022). Role of poroelasticity during the early postseismic deformation of the 2010 Maule megathrust earthquake, *Geophys. Res. Lett.* **49,** no. 9, e2022GL098144, doi: 10.1029/2022GL098144.

Pérez-Gussinyé, M., A. R. Lowry, J. P. Morgan, and A. Tassara (2008). Effective elastic thickness variations along the Andean margin and their relationship to subduction geometry, *Geochem. Geophys. Geosys.* **9,** no. 2, doi: 10.1029/2007GC001786.

Qiu, Q., J. D. P. Moore, S. Barbot, L. Feng, and E. M. Hill (2018). Transient rheology of the Sumatran mantle wedge revealed by a decade of great earthquakes, *Nat. Commun.* **9,** no. 1, 995.

Pollitz, F. F. (2015). Postearthquake relaxation evidence for laterally variable viscoelastic structure and water content in the Southern California mantle, *J. Geophys. Res.* **120,** no. 4, 2672–2696.

Pollitz, F. F. (2019). Lithosphere and shallow asthenosphere rheology from observations of post-earthquake relaxation, *Phys. Earth Planet. Int.* **293,** 106271.

Rodriguez Piceda, C., Y. J. Gao, M. Cacace, M. Scheck-Wenderoth, J. Bott, M. Strecker, and F. Tilmann (2023). The influence of mantle hydration and flexure on slab seismicity in the southern central Andes, *Commun. Earth Environ.* **4,** no. 1, 79.

Rosenbaum, G., J. T. Caulfield, T. Ubide, J. F. Ward, D. Sandiford, and M. Sandiford (2021). Spatially and geochemically anomalous arc magmatism: Insights from the Andean arc, *Geochem. Geophys. Geosyst.* **22,** no. 6, e2021GC009688.

Shao, Z., W. Zhan, L. Zhang, and J. Xu (2016). Analysis of the far-field co-seismic and post-seismic responses caused by the 2011 M_W 9.0 Tohoku-Oki earthquake, *Pure Appl. Geophys.* **173,** no. 2, 411–424.

Shapiro, N. M., M. H. Ritzwoller, and E. R. Engdahl (2008). Structural context of the great Sumatra-Andaman Islands earthquake, *Geophys. Res. Lett.* **35,** no. 5, doi: 10.1029/2008GL033381.

So, B., and F. A. Capitanio (2016). The emergence of seismic cycles from stress feedback between intra-plate faulting and far-field tectonic loading, *Earth Planet. Sci. Lett.* **447,** 112–118.

So, B., and F. A. Capitanio (2017). The effect of plate-scale rheology and plate interactions on intraplate seismicity, *Earth Planet. Sci. Lett.* **478,** 121–131.

Suito, H. (2017). Importance of rheological heterogeneity for interpreting viscoelastic relaxation caused by the 2011 Tohoku-Oki earthquake, *Earth Planets Space* **69,** no. 1, 1–12.

Sun, T., K. Wang, and J. He (2024). Geodetic signature of a weak lithosphere-asthenosphere boundary in postseismic deformation of large subduction earthquakes, *Earth Planet. Sci. Lett.* **630,** 118,619.

Sun, T., K. Wang, T. Iinuma, R. Hino, J. He, H. Fujimoto, M. Kido, Y. Osada, S. Miura, Y. Ohta, *et al.* (2014). Prevalence of viscoelastic relaxation after the 2011 Tohoku-Oki earthquake, *Nature* **514,** no. 7520, 84–87.

Syracuse, E. M., P. E. van Keken, and G. A. Abers (2010). The global range of subduction zone thermal models, *Phys. Earth Planet. Int.* **183,** 73–90.

Tagami, A., M. Matsuno, T. Okada, S. I. Sakai, M. Ohzono, K. Katsumata, and , and Group for the aftershock observations of the 2011 off the Pacific coast of Tohoku Earthquake (2024). Stress field in northeastern Japan and its relationship with faults of recent earthquakes, *Earth Planets Space* **76,** no. 1, 39.

Thybo, H. (2006). The heterogeneous upper mantle low velocity zone, *Tectonophysics* **416,** 53–79.

Tian, Z., J. T. Freymueller, Y. He, G. Ji, S. Wang, and Z. Li (2024). Postseismic deformation due to the 2021 M_w 7.4 Maduo (China) earthquake and implications for regional rheology and seismic hazards around the Bayan Har block, *Earth Planet. Sci. Lett.* **647,** 119,059.

Toda, S., R. S. Stein, and J. Lin (2011). Widespread seismicity excitation throughout central Japan following the 2011 M = 9.0 Tohoku earthquake and its interpretation by Coulomb stress transfer, *Geophys. Res. Lett.* **38,** L00G03, doi: 10.1029/2011GL047834.

Trubienko, O., J.-D. Garaud, and L. Fleitout (2014). Models of postseismic deformation after megaearthquakes: The role of various rheological and geometrical parameters of the subduction zone, *Solid Earth Discuss.* **6,** no. 1, 427–466.

van Keken, P. E., B. R. Hacker, E. M. Syracuse, and G. A. Abers (2011). Subduction factory: 4. Depth-dependent flux of H2O from subducting slabs worldwide, *J. Geophys. Res.* **116,** no. B1, doi: 10.1029/2010JB007922.

van Keken, P. E., S. Kita, and J. Nakajima (2012). Thermal structure and intermediate-depth seismicity in the Tohoku-Hokkaido subduction zones, *Solid Earth* **3,** no. 2, 355–364.

Völker, D., and M. Stipp (2015). Water input and water release from the subducting Nazca plate along southern central Chile (33°S–46°S), *Geochem. Geophys. Geosys.* **16,** no. 6, 1825–1847.

Wada, I., and K. Wang (2009). Common depth of slab-mantle decoupling: Reconciling diversity and uniformity of subduction zones, *Geochem. Geophys. Geosyst.* **10,** Q10009.

Wang, K., and J. He (2008). Effects of frictional behaviour and geometry of subduction fault on coseismic seafloor deformation, *Bull. Seismol. Soc. Am.* **98,** no. 2, 571–579.

Wang, K., Y. Hu, and J. He (2012). Deformation cycles of subduction earthquakes in a viscoelastic Earth, *Nature* **484,** no. 7394, 327–332.

Watanabe, S., M. Sato, M. Fujita, T. Ishikawa, Y. Yokota, N. Ujihara, and A. Asada (2014). Evidence of viscoelastic deformation following the 2011 Tohoku-Oki earthquake revealed from seafloor geodetic observation, *Geophys. Res. Lett.* **41,** no. 16, 5789–5796.

Weiss, J. R., Q. Qiu, S. Barbot, T. J. Wright, J. H. Foster, A. Saunders, B. Brooks, M. Bevis, E. Kendrick, T. L. Ericksen, *et al.* (2019). Illuminating subduction zone rheological properties in the wake of a giant earthquake, *Sci. Adv.* **5,** no. 12, eaax6720, doi: 10.1126/sciadv.aax6720.

Wiseman, K., R. Bürgmann, A. M. Freed, and P. Banerjee (2015). Viscoelastic relaxation in a heterogeneous Earth following the 2004 Sumatra–Andaman earthquake, *Earth Planet. Sci. Lett.* **431,** 308–317.

Yuen, D. A., R. Sabadini, and E. Boschi (1982). Mantle rheology from a geodynamical standpoint, *Riv. Nuovo Cimento (1978-1999)* **5,** no. 8, 1–35.

Manuscript received 9 May 2025
Published online 22 August 2025

A Single-Station Earthquake Catalog for the Endeavour Segment of the Juan de Fuca Ridge (2011–2016): Challenges and Implications for the Spreading Cycle

Zoe Krauss*[1], Christian Baillard[2], William S. D. Wilcock[1], Martin Heesemann[3], Angela Schlesinger[3], and Jacob Kukovica[3,4]

Abstract

The Endeavour segment of the Juan de Fuca ridge oceanic spreading center has been intermittently monitored by ocean-bottom seismometer (OBS) networks for three decades. The available long-term earthquake record is influenced by magmatic, tectonic, and hydrothermal processes surrounding a sequence of dike emplacements from 1999 to 2005. Background seismicity decreased at the end of this sequence and was low a decade later in 2016 when multistation monitoring began with the Ocean Networks Canada NEPTUNE cabled observatory. Because of a gap in the catalog, it is unknown whether the rates were consistently low from 2006 to 2016. We expand the catalog to include 2011–2016 using a single OBS on the NEPTUNE cabled observatory. We perform single-station earthquake detection and explore earthquake localization using *P*-wave polarization and *P*- and *S*-wave differential arrival times. We assess the accuracy of these techniques by comparison to traditional network methods in 2016–2017. We find that distances between the earthquake and station are estimated well using a single station, but for most stations, *P* waves display a strongly preferred polarization direction that is independent of earthquake source azimuth. This is only observed for stations within the highly fractured axial graben. We propose that this effect is intrinsic to the midocean ridge environment and is a result of shallow fracture-induced scattering very near the OBS. Although this prevents us from calculating earthquake hypocenters, we present earthquake counts, ranges, and moments for 2011–2016 in comparison to the multistation catalog that begins in 2016. We show that seismicity rates remain consistently low both in the segment center and segment ends for 2011–2016. Our results provide further evidence that the 1999–2005 dike emplacements relieved most of the extensional strain on the segment.

Cite this article as Krauss, Z., C. Baillard, W. S. D. Wilcock, M. Heesemann, A. Schlesinger, and J. Kukovica (2025). A Single-Station Earthquake Catalog for the Endeavour Segment of the Juan de Fuca Ridge (2011–2016): Challenges and Implications for the Spreading Cycle, *Seismol. Res. Lett.* **97,** 369–382, doi: 10.1785/0220240427.

Supplemental Material

Introduction and Motivation

Short-range observations are necessary to observe small magnitude earthquakes. Unfortunately, it is not atypical in a marine setting to have sparse ocean-bottom seismometer (OBS) networks comprising only one or two stations, or unideal network geometries such that small earthquakes are only recorded on 1–2 stations. Nevertheless, the value of sparse seafloor observations has been shown repeatedly: even one OBS can significantly expand the capability of onshore networks to detect small earthquakes (Sgroi *et al.*, 2007; D'Alessandro *et al.*, 2013; Monna *et al.*, 2014; Tréhu *et al.*, 2018) and improve earthquake locations and source mechanism constraints (Romanowicz *et al.*, 2006; Frontera *et al.*, 2010; Sgroi *et al.*, 2021).

If only one seismometer records earthquakes, single-station localization techniques can still allow tectonic characterization in the absence of a larger network (Frohlich and Pulliam, 1999). With three components of particle motion, one can extract the polarization direction of the incoming *P* wave (Park *et al.*, 1987; Jurkevics, 1988; Roberts *et al.*, 1989); in

1. School of Oceanography, University of Washington, Seattle, Washington, U.S.A., https://orcid.org/0000-0002-5933-6823 (ZK); https://orcid.org/0000-0001-7224-7246 (WSDW); 2. Daimler Trucks AG, Leinfelden-Echterdingen, Germany; 3. Ocean Networks Canada, University of Victoria, Victoria, British Columbia, Canada, https://orcid.org/0000-0002-6877-6062 (MH); https://orcid.org/0000-0002-8195-0221 (AS); 4. Nanometrics Inc., Kanata, Ontario, Canada

*Corresponding author: zkrauss@uw.edu

the absence of significant scattering near the receiver, the polarization direction points in the horizontal direction of the epicenter. With earthquake azimuth calculated, an epicenter can be constrained with a single seismometer by calculating distance with differential *S*- and *P*-wave arrival times. Pioneering authors showed three-component-based localization methods to be effective by comparing solutions to network locations for local earthquakes (Alessandrini *et al.*, 1994), regional earthquakes (Magotra *et al.*, 1989), and explosions (Ruud *et al.*, 1988; Kim and Gao, 1997). Polarization methods have also been valuable in extending the reach of limited networks using standalone stations (Agius and Galea, 2011; Gómez-Arredondo *et al.*, 2016) and show potential in constraining rupture propagation in near-real time (Bayer *et al.*, 2012).

Single-station techniques have also been successfully applied to OBS. Offshore Palermo, D'Alessandro *et al.* (2013) were able to detect earthquakes unseen by land-based networks down to $M_L - 0.5$ and determine epicenters and hypocentral depths via polarization methods and emergence angle of the *P* wave. Similar results were reported by Sgroi *et al.* (2007) for a subset of earthquakes recorded by an OBS offshore Sicily. Both studies calculated single-station locations that agree well with known tectonic patterns. At the Southwest Indian ridge, Liu *et al.* (2019) calculated well-clustered hypocenters for both volcanotectonic earthquakes and regional earthquakes using single-station polarization methods.

At the Endeavour segment of the Juan de Fuca midocean spreading ridge, there are five years of seismic data suitable for single-station analysis. The data set comes from an OBS on the Ocean Networks Canada (ONC) North-East Pacific Time-series Undersea Network Experiments (NEPTUNE) cabled observatory, which provides real-time streaming data from and long-term power to seafloor instruments (Heesemann *et al.*, 2014). The observatory came online in 2011 and supported a maximum of two OBS at once until 2016 (Fig. 1a). Seismic data from the multistation network installed in 2016 have been analyzed to produce an earthquake catalog that extends through 2021 (Krauss *et al.*, 2023) and beyond (Krauss and Wilcock, 2021). The single-station sites remain instrumented following the installation of the multistation network in 2016, providing an opportunity to verify single-station methods against the multistation catalog.

The Endeavour segment is a 90 km portion of the intermediate-rate Juan de Fuca ridge oceanic spreading center. The axial graben ranges in width from 0.4 to 1 km, increasing from south to north (Clague *et al.*, 2014, 2020). Along the central 10 km of the segment, there are five main high-temperature hydrothermal vent sites within the graben (Kelley *et al.*, 2012). The Endeavour segment is capped at both ends by left-stepping overlapping spreading centers (OSCs) that are propagating toward the segment center (Fig. 1b). Complex plate boundary reorganization in the region (Johnson *et al.*, 1983; Karsten *et al.*, 1986; Shoberg *et al.*, 1991; Dziak, 2006), hydrothermal circulation, and seafloor extension all lead to extensive small-magnitude seismicity on the segment. Earthquakes at the Endeavour segment have been characterized using networks of OBSs for three decades, starting in 1995 and continuing into the foreseeable future with a near-real-time catalog from the NEPTUNE cabled network (Wilcock *et al.*, 2002; Weekly *et al.*, 2013; Krauss *et al.*, 2023).

The Endeavour segment is expected to undergo extensional rupture episodes in the form of dike emplacements ("spreading" events) every ~20 yr (Krauss *et al.*, 2023). The last extensional episode occurred as a series of spreading events from 1999 to 2005 (Weekly *et al.*, 2013), with seismicity increasing prior to dike emplacements, and dying off nearly completely afterward. Krauss *et al.* (2023) showed that seismicity rates remained low in 2016, comparable to rates seen in 2005 immediately following rupture, and then began to increase in the following years. Whether these low rates persisted during 2011–2016 is unclear without analysis of the single-station period. Krauss *et al.* (2023) also suggested that the opposing limbs of the overlapping ridge segments on either end of the Endeavour may have undergone further spreading events between 2006 and 2016; even with one station, we could expect to record such an event if it occurred.

Using a single station to make earthquake observations can introduce higher location uncertainty due to a lack of multiple observations and unstable azimuth calculations (Sgroi *et al.*, 2007; Agius and Galea, 2011). However, one station can still constrain earthquake rates and the general locations of seismically active areas. Earthquake rates within vent fields are often correlated to changes in hydrothermal venting character and are therefore useful to document (Sohn *et al.*, 1998; Kellogg, 2011; Arnoux *et al.*, 2017). In this study, we take advantage of the single OBS at the Endeavour segment for 2011–2016 and apply single-station earthquake detection and localization techniques. The value of this work is twofold: it (1) informs technical methods of single-station localization on midocean ridges and (2) augments our understanding of interrupture seismicity patterns by completing the analysis of available seismic observations at the Endeavour segment.

Data

ONC cabled network

The first OBS on the Endeavour segment node of the ONC NEPTUNE cabled observatory (Heesemann *et al.*, 2014) came online at the High Rise site (station code NCHR) in November 2010. Until June 2016, a maximum of two short-period OBS were functioning at one time, either at High Rise or the Main Field site (KEMF), with only a brief overlap period from September 2011 to May 2012 (Fig. 1a). The KEMF site provides five years of continuous single-station observations that then continued as part of the multistation network from June 2016. The KEMF site underwent instrumentation changes in March 2013 and May 2014 (Fig. 1a). For validation of our

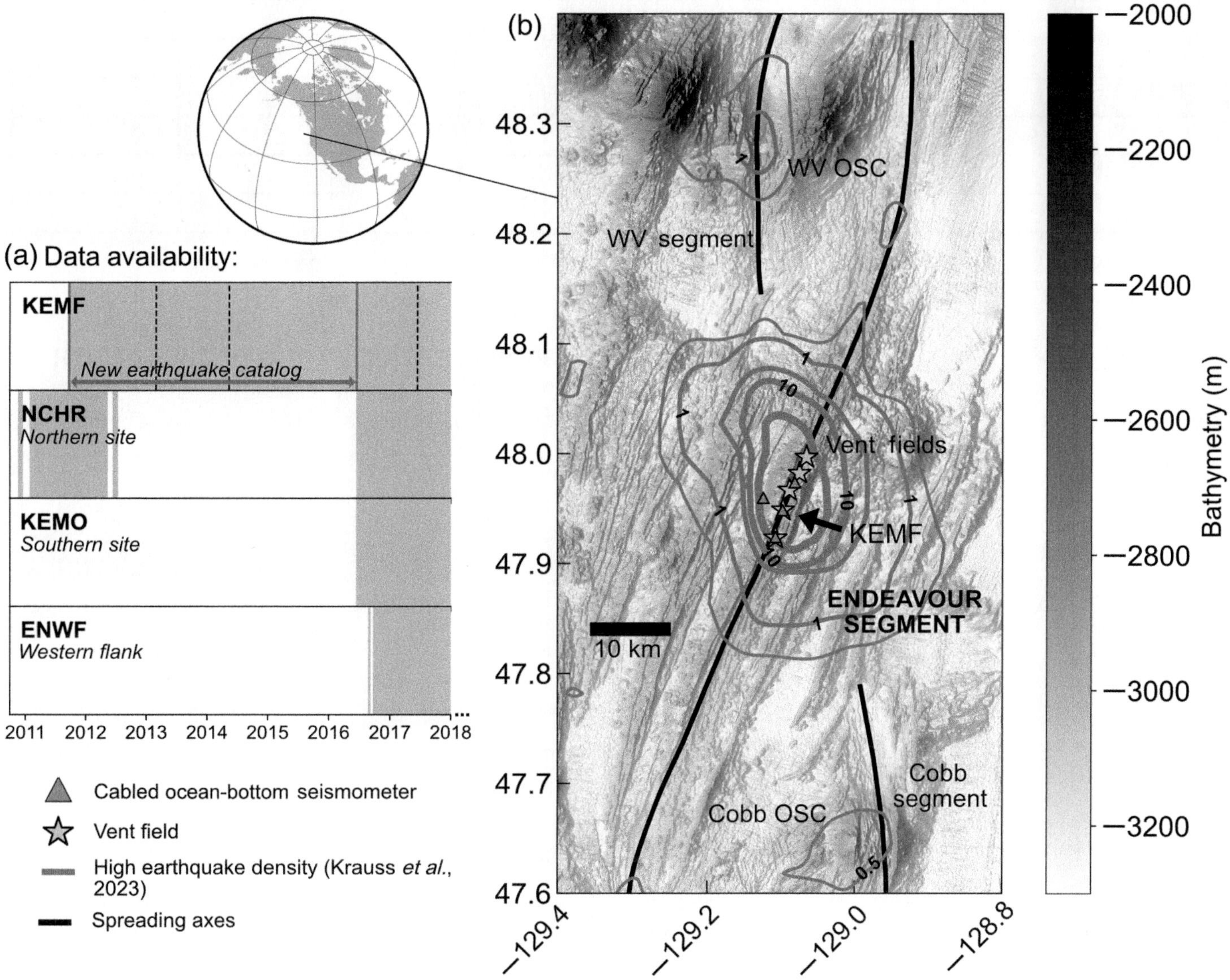

single-station detection rates and localization method, we compare our single-station detections and locations to the multi-station detections and locations of Krauss *et al.* (2023) for October 2016 to December 2017, a period when four stations were in operation without instrument changes.

Figure 1. Summary of study site and data availability. (a) Timeline showing when data are available (green) for the four main ocean-bottom seismometer (OBS) sites on the Ocean Networks Canada (ONC) NEPTUNE cabled observatory operating before 2018. Times when the KEMF site underwent a change are marked with black-dashed vertical lines: in 2017, the LED lights were turned on; all other times are an instrument change. The period for which we present new earthquake information is bounded by pink-solid vertical lines and labeled with an arrow. (b) Map of the Endeavour segment with the inset showing its global location. Bathymetry is shown in gray scale with the main features annotated. WV, West Valley. Spreading axes are shown with black lines, vent fields with gold stars, and seismic stations with green triangles. The station in place from 2011 to 2016, KEMF, is labeled. The distribution of seismicity for 2016–2021 (Krauss *et al.*, 2023) is shown using pink contours, with the contours at 0.5, 1, 5, 10, and 25 earthquakes per squared kilometer, in order of increasing thickness. The color version of this figure is available only in the electronic edition.

Velocity models

For earthquake localization, we use 3D velocity models for both *P* and *S* waves generated from a marine active seismic experiment (Arnoux *et al.*, 2019b; Kim *et al.*, 2019b). The velocity models extend over a volume of $60 \times 90 \times 9$ km^3 with a grid spacing of 0.2 km.

Methods

Automatic earthquake detection, phase picking, and moment calculation

Three-component seismic time-series data are processed for a single station using detection algorithms developed for use on Axial Seamount (Wilcock *et al.*, 2016) and adapted for the Endeavour segment. As detailed in Krauss *et al.* (2023),

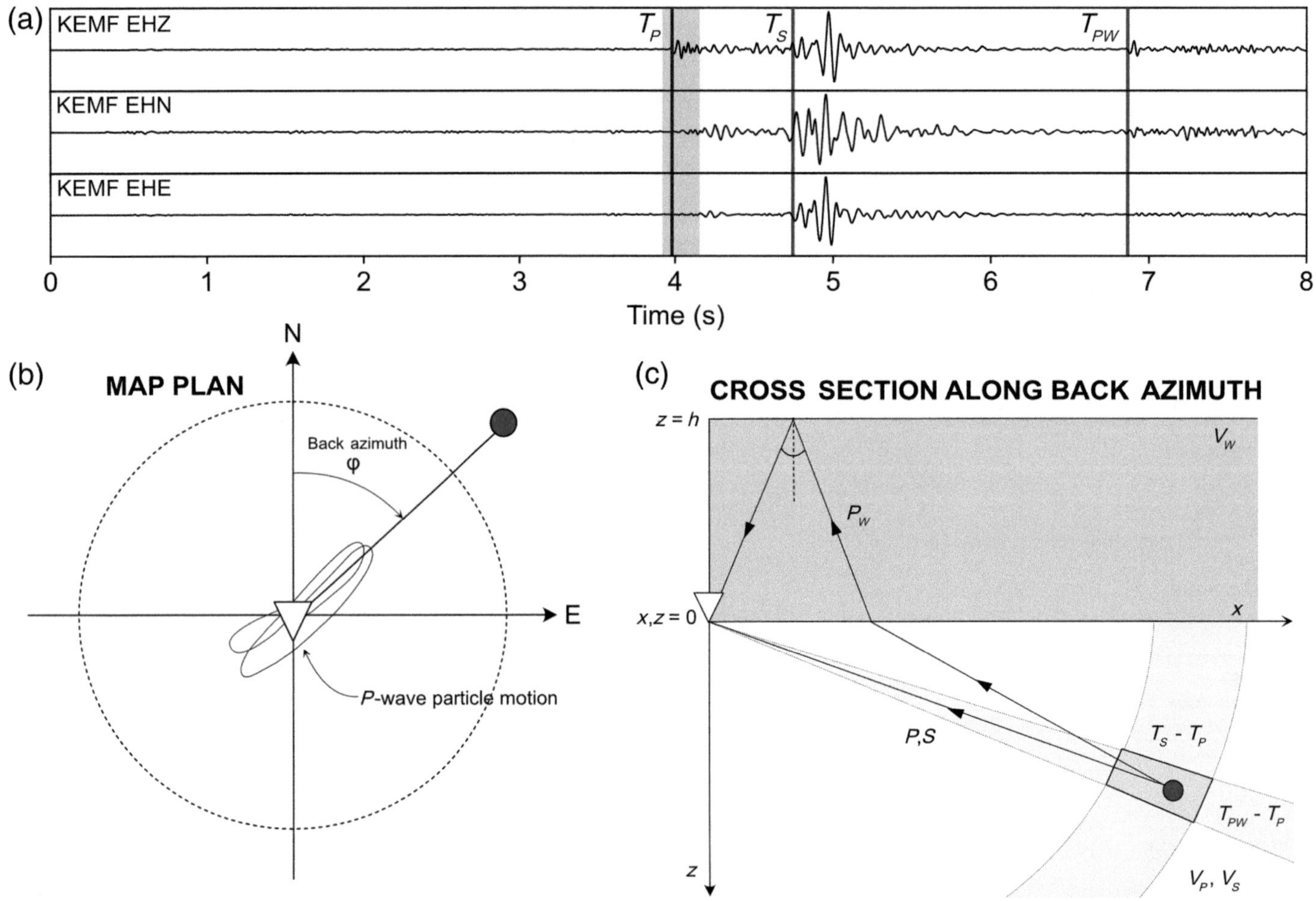

Figure 2. Illustration of a single-station location method for an OBS. As discussed in the Single-station earthquake ranging and localization section, we were only able to partially implement this method to constrain the horizontal range to earthquakes. (a) Filtered waveform of a local microearthquake with high signal-to-noise ratio (SNR), with arrival times *T*, of *P*, *S*, and P_W arrivals annotated and marked by blue, red, and green vertical lines, respectively. The window used to measure *P*-wave polarity, 0.05 s before and 0.12 s after the arrival, is shown in gray. (b) Plan view showing how *P*-wave particle motion calculated using the gray window in panel (a) relates to the azimuth of the earthquake source. In panels (b,c), the inverted-white triangle represents the seismometer, and the red circle represents the earthquake source. (c) Cross section along the azimuth in panel (b) showing how relative arrival times of the *P*, *S*, and P_W waves could be used to calculate an earthquake location. The seafloor is at $z = 0$. The blue region between $z = 0$ and $z = h$ is the water column, which has a *P*-wave velocity of V_W, and the bottom portion below $z = 0$ is the crust for which *P*- and *S*-wave velocities (V_P, V_S) are from a 3D velocity model. The color version of this figure is available only in the electronic edition.

impulsive signals are identified using a short-term long-term root mean square triggering algorithm, associated across the three components on a single seismometer, and then classified as earthquakes, whale calls, or noise based on their frequency content and similarity across channels. For events flagged as earthquakes, *P*- and *S*-wave arrival times are picked iteratively with a short-term long-term average approach (Krauss *et al.*, 2023) and then refined using Kurtosis (Baillard *et al.*, 2014).

Single-station earthquake ranging and localization

Full earthquake localization with a single seismometer is, in principle, possible in the marine setting via the approach depicted in Figure 2. The back azimuth to the earthquake can be determined using the particle motions of the *P* wave. The horizontal range and depth of the earthquake can then be obtained via the relative arrival times of *P*, *S*, and P_W (the sea-surface reflection of the *P* wave). This was the initial objective of our single-station analysis. However, we were unable to calculate reliable back azimuths for the earthquakes (see the Single-station earthquake method validation section), and as a result, could not determine the water depth where the P_W ray path crossed the seafloor accurately enough for P_W arrivals to constrain earthquake depths (Text S1, available in the supplemental material to this article). Instead, we determined horizontal ranges to earthquakes by assuming the earthquake depths and modeling the *S*–*P* arrival times. We describe this simplified approach here.

First, the three-component seismogram was retrieved from 4 s before the *P*-wave pick to 4 s after the *S*-wave pick. The horizontal components of the seismogram were rotated to north and east using the OBS orientation and then detrended, tapered using a Hann window applied to the first and last 5% of the window, and band-pass filtered between 8 and 35 Hz. The instrument responses were then removed and the seismogram was converted to displacement.

We attempted to estimate earthquake azimuth by calculating the principal component of the *P*-wave first motion (Fig. 2a,b). Because the *P* wave is a rectilinear wave, its particle motion is polarized along the vertical plane connecting the source and the receiver. Therefore, its principal component should point down along the source azimuth of the earthquake. We applied the method of Jurkevics (1988), which takes the eigendecomposition of the covariance matrix of the three-component time series, to a short-window cut 0.05 s before and 0.12 s after the *P*-wave arrival. This window length, along with the frequency band of 8–35 Hz, was chosen to maximize the rectilinearity of the waveforms (Text S2). Rectilinearity is a measure between 0 and 1 calculated using the eigenvalues of the covariance matrix. Pure body waves have a rectilinearity equal to 1. Azimuths with rectilinearity <0.5 are discarded. Azimuthal error is defined as the product of 360° and the difference between the rectilinearity and 1, such that the higher the rectilinearity, the smaller the azimuthal error.

As detailed in further sections, we found that our calculated azimuths were inconsistent with expected earthquake locations. We therefore fix earthquake depths and simply estimate the horizontal range of earthquakes. To do so in a way that is largely independent of earthquake azimuth, we generated depth-averaged versions of the 3D *P*- and *S*-velocity models (Arnoux *et al.*, 2019b; Kim *et al.*, 2019b). We created travel-time grids for these depth-averaged models using NonLinLoc's Grid2Time software (Lomax *et al.*, 2009), which solves the forward problem using a finite-difference method (Podvin and Lecomte, 1991) and assumes a flat seafloor. Using an *S–P* differenced travel-time grid, ranges are obtained by matching the observed *S–P* time to the predicted *S–P* time for a fixed earthquake depth: 2 km depth for earthquakes <2 km from the station (within the vicinity of the vent fields), or 3 km depth for earthquakes farther away, following Krauss *et al.* (2023).

Using the estimated range, *P*- and *S*-wave moments for each earthquake are calculated using the method described in Krauss *et al.* (2023). Moment magnitude is computed for each earthquake using the mean of *P*- and *S*-wave moments following Hanks and Kanamori (1979).

Results

Single-station earthquake method validation

To evaluate the efficacy of single-station localization, we apply our simplified technique of earthquake azimuth and range calculation to all four available OBS time series for 1 October 2016 to 31 December 2017, an interval with stable network geometry (Fig. 1). We then compare our single-station azimuths and ranges to those calculated by the traditional multistation methods of Krauss *et al.* (2023; Fig. 3). We only present comparisons between multistation earthquake detections and single-station earthquake detections that have both *P* and *S* arrivals on the same station that agree within 0.5 s.

For three of four stations, earthquake azimuths calculated using *P* polarization show a preferred direction that is inconsistent with the corresponding multistation locations despite high rectilinearities (>0.85; Fig. 3). For KEMF (3563 arrivals), 75% of *P* arrivals yield an azimuth within 20° of the median of 182° (Fig. 3a,f). *P* arrivals display a different preferred polarization on NCHR (3448 arrivals), with 58% yielding an azimuth within 20° of the median of 117°. For KEMO, the polarization preference is weaker, with only 21% of arrivals within 20° of the median azimuth of 295°; but, there are fewer multistation locations with both a *P* and *S* pick (1135 arrivals). In contrast, *P* arrivals to ENWF yield earthquake azimuths that are broadly consistent with multistation locations (Fig. 3i).

Ranges calculated using a single station are consistent with corresponding multistation locations (Fig. 3b,c,d,e). The median absolute difference between range calculated using a single station and that calculated with the multistation network is 1.60 km for KEMF, 1.75 km for NCHR, 1.85 km for KEMO, and 1.51 km for ENWF. Single-station ranges appear to slightly underestimate multistation ranges for all stations, with KEMF single-station ranges on average 1.26 km lower than the corresponding multistation range. This systematic difference is consistent with that expected from the variation in travel-time grids used between the single-station and multistation locations (see Text S3). Uncertainties in ranges, calculated using bootstrapping, do not increase with range and have a median of 1.7 km and maximum of 3.3 km for the KEMF station; these uncertainties do not account for errors in the velocity model.

For all stations, there are some earthquakes at ranges <10 km that are incorrectly given 0 km range by the single-station localization algorithm (Fig. 4c). This is likely a result of fixing the depth. Although we fix earthquake depths to 2 km for earthquakes within 2 km of the station and 3 km for farther earthquakes, we know from the multistation catalog that many of the small earthquakes within 2 km of KEMF are shallower (23% have depths <1 km; Krauss *et al.*, 2023). When the fixed depth is too deep, the predicted *S–P* time is too large, and the earthquake location moves closer to the station to compensate. This leads to some 0 km ranges. In contrast, for multistation localizations, when the fixed depth is too deep, the final location balances travel-time misfits between phase picks on all stations, rather than placing earthquakes beneath KEMF.

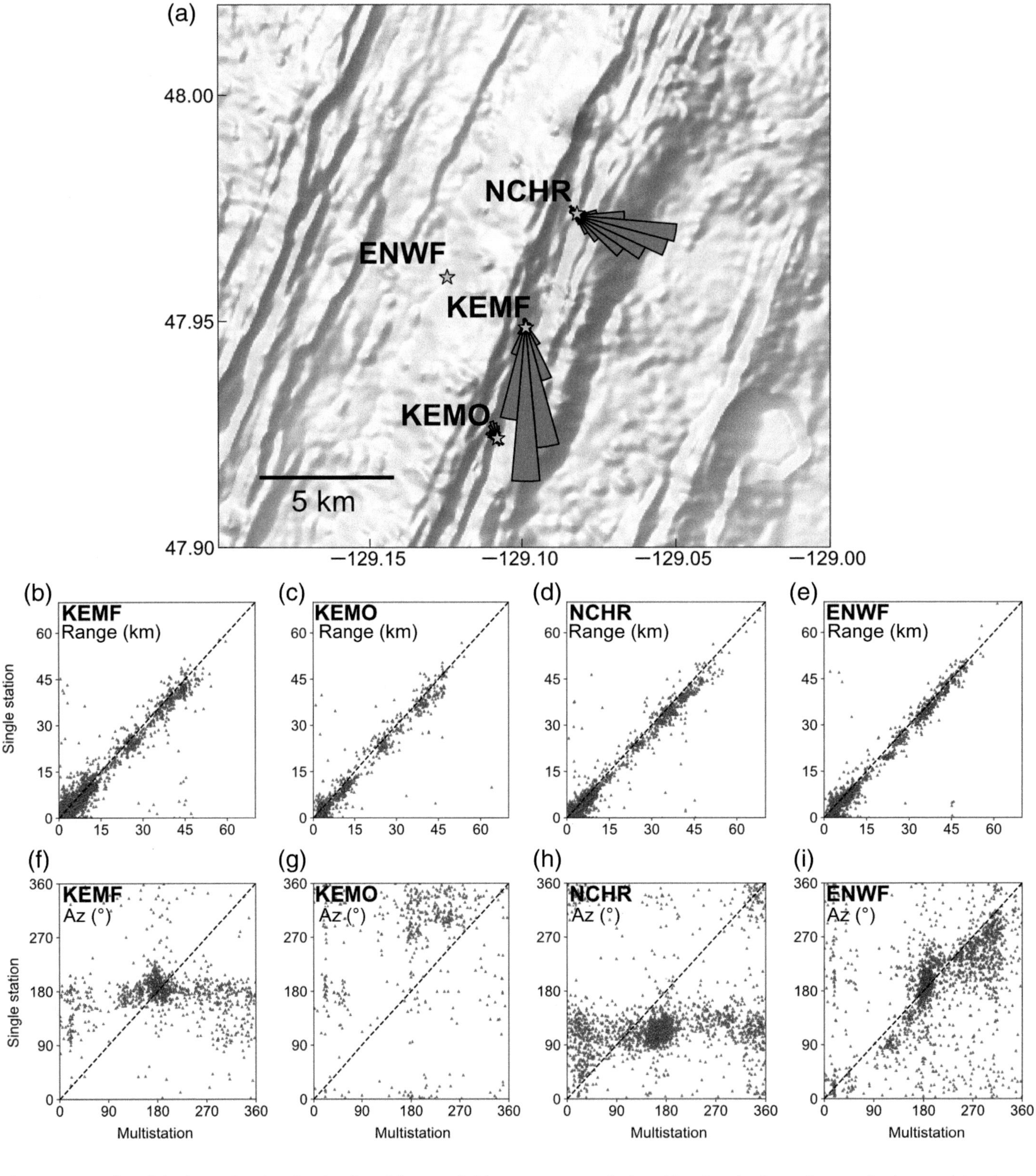

Figure 3. Results of single-station localization for all four available stations from October 2016 to December 2018 compared to multistation localization. For each station, results are only shown if the multistation location had both a *P* and *S* pick on that station. (a) Map showing station locations and single-station azimuths as a rose plot for the three stations that show a near constant polarization direction. The rose plot radii are scaled such that the maximum radius corresponds to 950 observations. The rose plot for KEMO is small because the station recorded comparatively few arrivals. (b–e) Scatter plots comparing earthquake ranges calculated by the single-station method to multistation locations for earthquakes detected from October 2016 to December 2018. The dashed line shows ranges that match (slope of 1). (f–i) Scatter plots comparing earthquake azimuths (as degrees clockwise from north) calculated by the single-station method to multistation locations. Results are shown for events with a *P*-wave SNR ≥ 3 and rectilinearity ≥ 0.85. The dashed line shows azimuths that match (slope of 1). The color version of this figure is available only in the electronic edition.

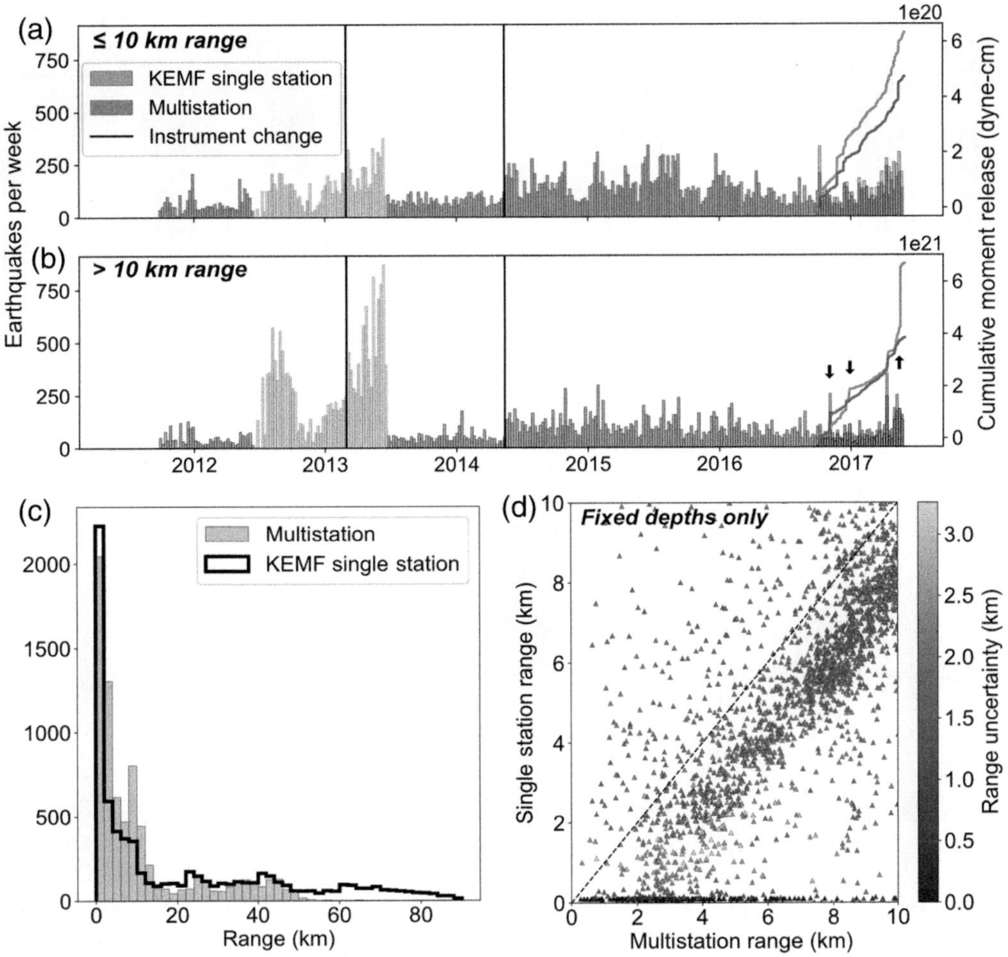

Figure 4. Results of single-station detection using KEMF, and a comparison to the multistation network from October 2016 to June 2017. (a) Histogram showing earthquake counts in 2-week bins with ranges from KEMF < 10 km for single-station detections (gray) and the unadjusted multistation catalog (orange). The cumulative moment release is overlain for the overlap period. Black-vertical lines in 2013 and 2014 indicate times when the instrument at the KEMF site was changed. Lighter shading for the KEMF detections indicates the interval when earthquake detection was corrupted by noise. (b) Same as panel (a) but for earthquakes with ranges from KEMF >10 km. Black arrows mark discrepancies in the moment release noted in the text. (c) Histogram comparing the distribution of source-to-station ranges for all earthquakes detected during the 2016–2017 overlap period by the multistation network (orange) and KEMF (overlain in black), with bin sizes of 2 km. (d) Comparison between multi- and single-station ranges for earthquakes <10 km from the station. This is a zoomed-in version of Figure 3b, except scatter points are colored by range uncertainty and only earthquakes for which depths were fixed in the multistation catalog are shown. The dashed line has a slope of 1. The color version of this figure is available only in the electronic edition.

properly detects earthquakes (Fig. S6d), but there is no straightforward way to automatically discriminate these from noise. The NCHR-only catalog for 2011–2012 is dominated by misdetections; of the earthquakes in the NCHR catalog during times that overlap KEMF (Fig. 1a), only 4% had a *P* pick within 5 s of a *P* pick on KEMF. For this reason, we only report single-station results for KEMF.

Comparison of 2016–2017 overlap period. To understand the confidence with which we can interpret single-station detections, we compare the earthquake catalogs calculated using KEMF and the multistation network for October 2016 to June 2017; after this timeframe, lights on the KEMF station were accidentally left on, which created pulsating noise that led to many spurious detections. These could not be removed without arrival-time context from other stations. We present earthquakes at ranges <10 km and ranges >10 km separately because there appears to be a change in the sensitivity of the single-station detections near this threshold (Fig. S7). This threshold also partitions the seismicity between the vent field region and the OSCs (Fig. 1).

Within 10 km of KEMF, the multistation catalog includes 5181 earthquakes during the overlap period (Fig. 4a), and the KEMF catalog includes 3959 earthquakes (Fig. 4a). We do not expect the KEMF catalog to include all earthquakes in the multistation catalog, only the ones with both a *P* and *S* pick on the KEMF station, and more specifically, a clear *P* arrival. Therefore, for comparison, we create an adjusted multistation catalog with only earthquakes that have both a *P* and *S* pick on KEMF and require that the *P* pick have a location weight >0.4. There are 2887 earthquakes in this "adjusted"

Seismicity from 2011 to 2016

The lack of azimuth constraints on NHCR and KEMF means that we are unable to obtain earthquake localizations for 2011–2016. However, we can still calculate earthquake detection counts and ranges. Manual examination of the automatic detections on NCHR for November 2010 to May 2012 shows that the instrument is often plagued by high-frequency noise that is either falsely identified as earthquakes or obscures *P*-wave arrivals (Fig. S6a–c). There are times when the algorithm

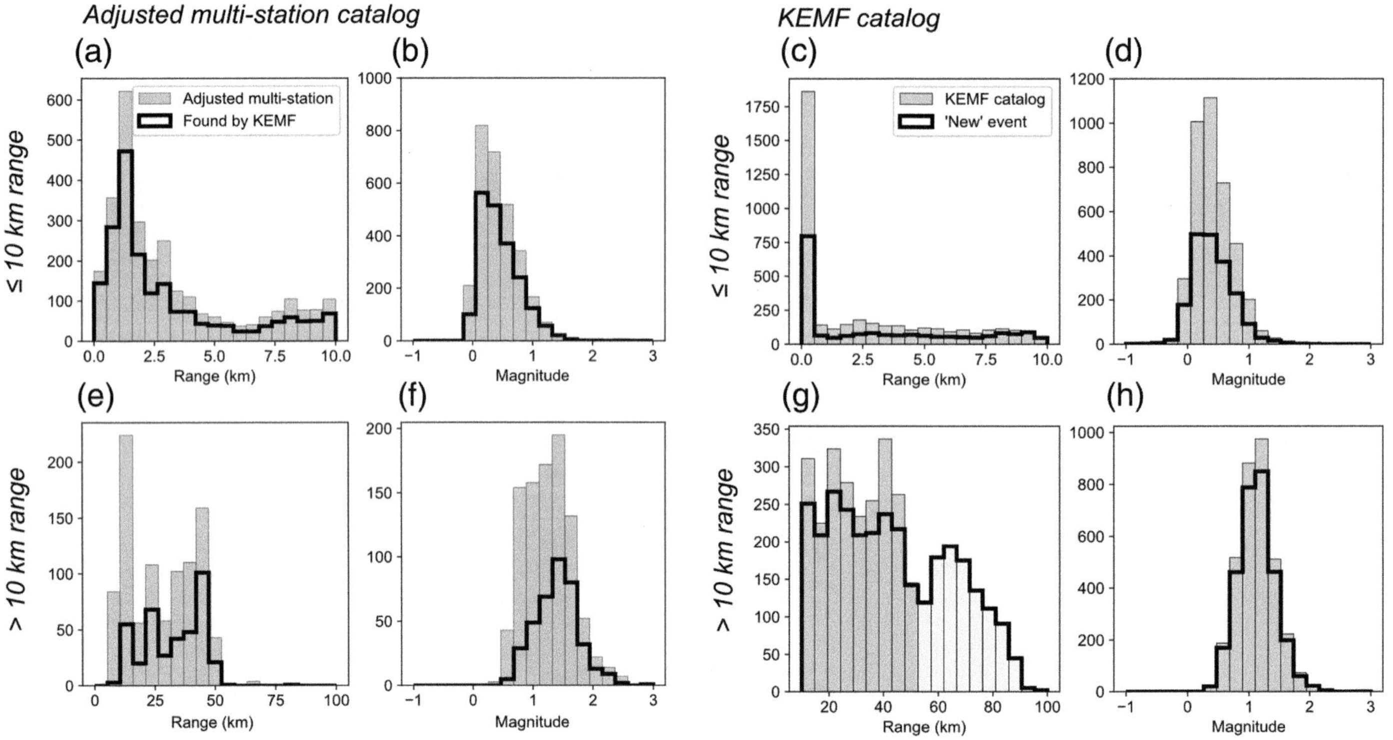

Figure 5. Comparison of earthquake characteristics between the adjusted multistation and single-station KEMF catalogs. The upper row of subplots shows earthquakes ≤10 km from the station and the bottom row shows earthquakes >10 km. (a,b,e,f) Comparison between all earthquakes in the adjusted multistation catalog and those that are also found by the KEMF catalog for 2016–2017, showing (a,e) range distribution and (b,f) magnitude distribution. (c,d,g,h) Earthquakes in the KEMF catalog overlain by earthquakes that are "new" (not in the adjusted multistation catalog based on origin times within 1 s). The range distribution is shown in panels (c,g) and magnitude distribution is shown in panels (d,h). In panel (g), earthquakes >50 km are shown with lighter shading because they are not included in the final earthquake count (see the Extending the earthquake time series for the Endeavour segment section). The color version of this figure is available only in the electronic edition.

multistation catalog. Counting events as the same if they have an origin time within 1 s, the KEMF catalog includes 70% of the earthquakes in the adjusted multistation catalog (Fig. 5a,b).

Only 51% of the earthquakes in the KEMF catalog have origin times, calculated using the estimated travel time of the *P* wave, matched within 1 s to origin times of earthquakes in the adjusted multistation catalog. This is not a result of mispicked arrivals because the proportion does not increase significantly if origin times are matched to only within 5 s. Most of the "new" unmatched earthquakes have ranges <1 km (Fig. 5c), which suggests that they are small earthquakes very near KEMF that were not included in the multistation catalog due to a lack of picked arrivals on neighboring stations.

The cumulative moment release within 10 km of KEMF for the KEMF catalog is 25% less than the unadjusted multistation catalog, but increases in moment release occur at the same times (Fig. 4a). For individual matched earthquakes, the calculated moment is slightly larger in the KEMF catalog; the median ratio of multistation to KEMF moments is 0.85 (Fig. S7).

At ranges >10 km from KEMF, the multistation catalog includes 2275 earthquakes in the overlap period (Fig. 4b) whereas the KEMF catalog contains 3430 (Fig. 4b). The adjusted multistation catalog (only events with a *P* weight >0.4 on KEMF) includes 954 earthquakes. The KEMF catalog includes only 41% of earthquakes in the adjusted multistation catalog (Fig. 5e,f) and tends to include those with higher magnitudes (Fig. 5f). The KEMF catalog may miss many of these lower-magnitude earthquakes because events farther from the network tend to have arrivals that are less clear (low signal-to-noise ratio [SNR] or emergent character) and so are more often missed or mispicked (Fig. S8). Matched earthquakes account for only 11% of the KEMF catalog (Fig. 5g,h). Of the new events, 37% have ranges >50 km (Fig. 5g). In the multistation catalog, earthquakes are generally not located this far away because the localization algorithm effectively limits the maximum *S–P* time. From inspecting a sample of these distant events in the KEMF catalog, at least 50% are mispicked true earthquakes with falsely large *S–P* times or, occasionally, instrument noise (Fig. S8).

The total moment release for the KEMF catalog at >10 km range is 42% less than the unadjusted multistation catalog total moment release. The cumulative moment release rates match well until 19 May 2017, when a magnitude 3.5 earthquake

~82 km from the network was anomalously captured by the multistation catalog but not the KEMF catalog (Fig. 4b). There are also discrepancies on 2 November 2016, from a swarm located ~30 km west of the center of the segment, and from 17 to 27 December 2016, from a swarm located ~40 km north of the network on the West Valley segment (Fig. 4b). For individual matched earthquakes at ranges >10 km, the KEMF catalog has slightly smaller moments than the multistation catalog; the median ratio of multistation to KEMF moments is 1.2 (Fig. S7).

Detections from 2011 to 2016. For the 5 yr preceding the multistation network, September 2011 to June 2016, the KEMF catalog includes 69,776 earthquakes. Two apparent changes in earthquake rates, in March 2013 and May 2014, are contemporaneous with changes in the instrument and thus presumably artifacts of detection sensitivity (Fig. 4a,b). In June 2012, the rate of earthquakes increases markedly and then decreases in June 2013. During this interval, the catalog includes many more earthquakes at >50 km range (Fig. S9). Examination of this interval reveals many misdetections on an instrumental noise source that repeats every ~3 hr (Fig. S10). This noise is associated with a subsea junction box near the instrument, which failed in June 2012 and was then disconnected in June 2013. The timing of the noise was not consistent enough to allow automated removal of these misdetections. We therefore exclude June 2012–June 2013 from our interpretation.

Discussion

Implications of the observed azimuthal bias

The preferred polarization directions we see for the ridge-axis stations (Fig. 3) are independent of earthquake magnitudes, ranges, and source azimuths. It is unlikely that these preferred polarizations are a result of methodological choices. Polarization characteristics change with frequency, such that the same seismic waveform filtered with different frequency bands may show different polarization strength or direction due to different noise sources such as anthropogenic sources or microseisms (Koper and Hawley, 2010). However, we carefully iterated on the choice of our frequency band (8–35 Hz) to maximize rectilinearity (Text S2). Varying this frequency band reduced overall rectilinearity but still yielded the same preferred polarizations. Another contribution to misdiagnosed polarization could be mistakenly including the coda of the *P* wave, which tends to have random polarization (Menke *et al.*, 1990). We chose the length of our polarization window (0.05–0.12 s around the *P* arrival) to ensure maximum rectilinearity values. The polarizations shown in Figure 3 are all for *P* waves with rectilinearities >0.85, indicating we are capturing only the truly polarized arrival. Perhaps the strongest indication that the source of the preferred polarizations is not methodological is that our technique works for station ENWF (Fig. 3), the only station not within the axial graben and the only station buried in thin sediments. We therefore suggest that the preferred polarizations are site dependent and related to deployments on bare rock in the central ridge axial graben.

Site-specific preferred ground-motion direction was investigated by Bonamassa *et al.* (1991), Bonamassa and Vidale (1991), and Vidale *et al.* (1991) following the 1989 Loma Prieta earthquake. They observed that seismometers as close as 25 m displayed significantly different preferred directions of *S*-wave ground motion, regardless of earthquake source azimuths or focal mechanisms. Bonamassa and Vidale (1991) suggested that amplified motion of scattered waves in one preferred direction effectively overrode motion in the orthogonal direction. Xu *et al.* (1996) used polarization estimates from explosions near the same sites to show that the site-specific preferred direction effect is also seen with *P* waves. They present simple models suggesting this observation is a result of scattering from shallow-dipping velocity heterogeneities near the station.

In some locations, the direction and strength of preferred ground motion appears to be influenced by local scattering from proximal fracture zones. Preferred orientation directions are commonly at a high angle or orthogonal to the strike of the fault zone (Rigano *et al.*, 2008; Di Giulio *et al.*, 2009; Pischiutta *et al.*, 2012). Near the Hayward fault, Pischiutta *et al.* (2012) observed preferred directionality of ground motion only on stations very close to the fault zone; this effect disappears at a distance of only 200 m from the fault damage zone. At Mt. Etna, Di Giulio *et al.* (2009) similarly observed directional resonance only for stations near a highly deformed rift. Pischiutta *et al.* (2012) attribute the preferred directions to the anisotropic reduction of the Young's modulus normal to the damaged zone; as the angle from the orientation of cracks increases, compliance of the substrate increases, which leads to amplified motion in the fault-orthogonal direction.

We infer that the preferred ground-motion directions on stations NCHR, KEMF, and KEMO, which are all located within the region of highest fracturing in the axial graben, arise from local scattering. The only site that does not display a preferred polarization direction (ENWF) is located ~2 km west of the axial graben (Fig. 3). However, the preferred motion directions for on-axis stations are not clearly related to the dominant fracture orientation within the axial graben. High-resolution bathymetry shows predominantly ridge-parallel cracks at all sites (Clague *et al.*, 2020), but our observed directions of preferred polarization are not consistently ridge parallel (Fig. 3). Preferred polarizations also change significantly between the NCHR, KEMF, and KEMO sites. This suggests that the subsurface structures that cause scattered waves to have a preferred direction are extremely localized, rather than the fissures that define the axial valley on the scale of tens of meters. This could include, for example, fractures or boundaries between pillow lavas within meters of the instrument. At this small scale, the scattering mechanism could be equivalently viewed as the rocking of a block of crust.

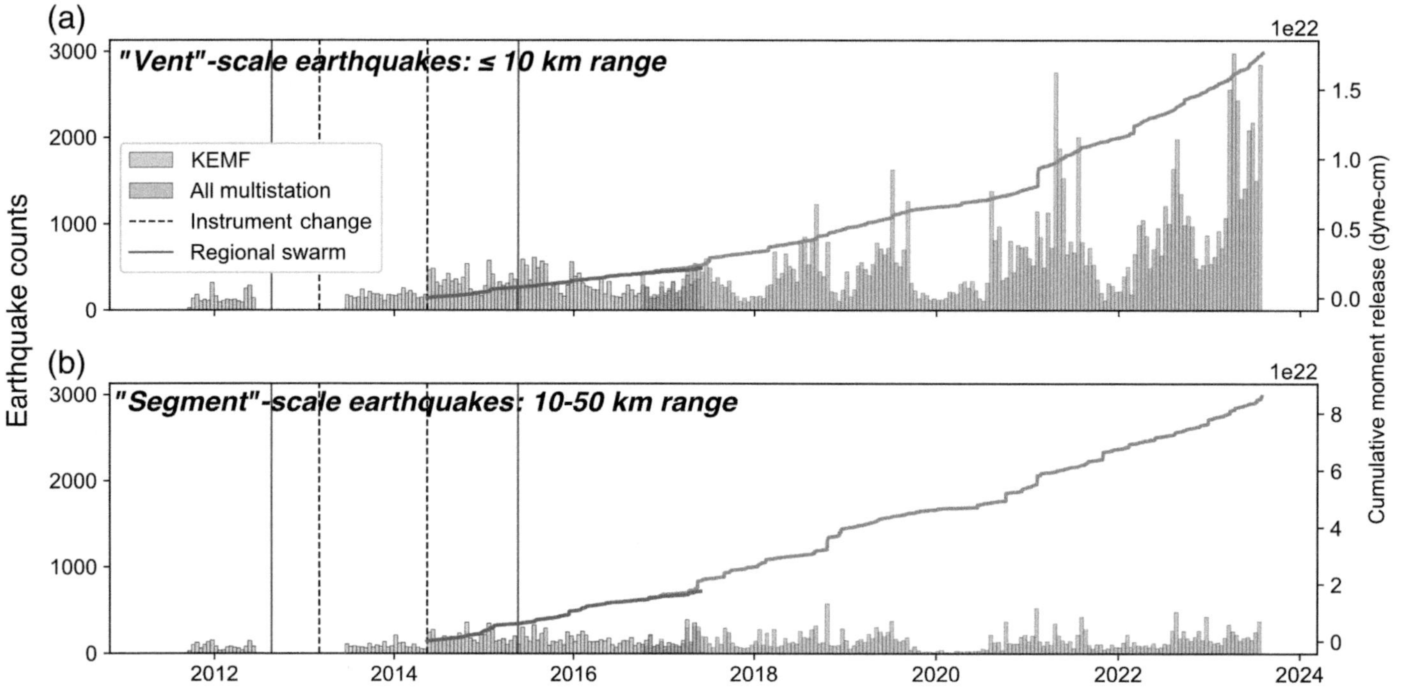

Figure 6. Time series of earthquake counts and moment release for 2011–2023 for (a) earthquakes within 10 km of the KEMF station and (b) earthquakes with ranges 10–50 km. For the multistation catalog as shown, we do not apply the station-specific corrections for network changes from Krauss *et al.* (2023), and we update their catalog to show earthquake rates up to August 2023. Earthquake counts are shown as a histogram with bin sizes of two weeks. Instrument changes during the single-station period are shown using vertical-gray-dashed lines, and the regional swarms cited as potential segment-end spreading events by Krauss *et al.* (2023) are marked using vertical-magenta lines. Decreases in detections during winter months are due to increased noise from fin whale calls. The color version of this figure is available only in the electronic edition.

The observation that the off-axis station does not exhibit preferred polarization supports that complex subsurface fracturing begins to heal significantly within several kilometers of the axial walls (Fig. 3). This is consistent with *P*-wave anisotropy observed at the ridge: the strength of anisotropy, interpreted to represent the dominance of unfilled cracks, drops off significantly at 5 km off-axis and diminishes by >50% between 5 and 10 km off-axis (Weekly *et al.*, 2014). Further, the deployment of the instrument in (or on) a few meters of sediment may lead to a more homogenous subsurface near the instrument, diminishing the preferred polarization effect.

Observations from other sites near midocean ridges and seafloor volcanic features show that preferred ground-motion directions are commonly observed. Bohidar (2023) attempted to orient short-period OBS at various volcanic sites using *P*-wave polarization for local earthquakes. Despite varying earthquake locations, they often observed a near-constant calculated azimuth. This appears to be correlated with stations at highly fractured sites. For several experiments, a preferred azimuth is seen on only some stations within a network: at Mayotte, only stations closest to the main volcanic ridge demonstrated a preferred azimuth; at Rainbow hydrothermal field, the sole station that did not show a preferred azimuth was in a deeper site farther from fracturing associated with active venting; and at Axial Seamount, stations near the caldera walls showed preferred polarizations but a station in the central, less fractured caldera did not. In their study, it is unclear how much the preferred polarization directions varied between nearby sites because most station orientations are unknown.

Preferred polarizations may also have biased the earthquake locations obtained by Liu *et al.* (2019) using a single-broadband OBS at the Southwest Indian ridge. The earthquake locations, which were made using *P*-wave polarization, have a consistent azimuth with respect to the station (see their fig. 8). Their polarized *P*-wave arrivals have high rectilinearities and their resulting earthquake locations show good clustering, but the locations do not agree with those obtained from earlier multistation network deployments (Schlindwein and Schmid, 2016; Schmid and Schlindwein, 2016). The relatively small and tight distribution of earthquakes that Liu *et al.* (2019) observed in comparison to the much broader distribution seen by the previous studies suggests that they may be seeing a similar preferred polarization effect.

Extending the earthquake time series for the Endeavour segment

We extend the time series of multistation earthquake counts and moment release for the Endeavour segment by five years to include 2011–2016 (Fig. 6). For comparison to the multistation catalog, we present these results separately for vent-scale earthquakes <10 km range from KEMF (Fig. 6a) and segment-scale earthquakes between 10 and 50 km range (Fig. 6b). We exclude earthquakes farther than 50 km because they are usually not captured by the multistation catalog and in the KEMF catalog, many of these appear to be spurious picks (Fig. 5g). We also exclude earthquakes between June 2012 and June 2013 that are impacted by instrumental noise (Figs. S8, S9). Following comparison to the multistation catalog, we correct the moment release rates in the KEMF catalog by factors of 0.85 and 1.2 for earthquakes closer and farther than 10 km from KEMF, respectively (see the Comparison of 2016-2017 overlap period section). We only present moment release rates calculated using the KEMF instrument that is in place during the multistation overlap period, which was deployed in 2014 (Fig. 6). Seasonally reduced detections during winter months in both catalogs (Fig. 6) are due to increased noise from fin whale calls (Krauss *et al.*, 2023).

During the overlap period of October 2016 to June 2017, "vent"-scale earthquake detection numbers are slightly underestimated by the KEMF catalog but are roughly comparable, with 5181 found in the multistation catalog and 3959 found in the KEMF catalog (Fig. 6a); these catalogs have equivalent magnitudes of completeness (M_c), suggesting that our moment release correction factor is appropriate and the KEMF catalog approximates well seismicity at <10 km (Fig. S11a). For earthquakes ≥10 km from KEMF, the KEMF catalog instead slightly overestimates earthquake counts, with 2275 in the multistation catalog and 3430 in the KEMF catalog (Fig. 6b). This discrepancy reflects a higher M_c for the multistation catalog, which is likely due to the requirement that more stations have clear arrivals (Fig. S11b).

Within the KEMF catalog from 2011 to 2014, abrupt changes in seismicity rates coincide with instrument changes in 2013 and 2014 (Fig. 6). Lower seismicity rates prior to the 2013 instrument change can be attributed to a lower detection sensitivity, as evidenced by a higher M_c (Fig. S11c,d). However, calculated M_c for 2013–2014 and 2014–onward is equivalent despite an obvious abrupt shift in seismicity rates (Fig. 6 and Fig. S11c,d). This suggests that the moments calculated using the KEMF instrument in 2013–2014 are overestimates compared to the instrument deployed later and provides further support for only considering moment release rates from 2014 onward (Fig. 6).

Krauss *et al.* (2023) suggested that the opposing limbs of the OSCs (Fig. 1) may have undergone further spreading events between 2006 and 2016 and pointed to several large earthquakes and swarms detected via land-based networks as candidates for such events. However, there is no indication that the candidate events during our observation period were associated with spreading events on the opposing limbs of the OSCs (see magenta lines in Fig. 6). We would expect to see a clear uptick in earthquakes >10 km from the station leading up to and during an event of that type, with a decrease in background seismicity levels afterward, which should appear regardless of variable M_c (Fig. S11d). Rather, seismicity appears at a relatively low rate consistent with the multistation rates seen in 2016. We also visually inspected the excluded data for the late 2012 regional swarm to confirm that no anomalous activity occurred (Fig. 6). If the opposing limbs did undergo further spreading events post 2006, then, it likely occurred prior to 2011.

The extended time series of Endeavour segment seismicity shows that low rates of seismicity have continued at the segment ends for at least 12 yr (Fig. 6b), with vent-scale seismicity rates near the segment center remaining relatively low until a significant uptick started in ~2018 (Fig. 6a). The seismicity rates remain overall low from 2011 to 2016 in our observations, which leaves the prediction of Krauss *et al.* (2023), that the central portion of the segment will be the first to undergo a repeated extensional dike intrusion event, unchanged. This also supports the interpretation that the 2005 rupture of the Endeavour segment largely relieved extensional stresses along the entirety of the main segment (Krauss *et al.*, 2023). Our extended vent-scale seismicity time series suggests that earthquake rates pick up exponentially rather than linearly in relation to increasing extension (Fig. 6a), similarly to trends seen at Axial Seamount (Chadwick *et al.*, 2022) and as expected for a system responding to increased stress levels (Kilburn, 2012).

Conclusions

Using only one OBS, we have extended the available time series of earthquake rates for the Endeavour segment by five years to include 2011–2016 (Fig. 6). We attempted to perform single-station localization for this period using *P*-wave polarizations to constrain earthquake azimuth and differential *P*- and *S*-wave arrival times to constrain earthquake range. Unfortunately, comparison of azimuth estimates to multistation locations shows that for most stations, *P* waves are polarized in a single preferred direction independent of earthquake source azimuth. This preferred polarization is only observed for stations within the highly fractured axial graben. The orientation of the polarization varies widely between stations only ~2 km apart and does not correlate with fracture patterns observed in high-resolution bathymetry. Because similar phenomena have also been observed at other midocean ridge sites, we propose that this effect is inherent to the midocean ridge setting and is a result of near-surface scattering from highly fractured material. We observed that *P*-wave polarizations agree with multistation locations for a station outside of the axial graben, suggesting that this scattering diminishes within ~2 km of the ridge axis at the Endeavour segment.

Although we are unable to obtain earthquake hypocenters for 2011–2016, we present earthquake counts, ranges, and moment release rates in comparison to the multistation catalog (Fig. 6), including the overlapping period between single- and multistation catalogs in 2016 and 2017. We find that single-station earthquake detection occasionally mispicks earthquake arrivals due to a lack of relative timing information from other stations. Despite this, single-station earthquake detection approximates earthquake counts, earthquake ranges, and moment release rates quite well when compared to the multistation catalog. For earthquakes both near the segment center (<10 km from the station) and near the segment ends (10–50 km), seismicity rates remain low with no significant changes during 2011–2016 (Fig. 6). This provides further support that the 1999–2005 extensional dike emplacement events relieved most of the extension along the segment, and only after ~20 yr did stresses rebuild to the point that seismicity rates were significantly enhanced.

Data and Resources

The seismic waveform data for the Ocean Networks Canada (ONC) NEPTUNE network (network code NV; Ocean Networks Canada, 2009) are available through the Incorporated Research Institutions for Seismology (IRIS) webservices (https://service.iris.edu/) via doi: 10.7914/SN/NV. The *P*-wave velocity model used for earthquake location is available through the Marine Geoscience Data System via doi: 10.1594/IEDA/324849 (Arnoux *et al.*, 2019a). The *S*-wave velocity model used for earthquake location is available through the Marine Geoscience Data System via doi: 10.1594/IEDA/324623 (Kim *et al.*, 2019a). The Vel2Grid software used to calculate travel-time grids is available at https://github.com/alomax/NonLinLoc under the GNU Lesser General Public License. The multistation earthquake catalog that served as comparison to this study is available through the Marine Geoscience Data System via doi: 10.26022/IEDA/330498 (Krauss and Wilcock, 2021). The finalized single-station earthquake catalog presented in Figure 6 is available through the Marine Geoscience Data System via doi: 10.60521/IEDA/331527 (Krauss and Wilcock, 2024). The ongoing catalog is available through ONC via https://data.oceannetworks.ca/EndeavourEarthquakeCatalog. The supplemental material for this article includes a description of theoretical single-station earthquake location using the P_W arrival (Text S1, Fig. S1), a description of the tuning of the single-station method (Text S2, Figs. S2 and S3), a description of travel-time grid differences (Text S3, Fig. S4), examples of P_W arrival picks (Fig. S5), examples of noise waveforms on station NCHR (Fig. S6), scatter plots showing moment comparison between the multistation and single-station catalogs (Fig. S7), example waveforms of mispicked large-range KEMF detections (Fig. S8), scatter plots showing temporal magnitude and range distributions of the KEMF catalog (Fig. S9), a spectrogram of the junction box noise observed on KEMF (Fig. S10), and plots of magnitude of completeness for different portions of the catalog (Fig. S11).

Declaration of Competing Interests

The authors acknowledge that there are no conflicts of interest recorded.

Acknowledgments

The data analysis was supported by the National Science Foundation (NSF) under Grant Number OCE-1833419 and through a National Defense and Science and Engineering Graduate Fellowship to Z. K. The authors thank two anonymous reviewers for constructive feedback that improved the article.

References

Agius, M. R., and P. Galea (2011). A single-station automated earthquake location system at Wied Dalam Station, Malta, *Seismol. Res. Lett.* **82,** no. 4, 545–559, doi: 10.1785/gssrl.82.4.545.

Alessandrini, B., M. Cattaneo, M. Demartin, M. Gasperini, and V. Lanza (1994). A simple P-wave polarization analysis: Its application to earthquake location, *Ann. Geofis.* **XXXVII,** no. 5, doi: 10.4401/ag-4181.

Arnoux, G., D. Toomey, E. Hooft, and W. Wilcock (2019a). Crustal and topmost mantle velocity structure of the Endeavour segment, Juan de Fuca ridge [Dataset], *IEDA*, doi: 10.1594/IEDA/324849.

Arnoux, G. M., D. R. Toomey, E. E. Hooft, and W. S. D. Wilcock (2019b). Seismic imaging and physical properties of the Endeavour segment: Evidence that skew between mantle and crustal magmatic systems governs spreading center processes, *Geochem. Geophys. Geosys.* **20,** no. 3, 1319–1339, doi: 10.1029/2018GC007978.

Arnoux, G. M., D. R. Toomey, E. E. Hooft, W. S. D. Wilcock, J. Morgan, M. Warner, and B. P. Van der Beek (2017). Seismic evidence that black smoker heat flux is influenced by localized magma replenishment and associated increases in crustal permeability: Magma recharge governs heat flux, *Geophys. Res. Lett.* **44,** no. 4, 1687–1695, doi: 10.1002/2016GL071990.

Baillard, C., W. C. Crawford, V. Ballu, C. Hibert, and A. Mangeney (2014). An automatic kurtosis-based P-and S-phase picker designed for local seismic networks, *Bull. Seismol. Soc. Am.* **104,** no. 1, 394–409.

Bayer, B., R. Kind, M. Hoffmann, X. Yuan, and T. Meier (2012). Tracking unilateral earthquake rupture by P-wave polarization analysis: Tracking unilateral earthquake, *Geophys. J. Int.* **188,** no. 3, 1141–1153, doi: 10.1111/j.1365-246X.2011.05304.x.

Bohidar, S. (2023). A seismological study of Lucky Strike volcano and hydrothermal field, Mid-Atlantic Ridge, *Doctoral Dissertation*, Université Paris Cité.

Bonamassa, O., and J. E. Vidale (1991). Directional site resonances observed from aftershocks of the 18 October 1989 Loma Prieta earthquake, *Bull. Seismol. Soc. Am.* **81,** no. 5, 1945–1957, doi: 10.1785/BSSA0810051945.

Bonamassa, O., J. E. Vidale, H. Houston, and S. Y. Schwartz (1991). Directional site resonances and the influence of near-surface geology on ground motion, *Geophys. Res. Lett.* **18,** no. 5, 901–904, doi: 10.1029/91GL01063.

Chadwick, W. W., Jr, W. S. D. Wilcock, S. L. Nooner, J. W. Beeson, A. M. Sawyer, and T.-K. Lau (2022). Geodetic monitoring at Axial Seamount since its 2015 eruption reveals a waning magma supply and tightly linked rates of deformation and seismicity, *Geochem. Geophys. Geosys.* **23,** no. 1, e2021GC010153, doi: 10.1029/2021GC010153.

Clague, D. A., B. M. Dreyer, J. B. Paduan, J. F. Martin, D. W. Caress, J. B. Gill, *et al.* (2014). Eruptive and tectonic history of the Endeavour Segment, Juan de Fuca Ridge, based on AUV mapping data and lava flow ages, *Geochem. Geophys. Geosys.* **15,** no. 8, 3364–3391.

Clague, D. A., J. F. Martin, J. B. Paduan, D. A. Butterfield, J. W. Jamieson, M. SaoutLe, *et al.* (2020). Hydrothermal chimney distribution on the Endeavour segment, Juan de Fuca Ridge, *Geochem. Geophys. Geosys.* **21,** no. 6, e2020GC008917, doi: 10.1029/2020GC008917.

D'Alessandro, A., G. Mangano, G. D'Anna, and D. Luzio (2013). Waveforms clustering and single-station location of microearthquake multiplets recorded in the northern Sicilian offshore region, *Geophys. J. Int.* **194,** no. 3, 1789–1809, doi: 10.1093/gji/ggt192.

Di Giulio, G., F. Cara, A. Rovelli, G. Lombardo, and R. Rigano (2009). Evidences for strong directional resonances in intensely deformed zones of the Pernicana fault, Mount Etna, Italy, *J. Geophys. Res.* **114,** no. B10, doi: 10.1029/2009JB006393.

Dziak, R. P. (2006). Explorer deformation zone: Evidence of a large shear zone and reorganization of the Pacific–Juan de Fuca–North American triple junction, *Geology* **34,** no. 3, 213–216.

Frohlich, C., and J. Pulliam (1999). Single-station location of seismic events: A review and a plea for more research, *Phys. Earth Planet. In.* **113,** no. 1, 277–291, doi: 10.1016/S0031-9201(99)00055-2.

Frontera, T., A. Ugalde, C. Olivera, J. A. Jara, and X. Goula (2010). Seismic ambient noise characterization of a new permanent broadband ocean bottom seismometer site offshore Catalonia (Northeastern Iberian Peninsula), *Seismol. Res. Lett.* **81,** no. 5, 740–749, doi: 10.1785/gssrl.81.5.740.

Gómez-Arredondo, C. M., J. C. Montalvo-Arrieta, A. Iglesias-Mendoza, and V. H. Espíndola-Castro (2016). Relocation and seismotectonic interpretation of the seismic swarm of August–December of 2012 in the Linares area, northeastern Mexico, *Geofís. Int.* **55,** no. 2, doi: 10.22201/igeof.00167169p.2016.55.2.1714.

Hanks, T. C., and H. Kanamori (1979). A moment magnitude scale, *J. Geophys. Res.* **84,** no. B5, 2348–2350.

Heesemann, M., T. L. Insua, M. Scherwath, K. S. JUNIPER, and K. Moran (2014). Ocean Networks Canada: From geohazards research laboratories to smart ocean systems, *Oceanography* **27,** no. 2, 151–153, doi: 10.5670/oceanog.2014.50.

Johnson, H. P., J. L. Karsten, J. R. Delaney, E. E. Davis, R. G. Currie, and R. L. Chase (1983). A detailed study of the Cobb offset of the Juan de Fuca Ridge: Evolution of a propagating rift, *J. Geophys. Res.* **88,** no. B3, 2297–2315.

Jurkevics, A. (1988). Polarization analysis of three-component array data, *Bull. Seismol. Soc. Am.* **78,** no. 5, 1725–1743.

Karsten, J. L., S. R. Hammond, E. E. Davis, and R. G. Currie (1986). Detailed geomorphology and neotectonics of the Endeavour segment, Juan de Fuca Ridge: New results from Seabeam swath mapping, *Geol. Soc. Am. Bull.* **97,** no. 2, 213–221.

Kelley, D. S., S. M. Carbotte, D. W. Caress, D. A. Clague, J. R. Delaney, J. B. Gill, H. Hadaway, J. F. Holden, E. E. E. Hooft, J. P. Kellogg, *et al.* (2012). Endeavour segment of the Juan de Fuca Ridge: One of the most remarkable places on earth, *Oceanography* **25,** no. 1, 44–61.

Kellogg, J. P. (2011). *Temporal and Spatial Variability of Hydrothermal Fluxes Within a Mid-Ocean Ridge Segment*, ProQuest Dissertations and Thesis, University of Washington.

Kilburn, C. (2012). Precursory deformation and fracture before brittle rock failure and potential application to volcanic unrest: Precursors to brittle rock failure, *J. Geophys. Res.* **117,** no. B2, doi: 10.1029/2011JB008703.

Kim, E., D. Toomey, E. Hooft, W. Wilcock, R. Weekly, S. Lee, and Y. Kim (2019a). ETOMO: Three-dimensional (3-D) P-wave and S-wave velocity structure of the upper crust beneath the Endeavour segment of the Juan de Fuca Ridge [Dataset], *IEDA*, doi: 10.1594/IEDA/324623.

Kim, E., D. R. Toomey, E. E. Hooft, W. S. D. Wilcock, R. T. Weekly, S.-M. Lee, and Y. H. Kim (2019b). Upper crustal Vp/Vs ratios at the Endeavour segment, Juan de Fuca Ridge, from joint inversion of P and S traveltimes: Implications for hydrothermal circulation, *Geochem. Geophys. Geosys.* **20,** no. 1, 208–229.

Kim, S. G., and F. Gao (1997). Study on some characteristics of earthquakes and explosions using the polarization method, *J. Phys. Earth* **45,** no. 1, 13–27, doi: 10.4294/jpe1952.45.13.

Koper, K. D., and V. L. Hawley (2010). Frequency dependent polarization analysis of ambient seismic noise recorded at a broadband seismometer in the central United States, *Earthq. Sci.* **23,** no. 5, 439–447, doi: 10.1007/s11589-010-0743-5.

Krauss, Z., and W. S. D. Wilcock (2021). Microseismicity earthquake catalog, Endeavour Segment, Juan de Fuca ridge, 1995-2023 [Dataset], *MGDS*, doi:10.26022/IEDA/330498.

Krauss, Z., and W. S. D. Wilcock (2024). Single-station microseismicity earthquake catalog, station KEMF, Endeavour Segment, Juan de Fuca ridge, 2011-2017 [Dataset], *MGDS*, doi: 10.60521/331527.

Krauss, Z., W. S. D. Wilcock, M. Heesemann, A. Schlesinger, J. Kukovica, and J. J. Farrugia (2023). A long-term earthquake catalog for the Endeavour segment: Constraints on the extensional cycle and evidence for hydrothermal venting supported by propagating rifts, *J. Geophys. Res.* **123,** e2022JB025662, doi: 10.1029/2022JB025662.

Liu, Y., C. Tao, C. Liu, L. Qiu, V. Schlindwein, H. Zhang, Y. Tian, and H. Wang (2019). Seismic activity recorded by a single OBS/H near the active Longqi hydrothermal vent at the ultraslow spreading Southwest Indian Ridge (49°39′ E), *Mar. Geores. Geotechnol.* **37,** no. 2, 201–211, doi: 10.1080/1064119X.2017.1420114.

Lomax, A., A. Michelini, and A. Curtis (2009). Earthquake location, direct, global-search methods, in *Encyclopedia of Complexity and Systems Science: Assembles for the First Time the Concepts and Tools for Analyzing Complex Systems in a Wide Range of Fields*, 1st ed., Springer, 2449–2473.

Magotra, N., N. Ahmed, and E. Chael (1989). Single-station seismic event detection and location, *IEEE Trans. Geosci. Remote Sens.* **27,** no. 1, 15–23, doi: 10.1109/36.20270.

Menke, W., A. Lerner-Lam, B. Dubendorff, and J. Pacheco (1990). Polarization and coherence of 5 to 30 Hz seismic wave fields at a hard-rock site and their relevance to velocity heterogeneities in the crust, *Bull. Seismol. Soc. Am.* **80,** doi: 10.1785/BSSA0800020430.

Monna, S., G. Falcone, L. Beranzoli, F. Chierici, G. Cianchini, M. De Caro, A. De Santis, D. Embriaco, F. Frugoni, G. Marinaro, *et al.* (2014). Underwater geophysical monitoring for European multidisciplinary seafloor and water column observatories, *J. Mar. Syst.* **130,** 12–30, doi: 10.1016/j.jmarsys.2013.09.010.

Ocean Networks Canada (2009). NEPTUNE seismic stations [Dataset], *International Federation of Digital Seismograph Networks*, doi: 10.7914/SN/NV.

Park, J., F. L. Vernon, and C. R. Lindberg (1987). Frequency dependent polarization analysis of high-frequency seismograms, *J. Geophys. Res.* **92,** no. B12, 12,664, doi: 10.1029/JB092iB12p12664.

Pischiutta, M., F. Salvini, J. Fletcher, A. Rovelli, and Y. Ben-Zion (2012). Horizontal polarization of ground motion in the

Hayward fault zone at Fremont, California: dominant fault-high-angle polarization and fault-induced cracks, *Geophys. J. Int.* **188,** no. 3, 1255–1272, doi: 10.1111/j.1365-246X.2011.05319.x.

Podvin, P., and I. Lecomte (1991). Finite difference computation of traveltimes in very contrasted velocity models: A massively parallel approach and its associated tools, *Geophys. J. Int.* **105,** no. 1, 271–284, doi: 10.1111/j.1365-246X.1991.tb03461.x.

Rigano, R., F. Cara, G. Lombardo, and A. Rovelli (2008). Evidence for ground motion polarization on fault zones of Mount Etna volcano, *J. Geophys. Res.* **113,** no. B10, doi: 10.1029/2007JB005574.

Roberts, R. G., A. Christoffersson, and F. Cassidy (1989). Real-time event detection, phase identification and source location estimation using single station three-component seismic data, *Geophys. J. Int.* **97,** no. 3, 471–480, doi: 10.1111/j.1365-246X.1989.tb00517.x.

Romanowicz, B., D. Stakes, D. Dolenc, D. Neuhauser, P. McGill, R. Uhrhammer, and T. Ramirez (2006). The Monterey Bay broadband ocean bottom seismic observatory, *Ann. Geophys.* **49,** nos. 2/3, doi: 10.4401/ag-3132.

Ruud, B. O., E. S. Husebye, S. F. Ingate, and A. Christoffersson (1988). Event location at any distance using seismic data from a single, three-component station, *Bull. Seismol. Soc. Am.* **78,** no. 1, 308–325, doi: 10.1785/BSSA0780010308.

Schlindwein, V., and F. Schmid (2016). Mid-ocean-ridge seismicity reveals extreme types of ocean lithosphere, *Nature* **535,** no. 7611, 276–279, doi: 10.1038/nature18277.

Schmid, F., and V. Schlindwein (2016). Microearthquake activity, lithospheric structure, and deformation modes at an amagmatic ultraslow spreading Southwest Indian Ridge segment, *Geochem. Geophys. Geosys.* **17,** no. 7, 2905–2921, doi: 10.1002/2016GC006271.

Sgroi, T., G. Barberi, and A. Marchetti (2021). The contribution of the NEMO-SN1 seafloor observatory to improve the seismic locations in the Ionian Sea (Italy), *Ann. Geophys.* **64,** no. 6, SE655, doi: 10.4401/ag-8575.

Sgroi, T., L. Beranzoli, G. Di Grazia, A. Ursino, and P. Favali (2007). New observations of local seismicity by the SN-1 seafloor observatory in the Ionian Sea, off-shore Eastern Sicily (Italy), *Geophys. J. Int.* **169,** no. 2, 490–501, doi: 10.1111/j.1365-246X.2007.03348.x.

Shoberg, T., S. Stein, and J. Karsten (1991). Constraints on rift propagation history at the Cobb Offset, Juan de Fuca Ridge, from numerical modeling of tectonic fabric, *Tectonophysics* **197,** nos. 2/4, 295–308.

Sohn, R. A., D. J. Fornari, K. L. Von Damm, J. A. Hildebrand, and S. C. Webb (1998). Seismic and hydrothermal evidence for a cracking event on the East Pacific Rise crest at 9 50′ N, *Nature* **396,** no. 6707, 159–161.

Tréhu, A. M., W. S. D. Wilcock, R. Hilmo, P. Bodin, J. Connolly, E. C. Roland, and J. Braunmiller (2018). The role of the ocean observatories initiative in monitoring the offshore earthquake activity of the Cascadia subduction zone, *Oceanography* **31,** no. 1, 104–113.

Vidale, J. E., O. Bonamassa, and H. Houston (1991). Directional site resonances observed from the 1 October 1987 Whittier Narrows, California, earthquake and the 4 October aftershock, *Earthq. Spectra* **7,** no. 1, 107–125.

Weekly, R. T., W. S. D. Wilcock, E. E. E. Hooft, D. R. Toomey, P. R. McGill, and D. S. Stakes (2013). Termination of a 6 year ridge-spreading event observed using a seafloor seismic network on the Endeavour Segment, Juan de Fuca Ridge: Spreading event on the Endeavour Segment, *Geochem. Geophys. Geosys.* **14,** no. 5, 1375–1398, doi: 10.1002/ggge.20105.

Weekly, R. T., W. S. D. Wilcock, D. R. Toomey, E. E. Hooft, and E. Kim (2014). Upper crustal seismic structure of the Endeavour segment, Juan de Fuca Ridge from traveltime tomography: Implications for oceanic crustal accretion, *Geochem. Geophys. Geosys.* **15,** no. 4, 1296–1315.

Wilcock, W. S. D., S. D. Archer, and G. M. Purdy (2002). Microearthquakes on the Endeavour segment of the Juan de Fuca Ridge, *J. Geophys. Res.* **107,** no. B12, EPM-4.

Wilcock, W. S. D., M. Tolstoy, F. Waldhauser, C. Garcia, Y. J. Tan, D. R. Bohnenstiehl, J. Caplan-Auerbach, R. P. Dziak, A. F. Arnulf, and M. E. Mann (2016). Seismic constraints on caldera dynamics from the 2015 Axial Seamount eruption, *Science* **354,** no. 6318, 1395–1399.

Xu, Z., S. Y. Schwartz, and T. Lay (1996). Seismic wave-field observations at a dense, small-aperture array located on a landslide in the Santa Cruz Mountains, California, *Bull. Seismol. Soc. Am.* **86,** no. 3, 655–669, doi: 10.1785/BSSA0860030655.

Manuscript received 23 October 2024
Published online 23 July 2025

Seismogenic Potential of Hydraulic Fracturing in the South Montney Play, Northeast British Columbia: A Seismogenic Index Approach

OPEN ACCESS

Ramin M. H. Dokht[*1], Honn Kao[1,2], and Ryan Visser[1]

Abstract

Understanding the seismogenic potential of fluid injection, such as hydraulic fracturing (HF), is essential for the assessment of seismic hazards of unconventional reservoirs. This study integrates statistical and seismotectonic analyses to characterize induced seismicity and quantify its potential impact associated with the South Montney Play. A comprehensive earthquake catalog, combined with detailed HF operation records, is analyzed using density-based spatial clustering and frequency–magnitude distributions. The results indicate that seismicity is predominantly associated with HF targeting the Lower-Middle Montney (LMM) formation, which accounts for more than 90% of the induced events. The classic Gutenberg–Richter relation and the lower-bound approach were employed to analyze the spatial variations of the *b*-value, revealing significant variability ranging from approximately 0.5 to 2.5. The lowest *b*-values, concentrated in LMM-associated clusters, suggest an elevated probability of larger-magnitude events. A significant negative correlation is observed between *b*-values and the maximum magnitudes of induced earthquake clusters, reinforcing the importance of *b*-value in hazard forecasting. The seismogenic index further quantifies the susceptibility of different clusters to induced seismicity, providing a statistical basis for earthquake forecasting models. The strong agreement between observed and forecasted seismicity validates the applicability of statistical models derived from seismogenic index to assess the seismic hazard induced by HF. These findings establish a robust framework for seismic risk mitigation, emphasizing the importance of statistical seismology in improving hazard forecasting and regulatory decision-making in unconventional resource development.

Cite this article as Dokht, R. M. H., H. Kao, and R. Visser (2025). Seismogenic Potential of Hydraulic Fracturing in the South Montney Play, Northeast British Columbia: A Seismogenic Index Approach, *Seismol. Res. Lett.* **97**, 383–398, doi: 10.1785/0220250130.

Supplemental Material

Introduction

Induced seismicity within the Western Canada Sedimentary Basin (WCSB) has garnered significant attention in recent studies, particularly as the number of hydraulic fracturing (HF) operations targeting the Montney formation of northeastern British Columbia (NE BC) has increased over the past decade (BC Energy Regulator [BCER], 2014; Schultz *et al.*, 2020; Wozniakowska and Eaton, 2020; Mehrabifard *et al.*, 2025). The Montney formation is a Lower Triassic unit within the WCSB. It unconformably overlies Permian or Carboniferous strata, such as the Belloy formation, and ultimately rests above the Precambrian crystalline basement (Edwards *et al.*, 1990). The depositional patterns and subsequent structural deformation of the Montney formation have been significantly influenced by basement-rooted fault systems. Notably, the Dawson Creek Graben Complex and the Hay River fault zone are well-documented reactivated structures in NE BC that underlie the Montney formation (Davies *et al.*, 2018). The presence of such faults is particularly pertinent to induced seismicity because they may serve as conduits for fluid migration and stress transmission from HF operations within the Montney formation to deeper, seismically active structures (Wang *et al.*, 2021). Among the identified induced seismicity hotspots, the Dawson-Septimus area has experienced a marked increase in

1. Natural Resources Canada, Geological Survey of Canada, Sidney, British Columbia, Canada, https://orcid.org/0000-0002-3127-363X (RMHD); https://orcid.org/0000-0001-9150-9416 (HK); 2. School of Earth and Ocean Sciences, University of Victoria, Victoria, British Columbia, Canada

*Corresponding author: ramin.mohammadhosseinidokht@NRCan-RNCan.gc.ca

seismic activity since the mid-2000s (Yu *et al.*, 2019), coinciding with extensive HF activities aimed at developing unconventional hydrocarbon resources.

Several significant seismic events have been documented within the Montney formation of NE BC, with magnitudes reaching or exceeding the established red-light threshold of M_L 4.0. The most notable include the M_w 4.6 earthquake on 17 August 2015 and the 30 November 2018 events that registered a magnitude of 4.5 (Babaie Mahani *et al.*, 2017; Yaghoubi *et al.*, 2022). These events are part of a broader trend of increasing M_w 3+ seismicity in NE BC attributed to HF operations (Schultz *et al.*, 2020; Roth *et al.*, 2022), which is significant not only due to their magnitudes but also because of their implications for the potential occurrence of larger seismic events, particularly in regions where geological conditions may be conducive to fault reactivation. In addition, it has been documented that the increase in seismicity is not solely attributable to HF but may also involve fluid injection from disposal wells, further complicating the understanding of causative factors (BCER, 2014; Wang *et al.*, 2023). As the regulatory frameworks and risk mitigation strategies demand the distinction between the effects of HF and those of wastewater disposal (WD), spatiotemporal correlation of seismic events with injection activities demonstrates that the increase in seismic activity in the WCSB is primarily due to HF operations despite the relatively low volumes of injected fluid compared to WD (Atkinson *et al.*, 2016; Roth *et al.*, 2023; Wang *et al.*, 2023).

The mechanisms of HF-induced seismicity in the Montney formation are complex and primarily involve pore pressure increase, which reduces effective stress on pre-existing faults, triggering slip, particularly in optimally oriented fault systems (Schultz *et al.*, 2017; Eaton and Schultz, 2018; Eyre *et al.*, 2019). Hydraulic communication between fractures and faults can further transmit fluid pressure, as reported in the M_w 4.5 event on 30 November 2018, where fluid migrated through a high-permeability conduit to a basement fault (Deng *et al.*, 2016; Peña Castro *et al.*, 2020). Beyond fluid diffusion, poroelastic stress transfer plays a role in seismicity occurring at greater distances, as stress redistribution through the fluid and solid matrix can induce rapid seismic responses (Goebel and Brodsky, 2018; Kozlowska *et al.*, 2018). Machine-learning-based analyses have identified cumulative injection volume, fracking stages, proximity to the Fort St. John Graben (FSJG), and depth-related metrics as key factors influencing seismogenic potential (Wang, Kao, Yu, *et al.*, 2022; Esfahani *et al.*, 2024; Wang *et al.*, 2024). These findings highlight regional variability in seismic susceptibility and provide critical insights for risk mitigation and regulatory strategies.

The seismic hazard implications of injection-induced seismicity associated with the Montney Play are substantial. Observational studies have shown that moderate-magnitude induced earthquakes can produce unexpectedly strong ground motions due to their shallow focal depths, potentially leading to localized damage, particularly in regions where infrastructure was not designed for significant seismic loading (Atkinson *et al.*, 2015). Statistical analyses of injection-induced sequences suggest that the size of induced events is governed more by regional tectonic conditions than by the specifics of injection itself (Van der Elst *et al.*, 2016). Indeed, induced events are often as large as those expected from the Gutenberg–Richter (GR) distribution for natural earthquakes, implying that seismic hazard from induced sources may approach levels observed in tectonically active regions when seismicity becomes prolific (Rubinstein and Mahani, 2015; Atkinson *et al.*, 2016; Bommer, 2022). The potential for M_w 5+ events associated with the Montney Play underscores the need for rigorous hazard assessment, as current mitigation measures, such as traffic-light protocols, may not fully account for delayed or anomalously large seismic responses (Chapman, 2021).

Despite these concerns, many probabilistic seismic hazard assessments of induced seismicity rely on simplified assumptions that do not fully capture the dynamic nature of anthropogenic earthquake sequences. Traditional models often treat induced seismicity as a stationary Poisson process with constant seismicity rate and frequency–magnitude (FM) distribution parameters, typically assuming an unbounded maximum magnitude (McGarr, 2014; Boitz *et al.*, 2024). However, induced seismicity is nonstationary by nature and strongly tied to temporal variations in injection activity (Hajati *et al.*, 2015). As Reyes Canales (2020) highlights, the use of fixed FM distribution parameters can result in misestimation of seismic hazard, particularly for larger magnitude events, necessitating adaptive modeling strategies and declustering approaches. Moreover, assuming spatial and temporal homogeneity may be especially limiting in geologically complex regions such as the FSJG, where mixed faulting regimes and subsurface heterogeneity further complicate seismic hazard modeling (Salvage and Eaton, 2022). These limitations emphasize the need for more refined, dynamic hazard frameworks that incorporate operational parameters, geological variability, and fault-specific behavior.

To effectively mitigate the risks associated with induced seismicity, detailed spatiotemporal analyses of FM distributions and the application of a seismogenic index are essential. Such analyses can provide critical insights into the patterns of seismicity and help identify areas of heightened risk (Wozniakowska and Eaton, 2020; Khajehdehi *et al.*, 2022; Muntendam-Bos and Grobbe, 2022). The seismogenic index, which quantifies the potential for seismic events based on geological and operational parameters, can be particularly useful in forecasting future seismic occurrences (Shapiro *et al.*, 2010; Reyes Canales *et al.*, 2022). By integrating geological susceptibility with operational data, researchers can refine hazard forecasts and develop targeted monitoring strategies, ultimately enhance our understanding of the seismic landscape, and improve regulatory frameworks to minimize the impacts of induced seismicity on communities and infrastructure (Langenbruch *et al.*, 2018; Pawley *et al.*, 2018; Salvage *et al.*, 2021).

The interplay between HF and induced seismicity associated with the Montney Play underscores the need for a comprehensive understanding of the risks and mitigation strategies associated with this phenomenon. As the demand for unconventional resource extraction continues to grow, addressing the implications of induced seismicity will be critical for ensuring the safety and sustainability of these operations. In this study, we focus on the southern Montney Play, which aligns with the Kiskatinaw Seismic Monitoring and Mitigation Area (KSMMA). Established by the BC Energy Regulator (BCER), the KSMMA addresses induced seismicity resulting from HF activities in the Farmington and Tower Lake areas of NE BC. This region benefits from enhanced seismic network coverage, facilitating accurate detection, and characterization of seismic events. In addition, the high concentration of HF operations provides a robust dataset for analyzing the relationship between injection activities and seismic responses. The proximity to major communities, such as Fort St. John and Dawson Creek, underscores the importance of understanding induced seismicity to ensure public safety and informed regulatory practices. Through this study, we aim to elucidate the interplay between HF operations and induced seismicity associated with the southern Montney Play, contributing to the development of more effective mitigation strategies and regulatory frameworks to manage seismic risks associated with HF activities.

Earthquake and Injection Datasets

The dataset used in this study comprises earthquake catalogs compiled by the Geological Survey of Canada (Visser *et al.*, 2017, 2021; Goerzen *et al.*, 2024) and the National Earthquake Database (available at the Earthquakes Canada website, see Data and Resources) between January 2017 and September 2023. After removing duplicate events, the final dataset consists of 41,586 events, of which 38,706 occurred within the southern Montney Play with earthquake magnitudes ranging from −1.8 to 4.2 and an average reported depth of 2 km (Fig. 1, Fig. S1a, available in the supplemental material to this article). This comprehensive dataset provides a robust foundation for detailed statistical analysis to delineate the spatial and temporal patterns of induced seismicity associated with HF operations in the study area.

The BCER Data Center reports 1456 active HF wells in this area during the study period (see Fig. 1). The South Montney stratigraphic dataset reveals that 972 and 128 HF wells target the Upper Montney (UM) and Upper-Middle Montney (UMM) formations, respectively, whereas 350 wells focus on the Lower-Middle Montney (LMM) and only 6 wells on the Lower Montney (LM). To investigate the spatiotemporal occurrence of the injection-induced seismicity at different injection sites, we employ the Density-Based Spatial Clustering of Applications with Noise (DBSCAN; Ester *et al.*, 1996) algorithm to group the HF injection wells based on their (1) target formations, (2) well surface locations, and (3) activity times. The DBSCAN algorithm is a widely used clustering method that identifies clusters as regions of high point density separated by regions of lower density. Unlike traditional partitioning methods, DBSCAN does not require the number of clusters to be specified in advance and can detect clusters of arbitrary shape (Borah and Bhattacharyya, 2004). This clustering approach allows for a more refined analysis, accounting for potential variations in seismicity patterns based on the target formation.

The reported horizontal and depth uncertainties in earthquake locations within the South Montney Play provide critical context for associating seismicity with HF operations. The average horizontal and depth uncertainties are approximately 0.9 and 0.7 km, respectively (Fig. 2, Fig. S1b). Notably, the central region exhibits significantly lower uncertainties (Fig. 2) likely due to the presence of a denser seismic network in the center of the monitoring area. These spatial uncertainties emphasize the need for a robust spatial threshold when correlating seismic events with HF operations. We follow the approach proposed by Schultz *et al.* (2018) and Wang *et al.* (2024) to establish the spatiotemporal correlation between injection-induced earthquakes (IIEs) and HF operations. To attribute each IIE to its corresponding HF well, the induced event should occur within a time window bounded by the completion of the first fracking stage and 7 days after the completion of the final stage. In addition, we consider a maximum distance of 5 km between the IIE and the HF well as the spatial threshold. This distance accounts for potential uncertainties in earthquake locations reported in the original earthquake catalogs, ensuring that the reliability of the well-seismicity association is not undermined by location uncertainty. An induced event is associated with a specific injection site if it satisfies both the temporal and spatial criteria outlined above. It should be noted that due to overlapping injection activities and inherent uncertainties in earthquake locations, induced events could be associated with clusters of nearby HF wells rather than individual wells.

Methods

GR relationship and lower-bound method

Induced seismicity research typically employs statistical approaches to analyze the frequency and magnitude of induced events in response to injection operations. The GR relation is a fundamental empirical law that describes the statistical distribution of earthquake magnitudes within a given area and time period as $\log_{10}(N_{\geq M}) = a - bM$, in which N is the number of earthquakes with magnitude $\geq M$ and a and b are characteristic constants of regional seismicity. The b-value of the GR relation is a critical parameter that indicates how the occurrence of small earthquakes compares to larger ones and provides insights into the underlying seismotectonic processes, stress

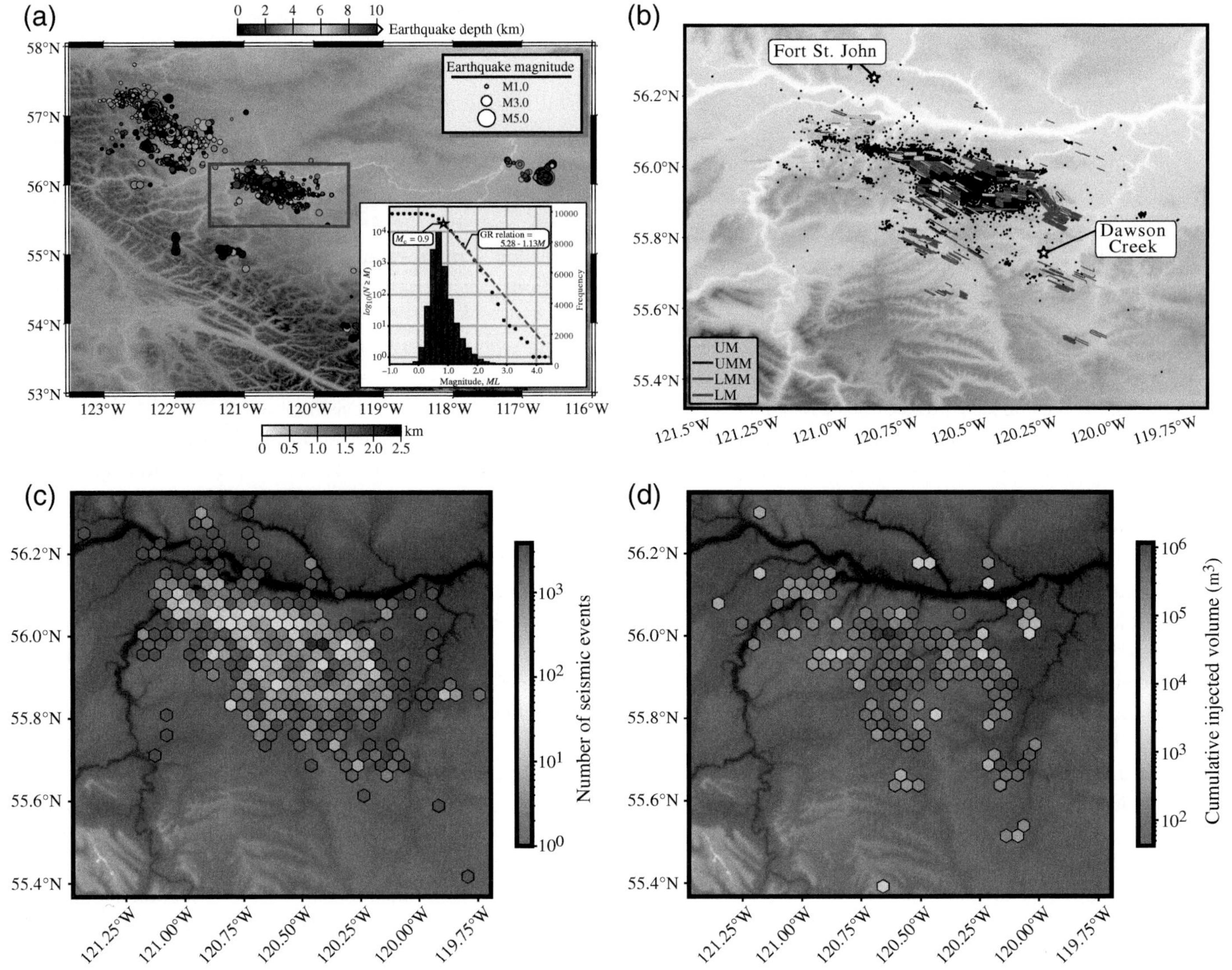

Figure 1. (a) Spatial distribution of seismicity in western Canada recorded between January 2017 and September 2023. Cold and warm colors represent shallow and deep earthquakes. The inset figure shows the frequency–magnitude (FM) distribution and the corresponding Gutenberg–Richter (GR) relation parameters for seismicity within the South Montney Play (outlined by the red rectangle). (b) Distribution of the hydraulic fracturing (HF) wells operating during the study period within the South Montney Play. Different colors represent different target formations; LM, Lower Montney; LMM: Lower-Middle Montney; UM, Upper Montney; and UMM, Upper-Middle Montney. Black dots represent the background seismicity. (c,d) Hexagonal binned plots showing the earthquake counts and cumulative injected volumes, respectively, for the entire study period. The color version of this figure is available only in the electronic edition.

regimes, and potential seismic hazard (Fiedler *et al.*, 2018; Geffers *et al.*, 2022).

Although b-value estimations provide important insights into seismic behavior, their reliability depends on the completeness and quality of the seismicity catalog and the limitations of the GR model, particularly in representing the occurrence of larger events, introduce uncertainties that warrant careful interpretation. The GR relationship, although widely utilized in seismology, has notable limitations when applied to induced seismicity. The GR model assumes an infinite seismotectonic continuum, which fails to account for the finite, stimulated volume associated with induced seismic events (Shapiro *et al.*, 2011; Eaton *et al.*, 2014; Urban *et al.*, 2016; Boitz *et al.*, 2024). This often leads to an overestimation of the b-value. To address this limitation, Boitz *et al.* (2024) introduced the lower-bound (LB) method incorporating the spatially constrained nature of induced seismicity, focusing on the reservoir layer where rupture surfaces are confined within the stimulated volume. This approach results in a different FM distribution, typically characterized by a scarcity of larger events. The LB method integrates the reservoir and rupture geometry to yield a more accurate b-value and a physically constrained upper-magnitude limit for induced seismicity. This approach better captures magnitude scaling within the finite, stimulated volume and typically results in lower b-values

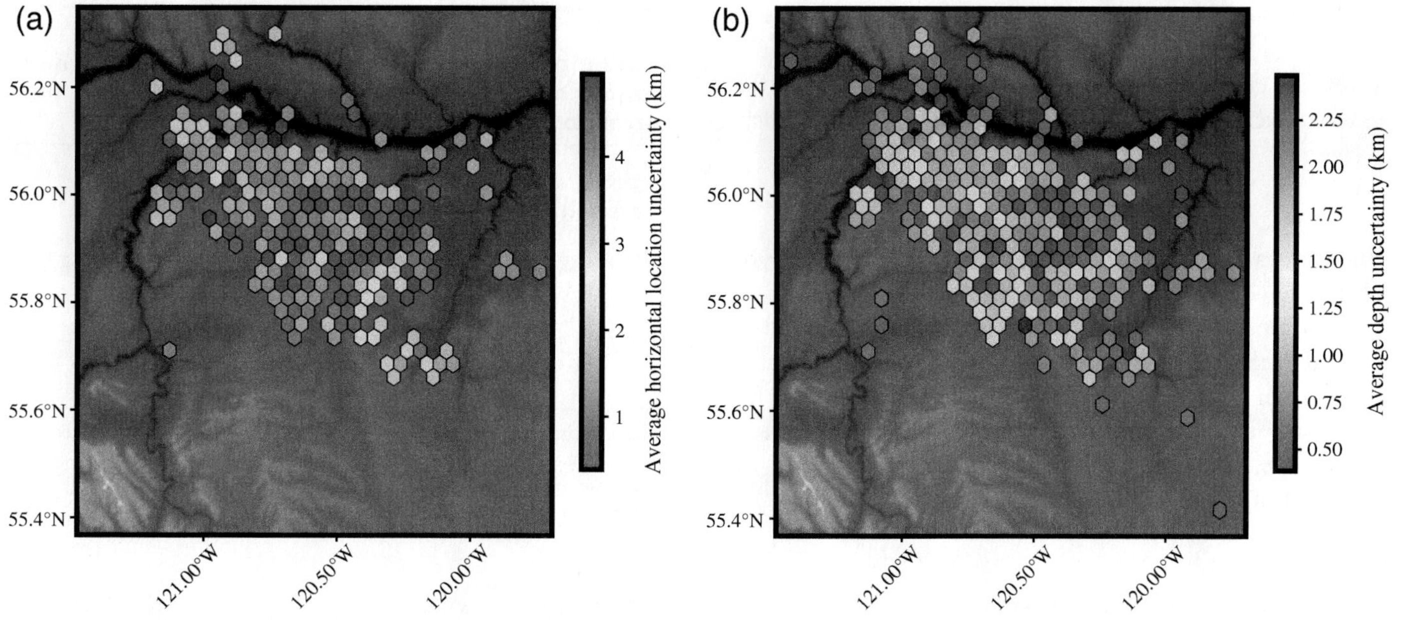

Figure 2. Heat maps showing the spatial distributions of the average (a) horizontal and (b) depths uncertainties in earthquake locations. The color version of this figure is available only in the electronic edition.

than those obtained from the classical GR relationship (Boitz *et al.*, 2024):

$$\log_{10}(N_M) = a - bM + 2\log_{10}\left(1 - 10^{\frac{M-M_Y}{2}}\right), \quad (1)$$

in which M_Y is the maximum magnitude for a reservoir-limited rupture and can be estimated using the effective rupture length X_Y and an estimate of stress drop $\Delta\sigma$:

$$M_Y = \log_{10}(X_Y^2) + \frac{2}{3}\log_{10}(\Delta\sigma) - 6.07. \quad (2)$$

It is important to note that the method proposed by Boitz *et al.* (2024) assumes that fault ruptures are confined within the reservoir interval. However, in the Montney Play, a few studies (e.g., Esmaeilzadeh and Eaton, 2022) have documented faults that may extend into the underlying basement. As a result, this assumption may not universally hold and could introduce uncertainties in the estimated b-values due to the potential for larger rupture dimensions associated with basement-penetrating faults.

Seismogenic index and forecasting the largest IIE

Although the GR relation provides a statistical framework to describe the FM distribution of induced earthquakes, it does not explicitly incorporate operational parameters such as fluid injection. The seismogenic index Σ introduced by Shapiro *et al.* (2010) extends the GR relation by quantifying the susceptibility of a region to injection-induced seismicity per unit volume of injected fluid. The seismogenic index provides a means to estimate the occurrence probability of earthquakes with a given magnitude induced during fluid injection (Shapiro *et al.*, 2010; Dinske and Shapiro, 2013), making it a crucial parameter for assessing and mitigating seismic hazard associated with HF operations. The modified GR relation, incorporating the seismogenic index, relates the temporal changes in seismicity to the cumulative injected volume until time t, $Qc(t)$, as

$$\log_{10}(N_M(t)) = \log_{10}(Qc(t)) + \Sigma - bM, \quad (3)$$

in which $N_M(t)$ represents the number of induced events with magnitudes larger than M after time t, and b is the b-value of the GR relation. Under the assumption of a constant b-value, Σ remains time independent and captures spatial variations in seismogenic potential that stem from local geological conditions, stress regime, and operational practices. Regions with higher Σ values exhibit greater seismogenic productivity and are thus more susceptible to larger induced events (Dinske and Shapiro, 2013; Langenbruch and Zoback, 2016). Mapping the spatial distribution of Σ across seismicity clusters enables the identification of zones where the combination of injection operations and subsurface conditions elevates seismic hazard.

In addition to describing the seismic response to fluid injection, the seismogenic index facilitates statistical forecasting of the largest expected IIE. Assuming that induced seismicity follows a Poisson distribution, for which events occur independently (Langenbruch *et al.*, 2011), we can statistically estimate the absence probability of an event with a magnitude greater than M over a given injection interval t as (Shapiro *et al.*, 2010)

$$P(M,t) = \exp(-Qc(t)10^{\Sigma-bM}). \quad (4)$$

The absence probability functions provide a means to estimate the largest expected magnitudes $M_{\mathrm{Max}}^{\Sigma\chi}$ within a cluster at different confidence levels χ by assessing the likelihood that no event exceeds a given magnitude within a given seismicity cluster:

$$M_{\mathrm{Max}}^{\Sigma\chi} = \frac{\Sigma - \log_{10}\left(\frac{-\ln\chi}{Qc(t)}\right)}{b}. \quad (5)$$

This framework provides a probabilistic upper bound on induced earthquake magnitude, grounded in observed seismicity, injection history, and local seismogenic characteristics. It is particularly useful for identifying clusters for which elevated values of Σ and injection volume combine to increase the likelihood of significant seismic events.

Results

Recent advancements in seismic monitoring and the availability of comprehensive earthquake and injection datasets have significantly improved our ability to conduct detailed analyses of induced seismicity in the South Montney Play. The spatial distribution of seismicity shows an average horizontal distance of approximately 0.5 km between induced events and their corresponding injection points (Fig. S2). This is consistent with previous observations of induced seismicity occurring up to ~1.5 km from HF operations within the WCSB (Li *et al.*, 2023). To investigate the relationship between HF and induced seismicity within the South Montney Play, we apply DBSCAN to group the HF wells and associated induced seismicity events, which helps identify seismogenic clusters. This clustering approach allows for a focused analysis of induced seismicity tied to specific HF operations. Each identified cluster will be characterized by its spatial extent, number of events, and injection parameters. The DBSCAN clustering process identified a total of 535 HF injection clusters from which seismicity data were further analyzed using the spatiotemporal criteria established by Schultz *et al.* (2018) and Wang *et al.* (2024) to associate IIEs with specific clusters. Remarkably, nearly 92% of seismicity (33,223 events) was linked to HF operations targeting the LMM formation, despite this formation having the second largest cumulative injected volume compared to injection at the UM formation over the entire study period (Fig. S3). In contrast, only ~6% (2201 events) and 2% (639 events) of seismicity were associated with HF operations targeting the UM and UMM formations, respectively. No induced seismicity was detected in association with HF operations targeting the LM formation, for which the cumulative injected volume over the entire study period remains insignificant compared to other formations (12×10^4 m^3; see Fig. S3). To ensure statistical robustness and focus the analysis on seismogenic behavior, only clusters with more than 100 associated IIEs were considered for further evaluation. This criterion yielded 75 seismogenic clusters, the majority of which were associated with injection operations targeting the LMM formation (62 clusters), followed by the UM (10 clusters), and UMM (3 clusters) formations (see Table 1). This distribution underscores the dominant role of the LMM formation in causing seismogenic activity in the study area.

TABLE 1
Number of Individual HF Wells (Second Column) and Number of HF Clusters (Third Column) Based on the Corresponding Target Formation

Target Formation	Number of HF Wells	Number of HF Clusters
UM	972	10
UMM	128	3
LMM	350	62
LM	6	0

To identify seismogenic clusters, we only consider those clusters that have more than 100 IIEs associated with them. HF, hydraulic fracturing; IIEs, injection-induced earthquakes; LM, Lower Montney; LMM, Lower-Middle Montney; UM, Upper Montney; and UMM, Upper-Middle Montney.

To characterize the FM distribution of HF-induced seismicity, we applied both the classical GR relation and the LB method to 75 seismogenic clusters. For each cluster identified using the DBSCAN algorithm, the magnitude of completeness (M_c) was first determined using the maximum-curvature method, which identifies the point of steepest slope on the FM distribution curve. This ensured that GR b-values were computed only from the complete portion of the seismic catalog. Classical GR b-values were then estimated using the maximum-likelihood method (Aki, 1965; Utsu, 1966) applied to events above M_c. To quantify uncertainties, a bootstrap resampling technique with 200 replicates was employed (Efron, 1982; Schorlemmer *et al.*, 2003).

In parallel, b-values were also derived using the LB-statistic model (Boitz *et al.*, 2024), which modifies the GR relation by incorporating a physically constrained upper-bound magnitude. This approach accounts for the finite extent of the stimulated volume and the observed scarcity of large-magnitude events in induced seismicity. The upper-magnitude limit was estimated using reservoir geometry and stress-drop assumptions. We adopted a fault dip angle of 50°, consistent with focal mechanism studies in South Montney indicating that faults in the region are steeply dipping (Babaie Mahani *et al.*, 2020) and a uniform average stress drop of ~80 MPa. Although this stress drop may seem relatively high, particularly for induced events at shallow depths, it is not without precedent in the WCSB. This value falls within the observed range for induced events in the Montney Play (~0.1 to 80 MPa; Zhang *et al.*, 2016), including the highest estimates (54–120 MPa) reported by Holmgren *et al.* (2019) for the November 2018 M_w 4.3 event. It also provides a conservative upper-bound estimate for the maximum-

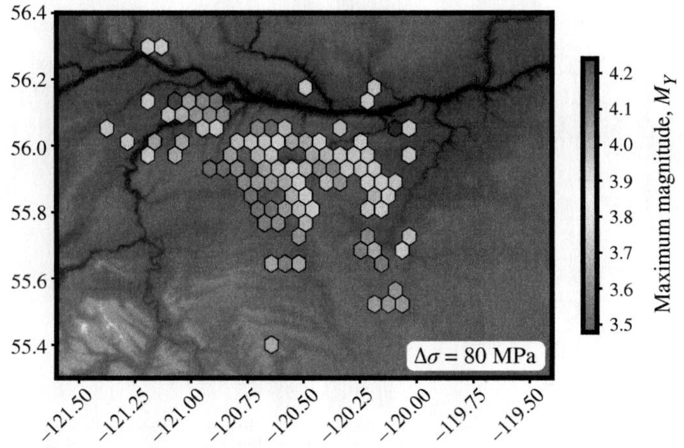

Figure 3. Spatial distribution of the maximum magnitude for a reservoir-limited rupture M_Y obtained using equation (2). The color version of this figure is available only in the electronic edition.

magnitude scenario, assuming rupture propagation throughout the entire reservoir thickness. Spatially varying rupture lengths based on mapped reservoir thickness (Figs. S4, S5) were used to calculate the upper limit for the maximum-possible magnitude M_Y (Fig. 3). Incorporating this constraint, the LB-statistic parameters were obtained through fitting equation (1) (Fig. S6 shows examples of LB fits to FM distributions of two representative IIE clusters).

The application of both the classical GR relation and the LB method to clusters of HF-induced seismicity provides valuable insights into the statistical characterization of induced events. The FM distributions reveal considerable variability in *b*-values across the study area ranging from approximately 0.5 to 2.5. These variations reflect differences in local stress regimes, geological heterogeneity, and HF operational conditions influencing seismogenic behavior. In contrast, M_c values remain relatively consistent across all clusters and target formations, typically ranging between 0.6 and 1.4 (Fig. 4a), indicating uniform detection capabilities within the seismic network. A direct comparison shows that *b*-values derived using the LB-statistic model are, on average, ~25% smaller than those estimated via the classical GR relation (Fig. 4b). This systematic difference is consistent with the theoretical expectation that the LB model better accounts for the constrained seismic volume and truncation of large events.

Clusters targeting the LMM formation exhibit the widest range of seismogenic behavior, with both the lowest and highest *b*-values observed and maximum magnitudes ranging from approximately 1.5 to 4.2 (Fig. 4c). In contrast, clusters associated with the UM and UMM formations generally show higher *b*-values ($b > 1.0$) and lower-maximum magnitudes ($M < 2.5$), indicating a predominance of smaller events. These formation-specific patterns emphasize the role of the geological context in shaping the FM characteristics of HF-induced seismicity. A significant negative correlation (correlation coefficient of −0.7) between *b*-values and maximum-observed magnitudes further supports the inverse relationship between these parameters across the clusters. In addition, a weak positive correlation (correlation coefficient of ~0.3; Fig. S7) is observed between the LMM reservoir thickness and maximum magnitude, suggesting that while reservoir thickness may influence rupture potential, other geological and operational factors likely play a more crucial role in controlling the upper-magnitude limit.

Spatial distributions of average *b*-values and M_cs reveal pronounced lateral variations across the study area (Figs. 5a, 6b), with corresponding uncertainties of up to $\sim \pm 0.25$ (Fig. 5c,d). These lateral anomalies underscore the heterogeneity in seismic responses, with the western region characterized by the highest *b*-value exceeding 2.2, indicating a greater likelihood of smaller seismic events, and the northwestern region exhibiting the lowest *b*-values ($b < 1.0$), suggesting a higher likelihood of larger seismic events.

By integrating *b*-values, M_cs, and spatiotemporal correlations between seismicity and cumulative injected volumes, seismogenic indices (Σ) were estimated for each injection site. We observed a moderate positive correlation (correlation coefficient of ~0.4) between seismogenic indices and *b*-values, particularly within the LMM formation, highlighting its distinctive seismogenic behavior (Fig. 6a,b). On average, the Σ-values derived using LB-based *b*-values are 0.3 units lower than those obtained from the classical GR approach (Fig. 6c), primarily because LB model yields smaller *b*-values, which directly influence the resulting seismogenic indices. Nonetheless, both approaches show consistent spatial trends across different clusters. In contrast to the spatial distribution of *b*-values, the spatial distribution of the seismogenic indices shows a clear lateral pattern, with larger indices (closer to 0) predominantly observed in the southern areas, whereas smaller indices ($\Sigma < -1.0$) are found in the northern region (Fig. 7). Unusually high seismogenic index values are rare in western Canada and generally fall outside the typical range of −4.5 to −1.5 reported for HF operations (Dokht *et al.*, 2021). However, recent studies have documented exceptional cases, such as $\Sigma \approx -0.5$, in parts of the Montney formation of NE BC (Li *et al.*, 2022). These cases are associated with a combination of high tectonic stress, overpressured formations, and operational factors such as episodic injection and limited pressure dissipation. Collectively, these conditions can elevate seismic productivity, making high Σ values uncommon but plausible under specific geologic and operational scenarios. Uncertainties in Σ are generally low, remaining below ± 0.2 across the study area. These spatial trends reflect the localized geological and operational influences on induced seismicity in the South Montney Play and lay the groundwork for spatially resolved hazard assessment.

Despite the systematic differences in *b*-value and Σ estimation between the LB and classical GR methods, both yield

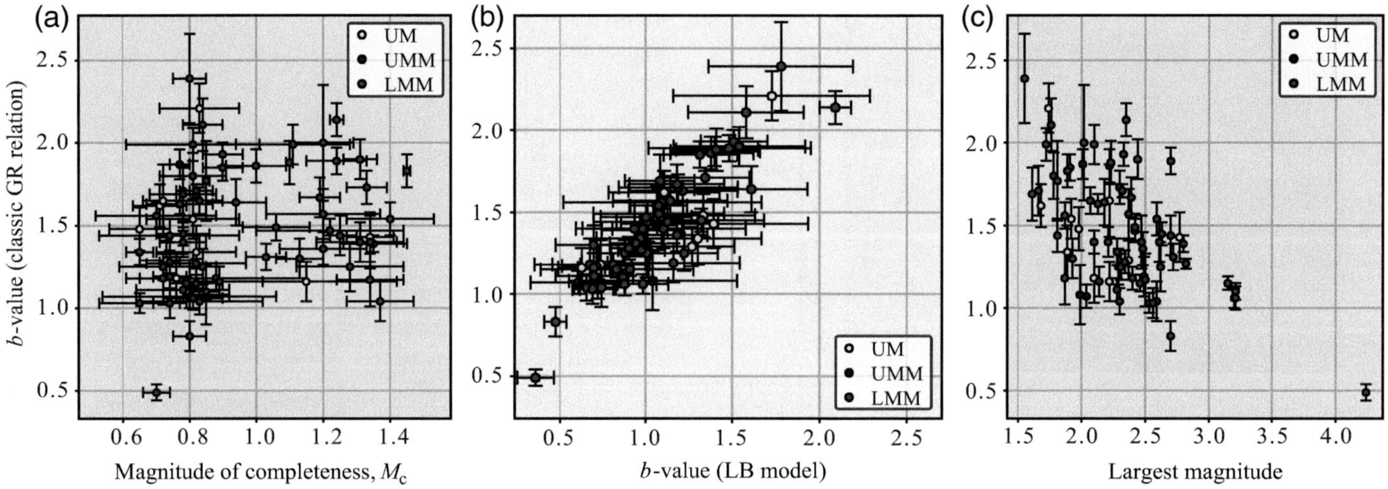

Figure 4. Variations in the GR relation *b*-values with respect to (a) FM distributions' M_cs, (b) *b*-values from the lower-bound (LB) model, and (c) the largest magnitudes of individual clusters. Horizontal and vertical bars represent one standard deviation for each parameter. Different marker colors indicate the target formations. The color version of this figure is available only in the electronic edition.

nearly identical goodness-of-fit statistics when applied to the FM distributions. The average correlation coefficients of ~0.98 for the GR fit and ~0.99 for the LB fit indicate that both models provide an excellent statistical representation of the observed seismicity. Although the LB model introduces physically motivated constraints, such as a finite upper-magnitude limit, and improves interpretability, both approaches perform similarly in modeling the overall FM trends of HF-induced seismicity. It should be emphasized that the occurrence of earthquakes within the basement challenges the LB model's underlying assumption that ruptures are confined to the stimulated reservoir. However, significant depth uncertainties in the earthquake catalog hinder us from further evaluating its potential limitations.

To evaluate the predictive capability of the seismogenic index framework, we compare the largest observed magnitudes ($M_{\mathrm{Max}}^{\mathrm{Obs}}$) with the largest expected magnitudes at a 68% confidence level ($M_{\mathrm{Max}}^{\Sigma 68}$) across all seismicity clusters (Figs. 8a, 9). The forecasted magnitudes are, on average, ~15% larger than the observed values, consistent with the conservative nature of probabilistic forecasting based on absence probability functions. This overestimation is particularly characteristic of forecasts made at higher absence probability levels, for which more conservative magnitude estimates are inherently expected. Importantly, the spatial patterns of $M_{\mathrm{Max}}^{\mathrm{Obs}}$ and $M_{\mathrm{Max}}^{\Sigma 68}$ are in close agreement, and the two exhibit a high correlation (correlation coefficient of about 0.9), underscoring the model's reliability. In addition, we compare the most probable maximum magnitudes estimated using the Van der Elst *et al.* (2016) formulation and the observed maximum magnitude across all clusters. These estimates, calculated as $\widehat{M}_{\mathrm{Max}} = \frac{1}{b}\left(\Sigma + \log_{10} Qc(t)\right)$ and corresponding to a 63% exceedance probability under a Poisson distribution framework, were found to be on average ~4% higher than the observed values. However, for clusters with larger maximum magnitudes, these estimates were slightly lower by less than 2%, indicating a mild underestimation in the upper magnitude range (Fig. 8b). These experiments serve as a retrospective validation of the GR law and the seismogenic index approach against the observed earthquake catalog, and their results demonstrate that the seismogenic index framework—when combined with spatiotemporal injection data and FM parameters—provides an effective and robust means to forecast the upper bounds of HF-induced seismicity in the South Montney Play.

Seismogenic Controls in the LMM

HF-induced seismicity within the Montney formation has shown considerable spatiotemporal and stratigraphic variability. Although the Montney formation is a stacked play with multiple horizontal wells drilled into different depth levels, the LMM formation stands out as a key seismogenic horizon within the Montney Play (Nieto *et al.*, 2018). Recent studies have shown that although the LMM represents a subset of the HF-targeted reservoir volume, it accounts for the majority of M_w 3+ earthquakes induced by HF in NE BC (Wozniakowska and Eaton, 2023; Wang *et al.*, 2024). This seismogenic behavior is attributed to a convergence of geological, geomechanical, and operational factors unique to this stratigraphic interval.

From geological and stratigraphical perspectives, the LMM lies at a greater depth than the UM and is adjacent to formations with enhanced fault connectivity, such as Debolt and Belloy formations, and in some areas directly overlies the crystalline basement (Barclay *et al.*, 1990; Fox and Watson, 2019; Peña Castro *et al.*, 2020). As a result, fluid pressure perturbations from HF operations in the LMM can more readily migrate to critically stressed fault systems, especially in regions underlain by the FSJG, a zone of pervasive faulting and historical structural extension (Salvage and Eaton, 2022). The FSJG's dense fault network intersects the LMM at steep angles, providing permeable

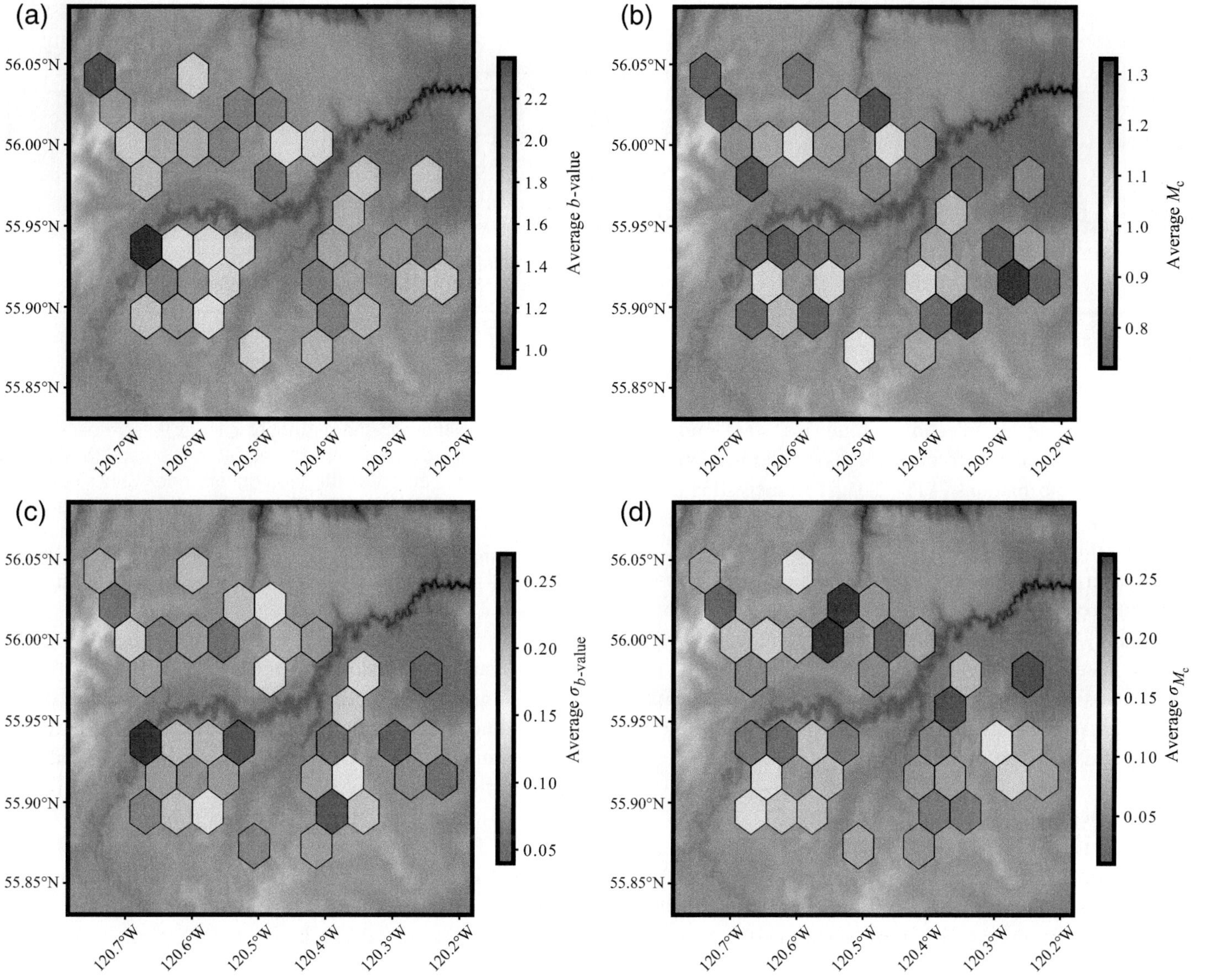

Figure 5. Hexagonal heat maps showing the spatial distributions of the (a) GR relation *b*-values and (b) magnitudes of completeness, obtained from seismogenic injection clusters using the maximum-likelihood method. (c,d) Corresponding uncertainties obtained using the bootstrap resampling algorithm. The color version of this figure is available only in the electronic edition.

conduits that facilitate rapid pressure diffusion into the basement, where induced earthquakes of significant magnitudes are ultimately located (Babaie Mahani *et al.*, 2019; Peña Castro *et al.*, 2020). Spatial analyses further support this connection, showing that HF pads within or proximal to the FSJG are significantly more seismogenic than those in surrounding structural blocks (Wang, Kao, Dokht, *et al.*, 2022; Wozniakowska and Eaton, 2023). In addition, the LMM hosts key lithologic members, such as the calcite-rich Altares and Pocketknife members, which exhibit high-mechanical stiffness and low-ductile behavior compared to the overlying shales of the UM (Sanders *et al.*, 2018; Wang *et al.*, 2024), where higher clay and total organic carbon content contribute to more ductile failure and aseismic accommodation of strain. This stratigraphic brittleness not only enhances rupture nucleation within the LMM but also promotes efficient stress transfer to underlying fault systems.

From a geomechanical standpoint, the regional stress regime in NE BC is predominantly strike slip, characterized by critically stressed faults that are oriented subparallel to the maximum horizontal stress (Babaie Mahani *et al.*, 2020; Eyre *et al.*, 2022). These faults are further brought closer to failure due to overpressure conditions within the LMM, which reduce the effective normal stress—an effect that becomes more pronounced when HF-induced pore pressure perturbations are superimposed on an already near-critical stress state (Fox and Watson, 2019; Holmgren *et al.*, 2019; Yu *et al.*, 2020). Operational practices further compound these geological and geomechanical susceptibilities. These practices can increase the likelihood of reaching fault activation thresholds, especially when injections are conducted continuously or in close temporal proximity (Wang, Kao, Yu, *et al.*, 2022). However, even

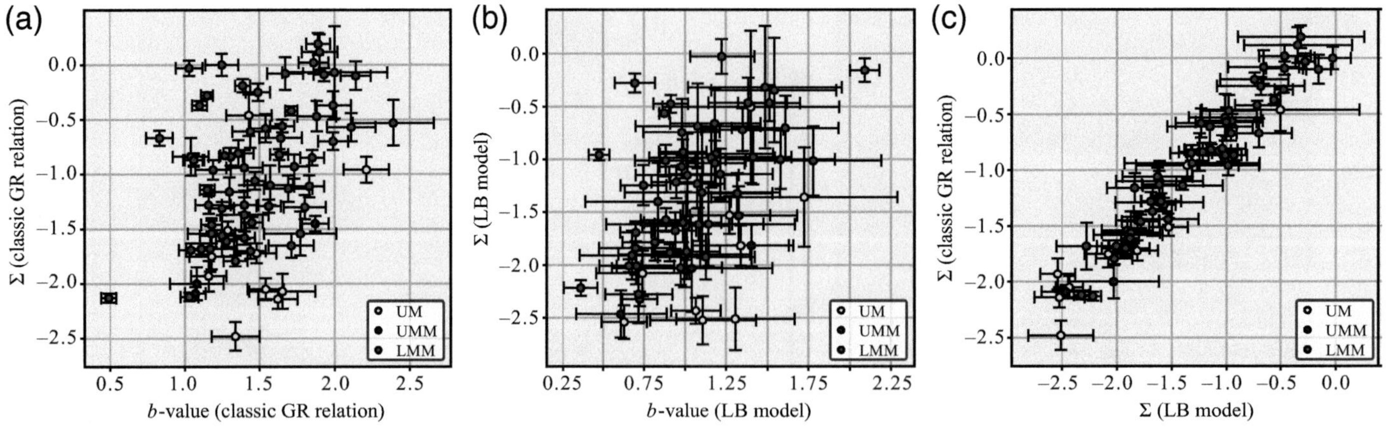

Figure 6. Variations in the seismogenic index with respect to the *b*-values obtained from (a) the classic GR relation and (b) the LB model. (c) Comparison of the seismogenic index values derived from the GR relation and the LB model. Horizontal and vertical bars represent one standard deviation for each parameter. Different marker colors indicate the target formations. The color version of this figure is available only in the electronic edition.

after normalizing for injection volume per stage and stage count, the LMM shows comparable results to those obtained from other subformations (Table 2, Fig. S8), suggesting that its seismogenic behavior is rooted in intrinsic geological characteristics rather than operational intensity alone.

Together, these findings suggest that the LMM represents a unique convergence of deep-seated fault proximity, brittle stratigraphy, critical stress conditions, and high-volume HF activity. Its elevated seismic productivity underscores the need for targeted mitigation strategies that account for formation-specific hazard, such as tailored injection protocols, seismic risk zoning, and real-time monitoring.

Seismogenic Parameters and Probabilistic Hazard Assessment

Probabilistic seismic hazard assessments require reliable estimates of the FM distribution parameters to measure the likelihood of different magnitude seismic events, particularly in the context of induced seismicity. Changes in *b*-value can reflect the impact of fluid injection and HF on seismicity (Babaie Mahani, 2021) and provide insights into distinguishing seismicity induced by the creation of new fractures versus the reactivation of pre-existing faults (Mousavi *et al.*, 2017). However, the broad range of *b*-values reported for induced events complicates this distinction. Our cluster analysis reveals significant spatiotemporal variations in *b*-values, ranging from ~0.5 to 2.5 within the South Montney Play, which are in accordance with those previously reported for the same area. Babaie Mahani (2021) employed a catalog of distance-corrected magnitudes and reported an average *b*-value of 1.37 (with spatial variations between 0.8 and 2.3) for southern Montney with annual temporal changes ranging between 1.4 and 1.8 during the period from 2014 to 2018 for the entire area. This study also noted a depth dependence, with *b*-values >2 in clusters with shallower depths (<2.2 km), and lower *b*-values ($b < 1.4$) in clusters with deeper depths (>2.7 km). This is in agreement with our estimate of a *b*-value of ~0.5(± 0.05) for the 30 November 2018 M_w 4.2 HF-induced earthquake sequence, which had the largest event occurring at a depth of ~4.5 km within the crystalline basement (Peña Castro *et al.*, 2020). The *b*-value has been also linked to the stress regime of a region, and it has been observed that different tectonic settings exhibit variations in *b*-values (Mehrabifard and Eberhardt, 2023). An empirical study by Amini and Eberhardt (2019) investigates the influence of tectonic regime on the *b*-value and reported that the thrust regime of the Montney Play shows a lower *b*-value (<1.0) compared to the one obtained from the strike-slip stress regime in the midcontinent. Other studies focusing on the KSMMA of southern Montney have reported a wide range of *b*-values using a dense local array, from as low as 0.61 to as high as ~2.0 (Salvage *et al.*, 2021; Salvage and Eaton, 2022), which further supports our *b*-value estimates (see Figs. 4, 5).

The Σ estimates obtained for the South Montney clusters in this study, ranging between approximately −2.5 and 0, are broadly consistent with previous studies across western Canada. (Amini *et al.*, 2024) reported the seismogenic indices of ~−2.0 to −0.8 for HF wells across the entire Montney region. The previous spatiotemporal analysis of induced seismicity within the WCSB reports the highest Σ-values for two major clusters of the Montney formation with an average estimate of approximately 2.0– (Dokht *et al.*, 2021). These elevated values were often associated with deeper HF operations and large cumulative injection volumes. Comparisons with other HF and WD sites in western Canada also show typical values between −4.0 and −1.5 (Schultz *et al.*, 2014; Bao and Eaton, 2016; Verdon and Budge, 2018). More specifically, Salvage and Eaton (2022) estimated Σ-value of approximately −0.5 for the HF wells associated with the 30 November 2018 Fort St. John M_L 4.5 IIE sequence, suggesting that the South Montney Play exhibits a relatively high seismogenic potential within the regional context. These estimates align

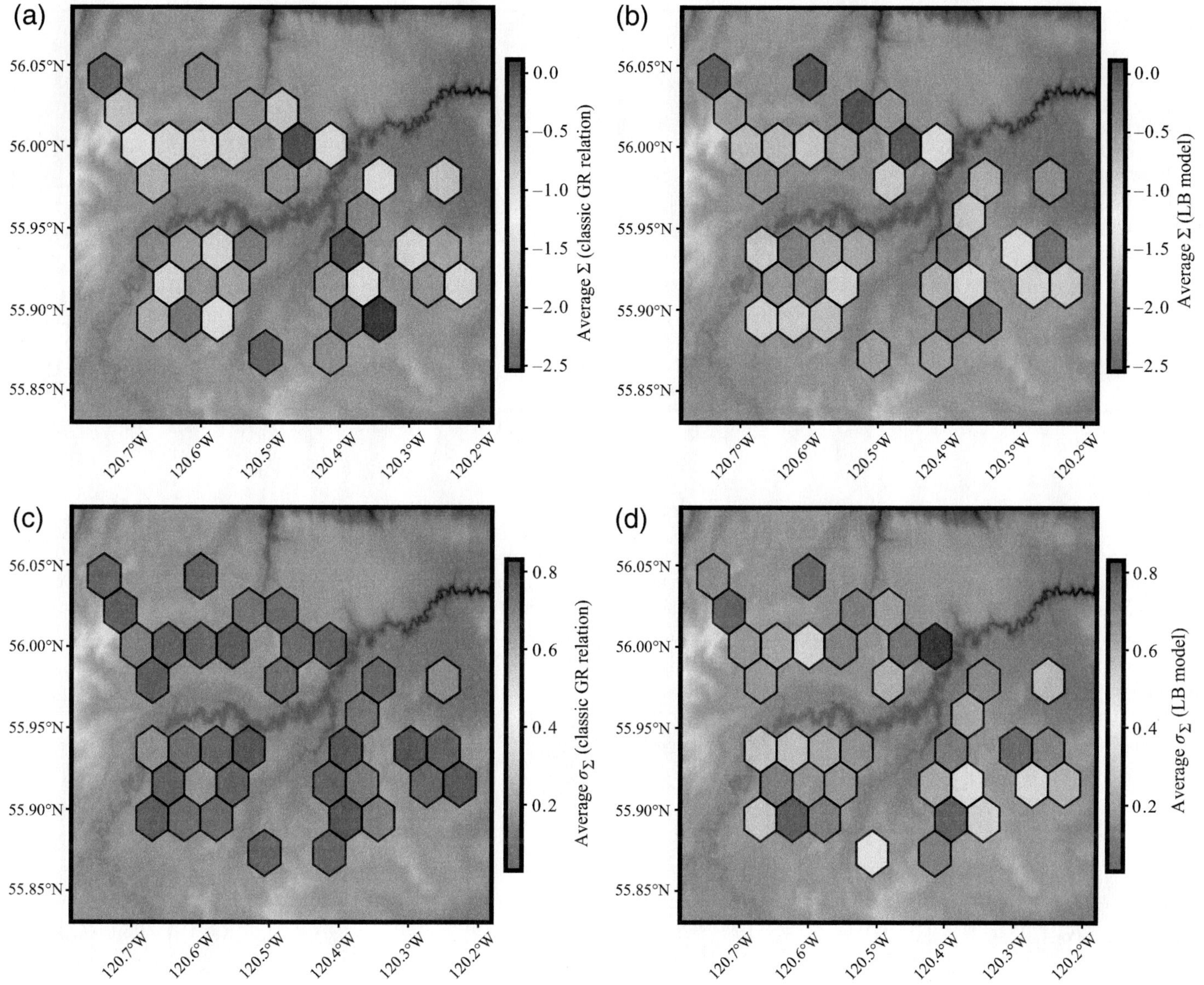

Figure 7. Spatial distribution of the average seismogenic index estimates obtained from (a) the classic GR relation and (b) the LB model. The corresponding uncertainties are shown in panels (c) and (d). The color version of this figure is available only in the electronic edition.

well with the upper end of the Σ range derived in this study, reinforcing the interpretation that certain zones within the South Montney Play, particularly those with deeper completions and favorable fault geometries, exhibit a heightened capacity for induced seismicity per unit of injected fluid (see Fig. 6).

These findings reinforce the broader understanding that spatial variations in Σ offer valuable insight into the concentration of pre-existing fractures and the local state of stress at injection sites (Shapiro *et al.*, 2010; Boitz *et al.*, 2024). Such variations can help identify regions more susceptible to induced seismicity, particularly given the observed positive correlation between Σ and the level of tectonic activity in some areas (Dokht *et al.*, 2021). Incorporated into the modified GR models, the seismogenic index enables the estimation of earthquake probabilities above regulatory thresholds and supports real-time mitigation strategies such as traffic-light systems (Kao *et al.*, 2018). It is also instrumental in adapting probabilistic seismic hazard analysis frameworks to account for the nonstationary nature of injection-driven seismicity (Reyes Canales, 2020). Beyond reflecting subsurface fault structures and geomechanical conditions, Σ also serves as a forecasting tool for estimating future seismicity rates. The exceedance probability functions, which represent the probability of inducing events with magnitudes greater than M, defined as $EP(M,t) = 1-P(M,t)$ (see equation 4), enable us to estimate the number of IIEs exceeding magnitude M, $N_M = -\ln(1 - EP)$. Figure 10 presents a spatial comparison between the observed and expected numbers of IIEs at different magnitude thresholds. The comparison reveals that the forecasting model generally captures the spatial distribution of seismicity across the study area. However, the model exhibits a slight

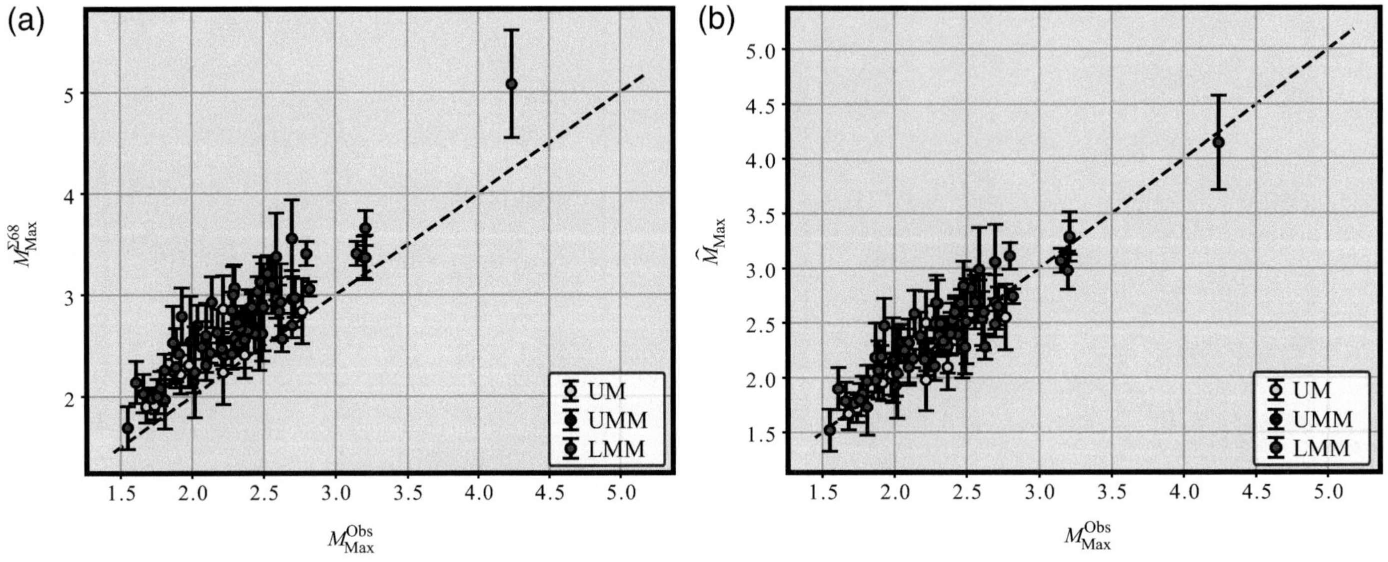

Figure 8. (a) Comparison of forecasted maximum magnitudes ($M_{\mathrm{Max}}^{\Sigma 68}$), derived at 68% confidence intervals, and observed largest injection-induced earthquakes (IIEs) ($M_{\mathrm{Max}}^{\mathrm{Obs}}$). Vertical lines indicate uncertainties associated with the forecasted magnitudes. (b) Same as panel (a), but the most probable maximum magnitudes ($\widehat{M}_{\mathrm{Max}}$) are estimated using the formulation proposed by Van der Elst *et al.* (2016), corresponding to a 63% exceedance probability. The color version of this figure is available only in the electronic edition.

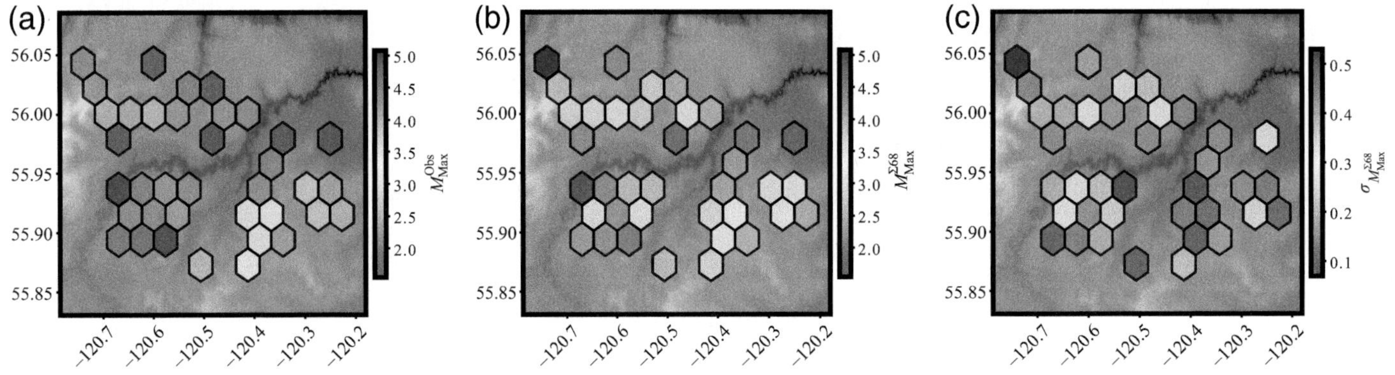

Figure 9. Heat maps illustrating the spatial distributions of (a) observed and (b) forecasted largest IIEs obtained at 68% confidence intervals. Panel (c) shows the uncertainties associated with the forecasted magnitudes. The color version of this figure is available only in the electronic edition.

underestimation at lower magnitude thresholds (Fig. 10a,d), suggesting that while the overall trends align, localized discrepancies exist. At larger magnitude thresholds, the agreement between expected and observed numbers of IIEs becomes more consistent and the model performs more accurately, effectively capturing the rare nature of stronger induced earthquakes. The improved consistency at larger magnitudes highlights the predictive strength of statistical modeling for seismic hazard assessments, emphasizing its utility in regulating HF operations and mitigating seismic risks in seismically active regions.

These findings underscore the importance of incorporating seismogenic parameters into probabilistic hazard models for fluid-induced seismicity. The seismogenic index, in particular,

TABLE 2
Average Number of Stages per HF Well (Second Column) and Average Injection Volume per Stage (Third Column) for Different Target Formations

Target Formation	Average Number of Stages per Well	Average Injected Volume per Stage (m^3)
UM	30	560
UMM	35	585
LMM	32	580

HF, hydraulic fracturing; LMM, Lower-Middle Montney; UM, Upper Montney; and UMM, Upper-Middle Montney.

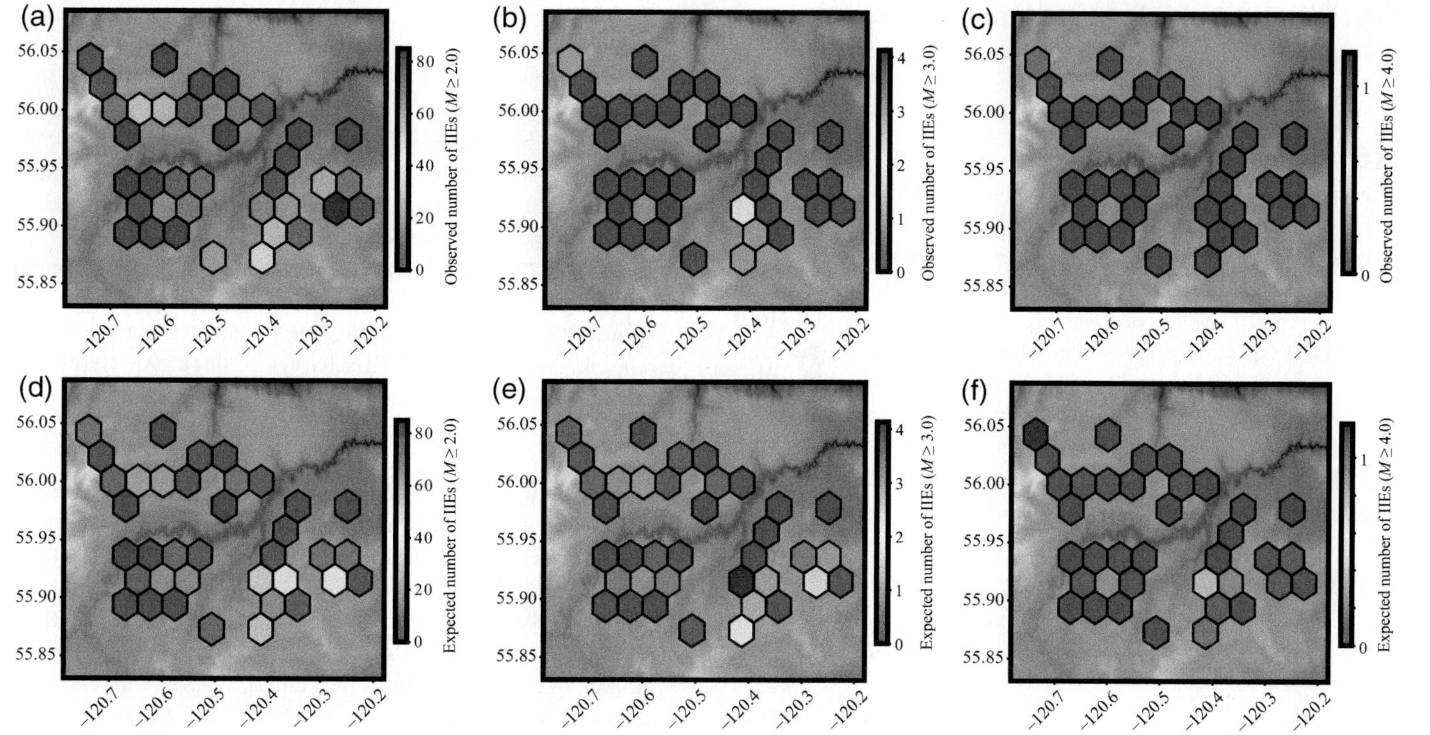

Figure 10. Heat maps comparing (a–c) observed and (d–f) expected number of IIEs at different magnitude thresholds. The color version of this figure is available only in the electronic edition.

provides a valuable linkage between operational factors and the underlying seismotectonic setting, enabling the estimation of both the likelihood and magnitude of induced earthquakes. This information is essential for effective risk management, informed regulatory oversight, and the sustainable development of subsurface energy resources.

Conclusions

In this study, we provide a comprehensive assessment of HF-induced seismicity in the South Montney Play, emphasizing the application of the seismogenic index for quantifying seismic hazard and forecasting induced event occurrences. The results confirm that the seismogenic index is a robust statistical tool for assessing the likelihood of induced seismicity across different geological formations and injection conditions. Spatial variations in seismogenic indices highlight localized differences in seismic productivity, with certain clusters exhibiting a significantly higher induced event rate per unit injection volume, underscoring the combined influence of geological and operational factors on seismic hazard. LMM's high seismogenic behavior is likely more related to intrinsic geological characteristics rather than fluid injection operational intensity alone.

The strong correlation between seismogenic index values and observed seismic productivity further confirms the predictive capability of seismogenic index-based models in assessing seismic hazard. Our results show a significant negative correlation between b-values and the observed maximum magnitudes of induced seismicity clusters, indicating that clusters with lower b-values are more likely to host larger induced events. A moderate positive correlation exists between seismogenic indices and b-values, suggesting interconnected controls between statistical seismogenic parameters and rupture potential. The application of seismogenic index-derived statistical models for earthquake forecasting demonstrates their effectiveness in predicting both the number of expected events and the likelihood of larger magnitude occurrences. The forecasted maximum magnitudes are, on average, 15% higher than the observed magnitudes, consistent with the conservative nature of probabilistic forecasting.

Overall, the consistency between observed and predicted seismicity trends emphasizes the value of seismogenic index-derived models in both regulatory decision-making and seismic risk mitigation. These findings contribute to the development of more refined hazard assessment frameworks and highlight the importance of incorporating geological, operational, and statistical factors in the safe and sustainable development of unconventional resources.

Data and Resources

Earthquake data are publicly available through the Geological Survey of Canada Open-File reports (Visser *et al.*, 2017, 2021; Goerzen *et al.*, 2024). Hydraulic fracturing (HF) datasets were obtained from the British Columbia Energy Regulator (BC ER) at https://www.bc-er.ca/data-reports/data-centre/ (last accessed April 2025). The Earthquakes Canada website is available at https://www.earthquakescanada.nrcan.gc.ca (last accessed July 2025). The supplemental material for this article includes two tables and eight figures.

Declaration of Competing Interests

The authors acknowledge that there are no conflicts of interest recorded.

Acknowledgments

The authors are grateful to Stu Venables, Michelle Gaucher, the *Seismological Research Letters* (*SRL*) Editor-in-Chief Allison Bent, Cornelius Langenbruch, and an anonymous reviewer for insightful suggestions and constructive comments. The authors would like to thank Jeremy Gosselin for serving as the Natural Resources Canada (NRCan) internal reviewer of this article with insightful comments and valuable discussions that helped improve the quality of this work. This study is supported by the Induced Seismicity Research Project, Environmental Geoscience Program of NRCan and a BCOGRIS (BC Oil and Gas Research and Innovation Society) research grant to the University of Victoria.

References

Aki, K. (1965). Maximum likelihood estimate of b in the formula log n=a-bm and its confidence limits, *Bull. Earthq. Res. Inst. Univ. Tokyo* **43,** 237–239.

Amini, A., and E. Eberhardt (2019). Influence of tectonic stress regime on the magnitude distribution of induced seismicity events related to hydraulic fracturing, *J. Petrol. Sci. Eng.* **182,** 106,284.

Amini, A., E. Eberhardt, and A. Mehrabifard (2024). Application of supervised machine learning to assess and manage fluid-injection-induced seismicity hazards based on the montney region of northeastern British Columbia, *Comput. Geosci.* **28,** 1251–1277.

Atkinson, G. M., D. W. Eaton, H. Ghofrani, D. Walker, B. Cheadle, R. Schultz, and H. Kao (2016). Hydraulic fracturing and seismicity in the western canada sedimentary basin, *Seismol. Res. Lett.* **87,** no. 3, 631–647.

Atkinson, G. M., H. Ghofrani, and K. Assatourians (2015). Impact of induced seismicity on the evaluation of seismic hazard: Some preliminary considerations, *Seismol. Res. Lett.* **86,** no. 3, 1009–1021.

Babaie Mahani, A. (2021). Seismic *b* value within the montney play of northeastern British Columbia, Canada, *Can. J. Earth Sci.* **58,** no. 8, 720–730.

Babaie Mahani, A., F. Esfahani, H. Kao, M. Gaucher, M. Hayes, R. Visser, and S. Venables (2020). A systematic study of earthquake source mechanism and regional stress field in the southern montney unconventional play of northeast British Columbia, Canada, *Seismol. Res. Lett.* **91,** no. 1, 195–206.

Babaie Mahani, A., H. Kao, G. M. Atkinson, K. Assatourians, K. Addo, and Y. Liu (2019). Ground-motion characteristics of the 30 November 2018 injection-induced earthquake sequence in northeast British Columbia, Canada, *Seismol. Res. Lett.* **90,** no. 4, 1457–1467.

Babaie Mahani, A., H. Kao, J. Johnson, and C. Salas (2017). Ground motion from the august 17, 2015, moment magnitude 4.6 earthquake induced by hydraulic fracturing in northeastern British Columbia, *Geoscience BC Summary of Activities 2016, Volume Rept. 2017-01*, 9–14. Geoscience BC.

Bao, X., and D. W. Eaton (2016). Fault activation by hydraulic fracturing in western Canada, *Science* **354,** no. 6318, 1406–1409.

Barclay, J., F. Krause, R. Campbell, and J. Utting (1990). Dynamic casting and growth faulting: Dawson Creek graben complex, Carboniferous–Permian Peace River embayment, western Canada, *Bull. Can. Petrol. Geol.* **38,** no. 1, 115–145.

BC Energy Regulator (BCER) (2014). Investigation of observed seismicity in the Montney Trend, available at https://www.bc-er.ca/node/12291/ (last accessed April 2025).

Boitz, N., C. Langenbruch, and S. A. Shapiro (2024). Production-induced seismicity indicates a low risk of strong earthquakes in the Groningen gas field, *Nat. Commun.* **15,** no. 1, 329.

Bommer, J. J. (2022). Earthquake hazard and risk analysis for natural and induced seismicity: Towards objective assessments in the face of uncertainty, *Bull. Earthq. Eng.* **20,** no. 6, 2825–3069.

Borah, B., and D. K. Bhattacharyya (2004). An improved sampling-based DBSCAN for large spatial databases, *Int. Conf. on Intelligent Sensing and Information Processing, 2004*, Proceedings of IEEE, 92–96.

Chapman, A. R. (2021). Hydraulic fracturing, cumulative development and earthquakes in the peace river region of British Columbia, Canada, *J. Geosci. Environ. Protect.* **9,** no. 5, 55–82.

Davies, G. R., N. Watson, T. F. Moslow, and J. A. MacEachern (2018). Regional subdivisions, sequences, correlations and facies relationships of the lower Triassic Montney formation, west-central Alberta to northeastern British Columbia, Canada–with emphasis on role of paleostructure, *Bull. Can. Petrol. Geol.* **66,** no. 1, 23–92.

Deng, K., Y. Liu, and R. M. Harrington (2016). Poroelastic stress triggering of the December 2013 Crooked Lake, Alberta, induced seismicity sequence, *Geophys. Res. Lett.* **43,** no. 16, 8482–8491.

Dinske, C., and S. A. Shapiro (2013). Seismotectonic state of reservoirs inferred from magnitude distributions of fluid-induced seismicity, *J. Seismol.* **17,** 13–25.

Dokht, R. M., H. Kao, A. Babaie Mahani, and R. Visser (2021). Spatiotemporal analysis of seismotectonic state of injection-induced seismicity clusters in the western Canada sedimentary basin, *J. Geophys. Res.* **126,** no. 4, e2020JB021362, doi: 10.1029/2020JB021362.

Eaton, D. W., J. Davidsen, P. K. Pedersen, and N. Boroumand (2014). Breakdown of the Gutenberg–Richter relation for microearthquakes induced by hydraulic fracturing: Influence of stratabound fractures, *Geophys. Prospect.* **62,** no. 4, 806–818.

Eaton, D. W., and R. Schultz (2018). Increased likelihood of induced seismicity in highly overpressured shale formations, *Geophys. J. Int.* **214,** no. 1, 751–757.

Edwards, D., J. Barclay, D. Gibson, G. Kvill, and E. Halton (1990). Triassic strata of the Western Canada sedimentary basin, *Bull. Can. Petrol. Geol.* **38,** no. 1, 163–163.

Efron, B. (1982). *The Jackknife, the Bootstrap and Other Resampling Plans*, Society for Industrial and Applied Mathematics, Philadelphia.

Esfahani, F., A. Babaie Mahani, and H. Kao (2024). Analysis of the influential factors controlling the occurrence of injection-induced earthquakes in northeast British Columbia, Canada, using machine-learning-based algorithms, *J. Seismol.* **28,** no. 6, 1489–1504.

Esmaeilzadeh, Z., and D. Eaton (2022). Investigating fault sealing effects on induced seismicity and pore pressure distribution in NEBC, *GeoConvention Conference*, Calgary, Canada, June 2022.

Ester, M., H. P. Kriegel, J. Sander, and X. Xu (1996). A density-based algorithm for discovering clusters in large spatial databases with noise, *Knowledge Discovery and Data Mining*, Vol. 96, 226–231.

Eyre, T. S., D. W. Eaton, D. I. Garagash, M. Zecevic, M. Venieri, R. Weir, and D. C. Lawton (2019). The role of aseismic slip in hydraulic fracturing–induced seismicity, *Sci. Adv.* **5,** no. 8, eaav7172, doi: 10.1126/sciadv.aav7172.

Eyre, T. S., S. Samsonov, W. Feng, H. Kao, and D. W. Eaton (2022). InSAR data reveal that the largest hydraulic fracturing-induced earthquake in Canada, to date, is a slow-slip event, *Sci. Rep.* **12,** no. 1, 2043.

Fiedler, B., S. Hainzl, G. Zöller, and M. Holschneider (2018). Detection of Gutenberg–Richter *b*-value changes in earthquake time series, *Bull. Seismol. Soc. Am.* **108,** no. 5A, 2778–2787.

Fox, A., and N. Watson (2019). Induced seismicity study in the Kiskatinaw seismic monitoring and mitigation area, British Columbia, *Technical Rept.*, available at https://www.bc-er.ca/files/documents/final-report-enlighten-geoscience-kssma-phase-1-study-2019w-appendices-links.pdf (last accessed July 2025).

Geffers, G. M., I. G. Main, and M. Naylor (2022). Biases in estimating b-values from small earthquake catalogues: How high are high b-values? *Geophys. J. Int.* **229,** no. 3, 1840–1855.

Goebel, T. H., and E. E. Brodsky (2018). The spatial footprint of injection wells in a global compilation of induced earthquake sequences, *Science* **361,** no. 6405, 899–904.

Goerzen, C., H. Kao, R. Visser, R. M. H. Dokht, and S. Venables (2024). A comprehensive earthquake catalogue for northeastern British Columbia, 2021 and 2022, *Technical Rept. Geol. Surv. Canada Open-File 9160*, 17 pp., doi: 10.4095/332532.

Hajati, T., C. Langenbruch, and S. Shapiro (2015). A statistical model for seismic hazard assessment of hydraulic-fracturing-induced seismicity, *Geophys. Res. Lett.* **42,** no. 24, 10–601.

Holmgren, J. M., G. M. Atkinson, and H. Ghofrani (2019). Stress drops and directivity of induced earthquakes in the western Canada sedimentary basin, *Bull. Seismol. Soc. Am.* **109,** no. 5, 1635–1652.

Kao, H., R. Visser, B. Smith, and S. Venables (2018). Performance assessment of the induced seismicity traffic light protocol for northeastern British Columbia and western Alberta, *The Leading Edge* **37,** no. 2, 117–126.

Khajehdehi, O., D. W. Eaton, and J. Davidsen (2022). Spatiotemporal clustering of seismicity in the Kiskatinaw seismic monitoring and mitigation area, *Front. Earth Sci.* **10,** 894,549.

Kozlowska, M., M. R. Brudzinski, P. Friberg, R. J. Skoumal, N. D. Baxter, and B. S. Currie (2018). Maturity of nearby faults influences seismic hazard from hydraulic fracturing, *Proc. Natl. Acad. Sci.* **115,** no. 8, E1720–E1729.

Langenbruch, C., and M. D. Zoback (2016). How will induced seismicity in oklahoma respond to decreased saltwater injection rates? *Sci. Adv.* **2,** no. 11, e1601542, doi: 10.1126/sciadv.1601542.

Langenbruch, C., C. Dinske, and S. A. Shapiro (2011). Inter event times of fluid induced earthquakes suggest their Poisson nature, *Geophys. Res. Lett.* **38,** no. 21, doi: 10.1029/2011GL049474.

Langenbruch, C., M. Weingarten, and M. D. Zoback (2018). Physics-based forecasting of man-made earthquake hazards in Oklahoma and Kansas, *Nat. Commun.* **9,** no. 1, 3946.

Li, Q., E. Konstantinovskaya, A. Zhmodik, and C. Ibelegbu (2023). Interaction of natural and hydraulic fractures: The impact on reservoir pressure buildup and risk of shear fault reactivation in the Upper Devonian Duvernay Formation, Fox Creek, Alberta, *Geomech. Geophys. Geo-Energy Geo-Resour.* **9,** no. 1, 21.

Li, Z., D. Eaton, and J. Davidsen (2022). Short-term forecasting of Mmax during hydraulic fracturing, *Sci. Rep.* **12,** no. 1, 12,509.

McGarr, A. (2014). Maximum magnitude earthquakes induced by fluid injection, *J. Geophys. Res.* **119,** no. 2, 1008–1019.

Mehrabifard, A., and E. Eberhardt (2023). Reliability of earthquake-size distribution and stress regime relationships for fluid-injection-induced seismicity, *Geoenergy Sci. Eng.* **226,** 211,776.

Mehrabifard, A., S. Rogers, C. Byrne, and E. Eberhardt (2025). Induced seismicity in the Kiskatinaw area of northeastern British Columbia, Canada: Empirical investigation of hydraulic diffusivity and induced seismic response of the fractured reservoir, *Geoenergy Sci. Eng.* **244,** 213,458.

Mousavi, S. M., P. O. Ogwari, S. P. Horton, and C. A. Langston (2017). Spatio-temporal evolution of frequency-magnitude distribution and seismogenic index during initiation of induced seismicity at Guy-Greenbrier, Arkansas, *Phys. Earth Planet. In.* **267,** 53–66.

Muntendam-Bos, A. G., and N. Grobbe (2022). Data-driven spatio-temporal assessment of the event-size distribution of the Groningen extraction-induced seismicity catalogue, *Sci. Rep.* **12,** no. 1, 10,119.

Nieto, J., B. Bialowas, B. Batlai, and G. Janega (2018). Managing induced seismicity in canbriam's altares field in the Montney formation, ne British Columbia–an update, *CSEG Recorder*, Vol. 43, no. 7, available at https://csegrecorder.com/articles/view/managing-induced-seismicity-in-canbriams-altares-field-in-the-montney-fm (last accessed July 2025).

Pawley, S., R. Schultz, T. Playter, H. Corlett, T. Shipman, S. Lyster, and T. Hauck (2018). The geological susceptibility of induced earthquakes in the Duvernay play, *Geophys. Res. Lett.* **45,** no. 4, 1786–1793.

Peña Castro, A. F., M. P. Roth, A. Verdecchia, J. Onwuemeka, Y. Liu, R. M. Harrington, and H. Kao (2020). Stress chatter via fluid flow and fault slip in a hydraulic fracturing-induced earthquake sequence in the Montney formation, British Columbia, *Geophys. Res. Lett.* **47,** no. 1, e2020GL087254, doi: 10.1029/2020GL087254.

Reyes Canales, M. (2020). Probabilistic seismic hazard analysis for induced seismicity, *Ph.D. Thesis*, University of Alberta, Alberta.

Reyes Canales, M., G. Rodriguez-Pradilla, J. Yusifbayov, and M. van der Baan (2022). The rise, peak and decline of the seismic hazard related to hydraulic fracturing activities in the Duvernay play, Fox Creek area, Alberta, *J. Geophys. Res.* **127,** no. 1, e2021JB023060, doi: 10.1029/2021JB023060.

Roth, M. P., K. B. Kemna, R. M. Harrington, and Y. Liu (2022). Source properties of hydraulic-fracturing-induced earthquakes in the Kiskatinaw area, British Columbia, Canada, *J. Geophys. Res.* **127,** no. 3, e2021JB022750, doi: 10.1029/2021JB022750.

Roth, M. P., A. Verdecchia, R. Harrington, and Y. Liu (2023). Inferring rock strength and fault activation from high-resolution in situ VP/VS estimates surrounding induced earthquake clusters, *Seismica* **2,** no. 2, doi: 10.26443/seismica.v2i2.498.

Rubinstein, J. L., and A. B. Mahani (2015). Myths and facts on wastewater injection, hydraulic fracturing, enhanced oil recovery, and induced seismicity, *Seismol. Res. Lett.* **86,** no. 4, 1060–1067.

Salvage, R. O., J. Dettmer, T. H. A. Swinscoe, K. MacDougall, D. W. Eaton, M. Stacey, and J. Rhie (2021). Real-time monitoring of seismic activity in the kiskatinaw area, northeastern British Columbia (NTS 093p, 094a), *Geoscience BC Summary of Activities 2020: Energy and Water, Geoscience BC Rept. 2021*, Vol. 2, 17–30.

Salvage, R. O., and D. W. Eaton (2022). The influence of a transitional stress regime on the source characteristics of induced seismicity and fault activation: Evidence from the 30 November 2018 Fort St. John ML 4.5 induced earthquake sequence, *Bull. Seismol. Soc. Am.* **112,** no. 3, 1336–1355.

Sanders, S., C. Etienne, A. Gegolick, D. Kelly, and J. P. Zonneveld (2018). The middle montney altares member: Lithology, depositional setting and significance for horizontal drilling and completion in the Altares Field, British Columbia, *Bull. Can. Petrol. Geol.* **66,** no. 1, 318–337.

Schorlemmer, D., G. Neri, S. Wiemer, and A. Mostaccio (2003). Stability and significance tests for b-value anomalies: Example from the Tyrrhenian sea, *Geophys. Res. Lett.* **30,** no. 16, doi: 10.1029/2003GL017335.

Schultz, R., G. Atkinson, D. W. Eaton, Y. J. Gu, and H. Kao (2018). Hydraulic fracturing volume is associated with induced earthquake productivity in the Duvernay play, *Science* **359,** no. 6373, 304–308.

Schultz, R., R. J. Skoumal, M. R. Brudzinski, D. Eaton, B. Baptie, and W. Ellsworth (2020). Hydraulic fracturing-induced seismicity, *Rev. Geophys.* **58,** no. 3, e2019RG000695, doi: 10.1029/2019RG000695.

Schultz, R., V. Stern, and Y. J. Gu (2014). An investigation of seismicity clustered near the Cordel Field, west central Alberta, and its relation to a nearby disposal well, *J. Geophys. Res.* **119,** no. 4, 3410–3423.

Schultz, R., R. Wang, Y. J. Gu, K. Haug, and G. Atkinson (2017). A seismological overview of the induced earthquakes in the duvernay play near Fox Creek, Alberta, *J. Geophys. Res.* **122,** no. 1, 492–505.

Shapiro, S. A., C. Dinske, C. Langenbruch, and F. Wenzel (2010). Seismogenic index and magnitude probability of earthquakes induced during reservoir fluid stimulations, *The Leading Edge* **29,** no. 3, 304–309.

Shapiro, S. A., O. S. Krüger, C. Dinske, and C. Langenbruch (2011). Magnitudes of induced earthquakes and geometric scales of fluid-stimulated rock volumes, *Geophysics* **76,** no. 6, WC55–WC63.

Urban, P., S. Lasocki, P. Blascheck, A. F. Do Nascimento, N. Van Giang, and G. Kwiatek (2016). Violations of Gutenberg–Richter relation in anthropogenic seismicity, *Pure Appl. Geophys.* **173,** 1517–1537.

Utsu, T. (1966). A statistical significance test of the difference in b-value between two earthquake groups, *J. Phys. Earth* **14,** no. 2, 37–40.

Van der Elst, N. J., M. T. Page, D. A. Weiser, T. H. Goebel, and S. M. Hosseini (2016). Induced earthquake magnitudes are as large as (statistically) expected, *J. Geophys. Res.* **121,** no. 6, 4575–4590.

Verdon, J. P., and J. Budge (2018). Examining the capability of statistical models to mitigate induced seismicity during hydraulic fracturing of shale gas reservoirs, *Bull. Seismol. Soc. Am.* **108,** no. 2, 690–701.

Visser, R., H. Kao, R. M. H. Dokht, A. B. Mahani, and S. Venables (2021). A comprehensive earthquake catalogue for Northeastern British Columbia: The northern Montney trend from 2017 to 2020 and the kiskatinaw seismic monitoring and mitigation area from 2019 to 2020, *Technical Rept. Geol. Surv. Canada*, doi: 10.4095/329078.

Visser, R., H. Kao, B. Smith, C. Goerzen, B. Kontou, R. M. H. Dokht, J. Hutchinson, F. Tan, and A. B. Mahani (2017). A comprehensive earthquake catalogue for the Fort St. John–Dawson creek region, British Columbia, *Technical Rept. Geol. Surv. Canada*, doi: 10.4095/326015.

Wang, B., H. Kao, R. M. Dokht, R. Visser, and H. Yu (2022). Delineating the controlling factors of hydraulic fracturing–induced seismicity in the northern montney play, northeastern British Columbia, Canada, with machine learning, *Seismol. Res. Lett.* **93,** no. 5, 2439–2450.

Wang, B., H. Kao, H. Yu, G. Li, R. M. Dokht, and R. Visser (2024). Unveiling key factors governing seismogenic potential and seismogenic productivity of hydraulic fracturing pads: Insights from machine learning in the southern Montney play, *Earth Planet. Sci. Lett.* **626,** 118,511.

Wang, B., H. Kao, H. Yu, R. Visser, and S. Venables (2022). Physical factors controlling the diverse seismogenic behavior of fluid injections in western Canada, *Earth Planet. Sci. Lett.* **589,** 117,555.

Wang, B., H. Kao, H. Yu, R. Visser, and A. Verdecchia (2023). Quantitative evaluation of the competing effects of wastewater disposal and hydraulic fracturing on causing induced earthquakes: A case study of an M3.1 earthquake sequence in western Canada, *J. Geophys. Res.* **128,** no. 2, e2022JB025048, doi: 10.1029/2022JB025048.

Wang, B., A. Verdecchia, H. Kao, R. M. Harrington, Y. Liu, and H. Yu (2021). A study on the largest hydraulic fracturing induced earthquake in Canada: Numerical modeling and triggering mechanism, *Bull. Seismol. Soc. Am.* **111,** no. 3, 1392–1404.

Wozniakowska, P., and D. W. Eaton (2020). Machine learning–based analysis of geological susceptibility to induced seismicity in the Montney formation, Canada, *Geophys. Res. Lett.* **47,** no. 22, e2020GL089651, doi: 10.1029/2020GL089651.

Wozniakowska, P., and D. W. Eaton (2023). Testing hypotheses for geological controls on hydraulic-fracturing-induced seismicity in the Montney formation, Canada, *Energies* **16,** no. 14, 5322.

Yaghoubi, A., M. B. Dusseault, and Y. Leonenko (2022). Injection-induced fault slip assessment in montney formation in western Canada, *Sci. Rep.* **12,** no. 1, 11,551.

Yu, H., R. M. Harrington, H. Kao, Y. Liu, R. E. Abercrombie, and B. Wang (2020). Well proximity governing stress drop variation and seismic attenuation associated with hydraulic fracturing induced earthquakes, *J. Geophys. Res.* **125,** no. 9, e2020JB020103, doi: 10.1029/2020JB020103.

Yu, H., R. M. Harrington, Y. Liu, and B. Wang (2019). Induced seismicity driven by fluid diffusion revealed by a near-field hydraulic stimulation monitoring array in the Montney basin, British Columbia, *J. Geophys. Res.* **124,** no. 5, 4694–4709.

Zhang, H., D. W. Eaton, G. Li, Y. Liu, and R. M. Harrington (2016). Discriminating induced seismicity from natural earthquakes using moment tensors and source spectra, *J. Geophys. Res.* **121,** no. 2, 972–993.

Manuscript received 28 April 2025
Published online 13 August 2025

Systematics of the Fault-Zone Seismogenic Width of Strike-Slip Plate Boundaries

Shaked Engelberg*[1,2], Amotz Agnon[2], Amir Sagy[1], and Nadav Wetzler[1]

Abstract

Strike-slip plate boundaries commonly exhibit elevated seismicity that tapers with distance from the area of high strain about the plate boundary faults. Although this typical seismicity pattern is well documented for the entire seismogenic depth, the variation of the fault-zone seismogenic width (FZSW) with depth is unclear. Here, we examine earthquake catalogs along twenty-three segments of four major strike-slip plate boundaries: the San Andreas, the Dead Sea, the North Anatolian, and the East Anatolian faults. For each segment catalog, we calculate the seismicity densities normal to the faults and stack events on one side of the fault. We define the FZSW as the distance of 30% of the peak density from the fault. First, we calculate the FZSW represented by the entire catalog. Then, to examine the influence of distinct events, we compare the density pattern of declustered catalogs with clustered events. This analysis reveals that the declustered catalog presents a systematic density decay pattern, which can be diluted by large events that trigger aftershocks at nearby faults. We exclude all aftershocks and measure the FZSW at two depth intervals with respect to the median depths of each fault segment. Our analysis reveals a general decrease of the seismogenic width with depth from 5 to 13.5 km in the shallow sections to a systematic width of 3 to 5 km. Segments with a width >5 km at both depth intervals indicate fault segmentation or activity on concealed faults. This study provides an independent measurement of the seismogenic damage zone around strike-slip faults and is useful for fault and seismic hazard modeling.

Cite this article as Engelberg, S., A. Agnon, A. Sagy, and N. Wetzler (2025). Systematics of the Fault-Zone Seismogenic Width of Strike-Slip Plate Boundaries, *Seismol. Res. Lett.* **97**, 399–408, doi: 10.1785/0220250060.

Supplemental Material

Introduction

Fault zones are regions where rocks are damaged and deformed due to the strain associated with fault movements (e.g., Sibson, 1983; Wibberley *et al.*, 2008). However, identifying and measuring these zones, in particular their spatial variations in width and depth, has long posed a challenge for geologists. Measurements of the damage zone have been conducted near the surface, which does not necessarily reflect the deformation structure and width at depth (Sibson, 2003; Mitchell and Faulkner, 2009; Stefanov and Bakeev, 2015). Mechanical models, for example, suggest that brittle deformation near large strike-slip faults is more localized below the first ~5 km from the surface (e.g., Finzi *et al.*, 2009). In addition, exhumation and erosion processes might affect fracture density (Eppes *et al.*, 2018), and in many cases, measurements normal to the fault are limited by the exposure amount and by the effects of other faults. Variations in the measurements of damage zones can be attributed to the measurement methods, making it difficult to compare damage zones consistently (Wu and Pollard, 2002). Finally, geological measurements of damage zones near faults integrate damage generated during different periods (Tal and Faulkner, 2022) and may not necessarily represent the current damage zone at depth, which can be altered due to damage evolution and healing processes (Karner *et al.*, 1997; Finzi *et al.*, 2011).

In a complementary manner, earthquake seismicity patterns can potentially reflect the current active periphery and the stress–strain fields near the examined fault. A study analyzing the seismicity in the vicinity of fault segments in California revealed a finite width of seismicity around the fault (Powers and Jordan, 2010). They categorized faults according to size, productivity, and location, and stacked seismicity decay from the faults for each category, resulting in a fault-zone seismogenic width (FZSW) ranging from 3 to 6 km. Powers and Jordan (2010) established the relationships between variations in the depth-independent FZSW and three factors: cumulative offset, seismic productivity, and aseismic slip. A much narrower FZSW (~100 m) was reported for the Calaveras fault

1. Geological Survey of Israel, Jerusalem, Israel, https://orcid.org/0009-0001-9301-9143 (SE); https://orcid.org/0000-0002-7552-0866 (NW); 2. Hebrew University, Jerusalem, Israel, https://orcid.org/0000-0002-0232-8574 (AA)

*Corresponding author: shakedeng@gmail.com

in California (Kocharyan *et al.*, 2011). Hauksson (2010) showed that aftershock sequences in the vicinity of strike-slip faults in California are tightly clustered around the fault, at a normal distance of 2.5 km. Perrin *et al.* (2021) inferred that the distribution of density of aftershock sequences decreases with geological fault slip. Both studies suggest that localization increases with cumulative offset. However, the examinations of these trends were not tested beyond California.

In this study, we present new measurements of the seismicity near major strike-slip plate boundary faults and present a new analysis for revealing their damage zone represented by a depth-dependent FZSW. We select coherent fault segments of four strike-slip plate boundaries: the San Andreas fault (SAF), the Dead Sea Fault (DSF), the North Anatolian fault (NAF) in the Marmara region, and the East Anatolian fault (EAF). The selected plate boundaries provide a range of tectonic conditions, slip rates, and geological complexities (Table S1, available in the supplemental material to this article). For example, the tectonic activity of the SAF initiated ~23 Ma (Revenaugh and Reasoner, 1997), compared with the younger faulting along the western NAF dated to ~3.5 Ma (Yaltırak *et al.*, 1998; Alpar and Yaltırak, 2002). Fault plate motion rates of the segments also indicate large variations ranging from ~5 mm/yr along the DSF (Sadeh *et al.*, 2012) to 28 mm/yr in the southern segments of the SAF (Zeng and Shen, 2016). In addition, the seismogenic depths vary between these faults and highlight the intrinsic rheological and thermal characteristics of each region, with the SAF and NAF being more similar, reaching ~20 km (Lin *et al.*, 2007; Smith-Konter *et al.*, 2011; Wollin *et al.*, 2018) compared with the DSF, with seismicity that tapers below 30 km depth (Wetzler and Kurzon, 2016). In the EAF, the seismogenic depth extends to around 20 km in most of the fault zone (Bulut *et al.*, 2012), though in certain areas, it reaches a depth of up to 25 km (Ezgi Güvercin, 2024).

We measure seismicity density variations at normal distances to the mapped traces of the faults. We extend our analysis to test the influence of aftershocks on the measurements by comparing the FZSW of the declustered catalog with the aftershock population. To obtain information on the vertical dimension, we investigate the FZSW at two intervals with respect to the median depth of the seismicity in each segment.

Methods

Identifying and selecting fault segments

We first select seismically active fault segments in which the seismicity is visibly associated with the main trace (Fig. 1). To prevent bias by undersampled segments, we choose 50 recorded earthquakes as the minimum. We restrict our selection to distinct strike-slip faults, including single steeply dipping subvertical fault segments, partitioned fault zones (basins), faults that are located adjacent to other fault traces, and faults with nonvertical dip angles (Table S1; Shulman *et al.*, 2004; Plesch *et al.*, 2007; Hofstetter *et al.*, 2012; Olson *et al.*, 2014).

To equalize the measurements and identify spatial variations along the plate boundaries, we separate traces larger than 70 km into segments (e.g., NAF and EAF, Fig. 1b,d), resulting in equivalent lengths ranging from 35 to 70 km. The choice of this size limit resulted in a total of twenty-three strike-slip fault segments representing diverse characteristics of seismogenic depths, ages, plate motion rates, and so forth (Table S1).

Dataset

We use three regional earthquake catalogs: (1) southern California (32.0°–37.0° N; 144°–122.0° W) from 1985 to 2018; (2) Türkiye (35.0°–44.0° N; 25°–46.0° E) from 1980 to 2018; and (3) Israel (27.2°–35.6° N; 31.76°–38.36° E) from 1983 to 2023 (see Data and Resources). In each catalog, we retain all earthquakes above the regional magnitude of completeness (M_c), computed iteratively using the Kolmogorov–Smirnov test between the observed and theoretical Gutenberg–Richter distributions (e.g., Goebel *et al.*, 2017). The resulting M_c-values are: 2.1 in the DSF, 2.4 in California, and 2.9 in the NAF and EAF.

The uncertainty of earthquake location varies between the catalogs. For the case of the DSF catalog, the uncertainty reported in the relocated catalog is ±0.5 km on the horizontal dimensions and ±1.2 km in the vertical dimension (Wetzler *et al.*, 2024). For the SAF, the uncertainty is ±2 km, and ±4 km in the horizontal and vertical dimensions, respectively (Hauksson and Shearer, 2005; Powers and Jordan, 2010). For the catalog of Türkiye, the uncertainty is estimated using the root mean square (rms) values, indicating an average rms of ~0.5 s, which translates to ±3 km for the average seismic velocity of 6 km/s.

Determining the FZSW

The FZSW is determined from the decay of earthquake density as a function of normal distance from the fault trace, counted at 0.5 km intervals up to a distance of 20 km normal to the fault. We fit the seismicity density to a smoothed trend using the polynomial algorithm of Savitzky–Golay (Savitzky and Golay, 1964). Considering that the fault geometry involves subvertical fault segments (Shulman *et al.*, 2004; Plesch *et al.*, 2007; Hofstetter *et al.*, 2012; Olson *et al.*, 2014), we stack the two sides of the fault. The FZSW was determined according to a threshold of 30% of peak density, which was found to capture the intersection of the seismicity density fall-off from the fault with the background level. We also tested 25% and 35% values to examine the stability of this threshold.

The occurrence of larger mainshocks can potentially influence the calculation of the FZSW, increasing the distance by statically or dynamically triggered aftershocks at neighboring faults (Freed, 2005; van der Elst and Shaw, 2015; Inbal *et al.*, 2023). To test the influence of aftershocks on the measured FZSW, we decluster the earthquake catalog into two main populations: background seismicity combined with the mainshock population, and aftershocks. We use the declustering method

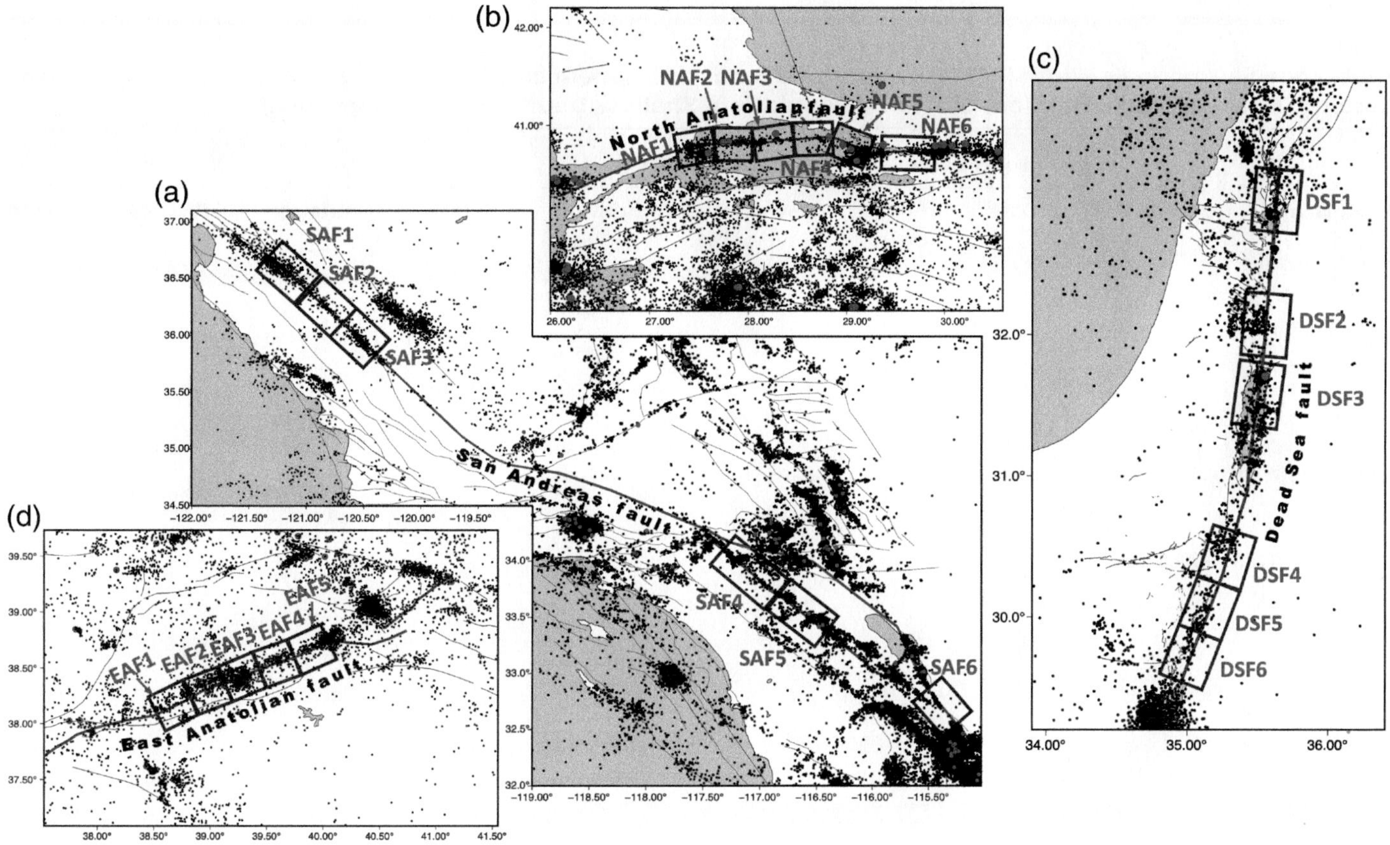

of Zaliapin and Ben-Zion (2013) based on the metric of Baiesi and Paczuski (2004). The determination of the decision boundary between the clustered and background populations provides two subgroups from each catalog, allowing the systematic characterization of the two populations.

Figure 1. Maps of four strike-slip faults used in this research: (a) San Andreas fault (SAF); (b) North Anatolian fault (NAF); (c) Dead Sea fault (DSF); and (d) East Anatolian fault (EAF). Segments used for the analysis are marked by blue rectangles. The main strike-slip fault trace is marked in red. The color version of this figure is available only in the electronic edition.

Results

Our method describes an FZSW for twenty of the selected fault segments (Table 1, Fig. S1). Only three segments indicate seismicity density that does not decrease below the 30% threshold (Table 1, Fig. S1b_5,c_2,d_1). Twelve fault segments show consistent gradual decay of the density pattern (Fig. S1$a_1 - a_4$,a_6,b_1,b_2,b_4,b_6,c_3,c_4,c_6). For these segments, the FZSW ranges from 3 km (Fig. S1a_6) to 8 km (Fig. S1c_3). For other segments, the seismicity density departs from the general decay and peaks with a hump at a distance ranging from ~2 to 10 km from the fault trace (e.g., Fig. S1$d_1 - d_4$). Some segments present a bimodal pattern with a secondary density increase (e.g., Fig. S1a_5,b_5,c_1,c_2,c_5,c_6,d_5). Overall, the FZSW of the entire population ranges between 3 and 14.5 km.

Aftershock effects on the FZSW

We find notable differences in the density patterns when comparing the declustered catalog and the clustered population. For eight segments, the seismicity density departs from the general decay for the clustered population (Table 1, Fig. S2). We associate this observation with the temporary activation of off-fault structures due to stress changes induced by the main rupture, rather than direct association with the damage zone of a specific plate boundary (Das and Scholz, 1981). Temporary off-fault activities can also occur due to other mechanisms. For example, in the northern segment of our DSF catalog (Fig. 1c, DSF1), peak seismicity density is found 3 km from the main fault, and an FZSW of 7 km (Fig. 2a). However, for the declustered catalog, peak density is located on the fault with a decreased FZSW of 5.5 km (Fig. 2b). This is due to the exclusion of swarm sequences that occurred in 2013 and 2018 along peripheral faults (e.g., Wetzler *et al.*, 2019). Another such case appears in NAF1 (Fig. S2) in which a large earthquake took place (Ambraseys and Jackson, 2000), and the FZSW is decreased for the declustered seismicity along with a change in the seismicity pattern.

To conclude, we find the declustered population more suitable to represent the general damage zone by FZSW (green dots, Fig. S2). Therefore, we exclude the clustered population from the catalogs for further statistical analysis, retaining only the background seismicity and mainshocks.

TABLE 1
Fault-Zone Seismogenic Width (FZSW) Determined for Each Segment and for Every Stage of the Analysis (Entire Catalog, Declustered Population, Clustered Population, Shallow Depth, and Deep Interval)

		Fault Zone Seismogenic Width (km)				
Fault Name	**Segment ID**	**Entire Catalog**	**Declustered Population**	**Clustered Population**	**Shallow**	**Deep**
SAF	SAF1	3.5	4.0	3.0	3	7
	SAF2	3.5	3.0	5.0	3	3
	SAF3	4.0	4.0	6.0	3.5	4
	SAF4	4.0	3.5	4.5	5.5	3.5
	SAF5	10.5	9.5	10.0	16.5	7.5
	SAF6	3.0	3.0	2.5	3	3
NAF	NAF1	10.0	7.5	14.5	9	4
	NAF2	4.5	5.0	4.5	5.5	4.5
	NAF3	5.5	5.5	8.0	5.5	5
	NAF4	4.5	4.5	5.5	5	3
	NAF5	–	–	–	–	6
	NAF6	6.5	8.0	6.5	6.5	7.5
DSF	DSF1	7.0	5.5	7.0	6.5	5
	DSF2	–	–	–	–	7.5
	DSF3	8.0	8.5	8.5	13.5	5
	DSF4	10.0	13.5	3.5	8.5	11.5
	DSF5	7.5	8.0	7.5	7	12.5
	DSF6	7.5	7.5	8.5	10	4.5
EAF	EAF1	–	4.0	15.5	14	–
	EAF2	14.5	13.0	12.5	12.5	14.0
	EAF3	11.0	8.5	11.0	11	11
	EAF4	10.0	7.5	10	8.5	10.5
	EAF5	5.5	7.5	11.0	11	11

DSF, Dead Sea fault; EAF, East Anatolian fault; NAF, North Anatolian fault; and SAF, San Andreas fault.

FZSW and seismogenic depth

The dependence of the depth on the FZSW is evaluated for two depth sections based on depth distribution for each segment: shallow (surface to median), and deep; the seismogenic depth is determined by the 99th percentile of the seismicity depths at each zone for the background population (Fig. S3, Table S1). The calculated seismogenic depths range between 15 and 33 km, with the shallowest being the segment NAF6 (Fig. S3b_6) and the deepest being DSF4 (Fig. S3c_4). The median depths range between 5 and 16 km, representing ~40% of the entire seismogenic depth, on average (Table S1).

We now compare the calculated FZSW for the two depth intervals. At this stage, for eleven segments, a systematic pattern and FZSW of the values 3–5 km appear at depth (Fig. 3a–p, Fig. S4). For eight out of the eleven segments, we find the FZSW to decrease at depth, whereas in the shallow part it increases significantly, in 1–8.5 km. Three segments show uniform width for the two depth intervals (Fig. 3a,e,m). Along the DSF, we identify relatively larger differences between the shallow and the deep depth intervals, with 8.5 km in the Dead Sea basin (Fig. 3g) and 5.5 km in the southern part of the fault (Fig. 3k). To investigate segment DSF3 with the largest difference, we reanalyzed it for three depth intervals, revealing a narrowing width (Fig. S5). The other twelve segments present density patterns resulting in FZSWs larger than 5 km at depth (e.g., Fig. S4a_4,b_6). In eight of these segments, the peak density at depth is located 2–8 km from the fault (e.g., Fig. S4b_5,c_2,d_2); the others present mild decay (e.g., Fig. S4a_1,a_5).

To highlight the differences between the shallow and deep populations, we calculated the mean difference between the

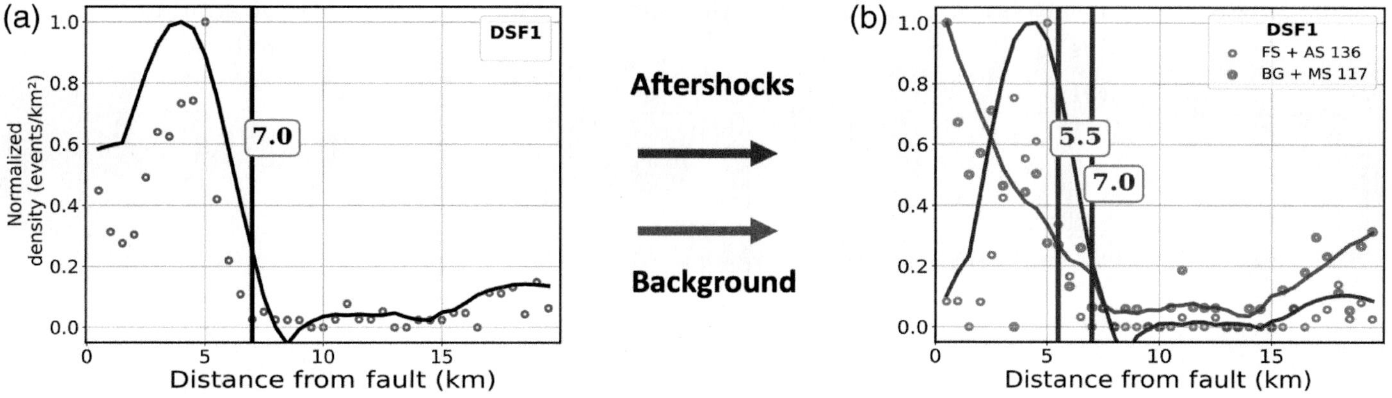

Figure 2. The calculated fault-zone seismogenic width (FZSW) (vertical line) is shown for segment DSF1 for the entire catalog (a), and for the declustered (dark green) and clustered (purple) populations (b). The color version of this figure is available only in the electronic edition.

two smoothed density functions, Δf, up to a distance of 10 km (Fig. 3). We find that the difference between the two density functions increases with the seismogenic depth (Fig. S6). In the central and southern DSF, where the seismogenic depth is the largest (Fig. 3g,k), the difference between the FZSW is larger than 4 km, whereas, in the segments of the SAF, NAF, and the shallower segment of the DSF located at its northern part (DSF1), the difference does not reach 4 km.

Stability of the calculated FZSW

To evaluate the stability of the calculated FZSW with respect to the 30% threshold, we tested two additional thresholds of 30% ±5% for the eleven segments with the localized pattern at depth. Lowering the threshold by 5% resulted in a wider FZSW with an average increase of 0.2 km at the deep interval, compared with the 30% (Fig. S7). At 35%, the average FZSW decreases by 0.3 km (Fig. S8). For the three considered thresholds, the FZSW is found to decrease with depth. Overall, 30% appears to capture the main decay envelope of seismicity without overfitting to noise or underrepresenting width (Fig. 3), providing consistent and realistic boundaries across the inspected fault segments.

To test the effect of location uncertainty, we calculated the FZSW for 1000 perturbed catalogs generated for each segment. Catalogs' locations were randomly perturbed according to a Gaussian function with a standard deviation equal to the location uncertainty attributed in the methods section for each catalog. The average standard deviation measured for the SAF and DSF segments, with reported uncertainties of ±2 km, is on average ±0.5 km for the deep interval and ±1 km for the shallow interval (Fig. S9). In the NAF segments, uncertainties increase to ±3 km, with an average standard deviation of ±1.4 km. Our test demonstrates that the seismogenic FZSWs are mostly stable within the range of the uncertainty of the catalogs.

Discussion

Patterns of localized seismicity

Our results establish a method for defining the FZSW of a segment along a major strike-slip plate boundary. We filter a group of well-localized plate boundary strike-slip faults based on an FZSW lower than 5 km at depth (Fig. 3, Table 2). For this group, the width at depth is relatively similar despite the differences in age, tectonic plate motion rate, and seismicity rate of the considered plate boundaries (Table S1). However, we acknowledge that differences may exist and are potentially hidden within the uncertainties.

Our results show that aftershocks tend to increase the FZSW with more complicated density patterns compared with the typical decrease of localized faults, shown by the declustered catalog. Moreover, the FZSW and density patterns are found to be sensitive to fault structure, enabling the identification of geometry at depth.

To evaluate the conditions for localized seismicity along the plate boundaries, we conduct the Pearson test (Pearson, 1895) to quantify the linear correlation between the raw data and the smoothed curves in the range of the FZSW. Our analysis revealed that all localized patterns with effective FZSWs smaller than 5 km showed correlation values exceeding 0.7, with one representing a perfect correlation (Table S1, Fig. S10). However, identifying a clear pattern for the complex segments proved more challenging because they exhibit diverse structures and varying levels of complexity (Table S1).

We note some similarities and differences in the measured FZSW compared with the depth-independent FZSW measured by Powers and Jordan (2010). Comparable results are found for the full catalog (Fig. S1), showing similar values of the measured FZSW for northern California of 3 km. However, differences are found in the southern segments at SAF4 and SAF6 (Fig. 1a), resulting in half of the width recognized by Powers and Jordan (2010). We attribute these differences to three main reasons: first, the study of Powers and Jordan included seismicity from the entire seismogenic zone. We observe that diffused shallow seismicity may inflate the overall

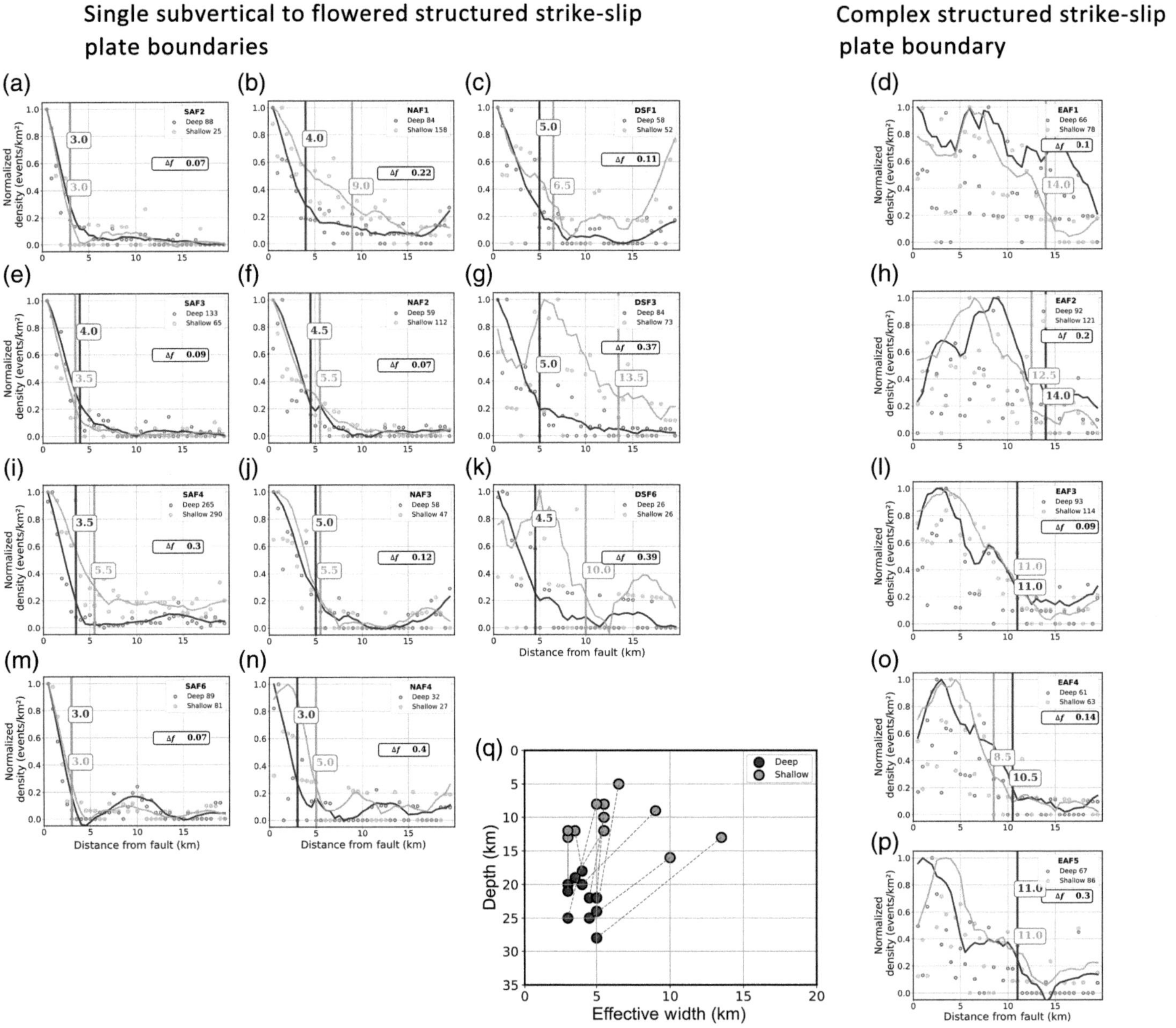

measured FZSW of the entire seismogenic zone (e.g., Fig. S4, SAF4). Second, stacking seismicity from several fault segments (Powers and Jordan, 2010) may mask the seismicity patterns of the individual faults, resulting in a larger FZSW. Moreover, faults with a limited amount of data might be diluted by the fit of the more active segments.

In addition, Perrin *et al.* (2021) found a localization of the seismicity width with fault cumulative displacement, which we miss out. However, a direct comparison with their results is not straightforward, as Perrin *et al.* (2021) include aftershocks, which are omitted from our analysis.

The density function of localized plate boundaries is consistent with structural observations of strike-slip fault zones showing typical localization patterns at depth, with widening toward the surface (Beidinger and Decker, 2011). This pattern is commonly attributed to the reduction in stress near the

Figure 3. The FZSWs (vertical lines, color key explained below) are shown for the sixteen fault segments considered for declustered catalogs: San Andreas fault (SAF) (a,e,i,m), NAF (b,f,j,n), DSF (c,g, k), and the EAF (d,h,l,o,p), and defined according to 30% of peak density. Earthquake density (ordinate) is calculated with the horizontal distances respective to the plate boundaries (red line, Fig. 1), for two depth intervals from the depth distributions: the shallow part between 0 and 0.5 quantile (orange) and the deep part between 0.5 and 0.99 quantile (green). The raw data of the density are presented by the dots and their smoothed curve by the corresponding line. The difference between the root mean square (rms) of the two smoothed functions at a distance between 0 and 10 km from the plate boundary, Δf, is labeled (black boxes, in kilometers). The FZSW measured for the two depth sections of the localized faults is plotted according to the depths of the 0.5 and 0.99 quantiles (q). The color version of this figure is available only in the electronic edition.

TABLE 2
Classification of the Segments into Four Categories According to the Fault-Zone Seismogenic Width (FZSW)

	Strike-Slip Plate Boundaries			
FZSW	**Single Subvertical Sharp Plate Boundary**	**Flower-Structured Plate Boundary**	**Complex Structured Plate Boundary**	**Shallow Single Subvertical Plate Boundary**
Deep fault zone seismogenic width	EW < 5 km	EW < 5 km	EW > 5 km	EW > 5 km
Shallow fault zone seismogenic width	EW < 5 km	EW > 5 km	EW > 5 km	EW < 5 km
Segments	SAF2, SAF3, and SAF6	SAF4, NAF1, NAF2, NAF3, and NAF4	SAF5, NAF5, NAF6, DSF2, DSF5, EAF1, EAF2, EAF3, EAF4, and EAF5	SAF1 and DSF4

DSF, Dead Sea fault; EAF, East Anatolian fault; EW, east–west; NAF, North Anatolian fault; and SAF, San Andreas fault.

surface (Sylvester, 1988), as was demonstrated by numerical models (e.g., Finzi *et al.* 2009). The FZSW of localized faults compares well with the 1–2 km wide low-velocity zone measured around the fault activated in the 2019 M_w 7.1 Ridgecrest, California, earthquake (Qiu *et al.*, 2021).

Field measurements have shown that fault zones can be simplified to fault core surrounded by a broad damage zone, in which damage intensity decreases toward the host rocks (e.g., Sibson, 1977; Chester *et al.*, 1993; Mitchell and Faulkner, 2009). Similarly, our observations of plate boundary faults reveal a comparable pattern of seismicity decay away from the fault.

Because seismicity reflects brittle failure, it is reasonable to assume that the gradual increase in strain near a plate boundary fault during the interseismic stage (see chapter 2 in Segall, 2010) and the heterogeneity of the fault zone (e.g., Goebel *et al.*, 2014) are the primary drivers of this characteristic distribution.

In addition, our findings indicate that large fault damage zones extend up to several kilometers at seismogenic depths. These length scales align with the widest fault zones observed in field studies (Childs *et al.*, 2009). We therefore suggest that while large earthquakes generate intensive wear and pulverization zones dynamically (Reches and Dewers, 2005), ongoing seismicity (represented by background) might be an important factor in shaping the characteristics of wide damage zones near faults.

Patterns of diffuse seismicity

Certain plate boundary segments result in density curves that depart from the expected trend of peak seismicity at the main fault trace, reflecting a more complex structure. In most of these cases, the seismicity density peak is shifted from the trace of the main fault and results in a wider FZSW. For example, in four out of five segments of the EAF, the FZSW is found to be wider than 8 km, with a peak density shift at up to 9 km away from the fault trace (Fig. 3d,h,l,o,p). Wider FZSW may suggest a plate boundary of complex structure and a damage zone. Previous seismological observations show that most earthquakes that occur on the plate boundary of the EAF (Fig. 1d) are located north of the main trace, distributed across smaller subparallel faults (Bulut *et al.*, 2012). The offset of the seismicity from the main trace and the large FZSW may alternatively indicate nonvertical planes of the fault segments. The EAF is characterized by dip angles of 40°–70° at depths greater than 7.5 km (Güvercin *et al.*, 2022). However, it is difficult to attribute the complex density patterns of the EAF to the dipping plane due to the lack of a depth-dependent shift in the peak density. Nevertheless, the EAF is found to possess a relatively large FZSW that we attribute to fault complexity. A clearer example of the relationship between the seismicity patterns and fault geometry is found for the San Jacinto fault in segments SAF4, where the fault dips at 70° down to 10 km depth (Ross *et al.*, 2017). Our analysis is consistent with the estimated fault geometry showing a relatively large FZSW (Fig. S4).

Another example of diffused seismicity is at the south of the DSF, where the FZSW of the segment increases to 12.5 km at depth (Fig. S4c_5). However, previous studies concluded that this segment is well localized from geological observations (Kesten *et al.*, 2008), geodetic measurements (Le Beon *et al.*, 2008; Masson *et al.*, 2015), and high-resolution seismic profiles (Haberland *et al.*, 2007; Ryberg *et al.*, 2007). We suggest that the increase in the FZSW is attributed to an interaction of the main plate boundary (Arava fault), with subparallel and transverse secondary faults.

We can correlate the main cases of density patterns observed in the study with three types of strike-slip faults (Fig. 4, Table 2): (1) well-localized faults, for example, SAF or NAF (Fig. 4a), forming a consistent FZSW across the seismogenic zone; (2) pull-apart basin structures, for example, the Dead Sea basin (Fig. 4b), deflecting the seismicity to the longitudinal boundary faults, expanding the FZSW at shallow depth which decreases and becomes more localized at depth; (3) segmented strike-slip faults, for example, the EAF (Fig. 4c) with

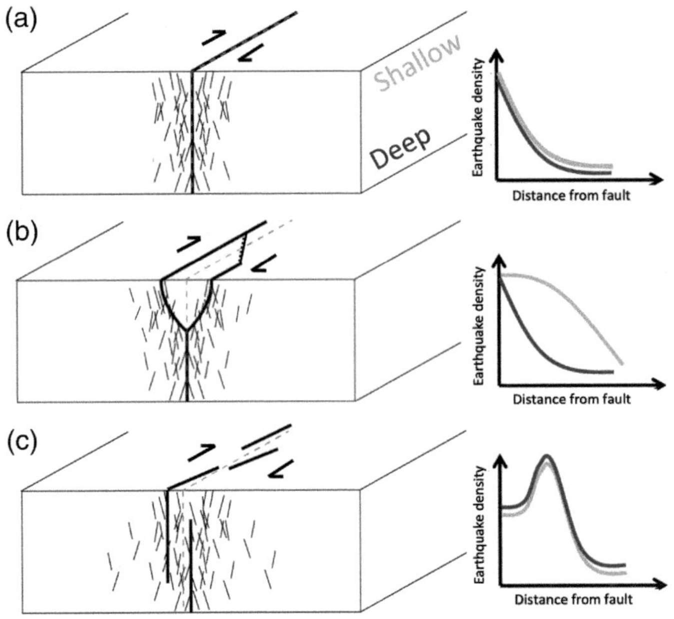

Figure 4. Typical strike-slip fault structures and their predicted earthquake density curves: (a) a well-localized fault, and its density curves of two depth intervals; a (b) a typical cross section of a flower-type structure on the shallow part of the fault, and (c) a complex strike-slip partitioning between subparallel segments. The color version of this figure is available only in the electronic edition.

subparallel faulting patterns at both depth interval, lacking localization at depth.

Conclusions

We systematically measure the FZSW for twenty-three segments of four different strike-slip plate boundaries. Our methodology includes the removal of clustered events, which reveal a long-term pattern of the seismicity. This is demonstrated when comparing the declustered catalog with the aftershock population that activates seismicity at larger distances and, in some cases, controls the pattern. As a result, the FZSWs measured reflect long-term tectonic behavior, unbiased by infrequent large events, and help resolve and define fault structure.

The FZSW is a useful tool to characterize fault properties and structure because it is found sensitive to the structural complexity of the faults, highlighting pull-apart basins and fault segmentation. The FZSW reveals localization of the SAF, NAF, and DSF at depth, with comparable deformation zones of 3–5 km at depth (symmetrically to the fault), suggesting a finite deformation zone of large plate boundaries. In contrast, the EAF is not localized close to the surface nor in-depth, and consistent with previous observations that the fault is characterized by branches adjacent to the main trace.

Because we understand the applications and information revealed by the FZSW measurements, it is essential to address the limitations associated with the standard catalogs to be used in this type of research. Enhancing precision and emphasizing variations across plate boundaries can be achieved using relocated catalogs, which may reveal if differences between the segments are hidden within the stated uncertainty of measurements.

Data and Resources

The workflow and detailed explanations of the nearest-neighbor clustering method by Zaliapin and Ben-Zion (2013) are available at https://github.com/tgoebel/clustering-analysis (last accessed August 2024). The earthquake data are from the Geological Survey of Israel at https://eq.gsi.gov.il/en/earthquake/accEarthquakes.php (last accessed January 2025) (Wetzler *et al.*, 2024). Earthquake data for California were accessed through the Southern California Earthquake Data Center (SCEDC; doi: 10.7909/C3WD3xH1). For Türkiye, we used the earthquake catalog of Tan (2021). The maps in this article were made by the PyGMT (Uieda *et al.*, 2021). The code for calculating the Gutenberg–Richter magnitude distribution is available at https://github.com/tgoebel/magnitude-distribution (last accessed August 2024). The code for calculating the density function is available at https://github.com/shkud/Earthquakes-density.git (last accessed August 2024). The supplemental material includes eleven supporting figures and one table.

Declaration of Competing Interests

The authors acknowledge that there are no conflicts of interest recorded.

Acknowledgments

The authors would like to thank Professor Emily Brodsky for her helpful comments and suggestions. The authors also thank *SRL* Editor-in-Chief Allison Bent, Peter Powers, and an anonymous reviewer for their valuable remarks, which significantly improved the article. This work was supported by the Israel Science Foundation (Grant Numbers 363/20).

References

Alpar, B., and C. Yaltırak (2002). Characteristic features of the North Anatolian fault in the eastern Marmara region and its tectonic evolution, *Mar. Geol.* **190,** nos. 1/2, 329–350, doi: 10.1016/S0025-3227(02)00353-5.

Ambraseys, N. N., and J. A. Jackson (2000). Seismicity of the Sea of Marmara (Turkey) since 1500, *Geophys. J. Int.* **141,** no. 3, F1–F6, doi: 10.1046/j.1365-246x.2000.00137.x.

Baiesi, M., and M. Paczuski (2004). Scale-free networks of earthquakes and aftershocks, *Phys. Rev. E* **69,** no. 6, 066106, doi: 10.1103/PhysRevE.69.066106.

Beidinger, A., and K. Decker (2011). 3D geometry and kinematics of the Lassee flower structure: Implications for segmentation and seismotectonics of the Vienna basin strike–slip fault, Austria, *Tectonophysics* **499,** nos. 1/4, 22–40, doi: 10.1016/j.tecto.2010.11.006.

Bulut, F., M. Bohnhoff, T. Eken, C. Janssen, T. Kılıç, and G. Dresen (2012). The East Anatolian fault zone: Seismotectonic setting and spatiotemporal characteristics of seismicity based on precise earthquake locations, *J. Geophys. Res.* **117,** no. B7, doi: 10.1029/2011JB008966.

Chester, F. M., J. P. Evans, and R. L. Biegel (1993). Internal structure and weakening mechanisms of the San Andreas fault, *J. Geophys. Res.* **98,** no. B1, 771–786, doi: 10.1029/92JB01866.

Childs, C., T. Manzocchi, J. J. Walsh, C. G. Bonson, A. Nicol, and M. P. Schöpfer (2009). A geometric model of fault zone and fault rock thickness variations, *J. Struct. Geol.* **31,** no. 2, 117–127, doi: 10.1016/j.jsg.2008.08.009.

Das, S., and C. H. Scholz (1981). Off-fault aftershock clusters caused by shear stress increase? *Bull. Seismol. Soc. Am.* **71,** 1669–1675, doi: 10.1785/BSSA0710051669.

Eppes, M. C., G. S. Hancock, X. Chen, J. Arey, T. Dewers, J. Huettenmoser, S. Kiessling, F. Moser, N. Tannu, B. Weiserbs, *et al.* (2018). Rates of subcritical cracking and long-term rock erosion, *Geology* **46,** no. 11, 951–954 10.1130/G45256.1.

Ezgi Güvercin, S. (2024). 2023 earthquake doublet in Türkiye reveals the complexities of the East Anatolian fault zone: Insights from aftershock patterns and moment tensor solutions, *Seismol. Res. Lett.* **95,** no. 2A, 664–679, doi: 10.1785/0220230317.

Finzi, Y., E. H. Hearn, Y. Ben-Zion, and V. Lyakhovsky (2009). Structural properties and deformation patterns of evolving strike-slip faults: Numerical simulations incorporating damage rheology, *Pure Appl. Geophys.* **166,** nos. 10/11, 1537–1573, doi: 10.1007/s00024-009-0522-1.

Finzi, Y., E. H. Hearn, V. Lyakhovsky, and L. Gross (2011). Fault-zone healing effectiveness and the structural evolution of strike-slip fault systems, *Geophys. J. Int.* **186,** 963–970, doi: 10.1111/j.1365-246X.2011.05099.x.

Freed, A. M. (2005). Earthquake triggering by static, dynamic, and postseismic stress transfer, *Annu. Rev. Earth Planet. Sci.* **33,** no. 1, 335–367, doi: 10.1146/annurev.earth.33.092203.122505.

Goebel, T. H., G. Kwiatek, T. W. Becker, E. E. Brodsky, and G. Dresen (2017). What allows seismic events to grow big?: Insights from b-value and fault roughness analysis in laboratory stick-slip experiments, *Geology* **45,** no. 9, 815–818, doi: 10.1130/G39147.1.

Goebel, T. H. W., T. Candela, C. G. Sammis, T. W. Becker, G. Dresen, and D. Schorlemmer (2014). Seismic event distributions and off-fault damage during frictional sliding of saw-cut surfaces with pre-defined roughness, *Geophys. J. Int.* **196,** no. 1, 612–625.

Güvercin, S. E., H. Karabulut, A. Ö. Konca, U. Doğan, and S. Ergintav (2022). Active seismotectonics of the East Anatolian fault, *Geophys. J. Int.* **230,** no. 1, 50–69, doi: 10.1093/gji/ggac045.

Haberland, C., N. Maercklin, D. Kesten, T. Ryberg, C. Janssen, A. Agnon, M. Weber, A. Schulze, I. Qabbani, and R. El-Kelani (2007). Shallow architecture of the Wadi Araba fault (Dead Sea Transform) from high-resolution seismic investigations, *Tectonophysics* **432,** no. 1/4, 37–50, doi: 10.1016/j.tecto.2006.12.006.

Hauksson, E. (2010). Spatial separation of large earthquakes, aftershocks, and background seismicity: Analysis of interseismic and coseismic seismicity patterns in southern California, *Pure Appl. Geophys.* 167, no. 8, 979–997, doi: 10.1007/978-3-0346-0500-7_10.

Hauksson, E., and P. Shearer (2005). Southern California hypocenter relocation with waveform cross-correlation, part 1: Results using the double-difference method, *Bull. Seismol. Soc. Am.* **95,** no. 3, 896–903, doi: 10.1785/0120040167.

Hofstetter, R., C. Dorbath, and M. Calò (2012). Crustal structure of the Dead Sea basin from local earthquake tomography, *Geophys. J. Int.* **189,** no. 1, 554–568, doi: 10.1111/j.1365-246X.2012.05369.x.

Inbal, A., A. Ziv, I. Lior, R. N. Nof, and A. S. Eisermann (2023). Non-triggering and then triggering of a repeating aftershock sequence in the Dead Sea by the 2023 Kahramanmaraş earthquake pair: Implications for the physics of remote delayed aftershocks, *Geophys. Res. Lett.* **50,** no. 18, e2023GL104908, doi: 10.1029/2023GL104908.

Karner, S. L., C. Marone, and B. Evans (1997). Laboratory study of fault healing and lithification in simulated fault gouge under hydrothermal conditions, *Tectonophysics* **277,** nos. 1/3, 41–55, doi: 10.1016/S0040-1951(97)00077-2.

Kesten, D., M. Weber, C. Haberland, C. Janssen, A. Agnon, Y. Bartov, I. Rabba, and , and Desert Group (2008). Combining satellite and seismic images to analyse the shallow structure of the Dead Sea Transform near the DESERT transect, *Int. J. Earth Sci.* **97,** 153–169, doi: 10.1007/s00531-006-0168-5.

Kocharyan, G. G., S. B. Kishkina, and A. A. Ostapchuk (2011). Seismogenic width of a fault zone, in *Doklady Earth Sciences*, Vol. 437, SP MAIK Nauka/Interperiodica, doi: 10.1134/S1028334X11030147, 412–415.

Le Beon, M., Y. Klinger, A. Q. Amrat, A. Agnon, L. Dorbath, G. Baer, Ruegg, J.-C. Charade, and O. Mayyas (2008). Slip rate and locking depth from GPS profiles across the southern Dead Sea Transform, *J. Geophys. Res.* **113,** no. B11, doi: 10.1029/2007JB005280.

Lin, G., P. M. Shearer, and E. Hauksson (2007). Applying a three-dimensional velocity model, waveform cross correlation, and cluster analysis to locate southern California seismicity from 1981 to 2005, *J. Geophys. Res.* **112,** no. B12, doi: 10.1029/2007JB004986.

Masson, F., Y. Hamiel, A. Agnon, Y. Klinger, and A. Deprez (2015). Variable behavior of the Dead Sea fault along the southern Arava segment from GPS measurements, *C. R. Geosci.* **347,** no. 4, 161–169, doi: 10.1016/j.crte.2014.11.001.

Mitchell, T. M., and D. R. Faulkner (2009). The nature and origin of off-fault damage surrounding strike-slip fault zones with a wide range of displacements: A field study from the Atacama fault system, northern Chile, *J. Struct. Geol.* **31,** no. 8, 802–816, doi: 10.1016/j.jsg.2009.05.002.

Olson, C. J., J. J. Becker, and D. T. Sandwell (2014). A new global bathymetry map at 15 arcsecond resolution for resolving seafloor fabric: SRTM15_PLUS, *AGU Fall Meeting Abstracts*, Vol. 2014, OS34A-03 pp.

Pearson, K. (1895). Contributions to the mathematical theory of evolution. III. Regression, heredity, and panmixia, *Proc. Math. Phys. Sci.* **59,** 69–71.

Perrin, C., F. Waldhauser, and C. H. Scholz (2021). The shear deformation zone and the smoothing of faults with displacement, *J. Geophys. Res.* **126,** no. 5, e2020JB020447, doi: 10.1029/2020JB020447.

Plesch, A., J. H. Shaw, C. Benson, W. A. Bryant, S. Carena, M. Cooke, J. Dolan, G. Fuis, E. Gath, L. Grant, *et al.* (2007). Community fault model (CFM) for southern California, *Bull. Seismol. Soc. Am.* **97,** no. 6, 1793–1802, doi: 10.1785/0120050211.

Powers, P. M., and T. H. Jordan (2010). Distribution of seismicity across strike-slip faults in California, *J. Geophys. Res.* **115,** no. B5, doi: 10.1029/2008JB006234.

Qiu, H., Y. Ben-Zion, R. Catchings, M. R. Goldman, A. A. Allam, and J. Steidl (2021). Seismic imaging of the M_w 7.1 Ridgecrest earthquake rupture zone from data recorded by dense linear arrays,

J. Geophys. Res. **126,** no. 7, e2021JB022043, doi: 10.1029/2021JB022043.

Reches, Z. E., and T. A. Dewers (2005). Gouge formation by dynamic pulverization during earthquake rupture, *Earth Planet. Sci. Lett.* **235,** nos. 1/2, 361–374, doi: 10.1016/j.epsl.2005.04.009.

Revenaugh, J., and C. Reasoner (1997). Cumulative offset of the San Andreas fault in central California: A seismic approach, *Geology* **25,** no. 2, 123–126.

Ross, Z. E., E. Hauksson, and Y. Ben-Zion (2017). Abundant off-fault seismicity and orthogonal structures in the San Jacinto fault zone, *Sci. Adv.* **3,** no. 3, e1601946, doi: 10.1126/sciadv.1601946.

Ryberg, T., M. H. Weber, Z. Garfunkel, and Y. Bartov (2007). The shallow velocity structure across the Dead Sea Transform fault, Arava Valley, from seismic data, *J. Geophys. Res.* **112,** no. B8, doi: 10.1029/2006JB004563.

Sadeh, M., Y. Hamiel, A. Ziv, Y. Bock, P. Fang, and S. Wdowinski (2012). Crustal deformation along the Dead Sea Transform and the Carmel fault inferred from 12 years of GPS measurements, *J. Geophys. Res.* **117,** no. B8, doi: 10.1029/2012JB009241.

Savitzky, A., and M. J. Golay (1964). Smoothing and differentiation of data by simplified least squares procedures, *Anal. Chem.* **36,** no. 8, 1627–1639, doi: 10.1021/ac60214a047.

Segall, P. (2010). *Earthquake and Volcano Deformation*, STU-Student edition, Princeton University Press, Princeton, New Jersey.

Shulman, H., M. Reshef, and Z. Ben-Avraham (2004). The structure of the Golan Heights and its tectonic linkage to the Dead Sea Transform and the Palmyrides folding, *Israel J. Earth Sci.* **53,** doi: 10.1134/S1069351315040114.

Sibson, R. H. (1977). Fault rocks and fault mechanisms, *J. Geol. Soc.* **133,** no. 3, 191–213, doi: 10.1144/gsjgs.133.3.0191.

Sibson, R. H. (1983). Continental fault structure and the shallow earthquake source, *J. Geol. Soc. Lond.* **140,** no. 5, 741–767, doi: 10.1144/gsjgs.140.5.0741.

Sibson, R. H. (2003). Thickness of the seismic slip zone, *Bull. Seismol. Soc. Am.* **93,** no. 3, 1169–1178, doi: 10.1785/0120020061.

Smith-Konter, B. R., D. T. Sandwell, and P. Shearer (2011). Locking depths estimated from geodesy and seismology along the San Andreas fault system: Implications for seismic moment release, *J. Geophys. Res.* **116,** no. B6, doi: 10.1029/2010JB008117.

Stefanov, Y. P., and R. A. Bakeev (2015). Formation of flower structures in a geological layer at a strike-slip displacement in the basement, *Izv. Phys. Solid Earth* **51,** 535–547.

Sylvester, A. G. (1988). Strike-slip faults, *Geol. Soc. Am. Bull.* **100,** no. 11, 1666–1703.

Tal, Y., and D. Faulkner (2022). The effect of fault roughness and earthquake ruptures on the evolution and scaling of fault damage zones, *J. Geophys. Res.* **127,** no. 1, e2021JB023352, doi: 10.1029/2021JB023352.

Tan, O. (2021). A homogeneous earthquake catalogue for Turkey, *Nat. Hazards Earth Syst. Sci.* **21,** no. 7, 2059–2073.

Uieda, L., D. Tian, W. J. Leong, L. Toney, W. Schlitzer, M. Grund, D. Newton, M. Ziebarth, M. Jones, and P. Wessel (2021). PyGMT: A Python interface for the Generic Mapping Tools, *Zenodo.*

van der Elst, N. J., and B. E. Shaw (2015). Larger aftershocks happen farther away: Nonseparability of magnitude and spatial distributions of aftershocks, *Geophys. Res. Lett.* **42,** no. 14, 5771–5778, doi: 10.1002/2015GL064734.

Wetzler, N., and I. Kurzon (2016). The earthquake activity of Israel: Revisiting 30 years of local and regional seismic records along the Dead Sea transform, *Seismol. Res. Lett.* **87,** no. 1, 47–58, doi: 10.1785/0220150157.

Wetzler, N., I. Kurzon, and G. Yagoda-Biran (2024). A relocated catalog for the Dead Sea Fault region and its periphery for probabilistic seismic hazard analysis in Israel, *TR-GSI/02/2024*, 6 pp., doi: 10.13140/RG.2.2.19755.66089.

Wetzler, N., E. Shalev, T. Göbel, F. Amelung, I. Kurzon, V. Lyakhovsky, and E. E. Brodsky (2019). Earthquake swarms triggered by groundwater extraction near the Dead Sea fault, *Geophys. Res. Lett.* **46,** 2019GL083491, doi: 10.1029/2019GL083491.

Wibberley, C. A., G. Yielding, and G. Di Toro (2008). Recent advances in the understanding of fault zone internal structure: A review, doi: 10.1144/SP299.2.

Wollin, C., M. Bohnhoff, P. Martínez-Garzón, L. Küperkoch, and C. Raub (2018). A unified earthquake catalogue for the Sea of Marmara region, Turkey, based on automatized phase picking and travel-time inversion: Seismotectonic implications, *Tectonophysics* **747,** 416–444, doi: 10.13140/RG.2.2.19755.66089.

Wu, H., and D. D. Pollard (2002). Imaging 3-D fracture networks around boreholes, *AAPG Bull.* **86,** no. 4, 593–604, doi: 10.1306/61EEDB52-173E-11D7-8645000102C1865D.

Yaltırak, C., B. Alpar, and H. Yüce (1998). Tectonic elements controlling the evolution of the Gulf of Saros (northeastern Aegean Sea, Turkey), *Tectonophysics* **300,** nos. 1/4, 227–248, doi: 10.1016/S0040-1951(98)00242-X.

Zaliapin, I., and Y. Ben-Zion (2013). Earthquake clusters in southern California I: Identification and stability, *J. Geophys. Res.* **118,** no. 6, 2847–2864, doi: 10.1002/jgrb.50179.

Zeng, Y., and Z. K. Shen (2016). A fault-based model for crustal deformation, fault slip rates, and off-fault strain rate in California, *Bull. Seismol. Soc. Am.* **106,** no. 2, 766–784, doi: 10.1785/0120140250.

Manuscript received 21 February 2025
Published online 15 August 2025

Illuminating Subsurface Structures Beneath Lake George Fault Zone, Southeast Australia with Traffic Noise

Chengxin Jiang*[1] and Meghan S. Miller[1]

Abstract

Mapping fault-zone properties is crucial for mitigating seismic hazards, particularly in urban settings. This process often requires high-resolution seismic imaging, which depends on dense data coverage and high-frequency seismic energy sensitive to shallow structures, with traffic noise providing an ideal source. However, extracting coherent phases from traffic noise remains challenging due to the complex conditions of variable sources and array configurations. Although array seismology techniques enhance coherence, they can limit model resolution. In this study, we demonstrate that high-quality surface Rayleigh-wave dispersions (2.5–10 Hz) can be extracted from single-station-pair cross correlations using a meticulously designed dense nodal array near a highway in the Lake George fault zone, southeast Australia. By analyzing the complete nine-component cross-correlation tensor, we find that radial–radial correlations, rather than conventional vertical–vertical correlations, yield the strongest dispersion signals. These high-frequency dispersion measurements enable surface-wave tomography, providing the first detailed velocity structure of the top 800 m of the fault zone. The mapped Lake George fault zone displays seismic characteristics similar to those of several major active fault systems worldwide. It represents a long-lived damage zone capable of hosting significant seismic events. These results provide new insights into the application of traffic noise for near-surface imaging and monitoring in urban environments, and they have significant implications for considering the directionality of distributed acoustic sensing data in future work.

Cite this article as Jiang, C., and M. S. Miller (2025). Illuminating Subsurface Structures Beneath Lake George Fault Zone, Southeast Australia with Traffic Noise, *Seismol. Res. Lett.* **97**, 409–424, doi: 10.1785/0220250046.

Supplemental Material

Introduction

High-precision mapping of shallow seismic structures within the upper few hundred meters is crucial for urban development and seismic hazard assessments, where hidden faults and subsurface structural variability pose significant risks from ground shaking. Traditional methods, such as drilling and active source geophysical surveys, offer precise information but are often expensive, invasive, and limited in spatial coverage. As an alternative, seismic ambient noise provides a sustainable, noninvasive, and continuous energy source for subsurface imaging. Ambient noise is generated by background vibrations from natural sources, such as oceans and human activities (Campillo and Paul, 2003; Shapiro and Campillo, 2004; Sabra *et al.*, 2005), making it ideal for long-term monitoring and dense spatial coverage without disrupting the environment. Since its first successful application in 2005 (Shapiro *et al.*, 2005), ambient noise tomography has become a widely used technique for characterizing geological structures from the crust to the upper mantle and has contributed to our understanding of tectonic processes, lithospheric evolution, and seismic hazards in diverse settings (Yao *et al.*, 2006; Brenguier *et al.*, 2007; Yang *et al.*, 2007; Lin *et al.*, 2008; Prieto and Beroza, 2008; Nishida *et al.*, 2009; Saygin and Kennett, 2010; Ward *et al.*, 2013; Denolle *et al.*, 2014; Mordret *et al.*, 2015; Boué *et al.*, 2016; Wang *et al.*, 2020; Zhao *et al.*, 2024).

During its initial decade, several pioneering studies demonstrated the feasibility of using ambient noise to image the shallow crust (Draganov *et al.*, 2009; Picozzi *et al.*, 2009; Behm *et al.*, 2014). However, progress was initially constrained by the availability of dense data, which restricted investigations to kilometer-scale depths or narrow regions. Recent advances in seismic instrumentation, such as the development of nodal sensors (e.g., Lin *et al.*, 2013) and distributed acoustic sensing (DAS) techniques (e.g., Zhan, 2020), have significantly

1. Research School of Earth Sciences, Australian National University, Canberra, Australia, https://orcid.org/0000-0002-8768-2782 (CJ); https://orcid.org/0000-0001-5494-2296 (MSM)

*Corresponding author: chengxin.jiang1@anu.edu.au

transformed this field. These innovations have enabled the deployment of large-N arrays comprising hundreds to thousands of sensors in a single experiment, achieving interstation spacing as fine as meters to tens of meters. This enhanced spatial resolution creates new opportunities for high-resolution near-surface seismic imaging that benefit mineral and energy exploration (Tomar *et al.*, 2018; Chmiel *et al.*, 2019; Cheng *et al.*, 2021; Olivier *et al.*, 2024), urban subsurface investigation (Dou *et al.*, 2017; Lai *et al.*, 2024), and geohazard mitigation (Spica *et al.*, 2020; Castellanos and Clayton, 2021).

Traffic noise is a key source of micro tremors in urban areas, offering higher frequencies of seismic energy than microseismic signals commonly used in ambient noise studies. For decades, this noise has been part of broad-range signals used in traditional methods such as SPatial Autocorrelation Analysis (SPAC; Aki, 1957) and the horizontal-to-vertical spectral ratio method (Nakamura, 1989) to characterize local structures and/or site amplification. Recent advances in seismic interferometry have led to innovative approaches for extracting high-frequency seismic signals from traffic noise for imaging and monitoring (e.g., Nakata *et al.*, 2011; Brenguier *et al.*, 2019). For example, Nakata *et al.* (2015) extract pairwise body-wave information from ambient noise recorded by over 5000 nodal sensors in Long Beach, California, to create a detailed 3D map of shallow structures up to 1 km deep. These technical and application developments align with theoretical advances that exploit nonideal noise sources for seismic imaging and monitoring. The key insight is that uniformly distributed noise sources are not essential; instead, noise sources need to be situated in specific, confined areas known as stationary phase zones. Both theoretical and numerical simulations indicate that the cross correlation approximating the derivative of Green's functions remains valid under these conditions (Colombi *et al.*, 2014; Boschi and Weemstra, 2015; Nakata *et al.*, 2019). Because more dense and noninvasive networks of nodal sensors and DAS systems expand in urban environments, the utility of traffic signals for shallow-earth imaging is increasingly evident. Successful applications include retrieving reflection profiles (Draganov *et al.*, 2009; Nakata *et al.*, 2011; Viens *et al.*, 2022), imaging 3D *P*- or *S*-wave velocity structures (Zhang *et al.*, 2020; Castellanos and Clayton, 2021; Yang *et al.*, 2022), inferring attenuation properties (Meng *et al.*, 2021), and continuous groundwater and fault activity monitoring (Sheng *et al.*, 2023; Shen, *et al.*, 2024).

In utilizing traffic noise for subsurface imaging, two primary configurations for array setups relative to roadways have emerged: parallel and perpendicular arrangements with respect to traffic flow. Although both configurations have demonstrated varying degrees of success (Nakata *et al.*, 2011; Behm *et al.*, 2014; Quiros *et al.*, 2016; Dou *et al.*, 2017; Zhang *et al.*, 2020), the predominant reliance on array seismology techniques (Rost and Thomas, 2002) to enhance and isolate coherent phases from the intricate wavefield is evident in nearly all seismic imaging applications utilizing traffic noise. This technique is essential for handling the complex wavefields observed in cross correlations, which are often influenced by significant heterogeneities within the shallow crust and the dynamics of multiple moving noise sources. However, the application of array seismology mandates spatial averaging of the resulting seismic images, which inherently restricts resolution capabilities. The challenge of extracting dispersion information from traffic noise using single-station pairs has proven to be markedly difficult, with only a handful of successful instances documented in the literature (e.g., Picozzi *et al.*, 2009; Zigone *et al.*, 2019). This study seeks to address these challenges through a meticulously designed experiment that incorporates a targeted source–receiver configuration, along with a relatively controlled traffic source from a busy highway near a city. The investigation narrows its focus to a single traffic lane to minimize potential interference. Furthermore, employing three-component sensors presents an exceptional opportunity to comprehensively analyze the ambient noise wavefield generated by traffic, thereby facilitating the extraction of reliable seismic signals for enhanced imaging applications.

Data and Methods

The Lake George fault zone is one of the three major fault systems near Canberra, putting this capital city of Australia at high hazard risk (Griffin *et al.*, 2023). The fault zone stretches about 80 km north–south, and geomorphological analysis indicates that the fault zone has undergone over 250 m of relief change due to deformation in the last 4 Ma (Clark *et al.*, 2017). The fault is still regarded as active today. The Geoscience Australia earthquake catalog contains about 50 events ranging in magnitudes from 1 to 3.5 within about 5 km of this fault in the last 60 yr. The Lake George basin, situated at the northern end of the fault zone, has undergone significant periods of filling and drying throughout its geological history, documenting continuous hydrological changes in Australia over the past 5 million years (Barrow, 2013). The sediments within the basin range in age from Neogene to Quaternary, with the primary lithologies being sandstone and clay, with some minor silt content (Abell, 1991; Macphail *et al.*, 2015). Drill holes conducted by the Bureau of Mineral Resources in the 1990s (now known as Geoscience Australia) indicate that the sediment thickness varies from 60 to 160 m (Abell, 1991). Beneath this sediment, Paleozoic basement rocks, composed of quartz-rich turbidites and volcanoclastics, are present (Abell, 1991; Macphail *et al.*, 2015).

The Lake George nodal array was a short-term seismic experiment in the then-dry bed of Lake George (Fig. 1a,b). The array comprises 97 three-component SmartSolo sensors (16HR-3C with a corner frequency of 5 Hz) arranged in five east–west lines perpendicular to the Federal Highway, which is the main thoroughfare connecting Canberra to Sydney. Five stations were positioned west of the highway on the Lake

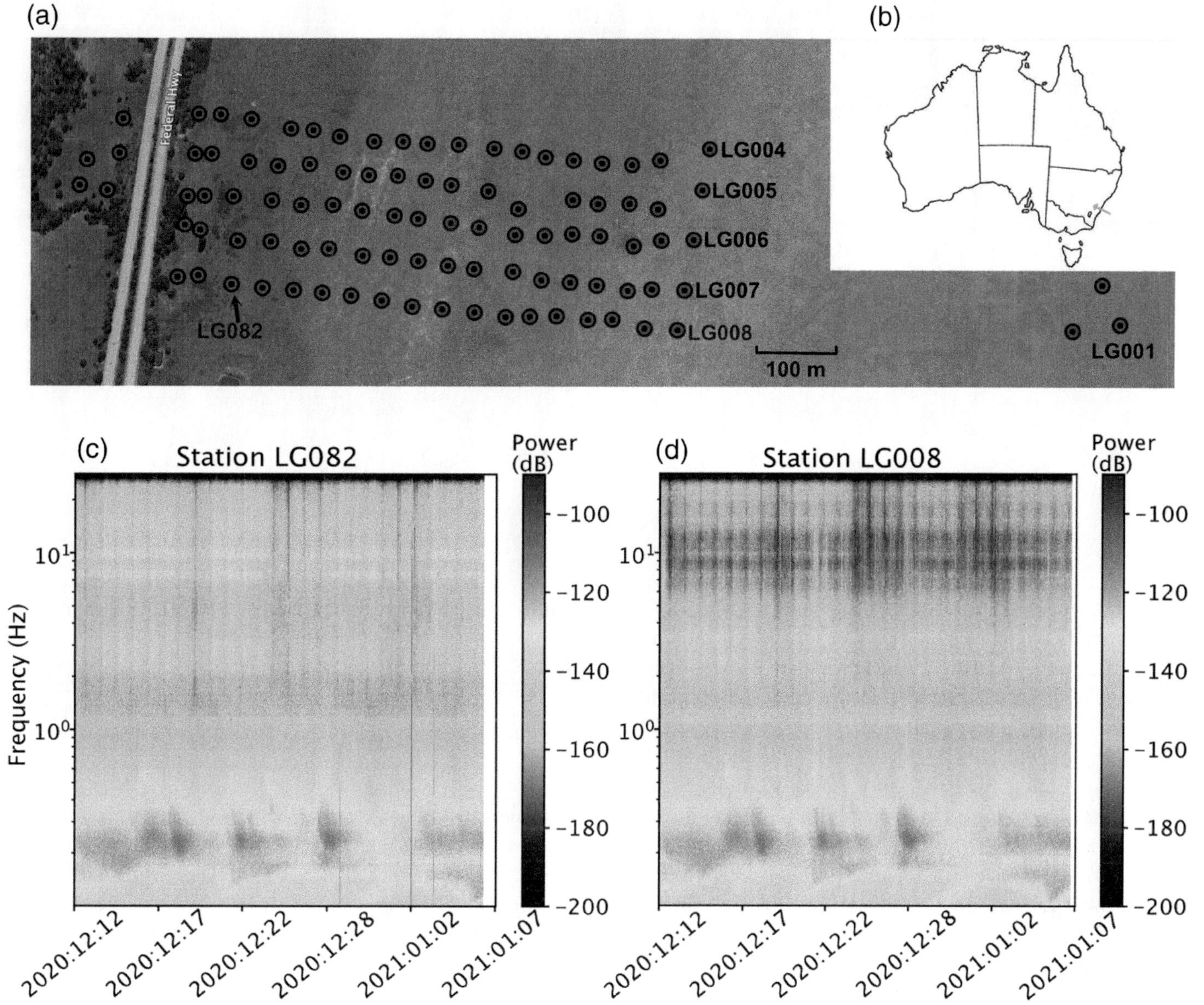

Figure 1. (a) The station distribution of the Lake George nodal array with example station names. (b) The regional context of the study region relative to the Australian continent. (c,d) Spectrogram of two stations, LG087 and LG001, over the entire duration. The spectrogram is calculated using a time window length of 1800 s with a 450 s overlap between windows, covering the entire experiment duration. The blank stripes indicate data gaps. The color version of this figure is available only in the electronic edition.

George fault scarp flank, whereas the remaining stations were located to the east in the dry lakebed. The array recorded continuous data for about four weeks from December 2020 to January 2021, with a sampling rate of 250 Hz and an average interstation spacing of 30–40 m.

Characteristics of seismic data

To understand the general characteristics of the recorded seismic signals, Figure 1c,d presents the spectrograms of the continuous data at two stations, LG082 and LG008, located on the far west and east sides of the array, respectively. Both stations exhibit similar microseismic energy in the 0.15–0.5 Hz frequency range with strong daily variations. Above 1 Hz, two strong bands of seismic energy are observed at station LG082: one centered in the 2–6 Hz frequency range and another above 9 Hz. The strong weekly patterns of these signals indicate a close relationship with anthropogenic sources, which we identify as traffic signals. At station LG008, ~600 m from the highway, the lower-frequency energy (1–5 Hz) persists, whereas most of the high-frequency energy is absent, most likely due to attenuation. We follow the scheme described in Harmon *et al.* (2010) to calculate the beamforming image based on the stacked cross-correlation functions (CCFs) introduced in the following section. The beamforming images (Fig. 2) confirm the dominant source direction from the highway in the west, though much simpler wavefields can be observed from the RR component than from the ZZ component.

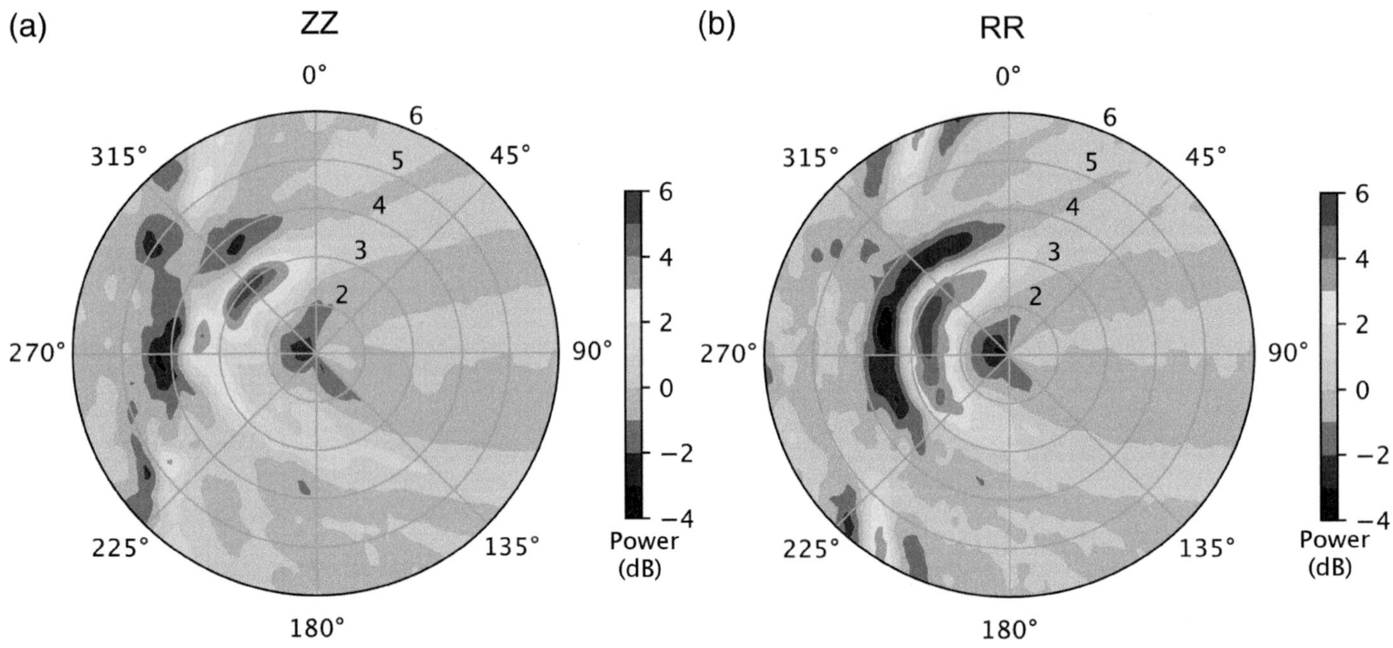

Figure 2. Beamforming analysis upon the (a) ZZ and (b) RR components of cross-correlation functions (CCFs) for all station pairs within 300 m centered at the station LG008. The waveforms are filtered within the 2.5–10 Hz frequency band before analysis. The color version of this figure is available only in the electronic edition.

Ambient noise data processing

To process the ambient noise data, we adopt the high-performance open-source Python package *NoisePy* (Jiang and Denolle, 2020), which is specifically designed for high-performance ambient noise seismology. The calculation of CCFs follows Bensen *et al.* (2007) with minor modifications to fulfill our main interests in high-frequency signals. Continuous noise data are first downsampled to 50 Hz before being cut into 8-hr-long traces. Each trace is further divided into 15-min segments with a 75% overlap between adjacent segments to increase the final stacking's signal-to-noise ratio (SNR). All time series are demeaned, detrended, and prefiltered between 0.05 and 24 Hz with instrument response removed. The CCFs are calculated in the frequency domain using the coherency method (Prieto *et al.*, 2009), for which the spectrum is whitened with a moving window length of 40 samples. Finally, the cross correlations of the small time windows are linearly stacked for each station pair, resulting in 4656 stacked CCFs across the array. Because these procedures are applied to all three-component data, each station pair yields nine cross correlations, forming a complete correlation tensor.

Figure 3 presents moveout plots for the nine-component correlation tensor, averaged across the array and filtered in the 1–15 Hz frequency range. The dominant energy in the negative lag is again identified as traffic noise coming from the west. In general, the correlations between horizontal and vertical channels (e.g., ZT and RT) exhibit more complex features than those observed in the ZZ, RR, and TT components. Specifically, the waveforms associated with these cross components predominantly feature high-frequency energy, in contrast to the relatively lower-frequency signals found in the RR and TT components during the same time windows. The subsequent frequency–time analysis indicates that much of this high-frequency energy represents body waves, and their appearance in the later travel-time windows may be related to potential scattering effects. Upon closer inspection of the ZZ, RR, and TT components, their waveforms display different characteristics. For example, the ZZ component exhibits a clear high-frequency phase (>9 Hz) near time zero, with an average moveout velocity of approximately 2 km/s (cyan-dashed line in Fig. 3). However, this signal is absent in both the RR and TT components. Frequency–time analysis (Fig. 4a) suggests that this phase is nondispersive, characteristic of a body wave. At the same time, the relatively lower frequency and slower energy correspond to surface waves with strong dispersion features (Fig. 4a). The dominant surface-wave energy in the ZZ component has an average group velocity of about 370 m/s, significantly faster than that in the RR and TT components, which have an average speed of approximately 200 m/s. We note that this feature does not conflict with the beamforming images shown in Figure 2, which considers CCFs limited to a distance range of 300 m. The moveout plots for individual virtual sources (see Fig. S1, available in the supplemental material to this article) indicate the presence of spurious seismic phases occurring between time zero and the fundamental-mode surface wave, which complicates the wavefields. These spurious phases exhibit scattering signatures that could be attributed to local structural boundaries (Retailleau and Beroza, 2021), as observed in our study region. Numerical simulations may

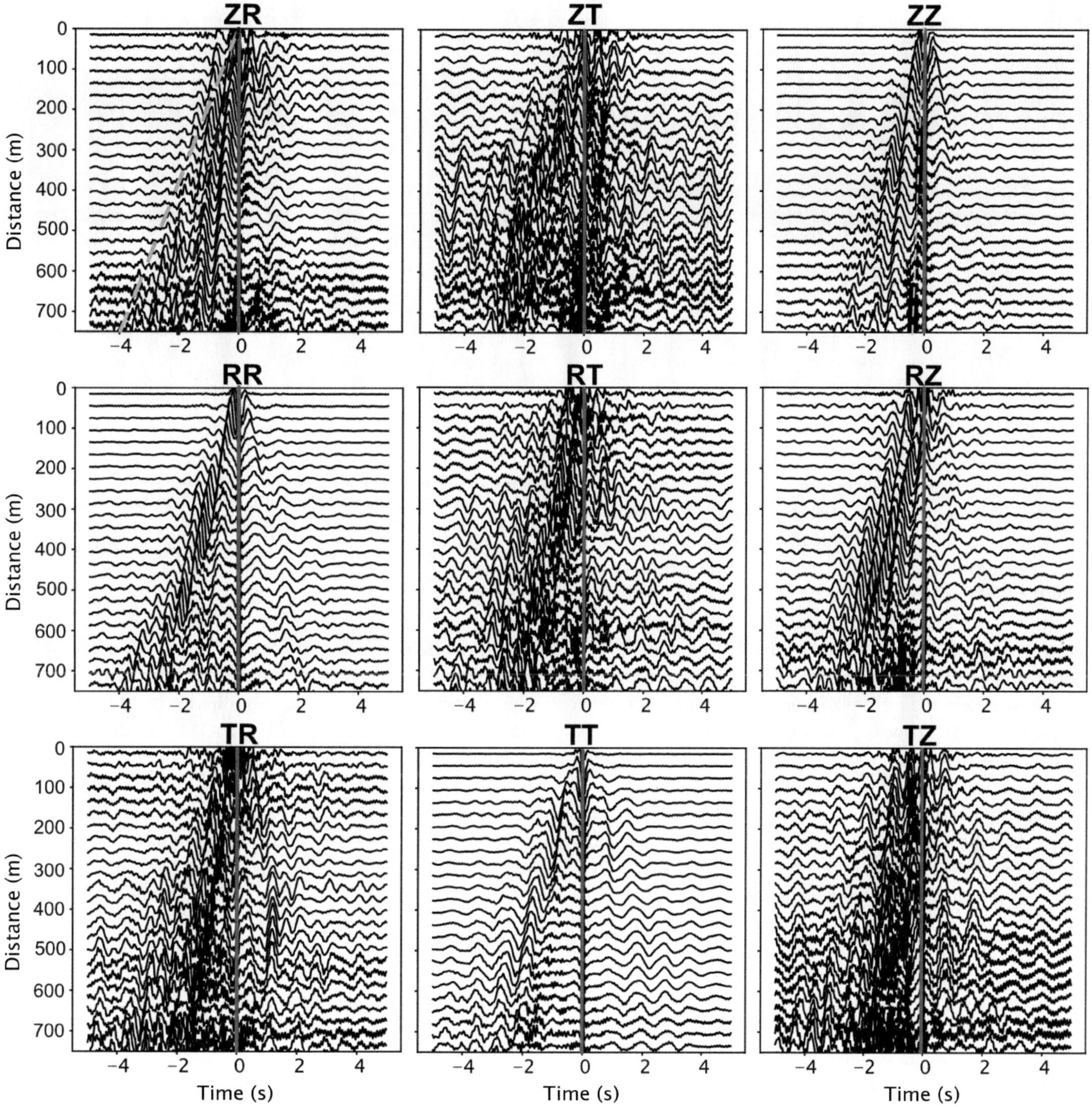

help verify this observation and will be the subject of our future study. Notably, this feature is only apparent in the ZZ component. Kennett *et al.* (2023) applied a particle motion filter to suppress the faster wave energy for improved dispersion extraction using array seismology.

In contrast to the complex wavefields observed in the ZZ component, the RR component exhibits cleaner waveforms of surface-wave signals. The dominant seismic phase in the RR component has a group speed that matches the slower branch seen in the ZZ and TT components, suggesting it may represent the fundamental-mode surface wave. To investigate

Figure 3. Moveout plot for the nine-component correlation tensor averaged over all station pairs of the array. The waveforms are filtered at the 1–15 Hz frequency range. Each waveform represents the average of the waveforms from station pairs within a distance range of 30 m. The red line marks time zero, and the blue- and green-dashed lines denote a group velocity of 375 and 187.5 m/s, respectively. The cyan-dashed line in ZZ component highlights the body-wave energy, which has relatively higher frequencies and much faster group speeds compared to those between the blue- and green-dashed lines. The color version of this figure is available only in the electronic edition.

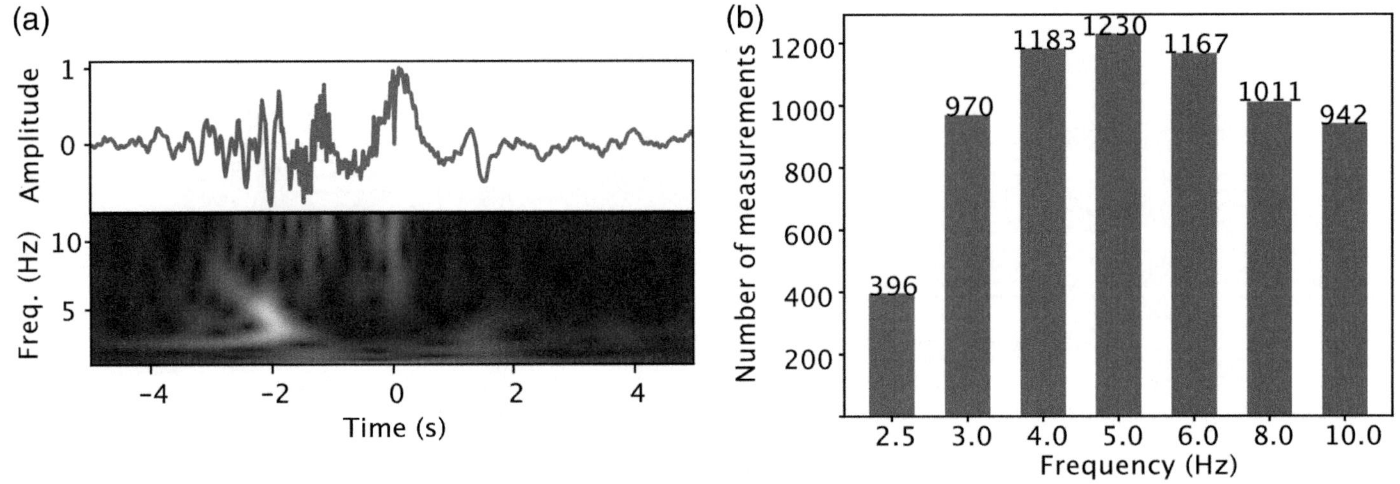

Figure 4. (a) Frequency–time analysis for the CCF of LG008–LG082. The upper panel shows the normalized CCF, and the lower panel displays the frequency–time image from *S* transform. (b) Number of dispersion measurements at different frequency bands. Note that the interval along the *x* axis is not uniform. The color version of this figure is available only in the electronic edition.

this further, we analyze the coherent phases in the wavefield using the classical SPAC method (Aki, 1957). The resulting dispersion image for the RR component (see Fig. S2a) confirms that the fundamental-mode surface wave predominates the wavefield, with its energy distinctly separated from higher-mode counterparts, which are much weaker in energy. We also apply the SPAC method to the ZZ and TT components (Fig. S2b,c), and the results indicate minimal leakage of seismic energy from the TT component into the RR component. This finding supports the use of the RR component for dispersion extraction. The image for the ZZ component shows a sudden change in seismic velocity around 0.25 s, which could be related to the complex wavefield caused by scattering, as described earlier. However, this complexity is not present in the RR component, reinforcing our choice to utilize RR-component data for analysis. Individual CCFs show high-quality signals upon visual inspection (Fig. 4a) and provide unprecedented opportunities to extract dispersion data based on a single station. Using the image transformation method (Yao *et al.*, 2006), dispersion data within the 2.5–10 Hz range are successfully extracted. The image transformation method is chosen here for its flexibility and convenience in manually selecting each dispersion data set, offering essential quality control when handling high-frequency signals.

To assist in dispersion selection and to avoid potential contamination from higher modes, we utilize the dispersion images derived from the SPAC method. We extract the averaged dispersion information from these images, which serve as a reference model to guide dispersion selection for the station-pair-based data. To account for the potentially strong heterogeneity in the region, we construct two reference dispersion curves: one for the eastern half of the seismic array and another for the western half. During the manual selection process, we choose the dispersion energies that align with the reference values and eliminate those that deviate significantly from the reference over the periods or exhibit sharp velocity changes across these periods. This process produces an averaged dispersion for the region (white dots in Fig. S2a) that is consistent with the SPAC-derived dispersion image. In addition, to address the effects of noise-source distribution, we select only the station pairs that align with the traffic noise direction, that is, those pairs within an azimuthal range of 225°–330°, as determined by beamforming analysis (Fig. 2). This azimuthal range approximates the general stationary zones based on the station geometry in our study. However, it is important that for station pairs crossing the highway, the seismic noise sources lie between the stations, causing their cross correlation to deviate significantly from the assumptions for seismic interferometry. Therefore, these station pairs have been excluded from further analysis. Consequently, more than 1000 high-quality dispersions are obtained within the 2.5–10 Hz frequency range (Fig. 4b) across most frequency bands, enabling high-resolution ambient noise tomography at this shallow and compact scale.

Shear-wave velocity modeling

We employ a two-step approach to develop a near-surface 3D V_S model using the extracted dispersion curves from above, including surface-wave tomography and a subsequent local shear-wave velocity model inversion.

Surface-wave tomography. Dispersion measurements that met the following criteria are selected to invert for 2D phase velocity maps, including (1) the SNR, defined in Yao *et al.* (2006) greater than 5, (2) the interstation distance larger than 1.5 times the corresponding wavelength, and (3) a manual screening process. Eventually, more than 1000 dispersions are retained throughout most periods (Fig. 4b). For the surface-wave tomography, we follow Jiang *et al.* (2023) to employ a Poisson

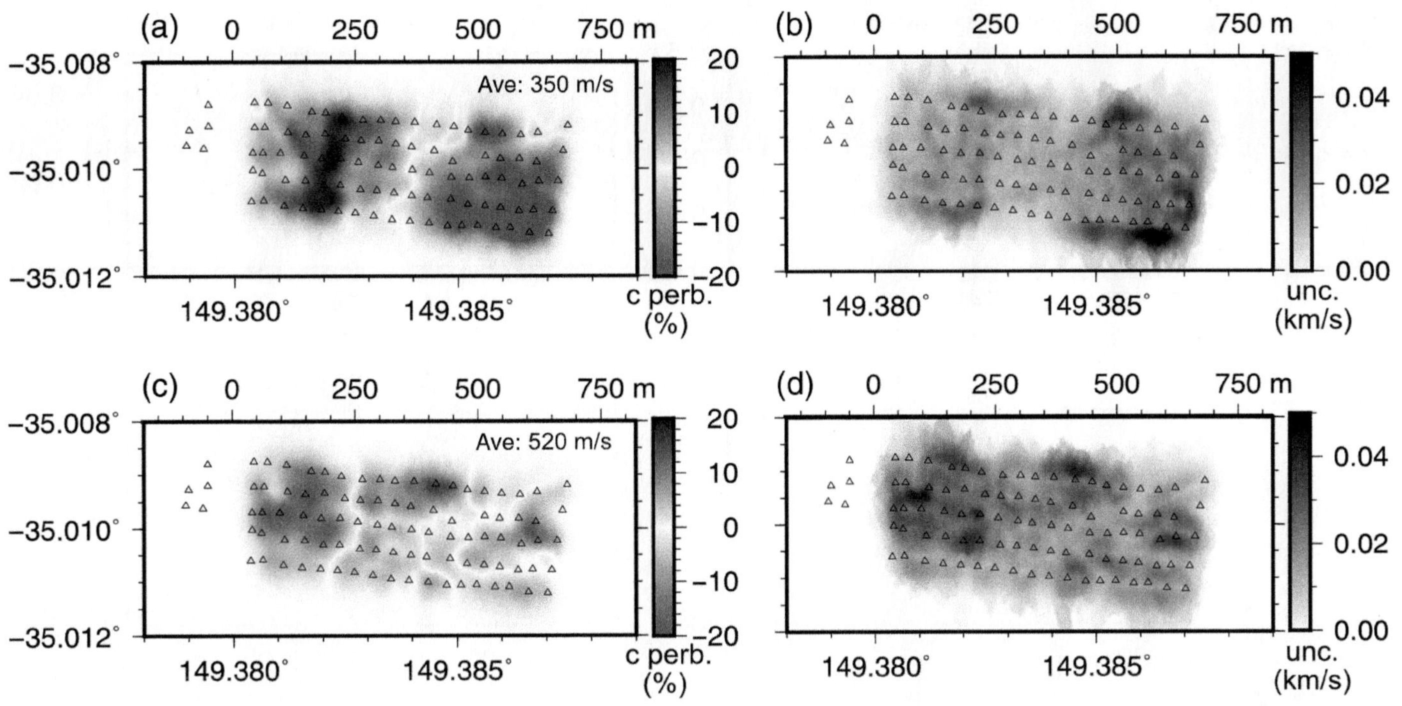

Figure 5. (a) Phase velocity map at 6.25 Hz, plotting as a perturbation in percentage. The hollow triangles denote the seismic stations. (b) The associated uncertainty of the phase velocity map. (c) Same as panel (a) but for 2.5 Hz. (d) Same as panel (b) but for 2.5 Hz. Note that the distance axis of the figures is calculated relative to the highway at a longitude of 149.380°. The color version of this figure is available only in the electronic edition.

Voronoi (PV) projection-based method (Fang *et al.*, 2020), which projects the original 2D space on a regular grid into low-dimensional subspaces formed by PV cells (Sambridge *et al.*, 1995). In each subspace, the low-dimensional image is optimized efficiently, making the process computationally practical and eliminating the need for explicit smoothing regularization, whereas damping regularization could still be employed in each subspace minimization to avoid significant velocity deviations from the mean of the observational travel-time data. We use the least-squares method of Paige and Saunders (1982) to solve the minimization problem. The final solution can be obtained by averaging all solutions from low-dimensional subspaces by conducting such inversions multiple times (several tens to a few hundred), each with a random distribution of Voronoi cells. The ensemble solution also allows for the quantification of model parameter uncertainties (Fang *et al.*, 2020).

Phase velocity map inversions were conducted for Rayleigh waves at 2.5–10 Hz with the 2D model space at each period parameterized with 400 Voronoi cells. We conducted 100 low-dimensional inversions and used their average and standard deviation as the basis for the final model. The number of Voronoi cells and low-dimensional inversions has a minor effect on the inversion results, provided they are within a certain range, beyond 200 and 70, respectively, in this case. In each low-dimensional inversion, the travel-time wavefield is calculated using the ray-based pyKonal package (White *et al.*, 2020).

Figure 5 presents phase velocity maps and associated model uncertainties at two example frequencies, 6.25 and 2.5 Hz, which reveal several interesting velocity features in the study region. At 6.25 Hz (Fig. 5a), for which phase velocities are sensitive to depths of approximately 60–100 m, the study region is split into two components, with the western region exhibiting significantly faster velocities (>30%) compared to those in the east. At 2.5 Hz (Fig. 5c), the velocities represent structures greater than 200 m deep, where the velocity pattern is reversed: the western half displays slower velocity anomalies relative to the east. However, the velocity contrast decreases to about 20% at this frequency. The observed velocity features are well resolved with velocity variations beyond the associated uncertainties (Fig. 5b–d). The travel-time residuals before and after the tomography at these two frequencies are summarized in Figure S2, demonstrating a much-improved fit of the inverted model.

Synthetic resolution tests. We perform resolution tests to assess the general resolution of our tomography results using synthetic data. We design synthetic spike models with alternate slow and fast anomalies of size of 0.006° × 0.006° (approximately 54 m × 54 m) and an absolute amplitude of 10%. A space with the same dimension as the anomaly separates the velocity anomalies. Such tests are suggested to provide more realistic estimations of the model's resolvability compared to the traditional checkerboard tests, according to Rawlinson and Spakman (2016). To synthesize the travel-time data, we input the spike model into the Pykonal package (White *et al.*, 2020) and calculate the surface-wave travel time between

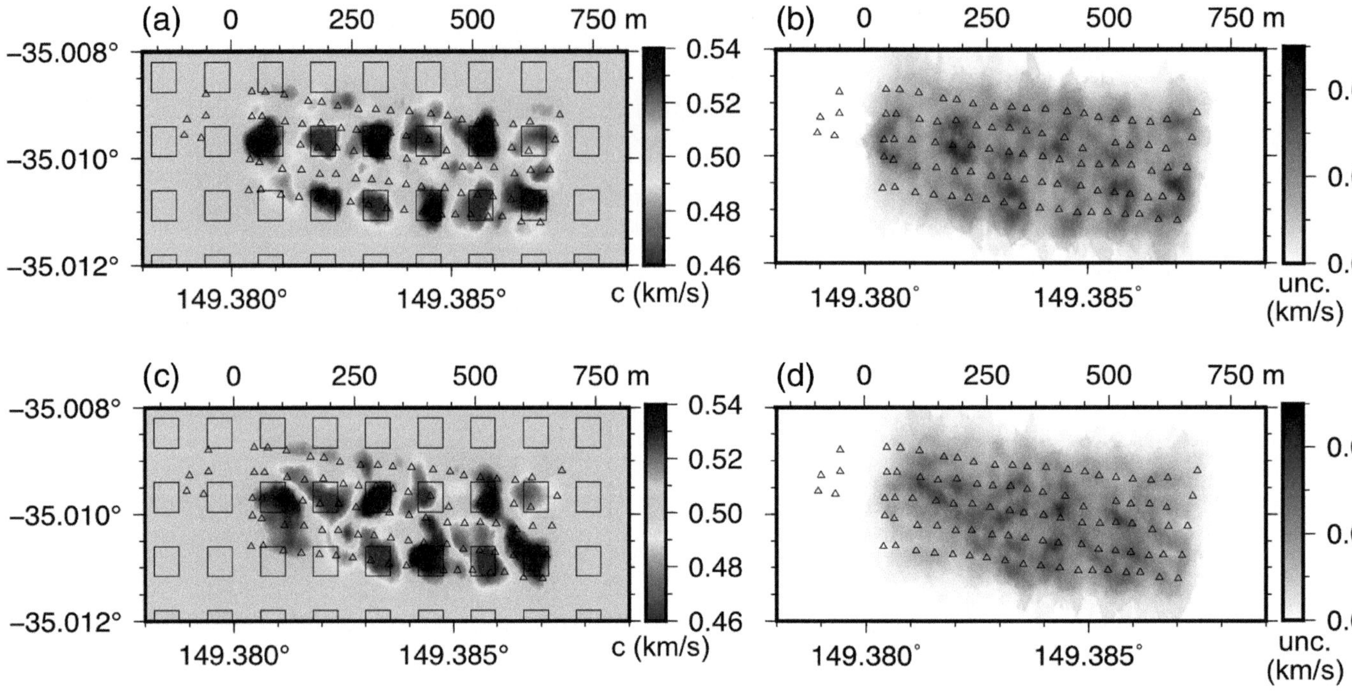

Figure 6. Spike test results and the associated model uncertainty at (a,b) 6.25 and (c,d) 2.5 Hz, respectively. The thin-black lines in panels (a) and (c) denote the input spikes with sizes of 54 m × 54 m. The same dimension separates them and has an amplitude of 10%. The hollow triangles show the station distribution. Note that the distance axis of the figures is calculated relative to the highway at a longitude of 149.380°. The color version of this figure is available only in the electronic edition.

the stations used in the real data. We add a Gaussian noise with a standard deviation of 0.01 s in the travel time to approximate the uncertainty observed in the real data (Fig. S3). Figure 6 summarizes the spike test results at two example frequencies of 6.25 and 2.5 Hz, respectively. The input models at both frequencies are generally well recovered, including their shape and amplitude. However, some smearing effects can be observed at the model edges, particularly on the western edge, where there is less path coverage. Based on the test, we estimate that the tomography results have a general resolution of around 50 m in the lateral dimension. The velocity anomalies resolved in the tomography with real data (Fig. 5) are much larger than the synthetic anomalies. Therefore, our results are considered to be highly accurate.

Inversion of 1D V_S profiles. Phase velocity maps are used as inputs for local 1D V_S inversions and then combined to form a comprehensive 3D velocity model. First, local dispersion curves at 2.5–10 Hz were extracted from the regional phase velocity maps at a 0.0002° × 0.0002° grid (approximately 18 m × 18 m). Such dispersion enables good constraints of V_S from the surface to a depth of about 800 m. A Bayesian Markov chain Monte Carlo (MCMC) inversion method based on Shen *et al.* (2013) was then used to invert local 1D V_S profiles on these grid points. The details of this inversion method can be found in Shen *et al.* (2013) and Jiang *et al.* (2023) and are briefly described subsequently.

The inversion framework explores the model space through a series of 1D V_S profiles that extend from the surface to a depth of 5 km, represented by seven free parameters. This includes five B-spline coefficients defining a continuous V_S in the slow sediments, a parameter denoting the local depth of sediment–crystalline crust, and a V_S of the basement rock, respectively. The weathered bedrock is treated as a part of the sediment here, considering the relatively low shear-wave velocity. Uniform prior distributions are used for all parameters, as shown in Table S1. During the inversion, V_P and density of the 1D profile are scaled to V_S according to the empirical relations 1 and 9 of Brocher (2005). Attenuation effects on surface-wave dispersion are corrected following Kanamori and Anderson (1977). In this study, each 1D inversion contains 0.7 million iterations, and the final average model and uncertainty are calculated from the mean of the best 2000 models with the associated standard deviation approximating the corresponding model uncertainty.

Results

Figures 7 and 8 present horizontal and vertical slices through our 3D velocity model, revealing significant velocity variations in the top 800 m. Generally, velocities range from 300 to 400 m/s near the surface to around 1 km/s at 200–300 m depth before stabilizing near 1.2 km/s at depths of 400–600 m. The model uncertainty is within 40 m/s (10% relative to the regional average V_S) in the top 200 m but increases significantly to approximately 200 m/s below 500–600 m depths (Fig. 9).

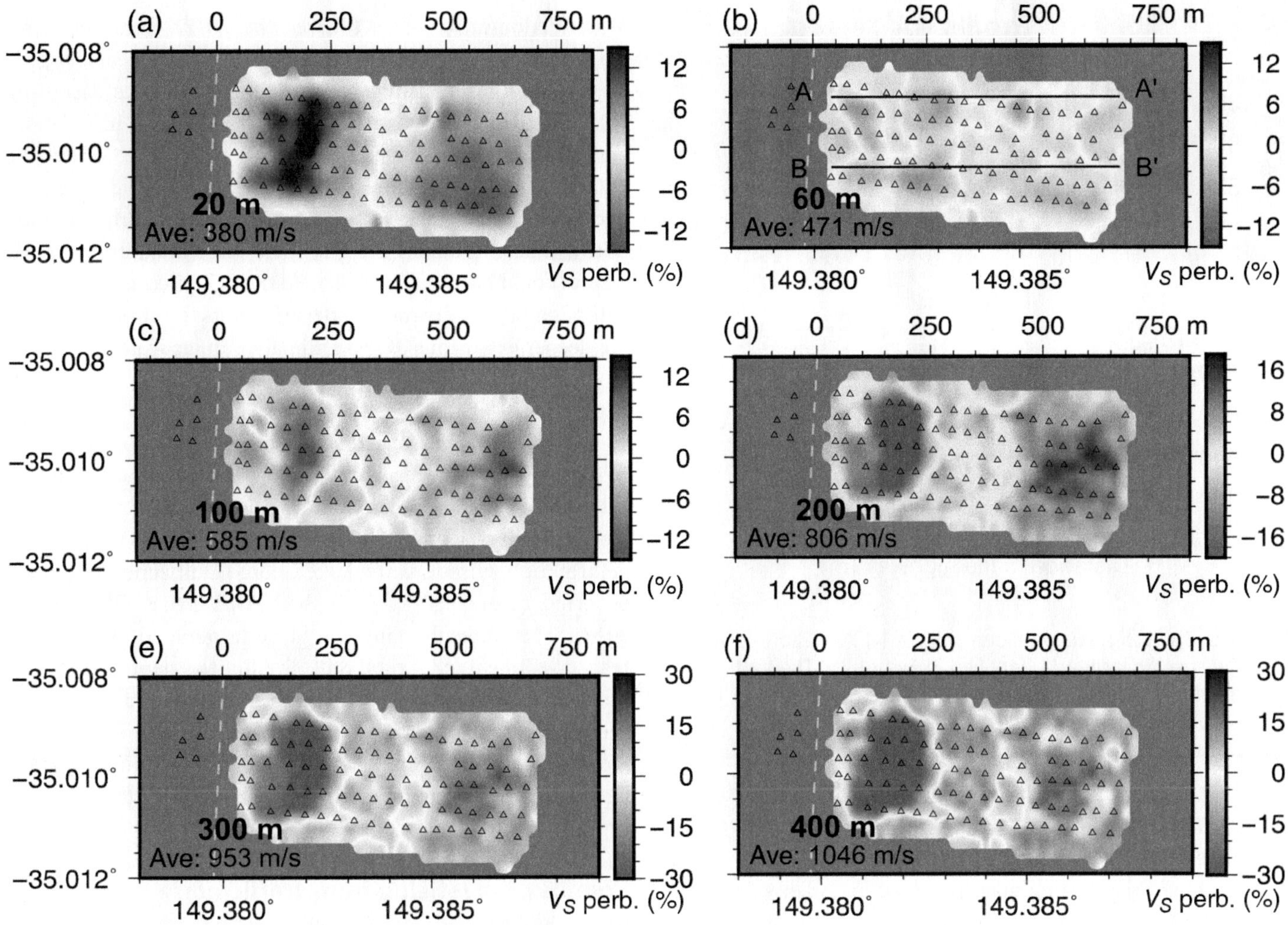

Figure 7. Shear-wave velocity maps for horizontal slices at (a) 20, (b) 60, (c) 100, (d) 200, (e) 300, and (f) 400 m depths. The lower left text in each panel shows the regionally averaged V_S at each depth, based on which perturbations are calculated. The cyan-dashed lines denote the highway. The locations of the two vertical profiles shown in Figure 8 are labeled in panel (b). The color version of this figure is available only in the electronic edition.

At shallow depths, for example, 20 and 60 m (Fig. 7a,b), there is a marked north–south-striking contrast in velocity, with low velocities concentrated in the eastern half of the model, contrasting with higher velocities in the west. The high velocities extend from the highway to about 350 m eastward and extend beyond a depth of 60 m. Despite the significant velocity contrast, velocities at these depths remain below 500 m/s, indicating the presence of unconsolidated sedimentary rocks. We attribute the 20% lower velocity on the east side to more weathered sediments, consistent with much softer soil conditions near the surface. The velocity contrast diminishes with depth, likely reflecting reduced fractures and/or weathering due to compaction. Although our data lack direct constraints on the basement depth due to the smooth sensitivities of surface waves, borehole data from a nearby site suggest a depth of about 100 m to the weathered regolith (Clark *et al.*, personal comm., 2024). This corresponds well to the change of velocity features at deeper depths, as shown in our model. Secondary features, such as velocity variations within the high-velocity anomaly in the west, are also observed at this depth.

At greater depths of 100–400 m (Fig. 7c–f), the velocity pattern reverses, with lower velocities shifting to the western side of this north–south-trending feature. In contrast, relatively higher velocities emerge beneath the slow sediments in the east. Interestingly, the magnitude of this velocity contrast intensifies with depth, increasing from −10% at 100 m to over −25% at 400 m. The cross section (Fig. 8) shows that the low-velocity zone (LVZ) extends much deeper, with an amplitude exceeding 35% at 600–800 m. This extensive LVZ has a lateral dimension of approximately 200 m at a depth of 200 m and narrows gradually at depth, extending beyond the resolution of our model. Further eastward, another similar LVZ with a smaller lateral extent and slightly less velocity reduction is observed (at a distance range of 400–450 m; Fig. 7f), though it has much higher uncertainty (Fig. 9).

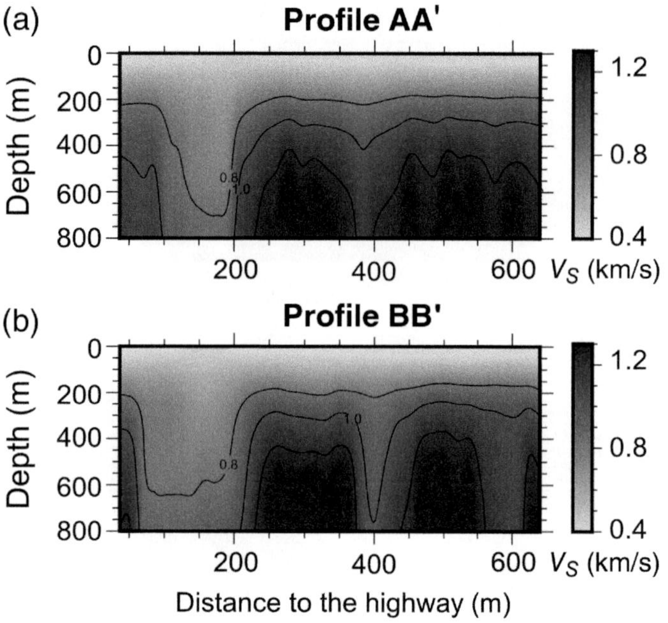

Figure 8. The cross section along profiles (a) A–A′ and (b) B–B′ with the specific locations identified in Figure 7b. The sections have a vertical–horizontal ratio of 3:1. The color version of this figure is available only in the electronic edition.

Discussion

Lake George fault-zone structures

This study analyzes traffic noise recorded by a dense array to construct a high-resolution 3D shear-wave velocity of the Lake George fault zone. Our work represents one of the few successful local ambient noise surface-wave tomography using high-quality dispersion (up to 10 Hz) derived from traffic noise. The resulting 3D velocity model provides unprecedented insights into the structural characteristics of the Lake George fault zone for the first time.

Our primary finding reveals that the Lake George fault zone contains a pronounced north–south-striking LVZ with an average velocity reduction of 30%–40% relative to the surrounding rock (Fig. 7c,d). This LVZ extends laterally approximately 200 m in the east–west direction and appears at depths greater than 100 m (Fig. 8). Its depth rules out the possibility that it represents near-surface sediments, previously suggested as a complicating factor in identifying fault-zone structures (e.g., Yang *et al.*, 2020). The dimensions and velocity reduction of this LVZ are comparable to those observed in other major active fault systems, such as several southern branches of the San Jacinto fault zone (SJFZ; Yang *et al.*, 2014; Share *et al.*, 2017; Qiu *et al.*, 2020) and the Parkfield section of the San Andreas fault (Li *et al.*, 2004) in central California, as well as the Longmenshan fault zone in southwestern China (Li *et al.*, 2013). For example, waveform inversions of trapped waves within the SJFZ at Blackburn Saddle indicate the presence of a structure approximately 200 m wide, accompanied by a V_S reduction of 30%–40% (Share *et al.*, 2017). Comprehensive paleoseismic studies suggest that the SJFZ has repeatedly generated significant seismic events, with magnitudes exceeding 7.0, over the past 4000 yr (Rockwell *et al.*, 2015). In addition, core samples from the Longmenshan fault zone, where the 2008 M_w 7.9 Wenchuan earthquake ruptured, have an identified fault damage zone ranging from 100 to 200 m (Li *et al.*, 2013). These parallels suggest that large-magnitude earthquakes could have similarly shaped the Lake George fault zone. Although our observational aperture limits the ability to detect the deeper extensions of this anomaly, similar scale fault zones in southern California suggest that the fault might extend to depths of 3–4 km.

We note that the imaged LVZ exhibits low-velocity characteristics over 100 m below the subsurface, with the depth and extent that could help constrain the timing of the fault's most recent activity. Geomorphological studies indicate that the last deformation episode at the Lake George fault zone most likely occurred before 780 ka (Macphail *et al.*, 2015; Clark *et al.*, 2017). Therefore, the fault might be terminated at the more recent sedimentary layers. Still, the limited depth resolution (~50 m) prevents us from making further interpretations at these depths. If confirmed, this study's pronounced velocity reduction and geographic extent support the interpretation that the Lake George fault zone is a long-lived damage zone capable of significant earthquakes.

Complex wavefields from traffic noise and implications for future near-surface imaging

Compared to urban settings, where traffic noise varies considerably, highways outside cities offer a simpler setting with fewer constraints. This makes them ideal for conducting seismic experiments. For example, several seismic experiments with similar array configurations have targeted the southern branches of the SJFZ in southern California (e.g., Ben-Zion *et al.*, 2015; Zigone *et al.*, 2019; Qiu *et al.*, 2020) and the Bingchuan fault zone in western China (e.g., Yang *et al.*, 2020). Building on these previous efforts, our study introduces several improvements that enable the extraction of high-quality, high-frequency dispersion for ambient noise surface-wave tomography. These improvements have significant implications for future nodal and DAS imaging experiments.

One key advancement in this study is the use of a three-component nodal array, which enables the computation of a complete correlation tensor. This allows for high-quality dispersion measurements from station pairs and traditional ambient noise tomography applications. Although three-component sensors have been used in previous studies, there has been limited investigation into the nine-component tensor, possibly due to the computational costs associated with it. Initially, we focused on the vertical component of the cross correlation for data analysis. However, the complex wavefields make it challenging to obtain high-quality dispersion

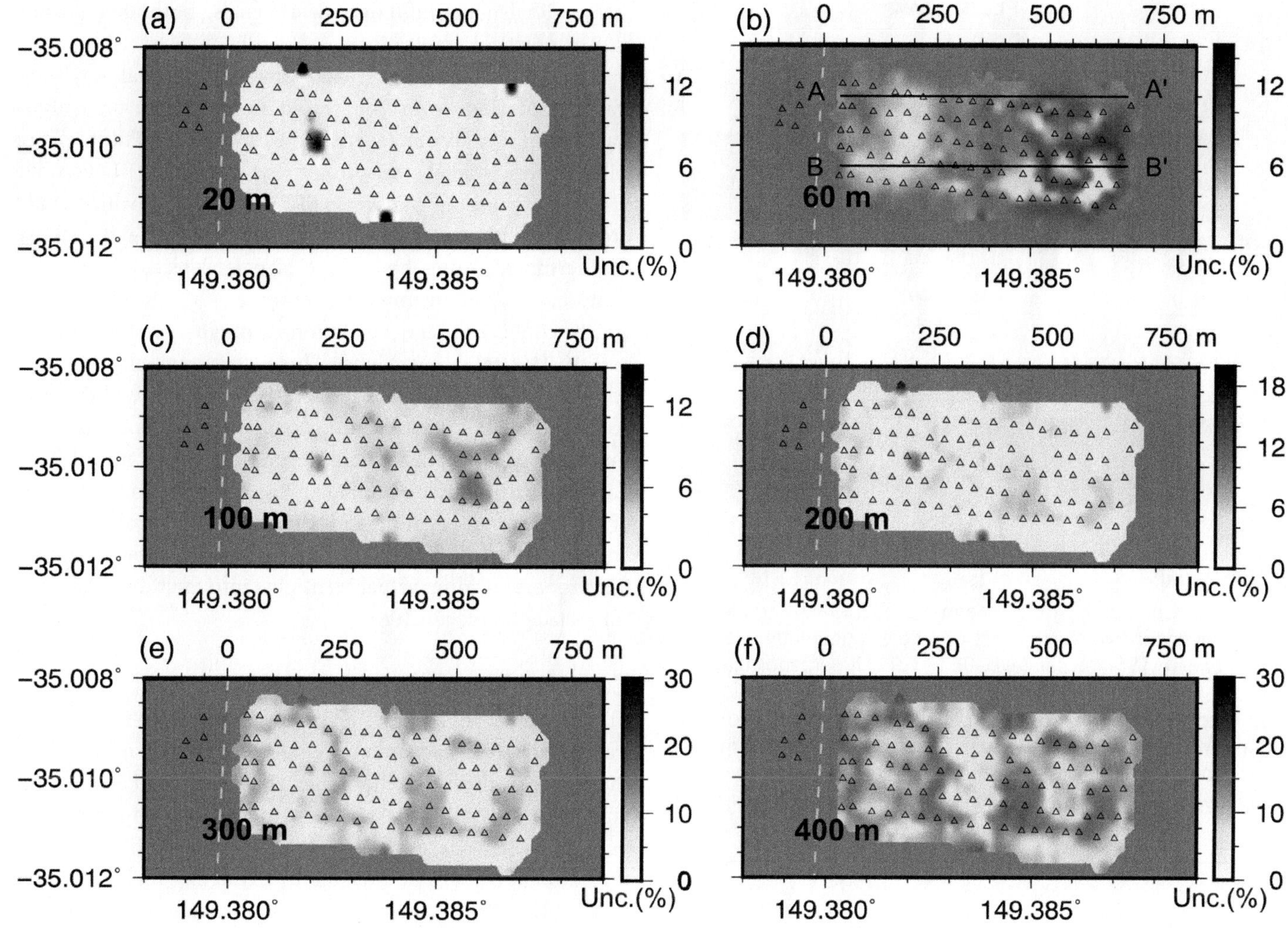

Figure 9. Shear-wave velocity model uncertainties at horizontal slices at (a) 20, (b) 60, (c) 100, (d) 200, (e) 300, and (f) 400 m depths. The uncertainties are perturbations based on the averaged V_S at each depth, as noted in Figure 7. The cyan-dashed lines denote the highway. The color version of this figure is available only in the electronic edition.

data from single-station pairs, despite applying a particle motion filter to clean the waveform (Kennett *et al.*, 2023). We gain a better understanding of the wavefield by examining the entire correlation tensor, particularly the vertical (ZZ) and radial (RR) components. Notably, the ZZ component reveals dominant energy that does not correspond to direct surface waves or their higher modes; we interpret this as scattering from the sharp boundaries of the fault zone. Our method provides significantly higher resolution compared to those from array seismology techniques. For example, the dispersion data from array-based analysis of the Lake George data (Kennett *et al.*, 2023) achieved a resolution of approximately 200 m. In contrast, this study has a lateral resolution of ~50 m.

The clearer and simpler waveforms observed in the RR component are noteworthy. Although this component is less explored in seismic noise studies using nodes, the cross correlation of DAS data technically represents an RR component due to its along-axis sensitivity. The key difference in the DAS setup lies in the geometry of the parallel seismic array relative to the traffic flow. In our configuration, the array was oriented perpendicular to the traffic and positioned on one side of the roadway. This arrangement aligns with theoretical frameworks, such as those derived by Kennett *et al.* (2023), which suggest that perpendicular arrays enhance contributions from stationary zones where moving vehicles produce consistent energy. Although parallel configurations can also be effective, the perpendicular layout offers distinct advantages in capturing strong and consistent energy between stations. For instance, previous seismic monitoring efforts have designed arrays perpendicular to train tracks to utilize train noise for extracting fault-zone-sensitive body waves (Brenguier *et al.*, 2019; Sheng *et al.*, 2024). In our study, the limited array configuration along the traffic flow makes it challenging to conduct a quantitative analysis for comparison. Nonetheless, it is generally observed that station pairs oriented

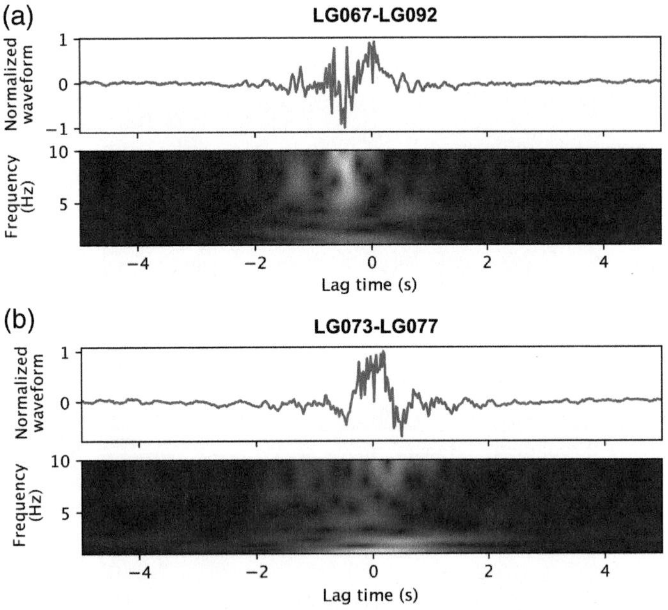

Figure 10. Comparison of CCFs and their associated frequency–time analysis for two station pairs of different geometry relative to the roadway. Station pair (a) LG067–LG092 is perpendicular to the road, whereas (b) LG073–LG077 is almost parallel. The upper panel shows the normalized RR component of the cross-correlation tensor, and the lower panel shows the frequency–time image computed using the *S* transform. See Figure 11a for the locations of the corresponding stations. The color version of this figure is available only in the electronic edition.

in the north–south direction (i.e., parallel to traffic) exhibit more complex waveform and dispersion characteristics than those aligned east–west (Fig. 10). To further demonstrate this point, we conducted a slant-stacking of CCFs from two linear subarrays close to the highway, one parallel to the traffic and the other perpendicular. The resulting dispersion images (Fig. 11) indicate that the configuration with the perpendicular array is significantly clearer than the one with the parallel configuration. These results highlight the potential for optimizing nodal array configurations to improve imaging efficiency in seismic monitoring.

In DAS applications, wavefield complexity is even greater due to the along-fiber sensitivities, which can result in the contamination of CCFs by Rayleigh and Love waves from off-axis sources near the fiber (Song *et al.*, 2021). Therefore, careful interpretation is essential when using DAS data for subsurface imaging. Some studies have successfully combined nodal and DAS arrays to jointly constrain subsurface structures, with nodal arrays providing critical insights into wavefield characteristics (Obermann *et al.*, 2022; Benjumea *et al.*, 2024). Incorporating three-component seismometers alongside DAS systems is highly recommended for such studies. Alternatively, Luo *et al.* (2020) demonstrate that using waveforms from horizontally orthogonal DAS arrays can reliably extract Rayleigh- and Love-wave signals, both theoretically and in practical applications.

This study focused on extracting fundamental Rayleigh-wave dispersion from the traffic noise. However, only a fraction of the available energy was utilized. Future work will explore radial anisotropy by extracting Love-wave dispersion from the transverse (TT) component, which could provide additional constraints on the fault-zone structures. Furthermore, strong body-wave signals detected in the ZZ component hold promise for refining V_P velocity models, which could enhance resolution through V_P tomography and V_P/V_S ratio inversions. These developments will offer complementary insights into the internal structure of the fault zone and further expand the capabilities of ambient noise tomography. This study's high-resolution 3D V_S model facilitates waveform simulation, enabling a deeper understanding of body-wave propagation and scattering. This capability could illuminate the complex interactions of seismic waves within the fault zone, providing valuable insights into fault dynamics and subsurface heterogeneity.

Conclusions

In this study, we conduct a seismic experiment that utilizes traffic noise to accurately characterize the near-surface shear-wave velocity in the upper 800 m of the Lake George fault zone in southeast Australia. Our tomography represents one of the few successful efforts to enhance traffic noise for high-resolution seismic imaging by extracting high-frequency (2.5–10 Hz) surface-wave dispersion information based on single-station pairs. The mapped Lake George fault zone extends laterally for 200 m and exhibits a 30% reduction in velocity, reflecting seismic characteristics akin to numerous prominent active fault systems in Southern California and Western China. This reflects it as a long-standing damage zone capable of producing significant seismic activity. Our research provides new insights into one of eastern Australia's most active Quaternary fault zones and presents important implications for hazard assessment in near-urban settings and utilizing traffic noise for near-surface imaging and monitoring.

Data and Resources

The Lake George seismic nodal array is available from AusPass (https://auspass.edu.au, last accessed October 2024): Australian Passive Seismic Server for network 1 G (doi: 10.7914/t2z3-2m87). Figures were produced using the Generic Mapping Tools (GMT; Wessel and Smith, 1991) and Matplotlib. NoisePy used in this study can be obtained from https://github.com/chengxinjiang/NoisePy (last accessed December 2024). The supplemental material includes one table and three figures referenced in the Data and Methods section.

Declaration of Competing Interests

The authors acknowledge that there are no conflicts of interest recorded.

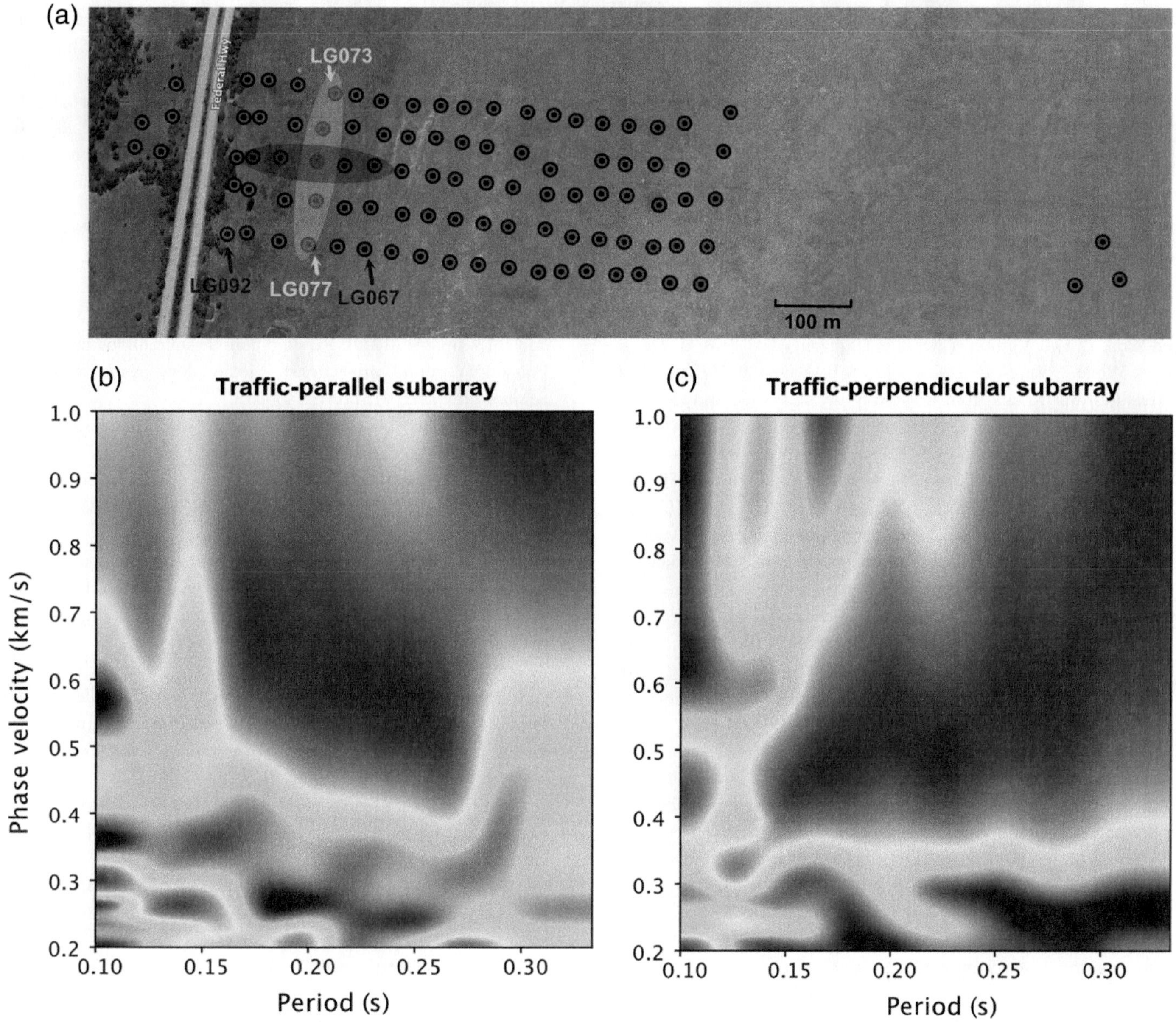

Figure 11. Comparison of resulting dispersion images for two subarrays configured differently in relation to the traffic flow. Panel (a) displays the locations of the two subarrays, which contain the same number of stations. It also shows the stations referenced in Figure 10. The dispersion image for the cyan-shaded subarray, which is parallel to the traffic, is shown in panel (b); whereas the result for the blue-shaded subarray, which is oriented perpendicular to the traffic, is presented in panel (c). Note that the *x* axis in panels (b,c) represents the period range and more coherent energy are generally observed in panel (c). The color version of this figure is available only in the electronic edition.

Acknowledgments

This project was enabled by AuScope and the Australian Government via the National Collaborative Research Infrastructure Strategy (NCRIS). C. J. acknowledges the financial support from an Australian Research Council Discovery Early Career Researcher Award (DE220100907). The Lake George experiment was impossible without Brad Pillans and Simon Haberle's help with land access issues. The authors thank Brad Pillans, Robert Pickle, Voon Hui Lai, and Kimberley Berends for their invaluable fieldwork assistance at Lake George. This study benefits from discussions with Brian Kennett, Brad Pillans, and Dan Clark. The authors thank Huajian Yao for sharing his image transformation code for the dispersion extraction in this study.

References

Abell, R. S. (1991). Geology of the Canberra 1:100 000 sheet area, new south wales and Australian capital territory, *Bull. Australia Bur. Mineral Resour. Geol. Geophys.* **233,** 1–135.

Aki, K. (1957). Space and time spectra of stationary stochastic waves, with special reference to microtremors, *Bull. Earthq. Res. Inst.* **35,** 415–456.

Barrow, G. (2013). *'Magnificent': Lake George: The Biography*, Dagraja Press, Canberra, Australia.

Behm, M., G. M. Leahy, and R. Snieder (2014). Retrieval of local surface wave velocities from traffic noise–an example from the la barge basin (Wyoming), *Geophys. Prospect.* **62,** no. 2, 223–243.

Benjumea, B., B. Gaite, M. Schimmel, F. Bohoyo, Z. Spica, F. Mancilla, Y. Li, J. Almendros, and J. Morales (2024). Subsurface imaging in urban areas with ambient noise using das and seismometer data sets: Granada, Spain, *J. Geophys. Res.* **129,** no. 11, e2024JB029820, doi: 10.1029/2024JB029820.

Bensen, G., M. Ritzwoller, M. Barmin, A. L. Levshin, F. Lin, M. Moschetti, N. Shapiro, and Y. Yang (2007). Processing seismic ambient noise data to obtain reliable broad-band surface wave dispersion measurements, *Geophys. J. Int.* **169,** no. 3, 1239–1260.

Ben-Zion, Y., F. L. Vernon, Y. Ozakin, D. Zigone, Z. E. Ross, H. Meng, M. White, J. Reyes, D. Hollis, and M. Barklage (2015). Basic data features and results from a spatially dense seismic array on the san Jacinto fault zone, *Geophys. J. Int.* **202,** no. 1, 370–380.

Boschi, L., and C. Weemstra (2015). Stationary-phase integrals in the cross correlation of ambient noise, *Rev. Geophys.* **53,** no. 2, 411–451.

Boué, P., M. Denolle, N. Hirata, S. Nakagawa, and G. C. Beroza (2016). Beyond basin resonance: Characterizing wave propagation using a dense array and the ambient seismic field, *Geophys. J. Int.* **206,** no. 2, 1261–1272.

Brenguier, F., P. Boué, Y. Ben-Zion, F. Vernon, C. W. Johnson, A. Mordret, O. Coutant, P.-E. Share, E. Beaucé, D. Hollis, *et al.* (2019). Train traffic as a powerful noise source for monitoring active faults with seismic interferometry, *Geophys. Res. Lett.* **46,** no. 16, 9529–9536.

Brenguier, F., N. M. Shapiro, M. Campillo, A. Nercessian, and V. Ferrazzini (2007). 3-d surface wave tomography of the piton de la Fournaise volcano using seismic noise correlations, *Geophys. Res. Lett.* **34,** no. 2, doi: 10.1029/2006GL028586.

Brocher, T. M. (2005). Empirical relations between elastic wavespeeds and density in the earth's crust, *Bull. Seismol. Soc. Am.* **95,** no. 6, 2081–2092.

Campillo, M., and A. Paul (2003). Long-range correlations in the diffuse seismic coda, *Science* **299,** 547–549.

Castellanos, J. C., and R. W. Clayton (2021). The fine-scale structure of Long Beach, California, and its impact on ground motion acceleration, *J. Geophys. Res.* **126,** no. 12, e2021JB022462, doi: 10.1029/2021JB022462.

Cheng, F., J. Xia, J. B. Ajo-Franklin, M. Behm, C. Zhou, T. Dai, C. Xi, J. Pang, and C. Zhou (2021). High-resolution ambient noise imaging of geothermal reservoir using 3c dense seismic nodal array and ultra-short observation, *J. Geophys. Res.* **126,** no. 8, e2021JB021827, doi: 10.1029/2021JB021827.

Chmiel, M., A. Mordret, P. Boué, F. Brenguier, T. Lecocq, R. Courbis, D. Hollis, X. Campman, R. Romijn, and W. Van der Veen (2019). Ambient noise multimode Rayleigh and love wave tomography to determine the shear velocity structure above the Groningen gas field, *Geophys. J. Int.* **218,** no. 3, 1781–1795.

Clark, D., A. McPherson, B. Pillans, D. White, and D. Macfarlane (2017). Potential geologic sources of seismic hazard in Australia's south-eastern highlands: What do we know, *Australian Earthquake Engineering Society 2017 Conference*, 24–26.

Colombi, A., L. Boschi, P. Roux, and M. Campillo (2014). Green's function retrieval through cross-correlations in a two-dimensional complex reverberating medium, *J. Acoust. Soc. Am.* **135,** no. 3, 1034–1043.

Denolle, M. A., E. M. Dunham, G. A. Prieto, and G. C. Beroza (2014). Strong ground motion prediction using virtual earthquakes, *Science* **343,** 399–403.

Dou, S., N. Lindsey, A. M. Wagner, T. M. Daley, B. Freifeld, M. Robertson, J. Peterson, C. Ulrich, E. R. Martin, and J. B. Ajo-Franklin (2017). Distributed acoustic sensing for seismic monitoring of the near surface: A traffic-noise interferometry case study, *Sci. Rep.* **7,** no. 1, 11,620.

Draganov, D., X. Campman, J. Thorbecke, A. Verdel, and K. Wapenaar (2009). Reflection images from ambient seismic noise, *Geophysics* **74,** no. 5, A63–A67.

Fang, H., R. D. Van Der Hilst, M. V. de Hoop, K. Kothari, S. Gupta, and I. Dokmanić (2020). Parsimonious seismic tomography with Poisson Voronoi projections: Methodology and validation, *Seismol. Res. Lett.* **91,** no. 1, 343–355.

Griffin, J., T. Allen, D. Clark, P. Cummins, H. Ghasemi, and R. Ebrahimi (2023). The 2023 national seismic hazard assessment of Australia: Rationale for changes in hazard, *Australian Earthquake Engineering Society 2023 Conference*, 23–25 November 2023, Brisbane, Queensland, Australia.

Harmon, N., C. Rychert, and P. Gerstoft (2010). Distribution of noise sources for seismic interferometry, *Geophys. J. Int.* **183,** no. 3, 1470–1484.

Jiang, C., and M. A. Denolle (2020). Noisepy: A new high-performance python tool for ambient-noise seismology, *Seismol. Res. Lett.* **91,** no. 3, 1853–1866.

Jiang, C., B. Schmandt, G. A. Abers, E. Kiser, and M. S. Miller (2023). Segmentation and radial anisotropy of the deep crustal magmatic system beneath the cascades arc, *Geochem. Geophys. Geosys.* **24,** no. 3, e2022GC010738, doi: 10.1029/2022GC010738.

Kanamori, H., and D. L. Anderson (1977). Importance of physical dispersion in surface wave and free oscillation problems, *Rev. Geophys.* **15,** no. 1, 105–112.

Kennett, B., C. Jiang, and K. Smolinski (2023). Local station correlation: Large n-arrays and das, *Seismica* **2,** no. 2, doi: 10.26443/seismica.v2i2.389.

Lai, V. H., M. S. Miller, C. Jiang, Y. Yang, F. Magrini, Z. Zhan, and H. McQueen (2024). Passive seismic imaging of urban environments using distributed acoustic sensing: A case study from Melbourne, Australia, *Seism. Record* **4,** no. 4, 308–317.

Li, H., H. Wang, Z. Xu, J. Si, J. Pei, T. Li, Y. Huang, S.-R. Song, L.-W. Kuo, Z. Sun, *et al.* (2013). Characteristics of the fault-related rocks, fault zones and the principal slip zone in the Wenchuan earthquake fault scientific drilling project hole-1 (wfsd-1), *Tectonophysics* **584,** 23–42.

Li, Y.-G., J. E. Vidale, and E. S. Cochran (2004). Low-velocity damaged structure of the San Andreas fault at Parkfield from fault zone trapped waves, *Geophys. Res. Lett.* **31,** no. 12, doi: 10.1029/2003GL019044.

Lin, F.-C., D. Li, R. W. Clayton, and D. Hollis (2013). High-resolution 3d shallow crustal structure in Long Beach, California: Application of ambient noise tomography on a dense seismic array, *Geophysics* **78,** Q45–Q56.

Lin, F.-C., M. P. Moschetti, and M. H. Ritzwoller (2008). Surface wave tomography of the western United States from ambient seismic noise: Rayleigh and Love wave phase velocity maps, *Geophys. J. Int.* **173,** 281–298.

Luo, B., W. Trainor-Guitton, E. Bozdağ, L. LaFlame, S. Cole, and M. Karrenbach (2020). Horizontally orthogonal distributed acoustic

sensing array for earthquake-and ambient-noise-based multichannel analysis of surface waves, *Geophys. J. Int.* **222,** no. 3, 2147–2161.
Macphail, M., L. K. Fifield, B. Pillans, M. Davies, and G. Hope (2015). Lake George revisited: New evidence for the origin and evolution of a large closed lake, southern tablelands, NSW, Australia, *Aust. J. Earth Sci.* **62,** no. 7, 853–871.
Meng, H., Y. Ben-Zion, and C. W. Johnson (2021). Analysis of seismic signals generated by vehicle traffic with application to derivation of subsurface q-values, *Seismol. Res. Lett.* **92,** no. 4, 2354–2363.
Mordret, A., D. Rivet, M. Landès, and N. M. Shapiro (2015). Three-dimensional shear velocity anisotropic model of piton de la Fournaise volcano (la Réunion island) from ambient seismic noise, *J. Geophys. Res.* **120,** no. 1, 406–427.
Nakamura, Y. (1989). A method for dynamic characteristics estimation of subsurface using microtremor on the ground surface, *Quarterly Reports*, Vol. 30, Railway Technical Research Institute.
Nakata, N., J. P. Chang, J. F. Lawrence, and P. Boué (2015). Body wave extraction and tomography at Long Beach, California, with ambient-noise interferometry, *J. Geophys. Res.* **120,** no. 2, 1159–1173.
Nakata, N., L. Gualtieri, and A. Fichtner (2019). *Seismic Ambient Noise*. Cambridge University Press, Cambridge, United Kingdom.
Nakata, N., R. Snieder, T. Tsuji, K. Larner, and T. Matsuoka (2011). Shear wave imaging from traffic noise using seismic interferometry by cross-coherence, *Geophysics* **76,** no. 6, SA97–SA106.
Nishida, K., J.-P. Montagner, and H. Kawakatsu (2009). Global surface wave tomography using seismic hum, *Science* **326,** no. 5949, 112–112.
Obermann, A., P. Sánchez-Pastor, S.-M. Wu, C. Wollin, A. F. Baird, M. P. Isken, J. Clinton, B. P. Goertz-Allmann, T. Dahm, A. Wuestefeld, *et al.* (2022). Combined large-n seismic arrays and das fiber optic cables across the Hengill geothermal field, Iceland, *Seismol. Res. Lett.* **93,** no. 5, 2498–2514.
Olivier, G., G. Heinson, B. Kay, G. Boren, Y. Liu, S. Carter, T. Jones, P. Dales, R. Abel, L. Vella, *et al.* (2024). Ambient noise tomography of an iron-oxide copper–gold (IOCG) deposit under thick cover, *Explor. Geophys.* **55,** no. 6, 667–677.
Paige, C. C., and M. A. Saunders (1982). LSQR: An algorithm for sparse linear equations and sparse least squares, *ACM Trans. Math. Softw.* **8,** no. 1, 43–71.
Picozzi, M., S. Parolai, D. Bindi, and A. Strollo (2009). Characterization of shallow geology by high-frequency seismic noise tomography, *Geophys. J. Int.* **176,** no. 1, 164–174.
Prieto, G., J. Lawrence, and G. Beroza (2009). Anelastic earth structure from the coherency of the ambient seismic field, *J. Geophys. Res.* **114,** no. B7, doi: 10.1029/2008JB006067.
Prieto, G. A., and G. C. Beroza (2008). Earthquake ground motion prediction using the ambient seismic field, *Geophys. Res. Lett.* **35,** L14304, doi: 10.1029/2008GL034428.
Qiu, H., A. A. Allam, F.-C. Lin, and Y. Ben-Zion (2020). Analysis of fault zone resonance modes recorded by a dense seismic array across the San Jacinto fault zone at Blackburn saddle, *J. Geophys. Res.* **125,** no. 10, e2020JB019756, doi: 10.1029/2020JB019756.
Quiros, D. A., L. D. Brown, and D. Kim (2016). Seismic interferometry of railroad induced ground motions: Body and surface wave imaging, *Geophys. J. Int.* **205,** no. 1, 301–313.
Rawlinson, N., and W. Spakman (2016). On the use of sensitivity tests in seismic tomography, *Geophys. J. Int.* **205,** no. 2, 1221–1243.
Retailleau, L., and G. C. Beroza (2021). Towards structural imaging using seismic ambient field correlation artefacts, *Geophys. J. Int.* **225,** no. 2, 1453–1465.
Rockwell, T. K., T. E. Dawson, J. Young Ben-Horin, and G. Seitz (2015). A 21-event, 4,000-year history of surface ruptures in the Anza seismic gap, San Jacinto fault, and implications for long-term earthquake production on a major plate boundary fault, *Pure Appl. Geophys.* **172,** 1143–1165.
Rost, S., and C. Thomas (2002). Array seismology: Methods and applications, *Rev. Geophys.* **40,** no. 3, 2–1.
Sabra, K. G., P. Gerstoft, P. Roux, W. A. Kuperman, and M. C. Fehler (2005). Extracting time-domain Green's function estimates from ambient seismic noise, *Geophys. Res. Lett.* **32,** L03310, doi: 10.1029/2004GL021862.
Sambridge, M., J. Braun, and H. McQueen (1995). Geophysical parametrization and interpolation of irregular data using natural neighbours, *Geophys. J. Int.* **122,** no. 3, 837–857.
Saygin, E., and B. L. Kennett (2010). Ambient seismic noise tomography of Australian continent, *Tectonophysics* **481,** nos. 1/4, 116–125.
Shapiro, N. M., and M. Campillo (2004). Emergence of broadband Rayleigh waves from correlations of the ambient seismic noise, *Geophys. Res. Lett.* **31,** L07614, doi: 10.1029/2004GL019491.
Shapiro, N. M., M. Campillo, L. Stehly, and M. H. Ritzwoller (2005). High-resolution surface-wave tomography from ambient seismic noise, *Science* **307,** no. 5715, 1615–1618.
Share, P.-E., Y. Ben-Zion, Z. E. Ross, H. Qiu, and F. L. Vernon (2017). Internal structure of the San Jacinto fault zone at Blackburn saddle from seismic data of a linear array, *Geophys. J. Int.* **210,** no. 2, 819–832.
Shen, W., M. H. Ritzwoller, V. Schulte-Pelkum, and F.-C. Lin (2013). Joint inversion of surface wave dispersion and receiver functions: A Bayesian Monte-Carlo approach, *Geophys. J. Int.* **192,** no. 2, 807–836.
Shen, Z., Y. Yang, X. Fu, K. H. Adams, E. Biondi, and Z. Zhan (2024). Fiber-optic seismic sensing of vadose zone soil moisture dynamics, *Nat. Commun.* **15,** no. 1, 6432.
Sheng, Y., F. Brenguier, A. Mordret, Q. Higueret, C. Aubert, L. Pinzon-Rincon, D. Hollis, F. Vernon, F. Wyatt, and Y. Ben-Zion (2024). In situ velocity-strain sensitivity near the San Jacinto fault zone analyzed through train tremors, *Geophys. Res. Lett.* **51,** no. 15, e2024GL110113, doi: 10.1029/2024GL110113.
Sheng, Y., A. Mordret, F. Brenguier, P. Boué, F. Vernon, T. Takeda, Y. Aoki, T. Taira, and Y. Ben-Zion (2023). Seeking repeating anthropogenic seismic sources: Implications for seismic velocity monitoring at fault zones, *J. Geophys. Res.* **128,** no. 1, e2022JB024725, doi: 10.1029/2022JB024725.
Song, Z., X. Zeng, and C. H. Thurber (2021). Surface-wave dispersion spectrum inversion method applied to love and Rayleigh waves recorded by distributed acoustic sensing, *Geophysics* **86,** no. 1, EN1–EN12.
Spica, Z. J., M. Perton, E. R. Martin, G. C. Beroza, and B. Biondi (2020). Urban seismic site characterization by fiber-optic seismology, *J. Geophys. Res.* **125,** no. 3, e2019JB018656, doi: 10.1029/2019JB018656.
Tomar, G., E. Stutzmann, A. Mordret, J.-P. Montagner, S. C. Singh, and N. M. Shapiro (2018). Joint inversion of the first overtone and

fundamental mode for deep imaging at the Valhall oil field using ambient noise, *Geophys. J. Int.* **214,** no. 1, 122–132.

Viens, L., C. Jiang, and M. A. Denolle (2022). Imaging the Kanto basin seismic basement with earthquake and noise autocorrelation functions, *Geophys. J. Int.* **230,** no. 2, 1080–1091.

Wang, K., C. Jiang, Y. Yang, V. Schulte-Pelkum, and Q. Liu (2020). Crustal deformation in southern California constrained by radial anisotropy from ambient noise adjoint tomography, *Geophys. Res. Lett.* **47,** no. 12, e2020GL088580, doi: 10.1029/2020GL088580.

Ward, K. M., R. C. Porter, G. Zandt, S. L. Beck, L. S. Wagner, E. Minaya, and H. Tavera (2013). Ambient noise tomography across the Central Andes, *Geophys. J. Int.* **194,** no. 3, 1559–1573.

Wessel, P., and W. H. Smith (1991). Free software helps map and display data, *Eos Trans. AGU* **72,** no. 41, 441–446.

White, M. C., H. Fang, N. Nakata, and Y. Ben-Zion (2020). Pykonal: A python package for solving the Eikonal equation in spherical and cartesian coordinates using the fast marching method, *Seismol. Res. Lett.* **91,** no. 4, 2378–2389.

Yang, H., Y. Duan, J. Song, X. Jiang, X. Tian, W. Yang, W. Wang, and J. Yang (2020). Fine structure of the Chenghai fault zone, Yunnan, china, constrained from teleseismic travel time and ambient noise tomography, *J. Geophys. Res.* **125,** no. 7, e2020JB019565, doi: 10.1029/2020JB019565.

Yang, H., Z. Li, Z. Peng, Y. Ben-Zion, and F. Vernon (2014). Low-velocity zones along the San Jacinto fault, Southern California, from body waves recorded in dense linear arrays, *J. Geophys. Res.* **119,** no. 12, 8976–8990.

Yang, Y., J. W. Atterholt, Z. Shen, J. B. Muir, E. F. Williams, and Z. Zhan (2022). Sub-kilometer correlation between near-surface structure and ground motion measured with distributed acoustic sensing, *Geophys. Res. Lett.* **49,** no. 1, e2021GL096503, doi: 10.1029/2021GL096503.

Yang, Y., M. H. Ritzwoller, A. L. Levshin, and N. M. Shapiro (2007). Ambient noise rayleigh wave tomography across Europe, *Geophys. J. Int.* **168,** no. 1, 259–274.

Yao, H., R. D. van Der Hilst, and M. V. De Hoop (2006). Surface-wave array tomography in se Tibet from ambient seismic noise and two-station analysis—I. Phase velocity maps, *Geophys. J. Int.* **166,** no. 2, 732–744.

Zhan, Z. (2020). Distributed acoustic sensing turns fiber-optic cables into sensitive seismic antennas, *Seismol. Res. Lett.* **91,** no. 1, 1–15.

Zhang, K., H. Li, X. Wang, and K. Wang (2020). Retrieval of shallow s-wave profiles from seismic reflection surveying and traffic-induced noise, *Geophysics* **85,** no. 6, EN105–EN117.

Zhao, K., Y. Yang, and Y. Luo (2024). Broadband love wave phase velocity maps based on modified double-beamforming of ambient noise cross-correlations, *J. Geophys. Res.* **129,** no. 3, e2023JB026871, doi: 10.1029/2023JB026871.

Zigone, D., Y. Ben-Zion, M. Lehujeur, M. Campillo, G. Hillers, and F. L. Vernon (2019). Imaging subsurface structures in the San Jacinto fault zone with high-frequency noise recorded by dense linear arrays, *Geophys. J. Int.* **217,** no. 2, 879–893.

Manuscript received 8 February 2025
Published online 26 August 2025

Unsupervised Deep Clustering of Microseismic Signals from the Dalk Glacier in East Antarctica

Lei Zhao[1], Lei Fu[*1], Jingxue Guo[2], Yanlan Hu[3], Zefeng Li[3], Kai Lu[2], Ruijia Wang[4], and Xiangyun Hu[1]

Abstract

In Antarctica, seismic monitoring and detection is significant for understanding long-term glacier activity, glacial melting, and other related scientific issues. We deployed 8 three-component short-period seismometers near the grounding line of the Dalk Glacier ice tongue in Southeast Antarctica, collecting seismic signals from 19 October 2022 to 28 February 2023. We applied unsupervised deep learning, using an autoencoder to encode the features of the input spectrograms into low-dimensional latent vectors, which were then input into a Gaussian mixture model for clustering. We ultimately identified four groups of microseismic signals: Group A wideband events (20–100 Hz) are associated with temperature variation; it is a group of crevasse events. Group B includes low-frequency (< 20 Hz) events that may be resonances generated by fluid-filled subglacial fractures, corresponding to the minimum and maximum tidal speeds at the Dalk Glacier coast. Group C events are vibrations caused by wind, and group D events are noise from commuter vehicles. In particular, we discuss the high-energy pulse events included in group A as well as the possible potential sources of group B events. Our research results indicate that deep clustering can effectively identify various types of microseismic signals. The icequakes are closely related to glacier activity driven by environmentally related factors. This may improve further study on the internal structure of glaciers.

Cite this article as Zhao, L., L. Fu, J. Guo, Y. Hu, Z. Li, K. Lu, R. Wang, and X. Hu (2025). Unsupervised Deep Clustering of Microseismic Signals from the Dalk Glacier in East Antarctica, *Seismol. Res. Lett.* **97**, 425–438, doi: 10.1785/0220250052.

Supplemental Material

Introduction

In recent decades, seismological techniques have been increasingly applied to seismic monitoring in Antarctica, providing new insights into glacier structural changes, iceberg calving, and ice flow dynamics (Blankenship *et al.*, 1986; Anandakrishnan and Bentley, 1993; Bassis *et al.*, 2008; Podolskiy and Walter, 2016). Previous studies on glacier change processes have identified a range of icequake signals, such as iceberg calving, basal sliding, and tremor (Bartholomaus *et al.*, 2013; Röösli *et al.*, 2014; Helmstetter *et al.*, 2015), which have continuously enriched our understanding of glacier dynamics and the cryosphere system (Aster and Winberry, 2017). The generation of icequake signals is closely related to the state of glaciers. In Antarctica, ice mass loss mainly results from coastal glacier calving (Smith *et al.*, 2020). Monitoring glacial activity helps identify large-scale crevasses and calving events (Paul Winberry *et al.*, 2013), thereby understanding glacial stability. Traditional seismic signal processing methods have struggled to handle the large volume of Antarctic data in recent years (Jenkins *et al.*, 2021). At the same time, deep learning methods have been applied to almost every subfield of seismology and have demonstrated superior capabilities in denoising, seismic location, phase picking, and other areas compared to classical methods (Perol *et al.*, 2018; Ross *et al.*, 2018; Mousavi, Sheng, *et al.*, 2019; Wang *et al.*, 2019).

Unsupervised deep learning can efficiently classify seismic data without event labels and prior knowledge (Kinzel *et al.*, 2024). Seydoux *et al.* (2020) used deep scattering networks and Gaussian mixture models (GMMs) to detect and cluster precursory signals of landslides, validating the capability of deep learning techniques to explore large seismic data sets.

1. Hubei Subsurface Multiscale Imaging Key Laboratory, School of Geophysics and Geomatics, China University of Geosciences, Wuhan, People's Republic of China, https://orcid.org/0009-0009-8431-3680 (LZ); https://orcid.org/0000-0001-9709-520X (LF); 2. Key Laboratory for Polar Science, MNR, Polar Research Institute of China, Shanghai, People's Republic of China, https://orcid.org/0000-0001-7761-8819 (JG); https://orcid.org/0000-0002-9761-3457 (KL); 3. Laboratory of Seismology and Physics of Earth's Interior, School of Earth and Space Sciences, University of Science and Technology of China, Hefei, People's Republic of China, https://orcid.org/0009-0000-0842-210X (YH); https://orcid.org/0000-0003-4405-8872 (ZL); 4. Department of Earth and Space Sciences, Southern University of Science and Technology, Shenzhen, People's Republic of China, https://orcid.org/0000-0002-1757-5113 (RW)

*Corresponding author: fulei@cug.edu.cn

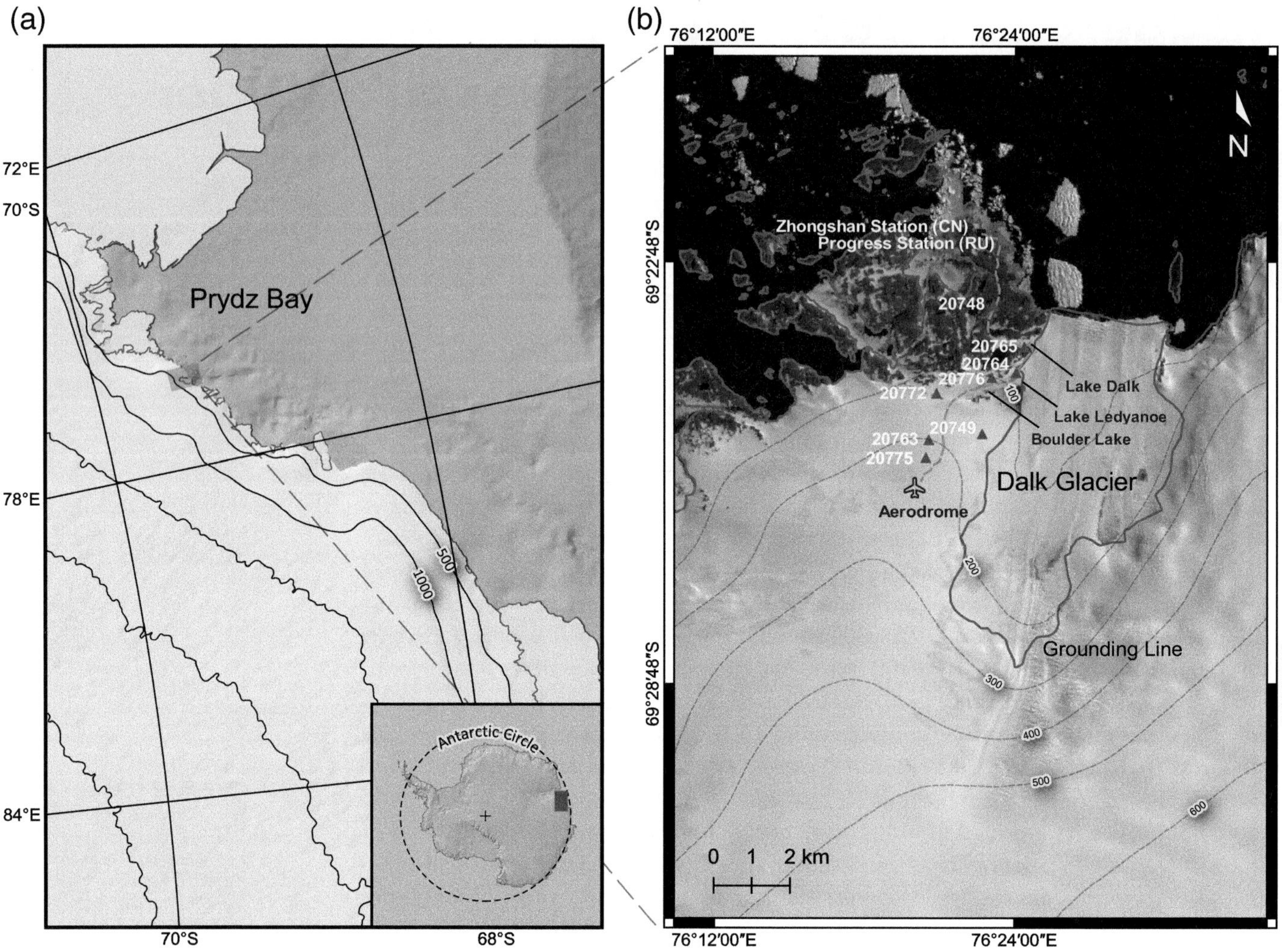

Figure 1. Study area and the locations of the short-period three-component node seismometers. (a) The coastline of Prydz Bay in East Antarctica, with the red box representing the study area. The red part of the illustration in bottom right corner represents the location of the panel (a) in Antarctica. (b) The Dalk Glacier, which has an outlet approximately 3.3 km wide, flowing north into the Southern Ocean. The node seismometers used are indicated by red triangles, and the yellow-dashed line represents the commuting route. Contour lines and grounding line are also marked. All data sources can be found in Data and Resources. The color version of this figure is available only in the electronic edition.

Mousavi, Zhu, *et al.* (2019) utilized autoencoders for unsupervised clustering of seismic data, successfully distinguishing waveforms recorded at different source distances and those with varying first-motion polarities. Jenkins *et al.* (2021) used autoencoders for feature compression and dimensionality reduction of seismic signals from the Ross Ice Shelf in Antarctica. They evaluated the performance of two deep unsupervised methods: deep embedded clustering and GMMs. Hu *et al.* (2024) conducted a study on microseismic signals from the southern Dalk Glacier in East Antarctica using unsupervised clustering methods and GMM. They identified several event types associated with environmental factors.

In Hu *et al.* (2024), the station array was located far from the Dalk Glacier front, causing some icequakes being detected by only part of the stations. To further study icequake events from the Dalk Glacier itself, we have deployed seismic stations near bedrock outcrops and on the glacier's western snowy side (Fig. 1). These stations will receive more energy radiated from potential seismic sources, and high-quality data aid in explaining the causes of icequake events, enhancing our understanding of the Dalk Glacier and the activity patterns of other major Antarctic outlet glaciers.

Data

From 19 October 2022 to 28 February 2023, 8 three-component short-period Smart Solo IGU-16HR 3C node seismometers were deployed on the western side of the Dalk Glacier near Zhongshan Station in Antarctica. The sampling rate of these seismometers is 250 Hz, and they are arranged approximately along the driving route from Zhongshan Station to the aerodrome. The stations located on bedrock (20765, 20748, 20764, and 20776) are deployed at the surface, whereas the remaining four stations are positioned at a depth of about 0.5 m below the

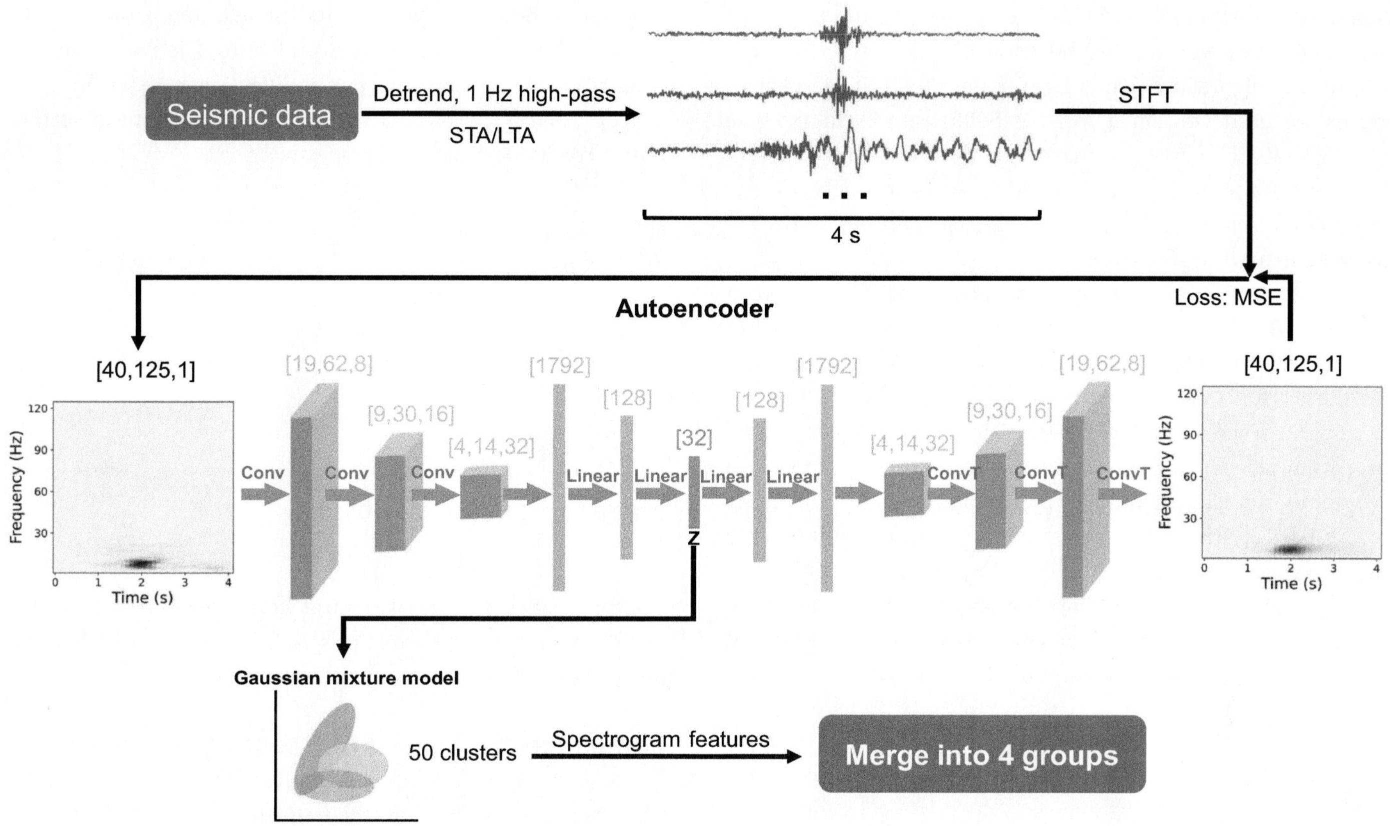

Figure 2. Deep clustering workflow used in the study. It includes the preprocessing steps of detrending, 1 Hz high-pass filtering, short-term average/long-term average (STA/LTA), and short-time Fourier transform (STFT), encoding the spectrogram into latent features Z, followed by an autoencoder that reconstructs the input from Z. In addition, it incorporates Gaussian mixture model (GMM) and a manual merging component. MSE, mean squared error. The color version of this figure is available only in the electronic edition.

snow surface. The distance between the stations ranges from 0.5 to 2 km (Fig. 1b).

To investigate the potential factors influencing icequake activity, we collected wind speed and temperature measurement data recorded at Zhongshan Station. Using the MATLAB package tide model driver (TMD3.0; Greene *et al.*, 2024) and the CATS2008a tidal model (Padman *et al.*, 2002), we simulated the tidal levels in the waters near the Dalk Glacier and calculated the hourly tidal velocity over the study period.

Method

Data preprocessing

We focused only on the vertical component, applying detrending and 1 Hz high-pass filtering to the waveforms. We utilized a short-term average/long-term average (STA/LTA) algorithm (with a short window of 0.5 s, a long window of 30 s, a trigger threshold of 10, and a detrigger threshold of 3) to detect icequake events (Allen, 1982; Hu *et al.*, 2024), resulting in a total of 273,789 events. For each detected event, the waveform was transformed into a time–frequency spectrogram using the short-time Fourier transform (STFT), resulting in a frequency range of up to 125 Hz and 40 time bins (4 s). Next, we interpolated the obtained frequency range into a uniform interval from 1 to 125 Hz, resulting in a spectrogram of size 125 × 40. Before inputting the spectrograms into the autoencoder, we extracted a 4 s time window by taking two seconds before and after the peak amplitude and normalized the maximum energy values to facilitate subsequent training (Fig. 2). Once the training is complete, the extracted latent features are input into the GMM for clustering.

Deep GMM clustering

The deep clustering process consists of two main steps: feature extraction using autoencoders and clustering using GMM (Fig. 2). An autoencoder is a type of unsupervised learning neural network primarily used for data compression and feature learning (Kramer, 1991). It consists of two parts: the encoder and the decoder. The autoencoder compresses the input data into a lower-dimensional representation through a series of nonlinear transformations, known as the bottleneck layer. The decoder then reconstructs this low-dimensional representation back into the original data. We divided the data into training and validation sets in an 80%–20% ratio, respectively, labeled as the training and validation sets. During the training process, batch normalization (applied to each layer) and a dropout rate of 0.1 (randomly deactivating 10% of the neurons) were employed to reduce overfitting. The activation function used was Rectified Linear Unit (ReLU), and the training parameters were optimized using the Adaptive Moment Estimation algorithm (Kingma and Ba, 2017). The spectrograms we used contain a total of 5000 features in the size of 125 × 40. The encoder maps the input data into a latent feature space Z with 32 embedded features through a series of convolutional layers. Subsequently, the decoder utilizes Z to reconstruct the input data.

Finally, we minimized the mean squared error (MSE) between the input data x_m and the reconstructed data x_m' as shown in equation (1). For a batch containing N samples in the entire data set, the loss function can be expressed as in equation (2). The loss is calculated across multiple batches in the training set. After processing all batches in the current epoch, the validation set is used to evaluate the model's performance before proceeding to the next epoch. This process is repeated continuously until the predetermined number of training epochs is completed. We set a condition to terminate training early if the validation loss does not improve for seven consecutive epochs, to prevent the autoencoder from overfitting the training data.

$$\ell(x,x') = \frac{1}{M}\sum_{M=1}^{M}(x_m - x_m')^2, \quad (1)$$

$$L = \frac{1}{N}\sum_{N=1}^{N}\ell(x_n,x_n'). \quad (2)$$

After obtaining the latent features Z, we used a GMM for clustering. The GMM assumes that the data are composed of multiple overlapping Gaussian distributions (normal distributions), with each Gaussian distribution representing a potential cluster within the data space (Reynolds, 2015). If z represents the multidimensional data points to be modeled, we set the number of component Gaussian distributions (clusters) as K, Let $\mathcal{N}(z|\mu_k,\sum_K)$ denote the Kth Gaussian distribution, in which μ_k is the mean, π_k (satisfying $\sum_{k=1}^{K}\pi_k = 1$ and $0 \le \pi_k \le 1$) is the mixture weight, and $\sum_k$ is the covariance matrix. The probability density function of the GMM is given by

$$P(z) = \sum_{k=1}^{K}\pi_k\mathcal{N}(z|\mu_k,\sum_K). \quad (3)$$

The model training is typically performed using the expectation–maximization algorithm to maximize the log-likelihood function of the observed data (Jordan and Xu, 1995). It mainly consists of two steps.

1. Expectation step (E-step): using the given initial parameters, calculate the posterior probability (responsibility weight) that each data point z belongs to each Gaussian component K:

$$r_{ik} = \frac{\pi_k\mathcal{N}(z_i \mid \mu_k,\sum_k)}{\sum_{j=1}^{K}\pi_j\mathcal{N}(z_i \mid \mu_j,\sum_j)}. \quad (4)$$

2. Maximization step (M-step): in this step, the parameters are updated by maximizing the expected log-likelihood function based on the computed responsibilities. Here, $N_k = \sum_{i=1}^{N} r_{ik}$, π_k, μ_k, and $\sum_k$ represent the mixture weights, mean vectors, and covariance matrices, respectively.

$$\pi_k = \frac{1}{N}\sum_{i=1}^{N} r_{ik}, \quad (5)$$

$$\mu_k = \frac{1}{N_k}\sum_{i=1}^{N} r_{ik}z_i, \quad (6)$$

$$\sum_k = \frac{1}{N_k}\sum_{i=1}^{N} r_{ik}(z_i - \mu_k)(z_i - \mu_k)^T. \quad (7)$$

Repeat steps (1) and (2) until convergence (or until the maximum number of iterations is reached), at which point the training of the algorithm is complete.

Manual merging based on spectrogram feature

We established two criteria to identify similar clusters. First, we define the peak frequency as the frequency corresponding to the peak energy in the spectrum. Second, in the time direction, because the spectral peak has been normalized to the center of the spectrogram, we instead calculate the median absolute deviation (MAD) of the energy to assess its dispersion. The required array is defined as the maximum energy value corresponding to each time value in the time direction, with a size of 40 × 1.

The MAD estimation is quite robust when dealing with data that contain outliers (Leys *et al.*, 2013). The process of calculating MAD can be summarized as first computing the deviation of the data from the median of the data and then finding the median of the absolute values of these deviations. Where the x_i denotes the ith element in the data set X, M stands for the operation of taking the median (equation 8). Because it does not involve excluding outliers, we simply define the coefficient b as 1.

$$\mathrm{MAD} = bM(|x_i - M(X)|). \quad (8)$$

Result and Discussion

We calculated the MAD and peak frequency of all spectral graphs in 50 clusters and plotted scatter diagrams, resulting in four groups of events: A–D (Fig. 3 and Fig. S1, available in the supplemental material to this article). Among them, groups A and B each contain two distinct subclasses, which we labeled as A1, A2 and B1, B2 (Fig. 4).

Group A: short-duration and broadband events

The two subclasses of events in group A exhibit characteristics of short duration (~0.5 s) and broadband energies (20–100 Hz). In group A, the number of A1 events is significantly greater

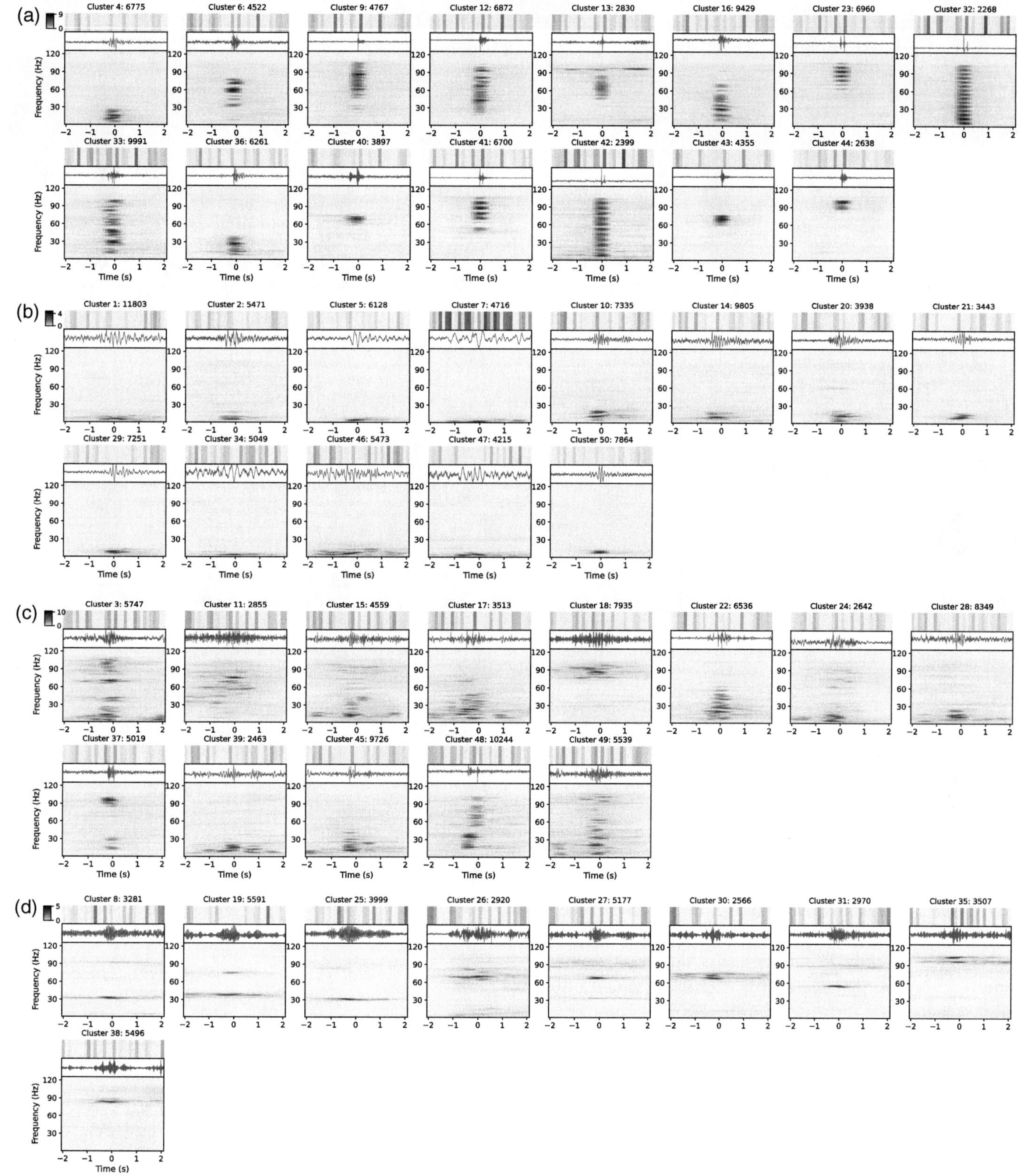

than that of A2 events. Events of A2 are concentrated in clusters 32 and 42; the rest of the clusters are A1 (Fig. 3a). The seismic phase of A1 events is composed primarily of surface waves, with the arrival of *P* waves being either unclear or absent, and there are no obvious *S*-wave phases (Fig. 4a). The particle motion shows a retrograde ellipsoid motion (Li *et al.*, 2021; Fig. S2).

Figure 3. Cluster number and event count, latent features, waveforms, and spectrograms of four groups center events for the (a–d) four groups, all possible repeated events are retained, and the form of the plot follows Hu *et al.* (2024). The central event is defined as the one with the smallest Euclidean distance to the average latent feature vector of the cluster. The color version of this figure is available only in the electronic edition.

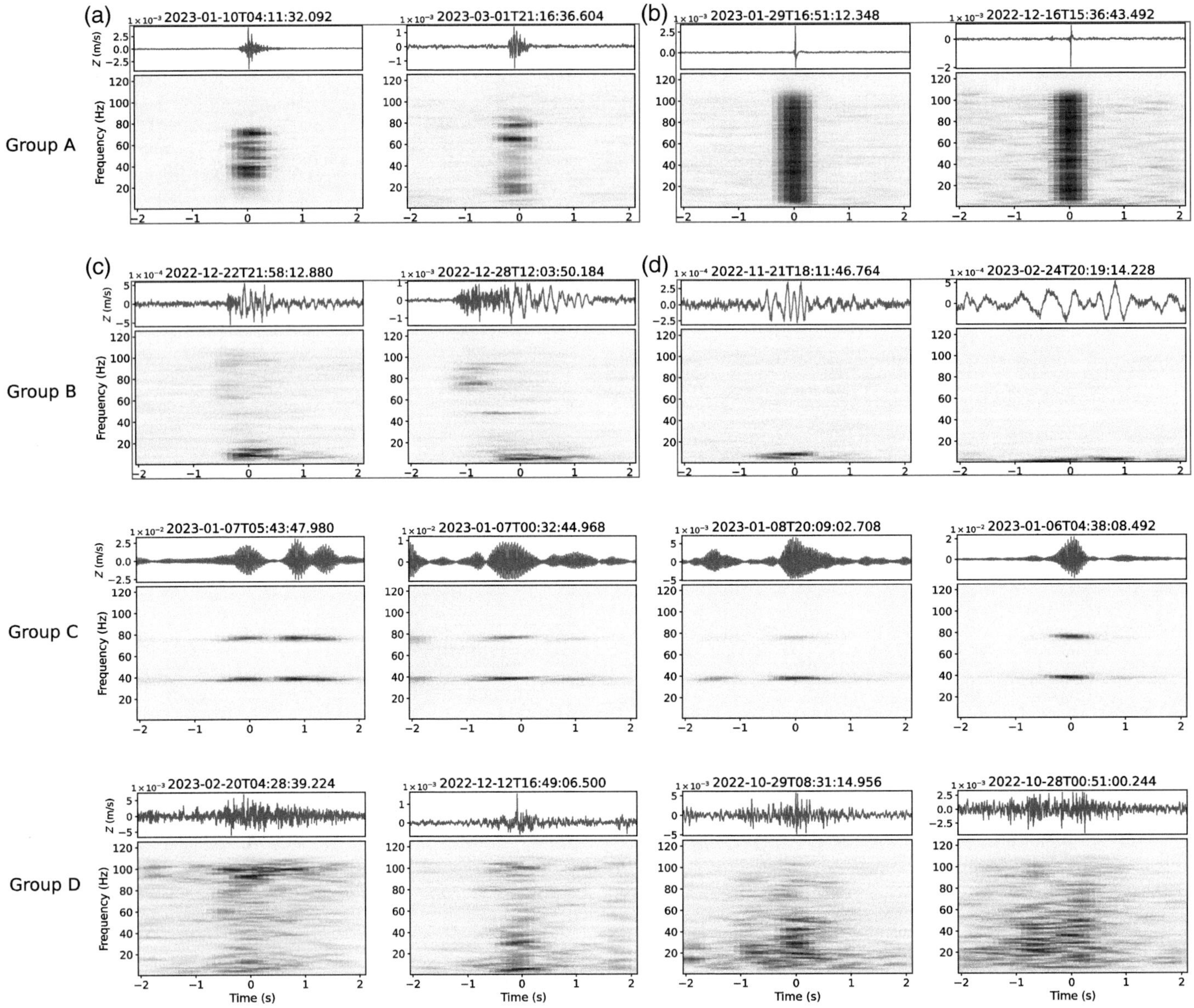

Figure 4. Representative cases of the four event groups: A, B, C, and D. (a,b) Two subclasses A1 and A2 of group A, and (c,d) two subclasses B1 and B2 of group B. Each subclass is marked with a red box. The subplot titles indicate the UTC time corresponding to the zero moment. The color version of this figure is available only in the electronic edition.

From a spatial perspective, the number of recorded events is antiproportional to the station distance of the glacier and the total number of effective sources varies significantly among stations, indicating that the source is close to station 20765 and that the energy attenuates quickly (Fig. 5d). These events significantly increase during periods of low temperatures, peaking at the lowest temperatures and frequently occurring during the transition between day and night (Fig. 5e). Previous studies have provided a clear explanation of its generation mechanism, indicating that under extremely cold conditions, low temperatures can cause the brittleness of ice (Walter *et al.*, 2009; Podolskiy *et al.*, 2018; Winter *et al.*, 2021). When the tensile stress (or the equivalent strain rate) exceeds a depth-dependent fracture criterion, cracks form on the glacier surface, leading to the occurrence of icequakes (Colgan *et al.*, 2016; Podolskiy and Walter, 2016; Olinger *et al.*, 2019). Therefore, we interpret class A1 events as surface crevasse icequakes.

Taking 30 January 2023 as an example, we manually selected A1 events recorded by three or more stations. For each phase, the arrival time was determined using the STA/LTA method. Subsequently, the study area was divided into a 50 × 50 grid, and the MSE of travel-time residuals was calculated for each grid node. For each event, the grid position with the minimum MSE was recorded as the optimal source location. We present the preliminary localization results, for which the source locations can be broadly categorized into two clusters (Fig. S8): the S1 cluster in the northeastern direction and the S2 cluster in the southwestern direction. These icequake events exhibit characteristics of high-

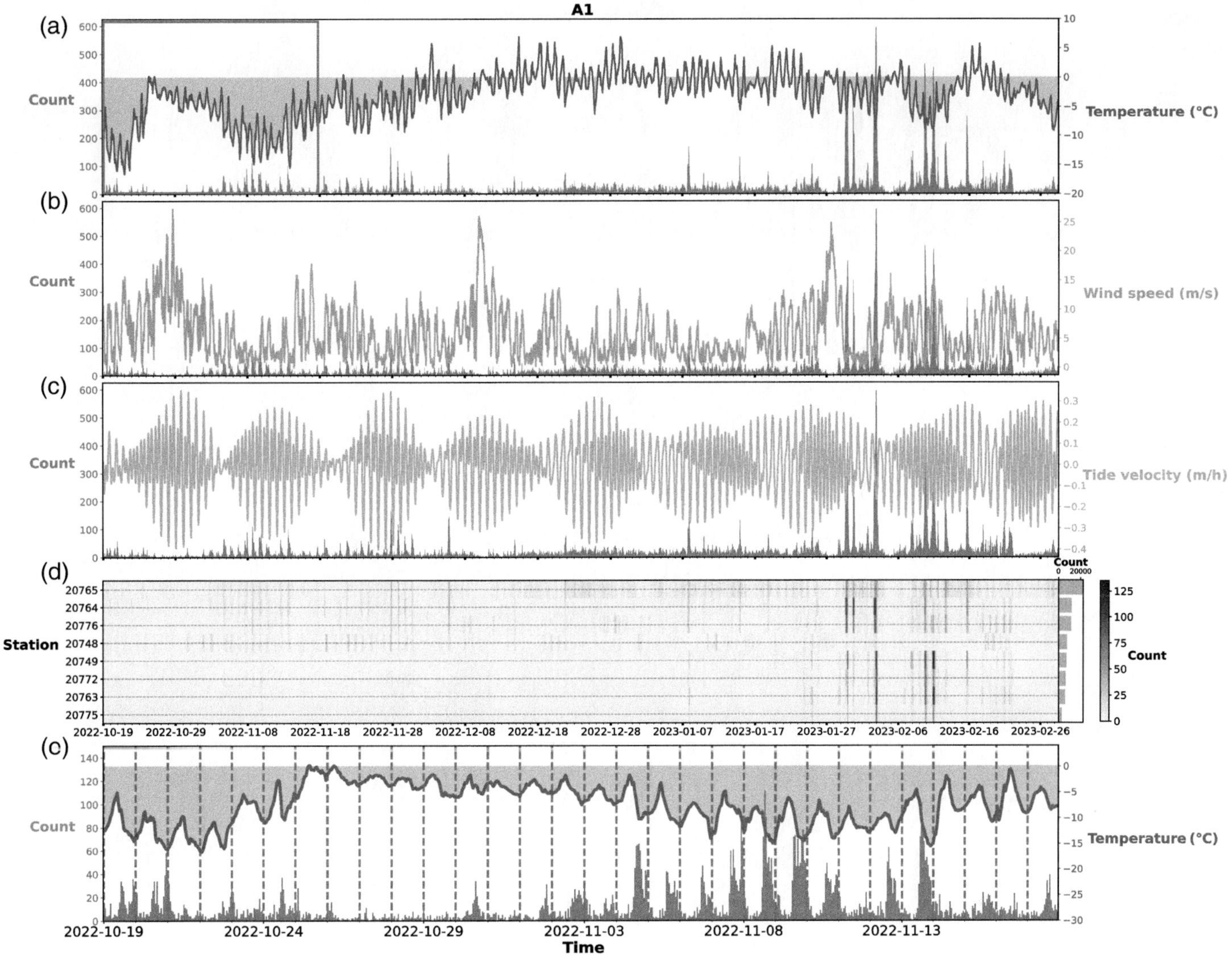

Figure 5. Comparison of the temperature recorded at (a) Zhongshan Station, (b) wind speed, (c) simulated hourly tidal velocity at Dalk Glacier coast, and (d) the hourly event counts of A1 along with the station distribution. The vertical axis (count) represents the number of recorded events per hour in panels (a–c) and (e). In panel (a), the temperature range below zero degrees is filled with light blue, and on the right side of panel (d) is a horizontally sorted bar chart showing the number of records from each station. (e) Partial (one month) enlarged view of the red box in panel (a). The color version of this figure is available only in the electronic edition.

frequency, rapid attenuation, and short-propagation distances, typically being recorded by no more than three stations (stations can only detect such events within a 1–2 km radius). Consequently, these events are predominantly distributed in areas with good station coverage. Regarding more precise determinations of icequake locations and source mechanism analyses, we intend to prioritize these aspects in future studies.

The duration of A2 events is very short (~0.1 s), and their energy is significantly greater than that of A1 events, exhibiting pulse *P* waves (Fig. 4b) and linear polarization characteristics (Fig. S3). Polarization analysis indicated a source direction of ~300° and an incidence angle of ~10° (Fig. 6d; Li *et al.*, 2021). Observing the hologram overlay that the source is almost directly beneath station 20764 (Fig. S4). These events often occur within a few hours of the highest daily temperatures, showing a correlation with glacier melting (Fig. 6e).

It is worth noting that there are a series of supraglacial lakes near station 20764, such as Dalk Lake, Boulder Lake, and Lake Ledyanoe (Boronina *et al.*, 2021; Fig. 1b), these lakes are close to the glacier grounding line and are almost always covered by ice. During the Antarctic summer, areas near the bedrock may melt, causing meltwater to accumulate in the lake region, which can result in the formation of water layers on the lake surface (Boronina *et al.*, 2021). Mishra *et al.* (2024) found that several supraglacial lakes located near the grounding line of the Dalk Glacier's eastern area experienced continuous melting and drainage during the summer months from 2017 to 2023. We speculate that the supraglacial lakes near station 20764 likely also experienced intense melting and drainage activities, which led to the occurrence of the A2 event. Because sufficient meltwater injected into the cracks will increase the subglacial

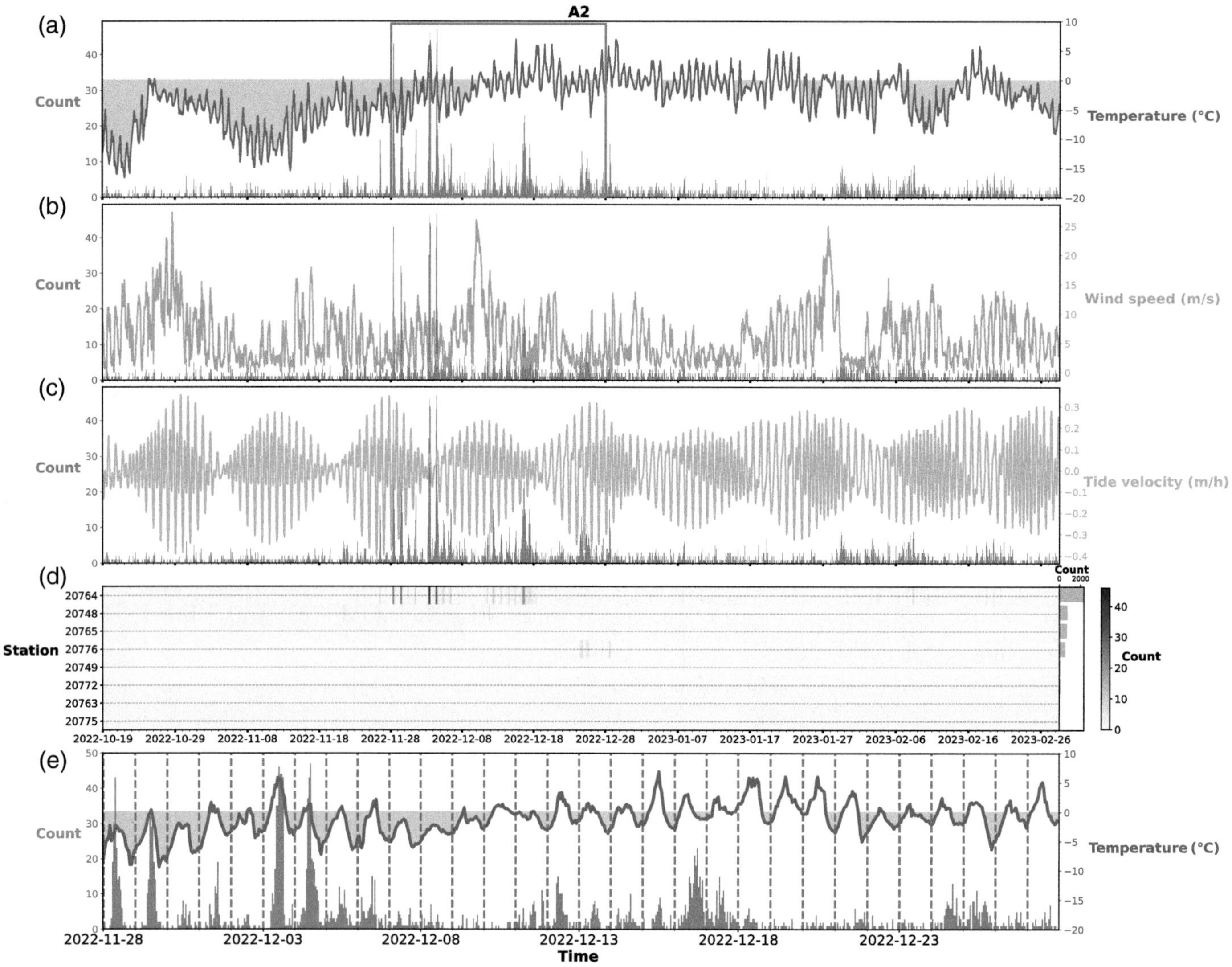

Figure 6. Comparison of the temperature recorded at (a) Zhongshan Station, (b) wind speed, (c) simulated hourly tidal velocity at Dalk Glacier coast, and (d) the hourly event counts of A2 along with the station distribution. The vertical axis (count) represents the number of recorded events per hour in panels (a–c) and (e). In panel (a), the temperature range below zero degrees is filled with light blue, and on the right side of panel (d) is a horizontally sorted bar chart showing the number of records from each station. (e) Partial (one month) enlarged view of the red box in panel (a). The color version of this figure is available only in the electronic edition.

water pressure, the ice fractures can develop deeper under the influence of hydrofracturing (Benn and Evans, 2014; Hudson *et al.*, 2020). Thus, we speculate that the A2 event may have been generated by extensional faults, representing a type of crevasse event occurring in the mid-to-deep regions driven by hydraulic forces.

During the process of the outlet glacier crossing the grounding line and transitioning from a land-based ice to a floating glacier, damage will increase significantly. Near the glacier's sidewalls, especially where the grounding line intersects the sidewalls, there will be regions of intense damage (Sun *et al.*, 2017). The difference in flow velocities between the center and the edges of the glacier, along with the bedrock obstruction at the glacier's terminus, can lead to localized stress concentrations. When the glacier is actively moving, this stress is released, resulting in the formation of fractures. Mishra *et al.* (2024) observed the ice velocities of Dalk Glacier from 2017 to the end of 2022, indicating that apart from the glacier terminus (the part close to the ocean), the flow velocity of the glacier body exhibits significant seasonal variations, with acceleration occurring during the summer months. Ai *et al.* (2019) found that Dalk Glacier's ice flow speed increased significantly in the 2009 summer, far exceeding the annual average increase. Previous studies on the dynamics of typical outlet glaciers in East Antarctica have also observed these characteristics (Greene *et al.*, 2018; Liang *et al.*, 2019). From December 2022 to January 2023, the temperature near Dalk experienced a period of sustained increase, and the temperature began to reach above zero degrees. It is evident that this period corresponds to the frequent occurrence of A2 events.

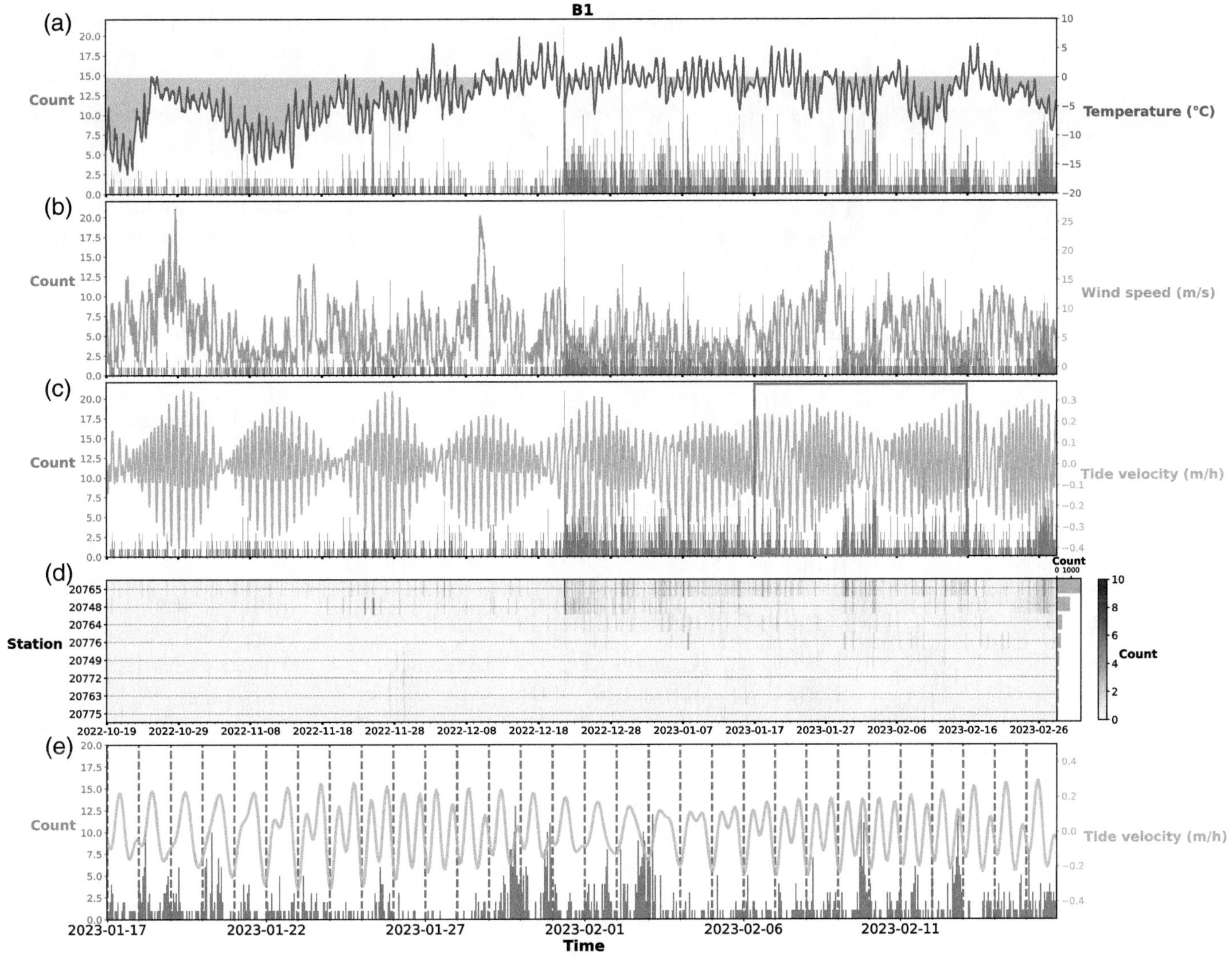

Figure 7. Comparison of the temperature recorded at (a) Zhongshan Station, (b) wind speed, (c) simulated hourly tidal velocity at Dalk Glacier coast, and (d) the hourly event counts of B1 along with the station distribution. The vertical axis (count) represents the number of recorded event per hour in panels (a–c) and (e). In panel (a), the temperature range below zero degrees is filled with light blue, and on the right side of panel (d) is a horizontally sorted bar chart showing the number of records from each station. (e) Partial (one month) enlarged view of the red box in panel (c). The color version of this figure is available only in the electronic edition.

Therefore, we hypothesize that the changes in flow speed of the Dalk Glacier in Antarctica during the summer exacerbate the internal damage in the grounded sections of the glacier's side walls, promoting the development of deep fissures. This may be one of the reasons for the concentration of A2 events.

Group B: low-frequency long-duration events

Group B events have varying durations, all longer than 1 s, with frequencies less than 20 Hz (Fig. 4c,d), and are observed at eight stations. In group B, events of B1 are concentrated in cluster 20, the rest of the clusters are B2 (Fig. 3b). The peaks in quantity correspond to the daily minimum and maximum tidal velocities, demonstrating a correlation with the diurnal tidal cycle (Fig. 7e and Fig. S5).

Taking the same group B event recorded by eight stations as an example, we found that the B1 event was mainly recorded by stations 20748 and 20765 (Fig. 7d). They have almost identical arrival times, featuring a weak high-frequency onset followed closely by a low-frequency surface wave (Fig. 8). The rapid attenuation of high-frequency energy indicates that the source is located east of stations 20748 and 20765, likely near the grounding line close to the coast. The sequence in which the waveforms arrive at the four southern stations also supports this, showing that most of the B2 events are residual waveforms that occur after the high-frequency component of the B1 event has attenuated. Based on previous results (Hammer *et al.*, 2015; Hu *et al.*, 2024), we believe this is a type of mixed event, with the mechanism involving the underwater portion of the glacier, where tidal fluctuations of the water and the gravitational effects of the ice interact to cause cracks in the grounding zone. Subsequently, seawater flows into the opened cracks, leading to water resonance.

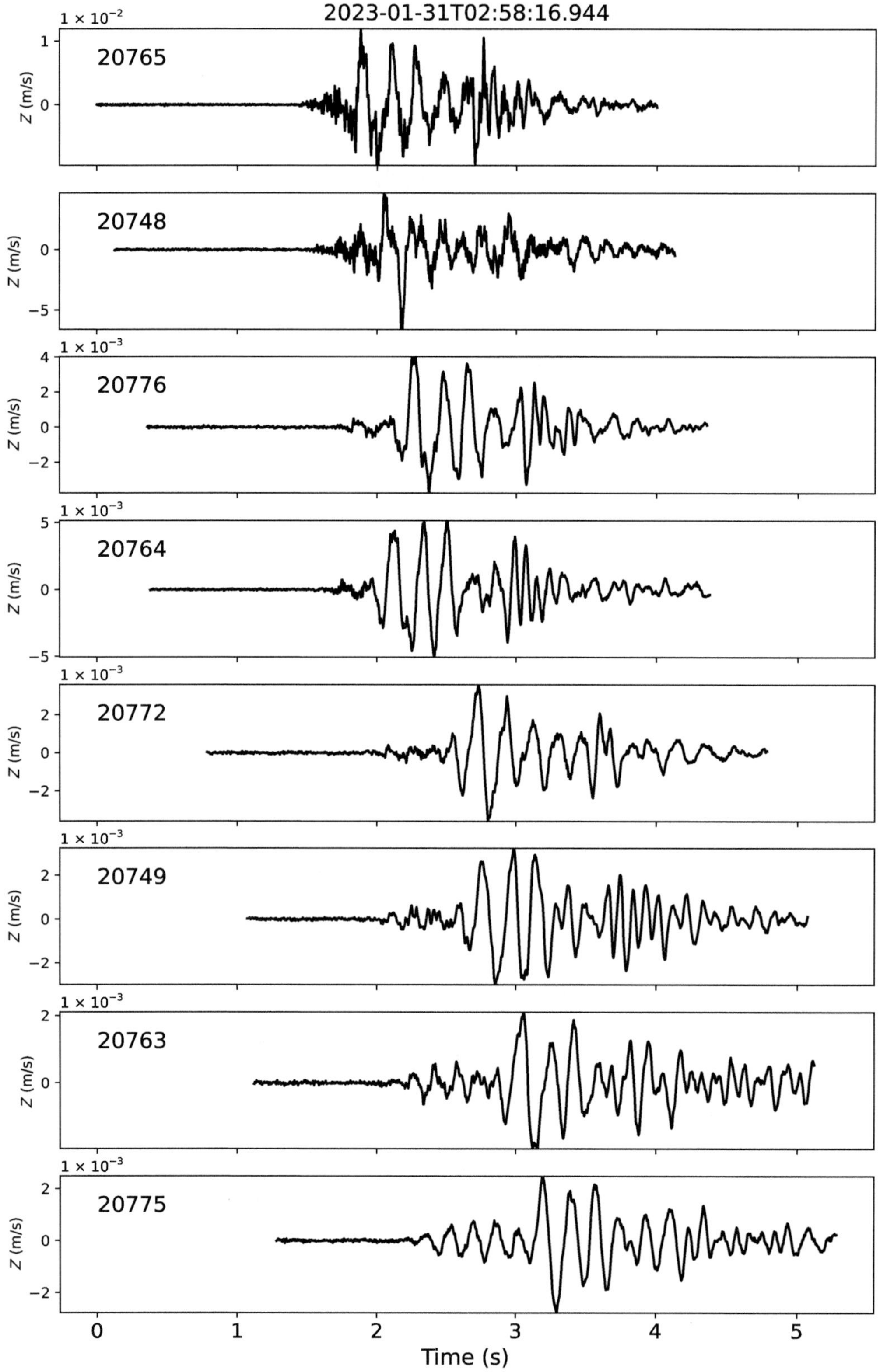

Figure 8. The same B group event recorded by all eight stations. The events are sorted according to the time points corresponding to the peaks of the event spectrum, with the earliest starting time marked.

After mid-December 2022, the overall number of group B events increased (Fig. 7d and Fig. S5). This period corresponds to the summer season in Antarctica, where temperatures began to fluctuate around the freezing point, making the glaciers more active and exacerbating the disintegration of the glacier front. The relatively increased sea surface temperature in the summer in Antarctica can also reduce the strength of the ice shelves, making fractures more likely to occur, particularly in the grounding zone where damage is more easily sustained. Based on the orientation of the source, it can be inferred that some isolated B2 events lasting from a few seconds to several tens of seconds may also represent discrete occurrences of calving events (Amundson *et al.*, 2012; Walter *et al.*, 2012; Bartholomaus *et al.*, 2013). They are similar to low-frequency microtsunami events generated by calving events with a long duration (MacAyeal *et al.*, 2009). Calving events may also regulate the occurrence of B1 events because the breaking of icebergs can generate locally destructive waves that lead to fatigue in the grounded ice (MacAyeal *et al.*, 2009), promoting the formation of fractures.

Groups C and D: wind-induced vibrations and vehicle signals

Group C events have a broad frequency range of 1–120 Hz, and the triggering of these events is closely related to changes in wind speed, which is consistent with the observations of Frankinet *et al.* (2021; Fig. 9). No correlation between

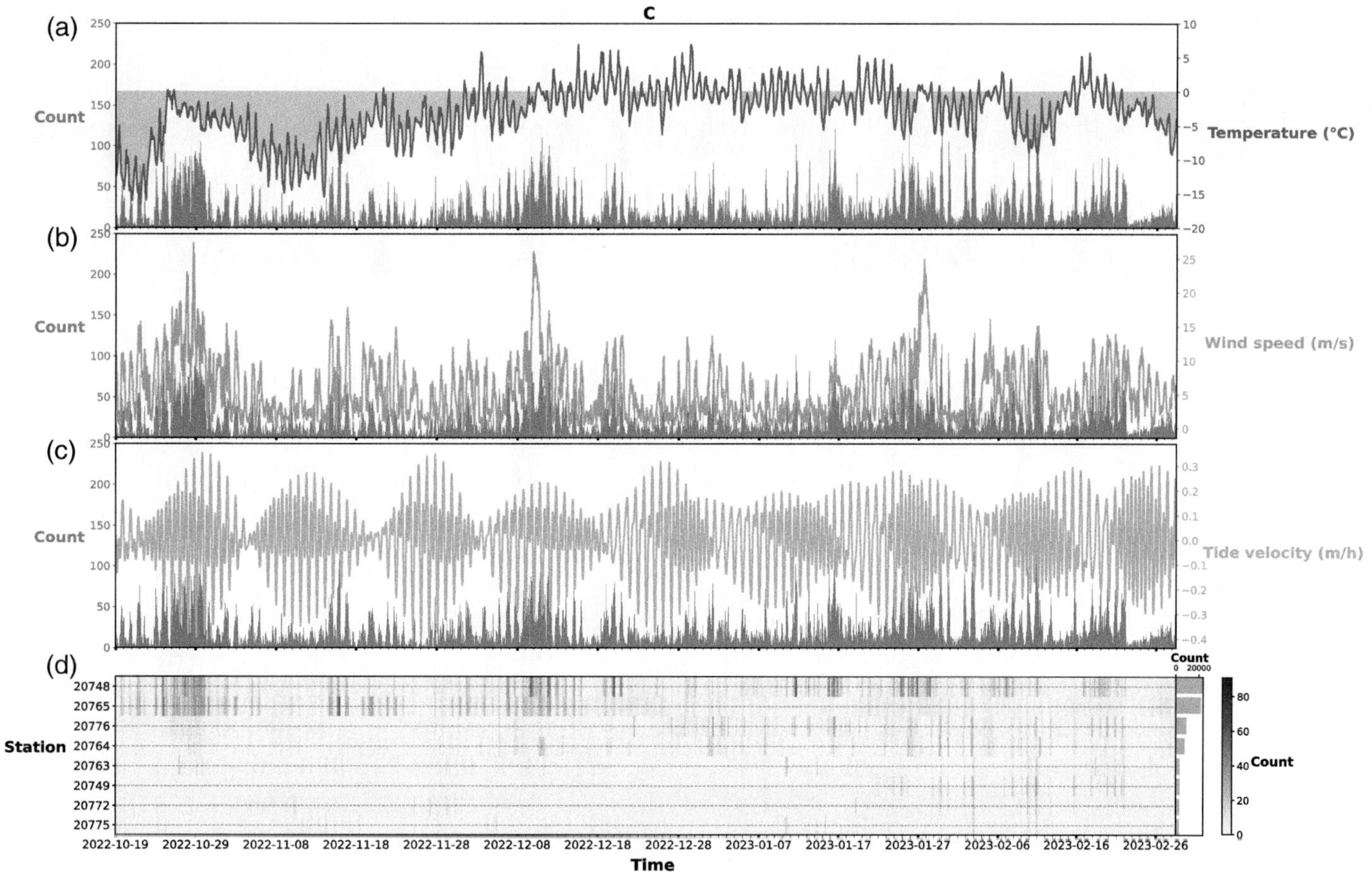

Figure 9. Comparison of the temperature recorded at (a) Zhongshan Station, (b) wind speed, (c) simulated hourly tidal velocity at Dalk Glacier coast, and (d) the hourly event counts of C along with the station distribution. The vertical axis (count) represents the number of recorded events per hour in panels (a–c). In panel (a), the temperature range below zero degrees is filled with light blue, and on the right side of panel (d) is a horizontally sorted bar chart showing the number of records from each station. The color version of this figure is available only in the electronic edition.

the events was observed, and each event was recorded by only a single station, indicating that the source is relatively close to the station. The majority of events were recorded by the stations 20748, 20765, 20776, and 20764, which are located on bedrock, whereas very few were recorded by the four stations located on snow. This aligns with our expectations, as the statistical count of wind direction by hour during the study period shows that most of the wind comes from the ocean (northeast) and the inland direction of the Dalk Glacier. The bedrock outcrops serve as prominent wind barriers facing the wind direction (Fig. S6), inevitably generating a large amount of wind noise.

Group D events are almost all concentrated at station 20748 (Fig. 10), and their waveforms are similar to vehicle noise (Ghosh *et al.*, 2015), with energy concentrated at 35 and 75–100 Hz. In January 2023, we obtained a large number of recordings. We created a heatmap (Fig. S7) for that month and found that the peak occurrence of events is closely related to the activity times of the research team at Zhongshan Station. Therefore, we can conclude that group D events are anthropogenic vehicle noise.

In our study, seismic stations are not configured in a linear array. Therefore, our unsupervised clustering analysis focused on waveform data from individual stations without incorporating information from adjacent stations. If the array was linearly arranged, spatial correlations between neighboring stations could be leveraged during unsupervised clustering analysis. For instance, the frequency–wavenumber (*f-k*) transform could be utilized to derive spectral features with spatial correlations, which might produce more favorable results.

Summary and Conclusion

We used unsupervised deep clustering to classify various seismic events near the Dalk Glacier in the Larsmann Hills of East Antarctica. Subsequently, based on similar spectral characteristics of certain classes, we combined all the events into four groups.

Group A consists of short-duration broadband events and has two subclasses. Subclass A1 consists of surface-wave seismic events, which represent surface crevasse icequakes; subclass A2 consists of high-frequency events with large impulsive energy, possibly corresponding to medium and deep crevasse icequakes driven by hydraulic fracturing and seasonal variations in glacial flow velocity. Group B contains low-

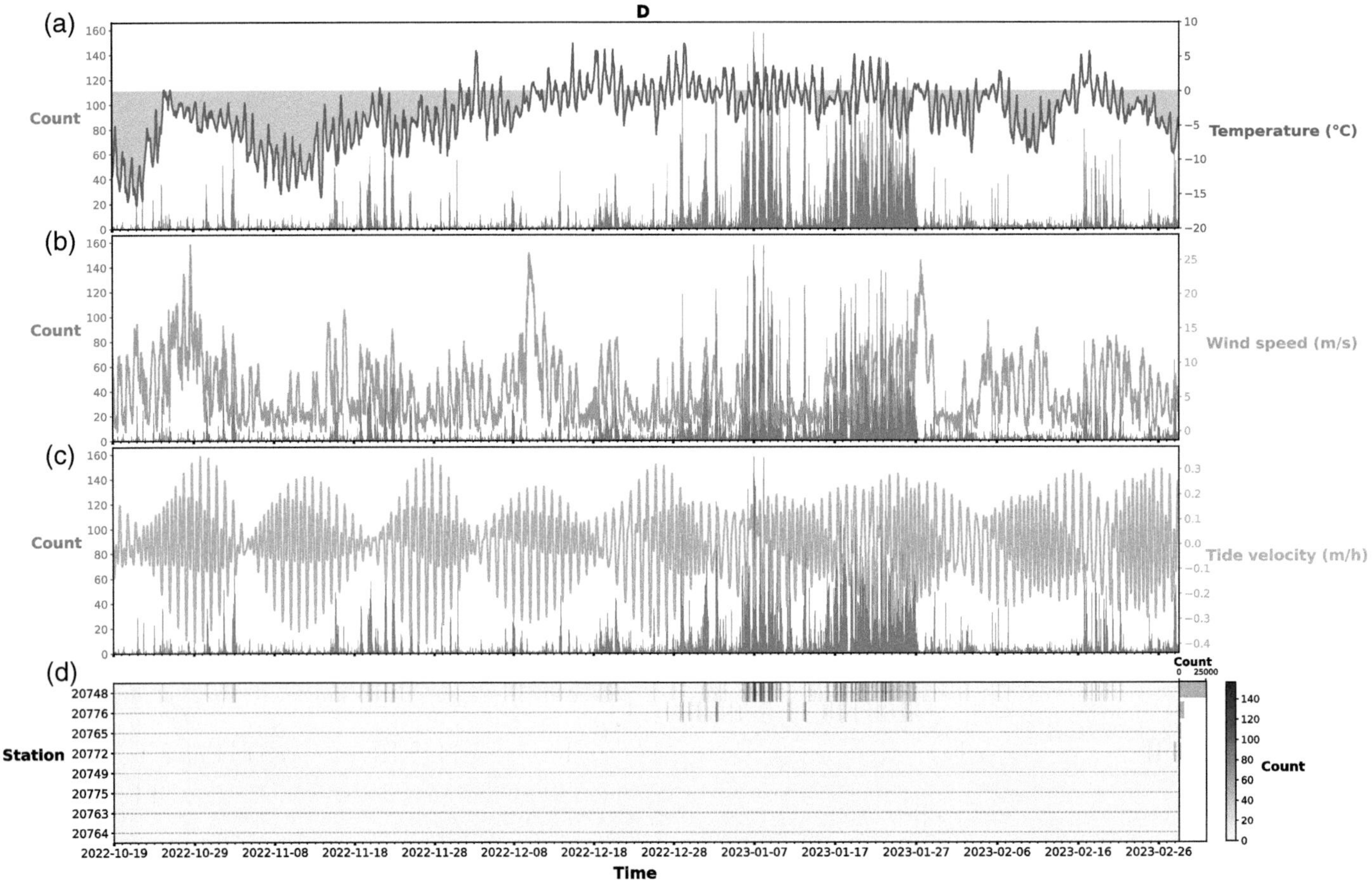

Figure 10. Comparison of the temperature recorded at (a) Zhongshan Station, (b) wind speed, (c) simulated hourly tidal velocity at Dalk Glacier coast, and (d) the hourly event counts of D along with the station distribution. The vertical axis (count) represents the number of recorded events per hour in panels (a–c). In panel (a), the temperature range below zero degrees is filled with light blue, and on the right side of panel (d) is a horizontally sorted bar chart showing the number of records from each station. The color version of this figure is available only in the electronic edition.

frequency, long-duration events and also has two subclasses. B1 is a mixed event characterized by weak high-frequency onsets followed by low-frequency tail waves, representing the resonance caused by fluid-filled ice-bottom cracks. The majority of B2 consists of the remaining waveforms after the high-frequency portion of B1 has attenuated, with a small portion possibly indicating the occurrence of calving events. Group C events are associated with vibrations caused by wind. Group D events are associated with vehicle noise near the Zhongshan Station.

The unsupervised deep clustering process successfully classified the complex seismic signals within the glacier system. We identified typical wind and vehicle noise signals. This inspired future station deployment strategies: seismic instruments should be placed in snow-covered, buried >0.5 m deep and away from human activities. The study of the epicentral directions, typical waveforms, and environmental drivers of events in groups A and B has led us to focus on potential sources located at the glacier grounding line. Setting up a denser network of observation stations there, along with longer periods of observation, will greatly enrich the data and offer new perspectives and understanding for the study of the internal structure of glaciers.

Data and Resources

The foundational code used is derived from Hu's work (https://github.com/nintynine0/Unsupervised-clustering; Hu *et al.*, 2024). The microseismic events and meteorological data used can be obtained from Harvard Dataverse by doi: 10.7910/DVN/UG9R61. The coastline and grounding line data for the study area are derived from the Scientific Committee on Antarctic Research (SCAR) Antarctic Digital Database (ADD; Gerrish *et al.*, 2023). Satellite imagery is sourced from the Landsat Image Mosaic of Antarctica (Bindschadler *et al.*, 2008). Contour data are obtained from the Radarsat Antarctic Mapping Project Digital Elevation Model (DEM), Version 2 (Liu *et al.*, 2015). The basemap data come from The Reference Elevation Model of Antarctica (REMA) and The International Bathymetric Chart of the Southern Ocean Version 2 (IBCSO v2; Howat *et al.*, 2019; Dorschel *et al.*, 2022). The mapping was conducted using QGIS3.16 (https://qgis.org) and the geospatial data package Quanktica32 (Matsuoka *et al.*, 2021). Tide level data were generated using the MATLAB tide model driver (TMD3.0; Greene *et al.*, 2024) and the CATS2008a tidal model (Padman *et al.*, 2002). Seismic data were processed using ObsPy software (Beyreuther *et al.*, 2010), and the autoencoder model was developed using PyTorch (https://pytorch.org). The experimental results were generated using MATLAB (https://www.mathworks.com) and Matplotlib (https://matplotlib.org). All websites were last accessed in August 2025. The supplemental material contains Figures S1–S8.

Declaration of Competing Interests

The authors acknowledge that there are no conflicts of interest recorded.

Acknowledgments

The authors thank the Polar Research Institute of China for logistical support during the data collection. This work was supported by the National Natural Science Foundation of China (Grant Numbers 42474079 and 42327803) and the "CUG Scholar" Scientific Research Funds at the China University of Geosciences (Wuhan) (Project Number 2022132).

References

Ai, S., S. Wang, Y. Li, G. Moholdt, C. Zhou, L. Liu, and Y. Yang (2019). High-precision ice-flow velocities from ground observations on Dalk Glacier, Antarctica, *Polar Sci.* **19,** 13–23, doi: 10.1016/j.polar.2018.09.003.

Allen, R. (1982). Automatic phase pickers: Their present use and future prospects, *Bull. Seismol. Soc. Am.* **72,** no. 6B, S225–S242, doi: 10.1785/BSSA07206B0225.

Amundson, J. M., J. F. Clinton, M. Fahnestock, M. Truffer, M. P. Lüthi, and R. J. Motyka (2012). Observing calving-generated ocean waves with coastal broadband seismometers, Jakobshavn Isbræ, Greenland, *Ann. Glaciol.* **53,** no. 60, 79–84, doi: 10.3189/2012/AoG60A200.

Anandakrishnan, S., and C. R. Bentley (1993). Micro-earthquakes beneath Ice Streams B and C, West Antarctica: Observations and implications, *J. Glaciol.* **39,** no. 133, 455–462, doi: 10.3189/S0022143000016348.

Aster, R. C., and J. P. Winberry (2017). Glacial seismology, *Rep. Prog. Phys.* **80,** no. 12, 126801, doi: 10.1088/1361-6633/aa8473.

Bartholomaus, T. C., C. F. Larsen, and S. O'Neel (2013). Does calving matter? Evidence for significant submarine melt, *Earth Planet. Sci. Lett.* **380,** 21–30, doi: 10.1016/j.epsl.2013.08.014.

Bassis, J. N., H. A. Fricker, R. Coleman, and J.-B. Minster (2008). An investigation into the forces that drive ice-shelf rift propagation on the Amery Ice Shelf, East Antarctica, *J. Glaciol.* **54,** no. 184, 17–27, doi: 10.3189/002214308784409116.

Benn, D., and D. J. A. Evans (2014). *Glaciers and Glaciation*, Second Ed., Routledge, London, doi: 10.4324/9780203785010.

Beyreuther, M., R. Barsch, L. Krischer, T. Megies, Y. Behr, and J. Wassermann (2010). ObsPy: A python toolbox for seismology, *Seismol. Res. Lett.* **81,** no. 3, 530–533, doi: 10.1785/gssrl.81.3.530.

Bindschadler, R., P. Vornberger, A. Fleming, A. Fox, J. Mullins, D. Binnie, S. Paulsen, B. Granneman, and D. Gorodetzky (2008). The Landsat image mosaic of Antarctica, *Remote Sens. Environ.* **112,** no. 12, 4214–4226, doi: 10.1016/j.rse.2008.07.006.

Blankenship, D. D., C. R. Bentley, S. T. Rooney, and R. B. Alley (1986). Seismic measurements reveal a saturated porous layer beneath an active Antarctic ice stream, *Nature* **322,** no. 6074, 54–57, doi: 10.1038/322054a0.

Boronina, A., S. Popov, G. Pryakhina, A. Chetverova, E. Ryzhova, and S. Grigoreva (2021). Formation of a large ice depression on Dålk Glacier (Larsemann Hills, East Antarctica) caused by the rapid drainage of an englacial cavity, *J. Glaciol.* **67,** no. 266, 1121–1136, doi: 10.1017/jog.2021.58.

Colgan, W., H. Rajaram, W. Abdalati, C. McCutchan, R. Mottram, M. S. Moussavi, and S. Grigsby (2016). Glacier crevasses: Observations, models, and mass balance implications, *Rev. Geophys.* **54,** no. 1, 119–161, doi: 10.1002/2015RG000504.

Dorschel, B., L. Hehemann, S. Viquerat, F. Warnke, S. Dreutter, Y. Schulze Tenberge, D. Accettella, L. An, F. Barrios, E. A. Bazhenova, *et al.* (2022). The International Bathymetric Chart of the Southern Ocean Version 2 (IBCSO v2), PANGAEA, 52 data points, doi: 10.1594/PANGAEA.937574.

Frankinet, B., T. Lecocq, and T. Camelbeeck (2021). Wind-induced seismic noise at the Princess Elisabeth Antarctica Station, *Cryosphere* **15,** no. 10, 5007–5016, doi: 10.5194/tc-15-5007-2021.

Gerrish, L., L. Ireland, P. Fretwell, and P. Cooper (2023). High resolution vector polylines of the Antarctic coastline—VERSION 7.8, NERC EDS UK Polar Data Centre, 2 files, 157 MB, doi: 10.5285/98D7C98C-B223-4774-B20E-886630632B12.

Ghosh, R., A. Akula, S. Kumar, and H. K. Sardana (2015). Time–frequency analysis based robust vehicle detection using seismic sensor, *J. Sound Vib.* **346,** 424–434, doi: 10.1016/j.jsv.2015.02.011.

Greene, C. A., S. Erofeeva, L. Padman, S. L. Howard, T. Sutterley, and G. Egbert (2024). Tide model driver for MATLAB, *JOSS* **9,** no. 95, 6018, doi: 10.21105/joss.06018.

Greene, C. A., D. A. Young, D. E. Gwyther, B. K. Galton-Fenzi, and D. D. Blankenship (2018). Seasonal dynamics of Totten Ice Shelf controlled by sea ice buttressing, *Cryosphere* **12,** 2869–2882.

Hammer, C., M. Ohrnberger, and V. Schlindwein (2015). Pattern of cryospheric seismic events observed at Ekström Ice Shelf, Antarctica, *Geophys. Res. Lett.* **42,** no. 10, 3936–3943, doi: 10.1002/2015GL064029.

Helmstetter, A., B. Nicolas, P. Comon, and M. Gay (2015). Basal icequakes recorded beneath an Alpine glacier (Glacier d'Argentière, Mont Blanc, France): Evidence for stick-slip motion? *J. Geophys. Res.* **120,** no. 3, 379–401, doi: 10.1002/2014JF003288.

Howat, I. M., C. Porter, B. E. Smith, M.-J. Noh, and P. Morin (2019). The reference elevation model of Antarctica, *Cryosphere* **13,** no. 2, 665–674, doi: 10.5194/tc-13-665-2019.

Hu, Y., Z. Li, L. Fu, and X. Liu (2024). Environment-modulated glacial seismicity Near Dålk Glacier in East Antarctica revealed by deep clustering, *J. Geophys. Res.* **129,** no. 4, e2023JF007593, doi: 10.1029/2023JF007593.

Hudson, T. S., A. M. Brisbourne, R. S. White, J. M. Kendall, R. Arthern, and A. M. Smith (2020). Breaking the ice: Identifying hydraulically forced crevassing, *Geophys. Res. Lett.* **47,** no. 21, e2020GL090597, doi: 10.1029/2020GL090597.

Jenkins, W. F., P. Gerstoft, M. J. Bianco, and P. D. Bromirski (2021). Unsupervised deep clustering of seismic data: monitoring the Ross Ice Shelf, Antarctica, *J. Geophys. Res.* **126,** no. 9, e2021JB021716, doi: 10.1029/2021JB021716.

Jordan, M. I., and L. Xu (1995). Convergence results for the EM approach to mixtures of experts architectures, *Neural Netw.* **8,** no. 9, 1409–1431, doi: 10.1016/0893-6080(95)00014-3.

Kingma, D. P., and J. Ba (2017). Adam: A method for stochastic optimization, doi: 10.48550/arXiv.1412.6980.

Kinzel, L., T. Fromm, V. Schlindwein, and P. Maass (2024). Unsupervised deep feature learning for icequake discrimination at Neumayer Station, Antarctica, *Seismol. Res. Lett.* **95,** no. 3, 1834–1848.

Kramer, M. A. (1991). Nonlinear principal component analysis using autoassociative neural networks, *AIChE J.* **37,** no. 2, 233–243, doi: 10.1002/aic.690370209.

Leys, C., C. Ley, O. Klein, P. Bernard, and L. Licata (2013). Detecting outliers: Do not use standard deviation around the mean, use absolute deviation around the median, *J. Exp. Social Psychol.* **49,** no. 4, 764–766, doi: 10.1016/j.jesp.2013.03.013.

Li, H., K. Qu, W. Rong, X. Tuo, J. Lu, R. Wang, X. Wang, and J. Courtois (2021). PolarGUI: A MATLAB-based tool for polarization analysis of the three-component seismic data using different algorithms, *Seismol. Res. Lett.* **92,** no. 6, 3821–3831, doi: 10.1785/0220200439.

Liang, Q., C. Zhou, I. M. Howat, S. Jeong, R. Liu, and Y. Chen (2019). Ice flow variations at Polar Record Glacier, East Antarctica, *J. Glaciol.* **65,** no. 250, 279–287, doi: 10.1017/jog.2019.6.

Liu, H., K. Jezek, B. Li, and Z. Zhao (2015). Radarsat Antarctic mapping project digital elevation model, version 2, NASA National Snow and Ice Data Center distributed active archive center, doi: 10.5067/8JKNEW6BFRVD.

MacAyeal, D. R., E. A. Okal, R. C. Aster, and J. N. Bassis (2009). Seismic observations of glaciogenic ocean waves (micro-tsunamis) on icebergs and ice shelves, *J. Glaciol.* **55,** no. 190, 193–206, doi: 10.3189/002214309788608679.

Matsuoka, K., A. Skoglund, G. Roth, J. De Pomereu, H. Griffiths, R. Headland, B. Herried, K. Katsumata, A. Le Brocq, K. Licht, *et al.* (2021). Quantarctica, an integrated mapping environment for Antarctica, the Southern Ocean, and sub-Antarctic islands, *Environ. Modell. Softw.* **140,** 105015, doi: 10.1016/j.envsoft.2021.105015.

Mishra, P., N. Tripathi, S. K. Singh, S. R. Oza, P. M. Solanki, and N. Y. Bhatt (2024). Comprehending the surface melt characteristics, calving processes, and seasonal ice velocity of Dålk glacier in Larsemann Hills, East Antarctica, *Polar Sci.* 101081, doi: 10.1016/j.polar.2024.101081.

Mousavi, S. M., Y. Sheng, W. Zhu, and G. C. Beroza (2019). STanford EArthquake Dataset (STEAD): A global data set of seismic signals for AI, *IEEE Access* **7,** 179,464–179,476, doi: 10.1109/ACCESS.2019.2947848.

Mousavi, S. M., W. Zhu, W. Ellsworth, and G. Beroza (2019). Unsupervised clustering of seismic signals using deep convolutional autoencoders, *IEEE Geosci. Remote Sens. Lett.* **16,** no. 11, 1693–1697, doi: 10.1109/LGRS.2019.2909218.

Olinger, S. D., B. P. Lipovsky, D. A. Wiens, R. C. Aster, P. D. Bromirski, Z. Chen, P. Gerstoft, A. A. Nyblade, and R. A. Stephen (2019). Tidal and thermal stresses drive seismicity along a major Ross Ice Shelf Rift, *Geophys. Res. Lett.* **46,** no. 12, 6644–6652, doi: 10.1029/2019GL082842.

Padman, L., H. A. Fricker, R. Coleman, S. Howard, and L. Erofeeva (2002). A new tide model for the Antarctic ice shelves and seas, *Ann. Glaciol.* **34,** 247–254, doi: 10.3189/172756402781817752.

Paul Winberry, J., S. Anandakrishnan, D. A. Wiens, and R. B. Alley (2013). Nucleation and seismic tremor associated with the glacial earthquakes of Whillans Ice Stream, Antarctica, *Geophys. Res. Lett.* **40,** no. 2, 312–315, doi: 10.1002/grl.50130.

Perol, T., M. Gharbi, and M. Denolle (2018). Convolutional neural network for earthquake detection and location, *Sci. Adv.* **4,** no. 2, e1700578, doi: 10.1126/sciadv.1700578.

Podolskiy, E. A., and F. Walter (2016). Cryoseismology, *Rev. Geophys.* **54,** no. 4, 708–758, doi: 10.1002/2016RG000526.

Podolskiy, E. A., K. Fujita, S. Sunako, A. Tsushima, and R. B. Kayastha (2018). Nocturnal thermal fracturing of a Himalayan debris-covered glacier revealed by ambient seismic noise, *Geophys. Res. Lett.* **45,** no. 18, 9699–9709, doi: 10.1029/2018GL079653.

Reynolds, D. (2015). Gaussian mixture models, in *Encyclopedia of Biometrics*, S. Z. Li and A. K. Jain (Editors), Springer US, Boston, Massachusetts, 827–832, doi: 10.1007/978-1-4899-7488-4_196.

Röösli, C., F. Walter, S. Husen, L. C. Andrews, M. P. Lüthi, G. A. Catania, and E. Kissling (2014). Sustained seismic tremors and icequakes detected in the ablation zone of the Greenland ice sheet, *J. Glaciol.* **60,** no. 221, 563–575, doi: 10.3189/2014JoG13J210.

Ross, Z. E., M.-A. Meier, E. Hauksson, and T. H. Heaton (2018). Generalized seismic phase detection with deep learning, *Bull. Seismol. Soc. Am.* **108,** no. 5A, 2894–2901, doi: 10.1785/0120180080.

Seydoux, L., R. Balestriero, P. Poli, M. D. Hoop, M. Campillo, and R. Baraniuk (2020). Clustering earthquake signals and background noises in continuous seismic data with unsupervised deep learning, *Nat. Commun.* **11,** no. 1, 3972, doi: 10.1038/s41467-020-17841-x.

Smith, B., H. A. Fricker, A. S. Gardner, B. Medley, J. Nilsson, F. S. Paolo, N. Holschuh, S. Adusumilli, K. Brunt, B. Csatho, *et al.* (2020). Pervasive ice sheet mass loss reflects competing ocean and atmosphere processes, *Science* **368,** no. 6496, 1239–1242, doi: 10.1126/science.aaz5845.

Sun, S., S. L. Cornford, J. C. Moore, R. Gladstone, and L. Zhao (2017). Ice shelf fracture parameterization in an ice sheet model, *Cryosphere* **11,** no. 6, 2543–2554, doi: 10.5194/tc-11-2543-2017.

Walter, F., J. M. Amundson, S. O'Neel, M. Truffer, M. Fahnestock, and H. A. Fricker (2012). Analysis of low-frequency seismic signals generated during a multiple-iceberg calving event at Jakobshavn Isbræ, Greenland, *J. Geophys. Res.* **117,** no. F1, 2011JF002132, doi: 10.1029/2011JF002132.

Walter, F., J. F. Clinton, N. Deichmann, D. S. Dreger, S. E. Minson, and M. Funk (2009). Moment tensor inversions of icequakes on Gornergletscher, Switzerland, *Bull. Seismol. Soc. Am.* **99,** no. 2A, 852–870, doi: 10.1785/0120080110.

Wang, J., Z. Xiao, C. Liu, D. Zhao, and Z. Yao (2019). Deep learning for picking seismic arrival times, *J. Geophys. Res.* **124,** no. 7, 6612–6624, doi: 10.1029/2019JB017536.

Winter, K., D. Lombardi, A. Diaz-Moreno, and R. Bainbridge (2021). Monitoring icequakes in East Antarctica with the Raspberry Shake, *Seismol. Res. Lett.* **92,** no. 5, 2736–2747, doi: 10.1785/0220200483.

Manuscript received 15 February 2025
Published online 27 August 2025

Characterizing Seismic Events in an Industrial Corridor of the Chicago Area

Ann Mariam Thomas*[1], Omkar Ranadive[1], and Suzan van der Lee[1]

Abstract

Urban and industrial environments present a major challenge for seismic event detection and classification. Anthropogenic events can closely resemble tectonic signals and reduce their signal-to-noise ratios, leading to misclassifications of earthquakes and tremors. By detecting and characterizing these anthropogenic events, we can improve detection algorithms and motivate new applications in seismic monitoring and imaging. In this study, we develop a workflow to detect and cluster anomalous seismic events, recorded by a broadband seismic station installed in a unique industrial corridor of the Chicago area. Our workflow consists of (1) a power spectral density (PSD) misfit detector to detect anomalous events in continuous data and (2) a *k*-means clustering model to generate clusters of anomalous events. We discuss our workflow development, where we select parameters and generalizable model features to maximize the coherence and interpretability of generated clusters. When applied to two years of continuous seismic data, our workflow successfully identified several classes of events, including surface quarry blasts, underground blasts, and machinery operations. Using our results, we created a labeled data set of 1000+ man-made seismic events in the Chicago area. Our study demonstrates how a simple PSD detector and clustering model can be used to efficiently mine through a noisy multiyear data set and create an event catalog.

Cite this article as Thomas, A. M., O. Ranadive, and S. van der Lee (2025). Characterizing Seismic Events in an Industrial Corridor of the Chicago Area, *Seismol. Res. Lett.* **97**, 439–450, doi: 10.1785/0220250109.

Introduction

Urban and industrial environments are characterized by dynamic, high-amplitude seismic noise, which can pose a serious challenge for earthquake detection and discrimination. Persistent anthropogenic noise—seismic noise from human-generated activities like traffic or construction—can decrease the signal-to-noise ratios of seismic events, leading to missed detections of earthquakes and other signals of interest. Impulsive anthropogenic events (e.g., quarry blasts, train signals) have also been falsely detected as earthquakes or tremors (e.g., Li *et al.*, 2018; Maher *et al.*, 2024). With rapid urbanization and industrialization, these detection challenges within built environments are growing in number and complexity. In response, recent studies have developed new algorithms to remove persistent anthropogenic noise from seismic data (e.g., Karasözen and West, 2022; Yang *et al.*, 2022). However, due to the broad spectrum and diversity of anthropogenic noise, further research is needed to develop robust algorithms that can accommodate diverse detection environments. Developers and other stakeholders have recommended expanding labeled data sets with dynamic anthropogenic noise, to develop and refine such algorithms (Mousavi *et al.*, 2020; Maher *et al.*, 2024).

With a growing number of studies that address the challenge of anthropogenic noise, there is also a growing body of research that harnesses this "noise" for innovative seismological applications. Recent studies have shown that urban seismometers can offer a cost-effective, less-invasive means of monitoring vehicular and even foot traffic (e.g., Díaz *et al.*, 2017; Jakkampudi *et al.*, 2020; Li *et al.*, 2023). Traffic noise has also shown great potential as a passive source for near-surface imaging (e.g., Quiros *et al.*, 2016; Zhang *et al.*, 2019). Within education and outreach, urban seismic events—especially those from major cultural activities like concerts and sports games—can capture mass media interest, showcasing the field of seismology to a wider audience (e.g., Díaz *et al.*, 2017, 2020; Caplan-Auerbach *et al.*, 2024).

These diverse applications of anthropogenic noise motivate exploratory research in built environments. Whether the aim is to harness or remove anthropogenic noise, it is valuable to identify the seismic signatures of dominant man-made signals. Previous studies have characterized seismic data within densely populated cities such as Long Beach (Riahi and Gerstoft, 2015; Snover *et al.*, 2020), Bucharest (Ritter *et al.*, 2005), Auckland (Boese *et al.*, 2015), and London (Green

1. Northwestern University, Earth and Planetary Sciences, Evanston, Illinois, U.S.A., https://orcid.org/0000-0001-6271-1738 (AMT); https://orcid.org/0000-0003-1884-1185 (SL)

*Corresponding author: annthomas2025@u.northwestern.edu

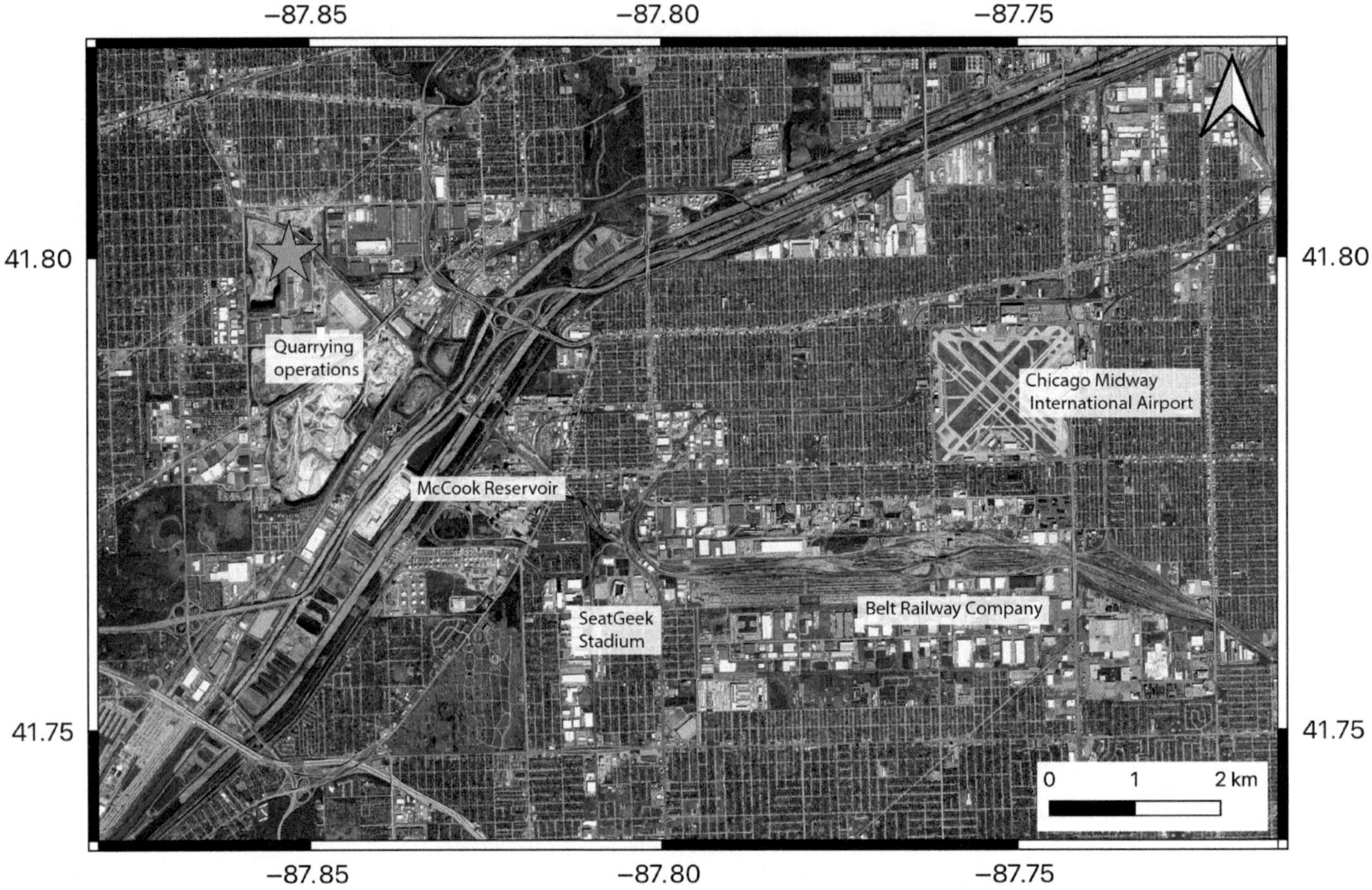

Figure 1. Map of southwest Chicago and suburbs, showing the locations of station NW.HQIL (star at 41.80° N, 87.85° W) and local noise sources. Figure was created with QGIS using ESRI Satellite Imagery. The color version of this figure is available only in the electronic edition.

et al., 2016). In this study, we explore seismic data from a broadband seismometer (NW.HQIL) installed in a unique industrial corridor of the Chicago area. The station was installed shortly after a magnitude 3.2 earthquake in 2013, near its epicenter to search for aftershocks and was operational until December 2019. Its noisy location—within a few kilometers of dense residential districts, quarrying operations, a flood-control reservoir, major highways, railroads, a sports stadium, and a commercial airport (Fig. 1)—generates thousands of transient events in just a few days of data. This combination of urban and industrial features makes station HQIL a unique site for exploratory research.

Manually exploring the rich, heterogeneous data of this station is time-consuming and challenging, especially when attempting to find patterns and groups of repeating events. Here, we present a semiautomated approach to identify clusters of anomalous seismic events in continuous, three-component data. Our approach is divided into two stages: (1) applying a power spectral density (PSD) misfit detector to identify anomalous events in continuous data and (2) applying an unsupervised learning model (k-means clustering) to group the anomalous events detected in stage 1. Using the results of our clustering analysis, we created a labeled data set of 1262 man-made signals recorded in HQIL data, placing a special emphasis on impulsive events that have earthquake-like characteristics.

PSD Misfit Detector

Our two-stage methodology is outlined in the concept map of Figure 2. The workflow begins by applying a PSD misfit detector to detect anomalous events in continuous data. A PSD misfit detector measures the difference (or misfit) between the PSD of a given time window and the PSD of background noise. "Detected" anomalous events are windows with PSD misfits above a selected threshold. Unlike the short-term average/long-term average (STA/LTA) ratio method (Allen, 1978), which is commonly used for event subselection in machine learning workflows, the PSD misfit detector can detect anomalous events with low signal-to-noise ratios (SNRs) (Vaezi and Van der Baan, 2015). PSD-based approaches are particularly beneficial in urban and industrial areas where persistent man-made noise (e.g., noise from construction and machinery operation) can decrease the SNR of anomalous events. PSD misfit approaches have been shown to detect a wide range of events, including weak microseismic events (Vaezi and Van der Baan, 2015) and industrial operations (Guenaga *et al.*, 2021).

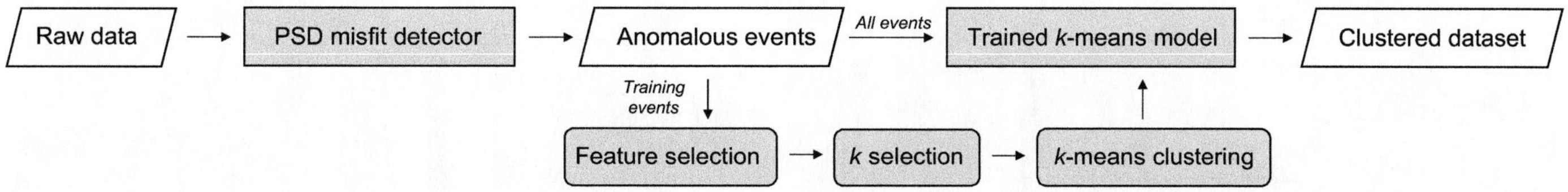

Figure 2. Concept map of study methodology for detecting and clustering anomalous events in continuous, single-station data. PSD, power spectral density.

Methodology

Our PSD misfit approach is based on the methodology of Vaezi and Van der Baan (2015) with some modifications. We first computed PSDs of overlapping (50%) 10 s windows in continuous HQIL data using the Welch method (Welch, 1967). Waveforms were processed with the following procedure prior to PSD computation: filling gaps via linear interpolation, linear detrending, and response correction to convert from counts to ground acceleration. Note that the gap-filling step was performed prior to this study when saving the raw data as local files. This step can be omitted with minimal impact on the results. Using a methodology similar to McNamara and Buland (2004), PSDs of each 10 s window were computed by taking the average PSD of 13 overlapping (50%) subsegments of 2.5 s. This subsegmentation and averaging procedure reduce the variance of each power measurement, providing a more stable PSD estimate of each 10 s window. We then computed the weighted difference $u[f]$ between the PSD of the 10 s window, $\mathrm{PSD}[f]$, and the PSD of a "background noise" window, $\mathrm{PSD}_{\mathrm{bg}}[f]$, using the following equation:

$$u[f] = \frac{\mathrm{PSD}[f] - \mathrm{PSD}_{\mathrm{bg}}[f]}{\sigma_{\mathrm{bg}}[f]}, \tag{1}$$

in which σ_{bg} is a standard deviation estimate of the "background noise" PSD at a given frequency f. The Dynamic background noise section describes how we estimated $\mathrm{PSD}_{\mathrm{bg}}[f]$ and $\sigma_{\mathrm{bg}}[f]$ for HQIL noise.

Following the methodology of Vaezi and Van der Baan (2015), we set $u(f)$-values below 1 as zero:

$$u'[f] = \begin{cases} u[f] & \text{if } u[f] > 1 \\ 0 & \text{if } u[f] \leq 1. \end{cases} \tag{2}$$

Finally, we computed the PSD misfit Λ of each 10 s window:

$$\Lambda = \frac{1}{N}\sum_{f=0}^{N} u'[f], \tag{3}$$

in which N is the number of all discrete frequencies that comprose the PSD estimate $\mathrm{PSD}[f]$. In summary, our PSD misfit Λ is the average value of the adjusted difference $u'[f]$ between the PSD of a 10 s window and the PSD of a "background noise" window.

Dynamic background noise

Selecting an appropriate background noise PSD for urban/industrial environments is particularly challenging due to their strongly heterogeneous and time-dependent noise. Noise levels typically peak during daytime hours of the workweek and decrease during evening and night hours. Because of this dynamic nature of man-made noise, we implemented a dynamic or time-dependent background noise window for our misfit detector. Depending on the following four times of day, a different background noise PSD, $\mathrm{PSD}_{\mathrm{bg}}[f]$, and standard deviation estimate, $\sigma_{\mathrm{bg}}[f]$, will be selected:

1. Night: 12:00 a.m.–6:00 a.m.
2. Morning: 06:00 a.m.–12:00 p.m.
3. Afternoon: 12:00 p.m.–06:00 p.m.
4. Evening: 06:00 p.m.–12:00 a.m.

All times are with respect to the local Chicago time (US/central time zone). Compared to a static or time-constant background noise window, a dynamic PSD is better suited to detect anomalous events during low-noise periods (e.g., nighttime).

To estimate the four background noise PSDs and their standard deviations, we randomly selected 50 days in the time period of July 2014 to December 2019, excluding select days with poor or incomplete data. We then computed 1 hr PSDs for each station component using the same methodology of McNamara and Buland (2004), omitting the smoothing procedure. For each of the four time periods, we computed the average and standard deviation of all 1 hr PSDs that occurred with that period. The average PSD and standard deviation are then smoothed using the 1/8 octave smoothing procedure implemented by McNamara and Buland (2004) and decimated to have the same frequency resolution of the 10 s PSDs. The processed averages and standard deviations became the background noise PSDs, $\mathrm{PSD}_{\mathrm{bg}}[f]$, and the standard deviation estimates, $\sigma_{\mathrm{bg}}[f]$, for our misfit detector. Figure 3 shows the background noise PSDs, $\mathrm{PSD}_{\mathrm{bg}}[f]$, we used for all three station components and four times of day.

Threshold selection

Our dynamic PSD misfit detector was applied to overlapping (50%) 10 s windows that span about two years of HQIL data (June 2017 to June 2019). After manually inspecting a subset of 10 s windows and comparing their PSD misfit values, we

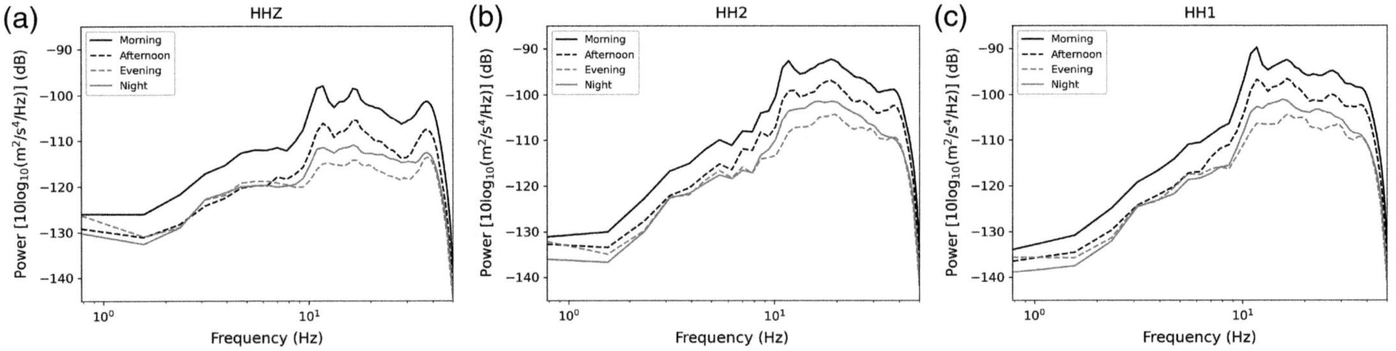

Figure 3. Background noise power spectral densities PSD_{bg} used in the PSD misfit detector for each component of station HQIL: (a) HHZ, (b) HH1, and (c) HH2. PSD_{bg} are estimated for four times of day: night (12:00 a.m.–06:00 a.m.), morning (06:00 a.m.–12:00 p.m.), afternoon (12:00 p.m.–06:00 p.m.), and evening (06:00 p.m.–12:00 a.m.). All times are with respect to local Chicago time (US/central).

decided on a misfit threshold of 1.0 standard deviation; if the PSD misfit of any component of a 10 s window is above 1.0 standard deviation, then it is detected as an anomalous event and passed to the clustering model. With this threshold, about 5% of all overlapping windows in the two-year data set are detected. As will be discussed in the Application and Analysis section, the PSD misfit detector identified a diverse range of events in our two-year data set, including both narrowband and broadband anomalies spanning a wide range of SNRs.

K-means Clustering

After detecting anomalous events using the PSD detector, we applied the *k*-means clustering algorithm to identify groups (clusters) of repeating anomalous events of the same source. The *k*-means algorithm (also known as Lloyd's algorithm, Lloyd, 1982) is an unsupervised learning algorithm that groups unlabeled data into *k* number of clusters. The algorithm aims to assign cluster labels that minimize the following criterion known as inertia J:

$$J = \sum_{k=1}^{k} \sum_{i=1}^{n} \| (x_i - \mu_k) \|^2, \tag{4}$$

in which k is the number of clusters, n is the number of data points, x_i is the ith data point, and u_k is the kth centroid. The algorithm begins by setting an initial guess of cluster centroids and assigning each data sample with the cluster label of its closest centroid. Cluster centroids are then reset to be the average of all assigned data samples in that cluster. This process of assigning cluster labels and resetting cluster centroids is repeated until the centroids are stable (Watt *et al.*, 2016; Yuan and Yang, 2019). With this simple iterative procedure, the *k*-means algorithm is a powerful and widely used tool in seismology for exploratory data analysis (Johnson *et al.*, 2020; Mousavi and Beroza, 2023; Saadia and Fotopoulos, 2023). It is critical to carefully select model features and a *k*-value for the algorithm to produce meaningful and well-separated clusters.

Feature selection

Table 1 details the features we explored and selected for our final clustering model. The majority of the features are statistical and are motivated by our previous work on earthquake detection in the Chicago area (Thomas *et al.*, 2023). For each 10 s window detected by the PSD misfit detector, we computed its STA/LTA (Allen, 1978) ratio using the 10 s detection as the short-term (ST) window and a preceding 40 s window as the long-term (LT) window. We also computed the skewness and kurtosis of the 10 s window. Each statistical feature was computed on waveforms that were processed with the following procedure: filling gaps via linear interpolation, linear detrending, and division by the stage zero sensitivity to convert to units of velocity. Additional features include the previously computed PSD misfit values, the hour of day, and the day of the week corresponding to each 10 s detection. Excluding the two temporal features (hour and day of the 10 s window), each feature is computed on each of the three channel components (HHZ, HH1, and HH2).

Our feature selection was informed by the observed temporal characteristics of urban and industrial noise in the Chicago area. As expected, man-made noise dominates the seismic record during daytime hours of the weekday. Events like quarry blasts consistently occur at the same few hours of the early afternoon, likely due to a routine blasting schedule. Events of different noise sources can also be differentiated by their event duration. Compared to blastlike events, construction noise and machinery operation tend to be longer in duration (≥10 s), resulting in a distinct skewness and kurtosis value for a 10 s window. Using a combination of statistical and time-based features, we aimed to maximize the separation between noise events of different sources.

From this initial list of 14 total features, we selected a subset of 10 model features using a simple correlation analysis. Because highly correlated features can introduce unnecessary complexity into a clustering algorithm, we aimed to remove redundant features from the initial list. For three weeks of

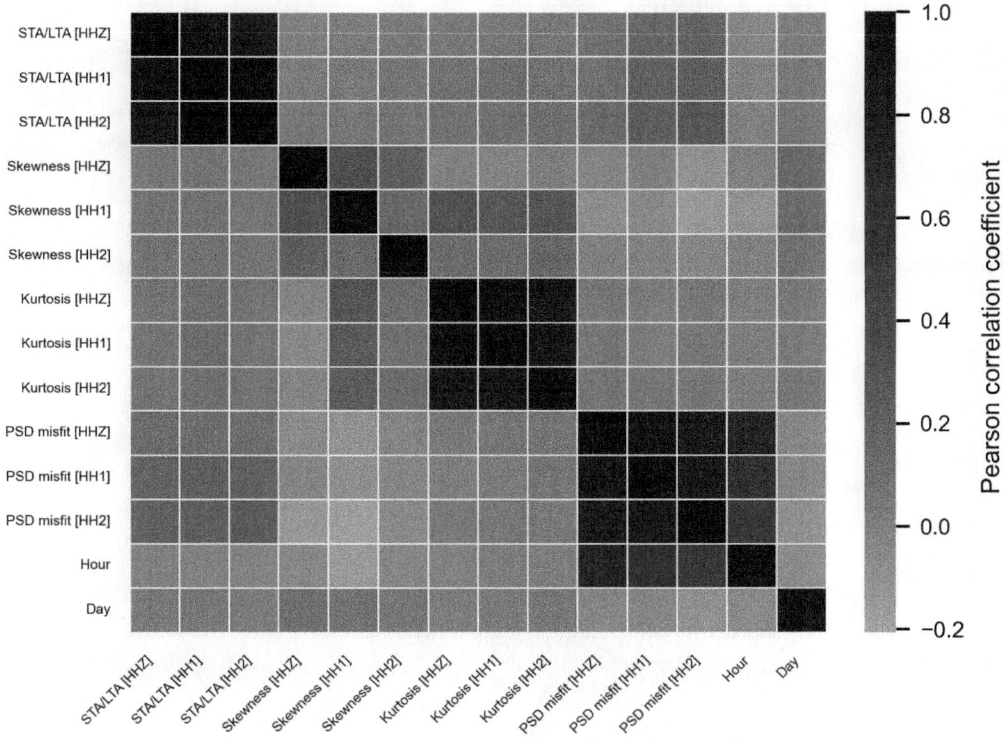

Figure 4. Correlation matrix of the 14 features, detailed in Table 1, corresponding to anomalous events detected in 3 weeks of HQIL data. The following features were omitted in the final model to eliminate any feature pairs with correlations greater than 0.85: STA/LTA [HH1], PSD misfit [HH1], Kurtosis [HHZ], and Kurtosis [HH2]. The color version of this figure is available only in the electronic edition.

HQIL data (1–21 August 2017), we applied the PSD misfit detector and computed all 14 features for the detected events. We then computed the correlation coefficient of each pair of features. Figure 4 shows the correlation matrix of the 14 features computed for the three-week data set. We removed four features to eliminate any feature pairs with correlations greater than 0.85: a threshold determined through empirical testing to balance redundancy reduction and feature retention. See Table 1 for all features included in the final model.

Number of clusters

We explored both quantitative and qualitative methods to determine the number of clusters k to use in our model. For events detected by the PSD misfit detector in three weeks of HQIL data (1–21 August 2017), we applied the k-means clustering algorithm for k-values ranging from 2 to 20. We implemented Lloyd's k-means algorithm using the Python package *scikit-learn* and its default hyperparameters (greedy k-means++ algorithm for cluster centroid initialization, 300 maximum iterations) (Pedregosa *et al.*, 2011).

As a quantitative method, we computed the silhouette coefficient—a measure of intracluster similarity and intercluster separation (Yuan and Yang, 2019)—for each k-value. We also applied the elbow method, which identifies the optimal k-value as the value that corresponds to an "elbow" or an inflection

TABLE 1
Features Explored and Selected for the Clustering Model

Feature	Description	Equation	HHZ	HH1	HH2
STA/LTA	Ratio of the average absolute amplitude in the 10 s short-term (ST) window to the average absolute amplitude in a preceding 40 s long-term (LT) window	$\frac{\frac{1}{N_S}\sum_{n=N_L}^{N_S+N_L-1}\lvert y[n]\rvert}{\frac{1}{N_L}\sum_{n=0}^{N_L-1}\lvert y[n]\rvert}$	Yes	No	Yes
Skewness	Skewness of the amplitude distribution in the 10 s window	$\sqrt{N_S}\frac{\sum_{n=N_L}^{N_S+N_L-1}(y[n]-\bar{y})^3}{\left(\sum_{n=N_L}^{N_S+N_L-1}(y[n]-\bar{y})^2\right)^{3/2}}$	Yes	Yes	Yes
Kurtosis	Kurtosis of the amplitude distribution in the 10 s window	$N_S\frac{\sum_{n=N_L}^{N_S+N_L-1}(y[n]-\bar{y})^4}{\left(\sum_{n=N_L}^{N_S+N_L-1}(y[n]-\bar{y})^2\right)^{2}}$	No	Yes	No
PSD misfit	Misfit between the power spectral density (PSD) of the 10 s window and a background noise PSD	See equation (3)	Yes	No	Yes
Hour	Hour of day in local time corresponding to the 10 s window. Value is an integer within the interval [0, 23].	N/A	Yes		
Day	Day of the week corresponding to the 10 s window. Value is an integer within the interval [1,7], in which 1 is Monday and 7 is Sunday.	N/A	Yes		

The discrete time series $y[n]$ includes amplitudes of the 10 s window detected by the PSD misfit detector and a preceding 40 s window. N_S is the number of samples within the 10 s window and N_L is the number of samples within the 40 s window. STA/LTA, short-term average/long-term average.

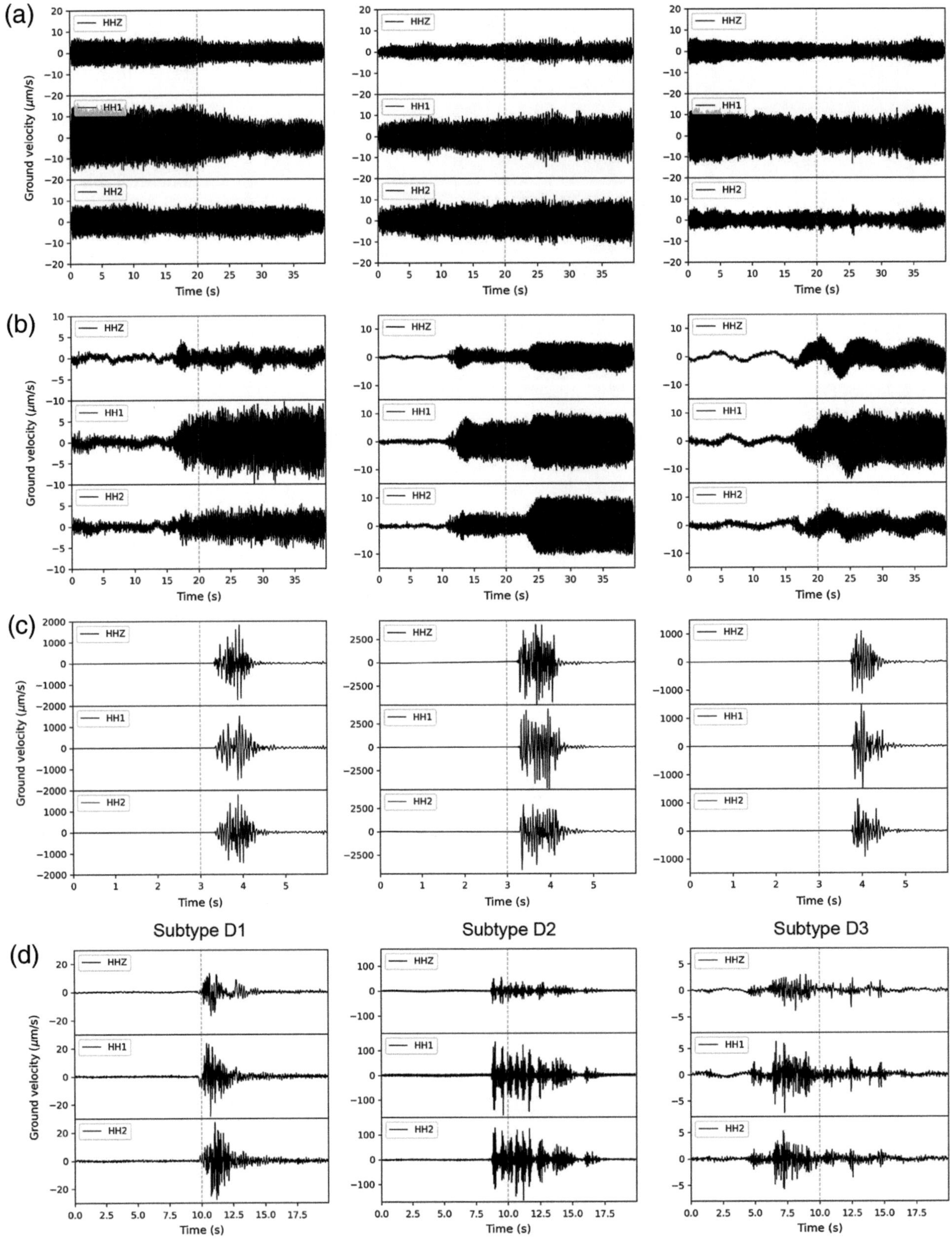

point within an inertia versus k plot (Yuan and Yang, 2019). Both methods suggested k-values below 7.

As our qualitative approach, we visualized a subset of events in every cluster for each tested k-value. We found that a k-value of 12 consistently produced a cluster of signals that indicated an operational change (i.e., machinery turning ON and

Figure 5. (a–d) Examples of HQIL anomalous events in the four event types (A–D) described in Table 2. The gray dashed lines indicates the start of the 10 s window, detected as an anomalous event by the PSD misfit detector. Note the changes in times and amplitude scaling for each example.

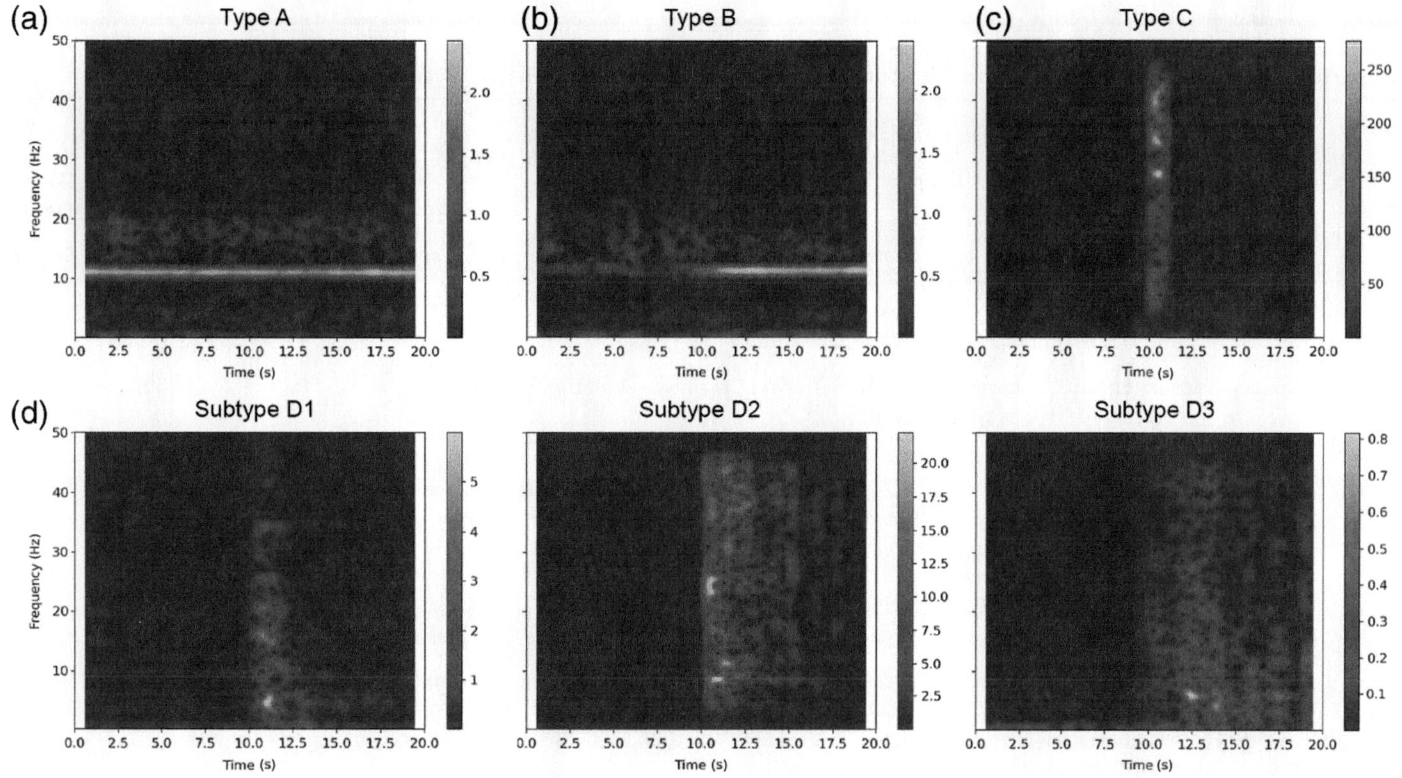

Figure 6. Examples of vertical-component spectrograms for event types (a–d) A–D described in Table 2. Each spectrogram shows 10 s before and after the event onset. Raw waveforms were linearly detrended and converted from counts to ground velocity by dividing by the stage-zero sensitivity. Color scales are in units of micrometers per second. The color version of this figure is available only in the electronic edition.

producing a sudden change in relative amplitude, see Fig. 5b). These signals are of special interest because they have been commonly misclassified as earthquakes by earthquake detection algorithms; they constituted about 20% of EQTransformer (Mousavi *et al.*, 2020) detections for station HQIL in 2015 (Thomas *et al.*, 2023). For lower *k*-values, these transitional signals were combined into large clusters (>3000 events) of high-amplitude long-duration events.

Selecting a *k*-value of 12 resulted in a silhouette score of 0.36, which indicates fair clustering structure but strong overlapping. This overlapping quality was evident in our visualization analysis because a few small clusters (<30 events) contained similar blast events. Although choosing a smaller *k* would reduce this overlapping and produce a higher silhouette coefficient, we decided to compromise on this consequence in exchange for a strong, distinct cluster of transitional signals. It is less time-consuming to manage multiple small clusters, which ideally should be combined, compared to sifting through large clusters to find a few signals of interest. Hence, we finalized our workflow with a *k*-value of 12, as supported by our qualitative approach.

Model fitting

Our final *k*-means clustering model was trained on 21,293 anomalous events detected by the PSD misfit detector in 3 weeks of HQIL data (1–21 August 2017). We used the 10 features listed in Table 1 and a *k*-value of 12. We trained the final model using *scikit-learn* (Pedregosa *et al.*, 2011) and its default parameters for *k*-means clustering (*k*-means++ initialization of cluster centroids, Lloyd's algorithm). Hereafter, we refer to this model as the pretrained model.

Application and Analysis

We applied the pretrained clustering model to 654,410 ten-second windows of anomalous events detected by the PSD misfit detector in two years of HQIL data (June 2017–June 2019). Applying the pretrained model to both the 3-week training data set and the full two-year data set produced similar clusters and cluster distributions. During workflow development, we also evaluated the clustering performance of a *k*-means model trained on the full two-year data set. Our decision to use the pretrained model in the final workflow is described in detail in the Discussion section.

To characterize each cluster and identify potential noise sources, we analyzed the average spectra and a subset of waveforms in each cluster of the two-year data set. We also examined their temporal occurrences using heat maps. This analysis identified four major event types that characterize one or multiple clusters in our data set. Table 2 provides descriptions of the four event types and their distribution in both the

TABLE 2
Description, Potential Sources, and Cluster Distribution of Detected Event Types

Type	Description	Potential Source(s)	Cluster Label(s)	Distribution: Training	Distribution: All Data
A	Long-duration (>10 s) man-made noise, dominated by 11 Hz energy (characteristic of eight-pole motors). Predominantly occurs during weekday daytime hours.	Operation of industrial machinery (e.g., conveyor belt with an eight-pole motor)	0,2,5,7,10	98.5%	98.6%
B	Transitional signals (turning ON signals) with similar waveform and spectral features as type A events. Signals typically have high STA/LTA ratios.	Turning ON of type A machinery	11	1.35%	1.20%
C	High-amplitude, short-duration (<10 s) blasts, dominated by high-frequency energy (>30 Hz). Signals typically have a maximum amplitude on the order of 0.001 m/s across all components. Predominantly occurs between 11:00 a.m. and 02:00 p.m. local time on weekdays.	Surface blasts at the nearest quarry (<1 km from HQIL)	1,4,6,8,9	0.06%	0.10%
D	Low-amplitude blast-like events of mixed sources. Signals have a maximum amplitude that are about 1–3 orders of magnitude lower than type C signals. Occurs during a wide range of hours, but predominantly from 12:00 p.m. to 02:00 p.m. local time.	Quarry blasts with source distances ≥1 km from station HQIL (D1), underground explosions at the nearest quarry (D2), wind interaction with local structures (D3)	3	0.06%	0.11%

STA/LTA, short-term average/long-term average.

training set (1–21 August 2017) and the entire two-year data set. Figures 5 and 6 show example waveforms and spectrograms, respectively, of each event type.

Our visual analysis of the two-year data set revealed a moderately strong degree of cluster coherence. With the exception of cluster 3 (event type D), events within a cluster generally had similar spectral features and likely originated from the same source (e.g., industrial machinery, surface quarry blasts). However, some cluster overlapping was observed. When visualizing a randomized subset of events, about 70% of the events in each cluster matched the description given in Table 2; the remaining events were either misclassified or consisted of signals not clearly associated with any of the event types described in Table 2.

As discussed in the Number of clusters section, selecting a high k-value of 12 resulted in multiple clusters containing the same event type. These events were likely grouped into different clusters based on their temporal occurrence. For example, clusters 0 and 2 contain events with similar waveforms and spectra, indicating a similar source or event type. However, cluster 0 events predominately occur between 12:00 and 03:00 p.m. local time while cluster 2 events predominately occur between 06:00 and 08:00 p.m. local time. These temporal distinctions are of minor significance to our analysis and discussion. Therefore, we will proceed by referring to events based on their event types rather than their assigned cluster labels.

As detailed in Table 2, type A events are characterized by monochromatic waveforms, long durations (>10 s), and a peak frequency at 11 Hz, indicative of an eight-pole motor (Groos and Ritter, 2009). A potential source is the operation of heavy industrial machinery, such as a conveyor belt, at the nearest quarry operation. Type B events are similar in spectral and temporal features to type A events, but they are transitional signals (i.e., turning ON of machinery). Type C events are the highest-amplitude events recorded in station HQIL. They are short-duration (<10 s) events, dominated by energy at frequencies >30 Hz. From previous correspondence with local quarry representatives and residents, a few type C events have been confirmed as surface blasts from the nearest quarry operation to HQIL.

Type D events consist of blastlike events with diverse waveforms, which are generally lower in amplitude and longer in duration than type C blasts. They are of special interest because many type D events have waveform features that are similar to local earthquakes. Although there are at least five different types of event waveforms (and thus sources) within type D, the majority of D events can be grouped into two subtypes: subtype D1) waveforms of a 3–4 s duration that are dominated by frequencies below 20 Hz (Fig. 5d, left panel) and subtype D2) waveforms of a 5–10 s duration and peak frequencies above 20 Hz (Fig. 5d, center panel). D1 and D2 events make up about 17% and 46% of all D events, respectively. Both D1 and D2 events occur predominately during early afternoon hours of weekdays.

D1 events have similar waveforms and timing to type C blasts but are longer in duration and lower in amplitude, suggesting they may also be quarry blasts but from a farther distance. Many D1 events show signs of air-wave arrivals that occur between 2.5 and 3.5 s after the first arrival, indicating source distances of about 1 km. There are two quarry operations within a 5 km radius of HQIL. Type C events are surface blasts from the nearest operation and D1 events are likely surface blasts from the second operation.

Compared to D1 events, D2 events have a more complex seismic signature. Generally, D2 events are composed of 5–15 bursts with variable time intervals between bursts. From previous correspondence with local quarry representatives, one D2 event was confirmed as an underground blast at the nearest quarry operation. To further test this potential source of D2 events, we applied our PSD misfit detector and pretrained model to the 6-month period preceding the quarry's official transition to underground blasting. When analyzing cluster 3 (type D) events, we did not detect any events that strongly resembled D2 events, indicating that underground explosions are the likely source for D2 events.

Although few in number, we also detected 11 events (D3 events, Fig. 5d, right panel) that have features that look like *P*- and *S*-wave arrivals. All D3 detections occurred during late afternoon or early evening hours. This temporal trend and their high-frequency content suggests that D3 events are not earthquakes. D3 events closely resemble wind-generated signals characterized in Johnson *et al.* (2019, see their fig. 9). The earthquake-like signals of the 2019 study are generated from wind interaction with local vegetation and structures (Johnson *et al.*, 2019). An independent investigation is needed to verify that D3 events are indeed wind-generated.

Labeled Data Set

Using the results of our clustering analysis, we created a labeled data set of 1262 events recorded by station HQIL. Links to metadata and three-component seismograms (stored as miniSEED files) are provided in Data and Resources. Each miniSEED file is 20 s in duration, containing 10 s before and after the onset of each event. The data set contains all type C and type D1-3 events detected during our two-year study period. There are 176 type C, 75 type D1, 199 type D2, and 12 type D3 events. We also include a subset of type A and type B events (400 events each). Note that our workflow detected thousands of types A and B events in our two-year data set. However, due to the manual inspection procedure described subsequently, we only included a subset of these events.

For each event in the data set, we manually inspected their waveforms and spectrograms to (1) confirm that the event type matches the description given in Table 2, (2) check for any hidden transient event signals in both the 10 s detection window and the preceding 10 s window, and (3) manually pick the onset time for each event. Because we used overlapping (50%) 10 s windows, the window start time of an event may not coincide with its real onset (or first wave arrival) (see Fig 5). Onset times are not applicable for type A events, so their "onset times" are the same as their window start times.

Discussion

Our motivation and methodology for seismic exploration in built environments are similar to those of Saadia and Fotopoulos (2023) and Chai *et al.* (2025), who also apply an unsupervised learning approach to an urban or industrial setting. In this study, we develop and apply our workflow to a longer, multiyear data set in a unique urban and industrial environment. Unlike previous studies, we place a special focus on impulsive, blast- and earthquake-like signals and create a labeled data set that can be used to improve future earthquake detection and discrimination methods.

In designing our workflow, our guiding philosophy was to start with the simplest approach and to iteratively add complexity until we were satisfied with the clustering performance on three weeks of continuous HQIL data. In particular, we visually inspected the waveforms of clustered events after each addition or modification to confirm that they produced a visually discernable improvement in cluster coherence and interpretability. As an example, early iterations of our workflow did not have a detection stage: we initially applied *k*-means to all overlapping windows in continuous HQIL data. Implementing the PSD misfit detector prior to clustering produced one of the most substantial improvements in our results. Without this detection stage, *k*-means primarily generated small clusters of high-amplitude surface blasts (type C), with smaller-amplitude blastlike events (type D) and transitional signals (type B) hidden in large clusters of mixed waveforms.

In line with our guiding philosophy, we began and ultimately finalized our workflow with one of the simplest clustering algorithms: *k*-means. After including a detection stage and expanding our feature space with higher-order statistics (skewness and kurtosis), the *k*-means algorithm consistently generated coherent, interpretable clusters of diverse anomalous events in our data set. In the past decade, more advanced clustering methods (e.g., HDBSCAN as used by Chai *et al.*, 2025) have been developed to provide a more robust approach for exploratory data analysis (e.g., Campello *et al.*, 2013). Implementing such clustering algorithms may further improve our clustering performance and alleviate some of our major challenges (*k*-selection and type D subclustering). Comparing the implementation and performance of different unsupervised learning approaches is a promising direction for our future work. Our labeled data set and the complex built environment of station HQIL offers a unique testbed for such comparisons.

As mentioned in the Application and Analysis section, we explored two options for clustering our two-year data set: (1) applying the pretrained model (model trained on the three-week data set) and (2) training a new k-means model on the full two-year data set using the same parameters as the pretrained model. Option 2 was theoretically ideal because it incorporates the full variability of anomalous events in the two-year data set. However, when we visualized the clusters of option 2, we found that the transitional signals (type B) were hidden in large clusters of type A events. This is understandable because the features differences between type A and type B events are relatively small compared to the differences between these events and higher-amplitude blastlike events (types C and D). It is possible that a different k-value or set of initial centroids may generate a well-separated cluster of type B events for a model trained on the two-year data set. We finalized our workflow with the pretrained model because it produced clusters of similar coherence to the clusters of the 3-week training data set. This analysis indicates that our workflow may be highly sensitive to clustering parameters, particularly the k-value. At the same time, it also demonstrates the success of our parameter selection process, which produced a clustering model that generalizes well to a larger data set. When adapting our workflow to a different built environment, we strongly recommend following a similar procedure of qualitatively assessing clustering performance across different k-values. We also suggest exploring local news sources and collaborating with local entities to ensure that no major disruptions or transitions (e.g., moving from surface to underground mining) occurred during the period used to train the clustering model. If prior knowledge of local operations is limited, it will be beneficial to tune and train the clustering model on a larger, randomized subset of days within your desired study period.

Another promising area for workflow improvement and comparison is with respect to the dynamic PSD misfit detector. Our approach accommodates the most prominent source of variation in HQIL data: diurnal fluctuations. However, weekday–weekend and seasonal variations also impact HQIL noise, although to a lesser extent. Incorporating these additional variations into the PSD misfit detector may produce a more diverse range of detections (e.g., sports stadium events, aircraft signals, etc.), particularly on low-noise days such as Sundays. During our workflow development, we considered using separate background PSDs for weekdays and weekends. However, we ultimately omitted this distinction after observing that the local quarry frequently operates on Saturdays.

Our relatively simple workflow produced coherent, interpretable clusters in a noisy two-year data set. With only one exception, the majority of events in each cluster shared similar waveforms and thus the same source. Cluster 3 (type D) events needed to be manually subdivided for analysis. It is possible to automate this process by training another clustering model only on type D events. Incorporating frequency-based features into the original clustering model may also achieve cluster separation for type D events.

Despite the heterogeneous setting of station HQIL (Fig. 1), the majority of detected events were related to the nearest quarrying operation. This is understandable as the quarry is the closest noise source and their blasts produce the largest shaking events in the area. In addition to different types of blasts, our workflow detected low-amplitude machinery operations, notably type A events, which do not have a sudden amplitude change in the detected 10 s window or a preceding 40 s window. These types of events would not have been detected by strictly amplitude-based methods like the STA/LTA ratio method (Allen, 1978), which require high relative amplitudes with respect to a preceding "noise" window. Using a PSD detector in our workflow, we were able to detect and characterize a diverse range of operations at the local quarrying facility. Thus, similar to Chai *et al.* (2025), our study demonstrates how seismometers can be a cost-effective and multiuse tool for industrial facility monitoring. When coupled with additional sensors, our workflow can be adapted to identify and locate anomalous operations in an industrial setting.

Finally, by building a labeled data set of 1262 events with their potential sources, we demonstrate how our workflow can be used to extract interpretable clusters of signals in a noisy data set and create an event catalog. With the persistent challenge of earthquake and tremor detection in built environments, it can be critical to create/expand catalogs of dynamic nontectonic events, such as the Exotic Seismic Events Catalog (Bahavar *et al.*, 2019). Nontectonic catalogs can be used to train or refine detection algorithms to better accommodate man-made events with quake- or tremorlike features. They can also be used to identify the sources of unknown events and potentially motivate new applications in urban and environmental seismology. Because our workflow is based on a single-station approach, we acknowledge that our simple data set is limited in its attributes and capacity. We cannot provide reliable source locations for our events. In the future, we hope to install a small network of sensors in the same environment and apply our workflow to create a robust catalog of located events. We plan to add these located events to the Exotic Seismic Events Catalog (Bahavar *et al.*, 2019) for the community to easily access and visualize.

Conclusions

To explore the seismic landscape of a unique urban and industrial environment of the Chicago area, we developed a workflow to detect and cluster anomalous events in continuous data from a single broadband seismometer. Our workflow uses a PSD misfit detector and a k-means clustering model for detecting and clustering, respectively. The workflow utilizes simple and intuitive features, which can be applied to other built environments. When applied to 2 yr of continuous single-station data in the Chicago area, we detected and clustered over 650,000 windows of anomalous events. With one exception, our workflow produced coherent clusters of events with similar waveforms and likely the same source. One cluster needed to be manually subdivided into individual subclusters for event characterization. By analyzing the temporal and spectral features of each cluster and subcluster, we successfully identified several sources for our detections, including industrial machinery operations, surface quarry blasts, underground blasts, and earthquake-like signals that are potentially wind-generated. Using our results, we created a labeled data set of 1262 anomalous events. Expanding seismic catalogs to include dynamic nontectonic events is critical for improving earthquake detection and discrimination in noisy built environments. Our study demonstrates how a simple two-stage workflow can be used to efficiently mine a noisy multiyear data set and build a labeled catalog of dynamic nontectonic events.

Data and Resources

The code used in this study is available on GitHub at https://github.com/am-thomas/SeismoExplore-Chicago and has been archived on Zenodo at https://zenodo.org/records/15047293. Both websites were last updated on March 2025. Metadata and waveforms of their labeled data set can be accessed on Zenodo at https://zenodo.org/records/15047874 (last modified May 2025). HQIL waveforms and metadata are publicly available; they were accessed using the facilities of EarthScope Consortium. These services are funded through the National Science Foundation's Seismological Facility for the Advancement of Geoscience (SAGE) Award under Cooperative Agreement EAR-1724509. Their code is written in Python and utilizes tools from NumPy (Harris *et al.*, 2020), SciPy (Virtanen *et al.*, 2020), ObsPy (Beyreuther *et al.*, 2010), and Scikit-learn (Pedregosa *et al.*, 2011). Visualizations were created using Matplotlib (Hunter, 2021) and Seaborn (Waskom, 2021).

Declaration of Competing Interests

The authors acknowledge that there are no conflicts of interest recorded.

Acknowledgments

The authors would like to express their gratitude to the local quarry representatives for allowing the broadband station HQIL to be installed on their land and for valuable discussion. The authors also thank the EarthScope Primary Instrument Center (EPIC, formerly The Incorporated Research Institutions for Seismology [IRIS] Program for the Array Seismic Studies of the Continental Lithosphere [PASSCAL] Instrument Center) for loaning auxiliary and primary instrumentation. For their analysis, the authors thank Christopher W. Johnson for his feedback during the Fall 2024 Meeting of the American Geophysical Union, particularly in suggesting that some of their unknown earthquake-like events may be wind-generated. The authors are also grateful to Caio Ciardelli for his helpful feedback and suggestions during the development of their workflow and presentation of results. This research was supported in part through the computational resources and staff contributions provided for the Quest high-performance computing facility at Northwestern University which is jointly supported by the Office of the Provost, the Office for Research, and Northwestern University Information Technology.

References

Allen, R. V. (1978). Automatic earthquake recognition and timing from single traces, *Bull. Seismol. Soc. Am.* **68,** no. 5, 1521–1532, doi: 10.1785/BSSA0680051521.

Bahavar, M., K. E. Allstadt, M. Van Fossen, S. D. Malone, and C. Trabant (2019). Exotic seismic events catalog (ESEC) data product, *Seismol. Res. Lett.* **90,** no. 3, 1355–1363, doi: 10.1785/0220180402.

Beyreuther, M., R. Barsch, L. Krischer, T. Megies, Y. Behr, and J. Wassermann (2010). ObsPy: A python toolbox for seismology, *Seismol. Res. Lett.* **81,** no. 3, 530–533, doi: 10.1785/gssrl.81.3.530.

Boese, C. M., L. Wotherspoon, M. Alvarez, and P. Malin (2015). Analysis of anthropogenic and natural noise from multilevel borehole seismometers in an urban environment, Auckland, New Zealand, *Bull. Seismol. Soc. Am.* **105,** no. 1, 285–299, doi: 10.1785/0120130288.

Caplan-Auerbach, J., K. Marczewski, and G. S. Bullock (2024). Beast quake (Taylor's version): Analysis of seismic signals recorded during two Taylor swift concerts in Seattle, July 2023, *GSA Today* **34,** 4–10, doi: 10.1130/GSATG589A.1.

Campello, R. J. G. B., D. Moulavi, and J. Sander (2013). Density-based clustering based on hierarchical density estimates, in *Advances in Knowledge Discovery and Data Mining*, J. Pei, V. S. Tseng, L. Cao, H. Motoda, and G. Xu (Editors), Springer, Berlin, Heidelberg, 160–172, ISBN 978-3-642-37456-2, doi: 10.1007/978-3-642-37456-2_14.

Chai, C., O. Marcillo, M. Maceira, J. Park, S. Arrowsmith, J. O. Thomas, and J. Cunningham (2025). Exploring continuous seismic data at an industry facility using unsupervised machine learning, *Seism. Rec.* **5,** no. 1, 64–72, doi: 10.1785/0320240046.

Díaz, J., M. Ruiz, P. S. Sánchez-Pastor, and P. Romero (2017). Urban seismology: On the origin of earth vibrations within a city, *Sci. Rep.* **7,** no. 1, 15296, doi: 10.1038/s41598-017-15499-y.

Díaz, J., M. Schimmel, M. Ruiz, and R. Carbonell (2020). Seismometers within cities: A tool to connect earth sciences and society, *Front. Earth Sci.* **8,** doi: 10.3389/feart.2020.00009.

Green, D. N., I. D. Bastow, B. Dashwood, and S. E. J. Nippress (2016). Characterizing broadband seismic noise in central London, *Seismol. Res. Lett.* **88,** no. 1, 113–124, doi: 10.1785/0220160128.

Groos, J. C., and J. R. R. Ritter (2009). Time domain classification and quantification of seismic noise in an urban environment, *Geophys. J. Int.* **179,** no. 2, 1213–1231, doi: 10.1111/j.1365-246X.2009.04343.x.

Guenaga, D. L., C. Chai, M. Maceira, O. E. Marcillo, and A. A. Velasco (2021). Seismically detecting nuclear reactor operations using a power spectral density (PSD) misfit detector, *Bull. Seismol. Soc. Am.* **111,** no. 3, 1378–1391, doi: 10.1785/0120200267.

Harris, C. R., K. J. Millman, S. J. van der Walt, R. Gommers, P. Virtanen, D. Cournapeau, E. Wieser, J. Taylor, S. Berg, N. J. Smith, *et al.* (2020). Array programming with NumPy, *Nature* **585,** no. 7825, 357–362, doi: 10.1038/s41586-020-2649-2.

Hunter, J. D. (2021). Matplotlib: A 2d graphics environment, *Comput. Sci. Eng.* **9,** no. 3, 90–95, doi: 10.1109/MCSE.2007.55.

Jakkampudi, S., J. Shen, W. Li, A. Dev, T. Zhu, and E. R. Martin (2020). Footstep detection in urban seismic data with a convolutional neural network, *The Leading Edge* **39,** no. 9, 654–660, doi: 10.1190/tle39090654.1.

Johnson, C. W., Y. Ben-Zion, H. Meng, and F. Vernon (2020). Identifying different classes of seismic noise signals using unsupervised learning, *Geophys. Res. Lett.* **47,** no. 15, e2020GL088353, doi: 10.1029/2020GL088353.

Johnson, C. W., H. Meng, F. Vernon, and Y. Ben-Zion (2019). Characteristics of ground motion generated by wind interaction with trees, structures, and other surface obstacles, *J. Geophys. Res.* **124,** no. 8, 8519–8539, doi: 10.1029/2018JB017151.

Karasözen, E., and M. E. West (2022). An adaptive spectral subtraction algorithm to remove persistent cultural noise, *Bull. Seismol. Soc. Am.* **112,** no. 5, 2297–2311, doi: 10.1785/0120210317.

Li, C., Z. Li, Z. Peng, C. Zhang, N. Nakata, and T. Sickbert (2018). Long-period long-duration events detected by the IRIS community wavefield demonstration experiment in Oklahoma: Tremor or train signals? *Seismol. Res. Lett.* **89,** no. 5, 1652–1659, doi: 10.1785/0220180081.

Li, Y. E., E. A. Nilot, Y. Zhao, and G. Fang (2023). Quantifying urban activities using nodal seismometers in a heterogeneous urban space, *Sensors* **23,** no. 3, 1322, doi: 10.3390/s23031322.

Lloyd, S. (1982). Least squares quantization in PCM, *IEEE Trans. Inf. Theory* **28,** no. 2, 129–137, doi: 10.1109/TIT.1982.1056489.

Maher, S. P., M. E. Glasgow, E. S. Cochran, and Z. Peng (2024). Distinguishing natural sources from anthropogenic events in seismic data, *Seismol. Res. Lett.* **96,** no. 1, 1–6, doi: 10.1785/0220240330.

McNamara, D., and R. Buland (2004). Ambient noise levels in the continental United States, *Bull. Seismol. Soc. Am.* **94,** 1517–1527, doi: 10.1785/012003001.

Mousavi, S. M., and G. C. Beroza (2023). Machine learning in earthquake seismology, *Annu. Rev. Earth Planet. Sci.* **51,** 105–129, doi: 10.1146/annurev-earth-071822-100323.

Mousavi, S. M, W. L. Ellsworth, W. Zhu, L. Y. Chuang, and G. C. Beroza (2020). Earthquake transformer—An attentive deep-learning model for simultaneous earthquake detection and phase picking, *Nat. Commun.* **11,** no. 1, 3952, doi: 10.1038/s41467-020-17591-w.

Pedregosa, F., G. Varoquaux, A. Gramfort, V. Michel, B. Thirion, O. Grisel, M. Blondel, P. Prettenhofer, R. Weiss, V. Dubourg, *et al.* (2011). Scikit-learn: Machine learning in Python, *J. Machine Learn. Res.* **12,** 2825–2830, doi: 10.48550/arXiv.1201.0490.

Quiros, D. A., L. D. Brown, and D. Kim (2016). Seismic interferometry of railroad induced ground motions: body and surface wave imaging, *Geophys. J. Int.* **205,** no. 1, 301–313, doi: 10.1093/gji/ggw033.

Riahi, N., and P. Gerstoft (2015). The seismic traffic footprint: Tracking trains, aircraft, and cars seismically, *Geophys. Res. Lett.* **42,** no. 8, 2674–2681, doi: 10.1002/2015GL063558.

Ritter, J. R. R., S. F. Balan, K.-P. Bonjer, T. Diehl, T. Forbriger, G. Mărmureanu, F. Wenzel, and W. Wirth (2005). Broadband urban seismology in the Bucharest metropolitan area, *Seismol. Res. Lett.* **76,** no. 5, 574–580, doi: 10.1785/gssrl.76.5.574.

Saadia, B., and G. Fotopoulos (2023). Unsupervised clustering of ambient seismic noise in an urban environment, *Comput. Geosci.* **179,** 105432, doi: 10.1016/j.cageo.2023.105432.

Snover, D., C. W. Johnson, M. J. Bianco, and P. Gerstoft (2020). Deep clustering to identify sources of urban seismic noise in Long Beach, California, *Seismol. Res. Lett.* **92,** no. 2, 1011–1022, doi: 10.1785/0220200164.

Thomas, A. M., O. Ranadive, and S. van der Lee (2023). Towards detecting small, local earthquakes in greater Chicago using single-station data, *AGU Fall Meeting Abstracts* (S31D–0377).

Vaezi, Y., and M. Van der Baan (2015). Comparison of the STA/LTA and power spectral density methods for microseismic event detection, *Geophys. J. Int.* **203,** no. 3, 1896–1908, doi: 10.1093/gji/ggv419.

Virtanen, P., R. Gommers, T. E. Oliphant, M. Haberland, T. Reddy, D. Cournapeau, E. Burovski, P. Peterson, W. Weckesser, J. Bright, *et al.* (2020). SciPy 1.0: Fundamental algorithms for scientific computing in python, *Nat. Methods* **17,** no. 3, 261–272, doi: 10.1038/s41592-019-0686-2.

Waskom, M. L. (2021). Seaborn: statistical data visualization, *J. Open Source Software* **6,** no. 60, 3021, doi: 10.21105/joss.03021.

Watt, J., R. Borhani, and A. K. Katsaggelos (2016). *Machine Learning Refined: Foundations, Algorithms, and Applications*, Cambridge University Press, First Ed., ISBN 978-1-107-12352-6.

Welch, P. (1967). The use of fast Fourier transform for the estimation of power spectra: A method based on time averaging over short, modified periodograms, *IEEE Trans. Audio Electroacoust.* **15,** no. 2, 70–73, doi: 10.1109/TAU.1967.1161901.

Yang, L., X. Liu, W. Zhu, L. Zhao, and G. C. Beroza (2022). Toward improved urban earthquake monitoring through deep-learning-based noise suppression, *Sci. Adv.* **8,** no. 15, eabl3564, doi: 10.1126/sciadv.abl3564.

Yuan, C., and H. Yang (2019). Research on k-value selection method of k-means clustering algorithm, *Multidisciplinary Scientific J.* **2,** no. 2, 226–235, doi: 10.3390/j2020016.

Zhang, Y., Y. E. Li, H. Zhang, and T. Ku (2019). Near-surface site investigation by seismic interferometry using urban traffic noise in Singapore, *Geophysics* **84,** no. 2, B169–B180, doi: 10.1190/geo2017-0798.1.

Manuscript received 26 March 2025
Published online 1 August 2025

Revisiting Seismological Discoveries of the Inner Core

OPEN ACCESS

Adam T. Ringler[*1], Pritwiraj Moulik[2,3], Thomas Lee[2,4], David C. Wilson[1], and Robert E. Anthony[1]

Abstract

Seismology has been used as a tool for understanding the current physical properties of the interior of the Earth and its dynamic evolution with remarkable success over the last century. Much of this progress is due to the ever-expanding set of high-quality quantitative observations of teleseismic waveforms recorded at seismographic stations worldwide. In this work, we revisit historical seismological studies that helped first identify a core distinct in physical properties from the overlying mantle, followed by the detection of an inner core that was eventually verified to be solid based on normal-mode eigenperiods. Along with a brief overview of past studies of the Earth's inner core, we examine the reproducibility of these results and discuss how historical data compare against modern observations. After accounting for past normal-mode misidentifications, we confirm that introducing a solid inner core is required to afford significant improvements in fits to both radial modes and core-sensitive spheroidal overtones. Strong shear dissipation in the inner core of the radial reference Earth model, REM1D ($Q_\mu = 89.54$), fits the reference datasets of both normal-mode eigenperiods and quality factors accounting for physical dispersion. Because a liquid region would only have bulk dissipation, a narrow range of low Q_μ values that are preferred by the reference datasets affords additional evidence of a solid inner core. In addition, we find that there is little systematic bias in the timing accuracy of historical data, although large variances exist. Investigations into the temperature, composition, and evolution of the inner core, as well as the reproducibility of past studies, can benefit from the reconciliation of historical and modern seismological datasets.

Cite this article as Ringler, A. T., P. Moulik, T. Lee, D. C. Wilson, and R. E. Anthony (2025). Revisiting Seismological Discoveries of the Inner Core, *Seismol. Res. Lett.* **97**, 451–470, doi: 10.1785/0220250069.

Introduction

Probing the interior structure of the Earth has been a fundamental application of seismology starting at the turn of the twentieth century. Such work arguably began with Oldham (1906), where he used the identification of two distinct travel-time curves to suggest that the interior of the Earth contains a core. Extending this work, Gutenberg (1913) was able to quantify the radius of the core to be 3471 km, an estimate remarkably close (±0.2%) to the modern reference value of 3480 km (Dziewonski and Anderson, 1981; Moulik and Ekström, 2025a,b). These pioneering works motivated the use of seismic waves from earthquakes to characterize the physical properties of the Earth. Following this line of inquiry, Lehmann (1936) provided the first unambiguous observational evidence of an inner core. Observed arrival times of core-traversing compressional waves (*PKP*) were shown to be better explained by introducing a discontinuity in the core with a radius of 1404 km and a higher compressional velocity (Fig. 1). Introducing this structural complexity also explains the core phase triplication where three distinct branches of the compressional wave (PKP_{ab}, PKP_{bc}, and PKP_{df}) follow slightly different trends based on their bottoming depths within the core (e.g., d_{bot} for *PKP* branches follow $ab < bc < df$; Fig. 2). The naming convention of PKP_{ab}, PKP_{bc}, and PKP_{df} were introduced by Jeffreys and Bullen (1940). Before this Gutenberg and Richter (1938) introduced them as P_1', P_2', and P''. For a detailed discussion on the naming convention of body-wave phases, we refer the reader to Bormann *et al.* (2013). The lack of modern seismological techniques such as ray tracing (Buland and Chapman, 1983; Crotwell *et al.*, 1999) or radially varying velocity models (Fig. 1; e.g., Dziewonski and Anderson, 1981;

1. U.S. Geological Survey, Albuquerque Seismological Laboratory, Albuquerque, New Mexico, U.S.A., https://orcid.org/0000-0002-9839-4188 (ATR); https://orcid.org/0000-0001-7089-8846 (REA); 2. Department of Geosciences, Princeton University, Princeton, New Jersey, U.S.A., https://orcid.org/0000-0002-9976-8938 (PM); https://orcid.org/0000-0002-0227-8239 (TL); 3. Lamont-Doherty Earth Observatory of Columbia University, Palisades, New York, U.S.A.; 4. Geology Department, College of Natural and Health Sciences, University of Hawai'i at Hilo, Hilo, Hawai'i, U.S.A.

*Corresponding author: aringler@usgs.gov

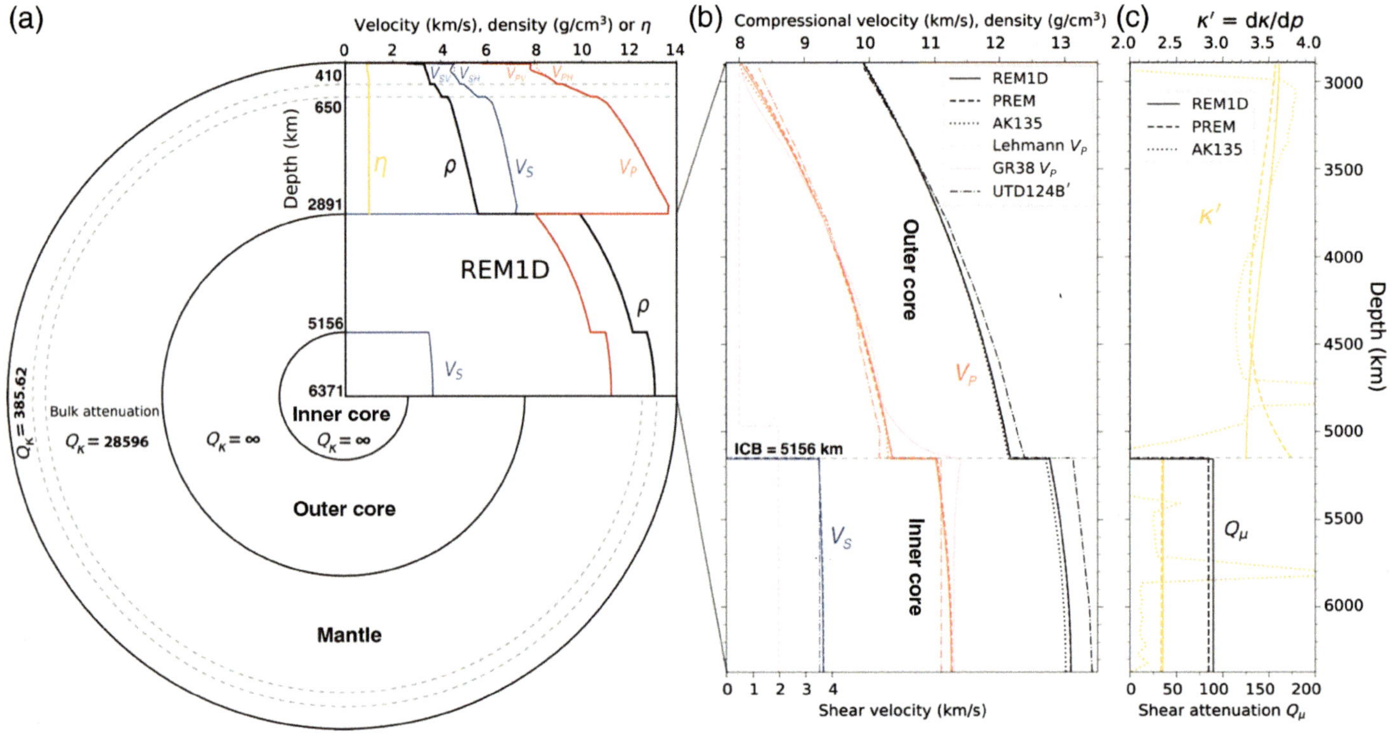

Figure 1. Core properties from the radial reference Earth model (REM1D) (Moulik and Ekström, 2025a,b). Values of radially anisotropic parameters, bulk attenuation (Q_κ), and density for (a) the whole Earth and (b) core, including Lehmann (1936), Gutenberg and Richter (1938), and Dziewonski and Gilbert (1972, UTD124B′). (c) Shear attenuation (Q_μ) and pressure derivative of bulk modulus $\kappa' = d\kappa/dp$. The ostensibly minor deviations (<1%) relative to the preliminary reference Earth model (PREM; Dziewonski and Anderson, 1981) and body-wave velocity model (AK135; Kennett *et al.*, 1995) lead to significant differences in data fits and thermochemical interpretations.

Kennett *et al.*, 1995; Moulik and Ekström, 2025a,b) complicated the testing of various hypotheses on the thermochemical state of the inner core. Despite these limitations, Gutenberg and Richter (1938) estimated the radius of the inner core to be ~1200 km, close (±1%) to the modern reference value of 1215 km (Moulik and Ekström, 2025a,b). Following this work, Birch (1940, 1952) suggested the possibility of a solid inner core and provided the possible quantitative parameters. In addition, Bullen (1950) estimated travel times for the possibility of shear waves in the inner core, which began the search for the elusive *PKJKP* phase (e.g., Okal and Cansi, 1998) that could provide direct body-wave evidence for the solidity of the inner core. However, direct observations have proven difficult because of the small amplitude of the signals (Shearer *et al.*, 2011). More recently, groups have attempted to use various stacking methods from arrays (e.g., Tkalčić *et al.*, 2022).

In the context of normal-mode theory (e.g., Dahlen and Tromp, 1998), body waves can be understood as various superpositions of spheroidal (*P–SV* phases; e.g., *PKP*) and toroidal modes (*SH* phases; e.g., *ScS*). The normal modes excited by an earthquake are categorized as spheroidal modes ${}_nS_l$ (*P–SV* motion) or toroidal modes ${}_nT_l$ (*SH* motion) with radial order n and angular order l. Large earthquakes ($M_w > 7.5$) strongly excite overtones ($n > 0$) that propagate as body waves that traverse the entire mantle and core (e.g., *PKIKP*-equivalent modes ${}_9S_0$, ${}_8S_1$). The superposition and interactions of several mode overtones that propagate with similar group velocities manifest as relatively impulsive body-wave arrivals in the time domain, which are recorded in various seismic catalogs (e.g., U.S. Geological Survey, International Seismological Centre [ISC]). In addition to identifying the arrival times of body-wave phases in time-domain seismograms, measuring the eigenperiods/eigenfrequencies and amplitude decay (e.g., quality factor Q) of the corresponding normal modes in the frequency domain is crucial for understanding the core structure.

Using normal-mode eigenperiods calculated for Earth models with either a solid or a liquid inner core and comparing them to the observations, Dziewonski and Gilbert (1971) provided observational verification of the solid inner core. Later still, the anisotropic nature of the inner core was identified using observations of anomalously split normal modes (e.g., Woodhouse *et al.*, 1986; Tromp, 1995). Although normal modes inform our understanding of the bulk properties of the inner core, much of the finer-scale structure is constrained using shorter-period body waves (<50 s dominant period; e.g., PKP_{df}, PKP_{ab}, and PKP_{bc}). Short-period body waves are used for this purpose because they are sensitive to small-scale structure and discontinuities, whereas longer-period body waves can have a Fresnel zone that is larger

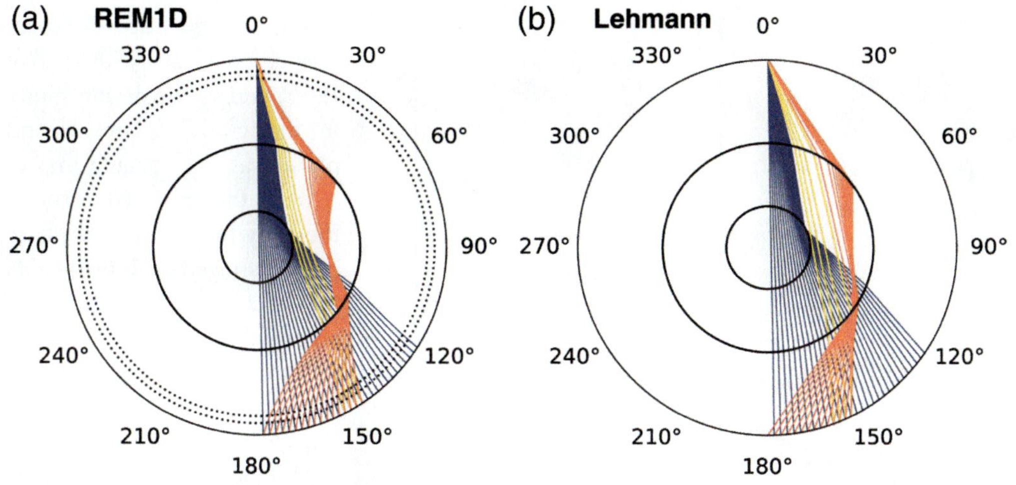

Figure 2. (a) Triplication of the core-traversing *PKP* phase. PKP_{ab} (solid red), PKP_{bc} (solid yellow), and $PKP_{df}/PKIKP$ (solid blue) through (a) the radial REM1D (Moulik and Ekström, 2025a,b). (b) Same as (a) but for the piecewise constant velocity model from Lehmann (1936). Note that the core radius is 1215 km in REM1D and 1404 km in the Lehmann model. The source lies at the surface on the equator, ellipticity is ignored, and the ray is traced at epicentral distances between 118° and 180° spaced 2° apart. Note that the body waves in the Lehmann model do not follow curved paths and $PKP_{ab/bc}$ branches bottom shallower in the outer core (4186 km depth at ~152° for bc) relative to REM1D (5075 km depth).

than the inner core (Deuss, 2014). For example, recent studies have used short-period body waves to propose 3D tomographic models of the uppermost inner core, efforts enabled by digital datasets of increasing size and quality as well as improved computational resources (e.g., Burdick *et al.*, 2019). However, even with the availability of high-quality data, some studies report using less than 10% of the available data because many records do not meet quality control criteria (e.g., Waszek and Deuss, 2013). This suggests that many studies are still relatively data-limited, as very few events meet the various quality control methods necessary to make robust observations.

Beyond understanding the thermochemical state of the inner core, seismological studies have also proposed the detection of temporal changes in the travel time of waves passing through the inner core based on several decades of global instrumentation (e.g., Song and Richards, 1996). These observations have sometimes been interpreted as changes in the rotation rate of the inner core. Such a change in relative rotation rate would imply that the inner core is not gravitationally locked to the mantle, in contrast to some dynamical expectations (e.g., Buffett, 1996). Although there are multiple data and modeling issues that could be producing inconsistencies (e.g., Tkalčić, 2024), temporal changes in the inner core would manifest as subtle signals and require very high-precision timing over long-time spans for a robust detection (Cormier *et al.*, 2021). Accurate estimation of the rotation of the inner core will require reconciliation with changes in the underlying physical properties (e.g., anisotropy or density changes; Richards, 2000; Krasnoshchekov *et al.*, 2005).

The goal of this work is to investigate the reproducibility of historical work by reviewing a few steps that led to the current understanding of the inner core and to quantify some of the limitations arising from data and processing methodologies. Instead of providing a comprehensive review, we refer the reader to Kölbl-Ebert (2001) for an overview of Lehmann (1936), while general overviews of the seismology of the core can be found in Bolt (1982), Souriau and Calvet (2015), Tkalčić (2017), and Cormier *et al.* (2021). Modern reference values of core properties based on full-spectrum tomography, which incorporates diverse astronomic–geodetic, surface-wave, normal-mode, and body-wave observations (~1–3200 s), are described by the radial reference Earth model (REM1D; Moulik and Ekström, 2025a,b). REM1D affords the average physical properties (V_P, V_S, radial anisotropy, density, shear, and bulk attenuation) of the heterogeneous Earth and serves as the update of the preliminary reference Earth model (PREM; Dziewonski and Anderson, 1981). The arrivals of major core phases (e.g., *PKIKP*) predicted by anisotropic REM1D are consistent (±0.25 s) with the isotropic body-wave model AK135 (Kennett *et al.*, 1995) that was optimized for earthquake location. Properties in the upper crust are extended to the surface, and the ocean is removed when tracing body waves through REM1D in the rest of the article. We first look at the arrival tables of Oldham (1906) and point out a curiosity in the identified phases. Next, we revisit the work of Lehmann (1936) and compare her velocity model and data to modern data, and find that much of the data provided at the time is consistent with the modern data but has a larger spread in the arrival-time residuals. We then revisit the work of Dziewonski and Gilbert (1971) and compare the historically reported mode eigenfrequencies to those estimated as part of the new reference dataset (Moulik and Ekström, 2025a). We also report new inner-core solidity experiments with shear attenuation (Q_μ) based on the quality factor (Q) measurements of normal modes. Finally, we point out some of the limitations in inner-core body-wave rotation studies when various simplifications in processing are used and how these could potentially introduce errors in the arrival times.

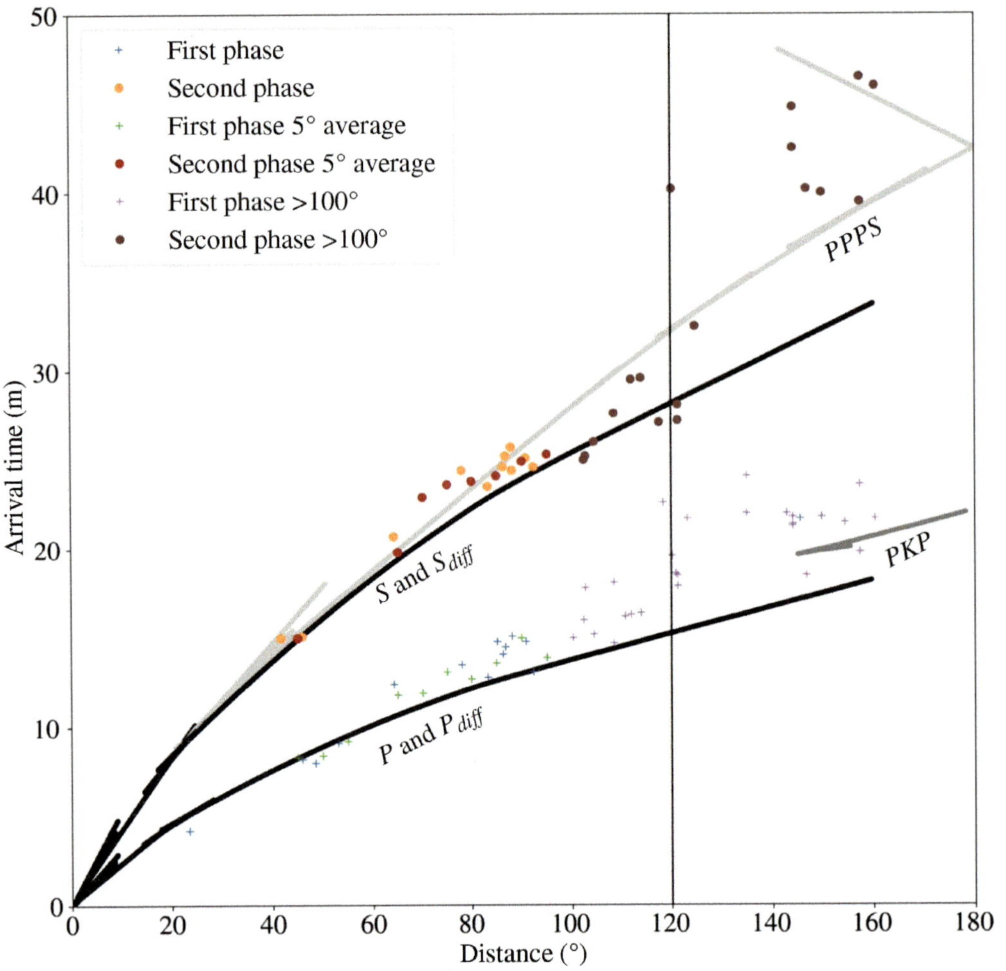

Figure 3. First arrival phases of Oldham (1906) as well as averages are shown as plus signs, and second phase arrivals are shown as circles. For reference, we have included arrival times from the radial REM1D (Moulik and Ekström, 2025a,b) for *P* and P_{diff} (black), *S* and S_{diff} (black), and *PPPS* and *PKP* (gray).

Discovery of the Core

Oldham (1906) provided seismic evidence for the existence of a core. He did this by identifying two different phase arrivals that he referred to as the first and second phase (Fig. 3), which were likely P/P_{diff} and S/S_{diff}. However, for the second phase, he also used several arrivals that were likely *PPPS* or other bounce phases that did not travel through the core. Oldham (1906) argued that the discontinuity in the second phase could be explained by the existence of a core with a slower velocity. He did not attempt to explain the composition of the core and even conceded that the data were too limited at the time to warrant further interrogation of the core.

Curiously, all the arrivals used by Oldham (1906) were consistently late relative to the modern REM1D, with a mean residual of 1.5 min for the first phase and 0.9 min for the second phase. Oldham (1906) acknowledged several possible sources of error, such as picking errors or earthquake time and location errors. It is possible that he misidentified the second phase at distances greater than 120° with that of *PPPS*, and so the discontinuity in the arrival of the second phase was not actually that of a wave that traveled through the core, but a different phase branch altogether. It is possible that his distant first phase arrivals (e.g., >140°) were *PKP* and did travel through the core along relatively straight ray paths. Oldham (1906) did suggest the possibility that the second phase was unable to travel through the core, but he rejected this in favor of the hypothesis that the core produced a slower velocity of 4.5 km/s for the second phase.

Although Oldham (1906) was data-limited due to large uncertainties in arrival times and earthquake locations, he introduced the concept of using seismic data to study the interior of the Earth and reported evidence for the existence of a core. However, we contend that his line of reasoning for the existence of the core was likely predicated on misidentified body-wave phases. Muir and Tsai (2020) also point out that the scatter in the data used in Oldham (1906) is problematic for making interpretations, and Brush (1980) pointed out that some of the data recorded at large distances are unreliable. However, this work did open the door to understanding these radial transitions in the Earth as well as the composition of various regions (Jeffreys, 1926).

The Inner Core

The discovery of the inner core was made by introducing a discontinuity that helped explain the triplicated phase branch PKP_{ab}, PKP_{bc}, and PKP_{df} (Fig. 2). Before the work of Lehmann (1936), the Earth was assumed to contain an entirely liquid core at a depth of 2900 km. Lehman calculated that no *PKP* phases would be observed with this kind of Earth model until an epicentral distance of 153.9° (e.g., orange and yellow curves in Fig. 2b). However, she noted that this conflicts with recordings of *PKP* phases at shorter distances (down to ~120°) that, due to advances in seismic instrumentation at the time,

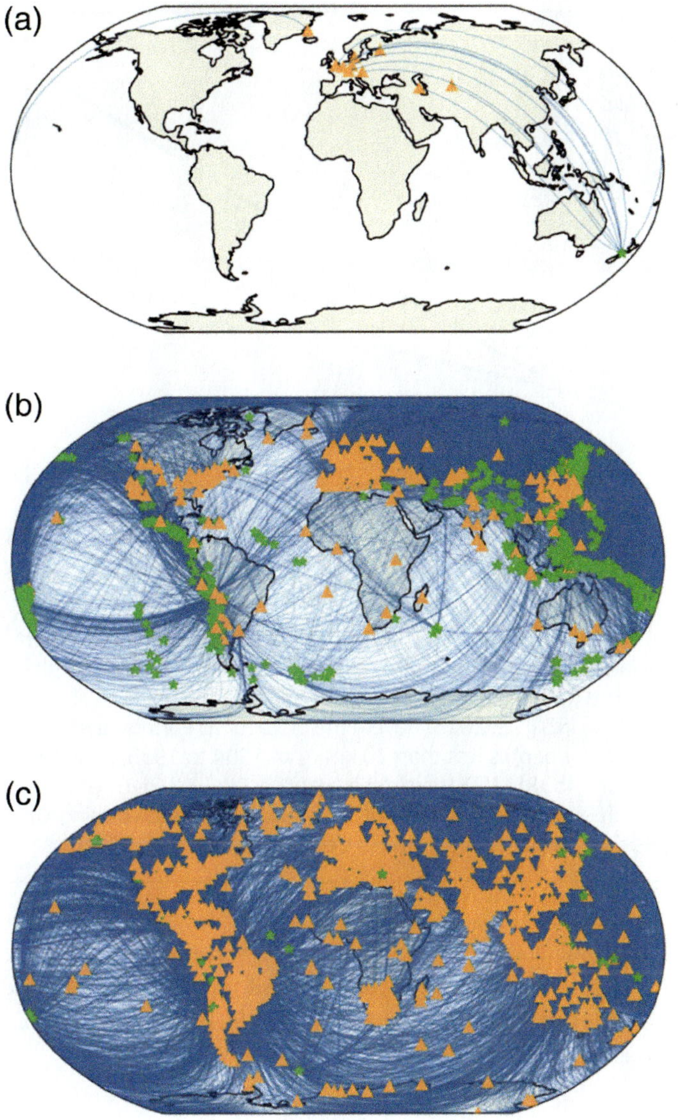

Figure 4. (a) Great-circle paths (blue) from earthquakes (green stars) to stations (orange triangles) for the 10 arrivals found in the International Seismological Centre (ISC) (ISC, 2025) bulletin used in Lehmann (1936). (b) Same as (a) but for the 7177 PKP_{df}, PKP_{ab}, and PKP_{bc} arrivals in the ISC (2025) bulletin between 1904 and 1935. (c) Same as (b) but for the 12,444 arrivals of *M* 7.0 and greater earthquakes between 1 January 2019 and 31 December 2021 in the ISC (2025) catalog.

had recently been observed. To explain this observation, Lehmann (1936) proposed that an inner core with a higher seismic velocity than the outer core must exist.

To evaluate this hypothesis, Lehmann (1936) studied a very limited number of high-quality records at an epicentral distance near 150° from the 1929 M_s 7.9 Murchison earthquake off the South Island of New Zealand (Fig. 4a, Table 1). We emphasize that these triplication phases are difficult to correctly identify and pick, even with modern data and the knowledge of arrival times (Fig. 5). For example, the readings identified as PKP_{df} by the ISC in the distance range from ~145° to 153° are often PKP_{bc} arrivals (Anderssen and Cleary, 1980). This is because amplitudes of PKP_{bc} arrivals are nearly an order of magnitude greater than those of $PKP_{df}/PKIKP$. After all, the latter encounters an additional reflection/transmission of energy at the inner-core boundary. In this study, we have focused on the arrival-time variations in historical studies, which are sufficiently modeled using ray theory within the distance ranges of observational interest. Although the triplication in *PKP* arrival times is well understood from ray theory, full-wave (or normal-mode) theory is necessary to interpret the intricate details of amplitude variations (e.g., Brekhovskikh, 1960; Aki and Richards, 2002).

Although Lehmann (1936) used a very limited dataset comprising 11 stations and one event (Fig. 4a), there was decent station coverage at this time with 279 stations reporting to the ISC (Fig. 4b). However, this is an order of magnitude smaller than current station coverage; 2673 stations reported the triplicated phases in the ISC (2025) catalog between 1 January 2019 and 31 December 2021 (Fig. 4c). Although Lehmann (1936) did not attempt to estimate the radius or properties of the inner core because her work was limited to explaining the PKP_{df} arrivals at short distances, her work was widely accepted and paved the way for further detailed analysis such as the radius of the inner core which was estimated only a few years later (Gutenberg and Richter, 1938). Nevertheless, she did introduce a velocity model to explain her *PKP* observations (Figs. 1b and 6). Although the absolute timing of her velocity model requires a relatively large correction of −171.83 s at a distance of 124° to match the REM1D predictions (Fig. 7), the phase branches line up relatively well, given the lack of modern ray tracing or computers at the time.

One interesting feature of the Lehmann (1936) model is an offset (3.8 s) in arrival times between *PKP* (*ab*/*bc*) and *df* (*PKIKP*) branches at ~154° due to the uniform V_P throughout the outer core in her model, which is significantly greater than the minor offset for REM1D (~0.5 s) at ~146° (Fig. 7). It is now known that the increase in velocities with depth in the outer core can be adequately expressed as second-order polynomial to fit reference datasets and match expectations from mineral physics (Moulik and Ekström, 2025a). This leads to two changes in *PKP* phases compared to Lehmann (1936): (1) ray paths curve downward till they reach a bottoming depth (d_{bot}) based on slowness/epicentral distance and relatedly; (2) they sample faster, deeper velocities and accrue less travel time (Fig. 2). Per Fermat's principle, absent gradual V_P gradients in Lehmann's model, the ray paths for *ab* and *bc* branches travel the shortest, linear path across the outer core with uniform velocity. At an epicentral distance ~152°, the *bc* branch bottoms at a relatively shallow depth of $d_{bot} = 4186$ km and travels at a much slower outer-core velocity than in the "real" Earth represented by REM1D, where the ray bottoms at $d_{bot} = 5075$ km. This path will be substantially different from the *df* branch in the case of Lehmann (1936), and the relative difference between inner–outer-core velocities that the two branches travel through

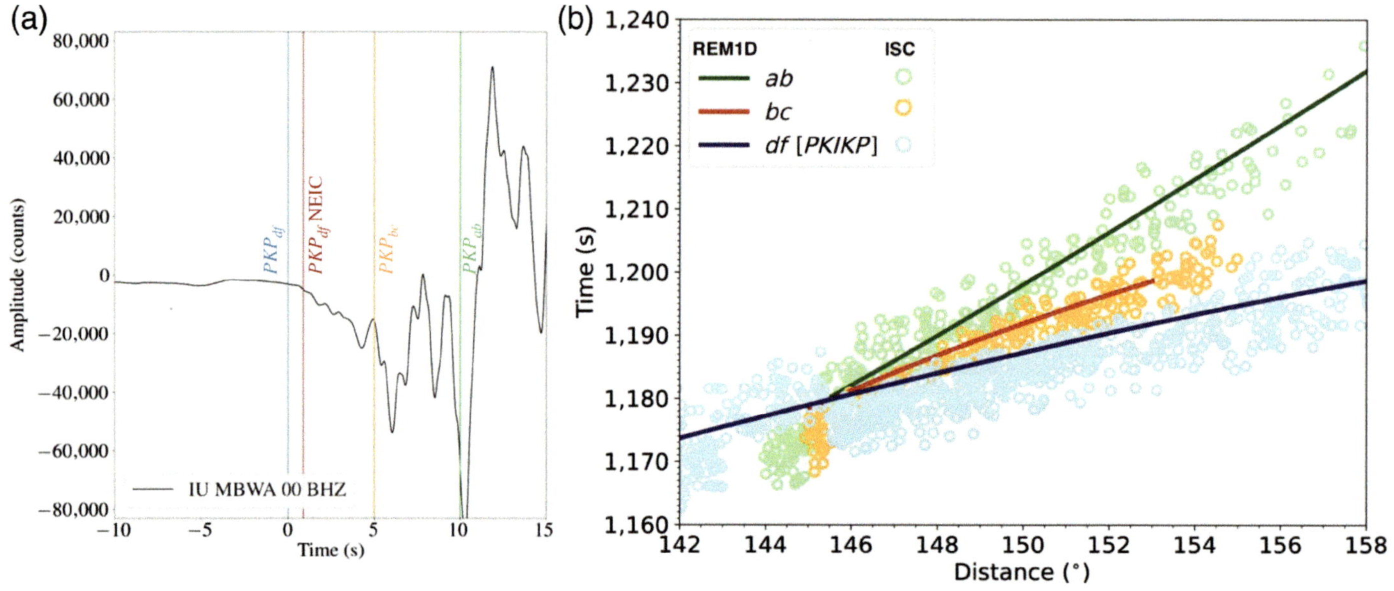

Figure 5. (a) Time-series data from the primary (location code 00) vertical-component broadband (channel BHZ) Incorporated Research Institutions for Seismology (IRIS) U.S. Geological Survey (USGS) station MBWA (Marble Bar, Western Australia) for the 26 June 2019 07:41:14.36 M_w 8.0 Peru earthquake. For reference, we have included the theoretical arrival times from the triplication PKP_{df} (blue), PKP_{bc} (orange), and PKP_{ab} (green) from radial REM1D (Moulik and Ekström, 2025a,b). Properties in the upper crust are extended to the surface, and the ocean is removed when tracing body waves through REM1D. The PKP_{df} arrival-time pick from the National Earthquake Information Center (NEIC) is shown in red. (b) ISC (ISC, 2025) travel-time picks for all earthquakes with hypocenter depths less than 20 km from 1904 to 1935, as shown in Figure 4b. REM1D travel-time branches are included for reference. It should be pointed out that during the initial picking of these phases, they would have been picked as P'.

will create an offset in arrival time. In contrast, ray paths and the outer-core V_P structure sampled by *PKP* in the REM1D model are more similar for *bc* and *df* branches, especially for the outer-core caustic at ~146°, which leads to the minor offset in arrival time. Understandably, Lehmann (1936) was not able to resolve the details of the *PKP* triplication and V_P gradients because arrivals of only a single branch (i.e., *df* or *PKIKP*) were employed in her analysis.

TABLE 1
Phase Arrival Times from the International Seismological Centre (ISC, 2025) Bulletin Used in Lehmann (1936)

Station Code	Latitude	Longitude	Distance (°)	Arrival Time (yyyy/mm/dd hh:mm:ss.ss)	Table
SCO	70.4833	−21.95	150.51	1929/06/16 23:07:06.00	5
PUL	59.7728	30.322	150.74	1929/06/16 23:07:09.00	5
COP	55.6853	12.4325	161.07	1929/06/16 23:07:19.00	6
VIE	48.2483	16.3617	162	1929/06/16 23:07:24.00	6
GTT	51.5464	9.9642	164.66	1929/06/16 23:07:35.00	6
STR	48.5845	7.7658	167.33	1929/06/16 23:07:32.00	6
UCC	50.7983	4.3594	167.93	1929/06/16 23:07:33.00	6
KEW	51.4683	−0.3131	169.28	1929/06/16 23:07:38.00	6
IRK	52.2431	104.2711	110.78	1929/06/16 23:01:57.00	7
TAS	41.325	69.295	124.45	1929/06/16 23:06:21.00	7
BAK	40.372	49.818	137.45	1929/06/16 23:06:45.00	7

First column is the station code; the second column is the station latitude; the third column is the station longitude; the fourth column is the distance of the station to the 16 June 1929 M_s 7.9 Murchison earthquake; the fifth column is the arrival time of PKP_{df}; and the sixth column is the corresponding table in Lehmann (1936).

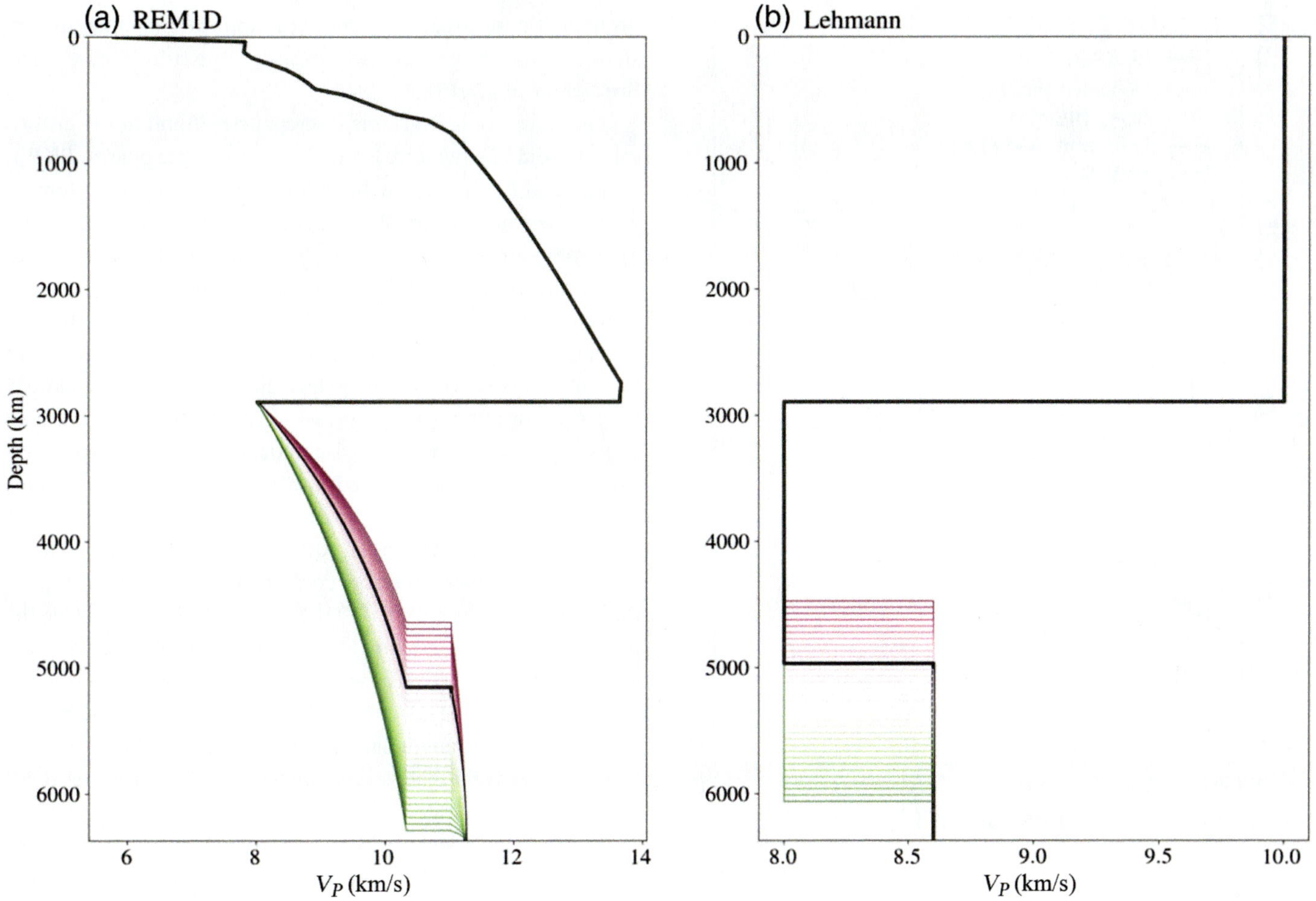

Figure 6. (a) Perturbations of the depth of the inner core and the profile of compressional velocity from radial REM1D (black; Moulik and Ekström, 2025a,b). Perturbations range from 5% shallower (pink) to 15% deeper (green). (b) Same as (a), but for the velocity model used in Lehmann (1936). The perturbed models are used to evaluate the optimal depth of the inner core based on various subsets of *PKP* datasets in Figure 8. Properties in the upper crust are extended to the surface, and the ocean is removed when tracing body waves through REM1D.

Although Lehmann (1936) used a very limited dataset of only the highest-quality records, the set of all available triplicated phases at the time is remarkably good. For example, if we perturb the REM1D inner core to fit her limited dataset (Fig. 4a) in a least-squares sense, it would yield an inner-core radius of ~1190 km, which would be ~2% deviation from the radius of 1215 km in REM1D (Fig. 8a). However, employing her piecewise constant velocity model results in a substantially larger inner-core radius that is off by more than 35% (Fig. 8b), primarily due to the trade-offs between (an overall slower outer core) velocity and (shallower) inner-core boundary while modeling arrival-time observations. Although she made use of a very limited number of stations and one earthquake, using all 7177 *PKP* phase picks available in the ISS and ISC bulletins (ISC, 2025) circa 1936 (Fig. 4b) produces a very consistent inner-core radius of 1208 km (<0.6% deviation, Fig. 8c). Note, however, that even if one assumes that Lehmann had access to the full set of bulletins, quite a feat without the data accessibility granted by modern library science and technology, processing of such a large dataset would have been difficult. Nonetheless, using about 250 events that occurred between 1918 and 1932, Gutenberg and Richter (1938) estimated the inner-core radius to be 1200 km, a result very consistent with that obtained by processing the full 1930s-era dataset with modern resources. Naturally, when a modern dataset is used, a consistent estimate of the inner-core radius is found (Fig. 8e), whereas the velocity model of Lehmann (1936) would result in an inner core with a radius ~560 km larger than modern reference values. Although the velocity models, data accessibility, and computational resources were limited at the time, given modern resources, seismologists of the 1930s would have been able to provide reasonable estimates of the inner-core radius with the datasets of the time.

We can investigate the potential biases in these datasets by looking at their statistical distributions. Figure 9 reports histograms of the residual travel times between PKP_{df}, PKP_{ab}, and PKP_{bc} picks from the ISC bulletin and those predicted from REM1D for each of the three datasets. Using the Lehmann (1936) dataset, which is composed entirely of PKP_{df} phases,

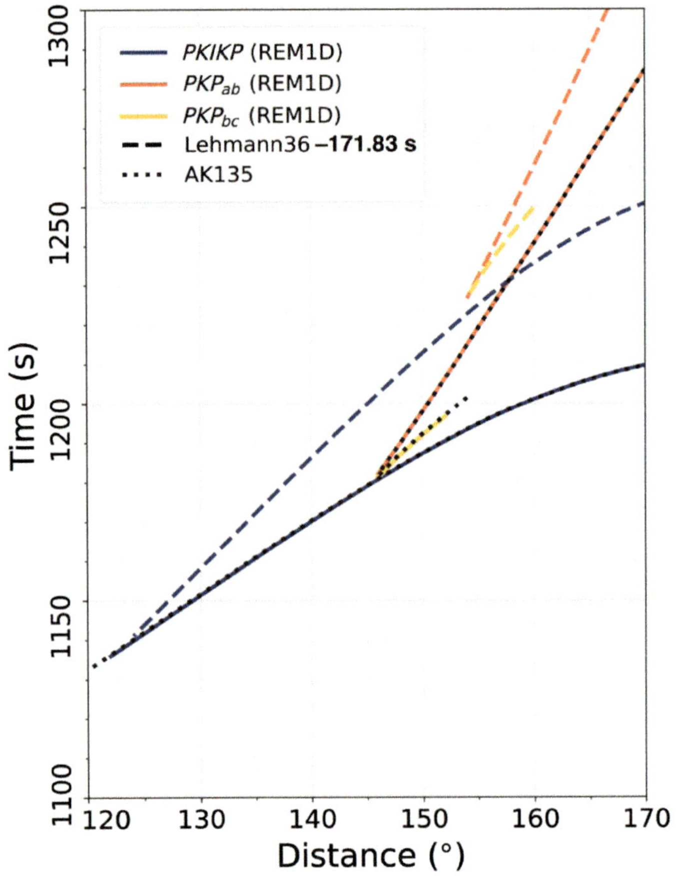

Figure 7. Arrival times as a function of distance for the triplication PKP_{ab} (solid red), PKP_{bc} (solid yellow), and $PKP_{df}/PKIKP$ (solid blue) through the radial REM1D (Moulik and Ekström, 2025a,b). Arrivals (*ab,df*) from the anisotropic REM1D model are consistent (±0.25 s) with the isotropic body-wave model AK135 (Kennett *et al.*, 1995; black dashed). We have shifted the arrivals for the model from Lehmann (1936) by −171.83 s to match the REM1D arrival-time curve at 124°. The source is a surface-focus earthquake located at the equator, and the ellipticity correction is not applied. The large offset between *PKP*(*ab/bc*) and *df* (*PKIKP*) branches at ~152° (3.8 s) is due to the constant outer-core velocity (8 km/s) in Lehmann's model (Fig. 2).

we find that the mean deviation between the expected arrival time and the observed is 4.6 s with a standard deviation of 4.1 s (Fig. 9a,d). For the historical dataset of arrivals between 1904 and 1935, we find that the mean deviation is −0.44 s with a standard deviation of 4.0 s (Fig. 9b,e). Finally, the ISC dataset from 1 January 2019 to 31 December 2020, has a mean residual of 0.029 s with a standard deviation of 1.83 s (Fig. 9c,f). The spread of the residuals suggests that there was more variance in the historical data (Fig. 9d,e) compared to modern arrival times (Fig. 9f). Although there is some systematic bias in all historical data with a mean deviation of −0.44 s (Fig. 9b,e), the spread in data is relatively large with a standard deviation of 4.03 s. It is worth noting that the mean offset of nearly 0.5 s in historical data is still enough to produce problematic residuals for modern applications like understanding the finer-scale structure of the inner core (e.g., Burdick *et al.*, 2019).

The source of arrival-time discrepancies found in the historical data could be twofold. First, picking the three phases, PKP_{df}, PKP_{ab}, and PKP_{bc} can be difficult because of the triplication, as well as their similar arrival times at certain distances (Figs. 5 and 7). Timing errors are a likely second source, including the practice of picking arrivals to the nearest 1 s, which was common in historical data (Wood, 1921). Although timing errors are still present in modern data (Ringler *et al.*, 2021), they appear to be much smaller (mean error less than 10 ms). For example, we can still see timing errors present in several ISC (2025) arrival picks (Fig. 9f). However, the systematic bias has reduced substantially in modern data, and the mean residual is only 0.029 s. This suggests that the dataset spanning 1 January 2019 to 31 December 2020 fits the radial REM1D very well, which is to be expected. The observed errors could be from stations with poor timing (e.g., Ringler *et al.*, 2021) or a misidentification of the phase. Although Lehmann (1936) mentioned only using very carefully picked arrivals, we found that the entire dataset available in ISC (2025) circa 1935 could likely have been used if sufficient computational resources were available because very few arrivals had exceptionally large outlier residuals (>5 s; Fig. 9b,e).

Many of the seismic stations used by Lehmann (1936) operated for several decades after the 1929 event used in her study. This provides an opportunity to look at changes in the mean deviation of the observed arrivals compared to the predicted arrivals as a function of time at each of these stations (Fig. 10). At a number of stations, we found decreasing residuals as a function of time. For example, station UCC (Uccle, Belgium) goes from a median residual for a decadal window centered on 1921 of 1.12–0.3 s for the decadal window centered around 2011. Looking at the medians of all stations, we note a varying but relatively constant median value (Fig. 11a). However, there is an overall trend of the standard deviations decreasing as a function of time (Fig. 11b). This suggests that observed arrival times of more recent data more closely match predicted times from the modern REM1D. Although the data before 1936 contained small systematic biases, the most dramatic improvement made in subsequent decades has been the substantial decrease in variance. Even with the improvements in accuracy, it is worth noting that even modern body-wave arrivals would not be able to identify the temperature and composition of the inner core because of their insensitivity to density structure and the difficulty in identifying phases that confirm the inner core being solid (e.g., *PKJKP*). The *PKJKP* phase is difficult to observe directly on seismograms because it loses energy when converting to the *J* phase and due to the high shear dissipation in the inner core (Shearer *et al.*, 2011), suggesting that other approaches may be necessary (e.g., arrays; Tkalčić *et al.*, 2022).

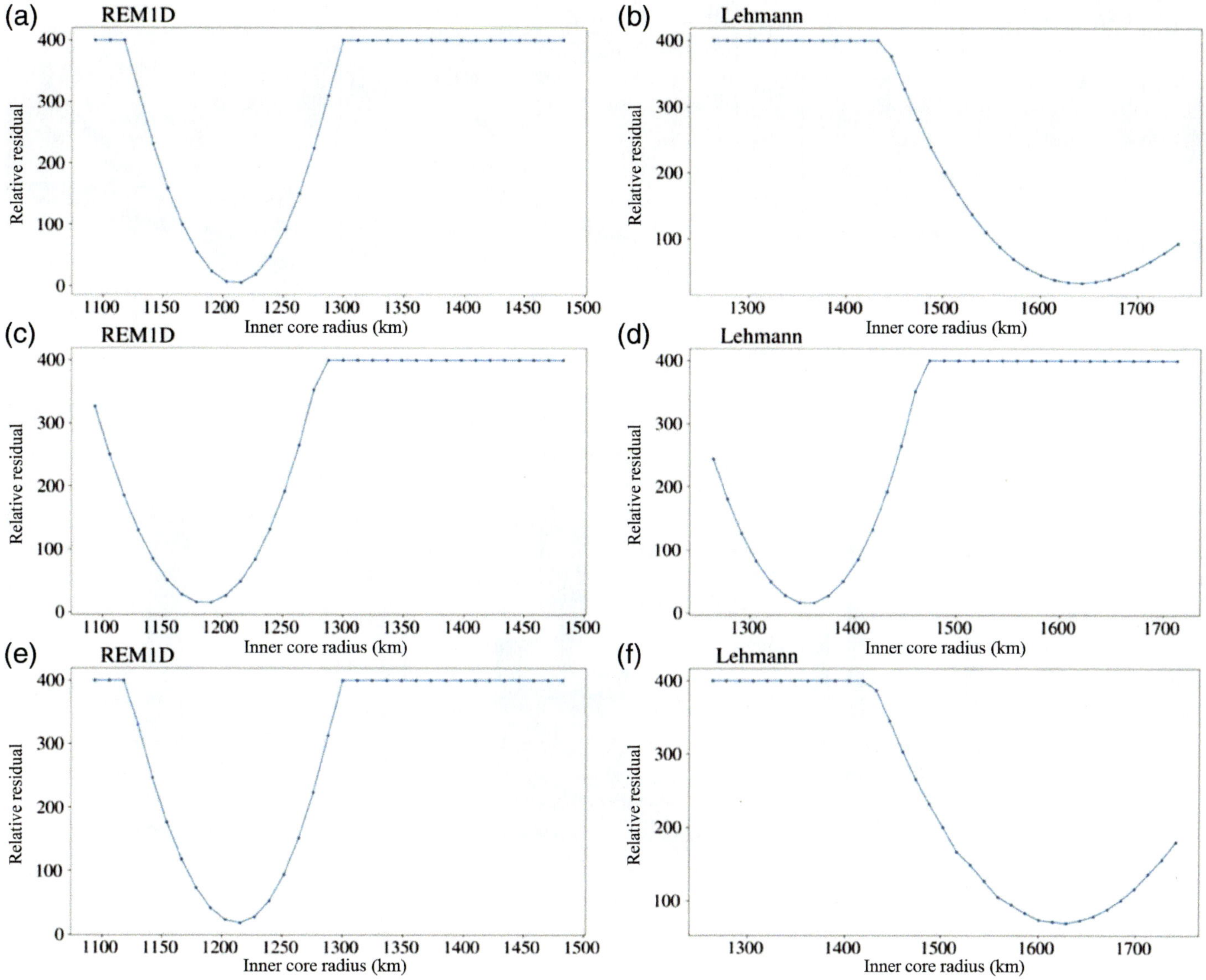

Figure 8. (a) Relative residual as a function of varying the inner-core radius of radial REM1D (Moulik and Ekström, 2025a,b) for the 11 arrivals found in the ISC (ISC, 2025) bulletin used in Lehmann (1936). (b) Same as (a) but using the velocity model from Lehmann (1936). (c) Same as (a) but for the 7177 PKP_{df}, PKP_{ab}, and PKP_{bc} arrivals in the ISC (2025) bulletin between 1904 and 1935. (d) Same as (c) but using the velocity model from Lehmann (1936). (e) Same as (c) and (f) is the same as (d) but for the 12,444 arrivals of 43 M 7.0 and greater earthquakes between 1 January 2019 and 31 December 2021 in the ISC (2025) catalog. Relative residuals are defined as the ratio of the data residual from perturbed models to that of the original velocity model (Fig. 6). Relative residuals greater than 400 have been fixed at 400 to aid interpretations.

A Solid Inner Core

After the 27 March 1964 M_w 9.2 Alaska earthquake, Dziewonski and Gilbert (1972) were able to estimate the eigenperiods/eigenfrequencies of several normal modes using analog records (digitized by hand) from stations of the WWSSN (Peterson and Hutt, 2014), a predecessor to the modern Global Seismographic Network. Based on the measurements of radial modes ${}_1S_0$, ${}_2S_0$, ${}_3S_0$, ${}_4S_0$, and spheroidal overtones ${}_2S_2$, ${}_5S_2$, ${}_6S_1$, ${}_7S_3$ ${}_8S_1$, they were able to show that the velocity model UTD124B′ with a liquid inner core was inconsistent with observations and that a solid inner core was required (Dziewonski and Gilbert, 1971). We point out that a possible piece of confusion is that the radial order n of the spheroidal-mode ${}_nS_l$ is indexed assuming no inner-core modes in Dziewonski and Gilbert (1971, 1972; Guy Masters, University of California, San Diego, personal comm., 2024). To assess this indexing issue, we calculated a dispersion diagram for the spheroidal and radial modes predicted by the radial REM1D and UTD124B′ modified to have a liquid inner core (Fig. 12). The modified UTD124B′ model does not predict the J_{SV} modes with the very high group velocities (i.e., steep slopes $d\omega/dk$ in the dispersion diagram, in which k is wavenumber) that are confined to the solid inner core in REM1D. The changes in the radial order, along with predicted mode eigenperiods from various models, are shown in

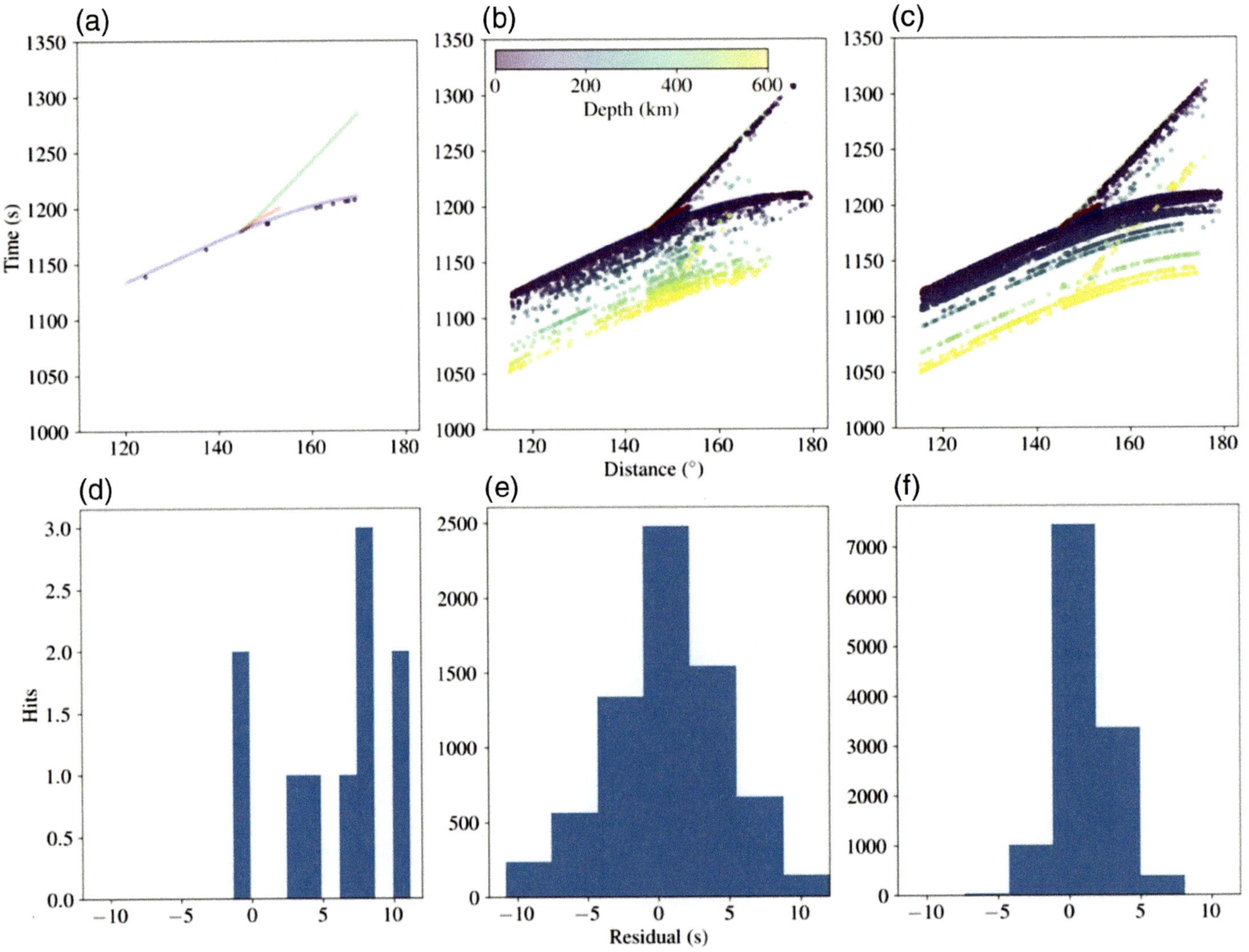

Figure 9. (a) Distances and arrival times of the phases used in Lehmann (1936) are shown in purple. The travel-time curves for PKP_{df} (blue), PKP_{ab} (green), and PKP_{bc} (red) from radial REM1D (Moulik and Ekström, 2025a,b) are also shown for reference for an event at a depth of 0 km. (b,c) Same as (a), but for the 7,177 PKP_{df}, PKP_{ab}, and PKP_{bc} arrivals in the ISC (2025) bulletin between 1904 and 1935 and for the 12,444 arrivals of M 7.0 and greater earthquakes between 1 January 2019 and 31 December 2021, in the ISC (2025) catalog, respectively. In (b) and (c), we have colored the arrival times by the depth of the event. (d) Histogram of the travel-time residuals from velocity model REM1D using the phase arrivals used in Lehmann (1936). (e) and (f) are the same as (d) but for the datasets used in (b) and (c), respectively. A zoomed-in version of (b) for shallow earthquakes is provided in Figure 5b.

Table 2; indexing with the inclusion of J_{SV} modes results in the spheroidal overtones of Dziewonski and Gilbert (1971) to correspond to ${}_3S_2$, ${}_7S_2$, ${}_8S_1$, ${}_9S_3$, and ${}_{11}S_1$ in the "real" Earth represented by REM1D. In the rest of this article, we will denote the mode from fluid inner-core models (second column of Table 2) by a prime (e.g., ${}_7S_2'$) to distinguish them from "real" Earth modes observed in the spectra of seismograms and predicted by REM1D (first column in Table 2).

Figure 13 provides the sensitivity kernels of some core-sensitive normal modes, which are functions of their displacement eigenfunctions at various depths and can be derived for the radially anisotropic REM1D model using the expressions from Mochizuki (1986). Overtone radial modes (${}_nS_0$ with $n > 0$) considered here are equivalent to radially propagating *PKIKP* waves and afford sensitivity to compressional velocity (V_P) in the whole Earth. Some spheroidal overtones are also *PKIKP* equivalent with sensitivities similar to that of the radial modes (e.g., ${}_8S_1$). When the values of the V_P sensitivity kernel are positive in the inner core, an increase in V_P within this region would cause an increase in eigenfrequencies and phase velocities and a corresponding decrease in travel time (Jeans, 1927). Note that the radial modes have large quality factors and, therefore, the decay in amplitude is substantially slower with time compared to other modes. If sufficiently long seismograms with accurate timing are available, as is the case for modern networks, the eigenperiods of these modes can be measured with high precision as reported by the new reference

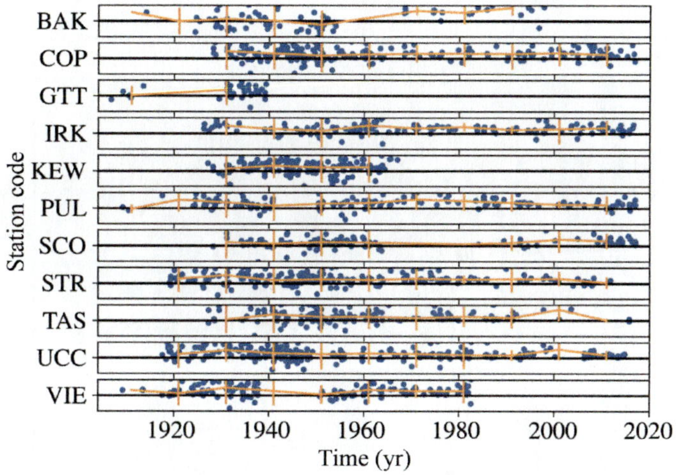

Figure 10. Station arrival-time residuals for the stations used in Lehmann (1936). The blue circles indicate individual residuals of PKP_{df} from ISC (2025) as compared to the radial REM1D (Moulik and Ekström, 2025a,b). The 10-year running medians of the arrival-time residuals, along with error bars (2.5 standard deviations), are shown in orange. The vertical window for each station is ±6 s.

dataset (Table 2; Moulik and Ekström, 2025a). This reference dataset reconciles measurements from various techniques of measuring normal-mode eigenfrequencies and quality factors, and the values are significantly different ($>2\sigma$) from the eigenperiod observations employed by Dziewonski and Gilbert (1971, 1972).

Some observed eigenfrequencies in fluid-core models by Dziewonski and Gilbert (1971) were indexed as ${}_2S_2'$ and ${}_7S_3'$, which correspond to ${}_3S_2$ and ${}_9S_3$ in models with a solid inner core. In the "real" Earth, ${}_2S_2$ and ${}_7S_3$ are J_{SV}-equivalent modes (i.e., similar in character to *PKJKP*, *SKJKS*, or *SKSKP*) and are predominantly sensitive to the shear wavespeed in the solid inner core (Fig. 13). Because J_{SV}-equivalent modes are difficult to measure due to the limited displacements at the surface, these two modes were not used in the construction of the PREM model (Dziewonski and Anderson, 1981) around a decade later, and remain excluded from the modern reference dataset and the radial REM1D. Based on the mode-ray duality, the low surface displacements of these overtone modes provide an explanation why the detection of related body-wave phases that traverse the inner core as shear waves (e.g., *PKJKP*) has remained elusive in observational seismology. Although techniques are being developed to iteratively fit spectra and glean information on these kinds of modes through coupling/resonance with other modes, these are strongly nonlinear inversions that require good starting source mechanisms and REM1Ds that have only materialized relatively recently.

Based on our calculations of modes for various inner-core scenarios, we found that ${}_7S_1'$ and ${}_9S_1'$ in fluid-core models were misidentified as ${}_6S_1'$ and ${}_8S_1'$, respectively by Dziewonski and Gilbert (1971, 1972). Throughout the article, we use ${}_nS_l'$ to denote a spheroidal mode of radial order n and angular degree l as produced by a model with a fluid core. This is evident based on our calculated eigenperiods of ${}_6S_1'$ and ${}_8S_1'$ for a modified liquid-core UTD124B′ model, which are substantially different 50<) s) from the reported eigenperiods (compare with table 1 in Dziewonski and Gilbert, 1971), while predictions for ${}_7S_1'$ and ${}_9S_1'$ are more consistent. The corresponding modes in the "real" Earth with a solid inner core are ${}_8S_1$ and ${}_{11}S_1$, respectively (Fig. 12, Table 2). It is worth noting that Dziewonski and Gilbert (1971, 1972) reported the eigenperiods of the appropriately indexed mode for solid inner-core scenarios, even though only the modes indexed with fluid inner cores are listed, albeit with the misidentification of ${}_6S_1'$ and ${}_8S_1'$. The use of correct modes for both solid/liquid inner-core scenarios helps us reproduce the trends in their reported calculations (compare with table 1 in Dziewonski and Gilbert, 1971). We document this explicitly in Table 2 to hopefully help future readers avoid this confusion.

Given the issues with the mode identification and quality of measurements employed by Dziewonski and Gilbert (1971, 1972) for their validation of a solid inner core, we reinvestigate their results using modern reference datasets and models. We calculate the eigenperiods for the modes used in Dziewonski and Gilbert (1972) for several radial models, first with a solid inner core (UTD124B′, PREM, and REM1D), and then with a liquid inner core ($V_S = 0$, $Q_\mu = 0$) retaining other parameters elsewhere in the Earth (Table 2). We find that the chi-square misfit between the reference dataset (Moulik and Ekström, 2025a) and the eigenperiods predicted by REM1D with the solid inner core ($\chi^2/N = 200$) is significantly lower than for a liquid inner core ($\chi^2/N \sim 500{,}000$), which is significant at the 99% confidence level. Only contemporary models with a solid inner core (PREM, REM1D) afford reasonable fits ($\chi^2/N \leq 200$) to the modern reference measurements of the "real" Earth modes employed by Dziewonski and Gilbert (1971).

Starting from a model with a solid outer core, the rigidity may be decreased to approach a zero value should observations require it. Several spheroidal overtones (${}_8S_1$, ${}_{11}S_1$) and radial modes are mostly compressional energy with some negative kernel values for inner-core V_S perturbations; these types of modes were categorized as group I by Dziewonski and Gilbert (1971, 1972) and would show an increase in eigenfrequency (and decrease in eigenperiod) as $V_S \to 0$ (Fig. 13). In contrast, eigenperiods of the other spheroidal overtones (group 2) would increase for a liquid inner core (Table 2). The only way to reverse the trend in eigenperiods due to $V_S \to 0$ is to reduce inner-core density relative to outer core for group 1 modes and increase the V_P (or bulk modulus) for group 2 modes (i.e., positive kernels in Fig. 13). The former scenario can be disfavored based on purely physical considerations, whereas the latter leads to inconsistencies with body-wave phases that

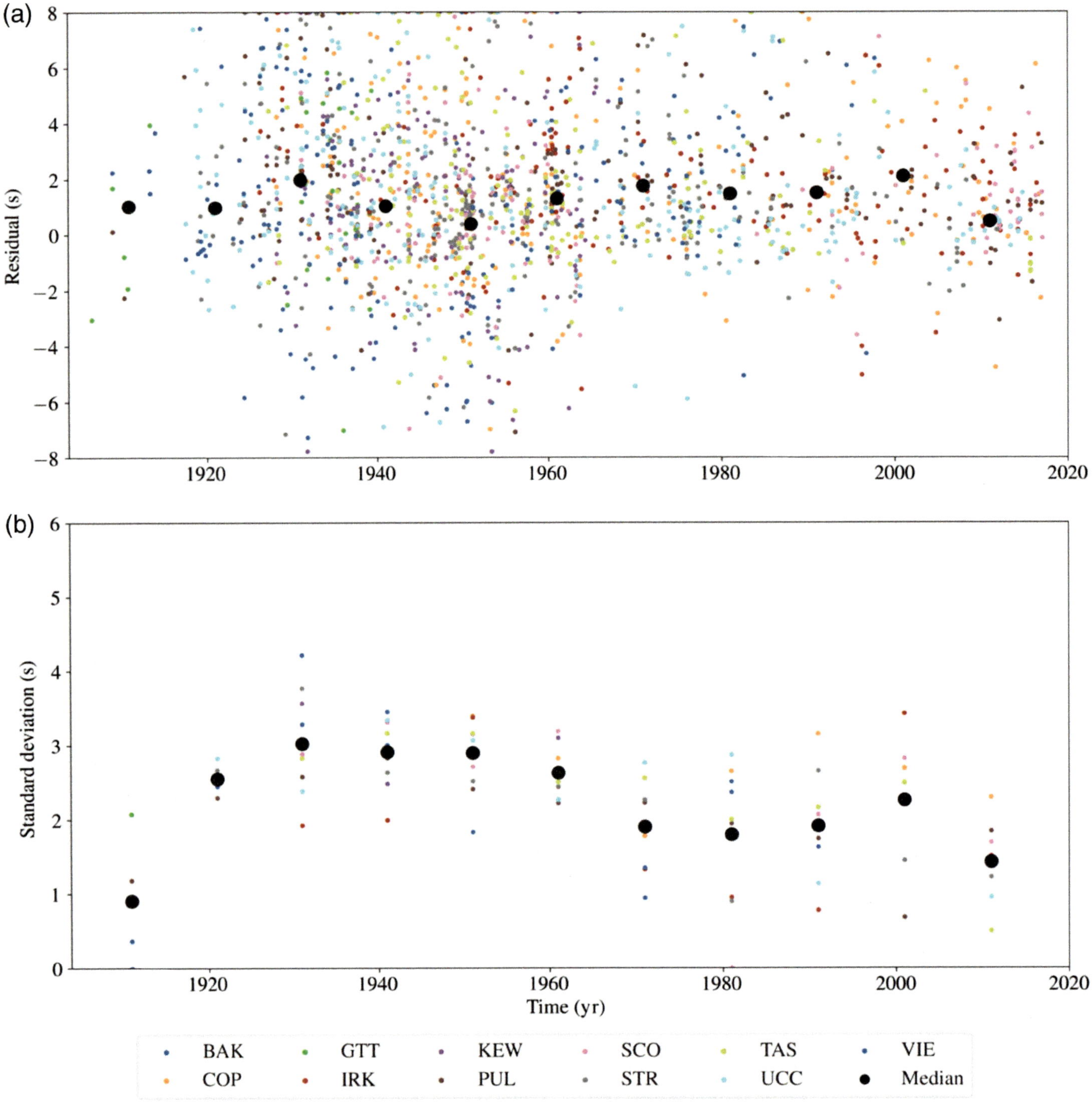

Figure 11. (a) Residuals from arrival times of PKP_{df} from the ISC (2025) as compared to the radial REM1D (Moulik and Ekström, 2025a,b) for the stations used in Lehmann (1936), which are listed in the legend. The black circle denotes the median of all stations using the 10-year medians of the mean values for each station. (b) Standard deviations using 10-year windows for each station. The median of the year windows for all stations is shown in black.

constrain the V_P structure in the inner core relatively well. Based on this trade-off during the fitting process, the basic premise of Dziewonski and Gilbert (1971, 1972) still holds true that jointly fitting the radial modes and inner-core sensitive spheroidal overtones requires invoking a solid inner core with nonzero values of V_S and shear modulus μ. It can be confusing to a reader that Dziewonski and Gilbert (1971, 1972) discuss the sensitivities of J_{SV} modes ${}_2S_2$ and ${}_7S_3$ that are not readily observed to support their solid inner-core arguments; the issue becomes clearer when their observations are attributed instead to the fluid-core modes ${}_2S_2'$ and ${}_7S_3'$ that correspond to ${}_3S_2$ and ${}_9S_3$ in the "real" Earth. Even in the absence of direct eigenperiod measurements of J_{SV} modes, other spheroidal overtones identified in our group 2 category (e.g., ${}_7S_2$) also have strong positive

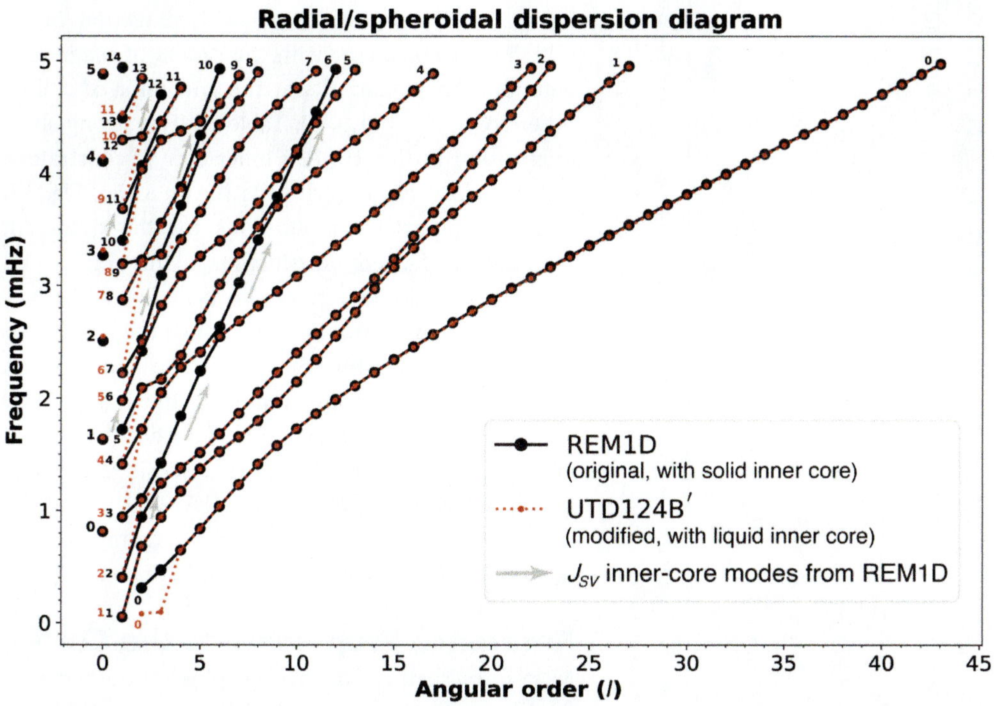

Figure 12. Dispersion diagram showing the spheroidal and radial modes predicted by the radial REM1D (Moulik and Ekström, 2025a,b). All $_nS_l$ modes below 5 mHz (eigenperiods > 200 s) are plotted versus the angular order l. Small numbers of left label denote the radial modes ($l = 0$) and the repeated numbers 0–14 denote the low frequency and high frequency ends of various overtone branches (n). Note that the modified UTD124B′ model with a liquid inner core (compare with table 1 in Dziewonski and Gilbert, 1971) does not predict the J_{SV} waves with the very high group velocities (i.e., slopes $d\omega/dk$) that are confined to the solid inner core in REM1D. Correct indexing with the inclusion of J_{SV} modes helps identify misidentified modes (Table 2).

V_S kernels in the inner core albeit with additional sensitivity to shallower structure (Fig. 13). In conjunction with other complementary datasets such as surface waves and body waves, the modern radial REM1D is able to exclude trade-offs with shallow sensitivities and robustly constrain the inner-core variations (Moulik and Ekström, 2025a,b).

Since Dziewonski and Gilbert (1972) started their work on verifying the solidity of the inner core with a starting model in which the inner core was solid, sensitivity kernels of misidentified spectral peaks (e.g., $_6S_1^{'}$ and $_8S_1^{'}$) would influence the structural inversion. For example, the misidentification and structural modeling of $_8S_1$ in observed spectra as $_6S_1^{'}$ in liquid-core models (in lieu of $_7S_1^{'}$) by Dziewonski and Gilbert (1971) may explain the substantially larger residuals from UTD124B′ ($\chi = -55$) compared to REM1D ($\chi = -8$). Conflating two modes with different structural sensitivities during identification from waveform spectra can lead to large data residuals. In addition, these calculations were all done before Woodhouse (1976) suggested a correction to Backus and Gilbert (1968) for normal-mode frequency and perturbation calculations. This historical error in perturbation theory could have led Dziewonski and Gilbert (1971, 1972) to inaccurately assess their resolving power and attribute data residuals to a less-than-optimal structure. However, as outlined by Woodhouse (1976), the normal modes for the derived models (e.g., with solid and liquid inner cores) could be solved by a direct calculation (e.g., Fig. 12) and checked for data fits (e.g., Table 2), so it is very unlikely there were gross errors in historical studies due to this past issue in perturbation theory.

It is now possible to look at the attenuation of core-sensitive modes, which would have been difficult in historical studies because of the limited instrumentation. Modern studies agree on a relatively high amount of shear dissipation in the inner core ($Q_\mu \sim 90$–100) based on the amplitude decay of radial and other *PKIKP*-equivalent modes (e.g., Widmer *et al.*, 1991; Moulik and Ekström, 2025b). An even more dissipative inner core would correspond to the high-attenuation limit $1/Q_\mu \rightarrow \infty$ (or $Q_\mu \rightarrow 0$) and reduce the velocity "sensed" by a long-period normal mode ($V_S \rightarrow 0$) even in case of slight rigidity (nonzero V_S and μ at the reference period of 1 s) due to physical dispersion in an anisotropic region (compare with equation 8 in Moulik and Ekström, 2025b). Figure 14 extends the inversion results in Moulik and Ekström (2025b) by performing a grid search around the reference $Q_\mu = 89.54$ in the REM1D inner core. Because of physical dispersion, a perturbed V_S profile that differs by up to ~150 m/s from the REM1D profile (valid at the reference period of 1 s) is "seen" by core-sensitive modes with longer eigenperiods (~400 s for $_7S_2$).

Figure 15 reports the chi-square misfits of the reference datasets from Moulik and Ekström (2025a) to scenarios that either suppress (higher Q_μ) or accentuate (lower Q_μ) the amount of shear dissipation in the inner core (Fig. 14). The optimal range of Q_μ, which corresponds to the minima in misfits for all modes and the subset of core-sensitive spheroidal overtones, is consistent with REM1D estimates. Both lower and higher dissipation than REM1D in the inner core leads to deterioration of fits to eigenperiods and quality factors. The significant deterioration in fits of eigenfrequencies (up to ~1000 times in Fig. 15), due to the relatively minor reduction

TABLE 2
Eigenperiods of Normal Modes Used in Dziewonski and Gilbert (1971)

"Real" Earth Solid IC Mode	D and G (1971) Liquid-Core Mode	D and G (1971) Observed	Reference Observation ± Uncertainty	Solid Inner Core (Column I, $_nS_l$)			Liquid Inner Core (Column II, $_nS'_l$)		
				UTD124B′ [χ]	PREM [χ]	REM1D [χ]	UTD124B′ [χ]	PREM [χ]	REM1D [χ]
$_1S_0$	$_1S'_0$	613.57 s	612.925 ± 0.030 s	614.64 s [−57]	612.87 s [2]	612.77 s[5]	607.44 s [183]	605.57 s [245]	605.47 s [249]
$_2S_0$	$_2S'_0$	398.54 s	398.579 ± 0.084 s	397.70 s [10]	398.27 s [4]	398.64 s [−0.7]	392.42 s [73]	392.77 s [69]	393.16 s [65]
$_3S_0$	$_3S'_0$	305.84 s	305.571 ± 0.003 s	306.11 s [−181]	305.66 s [−28]	305.63 s [−20]	301.48 s [1365]	300.83 s [1580]	300.80 s [1592]
$_4S_0$	$_4S'_0$	243.95 s	243.518 ± 0.002 s	243.92 s [−203]	243.55 s [−16]	243.59 s [−35]	241.23 s [1143]	240.78 s [1370]	240.80 s [1358]
$_3S_2$	$_2S'_2$	904.23 s	904.037 ± 0.106 s	904.54 [−5]	904.08 s [−0.4]	904.85 s [−8]	915.08 s [−104]	914.45 s [−98]	915.40 s [−107]
$_7S_2$	$_5S'_2$	397.36 s	396.723 ± 0.129 s	397.24 [−4]	397.25 s [−4]	397.07 s [−3]	400.18 s [−27]	399.64 s [−23]	399.49 s [−21]
$_8S_1$	$_7S'_1\{_6S'_1\}$	348.41 s	348.117 ± 0.006 s	348.45 [−55]	348.04 s [12]	348.16 s [−8]	347.33 s [132]	346.85 s [211]	347.02 s [183]
$_9S_3$	$_7S'_3$	281.37 s	281.174 ± 0.015 s	281.80 [−42]	281.34 s [−11]	281.19 s [−1]	282.99 s [−121]	282.38 s [−81]	282.26 s [−72]
$_{11}S_1$	$_9S'_1\{_8S'_1\}$	272.10 s	271.172 ± 0.043 s	271.97 [−19]	271.34 s [−4]	271.30 s [−3]	271.19 s [−0.4]	270.42 s [18]	270.43 s [17]
			χ^2/N =	9,195	154	200	361,213	500,000	499,448

Predictions by reference Earth model (REM1D) (Moulik and Ekström, 2025a,b) and historical models ($_nS_l$), and with the introduction of a liquid inner core ($_nS'_l$). Mean chi-square fit χ^2/N in which $\chi = [T_{obs} - T_{pred}]/\sigma$ for this subset ($N = 9$) of reference observations from REM1D. Modes misidentified by Dziewonski and Gilbert (1971) are denoted within {}. PREM, preliminary reference Earth model.

in V_S (~150 m/s) associated with reduction in Q_μ (Fig. 14), is consistent with the orders of magnitude deterioration in data fits at the end limit of a fluid inner core ($V_S = Q_\mu = 0$; Table 2). The strong shear attenuation in the REM1D inner core is constrained well based on our experiments ($Q_\mu = 89.54$; Fig. 15) and has important implications for the dominant mechanism of energy dissipation in this region that needs to be explored in future work. Note that the substantial changes in fits to eigenperiods are purely due to physical dispersion caused by shear dissipation because velocity/density structure is fixed at REM1D values in this experiment. Fits afforded by PREM are significantly worse for all core-sensitive datasets; a detailed comparison between REM1D and other radial models is provided elsewhere (compare with section 2.4 and table 2 in Moulik and Ekström, 2025b).

Reference Properties of the Core

Modern estimates of the average physical properties in the inner core are reported by REM1D (Fig. 1; Moulik and Ekström, 2025a,b). REM1D is constructed using a new reference dataset comprising normal-mode eigenfrequencies and quality factors, surface-wave dispersion curves, impedance constraints, and travel-time curves from body waves, and astronomic–geodetic observations. The inner core is a principal region that is 1215 km in radius (depth 5156–6371 km) with physical properties that increase with depth as a polynomial up to order 3. The range of REM1D physical properties in the inner core is compressional velocity ($V_P \sim 11.02$–11.25 km/s), shear velocity ($V_S \sim 3.49$–3.66 km/s), density ($\rho \sim 12.77$–13.09 g/cc), and a constant shear attenuation ($Q_\mu = 89.54$). REM1D accounts for the intertwined aspects of (an)elastic structure due to physical dispersion, affording orders of magnitude improvements in fits compared to earlier radial models of the core. REM1D is radially anisotropic in the upper mantle and is optimized to fit body-wave arrival times in agreement with widely used but theoretically incomplete isotropic models optimized for earthquake location (e.g., AK135). Historical estimates of core properties are broadly consistent with REM1D (Fig. 1); the strongest agreement (±0.2%) is on the depth of the core–mantle boundary at 3480 km while the gradients of velocities with depth and the related derivative properties (Fig. 1c) are most inconsistent due to limitations in past studies (Moulik and Ekström, 2025a).

Physical properties of the inner core derived from seismology have important implications for the temperature and composition of the Earth. Equations of state (EoS), which are used to calculate properties of minerals at high-pressure and temperature conditions (e.g., bulk

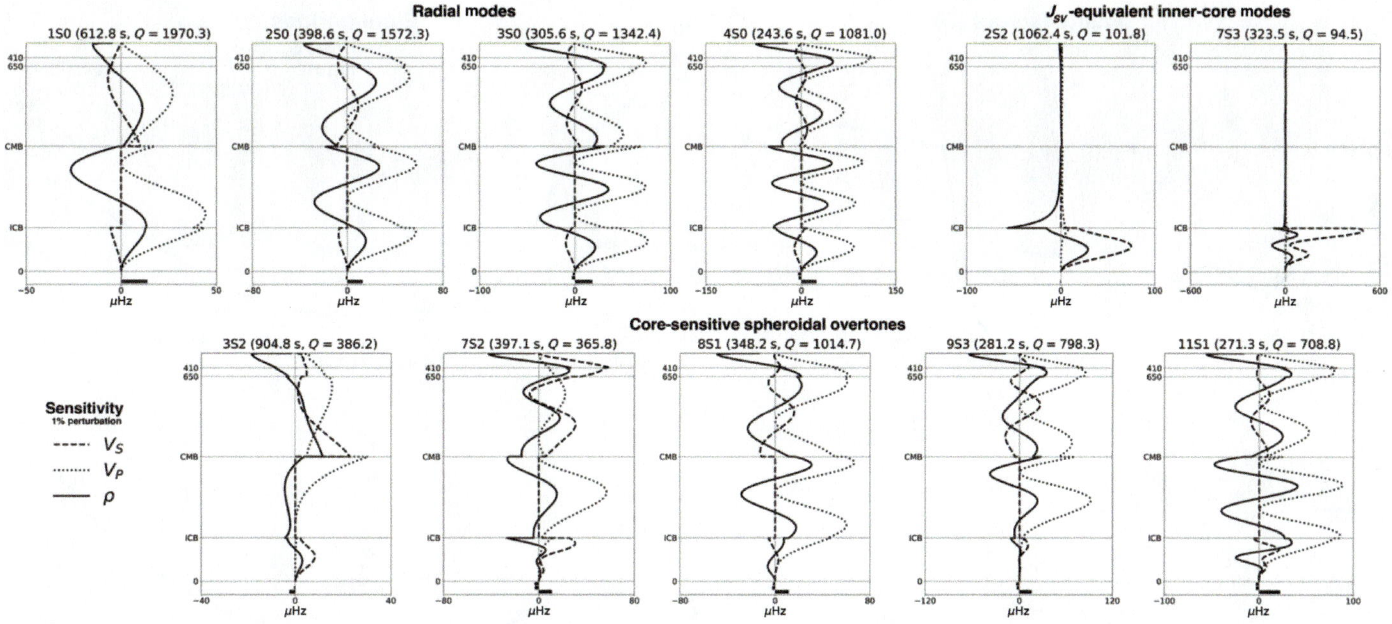

Figure 13. Sensitivity kernels of the inner-core sensitive modes employed by Dziewonski and Gilbert (1971). The kernels are calculated for perturbations of 1% using the radial REM1D (Moulik and Ekström, 2025a,b). The thick horizontal bars beneath the kernels show the mode's sensitivity (from top to bottom) to depth perturbations of the 410 and 650 km discontinuities and the core–mantle boundary. (a) Radial and (c) several spheroidal overtones are *PKIKP*-equivalent and afford V_P sensitivity. (b) J_{SV}-equivalent modes in the "real" Earth (${}_2S_2$ and ${}_7S_3$) are primarily sensitive to V_S in the solid inner core and have not been measured; ${}_2S_2'$ and ${}_7S_3'$ in the fluid-core models correspond to ${}_3S_2$ and ${}_9S_3$ and have been measured (Table 2).

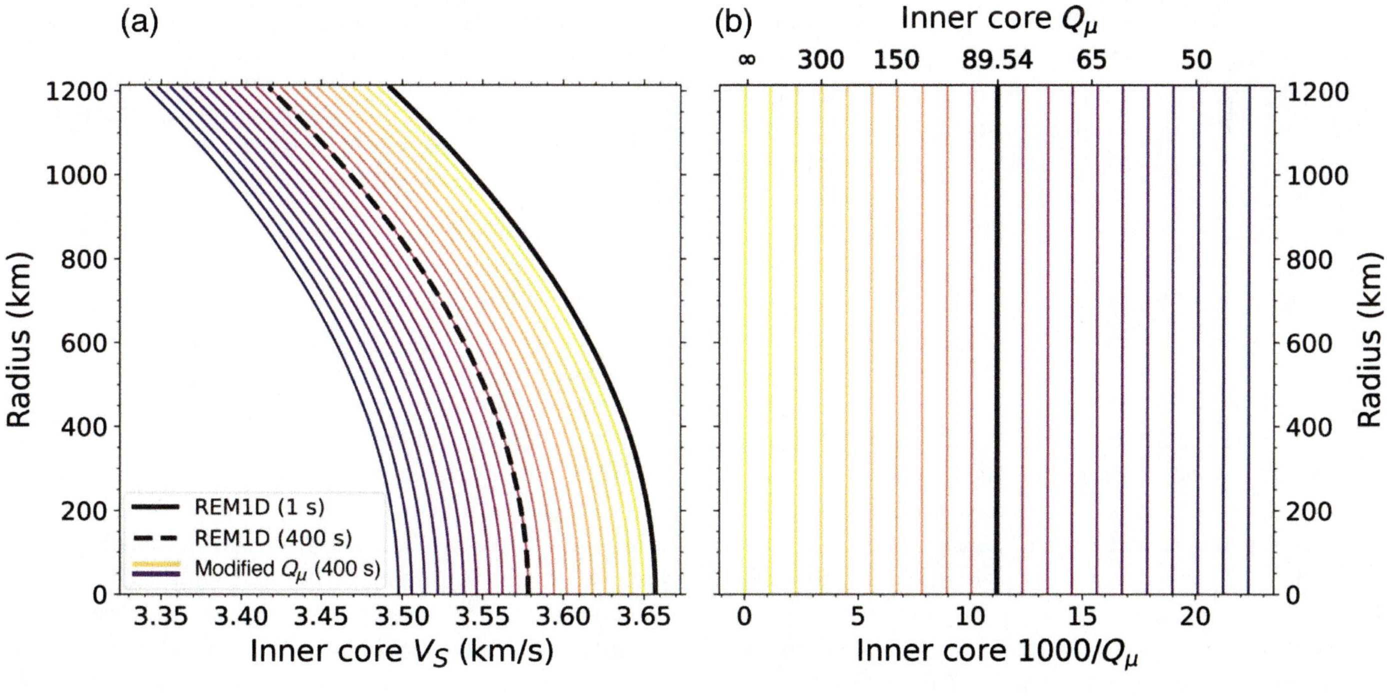

Figure 14. Various scenarios of shear dissipation in the (a,b) inner core. Low (and high) shear attenuation is marked by yellow (and purple) colors. Reference inner core $Q_\mu = 89.54$ and radially varying V_S profile from REM1D, defined at the reference period of 1 s are plotted as black curves. Because of the effects of physical dispersion, a perturbed V_S profile different from REM1D by up to ~150 m/s (black dashed curve) is "seen" by a typical core-sensitive mode at an eigenperiod ~400 s (Fig. 13). Physical dispersion allows the mode eigenperiods to provide additional constraints on the optimal Q_μ in the inner core (Fig. 15).

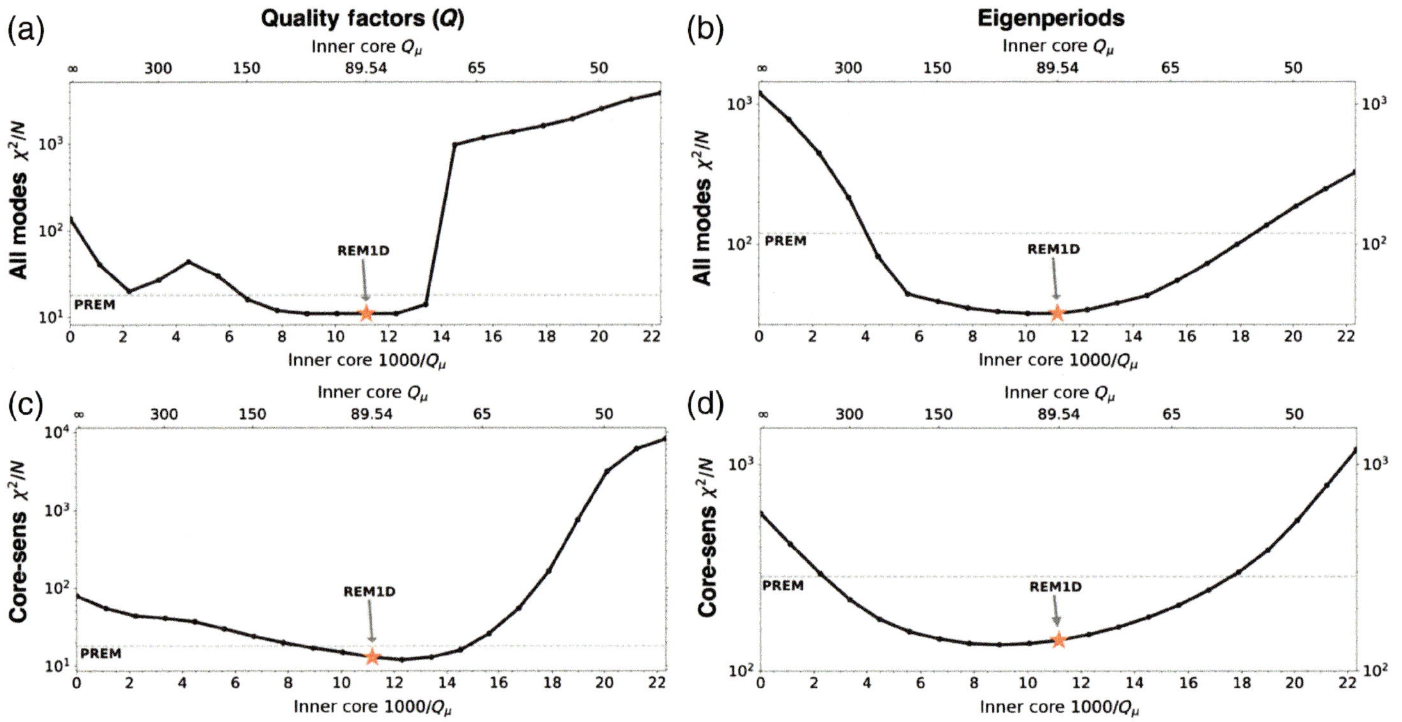

Figure 15. Evidence of strong shear dissipation in the inner core. Chi-square misfits are provided in semilog plots to all normal-mode quality factors (a,c) and eigenperiods (b,d), and the subset of core-sensitive modes (c,d) from the reference dataset, while accounting for the nonlinear crustal contributions to fundamental modes (Moulik and Ekström, 2025a,b). Perturbations are evenly spaced in $1000/Q_\mu$ relative to the REM1D inner-core $Q_\mu = 89.54$. REM1D fits all observations (red star) significantly better than PREM (gray dashed line). Note that the substantial changes in fits to eigenperiods are purely due to physical dispersion caused by shear dissipation (Fig. 14) because velocity/density structure is fixed at REM1D values.

modulus κ and its pressure derivative $\kappa' = d\kappa/dp$), are valid for an adiabatic region of uniform composition. Based on EoS predictions for a well-mixed isochemical region, the curvature κ'' should remain negative over the entire pressure range, decreasing in magnitude to zero at high pressures ($p \to \infty$) and therefore greater depths in a region of the Earth. REM1D removes the positive κ'' in the deepest ~1000 km of the outer core, which is an anomalous feature of PREM and body-wave models like AK135 (Fig. 1c). Deviations in earlier models were due to artifacts from parameterization and limitations of body-wave datasets (Moulik and Ekström, 2025a). EoS for various bulk compositions can be calibrated against seismological models, and past studies have argued for a solid inner core composed of a crystalline phase of iron with some light elements, and a liquid outer core comprising additional lighter alloying elements (e.g., C, H, S, Si, or O; Birch 1952, 1964; Jephcoat and Olson, 1987; Hirose *et al.*, 2013). REM1D finds κ' values in the inner core that are marginally higher (2.35–2.36) than PREM (2.33–2.34), which are features related to the 0.1%–0.5% reduction in velocities. The elastic and density variations in the REM1D inner and outer core follow closely the Adams–Williamson equation (e.g., stratification parameter $\eta_B = 1$; Bullen, 1963) with a negative κ'' throughout each region. Modern reference estimates of the physical properties are consistent with an iron-rich crystalline inner core and a neutrally stable outer core comprising a well-mixed iron alloy undergoing adiabatic compression (Moulik and Ekström, 2025b).

Discussion and Conclusion

We have revisited several historical studies that have helped shape our current understanding of the inner core from a seismological point of view. Although Oldham (1906) was able to identify a core, he did not speculate on its temperature or composition. It is possible that he misidentified the second phase as a late-arriving core phase instead of a bounce phase. Curiously, his data were biased toward late arrivals, which would suggest slower velocities than modern velocity models (Fig. 2). The problem of baseline differences in absolute arrivals and the overall slopes of teleseismic travel-time curves in early studies is well known. His observations were of limited quality and quantity (Muir and Tsai, 2020), and they likely contained errors in picking, earthquake time, and location. Although modern processing methods have improved earthquake characterization, leading to reduced baseline errors, discrepancies in arrival times across various filter bands and techniques persist and are being reconciled in collaboration with the seismological community (Moulik and The 3D Reference Earth Model [REM3D] Consortium, 2022).

In contrast to the data in Oldham (1906), we found that the data used by Lehmann (1936) and available in ISC (2025) for the time span of 1904–1935 feature relatively accurate timing. If modern ray-tracing techniques were available, it would have been possible to estimate the inner core to within 2% with the entire dataset. Although there was a large spread in the historical data with a standard deviation of 4.03 s, we found relatively little systematic bias. Finally, we note that the modern phase arrival data are considerably more precise with a standard deviation of 1.83 s, and very accurate with a mean systematic deviation of 0.029 s, an order of magnitude better than the historical data spanning 1904–1935. Although this trend is an overall improvement for seismology, it does suggest that historical data cannot automatically be used for studying the interior of the Earth. Historical datasets would likely need to be digitally scanned so that new arrival times can be estimated with the high resolution afforded by modern scanners and the high consistency and reproducibility afforded by computer algorithms.

Although there is demonstrated value in scanning and digitizing historical seismic data, there are also several complications. For example, the simple task of scanning and digitizing these records will require a large effort (e.g., Alejandro *et al.*, 2018). Even after the scanning and digitization, it will be important to understand the timing quality of the records as well as the fidelity and quality of the scans and how these factors may be determined by how the data were recorded, written, and stored (Lee *et al.*, 2020, 2022). For example, errors may be related to historical operating practices, such as errors in the historical absolute-time corrections to clock drift made with radio time (e.g., Agnew, 2020), equipment, for example, nonlinear time drift caused by rotation changes in the drum or scanning errors (Lee *et al.*, 2023), or storage, for example, distortion of physical paper or film media that analog data are stored on over time (e.g., Lee *et al.*, 2022). Many of these records will also be complicated to analyze because of their time-varying responses and the lack of metadata in modern formats (Ringler *et al.*, 2020). Our analysis of the same stations used by Lehmann (1936) suggests that many of the large arrival residuals persist in modern records. Based on a ten-year window centered around 2000, the standard deviation of residuals generally decreases, but there can be substantial periods of time with large amounts of outlier data (Figs. 10 and 11). This suggests that scanning and digitizing a large number of records would likely be necessary because the spread of the residuals could be large and potentially biased if only a few stations are used. Despite current limitations in the timing and resolution of historical stations, such a change would accrue over decades and could potentially be detected with fidelity in long-term records (e.g., 1.07 s change in 100 yr). Such work is especially promising if the large spread in the residuals of stations (Fig. 11b) is reduced. Such a reduction in uncertainty may be achieved through the repicking of phases using modern resources and techniques because changes in median arrival times larger than 1 s over time may be due to errors in the original picks or instrumentation (e.g., Röhm *et al.*, 1999).

Historically, identification of normal-mode multiplets in digitized seismograms for radial structure was done with coarse sampling rates of ~2–16 samples per second. However, a mode multiplet (and its constitutive singlets) may split due to Earth's heterogeneity and remain in resonance with other modes, resulting in complicated spectral signatures. Several inner-core sensitive normal modes are observed to split in a way that is consistent with a transversely isotropic inner core with a symmetry axis parallel to that of the Earth's rotation (e.g., Woodhouse *et al.*, 1986; Tromp, 1995). The estimation of splitting parameters from waveform spectra requires high-frequency resolution and timing accuracies in continuous time series (without gaps) spanning multiple hours and days (~1.1 Q cycles per mode; Dahlen, 1982), a requirement that needs to be met during the digitization of historical records for this application. The Q cycle corresponds to the time required for the modal signal to decay by $e^{-\pi}$ and is defined as the quality factor Q of the mode multiplied by its eigenperiod in seconds. The processing for several higher-order overtones is often attempted after removing the first several (up to 15 or 20) hours of each seismogram to leverage the property of the Earth as an attenuation filter (e.g., Dratler *et al.*, 1971). This process removes the fundamental modes and other modes with shorter Q cycles that attenuate after the first few hours, but it also necessitates long records. So long as archives of historical seismograms continue to exist and remain accessible, expanding mode-splitting datasets with historical data may be a valuable prospect given that the methods by which historical analog data can be recovered and digitized have improved significantly in the last half-century (e.g., Ishii and Ishii, 2022).

Modern observational seismology leverages a combination of theoretical advancements in wave propagation and large-scale computational resources that were unthinkable at the time of the discovery and early physical characterization of the inner core. Nevertheless, there could still be value in many of the historical records used in these efforts because the quality of the data in certain respects is not substantially different than modern records. Although it may remain challenging to use these historical data for applications that require high precision ($\ll$1 s), their utility is clear for certain applications where an extended time record is necessary even with only coarse timing. For example, changes in ocean-generated microseism amplitudes can be investigated with the sampling rate of a minute and power spectral densities (Lecocq *et al.*, 2020). Finally, while modern observational seismology has come a long way with recent studies involving massive datasets (e.g., Moulik *et al.*, 2022), many of the fundamental observations that have improved our understanding of the Earth's interior were made using careful analysis of only a few records. The work of Lehmann (1936) fits into this category and was truly revolutionary for the era in which she worked. The combined analysis of historical records that provide invaluable temporal coverage in conjunction with the ever-expanding sets of high-precision and high-accuracy observations from global seismographic networks may help detect new structural features of the Earth and refine previous estimates.

Based on the eigenfrequencies of normal modes, it is now well established that the inner core is solid. Although an inner core distinct in V_P structure was detected using *PKP* waves (Lehmann, 1936), it could only be validated as a solid region using the additional V_S and density sensitivity afforded by normal modes (Dziewonski and Gilbert, 1971). Two spheroidal overtones (${}_6S_1'$ and ${}_8S_1'$) were likely misidentified by this study, and discrepancies exist between the reported eigenperiods and modern reference estimates (Moulik and Ekström, 2025a). Nevertheless, the underlying conclusion holds true because the rigidity of the core provides the only way to jointly fit the eigenperiod observations of both radial modes and core-sensitive spheroidal overtones. Moreover, the strong shear dissipation in REM1D ($Q_\mu = 89.54$) affords a clear and optimal fit to the modern reference datasets of mode eigenperiods and quality factors accounting for physical dispersion. Because a liquid region would only have bulk dissipation, the narrow range of low Q_μ estimates from reference datasets supports the earlier conclusion based on eigenperiods alone that the inner core is solid (Dziewonski and Gilbert, 1971, 1972). Although several articles have reported observations of shear body-wave phases through the inner core, these observations are difficult to make because of their small amplitudes and interactions with other incoming phases arriving simultaneously.

Despite the limitations of theory and computational resources at the time, early seismological studies fundamentally shaped our understanding of the Earth's interior and motivated new research. Although the availability of data was limited in historical studies, it was adequate to discern the first-order features, and gross errors in early studies are remarkably low. Modern estimates of the average physical properties in the inner core are reported by the radial REM1D (Fig. 1; Moulik and Ekström, 2025a,b). The inner core is now considered a region 1215 km in radius with nonzero, radially varying shear and compressional velocities, and a strong, uniform shear attenuation ($Q_\mu = 89.54$). Reconciliation of historical and modern seismological datasets holds immense promise for future discoveries on inner-core structure.

Data and Resources

The reference dataset, radial reference Earth model (REM1D; Moulik and Ekström, 2025a,b), and codes to evaluate physical parameters at arbitrary locations are available from the project webpage (http://rem3d.org, last accessed August 2025) and are permanently archived on Zenodo (doi: 10.5281/zenodo.8407693; Moulik, 2025). Normal-mode calculations accounting for new astronomic–geodetic constants and ray tracing through both anisotropic (e.g., REM1D) and isotropic models (e.g., AK135) were performed using the open-source AVNI toolkit (http://avni.globalseismology.org, last accessed July 2025; Moulik *et al.*, 2023), which extends the anisotropic formulations of Woodhouse (1981, 1988). Code to reproduce all other figures will be published at https://code.usgs.gov/asl/papers/ringler (last accessed July 2025). The authors made extensive use of the Python packages Matplotlib (Hunter, 2007), ObsPy (Megies *et al.*, 2011), and Cartopy (Met Office, 2015). This work was supported by the Gordon and Betty Moore Foundation Award GBMF12801 (doi: 10.37807/GBMF12801).

Declaration of Competing Interests

The authors acknowledge that there are no conflicts of interest recorded.

Acknowledgments

The authors thank an anonymous reviewer, Duncan Agnew, Kristen Marra, Guust Nolet, and Brian Shiro for helpful reviews that improved this article. The authors also thank Paul Richards for reviewing this work and suggesting a number of additional pieces focused on body-wave observations. This work benefited from an early review by Paul Earle. The authors thank Duncan Agnew for providing several historical references that helped in the identification of stations as well as answering many questions. The authors thank Guy Masters, Fredrick Pollitz, Frederik Simons, and Joe Steim for helping track down some of the normal-mode frequencies. The authors thank Tyler Storm for providing several PKP_{df} phase examples. Adam T. Ringler supported the initial conception, formal analysis, data curation, visualization, writing—original draft, and writing—reviewing and editing. Pritwiraj Moulik supported the data curation, formal analysis, visualization, methodology, writing—original draft, and writing—reviewing and editing. Thomas L. Lee supported the methodology, writing—original draft, and writing—reviewing and editing. David C. Wilson supported the methodology, writing—original draft, and writing—reviewing and editing. Robert E. Anthony supported the methodology, writing—original draft, and writing—reviewing and editing.

References

Agnew, D. C. (2020). Time marks and clock corrections: A century of seismological timekeeping, *Seismol. Res. Lett.* **91,** no. 3, 1417–1429, doi: 10.1785/0220190284.

Aki, K., and P. Richards (2002). *Quantitative Seismology: Second Edition*, University Science Books, Sausalito, 700 pp.

Alejandro, A. C. B., C. R. Hutt, A. T. Ringler, S. V. Moore, R. E. Anthony, and D. C. Wilson (2018). The Albuquerque Seismological Lab WWSSN film chip preservation project, *Seismol. Res. Lett.* **90,** no. 1, 401–408, doi: 10.1785/0220180275.

Anderssen, R. S., and J. R. Cleary (1980). Estimation of *PKP* times from ISC data, *Phys. Earth Planet. Int.* **23,** 207–214, doi: 10.1016/0031-9201(80)90110-7.

Backus, G., and F. Gilbert (1968). The resolving power of gross Earth data, *Geophys. J. Int.* **16,** no. 2, 169–205, doi: 10.1111/j.1365-246X.1968.tb00216.x.

Birch, F. (1940). The alpha-gamma transformation of iron at high pressures, and the problem of the Earth's magnetism, *Am. J. Sci.* **238,** no. 3, 192–211, doi: 10.2475/ajs.238.3.192.

Birch, F. (1952). Elasticity and constitution of the Earth's interior, *J. Geophys. Res.* **57,** no. 2, 227–286, doi: 10.1029/JZ057i002p00227.

Birch, F. (1964). Density and composition of mantle and core, *J. Geophys. Res.* **69,** no. 20, 4377–4388, doi: 10.1029/jz069i020p04377.

Bolt, B. A. (1982). *Inside the Earth: Evidence from Earthquakes*, W. H. Freeman and Company, New York, 191 pp., doi: 10.1016/0191-8141(83)90063-9.

Bormann, P., D. A. Storchak, and J. Schweitzer (2013). The IASPEI standard nomenclature of seismic phases, in *New Manual of Seismological Observatory Practice 2*, Geutsches GeoForschungsZentrum GFAZ, Potsdam, Germany, 20 pp., doi: 10.2312/GFZ.NMSOP-2_IS_2.1.

Brekhovskikh, L. M. (1960). *Waves in Layered Media*, Academic Press, London, 561 pp.

Brush, S. G. (1980). Discovery of the Earth's core, *Am. J. Phys.* **48,** 705–724, doi: 10.1119/1.12026.

Buffet, B. A. (1996). A mechanism for decade fluctuations in the length of day, *Geophys. Res. Lett.* **23,** no. 25, 3803–3806, doi: 10.1029/96GL03571.

Buland, R., and C. H. Chapman (1983). The computation of seismic travel times, *Bull. Seismol. Soc. Am.* **73,** no. 5, 1271–1302, doi: 10.1785/BSSA0730051271.

Bullen, K. E. (1950). Theoretical travel-times of S waves in the Earth's inner core, *Geophys. J. Int.* **6,** no. s2, 125–128, doi: 10.1111/j.1365-246X.1950.tb02986.x.

Bullen, K. E. (1963). An index of degree of chemical inhomogeneity in the earth, *Geophys. J. Int.* **7,** no. 5, 584–592, doi: 10.1111/j.1365-246X.1963.tb03823.x.

Burdick, S., L. Waszek, and V. Lekić (2019). Seismic tomography of the uppermost inner core, *Earth Planet. Sci. Lett.* **528,** 115,789, doi: 10.1016/j.epsl.2019.115789.

Cormier, V. F., M. I. Bergman, and P. L. Olson (2021). *Earth's Core: Geophysics of a Planet's Deepest Interior*, Elsevier, Amsterdam, The Netherlands, 324 pp.

Crotwell, H. P., T. J. Owens, and Ritsema (1999). The TauP toolkit: Flexible seismic travel-time and ray-path utilities, *Seismol. Res. Lett.* **70,** no. 2, 154–160, doi: 10.1785/gssrl.70.2.154.

Dahlen, F. A. (1982). The effect of data windows on the estimation of free oscillation parameters, *Geophys. J. Int.* **69,** no. 2, 537–549, doi: 10.1111/J.1365-246X.1982.tb04964.x.

Dahlen, F. A., and J. Tromp (1998). *Theoretical Global Seismology*, Princeton University Press, New Jersey, 1025 pp., doi: 10.2307/j.ctv131bvfd.

Deuss, A. (2014). Heterogeneity and anisotropy of Earth's inner core, *Annu. Rev. Earth Planet. Sci.* **42,** 103–126, doi: 10.1146/annurev-earth-060313-054658.

Dratler, J., W. E. Farrell, B. Block, and F. Gilbert (1971). High-Q overtone modes of the Earth, *Geophys. J. Int.* **23,** no. 4, 399–410, doi: 10.1111/j.1365-246X.1971.tb01832.x.

Dziewonski, A. M., and D. L. Anderson (1981). Preliminary reference Earth model, *Phys. Earth Planet. Inter.* **25,** no. 4, 297–356, doi: 10.1016/0031-9201(81)90046-7.

Dziewonski, A. M., and F. Gilbert (1971). Solidity of the inner core of the Earth inferred from normal mode observations, *Nature* **234,** no. 5330, 465–466, doi: 10.1038/234465a0.

Dziewonski, A. M., and F. Gilbert (1972). Observations of normal modes from 84 recordings of the Alaska earthquake of 1964 March 28, *Geophys. J. Int.* **27,** no. 4, 393–446, doi: 10.1111/j.1365-246X.1972.tb06100.x.

Gutenberg, B. (1913). Über die konstituion des Erdinnern, erschlossen aus Erdbebenbeobachtungen, *Z. Geophys.* **14,** 1217–1218 (in German).

Gutenberg, B., and C. F. Richter (1938). P′ and the Earth's core, *Geophys. Suppl. Mon. Notices Roy. Astron. Soc.* **4,** no. 5, 363–372, doi: 10.1111/J.1365-246X.1938.tb01761.x.

Hirose, K., S. Labrosse, and J. Hernlund (2013). Composition and state of the core, *Annu. Rev. Earth Planet. Sci.* **41,** 657–691, doi: 10.1146/annurev-earth-050212-124007.

Hunter, J. D. (2007). Matplotlib: A 2D graphics environment, *Comput. Sci. Eng.* **9,** no. 3, 90–95, doi: 10.1109/MCSE.2007.55.

International Seismological Centre (ISC) (2025). *Online bulletin*, doi: 10.31905/D808B830.

Ishii, M., and H. Ishii (2022). DigitSeis: Software to extract time series from analogue seismograms, *Progr. Earth Planet. Sci.* **9,** no. 1, 50, doi: 10.1186/s40645-022-00508-0.

Jeans, J. (1927). The propagation of earthquake waves, *Proc. Math. Phys. Sci.* **102,** 554–574, doi: 10.1098/rspa.1923.0015.

Jeffreys, H. (1926). The rigidity of the Earth's central core, *Geophys. Suppl. Mon. Notices Roy. Astron. Soc.* **1,** 371–383, doi: 10.1111/j.1365-246X.1926.tb05385.x.

Jeffreys, H., and K. E. Bullen (1940). *Seismological Tables, British Association for the Advancement of Science*, Gray Milne Trust, London, 50 pp.

Jephcoat, A., and P. Olson (1987). Is the inner core of the Earth pure iron?, *Nature* **325,** no. 6102, 332–335, doi: 10.1038/325332a0.

Kennett, B. L. N., E. R. Engdahl, and R. Buland (1995). Constraints on seismic velocities in the Earth from traveltimes, *Geophys. J. Int.* **122,** no. 1, 108–124, doi: 10.1111/j.1365-246X.1995.tb03540.x.

Kölbl-Ebert, M. (2001). Inge Lehmann's paper: "P′" (1936), *Episodes* **24,** 262–267, doi: 10.18814/epiiugs/2001/v24i4/007.

Krasnoshchekov, D. N., P. B. Kaazik, and V. M. Ovtchinnikov (2005). Seismological evidence for mosaic structure of the surface of the Earth's inner core, *Nature* **435,** 483–487, doi: 10.1038/nature03613.

Lecocq, T., F. Ardhuin, F. Collin, and T. Camelbeeck (2020). On the extraction of microseismic ground motion from analog seismograms for the validation of ocean-climate models, *Seismol. Res. Lett.* **91,** no. 3, 1518–1530, doi: 10.1785/0220190276.

Lee, T., M. Ishii, and P. Okubo (2020). Relative time corrections for historical analog seismograms using the single-day ambient noise correlation function, *Bull. Seismol. Soc. Am.* **110,** no. 6, 3185–3195, doi: 10.1785/0120190313.

Lee, T., M. Ishii, and P. Okubo (2022). Assessing the fidelity of seismic records from microfilm and paper media, *Seismol. Res. Lett.* **93,** no. 6, 3444–3453, doi: 10.1785/0220220134.

Lee, T. A., A. T. Ringler, R. E. Anthony, and M. Ishii (2023). Comparison of corecorded analog and digital systems for characterization of responses and uncertainties, *Seismol. Res. Lett.* **94,** no. 5, 2301–2312, doi: 10.1785/0220230129.

Lehmann, I. (1936). P′, *Bureau Central Seismol. Int.* **14,** 87–115.

Megies, T., M. Beyreuther, R. Barsch, L. Krischer, and J. Wassermann (2011). ObsPy – What can it do for data centers and observatories?, *Ann. Geophys.* **54,** no. 1, 47–58, doi: 10.4401/ag-4838.

Met Office (2015). Cartopy: A cartographic Python library with a Matplotlib interface, Exter, Devon, available at http://scitools.org.uk/cartopy (last accessed October 2019).

Mochizuki, E. (1986). The free oscillations of an anisotropic and heterogeneous Earth, *Geophys. J. Int.* **86,** no. 1, 167–176, doi: 10.1111/j.1365-246X.1986.tb01078.x.

Moulik, P. (2025). Dataset and software for the radial reference earth model REM1D, *Phys. Earth Planet. Int. (v1.0). Zenodo*, doi: 10.5281/zenodo.8407693.

Moulik, P., and , and The 3D Reference Earth Model (REM3D) Consortium (2022). *Three Dimensional Reference Earth Model Project: Data, Techniques, Models & Tools*, American Geophysical Union Fall Meeting, Chicago, Illinois, doi: 10.5281/zenodo.7883683.

Moulik, P., and G. Ekström (2025a). Radial structure of the Earth: [I] Model concepts and data, *Phys. Earth Planet. Int.* pp. 1–123, 107,319, doi: 10.1016/j.pepi.2025.107319.

Moulik, P., and G. Ekström (2025b). Radial structure of the Earth: [II] Model features and interpretations, *Phys. Earth Planet. Int.* 107,320, doi: 10.1016/j.pepi.2025.107320.

Moulik, P., V. Lekic, B. Romanowicz, Z. Ma, A. Schaeffer, T. Ho, E. Beucler, D. Debayle, A. Deuss, S. Durand, *et al.* (2022). Global reference seismological data sets: Multimode surface wave dispersion, *Geophys. J. Int.* **228,** no. 3, 1808–1849, doi: 10.1093/gji/ggab418.

Moulik, P., R. Maguire, R. Gassmoeller, and C. Havlin (2023). AVNI: Analysis and visualization toolkit for planetary inferences, doi: 10.5281/zenodo.10035731.

Muir, J. B., and V. C. Tsai (2020). Did Oldham discover the core after all? Handing imprecise historical data with hierarchical Bayesian model selection methods, *Seismol. Res. Lett.* **91,** no. 3, 1377–1383, doi: 10.1785/0220190266.

Okal, E., and Y. Cansi (1998). Detection of *PKJKP* at intermediate periods by progressive multi-channel correlation, *Earth Planet. Sci. Lett.* **164,** 23–30, doi: 10.1016/S0012-821X(89)00210-6.

Oldham, R. D. (1906). The constitution of the interior of the Earth, as revealed by earthquakes, *Q. J. Geol. Soc.* **62,** 456–475, doi: 10.1144/GSL.JGS.1906.062.01-04.21.

Peterson, J, and C. R. Hutt (2014). World-wide standardized seismograph network—A data users guide, *U.S. Geol. Surv. Open-File Rept. 2014-1218* , 74 pp., doi: 10.3133/ofr20141218.

Richards, P. G. (2000). Earth's inner core-discoveries and conjectures, *Astron. Geophys.* **41,** no. 1, 1.20–1.24, doi: 10.1046/j.1468-4004-2000.00020.x.

Ringler, A. T., R. E. Anthony, D. C. Wilson, D. Auerbach, S. Bargabus, P. Davis, M. Gunnels, K. Hafner, J. F. Holland, A. Kearns, and E. Klimczak (2021). A review of timing accuracy across the Global Seismographic Network, *Seismol. Res. Lett.* **92,** no. 4, 2270–2281, doi: 10.1785/0220200394.

Ringler, A. T., D. C. Wilson, E. Wolin, T. Storm, and L. Sandoval (2020). Calibration analysis and noise estimates of WWSSN station ALQ (Albuquerque, New Mexico), *Seismol. Res. Lett.* **91,** no. 3, 1359–1366, doi: 10.1785/0220190201.

Röhm, A. H. E., J. Trampert, H. Paulssen, and R. K. Snider (1999). Bias in reported seismic arrival times deduced from the ISC Bulletin, *Geophys. J. Int.* **137,** no. 1, 163–174, doi: 10.1046/j.1365-246x.1999.00774.x.

Shearer, P. M., C. A. Rychert, and Q. Liu (2011). On the visibility of the inner-core shear wave phase PKJKP at long periods, *Geophys. J. Int.* **185,** 1379–1383, doi: 10.1111/j.1365-246X.2011.05011.x.

Song, X., and P. G. Richards (1996). Seismological evidence for differential rotation of the Earth's inner core, *Nature* **382,** no. 6588, 221–224, doi: 10.1038/382221a0.

Souriau, A., and M. Calvet (2015). Deep Earth structure: The Earth's core, in *Treatise on Geophysics*, Second Ed., G. Schubert (Editor), Vol. 1, Elsevier, Amsterdam, The Netherlands, 655–693, doi: 10.1016/B978-0-444-53802-4.00020-8.

Tkalčić, H. (2017). *The Earth's Inner Core Revealed by Observational Seismology*, Cambridge University Press, Cambridge, 234 pp., doi: 10.1017/0781139583954.

Tkalčić, H. (2024). On the inner-core differential-rotation (un)resolvability from earthquake doublets: The traps of data selection, *Geophys. Res. Lett.* **51,** no. 6, e2023GL107043, doi: 10.1029/2023GL107043.

Tkalčić, H., S. Wang, and T. -S. Phan (2022). Shear properties of Earth's inner core, *Annu. Rev. Earth Planet. Sci.* **50,** 153–181, doi: 10.1146/annurev-earth-071521-063942.

Tromp, J. (1995). Normal-mode splitting due to inner-core anisotropy, *Geophys. J. Int.* **121,** no. 3, 963–968, doi: 10.1111/j.1365-246X.1995.tb06451.x.

Waszek, L., and A. Deuss (2013). A low attenuation layer in the Earth's uppermost inner core, *Geophys. J. Int.* **195,** no. 3, 2005–2015, doi: 10.1093/gji/ggt368.

Widmer, R., G. Masters, and F. Gilbert (1991). Spherically symmetric attenuation within the Earth from normal mode data, *Geophys. J. Int.* **104,** no. 3, 541–553, doi: 10.1111/j.1365-246X.1991.tb05700.x.

Wood, H. O. (1921). A list of seismologic stations of the world, *Bull. Natl. Res Counc.* **2,** no. 15, 397–538.

Woodhouse, J. (1988). The calculation of the eigenfrequencies and eigenfunctions of the free oscillations of the earth and the sun, in *Seismological Algorithms: Computational Methods and Computer Programs*, D. J. Doornbos (Editor), Academic Press, San Diego, California, pp. 321.

Woodhouse, J. H. (1976). On Rayleigh's principle, *Geophys. J. Int.* **46,** no. 1, 11–22, doi: 10.1111/j.1365-246X.1976.tb01629.x.

Woodhouse, J. H. (1981). A note on the calculation of travel times in a transversely isotropic Earth model, *Phys. Earth Planet. Int.* **25,** no. 4, 357–359, doi: 10.1016/0031-9201(81)90047-9.

Woodhouse, J. H., D. Giardini, and X. -D. Li (1986). Evidence for inner core anisotropy from free oscillations, *Geophys. Res. Lett.* **13,** no. 13, GL013i013p01549, 1549–1552, doi: 10.1029/GL013i013p01549.

Manuscript received 24 February 2025
Published online 10 September 2025

Evaluation of Seismic Artificial Intelligence with Uncertainty

Samuel Myren[*1,2], Nidhi Parikh[2], Rosalyn Rael[2], Garrison Flynn[2], Dave Higdon[1], and Emily Casleton[2]

Abstract

Artificial intelligence has transformed the seismic community with deep learning models (DLMs) that are trained to complete specific tasks within workflows. However, there is still a lack of robust evaluation frameworks for evaluating and comparing DLMs. We address this gap by designing an evaluation framework that jointly incorporates two crucial aspects: performance uncertainty and learning efficiency. To target these aspects, we meticulously construct the training, validation, and test splits using a clustering method tailored to seismic data and enact an expansive training design to segregate performance uncertainty arising from stochastic training processes and random data sampling. The framework's ability to guard against misleading declarations of model superiority is demonstrated through the evaluation of PhaseNet (Zhu and Beroza, 2018), a popular seismic phase picking DLM, under three training approaches. Our framework helps practitioners choose the best model for their problem and set performance expectations by explicitly analyzing model performance with uncertainty at varying budgets of training data.

Cite this article as Myren, S., N. Parikh, R. Rael, G. Flynn, D. Higdon, and E. Casleton (2025). Evaluation of Seismic Artificial Intelligence with Uncertainty, *Seismol. Res. Lett.* **97**, 471–486, doi: 10.1785/0220240444.

Introduction

In the last 20 years, seismology has entered the big data regime (Arrowsmith *et al.*, 2022), which has resulted in an explosion of interest in automating seismic tasks through artificial intelligence (AI), particularly using deep learning models (DLMs) (Yu and Ma, 2021; Mousavi and Beroza, 2022; Mousavi *et al.*, 2024). However, different published models are often trained and evaluated using datasets that differ in important characteristics, making it hard to compare them directly. Although the growing availability of open-source benchmark data sets and software packages, such as SeisBench (Woollam *et al.*, 2022), has enabled researchers to compare popular models on the same datasets (Münchmeyer *et al.*, 2022), we still lack robust evaluation methods to fairly evaluate and compare DLMs. Without a robust evaluation approach, we are unable to determine whether new technological developments are truly state of the art, we lack diagnostics that assist developers in pinpointing areas for model improvement, and we fail to convey the scenarios under which a model can be trusted. In this research, we address this gap by identifying two fundamental evaluation aspects for DLMs and uniting them under a single evaluation framework.

The first and perhaps most important evaluation aspect is performance uncertainty in terms of benchmarking. Two identical DLM architectures with identical training approaches will realize different performance metrics when tested on a benchmark dataset as a result of different initializations and random batching during training (Reimers and Gurevych, 2017; Bouthillier *et al.*, 2021). We refer to this as training uncertainty. Furthermore, the training data sample has drastic random effects on performance metrics (Bouthillier *et al.*, 2021). We refer to this as data uncertainty. Determining algorithmic superiority in light of both sources of uncertainty is a known issue (Goldstein and Spiegelhalter, 1996; Dietterich, 1998; Dehghani *et al.*, 2021; Wein *et al.*, 2023) and, to our knowledge, has not been explored for the seismic AI community. We note that our aim is not to quantify prediction uncertainty, which entails relating model variability in predictions to the prediction errors quantitatively, typically using statistical confidence or credible intervals.

The second vital, yet often unexplored, evaluation aspect is the model's learning efficiency in terms of data utilization. Adding redundant data (too many similar examples) does not necessarily add new information, making model training inefficient. So, here, learning efficiency is defined as the relationship between the gain in performance as a result of the additional training data and data diversity required (see also

1. Department of Statistics, Virginia Tech, Blacksburg, Virginia, U.S.A., https://orcid.org/0000-0001-7135-5923 (SM); https://orcid.org/0009-0009-5880-948X (DH); 2. Los Alamos National Laboratory, Los Alamos, New Mexico, U.S.A., https://orcid.org/0000-0002-5707-6124 (NP); https://orcid.org/0000-0003-0172-4716 (RR); https://orcid.org/0000-0002-5612-4948 (GF); https://orcid.org/0000-0003-2909-5704 (EC)

*Corresponding author: myrenst@lanl.gov

Hlynsson *et al.*, 2019). Understanding a model's learning efficiency helps decision makers compute the cost-to-benefit ratio of acquiring additional and more diverse data to meet a problem's performance requirements, especially in data-scarce scenarios (Alzubaidi *et al.*, 2023). It is particularly important in the context of transfer learning (TL), for which models trained in one context are fine-tuned with smaller, targeted datasets for another context (Bornstein *et al.*, 2024), and the models that best adapt are preferred.

Measuring learning efficiency while accounting for uncertainty may appear to be simple at first. One might train two models on different budgets of randomly sampled training data, compare their performances, and repeat under resampled data to account for data uncertainty. However, randomly sampling data does not take correlations between seismic data into account. Waveforms may share similar signal properties if they originate from similar sources, come from nearby stations, or follow similar paths. This is a form of data leakage (Ferrer Florensa *et al.*, 2024), for which one dataset contains overlapping information from another dataset. Data leakage can influence all aspects of model evaluation. For example, when identical or nearly identical data points exist in both training and test datasets, model performance can be overestimated. Failing to account for data leakage when choosing training budgets can lead to inaccurate measurements of learning efficiency. This is because, as more data is added, there is no control over how much new information (or diversity) is being added. That is, without controlling for data leakage in developing training budgets, one may fail to systematically expose the models to more data diversity. Finally, failure to account for it can induce unrealistic representation of uncertainty arising from data sampling, potentially underestimating its impact by downplaying bias in the sampling procedure. In this work, we mitigate data leakage to more directly measure learning efficiency and better represent realistic data uncertainty using stratified sampling to construct the training data budgets.

This research develops an evaluation framework for seismic DLMs that considers two aspects: performance uncertainty arising from data and training, and learning efficiency. We utilize concepts from statistical experimental design to measure each aspect in turn. We demonstrate our framework using a seismic DLM to directly compare three training approaches: training from scratch and two TL approaches. We measure uncertainty through deep ensembles and random data selection processes, and learning efficiency through careful data splitting and varying data amounts. Finally, we cast all performance results into a statistical framework for direct comparison with uncertainty.

We use a popular seismic DLM to demonstrate the evaluation framework. A plethora of research in applying DLMs to the cardinal task of phase-picking provides a strong basis for our demonstration. Phase picking is the task of identifying the time that event-related signatures arrive, typically the primary and/or secondary phases (*P* and *S* arrivals, respectively), at a seismic station. Phase picking is a vital task for detecting, locating, and characterizing seismic events such as earthquakes or explosions. It can be a cumbersome task, motivating researchers to actively construct better deep learning (DL) phase picking models (referred to as pickers hereafter; Ross *et al.*, 2018; Zhu and Beroza, 2018; Zhu *et al.*, 2019, 2022; Mousavi *et al.*, 2020; Chen and Li, 2022; Tokuda and Nagao, 2023; Bornstein *et al.*, 2024; Niksejel and Zhang, 2024) and others are using these pickers to expedite workflows and create catalogs (Cianetti *et al.*, 2021; Park *et al.*, 2022; Armstrong *et al.*, 2023; Yoon *et al.*, 2023). Of course, the best-performing and most robust picker is preferred, but determining which picker is best for a given context remains a challenge that our framework is positioned to address.

The article is formulated as follows. We first introduce the data sets and how the data splits are constructed to incorporate the two fundamental evaluation aspects. Then, we briefly introduce the model architecture and training scheme, including curating the inputs and targets, and provide a detailed review of the three training approaches used for comparison. This is followed by the evaluation approach, including the statistical framework that distills the different model performances for digestible comparison with uncertainty. Finally, we present the results in terms of performance and uncertainty and finish with concluding remarks and future work.

Data

We use two publicly available, labeled, noncontinuous waveform datasets: the Stanford Earthquake Dataset (STEAD; Mousavi *et al.*, 2019) and the Italian seismic dataset for machine learning (INSTANCE; Michelini *et al.*, 2021), both accessed through the Python seismic deep learning package, SeisBench. STEAD is used for pretraining, and INSTANCE for subsequent fine-tuning and testing. STEAD contains ~235k noise waveforms and ~1.03M earthquake waveforms representing ~441k unique sources. For the INSTANCE dataset, we use the version measured in counts (InstanceCountsCombined in SeisBench documentation). In addition, we use the instrument response deconvolved traces in velocity without redundant measurements in acceleration. The resulting INSTANCE set includes ~132k noise waveforms and ~824k earthquake waveforms arising from ~54k unique sources. An example waveform from INSTANCE is shown in Figure 1 along with the labeled *P* and *S* arrivals.

Training, validation, and test splits

We use the default splits provided in SeisBench for STEAD for pretraining the models, which we then fine-tune using INSTANCE data. We implement a more meticulous splitting process that is meant to reduce data leakage for INSTANCE because we use it to measure learning efficiency with uncertainty. We construct the splits using stratified sampling on

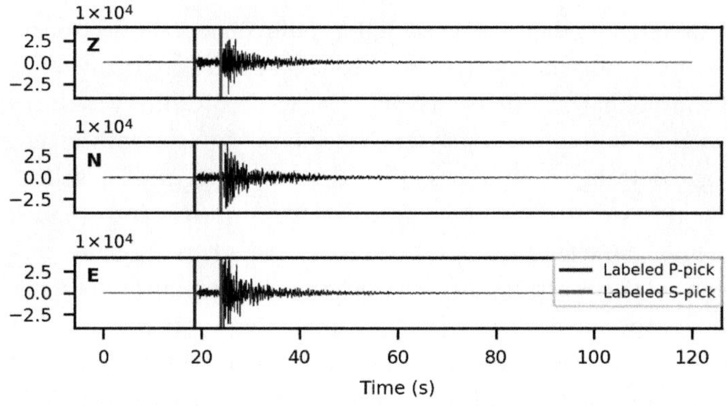

Figure 1. An example waveform from the INSTANCE dataset showing the three-component response in counts (Z, top; N, middle; E, bottom) with the labeled *P* arrival (vertical-blue line) and labeled *S* arrival (vertical-red line). The color version of this figure is available only in the electronic edition.

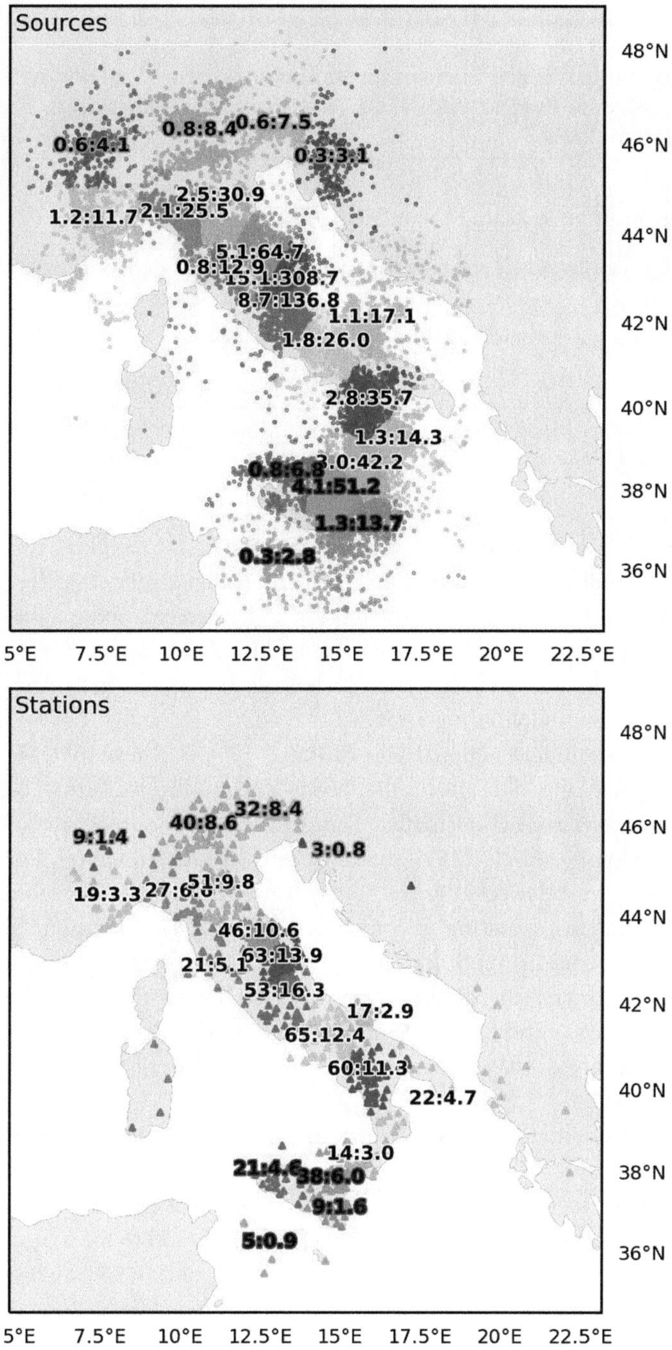

Figure 2. INSTANCE data with 20 colored clusters for the (a) sources (circles) and the (b) stations (triangles). For the sources, the numbers indicate the number of sources in thousands, followed by the number of waveforms in thousands. For the stations, the numbers indicate the number of stations and the number of noise waveforms, both in thousands. The colored text outline designates the group: the north test group is cyan, the training and validation group is white, and the south test group is red. The color version of this figure is available only in the electronic edition.

source locations. We chose location as a stratifying feature because it was an easy-to-implement first-order way to segregate the data such that it captures some diversity and represents how seismic datasets are often constrained to specific geographic regions, thereby roughly mimicking a realistic data sampling procedure. For example, many of the publicly available benchmark datasets in SeisBench are sourced from specific geographical regions. In practice, one might want to consider how model performance improves with the inclusion of data from new regions, or how a model might perform when predicting activity in a new region with limited data.

To accomplish our stratification, we cluster the INSTANCE sources spatially based on their latitude and longitude using the k-means algorithm from the Python package, Scikit-learn (Pedregosa *et al.*, 2018). K-means is an iterative, centroid-based clustering algorithm. Initially, all cluster centroids are selected at random, and all data points are assigned to the cluster closest to them. Next, in each iteration, a new centroid is estimated for each cluster based on the mean of all points assigned to this cluster, and then these new centroids are used to assign clusters for each point (i.e., based on the nearest cluster centroid). This process continues until convergence. We chose 20 clusters because they provided clusters large enough to feasibly represent the region's activity, yet small enough to explore model performance in limited data settings. To assign the noise waveforms, which have no corresponding source locations, to the established clusters, we use the trained k-means model to predict its associated cluster based on its station location. The clusters and number of sources, stations, and waveforms are shown in Figure 2. Table 1 summarizes the amount of data in the training, validation, and test splits, and the construction of the splits is described next.

To construct the INSTANCE splits, we first segregate the clusters into two groups: a training and validation pool and a test pool. We select the 12 central clusters to be the pool from which the training and validation data will be constructed, and eight clusters—the four northern most and four southern most —to be the test clusters (see Fig. 2). Choosing the test clusters

TABLE 1
Data Splits are Summarized Showing the Number of Sources, Earthquake (EQ) Waveforms (WFs), and Noise WFs

Data Split	Sources	EQ WFs	Noise WFs
Training	636 × number of clusters	8,878 × number of clusters	1,106 × number of clusters
Validation	1,908	27,169	3,312
Test	4,538	49,516	5,644

For the training split, values should be multiplied by the number of clusters used in the training design.

from northern and southern regions allows us to explore two different concepts. First, they help to evaluate model performance on semi-out-of-distribution data. Second, these splits represent a situation where we may know how a model performs in a certain region, and we want to measure its consistency for neighboring regions.

To mitigate regional bias in the INSTANCE test split, we balance the data from the north and south regions. The northern region is smaller, comprising 2269 sources, so we randomly sample 2269 sources from the southern region. For each source selected in the test split, we include all associated waveforms, resulting in a test set totaling 49,516 earthquake waveforms: 23,086 from the north and 26,430 from the south. To maintain the overall ratio of 11.4% noise to earthquake waveform ratio originally in INSTANCE, we randomly select 2822 noise waveforms from each of the south and north regions.

We aim for an 80:20 ratio for the training to validation splits, and we desire an equal number of sources from each cluster to reduce bias. Because the smallest of the 12 central clusters has 795 sources, we randomly sample 159 sources from each cluster for the validation set. This totals 1908 sources encompassing 27,169 earthquake waveforms. Maintaining a ~11.4% Earthquake to noise ratio, we then randomly sample 276 noise waveforms per cluster, totaling 3312 noise waveforms for the validation split.

After removing the INSTANCE validation set from the central clusters, the remaining waveforms become the pool from which we build the training splits. When training models, the amount of training data is specified by the number of clusters used for training. However, to keep data amounts relatively constant across clusters, each time a cluster is selected to be included in training data, we randomly select 636 sources (80% of 795, the smallest number of sources in any cluster), which on average results in 8878 earthquake waveforms and 1106 noise waveforms per cluster.

In our stratification, we aimed to choose a realistic feature that captures data diversity, mimics data sampling variability, and mitigates data leakage and thus reducing bias in measuring learning efficiency. We acknowledge that there are many other features that seismologists may use to stratify the waveform data, including time, network, geological faults or other geological features, source–station distance, magnitude, instrument type, earthquake type, signal-to-noise ratio (SNR), signal characteristics, and possibly many others. We also recognize that partitioning data on any single feature does not fully capture all forms of data diversity. However, we find that partitioning on source locations induces some segregation in these other data features. Figure 3 provides deeper insight into how the geographical clustering impacts the distributions of selected metadata features derived from the INSTANCE dataset. More details and figures showing distributions of other data features and waveform signal properties of the clusters are provided in the appendix (Figs. A1–A5). Other details regarding INSTANCE data, including geographical visualizations of source focal mechanisms and magnitudes, can be found in Michelini *et al.* (2021).

Methods—Model Architecture and Three Training Approaches

We develop a unifying framework for evaluating AI models that considers performance uncertainty and learning efficiency to guide model selection. We demonstrate our framework by comparing three training approaches outlined in Table 2: training from scratch (the standard DL approach) and two TL approaches with varying numbers of free parameters. However, the framework presented is sufficiently broad for one could explore the impacts of any aspect of interest, such as different hyperparameters, training approaches, or new architectures altogether. We first review the model architecture and other commonalities among the models, and then we review the uniqueness of each model and how the training design allows for estimation of data and training uncertainty.

All models use the PhaseNet deep learning architecture which has been extensively utilized for phase picking (Münchmeyer *et al.*, 2022; Kim *et al.*, 2023; Bornstein *et al.*, 2024) and features a U-Net type architecture (Ronneberger *et al.*, 2015). PhaseNet intakes three-component waveforms of dimension 3001 and is trained to output probabilities of *P*, *S* arrivals, and noise for each time point in the waveform.

We curate the training inputs by applying a 30 s window randomly around the 100 Hz sampled three-component waveform. For earthquake waveforms, we require the window to include the labeled *P* arrival. The windows are re-randomized every epoch. Then, each waveform component is independently zero-meaned and scaled to unit variance. Because of the data curation of STEAD and INSTANCE, the *P* arrivals tend to appear early in the waveforms, most often within the first 15 s. As such, the random windowing reduces some temporal bias, but some remains, and this is a source of bias induced by the training process. There has been some work

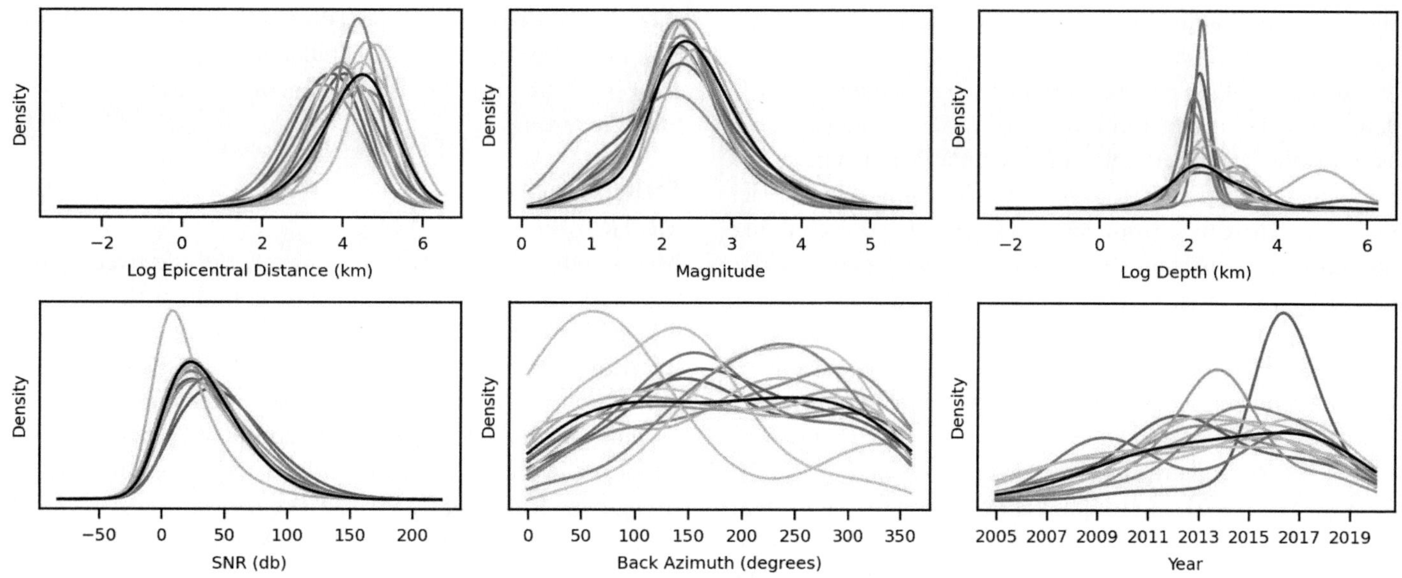

Figure 3. Distributions of selected data features (log epicentral distance, magnitude, log depth, signal-to-noise ratio (SNR) averaged over the three components, back azimuth, and source year) for each of the 12 training clusters (nonblack curves corresponding to Fig. 2) and the testing set comprising the four northern and four southern clusters (black curve). These features are provided as metadata in the INSTANCE dataset found in SeisBench. All curves are normalized for comparison, ensuring they integrate to 1. The color version of this figure is available only in the electronic edition.

inspecting how windowing and overlap can impact predictions (Park *et al.*, 2022, 2024; Pita-Sllim *et al.*, 2023), but this is not a focus of this work. Furthermore, we recognize the challenge of waveforms containing multiple unlabeled arrivals and how data augmentation can help mitigate this issue, but no other data augmentation was implemented because our focus is in the evaluation framework as opposed to progressing picker technology.

For the training targets, we follow a process similar to Zhu and Beroza (2018), for which we construct the *P*- and *S*-training targets using a normal distribution centered at the labeled picks with a standard deviation of 0.1 s. For the noise component, we simply subtract the *P*- and *S*-target components from a vector of ones. Because our goal is to demonstrate the evaluation framework, we focus only on the *P*-arrival predictions and discard the *S* arrival and noise predictions for all subsequent analysis.

To demonstrate our evaluation framework, we compare three training approaches: the standard approach for deep learning and two TL approaches. The standard approach entails randomly initializing model weights and pulling the training, validation, and test splits all from the dataset of interest, in this case, INSTANCE. Thus, the standard model represents this approach.

The two TL approaches are thought to be useful when a small amount of labeled data is available from the region of interest, but a large amount of labeled training data can be obtained from other regions. As such, one first trains a model with data from the other regions (we call it an upstream model), then switches to data from the region of interest to continue learning, thereby transferring the accumulated knowledge to the new domain. In our case, we first train PhaseNet using STEAD and then fine-tune using INSTANCE. We explore two options. The first allows all weights to change during the INSTANCE training phase, as similarly performed in Chai *et al.* (2020). The second fixes the weights of the input and convolution layers (i.e., the left half, or encoder side, of the network). Previous work exploring optimal layer freezing for U-Net architectures for medical image segmentation demonstrates that this choice may be nonoptimal (Amiri *et al.*, 2020), but our objective is model evaluation, not finding the optimal approach for TL. The TL models that have fully free weights are denoted as free, and those with some fixed weights are denoted as frozen. All three models (the

TABLE 2

Details of the Three Models Are Given in Each Row, Including Their Names, If the Model Is Initialized Randomly or Using Weights from an Upstream Model Trained on STEAD, and Whether Weights Were Frozen

Name	**Initialization**	**Weights**
Standard	Random	Free
TL free	STEAD	Free
TL frozen	STEAD	Half-frozen

STEAD, Stanford Earthquake Dataset; TL, transfer learning.

standard model and two TL models) are validated and tested using INSTANCE data.

To evaluate learning efficiency, we train each model using 1, 3, 6, 9, and 12 clusters from the INSTANCE training clusters. To measure data uncertainty at a given number of clusters, we randomly select the cluster set 12 times, training the model each time. Then, to separate the data uncertainty from training uncertainty, we use four deep ensembles (Huang *et al.*, 2017; Lakshminarayanan *et al.*, 2017; Ganaie *et al.*, 2022). That is, for each of the 12 cluster sets at a given quantity of clusters, we retrain the model four different times under different initializations, holding the training data sample fixed, to obtain four model instances for evaluation. To obtain different initializations for the standard model, we simply randomly reset the weights. For the TL models that are seeded by weights from an upstream model, we first train 48 upstream models with STEAD starting from random initializations. Then, we initialize the TL models by pulling the set of weights from one randomly selected upstream model.

In our deep ensemble implementation, we loosely follow the snapshot ensemble approach of Huang *et al.* (2017), which boasts computational advantages in finding different parameter states that minimize loss. We implement a cosine annealing learning schedule with 4 restarts, with an initial learning rate of 0.01 and final rate of 0. These learning parameters exhibited the best performance in preliminary training experiments, especially for models with the smallest number of clusters (one cluster). However, simple rate resets routinely failed to push models with small training sets into new basins of attraction, so we altered the approach toward the classical deep ensemble method (Lakshminarayanan *et al.*, 2017) by fully reprogramming the model weights at each scheduled rate reset rather than relying on rate resets alone. Depending on the model being trained, this reprogramming may be a complete randomized reset (for the standard model) or replacing weights by randomly pulling from one of the 48 upstream models (for the TL models).

For ease of discussion, we define a single "model instance" as the combination of model, quantity of clusters, cluster set (random selection of those clusters), and initialization (ensemble). For example, a single model instance of the standard model could be trained using three clusters randomly chosen—about Figure 2—to be clusters red, blue, and light green, and the third initialization. With the standard model and two TL models each trained using five quantities of clusters over 12 random cluster sets with four initializations, we obtain 720 model instances.

We train all models with the deep learning Python package, PyTorch (Paszke *et al.*, 2019), using a sufficient number of epochs to allow full convergence. The standard models reached convergence within 50 epochs, and the TL models reached convergence within 12 epochs. We selected the model instance for evaluation that exhibited the lowest loss on the validation data within a cosine annealing cycle. We used cross-entropy loss, the Adam optimizer (Kingma and Ba, 2017), and a constant batch size of 128 due to its superior performance in preliminary testing.

Evaluation

Metrics

Because our main goal is to demonstrate the effectiveness and versatility of our evaluation framework, we limit the scope of the evaluation of the pickers by displaying just a couple of classification metrics and one function-based regression metric. In this section, we briefly outline how we calculate these metrics. To motivate the specific metrics we consider, we note that it is important in evaluation of pickers to consider both the model's strength in identifying if a *P* arrival occurs (e.g., alerting) and, if so, the associated accuracy of the pick (e.g., how close is the predicted pick to the labeled *P* arrival).

In general, we implement techniques similar to those found in Zhu and Beroza (2018), Münchmeyer *et al.* (2022), and Kim *et al.* (2023) to obtain model outputs and picks for each test waveform. More specifically, we feed test waveforms through the model in 30 s intervals with 28 s of overlap and no end padding. Then, we take the mean of the model outputs at each time point to form a single vector of *P*-arrival probabilities as a function of time for each waveform. Given a defined threshold (described later), we define a pick as the discrete locations in time that a *P* arrival is predicted by the model by taking the argmax of groups of samples that contiguously exceed the threshold.

Evaluating the model's alerting capability is typically done using classification metrics defined from the picks (Zhu and Beroza, 2018; Münchmeyer *et al.*, 2022; Kim *et al.*, 2023; Yu *et al.*, 2023). We define a pick as a true positive (TP) if it falls within a TP window of ± 0.3 s of the labeled *P* arrival. False positives (FPs) are assigned to picks outside the window or to extra picks that are not TPs. False negatives (FNs) occur if no picks occur within the window. True negatives are not informative in this context and are not recorded. An example of a model prediction featuring classified picks is shown in Figure 4.

In our display, we consider summary metrics including $\mathrm{Recall} = \frac{\mathrm{TP}}{\mathrm{TP+FN}}$ and $\mathrm{F1} = \frac{2\mathrm{TP}}{2\mathrm{TP+FP+FN}}$, which are only applied to earthquake waveforms. For noise waveforms, we calculate noise percent correct as the number of noise waveforms containing no predicted picks ($\mathrm{TN}_{\mathrm{noise}}$) divided by the total number of noise waveforms (n_{noise}). That is, $\mathrm{Noise\%Correct} = \frac{\mathrm{TN}_{\mathrm{noise}}}{n_{\mathrm{noise}}}$. We recognize that classifying noise waveforms is a relatively trivial task and that analysts may be interested in different metrics beyond the ones analyzed here.

Evaluating accuracy is typically dependent on the classification results and is done using regression-based metrics (Zhu and Beroza, 2018; Münchmeyer *et al.*, 2022; Kim *et al.*, 2023; Yu *et al.*, 2023). If a pick is classified as a TP, then we obtain a residual defined as the difference in time between

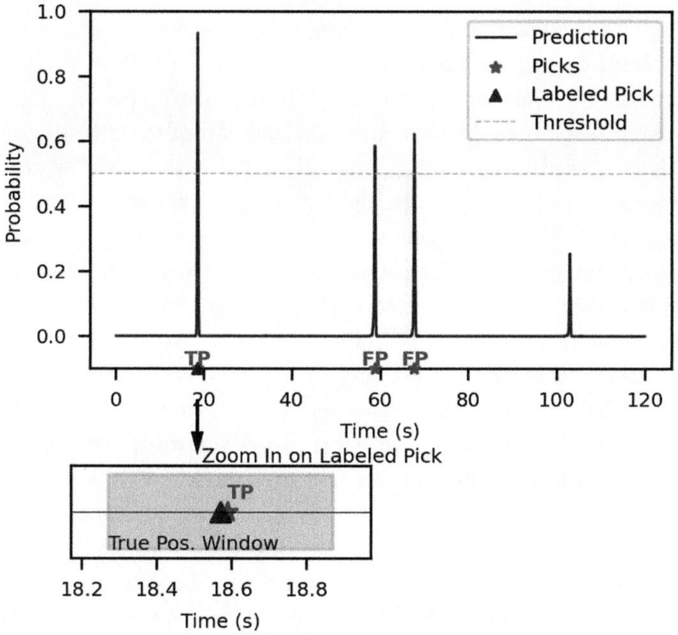

Figure 4. An example of a model output for a test waveform showing the predicted probability of the *P* arrival at each time point. The labeled *P* arrival is displayed on the *x-axis* as a blue triangle along with three predicted picks (green stars) and labels classifying the pick as either a false positive (FP) or true positive (TP). An inset plot zooms in on the TP window (orange box: ± 0.3 s around the labeled *P* arrival) to show the TP. Here, an arbitrary threshold of 0.5 (orange line) was used for example purposes. The color version of this figure is available only in the electronic edition.

the labeled *P* pick and the predicted *P* pick. Because different models can produce different numbers of TPs, typical regression metrics like the root mean square residual (rmsr; the square root of the sum of the residuals divided by the number of TPs) fail to convey the full story. Therefore, function-based metrics like cumulative rmsr, defined as rmsr calculated using only the residuals for which magnitudes are below some value, are more informative.

We define a different threshold for each model instance by choosing the threshold that maximizes the mean of F1 and Noise%Correct on the validation set to seek a balanced performance between noise and earthquake classes. However, this is an arbitrary decision, and the choice is typically dependent on the analyst's goals.

Statistical framework for evaluation

In this section, we present a statistical framework for comparing models in terms of their performance and uncertainty arising from data sampling and model training. The statistical framework can be thought of as a mixed effects model or a completely randomized design with subsampling. It allows us to distinguish performance effects with uncertainty between the three models and different data training budgets. Furthermore, we can segregate and estimate the two sources of variation with uncertainty.

For a given metric that summarizes the outcomes of a model instance, denoted y_{madi}, in which y is the metric (e.g., Recall), we set up the statistical model

$$y_{madi} = \gamma + \mu_m + \alpha_a + \theta_{ma} + \epsilon^{\text{data}}_{mad} + \epsilon^{\text{train}}_{madi}, \tag{1}$$

in which $m = \{1\ldots3\}$ indexes the three model training approaches, $a = \{1,\ldots,5\}$ indexes the five quantities of clusters (representing the amount of data) at levels $\{1,3,6,9,12\}$, $d = \{1,\ldots,12\}$ indexes the randomly selected cluster set (i.e., the data choice selected to train the model), and $i = \{1,2,3,4\}$ indexes the four model initializations. Here, γ is the grand mean, μ_m is the effect of model m, α_a is the effect of the ath quantity of clusters, and θ_{ma} is the interaction term.

The uncertainty associated with data sampling and training is segregated into two independent random terms each assuming a zero mean independent and identically distributed Gaussian with variance inherent to a given model and quantity of clusters: $\epsilon^{\text{data}}_{mad} \sim \mathcal{N}(0,\sigma^{2\text{data}}_{ma})$ and $\epsilon^{\text{train}}_{madi} \sim \mathcal{N}(0,\sigma^{2\text{train}}_{ma})$. The distribution of the error terms implies a distribution of the metric as $y_{madi} \sim \mathcal{N}(\gamma + \mu_m + \alpha_a + \theta_{ma}, \sigma^{2\text{data}}_{ma} + \sigma^{2\text{train}}_{ma})$. We recognize that metrics such as recall are bounded between [0,1], so the Gaussian assumption theoretically cannot hold. However, in practice, the metrics are calculated from a large number of test waveforms, which provides theoretical support for the Gaussian assumption through the central limit theorem. In addition, we find that the variances of these metrics are small compared to the range of the metrics' bounds. Furthermore, these assumptions are reasonable because the Gaussian distribution is capable of approximating confidence even when the error distribution is not strictly Gaussian. In addition, we verified the assumptions through visual inspection of quantile–quantile plots that compare the sorted residuals as a function of the theoretical quantiles for all metrics of interest. An example of this check for the F1 score is shown in Figure 5, demonstrating strong support for the theoretical assumptions.

Using these models, we estimate the effect of each model and quantity of clusters on the metric by computing the mean over the 12 cluster sets and the 4 initializations. Then, we compute 90% confidence intervals around those estimates using the Gaussian assumptions. The intervals are influenced more heavily by the cluster set (data choice) uncertainty because at each cluster set, we average over the initializations, thereby reducing training uncertainty influence.

Results

After training the 720 model instances, computing the performance metrics, and organizing them through the statistical framework, we are ready to compare the performance of the models.

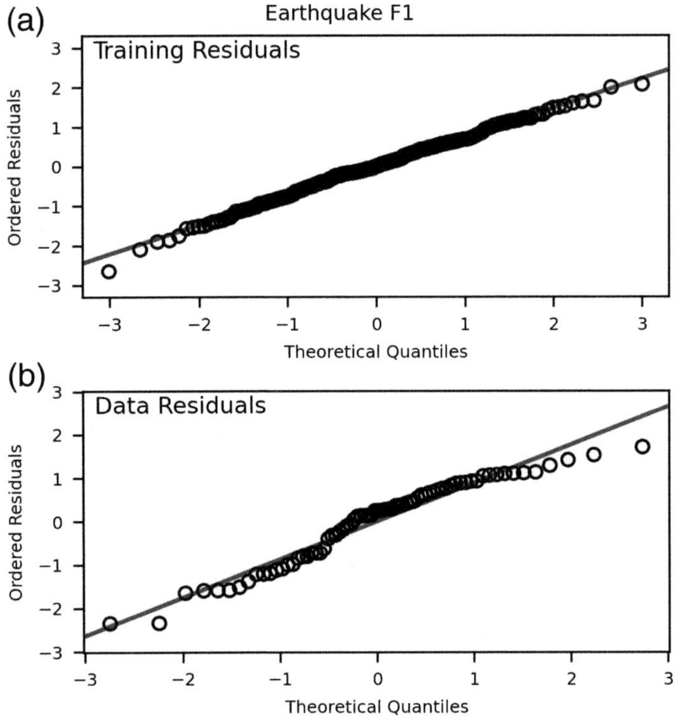

Figure 5. Gaussian assumptions are visually verified through quantile–quantile plots. As an example, the sorted (a) training and (b) data residuals for the F1 score are seen to align closely with the theoretical quantiles as defined by the statistical framework, as seen in how the points follow the red line. The color version of this figure is available only in the electronic edition.

The classification-based summary metrics of recall and noise percent correct are presented in Figure 6 along with 90% confidence intervals for the standard, TL free, and TL frozen models, showing their performance as a function of the quantity of clusters used in training. All models improve in recall because more data are added, with the largest gains between 1 and 3 clusters, followed by diminishing returns. The trend is less consistent for noise percent correct, where, in contrast to expectations, the TL frozen model performs slightly worse with increasing data. The uncertainty in performances decreases for all models as more training data are added.

The functional regression-based metric of cumulative rmsr, demonstrating the evaluation's framework versatility and importance, is shown in Figure 7 for the three models with 90% confidence intervals (ribbons) for 1, 6, and 12 quantities of clusters. To compute these, we apply the statistical framework (1), treating each discretized element along the domain as a standalone metric. Stark performance differences can be seen between each model, especially as more training data are added, as seen through tightening confidence intervals. The cumulative rmsr ends at 0.3 s because that is the half-width of the TP window.

In Figures 6 and 7, we see that there is no clear winner in terms of learning efficiency for all training budgets. The TL free model demonstrates superiority in the mean performance for recall and cumulative rmsr for the smallest data size of 1 cluster, but is surpassed by the standard model at three clusters and beyond. These results would help practitioners choose the model for their given problem. Depending on the availability of training data and how they prioritize performance metrics, their choice would change.

Our evaluation framework allows for estimation of two sources of performance uncertainty, including random data

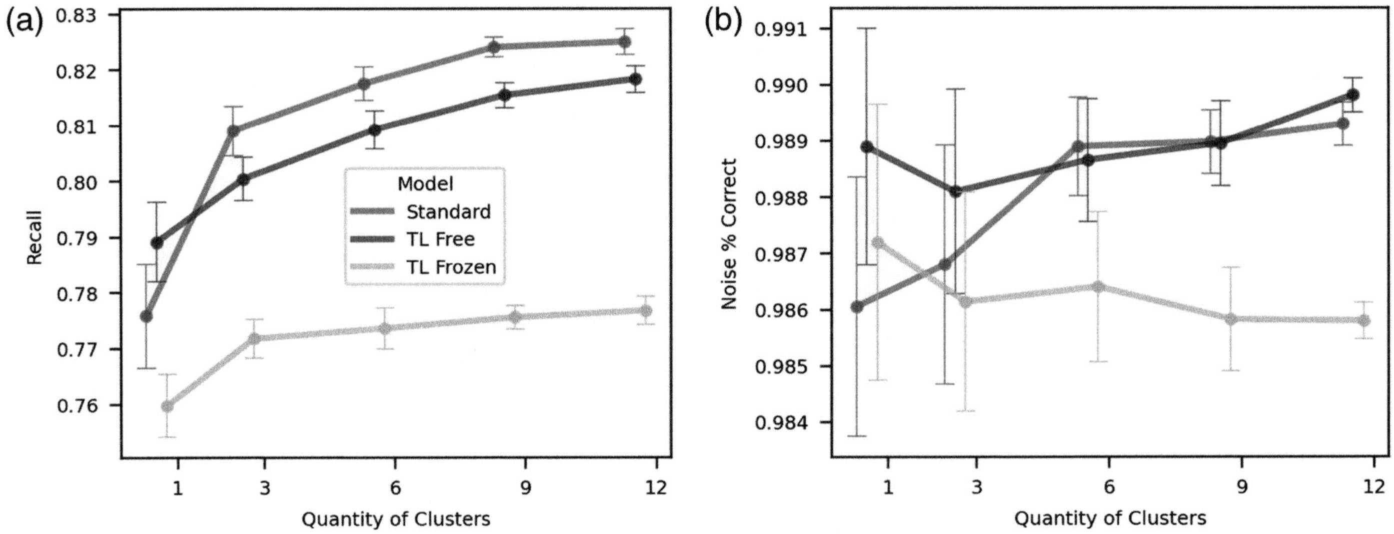

Figure 6. Statistical framework is used to summarize classification results, including earthquake (a) recall and (b) noise percent correct as a function of the number of clusters used for training for the three training approaches. Vertical bars represent 90% confidence intervals. Largest performance gains occur as the quantity of clusters increases from 1 to 3, and crossing lines indicate different training approaches are superior for different budgets of training data. TL, transfer learning. The color version of this figure is available only in the electronic edition.

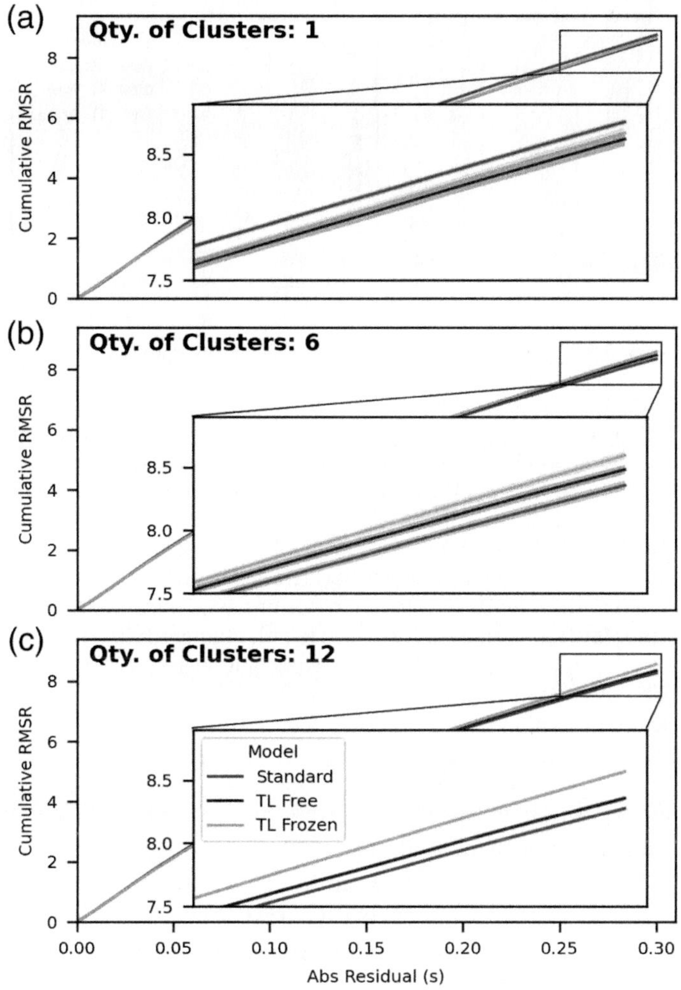

Figure 7. Statistical framework is used to summarize the regression-based functional metric of cumulative root mean square residual (rmsr) for (a) 1, (b) 6, and (c) 12 clusters for the three models. Ribbons indicate 90% confidence intervals. Inset plots zoom into the tails to show how the relative positions of the model curves change as more training data are added, indicating that no model is the most efficient learner for all training data budgets. The color version of this figure is available only in the electronic edition.

sampling and stochastic training processes. As an example, Figure 8 shows these estimates for F1 for the three models across the training data budgets with 90% confidence intervals. We see that training and data variance decrease as more training data are added, and we see some differentiation in the estimated variances for each model. The data variance (middle panel) shrinks quickly toward zero as more data are added and is often estimated as negative. These negative estimates are not shown because negative variance estimates are theoretically impossible. This is a known challenge in these classical statistical frameworks, but negative values essentially mean the data variance component is very small relative to the training variance.

Figure 8c shows the relative contributions of each source of uncertainty through bar plots, for which the opaque and transparent bars are the contributions of data and training variances, respectively. The total variance for all models trends downward with more data, with diminishing returns. The uncertainty is mostly dominated by the stochastic training processes when the number of clusters is 3 or more. Practitioners can use this information to target specific sources of variation that they suspect might dominate their problem, perhaps by running more initializations or strategically labeling data.

We provide an example that emphasizes the risk of evaluating models without considering uncertainty in performance. We consider the scenario in which a practitioner is deciding among the three training approaches to incorporate into their workflow. They are equipped with a single cluster set, say one cluster's worth of data. To make their decision, we imagine that they train one instance of each model using the fixed data. We did exactly this in our training design, but we went further by training each model four times under different initializations, not just once. As such, we imagine the practitioner is equally likely to get one of the four recall scores we obtained for each model. Thus, with three models and four equally likely results for each, there are $4^3 = 64$ equally likely possible outcomes that the practitioner could realize. If the practitioner ranks each model based on recall score (e.g., first place, second place, and third place), due to stochastic training processes, we might expect these rankings to change if the practitioner ran the experiment a second time. The important question then becomes, what is the probability that each model gets each rank?

Using our three models, each initialized four times for a fixed quantity of clusters, we calculate the exact probabilities that each model is ranked in first, second, or third place. Furthermore, because we have 12 cluster sets for each quantity of clusters, we conduct these calculations for each of the 12 sets and take the mean to mitigate data bias. The results of this simulation are presented in Figure 9, for which the probability estimates of ranking each model based on recall in first, second, or third place are shown for 1 and 12 cluster quantities.

Figure 9 shows that, due to training and data uncertainty, there is a substantial risk of choosing a model that performs more poorly on average. For example, for 1 cluster (Fig. 9a), there is a 2.0% chance that TL Frozen has the best recall score. In light of the recall results in Figure 6a for 1 cluster, we know that TL frozen performs substantially worse than the other two models on average. In our case, based purely on recall, it would be a mistake if the practitioner were to choose this model for their workflow. In a similar light, claiming that the TL frozen model is the state of the art compared to the other two would be a grave mistake because it could encourage technological development in a dead end. Our framework helps guard against such mistakes.

Discussion

We present results that will be increasingly relevant for developers of DLMs for the seismic community. In inspecting the results presented in Figure 6, we see overall poor performance

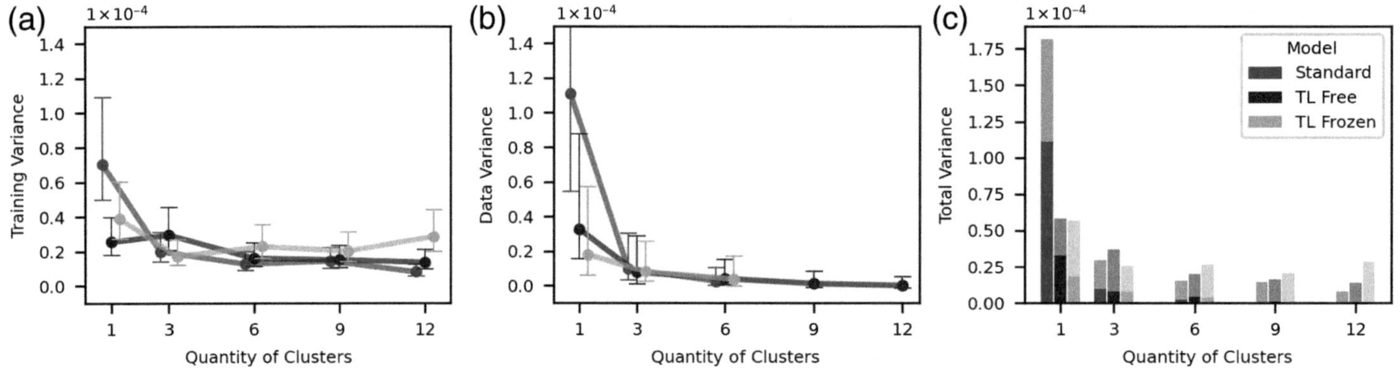

in the TL frozen model. We hypothesized that freezing half the model at the learned weights from the global dataset would produce the best model for small training data amounts. However, the results negate this hypothesis in our case for datasets comprising 10,000 waveforms (approximately the number of waveforms in a single cluster) or more for the PhaseNet architecture. In a similar vein, we see that models trained from scratch perform better than TL when the data size approaches 30,000 waveforms (three clusters). This suggests that TL might not always lead to better performance and emphasizes the need to continue comparing TL with traditional training approaches.

Figure 8. (a) Training variance and (b) data sampling variance are estimated with 90% confidence intervals (vertical bars) for F1 for the three training approaches. (c) Bar plots are constructed as the sum of the estimates of training and data variances. The different transparency levels show the contribution of each component, for which the training contribution is transparent and the data contribution is opaque. Estimating performance uncertainty and attributing the source is informative to practitioners during model selection for setting performance expectations and risk mitigation. The color version of this figure is available only in the electronic edition.

Our results show that there is no one model that performs the best across all training data quantities. The optimal model choice may depend on the amount of labeled data available for training, especially in low-data scenarios. Another valuable result for the seismic AI community is that expending effort to acquire larger and larger labeled training datasets may be wasteful. This is exhibited by Figure 6, for which we see diminishing improvement as the amount of training data increases. This suggests relatively smaller datasets (~30,000 or ~60,000 waveforms in our case) may be sufficient for reasonable model performance even when training models from scratch. This is good news because large labeled datasets are expensive and sometimes unattainable. We acknowledge that these conclusions may change depending on how a given analyst or developer chooses their data, model architecture, training process, data augmentations, and metric formulations. Estimating learning efficiency could help understand the cost and benefit trade-off for obtaining more data in this situation.

We emphasized evaluation of models in terms of their learning efficiency while accounting for training and data uncertainty in the metrics of interest. These aspects are valuable for a more holistic, robust evaluation, but there are more aspects that could supplement our framework by providing context to the raw performance metrics. Some examples of these aspects include the amount of training and computing resources, the intricacy of data augmentations, robustness to noise, predictive uncertainty coverage, architecture complexity, energy efficiency, and model transparency or interpretability. Although these important evaluation aspects are not covered in our exposition, our evaluation framework can assist with a fair comparison of them going forward.

In this work, we emphasized the importance of controlling data leakage when splitting the data into training, validation and test sets to better measure learning efficiency and represent data uncertainty. We constructed our splits by clustering using source locations as a simple and potentially representative approach to how seismic datasets are often geographically constrained. However, clustering on different features informed by domain experts may provide greater control over data leakage, better representation of data sampling procedures, and can target specific performance goals like performance on out-of-distribution test data.

The optimal number of clusters is something to be considered alongside estimating data variance. We noted that some data variances are estimated as negative because they are small relative to training variance. One way to more precisely estimate data variance is to increase the number of cluster sets (i.e., from 12 randomly chosen cluster sets to 30). However, we would not see much variation in the cluster sets for large quantities of clusters (e.g., 9 or 12) because we do not sample with replacement. Sampling with replacement would allow larger cluster quantities to have more variety in their cluster compositions. But, this also has a drawback in that some models may get biased toward a specific cluster if it appears multiple times in the cluster set and may not best represent data sampling uncertainty. Another option is to create more clusters such that each cluster set is more likely to be a unique combination of clusters, and the probability of a single cluster appearing multiple times is diminished. However, we are limited in decreasing

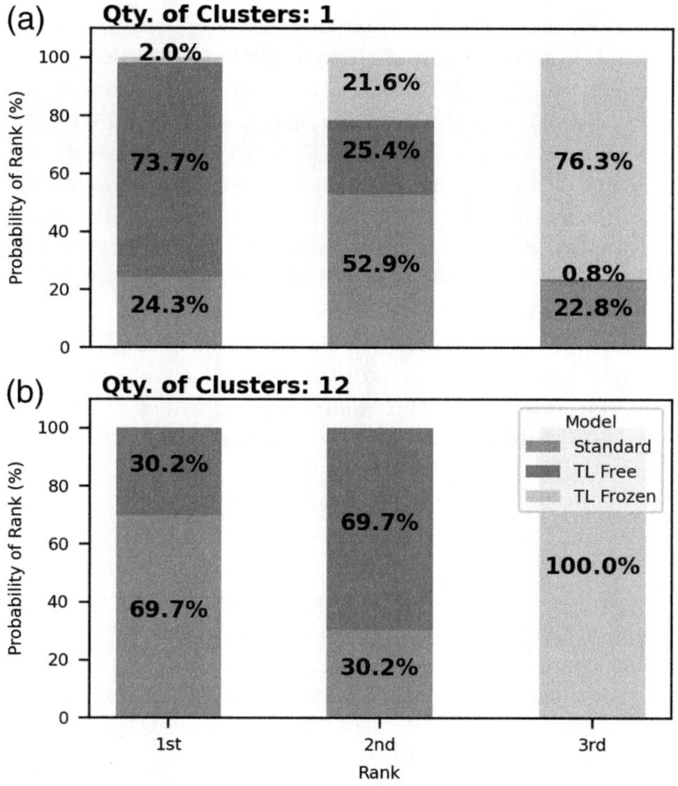

Figure 9. To demonstrate the importance of considering uncertainty in the evaluation framework, the probability of ranking the three training approaches based on recall in first, second, or third place is shown for (a) 1 and (b) 12 quantities of clusters. The numbers and height of bars indicate the probability of ranking the associated model in each place if one were to only train one model instance. Numbers less than 100% indicate that misranking the models is a risk that is detrimental to model selection. The color version of this figure is available only in the electronic edition.

the cluster sizes because as the total number of clusters approaches the number of sources, the issue of data leakage resurfaces. Determining the best solution to this issue is a fruitful topic for future research.

In our display, we leverage deep ensembles to obtain training uncertainty for performance for a few reasons. Fundamentally, deep ensembles are easy to understand and implement, and they only require extending training time. This is in contrast to other uncertainty methods that attempt to estimate prediction uncertainty or approximate the posterior distribution of a given prediction. These methods include Bayesian neural networks (Lampinen and Vehtari, 2001) and approximations thereof, including dropout (Gal and Ghahramani, 2016), stochastic weight averaging-Gaussian (SWAG; Maddox *et al.*, 2019), and many others (Gawlikowski *et al.*, 2022). However, these approaches enforce distributional assumptions of the model weights, make strong or arbitrary decisions (e.g., dropout), rarely consider different basins of attraction, and are generally more difficult to interpret. However, some methods, such as MultiSWAG (Wilson and Izmailov, 2022; see Armstrong *et al.*, 2023 for a seismic-based implementation), offer a strong balance between the complex Bayesian assumptions and the simpler empirical ensembles and offer strong promise for estimating performance uncertainty.

There are also avenues for improvement for the statistical framework. A Bayesian framework could assist when comparing models with similar characteristics through hierarchical sharing of information. In addition, it could also address the issue of estimating negative data variances through constrained priors.

Inspired by the remarkable success of foundation models (FMs), a subset of AI (typically DL) models trained on vast amounts of data in a self-supervised fashion that can be adapted for various downstream tasks using relatively smaller labeled datasets (Bommasani *et al.*, 2022), in the areas of natural language processing and computer vision, FMs are actively being developed for seismology (Gao *et al.*, 2024; Liu *et al.*, 2024; Si *et al.*, 2024). As the seismic community prepares to assess the utility of seismic FMs, our work provides some useful directions. Because FMs are pretrained using a large general dataset and fine-tuned (typically, weights for the last couple of layers are set to be updated) using tailored datasets to accomplish downstream tasks, our work highlights the importance of assessing the utility of seismic FMs by comparing them to traditional models. Our results also fortify the importance of learning efficiency as an aspect of future FM evaluation. Because the best model depends on the amount of training data, knowing which model or training approach performs better with less data is valuable information during model selection. And, as our results show, it may not be a simple one-model-takes-all, but rather a dynamic choice for a given situation.

Conclusion

We present an evaluation framework for seismic DLMs that simultaneously considers performance uncertainty and learning efficiency. We demonstrate our evaluation framework using PhaseNet—a popular phase picking DLM to compare three training approaches (training from scratch and two TL approaches). We implement an extensive training design utilizing deep ensembles and meticulously constructed training splits that partially control for data leakage. We summarize the resulting 720 model instances through a statistical framework to compare the three training approaches across the training budgets with uncertainty.

We demonstrate the effectiveness and versatility of the evaluation framework by comparing classification and functional regression metrics. We show how no model is a global winner in terms of learning efficiency; it depends on the total amount of training data used. By providing estimates for the data and training uncertainty, a developer or practitioner can better target their efforts to mitigate sources they deem most important for their problem. We show that without the evaluation framework, there is a significant risk of model misranking. Finally, our results demonstrate how TL may not always be the best choice in limited data scenarios, which is particularly important as the seismic community invests in seismic FMs and emphasizes the importance of comparing FMs to their simpler DLM counterparts and inspecting how training data budgets influence model performance. We hope that this research helps practitioners and developers by providing an evaluation framework for robust model comparison.

Data and Resources

All data used in this article came from published sources listed in the references.

Declaration of Competing Interests

The authors acknowledge that there are no conflicts of interest recorded.

Acknowledgments

This work was performed under the U.S. Department of Energy, National Nuclear Security Administration's Office of Defense Nuclear Nonproliferation Research and Development. This work is approved for public release under LA-UR-24-31133. The authors would like to thank Chengping Chai (Oak Ridge National Laboratory), Lisa Linville (Sandia National Laboratory), and Leanna House (Virginia Tech) for their advice and/or edits.

References

Alzubaidi, L., J. Bai, A. Al-Sabaawi, J. Santamaría, A. S. Albahri, B. S. N. Al-dabbagh, M. A. Fadhel, M. Manoufali, J. Zhang, A. H. Al-Timemy, *et al.* (2023). A survey on deep learning tools dealing with data scarcity: Definitions, challenges, solutions, tips, and applications. *J. Big Data* **10**, no. 1, 46.

Amiri, M., R. Brooks, and H. Rivaz (2020). Fine-tuning U-Net for ultrasound image segmentation: Different layers, different outcomes, *IEEE Trans. Ultrason. Ferroelect. Freq. Contr.* **67**, no. 12, 2510–2518.

Armstrong, A. D., Z. Claerhout, B. Baker, and K. D. Koper (2023). A deep-learning phase picker with calibrated Bayesian-derived uncertainties for earthquakes in the Yellowstone volcanic region, *Bull. Seismol. Soc. Am.* **113**, no. 6, 2323–2344.

Arrowsmith, S. J., D. T. Trugman, J. MacCarthy, K. J. Bergen, D. Lumley, and M. B. Magnani (2022). Big data seismology, *Rev. Geophys.* **60**, no. 2, e2021RG000769, doi: 10.1029/2021RG000769.

Bommasani, R., D. A. Hudson, E. Adeli, R. Altman, S. Arora, S. von Arx, M. S. Bernstein, J. Bohg, A. Bosselut, E. Brunskill, *et al.* (2022). On the opportunities and risks of foundation models, available at http://arxiv.org/abs/2108.07258 (last accessed January 2025).

Bornstein, T., D. Lange, J. Münchmeyer, J. Woollam, A. Rietbrock, G. Barcheck, I. Grevemeyer, and F. Tilmann (2024). PickBlue: Seismic phase picking for ocean bottom seismometers with deep learning, *Earth Space Sci.* **11**, no. 1, e2023EA003332, doi: 10.1029/2023EA003332.

Bouthillier, X., P. Delaunay, M. Bronzi, A. Trofimov, B. Nichyporuk, J. Szeto, N. Sepah, E. Raff, K. Madan, V. Voleti, *et al.* (2021). Accounting for variance in machine learning benchmarks, available at http://arxiv.org/abs/2103.03098 (last accessed December 2024).

Chai, C., M. Maceira, H. J. Santos-Villalobos, S. V. Venkatakrishnan, M. Schoenball, W. Zhu, G. C. Beroza, C. Thurber, and , and EGS Collab Team (2020). Using a deep neural network and transfer learning to bridge scales for seismic phase picking, *Geophys. Res. Lett.* **47**, no. 16, e2020GL088651, doi: 10.1029/2020GL088651.

Chen, G., and J. Li (2022). CubeNet: Array-based seismic phase picking with deep learning, *Seismol. Res. Lett.* **93**, no. 5, 2554–2569.

Cianetti, S., R. Bruni, S. Gaviano, D. Keir, D. Piccinini, G. Saccorotti, and C. Giunchi (2021). Comparison of deep learning techniques for the investigation of a seismic sequence: An application to the 2019, Mw 4.5 Mugello (Italy) earthquake, *J. Geophys. Res.* **126**, no. 12, e2021JB023405, doi: 10.1029/2021JB023405.

Dehghani, M., Y. Tay, A. A. Gritsenko, Z. Zhao, N. Houlsby, F. Diaz, D. Metzler, and O. Vinyals (2021). The benchmark lottery, available at http://arxiv.org/abs/2107.07002 (last accessed November 2024).

Dietterich, T. G. (1998). Approximate statistical tests for comparing supervised classification learning algorithms, *Neural Comput.* **10**, no. 7, 1895–1923.

Ferrer Florensa, A., J. Almagro Armenteros, H. Nielsen, F. Aarestrup, and P. Clausen (2024). SpanSeq: Similarity-based sequence data splitting method for improved development and assessment of deep learning projects, *NAR Genomics Bioinf.* **6**, no. 3, lqae106, doi: 10.1093/nargab/lqae106.

Gal, Y., and Z. Ghahramani (2016). Dropout as a Bayesian approximation: Representing model uncertainty in deep learning, available at http://arxiv.org/abs/1506.02142 (last accessed March 2024).

Ganaie, M., M. Hu, A. Malik, M. Tanveer, and P. Suganthan (2022). Ensemble deep learning: A review, *Eng. Appl. Artif. Intell.* **115,** 105,151.

Gao, H., X. Wu, L. Liang, H. Sheng, X. Si, G. Hui, and Y. Li (2024). A foundation model enpowered by a multi-modal prompt engine for universal seismic geobody interpretation across surveys, available at http://arxiv.org/abs/2409.04962 (last accessed February 2025).

Gawlikowski, J., C. R. N. Tassi, M. Ali, J. Lee, M. Humt, J. Feng, A. Kruspe, R. Triebel, P. Jung, R. Roscher, *et al.* (2022). A survey of uncertainty in deep neural networks, available at http://arxiv.org/abs/2107.03342 (last accessed October 2024).

Goldstein, H., and D. J. Spiegelhalter (1996). League tables and their limitations: Statistical issues in comparisons of institutional performance, *J. Roy. Stat. Soc. A* **159**, no. 3, 385.

Hlynsson, H. D., A. N. Escalante-B, and L. Wiskott (2019). Measuring the data efficiency of deep learning methods, *Proc. of the 8th International Conference on Pattern Recognition Applications and Methods*, 691–698, available at http://arxiv.org/abs/1907.02549 (last accessed January 2025).

Huang, G., Y. Li, G. Pleiss, Z. Liu, J. E. Hopcroft, and K. Q. Weinberger (2017). Snapshot ensembles: Train 1, get M for free, available at http://arxiv.org/abs/1704.00109 (last accessed May 2024).

Kim, A., Y. Nakamura, Y. Yukutake, H. Uematsu, and Y. Abe (2023). Development of a high-performance seismic phase picker using deep learning in the Hakone volcanic area, *Earth Planets Space* **75**, no. 1, 85.

Kingma, D. P., and J. Ba (2017). Adam: A method for stochastic optimization, available at http://arxiv.org/abs/1412.6980 (last accessed January 2025).

Lakshminarayanan, B., A. Pritzel, and C. Blundell (2017). Simple and scalable predictive uncertainty estimation using deep ensembles, available at http://arxiv.org/abs/1612.01474 (last accessed May 2024).

Lampinen, J., and A. Vehtari (2001). Bayesian approach for neural networks—Review and case studies, *Neural Networks* **14**, no. 3, 257–274.

Liu, T., J. Münchmeyer, L. Laurenti, C. Marone, M. V. d. Hoop, and I. Dokmanić (2024). SeisLM: A foundation model for seismic waveforms, available at http://arxiv.org/abs/2410.15765 (last accessed February 2025).

Maddox, W., T. Garipov, P. Izmailov, D. Vetrov, and A. G. Wilson (2019). A simple baseline for Bayesian uncertainty in deep learning, available at http://arxiv.org/abs/1902.02476 (last accessed December 2024).

Michelini, A., S. Cianetti, S. Gaviano, C. Giunchi, D. Jozinović, and V. Lauciani (2021). INSTANCE—The Italian seismic dataset for machine learning, *Earth Syst. Sci. Data* **13**, no. 12, 5509–5544.

Mousavi, S. M., and G. C. Beroza (2022). Deep-learning seismology, *Science* **377**, no. 6607, eabm4470, doi: 10.1126/science.abm4470.

Mousavi, S. M., G. C. Beroza, T. Mukerji, and M. Rasht-Behesht (2024). Applications of deep neural networks in exploration seismology: A technical survey, *Geophysics* **89**, no. 1, WA95–WA115.

Mousavi, S. M., W. L. Ellsworth, W. Zhu, L. Y. Chuang, and G. C. Beroza (2020). Earthquake transformer—An attentive deep-learning model for simultaneous earthquake detection and phase picking, *Nat. Commun.* **11**, no. 1, 3952.

Mousavi, S. M., Y. Sheng, W. Zhu, and G. C. Beroza (2019). STanford EArthquake Dataset (STEAD): A global data set of seismic signals for AI, *IEEE Access* **7**, 179,464–179,476.

Münchmeyer, J., J. Woollam, A. Rietbrock, F. Tilmann, D. Lange, T. Bornstein, T. Diehl, C. Giunchi, F. Haslinger, D. Jozinović, *et al.* (2022). Which picker fits my data? A quantitative evaluation of deep learning based seismic pickers, *J. Geophys. Res.* **127**, no. 1, e2021JB023499, doi: 10.1029/2021JB023499.

Niksejel, A., and M. Zhang (2024). OBSTransformer: A deep-learning seismic phase picker for OBS data using automated labelling and transfer learning, *Geophys. J. Int.* **237**, no. 1, 485–505.

Park, Y., G. C. Beroza, and W. L. Ellsworth (2022). Basement fault activation before larger earthquakes in Oklahoma and Kansas, *Seism. Record* **2**, no. 3, 197–206.

Park, Y., B. G. Delbridge, and D. R. Shelly (2024). Making phase-picking neural networks more consistent and interpretable, *Seism. Record* **4**, no. 1, 72–80.

Paszke, A., S. Gross, F. Massa, A. Lerer, J. Bradbury, G. Chanan, T. Killeen, Z. Lin, N. Gimelshein, L. Antiga, *et al.* (2019). PyTorch: An imperative style, high-performance deep learning library, available at http://arxiv.org/abs/1912.01703 (last accessed November 2022).

Pedregosa, F., G. Varoquaux, A. Gramfort, V. Michel, B. Thirion, O. Grisel, M. Blondel, A. Müller, J. Nothman, G. Louppe, *et al.* (2018). Scikit-learn: Machine learning in Python, available at http://arxiv.org/abs/1201.0490 (last accessed December 2024).

Pita-Sllim, O., C. J. Chamberlain, J. Townend, and E. Warren-Smith (2023). Parametric testing of EQTransformer's performance against a high-quality, manually picked catalog for reliable and accurate seismic phase picking, *Seism. Record* **3**, no. 4, 332–341.

Reimers, N., and I. Gurevych (2017). Reporting score distributions makes a difference: Performance study of LSTM-networks for sequence tagging, *Proc. 2017 Conference on Empirical Methods in Natural Language Processing, Volume Proceedings of the 2017 Conference on Empirical Methods in Natural Language Processing*, Copenhagen, Denmark, 338–348.

Ronneberger, O., P. Fischer, and T. Brox (2015). U-Net: Convolutional networks for biomedical image segmentation, in *Medical Image Computing and Computer-Assisted Intervention - MICCAI 2015*, N. Navab, J. Hornegger, W. M. Wells, and A. F. Frangi (Editors), Vol. 9351, Lecture Notes in Computer Science, Springer International Publishing. Cham, Switzerland, 234–241.

Ross, Z. E., M. Meier, E. Hauksson, and T. H. Heaton (2018). Generalized seismic phase detection with deep learning, *Bull. Seismol. Soc. Am.* **108**, no. 5A, 2894–2901.

Si, X., X. Wu, H. Sheng, J. Zhu, and Z. Li (2024). SeisCLIP: A seismology foundation model pre-trained by multimodal data for multipurpose seismic feature extraction, *IEEE Trans. Geosci. Remote Sens.* **62,** 1–13.

Tokuda, T., and H. Nagao (2023). Seismic-phase detection using multiple deep learning models for global and local representations of waveforms, *Geophys. J. Int.* **235**, no. 2, 1163–1182.

Wein, S., C. Homan, L. Aroyo, and C. Welty (2023). Follow the leader(-board) with confidence: Estimating p-values from a single test set with item and response variance, in *Findings of the Association for Computational Linguistics: ACL 2023*, A. Rogers, J. Boyd-Graber, and N. Okazaki (Editors), Association for Computational Linguistics, Toronto, Canada, 3138–3161.

Wilson, A. G., and P. Izmailov (2022). Bayesian deep learning and a probabilistic perspective of generalization, available at http://arxiv.org/abs/2002.08791 (last accessed January 2025).

Woollam, J., J. Münchmeyer, F. Tilmann, A. Rietbrock, D. Lange, T. Bornstein, T. Diehl, C. Giunchi, F. Haslinger, D. Jozinović, *et al.* (2022). SeisBench—A toolbox for machine learning in seismology, *Seismol. Res. Lett.* **93**, no. 3, 1695–1709.

Yoon, C. E., E. S. Cochran, E. A. Vanacore, V. Huerfano, G. Báez-Sánchez, J. D. Wilding, and J. Smith (2023). A detailed view of the 2020–2023 Southwestern Puerto Rico seismic sequence with deep learning, *Bull. Seismol. Soc. Am.* **113**, no. 6, 2377–2415.

Yu, S., and J. Ma (2021). Deep learning for geophysics: Current and future trends, *Rev. Geophys.* **59**, no. 3, e2021RG000742, doi: 10.1029/2021RG000742.

Yu, Z., W. Wang, and Y. Chen (2023). Benchmark on the accuracy and efficiency of several neural network based phase pickers using datasets from China Seismic Network, *Earthq. Sci.* **36**, no. 2, 113–131.

Zhu, L., Z. Peng, J. McClellan, C. Li, D. Yao, Z. Li, and L. Fang (2019). Deep learning for seismic phase detection and picking in the aftershock zone of 2008 M 7.9 Wenchuan earthquake, *Phys. Earth Planet. In.* **293,** 106,261.

Zhu, W., and G. C. Beroza (2018). PhaseNet: A deep-neural-network-based seismic arrival time picking method, *Geophys. J. Int.* **216,** no. 1, 261–273, doi: 10.1093/gji/ggy423.

Zhu, W., K. S. Tai, S. M. Mousavi, P. Bailis, and G. C. Beroza (2022). An end-to-end earthquake detection method for joint phase picking and association using deep learning, *J. Geophys. Res.* **127**, no. 3, e2021JB023283, doi: 10.1029/2021JB023283.

Appendix

Data splits and cluster distributions

Figures A1–A4 aim to provide a deeper view into how the clustering impacts the distributions of various signal properties of the waveforms. Because this work focuses primarily on *P* picking, we use a 10 s window starting at the labeled *P* arrival for

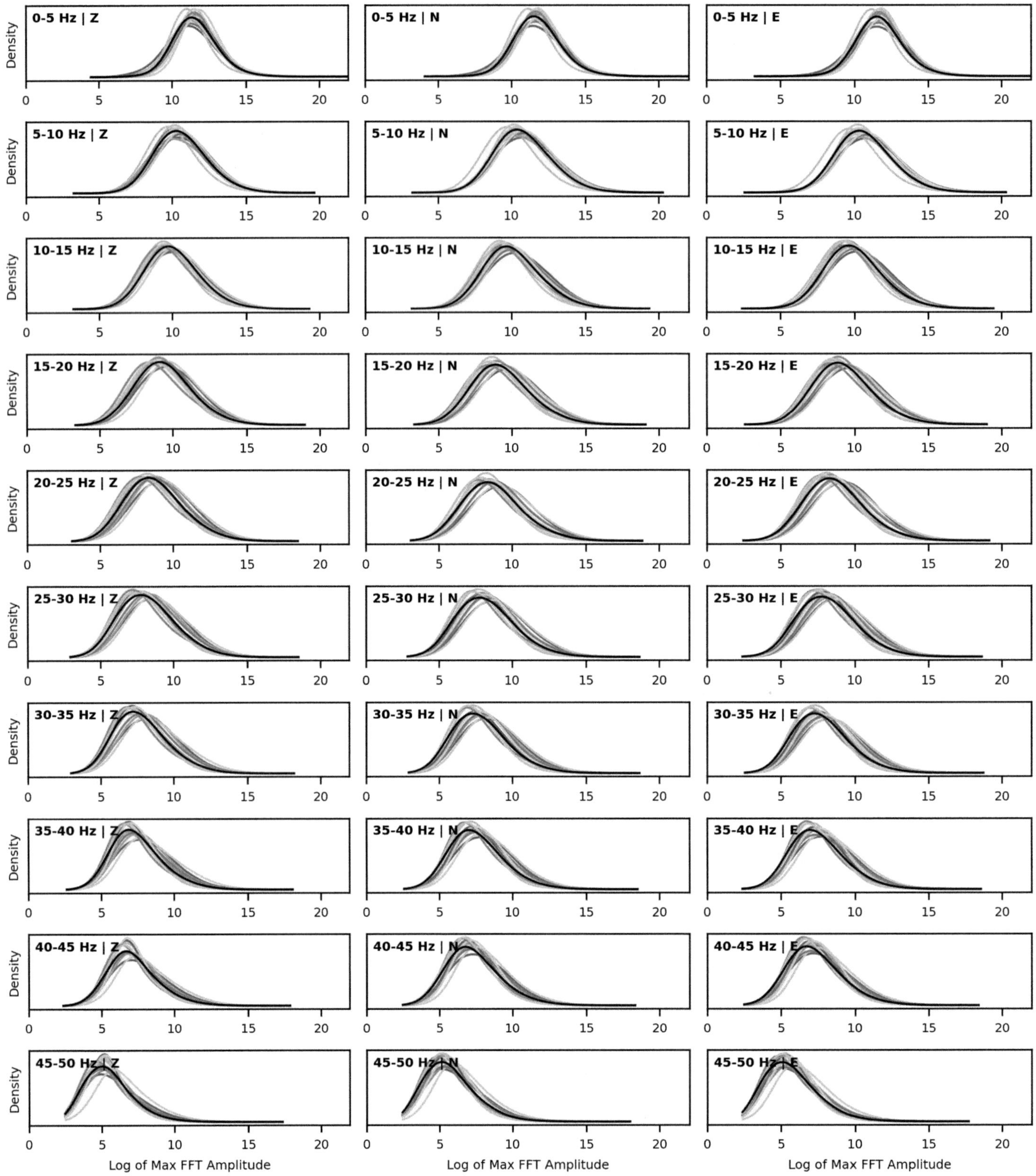

Figure A1. Distributions of the maximum log fast Fourier transform (FFT) amplitude within each 5 Hz frequency bin (rows) are shown for the three components (columns) for each cluster (nonblack curves) and the testing set (black curve). The color version of this figure is available only in the electronic edition.

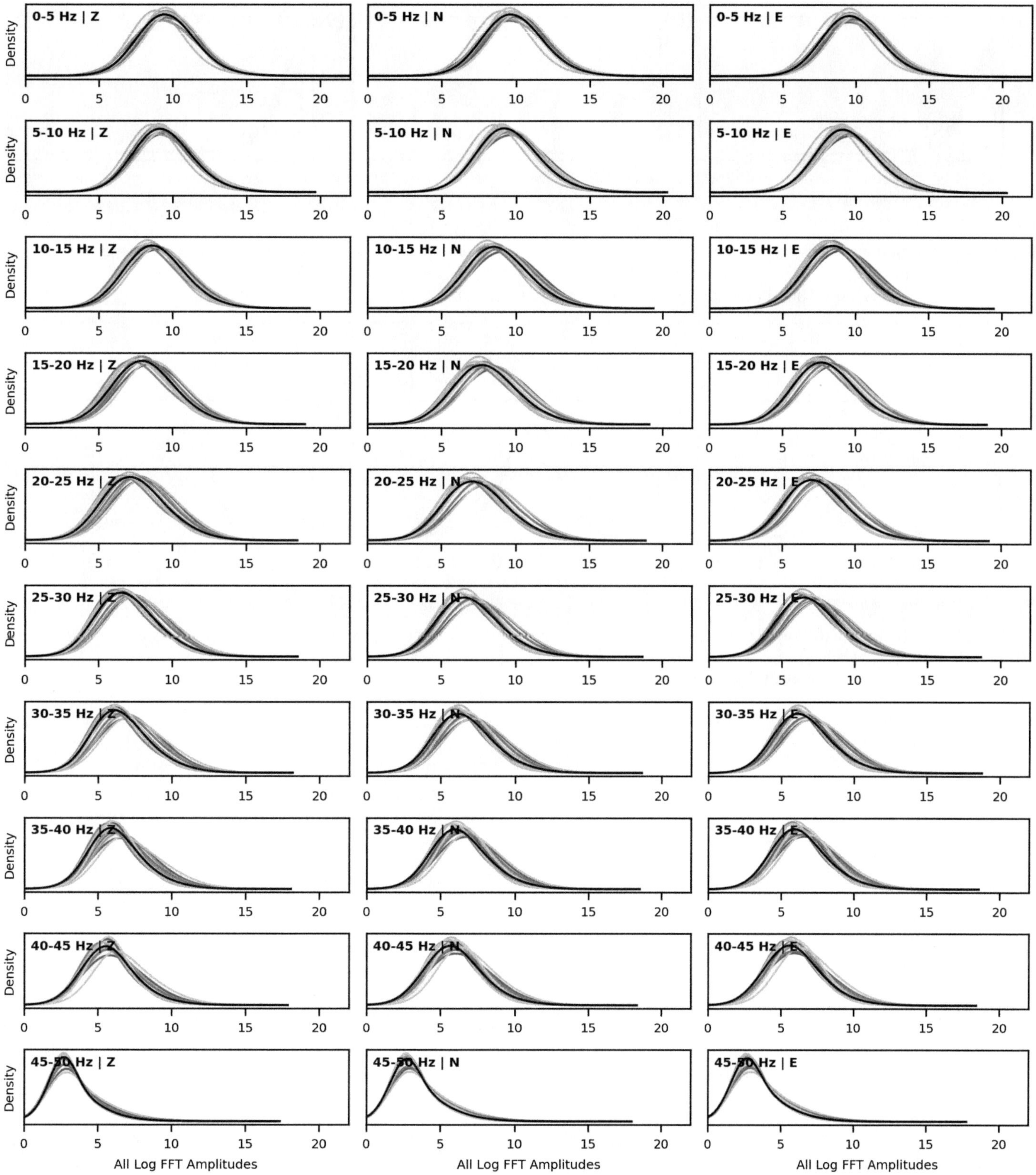

Figure A2. Distributions of all FFT amplitudes within each 5 Hz frequency bin (rows) are shown for the three components (columns) for each cluster (nonblack curves) and the testing set (black curve). The color version of this figure is available only in the electronic edition.

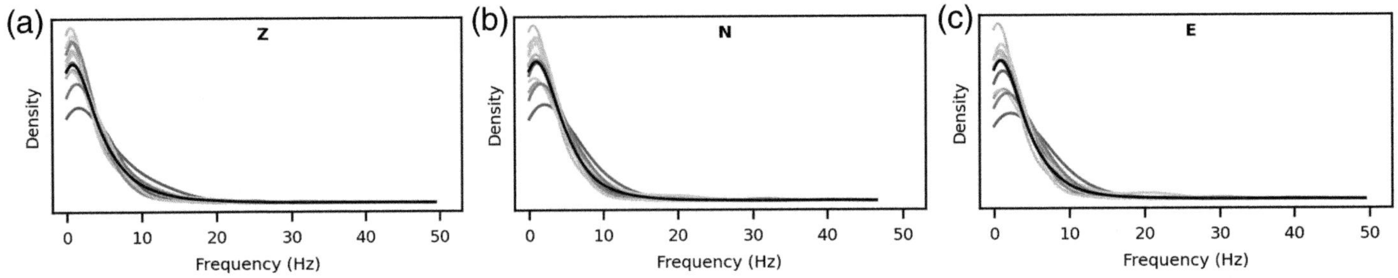

Figure A3. Distributions of the frequencies coinciding with the maximum FFT amplitudes (i.e., the argmax) within a 10 s window starting at the labeled *P* arrival are shown for the (a) Z, (b) N, and (c) E components for each cluster (nonblack curves) and the testing set (black curve). The color version of this figure is available only in the electronic edition.

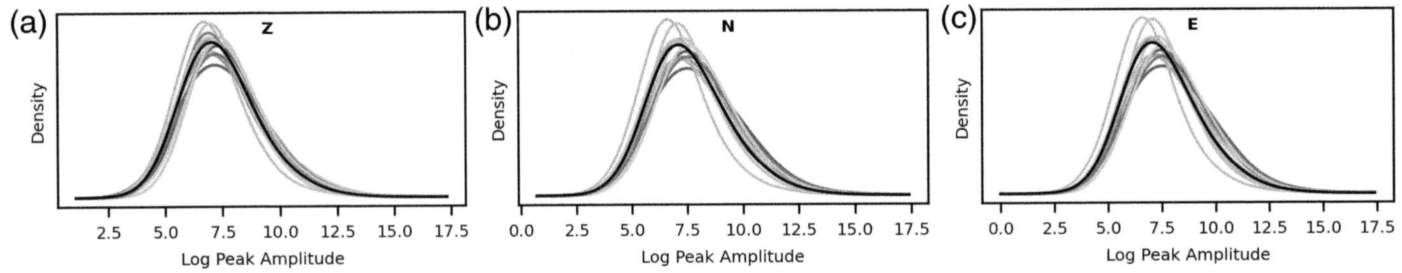

Figure A4. Distributions of the log of the peak amplitudes within a 10 s window starting at the labeled *P* arrival are shown for the (a) Z, (b) N, and (c) E components for each cluster (nonblack curves) and the testing set (black curve). The color version of this figure is available only in the electronic edition.

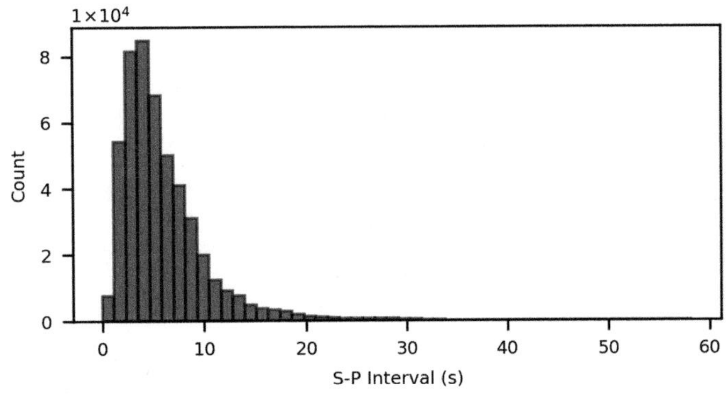

Figure A5. Distribution of the *S-P* intervals in seconds is shown for the INSTANCE data for which there are labeled *S* arrivals. Only about 60% of the 824,135 waveforms contain a labeled *S* arrival.

these signal properties. In all figures, the testing set is shown in black, and each nonblack curve coincides with the identically colored clusters in the main article (Fig. 2). All curves are normalized for comparison such that they integrate to 1. A 10 s window was chosen because only about 60% of the 824,135 waveforms have a labeled *S* wave, so an adaptive *S–P* interval window that captures only *P*-wave information was infeasible without further analysis. In addition, Figure A5 shows the distribution of *S–P* intervals for those waveforms that contain labeled *S* arrivals. About 87% of the waveforms have *S–P* intervals less than 10 s, so most or all of the *P*-wave information is captured in the majority of the waveforms, without including *S*-wave information for particularly long *S–P* intervals.

Manuscript received 4 November 2024
Published online 29 July 2025

Cardinal: Seismic and Geoacoustic Array Processing

Miro Ronac Giannone*[1,2], Stephen J. Arrowsmith[2], and Elizabeth A. Silber[1]

Abstract

Data collected via seismic and infrasound array deployments are leveraged in the geosciences to detect and characterize a myriad of natural and anthropogenic sources. These deployments consist of numerous sensors placed in a predetermined configuration to amplify signal strength and improve the efficacy of array processing techniques used to measure signal directionality and waveform coherence. High-fidelity feature extraction is often predicated on interstation distance as well as the frequency content and wavelength of an incident signal. Numerous array processing softwares analyze data in sequential frequency bands to obtain a more detailed characterization of a signal. However, current algorithms are limited in their ability to determine optimal array configuration for each band. We introduce an open-source Python code, called Cardinal, to process seismic and infrasound array data in discretized time–frequency space with the option of applying an adaptive array design to determine optimal subarray configuration for each frequency band. To reduce computational time, the array processing step can be run in parallel using multithreading. Moreover, the software has the capability to aggregate array processing results from different time–frequency pixels to produce separate sets of detections, or families, with added utility via the application of an adaptive semblance threshold, which aids in isolating signals-of-interest from coherent background noise. Upon appropriate configuration, Cardinal exhibits the potential to combine distinct seismic and infrasound phases into separate families.

Cite this article as Ronac Giannone, M., S. J. Arrowsmith, and E. A. Silber (2025). Cardinal: Seismic and Geoacoustic Array Processing, *Seismol. Res. Lett.* **97**, 487–500, doi: 10.1785/0220240434.

Supplemental Material

Introduction

Array deployments are commonly used in seismology and infrasound to record wavefields. Correspondingly, arrays are the groupings of sensors with spatial samplings designed based on target signal wavelengths. As opposed to processing single sensor data, array processing allows for the implementation of various beamforming methods, which involve the use of differential travel times measured between individual sensors to shift and sum the array data (Rost and Thomas, 2002). Beamforming leverages constructive interference of coherent signals during summation, whereas incoherent noise destructively interferes, thus boosting signal-to-noise ratio (SNR). In addition, this method provides directionality estimates, which can be useful for event location. When applying this approach to infrasound arrays, its effectiveness is dependent upon noise conditions, array design, and signal wavelength. In comparison to the solid earth, the comparatively lower lateral heterogeneity in the atmosphere means that directionality estimates from infrasound array data are often more useful than from seismic data. Both seismic and infrasound arrays are utilized extensively on a global scale as part of the International Monitoring System (IMS) to detect and locate nuclear explosions for international treaty verification (Christie and Campus, 2010).

Within the infrasound community, the progressive multichannel correlation (PMCC) algorithm is one of the most common methods used to process array data (Cansi, 1995; Cansi and Le Pichon, 2008). Its utility lies in its ability to process over multiple frequency bands and relax the requirements of the rigid plane-wave model via subarray processing. In addition, frequency–wavenumber (*f-k*) analysis is a frequently used array processing method for both seismic and infrasound data (Capon, 1969; Rost and Thomas, 2002, 2009). *f-k* analysis allows for the measurement of the complete slowness vector simultaneously via a grid search over trial slownesses in the frequency domain. As an alternative to *f-k* processing, least-squares beamforming has recently been explored to estimate directionality, although it is typically less robust for low SNR signals (Szuberla and Olson, 2004; Bishop *et al.*, 2020). A recent study introduced an open-source Python software package, which applies least-squares processing over multiple

1. Sandia National Laboratories, Albuquerque, New Mexico, U.S.A., https://orcid.org/0000-0001-8752-2263 (MRG); https://orcid.org/0000-0003-4778-1409 (EAS); 2. Department of Earth Science, Southern Methodist University, Dallas, Texas, U.S.A., https://orcid.org/0000-0002-9150-0363 (SJA)

*Corresponding author: mnronac@sandia.gov; mronacgiannone@smu.edu narrow-frequency bands (Iezzi *et al.*, 2022). The authors note improvements in detection capabilities over broadband processing. Although a few multifrequency array processing softwares are utilized in the geosciences, these algorithms lack a detailed approach for determining optimal subarray configuration for each frequency band when processing data from multiscale arrays.

In this article, we demonstrate the advantage of implementing an adaptive array selection procedure for robustly detecting and capturing the properties of signals. We describe the processing flow of Cardinal—a multifrequency array processing software with adaptive array design capabilities—and apply the software package to several ground-based and air-based events. In addition, within some of the examples, we illustrate when the adaptive array design can be implemented to improve processing results. Cardinal consists of four integral components: (1) the Segmentor, which discretizes time–frequency space, (2) the Adaptive Array, which uses both unsupervised and supervised machine learning algorithms to determine optimal subarray configuration for each sequential frequency band, (3) the Array Processor, which applies an array processing method to each pixel in time–frequency space, and (4) the Aggregator, which compiles pixels into sets of detections via a weighted distance and semblance threshold, with adaptive capabilities.

Preprocessing

Motivated by the work done by Park *et al.* (2023), the software package provides steps to preprocess array data prior to implementing the standard Cardinal processing algorithm. The approach begins by constructing power spectral densities (PSDs) to assess sensor state of health. Any flat PSD is automatically removed. A PSD is considered flat if the slope of the line of best fit to the frequencies and power spectral values are below a specified slope threshold (defaults to 0.1). In addition, the function utilizes density-based spatial clustering of applications with noise (DBSCAN) to identify any outlier sensors (Ester *et al.*, 1996). The outlier distance threshold for DBSCAN is based on the number of standard deviations from the mean of the power spectral values (defaults to 1). Waveform cross-correlation is then applied to the array data to check for inverted polarities. The program cross-correlates sensor data with a predetermined reference sensor. Any sensor with a correlation coefficient below a specified value is highlighted (defaults to −0.95). Finally, data availability rates are quantified for each sensor. The program automatically removes sensors with data gaps that exceed a specified percent threshold (defaults to 20%). We exemplify the preprocessing approach by introducing array data associated with an infrasonic bolide detection at the I07AU array (Fig. 1). We manually add noise to sensor H2 and invert the polarity at H3 (Fig. 1a). Figure 1b,c exhibits the program's capabilities at identifying the faulty sensor and inverted polarity, respectively. Figure 1d displays the data availability rates for each sensor.

Algorithm

Segmentor

Array data are processed by Cardinal in discrete time–frequency blocks. The Segmentor provides the discretized specification of processing time–frequency blocks. Deriving optimal time windows and frequency bands is predicated on a given array configuration and the signals-of-interest. Correspondingly, time windows should be determined based on array spacing and dominant signal period. It is imperative to choose a time window that provides sufficient temporal resolution for the largest period in a given filter band while also preventing the presence of multiple phases. In PMCC, for example, the minimum time window is twice the size of the maximum period within sequential bands. The use of multiple time–frequency blocks in Cardinal enables a more general processing scheme for application to signals with different temporal and spectral characteristics. However, based on the work of Iezzi *et al.* (2022), we suggest initially applying Cardinal using one-third octave frequency bands for interactive analysis because narrower bands allow for a more detailed characterization of seismic and infrasound signals. Cardinal provides utility functions that can generate frequency bands in a variety of ways with associated time windows. These functions include:

- *pmcc_fbands*: Returns the PMCC frequency band configuration (e.g., Matoza *et al.*, 2013). These bands are logarithmic, with time window based on the largest period of each frequency band that extends in totality from 0.01 to 5 Hz.
- *extend_pmcc_fbands*: Returns an extended PMCC configuration to a higher maximum frequency set by the user. This function retains logarithmic frequency band spacing and constructs window lengths corresponding to a linearly proportional relationship with period.
- *make_custom_fbands*: This function returns sequential frequency bands spaced as a function of decadal, octave, or one-third octave ratios (Garcés, 2013). The relationship between time window and frequency band is assumed linear with period and fit by constructing a straight line between the points defined by (*maximum period, maximum window length*) and (*minimum period, minimum window length*).

Adaptive array

The performance of an array for resolving a plane wave with specific wavelength is mathematically described by the array response function (ARF) (Rost and Thomas, 2002). Thus, we use the ARF as a starting point for quantifying how well a given array configuration fits a specific frequency band. The ARF is described by

$$A(\vec{k}) = \left| \frac{1}{N} \sum_{n=1}^{N} e^{-i\vec{k}\cdot\vec{r}_n} \right|^2, \tag{1}$$

in which N represents the number of sensors within the array, $\vec{r}_n$ is the positional vector for sensor, n, and $\vec{k}$ is the wavenumber vector defined by

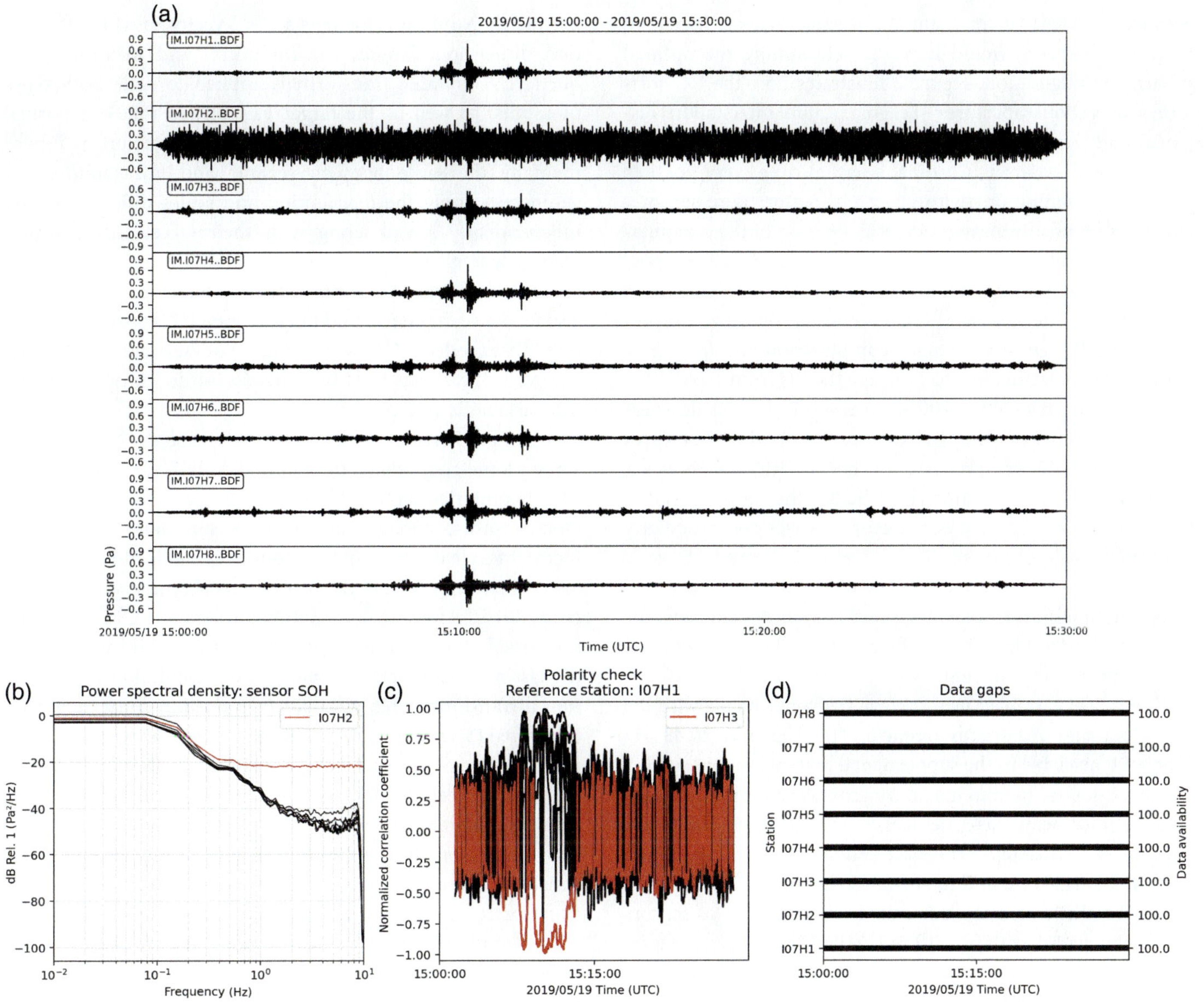

$$\vec{k} = w \times \vec{u}, \tag{2}$$

with ω and $\vec{u}$ representing angular frequency and slowness, respectively. Because the magnitude of the slowness vector is the reciprocal of velocity, angular frequency can thus be described as

$$w = \frac{2\pi v}{\lambda}, \tag{3}$$

in which v denotes velocity and λ represents wavelength. Because of the inverse relationship between frequency and wavelength, multifrequency array processing with multiscale arrays necessitates a search for an optimal subarray geometry for sequential frequency bands and a designated wavespeed.

Our generalized optimum selection problem requires our algorithm to determine the subarray configuration that gives the optimal ARF. We quantify the optimal response by constructing a single metric that we label as the response criterion (RC). The RC aggregates statistical characteristics of the ARF,

Figure 1. Cardinal's preprocessing routine applied to a bolide recorded by I07AU infrasound array. (a) The infrasound array data in which sensors H2 and H3 were modified to highlight how the function characterizes sensor state of health. (b) The power spectral densities of each sensor. (c) The cross-correlation results which check for inverted polarities. (d) Data availability.

including the normalized mean (average beam power, μ) and normalized standard deviation (spread of energy, σ), as well as the maximum of the absolute power (array gain, p_{max}). The relationship is given by

$$\mathrm{RC} = \frac{\mu + \sigma}{p_{max}}. \tag{4}$$

In this approach, our objective is to minimize RC. The standard deviation operates to filter out linearities within the ARF, whereas the mean functions to remove responses consisting of large main lobes. We include the p_{max} term in equation (4) because we want to maintain the impact that an increased number of sensors would have on determining the optimal subarray configuration. Figure 2 illustrates how the RC sorts arrays of various apertures (i.e., maximum interstation distance) and configurations.

For any given array, Cardinal searches over every possible subarray configuration (with at least three or more sensors) and assesses effectiveness via the RC. Because of the computational loading associated with generating an ARF for every possible subarray configuration, the software implements a pretrained neural network (RC ConvFormer) optimized at predicting the RC given a subarray configuration and frequency band. The processing time to compute the RC from an ARF for 3 sensors within a 200 × 200 slowness grid and 50 slowness steps takes 100 ms using the Central Processing Unit cores of an Apple M2 Pro processor. Whereas, RC ConvFormer, consisting of 58,267 parameters, executes the same operation in under 0.05 ms. The use of the neural network is particularly important for applications of the Adaptive Array to large-N arrays or for site selection, in which the number of possible array combinations to evaluate grows combinatorially according to the sum of binomial coefficients from 3 to n, in which n is the total number of sensors.

The model is trained using octave frequency bands with the minimum and maximum frequency of 0.02 and 20.48 Hz (Table S1, available in the supplemental material to this article). Octave bands are used to maximize generalization performance to both third-octave and decadal bands. Synthetic multiscale seismic and infrasound arrays are produced for training. Both contain a small-scale and large-scale aperture, which can have up to five elements each. Infrasound arrays consist of sensors randomly spaced within a 0.2 × 0.2 km and 5 × 5 km grid for both small- and large-scale configurations, respectively. Furthermore, seismic array elements are spaced within a 2 × 2 km and 50 × 50 km grid. The difference in scales between seismic and infrasound arrays functions to emulate the order of magnitude difference in associated propagation velocities. Each array can have a minimum of 3 and a maximum of 10 elements. In total, 250,000 synthetic seismic and 250,000 synthetic infrasound array geometries are compiled and randomly distributed across the 10 octave frequency bands. The coordinates within each array geometry are modified to be relative to a randomly selected reference element. ARFs are computed for each synthetic array, whereas the corresponding RC is stored as the neural network's target variable for training. Each ARF is plotted on a 200 × 200 slowness grid using 50 slowness steps with minimum phase velocities for both regional seismic (3000 m/s) and infrasound (340 m/s) signals.

To maintain a fixed input feature vector length, each array geometry is center padded. Thus, each input array geometry sustains a fixed dimension of 10 × 2, in which the first dimension represents the number of elements in the array, and the second dimension represents corresponding XY coordinates. Frequency bands are stored as a 1 × 2 vector in which the second dimension denotes the minimum and maximum frequency. A quantile transform is applied to scale both types of inputs, as well as the target variable, to follow a normal distribution. Because the underlying data structure is fundamentally the same between seismic and infrasound input geometries (only the distribution and scales differ), they are independently scaled along with their target variables and fed into a single model instead of creating two separate models for each data type. To improve the model's capacity to differentiate between them, an additional branch is constructed for a one-hot-encoded (OHE) variable. For seismic inputs, the categorical variable is [1,0], whereas for infrasound inputs, the variable is [0,1].

RC ConvFormer consists of three separate branches for array geometries, frequency bands, and OHE variables (Fig. 3). The geometries branch begins with preactivated residual blocks with convolutional layers to simultaneously extract hierarchical features from the input data and facilitate efficient backpropagation to the shallower layers (Lecun *et al.*, 1998; He *et al.*, 2016). After the convolutional layers, the OHE categorical variables are concatenated channel-wise with the output of the last residual block. The merged representation is then fed into a transformer block to aid in modeling contextual relationships (Vaswani *et al.*, 2017). In this architecture, the residual convolutional blocks operate to extract local spatial patterns between nearby sensors, whereas the transformer captures global relationships such as long-range dependencies between sensor positions and OHE categorical variables. Two dense layers are then added to improve the nonlinear mapping from inputs to outputs. The frequency band branch is simply fed through two dense layers. The respective outputs are then fused via a gated multimodal unit to generate an intermediate representation between the two (Arevalo *et al.*, 2020). Two dense layers are added again, and a final predictions layer with linear activation concludes the neural network. The linear activation function operates to keep the predictions unbounded for the corresponding regression task. To mitigate for overfitting during training, L2 kernel regularization is implemented throughout the model with increasing strength. K-fold cross-validation results using five splits are displayed in Figure S1. The model with the lowest mean square error is deployed within Cardinal.

ARF's assume a perfectly coherent plane wave across all array elements. However, this assumption may not hold in all cases, especially when the signal-of-interest contains higher frequencies. Consequently, to help mitigate for this waveform decorrelation, a gating mechanism is invoked to control the groupings of subarrays that RC ConvFormer searches over for each frequency band. The initial stage of the gating mechanism involves clustering subarrays by aperture using the K-means approach (MacQueen, 1967). The total number of clusters is suggested automatically within Cardinal via the

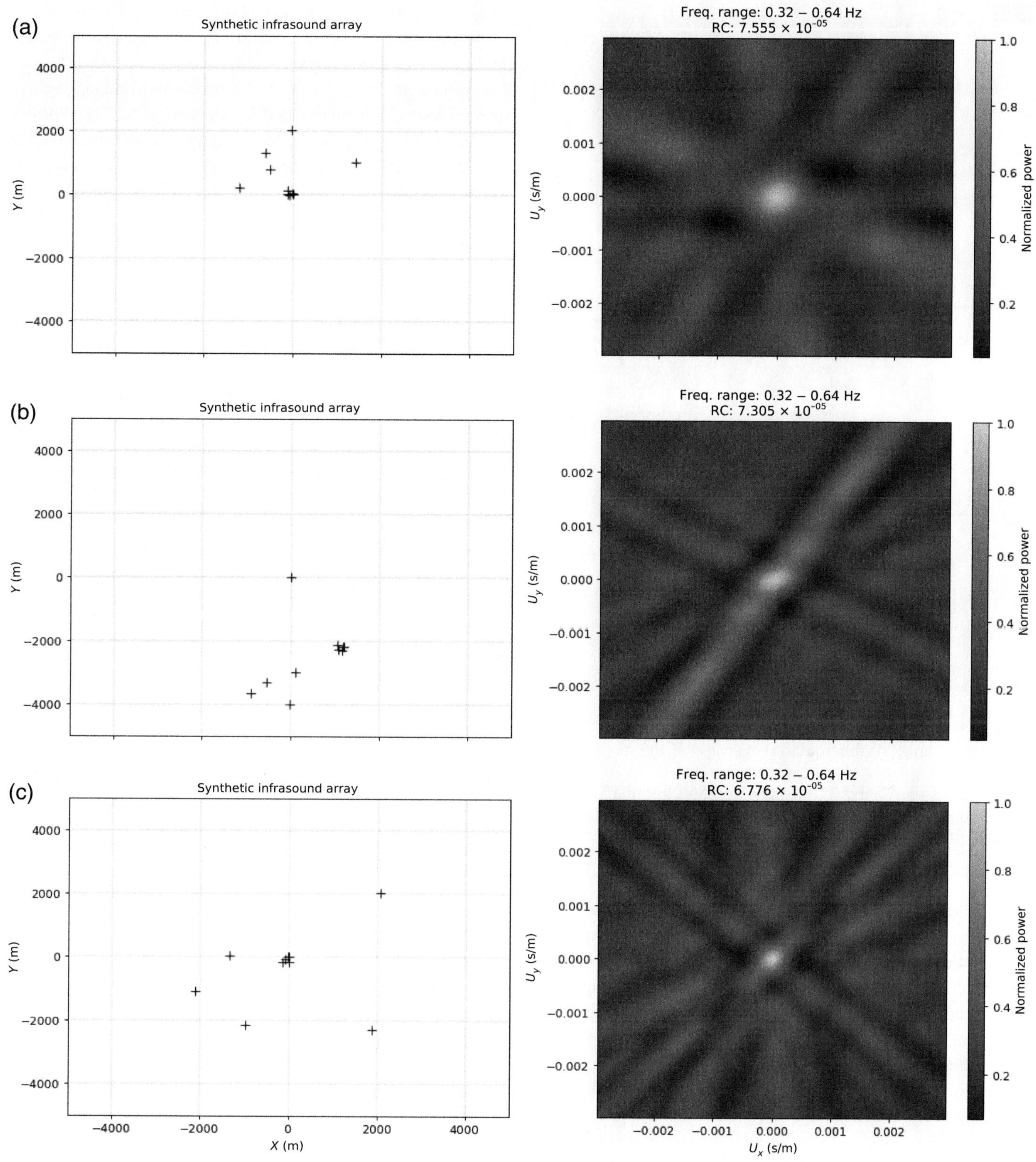

Figure 2. Response criterion (RC)-sorted array response functions (ARFs) for synthetically generated infrasound array geometries within the 0.32–0.64 Hz frequency band. First and second image columns display array geometries and associated ARFs, respectively. Each row consists of 10 randomly spaced sensors, in which 5 are included in a smaller central array configuration (0.2 × 0.2 km grid) and the remaining 5 constitute a larger outer array configuration (5 × 5 km grid). (a) The highest RC value. (b) A comparatively lower value due to an increased aperture resulting in a more focused and tighter main lobe, and (c) the lowest RC value by further removing the linearities within panel (b). The color version of this figure is available only in the electronic edition.

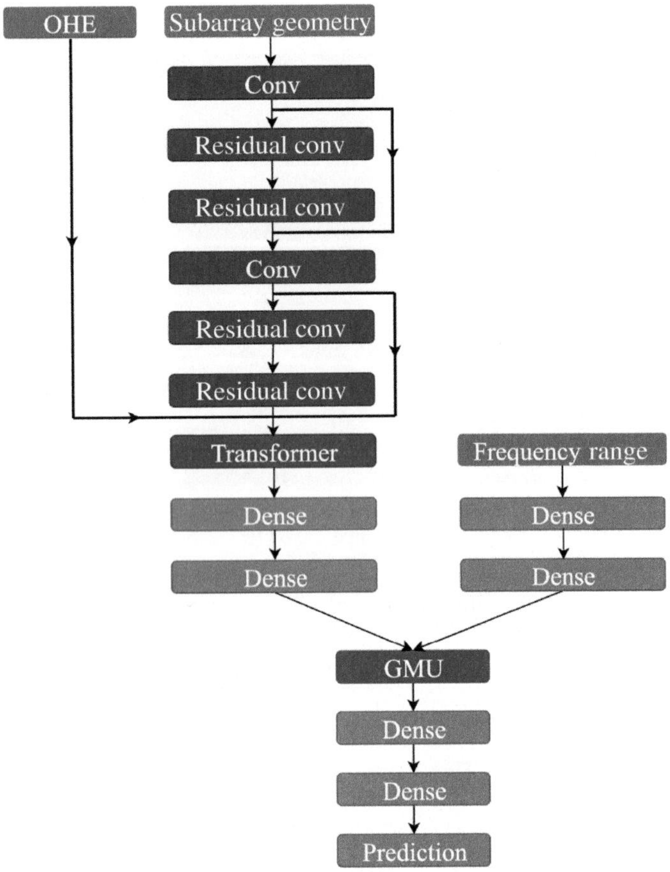

Figure 3. RC ConvFormer, a convolutional transformer network trained to predict RC, a single continuous variable, using relative array geometries, frequency bands, and one-hot-encoded (OHE) variables as input. A more detailed overview of the model, including the number of hidden units and embedding dimensions, can be seen on the GitHub page (for more information visit Data and Resources). GMU, gated multimodal unit. The color version of this figure is available only in the electronic edition.

hierarchical clustering dendrograms of interelement distances (e.g., Fig. S3b,d). The algorithm iterates over each frequency band, starting with the lowest frequency, and measures the maximum resolvable wavelength by dividing a designated wavespeed (340 m/s for infrasound and 3000 m/s for seismic) by the minimum frequency within the band. The operation begins with the cluster with the largest apertures and cycles to the following cluster once the maximum aperture within the grouping is larger than half of the maximum resolvable wavelength. This is done to facilitate reconstruction of the spatial characteristics of the wavefield. The RC is predicted for each subarray within the cluster and for each frequency band using the trained neural network. The subarray with the minimum RC is chosen as the optimal configuration for that band.

It is suggested to utilize the Adaptive Array's algorithm for regional events at regional distances recorded by multiscale arrays (e.g., Fig. S3a,c). In addition, it is imperative to not use frequency bands outside the frequency ranges used to train the model (i.e., do not use frequencies below 0.02 Hz and above 20.48 Hz). To maximize its application, frequency bands should be constructed following a three order of magnitude difference between minimum and maximum frequencies to aid in the characterization of broadband signals. Moreover, RC ConvFormer can be used pre-deployment to search over and determine optimal array configuration prior to an experiment. The model is versatile insofar as it is able to search over a wider range of array configurations, instead of being limited to the minimum of three sensors per array.

Array processor

Once time–frequency space has been discretized and optimal array geometries determined, Cardinal will execute the Array Processor and apply an array processing routine to each time–frequency block of data separately. In addition, Cardinal provides a slowness correction option which time-shifts the signals for a given slowness direction prior to processing. This enables the user to choose a shorter time window than required by the physical separation of the sensors for processing signals from a particular direction. The Array Processor also requires the ObsPy Stream object containing the waveform data for the array, and element coordinates. If the Adaptive Array was used prior to array processing, the output list of subarray ObsPy Stream objects will be used as substitute. The frequency bands, which are output by the Segmentor, are also required as input. Finally, the program requires slowness plane parameter inputs, which are initialized based on the array configuration and the anticipated wavespeed.

Cardinal is configured to apply the standard ObsPy *f-k* algorithm to the full array, or each subarray, across all frequency bands (Beyreuther *et al.*, 2010). For each time–frequency block, the discrete Fourier transform (DFT) is first applied to each time window using a cosine taper. The 22% taper, which tapers 11% from the start and 11% from the end, is an ObsPy default. Only the DFT for frequencies within the specified band is extracted. The method works by defining a slowness grid over all trial values of $u = (u_x, u_y)$ and estimating the power of beamformed signal for each trial value of slowness. The slowness grid should cover a plane over slowness values that extend out at least to the medium slowness, u_0. It is imperative that the slowness plane parameters are configured to encompass the characteristic slowness values of a signal-of-interest.

The output of array processing is a vector of times and matrices that contain the back azimuth, trace velocity, and semblance (i.e., power of the beam normalized by the total power in the waveforms). These matrices have dimension (N_f, N_t), in which N_f is the number of frequency bands and N_t is the number of time windows in the highest frequency band. The results from frequency bands with longer time windows are resampled onto the shortest time-window spacing. Cardinal provides the user various utility plotting functions to help visualize the processing results.

Aggregator

Cardinal further analyzes array processing results via the Aggregator by building sets of detections, or families. The term "families" is derived from PMCC and is based on the concept of aggregating array processing results from individual time–frequency blocks, referred to as "pixels" below, to form a detection representing an individual phase arrival (Cansi and Klinger, 1997). The process involves applying a semblance threshold to filter out values below a set limit. Thereafter, resultant pixels are clustered via a weighted distance threshold. The equations governing the weighted distance are as follows:

$$d_f = \frac{(f_i - f_j)^2}{\sigma_f^2}, \quad (5)$$

$$d_t = \frac{(t_i - t_j)^2}{\sigma_t^2}, \quad (6)$$

$$d_b = \frac{(b_i - b_j)^2}{\sigma_b^2}, \quad (7)$$

$$d = \sqrt{d_f + d_t + d_b}, \quad (8)$$

in which f_i, t_i, b_i, and f_j, t_j, b_j refer to the frequency, time, and back azimuth values of the ith and jth pixel, respectively, above some semblance threshold. The σ represents the standard deviation in frequency, time, and back-azimuth indices for clustering. These parameters can all be defined by the user prior to clustering. Furthermore, Cardinal provides added utility by allowing the user to apply a threshold minimum number of pixels for a family (Cansi and Klinger, 1997).

Finally, Cardinal is capable of applying an adaptive semblance threshold to mitigate for detections in bands with continuous coherent signals (e.g., microbaroms). These undesirable signals have the potential to obfuscate detections from other signals-of-interest. Simply raising the semblance threshold causes good detections to get missed in frequency bands without continuous background signals. Consequently, when making families, the user has the option to apply a p-value threshold, which operates to define a distinct semblance threshold for each frequency band that is weighted by the ambient coherence in that band. This form of anomaly detection is executed by estimating the background distribution of semblances in a frequency band using kernel density estimation (KDE) and then looking for outliers on the right tail based on the KDE fit (p-value threshold).

Results

To exhibit Cardinal's capabilities at detecting signals from various seismic and infrasonic sources, the software is applied to four events with distinct characteristics and associated array designs. First, we demonstrate the utility of combining Cardinal's adaptive array design and adaptive semblance threshold, citing improvements in both broadband detection and directionality estimates on two multiscale arrays, sampled at 20 Hz, which capture infrasound from two separate bolide events documented in National Aeronautics and Space Administration's Center for Near Earth Object Studies (CNEOS) database (Tagliaferri *et al.*, 1994). Following, the software is applied to infrasound generated by the 2024 Noto earthquake. Data were obtained via a high-frequency array in Korea sampled at 100 Hz. The Aggregator is employed to cluster sets of detections into families and filter out continuous coherent background noise by incorporating the adaptive semblance threshold. Finally, we apply Cardinal's adaptive array algorithm to the KSRS seismic array in Korea, which captured detections from the Democratic People's Republic of Korea's (DPRK) declared underground nuclear explosion (UNE) in September 2017. We report improvements in the characterization of the higher frequency components associated with the seismic phases as well as the signals corresponding to the subsequent cavity collapse. We limit our analysis to IMS stations for the detection and characterization of bolide infrasound. For the Noto earthquake, we use one of the many arrays that have been installed, maintained, and operated jointly by Southern Methodist University and the Korea Institute of Geoscience and Mineral Resources to improve source identification and quantify propagation path effects within the Korean Peninsula (Stump *et al.*, 2022). Third-octave frequency bands are applied ubiquitously throughout the remainder of the article.

Bolide infrasound

The interaction of a meteoroid with dense regions of the Earth's atmosphere generates luminous phenomena, or a meteor, through a number of physical and chemical processes, including sputtering, ablation, and sometimes fragmentation (Ceplecha *et al.*, 1998; Silber *et al.*, 2018). Fireballs are generally brighter than Venus (magnitude −4), whereas bolides typically refer to detonating fireballs. There are two main avenues through which infrasound can be generated by these types of atmospheric events. The first is through ballistic shock waves due to cylindrical line source geometry dominating the object's hypersonic flight within the continuum flow regime (ReVelle, 1976; Silber and Brown, 2014). Infrasound may also be generated via shock waves resulting from a fragmentation event, which could have spherical or quasi-spherical geometry (Silber, 2024).

We provide Cardinal array processing results from infrasound generated by two bolide events occurring on 19 May 2019 (Fig. 4a,c,e) and 26 February 2015 (Fig. 4b,d,e). Although classifying whether the observations are dominated by either spherical or cylindrical line source geometries is outside the scope of this article, we do note improvements in broadband detection, specifically detections at higher frequencies, for both bolides and improvements in directionality estimates with the 2015 event. Figure 4a,b displays results using Cardinal's default algorithm, which uses the entire array to process data for sequential frequency bands. Figure 4c,d displays results after implementing

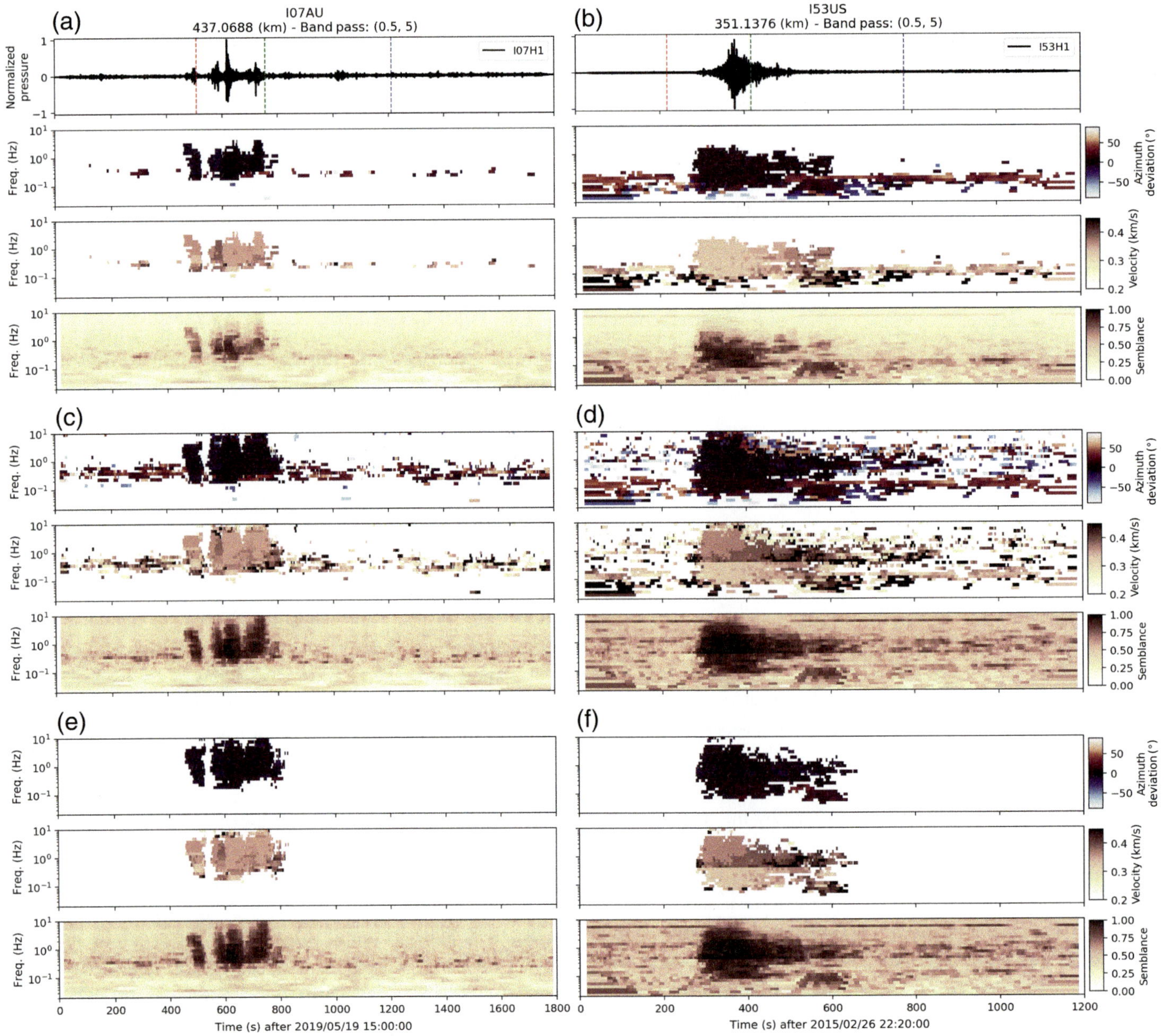

Figure 4. Cardinal array processing results from two distinct bolides recorded by International Monitoring System (IMS) stations I07AU (a,c,e) and I53US (b,d,f). For (a) and (b), the first panel plots the normalized filtered waveforms from a select reference station, the second panel plots the azimuth deviation relative to the location provided by Center for Near Earth Object Studies (CNEOS), the third panel displays associated trace velocity, and the last panel plots the semblance. The vertical red, green, and blue lines in the first panel represent theoretical delays for tropospheric (340 m/s), stratospheric (285 m/s), and thermospheric arrivals (220 m/s), respectively, based on the time and location corresponding to the peak brightness measured by CNEOS. We remove the first panel from successive subfigures for simplicity. The first row displays processing results using every sensor at each array for each frequency band (Cardinal's default setting). The second row showcases refined results after applying the Adaptive array. The final row displays further improvements after implementing Cardinal's Aggregator with adaptive semblance threshold. For results omitting the Aggregator, the semblance threshold was set to 0.5.

the Adaptive Array, which searches for an optimal subarray configuration for each frequency band. Refinements in directionality are showcased in the first panel of Figure 4d. Event maps for each bolide are displayed in Figure S2. Array configurations and associated dendrograms are shown in Figure S3. Subarray configurations used for each frequency band at I07AU and I53US are plotted in Figures S4 and S5, respectively. The frequency bands used to process the data are displayed in Table S2.

Axiomatically, waveform coherence will increase because array aperture decreases. This feature manifests as coherent background noise in Figure 4c,d at back azimuths discordant with the signals-of-interest. To filter out these undesirable detections, we implement Cardinal's Aggregator with p-value thresholds of 0.2 and 0.4 for each bolide, respectively (Fig. 4e,f). The adaptive semblance threshold effectively filters out continuous signals with semblance values comparable to the signals-of-interest. Values for each of the Aggregator's parameters are displayed in Table S3, and the families results are shown in Table S4. These results exhibit Cardinal's capability at comprehensively detecting infrasound from air-based events with characteristic broadband frequency contents in the presence of coherent background noise.

Earthquake infrasound

Infrasound from earthquakes is a comparatively less understood phenomenon due to the complexities associated with the interaction between the ground and atmosphere during the transfer of energy. Advancements in the understanding of this type of mechanical wave emission and propagation dates back to the mid-1900s when vertical ground motion on a seismometer was correlated to the generation of infrasound by local Rayleigh waves from the Great Alaskan earthquake of 1964 (Bolt, 1964). Subsequent studies were able to corroborate additional infrasound detections to an acoustic source near the earthquake epicenter (Mikumo, 1968; Young and Greene, 1982). It was also found that the propagation of seismic waves through mountain ranges has the capacity to emit yet another variety of earthquake infrasound via topographic vibrations (Young and Greene, 1982; Arrowsmith *et al.*, 2009). These subcategories of earthquake infrasound have been referred to as local, epicentral, and secondary infrasound, respectively (Arrowsmith *et al.*, 2010).

On 1 January 2024 (07:10:09 UTC), a 7.5 magnitude earthquake occurred off the Noto Peninsula in Japan with an epicentral location of 37.487° N and 137.271° E. These measurements were documented by the U.S. Geological Survey. Infrasound observations associated with the event, as well as the aftershock, were captured by a high-frequency array, labeled CHHAR, located toward the center of the Korean Peninsula ~894 km from the source. Event map and array design are visualized in Figures S6 and S7, respectively. Cardinal was applied to the CHHAR data and results shown in Figure 5. Frequency bands used to process the data are displayed in Table S5. Although it remains outside the scope of this study to determine whether associated infrasound observations are epicentral or secondary in nature, it is evident that the detections are partially obfuscated by microbaroms with similar back-azimuth values (Fig. 5a). To filter out these signals, we apply Cardinal's Aggregator with adaptive semblance threshold and display improved results in Figure 5b. The algorithm clustered detections from the signals-of-interest into two distinct families, or phases, associated with both the initial earthquake and the subsequent aftershock. Aggregator parameters and corresponding families' detections are visualized in Tables S6 and S7, respectively.

Explosion seismology

Explosions from anthropogenic activity, including industrial, military, nuclear testing, and mining operations, excite the seismoacoustic wavefield via the synchronous emission of mechanical waves that propagate through the ground and air. The proclivity for explosions to preferentially excite *P*-wave energy, as opposed to *S*-wave energy, is a key feature for discrimination between natural and anthropogenic activity (Stump *et al.*, 2002). Researchers have demonstrated the effectiveness of using ratios of *P/S* amplitudes at high frequencies to discriminate man-made explosions from earthquakes (Walter *et al.*, 1995). Moreover, recent studies have illustrated the utility of implementing *P/S* amplitude ratios within the 2–4 Hz frequency band for distinguishing between earthquakes and the DPRK declared nuclear tests (Walter *et al.*, 2018). Corresponding authors also found that using *Lg* cross-spectral ratios within the 2–4 Hz and 4–6 Hz bands accurately identified the cavity collapse, which followed DPRK's 2017 UNE, distinguishing it from regional earthquakes. Evidently, a detailed classification of a signal's frequency content, including its estimated directionality, trace velocity, and coherence, is imperative for high-fidelity explosion seismology source characterization.

On 3 September 2017 (03:30:01 UTC) DPRK conducted its sixth declared UNE with an estimated geographic location of 41.2999° N and 129.0790° E (Myers *et al.*, 2018). We apply Cardinal to corresponding seismic observations captured by a seismic array (KSRS), ~437 km from the source. Event map is plotted in Figure S8. Data are made available from 19 sensors with associated array configuration shown in Figure S9a. The sensors are spaced fairly equally; thus we modify the array to accommodate the Adaptive Array's requirement of a multiscale array (Fig. S9b). Subsequent interelement spacing dendrogram is displayed in Figure S9c. The same frequency bands used in the bolide examples are implemented here. Cardinal's default processing implementation, which incorporates all array elements for each frequency band, is applied to a 15 min segment of the array data (Fig. 6a). Thereafter, the Adaptive Array is applied to the modified array configuration. Resultant optimal subarray configurations for each frequency band are shown in Figure S10. In Figure 6b, we note improvements in the characterization of higher frequency components across a majority of the time window, especially with detections associated with the cavity collapse, which occurred ~8.5 min after the UNE (Myers *et al.*, 2018).

Discussion

In this study, we introduce a multifrequency array processing software capable of detecting and characterizing both seismic and infrasonic signals. We describe numerous utility functions within the Segmentor that discretize time–frequency space and

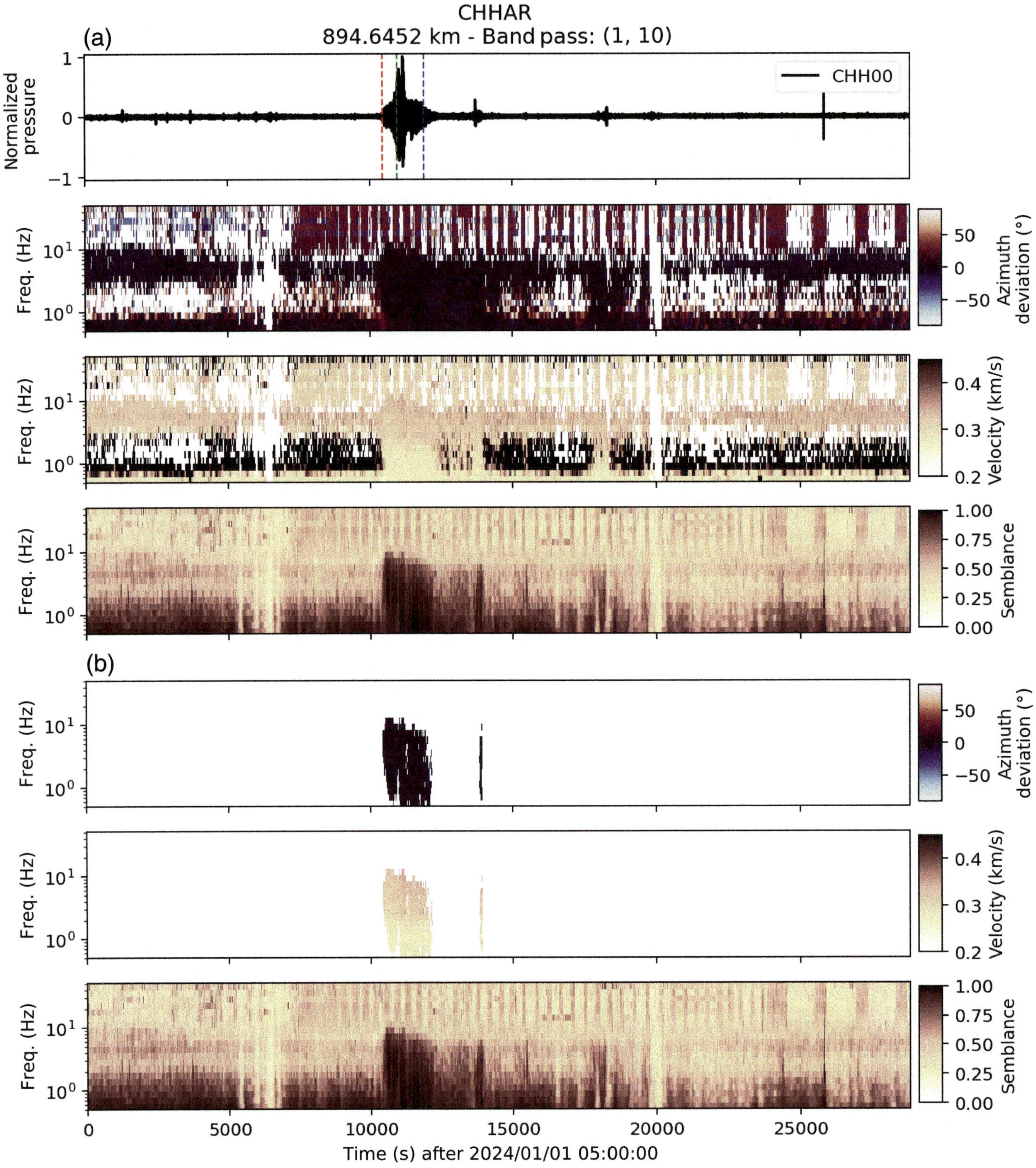

Figure 5. (a) Cardinal processing results using default settings (i.e., no Adaptive Array or Aggregator implementation). The first panel plots the normalized filtered waveforms from reference station CHH00, the second panel plots the azimuth deviation relative to the epicentral location as documented by the U.S. Geological Survey (USGS), the third panel displays corresponding trace velocities, and the last panel plots associated semblance values. Subfigure (b) presents refined results after applying Cardinal's Aggregator with adaptive semblance threshold. We only plot azimuth, velocity, and semblance results for simplicity.

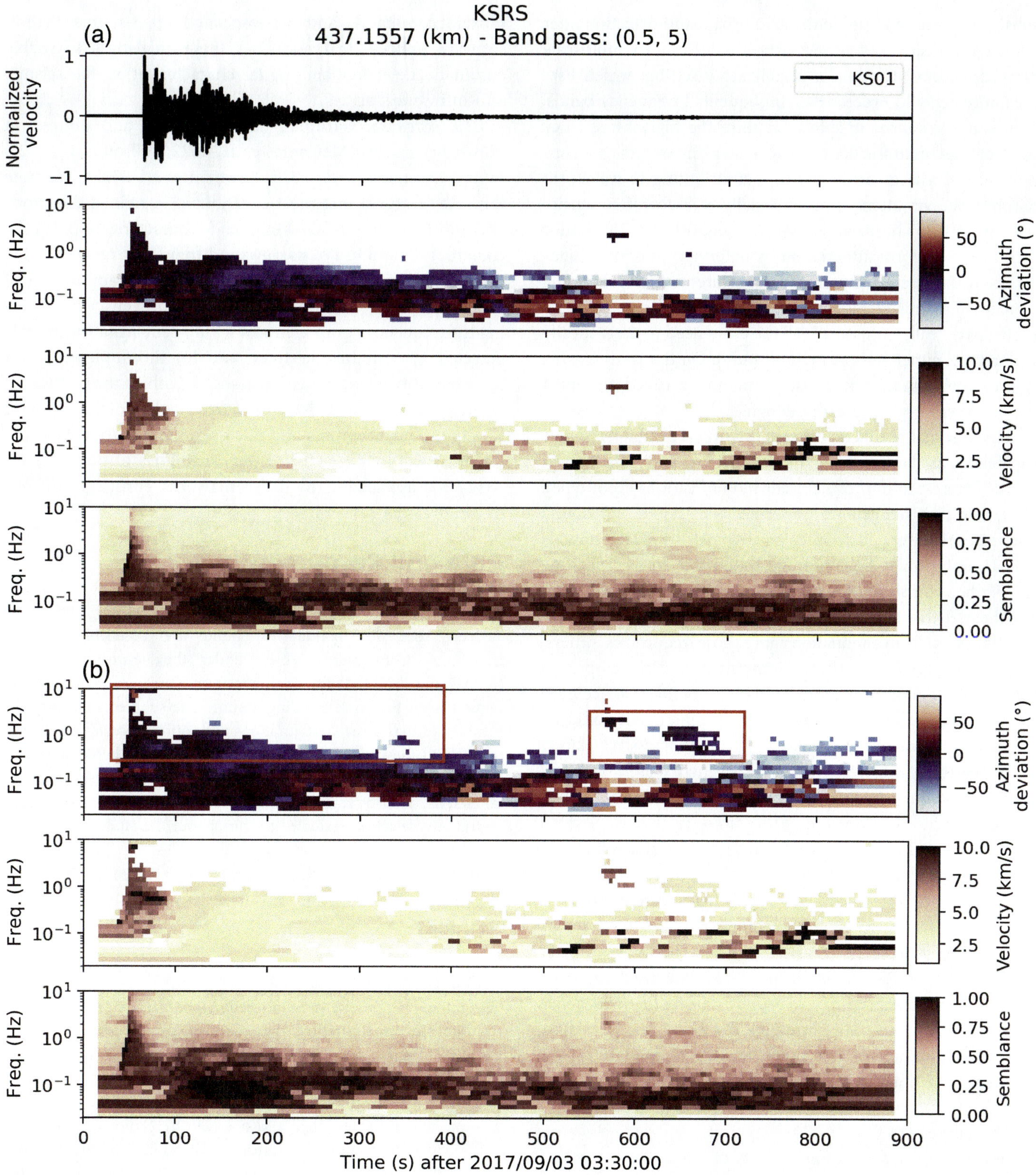

Figure 6. (a) Cardinal seismic array processing results for KSRS's detections of Democratic People's Republic of Korea's (DPRK) aforementioned 2017 underground nuclear explosion (UNE). First panel plots normalized waveforms band-pass filtered from 0.5 to 5 Hz. Second panel plots azimuth deviation relative to location estimates from Myers *et al.* (2018). Third panel plots corresponding trace velocity and the final panel displays the semblance. (b) Processing results after implementing Cardinal's Adaptive Array. Leftmost and rightmost red boxes highlight improvements in the characterization of higher frequencies and the subsequent cavity collapse, respectively. A semblance threshold of 0.5 was used for both panels (a) and (b).

subsequently note improvements in broadband detection after applying Cardinal's adaptive array algorithm to multiscale array detections. Cardinal's default array setting, which uses the entire array to process data in sequential frequency bands, is in some instances unable to capture the higher frequency components of an incident signal. This likely occurs as a consequence of a large array aperture contributing to waveform decoherence via attenuation, especially at higher frequencies (Green, 2015). The Adaptive Array's algorithm mitigates for increased waveform attenuation by determining optimal subarrays with successively smaller apertures when processing data in sequentially higher frequency bands. The algorithm is effectively fully automated; all the users need to do is specify a data type, either seismic or infrasound. On the contrary, the Aggregator's parameters must be manually tuned to suit a specific event type and array design.

The Cardinal results reported in this article exhibit its unique capabilities at characterizing array detections and isolating signals-of-interest to improve classification of various event types. We show that frequencies associated with bolide infrasound above 2 Hz were not initially detected by IMS stations I07AU and I53US when running traditional array processing (i.e., without incorporating our novel adaptive array algorithm). We theorize that this is due to the array aperture being too large such that waveform attenuation above those frequencies is inevitable across the entire array. Furthermore, we cite improved infrasound directionality estimates with the bolide that occurred in 2015. We speculate that this may be a consequence of exacerbated local wind noise associated with progressively larger array apertures, thus resulting in increasingly biased back-azimuth measurements. Following, we present earthquake infrasound detections from the 2024 Noto earthquake, which were obfuscated by coherent background noise (microbaroms) emanating from a similar back azimuth. The utility of the adaptive semblance threshold within Cardinal's Aggregator was demonstrated by successfully isolating array processing results corresponding to the signals-of-interest. Finally, Cardinal's application to DPRK's declared 2017 UNE showcased improved body-wave characterization, especially for frequencies above 0.5 Hz and for detections corresponding to the cavity collapse. Be that, as it may, the UNE example was slightly inhibited by the uniformity of KSRS's array configuration.

Conclusions

Detecting and characterizing a variety of signals on infrasound or seismic arrays benefit from processing data using multiple narrowband frequency ranges that span a wide bandwidth. Consequently, one can detect a diversity of signals across a wideband and simultaneously characterize detailed time–frequency components of each signal (Iezzi *et al.*, 2022). However, processing data in this way introduces challenges because both the array response and the ambient wavefield coherence vary as a function of frequency band. Here, we introduce methods and an associated open-source Python software package that addresses these challenges to enable automatic detection and signal characterization for seismic and infrasound arrays.

The software, Cardinal, has been cited and utilized in numerous articles (McComas *et al.*, 2022; Wilson *et al.*, 2023; Ronac Giannone *et al.*, 2024; Bowman *et al.*, 2025). We note three key features that most contributed to refined directionality estimates and detailed frequency characterization: (1) the construction and use of narrowband frequency ranges for the discretization of time–frequency space, (2) the application of an adaptive array algorithm to aid in comprehensively analyzing the frequency components of an incident signal-of-interest detected by a multiscale array, and (3) the implementation of an adaptive semblance threshold within the software's Aggregator to isolate detections from coherent background noise (e.g., microbaroms and microseisms). Future versions of Cardinal will look to expand the capabilities of the Adaptive Array for application to dense networks consisting of tens to hundreds of sensors.

Data and Resources

The Cardinal repository is publicly accessible on Github (https://github.com/sjarrowsmith/cardinal, last accessed April 2025). The datasets used for bolide infrasound are accessible on the Earthscope Consortium website under the network codes IM (I07AU and I53US). Additional data from Korea are available upon request from the corresponding author. The supplemental material includes various array configurations and source–receiver maps used throughout the study. The authors also provide the k-fold cross-validation results used to assess model training. Tables in the supplemental material describe various frequency bands, Aggregator parameters, and family detections referred to throughout the study.

Declaration of Competing Interests

The authors acknowledge that there are no conflicts of interest recorded.

Acknowledgments

The authors would like to acknowledge Jonathan Reiter for his contribution in incorporating the adaptive p-value threshold into Cardinal's Aggregator. The authors would also like to thank Robin Matoza and an additional anonymous reviewer for their constructive comments and suggestions. Sandia National Laboratories is a multimission laboratory managed and operated by National Technology and Engineering Solutions of Sandia, LLC (NTESS), a wholly owned subsidiary of Honeywell International Inc., for the U.S. Department of Energy's National Nuclear Security Administration (DOE/NNSA) under Contract DE-NA0003525. This written work is authored by an employee of NTESS. The employee, not NTESS, owns the right, title, and interest in and to the written work and is responsible for its contents. Any subjective views or opinions that might be expressed in the written work do not necessarily represent the views of the U.S. Government. The publisher acknowledges that the U.S. Government retains a nonexclusive, paid-up, irrevocable, worldwide license to publish or reproduce the published form of this written work or allow others to do so, for U.S. Government purposes. The DOE will provide public access to results of federally sponsored research in accordance with the DOE Public Access Plan. This study incorporates work from different funding sources. Portions of this research were supported by the Laboratory Directed Research and Development (LDRD) program at Sandia National Laboratories, a multimission laboratory managed and operated by National Technology and Engineering Solutions of Sandia, LLC., a wholly owned subsidiary of Honeywell International, Inc., for the U.S. DOE's National Nuclear Security Administration under Contract DE-NA-0003525. Portions of the research were also funded by the U.S. Army Corps of Engineers, Engineer Research and Development Center under Broad Agency Announcement Grant Number 0622146/AR9/01.

References

Arevalo, J., T. Solorio, M. Montes-y-Gomez, and F. A. González (2020). Gated multimodal networks, *Neural Comput. Appl.* **32,** 10,209–10,228.

Arrowsmith, S. J., R. Burlacu, R. Whitaker, and G. Randall (2009). A repeating secondary source of infrasound from the Wells, Nevada, earthquake sequence, *Geophys. Res. Lett.* **36,** doi: 10.1029/2009GL038363.

Arrowsmith, S. J., J. B. Johnson, D. P. Drob, and M. A. Hedlin (2010). The seismoacoustic wavefield: A new paradigm in studying geophysical phenomena, *Rev. Geophys.* **48,** doi: 10.1029/2010RG000335.

Beyreuther, M., R. Barsch, L. Krischer, T. Megies, Y. Behr, and J. Wassermann (2010). ObsPy: A Python toolbox for seismology, *Seismol. Res. Lett.* **81**, 530–533.

Bishop, J. W., D. Fee, and C. A. L. Szuberla (2020). Improved infrasound array processing with robust estimators, *Geophys. J. Int.* **221**, 2058–2074.

Bolt, B. A. (1964). Seismic air waves from the great 1964 Alaskan earthquake, *Nature* **202,** 1095–1096.

Bowman, D. C., E. A. Silber, M. Ronac Giannone, S. A. Albert, T. Edwards, F. K. Dannemann Dugick, and R. S. Longenbaugh (2025). Acoustic waves from the 2023 April 20 spacex starship rocket explosion travelling in the elevated 'Atmosofar' channel, *Geophys. J. Int.* **241,** no. 2, 1053–1065.

Cansi, Y. (1995). An automatic seismic event processing for detection and location: The P.M.C.C. method, *Geophys. Res. Lett.* **22,** 1021–1024.

Cansi, Y., and Y. Klinger (1997). An automated data processing method for mini-arrays, *News Lett* **11,** 2–4.

Cansi, Y., and A. Le Pichon (2008). Infrasound event detection using the progressive multi-channel correlation algorithm, in *Handbook of Signal Processing in Acoustics*, D. Havelock, S. Kuwano, and M. Vorlander (Editors), Springer Nature, New York, 1425–1435.

Capon, J. (1969). High-resolution frequency-wavenumber spectrum analysis, *Proc. IEEE* **57,** no. 8, 1408–1418.

Ceplecha, Z., J. Borovička, W. G. Elford, D. O. Revelle, R. L. Hawkes, V. Porubčan, and M. Šimek (1998). Meteor phenomena and bodies, *Space Sci. Rev.* **84,** 327–471.

Christie, D. R., and P. Campus (2010). The IMS infrasound network: Design and establishment of infrasound stations, in *Infrasound Monitoring for Atmospheric Studies*, A. Le Pichon, E. Blanc, and A. Hauchecorne (Editors), Springer, Dordrecht, The Netherlands, pp. 29–75.

Ester, M., H.-P. Kriegel, J. Sander, and X. Xu (1996). A density-based algorithm for discovering clusters in large spatial databases with noise, *Proc. of the Second International Conf. on Knowledge Discovery and Data Mining, KDD'96*, AAAI Press, pp. 226–231.

Garcés, M. A. (2013). On infrasound standards, part 1 time, frequency, and energy scaling, *InfraMatics* **2,** no. 2, 13–35.

Green, D. N. (2015). The spatial coherence structure of infrasonic waves: Analysis of data from international monitoring system arrays, *Geophys. J. Int.* **201,** no. 1, 377–389.

He, K., X. Zhang, S. Ren, and J. Sun (2016). Deep residual learning for image recognition, *Proc. of the IEEE Computer Society Conf. on Computer Vision and Pattern Recognition*, pp. 770–778, IEEE Computer Society.

Iezzi, A. M., R. S. Matoza, J. W. Bishop, S. Bhetanabhotla, and D. Fee (2022). Narrow-band least-squares infrasound array processing, *Seismol. Res. Lett.* **93,** 2818–2833.

Lecun, Y., L. Bottou, Y. Bengio, P. Haffner, and E. Bottou (1998). Gradient-based learning applied to document recognition, *Proc. IEEE* **86,** 2278–2324.

MacQueen, J. (1967). Some methods for classification and analysis of multivariate observations, in *Proceedings of the Fifth Berkeley Symposium on Mathematical Statistics and Probability, Volume I*, L. M. Le Cam and J. Neyman (Editors), University of California Press, Berkeley, California, 281–298.

Matoza, R. S., M. Landès, A. L. Pichon, L. Ceranna, and D. Brown (2013). Coherent ambient infrasound recorded by the international monitoring system, *Geophys. Res. Lett.* **40,** 429–433.

McComas, S., S. Arrowsmith, C. Hayward, B. Stump, and M. H. McKenna Taylor (2022). Quantifying low-frequency acoustic fields in urban environments, *Geophys. J. Int.* **229,** no. 2, 1152–1174.

Mikumo, T. (1968). Atmospheric pressure waves and tectonic deformation associated with the Alaskan earthquake of March 28, 1964, *J. Geophys. Res.* **73,** no. 6, 2009–2025, doi: 10.1029/JB073i006p02009.

Myers, S. C., S. R. Ford, R. J. Mellors, S. Baker, and G. Ichinose (2018). Absolute locations of the North Korean nuclear tests based on differential seismic arrival times and InSAR, *Seismol. Res. Lett.* **89,** no. 6, 2049–2058.

Park, J., C. Hayward, B.-I. Kim, B. Stump, I.-Y. Che, S. Arrowsmith, and K. Kim (2023). Data quality control tools used to monitor seismoacoustic research arrays in South Korea, *J. Seismol.* **27,** no. 4, 659–679.

ReVelle, D. O. (1976). On meteor-generated infrasound, *J. Geophys. Res.* **81,** 1217–1230.

Ronac Giannone, M., S. Arrowsmith, J. Park, B. Stump, C. Hayward, E. Larson, and I.-Y. Che (2024). Deep multimodal learning for seismoacoustic fusion to improve earthquake-explosion discrimination within the Korean peninsula, *Geophys. Res. Lett.* **51,** no. 14, doi: 10.1029/2024GL109404.

Rost, S., and C. Thomas (2002). Array seismology: Methods and applications, *Rev. Geophys.* **40,** 2-1–2-27.

Rost, S., and C. Thomas (2009). Improving seismic resolution through array processing techniques, *Surv. Geophys.* **30,** 271–299.

Silber, E. A. (2024). The utility of infrasound in global monitoring of extraterrestrial impacts: A case study of the 2008 July 23 Tajikistan bolide, *Astron. J.* **168,** no. 1, 17.

Silber, E. A., and P. G. Brown (2014). Optical observations of meteors generating infrasound-I: Acoustic signal identification and phenomenology, *J. Atmos. Sol. Terr. Phys.* **119,** 116–128.

Silber, E. A., M. Boslough, W. K. Hocking, M. Gritsevich, and R. W. Whitaker (2018). Physics of meteor generated shock waves in the Earth's atmosphere—A review, *Adv. Space Res.* **62,** no. 3, 489–532.

Stump, B. W., C. Hayward, P. Golden, J. Park, R. Kubacki, C. Cain, S. Arrowsmith, M. H. M. Taylor, S. J. Jeong, T. Ivey, *et al.* (2022). Seismic and infrasound data recorded at regional seismoacoustic research arrays in South Korea from the six DPRK underground nuclear explosions, *Seismol. Res. Lett.* **93,** 2389–2400.

Stump, B. W., M. A. Hedlin, D. C. Pearson, and V. Hsu (2002). Characterization of mining explosions at regional distances: Implications with the international monitoring system, *Rev. Geophys.* **40,** 2-1–2-21.

Szuberla, C. A. L., and J. V. Olson (2004). Uncertainties associated with parameter estimation in atmospheric infrasound arrays, *J. Acoust. Soc. Am.* **115,** 253–258.

Tagliaferri, E., R. Spalding, C. Jacobs, S. P. Worden, and A. Erlich (1994). Detection of meteoroid impacts by optical sensors in earth orbit, in *Hazards Due to Comets and Asteroids*, T. Gehrels, M. S. Matthews, and A. M. Schumann (Editors), University of Arizona Press, Tucson, Arizona, 199 pp.

Vaswani, A., N. Shazeer, N. Parmar, J. Uszkoreit, L. Jones, A. N. Gomez, Ł. Kaiser, and I. Polosukhin (2017). Attention is all you need, *Proc. of the 31st Conf. on Neural Information Processing Systems*, 1–11.

Walter, W., D. Dodge, G. Ichinose, S. Myers, M. Pasyanos, and S. Ford (2018). Body-wave methods of distinguishing between explosions, collapses, and earthquakes: Application to recent events in North Korea, *Seismol. Res. Lett.* **89,** 2131–2138.

Walter, W. R., K. M. Mayeda, and H. J. Patton (1995). Phase and spectral ratio discrimination between NTS earthquakes explosions. Part I: Empirical observations, *Bull. Seismol. Soc. Am.* **85,** 1050–1067.

Wilson, T. C., C. E. Petrin, and B. R. Elbing (2023). Infrasound and low-audible acoustic detections from a long-term microphone array deployment in Oklahoma, *Remote Sens.* **15,** no. 5, doi: 10.3390/rs15051455.

Young, J. M., and G. E. Greene (1982). Anomalous infrasound generated by the Alaskan earthquake of 28 March 1964, *J. Acoust. Soc. Am.* **71,** 334–339.

Manuscript received 29 October 2024
Published online 17 July 2025

Electronic Seismologist

OPEN ACCESS

MaxMagMod: A Web-Based Application for Next Largest Magnitude Forecasting in Enhanced Geothermal Systems

Sadegh Karimpouli*[1], Tomasz Balawajder[2], Joanna Kocot[2], and Grzegorz Kwiatek[1,3]

Abstract

Enhanced geothermal systems offer a promising solution for sustainable energy by injecting water into hot underground reservoirs to generate electricity or heat. However, the process often induces significant seismic activity, posing challenges for public acceptance and safety. This study introduces MaxMagMod, a web-based application designed to forecast the next largest magnitude of induced seismic events in near-real time. Integrated with a user interface into the EPISODES platform, the application utilizes both deterministic and probabilistic models available in the literature, providing the next largest magnitude forecasts using seismic and hydraulic data. The application's performance is validated through case studies from the St1 project in Helsinki, Finland, and the Cooper basin in Australia, demonstrating its reliability and effectiveness.

Cite this article as Karimpouli, S., T. Balawajder, J. Kocot, and G. Kwiatek (2025). MaxMagMod: A Web-Based Application for Next Largest Magnitude Forecasting in Enhanced Geothermal Systems, *Seismol. Res. Lett.* **97**, 501–513, doi: 10.1785/0220240468.

Introduction

Enhanced geothermal systems (EGSs) involve injecting water into hot underground areas to produce hot water that can be brought to the surface and used for electricity generation or heating. These systems are termed "enhanced" because they require human-made fractures to be created in low-permeability reservoirs to enable fluid circulation between injection and extraction wells (Mohamed, 2024). EGS has become increasingly popular globally due to its potential as a clean and renewable energy source, applicable across diverse geological conditions (Liu *et al.*, 2024). However, creating EGS reservoirs using hydraulic stimulation for enhancing permeability and further exploitation of the created reservoir by continuous fluid circulation and heat exchange could be associated with significant seismic activity (here we mean at least felt by the population). Pumping high-pressure fluids into the geothermal reservoir disturbs the stress state (pore-fluid pressure diffusion, and poroelastic stresses), leading to the formation of new fractures and reactivation of the pre-existing fracture network or major faults, inducing and triggering seismicity. In Basel in Switzerland (Deichmann and Giardini, 2009) and Pohang in South Korea (Park *et al.*, 2020) occurrence of large seismic events was directly attributed to fluid injection, resulting in the shutdown of the corresponding geothermal projects. These cases posed a significant negative socioeconomic impact by endangering local infrastructure and people's safety, which in turn affects an overall public perception and acceptance of EGS projects worldwide (Senyapar and Bayindir, 2023; Abdi *et al.*, 2024; Kwiatek *et al.*, 2024).

Efforts to understand seismomechanical processes related to fluid injection, forecast, and mitigate induced seismicity during geothermal operations have a long history, dating back to the 1970s (Raleigh *et al.*, 1976; Li *et al.*, 2022). Of particular interest is the assessment of the maximum possible magnitude, or in other words, the next largest magnitude expected based on seismicity and fluid injection operations. Such assessment can be performed in many ways using probabilistic or deterministic methods while including various seismomechanics-based concepts (see e.g., Kwiatek *et al.*, 2024, for a brief overview). McGarr (2014) related the maximum expected seismic moment to the total injected fluid volume into the reservoir. Hallo *et al.* (2014) modified McGarr's formula (McGarr, 1976) and introduced the seismic efficiency ratio (SER), the scalar parameter as a reservoir property (Hallo *et al.*, 2012, 2014).

1. GFZ Helmholtz Centre for Geosciences, Potsdam, Germany, https://orcid.org/0000-0003-1781-9760 (SK); https://orcid.org/0000-0003-1076-615X (GK); 2. ACC Cyfronet, AGH, Krakow, Poland, https://orcid.org/0000-0002-9824-7962 (JK); 3. GMuG Gesellschaft für Materialprüfung und Geophysik mbH, Bad Nauheim, Germany

*Corresponding author: sadegh.karimpouli@gfz.de

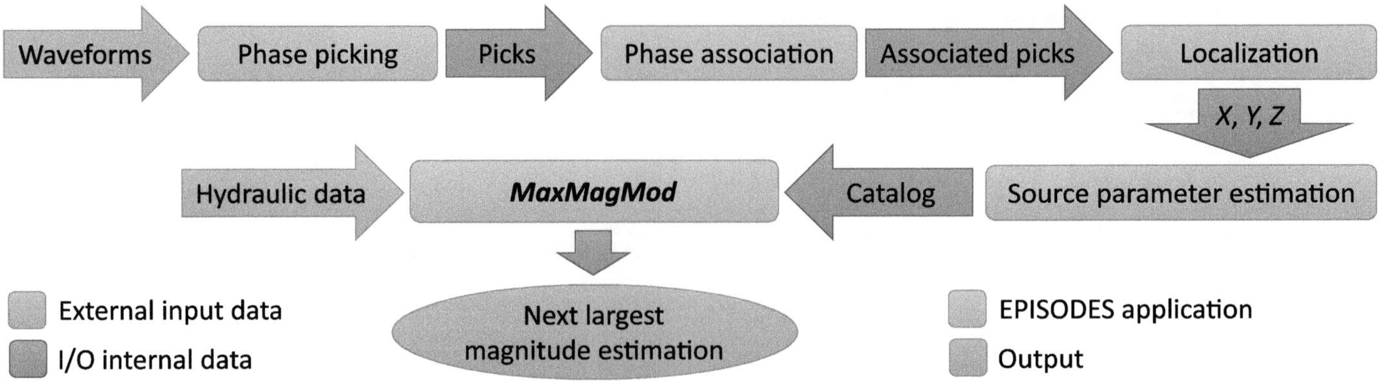

Figure 1. Workflow (III) of digital component twin for anthropogenic geophysical extremes forecasting (DTC-AGEF) in a digital twin for geophysical (DT-GEO) extremes project for modeling of the largest magnitude. Application of maximum magnitude deterministic and probabilistic models (MaxMagMod) is the last part of the workflow uses catalog and hydraulic data to estimate next largest magnitudes. The color version of this figure is available only in the electronic edition.

Li *et al.* (2022) modified further Hallo's model by incorporating the relaxation of stored elastic deformation in preceding seismic events. Recently, Drif *et al.* (2024) proposed a similar model, but with a different method for estimating total seismic moment, which is based on hydraulic energy. Shapiro *et al.* (2013) statistically derived the probability for the largest possible magnitude of an induced earthquake based on the stimulated volume of rock by fluid injection volume. van der Elst *et al.* (2016) introduced the bounds on the expected maximum magnitude as a function of the number of events, seismogenic index (Shapiro *et al.*, 2010), and GR b-value under an assumed confidence level. Finally, using the size of ruptures induced by localized pore-pressure perturbations and propagating on prestressed faults, Galis *et al.* (2017) developed a geomechanics-based model, which was further modified for effective bulk modulus by Orlecka-Sikora and Cielesta (2020). Using a rate and state friction framework, Im and Avouac (2024) derived an expression for maximum magnitude evolution, which has been confirmed by numerical simulations. Substantial variability in the next largest magnitude forecasts, even in the case of a single geothermal reservoir, has been reported while using different models (Kwiatek *et al.*, 2024). These differences were attributed to models' boundary conditions, parameterization, and limitations of key model parameters. It is important to realize that potential discrepancies do exist between the models and that these discrepancies need to be properly understood and handled. In applied environments, appropriate software tools that enable calculation of maximum magnitude during ongoing fluid injection in close to real time would be of benefit to provide first-order information on expected maximum magnitude under different forecasting models.

In the frame of a digital twin for geophysical extremes (DT-GEO) project funded by the Horizon Europe program, a collaborative research team develops a so-called digital component twin for anthropogenic geophysical extremes forecasting (DTC-AGEF). The DTC-AGEF aims to perform a near-real-time assessment of different aspects of anthropogenic seismic hazard. It is composed of four workflows related to forecasting (I) long-range and (II) late seismic responses of georeservoirs, modeling of the largest magnitude (III), and induced seismic hazard map estimation (IV). The workflows are being implemented within the EPISODES platform, a web-based/cloud computing environment of the EPOS thematic core service anthropogenic hazards (Orlecka-Sikora *et al.*, 2020).

We developed a web-based maximum magnitude deterministic and probabilistic models application (MaxMagMod) that constitutes the last part of the workflow (III) modeling of the largest magnitude (Fig. 1). The application provides forecasting of the next largest magnitude using a variety of deterministic and probabilistic models of the maximum magnitude available in the literature. An important consideration is that all these models are built upon specific assumptions, such as the events are more probable on rupture surfaces contained within the stimulated volume (Shapiro *et al.*, 2013) or that the seismic response to injection can be described with the Gutenberg–Richter power law, and for example, a commonly assumed b-value of 1 can be used (McGarr, 2014). Primarily, the developed application is suitable for case studies of pressure-controlled induced seismicity (e.g., Kwiatek *et al.*, 2019, 2022), in which the seismicity is solely related to fluid injection, and the maximum seismic moment is confined by self-arrested ruptures (e.g., Galis *et al.*, 2017). The application may not produce reliable results in scenarios in runaway scenarios, due to, for example, the presence of a stressed pre-existing fault, or active tectonics (Bentz *et al.*, 2020; Martínez-Garzón *et al.*, 2020). The application uses the seismic catalog and hydraulic data as input (Fig. 1), and is primarily developed for the near-real-time processing during workflow execution (with continuously growing hydraulic data and seismic catalog). However, it may also be executed interactively for the already existing offline data. We start with presenting the processing methodology and then discuss application implementation on the EPISODES platform. We finally validate the application and test its performance using two complete case studies of fluid-induced seismicity from the St1 Deep Heat project in Finland (Kwiatek *et al.*, 2019) and Cooper basin in Australia (Baisch *et al.*, 2006, 2009) and compare them to the outcomes of other studies.

Resources and Methods

EPISODES platform

The EPISODES platform (see Data and Resources) is an open-access virtual laboratory that provides access to the research infrastructure of the EPOS TCS AH (Orlecka-Sikora *et al.*, 2020). It facilitates collaborative scientific research on anthropogenic hazards by providing open access to the integrated data, computational tools, computational resources, and documents related to the subject. The provided data sets include seismic data (catalogs, waveforms), industrial data (e.g., temporal series of injection rate), associated geodata (e.g., well tracks), and supplementary data. Important for this study, EPISODES provides access to over 75 web-based applications for the processing of data of anthropogenic seismicity, a private used workspace to perform research online, team-working features to share the results and make the dissemination of knowledge easier, as well as a document repository. An end-user is able to analyze anthropogenic seismicity and related hazards, assess the potential impact of georesources exploitation, or use the platform as an educational resource to study and learn about anthropogenic hazards.

Application structure

The application is developed in the Python programming language. Generally, there are two types of inputs: input data and input parameters. The input data consists of seismicity catalog and hydraulic data (Fig. 1). The application is designed for integration into automated workflows, where it continuously updates the earthquake catalog, and for research and educational purposes. In ongoing projects, catalog data is automatically processed in near-real time during earlier stages of the workflow (not discussed here). In research and educational settings, these data can be imported either internally from the EPISODES platform or externally by the user in an "offline" mode. The application uses the hypocentral location, origin time, and earthquake magnitude from the earthquake catalog. Input hydraulic data are injection rates, and they are provided as time series. Input parameters depend on the maximum magnitude model and are introduced and discussed in the following sections. The main data outputs are estimations of the next largest magnitudes from a number of deterministic and probabilistic models (Fig. 1). It is important to note that this application is not a comprehensive tool for seismic hazard and risk analysis. As highlighted in a recent review by Zhou *et al.* (2024) effective seismic risk management in enhanced geothermal systems (EGS) requires considerations in multiple aspects, including (1) framework, (2) prescreening, (3) evaluation, (4) protocol design, (5) monitoring, and (6) communication. This application provides a first-order estimation of the next largest magnitude based on selected models, serving as a resource for expert users engaged in seismic hazard and risk management. In addition, researchers and educators can utilize the application to explore what could be expected in various injection scenarios using different models, while modifying various model parameters to compare results.

Forecasting models

The evaluation of the next largest magnitude during fluid injection operations can be conducted through either probabilistic or deterministic approaches, often employing principles grounded in physics, for example an elastic medium (Kwiatek *et al.*, 2024). Here discussed models compute directly the maximum moment magnitude, but some others compute maximum seismic moment (M_0), which is then converted to moment magnitude (M_w) using (Bormann and Di Giacomo, 2011)

$$M_w = (\log_{10} M_0 - 9.1)/1.5. \quad (1)$$

McGarr (2014) introduced a simple model that forecasts the next largest magnitude as

$$M_0^{max} = \frac{(1-B)}{B}\frac{2\mu(3\lambda + 2G)}{3}\Delta V, \quad (2)$$

in which $B = 2b/3$, b is the Gutenberg–Richter (GR) b-value, λ and G are Lame's elastic parameters of the geothermal reservoir, G is the modulus of rigidity, μ is the friction coefficient, and ΔV is the cumulative injected fluid. When $\lambda = G$, $\mu = 0.6$, and $b = 1$, the model simplifies to

$$M_0^{max} = G\Delta V. \quad (3)$$

McGarr's model is considered conservative because it assumes the worst-case scenario—whole deformation related to fluid injection may be converted to the seismic deformation, thus the next largest magnitude estimated using equations (2) or (3) is likely an upper bound to the maximum magnitude.

Hallo *et al.* (2012) introduced the SER that accounts for the partitioning of the elastic strain energy release ($\sum M_0$) associated with fluid injection into seismic and aseismic processes about the theoretical total seismic moment ($\sum M_{TOT}$):

$$SER = \sum M_0 / \sum M_{TOT}. \quad (4)$$

Having the SER, which is essentially a geothermal reservoir property, Hallo *et al.* (2014) defined the next largest magnitude as a product of SER and a conservative "upper bound" formulation of McGarr (2014):

$$\sum M_{TOT} = 2G\Delta V, \quad (5)$$

$$M_0^{max} = \text{SER}\frac{1-B}{B}\frac{2\mu(3\lambda+2G)}{3}\Delta V. \quad (6)$$

Li *et al.* (2022) introduced further modifications to the approach of Hallo *et al.* (2014). They define dM_0 as the difference between the upper limit of the $\sum M_0^{upper}$ and the observed $\sum M_0^{observed}$ from the earthquake catalog. Then, they assume dM_0 is stored energy that could potentially be released as a residual event with seismic moment in a single rupture, generating an event with magnitude:

$$M_0^{max} = \text{SER} \times 2G\Delta V - \sum M_0^{observed}. \quad (7)$$

van der Elst *et al.* (2016) proposed that the distribution of M_w^{max} is a heavy-tailed distribution, just like the GR distribution. They inverted the cumulative density function of M_w^{max} to get the bounds on the expected maximum magnitude as

$$M_{w(cl)}^{max} = \frac{1}{b}(\Sigma + \log_{10}\Delta V - \log_{10}[N(1 - cl^{1/N})]), \quad (8)$$

in which $M_{w(cl)}^{max}$ is the magnitude corresponding to some confidence level cl. Σ and b are the seismogenic index (Shapiro *et al.*, 2010) and GR b-value, and N is the number of events. In general, if an event occurs on average once per interval, and the events follow a Poisson distribution, then the probability of exactly one event in the next interval is equal to 37%.

The so-called "lower-bound" formulation of Shapiro *et al.* (2013) results in a maximum magnitude equal to

$$M_w^{max} = \log_{10} L^2 + 2/3(\log_{10}\Delta\sigma - \log_{10} C) - 6.07, \quad (9)$$

in which L denotes a characteristic length scale of the stimulated volume, $\Delta\sigma$ is a static stress drop, and C is a geometrical constant close to 1. Shapiro *et al.* (2013) stated that L expresses volume perturbed by fluid injection, which can be estimated by the distribution of earthquake hypocenters, and computed, for example, by surrounding the hypocenters with an ellipsoid. They found that the maximum observed magnitude is typically well approximated by the smallest semiaxis of the ellipsoid (see the Characteristic length scale section).

Selected models represent two major families of maximum magnitude models, where the maximum seismic moment scales as $M_{0,max} \propto \Delta V^1$or $M_{0,max} \propto \Delta V^{3/2}$ with the total volume of fluid injected. In addition, our model selection incorporates two major parameters driving the maximum magnitude. The original models of McGarr (2014), Hallo *et al.* (2012), and Li *et al.* (2022) all use the total volume of fluid injected into the reservoir as a main driver of the maximum magnitude estimate. However, the model of Shapiro *et al.* (2013) takes a different approach, with the maximum magnitude capped by the volume perturbed by fluid injection, rather than the volume of fluid injected. In addition, the selected models incorporate different steps in the partitioning of the elastic strain energy into the seismic and out-of-the-seismic band processes (see extended discussion in Drif *et al.*, 2024).

We selected maximum magnitude models that require a limited number of constant parameters and as many remaining parameters to be directly calculated from input data, rather than ad hoc specified by the user. This excluded the initial model of Galis *et al.* (2017) because it uses a notable number of input parameters to estimate a critical g parameter, whereas an alternative parameterization of γ through Σ suffers from persistent overestimation of the maximum magnitude (see discussion in Kwiatek et al., 2024, and Orlecka-Sikora and Cielesta 2020). However, the model of Galis *et al.* (2017) was found to provide qualitatively comparable results as the model of van der Elst *et al.* (2016) and Shapiro *et al.* (2013), which are here included. Likewise, the model of Im and Avouac (2024) at high injection rates is comparable to Galis *et al.* (2017). Finally, the recently developed model of Drif *et al.* (2024) considers seismic injection efficiency as a parameter guiding the balance between the seismic energy and available energy, being in bulk comparable to the here incorporated Hallo's SER parameter or Shapiro's Σ, thus it has not been taken into account as well. We note that the modular structure of the application allows us to incorporate these models in the future.

Models' parameters

The presented models of maximum magnitude introduce and use several parameters that need to be estimated or assumed. Some of these parameters are constant values that are believed to be representative of the whole reservoir, such as elastic parameters (λ and G), friction coefficient (μ), or average static stress drop ($\Delta\sigma$). However, some other parameters, such as b-value, seismogenic index Σ, and characteristic length scale L change, and are in principle time dependent, for example, during an ongoing EGS project. This means they should be updated for each new input (or a new input time window).

Gutenberg–Richter *b*-value

The original GR frequency–magnitude distribution (FMD) describes the relationship between the earthquake magnitude (M) and the number of earthquakes (N) below this magnitude:

$$\log_{10} N(M) = a + bM, \quad (10)$$

in which a and b are constant values (known as a-value and b-value). b-value is typically around 1 for tectonic seismicity due to natural processes governing earthquake occurrences (Varotsos *et al.*, 2004; Schorlemmer *et al.*, 2005). However, variation in b-value can occur due to changes in local stress distributions, leading to variations in seismic activity patterns (Ma, 1978; Geffers *et al.*, 2022). For example, for seismicity related to hydraulic fracturing and geothermal reservoirs, the b-value is often larger than 1, typically 1.1–1.7 (Schorlemmer *et al.*, 2005; Geffers *et al.*, 2022).

To calculate b-value, Aki (1965) assumed the FMD follows a power law and introduced the maximum-likelihood estimation (MLE) of b-value and corresponding standard error (σ_b) as

$$b = \frac{1}{(\overline{m} - m_c)\ln(10)}, \tag{11}$$

$$\sigma_b = \frac{b}{\sqrt{N}}, \tag{12}$$

in which m_c is the magnitude of completeness of the seismic catalog, $\overline{m}$ is the mean magnitude calculated from those events that are above m_c, and N is the number of events above m_c.

Van der Elst (2021) noted that the MLE of b-value strongly depends on the completeness magnitude, which may change in time (Knopoff *et al.*, 1982; Kagan, 2004). To account for potential biases introduced due to short-term catalog incompleteness, he uses the differences in magnitude between successive earthquakes and introduces a new estimator, "b-positive," which is based only on the positive differences. These differences have a double-exponential (Laplace) distribution, and the b-value is described similarly to the magnitude distribution itself. Accordingly, the Laplace estimator is

$$b^+ = \frac{1}{(\overline{m'} - m'_c)\ln(10)} \quad m' \geq m'_c, \tag{13}$$

in which $\overline{m'}$ is the sample mean of the magnitude of positive differences (in case of b^+), and m'_c is a minimum magnitude difference. The standard error is calculated using bootstrapping (see appendix in van der Elst, 2021).

Rotondi and Varini (2022) showed that the best-fitting FMD varies in time. For example, from foreshock to aftershock sequences, they may change from light-tailed distributions such as tapered GR (Pareto) distribution (TGR) to heavy-tailed distributions such as Gamma distribution (Kagan, 2002). Compared to truncated distributions, the TGR has an exponential taper applied to the cumulative number of events with seismic moments larger than M. According to Kagan (2002), the logarithm of the likelihood function for the TGR distribution is

$$\ell = nB\ln M_t + \frac{1}{M_x}\left(nM_t - \sum_{i=1}^{n} M_i\right) - B\sum_{i=1}^{n}\ln M_i + \sum_{i=1}^{n}\ln\left(\frac{B}{M_i} + \frac{1}{M_x}\right), \tag{14}$$

in which $B = 2b/3$, M is the seismic moment and M_t and M_x are the lower and upper bound seismic moments of the TGR distribution. The MLE estimates the B, M_x, and their standard errors.

In what follows, we use the "b-value options," which we mean that b-value could be either assumed as a constant value of 1 or computed using MLE for different FMD options such as exponential (GR), Laplace (of magnitude differences), and tapered GR (TGR) distribution.

Seismogenic index

In increasing or constant injection scenarios, Shapiro *et al.* (2010) state that the event probability is related to the pore-pressure perturbation. It means, the cumulative number of induced seismic events (N) depends on the cumulative injected fluid volume (Q), poroelastic storage coefficient (S), and tectonic potential (F), which is a measure of seismic activity in the region of injection. Assuming a G-R FMD, the number of events with magnitude larger than M is

$$\log_{10} N = \log_{10} Q - bM + a - \log_{10} FS. \tag{15}$$

Accordingly, they define a new quantity, seismogenic index, as

$$\Sigma = a - \log_{10} FS = \log_{10} N - \log_{10} Q + bM, \tag{16}$$

which is independent of injection properties and is a geothermal reservoir property characterizing the expected level of seismic activity. Higher seismogenic index means that the probability of an induced event of magnitude larger than the specified magnitude is higher.

Characteristic length scale

Following Shapiro *et al.* (2011, 2013), the stimulated volume can be approximated with the ellipsoid with principal axes of $L_{min} < L_{int} < L_{max}$ with at least 20–30 well-distributed points. Shapiro *et al.* (2011) showed that the characteristic length of the seismic cloud:

$$L = \left[\frac{1}{3}(1/L_{min}^3 + 1/L_{int}^3 + 1/L_{max}^3)\right]^{-1/3}, \tag{17}$$

can be used to assess the next maximum magnitude. The ellipsoid semiaxes are approximated using principal component analysis and earthquake hypocenters as input, while assuming for example, 95% of earthquakes must be within the ellipsoid. This procedure results in semiaxes lengths (L_{min}, L_{int}, and L_{max}) of the fitted ellipsoid. Shapiro *et al.* (2013) showed that if L_{min} is small enough, it has a dominant contribution to the length scale, which means $L \sim L_{min}$, thus L_{min} is typically used in equation (8) to calculate the next largest magnitude.

Error propagation

On the one hand, the asymptotic normality of MLE has not been universally established, raising questions about the normality of b-value error distribution (Bücher and Segers, 2017). On the other hand, it is not clear how the error deviates from the normal distribution and how such a deviation affects the error propagation. However, assuming the (near-) normality of

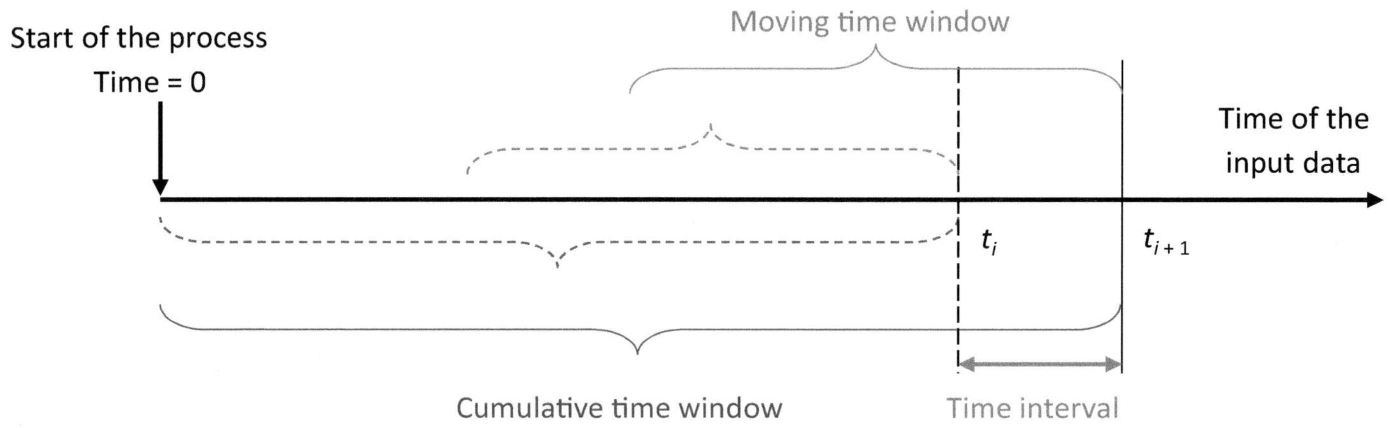

Figure 2 A schematic illustration of catalog data selection in the application. For injection data, cumulative injected volume is used in each step. Models are computed for inputs selected by time window and may proceed in each step with a time interval. Accordingly, the time window could be a moving or cumulative time window. The color version of this figure is available only in the electronic edition.

the MLE errors (σ_β), the standard errors are propagated to the subsequent parameters and models as Table 1.

Maximum Magnitude Models Application

Two main inputs of the MaxMagMod application are catalog and injection data, which should be prepared in a format compliant with the EPISODES platform formats specification (see Data and Resources). For catalog data, location (m), time (s), and magnitude of events are used. Locations are expected to be in the Cartesian coordinate system; however, geographical coordinates are also accepted and automatically converted to a relative Cartesian coordinate scale using the GeoPy library in Python. The time of the first event in the catalog is set to be the start of the process (Fig. 2), and results are produced in time starting from this origin. Magnitudes are assumed to be moment magnitude (M_w). However, the application accepts local magnitude as an input, assuming that the user is aware of potential discrepancies between the local and moment magnitude scale for the considered seismic catalog. For injection time series, the injection rate (l/min) is used.

To be flexible for different types of computations, we define some input parameters (e.g., time window and time interval), allowing the selection of all or part of the catalog data. The application uses input data, including only the time window, to estimate the next largest magnitude. The next time step is defined by a time interval parameter (Fig. 2), and the procedure is repeated until all intervals are met. As an example, computation could be repeated every 2 hr (time interval = 2), preparing 12 values per day. In addition, the time window could be fixed, for example, 24 hr (time length = 24), allowing to capture of recent variations in the input data. Otherwise, it could be an extended time window from the start of the project to capture the cumulative variability of the input data (Fig. 2). The calculation is performed if only a suitable number of events with a magnitude larger than the completeness magnitude are available for that particular time window. This is because, for example, the b-value or characteristic length scale (in Shapiro's model) needs roughly a minimum of 20–30 events to be reliably computed (albeit with larger uncertainties when the input number of events is low). When a short fixed time window is selected, it is more probable that it does not contain enough seismicity. If this is met only in some intervals, the application does not return values only for those intervals. However, if this happens in all intervals leading to empty results, the application warns this and prepares possible solutions and suggests, for example, to increase the "time window," decrease the "minimum number of events," or "completeness magnitude." When extending the window is used, even a short one, such limitations may only be observed in the first intervals when there is small seismicity.

Although the main output is the next largest magnitude generated by different models, we report related key input parameters as well, including, for example, b-value, SER (equation 4), Σ (equation 16), L (equation 17), cumulative number of events, and cumulative injected volume. Uncertainty estimations are calculated as well, following equations 18–21.

Accordingly, we developed a user interface (Fig. 3) that simplifies the selection of input data, model parameters, and other related options.

The plotting tool of the MaxMagMod prepares an interactive environment allowing for evaluation and interpretation of the

TABLE 1
Error Terms of the Models and Parameters

Model	Error Term	Equation Number
McGarr model	$\sigma_{M_w^{max}} = \frac{\sigma_\beta}{(\frac{3}{2}b-b^2)\ln(10)}$	(18)
Hallo model	$\sigma_{M_w^{max}} = \frac{SER\sigma_\beta}{(\frac{3}{2}b-b^2)\ln(10)}$	(19)
Seismogenic index	$\sigma_\Sigma = m_c\sigma_\beta$	(20)
van der Elst model	$\sigma_{M_w^{max}} = \lvert -\frac{\ln(N^2(1-c^{1/N}))}{b^2}\rvert\sigma_\beta$	(21)

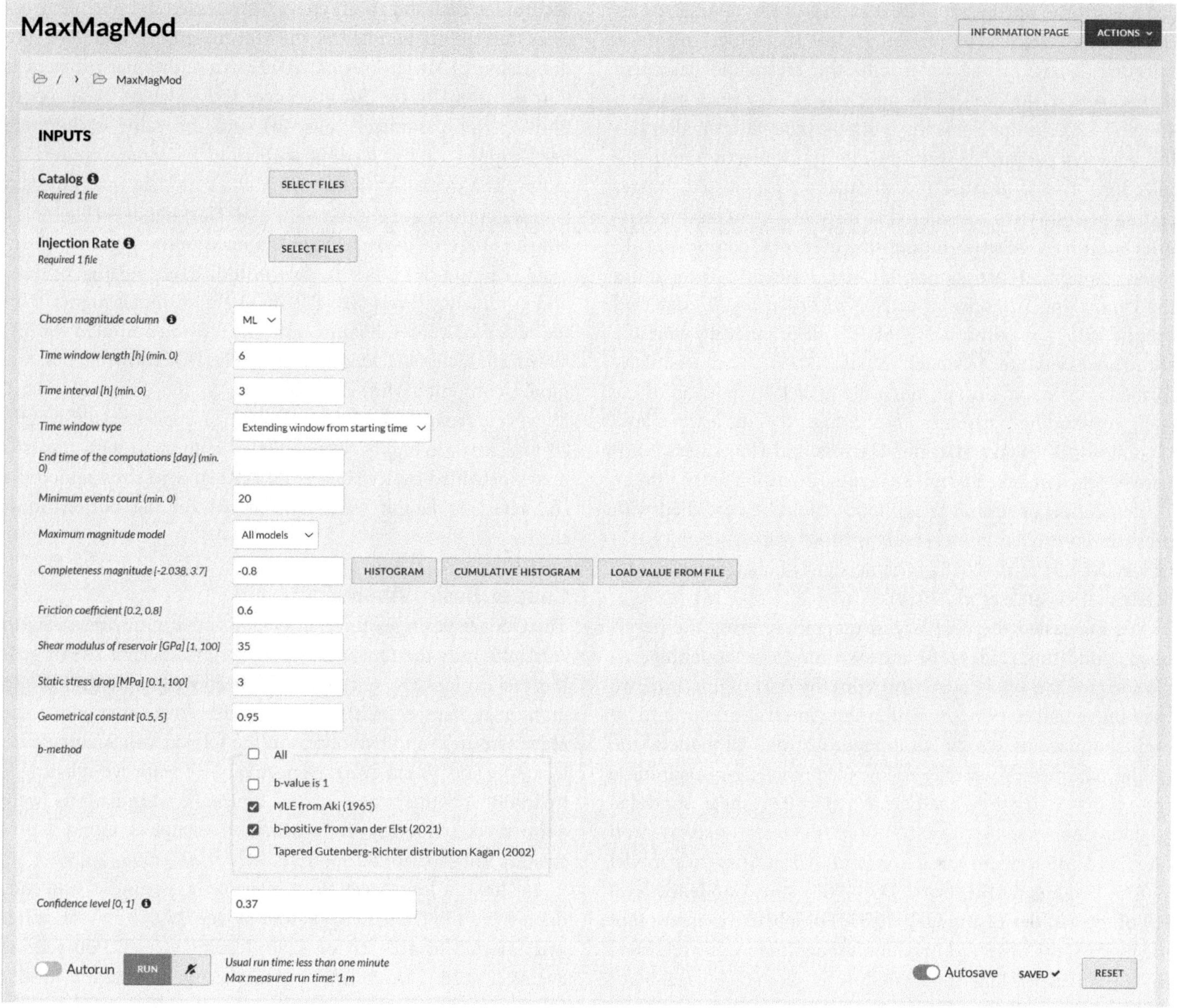

Figure 3. The application interface consists of input files and parameters (general and model parameters). The color version of this figure is available only in the electronic edition.

results by comparing them with the original values. However, evaluation of maximum magnitude models is not straightforward because: (1) Underestimation of an upcoming jump in the maximum observed magnitude is treated as a failure of a given model, and (2) overestimation of the evolving maximum observed magnitude should be minimal. Accordingly, Kwiatek *et al.* (2024) defined the best-performing model as the model with minimal yet positive deviation from the observed magnitude (i.e., slight overestimation of the next largest magnitude is preferred). This means that, interpretation of these results is usually qualitative, which is based on the background knowledge of an expert regarding the target injection well.

On the other hand, a best-performing model in one well is not guaranteed to be the best-performing model in another well on the same reservoir, even with about 500 m distance away (Kwiatek *et al.*, 2024). This may be induced by heterogeneity of subsurface material and structure, as well as variation in operational parameters. Because the results of the models are very case sensitive, in the first step, all models are suggested to be used to generate the estimations ("All models" option in the app). An expert could qualitatively evaluate the results and select the best-performing model(s). In the second step, the best-performing model could be manipulated to find the best set of model parameters by producing results for that specific model(s). See the case studies as two examples.

Case Studies

St1 Helsinki, Finland

The OTN-3 well at the St1 Helsinki site reached a depth of 6.1 km, with its last 1 km being an open-hole section inclined

45° toward the northeast. In 2018, a massive hydraulic stimulation campaign was performed in five stages over 60 days, injecting 18,160 m^3 of water into the crystalline basement rocks around the well. The injection rates varied between 400 and 1200 l/min, following a quasi-cyclic pattern, alternating between periods of constant-rate fluid injection and no-injection phases. Because the stimulation progressed, longer resting periods were considered in response to increasing seismic hazard. A seismic monitoring network comprising 12 three-component geophones tracked seismicity throughout the campaign. The seismic catalog recorded 55,707 detected events, with a maximum M_w of 1.7, all originating near the stimulated volume (Kwiatek *et al.*, 2019). The seismicity formed four major clusters along the final 1 km portion of the well, expanding spatially according to diffusion laws (Leonhardt, Kwiatek, Martínez-Garzón, and Heikkinen, 2021; Leonhardt, Kwiatek, Martínez-Garzón, Bohnhoff, *et al.*, 2021). The evolution of seismic magnitudes could be described with pressure-controlled models such as those of Galis *et al.* (2017) or van der Elst *et al.* (2016), with no signs of unstable, runaway behavior (Kwiatek *et al.*, 2024).

We forecasted the next largest magnitude using the developed application (Fig. 4). Because we aim to generate the estimations for the whole operation from the start of injection, we used the extended window with a time interval of 2 hr and 20 events limitations. As shown in Figure 2, for "All models" the model parameters were as follows: completeness magnitude (M_c) = −0.5, friction coefficient (μ) = 0.6, shear modulus (rigidity) of reservoir rock (G) = 35 GPa, static stress drop ($\Delta\sigma$) = 3 MPa, geometrical constant (C) of Shapiro's model = 0.95, b-value = MLE from Aki (1965) and confidence level (cl) of the van der Elst model = 0.37. For a better evaluation of the models, the observed maximum magnitude value recorded in the corresponding time window is plotted with a black dashed line in all the plots. Overall, the obtained results are comparable to that from a separate study of Kwiatek *et al.* (2024, their figs. 2 and 4). The only difference is the outcomes for Shapiro's model (Fig. 4a,f). The discrepancy is related to the different way the characteristic lengths are calculated. Here, the characteristic length was calculated from all clusters of seismicity (whole seismic activity), whereas Kwiatek *et al.* (2024) used only the extent of the largest bottom-most cluster.

Although Li's model (Fig. 4a,d) seems at times very close to the observed values of maximum magnitudes, there are large time intervals that this model severely underestimates the observed magnitudes, or it cannot be calculated (see equation 7). With this definition, Hallo's model (Fig. 4a,c) is the best-performing model for the St1 Helsinki stimulation. McGarr models (calculated with different b-value options, Fig. 4a,b) severely overestimate the next largest magnitude. This is expected because the St1 Helsinki stimulation is characterized by low seismic injection efficiency (Kwiatek *et al.*, 2019, 2022), suggesting that a significant portion of the accumulated elastic strain energy is released in aseismic processes that are not handled by the McGarr model (compare with discussion in Kwiatek *et al.*, 2024). An additional problem is that occasionally the b-value exceeds 1.5, which is an upper limit to this parameter (Fig. 4b), and the value is therefore hard-capped to 1.5, leading to bias in next magnitude estimates. The overall variations in Hallo's models with different b-value options are similar to the McGarr models (Fig. 4b,c), but the SER effectively reduces the maximum magnitude forecasts. The van der Elst's models with different b-value options and confidence levels (see Fig. 4a,e) are all much higher than the observed values. Shapiro's model is also computed for different characteristic length scales (Fig. 4f), showing that the model computed with L_{min} is closer to the observed values. However, regardless of the selection of characteristic length, all forecasts are highly overestimated compared with the estimates provided by Kwiatek *et al.* (2024), who constrained the characteristic length estimation based on the bottom-most cluster.

Cooper Basin, Australia

The Cooper basin geothermal field, located in northeast South Australia near the Queensland border, has been a site of geothermal exploration since 2002. Six deep wells were drilled into granite at depths 3629–4852 m, with four situated in the Habanero field and two others in the Jolokia and Savina fields, located 9 and 18 km away, respectively. To improve subsurface hydraulic conductivity, several hydraulic stimulations were performed, triggering the significant seismicity along a pre-existing sub-horizontal fault (Baisch *et al.*, 2006, 2009).

In 2003, a long-term fluid-injection experiment was conducted in the Habanero#1 well. Over 20,000 m^3 of water was injected at a depth of 4250, leading to ~27,000 seismic events (10,147 located). The seismicity outlined a nearly sub-horizontal planar structure extending 2 × 1.5 km with an apparent thickness of 150–200 m. The seismic activity showed clear spatiotemporal patterns: (I) migration beyond the immediate vicinity of the well, and (II) cessation of activity in previously activated areas. Analysis of event clusters revealed that the geothermal reservoir is dominated by a single fracture zone, with localized areas showing a reduced apparent thickness of just a few tens of meters (Baisch *et al.*, 2006, 2009).

Likewise, for St1 stimulation, we used the available 2003 catalog and injection data (IS-EPOS, 2020) from Cooper basin to forecast the next largest magnitude using all possible maximum magnitude models (Fig. 5). Almost all model parameters are similar to the St1 Helsinki case; however, we used local magnitude (M_L) with a completeness of −0.7. Comparing all models with the observed maximum magnitudes (black dashed line in Fig. 5a) reveals that the best-performing models are those of McGarr and Hallo's, but with different b-value options. The McGarr model (Fig. 5b) with a constant b-value equal to 1 produces the best estimation, whereas for Hallo's

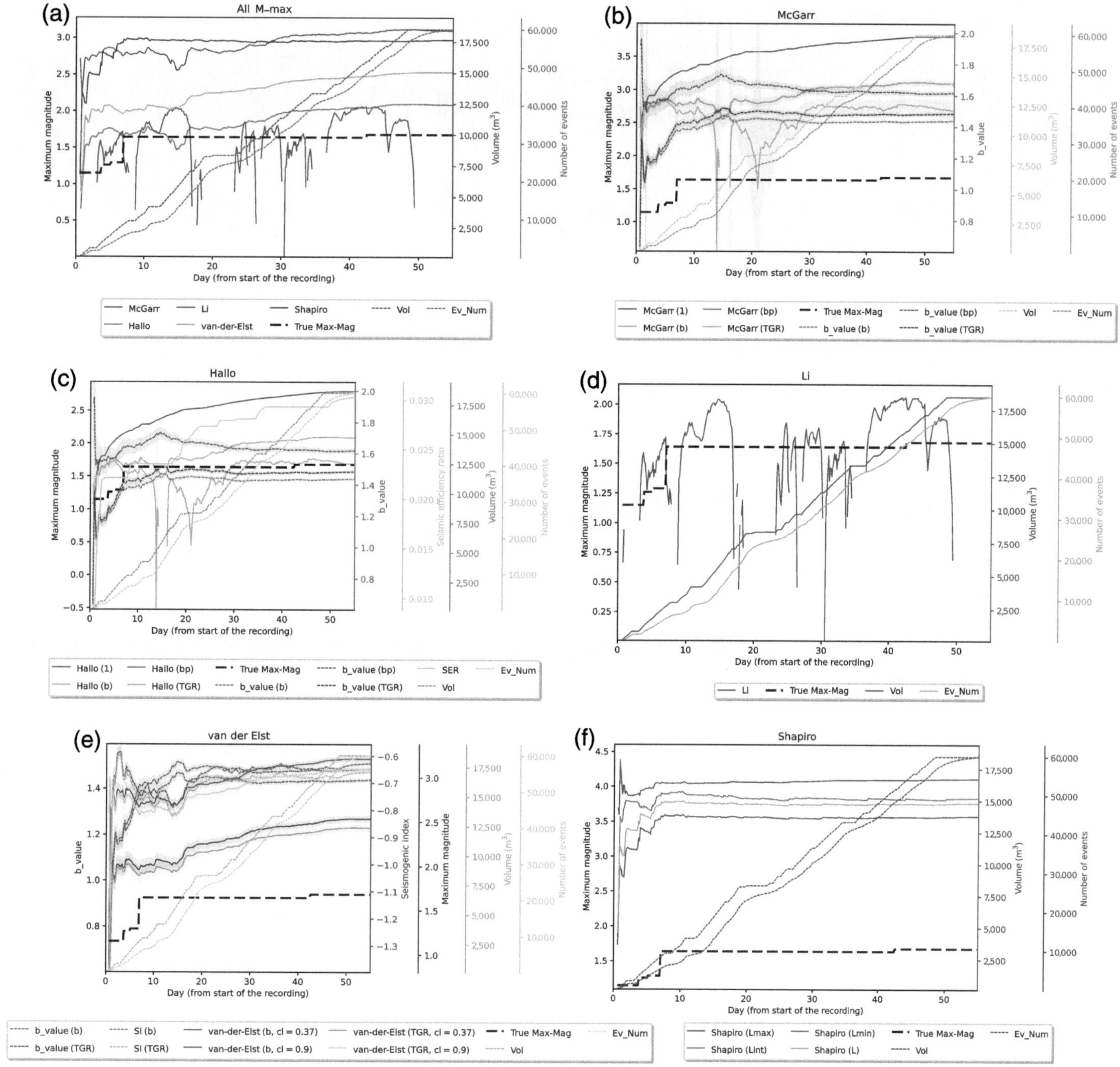

Figure 4. The application outputs for the St1 Helsinki injection campaign in OTN-3 well in 2018 (see Kwiatek *et al.*, 2019, 2022, 2024, for details). (a) Comparison of all models of next largest magnitude forecasts, (b–e) detailed view for each model using different model parameters: (b) McGarr model (with different *b*-value options), (c) Hallo model (same as McGarr), (d) Li model, (e) van der Elst (showcase of different *b*-value options and confidence intervals), and (f) Shapiro' model (showcase of the effects of characteristic lengths on the model). In all plots, maximum magnitude models and observed maximum magnitudes are shown with solid lines and a black dashed line, respectively. Other parameters are plotted with small dashed lines. The options of *b*-value estimation are either a constant value of one (1) or maximum-likelihood estimation (MLE) of exponential (GR) distribution (b), Laplace distribution of positive magnitude differences (bp) and tapered GR distribution (TGR). Other abbreviations are cl, confidence level; Ev_Num, cumulative number of events; L, characteristic length scale; SI, seismogenic index; SER, seismic efficiency ratio; and Vol, cumulative injected volume. The color version of this figure is available only in the electronic edition.

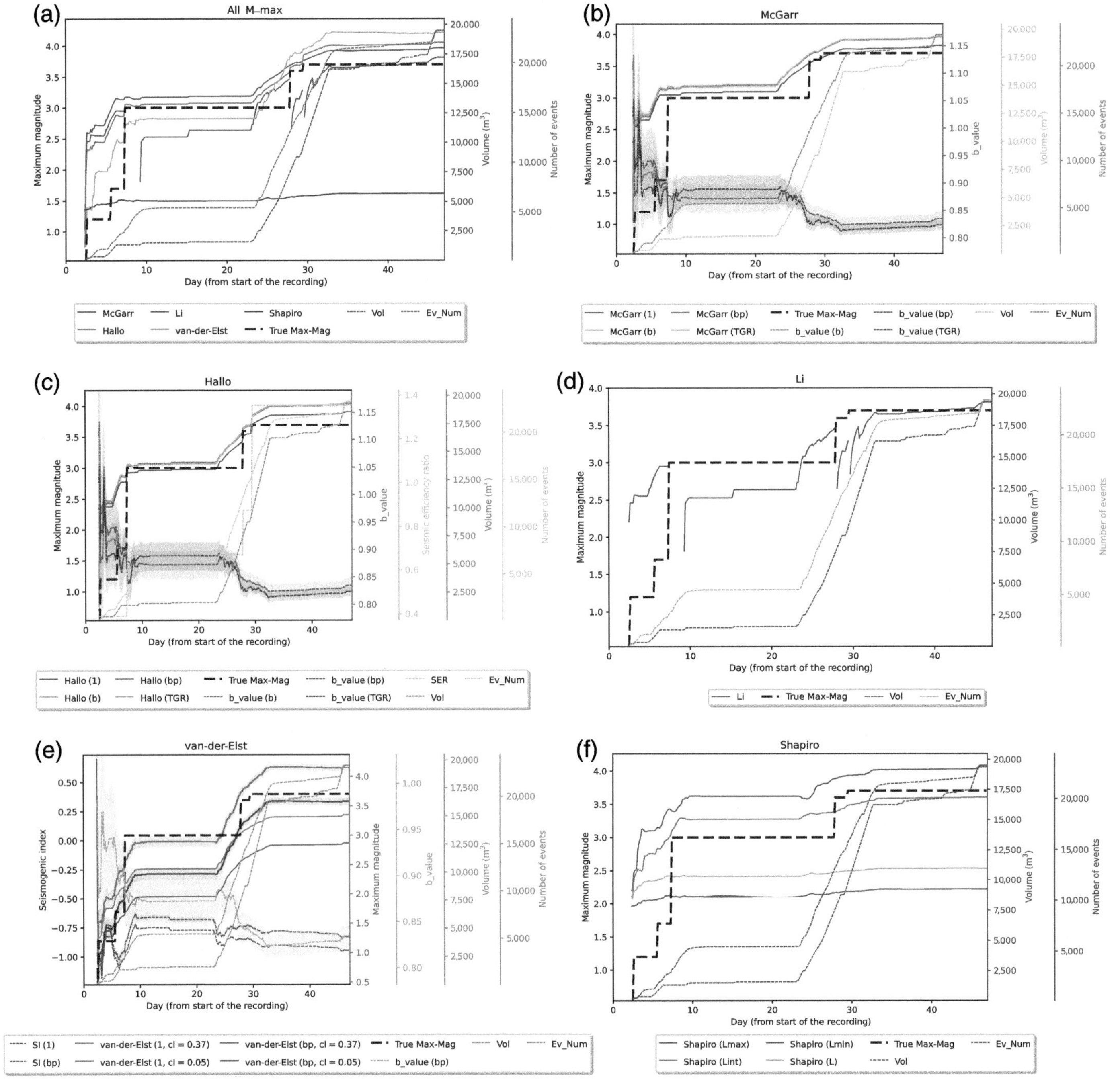

Figure 5. Similar to Figure 4, but for the Cooper basin. The color version of this figure is available only in the electronic edition.

(Fig. 5c), it is obtained using a time-dependent *b*-value. Li's model (Fig. 5a,d) shows the same variations as we discussed in St1 and always underestimates the next largest magnitude. On the other hand, van der Elst's model (Fig. 5e) provides better estimates for the Cooper basin than for the St1, especially once the *b*-positive method is used with a confidence level of 0.37. Interestingly, Shapiro's models with different characteristic lengths show that now L_{max} provides a reasonable assessment of the next largest magnitude (small, but positive overestimation), whereas the L_{int} starts to underestimate the magnitude in later stages of the injection. This discrepancy may be due to the spatially constrained distribution of seismicity in the Cooper basin that spreads over a thin fault zone (Király *et al.*, 2014). Therefore, L_{min} (and L likewise) are seemingly too small to characterize appropriately the characteristic length scale, in which the cluster-like distribution is in general, expected. It is conceivable that one has to select the semiaxes of the ellipsoid that correspond best to the slip direction of earthquakes, which in the case of the Cooper basin, corresponds roughly to the longest semiaxis length.

Discussion and Summary

We provide a new open-access web-based application of MaxMagMod, which was integrated into the EPISODES platform. This application forecasts the maximum magnitude earthquake, which may be triggered by injecting fluid into a reservoir in an EGS project. The user-friendly interface of the application allows all users of the EPISODES platform to use geodata of the platform or personal data to generate forecasts of the next largest magnitude using a variety of existing models of the maximum magnitude. The outputs are accessible either as a data sheet or a plot image.

We test the application on two case studies of induced seismicity associated with fluid injection in the St1 Deep Heat project, Finland, and the Cooper Basin, Australia. We show that, based on MaxMagMod, some models produce reliable results that are in agreement with independent studies. The presented case studies highlight the usefulness of the developed application in providing a quick, yet comprehensive overview of maximum magnitude forecasts from different statistical and deterministic models of the maximum magnitude. This is primarily achieved by an interactive environment that allows for quick changes to the input parameters and calculation conditions.

At the same time, the presented case studies clearly emphasize the importance of understanding model limitations, optimization, and the importance of model parameters as well as the processing workflow, to improve the performance of the next largest maximum magnitude forecasts using deterministic approaches. Interpretation of results, especially if they may vary significantly owing to hardly constrainable factors without the substantial aid of statistical tools, may not be straightforward. Instead, the interpretation is usually qualitative, while requiring substantial input of expert knowledge (even at the level of a single injection campaign) to constrain which particular model(s) will give the best answer. On the level of the single maximum magnitude model, a possible solution to empower deterministic techniques is to incorporate sampling or bootstrapping techniques (see Kwiatek *et al.*, 2024) to learn about the possible variety of maximum magnitude outputs. However, the selection of the most trustworthy model out of the handful of models, especially in advance of injection operations, is difficult. First of all, one should be aware that the models are primarily designed for stable, pressure-controlled injection without significant external input from tectonic stresses, and do not consider runaway conditions. From the perspective of the earthquake catalog, this means pressure-controlled seismic catalogs should display the properties of a quasi-stationary Poissonian process with limited variations in b-value and seismic activity driven (solely) by injection operations (compare with discussion in Kwiatek *et al.*, 2022). Any deviation from this behavior should trigger caution (Bentz *et al.*, 2020) and reassessment of injection operations. If prior seismic data are available, for example, from stimulation campaigns in neighboring injection wells, one should analyze their potential for unstable ruptures (e.g., Martínez-Garzón *et al.*, 2020). Such check-ups should be implemented during stimulation as well, especially if changes in structural conditions (e.g., faults) are expected.

During stimulation, the models provide (presumably) highly varying assessments of the maximum magnitude, which may be discouraging at first. Nevertheless, the evolution of maximum magnitude, or equivalently, a cumulative seismic moment release, provides first break information on whether the seismicity associated with (pending) injection is pressure controlled. As indicated in Bentz *et al.* (2020), higher exponents $\alpha > 3/2$ in $M_{0,\max} \propto \Delta V^{\alpha}$ are primarily not expected for stable, pressured-controlled seismicity and should trigger caution reassessment of injection operations. Contrary, evolution with $\alpha < 1$ is likely considered safe (Karimpouli *et al.*, 2025), likewise, the stationary maximum magnitude despite continuous fluid injection. The latter evolutions can be tracked with input parameters as well, including b-value, seismogenic index, and SER. It is expected that these parameters do not change dramatically during pressure-controlled injection. It is worth remembering McGarr (2014) estimate is an upper-bound limit to the maximum magnitude. Exceedance of this estimate suggests the runaway regime or problems with boundary conditions and/or input parameters. For example, Shapiro's next largest magnitude estimate is proxied by the characteristic length calculated for a single cluster of seismicity. Ignoring this assumption overestimates the key L parameters, leading to overestimation of the next largest magnitude.

Data and Resources

The application is available as an open-access tool on the EPISODES platform (https://EpisodesPlatform.eu/#app:MaxMagnitudeDPModels). Seismic and hydraulic data for the Cooper basin case are accessible on the geodata repository of the EPISODES platform (doi: 10.25171/InstGeoph_PAS_ISEPOS-2020-001). The St1 Deep Head data are available from Leonhardt, Kwiatek, Martínez-Garzón, and Heikkinen (2021) (doi: 10.5880/GFZ.4.2.2021.001). The EPISODES platform is available at https://EpisodesPlatform.eu and their formats specification is available at https://docs.cyfronet.pl/display/ISDOC/Data+formats. All websites were last accessed in July 2015.

Declaration of Competing Interests

The authors acknowledge that there are no conflicts of interest recorded.

Acknowledgments

This work was performed in the frame of the EU HORIZON DT-GEO project (HORIZON-INFRA-2021-TECH-01, Project Number 101058129). The authors gratefully acknowledge the Polish high-performance computing infrastructure PLGrid (HPC Center: ACK Cyfronet AGH) for providing computer facilities and support within computational Grant Number PLG/2024/017279. The described application was developed using Application Workbench, a tool developed in the frame of the Project EPOS-PL (No POIR.04.02.00-14-A003/16), cofinanced by the European Union from the funds of the European Regional Development Fund (ERDF).

References

Abdi, A. M., T. Murayama, S. Nishikizawa, and K. Suwanteep (2024). Social acceptance and associated risks of geothermal energy development in East Africa: Perspectives from geothermal energy developers, *Clean Energy* **8,** no. 5, 20–33, doi: 10.1093/CE/ZKAE051.

Aki, K. (1965). Maximum likelihood estimate of b in the formula log N= a-bM and its confidence limits, *Bull. Earthq. Res. Inst. Tokyo Univ.* **43,** 237–239.

Baisch, S., R. Vörös, R. Weidler, and D. Wyborn (2009). Investigation of fault mechanisms during geothermal reservoir stimulation experiments in the Cooper basin, Australia, *Bull. Seismol. Soc. Am.* **99,** no. 1, 148–158, doi: 10.1785/0120080055.

Baisch, S., R. Weidler, R. Vörös, D. Wyborn, and L. de Graaf (2006). Induced seismicity during the stimulation of a geothermal HFR reservoir in the Cooper basin, Australia, *Bull. Seismol. Soc. Am.* **96,** no. 6, 2242–2256, doi: 10.1785/0120050255.

Bentz, S., G. Kwiatek, P. Martínez-Garzón, M. Bohnhoff, and G. Dresen (2020). Seismic moment evolution during hydraulic stimulations, *Geophys. Res. Lett.* **47,** no. 5, e2019GL086185, doi: 10.1029/2019GL086185.

Bormann, P., and D. Di Giacomo (2011). The moment magnitude M_w and the energy magnitude M_e: Common roots and differences, *J. Seismol.* **15,** no. 2, 411–427, doi: 10.1007/S10950-010-9219-2.

Bücher, A., and J. Segers (2017). On the maximum likelihood estimator for the generalized extreme-value distribution, *Extremes (Boston)* **20,** no. 4, 839–872, doi: 10.1007/S10687-017-0292-6.

Deichmann, N., and D. Giardini (2009). Earthquakes induced by the stimulation of an enhanced geothermal system below Basel (Switzerland), *Seismol. Res. Lett.* **80,** no. 5, 784–798, doi: 10.1785/GSSRL.80.5.784.

Drif, K., O. Lengliné, J. Kinscher, and J. Schmitbuhl (2024). Induced seismicity controlled by injected hydraulic energy: The case study of the EGS Soultz-Sous-Forêts site, *J. Geophys. Res.* **129,** no. 6, e2023JB028190, doi: 10.1029/2023JB028190.

Galis, M., J. P. Ampuero, P. M. Mai, and F. Cappa (2017). Induced seismicity provides insight into why earthquake ruptures stop, *Sci. Adv.* **3,** no. 12, eaap7528, doi: 10.1126/sciadv.aap7528.

Geffers, G. M., I. G. Main, and M. Naylor (2022). Biases in estimating b-values from small earthquake catalogues: How high are high b-values? *Geophys. J. Int.* **229,** no. 3, 1840–1855, doi: 10.1093/GJI/GGAC028.

Hallo, M., L. Eisner, and M. Y. Ali (2012). Expected level of seismic activity caused by volumetric changes, *First Break* **30,** no. 7, 97–100, doi: 10.3997/1365-2397.30.7.60350.

Hallo, M., I. Oprsal, L. Eisner, and M. Y. Ali (2014). Prediction of magnitude of the largest potentially induced seismic event, *J. Seismol.* **18,** no. 3, 421–431, doi: 10.1007/S10950-014-9417-4.

Im, K., and J. Avouac (2024). Maximum magnitude of induced earthquakes in rate and state friction framework, *Seismol. Res. Lett.* doi: 10.1785/0220240382.

IS-EPOS (2020). Episode: COOPER BASIN, doi: 10.25171/InstGeoph_PAS_ISEPOS-2020-001.

Kagan, Y. Y. (2002). Seismic moment distribution revisited: I. Statistical results, *Geophys. J. Int.* **148,** no. 3, 520–541, doi: 10.1046/J.1365-246X.2002.01594.X.

Kagan, Y. Y. (2004). Short-term properties of earthquake catalogs and models of earthquake source, *Bull. Seismol. Soc. Am.* **94,** no. 4, 1207–1228, doi: 10.1785/012003098.

Karimpouli, S., G. Kwiatek, P. Martinez-Garzon, D. Caus, L. Wang, G. Dresen, and M. Bohnhoff (2025). Forecasting induced seismicity in enhanced geothermal systems using machine learning: Challenges and opportunities, *Geophys. J. Int.* **242,** 1–13, doi: 10.1093/gji/ggaf155.

Király, E., V. Gischig, D. Karvounis, and S. Weimer (2014). Validating models to forecasting induced seismicity related to deep geothermal energy projects, *39th Workshop on Geothermal Reservoir Engineering*, Stanford, California, 24–26 February 2014, 1–9.

Knopoff, L., Y. Y. Kagan, and R. Knopoff (1982). b Values for foreshocks and aftershocks in real and simulated earthquake sequences, *Bull. Seismol. Soc. Am.* **72,** no. 5, 1663–1676, doi: 10.1785/BSSA0720051663.

Kwiatek, G., I. Grigoratos, and S. Wiemer (2024). Variability of seismicity rates and maximum magnitude for adjacent hydraulic stimulations, *Seismol. Res. Lett.* doi: 10.1785/0220240043.

Kwiatek, G., P. Martínez-Garzón, J. Davidsen, P. Malin, A. Karjalainen, M. Bohnhoff, and G. Dresen (2022). Limited earthquake interaction during a geothermal hydraulic stimulation in Helsinki, Finland, *J. Geophys. Res.* **127,** no. 9, e2022JB024354, doi: 10.1029/2022JB024354.

Kwiatek, G., T. Saarno, T. Ader, F. Bluemle, M. Bohnhoff, M. Chendorain, G. Dresen, P. Heikkinen, I. Kukkonen, P. Leary, *et al.* (2019). Controlling fluid-induced seismicity during a 6.1-km-deep geothermal stimulation in Finland, *Sci. Adv.* **5,** no. 5, doi: 10.1126/SCIADV.AAV7224.

Leonhardt, M., G. Kwiatek, P. Martínez-Garzón, M. Bohnhoff, T. Saarno, P. Heikkinen, and G. Dresen (2021). Seismicity during and after stimulation of a 6.1 km deep enhanced geothermal system in Helsinki, Finland, *Solid Earth* **12,** no. 3, 581–594, doi: 10.5194/SE-12-581-2021.

Leonhardt, M., G. Kwiatek, P. Martínez-Garzón, and P. Heikkinen (2021). Earthquake catalog of induced seismicity recorded during and after stimulation of enhanced geothermal system in Helsinki, Finland, doi: 10.5880/GFZ.4.2.2021.001.

Li, Z., D. Eaton, and J. Davidsen (2022). Short-term forecasting of Mmax during hydraulic fracturing, *Sci. Rep.* **12,** no. 1, 1–12, doi: 10.1038/s41598-022-15365-6.

Liu, J., C. Shao, B. Yang, M. Ramadhani Ngata, M. Mwangomba, S. Josephat, and M. Dahiru Aminu (2024). Advances in enhanced geothermal systems: Integrating laboratory, numerical and field insights, *Appl. Therm. Eng.* **249,** 123350, doi: 10.1016/J.APPLTHERMALENG.2024.123350.

Ma, H. (1978). Variations of the b-values before several large earthquakes occurred in North China, *Acta Geophys. Sinica* **21,** 126–141.

Martínez-Garzón, P., G. Kwiatek, S. Bentz, M. Bohnhoff, and G. Dresen (2020). Induced earthquake potential in geothermal reservoirs: Insights from The Geysers, California, *The Leading Edge* **39,** no. 12, 873–882, doi: 10.1190/TLE39120873.1.

McGarr, A. (2014). Maximum magnitude earthquakes induced by fluid injection, *J. Geophys. Res.* **119,** no. 2, 1008–1019, doi: 10.1002/2013JB010597.

McGarr, A. (1976). Seismic moments and volume changes, *J. Geophys. Res.* **81,** no. 8, 1487–1494, doi: 10.1029/JB081I008P01487.

Mohamed, E. A. (2024). Enhanced geothermal energy systems, in *Encyclopedia of Renewable Energy, Sustainability and the Environment,* 1st edition, M. R. Rahimpour (Editor), Elsevier, Amsterdam, Netherlands, 235–248, doi: 10.1016/B978-0-323-93940-9.00226-7.

Orlecka-Sikora, B., and S. Cielesta (2020). Evidence for subcritical rupture of injection-induced earthquakes, *Sci. Rep.* **10,** no. 1, 1–15, doi: 10.1038/s41598-020-60928-0.

Orlecka-Sikora, B., S. Lasocki, J. Kocot, T. Szepieniec, J. R. Grasso, A. Garcia-Aristizabal, M. Schaming, P. Urban, G. Jones, I. Stimpson, *et al.* (2020). An open data infrastructure for the study of anthropogenic hazards linked to georesource exploitation, *Sci. Data* **7,** no. 1, 1–16, doi: 10.1038/s41597-020-0429-3.

Park, S., K. Il Kim, L. Xie, H. Yoo, K. B. Min, M. Kim, B. Yoon, K. Y. Kim, G. Zimmermann, F. Guinot, *et al.* (2020). Observations and analyses of the first two hydraulic stimulations in the Pohang geothermal development site, South Korea, *Geothermics* **88,** 101905, doi: 10.1016/J.GEOTHERMICS.2020.101905.

Raleigh, C. B., J. H. Healy, and J. D. Bredehoeft (1976). An experiment in earthquake control at Rangely, Colorado, *Science (1979)* **191,** no. 4233, 1230–1237, doi: 10.1126/SCIENCE.191.4233.1230.

Rotondi, R., and E. Varini (2022). Temporal variations of the probability distribution of voronoi cells generated by earthquake epicenters, *Front Earth Sci (Lausanne)* **10,** 928348, doi: 10.3389/FEART.2022.928348.

Schorlemmer, D., S. Wiemer, and M. Wyss (2005). Variations in earthquake-size distribution across different stress regimes, *Nature* **437,** no. 7058, 539–542, doi: 10.1038/nature04094.

Senyapar, H. N. D., and R. Bayindir (2023). The negative social impacts of renewable energy: A key consideration for a successful energy transition, *12th IEEE International Conf. on Renewable Energy Research and Applications, ICRERA 2023,* Oshawa, Ontario, Canada, 6 October 2023, 591–596, doi: 10.1109/ICRERA59003.2023.10269411.

Shapiro, S. A., C. Dinske, C. Langenbruch, and F. Wenzel (2010). Seismogenic index and magnitude probability of earthquakes induced during reservoir fluid stimulations, *The Leading Edge* **29,** no. 3, 304–309, doi: 10.1190/1.3353727.

Shapiro, S. A., O. S. Krüger, and C. Dinske (2013). Probability of inducing given-magnitude earthquakes by perturbing finite volumes of rocks, *J. Geophys. Res.* **118,** no. 7, 3557–3575, doi: 10.1002/JGRB.50264.

Shapiro, S. A., O. S. Krüger, C. Dinske, and C. Langenbruch (2011). Magnitudes of induced earthquakes and geometric scales of fluid-stimulated rock volumes, *Geophysics* **76,** no. 6, doi: 10.1190/GEO2010-0349.1.

van der Elst, N. J. (2021). B-positive: A robust estimator of aftershock magnitude distribution in transiently incomplete catalogs, *J. Geophys. Res.* **126,** no. 2, e2020JB021027, doi: 10.1029/2020JB021027.

van der Elst, N. J., M. T. Page, D. A. Weiser, T. H. W. Goebel, and S. M. Hosseini (2016). Induced earthquake magnitudes are as large as (statistically) expected, *J. Geophys. Res.* **121,** no. 6, 4575–4590, doi: 10.1002/2016JB012818.

Varotsos, P. A., N. V. Sarlis, E. S. Skordas, and H. Tanaka (2004). A plausible explanation of the b-value in the Gutenberg-Richter law from first principles, *Proc. Jpn. Acad. Ser B* **80,** no. 9, 429–434, doi: 10.2183/PJAB.80.429.

Zhou, W., F. Lanza, I. Grigoratos, R. Schultz, J. Cousse, E. Trutnevyte, A. Muntendam-Bos, and S. Wiemer (2024). Managing induced seismicity risks from enhanced geothermal systems: A good practice guideline, *Rev. Geophys.* **62,** no. 4, e2024RG000849, doi: 10.1029/2024RG000849.

Manuscript received 4 December 2024
Published online 29 July 2025

PySolate: A Python-Based Thresholding Tool to Denoise or Designal Seismic Waveforms Based on the Continuous Wavelet Transform

Ana C. Aguiar*[1], Andrea Chiang[1], and Stephen C. Myers[1]

Abstract

***PySolate* is a Python-based toolset that implements the continuous wavelet transform and nonlinear thresholding operations to denoise or designal seismic data, following Langston and Mousavi (2019). This filtering approach can remove microseismic noise to isolate intermediate-period seismic signals that are key to enabling full-waveform modeling and analysis of smaller-magnitude regional events. This approach is best for the application to signals with frequency or time separation of signal and noise, in contrast to Fourier analysis, which is effective when signal and noise are separated in frequency. We demonstrate the Python toolset using the six announced Democratic People's Republic of Korea declared nuclear tests, showing the effectiveness of isolating the seismic signal compared to standard bandpass filtering. We also demonstrate the ease of using the toolset with any Python processing tools.**

Cite this article as Aguiar, A. C., A. Chiang, and S. C. Myers (2025). *PySolate*: A Python-Based Thresholding Tool to Denoise or Designal Seismic Waveforms Based on the Continuous Wavelet Transform, *Seismol. Res. Lett.* **97**, 514–523, doi: 10.1785/0220250034.

Introduction

Distinguishing signal from noise in seismograms is an enduring challenge. Although this challenge applies across the broadband of signal and noise frequencies used in seismological analysis, it is particularly evident in the microseismic band from approximately 5 to 10 s. Data in this band may be used for analysis of larger events but tends to be discarded for analysis of smaller events because signal-to-noise ratio (SNR) is low and conventional Fourier-based filtering is generally ineffective at separating signal from noise in a common frequency band. Effective separation of signal from noise may enable analysis of small events using full waveform fitting and other modern methods, which could lower detection thresholds, as well as improve event characterization and determination of earth structure.

Band-pass filtering using the principles of Fourier analysis is the most common method for enhancing signals, but it is well known that Fourier-based methods can be ineffective when signal and noise frequencies overlap. More recently developed methods explored time–frequency representations (TFRs) of the seismic signals. Mousavi and Langston (2017) have explored several types of signal transforms in the search of efficacy and computational efficiency. However, generation of short-time window Fourier transform (also known as spectrograms) can become increasingly computationally expensive (Mousavi and Langston, 2016a), and accurate identification of spectral peaks can be difficult, due to a trade-off in time–frequency resolution (Tary *et al.*, 2014). To address computational efficiency due to the need of processing large amounts of data, many studies have also explored and successfully applied machine learning methods including deep neural networks (DNNs), but these tend to have limitations dependent on the data sets used to train the models (Wang and Nealon, 2019; Zhu *et al.*, 2019; Tibi *et al.*, 2021; Mousavi *et al.*, 2024).

Other examples that also explore TFRs, are the continuous wavelet transform (CWT) and synchrosqueezed CWT (Mousavi and Langston, 2016b), for which time-series data can be represented in a more compact form. CWT allows efficient decomposition of the signal into timescale, nonstationary basis functions, which can more effectively isolate superimposed components of the waveform, including individual phases (Herrera *et al.*, 2014). Therefore, the CWT approach can be used for denoising or designaling seismic data as well as other applications, including seismic-wave partitioning and template correlation with applications to local and near regional data

1. Lawrence Livermore National Laboratory, Livermore, California, U.S.A., https://orcid.org/0000-0001-5277-3337 (ACA); https://orcid.org/0000-0001-8513-4363 (AC); https://orcid.org/0000-0002-0315-5599 (SCM)

*Corresponding author: aguiarmoya1@llnl.gov

(Langston and Mousavi, 2019; Tibi *et al.*, 2023) and has been shown to be useful in DNN applications using the CWT as input to the model (Quinones and Tibi, 2024).

The application of a filtering method that removes microseismic noise, isolating the seismic signal, will be key to better utilization of short-period waveforms in seismic analysis, including fitting simulated waveforms to signals from low-magnitude events. Contributing to this effort, we developed an open-source, easy-to-use Python-based toolset that implements the CWT-based, nonlinear thresholding operations (Langston and Mousavi, 2019) to denoise or designal seismic data. We focus this study on the introduction of a new implementation of CWT-based denoising and aim to show its applicability as an open-source option and its possibility of integration into any Python workflow while focusing on several examples where this type of denoising can provide improvement.

Method

CWT is based on a transient wavelet, compared to Fourier analysis, which is based on continuous basis functions. To replicate any time series, the CWT wavelet is replicated, scaled in amplitude, shifted in time, and added to other wavelets originating from the same base function. As a result, CWT has two independent variables, scale a, and time lag τ, which produces a map of amplitude at scale versus time lag for the signal. Based on the Langston and Mousavi (2019) extensive analysis of the Morlet wavelet due to its harmonic nature, we also use the Morlet–Grossman definition of the CWT (Grossmann *et al.*, 1989; Starck *et al.*, 2010) as the mother wavelet in the examples for this article. The CWT is represented by relating the scale to Fourier period with the following equation:

$$W(a,\tau) = \frac{1}{\sqrt{a}} \int_{-\infty}^{+\infty} f(t)\psi^*\left(\frac{t-\tau}{a}\right)\mathrm{d}t, \tag{1}$$

in which * is the complex conjugate and CWT is the correlation of the signal, $f(t)$ with a scaled basis function $\psi(t)$ with inverse:

$$f(t) = \frac{1}{C}\int_{-\infty}^{+\infty}\int_{0}^{\infty}\frac{1}{\sqrt{a}}W(a,\tau)\psi\left(\frac{t-\tau}{a}\right)\frac{\mathrm{d}a\mathrm{d}\tau}{a^2}, \tag{2}$$

and

$$C = \int_0^{\infty}\frac{\hat{\psi}^*(\omega)\hat{\psi}(\omega)}{\omega}\mathrm{d}\omega. \tag{3}$$

Once the raw or instrument corrected time-series data are transformed into CWT domain, we can form a map of wavelet amplitude as a function of scale and time lag. Because of the transient wavelet function, transient signals and noise may be more easily partitioned in time, compared to Fourier analysis. First, the noise amplitude spectrum can be computed by summing the absolute value of the amplitude of the coefficients at each scale over time lag in a time window before the event's first arrival. As Langston and Mousavi (2019), we assume that most seismic signals have a clear onset in time for the selected scale band. This allows the selection of the pre-event time window as the distinct window to compute the noise model. We follow this assumption across the analysis. Using the first announced Democratic People's Republic of Korea (DPRK) nuclear tests in 2006 as an example (DPRK1), Figure 1 shows the CWT scalogram and noise model computed using a 50 s window before the event's first arrival.

Second, as shown in Langston and Mousavi (2019), from Donoho *et al.* (1995) the assumed noise contribution can be removed by applying a "hard thresholding" or "soft thresholding" to the wavelet. Hard thresholding keeps wavelet coefficients if they are greater than a threshold criterion $\beta(a)$; otherwise, they are set to zero as follows:

$$\tilde{W}(a,\tau) = \begin{cases} W(a,\tau) & \text{if } |W(a,\tau)| \geq \beta(a) \\ 0 & \text{otherwise.} \end{cases}. \tag{4}$$

Soft thresholding can be applied by scaling all coefficients that pass hard thresholding by the inferred noise level (Weaver *et al.*, 1991; Langston and Mousavi, 2019), represented as follows:

$$\tilde{W}(a,\tau) = \begin{cases} \mathrm{sign}[W(a,\tau)](|W(a,\tau)| - \beta(a)) & \text{if } |W(a,\tau)| \geq \beta(a) \\ 0 & \text{otherwise} \end{cases}, \tag{5}$$

in which

$$\mathrm{sign}[W(a,\tau)] = \frac{W(a,\tau)}{|W(a,\tau)|}. \tag{6}$$

This second option performs better than hard thresholding because, as stated in Langston and Mousavi (2019), noise outliers just above the threshold amplitude will have an effective SNR close to unity and will be diminished compared to high-SNR coefficients.

Langston and Mousavi (2019) also suggest a simpler way to estimate the nonlinear thresholding by estimating the noise model from the pre-event window. In using a pre-event segment of the waveform to estimate the nonlinear threshold for thresholding, it is assumed that noise is stationary throughout the waveform. Assuming Gaussian noise, the threshold can then be computed as

$$\beta(a) = \mathrm{mean}(|W(a,\tau)|) + c\,\mathrm{stdv}(|W(a,\tau)|), \tag{7}$$

which are the mean and standard deviation of the absolute value wavelet transform at each scale a and c can be estimated as

$$c = \sqrt{2\log_{10} N}, \tag{8}$$

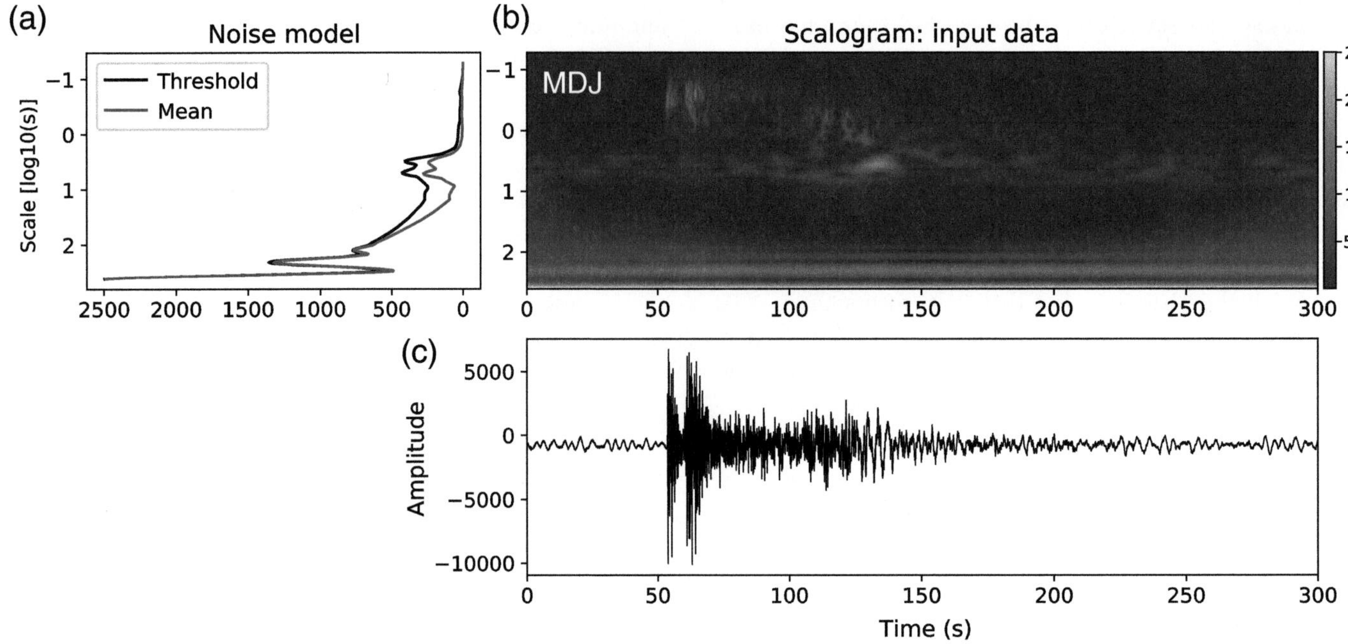

Figure 1. (a) The noise model estimated from 50 s prior to the first arrival of the event using the soft-thresholding approach. (b) Example of the continuous wavelet transform (CWT) scalogram (c) for the first Democratic People's Republic of Korea (DPRK) announced nuclear test (DPRK1) in 2006 on station MDJ in Mudanjiang, China. The color version of this figure is available only in the electronic edition.

as proposed by Donoho *et al.* (1995) in which N is the number of noise samples at each scale. But the noise distribution in real-seismic data is more complex that the Gaussian assumption; therefore, Langston and Mousavi (2019) instead use the empirical cumulative distribution function with 99% confidence. So the threshold function then becomes the inverse cumulative distribution as follows:

$$\beta(a) = \mathrm{ECDF}_a^{-1}(P = 0.99). \tag{9}$$

It is important that the type of thresholding selected may have implications on the resulting waveforms. Comprehensive studies have shown that the different types of thresholding might produce changes in amplitude and polarity (Mousavi and Langston, 2016b; Langston and Mousavi, 2019; Yang *et al.*, 2020; Tibi *et al.*, 2023; Zeng *et al.*, 2024). It has also been shown that this method can be sensitive to the choice of mother wavelet, which can have implications on noise suppression and changes in the signal (Mousavi and Langston, 2017; Tibi *et al.*, 2023) and should be given some consideration depending on the application. We refer the reader to the full text of Langston and Mousavi (2019) for further details on the method and instead focus this article on the Python toolset and examples of denoising. Both methods of thresholding presented here are available in the Python toolset.

Implementation

PySolate is written in Python and is an adaptation of the Langston and Mousavi (2019) MATLAB-based Block Choice Seismic Analysis (BCseis, version 1.1; see Data and Resources for link to the code). *PySolate* is entirely written in Python and it is open source, so users do not need to purchase a software license. It performs the same denoise and designal operations as BCseis and it can be incorporated easily into other Python workflows for additional analysis of seismic data. The forward and inverse CWT functions are based on the Synchrosqueezing toolbox by Thakur *et al.* (2013) and Daubechies *et al.* (2011). In addition to the standard Python installation, *PySolate* requires modules *ObsPy* (Beyreuther *et al.*, 2010), *matplotlib* (Hunter, 2007), *pyasdf* (Krischer *et al.*, 2016), and their dependences. *PySolate* is an open-source tool distributed under the terms of the Massachusetts Institute of Technology (MIT) license (see Data and Resources). We refer the reader to the GitHub page for details on installation as well as an example on the implementation of the tool.

PySolate has four core modules:

1. **Block:** the main core module to read and store the waveform files.
   a. In addition to *ObsPy* compatible waveform data formats, a HDF5 format data files can also be read.
   b. The parameter class determines the user-defined processes and CWT operations to be applied to the seismograms.
2. **Waveforms:** module that includes the routines for handling seismic waveform data, based on *ObsPy* stream objects for station and data information.
3. **Wavelet:** the routines to perform the wavelet transform with four different types of wavelets to select from. The module includes functions to

a. apply band reject filter to modify the wavelet coefficients over a scale bandpass,
b. the CWT using the wavelet function,
c. the inverse CWT,
d. the wavelet transform function of the wavelet filter in Fourier domain, and
e. the Fourier transform of the wavelet function.

4. **Threshold:** nonlinear thresholding operations using the CWT. These include functions to
   a. compute SNR for the CWT thresholding,
   b. compute the empirical cumulative probability distribution,
   c. calculate the noise model and threshold function,
   d. apply hard and soft thresholding to the noise (removing noise), and
   e. apply hard and soft thresholding to the signal (removing signal).

The available wavelet parameters that can be set within the tool are the following:

- **wave_type:** wavelet filter type with options "morlet," "shannon," "mhat," "hhat." Default is "morlet" and additional wavelet options are Shannon, Mexican hat wavelet (mhat), and Hermitian hat (hhat).
- **nvoices:** number of voices, that is, the sampling of CWT in scale. Higher number of voices give finer resolution. Default is 16.
- **Bandpass_blocking:** option to apply a band rejection filter for which wavelet coefficients are modified over a scale range (e.g., between 1 and 200 s).
- **scale_min:** minimum timescale for band-pass blocking. Default is 1.
- **scale_max:** maximum timescale for band-pass blocking. Default is 200.
- **block_threshhold:** percent amplitude adjustment to the wavelet coefficients within scale_min and scale_max. For example, a threshold of 5% means the wavelet coefficients in the band will be multiplied by 1.05. Default is 0.
- **estimate_noise:** flag to compute the noise model, default is True.
- **noise_starttime:** noise start time, default is 0 s.
- **noise_endtime:** noise end time, default is 60 s.
- **noise_threshold:** type of noise thresholding to be applied, the options are "hard" for hard thresholding and "soft" for soft thresholding. Default is None.
- **signal_threshold:** type of signal thresholding to be applied, the options are "hard" for hard thresholding, and "soft" for soft thresholding. Default is None.
- **nsigma_method:** method to determine the number of standard deviations for block thresholding. "donoho" for Donoho's Threshold criterion and "ECDF" for empirical cumulative probability distribution method. You can also specify the number of standard deviations by entering a number. The ECDF method assumes Gaussian statistic. The default method "ECDF" is recommended.
- **snr_detection:** flag to apply the SNR detection method, default is *False*. If *True* it will be applied before hard thresholding. The SNR detection is an event detector based on SNR. The empirical detector is applied by dividing the CWT parameters with the noise estimate (absolute value of the noise plus a percentage of the maximum value of the noise).
- **snr_lowerbound:** noise level percent lower bound. Default is 1.0. This parameter controls the percentage of maximum value of the noise applied in the detection.

TABLE 1
DPRK Event Dates and Estimated Magnitudes from IDC

Event	Date (yyyy/mm/dd)	Estimated M_b (IDC)
DPRK1	2006/10/09	$m_b \sim 4.1$
DPRK2	2009/05/25	$m_b \sim 4.5$
DPRK3	2013/02/12	$m_b \sim 4.9$
DPRK4	2016/01/06	$m_b \sim 4.8$
DPRK5	2016/09/09	$m_b \sim 5.1$
DPRK6	2017/10/03	$m_b \sim 6.1$

DPRK, Democratic People's Republic of Korea; IDC, International Data Centre for the Comprehensive Test-Ban Treaty Organization Preparatory Commission.

Although exploring the effects of the different parameters on seismic data is beyond the scope of this study, we refer the reader to the example on the GitHub page where these can be explored in detail.

Example Application to Seismic Data

We demonstrate *PySolate* using the six announced nuclear tests by the DPRK (Table 1).

Absolute locations for the events show that DPRK1 event is about 3 km away from the other events, which are within a 1 km radius of each other (Myers *et al.*, 2018). DPRK1 is also the smallest of the events (Fig. 2).

Close event proximity, similar explosion source, recordings at common stations, and varying SNR enable us to directly compare denoised low-SNR signals to high-SNR signals. Here, we present examples for two stations that recorded these events, stations MDJ in Mudanjiang, Heilongjiang Province, China with epicentral distance of about 370 km and BJT in Baijiatuan, Beijing, China (Fig. 3), at approximately 1100 km from the events. These two stations allow us to explore the issues that may arise when signal and noise separation in frequency and time is not straightforward.

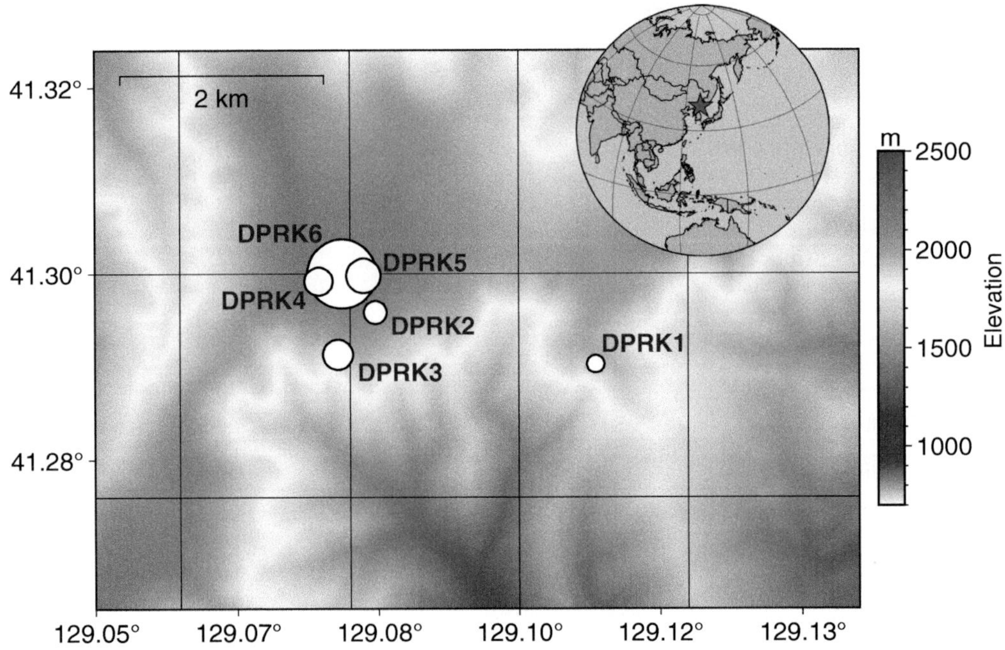

Figure 2. Map of DPRK event locations and estimated size in m_b as shown in Table 1 and reported by the International Data Centre (IDC). The color scale shows topographic elevation from Scripps' SRTM15 + V2.5.5 grid (Tozer *et al.*, 2019). Inset map shows general location of all the events on a larger scale. The color version of this figure is available only in the electronic edition.

Denoising the signal still allows a broad spectrum of frequencies to be present but seismic analysis frequently requires standard filtering to accentuate specific phases of interest. To understand the difference between denoising and standard (Fourier-based) filtering, we first use standard *ObsPy* tools to low-pass filter the raw data with a filter corner at 10 s (blue trace, Fig. 6). We then perform the same low-pass filter to the previously denoised waveform (red trace, Fig. 6) and compare the two in Figure 6.

There is a significant difference in the waveform after the two processing methods, and we can now clearly see the first arrival of the DPRK1 event in the low-pass and denoised trace (Fig. 6b), which is not

Waveform signals are similar when amplitudes are normalized (Fig. 4a), but signal amplitudes differ by orders of magnitude (Fig. 4b), resulting in a wide range of SNR. The 2006 event (DPRK1) is not observable at the same scales as later events (especially DPRK4-6; Fig. 4b) creating a challenge to compare this event with the others.

Using the *PySolate* soft thresholding option, we denoise the seismogram for all six events using a noise model computed from a 50 s window before the first *P*-wave arrival of each trace. Figure 5 shows the scalogram for DPRK1 data at station MDJ.

To create the plots in Figure 5, we read the data using *ObsPy* stream (st) and the steps in Algorithm 1:

ALGORITHM 1

1. Define the variable Parameters:

params = **bcs. Parameter**(

bandpass_blocking = False,

noise_endtime = 50.,

noise_threshold = "soft",

)

blocks = []

block = **bcs.read**(**params** = **params**, **data** = **st**)

(Continued next column.)

ALGORITHM 1 (continued)

block.run()

blocks.append(**block**)

2. Get the noise model for this trace:

block = **blocks**[0]

tag = **block.noise_model_tag**

3. Select the CWT for a specific station (MDJ) and the first DPRK event:

wave = **block.get_wavelets**(**tag**).select(**station**="MDJ")[0]

4. Seismograms can be selected in the same way:

tr = **block.waveforms.data**[**tag**].select(**station**="MDJ")[0]

5. Select the scales for the first event needed to plot:

scales = **np.log10**(**wave.scales**)

threshold = **wave.noise_model.P**

mean = **wave.noise_model.M**

6. Plot the denoised data and its scalogram (this creates Fig. 5):

block.plot("noise_removed", **station** = "MDJ")

7. Save the denoised data in SAC format; other formats are available:

tag = "noise_removed"

output = "waveforms"

block.write(**tag**, **output** = output, **format** = "SAC")

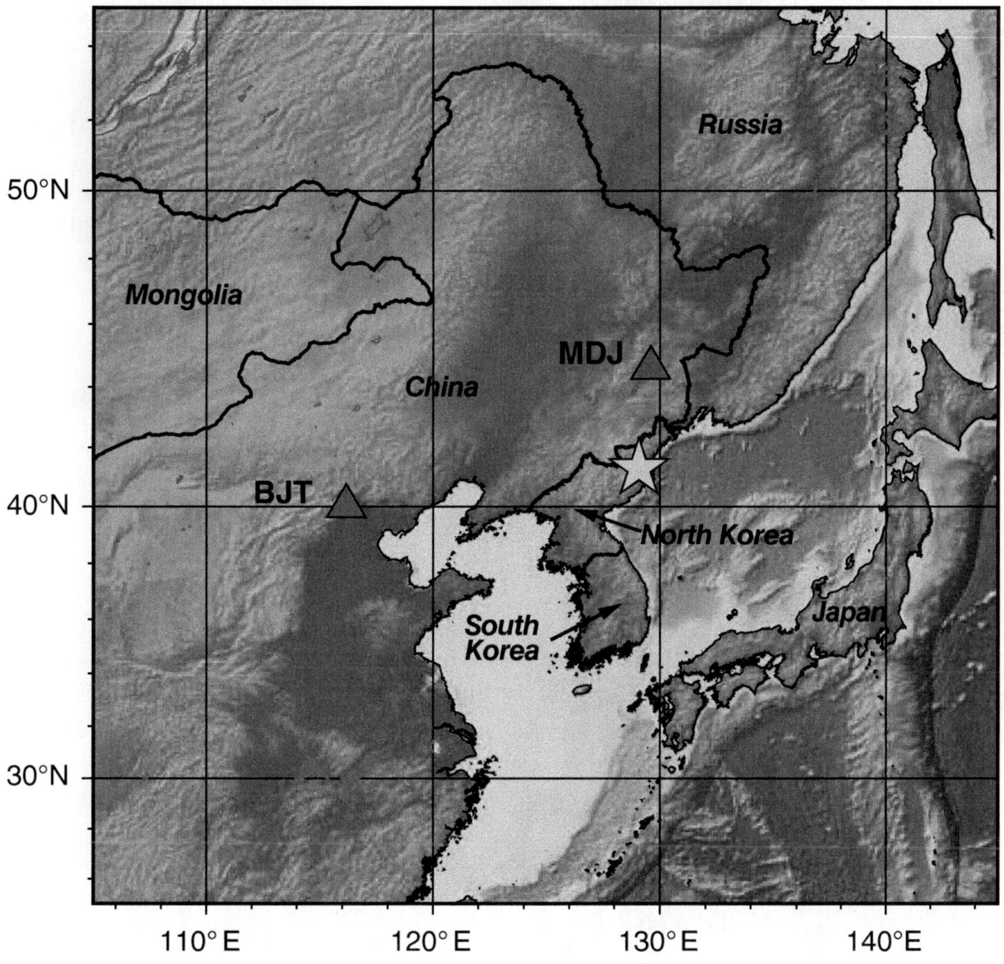

Figure 3. Map of the two stations in China used in the examples in this section and the general location of all DPRK events marked by a yellow star. The color version of this figure is available only in the electronic edition.

observable in the low-pass trace (Fig. 6a).

To further compare the two methods, we apply the same processing (filter-only vs. denoise and filter) for all other DPRK events. Because DPRK events have very similar waveforms, for simplicity, only two of the events are shown in Figure 7; DPRK1 (9 October 2006), which is the smallest event and used in the aforementioned denoising example, and DPRK5 (9 September 2016) which has waveforms similar to unplotted DPRK-event signals.

The low-pass (long-period) signal for DPRK1 would be much more difficult to model than the other higher-SNR signals from other DPRK events (Fig. 7a), due to the interference of microseismic noise. Figure 7b shows that wavelet-based denoising results in a DPRK1 waveform that is similar to waveforms for larger events with higher SNR. We do note a difference in the waveform for the DPRK1 after denoising, but this difference is apparent

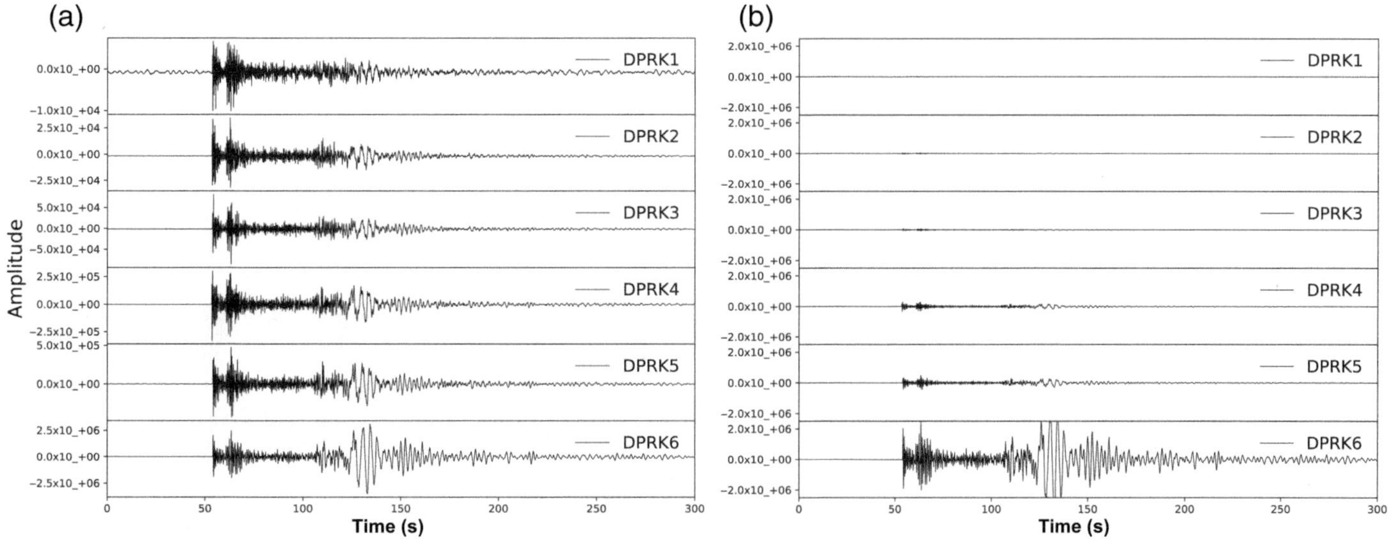

Figure 4. Records of the six DPRK announced nuclear tests at station MDJ, China. (a) Amplitude normalized and (b) common amplitude, scaled to the largest event in 2016 (DPRK6).

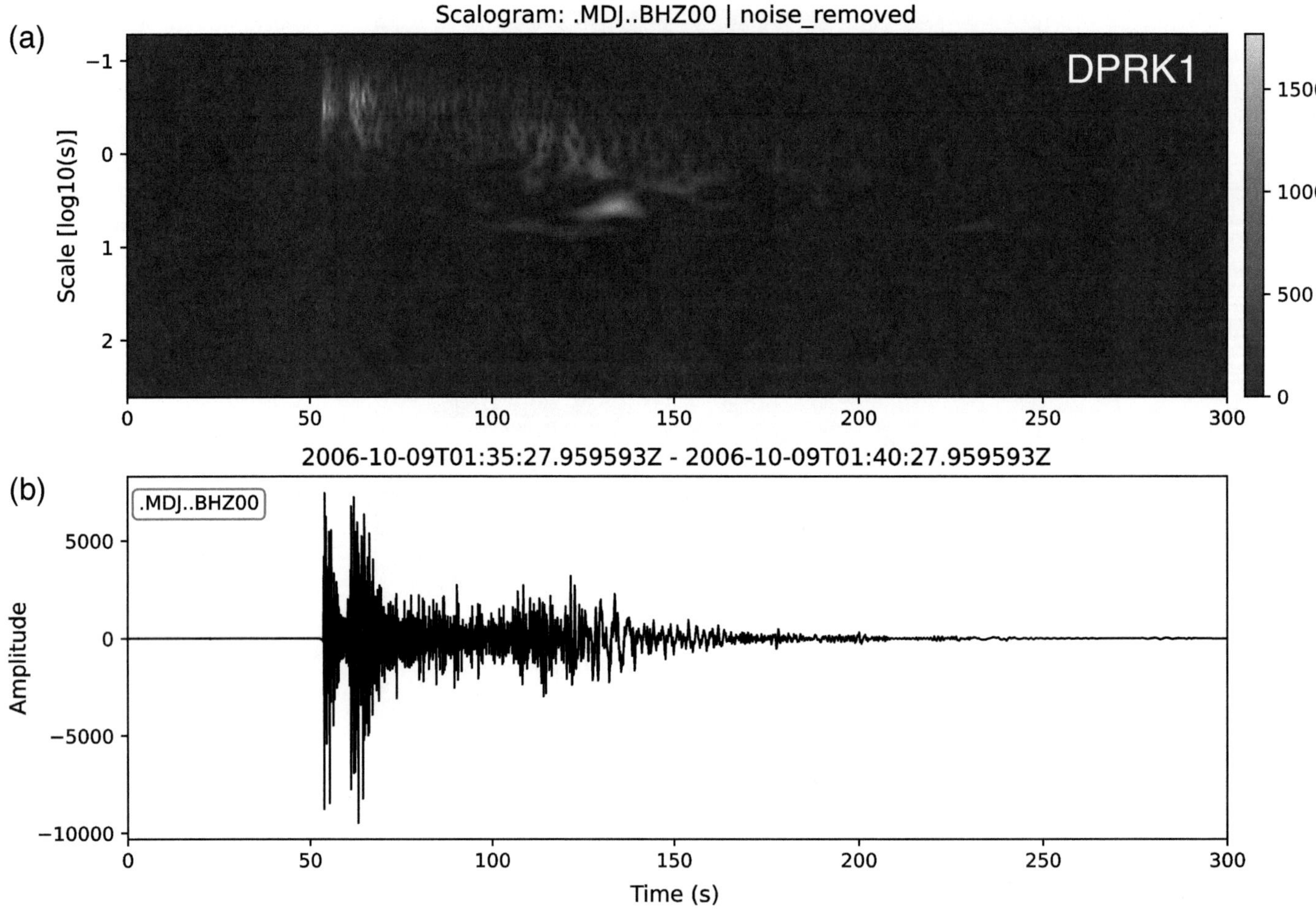

Figure 5. Example of denoised DPRK 1 data recorded at station MDJ using *PySolate*. (a) Scalogram and (b) denoised data using this method. The color version of this figure is available only in the electronic edition.

before denoising and is likely due to the difference in event location compared to the other events (Fig. 2).

We also look at station BTJ, in Beijing, China. This station is further away (~1100 km) from the DPRK tests than station MDJ, resulting in very low SNR for DPRK1 but with relatively clear signals for the other DPRK events. We expect the signal at BJT to have lower SNR as the path has to cross bay sediments, unlike station MDJ, which is in a mountainous region. Figure 8 shows the unfiltered seismogram, scalogram, and noise model for DPRK1 recorded at station BJT.

We also compare applications of CWT and standard filtering to seismograms recorded at station BJT, similar processing procedures as described for MDJ processing were applied to generate the results. Figure 9 shows a low-pass filter at 0.1 Hz and denoised data for only two of the DPRK events. As before, this is done for brevity as most of the events, except for the smallest (DPRK1) have very similar waveforms as shown in Figure 4.

Again, denoising results in a clearer surface wave that may be used for waveform modeling. We also observe some differences in the DPRK1 waveform, likely a result of the event location difference. We note that after standard filtering, station BJT seems to result in a noisier signal, which could be due to that epicentral distance is larger for this station. Denoising seems to improve the signal significantly, despite this distance.

Although the scope of this study does not extend to developing metrics for filter performance; we do validate our toolset with the MATLAB implementation of the method. We find that our toolset performs as expected and results are comparable to those from the MATLAB tool BCSeis version 1.1 (Langston and Mousavi, 2019; see Data and Resources for the link to this code) while using their test data set. We also implemented parallel processing in our toolset to allow for multithreading on larger data sets. We tested performance for a series of larger data sets and find that if one noise model is used for processing of over 100 earthquakes, execution time then scales linearly with the number of events as expected. The processing for a population of about 150 events on a 16 core stand-alone machine is 51 s. Here, we assume that noise characteristics for one station do not change substantially for a period of time, allowing us to use a single-noise model for this

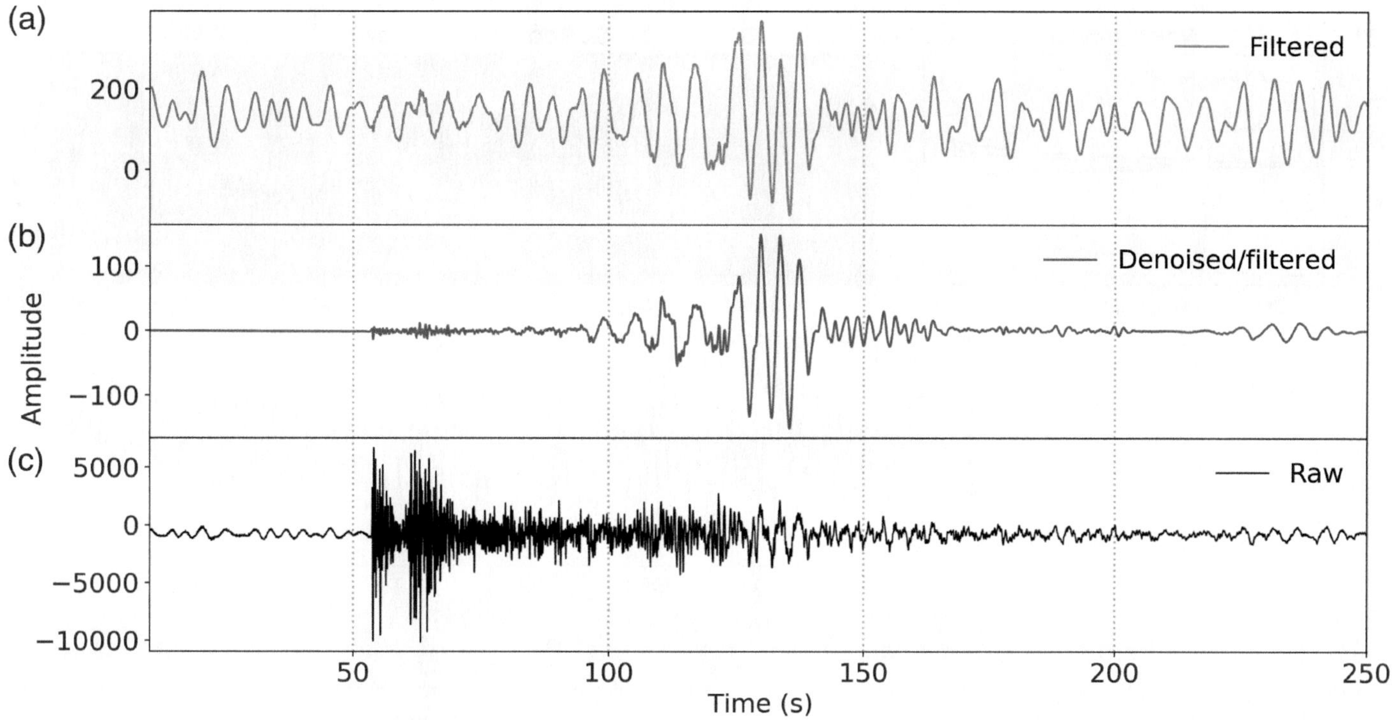

Figure 6. Example of DPRK1 compared to standard Fourier filtering. (a) Low-pass filter at 0.1 Hz, (b) denoised and filtered to the same frequencies as panel (a), and (c) original raw data. The color version of this figure is available only in the electronic edition.

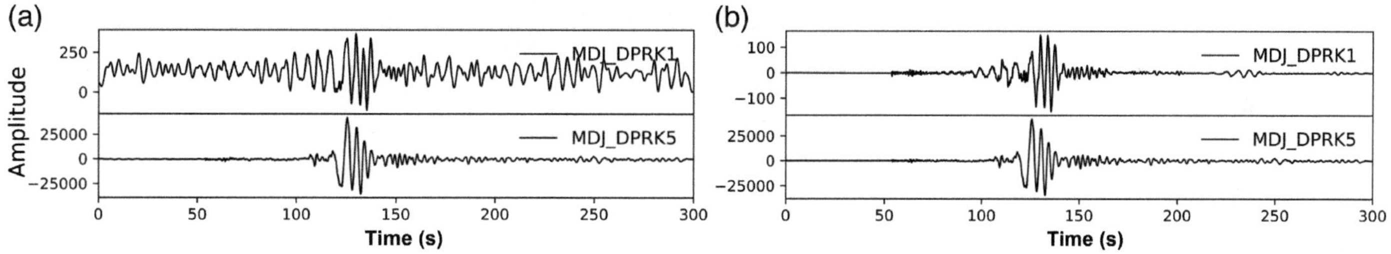

Figure 7. Station MDJ showing two DPRK events using (a) only conventional filtering and (b) using the wavelet-based filtering method in the toolkit.

data set. Testing how long in time a noise model can be used is outside of the scope of this study.

Conclusions

PySolate is a Python-based toolset that implements the CWT-based nonlinear thresholding operations to denoise or designal seismic data following the CWT MATLAB-based application of Langston and Mousavi (2019). A significant advantage of *PySolate* is that it is open source and does not require a licensed software platform. In addition, *PySolate* is modular and each component is easily incorporated into other Python workflows or libraries for seismological tools, making this an easy-to-use toolset for any Python user in the geophysics community. The tool set also has useful features to save and read the denoised data, the noise model, and all input parameters, which facilitates reproducibility and reuse of parameters and models. Plotting features are also available to visualize results.

We provide examples of raw, filtered (Fourier-based), and denoise seismogram recordings of the six announced DPRK nuclear tests to show the applicability and implementation of *PySolate*. In these examples, we highlight low-SNR surface waves of DPRK1 at regional stations MDJ and BJT, which are marginally usable for waveform modeling especially at larger epicentral distances, which is the case for station BJT. Conventional Fourier-based filtering is ineffective for

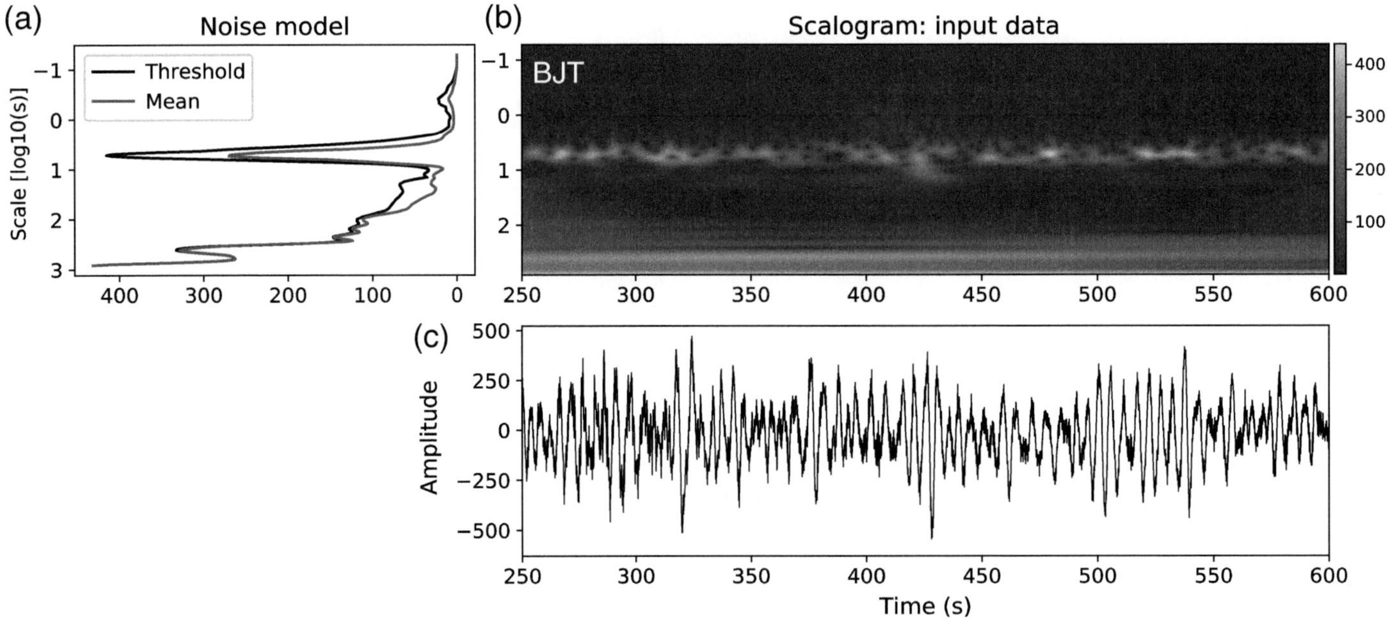

Figure 8. Example for station BJT in Baijiatuan, Beijing, China. (a) Noise model computed from the first 80 s of the trace shown in panel (c), (b) scalogram, and (c) raw data for station BJT. The color version of this figure is available only in the electronic edition.

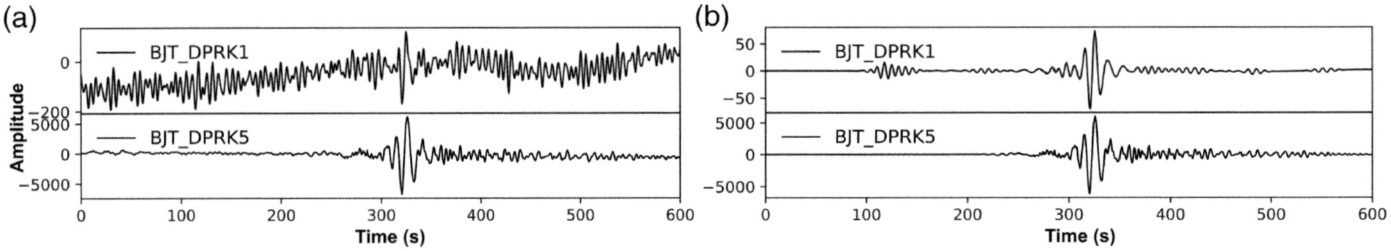

Figure 9. Station BJT showing two DPRK events using (a) only conventional filtering (low-pass filter at 0.1 Hz) and (b) using the *PySolate* wavelet-based filtering method before low-pass filtering.

boosting surface-wave SNR because the dominant frequency overlaps with the high-noise microseismic band. CWT denoising results in much higher SNR surface waves at 10 s, which may enable waveform modeling of smaller events that do not generate longer-period surface waves. CWT denoising offers a complement to traditional Fourier-based filtering and can be easily implemented using *PySolate*.

Data and Resources

All the seismic data used for this study were accessed through the EarthSscope Data Management Center (DMC) Data Services using the Python *ObsPy* package (Krischer *et al.*, 2015). BCSeis 1.1 can be found at http://www.ceri.memphis.edu/people/clangstn/software.html (last accessed May 2025). *PySolate* can be found at https://github.com/LLNL/pysolate (last accessed June 2025). MATLAB (www.mathworks.com/products/matlab, last accessed May 2024).

Declaration of Competing Interests

The authors acknowledge that there are no conflicts of interest recorded.

Acknowledgments

The authors thank Rigo Tibi and S. Mostafa Mousavi for very useful and constructive suggestions in the review process that have ultimately resulted in an improved article. This Low-Yield Nuclear Monitoring (LYNM) research was funded by the National Nuclear Security Administration, Defense Nuclear Nonproliferation Research and Development (NNSA DNN R&D). The authors acknowledge important interdisciplinary collaboration with scientists and engineers from the Los Alamos National Laboratory (LANL), Lawrence Livermore National Laboratory (LLNL), Nevada National Security Site (NNSS), Pacific Northwest National Laboratory (PNNL), and Sandia national Laboratory

(SNL). This work was performed under the auspices of the U.S. Department of Energy by LLNL under Contract DE-AC52-07NA27344. LLNL-JRNL-868619.

References

Beyreuther, M., R. Barsch, L. Krischer, T. Megies, Y. Behr, and J. Wassermann (2010). ObsPy: A python toolbox for seismology, *Seismol. Res. Lett.* **81,** no. 3, 530–533.

Daubechies, I., J. F. Lu, and H. T. Wu (2011). Synchrosqueezed wavelet transforms: An empirical mode decomposition-like tool, *Appl. Comput. Harmon. Anal.* **30,** no. 2, 243–261.

Donoho, D. L., I. M. Johnstone, G. Kerkyacharian, and D. Picard (1995). Wavelet shrinkage: Asymptopia? *J. Roy. Stat. Soc.* **57,** no. 2, 301–369.

Grossmann, A., R. Kronland-Martinet, and J. Morlet (1989). *Reading and Understanding Continuous Wavelet Transforms*, Springer, Berlin, Heidelberg.

Herrera, R. H., J. J. Han, and M. van der Baan (2014). Applications of the synchrosqueezing transform in seismic time-frequency analysis, *Geophysics* **79,** no. 3, V55–V64.

Hunter, J. D. (2007). Matplotlib: A 2D graphics environment, *Comput. Sci. Eng.* **9,** no. 3, 90–95.

Krischer, L., T. Megies, R. Barsch, M. Beyreuther, T. Lecocq, C. Caudron, and J. Wassermann (2015). ObsPy: A bridge for seismology into the scientific Python ecosystem, *Comput. Sci. Discov.* **8,** no. 1, 014003.

Krischer, L., J. Smith, W. J. Lei, M. Lefebvre, Y. Y. Ruan, E. S. de Andrade, N. Podhorszki, E. Bozdağ, and J. Tromp (2016). An adaptable seismic data format, *Geophys. J. Int.* **207,** no. 2, 1003–1011.

Langston, C. A., and S. M. Mousavi (2019). Separating signal from noise and from other signal using nonlinear thresholding and scale-time windowing of continuous wavelet transforms, *Bull. Seismol. Soc. Am.* **109,** no. 5, 1691–1700.

Mousavi, S. M., and C. A. Langston (2016a). Adaptive noise estimation and suppression for improving microseismic event detection, *J. Appl. Geophys.* **132,** 116–124.

Mousavi, S. M., and C. A. Langston (2016b). Hybrid seismic denoising using higher-order statistics and improved wavelet block thresholding, *Bull. Seismol. Soc. Am.* **106,** no. 4, 1380–1393.

Mousavi, S. M., and C. A. Langston (2017). Automatic noise-removal/signal-removal based on general cross-validation thresholding in synchrosqueezed domain and its application on earthquake data, *Geophysics* **82,** no. 4, V211–V227.

Mousavi, S. M., G. C. Beroza, T. Mukerji, and M. BeheshtRasht (2024). Applications of deep neural networks in exploration seismology: A technical survey, *Geophysics* **89,** no. 1, WA95–WA115.

Myers, S. C., S. R. Ford, R. J. Mellors, G. Ichinose, and S. Baker (2018). Absolute locations of the North Korean nuclear tests based on differential seismic arrival times and InSAR, *Seismol. Res. Lett.* **89,** no. 6, 2049–2058.

Quinones, L., and R. Tibi (2024). Denoising seismic waveforms using a wavelet-transform-based machine-learning method, *Bull. Seismol. Soc. Am.* **114,** no. 4, 1777–1788.

Starck, J.-L., F. Murtagh, and J. M. Fadili (2010). *Sparse Image and Signal Processing: Wavelets, Curvelets, Morphological Diversity*, Cambridge University Press, Cambridge, United Kingdom.

Tary, J. B., R. H. Herrera, J. Han, and M. van der Baan (2014). Spectral estimation—What is new? What is next? *Rev. Geophys.* **52,** no. 4, 723–749.

Thakur, G., E. Brevdo, N. S. Fuckar, and H. T. Wu (2013). The Synchrosqueezing algorithm for time-varying spectral analysis: Robustness properties and new paleoclimate applications, *Signal Process.* **93,** no. 5, 1079–1094.

Tibi, R., P. Hammond, R. Brogan, C. J. Young, and K. Koper (2021). Deep learning denoising applied to regional distance seismic data in Utah, *Bull. Seismol. Soc. Am.* **111,** no. 2, 775–790.

Tibi, R., C. J. Young, and R. W. Porritt (2023). Comparative study of the performance of seismic waveform denoising methods using local and near-regional data, *Bull. Seismol. Soc. Am.* **113,** no. 2, 548–561.

Tozer, B., D. T. Sandwell, W. H. F. Smith, C. Olson, J. R. Beale, and P. Wessel (2019). Global bathymetry and topography at 15 Arc Sec: SRTM15+, *Earth Space Sci.* **6,** no. 10, 1847–1864.

Wang, E., and J. Nealon (2019). Applying machine learning to 3D seismic image denoising and enhancement, *Interpretation* **7,** no. 3, SE131–SE139.

Weaver, J. B., Y. Xu, D. M. Healy Jr., and L. D. Cromwell (1991). Filtering noise from images with wavelet transforms, *Magn. Reson. Med.* **21,** no. 2, 288–295.

Yang, Y., C. Liu, and C. A. Langston (2020). Processing seismic ambient noise data with the continuous wavelet transform to obtain reliable empirical Green's functions. *Geophys. J. Int.* **222,** no. 2, 1224–1235.

Zeng, Z., P. Han, W. Zhang, Y. Zhou, X. Deng, D. Zhang, Y. Shi, Y. Chang, H. Ji, R. Dai, *et al.* (2024). An adaptive parameter-free seismic data denoising approach by combining general cross-validation thresholding and pixel connectivity in synchrosqueezed domain, *Earth Planets Space* **76,** no. 1, 134.

Zhu, W., S. M. Mousavi, and G. C. Beroza (2019). Seismic signal denoising and decomposition using deep neural networks, *IEEE Trans. Geosci. Remote Sens.* **57,** no. 11, 9476–9488.

Manuscript received 27 January 2025
Published online 15 August 2025

HypoNet Nankai: Rapid Hypocenter Determination Tool for the Nankai Trough Subduction Zone Using Physics-Informed Neural Networks

Ryoichiro Agata*[1], Satoru Baba[1,2], Ayako Nakanishi[1], and Yasuyuki Nakamura[1]

Abstract

Accurate hypocenter determination in the Nankai trough subduction zone is essential for hazard assessment and advancing our understanding of seismic activity in the region. Therefore, a handy hypocenter determination tool incorporating a realistic 3D velocity structure, accessible to the scientific community, is beneficial. In this study, we developed HypoNet Nankai, a rapid hypocenter determination tool based on a physics-informed neural network (PINN) emulator (surrogate model) for travel-time calculations. This tool leverages a PINN trained to predict *P*-wave travel times between arbitrary underground sources and surface receivers with a realistic 3D *P*-wave velocity structure model of the Nankai trough subduction zone that incorporates marine seismic survey data. The PINN embeds physical laws, namely, the Eikonal equation, directly into the loss function of training and circumvents the need for labeled training data. To address the training challenges posed by small-scale features in the velocity model, we employed a simple domain decomposition approach and Fourier feature embedding. Once trained, the PINN can immediately perform inference of the *P*-wave travel time, enabling rapid hypocenter determination. The data size required to store neural networks for travel-time calculations is significantly smaller than those of conventional travel-time tables. HypoNet Nankai provides high flexibility for the addition of new observation points. We verified HypoNet Nankai by comparing its performance with a widely used grid-based numerical method for forward travel-time calculations and synthetic hypocenter determination. In both tests, HypoNet Nankai provided results consistent with those for the conventional method. HypoNet Nankai offers a rapid, accurate, and easy-to-use hypocenter determination method for the Nankai trough subduction zone, with greater data efficiency and extendibility compared to conventional approaches.

Cite this article as Agata, R., S. Baba, A. Nakanishi, and Y. Nakamura (2025). HypoNet Nankai: Rapid Hypocenter Determination Tool for the Nankai Trough Subduction Zone Using Physics-Informed Neural Networks, *Seismol. Res. Lett.* **97**, 524–536, doi: 10.1785/0220240377.

Supplemental Material

Introduction

The Nankai trough subduction zone is one of the most active subduction zones in the world, having experienced repeated megathrust earthquakes with magnitudes ranging from M 8 to 9 (Ando, 1975). The 30-yr occurrence probability of such a large Nankai megathrust earthquake is estimated to be 70%–80% (Earthquake Research Committee, 2024). Therefore, achieving accurate hypocenter determination in such an active subduction zone to precisely understand the seismic activity is crucial for both hazard assessment and advancing scientific understanding.

The foundation of hypocenter determination analysis lies in the theoretical calculations of travel times from the seismic source in the Earth's interior to seismological observation points on the Earth's surface. Classic methods based on simple velocity structure models that are easy to handle (e.g., 1D structures) have been widely used (e.g., Klein, 1978; Hirata and Matsu'ura, 1987). However, it is evident that incorporating more realistic 3D velocity structure models has a substantial impact on the accuracy of hypocenter determination, particularly in regions with complex underground seismic velocity structures such as subduction zones and volcanoes (e.g.,

1. Japan Agency for Marine-Earth Science and Technology (JAMSTEC), Yokohama, Japan, https://orcid.org/0000-0002-4866-8267 (RA); https://orcid.org/0000-0002-5828-8030 (SB); https://orcid.org/0000-0001-5097-7248 (AN); https://orcid.org/0000-0001-6750-2791 (YN); 2. Now at Kyushu University, Fukuoka, Japan

*Corresponding author: agatar@jamstec.go.jp

Lomax *et al.*, 2001; Johnson and Vincent, 2002; Katsumata, 2015; Nakano *et al.*, 2015). Therefore, it is crucial to prepare appropriate 3D velocity structure models and perform 3D travel-time calculations aiming at accurate hypocenter determination.

Although establishing an appropriate 3D velocity structure model is challenging, research on velocity structures has made significant progress in the Nankai trough region. Consequently, multiple realistic 3D velocity structure models have been proposed for this region (Koketsu *et al.*, 2009, 2012; Yamamoto *et al.*, 2017; Nakanishi *et al.*, 2018; Arnulf *et al.*, 2022). Three-dimensional travel-time calculations have been established using methods such as raytracing (Julian and Gubbins, 1977; Um and Thurber, 1987), grid-based shortest path algorithms (Moser, 1991), and grid-based finite-difference calculations (Sethian, 1996; Zhao, 2005), with many open-source programs available for these approaches (e.g., White *et al.*, 2020; Giroux, 2021). Nevertheless, it is still common to observe simple structures, such as 1D models, being used in many studies, suggesting significant computational costs and effort required for 3D travel-time calculations in practice. Making accessible tools with which users can easily obtain results is essential for facilitating the adoption and widespread use of 3D velocity structure models for travel-time calculations and hypocenter determination.

A traditional approach that can be considered a solution is to precompute and store travel-time tables from underground grid points, which are assumed to be hypothetical hypocenter locations at each observation station (e.g., Katsumata, 2015). Utilizing these tables, users can interpolate and calculate travel times from the desired hypocenter locations. However, this approach has several limitations. For instance, dense grid points are required to ensure accurate interpolation, which results in an enormous amount of data. In addition, when new observation stations are added, especially in high-density settings, such as distributed acoustic sensing (DAS), additional costly travel-time calculations are required. Therefore, this approach can be considered suboptimal for tools available to the public. A more modern approach involves machine learning models, such as deep neural networks (DNNs), to produce an emulator (surrogate model) that bypasses expensive calculation in modeling the nonlinear relationship between inputs (i.e., source and receiver locations) and outputs (i.e., travel times). A trained DNN-based emulator enables travel time to be obtained rapidly via inference in forward pass. The amount of data required to store the DNN is much smaller than that required for a travel-time table. However, when utilizing such machine learning methods, it is necessary to prepare a large amount of labeled training data consisting of input and output pairs. This eventually requires an enormous number of theoretical 3D travel-time calculations.

Recently, physics-informed neural networks (PINNs; Raissi *et al.*, 2019) have gained attention as a new approach to solving partial differential equations (PDEs). PINN can incorporate physical laws described by PDEs, such as the Eikonal equation for travel-time calculation, into a loss function for training DNNs, eliminating the need for labeled training data. This allows the development of a neural network model that captures the nonlinear physical relationships between the source location, receiver location, and travel time without requiring the preparation of labeled data. PINN for the rapid calculation of travel time has been successfully developed (Smith *et al.*, 2021; Waheed *et al.*, 2021; Grubas *et al.*, 2023) and applied to developing emulators of travel-time calculations for a real-world velocity structure at a global scale (GlobeNN; Taufik *et al.*, 2023) and in the Southern California region (Smith *et al.*, 2022). The latter was further integrated into a Bayesian hypocenter determination tool called HypoSVI. Although these neural network (NN)-based models have been verified based on the residuals of the Eikonal equation, their performance in terms of accuracy of inferred travel times and hypocenter determination has not been assessed in detail.

To address the need for rapid and accurate hypocenter determination in the Nankai trough subduction zone, we developed HypoNet Nankai, a rapid hypocenter determination tool that employs PINNs. This tool utilizes a PINN-based emulator model trained to predict travel times between arbitrary source and receiver pairs within a 3D *P*-wave velocity structure model of the Nankai trough subduction zone (Nakanishi *et al.*, 2018). This velocity model is based on previous marine active-source seismic data and provides the foundation for the tool's application. We tested the accuracy of the PINN-based emulator and HypoNet Nankai by comparing them with a grid-based numerical calculation method for forward travel-time calculations and synthetic hypocenter determination problems, respectively.

Theory of PINN for Travel-Time Prediction

We first explain the PINN formulation for travel-time calculation (Smith *et al.*, 2021; Waheed *et al.*, 2021; Grubas *et al.*, 2023), which was slightly modified by Agata *et al.* (2023). The Eikonal equation relates the spatial derivative of the travel-time field to the velocity structure as follows:

$$|\nabla T(\mathbf{x},\mathbf{x}_s)|^2 = \frac{1}{v^2(\mathbf{x})}, \qquad \forall \mathbf{x} \in \Omega, \tag{1}$$

$$T(\mathbf{x}_s,\mathbf{x}_s) = 0, \tag{2}$$

in which Ω is an $\mathbb{R}^d$ domain, d is the space dimension, $T(\mathbf{x},\mathbf{x}_s)$ is the travel time at the point $\mathbf{x}$ from the source $\mathbf{x}_s$, $v(\mathbf{x})$ is the velocity defined in Ω, and ∇ denotes the gradient operator with respect to $\mathbf{x}$. The second equation defines the point-source condition. To avoid singularities in this condition, previous studies modeling travel time using PINN have introduced the following factored form (Smith *et al.*, 2021; Waheed *et al.*, 2021):

$$T(\mathbf{x},\mathbf{x}_s) = T_0(\mathbf{x},\mathbf{x}_s)\tau(\mathbf{x},\mathbf{x}_s), \tag{3}$$

in which T_0 is defined as

$$T_0(\mathbf{x},\mathbf{x}_s) = |\mathbf{x} - \mathbf{x}_s|. \tag{4}$$

This factorization automatically satisfies the point-source condition. We introduce an NN to predict the travel time for a given velocity structure. The NN constructs a function f_T characterized by the weight parameters $\boldsymbol{\theta}$. We define the NN-based function to approximate travel time as

$$T(\mathbf{x},\mathbf{x}_s) \simeq f_T(\mathbf{x},\mathbf{x}_s,\boldsymbol{\theta}), \tag{5}$$

$$= T_0(\mathbf{x},\mathbf{x}_s)/f_{\tau^{-1}}(\mathbf{x},\mathbf{x}_s,\boldsymbol{\theta}), \tag{6}$$

in which $f_{\tau^{-1}}$ is the output of the NN used to approximate $1/\tau(\mathbf{x},\mathbf{x}_s)$ instead of directly approximating τ. We use fully connected feedforward networks with Fourier feature embedding (Tancik *et al.*, 2020; Hennigh *et al.*, 2021) as explained in the Strategy for accurate training of PINN section to implement $f_{\tau^{-1}}$. Additional operations are applied to normalize the input and output of NNs, improve the convergence performance, and set the upper and lower limits of the final output values. Furthermore, the reciprocity condition (i.e., $T(\mathbf{x},\mathbf{x}_s) = T(\mathbf{x}_s,\mathbf{x})$) is imposed following Grubas *et al.* (2023) to improve the convergence of the solution to the Eikonal equation.

The NNs are trained using the following loss functions:

$$L(\boldsymbol{\theta}) = \frac{1}{N_c}\sum_{i=1}^{N_c}\left(v(\mathbf{x}_c^{(i)}) - \frac{1}{|\nabla f_T(\mathbf{x}_c^{(i)},\mathbf{x}_s^{(i)};\boldsymbol{\theta})|}\right)^2, \tag{7}$$

in which N_c is the number of collocation- and source-point pairs. $\mathbf{x}_c$ and $\mathbf{x}_s$ are the coordinates of the collocation and source points, respectively. The collocation points were set as the evaluation points for the PDE residuals (Raissi *et al.*, 2019). The loss function, which incorporates physics-informed constraints, consists of the sum of the squared residuals for each pair of source and collocation points. $\mathbf{x}_c^{(i)}$, which corresponds to $\mathbf{x}$ in equation (1), must cover the entire domain to ensure that the Eikonal equation is satisfied everywhere, regardless of how limited the distribution of receivers is to a small domain. In contrast, the distribution of $\mathbf{x}_s^{(i)}$ in equation (7), which corresponds to $\mathbf{x}_s$ in equation (1), can be taken arbitrarily for the domain of interest regarding the source distribution. $f_T(\mathbf{x}_c,\mathbf{x}_s;\boldsymbol{\theta}^*)$ with the optimized NN weight parameters $\boldsymbol{\theta}^* = \mathrm{argmin}_{\boldsymbol{\theta}} L(\boldsymbol{\theta})$ can serve as an emulator, which can infer travel time between any in-distribution receiver–source pair.

Our objective was to develop a PINN-based emulator that instantly infers the travel time between a source point anywhere in the given 3D velocity model and a receiver point anywhere on the Earth's surface within the velocity model domain. The distribution of the receiver points is considerably more limited than that of the source points. However, as stated previously, training f_T is easier when the distribution of the source points is limited, which is the opposite of our case. Leveraging the reciprocity of the sources and receivers in the Eikonal equation, we used the Earth's surface points as $\mathbf{x}_s^{(i)}$ and the points from the velocity model as $\mathbf{x}_c^{(i)}$ in the training stage (Fig. 1).

3D *P*-Wave Velocity Structure Model and Bathymetric Data

We used the *P*-wave velocity model proposed by Nakanishi *et al.* (2018; hereafter called N2018 model), which covers the entire domain of the Nankai trough subduction zone, to develop an NN model for travel-time calculations. This model was created by merging 2D *P*-wave velocity profiles obtained from previous wide-angle seismic reflection surveys using ocean-bottom seismometer arrival-time data (JAMSTEC, 2004) and a 3D velocity model obtained by seismic tomography using natural earthquakes (Yamamoto *et al.*, 2013, 2014). Because the N2018 model prioritizes the accurate modeling of offshore structures, this study focuses on developing a PINN specifically for travel-time calculations in the offshore region, which covers a horizontal area of 900 km × 300 km and a depth extent of 60 km (Fig. 2). We prepared $\mathbf{x}_c^{(i)}$ based on 3D point cloud data comprising the latitude, longitude, depth, and *P*-wave velocity, which constitute the N2018 model (Fig. 1a). The point locations are structured only in the vertical direction. We transformed them into a topocentric cartesian coordinate system, the origin of which was located at (136° N, 33° E, 0), without using map projection. The geoid data from Earth Gravitational Model (EGM) 2008 (Pavlis *et al.*, 2012) were used for this transformation. Furthermore, we translated and rotated the system to facilitate the use of the calculation grid in the grid-based travel-time calculations used in the comparisons. On average, the N2018 model sampled points every 0.5 km in the horizontal direction and 0.1 km in the vertical direction. Although dense sampling in the vertical direction helps capture sudden velocity jumps, such as those at the Moho, it oversamples other regions with moderate velocity changes. In the regions where the vertical velocity gradient was less than 0.1 s^{-1}, we downsampled the points to achieve a grid spacing of 1 km. This approach enables the optimization of computational resources by focusing on learning the travel-time function in regions with significant vertical velocity changes. The total number of data points after this approach was approximately 150 million, all of which were used for the minibatch training of the PINN. Because grid-based travel-time calculation methods can provide reference solutions for verification in our target calculation, we did not divide the data for validation and testing, which is typical in machine learning training methods.

We used the General Bathymetric Chart of the Oceans (GEBCO) Gridded Bathymetry Data (GEBCO Compilation Group, 2023) and the EGM2008 geoid data (Pavlis *et al.*, 2012) to compose the data of the receiver locations that were introduced into the training as $\mathbf{x}_s^{(i)}$ (Fig. 1a). Similar to the

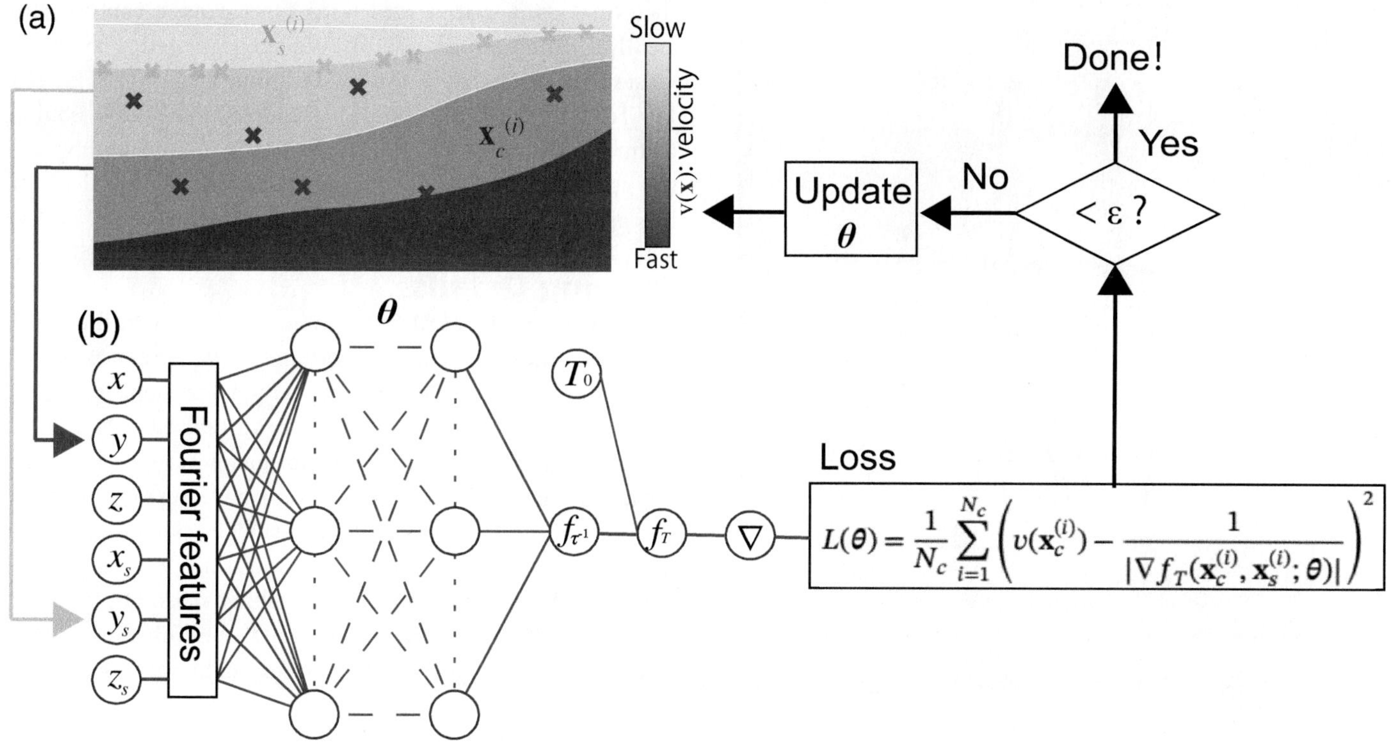

velocity model, we transformed the original data consisting of latitude, longitude, and elevation into the cartesian coordinate system. When sampling the data, we randomly generated points in the horizontal domain and obtained the vertical positions of the points by nearest-neighbor interpolation.

Strategy for Accurate Training of PINN

Previous studies using PINN for travel time in real-world problems, namely GlobeNN (Taufik *et al.*, 2023) and HypoSVI (Smith *et al.*, 2022), employed a single NN to infer the travel-time function in the entire target domain. GlobeNN was trained using GLAD-M25 (Lei *et al.*, 2020), a global velocity model derived from global adjoint tomography. The spatial resolution of this model varies with depth but is generally at least 100 km. The PINN incorporated into HypoSVI was trained for a relatively small region in Southern California, covering approximately 200 km × 200 km, horizontally. In contrast, the N2018 model covers the entire Nankai trough subduction zone (approximately 900 km × 300 km horizontally), derived from marine active-source seismic exploration. The typical model resolution beneath the survey lines is on the order of 10^0–10^1 km. This scale contrast, which is likely larger than those in the velocity structure models adopted in previous studies, possibly leads to a phenomenon known as "spectral bias" (Rahaman *et al.*, 2019): PINN formulations with fully connected feedforward NNs exhibit poor performance when the target functions include high-frequency or multiscale features (Wang *et al.*, 2021). Based on preliminary training, we found that the spectral bias can significantly degrade the accuracy of travel-time inference near the source (≤around 100 km). We adopted two approaches to mitigate this effect, namely, domain decomposition and Fourier feature embedding (Tancik *et al.*, 2020).

Figure 1. Overview of training physics-informed neural network (PINN)-based emulator for travel-time calculations using velocity structure model. (a) A 2D schematic of sampling of training points. Dark- and light-gray cross marks indicate the collocation and Earth's surface points $\mathbf{x}_c$ and $\mathbf{x}_s$, respectively. The light-blue domain indicates seawater. (b) Schematic view of the neural network formulation and training based on the physics-informed loss function. Although T_0 is also a function of $\mathbf{x} = (x,y,z)^T$ and $\mathbf{x}_s = (x_s,y_s,z_s)^T$, we do not describe this dependency here for simplicity. The dark- and light-gray points $\mathbf{x}_c$ and $\mathbf{x}_s$ in panel (a) are used as the input coordinates $\mathbf{x}$ and $\mathbf{x}_s$ of the neural network, leveraging the reciprocity of the Eikonal equation. The color version of this figure is available only in the electronic edition.

The core concept of our domain-decomposition approach is to introduce smaller, additional NNs to more accurately represent the travel-time function in a localized area near the source. Limiting the size of the domain makes high-frequency components that were present in the original larger domain become midfrequency components, mitigating the effects of spectral bias (Moseley *et al.*, 2023). The additional NNs were introduced to the travel-time function in overlapping subdomains in addition to the NN for the entire domain (hereafter called the global domain). Each subdomain spans 225 km × 150 km in the horizontal direction, with the same thickness as the global domain in the vertical direction. We generated 5 × 7 subdomains in the global domain. In inference, the travel

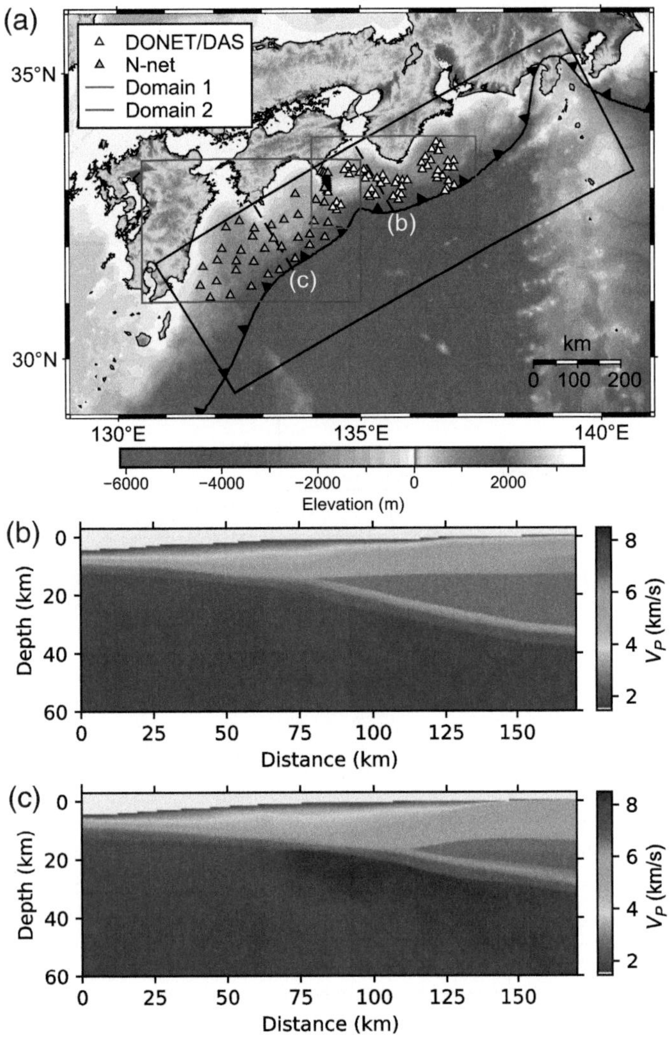

Figure 2. (a) Map of the study area. The black-solid rectangle denotes the modeling domain of the PINN employed in HypoNet Nankai. Domains 1 and 2 are the domains visualized in Figure 7a, b, which show the results of the numerical experiments of hypocenter determination using the locations of the Dense Oceanfloor Network system for Earthquakes and Tsunamis/distributed acoustic sensing (DONET and DAS) and N-net observation points, respectively. (b,c) *P*-wave velocity profiles along black-dashed lines plotted in panel (a). The color version of this figure is available only in the electronic edition.

time in the subdomain was inferred using the subdomain NN for which horizontal position of the central point was closest to that of the source. Those outside the subdomain were inferred using a global-domain NN (Fig. 3). This is a simpler but similar approach to that of the PINN variations proposed by Jagtap and Karniadakis (2020) and Moseley *et al.* (2023) who introduced compatible domain decomposition to the PINN formulation.

The fundamental idea of Fourier feature embedding is to apply a transformation to the input coordinates using a set of sinusoidal functions and encode higher-frequency variations that fully connected feedforward NNs cannot capture efficiently (Tancik *et al.*, 2020). We incorporated a trainable version of it (Hennigh *et al.*, 2021) into each NN (Fig. 1b). For NNs in the subdomains, we adopted multiscale Fourier feature embedding (Wang *et al.*, 2021) to further improve the convergence (see the supplemental material available to this article).

Training Details

We applied feedforward fully connected NNs with the Swish activation function (Ramachandran *et al.*, 2018) that was used in each layer except for the output function, for which linear activation was specified. We introduced NN models of nearly maximum possible size to maintain high-expressive power. Studies on image recognition have revealed that, in the absence of additional structures such as skip connections, the maximum number of hidden layers that can be trained without suffering from gradient vanishing is around 20 layers (He *et al.*, 2016). Therefore, we set the number of hidden layers used here to 20. For the global domain, we set the width of the NN to 512, which is nearly the largest size used in previous studies on PINN (Wang *et al.*, 2023). For subdomains, we set the width to 384, because a smaller size should be sufficient to ensure adequate expressive power. As demonstrated in the Verification through comparison with a grid-based travel-time calculation method section, these models are efficient enough for rapid hypocenter determination and are suitable for real-time processing despite their large sizes. The weight parameters of the velocity NN were initialized using the He's method (He *et al.*, 2015). The input for the NN was 3D coordinate of the source and receiver locations. The trainable parameters in the Fourier feature embeddings were initialized using a zero-mean normal distribution with $\sigma = 0.1$. The Yogi optimizer (Zaheer *et al.*, 2018) with an initial learning rate of 3×10^{-4} was used for all the training. Furthermore, we used an exponential decay rate of 0.9 every 20,000 steps, following Wang *et al.* (2023). All training was conducted with single precision.

The global-domain NN was trained for 350 epochs with a batch size of 400,000. The data size was the same as the number of points in the velocity model after downsampling. We used eight NVIDIA A100 graphical processing units (GPUs) equipped with Earth Simulator, made available by the Japan Agency for Marine-Earth Science and Technology (JAMSTEC), for 21 hr. The subdomain NNs were trained for 300 epochs with a batch size of 64,000. The data size was the number of points in the velocity model included in the subdomains, which averaged 20 million. In most cases, two NVIDIA A100 GPUs were used for an average of 12 hr to train each NN. Some additional trainings were conducted using a NVIDIA H100 GPU made available by the TSUBAME4.0 supercomputer at Science Tokyo. Table 1 summarizes the training details.

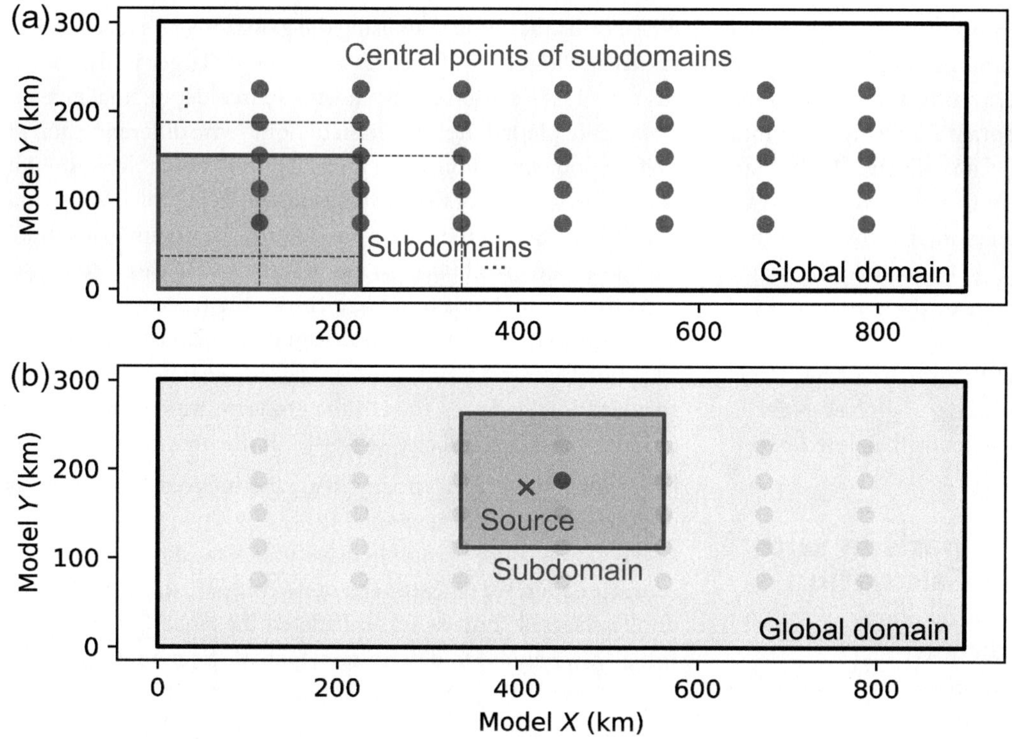

Figure 3. Illustration of our simple subdomain-based approach. (a) Subdomain decomposition. The light-blue domain surrounded by the red rectangle is the subdomain of the bottom-left central point. (b) Example of source-point inference using the subdomain-based approach. The highlighted central point represents the nearest point to the source in the horizontal plane. The light-blue domain surrounded by a red rectangle is the subdomain corresponding to the central point, in which the travel time is inferred using the subdomain neural network (NN). The light-yellow domain is the global domain, in which the travel time is inferred by the global domain NN. The color version of this figure is available only in the electronic edition.

Hypocenter Determination Method

For hypocenter determination using the *P*-wave arrival time, we adopted a maximum a posteriori (MAP) estimation, an approach similar to that used by Hirata and Matsu'ura (1987). This method enables uncertainty quantification from a Bayesian perspective with a Laplace approximation by fitting the posterior probability distribution using a Gaussian distribution. The posterior probability density function (PDF) for the hypocenter location $\mathbf{m}$, namely, longitude, latitude, and depth, is formulated using Bayes' theorem as follows:

$$P(\mathbf{m}|\mathbf{d}) \propto P(\mathbf{d}|\mathbf{m})P(\mathbf{m}), \qquad (8)$$

in which $P(\mathbf{m}|\mathbf{d})$, $P(\mathbf{d}|\mathbf{m})$, and $P(\mathbf{m})$ represent the posterior PDF of the hypocenter parameters, likelihood function, and prior PDF, respectively. $\mathbf{d}$ is a data vector, which is the scalar value of the observed arrival time t^{obs} in this specific case. We use a likelihood function that eliminates the origin time of the event from the formulation in Ryberg and Haberland (2019):

$$P(\mathbf{d}|\mathbf{m}) = \frac{1}{Z}\exp\left[-\frac{1}{2}\sum_{i=1}^{N_{obs}}\frac{(\Delta t_i - \langle \Delta t\rangle)^2}{\sigma_{data}^2}\right], \qquad (9)$$

in which i is an index for observation points, N_{obs} is the number of observation points, $\Delta t_i = T_i^{calc}(\mathbf{m}) - t_i^{obs}$, and $\langle \Delta t\rangle = \frac{1}{N_{obs}}\sum_{i=1}^{N_{obs}} \Delta t_i$. $T^{calc}(\mathbf{m})$ is the calculated *P*-wave travel time dependent on $\mathbf{m}$, which is rapidly inferred using the PINN-based emulator incorporated in HypoNet Nankai. The standard deviation of the data error σ_{data} is determined as

$$\sigma_{data}^2 = \sigma_{obs}^2 + \sigma_{pred}^2, \qquad (10)$$

in which σ_{obs} denotes the observation error defined by the user. σ_{pred} represents the model prediction error, which was determined following Smith *et al.* (2022) by incorporating the error proportional to the travel-time observation (see the supplemental material). We use a uniform prior for $P(\mathbf{m})$ with user-specified upper and lower bounds.

TABLE 1
Summary of the Hyperparameters and Computational Resources Employed in the Training of the PINN-Based Emulator for HypoNet Nankai

Parameters	Subdomains	Global Domain
Number of hidden layers	20	20
Number of neurons per layer	384	512
Encoding	Multiscale FF	Trainable FF
Activation function	Swish	
Optimization algorithm	Yogi	
Initial learning rate	3×10^{-4}	
Number of data points	~20,000,000	156,196,312
Batch size	64,000	400,000
Number of epochs	300	350
Hardware	A100 × 2	A100 × 8
Training time	~12 hr	21 hr

FF, Fourier feature; PINN, physics-informed neural network.

MAP estimation is a nonlinear optimization problem solved using the limited-memory BFGS optimizer (Liu and Nocedal, 1989). During the optimization stage, an invertible logarithmic transform was applied to **m** to incorporate a uniform prior into the gradient-based algorithm (Zhang and Curtis, 2020; Stan Development Team, 2024). The Hessian matrix for the MAP estimate, which is computable using automatic differentiation available in PyTorch (Paszke *et al.*, 2017), was used to exploit the approximated analytical expression of the posterior PDF representing estimation uncertainty.

In addition, a Python module for PINN-based travel-time calculation was made available alongside HypoNet Nankai. Users can utilize this module to implement their own hypocenter determination algorithms.

Verification Through Comparison with a Grid-Based Travel-Time Calculation Method

Verification 1: travel-time prediction

We set verification problems to compare the travel time inferred by the trained PINN with the results obtained using the fast marching method (FMM; Sethian, 1996), which is one of the most widely used grid-based finite-difference numerical calculation methods. Verification 1 targets the trained PINN only, and the hypocenter determination algorithm based on the MAP estimation and Laplace approximation are tested in verification 2. FMM calculations were conducted using Pykonal (White *et al.*, 2020). We generated random seismic sources within the target 3D domain and computed the travel times for each source at virtual receiver points distributed at 1 km intervals on the Earth's surface. In FMM calculation, the grid intervals were 0.5 km in the horizontal direction and 0.1 km in the vertical direction, which were equivalent to the data points in the N2018 velocity model. These grid intervals have been verified through preliminary runs to be fine enough to provide a reliable reference solution.

The travel-time functions on the Earth's surface for five sources, calculated using both PINN and FMM, show good agreement at the macroscopic level (Fig. 4a). The root mean square deviation (rmsd) of the travel time in each case is calculated as follows:

$$\mathrm{Rmsd} = \sqrt{\frac{1}{N}\sum_{i=1}^{N}(T_i^{\mathrm{PINN}} - T_i^{\mathrm{FMM}})^2}, \tag{11}$$

in which $T_i^{\mathrm{PINN/FMM}}$ is the travel time in the *i*th surface point calculated using either PINN or FMM, and N is the number of surface points. The rmsds are within the range of 0.1 and 0.3 s. Figure 4a presents the rmsd for each case. A discontinuous decrease in the absolute error in the rectangular region, including the horizontal source location, was apparent for some sources. This implies that travel-time inference using subdomain NNs is more accurate than using the global NN as expected. The rmsds and absolute differences were slightly larger in the fourth case in Figure 4 with the shallowest source depth smaller than 10 km. We plotted the histogram of point-wise differences for all surface points, including the median, 10th percentile, and 90th percentile, for each of the five cases shown in Figure 5. We found a significant bias of the differences toward the negative direction, with a skewed distribution shape, in most cases. This result indicates that PINN tends to underestimate the travel time slightly, likely due to its tendency to infer smoother travel-time function because of spectral bias: smoother travel-time function results in smaller PINN-inferred travel-time gradient, which corresponds to larger predicted velocity $\frac{1}{|\nabla f_T(\mathbf{x},\mathbf{x}_s;\boldsymbol{\theta})|}$. If the predicted velocity is larger than the actual velocity $v(\mathbf{x})$, the inferred travel time is underestimated (see equation 7).

To gain a more comprehensive understanding of the error characteristics, we repeated the same comparisons for 100 randomly selected sources and calculated the rmsd for each case. Initially, we aimed to determine which of the model axes (x, y, or z) showed the largest correlation with rmsd. However, the calculated correlations for these axes were relatively similar and moderate, the absolute values of which range from 0.3 to 0.4 (Fig. S1). To further refine our analysis, we conducted an optimization to find the spatial axis along which the correlation with rmsd values is maximized. This resulted in a direction vector $\mathbf{e} = (-0.064, -0.190, 0.980)$ in the model coordinate system and a correlation coefficient of 0.590 (Fig. 6). This result suggests that higher rmsd values tend to correspond to sources located in the shallower (z positive) and seaward (y negative) portions of the velocity model, as exemplified by the fourth source presented in Figure 4a. These regions are characterized by significant spatial variations in velocity (see Fig. 2b,c). This finding indicates that errors in PINN-inferred travel times are generally larger when the source is located in areas with substantial velocity variation.

These comparison results, which show only small differences, imply that our PINN provides results that are as accurate as FMM. However, the effect of these differences on the target application of our PINN, that is, hypocenter determination, remains unclear. Synthetic experiments to investigate these effects based on hypocenter determination are presented in the following section.

Verification 2: numerical experiment of hypocenter determination

We conducted synthetic tests for hypocenter determination using *P*-wave arrival times, assuming the use of seafloor seismic observation systems in the Nankai trough subduction zone. We focused on two domains in the Nankai trough subduction zone where real-time seismological observations are or will be operational. Domain 1 is a region with seismometers equipped in Dense Oceanfloor Network system for Earthquakes and

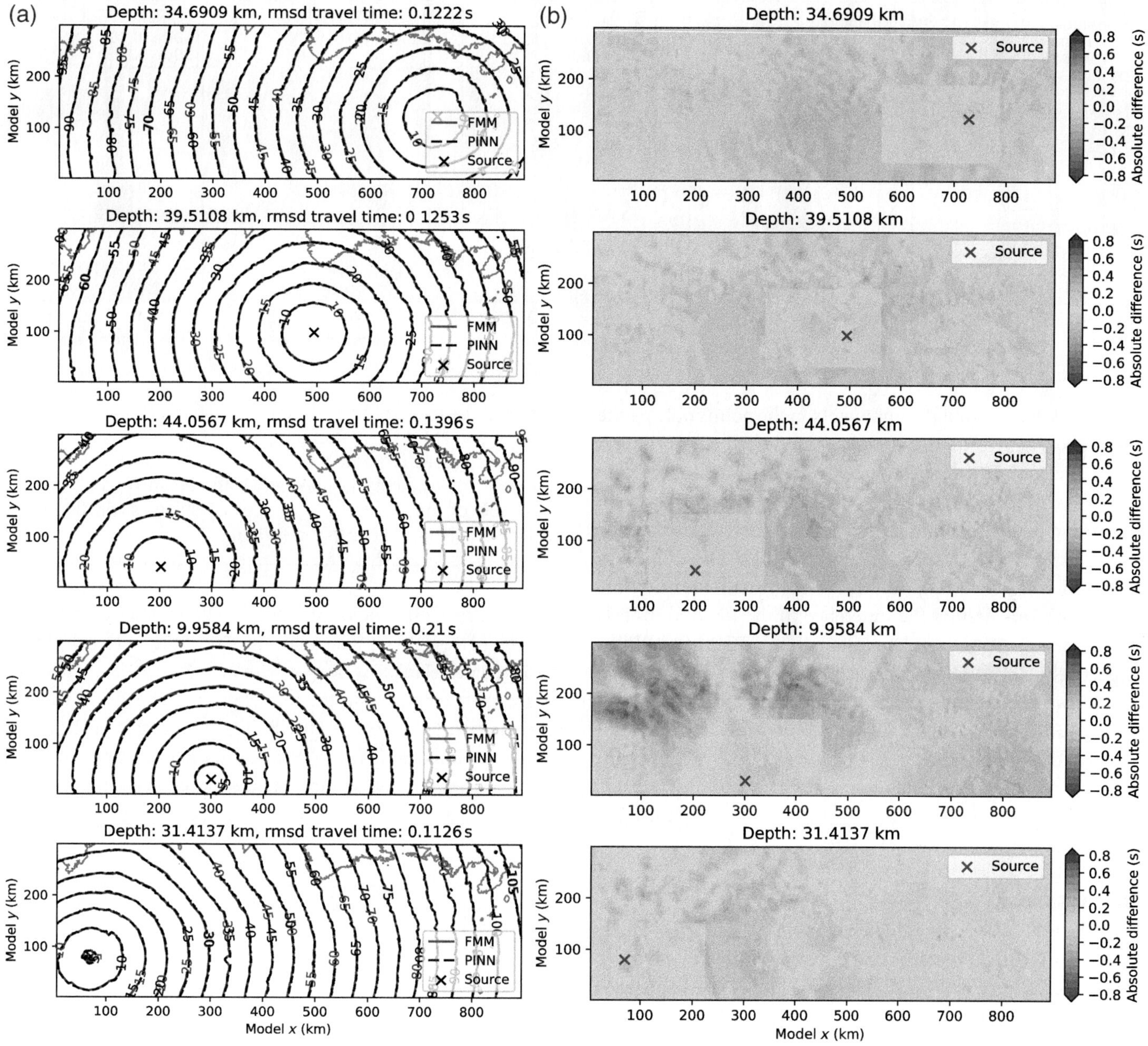

Figure 4. Five examples of (a) comparison of calculated (inferred) travel time at the Earth's surface from randomly chosen underground sources obtained using PINN and fast marching method (FMM) and (b) their absolute difference (PINN subtracted by FMM). Rmsd, root mean square deviation. The color version of this figure is available only in the electronic edition.

Tsunamis (DONET) (Kaneda *et al.*, 2015; Aoi *et al.*, 2020), and real-time DAS observation points used for the analysis of Baba *et al.* (2023) off Cape Muroto (Fig. 2). Domain 2 is the region where Nankai trough Seafloor Observation Network for Earthquakes and Tsunami (N-net) is being constructed (Aoi *et al.*, 2023). We extracted hypocenter models from the 2021 version of the Japanese Meteorological Agency (JMA) earthquake catalog by applying certain magnitude thresholds to ensure a relatively even horizontal distribution of hypocenters. We calculated the synthetic travel-time data between these hypocenter models and the DONET, DAS, and N-net points using FMM and used them as artificial observation data. Artificial noise was not added to the data. We then performed hypocenter determination using HypoNet Nankai to determine how the sources were inverted. These numerical experiments were conducted separately in domains 1 and 2. Table 2 summarizes the number of observation points and hypocenter models employed in each experiment. Other parameters used in the experiments can be found in the supplemental material.

The MAP-estimated horizontal locations of the hypocenters inside the observation network were accurate and precise in domains 1 and 2 (Fig. 7a,c). The depth components in most

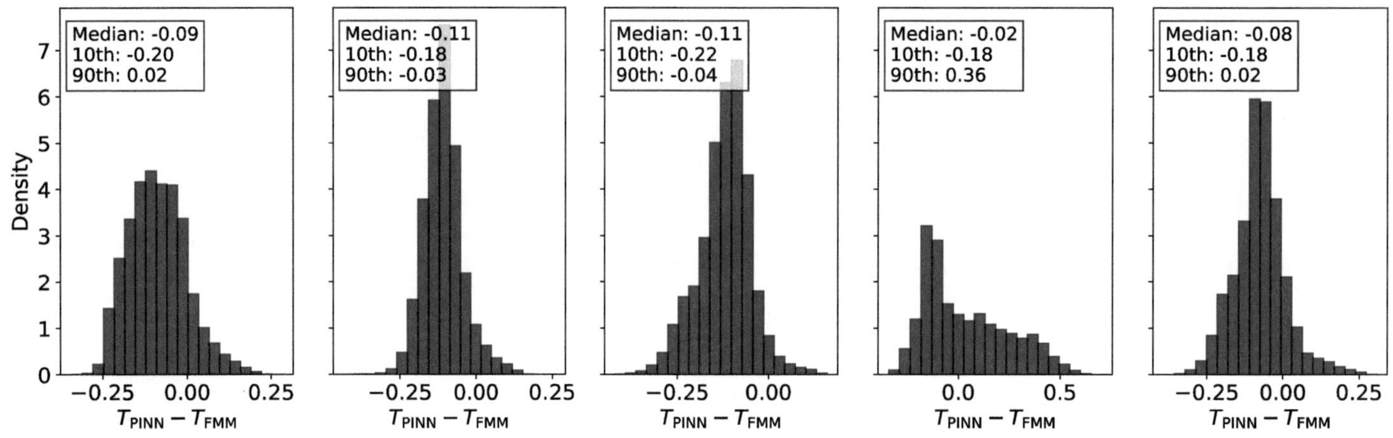

Figure 5. Histograms of the point-wise difference between PINN-inferred and FMM-calculated travel time (T_{PINN} and T_{FMM}) for the five source cases presented in Figure 4. Each panel includes statistical information: the median, 10th percentile, and 90th percentile of the distribution. The color version of this figure is available only in the electronic edition.

points and the horizontal components in the points outside the observation network tended to show larger estimation uncertainties, which were derived based on the Laplace approximation (Fig. 7a–d). Although the differences between the mean and true models for some of these events are larger, they fall within the range of estimation uncertainties. These findings suggest that the inverting models are consistent with the true model locations despite the difference in the forward models used in data generation and inversion, that is, FMM and PINN, respectively. The estimation of each hypocenter was completed within two-six seconds using eight central processing unit cores of AMD EPYC 7742 in Earth Simulator at JAMSTEC. Compared to the specifications of a widely referenced automatic hypocenter determination system (Matsumura *et al.*, 2006), this computation time can be considered sufficiently short to be applicable to such systems.

Discussion

Once the PINN-based training was completed, HypoNet Nankai required a short-computation time for travel-time inference in hypocenter determination. However, an FMM-based approach with an ideal travel-time table created beforehand would require an even shorter time for hypocenter determination when data-loading time for the table is not considered. Advantages of introducing an NN-based emulator for hypocenter determination lie rather in other aspects. One advantage of NN-based methods is that they can add new observation points to hypocenter determination systems without much effort. For example, among the seafloor seismic observation networks used in this study, the operational time of DONET is a decade longer than that of the DAS system off Muroto. The development of N-net was only recently completed in 2025. If we consider to adapt a hypocenter determination system originally created for DONET to DAS and N-net, an FMM-based system would require new travel-time calculations to expand the travel-time table. In contrast, a system based on HypoNet Nankai can be applied to newly installed points without any modification. When planning the installation of new observation points, HypoNet Nankai can be readily applied to feasibility studies of multiple scenario configurations for these new observation points as well. Another advantage is the size of the data set. The total data size of the 36 NNs included in HypoNet Nankai was approximately 500 MB, whereas the FMM table employed in the numerical experiment for domain 1 alone reached a size of 80 GB. This size is not negligible in terms of data-loading time when real-time processing is considered. However, reducing the data size sacrifices accuracy. When developing a tool for public use, developers would never know

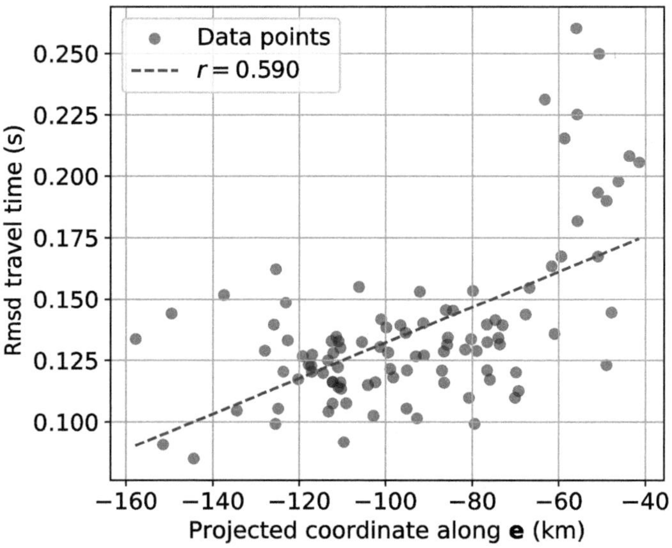

Figure 6. Relationship between rmsds of 100 sources and the projected coordinate along the estimated optimal direction $\mathbf{e} = (-0.064, -0.190, 0.980)$. The red-dashed line indicates the results of linear regression fitted to the data, with the Pearson correlation coefficient *r* shown in the legend. The color version of this figure is available only in the electronic edition.

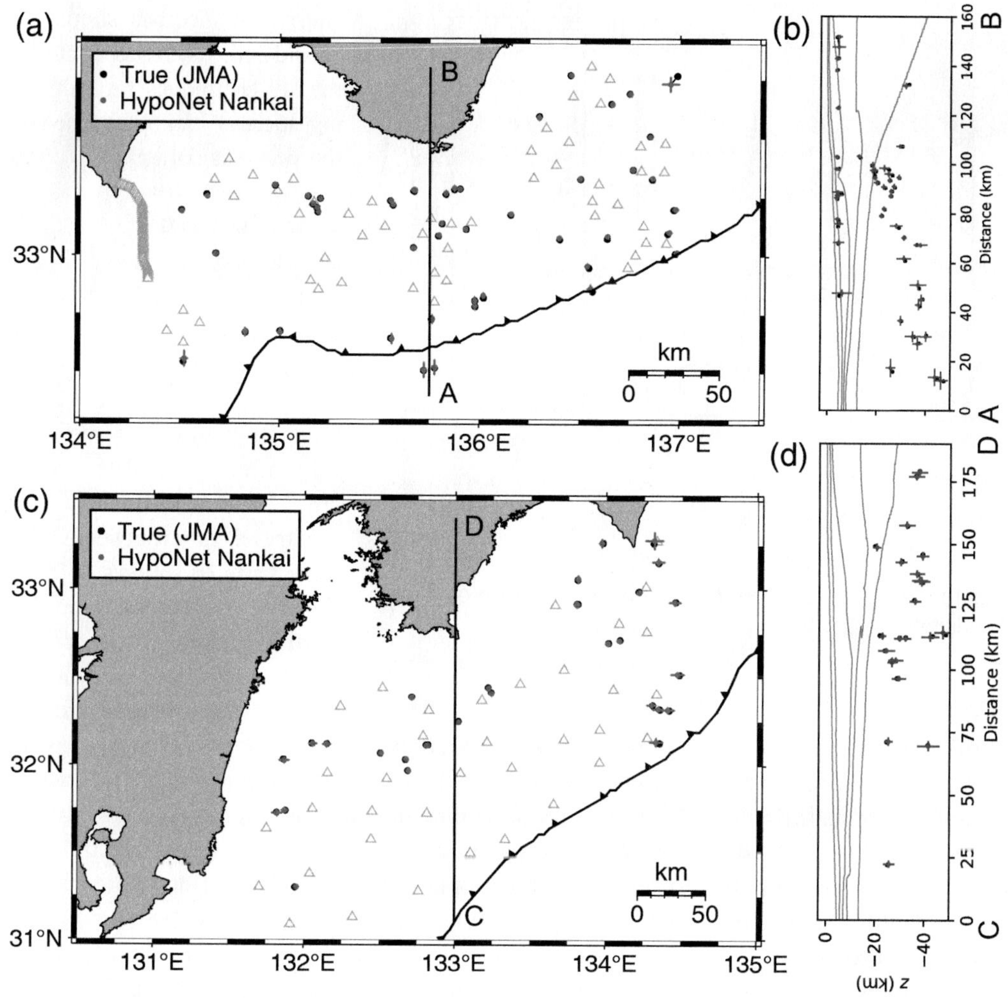

Figure 7. Results of the numerical experiments for hypocenter determination using HypoNet Nankai. (a) Results for domain 1 using DONET and DAS. (b) Plots of cross-section AB described in panel (a). (c) Results for domain 2 with N-net. (d) Those plotted on the cross-section CD described in panel (c). The magenta crossbar indicates the $2-\sigma$ confidence interval. JMA, Japanese Meteorological Agency. The color version of this figure is available only in the electronic edition.

where potential users would want to place observation points for their calculations. Therefore, providing a tool that supports a compact data size and a flexible choice of observation points leveraging NNs is advantageous for this purpose.

To demonstrate the impact of introducing the 3D velocity structure model, we performed a hypocenter determination analysis based on a layered (1D) velocity structure (Nakano *et al.*, 2013) using the synthetic observational data used in the previous section (see the supplemental material). We found a significant discrepancy between the estimated and true hypocenter locations beyond the estimation uncertainty in the horizontal locations of the hypocenters outside the observation network and the depth components of many hypocenters (Fig. 8). These patterns of discrepancies are consistent with previous comparisons of hypocenter determinations in 3D versus layered velocity structures (Nakano *et al.*, 2013). The impact of replacing a simple layered velocity model with a realistic 3D model is evident. However, we should also note that the comparison presented here does not reflect the best estimation performance using a 1D model in a practical application. This is because station corrections are usually applied to hypocenter determination with 1D models to reduce bias in the estimation originating from model errors. From the same perspective, note that the 3D model introduced in this study is imperfect in principle. This includes regions with sparse seismic survey lines, those beyond the reach of the ray path from the active-seismic source, and junction points with onshore regions, where the estimation accuracy of the velocity structure is low (Nakanishi *et al.*, 2018). Even in the case of 3D model-based approaches, it may be necessary to implement measures to improve hypocenter determination accuracy, such as estimating station corrections and properly setting model errors in the Bayesian estimation scheme.

Nakanishi *et al.* (2018) conducted a validation study on the western part of the N2018 *P*-wave velocity model, which prioritizes marine seismic survey data. Their validation study involved hypocenter determination using real-earthquake data and compared the results with another study that determined hypocenters using double-difference tomography directly (Yamamoto *et al.*, 2013). However, this validation study suggested that there is still potential for improvement in the

TABLE 2
Summary of the Number of Hypocenters and Observation Points Employed in the Numerical Experiments for Hypocenter Determination

	Domain 1	Domain 2
Number of hypocenters	47	30
Number of observation points	106	36

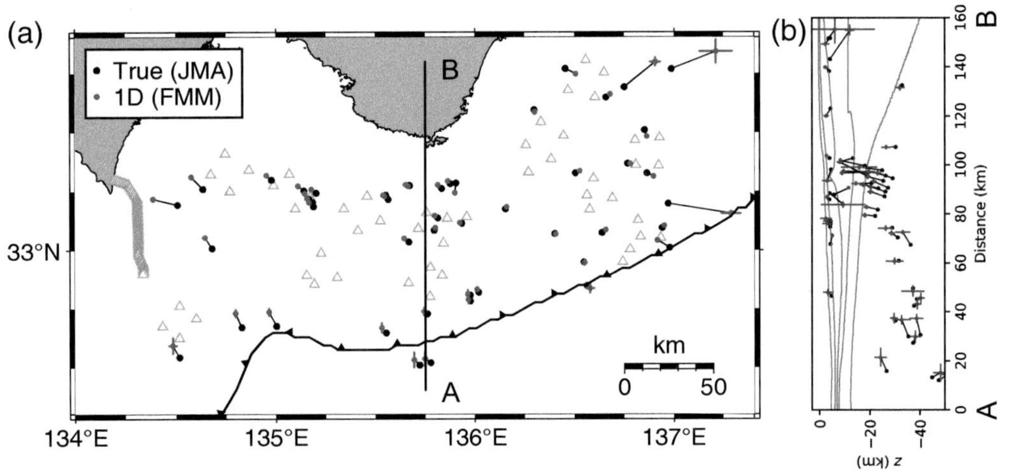

Figure 8. Results of numerical experiments of hypocenter determination using 1D velocity structure and FMM. (a) Results for domain 1 using DONET and DAS. (b) Plots of cross-section AB described in panel (a). The magenta crossbar indicates the $2-\sigma$ confidence interval. The color version of this figure is available only in the electronic edition.

model, particularly in the portion beneath the onshore region. For example, information from models based on the inversion of both seismic survey data and local natural earthquakes with both offshore and onshore first-arrival pick data (Arnulf *et al.*, 2022) and onshore structures that are well validated using waveform simulations (Koketsu *et al.*, 2009, 2012) should be incorporated to further improve accuracy. These improvements would enable the expansion of the target region for travel-time modeling from primarily offshore areas to include onshore regions as well. Travel-time calculations for the *S*-wave velocity structure are also essential for better constraining hypocenters, especially for slow earthquakes (Maeda and Obara, 2009). Therefore, constructing an *S*-wave velocity structure model for the entire domain of the Nankai trough subduction zone is anticipated. Furthermore, HypoNet Nankai should follow these updates to the 3D velocity structure model in the future. Notably, if the target region is expanded or if a significant contrast in the seismic velocity are introduced owing to updates in the target velocity structure, the issue of spectral bias may become more pronounced. To address this issue, the continuous integration of state-of-the-art techniques to mitigate spectral bias, which image recognition experts are actively developing into PINN (e.g., hash encoding, Müller *et al.*, 2022; Huang and Alkhalifah, 2024), is essential.

The discontinuity in the travel-time function, visible in Figure 4b, arises at the boundaries where predictions switch between subdomain and global domain methods. Although this effect was not significant in the current analysis, it could degrade the convergence of the quasi-Newton optimization used by HypoNet Nankai to estimate the hypocenter in some cases. These discontinuities are inherent to the current domain decomposition approach. To mitigate them and improve accuracy, alternative methods should be considered, such as state-of-the-art techniques for mitigating spectral bias mentioned in the previous paragraph.

Conclusion

We developed a rapid hypocenter determination tool for the Nankai trough subduction zone, named HypoNet Nankai, based on a PINN-based emulator for travel-time calculation. The PINN-based emulator was designed to learn the travel time between arbitrary pairs of sources in a 3D volume and receivers on the Earth's surface in the domain of interest. We used a 3D velocity structure model for the Nankai trough subduction zone that prioritizes marine seismic survey data (Nakanishi *et al.*, 2018) to train the PINN. To cope with the training difficulty due to the small-scale features included within the velocity model, specifically spectral bias, we employed a simple domain decomposition approach and Fourier feature embedding. We performed two verification tests to assess the accuracy of the PINN-based emulator and HypoNet Nankai by comparing them against grid-based numerical calculation methods. In the comparison of forward travel-time calculations, we found good agreement in the travel-time functions on the Earth's surface for some random sources. In the numerical experiment for hypocenter determination, results indicate that hypocenters estimated using HypoNet Nankai are consistent with those obtained using FMM within the range of estimation uncertainty. We confirmed that HypoNet Nankai is a fast, accurate, and easy-to-use tool for hypocenter determination for offshore events in the Nankai trough subduction zones. It is a data efficient and highly extendible alternative to conventional methods using grid-based travel-time calculations.

Data and Resources

HypoNet Nankai is available at https://github.com/eagleray2020/HypoNet_Nankai_P.git. Earthquake catalogs used in this study are archived by the Japan Meteorological Agency (JMA, https://www.data.jma.go.jp/eqev/data/bulletin/hypo_e.html). The data usage application for the 3D *P*-wave velocity structure model of Nakanishi *et al.* (2018) can be made at https://www.jamstec.go.jp/obsmcs_db/j/Nankai_3D_model-j.html. The coordinates of the data points for distributed acoustic sensing (DAS) were made available by Baba *et al.* (2023) at https://zenodo.org/records/7935235. Those for N-net were obtained by digitizing the figure described in Aoi *et al.* (2023). All websites were last accessed in July 2025. The supplemental material provides some technical details on the training of physics-informed neural network (PINN), the hypocenter determination algorithm, and the problem setting of a numerical experiment.

Declaration of Competing Interests

The authors acknowledge that there are no conflicts of interest recorded.

Acknowledgments

This study was supported by JSPS KAKENHI Grant-in-Aid for Scientific Research on Transformative Research Areas (A) "Science of Slow-to-Fast earthquakes" (24H01042). The calculations were carried out using Earth Simulator at the Japan Agency for Marine-Earth Science and Technology (JAMSTEC) and the TSUBAME4.0 supercomputer at Science Tokyo. Some figures were produced using PyGMT (Uieda *et al.*, 2021), namely, a Pythonic interface for Generic Mapping Tools 6 (GMT6; Wessel *et al.*, 2019).

References

Agata, R., K. Shiraishi, and G. Fujie (2023). Bayesian seismic tomography based on velocity-space stein variational gradient descent for physics-informed neural network, *IEEE Trans. Geosci. Remote Sens.* **61,** 1–17.

Ando, M. (1975). Source mechanisms and tectonic significance of historical earthquakes along the Nankai Trough, Japan, *Tectonophysics* **27,** no. 2, 119–140.

Aoi, S., Y. Asano, T. Kunugi, T. Kimura, K. Uehira, N. Takahashi, H. Ueda, K. Shiomi, T. Matsumoto, and H. Fujiwara (2020). Mowlas: Nied observation network for earthquake, tsunami and volcano, *Earth Planets Space* **72,** no. 1, 1–31.

Aoi, S., T. Takeda, T. Kunugi, M. Shinohara, T. Miyoshi, K. Uehira, M. Mochizuki, and N. Takahashi (2023). Development and Construction of Nankai Trough seafloor observation network for earthquakes and tsunamis: N-net, *2023 IEEE Underwater Technology (UT)*, IEEE, 1–5.

Arnulf, A. F., D. Bassett, A. J. Harding, S. Kodaira, A. Nakanishi, and G. Moore (2022). Upper-plate controls on subduction zone geometry, hydration and earthquake behavior, *Nature Geosci.* **15,** no. 2, 143–148.

Baba, S., E. Araki, Y. Yamamoto, T. Hori, G. Fujie, Y. Nakamura, T. Yokobiki, and H. Matsumoto (2023). Observation of shallow slow earthquakes by distributed acoustic sensing using offshore fiber-optic cable in the Nankai Trough, Southwest Japan, *Geophys. Res. Lett.* **50,** no. 12, e2022GL102678, doi: 10.1029/2022GL102678.

Earthquake Research Committee (2024). List of long-term evaluation of earthquake occurrence along major active faults and subduction, available at https://www.jishin.go.jp/evaluation/long_term_evaluation/lte_summary (last accessed July 2024) (in Japanese).

GEBCO Compilation Group (2023). GEBCO 2023 grid, available at https://www.gebco.net/data-products/gridded-bathymetry-data (last accessed July 2025).

Giroux, B. (2021). ttcrpy: A python package for traveltime computation and raytracing, *SoftwareX* **16,** 100,834.

Grubas, S., A. Duchkov, and G. Loginov (2023). Neural Eikonal solver: Improving accuracy of physics-informed neural networks for solving Eikonal equation in case of caustics, *J. Comput. Phys.* **474,** 111,789.

He, K., X. Zhang, S. Ren, and J. Sun (2015). Delving deep into rectifiers: Surpassing human-level performance on imagenet classification, *Proc. of the IEEE International Conf. on Computer Vision*, 1026–1034.

He, K., X. Zhang, S. Ren, and J. Sun (2016). Deep residual learning for image recognition, *2016 IEEE Conf. on Computer Vision and Pattern Recognition (CVPR)*, 770–778.

Hennigh, O., S. Narasimhan, M. A. Nabian, A. Subramaniam, K. Tangsali, Z. Fang, M. Rietmann, W. Byeon, and S. Choudhry (2021). NVIDIA SimNet™: An AI-accelerated multi-physics simulation framework, *Int. Conf. on Computational Science*, Springer, 447–461.

Hirata, N., and M. Matsu'ura (1987). Maximum-likelihood estimation of hypocenter with origin time eliminated using nonlinear inversion technique, *Phys. Earth Planet. In.* **47,** 50–61.

Huang, X., and T. Alkhalifah (2024). Efficient physics-informed neural networks using hash encoding, *J. Comput. Phys.* **501,** 112,760.

Jagtap, A. D., and G. E. Karniadakis (2020). Extended physics-informed neural networks (XPINNs): A generalized space-time domain decomposition based deep learning framework for nonlinear partial differential equations, *Comm. Comput. Phys.* **28,** no. 5.

JAMSTEC (2004). JAMSTEC seismic survey database, doi: 10.17596/0002069.

Johnson, M., and C. Vincent (2002). Development and testing of a 3D velocity model for improved event location: A case study for the India-Pakistan region, *Bull. Seismol. Soc. Am.* **92,** no. 8, 2893–2910.

Julian, B., and D. Gubbins (1977). Three-dimensional seismic ray tracing, *J. Geophys.* **43,** no. 1, 95–113.

Kaneda, Y., K. Kawaguchi, E. Araki, H. Matsumoto, T. Nakamura, S. Kamiya, K. Ariyoshi, T. Hori, T. Baba, and N. Takahashi (2015). Development and application of an advanced ocean floor network system for megathrust earthquakes and tsunamis, in *Seafloor Observatories*, Springer Science & Business Media, Berlin, Germany, 643–662.

Katsumata, A. (2015). Fast hypocenter determination in an inhomogeneous velocity structure using a 3D travel-time table, *Bull. Seismol. Soc. Am.* **105,** no. 6, 3203–3208.

Klein, F. W. (1978). *Hypocenter location program HYPOINVERSE: Part I. Users guide to versions 1, 2, 3, and 4. Part II. Source listings and notes, Technical Rept. U.S. Geol. Surv*, doi: 10.3133/ofr78694.

Koketsu, K., H. Miyake, and H. Suzuki (2012). Japan integrated velocity structure model version 1, *Proc. 15th World Conf. on Earthquake Engineering*, Lisbon, Portugal, September 2012.

Koketsu, K., H. Miyake, Afnimar, and Y. Tanaka (2009). A proposal for a standard procedure of modeling 3-D velocity structures and its application to the Tokyo metropolitan area, Japan, *Tectonophysics* **472,** nos. 1/4, 290–300.

Lei, W., Y. Ruan, E. Bozdağ, D. Peter, M. Lefebvre, D. Komatitsch, J. Tromp, J. Hill, N. Podhorszki, and D. Pugmire (2020). Global adjoint tomography—Model GLAD-M25, *Geophys. J. Int.* **223,** no. 1, 1–21.

Liu, D. C., and J. Nocedal (1989). On the limited memory BFGS method for large scale optimization, *Math. Program.* **45,** no. 1, 503–528.

Lomax, A., A. Zollo, P. Capuano, and J. Virieux (2001). Precise, absolute earthquake location under Somma–Vesuvius volcano using a new three-dimensional velocity model, *Geophys. J. Int.* **146,** no. 2, 313–331.

Maeda, T., and K. Obara (2009). Spatiotemporal distribution of seismic energy radiation from low-frequency tremor in western Shikoku, Japan, *J. Geophys. Res.* **114,** no. B10, doi: 10.1029/2008JB006043.

Matsumura, M., Y. Ito, H. Kimura, K. Obara, S. Sekiguchi, S. Hori, and K. Kasahara (2006). Development of accurate and quick analysis system for source parameters (AQUA), *Zisin* **59**, no. 2, 167–184 (in Japanese with English abstract).

Moseley, B., A. Markham, and T. Nissen-Meyer (2023). Finite basis physics-informed neural networks (fbpinns): A scalable domain decomposition approach for solving differential equations, *Adv. Comput. Math.* **49,** no. 4, 62.

Moser, T. (1991). Shortest path calculation of seismic rays, *Geophysics* **56,** no. 1, 59–67.

Müller, T., A. Evans, C. Schied, and A. Keller (2022l). Instant neural graphics primitives with a multiresolution hash encoding, *ACM Trans. Graph.* **41,** no. 4, 1–5.

Nakanishi, A., N. Takahashi, Y. Yamamoto, T. Takahashi, S. O. Citak, T. Nakamura, K. Obana, S. Kodaira, and Y. Kaneda (2018). Three-dimensional plate geometry and P-wave velocity models of the subduction zone in SW Japan: Implications for seismogenesis, in *Geology and Tectonics of Subduction Zones: A Tribute to Gaku Kimura*, T. Byrne, M. B. Underwood, D. Fisher, L. McNeill, D. Saffer, K. Ujiie, and A. Yamaguchi (Editors), Vol. 534, Geological Society of America, Boulder, Colorado, 69.

Nakano, M., T. Nakamura, S. Kamiya, M. Ohori, and Y. Kaneda (2013). Intensive seismic activity around the Nankai trough revealed by Donet ocean-floor seismic observations, *Earth Planets Space* **65,** 5–15.

Nakano, M., T. Nakamura, and Y. Kaneda (2015). Hypocenters in the Nankai trough determined by using data from both ocean-bottom and land seismic networks and a 3D velocity structure model: Implications for seismotectonic activity, *Bull. Seismol. Soc. Am.* **105,** no. 3, 1594–1605.

Paszke, A., S. Gross, S. Chintala, G. Chanan, E. Yang, Z. DeVito, Z. Lin, A. Desmaison, L. Antiga, and A. Lerer (2017). Automatic differentiation in PyTorch, *NeurIPS 2017 Workshop Autodiff*, Los Angeles, California, 9 December 2017.

Pavlis, N. K., S. A. Holmes, S. C. Kenyon, and J. K. Factor (2012). The development and evaluation of the Earth Gravitational Model 2008 (EGM2008), *J. Geophys. Res.* **117,** no. B4, doi: 10.1029/2011JB008916.

Rahaman, N., A. Baratin, D. Arpit, F. Draxler, M. Lin, F. Hamprecht, Y. Bengio, and A. Courville (2019). On the spectral bias of neural networks, *International Conf. on Machine Learning*, PMLR, 5301–5310.

Raissi, M., P. Perdikaris, and G. E. Karniadakis (2019). Physics-informed neural networks: A deep learning framework for solving forward and inverse problems involving nonlinear partial differential equations, *J. Comput. Phys.* **378,** 686–707.

Ramachandran, P., B. Zoph, and Q. V. Le (2018). Searching for activation functions, *International Conf. on Learning Representations*, Vancouver, Canada, May 2018.

Ryberg, T., and C. Haberland (2019). Bayesian simultaneous inversion for local earthquake hypocentres and 1-D velocity structure using minimum prior knowledge, *Geophys. J. Int.* **218,** no. 2, 840–854.

Sethian, J. A. (1996). A fast marching level set method for monotonically advancing fronts, *Proc. Natl. Acad. Sci.* **93,** no. 4, 1591–1595.

Smith, J. D., K. Azizzadenesheli, and Z. E. Ross (2021). Eikonet: Solving the Eikonal equation with deep neural networks, *IEEE Trans. Geosci. Remote Sens.* **59,** no. 12, 10,685–10,696.

Smith, J. D., Z. E. Ross, K. Azizzadenesheli, and J. B. Muir (2022). HypoSVI: Hypocentre inversion with Stein variational inference and physics informed neural networks, *Geophys. J. Int.* **228,** no. 1, 698–710.

Stan Development Team (2024). Stan modeling language users guide and reference manual, version 2.35, available at https://mc-stan.org (last accessed July 2024).

Tancik, M., P. Srinivasan, B. Mildenhall, S. Fridovich-Keil, N. Raghavan, U. Singhal, R. Ramamoorthi, J. Barron, and R. Ng (2020). Fourier features let networks learn high frequency functions in low dimensional domains, *Adv. Neural Inform. Process. Syst.* **33,** 7537–7547.

Taufik, M. H., U. B. Waheed, and T. A. Alkhalifah (2023). A neural network based global traveltime function (GlobeNN), *Sci. Rep.* **13,** no. 1, 7179.

Uieda, L., D. Tian, W. J. Leong, L. Toney, W. Schlitzer, J. Yao, M. Grund, M. Jones, K. Materna, T. Newton, M. Ziebarth, and P. Wessel (2021). PyGMT: A Python interface for the generic mapping tools, doi: 10.5281/zenodo.3781524.

Um, J., and C. Thurber (1987). A fast algorithm for two-point seismic ray tracing, *Bull. Seismol. Soc. Am.* **77,** no. 3, 972–986.

Waheed, U. B., E. Haghighat, T. Alkhalifah, C. Song, and Q. Hao (2021). PINNeik: Eikonal solution using physics-informed neural networks, *Comput. Geosci.* **155,** 104,833.

Wang, S., S. Sankaran, H. Wang, and P. Perdikaris (2023). An expert's guide to training physics-informed neural networks, arXiv preprint, doi: 10.48550/arXiv.2308.08468.

Wang, S., H. Wang, and P. Perdikaris (2021). On the eigenvector bias of Fourier feature networks: From regression to solving multi-scale PDEs with physics-informed neural networks, *Comput. Methods Appl. Mech. Eng.* **384,** 113,938.

Wessel, P., J. Luis, L. Uieda, R. Scharroo, F. Wobbe, W. H. Smith, and D. Tian (2019). The generic mapping tools version 6, *Geochem. Geophys. Geosys.* **20,** no. 11, 5556–5564.

White, M. C., H. Fang, N. Nakata, and Y. Ben-Zion (2020). PyKonal: A Python package for solving the Eikonal equation in spherical and Cartesian coordinates using the fast marching method, *Seismol. Res. Lett.* **91,** no. 4, 2378–2389.

Yamamoto, Y., K. Obana, T. Takahashi, A. Nakanishi, S. Kodaira, and Y. Kaneda (2013). Imaging of the subducted Kyushu-Palau Ridge in the Hyuga-nada region, western Nankai Trough subduction zone, *Tectonophysics* **589,** 90–102.

Yamamoto, Y., K. Obana, T. Takahashi, A. Nakanishi, S. Kodaira, and Y. Kaneda (2014). Seismicity and structural heterogeneities around the western Nankai Trough subduction zone, southwestern Japan, *Earth Planet. Sci. Lett.* **396,** 34–45.

Yamamoto, Y., T. Takahashi, Y. Kaiho, K. Obana, A. Nakanishi, S. Kodaira, and Y. Kaneda (2017). Seismic structure off the Kii Peninsula, Japan, deduced from passive-and active-source seismographic data, *Earth Planet. Sci. Lett.* **461,** 163–175.

Zaheer, M., S. Reddi, D. Sachan, S. Kale, and S. Kumar (2018). Adaptive methods for nonconvex optimization, in *Advances in Neural Information Processing Systems*, S. Bengio, H. Wallach, H. Larochelle, K. Grauman, N. Cesa-Bianchi, and R. Garnett (Editors), *NeurIPS 2018*, Montréal, Canada, December 2018.

Zhang, X., and A. Curtis (2020). Variational full-waveform inversion, *Geophys. J. Int.* **222,** no. 1, 406–411.

Zhao, H. (2005). A fast sweeping method for Eikonal equations, *Math. Comput.* **74,** no. 250, 603–627.

Manuscript received 9 October 2024
Published online 7 August 2025

Parallel Seismic Data Processing Performance with Cloud-Based Storage

Sasmita Mohapatra*[1], Weiming Yang[2], Zhengtang Yang[2], Chenxiao Wang[2], Jinxin Ma[3], Gary L. Pavlis[4], and Yinzhi Wang[2]

Abstract

This article introduces a general processing framework to effectively utilize waveform data stored on modern cloud platforms. The focus is hybrid processing schemes for which a local system drives processing. We show that downloading files and doing all processing locally is problematic even when the local system is a high-performance computing (HPC) cluster. Benchmark tests with parallel processing show that approach always creates a bottleneck as the volume of data being handled increases with more processes pulling data. We find a hybrid model for which processing to reduce the volume of data transferred from the cloud servers to the local system can dramatically improve processing time. Tests implemented with the Massively Parallel Analysis System for Seismology (MsPASS) utilizing Amazon Web Service's (AWS) Lambda service yield throughput comparable to processing day files on a local HPC file system. Given the ongoing migration of seismology data to cloud storage, our results show doing some or all processing on the cloud will be essential for any processing involving large volumes of data.

Cite this article as Mohapatra, S., W. Yang, Z. Yang, C. Wang, J. Ma, G. L. Pavlis, and Y. Wang (2025). Parallel Seismic Data Processing Performance with Cloud-Based Storage, *Seismol. Res. Lett.* **97**, 537–547, doi: 10.1785/0220250115.

Introduction

Cloud computing is revolutionizing scientific computing with large data sets. Information Technology jargon and blatant sales pitches found on the internet obscure some simple facts about what "cloud computing" really means. Some anchor points that may prove useful to this community are as follows.

1. A cloud system is conceptually the same as high-performance computing (HPC) clusters operated by many universities and national centers like the Texas Advanced Computing Center (TACC). Both are collections (clusters) of many interconnected computers. The main difference is that the hardware and software of cloud systems is optimized for data handling whereas HPC systems are tuned to running large simulation jobs.
2. The software that manages scheduling jobs on a cloud system and an HPC system are radically different. That means not only CPU and memory resources but also how data are accessed by both cloud and HPC systems.
3. A fundamental concept in all current generation cloud systems is "virtualization." A simple perspective on what that means is that the definition of all the components that define the cluster are abstracted as "virtual machines" that define the environment a workflow runs in. In contrast, virtual machines can be used in an HPC environment, but they are not essential.

The key point is that a cloud system is a platform for massively parallel computing, but a cloud system has different software and hardware environments than HPC clusters.

Until recently, the software infrastructure of seismology had no generic capability of handling large data sets with parallel processing at all, let alone modern cluster systems. Existing software such as ObsPy and Seismic Analysis Code (SAC) are designed to process one waveform file at a time, which becomes inefficient for large data sets. This file-by-file approach limits scalability and slows down seismic analysis workflows. The rise of cloud computing also fueled the development of data formats optimal for cloud native storage and parallel throughput. The combination of cloud-native data formats and horizontal scaling of cloud computing architecture is an attractive solution for seismological research. It is impacted by the recent emergence of applications of big data, cloud computing, and machine learning to earthquake seismology. Addair *et al.* (2014) first demonstrated

1. High Performance Research Computing, ORI, The University of Texas at Dallas, Richardson, Texas, U.S.A., https://orcid.org/0000-0001-6765-2714 (SM); 2. Texas Advanced Computing Center, The University of Texas at Austin, Austin, Texas, U.S.A., https://orcid.org/0009-0008-4031-1782 (CW); https://orcid.org/0000-0001-8505-0223 (YW); 3. The University of Texas at Austin, Austin, Texas, U.S.A.; 4. Department of Earth and Atmospheric Sciences, Indiana University, Bloomington, Indiana, U.S.A.

*Corresponding author: sasmita.mohapatra5@gmail.com;sasmita@utdallas.edu the applicability of the Hadoop software framework to large-scale seismic data processing. Articles by Mohammadzaheri *et al.* (2013), Dodge and Walter (2015), Chen *et al.* (2016), Magana-Zook *et al.* (2016), Junek *et al.* (2017), Choubik *et al.* (2020), and Clements and Denolle (2021) demonstrate that the MapReduce concept is an efficient programming model for many forms of seismic data processing. A large fraction of seismology data processing amounts to the application of a sequence of algorithms to subsets of data. Such processing workflows are well suited for parallelization, in general, and the optimal design for cloud computing, in particular, as discussed by MacCarthy *et al.* (2020).

The volume of data available for seismology research has outgrown the software infrastructure for handling that data. One of the major bottlenecks today is data delivery from the current generation of archival storage. MacCarthy *et al.* (2020) all report that downloading all three-component, broadband seismic data from the USArray Transportable Array would take nearly a month to download, and "US Regional" data (from the Incorporated Research Institutions for Seismology Data Management Center Data Statistics, see Data and Resources) would take a year, assuming uninterrupted acquisition. Our experience was even worse. Around the same time period, we used ObsPy's mass download procedure (procedure; see Data and Resources) to download all broadband data for teleseismic events within the footprint of the USArray deployment. It took us six months to complete that task. We concur with the assertion by MacCarthy *et al.* (2020) that these retrieval costs inhibit "survey scale" research and that the problem will continue to grow as high sample-rate instruments, such as nodal seismometers, and large research data sets become more common (Incorporated Research Institutions for Seismology, 2019). MacCarthy *et al.* (2020) also argue that one solution to this problem is handling raw data at its point of storage using cloud computing. This article explores that issue by considering trade-offs in performance with respect to the kinds of processing best done within a cloud system. We cast the problem in terms of generic solutions for working with a system for which data centers are hosted in the cloud. The generic models we describe here are an important contribution because we show how they can be made concrete using the Massively Parallel Analysis System for Seismology (MsPASS) software framework (Wang *et al.*, 2021). In addition, the performance tests we describe using MsPASS and Amazon Web Service (AWS) provide important baseline data for designing data processing workflows that can effectively utilize cloud storage.

Although EarthScope is in the process of migrating all the seismic archive to the cloud, the testing we report here was done on the only large data set currently openly available on the cloud at the time this work was completed: the Southern California Earthquake Data Center (SCEDC) archive hosted on AWS (Yu *et al.*, 2021). In addition to EarthScope, other U.S. data centers like the Northern California Earthquake Data Center are also contributing to this shift, with resources such as their AWS Open Dataset for Northern California earthquakes. We find that in that environment there is at least an order of magnitude increase in throughput if the data are windowed using the AWS "lambda" capability before the data are transferred to local storage. The implications are not surprising but important. That is, the unambiguous role of cloud computing, at present, is preprocessing the data as much as possible to reduce the volume of data to be transferred over a long-haul internet connection to a home institution.

Conceptual Models for Modern Data Processing

This article addresses a small subset of the larger world of cloud computing that is of current interest to most seismologists. The generic issue is how the community can make a more effective use of the large archive of seismology data managed by EarthScope and other groups now being moved to the cloud. The results of this article apply to that problem with these assumptions to reduce the scope of the problem:

1. The size of the waveform archive is the primary issue. Everything else EarthScope curates is tiny by comparison.
2. A critical community need is multiple ways to access that data to support research. Mission agencies with fixed data requirements are secondary, that is, in this article we are addressing issues important for a scientist working on basic research problems not the needs of an operational system like a seismic network operator.
3. All scientists have home computing systems for which they need to do their research. Research needs on that system can span a range of tasks that could be done on a desktop or laptop computer to something that would require the most advanced HPC cluster. The key assumption is "home" today is almost guaranteed to not be on the cloud. Furthermore, there will always be a role of a local system to produce the final products that go into a published article, so all processing eventually ends up with at least one stop occurring on premises.
4. The reason data centers like EarthScope and assorted Federation of Digital Seismograph Networks (FDSN) data centers exist is to support science using the data they curate. The data holdings of all such centers is huge compared to what most, if not all, institutions could absorb. For that reason, a universal first step in any research project is selecting a subset of data from the archive. That starts as a recipe for what needs to be selected. However, it continues in stages until a product is produced that forms the basis for a scientific result.

With those assumptions, we suggest that every example we know for interaction with data centers can be reduced to three distinct tasks: (1) read some data from the archive, (2) do some first-order processing of the waveform data, and (3) save the data to the "home" system for the research project of interest. There are two end members implementing this conceptual model. The first, which is the status quo today, can be called the "download model." That is, step 1 is a request for data from the archive that is delivered by some mechanism to local storage. One then does all waveform processing on their "home" system, so the entire waveform subset needs to at least reside temporarily on the home system. The other end member is to just do all your work on the cloud. Although that end member is feasible today, there is little question the training barrier required for most of the community is currently far too high for that to be a realistic solution. That may change with facilities such as the GeoLab gateway at EarthScope and related cloud training material (see Data and Resources). However, at this time that barrier is real. In addition, as we discuss later, there are major economic implications for that model as all cloud systems are commercial entities. As a result, we assert that for the foreseeable future the optimal solution is a hybrid where "first-order processing" is between the end members of nothing for the download model and everything for the cloud only model.

With that background, what defines "first-order processing"? Some examples are predictable, and EarthScope and other data centers may well provide turnkey solutions for them. Examples are prewindowed event data or some basic signal processing steps like demean operators. However, a fundamental issue is that research by definition needs to be flexible, and turnkey solutions may limit innovation. As a result, the range of what defines "first-order" processing is problem dependent and thus needs to be flexible.

In this article, we describe tests relevant to the two conceptual models of hybrid cloud processing illustrated in Figure 1. Figure 1a,b illustrates what we will call the cloud storage model. This model is an instance of something most readers of this article have likely experienced. That is, all cell phones and many laptop computers have tightly integrated cloud storage systems hidden behind applications that run on the device. Those applications do not store all the data they consume locally but fetch the fraction of data needed driven by a request. Future developments of data centers may provide other abstractions that provide alternatives, but the model we used in this article is the traditional file-system model. That is, we aim to access data stored in files on the AWS Simple Storage Service (S3) cloud storage. Other cloud systems have similar functionality, but with a different Application Programmer's Interface (API). The general idea is to use the cloud equivalent of low-level IO operations: (a) open file, (b) optional seek, (c) read, and (d) close file. That concept is illustrated in Figure 1a for a parallel processing instance with three "workers." In that context a scheduler, which is illustrated as a box in that figure, sends instructions to each worker telling it which data file to read, how far to seek, and how many bytes it should read. A key point is this conceptual model uses an abstraction that allows interaction of the cloud store as if it were a local file system.

Figure 1b illustrates a second conceptual model for cloud processing we will refer to as the "shared processing model." The basic idea is to offload some or all waveform processing to the cloud system. Figure 1b illustrates that idea by showing processing "workers" running on both the "home" and "cloud system." In this model a particular waveform is handled as follows.

1. The scheduler sends instructions to a cloud-side worker to read the data that defines a particular waveform stored in the archive.
2. A reader running on the cloud system loads the requested data into its memory.
3. The cloud instance runs a sequence of processing algorithms on that waveform. The result of the cloud processing is returned via an open internet connection to the local system.

   In this article, it is assumed to be a seismic data object, but it would not have to be, for example, it could be an arrival-time estimate produced by an automated picker.
4. The scheduler passes the return to a local worker process. That worker may do additional work on the result or just write it to local storage.

The approach in Figure 1b makes the most sense if step 3 produces a significant reduction in data volume that is returned through the internet connection to the "home system."

Prototype Implementations

Software framework

A fundamental problem today with working on cloud systems is that most of the software in common use in our community is not compatible with constraints imposed by the environment. Even worse is that fact that even if one made the effort to port a common tool like SAC to the cloud environment, it would be fundamentally incapable of fully exploiting the massive parallelization capabilities that characterize cloud systems. The only generic solution to this problem that exists today is the MsPASS framework (Wang *et al.*, 2021) we used for the work reported in this article. Features of MsPASS that made it the tool of choice for this study are as follows.

1. MsPASS is containerized, which is the standard method today to create the virtual environment that defines a cloud system.
2. MsPASS parallelism is scalable and can run on a single desktop machine to a cluster like AWS with nearly unlimited numbers of processors.
3. The portability of the package makes it possible to run MsPASS on both ends of hybrid setups like that illustrated in Figure 1b.
4. MsPASS has an integrated database system that is essential for managing large data volumes.

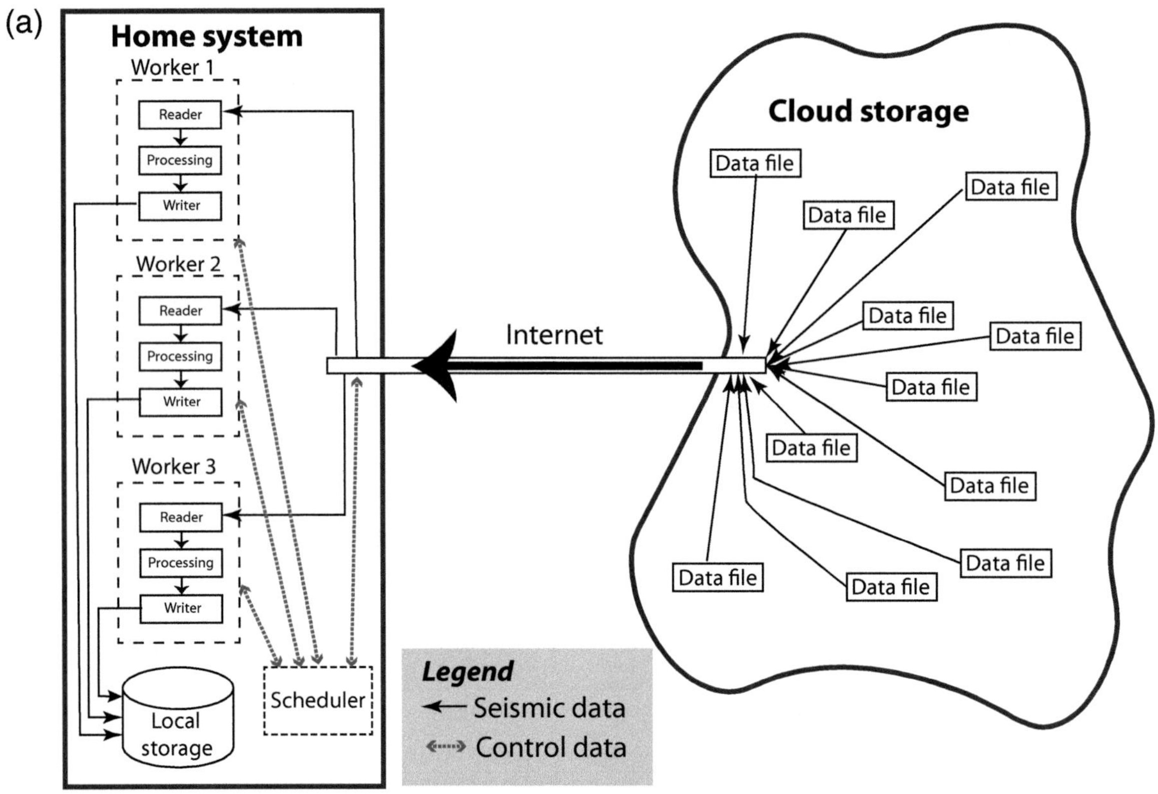

Figure 1. Generic models for parallel data processing with cloud data storage prototype and shared processing prototype. Panel (a) illustrates how parallel processing can work with data stored on the cloud and downloaded as needed. In the implementation described in the Cloud storage prototype section, this is the model we refer to as "S3" (Simple Storage Service) because the implementation uses Amazon Web Service (AWS) S3 cloud storage. The large box on the left illustrates the hardware of a system in which processing is performed, and the irregular polygon at the right is an abstraction of a cloud system. The example illustrates three worker processes running on a local system that request data and retrieve files through a common internet connection to a cloud server. In this case, the parallel scheduler only needs to interact with the local processes as illustrated by the red lines with arrowheads. Workers then request data (reader box) from the cloud, and they receive the data through a common internet connection as illustrated with the heavy black array. Processing functions (Processing box) may do some work on the data before saving the results to local storage (Writer box). Panel (b) illustrates what we call a hybrid model in which some of the processing is done on the cloud system before being transferred to a local system. The illustration is an example with three workers running on the local system and three workers running on the cloud system. That generic approach would allow different numbers of workers on both sides to optimize performance. A key difference in this model compared to panel (a) is that the scheduler running on the local system has to send control messages to manage not only local but also remote processes running on the cloud system. That is illustrated here by red-dashed lines with arrowheads on both the local and cloud side of the system connected via the internet connection. A difference in this model is the reader box is on the cloud side, and data would be reduced in size with the box labeled "Cloud System Processing" before being transmitted across the long distance internet connection. The color version of this figure is available only in the electronic edition.(*Continued*)

Data Index Abstraction

We used the MsPASS framework (Wang *et al.*, 2021) to implement prototypes for the two cloud data processing models illustrated in Figure 1. The tests all accessed the SCEDC data set stored on AWS (MacCarthy *et al.*, 2020; Yu *et al.*, 2021). The archive contains waveform data from the Southern California Seismic Network going back to the year 2000. The data are stored as miniSEED day files and event files with a total data volume ~100 TB. The storage is abstracted as what Amazon calls an "S3 bucket".

The first step for interacting with data stored on S3 is to build an index to enable efficient querying and access to relevant waveform files. We treated this issue as a problem independently from data processing. The assumption is that if one were doing a full-scale data preprocessing workflow, the index would be already available by some mechanism. For our tests we had to build one, but the expectation is that a more efficient mechanism will need to be developed in the future to supply the index for the massive EarthScope and related FDSN archives.

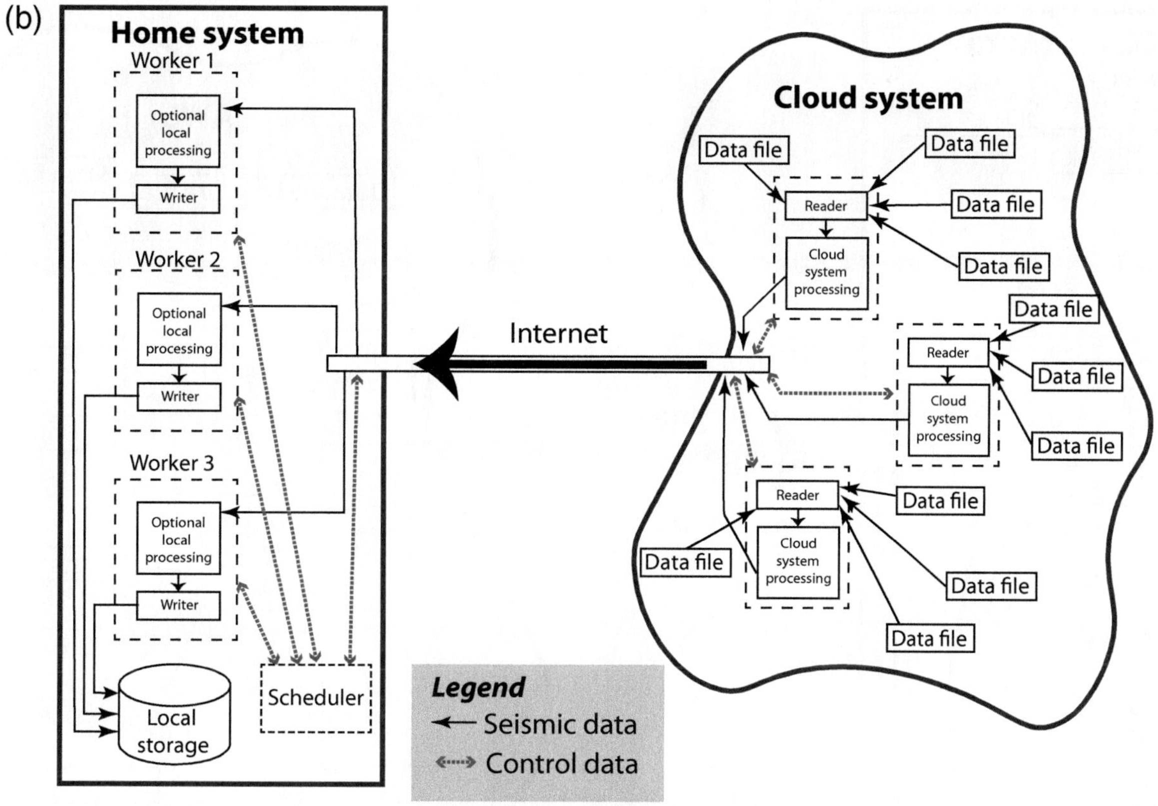

Figure 1. Continued

For the SCEDC data, we developed a prototype for building an index to their continuous and event files stored on S3. The prototype code was implemented as part of the MsPASS Database class used in MsPASS to abstract all waveform IO operations. In particular, the index we constructed is stored as a MongoDB document that when loaded using the Python API (PyMongo) creates a Python dictionary that can be used to drive the reader. The Database class method called read_data abstracts the read operation to load a single channel of data stored in a particular S3 file for each document defined in the indexing documents. The prototype is not generic, but once the EarthScope system is fully released we expect to make the prototype more generic to allow reading any miniSEED format archive stored on S3. In particular, the MongoDB document index document contains all the information needed to access a particular waveform and is easily extended to support any S3 indexing scheme.

The abstraction we used allows us to read data on S3 with a Python script. The script needs only instantiate an instance of a Database object that holds the index, query MongoDB to define the subset of data desired, and then construct the data set with one channel of waveform data per document returned by the query. The only complication in reading from S3 is that the script must define the credentials needed to access the requested data via a pair of "access keys" that AWS uses for access control. The tests described in this article all use an index stored in a local (home) database. However, we note that the abstraction we use could allow the query mechanism to be done by the data provider with a minor modification. That is, the provider need only allow read access to their waveform relational database. There are standard "big data" tools for querying relational database servers in the Dask (see Data and Resources) and Spark (see Data and Resources) schedulers used in MsPASS. Converting the output of an SQL server to input to drive a MsPASS workflow requires only a few lines of Python code.

Cloud Storage Prototype

For the SCEDC data we used Amazon's boto3 Python package (see Data and Resources) to interact with AWS. The approach we used was more or less a cloud version of the download model. That is, the index document contains the equivalent of a file name that the reader uses to download the entire file it references into the local system's memory. The usage is very similar to the web service download functions in ObsPy that may be familiar to many readers. The MsPASS reader then translates the miniSEED binary data into the internal MsPASS data structure called a "TimeSeries" object for which

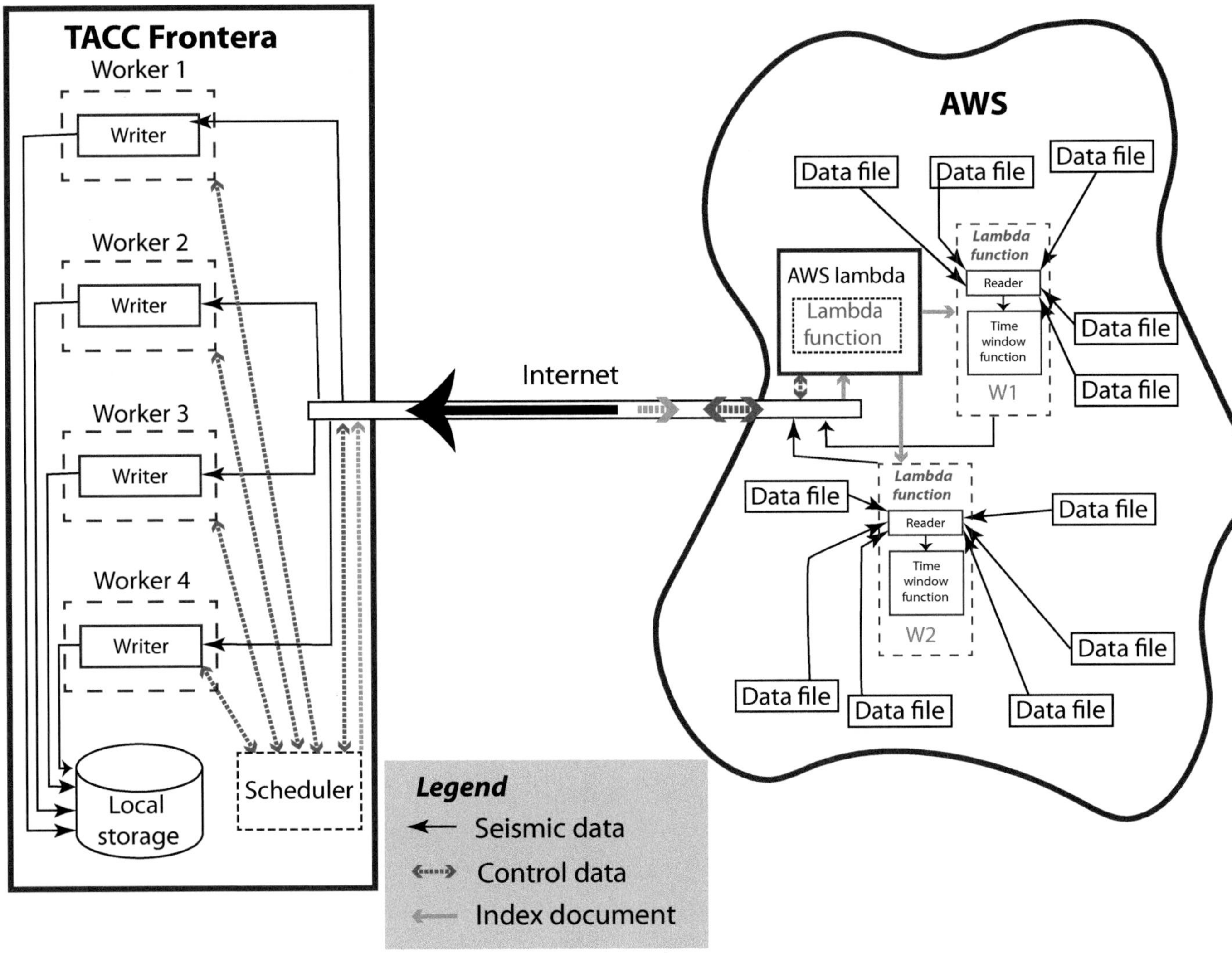

additional processing functions can be applied to the data before it is saved locally. A serial version of that process is conceptually identical to an ObsPy processing loop driven by webservice calls to download and process one waveform at a time. A key difference MsPASS provides is the parallel processing capability illustrated conceptually in Figure 1a. For the tests in this article, we used the parallel scheduling framework called Dask (see Data and Resources). Parallel processing in our test is driven by a parallel data structure Dask calls a "bag," which is conceptually a Python list of things that do not necessarily fit in system memory. The "scheduler" illustrated in Figure 1a, in this context, more-of-less sends waveform index documents to each "worker" process. Each worker then uses boto3 to download the file the document defines, process the result, and save the (reduced size) result locally.

Shared Processing Prototype

The conceptual model of Figure 1b could be implemented in a number of ways. Our prototype implementation is illustrated in Figure 2. The prototype uses a feature in AWS that Amazon refers to as a "lambda service" (see Data and Resources). Readers familiar with "lambda functions," which is standardized in most modern computing languages including Python, can appreciate the name. Conceptually, AWS lambda allows a single Python function to be callable as a remote service from an

Figure 2. Implementation of hybrid processing using AWS lambda service. This figure is directly comparable to the generic form of this concept illustrated in Figure 1b. Note the difference in that the cloud side is implemented through a specific approach available on AWS called a lambda service (see the Shared processing prototype section). The lambda service automatically scales worker processes to handle load up to a limit imposed by a cost structure. We illustrate that here through two worker boxes labeled "W1" and "W2." Each AWS worker handles files assigned at AWS by their schedule. The local side only sends requests illustrated here by an orange arrow labeled "Index document." In our implementation, the index document drives a Python reader running as the lambda function at AWS. In tests presented in the article that also function as windows data to reduce the size of what is returned. The output of the lambda function is returned to the local (Texas Advanced Computing Center [TACC] Frontera) side as illustrated by the black lines with arrowheads. As in Figure 1, the red-dashed lines with arrowheads illustrate control data paths used by the scheduler running on Frontera. The color version of this figure is available only in the electronic edition.

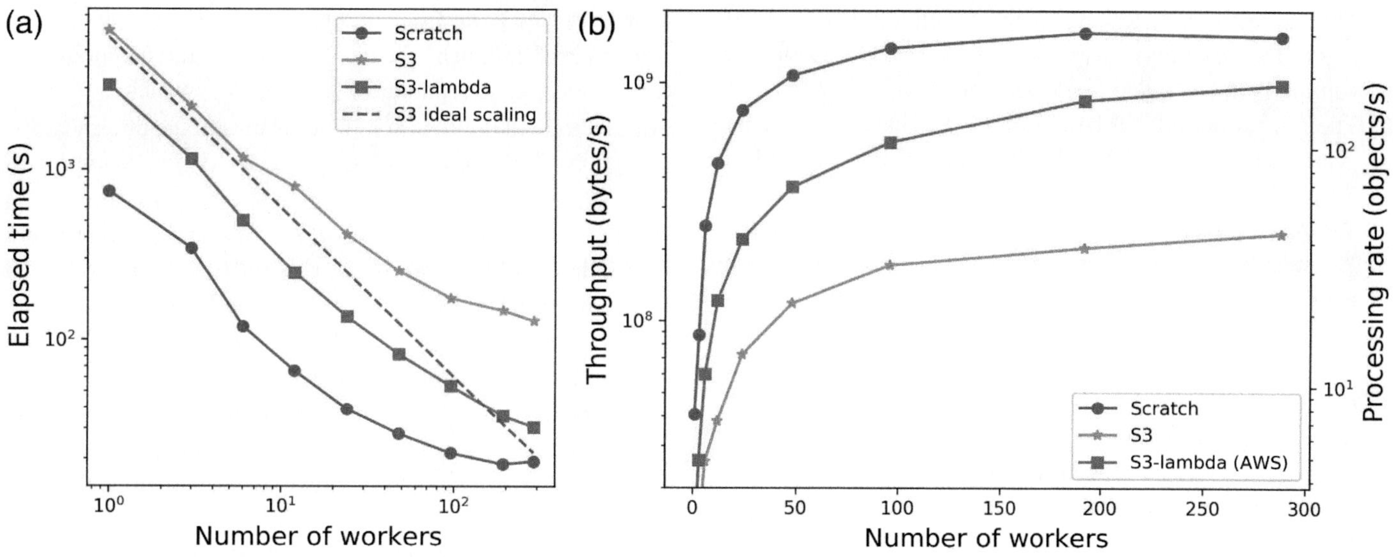

Figure 3. Performance results reading Southern California Earthquake Data Center (SCEDC) day file data from AWS on Frontera with different processing approaches. All results are for the same processing sequence involving only reading, unpacking miniSEED data, and windowing the data to a 5 min long segment. The data files used for these tests are 40 samples per second day files, of the order of 5 MB size, with read times of the order of 10 ms. (a) Displays the data as elapsed time as a function of the number of serial and parallel workers. The tag name in the legend defines the three algorithms discussed in the Cloud storage prototype and Shared processing prototype sections. The red-dashed line is the S3 benchmark time with Dask running one worker. (b) Same data as panel (a) but converted to throughput and plotted with a logarithmic *y* axis and a linear *x* axis. The ideal scaling curve is omitted. Panel (b) has a second logarithmic axis on the right with the data converted to the number of files (objects) processed per second. The color version of this figure is available only in the electronic edition.

application. That function can be anything provided it is stateless, meaning all relevant parameters describing its behavior must be sent to it. In the implementation for this article that function is an MsPASS function driven by a waveform index document that defines an S3 object (file). For this article that lambda function does three things: (1) use the input document to construct an MsPASS TimeSeries object from the miniSEED data, (2) window the data from day files to a specified interval, and (3) return the windowed data to the local system. It is important to realize that step 2 was intentionally made simple so we could evaluate input–output performance. In most applications, additional processing functions would likely be called within the lambda function. Windowing alone is best thought of as an end-member example. We discuss the implications of this below in terms of load balancing and economics after showing the results focused on input–output performance (Figs. 1b, 2).

The key difference between Figures 1b and 2 is how the cloud system manages load balancing. The generic model of Figure 1b shows the general problem the overall system must handle. That is, in a parallel processing environment the workers on the local system need to be balanced with the workers on the cloud system. Figures 1b and 2 show the naïve concept of matching workers one-to-one on the local and cloud sides. However, the AWS lambda service does a sensible thing. The AWS cloud management system takes care of the load balancing automatically. That is, it adds workers behind the scenes to run instances of the lambda function as requests come in. That scaling occurs automatically but is limited by economics. That is, the service scales up to a limit. Adding performance requires paying more money to Amazon. That idea is illustrated in Figure 2 by showing different numbers of workers on the two sides of the connection.

Performance Tests

Our primary goal was (Fig. 3) to evaluate the throughput possible in a world with data stored on a cloud system like AWS. To address that we focus on a processing end member that does minimal processing but reduces data volume significantly. That is, our test workflow does one and only one data handling step: time windowing. Related benchmarks with MsPASS indicate that the time spent on the windowing function alone can be largely neglected. Specifically, we found the windowing function from a typical SCEDC day-long waveform segment on TACC's Frontera system (Stanzione *et al.*, 2020) is ~67 microseconds(μs) per call.

The test results were designed to appraise performance scaling with the number of processors dedicated to processing. Hence, we scaled the workflow from a single worker to 384 workers distributed across up to eight compute nodes. For the TACC's Frontera system more than one node is used when the number of workers exceeds 56, which is the number of cores on a single node. We ran the tests using both the Dask and Spark scheduler to appraise their relative performance. However, the differences between Dask and Spark were negligible, and results here are reported only for the Dask runs.

Figure 3a shows elapsed time data on previously indexed day files run three different ways.

1. The figures tagged "S3" are results running in the mode of Figure 1a; the cloud storage prototype for which the full day volume is downloaded for local processing.
2. The figures tagged "S3 lambda" use the shared processing prototype implemented with AWS lambda as illustrated in Figure 2.
3. The results labeled "Scratch" are a control test. That is, the "Scratch" timing data were produced by running the same windowing workflow but with the miniSEED files previously loaded and indexed on TACC's Frontera cluster. The "Scratch" label is a detail that the file system on which the data were stored is the Lustre file system on Frontera with that label. Scratch is a large virtual disk farm shared by all Frontera users for staging large datasets. The point is that Frontera "Scratch" is a state-of-the-art local file system for an HPC cluster. The "Scratch" results thus provide a measure of ultimate performance we could expect the other tests to, at best, approach.

Our results illustrated in Figure 3a show elapsed time for windowing 5660-day files from the SCEDC open data stored on AWS S3 (MacCarthy *et al.*, 2020; Yu *et al.*, 2021). The approximate total size of data accessed is 28 GB.

Results

Figure 3a shows that the performance of all three workflows improve (elapsed time decreases) as the number of workers increases. However, the scaling in all cases departs significantly from the ideal scaling line illustrated in the figure. That is not unexpected, but it is important for the reader to understand what we do and do not know about what shapes those curves.

In the context of Figure 3a, the elapsed time can be expressed as

$$T = T_s(N) + \frac{T_P(N)}{N}, \tag{1}$$

in which T_s is a serial portion of the code that cannot be parallelized, T_P is the time to execute a fully parallel algorithm, and N is the number of workers running the parallel algorithm. In our tests all are functions of N. In all cases, T_s is dominated by Dask or Spark scheduling overhead. Profiling we have done and the Dask documentation indicate the T_s is probably under 1 s for all tests. If so, T_s is likely small for all but the largest values of N for the control (scratch) test.

The factors controlling T_p are different for the different tests and all, as noted, are largely controlled by IO performance. However, in all cases T_p can be expanded as

$$T_p = T_{\text{open}} + T_{\text{read}} + T_{\text{unpack}} + T_w + T_{\text{close}}, \tag{2}$$

in which each of the terms in the sum on the right side defines a generic concept that is implemented in different ways in each of these tests. The term T_{open} for a file system read (scratch) is the time required to "open" the file. For both S3 and S3 lambda we know of no way to separate T_{open} from T_{read}, which is the time required to read the stream of bytes from storage into memory. T_{unpack} is the time required to convert the compressed miniSEED packets into an array in memory for processing and T_w is the time to run the window function. Independent timing tests with 1000 trials show the median value of T_{unpack} is 50 ms and the median value of T_w, as noted earlier, is 0.05 ms. The sum $T_{\text{unpack}} + T_w$ is approximately 50 ms, and we can assume it is nearly constant for all tests. Variations can be expected only for hardware differences, which as best can tell are not dramatically different between Frontera and the hardware at AWS where we ran these tests. Finally, T_{close} is the time required to close a file or to end an AWS transaction. For the scratch control test, T_{close} is the file close time, which can be neglected. For S3 it can also be neglected as it is, at most, the time to release the memory held by miniSEED file image in memory. For S3 lambda, T_{close} is something very different. It is the time to transfer the output of the window function back to Frontera.

That framework provides a model to explain the form of the curves in Figure 3. Consider the control experiment first as that model is likely familiar to most readers. File open and close times on a system like Frontera are tiny and of the order of 1 ms or less in normal conditions. For these tests, we used only the 40 samples per second day files, which are of the order of 5 MB in size with read times of the order of 10 ms. As aforementioned, $T_{\text{unpack}} + T_w$ is approximately constant for all files. If all the terms were independent of N, equation (1) says the elapsed time plot in Figure 3 would be approximately linear at low values of N but asymptotic to log T_s as N gets large. For the "Scratch" control, T_s can be neglected and the ideal scaling on the log–log plot of Figure 3a would be a linear curve passing through the serial processing time (one worker). The S3 curve begins to flatten at tens of workers, indicating diminishing returns in performance as parallelism increases and highlighting a departure from ideal linear scaling. The reason is best understood by the alternative representation of these data plotted in Figure 3b expressed as throughput = D/T, in which D is the data volume (30 GB for these tests) and T is the elapsed time. Even on an HPC cluster like Frontera 300+ processes actively doing IO operations can reduce throughput, that is, open, close, and read times all are likely to increase on an IO bound task like this as N increases. We conclude for the control experiments, our tests with larger numbers of workers are saturating the Frontera scratch file systems read bandwidth.

The S3 and S3 lambda tests are subject to similar issues, but the controlling factors are different. For S3, we devised a set of independent tests to measure the different terms in equation (2). First, we ran independent measurement of $T_{\text{open}} + T_{\text{read}}$ without the complication of N workers screaming for data at the same time. We found such transfers took an average of

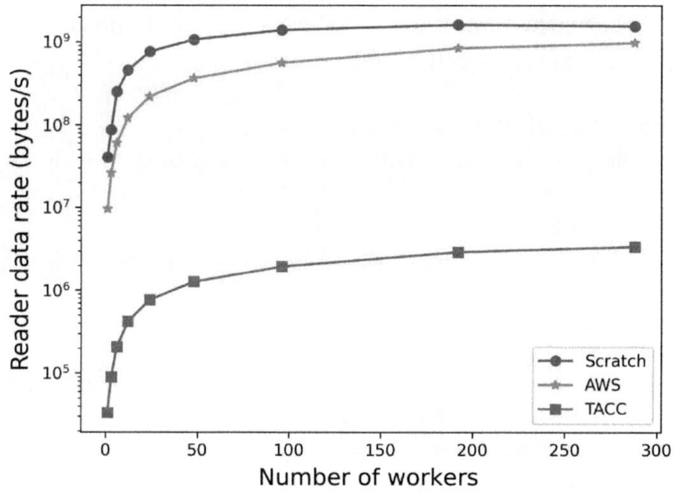

Figure 4. Processing data volume scaling for different algorithms. This plot is similar to Figure 3b, but the curves represent the data being handled by different instances of the processing code. As in Figure 3, "Scratch" is the data being read and processed on Frontera in the control experiment reading from a high-performance local file system. The curve labeled "Frontera" is the data being handled on Frontera when reading from AWS with the lambda service handling the miniSEED unpacking and windowing. The curve labeled "AWS" is the data rate AWS has to sustain to feed the lambda data sent to the processes running on Frontera. The "Frontera" curve is the same as "AWS" but offset by a factor of the ratio 86,400/300 (1 day/5 min). The color version of this figure is available only in the electronic edition.

0.75 s with a variance of less than 1% in 1000 trials. Because $T_{unpack} + T_w$ is approximately constant (approximately 50 s) and T_{close} is approximately zero, we can project an ideal scaling assuming $T_{unpack} + T_w$ is independent of N as the line illustrated in Figure 3a. The intercept is the S3 benchmark time with Dask running one worker. At $N = 1$ with T_s and T_p constant equation (1) reduces to $T_s + T_p$. We point out that simple relationship because, to make the ideal scaling curve match S3, either T_s or T_p must be larger than our model values. The more important issue is that the S3 curve departs strongly from the model prediction, which is close to linear on the log–log plot of Figure 3a. Similar to the control experiment, however, Figure 3b provides the most likely explanation for that scaling. That figure shows that the Scratch throughput flattens at approximately 300 MB/s whereas the S3 throughput flattens at around 30 MB/s. Both are of the order of the IO bandwidth through which those data are read: scratch file system and internet connection, respectively, on Frontera. Hence, we conclude that the performance for scratch and S3 in these tests are IO limited when N is of the order of 10 or more.

The limiting factor for the S3 lambda case is different. The justification for this claim is found in Figure 4. There we represent the timing data in terms of the data volume the readers on the two sides of the system illustrated in Figure 2 must handle in these tests. The "Frontera" curve shows the throughput that must be handled at Frontera compared to what AWS had to handle under the hood to feed that data to Frontera at that rate. The two curves have exactly the same form but are offset on the y axis by a factor of 300/86,400 (5 min/1 day). The volume of data transferred is drastically reduced because of the windowing operation applied to day volumes. Because the y axis in Figure 2b is logarithmic, the Frontera curve is then a simple downward shift from the AWS curve. A key point is that the Frontera data rate is several orders of magnitude less than the IO bandwidth of the internet bandwidth at Frontera as measured roughly by the S3 curve of Figure 3b. We plot the control data read rate for scratch in Figure 4, and curve is similar in shape and only slightly offset from larger than the curve with the tag "AWS." That suggests that a similar saturation of the IO bandwidth is occurring in these tests on the AWS server side. Given that Frontera's scratch is a state-of-the-art cluster file system, that hypothesis is reasonable.

An issue with the scaling of S3 Lambda that is important to understand at this point is the resources allocated to the lambda service at AWS. S3 Lambda automatically scales in response to incoming requests, adjusting to traffic volume while being billed based on execution time and memory usage. It has a 15-min run limit, along with concurrency thresholds and potential cold starts that may cause latency. Cloud services like AWS are "elastic" meaning the performance can be improved by increasing resources dedicated to the task on AWS. However, increased performance comes at a cost. With this model, a research project using an AWS lambda service would need to pay more money if the project required improved performance to be feasible.

Discussion and Conclusion

The first thing all readers should recognize is that the modified download model as described in the Cloud storage prototype section (Fig. 1a) "S3" is not an effective solution for processing very large datasets. A case in point is the extended USArray data set we mentioned in the Introduction made up of P-wave records of all broadband stations in the lower 48 states for the USArray recording period. The data set is of the order of 40 million waveforms. It took us about 6 months to download that data set with ObsPy and webservices. From the aforementioned timing data, if we did the same operation on Frontera with one worker using MsPASS and the S3 algorithm, the job would run for 462 days. Figure 3b shows that parallelization with the "S3" tests with a rate approximately 20 times faster than a single worker. Hence, that same data set would still take the order of 20 days to assemble with 50 active workers. That is feasible, but an important warning is the times could be orders of magnitude slower due to local network performance if run else where. We ran these tests on Frontera, which has about as fast a connection to the internet as possible. Time to assemble a large data set like the extended USArray example would, at best, remain painfully long using the S3 approach. Hence, the version of hybrid models of Figures 1b or 2 seems essential for working with massive datasets.

The current fundamental problem to implement a hybrid processing scheme such as Figures 1b or 2 is software. Our tests show MsPASS can be used to do that with the AWS Lambda service. MsPASS is generic enough that other ways to implement the more general approach of Figure 1b are feasible. In any case, the implementation is currently far from easy as it requires understanding of all the pieces of a complex collection of software. One possible solution may be a science gateway under development by the Seismic Computational Platform for Empowering Discovery (SCOPED) project (see Data and Resources). Smaller datasets may be handled with EarthScope's GeoLab (see Data and Resources), but at present that gateway is limited to four processors and provides limited cloud storage to save processed data. Until then, those needing to handle huge datasets either need to be very patient or be hardy enough to work with the MsPASS framework.

Our tests were run on the SCEDC data, but how will this work with the unified archive now staged to AWS by EarthScope? The current development plans to use S3 bucket storage with a webservice API to query the archive to retrieve index information (Chad Trabant, 2025, personal comm.). That setup will allow use of a lambda service like that in our prototype for cloud-side preprocessing. The main differences are in how the data index is acquired and differences in credential validation for EarthScope and SCEDC. We suggest the lambda service model used here should be a standard way to handle preprocessing of large data volumes to assemble a research ready data set. That approach is not well matched to the GeoLab gateway but is possible with MsPASS, as our tests demonstrate.

A final point about the hybrid model using lambda service or S3 is economics. AWS and other cloud providers are commercial entities that charge real money for their services. Someone has to pay, and there is little doubt the days of unlimited, free data access will disappear with the transition to cloud storage. The cheapest solution as described in the Cloud storage prototype section for the foreseeable future is likely to remain the "S3" model of Figure 1a. In that case, the data center needs only feed data in response to user requests, and the costs are the fixed storage costs and any computing that the data center pays. The hybrid model of Figures 1b or 2 changes the economics. The cost for the AWS Lambda service, for example, scales with the maximum number of processors allocated when the service is launched. The greater the computation workload shifted to the cloud, the higher the cost the task will incur from the provider. Hence, the economics of a hybrid system will be a trade-off of local fixed costs to maintain research computing hardware versus the cost of doing your work through a commercial provider. All you can predict for sure about that problem is that it is subject to large changes with time. However, transition to that model seems inevitable because it is essential to provide a mechanism for processing large data volumes obtained from the international archives.

Data and Resources

The documentation of the Massively Parallel Analysis System for Seismology (MsPASS) is available at https://www.mspass.org/user_manual. The MsPASS source code is available at https://github.com/mspass-team/mspass and the containerized distribution can be found in https://hub.docker.com/r/mspass/mspass. The information about GridFS is available at https://docs.mongodb.com/manual/core/gridfs. Comparison with Spark is available at https://docs.dask.org/en/latest/spark.html. Examples of using the MsPASS implementation for Simple Storage Service (S3) on Amazon Web Service (AWS) can be found in https://www.mspass.org/user_manual/importing_data.html. Several examples of automated script of the lambda function can be found here: https://github.com/SCEDC/cloud/tree/master/pds-lambda-example. For basic usage of S3 bucket for the Southern California Earthquake Data Center (SCEDC) data can be found here: https://scedc.caltech.edu/data/getstarted-pds.html. For basic usage of lambda, one can refer to https://scedc.caltech.edu/data/lambda.html. The SCOPED Gateway enables users to run seismology applications on high-performance computing (HPC) or Cloud through tapis: https://seisscoped.org/tapis-ui. Mass downloader for the Federation of Digital Seismograph Networks (FDSN) compliant webservices is available at https://docs.obspy.org/packages/autogen/obspy.clients.fdsn.mass_downloader.html. The cloud training material is available at https://arxiv.org/abs/2409.19147. The Dask dataframe is available at https://docs.dask.org/en/stable/generated/dask.dataframe.read_sql.html, and the Spark documentation is available at https://spark.apache.org/docs/3.5.3/sql-ref.html. Amazon's boto3 Python package is available at https://boto3.amazonaws.com/v1/documentation/api/latest/index.html. The Dask website is available at https://www.dask.org/. AWS lambda documentation is available at https://docs.aws.amazon.com/lambda/. EarthScope gateway is available at https://www.earthscope.org/gateway. EarthScope's GeoLab is available at https://www.earthscope.org/data/geolab/. All websites were last accessed in July 2025.

Declaration of Competing Interests

The authors acknowledge that there are no conflicts of interest recorded.

Acknowledgments

This work is supported by the National Science Foundation (NSF) through Awards OAC-2103494 and OAC-1931352.

References

Addair, T. G., D. A. Dodge, W. R. Walter, and S. D. Ruppert (2014). Large-scale seismic signal analysis with Hadoop, *Comput. Geosci.* **66,** 145–154, doi: 10.1016/j.cageo.2014.01.014.

Chen, P., N. J. Taylor, K. G. Dueker, I. S. Keifer, A. K. Wilson, C. L. McGuffy, C. G. Novitsky, A. J. Spears, and W. S. Holbrook (2016). pSIN: A scalable, Parallel algorithm for Seismic INterferometry of large-N ambient-noise data, *Comput. Geosci.* **93,** 88–95, doi: 10.1016/j.cageo.2016.05.003.

Choubik, Y., A. Mahmoudi, M. M. Himmi, and L. El Moudnib (2020). STA/LTA trigger algorithm implementation on a seismological dataset using Hadoop MapReduce, *IAES Int. J. Artif. Intell.* **9,** no. 2, 269–275, doi: 10.11591/ijai.v9.i2.pp269-275.

Clements, T., and M. A. Denolle (2021). SeisNoise.jl: Ambient seismic noise cross correlation on the CPU and GPU in Julia, *Seismol. Res. Lett.* **92,** no. 1, 517–527, doi: 10.1785/0220200192.

Dodge, D. A., and W. R. Walter (2015). Initial global seismic crosscorrelation results: Implications for empirical signal detectors, *Bull. Seismol. Soc. Am.* **105,** no. 1, 240–256, doi: 10.1785/0120140166.

Incorporated Research Institutions for Seismology (2019). IRIS PASSCAL to expand pool of seismic instruments, available at https://www.iris.edu/hq/news/story/iris_passcal_to_expand_pool_of_seismic_instruments (last accessed October 2019).

Junek, W. N., C. A. Houchin, J. A. Wehlen III, J. E. Highcock II, and M. Waineo (2017). Acquisition of seismic, hydroacoustic, and infrasonic data with Hadoop and Accumulo, *Seismol. Res. Lett.* **88,** no. 6, 1553–1559, doi: 10.1785/0220170056.

MacCarthy, J., O. Marcillo, and C. Trabant (2020). Seismology in the cloud: A new streaming workflow, *Seismol. Res. Lett.* **91,** 1804–1812, doi: 10.1785/0220190357.

Magana-Zook, S., J. M. Gaylord, D. R. Knapp, D. A. Dodge, and S. D. Ruppert (2016). Large-scale seismic waveform quality metric, *Comput, Geosci.* 94, 18–30, doi: 10.1016/j.cageo.2016.05.012.

Mohammadzaheri, A., H. Sadeghi, S. K. Hosseini, and M. Navazandeh (2013). DISRAY: A distributed ray tracing by map reduce, *Comput. Geosci.* **52,** 453–458, doi: 10.1016/j.cageo.2012.10.009.

Stanzione, D., J. West, R. T. Evans, T. Minyard, O. Ghattas, and D. K. Panda (2020). Frontera: The evolution of leadership computing at the national science foundation, *PEARC '20: Practice and Experience in Advanced Research Computing 2020: Catch the Wave*, Association for Computing Machinery, New York, New York, 106–111, doi: 10.1145/3311790.3396656.

Wang, Y., G. L. Pavlis, W. Yang, and J. Ma (2021). MsPASS: A data management and processing framework for seismology, *Seismol. Res. Lett.* **93,** 426–434.

Yu, E., A. Bhaskaran, S. Chen, Z. E. Ross, E. Hauksson, and R. W. Clayton (2021). Southern California earthquake data now available in the AWS Cloud, *Seismol. Res. Lett.* doi: 10.1785/0220210039.

Manuscript received 8 April 2025
Published online 20 August 2025

Historical Seismologist

OPEN ACCESS

Reflections on a Trio of North American Earthquakes in 1925

Susan E. Hough[*1], Maurice Lamontagne[2], John Ebel[3], and Laurie Baise[4]

Abstract

In 1925, three moderately large damaging earthquakes occurred in North America over four months: the 28 February (local time; LT) M 6.2 Charlevoix, 27 June (LT) M 6.6 Montana, and 29 June M 6.5 Santa Barbara earthquakes. The centennial anniversaries of these events motivated this retrospective consideration focused on the ground motions generated by the three events, including a reconsideration of early intensity assignments for the Montana earthquake. At the time, these three earthquakes appeared to support the arguments of some geologists who downplayed the severity of seismic hazard in southern California relative to other parts of the country. Some of the arguments advanced at that time, for example that Los Angeles "has the least to fear from 'Acts of God' of any city under the American flag," (Hill, 1928) sound naïve if not laughable now, but a comparison of well-constrained shaking distributions for the three earthquakes reveals the dramatic difference in wave propagation efficiency in western versus eastern North America (ENAM), which leads to moderate ENAM events being felt to much larger distances. At M 6.2, the 1925 Charlevoix earthquake was a notably large event in ENAM. This earthquake was the largest event in eastern Canada since 1870 and caused damage in the epicentral region in addition to towns as far away as 200 km, with felt shaking extending over 1000 km. In contrast, felt shaking from the Santa Barbara earthquake barely extended beyond ~200 km. Compiling published intensity distributions for larger ENAM earthquakes, we show that perceptible earthquake shaking is not uncommon in ENAM over century time scales, but experience with weakly felt shaking may incline people to downplay potential earthquake risk.

Cite this article as Hough, S. E., M. Lamontagne, J. Ebel, and L. Baise (2025). Reflections on a Trio of North American Earthquakes in 1925, *Seismol. Res. Lett.* **97**, 548–563, doi: 10.1785/0220250149.

Introduction

The severity of earthquake hazard in the greater Los Angeles area was debated in the early twentieth century (Wood, 1916; Hill, 1928; also see Geschwind, 2003; Hough, 2020), even after most of the San Andreas fault was mapped in the aftermath of the 1906 San Francisco earthquake (Lawson *et al.*, 1908), and several major fault zones had been mapped in the greater Los Angeles area (Willis, 1923).

In a book published in 1928, geologist Robert T. Hill, sometimes hailed as the Father of Texas Geology (Alexander, 1976), acknowledged that earthquake occurrence was associated with "regions of late mountain-making" (Hill, 1928, p. 13), including California, but went on to summarize reasons why earthquake shaking and hazard in the Los Angeles area was not expected to be severe. A statement on the book's dust cover included the assertion that Los Angeles "has the least to fear from 'Acts of God' of any city under the American flag." Assertions within the book included the statement, "it cannot be said that there is any great menace from the Newport line" (Hill, 1928; p. 40). Here, Hill referred to the structure now known as the Newport–Inglewood–Rose Canyon fault zone, on which the damaging Long Beach earthquake occurred just five years later (Wood, 1933). In his chapter on the Long Beach earthquake, Richter (1958) noted the earthquake "put an end to efforts by incompletely informed or misguided interests to deny…the existence of serious earthquake hazard in California." Among the reasons cited for the claims by Hill and a few of his contemporaries (see Hough, 2020) was the recognition that severe shaking is concentrated in proximity to fault rupture. By 1925, the San Andreas fault had been mapped in southern as well as northern California; the fault was known to be farther away from the Los Angeles area than it is from the San Francisco peninsula. Shaking effects from past earthquakes in California were also limited in extent compared to the effects of large earthquakes

1. U.S. Geological Survey, Pasadena, California, U.S.A., https://orcid.org/0000-0002-5980-2986 (SEH); 2. Carleton University, Ottawa, Canada; 3. Weston Observatory, Boston College, Boston, Massachusetts, U.S.A., https://orcid.org/0000-0003-1064-0629 (JE); 4. Tufts University, Medford, Massachusetts, U.S.A.

*Corresponding author: hough@usgs.gov

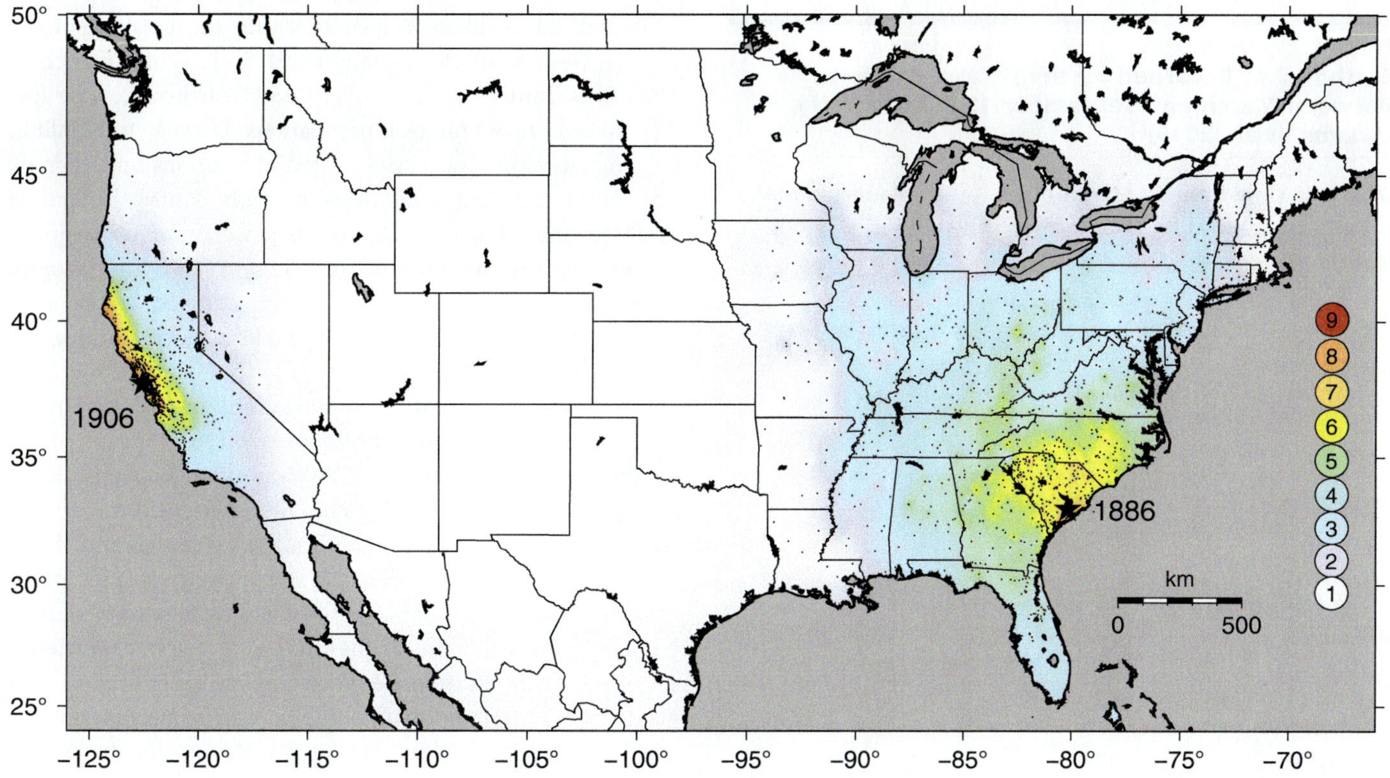

Figure 1. Interpolated shaking intensities for the 1886 Charleston and 1906 San Francisco earthquakes. Small black dots indicate locations for which intensity values are estimated. Intensities from Hough and Bilham (2024) and Boatwright and Bundock (2006).

in the central and eastern United States. Before the earthquake magnitude scale was introduced by Richter (1935), scientists ranked the principal 1811–1812 New Madrid mainshocks among the "greatest earthquakes in known history" (Heck, 1934, p. 115). Popular articles about damaging earthquakes mentioned the 1906 San Francisco earthquake together with eastern North America (ENAM) events, including the 1811–1812 New Madrid sequence and the 1886 Charleston earthquake (Times-Picayune, 1925). As late as 1969, the Los Angeles, California, and greater Boston areas were assigned the same level of hazard in seismic zonation maps (Algermissen, 1969).

Extensive archival accounts of the 1886 **M** 7.0–7.2 Charleston and 1906 **M** 7.9 San Francisco earthquakes have been used to determine shaking distributions for each event (Boatwright and Bundock, 2006; Hough and Bilham, 2024) using the modified Mercalli intensity (MMI) scale (Wood and Neumann, 1931). These results provide a modern visualization (Fig. 1) of observations that were appreciated qualitatively at the time. Scientists, including Hill and others, grappled with a conundrum: although earthquakes were thought to be associated with mountain–building and known to be more frequent in California than earthquakes in the east (Hill, 1928), the most widely felt earthquakes over the past century or so had occurred in the central and eastern United States. Although the 1906 earthquake caused significant damage in San Francisco and its environs, its overall felt extent was modest compared to that of the 1886 Charleston earthquake (Fig. 1). Ground motions in general were poorly understood before the advent of strong-motion accelerometers in the early 1930s (Heck, 1934).

Thus was the stage set for 1925, a year when a trio of moderately large earthquakes struck North America (Table 1). All three events were recorded instrumentally at regional to teleseismic distances. However, with the introduction of the magnitude scale (Richter, 1935) still a decade away, the shaking effects of these three earthquakes (discussed in this article) did appear to lend further credence to the argument that seismic hazard in California is not inordinately high relative to the rest of the country (Hill, 1928). Later studies used available instrumental data to determine magnitude values for all three events. Ebel *et al.* (1986) estimated a surface-wave magnitude M_s of 6.4 for the Charlevoix earthquake; Bent (1992) later estimated moment magnitude **M** 6.2, the current catalog value. Doser (1989) estimated **M** 6.6 for the Montana earthquake. Hough and Martin (2018) estimated the Santa Barbara earthquake to be **M** 6.5 from joint consideration of macroseismic intensities and network bulletin data; as of this writing, the accepted U.S. Geological Survey (USGS) catalog magnitude is 6.8 (U.S. Geological Survey, Earthquake Hazards Program [USGS], 2017). In addition to a retrospective summary of a pivotal time for earthquake science in North America, in this report, we summarize what is known about the shaking

TABLE 1
Earthquakes Recorded by the Ottawa Station Between March and September 1925 Inclusively (Adams *et al.*, 2015)

Date and Time (mm/dd hh:mm)	Magnitude (M_L)
03/01 02:19	6.2 (**M**) (mainshock)
03/01 04:30	5.0 (4.6 **M**)
03/01 06:25	4.0
03/01 02:30	4.0
03/01 13:21	3.7
03/07 02:30	4.0
03/14 10:18	3.7
03/17 14:45	3.7
03/18 13:15	3.7
03/21 15:22	5.0 (4.6 **M**)
04/10 09:30	3.0
04/11 11:30	3.0
04/26 04:50	3.7
05/31 03:57	3.0
07/06 21:33	3.7
07/27 02:20	3.7
07/27 09:00	3.0

Times and dates in UTC. The tendency for times to be reported to even multiples of 5 min likely reflects the imprecision of early clocks.

distributions of each of these earthquakes. No strong-motion data exist for any of the earthquakes, which predated the development of strong-motion instrumentation (Heck, 1934). The three earthquakes also predated a program launched by the United States Coast and Geodetic Survey to collect macroseismic data using postcard questionnaires (Byerly and Dyk, 1936). Extensive macroseismic data sets have been compiled, however, for all three events, drawing from archival sources such as newspapers and intensity surveys undertaken following the events (Pardee, 1927; Hodgson, 1950). In addition, Ebel and Hart (2001) compiled detailed accounts of shaking felt across the greater Boston, Massachusetts, region, data that we reconsider here.

Charlevoix, Quebec

The 28 February (LT) 1925 **M** 6.2 Charlevoix, Quebec, earthquake was widely felt throughout eastern Canada and the northeastern United States to more than 1000 km. (e.g., Bruneau and Lamontagne, 1994; Cajka, 1999; Lamontagne, 2020; Lamontagne *et al.*, 2021). In some older reports, this earthquake was also known as the 1925 St. Lawrence earthquake or the 1925 La Malbaie earthquake (Cajka, 1999). This earthquake likely helped motivate the creation of the Eastern Section of the Seismological Society of America in 1926 (see Chiu *et al.*, 1999). The 1925 earthquake also had a profound impact on local populations. Damage to buildings and infrastructure was concentrated in locations underlain by postglacial clay and sand deposits, with damage extending as far as Shawinigan (260 km distance), and on artificial fill in the seaport of Quebec City, at 150 km distance (Hodgson, 1950). In addition to the damage, a sustained aftershock sequence continued to stoke concern among the population (Hodgson, 1950).

Contemporary scientific investigations of the earthquake included a total of six post-earthquake field surveys undertaken by the Canadian Dominion Observatory seismologist E. A. Hodgson (Hodgson, 1950). The first two field excursions focused on identifying the earthquake epicenter and documenting the damage. The last four had more specific goals, such as looking for a suitable site for a seismograph station, but Hodgson made use of these visits to better characterize the effects of the earthquake. The complete set of photographs taken by E. A. Hodgson in the field and some descriptions can be found in Lamontagne (2020). Because of the fear of the adverse impact on industrial investments and tourism in the Province of Quebec (Lamontagne *et al.*, 2021), the scientific report of the earthquake was not released until 1950 (Hodgson, 1950). Even as some in southern California sought to downplay the severity of local earthquake hazard compared to that in the east, local government officials did not want business leaders to believe that Quebec's earthquake risk was similar to that in California (Lamontagne *et al.*, 2021).

The 1925 earthquake was also investigated with early instrumental data. Although there were seismograph records of this earthquake, they were mostly at regional or teleseismic distances (Ebel *et al.*, 1986; Bent, 2009). However, these records were sufficient to determine that the earthquake occurred in the northeast part of the active zone, one of the two subareas where recent earthquakes tend to concentrate (Lamontagne and Ranalli, 1997). To refine the epicenter, Hodgson (1950) used the distribution of damage determined from field surveys. Both the damage distribution and the number of locally felt aftershocks indicated the earthquake had been centered near Charlevoix (Hodgson, 1950). Following the 1935 introduction of the magnitude scale (Richter, 1935), the earliest analysis of seismic data yielded a magnitude estimate of 7 (Gutenberg and Richter, 1954). In retrospect, the estimate was biased by a lack of calibration events for large ENAM earthquakes. Later, Bent (1992) estimated **M** 6.2 from well-calibrated instrumental records.

The Charlevoix seismic zone (CSZ), the focus of extensive modern investigations (e.g., Buchbinder *et al.*, 1988; Lamontagne and Ranalli, 1997; Tuttle and Atkinson, 2010), parallels the St. Lawrence River, and the 1925 earthquake caused damage on both shores of the River. It is now accepted

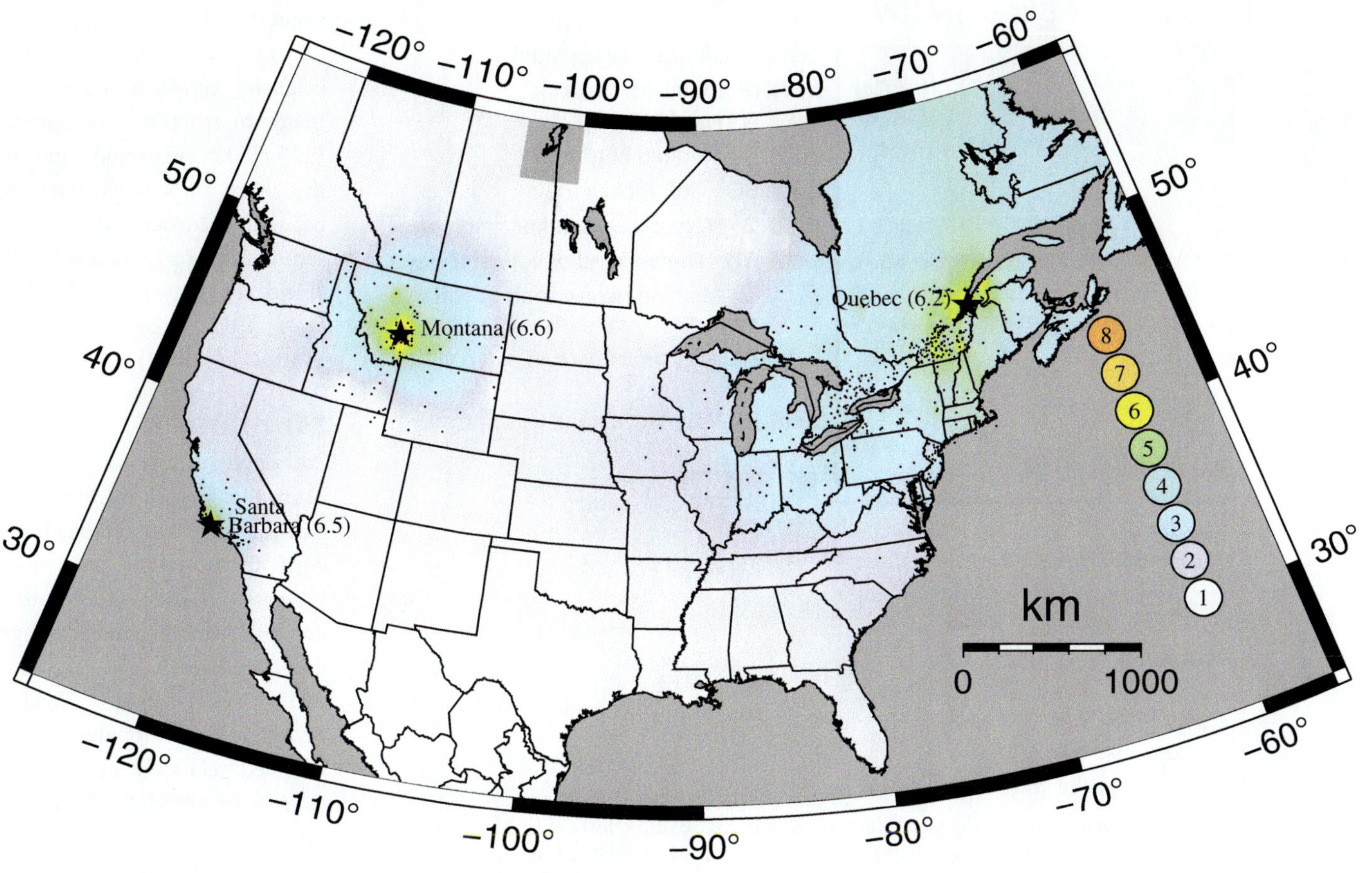

that the epicenter was located in the northeast part of the CSZ with a shallow (~10 km) focal depth (Bent, 2009).

The 1925 earthquake is one of the five earthquakes of magnitude 6 or more to occur in the Charlevoix area during historical times: 1663 **M**~7 to 7.5, 1791 **M**~5.5, 1860 **M**~6, and 1870 **M**~6 to 6.5 (Bent, 2009; Ebel, 2011; Ebel *et al.*, 2013). Because of these damaging earthquakes and the frequent lower magnitude earthquakes, the CSZ is recognized as the most active seismic zone of eastern Canada (Adams *et al.*, 2015).

Macroseismic observations provide the only data to characterize ground motions from the earthquake. Lamontagne *et al.* (2021) reviewed macroseismic data from Canadian felt reports originally compiled by Cajka (1999), expanding the compilation with images of damage and local impact descriptions. Shaking was felt from Newfoundland to the east to Sault Ste. Marie, Ontario, to the west, and as far south as Virginia, more than 1000 km from the epicenter (Lamontagne *et al.*, 2021). Macroseismic data are also useful to characterize the aftershock sequence (Lamontagne *et al.*, 2021). The largest of those were recorded by the Ottawa seismograph, for which their local magnitudes were later estimated to be between 3.7 and 5.0 (the latter corresponds to **M** 4.6; Table 1; Lamontagne *et al.*, 2021).

Given the recency and thoroughness of these studies, we do not revisit intensity assignments, referring the reader to Lamontagne (2020) and Lamontagne *et al.* (2021). Numerical intensity values are available at a total of 639 intensity data points (IDPs) in Canada and the United States. Figure 2 shows the interpolated intensity distribution, generated using a Laplacian operator with a tension factor of 1, with no maxima or minima possible except at control points (see Data and Resources). Unlike USGS ShakeMaps (e.g., Wald *et al.*, 2021) the interpolated intensity field does not consider predicted site response, but provides a good first-hand characterization of the shaking distributions. Because there was no overlap between the felt areas of the three earthquakes considered in this study it is possible to plot all of them on a single map (Fig. 2). The intensity distribution for the Quebec event provides a good characterization of ground motions at local and regional distances, although observations are limited north of the epicenter due to sparse population density.

Figure 2. Contoured shaking intensities (modified Mercalli intensity [MMI]; color scale shown) for the three earthquakes considered in this study: Quebec (1 March), Montana (27 June), and Santa Barbara (28 June). Locations of individual intensity data points (IDPs) are indicated with small black dots. Although the Santa Barbara earthquake caused severe damage locally, the damage was concentrated in an area smaller than the event symbol.

In addition to the overall characterization of intensities, Ebel and Hart (2001) undertook a focused study of shaking felt across the Boston, Massachusetts, area, determined from

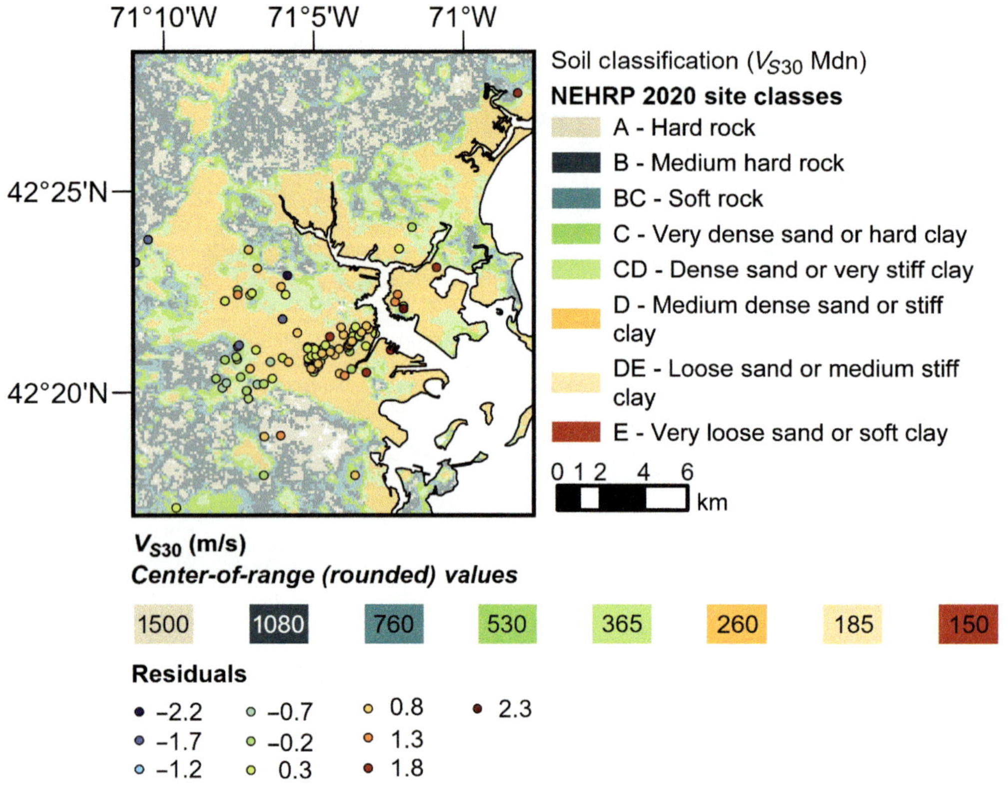

Figure 3. Intensity residuals (directly estimated minus predicted; Ebel and Hart, 2001) for the 1925 Quebec earthquake across the Boston area. Color scale for residuals is from +2.3 (estimated MMI 6.5) to −2.2 (MMI 2). Shaking was generally stronger in parts of Boston, including East Boston (EB), underlain by artificial fill (Ebel and Hart, 2001; Baise *et al.*, 2016; Yilar *et al.*, 2017), with weakly felt shaking in regions underlain by stiffer sediments and rock. NEHRP, National Earthquake Hazards Reduction Program.

site-specific damage reports included in local newspaper articles. The overall estimated intensity level in the Boston area was near 4 (see Fig. 1), but estimated intensities for detailed damage accounts ranged from 2 to 6.5 (Ebel and Hart, 2001). A single value of 6.5 was assigned for a building that reportedly collapsed, with no reports of the collapse of neighboring buildings. Apart from that, damage was limited to a few instances of damage to plaster, indicating MMI 6. Newspaper articles noted that the most severe shaking was concentrated along the Charles River embankment and in other areas underlain by artificial fill (Boston Herald, 1925). Figure 3 presents a map of intensity residuals, defined as observed minus predicted intensity (MMI 4.2; Ebel and Hart, 2001) for the 1925 earthquake across the greater Boston area, using data from Ebel and Hart (2001). Intensities values as high as 5–6 are estimated for locations underlain by National Earthquake Hazards Reduction Program (NEHRP) Class D sediments (see Dobry *et al.*, 2000), with weakly felt shaking (MMI 3–4) in areas underlain by stiffer sediments or rock (Baise *et al.*, 2016; Yilar *et al.*, 2017; Fig. 3). The visualization suggests that the distribution of widely felt weak shaking across the Boston region can be useful for microzonation, as suggested by Ebel and Hart (2001). Differences in shaking intensity across a number of major metropolitan regions in ENAM are expected due to the sharp impedance contrast between bedrock and glacial sediments or artificial fill (Field *et al.*, 1990; Fischer *et al.*, 1995; Baise *et al.*, 2016; Pratt *et al.*, 2017).

Montana

Although estimated to have been the largest of the three earthquakes considered here, with instrumental data analyzed by Doser (1989), the ground motions and damage associated with the 27 June 1925 Clarkston Valley Montana earthquake have received relatively little attention in the modern literature. Stickney (2022) provided an overview of the earthquake and other notable events in Montana. MMI values assigned following modern conventions have not been previously available for the Clarkston Valley earthquake. A 1927 USGS report summarized the damage in some detail (Pardee, 1927). Brick and stone school buildings in several towns close to the epicenter sustained significant damage, with damage in many towns within a radius of ~120 km (75 miles; Pardee, 1927). Damage to school buildings left an estimated 1000 children without school facilities (Bozeman Courier, 1925).

Pardee (1927) assigned intensity values using the Rossi–Forel (RF) scale (de Rossi, 1883). We review and revise assignments using the MMI scale, relying on documented effects on the built environment rather than environmental effects such as rock falls that may not by themselves be reliable indicators of shaking severity (Ambraseys and Jackson, 2003). Table 2 preserves place names and coordinates from Pardee (1927), as well as summary effects, and the ordering of the table (generally sorted by intensity level within states and Canadian provinces). Pardee (1927) gives locations to the nearest arc minute, implying measurement accuracy of 1–2 km. Because the footprints of towns are generally larger than 2 km, and modern town centers may not be the same as historic town centers, we do not attempt to refine IDP locations. We assign numerical MMI values at a total of 154 IDPs, including 36 at which Pardee (1927) indicates a "negative

TABLE 2
Felt Effects of 28 February (LT) 1925 Montana Earthquake (Pardee, 1927)

Location*	Longitude	Latitude	RF	MMI	Summary
Cardinal	111° 22′	46° 7′	9+	8.0	Heavy stove moved, extensive rockfalls.
Stockburger's	111° 20′	46° 8′	9+	9	Furniture in a small house is thrown around violently. Cracks in the ground. Log buildings are distorted.
Deer Park	111° 19′	46° 8′	9+	8.5	Extensive rockfalls and slides. The heavy stove moved. Other furniture in the small house was thrown about.
Garden Gulch	111° 20′	46° 6′	9+	9.5	Loose clods in a plowed field "danced and shuffled about." The stove in the cabin was thrown over. The log cabin sprang out of shape.
Dave Johnsons'	111° 21′	46° 9′	9+	7.5	Ground cracks. All loose objects in a small frame house are thrown about violently.
Lombard	111° 24′	46° 8′	9+	9	Extensive rockfalls. Heavy steel safe in the depot was moved. Swells formed on the railroad track.
Perugin's	111° 22′	46° 15′	9	8	Stove door jerked off.
Clarkston	111° 24′	46° 02′	9+	NA	Ground cracks and sand spout. Visible ground waves.
Jacob's	111° 22′	46° 15′	9	9	The small frame house was distorted. Furniture was thrown about.
Denzer's	111° 23′	46° 17′	9+	8	Doors jerked off their hinges. Furniture, and so forth, thrown about and wrecked. Ground cracks.
Stillman's	111° 17′	46° 04′	9	7.5	All loose articles in a small house are thrown about.
Trident	111° 29′	45° 57′	9	8	All chimneys are broken or thrown down. Cement walls and foundations seriously damaged.
Three Forks	111° 33′	45° 56′	9	8.5	Brick and stone buildings were seriously damaged; some were partially wrecked.
Manhattan	111° 20′	45° 42′	9	8.5	Several brick and stone buildings were seriously damaged; some were partly wrecked.
Logan	111° 26′	45° 53′	9	8.5	The brick schoolhouse was partly wrecked. Chimneys generally overturned.
Toston	111° 26′	46° 10′	9	7.5	Many chimneys were overthrown. Piano moved. Loose objects on the shelves fell.
Mockel's	111° 36′	46° 08′	8+	7.5	Chimneys overthrown.
Madison River Valley	111° 32′	45° 46′	8	7.5	Rock falls. Chimneys overthrown. Cracks opened in the cliffs. Water is thrown out of troughs.
Gallatin Valley	111° 20′	45° 50′	8+	7.5	Chimneys overthrown.
Maudlow	111° 10′	46° 08′	8	7	Some chimneys were overthrown. Loose articles fell from the shelves.
Accola	111° 13′	45° 54′	8+	NA	Rockfalls.
Menard	111° 12′	45° 58′	8+	7.5	Chimneys overthrown.
Radersburg	111° 39′	46° 13′	8+	8.0	Chimneys overthrown. Some brick and stone buildings were seriously damaged.
Walbert's	111° 38′	46° 02′	8+	NA	Visible ground waves. Water is thrown out of the trough.
Doherty's	111° 25′	46° 18′	8+	8.0	A heavy tractor was thrown off of timbers on which it had been blocked up. Chimneys overthrown.
Thompson's	111° 25′	46° 19′	8+	7.0	The doors on a one-story frame house swung violently. Some chimneys overthrown.

MMI, modified Mercalli intensity; NF, not felt report.
*Locations in Montana unless otherwise indicated.
(Continued next page.)

TABLE 2 (continued)
Felt Effects of 28 February (LT) 1925 Montana Earthquake (Pardee, 1927)

Location*	Longitude	Latitude	RF	MMI	Summary
Willow Creek	111° 39′	45° 40′	8+	7.5	The brick schoolhouse was seriously damaged. Some chimneys were overthrown. Plate-glass windows are broken. Visible Earth waves. Goods fell from the shelves.
Steingruber's	111° 39′	45° 53′	8	6	Loose articles thrown about. Rockfalls.
Belgrade	111° 11′	45° 02′	8	7.5	The cornice on the brick schoolhouse fell. Some chimneys were overthrown. Brick and stone walls cracked.
Carroll's	111° 6′	46° 02′	8	6.0	Loose articles thrown from shelves. Chimneys broken.
Helena	112° 0′	46° 36′	7	6.0	Slight damage to some buildings and a few chimneys was wrecked. Loose articles fell from shelves in several stores.
Whitehall	112° 6′	45° 48′	7	6	The top of the two-story brick wall fell off. Chimneys damaged. Some loose articles fell from the shelves. Parked cars rolled back and forth.
Jefferson Island	111° 57′	45° 47′	7	5	Buildings and other objects swayed alarmingly.
Bozeman	111° 03′	45° 41′	7	6.5	A few chimneys were overthrown. A few brick buildings were seriously damaged. Chandeliers swung violently. The heavy steel safe moved a few inches.
White Sulfer Springs	110° 54′	46° 33′	7	7.0	A few brick or stone buildings were seriously damaged. Several chimneys were overthrown. Water splashed out of the trough.
Doggett's	111° 12′	46° 43′	6+	6.0	Buildings swayed. Some chimneys cracked; one fell.
Fort Logan	111° 11′	46° 42′	7	5.0	Buildings swayed alarmingly
House northeast of Bozeman	110° 53′	45° 50′	6+	6.0	Buildings swayed. Some chimneys cracked; one fell.
Clyde Park	110° 37′	45° 53′	7	6.5	The plaster cracked. Some chimneys were overthrown.
Wilsall	110° 39′	46° 00′	6+	5.0	Some loose objects were thrown from the shelves.
Ringling	110° 49′	46° 16′	7	6.0	Cracks in plaster and chimneys.
Canyon Ferry	111° 42′	46° 39′	7+	6.5	Some chimneys were overthrown. Surges on Lake Sewell. Ground cracks. Earth banks fell.
Clancy	111° 58′	46° 28′	7	6.5	Several chimneys were thrown down. The flow of hot springs increased.
Norris	111° 42′	45° 34′	7+	7.0	Chimneys damaged; some overthrown. The school bell rang.
Harrison	111° 48′	45° 42′	7+	6.0	Cement walls cracked. The chimneys were damaged, and plaster cracked. Visible earth waves.
Livingston	110° 34′	45° 40′	6+	6.0	Some chimneys cracked. Loose objects fell.
Eldridge	111° 14′	45° 12′	6	5.0	The log house shook strongly. Loose objects moved or rattled.
Ennis	111° 44′	45° 21′	6	4.5	Hanging lamps swung. A few loose bricks fell from the top of the wall.
Virginia City	111° 56′	45° 18′	6+	6.0	Old stone walls and chimneys cracked. A few chimneys down. The plaster cracked. A few bricks were sheared from the cornices of some buildings.
Twin Bridges	112° 20′	45° 33′	6+	6.5	Several chimneys were damaged and a few were overthrown.
Butte	112° 33′	48° 00′	6+	6.5	Some old brick walls and chimneys are cracked or fallen. Chandeliers swung. Vases and similar objects toppled.
Sieben	112° 08′	45° 54′	6	4.5	The small house was strongly shaken.

MMI, modified Mercalli intensity; NF, not felt report.
*Locations in Montana unless otherwise indicated.
(Continued next page.)

TABLE 2 (continued)
Felt Effects of 28 February (LT) 1925 Montana Earthquake (Pardee, 1927)

Location*	Longitude	Latitude	RF	MMI	Summary
Wolf Creek	112° 04′	47° 01′	5+	4.0	Chandeliers swung.
Drummond	113° 08′	46° 40′	5+	4.0	The house shook. Hanging lamps swung.
Great Falls	111° 17′	47° 30′	5	5.0	Chandeliers swung. A few vases, and so forth, toppled. Buildings swayed.
Neihart	110° 43′	46° 15′	5+	4.5	Loose articles moved but did not topple. Bricks fell from the old chimney.
Belt	110° 56′	47° 22′	5	4.5	Hanging lamps swung. Posts, and so forth, swayed. The old, cracked chimney was torn down.
Barker	110° 37′	47° 04′	5	4.0	Buildings swayed.
Monarch	110° 50′	47° 06′	5	4.5	Posts swayed. Loose articles moved.
Cascade	110° 42′	47° 15′	5	5.0	Loose objects moved. A few articles fell from the shelves.
Anaconda	112° 57′	46° 07′	6	5.5	Buildings swayed; some loose bricks fell. Some dishes and vases were overturned. Cars in garages moved back and forth. Water splashed out of pails. A "dead" motor or railway track moved.
Philipsburg	113° 18′	46° 20′	6	6.0	Buildings swayed alarmingly. Some plaster cracked, and loose bricks were shaken from the tops of some walls. The courthouse clocks stopped.
Columbus	109° 15′	45° 38′	6	6.0	Felt by nearly everyone. Some foundations settled, and some chimneys toppled.
Hutchens′	111° 37′	44° 51′	5	4.5	Hanging pictures shifted awry.
Gardiner	110° 44′	45° 03′	5	4.5	Strong shock. Hanging lamps, and so forth, swung.
Missoula	114° 00′	46° 53′	5	5.5	Generally felt. Hanging lamps swung moderately. A few cracks in plaster.
Superior	114° 59′	47° 12′	4	4.0	Chandeliers swung. Walls creaked. Felt distinctly for several seconds.
Roundup	108° 03′	46° 27′	5	5.0	Felt by nearly everyone indoors and out. Lamps swung. Loose objects moved.
Fort Benton	110° 41′	47° 50′	4	4.0	Felt by several persons outdoors. Loose objects moved. The frame building creaked.
Grangeville, Idaho	111° 03′	45° 50′	4	4.0	Felt by many. Houses creaked and beds "wiggled."
Moscow, Idaho	117° 00′	46° 42′	4	4.0	Hanging lamps swung. Loose objects moved or rattled. Two water pipe connections are broken.
Shelby, Idaho	111° 52′	48° 30′	4	4.0	Felt generally. Hanging lamps and pictures swung. Doors and windows rattled.
Havre, Idaho	109° 40′	48° 33′	4	4.0	Felt by nearly all. Hanging objects swung. Doors and windows rattled.
Cody, Wyoming	109° 03′	44° 33′	4	3.5	Generally felt indoors. Hanging lamps, and so forth, swung.
Salmon, Idaho	113° 53′	45° 10′	4+	4.0	Felt by everyone. Loose objects moved or rattled. Lamps swung.
Mackay, Idaho	113° 37′	43° 56′	3+	3.5	Noticed by several people indoors. Windows, and so forth, rattled slightly.
Nezperce, Idaho	116° 15′	46° 12′	3	3.0	Noticed by several persons indoors. Windows, and so forth, rattled slightly.
Pullman, Washington	117° 11′	46° 44′	3	3.5	Noticed by several persons indoors. Windows rattled.
Malta, Idaho	107° 52′	48° 22′	–	3.0	Noticed by several persons indoors. Hanging lamps swung.
Challis, Idaho	114° 14′	44° 30′	4	4.0	Noticed by nearly everyone indoors. Hanging lamps swung and windows rattled.
Dubois, Idaho	112° 15′	44° 10′	3	3.0	Felt by several persons indoors.

MMI, modified Mercalli intensity; NF, not felt report.
*Locations in Montana unless otherwise indicated.
(Continued next page.)

TABLE 2 (continued)
Felt Effects of 28 February (LT) 1925 Montana Earthquake (Pardee, 1927)

Location*	**Longitude**	**Latitude**	**RF**	**MMI**	**Summary**
Lethbridge, Alberta	112° 52′	49° 43′	3+	3.5	Felt indoors only. Lasted 30 s. Lights and hanging objects in store swayed. Flower pots fell from ledge. Piano moved perceptibly.
Macleod, Alberta	113° 23′	49° 44′	3+	4.0	Felt by many, some outdoors. Hanging objects swung and windows rattled.
Forsyth	106° 38′	46° 16′	4	3.5	Felt on the ground floor. Loose objects moved or rattled.
Baker, Oregon	117° 52′	44° 47′	3	3.5	Felt by several persons indoors only. Chains and saws in the hardware store rattled.
Colfax, Washington	117° 24′	46° 41′	3	3.5	Felt by several persons indoors only. Windows rattled. Bench and bed moved perceptibly.
Medicine Hat, Alberta	110° 40′	50° 00′	2+	3.0	Felt by several persons indoors only. Hanging lamps swayed slightly. People sitting felt a swinging motion.
Cardston, Alberta	113° 20′	49° 11′	3	3.5	Felt by several, some of whom were outdoors. Two tremors felt. Furniture moved "nervously."
Maple Creek, Saskatchewan	109° 27′	49° 55′	2+	3.5	Felt by several persons, some of whom were outdoors.
Swift Current, Saskatchewan	107° 49′	50° 17′	2	2.5	Felt by several indoors only. Slight on the ground floor, fairly distinct on the upper floors. Dishes rattled in the fourth-floor apartment.
Glacier Park	113° 12′	48° 26′	3	3.0	Felt by most indoors. Hanging lamps swung slightly.
Wibaux	104° 11′	46° 41′	2+	2.0	Felt by a few persons on the upper floors. Rocking sensation. Windows rattled.
Casper, Wyoming	106° 17′	42° 52′	2	2.0	Felt on the fifth floor. Loose objects rattled.
Lewiston, Washington	117° 01′	46° 23′	2+	3.5	Felt by a few persons indoors only. Loose objects rattled slightly.
St. Anthony, Idaho	111° 43′	43° 58′	2	2.0	Felt by several persons indoors only.
Weiser, Idaho	116° 58′	44° 15′	3	3.0	Felt by a few people inside. Lamps swung, and loose objects rattled.
Warm Springs	112° 47′	46° 11′	6	5.5	Some brick veneer fell, and some walls cracked.
Hamilton	114° 10′	46° 15′	5+	5.5	Some merchandise was shaken from the shelves. Some plaster cracked. People rushed out.
Kalispell	114° 17′	48° 12′	3+	3.0	Shocks lasting 10 s.
Dillon	112° 38′	45° 14′	6+	5.5	Some plaster fell and dishes were broken. People were alarmed and ran outside.
Lima	112° 36′	44° 38′	5+	4.0	People ran outside.
Miles City	105° 51′	46° 24′	3+	3.5	Pictures and chandeliers swung. Some ran outdoors.
Boise, Idaho	116° 12′	43° 37′	2+	3.0	Slight alarm on the upper floors of hotels.
Sheridan, Wyoming	106° 54′	44° 48′	3+	3.0	Small shock felt in several widely scattered localities.
Thermopolis, Wyoming	108° 12′	43° 38′	3+	3.0	Light shock felt.
Southern Cross	113° 15′	46° 12′	5+	5.0	Water in the pool splashed. A large rock rolled down hill. Trees waved.
Billings	108° 30′	45° 47′	6	5.5	Cracks in some old-brick buildings. Some old-wood-block paving buckled. Mild panic.
Spokane, Washington	117° 25′	47° 40′	2+	2.5	Registered on the seismograph at Gonzaga. Felt in homes and downtown office buildings.
Sand Point, Idaho	116° 32′	48° 17′	3	3.0	Tremors lasting 2 or 3 min.

MMI, modified Mercalli intensity; NF, not felt report.
*Locations in Montana unless otherwise indicated.
(Continued next page.)

TABLE 2 (continued)
Felt Effects of 28 February (LT) 1925 Montana Earthquake (Pardee, 1927)

Location*	Longitude	Latitude	RF	MMI	Summary
Bonners Ferry, Idaho	116° 20′	48° 42′	3	3.0	Tremors lasting 2 or 3 min.
St. Maries, Idaho	116° 33′	47° 19′	3	3.0	Tremors lasting 2 or 3 min.
Carmangay, Alberta	113° 06′	50° 05′	3	3.0	Lasted 15–30 s. Rocking motion felt upstairs in a 1.5-story house.
Taber, Alberta	112° 08′	49° 39′	3	3.0	Lasted 3–4 s. Lights swayed. Counter swayed. The house swayed gently.
Calgary, Alberta	114° 05′	51° 04′	2	2.0	Felt in high buildings only. Clocks stopped.
Moose Jaw, Saskatchewan	105° 32′	50° 24′	2	2.0	Felt by several. Dishes danced on the table on the fourth floor.
East End, Saskatchewan	108° 50′	49° 35′	2	NA	The clock in the railroad station stopped.
Assiniboia, Saskatchewan	106° 00′	49° 41′	3	3.0	Distinct, lasted 8 s.
Regina, Saskatchewan	104° 35′	50° 27′	NF	1.0	Negative report received
High River, Alberta	113° 52′	50° 35′	NF	1.0	Negative report received
Rossland, British Columbia	117° 37′	49° 4′	NF	1.0	Negative report received
Cranbrook, British Columbia	115° 46′	49° 30′	NF	1.0	Negative report received
Culbertson	115° 46′	48° 9′	NF	1.0	Negative report received
Plentywood	104° 35′	48° 46′	NF	1.0	Negative report received
Baker	104° 15′	46° 23′	NF	1.0	Negative report received
Ekalaka, Montana	104° 33′	45° 53′	NF	1.0	Negative report received
Sundance, Wyoming	104° 20′	44° 24′	NF	1.0	Negative report received
Newcastle, Wyoming	104° 10′	43° 52′	NF	1.0	Negative report received
Lander, Wyoming	108° 43′	42° 50′	NF	1.0	Negative report received
Evanston, Wyoming	110° 57′	41° 15′	NF	1.0	Negative report received
Kemmerer, Wyoming	110° 32′	41° 48′	NF	1.0	Negative report received
Green River, Wyoming	109° 28′	41° 32′	NF	1.0	Negative report received
Paris, Idaho	111° 24′	42° 13′	NF	1.0	Negative report received
Montpelier, Idaho	111° 18′	42° 18′	NF	1.0	Negative report received
Preston, Idaho	111° 39′	42° 6′	NF	1.0	Negative report received
Twin Falls, Idaho	114° 49′	42° 34′	NF	1.0	Negative report received
Gooding, Idaho	114° 43′	42° 56′	NF	1.0	Negative report received
Rupert, Idaho	113° 41′	42° 37′	NF	1.0	Negative report received
Idaho Falls, Idaho	112° 4′	43° 29′	NF	1.0	Negative report received
American Falls, Idaho	104° 35′	50° 27′	NF	1.0	Negative report received
Shoshone, Idaho	114° 24′	42° 56′	NF	1.0	Negative report received
Blackfoot, Idaho	112° 21′	43° 11′	NF	1.0	Negative report received
Pocatello, Idaho	112° 26′	42° 52′	NF	1.0	Negative report received
Hailey, Idaho	114° 18′	43° 30′	NF	1.0	Negative report received
Silver City, Idaho	116° 42′	43° 00′	NF	1.0	Negative report received
Council, Idaho	116° 25′	44° 44′	NF	1.0	Negative report received

MMI, modified Mercalli intensity; NF, not felt report.
*Locations in Montana unless otherwise indicated.
(Continued next page.)

TABLE 2 (continued)
Felt Effects of 28 February (LT) 1925 Montana Earthquake (Pardee, 1927)

Location*	Longitude	Latitude	RF	MMI	Summary
Logan, Idaho	111° 50′	41° 45′	NF	1.0	Negative report received
Brigham, Idaho	112° 01′	41° 30′	NF	1.0	Negative report received
La Grande, Oregon	118° 07′	45° 20′	NF	1.0	Negative report received
Enterprise, Oregon	117° 18′	45° 25′	NF	1.0	Negative report received
Pomeroy, Washington	117° 42′	46° 28′	NF	1.0	Negative report received
Walla Walla, Washington	118° 22′	46° 04′	NF	1.0	Negative report received
Dayton, Washington	117° 59′	46° 17′	NF	1.0	Negative report received
Rawlins, Wyoming	107° 14′	41° 47′	NF	1.0	Negative report received

MMI, modified Mercalli intensity; NF, not felt report.
*Locations in Montana unless otherwise indicated.

report," that is, that shaking was not noticed at that location. (Table 2; Fig. 2). Our assigned MMI values are generally comparable to but slightly lower than the Pardee (1927) RF assignments, on average lower by 0.4 units. Shaking from the Montana earthquake was felt throughout six western U.S. states and three Canadian provinces, a felt extent radius of ~600 km (Fig. 2). The intensity distribution (Fig. 2) is asymmetrical, with shaking felt to greater distances in the plains to the east of the earthquake than across the Cordillera to the west. This example shows that the long-noted differences in attenuation across North America (e.g., Nuttli, 1973) can sometimes explain the shaking distributions for individual earthquakes. However, we do note that impressions can be skewed by conventional map projections: the size of the intensity distribution of the Montana earthquake relative to Santa Barbara is distorted on a Mercator-projection map, conveying the impression of an even larger relative felt area.

Santa Barbara

The 29 June 1925 Santa Barbara earthquake occurred approximately 14 hr after the Montana earthquake, leading to speculation even at the time about possible triggering (New York Times, 30 June 1925). Today, scientists recognize the potential for earthquakes to trigger other earthquakes beyond the immediate aftershock zone (e.g., Hill *et al.*, 1992), but without modern data, it remains difficult, if not impossible, to explore a causal relationship between the two events. The Santa Barbara earthquake predated the advent of regional monitoring in Southern California (e.g., Hutton *et al.*, 2010) but was recorded at regional-to-teleseismic distances; Hough and Martin, 2018) estimated a preferred magnitude, effectively a surface-wave magnitude of 6.5 from a combination of macroseismic data and network bulletin data. The Santa Barbara earthquake caused heavy damage to masonry buildings and chimneys in the city of Santa Barbara (Dewell and Willis, 1925), with felt shaking extending over much of southern California (Hough and Martin, 2018). We use the MMI values determined by Hough and Martin (2018), available for a total of 227 IDPs, all within California (Fig. 2). The radius of perceptible shaking (MMI II or greater) was on the order of 300 km, with felt shaking generally limited to distances on the order of 200 km.

Although the Santa Barbara earthquake did not cause damage in the greater Los Angeles area, shaking was strongly felt, and reports of damage were headline news in newspapers across the country (e.g., New York Times, 1925). Earthquake professionals, including Bailey Willis and Harry Wood, capitalized on the opportunity to raise awareness of earthquake risk in the region and the need for building codes (e.g., Geschwind, 2003; Hough, 2020). Following the earthquake, local building codes were adopted by Santa Barbara and Palo Alto, with increased attention to earthquake-resistant design (Geschwind, 2003). The earthquake also provided impetus for the development of the local seismic network, which began in 1927 (Geschwind, 2003). Progress toward wider statewide adoption of building codes stalled out, however, as the severity of the hazard in the greater Los Angeles area continued to be debated (Geschwind, 2003; Hough, 2020).

What's Shaking, North America?

Shaking from the three moderate-to-strong earthquakes in 1925 was reported at some locations in all but 17 of the contiguous 48 U.S. states, and much of southeastern Canada (Fig. 2). In retrospect, the occurrence of these three earthquakes within a single calendar year was unusual. Considering earthquake activity since 1900, California has experienced 26 earthquakes $\mathbf{M} \geq 6.5$, on average once every ~5 yr (USGS, 2017). Six $\mathbf{M} \geq 6.5$ earthquakes have occurred since 1900 in the intermountain west region, an average rate of one every ~21 yr (USGS, 2017). In ENAM, only five $\mathbf{M} \geq 6.0$ earthquakes have occurred between 1900 and 2024 throughout the entire region east of 93° W; of these events, two were well offshore, and one, the 1989 Ungava

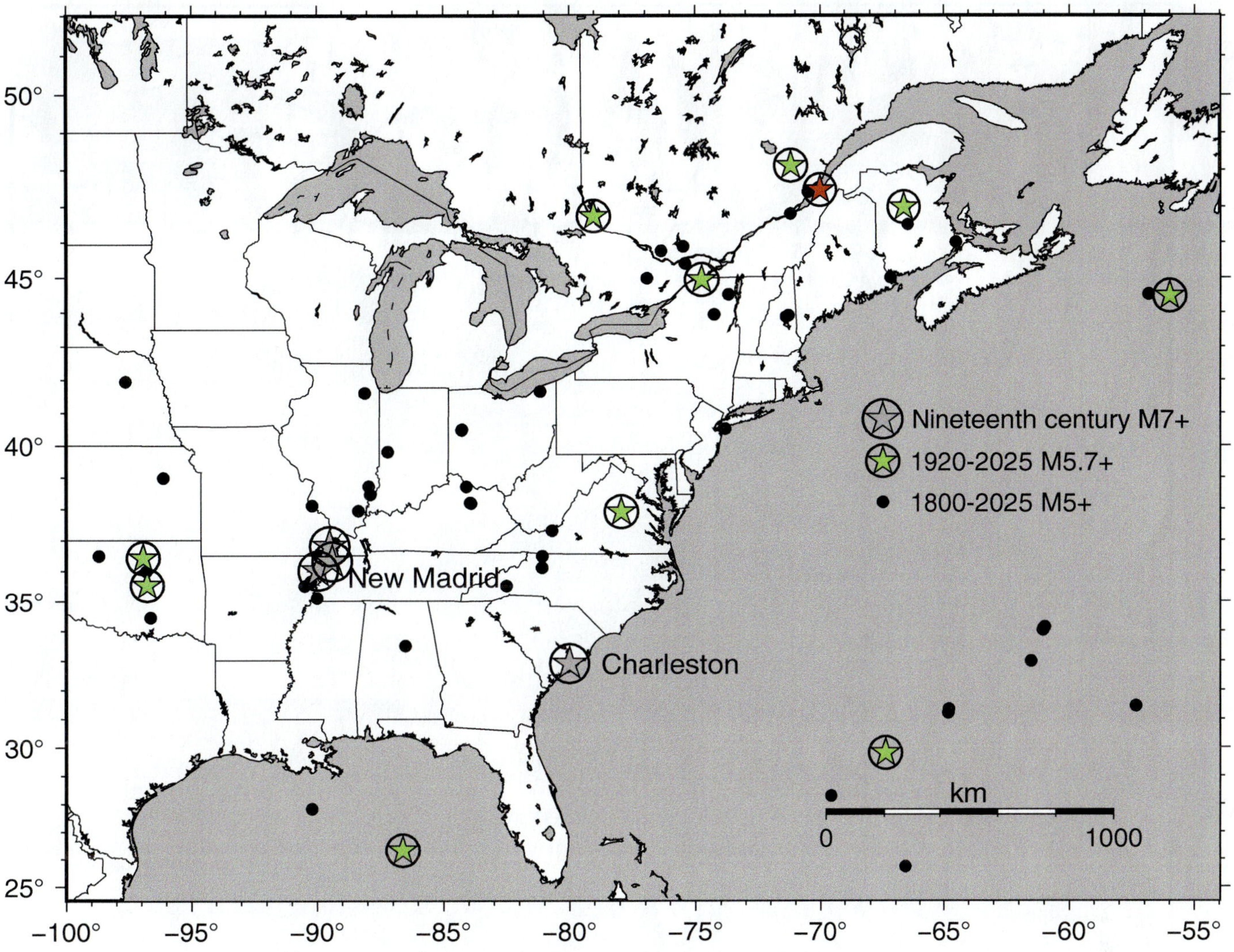

Figure 4. Moderately large earthquakes in the United States and southern Canada, including **M** 5.7+ events since 1920 (circled green stars; red star indicating 1925 Quebec earthquake) for which instrumental data are generally available, large historic events (circled gray stars), and **M** 5+ earthquakes. The map does not distinguish between tectonic events and earthquakes that may have been induced by anthropogenic activities (Keranen *et al.*, 2013).

earthquake (Bent, 1994), was in a northern part of eastern Canada. Going back to 1800, a total of 16 earthquakes have occurred in the map area (Fig. 4) for which modern catalog estimates are **M** ≥ 6.0, eight of which were part of the 1811–1812 New Madrid sequence (USGS, 2017; Fig. 4). Catalog magnitudes for historical events may be overestimated (e.g., Hough and Page, 2011), and in any case are more uncertain than magnitudes of instrumentally recorded earthquakes (Lucas *et al.*, 2023). However, based on past seismicity, one **M** ≥ 6.0 earthquake (including aftershocks) is likely to occur in ENAM every 15–25 yr. Although this number is buoyed by the 1811–1812 New Madrid sequence and the 1886 Charleston earthquake, since 1920, roughly the start of the instrumental era, a total of eight **M** ≥ 5.7 earthquakes have occurred in ENAM east of 95° W longitude, a rate of one every ~13 yr.

Earthquakes above **M** 6 have been reliably catalogued since around 1900 (e.g., Engdahl and Villaseñor, 2002), although earthquakes around and even above **M** 6 escaped detection in remote regions, including the Canadian Arctic which had an estimated detection threshold of **M** 6.8 in 1925 (Lamontagne and Bent, 2021).

Instrumental magnitudes are available for teleseismically recorded events since the late nineteenth century (e.g., Abe, 1994). Varying collections of macroseismic data exist for larger events. The 1999 introduction of the USGS “Did You Feel It?” (DYFI; Wald *et al.*, 1999) system provides a systematic catalog of macroseismic intensities in the United States and southernmost Canada over the past 25 yr. Since 2009, the Geological Survey of Canada has collected felt reports, providing more spatially rich sampling within Canada (see Data and Resources). Over the past 25 yr, as in 1925 alone, earthquakes generated perceptible shaking throughout most U.S. States and Canadian provinces (Quitoriano and Wald, 2020).

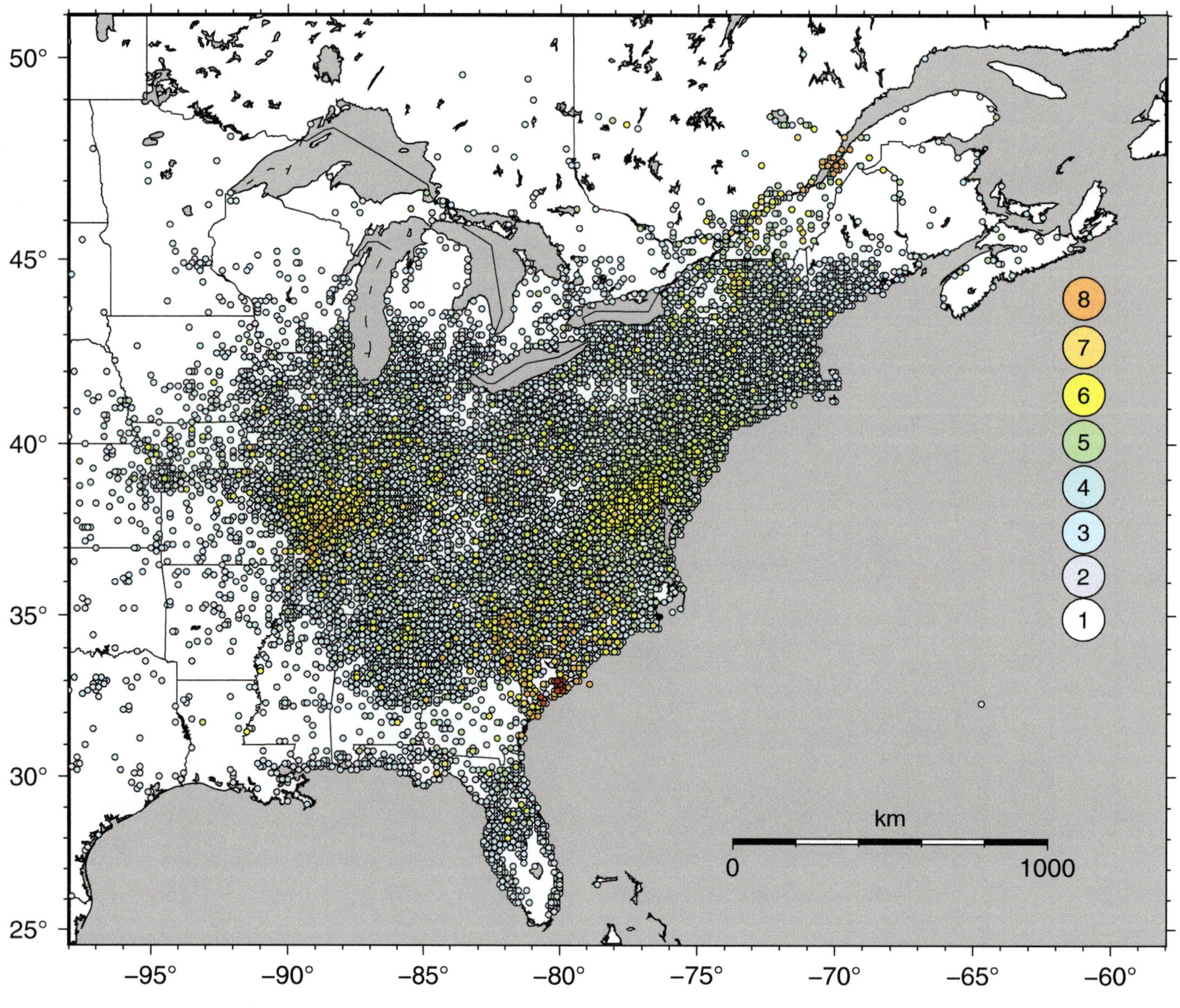

Figure 5. Maximum estimated historical intensities in the eastern United States and southeastern Canada (0.1° grid cells) among the 13 earthquakes listed in Table 3.

At present, there is no systematically compiled and reviewed database of macroseismic intensities for central and ENAM. However, we can consider published intensity distributions for some of the most notable known earthquakes in ENAM (east of 98° W) since 1800 (Table 3). Maximum-estimated intensities within 0.1° grid cells are shown in Figure 5. Figure 5 reveals some of the potential challenges associated with the completeness of a macroseismic database for a low-seismicity region. For example, the 1886 Charleston earthquake likely generated maximum historically felt intensities throughout the State of South Carolina (Hough and Bilham, 2024), but for many grid cells in South Carolina, maximum-estimated intensities were generated by a more moderate regional earthquake in 2020 (Table 3). It is moreover possible that moderate earthquakes have generated the strongest historically observed shaking levels in some regions. A full statistical analysis, as has been done in other regions (Salditch *et al.*, 2024) is therefore expected to be challenging.

Conclusions

We have presented shaking distributions for a trio of damaging earthquakes that occurred in North America in 1925, including an updated distribution for the 27 June 1925 Montana earthquake. A modern consideration of shaking effects illustrates the by-now well-established difference in wave propagation in eastern versus central versus western North America. In 1925, the disparate extents of the three earthquakes lent credence to arguments that earthquake hazard in California was not inordinately high compared to the rest of the country (e.g., Hill, 1928). Although earthquakes as large as the 1925 Quebec event do not occur commonly in ENAM, our consideration of

TABLE 3
Selected Notable North American Earthquakes East of 98° W

Date (yyyy/mm/dd)	M	Location	IDPs	Source of Intensities
1811/12/16	–*	New Madrid (mainshock)	46	Hough and Page (2011)
1811/12/16	–*	New Madrid (aftershock)	86	Hough and Martin (2002)
1812/01/23	–*	New Madrid	49	Hough and Page (2011)
1812/02/07	–*	New Madrid	46	Hough and Page (2011)
1886/09/01	–*	South Carolina	1293	Hough and Bilham (2024)
1895/10/31	–*	Missouri	771	Hough and Martin (2019)
1925/02/27	6.2	Quebec	1014	Lamontagne (2020)
1968/11/09	5.3	Illinois	1288	Hough and Martin (2019)
2002/06/18	4.6	Indiana	2152	DYFI
2008/04/18	5.2	Illinois	3601	DYFI
2011/08/23	5.8	Virginia	8626	DYFI
2020/08/09	5.1	North Carolina	3233	DYFI
2024/04/05	4.8	New Jersey	4393	DYFI

This table includes only instrumentally constrained moment magnitude estimates (Wald *et al.*, 1999). DYFI, "Did You Feel It?"; IDPs, intensity data points.
*Pre-instrumental events.

historically observed intensities reveals that felt shaking has extended over most of the eastern United States over the past ~200 yr, with damaging shaking (MMI ~6 and above) extending across a number of states. However, the combination of low-seismicity rates and low attenuation poses a challenge for the communication of earthquake hazard. Although small-to-moderate felt events such as the 5 April 2020 **M** 4.8 Tewksbury, New Jersey, and 17 December 2023 **M** 4.0 Saint-Boniface, Quebec, earthquakes remind people that earthquakes do occur in their area, experience with weakly felt shaking can lead to a false feeling of security (Chauffeur *et al.*, 2025). This effect is expected to be exacerbated in ENAM, where weakly felt shaking extends over larger areas than in the west. With felt shaking occurring overwhelmingly at weak-to-moderate intensity levels, earthquakes can be perceived to be no worse than occasionally surprising. Anniversaries of notable earthquakes provide opportunities to raise awareness of possible larger and potentially more damaging events.

Data and Resources

Macroseismic data and previously published interpreted intensity values used in this study are from published sources, as cited. Figures 1, 2, 4, and 5 were generated using Generic Mapping Tools (GMT; https://www.generic-mapping-tools.org/, last accessed June 2025), with interpolation using the *surface* module.

Declaration of Competing Interests

The authors acknowledge that there are no conflicts of interest recorded

Acknowledgments

The authors thank Michael Blanpied, Diane Dozer, Shane Detweiller, and Editor-in-Chief Allison Bent for constructive feedback that improved this article and Allison Bent for her continued stewardship of the journal.

Any use of trade, firm, or product names is for descriptive purposes only and does not imply endorsement by the U.S. Government.

References

Abe, K. (1994). Instrumental magnitudes of historical earthquakes, 1892-1898, *Bull. Seismol. Soc. Am.* **84,** no. 2, 415–425, doi: 10.1785/BSSA0840020415.

Adams, J., S. Halchuk, T. Allen, and G. Rogers (2015). Canada's 5th generation seismic hazard model, as prepared for the 2015 National Building Code of Canada, *11th Canadian Conference on Earthquake Engineering*, 21–24.

Alexander, N. S. (1976). *The Father of Texas Geology*, Southern Methodist University Press, Dallas, Texas, 317 pp.

Algermissen, S. T. (1969). Seismic risk studies in the United States, *Fourth World Conference on Earthquake Engineering*, Santiago, Chile, 13–18 January.

Ambraseys, N., and J. A. Jackson (2003). A note on early earthquakes in northern India and southern Tibet, *Curr. Sci.* **84,** no. 4, 570–582.

Baise, L. G., J. Kaklamanos, B. M. Berry, and E. M. Thompson (2016). Soil amplification with a strong impedance contrast: Boston, Massachusetts, *Eng. Geol.* **202,** 1–13, doi: 10.1016/j.enggeo.2015.12.016.

Bent, A. L. (1992). A re-examination of the 1925 Charlevoix, Quebec earthquake, *Bull. Seismol. Soc. Am.* **82,** no. 5, 2097–2113, doi: 10.1785/BSSA0820052097.

Bent, A. L. (1994). The 1989 (Ms 6.3) Ungava, Quebec, earthquake: A complex intraplate event, *Bull. Seismol. Soc. Am.* **84,** no. 4, 1075–1088, doi: 10.1785/BSSA0840041075.

Bent, A. L. (2009). A moment magnitude catalog for the 150 largest eastern Canadian earthquakes, *Geol. Surv. Canada Open-File Rept. 6080*, 23 pp.

Boatwright, J., and H. Bundock (2006). The distribution of modified Mercalli intensity in the 18 April 1906 San Francisco earthquake, *Bull. Seismol. Soc. Am.* **98,** no. 2, 890–900, doi: 10.1785/0120060404.

Boston Herald (1925). Local shocks worst in south Boston, 1 March, pg 1, col 7-8.

Bozeman Courier (1925). 1,000 children are without school facilities, no. 30, pg 1, col. 3, 8 July.

Bruneau, M., and M. Lamontagne (1994). Damage from 20th century earthquakes in eastern Canada and seismic vulnerability of unreinforced masonry buildings, *Can. J. Civil Eng.* **21,** no. 4, 643–662, doi: 10.1139/l94-065.

Buchbinder, G. G. R., A. Lambert, R. D. Kurtz, D. R. Bower, F. M. Anglin, and J. Peters (1988). Twelve years of geophysical research in the Charlevoix seismic zone, *Tectonophysics* **156,** nos. 3/4, 193–224.

Byerly, P., and H. Dyk (1936). The questionnaire program for collection earthquake data, Earthquake Investigations in California, *U.S. Department of Commerce Coast and Geodetic Surv. 1934-1935*, 43–48.

Cajka, M. G. (1999). The 1925 Charlevoix, Quebec earthquake: Re-evaluation of the Canadian intensity data using the Modified Mercalli Scale, *Geol. Surv. of Canada Open-File Rept. 3786*, 70 pp., doi: 10.4095/211009.

Chauffeur, J. M., J. K. Saunders, S. E. Minson, A. S. Baltay, E. S. Cochran, S. E. Hough, V. Quitoriano, M. Page, and J. L. Blair (2025). What 25+ years of "Did you feel it" intensities tell us about shaking in California, *Seismol. Res. Lett.* doi: 10.1785/0220240393.

Chiu, J.-M., G. Atkinson, M. Lamontagne, W. Person, and C. Powell. (1999). History of the eastern section of the Seismological Society of America, available at https://www.seismosoc.org/inside-eastern-section/eastern-section-history/ (last accessed February 2025).

de Rossi, M. S. (1883). Il terremoto dell'isola d'Ischia, *Bollettino della Società Geografica Italiana*, 621–633 (in Italian).

Dewell, H. D., and B. Willis (1925). Earthquake damage to buildings, *Bull. Seismol. Soc. Am.* **15,** no. 4, 282–301, doi: 10.1785/BSSA0150040282.

Dobry, R., R. D. Borcherdt, C. B. Crouse, I. M. Idriss, W. B. Joyner, G. R. Martin, M. S. Power, E. E. Rinne, and R. B. Seed (2000). New site coefficients and site classification used in recent seismic building code provisions, *Earthq. Spectra* **16,** no. 1, 41–67, doi: 10.1193/1.1486082.

Doser (1989). Source parameters of Montana earthquakes (1925-1964) and tectonic deformation in the northern Intermountain Seismic Belt, *Bull. Seismol. Soc. Am.* **79,** no. 1, 31–50, doi: 10.1785/BSSA0780010031.

Ebel, J. E. (2011). A new analysis of the magnitude of the February 1663 earthquake at Charlevoix, Quebec, *Bull. Seismol. Soc. Am.* **101,** 1024–1038.

Ebel, J. E., and K. A. Hart (2001). Earthquake ground motions in Boston & vicinity, Civil Engineering Practice, Fall/Winter, 5–16.

Ebel, J. E., M. Dupuy, and W. H. Bakun (2013). Assessing the location and magnitude of the 20 October 1870 Charlevoix, Quebec earthquake, *Bull. Seismol. Soc. Am.* **103,** no. 1, 589–594, doi: 10.1785/0120110063.

Ebel, J. E., P. G. Somerville, and J. D. McIver (1986). A study of the source parameters of some large earthquakes of northeastern North America, *J. Geophys. Res.* **91,** no. B8, 8231–8247, doi: 10.1029/JB091iB08p08231.

Engdahl, R., and A. Villaseñor (2002). Global seismicity: 1900-1999, *Int. Geophys.* **81,** no. A, 665–690, doi: 10.1016/S0074-6142(02)80244-3.

Field, E. H., S. E. Hough, and K. H. Jacob (1990). Using microtremors to assess potential earthquake site response: A case study in Flushing Meadows, New York City, *Bull. Seismol. Soc. Am.* **80,** no. 6A, 1456–1480, doi: 10.1785/BSSA08006A1456.

Fischer, K. M., L. A. Salvati, S. E. Hough, E. Gonzalez, C. E. Nelson, and E. G. Roth (1995). Sediment-induced amplification in the northeastern United States: A case study in Providence, Rhode Island, *Bull. Seismol. Soc. Am.* **85,** no. 5, 1388–1397, doi: 10.1785/BSSA0850051388.

Geschwind, C. H. (2003) *California Earthquakes: Science, Risk, and the Politics of Hazard Mitigation*, John Hopkins University Press.

Gutenberg, B., and C. F. Richter (1954). *Seismicity of the Earth and Associated Phenomena*. Princeton University Press, Princeton, New Jersey.

Heck, N. H. (1934). On the earthquake strong-motion program, *Seismol. Res. Lett.* **6,** no. 3, 1–7, doi: 10.1785/gssrl.6.3.1.

Hill, D. P., P. A. Reasenberg, A. Michael, J. Arabaz, G. Beroza, D. Brumbaugh, J. N. Brune, R. Castro, S. Davis, D. dePolo, *et al.* (1992). Seismicity remotely triggered by the magnitude 7.3 Landers, California, earthquake, *Science* **260,** no. 5114, 1617–1623, doi: 10.1126/science.260.5114.1617.

Hill, R. T. (1928). Southern California geology and Los Angeles earthquakes, Southern California Academy of Sciences, Los Angeles, California, 100 pp.

Hodgson, E. A. (1950). The Saint Lawrence earthquake, March 1, 1925, Dominion Observatory Publications, Ottawa, Canada, Vol. 7, 361–436.

Hough, S. E. (2020). *The Great Quake Debate*, University of Washington Press, Seattle, Washington, 317 pp.

Hough, S. E., and R. Bilham (2024). The 1886 Charleston, South Carolina, earthquake: Intensities and ground motions, *Bull. Seismol. Soc. Am.* **114,** 1658–1679, doi: 10.1785/0120230224.

Hough, S. E., and S. Martin (2002). Magnitude estimates of two large aftershocks of the 16 December 1811 New Madrid earthquake, *Bull. Seismol. Soc. Am.* **92,** no. 8, 3259–3268, doi: 10.1785/0120010225.

Hough, S. E., and S. Martin (2018). A proposed rupture scenario for the 1925 Mw Santa Barbara, California, earthquake, *Tectonophysics* **747-748,** 211–224, doi: 10.1016/j.tecto.2018.09.012.

Hough, S. E., and S. Martin (2019). Where was the 31 October 1895 Charleston, Missouri, earthquake? *Bull. Seismol. Soc. Am.* **109,** no. 4, 1479–1497, doi: 10.1785/0120180328.

Hough, S. E., and M. Page (2011). Towards a consistent model for strain accrual and release for the New Madrid Seismic Zone, central United States, *J. Geophys. Res.* **116,** no. B3, doi: 10.1029/2010JB007783.

Hutton, K., J. Woessner, and E. Hauksson (2010). Earthquake monitoring in southern California for seventy-seven years (1932-2008), *Bull. Seismol. Soc. Am.* **100,** no. 2, 423–446, doi: 10.1785/0120090130.

Keranen, K., M. Savage, G. A. Abers, and E. Cochran (2013). Potentially induced earthquakes in Oklahoma, USA: Links between wastewater injection and the 2011 Mw 5.7 earthquake sequence, *Geology* **41,** no. 6, 699–702, doi: 10.1130/G34045.1.

Lamontagne, M. (2020). Photographs taken in the field by E. A. Hodgson following the 1925 magnitude 6.2 Charlevoix, Quebec, earthquake, *Geol. Surv. Canada Open-File 8737,* 33 pp., doi: 10.4095/326932.

Lamontagne, M., and A. L. Bent (2021). Earthquakes in the Eastern Canadian Arctic: Past occurrences, present hazard, and future risk, *Seismol. Res. Lett.* **92,** no. 5, 2824–2837, doi: 10.1785/0220210014.

Lamontagne, M., and G. Ranalli (1997). Faults and spatial clustering of earthquakes near La Malbaie, Charlevoix seismic zone, Canada, *Seismol. Res. Lett.* **68,** no. 2, 337–352, doi: 10.1785/gssrl.68.2.337.

Lamontagne, M., K. B. S. Burke, P. Archambault, and L. Olson (2021). Felt reports and damage accounts for the 1925 moment magnitude 6.2 Charlevoix, Quebec earthquake, *Geol. Surv. Canada, Open File 8775,* available at https://publications.gc.ca/collections/collection_2022/rncan-nrcan/m183-2/M183-2-8775-eng.pdf (last accessed March 2025).

Lawson, A. C., A. Cowper, and H. F. Ried. (1908). Report of the State earthquake investigation commission, Carnegie Institution, Washington D.C., Vol. 1, X pp.

Lucas, M. C., S. E. Hough, S. Stein, L. Salditch, M. M. Gallahue, J. S. Neely, and N. Abrahamson (2023). Uncertainties in intensity-based earthquake magnitude estimates, *Seismol. Res. Lett.* **94,** 2202–2214.

New York Times (1925). Severe earthquake wrecks Santa Barbara; hotels collapse; business area in ruins; 12 persons killed; property loss of millions, 30 June, v. LXXIV, no 24,629, pg 1, cols 4-7.

Nuttli, O. W. (1973). Seismic wave attenuation and magnitude relations for eastern North America, *J. Geophys. Res.* **78,** no. 5, 876–885, doi: 10.1029/JB078i005p00876.

Pardee, J. T. (1927). The Montana earthquake of June 27, 1925, *U.S. Geol. Surv. Profess. Pap. 147,* doi: 10.3133/pp147B.

Pratt, T. L., J. W. Horton Jr., J. Muñoz, S. E. Hough, M. C. Chapman, and C. G. Olgun (2017). Amplification of earthquake ground motions in Washington DC, and implications for hazard assessments in central and eastern North America, *Geophys. Res. Lett.* **44,** 12,150–12,160, doi: 10.1002/2017GL075517.

Quitoriano, V., and D. J. Wald (2020). USGS "Did you feel it?"—Science and lessons from 20 years of citizen-based seismology, *Front. Earth Sci.* **8,** 120, doi: 10.3389/feart-08-00120.

Richter, C. F. (1935). An instrumental earthquake magnitude scale, *Bull. Seismol. Soc. Am.* **25,** no. 1, 1–32, doi: 10.1785/BSSA0250010001.

Richter, C. F. (1958). *Elementary Seismology,* W.H. Freeman, San Francisco, California, 568 pp.

Salditch, L., M. M. Gallahue, S. Stein, J. S. Neely, N. Abrahamson, and S. E. Hough (2024). Why do seismic hazard models worldwide appear to overpredict historical intensity observations? *Sci. Adv.* **10,** doi: 10.1126/sciadv.adj9291.

Stickney, M. C. (2022). Earthquakes and seismic monitoring in Montana, Montana Bur. Mines Geol. Special Publication 122: Geology of Montana, v. 2, special topics, available at https://mbmg.mtech.edu/pdf/geologyvolume/StickneyEarthquakesFinal.pdf (last accessed June 2025).

Times-Picayune (1925). Science sees New York City menaced by earthquakes, 18 May, 4 pp., col. 5-6.

Tuttle, M. P., and G. M. Atkinson (2010). Localization of large earthquakes in the Charlevoix Seismic Zone, *Seismol. Res. Lett.* **81,** no. 1, 140–147.

U.S. Geological Survey, Earthquake Hazards Program (USGS) (2017). Advanced National Seismic System (ANSS) comprehensive catalog of earthquake events and products: Various, doi: 10.5066/F7MS3QZH.

Wald, D. J., V. Quitoriano, L. Dengler, and J. W. Dewey (1999), Utilization of the internet for rapid community intensity maps, *Seismol. Res. Lett.* **70,** no. 6, 680–697, doi: 10.1785/gssrl.70.6.680.

Wald, D. J., C. B. Worden, E. M. Thompson, and M. Hearne (2021). ShakeMap operations, policies, and procedures, *Earthq. Spectra* **38,** no. 1, doi: 10.1177/87552930211030298.

Willis, B. (1923). A fault map of California, *Bull. Seismol. Soc. Am.* **13,** no. 1, 1–12, doi: 10.1785/BSSA0130010001.

Wood, H. O. (1916). The earthquake problem in the western United States, *Bull. Seismol. Soc. Am.* **6,** no. 4, 197–217, doi: 10.1785/BSSA0060040197.

Wood, H. O. (1933). Preliminary report on the Long Beach earthquake, *Bull. Seismol. Soc. Am.* **43,** no. 2, 43–56, doi: 10.1785/BSSA0230020043.

Wood, H. O., and F. Neumann (1931). Modified Mercalli intensity scale, *Bull. Seismol. Soc. Am.* **21,** no. 4, 277–283, doi: 10.1785/BSSA0210040277.

Yilar, E., L. G. Baise, and J. E. Ebel (2017). Using H/V measurements to determine depth to bedrock and Vs30 in Boston, Massachusetts, *Eng. Geol.* **217,** 12–22, doi: 10.1016/j.enggeo.2016.12.002.

Manuscript received 8 May 2025
Published online 25 July 2025

Early Macroseismic Intensity Observations, Isoseismal Maps, and Instrumental Recordings of Earthquakes in Mexico (1888–1934): A Review

Max Suter*[1]

Abstract

The macroseismic intensity observations and isoseismal maps by the Observatorio Meteorológico Central de México and the instrumental recordings of earthquakes by the Observatorio Astronómico Nacional, now mostly in oblivion, are a rich data source documenting late nineteenth–early twentieth-century earthquakes in Mexico and Guatemala. During 1877–1912, the meteorological observatory collected macroseismic data through the staff of its weather stations. Between July 1888 and November 1909, the observations were published in the seismology section of the *Boletín del Observatorio Meteorológico-Magnético Central de México* together with isoseismal maps for major earthquakes in southern Mexico and Guatemala such as the 18 April 1902 Guatemala, 23 September 1902 Chiapas, and 13 January 1903 offshore Chiapas earthquakes, and several earthquakes in Guerrero between 1902 and 1908. The Observatorio Astronómico Nacional recorded earthquakes on two Bosch–Omori seismometers (horizontal components) and a Schmidt trifilar gravimeter (vertical component). The readings (time, various phases, period, and amplitude) and the estimated distance of the focus appeared 1905–1908 in the annual catalogs of the International Seismological Association and were published from 1909 on in Mexican earthquake station bulletins. As a part of this review, facsimiles of the seismology sections in the *Boletín del Observatorio Meteorológico-Magnético Central de México* (1888–1909), including its isoseismal maps, as well as descriptive catalogs of Mexican earthquakes before 1888; annual catalogs (1889–1912); contemporary seismicity maps (1858–1927); and earthquake questionnaires (1863–1904) have been deposited in the Open Science Framework (OSF) storage, whereas the early Mexican station bulletins (1909–1934) have been contributed to the Electronic Archive of Printed Station/Network Bulletins recently created by the International Seismological Centre. They will be of value in modern studies of historical earthquakes and to historians of earthquake science.

Cite this article as Suter, M. (2025). Early Macroseismic Intensity Observations, Isoseismal Maps, and Instrumental Recordings of Earthquakes in Mexico (1888–1934): A Review, *Seismol. Res. Lett.* **97**, 564–577, doi: 10.1785/0220250157.

Introduction and Review Outline

The last third of the nineteenth century was in Mexico a time of scientific renovation. Education and research were encouraged by the scientific positivism of the time and became institutionalized during the governments of Benito Juárez and Porfirio Díaz (Saldaña and Azuela, 1994; Trabulse, 1994; Saldaña and Cuevas Cardona, 1999). Several newly created governmental institutions were involved in the study of earthquakes: The Observatorio Meteorológico Central de México (the Mexican national weather service), which was inaugurated in 1877, included a seismology section (Bárcena *et al.*, 1877); the Observatorio Astronómico Nacional, which was established in 1877 (Jiménez and Anguiano, 1877), recorded earthquakes instrumentally as early as 1882; the Instituto Geológico de México, inaugurated in 1891 (Azuela, 2016; Morelos Rodríguez, 2016, 2021, 2022), carried out field studies of

1. Instituto de Geología, Universidad Nacional Autónoma de México (UNAM), Estación Regional del Noroeste, Hermosillo, Mexico, https://orcid.org/0000-0002-8815-1086 (MS)

*Corresponding author: Sutermax@AlumniBasel.ch

earthquakes and eventually was put in charge of the Servicio Sismológico Nacional (Mexican Seismological Service), which was created in April 1908 (Aguilera, 1910).

The major purpose of this article is a review of the contributions to earthquake science by the Observatorio Meteorológico Central de México and the Observatorio Astronómico Nacional. The publications of the meteorological observatory, now mostly in oblivion, are a rich data source documenting late nineteenth–early twentieth-century Mexican earthquakes. During 1877–1912, the observatory collected macroseismic data through the staff of its weather stations. This is the only period with a methodically organized macroseismic data record of Mexican earthquakes, at a time when instrumental earthquake recordings and their analysis were only coming into existence. Between July 1888 and November 1909, the observations were published in the seismology section of the newly created monthly *Boletín del Observatorio Meteorológico-Magnético Central de México* together with isoseismal maps for major earthquakes in southern Mexico and Guatemala such as the 18 April 1902 Guatemala, 23 September 1902 Chiapas, and 13 January 1903 offshore Chiapas earthquakes, as well as several earthquakes in Guerrero between 1902 and 1908 (Table 1). Facsimiles of the seismology sections are included in the supplemental material (see Data and Resources).

This paper also provides an overview of the published early twentieth-century bulletins of seismological stations in Mexico (Table 2), of which facsimiles were provided to the "Electronic Archive of Printed Station/Network Bulletins" created by the International Seismological Centre (di Giacomo *et al.*, 2022) (see Data and Resources). The Observatorio Astronómico Nacional recorded earthquakes with two Bosch–Omori seismometers (east–west and north–south components) and a Schmidt trifilar gravimeter (vertical component). The readings (time, various phases, period, and amplitude) and the estimated distance of the focus were first reported in the annual catalogs of the International Seismological Association from 1905 to 1908 and subsequently published in Mexican earthquake station/network bulletins starting from 1909 (Table 2). Finally, the contemporary interpretations of the data gathered by these two Mexican observatories and the Instituto Geológico de México are also briefly reviewed.

Macroseismic Observations

The Observatorio Meteorológico Central de México (the Mexican national weather service) was inaugurated in 1877, only seven years after the Weather Bureau of the United States, which it tried to emulate. The observatory, which included a seismology section, was headed by Mariano Bárcena from its inauguration until 1899 (Saldaña and Azuela, 1994). Bárcena had a vested interest in earthquake studies (Morelos Rodríguez, 2012); prior to his position at the observatory, he had compiled a regional earthquake catalog for the Colima–Jalisco region (west-central Mexico) (Bárcena, 1875). Bárcena also belonged to the working group that studied the 11 February 1875 continental San Cristóbal, Jalisco, earthquake (Iglesias *et al.*, 1877). In 1879, at a meeting of the Sociedad Mexicana de Historia Natural (Mexican Society of Natural History, founded in 1868), Bárcena made an oral presentation about the periodicity and direction of Mexican earthquakes (Velasco, 1881, p. 156; Trabulse, 1992). After Bárcena died in 1899, the Observatorio Meteorológico Central de México was headed by Manuel Pastrana, who wrote a monograph about the observatory for the St. Louis, Missouri, Universal Exposition of 1904 (Pastrana, 1906).

During 1877–1909, the observatory collected macroseismic data through the skilled staff of its nationwide network of weather stations, many of them being installed at telegraph stations. The observations included the approximate time when the ground motion began, the type of motion, and its intensity and approximate duration (Pastrana, 1906, p. 26). The related 1883 instructions by the observatory, as well as an earlier earthquake questionnaire by the Smithsonian Institution, published in Mexico in 1863, and an 1886 questionnaire, issued by the U.S. Geological Survey (USGS) after the 31 August 1886 Charleston, South Carolina, earthquake (Hough and Bilham, 2024), and reused after the 3 May 1887 M_w 7.5 Sonora, Mexico, earthquake (Aguilera, 1888; Suter, 2006) has been included in the supplemental material (see Data and Resources). In 1903, earthquakes were reported from 65 stations of the nationwide network of weather stations (appendix 2 in Rudolph, 1905). At its peak, in December 1909, the network counted 210 stations.

The Boletín del Observatorio Meteorológico-Magnético Central de México

The macroseismic earthquake observations by the observatory were originally published in the governmental official newspaper *Diario Oficial*, and from 3 July 1877 until 10 July 1886 in the new journal *Boletín del Ministerio de Fomento* (volumes 1–10) (see Data and Resources). Subsequently, from July 1888 until May 1890 and, after a hiatus, again from January 1895 until November 1909, the observations were published in the seismology section of the new monthly *Boletín del Observatorio Meteorológico-Magnético Central de México* (hereupon the *Boletín*).

In a terse statement in the December 1909 issue of the *Boletín*, the weather stations were asked to report their earthquake observations not to the observatory anymore but instead to the Instituto Geológico de México, which published annual catalogs of macroseismic observations in its journal *Parergones* from 1904 until 1912. Apparently, no systematic collection of macroseismic data was undertaken after 1912. The time between 1877 and 1912, therefore, is the only period with a methodically organized macroseismic data record of Mexican earthquakes, at a time when instrumental earthquake recordings and their analysis were still in an early phase of development.

Surprisingly, the earthquake data in the *Boletín* are underutilized, if not unknown, in the more recent literature. Whereas

TABLE 1
Isoseismal Maps of Earthquakes in Mexico and Guatemala by the Observatorio Meteorológico Nacional

Origin (yyyy/mm/dd)	Geographic Location	Reference	Number of Intensity Data Points in the *Boletín*	Location of Extensive Damage	Magnitude	Inferred Source Type
1902/01/16	Guerrero	*Boletín,* Año de 1902, no. 1, after p. 56, plate 7	48; (additional ones for the epicentral region in Böse and Angermann (1904)	Chilapa, Tixtla, Chilpancingo, and Iguala (Böse and Angermann, 1904)	M_l 6.2 (Suárez *et al.*, 2020)	Motion along an east–west-striking fault (Böse and Angermann, 1904). Subduction in-slab earthquake (Suárez *et al.*, 2020)
1902/01/24	Guerrero	*Boletín,* Año de 1902, no. 1, after p. 56, plate 8	33	No major damage	M_l 6.6 (Suárez *et al.*, 2020)	Subduction interface (Suárez *et al.*, 2020)
1902/04/19	Guatemala	*Boletín,* Año de 1902, no. 4, after p. 226, plate 4; Sapper (1902, plate 17)	23; additional ones in Sapper (1902); Eisen (1903); Ambraseys and Adams (2001)	Extensive damage in the San Marcos and Quetzaltenango districts. Sporadic damage extended to Guatemala City	M_s 7.5 (Ambraseys and Adams, 2001)	Subduction zone (White *et al.*, 2004). Macroseismic effects suggest a shallow focus (Ambraseys and Adams, 2001)
1902/09/23	Chiapas	*Boletín,* Año de 1902, no. 10, after p. 507, plate 4; Böse (1903)	31 (mostly far field); additional ones (near field) in Böse (1903)	Zone of major destruction (between San Bartolomé de los Llanos and Acala) is 100 km long and 25 km wide (Böse, 1903)	M_s 7.6 (Ambraseys and Adams, 2001)	Subduction zone (White *et al.*, 2004). Crustal source: (Böse, 1903; Ambraseys and Adams, 2001).
1903/01/14	Off the coast of Chiapas (Gulf of Tehuantepec)	*Boletín,* Año de 1902, no. 3, after p. 186, plate 4	16; additional ones in Rudolph (1905), Sapper (1905), Nishenko and Singh (1987)	No damage	M_s 7.8 (Ambraseys and Adams 2001)	Subduction intraplate (in-slab) (Ambraseys and Adams, 2001)
1907/04/15	Guerrero	*Boletín,* Año de 1907, no. 5, after p. 268	>50; additional ones (epicentral region) in Böse *et al.* (1908)	Devastating in Ayutla, major damage in San Marcos, Chilapa, and Chilpancingo (Böse *et al.*, 1908)	M_w 7.8 ± 0.4; depth: 30 ± 3.9 km (ISC-GEM catalog, version 11, 2024).	Interplate thrust earthquake (Anderson *et al.*, 1989)
1908/03/26	Guerrero-Oaxaca	Miranda y Marrón (1910)	>90; additional ones in Miranda y Marrón (1910)	Destructive in Chilapa and Ometepec (Guerrero) and in Silacayoapan (Oaxaca)	M_w 7.46 ± 0.3; depth: 25 ± 12.2 km (ISC-GEM catalog, version 11, 2024)	Interplate thrust earthquake (Anderson *et al.*, 1989)
1911/06/07	Michoacán	Miranda y Marrón (1912, plate 2)	55 in Instituto Geológico de México (1913); additional ones in García Acosta and Suárez Reynoso (1996)	Devastating in Ciudad Guzmán, Jalisco (Miranda y Marrón, 1912; Castolo, 2011). Moderate-to-severe damage in Mexico City (Rodríguez, 2020)	M_w 7.6 ± 0.4; depth: 30 ± 25.4 km (ISC-GEM catalog, version 11, 2024).	Interplate thrust earthquake (Anderson *et al.*, 1989)

Facsimiles of the isoseismal maps are provided in the supplemental material (see Data and Resources). ISC-GEM, International Seismological Centre–Global Earthquake Model.

TABLE 2
Station Bulletins and Catalogs that Include Mexican Phase Readings (1905–1934)

Period Covered	Reference	Stations Included	Type of Readings	Parameters Calculated
1905	Catalogs of the International Seismological Association (Szirtes, 1909a,b)	TAC	Type of instrument, various phases, time, and duration	Epicentral distance in kilometer and azimuth, and epicenter position (for major earthquakes only)
1906	Catalogs of the International Seismological Association (Szirtes, 1910a,b)	TAC	Type of instrument, various phases, and time	Epicentral distance in kilometer and azimuth, and epicenter position (for major earthquakes only)
1907	Catalogs of the International Seismological Association (Szirtes, 1912a,b)	TAC	Type of instrument, various phases, and time	Epicentral distance in kilometer and azimuth, and epicenter position (for major earthquakes only)
1908	Catalog of the International Seismological Association (Szirtes, 1913)	TAC	Type of instrument, various phases, time, and felt reports	None (catalog of major earthquakes remained unpublished)
1909	Instituto Geológico de México (1909b, 1911a)	TAC	Type of instrument, various phases, time, duration, and amplitude	Distance to focus in kilometer
1910	Instituto Geológico de México (1911b)	TAC, MAZ, and OAX (the latter two from August on)	Type of instrument, various phases, time, duration, and amplitude	Distance to focus in kilometer
1911	Instituto Geológico de México (1912)	TAC	Type of instrument, various phases, time, duration, and amplitude	Distance to focus in kilometer
1911	Instituto Geológico de México (1913)	MAZ, MER, and OAX	Type of instrument, various phases, time, period, duration, and amplitude	Distance to focus in kilometer
1912	Instituto Geológico de México (1914)	MAZ, MER, OAX, and ZAIG	Type of instrument, various phases, time, period, duration, and amplitude	Distance to focus in kilometer
1915/07–1918/03*	*Boletín mensual del Observatorio Meteorológico y Sismológico Central de México*	TAC	Type of instrument, various phases, time, period, duration, and amplitude	Distance to focus in kilometer
1918	*The International Seismological Summary*	TAC	Various phases, and time	Time at origin, epicentral distance in kilometer and azimuth, and epicenter position
1920	*The International Seismological Summary*	TAC, MAZ, OAX	Various phases and time	Time at origin, epicentral distance in kilometer and azimuth, epicenter position, and focal depth
1920	Instituto Geológico de México (1923)	TAC, MAZ, OAX	Type of instrument, various phases, time, period, duration, and amplitude	Distance to focus

These station bulletins are preserved in digital form at the International Seismological Centre (ISC) Electronic Archive of Printed Station / Network Bulletins (see Data and Resources), the ones for 1905–1908 under "Strasbourg," the International Seismological Summary for 1918 and 1920 under "ISC," the remainder under "Mexico City" or "Tacubaya." CHH, Chihuahua; CMX, Colima; GUM, Guadalajara; MAZ, Mazatlán; MER, Mérida; MNZ, Manzanillo; OAX, Oaxaca; PUE, Puebla; VCM, Veracruz; ZAIG, Zacatecas.

*No Mexican station bulletins were published for the periods January 1913–June 1915; August 1915–10 November 1915; and April 1918–December 1919.

†From July 1932 on, additionally the station "La Hacienda de Sta. Barbara," located in the southeastern part of the Mexico City basin (apparently not included in the International Seismograph Station Registry). The initial equipment at TAC was two Bosch–Omori seismometers and a Schmidt trifilar gravimeter. In addition, several Wiechert seismometers were recording from 20 May 1910 on at TAC and eventually also at the other stations.

(Continued next page.)

TABLE 2 (continued)
Station Bulletins and Catalogs that Include Mexican Phase Readings (1905–1934)

Period Covered	Reference	Stations Included	Type of Readings	Parameters Calculated
1921/01–1927/12	*Instituto Geológico de México, Catálogo de los temblores registrados en la Red Sismológica Mexicana*	TAC, CMX (until November 1923), CHH (from October 1927), GUM (from May 1925), MAZ, MER, MNZ (from November 1923), OAX, PUE, and VCM	Type of instrument, various phases, time, period, duration, and amplitude	Distance to focus
1928/01–1934/12	*Universidad Nacional de México, Instituto de Geología, Catálogo de los temblores registrados en la Red Sismológica Mexicana*	TAC, CHH, GUM, MAZ, MER, MNZ, OAX, PUE, and VCM†	Type of instrument, various phases, time, period, duration, and amplitude	Distance to focus, position of the epicenter (from January 1931 on), felt reports

These station bulletins are preserved in digital form at the International Seismological Centre (ISC) Electronic Archive of Printed Station / Network Bulletins (see Data and Resources), the ones for 1905–1908 under "Strasbourg," the International Seismological Summary for 1918 and 1920 under "ISC," the remainder under "Mexico City" or "Tacubaya." CHH, Chihuahua; CMX, Colima; GUM, Guadalajara; MAZ, Mazatlán; MER, Mérida; MNZ, Manzanillo; OAX, Oaxaca; PUE, Puebla; VCM, Veracruz; ZAIG, Zacatecas.
*No Mexican station bulletins were published for the periods January 1913–June 1915; August 1915–10 November 1915; and April 1918–December 1919.
†From July 1932 on, additionally the station "La Hacienda de Sta. Barbara," located in the southeastern part of the Mexico City basin (apparently not included in the International Seismograph Station Registry). The initial equipment at TAC was two Bosch–Omori seismometers and a Schmidt trifilar gravimeter. In addition, several Wiechert seismometers were recording from 20 May 1910 on at TAC and eventually also at the other stations.

this author has incorporated them in his regional catalogs of historical earthquakes for northwestern Mexico (Suter, 2001) and Baja California (Suter, 2018), this data source was, for example, taken into account neither in the catalog of historical Mexican earthquakes by García Acosta and Suárez Reynoso (1996), which reaches up to 1912, nor in the description and evaluation of historical earthquakes felt from 1500 through 1899 in Chiapas (southeastern Mexico) by Feldman (1993) and the catalog of earthquakes in central America and Chiapas (1898–1995) by Ambraseys and Adams (2001). Facsimiles of the seismology sections of the *Boletín* (1888–1909) are included for that reason in the supplemental material (see Data and Resources). They will be of value in modern studies of the earthquakes of that period and to historians of earthquake science.

Other earth science observations included in the *Boletín*

Beginning with its April 1902 issue, the *Boletín* additionally includes, until its January 1903 issue, earthquake observations made by the Laboratorio Químico Central de Guatemala. Chronologically, these follow the macroseismic observations published by the same institution for the years 1898–1902 in their journal *Observaciones Meteorológicas* (see Data and Resources). The *Boletín* also included a catalog of historical earthquakes for the Zapotlán el Grande (now Ciudad Guzmán, Jalisco) region (Arreola, 1894; Suter, 2019) as well as a catalog of the earthquakes recorded at the Puebla Jesuit observatory 1877–1906 (Heredia, 1907; Suter, 2022) (see below).

Besides weather and earthquake observations, the *Boletín* also published information about volcanoes. A new section, "Vulcanología" appeared from December 1895 on with detailed observations of Colima volcano by the two observatories of the Seminario Conciliar in Zapotlán el Grande and Colima (see Data and Resources). These observations were eventually put together in a 1893–1905 catalog presented at the tenth International Geological Congress by Díaz (1907). Worth to be noted are also the reported thickness measurements of the ash spread in Mexico by the October 1902 Plinian eruption of Santa María volcano in western Guatemala and a related isopach map (Anonymous, 1903), a data source that adds, together with related observations in the aforementioned journal *Observaciones Meteorológicas*, to the numerous sources taken into account in the study of this eruption by Berry *et al.* (2021).

Annual catalogs of macroseismic observations in Mexico (1888–1912)

Before the formation of annual catalogs, Orozco y Berra (1888a, b) had compiled an earthquake catalog from prehispanic times to A.D. 1887, which for southern Mexico is mostly based on the unpublished catalog by Martínez Gracida (1886). Subsequently, the monthly earthquake reports by the *Boletín* were assembled into annual catalogs of Mexican earthquakes by Orozco y Berra (1888c) for 1888, Beltrán y Puga and Aguilar y Santillán (1891) for 1889, and Aguilar y Santillán and Beltrán y Puga (1891) for 1890, whereas no annual catalogs seem to exist for the period 1891–1902. A detailed list of Mexican earthquakes during 1903 (entitled "Temblores verificados en la República Mexicana durante el año de 1903, según los datos que obran en el Observatorio Meteorológico Central

Tacubaya") was incorporated into the worldwide earthquake catalog for 1903 by Rudolph (1905). Like the earthquake data reported in the *Boletín*, these annual catalogs are virtually unknown. For example, not even one of them was incorporated in the most detailed descriptive catalog of historical Mexican earthquakes presently available (García Acosta and Suárez Reynoso, 1996). Subsequently, the Instituto Geológico de México catalogued the macroseismic observations of Mexican earthquakes that had occurred 1904–1908 (Instituto Geológico de México, 1909a), mostly based on the information already published in the *Boletín*. Several more annual catalogs of macroseismic observations were assembled by the Instituto Geológico de México for the period 1909–1912 (Instituto Geológico de México, 1909b, 1911a,b, 1913, 1914), when the publication of annual macroseismicity catalogs was discontinued. Because of their difficult availability, these annual catalogs, as well as the prior catalogs by Martínez Gracida (1886) and Orozco y Berra (1888a, b), have been included in the supplemental material (see Data and Resources).

Isoseismal Maps

In addition to listings of macroseismic observations, the *Boletín* also published isoseismal maps for six significant earthquakes between 1902 and 1907 in southern Mexico and Guatemala, such as the 18 April 1902 Guatemala, 23 September 1902 Chiapas, and 13 January 1903 offshore Chiapas earthquakes, as well as several earthquakes in Guerrero between 1902 and 1908 (Table 1). Subsequently, isoseismal maps based on data provided by the Observatorio were published elsewhere for major earthquakes in 1908 (Miranda y Marrón, 1910) and 1911 (Miranda y Marrón, 1912) (Table 1). Facsimiles of these isoseismal maps can be found in the supplemental material (see Data and Resources). Table 1 provides for each of these earthquakes not only the number of intensity data points listed in the *Boletín* and in additional macroseismic data sources but also indicates the location of extensive damage and the source type inferred in the literature. However, an analysis of these legacy isoseismal maps and the underlying macroseismic data is beyond the scope of this review article, and no attempt is made here to discuss the seismotectonic significance of these earthquakes. Suffice it to say that the data and isoseismal maps published in the *Boletín* have not been taken into account in any case study of these earthquakes (Table 1).

Instrumentation and Instrumental Earthquake Recordings

Instrumentation at the Observatorio Meteorológico Central de México

The installation of three vertical pendulum seismoscopes at the newly created Observatorio Meteorológico Central de México in 1877 is reported by Bárcena *et al.* (1877, p. 28). However, the design details, such as the length and period of the instruments, were not provided. In 1890, a Palmieri chrono-seismoscope was added (newspaper *La Voz de México*, 4 December 1890 issue). Several seismoscope tracings were documented graphically in the *Boletín* from 1902 on, and the amplitude and long-axis orientation of the ellipses traced by the pendulum were noted as well as the duration of its motion. The tracings indicate the initial direction of ground motion. However, it is unknown what phase of the earthquake waves is indicated by the pendulum motion and what minimum ground motion was required to trigger the pendulum.

A Mexico City station (besides other North American stations in Victoria, British Columbia; Toronto; Baltimore; and Philadelphia) of the worldwide station network of the British Association for the Advancement of Science (also known as Milne seismograph network) is marked on a map included with the proceedings of the first international seismological conference, held in Strassburg in 1901 (Weigand, 1902) and on the worldwide earthquake district map by Milne (1903). A three-component Milne horizontal seismograph (Dewey and Byerly, 1969) was forwarded to Mexico in 1899 (Milne, 1899). The equipment is included in the inventory of instruments at the Observatorio Meteorológico Central de México in June 1904 by Pastrana (1906, p. 50 and 61). In 1935, this Milne seismograph still appeared in the inventory of the Puebla observatory of the Mexican Seismological Service (Muñoz-Lumbier, 1935, p. 101). However, no station recordings from Mexico are included in the Milne network catalogs for 1899–1903 (Milne, 1911), 1904–1909 (Milne, 1912), and 1910 (Milne, 1913).

Instrumental earthquake observations in Puebla at the Observatorio Astronómico del Colegio Católico del Sagrado Corazón de Jesús

Regular earthquake observations with a vertical pendulum seismoscope began at this Jesuit observatory in Puebla (east-central Mexico) in 1877, in the same year as at the Observatorio Meteorológico Nacional in Mexico City. In 1904, three seismographs were operating at the observatory (Carrasco, 1906). Each recorded the motion traced by a vertical pendulum on a smoked glass (Anonymous, 1905). The observations were continuous until 1914, when the observatory was closed due to the Mexican Revolution (Udías and Stauder, 2002; Udías, 2003). A catalog documents the recordings 1877–1906 (Heredia, 1907) (see supplemental material; Data and Resources), and an updated version extends to 1909 (Heredia, 1910). According to Heredia (1907), the dominant orientation of the recordings is north-northeast–south-southwest, and all the recordings coincide with earthquakes of major intensity in Oaxaca and Guerrero.

Instrumentation at the Observatorio Astronómico Nacional

My summary of the early seismographic instrumentation at the Observatorio Astronómico Nacional is mostly based on the annual reports in their journal *Anuario del Observatorio*

Astronómico (hereupon the *Anuario*), which was published from 1881 on. Originally, astronomers recorded the changes in the orientation of pendulums to track ground motions caused by the gravitational effect of celestial bodies (von Rebeur-Paschwitz, 1892; Schweitzer and Lay, 2019). The French astronomer Anatole Bouquet de la Grye, together with Ángel Anguiano and Felipe Valle of the Observatorio Astronómico Nacional, made for that purpose pendulum recordings at Fuerte de Loreto in Puebla, Mexico, while observing there the transit of Venus on 6 December 1882. Bouquet de la Grye (1884) provides a technical description and a drawing of the seismoscope they used (his séismographe multiplicateur); a pendulum connected to scales with an amplification factor of 56, which Bouquet de la Grye had devised and which he donated to the Observatorio. During their 29 days of observation in Puebla, the team recorded several changes in pendulum orientation that they could not explain by planetary motions and which were consistently oriented northwest–southeast. One of these changes, on 7 December 1882, coincided with an earthquake felt in Puebla, which was also recorded there at the local Jesuit observatory (Heredia, 1907). In 1889, Felipe Valle visited several astronomical observatories in the United States (*Anuario*, 1890, p. 131–310), such as the Lick observatory in California, from which the Observatorio Astronómico Nacional received an Ewing duplex pendulum seismometer for horizontal motion (Holden, 1898, p. 21). In 1896, the Observatorio was invited by Dr. Gerland of the University of Strassburg, Germany (now Strasbourg, France), to cooperate in the formation of an international association for the study of seismic motions (*Anuario*, 1896, p. 240).

From 1904 on, the observatory recorded the east–west and north–south components of earthquakes on two Bosch–Omori seismographs made by the instrument manufacturers J. & A. Bosch in Strassburg (Dewey and Byerly, 1969; Schweitzer and Lee, 2003, their fig. 17), and their vertical component on a Schmidt trifilar gravimeter (Schmidt, 1900, 1902; Sieberg, 1904, p. 219; Muñoz-Lumbier, 1919, p. 29). A rigorous theoretical analysis of these instruments and their response is given by Berlage (1932). It is noteworthy that only very few stations at that time used instruments recording vertical motions (Ou *et al.*, 2025) and, based on the catalogs of the International Seismological Association (Table 2), no other seismological station worldwide used a Schmidt trifilar gravimeter for that purpose. According to Mejía *et al.* (n.d.), some of the seismograms recorded between 1904 and 1908 are preserved at Archivo Histórico de la Universidad Nacional Autónoma de México (Fondo Observatorio Astronómico Nacional, expedientes 101–107). Recently, attempts have been initiated to digitize the legacy analog seismograms preserved in Mexico (Pérez-Campos *et al.*, 2020).

In this context, it is also worth mentioning that the earliest recording of a Mexican earthquake at teleseismic distance seems to be a 2 November 1894 subduction-zone shock near the Pacific coast of southern Mexico (Singh *et al.*, 1981; Suárez *et al.*, 2020), which was recorded at Nicolajew (Ukraine) and in Rome (Italy) (von Rebeur-Paschwitz, 1895, p. 528). The worldwide station network of the British Association for the Advancement of Science (also known as the Milne seismograph network) located Mexican earthquakes 1897–1910 (Milne, 1899, 1911, 1912, 1913).

The Servicio Sismológico Nacional

At the beginning of 1909, the Instituto Geológico de México began to operate the instruments previously used by the Observatorio Astronómico Nacional (Pérez-Campos *et al.*, 2018). New Wiechert instruments, manufactured by Spindler and Hoyer in Göttingen, Germany, were added the same year (Aguilera, 1910). The earliest recordings by Wiechert instruments listed in the station bulletins date from 20 May 1910 (Instituto Geológico de México, 1911b).

The early development of the Servicio Sismológico Nacional (SSN), operated by the Instituto Geológico, was much influenced by political, social, and economic constraints as well as the occurrence of some specific earthquakes. The original network, inaugurated on 5 September 1910, had stations in Mazatlán, Mérida, Oaxaca, Zacatecas, and the central station at Tacubaya, Distrito Federal. It was put to the test by a 7 June 1911 M_w 7.6 subduction zone earthquake (Table 1), which occurred only a few hours before the triumphant entry in Mexico City of the revolutionaries who overthrew President Porfirio Díaz (Posada, 1911). Additional SSN network stations were installed in Guadalajara in 1912 because of an earthquake series in that region (Ordóñez, 1912) and Monterrey in 1913 (Muñoz-Lumbier, 1919). However, recordings from Guadalajara only appear in the network bulletins from 1925 on, and no recordings from Monterrey were ever included within the time range of this study, which ends in 1934 (Table 2).

In 1915, the scientific institutions in Mexico were paralyzed by political and social turmoil. The Instituto Geológico stayed closed between February and September 1915, and most of its research staff were dismissed (Morelos Rodríguez, 2022). From August to November 1915, the central SSN station at Tacubaya remained closed. In an organizational turnaround, the operation of the network was transferred in late 1915 from the Instituto Geológico to the Observatorio Astronómico Nacional, and eventually to the Observatorio Meteorológico, and was mostly limited to the station at Tacubaya (Muñoz-Lumbier, 1923). The transfer of duties to the Servicio Meteorológico likely emulated the organization in the United States, where the Weather Bureau had the official responsibility for earthquake monitoring from the end of 1914 until 1925 (Schweitzer and Lee, 2003, p. 1686).

As a consequence of a major crustal earthquake in the Jalapa, Veracruz region in 1920 (Comisiones del Instituto Geológico de México, 1922), the responsibility for the SSN seismographic network was moved back to the Instituto Geológico, the stations at Guadalajara, Mazatlán, Mérida, and Oaxaca were put back into service, and new stations were added in 1921 at Colima, Puebla, and Veracruz (Table 2). In 1923, the Colima station was moved to Manzanillo. Furthermore, because of the crustal earthquakes that occurred in 1925 in northern Mexico, in the regions of Parral, Chihuahua, and Chalchihuites, Zacatecas (Suter and Morelos-Rodríguez, 2025), a new station was established in the town of Chihuahua in 1927 (Muñoz-Lumbier, 1928).

Early station and network bulletins (1905–1934)

Like the earthquake-related publications of the meteorological observatory, the early Mexican station bulletins are now mostly in oblivion. The bulletins for 1909–1934 have been contributed for that reason to the Electronic Archive of Printed Station/Network Bulletins recently created by the International Seismological Centre (Di Giacomo *et al.*, 2022) (see Data and Resources). For important shocks recorded during that period at the Tacubaya observatory, the parametric data stored in these bulletins are the only record left because their seismograms are missing (Singh *et al.*, 1984, p. 278).

The earliest published parameter readings from the Tacubaya station, such as the onsets of *P*, *S*, and surface waves, and the estimated distance to the focus, were tabulated from 1905 to 1908 in the annual catalogs of the International Seismological Association (Table 2), which was founded in 1904 (Schweitzer and Lay, 2019). From 1909 to 1912, the parameters, now additionally including amplitude readings, were published by the Instituto Geológico de México in their journal *Parergones*, and from 1915 to 1919 by the Observatorio Meteorológico y Sismológico Central de México in their *Boletín* (Table 2). The bulletins also include the instrumental constants for the Bosch–Omori and Wiechert instruments (period, magnification, and damping ratio) (e.g., Instituto Geológico de México, 1911b, p. 547) but not for the Schmidt trifilar gravimeter. They sometimes indicate what seismic travel-time table was used in the calculation of the focal distance. More detailed information about the travel-time tables in use in Mexico at that time can be found in Böse (1909, p. 98–124), Muñoz-Lumbier (1918, p. 39), and Muñoz-Lumbier (1927).

The *International Seismological Summary* (ISS), which was initiated in 1918 (Schweitzer and Lay, 2019), includes for the year 1918 records from Tacubaya but not from any other Mexican station, whereas the ISS for 1919 does not include any Mexican records, not even from Tacubaya. The ISS for 1920 includes records from TAC, MAZ, and OAX (Table 2). From 1920 on, the seismogram parameter readings of the network, as well as the estimated distance from the recording stations to the focus, were published again in annual bulletins by the Instituto Geológico de México, which in 1929 was incorporated into the newly created Instituto de Geología, Universidad Nacional Autónoma de México (Morelos Rodríguez, 2021). From January 1931 on, the bulletins included, for some earthquakes, an estimate of their epicenter location (Table 2). The earliest detailed Mexican seismicity map (Muñoz-Lumbier, 1927) (see supplemental material; Data and Resources) is based on 16 yr of instrumental recordings by the Servicio Sismológico Nacional. Because of the small scale of the map, Muñoz-Lumbier (1927) averaged epicenters located within 10 km of each other into just one event. The map shows 199 earthquake epicenters, each with a reference number. In the explanations that accompany the map, the coordinates and the distance from Tacubaya are provided for each focus.

Early Interpretations of Mexican Earthquakes

A highlight of the late nineteenth-century earthquake research in Mexico is the groundbreaking study of the major 1887 Sonora (Basin and Range Province) earthquake by Aguilera (1888), who mapped its surface rupture and documented its macroseismic intensity distribution with an isoseismal map (facsimiles in Suter, 2006). Trained as an engineer at the School of Mines in Mexico City, Aguilera stayed during the mid-1880s at the Smithsonian Institution in Washington, D.C. He likely was informed about the studies of the 1886 Charleston earthquake by the staff of the USGS, which had its offices there (Yochelson, 1985). Aguilera's study was ahead of his time in many aspects. Based on his geological mapping of the epicentral region (facsimile in Suter, 2007), he realized that the 1887 Sonora earthquake was caused by the reactivation of a normal-fault zone and understood that faulting was the primary earthquake process. He was likely influenced by Gilbert (1884), who had introduced a conceptual spring-block model to explain tectonic earthquakes by the recurrent frictional stick-slip behavior during the growth of faults. Aguilera's surface rupture map shows northward bifurcations of the rupture scarp at many places, from which he inferred a northward direction of rupture propagation (Suter, 2015). The isoseismals he drew are elongated in north-northwest–south-southeast direction, which he explained by directional differences in the intensity attenuation properties of the rocks (Aguilera, 1888, p. 37–38).

The tinted worldwide seismicity distribution map by Mallet (1858), which is based on his catalog with nearly 7000 entries up to A.D. 1842, provides the earliest visualization of the earthquake distribution in Mexico (facsimile in the supplemental material, see Data and Resources). The map already clearly shows the band of seismicity along the Pacific margin of Mexico. de Montessus de Ballore (1892; his plate 2) made a seismicity map of Mexico by graphing the intensity observation points from Orozco y Berra (1888a, b). In an update, de Montessus de Ballore (1900; his plate 2) additionally included data from the *Boletín*. The same plate includes the earliest earthquake zonation map of Mexico, which is based on his quantitative analysis of the intensity observations. Facsimiles of these two maps have been included in the supplemental material (see Data and Resources). In a different approach, Deckert (1902) defined and graphically compared felt areas for several major historical shocks in Mexico. For example, he could show that the felt area of a 24 January 1899 earthquake (Milne, 1899, p. 208) was larger than that of the 16 January 1902 subduction-zone earthquake (Table 1) with focus in the same region. The earliest of the several maps of the worldwide earthquake distribution from instrumental observations made by John Milne is based on the recordings of his network since 1899 (Milne, 1903). On his map, the region of Mexico is defined as earthquake district B, with 14 megaseisms having originated from this district since 1899, and in his catalog for 1899–1903 (Milne, 1911), he provides their epicenters. The map included with his earthquake catalog for 1904–1909 (Milne, 1912) shows numerous epicenters of worldwide recorded Mexican earthquakes, which are tagged with their reference number in the *Shide Register*, the related network bulletin published by the British Association for the Advancement of Science. Facsimiles of these two maps by John Milne have also been included in the supplemental material (see Data and Resources).

In the autumn of 1906, the tenth International Geological Congress took place in Mexico (Puche Riart and Mazadiego Martínez, 2011), only a few months after the 18 April M_w 7.7 San Francisco earthquake, and the congress served as a platform for the presentation of the earliest research results about this earthquake by Andrew Lawson (Anonymous, 1907, p. 145). After a talk by Heilprin (1907) about the concurrence and interrelation of volcanic and seismic phenomena, Harry Reid and Andrew Lawson intervened in the ensuing discussion, recorded in the congress proceedings (Anonymous, 1907, p. 125), and Andrew Lawson explained how the 1872 Inyo (Owens Valley), 1887 Sonora, and 1906 California earthquakes were caused by faulting and did not have any connection with volcanic activity. In his talk about volcanism and seismicity in Mexico, Aguilera (1907) showed an earthquake zonation map (included in the supplemental material; see Data and Resources), for which compilation he gives credit to Ezequiel Ordóñez.

The congress led to significant scientific advances in Mexico. Tacubaya seismograms were contributed to the monographs about the 18 April 1906 M_w 7.7 San Francisco (Reid, 1910) and 16 August 1906 M_w 8.3 Chile (Rudolph and Tams, 1907) earthquakes. These monographs were emulated in a detailed Mexican study of the 14 April 1907 M_w 7.8 Guerrero earthquake (Table 1) by Böse *et al.* (1908), which includes a compilation of worldwide instrumental recordings, a detailed field study of the construction damage in the epicentral region, as well as a regional catalog of the historical seismicity (A.D. 1697–1906), which was also the earliest catalog that gathered information about tsunamis on the Pacific coast of Mexico. Aguilera (1907) and Böse (1909) realized, based on their prior field observations of active continental faults in the Basin and Range Province of Sonora (Aguilera, 1888), in the Rhinegraben (Böse, 1898), and in southern Mexico (Böse, 1903), that the frequent earthquakes along the Pacific margin are not caused by a point source and explained them by a hypothetical offshore fault. A similar hypothesis had been made as early as 1840 by the geologist Charles Darwin to explain the 1835 seaquake in Chile (Darwin, 1840; Oeser, 2003, p. 70; Castaños and Lomnitz, 2013). Eventually, their hypothesis was supported by the discovery of the Middle America trench (Heck, 1924) and became confirmed around the mid-twentieth century, when instrumental earthquake recordings had gained enough spatial resolution to document the cross-sectional geometry of the causative Middle America subduction-zone plate interface (Benioff, 1954).

Conclusions

There is a trove of macroseismic and instrumental data about Mexican earthquakes of the late nineteenth century and early twentieth century created by the Observatorio Meteorológico Central de México (the Mexican national weather service) and the Observatorio Astronómico Nacional that has remained underused, if not outright unknown. In this study, the sources of these data have been reviewed, and facsimiles of most of the data have been made available online (see Data and Resources) to encourage their use. They include the macroseismic intensity observations, isoseismal maps, and instrumental recordings of earthquakes in Mexico and Guatemala by the Observatorio Meteorológico-Magnético Central de México (1877–1909), which were published between July 1888 and November 1909 in the seismology section of the newly created monthly *Boletín del Observatorio Meteorológico-Magnético Central de México*, a data source not taken into account either in recent catalogs of historical earthquakes in Mexico and central America or in modern studies of earthquakes of that period. The early Mexican station/network bulletins (1909–1934), another important major data set, have been contributed to the Electronic Archive of Printed Station/Network Bulletins of the International Seismological Centre.

A highlight of the late nineteenth-century earthquake research in Mexico is the groundbreaking study of the 1887 M_w 7.5 earthquake in the Basin and Range Province of Sonora by Aguilera (1888), who documented its surface rupture and its macroseismic intensity distribution. During the early twentieth century, the instrumental recordings by the Observatorio Astronómico Nacional with two Bosch–Omori seismometers and a Schmidt trifilar gravimeter and the publication of the readings 1905–1908 in the annual catalogs of the International Seismological Association were an important advance. Earthquake research in Mexico was likely encouraged by the tenth International Geological Congress, held in Mexico City only a few months after the 18 April 1906 M_w 7.7 San Francisco earthquake. Tacubaya seismograms were contributed to the monographs about that earthquake and the 16 August 1906 M_w 8.3 Chile earthquake. These analyses were emulated in a detailed Mexican study of the 14 April 1907 M_w 7.8 Guerrero earthquake by Böse *et al.* (1908). Aguilera

(1907) and Böse (1909) realized that the frequent earthquakes along the Pacific margin are not caused by a point source and explained them by a hypothetical offshore fault. A similar hypothesis had already been made by Darwin (1840) to explain the 1835 seaquake in Chile. Eventually, their hypothesis was confirmed by Benioff (1954) when the instrumental recordings had gained enough spatial resolution to document the cross-sectional geometry of the causative Middle America subduction-zone plate interface.

Data and Resources

The data about historical Mexican earthquakes in the supplemental material are available from Open Science Framework (OSF) storage, a free open-source service maintained by the Center for Open Science, at https://osf.io/6xm48/. It includes facsimiles of the earthquake information in the journal *Boletín del Ministerio de Fomento* (1877–1886); major descriptive catalogs of earthquakes prior to 1888 by Martínez Gracida (1886) and Orozco y Berra (1888a, b); the seismology and volcanology sections in the *Boletín del Observatorio Meteorológico-Magnético Central de México* (July 1888–November 1909); the isoseismal maps for major earthquakes in southern Mexico and Guatemala (1902–1911) published in there (Table 1); annual catalogs of the macroseismic observations in Mexico (1889–1912); the seismology sections of the Guatemalan journal *Observaciones Meteorológicas* (1898–1902); the catalog of the earthquakes recorded at the Jesuit observatory in Puebla 1877–1906 (Heredia, 1907); contemporary seismicity maps (1858–1907); technical descriptions of the séismographe multiplicateur designed by Bouquet de la Grye (1884), the pendulum seismoscope designed by Heredia (Anonymous, 1905), and the trifilar gravimeter designed by Schmidt (1900) as well as instrument catalogs by Spindler and Hoyer and J. and A. Bosch; and several earthquake questionnaires issued by the Smithsonian Institution, the U.S. Geological Survey, and the Observatorio Meteorológico Central de México (1863–1904). The early Mexican station bulletins (1909–1934) (Table 2) are preserved in digital form at the Electronic Archive of Printed Station/Network Bulletins of the International Seismological Centre (http://www.isc.ac.uk/printedStnBulletins/index.php) (di Giacomo *et al.*, 2022), the ones for 1905–1908 under "Strasbourg," the ones of the *International Seismological Summary* for 1918 and 1920 under "ISC," the remainder under "Mexico City" or "Tacubaya." Several of the cited publications by the International Seismological Association can be consulted at the website of the International Association of Seismology and Physics of the Earth's Interior (IASPEI) at http://iaspei.org/documents/publications. Facsimiles of the catalogs of the International Seismological Association and the British Association for the Advancement of Science (Milne, 1911, 1912, 1913) are included in the *International Handbook of Earthquake and Engineering Seismology* (Lee *et al.*, 2003) on the Handbook CD #3 (Schweitzer, 2003; Schweitzer and Lee, 2003). The magnitudes in Table 2 are in part from the International Seismological Centre-Global Earthquake Model (ISC-GEM) catalog, version 11, 2024 (di Giacomo *et al.*, 2018), doi: 10.31905/d808b825. All websites were last accessed in April 2025.

Declaration of Competing Interests

The author acknowledges that there are no conflicts of interest recorded with respect to the research, authorship, and/or publication of this article. The author declares that he has no known competing financial interests or personal relationships that could have appeared to influence the work reported in this article.

Acknowledgments

The comments by Associate Editor John Ebel and an anonymous reviewer helped clarify the content. The author is thankful to Lucero Morelos Rodríguez for thought-provoking discussions and for sharing some of the attached source documents. Alfredo Miguel (Instituto de Geología, UNAM) provided a photograph of the 1927 seismicity map by Manuel Muñoz Lumbier. My thanks and appreciation to the staff at the various libraries that made available the data sources included in this review: Biblioteca Nacional de México (Mexico City); University of Arizona Libraries Special Collections (Tucson, Arizona); Universitätsbibliothek Basel (Switzerland); Bibliothek vonRoll (Bern, Switzerland); and Ibero-Amerikanisches Institut (Berlin, Germany).

References

Aguilar y Santillán, R., and G. Beltrán y Puga (1891). Catálogo de los temblores de tierra y fenómenos volcánicos verificados en la República Mexicana durante el año de 1890, *Memorias de la Sociedad Científica "Antonio Alzate"* **4,** 323–329 (in Spanish).

Aguilera, J. G. (1888). Estudio de los fenómenos séismicos del 3 de mayo de 1887, *Anales del Ministerio de Fomento de la República Mexicana* **10,** 5–56 (in Spanish).

Aguilera, J. G. (1907). Les volcans du Mexique dans leurs relations avec le relief et la tectonique générale du pays, *Xème Session du Congrès Géologique International (Mexico, 1906), Compte Rendu*, 1155–1168 and 1:5,000,000 scale volcanotectonic and seismic zonation maps (in French).

Aguilera, J. G. (1910). Rapport préliminaire sur l'établissement du Service Séismologique du Mexique, in *Comptes-rendus des séances de la troisième réunion de la commission permanente de l'Association Internationale de Sismologie*, R. de Kövesligethy (Editor), Hornyánszky, Budapest, Hungary, 106–108 (in French).

Ambraseys, N. N., and R. D. Adams (2001). *The seismicity of Central America. A descriptive catalogue 1898-1995*, Imperial College Press, London, United Kingdom, 309 pp.

Anderson, J. G., S. K. Singh, J. M. Espindola, and J. Yamamoto (1989). Seismic strain release in the Mexican subduction thrust, *Phys. Earth Planet. In.* **58,** 307–322.

Anonymous (1903). La lluvia de cenizas en territorio mexicano, ocurrida los días del 25 al 28 de octubre del año de 1902, motivada por la erupción del 24 del mismo mes, del volcán Santa María, de la República de Guatemala, *Boletín Mensual del Observatorio Meteorológico-Magnético Central de México*, año de **1903,** no. 7, 386–393.

Anonymous (1905). El seismógrafo inventado por el Sr. Pbro. J. Gustavo Heredia, S. J., *Bol. Soc. Astron. Mex.* **40,** 597–599 (in Spanish).

Anonymous (1907). Xème Session du Congrès Géologique International (Mexico, 1906), *Compte Rendu*, 1358 pp. (in French).

Arreola, J. M. (1894). Datos de los temblores, erupciones, lluvias y otros fenómenos notables observados en Zapotlan y referidos al que subscribe por testigos oculares y auriculares, preguntados cuidadosamente, *Boletín Mensual del Observatorio Meteorológico-Magnético Central de México* **3,** 307–308.

Azuela, L. F. (2016). *Towards a Nationwide Geological Survey in Nineteenth Century Mexico*, Geological Society, London, Special Publications 442, 289–301, doi: 10.1144/SP442.11.

Bárcena, M. (1875). Los terremotos de Jalisco, *Boletín de la Sociedad Mexicana de Geografía y Estadística*, 3a época **2,** 240–248 (in Spanish).

Bárcena, M., V. Reyes, and M. Pérez (1877). Boletín Meteorológico del Observatorio Central de México, mes de marzo de 1877, *Anales del Ministerio de Fomento de la República Mexicana* **3,** 5–59 (in Spanish).

Beltrán y Puga, G., and R. Aguilar y Santillán (1891). Catálogo de los temblores de tierra y fenómenos volcánicos verificados en la República Mexicana durante el año de 1889, *Memorias de la Sociedad Científica "Antonio Alzate"* **4,** 179–191 (in Spanish).

Benioff, H. (1954). Orogenesis and deep crustal structure–Additional evidence from seismology, *Geol. Soc. Am. Bull.* **65,** no. 5, 385–400.

Berlage, H. P., Jr (1932). Seismometer, in *Handbuch der Geophysik*, B. Gutenberg (Editor), Vol. 4, Verlag Bornträger, Berlin, Germany, 299–526 (in German).

Berry, H. C., K. V. Cashman, and C. H. Williams (2021). The 1902 Plinian eruption of Santa María volcano: A new assessment of magnitude and impact using historical sources, *J. Volcanol. Geotherm. Res.* **414,** 107167, doi: 10.1016/j.jvolgeores.2020.107167.

Böse, E. (1898). Das Erdbeben in der Gegend von Freiburg am 17. November 1891, *Verhandlungen des naturwissenschaftlichen Vereins zu Karlsruhe* 12**,** 29 pp. (in German).

Böse, E. (1903). *Los temblores de Zanatepec, Oaxaca a fines de septiembre de 1902*, Instituto Geológico de México, Parergones, Vol. 1, 5–19 (in Spanish).

Böse, E. (1909). Die Erdbeben, in *Die Natur (Eine Sammlung naturwissenschaftlicher Monographien)*, W. Schoenichen (Editor), Verlag von A. W. Zwickfeldt, Osterwieck, Harz, Germany, Vol. 7, 146 pp. (in German).

Böse, E., and E. Angermann (1904). *Estudio sobre el temblor del 16 de enero de 1902 en el Estado de Guerrero*, Instituto Geológico de México, Parergones, Vol. 1, 124–131 (in Spanish).

Böse, E., A. Villafaña, and J. García y García (1908). *El temblor del 14 de abril de 1907*, Instituto Geológico de México, Parergones, Vol. 2, 135–258 (in Spanish).

Bouquet de la Grye, A. (1884). Etude sur les déviations du pendule au Mexique, *Comptes Rendus hebdomadaires de séances de l'Académie des sciences* **99,** no. 4, 170–174 (in French).

Carrasco, G. (1906). Observatorio Astronómico del Colegio Católico del Sagrado Corazón de Jesús de Puebla, in *El Servicio Meteorológico de la República Mexicana*, M. E. Pastrana (Editor), Secretaría de Fomento, Mexico City, 86–87 (in Spanish).

Castaños, H., and C. Lomnitz (2013). Charles Darwin and the 1835 Chile earthquake: Prograde ground motion, mountain building, and tsunamis, *Seismol. Res. Lett.* **84,** no. 1, 19–23, doi: 10.1785/0220120072.

Castolo, F. G. (2011). 1911. Documentos sobre la tragedia, Ediciones del Archivo Histórico Municipal de Zapotlán el Grande, Jalisco, Mexico, 99 pp. (in Spanish).

Comisiones del Instituto Geológico de México (1922). *Memoria relativa al terremoto mexicano del 3 de enero de 1920*, Instituto Geológico de México, Boletín, Vol. 38, 106 pp. (in Spanish).

Darwin, C. (1840). On the connexion of certain volcanic phenomena in South America; and on the formation of mountain chains and volcanos, as the effect of the same power by which continents are elevated, *Trans. Geol. Soc. Lond.* **5,** 601–631.

de Montessus de Ballore, F. (1892). México séismico, *Memorias de la Sociedad Científica "Antonio Alzate"* **6,** 49–60 (in Spanish).

de Montessus de Ballore, F. (1900). Le Mexique sismique, in *Archives des Sciences physiques et naturelles (Genève, Switzerland), quatrième période*, Vol. 9, 253–268 (in French).

Deckert, E. (1902). Die Erdbebenherde und Schüttergebiete von Nord-Amerika in ihren Beziehungen zu den morphologischen Verhältnissen, *Zeitschrift der Gesellschaft für Erdkunde zu Berlin* **1902,** 367–389 (in German).

Dewey, J., and P. Byerly (1969). The early history of seismometry (to 1900), *Bull. Seismol. Soc. Am.* **59,** no. 1, 183–227.

Di Giacomo, D., E. R. Engdahl, and D. A. Storchak (2018). The ISC-GEM earthquake catalogue (1904–2014): Status after the extension project, *Earth Syst. Sci. Data* **10,** 1877–1899, doi: 10.5194/essd-10-1877-2018.

Di Giacomo, D., D. Olaru, A. Armstrong, J. Harris, and D. A. Storchak (2022). The ISC electronic archive of printed station and network bulletins, *Seismol. Res. Lett.* **93,** 749–752, doi: 10.1785/0220210262.

Díaz, S. (1907). Efemérides del volcán de Colima según las observaciones practicadas en los observatorios de Zapotlán y Colima de 1893 a 1905, *Xème Session du Congrès Géologique International (Mexico, 1906), Compte Rendu*, 763–960 (in Spanish).

Eisen, G. (1903). The earthquake and volcanic eruption in Guatemala in 1902, *Bull. Am. Geogr. Soc.* **35,** no. 4, 325–352.

Feldman, L. H. (1993). *Mountains of Fire, Lands that Shake. Earthquakes and Volcanic Eruptions in the Historic Past of Central America (1505-1899)*, Labyrinthos, Culver City, California, 295 pp.

García Acosta, V., and G. Suárez Reynoso (1996). *Los sismos en la historia de México*, Vol. 1, Universidad Nacional Autónoma de México, Centro de Investigaciones y Estudios Superiores en Antropología Social, and Fondo de Cultura Económica, Mexico City, 718 pp. (in Spanish).

Gilbert, G. K. (1884). A theory of the earthquakes of the Great Basin, with a practical application, *Am. J. Sci.* **27,** 49–53.

Heck, N. H. (1924). A deep off the coast of Mexico and central America, *Bull. Seismol. Soc. Am.* **14,** no. 3, 200.

Heilprin, A. (1907). The concurrence and interrelation of volcanic and seismic phenomena, *Xème Session du Congrès Géologique International (Mexico, 1906), Compte Rendu*, 187–196.

Heredia, G. (1907). Perturbaciones seísmicas registradas en Puebla, 1877-1906, *Boletín mensual del Observatorio Meteorológico-Magnético Central de México*, año meteorológico de **1907,** no. 2, 90–91 (in Spanish).

Heredia, G. (1910). Catálogo de temblores registrados en el Observatorio Astronómico del Colegio Católico del Sagrado Corazón de Jesús de Puebla, desde 1877 hasta 1909, *La Espiga de Oro, Semanario religioso y literario ilustrado* **2,** no. 9, 24 (in Spanish).

Holden, S. E. (1898). A catalogue of earthquakes on the Pacific coast 1769 to 1897, *Smithsonian Miscellaneous Collections* **37,** 253 pp.

Hough, S. E., and R. Bilham (2024). The 1886 Charleston, South Carolina, earthquake: Intensities and ground motions, *Bull. Seismol. Soc. Am.* **114,** no. 3, 1658–1679, doi: 10.1785/0120230224.

Iglesias, M., M. Bárcena, and J. I. Matute (1877). Informe sobre los temblores de Jalisco, *Anales del Ministerio de Fomento* **1,** 115–204 (in Spanish).

Instituto Geológico de México (1909a). *Catálogo de los temblores (macrosismos) sentidos en la República Mexicana durante los años de 1904 a 1908*, Instituto Geológico de México, Parergones, Vol. 2, 389–467 (in Spanish).

Instituto Geológico de México (1909b). *Catálogo de los temblores (macro y microseismos) sentidos en la República Mexicana durante el primer semestre de 1909*, Instituto Geológico de México, Parergones, Vol. 3, no. 3, 173–199 (in Spanish).

Instituto Geológico de México (1911a). *Catálogo de los temblores (macroseismos) sentidos en la República Mexicana y microseísmos registrado en la Estación Seismológica Central, Tacubaya, D. F., durante el segundo semestre de 1909*, Instituto Geológico de México, Parergones, Vol. 3, no. 8, 435–496 (in Spanish).

Instituto Geológico de México (1911b). *Catálogo de los temblores (macroseismos) sentidos en la República Mexicana y microseismos registrados en la Estación Sismológica Central, Tacubaya, D. F., durante el año de 1910 y en las de Mazatlán y Oaxaca de agosto a diciembre de 1910*, Instituto Geológico de México, Parergones, Vol. 3, 528–587 (in Spanish).

Instituto Geológico de México (1912). *Catálogo de los microseismos registrados en la Estación Seismológica Central durante el año de 1911*, Instituto Geológico de México, Parergones, Vol. 4, 33–85 (in Spanish).

Instituto Geológico de México (1913). *Catálogo de los movimientos registrados en las Estaciones Seismológicas de Mérida, Mazatlán, Oaxaca y de los macroseismos sentidos en la República Mexicana durante el año de 1911*, Instituto Geológico de México, Parergones, Vol. 5, 1–79 (in Spanish).

Instituto Geológico de México (1914). *Catálogo de los seísmos registrados en la Estación Seismológica Central y en las de Mérida, Zacatecas, Oaxaca y Mazatlán, y de los macroseismos sentidos en la República Mexicana durante el año de 1912*, Instituto Geológico de México, Parergones, Vol. 5, 225–349 (in Spanish).

Instituto Geológico de México (1923). Catálogo de los temblores registrados en la Red Sismológica Mexicana durante el año de 1920, Imprenta de la Dirección de Estudios Geográficos y Climatológicos, Tacubaya, Mexico, unpaginated (in Spanish).

Jiménez, F., and A. Anguiano (1877). Memoria sobre el establecimiento del Observatorio Astronómico Central, in *Memoria presentada al Congreso de la Unión por el Secretario de Estado y del Despacho de Fomento, Colonización, Industria y Comercio Vicente Riva Palacio, corresponde al año trascurrido de diciembre de 1876 á noviembre de 1877*, Imprenta de Francisco Díaz de León, Mexico City, 495–513.

Lee, W. H. K., H. Kanamori, P. C. Jennings, and C. Kisslinger (2003) (Editors). *International Handbook of Earthquake and Engineering Seismology*, Academic Press, San Diego, California, part A, p. 1-934 and Handbook CD #1; part B, p 935–1945 and Handbook CDs #2 and #3.

Mallet, R. (1858). Fourth report upon the facts and theory of earthquake phenomena, *Report of the 28th Meeting of the British Association for the Advancement of Science*, 1–136.

Martínez Gracida, M. (1886). Catálogo de terremotos desde 1507 hasta 1885, in *Cuadros sinópticos, geográficos y estadísticos de Oaxaca*, unpublished manuscript dated 15 May 1886, preserved at Biblioteca Pública Central "Margarita Maza de Juárez", Oaxaca, Mexico, 70 pp. (in Spanish).

Mejía, F., C. Siqueiros, D. Zaragoza, and S. Biro (n.d.). *Fondo Observatorio Astronómico Nacional, catálogo, cajas 1-256*, Archivo Histórico de la Universidad Nacional Autónoma de México, Mexico City, unpublished, unpaginated archival inventory (in Spanish).

Milne, J. (1899). Seismological investigations, Fourth Report of the Committee, *Report of the Sixty-Ninth Meeting of the British Association for the Advancement of Science*, 161–238.

Milne, J. (1903). Seismological observations and earth physics, *Geogr. J.* **21,** no. 1, 1–22.

Milne, J. (1911). Seismological investigations – Sixteenth Report of the Seismological Committee, List of earthquakes 1899-1903 inclusive, *Report of the Eightieth Meeting of the British Association for the Advancement of Science*, 30–67.

Milne, J. (1912). Seismological investigations – Seventeenth Report of the Seismological Committee, Seismic activity, 1904 to 1909 inclusive, *Report of the Eighty-Second Meeting of the British Association for the Advancement of Science*, 70–88.

Milne, J. (1913). Seismological investigations – Eighteenth Report of the Seismological Committee, Seismic activity in 1910, *Report of the Eighty-Third meeting of the British Association for the Advancement of Science*, 46–51.

Miranda y Marrón, M. S. A. (1910). Los terremotos del año de 1908, in *Memorias de la Sociedad Científica "Antonio Alzate"*, Vol. 28, 93–153 (in Spanish).

Miranda y Marrón, M. S. A. (1912). El temblor del 7 de junio de 1911, *Memorias de la Sociedad Científica "Antonio Alzate"*, Vol. 32, Mexico, 27–66 (in Spanish).

Morelos Rodríguez, L. (2012). La geología mexicana en el siglo XIX. Una revisión histórica de las obras de Antonio del Castillo, Santiago Ramírez y Mariano Bárcena, Secretaría de Cultura del Estado de Michoacán, Morelia, Michoacán, and Plaza y Valdés Editores, Mexico City, 356 pp. (in Spanish).

Morelos Rodríguez, L. (2016). Brief history of geological and mining exploration in nineteenth century Mexico, in *History of Geoscience: Celebrating 50 Years of INHIGEO*, W. Mayer, R. M. Clary, L. F. Azuela, T. S. Mota, and S. Wołkowicz (Editors), Geological Society, London, Special Publication 442, 303–313, doi: 10.1144/SP442.8.

Morelos Rodríguez, L. (2021). *The Institute of Geology of Mexico and Its Precedents: History and Legacy*, Oxford Research Encyclopedias, Oxford University Press, Latin American History, doi: 10.1093/acrefore/9780199366439.013.656.

Morelos Rodríguez, L. (2022). La Sociedad Geológica Mexicana en sus primeros años (1904-1912), *Bol. Soc. Geol. Mex.* **74,** no. 1, A301121, doi: 10.18268/BSGM2022v74n1a301121 (in Spanish).

Muñoz-Lumbier, M. (1918). La seismología en México hasta 1917, *Bol. Inst. Geol. de Méx.* **36,** 102 pp. (in Spanish).

Muñoz-Lumbier, M. (1919). Descripción histórica de la red sismológica, *Bol. Inst. Geol. de Méx.* **18,** 68 pp. (in Spanish).

Muñoz-Lumbier, M. (1923). Advertencia, in *Instituto Geológico de México, Catálogo de los temblores registrados en la red sismológica mexicana durante el año 1921*, Secretaría de Industria, Comercio y Trabajo, Departamento de Exploraciones y Estudios Geológicos, Tacubaya, Mexico, unpaginated (in Spanish).

Muñoz-Lumbier, M. (1927). *Memoria descriptiva de la Carta sísmica de México (con datos obtenidos hasta 1926)*, 1 map, scale 1:2,000,000,

and explanatory text (16 pp.), Imprenta de la Dirección de Estudios Geográficos y Climatológicos, Tacubaya, Mexico (in Spanish).
Muñoz-Lumbier, M. (1928). La estación sismológica de Chihuahua, in *Instituto Geológico de México. Catálogo de los temblores registrados en la red sismológica mexicana durante el año 1927*, Secretaría de Industria, Comercio y Trabajo, Departamento de Exploraciones y Estudios Geológicos, Tacubaya, Mexico, unpaginated (in Spanish).
Muñoz-Lumbier, M. (1935). *Geografía sísmica con aplicaciones a la República Mexicana. Contribución a la Carta Mundial de Calamidades*, Secretaría de la Economía Nacional, Oficina de Geografía Económica, Mexico City, 126 pp., 2 maps (in Spanish).
Nishenko, S. P., and S. K. Singh (1987). Relocation of the great Mexican earthquake of 14 January 1903, *Bull. Seismol. Soc. Am.* **77,** 256–259.
Oeser, E. (2003). Historische Erdbebentheorien von der Antike bis zum Ende des 19. Jahrhunderts, *Abhandlungen der geologischen Bundesanstalt* (Vienna) **58,** 204 pp. (in German).
Ordóñez, E. (1912). The recent Guadalajara earthquakes, *Bull. Seismol. Soc. Am.* **2,** no. 2, 134–137.
Orozco y Berra, J. (1888a). Efemérides séismicas mexicanas, *Memorias de la Sociedad Científica "Antonio Alzate"* **1,** 303–541 (in Spanish).
Orozco y Berra, J. (1888b). Efemérides séismicas mexicanas, *Memorias de la Sociedad Científica "Antonio Alzate"* **2,** 261–288 (in Spanish).
Orozco y Berra, J. (1888c). Efemérides séismicas mexicanas, *Memorias de la Sociedad Científica "Antonio Alzate"* **2,** 253–260 (in Spanish).
Ou, Q., G. Kulikova, and F. Krüger (2025). Earthquake source parameters determination using analog seismic records, in *Understanding Past Earthquakes*, A. Elliott and C. Gruetzner (Editors), Springer Nature, Switzerland, Cham, doi: 10.1007/978-3-031-73580-6_2.
Pastrana, M. E. (1906). *El Servicio Meteorológico de la República Mexicana, monografía formada para la Exposición Universal de San Louis Missouri por el director del observatorio*, Imprenta y Fototipía de la Secretaría de Fomento, Mexico City, 138 pp. (in Spanish).
Pérez-Campos, X., S. Armendáriz-Sánchez, V. H. Espíndola, M. Castro-Escamilla, J. Pérez, L. M. Casiano, I. Rodríguez Rasilla, C. Cárdenas Monroy, and A. Cárdenas (2020). Preservation and reuse of historical seismic data in Mexico: SISMOMex and the online "National seismogram library," *Seismol. Res. Lett.* **91,** no. 3, 1482–1487, doi: 10.1785/0220190340.
Pérez-Campos, X., V. H. Espíndola, J. Pérez, J. A. Estrada, C. Cárdenas Monroy, D. Bello, A. González-López, D. González Ávila, M. G. Contreras Ruiz Esparza, R. Maldonado, *et al.* (2018). The Mexican national seismological service: An overview, *Seismol. Res. Lett.* **89,** no. 2A, 318–323, doi: 10.1785/0220170186.
Posada, J. G. (1911). *Cantos populares Maderistas. ¡Hasta la tierra tembló!*, Antonio Vanegas Arroyo's printing house, Mexico City, broadsheet (in Spanish), preserved at Ibero-Amerikanisches Institut Preussischer Kulturbesitz, Berlin, Germany, available at https://digital.iai.spk-berlin.de/viewer/image/1012649873/1/#topDocAnchor (last accessed August 2025).
Puche Riart, O., and L. F. Mazadiego Martínez (2011). The 10th International Geological Congress, Mexico (1906), *Episodes* **34,** no. 3, 197–207.
Reid, H. F. (1910). *The California Earthquake of April 18, 1906. Vol. 2, The mechanics of the Earthquake, Report of the State Earthquake Investigation Commission in two volumes and Atlas*, Carnegie Institution of Washington, Washington, D. C., Publication no. 87, Vol. 2, 192 pp.
Rodríguez, M. (2020). 'Tres tamaños temblores' en la memoria de la Ciudad de México, in *Historiar las catástrofes*, M. D. Lorenzo, M. Rodríguez, and D. Marcilhacy (Editors), Universidad Nacional Autónoma de México, Instituto de Investigaciones Históricas, Mexico City, 123–162 (in Spanish).
Rudolph, E. (1905). Katalog der im Jahre 1903 bekannt gewordenen Erdbeben, *Beiträge zur Geophysik, Zeitschrift für physikalische Erdkunde*, Ergänzungsband **3**, XVII and 674 pp. Available at https://www.deutsche-digitale-bibliothek.de (in German).
Rudolph, E., and E. Tams (1907). *Seismogramme des nordpazifischen und südamerikanischen Erdbebens am 16. August 1906*, Zentralbureau der Internationalen Seismologischen Assoziation und kaiserliche Hauptstation für Erdbebenforschung, Straßburg im Elsass, Deutschland (now Strasbourg, France), 98 pp. Available at http://iaspei.org/documents/publications (in German).
Saldaña, J. J., and L. F. Azuela (1994). De amateurs a profesionales. Las sociedades científicas mexicanas en el siglo XIX, Sociedad Mexicana de la Ciencia y de la Tecnología, Quipu, Vol. 11, 135–172 (in Spanish).
Saldaña, J. J., and C. Cuevas Cardona (1999). La invención en México de la investigación científica profesional: El Museo Nacional 1868-1908, Sociedad Mexicana de la Ciencia y de la Tecnología, Quipu, Vol. 12, 309–332 (in Spanish).
Sapper, K. (1902). Das Erdbeben in Guatemala vom 18. April 1902, *Petermanns Geographische Mitteilungen* **48,** no. 9, 193–195 and plate 17 (in German).
Sapper, K. (1905). *In den Vulcangebieten Mittelamericas und Westindiens*, E. Schweizerbartsche Verlagshandlung, Stuttgart, Germany, 334 pp. (in German).
Schmidt, A. (1900). Das Trifilargravimeter, *Beiträge zur Geophysik* **4,** 109–115 (in German).
Schmidt, A. (1902). Das Trifilargravimeter, *Beiträge zur Geophysik*, Ergänzungsband **1**, 254–258 (in German).
Schweitzer, J., (2003). Early German contributions to modern seismology, in *International Handbook of Earthquake and Engineering Seismology*, W. H. K. Lee, H. Kanamori, P. C. Jennings, and C. Kisslinger (Editors), Academic Press, San Diego, California, chapter 79.24, part A, 58 pp. on attached Handbook CD #2.
Schweitzer, J., and T. Lay (2019). IASPEI: Its origins and the promotion of global seismicity, *Hist. Geo Space Sci.* **10,** 173–180, doi: 10.5194/hgss-10-173-2019.
Schweitzer, J., and W. H. K. Lee (2003). Old seismic bulletins to 1920: A collective heritage from early seismologists, in *International Handbook of Earthquake & Engineering Seismology*, W. H. K. Lee, H. Kanamori, P. C. Jennings, and C. Kisslinger (Editors), Academic Press, San Diego, California, part B, 1665–1723 and chapter 88 on attached Handbook CD #3.
Sieberg, A. (1904). *Handbuch der Erdbebenkunde*, Vieweg Verlag, Braunschweig, Germany, 362 pp. (in German).
Singh, S. K., L. Astiz, and J. Havskov (1981). Seismic gaps and recurrence periods of large earthquakes along the Mexican subduction zone: A reexamination, *Bull. Seismol. Soc. Am.* **71,** no. 3, 827–843.
Singh, S. K., M. Rodríguez, and J. Havskov (1984). A catalog of shallow earthquakes of Mexico from 1900 to 1981, *Bull. Seismol. Soc. Am.* **74,** no. 1, 267–279.

Suárez, G., D. Ruiz-Barón, C. Chico-Hernández, and F. R. Zúñiga (2020). Catalog of preinstrumental earthquakes in central Mexico: Epicentral and magnitude estimations based on macroseismic data, *Bull. Seismol. Soc. Am.* **110,** no. 6, 3021–3036, doi: 10.1785/0120200127.

Suter, M. (2001). The historical seismicity of northeastern Sonora and northwestern Chihuahua, Mexico (28-32° N, 106-111° W), *J. South Am. Earth Sci.* **14,** 521–532, doi: 10.1016/S0895-9811(01)00050-5.

Suter, M. (2006). Contemporary studies of the 3 May 1887 M_W 7.5 Sonora, Mexico (Basin and Range Province) earthquake, *Seismol. Res. Lett.* **77,** no. 2, 134–147.

Suter, M. (2007). The first geologic map of Sonora, *Bol. Soc. Geol. Mex.* **59,** 1–7.

Suter, M. (2015). The surface rupture of the 1887 M_W 7.5 Sonora, Mexico earthquake (southern Basin-and-Range Province) along the Pitáycachi fault: Rupture kinematics and epicenter inferred from rupture branching patterns, *J. Geophys. Res.* **120,** 617–641, doi: 10.1002/2014JB011244.

Suter, M. (2018). The historical seismicity of the Loreto region, Baja California peninsula, Mexico (1684-1878), *Seismol. Res. Lett.* **89,** no. 1, 202–209, doi: 10.1785/0220170204.

Suter, M. (2019). Macroseismic study of the devastating 22–23 October 1749 earthquake doublet in the northern Colima graben (trans-Mexican volcanic belt, western Mexico), *Seismol. Res. Lett.* **90,** no. 6, 2304–2317, doi: 10.1785/0220190162.

Suter, M. (2022). The historical seismicity of the Puebla-Tlaxcala region (trans-Mexican volcanic belt) during early Novohispanic times (A.D. 1542–1740) and the structure of the Tlaxcala-Huamantla half-graben, *Seismol. Res. Lett.* **93,** no. 1, 296–314, doi: 10.1785/0220210200.

Suter, M., and L. Morelos-Rodríguez (2025). Seismotectonics of North-Central Mexico (Basin and Range Province) and the 3 April 1925 M_I 4.9 Chalchihuites, Zacatecas, earthquake, *Seismol. Res. Lett.* **96**, no. 4, 2152–2166, doi: 10.1785/0220240475.

Szirtes, S. (1909a). *Katalog der im Jahre 1905 registrierten seismischen Störungen. I. Teil,* Veröffentlichungen des Zentral-Bureaus der Internationalen Seismologischen Assoziation, Serie B, Kataloge, Strassburg, Germany (now Strasbourg, France), 193 pp. (in German).

Szirtes, S. (1909b). *Katalog der im Jahre 1905 registrierten seismischen Störungen. II. Teil,* Veröffentlichungen des Zentral-Bureaus der Internationalen Seismologischen Assoziation, Serie B, Kataloge, Strassburg, Germany (now Strasbourg, France), 68 pp. (in German).

Szirtes, S. (1910a). *Katalog der im Jahre 1906 registrierten seismischen Störungen. I. Teil,* Die schwächeren und weniger ausgeprägten Störungen, Veröffentlichungen des Zentral-Bureaus der Internationalen Seismologischen Assoziation, Serie B, Kataloge, Strassburg, Germany (now Strasbourg, France), 109 pp. (in German).

Szirtes, S. (1910b). *Katalog der im Jahre 1906 registrierten seismischen Störungen. II. Teil, Die grossen und gut ausgeprägten Störungen, Veröffentlichungen des Zentral-Bureaus der Internationalen Seismologischen Assoziation,* Serie B, Kataloge, Strassburg, Germany (now Strasbourg, France), 85 pp. (in German).

Szirtes, S. (1912a). *Katalog der im Jahre 1907 registrierten seismischen Störungen,* Veröffentlichungen des Zentral-Bureaus der Internationalen Seismologischen Assoziation, Serie B, Kataloge, Strassburg, Germany (now Strasbourg, France), 120 pp. (in German).

Szirtes, S. (1912b). Registrierungen der besser ausgeprägten sesmischen Störungen des Jahres 1907, in *Ergänzungen zum mikroseismischen Katalog,* Veröffentlichungen des Zentral-Bureaus der Internationalen Seismologischen Assoziation, Serie B, Kataloge, Strassburg, Germany (now Strasbourg, France), 111 pp. (in German).

Szirtes, S. (1913). *Katalog der im Jahre 1908 registrierten seismischen Störungen,* Veröffentlichungen des Zentral-Bureaus der Internationalen Seismologischen Assoziation, Serie B, Kataloge, Strassburg, Germany (now Strasbourg, France), 132 pp. (in German).

Trabulse, E. (1992). *José María Velasco, un paisaje de la ciencia en México,* Instituto Mexiquense de Cultura, Toluca, Mexico, 332 pp. (in Spanish).

Trabulse, E. (1994). *Historia de la ciencia en México (versión abreviada),* Consejo Nacional de Ciencia y Tecnología and Fondo de Cultura Económica, Mexico City, 542 pp. (in Spanish).

Udías, A. (2003). *Searching the Heavens and the Earth: The History of Jesuit Observatories,* Kluwer Academic Publishers, Dordrecht, The Netherlands, 369 pp.

Udías, A., and W. Stauder (2002). The Jesuit contribution to seismology, in *International Handbook of Earthquake and Engineering Seismology,* W. H. K. Lee, H. Kanamori, P. C. Jennings, and C. Kisslinger (Editors), Academic Press, San Diego, California, 19–27.

Velasco, J. M. (1881). Informe que rinde el primer secretario a la Sociedad Mexicana de Historia Natural de los trabajos presentados en los años de 1879 y 1880, *La Naturaleza* **5,** 149–168 (in Spanish).

von Rebeur-Paschwitz, E. (1892). Das Horizontalpendel und seine Anwendung zur Beobachtung der absoluten und relativen Richtungs-Änderungen der Lothlinie, *Nova Acta der Ksl. Leop.-Carol. Deutschen Akademie der Naturforscher* **60,** no. 1, 216 (in German).

von Rebeur-Paschwitz, E. (1895). Horizontalpendel-Beobachtungen auf der kaiserlichen Universitäts-Sternwarte zu Strassburg 1892-1894, *Beiträge zur Geophysik* **2,** 211–536 (in German).

Weigand, B. (1902). Ausbreitungen der mikroseismischen Beobachtungen, *Beiträge zur Geophysik, Ergänzungsband* **1,** 183–188 (in German).

White, R. A., J. P. Ligorría, and I. L. Cifuentes (2004). Seismic history of the Middle America subduction zone along El Salvador, Guatemala, and Chiapas, Mexico: 1526–2000, in *Natural hazards in El Salvador,* W. I. Rose, J. J. Bommer, D. L. López, M. J. Carr, and J. J. Major (Editors), Geological Society of America, Special Paper 375, Mexico, 379–396.

Yochelson, E. L. (1985). The role and development of the Smithsonian Institution in the American geological community, in *Geologists and Ideas: A history of North American Geology,* Geological Society of America, Centennial Special Vol. 1, 337–354.

Manuscript received 9 May 2025
Published online 15 August 2025

Introducing Novices to Active-Source Seismology via SeismicUnixGui

Juan M. Lorenzo*[1], Mike Hubenthal[2], Nathan W. Benton[3], and Emilio E. Vera[4]

Abstract

Since its origin in 1998, the Incorporated Research Institutions for Seismology Undergraduate Research Internship Program, which has now been integrated into EarthScope, has benefited 262 students, helping them to initiate their careers in research and industry. From 2006 onward, interns have participated in a weeklong introductory program in active-source and earthquake seismology that emphasized field data collection, analysis, and interpretation in the classroom. Here, we describe an active-source seismology experience in which we adopted the well-known 2D, seismic reflection processing software package, Seismic Unix (SU). To encourage critical understanding of the seismic data, within the limited time frame of the instructional program, we created a new graphical user interface (GUI): SeismicUnixGui (SUG). SUG facilitates interactive testing of parameters on visual outputs, with single, mouse-driven clicks. SUG software is free, open-source with cross-platform capability. SUG runs on Linux-based systems such as Ubuntu or the Microsoft Windows Subsystem for Linux. SUG for Windows Desktop and older Apple PC platforms that use Intel processors is distributed as a Docker image. Development of SUG for more recent Apple silicon-based platforms is currently underway. Perl-based software wrappers give access to 290 SU and third-party programs that are used for a range of fundamental signal analysis functions including data format manipulation, integral transforms, seismic-waveform modeling, poststack time migration, and various image displays and manual data picking. SUG enforces a manageable, predefined directory structure to generate shareable bash and Perl scripts, which work independently of the GUI itself. The free, open, and downloadable code is accompanied by an installation manual, a demonstration field data set collected by student interns, and a tutorial with examples of the working scripts employed by the students to process the data during orientation week.

Cite this article as Lorenzo, J. M., M. Hubenthal, N. W. Benton, and E. E. Vera (2025). Introducing Novices to Active-Source Seismology via SeismicUnixGui, *Seismol. Res. Lett.* **97**, 578–584, doi: 10.1785/0220250080.

Supplemental Material

Introduction

During the week-long orientation of the Incorporated Research Institutions for Seismology (IRIS) Undergraduate Research Internship Program, now integrated into EarthScope's "Research Experiences in Solid Earth Sciences for Students" (RESESS; Research Experiences in Solid Earth Sciences for Students [RESESS], 2024), participants keen to gain experience in seismology participated in more than 30 hr of instruction focused on both passive-(~17 hr) and active-source (~15 hr) seismology. Broadband sensors, on loan from the National Science Foundation (NSF) Seismological Facility for the Advancement of Geoscience (SAGE) EarthScope Primary Instrument Center (EPIC) Facility (EarthScope Primary Instrument Center [EPIC], 2024; formerly the Program for Array Seismic Studies of the Continental Lithosphere [PASSCAL] Instrument Center) were deployed by the participants (~3 hr) and the data were recovered several days later. Analysis of the data collected, along with data from the SAGE Facility, used Linux-based commercial software, Jupyter Notebooks, and Python-based libraries (e.g., ObsPy; Beyreuther *et al.*, 2010) to explore regional and whole-Earth structures through a mixture of lecture and hands-on learning opportunities. The active-source instructional component also involved data collection, digital signal analysis, as well as experiment design, and led students to consider the role of shallow structures in the data they had acquired. Over roughly 5 hr, students laid out a static linear array of geophones and conducted a

1. Department of Geology and Geophysics, Louisiana State University, Baton Rouge, Louisiana, U.S.A.; 2. EarthScope Corporate Headquarters, Washington, D.C., U.S.A., https://orcid.org/0000-0002-2790-7054 (MH); 3. Department of Geology and Geophysics, Louisiana State University, Baton Rouge, Louisiana, U.S.A.; 4. Facultad de Ciencias Físicas y Matemáticas, Universidad de Chile, Santiago, Chile

*Corresponding author: gllore@lsu.edu

TABLE 1

Between 2017 and 2023 Collection of Student Responses Guided and Drove Development of the SeismicUnixGui (SUG)

Questionnaire Results on Usage of SUG				
Question and Sample Size (*n*)	**Yes**	**A Little (%)**	**A Lot (%)**	**The Same (%)**
The active-source experiment is one of the best parts of the orientation week (*n*-54)	56%			
My understanding of seismic data collection (station install and active-source collection) has improved (*n*-52)		33	62	5
My understanding of reflection and refraction theory (reflection coefficient, attenuation, resolution, etc.) has improved (*n*-52)		56	27	17
My ability to analyze reflection data in Seismic Unix (SU) has improved (*n*-51)		49	31	20

Years 2021 and 2022 were not held because of COVID.

simplified, horizontal shear-wave (S_H), common-midpoint seismic reflection survey.

Near-surface seismology has numerous applications, including studying the relationship between regional weathering patterns and stress fields (St. Clair *et al.* 2015), and geotechnical and engineering problems (Miller *et al.* 2010), such as seismic analysis of dams (Butler *et al.* 2019) and levees (Lorenzo *et al.* 2014, Wodajo *et al.* 2019), and seismic site characterization (e.g., Parolai *et al.*, 2022). Because the active seismology component of the instruction targeted the upper 40 m of the subsurface, postacquisition data processing and interpretation commonly led to discussions of near-surface processes in the upper-most portion of the critical zone (Slater *et al.* 2006).

Since inception, instruction on the analysis of active-source seismic data has transitioned from early use of commercial software toward the adoption of free and open-source software. Commercial packages, although fully featured, included content that far exceeded the instructional needs of this orientation week. As a result, in 2014 we began to use Seismic Unix (SU; Stockwell, 1999), the well-known 2D, seismic reflection processing software package that runs under a Linux-family operating system (OS). The highly modular and reliable nature of the SU package requires writing shell scripts (e.g., using the bash language) to run small independent programs and exchange output via standard input and output line commands from any Linux OS. Although extensive documentation and instructional materials exist for SU (Forel *et al.*, 2005), shell-scripted workflows remain difficult for novice students, generally with limited-to-no prior coding experience, to learn in the instructional sessions available during the orientation week. As a result, instruction often had to prioritize programming skills over fundamental geophysical concepts or science discussions to interpret the subsurface data. Complex interactive processing stages, for example, selection of optimal stacking velocities, removal of bad data traces, or spectral analysis also required advanced coding beyond the scope of such introductory classes.

To compensate for this limitation and to encourage critical understanding of the seismic data, within the limited time frame of the instructional program, we opted to start development of a graphical user interface (GUI) for SU (Lorenzo, 2017). During the following 6 yr (Table 1), IRIS interns used the software during instruction. The opportunity to see sets of beginners interact with the interface provided invaluable feedback and drove the continuous development and improvement of the interface (Lorenzo, 2018, 2019). Here, we present SeismicUnixGui (SUG) that addresses the challenges novices face by removing the immediate need for shell scripting and facilitate interactive testing of parameters on visual outputs, with single, mouse-driven clicks. The latest SUG is open-source and free software, available for Ubuntu, a popular and free Linux OS and the Windows OS Linux subsystem via the Docker Desktop application (see Data and Resources). Docker software provides both the frontend user interface and backend, pre-compiled SU software in the same installation step.

SU, the SUG Interface, and Open-Source Software

SUG (see Data and Resources) consists of a primary interactive window used to assemble sequences of independent programs from the SU software package and assign their appropriate geophysical parameters (Fig. 1). SU (see Data and Resources) is a seismic reflection software package that permits the processing of moderate sized 2D seismic or ground-penetrating radar data sets (Rousset and the Seismic Unix Users Group, 2020). The SUG interface (Fig. 1) currently accesses 290 SU programs that are used for a range of fundamental signal analysis functions including data format manipulation, integral transforms, seismic-waveform modeling, poststack time migration, and various image displays and manual data picking.

SU pioneered the open-software concept for seismic reflection processing software. SUG follows using an open-source approach and in the development of its graphical interface using open-source packages. TkSu (Equipment News, 2003) and Botoseis (Lima *et al*, 2009) are early examples of graphically driven interactive software, both employing Tcl/Tk (Ousterhout, 1993) and using SeismicUnix modules as their engine. Other examples

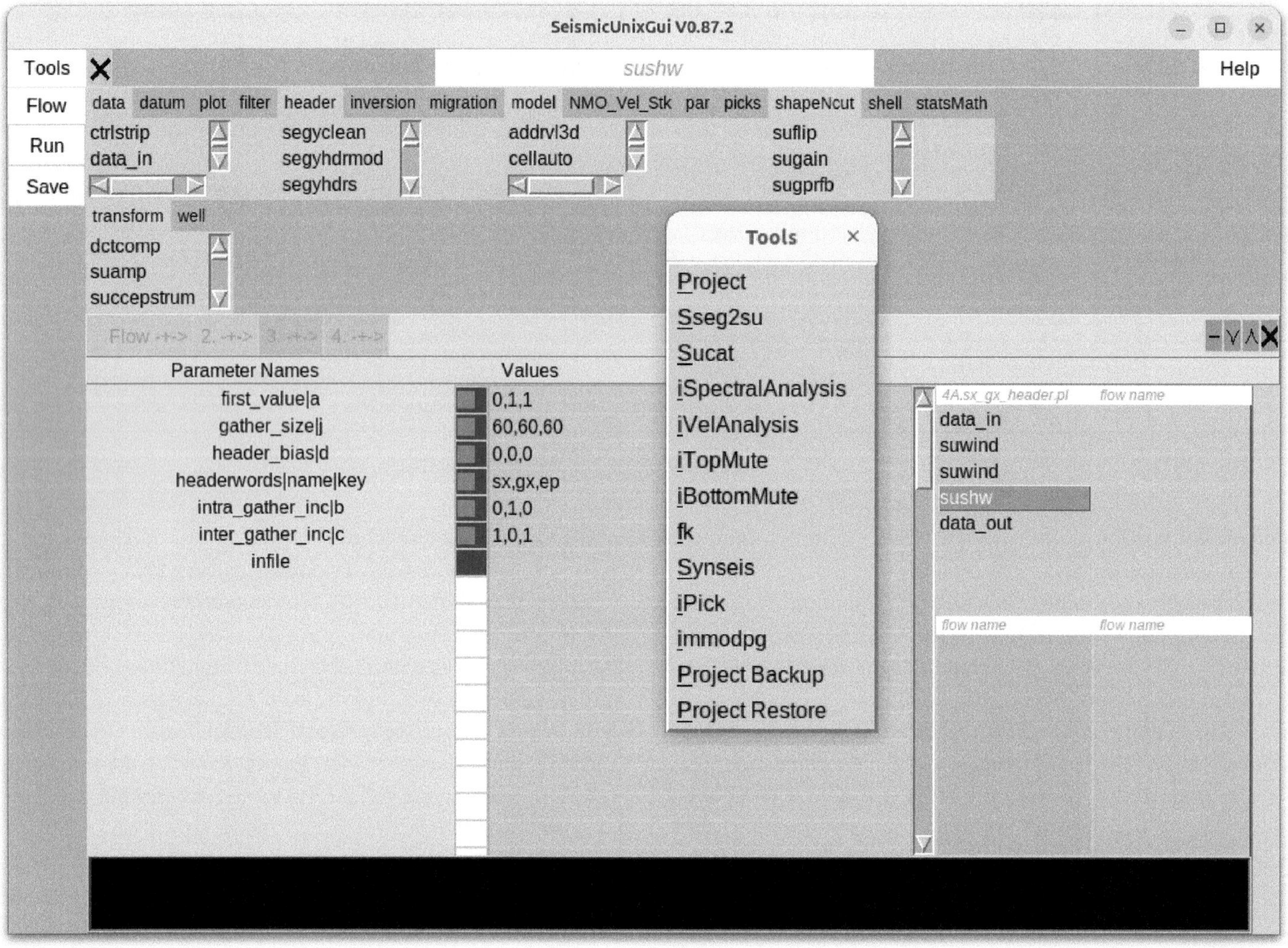

Figure 1. A brief tour of the SeismicUnixGui (SUG) graphical user interface (GUI). One main user interface handles input parameters for most programs. Four colored windows (right side) are used to compose and run four independent sets of sequential instructions. A pull-down menu ("Tools," top-left menu, and also shown detached) contains pre-existing tools built upon complex combinations of Seismic Unix (SU) programs, including management tools ("Project," "Project Backup," and "Project Restore"), third-party format conversion ("Sseg2su"), simple synthetic seismograms ("Synseis"), raytracing ("immodpg"), and interactive spectral, velocity analysis and data removal ("mute"), frequency–wavenumber (*f-k*) analysis, and data digitization ("iPick"). Traditional SU help installation manuals are available (via click of the third mouse button), as well as access to tutorial and installation manuals ("Help"). SU modules are classified within 16 scrollable windows (upper rows of interface, e.g., "data," "datum," "plot," "filter," "header," etc.). Behind the "Tools" menu, the main interface displays an example of "parameter values" for one specific SU module ("sushw"), belonging to the "header" category. Software wrappers facilitate the addition of descriptive parameter names as well as the original variable names from SU (e.g., "first_value or a"). The color version of this figure is available only in the electronic edition.

include OpenSeaSeis (Olofsson, 2012), based on a Java interface (Table 2) or Visual_SUNT (2024), a commercial package under the Windows OS. Additional open-source seismic reflection codes (Table 2) exist that have been developed in either academic, for example, Madagascar (Fomel *et al.*, 2013), or commercial settings such as FreeUSP (BP-Amoco, 2024), or Conoco Philips Seismic processing software (CPSEIS; Conoco Philips Seismic processing software [CPSEIS], 2024), but these do not rely on SU software modules.

Design Strategy for SUG and Project Management

SUG primarily uses extensible modules written in Perl (Simmons and Rézic, 2024) to "wrap" (Fig. 2) themselves around modular, independent units of compiled C or Fortran code. The wrapper code provides an additional layer of abstraction between the user and the running code. This layer helps simplify code usability and adds tailored functionality that is not directly available from some versions of SU code. For example, one standard SU module ("sukill") is used for deleting unwanted data traces within a seismic data file. However, if the unwanted traces are irregularly spaced the task becomes repetitive and cumbersome for the user.

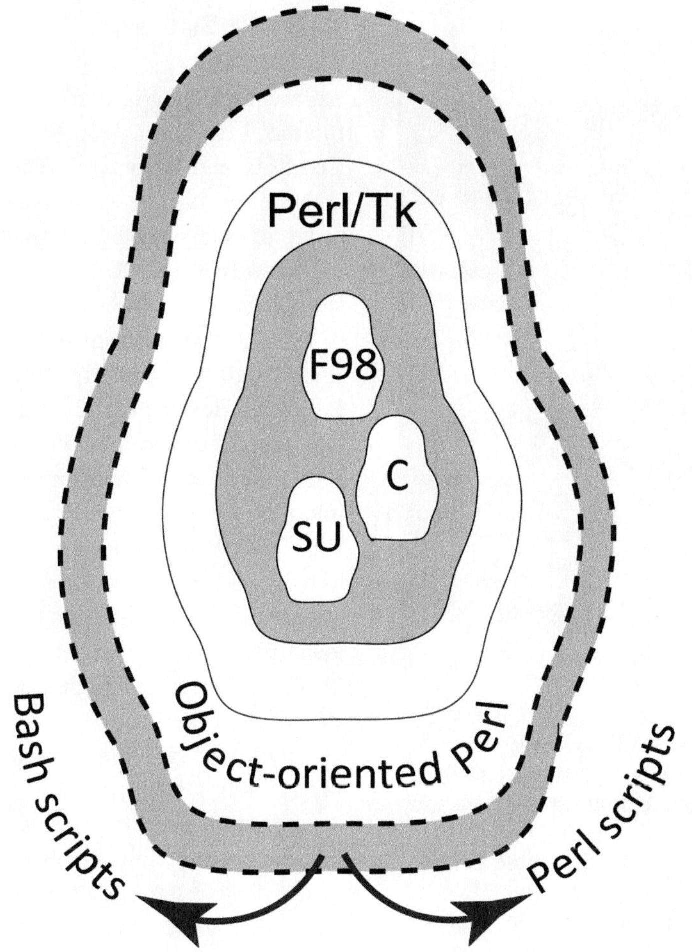

Figure 2. Schematic outline (inspired by nested Russian folk dolls), of the SUG architecture. SUG shows that both Perl and bash scripts are generated to run sequences of SU modules from the interface or command line. Perl integrates (Simmons and Rézic, 2024) the Tk toolkit, with background third-party software written in C (SU) and Fortran (F98); see the supplemental material. The color version of this figure is available only in the electronic edition.

Instead, the wrapper introduces a new option for the program that allows unwanted data traces to be specified more simply in a text-based list. The wrapper handles the process of data removal in a manner that is seamless to the user.

Software wrappers permit integration of varied and tested software into SUG. Although SU already has a SEG2 (Pullan, 1990)-to-SEG-Y (Levin and New, 2024) seismic format conversion module, one SUG wrapper incorporates data format conversion from another open-seismic processing software, Scripps Institute of Oceanography Seismic processing system (SIOSEIS; Scripps Institute of Oceanography Seismic processing system [SIOSEIS], 2011). Students can improve and develop their understanding of geological models via forward modeling of reflected and refracted seismic arrival data (e.g., Song and Ten Brink, 2004). For this purpose, SUG tool uses Perl wrappers to run an interactive raytracing program for a 1D layered earth model that is written entirely in Fortran 77 and 95. Perl scripts communicate asynchronously with the Fortran code via text messaging, and the Fortran dynamically updates data and calculations in response to button clicks and data input within the GUI. Perl can also readily incorporate Linux shell programs into its interface such as "evince," an open-source document viewer.

SUG forces data and generated Perl scripts into a prescribed directory structure. Directories and minimal files needed by SUG are created automatically at the start of each newly named Project using a "Project Selector" tool. Because Linux commands allow free navigation throughout the directories, the user can add new subdirectories within the existing file structure, without affecting SUG behavior. The default SUG Project directory structure allows multiple students to share one Project directory structure, while keeping independent copies of their scripts and data. This centralized location of student work on a hard drive has proven convenient for managing and supervising class exercises.

Shareable SUG Scripts

With SUG, a user populates a parameter sheet and runs a sequence of programs. Beneficially, SUG also provides

TABLE 2
List of Open-Source Seismic Reflection Processing Programs with Graphical User Interfaces That Interface with Seismic Unix (SU) Modules

Additional SU-Related Software

Name	Prerequisites	Source	License	Reference Author
BotoSeis	Java SE Runtime >6.0, Ubuntu 16.04	https://github.com/botoseis/BotoSeis	GNU General Public License v3.0. (GPL)	Lima *et al.* (2009)
GeBR	Gtk+, Java	https://www.ime.unicamp.br/~biloti/gebrproject/	GPLv2.0	Biloti (2012)
TkSU	C, Motif, Linux 2.2.14	http://www.henrythorson.com/software.htm	GPL	Equipment News (2003)
OpenSeaSeis	Java	https://github.com/JohnWStockwellJr/OpenSeaSeis	GPL	Olofsson (2012)

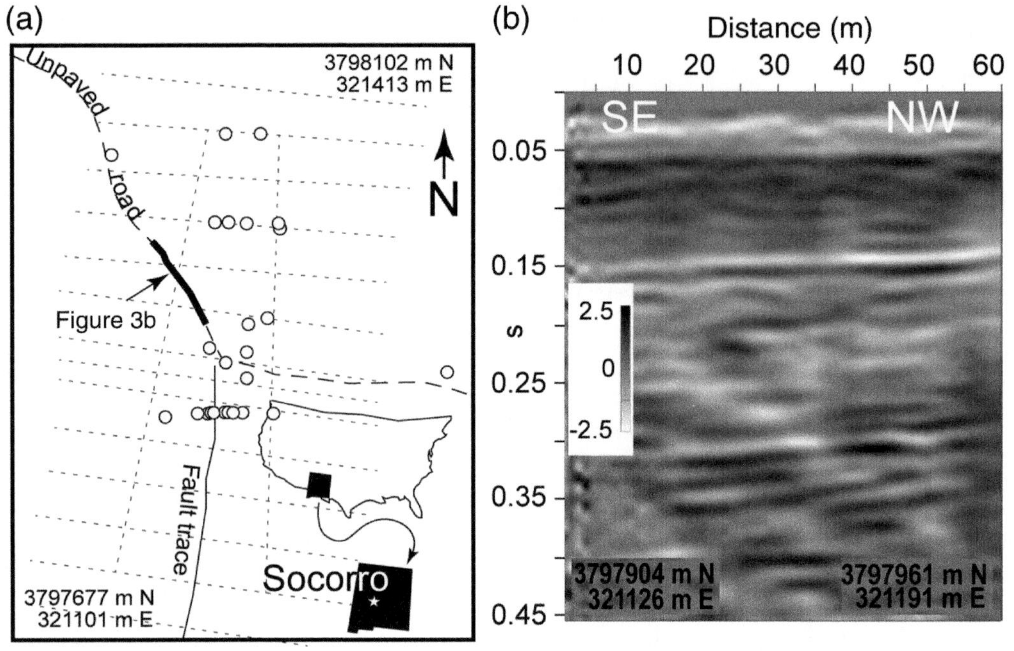

Figure 3. (a) Seismic line transect (thick-black line) along unpaved road in Servilleta National Wildlife Refuge, ~30 km north of Socorro, New Mexico, United States (UTM Z = 13, see inset). Straight dashed lines locate direct current resistivity profiles and open circles mark well locations also from prior study by Barnes *et al.*, (2021). (b) Output example from tutorial (step 9, flow 8A; see Data and Resources) displays a final stacked section that is produced by students. A linear stacking velocity gradient model ranging from 100 to 250 m/s is applied together with a low-pass filter (below 60 Hz) and automatically scaled amplitudes for the display. The reflector at approximately 0.14 s of two-way travel time can be interpreted to represent an erosional surface between sediments of the Rio Grande (below) and Rio Salado (above). The color version of this figure is available only in the electronic edition.

executable bash and Perl script versions of the command sequences, self-documented with a simple-to-use Perl markup language. Every bash script run from SUG is logged to a text file, which includes a time stamp and version number of the SUG that was used. Once generated, bash scripts can be recovered from the logging file and executed on the command line. Similarly, the generated Perl script can later be run from the command line directly or reapplied from within the GUI. Given the predefined directory structure, unmodified scripts also serve as a useful reproducible record of the processing steps that can be readily shared between students.

An advantage of the generated scripts is that they can be readily modified by a user to develop more elaborate, complex sophisticated interactive tools. Such added-on-tools that amalgamate the functionality of several SU modules are available under a drop-down menu ("Tools"; Fig. 1). These tools also can be run from the command line for convenience but are attached to the menu options in the GUI. We find that complex interactive processing stages, for example, selection of optimal stacking velocities, killing bad data traces, or spectral analysis, requires these more prebuilt tools because complex flows are beyond the scope of introductory classes.

A Data Set and Tutorial

An accompanying data set and tutorial is available for SUG (see Data and Resources). The data set was collected over half a day of field work by student participants in the IRIS internship program with the assistance of EPIC instrument center staff (EPIC, 2024; formerly the PASSCAL Instrument Center) and processed over a period of a few hours during the summer internship orientation week. Between 2018 and 2019, we collected S_H seismic reflection data across a nearby outcropping fault (Fig. 3a; Barnes *et al*, 2021). For planning and discussion of the experimental design of the survey, the Loma Blanca fault is readily identified in satellite imagery. In the field, the fault zone appears as a weathering-resistant ridge indurated by calcite cementation. The subsurface is well characterized by core samples from 29 boreholes and 16 direct-current electrical resistivity profiles in a small area approximately 100 m × 400 m in rectangular extent (Fig. 3a). Moreover, a sharp acoustic impedance contrast that exists at shallow depths of ~7 m (0.14 s at 100 m/s; Fig. 3b) provides readily recognizable reflection hyperbolae for velocity analysis and quick stacking.

Shear-wave data were collected because they were easier to separate by muting (see the supplemental material) from accompanying surface waves than traditional higher-velocity *P* waves. Further details of the acquisition geometry are included in the tutorial. Additional processing was required to stack pairs of shotpoint gathers with opposite polarities. At each S_H shot point location we generate two data sets of opposite polarities by hitting a small, embedded I-beam on opposite sides. Differencing the data sets attempts to double the amplitude of true S_H arrivals while attenuating converted *P*-wave modes (Helbig, 1986). Students' exercises transition from the stage of raw field data to the final stacked section in approximately eight steps, and interact with the effects of the multiple processing parameters along the way guided by the instructor.

Future of SUG

The new EarthScope program continues to evolve while incorporating prior internship programs from the former UNAVCO;

the hands-on seismic experimentation will remain an integral part of the weeklong internship program. SUG exposes students to tailored and function open-source software they can continue to use during relevant research experiences. We hope that SUG or other similar projects will help introduce near-surface seismology to future generations of geophysicists. Continuous updates to the SUG will be available at three public sites (see Data and Resources) and enquiries can be directed to the first author. Changes will be dictated based on future student needs and responses from potential users.

Data and Resources

Source code for the SeismicUnixGui (SUG) program, which is intended for use under an Ubuntu version of the Linux operating system (OS), is available from two different internet locations. (1) The complete SUG package can be downloaded and installed free of charge, under the Artistic and General Public license, from https://github.com/gllore/App/SeismicUnixGui (last accessed June 2025). (2) SUG is also publicly available from the Comprehensive Perl Archive Network (https://www.cpan.org, last accessed June 2025) and can be installed automatically using the "cpan" utility in Perl. This automatic installation will detect and install missing modules and test the code during the installation process. For Windows OS and Apple PC users, a Docker image is available for free from https://hub.docker.com/r/nathanbenton/sug (last accessed July 2025). The current SUG will run on older Apple PCs that use Intel chipsets. Development of SUG for more recent Apple silicon-based platforms is underway. The docker image contains a precompiled, fully working version of SUG, Seismic Unix (SU), and other third-party software libraries (C and Fortran) that run seamlessly within the Windows Subsytem for Linux (WSL2). Docker is an open-source containerization software analogous to Anaconda (for Python, 2024) that allows for exchange of prefabricated software systems. Both a tutorial for the accompanying data set and an extensive manual explaining how to install SUG, SU, and third-party software such as SIOSEIS are available from: https://github.com/gllore/App-SeismicUnixGui/tree/V0.87.3/lib/App/SeismicUnixGui/doc (last accessed June 2025). Once SUG is installed, this document is also available under the "Help" button. Because the tutorial scripts and data set used are quite large in size, they are included separately as a single compressed file (~364 MB) from a different Zenodo site (doi: 10.5281/zenodo.13401754). Zenodo is general-purpose open-research repository (https://zenodo.org/). These data were collected by students and analyzed during the 2018 Undergraduate Research Internships in Seismology (URISE; Undergraduate Research Internships in Seismology [URISE], 2024) orientation week. The supplemental material for this article includes an example image output from the online tutorial and technical details of the design strategy for SUG. SUG is designed to interact with modules from SU, a free, open-software package, licensed under a New Berkeley Source Distribution. For purely Linux-based OS, the SU package should be installed separately and is available from https://github.com/JohnWStockwellJr/SeisUnix (last accessed July 2025).

Declaration of Competing Interests

The authors acknowledge that there are no conflicts of interest recorded.

Acknowledgments

The authors are grateful to John Stockwell and the Colorado School of Mines for developing Seismic Unix (SU) and to D. Roussset (Univ. Pau) for promoting growth and distribution of the SU. The former Incorporated Research Institutions for Seismology (IRIS/URISE) program was supported by the National Science Foundation (NSF) Awards EAR-1852339 and EAR-1724509. This funding supported numerous students who, with the assistance of New Mexico Institute of Mining and Technology (NMT) faculty including S. Bilek, and G. Spinelli, and the Program for Array Seismic Studies of the Continental Lithosphere (PASSCAL) instrumentation facility staff, especially G. Chavez, collected the tutorial data set and tested early versions of the SeismicUnixGui (SUG). Many funded research activities and graduate student projects also motivated code development, including Codelco Chile, ExxonMobil Upstream Research, DOE/LEQSF (2004-7)-L, USDS-Fulbright, K. Hayashi at Geometrics Inc., Louisiana Sea Grant, Southeast Louisiana Flood Protection Authorities, American Petroleum Institute (API) Delta Chapter- New Orleans, New Orleans Geological Society (NOGS), Southeastern Geophysical Society (SGS), and above all the Louisiana State University (LSU) Department of Geology & Geophysics for its active support of graduate student research. The original article benefitted from the highly constructive reviews of A. Kafka and an anonymous reviewer.

References

Barnes, H., J. R. Hinojosa, G. A. Spinelli, P. S. Mozley, D. Koning, T. G. Sproule, and J. L. Wilson (2021). Detecting fault zone characteristics and paleovalley incision using electrical resistivity: Loma Blanca Fault, New Mexico, *Geophysics* **86,** B209–B221.

Beyreuther, M., R. Barsch, L. Krischer, T. Megies, Y. Behr, and J. Wassermann (2010). ObsPy: A python toolbox for seismology, *Seismol. Res. Lett.* **81,** 530–533.

Biloti, R. (2012). GeBR:A free seismic processing interface, *74th EAGE Conference and Exhibition - Workshops*, July 2012, cp-295-00129, EAGE.

BP-Amoco (2024). BP-Amoco software, available at https://stuartschmitt.com/FreeUSP/FreeUSP_License.html (last accessed October 2024).

Butler, K. E., D. B. McLean, C. Cosma, and N. Enescu (2019). A borehole seismic reflection survey in support of seepage surveillance at the abutment of a large embankment dam, in *Levees and Dams: Advances in Geophysical Monitoring and Characterization*, J. M. Lorenzo and W. Doll (Editors), Springer International Publishing, Cham, Switzerland, 41–67.

Conoco Philips Seismic processing software (CPSEIS) (2024). ConocoPhillips seismic processing software, available at https://sourceforge.net/projects/cpseis/ (last accessed October 2024).

EarthScope Primary Instrument Center (EPIC) (2024). EarthScope primary instrument center, available at https://www.epic.earthscope.org/ (last accessed October 2024).

Equipment News (2003). *Seismol. Res. Lett.* **74,** no. 1, 50, doi: 10.1785/gssrl.74.1.50.

Fomel, S., P. Sava, I. Vlad, Y. Liu, and V. Bashkardin (2013). Madagascar: Open-source software project for multidimensional data analysis and reproducible computational experiments, *J. Open Res. Softw.* **1,** 1.

Forel, D., T. Benz, and W. D. Pennington (2005). *Seismic Data Processing with Seismic Un*x: A 2D Seismic Data Processing Primer*, Society of Exploration Geophysicists, Tulsa, Oklahoma.

Helbig, K. (1986). Shear waves- What they are and how they can be used, in *Shear-Wave Exploration Geophysical Development Series*, S. H. Danbom and S. N. Domenico (Editors), Society of Exploration Geophysicists, Tulsa, Oklahoma, 19–36.

Levin, S. A., and S. New (Editors) (2024). *SEG-Y_r2.1: SEG-Y revision 2.1 Data Exchange format*, Society of Exploration Geophysicists, available at https://library.seg.org/pb-assets/technical-standards/seg_y_rev2_1-oct2023.pdf (last accessed October 2024).

Lima, W., G. Garabito, and J. C. R. Cruz (2009). BOTOSEIS: A new Seismic Unix based interactive platform for seismic data processing, *11th Int. Congress of the Brazilian Geophysical Society and EXPOGEF 2009*, Salvador, Bahia, Brazil, 24–28 August 2009, 1507–1510.

Lorenzo, J. M. (2017). TkPl_SU: An Open-source Perl Script Builder for Seismic Unix, (263077/ NS41B-0014). Th., 14 December, *AGU Fall Meeting*, E. Morial Convention Center, 08:00-12:20, Hall D-F, New Orleans.

Lorenzo, J. M. (2018). L_SU (V 0.3.2)- a graphical user interface useful for building seismic flows from Seismic Unix, *Abstract presented at 2018 Fall Meeting, AGU*, Washington, D.C., 14 December.

Lorenzo, J. M. (2019). L_SU (V0.3.9): A graphical user interface useful for building seismic flows from Seismic Unix, *AGU Fall Meeting 2019*, San Francisco, California.

Lorenzo, J. M., J. Hicks, and E. E. Vera (2014). Integrated seismic and cone penetration test observations at a distressed earthen levee: Marrero, Louisiana, U.S.A, *Eng. Geol.* **168,** 59–68.

Miller, R. D., J. H. Bradford, and K. Holliger (Editors) (2010). *Advances in Near-Surface Seismology and Ground-Penetrating Radar*, Society of Exploration Geophysicists, American Geophysical Union, Environmental and Engineering Geophysical Society, Oklahoma; Washington, D.C.

Olofsson, B. (2012). SeaSeis: A simple open-source seismic data processing system, *74th EAGE Conference and Exhibition - Workshops*, July 2012, cp-295-00126, European Association of Geoscientists & Engineers.

Ousterhout, J. K. (1993). *Tcl and the Tk Toolkit*, Addison-Wesley Professional Computing Series, Addison-Wesley Publishing, Reading, Massachusetts.

Parolai, S., C. G. Lai, I. Dreossi, O.-J. Ktenidou, and A. Yong (2022). A review of near-surface QS estimation methods using active and passive sources, *J. Seismol.* **26,** 823–862.

Pullan, S. (1990). Recommended standard for seismic (/radar) data files in the personal computer environment, *Geophysics* **55,** 1260–1271.

Python (2024). available at https://www.python.org/ (last accessed October 2024).

Research Experiences in Solid Earth Sciences for Students (RESESS) (2024). Research experiences in solid earth sciences for students, available at https://resess.unavco.org/ (last accessed October 2024).

Rousset, D., and , and the Seismic Unix Users Group (2020). Seismic Unix, a valuable tool for seismic processing, *18th International Conf. on Ground Penetrating Radar*, Golden, Colorado, 14–19 June 2020, 251–254.

Simmons, N.-I., and S. Rézic (2024). Tk- A graphical user interface toolkit for Perl., available at https://metacpan.org/dist/Tk/view/Tk.pod (Version 804.036., last accessed October 2024).

Scripps Institute of Oceanography Seismic processing system (SIOSEIS) (2011). A computer system for enhancing and manipulating marine seismic reflection and refraction data, available at https://sioseis.com (last accessed October 2024).

Slater, L., R. Knight, K. Singha, A. Binley, and E. Atekwana (2006). Near-surface geophysics: A new focus group, *Eos Trans. AGU* **87,** 249–249.

Song, J.-L., and U. Ten Brink (2004). *RayGUI 2.0—A graphical user interface for interactive forward and inversion ray-tracing, U.S. Geol. Surv. Open-File Rept. 1426.*

St. Clair, J., S. Moon, W. Holbrook, J. Perron, C. Riebe, S. Martel, B. Carr, C. Harman, K. Singha, and D. Richter (2015). Geophysical imaging reveals topographic stress control of bedrock weathering, *Science* **350,** 534–538.

Stockwell, J. W. (1999). The CWP/SU: Seismic Unix package, *Comput. Geosci.* **25,** 415–419.

Undergraduate Research Internships in Seismology (URISE) (2024). Undergraduate research internships in seismology, available at https://www.iris.edu/hq/internship/ (last accessed October 2024).

Visual_SUNT (2024). Seismic Reflection processing, graphical interface for SEISMIC UNIX* for Windows, available at http://www.wgeosoft.ch/PDF/Visual_SUNT_Pro_Data.html (last accessed October 2024).

Wodajo, L. T., C. J. Hickey, and T. C. Brackett (2019). Application of seismic refraction and electrical resistivity cross-plot analysis: A case study at Francis levee site, levees and dams, in *Levees and Dams: Advances in Geophysical Monitoring and Characterization*, J. M. Lorenzo and W. Doll (Editors), Advances in Geophysical Monitoring and Characterization, Springer International Publishing, Cham, Switzerland, 23–40.

Manuscript received 4 March 2025
Published online 15 August 2025

Data Mine

LAB2022: A New Nodal Seismic Array Spanning the Los Angeles Basin

Fan-Chi Lin*[1], Robert W. Clayton[2], Heather A. Ford[3], Amir Allam[1], Konstantinos Gkogkas[1], Valeria Villa[2], and HyeJeong Kim[1]

Abstract

LAB2022 is a new temporary array consisting of 273 geophones that was deployed in the Los Angeles basin for one month during the summer of 2022. The array was designed to improve the 3D seismic velocity model of the basin through passive seismic imaging, which is crucial for both earthquake hazard assessment and the understanding of the region's tectonic evolution. The sensors are 3C 5 Hz Zland and Smart Solo instruments. The data has been archived at the EarthScope SAGE Data Management Center and will be publicly available in summer 2025.

Cite this article as Lin, F.-C., R. W. Clayton, H. A. Ford, A. Allam, K. Gkogkas, V. Villa, and H. Kim (2025). LAB2022: A New Nodal Seismic Array Spanning the Los Angeles Basin, *Seismol. Res. Lett.* **97**, 585–590, doi: 10.1785/0220250082.

Introduction

In the summer of 2022, we deployed a 273 nodal geophone seismic array across the Los Angeles basin (LAB) for approximately one month (5 June–7 July). The experiment is named LAB2022 (network: 6W; Lin *et al.*, 2022) and the station locations are shown in Figure 1. The purpose is to image the basin and crustal structure to better understand the tectonics of the basin formation (Wright, 1991; Ingersoll and Rumelhart, 1999) and seismic hazard (Filippitzis *et al.*, 2021). Teams from the University of Utah, Caltech, and the University of California, Riverside, deployed the array in two days with the help of ~30 volunteers consisting of graduate students, faculty/staff members, and private citizens from the broad Southern California Earthquake Center (SCEC) community. The array was retrieved in about the same amount of time. This array temporarily increases the density of the seismic station coverage in the LAB by about a factor of 10. The experiment was funded by SCEC and is the continuation of the effort to increase the density of seismic observations in the basins in the Los Angeles area (Clayton *et al.*, 2019).

The array consists of two northeast–southwest dense lines with 44 and 49 nodes each (0.7 km spacing) and a distributed shotgun array of 185 nodes, roughly evenly distributed across the LAB area with ~2.5 km spacing. The linear arrays were instrumented with SmartSolo 3C 5 Hz nodes, with the west line using nodes from the EarthScope Primary Instrument Center (EPIC, formerly The IRIS PASSCAL Instrument Center) and the east line using nodes from the University of California, Riverside. The shotgun array was deployed with equivalent Zland 3C 5 Hz nodes owned by the University of Utah. The deployers were given a set of computer-generated locations with instructions to find sites within 0.25 km of these positions. Most were deployed at private houses, but in commercial and industrial portions of the city, nodes were placed in decorative landscaping associated with malls, parks, and businesses, or in the public right-of-way on the sides of roads. Nodes were buried when feasible, although many were simply spiked into the ground to minimize disturbance. The battery life of these nodes lasted about 30 days. A total of nine nodes were lost or damaged during the survey, primarily due to theft and vandalism. The data recovery from the nodes were nearly 100% without any data gap and no apparent issues with the clock synchronization based on the preliminary ambient noise and earthquake analyses.

Data Quality and Availability

Data from the experiment are uploaded to the EarthScope SAGE Data Management Center (DMC). We examine the data quality by comparing two pairs of close by stations (Fig. 1). The four stations, CI.LAF, 6W.W39, 6W.S453, and 6W.E13, we used for comparison have the instrument types of STS-2.5, SmartSolo, Zland, and SmartSolo, respectively, and station CI.LAF is a permanent broadband station. First, we compare the vertical displacement waveforms from two earthquakes, one teleseismic (**M** 6.5 Peru earthquake on 8 June 2022) and one regional (**M** 5.2 Mexico earthquake on 18 June

1. Department of Geology and Geophysics, University of Utah, Salt Lake City, Utah, U.S.A., https://orcid.org/0000-0003-0394-6830 (F-CL); https://orcid.org/0000-0002-6447-0779 (AA); https://orcid.org/0000-0002-8271-4319 (HK); 2. Seismological Laboratory, California Institute of Technology, Pasadena, California, U.S.A., https://orcid.org/0000-0003-3323-3508 (RWC); https://orcid.org/0000-0002-0518-9143 (VV); 3. Department of Earth and Planetary Sciences, University of California, Riverside, California, U.S.A.

*Corresponding author: FanChi.Lin@utah.edu

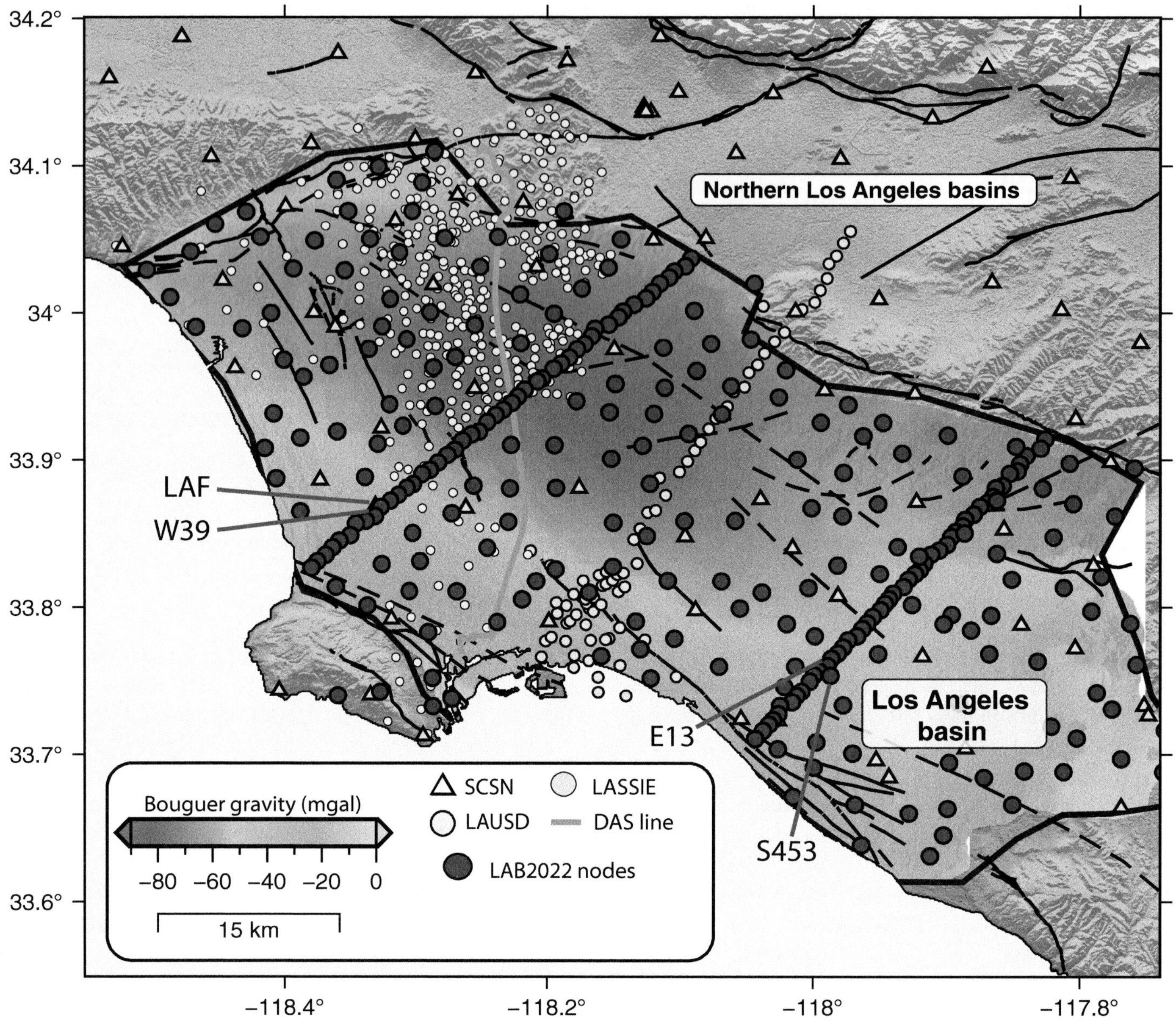

Figure 1. Los Angeles basin (LAB) survey. The red dots represent the LAB2022 survey conducted in 2022, consisting of 273 node stations. The white triangles indicate the permanent Southern California Seismic Network (SCSN) broadband network. The white dots correspond to the LAUSD/Community Seismic Network (CSN) array, which had ~400 stations at the time of the Ridgecrest earthquake and has since expanded to about 600 stations. The yellow dots represent the LASSIE survey. The pink line denotes the Alameda distributed acoustic sensing (DAS) array. The background color illustrates the observed Bouguer gravity with the main faults shown by black lines. The four stations used for comparison in Figure 2 are labeled with their station names. The color version of this figure is available only in the electronic edition.

2022). We band pass the waveforms by 0.1–1.0 Hz for the teleseismic and 0.5–2.0 Hz for the regional event after removing the instrument response to highlight the seismic signal (Fig. 2a, d,g,j). Despite the 5 Hz natural frequency of the geophone sensors, there is good agreement in all comparisons. The slight waveform difference for the regional event can be attributed to the slight difference in station location and ground coupling.

We also assess the data quality using the power spectral density probability density function (PSDPDF) of the four stations (Fig. 2b,c,e,f,h,i,k,l). We compute the PSDPDF using data throughout the deployment for 6W network stations and use data from 6 June to 4 July 2022 for CI.LAF. All stations have similar noise levels in periods shorter than 6 s. The urban environment results in noise levels higher than the high noise model (Peterson, 1993) at periods shorter than 1 second. The noise level difference between the geophones and the broadband station becomes apparent particularly above 10 s periods, consistent with previous observations (Sweet *et al.*, 2018) and likely due to geophones' insensitivity to long-period signals. We also randomly check the PSDPDFs of other nodal

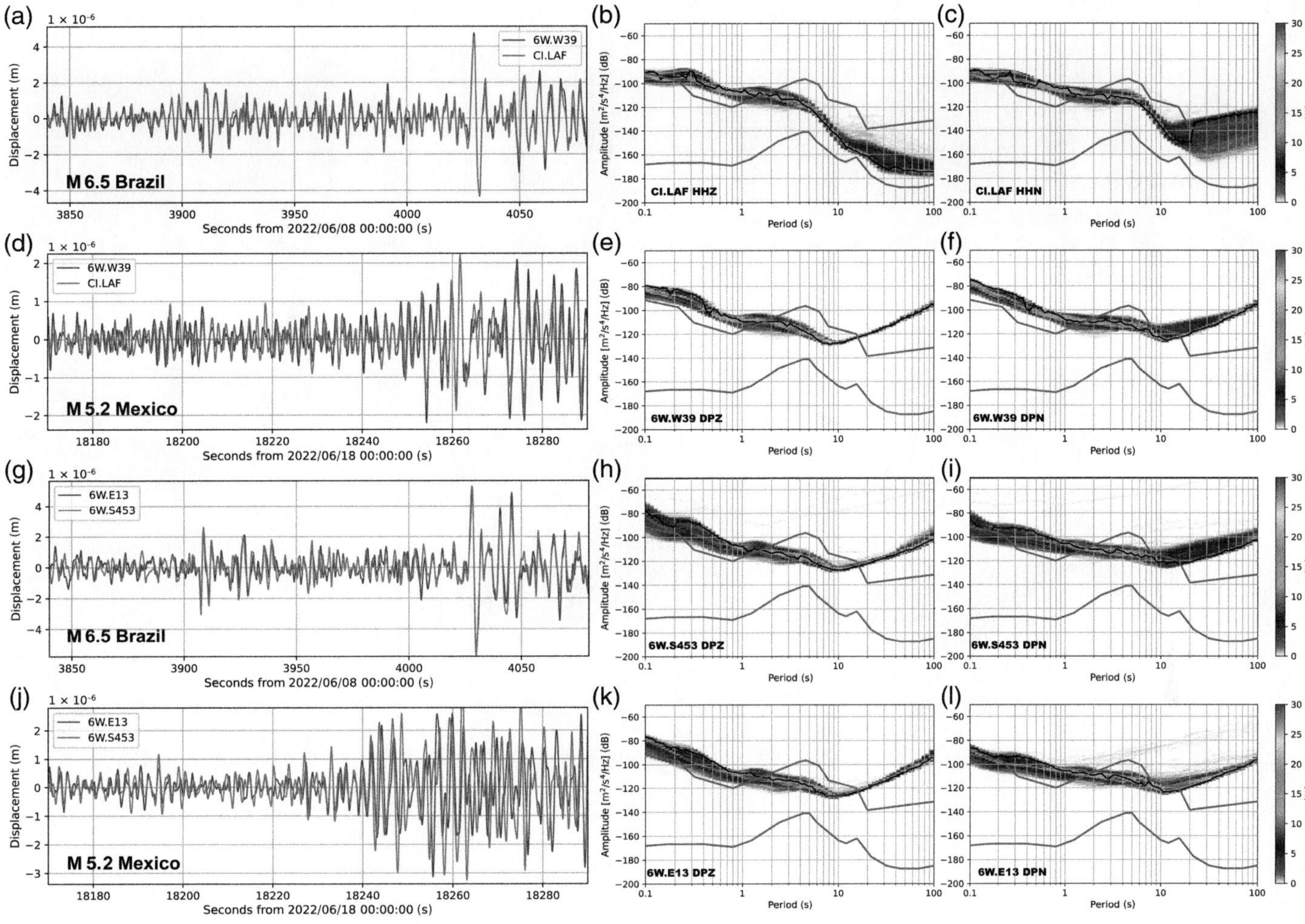

Figure 2. Waveform and noise level comparisons between two different pairs of stations (CI.LAF versus 6W.W39 and 6W.S453 versus 6W.E13; Fig. 1). (a) The 0.1–1.0 Hz band-passed vertical-component waveforms of the **M** 6.5 Peru event recorded by 6W.W39 (red) and CI.LAF (blue). (d) Same as (a), but for the **M** 5.2 Mexico event, band passed between 0.5 and 2.0 Hz. (g,j) Same as (a,d), but for station 6W.E13 (red) and 6W.S453 (blue). (b,e,h,k) The monthly vertical-component power spectral density probability density functions (PSDPDFs) of stations CI.LAF, 6W.W39, 6W.S453, and 6W.E13. (c,f,i,l) Same as (b,e,h,k), but for the north component. The solid dark gray lines represent the low-noise and high-noise models from Peterson (1993). The color version of this figure is available only in the electronic edition.

stations calculated by the DMC Modular Utility for STAtistical kNowledge Gathering service (MUSTANG; Casey *et al.*, 2018). The results are quite consistent with those shown in Figure 2b, c,e,f,h,i,k,l.

Initial Analysis

Ambient noise cross correlation

Figure 3 shows an example of the noise cross correlations calculated using data recorded by this array. Clear surface-wave signals are observed in the multicomponent correlations spanning the entire basin with both fundamental and first overtone of Rayleigh waves observed in the vertical (Z) and radial components (R) and Love waves observed in the transverse (T) component (Berg *et al.*, 2018; Qiu *et al.*, 2019; Li *et al.*, 2023). The correlations have useful signal down to 0.1 Hz, and hence we will be able to determine the shear-wave velocity to about 10 km depth. One advantage of the array's distribution and density is that short-period ambient noise surface-wave studies can be conducted using only stations within the basin, avoiding complications from wavepaths that cross the basin boundary (Zeng *et al.*, 2024). The dense station distribution also improves the coverage of station-specific measurements, such as Rayleigh-wave ellipticity (e.g., Berg *et al.*, 2021). The dense linear arrays will make it possible to image high-resolution 2D shear-wave velocity profiles through linear array processing methods (e.g., Gkogkas *et al.*, 2021). We will aim to update the community velocity models (CVMs) for southern California in the LAB area (Jia and Clayton, 2021; Muir *et al.*, 2022).

Teleseismic receiver function

Figure 4 shows the recording of the 8 June 2022 **M** 6.5 Peru event across the western linear array, which we plan to use along with another event that occurred when 60% of the array was deployed, to perform receiver function analysis to

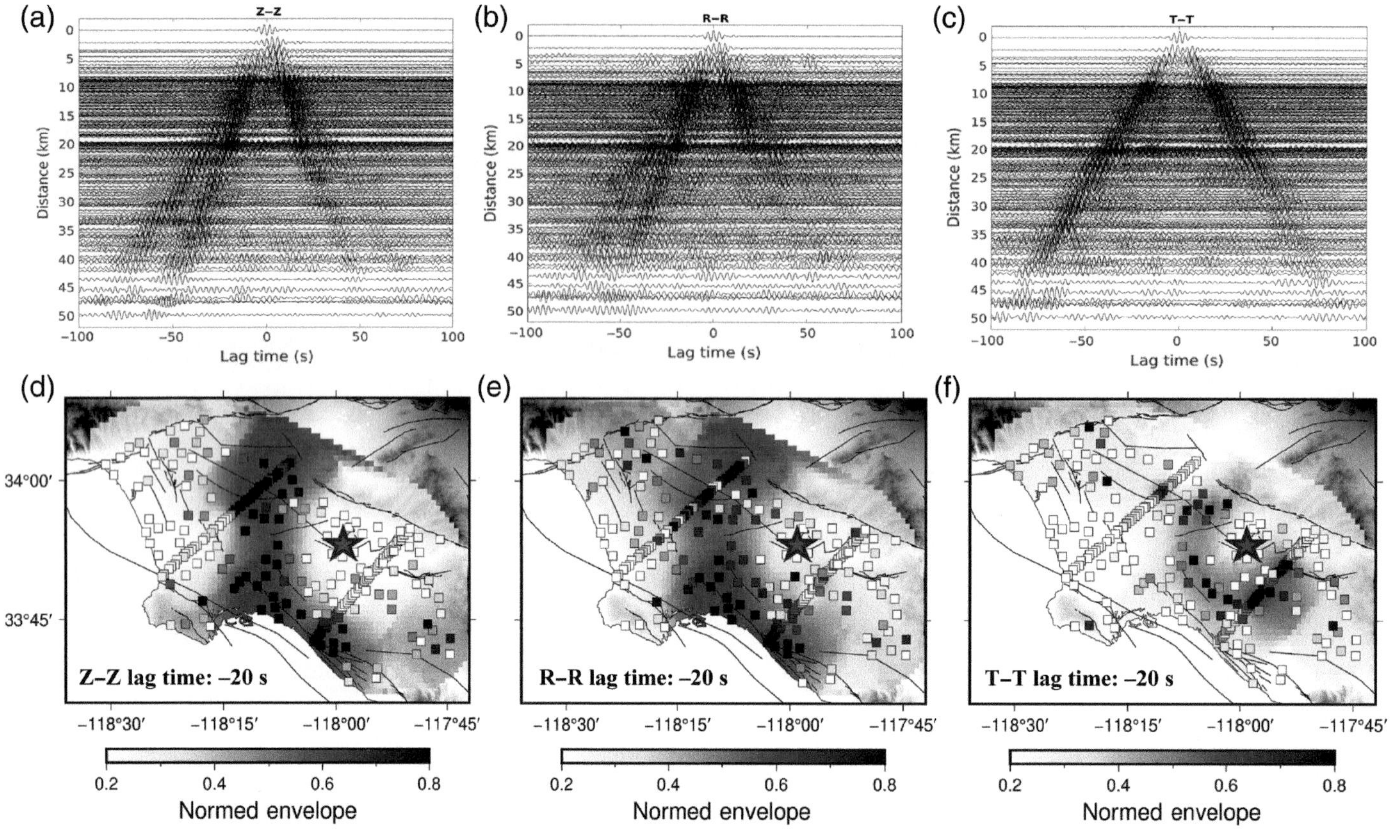

Figure 3. Noise cross correlations. Example cross-correlation record sections are shown in the top panel. The ZZ and RR record sections (a,b) display both the fundamental- and higher-mode Rayleigh-wave moveout, and the TT record section (c) shows the fundamental-mode Love wave moveout. The normalized envelope amplitude maps in the lower panels present a snapshot of the (d,e) Rayleigh- and (f) Love-wave packets at −20 s lag time, with the red star marking the common correlation source station. A Gaussian smoothing is applied to interpolate the observed amplitudes at the station locations. The color version of this figure is available only in the electronic edition.

determine crustal interfaces (e.g., depth of the basin and the Moho). The basin base and Moho have been imaged by receiver functions from the LASSIE array (see Fig. 1) (Ma and Clayton, 2016), and we plan to extend this over the whole basin. A preliminary estimate of the LAB depth based on the Peru event (Fig. 4), is shown in Figure 5. Many of the current models constrain the basin depth and shape based on gravity (McCulloh, 1960; Wright, 1991), and hence are subject to the uncertainty with the unknown density at depth and a regional gravity correction. Knowing the depth of the basin and Moho will allow us to determine the stretching factor of the basin (McKenzie, 1978; Turcotte and McAdoo, 1979) and with that, an estimate of the thermal history. The basin shape and depth along with the shear velocity of the sediments contained within, controls the resonance properties, which causes enhanced motions for the tall buildings in downtown LA. As demonstrated by the 2019 Ridgecrest earthquake, the basin amplifies long-period motions. For example, 6 s waves are amplified by a factor of five compared to the surrounding bedrock (Filippitzis *et al.*, 2021). The combination of surface wave and receiver function inversions should allow the construction of a much more detailed map of the basin resonance. The use of gravity will help in the identification of the converted phases on the receiver functions (Villa *et al.*, 2023). We also plan to use autocorrelations of ambient noise to detect internal layering in the LAB for the San Gabriel and San Bernardino basins (Zou and Clayton, 2024).

Local earthquakes. The array recorded several local events in the magnitude range 1.0–2.4, during its deployment, and a few of these were below the LAB itself. They were also well recorded by the Community Seismic Network (CSN). A number of these events have a clear basin-bottom converted (*Sp*) phase that allow for an independent estimate for the depth of the basin (Yang and Clayton, 2024), which also used data from LAB2022. The improved network coverage will likely lower the detection threshold for local earthquakes (Yang and Clayton, 2023), which will be the subject of a future study.

Other available data in LAB. The LAB is also covered by 40 permanent stations from the Southern California Seismic Network (SCSN), and by 581 permanent stations of the CSN. The former are stations with broadband sensors and

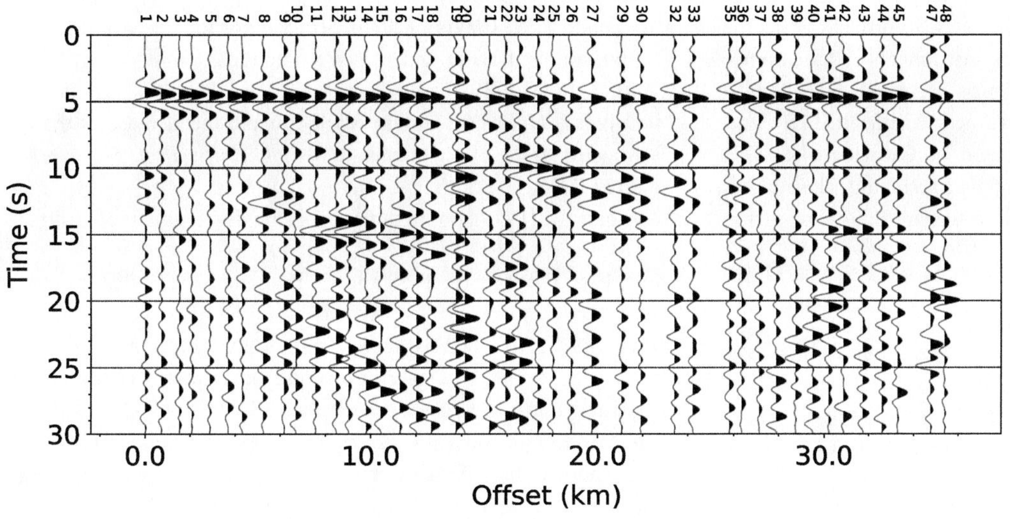

Figure 4. An example of a teleseismic event: the **M** 6.3 earthquake that occurred on 8 June 2023, near the Peru–Brazil border. The stations are along the western linear array, with zero offset at the northeastern end. A band-pass filter between 0.01 and 1.0 Hz was applied, and the traces are aligned relative to the origin time of the event.

strong-motion accelerometers. The latter are low-sensitivity accelerometers. Note the noise floor of the CSN instruments are higher than the ambient noise levels, and hence they cannot produce good noise correlations, but they do detect earthquakes in the basin region that are **M** 3.5+. There is also a DAS cable along the Almeda transportation corridor, that started recording in mid-2023. The method for distributing the DAS data is still being developed, but at least the event-based data will likely be made publicly available.

Data and Resources

The continuous data from the LAB2022 deployment are archived at the EarthScope Data Management Center (doi: 10.7914/36n1-zm78; network: 6W; Lin *et al.*, 2022), and will be publicly available in summer 2025. The data from Southern California Seismic Network (SCSN) broadband network are available from Southern California Earthquake Data Center (SCEDC) (https://scedc.caltech.edu, doi: 10.7909/C3WD3xH1, under the network ID CI). The Community Seismic Network (CSN) data are available on a per event basis form (https://csn.caltech.edu/data, with network ID CJ. doi: 10.7909/ce154f0q). The Alameda distributed acoustic sensing (DAS) array is in the process of developing a data retrieval mechanism and will likely be accessed through the SCEDC. All websites were last accessed in June 2025.

Declaration of Competing Interests

The authors acknowledge that there are no conflicts of interest recorded.

Acknowledgments

This study was supported by the U. S. Department of Energy (Award DE-SC0016520). Some preliminary analyses and data archiving efforts were supported by the U.S. National Science Foundation (Grants EAR-2438772 and EAR-2438773). The research benefitted from discussions facilitated by the Statewide California Earthquake Center (SCEC). K. G. acknowledges a scholarship by the Alexander S. Onassis Foundation (Scholarship ID: F ZO 02-1/2018–2019). V. V. was partially supported by a National Science Foundation (NSF) Graduate Fellowship. The

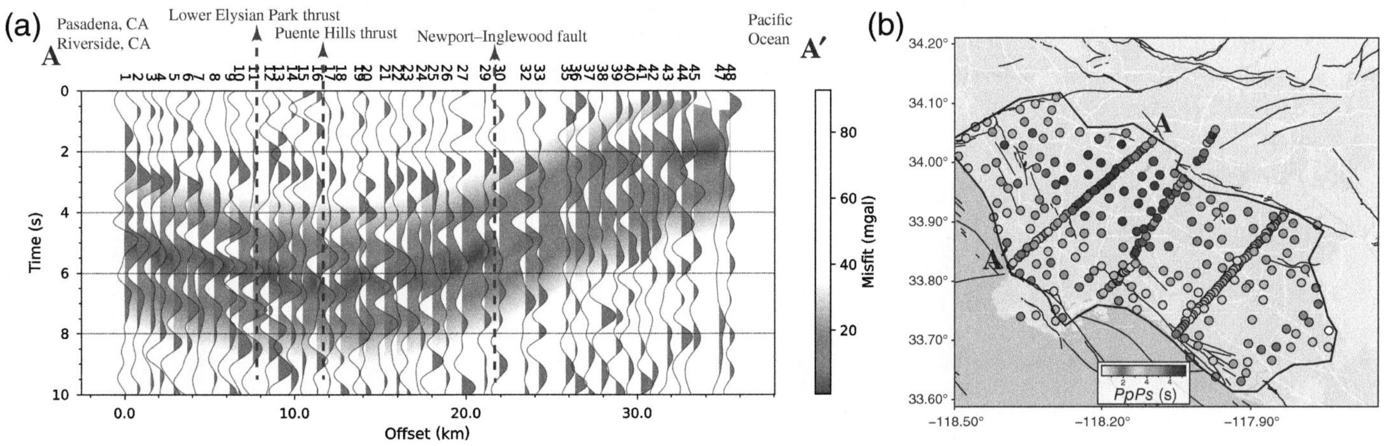

Figure 5. Receiver functions (RFs). (a) The RF picks along the western node line. The wiggle traces represent the raw RFs, and the colored zones indicate the penalty function derived from gravity (see Villa *et al.*, 2023). (b) The figure extends this analysis to all node stations in the Los Angeles (LA) basin, clearly highlighting the deep portion of the central basin. The color version of this figure is available only in the electronic edition.

authors are grateful to the numerous volunteers from the SCEC community who helped deploy and retrieve the instruments and the homeowners who hosted the nodes. The authors would also like to acknowledge EarthScope Primary Instrument Center (EPIC) and Seismological Facility for the Advancement of Geoscience (SAGE) for their help with the instrumentation and data archiving. The authors thank two anonymous reviewers and the Associate Editor for giving suggestions to improve the article.

References

Berg, E., F.-C. Lin, A.A. Allam, H. Qiu, W. Shen, and Y. Ben-Zion (2018). Tomography of southern California via Bayesian joint inversion of Rayleigh wave ellipticity and phase velocity from ambient noise cross-correlations, *J. Geophys. Res.* **123,** 9933–9949, doi: 10.1029/2018JB016269.

Berg, E. M., F.-C. Lin, V. Schulte-Pelkum, A. Allam, H. Qiu, and K. Gkogkas (2021).Shallow crustal shear velocity and V_p/V_s across southern California: Joint inversion of short-period Rayleigh wave ellipticity, phase velocity, and teleseismic receiver functions, *Geophys. Res. Lett.* **48,** e2021GL092626, doi: 10.1029/2021GL092626.

Casey, R., M. E. Templeton, G. Sharer, L. Keyson, B. R. Weertman, and T. Ahern (2018). Assuring the quality of IRIS data with MUSTANG, *Seismol. Res. Lett.* **89,** no. 2A, 630–639, doi: 10.1785/0220170191.

Clayton, R., P. Persaud, M Denolle, and J. Polet (2019). Exposing Los Angeles's shakey geologic underbelly, *Eos* **100,** doi: 10.1029/2019EO135099.

Filippitzis, F., M. Kohler, T. Heaton, R. Graves, R. Clayton, R. Guy, J. Bunn, and M. Chandy (2021). Ground motion response in urban Los Angeles from the 2019 Ridgecrest earthquake sequence, *Earthq. Spectra* doi: 10.1177/87552930211003916.

Gkogkas, K., F.C. Lin, A. A. Allam, and Y. Wang (2021). Shallow damage zone structure of the Wasatch fault in Salt Lake City from ambient-noise double beamforming with a temporary linear array, *Seismol. Res. Lett.* **92,** no. 4, 2453–2463, doi: 10.1785/0220200404.

Ingersoll, R. V., and P. E. Rumelhart (1999). Three-stage evolution of the Los Angeles basin, southern California, *Geology* **27,** no. 7, 593–596.

Jia, Z., and R. W. Clayton (2021). Determination of near surface shear-wave velocities in the central Los Angeles basin with dense arrays, *J. Geophys. Res.* **126,** no. 5, e2020JB021369, doi: 10.1029/2020JB021369.

Li, Y., V. Villa, R. W. Clayton, and P. Persaud (2023). Shear Wave Velocities in the San Gabriel and San Bernardino basins, California, *J. Geophys. Res.* **128,** e2023JB026488, doi: 10.1029/2023JB026488.

Lin, F.-C., R. Clayton, H. Ford, A. Allam, K. Gkogkas, and H. Kim (2022). LAB2022 [Dataset], *International Federation of Digital Seismograph Networks*, doi: 10.7914/36n1-zm78.

Ma, Y., and R.W. Clayton (2016). Structure of the Los Angeles basin from ambient noise and receiver functions, *Geophys. J. Int.* **206,** no. 3, 1645–1651.

McCulloh, J. H. (1960). Gravity Variation and the Geology of the Los Angeles Basin of California, *U.S. Geol. Surv. Prof. Paper 400B, B320-B325.*

McKenzie, D. (1978). Some remarks on the development of sedimentary basins, *Earth Planet. Sci. Lett.* **40,** 25–32.

Muir, J., R. Clayton, V. Tsai, and Q. Brissaud (2022). Parsimonious velocity inversion applied to the Los Angeles basin, CA, *J. Geophys. Res.* **127,** e2021JB023103, doi: 10.1029/2021JB023103.

Peterson, J. R. (1993). Observations and modeling of seismic background noise, *U.S. Geol. Surv. Open-File Rept. 93-322*, 142 pp.

Qiu, H., F-C. Lin, and Y. Ben-Zion (2019). Eikonal tomography of the southern California plate boundary region, *J. Geophys. Res.* **124,** doi: 10.1029/2019JB017806.

Sweet, R.J., K.R. Anderson, S. Bilek, M. Brudzinski, X. Chen, H. DeShon, C. Hayward, M. Karplus, K. Keranen, C. Langston, *et al.* (2018). A community experiment to record the full seismic wavefield in Oklahoma, *Seismol. Res. Lett.* doi: 10.1785/0220180079.

Turcotte, D., and D. McAdoo (1979). Thermal subsidence and petroleum generation in the southwestern block of the Los Angeles basin, California, *J. Geophys. Res.* **84,** 3460–3464.

Villa, V., Y. Li, R. W. Clayton, and P. Persaud (2023). Three-dimensional basin depth map of the northern Los Angeles from gravity and seismic measurements, *J. Geophys. Res.* **128,** e2022JB025425, doi: 10.1029/2022JB025425.

Wright, T. L. (1991). Structural geology and tectonic evolution of the Los Angeles basin, California, in *Active Margin Basins*, K. T. Biddle (Editor), Vol. 52, 35–134, doi: 10.1306/M52531C3.

Yang, Y., and R. Clayton (2023). Shallow seismicity in the Long Beach–Seal Beach, California area, *Seismol. Res. Lett.* **94,** no. 4, 1948–1956, doi: 10.1785/0220220358.

Yang, Y., and R. Clayton (2024). Mapping Los Angeles basin depth with *Sp* converted phases, *Geophys. Res. Lett.* **51,** e2024GL111135, doi: 10.1029/2024GL111135.

Zeng, Q., F. C. Lin, and V. C. Tsai (2024). Spurious Rayleigh-wave apparent anisotropy near major structural boundaries: A numerical and theoretical investigation, *Geophys. J. Int.* **239,** no. 2, 901–913, doi: 10.1093/gji/ggae305.

Zou, C., and R. Clayton (2024). Imaging the Northern Los Angeles basins with autocorrelations, *Seismol. Res. Lett.* **96,** no. 3, 1791–1801, doi: 10.1785/0220240140.

Manuscript received 5 March 2025
Published online 29 July 2025

Data Mine

OPEN ACCESS

Active and Passive Seismic Surveys over the Grounding Zone of Eastwind Glacier, Antarctica

Ronan S. Agnew[*†1,2], Emma Pearce[†2,3], Marianne Karplus[4], Meghana Ranganathan[5], Andrew O. Hoffman[6], Madeline Hunt[7,8], Andrew Pretorius[1], Sooraj E. Shanly[1,9], Mitchel Beres[10], Kaushik K. Pradhan[4], Yeshey Seldon[4,11], Adam D. Booth[1], Roger A. Clark[1], and Tun Jan Young[12]

Abstract

The grounding zone of a marine-terminating glacier, where ice begins to float, is a key control on glacier stability and ice discharge. Seismic deployments are a powerful means of studying both the geometry and processes of grounding zones; however, these regions are frequently inaccessible and dangerous for field work, and as a result are underrepresented in field studies. We report new data sets acquired at Eastwind Glacier, Antarctica, a relatively accessible grounding zone near McMurdo Station and Scott Base, as part of the Eastwind Glacier Geophysical Surveys on Top of an Antarctic Ice Shelf Transition, EGGS on TOAST, project. These data sets comprise a deployment of three-component seismic nodes and distributed acoustic sensing. The nodal deployment consisted of 330 nodes crossing the grounding zone, with all 330 nodes continuously recording for at least nine days, and 150 nodes recording for 19 days, in the austral summer of 2022/2023. Hammer-and-plate sources were recorded, with densely spaced shots along flow through the center of the array and shots located at every node. In 2023/2024, a 2.2 km fiber-optic cable was deployed for active source imaging by distributed acoustic sensing along and across flow, immediately downstream of the grounding line, for a period of 2 hr. Analysis of active source data recorded by the nodal array locates the point of flotation within the grounding zone and provides ice thickness estimates. We present initial analyses of passive source data, including icequake detection and location, and ambient noise analysis. We expect this data set to be of significant value to provide insight into fundamental grounding zone processes and as an event-rich cryoseismological data set on which to test novel methods of seismic analysis.

Cite this article as Agnew, R. S., E. Pearce, M. Karplus, M. Ranganathan, A. O. Hoffman, M. Hunt, A. Pretorius, S. E. Shanly, M. Beres, K. K. Pradhan, *et al.* (2025). Active and Passive Seismic Surveys over the Grounding Zone of Eastwind Glacier, Antarctica, *Seismol. Res. Lett.* **97**, 591–605, doi: 10.1785/0220250024.

Supplemental Material

Introduction

Dynamics of marine-terminating glaciers and ice sheets are influenced by both their geometry and physical processes at grounding zones, where the ice transitions from grounded on land to floating on water (Weertman, 1974; Hughes, 1975; Conway *et al.*, 1999; Schoof, 2007). The locations of grounding zones define the point at which ice no longer responds to friction associated with basal sliding, and are also a measure of glacier extent, bounding the interior grounded region of an ice sheet that can contribute to sea level. Glacier grounding zones are dynamic environments in which the flotation point advances and retreats in response to both short-term tidal variation (e.g., Freer *et al.*, 2023) and to longer-term glaciological and oceanographic forcings (e.g., Gudmundsson *et al.*, 2012; Robel *et al.*, 2014; Neuhaus *et al.*, 2021; Haseloff and Sergienko, 2022). Primary controls on a

1. University of Leeds, Leeds, United Kingdom, https://orcid.org/0009-0000-3609-6815 (RSA); https://orcid.org/0000-0002-8166-9608 (ADB); https://orcid.org/0000-0002-3508-8183 (RAC); 2. British Antarctic Survey, Cambridge, United Kingdom, https://orcid.org/0000-0001-5696-8465 (EP); 3. University of Strasbourg/CNRS Institut Terre and Environment of Strasbourg (ITES), Strasbourg, France; 4. University of Texas at El Paso, El Paso, Texas, U.S.A., https://orcid.org/0000-0001-6007-5790 (MK); https://orcid.org/0000-0001-7722-0106 (KKP); https://orcid.org/0009-0007-1389-2924 (YS); 5. University of Chicago, Chicago, Illinois, U.S.A., https://orcid.org/0000-0002-8099-4775 (MR); 6. Lamont-Doherty Earth Observatory, Palisades, New York, U.S.A., https://orcid.org/0000-0003-1236-5704 (AOH); 7. Earthscope Consortium, Socorro, New Mexico, U.S.A., https://orcid.org/0009-0005-6364-318X (MH); 8. Boise State University, Boise, Idaho, U.S.A.; 9. Peak Processing, Wroxham, United Kingdom; 10. Montana State University, Bozeman, Montana, U.S.A.; 11. Southern Methodist University, Dallas, Texas, U.S.A.; 12. University of St Andrews, St Andrews, Scotland, https://orcid.org/0000-0001-5865-3459 (TJY)

*Corresponding author: rognew91@bas.ac.uk

†These authors contributed equally to the work.

glacier grounding zone include the glacier geometry and ice volume, bed characteristics beneath the glacier, sea level and ocean tidal effects, and sea floor topography and materials (Fricker *et al.*, 2009; Brunt *et al.*, 2010).

Numerous observational studies have suggested that present-day grounding zones across the Antarctic ice sheet are in long-term retreat, increasing their contribution to sea-level rise and potentially influencing instabilities that could affect large portions of the ice sheet (Joughin *et al.*, 2014; Rignot *et al.*, 2014; Jenkins *et al.*, 2018; Graham *et al.*, 2022; Reese *et al.*, 2023). These observations make mapping and understanding grounding zone processes of great importance to understand the present and future behavior of the Antarctic ice sheet. Geophysical techniques are valuable tools with which to observe these processes.

In recent years, dense seismic monitoring of glaciers has become increasingly commonplace because technological advances now make it possible to deploy large numbers (100 s–1000 s) of three-component, lightweight seismic nodes on glaciers; these include geophones and digitizers with built-in batteries lasting up to 35 days (e.g., Karplus and Schmandt, 2018; Gimbert *et al.*, 2021; Veitch *et al.*, 2021; Nanni *et al.*, 2022; Karplus *et al.*, 2024). Using data from these networks, a suite of seismic imaging methods can be used to improve our understanding of glacier structure and processes. This includes analysis of impulsive sources such as icequakes and of ambient noise. Icequakes are microseismic events associated with basal stick-slip or englacial fracturing and are a widespread phenomenon; basal seismicity beneath marine-terminating glaciers and ice streams has been linked to tidal cycles (e.g., Anandakrishnan and Alley, 1997; Zoet *et al.*, 2012; Podolskiy *et al.*, 2016; Minowa *et al.*, 2019; Lucas *et al.*, 2023). Studying icequakes using dense seismic networks has provided insight into glacier basal stick-slip mechanics (Gimbert *et al.*, 2021), crevasse location (Nanni *et al.*, 2022), and ice deformation at a grounding zone related to tidal cycles (Le Bris *et al.*, 2024). Ambient noise sources have been used to study subglacial hydrology (van Ginkel *et al.*, 2025), as well as the structure and anisotropy of firn and ice (Chaput *et al.*, 2023; Pearce *et al.*, 2024). Using ambient noise techniques with a dense seismic array, Nanni *et al.* (2021) demonstrated the potential of dense seismic monitoring to study the subglacial environment, mapping a subglacial hydrological system in great detail. A dense array spanning a glacier grounding zone therefore has the potential to provide insight into the complex processes occurring in and beneath the ice in this dynamic environment and to investigate structural features of the ice column.

Distributed acoustic sensing (DAS) is a complementary method to traditional seismic deployments. Fiber-optic cables can be deployed on the surface or in pre-existing boreholes, offering an efficient means to investigate glacial structures at extremely high resolution. In Greenland and Antarctica, fiber-optic methods have been used to record anthropogenic noise (Fichtner, Hofstede, Kennett, *et al.*, 2023), and for active-source surveying (Booth *et al.*, 2020; Brisbourne *et al.*, 2021; Fichtner, Hofstede, Gebraad, *et al.*, 2023) to constrain internal ice structure and basal properties. Other workers have used naturally occurring seismicity to monitor englacial deformation (Fichtner *et al.*, 2025) and basal processes (Hudson *et al.*, 2021), demonstrating the versatility of DAS as a glacier geophysical tool (see Brisbourne *et al.*, 2024, for an overview of recent advances in glaciological DAS studies).

Although field geophysical campaigns on Antarctic ice streams have advanced our understanding of grounding zones (Anandakrishnan *et al.*, 2003; Christianson *et al.*, 2013; Hulbe *et al.*, 2016; Horgan *et al.*, 2021; Davis *et al.*, 2023), many questions remain about ice–ocean interactions, ice mechanics, and sediment deposition in these environments (Begeman *et al.*, 2020; Drews *et al.*, 2021; Davis *et al.*, 2023). In this article, we describe data collected as part of the Eastwind Glacier Geophysical Surveys oN Top of an Antarctic Ice Shelf Transition, EGGS on TOAST, project. The project aims to investigate the geometry and processes of the grounding zone of Eastwind Glacier using active- and passive-source seismic and DAS data collected over two field seasons during the 2022–2023 and 2023–2024 austral summers. Ice-penetrating radar and geodetic data were also collected during the same season and are reported elsewhere (Hoffman *et al.*, 2025). We selected this suite of techniques to illuminate all parts of the grounding zone, including the snow, firn, ice, bed, ocean, and seafloor, in detail and in three dimensions. Although there is a long history of seismic recording on and near Ross Island (Stern *et al.*, 1991; Rowe *et al.*, 2000), this is the first seismic deployment on Eastwind Glacier (EG) and the first seismic survey crossing the grounding zone of a Ross Island glacier. We believe this deployment is the most extensive nodal array to date at a glacier grounding zone.

Study Area

EG is an $\sim$30 km^2 glacier that drains the south slope of Mount Terror on Ross Island flowing with a maximum velocity of $\sim$300 $m\,yr^{-1}$ (Fig. 1). It flows southwest from Mount Terror before merging with Terror Glacier along its western edge and flowing into Fog Bay, a small bay in Windless Bight, feeding the McMurdo Ice Shelf. Ross Island is located near the southern end of the Terror rift within the West Antarctic rift system (Behrendt, 1999). The island formed with the emplacement of basaltic shield volcanoes Mount Bird (1765 m) and Mount Terror (3230 m) between 4.6 and 3.8 Ma and 1.7 and 1.3 Ma, respectively, and has continued to evolve over the past 1 Ma with the formation of the $\sim$3795 m high composite edifice of Mount Erebus during its current eruptive phase. The persistent convecting lava lake near the summit of Erebus is connected to a magma-filled conduit system with surface vents and fumaroles, which contributes to various eruptive seismic signals, including very long-period signals (Aster *et al.*, 2003; Dibble *et al.*, 2008).

Figure 1 shows the study area in the wider context of Ross Island and the Antarctic continent. The grounding zone of EG

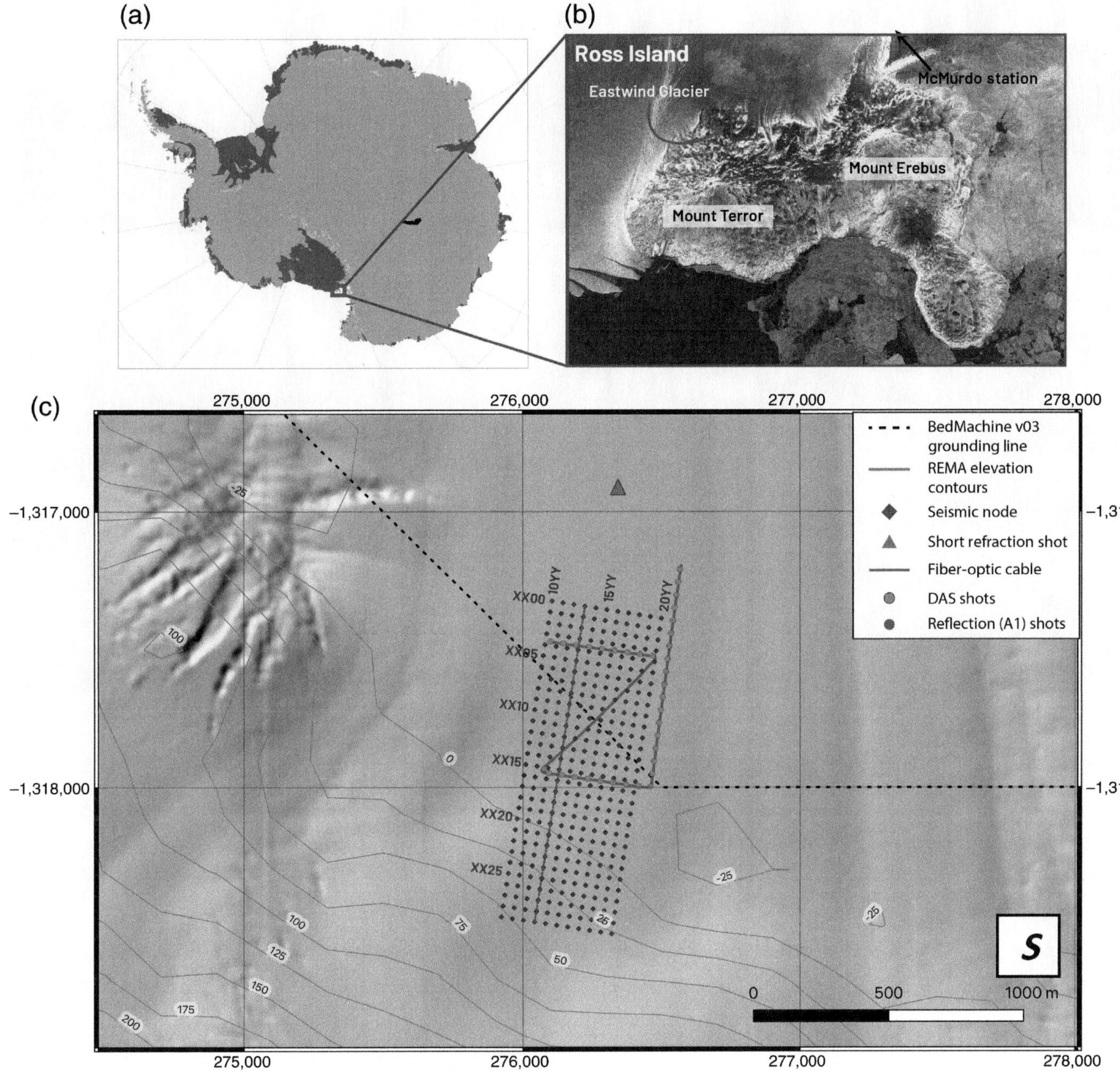

Figure 1. (a) Map of Antarctica from Morlighem *et al.* (2020), with grounded ice in light gray, floating ice in dark gray, and Ross Island denoted by a red box. (b) Map of Ross Island, with Eastwind Glacier denoted by a red box. Imagery is from Sentinel 1A data, converted to reflection backscatter using the SNAP toolbox. (c) Topographic map of the study area, with ice flow from bottom to top. The dotted arrow points in the direction of flow. Locations of seismic nodes are shown by red diamonds, and seismic reflection shot points (acquisition A1) are shown by purple dots. Also shown are the distributed acoustic sensing (DAS) cable (blue line) and associated shots (green dots) and shot location for short refraction survey (blue triangle). Surface elevation contours are from the reference elevation model for Antarctica (REMA; Howat *et al.*, 2019). The grounding line shown is from BedMachine v03 (Morlighem *et al.*, 2020; Morlighem *et al.*, 2022). Note this grounding line is downstream of the topographic minimum and expected grounding line from surface topography. The color version of this figure is available only in the electronic edition.

is ~5 km north from "Cozy Camp" (77.693° S 168.087° E), ~50 km from Scott Base and McMurdo stations, and it is easily accessible by snowmobile and PistenBully. The main trunk of the glacier is ~1.5 km wide, and its shear margins contain active crevassing and icefall features. Despite this, there is a limited surface crevassing on the main trunk of the glacier and nearby shelf, so the area is therefore relatively safe for in situ geophysical surveying compared with other grounding zones, which frequently exhibit more deformation and surface crevassing. This study area was chosen due to its relative

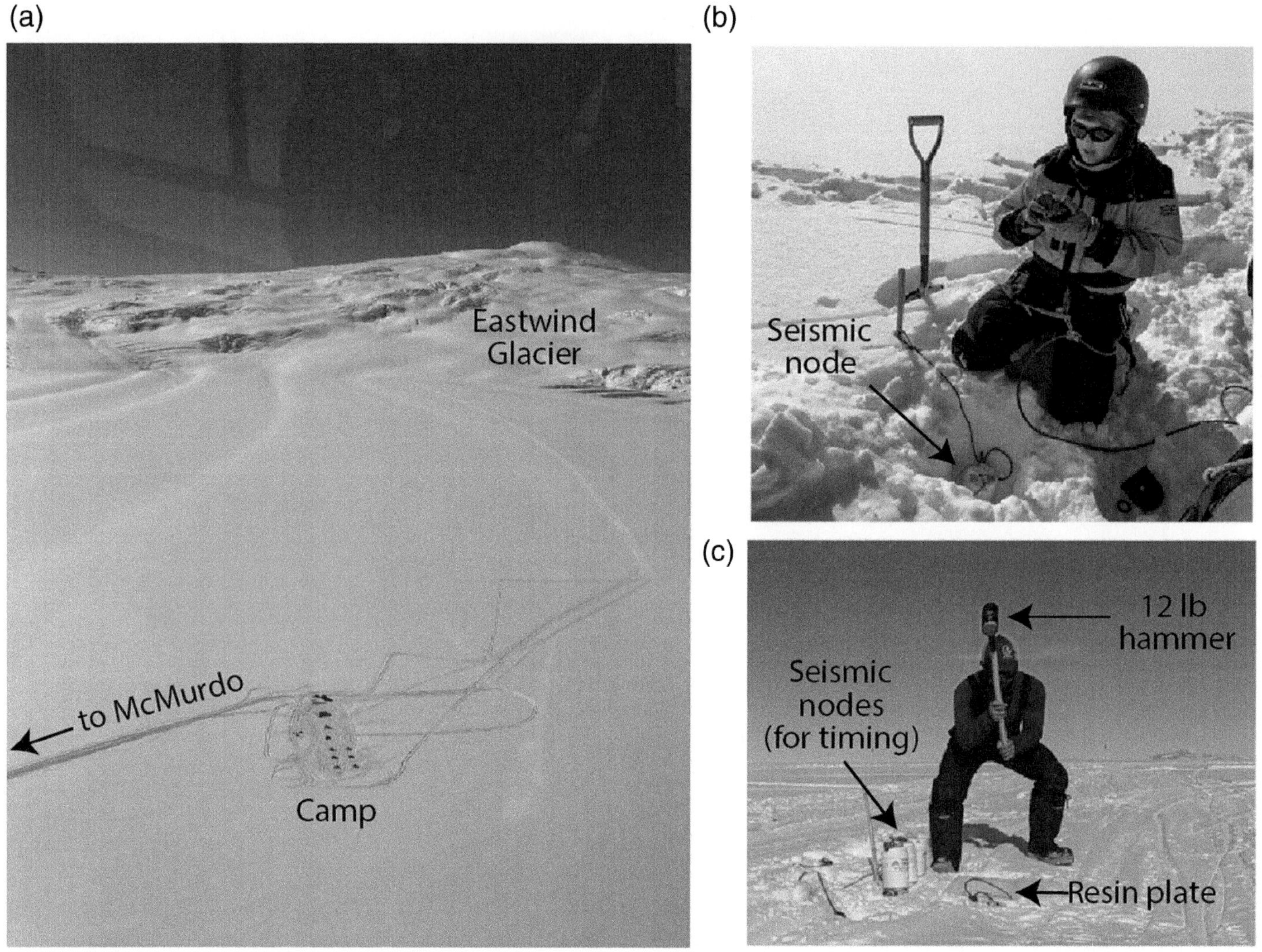

Figure 2. (a) Aerial photo of Cozy Camp, with vehicle track leading to Eastwind Glacier and the nodal array (Photograph credit: Jenny Cunningham). (b) Field deployment of a three-component seismic node at ~25 cm depth. (c) Hammer strikes on resin plate to create seismic source, with timing nodes nearby. The color version of this figure is available only in the electronic edition.

accessibility, safety, scale, and the ability to observe a complete grounding zone with relative logistical simplicity.

Data Acquisition and Availability

Nodal array

During the first field season (2022–2023), we deployed a nodal array across the grounding zone of EG, as defined loosely from surface topography and supported by ice-penetrating radar data acquired in late 2022 (Hoffman *et al.*, 2025). An expected grounding line position was identified upstream of a minimum in surface elevation, which occurs where ungrounded ice forms a depression immediately downstream of the flotation point before adjusting to isostatic equilibrium. It was therefore expected that the array would span both grounded ice and ice shelf.

A total of 330 Magseis Fairfield Z-Land Generation 25 Hz three-component nodes were deployed in an array between 11 and 13 January 2023 (Fig. 2). The nodes were deployed in eleven lines aligned along the flow of the glacier, with the naming convention of XXYY, in which XX represents the across flow line number. YY represents the position along flow in that line, sequenced opposite to the flow direction (i.e., station XX00 is positioned farthest downstream in line XX). Each line was composed of 30 nodes. Nodes were spaced 40 m apart in both the along- and across-flow directions to allow sufficient spatial coverage both along and across flow, while also allowing the recovery of wavelengths down to 80 m; this is sufficient for the recording and use of ambient noise data to image the shallow subsurface. The array spanned a 400 m by 1160 m grid covering the approximate location of the grounding zone, with the true north end of the grid upstream on the grounded ice and the south end of the grid downstream on the ice shelf. All nodes recorded at a sampling rate of 1 kHz and a preamp gain of 12 dB. Nodes were oriented to true north using a magnetic declination of 138° E and buried at an average depth of 25 cm

TABLE 1
Timeline of Activities Conducted at the Field Site in January/February 2023

Date (mm/dd)	Activity
01/11–01/13	Installed seismic nodes
01/14–01/16	Refraction survey (Hoffman *et al.*, 2025)
01/16	Snowmobile grooming of survey region
01/17	2D active source survey (acquisition A1)
01/18–01/21	3D active source survey (acquisition A2)
01/22	Decommissioned 180 seismic nodes
01/23	Camp pullout
01/24–01/31	Seismic nodes recording for "quiet period"
02/01–02/02	Uplift of remaining seismic nodes

from the snow surface to the top of the node. Bamboo poles were installed roughly 0.5 m west of each node to mitigate wind noise, and a 1.5 m length of string was tied between the bamboo and the node to aid in rapid node recovery (Fig. 2b). All stations were located using a real-time kinematic (RTK) Global Navigation Satellite Systems receiver (Stonex S900) prior to node deployment, with relative positions to a base station located at station 1414 determined to within a few centimeters. A timeline of activity around the deployment is shown in Table 1.

One hundred eighty nodes (along-flow lines 13, 14, 15, 17, and 18; stations 13YY, 14YY, 15YY, 17YY, 18YY, and 19YY) were retrieved on 22 January 2023, after 9–11 days of recording. The remaining 150 nodes (lines 10YY, 11YY, 12YY, 16YY, and 20YY) were retrieved on 1–2 February 2023, after 19–22 days of recording. Nodes retrieved on 22 January were chosen to maximize variation of distances between remaining stations. Data were offloaded in Fairfield continuous (fcnt) format and then converted to PH5 format using Earthscope PH5 tools. All PH5 data are archived at the Earthscope Data Management Center with the network code XS (Young *et al.*, 2023).

Active source experiments

The January–February 2023 nodal array was designed to facilitate joint passive and active acquisitions. Sources were generated by a 12 lb sledgehammer striking a 30 × 30 × 2 cm resin plate placed at the snow surface (Fig. 2c). At least five good-quality hammer strikes (good coupling with the plate and no double bounce of the hammer) were conducted at each source location. A node was deployed (station number 1334) at each source location and carried between source locations to record shot times at zero offset. Source times were recorded to the nearest second, so the exact time must be estimated from the timer node record in further analysis. Hammer strikes were at least 10 s apart to ensure the individual shots could be identified in the seismic record without interference from adjacent shots in the sequence.

Data from two groups of seismic sources, which we refer to as A1 and A2, were recorded at the node grid: (A1) a 2D reflection profile and (A2) a 3D acquisition. The 2D reflection profile (A1) was acquired along line 13 of the node grid on 17 January 2023 and consisted of a total of one hundred seventeen sources, spaced at 10 m intervals between stations 1300 and 1329. The sources for acquisition A2 were located at every station in the node grid along lines 10 to 20 (330 source locations in total). These data were collected from 18–21 January 2023. In addition to this, short refraction surveys, recorded with conventional geophones on a Geometrics Geode system, were conducted on 14–16 January 2023 and are reported by Hoffman *et al.* (2025).

DAS

During the second field season (2023–2024), we acquired DAS seismic data along a fiber-optic cable, immediately downstream of the grounding line. We deployed ~2.2 km of Linden SPE-7196 single-mode fiber-optic cable using a fiber-optic cable-laying sled towed behind a snowmobile. The sled included a spool holding the fiber-optic cable and a metal keel with a hollow metal tube to simultaneously dig a trench 30 cm deep and unspool the cable into the trench as the sled was towed. The fiber-optic cable was deployed in a layout that provides seismic recording parallel to the long and short axes of the 2022–2023 nodal grid (Fig. 1). The first section of cable extended in a northerly direction from the interrogator, parallel to the long axis of the grid, then turned east to cross its short axis. The cable then tracked diagonally southwest across the grid, with a final span again traversing east across the short axis of the grid close to its southern extent. The total length of fiber-optic cable is 3.4 km. This comprises, in order, (1) a 1 km launch lead (included to ensure faithful recording of amplitudes along the whole cable length), (2) the main 2.2 km of fiber under test, and (3) 200 m of redundant fiber remaining spooled on a cable drum. Channels 1–625 therefore compose launch lead and channels 2076–2200 compose redundant cable. The cable was buried on 5 February 2024 and left for two days to sinter in to improve coupling to the soft snow.

On 7 February 2024, we recorded continuous data with a Febus Optics A1-R interrogator over a 2 hr period. The system was powered by a 2 kHz portable generator with an uninterruptable power supply, which set a limit on continuous recording time due to the necessity of refueling. The interrogator and PC monitor were kept in a tent to keep snow out and keep the system warm. Because the cable was trenched at a consistent depth in the snow to isolate it from wind noise, we expect coupling and noise to be consistent along the cable, and reflective of the coupling achieved by the nodes buried at approximately the same depth. Generator noise was mitigated by placing the

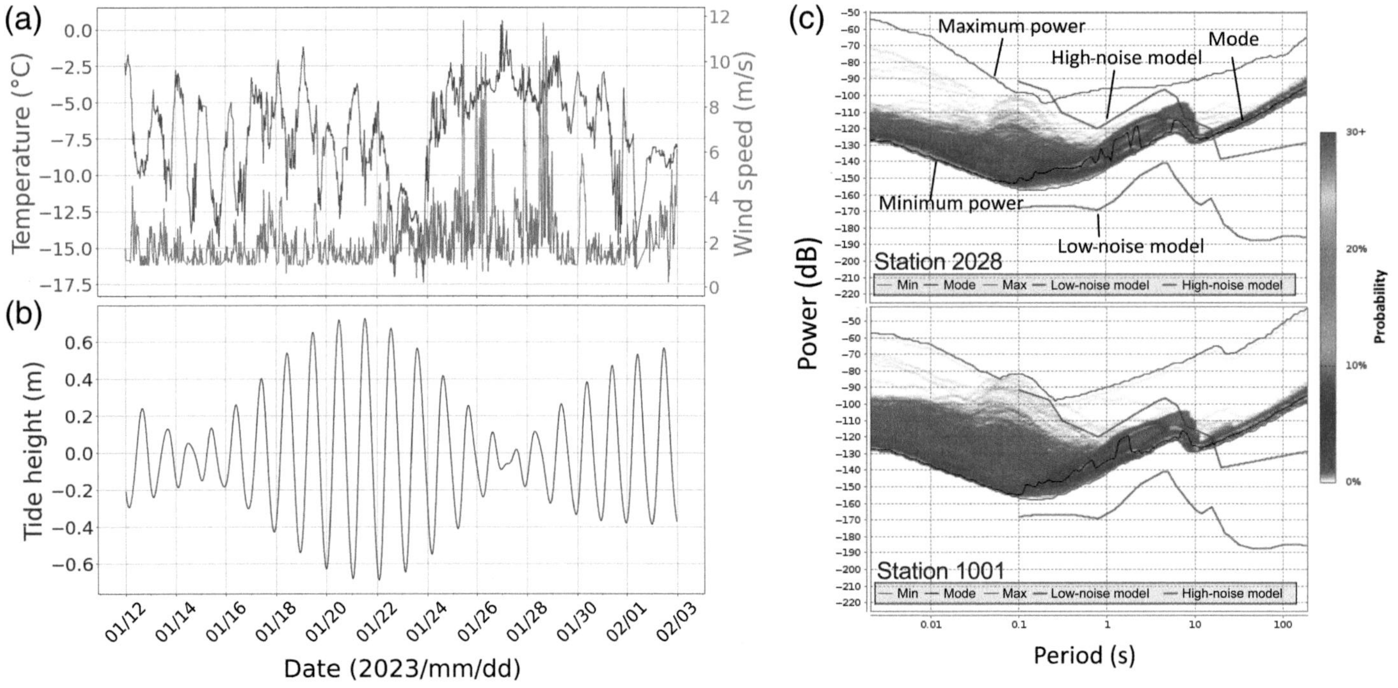

Figure 3. (a) Wind speed and temperature for the 2023 period of node deployment, from the Windless Bight Automatic Weather Station. (b) Tidal data for the period of node deployment, from the CATS2008 tidal model (Padman *et al.*, 2002). (c) Noise probability density functions (PDFs) derived from power spectral density (PSD) for vertical components across all stations, from the Incorporated Research Institutions for Seismology (IRIS) Modular Utility for STAtistical kNowledge Gathering (Casey *et al.*, 2018). The color scale represents the probability density of a specific power level at a certain frequency. The red line represents the minimum power at each period, the blue line represents the maximum power, and the black line represents mode. The brown lines represent a low- and high-noise model for the entire array (Peterson, 1993). The color version of this figure is available only in the electronic edition.

generator on foam pads and situating it roughly 15 m from the end of the fiber. The measurement of strain rate was calculated in a 10 m gauge length. The output data set has a 1 ms sampling interval and a 1.6 m trace interval.

Hammer strikes were recorded at thirty-six locations along the length of the fiber-optic cable, with a distance of 47 m between the shot locations, and no shots recorded along the diagonal section of the cable (Fig. 1). Shot points were surveyed by RTK Global Positioning System (GPS). Up to seven repeat shots were taken at each location to facilitate stacking and increase signal-to-noise ratio (SNR). Shot times are estimated directly from the DAS data, which has GPS timing, by observing the earliest arrival of seismic energy at the appropriate position along the cable. DAS data are available at the United Kingdom Natural Environment Research Council Polar Data Centre.

Environment

As context for further analyses of the nodal data acquired in January–February 2023, we show data from the Windless Bight Automatic Weather Station (Lazzara *et al.*, 2012), along with tidal data obtained from the CATS2008 high-resolution regional inverse model of the entire circum-Antarctic ocean (Padman *et al.*, 2002). The deployment covered most of the period of a spring-neap tidal cycle and hence could record signals due to tidal mixing or grounding line migration associated with the change in tide height (e.g., Minowa *et al.*, 2019; Nanni *et al.*, 2022).

Figure 3a,b shows a summary of wind speed, temperature, and tide height for the period of deployment. Temperatures ranged from −17.4°C to +0.6°C, averaging −7°C ± 3°C. Wind speeds ranged from 0.2 to 11.8 $\mathrm{m\,s^{-1}}$, with maximum speeds recorded between 25 and 29 January. The average wind speed for the period of node deployment was 2.4 $\mathrm{m\,s^{-1}}$. During node retrieval, we noted that more than 30 cm of snow had accumulated on top of the nodes between 23 January and 1 February 2023. Nodes were deployed for the majority of a monthly tidal cycle, with a maximum tidal amplitude of 1.4 m.

Figure 3c shows aggregated noise probability density functions (PDFs) for representative "quiet" (station 2028) and "noisy" (station 1001) stations for the period of deployment. The PDF is derived from power spectral density estimates (McNamara and Buland, 2004) for the nodes using the method of Casey *et al.* (2018). Lines representing models of typical global background seismic noise are plotted alongside the PDF and are marked as "high noise model" and "low noise model" (Peterson, 1993). The maximum and minimum power as a function of period are shown as the blue and red lines, respectively. The primary microseism peak, likely produced by the direct interaction of ocean waves with the coastline, is probably obscured by the self-noise of the nodes. The

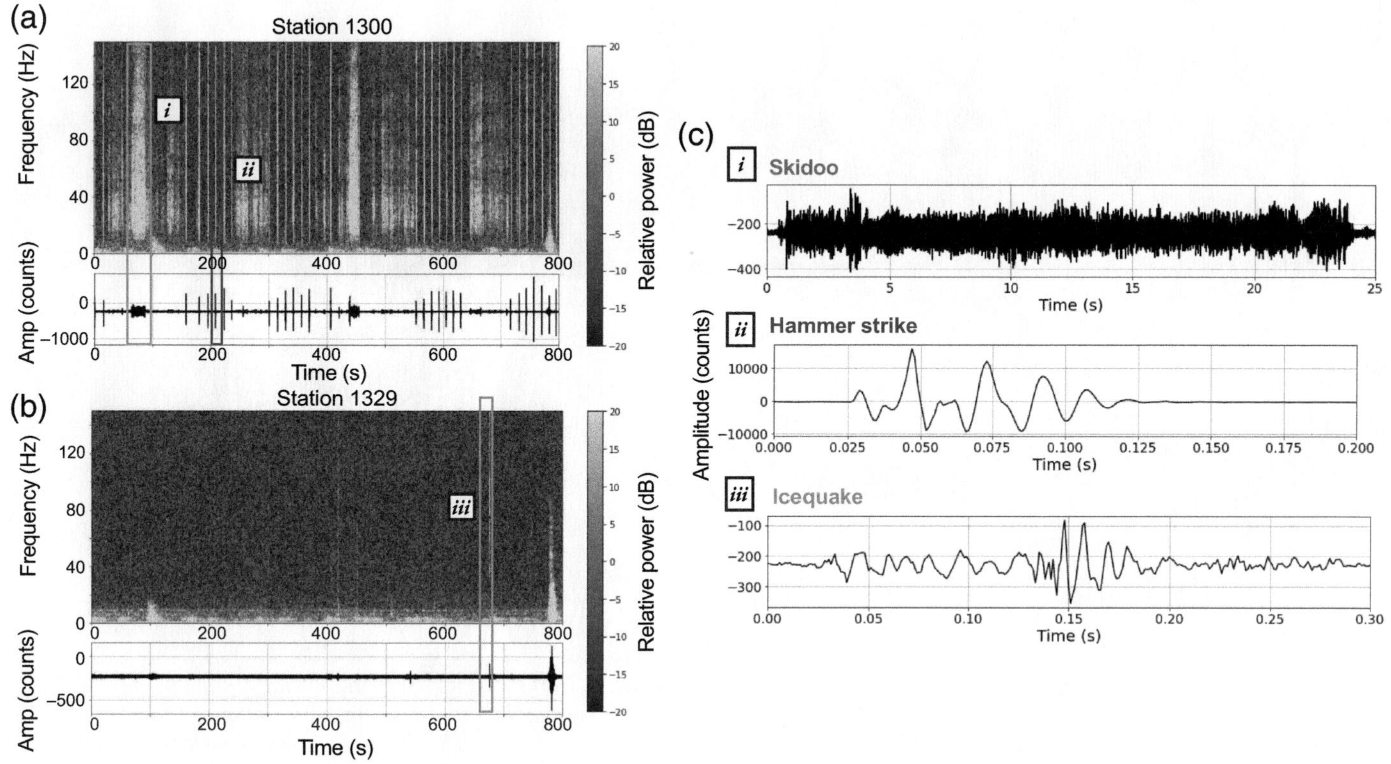

secondary microseism (half the period of the primary) results from the interaction of direct and reflected ocean waves (Longuet-Higgins, 1950) and can be seen at a period of ~5–10 s. The PDF from these data generally falls between the low- and high-noise models (Peterson, 1993) for the expected frequencies for the nodes, indicating generally expected background noise levels for the sensors.

Figure 4. Example signals recorded by the deployed array on 17 January 2023. (i) Skidoo noise, (ii) Hammer strike from active source surveying, and (iii) icequake. (a,b) Spectrograms and vertical-component traces for stations 1300 (downstream) and 1329 (upstream) for the exact same time period. Plots on the right side (c) show a zoom of the event signals (vertical component). Skidoo and hammer strike traces are shown from station 1300. Icequake signal is shown from station 1329. The color version of this figure is available only in the electronic edition.

Data Snapshots

Example events

A wide variety of seismic signals were recorded by the nodal array; examples are shown in Figure 4. Figure 4a,b shows spectrograms for an 800 s period on 17 January 2023, for stations 1300 and 1329, which are at opposite ends of the array (downstream/upstream, respectively). The signals shown for this time period include both active (i, ii) and passive source (iii, iv) signals. Event (i) consists of skidoo noise, and (ii) shows a hammer-and-plate source. We interpret signal (iii) as an icequake, recorded only at the upstream station (over grounded ice).

Seismic reflection (hammer-and-plate node data)

Shot times were precisely found by picking shots from the timer node record. Shot gathers were then extracted from the PH5 volume and stacked to improve the SNR. Data were then processed as common receiver gathers because of the unconventional shooting geometry combining sparse receiver coverage with dense source spacing. Preprocessing followed a workflow that involved static corrections to correct for surface topography, spiking deconvolution (minimum phase, operator length 20 ms), and frequency–wavenumber (*f-k*) filtering to remove interference from groundroll. The *f-k* filter was chosen to remove phases with apparent velocities less than 3.5 km s^{-1}, and 200 Hz noise with zero apparent velocity prominent on near-offset channels. An Ormsby band-pass filter (frequencies 25–50–250–300 Hz) was then applied. The dominant frequency of the reflected wavelet is 84 Hz, with a normal-incidence Fresnel radius at the ice base of ~74 m. Figure 5 shows two preprocessed common receiver gathers from the acquisition (unprocessed receiver gathers can be found in the supplemental material, available to this article). Figure 5a shows a receiver gather from station 1300, at the far downstream end of the array, assumed to be on the shelf. Inset is an example wavelet of a diving wave first arrival to highlight the polarity convention. The ice-base reflection (two-way travel time ≃0.15 s) at this point is a reversed polarity wavelet (label 1), indicating a downward change in acoustic impedance consistent with an ice–water interface. This is followed at 0.31 s by the ice–base multiple (label 2), and at 0.34 s by the normal-polarity seabed reflection (label 3). At the shelf end of the line, there is an interference between the seabed primary reflection

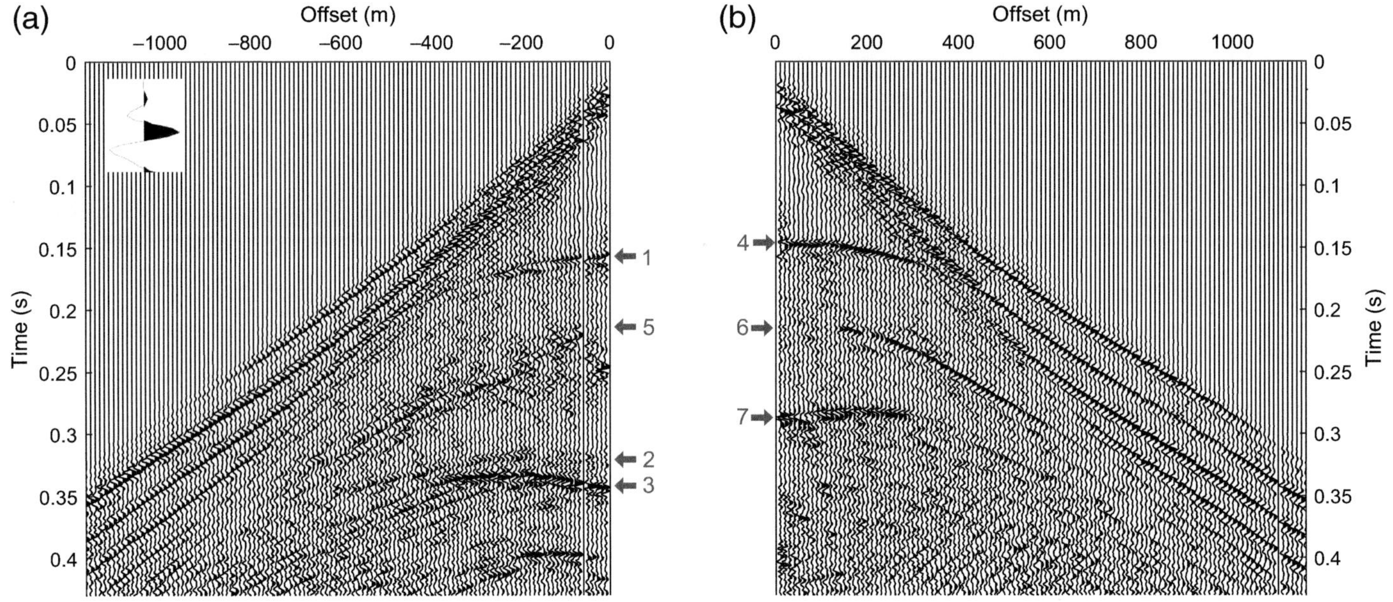

Figure 5. Common receiver gathers from (a) station 1300, at the far downstream end of the array, and (b) station 1329, at the far upstream end. Main reflected phases visible are labeled as (1) ice–water interface (reverse polarity), (2) ice–water multiple, (3) seabed reflection, (4) ice–bed interface (normal polarity), (5), (6) converted wave, and (7) ice–bed multiple. Data shown are preprocessed receiver gathers shown with an automatic gain control (window length 100 ms) for display only. Inset in (a) shows a diving wavelet to highlight the polarity convention. The color version of this figure is available only in the electronic edition.

and the ice–water first multiple. Figure 5b shows a common-receiver gather from station 1329, at the far upstream end of the line. The ice–base reflection here is of normal polarity, which is consistent with an ice–bedrock/stiff sediment interface (label 4). There is an arrival (two-way travel time ~0.2 s; label 5) with significant energy between the ice–base primary and its multiple (label 6), which may be a *P-to-S* converted wave detected on the vertical component due to the basal and surface topography.

DAS

Hammer strikes were recorded by the DAS interrogator (Fig. 6). The strain-rate response to the shot was observed in the fiber-optic cable roughly 200 m either side of the shot points. Hammer strikes are impulsive signals with frequency content from ~50 to 300 Hz. Figure 6a,b shows example windows of multichannel DAS data, along with an example of a single trace (channel 719, 9.5 m source–receiver offset), both raw and with a band-pass filter applied (Fig. 6c). Figure 6d shows a spectrogram of a recorded trace.

First Results

Reflection imaging

Preprocessed data were corrected for normal moveout and stacked. Figure 7a shows the surface topography obtained from RTK GPS surveys and Figure 7b an unmigrated time section obtained from the hammer-and-plate source node data. Ice flow is from right to left. Labeled on the section are the clearly visible ice–water and ice–bedrock interfaces (1 and 2, respectively), the seabed (3 and 4), and the ice-bottom multiple (5). Apparent features in the ice column arriving before the ice–base reflection consist of residual groundroll and *f-k* artefacts.

The grounding zone location is identifiable as the point in the profile where the ice–base reflection changes polarity from reversed to normal. We do not analyze absolute reflectivity; however, we note that the positive polarity reflection from the ice–bed interface must come from a positive impedance contrast and is therefore indicative of a relatively hard bed (encompassing materials from stiff sediment to bedrock). This occurs 700 ± 40 m upstream from station 1300. This is consistent with inferences made from surface topography, where the point of flotation is expected to be a short distance upstream of the topographic minimum (560 m upstream from station 1300, at station 1314), but is ~300 m upstream of the BedMachine picked grounding line. We image the seabed along two portions of the profile: from 0 to 300 m, and from 600 m to the grounding zone. Interference between the ice–water multiple and the seabed reflection results in ambiguity between these events at $x \simeq 200$ m; however, the dip and normal polarity of the seabed reflection enables its identification (the ice–base multiple has a reversed polarity). Taking an average velocity in the firn and ice of 3610 ± 30 ms^{-1} from short refraction surveys (Hoffman *et al.*, 2025), the ice thickness is 280 ± 10 m at the downstream end of the array and 258 ± 10 m at the upstream end. The ice thins to 233 ± 10 m as it crosses the grounding line. Assuming a seawater velocity of 1500 ms^{-1}, the water column thickness is 140 m beneath station 1300.

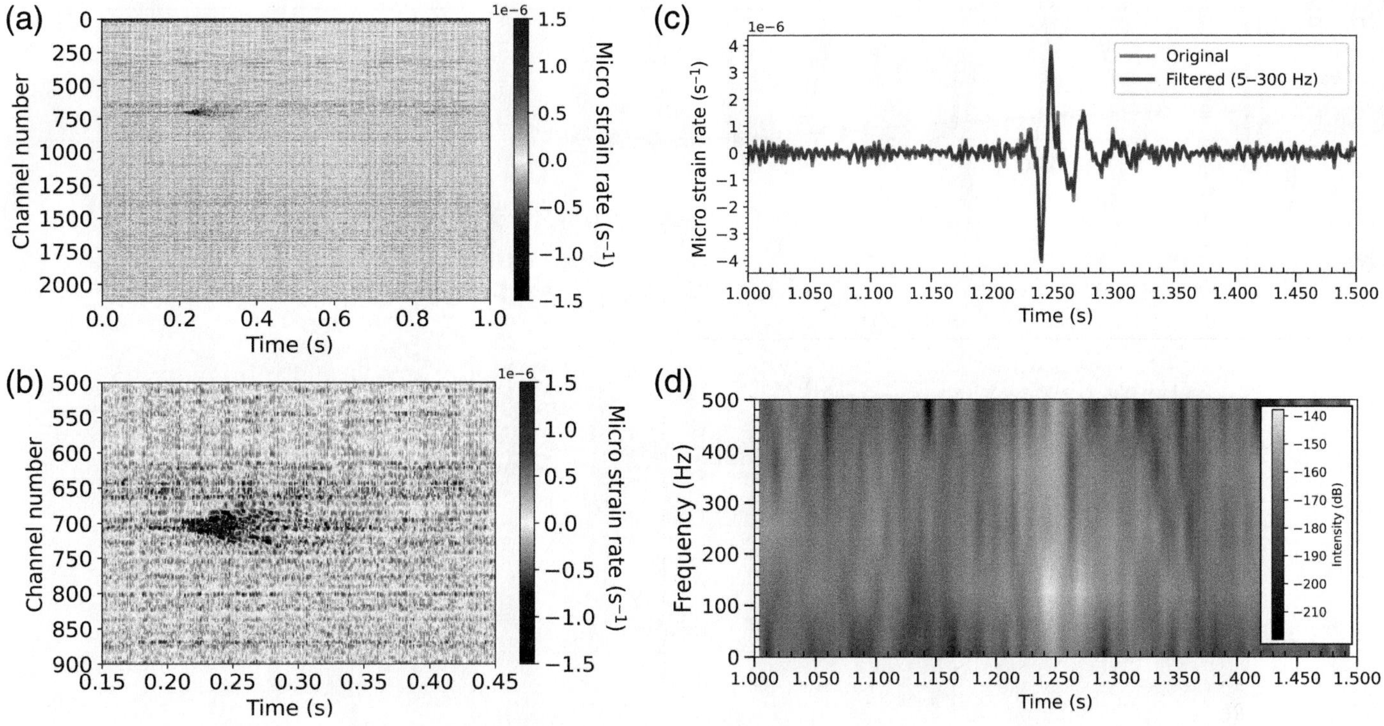

Figure 6. (a) One second of DAS strain-rate data recorded on 3.4 km of fiber-optic cable, showing one hammer strike. (b) Zoom of 0.3 s of the DAS data displayed in (a), from channels 500 to 900. Main cable layout is from channel 626. (c) Example trace from channel 719 (9.5 m source–receiver offset), displayed raw (gray line) and with a 5–300 Hz band-pass filter (red line). Sampling rate is 1 kHz. (d) Spectrogram for 0.5 s strain-rate data for channel 719. Displayed data are from the file EWG_ACTIVE_2024-02-06_23-53-07_UTC. The color version of this figure is available only in the electronic edition.

Where we do not image the seabed, there is a seabed elevation change of 80 m over a horizontal distance of 270 m, implying a steep dip of roughly 17°.

Analysis of active source data from the 3D acquisition (A2) will provide insights into the 3D structure and deformation of the grounding zone, including crystal orientation fabric, azimuthal anisotropy, and 3D bed topography. Tides at this site are small in the context of the Antarctic continent (∼1.4 m); this fact combined with the steep bed topography leads us to expect little grounding line migration. This data set may therefore provide a useful control to study glaciological processes where the grounding zone geometry may be relatively static, and provide context for further studies in areas such as the Weddell Sea where grounding lines migrate large distances (e.g., Freer *et al.*, 2023).

Ambient noise analysis

Ambient noise techniques reconstruct virtual active sources at each station location by cross-correlating continuous seismic noise records between every pair of stations. Ambient noise processing followed Pearce *et al.* (2024). Optimization for ambient noise data acquisition ensured varying interstation distances to record waves of different frequencies that sample a wide range of depths. Over 54,000 Green's functions were extracted from nine days of recordings for interstation cross correlations, with interstation distances ranging from ∼40 to 1200 m. We used continuous data from all 330 stations for nine days of recording between 13 and 21 January 2023. Data preprocessing involved down-sampling to 100 Hz and high-pass filtering at 0.04 Hz. Subsequently, the data were segmented into 15 min intervals. For each segment, processing was conducted to remove any impulsive events unrelated to the ambient noise field (e.g., volcanic or icequake signals).

Cross-correlation functions were computed in the frequency domain between all station pairs using the processed 15 min segments, following the approach of Bensen *et al.* (2007). Correlation functions from all segments in a day were averaged to obtain a single daily correlation function for each station pair. Nine intercomponent correlation functions corresponding to the elastic Green's tensor were computed. The Green's correlation tensor was rotated along the interstation azimuth to provide correlation functions between the radial (R), transverse (T), and vertical (Z) components (Fig. 8).

The observed arrivals primarily consist of dispersive surface waves traveling between station pairs; this is clear from the frequency dependence of the reconstructed wave velocity. Rayleigh waves are observed on the RR, ZZ, RZ, and ZR components, whereas Love waves are apparent on the TT correlation term.

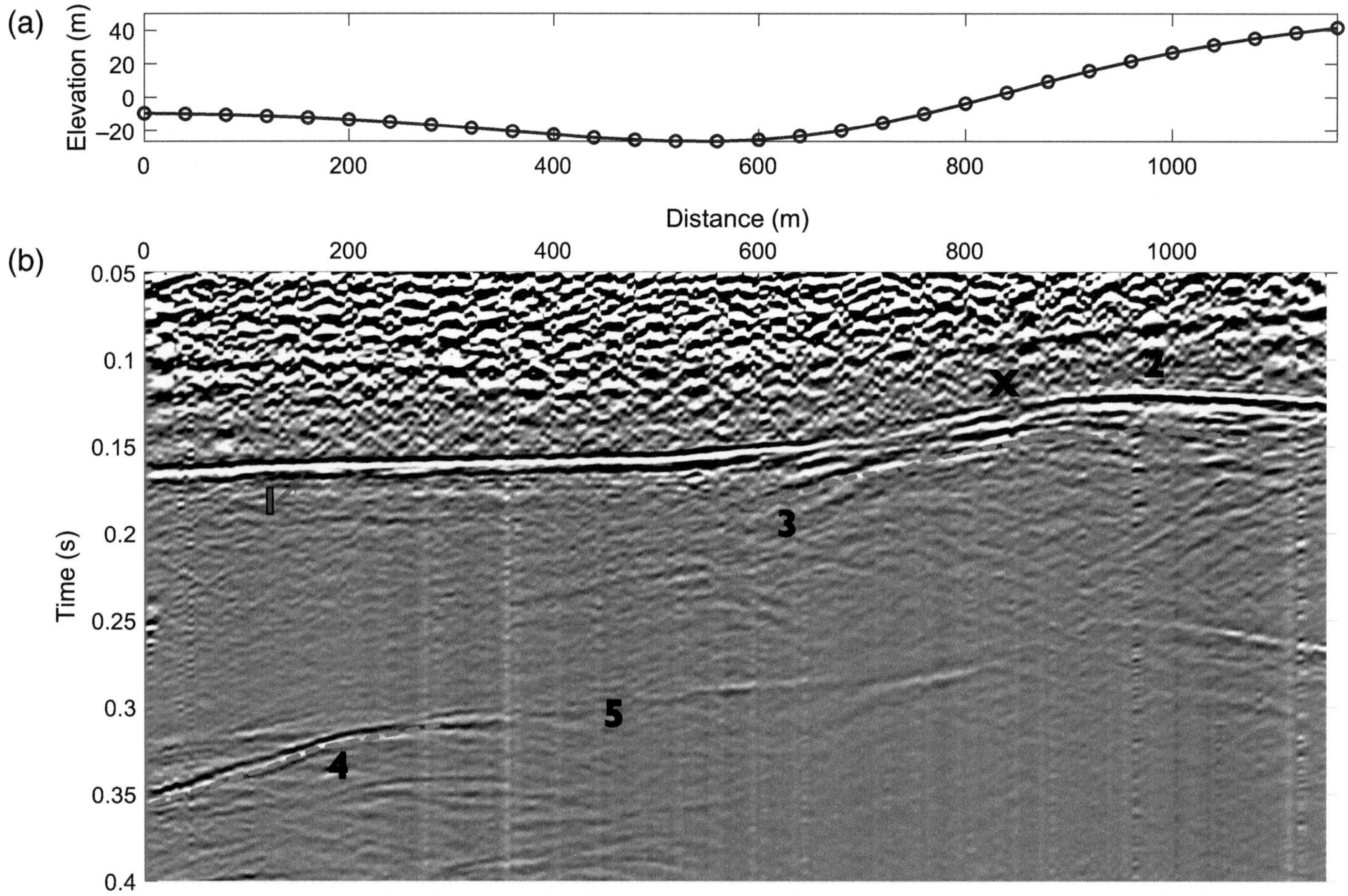

Figure 7. (a) Surface elevation over grounding zone from real-time kinematic (RTK) Global Positioning System (GPS) surveying. The circles indicate node locations. (b) Unmigrated time section of seismic data over the grounding zone. Time axis is two-way travel time. Features indicated are (1) ice–water interface, (2) ice–bedrock interface, (3) seabed close to grounding zone, (4) seabed beneath the ice shelf, and (5) ice–water multiple. "X" marks the location of the grounding line at time of survey. Interpreted seabed is marked with the overlaid line, with the central section hypothesized steeply dipping and not imaged. Apparent features arriving before the ice–base reflection consist of residual groundroll and *f-k* artefacts. Flow is right to left. The color version of this figure is available only in the electronic edition.

Icequake detection and location

Icequakes are seismic events generated from fracturing in the ice column or stick slip at the ice–bed interface. As shown in Figure 4, there were a variety of events detected by the EG array. We show here a more detailed example of one such event detected using QuakeMigrate (Winder *et al.*, 2022), using a 19-station subset of the array. QuakeMigrate calculates probable source locations by moving through the travel-time curves for both *P* and *S* waves. These locations and times are mapped into a common coordinate system to form a coalescence function—the maximum of the normalized coalescence represents the most likely event location. Figure 9 shows the output of QuakeMigrate for a single event detected at the EG array. Figure 9a shows the coalescence value in latitude/longitude, latitude/depth, and longitude/depth axes, locating the event to ~100 m southeast of the array, at ~50 m depth (i.e., in the ice column). Figure 9b shows waveforms for all three components, along with modeled compressional- and shear-wave arrival times. Figure 9c shows the maximum coalescence over time for this event pick.

We detect and locate events for a 24 hr period on 24 January 2023, on the 19-station subset of our array. We detect events between 5 and 120 Hz for *P*-wave arrivals and 5–50 Hz for *S*-wave arrivals. During this 24 hr period, ~26,000 events were detected. Note that this catalog has not been robustly validated, so this is likely an overestimate. We cluster these events into bins of size 100 × 150 m. Figure 10 shows the event density (events per bin) for the period. The event density is high within the array (~200 events per bin per day), but the highest density of events (>400 events per bin per day) coincides with the shear margin to the southeast of the array. This suggests that the data set contains abundant surface and crevassing events. Although we do not locate any volcanic events associated with the position of Mt Erebus, we expect this is due to the parameterization of QuakeMigrate, which was tuned for the detection of icequakes, which are of higher frequency than typical volcanic signals. Further analysis of

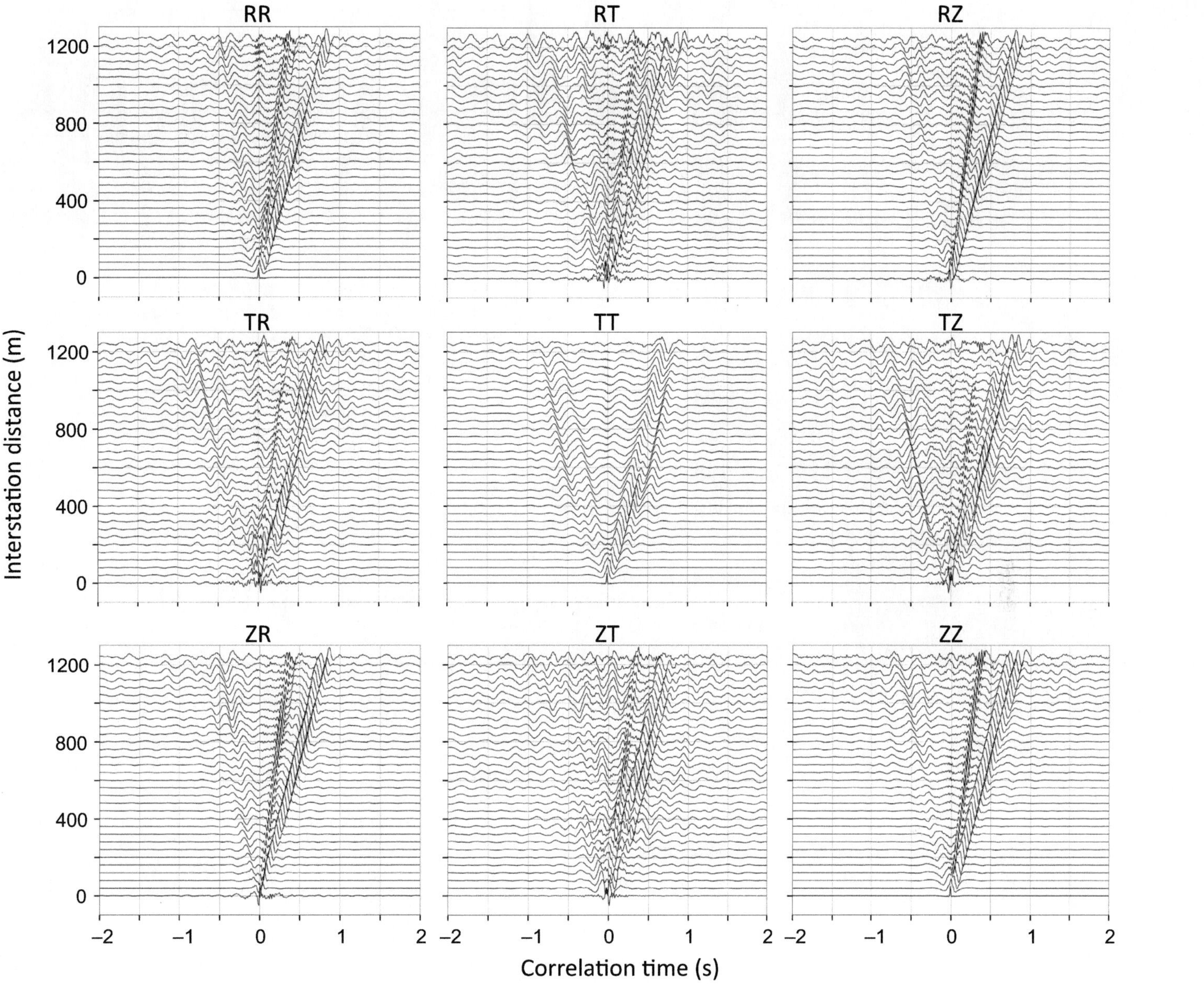

Figure 8. Correlograms obtained from the 54,000 interstation Green's functions, stacked based on interstation distance.

icequakes will allow the identification of basal events and may provide more information about the extent and character of tidal grounding line migration.

Summary

We have described data sets that comprise active and passive seismic surveys undertaken with a dense array of 330 seismic nodes in 2022/2023 and DAS in 2023/2024. This data set represents a comprehensive survey of the structure and seismic activity of a grounding zone over a tidal cycle. We have imaged the seabed downstream of the grounding zone and located the point of flotation using hammer-and-plate active seismics. The data set contains events from a variety of sources, including hammer shots, icequakes, and skidoos. Preliminary analysis of icequakes detected suggests a high proportion of surface events. Further analyses of these data sets will provide fundamental insights into grounding zone processes and the grounding zone's 3D structure, informing studies of grounding zone dynamics around the Antarctic continent.

Data and Resources

Node data have been archived at the Incorporated Research Institutions for Seismology (IRIS) Data Management Center (DMC) with the network code XS (Young *et al.*, 2023). Metadata are available at https://ds.iris.edu/mda/XS/?timewindow=2023-2023 (last accessed July 2025). Note stations 1334, 1335, and 1336 are timer nodes. 1335 and 1336 did not record all shots. The supplemental material includes one pdf file showing unprocessed receiver gathers and two csv files containing approximate shot times for the 2D and 3D active source surveys (acquisitions A1 and A2). Distributed acoustic sensing data are archived with the United Kingdom Natural Environment

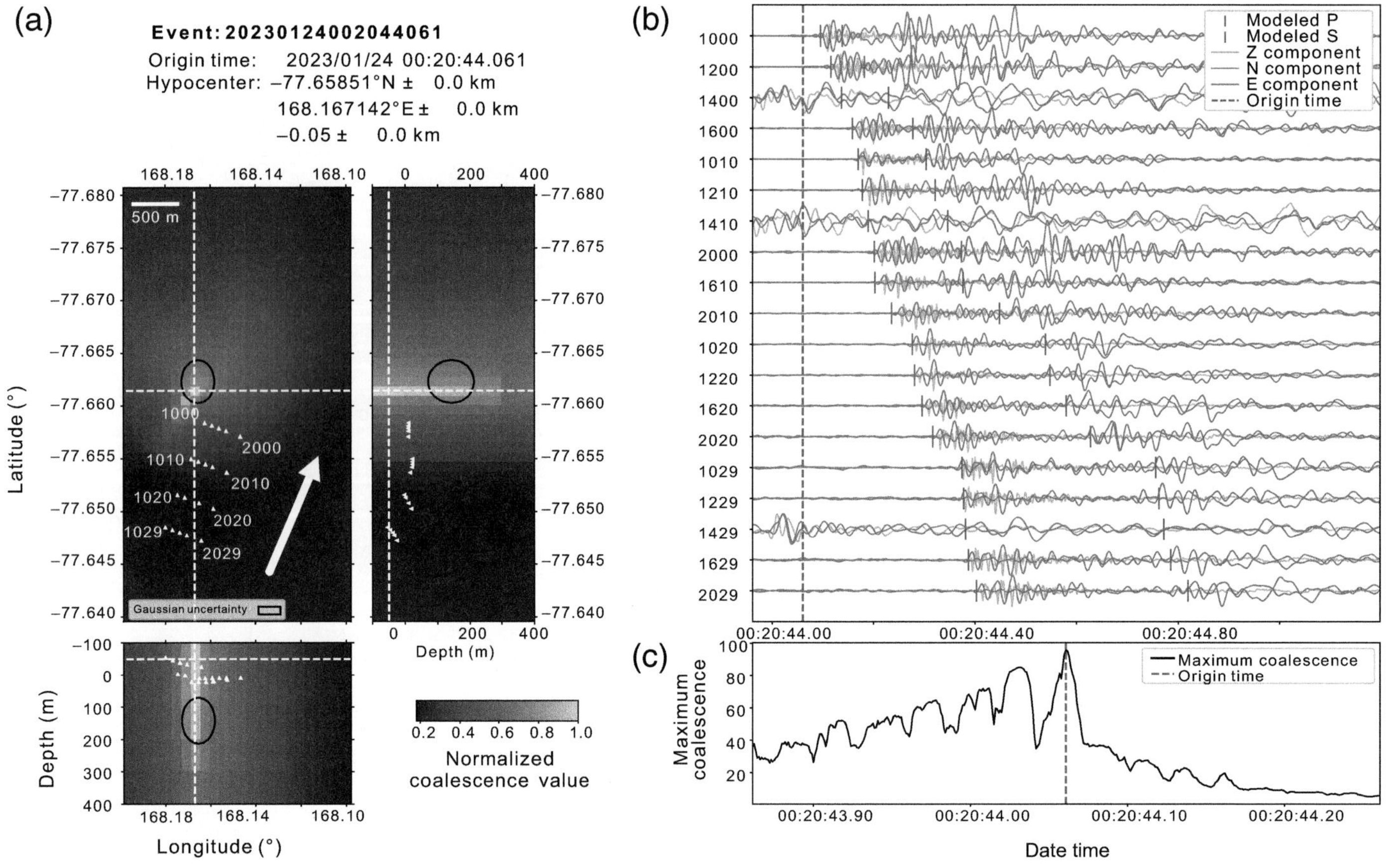

Figure 9. Output of Quakemigrate event detection and location for a single surface event. (a) An energy distribution map showing coalescence of a single event on all receivers. High normalized coalescence indicates the most likely source location and depth for the picked event. Ice flow direction is indicated by the arrow. (b) The modeled compressional (*P*)- and shear (*S*)-wave arrival time for the picked event used for the event location, shown alongside detected waveforms. (c) Maximum coalescence over time. The red dashed line shows the estimated origin time of the event. The color version of this figure is available only in the electronic edition.

Research Council (NERC) Polar Data Centre, doi: 10.5285/23dbd529-3a57-4933-bb9d-16ee1c85fda0.

Declaration of Competing Interests

The authors acknowledge that there are no conflicts of interest recorded.

Acknowledgments

Eastwind Glacier Geophysical Surveys on Top of an Antarctic Ice Shelf Transition (EGGS on TOAST) was supported through a National Science Foundation (NSF) Emerging Tasking Identification and is part of the Thwaites Interdisciplinary Margin Evolution (TIME) project, a component of the International Thwaites Glacier Collaboration (ITGC). Support from NSF (Grant 1739027) and Natural Environment Research Council (NERC: Grants NE/S006788/1 and NE/S00677X/1). Logistics were provided by NSF-U.S. Antarctic Program and NERC-British Antarctic Survey. ITGC Contribution Number ITGC-141. Preparatory surveys of Eastwind Glacier were conducted through the EAGER project (Project number NSF 2027579). Seismic instruments were provided by EarthScope Consortium through PASSCAL Polar Support Services, by the University of Texas at El Paso, and by the University of Oklahoma. The facilities of EarthScope Consortium are supported by NSF's Seismological Facility for the Advancement of Geoscience (SAGE) Award (Cooperative Support Agreement OPP-1851037). Geodetic instruments were provided by the GAGE Facility, operated by EarthScope Consortium, with support from NSF, National Aeronautics and Space Administration (NASA), and the U.S. Geological Survey (NSF Cooperative Agreement EAR-1724794). Febus Optics A1-R Distributed acoustic sensing interrogator was loaned from the University of Leeds Fibre Optic Facility, under loan Agreement UOL-FOF-0004. The authors acknowledge the support of the University of Wisconsin–Madison Automatic Weather Station Program for the AWS data (NSF Grant 2301362) and the Polar Geospatial Center for mapping support. S. E. S. performed initial processing of seismic reflection data as part of the MSc Exploration Geophysics at the University of Leeds. Seismic data were processed with Halliburton–Landmark ProMAX software under academic license to British Antarctic Survey. The authors thank Jenny Cunningham for logistical support and Kelly M. Brunt for facilitating implementation of the Emerging Tasking Identification; Greg Runyan, Ema Mayo, and Hannah Miner for assistance in the field; Knut Christianson, Andy Smith, and Galen Kaip for advising on data acquisition; Ash Goverman for advising

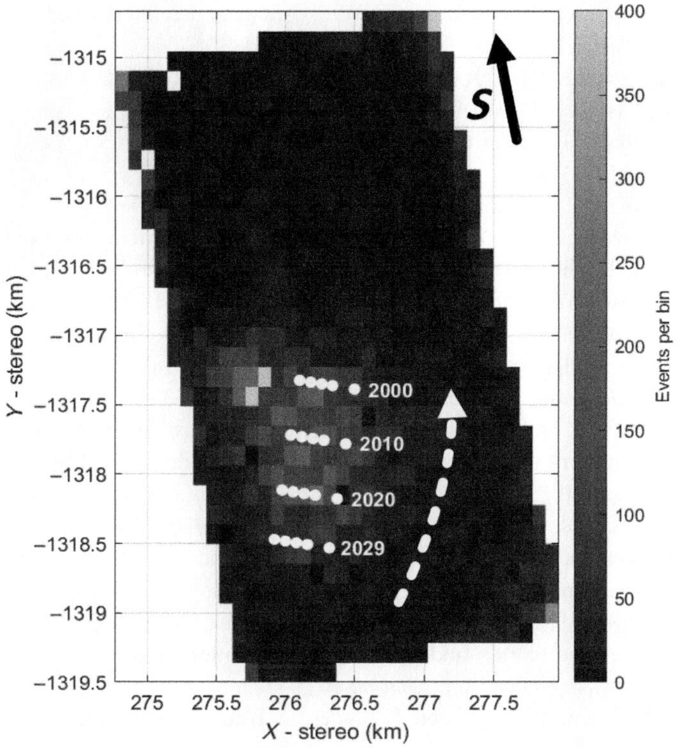

Figure 10. Event density for 1 day of data, 24 January 2023, clustered into 100 × 150 m bins. Approximately 26,000 seismic events were detected for the 24 hr period. The dashed arrow indicates ice flow direction. There is a high density of events in the shear margin southeast of the array. The color version of this figure is available only in the electronic edition.

on field planning. The authors are grateful to Florent Gimbert, Nicolas Paris, one anonymous reviewer, and the editor, whose feedback improved the article.

References

Anandakrishnan, S., and R. B. Alley (1997). Tidal forcing of basal seismicity of Ice Stream C, West Antarctica, observed far inland, *J. Geophys. Res.* **102,** no. B7, 15,183–15,196.

Anandakrishnan, S., D. Voigt, R. Alley, and M. King (2003). Ice stream D flow speed is strongly modulated by the tide beneath the Ross Ice Shelf, *Geophys. Res. Lett.* **30,** 1361.

Aster, R., S. Mah, P. Kyle, W. McIntosh, N. Dunbar, J. Johnson, M. Ruiz, and S. McNamara (2003). Very long period oscillations of Mount Erebus Volcano, *J. Geophys. Res.* **108,** 2522.

Begeman, C., S. Tulaczyk, L. Padman, M. King, M. Siegfried, T. Hodson, and H. Fricker (2020). Tidal pressurization of the ocean cavity near an Antarctic ice shelf grounding line, *J. Geophys. Res.* **125,** no. 4, doi: 10.1029/2019JC015562.

Behrendt, J. (1999). Crustal and lithospheric structure of the West Antarctic rift system from geophysical investigations—A review, *Global Planet. Change* **23,** nos. 1/4, 25–44.

Bensen, G., M. Ritzwoller, M. Barmin, A. L. Levshin, F. Lin, M. Moschetti, N. Shapiro, and Y. Yang (2007). Processing seismic ambient noise data to obtain reliable broad-band surface wave dispersion measurements, *Geophys. J. Int.* **169,** no. 3, 1239–1260.

Booth, A. D., P. Christoffersen, C. Schoonman, A. Clarke, B. Hubbard, R. Law, S. H. Doyle, T. R. Chudley, and A. Chalari (2020). Distributed acoustic sensing of seismic properties in a borehole drilled on a fast-flowing greenlandic outlet glacier. *Geophys. Res. Lett.* **47,** no. 13, e2020GL088148, doi: 10.1029/2020GL088148.

Brisbourne, A. M., T. S. Hudson, and J. M. Kendall (2024). *Borehole and Surface Applications of Distributed Acoustic Sensing for Characterization of the Cryosphere and Glacial Environments,* American Geophysical Union (AGU), Washington, D.C., 225–237.

Brisbourne, A. M., M. Kendall, S.-K. Kufner, T. S. Hudson, and A. M. Smith (2021). Downhole distributed acoustic seismic profiling at Skytrain Ice Rise, West Antarctica, *Cryosphere* **15,** no. 7, 3443–3458.

Brunt, K., H. Fricker, L. Padman, T. Scambos, and S. O'Neel (2010). Mapping the grounding zone of the Ross Ice Shelf, Antarctica, using ICESat laser altimetry, *Ann. Glaciol.* **51,** no. 55, 71–79.

Casey, R., M. E. Templeton, G. Sharer, L. Keyson, B. R. Weertman, and T. Ahern (2018). Assuring the quality of IRIS data with MUSTANG, *Seismol. Res. Lett.* **89,** no. 2A, 630–639.

Chaput, J., R. Aster, M. Karplus, N. Nakata, P. Gerstoft, P. Bromirski, A. Nyblade, R. Stephen, and D. Wiens (2023). Near-surface seismic anisotropy in Antarctic glacial snow and ice revealed by high-frequency ambient noise, *J. Glaciol.* **69,** no. 276, 773–789.

Christianson, K., B. Parizek, R. Alley, H. Horgan, R. Jacobel, S. Anandakrishnan, B. Keisling, B. Craig, and A. Muto (2013). Ice sheet grounding zone stabilization due to till compaction, *Geophys. Res. Lett.* **40,** 5406–5411.

Conway, H., B. Ball, G. H. Denton, A. Gades, and E. Waddington (1999). Past and future grounding-line retreat of the West Antarctic ice sheet, *Science* **286,** 280–283.

Davis, P., K. Nicholls, D. M. Holland, B. E. Schmidt, P. Washam, K. L. Riverman, R. J. Arthern, I. Vaňková, C. Eayrs, J. A. Smith, *et al.* (2023). Suppressed basal melting in the eastern Thwaites Glacier grounding zone, *Nature* **614,** 479–485.

Dibble, R., P. Kyle, and C. Rowe (2008). Video and seismic observations of Strombolian eruptions at Erebus volcano, Antarctica, *J. Volcanol. Geotherm. Res.* **177,** 619–634.

Drews, R., C. Wild, O. Marsh, W. Rack, T. Ehlers, N. Neckel, and V. Helm (2021). Grounding-zone flow variability of Priestley Glacier, Antarctica, in a diurnal tidal regime, *Geophys. Res. Lett.* **48,** e2021GL093853, doi: 10.1029/2021GL093853.

Fichtner, A., C. Hofstede, L. Gebraad, A. Zunino, D. Zigone, and O. Eisen (2023). Borehole fibre-optic seismology inside the Northeast Greenland Ice Stream, *Geophys. J. Int.* **235,** no. 3, 2430–2441.

Fichtner, A., C. Hofstede, B. L. N. Kennett, N. F. Nymand, M. L. Lauritzen, D. Zigone, and O. Eisen (2023). Fiber-optic airplane seismology on the northeast Greenland Ice Stream, *Seism. Rec.* **3,** no. 2, 125–133.

Fichtner, A., C. Hofstede, B. L. N. Kennett, A. Svensson, J. Westhoff, F. Walter, J.-P. Ampuero, E. Cook, D. Zigone, D. Jansen, *et al.* (2025). Hidden cascades of seismic ice stream deformation, *Science* **387,** no. 6736, 858–864.

Freer, B. I. D., O. J. Marsh, A. E. Hogg, H. A. Fricker, and L. Padman (2023). Modes of Antarctic tidal grounding line migration revealed by Ice, Cloud, and land elevation satellite-2 (ICESat-2) laser altimetry, *Cryosphere* **17,** no. 9, 4079–4101.

Fricker, H., R. Coleman, L. Padman, T. Scambos, J. Bohlander, and K. Brunt (2009). Mapping the grounding zone of the Amery Ice Shelf, east Antarctica using InSAR, MODIS and ICESat, *Antarct. Sci.* **21,** 515–532.

Gimbert, F., U. Nanni, P. Roux, A. Helmstetter, S. Garambois, A. Lecointre, A. Walpersdorf, B. Jourdain, M. Langlais, O. Laarman, *et al.* (2021). A multi-physics experiment with a temporary dense seismic array on the Argentière Glacier, French Alps: The RESOLVE project, *Seismol. Res. Lett.* **92,** no. 2A, 1185–1201.

Graham, A., A. Wahlin, K. A. Hogan, F. O. Nitsche, K. J. Heywood, R. L. Totten, J. A. Smith, C. D. Hillenbrand, L. M. Simkins, J. B. Anderson, *et al.* (2022). Rapid retreat of Thwaites Glacier in the pre-satellite era, *Nature Geosci.* **15,** 706–713.

Gudmundsson, G., J. Krug, G. Durand, L. Favier, and O. Gagliardini (2012). The stability of grounding lines on retrograde slopes, *Cryosphere* **6,** 1497–1505.

Haseloff, M., and O. Sergienko (2022). Effects of calving and submarine melting on steady states and stability of buttressed marine ice sheets, *J. Glaciol.* 1–18.

Hoffman, A. O., K. Christianson, M. S. Karplus, R. S. Agnew, E. Pearce, M. Ranganathan, S. Anandakrishnan, S. A. Cortez, M. Beres, R. Bingham, *et al.* (2025). Geophysical surveys and instrument incubation program across a glacier grounding zone: Eastwind Glacier's contribution to McMurdo ice shelf mass balance, ESS Open Archive, doi: 10.22541/essoar.173687398.85162904/v1.

Horgan, H., L. van Gaastrecht, R. Alley, S. Anandakrishnan, L. Beem, K. Christianson, A. Muto, and M. Siegfried (2021). Grounding zone subglacial properties from calibrated active-source seismic methods, *Cryosphere* **15,** 1863–1880.

Howat, I. M., C. Porter, B. E. Smith, M.-J. Noh, and P. Morin (2019). The reference elevation model of Antarctica, *Cryosphere* **13,** no. 2, 665–674.

Hudson, T. S., A. F. Baird, J. M. Kendall, S. K. Kufner, A. M. Brisbourne, A. M. Smith, A. Butcher, A. Chalari, and A. Clarke (2021). Distributed acoustic sensing (DAS) for natural microseismicity studies: A case study from Antarctica, *J. Geophys. Res.* **126,** no. 7, e2020JB021493, doi: 10.1029/2020JB021493.

Hughes, T. (1975). The West Antarctic Ice Sheet: Instability, disintegration, and initiation of ice ages, *Rev. Geophys.* **13,** 502–526.

Hulbe, C. L., M. Klinger, M. Masterson, G. Catania, K. Cruikshank, and A. Bugni (2016). Tidal bending and strand cracks at the kamb ice stream grounding line, West Antarctica, *J. Glaciol.* **62,** no. 235, 816–824.

Jenkins, A., D. Shoosmith, P. Dutrieux, S. Jacobs, T. Kim, S. Lee, H. Ga, and S. Stammerjohn (2018). West Antarctic Ice Sheet retreat in the Amundsen Sea driven by decadal oceanic variability, *Nature Geosci.* **11,** 733–738.

Joughin, I., B. Smith, and B. Medley (2014). Marine ice sheet collapse potentially under way for the Thwaites Glacier basin, *West Antarctica Sci.* **344,** 735–738.

Karplus, M., and B. Schmandt (2018). Preface to the focus section on geophone array seismology, *Seismol. Res. Lett.* **89,** no. 5, 1597–1600.

Karplus, M. S., N. Nakata, G. M. Kaip, S. H. Harder, L. F. Gonzalez, A. D. Booth, E. C. Smith, S. A. Veitch, J. I. Walter, and P. Christoffersen (2024). Signal characteristics of surface seismic explosive sources near the West Antarctic Ice Sheet divide, *J. Glaciol.* **70,** e16.

Lazzara, M. A., G. A. Weidner, L. M. Keller, J. E. Thom, and J. J. Cassano (2012). Antarctic automatic weather station program: 30 years of polar observation, *Bull. Am. Meteorol. Soc.* **93,** no. 10, 1519–1537.

Le Bris, T., G. Barruol, F. Gimbert, E. Le Meur, D. Zigone, A. Togaibekov, and D. Lombardi (2024). Spatial and temporal variability in tide-induced icequake activity at the Astrolabe Glacier, East Antarctica, ESS Open Archive, doi: 10.22541/essoar.173324864.46462523/v1.

Longuet-Higgins, M. (1950). A theory of the origin of microseisms, *Phil. Trans. Roy. Soc. Lond. A* **243,** no. 857, 1–35.

Lucas, E. M., A. A. Nyblade, R. C. Aster, D. A. Wiens, T. J. Wilson, J. P. Winberry, and A. D. Huerta (2023). Tidally modulated glacial seismicity at the Foundation Ice Stream, West Antarctica, *J. Geophys. Res.* **128,** no. 7, e2023JF007172, doi: 10.1029/2023JF007172.

McNamara, D., and R. Buland (2004). Ambient noise levels in the continental united states, *Bull. Seismol. Soc. Am.* **94,** no. 4, 1517–1527.

Minowa, M., E. A. Podolskiy, and S. Sugiyama (2019). Tide-modulated ice motion and seismicity of a floating glacier tongue in East Antarctica, *Ann. Glaciol.* **60,** no. 79, 57–67.

Morlighem, M., E. Rignot, T. Binder, D. Blankenship, R. Drews, G. Eagles, O. Eisen, F. Ferraccioli, R. Forsberg, and P. Fretwell, *et al.* (2020). Deep glacial troughs and stabilizing ridges unveiled beneath the margins of the Antarctic ice sheet, *Nature Sci.* 13, 132–137, doi: 10.1038/s41561-019-0510-8.

Morlighem, M., E. Rignot, T. Binder, D. Blankenship, R. Drews, G. Eagles, O. Eisen, F. Ferraccioli, R. Forsberg, P. Fretwell, *et al.* (2020). Deep glacial troughs and stabilizing ridges unveiled beneath the margins of the Antarctic ice sheet, *Nature Geosci.* **13,** no. 2, 132–137.

Nanni, U., F. Gimbert, P. Roux, and A. Lecointre (2021). Observing the subglacial hydrology network and its dynamics with a dense seismic array, *Proc. Natl. Acad. Sci. Unit. States Am.* **118,** no. 28, e2023757118, doi: 10.1073/pnas.2023757118.

Nanni, U., P. Roux, F. Gimbert, and A. Lecointre (2022). Dynamic imaging of glacier structures at high-resolution using source localization with a dense seismic array, *Geophys. Res. Lett.* **49,** no. 6, e2021GL095996, doi: 10.1029/2021GL095996.

Neuhaus, S. U., S. M. Tulaczyk, N. D. Stansell, J. J. Coenen, R. P. Scherer, J. A. Mikucki, and R. D. Powell (2021). Did holocene climate changes drive West Antarctic grounding line retreat and readvance? *Cryosphere* **15,** no. 10, 4655–4673.

Padman, L., H. A. Fricker, R. Coleman, S. Howard, and L. Erofeeva (2002). A new tide model for the Antarctic ice shelves and seas, *Ann. Glaciol.* **34,** 247–254.

Pearce, E., D. Zigone, C. Hofstede, A. Fichtner, J. Rimpot, S. O. Rasmussen, J. Freitag, and O. Eisen (2024). Firn seismic anisotropy in the northeast Greenland Ice Stream from ambient-noise surface waves, *Cryosphere* **18,** no. 10, 4917–4932.

Peterson, J. (1993). Observations and modeling of seismic background noise, *U.S. Geol. Surv. Open-File Rept. 93-322,* 94 pp.

Podolskiy, E. A., S. Sugiyama, M. Funk, F. Walter, R. Genco, S. Tsutaki, M. Minowa, and M. Ripepe (2016). Tide-modulated ice flow variations drive seismicity near the calving front of Bowdoin Glacier, Greenland, *Geophys. Res. Lett.* **43,** no. 5, 2036–2044.

Reese, R., J. Garbe, E. Hill, B. Urruty, K. Naughten, O. Gagliardini, G. Durand, F. Gillet-Chaulet, G. Gudmundsson, D. Chandler, *et al.* (2023). The stability of present-day Antarctic grounding lines - Part 2: Onset of irreversible retreat of Amundsen Sea glaciers under current climate on centennial timescales cannot be excluded, *Cryosphere* **17,** 3761–3783.

Rignot, E., M. Mouginot, M. Morlighem, H. Seroussi, and B. Scheuchl (2014). Widespread, rapid grounding line retreat of Pine Island, Thwaites, Smith, and Kohler glaciers, West Antarctica, from 1992 to 2011, *Geophys. Res. Lett.* **41,** 3502–3509.

Robel, A., C. Schoof, and E. Tziperman (2014). Rapid grounding line migration induced by internal ice stream variability, *J. Geophys. Res.* **119,** 2430–2447.

Rowe, C., R. Aster, P. Kyle, R. Dibble, and J. Schlue (2000). Seismic and acoustic observations at Mount Erebus Volcano, Ross Island, Antarctica, *J. Volcanol. Geotherm. Res.* **101,** 105–128.

Schoof, C. (2007). Ice sheet grounding line dynamics: Steady states, stability, and hysteresis, *J. Geophys. Res.* **112,** F03S28, doi: 10.1029/2006JF000664.

Stern, T., F. Davey, and G. Delisle (1991). Lithospheric flexure induced by the load of the Ross archipelago, southern Victoria Land, Antarctica, *Proceedings of the Fifth International Symposium on Antarctic Earth Sciences*, Cambridge, August 1987, 323–328.

van Ginkel, J., F. Walter, F. Lindner, M. Hallo, M. Huss, and D. Fäh (2025). Spectral characteristics of seismic ambient vibrations reveal changes in the subglacial environment of glacier de la plaine morte, switzerland, *Cryosphere* **19,** no. 3, 1469–1490.

Veitch, S. A., M. Karplus, G. Kaip, L. F. Gonzalez, J. M. Amundson, and T. C. Bartholomaus (2021). Ice thickness estimates of Lemon Creek Glacier, Alaska, from active-source seismic imaging, *J. Glaciol.* **67,** no. 265, 824–832.

Weertman, J. (1974). Stability of the junction of an ice sheet and an ice shelf, *J. Glaciol.* **13,** 3–13.

Winder, T., C. Bacon, J. Smith, T. Hudson, T. Greenfield, and R. White (2022). QuakeMigrate: A modular, open-source python package for automatic earthquake detection and location, Authorea, doi: 10.1002/essoar.10505850.1.

Young, T. J., R. Agnew, M. Hunt, E. Pearce, and M. Karplus (2023). *Eastwind Glacier Geophysical Surveys on Top Of Antarctic iceShelf Transition* [Data Set], International Federation of Digital Seismograph Networks, doi: 10.7914/jah0-9856.

Zoet, L. K., S. Anandakrishnan, R. B. Alley, A. A. Nyblade, and D. A. Wiens (2012). Motion of an Antarctic glacier by repeated tidally modulated earthquakes, *Nature Geosci.* **5,** no. 9, 623–626.

Manuscript received 17 January 2025
Published online 22 August 2025

Data Mine

Preliminary Analysis of Distributed Acoustic Sensing (DAS) Data Using a Submarine Fiber-Optic Cable Across the North Anatolian Fault

Ji Zhang*[1], Aitaro Kato[1], Ahmet Anil Dindar[2], Wei Wang[3,4], Shigeki Nakagawa[1], Yosuke Aoki[1], Masanao Shinohara[1], Yoshiyuki Kaneda[5], and Süleyman Tunç[2]

Abstract

Distributed acoustic sensing (DAS) is an emerging technique that uses fiber-optic cables to detect ground vibrations. DAS can record vibrations similarly to a dense network of seismic stations, aiding earthquake detection and the analysis of subsurface structures. Although terrestrial DAS setups are relatively accessible, there are few submarine optical cables available for use. As a result, most DAS data currently come from terrestrial cables. We started monitoring earthquakes using a communication cable that crosses the North Anatolian fault in the Marmara Sea for the first time. This cable crosses a bay that contains a trench that is related to deformation along the North Anatolian fault, creating a unique and complex observational environment. We present overviews of seismic data from local, regional, and teleseismic events retrieved using the new DAS system and make these data publicly available. The analysis of waveforms from nearby seismic stations and DAS instruments highlights the potential seismic applications of DAS data in the Marmara Sea.

Cite this article as Zhang, J., A. Kato, A. Anil Dindar, W. Wang, S. Nakagawa, Y. Aoki, M. Shinohara, Y. Kaneda, and S. Tunç (2025). Preliminary Analysis of Distributed Acoustic Sensing (DAS) Data Using a Submarine Fiber-Optic Cable Across the North Anatolian Fault, *Seismol. Res. Lett.* **97**, 606–615, doi: 10.1785/0220250049.

Introduction

Distributed acoustic sensing (DAS) is a rapidly advancing technique that uses standard fiber-optic cables as dense arrays of virtual sensors. By sending short laser pulses along the cable and measuring the light that is backscattered due to inherent imperfections, DAS captures strain from external forces, including seismic waves and acoustic vibrations. This strain causes small phase shifts in the backscattered light, which the DAS system records as changes in strain over time. This process effectively converts a fiber-optic cable into a series of virtual sensors, often achieving a spatial resolution of ~1 m and sampling rate of several kilohertz. DAS enables the measurement of transient ground deformations (strain and strain rate) along the optical cables that are used for internet connections on land and underwater at almost every point on Earth. Unlike traditional point sensors, such as seismometers, accelerometers, and Global Navigation Satellite System stations, DAS provides spatially dense measurements along the length of the fiber, typically every 10 m over distances of 80–150 km, depending on the DAS interrogator. By continuously monitoring an entire fiber-optic cable, DAS can function as a high-resolution distributed strain and vibration sensing array, offering extensive coverage over long distances (Zhan, 2019). DAS offers high spatial resolution along the cable, enabling detailed investigations of strain fields and providing a cost-effective alternative to deploying individual sensors. Standard pre-existing submarine telecom fibers can be used in offshore regions for seismic monitoring (Lindsey *et al.*, 2017; Sladen *et al.*, 2019; Shinohara *et al.*, 2022; Mata Flores *et al.*, 2023), eliminating the need for specialized hardware and enabling continuous large-scale monitoring of seismic wavefields.

In recent years, the unique capabilities of DAS have proven valuable for a variety of seismological applications, including earthquake analysis and subsurface imaging (Ajo-Franklin *et al.*, 2019). By transforming segments of fiber-optic cables into single-component strain meters, DAS captures coherent

1. Earthquake Research Institute, The University of Tokyo, Bunkyō, Japan, https://orcid.org/0000-0003-1327-509X (MS); 2. MARTEST Research and Training Center, Gebze Technical University, Darıca, Türkiye, https://orcid.org/0000-0003-3168-8322 (AAD); https://orcid.org/0000-0001-7336-425X (ST); 3. Key Laboratory of Earth and Planetary Physics, Institute of Geology and Geophysics, Chinese Academy of Sciences, Beijing, China, https://orcid.org/0000-0002-5934-4268 (WW); 4. College of Earth and Planetary Sciences, University of Chinese Academy of Sciences, Beijing, China; 5. Kagawa University, Takamatsu, Japan

*Corresponding author: zhangj@eri.u-tokyo.ac.jp

signals with high sensitivity and accuracy across thousands of virtual channels. DAS arrays, often spanning tens of kilometers, serve as dense seismic arrays, providing excellent spatial resolution and revealing important regional seismic structures (Ajo-Franklin *et al.*, 2019; Spica *et al.*, 2020, 2022; Cheng *et al.*, 2021; Viens *et al.*, 2022; Yang *et al.*, 2022). DAS is also effective for local earthquake detection (Li and Zhan, 2018; Atterholt *et al.*, 2022) and can detect seismic signals from various sources (Williams *et al.*, 2019; Wang *et al.*, 2020; Zhan *et al.*, 2021). The near-real-time operational capability makes DAS particularly well suited for applications that require a rapid response, such as earthquake monitoring, oil and gas exploration, and structural damage assessment. DAS data are valuable for scientific research, with many open-source DAS data sets being available. Most open-source DAS data sets are terrestrial (e.g., PubDAS; Spica *et al.*, 2023); however, growing interest in the oceanic environment has led to an increasing number of studies using DAS for underwater observations (e.g., Lindsey *et al.*, 2019; Lior *et al.*, 2021; Bouffaut *et al.*, 2022; Smith *et al.*, 2023; Wilcock *et al.*, 2023; Glover *et al.*, 2024). Deploying and processing terrestrial fiber-optic networks is relatively straightforward, whereas the availability of submarine dark fibers is limited, and data acquisition is more challenging.

We have used DAS to record seismic data from the North Anatolian fault over an extended period using a submarine cable in the Marmara Sea. We selected DAS data for notable seismic events at varying hypocentral distances. The waveforms recorded by DAS offer valuable insights into both the location of the fiber-optic cable and the underlying submarine structure. We compared teleseismic waveforms from DAS with those recorded by nearby seismic stations. The results demonstrate the potential of DAS to contribute to the exploration of the deep structure of the Earth. We make these data available to facilitate in-depth analysis.

Fiber-Optic Cable and DAS Parameters

The northern strand of the North Anatolian fault trends east–west across the Marmara Sea. The fault system is complex, comprising active and inactive faults. Most faults are strike-slip, recording transpressional and transtensional movements (Şengör *et al.*, 2014; Gasperini *et al.*, 2021). This fault system is important for understanding the distribution of plate motions across multiple fault strands and how this distribution evolves over time (Kurt *et al.*, 2013). The North Anatolian fault zone has experienced several major historical earthquakes ($M > 7$; e.g., Barka *et al.*, 2002); however, no significant earthquakes have occurred over the past few hundred years along the Marmara segment (Parsons *et al.*, 2000), suggesting substantial stress accumulation in the area and the potential for a large earthquake (Ergintav *et al.*, 2014; Schmittbuhl *et al.*, 2016). Determining the seismic activity and stress changes in this region is important for disaster mitigation and preparedness. Various observational methods have been used in the region, including seismic reflection data from the KPR0807 data set provided by the Marine Geoscience Data System and regional seismic stations (Özkan *et al.*, 2024). All these data sets have been made open source to enhance our understanding of fault activity, stress states, and disaster mitigation along the North Anatolian fault zone and around the Marmara Sea; however, there are currently no available open-source DAS data. We address this gap by providing access to DAS observations.

We used a fiber-optic communication cable that spans from Darıca on the north coast of Izmit bay to Yalova on the south coast, crossing the easternmost bay of the Marmara Sea (Fig. 1a). The cable is located partially on land and partially beneath the sea. The submarine part crosses two active transpressive faults and a submarine trench. The detailed location of this seafloor cable is difficult to obtain, and Turk Telecom Company provides only five spot locations for the undersea cable (A–E in Fig. 1a). The bathymetry along the cable is shown in Figure 1b. We also do not know the location of the terrestrial part of the cable. Here, we analyze mainly DAS data from the submarine part of the cable. The total length of the cable is estimated to be 27 km end-to-end, with ~18 km (from A to E in Fig. 1a) beneath the sea.

We started DAS using this fiber-optic cable in May 2024. A DAS interrogator unit from the Nippon Electric Company was installed in Darıca, and strain-rate data are recorded for the 27 km length of the cable with a spatial resolution of 3.26 m and sampling frequency of 1000 Hz. The number of channels is 8275, and the gauge length is set to 6.4 m. The gauge length refers to the spatial resolution of the fiber-optic sensor, which is essentially the measurement interval or sampling distance along the fiber, and represents the segment of the fiber over which each measurement is averaged. The data were collected continuously from May 2024 to this date of writing (December 2024).

DAS Data Analysis

We computed spectra for each channel along the fiber using one day of DAS data, revealing distinct frequency responses at different locations (Fig. 2a). Figure 1b shows the bathymetry along the cable in the submarine section. Along the onshore section (0–7 km), energy is observed mainly in the high-frequency band (10–20 Hz), primarily from vehicle traffic. Although terrestrial noise remains prominent along the near-shore section, at a water depth of ~100 m (7–11 km), the energy gradually attenuates and shifts toward lower frequencies, mainly 5–10 Hz. Farther offshore, at a water depth of ~200 m (11–15 km), the dominant frequency decreases to ~1 Hz. In the fault zone (15–17 km), low-frequency energy is largely absent, possibly due to poor coupling between the fiber-optic cable and the seafloor. In the trench region, at a water depth of ~600 m (17–26 km), low-frequency energy

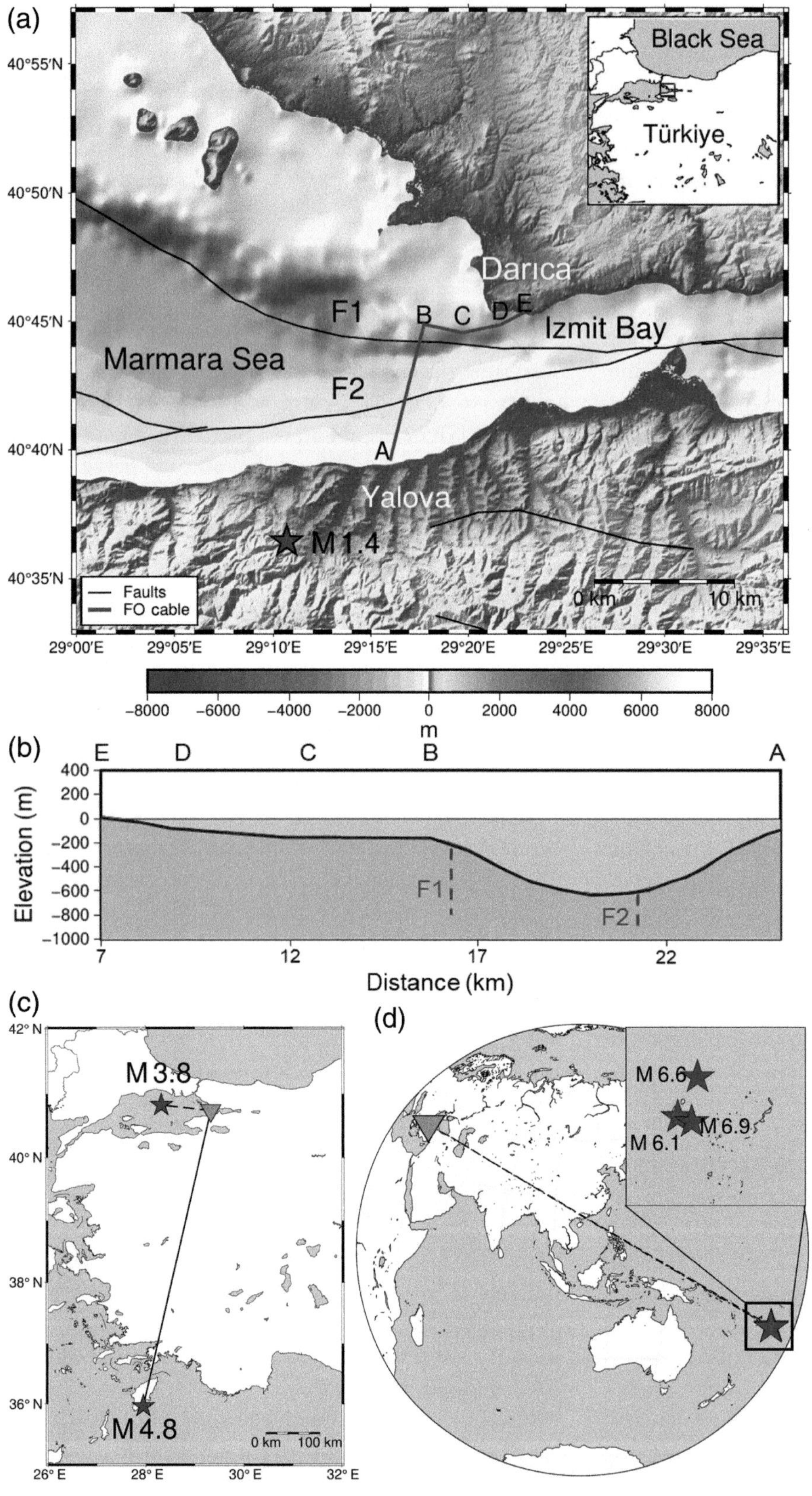

Figure 1. Study area and seismic event locations. (a) Geometry of the distributed acoustic sensing (DAS) system and location of the local event (*M* 1.4). The inset in (a) shows the location of the study area in northwestern Türkiye. (b) Bathymetry along the cable from points A to E. Location of (c) local (*M* 3.8) and regional (*M* 4.8) events, and (d) teleseismic events (*M* 6.1, 6.6, and 6.9) in Tonga. The inset in (d) provides a zoom-in view of the three teleseismic earthquakes. FO cable, fiber-optic cable. The color version of this figure is available only in the electronic edition.

remains centered around 2 Hz, suggesting stronger coupling or reduced ambient noise. At the far end of the array, where the cable reaches land again (>26 km), the dominant frequency returns to 10–20 Hz.

Although the submarine section of the array is affected by ocean dynamics (e.g., Guerin *et al.*, 2022; Shen and Wu, 2024; Shen *et al.*, 2024; Shi *et al.*, 2025), the Marmara Sea is a semienclosed inland sea where wind and wave activity are limited compared with the open ocean (Ying *et al.*, 2014). Consequently, ocean dynamics have a weaker effect on ambient noise levels, resulting in relatively high-quality seismic data. To illustrate the spatial variations in spectral characteristics, we present representative power spectral densities (PSDs) from the southern coast part (Fig. 2b). Near the southern coastline (~26 km), we observe a clear energy enhancement in the PSD around ~0.1 Hz, which is likely caused by ocean dynamics (Shi *et al.*, 2025). Because the distance from the coast increases (e.g., at 25.4 km), the low-frequency (~0.1 Hz) disturbance becomes relatively weaker. These observations indicate that regions with deeper water in the Marmara Sea tend to have more stable signals with less ocean noise. In addition, elevated PSD levels are also observed near 2 Hz, which may be associated with anthropogenic sources such as vessel activity or offshore infrastructure. Spectral and PSD analyses provide insights into why seismic signals observed in our DAS data are more

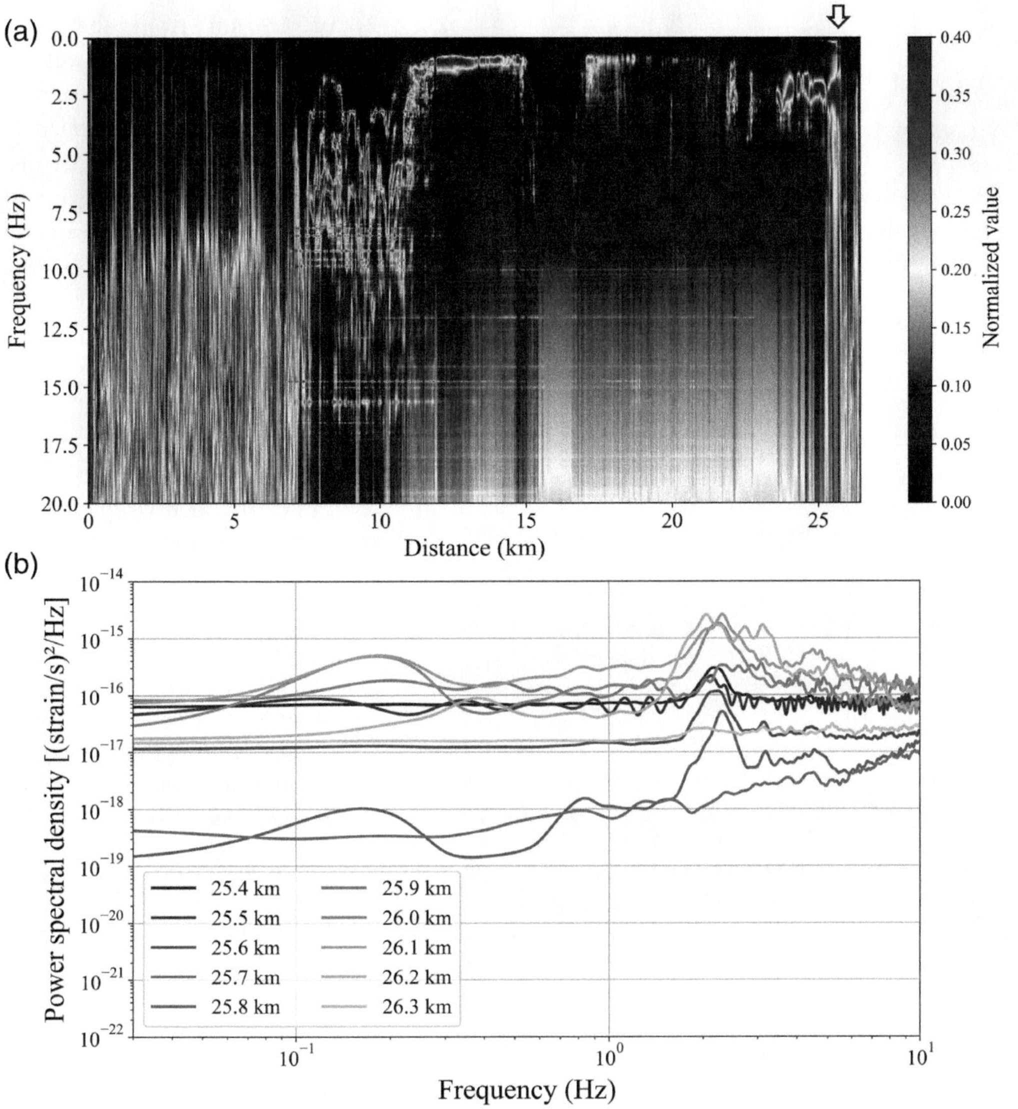

Figure 2. Spectrum and power spectral density. (a) Spectrum along the cable. (b) Power spectral density at locations corresponding to the arrow in (a). The color version of this figure is available only in the electronic edition.

clearly identifiable compared to those from other open-ocean DAS deployments.

Seismological Observations of Local, Regional, and Teleseismic Events

We obtained a large amount of data over a 6-month period, and we present some interesting seismic waveforms that help us better understand the subsurface structure and further demonstrate the broad applicability of DAS. We display data from local, regional, and teleseismic events, the details of which are taken from Disaster and Emergency Management Authority (AFAD) in Türkiye and U.S. Geological Survey (USGS) catalogs (Table 1). The wavefields shown have been filtered and normalized by the standard deviation of each individual trace in Figure 3. We used a band-pass filter between 1 and 15 Hz for local earthquakes, between 3 and 7 Hz for regional events, and between 2 and 3 Hz for teleseismic events.

The local event (M 1.4) occurred near point A on the fiber-optic cable, at a distance

TABLE 1
Event Information

Magnitude and Sources	Date and Time (UTC) (yyyy/mm/dd hh:mm:ss)	Latitude	Longitude	Depth (km)	Distance
1.4, AFAD	2024/06/05 16:57:29	40.607° N	29.178° E	9.2	16.2 km
3.8, AFAD	2024/05/26 21:38:18	40.828° N	28.319° E	7.0	82.0 km
4.8, AFAD	2024/06/12 19:19:10	35.962° N	27.947° E	59.0	542.1 km
6.9, USGS	2024/08/25 23:29:08	19.755° S	175.041° W	106.7	150.5°
6.1, USGS	2024/08/25 23:30:52	19.798° S	174.918° W	106.5	150.6°
6.6, USGS	2024/05/26 20:47:10	19.418° S	174.867° W	127.1	150.3°

USGS, U.S. Geological Survey.

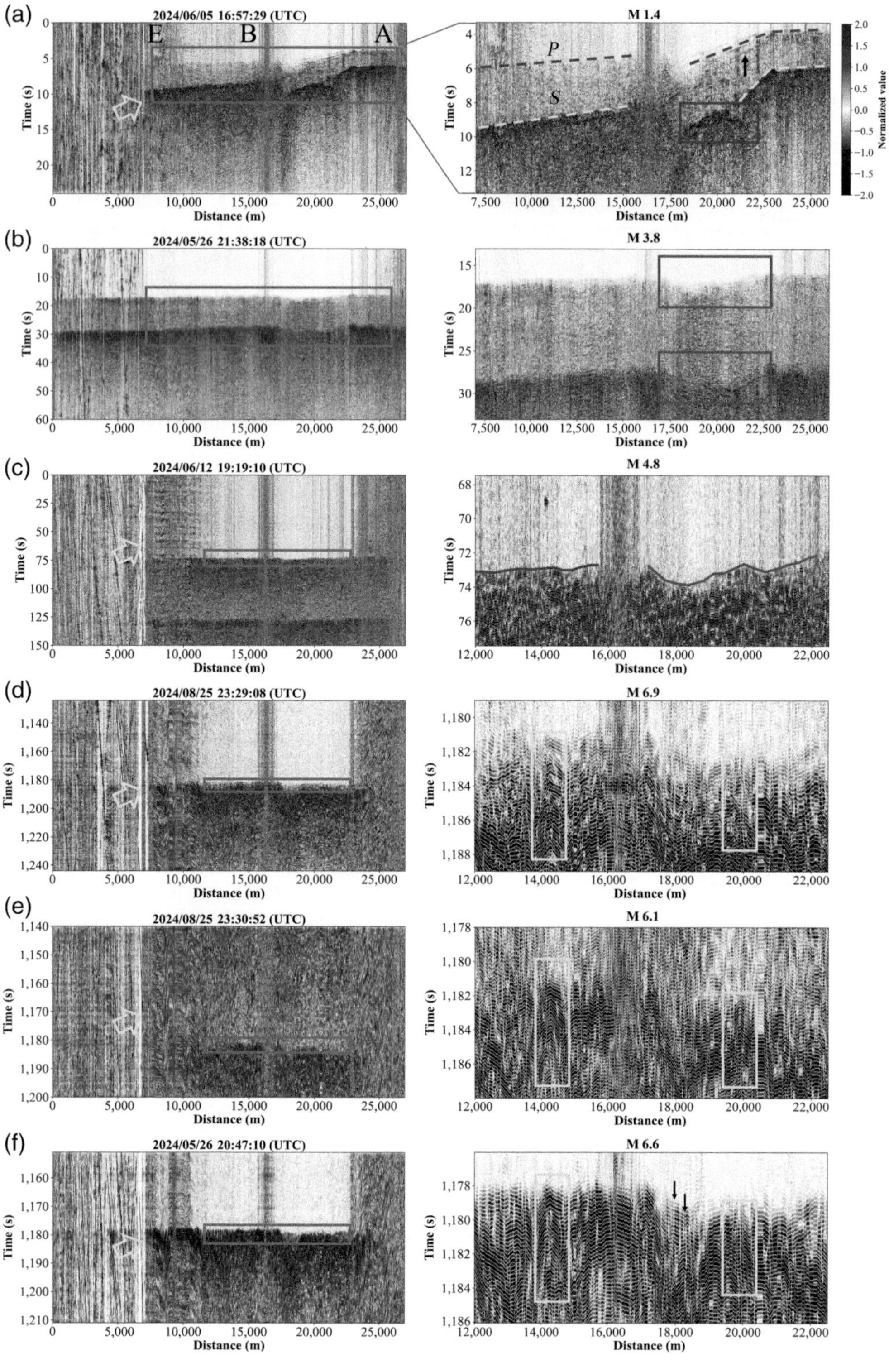

Figure 3. DAS data of different seismic events. The DAS data from *M* 1.4 (a), *M* 3.8 (b), *M* 4.8 (c), *M* 6.9 (d), *M* 6.1 (e), and *M* 6.6 (f) events. The vertical axis is the elapsed time from the origin time of each event. In each panel, the left side displays the entire data set, and the right side is a zoomed-in view of the green-boxed region from the left side, highlighting first arrivals. The blue arrow in (a) indicates noise channels, and yellow arrows in (a) and (c)–(f) indicate the boundary between the terrestrial and submarine records. The red-dashed and yellow-dashed lines denote the *P*- and *S*-wave arrivals, respectively, the red box in (a) indicates a hyperbolic shape, blue boxes in (b) indicate the area with delayed travel times, the red and blue lines in (c) denote first arrivals, and the yellow boxes in (d)–(f) indicate chevron-like shapes. The color version of this figure is available only in the electronic edition.

of 16 km from the cable (Fig. 1a). The waveform recorded by the DAS system for this event is illustrated in Figure 3a. The left panel displays a 60 s recording across all channels, providing an overview of the data captured, and the right panel zooms in on the section indicated by the green box in Figure 1a (7–26 km and 3–13 s), which captures the main seismic waveform. Near point A, we can clearly identify the *P*-wave (red-dashed lines) and *S*-wave (yellow-dashed lines) arrivals as shown in the right panel of Figure 3a; however, because the offset increases, there are abrupt changes in these seismic phases due to structural effects along the cable path. Other phase arrivals (black arrows) can also be observed due to the strong impedance contrast at the sediment–bedrock interface, which causes *P*-wave splitting (Trabattoni *et al.*, 2024).

Another local event (*M* 3.8) in the middle of the Marmara Sea, at a distance of 82 km, is shown in Figure 1c. The waveform display configuration of Figure 3b mirrors that of Figure 3a but covers a time of 14–34 s because of the increase in the *S*–*P* time. This event was stronger than the *M* 1.4 event, allowing us to clearly observe the *P* and *S* waves. Remarkably, these phases are identifiable even in the land section (0–7 km), despite significant vehicle noise. In the segment from 7 to 15 km, the inclination of the first arrival is influenced primarily by the cable geometry, which runs from point B to point E. Around the 20 km mark (blue boxes in

Fig. 3b), the waveform exhibits a concave pattern, mirroring the shape of the trench (Fig. 1b), likely due to the sedimentary structure around the trench. Clear *P*- and *S*-wave travel times increase our ability to determine accurate event locations when combined with seismic station data.

The *M* 4.8 regional event on Rhodes, Greece, was located 542 km from the cable (Fig. 1c). Unlike the clear recordings of local events, this event is only weakly recorded in DAS data (Fig. 3c). In particular, the near-shore sections (7–12 and 23–27 km) yield weak waveforms, with the signals obscured almost completely by noise generated by nearby human or industrial activities. The most significant waveforms, at 12–23 km along the cable and at 68–77 s, include identifiable *P*-wave arrivals, visible in the right panel in Figure 3c. For regional events such as this, the direct arrivals display uneven patterns (red and blue lines in the right panel in Fig. 3c). These patterns are affected less by the cable geometry and more by variations in the subsurface structure, including prominent low-velocity sedimentary layers. This structural effect causes noticeable inconsistencies in arrival times across the recorded segments.

The locations of the teleseismic *M* 6.1, 6.6, and 6.9 events from Tonga, located ~150° away, are illustrated in Figure 1d. The waveform of the *M* 6.9 event is shown in Figure 3d, where the first teleseismic arrival is distinguishable above the noise. A zoomed-in view from 12–23 km and 1179–1189s shows the *P*-wave arrivals from this teleseismic event. Although the signal is apparent above the background noise, the arrivals remain somewhat indistinct, making precise picking difficult.

Figure 3e displays the waveform from the *M* 6.1 event, which occurred <2 min after the *M* 6.9 event (Table 1). The first arrival is difficult to discern, although subtle differences are visible around 1182 s. In the zoomed-in view from 1178 to 1188 s, the first arrival is not prominent, both because this event is not large enough and because the first arrival is obscured by the coda waves generated by the *M* 6.9 event.

In contrast, the *M* 6.6 event was recorded more clearly by DAS (Fig. 3f). The first arrival is evident in the zoomed-in view, which highlights the clear onset. The presence of numerous coherent phases (the black arrows in Fig. 3f) suggests the existence of multiple distinct layers, which are likely associated with seafloor sedimentary deposits (e.g., the trench structure shown in Fig. 1b). The clear DAS data (Fig. 3f) from the *M* 6.6 event demonstrate the potential of DAS for capturing detailed seismic activity and stratigraphic information across long distances.

Discussion

There are distinct inclined lines in the 0–7 km section in Figure 2a,c–f (yellow arrows), which we interpret as vehicle noise, indicating that this portion of the data corresponds to the terrestrial part of the cable. In Figure 3b, we can observe the seismic phases clearly across all channels because this is a strong earthquake that occurred near the DAS cable. The seismic signal strength is much higher than the vehicle noise in the terrestrial part of cable. In contrast, there is a noticeable noise around the 16 km mark (blue arrow in Fig. 3a), likely due to the cable crossing the first fault (F1 in Fig. 1a,b), a transpressive fault with a large fault zone. The steep fault scarp with a large elevation difference causes poor coupling between the cable and the seafloor, resulting in higher noise levels in this area. A hyperbolic shape is visible in the right panel of Figure 3a at ~20 km (the red box), which could be associated with the second fault (F2). When seismic waves encounter faults, they may generate new seismic sources or reflections. Previous studies have proposed that chevronlike patterns in seismic data can indicate fault structures (Lindsey *et al.*, 2017; Atterholt *et al.*, 2022). Similar chevronlike features in Figure 3d–f (yellow boxes) further support the presence of fault-related structures in these regions, reinforcing our hypothesis that these shapes may reflect geological discontinuities or faults. This inference is consistent with findings of Beyhan *et al.* (2009), who documented numerous positive and negative flower structures in the Marmara Sea using seismic reflection data.

Detecting and locating local events is crucial in seismology (Zhu *et al.*, 2023). Although phase-picking methods such as PhaseNet-DAS (Zhu *et al.*, 2023) have been developed and shown to be effective for terrestrial DAS data, their performance deteriorates significantly when applied to submarine DAS data. This is primarily due to the complexity of the seafloor environment, including converted phases and various types of oceanic noise. Moreover, the presence of low-velocity sedimentary layers beneath the seafloor necessitates the application of moveout corrections to account for structural effects and to improve earthquake location accuracy. The velocity structure beneath the DAS cable is also critical for enhancing location precision. Improving phase-picking accuracy for seafloor DAS data, applying precise moveout corrections, and constraining the subsurface velocity model beneath the cable are essential and challenging tasks for advancing earthquake location capabilities in marine environments. Here, however, we are interested in the teleseismic phases and their potential utility compared with data from seismic stations. Although the signal-to-noise ratio (SNR) of DAS data is lower than that of seismic data (Lindsey *et al.*, 2017), we observed teleseismic signals (Fig. 3d,e). Fortunately, we can suppress random noise and increase the SNR by stacking waveforms from nearby channels. We stack the records from the section spanning 14.20–14.75 km, where the seismic waveforms are consistent, indicating stable phases. There are time shifts between different channels due to the bathymetry (Fig. 1b). We use apparent velocities of 300–600 m/s (based on the trend of the same phase) to correct for the time difference and stack the data. From the stacked, time-shifted data, we select the waveform corresponding to the maximum amplitude. Finally, we apply a band-pass filter at 2–3 Hz. The stacked results for three teleseismic events are shown in Figure 4e, where the first three rows display waveforms stacked over a 20 s interval. A 10 s segment between 9 and 19 s in the fourth row shows that the waveforms are aligned, with minimal differences observed along similar propagation paths.

We calculated theoretical travel times for the teleseismic events using TauP (Crotwell *et al.*, 1999) and the iasp91 global 1D model (Kennett and Engdahl, 1991). In Figure 4e, the red vertical lines represent the theoretical *PKIKP* (the *P* wave that travels through both the outer and inner cores) arrivals, which closely align with the observed phase in the zoomed-in panel at right. In the waveform of the *M* 6.6 event, the green-dotted vertical line marks the theoretical *PKP* (the *P* wave that traverses the outer core) arrival, whereas in the data for the *M* 6.9 event, it indicates the theoretical *PKiKP* (the *P* wave that travels through the outer and reflects off the inner-core boundary [ICB]) arrival. The global 1D velocity model accounts for theoretical travel times, but the placement of the DAS array on the seafloor and the presence of low-velocity sedimentary layers result in a delay in the observed arrival of *P* waves relative to theoretical estimates; therefore, the theoretical *PKP* arrival precedes the actual arrival (black-dashed line). This is consistent with our expected results (Fig. 4e). The observed *PKiKP* arrival lags farther behind the theoretical *PKiKP* arrival, suggesting either that the ICB velocity in the iasp91 model is too fast or that the seismic waves encountered a low-velocity structure, causing a further delay. The velocity model for the ICB is complex, and discrepancies arising from a 1D velocity model are inevitable, but these remain within an acceptable range. Furthermore, for the *PKP* and *PKIKP* phases from the *M* 6.6 and 6.1 events, the theoretical arrival times should be nearly identical, given their similar epicentral distances and ray paths. However, there is a larger delay in the observed *PKP* phase from the *M* 6.6 event (depth = 127 km) than that from the *M* 6.1 event (depth = 106 km), despite occurring at approximately the same location. This discrepancy may be due to noise: although stacking enhances the signal, residual noise may still be present and contribute to the apparent delay. Alternatively, the difference could arise from subtle variations in the ray paths, for example, the ray from the *M* 6.6 event may have passed through a localized low-velocity zone, or conversely, the ray from the *M* 6.1 event may have traversed a high-velocity structure.

Using these travel-time differences, incorporating additional teleseismic data from DAS, minimizing noise, and integrating information from nearby seismic stations, we may be able to identify velocity anomalies and construct a more comprehensive velocity model for deep structural interfaces.

To assess the stability of seismic phases detected by DAS, we compared them with data from nearby seismic stations. This approach allows us to evaluate whether the arrival times and characteristics of seismic phases, including the *PKP* phase, are consistent between locations or whether discrepancies are due to local geological conditions. We obtained waveforms recorded by accelerometers close to the fiber-optic cable, the locations of which are shown in Figure 4a. We selected three-component waveforms from the *M* 6.6, 6.9, and 6.1 teleseismic events (Fig. 4b–d, respectively). The first arrivals for the *M* 6.6 and 6.9 events are clearly visible in the waveforms. The data for the *M* 6.1 event have a lower SNR, but the arrival can still be roughly identified at ~1180 s. We stacked the selected seismic station data for comparison with the DAS data, using only the Z component. We selected the section from 14.20 to 14.75 km on the northern side of the trench for stacking DAS data lies (Fig. 1b). Comparing these stacked data with the three components from nearby seismic stations indicates that the stacked signal is approximately equivalent to the Z component; therefore, using the Z component of the seismic data allows for a more straightforward comparison between the motion captured by both the DAS system and the seismic sensors. The strain rate can be converted to particle acceleration by multiplying by the apparent velocity (Yang *et al.*, 2021) or strain can be transformed into displacement (Trabattoni *et al.*, 2023). Given the small distance over which stack the data (14.20–14.75 km) and that we are using teleseismic waves, we assume that the apparent velocity is constant. The data are band-pass filtered between 2 and 3 Hz and then normalized by its absolute maximum value. After processing, we compare the DAS data directly with the seismic acceleration data. The stacked DAS data (solid red line) are displayed alongside the stacked seismic station data (blue-dashed line) in Figure 3f. The two data sets show match well, with only slight differences. This indicates that DAS data can detect teleseismic phases and have great potential in studies of deep Earth structures (Yu *et al.*, 2019). This comparison demonstrates that DAS data could be used effectively for seismic research, like traditional seismometer-based data, offering a promising alternative for monitoring and analyzing seismic events.

One of the key advantages of using DAS for seismic imaging is its ability to provide high spatial coverage, particularly in marine environments (Fontaine *et al.*, 2025). By repurposing existing submarine fiber-optic cables into dense seismic arrays, it is possible to achieve continuous and extensive monitoring over vast offshore regions (Lindsey *et al.*, 2019). This dense sensing network improves both the resolution and reliability of seismic imaging, offering substantial benefits for investigating tectonic structures and seismicity in previously underinstrumented oceanic areas.

Conclusions

We deployed a DAS system using a seafloor cable in the Marmara Sea, which crosses two active strands of the North Anatolian fault within a trench. The DAS data are unique and provide valuable insights, capturing signals from local, regional, and teleseismic events. These data allow for direct structural inferences based on the features observed in the

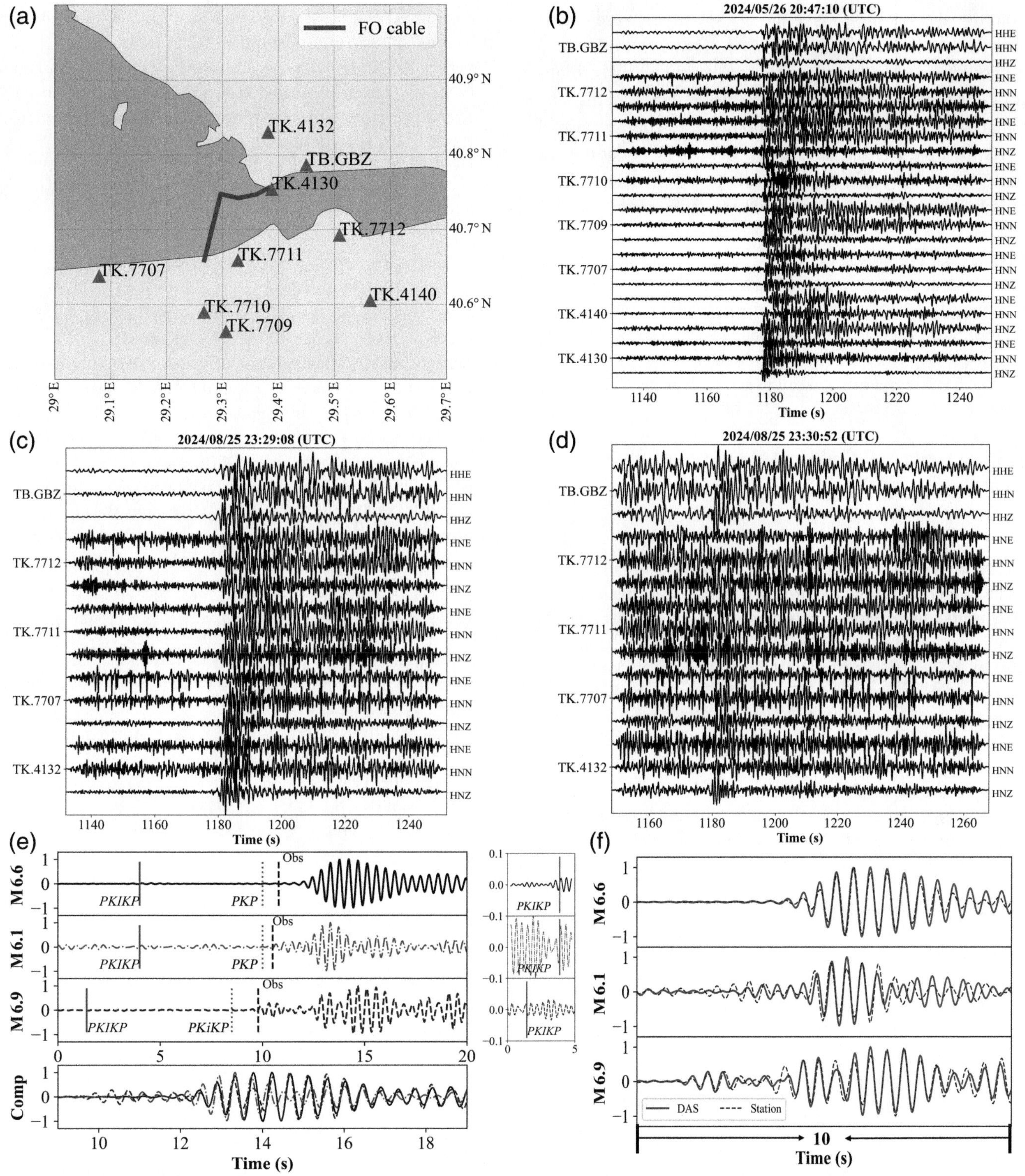

Figure 4. Analysis of teleseismic events. (a) Seismic station locations. The red line indicates the FO cable. The triangles represent seismic stations. Seismic data for *M* 6.6 (b), *M* 6.9 (c), and *M* 6.1 (d). (e) Stacked teleseismic DAS data. The solid black, dotted-dashed red, and blue-dashed lines represent DAS data from the *M* 6.6, 6.1, and 6.9 events, respectively. The solid red vertical line represents the theoretical *PKIKP* arrival, which is shown in detail at right. The green-dotted vertical line represents the theoretical *PKP* arrival, and the black-dashed line indicates the observed *PKP* arrival for the *M* 6.6 and 6.1 events. Similarly, the red-dotted vertical line denotes the theoretical *PKiKP* arrival, and the black-dashed line corresponds to the observed *PKiKP* arrival for the *M* 6.9 event. (f) Comparison of stacked teleseismic DAS (solid red line) and seismic station (blue-dashed line) data over a 10 s window. The color version of this figure is available only in the electronic edition.

seismic signals. We have made the DAS data for these events publicly available. Furthermore, the waveforms from the DAS data show good agreement with seismometer records, highlighting the potential of DAS as a complementary tool for seismic analysis. In the future, DAS could act as an effective virtual network for investigating deep Earth structures, including the outer and inner cores, further advancing our understanding of seismic phenomena and the internal structure of the Earth.

Data and Resources

The distributed acoustic sensing (DAS) data for these six events are available in the MARTEST Repository (https://zenodo.org/communities/satreps-martest/). The catalog of the study events can be found in AFAD (https://deprem.afad.gov.tr/event-catalog) and U.S. Geological Survey (USGS) (https://earthquake.usgs.gov/earthquakes/search/). All websites were last accessed in August 2025.

Declaration of Competing Interests

The authors acknowledge that there are no conflicts of interest recorded.

Acknowledgments

The authors sincerely thank the reviewers and the associate editor for their thoughtful and constructive suggestions, which greatly contributed to the improvement of this work. The authors thank the funding support by SATREPS (Grant Number JPMJSA2209) under the title "Establishment of a Research and Education Complex for Developing Disaster-resilient Societies–MARTEST of SATREPS." promoted by the Japan International Cooperation Agency (JICA) and Japan Science and Technology Agency (JST). The authors also thank Turk Telekom for providing the fiber-optic (FO) cable and hosting of distributed acoustic sensing (DAS) instrument. The authors thank AFAD and U.S. Geological Survey (USGS) for the open-source catalog.

References

Ajo-Franklin, J. B., S. Dou, N. J. Lindsey, I. Monga, C. Tracy, M. Robertson, V. Rodriguez Tribaldos, C. Ulrich, B. Freifeld, T. Daley, *et al.* (2019). Distributed acoustic sensing using dark fiber for near-surface characterization and broadband seismic event detection, *Sci. Rep.* **9,** no. 1, doi: 10.1038/s41598-018-36675-8.

Atterholt, J., Z. Zhan, and Y. Yang (2022). Fault zone imaging with distributed acoustic sensing: Body-to-surface wave scattering, *J. Geophys. Res.* **127,** no. 11, doi: 10.1029/2022jb025052.

Barka, A., H. S. Akyüz, E. Altunel, G. Sunal, Z. Cakir, A. Dikbas, B. Yerli, R. Armijo, B. Meyer, B. de Chabalier, *et al.* (2002). The surface rupture and slip distribution of the 17 August 1999 Izmit earthquake (M 7.4), North Anatolian fault, *Bull. Seismol. Soc. Am.* **92,** no. 1, 43–60, doi: 10.1785/0120000841.

Beyhan, G., H. H. Selim, and B. Özçiçek (2009). Tectonics related to the North Anatolian fault in the Sea of Marmara: evidence from seismic reflection data, *Marine Geophys. Res.* **30,** no. 4, 237–250, doi: 10.1007/s11001-010-9083-z.

Bouffaut, L., K. Taweesintananon, H. J. Kriesell, R. A. Rørstadbotnen, J. R. Potter, M. Landrø, S. E. Johansen, J. K. Brenne, A. Haukanes, O. Schjelderup, *et al.* (2022). Eavesdropping at the speed of light: Distributed acoustic sensing of Baleen Whales in the Arctic, *Front. Marine Sci.* **9,** doi: 10.3389/fmars.2022.901348.

Cheng, F., B. Chi, N. J. Lindsey, T. C. Dawe, and J. B. Ajo-Franklin (2021). Utilizing distributed acoustic sensing and ocean bottom fiber optic cables for submarine structural characterization, *Sci. Rep.* **11,** no. 1, 5613, doi: 10.1038/s41598-021-84845-y.

Crotwell, H. P., T. J. Owens, and J. Ritsema (1999). The TauP toolkit: Flexible seismic travel-time and ray-path utilities, *Seismol. Res. Lett.* **70,** no. 2, 154–160, doi: 10.1785/gssrl.70.2.154.

Ergintav, S., R. E. Reilinger, R. Çakmak, M. Floyd, Z. Cakir, U. Doğan, R. W. King, S. McClusky, and H. Özener (2014). Istanbul's earthquake hot spots: Geodetic constraints on strain accumulation along faults in the Marmara seismic gap, *Geophys. Res. Lett.* **41,** no. 16, 5783–5788, doi: 10.1002/2014gl060985.

Fontaine, N. K., M. Karrenbach, L. Dallachiesa, R. Ryf, V. Kamalov, E. F. Williams, A. I. Gunnarsson, Ö. Jonsson, A. A. Hlynsson, S. Hlynsson, *et al.* (2025). Global seismic monitoring using multiple operational trans-oceanic telecommunications cables, *Optical Fiber Communication Conference (OFC) Postdeadline Papers 2025*, Postdeadline Paper Digest, Optica Publishing Group, paper Th4C.1.

Gasperini, L., M. Stucchi, V. Cedro, M. Meghraoui, G. Ucarkus, and A. Polonia (2021). Active fault segments along the North Anatolian fault system in the Sea of Marmara: Implication for seismic hazard, *Mediterr. Geosci. Rev.* **3,** no. 1, 29–44, doi: 10.1007/s42990-021-00048-7.

Glover, H. E., M.E. Wengrove, and R. Holman (2024). Measuring hydrodynamics and exploring nearshore processes using distributed sensing of fiber-optic cable strain, *Coastal Eng.* **190,** 104,487, doi: 10.1016/j.coastaleng.2024.104487.

Guerin, G., D. Rivet, M P A van den Ende, E Stutzmann, A. Sladen, and J-P. Ampuero (2022). Quantifying microseismic noise generation from coastal reflection of gravity waves recorded by seafloor DAS, *Geophys. J. Int.* **231,** no. 1, 394–407, doi: 10.1093/gji/ggac200.

Kennett, B. L. N., and E. R. Engdahl (1991). Traveltimes for global earthquake location and phase identification, *Geophys. J. Int.* **105,** no. 2, 429–465, doi: 10.1111/j.1365-246x.1991.tb06724.x.

Kurt, H., C. C. Sorlien, L. Seeber, M. S. Steckler, D. J. Shillington, G. Cifci, M.-H. Cormier, J.-X. Dessa, O. Atgin, D. Dondurur, *et al.* (2013). Steady late quaternary slip rate on the Cinarcik section of the North Anatolian fault near Istanbul, Turkey, *Geophys. Res. Lett.* **40,** no. 17, 4555–4559, doi: 10.1002/grl.50882.

Li, Z., and Z. Zhan (2018). Pushing the limit of earthquake detection with distributed acoustic sensing and template matching: A case study at the Brady geothermal field, *Geophys. J. Int.* **215,** no. 3, 1583–1593, doi: 10.1093/gji/ggy359.

Lindsey, N. J., T. C. Dawe, and J. B. Ajo-Franklin (2019). Illuminating seafloor faults and ocean dynamics with dark fiber distributed acoustic sensing, *Science* **366,** no. 6469, 1103–1107, doi: 10.1126/science.aay5881.

Lindsey, N. J., E. R. Martin, D. S. Dreger, B. Freifeld, S. Cole, S. R. James, B. L. Biondi, and J. B. Ajo-Franklin (2017). Fiber-optic network observations of earthquake wavefields, *Geophys. Res. Lett.* **44,** no. 23, doi: 10.1002/2017gl075722.

Lior, I., A. Sladen, D. Rivet, J.-P. Ampuero, Y. Hello, C. Becerril, H. F. Martins, P. Lamare, C. Jestin, S. Tsagkli, *et al.* (2021). On the detection capabilities of underwater distributed acoustic sensing, *J. Geophys. Res.* **126,** no. 3, doi: 10.1029/2020jb020925.

Mata Flores, D., A. Sladen, J. Ampuero, E. Diego Mercerat, and D. Rivet (2023). Monitoring deep sea currents with seafloor distributed acoustic sensing, *Earth Space Sci.* **10,** no. 6, doi: 10.1029/2022ea002723.

Özkan, B., T. Eken, P. Gaebler, and T. Taymaz (2024). Coda-derived source properties estimated using local earthquakes in the Sea of Marmara, Türkiye, *Solid Earth* **15,** no. 11, 1303–1317, doi: 10.5194/se-15-1303-2024.

Parsons, T., S. Toda, R. Stein, A. Barka, and J. Dieterich (2000). Heightened odds of large earthquakes near Istanbul: An interaction-based probability calculation, *Science* **288,** 661–665.

Schmittbuhl, J., H. Karabulut, O. Lengline, and M. Bouchon (2016). Seismicity distribution and locking depth along the Main Marmara fault, Turkey, *Geochem. Geophys. Geosys* **17,** no. 3, 954–965, doi: 10.1002/2015gc006120.

Şengör, A. M. C., C. Grall, C. İmren, X. Le Pichon, N. Görür, P. Henry, H. Karabulut, and M. Siyako (2014). The geometry of the North Anatolian transform fault in the Sea of Marmara and its temporal evolution: Implications for the development of intracontinental transform faults, *Can. J. Earth Sci.* **51,** no. 3, 222–242, doi: 10.1139/cjes-2013-0160.

Shen, Z., and W. Wu (2024). Ocean bottom distributed acoustic sensing for oceanic seismicity detection and seismic ocean thermometry, *J. Geophys. Res.* **129,** no. 3, doi: 10.1029/2023jb027799.

Shen, Z., W. Wu, and Y.-T. Lin (2024). High-resolution observations of shallow-water acoustic propagation with distributed acoustic sensing, *J. Acoust. Soc. Am.* **156,** no. 4, 2237–2249, doi: 10.1121/10.0030400.

Shi, Q., E. F. Williams, B. P. Lipovsky, M. A. Denolle, W. S. D. Wilcock, D. S. Kelley, and K. Schoedl (2025). Multiplexed distributed acoustic sensing offshore Central Oregon, *Seismol. Res. Lett.* **96,** no. 2A, 784–800, doi: 10.1785/0220240460.

Shinohara, M., T. Yamada, T. Akuhara, K. Mochizuki, and S. Sakai (2022). Performance of seismic observation by distributed acoustic sensing technology using a Seafloor Cable Off Sanriku, Japan, *Front. Marine Sci.* **9,** doi: 10.3389/fmars.2022.844506.

Sladen, A., D. Rivet, J. P. Ampuero, L. De Barros, Y. Hello, G. Calbris, and P. Lamare (2019). Distributed sensing of earthquakes and ocean-solid Earth interactions on seafloor telecom cables, *Nat. Commun.* **10,** no. 1, 5777, doi: 10.1038/s41467-019-13793-z.

Smith, M. M., J. Thomson, M. G. Baker, R. E. Abbott, and J. Davis (2023). Observations of ocean surface wave attenuation in sea ice using seafloor cables, *Geophys. Res. Lett.* **50,** no. 20, doi: 10.1029/2023gl105243.

Spica, Z. J., J. Ajo-Franklin, G. C. Beroza, B. Biondi, F. Cheng, B. Gaite, B. Luo, E. Martin, J. Shen, C. Thurber, *et al.* (2023). PubDAS: A PUBlic distributed acoustic sensing datasets repository for geosciences, *Seismol. Res. Lett.* **94,** no. 2A, 983–998, doi: 10.1785/0220220279.

Spica, Z. J., J. C. Castellanos, L. Viens, K. Nishida, T. Akuhara, M. Shinohara, and T. Yamada (2022). Subsurface imaging with ocean-bottom distributed acoustic sensing and water phases reverberations, *Geophys. Res. Lett.* **49,** no. 2, doi: 10.1029/2021gl095287.

Spica, Z. J., K. Nishida, T. Akuhara, F. Pétrélis, M. Shinohara, and T. Yamada (2020). Marine sediment characterized by ocean-bottom fiber-optic seismology, *Geophys. Res. Lett.* **47,** no. 16, doi: 10.1029/2020gl088360.

Trabattoni, A., F. Biagioli, C. Strumia, F. Scotto, G. Festa, D. Rivet, A. Sladen, J. P. Ampuero, J.-P. Métaxian, *et al.* (2023). From strain to displacement: Using deformation to enhance distributed acoustic sensing applications, *Geophys. J. Int.* **235,** no. 3, 2372–2384, doi: 10.1093/gji/ggad365.

Trabattoni, A., C. Vernet, M. Baillet, Bertrand Potin, and D. Rivet (2024). Sediment corrections for distributed acoustic sensing, *J. Geophys. Res.* **129,** no. 10, doi: 10.1029/2024jb029054.

Viens, L., M. Perton, Z. J. Spica, K. Nishida, T. Yamada, and M. Shinohara (2022). Understanding surface wave modal content for high-resolution imaging of submarine sediments with distributed acoustic sensing, *Geophys. J. Int.* **232,** no. 3, 1668–1683, doi: 10.1093/gji/ggac420.

Wang, X., E. F. Williams, M. Karrenbach, Miguel González Herráez, Hugo Fidalgo Martins, and Z. Zhan (2020). Rose parade seismology: Signatures of floats and bands on optical fiber, *Seismol. Res. Lett.* **91,** no. 4, 2395–2398, doi: 10.1785/0220200091.

Wilcock, W. S. D., S. Abadi, and B. P. Lipovsky (2023). Distributed acoustic sensing recordings of low-frequency whale calls and ship noise offshore Central Oregon, *JASA Express Lett.* **3,** no. 2, doi: 10.1121/10.0017104.

Williams, E. F., M. R. Fernández-Ruiz, R. Magalhaes, R. Vanthillo, Z. Zhan, M. González-Herráez, and H. F. Martins (2019). Distributed sensing of microseisms and teleseisms with submarine dark fibers, *Nat. Commun.* **10,** no. 1, doi: 10.1038/s41467-019-13262-7.

Yang, Y., J. W. Atterholt, Z. Shen, J. B. Muir, E. F. Williams, and Z. Zhan (2021). Sub-kilometer correlation between near-surface structure and ground motion measured with distributed acoustic sensing, *Geophys. Res. Lett.* **49,** no. 1, doi: 10.1029/2021gl096503.

Yang, Y., Z. Zhan, Z. Shen, and J. Atterholt (2022). Fault zone imaging with distributed acoustic sensing: Surface-to-surface wave scattering, *J. Geophys. Res.* **127,** no. 6, doi: 10.1029/2022jb024329.

Ying, Y., C. J. Bean, and P. D. Bromirski (2014). Propagation of microseisms from the deep ocean to land, *Geophys. Res. Lett.* **41,** no. 18, 6374–6379, doi: 10.1002/2014gl060979.

Yu, C., Z. Zhan, N. J. Lindsey, J. B. Ajo-Franklin, and M. Robertson (2019). The potential of DAS in teleseismic studies: Insights from the goldstone experiment, *Geophys. Res. Lett.* **46,** no. 3, 1320–1328, doi: 10.1029/2018gl081195.

Zhan, Z. (2019). Distributed acoustic sensing turns fiber-optic cables into sensitive seismic antennas, *Seismol. Res. Lett.* **91,** no. 1, 1–15, doi: 10.1785/0220190112.

Zhan, Z., M. Cantono, V. Kamalov, A. Mecozzi, R. Müller, S. Yin, and J. C. Castellanos (2021). Optical polarization–based seismic and water wave sensing on transoceanic cables, *Sci.* **371,** no. 6532, 931–936, doi: 10.1126/science.abe6648.

Zhu, W., E. Biondi, J. Li, J. Yin, Z. E. Ross, and Z. Zhan (2023). Seismic arrival-time picking on distributed acoustic sensing data using semi-supervised learning, *Nat. Commun.* **14,** no. 1, doi: 10.1038/s41467-023-43355-3.

Manuscript received 13 February 2025
Published online 8 September 2025

Paul Andrew Spudich Fund Supports Scientific Travel to Japan

An SSA student and early-career member attended a seismology-advancing conference in Kochi, Japan—An experience made possible by donor generosity

Baoning Wu never met the late seismologist who inspired SSA's newest support program, but he knows his research well. One of Paul Spudich's widely cited papers is referenced throughout Wu's Ph.D. project on earthquake high-frequency radiation. In 2019, the project served as Wu's first major oral presentation. He was too nervous to absorb much of the other talks that day, but he remembers why one presentation drew more applause than the rest.

"It was an ovation for Paul Spudich," Wu says, explaining that the beloved scientist had died just a few months before the meeting, so his colleague Antonella Cirella presented Spudich's final paper (on modeling ground motions of the 2009 L'Aquila earthquake) on his behalf.

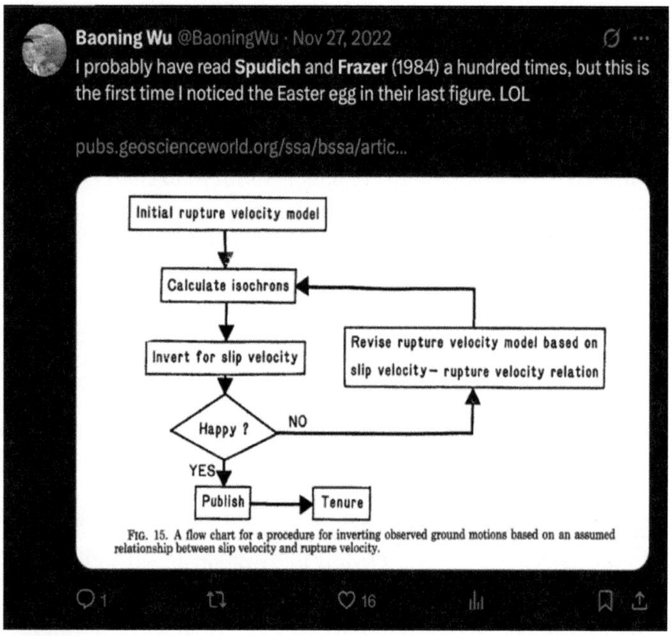

The widely cited *Bulletin of the Seismological Society of America* (BSSA) paper Spudich and Frazer (1984) is referenced many times in Wu's Ph.D. project, but he says he nearly overlooked the joke in the paper's final figure. "Good papers back then often did not read as seriously as those nowadays," Wu says. "Sometimes, you can even guess the personality of some authors from their writing. Paul Spudich is one of them. I really enjoy reading papers like those." The color version of this figure is available only in the electronic edition.

Today, SSA's Paul Andrew Spudich Fund continues to honor the giant in seismology by providing grants that support burgeoning studies in earthquake source physics or ground-motion prediction—areas Spudich made important contributions to during his distinguished career with the U.S. Geological Survey.

The fund just enabled Wu, an early-career theoretical geophysicist, and Jeena Yun, a Ph.D. candidate at Scripps Institution of Oceanography, to participate in the September 2025 International Joint Workshop on Slow-to-Fast Earthquakes in Kochi, Japan. Both SSA members returned from the workshop with new connections, ideas, and enthusiasm for their future projects.

Because Wu has worked on modeling slow earthquakes since his Ph.D., traveling to Japan to attend this leading conference for sharing slow-earthquake research had been on his scientific wish list for a long time. He found it especially meaningful to finally meet the slow-earthquake community in person, including scientists who have had a major impact on his work. "My abstract was selected for an oral presentation, and I gave a talk in front of Professor Ryosuke Ando, whose work my research is based on. Professor Satoshi Ide, whose ideas inspired my research, also sat in the front row," Wu says.

Yun was eager to attend the workshop because her recent research project focuses on understanding how an earthquake can affect the sequences of slow and fast earthquakes on a nearby megathrust interface. She appreciated the workshop's balance of contributions from different subdisciplines of geosciences, including seismology, geodesy, mineral physics, and petrology, and says the experience opened her eyes to both new projects and perspectives.

"I extended my knowledge on cutting-edge research on not only slow and fast earthquakes in various subduction zones, but also their structural and geological properties," she says, adding that she also built connections with possible collaborators from Japan, China, and Canada working on different aspects of subduction zone earthquakes.

Both researchers say their career-advancing experience was only possible because of the donor-funded grant program. "Without the support of the SSA Paul Andrew Spudich Travel Grant, I would not be able to attend this workshop due to the shortage of other funding," Yun says.

Wu feels particularly grateful for the travel grant's focus on theoretical research. "While I don't have tenure and probably won't have one in the foreseeable future, I often have to work on several observational or practical projects simultaneously to support myself in conducting those with more theoretical flavor," he says. "The SSA Paul Spudich Travel Grant offered great help to me, and I feel truly grateful."

Jeena Yun (right of fellow grant recipient Baoning Wu), says she welcomed the opportunity for in-person scientific exchange between scientists based in America and Japan, two highly active countries in earthquake research. "Thanks to the travel grant, I learned about a number of interesting projects led by Japanese colleagues, which I was not aware of before attending this workshop." The color version of this figure is available only in the electronic edition.

After receiving feedback at the workshop, Wu feels more prepared to wrap up his slow-earthquake models into publications. Yun has new contacts she can call on for projects aimed at advancing earthquake science and lowering seismic hazard.

The Paul Andrew Spudich Travel Grant program will welcome applications once again in February. "In this era of uncertain funding situations," Yun says, "I highly encourage my peers to apply and grab this invaluable opportunity."

For more information on SSA's Paul Andrew Spudich Travel Grant program, visit seismosoc.org/grants-and-fellowship/paul-andrew-spudich-travel-grants-2/.

Manuscript received 3 November 2025
Published online 2 December 2025

Corporate Members, Seismological Society of America

ExxonMobil
Sara Gates
22777 Springwoods Village Parkway
Spring, TX 77389
www.corporate.exxonmobil.com

GeoSIG Ltd
Talhan Biro
Wiesenstrasse 39
8952 Schlieren
Switzerland
www.geosig.com

Guralp Systems
James Lindsey
3 Midas House, Calleva Park Aldermaston
Berkshire RG7 8EA
United Kingdom
www.guralp.com

ISTI
Paul Friberg
5 Case Street
Saratoga Springs, NY 12866
www.isti.com

Kinemetrics, Inc.
Veronica Vera
222 Vista Avenue
Pasadena, CA 91107
www.kinemetrics.com

Lettis Consultants International, Inc.
Jeffrey Unruh
1981 N Broadway
Suite 330
Walnut Creek, CA 94596
www.lettisci.com

Moody's
Nilesh Shome
7575 Gateway Boulevard
Newark, CA 94560
www.moodys.com

Nanometrics
Alyssa Parks
250 Herzberg Road
Kanata, ON K2K 2A1
Canada
www.nanometrics.ca

Puerto Rico Strong Motion Program
Dr. José Martinez-Cruzado
Call Box 9000-Civil Engineering
Mayaguez, Puerto Rico 00681
www.prsmp.uprm.edu

Reftek Systems Inc.
Leonid Zimakov
75 MacDonald Avenue
Dartmouth, NS B3B 1T8
Canada
www.reftek.com

Seismology Research Centre
Adam Pascale
141 Palmer Street
Richmond, VIC 3121
Australia
www.src.com.au

SSA
Seismological
Society of America

The Seismological Society of America is an international scientific society devoted to the advancement of seismology and the understanding of earthquakes for the benefit of society.

www.seismosoc.org
www.srl-online.org

Seismological Society of America